Periodic Table of the Elements

Legend:
- 9 = Atomic number
- F
- Fluorine
- 19.00 = Atomic mass

1 / 1A	2 / 2A	3 / 3B	4 / 4B	5 / 5B	6 / 6B	7 / 7B	8	9 / 8B	10	11 / 1B	12 / 2B	13 / 3A	14 / 4A	15 / 5A	16 / 6A	17 / 7A	18 / 8A
1 **H** Hydrogen 1.008																	2 **He** Helium 4.003
3 **Li** Lithium 6.941	4 **Be** Beryllium 9.012											5 **B** Boron 10.81	6 **C** Carbon 12.01	7 **N** Nitrogen 14.01	8 **O** Oxygen 16.00	9 **F** Fluorine 19.00	10 **Ne** Neon 20.18
11 **Na** Sodium 22.99	12 **Mg** Magnesium 24.31											13 **Al** Aluminum 26.98	14 **Si** Silicon 28.09	15 **P** Phosphorus 30.97	16 **S** Sulfur 32.07	17 **Cl** Chlorine 35.45	18 **Ar** Argon 39.95
19 **K** Potassium 39.10	20 **Ca** Calcium 40.08	21 **Sc** Scandium 44.96	22 **Ti** Titanium 47.88	23 **V** Vanadium 50.94	24 **Cr** Chromium 52.00	25 **Mn** Manganese 54.94	26 **Fe** Iron 55.85	27 **Co** Cobalt 58.93	28 **Ni** Nickel 58.69	29 **Cu** Copper 63.55	30 **Zn** Zinc 65.39	31 **Ga** Gallium 69.72	32 **Ge** Germanium 72.59	33 **As** Arsenic 74.92	34 **Se** Selenium 78.96	35 **Br** Bromine 79.90	36 **Kr** Krypton 83.80
37 **Rb** Rubidium 85.47	38 **Sr** Strontium 87.62	39 **Y** Yttrium 88.91	40 **Zr** Zirconium 91.22	41 **Nb** Niobium 92.91	42 **Mo** Molybdenum 95.94	43 **Tc** Technetium (98)	44 **Ru** Ruthenium 101.1	45 **Rh** Rhodium 102.9	46 **Pd** Palladium 106.4	47 **Ag** Silver 107.9	48 **Cd** Cadmium 112.4	49 **In** Indium 114.8	50 **Sn** Tin 118.7	51 **Sb** Antimony 121.8	52 **Te** Tellurium 127.6	53 **I** Iodine 126.9	54 **Xe** Xenon 131.3
55 **Cs** Cesium 132.9	56 **Ba** Barium 137.3	57 **La** Lanthanum 138.9	72 **Hf** Hafnium 178.5	73 **Ta** Tantalum 180.9	74 **W** Tungsten 183.9	75 **Re** Rhenium 186.2	76 **Os** Osmium 190.2	77 **Ir** Iridium 192.2	78 **Pt** Platinum 195.1	79 **Au** Gold 197.0	80 **Hg** Mercury 200.6	81 **Tl** Thallium 204.4	82 **Pb** Lead 207.2	83 **Bi** Bismuth 209.0	84 **Po** Polonium (210)	85 **At** Astatine (210)	86 **Rn** Radon (222)
87 **Fr** Francium (223)	88 **Ra** Radium (226)	89 **Ac** Actinium (227)	104 **Rf** Rutherfordium (257)	105 **Db** Dubnium (260)	106 **Sg** Seaborgium (263)	107 **Bh** Bohrium (262)	108 **Hs** Hassium (265)	109 **Mt** Meitnerium (266)	110 **Ds** Darmstadtium (269)	111 **Rg** Roentgenium (272)	112	(113)	114	(115)	116	(117)	(118)

Lanthanides and Actinides:

58 **Ce** Cerium 140.1	59 **Pr** Praseodymium 140.9	60 **Nd** Neodymium 144.2	61 **Pm** Promethium (147)	62 **Sm** Samarium 150.4	63 **Eu** Europium 152.0	64 **Gd** Gadolinium 157.3	65 **Tb** Terbium 158.9	66 **Dy** Dysprosium 162.5	67 **Ho** Holmium 164.9	68 **Er** Erbium 167.3	69 **Tm** Thulium 168.9	70 **Yb** Ytterbium 173.0	71 **Lu** Lutetium 175.0
90 **Th** Thorium 232.0	91 **Pa** Protactinium (231)	92 **U** Uranium 238.0	93 **Np** Neptunium (237)	94 **Pu** Plutonium (242)	95 **Am** Americium (243)	96 **Cm** Curium (247)	97 **Bk** Berkelium (247)	98 **Cf** Californium (249)	99 **Es** Einsteinium (254)	100 **Fm** Fermium (253)	101 **Md** Mendelevium (256)	102 **No** Nobelium (254)	103 **Lr** Lawrencium (257)

Key:
- Metals
- Metalloids
- Nonmetals

The 1–18 group designation has been recommended by the International Union of Pure and Applied Chemistry (IUPAC) but is not yet in wide use. In this text we use the standard U.S. notation for group numbers (1A–8A and 1B–8B). No names have been assigned for elements 112, 114, and 116. Elements 113, 115, 117, and 118 have not yet been synthesized.

List of the Elements with Their Symbols and Atomic Masses*

Element	Symbol	Atomic Number	Atomic Mass[†]	Element	Symbol	Atomic Number	Atomic Mass[†]
Actinium	Ac	89	(227)	Mendelevium	Md	101	(256)
Aluminum	Al	13	26.98	Mercury	Hg	80	200.6
Americium	Am	95	(243)	Molybdenum	Mo	42	95.94
Antimony	Sb	51	121.8	Neodymium	Nd	60	144.2
Argon	Ar	18	39.95	Neon	Ne	10	20.18
Arsenic	As	33	74.92	Neptunium	Np	93	(237)
Astatine	At	85	(210)	Nickel	Ni	28	58.69
Barium	Ba	56	137.3	Niobium	Nb	41	92.91
Berkelium	Bk	97	(247)	Nitrogen	N	7	14.01
Beryllium	Be	4	9.012	Nobelium	No	102	(253)
Bismuth	Bi	83	209.0	Osmium	Os	76	190.2
Bohrium	Bh	107	(262)	Oxygen	O	8	16.00
Boron	B	5	10.81	Palladium	Pd	46	106.4
Bromine	Br	35	79.90	Phosphorus	P	15	30.97
Cadmium	Cd	48	112.4	Platinum	Pt	78	195.1
Calcium	Ca	20	40.08	Plutonium	Pu	94	(242)
Californium	Cf	98	(249)	Polonium	Po	84	(210)
Carbon	C	6	12.01	Potassium	K	19	39.10
Cerium	Ce	58	140.1	Praseodymium	Pr	59	140.9
Cesium	Cs	55	132.9	Promethium	Pm	61	(147)
Chlorine	Cl	17	35.45	Protactinium	Pa	91	(231)
Chromium	Cr	24	52.00	Radium	Ra	88	(226)
Cobalt	Co	27	58.93	Radon	Rn	86	(222)
Copper	Cu	29	63.55	Rhenium	Re	75	186.2
Curium	Cm	96	(247)	Rhodium	Rh	45	102.9
Darmstadtium	Ds	110	(269)	Roentgenium	Rg	111	(272)
Dubnium	Db	105	(260)	Rubidium	Rb	37	85.47
Dysprosium	Dy	66	162.5	Ruthenium	Ru	44	101.1
Einsteinium	Es	99	(254)	Rutherfordium	Rf	104	(257)
Erbium	Er	68	167.3	Samarium	Sm	62	150.4
Europium	Eu	63	152.0	Scandium	Sc	21	44.96
Fermium	Fm	100	(253)	Seaborgium	Sg	106	(263)
Fluorine	F	9	19.00	Selenium	Se	34	78.96
Francium	Fr	87	(223)	Silicon	Si	14	28.09
Gadolinium	Gd	64	157.3	Silver	Ag	47	107.9
Gallium	Ga	31	69.72	Sodium	Na	11	22.99
Germanium	Ge	32	72.59	Strontium	Sr	38	87.62
Gold	Au	79	197.0	Sulfur	S	16	32.07
Hafnium	Hf	72	178.5	Tantalum	Ta	73	180.9
Hassium	Hs	108	(265)	Technetium	Tc	43	(99)
Helium	He	2	4.003	Tellurium	Te	52	127.6
Holmium	Ho	67	164.9	Terbium	Tb	65	158.9
Hydrogen	H	1	1.008	Thallium	Tl	81	204.4
Indium	In	49	114.8	Thorium	Th	90	232.0
Iodine	I	53	126.9	Thulium	Tm	69	168.9
Iridium	Ir	77	192.2	Tin	Sn	50	118.7
Iron	Fe	26	55.85	Titanium	Ti	22	47.88
Krypton	Kr	36	83.80	Tungsten	W	74	183.9
Lanthanum	La	57	138.9	Uranium	U	92	238.0
Lawrencium	Lr	103	(257)	Vanadium	V	23	50.94
Lead	Pb	82	207.2	Xenon	Xe	54	131.3
Lithium	Li	3	6.941	Ytterbium	Yb	70	173.0
Lutetium	Lu	71	175.0	Yttrium	Y	39	88.91
Magnesium	Mg	12	24.31	Zinc	Zn	30	65.39
Manganese	Mn	25	54.94	Zirconium	Zr	40	91.22
Meitnerium	Mt	109	(266)				

*All atomic masses have four significant figures. These values are recommended by the Committee on Teaching of Chemistry, International Union of Pure and Applied Chemistry.
[†]Approximate values of atomic masses for radioactive elements are given in parentheses.

Fundamental Constants

Avogadro's number	6.0221367×10^{23}
Electron charge (e)	1.6022×10^{-19} C
Electron mass	9.109387×10^{-28} g
Faraday constant (F)	96,485.3 C/mol e^-
Gas constant (R)	8.314 J/K · mol (0.08206 L · atm/K · mol)
Planck's constant (h)	6.6256×10^{-34} J · s
Proton mass	1.672623×10^{-24} g
Neutron mass	1.674928×10^{-24} g
Speed of light in vacuum	2.99792458×10^8 m/s

Useful Conversion Factors and Relationships

1 lb = 453.6 g

1 in = 2.54 cm (exactly)

1 mi = 1.609 km

1 km = 0.6215 mi

1 pm = 1×10^{-12} m = 1×10^{-10} cm

1 atm = 760 mmHg = 760 torr − 101,325 N/m^2 = 101,325 Pa

1 cal = 4.184 J (exactly)

1 L atm = 101.325 J

1 J = 1 C × 1 V

$$?°C = (°F - 32°F) \times \frac{5°C}{9°F}$$

$$?°F = \frac{9°F}{5°C} \times (°C) + 32°F$$

$$?K = (°C + 273.15°C)\left(\frac{1\ K}{1°C}\right)$$

Color Codes for Molecular Models

H

B

C

N

O

F

P

S

Cl

Br

I

Some Prefixes Used with SI Units

tera (T)	10^{12}	centi (c)	10^{-2}
giga (G)	10^{9}	milli (m)	10^{-3}
mega (M)	10^{6}	micro (μ)	10^{-6}
kilo (k)	10^{3}	nano (n)	10^{-9}
deci (d)	10^{-1}	pico (p)	10^{-12}

Index of Important Figures and Tables

Chemistry

Ninth Edition

Raymond
CHANG

Williams College

 Higher Education

Boston   Burr Ridge, IL   Dubuque, IA   Madison, WI   New York   San Francisco   St. Louis
Bangkok   Bogotá   Caracas   Kuala Lumpur   Lisbon   London   Madrid   Mexico City
Milan   Montreal   New Delhi   Santiago   Seoul   Singapore   Sydney   Taipei   Toronto

Higher Education

CHEMISTRY, NINTH EDITION

Published by McGraw-Hill, a business unit of The McGraw-Hill Companies, Inc., 1221 Avenue of the Americas, New York, NY 10020. Copyright © 2007 by The McGraw-Hill Companies, Inc. All rights reserved. No part of this publication may be reproduced or distributed in any form or by any means, or stored in a database or retrieval system, without the prior written consent of The McGraw-Hill Companies, Inc., including, but not limited to, in any network or other electronic storage or transmission, or broadcast for distance learning.

Some ancillaries, including electronic and print components, may not be available to customers outside the United States.

This book is printed on acid-free paper.

2 3 4 5 6 7 8 9 0 DOW/DOW 0 9 8 7

ISBN-13   978–0–07–326827–9
ISBN-10   0–07–326827–5

Publisher: *Thomas D. Timp*
Managing Developmental Editor: *Shirley R. Oberbroeckling*
Senior Marketing Manager: *Tamara L. Good-Hodge*
Director Secondary Marketing: *Jim Lewis*
Senior Project Manager: *Gloria G. Schiesl*
Senior Production Supervisor: *Kara Kudronowicz*
Lead Media Project Manager: *Judi David*
Lead Media Producer: *John J. Theobald*
Senior Designer: *David W. Hash*
Cover/Interior Designer: *Jamie E. O'Neal*
Senior Photo Research Coordinator: *John C. Leland*
Photo Research: *Chris Hammond/PhotoFind, LLC*
Supplement Producer: *Tracy L. Konrardy*
Compositor: *TechBooks/GTS, Los Angeles, CA*
Typeface: *10/12 Times Roman*
Printer: *R. R. Donnelley Willard, OH*

The credits section for this book begins on page C-1and is considered an extension of the copyright page.

www.mhhe.com

About the Author

Raymond Chang was born in Hong Kong and grew up in Shanghai and Hong Kong. He received his B.Sc. degree in chemistry from London University, England, and his Ph.D. in chemistry from Yale University. After doing postdoctoral research at Washington University and teaching for a year at Hunter College of the City University of New York, he joined the chemistry department at Williams College, where he has taught since 1968.

Professor Chang has served on the American Chemical Society Examination Committee, the National Chemistry Olympiad Examination Committee, and the Graduate Record Examinations (GRE) Committee. He is an editor of *The Chemical Educator*. Professor Chang has written books on physical chemistry, industrial chemistry, and physical science. He has also coauthored books on the Chinese language, children's picture books, and a novel for young readers.

For relaxation, Professor Chang maintains a forest garden; plays tennis, Ping-Pong, and the harmonica; and practices the violin.

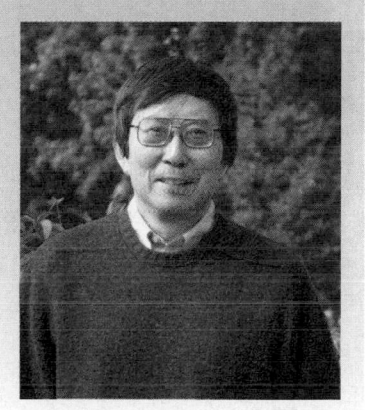

Cover Images

Left: Pb^{2+}–EDTA complex. Middle: Electrostatic potential map showing the formation of H_2 from two H atoms. Right: The α-helical structure of a protein molecule.

Contents

Chemistry: The Study of Change 2

Atoms, Molecules, and Ions 40

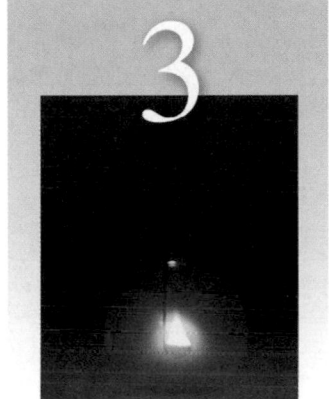

Mass Relationships in Chemical Reactions 76

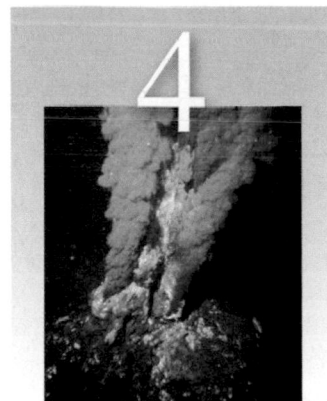

Reactions in Aqueous Solutions 118

CHEMICAL *Mystery*
Who Killed Napoleon? 166

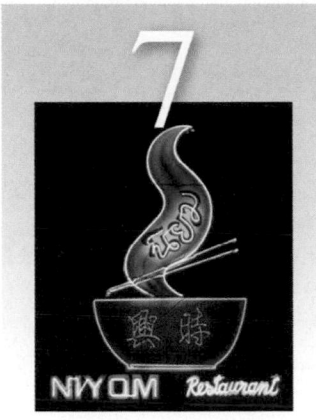

Quantum Theory and the Electronic Structure of Atoms 266

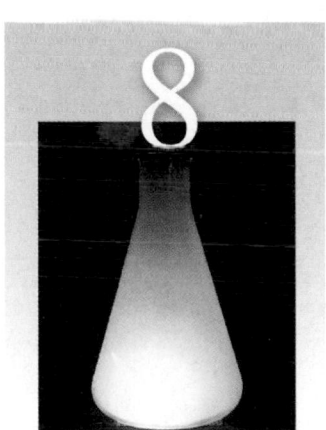

Periodic Relationships Among the Elements 314

Chemical Bonding I: Basic Concepts 356

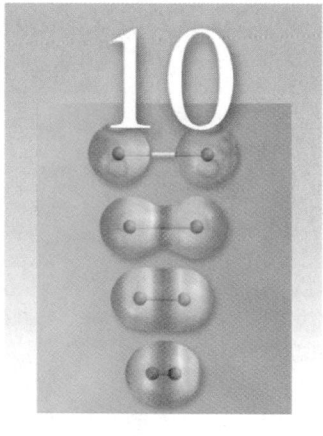

Chemical Bonding II: Molecular Geometry and Hybridization of Atomic Orbitals 398

Intermolecular Forces and Liquids and Solids 450

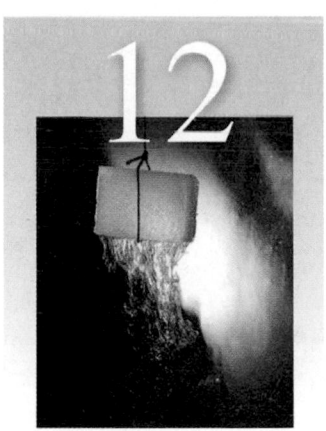

Physical Properties of Solutions 502

Chemical Kinetics 544

Chemical Equilibrium 600

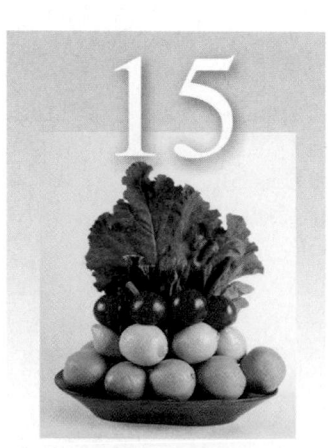

Acids and Bases 644

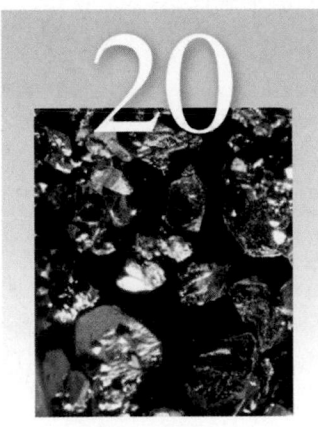

Metallurgy and the Chemistry of Metals 866

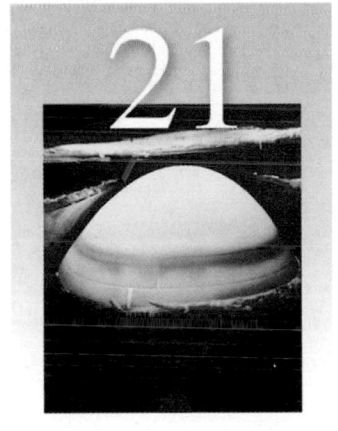

Nonmetallic Elements and Their Compounds 894

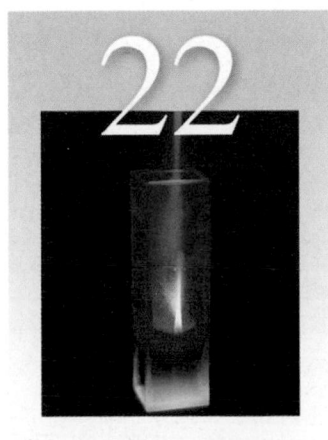

Transition Metal Chemistry and Coordination Compounds 934

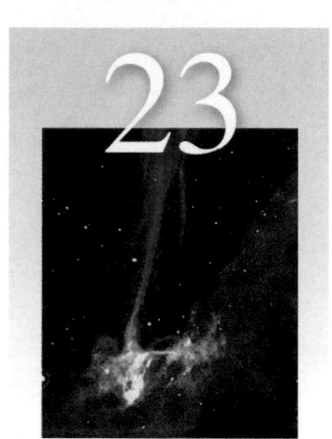

Nuclear Chemistry 966

Organic Chemistry 1002

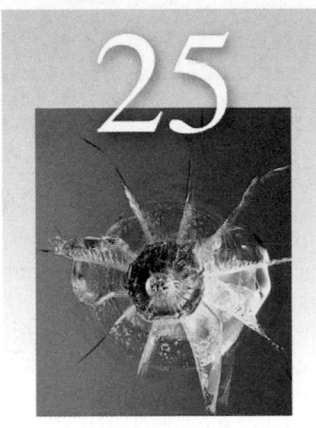

Synthetic and Natural Organic Polymers 1038

List of Applications

The opening sentence of this text is, "Chemistry is an active, evolving science that has vital importance to our world, in both the realm of nature and the realm of society." Throughout the text, Chemistry in Action and Chemical Mysteries give specific examples of chemistry as active and evolving in all facets of our lives.

CHEMISTRY *in Action*

CHEMICAL *Mystery*

List of Animations

 The animations listed here are correlated to *Chemistry* within each chapter in two ways. The first is the Interactive Activity Summary found on the opening pages of every chapter. Then within the chapter are icons letting the student and instructor know that an animation is available for a specific topic and where to find the animation for viewing. For the instructor, the animations are also available on the Chemistry Animations Library.

Chang Animations

Absorption of color (22.5)
Acid-base titrations (16.4)
Acid ionization (15.5)
Activation energy (13.4)
Alpha, beta, and gamma rays (2.2)
Alpha-particle scattering (2.2)
Atomic and ionic radius (8.3)
Base ionization (15.6)
Buffer solutions (16.3)
Catalysis (13.6)
Cathode ray tube (2.2)
Chemical equilibrium (14.1)
Chirality (22.4 and 24.2)
Collecting a gas over water (5.6)
Diffusion of gases (5.7)
Dissolution of an ionic and a covalent compound (12.2)
Electron configurations (7.8)
Emission spectra (7.3)
Equilibrium vapor pressure (11.8)
Formal charge calculations (9.7)
Galvanic cells (19.2)
The gas laws (5.3)
Heat flow (6.4)
Hybridization (10.4)
Hydration (4.1)
Ionic vs. covalent bonding (9.2)
Le Chatelier's principle (14.5)
Limiting reagent (3.9)
Making a solution (4.5)
Millikan oil drop (2.2)
Nuclear fission (23.5)
Neutralization reactions (4.3)
Orientation of collision (13.4)
Osmosis (12.6)

Oxidation-reduction reactions (4.4)
Packing spheres (11.4)
Polarity of molecules (10.2)
Precipitation reactions (4.2)
Preparing a solution by dilution (4.5)
Radioactive decay (23.3)
Resonance (9.8)
Sigma and pi bonds (10.5)
Strong electrolytes, weak electrolytes, and nonelectrolytes (4.1)
VSEPR (10.1)

McGraw-Hill Animations

Atomic line spectra (7.3)
Charles' law (5.3)
Cubic unit cells and their origins (11.4)
Dissociation of strong and weak acids (15.5)
Dissolving table salt (4.1)
Electronegativity (9.5)
Equilibrium (14.1)
Exothermic and endothermic reactions (6.2)
Formation of an ionic compound (9.2)
Formation of the covalent bond in H_2 (10.3)
Half-life (13.3)
Influence of shape on polarity (10.2)
Law of conservation of mass (2.1)
Molecular shape and orbital hybridization (10.4)
Nuclear medicine (23.7)
Operation of voltaic cell (19.2)
Oxidation-reduction reaction (4.4 and 19.1)
Phase diagrams and the states of matter (11.9)
Reaction rate and the nature of collisions (13.4)
Three states of matter (1.5)
Using a buffer (16.3)
VSEPR theory and the shapes of molecules (10.1)

Simulations

Stoichiometry (Chapter 3)
Ideal gas law (Chapter 5)
Kinetics (Chapter 13)
Equilibrium (Chapter 14)
Titration (Chapter 16)
Electrochemistry (Chapter 19)
Nuclear (Chapter 23)

Reinforced Binding

What does it mean?

For adopting schools this means these texts can be expected to be more durable and last longer when subjected to daily classroom use in a school environment where textbooks are adopted for multiple years.

This text has been widely adopted by colleges and universities yet is often used in high schools for teaching Advanced Placement,* honors, elective, and college prep courses. Because advanced high school program adoption periods often last several years and a text must stand up to usage by multiple students, McGraw-Hill has elected to manufacture this text in a manner compliant with the "Manufacturing Standards and Specifications for Textbooks" (MSST) published by the "National Association of State Textbook Administrators" (NASTA). The MSST manufacturing guidelines provide guidance and minimum standards for the binding, paper type, and other physical characteristics of a text with the goal of making it more durable in a school environment. These manufacturing standards are in common use for manufacturing of basal level texts. For full production specification detail visit: www.NASTA.org

From the first edition, my aim has been to write a general chemistry text that provides a firm foundation in chemical concepts and principles and to instill in students an appreciation of the vital part chemistry plays in our daily lives. It is the responsibility of the textbook author to assist both instructors and their students in their pursuit of this objective by presenting a broad range of topics in a clear, logical manner. I have tried to strike a balance between theory and application and to illustrate basic principles with everyday examples whenever possible. And above all, I have placed the highest priority on writing a lucid and readable text.

With each new edition, I have strived to refine the pedagogy to develop students' problem-solving and critical thinking skills and find new and more effective ways to present abstract chemical concepts. At the same time, my publisher and I employ the many tools technology has to offer to help students visualize chemistry and explore ideas in an interactive environment. The integration of these tools in this edition serves to inspire the students in their learning process, and takes them beyond the confines of the traditional textbook.

What's New in This Edition?

Many sections have been revised and updated based on the comments from reviewers and users. Some examples are:

- The chapter opening pages include a new feature titled: "A Look Ahead," providing students with an overview of what will be coming up in the chapter.

- All key equations and answers to most Worked Examples have been shaded for easy visual access.

- An introduction to organic compounds has been added to Section 2.8.

- Reaction types (precipitation and acid-base) in Chapter 4 have been revised.

- The treatment of gas diffusion and effusion has been expanded in Section 5.7.

- Section 13.3 now also discusses zero-order reactions in addition to first- and second-order reactions.

- Section 15.3 compares the definition of pH using concentration and activity.

- A number of Chemistry in Action essays have been updated and two new ones have been added in Chapters 11 and 19.

- A new Chemical Mystery has been added in Chapter 7.

- As in the previous edition, there is a good mix of easy, intermediate, and difficult problems at the end of each chapter. In addition, Special Problems is a new category that contains more challenging problems.

- The ARIS electronic homework system is available for the ninth edition. ARIS will enhance the student learning experience, administer assignments, track student progress, and administer an instructor's course. Students can locate the animations and interactives noted in the text margins in ARIS. Quizzing and homework assigned by the instructor is available in the ARIS electronic homework program.

*Pre-AP, AP, and Advanced Placement program are registered trademarks of the College Entrance Examination Board, which was not involved in the production of and does not endorse these products.

Art

As always, I strive for a clean but visual design. Each chapter opens with a two-page spread containing a photo with accompanying molecular models to illustrate the chemical or physical process at the molecular level.

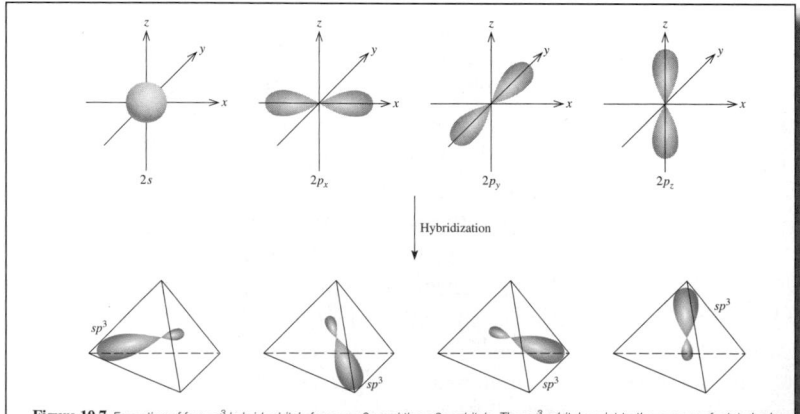

Many of the line art drawings have a new look while still maintaining accurate chemical information. For example, the hybrid orbitals in Chapter 10 have a new and updated visual look.

I have also added new molecular art to line drawings and photos and to a number of end-of-chapter problems. In addition, we have updated the photo program to complement the visual layout of the design. Finally, we have updated the format of the periodic table throughout the text.

Figure 10.7 *Formation of four sp^3 hybrid orbitals from one 2s and three 2p orbitals. The sp^3 orbitals point to the corners of a tetrahedron.*

Problems

The development of problem-solving skills has always been a major objective of this text. For example, in Section 3.8 the general approach for solving stoichiometry problems is broken down in a numbered step-by-step process. Immediately following is Example 3.13 using this approach. Example 3.14 then requires the students to use this same type of process on their own.

Marginal references enable students to apply new skills to other, similar problems at the end of the chapter. Each Worked Example is followed by a Practice Exercise that asks the students to solve a similar problem on their own. The answers to the Practice Exercises are provided after the end-of-chapter problems in each chapter.

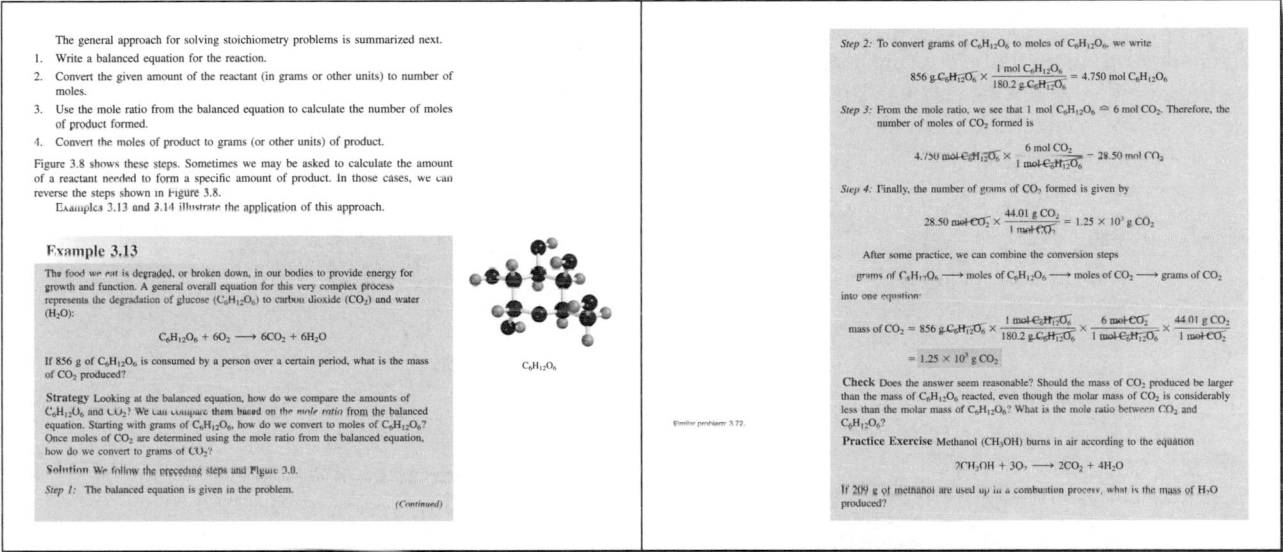

As an instructor, I often tell my students that a good learning tool is to sketch out the inner workings of a problem. In some of the Worked Examples, I have included this type of drawing (for example, see Example 16.10 on p. 724). It is what a scientist would do as he/she works out a problem.

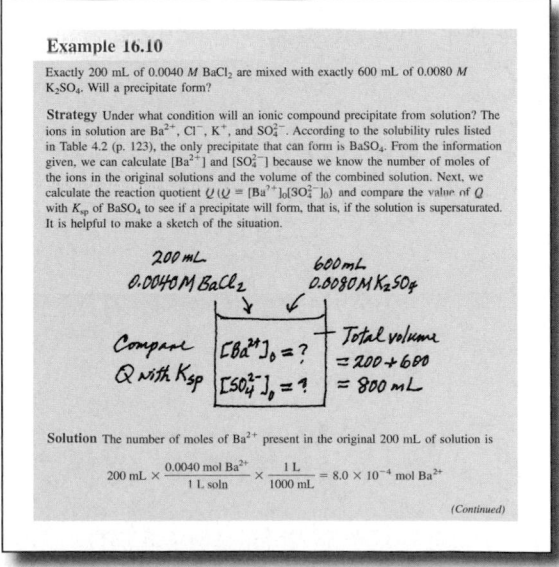

New to this edition! "Special Problems" have been written to challenge the student. A number of these problems have been included at the end of each chapter.

Special Problems

1.94 A bank teller is asked to assemble "one-dollar" sets of coins for his clients. Each set is made of three quarters, one nickel, and two dimes. The masses of the coins are: quarter: 5.645 g; nickel: 4.967 g; dime: 2.316 g. What is the maximum number of sets that can be assembled from 33.871 kg of quarters, 10.432 kg of nickels, and 7.990 kg of dimes? What is the total mass (in g) of this collection of coins?

1.98 A chemist mixes two liquids A and B to form a homogeneous mixture. The densities of the liquids are 2.0514 g/mL for A and 2.6678 g/mL for B. When she drops a small object into the mixture, she finds that the object becomes suspended in the liquid; that is, it neither sinks nor floats. If the mixture is made of 41.37 percent A and 58.63 percent B by volume, what is the density of the metal? Can this procedure be used in general to determine the densities of solids? What assumptions must be made in applying this method?

Pedagogy

Each chapter opening section contains the new "A Look Ahead," providing the students with an overview of the topics to be presented within the chapter. The Interactive Activity Summary shows the available media to further enhance students' ability to understand a concept.

2

Colored images of the radioactive emission of radium (Ra). The models show the nuclei of radium and the radioactive decay products—radon (Rn) and an alpha particle, which has two protons and two neutrons. Study of radioactivity helped to advance scientists' knowledge about atomic structure.

Atoms, Molecules, and Ions

2.1   The Atomic Theory
2.2   The Structure of the Atom
2.3   Atomic Number, Mass Number, and Isotopes
2.4   The Periodic Table
2.5   Molecules and Ions
2.6   Chemical Formulas
2.7   Naming Compounds
2.8   Introduction to Organic Compounds

A LOOK AHEAD

- We begin with a historical perspective of the search for the fundamental units of matter. The modern version of atomic theory was laid by John Dalton in the nineteenth century, who postulated that elements are composed of extremely small particles, called atoms. All atoms of a given element are identical, but they are different from atoms of all other elements. (2.1)

- We note that, through experimentation, scientists have learned that an atom is composed of three elementary particles: proton, electron, and neutron. The proton has a positive charge, the electron has a negative charge, and the neutron has no charge. Protons and neutrons are located in a small region at the center of the atom, called the nucleus, while electrons are spread out about the nucleus at some distance from it. (2.2)

- We will learn the following ways to identify atoms. Atomic number is the number of protons in a nucleus; atoms of different elements have different atomic numbers. Isotopes are atoms of the same element having a different number of neutrons. Mass number is the sum of the number of protons and neutrons in an atom. Because an atom is electrically neutral, it contains an equal number of protons and electrons. (2.3)

- Next we will see how elements can be grouped together according to their chemical and physical properties in a chart called the periodic table. The periodic table enables us to classify elements (as metals, metalloids, and nonmetals) and correlate their properties in a systematic way. (2.4)

- We will see that atoms of most elements interact to form compounds, which are classified as molecules or ionic compounds made of positive (cations) and negative (anions) ions. (2.5)

- We then learn to use chemical formulas (molecular and empirical) to represent molecules and ionic compounds and models to represent molecules. (2.6)

- We learn a set of rules that help us name the inorganic compounds. (2.7)

- This chapter ends with a brief introduction to the organic world to which we will return in Chapter 24. (2.8)

Interactive Activity Summary

1. Animation: Cathode Ray Tube (2.2)
2. Animation: Millikan Oil Drop (2.2)
3. Animation: Alpha, Beta, and Gamma Rays (2.2)
4. Animation: α-Particle Scattering (2.2)

Since ancient times humans have pondered the nature of matter. Our modern ideas of the structure of matter began to take shape in the early nineteenth century with Dalton's atomic theory. We now know that all matter is made of atoms, molecules, and ions. All of chemistry is concerned in one way or another with these species.

41

Marginal notes provide additional information to the student regarding quick facts; referring a student forward to a section in which the concept will be further detailed or linking back to a section they can use to review the material.

There is a plethora of molecular art in the margin, enabling students to "see" the molecule under discussion.

The periodic table icon in the margin illustrates the properties of elements according to their positions in the periodic table.

Elements that exist as diatomic molecules.

Also in the margin, the student will find the icon highlighting the media (animations and interactives) that can be used to understand the concept presented.

The end of the chapter provides further study aids with the Summary of Facts and Concepts and also the Key Words. They give the student a quick snapshot of the chapter in review.

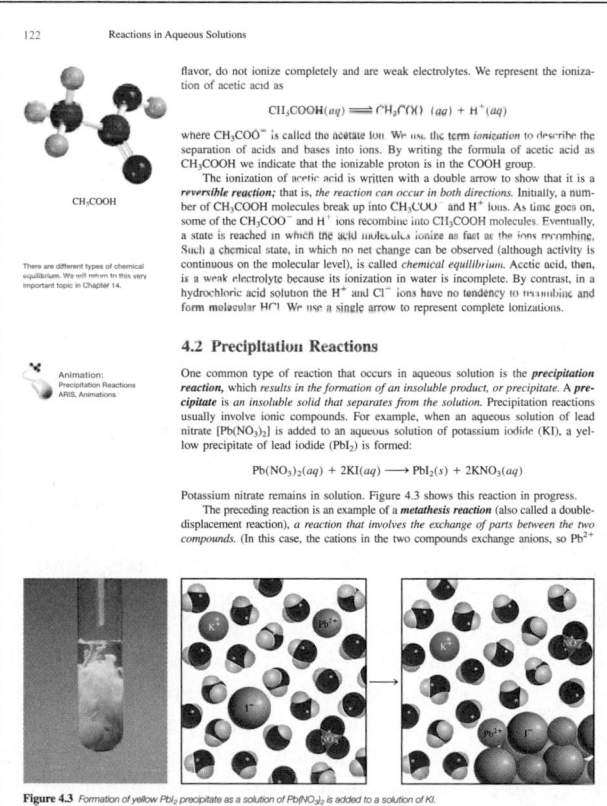

122   Reactions in Aqueous Solutions

CH_3COOH

There are different types of chemical equilibrium. We will return to this very important topic in Chapter 14.

flavor, do not ionize completely and are weak electrolytes. We represent the ionization of acetic acid as

$$CH_3COOH(aq) \rightleftharpoons CH_3COO^-(aq) + H^+(aq)$$

where CH_3COO^- is called the acetate ion. We use the term *ionization* to describe the separation of acids and bases into ions. By writing the formula of acetic acid as CH_3COOH we indicate that the ionizable proton is in the COOH group.

The ionization of acetic acid is written with a double arrow to show that it is a *reversible reaction;* that is, *the reaction can occur in both directions.* Initially, a number of CH_3COOH molecules break up into CH_3COO^- and H^+ ions. As time goes on, some of the CH_3COO^- and H^+ ions recombine into CH_3COOH molecules. Eventually, a state is reached in which the acid molecules ionize as fast as the ions recombine. Such a chemical state, in which no net change can be observed (although activity is continuous on the molecular level), is called *chemical equilibrium.* Acetic acid, then, is a weak electrolyte because its ionization in water is incomplete. By contrast, in a hydrochloric acid solution the H^+ and Cl^- ions have no tendency to recombine and form molecular HCl. We use a single arrow to represent complete ionizations.

4.2 Precipitation Reactions

Animation:
Precipitation Reactions
ARIS, Animations

One common type of reaction that occurs in aqueous solution is the *precipitation reaction,* which results in the formation of an insoluble product, or precipitate. A *precipitate* is an insoluble solid that separates from the solution. Precipitation reactions usually involve ionic compounds. For example, when an aqueous solution of lead nitrate [$Pb(NO_3)_2$] is added to an aqueous solution of potassium iodide (KI), a yellow precipitate of lead iodide (PbI_2) is formed:

$$Pb(NO_3)_2(aq) + 2KI(aq) \longrightarrow PbI_2(s) + 2KNO_3(aq)$$

Potassium nitrate remains in solution. Figure 4.3 shows this reaction in progress.

The preceding reaction is an example of a *metathesis reaction* (also called a double-displacement reaction), *a reaction that involves the exchange of parts between the two compounds.* (In this case, the cations in the two compounds exchange anions, so Pb^{2+}

Figure 4.3 *Formation of yellow PbI_2 precipitate as a solution of $Pb(NO_3)_2$ is added to a solution of KI.*

Media

The Interactive Activity Summary in the chapter opening pages enables the student and instructor to see at a glance the media that can be incorporated into the learning process. Within the text, an icon shows the student where the concept in the animation or interactive is introduced. The icon directs the student to the ARIS website for viewing. For the instructor, there are also directions for finding the animation or interactive in the instructor materials.

- **Animations**

  We have created six NEW animations to accompany the library of animations that support the ninth edition. The animations visually bring to life the areas in chemistry that are difficult to understand by reading alone. The animations are marked by an icon and located within ARIS for student use.

- **Interactives**

  Two sets of interactives are available with *Chemistry.* The interactives enable the student to manipulate several variables. The student can "see" how changes affect the topic being studied. The seven topics include stoichiometry, gas laws, kinetics, equilibrium, acid/base, nuclear reactions and radioactivity, and the electrochemical cell. The other set of interactives is simple and fun learning tools that encompass a broad range of topics. All of these interactives are marked by the Interactive Activity icon.

Instructor's Resources

Advanced Placement Chemistry Instructor's Manual

This comprehensive resource was developed specifically for the AP Chemistry course. Each chapter includes a chapter overview highlighting important topics for an Advanced Placement course, detailed chapter discussions, "Math Skills," suggested problems, labs and demonstrations, and numerous figures and illustrations.

Instructor's Testing and Resource CD-ROM

The *Test Bank* is written by John Adams (University of Missouri) and the *Instructor's Solution Manual* is written by Brandon J. Cruickshank (Northern Arizona University) and Raymond Chang. The Test Bank contains over 2000 multiple-choice and short-answer questions. The questions, which are graded in difficulty, are comparable to the problems in the text and include multistep problems that require conceptual analysis. The Test Bank also includes over 200 algorithmically based questions that instructors can edit to create their own test templates. The Test Bank is formatted for integration into the following course management systems: Blackboard and PageOut.

The Instructor's Testing and Resource CD-ROM also contains the electronic file of the **Instructor's Solution Manual.** The solutions to all of the end-of-chapter problems are given in the Manual. This Manual is included on the Instructor's Testing and Resource CD and on ARIS.

ARIS (Assessment, Review, and Instruction System)

McGraw-Hill's Assessment, Review, and Instruction System for *Chemistry* is a complete electronic homework and course management system, designed for greater ease of use than any other system available. Students can access the site for quizzing and viewing the animations and interactives as marked by the icons in the text.

Instructors can create and share course materials and assignments with colleagues with a few clicks of the mouse. Instructors can edit questions, import their own content, and create announcements and due dates for assignments. ARIS has automatic grading and reporting of easy-to-assign homework, quizzing, and testing. Once a student is registered in the course, all student activity within McGraw-Hill's ARIS is automatically recorded and available to the instructor through a fully integrated grade book that can be downloaded to Excel. The book-specific website is found at www.mhhe.com/chang.

McGraw-Hill's ARIS for *Chemistry* contains many useful tools for empowering both students and instructors.

- All assignments and questions are directly tied to text-specific materials in *Chemistry*, but you can edit questions and algorithms, import your own content, and create announcements and due dates for assignments.

- A secured Instructor Center stores your course materials, saving you preparation time.

- ARIS provides you with access to these essential instructor resources for each chapter: PowerPoint lecture outlines, *Instructor's Solution Manual,* and animations.

- ChemSkill Builder, McGraw-Hill's powerful electronic homework system, gives students the tutorial practice they need to master concepts covered in your general chemistry course. *ChemSkill Builder* contains more than 1500 algorithmically generated questions as well as interactive exercises, quizzes, animations, and study tools that correlate directly with each chapter of the text. A record of student work is maintained in an online gradebook so that homework can be easily assigned and factored into the course syllabus.

Overhead Transparencies

Approximately 260 full-color text illustrations are reproduced on acetate for overhead projection.

Chemistry Animations Library

This instructor's DVD enables you to use animations in your classroom in the way that works best for you. Included are over 300 animations and interactives that can be played directly from the DVD or can be imported easily into your own lecture presentation. The animation library is fully searchable, and many animations are included at full-screen size.

Six **NEW** animations have been created by Brandon J. Cruickshank (Northern Arizona University) and added to the current thirty-nine Chang animations. The animations are interactive and specifically support content and concepts in *Chemistry*. The interactive summary and icons in the text show which concepts are animated. Animations are available for use in lecture and PowerPoint presentations and can be used by both instructors and students within ARIS.

Digital Content Library

This multimedia collection of visual resources, available on DVD or CD-ROM, enables instructors to utilize artwork from the text in multiple formats to create customized classroom presentations, visually based tests and quizzes, dynamic course website content, or attractive printed support material. The digital assets on this cross-platform CD-ROM are grouped by chapter within easy-to-use folders. Available are all figures, tables, many photographs, Active Art, Text Edit Art and the PowerPoint lecture presentation.

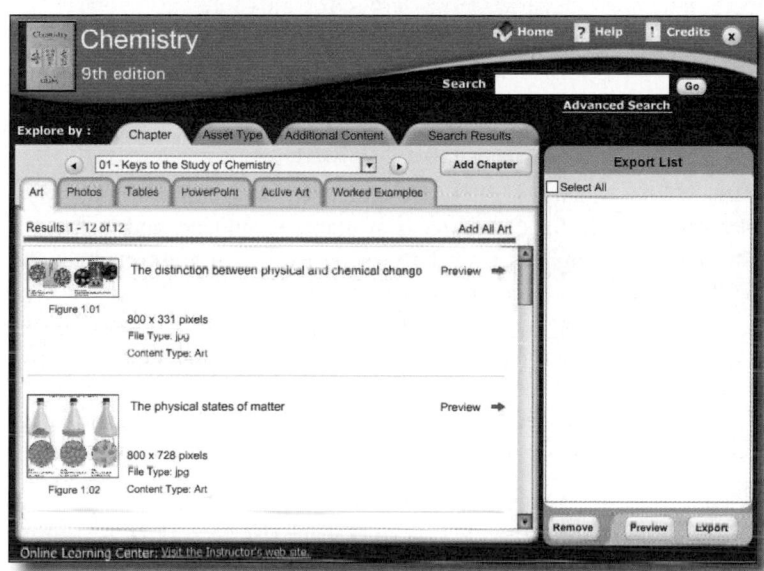

- All **figures, photos, tables,** and **Worked Examples** are provided.
- **Active Art** by Eric Johnson (Ball State University). Active Art presents key art pieces as a series of PowerPoint slides that illustrate difficult concepts in a step-by-step manner. Artwork is broken into small, digestible frames, enabling the instructor to bring each piece into lecture in whatever sequence or format is desired. The figures can be customized in almost any way imaginable. Because every Active Art image is completely ungroupable, any part of an Active Art slide can be used as a "chemical clipart" in any other PowerPoint presentation, or as a component in your own rendition of a figure. The Active Art is available on the Digital Content Manager DVD or CD-ROM.
- **Text Edit Art** enables an instructor to revise or delete labels on a figure as desired within PowerPoint to create customized presentations or for use in tests. Labels can be moved, deleted, or revised; the leader lines can be moved or deleted, separate from the image and labels; and images can be stretched or enlarged. The Text Edit Art is available on the Digital Content Manager DVD or CD-ROM.
- **PowerPoint Lecture Presentation** by J. David Robertson (University of Missouri). Instructors who adopt *Chemistry* will find that this presentation not only saves time but also enables them to create a visually stunning lecture presentation. The web-based PowerPoint lecture includes notes for the entire course, visuals from the ninth edition, and animations embedded at the appropriate points in the program. Use this complete lecture outline, or revise the lecture to fit your own course. The PowerPoint Lecture Presentation is available on the Digital Content Manager DVD or CD-ROM.

Annotated Instructor's Edition

The Annotated Instructor's Edition includes all resources available to the instructor marked by icons located in the margins of the text. Information is provided with regard to the integration of media (animations, interactives, ARIS) and instructions as to where the instructor will find the various media. The difficulty level of the end-of-chapter problems and the various chemical disciplines to which the problems are related is indicated. Information on quality demonstration videos, tips for the instructor, and the icons marking the digital assets available on the Digital Content Manager are provided.

Course Management Systems

The Test Bank questions and end-of-chapter problems are available in Blackboard and PageOut. Ask your sales representative how to receive material in the system of your choice.

Course Specific PageOut

Designed specifically to help you with your individual course needs, PageOut will assist you in integrating your syllabus with chemistry, and state-of-the-art new media tools. At the heart of PageOut you will find integrated multimedia and a full-scale ARIS site. You can upload your original test questions and create your own custom designs. More than 60,000 professors have chosen PageOut to create customized course websites.

Primis LabBase

By Joseph Lagowski (the University of Texas of Austin). More than 40 general chemistry experiments are available in this database collection of general lab experiments from the *Journal of Chemical Education* and experiments used by Professor Lagowski at the University of Texas at Austin, enabling instructors to customize their lab manuals.

General Chemistry Laboratory Manual

By Petra A. M. van Koppen (University of California, Santa Barbara). This is the definitive lab manual for the two-semester general chemistry course. The manual contains 21 experiments that cover the most commonly assigned experiments for the introductory chemistry course.

Cooperative Chemistry Laboratory Manual

By Melanie Cooper (Clemson University). This innovative guide features open-ended problems designed to simulate experience in a research lab. Working in groups, students investigate one problem over a period of several weeks, so that they might complete three or four projects during the semester, rather than one preprogrammed experiment per class. The emphasis here is on experimental design, analysis problem solving, and communication.

Student Resources

Advanced Placement Chemistry Test Preparation Guide

Written specifically for students this Guide is designed to be used with the best selling college chemistry textbook authored by Raymond Chang. Coupled with Chemistry, 9th Edition this guide provides students with the necessary knowledge and skills to achieve a "5" on the Chemistry AP Exam.

This 3-part Guide includes:

- Two complete *practice exams* with answers and thorough explanations.
- Comprehensive tips on writing essays for the *free-response questions.*
- Practice questions with answers and complete explanations.
- Special "Take Note" sections for the most important material.
- Figures and tables to illustrate key points.
- Chapter concepts, skills and summaries that highlight and reinforce key chapter material.

Student Solutions Manual

By Brandon J. Cruickshank (Northern Arizona University) and Raymond Chang. This supplement contains detailed solutions and explanations for all even-numbered problems in the main text. The manual also includes a detailed discussion of different types of problems and approaches to solving chemical problems and tutorial solutions for many of the end-of-chapter problems in the text, along with strategies for solving them.

Student Study Guide

By Kim Woodrum (University of Kentucky). This valuable ancillary contains material to help the student practice problem-solving skills. For each section of a chapter, the author provides study objectives and a summary of the corresponding text. Following the summary are sample problems with detailed solutions. Each chapter has true-false questions and self-test, with all answers provided at the end of the chapter.

ARIS (Assessment, Review, and Instruction System)

McGraw-Hill's Assessment, Review, and Instruction System for *Chemistry* is available to students and instructors using this text. This user-friendly program enables students to complete their homework online, as assigned by their instructors. This text-specific website offers quizzing and animations for further study. For the students, ARIS also features interactive quizzes, animation center, interactive center for each chapter of the text, and an interactive glossary with audio.

- **Chang Animations**
  By Brandon J. Cruickshank (Northern Arizona University). Six new animations have been added to the current 39 animations. The animations are interactive and specifically support content and concepts in chemistry. The interactive summary and icons in the text show which concepts are animated. Animations can be used by both instructors and students within ARIS.

- **Interactives**
  The Interactives marked by an icon in the text are available within ARIS. They allow manipulation of variables for specific chemical concepts including stoichiometry, gas laws, kinetics, equilibrium, and acid/base. There are also available interactives that are simple and fun to help with learning many concepts.

Chang Chemistry Resource Card

Our resource card is an easy, quick source of information on general chemistry. The student will find the periodic table, basic tables, and key equations within reach without having to consult the text.

ChemSkill Builder

ChemSkill Builder generates questions for students for every topic in the general chemistry course. The questions are presented in a randomized fashion with a constant mix of variables so that no two students will receive the same questions. The application provides feedback for students when incorrect answers are entered, and the answers can be submitted online to an instructor for grading.

Understanding Chemistry by Lovett/Chang

This short text is specially written in a friendly and informative manner for easy learning of the most important chemical concepts. The authors break the information down into language for a nonscientist. Cartoons were created to provide a learning tool to remember basic concepts.

Acknowledgments

I would like to thank the following reviewers and symposium participants, whose comments were of great help to me in preparing this revision:

Rex D. Ackerson *Northern Oklahoma College*

Jeff Anderson *Murray State University*

Jeff Appling *Clemson University*

Elizabeth Arendt *Community College of Rhode Island*

Alexandru Balaban *Texas A & M University–Galveston*

David Ball *Cleveland State University*

Mufeed Basti *North Carolina A & T State University*

Alan Bates *University of Massachusetts–Dartmouth College*

Colin Bateman *Brevard Community College*

Sr. Joanne Bauer *Xavier University*

Paul Benoit *University of Arkansas*

Laine Berghout *Weber State University*

Conrad Bergo *East Stroudsburg University*

Richard Biagioni *Missouri State University*

Christine Bilicki *Pasadena City College*

Dan Black *Snow College*

John Blaha *Columbia State Community College*

Jeffrey O. Boles *Tennessee Technological University*

Wayne Bosma *Bradley University*

David Boyajain *Palomar College*

Robert G. Bryant *University of Virginia*

Brian Buffin *Western Michigan University*

Stuart Burris *Western Kentucky University*

Bindu Chakravarty *Houston Community College*

David Chatfield *Florida International University*

Joann Chickering *Bellevue Community College*

Paul Chirik *Cornell University*

Bill Cleaver *University of Vermont*

W. Lin Coker III *Campbell University*

Robert Cordell *Heidelberg College*

Ray Crawford *San Jacinto College, South*

Gary DeBoer *LeTorneau University*

Pat Delaney *Worcester Polytechnic Institute*

Yuanjian Deng *Texas Southern University*

Mary Kate Donais *Saint Anselm College*

Bill Durham *University of Arkansas*

Jeffrey Evans *University of Southern Mississippi*

Dr. Ewane *Houston Community College*

Ted Fickel *Los Angeles Valley College*

Neil Fitzgerald *Marist College*

Doug Flournoy *Indian Hills Community College*

Krishna Foster *California State University–Los Angeles*

Kristeen Fukunaga *Palomar College*

Daquing Gao *Queensborough Community College*

Roy Garvey *North Dakota State University*

Natarajan Geetha *Palomar College*

Alicia Glatfelter *Wilkes University*

Joel Goldberg *University of Vermont*

Harold Goldwhite *California State University–Los Angeles*

Lisa Goss *Idaho State University*

Gary Gray *University of Alabama–Birmingham*

Gregory R. Hale *University of Texas at Arlington*

Dale Hawley *Kansas State University*

Sherman Henzel *Monroe Community College*

Narayan Hosmane *Northern Illinois University*

Larry Houk *University of Memphis*

Byron Howell *Tyler Junior College*

Wendy Innis-Whitehouse *University of Texas–Pan American*

Richard Jarman *College of DuPage*

Eric Johnson *Ball State University*

Stacy Jones *Northwest Mississippi Community College*

Carolyn Judd *Houston Community College*

Don Jurkowitz *Community College of Rhode Island*

Kirk Kawagoe *Fresno City College*

Robert Keil *Moorpark College*

Neil Kestner *Louisiana State University*

Tracy Knowles *Lexington Community College*

Patrick Kolniak *Louisiana State University*

Gerald Korenowski *Rensselaer Polytechnic Institute*

Peter Krieger *Palm Beach Community College*

Bette A. Kreuz *University of Michigan–Dearborn*

Lennart H. Kullberg *Winthrop University*

Jothi V. Kumar *North Carolina A & T State University*
Brian Lamp *Truman State University*
John Larese *University of Tennessee–Knoxville*
Laurence Lavelle *University of California–Los Angeles*
Daniel Lawson *University of Michigan–Dearborn*
Clifford LeMaster *Boise State University*
Michael Lerner *Oregon State*
Shannon Lieb *Butler University*
Gerhard Lind *Metro State College of Denver*
Arthur Low *Tarleton University*
Rudy Luck *Michigan Technological University*
Yinfa Ma *University of Missouri–Rolla*
Mark Matthews *Jefferson Community College*
Richard Nafshun *Oregon State University*
Brian McBurnett *California State University–Chico*
Debbie McClinton *Brevard Community College*
Donald Mencer *Wilkes University*
Dave Metcalf *University of Virginia*
Joyce Miller *San Jacinto College*
Randy Miller *California State University–Chico*
Renee R. Muro *Oakland Community College*
Chip Nataro *LaFayette College*
David Newman *Bowling Green State University*
Anne Nickel *Milwaukee School of Engineering*
Daphne Norton *Emory University*
Greg Oswald *North Dakota State University*
Tom Otieno *Eastern Kentucky University*
Jason Overby *College of Charleston*
Gholam Pahlavan *Houston Community College*
Ruben Dario Parra *DePaul University*
Manoj Patil *Western Iowa Technical Community College*
Les Pesterfield *Western Kentucky University*
Karl Peterson *University of Wisconsin–River Falls*
Gary Pfeiffer *Ohio University–Athens*
Joanna Piotrwoska *Normandale Community College*
Henry Po *California State University–Long Beach*
Steve Pruett *Jefferson Community College*
Judy Ratliff *Murray State University*
Carey S. Reed *Penn State–Altoona*
Jerry Reed-Mundell *Cleveland State University*
Michelle Richards-Babb *West Virginia University*
B. Ken Robertson *University of Missouri–Rolla*
Rhonda Robertson *Jones Junior College*
Ellen Roskes *Villa Julie College*
Tim Royappa *University of West Florida*

James Rozell *Tyler Junior College*
Susan Rutkowsky *Drexel University*
Arthur Salido *Mercer University*
Karen Sanchez *Florida Community College at Jacksonville*
Dennis Sardella *Boston College*
Paul Schumacher *United States Military Academy*
Nelson Scott *California State Polytechnic University*
Will Seltzer *University of Alabama–Huntsville*
Supriya Sihi *Houston Community College*
Alka Shukla *Houston Community College*
Shyam Shukla *Lamar University*
Andy Slagle *Rose State College*
Sheila Smith *University of Michigan–Dearborn*
Kathie Snyder *Winthrop University*
Larry O. Spreer *University of the Pacific*
Alan Stolzenberg *West Virginia University*
Kathy Thrush *Villanova University*
Wayne Tikkanen *California State University–Los Angeles*
Richard Toomey *Northwest Missouri State University*
Frank Torre *Springfield College*
Anthony Toste *Missouri State University*
Kris Varazo *Francis Marion University*
Maria Villarba *Glendale Community College*
Dragic Vukomanovic *University of Massachusetts–Dartmouth*
Rosie Walker *Metropolitan State College of Denver*
Sheryl Wallace *South Plains College*
Jeffrey Wardeska *East Tennessee State University*
Phil Watson *Oregon State University*
David Weiss *University of Colorado at Colorado Springs*
Tracy Willis *Texas Southern University*
Klaus Woelk *University of Missouri–Rolla*
Frank Woodruff *University of Southern Mississippi*
John Young *Mississippi State University*
James Zimmerman *Missouri State University*

I would also like to thank the following individuals for for their contributions to the end-of-chapter problems:
Nancy Gardner *California State University–Long Beach*
John Hagen *California Polytechnic State University–San Luis Obispo*
Michael Jones *Texas Tech University*
Jason Overby *College of Charleston*
Philip Reid *University of Washington*

As always, I have benefited much from discussions with my colleagues at Williams College and correspondence with many instructors here and abroad.

It is a pleasure to acknowledge the support given to me by the following members of McGraw-Hill's College Division: Tammy Ben, Doug Dinardo, Chad Grall, Tracy Konrardy, Kara Kudronowicz, Marty Lange, Michael Lange, and Kurt Strand. In particular, I would like to mention Gloria Schiesl for supervising the production under the tight schedule, David Hash for the book design, John Leland for photo research, Jake Theobald and Judi David for the media, and Tami Hodge, the marketing manager, for her suggestions and encouragement. I also thank my sponsoring editor, Thomas Timp, and publisher, Kent Peterson, for their advice and assistance. Finally, my special thanks go to Shirley Oberbroeckling, the developmental editor, for her care and enthusiasm for the project, and supervision at every stage of the writing of this edition.

—*Raymond Chang*

A Note to the Student

General chemistry is commonly perceived to be more difficult than most other subjects. There is some justification for this perception. For one thing, chemistry has a very specialized vocabulary. At first, studying chemistry is like learning a new language. Furthermore, some of the concepts are abstract. Nevertheless, with diligence you can complete this course successfully, and you might even enjoy it. Here are some suggestions to help you form good study habits and master the material in this text.

- Attend classes regularly and take careful notes.

- If possible, always review the topics discussed in class the same day they are covered in class. Use this book to supplement your notes.

- Think critically. Ask yourself if you really understand the meaning of a term or the use of an equation. A good way to test your understanding is to explain a concept to a classmate or some other person.

- Do not hesitate to ask your instructor or your teaching assistant for help.

The ninth edition tools for *Chemistry* are designed to enable you to do well in your general chemistry course. The following guide explains how to take full advantage of the text, technology, and other tools.

- Before delving into the chapter, read the chapter *outline* and the chapter *introduction* to get a sense of the important topics. Use the outline to organize your notetaking in class.

- Use the *Interactive Activity Icon* as a guide to review challenging concepts in motion. The animations and interactives are valuable in presenting a concept and enabling the student to manipulate or choose steps so full understanding can happen.

- At the end of each chapter you will find a summary of facts and concepts, and a list of key words, all of which will help you review for exams.

- Definitions of the key words can be studied in context on the pages cited in the end-of-chapter list or in the glossary at the back of the book.

- ARIS houses an extraordinary amount of resources. Go to www.mhhe.com/physsci/chemistry/chang and click on the appropriate cover to explore chapter quizzes, animations, interactivities, simulations, and more.

- Careful study of the worked-out examples in the body of each chapter will improve your ability to analyze problems and correctly carry out the calculations needed to solve them. Also take the time to work through the practice exercise that follows each example to be sure you understand how to solve the type of problem illustrated in the example. The answers to the practice exercises appear at the end of the chapter, following the homework problems. For additional practice, you can turn to similar homework problems referred to in the margin next to the example.

- The questions and problems at the end of the chapter are organized by section.

- For even more practice problems, use *ChemSkill Builder*. ChemSkill Builder is a problem-solving tutorial with hundreds of problems that include feedback.

- The back inside cover shows a list of important figures and tables with page references. This index makes it convenient to quickly look up information when you are solving problems or studying related subjects in different chapters.

If you follow these suggestions and stay up-to-date with your assignments, you should find that chemistry is challenging, but less difficult and much more interesting than you expected.

—*Raymond Chang*

Chemistry

1

A hydrogen-filled balloon exploding when heated with a flame. The hydrogen gas reacts with oxygen in air to form water vapor. Chemistry is the study of the properties of matter and the changes it undergoes. The models show hydrogen, oxygen, and water molecules.

Chemistry
The Study of Change

A LOOK AHEAD

- We begin with a brief introduction to the study of chemistry and describe its role in our modern society. (1.1 and 1.2)

- Next, we become familiar with the scientific method, which is a systematic approach to research in all scientific disciplines. (1.3)

- We define matter and note that a pure substance can either be an element or a compound. We distinguish between a homogeneous mixture and a heterogeneous mixture. We also learn that, in principle, all matter can exist in one of three states: solid, liquid, and gas. (1.4 and 1.5)

- To characterize a substance, we need to know its physical properties, which can be observed without changing its identity and chemical properties, which can be demonstrated only by chemical changes. (1.6)

- Being an experimental science, chemistry involves measurements. We learn the basic SI units and use the SI-derived units for quantities like volume and density. We also become familiar with the three temperature scales: Celsius, Fahrenheit, and Kelvin. (1.7)

- Chemical calculations often involve very large or very small numbers and a convenient way to deal with these numbers is the scientific notation. In calculations or measurements, every quantity must show the proper number of significant figures, which are the meaningful digits. (1.8)

- Finally, we learn that dimensional analysis is useful in chemical calculations. By carrying the units through the entire sequence of calculations, all the units will cancel except the desired one. (1.9)

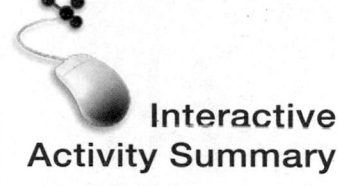

Interactive Activity Summary

1. Interactivity: Substances and Mixtures (1.4)
2. Interactivity: Elements (1.4)
3. Interactivity: SI Base Units (1.7)
4. Interactivity: Unit Prefixes (1.7)
5. Interactivity: Density (1.7)
6. Interactivity: Accuracy and Precision (1.8)
7. Interactivity: Dimensional Analysis (1.9)

Chemistry is an active, evolving science that has vital importance to our world, in both the realm of nature and the realm of society. Its roots are ancient, but as we will soon see, chemistry is every bit a modern science.

We will begin our study of chemistry at the macroscopic level, where we can see and measure the materials of which our world is made. In this chapter we will discuss the scientific method, which provides the framework for research not only in chemistry but in all other sciences as well. Next we will discover how scientists define and characterize matter. Then we will familiarize ourselves with the systems of measurement used in the laboratory. Finally, we will spend some time learning how to handle numerical results of chemical measurements and solve numerical problems. In Chapter 2 we will begin to explore the microscopic world of atoms and molecules.

The Chinese characters for chemistry mean "The study of change."

1.1 Chemistry: A Science for the Twenty-First Century

Chemistry is *the study of matter and the changes it undergoes.* Chemistry is often called the central science, because a basic knowledge of chemistry is essential for students of biology, physics, geology, ecology, and many other subjects. Indeed, it is central to our way of life; without it, we would be living shorter lives in what we would consider primitive conditions, without automobiles, electricity, computers, CDs, and many other everyday conveniences.

Although chemistry is an ancient science, its modern foundation was laid in the nineteenth century, when intellectual and technological advances enabled scientists to break down substances into ever smaller components and consequently to explain many of their physical and chemical characteristics. The rapid development of increasingly sophisticated technology throughout the twentieth century has given us even greater means to study things that cannot be seen with the naked eye. Using computers and special microscopes, for example, chemists can analyze the structure of atoms and molecules—the fundamental units on which the study of chemistry is based—and design new substances with specific properties, such as drugs and environmentally friendly consumer products.

As we enter the twenty-first century, it is fitting to ask what part the central science will have in this century. Almost certainly, chemistry will continue to play a pivotal role in all areas of science and technology. Before plunging into the study of matter and its transformation, let us consider some of the frontiers that chemists are currently exploring (Figure 1.1). Whatever your reasons for taking general chemistry, a good knowledge of the subject will better enable you to appreciate its impact on society and on you as an individual.

Health and Medicine

Three major advances in the past century have enabled us to prevent and treat diseases. They are public health measures establishing sanitation systems to protect vast numbers of people from infectious disease; surgery with anesthesia, enabling physicians to cure potentially fatal conditions, such as an inflamed appendix; and the introduction of vaccines and antibiotics that make it possible to prevent diseases spread by microbes. Gene therapy promises to be the fourth revolution in medicine. (A gene is the basic unit of inheritance.) Several thousand known conditions, including cystic fibrosis and hemophilia, are carried by inborn damage to a single gene. Many other ailments, such as cancer, heart disease, AIDS, and arthritis, result to an extent from impairment of one or more genes involved in the body's defenses. In gene therapy, a selected healthy gene is delivered to a patient's cell to cure or ease such disorders. To carry out such a procedure, a doctor must have a sound knowledge of the chemical properties of the molecular components involved. The decoding of the human genome, which comprises all of the genetic material in the human body and plays an essential part in gene therapy, relies largely on chemical techniques.

Chemists in the pharmaceutical industry are researching potent drugs with few or no side effects to treat cancer, AIDS, and many other diseases as well as drugs to increase the number of successful organ transplants. On a broader scale, improved understanding of the mechanism of aging will lead to a longer and healthier life span for the world's population.

Energy and the Environment

Energy is a by-product of many chemical processes, and as the demand for energy continues to increase, both in technologically advanced countries like the United

Figure 1.1 *(a) The output from an automated DNA sequencing machine. Each lane displays the sequence (indicated by different colors) obtained with a separate DNA sample. (b) Photovoltaic cells. (c) A silicon wafer being processed. (d) The leaf on the left was taken from a tobacco plant that was not genetically engineered but was exposed to tobacco horn worms. The leaf on the right was genetically engineered and is barely attacked by the worms. The same technique can be applied to protect the leaves of other types of plants.*

States and in developing ones like China, chemists are actively trying to find new energy sources. Currently the major sources of energy are fossil fuels (coal, petroleum, and natural gas). The estimated reserves of these fuels will last us another 50–100 years, at the present rate of consumption, so it is urgent that we find alternatives.

Solar energy promises to be a viable source of energy for the future. Every year Earth's surface receives about 10 times as much energy from sunlight as is contained in all of the known reserves of coal, oil, natural gas, and uranium combined. But much of this energy is "wasted" because it is reflected back into space. For the past 30 years, intense research efforts have shown that solar energy can be harnessed effectively in two ways. One is the conversion of sunlight directly to electricity using devices called *photovoltaic cells.* The other is to use sunlight to obtain hydrogen from water. The hydrogen can then be fed into a *fuel cell* to generate electricity. Although our understanding of the scientific process of converting solar energy to electricity has advanced, the technology has not yet improved to the point where we can produce electricity on a large scale at an economically acceptable cost. By 2050, however, it has been predicted that solar energy will supply over 50 percent of our power needs.

Another potential source of energy is nuclear fission, but because of environmental concerns about the radioactive wastes from fission processes, the future of the nuclear industry in the United States is uncertain. Chemists can help to devise better ways to dispose of nuclear waste. Nuclear fusion, the process that occurs in the sun and other stars, generates huge amounts of energy without producing much dangerous radioactive waste. In another 50 years, nuclear fusion will likely be a significant source of energy.

Energy production and energy utilization are closely tied to the quality of our environment. A major disadvantage of burning fossil fuels is that they give off carbon dioxide, which is a *greenhouse gas* (that is, it promotes the heating of Earth's atmosphere), along with sulfur dioxide and nitrogen oxides, which result in acid rain and smog. (Harnessing solar energy has no such detrimental effects on the environment.) By using fuel-efficient automobiles and more effective catalytic converters, we should be able to drastically reduce harmful auto emissions and improve the air quality in areas with heavy traffic. In addition, electric cars, powered by durable, long-lasting batteries, and hybrid cars, powered by both batteries and gasoline, should become more prevalent, and their use will help to minimize air pollution.

Materials and Technology

Chemical research and development in the twentieth century have provided us with new materials that have profoundly improved the quality of our lives and helped to advance technology in countless ways. A few examples are polymers (including rubber and nylon), ceramics (such as cookware), liquid crystals (like those in electronic displays), adhesives (used in your Post-It notes), and coatings (for example, latex paint).

What is in store for the near future? One likely possibility is room-temperature *superconductors.* Electricity is carried by copper cables, which are not perfect conductors. Consequently, about 20 percent of electrical energy is lost in the form of heat between the power station and our homes. This is a tremendous waste. Superconductors are materials that have no electrical resistance and can therefore conduct electricity with no energy loss. Although the phenomenon of superconductivity at very low temperatures (more than 400 degrees Fahrenheit below the freezing point of water) has been known for over 80 years, a major breakthrough in the mid-1980s demonstrated that it is possible to make materials that act as superconductors at or near room temperature. Chemists have helped to design and synthesize new materials that show promise in this quest. The next 30 years will see high-temperature superconductors being applied on a large scale in magnetic resonance imaging (MRI), levitated trains, and nuclear fusion.

If we had to name one technological advance that has shaped our lives more than any other, it would be the computer. The "engine" that drives the ongoing computer revolution is the microprocessor—the tiny silicon chip that has inspired countless inventions, such as laptop computers and fax machines. The performance of a microprocessor is judged by the speed with which it carries out mathematical operations, such as addition. The pace of progress is such that since their introduction, microprocessors have doubled in speed every 18 months. The quality of any microprocessor depends on the purity of the silicon chip and on the ability to add the desired amount of other substances, and chemists play an important role in the research and development of silicon chips. For the future, scientists have begun to explore the prospect of "molecular computing," that is, replacing silicon with molecules. The advantages are that certain molecules can be made to respond to light, rather than to electrons, so that we would have optical computers rather than electronic computers. With proper genetic engineering, scientists can synthesize such molecules using microorganisms instead of large factories. Optical computers also would have much greater storage capacity than electronic computers.

Food and Agriculture

How can the world's rapidly increasing population be fed? In poor countries, agricultural activities occupy about 80 percent of the workforce, and half of an average family budget is spent on foodstuffs. This is a tremendous drain on a nation's resources. The factors that affect agricultural production are the richness of the soil, insects and diseases that damage crops, and weeds that compete for nutrients. Besides irrigation, farmers rely on fertilizers and pesticides to increase crop yield. Since the 1950s, treatment for crops suffering from pest infestations has sometimes been the indiscriminate application of potent chemicals. Such measures have often had serious detrimental effects on the environment. Even the excessive use of fertilizers is harmful to the land, water, and air.

To meet the food demands of the twenty-first century, new and novel approaches in farming must be devised. It has already been demonstrated that, through biotechnology, it is possible to grow larger and better crops. These techniques can be applied to many different farm products, not only for improved yields, but also for better frequency, that is, more crops every year. For example, it is known that a certain bacterium produces a protein molecule that is toxic to leaf-eating caterpillars. Incorporating the gene that codes for the toxin into crops enables plants to protect themselves so that pesticides are not necessary. Researchers have also found a way to prevent pesky insects from reproducing. Insects communicate with one another by emitting and reacting to special molecules called pheromones. By identifying and synthesizing pheromones used in mating, it is possible to interfere with the normal reproductive cycle of common pests; for example, by inducing insects to mate too soon or tricking female insects into mating with sterile males. Moreover, chemists can devise ways to increase the production of fertilizers that are less harmful to the environment and substances that would selectively kill weeds.

1.2 The Study of Chemistry

Compared with other subjects, chemistry is commonly believed to be more difficult, at least at the introductory level. There is some justification for this perception; for one thing, chemistry has a very specialized vocabulary. However, even if this is your first course in chemistry, you already have more familiarity with the subject than you may realize. In everyday conversations we hear words that have a chemical connection, although they may not be used in the scientifically correct sense. Examples are "electronic," "quantum leap," "equilibrium," "catalyst," "chain reaction," and "critical mass." Moreover, if you cook, then you are a practicing chemist! From experience gained in the kitchen, you know that oil and water do not mix and that boiling water left on the stove will evaporate. You apply chemical and physical principles when you use baking soda to leaven bread, choose a pressure cooker to shorten the time it takes to prepare soup, add meat tenderizer to a pot roast, squeeze lemon juice over sliced pears to prevent them from turning brown or over fish to minimize its odor, and add vinegar to the water in which you are going to poach eggs. Every day we observe such changes without thinking about their chemical nature. The purpose of this course

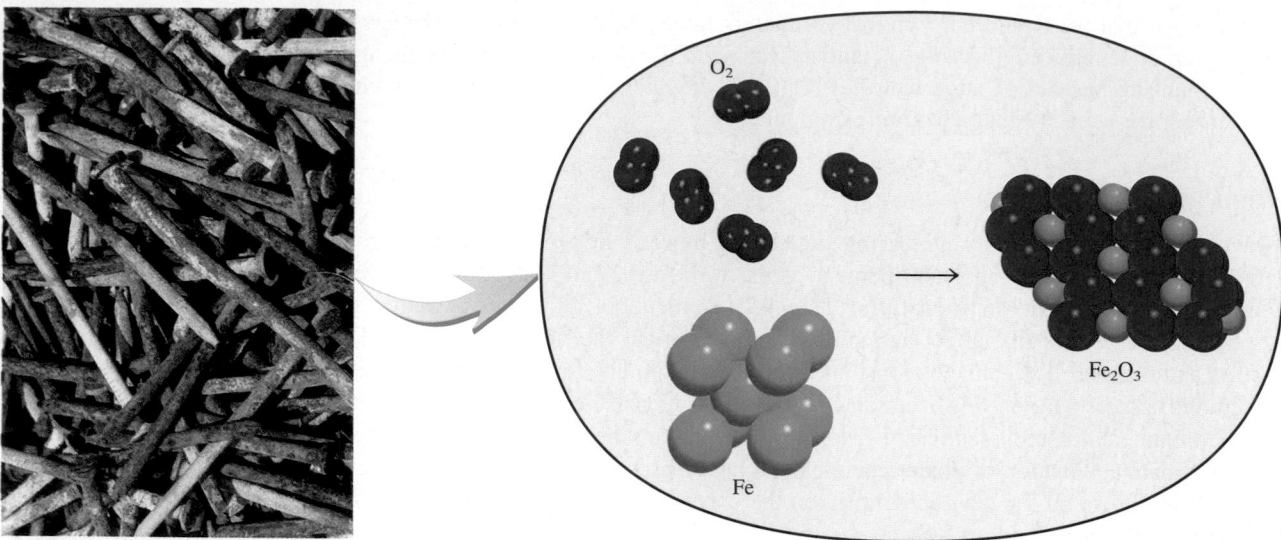

Figure 1.2 *A simplified molecular view of rust (Fe$_2$O$_3$) formation from iron atoms (Fe) and oxygen molecules (O$_2$). In reality, the process requires water and rust also contains water molecules.*

is to make you think like a chemist, to look at the *macroscopic world*—the things we can see, touch, and measure directly—and visualize the particles and events of the *microscopic world* that we cannot experience without modern technology and our imaginations.

At first some students find it confusing that their chemistry instructor and textbook seem to be continually shifting back and forth between the macroscopic and microscopic worlds. Just keep in mind that the data for chemical investigations most often come from observations of large-scale phenomena, but the explanations frequently lie in the unseen and partially imagined microscopic world of atoms and molecules. In other words, chemists often *see* one thing (in the macroscopic world) and *think* another (in the microscopic world). Looking at the rusted nails in Figure 1.2, for example, a chemist might think about the basic properties of individual atoms of iron and how these units interact with other atoms and molecules to produce the observed change.

1.3 The Scientific Method

All sciences, including the social sciences, employ variations of what is called the **scientific method,** *a systematic approach to research.* For example, a psychologist who wants to know how noise affects people's ability to learn chemistry and a chemist interested in measuring the heat given off when hydrogen gas burns in air would follow roughly the same procedure in carrying out their investigations. The first step is to carefully define the problem. The next step includes performing experiments, making careful observations, and recording information, or *data,* about the system—the part of the universe that is under investigation. (In the examples just discussed, the systems are the group of people the psychologist will study and a mixture of hydrogen and air.)

The data obtained in a research study may be both **qualitative,** *consisting of general observations about the system,* and **quantitative,** *comprising numbers obtained*

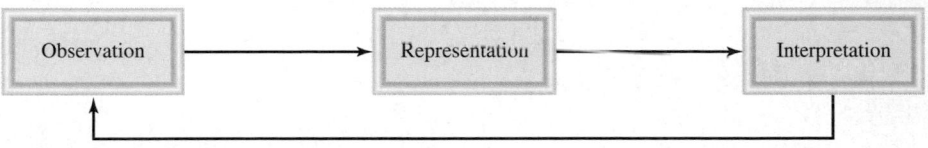

Figure 1.3 *The three levels of studying chemistry and their relationships. Observation deals with events in the macroscopic world; atoms and molecules constitute the microscopic world. Representation is a scientific shorthand for describing an experiment in symbols and chemical equations. Chemists use their knowledge of atoms and molecules to explain an observed phenomenon.*

by various measurements of the system. Chemists generally use standardized symbols and equations in recording their measurements and observations. This form of representation not only simplifies the process of keeping records, but also provides a common basis for communication with other chemists.

When the experiments have been completed and the data have been recorded, the next step in the scientific method is interpretation, meaning that the scientist attempts to explain the observed phenomenon. Based on the data that were gathered, the researcher formulates a ***hypothesis,*** *a tentative explanation for a set of observations.* Further experiments are devised to test the validity of the hypothesis in as many ways as possible, and the process begins anew. Figure 1.3 summarizes the main steps of the research process.

After a large amount of data has been collected, it is often desirable to summarize the information in a concise way, as a law. In science, a ***law*** *is a concise verbal or mathematical statement of a relationship between phenomena that is always the same under the same conditions.* For example, Sir Isaac Newton's second law of motion, which you may remember from high school science, says that force equals mass times acceleration ($F = ma$). What this law means is that an increase in the mass or in the acceleration of an object will always increase its force proportionally, and a decrease in mass or acceleration will always decrease the force.

Hypotheses that survive many experimental tests of their validity may evolve into theories. A ***theory*** *is a unifying principle that explains a body of facts and/or those laws that are based on them.* Theories, too, are constantly being tested. If a theory is disproved by experiment, then it must be discarded or modified so that it becomes consistent with experimental observations. Proving or disproving a theory can take years, even centuries, in part because the necessary technology may not be available. Atomic theory, which we will study in Chapter 2, is a case in point. It took more than 2000 years to work out this fundamental principle of chemistry proposed by Democritus, an ancient Greek philosopher. A more contemporary example is the Big Bang theory of the origin of the universe discussed on page 10.

Scientific progress is seldom, if ever, made in a rigid, step-by-step fashion. Sometimes a law precedes a theory; sometimes it is the other way around. Two scientists may start working on a project with exactly the same objective, but will end up taking drastically different approaches. Scientists are, after all, human beings, and their modes of thinking and working are very much influenced by their background, training, and personalities.

The development of science has been irregular and sometimes even illogical. Great discoveries are usually the result of the cumulative contributions and experience of many workers, even though the credit for formulating a theory or a law is usually given to only one individual. There is, of course, an element of luck involved in scientific discoveries, but it has been said that "chance favors the prepared mind." It takes an alert and well-trained person to recognize the significance of an accidental discovery and to take full advantage of it. More often than not, the public learns only of spectacular scientific breakthroughs. For every success story, however, there are hundreds of cases in which scientists have spent years working on projects that

CHEMISTRY
in Action

Primordial Helium and the Big Bang Theory

Where did we come from? How did the universe begin? Humans have asked these questions for as long as we have been able to think. The search for answers provides an example of the scientific method.

In the 1940s the Russian-American physicist George Gamow hypothesized that our universe burst into being billions of years ago in a gigantic explosion, or *Big Bang*. In its earliest moments, the universe occupied a tiny volume and was unimaginably hot. This blistering fireball of radiation mixed with microscopic particles of matter gradually cooled enough for atoms to form. Under the influence of gravity, these atoms clumped together to make billions of galaxies including our own Milky Way Galaxy.

Gamow's idea is interesting and highly provocative. It has been tested experimentally in a number of ways. First, measurements showed that the universe is expanding; that is, galaxies are all moving away from one another at high speeds. This fact is consistent with the universe's explosive birth. By imagining the expansion running backward, like a movie in reverse, astronomers have deduced that the universe was born about 13 billion years ago. The second observation that supports Gamow's hypothesis is the detection of *cosmic background radiation*. Over billions of years, the searingly hot universe has cooled down to a mere 3 K (or −270°C)! At this temperature, most energy is in the microwave region. Because the Big Bang would have occurred simultaneously throughout the tiny volume of the forming universe, the radiation it generated should have filled the entire universe. Thus, the radiation should be the same in any direction that we observe. Indeed, the microwave signals recorded by astronomers are *independent* of direction.

The third piece of evidence supporting Gamow's hypothesis is the discovery of primordial helium. Scientists believe that helium and hydrogen (the lightest elements) were the first elements formed in the early stages of cosmic evolution. (The heavier elements, like carbon, nitrogen, and oxygen, are thought to have originated later via nuclear reactions involving hydrogen and helium in the center of stars.) If so, a diffuse gas of hydrogen and helium would have spread through the early universe before much of the galaxies formed. In 1995

A color photo of some distant galaxy, including the position of a quasar.

astronomers analyzed ultraviolet light from a distant *quasar* (a strong source of light and radio signals that is thought to be an exploding galaxy at the edge of the universe) and found that some of the light was absorbed by helium atoms on the way to Earth. Because this particular quasar is more than 10 billion light-years away (a light-year is the distance traveled by light in a year), the light reaching Earth reveals events that look place 10 billion years ago. Why wasn't the more abundant hydrogen detected? A hydrogen atom has only one electron, which is stripped by the light from a quasar in a process known as *ionization*. Ionized hydrogen atoms cannot absorb any of the quasar's light. A helium atom, on the other hand, has two electrons. Radiation may strip a helium atom of one electron, but not always both. Singly ionized helium atoms can still absorb light and are therefore detectable.

Proponents of Gamow's explanation rejoiced at the detection of helium in the far reaches of the universe. In recognition of all the supporting evidence, scientists now refer to Gamow's hypothesis as the Big Bang theory.

ultimately led to a dead end, and in which positive achievements came only after many wrong turns and at such a slow pace that they went unheralded. Yet even the dead ends contribute something to the continually growing body of knowledge about the physical universe. It is the love of the search that keeps many scientists in the laboratory.

1.4 Classifications of Matter

We defined chemistry at the beginning of the chapter as the study of matter and the changes it undergoes. *Matter* is *anything that occupies space and has mass.* Matter includes things we can see and touch (such as water, earth, and trees), as well as things we cannot (such as air). Thus, everything in the universe has a "chemical" connection.

Chemists distinguish among several subcategories of matter based on composition and properties. The classifications of matter include substances, mixtures, elements, and compounds, as well as atoms and molecules, which we will consider in Chapter 2.

Substances and Mixtures

A **substance** is *a form of matter that has a definite (constant) composition and distinct properties.* Examples are water, ammonia, table sugar (sucrose), gold, and oxygen. Substances differ from one another in composition and can be identified by their appearance, smell, taste, and other properties.

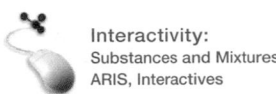

Interactivity:
Substances and Mixtures
ARIS, Interactives

A **mixture** is *a combination of two or more substances in which the substances retain their distinct identities.* Some familiar examples are air, soft drinks, milk, and cement. Mixtures do not have constant composition. Therefore, samples of air collected in different cities would probably differ in composition because of differences in altitude, pollution, and so on.

Mixtures are either homogeneous or heterogeneous. When a spoonful of sugar dissolves in water we obtain a **homogeneous mixture** in which *the composition of the mixture is the same throughout.* If sand is mixed with iron filings, however, the sand grains and the iron filings remain separate (Figure 1.4). This type of mixture is called a **heterogeneous mixture** because *the composition is not uniform.*

Any mixture, whether homogeneous or heterogeneous, can be created and then separated by physical means into pure components without changing the identities of the components. Thus, sugar can be recovered from a water solution by heating the solution and evaporating it to dryness. Condensing the vapor will give us back the water component. To separate the iron-sand mixture, we can use a magnet to remove

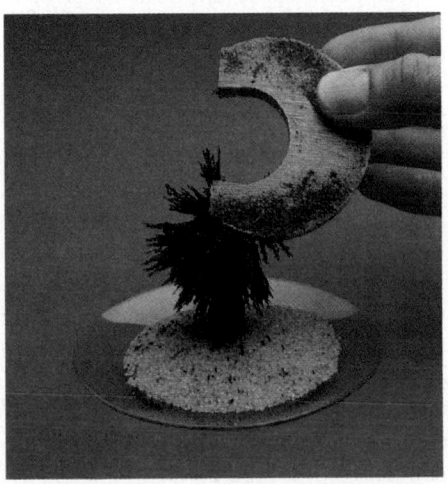

(a)   (b)

Figure 1.4 *(a) The mixture contains iron filings and sand. (b) A magnet separates the iron filings from the mixture. The same technique is used on a larger scale to separate iron and steel from nonmagnetic objects such as aluminum, glass, and plastics.*

TABLE 1.1	Some Common Elements and Their Symbols				
Name	**Symbol**	**Name**	**Symbol**	**Name**	**Symbol**
Aluminum	Al	Fluorine	F	Oxygen	O
Arsenic	As	Gold	Au	Phosphorus	P
Barium	Ba	Hydrogen	H	Platinum	Pt
Bismuth	Bi	Iodine	I	Potassium	K
Bromine	Br	Iron	Fe	Silicon	Si
Calcium	Ca	Lead	Pb	Silver	Ag
Carbon	C	Magnesium	Mg	Sodium	Na
Chlorine	Cl	Manganese	Mn	Sulfur	S
Chromium	Cr	Mercury	Hg	Tin	Sn
Cobalt	Co	Nickel	Ni	Tungsten	W
Copper	Cu	Nitrogen	N	Zinc	Zn

the iron filings from the sand, because sand is not attracted to the magnet [see Figure 1.4(b)]. After separation, the components of the mixture will have the same composition and properties as they did to start with.

Elements and Compounds

Interactivity:
Elements
ARIS, Interactives

Substances can be either elements or compounds. An **element** is *a substance that cannot be separated into simpler substances by chemical means.* To date, 114 elements have been positively identified. Most of them occur naturally on Earth. The others have been created by scientists via nuclear processes, which are the subject of Chapter 23 of this text.

For convenience, chemists use symbols of one or two letters to represent the elements. The first letter of a symbol is *always* capitalized, but any following letters are not. For example, Co is the symbol for the element cobalt, whereas CO is the formula for the carbon monoxide molecule. Table 1.1 shows the names and symbols of some of the more common elements; a complete list of the elements and their symbols appears inside the front cover of this book. The symbols of some elements are derived from their Latin names—for example, Au from *aurum* (gold), Fe from *ferrum* (iron), and Na from *natrium* (sodium)—whereas most of them come from their English names. Appendix 1 gives the origin of the names and lists the discoverers of most of the elements.

Atoms of most elements can interact with one another to form compounds. Hydrogen gas, for example, burns in oxygen gas to form water, which has properties that are distinctly different from those of the starting materials. Water is made up of two parts hydrogen and one part oxygen. This composition does not change, regardless of whether the water comes from a faucet in the United States, a lake in Outer Mongolia, or the ice caps on Mars. Thus, water is a **compound,** *a substance composed of atoms of two or more elements chemically united in fixed proportions.* Unlike mixtures, compounds can be separated only by chemical means into their pure components.

The relationships among elements, compounds, and other categories of matter are summarized in Figure 1.5.

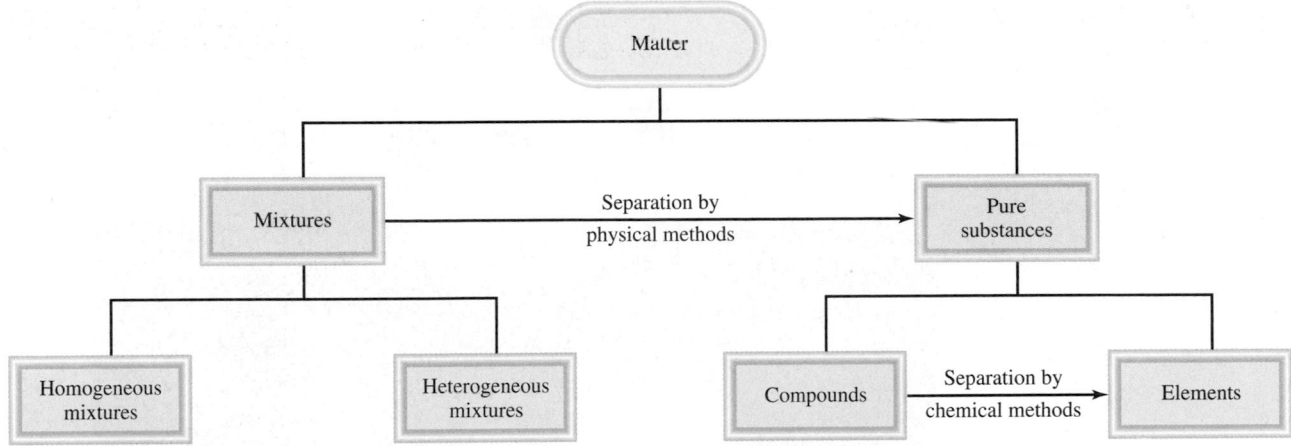

Figure 1.5 *Classifications of matter.*

1.5 The Three States of Matter

All substances, at least in principle, can exist in three states: solid, liquid, and gas. As Figure 1.6 shows, gases differ from liquids and solids in the distances between the molecules. In a solid, molecules are held close together in an orderly fashion with little freedom of motion. Molecules in a liquid are close together but are not held so rigidly in position and can move past one another. In a gas, the molecules are separated by distances that are large compared with the size of the molecules.

The three states of matter can be interconverted without changing the composition of the substance. Upon heating, a solid (for example, ice) will melt to form a liquid (water). (The temperature at which this transition occurs is called the *melting point.*) Further heating will convert the liquid into a gas. (This conversion takes place at the *boiling point* of the liquid.) On the other hand, cooling a gas will cause it to condense into a liquid. When the liquid is cooled further, it will freeze into the solid

Figure 1.6 *Microscopic views of a solid, a liquid, and a gas.*

Solid   Liquid   Gas

Figure 1.7 *The three states of matter. A hot poker changes ice into water and steam.*

form. Figure 1.7 shows the three states of water. Note that the properties of water are unique among common substances in that the molecules in the liquid state are more closely packed than those in the solid state.

1.6 Physical and Chemical Properties of Matter

Substances are identified by their properties as well as by their composition. Color, melting point, and boiling point are physical properties. A ***physical property*** *can be measured and observed without changing the composition or identity of a substance.* For example, we can measure the melting point of ice by heating a block of ice and recording the temperature at which the ice is converted to water. Water differs from ice only in appearance, not in composition, so this is a physical change; we can freeze the water to recover the original ice. Therefore, the melting point of a substance is a physical property. Similarly, when we say that helium gas is lighter than air, we are referring to a physical property.

On the other hand, the statement "Hydrogen gas burns in oxygen gas to form water" describes a ***chemical property*** of hydrogen, because *to observe this property we must carry out a chemical change,* in this case burning. After the change, the original chemical substance, the hydrogen gas, will have vanished, and all that will be left is a different chemical substance—water. We *cannot* recover the hydrogen from the water by means of a physical change, such as boiling or freezing.

Every time we hard-boil an egg, we bring about a chemical change. When subjected to a temperature of about 100°C, the yolk and the egg white undergo changes that alter not only their physical appearance but their chemical makeup as well. When eaten, the egg is changed again, by substances in our bodies called *enzymes*. This digestive action is another example of a chemical change. What happens during digestion depends on the chemical properties of both the enzymes and the food.

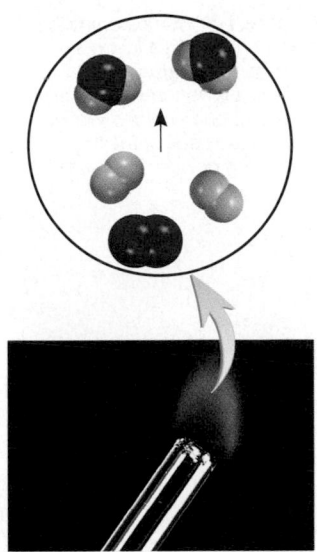

All measurable properties of matter fall into one of two additional categories: extensive properties and intensive properties. The measured value of an **extensive property** *depends on how much matter is being considered.* **Mass,** which is *the quantity of matter in a given sample of a substance,* is an extensive property. More matter means more mass. Values of the same extensive property can be added together. For example, two copper pennies will have a combined mass that is the sum of the masses of each penny, and the length of two tennis courts is the sum of the lengths of each tennis court. **Volume,** defined as *length cubed,* is another extensive property. The value of an extensive quantity depends on the amount of matter.

Hydrogen burning in air to form water.

The measured value of an **intensive property** *does not depend on how much matter is being considered.* **Density,** defined as *the mass of an object divided by its volume,* is an intensive property. So is temperature. Suppose that we have two beakers of water at the same temperature. If we combine them to make a single quantity of water in a larger beaker, the temperature of the larger quantity of water will be the same as it was in two separate beakers. Unlike mass, length, and volume, temperature and other intensive properties are not additive.

1.7 Measurement

The measurements chemists make are often used in calculations to obtain other related quantities. Different instruments enable us to measure a substance's properties: The meterstick measures length or scale; the buret, the pipet, the graduated cylinder, and the volumetric flask measure volume (Figure 1.8); the balance measures mass; the thermometer measures temperature. These instruments provide measurements of **macroscopic properties,** which *can be determined directly.* **Microscopic properties,** *on the atomic or molecular scale, must be determined by an indirect method,* as we will see in Chapter 2.

A measured quantity is usually written as a number with an appropriate unit. To say that the distance between New York and San Francisco by car along a certain route is 5166 is meaningless. We must specify that the distance is 5166 kilometers. The same is true in chemistry; units are essential to stating measurements correctly.

SI Units

For many years scientists recorded measurements in *metric units,* which are related decimally, that is, by powers of 10. In 1960, however, the General Conference of Weights and Measures, the international authority on units, proposed a revised metric system called the **International System of Units** (abbreviated **SI,** from the French *Système Internationale d'Unites*). Table 1.2 shows the seven SI base units. All

Interactivity:
SI Base Units
ARIS, Interactives

Figure 1.8 *Some common measuring devices found in a chemistry laboratory. These devices are not drawn to scale relative to one another. We will discuss the uses of these measuring devices in Chapter 4.*

Buret   Pipet   Graduated cylinder   Volumetric flask

Interactivity:
Unit Prefixes
ARIS, Interactives

other units of measurement can be derived from these base units. Like metric units, SI units are modified in decimal fashion by a series of prefixes, as shown in Table 1.3. We will use both metric and SI units in this book.

Measurements that we will utilize frequently in our study of chemistry include time, mass, volume, density, and temperature.

Mass and Weight

The terms "mass" and "weight" are often used interchangeably, although, strictly speaking, they are different quantities. Whereas mass is a measure of the amount of matter in an object, *weight,* technically speaking, is *the force that gravity exerts on an object.* An apple that falls from a tree is pulled downward by Earth's gravity. The mass of the apple is constant and does not depend on its location, but its weight does. For example, on the surface of the moon the apple would weigh only one-sixth what it does on Earth, because

An astronaut jumping on the surface of the moon.

TABLE 1.2	SI Base Units	
Base Quantity	**Name of Unit**	**Symbol**
Length	meter	m
Mass	kilogram	kg
Time	second	s
Electrical current	ampere	A
Temperature	kelvin	K
Amount of substance	mole	mol
Luminous intensity	candela	cd

TABLE 1.3		Prefixes Used with SI Units	
Prefix	Symbol	Meaning	Example
tera-	T	$1,000,000,000,000$, or 10^{12}	1 terameter (Tm) $= 1 \times 10^{12}$ m
giga-	G	$1,000,000,000$, or 10^9	1 gigameter (Gm) $= 1 \times 10^9$ m
mega-	M	$1,000,000$, or 10^6	1 megameter (Mm) $= 1 \times 10^6$ m
kilo-	k	$1,000$, or 10^3	1 kilometer (km) $= 1 \times 10^3$ m
deci-	d	$1/10$, or 10^{-1}	1 decimeter (dm) $= 0.1$ m
centi-	c	$1/100$, or 10^{-2}	1 centimeter (cm) $= 0.01$ m
milli-	m	$1/1,000$, or 10^{-3}	1 millimeter (mm) $= 0.001$ m
micro-	μ	$1/1,000,000$, or 10^{-6}	1 micrometer (μm) $= 1 \times 10^{-6}$ m
nano-	n	$1/1,000,000,000$, or 10^{-9}	1 nanometer (nm) $= 1 \times 10^{-9}$ m
pico-	p	$1/1,000,000,000,000$, or 10^{-12}	1 picometer (pm) $= 1 \times 10^{-12}$ m

the moon's gravity is only one-sixth that of Earth. The moon's smaller gravity enabled astronauts to jump about rather freely on its surface despite their bulky suits and equipment. Chemists are interested primarily in mass, which can be determined readily with a balance; the process of measuring mass, oddly, is called *weighing*.

The SI unit of mass is the *kilogram* (kg). Unlike the units of length and time, which are based on natural processes that can be repeated by scientists anywhere, the kilogram is defined in terms of a particular object (Figure 1.9). In chemistry, however, the smaller *gram* (g) is more convenient:

$$1 \text{ kg} = 1000 \text{ g} = 1 \times 10^3 \text{ g}$$

Figure 1.9 *The prototype kilogram is made of a platinum-iridium alloy. It is kept in a vault at the International Bureau of Weights and Measures in Sèvres, France.*

Volume

The SI unit of length is the *meter* (m), and the SI-derived unit for volume is the *cubic meter* (m^3). Generally, however, chemists work with much smaller volumes, such as the cubic centimeter (cm^3) and the cubic decimeter (dm^3):

$$1 \text{ cm}^3 = (1 \times 10^{-2} \text{ m})^3 = 1 \times 10^{-6} \text{ m}^3$$
$$1 \text{ dm}^3 = (1 \times 10^{-1} \text{ m})^3 = 1 \times 10^{-3} \text{ m}^3$$

Another common unit of volume is the liter (L). A **liter** is *the volume occupied by one cubic decimeter.* One liter of volume is equal to 1000 milliliters (mL) or 1000 cm^3:

$$\begin{aligned} 1 \text{ L} &= 1000 \text{ mL} \\ &= 1000 \text{ cm}^3 \\ &= 1 \text{ dm}^3 \end{aligned}$$

and one milliliter is equal to one cubic centimeter:

$$1 \text{ mL} = 1 \text{ cm}^3$$

Figure 1.10 compares the relative sizes of two volumes. Even though the liter is not an SI unit, volumes are usually expressed in liters and milliliters.

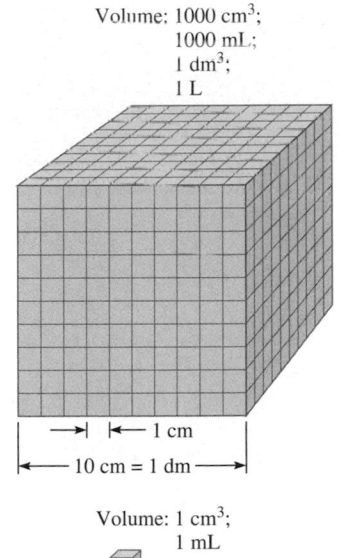

Volume: 1000 cm^3;
1000 mL;
1 dm^3;
1 L

1 cm

10 cm = 1 dm

Volume: 1 cm^3;
1 mL

1 cm

Figure 1.10 *Comparison of two volumes, 1 mL and 1000 mL.*

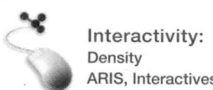

Density

The equation for density is

$$\text{density} = \frac{\text{mass}}{\text{volume}}$$

or

$$d = \frac{m}{V} \tag{1.1}$$

TABLE 1.4

Densities of Some Substances at 25°C

Substance	Density (g/cm³)
Air*	0.001
Ethanol	0.79
Water	1.00
Mercury	13.6
Table salt	2.2
Iron	7.9
Gold	19.3
Osmium†	22.6

*Measured at 1 atmosphere.
†Osmium (Os) is the densest element known.

where d, m, and V denote density, mass, and volume, respectively. Because density is an intensive property and does not depend on the quantity of mass present, for a given substance the ratio of mass to volume always remains the same; in other words, V increases as m does.

The SI-derived unit for density is the kilogram per cubic meter (kg/m^3). This unit is awkwardly large for most chemical applications. Therefore, grams per cubic centimeter (g/cm^3) and its equivalent, grams per milliliter (g/mL), are more commonly used for solid and liquid densities. Because gas densities are often very low, we express them in units of grams per liter (g/L):

$$1 \text{ g/cm}^3 = 1 \text{ g/mL} = 1000 \text{ kg/m}^3$$
$$1 \text{ g/L} = 0.001 \text{ g/mL}$$

Table 1.4 lists the densities of several substances.
Examples 1.1 and 1.2 show density calculations.

Gold bars.

Similar problems: 1.21, 1.22.

Example 1.1

Gold is a precious metal that is chemically unreactive. It is used mainly in jewelry, dentistry, and electronic devices. A piece of gold ingot with a mass of 301 g has a volume of 15.6 cm³. Calculate the density of gold.

Solution We are given the mass and volume and asked to calculate the density. Therefore, from Equation (1.1), we write

$$d = \frac{m}{V}$$
$$= \frac{301 \text{ g}}{15.6 \text{ cm}^3}$$
$$= 19.3 \text{ g/cm}^3$$

Practice Exercise A piece of platinum metal with a density of 21.5 g/cm³ has a volume of 4.49 cm³. What is its mass?

Example 1.2

The density of mercury, the only metal that is a liquid at room temperature, is 13.6 g/mL. Calculate the mass of 5.50 mL of the liquid.

(Continued)

Solution We are given the density and volume of a liquid and asked to calculate the mass of the liquid. We rearrange Equation (1.1) to give

$$m = d \times V$$
$$= 13.6 \frac{g}{mL} \times 5.50\ mL$$
$$= \boxed{74.8\ g}$$

Practice Exercise The density of sulfuric acid in a certain car battery is 1.41 g/mL. Calculate the mass of 242 mL of the liquid.

Mercury.

Similar problems: 1.21, 1.22.

Temperature Scales

Three temperature scales are currently in use. Their units are °F (degrees Fahrenheit), °C (degrees Celsius), and K (kelvin). The Fahrenheit scale, which is the most commonly used scale in the United States outside the laboratory, defines the normal freezing and boiling points of water to be exactly 32°F and 212°F, respectively. The Celsius scale divides the range between the freezing point (0°C) and boiling point (100°C) of water into 100 degrees. As Table 1.2 shows, the *kelvin* is *the SI base unit of temperature:* it is the *absolute* temperature scale. By absolute we mean that the zero on the Kelvin scale, denoted by 0 K, is the lowest temperature that can be attained theoretically. On the other hand, 0°F and 0°C are based on the behavior of an arbitrarily chosen substance, water. Figure 1.11 compares the three temperature scales.

Note that the Kelvin scale does not have the degree sign. Also, temperatures expressed in kelvins can never be negative.

The size of a degree on the Fahrenheit scale is only 100/180, or 5/9, of a degree on the Celsius scale. To convert degrees Fahrenheit to degrees Celsius, we write

$$?°C = (°F - 32°F) \times \frac{5°C}{9°F} \tag{1.2}$$

The following equation is used to convert degrees Celsius to degrees Fahrenheit:

$$?°F = \frac{9°F}{5°C} \times (°C) + 32°F \tag{1.3}$$

373 K — 100°C ← Boiling point → 212°F
of water

310 K — 37°C ← Body → 98.6°F
temperature

298 K — 25°C ← Room → 77°F
temperature

273 K — 0°C ← Freezing point → 32°F
of water

Kelvin   Celsius   Fahrenheit

Figure 1.11 *Comparison of the three temperature scales: Celsius, Fahrenheit, and the absolute (Kelvin) scales. Note that there are 100 divisions, or 100 degrees, between the freezing point and the boiling point of water on the Celsius scale, and there are 180 divisions, or 180 degrees, between the same two temperature limits on the Fahrenheit scale. The Celsius scale was formerly called the centigrade scale.*

CHEMISTRY
in Action

The Importance of Units

In December 1998 NASA launched the 125-million dollar Mars Climate Orbiter, intended as the red planet's first weather satellite. After a 416-million mi journey, the spacecraft was supposed to go into Mars' orbit on September 23, 1999. Instead, it entered Mars' atmosphere about 100 km (62 mi) lower than planned and was destroyed by heat. The mission controllers said the loss of the spacecraft was due to the failure to convert English measurement units into metric units in the navigation software.

Engineers at Lockheed Martin Corporation who built the spacecraft specified its thrust in pounds, which is an English unit. Scientists at NASA's Jet Propulsion Laboratory, on the other hand, had assumed that thrust data they received were expressed in metric units, as newtons. Normally, pound is the unit for mass. Expressed as a unit for force, however, 1 lb is the force due to gravitational attraction on an object of that mass. To carry out the conversion between pound and newton, we start with 1 lb = 0.4536 kg and from Newton's second law of motion,

$$\text{force} = \text{mass} \times \text{acceleration}$$
$$= 0.4536 \text{ kg} \times 9.81 \text{ m/s}^2$$
$$= 4.45 \text{ kg m/s}^2$$
$$= 4.45 \text{ N}$$

because 1 newton (N) = 1 kg m/s². Therefore, instead of converting one pound of force to 4.45 N, the scientists treated it as 1 N.

The considerably smaller engine thrust expressed in newtons resulted in a lower orbit and the ultimate destruction of the spacecraft. Commenting on the failure of the Mars mission, one scientist said: "This is going to be the cautionary tale that will be embedded into introduction to the metric system in elementary school, high school, and college science courses till the end of time."

Artist's conception of the Martian Climate Orbiter.

Both the Celsius and the Kelvin scales have units of equal magnitude; that is, one degree Celsius is equivalent to one kelvin. Experimental studies have shown that absolute zero on the Kelvin scale is equivalent to −273.15°C on the Celsius scale. Thus, we can use the following equation to convert degrees Celsius to kelvin:

$$? \text{ K} = (°\text{C} + 273.15°\text{C}) \frac{1 \text{ K}}{1°\text{C}} \tag{1.4}$$

We will frequently find it necessary to convert between degrees Celsius and degrees Fahrenheit and between degrees Celsius and kelvin. Example 1.3 illustrates these conversions.

The Chemistry in Action essay above shows why we must be careful with units in scientific work.

Example 1.3

(a) Solder is an alloy made of tin and lead that is used in electronic circuits. A certain solder has a melting point of 224°C. What is its melting point in degrees Fahrenheit? (b) Helium has the lowest boiling point of all the elements at −452°F. Convert this temperature to degrees Celsius. (c) Mercury, the only metal that exists as a liquid at room temperature, melts at −38.9°C. Convert its melting point to kelvins.

Solution These three parts require that we carry out temperature conversions, so we need Equations (1.2), (1.3), and (1.4). Keep in mind that the lowest temperature on the Kelvin scale is zero (0 K); therefore, it can never be negative.

(a) This conversion is carried out by writing

$$\frac{9°F}{5°C} \times (224°C) + 32°F = \boxed{435°F}$$

(b) Here we have

$$(-452°F - 32°F) \times \frac{5°C}{9°F} = \boxed{-269°C}$$

(c) The melting point of mercury in kelvins is given by

$$(-38.9°C + 273.15°C) \times \frac{1\ K}{1°C} = \boxed{234.3\ K}$$

Practice Exercise Convert (a) 327.5°C (the melting point of lead) to degrees Fahrenheit; (b) 172.9°F (the boiling point of ethanol) to degrees Celsius; and (c) 77 K, the boiling point of liquid nitrogen, to degrees Celsius.

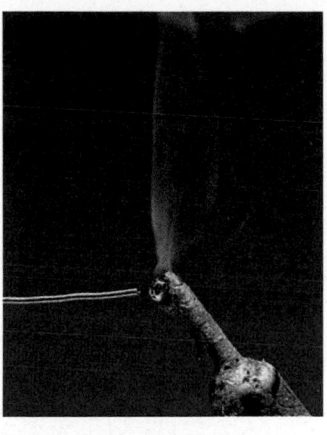

Solder is used extensively in the construction of electronic circuits.

Similar problems: 1.24, 1.25, 1.26.

1.8 Handling Numbers

Having surveyed some of the units used in chemistry, we now turn to techniques for handling numbers associated with measurements: scientific notation and significant figures.

Scientific Notation

Chemists often deal with numbers that are either extremely large or extremely small. For example, in 1 g of the element hydrogen there are roughly

$$602,200,000,000,000,000,000,000$$

hydrogen atoms. Each hydrogen atom has a mass of only

$$0.00000000000000000000000166\ g$$

These numbers are cumbersome to handle, and it is easy to make mistakes when using them in arithmetic computations. Consider the following multiplication:

$$0.0000000056 \times 0.00000000048 = 0.000000000000000002688$$

It would be easy for us to miss one zero or add one more zero after the decimal point. Consequently, when working with very large and very small numbers, we use a system called *scientific notation.* Regardless of their magnitude, all numbers can be expressed in the form

$$N \times 10^n$$

where N is a number between 1 and 10 and n, the exponent, is a positive or negative integer (whole number). Any number expressed in this way is said to be written in scientific notation.

Suppose that we are given a certain number and asked to express it in scientific notation. Basically, this assignment calls for us to find n. We count the number of places that the decimal point must be moved to give the number N (which is between 1 and 10). If the decimal point has to be moved to the left, then n is a positive integer; if it has to be moved to the right, n is a negative integer. The following examples illustrate the use of scientific notation:

(1) Express 568.762 in scientific notation:

$$568.762 = 5.68762 \times 10^2$$

Note that the decimal point is moved to the left by two places and $n = 2$.

(2) Express 0.00000772 in scientific notation:

$$0.00000772 = 7.72 \times 10^{-6}$$

Here the decimal point is moved to the right by six places and $n = -6$.

Any number raised to the power zero is equal to one.

Keep in mind the following two points. First, $n = 0$ is used for numbers that are not expressed in scientific notation. For example, 74.6×10^0 ($n = 0$) is equivalent to 74.6. Second, the usual practice is to omit the superscript when $n = 1$. Thus the scientific notation for 74.6 is 7.46×10 and not 7.46×10^1.

Next, we consider how scientific notation is handled in arithmetic operations.

Addition and Subtraction

To add or subtract using scientific notation, we first write each quantity—say N_1 and N_2—with the same exponent n. Then we combine N_1 and N_2; the exponents remain the same. Consider the following examples:

$$(7.4 \times 10^3) + (2.1 \times 10^3) = 9.5 \times 10^3$$
$$(4.31 \times 10^4) + (3.9 \times 10^3) = (4.31 \times 10^4) + (0.39 \times 10^4)$$
$$= 4.70 \times 10^4$$
$$(2.22 \times 10^{-2}) - (4.10 \times 10^{-3}) = (2.22 \times 10^{-2}) - (0.41 \times 10^{-2})$$
$$= 1.81 \times 10^{-2}$$

Multiplication and Division

To multiply numbers expressed in scientific notation, we multiply N_1 and N_2 in the usual way, but *add* the exponents together. To divide using scientific notation, we divide N_1 and N_2 as usual and subtract the exponents. The following examples show how these operations are performed:

$$(8.0 \times 10^4) \times (5.0 \times 10^2) = (8.0 \times 5.0)(10^{4+2})$$
$$= 40 \times 10^6$$
$$= 4.0 \times 10^7$$

$$(4.0 \times 10^{-5}) \times (7.0 \times 10^{3}) = (4.0 \times 7.0)(10^{-5+3})$$
$$= 28 \times 10^{-2}$$
$$= 2.8 \times 10^{-1}$$
$$\frac{6.9 \times 10^{7}}{3.0 \times 10^{-5}} = \frac{6.9}{3.0} \times 10^{7-(-5)}$$
$$= 2.3 \times 10^{12}$$
$$\frac{8.5 \times 10^{4}}{5.0 \times 10^{9}} = \frac{8.5}{5.0} \times 10^{4-9}$$
$$= 1.7 \times 10^{-5}$$

Significant Figures

Except when all the numbers involved are integers (for example, in counting the number of students in a class), it is often impossible to obtain the exact value of the quantity under investigation. For this reason, it is important to indicate the margin of error in a measurement by clearly indicating the number of *significant figures,* which are *the meaningful digits in a measured or calculated quantity.* When significant figures are used, the last digit is understood to be uncertain. For example, we might measure the volume of a given amount of liquid using a graduated cylinder with a scale that gives an uncertainty of 1 mL in the measurement. If the volume is found to be 6 mL, then the actual volume is in the range of 5 mL to 7 mL. We represent the volume of the liquid as (6 ± 1) mL. In this case, there is only one significant figure (the digit 6) that is uncertain by either plus or minus 1 mL. For greater accuracy, we might use a graduated cylinder that has finer divisions, so that the volume we measure is now uncertain by only 0.1 mL. If the volume of the liquid is now found to be 6.0 mL, we may express the quantity as (6.0 ± 0.1) mL, and the actual value is somewhere between 5.9 mL and 6.1 mL. We can further improve the measuring device and obtain more significant figures, but in every case, the last digit is always uncertain; the amount of this uncertainty depends on the particular measuring device we use.

Figure 1.12 shows a modern balance. Balances such as this one are available in many general chemistry laboratories; they readily measure the mass of objects to four decimal places. Therefore, the measured mass typically will have four significant figures (for example, 0.8642 g) or more (for example, 3.9745 g). Keeping track of the number of significant figures in a measurement such as mass ensures that calculations involving the data will reflect the precision of the measurement.

Guidelines for Using Significant Figures

We must always be careful in scientific work to write the proper number of significant figures. In general, it is fairly easy to determine how many significant figures a number has by following these rules:

1. Any digit that is not zero is significant. Thus, 845 cm has three significant figures, 1.234 kg has four significant figures, and so on.

2. Zeros between nonzero digits are significant. Thus, 606 m contains three significant figures, 40,501 kg contains five significant figures, and so on.

3. Zeros to the left of the first nonzero digit are not significant. Their purpose is to indicate the placement of the decimal point. For example, 0.08 L contains one significant figure, 0.0000349 g contains three significant figures, and so on.

4. If a number is greater than 1, then all the zeros written to the right of the decimal point count as significant figures. Thus, 2.0 mg has two significant figures,

Figure 1.12 *A single-pan balance.*

40.062 mL has five significant figures, and 3.040 dm has four significant figures. If a number is less than 1, then only the zeros that are at the end of the number and the zeros that are between nonzero digits are significant. This means that 0.090 kg has two significant figures, 0.3005 L has four significant figures, 0.00420 min has three significant figures, and so on.

5. For numbers that do not contain decimal points, the trailing zeros (that is, zeros after the last nonzero digit) may or may not be significant. Thus, 400 cm may have one significant figure (the digit 4), two significant figures (40), or three significant figures (400). We cannot know which is correct without more information. By using scientific notation, however, we avoid this ambiguity. In this particular case, we can express the number 400 as 4×10^2 for one significant figure, 4.0×10^2 for two significant figures, or 4.00×10^2 for three significant figures.

Example 1.4 shows the determination of significant figures.

Example 1.4

Determine the number of significant figures in the following measurements: (a) 478 cm, (b) 6.01 g, (c) 0.825 m, (d) 0.043 kg, (e) 1.310×10^{22} atoms, (f) 7000 mL.

Solution (a) Three, because each digit is a nonzero digit. (b) Three, because zeros between nonzero digits are significant. (c) Three, because zeros to the left of the first nonzero digit do not count as significant figures. (d) Two. Same reason as in (c). (e) Four, because the number is greater than one so all the zeros written to the right of the decimal point count as significant figures. (f) This is an ambiguous case. The number of significant figures may be four (7.000×10^3), three (7.00×10^3), two (7.0×10^3), or one (7×10^3). This example illustrates why scientific notation must be used to show the proper number of significant figures.

Similar problems: 1.33, 1.34.

Practice Exercise Determine the number of significant figures in each of the following measurements: (a) 24 mL, (b) 3001 g, (c) 0.0320 m^3, (d) 6.4×10^4 molecules, (e) 560 kg.

A second set of rules specifies how to handle significant figures in calculations.

1. In addition and subtraction, the answer cannot have more digits to the right of the decimal point than either of the original numbers. Consider these examples:

$$
\begin{array}{r}
89.332 \\
+\ 1.1 \quad \longleftarrow \text{one digit after the decimal point} \\
\hline
90.432 \longleftarrow \text{round off to } 90.4
\end{array}
$$

$$
\begin{array}{r}
2.097 \\
-0.12 \quad \longleftarrow \text{two digits after the decimal point} \\
\hline
1.977 \longleftarrow \text{round off to } 1.98
\end{array}
$$

The rounding-off procedure is as follows. To round off a number at a certain point we simply drop the digits that follow if the first of them is less than 5. Thus, 8.724 rounds off to 8.72 if we want only two digits after the decimal point. If the first digit following the point of rounding off is equal to or greater than 5, we add 1 to the preceding digit. Thus, 8.727 rounds off to 8.73, and 0.425 rounds off to 0.43.

2. In multiplication and division, the number of significant figures in the final product or quotient is determined by the original number that has the *smallest* number of significant figures. The following examples illustrate this rule:

$$2.8 \times 4.5039 = 12.61092 \quad \longleftarrow \quad \text{round off to } 13$$

$$\frac{6.85}{112.04} = 0.0611388789 \quad \longleftarrow \quad \text{round off to } 0.0611$$

3. Keep in mind that *exact numbers* obtained from definitions or by counting numbers of objects can be considered to have an infinite number of significant figures. For example, the inch is defined to be exactly 2.54 centimeters; that is,

$$1 \text{ in} = 2.54 \text{ cm}$$

Thus, the "2.54" in the equation should not be interpreted as a measured number with three significant figures. In calculations involving conversion between in and cm, we treat both "1" and "2.54" as having an infinite number of significant figures. Similarly, if an object has a mass of 5.0 g, then the mass of nine such objects is

$$5.0 \text{ g} \times 9 = 45 \text{ g}$$

The answer has two significant figures because 5.0 g has two significant figures. The number 9 is exact and does not determine the number of significant figures.

Example 1.5 shows how significant figures are handled in arithmetic operations.

Example 1.5

Carry out the following arithmetic operations to the correct number of significant figures: (a) 11,254.1 g + 0.1983 g, (b) 66.59 L − 3.113 L, (c) 8.16 m × 5.1355, (d) 0.0154 kg ÷ 88.3 mL, (e) 2.64×10^3 cm + 3.27×10^2 cm.

Solution In addition and subtraction, the number of decimal places in the answer is determined by the number having the lowest number of decimal places. In multiplication and division, the significant number of the answer is determined by the number having the smallest number of significant figures.

(a)   11,254.1 g
   +   0.1983 g
      11,254.2983 g $\longleftarrow$ round off to 11,254.3 g

(b)   66.59 L
   −   3.113 L
      63.477 L $\longleftarrow$ round off to 63.48 L

(c) 8.16 m × 5.1355 = 41.90568 m $\longleftarrow$ round off to 41.9 m

(d) $\dfrac{0.0154 \text{ kg}}{88.3 \text{ mL}}$ = 0.000174405436 kg/mL $\longleftarrow$ round off to 0.000174 kg/mL
                             or 1.74×10^{-4} kg/mL

(e) First we change 3.27×10^2 cm to 0.327×10^3 cm and then carry out the addition $(2.64 \text{ cm} + 0.327 \text{ cm}) \times 10^3$. Following the procedure in (a), we find the answer is 2.97×10^3 cm.

Similar problems: 1.35, 1.36.

Practice Exercise Carry out the following arithmetic operations and round off the answers to the appropriate number of significant figures: (a) 26.5862 L + 0.17 L, (b) 9.1 g − 4.682 g, (c) 7.1×10^4 dm × 2.2654×10^2 dm, (d) 6.54 g ÷ 86.5542 mL, (e) $(7.55 \times 10^4$ m$) - (8.62 \times 10^3$ m$)$.

The preceding rounding-off procedure applies to one-step calculations. In *chain calculations,* that is, calculations involving more than one step, we can get a different answer depending on how we round off. Consider the following two-step calculations:

First step: $A \times B = C$
Second step: $C \times D = E$

Let's suppose that $A = 3.66$, $B = 8.45$, and $D = 2.11$. Depending on whether we round off C to three or four significant figures, we obtain a different number for E:

Method 1	Method 2
$3.66 \times 8.45 = 30.9$	$3.66 \times 8.45 = 30.93$
$30.9 \times 2.11 = 65.2$	$30.93 \times 2.11 = 65.3$

However, if we had carried out the calculation as $3.66 \times 8.45 \times 2.11$ on a calculator without rounding off the intermediate answer, we would have obtained 65.3 as the answer for E. Although retaining an additional digit past the number of significant figures for intermediate steps helps to eliminate errors from rounding, this procedure is not necessary for most calculations because the difference between the answers is usually quite small. Therefore, for most examples and end-of-chapter problems where intermediate answers are reported, all answers, intermediate and final, will be rounded.

Accuracy and Precision

Interactivity:
Accuracy and Precision
ARIS, Interactives

In discussing measurements and significant figures it is useful to distinguish between *accuracy* and *precision*. **Accuracy** tells us *how close a measurement is to the true value of the quantity that was measured.* To a scientist there is a distinction between accuracy and precision. ***Precision*** *refers to how closely two or more measurements of the same quantity agree with one another* (Figure 1.13).

The difference between accuracy and precision is a subtle but important one. Suppose, for example, that three students are asked to determine the mass of a piece of copper wire. The results of two successive weighings by each student are

	Student A	Student B	Student C
	1.964 g	1.972 g	2.000 g
	1.978 g	1.968 g	2.002 g
Average value	1.971 g	1.970 g	2.001 g

The true mass of the wire is 2.000 g. Therefore, Student B's results are more *precise* than those of Student A (1.972 g and 1.968 g deviate less from 1.970 g than 1.964 g

Figure 1.13 *The distribution of darts on a dart board shows the difference between precise and accurate. (a) Good accuracy and good precision. (b) Poor accuracy and good precision. (c) Poor accuracy and poor precision. The blue dots show the positions of the darts.*

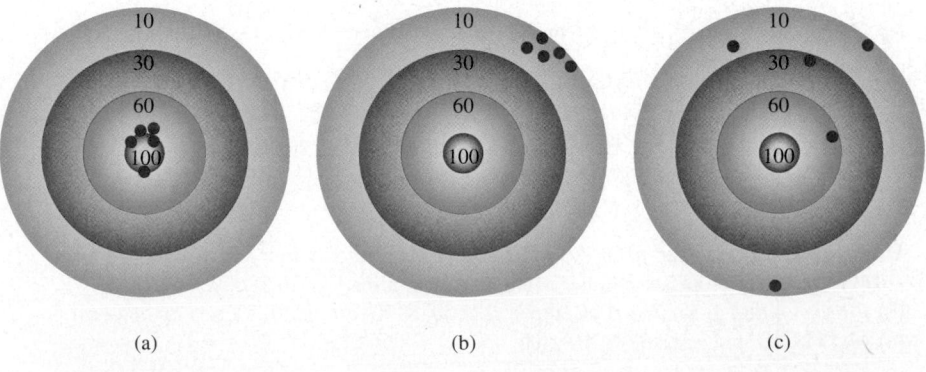

(a)   (b)   (c)

and 1.978 g from 1.971 g), but neither set of results is very *accurate.* Student C's results are not only the most *precise,* but also the most *accurate,* because the average value is closest to the true value. Highly accurate measurements are usually precise too. On the other hand, highly precise measurements do not necessarily guarantee accurate results. For example, an improperly calibrated meterstick or a faulty balance may give precise readings that are in error.

1.9 Dimensional Analysis in Solving Problems

Careful measurements and the proper use of significant figures, along with correct calculations, will yield accurate numerical results. But to be meaningful, the answers also must be expressed in the desired units. The procedure we use to convert between units in solving chemistry problems is called *dimensional analysis* (also called the *factor-label method*). A simple technique requiring little memorization, dimensional analysis is based on the relationship between different units that express the same physical quantity. For example, we know that the monetary unit "dollar" is different from the unit "penny." However, 1 dollar is *equivalent* to 100 pennies because they both represent the same amount of money; that is,

Dimensional analysis might also have led Einstein to his famous mass-energy equation ($E = mc^2$).

$$1 \text{ dollar} = 100 \text{ pennies}$$

This equivalence enables us to write a conversion factor

$$\frac{1 \text{ dollar}}{100 \text{ pennies}}$$

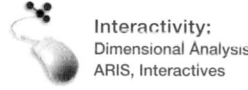

Interactivity:
Dimensional Analysis
ARIS, Interactives

if we want to convert pennies to dollars. Conversely, the conversion factor

$$\frac{100 \text{ pennies}}{1 \text{ dollar}}$$

enables us to convert dollars to pennies. A conversion factor, then, is a fraction whose numerator and denominator are the same quantity expressed in different units.

Now consider the problem

$$? \text{ pennies} = 2.46 \text{ dollars}$$

Because this is a dollar-to-penny conversion, we choose the conversion factor that has the unit "dollar" in the denominator (to cancel the "dollars" in 2.46 dollars) and write

$$2.46 \text{ dollars} \times \frac{100 \text{ pennies}}{1 \text{ dollar}} = 246 \text{ pennies}$$

Note that the conversion factor 100 pennies/1 dollar contains exact numbers, so it does not affect the number of significant figures in the final answer.

Next let us consider the conversion of 57.8 meters to centimeters. This problem can be expressed as

$$? \text{ cm} = 57.8 \text{ m}$$

By definition,

$$1 \text{ cm} = 1 \times 10^{-2} \text{ m}$$

Because we are converting "m" to "cm," we choose the conversion factor that has meters in the denominator,

$$\frac{1 \text{ cm}}{1 \times 10^{-2} \text{ m}}$$

and write the conversion as

$$? \text{ cm} = 57.8 \cancel{\text{ m}} \times \frac{1 \text{ cm}}{1 \times 10^{-2} \cancel{\text{ m}}}$$
$$= 5780 \text{ cm}$$
$$= 5.78 \times 10^3 \text{ cm}$$

Note that scientific notation is used to indicate that the answer has three significant figures. Again, the conversion factor $1 \text{ cm}/1 \times 10^{-2}$ m contains exact numbers; therefore, it does not affect the number of significant figures.

In general, to apply dimensional analysis we use the relationship

given quantity × conversion factor = desired quantity

and the units cancel as follows:

Remember that the unit we want appears in the numerator and the unit we want to cancel appears in the denominator.

$$\cancel{\text{given unit}} \times \frac{\text{desired unit}}{\cancel{\text{given unit}}} = \text{desired unit}$$

In dimensional analysis, the units are carried through the entire sequence of calculations. Therefore, if the equation is set up correctly, then all the units will cancel except the desired one. If this is not the case, then an error must have been made somewhere, and it can usually be spotted by reviewing the solution.

A Note on Problem Solving

At this point you have been introduced to scientific notation, significant figures, and dimensional analysis, which will help you in solving numerical problems. Chemistry is an experimental science and many of the problems are quantitative in nature. The key to success in problem solving is practice. Just as a marathon runner cannot prepare for a race by simply reading books on running and a pianist cannot give a successful concert by only memorizing the musical score, you cannot be sure of your understanding of chemistry without solving problems. The following steps will help to improve your skill at solving numerical problems.

1. Read the question carefully. Understand the information that is given and what you are asked to solve. Frequently it is helpful to make a sketch that will help you to visualize the situation.

2. Find the appropriate equation that relates the given information and the unknown quantity. Sometimes solving a problem will involve more than one step, and you may be expected to look up quantities in tables that are not provided in the problem. Dimensional analysis is often needed to carry out conversions.

3. Check your answer for the correct sign, units, and significant figures.

4. A very important part of problem solving is being able to judge whether the answer is reasonable. It is relatively easy to spot a wrong sign or incorrect units. But if a number (say 9) is incorrectly placed in the denominator instead of in the numerator, the answer would be too small even if the sign and units of the calculated quantity were correct.

5. One way to quickly check the answer is to make a "ball-park" estimate. The idea here is to round off the numbers in the calculation in such a way so as to simplify the arithmetic. This approach is sometimes called the "back-of-the-envelope calculation" because it can be done easily without using a calculator. The answer you get will not be exact, but it will be close to the correct one.

Example 1.6

A person's average daily intake of glucose (a form of sugar) is 0.0833 pound (lb). What is this mass in milligrams (mg)? (1 lb = 453.6 g.)

Strategy The problem can be stated as

$$? \text{ mg} = 0.0833 \text{ lb}$$

The relationship between pounds and grams is given in the problem. This relationship will enable conversion from pounds to grams. A metric conversion is then needed to convert grams to milligrams (1 mg = 1×10^{-3} g). Arrange the appropriate conversion factors so that pounds and grams cancel and the unit milligrams is obtained in your answer.

Solution The sequence of conversions is

$$\text{pounds} \longrightarrow \text{grams} \longrightarrow \text{milligrams}$$

Using the following conversion factors

$$\frac{453.6 \text{ g}}{1 \text{ lb}} \quad \text{and} \quad \frac{1 \text{ mg}}{1 \times 10^{-3} \text{ g}}$$

we obtain the answer in one step:

$$? \text{ mg} = 0.0833 \text{ lb} \times \frac{453.6 \text{ g}}{1 \text{ lb}} \times \frac{1 \text{ mg}}{1 \times 10^{-3} \text{ g}} = 3.78 \times 10^4 \text{ mg}$$

Check As an estimate, we note that 1 lb is roughly 500 g and that 1 g = 1000 mg. Therefore, 1 lb is roughly 5×10^5 mg. Rounding off 0.0833 lb to 0.1 lb, we get 5×10^4 mg, which is close to the preceding quantity.

Practice Exercise A roll of aluminum foil has a mass of 1.07 kg. What is its mass in pounds?

Conversion factors for some of the English system units commonly used in the United States for nonscientific measurements (for example, pounds and inches) are provided inside the back cover of this book.

Similar problem: 1.43.

As Examples 1.7 and 1.8 illustrate, conversion factors can be squared or cubed in dimensional analysis.

Example 1.7

An average adult has 5.2 L of blood. What is the volume of blood in m^3?

Strategy The problem can be stated as

$$? \text{ m}^3 = 5.2 \text{ L}$$

(Continued)

How many conversion factors are needed for this problem? Recall that $1\ L = 1000\ cm^3$ and $1\ cm = 1 \times 10^{-2}\ m$.

Solution We need two conversion factors here: one to convert liters to cm^3 and one to convert centimeters to meters:

$$\frac{1000\ cm^3}{1\ L} \quad \text{and} \quad \frac{1 \times 10^{-2}\ m}{1\ cm}$$

Because the second conversion factor deals with length (cm and m) and we want volume here, it must therefore be cubed to give

$$\frac{1 \times 10^{-2}\ m}{1\ cm} \times \frac{1 \times 10^{-2}\ m}{1\ cm} \times \frac{1 \times 10^{-2}\ m}{1\ cm} = \left(\frac{1 \times 10^{-2}\ m}{1\ cm}\right)^3$$

This means that $1\ cm^3 = 1 \times 10^{-6}\ m^3$. Now we can write

$$?\ m^3 = 5.2\ \cancel{L} \times \frac{1000\ cm^3}{1\ \cancel{L}} \times \left(\frac{1 \times 10^{-2}\ m}{1\ cm}\right)^3 = \boxed{5.2 \times 10^{-3}\ m^3}$$

Check From the preceding conversion factors you can show that $1\ L = 1 \times 10^{-3}\ m^3$. Therefore, 5 L of blood would be equal to $5 \times 10^{-3}\ m^3$, which is close to the answer.

Similar problem: 1.48(d).

Practice Exercise The volume of a room is $1.08 \times 10^8\ dm^3$. What is the volume in m^3?

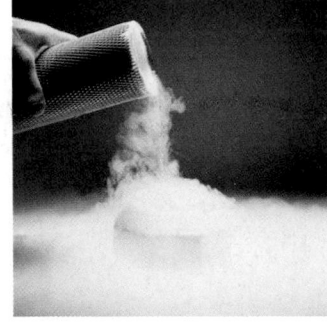

Liquid nitrogen

Example 1.8

Liquid nitrogen is obtained from liquefied air and is used to prepare frozen goods and in low-temperature research. The density of the liquid at its boiling point ($-196°C$ or 77 K) is $0.808\ g/cm^3$. Convert the density to units of kg/m^3.

Strategy The problem can be stated as

$$?\ kg/m^3 = 0.808\ g/cm^3$$

Two separate conversions are required for this problem: $g \longrightarrow kg$ and $cm^3 \longrightarrow m^3$. Recall that $1\ kg = 1000\ g$ and $1\ cm = 1 \times 10^{-2}\ m$.

Solution In Example 1.7 we saw that $1\ cm^3 = 1 \times 10^{-6}\ m^3$. The conversion factors are

$$\frac{1\ kg}{1000\ g} \quad \text{and} \quad \frac{1\ cm^3}{1 \times 10^{-6}\ m^3}$$

Finally,

$$?\ kg/m^3 = \frac{0.808\ \cancel{g}}{1\ \cancel{cm^3}} \times \frac{1\ kg}{1000\ \cancel{g}} \times \frac{1\ \cancel{cm^3}}{1 \times 10^{-6}\ m^3} = \boxed{808\ kg/m^3}$$

Check Because $1\ m^3 = 1 \times 10^6\ cm^3$, we would expect much more mass in $1\ m^3$ than in $1\ cm^3$. Therefore, the answer is reasonable.

Similar problem: 1.49.

Practice Exercise The density of the lightest metal, lithium (Li), is $5.34 \times 10^2\ kg/m^3$. Convert the density to g/cm^3.

Summary of Facts and Concepts

1. The study of chemistry involves three basic steps: observation, representation, and interpretation. Observation refers to measurements in the macroscopic world; representation involves the use of shorthand notation symbols and equations for communication; interpretations are based on atoms and molecules, which belong to the microscopic world.

2. The scientific method is a systematic approach to research that begins with the gathering of information through observation and measurements. In the process, hypotheses, laws, and theories are devised and tested.

3. Chemists study matter and the changes it undergoes. The substances that make up matter have unique physical properties that can be observed without changing their identity and unique chemical properties that, when they are demonstrated, do change the identity of the substances. Mixtures, whether homogeneous or heterogeneous, can be separated into pure components by physical means.

4. The simplest substances in chemistry are elements. Compounds are formed by the chemical combination of atoms of different elements in fixed proportions.

5. All substances, in principle, can exist in three states: solid, liquid, and gas. The interconversion between these states can be effected by changing the temperature.

6. SI units are used to express physical quantities in all sciences, including chemistry.

7. Numbers expressed in scientific notation have the form $N \times 10^n$, where N is between 1 and 10, and n is a positive or negative integer. Scientific notation helps us handle very large and very small quantities.

Key Words

Accuracy, p. 26	Homogeneous mixture, p. 11	Macroscopic property, p. 15	Quantitative, p. 8
Chemical property, p. 14	Hypothesis, p. 9	Mass, p. 15	Scientific method, p. 8
Chemistry, p. 4	Intensive property, p. 15	Matter, p. 11	Significant figures, p. 23
Compound, p. 12	International System of Units	Microscopic property, p. 15	Substance, p. 11
Density, p. 15	(SI), p. 15	Mixture, p. 11	Theory, p. 9
Element, p. 12	Kelvin, p. 19	Physical property, p. 14	Volume, p. 15
Extensive property, p. 15	Law, p. 9	Precision, p. 26	Weight, p. 16
Heterogeneous mixture, p. 11	Liter, p. 17	Qualitative, p. 8	

Questions and Problems

The Scientific Method

Review Questions

1.1 Explain what is meant by the scientific method.

1.2 What is the difference between qualitative data and quantitative data?

Problems

1.3 Classify the following as qualitative or quantitative statements, giving your reasons. (a) The sun is approximately 93 million mi from Earth. (b) Leonardo da Vinci was a better painter than Michelangelo. (c) Ice is less dense than water. (d) Butter tastes better than margarine. (e) A stitch in time saves nine.

1.4 Classify each of the following statements as a hypothesis, a law, or a theory. (a) Beethoven's contribution to music would have been much greater if he had married. (b) An autumn leaf gravitates toward the ground because there is an attractive force between the leaf and Earth. (c) All matter is composed of very small particles called atoms.

Classification and Properties of Matter

Review Questions

1.5 Give an example for each of the following terms: (a) matter, (b) substance, (c) mixture.

1.6 Give an example of a homogeneous mixture and an example of a heterogeneous mixture.

1.7 Using examples, explain the difference between a physical property and a chemical property.

1.8 How does an intensive property differ from an extensive property? Which of the following properties are intensive and which are extensive? (a) length, (b) volume, (c) temperature, (d) mass.

1.9   Give an example of an element and a compound. How do elements and compounds differ?

1.10 What is the number of known elements?

Problems

1.11 Do the following statements describe chemical or physical properties? (a) Oxygen gas supports combustion. (b) Fertilizers help to increase agricultural production. (c) Water boils below 100°C on top of a mountain. (d) Lead is denser than aluminum. (e) Uranium is a radioactive element.

1.12 Does each of the following describe a physical change or a chemical change? (a) The helium gas inside a balloon tends to leak out after a few hours. (b) A flashlight beam slowly gets dimmer and finally goes out. (c) Frozen orange juice is reconstituted by adding water to it. (d) The growth of plants depends on the sun's energy in a process called photosynthesis. (e) A spoonful of table salt dissolves in a bowl of soup.

1.13 Give the names of the elements represented by the chemical symbols Li, F, P, Cu, As, Zn, Cl, Pt, Mg, U, Al, Si, Ne. (See Table 1.1 and the inside front cover.)

1.14 Give the chemical symbols for the following elements: (a) potassium, (b) tin, (c) chromium, (d) boron, (e) barium, (f) plutonium, (g) sulfur, (h) argon, (i) mercury. (See Table 1.1 and the inside front cover.)

1.15 Classify each of the following substances as an element or a compound: (a) hydrogen, (b) water, (c) gold, (d) sugar.

1.16 Classify each of the following as an element, a compound, a homogeneous mixture, or a heterogeneous mixture: (a) seawater, (b) helium gas, (c) sodium chloride (table salt), (d) a bottle of soft drink, (e) a milkshake, (f) air in a bottle, (g) concrete.

Measurement
Review Questions

1.17 Name the SI base units that are important in chemistry. Give the SI units for expressing the following: (a) length, (b) volume, (c) mass, (d) time, (e) energy, (f) temperature.

1.18 Write the numbers represented by the following prefixes: (a) mega-, (b) kilo-, (c) deci-, (d) centi-, (e) milli-, (f) micro-, (g) nano-, (h) pico-.

1.19 What units do chemists normally use for density of liquids and solids? For gas density? Explain the differences.

1.20 Describe the three temperature scales used in the laboratory and in everyday life: the Fahrenheit scale, the Celsius scale, and the Kelvin scale.

Problems

1.21 Bromine is a reddish-brown liquid. Calculate its density (in g/mL) if 586 g of the substance occupies 188 mL.

1.22 The density of ethanol, a colorless liquid that is commonly known as grain alcohol, is 0.798 g/mL. Calculate the mass of 17.4 mL of the liquid.

1.23 Convert the following temperatures to degrees Celsius or Fahrenheit: (a) 95°F, the temperature on a hot summer day; (b) 12°F, the temperature on a cold winter day; (c) a 102°F fever; (d) a furnace operating at 1852°F; (e) -273.15°C (theoretically the lowest attainable temperature).

1.24 (a) Normally the human body can endure a temperature of 105°F for only short periods of time without permanent damage to the brain and other vital organs. What is this temperature in degrees Celsius? (b) Ethylene glycol is a liquid organic compound that is used as an antifreeze in car radiators. It freezes at -11.5°C. Calculate its freezing temperature in degrees Fahrenheit. (c) The temperature on the surface of the sun is about 6300°C. What is this temperature in degrees Fahrenheit? (d) The ignition temperature of paper is 451°F. What is the temperature in degrees Celsius?

1.25 Convert the following temperatures to kelvin: (a) 113°C, the melting point of sulfur, (b) 37°C, the normal body temperature, (c) 357°C, the boiling point of mercury.

1.26 Convert the following temperatures to degrees Celsius: (a) 77 K, the boiling point of liquid nitrogen, (b) 4.2 K, the boiling point of liquid helium, (c) 601 K, the melting point of lead.

Handling Numbers
Review Questions

1.27 What is the advantage of using scientific notation over decimal notation?

1.28 Define significant figure. Discuss the importance of using the proper number of significant figures in measurements and calculations.

Problems

1.29 Express the following numbers in scientific notation: (a) 0.000000027, (b) 356, (c) 47,764, (d) 0.096.

1.30 Express the following numbers as decimals: (a) 1.52×10^{-2}, (b) 7.78×10^{-8}.

1.31 Express the answers to the following calculations in scientific notation:

(a) $145.75 + (2.3 \times 10^{-1})$

(b) $79,500 \div (2.5 \times 10^{2})$

(c) $(7.0 \times 10^{-3}) - (8.0 \times 10^{-4})$

(d) $(1.0 \times 10^{4}) \times (9.9 \times 10^{6})$

1.32 Express the answers to the following calculations in scientific notation:

(a) $0.0095 + (8.5 \times 10^{-3})$

(b) $653 \div (5.75 \times 10^{-8})$

(c) $850,000 - (9.0 \times 10^5)$

(d) $(3.6 \times 10^{-4}) \times (3.6 \times 10^6)$

1.33 What is the number of significant figures in each of the following measurements?

(a) 4867 mi

(b) 56 mL

(c) 60,104 ton

(d) 2900 g

(e) 40.2 g/cm^3

(f) 0.0000003 cm

(g) 0.7 min

(h) 4.6×10^{19} atoms

1.34 How many significant figures are there in each of the following? (a) 0.006 L, (b) 0.0605 dm, (c) 60.5 mg, (d) 605.5 cm^2, (e) 960×10^{-3} g, (f) 6 kg, (g) 60 m.

1.35 Carry out the following operations as if they were calculations of experimental results, and express each answer in the correct units with the correct number of significant figures:

(a) $5.6792 \text{ m} + 0.6 \text{ m} + 4.33 \text{ m}$

(b) $3.70 \text{ g} - 2.9133 \text{ g}$

(c) $4.51 \text{ cm} \times 3.6666 \text{ cm}$

1.36 Carry out the following operations as if they were calculations of experimental results, and express each answer in the correct units with the correct number of significant figures:

(a) $7.310 \text{ km} \div 5.70 \text{ km}$

(b) $(3.26 \times 10^{-3} \text{ mg}) - (7.88 \times 10^{-5} \text{ mg})$

(c) $(4.02 \times 10^6 \text{ dm}) + (7.74 \times 10^7 \text{ dm})$

Dimensional Analysis

Problems

1.37 Carry out the following conversions: (a) 22.6 m to decimeters, (b) 25.4 mg to kilograms, (c) 556 mL to liters, (d) 10.6 kg/m^3 to g/cm^3.

1.38 Carry out the following conversions: (a) 242 lb to milligrams, (b) 68.3 cm^3 to cubic meters, (c) 7.2 m^3 to liters, (d) 28.3 μg to pounds.

1.39 The average speed of helium at 25°C is 1255 m/s. Convert this speed to miles per hour (mph).

1.40 How many seconds are there in a solar year (365.24 days)?

1.41 How many minutes does it take light from the sun to reach Earth? (The distance from the sun to Earth is 93 million mi; the speed of light = 3.00×10^8 m/s.)

1.42 A slow jogger runs a mile in 13 min. Calculate the speed in (a) in/s, (b) m/min, (c) km/h. (1 mi = 1609 m; 1 in = 2.54 cm.)

1.43 A 6.0-ft person weighs 168 lb. Express this person's height in meters and weight in kilograms. (1 lb = 453.6 g; 1 m = 3.28 ft.)

1.44 The current speed limit in some states in the United States is 55 miles per hour. What is the speed limit in kilometers per hour? (1 mi = 1609 m.)

1.45 For a fighter jet to take off from the deck of an aircraft carrier, it must reach a speed of 62 m/s. Calculate the speed in miles per hour (mph).

1.46 The "normal" lead content in human blood is about 0.40 part per million (that is, 0.40 g of lead per million grams of blood). A value of 0.80 part per million (ppm) is considered to be dangerous. How many grams of lead are contained in 6.0×10^3 g of blood (the amount in an average adult) if the lead content is 0.62 ppm?

1.47 Carry out the following conversions: (a) 1.42 light-years to miles (a light-year is an astronomical measure of distance—the distance traveled by light in a year, or 365 days; the speed of light is 3.00×10^8 m/s), (b) 32.4 yd to centimeters, (c) 3.0×10^{10} cm/s to ft/s.

1.48 Carry out the following conversions: (a) 185 nm to meters. (b) 4.5 billion years (roughly the age of Earth) to seconds. (Assume there are 365 days in a year.) (c) 71.2 cm^3 to m^3. (d) 88.6 m^3 to liters.

1.49 Aluminum is a lightweight metal (density = 2.70 g/cm^3) used in aircraft construction, high-voltage transmission lines, beverage cans, and foils. What is its density in kg/m^3?

1.50 The density of ammonia gas under certain conditions is 0.625 g/L. Calculate its density in g/cm^3.

Additional Problems

1.51 Give one qualitative and one quantitative statement about each of the following: (a) water, (b) carbon, (c) iron, (d) hydrogen gas, (e) sucrose (cane sugar), (f) table salt (sodium chloride), (g) mercury, (h) gold, (i) air.

1.52 Which of the following statements describe physical properties and which describe chemical properties? (a) Iron has a tendency to rust. (b) Rainwater in industrialized regions tends to be acidic. (c) Hemoglobin molecules have a red color. (d) When a glass of water is left out in the sun, the water gradually disappears. (e) Carbon dioxide in air is converted to more complex molecules by plants during photosynthesis.

1.53 In 2004, about 95.0 billion lb of sulfuric acid were produced in the United States. Convert this quantity to tons.

1.54 In determining the density of a rectangular metal bar, a student made the following measurements: length, 8.53 cm; width, 2.4 cm; height, 1.0 cm; mass, 52.7064 g. Calculate the density of the metal to the correct number of significant figures.

1.55   Calculate the mass of each of the following: (a) a sphere of gold with a radius of 10.0 cm [the volume of a sphere with a radius r is $V = (4/3)\pi r^3$; the density of gold = 19.3 g/cm^3], (b) a cube of platinum of edge length 0.040 mm (the density of platinum = 21.4 g/cm^3), (c) 50.0 mL of ethanol (the density of ethanol = 0.798 g/mL).

1.56   A cylindrical glass tube 12.7 cm in length is filled with mercury. The mass of mercury needed to fill the tube is 105.5 g. Calculate the inner diameter of the tube. (The density of mercury = 13.6 g/mL.)

1.57   The following procedure was used to determine the volume of a flask. The flask was weighed dry and then filled with water. If the masses of the empty flask and filled flask were 56.12 g and 87.39 g, respectively, and the density of water is 0.9976 g/cm^3, calculate the volume of the flask in cm^3.

1.58   The speed of sound in air at room temperature is about 343 m/s. Calculate this speed in miles per hour. (1 mi = 1609 m.)

1.59   A piece of silver (Ag) metal weighing 194.3 g is placed in a graduated cylinder containing 242.0 mL of water. The volume of water now reads 260.5 mL. From these data calculate the density of silver.

1.60   The experiment described in Problem 1.59 is a crude but convenient way to determine the density of some solids. Describe a similar experiment that would enable you to measure the density of ice. Specifically, what would be the requirements for the liquid used in your experiment?

1.61   A lead sphere has a mass of 1.20×10^4 g, and its volume is 1.05×10^3 cm^3. Calculate the density of lead.

1.62   Lithium is the least dense metal known (density: 0.53 g/cm^3). What is the volume occupied by 1.20×10^3 g of lithium?

1.63   The medicinal thermometer commonly used in homes can be read $\pm 0.1°$F, whereas those in the doctor's office may be accurate to $\pm 0.1°$C. In degrees Celsius, express the percent error expected from each of these thermometers in measuring a person's body temperature of 38.9°C.

1.64   Vanillin (used to flavor vanilla ice cream and other foods) is the substance whose aroma the human nose detects in the smallest amount. The threshold limit is 2.0×10^{-11} g per liter of air. If the current price of 50 g of vanillin is $112, determine the cost to supply enough vanillin so that the aroma could be detected in a large aircraft hangar with a volume of 5.0×10^7 ft^3.

1.65   At what temperature does the numerical reading on a Celsius thermometer equal that on a Fahrenheit thermometer?

1.66   Suppose that a new temperature scale has been devised on which the melting point of ethanol ($-117.3°$C) and the boiling point of ethanol (78.3°C) are taken as 0°S and 100°S, respectively, where S is the symbol for the new temperature scale. Derive an equation relating a reading on this scale to a reading on the Celsius scale. What would this thermometer read at 25°C?

1.67   A resting adult requires about 240 mL of pure oxygen/min and breathes about 12 times every minute. If inhaled air contains 20 percent oxygen by volume and exhaled air 16 percent, what is the volume of air per breath? (Assume that the volume of inhaled air is equal to that of exhaled air.)

1.68   (a) Referring to Problem 1.67, calculate the total volume (in liters) of air an adult breathes in a day. (b) In a city with heavy traffic, the air contains 2.1×10^{-6} L of carbon monoxide (a poisonous gas) per liter. Calculate the average daily intake of carbon monoxide in liters by a person.

1.69   The total volume of seawater is 1.5×10^{21} L. Assume that seawater contains 3.1 percent sodium chloride by mass and that its density is 1.03 g/mL. Calculate the total mass of sodium chloride in kilograms and in tons. (1 ton = 2000 lb; 1 lb = 453.6 g.)

1.70   Magnesium (Mg) is a valuable metal used in alloys, in batteries, and in the manufacture of chemicals. It is obtained mostly from seawater, which contains about 1.3 g of Mg for every kilogram of seawater. Referring to Problem 1.69, calculate the volume of seawater (in liters) needed to extract 8.0×10^4 tons of Mg, which is roughly the annual production in the United States.

1.71   A student is given a crucible and asked to prove whether it is made of pure platinum. She first weighs the crucible in air and then weighs it suspended in water (density = 0.9986 g/mL). The readings are 860.2 g and 820.2 g, respectively. Based on these measurements and given that the density of platinum is 21.45 g/cm^3, what should her conclusion be? (*Hint:* An object suspended in a fluid is buoyed up by the mass of the fluid displaced by the object. Neglect the buoyance of air.)

1.72   The surface area and average depth of the Pacific Ocean are 1.8×10^8 km^2 and 3.9×10^3 m, respectively. Calculate the volume of water in the ocean in liters.

1.73   The unit "troy ounce" is often used for precious metals such as gold (Au) and platinum (Pt). (1 troy ounce = 31.103 g.) (a) A gold coin weighs 2.41 troy ounces. Calculate its mass in grams. (b) Is a troy ounce heavier or lighter than an ounce? (1 lb = 16 oz; 1 lb = 453.6 g.)

1.74   Osmium (Os) is the densest element known (density = 22.57 g/cm^3). Calculate the mass in pounds and in kilograms of an Os sphere 15 cm in diameter (about the size of a grapefruit). See Problem 1.55 for volume of a sphere.

1.75   Percent error is often expressed as the absolute value of the difference between the true value and the experimental value, divided by the true value:

$$\text{percent error} = \frac{|\text{true value} - \text{experimental value}|}{|\text{true value}|} \times 100\%$$

The vertical lines indicate absolute value. Calculate the percent error for the following measurements: (a) The density of alcohol (ethanol) is found to be 0.802 g/mL. (True value: 0.798 g/mL.) (b) The mass of gold in an earring is analyzed to be 0.837 g. (True value: 0.864 g.)

1.76 The natural abundances of elements in the human body, expressed as percent by mass, are: oxygen (O), 65 percent; carbon (C), 18 percent; hydrogen (H), 10 percent; nitrogen (N), 3 percent; calcium (Ca), 1.6 percent; phosphorus (P), 1.2 percent; all other elements, 1.2 percent. Calculate the mass in grams of each element in the body of a 62-kg person.

1.77 The men's world record for running a mile outdoors (as of 1997) is 3 min 44.39 s. At this rate, how long would it take to run a 1500-m race? (1 mi = 1609 m.)

1.78 Venus, the second closest planet to the sun, has a surface temperature of 7.3×10^2 K. Convert this temperature to °C and °F.

1.79 Chalcopyrite, the principal ore of copper (Cu), contains 34.63 percent Cu by mass. How many grams of Cu can be obtained from 5.11×10^3 kg of the ore?

1.80 It has been estimated that 8.0×10^4 tons of gold (Au) have been mined. Assume gold costs $350 per ounce. What is the total worth of this quantity of gold?

1.81 A 1.0-mL volume of seawater contains about 4.0×10^{-12} g of gold. The total volume of ocean water is 1.5×10^{21} L. Calculate the total amount of gold (in grams) that is present in seawater, and the worth of the gold in dollars (see Problem 1.80). With so much gold out there, why hasn't someone become rich by mining gold from the ocean?

1.82 Measurements show that 1.0 g of iron (Fe) contains 1.1×10^{22} Fe atoms. How many Fe atoms are in 4.9 g of Fe, which is the total amount of iron in the body of an average adult?

1.83 The thin outer layer of Earth, called the crust, contains only 0.50 percent of Earth's total mass and yet is the source of almost all the elements (the atmosphere provides elements such as oxygen, nitrogen, and a few other gases). Silicon (Si) is the second most abundant element in Earth's crust (27.2 percent by mass). Calculate the mass of silicon in kilograms in Earth's crust. (The mass of Earth is 5.9×10^{21} tons. 1 ton = 2000 lb; 1 lb = 453.6 g.)

1.84 The diameter of a copper (Cu) atom is roughly 1.3×10^{-10} m. How many times can you divide evenly a piece of 10-cm copper wire until it is reduced to two separate copper atoms? (Assume there are appropriate tools for this procedure and that copper atoms are lined up in a straight line, in contact with each other. Round off your answer to an integer.)

1.85 One gallon of gasoline in an automobile's engine produces on the average 9.5 kg of carbon dioxide, which is a greenhouse gas, that is, it promotes the warming of Earth's atmosphere. Calculate the annual production of carbon dioxide in kilograms if there are 40 million cars in the United States and each car covers a distance of 5000 mi at a consumption rate of 20 miles per gallon.

1.86 A sheet of aluminum (Al) foil has a total area of 1.000 ft^2 and a mass of 3.636 g. What is the thickness of the foil in millimeters? (Density of Al = 2.699 g/cm^3.)

1.87 Comment on whether each of the following is a homogeneous mixture or a heterogeneous mixture: (a) air in a closed bottle and (b) air over New York City.

1.88 Chlorine is used to disinfect swimming pools. The accepted concentration for this purpose is 1 ppm chlorine, or 1 g of chlorine per million grams of water. Calculate the volume of a chlorine solution (in milliliters) a homeowner should add to her swimming pool if the solution contains 6.0 percent chlorine by mass and there are 2.0×10^4 gallons of water in the pool. (1 gallon = 3.79 L; density of liquids = 1.0 g/mL.)

1.89 The world's total petroleum reserve is estimated at 2.0×10^{22} J (joule is the unit of energy where 1 J = 1 kg m^2/s^2). At the present rate of consumption, 1.8×10^{20} J/yr, how long would it take to exhaust the supply?

1.90 In water conservation, chemists spread a thin film of certain inert material over the surface of water to cut down the rate of evaporation of water in reservoirs. This technique was pioneered by Benjamin Franklin three centuries ago. Franklin found that 0.10 mL of oil could spread over the surface of water of about 40 m^2 in area. Assuming that the oil forms a *monolayer*, that is, a layer that is only one molecule thick, estimate the length of each oil molecule in nanometers. (1 nm = 1×10^{-9} m.)

1.91 Fluoridation is the process of adding fluorine compounds to drinking water to help fight tooth decay. A concentration of 1 ppm of fluorine is sufficient for the purpose. (1 ppm means one part per million, or 1 g of fluorine per 1 million g of water.) The compound normally chosen for fluoridation is sodium fluoride, which is also added to some toothpastes. Calculate the quantity of sodium fluoride in kilograms needed per year for a city of 50,000 people if the daily consumption of water per person is 150 gallons. What percent of the sodium fluoride is "wasted" if each person uses only 6.0 L of water a day for drinking and cooking? (Sodium fluoride is 45.0 percent fluorine by mass. 1 gallon = 3.79 L; 1 year = 365 days; density of water = 1.0 g/mL.)

1.92 A gas company in Massachusetts charges $1.30 for 15.0 ft^3 of natural gas. (a) Convert this rate to dollars per liter of gas. (b) If it takes 0.304 ft^3 of gas to boil a liter of water, starting at room temperature (25°C), how much would it cost to boil a 2.1-L kettle of water?

1.93 Pheromones are compounds secreted by females of many insect species to attract mates. Typically, 1.0×10^{-8} g of a pheromone is sufficient to reach all targeted males within a radius of 0.50 mi. Calculate the density of the pheromone (in grams per liter) in a circular air space having a radius of 0.50 mi and a height of 40 ft.

Special Problems

1.94 A bank teller is asked to assemble "one-dollar" sets of coins for his clients. Each set is made of three quarters, one nickel, and two dimes. The masses of the coins are: quarter: 5.645 g; nickel: 4.967 g; dime: 2.316 g. What is the maximum number of sets that can be assembled from 33.871 kg of quarters, 10.432 kg of nickels, and 7.990 kg of dimes? What is the total mass (in g) of this collection of coins?

1.95 A graduated cylinder is filled to the 40.00-mL mark with a mineral oil. The masses of the cylinder before and after the addition of the mineral oil are 124.966 g and 159.446 g, respectively. In a separate experiment, a metal ball bearing of mass 18.713 g is placed in the cylinder and the cylinder is again filled to the 40.00-mL mark with the mineral oil. The combined mass of the ball bearing and mineral oil is 50.952 g. Calculate the density and radius of the ball bearing. [The volume of a sphere of radius r is $(4/3)\pi r^3$.]

1.96 Bronze is an alloy made of copper (Cu) and tin (Sn). Calculate the mass of a bronze cylinder of radius 6.44 cm and length 44.37 cm. The composition of the bronze is 79.42 percent Cu and 20.58 percent Sn and the densities of Cu and Sn are 8.94 g/cm³ and 7.31 g/cm³, respectively. What assumption should you make in this calculation?

1.97 A chemist in the nineteenth century prepared an unknown substance. In general, do you think it would be more difficult to prove that it is an element or a compound? Explain.

1.98 A chemist mixes two liquids A and B to form a homogeneous mixture. The densities of the liquids are 2.0514 g/mL for A and 2.6678 g/mL for B. When she drops a small object into the mixture, she finds that the object becomes suspended in the liquid; that is, it neither sinks nor floats. If the mixture is made of 41.37 percent A and 58.63 percent B by volume, what is the density of the metal? Can this procedure be used in general to determine the densities of solids? What assumptions must be made in applying this method?

1.99 You are given a liquid. Briefly describe steps you would take to show whether it is a pure substance or a homogeneous mixture.

1.100 Tums is a popular remedy for acid indigestion. A typical Tums tablet contains calcium carbonate plus some inert substances. When ingested, it reacts with the gastric juice (hydrochloric acid) in the stomach to give off carbon dioxide gas. When a 1.328-g tablet reacted with 40.00 mL of hydrochloric acid (density: 1.140 g/mL), carbon dioxide gas was given off and the resulting solution weighed 46.699 g. Calculate the number of liters of carbon dioxide gas released if its density is 1.81 g/L.

1.101 A 250-mL glass bottle was filled with 242 mL of water at 20°C and tightly capped. It was then left outdoors overnight, where the average temperature was −5°C. Predict what would happen. The density of water at 20°C is 0.998 g/cm³ and that of ice at −5°C is 0.916 g/cm³.

Answers to Practice Exercises

1.1 96.5 g. **1.2** 341 g. **1.3** (a) 621.5°F, (b) 78.3°C, (c) −196°C. **1.4** (a) Two, (b) four, (c) three, (d) two, (e) three or two. **1.5** (a) 26.76 L, (b) 4.4 g, (c) 1.6×10^7 dm², (d) 0.0756 g/mL, (e) 6.69×10^4 m. **1.6** 2.36 lb. **1.7** 1.08×10^5 m³. **1.8** 0.534 g/cm³.

C H E M I C A L
Mystery

The Disappearance of the Dinosaurs

Dinosaurs dominated life on Earth for millions of years and then disappeared very suddenly. To solve the mystery, paleontologists studied fossils and skeletons found in rocks in various layers of Earth's crust. Their findings enabled them to map out which species existed on Earth during specific geologic periods. They also revealed no dinosaur skeletons in rocks formed immediately after the Cretaceous period, which dates back some 65 million years. It is therefore assumed that the dinosaurs became extinct about 65 million years ago.

Among the many hypotheses put forward to account for their disappearance were disruptions of the food chain and a dramatic change in climate caused by violent volcanic eruptions. However, there was no convincing evidence for any one hypothesis until 1977. It was then that a group of paleontologists working in Italy obtained some very puzzling data at a site near Gubbio. The chemical analysis of a layer of clay deposited above sediments formed during the Cretaceous period (and therefore a layer that records events occurring *after* the Cretaceous period) showed a surprisingly high content of the element iridium (Ir). Iridium is very rare in Earth's crust but is comparatively abundant in asteroids.

This investigation led to the hypothesis that the extinction of dinosaurs occurred as follows. To account for the quantity of iridium found, scientists suggested that a large asteroid several miles in diameter hit Earth about the time the dinosaurs disappeared. The impact of the asteroid on Earth's surface must have been so tremendous that it literally vaporized a large quantity of surrounding rocks, soils, and other objects. The resulting dust and debris floated through the air and blocked the sunlight for months or perhaps years. Without ample sunlight most plants could not grow, and the fossil record confirms that many types of plants did indeed die out at this time. Consequently, of course, many plant-eating animals perished, and then, in turn, meat-eating animals began to starve. Dwindling food sources would obviously affect large animals needing great amounts of food more quickly and more severely than small animals. Therefore, the huge dinosaurs, the largest of which might have weighed as much as 30 tons, vanished due to lack of food.

Chemical Clues

1. How does the study of dinosaur extinction illustrate the scientific method?

2. Suggest two ways that would enable you to test the asteroid collision hypothesis.

3. In your opinion, is it justifiable to refer to the asteroid explanation as the theory of dinosaur extinction?

4. Available evidence suggests that about 20 percent of the asteroid's mass turned to dust and spread uniformly over Earth after settling out of the upper atmosphere. This dust amounted to about 0.02 g/cm^2 of Earth's surface. The asteroid very likely had a density of about 2 g/cm^3. Calculate the mass (in kilograms and tons) of the asteroid and its radius in meters, assuming that it was a sphere. (The area of Earth is $5.1 \times 10^{14} \, m^2$; 1 lb = 453.6 g,) (Source: *Consider a Spherical Cow—A Course in Environmental Problem Solving* by J. Harte, University Science Books, Mill Valley, CA 1988. Used with permission.)

Colored images of the radioactive emission of radium (Ra). The models show the nuclei of radium and the radioactive decay products—radon (Rn) and an alpha particle, which has two protons and two neutrons. Study of radioactivity helped to advance scientists' knowledge about atomic structure.

Atoms, Molecules, and Ions

A LOOK AHEAD

- We begin with a historical perspective of the search for the fundamental units of matter. The modern version of atomic theory was laid by John Dalton in the nineteenth century, who postulated that elements are composed of extremely small particles, called atoms. All atoms of a given element are identical, but they are different from atoms of all other elements. (2.1)

- We note that, through experimentation, scientists have learned that an atom is composed of three elementary particles: proton, electron, and neutron. The proton has a positive charge, the electron has a negative charge, and the neutron has no charge. Protons and neutrons are located in a small region at the center of the atom, called the nucleus, while electrons are spread out about the nucleus at some distance from it. (2.2)

- We will learn the following ways to identify atoms. Atomic number is the number of protons in a nucleus; atoms of different elements have different atomic numbers. Isotopes are atoms of the same element having a different number of neutrons. Mass number is the sum of the number of protons and neutrons in an atom. Because an atom is electrically neutral, it contains an equal number of protons and electrons. (2.3)

- Next we will see how elements can be grouped together according to their chemical and physical properties in a chart called the periodic table. The periodic table enables us to classify elements (as metals, metalloids, and nonmetals) and correlate their properties in a systematic way. (2.4)

- We will see that atoms of most elements interact to form compounds, which are classified as molecules or ionic compounds made of positive (cations) and negative (anions) ions. (2.5)

- We then learn to use chemical formulas (molecular and empirical) to represent molecules and ionic compounds and models to represent molecules. (2.6)

- We learn a set of rules that help us name the inorganic compounds. (2.7)

- This chapter ends with a brief introduction to the organic world to which we will return in Chapter 24. (2.8)

Interactive Activity Summary

1. Animation: Cathode Ray Tube (2.2)
2. Animation: Millikan Oil Drop (2.2)
3. Animation: Alpha, Beta, and Gamma Rays (2.2)
4. Animation: α-Particle Scattering (2.2)

Since ancient times humans have pondered the nature of matter. Our modern ideas of the structure of matter began to take shape in the early nineteenth century with Dalton's atomic theory. We now know that all matter is made of atoms, molecules, and ions. All of chemistry is concerned in one way or another with these species.

2.1 The Atomic Theory

In the fifth century B.C. the Greek philosopher Democritus expressed the belief that all matter consists of very small, indivisible particles, which he named *atomos* (meaning uncuttable or indivisible). Although Democritus' idea was not accepted by many of his contemporaries (notably Plato and Aristotle), somehow it endured. Experimental evidence from early scientific investigations provided support for the notion of "atomism" and gradually gave rise to the modern definitions of elements and compounds. It was in 1808 that an English scientist and school teacher, John Dalton,[†] formulated a precise definition of the indivisible building blocks of matter that we call atoms.

Dalton's work marked the beginning of the modern era of chemistry. The hypotheses about the nature of matter on which Dalton's atomic theory is based can be summarized as follows:

1. Elements are composed of extremely small particles called atoms.

2. All atoms of a given element are identical, having the same size, mass, and chemical properties. The atoms of one element are different from the atoms of all other elements.

3. Compounds are composed of atoms of more than one element. In any compound, the ratio of the numbers of atoms of any two of the elements present is either an integer or a simple fraction.

4. A chemical reaction involves only the separation, combination, or rearrangement of atoms; it does not result in their creation or destruction.

Figure 2.1 is a schematic representation of the last three hypotheses.

Dalton's concept of an atom was far more detailed and specific than Democritus'. The second hypothesis states that atoms of one element are different from atoms of all other elements. Dalton made no attempt to describe the structure or composition of atoms—he had no idea what an atom is really like. But he did realize that the different properties shown by elements such as hydrogen and oxygen can be explained by assuming that hydrogen atoms are not the same as oxygen atoms.

The third hypothesis suggests that, to form a certain compound, we need not only atoms of the right kinds of elements, but specific numbers of these atoms as well. This

---

[†]John Dalton (1766–1844). English chemist, mathematician, and philosopher. In addition to the atomic theory, he also formulated several gas laws and gave the first detailed description of color blindness, from which he suffered. Dalton was described as an indifferent experimenter, and singularly wanting in the language and power of illustration. His only recreation was lawn bowling on Thursday afternoons. Perhaps it was the sight of those wooden balls that provided him with the idea of the atomic theory.

Figure 2.1 *(a) According to Dalton's atomic theory, atoms of the same element are identical, but atoms of one element are different from atoms of other elements. (b) Compound formed from atoms of elements X and Y. In this case, the ratio of the atoms of element X to the atoms of element Y is 2:1. Note that a chemical reaction results only in the rearrangement of atoms, not in their destruction or creation.*

Atoms of element X   Atoms of element Y   Compounds of elements X and Y

(a)   (b)

idea is an extension of a law published in 1799 by Joseph Proust,[†] a French chemist. Proust's **law of definite proportions** states that *different samples of the same compound always contain its constituent elements in the same proportion by mass.* Thus, if we were to analyze samples of carbon dioxide gas obtained from different sources, we would find in each sample the same ratio by mass of carbon to oxygen. It stands to reason, then, that if the ratio of the masses of different elements in a given compound is fixed, the ratio of the atoms of these elements in the compound also must be constant.

Dalton's third hypothesis supports another important law, the **law of multiple proportions.** According to the law, *if two elements can combine to form more than one compound, the masses of one element that combine with a fixed mass of the other element are in ratios of small whole numbers.* Dalton's theory explains the law of multiple proportions quite simply: Different compounds made up of the same elements differ in the number of atoms of each kind that combine. For example, carbon forms two stable compounds with oxygen, namely, carbon monoxide and carbon dioxide. Modern measurement techniques indicate that one atom of carbon combines with one atom of oxygen in carbon monoxide and with two atoms of oxygen in carbon dioxide. Thus, the ratio of oxygen in carbon monoxide to oxygen in carbon dioxide is 1:2. This result is consistent with the law of multiple proportions (Figure 2.2).

Dalton's fourth hypothesis is another way of stating the **law of conservation of mass,**[‡] which is that *matter can be neither created nor destroyed.* Because matter is made of atoms that are unchanged in a chemical reaction, it follows that mass must be conserved as well. Dalton's brilliant insight into the nature of matter was the main stimulus for the rapid progress of chemistry during the nineteenth century.

Carbon monoxide

Carbon dioxide

Ratio of oxygen in carbon monoxide to oxygen in carbon dioxide: 1:2

Figure 2.2 *An illustration of the law of multiple proportions.*

2.2 The Structure of the Atom

On the basis of Dalton's atomic theory, we can define an **atom** as *the basic unit of an element that can enter into chemical combination.* Dalton imagined an atom that was both extremely small and indivisible. However, a series of investigations that began in the 1850s and extended into the twentieth century clearly demonstrated that atoms actually possess internal structure; that is, they are made up of even smaller particles, which are called *subatomic particles.* This research led to the discovery of three such particles—electrons, protons, and neutrons.

The Electron

In the 1890s many scientists became caught up in the study of **radiation,** *the emission and transmission of energy through space in the form of waves.* Information gained from this research contributed greatly to our understanding of atomic structure. One device used to investigate this phenomenon was a cathode ray tube, the forerunner of the television tube (Figure 2.3). It is a glass tube from which most of the air has been evacuated. When the two metal plates are connected to a high-voltage source, the negatively charged plate, called the *cathode,* emits an invisible ray. The cathode ray is drawn to the positively charged plate, called the *anode,* where it passes through a hole and continues traveling to the other end of the tube. When the ray strikes the specially coated surface, it produces a strong fluorescence, or bright light.

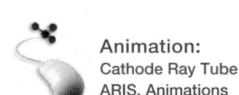

Animation:
Cathode Ray Tube
ARIS, Animations

[†]Joseph Louis Proust (1754–1826). French chemist. Proust was the first person to isolate sugar from grapes.

[‡]According to Albert Einstein, mass and energy are alternate aspects of a single entity called *mass-energy.* Chemical reactions usually involve a gain or loss of heat and other forms of energy. Thus, when energy is lost in a reaction, for example, mass is also lost. Except for nuclear reactions (see Chapter 23), however, changes of mass in chemical reactions are too small to detect. Therefore, for all practical purposes mass is conserved.

Figure 2.3 *A cathode ray tube with an electric field perpendicular to the direction of the cathode rays and an external magnetic field. The symbols N and S denote the north and south poles of the magnet. The cathode rays will strike the end of the tube at A in the presence of a magnetic field, at C in the presence of an electric field, and at B when there are no external fields present or when the effects of the electric field and magnetic field cancel each other.*

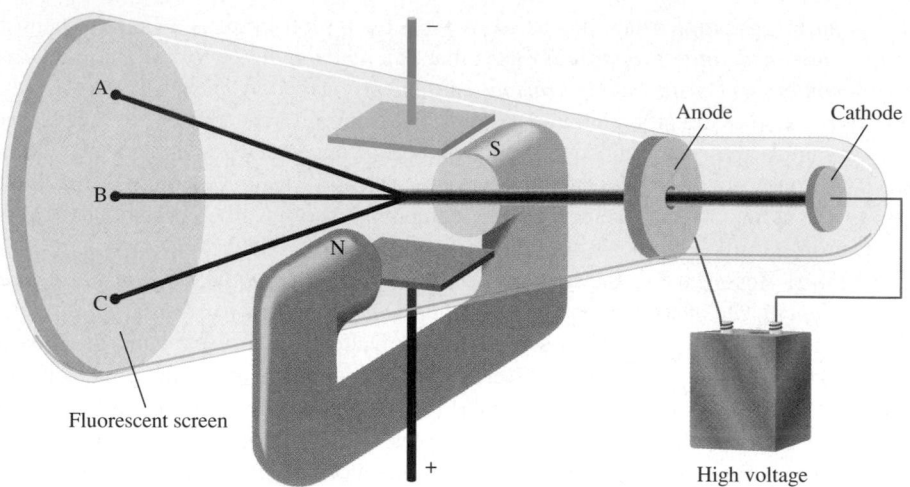

Electrons are normally associated with atoms. However, they can also be studied individually.

In some experiments, two electrically charged plates and a magnet were added to the *outside* of the cathode ray tube (see Figure 2.3). When the magnetic field is on and the electric field is off, the cathode ray strikes point A. When only the electric field is on, the ray strikes point C. When both the magnetic and the electric fields are off or when they are both on but balanced so that they cancel each other's influence, the ray strikes point B. According to electromagnetic theory, a moving charged body behaves like a magnet and can interact with electric and magnetic fields through which it passes. Because the cathode ray is attracted by the plate bearing positive charges and repelled by the plate bearing negative charges, it must consist of negatively charged particles. We know these *negatively charged particles* as **electrons.** Figure 2.4 shows the effect of a bar magnet on the cathode ray.

An English physicist, J. J. Thomson,[†] used a cathode ray tube and his knowledge of electromagnetic theory to determine the ratio of electric charge to the mass of an

(a)   (b)   (c)

Figure 2.4 *(a) A cathode ray produced in a discharge tube. The ray itself is invisible, but the fluorescence of a zinc sulfide coating on the glass causes it to appear green. (b) The cathode ray is bent downward when the north pole of the bar magnet is brought toward it. (c) When the polarity of the magnet is reversed, the ray bends in the opposite direction.*

[†]Joseph John Thomson (1856–1940). British physicist who received the Nobel Prize in Physics in 1906 for discovering the electron.

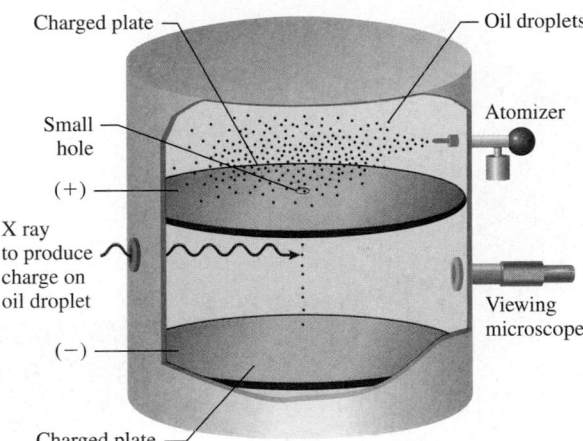

Figure 2.5 *Schematic diagram of Millikan's oil drop experiment.*

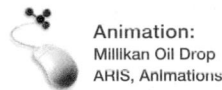

Animation:
Millikan Oil Drop
ARIS, Animations

individual electron. The number he came up with was -1.76×10^8 C/g, where C stands for *coulomb,* which is the unit of electric charge. Thereafter, in a series of experiments carried out between 1908 and 1917, R. A. Millikan[†] succeeded in measuring the charge of the electron with great precision. His work proved that the charge on each electron was exactly the same. In his experiment, Millikan examined the motion of single tiny drops of oil that picked up static charge from ions in the air. He suspended the charged drops in air by applying an electric field and followed their motions through a microscope (Figure 2.5). Using his knowledge of electrostatics, Millikan found the charge of an electron to be -1.6022×10^{-19} C. From these data he calculated the mass of an electron:

$$
\begin{aligned}
\text{mass of an electron} &= \frac{\text{charge}}{\text{charge/mass}} \\
&= \frac{-1.6022 \times 10^{-19}\ \text{C}}{-1.76 \times 10^8\ \text{C/g}} \\
&= 9.10 \times 10^{-28}\ \text{g}
\end{aligned}
$$

This is an exceedingly small mass.

Radioactivity

In 1895, the German physicist Wilhelm Röntgen[‡] noticed that cathode rays caused glass and metals to emit very unusual rays. This highly energetic radiation penetrated matter, darkened covered photographic plates, and caused a variety of substances to fluoresce. Because these rays could not be deflected by a magnet, they could not contain charged particles as cathode rays do. Röntgen called them X rays because their nature was not known.

Not long after Röntgen's discovery, Antoine Becquerel,[§] a professor of physics in Paris, began to study the fluorescent properties of substances. Purely by accident, he found that exposing thickly wrapped photographic plates to a certain uranium

[†]Robert Andrews Millikan (1868–1953). American physicist who was awarded the Nobel Prize in Physics in 1923 for determining the charge of the electron.

[‡]Wilhelm Konrad Röntgen (1845–1923). German physicist who received the Nobel Prize in Physics in 1901 for the discovery of X rays.

[§]Antoine Henri Becquerel (1852–1908). French physicist who was awarded the Nobel Prize in Physics in 1903 for discovering radioactivity in uranium.

Figure 2.6 *Three types of rays emitted by radioactive elements. β Rays consist of negatively charged particles (electrons) and are therefore attracted by the positively charged plate. The opposite holds true for α rays— they are positively charged and are drawn to the negatively charged plate. Because γ rays have no charges, their path is unaffected by an external electric field.*

Lead block

Radioactive substance

Animation:
Alpha, Beta, and Gamma Rays
ARIS, Animations

compound caused them to darken, even without the stimulation of cathode rays. Like X rays, the rays from the uranium compound were highly energetic and could not be deflected by a magnet, but they differed from X rays because they arose spontaneously. One of Becquerel's students, Marie Curie,[†] suggested the name ***radioactivity*** to describe this *spontaneous emission of particles and/or radiation.* Since then, any element that spontaneously emits radiation is said to be *radioactive.*

Three types of rays are produced by the *decay,* or breakdown, of radioactive substances such as uranium. Two of the three are deflected by oppositely charged metal plates (Figure 2.6). ***Alpha (α) rays*** consist of *positively charged particles,* called ***α particles,*** and therefore are deflected by the positively charged plate. ***Beta (β) rays,*** or ***β particles,*** are *electrons* and are deflected by the negatively charged plate. The third type of radioactive radiation consists of high-energy rays called ***gamma (γ) rays.*** Like X rays, γ rays have no charge and are not affected by an external field.

The Proton and the Nucleus

By the early 1900s, two features of atoms had become clear: they contain electrons, and they are electrically neutral. To maintain electric neutrality, an atom must contain an equal number of positive and negative charges. Therefore, Thomson proposed that an atom could be thought of as a uniform, positive sphere of matter in which electrons are embedded like raisins in a cake (Figure 2.7). This so-called "plum-pudding" model was the accepted theory for a number of years.

In 1910 the New Zealand physicist Ernest Rutherford,[‡] who had studied with Thomson at Cambridge University, decided to use α particles to probe the structure

Positive charge spread over the entire sphere

Figure 2.7 *Thomson's model of the atom, sometimes described as the "plum-pudding" model, after a traditional English dessert containing raisins. The electrons are embedded in a uniform, positively charged sphere.*

[†]Marie (Marya Sklodowska) Curie (1867–1934). Polish-born chemist and physicist. In 1903 she and her French husband, Pierre Curie, were awarded the Nobel Prize in Physics for their work on radioactivity. In 1911, she again received the Nobel prize, this time in chemistry, for her work on the radioactive elements radium and polonium. She is one of only three people to have received two Nobel prizes in science. Despite her great contribution to science, her nomination to the French Academy of Sciences in 1911 was rejected by one vote because she was a woman! Her daughter Irene, and son-in-law Frederic Joliot-Curie, shared the Nobel Prize in Chemistry in 1935.

[‡]Ernest Rutherford (1871–1937). New Zealand physicist. Rutherford did most of his work in England (Manchester and Cambridge Universities). He received the Nobel Prize in Chemistry in 1908 for his investigations into the structure of the atomic nucleus. His often-quoted comment to his students was that "all science is either physics or stamp-collecting."

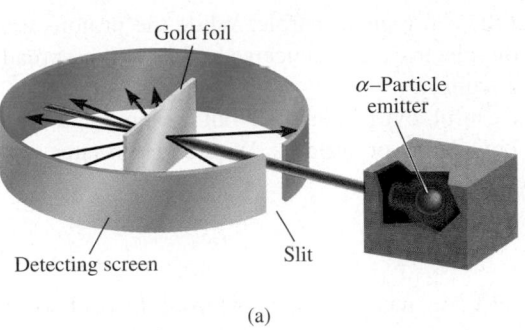

Gold foil

α–Particle
emitter

Detecting screen   Slit

(a)

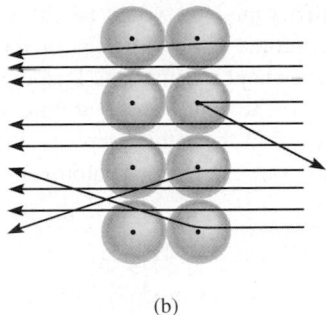

(b)

Figure 2.8 *(a) Rutherford's experimental design for measuring the scattering of α particles by a piece of gold foil. Most of the α particles passed through the gold foil with little or no deflection. A few were deflected at wide angles. Occasionally an α particle was turned back. (b) Magnified view of α particles passing through and being deflected by nuclei.*

of atoms. Together with his associate Hans Geiger[†] and an undergraduate named Ernest Marsden,[‡] Rutherford carried out a series of experiments using very thin foils of gold and other metals as targets for α particles from a radioactive source (Figure 2.8). They observed that the majority of particles penetrated the foil either undeflected or with only a slight deflection. But every now and then an α particle was scattered (or deflected) at a large angle. In some instances, an α particle actually bounced back in the direction from which it had come! This was a most surprising finding, for in Thomson's model the positive charge of the atom was so diffuse that the positive α particles should have passed through the foil with very little deflection. To quote Rutherford's initial reaction when told of this discovery: "It was as incredible as if you had fired a 15-inch shell at a piece of tissue paper and it came back and hit you."

Rutherford was later able to explain the results of the α-scattering experiment in terms of a new model for the atom. According to Rutherford, most of the atom must be empty space. This explains why the majority of α particles passed through the gold foil with little or no deflection. The atom's positive charges, Rutherford proposed, are all concentrated in the **nucleus,** which is *a dense central core within the atom.* Whenever an α particle came close to a nucleus in the scattering experiment, it experienced a large repulsive force and therefore a large deflection. Moreover, an α particle traveling directly toward a nucleus would be completely repelled and its direction would be reversed.

The positively charged particles in the nucleus are called **protons.** In separate experiments, it was found that each proton carries the same *quantity* of charge as an electron and has a mass of 1.67262×10^{-24} g—about 1840 times the mass of the oppositely charged electron.

At this stage of investigation, scientists perceived the atom as follows: The mass of a nucleus constitutes most of the mass of the entire atom, but the nucleus occupies only about $1/10^{13}$ of the volume of the atom. We express atomic (and molecular) dimensions in terms of the SI unit called the *picometer (pm),* where

$$1 \text{ pm} = 1 \times 10^{-12} \text{ m}$$

A typical atomic radius is about 100 pm, whereas the radius of an atomic nucleus is only about 5×10^{-3} pm. You can appreciate the relative sizes of an atom and its nucleus by imagining that if an atom were the size of a sports stadium, the volume

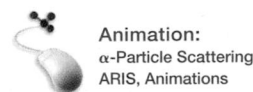

Animation:
α-Particle Scattering
ARIS, Animations

A common non-SI unit for atomic length is the angstrom (Å; 1 Å = 100 pm).

If the size of an atom were expanded to that of this sports stadium, the size of the nucleus would be that of a marble.

[†]Johannes Hans Wilhelm Geiger (1882–1945). German physicist. Geiger's work focused on the structure of the atomic nucleus and on radioactivity. He invented a device for measuring radiation that is now commonly called the Geiger counter.

[‡]Ernest Marsden (1889–1970). English physicist. It is gratifying to know that at times an undergraduate can assist in winning a Nobel Prize. Marsden went on to contribute significantly to the development of science in New Zealand.

of its nucleus would be comparable to that of a small marble. While the protons are confined to the nucleus of the atom, the electrons are conceived of as being spread out about the nucleus at some distance from it.

The concept of atomic radius is useful experimentally, but it should not be inferred that atoms have well-defined boundaries or surfaces. We will learn later that the outer regions of atoms are relatively "fuzzy."

The Neutron

Rutherford's model of atomic structure left one major problem unsolved. It was known that hydrogen, the simplest atom, contains only one proton and that the helium atom contains two protons. Therefore, the ratio of the mass of a helium atom to that of a hydrogen atom should be 2:1. (Because electrons are much lighter than protons, their contribution to atomic mass can be ignored.) In reality, however, the ratio is 4:1. Rutherford and others postulated that there must be another type of subatomic particle in the atomic nucleus; the proof was provided by another English physicist, James Chadwick,[†] in 1932. When Chadwick bombarded a thin sheet of beryllium with α particles, a very high-energy radiation similar to γ rays was emitted by the metal. Later experiments showed that the rays actually consisted of a third type of subatomic particles, which Chadwick named **neutrons,** because they proved to be *electrically neutral particles having a mass slightly greater than that of protons.* The mystery of the mass ratio could now be explained. In the helium nucleus there are two protons and two neutrons, but in the hydrogen nucleus there is only one proton and no neutrons; therefore, the ratio is 4:1.

Figure 2.9 shows the location of the elementary particles (protons, neutrons, and electrons) in an atom. There are other subatomic particles, but the electron, the proton, and the neutron are the three fundamental components of the atom that are important in chemistry. Table 2.1 shows the masses and charges of these three elementary particles.

[†]James Chadwick (1891–1972). British physicist. In 1935 he received the Nobel Prize in Physics for proving the existence of neutrons.

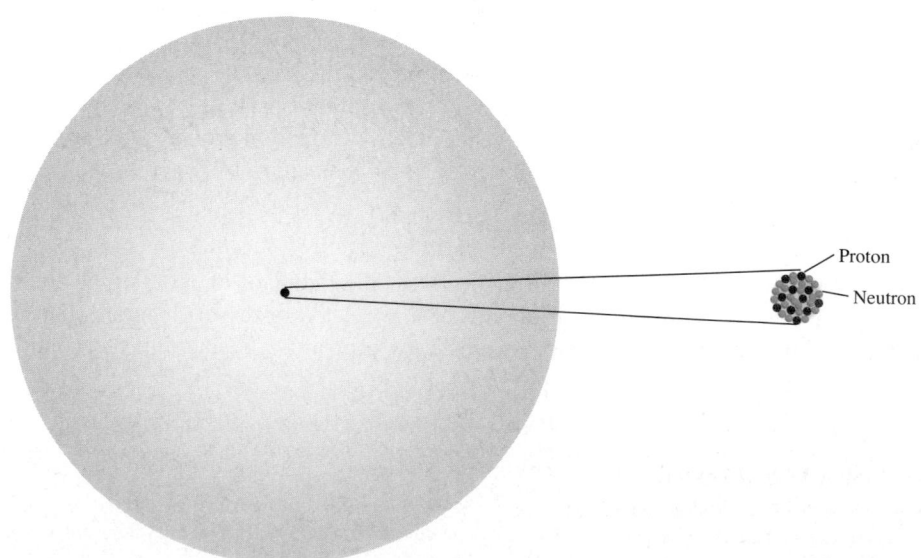

Figure 2.9 *The protons and neutrons of an atom are packed in an extremely small nucleus. Electrons are shown as "clouds" around the nucleus.*

Proton

Neutron

TABLE 2.1	Mass and Charge of Subatomic Particles		
		Charge	
Particle	**Mass (g)**	**Coulomb**	**Charge Unit**
Electron*	9.10939×10^{-28}	-1.6022×10^{-19}	-1
Proton	1.67262×10^{-24}	$+1.6022 \times 10^{-19}$	$+1$
Neutron	1.67493×10^{-24}	0	0

*More refined measurements have given us a more accurate value of an electron's mass than Millikan's.

2.3 Atomic Number, Mass Number, and Isotopes

All atoms can be identified by the number of protons and neutrons they contain. The *atomic number (Z)* is *the number of protons in the nucleus of each atom of an element.* In a neutral atom the number of protons is equal to the number of electrons, so the atomic number also indicates the number of electrons present in the atom. The chemical identity of an atom can be determined solely from its atomic number. For example, the atomic number of fluorine is 9. This means that each fluorine atom has 9 protons and 9 electrons. Or, viewed another way, every atom in the universe that contains 9 protons is correctly named "fluorine."

The *mass number (A)* is *the total number of neutrons and protons present in the nucleus of an atom of an element.* Except for the most common form of hydrogen, which has one proton and no neutrons, all atomic nuclei contain both protons and neutrons. In general, the mass number is given by

$$\text{mass number} = \text{number of protons} + \text{number of neutrons}$$
$$= \text{atomic number} + \text{number of neutrons}$$

The number of neutrons in an atom is equal to the difference between the mass number and the atomic number, or $(A - Z)$. For example, the mass number of fluorine is 19 and the atomic number is 9. Thus, the number of neutrons in an atom of fluorine is $19 - 9 = 10$. Note that the atomic number, number of neutrons, and mass number all must be positive integers (whole numbers).

Atoms of a given element do not all have the same mass. Most elements have two or more *isotopes,* *atoms that have the same atomic number but different mass numbers.* For example, there are three isotopes of hydrogen. One, simply known as hydrogen, has one proton and no neutrons. The *deuterium* isotope contains one proton and one neutron, and *tritium* has one proton and two neutrons. The accepted way to denote the atomic number and mass number of an atom of an element (X) is as follows:

$$\text{mass number} \searrow {}^{A}_{Z}\text{X}$$
$$\text{atomic number} \nearrow$$

Thus, for the isotopes of hydrogen, we write

$$\underset{\text{hydrogen}}{{}^{1}_{1}\text{H}} \qquad \underset{\text{deuterium}}{{}^{2}_{1}\text{H}} \qquad \underset{\text{tritium}}{{}^{3}_{1}\text{H}}$$

As another example, consider two common isotopes of uranium with mass numbers of 235 and 238, respectively:

$$^{235}_{92}\text{U} \qquad ^{238}_{92}\text{U}$$

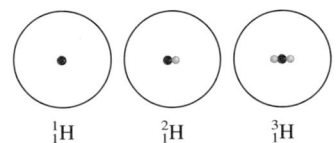

$$\underset{{}^{1}_{1}\text{H}}{} \qquad \underset{{}^{2}_{1}\text{H}}{} \qquad \underset{{}^{3}_{1}\text{H}}{}$$

The first isotope is used in nuclear reactors and atomic bombs, whereas the second isotope lacks the properties necessary for these applications. With the exception of hydrogen, which has different names for each of its isotopes, isotopes of elements are identified by their mass numbers. Thus, the preceding two isotopes are called uranium-235 (pronounced "uranium two thirty-five") and uranium-238 (pronounced "uranium two thirty-eight").

The chemical properties of an element are determined primarily by the protons and electrons in its atoms; neutrons do not take part in chemical changes under normal conditions. Therefore, isotopes of the same element have similar chemistries, forming the same types of compounds and displaying similar reactivities.

Example 2.1 shows how to calculate the number of protons, neutrons, and electrons using atomic numbers and mass numbers.

Example 2.1

Give the number of protons, neutrons, and electrons in each of the following species: (a) $^{17}_{8}O$, (b) $^{199}_{80}Hg$, and (c) $^{200}_{80}Hg$.

Strategy Recall that the superscript denotes mass number and the subscript denotes atomic number. Mass number is always greater than atomic number. (The only exception is $^{1}_{1}H$, where the mass number is equal to the atomic number.)

Solution

(a) The atomic number is 8, so there are 8 protons. The mass number is 17, so the number of neutrons is $17 - 8 = 9$. The number of electrons is the same as the number of protons, that is, 8.

(b) The atomic number is 80, so there are 80 protons. The mass number is 199, so the number of neutrons is $199 - 80 = 119$. The number of electrons is 80.

(c) Here the number of protons is the same as in (b), or 80. The number of neutrons is $200 - 80 = 120$. The number of electrons is also the same as in (b), 80. The species in (b) and (c) are chemically similar isotopes of mercury.

Practice Exercise How many protons, neutrons, and electrons are in the following isotope of copper: $^{63}_{29}Cu$?

Similar problems: 2.15, 2.16.

2.4 The Periodic Table

More than half of the elements known today were discovered between 1800 and 1900. During this period, chemists noted that many elements show strong similarities to one another. Recognition of periodic regularities in physical and chemical behavior and the need to organize the large volume of available information about the structure and properties of elemental substances led to the development of the *periodic table, a chart in which elements having similar chemical and physical properties are grouped together.* Figure 2.10 shows the modern periodic table in which the elements are arranged by atomic number (shown above the element symbol) in *horizontal rows* called *periods* and in *vertical columns* known as *groups* or *families,* according to similarities in their chemical properties. Note that elements 112, 114, and 116 have recently been synthesized, although they have not yet been named.

The elements can be divided into three categories—metals, nonmetals, and metalloids. A *metal* is *a good conductor of heat and electricity* while a *nonmetal* is usually *a poor conductor of heat and electricity.* A *metalloid has properties that are*

1 1A																	18 8A
1 H	2 2A											13 3A	14 4A	15 5A	16 6A	17 7A	2 He
3 Li	4 Be											5 B	6 C	7 N	8 O	9 F	10 Ne
11 Na	12 Mg	3 3B	4 4B	5 5B	6 6B	7 7B	8	9 8B	10	11 1B	12 2B	13 Al	14 Si	15 P	16 S	17 Cl	18 Ar
19 K	20 Ca	21 Sc	22 Ti	23 V	24 Cr	25 Mn	26 Fe	27 Co	28 Ni	29 Cu	30 Zn	31 Ga	32 Ge	33 As	34 Se	35 Br	36 Kr
37 Rb	38 Sr	39 Y	40 Zr	41 Nb	42 Mo	43 Tc	44 Ru	45 Rh	46 Pd	47 Ag	48 Cd	49 In	50 Sn	51 Sb	52 Te	53 I	54 Xe
55 Cs	56 Ba	57 La	72 Hf	73 Ta	74 W	75 Re	76 Os	77 Ir	78 Pt	79 Au	80 Hg	81 Tl	82 Pb	83 Bi	84 Po	85 At	86 Rn
87 Fr	88 Ra	89 Ac	104 Rf	105 Db	106 Sg	107 Bh	108 Hs	109 Mt	110 Ds	111 Rg	112	(113)	114	(115)	116	(117)	(118)

58 Ce	59 Pr	60 Nd	61 Pm	62 Sm	63 Eu	64 Gd	65 Tb	66 Dy	67 Ho	68 Er	69 Tm	70 Yb	71 Lu
90 Th	91 Pa	92 U	93 Np	94 Pu	95 Am	96 Cm	97 Bk	98 Cf	99 Es	100 Fm	101 Md	102 No	103 Lr

Metals

Metalloids

Nonmetals

Figure 2.10 *The modern periodic table. The elements are arranged according to the atomic numbers above their symbols. With the exception of hydrogen (H), nonmetals appear at the far right of the table. The two rows of metals beneath the main body of the table are conventionally set apart to keep the table from being too wide. Actually, cerium (Ce) should follow lanthanum (La), and thorium (Th) should come right after actinium (Ac). The 1–18 group designation has been recommended by the International Union of Pure and Applied Chemistry (IUPAC) but is not yet in wide use. In this text, we use the standard U.S. notation for group numbers (1A–8A and 1B–8B). No names have yet been assigned to elements 112, 114, and 116. Elements 113, 115, 117, and 118 have not yet been synthesized.*

intermediate between those of metals and nonmetals. Figure 2.10 shows that the majority of known elements are metals; only 17 elements are nonmetals, and 8 elements are metalloids. From left to right across any period, the physical and chemical properties of the elements change gradually from metallic to nonmetallic.

Elements are often referred to collectively by their periodic table group number (Group 1A, Group 2A, and so on). However, for convenience, some element groups have been given special names. *The Group 1A elements (Li, Na, K, Rb, Cs, and Fr) are called **alkali metals,** and the Group 2A elements (Be, Mg, Ca, Sr, Ba, and Ra) are called **alkaline earth metals.** Elements in Group 7A (F, Cl, Br, I, and At) are known as **halogens,** and elements in Group 8A (He, Ne, Ar, Kr, Xe, and Rn) are called **noble gases,*** or *rare gases.*

The periodic table is a handy tool that correlates the properties of the elements in a systematic way and helps us to make predictions about chemical behavior. We will take a closer look at this keystone of chemistry in Chapter 8.

The Chemistry in Action essay on p. 52 describes the distribution of the elements on Earth and in the human body.

CHEMISTRY
in Action

Distribution of Elements on Earth and in Living Systems

The majority of elements are naturally occurring. How are these elements distributed on Earth, and which are essential to living systems?

Earth's crust extends from the surface to a depth of about 40 km (about 25 mi). Because of technical difficulties, scientists have not been able to study the inner portions of Earth as easily as the crust. Nevertheless, it is believed that there is a solid core consisting mostly of iron at the center of Earth. Surrounding the core is a layer called the *mantle*, which consists of hot fluid containing iron, carbon, silicon, and sulfur.

Of the 83 elements that are found in nature, 12 make up 99.7 percent of Earth's crust by mass. They are, in decreasing order of natural abundance, oxygen (O), silicon (Si), aluminum (Al), iron (Fe), calcium (Ca), magnesium (Mg), sodium (Na), potassium (K), titanium (Ti), hydrogen (H), phosphorus (P), and manganese (Mn). In discussing the natural abundance of the elements, we should keep in mind that (1) the elements are not evenly distributed throughout Earth's crust, and (2) most elements occur in combined forms. These facts provide the basis for most methods of obtaining pure elements from their compounds, as we will see in later chapters.

The accompanying table lists the essential elements in the human body. Of special interest are the *trace elements*, such as iron (Fe), copper (Cu), zinc (Zn), iodine (I), and cobalt (Co), which together make up about 0.1 percent of the body's mass. These elements are necessary for biological functions such as growth, transport of oxygen for metabolism, and defense against disease. There is a delicate balance in the amounts of these elements in our bodies. Too much or too little over an extended period of time can lead to serious illness, retardation, or even death.

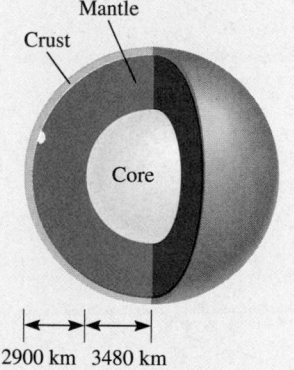

Structure of Earth's interior.

Essential Elements in the Human Body

Element	Percent by Mass*	Element	Percent by Mass*
Oxygen	65	Sodium	0.1
Carbon	18	Magnesium	0.05
Hydrogen	10	Iron	<0.05
Nitrogen	3	Cobalt	<0.05
Calcium	1.6	Copper	<0.05
Phosphorus	1.2	Zinc	<0.05
Potassium	0.2	Iodine	<0.05
Sulfur	0.2	Selenium	<0.01
Chlorine	0.2	Fluorine	<0.01

*Percent by mass *gives the mass of the element in grams present in a 100-g sample.*

(a) Natural abundance of the elements in percent by mass. For example, oxygen's abundance is 45.5 percent. This means that in a 100-g sample of Earth's crust there are, on the average, 45.5 g of the element oxygen. (b) Abundance of elements in the human body in percent by mass.

(a)

(b)

2.5 Molecules and Ions

Of all the elements, only the six noble gases in Group 8A of the periodic table (He, Ne, Ar, Kr, Xe, and Rn) exist in nature as single atoms. For this reason, they are called *monatomic* (meaning a single atom) gases. Most matter is composed of molecules or ions formed by atoms.

Molecules

A *molecule* is an *aggregate of at least two atoms in a definite arrangement held together by chemical forces* (also called *chemical bonds*). A molecule may contain atoms of the same element or atoms of two or more elements joined in a fixed ratio, in accordance with the law of definite proportions stated in Section 2.1. Thus, a molecule is not necessarily a compound, which, by definition, is made up of two or more elements (see Section 1.4). Hydrogen gas, for example, is a pure element, but it consists of molecules made up of two H atoms each. Water, on the other hand, is a molecular compound that contains hydrogen and oxygen in a ratio of two H atoms and one O atom. Like atoms, molecules are electrically neutral.

We will discuss the nature of chemical bonds in Chapters 9 and 10.

The hydrogen molecule, symbolized as H_2, is called a *diatomic molecule* because it *contains only two atoms*. Other elements that normally exist as diatomic molecules are nitrogen (N_2) and oxygen (O_2), as well as the Group 7A elements—fluorine (F_2), chlorine (Cl_2), bromine (Br_2), and iodine (I_2). Of course, a diatomic molecule can contain atoms of different elements. Examples are hydrogen chloride (HCl) and carbon monoxide (CO).

Elements that exist as diatomic molecules.

The vast majority of molecules contain more than two atoms. They can be atoms of the same element, as in ozone (O_3), which is made up of three atoms of oxygen, or they can be combinations of two or more different elements. *Molecules containing more than two atoms* are called *polyatomic molecules.* Like ozone, water (H_2O) and ammonia (NH_3) are polyatomic molecules.

Ions

An *ion* is *an atom or a group of atoms that has a net positive or negative charge.* The number of positively charged protons in the nucleus of an atom remains the same during ordinary chemical changes (called chemical reactions), but negatively charged electrons may be lost or gained. The loss of one or more electrons from a neutral atom results in a *cation,* an ion with a net positive charge. For example, a sodium atom (Na) can readily lose an electron to become a sodium cation, which is represented by Na^+:

In Chapter 8 we will see why atoms of different elements gain (or lose) a specific number of electrons.

Na Atom	Na$^+$ Ion
11 protons	11 protons
11 electrons	10 electrons

On the other hand, an *anion* is *an ion whose net charge is negative* due to an increase in the number of electrons. A chlorine atom (Cl), for instance, can gain an electron to become the chloride ion Cl^-:

Cl Atom	Cl$^-$ Ion
17 protons	17 protons
17 electrons	18 electrons

Sodium chloride (NaCl), ordinary table salt, is called an *ionic compound* because it is *formed from cations and anions.*

1 1A																	18 8A
	2 2A											13 3A	14 4A	15 5A	16 6A	17 7A	
Li⁺													C⁴⁻	N³⁻	O²⁻	F⁻	
Na⁺	Mg²⁺	3 3B	4 4B	5 5B	6 6B	7 7B	8	9 —8B—	10	11 1B	12 2B	Al³⁺		P³⁻	S²⁻	Cl⁻	
K⁺	Ca²⁺				Cr²⁺ Cr³⁺	Mn²⁺ Mn³⁺	Fe²⁺ Fe³⁺	Co²⁺ Co³⁺	Ni²⁺ Ni³⁺	Cu⁺ Cu²⁺	Zn²⁺				Se²⁻	Br⁻	
Rb⁺	Sr²⁺									Ag⁺	Cd²⁺		Sn²⁺ Sn⁴⁺		Te²⁻	I⁻	
Cs⁺	Ba²⁺									Au⁺ Au³⁺	Hg₂²⁺ Hg²⁺		Pb²⁺ Pb⁴⁺				

Figure 2.11 *Common monatomic ions arranged according to their positions in the periodic table. Note that the* Hg_2^{2+} *ion contains two atoms.*

An atom can lose or gain more than one electron. Examples of ions formed by the loss or gain of more than one electron are Mg^{2+}, Fe^{3+}, S^{2-}, and N^{3-}. These ions, as well as Na^+ and Cl^-, are called **monatomic ions** because they *contain only one atom*. Figure 2.11 shows the charges of a number of monatomic ions. With very few exceptions, metals tend to form cations and nonmetals form anions.

In addition, two or more atoms can combine to form an ion that has a net positive or net negative charge. **Polyatomic ions** such as OH^- (hydroxide ion), CN^- (cyanide ion), and NH_4^+ (ammonium ion) are *ions containing more than one atom.*

2.6 Chemical Formulas

Chemists use **chemical formulas** to *express the composition of molecules and ionic compounds in terms of chemical symbols.* By composition we mean not only the elements present but also the ratios in which the atoms are combined. Here we are concerned with two types of formulas: molecular formulas and empirical formulas.

Molecular Formulas

A **molecular formula** *shows the exact number of atoms of each element in the smallest unit of a substance.* In our discussion of molecules, each example was given with its molecular formula in parentheses. Thus, H_2 is the molecular formula for hydrogen, O_2 is oxygen, O_3 is ozone, and H_2O is water. The subscript numeral indicates the number of atoms of an element present. There is no subscript for O in H_2O because there is only one atom of oxygen in a molecule of water, and so the number "one" is omitted from the formula. Note that oxygen (O_2) and ozone (O_3) are allotropes of oxygen. An **allotrope** is *one of two or more distinct forms of an element.* Two allotropic forms of the element carbon—diamond and graphite—are dramatically different not only in properties but also in their relative cost.

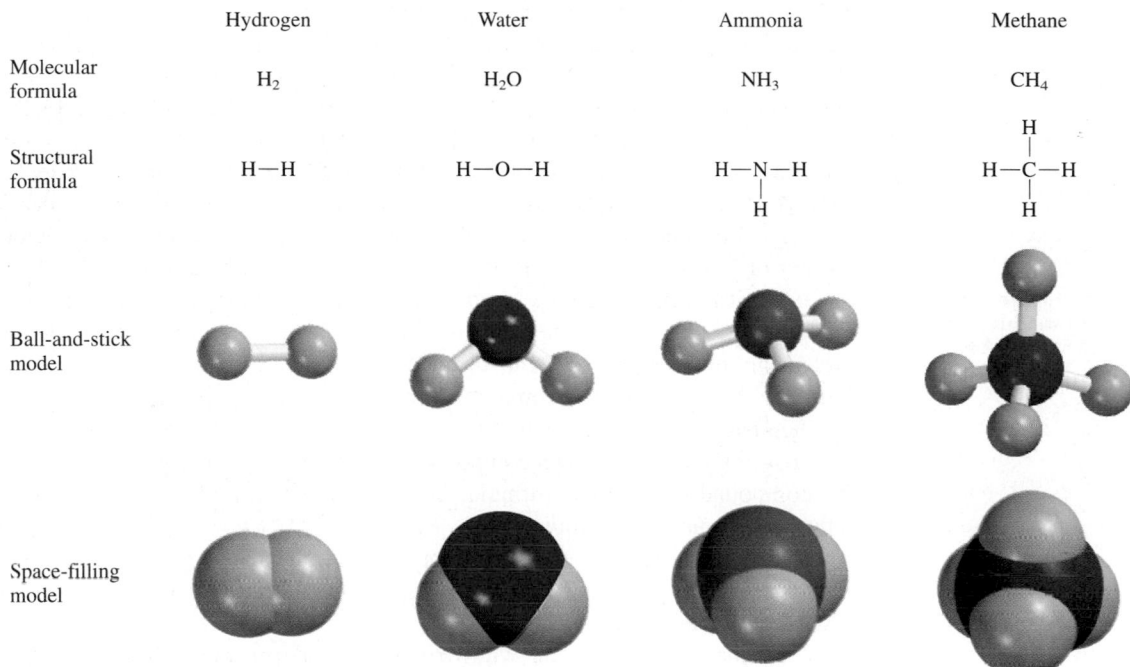

	Hydrogen	Water	Ammonia	Methane
Molecular formula	H_2	H_2O	NH_3	CH_4

Figure 2.12 *Molecular and structural formulas and molecular models of four common molecules.*

Molecular Models

Molecules are too small for us to observe directly. An effective means of visualizing them is by the use of molecular models. Two standard types of molecular models are currently in use: *ball-and-stick* models and *space-filling* models (Figure 2.12). In ball-and-stick model kits, the atoms are wooden or plastic balls with holes in them. Sticks or springs are used to represent chemical bonds. The angles they form between atoms approximate the bond angles in actual molecules. With the exception of the H atom, the balls are all the same size and each type of atom is represented by a specific color. In space-filling models, atoms are represented by truncated balls held together by snap fasteners, so that the bonds are not visible. The balls are proportional in size to atoms. The first step toward building a molecular model is writing the **structural formula,** which *shows how atoms are bonded to one another in a molecule.* For example, it is known that each of the two H atoms is bonded to an O atom in the water molecule. Therefore, the structural formula of water is H—O—H. A line connecting the two atomic symbols represents a chemical bond.

See back end paper for color codes for atoms.

Ball-and-stick models show the three-dimensional arrangement of atoms clearly, and they are fairly easy to construct. However, the balls are not proportional to the size of atoms. Furthermore, the sticks greatly exaggerate the space between atoms in a molecule. Space-filling models are more accurate because they show the variation in atomic size. Their drawbacks are that they are time-consuming to put together and they do not show the three-dimensional positions of atoms very well. We will use both models extensively in this text.

Empirical Formulas

The molecular formula of hydrogen peroxide, a substance used as an antiseptic and as a bleaching agent for textiles and hair, is H_2O_2. This formula indicates that each

H_2O_2

hydrogen peroxide molecule consists of two hydrogen atoms and two oxygen atoms. The ratio of hydrogen to oxygen atoms in this molecule is 2:2 or 1:1. The empirical formula of hydrogen peroxide is HO.Thus, the ***empirical formula*** *tells us which elements are present and the simplest whole-number ratio of their atoms,* but not necessarily the actual number of atoms in a given molecule.As another example, consider the compound hydrazine (N_2H_4), which is used as a rocket fuel.The empirical formula of hydrazine is NH_2. Although the ratio of nitrogen to hydrogen is 1:2 in both the molecular formula (N_2H_4) and the empirical formula (NH_2), only the molecular formula tells us the actual number of N atoms (two) and H atoms (four) present in a hydrazine molecule.

Empirical formulas are the *simplest* chemical formulas; they are written by reducing the subscripts in the molecular formulas to the smallest possible whole numbers.Molecular formulas are the *true* formulas of molecules.If we know the molecular formula, we also know the empirical formula, but the reverse is not true.Why, then, do chemists bother with empirical formulas?As we will see in Chapter 3, when chemists analyze an unknown compound, the first step is usually the determination of the compound's empirical formula.With additional information, it is possible to deduce the molecular formula.

For many molecules, the molecular formula and the empirical formula are one and the same.Some examples are water (H_2O), ammonia (NH_3), carbon dioxide (CO_2), and methane (CH_4).

Examples 2.2 and 2.3 deal with writing molecular formulas from molecular models and writing empirical formulas from molecular formulas.

The word "empirical" means "derived from experiment." As we will see in Chapter 3, empirical formulas are determined experimentally.

Methanol

Similar problems: 2.47, 2.48.

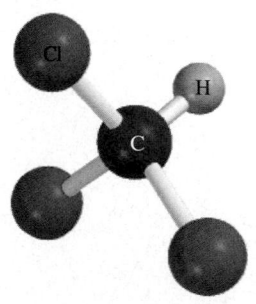

Chloroform

Example 2.2

Write the molecular formula of methanol, an organic solvent and antifreeze, from its ball-and-stick model, shown in the margin.

Solution Refer to the labels (also see back endpapers).There are four H atoms, one C atom, and one O atom.Therefore, the molecular formula is CH_4O. However, the standard way of writing the molecular formula for methanol is CH_3OH because it shows how the atoms are joined in the molecule.

Practice Exercise Write the molecular formula of chloroform, which is used as a solvent and a cleansing agent.The ball-and-stick model of chloroform is shown in the margin.

Example 2.3

Write the empirical formulas for the following molecules: (a) acetylene (C_2H_2), which is used in welding torches; (b) glucose ($C_6H_{12}O_6$), a substance known as blood sugar; and (c) nitrous oxide (N_2O), a gas that is used as an anesthetic gas ("laughing gas") and as an aerosol propellant for whipped creams.

Strategy Recall that to write the empirical formula, the subscripts in the molecular formula must be converted to the smallest possible whole numbers.

Solution

(a) There are two carbon atoms and two hydrogen atoms in acetylene.Dividing the subscripts by 2, we obtain the empirical formula CH.

(Continued)

(b) In glucose there are 6 carbon atoms, 12 hydrogen atoms, and 6 oxygen atoms. Dividing the subscripts by 6, we obtain the empirical formula CH_2O. Note that if we had divided the subscripts by 3, we would have obtained the formula $C_2H_4O_2$. Although the ratio of carbon to hydrogen to oxygen atoms in $C_2H_4O_2$ is the same as that in $C_6H_{12}O_6$ (1:2:1), $C_2H_4O_2$ is not the simplest formula because its subscripts are not in the smallest whole-number ratio.

(c) Because the subscripts in N_2O are already the smallest possible whole numbers, the empirical formula for nitrous oxide is the same as its molecular formula.

Similar problems: 2.45, 2.46.

Practice Exercise Write the empirical formula for caffeine ($C_8H_{10}N_4O_2$), a stimulant found in tea and coffee.

Formula of Ionic Compounds

The formulas of ionic compounds are usually the same as their empirical formulas because ionic compounds do not consist of discrete molecular units. For example, a solid sample of sodium chloride (NaCl) consists of equal numbers of Na^+ and Cl^- ions arranged in a three-dimensional network (Figure 2.13). In such a compound there is a 1:1 ratio of cations to anions so that the compound is electrically neutral. As you can see in Figure 2.13, no Na^+ ion in NaCl is associated with just one particular Cl^- ion. In fact, each Na^+ ion is equally held by six surrounding Cl^- ions and vice versa. Thus, NaCl is the empirical formula for sodium chloride. In other ionic compounds, the actual structure may be different, but the arrangement of cations and anions is such that the compounds are all electrically neutral. Note that the charges on the cation and anion are not shown in the formula for an ionic compound.

Sodium metal reacting with chlorine gas to form sodium chloride.

For ionic compounds to be electrically neutral, the sum of the charges on the cation and anion in each formula unit must be zero. If the charges on the cation and anion are numerically different, we apply the following rule to make the formula electrically neutral: *The subscript of the cation is numerically equal to the charge on the anion, and the subscript of the anion is numerically equal to the charge on the cation. If the charges are numerically equal, then no subscripts are necessary.* This rule follows from the fact that because the formulas of ionic compounds are usually empirical

(a)   (b)   (c)

Figure 2.13 *(a) Structure of solid NaCl. (b) In reality, the cations are in contact with the anions. In both (a) and (b), the smaller spheres represent Na^+ ions and the larger spheres, Cl^- ions. (c) Crystals of NaCl.*

formulas, the subscripts must always be reduced to the smallest ratios. Let us consider some examples.

- **Potassium Bromide.** The potassium cation K^+ and the bromine anion Br^- combine to form the ionic compound potassium bromide. The sum of the charges is $+1 + (-1) = 0$, so no subscripts are necessary. The formula is KBr.

- **Zinc Iodide.** The zinc cation Zn^{2+} and the iodine anion I^- combine to form zinc iodide. The sum of the charges of one Zn^{2+} ion and one I^- ion is $+2 + (-1) = +1$. To make the charges add up to zero we multiply the -1 charge of the anion by 2 and add the subscript "2" to the symbol for iodine. Therefore the formula for zinc iodide is ZnI_2.

- **Aluminum Oxide.** The cation is Al^{3+} and the oxygen anion is O^{2-}. The following diagram helps us determine the subscripts for the compound formed by the cation and the anion:

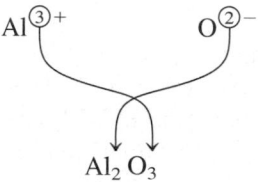

The sum of the charges is $2(+3) + 3(-2) = 0$. Thus, the formula for aluminum oxide is Al_2O_3.

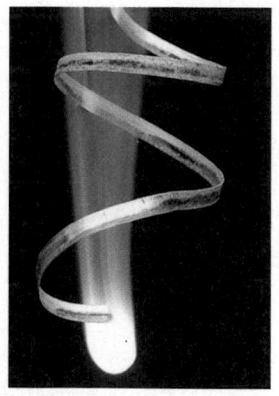

When magnesium burns in air, it forms both magnesium oxide and magnesium nitride.

Similar problems: 2.43, 2.44.

Example 2.4

Write the formula of magnesium nitride, containing the Mg^{2+} and N^{3-} ions.

Strategy Our guide for writing formulas for ionic compounds is electrical neutrality; that is, the total charge on the cation(s) must be equal to the total charge on the anion(s). Because the charges on the Mg^{2+} and N^{3-} ions are not equal, we know the formula cannot be MgN. Instead, we write the formula as Mg_xN_y, where x and y are subscripts to be determined.

Solution To satisfy electrical neutrality, the following relationship must hold:

$$(+2)x + (-3)y = 0$$

Solving, we obtain $x/y = 3/2$. Setting $x = 3$ and $y = 2$, we write

Check The subscripts are reduced to the smallest whole number ratio of the atoms because the chemical formula of an ionic compound is usually its empirical formula.

Practice Exercise Write the formulas of the following ionic compounds: (a) chromium sulfate (containing the Cr^{3+} and SO_4^{2-} ions) and (b) titanium oxide (containing the Ti^{4+} and O^{2-} ions).

2.7 Naming Compounds

When chemistry was a young science and the number of known compounds was small, it was possible to memorize their names. Many of the names were derived from their physical appearance, properties, origin, or application—for example, milk of magnesia, laughing gas, limestone, caustic soda, lye, washing soda, and baking soda.

Today the number of known compounds is well over 20 million. Fortunately, it is not necessary to memorize their names. Over the years chemists have devised a clear system for naming chemical substances. The rules are accepted worldwide, facilitating communication among chemists and providing a useful way of labeling an overwhelming variety of substances. Mastering these rules now will prove beneficial almost immediately as we proceed with our study of chemistry.

To begin our discussion of chemical *nomenclature,* the naming of chemical compounds, we must first distinguish between inorganic and organic compounds. ***Organic compounds*** *contain carbon, usually in combination with elements such as hydrogen, oxygen, nitrogen, and sulfur.* All other compounds are classified as ***inorganic compounds.*** For convenience, some carbon-containing compounds, such as carbon monoxide (CO), carbon dioxide (CO_2), carbon disulfide (CS_2), compounds containing the cyanide group (CN^-), and carbonate (CO_3^{2-}) and bicarbonate (HCO_3^-) groups are considered to be inorganic compounds. Section 2.8 gives a brief introduction to organic compounds.

To organize and simplify our venture into naming compounds, we can divide inorganic compounds into four categories: ionic compounds, molecular compounds, acids and bases, and hydrates.

Ionic Compounds

In Section 2.5 we learned that ionic compounds are made up of cations (positive ions) and anions (negative ions). With the important exception of the ammonium ion, NH_4^+, all cations of interest to us are derived from metal atoms. Metal cations take their names from the elements. For example,

The most reactive metals (green) and the most reactive nonmetals (blue) combine to form ionic compounds.

Element		Name of Cation	
Na	sodium	Na^+	sodium ion (or sodium cation)
K	potassium	K^+	potassium ion (or potassium cation)
Mg	magnesium	Mg^{2+}	magnesium ion (or magnesium cation)
Al	aluminum	Al^{3+}	aluminum ion (or aluminum cation)

Many ionic compounds are ***binary compounds,*** or *compounds formed from just two elements.* For binary compounds, the first element named is the metal cation, followed by the nonmetallic anion. Thus, NaCl is sodium chloride. The anion is named by taking the first part of the element name (chlorine) and adding "-ide." Potassium bromide (KBr), zinc iodide (ZnI_2), and aluminum oxide (Al_2O_3) are also binary compounds. Table 2.2 shows the "-ide" nomenclature of some common monatomic anions according to their positions in the periodic table.

The "-ide" ending is also used for certain anion groups containing different elements, such as hydroxide (OH^-) and cyanide (CN^-). Thus, the compounds LiOH and KCN are named lithium hydroxide and potassium cyanide, respectively. These and a number of other such ionic substances are called ***ternary compounds,*** meaning *compounds consisting of three elements.* Table 2.3 lists alphabetically the names of a number of common cations and anions.

Certain metals, especially the *transition metals,* can form more than one type of cation. Take iron as an example. Iron can form two cations: Fe^{2+} and Fe^{3+}. An older

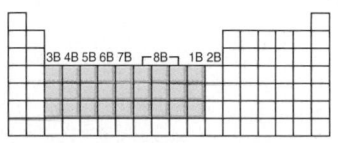

The transition metals are the elements in Groups 1B and 3B–8B (see Figure 2.10).

TABLE 2.2	The "-ide" Nomenclature of Some Common Monatomic Anions According to Their Positions in the Periodic Table			

Group 4A	Group 5A	Group 6A	Group 7A
C carbide (C^{4-})*	N nitride (N^{3-})	O oxide (O^{2-})	F fluoride (F^-)
Si silicide (Si^{4-})	P phosphide (P^{3-})	S sulfide (S^{2-})	Cl chloride (Cl^-)
		Se selenide (Se^{2-})	Br bromide (Br^-)
		Te telluride (Te^{2-})	I iodide (I^-)

*The word "carbide" is also used for the anion C_2^{2-}.

TABLE 2.3	Names and Formulas of Some Common Inorganic Cations and Anions

Cation	Anion
aluminum (Al^{3+})	bromide (Br^-)
ammonium (NH_4^+)	carbonate (CO_3^{2-})
barium (Ba^{2+})	chlorate (ClO_3^-)
cadmium (Cd^{2+})	chloride (Cl^-)
calcium (Ca^{2+})	chromate (CrO_4^{2-})
cesium (Cs^+)	cyanide (CN^-)
chromium(III) or chromic (Cr^{3+})	dichromate ($Cr_2O_7^{2-}$)
cobalt(II) or cobaltous (Co^{2+})	dihydrogen phosphate ($H_2PO_4^-$)
copper(I) or cuprous (Cu^+)	fluoride (F^-)
copper(II) or cupric (Cu^{2+})	hydride (H^-)
hydrogen (H^+)	hydrogen carbonate or bicarbonate (HCO_3^-)
iron(II) or ferrous (Fe^{2+})	hydrogen phosphate (HPO_4^{2-})
iron(III) or ferric (Fe^{3+})	hydrogen sulfate or bisulfate (HSO_4^-)
lead(II) or plumbous (Pb^{2+})	hydroxide (OH^-)
lithium (Li^+)	iodide (I^-)
magnesium (Mg^{2+})	nitrate (NO_3^-)
manganese(II) or manganous (Mn^{2+})	nitride (N^{3-})
mercury(I) or mercurous (Hg_2^{2+})*	nitrite (NO_2^-)
mercury(II) or mercuric (Hg^{2+})	oxide (O^{2-})
potassium (K^+)	permanganate (MnO_4^-)
rubidium (Rb^+)	peroxide (O_2^{2-})
silver (Ag^+)	phosphate (PO_4^{3-})
sodium (Na^+)	sulfate (SO_4^{2-})
strontium (Sr^{2+})	sulfide (S^{2-})
tin(II) or stannous (Sn^{2+})	sulfite (SO_3^{2-})
zinc (Zn^{2+})	thiocyanate (SCN^-)

*Mercury(I) exists as a pair as shown.

nomenclature system that is still in limited use assigns the ending "-ous" to the cation with fewer positive charges and the ending "-ic" to the cation with more positive charges:

$$Fe^{2+} \qquad \text{ferrous ion}$$
$$Fe^{3+} \qquad \text{ferric ion}$$

The names of the compounds that these iron ions form with chlorine would thus be

$$FeCl_2 \qquad \text{ferrous chloride}$$
$$FeCl_3 \qquad \text{ferric chloride}$$

This method of naming ions has some distinct limitations. First, the "-ous" and "-ic" suffixes do not provide information regarding the actual charges of the two cations involved. Thus, the ferric ion is Fe^{3+}, but the cation of copper named cupric has the formula Cu^{2+}. In addition, the "-ous" and "-ic" designations provide names for only two different elemental cations. Some metallic elements can assume three or more different positive charges in compounds. Therefore, it has become increasingly common to designate different cations with Roman numerals. This is called the Stock[†] system. In this system, the Roman numeral I indicates one positive charge, II means two positive charges, and so on. For example, manganese (Mn) atoms can assume several different positive charges:

$$Mn^{2+}: MnO \qquad \text{manganese(II) oxide}$$
$$Mn^{3+}: Mn_2O_3 \qquad \text{manganese(III) oxide}$$
$$Mn^{4+}: MnO_2 \qquad \text{manganese(IV) oxide}$$

These names are pronounced "manganese-two oxide," "manganese-three oxide," and "manganese-four oxide." Using the Stock system, we denote the ferrous ion and the ferric ion as iron(II) and iron(III), respectively; ferrous chloride becomes iron(II) chloride; and ferric chloride is called iron(III) chloride. In keeping with modern practice, we will favor the Stock system of naming compounds in this textbook.

Examples 2.5 and 2.6 illustrate how to name ionic compounds and write formulas for ionic compounds based on the information given in Figure 2.11 and Tables 2.2 and 2.3.

FeCl₂ (left) and FeCl₃ (right).

For names and symbols of the elements, see front endpapers.

Example 2.5

Name the following compounds: (a) $Cu(NO_3)_2$, (b) KH_2PO_4, and (c) NH_4ClO_3.

Strategy Note that the compounds in (a) and (b) contain both metal and nonmetal atoms, so we expect them to be ionic compounds. There are no metal atoms in (c) but there is an ammonium group, which bears a positive charge. So NH_4ClO_3 is also an ionic compound. Our reference for the names of cations and anions is Table 2.3. Keep in mind that if a metal atom can form cations of different charges (see Figure 2.11), we need to use the Stock system.

Solution

(a) The nitrate ion (NO_3^-) bears one negative charge, so the copper ion must have two positive charges. Because copper forms both Cu^+ and Cu^{2+} ions, we need to use the Stock system and call the compound copper(II) nitrate.

(Continued)

[†]Alfred E. Stock (1876–1946). German chemist. Stock did most of his research in the synthesis and characterization of boron, beryllium, and silicon compounds. He was the first scientist to explore the dangers of mercury poisoning.

(b) The cation is K^+ and the anion is $H_2PO_4^-$ (dihydrogen phosphate). Because potassium only forms one type of ion (K^+), there is no need to use potassium(I) in the name. The compound is potassium dihydrogen phosphate.

(c) The cation is NH_4^+ (ammonium ion) and the anion is ClO_3^-. The compound is ammonium chlorate.

Practice Exercise Name the following compounds: (a) PbO and (b) Li_2SO_3.

Similar problems: 2.57(b), (e), (f).

Example 2.6

Write chemical formulas for the following compounds: (a) mercury(I) nitrite, (b) cesium sulfide, and (c) calcium phosphate.

Strategy We refer to Table 2.3 for the formulas of cations and anions. Recall that the Roman numerals in the Stock system provide useful information about the charges of the cation.

Solution

(a) The Roman numeral shows that the mercury ion bears a +1 charge. According to Table 2.3, however, the mercury(I) ion is diatomic (that is, Hg_2^{2+}) and the nitrite ion is NO_2^-. Therefore, the formula is $Hg_2(NO_2)_2$.

(b) Each sulfide ion bears two negative charges, and each cesium ion bears one positive charge (cesium is in Group 1A, as is sodium). Therefore, the formula is Cs_2S.

(c) Each calcium ion (Ca^{2+}) bears two positive charges, and each phosphate ion (PO_4^{3-}) bears three negative charges. To make the sum of the charges equal zero, we must adjust the numbers of cations and anions:

$$3(+2) + 2(-3) = 0$$

Thus, the formula is $Ca_3(PO_4)_2$.

Similar problems: 2.59(a), (b), (d), (h), (i).

Practice Exercise Write formulas for the following ionic compounds: (a) rubidium sulfate and (b) barium hydride.

TABLE 2.4

Greek Prefixes Used in Naming Molecular Compounds

Prefix	Meaning
mono-	1
di-	2
tri-	3
tetra-	4
penta-	5
hexa-	6
hepta-	7
octa-	8
nona-	9
deca-	10

Molecular Compounds

Unlike ionic compounds, molecular compounds contain discrete molecular units. They are usually composed of nonmetallic elements (see Figure 2.10). Many molecular compounds are binary compounds. Naming binary molecular compounds is similar to naming binary ionic compounds. We place the name of the first element in the formula first, and the second element is named by adding -ide to the root of the element name. Some examples are

HCl	hydrogen chloride
HBr	hydrogen bromide
SiC	silicon carbide

It is quite common for one pair of elements to form several different compounds. In these cases, confusion in naming the compounds is avoided by the use of Greek prefixes to denote the number of atoms of each element present (Table 2.4). Consider the following examples:

CO	carbon monoxide
CO_2	carbon dioxide

SO_2	sulfur dioxide
SO_3	sulfur trioxide
NO_2	nitrogen dioxide
N_2O_4	dinitrogen tetroxide

The following guidelines are helpful in naming compounds with prefixes:

• The prefix "mono-" may be omitted for the first element. For example, PCl_3 is named phosphorus trichloride, not monophosphorus trichloride. Thus, the absence of a prefix for the first element usually means there is only one atom of that element present in the molecule.

• For oxides, the ending "a" in the prefix is sometimes omitted. For example, N_2O_4 may be called dinitrogen tetroxide rather than dinitrogen tetraoxide.

Exceptions to the use of Greek prefixes are molecular compounds containing hydrogen. Traditionally, many of these compounds are called either by their common, nonsystematic names or by names that do not specifically indicate the number of H atoms present:

B_2H_6	diborane
CH_4	methane
SiH_4	silane
NH_3	ammonia
PH_3	phosphine
H_2O	water
H_2S	hydrogen sulfide

Note that even the order of writing the elements in the formulas for hydrogen compounds is irregular. In water and hydrogen sulfide, H is written first, whereas it appears last in the other compounds.

Writing formulas for molecular compounds is usually straightforward. Thus, the name arsenic trifluoride means that there are three F atoms and one As atom in each molecule, and the molecular formula is AsF_3. Note that the order of elements in the formula is the same as in its name.

Example 2.7

Name the following molecular compounds: (a) $SiCl_4$ and (b) P_4O_{10}.

Strategy We refer to Table 2.4 for prefixes. In (a) there is only one Si atom so we do not use the prefix "mono."

Solution (a) Because there are four chlorine atoms present, the compound is silicon tetrachloride.

(b) There are four phosphorus atoms and ten oxygen atoms present, so the compound is tetraphosphorus decoxide. Note that the "a" is omitted in "deca."

Similar problems: 2.57(c), (i), (j).

Practice Exercise Name the following molecular compounds: (a) NF_3 and (b) Cl_2O_7.

Example 2.8

Write chemical formulas for the following molecular compounds: (a) carbon disulfide and (b) disilicon hexabromide.

(Continued)

Strategy Here we need to convert prefixes to numbers of atoms (see Table 2.4). Because there is no prefix for carbon in (a), it means that there is only one carbon atom present.

Solution (a) Because there are two sulfur atoms and one carbon atom present, the formula is CS_2.

(b) There are two silicon atoms and six bromine atoms present, so the formula is Si_2Br_6.

Practice Exercise Write chemical formulas for the following molecular compounds: (a) sulfur tetrafluoride and (b) dinitrogen pentoxide.

Similar problems: 2.59(g), (j).

Figure 2.14 summarizes the steps for naming ionic and binary molecular compounds.

Acids and Bases

Naming Acids

An **_acid_** can be described as _a substance that yields hydrogen ions (H^+) when dissolved in water._ (H^+ is equivalent to one proton, and is often referred to that way.)

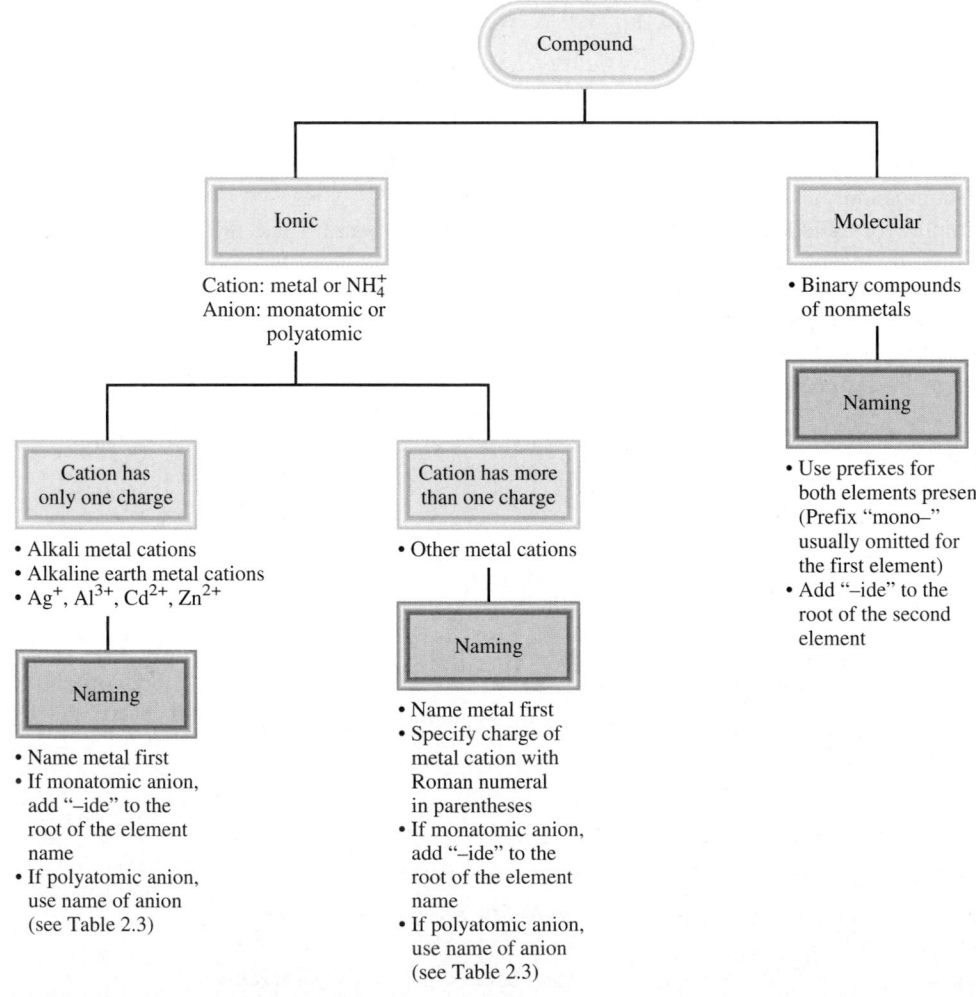

Figure 2.14 _Steps for naming ionic and binary molecular compounds._

TABLE 2.5	Some Simple Acids

Anion	Corresponding Acid
F⁻ (fluoride)	HF (hydrofluoric acid)
Cl⁻ (chloride)	HCl (hydrochloric acid)
Br⁻ (bromide)	HBr (hydrobromic acid)
I⁻ (iodide)	HI (hydroiodic acid)
CN⁻ (cyanide)	HCN (hydrocyanic acid)
S²⁻ (sulfide)	H₂S (hydrosulfuric acid)

F^- (fluoride); Cl^- (chloride); Br^- (bromide); I^- (iodide); CN^- (cyanide); S^{2-} (sulfide) → HF (hydrofluoric acid); HCl (hydrochloric acid); HBr (hydrobromic acid); HI (hydroiodic acid); HCN (hydrocyanic acid); H_2S (hydrosulfuric acid)

Note that these acids all exist as molecular compounds in the gas phase.

When dissolved in water, the HCl molecule is converted to the H^+ and Cl^- ions. The H^+ ion is associated with one or more water molecules, and is usually represented as H_3O^+.

Formulas for acids contain one or more hydrogen atoms as well as an anionic group. Anions whose names end in "-ide" form acids with a "hydro-" prefix and an "-ic" ending, as shown in Table 2.5. In some cases two different names seem to be assigned to the same chemical formula.

HCl	hydrogen chloride
HCl	hydrochloric acid

The name assigned to the compound depends on its physical state. In the gaseous or pure liquid state, HCl is a molecular compound called hydrogen chloride. When it is dissolved in water, the molecules break up into H^+ and Cl^- ions; in this state, the substance is called hydrochloric acid.

Oxoacids are acids that *contain hydrogen, oxygen, and another element (the central element)*. The formulas of oxoacids are usually written with the H first, followed by the central element and then O, as illustrated by the following examples:

HNO_3	nitric acid
H_2CO_3	carbonic acid
H_2SO_4	sulfuric acid
$HClO_3$	chloric acid

HNO_3

Often two or more oxoacids have the same central atom but a different number of O atoms. Starting with the reference oxoacids whose names end with "-ic," we use the following rules to name these compounds.

1. Addition of one O atom to the "-ic" acid: The acid is called "per . . . -ic" acid. Thus, adding an O atom to $HClO_3$ changes chloric acid to perchloric acid, $HClO_4$.

2. Removal of one O atom from the "-ic" acid: The acid is called "-ous" acid. Thus, nitric acid, HNO_3, becomes nitrous acid, HNO_2.

3. Removal of two O atoms from the "-ic" acid: The acid is called "hypo . . . -ous" acid. Thus, when $HBrO_3$ is converted to HBrO, the acid is called hypobromous acid.

The rules for naming *oxoanions, anions of oxoacids,* are as follows:

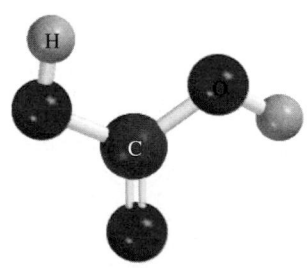

H_2CO_3

1. When all the H ions are removed from the "-ic" acid, the anion's name ends with "-ate." For example, the anion CO_3^{2-} derived from H_2CO_3 is called carbonate.

2. When all the H ions are removed from the "-ous" acid, the anion's name ends with "-ite." Thus, the anion ClO_2^- derived from $HClO_2$ is called chlorite.

Figure 2.15 *Naming oxoacids and oxoanions.*

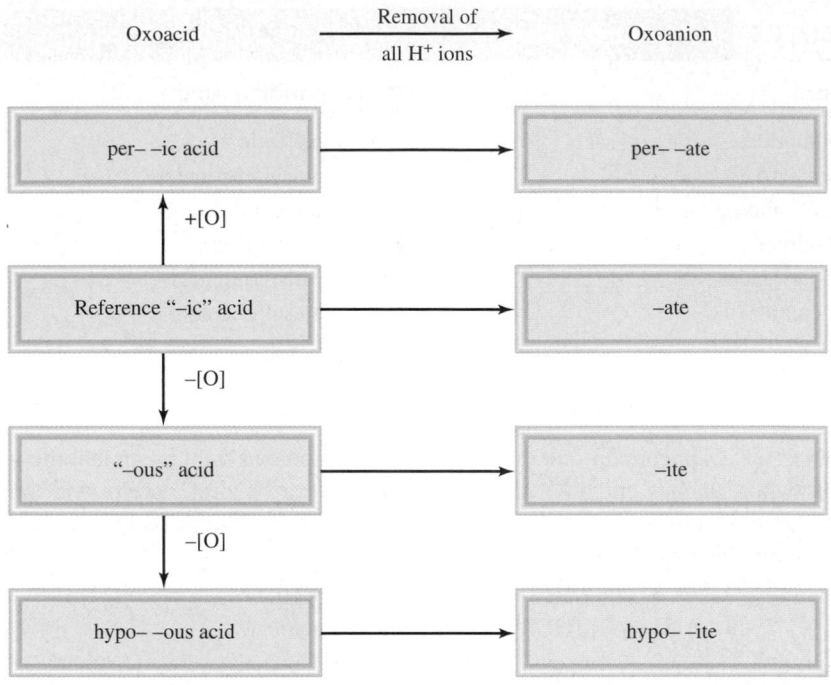

3. The names of anions in which one or more but not all the hydrogen ions have been removed must indicate the number of H ions present. For example, consider the anions derived from phosphoric acid:

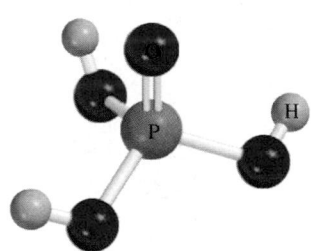

H_3PO_4

H_3PO_4	phosphoric acid
$H_2PO_4^-$	dihydrogen phosphate
HPO_4^{2-}	hydrogen phosphate
PO_4^{3-}	phosphate

Note that we usually omit the prefix "mono-" when there is only one H in the anion. Figure 2.15 summarizes the nomenclature for the oxoacids and oxoanions, and Table 2.6 gives the names of the oxoacids and oxoanions that contain chlorine.

Example 2.9 deals with the nomenclature for an oxoacid and an oxoanion.

Example 2.9

Name the following oxoacid and oxoanion: (a) H_3PO_3 and (b) IO_4^-.

Strategy To name the acid in (a), we first identify the reference acid, whose name ends with "ic," as shown in Figure 2.15. In (b), we need to convert the anion to its parent acid shown in Table 2.6.

Solution (a) We start with our reference acid, phosphoric acid (H_3PO_4). Because H_3PO_3 has one fewer O atom, it is called phosphorous acid.

(b) The parent acid is HIO_4. Because the acid has one more O atom than our reference iodic acid (HIO_3), it is called periodic acid. Therefore, the anion derived from HIO_4 is called periodate.

Similar problems: 2.57(h), 2.58(c).

Practice Exercise Name the following oxoacid and oxoanion: (a) HBrO and (b) HSO_4^-.

TABLE 2.6	Names of Oxoacids and Oxoanions That Contain Chlorine
Acid	**Anion**
$HClO_4$ (perchloric acid)	ClO_4^- (perchlorate)
$HClO_3$ (chloric acid)	ClO_3^- (chlorate)
$HClO_2$ (chlorous acid)	ClO_2^- (chlorite)
$HClO$ (hypochlorous acid)	ClO^- (hypochlorite)

Naming Bases

A **base** can be described as *a substance that yields hydroxide ions (OH^-) when dissolved in water.* Some examples are

NaOH	sodium hydroxide
KOH	potassium hydroxide
$Ba(OH)_2$	barium hydroxide

Ammonia (NH_3), a molecular compound in the gaseous or pure liquid state, is also classified as a common base. At first glance this may seem to be an exception to the definition of a base. But note that as long as a substance *yields* hydroxide ions when dissolved in water, it need not contain hydroxide ions in its structure to be considered a base. In fact, when ammonia dissolves in water, NH_3 reacts partially with water to yield NH_4^+ and OH^- ions. Thus, it is properly classified as a base.

Hydrates

Hydrates are *compounds that have a specific number of water molecules attached to them.* For example, in its normal state, each unit of copper(II) sulfate has five water molecules associated with it. The systematic name for this compound is copper(II) sulfate pentahydrate, and its formula is written as $CuSO_4 \cdot 5H_2O$. The water molecules can be driven off by heating. When this occurs, the resulting compound is $CuSO_4$, which is sometimes called *anhydrous* copper(II) sulfate; "anhydrous" means that the compound no longer has water molecules associated with it (Figure 2.16). Some other hydrates are

$BaCl_2 \cdot 2H_2O$	barium chloride dihydrate
$LiCl \cdot H_2O$	lithium chloride monohydrate
$MgSO_4 \cdot 7H_2O$	magnesium sulfate heptahydrate
$Sr(NO_3)_2 \cdot 4H_2O$	strontium nitrate tetrahydrate

Figure 2.16 *$CuSO_4 \cdot 5H_2O$ (left) is blue; $CuSO_4$ (right) is white.*

TABLE 2.7	Common and Systematic Names of Some Compounds	
Formula	**Common Name**	**Systematic Name**
H_2O	Water	Dihydrogen monoxide
NH_3	Ammonia	Trihydrogen nitride
CO_2	Dry ice	Solid carbon dioxide
NaCl	Table salt	Sodium chloride
N_2O	Laughing gas	Dinitrogen monoxide
$CaCO_3$	Marble, chalk, limestone	Calcium carbonate
CaO	Quicklime	Calcium oxide
$Ca(OH)_2$	Slaked lime	Calcium hydroxide
$NaHCO_3$	Baking soda	Sodium hydrogen carbonate
$Na_2CO_3 \cdot 10H_2O$	Washing soda	Sodium carbonate decahydrate
$MgSO_4 \cdot 7H_2O$	Epsom salt	Magnesium sulfate heptahydrate
$Mg(OH)_2$	Milk of magnesia	Magnesium hydroxide
$CaSO_4 \cdot 2H_2O$	Gypsum	Calcium sulfate dihydrate

CH_3OH

Familiar Inorganic Compounds

Some compounds are better known by their common names than by their systematic chemical names. Familiar examples are listed in Table 2.7.

2.8 Introduction to Organic Compounds

The simplest type of organic compounds is the *hydrocarbons,* which contain only carbon and hydrogen atoms. The hydrocarbons are used as fuels for domestic and industrial heating, for generating electricity and powering internal combustion engines, and as starting materials for the chemical industry. One class of hydrocarbons is called the *alkanes.* Table 2.8 shows the names, formulas, and molecular models of the first ten *straight-chain* alkanes, in which the carbon chains have no branches. Note that all the names end with *-ane.* Starting with C_5H_{12}, we use the Greek prefixes in Table 2.4 to indicate the number of carbon atoms present.

CH_3NH_2

The chemistry of organic compounds is largely determined by the *functional groups,* which consist of one or a few atoms bonded in a specific way. For example, when an H atom in methane is replaced by a hydroxyl group (—OH), an amino group (—NH_2), and a carboxyl group (—COOH), the following molecules are generated:

$$
\begin{array}{ccc}
\underset{\displaystyle \text{Methanol}}{H-\overset{\displaystyle H}{\underset{\displaystyle H}{C}}-OH} &
\underset{\displaystyle \text{Methylamine}}{H-\overset{\displaystyle H}{\underset{\displaystyle H}{C}}-NH_2} &
\underset{\displaystyle \text{Acetic acid}}{H-\overset{\displaystyle H}{\underset{\displaystyle H}{C}}-\overset{\displaystyle O}{\underset{}{\overset{\|}{C}}}-OH}
\end{array}
$$

CH_3COOH

The chemical properties of these molecules can be predicted based on the reactivity of the functional groups. Although the nomenclature of the major classes of organic compounds and their properties in terms of the functional groups will not be discussed until Chapter 24, we will frequently use organic compounds as examples to illustrate chemical bonding, acid-base reactions, and other properties throughout the book.

TABLE 2.8	The First Ten Straight-Chain Alkanes	
Name	Formula	Molecular Model
Methane	CH_4	
Ethane	C_2H_6	
Propane	C_3H_8	
Butane	C_4H_{10}	
Pentane	C_5H_{12}	
Hexane	C_6H_{14}	
Heptane	C_7H_{16}	
Octane	C_8H_{18}	
Nonane	C_9H_{20}	
Decane	$C_{10}H_{22}$	

Summary of Facts and Concepts

1. Modern chemistry began with Dalton's atomic theory, which states that all matter is composed of tiny, indivisible particles called atoms; that all atoms of the same element are identical; that compounds contain atoms of different elements combined in whole-number ratios; and that atoms are neither created nor destroyed in chemical reactions (the law of conservation of mass).

2. Atoms of constituent elements in a particular compound are always combined in the same proportions by mass (law of definite proportions). When two elements can combine to form more than one type of compound, the masses of one element that combine with a fixed mass of the other element are in a ratio of small whole numbers (law of multiple proportions).

3. An atom consists of a very dense central nucleus containing protons and neutrons, with electrons moving about the nucleus at a relatively large distance from it.

4. Protons are positively charged, neutrons have no charge, and electrons are negatively charged. Protons and neutrons have roughly the same mass, which is about 1840 times greater than the mass of an electron.

5. The atomic number of an element is the number of protons in the nucleus of an atom of the element; it determines the identity of an element. The mass number is the sum of the number of protons and the number of neutrons in the nucleus.

6. Isotopes are atoms of the same element with the same number of protons but different numbers of neutrons.

7. Chemical formulas combine the symbols for the constituent elements with whole-number subscripts to show the type and number of atoms contained in the smallest unit of a compound.

8. The molecular formula conveys the specific number and type of atoms combined in each molecule of a compound. The empirical formula shows the simplest ratios of the atoms combined in a molecule.

9. Chemical compounds are either molecular compounds (in which the smallest units are discrete, individual molecules) or ionic compounds, which are made of cations and anions.

10. The names of many inorganic compounds can be deduced from a set of simple rules. The formulas can be written from the names of the compounds.

11. Organic compounds contain carbon and elements like hydrogen, oxygen, and nitrogen. Hydrocarbon is the simplest type of organic compound.

Key Words

Acid, p. 64
Alkali metals, p. 51
Alkaline earth
    metals, p. 51
Allotrope, p. 54
Alpha (α) particles, p. 46
Alpha (α) rays, p. 46
Anion, p. 53
Atom, p. 43
Atomic number (Z), p. 49
Base, p. 67
Beta (β) particles, p. 46
Beta (β) rays, p. 46
Binary compound, p. 59

Cation, p. 53
Chemical formula, p. 54
Diatomic molecule, p. 53
Electron, p. 44
Empirical formula, p. 56
Families, p. 50
Gamma (γ) rays, p. 46
Groups, p. 50
Halogens, p. 51
Hydrate, p. 67
Inorganic compounds, p. 59
Ion, p. 53
Ionic compound, p. 53
Isotope, p. 49

Law of conservation
    of mass, p. 43
Law of definite
    proportions, p. 43
Law of multiple
    proportions, p. 43
Mass number (A), p. 49
Metal, p. 50
Metalloid, p. 50
Molecular formula, p. 54
Molecule, p. 53
Monatomic ion, p. 54
Neutron, p. 48
Noble gases, p. 51

Nonmetal, p. 50
Nucleus, p. 47
Organic compound, p. 59
Oxoacid, p. 65
Oxoanion, p. 65
Periods, p. 50
Periodic table, p. 50
Polyatomic ion, p. 54
Polyatomic molecule, p. 53
Proton, p. 47
Radiation, p. 43
Radioactivity, p. 46
Structural formula, p. 55
Ternary compound, p. 59

Questions and Problems

Structure of the Atom
Review Questions

2.1 Define the following terms: (a) α particle, (b) β particle, (c) γ ray, (d) X ray.

2.2 Name the types of radiation known to be emitted by radioactive elements.

2.3 Compare the properties of the following: α particles, cathode rays, protons, neutrons, electrons.

2.4 What is meant by the term "fundamental particle"?

2.5 Describe the contributions of the following scientists to our knowledge of atomic structure: J. J. Thomson, R. A. Millikan, Ernest Rutherford, James Chadwick.

2.6 Describe the experimental basis for believing that the nucleus occupies a very small fraction of the volume of the atom.

Problems

2.7 The diameter of a neutral helium atom is about 1×10^2 pm. Suppose that we could line up helium atoms side by side in contact with one another. Approximately how many atoms would it take to make the distance from end to end 1 cm?

2.8 Roughly speaking, the radius of an atom is about 10,000 times greater than that of its nucleus. If an atom were magnified so that the radius of its nucleus became

2.0 cm, about the size of a marble, what would be the radius of the atom in miles? (1 mi = 1609 m.)

Atomic Number, Mass Number, and Isotopes
Review Questions

2.9 Use the helium-4 isotope to define atomic number and mass number. Why does a knowledge of atomic number enable us to deduce the number of electrons present in an atom?

2.10 Why do all atoms of an element have the same atomic number, although they may have different mass numbers?

2.11 What do we call atoms of the same elements with different mass numbers?

2.12 Explain the meaning of each term in the symbol $_{Z}^{A}X$.

Problems

2.13 What is the mass number of an iron atom that has 28 neutrons?

2.14 Calculate the number of neutrons of ^{239}Pu.

2.15 For each of the following species, determine the number of protons and the number of neutrons in the nucleus:

$$_{2}^{3}\text{He}, \; _{2}^{4}\text{He}, \; _{12}^{24}\text{Mg}, \; _{12}^{25}\text{Mg}, \; _{22}^{48}\text{Ti}, \; _{35}^{79}\text{Br}, \; _{78}^{195}\text{Pt}$$

2.16 Indicate the number of protons, neutrons, and electrons in each of the following species:

$$_{7}^{15}\text{N}, \; _{16}^{33}\text{S}, \; _{29}^{63}\text{Cu}, \; _{38}^{84}\text{Sr}, \; _{56}^{130}\text{Ba}, \; _{74}^{186}\text{W}, \; _{80}^{202}\text{Hg}$$

2.17 Write the appropriate symbol for each of the following isotopes: (a) $Z = 11$, $A = 23$; (b) $Z = 28$, $A = 64$.

2.18 Write the appropriate symbol for each of the following isotopes: (a) $Z = 74$, $A = 186$, (b) $Z = 80$; $A = 201$.

The Periodic Table
Review Questions

2.19 What is the periodic table, and what is its significance in the study of chemistry?

2.20 State two differences between a metal and a nonmetal.

2.21 Write the names and symbols for four elements in each of the following categories: (a) nonmetal, (b) metal, (c) metalloid.

2.22 Define, with two examples, the following terms: (a) alkali metals, (b) alkaline earth metals, (c) halogens, (d) noble gases.

Problems

2.23 Elements whose names end with *ium* are usually metals; sodium is one example. Identify a nonmetal whose name also ends with *ium*.

2.24 Describe the changes in properties (from metals to nonmetals or from nonmetals to metals) as we move (a) down a periodic group and (b) across the periodic table from left to right.

2.25 Consult a handbook of chemical and physical data (ask your instructor where you can locate a copy of the handbook) to find (a) two metals less dense than water, (b) two metals more dense than mercury, (c) the densest known solid metallic element, (d) the densest known solid nonmetallic element.

2.26 Group the following elements in pairs that you would expect to show similar chemical properties: K, F, P, Na, Cl, and N.

Molecules and Ions
Review Questions

2.27 What is the difference between an atom and a molecule?

2.28 What are allotropes? Give an example. How are allotropes different from isotopes?

2.29 Describe the two commonly used molecular models.

2.30 Give an example of each of the following: (a) a monatomic cation, (b) a monatomic anion, (c) a polyatomic cation, (d) a polyatomic anion.

Problems

2.31 Which of the following diagrams represent diatomic molecules, polyatomic molecules, molecules that are not compounds, molecules that are compounds, or an elemental form of the substance?

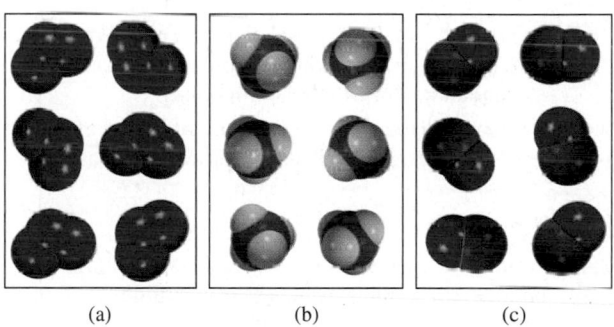

(a)   (b)   (c)

2.32 Which of the following diagrams represent diatomic molecules, polyatomic molecules, molecules that are not compounds, molecules that are compounds, or an elemental form of the substance?

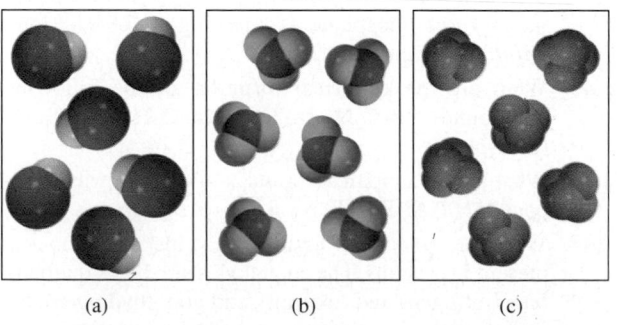

(a)   (b)   (c)

2.33 Identify the following as elements or compounds: NH_3, N_2, S_8, NO, CO, CO_2, H_2, SO_2.

2.34 Give two examples of each of the following: (a) a diatomic molecule containing atoms of the same element, (b) a diatomic molecule containing atoms of different elements, (c) a polyatomic molecule containing atoms of the same element, (d) a polyatomic molecule containing atoms of different elements.

2.35 Give the number of protons and electrons in each of the following common ions: Na^+, Ca^{2+}, Al^{3+}, Fe^{2+}, I^-, F^-, S^{2-}, O^{2-}, and N^{3-}.

2.36 Give the number of protons and electrons in each of the following common ions: K^+, Mg^{2+}, Fe^{3+}, Br^-, Mn^{2+}, C^{4-}, Cu^{2+}.

Chemical Formulas

Review Questions

2.37 What does a chemical formula represent? What is the ratio of the atoms in the following molecular formulas? (a) NO, (b) NCl_3, (c) N_2O_4, (d) P_4O_6

2.38 Define molecular formula and empirical formula. What are the similarities and differences between the empirical formula and molecular formula of a compound?

2.39 Give an example of a case in which two molecules have different molecular formulas but the same empirical formula.

2.40 What does P_4 signify? How does it differ from 4P?

2.41 What is an ionic compound? How is electrical neutrality maintained in an ionic compound?

2.42 Explain why the chemical formulas of ionic compounds are usually the same as their empirical formulas.

Problems

2.43 Write the formulas for the following ionic compounds: (a) sodium oxide, (b) iron sulfide (containing the Fe^{2+} ion), (c) cobalt sulfate (containing the Co^{3+} and SO_4^{2-} ions), and (d) barium fluoride. (*Hint:* See Figure 2.11.)

2.44 Write the formulas for the following ionic compounds: (a) copper bromide (containing the Cu^+ ion), (b) manganese oxide (containing the Mn^{3+} ion), (c) mercury iodide (containing the Hg_2^{2+} ion), and (d) magnesium phosphate (containing the PO_4^{3-} ion). (*Hint:* See Figure 2.11.)

2.45 What are the empirical formulas of the following compounds? (a) C_2N_2, (b) C_6H_6, (c) C_9H_{20}, (d) P_4O_{10}, (e) B_2H_6

2.46 What are the empirical formulas of the following compounds? (a) Al_2Br_6, (b) $Na_2S_2O_4$, (c) N_2O_5, (d) $K_2Cr_2O_7$

2.47 Write the molecular formula of glycine, an amino acid present in proteins. The color codes are: black (carbon), blue (nitrogen), red (oxygen), and gray (hydrogen).

2.48 Write the molecular formula of ethanol. The color codes are: black (carbon), red (oxygen), and gray (hydrogen).

2.49 Which of the following compounds are likely to be ionic? Which are likely to be molecular? $SiCl_4$, LiF, $BaCl_2$, B_2H_6, KCl, C_2H_4

2.50 Which of the following compounds are likely to be ionic? Which are likely to be molecular? CH_4, NaBr, BaF_2, CCl_4, ICl, CsCl, NF_3

Naming Inorganic Compounds

Review Questions

2.51 What is the difference between inorganic compounds and organic compounds?

2.52 What are the four major categories of inorganic compounds?

2.53 Give an example each for a binary compound and a ternary compound.

2.54 What is the Stock system? What are its advantages over the older system of naming cations?

2.55 Explain why the formula HCl can represent two different chemical systems.

2.56 Define the following terms: acids, bases, oxoacids, oxoanions, and hydrates.

Problems

2.57 Name the following compounds: (a) KH_2PO_4, (b) K_2HPO_4, (c) HBr (gas), (d) HBr (in water), (e) Li_2CO_3, (f) $K_2Cr_2O_7$, (g) NH_4NO_2, (h) HIO_3, (i) PF_5, (j) P_4O_6, (k) CdI_2, (l) $SrSO_4$, (m) $Al(OH)_3$.

2.58 Name the following compounds: (a) KClO, (b) Ag_2CO_3, (c) HNO_2, (d) $KMnO_4$, (e) $CsClO_3$, (f) KNH_4SO_4, (g) FeO, (h) Fe_2O_3, (i) $TiCl_4$, (j) NaH, (k) Li_3N, (l) Na_2O, (m) Na_2O_2.

2.59 Write the formulas for the following compounds: (a) rubidium nitrite, (b) potassium sulfide, (c) sodium hydrogen sulfide, (d) magnesium phosphate, (e) calcium hydrogen phosphate, (f) potassium dihydrogen phosphate, (g) iodine heptafluoride, (h) ammonium sulfate, (i) silver perchlorate, (j) boron trichloride.

2.60 Write the formulas for the following compounds: (a) copper(I) cyanide, (b) strontium chlorite, (c) perbromic acid, (d) hydroiodic acid, (e) disodium ammonium phosphate, (f) lead(II) carbonate, (g) tin(II) fluoride, (h) tetraphosphorus decasulfide, (i) mercury(II) oxide, (j) mercury(I) iodide, (k) selenium hexafluoride.

Additional Problems

2.61 A sample of a uranium compound is found to be losing mass gradually. Explain what is happening to the sample.

2.62 In which one of the following pairs do the two species resemble each other most closely in chemical properties? Explain. (a) $^{1}_{1}H$ and $^{1}_{1}H^{+}$, (b) $^{14}_{7}N$ and $^{14}_{7}N^{3-}$, (c) $^{12}_{6}C$ and $^{13}_{6}C$.

2.63 One isotope of a metallic element has mass number 65 and 35 neutrons in the nucleus. The cation derived from the isotope has 28 electrons. Write the symbol for this cation.

2.64 One isotope of a nonmetallic element has mass number 127 and 74 neutrons in the nucleus. The anion derived from the isotope has 54 electrons. Write the symbol for this anion.

2.65 The following table gives numbers of electrons, protons, and neutrons in atoms or ions of a number of elements. Answer the following: (a) Which of the species are neutral? (b) Which are negatively charged? (c) Which are positively charged? (d) What are the conventional symbols for all the species?

Atom or Ion of Element

	A	B	C	D	E	F	G
Number of electrons	5	10	18	28	36	5	9
Number of protons	5	7	19	30	35	5	9
Number of neutrons	5	7	20	36	46	6	10

2.66 What is wrong with or ambiguous about the phrase "four molecules of NaCl"?

2.67 The following phosphorus sulfides are known: P_4S_3, P_4S_7, and P_4S_{10}. Do these compounds obey the law of multiple proportions?

2.68 Which of the following are elements, which are molecules but not compounds, which are compounds but not molecules, and which are both compounds and molecules? (a) SO_2, (b) S_8, (c) Cs, (d) N_2O_5, (e) O, (f) O_2, (g) O_3, (h) CH_4, (i) KBr, (j) S, (k) P_4, (l) LiF

2.69 What is wrong with the name (in parentheses) for each of the following compounds: (a) $BaCl_2$ (barium dichloride), (b) Fe_2O_3 [iron(II) oxide], (c) $CsNO_2$ (cesium nitrate), (d) $Mg(HCO_3)_2$ [magnesium(II) bicarbonate]?

2.70 What is wrong with the chemical formula for each of the following compounds: (a) $(NH_3)_2CO_3$ (ammonium carbonate), (b) CaOH (calcium hydroxide), (c) $CdSO_3$ (cadmium sulfide), (d) $ZnCrO_4$ (zinc dichromate)?

2.71 Fill in the blanks in the following table:

Symbol		$^{54}_{26}Fe^{2+}$			
Protons	5			79	86
Neutrons	6		16	117	136
Electrons	5		18	79	
Net charge			-3		0

2.72 (a) Which elements are most likely to form ionic compounds? (b) Which metallic elements are most likely to form cations with different charges?

2.73 Write the formula of the common ion derived from each of the following: (a) Li, (b) S, (c) I, (d) N, (e) Al, (f) Cs, (g) Mg

2.74 Which of the following symbols provides more information about the atom: ^{23}Na or $_{11}Na$? Explain.

2.75 Write the chemical formulas and names of acids that contain Group 7A elements. Do the same for elements in Groups 3A, 4A, 5A, and 6A.

2.76 Of the 114 elements known, only two are liquids at room temperature (25°C). What are they? (*Hint:* One element is a familiar metal and the other element is in Group 7A.)

2.77 For the noble gases (the Group 8A elements), $^{4}_{2}He$, $^{20}_{10}Ne$, $^{40}_{18}Ar$, $^{84}_{36}Kr$, and $^{132}_{54}Xe$, (a) determine the number of protons and neutrons in the nucleus of each atom, and (b) determine the ratio of neutrons to protons in the nucleus of each atom. Describe any general trend you discover in the way this ratio changes with increasing atomic number.

2.78 List the elements that exist as gases at room temperature. (*Hint:* Most of these elements can be found in Groups 5A, 6A, 7A, and 8A.)

2.79 The Group 1B metals, Cu, Ag, and Au, are called coinage metals. What chemical properties make them specially suitable for making coins and jewelry?

2.80 The elements in Group 8A of the periodic table are called noble gases. Can you suggest what "noble" means in this context?

2.81 The formula for calcium oxide is CaO. What are the formulas for magnesium oxide and strontium oxide?

2.82 A common mineral of barium is barytes, or barium sulfate ($BaSO_4$). Because elements in the same periodic group have similar chemical properties, we might expect to find some radium sulfate ($RaSO_4$) mixed with barytes since radium is the last member of Group 2A. However, the only source of radium compounds in nature is in uranium minerals. Why?

2.83   List five elements each that are (a) named after places, (b) named after people, (c) named after a color. (*Hint:* See Appendix 1.)

2.84   Name the only country that is named after an element. (*Hint:* This country is in South America.)

2.85   Fluorine reacts with hydrogen (H) and deuterium (D) to form hydrogen fluoride (HF) and deuterium fluoride (DF), where deuterium (^2_1H) is an isotope of hydrogen. Would a given amount of fluorine react with different masses of the two hydrogen isotopes? Does this violate the law of definite proportion? Explain.

2.86   Predict the formula and name of a binary compound formed from the following elements: (a) Na and H, (b) B and O, (c) Na and S, (d) Al and F, (e) F and O, (f) Sr and Cl.

2.87   Identify each of the following elements: (a) a halogen whose anion contains 36 electrons, (b) a radioactive noble gas with 86 protons, (c) a Group 6A element whose anion contains 36 electrons, (d) an alkali metal cation that contains 36 electrons, (e) a Group 4A cation that contains 80 electrons.

2.88   Write the molecular formulas for and names of the following compounds.

2.89   Show the locations of (a) alkali metals, (b) alkaline earth metals, (c) the halogens, and (d) the noble gases

in the following outline of a periodic table. Also draw dividing lines between metals and metalloids and between metalloids and nonmetals.

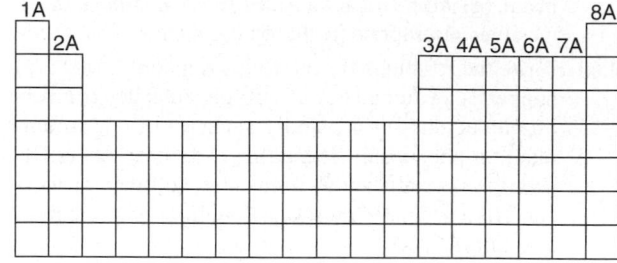

2.90   Fill the blanks in the following table.

Cation	Anion	Formula	Name
			Magnesium bicarbonate
		$SrCl_2$	
Fe^{3+}	NO_2^-		
			Manganese(II) chlorate
		$SnBr_4$	
Co^{2+}	PO_4^{3-}		
Hg_2^{2+}	I^-		
		Cu_2CO_3	
			Lithium nitride
Al^{3+}	S^{2-}		

2.91   Some compounds are better known by their common names than by their systematic chemical names. Give the chemical formulas of the following substances: (a) dry ice, (b) table salt, (c) laughing gas, (d) marble (chalk, limestone), (e) quicklime, (f) slaked lime, (g) baking soda, (h) washing soda, (i) gypsum, (j) milk of magnesia.

Special Problems

2.92   On p. 43 it was pointed out that mass and energy are alternate aspects of a single entity called *mass-energy.* The relationship between these two physical quantities is Einstein's famous equation, $E = mc^2$, where E is energy, m is mass, and c is the speed of light. In a combustion experiment, it was found that 12.096 g of hydrogen molecules combined with 96.000 g of oxygen molecules to form water and released 1.715×10^3 kJ of heat. Calculate the corresponding mass change in this process and comment on whether the law of conser-

vation of mass holds for ordinary chemical processes. (*Hint:* The Einstein equation can be used to calculate the change in mass as a result of the change in energy. 1 J = 1 kg m^2/s^2 and $c = 3.00 \times 10^8$ m/s.)

2.93   Draw all possible structural formulas of the following hydrocarbons: CH_4, C_2H_6, C_3H_8, C_4H_{10}, and C_5H_{12}.

2.94   (a) Describe Rutherford's experiment and how it led to the structure of the atom. How was he able to estimate the number of protons in a nucleus from the scattering of the α particles? (b) Consider the ^{23}Na atom. Given that the radius and mass of the nucleus are 3.04×10^{-15} m and 3.82×10^{-23} g, respectively, calculate the density of the nucleus in g/cm^3. The radius of a ^{23}Na atom is 186 pm. Calculate the density of the space occupied by the electrons in the sodium atom. Do your results support Rutherford's model of an atom? [The volume of a sphere of radius r is $(4/3)\pi r^3$.]

2.95 Draw two different structural formulas based on the molecular formula C_2H_6O. Is the fact that you can have more than one compound with the same molecular formula consistent with Dalton's atomic theory?

2.96 Ethane and acetylene are two gaseous hydrocarbons. Chemical analyses show that in one sample of ethane, 2.65 g of carbon are combined with 0.665 g of hydrogen, and in one sample of acetylene, 4.56 g of carbon are combined with 0.383 g of hydrogen. (a) Are these results consistent with the law of multiple proportions? (b) Write reasonable molecular formulas for these compounds.

2.97 A cube made of platinum (Pt) has an edge length of 1.0 cm. (a) Calculate the number of Pt atoms in the cube. (b) Atoms are spherical in shape. Therefore, the Pt atoms in the cube cannot fill all of the available space. If only 74 percent of the space inside the cube is taken up by Pt atoms, calculate the radius in picometers of a Pt atom. The density of Pt is 21.45 g/cm^3 and the mass of a single Pt atom is 3.240×10^{-22} g. [The volume of a sphere of radius r is $(4/3)\pi r^3$.]

2.98 A monatomic ion has a charge of $+2$. The nucleus of the parent atom has a mass number of 55. If the number of neutrons in the nucleus is 1.2 times that of the number of protons, what is the name and symbol of the element?

2.99 In the following 2×2 crossword, each letter must be correct four ways: horizontally, vertically, diagonally,

and by itself. When the puzzle is complete, the four spaces below will contain the overlapping symbols of 10 elements. Use capital letters for each square. There is only one correct solution.*

1.	2
3	4

Horizontal

1–2: Two-letter symbol for a metal used in ancient times
3–4: Two-letter symbol for a metal that burns in air and is found in Group 5A

Vertical

1–3: Two-letter symbol for a metalloid
2–4: Two-letter symbol for a metal used in U.S. coins

Single Squares

1: A colorful nonmetal
2: A colorless gaseous nonmetal
3: An element that makes fireworks green
4: An element that has medicinal uses

Diagonal

1–4: Two-letter symbol for an element used in electronics
2–3: Two-letter symbol for a metal used with Zr to make wires for superconducting magnets

2.100 Name the following acids:

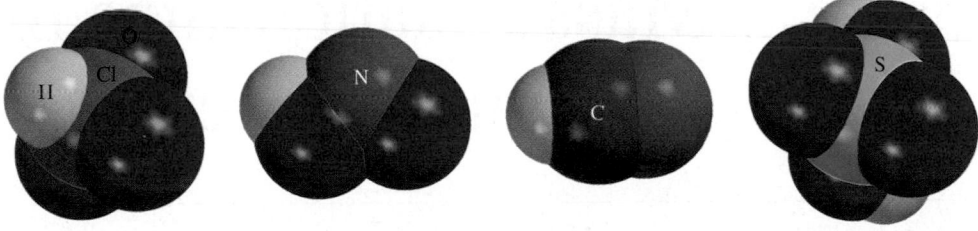

Answers to Practice Exercises

2.1 29 protons, 34 neutrons, and 29 electrons. **2.2** $CHCl_3$. **2.3** $C_4H_5N_2O$. **2.4** (a) $Cr_2(SO_4)_3$, (b) TiO_2. **2.5** (a) Lead(II) oxide, (b) lithium sulfite. **2.6** (a) Rb_2SO_4, (b) BaH_2.

2.7 (a) Nitrogen trifluoride, (b) dichlorine heptoxide. **2.8** (a) SF_4, (b) N_2O_5. **2.9** (a) Hypobromous acid, (b) hydrogen sulfate ion.

---

*Reproduced with permission of S. J. Cyvin of the University of Trondheim (Norway). This puzzle appeared in *Chemical & Engineering News*, December 14, 1987 (p. 86) and in *Chem Matters*, October 1988.

3

Sulfur burning in oxygen to form sulfur dioxide. About 50 million tons of SO_2 are released to the atmosphere every year. The models show elemental sulfur (S_8), and oxygen and sulfur dioxide molecules.

Mass Relationships in Chemical Reactions

A LOOK AHEAD

- We begin by studying the mass of an atom, which is based on the carbon-12 isotope scale. An atom of the carbon-12 isotope is assigned a mass of exactly 12 atomic mass unit (amu). To work with the more convenient scale of grams, we use the molar mass. The molar mass of carbon-12 has a mass of exactly 12 grams and contains an Avogadro's number (6.022×10^{23}) of atoms. The molar masses of other elements are also expressed in grams and contain the same number of atoms. (3.1 and 3.2)

- Our discussion of atomic mass leads to molecular mass, which is the sum of the masses of the constituent atoms present. We learn that the most direct way to determine atomic and molecular mass is by the use of a mass spectrometer. (3.3 and 3.4)

- To continue our study of molecules and ionic compounds, we learn how to calculate the percent composition of these species from their chemical formulas. (3.5)

- We will see how the empirical and molecular formulas of a compound are determined by experiment. (3.6)

- Next, we learn how to write a chemical equation to describe the outcome of a chemical reaction. A chemical equation must be balanced so that we have the same number and type of atoms for the reactants, the starting materials, and the products, the substances formed at the end of the reaction. (3.7)

- Building on our knowledge of chemical equations, we then proceed to study the mass relationships of chemical reactions. A chemical equation enables us to use the mole method to predict the amount of product(s) formed, knowing how much the reactant(s) was used. We will see that a reaction's yield depends on the amount of limiting reagent (a reactant that is used up first) present. (3.8 and 3.9)

- We will learn that the actual yield of a reaction is almost always less than that predicted from the equation, called the theoretical yield, because of various complications. (3.10)

Interactive Activity Summary

1. Interactivity: Molecular Mass (3.3)
2. Interactivity: Balance the Equation (3.7)
3. Interactivity: Balancing Chemical Equations (3.7)
4. Interactivity: The Mole Method (3.8)
5. Animation: Limiting Reagent (3.9)
6. Interactivity: Limiting Reactant Game (3.9)

In this chapter we will consider the masses of atoms and molecules and what happens to them when chemical changes occur. Our guide for this discussion will be the law of conservation of mass.

3.1 Atomic Mass

In this chapter we will use what we have learned about chemical structure and formulas in studying the mass relationships of atoms and molecules. These relationships in turn will help us to explain the composition of compounds and the ways in which composition changes.

Section 3.4 describes a method for determining atomic mass.

The mass of an atom depends on the number of electrons, protons, and neutrons it contains. Knowledge of an atom's mass is important in laboratory work. But atoms are extremely small particles—even the smallest speck of dust that our unaided eyes can detect contains as many as 1×10^{16} atoms! Clearly we cannot weigh a single atom, but it is possible to determine the mass of one atom *relative* to another experimentally. The first step is to assign a value to the mass of one atom of a given element so that it can be used as a standard.

One atomic mass unit is also called one dalton.

By international agreement, ***atomic mass*** (sometimes called *atomic weight*) is *the mass of the atom in atomic mass units (amu)*. One ***atomic mass unit*** is defined as *a mass exactly equal to one-twelfth the mass of one carbon-12 atom.* Carbon-12 is the carbon isotope that has six protons and six neutrons. Setting the atomic mass of carbon-12 at 12 amu provides the standard for measuring the atomic mass of the other elements. For example, experiments have shown that, on average, a hydrogen atom is only 8.400 percent as massive as the carbon-12 atom. Thus, if the mass of one carbon-12 atom is exactly 12 amu, the atomic mass of hydrogen must be 0.084×12.00 amu or 1.008 amu. Similar calculations show that the atomic mass of oxygen is 16.00 amu and that of iron is 55.85 amu. Thus, although we do not know just how much an average iron atom's mass is, we know that it is approximately 56 times as massive as a hydrogen atom.

Average Atomic Mass

When you look up the atomic mass of carbon in a table such as the one on the inside front cover of this book, you will find that its value is not 12.00 amu but 12.01 amu. The reason for the difference is that most naturally occurring elements (including carbon) have more than one isotope. This means that when we measure the atomic mass of an element, we must generally settle for the *average* mass of the naturally occurring mixture of isotopes. For example, the natural abundances of carbon-12 and carbon-13 are 98.90 percent and 1.10 percent, respectively. The atomic mass of carbon-13 has been determined to be 13.00335 amu. Thus, the average atomic mass of carbon can be calculated as follows:

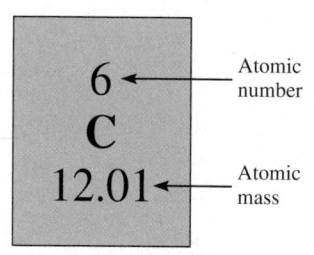

average atomic mass
of natural carbon $= (0.9890)(12.00000 \text{ amu}) + (0.0110)(13.00335 \text{ amu})$
$= 12.01 \text{ amu}$

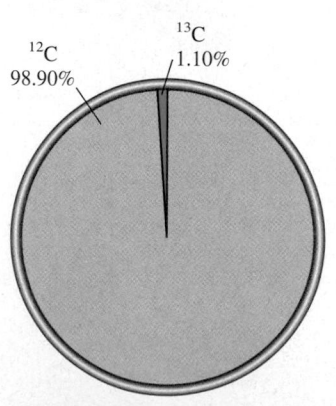

Natural abundances of C-12 and C-13 isotopes.

Note that in calculations involving percentages, we need to convert percentages to fractions. For example, 98.90 percent becomes 98.90/100, or 0.9890. Because there are many more carbon-12 atoms than carbon-13 atoms in naturally occurring carbon, the average atomic mass is much closer to 12 amu than to 13 amu.

It is important to understand that when we say that the atomic mass of carbon is 12.01 amu, we are referring to the *average* value. If carbon atoms could be examined individually, we would find either an atom of atomic mass 12.00000 amu or one of 13.00335 amu, but never one of 12.01 amu. Example 3.1 shows how to calculate the average atomic mass of an element.

Example 3.1

Copper, a metal known since ancient times, is used in electrical cables and pennies, among other things. The atomic masses of its two stable isotopes, $^{63}_{29}Cu$ (69.09 percent) and $^{65}_{29}Cu$ (30.91 percent), are 62.93 amu and 64.9278 amu, respectively. Calculate the average atomic mass of copper. The relative abundances are given in parentheses.

Strategy Each isotope contributes to the average atomic mass based on its relative abundance. Multiplying the mass of an isotope by its fractional abundance (not percent) will give the contribution to the average atomic mass of that particular isotope.

Solution First the percents are converted to fractions: 69.09 percent to 69.09/100 or 0.6909 and 30.91 percent to 30.91/100 or 0.3091. We find the contribution to the average atomic mass for each isotope, then add the contributions together to obtain the average atomic mass.

$$(0.6909)(62.93 \text{ amu}) + (0.3091)(64.9278 \text{ amu}) = 63.55 \text{ amu}$$

Check The average atomic mass should be between the two isotopic masses; therefore, the answer is reasonable. Note that because there are more $^{63}_{29}Cu$ than $^{65}_{29}Cu$ isotopes, the average atomic mass is closer to 62.93 amu than to 64.9278 amu.

Practice Exercise The atomic masses of the two stable isotopes of boron, $^{10}_{5}B$ (19.78 percent) and $^{11}_{5}B$ (80.22 percent), are 10.0129 amu and 11.0093 amu, respectively. Calculate the average atomic mass of boron.

Copper.

Similar problems: 3.5, 3.6.

The atomic masses of many elements have been accurately determined to five or six significant figures. However, for our purposes we will normally use atomic masses accurate only to four significant figures (see table of atomic masses inside the front cover). For simplicity, we will omit the word "average" when we discuss the atomic masses of the elements.

3.2 Avogadro's Number and the Molar Mass of an Element

Atomic mass units provide a relative scale for the masses of the elements. But because atoms have such small masses, no usable scale can be devised to weigh them in calibrated units of atomic mass units. In any real situation, we deal with macroscopic samples containing enormous numbers of atoms. Therefore, it is convenient to have a special unit to describe a very large number of atoms. The idea of a unit to denote a particular number of objects is not new. For example, the pair (2 items), the dozen (12 items), and the gross (144 items) are all familiar units. Chemists measure atoms and molecules in moles.

In the SI system the ***mole (mol)*** is *the amount of a substance that contains as many elementary entities (atoms, molecules, or other particles) as there are atoms in exactly 12 g (or 0.012 kg) of the carbon-12 isotope.* The actual number of atoms in 12 g of carbon-12 is determined experimentally. This number is called ***Avogadro's number (N_A),*** in honor of the Italian scientist Amedeo Avogadro.[†] The currently accepted value is

The adjective formed from the noun "mole" is "molar."

$$N_A = 6.0221367 \times 10^{23}$$

[†]Lorenzo Romano Amedeo Carlo Avogadro di Quaregna e di Cerreto (1776–1856). Italian mathematical physicist. He practiced law for many years before he became interested in science. His most famous work, now known as Avogadro's law (see Chapter 5), was largely ignored during his lifetime, although it became the basis for determining atomic masses in the late nineteenth century.

Figure 3.1 *One mole each of several common elements. Carbon (black charcoal powder), sulfur (yellow powder), iron (as nails), copper wires, and mercury (shiny liquid metal).*

Generally, we round Avogadro's number to 6.022×10^{23}. Thus, just as one dozen oranges contains 12 oranges, 1 mole of hydrogen atoms contains 6.022×10^{23} H atoms. Figure 3.1 shows samples containing 1 mole each of several common elements.

The enormity of Avogadro's number is difficult to imagine. For example, spreading 6.022×10^{23} oranges over the entire surface of Earth would produce a layer 9 mi into space! Because atoms (and molecules) are so tiny, we need a huge number to study them in manageable quantities.

In calculations, the units of molar mass are g/mol or kg/mol.

We have seen that 1 mole of carbon-12 atoms has a mass of exactly 12 g and contains 6.022×10^{23} atoms. This mass of carbon-12 is its ***molar mass (M),*** defined as *the mass (in grams or kilograms) of 1 mole of units* (such as atoms or molecules) of a substance. Note that the molar mass of carbon-12 (in grams) is numerically equal to its atomic mass in amu. Likewise, the atomic mass of sodium (Na) is 22.99 amu and its molar mass is 22.99 g; the atomic mass of phosphorus is 30.97 amu and its molar mass is 30.97 g; and so on. If we know the atomic mass of an element, we also know its molar mass.

The molar masses of the elements are given on the inside front cover of the book.

Knowing the molar mass and Avogadro's number, we can calculate the mass of a single atom in grams. For example, we know the molar mass of carbon-12 is 12.00 g and there are 6.022×10^{23} carbon-12 atoms in 1 mole of the substance; therefore, the mass of one carbon-12 atom is given by

$$\frac{12.00 \text{ g carbon-12 atoms}}{6.022 \times 10^{23} \text{ carbon-12 atoms}} = 1.993 \times 10^{-23} \text{ g}$$

We can use the preceding result to determine the relationship between atomic mass units and grams. Because the mass of every carbon-12 atom is exactly 12 amu, the number of atomic mass units equivalent to 1 gram is

$$\frac{\text{amu}}{\text{gram}} = \frac{12 \text{ amu}}{1 \text{ carbon-12 atom}} \times \frac{1 \text{ carbon-12 atom}}{1.993 \times 10^{-23} \text{ g}}$$
$$= 6.022 \times 10^{23} \text{ amu/g}$$

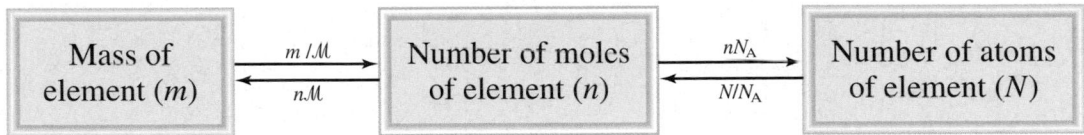

Figure 3.2 *The relationships between mass (m in grams) of an element and number of moles of an element (n) and between number of moles of an element and number of atoms (N) of an element. $\mathcal{M}$ is the molar mass (g/mol) of the element and N_A is Avogadro's number.*

Thus,

$$1 \text{ g} = 6.022 \times 10^{23} \text{ amu}$$

and

$$1 \text{ amu} = 1.661 \times 10^{-24} \text{ g}$$

This example shows that Avogadro's number can be used to convert from the atomic mass units to mass in grams and vice versa.

The notions of Avogadro's number and molar mass enable us to carry out conversions between mass and moles of atoms and between moles and number of atoms (Figure 3.2). We will employ the following conversion factors in the calculations:

$$\frac{1 \text{ mol X}}{\text{molar mass of X}} \quad \text{and} \quad \frac{1 \text{ mol X}}{6.022 \times 10^{23} \text{ X atoms}}$$

where X represents the symbol of an element. Using the proper conversion factors we can convert one quantity to another, as Examples 3.2–3.4 show.

Example 3.2

Helium (He) is a valuable gas used in industry, low-temperature research, deep-sea diving tanks, and balloons. How many moles of He atoms are in 6.46 g of He?

Strategy We are given grams of helium and asked to solve for moles of helium. What conversion factor do we need to convert between grams and moles? Arrange the appropriate conversion factor so that grams cancel and the unit moles is obtained for your answer.

Solution The conversion factor needed to convert between grams and moles is the molar mass. In the periodic table (see inside front cover) we see that the molar mass of He is 4.003 g. This can be expressed as

$$1 \text{ mol He} = 4.003 \text{ g He}$$

From this equality, we can write two conversion factors

$$\frac{1 \text{ mol He}}{4.003 \text{ g He}} \quad \text{and} \quad \frac{4.003 \text{ g He}}{1 \text{ mol He}}$$

The conversion factor on the left is the correct one. Grams will cancel, leaving the unit mol for the answer, that is,

$$6.46 \text{ g He} \times \frac{1 \text{ mol He}}{4.003 \text{ g He}} = 1.61 \text{ mol He}$$

Thus, there are 1.61 moles of He atoms in 6.46 g of He.

(Continued)

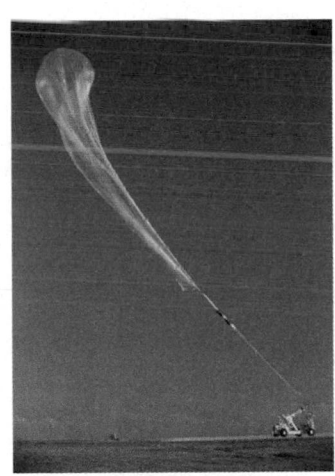

A scientific research helium balloon.

Similar problem: 3.15.

Check Because the given mass (6.46 g) is larger than the molar mass of He, we expect to have more than 1 mole of He.

Practice Exercise How many moles of magnesium (Mg) are there in 87.3 g of Mg?

Example 3.3

Zinc.

Zinc (Zn) is a silvery metal that is used in making brass (with copper) and in plating iron to prevent corrosion. How many grams of Zn are in 0.356 mole of Zn?

Strategy We are trying to solve for grams of zinc. What conversion factor do we need to convert between moles and grams? Arrange the appropriate conversion factor so that moles cancel and the unit grams are obtained for your answer.

Solution The conversion factor needed to convert between moles and grams is the molar mass. In the periodic table (see inside front cover) we see the molar mass of Zn is 65.39 g. This can be expressed as

$$1 \text{ mol Zn} = 65.39 \text{ g Zn}$$

From this equality, we can write two conversion factors

$$\frac{1 \text{ mol Zn}}{65.39 \text{ g Zn}} \quad \text{and} \quad \frac{65.39 \text{ g Zn}}{1 \text{ mol Zn}}$$

Similar problem: 3.16.

The conversion factor on the right is the correct one. Moles will cancel, leaving unit of grams for the answer. The number of grams of Zn is

$$0.356 \text{ mol Zn} \times \frac{65.39 \text{ g Zn}}{1 \text{ mol Zn}} = 23.3 \text{ g Zn}$$

Thus, there are 23.3 g of Zn in 0.356 mole of Zn.

Check Does a mass of 23.3 g for 0.356 mole of Zn seem reasonable? What is the mass of 1 mole of Zn?

Practice Exercise Calculate the number of grams of lead (Pb) in 12.4 moles of lead.

Example 3.4

Elemental sulfur (S₈) consists of eight S atoms joined in a ring.

Sulfur (S) is a nonmetallic element that is present in coal. When coal is burned, sulfur is converted to sulfur dioxide and eventually to sulfuric acid that gives rise to the acid rain phenomenon. How many atoms are in 16.3 g of S?

Strategy The question asks for atoms of sulfur. We cannot convert directly from grams to atoms of sulfur. What unit do we need to convert grams of sulfur to in order to convert to atoms? What does Avogadro's number represent?

Solution We need two conversions: first from grams to moles and then from moles to number of particles (atoms). The first step is similar to Example 3.2. Because

$$1 \text{ mol S} = 32.07 \text{ g S}$$

the conversion factor is

$$\frac{1 \text{ mol S}}{32.07 \text{ g S}}$$

(Continued)

Avogadro's number is the key to the second step. We have

$$1 \text{ mol} = 6.022 \times 10^{23} \text{ particles (atoms)}$$

and the conversion factors are

$$\frac{6.022 \times 10^{23} \text{ S atoms}}{1 \text{ mol S}} \quad \text{and} \quad \frac{1 \text{ mol S}}{6.022 \times 10^{23} \text{ S atoms}}$$

The conversion factor on the left is the one we need because it has number of S atoms in the numerator. We can solve the problem by first calculating the number of moles contained in 16.3 g of S, and then calculating the number of S atoms from the number of moles of S:

$$\text{grams of S} \longrightarrow \text{moles of S} \longrightarrow \text{number of S atoms}$$

We can combine these conversions in one step as follows:

$$16.3 \text{ g S} \times \frac{1 \text{ mol S}}{32.07 \text{ g S}} \times \frac{6.022 \times 10^{23} \text{ S atoms}}{1 \text{ mol S}} = 3.06 \times 10^{23} \text{ S atoms}$$

Thus, there are 3.06×10^{23} atoms of S in 16.3 g of S.

Check Should 16.3 g of S contain fewer than Avogadro's number of atoms? What mass of S would contain Avogadro's number of atoms?

Similar problems: 3.20, 3.21.

Practice Exercise Calculate the number of atoms in 0.551 g of potassium (K).

3.3 Molecular Mass

If we know the atomic masses of the component atoms, we can calculate the mass of a molecule. The **molecular mass** (sometimes called *molecular weight*) is *the sum of the atomic masses (in amu) in the molecule.* For example, the molecular mass of H_2O is

Interactivity:
Molecular Mass
ARIS, Interactives

$$2(\text{atomic mass of H}) + \text{atomic mass of O}$$

or

$$2(1.008 \text{ amu}) + 16.00 \text{ amu} = 18.02 \text{ amu}$$

In general, we need to multiply the atomic mass of each element by the number of atoms of that element present in the molecule and sum over all the elements. Example 3.5 illustrates this approach.

Example 3.5

Calculate the molecular masses (in amu) of the following compounds: (a) sulfur dioxide (SO_2) and (b) caffeine ($C_8H_{10}N_4O_2$).

Strategy How do atomic masses of different elements combine to give the molecular mass of a compound?

Solution To calculate molecular mass, we need to sum all the atomic masses in the molecule. For each element, we multiply the atomic mass of the element by the number of atoms of that element in the molecule. We find atomic masses in the periodic table (inside front cover).

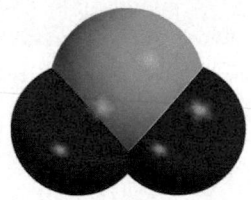

SO_2

(Continued)

(a) There are two O atoms and one S atom in SO_2, so that

$$\text{molecular mass of } SO_2 = 32.07 \text{ amu} + 2(16.00 \text{ amu})$$
$$= \boxed{64.07 \text{ amu}}$$

(b) There are eight C atoms, ten H atoms, four N atoms, and two O atoms in caffeine, so the molecular mass of $C_8H_{10}N_4O_2$ is given by

$$8(12.01 \text{ amu}) + 10(1.008 \text{ amu}) + 4(14.01 \text{ amu}) + 2(16.00 \text{ amu}) = \boxed{194.20 \text{ amu}}$$

Similar problems: 3.23, 3.24.

Practice Exercise What is the molecular mass of methanol (CH_4O)?

From the molecular mass we can determine the molar mass of a molecule or compound. The molar mass of a compound (in grams) is numerically equal to its molecular mass (in amu). For example, the molecular mass of water is 18.02 amu, so its molar mass is 18.02 g. Note that 1 mole of water weighs 18.02 g and contains 6.022×10^{23} H_2O *molecules,* just as 1 mole of elemental carbon contains 6.022×10^{23} carbon *atoms.*

As Examples 3.6 and 3.7 show, a knowledge of the molar mass enables us to calculate the numbers of moles and individual atoms in a given quantity of a compound.

CH_4

Methane gas burning on a cooking range.

Example 3.6

Methane (CH_4) is the principal component of natural gas. How many moles of CH_4 are present in 6.07 g of CH_4?

Strategy We are given grams of CH_4 and asked to solve for moles of CH_4. What conversion factor do we need to convert between grams and moles? Arrange the appropriate conversion factor so that grams cancel and the unit moles are obtained for your answer.

Solution The conversion factor needed to convert between grams and moles is the molar mass. First we need to calculate the molar mass of CH_4, following the procedure in Example 3.5:

$$\text{molar mass of } CH_4 = 12.01 \text{ g} + 4(1.008 \text{ g})$$
$$= 16.04 \text{ g}$$

Because

$$1 \text{ mol } CH_4 = 16.04 \text{ g } CH_4$$

the conversion factor we need should have grams in the denominator so that the unit g will cancel, leaving the unit mol in the numerator:

$$\frac{1 \text{ mol } CH_4}{16.04 \text{ g } CH_4}$$

We now write

$$6.07 \text{ g } \cancel{CH_4} \times \frac{1 \text{ mol } CH_4}{16.04 \text{ g } \cancel{CH_4}} = \boxed{0.378 \text{ mol } CH_4}$$

Thus, there is 0.378 mole of CH_4 in 6.07 g of CH_4.

(Continued)

Check Should 6.07 g of CH_4 equal less than 1 mole of CH_4? What is the mass of 1 mole of CH_4?

Similar problem: 3.26.

Practice Exercise Calculate the number of moles of chloroform ($CHCl_3$) in 198 g of chloroform.

Example 3.7

How many hydrogen atoms are present in 25.6 g of urea [$(NH_2)_2CO$], which is used as a fertilizer, in animal feed, and in the manufacture of polymers? The molar mass of urea is 60.06 g.

Strategy We are asked to solve for atoms of hydrogen in 25.6 g of urea. We cannot convert directly from grams of urea to atoms of hydrogen. What unit do we need to obtain first before we can convert to atoms? How should Avogadro's number be used here? How many atoms of H are in 1 molecule of urea?

Solution To calculate number of H atoms, we first must convert grams of urea to number of molecules of urea. This part is similar to Example 3.4. The molecular formula of urea shows there are four H atoms in one urea molecule. We need three conversion factors: the molar mass of urea, Avogadro's number, and the number of H atoms in 1 molecule of urea. We can combine these three conversions

Urea.

$$\text{grams of urea} \longrightarrow \text{moles of urea} \longrightarrow \text{molecules of urea} \longrightarrow \text{atoms of H}$$

into one calculation,

$$25.6 \text{ g } \cancel{(NH_2)_2CO} \times \frac{1 \text{ mol } \cancel{(NH_2)_2CO}}{60.06 \text{ g } \cancel{(NH_2)_2CO}} \times \frac{6.022 \times 10^{23} \text{ molecules } \cancel{(NH_2)_2CO}}{1 \text{ mol } \cancel{(NH_2)_2CO}}$$
$$\times \frac{4 \text{ H atoms}}{1 \text{ molecule } \cancel{(NH_2)_2CO}} = 1.03 \times 10^{24} \text{ H atoms}$$

The preceding method utilizes the ratio of molecules (urea) to atoms (hydrogen). We can also solve the problem by reading the formula as the ratio of moles of urea to moles of hydrogen using the following conversions

$$\text{grams of urea} \longrightarrow \text{moles of urea} \longrightarrow \text{moles of H} \longrightarrow \text{atoms of H}$$

Try it.

Check Does the answer look reasonable? How many atoms of H would 60.06 g of urea contain?

Similar problems: 3.27, 3.28.

Practice Exercise How many H atoms are in 72.5 g of isopropanol (rubbing alcohol), C_3H_8O?

Finally, note that for ionic compounds like NaCl and MgO that do not contain discrete molecular units, we use the term *formula mass* instead. The formula mass of NaCl is the mass of one formula unit in amu:

$$\text{formula mass of NaCl} = 22.99 \text{ amu} + 35.45 \text{ amu}$$
$$= 58.44 \text{ amu}$$

and its molar mass is 58.44 g.

3.4 The Mass Spectrometer

The most direct and most accurate method for determining atomic and molecular masses is mass spectrometry, which is depicted in Figure 3.3. In one type of a *mass spectrometer,* a gaseous sample is bombarded by a stream of high-energy electrons. Collisions between the electrons and the gaseous atoms (or molecules) produce positive ions by dislodging an electron from each atom or molecule. These positive ions (of mass m and charge e) are accelerated by two oppositely charged plates as they pass through the plates. The emerging ions are deflected into a circular path by a magnet. The radius of the path depends on the charge-to-mass ratio (that is, e/m). Ions of smaller e/m ratio trace a wider curve than those having a larger e/m ratio, so that ions with equal charges but different masses are separated from one another. The mass of each ion (and hence its parent atom or molecule) is determined from the magnitude of its deflection. Eventually the ions arrive at the detector, which registers a current for each type of ion. The amount of current generated is directly proportional to the number of ions, so it enables us to determine the relative abundance of isotopes.

The first mass spectrometer, developed in the 1920s by the English physicist F. W. Aston,[†] was crude by today's standards. Nevertheless, it provided indisputable evidence of the existence of isotopes—neon-20 (atomic mass 19.9924 amu and natural abundance 90.92 percent) and neon-22 (atomic mass 21.9914 amu and natural abundance 8.82 percent). When more sophisticated and sensitive mass spectrometers became available, scientists were surprised to discover that neon has a third stable isotope with an atomic mass of 20.9940 amu and natural abundance 0.257 percent (Figure 3.4). This example illustrates how very important experimental accuracy is to a quantitative science like chemistry. Early experiments failed to detect neon-21 because its natural abundance is just 0.257 percent. In other words, only 26 in 10,000 Ne atoms are neon-21. The masses of molecules can be determined in a similar manner by the mass spectrometer.

3.5 Percent Composition of Compounds

As we have seen, the formula of a compound tells us the numbers of atoms of each element in a unit of the compound. However, suppose we needed to verify the purity of a compound for use in a laboratory experiment. From the formula we could calculate what percent of the total mass of the compound is contributed by each element.

[†]Francis William Aston (1877–1945). English chemist and physicist. He was awarded the Nobel Prize in Chemistry in 1922 for developing the mass spectrometer.

Figure 3.3 *Schematic diagram of one type of mass spectrometer.*

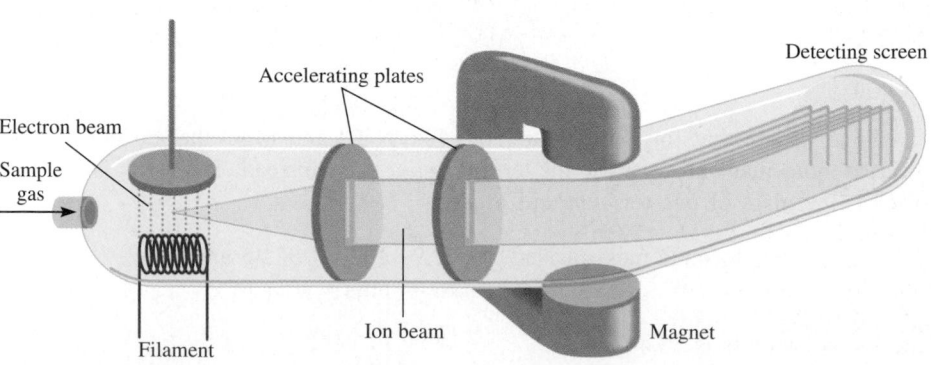

Detecting screen

Accelerating plates

Electron beam

Sample gas

Filament

Ion beam

Magnet

Figure 3.4 *The mass spectrum of the three isotopes of neon.*

Then, by comparing the result to the percent composition obtained experimentally for our sample, we could determine the purity of the sample.

The ***percent composition by mass*** is the *percent by mass of each element in a compound.* Percent composition is obtained by dividing the mass of each element in 1 mole of the compound by the molar mass of the compound and multiplying by 100 percent. Mathematically, the percent composition of an element in a compound is expressed as

$$\text{percent composition of an element} = \frac{n \times \text{molar mass of element}}{\text{molar mass of compound}} \times 100\% \qquad (3.1)$$

where n is the number of moles of the element in 1 mole of the compound. For example, in 1 mole of hydrogen peroxide (H_2O_2) there are 2 moles of H atoms and 2 moles of O atoms. The molar masses of H_2O_2, H, and O are 34.02 g, 1.008 g, and 16.00 g, respectively. Therefore, the percent composition of H_2O_2 is calculated as follows:

$$\%H = \frac{2 \times 1.008 \text{ g H}}{34.02 \text{ g } H_2O_2} \times 100\% = 5.926\%$$

$$\%O = \frac{2 \times 16.00 \text{ g O}}{34.02 \text{ g } H_2O_2} \times 100\% = 94.06\%$$

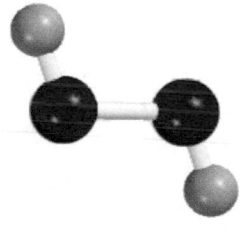

H_2O_2

The sum of the percentages is $5.926\% + 94.06\% = 99.99\%$. The small discrepancy from 100 percent is due to the way we rounded off the molar masses of the elements. If we had used the empirical formula HO for the calculation, we would have written

$$\%H = \frac{1.008 \text{ g H}}{17.01 \text{ g HO}} \times 100\% = 5.926\%$$

$$\%O = \frac{16.00 \text{ g O}}{17.01 \text{ g HO}} \times 100\% = 94.06\%$$

Because both the molecular formula and the empirical formula tell us the composition of the compound, it is not surprising that they give us the same percent composition by mass.

H_3PO_4

Similar problem: 3.40.

Example 3.8

Phosphoric acid (H_3PO_4) is a colorless, syrupy liquid used in detergents, fertilizers, toothpastes, and in carbonated beverages for a "tangy" flavor. Calculate the percent composition by mass of H, P, and O in this compound.

Strategy Recall the procedure for calculating a percentage. Assume that we have 1 mole of H_3PO_4. The percent by mass of each element (H, P, and O) is given by the combined molar mass of the atoms of the element in 1 mole of H_3PO_4 divided by the molar mass of H_3PO_4, then multiplied by 100 percent.

Solution The molar mass of H_3PO_4 is 97.99 g. The percent by mass of each of the elements in H_3PO_4 is calculated as follows:

$$\%H = \frac{3(1.008 \text{ g}) \text{ H}}{97.99 \text{ g } H_3PO_4} \times 100\% = 3.086\%$$

$$\%P = \frac{30.97 \text{ g P}}{97.99 \text{ g } H_3PO_4} \times 100\% = 31.61\%$$

$$\%O = \frac{4(16.00 \text{ g}) \text{ O}}{97.99 \text{ g } H_3PO_4} \times 100\% = 65.31\%$$

Check Do the percentages add to 100 percent? The sum of the percentages is (3.086% + 31.61% + 65.31%) = 100.01%. The small discrepancy from 100 percent is due to the way we rounded off.

Practice Exercise Calculate the percent composition by mass of each of the elements in sulfuric acid (H_2SO_4).

The procedure used in the example can be reversed if necessary. Given the percent composition by mass of a compound, we can determine the empirical formula of the compound (Figure 3.5). Because we are dealing with percentages and the sum of all the percentages is 100 percent, it is convenient to assume that we started with 100 g of a compound, as Example 3.9 shows.

The molecular formula of ascorbic acid is $C_6H_8O_6$.

Example 3.9

Ascorbic acid (vitamin C) cures scurvy. It is composed of 40.92 percent carbon (C), 4.58 percent hydrogen (H), and 54.50 percent oxygen (O) by mass. Determine its empirical formula.

Strategy In a chemical formula, the subscripts represent the ratio of the number of moles of each element that combine to form one mole of the compound. How can we convert from mass percent to moles? If we assume an exactly 100-g sample of the compound, do we know the mass of each element in the compound? How do we then convert from grams to moles?

Solution If we have 100 g of ascorbic acid, then each percentage can be converted directly to grams. In this sample, there will be 40.92 g of C, 4.58 g of H, and 54.50 g of O. Because the subscripts in the formula represent a mole ratio, we need to convert the grams of each element to moles. The conversion factor needed is the molar mass of each element. Let n represent the number of moles of each element so that

(Continued)

$$n_C = 40.92 \text{ g C} \times \frac{1 \text{ mol C}}{12.01 \text{ g C}} = 3.407 \text{ mol C}$$

$$n_H = 4.58 \text{ g H} \times \frac{1 \text{ mol H}}{1.008 \text{ g H}} = 4.54 \text{ mol H}$$

$$n_O = 54.50 \text{ g O} \times \frac{1 \text{ mol O}}{16.00 \text{ g O}} = 3.406 \text{ mol O}$$

Thus, we arrive at the formula $C_{3.407}H_{4.54}O_{3.406}$, which gives the identity and the mole ratios of atoms present. However, chemical formulas are written with whole numbers. Try to convert to whole numbers by dividing all the subscripts by the smallest subscript (3.406):

$$C: \frac{3.407}{3.406} \approx 1 \quad H: \frac{4.54}{3.406} = 1.33 \quad O: \frac{3.406}{3.406} = 1$$

where the $\approx$ sign means "approximately equal to." This gives $CH_{1.33}O$ as the formula for ascorbic acid. Next, we need to convert 1.33, the subscript for H, into an integer. This can be done by a trial-and-error procedure:

$$1.33 \times 1 = 1.33$$
$$1.33 \times 2 = 2.66$$
$$1.33 \times 3 = 3.99 \approx 4$$

Because 1.33×3 gives us an integer (4), we multiply all the subscripts by 3 and obtain $C_3H_4O_3$ as the empirical formula for ascorbic acid.

Check Are the subscripts in $C_3H_4O_3$ reduced to the smallest whole numbers?

Practice Exercise Determine the empirical formula of a compound having the following percent composition by mass: K: 24.75 percent; Mn: 34.77 percent; O: 40.51 percent.

Mass percent

↓ Convert to grams and divide by molar mass

Moles of each element

↓ Divide by the smallest number of moles

Mole ratios of elements

↓ Change to integer subscripts

Empirical formula

Figure 3.5 *Procedure for calculating the empirical formula of a compound from its percent compositions.*

Similar problems: 3.49, 3.50.

Chemists often want to know the actual mass of an element in a certain mass of a compound. For example, in the mining industry, this information will tell the scientists about the quality of the ore. Because the percent composition by mass of the elements in the substance can be readily calculated, such a problem can be solved in a rather direct way.

Example 3.10

Chalcopyrite ($CuFeS_2$) is a principal mineral of copper. Calculate the number of kilograms of Cu in 3.71×10^3 kg of chalcopyrite.

Strategy Chalcopyrite is composed of Cu, Fe, and S. The mass due to Cu is based on its percentage by mass in the compound. How do we calculate mass percent of an element?

Solution The molar masses of Cu and $CuFeS_2$ are 63.55 g and 183.5 g, respectively. The mass percent of Cu is therefore

$$\%Cu = \frac{\text{molar mass of Cu}}{\text{molar mass of } CuFeS_2} \times 100\%$$
$$= \frac{63.55 \text{ g}}{183.5 \text{ g}} \times 100\% = 34.63\%$$

(Continued)

Chalcopyrite.

To calculate the mass of Cu in a 3.71×10^3 kg sample of $CuFeS_2$, we need to convert the percentage to a fraction (that is, convert 34.63 percent to 34.63/100, or 0.3463) and write

$$\text{mass of Cu in } CuFeS_2 = 0.3463 \times (3.71 \times 10^3 \text{ kg}) = 1.28 \times 10^3 \text{ kg}$$

Check As a ball-park estimate, note that the mass percent of Cu is roughly 33 percent, so that a third of the mass should be Cu; that is, $\frac{1}{3} \times 3.71 \times 10^3$ kg $\approx 1.24 \times 10^3$ kg. This quantity is quite close to the answer.

Practice Exercise Calculate the number of grams of Al in 371 g of Al_2O_3.

Similar problem: 3.45.

3.6 Experimental Determination of Empirical Formulas

The fact that we can determine the empirical formula of a compound if we know the percent composition enables us to identify compounds experimentally. The procedure is as follows. First, chemical analysis tells us the number of grams of each element present in a given amount of a compound. Then, we convert the quantities in grams to number of moles of each element. Finally, using the method given in Example 3.9, we find the empirical formula of the compound.

As a specific example, let us consider the compound ethanol. When ethanol is burned in an apparatus such as that shown in Figure 3.6, carbon dioxide (CO_2) and water (H_2O) are given off. Because neither carbon nor hydrogen was in the inlet gas, we can conclude that both carbon (C) and hydrogen (H) were present in ethanol and that oxygen (O) may also be present. (Molecular oxygen was added in the combustion process, but some of the oxygen may also have come from the original ethanol sample.)

The masses of CO_2 and of H_2O produced can be determined by measuring the increase in mass of the CO_2 and H_2O absorbers, respectively. Suppose that in one experiment the combustion of 11.5 g of ethanol produced 22.0 g of CO_2 and 13.5 g of H_2O. We can calculate the mass of carbon and hydrogen in the original 11.5-g sample of ethanol as follows:

$$\text{mass of C} = 22.0 \text{ g } CO_2 \times \frac{1 \text{ mol } CO_2}{44.01 \text{ g } CO_2} \times \frac{1 \text{ mol C}}{1 \text{ mol } CO_2} \times \frac{12.01 \text{ g C}}{1 \text{ mol C}}$$
$$= 6.00 \text{ g C}$$
$$\text{mass of H} = 13.5 \text{ g } H_2O \times \frac{1 \text{ mol } H_2O}{18.02 \text{ g } H_2O} \times \frac{2 \text{ mol H}}{1 \text{ mol } H_2O} \times \frac{1.008 \text{ g H}}{1 \text{ mol H}}$$
$$= 1.51 \text{ g H}$$

Figure 3.6 *Apparatus for determining the empirical formula of ethanol. The absorbers are substances that can retain water and carbon dioxide, respectively.*

Thus, 11.5 g of ethanol contains 6.00 g of carbon and 1.51 g of hydrogen. The remainder must be oxygen, whose mass is

$$\begin{aligned} \text{mass of O} &= \text{mass of sample} - (\text{mass of C} + \text{mass of H}) \\ &= 11.5 \text{ g} - (6.00 \text{ g} + 1.51 \text{ g}) \\ &= 4.0 \text{ g} \end{aligned}$$

The number of moles of each element present in 11.5 g of ethanol is

$$\text{moles of C} = 6.00 \text{ g C} \times \frac{1 \text{ mol C}}{12.01 \text{ g C}} = 0.500 \text{ mol C}$$

$$\text{moles of H} = 1.51 \text{ g H} \times \frac{1 \text{ mol H}}{1.008 \text{ g H}} = 1.50 \text{ mol H}$$

$$\text{moles of O} = 4.0 \text{ g O} \times \frac{1 \text{ mol O}}{16.00 \text{ g O}} = 0.25 \text{ mol O}$$

The formula of ethanol is therefore $C_{0.50}H_{1.5}O_{0.25}$ (we round off the number of moles to two significant figures). Because the number of atoms must be an integer, we divide the subscripts by 0.25, the smallest subscript, and obtain for the empirical formula C_2H_6O.

Now we can better understand the word "empirical," which literally means "based only on observation and measurement." The empirical formula of ethanol is determined from analysis of the compound in terms of its component elements. No knowledge of how the atoms are linked together in the compound is required.

It happens that the molecular formula of ethanol is the same as its empirical formula.

Determination of Molecular Formulas

The formula calculated from percent composition by mass is always the empirical formula because the subscripts in the formula are always reduced to the smallest whole numbers. To calculate the actual, molecular formula we must know the *approximate* molar mass of the compound in addition to its empirical formula. Knowing that the molar mass of a compound must be an integral multiple of the molar mass of its empirical formula, we can use the molar mass to find the molecular formula, as Example 3.11 demonstrates.

Example 3.11

A sample of a compound contains 1.52 g of nitrogen (N) and 3.47 g of oxygen (O). The molar mass of this compound is between 90 g and 95 g. Determine the molecular formula and the accurate molar mass of the compound.

Strategy To determine the molecular formula, we first need to determine the empirical formula. How do we convert between grams and moles? Comparing the empirical molar mass to the experimentally determined molar mass will reveal the relationship between the empirical formula and molecular formula.

Solution We are given grams of N and O. Use molar mass as a conversion factor to convert grams to moles of each element. Let n represent the number of moles of each element. We write

$$n_N = 1.52 \text{ g N} \times \frac{1 \text{ mol N}}{14.01 \text{ g N}} = 0.108 \text{ mol N}$$

$$n_O = 3.47 \text{ g O} \times \frac{1 \text{ mol O}}{16.00 \text{ g O}} = 0.217 \text{ mol O}$$

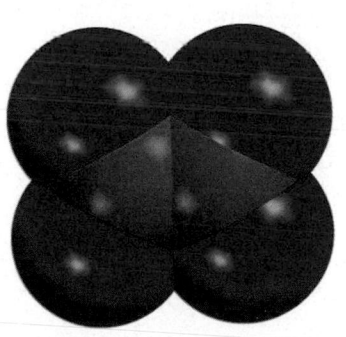

N_2O_4

(Continued)

Thus, we arrive at the formula $N_{0.108}O_{0.217}$, which gives the identity and the ratios of atoms present. However, chemical formulas are written with whole numbers. Try to convert to whole numbers by dividing the subscripts by the smaller subscript (0.108). After rounding off, we obtain NO_2 as the empirical formula.

The molecular formula might be the same as the empirical formula or some integral multiple of it (for example, two, three, four, or more times the empirical formula). Comparing the ratio of the molar mass to the molar mass of the empirical formula will show the integral relationship between the empirical and molecular formulas. The molar mass of the empirical formula NO_2 is

$$\text{empirical molar mass} = 14.01 \text{ g} + 2(16.00 \text{ g}) = 46.01 \text{ g}$$

Next, we determine the ratio between the molar mass and the empirical molar mass

$$\frac{\text{molar mass}}{\text{empirical molar mass}} = \frac{90 \text{ g}}{46.01 \text{ g}} \approx 2$$

The molar mass is twice the empirical molar mass. This means that there are two NO_2 units in each molecule of the compound, and the molecular formula is $(NO_2)_2$ or N_2O_4.

The actual molar mass of the compound is two times the empirical molar mass, that is, 2(46.01 g) or 92.02 g, which is between 90 g and 95 g.

Check Note that in determining the molecular formula from the empirical formula, we need only know the *approximate* molar mass of the compound. The reason is that the true molar mass is an integral multiple ($1\times, 2\times, 3\times, \ldots$) of the empirical molar mass. Therefore, the ratio (molar mass/empirical molar mass) will always be close to an integer.

Practice Exercise A sample of a compound containing boron (B) and hydrogen (H) contains 6.444 g of B and 1.803 g of H. The molar mass of the compound is about 30 g. What is its molecular formula?

Similar problems: 3.52, 3.53, 3.54.

3.7 Chemical Reactions and Chemical Equations

Having discussed the masses of atoms and molecules, we turn next to what happens to atoms and molecules in a ***chemical reaction,*** *a process in which a substance (or substances) is changed into one or more new substances.* To communicate with one another about chemical reactions, chemists have devised a standard way to represent them using chemical equations. A ***chemical equation*** *uses chemical symbols to show what happens during a chemical reaction.* In this section we will learn how to write chemical equations and balance them.

Writing Chemical Equations

Consider what happens when hydrogen gas (H_2) burns in air (which contains oxygen, O_2) to form water (H_2O). This reaction can be represented by the chemical equation

$$H_2 + O_2 \longrightarrow H_2O \tag{3.2}$$

where the "plus" sign means "reacts with" and the arrow means "to yield." Thus, this symbolic expression can be read: "Molecular hydrogen reacts with molecular oxygen to yield water." The reaction is assumed to proceed from left to right as the arrow indicates.

We use the law of conservation of mass as our guide in balancing chemical equations.

Equation (3.2) is not complete, however, because there are twice as many oxygen atoms on the left side of the arrow (two) as on the right side (one). To conform

Two hydrogen molecules   +   One oxygen molecule $\longrightarrow$ Two water molecules

$2H_2$ + O_2 $\longrightarrow$ $2H_2O$

Figure 3.7 *Three ways of representing the combustion of hydrogen. In accordance with the law of conservation of mass, the number of each type of atom must be the same on both sides of the equation.*

with the law of conservation of mass, there must be the same number of each type of atom on both sides of the arrow; that is, we must have as many atoms after the reaction ends as we did before it started. We can *balance* Equation (3.2) by placing the appropriate coefficient (2 in this case) in front of H_2 and H_2O:

$$2H_2 + O_2 \longrightarrow 2H_2O$$

When the coefficient is 1, as in the case of O_2, it is not shown.

This *balanced chemical equation* shows that "two hydrogen molecules can combine or react with one oxygen molecule to form two water molecules" (Figure 3.7). Because the ratio of the number of molecules is equal to the ratio of the number of moles, the equation can also be read as "2 moles of hydrogen molecules react with 1 mole of oxygen molecules to produce 2 moles of water molecules." We know the mass of a mole of each of these substances, so we can also interpret the equation as "4.04 g of H_2 react with 32.00 g of O_2 to give 36.04 g of H_2O." These three ways of reading the equation are summarized in Table 3.1.

We refer to H_2 and O_2 in Equation (3.2) as **reactants,** which are *the starting materials in a chemical reaction.* Water is the **product,** which is *the substance formed as a result of a chemical reaction.* A chemical equation, then, is just the chemist's shorthand description of a reaction. In a chemical equation, the reactants are conventionally written on the left and the products on the right of the arrow:

$$reactants \longrightarrow products$$

To provide additional information, chemists often indicate the physical states of the reactants and products by using the letters *g*, *l*, and *s* to denote gas, liquid, and solid, respectively. For example,

$$2CO(g) + O_2(g) \longrightarrow 2CO_2(g)$$
$$2HgO(s) \longrightarrow 2Hg(l) + O_2(g)$$

The procedure for balancing a chemical equation is shown in the next subsection.

To represent what happens when sodium chloride (NaCl) is added to water, we write

$$NaCl(s) \xrightarrow{H_2O} NaCl(aq)$$

TABLE 3.1	Interpretation of a Chemical Equation	
$2H_2$	$+ O_2$	$\longrightarrow 2H_2O$
Two molecules	+ one molecule	$\longrightarrow$ two molecules
2 moles	+ 1 mole	$\longrightarrow$ 2 moles
$2(2.02 \text{ g}) = 4.04 \text{ g}$	$+ 32.00 \text{ g}$	$\longrightarrow 2(18.02 \text{ g}) = 36.04 \text{ g}$
36.04 g reactants		36.04 g product

where *aq* denotes the aqueous (that is, water) environment. Writing H_2O above the arrow symbolizes the physical process of dissolving a substance in water, although it is sometimes left out for simplicity.

Knowing the states of the reactants and products is especially useful in the laboratory. For example, when potassium bromide (KBr) and silver nitrate ($AgNO_3$) react in an aqueous environment, a solid, silver bromide (AgBr), is formed. This reaction can be represented by the equation:

$$KBr(aq) + AgNO_3(aq) \longrightarrow KNO_3(aq) + AgBr(s)$$

If the physical states of reactants and products are not given, an uninformed person might try to bring about the reaction by mixing solid KBr with solid $AgNO_3$. These solids would react very slowly or not at all. Imagining the process on the microscopic level, we can understand that for a product like silver bromide to form, the Ag^+ and Br^- ions would have to come in contact with each other. However, these ions are locked in place in their solid compounds and have little mobility. (Here is an example of how we explain a phenomenon by thinking about what happens at the molecular level, as discussed in Section 1.2.)

Balancing Chemical Equations

Suppose we want to write an equation to describe a chemical reaction that we have just carried out in the laboratory. How should we go about doing it? Because we know the identities of the reactants, we can write their chemical formulas. The identities of products are more difficult to establish. For simple reactions it is often possible to guess the product(s). For more complicated reactions involving three or more products, chemists may need to perform further tests to establish the presence of specific compounds.

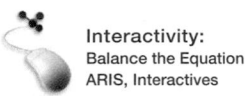

Interactivity:
Balance the Equation
ARIS, Interactives

Once we have identified all the reactants and products and have written the correct formulas for them, we assemble them in the conventional sequence—reactants on the left separated by an arrow from products on the right. The equation written at this point is likely to be *unbalanced;* that is, the number of each type of atom on one side of the arrow differs from the number on the other side. In general, we can balance a chemical equation by the following steps:

Interactivity:
Balancing Chemical Equations
ARIS, Interactives

1. Identify all reactants and products and write their correct formulas on the left side and right side of the equation, respectively.

2. Begin balancing the equation by trying different coefficients to make the number of atoms of each element the same on both sides of the equation. We can change the coefficients (the numbers preceding the formulas) but not the subscripts (the numbers within formulas). Changing the subscripts would change the identity of the substance. For example, $2NO_2$ means "two molecules of nitrogen dioxide," but if we double the subscripts, we have N_2O_4, which is the formula of dinitrogen tetroxide, a completely different compound.

3. First, look for elements that appear only once on each side of the equation with the same number of atoms on each side: The formulas containing these elements must have the same coefficient. Therefore, there is no need to adjust the coefficients of these elements at this point. Next, look for elements that appear only once on each side of the equation but in unequal numbers of atoms. Balance these elements. Finally, balance elements that appear in two or more formulas on the same side of the equation.

4. Check your balanced equation to be sure that you have the same total number of each type of atoms on both sides of the equation arrow.

Let's consider a specific example. In the laboratory, small amounts of oxygen gas can be prepared by heating potassium chlorate ($KClO_3$). The products are oxygen gas (O_2) and potassium chloride (KCl). From this information, we write

$$KClO_3 \longrightarrow KCl + O_2$$

(For simplicity, we omit the physical states of reactants and products.) All three elements (K, Cl, and O) appear only once on each side of the equation, but only for K and Cl do we have equal numbers of atoms on both sides. Thus, $KClO_3$ and KCl must have the same coefficient. The next step is to make the number of O atoms the same on both sides of the equation. Because there are three O atoms on the left and two O atoms on the right of the equation, we can balance the O atoms by placing a 2 in front of $KClO_3$ and a 3 in front of O_2.

$$2KClO_3 \longrightarrow KCl + 3O_2$$

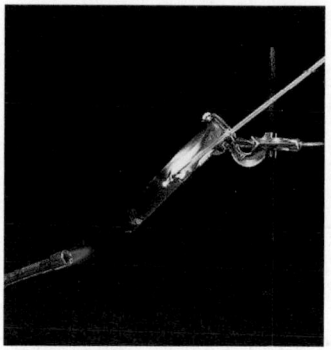

Heating potassium chlorate produces oxygen, which supports the combustion of wood splint.

Finally, we balance the K and Cl atoms by placing a 2 in front of KCl:

$$2KClO_3 \longrightarrow 2KCl + 3O_2 \tag{3.3}$$

As a final check, we can draw up a balance sheet for the reactants and products where the number in parentheses indicates the number of atoms of each element:

Reactants	Products
K (2)	K (2)
Cl (2)	Cl (2)
O (6)	O (6)

Note that this equation could also be balanced with coefficients which are multiples of 2 (for $KClO_3$), 2 (for KCl), and 3 (for O_2); for example,

$$4KClO_3 \longrightarrow 4KCl + 6O_2$$

However, it is common practice to use the *simplest* possible set of whole-number coefficients to balance the equation. Equation (3.3) conforms to this convention.

Now let us consider the combustion (that is, burning) of the natural gas component ethane (C_2H_6) in oxygen or air, which yields carbon dioxide (CO_2) and water. The unbalanced equation is

$$C_2H_6 + O_2 \longrightarrow CO_2 + H_2O$$

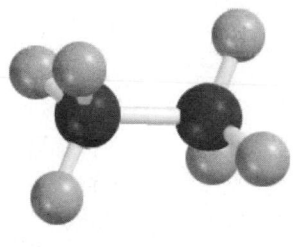

C_2H_6

We see that the number of atoms is not the same on both sides of the equation for any of the elements (C, H, and O). In addition, C and H appear only once on each side of the equation; O appears in two compounds on the right side (CO_2 and H_2O). To balance the C atoms, we place a 2 in front of CO_2:

$$C_2H_6 + O_2 \longrightarrow 2CO_2 + H_2O$$

To balance the H atoms, we place a 3 in front of H_2O:

$$C_2H_6 + O_2 \longrightarrow 2CO_2 + 3H_2O$$

At this stage, the C and H atoms are balanced, but the O atoms are not because there are seven O atoms on the right-hand side and only two O atoms on the left-hand side of the equation. This inequality of O atoms can be eliminated by writing $\frac{7}{2}$ in front of the O_2 on the left-hand side:

$$C_2H_6 + \tfrac{7}{2}O_2 \longrightarrow 2CO_2 + 3H_2O$$

The "logic" for using $\frac{7}{2}$ as a coefficient is that there were seven oxygen atoms on the right-hand side of the equation, but only a pair of oxygen atoms (O_2) on the left. To balance them we ask how many *pairs* of oxygen atoms are needed to equal seven oxygen atoms. Just as 3.5 pairs of shoes equal seven shoes, $\frac{7}{2}O_2$ molecules equal seven O atoms. As the following tally shows, the equation is now balanced:

Reactants	Products
C (2)	C (2)
H (6)	H (6)
O (7)	O (7)

However, we normally prefer to express the coefficients as whole numbers rather than as fractions. Therefore, we multiply the entire equation by 2 to convert $\frac{7}{2}$ to 7:

$$2C_2H_6 + 7O_2 \longrightarrow 4CO_2 + 6H_2O$$

The final tally is

Reactants	Products
C (4)	C (4)
H (12)	H (12)
O (14)	O (14)

Note that the coefficients used in balancing the last equation are the smallest possible set of whole numbers.

In Example 3.12 we will continue to practice our equation-balancing skills.

Example 3.12

When aluminum metal is exposed to air, a protective layer of aluminum oxide (Al_2O_3) forms on its surface. This layer prevents further reaction between aluminum and oxygen, and it is the reason that aluminum beverage cans do not corrode. [In the case of iron, the rust, or iron(III) oxide, that forms is too porous to protect the iron metal underneath, so rusting continues.] Write a balanced equation for the formation of Al_2O_3.

Strategy Remember that the formula of an element or compound cannot be changed when balancing a chemical equation. The equation is balanced by placing the appropriate coefficients in front of the formulas. Follow the procedure described on p. 94.

Solution The unbalanced equation is

$$Al + O_2 \longrightarrow Al_2O_3$$

In a balanced equation, the number and types of atoms on each side of the equation must be the same. We see that there is one Al atom on the reactants side and there are two Al atoms on the product side. We can balance the Al atoms by placing a coefficient of 2 in front of Al on the reactants side.

$$2Al + O_2 \longrightarrow Al_2O_3$$

(Continued)

There are two O atoms on the reactants side, and three O atoms on the product side of the equation. We can balance the O atoms by placing a coefficient of $\frac{3}{2}$ in front of O_2 on the reactants side.

$$2Al + \tfrac{3}{2}O_2 \longrightarrow Al_2O_3$$

This is a balanced equation. However, equations are normally balanced with the smallest set of *whole* number coefficients. Multiplying both sides of the equation by 2 gives whole number coefficients.

$$2(2Al + \tfrac{3}{2}O_2 \longrightarrow Al_2O_3)$$

or

$$4Al + 3O_2 \longrightarrow 2Al_2O_3$$

Check For an equation to be balanced, the number and types of atoms on each side of the equation must be the same. The final tally is

Reactants	Products
Al (4)	Al (4)
O (6)	O (6)

The equation is balanced. Also, the coefficients are reduced to the simplest set of whole numbers.

Similar problems: 3.59, 3.60.

Practice Exercise Balance the equation representing the reaction between iron(III) oxide, Fe_2O_3, and carbon monoxide (CO) to yield iron (Fe) and carbon dioxide (CO_2).

3.8 Amounts of Reactants and Products

A basic question raised in the chemical laboratory is "How much product will be formed from specific amounts of starting materials (reactants)?" Or in some cases, we might ask the reverse question: "How much starting material must be used to obtain a specific amount of product?" To interpret a reaction quantitatively, we need to apply our knowledge of molar masses and the mole concept. *Stoichiometry* is *the quantitative study of reactants and products in a chemical reaction.*

Whether the units given for reactants (or products) are moles, grams, liters (for gases), or some other units, we use moles to calculate the amount of product formed in a reaction. This approach is called the ***mole method,*** which means simply that *the stoichiometric coefficients in a chemical equation can be interpreted as the number of moles of each substance.* For example, the combustion of carbon monoxide in air produces carbon dioxide:

$$2CO(g) + O_2(g) \longrightarrow 2CO_2(g)$$

The stoichiometric coefficients show that two molecules of CO react with one molecule of O_2 to form two molecules of CO_2. It follows that the relative numbers of moles are the same as the relative numbers of molecules:

$2CO(g)$	$+$	$O_2(g)$	$\longrightarrow$	$2CO_2(g)$
2 molecules		1 molecule		2 molecules
$2(6.022 \times 10^{23}$ molecules)		6.022×10^{23} molecules		$2(6.022 \times 10^{23}$ molecules)
2 mol		1 mol		2 mol

Thus, this equation can also be read as "2 moles of carbon monoxide gas combine with 1 mole of oxygen gas to form 2 moles of carbon dioxide gas." In stoichiometric

Carbon monoxide burns in air to form carbon dioxide.

calculations, we say that two moles of CO are equivalent to two moles of CO_2, that is,

$$2 \text{ mol CO} \simeq 2 \text{ mol CO}_2$$

where the symbol $\simeq$ means "stoichiometrically equivalent to" or simply "equivalent to." The mole ratio between CO and CO_2 is 2:2 or 1:1, meaning that if 10 moles of CO are reacted, 10 moles of CO_2 will be produced. Likewise, if 0.20 mole of CO is reacted, 0.20 mole of CO_2 will be formed. This relationship enables us to write the conversion factors

$$\frac{2 \text{ mol CO}}{2 \text{ mol CO}_2} \quad \text{and} \quad \frac{2 \text{ mol CO}_2}{2 \text{ mol CO}}$$

Similarly, we have 1 mol $O_2 \simeq 2$ mol CO_2 and 2 mol CO $\simeq$ 1 mol O_2.

Let's consider a simple example in which 4.8 moles of CO react completely with O_2 to form CO_2. To calculate the amount of CO_2 produced in moles, we use the conversion factor that has CO in the denominator and write

$$\text{moles of CO}_2 \text{ produced} = 4.8 \ \cancel{\text{mol CO}} \times \frac{2 \text{ mol CO}_2}{2 \ \cancel{\text{mol CO}}}$$
$$= 4.8 \text{ mol CO}_2$$

Now suppose 10.7 g of CO react completely with O_2 to form CO_2. How many grams of CO_2 will be formed? To do this calculation, we note that the link between CO and CO_2 is the mole ratio from the balanced equation. So we need to first convert grams of CO to moles of CO, then to moles of CO_2, and finally to grams of CO_2. The conversion steps are

$$\text{grams of CO} \longrightarrow \text{moles of CO} \longrightarrow \text{moles of CO}_2 \longrightarrow \text{grams of CO}_2$$

First, we convert 10.7 g of CO to number of moles of CO, using the molar mass of CO as the conversion factor:

$$\text{moles of CO} = 10.7 \ \cancel{\text{g CO}} \times \frac{1 \text{ mol CO}}{28.01 \ \cancel{\text{g CO}}}$$
$$= 0.382 \text{ mol CO}$$

Next, we calculate the number of moles of CO_2 produced.

$$\text{moles of CO}_2 = 0.382 \ \cancel{\text{mol CO}} \times \frac{2 \text{ mol CO}_2}{2 \ \cancel{\text{mol CO}}}$$
$$= 0.382 \text{ mol CO}_2$$

Finally, we calculate the mass of CO_2 produced in grams using the molar mass of CO_2 as the conversion factor

$$\text{grams of CO}_2 = 0.382 \ \cancel{\text{mol CO}_2} \times \frac{44.01 \text{ g CO}_2}{1 \ \cancel{\text{mol CO}_2}}$$
$$= 16.8 \text{ g CO}_2$$

These three separate calculations can be combined in a single step as follows:

$$\text{grams of CO}_2 = 10.7 \ \cancel{\text{g CO}} \times \frac{1 \ \cancel{\text{mol CO}}}{28.01 \ \cancel{\text{g CO}}} \times \frac{2 \ \cancel{\text{mol CO}_2}}{2 \ \cancel{\text{mol CO}}} \times \frac{44.01 \text{ g CO}_2}{1 \ \cancel{\text{mol CO}_2}}$$
$$= 16.8 \text{ g CO}_2$$

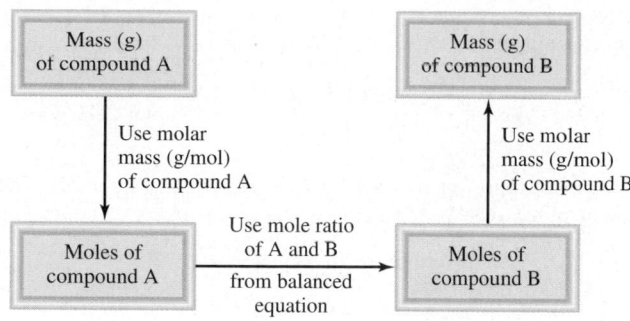

Similarly, we can calculate the mass of O_2 in grams consumed in this reaction. By using the relationship 2 mol CO $\rightleftharpoons$ 1 mol O_2, we write

$$\text{grams of } O_2 = 10.7 \text{ g } \cancel{CO} \times \frac{1 \text{ mol } \cancel{CO}}{28.01 \text{ g } \cancel{CO}} \times \frac{1 \text{ mol } \cancel{O_2}}{2 \text{ mol } \cancel{CO}} \times \frac{32.00 \text{ g } O_2}{1 \text{ mol } \cancel{O_2}}$$
$$= 6.11 \text{ g } O_2$$

The general approach for solving stoichiometry problems is summarized next.

1. Write a balanced equation for the reaction.
2. Convert the given amount of the reactant (in grams or other units) to number of moles.
3. Use the mole ratio from the balanced equation to calculate the number of moles of product formed.
4. Convert the moles of product to grams (or other units) of product.

Figure 3.8 shows these steps. Sometimes we may be asked to calculate the amount of a reactant needed to form a specific amount of product. In those cases, we can reverse the steps shown in Figure 3.8.

Examples 3.13 and 3.14 illustrate the application of this approach.

Example 3.13

The food we eat is degraded, or broken down, in our bodies to provide energy for growth and function. A general overall equation for this very complex process represents the degradation of glucose ($C_6H_{12}O_6$) to carbon dioxide (CO_2) and water (H_2O):

$$C_6H_{12}O_6 + 6O_2 \longrightarrow 6CO_2 + 6H_2O$$

If 856 g of $C_6H_{12}O_6$ is consumed by a person over a certain period, what is the mass of CO_2 produced?

$C_6H_{12}O_6$

Strategy Looking at the balanced equation, how do we compare the amounts of $C_6H_{12}O_6$ and CO_2? We can compare them based on the *mole ratio* from the balanced equation. Starting with grams of $C_6H_{12}O_6$, how do we convert to moles of $C_6H_{12}O_6$? Once moles of CO_2 are determined using the mole ratio from the balanced equation, how do we convert to grams of CO_2?

Solution We follow the preceding steps and Figure 3.8.

Step 1: The balanced equation is given in the problem.

(Continued)

Step 2: To convert grams of $C_6H_{12}O_6$ to moles of $C_6H_{12}O_6$, we write

$$856 \text{ g } C_6H_{12}O_6 \times \frac{1 \text{ mol } C_6H_{12}O_6}{180.2 \text{ g } C_6H_{12}O_6} = 4.750 \text{ mol } C_6H_{12}O_6$$

Step 3: From the mole ratio, we see that 1 mol $C_6H_{12}O_6 \simeq 6$ mol CO_2. Therefore, the number of moles of CO_2 formed is

$$4.750 \text{ mol } C_6H_{12}O_6 \times \frac{6 \text{ mol } CO_2}{1 \text{ mol } C_6H_{12}O_6} = 28.50 \text{ mol } CO_2$$

Step 4: Finally, the number of grams of CO_2 formed is given by

$$28.50 \text{ mol } CO_2 \times \frac{44.01 \text{ g } CO_2}{1 \text{ mol } CO_2} = 1.25 \times 10^3 \text{ g } CO_2$$

After some practice, we can combine the conversion steps

grams of $C_6H_{12}O_6 \longrightarrow$ moles of $C_6H_{12}O_6 \longrightarrow$ moles of $CO_2 \longrightarrow$ grams of CO_2

into one equation:

$$\text{mass of } CO_2 = 856 \text{ g } C_6H_{12}O_6 \times \frac{1 \text{ mol } C_6H_{12}O_6}{180.2 \text{ g } C_6H_{12}O_6} \times \frac{6 \text{ mol } CO_2}{1 \text{ mol } C_6H_{12}O_6} \times \frac{44.01 \text{ g } CO_2}{1 \text{ mol } CO_2}$$

$$= 1.25 \times 10^3 \text{ g } CO_2$$

Check Does the answer seem reasonable? Should the mass of CO_2 produced be larger than the mass of $C_6H_{12}O_6$ reacted, even though the molar mass of CO_2 is considerably less than the molar mass of $C_6H_{12}O_6$? What is the mole ratio between CO_2 and $C_6H_{12}O_6$?

Practice Exercise Methanol (CH_3OH) burns in air according to the equation

$$2CH_3OH + 3O_2 \longrightarrow 2CO_2 + 4H_2O$$

If 209 g of methanol are used up in a combustion process, what is the mass of H_2O produced?

Similar problem: 3.72.

Example 3.14

Lithium reacting with water to produce hydrogen gas.

All alkali metals react with water to produce hydrogen gas and the corresponding alkali metal hydroxide. A typical reaction is that between lithium and water:

$$2Li(s) + 2H_2O(l) \longrightarrow 2LiOH(aq) + H_2(g)$$

How many grams of Li are needed to produce 9.89 g of H_2?

Strategy The question asks for number of grams of reactant (Li) to form a specific amount of product (H_2). Therefore, we need to reverse the steps shown in Figure 3.8. From the equation we see that 2 mol Li $\simeq$ 1 mol H_2.

Solution The conversion steps are

grams of $H_2 \longrightarrow$ moles of $H_2 \longrightarrow$ moles of Li $\longrightarrow$ grams of Li

(Continued)

Combining these steps into one equation, we write

$$9.89 \text{ g } H_2 \times \frac{1 \text{ mol } H_2}{2.016 \text{ g } H_2} \times \frac{2 \text{ mol Li}}{1 \text{ mol } H_2} \times \frac{6.941 \text{ g Li}}{1 \text{ mol Li}} = \boxed{68.1 \text{ g Li}}$$

Check There are roughly 5 moles of H_2 in 9.89 g H_2, so we need 10 moles of Li. From the approximate molar mass of Li (7 g), does the answer seem reasonable?

Practice Exercise The reaction between nitric oxide (NO) and oxygen to form nitrogen dioxide (NO_2) is a key step in photochemical smog formation:

$$2NO(g) + O_2(g) \longrightarrow 2NO_2(g)$$

How many grams of O_2 are needed to produce 2.21 g of NO_2?

Similar problems: 3.66, 3.70.

3.9 Limiting Reagents

When a chemist carries out a reaction, the reactants are usually not present in exact *stoichiometric amounts*, that is, *in the proportions indicated by the balanced equation*. Because the goal of a reaction is to produce the maximum quantity of a useful compound from the starting materials, frequently a large excess of one reactant is supplied to ensure that the more expensive reactant is completely converted to the desired product. Consequently, some reactant will be left over at the end of the reaction. *The reactant used up first in a reaction* is called the **limiting reagent**, because the maximum amount of product formed depends on how much of this reactant was originally present. When this reactant is used up, no more product can be formed. *Excess reagents* are the *reactants present in quantities greater than necessary to react with the quantity of the limiting reagent.*

The concept of the limiting reagent is analogous to the relationship between men and women in a dance contest at a club. If there are 14 men and only 9 women, then only 9 female/male pairs can compete. Five men will be left without partners. The number of women thus *limits* the number of men that can dance in the contest, and there is an *excess* of men.

Consider the formation of nitrogen dioxide (NO_2) from nitric oxide (NO) and oxygen:

$$2NO(g) + O_2(g) \longrightarrow 2NO_2(g)$$

Suppose initially we have 8 moles of NO and 7 moles of O_2 (Figure 3.9). One way to determine which of the two reactants is the limiting reagent is to calculate the number of moles of NO_2 obtained based on the initial quantities of NO and O_2. From the preceding definition, we see that only the limiting reagent will yield the smaller amount of the product. Starting with 8 moles of NO, we find the number of moles of NO_2 produced is

$$8 \text{ mol NO} \times \frac{2 \text{ mol } NO_2}{2 \text{ mol NO}} = 8 \text{ mol } NO_2$$

and starting with 7 moles of O_2, the number of moles of NO_2 formed is

$$7 \text{ mol } O_2 \times \frac{2 \text{ mol } NO_2}{1 \text{ mol } O_2} = 14 \text{ mol } NO_2$$

Because NO results in a smaller amount of NO_2, it must be the limiting reagent. Therefore, O_2 is the excess reagent.

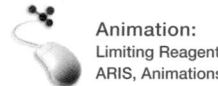

Animation:
Limiting Reagent
ARIS, Animations

Before reaction has started

After reaction is complete

Figure 3.9 *At the start of the reaction, there were eight NO molecules and seven O_2 molecules. At the end, all the NO molecules are gone and only three O_2 molecules are left. Therefore, NO is the limiting reagent and O_2 is the excess reagent. Each molecule can also be treated as one mole of the substance in this reaction.*

In stoichiometric calculations involving limiting reagents, the first step is to decide which reactant is the limiting reagent. After the limiting reagent has been identified, the rest of the problem can be solved as outlined in Section 3.8. Example 3.15 illustrates this approach.

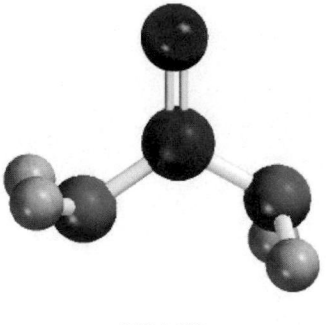

$(NH_2)_2CO$

Example 3.15

Urea $[(NH_2)_2CO]$ is prepared by reacting ammonia with carbon dioxide:

$$2NH_3(g) + CO_2(g) \longrightarrow (NH_2)_2CO(aq) + H_2O(l)$$

In one process, 637.2 g of NH_3 are treated with 1142 g of CO_2. (a) Which of the two reactants is the limiting reagent? (b) Calculate the mass of $(NH_2)_2CO$ formed. (c) How much excess reagent (in grams) is left at the end of the reaction?

(a) Strategy The reactant that produces fewer moles of product is the limiting reagent because it limits the amount of product that can be formed. How do we convert from the amount of reactant to amount of product? Perform this calculation for each reactant, then compare the moles of product, $(NH_2)_2CO$, formed by the given amounts of NH_3 and CO_2 to determine which reactant is the limiting reagent.

Solution We carry out two separate calculations. First, starting with 637.2 g of NH_3, we calculate the number of moles of $(NH_2)_2CO$ that could be produced if all the NH_3 reacted according to the following conversions:

$$\text{grams of } NH_3 \longrightarrow \text{moles of } NH_3 \longrightarrow \text{moles of } (NH_2)_2CO$$

Combining these conversions in one step, we write

$$\text{moles of } (NH_2)_2CO = 637.2 \text{ g } NH_3 \times \frac{1 \text{ mol } NH_3}{17.03 \text{ g } NH_3} \times \frac{1 \text{ mol } (NH_2)_2CO}{2 \text{ mol } NH_3}$$
$$= 18.71 \text{ mol } (NH_2)_2CO$$

Second, for 1142 g of CO_2, the conversions are

$$\text{grams of } CO_2 \longrightarrow \text{moles of } CO_2 \longrightarrow \text{moles of } (NH_2)_2CO$$

The number of moles of $(NH_2)_2CO$ that could be produced if all the CO_2 reacted is

$$\text{moles of } (NH_2)_2CO = 1142 \text{ g } CO_2 \times \frac{1 \text{ mol } CO_2}{44.01 \text{ g } CO_2} \times \frac{1 \text{ mol } (NH_2)_2CO}{1 \text{ mol } CO_2}$$
$$= 25.95 \text{ mol } (NH_2)_2CO$$

It follows, therefore, that NH_3 must be the limiting reagent because it produces a smaller amount of $(NH_2)_2CO$.

(b) Strategy We determined the moles of $(NH_2)_2CO$ produced in part (a), using NH_3 as the limiting reagent. How do we convert from moles to grams?

Solution The molar mass of $(NH_2)_2CO$ is 60.06 g. We use this as a conversion factor to convert from moles of $(NH_2)_2CO$ to grams of $(NH_2)_2CO$:

$$\text{mass of } (NH_2)_2CO = 18.71 \text{ mol } (NH_2)_2CO \times \frac{60.06 \text{ g } (NH_2)_2CO}{1 \text{ mol } (NH_2)_2CO}$$
$$= 1124 \text{ g } (NH_2)_2CO$$

Check Does your answer seem reasonable? 18.71 moles of product are formed. What is the mass of 1 mole of $(NH_2)_2CO$?

(Continued)

(c) Strategy Working backward, we can determine the amount of CO_2 that reacted to produce 18.71 moles of $(NH_2)_2CO$. The amount of CO_2 left over is the difference between the initial amount and the amount reacted.

Solution Starting with 18.71 moles of $(NH_2)_2CO$, we can determine the mass of CO_2 that reacted using the mole ratio from the balanced equation and the molar mass of CO_2. The conversion steps are

$$\text{moles of } (NH_2)_2CO \longrightarrow \text{moles of } CO_2 \longrightarrow \text{grams of } CO_2$$

so that

$$\text{mass of } CO_2 \text{ reacted} = 18.71 \text{ mol } (NH_2)_2CO \times \frac{1 \text{ mol } CO_2}{1 \text{ mol } (NH_2)_2CO} \times \frac{44.01 \text{ g } CO_2}{1 \text{ mol } CO_2}$$

$$= 823.4 \text{ g } CO_2$$

The amount of CO_2 remaining (in excess) is the difference between the initial amount (1142 g) and the amount reacted (823.4 g):

$$\text{mass of } CO_2 \text{ remaining} = 1142 \text{ g} - 823.4 \text{ g} = \boxed{319 \text{ g}}$$

Similar problem: 3.86.

Practice Exercise The reaction between aluminum and iron(III) oxide can generate temperatures approaching 3000°C and is used in welding metals:

$$2Al + Fe_2O_3 \longrightarrow Al_2O_3 + 2Fe$$

In one process, 124 g of Al are reacted with 601 g of Fe_2O_3. (a) Calculate the mass (in grams) of Al_2O_3 formed. (b) How much of the excess reagent is left at the end of the reaction?

Example 3.15 brings out an important point. In practice, chemists usually choose the more expensive chemical as the limiting reagent so that all or most of it will be consumed in the reaction. In the synthesis of urea, NH_3 is invariably the limiting reagent because it is much more expensive than CO_2.

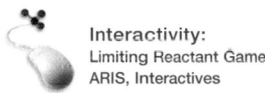

Interactivity:
Limiting Reactant Game
ARIS, Interactives

3.10 Reaction Yield

The amount of limiting reagent present at the start of a reaction determines the ***theoretical yield*** of the reaction, that is, *the amount of product that would result if all the limiting reagent reacted.* The theoretical yield, then, is the *maximum* obtainable yield, predicted by the balanced equation. In practice, the ***actual yield,*** or *the amount of product actually obtained from a reaction,* is almost always less than the theoretical yield. There are many reasons for the difference between actual and theoretical yields. For instance, many reactions are reversible, and so they do not proceed 100 percent from left to right. Even when a reaction is 100 percent complete, it may be difficult to recover all of the product from the reaction medium (say, from an aqueous solution). Some reactions are complex in the sense that the products formed may react further among themselves or with the reactants to form still other products. These additional reactions will reduce the yield of the first reaction.

To determine how efficient a given reaction is, chemists often figure the ***percent yield,*** which describes *the proportion of the actual yield to the theoretical yield.* It is calculated as follows:

$$\% \text{yield} = \frac{\text{actual yield}}{\text{theoretical yield}} \times 100\% \tag{3.4}$$

CHEMISTRY
in Action

Chemical Fertilizers

Feeding the world's rapidly increasing population requires that farmers produce ever-larger and healthier crops. Every year they add hundreds of millions of tons of chemical fertilizers to the soil to increase crop quality and yield. In addition to carbon dioxide and water, plants need at least six elements for satisfactory growth. They are N, P, K, Ca, S, and Mg. The preparation and properties of several nitrogen- and phosphorus-containing fertilizers illustrate some of the principles introduced in this chapter.

Nitrogen fertilizers contain nitrate (NO_3^-) salts, ammonium (NH_4^+) salts, and other compounds. Plants can absorb nitrogen in the form of nitrate directly, but ammonium salts and ammonia (NH_3) must first be converted to nitrates by the action of soil bacteria. The principal raw material of nitrogen fertilizers is ammonia, prepared by the reaction between hydrogen and nitrogen:

$$3H_2(g) + N_2(g) \longrightarrow 2NH_3(g)$$

(This reaction will be discussed in detail in Chapters 13 and 14.) In its liquid form, ammonia can be injected directly into the soil.

Alternatively, ammonia can be converted to ammonium nitrate, NH_4NO_3, ammonium sulfate, $(NH_4)_2SO_4$, or ammonium hydrogen phosphate, $(NH_4)_2HPO_4$, in the following acid-base reactions:

$$NH_3(aq) + HNO_3(aq) \longrightarrow NH_4NO_3(aq)$$
$$2NH_3(aq) + H_2SO_4(aq) \longrightarrow (NH_4)_2SO_4(aq)$$
$$2NH_3(aq) + H_3PO_4(aq) \longrightarrow (NH_4)_2HPO_4(aq)$$

Liquid ammonia being applied to the soil before planting.

Percent yields may range from a fraction of 1 percent to 100 percent. Chemists strive to maximize the percent yield in a reaction. Factors that can affect the percent yield include temperature and pressure. We will study these effects later.

In Example 3.16 we will calculate the yield of an industrial process.

The frame of this bicycle is made of titanium.

Example 3.16

Titanium is a strong, lightweight, corrosion-resistant metal that is used in rockets, aircraft, jet engines, and bicycle frames. It is prepared by the reaction of titanium(IV) chloride with molten magnesium between 950°C and 1150°C:

$$TiCl_4(g) + 2Mg(l) \longrightarrow Ti(s) + 2MgCl_2(l)$$

In a certain industrial operation 3.54×10^7 g of $TiCl_4$ are reacted with 1.13×10^7 g of Mg. (a) Calculate the theoretical yield of Ti in grams. (b) Calculate the percent yield if 7.91×10^6 g of Ti are actually obtained.

(a) Strategy Because there are two reactants, this is likely to be a limiting reagent problem. The reactant that produces fewer moles of product is the limiting reagent. How

(Continued)

Another method of preparing ammonium sulfate requires two steps:

$$2NH_3(aq) + CO_2(aq) + H_2O(l) \longrightarrow (NH_4)_2CO_3(aq) \quad (1)$$

$$(NH_4)_2CO_3(aq) + CaSO_4(aq) \longrightarrow$$
$$(NH_4)_2SO_4(aq) + CaCO_3(s) \quad (2)$$

This approach is desirable because the starting materials—carbon dioxide and calcium sulfate—are less costly than sulfuric acid. To increase the yield, ammonia is made the limiting reagent in Reaction (1) and ammonium carbonate is made the limiting reagent in Reaction (2).

The table lists the percent composition by mass of nitrogen in some common fertilizers. The preparation of urea was discussed in Example 3.15.

Percent Composition by Mass of Nitrogen in Five Common Fertilizers

Fertilizer	% N by Mass
NH_3	82.4
NH_4NO_3	35.0
$(NH_4)_2SO_4$	21.2
$(NH_4)_2HPO_4$	21.2
$(NH_2)_2CO$	46.7

Several factors influence the choice of one fertilizer over another: (1) cost of the raw materials needed to prepare the fertilizer; (2) ease of storage, transportation, and utilization; (3) percent composition by mass of the desired element; and (4) suitability of the compound, that is, whether the compound is soluble in water and whether it can be readily taken up by plants. Considering all these factors together, we find that NH_4NO_3 is the most important nitrogen-containing fertilizer in the world, even though ammonia has the highest percentage by mass of nitrogen.

Phosphorus fertilizers are derived from phosphate rock, called *fluorapatite,* $Ca_5(PO_4)_3F$. Fluorapatite is insoluble in water, so it must first be converted to water-soluble calcium dihydrogen phosphate [$Ca(H_2PO_4)_2$]:

$$2Ca_5(PO_4)_3F(s) + 7H_2SO_4(aq) \longrightarrow$$
$$3Ca(H_2PO_4)_2(aq) + 7CaSO_4(aq) + 2HF(g)$$

For maximum yield, fluorapatite is made the limiting reagent in this reaction.

The reactions we have discussed for the preparation of fertilizers all appear relatively simple, yet much effort has been expended to improve the yields by changing conditions such as temperature, pressure, and so on. Industrial chemists usually run promising reactions first in the laboratory and then test them in a pilot facility before putting them into mass production.

do we convert from amount of reactant to amount of product? Perform this calculation for each reactant, then compare the moles of product, Ti, formed.

Solution Carry out two separate calculations to see which of the two reactants is the limiting reagent. First, starting with 3.54×10^7 g of $TiCl_4$, calculate the number of moles of Ti that could be produced if all the $TiCl_4$ reacted. The conversions are

$$\text{grams of } TiCl_4 \longrightarrow \text{moles of } TiCl_4 \longrightarrow \text{moles of Ti}$$

so that

$$\text{moles of Ti} = 3.54 \times 10^7 \text{ g } TiCl_4 \times \frac{1 \text{ mol } TiCl_4}{189.7 \text{ g } TiCl_4} \times \frac{1 \text{ mol Ti}}{1 \text{ mol } TiCl_4}$$
$$= 1.87 \times 10^5 \text{ mol Ti}$$

Next, we calculate the number of moles of Ti formed from 1.13×10^7 g of Mg. The conversion steps are

$$\text{grams of Mg} \longrightarrow \text{moles of Mg} \longrightarrow \text{moles of Ti}$$

(Continued)

and we write

$$\text{moles of Ti} = 1.13 \times 10^7 \text{ g Mg} \times \frac{1 \text{ mol Mg}}{24.31 \text{ g Mg}} \times \frac{1 \text{ mol Ti}}{2 \text{ mol Mg}}$$

$$= 2.32 \times 10^5 \text{ mol Ti}$$

Therefore, $TiCl_4$ is the limiting reagent because it produces a smaller amount of Ti. The mass of Ti formed is

$$1.87 \times 10^5 \text{ mol Ti} \times \frac{47.88 \text{ g Ti}}{1 \text{ mol Ti}} = 8.95 \times 10^6 \text{ g Ti}$$

(b) Strategy The mass of Ti determined in part (a) is the theoretical yield. The amount given in part (b) is the actual yield of the reaction.

Solution The percent yield is given by

$$\%\text{yield} = \frac{\text{actual yield}}{\text{theoretical yield}} \times 100\%$$

$$= \frac{7.91 \times 10^6 \text{ g}}{8.95 \times 10^6 \text{ g}} \times 100\%$$

$$= 88.4\%$$

Similar problems: 3.89, 3.90.

Check Should the percent yield be less than 100 percent?

Practice Exercise Industrially, vanadium metal, which is used in steel alloys, can be obtained by reacting vanadium(V) oxide with calcium at high temperatures:

$$5Ca + V_2O_5 \longrightarrow 5CaO + 2V$$

In one process, 1.54×10^3 g of V_2O_5 react with 1.96×10^3 g of Ca. (a) Calculate the theoretical yield of V. (b) Calculate the percent yield if 803 g of V are obtained.

Industrial processes usually involve huge quantities (thousands to millions of tons) of products. Thus, even a slight improvement in the yield can significantly reduce the cost of production. A case in point is the manufacture of chemical fertilizers, discussed in the Chemistry in Action essay on pp. 104–5.

Summary of Facts and Concepts

1. Atomic masses are measured in atomic mass units (amu), a relative unit based on a value of exactly 12 for the C-12 isotope. The atomic mass given for the atoms of a particular element is the average of the naturally occurring isotope distribution of that element. The molecular mass of a molecule is the sum of the atomic masses of the atoms in the molecule. Both atomic mass and molecular mass can be accurately determined with a mass spectrometer.

2. A mole is Avogadro's number (6.022×10^{23}) of atoms, molecules, or other particles. The molar mass (in grams) of an element or a compound is numerically equal to its mass in atomic mass units (amu) and contains Avogadro's number of atoms (in the case of elements), molecules (in

the case of molecular substances), or simplest formula units (in the case of ionic compounds).

3. The percent composition by mass of a compound is the percent by mass of each element present. If we know the percent composition by mass of a compound, we can deduce the empirical formula of the compound and also the molecular formula of the compound if the approximate molar mass is known.

4. Chemical changes, called chemical reactions, are represented by chemical equations. Substances that undergo change—the reactants—are written on the left and the substances formed—the products—appear to the right of the arrow. Chemical equations must be balanced, in

accordance with the law of conservation of mass. The number of atoms of each element in the reactants must equal the number in the products.

5. Stoichiometry is the quantitative study of products and reactants in chemical reactions. Stoichiometric calculations are best done by expressing both the known and unknown quantities in terms of moles and then convert-ing to other units if necessary. A limiting reagent is the re-actant that is present in the smallest stoichiometric amount. It limits the amount of product that can be formed. The amount of product obtained in a reaction (the actual yield) may be less than the maximum possible amount (the theoretical yield). The ratio of the two mul-tiplied by 100 percent is expressed as the percent yield.

Key Words

Actual yield, p. 103
Atomic mass, p. 78
Atomic mass unit (amu), p. 78
Avogadro's number (N_A), p. 79
Chemical equation, p. 92

Chemical reaction, p. 92
Excess reagent, p. 101
Limiting reagent, p. 101
Molar mass ($\mathcal{M}$), p. 80
Mole (mol), p. 79

Mole method, p. 97
Molecular mass, p. 83
Percent composition
  by mass, p. 87
Percent yield, p. 103

Product, p. 93
Reactant, p. 93
Stoichiometric amount, p. 101
Stoichiometry, p. 97
Theoretical yield, p. 103

Questions and Problems

Atomic Mass
Review Questions

3.1   What is an atomic mass unit? Why is it necessary to introduce such a unit?

3.2   What is the mass (in amu) of a carbon-12 atom? Why is the atomic mass of carbon listed as 12.01 amu in the table on the inside front cover of this book?

3.3   Explain clearly what is meant by the statement "The atomic mass of gold is 197.0 amu."

3.4   What information would you need to calculate the av-erage atomic mass of an element?

Problems

3.5   The atomic masses of $^{35}_{17}Cl$ (75.53 percent) and $^{37}_{17}Cl$ (24.47 percent) are 34.968 amu and 36.956 amu, respectively. Calculate the average atomic mass of chlorine. The percentages in parentheses denote the relative abundances.

3.6   The atomic masses of $^{6}_{3}Li$ and $^{7}_{3}Li$ are 6.0151 amu and 7.0160 amu, respectively. Calculate the natural abun-dances of these two isotopes. The average atomic mass of Li is 6.941 amu.

3.7   What is the mass in grams of 13.2 amu?

3.8   How many amu are there in 8.4 g?

Avogadro's Number and Molar Mass
Review Questions

3.9   Define the term "mole." What is the unit for mole in calculations? What does the mole have in common with the pair, the dozen, and the gross? What does Avogadro's number represent?

3.10   What is the molar mass of an atom? What are the com-monly used units for molar mass?

Problems

3.11   Earth's population is about 6.5 billion. Suppose that every person on Earth participates in a process of count-ing identical particles at the rate of two particles per sec-ond. How many years would it take to count 6.0×10^{23} particles? Assume that there are 365 days in a year.

3.12   The thickness of a piece of paper is 0.0036 in. Suppose a certain book has an Avogadro's number of pages; cal-culate the thickness of the book in light-years. (*Hint:* See Problem 1.47 for the definition of light-year.)

3.13   How many atoms are there in 5.10 moles of sulfur (S)?

3.14   How many moles of cobalt (Co) atoms are there in 6.00×10^9 (6 billion) Co atoms?

3.15   How many moles of calcium (Ca) atoms are in 77.4 g of Ca?

3.16   How many grams of gold (Au) are there in 15.3 moles of Au?

3.17   What is the mass in grams of a single atom of each of the following elements? (a) Hg, (b) Ne.

3.18   What is the mass in grams of a single atom of each of the following elements? (a) As, (b) Ni.

3.19   What is the mass in grams of 1.00×10^{12} lead (Pb) atoms?

3.20   How many atoms are present in 3.14 g of copper (Cu)?

3.21   Which of the following has more atoms: 1.10 g of hy-drogen atoms or 14.7 g of chromium atoms?

3.22   Which of the following has a greater mass: 2 atoms of lead or 5.1×10^{-23} mole of helium.

Molecular Mass
Problems

3.23   Calculate the molecular mass or formula mass (in amu) of each of the following substances: (a) CH_4, (b) NO_2, (c) SO_3, (d) C_6H_6, (e) NaI, (f) K_2SO_4, (g) $Ca_3(PO_4)_2$.

3.24   Calculate the molar mass of the following substances: (a) Li_2CO_3, (b) CS_2, (c) $CHCl_3$ (chloroform), (d) $C_6H_8O_6$ (ascorbic acid, or vitamin C), (e) KNO_3, (f) Mg_3N_2.

3.25   Calculate the molar mass of a compound if 0.372 mole of it has a mass of 152 g.

3.26   How many molecules of ethane (C_2H_6) are present in 0.334 g of C_2H_6?

3.27   Calculate the number of C, H, and O atoms in 1.50 g of glucose ($C_6H_{12}O_6$), a sugar.

3.28   Urea [$(NH_2)_2CO$] is used for fertilizer and many other things. Calculate the number of N, C, O, and H atoms in 1.68×10^4 g of urea.

3.29   Pheromones are a special type of compound secreted by the females of many insect species to attract the males for mating. One pheromone has the molecular formula $C_{19}H_{38}O$. Normally, the amount of this pheromone secreted by a female insect is about 1.0×10^{-12} g. How many molecules are there in this quantity?

3.30   The density of water is 1.00 g/mL at 4°C. How many water molecules are present in 2.56 mL of water at this temperature?

Mass Spectrometry
Review Questions

3.31   Describe the operation of a mass spectrometer.

3.32   Describe how you would determine the isotopic abundance of an element from its mass spectrum.

Problems

3.33   Carbon has two stable isotopes, $^{12}_6C$ and $^{13}_6C$, and fluorine has only one stable isotope, $^{19}_9F$. How many peaks would you observe in the mass spectrum of the positive ion of CF_4^+? Assume that the ion does not break up into smaller fragments.

3.34   Hydrogen has two stable isotopes, ^1_1H and ^2_1H, and sulfur has four stable isotopes, $^{32}_{16}S$, $^{33}_{16}S$, $^{34}_{16}S$, and $^{36}_{16}S$. How many peaks would you observe in the mass spectrum of the positive ion of hydrogen sulfide, H_2S^+? Assume no decomposition of the ion into smaller fragments.

Percent Composition and Chemical Formulas
Review Questions

3.35   Use ammonia (NH_3) to explain what is meant by the percent composition by mass of a compound.

3.36   Describe how the knowledge of the percent composition by mass of an unknown compound can help us identify the compound.

3.37   What does the word "empirical" in empirical formula mean?

3.38   If we know the empirical formula of a compound, what additional information do we need to determine its molecular formula?

Problems

3.39   Tin (Sn) exists in Earth's crust as SnO_2. Calculate the percent composition by mass of Sn and O in SnO_2.

3.40   For many years chloroform ($CHCl_3$) was used as an inhalation anesthetic in spite of the fact that it is also a toxic substance that may cause severe liver, kidney, and heart damage. Calculate the percent composition by mass of this compound.

3.41   Cinnamic alcohol is used mainly in perfumery, particularly in soaps and cosmetics. Its molecular formula is $C_9H_{10}O$. (a) Calculate the percent composition by mass of C, H, and O in cinnamic alcohol. (b) How many molecules of cinnamic alcohol are contained in a sample of mass 0.469 g?

3.42   All of the substances listed below are fertilizers that contribute nitrogen to the soil. Which of these is the richest source of nitrogen on a mass percentage basis?

(a) Urea, $(NH_2)_2CO$

(b) Ammonium nitrate, NH_4NO_3

(c) Guanidine, $HNC(NH_2)_2$

(d) Ammonia, NH_3

3.43   Allicin is the compound responsible for the characteristic smell of garlic. An analysis of the compound gives the following percent composition by mass: C: 44.4 percent; H: 6.21 percent; S: 39.5 percent; O: 9.86 percent. Calculate its empirical formula. What is its molecular formula given that its molar mass is about 162 g?

3.44   Peroxyacylnitrate (PAN) is one of the components of smog. It is a compound of C, H, N, and O. Determine the percent composition of oxygen and the empirical formula from the following percent composition by mass: 19.8 percent C, 2.50 percent H, 11.6 percent N. What is its molecular formula given that its molar mass is about 120 g?

3.45   The formula for rust can be represented by Fe_2O_3. How many moles of Fe are present in 24.6 g of the compound?

3.46   How many grams of sulfur (S) are needed to react completely with 246 g of mercury (Hg) to form HgS?

3.47   Calculate the mass in grams of iodine (I_2) that will react completely with 20.4 g of aluminum (Al) to form aluminum iodide (AlI_3).

3.48 Tin(II) fluoride (SnF_2) is often added to toothpaste as an ingredient to prevent tooth decay. What is the mass of F in grams in 24.6 g of the compound?

3.49 What are the empirical formulas of the compounds with the following compositions? (a) 2.1 percent H, 65.3 percent O, 32.6 percent S, (b) 20.2 percent Al, 79.8 percent Cl.

3.50 What are the empirical formulas of the compounds with the following compositions? (a) 40.1 percent C, 6.6 percent H, 53.3 percent O, (b) 18.4 percent C, 21.5 percent N, 60.1 percent K.

3.51 The anticaking agent added to Morton salt is calcium silicate, $CaSiO_3$. This compound can absorb up to 2.5 times its mass of water and still remains a free-flowing powder. Calculate the percent composition of $CaSiO_3$.

3.52 The empirical formula of a compound is CH. If the molar mass of this compound is about 78 g, what is its molecular formula?

3.53 The molar mass of caffeine is 194.19 g. Is the molecular formula of caffeine $C_4H_5N_2O$ or $C_8H_{10}N_4O_2$?

3.54 Monosodium glutamate (MSG), a food-flavor enhancer, has been blamed for "Chinese restaurant syndrome," the symptoms of which are headaches and chest pains. MSG has the following composition by mass: 35.51 percent C, 4.77 percent H, 37.85 percent O, 8.29 percent N, and 13.60 percent Na. What is its molecular formula if its molar mass is about 169 g?

Chemical Reactions and Chemical Equations
Review Questions

3.55 Use the formation of water from hydrogen and oxygen to explain the following terms: chemical reaction, reactant, product.

3.56 What is the difference between a chemical reaction and a chemical equation?

3.57 Why must a chemical equation be balanced? What law is obeyed by a balanced chemical equation?

3.58 Write the symbols used to represent gas, liquid, solid, and the aqueous phase in chemical equations.

Problems

3.59 Balance the following equations using the method outlined in Section 3.7:
(a) $C + O_2 \longrightarrow CO$
(b) $CO + O_2 \longrightarrow CO_2$
(c) $H_2 + Br_2 \longrightarrow HBr$
(d) $K + H_2O \longrightarrow KOH + H_2$
(e) $Mg + O_2 \longrightarrow MgO$
(f) $O_3 \longrightarrow O_2$

(g) $H_2O_2 \longrightarrow H_2O + O_2$
(h) $N_2 + H_2 \longrightarrow NH_3$
(i) $Zn + AgCl \longrightarrow ZnCl_2 + Ag$
(j) $S_8 + O_2 \longrightarrow SO_2$
(k) $NaOH + H_2SO_4 \longrightarrow Na_2SO_4 + H_2O$
(l) $Cl_2 + NaI \longrightarrow NaCl + I_2$
(m) $KOH + H_3PO_4 \longrightarrow K_3PO_4 + H_2O$
(n) $CH_4 + Br_2 \longrightarrow CBr_4 + HBr$

3.60 Balance the following equations using the method outlined in Section 3.7:
(a) $N_2O_5 \longrightarrow N_2O_4 + O_2$
(b) $KNO_3 \longrightarrow KNO_2 + O_2$
(c) $NH_4NO_3 \longrightarrow N_2O + H_2O$
(d) $NH_4NO_2 \longrightarrow N_2 + H_2O$
(e) $NaHCO_3 \longrightarrow Na_2CO_3 + H_2O + CO_2$
(f) $P_4O_{10} + H_2O \longrightarrow H_3PO_4$
(g) $HCl + CaCO_3 \longrightarrow CaCl_2 + H_2O + CO_2$
(h) $Al + H_2SO_4 \longrightarrow Al_2(SO_4)_3 + H_2$
(i) $CO_2 + KOH \longrightarrow K_2CO_3 + H_2O$
(j) $CH_4 + O_2 \longrightarrow CO_2 + H_2O$
(k) $Be_2C + H_2O \longrightarrow Be(OH)_2 + CH_4$
(l) $Cu + HNO_3 \longrightarrow Cu(NO_3)_2 + NO + H_2O$
(m) $S + HNO_3 \longrightarrow H_2SO_4 + NO_2 + H_2O$
(n) $NH_3 + CuO \longrightarrow Cu + N_2 + H_2O$

Amounts of Reactants and Products
Review Questions

3.61 On what law is stoichiometry based? Why is it essential to use balanced equations in solving stoichiometric problems?

3.62 Describe the steps involved in the mole method.

Problems

3.63 Which of the following equations best represents the reaction shown in the diagram?
(a) $8A + 4B \longrightarrow C + D$
(b) $4A + 8B \longrightarrow 4C + 4D$
(c) $2A + B \longrightarrow C + D$
(d) $4A + 2B \longrightarrow 4C + 4D$
(e) $2A + 4B \longrightarrow C + D$

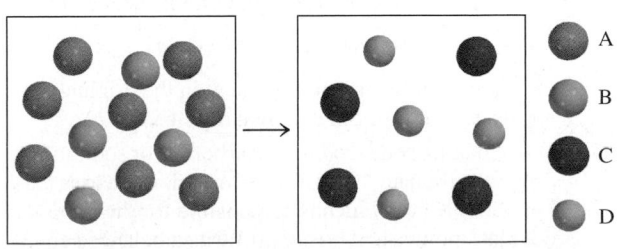

3.64 Which of the following equations best represents the reaction shown in the diagram?

(a) $A + B \longrightarrow C + D$

(b) $6A + 4B \longrightarrow C + D$

(c) $A + 2B \longrightarrow 2C + D$

(d) $3A + 2B \longrightarrow 2C + D$

(e) $3A + 2B \longrightarrow 4C + 2D$

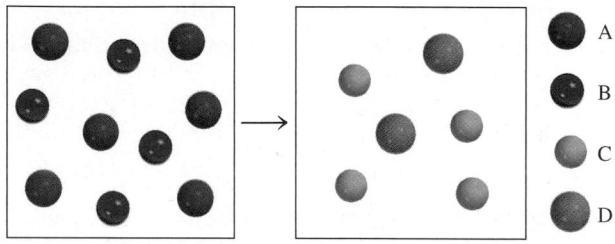

3.65 Consider the combustion of carbon monoxide (CO) in oxygen gas

$$2CO(g) + O_2(g) \longrightarrow 2CO_2(g)$$

Starting with 3.60 moles of CO, calculate the number of moles of CO_2 produced if there is enough oxygen gas to react with all of the CO.

3.66 Silicon tetrachloride ($SiCl_4$) can be prepared by heating Si in chlorine gas:

$$Si(s) + 2Cl_2(g) \longrightarrow SiCl_4(l)$$

In one reaction, 0.507 mole of $SiCl_4$ is produced. How many moles of molecular chlorine were used in the reaction?

3.67 Ammonia is a principal nitrogen fertilizer. It is prepared by the reaction between hydrogen and nitrogen.

$$3H_2(g) + N_2(g) \longrightarrow 2NH_3(g)$$

In a particular reaction, 6.0 moles of NH_3 were produced. How many moles of H_2 and how many moles of N_2 were reacted to produce this amount of NH_3?

3.68 Consider the combustion of butane (C_4H_{10}):

$$2C_4H_{10}(g) + 13O_2(g) \longrightarrow 8CO_2(g) + 10H_2O(l)$$

In a particular reaction, 5.0 moles of C_4H_{10} are reacted with an excess of O_2. Calculate the number of moles of CO_2 formed.

3.69 The annual production of sulfur dioxide from burning coal and fossil fuels, auto exhaust, and other sources is about 26 million tons. The equation for the reaction is

$$S(s) + O_2(g) \longrightarrow SO_2(g)$$

How much sulfur (in tons), present in the original materials, would result in that quantity of SO_2?

3.70 When baking soda (sodium bicarbonate or sodium hydrogen carbonate, $NaHCO_3$) is heated, it releases carbon dioxide gas, which is responsible for the rising of cookies, donuts, and bread. (a) Write a balanced equation for the decomposition of the compound (one of the products is Na_2CO_3). (b) Calculate the mass of $NaHCO_3$ required to produce 20.5 g of CO_2.

3.71 When potassium cyanide (KCN) reacts with acids, a deadly poisonous gas, hydrogen cyanide (HCN), is given off. Here is the equation:

$$KCN(aq) + HCl(aq) \longrightarrow KCl(aq) + HCN(g)$$

If a sample of 0.140 g of KCN is treated with an excess of HCl, calculate the amount of HCN formed, in grams.

3.72 Fermentation is a complex chemical process of wine making in which glucose is converted into ethanol and carbon dioxide:

$$\underset{\text{glucose}}{C_6H_{12}O_6} \longrightarrow \underset{\text{ethanol}}{2C_2H_5OH} + 2CO_2$$

Starting with 500.4 g of glucose, what is the maximum amount of ethanol in grams and in liters that can be obtained by this process? (Density of ethanol = 0.789 g/mL.)

3.73 Each copper(II) sulfate unit is associated with five water molecules in crystalline copper(II) sulfate pentahydrate ($CuSO_4 \cdot 5H_2O$). When this compound is heated in air above 100°C, it loses the water molecules and also its blue color:

$$CuSO_4 \cdot 5H_2O \longrightarrow CuSO_4 + 5H_2O$$

If 9.60 g of $CuSO_4$ are left after heating 15.01 g of the blue compound, calculate the number of moles of H_2O originally present in the compound.

3.74 For many years the recovery of gold—that is, the separation of gold from other materials—involved the use of potassium cyanide:

$$4Au + 8KCN + O_2 + 2H_2O \longrightarrow$$
$$4KAu(CN)_2 + 4KOH$$

What is the minimum amount of KCN in moles needed to extract 29.0 g (about an ounce) of gold?

3.75 Limestone ($CaCO_3$) is decomposed by heating to quicklime (CaO) and carbon dioxide. Calculate how many grams of quicklime can be produced from 1.0 kg of limestone.

3.76 Nitrous oxide (N_2O) is also called "laughing gas." It can be prepared by the thermal decomposition of ammonium nitrate (NH_4NO_3). The other product is H_2O. (a) Write a balanced equation for this reaction. (b) How many grams of N_2O are formed if 0.46 mole of NH_4NO_3 is used in the reaction?

3.77 The fertilizer ammonium sulfate [$(NH_4)_2SO_4$] is prepared by the reaction between ammonia (NH_3) and sulfuric acid:

$$2NH_3(g) + H_2SO_4(aq) \longrightarrow (NH_4)_2SO_4(aq)$$

How many kilograms of NH_3 are needed to produce 1.00×10^5 kg of $(NH_4)_2SO_4$?

3.78 A common laboratory preparation of oxygen gas is the thermal decomposition of potassium chlorate ($KClO_3$). Assuming complete decomposition, calculate the number of grams of O_2 gas that can be obtained from 46.0 g of $KClO_3$. (The products are KCl and O_2.)

Limiting Reagents

Review Questions

3.79 Define limiting reagent and excess reagent. What is the significance of the limiting reagent in predicting the amount of the product obtained in a reaction? Can there be a limiting reagent if only one reactant is present?

3.80 Give an everyday example that illustrates the limiting reagent concept.

Problems

3.81 Consider the reaction

$$2A + B \longrightarrow C$$

(a) In the diagram here that represents the reaction, which reactant, A or B, is the limiting reagent? (b) Assuming complete reaction, draw a molecular-model representation of the amounts of reactants and products left after the reaction. The atomic arrangement in C is ABA.

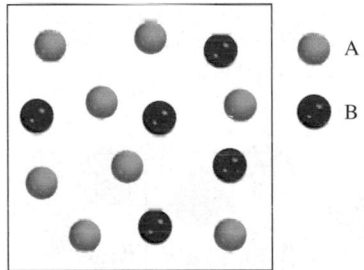

3.82 Consider the reaction

$$N_2 + 3H_2 \longrightarrow 2NH_3$$

Assuming each model represents 1 mole of the substance, show the number of moles of the product and the excess reagent left after the complete reaction.

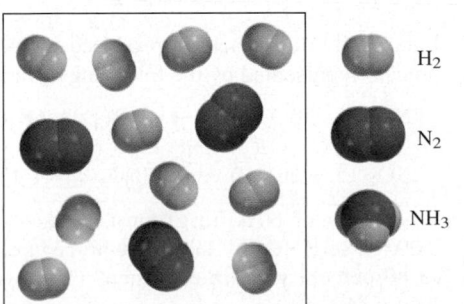

3.83 Nitric oxide (NO) reacts with oxygen gas to form nitrogen dioxide (NO_2), a dark-brown gas:

$$2NO(g) + O_2(g) \longrightarrow 2NO_2(g)$$

In one experiment 0.886 mole of NO is mixed with 0.503 mole of O_2. Calculate which of the two reactants is the limiting reagent. Calculate also the number of moles of NO_2 produced.

3.84 The depletion of ozone (O_3) in the stratosphere has been a matter of great concern among scientists in recent years. It is believed that ozone can react with nitric oxide (NO) that is discharged from the high-altitude jet plane, the SST. The reaction is

$$O_3 + NO \longrightarrow O_2 + NO_2$$

If 0.740 g of O_3 reacts with 0.670 g of NO, how many grams of NO_2 will be produced? Which compound is the limiting reagent? Calculate the number of moles of the excess reagent remaining at the end of the reaction.

3.85 Propane (C_3H_8) is a component of natural gas and is used in domestic cooking and heating. (a) Balance the following equation representing the combustion of propane in air:

$$C_3H_8 + O_2 \longrightarrow CO_2 + H_2O$$

(b) How many grams of carbon dioxide can be produced by burning 3.65 moles of propane? Assume that oxygen is the excess reagent in this reaction.

3.86 Consider the reaction

$$MnO_2 + 4HCl \longrightarrow MnCl_2 + Cl_2 + 2H_2O$$

If 0.86 mole of MnO_2 and 48.2 g of HCl react, which reagent will be used up first? How many grams of Cl_2 will be produced?

Reaction Yield

Review Questions

3.87 Why is the theoretical yield of a reaction determined only by the amount of the limiting reagent?

3.88 Why is the actual yield of a reaction almost always smaller than the theoretical yield?

Problems

3.89 Hydrogen fluoride is used in the manufacture of Freons (which destroy ozone in the stratosphere) and in the production of aluminum metal. It is prepared by the reaction

$$CaF_2 + H_2SO_4 \longrightarrow CaSO_4 + 2HF$$

In one process, 6.00 kg of CaF_2 are treated with an excess of H_2SO_4 and yield 2.86 kg of HF. Calculate the percent yield of HF.

3.90 Nitroglycerin ($C_3H_5N_3O_9$) is a powerful explosive. Its decomposition may be represented by

$$4C_3H_5N_3O_9 \longrightarrow 6N_2 + 12CO_2 + 10H_2O + O_2$$

This reaction generates a large amount of heat and many gaseous products. It is the sudden formation of these gases, together with their rapid expansion, that produces the explosion. (a) What is the maximum amount of O_2 in grams that can be obtained from 2.00×10^2 g of nitroglycerin? (b) Calculate the percent yield in this reaction if the amount of O_2 generated is found to be 6.55 g.

3.91 Titanium(IV) oxide (TiO_2) is a white substance produced by the action of sulfuric acid on the mineral ilmenite ($FeTiO_3$):

$$FeTiO_3 + H_2SO_4 \longrightarrow TiO_2 + FeSO_4 + H_2O$$

Its opaque and nontoxic properties make it suitable as a pigment in plastics and paints. In one process, 8.00×10^3 kg of $FeTiO_3$ yielded 3.67×10^3 kg of TiO_2. What is the percent yield of the reaction?

3.92 Ethylene (C_2H_4), an important industrial organic chemical, can be prepared by heating hexane (C_6H_{14}) at 800°C:

$$C_6H_{14} \longrightarrow C_2H_4 + \text{other products}$$

If the yield of ethylene production is 42.5 percent, what mass of hexane must be reacted to produce 481 g of ethylene?

3.93 When heated, lithium reacts with nitrogen to form lithium nitride:

$$6Li(s) + N_2(g) \longrightarrow 2Li_3N(s)$$

What is the theoretical yield of Li_3N in grams when 12.3 g of Li are heated with 33.6 g of N_2? If the actual yield of Li_3N is 5.89 g, what is the percent yield of the reaction?

3.94 Disulfide dichloride (S_2Cl_2) is used in the vulcanization of rubber, a process that prevents the slippage of rubber molecules past one another when stretched. It is prepared by heating sulfur in an atmosphere of chlorine:

$$S_8(l) + 4Cl_2(g) \longrightarrow 4S_2Cl_2(l)$$

What is the theoretical yield of S_2Cl_2 in grams when 4.06 g of S_8 are heated with 6.24 g of Cl_2? If the actual yield of S_2Cl_2 is 6.55 g, what is the percent yield?

Additional Problems

3.95 The following diagram represents the products (CO_2 and H_2O) formed after the combustion of a hydrocarbon (a compound containing only C and H atoms). Write an equation for the reaction. (*Hint:* The molar mass of the hydrocarbon is about 30 g.)

3.96 Consider the reaction of hydrogen gas with oxygen gas:

$$2H_2(g) + O_2(g) \longrightarrow 2H_2O(g)$$

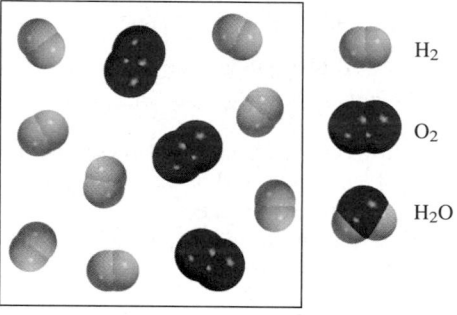

Assuming complete reaction, which of the diagrams shown next represents the amounts of reactants and products left after the reaction?

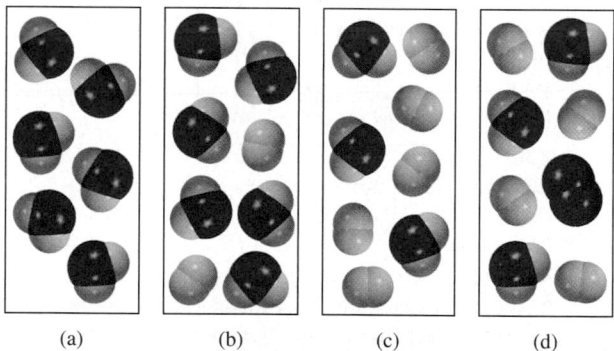

(a)   (b)   (c)   (d)

3.97 Industrially, nitric acid is produced by the Ostwald process represented by the following equations:

$$4NH_3(g) + 5O_2(g) \longrightarrow 4NO(g) + 6H_2O(l)$$
$$2NO(g) + O_2(g) \longrightarrow 2NO_2(g)$$
$$2NO_2(g) + H_2O(l) \longrightarrow HNO_3(aq) + HNO_2(aq)$$

What mass of NH_3 (in g) must be used to produce 1.00 ton of HNO_3 by the above procedure, assuming an 80 percent yield in each step? (1 ton = 2000 lb; 1 lb = 453.6 g.)

3.98 A sample of a compound of Cl and O reacts with an excess of H_2 to give 0.233 g of HCl and 0.403 g of H_2O. Determine the empirical formula of the compound.

3.99 The atomic mass of element X is 33.42 amu. A 27.22-g sample of X combines with 84.10 g of another element Y to form a compound XY. Calculate the atomic mass of Y.

3.100 How many moles of O are needed to combine with 0.212 mole of C to form (a) CO and (b) CO_2?

3.101 A research chemist used a mass spectrometer to study the two isotopes of an element. Over time, she recorded a number of mass spectra of these isotopes. On analysis, she noticed that the ratio of the taller peak (the more abundant isotope) to the shorter peak (the less abundant isotope) gradually increased with time. Assuming that the mass spectrometer was functioning normally, what do you think was causing this change?

3.102 The aluminum sulfate hydrate $[Al_2(SO_4)_3 \cdot xH_2O]$ contains 8.20 percent Al by mass. Calculate x, that is, the number of water molecules associated with each $Al_2(SO_4)_3$ unit.

3.103 Mustard gas ($C_4H_8Cl_2S$) is a poisonous gas that was used in World War I and banned afterward. It causes general destruction of body tissues, resulting in the formation of large water blisters. There is no effective antidote. Calculate the percent composition by mass of the elements in mustard gas.

3.104 The carat is the unit of mass used by jewelers. One carat is exactly 200 mg. How many carbon atoms are present in a 24-carat diamond?

3.105 An iron bar weighed 664 g. After the bar had been standing in moist air for a month, exactly one-eighth of the iron turned to rust (Fe_2O_3). Calculate the final mass of the iron bar and rust.

3.106 A certain metal oxide has the formula MO where M denotes the metal. A 39.46-g sample of the compound is strongly heated in an atmosphere of hydrogen to remove oxygen as water molecules. At the end, 31.70 g of the metal is left over. If O has an atomic mass of 16.00 amu, calculate the atomic mass of M and identify the element.

3.107 An impure sample of zinc (Zn) is treated with an excess of sulfuric acid (H_2SO_4) to form zinc sulfate ($ZnSO_4$) and molecular hydrogen (H_2). (a) Write a balanced equation for the reaction. (b) If 0.0764 g of H_2 is obtained from 3.86 g of the sample, calculate the percent purity of the sample. (c) What assumptions must you make in (b)?

3.108 One of the reactions that occurs in a blast furnace, where iron ore is converted to cast iron, is

$$Fe_2O_3 + 3CO \longrightarrow 2Fe + 3CO_2$$

Suppose that 1.64×10^3 kg of Fe are obtained from a 2.62×10^3-kg sample of Fe_2O_3. Assuming that the reaction goes to completion, what is the percent purity of Fe_2O_3 in the original sample?

3.109 Carbon dioxide (CO_2) is the gas that is mainly responsible for global warming (the greenhouse effect). The burning of fossil fuels is a major cause of the increased concentration of CO_2 in the atmosphere. Carbon dioxide is also the end product of metabolism (see Example 3.13). Using glucose as an example of food, calculate the annual human production of CO_2 in grams, assuming that each person consumes 5.0×10^2 g of glucose per day. The world's population is 6.5 billion, and there are 365 days in a year.

3.110 Carbohydrates are compounds containing carbon, hydrogen, and oxygen in which the hydrogen to oxygen ratio is 2:1. A certain carbohydrate contains 40.0 percent carbon by mass. Calculate the empirical and molecular formulas of the compound if the approximate molar mass is 178 g.

3.111 Which of the following has the greater mass: 0.72 g of O_2 or 0.0011 mole of chlorophyll ($C_{55}H_{72}MgN_4O_5$)?

3.112 Analysis of a metal chloride XCl_3 shows that it contains 67.2 percent Cl by mass. Calculate the molar mass of X and identify the element.

3.113 Hemoglobin ($C_{2952}H_{4664}N_{812}O_{832}S_8Fe_4$) is the oxygen carrier in blood. (a) Calculate its molar mass. (b) An average adult has about 5.0 L of blood. Every milliliter of blood has approximately 5.0×10^9 erythrocytes, or red blood cells, and every red blood cell has about 2.8×10^8 hemoglobin molecules. Calculate the mass of hemoglobin molecules in grams in an average adult.

3.114 Myoglobin stores oxygen for metabolic processes in muscle. Chemical analysis shows that it contains 0.34 percent Fe by mass. What is the molar mass of myoglobin? (There is one Fe atom per molecule.)

3.115 Calculate the number of cations and anions in each of the following compounds: (a) 8.38 g of KBr, (b) 5.40 g of Na_2SO_4, (c) 7.45 g of $Ca_3(PO_4)_2$.

3.116 A mixture of NaBr and Na_2SO_4 contains 29.96 percent Na by mass. Calculate the percent by mass of each compound in the mixture.

3.117 Aspirin or acetyl salicylic acid is synthesized by reacting salicylic acid with acetic anhydride:

$$\underset{\text{salicylic acid}}{C_7H_6O_3} + \underset{\text{acetic anhydride}}{C_4H_6O_3} \longrightarrow \underset{\text{aspirin}}{C_9H_8O_4} + \underset{\text{acetic acid}}{C_2H_4O_2}$$

(a) How much salicylic acid is required to produce 0.400 g of aspirin (about the content in a tablet), assuming acetic anhydride is present in excess? (b) Calculate the amount of salicylic acid needed if only 74.9 percent of salicylic acid is converted to aspirin. (c) In one experiment, 9.26 g of salicylic acid is reacted with 8.54 g of acetic anhydride. Calculate the theoretical yield of aspirin and the percent yield if only 10.9 g of aspirin is produced.

3.118 Calculate the percent composition by mass of all the elements in calcium phosphate [$Ca_3(PO_4)_2$], a major component of bone.

3.119 Lysine, an essential amino acid in the human body, contains C, H, O, and N. In one experiment, the complete combustion of 2.175 g of lysine gave 3.94 g CO_2 and 1.89 g H_2O. In a separate experiment, 1.873 g of lysine gave 0.436 g NH_3. (a) Calculate the empirical formula of lysine. (b) The approximate molar mass of lysine is 150 g. What is the molecular formula of the compound?

3.120 Does 1 g of hydrogen molecules contain as many H atoms as 1 g of hydrogen atoms?

3.121 Avogadro's number has sometimes been described as a conversion factor between amu and grams. Use the fluorine atom (19.00 amu) as an example to show the relation between the atomic mass unit and the gram.

3.122 The natural abundances of the two stable isotopes of hydrogen (hydrogen and deuterium) are ^1_1H: 99.985 percent and ^2_1H: 0.015 percent. Assume that water exists as either H_2O or D_2O. Calculate the number of D_2O molecules in exactly 400 mL of water. (Density = 1.00 g/mL.)

3.123 A compound containing only C, H, and Cl was examined in a mass spectrometer. The highest mass peak seen corresponds to an ion mass of 52 amu. The most abundant mass peak seen corresponds to an ion mass of 50 amu and is about three times as intense as the peak at 52 amu. Deduce a reasonable molecular formula for the compound and explain the positions and intensities of the mass peaks mentioned. (*Hint:* Chlorine is the only element that has isotopes in comparable abundances: $^{35}_{17}Cl$: 75.5 percent; $^{35}_{17}Cl$: 24.5 percent. For H, use ^1_1H; for C, use $^{12}_6C$.)

3.124 In the formation of carbon monoxide, CO, it is found that 2.445 g of carbon combine with 3.257 g of oxygen. What is the atomic mass of oxygen if the atomic mass of carbon is 12.01 amu?

3.125 What mole ratio of molecular chlorine (Cl_2) to molecular oxygen (O_2) would result from the breakup of the compound Cl_2O_7 into its constituent elements?

3.126 Which of the following substances contains the greatest mass of chlorine? (a) 5.0 g Cl_2, (b) 60.0 g $NaClO_3$, (c) 0.10 mol KCl, (d) 30.0 g $MgCl_2$, (e) 0.50 mol Cl_2.

3.127 A compound made up of C, H, and Cl contains 55.0 percent Cl by mass. If 9.00 g of the compound contain 4.19×10^{23} H atoms, what is the empirical formula of the compound?

3.128 Platinum forms two different compounds with chlorine. One contains 26.7 percent Cl by mass, and the other contains 42.1 percent Cl by mass. Determine the empirical formulas of the two compounds.

3.129 Heating 2.40 g of the oxide of metal X (molar mass of X = 55.9 g/mol) in carbon monoxide (CO) yields the pure metal and carbon dioxide. The mass of the metal product is 1.68 g. From the data given, show that the simplest formula of the oxide is X_2O_3 and write a balanced equation for the reaction.

3.130 A compound X contains 63.3 percent manganese (Mn) and 36.7 percent O by mass. When X is heated, oxygen gas is evolved and a new compound Y containing 72.0 percent Mn and 28.0 percent O is formed. (a) Determine the empirical formulas of X and Y. (b) Write a balanced equation for the conversion of X to Y.

3.131 The formula of a hydrate of barium chloride is $BaCl_2 \cdot xH_2O$. If 1.936 g of the compound gives 1.864 g of anhydrous $BaSO_4$ upon treatment with sulfuric acid, calculate the value of x.

3.132 It is estimated that the day Mt. St. Helens erupted (May 18, 1980), about 4.0×10^5 tons of SO_2 were released into the atmosphere. If all the SO_2 were eventually converted to sulfuric acid, how many tons of H_2SO_4 were produced?

3.133 A mixture of $CuSO_4 \cdot 5H_2O$ and $MgSO_4 \cdot 7H_2O$ is heated until all the water is lost. If 5.020 g of the mixture gives 2.988 g of the anhydrous salts, what is the percent by mass of $CuSO_4 \cdot 5H_2O$ in the mixture?

3.134 When 0.273 g of Mg is heated strongly in a nitrogen (N_2) atmosphere, a chemical reaction occurs. The product of the reaction weighs 0.378 g. Calculate the empirical formula of the compound containing Mg and N. Name the compound.

3.135 A mixture of methane (CH_4) and ethane (C_2H_6) of mass 13.43 g is completely burned in oxygen. If the total mass of CO_2 and H_2O produced is 64.84 g, calculate the fraction of CH_4 in the mixture.

3.136 Leaded gasoline contains an additive to prevent engine "knocking." On analysis, the additive compound is found to contain carbon, hydrogen, and lead (Pb) (hence, "leaded gasoline"). When 51.36 g of this compound are burned in an apparatus such as that shown in Figure 3.6, 55.90 g of CO_2 and 28.61 g of H_2O are produced. Determine the empirical formula of the gasoline additive.

3.137 Because of its detrimental effect on the environment, the lead compound described in Problem 3.136 has been replaced in recent years by methyl *tert*-butyl ether (a compound of C, H, and O) to enhance the performance of gasoline. (As of 1999, this compound is also being phased out because of its contamination of drinking water.) When 12.1 g of the compound are burned in an apparatus like the one shown in Figure 3.6, 30.2 g of CO_2 and 14.8 g of H_2O are formed. What is the empirical formula of the compound?

3.138 Suppose you are given a cube made of magnesium (Mg) metal of edge length 1.0 cm. (a) Calculate the number of Mg atoms in the cube. (b) Atoms are spherical in shape. Therefore, the Mg atoms in the cube cannot fill all of the available space. If only 74 percent of the space inside the cube is taken up by Mg atoms, calculate the radius in picometers of a Mg atom. (The density of Mg is 1.74 g/cm^3 and the volume of a sphere of radius r is $\frac{4}{3}\pi r^3$.)

3.139 A certain sample of coal contains 1.6 percent sulfur by mass. When the coal is burned, the sulfur is converted to sulfur dioxide. To prevent air pollution, this sulfur dioxide is treated with calcium oxide (CaO) to form calcium sulfite ($CaSO_3$). Calculate the daily mass (in kilograms) of CaO needed by a power plant that uses 6.60×10^6 kg of coal per day.

3.140 Air is a mixture of many gases. However, in calculating its "molar mass" we need consider only the three major components: nitrogen, oxygen, and argon. Given that one mole of air at sea level is made up of 78.08 percent nitrogen, 20.95 percent oxygen, and 0.97 percent argon, what is the molar mass of air?

3.141 A die has an edge length of 1.5 cm. (a) What is the volume of one mole of such dice? (b) Assuming that the mole of dice could be packed in such a way that they were in contact with one another, forming stacking layers covering the entire surface of Earth, calculate the height in meters the layers would extend outward. [The radius (r) of Earth is 6371 km and the area of a sphere is $4\pi r^2$.]

3.142 The following is a crude but effective method for estimating the order of magnitude of Avogadro's number using stearic acid ($C_{18}H_{36}O_2$). When stearic acid is added to water, its molecules collect at the surface and form a monolayer; that is, the layer is only one mole-cule thick. The cross-sectional area of each stearic acid molecule has been measured to be 0.21 nm^2. In one experiment it is found that 1.4×10^{-4} g of stearic acid is needed to form a monolayer over water in a dish of diameter 20 cm. Based on these measurements, what is Avogadro's number? (The area of a circle of radius r is πr^2.)

3.143 Octane (C_8H_{18}) is a component of gasoline. Complete combustion of octane yields H_2O and CO_2. Incomplete combustion produces H_2O and CO, which not only reduces the efficiency of the engine using the fuel but is also toxic. In a certain test run, 1.000 gal of octane is burned in an engine. The total mass of CO, CO_2, and H_2O produced is 11.53 kg. Calculate the efficiency of the process; that is, calculate the fraction of octane converted to CO_2. The density of octane is 2.650 kg/gal.

3.144 Industrially, hydrogen gas can be prepared by reacting propane gas (C_3H_8) with steam at about 400°C. The products are carbon monoxide (CO) and hydrogen gas (H_2). (a) Write a balanced equation for the reaction. (b) How many kilograms of H_2 can be obtained from 2.84×10^3 kg of propane?

3.145 A reaction having a 90 percent yield may be considered a successful experiment. However, in the synthesis of complex molecules such as chlorophyll and many anticancer drugs, a chemist often has to carry out multiple-step synthesis. What is the overall percent yield for such a synthesis, assuming it is a 30-step reaction with a 90 percent yield at each step?

Special Problems

3.146 (a) For molecules having small molecular masses, mass spectrometry can be used to identify their formulas. To illustrate this point, identify the molecule which most likely accounts for the observation of a peak in a mass spectrum at: 16 amu, 17 amu, 18 amu, and 64 amu. (b) Note that there are (among others) two likely molecules that would give rise to a peak at 44 amu, namely, C_3H_8 and CO_2. In such cases, a chemist might try to look for other peaks generated when some of the molecules break apart in the spectrometer. For example, if a chemist sees a peak at 44 amu and also one at 15 amu, which molecule is producing the 44-amu peak? Why? (c) Using the following precise atomic masses: ^{1}H (1.00797 amu), ^{12}C (12.00000 amu), and ^{16}O (15.99491 amu), how precisely must the masses of C_3H_8 and CO_2 be measured to distinguish between them?

3.147 Potash is any potassium mineral that is used for its potassium content. Most of the potash produced in the United States goes into fertilizer. The major sources of potash are potassium chloride (KCl) and potassium sulfate (K_2SO_4). Potash production is often reported as the potassium oxide (K_2O) equivalent or the amount of K_2O that could be made from a given mineral. (a) If KCl costs $0.55 per kg, for what price (dollar per kg) must K_2SO_4 be sold to supply the same amount of potassium on a per dollar basis? (b) What mass (in kg) of K_2O contains the same number of moles of K atoms as 1.00 kg of KCl?

3.148 A 21.496-g sample of magnesium is burned in air to form magnesium oxide and magnesium nitride. When the products are treated with water, 2.813 g of gaseous ammonia are generated. Calculate the amounts of magnesium nitride and magnesium oxide formed.

3.149 A certain metal M forms a bromide containing 53.79 percent Br by mass. What is the chemical formula of the compound?

3.150 A sample of iron weighing 15.0 g was heated with potassium chlorate ($KClO_3$) in an evacuated container. The oxygen generated from the decomposition of $KClO_3$ converted some of the Fe to Fe_2O_3. If the combined mass of Fe and Fe_2O_3 was 17.9 g, calculate the mass of Fe_2O_3 formed and the mass of $KClO_3$ decomposed.

3.151 A sample containing NaCl, Na_2SO_4, and $NaNO_3$ gives the following elemental analysis: Na: 32.08 percent; O: 36.01 percent; Cl: 19.51 percent. Calculate the mass percent of each compound in the sample.

Answers to Practice Exercises

3.1 10.81 amu. **3.2** 3.59 moles. **3.3** 2.57×10^3 g.
3.4 8.49×10^{21} K atoms. **3.5** 32.04 amu. **3.6** 1.66 moles.
3.7 5.81×10^{24} H atoms. **3.8** H: 2.055%; S: 32.69%;
O: 65.25%. **3.9** $KMnO_4$ (potassium permanganate).
3.10 196 g. **3.11** B_2H_6. **3.12** $Fe_2O_3 + 3CO \longrightarrow 2Fe +$
$3CO_2$. **3.13** 235 g. **3.14** 0.769 g. **3.15** (a) 234 g, (b) 234 g.
3.16 (a) 863 g, (b) 93.0%.

4

Black smokers form when superheated water, rich in minerals, flows out onto the ocean floor through the lava on an ocean volcano. The hydrogen sulfide present converts the metals to insoluble metal sulfides. The models show hydrogen sulfide, metal ions, and a metal sulfide.

Reactions in Aqueous Solutions

A LOOK AHEAD

- We begin by studying the properties of solutions prepared by dissolving substances in water, called aqueous solutions. Aqueous solutions can be classified as nonelectrolyte or electrolyte, depending on their ability to conduct electricity. (4.1)

- We will see that precipitation reactions are those in which the product is an insoluble compound. We learn to represent these reactions using ionic equations and net ionic equations. (4.2).

- Next, we learn acid-base reactions, which involve the transfer of proton (H^+) from an acid to a base. (4.3)

- We then learn oxidation-reduction (redox) reactions in which electrons are transferred between reactants. We will see that there are several types of redox reactions (4.4)

- To carry out quantitative studies of solutions, we learn how to express the concentration of a solution in molarity. (4.5)

- Finally, we will apply our knowledge of the mole method from Chapter 3 to the three types of reactions studied here. We will see how gravimetric analysis is used to study precipitation reactions, and the titration technique is used to study acid-base and redox reactions. (4.6, 4.7, and 4.8)

Many chemical reactions and virtually all biological processes take place in water. In this chapter we will discuss three major categories of reactions that occur in aqueous solutions: precipitation reactions, acid-base reactions, and redox reactions. In later chapters we will study the structural characteristics and properties of water—the so-called *universal solvent*—and its solutions.

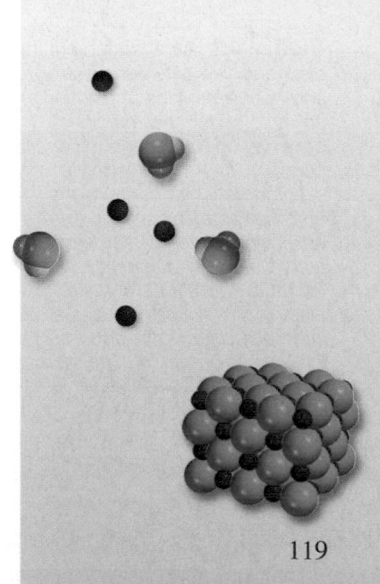

4.1 General Properties of Aqueous Solutions

A *solution* is *a homogeneous mixture of two or more substances.* The **solute** is *the substance present in a smaller amount,* and the **solvent** is *the substance present in a larger amount.* A solution may be gaseous (such as air), solid (such as an alloy), or liquid (seawater, for example). In this section we will discuss only **aqueous solutions,** in which *the solute initially is a liquid or a solid and the solvent is water.*

Electrolytic Properties

All solutes that dissolve in water fit into one of two categories: electrolytes and nonelectrolytes. An **electrolyte** is *a substance that, when dissolved in water, results in a solution that can conduct electricity.* A **nonelectrolyte** *does not conduct electricity when dissolved in water.* Figure 4.1 shows an easy and straightforward method of distinguishing between electrolytes and nonelectrolytes. A pair of inert electrodes (copper or platinum) is immersed in a beaker of water. To light the bulb, electric current must flow from one electrode to the other, thus completing the circuit. Pure water is a very poor conductor of electricity. However, if we add a small amount of sodium chloride (NaCl), the bulb will glow as soon as the salt dissolves in the water. Solid NaCl, an ionic compound, breaks up into Na^+ and Cl^- ions when it dissolves in water. The Na^+ ions are attracted to the negative electrode, and the Cl^- ions to the positive electrode. This movement sets up an electric current that is equivalent to the flow of electrons along a metal wire. Because the NaCl solution conducts electricity, we say that NaCl is an electrolyte. Pure water contains very few ions, so it cannot conduct electricity.

Comparing the lightbulb's brightness for the same molar amounts of dissolved substances helps us distinguish between strong and weak electrolytes. A characteristic of strong electrolytes is that the solute is assumed to be 100 percent dissociated into ions in solution. (By *dissociation* we mean the breaking up of the compound into cations and anions.) Thus, we can represent sodium chloride dissolving in water as

$$NaCl(s) \xrightarrow{\text{H}_2\text{O}} Na^+(aq) + Cl^-(aq)$$

This equation says that all sodium chloride that enters the solution ends up as Na^+ and Cl^- ions; there are no undissociated NaCl units in solution.

Figure 4.1 *An arrangement for distinguishing between electrolytes and nonelectrolytes. A solution's ability to conduct electricity depends on the number of ions it contains. (a) A nonelectrolyte solution does not contain ions, and the lightbulb is not lit. (b) A weak electrolyte solution contains a small number of ions, and the lightbulb is dimly lit. (c) A strong electrolyte solution contains a large number of ions, and the lightbulb is brightly lit. The molar amounts of the dissolved solutes are equal in all three cases.*

(a)

(b)

(c)

TABLE 4.1   Classification of Solutes in Aqueous Solution

Strong Electrolyte	Weak Electrolyte	Nonelectrolyte
HCl	CH_3COOH	$(NH_2)_2CO$ (urea)
HNO_3	HF	CH_3OH (methanol)
$HClO_4$	HNO_2	C_2H_5OH (ethanol)
H_2SO_4*	NH_3	$C_6H_{12}O_6$ (glucose)
NaOH	$H_2O^\dagger$	$C_{12}H_{22}O_{11}$ (sucrose)
$Ba(OH)_2$		
Ionic compounds		

*H_2SO_4 has two ionizable H^+ ions.
†Pure water is an extremely weak electrolyte.

Table 4.1 lists examples of strong electrolytes, weak electrolytes, and non-electrolytes. Ionic compounds, such as sodium chloride, potassium iodide (KI), and calcium nitrate [$Ca(NO_3)_2$], are strong electrolytes. It is interesting to note that human body fluids contain many strong and weak electrolytes.

Water is a very effective solvent for ionic compounds. Although water is an electrically neutral molecule, it has a positive region (the H atoms) and a negative region (the O atom), or positive and negative "poles"; for this reason it is a *polar* solvent. When an ionic compound such as sodium chloride dissolves in water, the three-dimensional network of ions in the solid is destroyed. The Na^+ and Cl^- ions are separated from each other and undergo **hydration,** *the process in which an ion is surrounded by water molecules arranged in a specific manner.* Each Na^+ ion is surrounded by a number of water molecules orienting their negative poles toward the cation. Similarly, each Cl^- ion is surrounded by water molecules with their positive poles oriented toward the anion (Figure 4.2). Hydration helps to stabilize ions in solution and prevents cations from combining with anions.

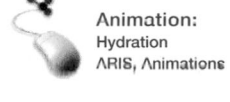

Animation:
Hydration
ARIS, Animations

Acids and bases are also electrolytes. Some acids, including hydrochloric acid (HCl) and nitric acid (HNO_3), are strong electrolytes. These acids are assumed to ionize completely in water; for example, when hydrogen chloride gas dissolves in water, it forms hydrated H^+ and Cl^- ions:

$$HCl(g) \xrightarrow{H_2O} H^+(aq) + Cl^-(aq)$$

In other words, *all* the dissolved HCl molecules separate into hydrated H^+ and Cl^- ions. Thus, when we write HCl(*aq*), it is understood that it is a solution of only $H^+(aq)$ and $Cl^-(aq)$ ions and that there are no hydrated HCl molecules present. On the other hand, certain acids, such as acetic acid (CH_3COOH), which gives vinegar its tart

Figure 4.2 *Hydration of Na^+ and Cl^- ions.*

CH$_3$COOH

There are different types of chemical equilibrium. We will return to this very important topic in Chapter 14.

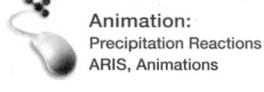

Animation:
Precipitation Reactions
ARIS, Animations

flavor, do not ionize completely and are weak electrolytes. We represent the ionization of acetic acid as

$$CH_3COOH(aq) \rightleftharpoons CH_3COO^-(aq) + H^+(aq)$$

where CH_3COO^- is called the acetate ion. We use the term *ionization* to describe the separation of acids and bases into ions. By writing the formula of acetic acid as CH_3COOH we indicate that the ionizable proton is in the COOH group.

The ionization of acetic acid is written with a double arrow to show that it is a **reversible reaction;** that is, *the reaction can occur in both directions.* Initially, a number of CH_3COOH molecules break up into CH_3COO^- and H^+ ions. As time goes on, some of the CH_3COO^- and H^+ ions recombine into CH_3COOH molecules. Eventually, a state is reached in which the acid molecules ionize as fast as the ions recombine. Such a chemical state, in which no net change can be observed (although activity is continuous on the molecular level), is called *chemical equilibrium.* Acetic acid, then, is a weak electrolyte because its ionization in water is incomplete. By contrast, in a hydrochloric acid solution the H^+ and Cl^- ions have no tendency to recombine and form molecular HCl. We use a single arrow to represent complete ionizations.

4.2 Precipitation Reactions

One common type of reaction that occurs in aqueous solution is the **precipitation reaction,** which *results in the formation of an insoluble product, or precipitate.* A **precipitate** *is an insoluble solid that separates from the solution.* Precipitation reactions usually involve ionic compounds. For example, when an aqueous solution of lead nitrate [Pb(NO$_3$)$_2$] is added to an aqueous solution of potassium iodide (KI), a yellow precipitate of lead iodide (PbI$_2$) is formed:

$$Pb(NO_3)_2(aq) + 2KI(aq) \longrightarrow PbI_2(s) + 2KNO_3(aq)$$

Potassium nitrate remains in solution. Figure 4.3 shows this reaction in progress.

The preceding reaction is an example of a **metathesis reaction** (also called a double-displacement reaction), *a reaction that involves the exchange of parts between the two compounds.* (In this case, the cations in the two compounds exchange anions, so Pb^{2+}

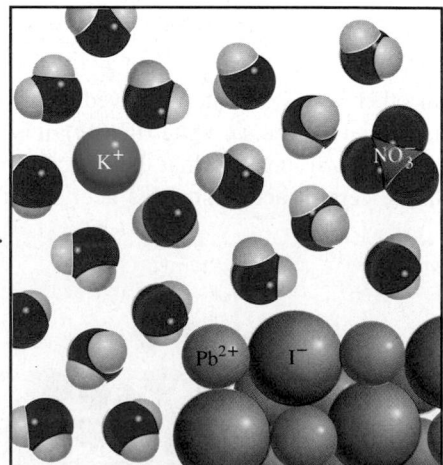

Figure 4.3 *Formation of yellow PbI$_2$ precipitate as a solution of Pb(NO$_3$)$_2$ is added to a solution of KI.*

TABLE 4.2	Solubility Rules for Common Ionic Compounds in Water at 25°C

Soluble Compounds	Exceptions
Compounds containing alkali metal ions (Li^+, Na^+, K^+, Rb^+, Cs^+) and the ammonium ion (NH_4^+)	
Nitrates (NO_3^-), bicarbonates (HCO_3^-), and chlorates (ClO_3^-)	
Halides (Cl^-, Br^-, I^-)	Halides of Ag^+, Hg_2^{2+}, and Pb^{2+}
Sulfates (SO_4^{2-})	Sulfates of Ag^+, Ca^{2+}, Sr^{2+}, Ba^{2+}, Hg_2^{2+}, and Pb^{2+}

Insoluble Compounds	Exceptions
Carbonates (CO_3^{2-}), phosphates (PO_4^{3-}), chromates (CrO_4^{2-}), sulfides (S^{2-})	Compounds containing alkali metal ions and the ammonium ion
Hydroxides (OH^-)	Compounds containing alkali metal ions and the Ba^{2+} ion

ends up with I^- as PbI_2 and K^+ ends up with NO_3^- as KNO_3.) As we will see, the precipitation reactions discussed in this chapter are examples of metathesis reactions.

Solubility

How can we predict whether a precipitate will form when a compound is added to a solution or when two solutions are mixed? It depends on the *solubility* of the solute, which is defined as *the maximum amount of solute that will dissolve in a given quantity of solvent at a specific temperature.* Chemists refer to substances as soluble, slightly soluble, or insoluble in a qualitative sense. A substance is said to be soluble if a fair amount of it visibly dissolves when added to water. If not, the substance is described as slightly soluble or insoluble. All ionic compounds are strong electrolytes, but they are not equally soluble.

Table 4.2 classifies a number of common ionic compounds as soluble or insoluble. Keep in mind, however, that even insoluble compounds dissolve to a certain extent. Figure 4.4 shows several precipitates.

Example 4.1 applies the solubility rules in Table 4.2.

Example 4.1

Classify the following ionic compounds as soluble or insoluble: (a) silver sulfate (Ag_2SO_4), (b) calcium carbonate ($CaCO_3$), (c) sodium phosphate (Na_3PO_4).

Strategy Although it is not necessary to memorize the solubilities of compounds, you should keep in mind the following useful rules: all ionic compounds containing alkali metal cations; the ammonium ion; and the nitrate, bicarbonate, and chlorate ions are soluble. For other compounds, we need to refer to Table 4.2.

(Continued)

Figure 4.4 *Appearance of several precipitates. From left to right: CdS, PbS, Ni(OH)₂, and Al(OH)₃.*

Similar problems: 4.19, 4.20.

Solution (a) According to Table 4.2, Ag₂SO₄ is insoluble.

(b) This is a carbonate and Ca is a Group 2A metal. Therefore, CaCO₃ is insoluble.

(c) Sodium is an alkali metal (Group 1A) so Na₃PO₄ is soluble.

Practice Exercise Classify the following ionic compounds as soluble or insoluble: (a) CuS, (b) Ca(OH)₂, (c) Zn(NO₃)₂.

Molecular Equations, Ionic Equations, and Net Ionic Equations

The equation describing the precipitation of lead iodide on page 122 is called a **molecular equation** because *the formulas of the compounds are written as though all species existed as molecules or whole units.* A molecular equation is useful because it identifies the reagents (that is, lead nitrate and potassium iodide). If we wanted to bring about this reaction in the laboratory, we would use the molecular equation. However, a molecular equation does not describe in detail what actually is happening in solution.

As pointed out earlier, when ionic compounds dissolve in water, they break apart into their component cations and anions. To be more realistic, the equations should show the dissociation of dissolved ionic compounds into ions. Therefore, returning to the reaction between potassium iodide and lead(II) nitrate, we would write

$$Pb^{2+}(aq) + 2NO_3^-(aq) + 2K^+(aq) + 2I^-(aq) \longrightarrow$$
$$PbI_2(s) + 2K^+(aq) + 2NO_3^-(aq)$$

The preceding equation is an example of an **ionic equation,** which *shows dissolved species as free ions.* To see whether a precipitate might form from this solution, we first combine the cation and anion from different compounds; that is, PbI₂ and KNO₃. Referring to Table 4.2, we see that PbI₂ is an insoluble compound and KNO₃ is soluble. Therefore, the dissolved KNO₃ remains in solution as separate K⁺ and NO₃⁻ ions, which are called **spectator ions,** or *ions that are not involved in the overall reaction.* Because spectator ions appear on both sides of an equation, they can be eliminated from the ionic equation

$$Pb^{2+}(aq) + 2\cancel{NO_3^-(aq)} + 2\cancel{K^+(aq)} + 2I^-(aq) \longrightarrow$$
$$PbI_2(s) + 2\cancel{K^+(aq)} + 2\cancel{NO_3^-(aq)}$$

Finally, we end up with the ***net ionic equation,*** which *shows only the species that actually take part in the reaction:*

$$Pb^{2+}(aq) + 2I^-(aq) \longrightarrow PbI_2(s)$$

Looking at another example, we find that when an aqueous solution of barium chloride ($BaCl_2$) is added to an aqueous solution of sodium sulfate (Na_2SO_4), a white precipitate is formed (Figure 4.5). Treating this as a metathesis reaction, the products are $BaSO_4$ and $NaCl$. From Table 4.2 we see that only $BaSO_4$ is insoluble. Therefore, we write the molecular equation as

$$BaCl_2(aq) + Na_2SO_4(aq) \longrightarrow BaSO_4(s) + 2NaCl(aq)$$

The ionic equation for the reaction is

$$Ba^{2+}(aq) + 2Cl^-(aq) + 2Na^+(aq) + SO_4^{2-}(aq) \longrightarrow$$
$$BaSO_4(s) + 2Na^+(aq) + 2Cl^-(aq)$$

Canceling the spectator ions (Na^+ and Cl^-) on both sides of the equation gives us the net ionic equation

$$Ba^{2+}(aq) + SO_4^{2-}(aq) \longrightarrow BaSO_4(s)$$

The following four steps summarize the procedure for writing ionic and net ionic equations:

1. Write a balanced molecular equation for the reaction, using the correct formulas for the reactant and product ionic compounds. Refer to Table 4.2 to decide which of the products is insoluble and therefore will appear as a precipitate.

2. Write the ionic equation for the reaction. The compound that does not appear as the precipitate should be shown as free ions.

3. Identify and cancel the spectator ions on both sides of the equation. Write the net ionic equation for the reaction.

4. Check that the charges and number of atoms balance in the net ionic equation.

These steps are applied in Example 4.2.

Interactivity:
Construct a Net Ionic Equation
ARIS, Interactives

Figure 4.5 *Formation of $BaSO_4$ precipitate.*

Example 4.2

Predict what happens when a potassium phosphate (K_3PO_4) solution is mixed with a calcium nitrate [$Ca(NO_3)_2$] solution. Write a net ionic equation for the reaction.

Strategy From the given information, it is useful to first write the unbalanced equation

$$K_3PO_4(aq) + Ca(NO_3)_2(aq) \longrightarrow ?$$

What happens when ionic compounds dissolve in water? What ions are formed from the dissociation of K_3PO_4 and $Ca(NO_3)_2$? What happens when the cations encounter the anions in solution?

Solution In solution, K_3PO_4 dissociates into K^+ and PO_4^{3-} ions and $Ca(NO_3)_2$ dissociates into Ca^{2+} and NO_3^- ions. According to Table 4.2, calcium ions (Ca^{2+}) and phosphate ions (PO_4^{3-}) will form an insoluble compound, calcium phosphate [$Ca_3(PO_4)_2$], while the other product, KNO_3, is soluble and remains in solution. Therefore, this is a precipitation reaction. We follow the stepwise procedure just outlined.

(Continued)

Precipitate formed by the reaction between $K_3PO_4(aq)$ and $Ca(NO_3)_2(aq)$.

CHEMISTRY *in Action*

An Undesirable Precipitation Reaction

Limestone ($CaCO_3$) and dolomite ($CaCO_3 \cdot MgCO_3$), which are widespread on Earth's surface, often enter the water supply. According to Table 4.2, calcium carbonate is insoluble in water. However, in the presence of dissolved carbon dioxide (from the atmosphere), calcium carbonate is converted to soluble calcium bicarbonate [$Ca(HCO_3)_2$]:

$$CaCO_3(s) + CO_2(aq) + H_2O(l) \longrightarrow Ca^{2+}(aq) + 2HCO_3^-(aq)$$

where HCO_3^- is the bicarbonate ion.

Water containing Ca^{2+} and/or Mg^{2+} ions is called *hard water,* and water that is mostly free of these ions is called *soft water.* Hard water is unsuitable for some household and industrial uses.

When water containing Ca^{2+} and HCO_3^- ions is heated or boiled, the solution reaction is reversed to produce the $CaCO_3$ precipitate

$$Ca^{2+}(aq) + 2HCO_3^-(aq) \longrightarrow CaCO_3(s) + CO_2(aq) + H_2O(l)$$

and gaseous carbon dioxide is driven off:

$$CO_2(aq) \longrightarrow CO_2(g)$$

Solid calcium carbonate formed in this way is the main component of the scale that accumulates in boilers, water heaters, pipes, and teakettles. A thick layer of scale reduces heat transfer and

Boiler scale almost fills this hot-water pipe. The deposits consist mostly of $CaCO_3$ with some $MgCO_3$.

decreases the efficiency and durability of boilers, pipes, and appliances. In household hot-water pipes it can restrict or totally block the flow of water. A simple method used by plumbers to remove scale deposits is to introduce a small amount of hydrochloric acid, which reacts with (and therefore dissolves) $CaCO_3$:

$$CaCO_3(s) + 2HCl(aq) \longrightarrow CaCl_2(aq) + H_2O(l) + CO_2(g)$$

In this way, $CaCO_3$ is converted to soluble $CaCl_2$.

Step 1: The balanced molecular equation for this reaction is

$$2K_3PO_4(aq) + 3Ca(NO_3)_2(aq) \longrightarrow Ca_3(PO_4)_2(s) + 6KNO_3(aq)$$

Step 2: To write the ionic equation, the soluble compounds are shown as dissociated ions:

$$6K^+(aq) + 2PO_4^{3-}(aq) + 3Ca^{2+}(aq) + 6NO_3^-(aq) \longrightarrow$$
$$6K^+(aq) + 6NO_3^-(aq) + Ca_3(PO_4)_2(s)$$

Step 3: Canceling the spectator ions (K^+ and NO_3^-) on each side of the equation, we obtain the net ionic equation:

$$3Ca^{2+}(aq) + 2PO_4^{3-}(aq) \longrightarrow Ca_3(PO_4)_2(s)$$

Step 4: Note that because we balanced the molecular equation first, the net ionic equation is balanced as to the number of atoms on each side and the number of positive ($+6$) and negative (-6) charges on the left-hand side is the same.

Similar problems: 4.21, 4.22.

Practice Exercise Predict the precipitate produced by mixing an $Al(NO_3)_3$ solution with a NaOH solution. Write the net ionic equation for the reaction.

The Chemistry in Action on p. 126 discusses some practical problems associated with precipitation reactions.

4.3 Acid-Base Reactions

Acids and bases are as familiar as aspirin and milk of magnesia although many people do not know their chemical names—acetylsalicylic acid (aspirin) and magnesium hydroxide (milk of magnesia). In addition to being the basis of many medicinal and household products, acid-base chemistry is important in industrial processes and essential in sustaining biological systems. Before we can discuss acid-base reactions, we need to know more about acids and bases themselves.

General Properties of Acids and Bases

In Section 2.7 we defined acids as substances that ionize in water to produce H^+ ions and bases as substances that ionize in water to produce OH^- ions. These definitions were formulated in the late nineteenth century by the Swedish chemist Svante Arrhenius[†] to classify substances whose properties in aqueous solutions were well known.

Acids

- Acids have a sour taste; for example, vinegar owes its sourness to acetic acid, and lemons and other citrus fruits contain citric acid.
- Acids cause color changes in plant dyes; for example, they change the color of litmus from blue to red.
- Acids react with certain metals, such as zinc, magnesium, and iron, to produce hydrogen gas. A typical reaction is that between hydrochloric acid and magnesium:

$$2HCl(aq) + Mg(s) \longrightarrow MgCl_2(aq) + H_2(g)$$

- Acids react with carbonates and bicarbonates, such as Na_2CO_3, $CaCO_3$, and $NaHCO_3$, to produce carbon dioxide gas (Figure 4.6). For example,

$$2HCl(aq) + CaCO_3(s) \longrightarrow CaCl_2(aq) + H_2O(l) + CO_2(g)$$
$$HCl(aq) + NaHCO_3(s) \longrightarrow NaCl(aq) + H_2O(l) + CO_2(g)$$

- Aqueous acid solutions conduct electricity.

Bases

- Bases have a bitter taste.
- Bases feel slippery; for example, soaps, which contain bases, exhibit this property.
- Bases cause color changes in plant dyes; for example, they change the color of litmus from red to blue.
- Aqueous base solutions conduct electricity.

Figure 4.6 *A piece of blackboard chalk, which is mostly $CaCO_3$, reacts with hydrochloric acid.*

[†]Svante August Arrhenius (1859–1927). Swedish chemist. Arrhenius made important contributions in the study of chemical kinetics and electrolyte solutions. He also speculated that life had come to Earth from other planets, a theory now known as *panspermia*. Arrhenius was awarded the Nobel Prize in Chemistry in 1903.

Figure 4.7 *Ionization of HCl in water to form the hydronium ion and the chloride ion.*

$$\text{HCl} \quad + \quad \text{H}_2\text{O} \quad \longrightarrow \quad \text{H}_3\text{O}^+ \quad + \quad \text{Cl}^-$$

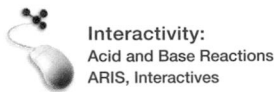
Brønsted Acids and Bases

Arrhenius's definitions of acids and bases are limited in that they apply only to aqueous solutions. Broader definitions were proposed by the Danish chemist Johannes Brønsted[†] in 1932; a **Brønsted acid** is *a proton donor,* and a **Brønsted base** is *a proton acceptor.* Note that Brønsted's definitions do not require acids and bases to be in aqueous solution.

Hydrochloric acid is a Brønsted acid because it donates a proton in water:

$$\text{HCl}(aq) \longrightarrow \text{H}^+(aq) + \text{Cl}^-(aq)$$

Note that the H^+ ion is a hydrogen atom that has lost its electron; that is, it is just a bare proton. The size of a proton is about 10^{-15} m, compared to a diameter of 10^{-10} m for an average atom or ion. Such an exceedingly small charged particle cannot exist as a separate entity in aqueous solution owing to its strong attraction for the negative pole (the O atom) in H_2O. Consequently, the proton exists in the hydrated form as shown in Figure 4.7. Therefore, the ionization of hydrochloric acid should be written as

$$\text{HCl}(aq) + \text{H}_2\text{O}(l) \longrightarrow \text{H}_3\text{O}^+(aq) + \text{Cl}^-(aq)$$

The *hydrated proton, H_3O^+,* is called the **hydronium ion.** This equation shows a reaction in which a Brønsted acid (HCl) donates a proton to a Brønsted base (H_2O).

Experiments show that the hydronium ion is further hydrated so that the proton may have several water molecules associated with it. Because the acidic properties of the proton are unaffected by the degree of hydration, in this text we will generally use $\text{H}^+(aq)$ to represent the hydrated proton. This notation is for convenience, but H_3O^+ is closer to reality. Keep in mind that both notations represent the same species in aqueous solution.

Acids commonly used in the laboratory include hydrochloric acid (HCl), nitric acid (HNO_3), acetic acid (CH_3COOH), sulfuric acid (H_2SO_4), and phosphoric acid (H_3PO_4). The first three are **monoprotic acids;** that is, *each unit of the acid yields one hydrogen ion upon ionization:*

$$\text{HCl}(aq) \longrightarrow \text{H}^+(aq) + \text{Cl}^-(aq)$$
$$\text{HNO}_3(aq) \longrightarrow \text{H}^+(aq) + \text{NO}_3^-(aq)$$
$$\text{CH}_3\text{COOH}(aq) \rightleftharpoons \text{CH}_3\text{COO}^-(aq) + \text{H}^+(aq)$$

As mentioned earlier, because the ionization of acetic acid is incomplete (note the double arrows), it is a weak electrolyte. For this reason it is called a weak acid (see Table 4.1). On the other hand, HCl and HNO_3 are strong acids because they are strong electrolytes, so they are completely ionized in solution (note the use of single arrows).

Sulfuric acid (H_2SO_4) is a **diprotic acid** because *each unit of the acid gives up two H^+ ions,* in two separate steps:

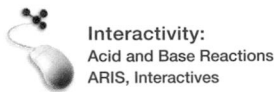

Electrostatic potential map of the H_3O^+ ion. In the rainbow color spectrum representation, the most electron-rich region is red and the most electron-poor region is blue.

[†]Johannes Nicolaus Brønsted (1879–1947). Danish chemist. In addition to his theory of acids and bases, Brønsted worked on thermodynamics and the separation of mercury into its isotopes.

$$H_2SO_4(aq) \longrightarrow H^+(aq) + HSO_4^-(aq)$$
$$HSO_4^-(aq) \rightleftharpoons H^+(aq) + SO_4^{2-}(aq)$$

H_2SO_4 is a strong electrolyte or strong acid (the first step of ionization is complete), but HSO_4^- is a weak acid or weak electrolyte, and we need a double arrow to represent its incomplete ionization.

Triprotic acids, which *yield three H^+ ions,* are relatively few in number. The best known triprotic acid is phosphoric acid, whose ionizations are

$$H_3PO_4(aq) \rightleftharpoons H^+(aq) + H_2PO_4^-(aq)$$
$$H_2PO_4^-(aq) \rightleftharpoons H^+(aq) + HPO_4^{2-}(aq)$$
$$HPO_4^{2-}(aq) \rightleftharpoons H^+(aq) + PO_4^{3-}(aq)$$

All three species (H_3PO_4, $H_2PO_4^-$, and HPO_4^{2-}) in this case are weak acids, and we use the double arrows to represent each ionization step. Anions such as $H_2PO_4^-$ and HPO_4^{2-} are found in aqueous solutions of phosphates such as NaH_2PO_4 and Na_2HPO_4. Table 4.3 lists several common strong and weak acids.

Table 4.1 shows that sodium hydroxide (NaOH) and barium hydroxide [$Ba(OH)_2$] are strong electrolytes. This means that they are completely ionized in solution:

$$NaOH(s) \xrightarrow{H_2O} Na^+(aq) + OH^-(aq)$$
$$Ba(OH)_2(s) \xrightarrow{H_2O} Ba^{2+}(aq) + 2OH^-(aq)$$

The OH^- ion can accept a proton as follows:

$$H^+(aq) + OH^-(aq) \longrightarrow H_2O(l)$$

Thus, OH^- is a Brønsted base.

Ammonia (NH_3) is classified as a Brønsted base because it can accept a H^+ ion (Figure 4.8):

$$NH_3(aq) + H_2O(l) \rightleftharpoons NH_4^+(aq) + OH^-(aq)$$

Ammonia is a weak electrolyte (and therefore a weak base) because only a small fraction of dissolved NH_3 molecules react with water to form NH_4^+ and OH^- ions.

The most commonly used strong base in the laboratory is sodium hydroxide. It is cheap and soluble. (In fact, all of the alkali metal hydroxides are soluble.) The most commonly used weak base is aqueous ammonia solution, which is sometimes erroneously called ammonium hydroxide; there is no evidence that the species NH_4OH actually exists. All of the Group 2A elements form hydroxides of the type $M(OH)_2$, where M denotes an alkaline earth metal. Of these hydroxides, only $Ba(OH)_2$ is soluble. Magnesium and calcium hydroxides are used in medicine and industry. Hydroxides of other metals, such as $Al(OH)_3$ and $Zn(OH)_2$ are insoluble and are not used as bases.

Example 4.3 classifies substances as Brønsted acids or Brønsted bases.

TABLE 4.3

Some Common Strong and Weak Acids

Strong Acids

Hydrochloric acid	HCl
Hydrobromic acid	HBr
Hydroiodic acid	HI
Nitric acid	HNO_3
Sulfuric acid	H_2SO_4
Perchloric acid	$HClO_4$

Weak Acids

Hydrofluoric acid	HF
Nitrous acid	HNO_2
Phosphoric acid	H_3PO_4
Acetic acid	CH_3COOH

Note that this bottle of aqueous ammonia is erroneously labeled.

Figure 4.8 *Ionization of ammonia in water to form the ammonium ion and the hydroxide ion.*

Example 4.3

Classify each of the following species in aqueous solution as a Brønsted acid or base: (a) HBr, (b) NO_2^-, (c) HCO_3^-.

Strategy What are the characteristics of a Brønsted acid? Does it contain at least an H atom? With the exception of ammonia, most Brønsted bases that you will encounter at this stage are anions.

Solution (a) We know that HCl is an acid. Because Br and Cl are both halogens (Group 7A), we expect HBr, like HCl, to ionize in water as follows:

$$HBr(aq) \longrightarrow H^+(aq) + Br^-(aq)$$

Therefore HBr is a Brønsted acid.

(b) In solution the nitrite ion can accept a proton from water to form nitrous acid:

$$NO_2^-(aq) + H^+(aq) \longrightarrow HNO_2(aq)$$

This property makes NO_2^- a Brønsted base.

(c) The bicarbonate ion is a Brønsted acid because it ionizes in solution as follows:

$$HCO_3^-(aq) \rightleftharpoons H^+(aq) + CO_3^{2-}(aq)$$

It is also a Brønsted base because it can accept a proton to form carbonic acid:

$$HCO_3^-(aq) + H^+(aq) \rightleftharpoons H_2CO_3(aq)$$

Comment The HCO_3^- species is said to be *amphoteric* because it possesses both acidic and basic properties. The double arrows show that this is a reversible reaction.

Practice Exercise Classify each of the following species as a Brønsted acid or base: (a) SO_4^{2-}, (b) HI.

Similar problems: 4.31, 4.32.

Acid-Base Neutralization

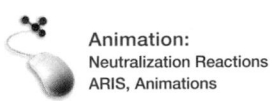

Animation:
Neutralization Reactions
ARIS, Animations

A ***neutralization reaction*** is *a reaction between an acid and a base.* Generally, aqueous acid-base reactions produce water and a ***salt,*** which is *an ionic compound made up of a cation other than H^+ and an anion other than OH^- or O^{2-}*:

$$\text{acid} + \text{base} \longrightarrow \text{salt} + \text{water}$$

The substance we know as table salt, NaCl, is a product of the acid-base reaction

Acid-base reactions generally go to completion.

$$HCl(aq) + NaOH(aq) \longrightarrow NaCl(aq) + H_2O(l)$$

However, because both the acid and the base are strong electrolytes, they are completely ionized in solution. The ionic equation is

$$H^+(aq) + Cl^-(aq) + Na^+(aq) + OH^-(aq) \longrightarrow Na^+(aq) + Cl^-(aq) + H_2O(l)$$

Therefore, the reaction can be represented by the net ionic equation

$$H^+(aq) + OH^-(aq) \longrightarrow H_2O(l)$$

Both Na^+ and Cl^- are spectator ions.

If we had started the preceding reaction with equal molar amounts of the acid and the base, at the end of the reaction we would have only a salt and no leftover acid or base. This is a characteristic of acid-base neutralization reactions.

A reaction between a weak acid such as hydrocyanic acid (HCN) and a strong base is

$$HCN(aq) + NaOH(aq) \longrightarrow NaCN(aq) + H_2O(l)$$

Because HCN is a weak acid, it does not ionize appreciably in solution. Thus, the ionic equation is written as

$$HCN(aq) + Na^+(aq) + OH^-(aq) \longrightarrow Na^+(aq) + CN^-(aq) + H_2O(l)$$

and the net ionic equation is

$$HCN(aq) + OH^-(aq) \longrightarrow CN^-(aq) + H_2O(l)$$

Note that only Na^+ is a spectator ion; OH^- and CN^- are not.

The following are also examples of acid-base neutralization reactions, represented by molecular equations:

$$HF(aq) + KOH(aq) \longrightarrow KF(aq) + H_2O(l)$$
$$H_2SO_4(aq) + 2NaOH(aq) \longrightarrow Na_2SO_4(aq) + 2H_2O(l)$$
$$HNO_3(aq) + NH_3(aq) \longrightarrow NH_4NO_3(aq)$$

The last equation looks different because it does not show water as a product. However, if we express $NH_3(aq)$ as $NH_4^+(aq)$ and $OH^-(aq)$, as discussed earlier, then the equation becomes

$$HNO_3(aq) + NH_4^+(aq) + OH^-(aq) \longrightarrow NH_4NO_3(aq) + H_2O(l)$$

Acid-Base Reactions Leading to Gas Formation

Certain salts like carbonates (containing the CO_3^{2-} ion), bicarbonates (containing the HCO_3 ion), sulfites (containing the SO_3^{2-} ion), and sulfides (containing the S^{2-} ion) react with acids to form gaseous products. For example, the molecular equation for the reaction between sodium carbonate (Na_2CO_3) and $HCl(aq)$ is

$$Na_2CO_3(aq) + 2HCl(aq) \longrightarrow 2NaCl(aq) + H_2CO_3(aq)$$

Carbonic acid is unstable and if present in solution in sufficient concentrations decomposes as follows:

$$H_2CO_3(aq) \longrightarrow H_2O(l) + CO_2(g)$$

Similar reactions involving other mentioned salts are

$$NaHCO_3(aq) + HCl(aq) \longrightarrow NaCl(aq) + H_2O(l) + CO_2(g)$$
$$Na_2SO_3(aq) + 2HCl(aq) \longrightarrow 2NaCl(aq) + H_2O(l) + SO_2(g)$$
$$K_2S(aq) + 2HCl(aq) \longrightarrow 2KCl(aq) + H_2S(g)$$

4.4 Oxidation-Reduction Reactions

Whereas acid-base reactions can be characterized as proton-transfer processes, the class of reactions called *oxidation-reduction,* or *redox, reactions* are considered *electron-transfer reactions.* Oxidation-reduction reactions are very much a part of the world around us. They range from the burning of fossil fuels to the action of household bleach. Additionally, most metallic and nonmetallic elements are obtained from their ores by the process of oxidation or reduction.

Figure 4.9 *Magnesium burns in oxygen to form magnesium oxide.*

Many important redox reactions take place in water, but not all redox reactions occur in aqueous solution. We begin our discussion with a reaction in which two elements combine to form a compound. Consider the formation of magnesium oxide (MgO) from magnesium and oxygen (Figure 4.9):

$$2Mg(s) + O_2(g) \longrightarrow 2MgO(s)$$

Magnesium oxide (MgO) is an ionic compound made up of Mg^{2+} and O^{2-} ions. In this reaction, two Mg atoms give up or transfer four electrons to two O atoms (in O_2). For convenience, we can think of this process as two separate steps, one involving the loss of four electrons by the two Mg atoms and the other being the gain of four electrons by an O_2 molecule:

$$2Mg \longrightarrow 2Mg^{2+} + 4e^-$$
$$O_2 + 4e^- \longrightarrow 2O^{2-}$$

Each of these steps is called a ***half-reaction,*** which *explicitly shows the electrons involved in a redox reaction.* The sum of the half-reactions gives the overall reaction:

$$2Mg + O_2 + 4e^- \longrightarrow 2Mg^{2+} + 2O^{2-} + 4e^-$$

or, if we cancel the electrons that appear on both sides of the equation,

$$2Mg + O_2 \longrightarrow 2Mg^{2+} + 2O^{2-}$$

Finally, the Mg^{2+} and O^{2-} ions combine to form MgO:

$$2Mg^{2+} + 2O^{2-} \longrightarrow 2MgO$$

A useful mnemonic for redox is OILRIG: Oxidation Is Loss (of electrons) and Reduction Is Gain (of electrons).

Oxidizing agents are always reduced and reducing agents are always oxidized. This statement may be somewhat confusing, but it is simply a consequence of the definitions of the two processes.

The term ***oxidation reaction*** refers to the *half-reaction that involves loss of electrons.* Chemists originally used "oxidation" to denote the combination of elements with oxygen. However, it now has a broader meaning that includes reactions not involving oxygen. A ***reduction reaction*** is a *half-reaction that involves gain of electrons.* In the formation of magnesium oxide, magnesium is oxidized. It is said to act as a ***reducing agent*** because it *donates electrons* to oxygen and causes oxygen to be reduced. Oxygen is reduced and acts as an ***oxidizing agent*** because it *accepts electrons* from magnesium,

Figure 4.10 *Metal displacement reactions in solution. (a) First beaker: A zinc strip is placed in a blue CuSO₄ solution. Immediately Cu²⁺ ions are reduced to metallic Cu in the form of a dark layer. Second beaker: In time, most of the Cu²⁺ ions are reduced and the solution becomes colorless. (b) First beaker: A piece of Cu wire is placed in a colorless AgNO₃ solution. Ag⁺ ions are reduced to metallic Ag. Second beaker: As time progresses, most of the Ag⁺ ions are reduced and the solution acquires the characteristic blue color due to the presence of hydrated Cu²⁺ ions.*

The Zn bar is in aqueous solution of CuSO₄

Cu²⁺ ions are converted to Cu atoms. Zn atoms enter the solution as Zn²⁺ ions.

(a)

When a piece of copper wire is placed in an aqueous AgNO₃ solution Cu atoms enter the solution as Cu²⁺ ions, and Ag⁺ ions are converted to solid Ag.

(b)

causing magnesium to be oxidized. Note that the extent of oxidation in a redox reaction must be equal to the extent of reduction; that is, the number of electrons lost by a reducing agent must be equal to the number of electrons gained by an oxidizing agent.

The occurrence of electron transfer is more apparent in some redox reactions than others. When metallic zinc is added to a solution containing copper(II) sulfate ($CuSO_4$), zinc reduces Cu^{2+} by donating two electrons to it:

$$Zn(s) + CuSO_4(aq) \longrightarrow ZnSO_4(aq) + Cu(s)$$

In the process the solution loses the blue color that characterizes the presence of hydrated Cu^{2+} ions (Figure 4.10):

$$Zn(s) + Cu^{2+}(aq) \longrightarrow Zn^{2+}(aq) + Cu(s)$$

The oxidation and reduction half-reactions are

$$Zn \longrightarrow Zn^{2+} + 2e^-$$
$$Cu^{2+} + 2e^- \longrightarrow Cu$$

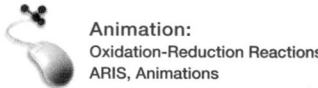

Animation:
Oxidation-Reduction Reactions
ARIS, Animations

Similarly, metallic copper reduces silver ions in a solution of silver nitrate ($AgNO_3$):

$$Cu(s) + 2AgNO_3(aq) \longrightarrow Cu(NO_3)_2(aq) + 2Ag(s)$$

or

$$Cu(s) + 2Ag^+(aq) \longrightarrow Cu^{2+}(aq) + 2Ag(s)$$

Oxidation Number

The definitions of oxidation and reduction in terms of loss and gain of electrons apply to the formation of ionic compounds such as MgO and the reduction of Cu^{2+} ions by Zn. However, these definitions do not accurately characterize the formation of hydrogen chloride (HCl) and sulfur dioxide (SO_2):

$$H_2(g) + Cl_2(g) \longrightarrow 2HCl(g)$$
$$S(s) + O_2(g) \longrightarrow SO_2(g)$$

Because HCl and SO_2 are not ionic but molecular compounds, no electrons are actually transferred in the formation of these compounds, as they are in the case of MgO. Nevertheless, chemists find it convenient to treat these reactions as redox reactions because experimental measurements show that there is a partial transfer of electrons (from H to Cl in HCl and from S to O in SO_2).

To keep track of electrons in redox reactions, it is useful to assign oxidation numbers to the reactants and products. An atom's **oxidation number,** also called **oxidation state,** signifies the *number of charges the atom would have in a molecule (or an ionic compound) if electrons were transferred completely.* For example, we can rewrite the above equations for the formation of HCl and SO_2 as follows:

$$\overset{0}{H_2}(g) + \overset{0}{Cl_2}(g) \longrightarrow \overset{+1-1}{2HCl}(g)$$
$$\overset{0}{S}(s) + \overset{0}{O_2}(g) \longrightarrow \overset{+4-2}{SO_2}(g)$$

The numbers above the element symbols are the oxidation numbers. In both of the reactions shown, there is no charge on the atoms in the reactant molecules. Thus, their oxidation number is zero. For the product molecules, however, it is assumed that complete electron transfer has taken place and that atoms have gained or lost electrons. The oxidation numbers reflect the number of electrons "transferred."

Oxidation numbers enable us to identify elements that are oxidized and reduced at a glance. The elements that show an increase in oxidation number—hydrogen and sulfur in the preceding examples—are oxidized. Chlorine and oxygen are reduced, so their oxidation numbers show a decrease from their initial values. Note that the sum of the oxidation numbers of H and Cl in HCl ($+1$ and -1) is zero. Likewise, if we add the charges on S ($+4$) and two atoms of O $[2 \times (-2)]$, the total is zero. The reason is that the HCl and SO_2 molecules are neutral, so the charges must cancel.

We use the following rules to assign oxidation numbers:

1. In free elements (that is, in the uncombined state), each atom has an oxidation number of zero. Thus, each atom in H_2, Br_2, Na, Be, K, O_2, and P_4 has the same oxidation number: zero.

2. For ions composed of only one atom (that is, monatomic ions), the oxidation number is equal to the charge on the ion. Thus, Li^+ ion has an oxidation number of $+1$; Ba^{2+} ion, $+2$; Fe^{3+} ion, $+3$; I^- ion, -1; O^{2-} ion, -2; and so on. All

alkali metals have an oxidation number of $+1$ and all alkaline earth metals have an oxidation number of $+2$ in their compounds. Aluminum has an oxidation number of $+3$ in all its compounds.

3. The oxidation number of oxygen in most compounds (for example, MgO and H_2O) is -2, but in hydrogen peroxide (H_2O_2) and peroxide ion (O_2^{2-}), it is -1.

4. The oxidation number of hydrogen is $+1$, except when it is bonded to metals in binary compounds. In these cases (for example, LiH, NaH, CaH_2), its oxidation number is -1.

5. Fluorine has an oxidation number of -1 in *all* its compounds. Other halogens (Cl, Br, and I) have negative oxidation numbers when they occur as halide ions in their compounds. When combined with oxygen—for example in oxoacids and oxoanions (see Section 2.7)—they have positive oxidation numbers.

6. In a neutral molecule, the sum of the oxidation numbers of all the atoms must be zero. In a polyatomic ion, the sum of oxidation numbers of all the elements in the ion must be equal to the net charge of the ion. For example, in the ammonium ion, NH_4^+, the oxidation number of N is -3 and that of H is $+1$. Thus the sum of the oxidation numbers is $-3 + 4(+1) = +1$, which is equal to the net charge of the ion.

7. Oxidation numbers do not have to be integers. For example, the oxidation number of O in the superoxide ion, O_2^-, is $-\frac{1}{2}$.

We apply the preceding rules to assign oxidation numbers in Example 4.4.

Example 4.4

Assign oxidation numbers to all the elements in the following compounds and ion: (a) Li_2O, (b) HNO_3, (c) $Cr_2O_7^{2-}$.

Strategy In general, we follow the rules just listed for assigning oxidation numbers. Remember that all alkali metals have an oxidation number of $+1$, and in most cases hydrogen has an oxidation number of $+1$ and oxygen has an oxidation number of -2 in their compounds.

Solution (a) By rule 2 we see that lithium has an oxidation number of $+1$ (Li^+) and oxygen's oxidation number is -2 (O^{2-}).

(b) This is the formula for nitric acid, which yields a H^+ ion and a NO_3^- ion in solution. From rule 4 we see that H has an oxidation number of $+1$. Thus the other group (the nitrate ion) must have a net oxidation number of -1. Oxygen has an oxidation number of -2, and if we use x to represent the oxidation number of nitrogen, then the nitrate ion can be written as

$$[N^{(x)}O_3^{(2-)}]^-$$

so that $$x + 3(-2) = -1$$

or $$x = +5$$

(c) From rule 6 we see that the sum of the oxidation numbers in the dichromate ion $Cr_2O_7^{2-}$ must be -2. We know that the oxidation number of O is -2, so all that remains is to determine the oxidation number of Cr, which we call y. The dichromate ion can be written as

$$[Cr_2^{(y)}O_7^{(2-)}]^{2-}$$

(Continued)

so that $2(y) + 7(-2) = -2$

or $y = +6$

Check In each case, does the sum of the oxidation numbers of all the atoms equal the net charge on the species?

Practice Exercise Assign oxidation numbers to all the elements in the following compound and ion: (a) PF_3, (b) MnO_4^-.

Similar problems: 4.47, 4.49.

Figure 4.11 shows the known oxidation numbers of the familiar elements, arranged according to their positions in the periodic table. We can summarize the content of this figure as follows:

- Metallic elements have only positive oxidation numbers, whereas nonmetallic elements may have either positive or negative oxidation numbers.

Figure 4.11 *The oxidation numbers of elements in their compounds. The more common oxidation numbers are in color.*

- The highest oxidation number an element in Groups 1A–7A can have is its group number. For example, the halogens are in Group 7A, so their highest possible oxidation number is $+7$.
- The transition metals (Groups 1B, 3B–8B) usually have several possible oxidation numbers.

Types of Redox Reactions

Among the most common oxidation-reduction reactions are combination, decomposition, combustion, and displacement reactions. A more involved type is called disproportionation reactions, which will also be discussed in this section.

Combination Reactions

A *combination reaction* is *a reaction in which two or more substances combine to form a single product.* Figure 4.12 shows some combination reactions. For example,

Not all combination reactions are redox in nature. The same holds for decomposition reactions.

$$\overset{0}{S}(s) + \overset{0}{O_2}(g) \longrightarrow \overset{+4\ -2}{SO_2}(g)$$

$$\overset{0}{2Al}(s) + \overset{0}{3Br_2}(l) \longrightarrow \overset{+3\ -1}{2AlBr_3}(s)$$

Decomposition Reactions

Decomposition reactions are the opposite of combination reactions. Specifically, a *decomposition reaction* is *the breakdown of a compound into two or more components* (Figure 4.13). For example,

$$\overset{+2\ -2}{2HgO}(s) \longrightarrow \overset{0}{2Hg}(l) + \overset{0}{O_2}(g)$$

$$\overset{+5\ -2}{2KClO_3}(s) \longrightarrow \overset{-1}{2KCl}(s) + \overset{0}{3O_2}(g)$$

$$\overset{+1\ -1}{2NaH}(s) \longrightarrow \overset{0}{2Na}(s) + \overset{0}{H_2}(g)$$

We show oxidation numbers only for elements that are oxidized or reduced.

(a) (b) (c)

Figure 4.12 *Some simple combination redox reactions. (a) Sulfur burning in air to form sulfur dioxide. (b) Sodium burning in chlorine to form sodium chloride. (c) Aluminum reacting with bromine to form aluminum bromide.*

Figure 4.13 *(a) On heating, mercury(II) oxide (HgO) decomposes to form mercury and oxygen. (b) Heating potassium chlorate (KClO₃) produces oxygen, which supports the combustion of the wood splint.*

(a)   (b)

Combustion Reactions

All combustion reactions are redox processes.

A ***combustion reaction*** is *a reaction in which a substance reacts with oxygen, usually with the release of heat and light to produce a flame.* The reactions between magnesium and sulfur with oxygen described earlier are combustion reactions. Another example is the burning of propane (C_3H_8), a component of natural gas that is used for domestic heating and cooking:

$$C_3H_8(g) + 5O_2(g) \longrightarrow 3CO_2(g) + 4H_2O(l)$$

Assigning an oxidation number to C atoms in organic compounds is more involved. Here, we focus only on the oxidation number of O atoms, which changes from 0 to -2.

Displacement Reactions

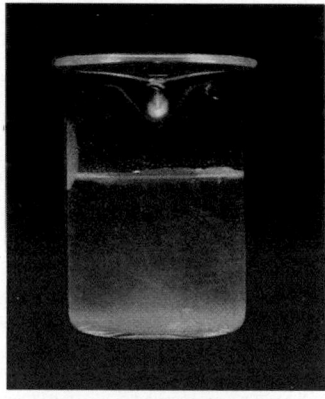

(a)

In a ***displacement reaction,*** *an ion (or atom) in a compound is replaced by an ion (or atom) of another element:* Most displacement reactions fit into one of three subcategories: hydrogen displacement, metal displacement, or halogen displacement.

1. Hydrogen Displacement. All alkali metals and some alkaline earth metals (Ca, Sr, and Ba), which are the most reactive of the metallic elements, will displace hydrogen from cold water (Figure 4.14):

$$\overset{0}{2Na}(s) + \overset{+1}{2H_2}O(l) \longrightarrow \overset{+1\ +1}{2NaOH}(aq) + \overset{0}{H_2}(g)$$

$$\overset{0}{Ca}(s) + \overset{+1}{2H_2}O(l) \longrightarrow \overset{+2\ +1}{Ca(OH)_2}(s) + \overset{0}{H_2}(g)$$

Many metals, including those that do not react with water, are capable of displacing hydrogen from acids. For example, zinc (Zn) and magnesium (Mg) do not react with cold water but do react with hydrochloric acid, as follows:

$$\overset{0}{Zn}(s) + \overset{+1}{2HCl}(aq) \longrightarrow \overset{+2}{ZnCl_2}(aq) + \overset{0}{H_2}(g)$$

$$\overset{0}{Mg}(s) + \overset{+1}{2HCl}(aq) \longrightarrow \overset{+2}{MgCl_2}(aq) + \overset{0}{H_2}(g)$$

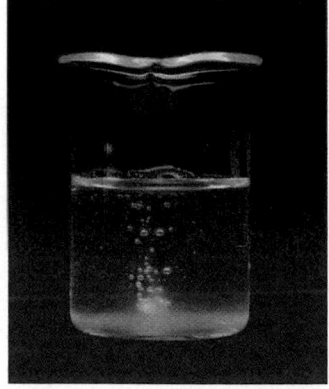

(b)

Figure 4.14 *Reactions of (a) sodium (Na) and (b) calcium (Ca) with cold water. Note that the reaction is more vigorous with Na than with Ca.*

Figure 4.15 shows the reactions between hydrochloric acid (HCl) and iron (Fe), zinc (Zn), and magnesium (Mg). These reactions are used to prepare hydrogen gas in the laboratory.

(a) (b) (c)

Figure 4.15 *Reactions of (a) iron (Fe), (b) zinc (Zn), and (c) magnesium (Mg) with hydrochloric acid to form hydrogen gas and the metal chlorides ($FeCl_2$, $ZnCl_2$, $MgCl_2$). The reactivity of these metals is reflected in the rate of hydrogen gas evolution, which is slowest for the least reactive metal, Fe, and fastest for the most reactive metal, Mg.*

2. Metal Displacement. A metal in a compound can be displaced by another metal in the elemental state. We have already seen examples of zinc replacing copper ions and copper replacing silver ions (see p. 133). Reversing the roles of the metals would result in no reaction. Thus, copper metal will not displace zinc ions from zinc sulfate, and silver metal will not displace copper ions from copper nitrate.

An easy way to predict whether a metal or hydrogen displacement reaction will actually occur is to refer to an *activity series* (sometimes called the *electrochemical series*), shown in Figure 4.16. Basically, an activity series is *a convenient summary of the results of many possible displacement reactions* similar to the ones already discussed. According to this series, any metal above hydrogen will displace it from water or from

Figure 4.16 *The activity series for metals. The metals are arranged according to their ability to displace hydrogen from an acid or water. Li (lithium) is the most reactive metal, and Au (gold) is the least reactive.*

Reducing strength increases →

$$Li \rightarrow Li^+ + e^-$$
$$K \rightarrow K^+ + e^-$$
$$Ba \rightarrow Ba^{2+} + 2e^-$$
$$Ca \rightarrow Ca^{2+} + 2e^-$$
$$Na \rightarrow Na^+ + e^-$$

React with cold water to produce H_2

$$Mg \rightarrow Mg^{2+} + 2e^-$$
$$Al \rightarrow Al^{3+} + 3e^-$$
$$Zn \rightarrow Zn^{2+} + 2e^-$$
$$Cr \rightarrow Cr^{3+} + 3e^-$$
$$Fe \rightarrow Fe^{2+} + 2e^-$$
$$Cd \rightarrow Cd^{2+} + 2e^-$$

React with steam to produce H_2

$$Co \rightarrow Co^{2+} + 2e^-$$
$$Ni \rightarrow Ni^{2+} + 2e^-$$
$$Sn \rightarrow Sn^{2+} + 2e^-$$
$$Pb \rightarrow Pb^{2+} + 2e^-$$
$$H_2 \rightarrow 2H^+ + 2e^-$$

React with acids to produce H_2

$$Cu \rightarrow Cu^{2+} + 2e^-$$
$$Ag \rightarrow Ag^+ + e^-$$
$$Hg \rightarrow Hg^{2+} + 2e^-$$
$$Pt \rightarrow Pt^{2+} + 2e^-$$
$$Au \rightarrow Au^{3+} + 3e^-$$

Do not react with water or acids to produce H_2

an acid, but metals below hydrogen will not react with either water or an acid. In fact, any metal listed in the series will react with any metal (in a compound) below it. For example, Zn is above Cu, so zinc metal will displace copper ions from copper sulfate.

Metal displacement reactions find many applications in metallurgical processes, the goal of which is to separate pure metals from their ores. For example, vanadium is obtained by treating vanadium(V) oxide with metallic calcium:

$$V_2O_5(s) + 5Ca(l) \longrightarrow 2V(l) + 5CaO(s)$$

Similarly, titanium is obtained from titanium(IV) chloride according to the reaction

$$TiCl_4(g) + 2Mg(l) \longrightarrow Ti(s) + 2MgCl_2(l)$$

In each case, the metal that acts as the reducing agent lies above the metal that is reduced (that is, Ca is above V and Mg is above Ti) in the activity series. We will see more examples of this type of reaction in Chapter 19.

The halogens.

3. Halogen Displacement. Another activity series summarizes the halogens' behavior in halogen displacement reactions:

$$F_2 > Cl_2 > Br_2 > I_2$$

The power of these elements as oxidizing agents decreases as we move down Group 7A from fluorine to iodine, so molecular fluorine can replace chloride, bromide, and iodide ions in solution. In fact, molecular fluorine is so reactive that it also attacks water; thus these reactions cannot be carried out in aqueous solutions. On the other hand, molecular chlorine can displace bromide and iodide ions in aqueous solution. The displacement equations are

$$\overset{0}{Cl_2}(g) + 2\overset{-1}{KBr}(aq) \longrightarrow 2\overset{-1}{KCl}(aq) + \overset{0}{Br_2}(l)$$
$$\overset{0}{Cl_2}(g) + 2\overset{-1}{NaI}(aq) \longrightarrow 2\overset{-1}{NaCl}(aq) + \overset{0}{I_2}(s)$$

The ionic equations are

$$\overset{0}{Cl_2}(g) + 2\overset{-1}{Br}(aq) \longrightarrow 2\overset{-1}{Cl^-}(aq) + \overset{0}{Br_2}(l)$$
$$\overset{0}{Cl_2}(g) + 2\overset{-1}{I^-}(aq) \longrightarrow 2\overset{-1}{Cl^-}(aq) + \overset{0}{I_2}(s)$$

Molecular bromine, in turn, can displace iodide ion in solution:

$$\overset{0}{Br_2}(l) + 2\overset{-1}{I^-}(aq) \longrightarrow 2\overset{-1}{Br^-}(aq) + \overset{0}{I_2}(s)$$

Reversing the roles of the halogens produces no reaction. Thus, bromine cannot displace chloride ions, and iodine cannot displace bromide and chloride ions.

The halogen displacement reactions have a direct industrial application. The halogens as a group are the most reactive of the nonmetallic elements. They are all strong oxidizing agents. As a result, they are found in nature in the combined state (with metals) as halides and never as free elements. Of these four elements, chlorine is by far the most important industrial chemical. In 2005 the amount of chlorine produced in the United States was about 25 billion pounds, making chlorine the tenth-ranking industrial chemical. The annual production of bromine is only one-hundredth that of chlorine, while the amounts of fluorine and iodine produced are even less.

Recovering the halogens from their halides requires an oxidation process, which is represented by

$$2X^- \longrightarrow X_2 + 2e^-$$

where X denotes a halogen element. Seawater and natural brine (for example, underground water in contact with salt deposits) are rich sources of Cl^-, Br^-, and I^- ions. Minerals such as fluorite (CaF_2) and cryolite (Na_3AlF_6) are used to prepare fluorine. Because fluorine is the strongest oxidizing agent known, there is no way to convert F^- ions to F_2 by chemical means. The only way to carry out the oxidation is by electrolytic means, the details of which will be discussed in Chapter 19. Industrially, chlorine, like fluorine, is produced electrolytically.

Bromine is prepared industrially by oxidizing Br^- ions with chlorine, which is a strong enough oxidizing agent to oxidize Br^- ions but not water:

$$2Br^-(aq) \longrightarrow Br_2(l) + 2e^-$$

One of the richest sources of Br^- ions is the Dead Sea—about 4000 parts per million (ppm) by mass of all dissolved substances in the Dead Sea is Br. Following the oxidation of Br^- ions, bromine is removed from the solution by blowing air over the solution, and the air-bromine mixture is then cooled to condense the bromine (Figure 4.17).

Iodine is also prepared from seawater and natural brine by the oxidation of I^- ions with chlorine. Because Br^- and I^- ions are invariably present in the same source, they are both oxidized by chlorine. However, it is relatively easy to separate Br_2 from I_2 because iodine is a solid that is sparingly soluble in water. The air-blowing procedure will remove most of the bromine formed but will not affect the iodine present.

Figure 4.17 *The industrial manufacture of liquid bromine by oxidizing an aqueous solution containing Br^- ions with chlorine gas.*

Bromine is a fuming red liquid.

Disproportionation Reaction

A special type of redox reaction is the disproportionation reaction. In a ***disproportionation reaction,*** *an element in one oxidation state is simultaneously oxidized and reduced.* One reactant in a disproportionation reaction *always* contains an element that can have at least three oxidation states. The element itself is in an intermediate oxidation state; that is, both higher and lower oxidation states exist for that element in the products. The decomposition of hydrogen peroxide is an example of a disproportionation reaction:

$$\overset{-1}{2H_2O_2}(aq) \longrightarrow \overset{-2}{2H_2O}(l) + \overset{0}{O_2}(g)$$

Here the oxidation number of oxygen in the reactant (-1) both increases to zero in O_2 and decreases to -2 in H_2O. Another example is the reaction between molecular chlorine and NaOH solution:

$$\overset{0}{Cl_2}(g) + 2OH^-(aq) \longrightarrow \overset{+1}{ClO^-}(aq) + \overset{-1}{Cl^-}(aq) + H_2O(l)$$

This reaction describes the formation of household bleaching agents, for it is the hypochlorite ion (ClO^-) that oxidizes the color-bearing substances in stains, converting them to colorless compounds.

Finally, it is interesting to compare redox reactions and acid-base reactions. They are analogous in that acid-base reactions involve the transfer of protons while redox reactions involve the transfer of electrons. However, while acid-base reactions are quite easy to recognize (because they always involve an acid and a base), there is no simple procedure for identifying a redox process. The only sure way is to compare the oxidation numbers of all the elements in the reactants and products. Any change in oxidation number *guarantees* that the reaction is redox in nature.

Elements that are most likely to undergo disproportionation.

Note that the oxidation number of H remains unchanged at +1.

The classification of different types of redox reactions is illustrated in Example 4.5.

Example 4.5

Classify the following redox reactions and indicate changes in the oxidation numbers of the elements:

(a) $2N_2O(g) \longrightarrow 2N_2(g) + O_2(g)$
(b) $6Li(s) + N_2(g) \longrightarrow 2Li_3N(s)$
(c) $Ni(s) + Pb(NO_3)_2(aq) \longrightarrow Pb(s) + Ni(NO_3)_2(aq)$
(d) $2NO_2(g) + H_2O(l) \longrightarrow HNO_2(aq) + HNO_3(aq)$

Strategy Review the definitions of combination reactions, decomposition reactions, displacement reactions, and disproportionation reactions.

Solution (a) This is a decomposition reaction because one reactant is converted to two different products. The oxidation number of N changes from $+1$ to 0, while that of O changes from -2 to 0.

(b) This is a combination reaction (two reactants form a single product). The oxidation number of Li changes from 0 to $+1$ while that of N changes from 0 to -3.

(c) This is a metal displacement reaction. The Ni metal replaces (reduces) the Pb^{2+} ion. The oxidation number of Ni increases from 0 to $+2$ while that of Pb decreases from $+2$ to 0.

(d) The oxidation number of N is $+4$ in NO_2 and it is $+3$ in HNO_2 and $+5$ in HNO_3. Because the oxidation number of the *same* element both increases and decreases, this is a disproportionation reaction.

Similar problems: 4.55, 4.56.

Practice Exercise Identify the following redox reactions by type:

(a) $Fe + H_2SO_4 \longrightarrow FeSO_4 + H_2$
(b) $S + 3F_2 \longrightarrow SF_6$
(c) $2CuCl \longrightarrow Cu + CuCl_2$
(d) $2Ag + PtCl_2 \longrightarrow 2AgCl + Pt$

The Chemistry in Action on p. 143 describes how law enforcement makes use of a redox reaction to apprehend drunk drivers.

4.5 Concentration of Solutions

To study solution stoichiometry, we must know how much of the reactants are present in a solution and also how to control the amounts of reactants used to bring about a reaction in aqueous solution.

The ***concentration of a solution*** is *the amount of solute present in a given quantity of solvent or solution.* (For this discussion, we will assume the solute is a liquid or a solid and the solvent is a liquid.) The concentration of a solution can be expressed in many different ways, as we will see in Chapter 12. Here we will consider one of the most commonly used units in chemistry, ***molarity (M),*** or ***molar concentration,*** which is *the number of moles of solute per liter of solution.* Molarity is defined as

$$\text{molarity} = \frac{\text{moles of solute}}{\text{liters of solution}} \tag{4.1}$$

CHEMISTRY
in Action

Breathalyzer

Every year in the United States about 25,000 people are killed and 500,000 more are injured as a result of drunk driving. In spite of efforts to educate the public about the dangers of driving while intoxicated and stiffer penalties for drunk driving offenses, law enforcement agencies still have to devote a great deal of work to removing drunk drivers from America's roads.

The police often use a device called a breathalyzer to test drivers suspected of being drunk. The chemical basis of this device is a redox reaction. A sample of the driver's breath is drawn into the breathalyzer, where it is treated with an acidic solution of potassium dichromate. The alcohol (ethanol) in the breath is converted to acetic acid as shown in the following equation:

$$3CH_3CH_2OH + 2K_2Cr_2O_7 + 8H_2SO_4 \longrightarrow$$

ethanol   potassium dichromate (orange yellow)   sulfuric acid

$$3CH_3COOH + 2Cr_2(SO_4)_3 + 2K_2SO_4 + 11H_2O$$

acetic acid   chromium(III) sulfate (green)   potassium sulfate

In this reaction, the ethanol is oxidized to acetic acid and the chromium(VI) in the orange-yellow dichromate ion is reduced to the green chromium(III) ion (see Figure 4.22). The driver's

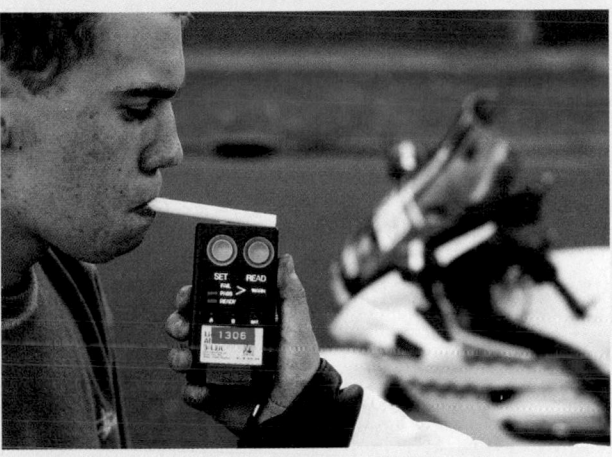

A driver being tested for blood alcohol content with a handheld breathalyzer.

blood alcohol level can be determined readily by measuring the degree of this color change (read from a calibrated meter on the instrument). The current legal limit of blood alcohol content in most states is 0.1 percent by mass. Anything higher constitutes intoxication.

Breath

Light source

$K_2Cr_2O_7$ solution

Filter

Photocell detector

Meter

Schematic diagram of a breathalyzer. The alcohol in the driver's breath is reacted with a potassium dichromate solution. The change in the absorption of light due to the formation of chromium(III) sulfate is registered by the detector and shown on a meter, which directly displays the alcohol content in blood. The filter selects only one wavelength of light for measurement.

Equation (4.1) can also be expressed algebraically as

$$M = \frac{n}{V} \qquad\qquad (4.2)$$

where n denotes the number of moles of solute and V is the volume of the solution in liters.

A 1.46 molar glucose ($C_6H_{12}O_6$) solution, written as 1.46 M $C_6H_{12}O_6$, contains 1.46 moles of the solute ($C_6H_{12}O_6$) in 1 L of the solution. Of course, we do not always work with solution volumes of 1 L. Thus, a 500-mL solution containing 0.730 mole of $C_6H_{12}O_6$ also has a concentration of 1.46 M:

$$\text{molarity} = \frac{0.730 \text{ mol } C_6H_{12}O_6}{500 \text{ mL soln}} \times \frac{1000 \text{ mL soln}}{1 \text{ L soln}} = 1.46 \; M \; C_6H_{12}O_6$$

Note that concentration, like density, is an intensive property, so its value does not depend on how much of the solution is present.

It is important to keep in mind that molarity refers only to the amount of solute originally dissolved in water and does not take into account any subsequent processes, such as the dissociation of a salt or the ionization of an acid. Consider what happens when a sample of potassium chloride (KCl) is dissolved in enough water to make a 1 M solution:

$$\text{KCl}(s) \xrightarrow{\text{H}_2\text{O}} \text{K}^+(aq) + \text{Cl}^-(aq)$$

Because KCl is a strong electrolyte, it undergoes complete dissociation in solution. Thus, a 1 M KCl solution contains 1 mole of K^+ ions and 1 mole of Cl^- ions, and no KCl units are present. The concentrations of the ions can be expressed as $[K^+] = 1 \; M$ and $[Cl^-] = 1 \; M$, where the square brackets [ ] indicate that the concentration is expressed in molarity. Similarly, in a 1 M barium nitrate $[Ba(NO_3)_2]$ solution

$$\text{Ba(NO}_3)_2(s) \xrightarrow{\text{H}_2\text{O}} \text{Ba}^{2+}(aq) + 2\text{NO}_3^-(aq)$$

we have $[Ba^{2+}] = 1 \; M$ and $[NO_3^-] = 2 \; M$ and no $Ba(NO_3)_2$ units at all.

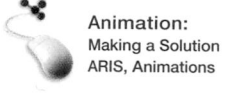

Animation:
Making a Solution
ARIS, Animations

The procedure for preparing a solution of known molarity is as follows. First, the solute is accurately weighed and transferred to a volumetric flask through a funnel (Figure 4.18). Next, water is added to the flask, which is carefully swirled to dissolve the solid. After *all* the solid has dissolved, more water is added slowly to bring the level of solution exactly to the volume mark. Knowing the volume of the solution in the flask and the quantity of compound (the number of moles) dissolved, we can calculate the molarity of the solution using Equation (4.1). Note that this procedure does not require knowing the amount of water added, as long as the volume of the final solution is known.

Examples 4.6 and 4.7 illustrate the applications of Equations (4.1) and (4.2).

A $K_2Cr_2O_7$ solution.

Example 4.6

How many grams of potassium dichromate ($K_2Cr_2O_7$) are required to prepare a 250-mL solution whose concentration is 2.16 M?

Strategy How many moles of $K_2Cr_2O_7$ does a 1-L (or 1000 mL) 2.16 M $K_2Cr_2O_7$ solution contain? A 250-mL solution? How would you convert moles to grams?

Solution The first step is to determine the number of moles of $K_2Cr_2O_7$ in 250 mL or 0.250 L of a 2.16 M solution. Rearranging Equation (4.1) gives

$$\text{moles of solute} = \text{molarity} \times \text{L soln}$$

(Continued)

Figure 4.18 *Preparing a solution of known molarity. (a) A known amount of a solid solute is transferred into the volumetric flask; then water is added through a funnel. (b) The solid is slowly dissolved by gently swirling the flask. (c) After the solid has completely dissolved, more water is added to bring the level of solution to the mark. Knowing the volume of the solution and the amount of solute dissolved in it, we can calculate the molarity of the prepared solution.*

(a)   (b)   (c)

Thus,

$$\text{moles of } K_2Cr_2O_7 = \frac{2.16 \text{ mol } K_2Cr_2O_7}{1 \text{ L soln}} \times 0.250 \text{ L soln}$$
$$= 0.540 \text{ mol } K_2Cr_2O_7$$

The molar mass of $K_2Cr_2O_7$ is 294.2 g, so we write

$$\text{grams of } K_2Cr_2O_7 \text{ needed} = 0.540 \text{ mol } K_2Cr_2O_7 \times \frac{294.2 \text{ g } K_2Cr_2O_7}{1 \text{ mol } K_2Cr_2O_7}$$
$$= 159 \text{ g } K_2Cr_2O_7$$

Check As a ball-park estimate, the mass should be given by [molarity (mol/L) × volume (L) × molar mass (g/mol)] or [2 mol/L × 0.25 L × 300 g/mol] = 150 g. So the answer is reasonable.

Practice Exercise What is the molarity of an 85.0-mL ethanol (C_2H_5OH) solution containing 1.77 g of ethanol?

Similar problems: 4.62, 4.63.

Example 4.7

In a biochemical essay, a chemist needs to add 3.81 g of glucose to a reaction mixture. Calculate the volume in milliliters of a 2.53 *M* glucose solution she should use for the addition.

Strategy We must first determine the number of moles contained in 3.81 g of glucose and then use Equation (4.2) to calculate the volume.

(Continued)

Note that we have carried an additional digit past the number of significant figures for the intermediate step.

Solution From the molar mass of glucose, we write

$$3.81 \text{ g C}_6\text{H}_{12}\text{O}_6 \times \frac{1 \text{ mol C}_6\text{H}_{12}\text{O}_6}{180.2 \text{ g C}_6\text{H}_{12}\text{O}_6} = 2.114 \times 10^{-2} \text{ mol C}_6\text{H}_{12}\text{O}_6$$

Next, we calculate the volume of the solution that contains 2.114×10^{-2} mole of the solute. Rearranging Equation (4.2) gives

$$V = \frac{n}{M}$$

$$= \frac{2.114 \times 10^{-2} \text{ mol C}_6\text{H}_{12}\text{O}_6}{2.53 \text{ mol C}_6\text{H}_{12}\text{O}_6/\text{L soln}} \times \frac{1000 \text{ mL soln}}{1 \text{ L soln}}$$

$$= 8.36 \text{ mL soln}$$

Check One liter of the solution contains 2.53 moles of $C_6H_{12}O_6$. Therefore, the number of moles in 8.36 mL or 8.36×10^{-3} L is $(2.53 \text{ mol} \times 8.36 \times 10^{-3})$ or 2.12×10^{-2} mol. The small difference is due to the different ways of rounding off.

Similar problem: 4.65.

Practice Exercise What volume (in milliliters) of a 0.315 *M* NaOH solution contains 6.22 g of NaOH?

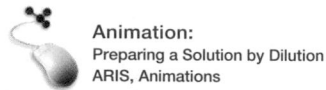

Animation:
Preparing a Solution by Dilution
ARIS, Animations

Two KMnO₄ solutions of different concentrations.

Dilution of Solutions

Concentrated solutions are often stored in the laboratory stockroom for use as needed. Frequently we dilute these "stock" solutions before working with them. *Dilution* is *the procedure for preparing a less concentrated solution from a more concentrated one.*

Suppose that we want to prepare 1 L of a 0.400 *M* KMnO₄ solution from a solution of 1.00 *M* KMnO₄. For this purpose we need 0.400 mole of KMnO₄. Because there is 1.00 mole of KMnO₄ in 1 L of a 1.00 *M* KMnO₄ solution, there is 0.400 mole of KMnO₄ in 0.400 L of the same solution:

$$\frac{1.00 \text{ mol}}{1 \text{ L soln}} = \frac{0.400 \text{ mol}}{0.400 \text{ L soln}}$$

Therefore, we must withdraw 400 mL from the 1.00 *M* KMnO₄ solution and dilute it to 1000 mL by adding water (in a 1-L volumetric flask). This method gives us 1 L of the desired solution of 0.400 *M* KMnO₄.

In carrying out a dilution process, it is useful to remember that adding more solvent to a given amount of the stock solution changes (decreases) the concentration of the solution without changing the number of moles of solute present in the solution (Figure 4.19). In other words,

moles of solute before dilution = moles of solute after dilution

Molarity is defined as moles of solute in one liter of solution, so the number of moles of solute is given by [see Equation (4.2)]

$$\underbrace{\frac{\text{moles of solute}}{\text{liters of soln}}}_{M} \times \underbrace{\text{volume of soln (in liters)}}_{V} = \underbrace{\text{moles of solute}}_{n}$$

(a)   (b)

Figure 4.19 *The dilution of a more concentrated solution (a) to a less concentrated one (b) does not change the total number of solute particles (18).*

or

$$MV = n$$

Because all the solute comes from the original stock solution, we can conclude that n remains the same; that is,

$$\underset{\substack{\text{moles of solute} \\ \text{before dilution}}}{M_i V_i} = \underset{\substack{\text{moles of solute} \\ \text{after dilution}}}{M_f V_f} \qquad (4.3)$$

where M_i and M_f are the initial and final concentrations of the solution in molarity and V_i and V_f are the initial and final volumes of the solution, respectively. Of course, the units of V_i and V_f must be the same (mL or L) for the calculation to work. To check the reasonableness of your results, be sure that $M_i > M_f$ and $V_f > V_i$.

We apply Equation (4.3) in Example 4.8.

Example 4.8

Describe how you would prepare 5.00×10^2 mL of a 1.75 M H_2SO_4 solution, starting with an 8.61 M stock solution of H_2SO_4.

Strategy Because the concentration of the final solution is less than that of the original one, this is a dilution process. Keep in mind that in dilution, the concentration of the solution decreases but the number of moles of the solute remains the same.

Solution We prepare for the calculation by tabulating our data:

$$M_i = 8.61\,M \qquad M_f = 1.75\,M$$
$$V_i = ? \qquad V_f = 5.00 \times 10^2\,\text{mL}$$

Substituting in Equation (4.3),

$$(8.61\,M)(V_i) = (1.75\,M)(5.00 \times 10^2\,\text{mL})$$
$$V_i = \frac{(1.75\,M)(5.00 \times 10^2\,\text{mL})}{8.61\,M}$$
$$= 102\,\text{mL}$$

Thus, we must dilute 102 mL of the 8.61 M H_2SO_4 solution with sufficient water to give a final volume of 5.00×10^2 mL in a 500-mL volumetric flask to obtain the desired concentration.

(Continued)

Similar problems: 4.71, 4.72.

Check The initial volume is less than the final volume, so the answer is reasonable.

Practice Exercise How would you prepare 2.00×10^2 mL of a 0.866 *M* NaOH solution, starting with a 5.07 *M* stock solution?

Now that we have discussed the concentration and dilution of solutions, we can examine the quantitative aspects of reactions in aqueous solution, or *solution stoichiometry*. Sections 4.6–4.8 focus on two techniques for studying solution stoichiometry: gravimetric analysis and titration. These techniques are important tools of *quantitative analysis*, which is *the determination of the amount or concentration of a substance in a sample.*

4.6 Gravimetric Analysis

Gravimetric analysis is *an analytical technique based on the measurement of mass.* One type of gravimetric analysis experiment involves the formation, isolation, and mass determination of a precipitate. Generally, this procedure is applied to ionic compounds. First, a sample substance of unknown composition is dissolved in water and allowed to react with another substance to form a precipitate. Then the precipitate is filtered off, dried, and weighed. Knowing the mass and chemical formula of the precipitate formed, we can calculate the mass of a particular chemical component (that is, the anion or cation) of the original sample. Finally, from the mass of the component and the mass of the original sample, we can determine the percent composition by mass of the component in the original compound.

A reaction that is often studied in gravimetric analysis, because the reactants can be obtained in pure form, is

$$AgNO_3(aq) + NaCl(aq) \longrightarrow NaNO_3(aq) + AgCl(s)$$

The net ionic equation is

$$Ag^+(aq) + Cl^-(aq) \longrightarrow AgCl(s)$$

This procedure would enable us to determine the purity of the NaCl sample.

The precipitate is silver chloride (see Table 4.2). As an example, let us say that we wanted to determine *experimentally* the percent by mass of Cl in NaCl. First, we would accurately weigh out a sample of NaCl and dissolve it in water. Next, we would add enough $AgNO_3$ solution to the NaCl solution to cause the precipitation of all the Cl^- ions present in solution as AgCl. In this procedure, NaCl is the limiting reagent and $AgNO_3$ the excess reagent. The AgCl precipitate is separated from the solution by filtration, dried, and weighed. From the measured mass of AgCl, we can calculate the mass of Cl using the percent by mass of Cl in AgCl. Because this same amount of Cl was present in the original NaCl sample, we can calculate the percent by mass of Cl in NaCl. Figure 4.20 shows how this procedure is performed.

Gravimetric analysis is a highly accurate technique, because the mass of a sample can be measured accurately. However, this procedure is applicable only to reactions that go to completion, or have nearly 100 percent yield. Thus, if AgCl were slightly soluble instead of being insoluble, it would not be possible to remove all the Cl^- ions from the NaCl solution and the subsequent calculation would be in error.

Example 4.9 shows the calculations involved in a gravimetric experiment.

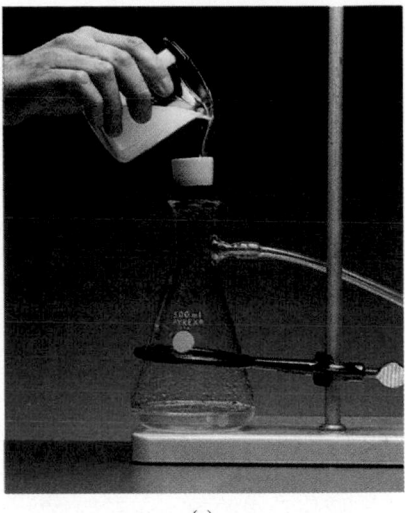

(a) (b) (c)

Figure 4.20 *Basic steps for gravimetric analysis. (a) A solution containing a known amount of NaCl in a beaker. (b) The precipitation of AgCl upon the addition of AgNO₃ solution from a measuring cylinder. In this reaction, AgNO₃ is the excess reagent and NaCl is the limiting reagent. (c) The solution containing the AgCl precipitate is filtered through a preweighed sintered disk crucible, which allows the liquid (but not the precipitate) to pass through. The crucible is then removed from the apparatus, dried in an oven, and weighed again. The difference between this mass and that of the empty crucible gives the mass of the AgCl precipitate.*

Example 4.9

A 0.5662-g sample of an ionic compound containing chloride ions and an unknown metal is dissolved in water and treated with an excess of AgNO₃. If 1.0882 g of AgCl precipitate forms, what is the percent by mass of Cl in the original compound?

Strategy We are asked to calculate the percent by mass of Cl in the unknown sample, which is

$$\%Cl = \frac{\text{mass of Cl}}{0.5662 \text{ g sample}} \times 100\%$$

The only source of Cl⁻ ions is the original compound. These chloride ions eventually end up in the AgCl precipitate. Can we calculate the mass of the Cl⁻ ions if we know the percent by mass of Cl in AgCl?

Solution The molar masses of Cl and AgCl are 35.45 g and 143.4 g, respectively. Therefore, the percent by mass of Cl in AgCl is given by

$$\%Cl = \frac{35.45 \text{ g Cl}}{143.4 \text{ g AgCl}} \times 100\%$$
$$= 24.72\%$$

Next, we calculate the mass of Cl in 1.0882 g of AgCl. To do so we convert 24.72 percent to 0.2472 and write

$$\text{mass of Cl} = 0.2472 \times 1.0882 \text{ g}$$
$$= 0.2690 \text{ g}$$

(Continued)

Because the original compound also contained this amount of Cl^- ions, the percent by mass of Cl in the compound is

$$\%Cl = \frac{0.2690 \text{ g}}{0.5662 \text{ g}} \times 100\%$$

$$= 47.51\%$$

Similar problem: 4.78.

Practice Exercise A sample of 0.3220 g of an ionic compound containing the bromide ion (Br^-) is dissolved in water and treated with an excess of $AgNO_3$. If the mass of the AgBr precipitate that forms is 0.6964 g, what is the percent by mass of Br in the original compound?

Note that gravimetric analysis does not establish the whole identity of the unknown. Thus, in Example 4.9 we still do not know what the cation is. However, knowing the percent by mass of Cl greatly helps us to narrow the possibilities. Because no two compounds containing the same anion (or cation) have the same percent composition by mass, comparison of the percent by mass obtained from gravimetric analysis with that calculated from a series of known compounds would reveal the identity of the unknown.

4.7 Acid-Base Titrations

Quantitative studies of acid-base neutralization reactions are most conveniently carried out using a technique known as titration. In *titration, a solution of accurately known concentration,* called a ***standard solution,*** *is added gradually to another solution of unknown concentration, until the chemical reaction between the two solutions is complete.* If we know the volumes of the standard and unknown solutions used in the titration, along with the concentration of the standard solution, we can calculate the concentration of the unknown solution.

Sodium hydroxide is one of the bases commonly used in the laboratory. However, it is difficult to obtain solid sodium hydroxide in a pure form because it has a tendency to absorb water from air, and its solution reacts with carbon dioxide. For these reasons, a solution of sodium hydroxide must be *standardized* before it can be used in accurate analytical work. We can standardize the sodium hydroxide solution by titrating it against an acid solution of accurately known concentration. The acid often chosen for this task is a monoprotic acid called potassium hydrogen phthalate (KHP), for which the molecular formula is $KHC_8H_4O_4$. KHP is a white, soluble solid that is commercially available in highly pure form. The reaction between KHP and sodium hydroxide is

Potassium hydrogen phthalate.

KHP is a weak acid.

$$KHC_8H_4O_4(aq) + NaOH(aq) \longrightarrow KNaC_8H_4O_4(aq) + H_2O(l)$$

and the net ionic equation is

$$HC_8H_4O_4^-(aq) + OH^-(aq) \longrightarrow C_8H_4O_4^{2-}(aq) + H_2O(l)$$

The procedure for the titration is shown in Figure 4.21. First, a known amount of KHP is transferred to an Erlenmeyer flask and some distilled water is added to make up a solution. Next, NaOH solution is carefully added to the KHP solution from a buret until we reach the ***equivalence point,*** that is, *the point at which the acid has completely reacted with or been neutralized by the base.* The equivalence point is

(a)   (b)

Figure 4.21 *(a) Apparatus for acid-base titration. A NaOH solution is added from the buret to a KHP solution in an Erlenmeyer flask. (b) A reddish-pink color appears when the equivalence point is reached. The color here has been intensified for visual display.*

usually signaled by a sharp change in the color of an indicator in the acid solution. In acid-base titrations, ***indicators*** are *substances that have distinctly different colors in acidic and basic media.* One commonly used indicator is phenolphthalein, which is colorless in acidic and neutral solutions but reddish pink in basic solutions. At the equivalence point, all the KHP present has been neutralized by the added NaOH and the solution is still colorless. However, if we add just one more drop of NaOH solution from the buret, the solution will immediately turn pink because the solution is now basic. Example 4.10 illustrates such a titration.

Example 4.10

In a titration experiment, a student finds that 23.48 mL of a NaOH solution are needed to neutralize 0.5468 g of KHP. What is the concentration (in molarity) of the NaOH solution?

Strategy We want to determine the molarity of the NaOH solution. What is the definition of molarity?

$$\text{molarity of NaOH} = \frac{\text{mol NaOH}}{\text{L soln}}$$

need to find

want to calculate

given

The volume of NaOH solution is given in the problem. Therefore, we need to find the number of moles of NaOH to solve for molarity. From the preceding equation for the reaction between KHP and NaOH shown in the text we see that 1 mole of KHP neutralizes 1 mole of NaOH. How many moles of KHP are contained in 0.5468 g of KHP?

(Continued)

Solution First we calculate the number of moles of KHP consumed in the titration:

$$\text{moles of KHP} = 0.5468 \text{ g KHP} \times \frac{1 \text{ mol KHP}}{204.2 \text{ g KHP}}$$

$$= 2.678 \times 10^{-3} \text{ mol KHP}$$

Because 1 mol KHP $\simeq$ 1 mol NaOH, there must be 2.678×10^{-3} mole of NaOH in 23.48 mL of NaOH solution. Finally, we calculate the number of moles of NaOH in 1 L of the solution or the molarity as follows:

$$\text{molarity of NaOH soln} = \frac{2.678 \times 10^{-3} \text{ mol NaOH}}{23.48 \text{ mL soln}} \times \frac{1000 \text{ mL soln}}{1 \text{ L soln}}$$

$$= 0.1141 \text{ mol NaOH/1 L soln} = 0.1141 \; M$$

Similar problems: 4.85, 4.86.

Practice Exercise How many grams of KHP are needed to neutralize 18.64 mL of a 0.1004 M NaOH solution?

The neutralization reaction between NaOH and KHP is one of the simplest types of acid-base neutralization known. Suppose, though, that instead of KHP, we wanted to use a diprotic acid such as H_2SO_4 for the titration. The reaction is represented by

$$2NaOH(aq) + H_2SO_4(aq) \longrightarrow Na_2SO_4(aq) + 2H_2O(l)$$

Because 2 mol NaOH $\simeq$ 1 mol H_2SO_4, we need twice as much NaOH to react completely with a H_2SO_4 solution of the *same* molar concentration and volume as a monoprotic acid like HCl. On the other hand, we would need twice the amount of HCl to neutralize a $Ba(OH)_2$ solution compared to a NaOH solution having the same concentration and volume because 1 mole of $Ba(OH)_2$ yields 2 moles of OH^- ions:

$$2HCl(aq) + Ba(OH)_2(aq) \longrightarrow BaCl_2(aq) + 2H_2O(l)$$

In calculations involving acid-base titrations, regardless of the acid or base that takes place in the reaction, keep in mind that the total number of moles of H^+ ions that have reacted at the equivalence point must be equal to the total number of moles of OH^- ions that have reacted.

Example 4.11 shows the titration of a NaOH solution with a diprotic acid.

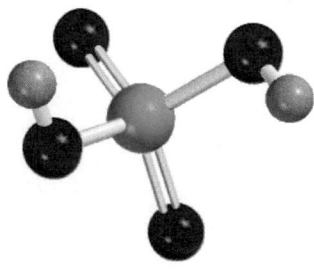

H_2SO_4 has two ionizable protons.

Example 4.11

How many milliliters (mL) of a 0.610 M NaOH solution are needed to neutralize 20.0 mL of a 0.245 M H_2SO_4 solution?

Strategy We want to calculate the volume of the NaOH solution. From the definition of molarity [see Equation (4.1)], we write

need to find

$$\text{L soln} = \frac{\text{mol NaOH}}{\text{molarity}}$$

want to calculate

given

(Continued)

From the equation for the neutralization reaction just shown, we see that 1 mole of H_2SO_4 neutralizes 2 moles of NaOH. How many moles of H_2SO_4 are contained in 20.0 mL of a 0.245 M H_2SO_4 solution? How many moles of NaOH would this quantity of H_2SO_4 neutralize?

Solution First we calculate the number of moles of H_2SO_4 in a 20.0 mL solution:

$$\text{moles } H_2SO_4 = \frac{0.245 \text{ mol } H_2SO_4}{1000 \text{ mL soln}} \times 20.0 \text{ mL soln}$$
$$= 4.90 \times 10^{-3} \text{ mol } H_2SO_4$$

From the stoichiometry we see that 1 mol $H_2SO_4 \cong$ 2 mol NaOH. Therefore, the number of moles of NaOH reacted must be $2 \times 4.90 \times 10^{-3}$ mole, or 9.80×10^{-3} mole. From the definition of molarity [see Equation (4.1)], we have

$$\text{liters of soln} = \frac{\text{moles of solute}}{\text{molarity}}$$

or

$$\text{volume of NaOH} = \frac{9.80 \times 10^{-3} \text{ mol NaOH}}{0.610 \text{ mol/L soln}}$$
$$= 0.0161 \text{ L or } 16.1 \text{ mL}$$

Similar problem: 4.87(b), (c).

Practice Exercise How many milliliters of a 1.28 M H_2SO_4 solution are needed to neutralize 60.2 mL of a 0.427 M KOH solution?

4.8 Redox Titrations

As mentioned earlier, redox reactions involve the transfer of electrons, and acid-base reactions involve the transfer of protons. Just as an acid can be titrated against a base, we can titrate an oxidizing agent against a reducing agent, using a similar procedure. We can, for example, carefully add a solution containing an oxidizing agent to a solution containing a reducing agent. The *equivalence point* is reached when the reducing agent is completely oxidized by the oxidizing agent.

Like acid-base titrations, redox titrations normally require an indicator that clearly changes color. In the presence of large amounts of reducing agent, the color of the indicator is characteristic of its reduced form. The indicator assumes the color of its oxidized form when it is present in an oxidizing medium. At or near the equivalence point, a sharp change in the indicator's color will occur as it changes from one form to the other, so the equivalence point can be readily identified.

There are not as many redox indicators as there are acid-base indicators.

Two common oxidizing agents are potassium permanganate ($KMnO_4$) and potassium dichromate ($K_2Cr_2O_7$). As Figure 4.22 shows, the colors of the permanganate and dichromate anions are distinctly different from those of the reduced species:

$$MnO_4^- \longrightarrow Mn^{2+}$$
purple   light
            pink

$$Cr_2O_7^{2-} \longrightarrow Cr^{3+}$$
orange   green
yellow

Figure 4.22 *Left to right: Solutions containing the MnO_4^-, Mn^{2+}, $Cr_2O_7^{2-}$, and Cr^{3+} ions.*

Thus, these oxidizing agents can themselves be used as *internal* indicator in a redox titration because they have distinctly different colors in the oxidized and reduced forms.

Redox titrations require the same type of calculations (based on the mole method) as acid-base neutralizations. The difference is that the equations and the stoichiometry tend to be more complex for redox reactions. The following is an example of a redox titration.

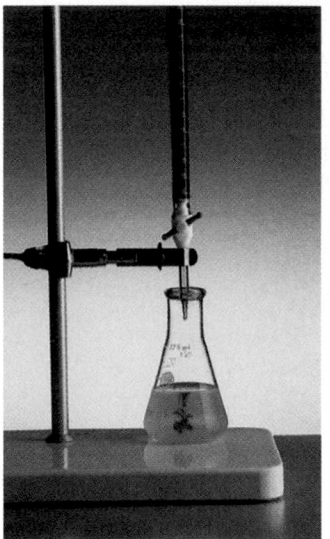

Addition of a $KMnO_4$ solution from a buret to a $FeSO_4$ solution.

Example 4.12

A 16.42-mL volume of 0.1327 *M* $KMnO_4$ solution is needed to oxidize 25.00 mL of a $FeSO_4$ solution in an acidic medium. What is the concentration of the $FeSO_4$ solution in molarity? The net ionic equation is

$$5Fe^{2+} + MnO_4^- + 8H^+ \longrightarrow Mn^{2+} + 5Fe^{3+} + 4H_2O$$

Strategy We want to calculate the molarity of the $FeSO_4$ solution. From the definition of molarity

$$\underset{\text{want to calculate}}{\text{molarity of } FeSO_4} = \frac{\overset{\text{need to find}}{\text{mol } FeSO_4}}{\underset{\text{given}}{\text{L soln}}}$$

The volume of the $FeSO_4$ solution is given in the problem. Therefore, we need to find the number of moles of $FeSO_4$ to solve for the molarity. From the net ionic equation, what is the stoichiometric equivalence between Fe^{2+} and MnO_4^-? How many moles of $KMnO_4$ are contained in 16.42 mL of 0.1327 *M* $KMnO_4$ solution?

Solution The number of moles of $KMnO_4$ in 16.42 mL of the solution is

$$\text{moles of } KMnO_4 = \frac{0.1327 \text{ mol } KMnO_4}{1000 \text{ mL soln}} \times 16.42 \text{ mL}$$
$$= 2.179 \times 10^{-3} \text{ mol } KMnO_4$$

From the net ionic equation we see that 5 mol $Fe^{2+} \simeq 1$ mol MnO_4^-. Therefore, the number of moles of $FeSO_4$ oxidized is

$$\text{moles } FeSO_4 = 2.179 \times 10^{-3} \text{ mol } KMnO_4 \times \frac{5 \text{ mol } FeSO_4}{1 \text{ mol } KMnO_4}$$
$$= 1.090 \times 10^{-2} \text{ mol } FeSO_4$$

(Continued)

CHEMISTRY
in Action

Metal from the Sea

Magnesium is a valuable, lightweight metal used as a structural material as well as in alloys, in batteries, and in chemical synthesis. Although magnesium is plentiful in Earth's crust, it is cheaper to "mine" the metal from seawater. Magnesium forms the second most abundant cation in the sea (after sodium); there are about 1.3 g of magnesium in a kilogram of seawater. The process for obtaining magnesium from seawater employs all three types of reactions discussed in this chapter: precipitation, acid-base, and redox reactions.

In the first stage in the recovery of magnesium, limestone ($CaCO_3$) is heated at high temperatures to produce quicklime, or calcium oxide (CaO):

$$CaCO_3(s) \longrightarrow CaO(s) + CO_2(g)$$

When calcium oxide is treated with seawater, it forms calcium hydroxide [$Ca(OH)_2$], which is slightly soluble and ionizes to give Ca^{2+} and OH^- ions:

$$CaO(s) + H_2O(l) \longrightarrow Ca^{2+}(aq) + 2OH^-(aq)$$

The surplus hydroxide ions cause the much less soluble magnesium hydroxide to precipitate:

$$Mg^{2+}(aq) + 2OH^-(aq) \longrightarrow Mg(OH)_2(s)$$

The solid magnesium hydroxide is filtered and reacted with hydrochloric acid to form magnesium chloride ($MgCl_2$):

$$Mg(OH)_2(s) + 2HCl(aq) \longrightarrow MgCl_2(aq) + 2H_2O(l)$$

After the water is evaporated, the solid magnesium chloride is melted in a steel cell. The molten magnesium chloride contains both Mg^{2+} and Cl^- ions. In a process called *electrolysis*, an

Magnesium hydroxide is obtained from seawater in settling ponds at the Dow Chemical Company in Freeport, Texas.

electric current is passed through the cell to reduce the Mg^{2+} ions and oxidize the Cl^- ions. The half-reactions are

$$Mg^{2+} + 2e^- \longrightarrow Mg$$
$$2Cl^- \longrightarrow Cl_2 + 2e^-$$

The overall reaction is

$$MgCl_2(l) \longrightarrow Mg(l) + Cl_2(g)$$

This is how magnesium metal is produced. The chlorine gas generated can be converted to hydrochloric acid and recycled through the process.

The concentration of the $FeSO_4$ solution in moles of $FeSO_4$ per liter of solution is

$$\text{molarity of } FeSO_4 = \frac{\text{mol } FeSO_4}{\text{L soln}}$$

$$= \frac{1.090 \times 10^{-2} \text{ mol } FeSO_4}{25.00 \text{ mL soln}} \times \frac{1000 \text{ mL soln}}{1 \text{ L soln}}$$

$$= 0.4360 \, M$$

Similar problems: 4.91, 4.92.

Practice Exercise How many milliliters of a 0.206 *M* HI solution are needed to reduce 22.5 mL of a 0.374 *M* $KMnO_4$ solution according to the following equation:

$$10HI + 2KMnO_4 + 3H_2SO_4 \longrightarrow 5I_2 + 2MnSO_4 + K_2SO_4 + 8H_2O$$

The Chemistry in Action above describes an industrial process that involves the types of reactions discussed in this chapter.

Summary of Facts and Concepts

1. Aqueous solutions are electrically conducting if the solutes are electrolytes. If the solutes are nonelectrolytes, the solutions do not conduct electricity.
2. Three major categories of chemical reactions that take place in aqueous solution are precipitation reactions, acid-base reactions, and oxidation-reduction reactions.
3. From general rules about solubilities of ionic compounds, we can predict whether a precipitate will form in a reaction.
4. Arrhenius acids ionize in water to give H^+ ions, and Arrhenius bases ionize in water to give OH^- ions. Brønsted acids donate protons, and Brønsted bases accept protons.
5. The reaction of an acid and a base is called neutralization.
6. In redox reactions, oxidation and reduction always occur simultaneously. Oxidation is characterized by the loss of electrons, reduction by the gain of electrons.
7. Oxidation numbers help us keep track of charge distribution and are assigned to all atoms in a compound or ion according to specific rules. Oxidation can be defined as an increase in oxidation number; reduction can be defined as a decrease in oxidation number.
8. Many redox reactions can be subclassified as combination, decomposition, combustion, displacement, or disproportionation reactions.
9. The concentration of a solution is the amount of solute present in a given amount of solution. Molarity expresses concentration as the number of moles of solute in 1 L of solution.
10. Adding a solvent to a solution, a process known as dilution, decreases the concentration (molarity) of the solution without changing the total number of moles of solute present in the solution.
11. Gravimetric analysis is a technique for determining the identity of a compound and/or the concentration of a solution by measuring mass. Gravimetric experiments often involve precipitation reactions.
12. In acid-base titration, a solution of known concentration (say, a base) is added gradually to a solution of unknown concentration (say, an acid) with the goal of determining the unknown concentration. The point at which the reaction in the titration is complete, as shown by the change in the indicator's color, is called the equivalence point.
13. Redox titrations are similar to acid-base titrations. The point at which the oxidation-reduction reaction is complete is called the equivalence point.

Key Words

Questions and Problems

Properties of Aqueous Solutions
Review Questions

4.1 Define solute, solvent, and solution by describing the process of dissolving a solid in a liquid.

4.2 What is the difference between a nonelectrolyte and an electrolyte? Between a weak electrolyte and a strong electrolyte?

4.3 Describe hydration. What properties of water enable its molecules to interact with ions in solution?

4.4 What is the difference between the following symbols in chemical equations: $\longrightarrow$ and $\rightleftharpoons$?

4.5 Water is an extremely weak electrolyte and therefore cannot conduct electricity. Why are we often cautioned not to operate electrical appliances when our hands are wet?

4.6 Lithium fluoride (LiF) is a strong electrolyte. What species are present in LiF(aq)?

Problems

4.7 The aqueous solutions of three compounds are shown in the diagram. Identify each compound as a nonelectrolyte, a weak electrolyte, and a strong electrolyte.

(a)   (b)   (c)

4.8 Which of the following diagrams best represents the hydration of NaCl when dissolved in water? The Cl$^-$ ion is larger in size than the Na$^+$ ion.

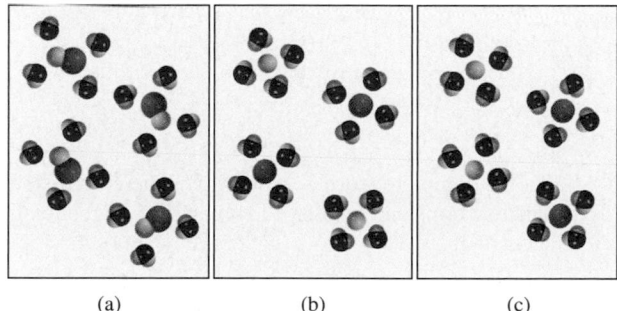

(a)   (b)   (c)

4.9 Identify each of the following substances as a strong electrolyte, weak electrolyte, or nonelectrolyte: (a) H_2O, (b) KCl, (c) HNO_3, (d) CH_3COOH, (e) $C_{12}H_{22}O_{11}$.

4.10 Identify each of the following substances as a strong electrolyte, weak electrolyte, or nonelectrolyte: (a) $Ba(NO_3)_2$, (b) Ne, (c) NH_3, (d) NaOH.

4.11 The passage of electricity through an electrolyte solution is caused by the movement of (a) electrons only, (b) cations only, (c) anions only, (d) both cations and anions.

4.12 Predict and explain which of the following systems are electrically conducting: (a) solid NaCl, (b) molten NaCl, (c) an aqueous solution of NaCl.

4.13 You are given a water-soluble compound X. Describe how you would determine whether it is an electrolyte or a nonelectrolyte. If it is an electrolyte, how would you determine whether it is strong or weak?

4.14 Explain why a solution of HCl in benzene does not conduct electricity but in water it does.

Precipitation Reactions
Review Questions

4.15 What is the difference between an ionic equation and a molecular equation?

4.16 What is the advantage of writing net ionic equations?

Problems

4.17 Two aqueous solutions of $AgNO_3$ and NaCl are mixed. Which of the following diagrams best represents the mixture?

(a)   (b)   (c)   (d)

4.18 Two aqueous solutions of KOH and $MgCl_2$ are mixed. Which of the following diagrams best represents the mixture?

(a)   (b)   (c)   (d)

4.19 Characterize the following compounds as soluble or insoluble in water: (a) $Ca_3(PO_4)_2$, (b) $Mn(OH)_2$, (c) $AgClO_3$, (d) K_2S.

4.20 Characterize the following compounds as soluble or insoluble in water: (a) $CaCO_3$, (b) $ZnSO_4$, (c) $Hg(NO_3)_2$, (d) $HgSO_4$, (e) NH_4ClO_4.

4.21 Write ionic and net ionic equations for the following reactions:
(a) $AgNO_3(aq) + Na_2SO_4(aq) \longrightarrow$
(b) $BaCl_2(aq) + ZnSO_4(aq) \longrightarrow$
(c) $(NH_4)_2CO_3(aq) + CaCl_2(aq) \longrightarrow$

4.22 Write ionic and net ionic equations for the following reactions:
(a) $Na_2S(aq) + ZnCl_2(aq) \longrightarrow$
(b) $K_3PO_4(aq) + 3Sr(NO_3)_2(aq) \longrightarrow$
(c) $Mg(NO_3)_2(aq) + 2NaOH(aq) \longrightarrow$

4.23 Which of the following processes will likely result in a precipitation reaction? (a) Mixing a $NaNO_3$ solution with a $CuSO_4$ solution. (b) Mixing a $BaCl_2$ solution with a K_2SO_4 solution. Write a net ionic equation for the precipitation reaction.

4.24 With reference to Table 4.2, suggest one method by which you might separate (a) K^+ from Ag^+, (b) Ba^{2+} from Pb^{2+}, (c) NH_4^+ from Ca^{2+}, (d) Ba^{2+} from Cu^{2+}. All cations are assumed to be in aqueous solution, and the common anion is the nitrate ion.

Acid-Base Reactions
Review Questions

4.25 List the general properties of acids and bases.

4.26 Give Arrhenius's and Brønsted's definitions of an acid and a base. Why are Brønsted's definitions more useful in describing acid-base properties?

4.27 Give an example of a monoprotic acid, a diprotic acid, and a triprotic acid.

4.28 What are the characteristics of an acid-base neutralization reaction?

4.29 What factors qualify a compound as a salt? Specify which of the following compounds are salts: CH_4, NaF, NaOH, CaO, $BaSO_4$, HNO_3, NH_3, KBr?

4.30 Identify the following as a weak or strong acid or base: (a) NH_3, (b) H_3PO_4, (c) LiOH, (d) HCOOH (formic acid), (e) H_2SO_4, (f) HF, (g) $Ba(OH)_2$.

Problems

4.31 Identify each of the following species as a Brønsted acid, base, or both: (a) HI, (b) CH_3COO^-, (c) $H_2PO_4^-$, (d) HSO_4^-.

4.32 Identify each of the following species as a Brønsted acid, base, or both: PO_4^{3-}, (b) ClO_2^-, (c) NH_4^+, (d) HCO_3^-.

4.33 Balance the following equations and write the corresponding ionic and net ionic equations (if appropriate):
(a) $HBr(aq) + NH_3(aq) \longrightarrow$
(b) $Ba(OH)_2(aq) + H_3PO_4(aq) \longrightarrow$
(c) $HClO_4(aq) + Mg(OH)_2(s) \longrightarrow$

4.34 Balance the following equations and write the corresponding ionic and net ionic equations (if appropriate):
(a) $CH_3COOH(aq) + KOH(aq) \longrightarrow$
(b) $H_2CO_3(aq) + NaOH(aq) \longrightarrow$
(c) $HNO_3(aq) + Ba(OH)_2(aq) \longrightarrow$

Oxidation-Reduction Reactions
Review Questions

4.35 Give an example of a combination redox reaction, a decomposition redox reaction, and a displacement redox reaction.

4.36 All combustion reactions are redox reactions. True or false? Explain.

4.37 What is an oxidation number? How is it used to identify redox reactions? Explain why, except for ionic compounds, oxidation number does not have any physical significance.

4.38 (a) Without referring to Figure 4.11, give the oxidation numbers of the alkali and alkaline earth metals in their compounds. (b) Give the highest oxidation numbers that the Groups 3A–7A elements can have.

4.39 How is the activity series organized? How is it used in the study of redox reactions?

4.40 Use the following reaction to define redox reaction, half-reaction, oxidizing agent, reducing agent:
$$4Na(s) + O_2(g) \longrightarrow 2Na_2O(s)$$

4.41 Is it possible to have a reaction in which oxidation occurs and reduction does not? Explain.

4.42 What is the requirement for an element to undergo disproportionation reactions? Name five common elements that are likely to take part in such reactions.

Problems

4.43 For the complete redox reactions given here, (i) break down each reaction into its half-reactions; (ii) identify the oxidizing agent; (iii) identify the reducing agent.
(a) $2Sr + O_2 \longrightarrow 2SrO$
(b) $2Li + H_2 \longrightarrow 2LiH$
(c) $2Cs + Br_2 \longrightarrow 2CsBr$
(d) $3Mg + N_2 \longrightarrow Mg_3N_2$

4.44 For the complete redox reactions given here, write the half-reactions and identify the oxidizing and reducing agents:
(a) $4Fe + 3O_2 \longrightarrow 2Fe_2O_3$
(b) $Cl_2 + 2NaBr \longrightarrow 2NaCl + Br_2$
(c) $Si + 2F_2 \longrightarrow SiF_4$
(d) $H_2 + Cl_2 \longrightarrow 2HCl$

4.45 Arrange the following species in order of increasing oxidation number of the sulfur atom: (a) H_2S, (b) S_8, (c) H_2SO_4, (d) S^{2-}, (e) HS^-, (f) SO_2, (g) SO_3.

4.46 Phosphorus forms many oxoacids. Indicate the oxidation number of phosphorus in each of the following acids: (a) HPO_3, (b) H_3PO_2, (c) H_3PO_3, (d) H_3PO_4, (e) $H_4P_2O_7$, (f) $H_5P_3O_{10}$.

4.47 Give the oxidation number of the underlined atoms in the following molecules and ions: (a) $\underline{Cl}F$, (b) $I\underline{F}_7$, (c) $\underline{C}H_4$, (d) $\underline{C}_2H_2$, (e) $\underline{C}_2H_4$, (f) $K_2\underline{Cr}O_4$, (g) $K_2\underline{Cr}_2O_7$, (h) $K\underline{Mn}O_4$, (i) $NaH\underline{C}O_3$, (j) $\underline{Li}_2$, (k) $Na\underline{I}O_3$, (l) $K\underline{O}_2$, (m) $\underline{P}F_6^-$, (n) $K\underline{Au}Cl_4$.

4.48 Give the oxidation number for the following species: H_2, Se_8, P_4, O, U, As_4, B_{12}.

4.49 Give oxidation numbers for the underlined atoms in the following molecules and ions: (a) $\underline{Cs}_2O$, (b) $Ca\underline{I}_2$, (c) $\underline{Al}_2O_3$, (d) $H_3\underline{As}O_3$, (e) $\underline{Ti}O_2$, (f) $\underline{Mo}O_4^{2-}$, (g) $\underline{Pt}Cl_4^{2-}$, (h) $\underline{Pt}Cl_6^{2-}$, (i) $\underline{Sn}F_2$, (j) $\underline{Cl}F_3$, (k) $\underline{Sb}F_6^-$.

4.50 Give the oxidation numbers of the underlined atoms in the following molecules and ions: (a) $Mg_3\underline{N}_2$, (b) $Cs\underline{O}_2$, (c) $Ca\underline{C}_2$, (d) $\underline{C}O_3^{2-}$, (e) $\underline{C}_2O_4^{2-}$, (f) $Zn\underline{O}_2^{2-}$, (g) $Na\underline{B}H_4$, (h) $\underline{W}O_4^{2-}$.

4.51 Nitric acid is a strong oxidizing agent. State which of the following species is *least* likely to be produced when nitric acid reacts with a strong reducing agent such as zinc metal, and explain why: N_2O, NO, NO_2, N_2O_4, N_2O_5, NH_4^+.

4.52 Which of the following metals can react with water? (a) Au, (b) Li, (c) Hg, (d) Ca, (e) Pt.

4.53 On the basis of oxidation number considerations, one of the following oxides would not react with molecular oxygen: NO, N_2O, SO_2, SO_3, P_4O_6. Which one is it? Why?

4.54 Predict the outcome of the reactions represented by the following equations by using the activity series, and balance the equations.
(a) $Cu(s) + HCl(aq) \longrightarrow$
(b) $I_2(s) + NaBr(aq) \longrightarrow$
(c) $Mg(s) + CuSO_4(aq) \longrightarrow$
(d) $Cl_2(g) + KBr(aq) \longrightarrow$

4.55 Classify the following redox reactions:
(a) $2H_2O_2 \longrightarrow 2H_2O + O_2$
(b) $Mg + 2AgNO_3 \longrightarrow Mg(NO_3)_2 + 2Ag$
(c) $NH_4NO_2 \longrightarrow N_2 + 2H_2O$
(d) $H_2 + Br_2 \longrightarrow 2HBr$

4.56 Classify the following redox reactions:
(a) $P_4 + 10Cl_2 \longrightarrow 4PCl_5$
(b) $2NO \longrightarrow N_2 + O_2$
(c) $Cl_2 + 2KI \longrightarrow 2KCl + I_2$
(d) $3HNO_2 \longrightarrow HNO_3 + H_2O + 2NO$

Concentration of Solutions
Review Questions

4.57 Write the equation for calculating molarity. Why is molarity a convenient concentration unit in chemistry?

4.58 Describe the steps involved in preparing a solution of known molar concentration using a volumetric flask.

Problems

4.59 Calculate the mass of KI in grams required to prepare 5.00×10^2 mL of a 2.80 M solution.

4.60 Describe how you would prepare 250 mL of a 0.707 M $NaNO_3$ solution.

4.61 How many moles of $MgCl_2$ are present in 60.0 mL of 0.100 M $MgCl_2$ solution?

4.62 How many grams of KOH are present in 35.0 mL of a 5.50 M solution?

4.63 Calculate the molarity of each of the following solutions: (a) 29.0 g of ethanol (C_2H_5OH) in 545 mL of solution, (b) 15.4 g of sucrose ($C_{12}H_{22}O_{11}$) in 74.0 mL of solution, (c) 9.00 g of sodium chloride (NaCl) in 86.4 mL of solution.

4.64 Calculate the molarity of each of the following solutions: (a) 6.57 g of methanol (CH_3OH) in 1.50×10^2 mL of solution, (b) 10.4 g of calcium chloride ($CaCl_2$) in 2.20×10^2 mL of solution, (c) 7.82 g of naphthalene ($C_{10}H_8$) in 85.2 mL of benzene solution.

4.65 Calculate the volume in mL of a solution required to provide the following: (a) 2.14 g of sodium chloride from a 0.270 M solution, (b) 4.30 g of ethanol from a 1.50 M solution, (c) 0.85 g of acetic acid (CH_3COOH) from a 0.30 M solution.

4.66 Determine how many grams of each of the following solutes would be needed to make 2.50×10^2 mL of a 0.100 M solution: (a) cesium iodide (CsI), (b) sulfuric acid (H_2SO_4), (c) sodium carbonate (Na_2CO_3), (d) potassium dichromate ($K_2Cr_2O_7$), (e) potassium permanganate ($KMnO_4$).

Dilution of Solutions
Review Questions

4.67 Describe the basic steps involved in diluting a solution of known concentration.

4.68 Write the equation that enables us to calculate the concentration of a diluted solution. Give units for all the terms.

Problems

4.69 Describe how to prepare 1.00 L of 0.646 M HCl solution, starting with a 2.00 M HCl solution.

4.70 Water is added to 25.0 mL of a 0.866 M KNO_3 solution until the volume of the solution is exactly 500 mL. What is the concentration of the final solution?

4.71 How would you prepare 60.0 mL of 0.200 M HNO_3 from a stock solution of 4.00 M HNO_3?

4.72 You have 505 mL of a 0.125 M HCl solution and you want to dilute it to exactly 0.100 M. How much water should you add?

4.73 A 35.2-mL, 1.66 M $KMnO_4$ solution is mixed with 16.7 mL of 0.892 M $KMnO_4$ solution. Calculate the concentration of the final solution.

4.74 A 46.2-mL, 0.568 M calcium nitrate $[Ca(NO_3)_2]$ solution is mixed with 80.5 mL of 1.396 M calcium nitrate solution. Calculate the concentration of the final solution.

Gravimetric Analysis

Review Questions

4.75 Describe the basic steps involved in gravimetric analysis. How does this procedure help us determine the identity of a compound or the purity of a compound if its formula is known?

4.76 Distilled water must be used in the gravimetric analysis of chlorides. Why?

Problems

4.77 If 30.0 mL of 0.150 M $CaCl_2$ is added to 15.0 mL of 0.100 M $AgNO_3$, what is the mass in grams of $AgCl$ precipitate?

4.78 A sample of 0.6760 g of an unknown compound containing barium ions (Ba^{2+}) is dissolved in water and treated with an excess of Na_2SO_4. If the mass of the $BaSO_4$ precipitate formed is 0.4105 g, what is the percent by mass of Ba in the original unknown compound?

4.79 How many grams of NaCl are required to precipitate most of the Ag^+ ions from 2.50×10^2 mL of 0.0113 M $AgNO_3$ solution? Write the net ionic equation for the reaction.

4.80 The concentration of Cu^{2+} ions in the water (which also contains sulfate ions) discharged from a certain industrial plant is determined by adding excess sodium sulfide (Na_2S) solution to 0.800 L of the water. The molecular equation is

$$Na_2S(aq) + CuSO_4(aq) \longrightarrow Na_2SO_4(aq) + CuS(s)$$

Write the net ionic equation and calculate the molar concentration of Cu^{2+} in the water sample if 0.0177 g of solid CuS is formed.

Acid-Base Titrations

Review Questions

4.81 Describe the basic steps involved in an acid-base titration. Why is this technique of great practical value?

4.82 How does an acid-base indicator work?

4.83 A student carried out two titrations using a NaOH solution of unknown concentration in the buret. In one titration she weighed out 0.2458 g of KHP (see p. 150) and transferred it to an Erlenmeyer flask. She then added 20.00 mL of distilled water to dissolve the acid. In the other titration she weighed out 0.2507 g of KHP

but added 40.00 mL of distilled water to dissolve the acid. Assuming no experimental error, would she obtain the same result for the concentration of the NaOH solution?

4.84 Would the volume of a 0.10 M NaOH solution needed to titrate 25.0 mL of a 0.10 M HNO_2 (a weak acid) solution be different from that needed to titrate 25.0 mL of a 0.10 M HCl (a strong acid) solution?

Problems

4.85 A quantity of 18.68 mL of a KOH solution is needed to neutralize 0.4218 g of KHP. What is the concentration (in molarity) of the KOH solution?

4.86 Calculate the concentration (in molarity) of a NaOH solution if 25.0 mL of the solution are needed to neutralize 17.4 mL of a 0.312 M HCl solution.

4.87 Calculate the volume in mL of a 1.420 M NaOH solution required to titrate the following solutions:
   (a) 25.00 mL of a 2.430 M HCl solution
   (b) 25.00 mL of a 4.500 M H_2SO_4 solution
   (c) 25.00 mL of a 1.500 M H_3PO_4 solution

4.88 What volume of a 0.500 M HCl solution is needed to neutralize each of the following:
   (a) 10.0 mL of a 0.300 M NaOH solution
   (b) 10.0 mL of a 0.200 M $Ba(OH)_2$ solution

Redox Titrations

Review Questions

4.89 What are the similarities and differences between acid-base titrations and redox titrations?

4.90 Explain why potassium permanganate ($KMnO_4$) and potassium dichromate ($K_2Cr_2O_7$) can serve as internal indicators in redox titrations.

Problems

4.91 Iron(II) can be oxidized by an acidic $K_2Cr_2O_7$ solution according to the net ionic equation:

$$Cr_2O_7^{2-} + 6Fe^{2+} + 14H^+ \longrightarrow$$
$$2Cr^{3+} + 6Fe^{3+} + 7H_2O$$

If it takes 26.0 mL of 0.0250 M $K_2Cr_2O_7$ to titrate 25.0 mL of a solution containing Fe^{2+}, what is the molar concentration of Fe^{2+}?

4.92 The SO_2 present in air is mainly responsible for the acid rain phenomenon. Its concentration can be determined by titrating against a standard permanganate solution as follows:

$$5SO_2 + 2MnO_4^- + 2H_2O \longrightarrow$$
$$5SO_4^{2-} + 2Mn^{2+} + 4H^+$$

Calculate the number of grams of SO_2 in a sample of air if 7.37 mL of 0.00800 M $KMnO_4$ solution are required for the titration.

4.93 A sample of iron ore (containing only Fe^{2+} ions) weighing 0.2792 g was dissolved in dilute acid solution, and all the Fe(II) was converted to Fe(III) ions. The solution required 23.30 mL of 0.0194 M $K_2Cr_2O_7$ for titration. Calculate the percent by mass of iron in the ore. (*Hint:* See Problem 4.91 for the balanced equation.)

4.94 The concentration of a hydrogen peroxide solution can be conveniently determined by titration against a standardized potassium permanganate solution in an acidic medium according to the following equation:

$$2MnO_4^- + 5H_2O_2 + 6H^+ \longrightarrow$$
$$5O_2 + 2Mn^{2+} + 8H_2O$$

If 36.44 mL of a 0.01652 M $KMnO_4$ solution are required to oxidize 25.00 mL of a H_2O_2 solution, calculate the molarity of the H_2O_2 solution.

4.95 Oxalic acid ($H_2C_2O_4$) is present in many plants and vegetables. If 24.0 mL of 0.0100 M $KMnO_4$ solution is needed to titrate 1.00 g of a sample of $H_2C_2O_4$ to the equivalence point, what is the percent by mass of $H_2C_2O_4$ in the sample? The net ionic equation is

$$2MnO_4^- + 16H^+ + 5C_2O_4^{2-} \longrightarrow$$
$$2Mn^{2+} + 10CO_2 + 8H_2O$$

4.96 A 15.0-mL sample of an oxalic acid solution requires 25.2 mL of 0.149 M NaOH for neutralization. Calculate the volume of a 0.122 M $KMnO_4$ solution needed to react with a second 15.0 mL sample of the oxalic acid solution. (*Hint:* Oxalic acid is a diprotic acid. See Problem 4.95 for redox equation.)

4.97 Iodate ion, IO_3^-, oxidizes SO_3^{2-} in acidic solution. The half-reaction for the oxidation is

$$SO_3^{2-} + H_2O \longrightarrow SO_4^{2-} + 2H^+ + 2e^-$$

A 100.0-mL sample of solution containing 1.390 g of KIO_3 reacts with 32.5 mL of 0.500 M Na_2SO_3. What is the final oxidation state of the iodine after the reaction has occurred?

4.98 Calcium oxalate (CaC_2O_4), the main component of kidney stones, is insoluble in water. For this reason it can be used to determine the amount of Ca^{2+} ions in fluids such as blood. The calcium oxalate isolated from blood is dissolved in acid and titrated against a standardized $KMnO_4$ solution as shown in Problem 4.95. In one test it is found that the calcium oxalate isolated from a 10.0-mL sample of blood requires 24.2 mL of 9.56×10^{-4} M $KMnO_4$ for titration. Calculate the number of milligrams of calcium per milliliter of blood.

Additional Problems

4.99 Classify the following reactions according to the types discussed in the chapter:

(a) $Cl_2 + 2OH^- \longrightarrow Cl^- + ClO^- + H_2O$

(b) $Ca^{2+} + CO_3^{2-} \longrightarrow CaCO_3$

(c) $NH_3 + H^+ \longrightarrow NH_4^+$

(d) $2CCl_4 + CrO_4^{2-} \longrightarrow$
$$2COCl_2 + CrO_2Cl_2 + 2Cl^-$$

(e) $Ca + F_2 \longrightarrow CaF_2$

(f) $2Li + H_2 \longrightarrow 2LiH$

(g) $Ba(NO_3)_2 + Na_2SO_4 \longrightarrow 2NaNO_3 + BaSO_4$

(h) $CuO + H_2 \longrightarrow Cu + H_2O$

(i) $Zn + 2HCl \longrightarrow ZnCl_2 + H_2$

(j) $2FeCl_2 + Cl_2 \longrightarrow 2FeCl_3$

4.100 Oxygen (O_2) and carbon dioxide (CO_2) are colorless and odorless gases. Suggest two chemical tests that would enable you to distinguish between these two gases.

4.101 Which of the following aqueous solutions would you expect to be the best conductor of electricity at 25°C? Explain your answer.

(a) 0.20 M NaCl

(b) 0.60 M CH_3COOH

(c) 0.25 M HCl

(d) 0.20 M $Mg(NO_3)_2$

4.102 A 5.00×10^2-mL sample of 2.00 M HCl solution is treated with 4.47 g of magnesium. Calculate the concentration of the acid solution after all the metal has reacted. Assume that the volume remains unchanged.

4.103 Calculate the volume of a 0.156 M $CuSO_4$ solution that would react with 7.89 g of zinc.

4.104 Sodium carbonate (Na_2CO_3) is available in very pure form and can be used to standardize acid solutions. What is the molarity of a HCl solution if 28.3 mL of the solution are required to react with 0.256 g of Na_2CO_3?

4.105 A 3.664-g sample of a monoprotic acid was dissolved in water. It took 20.27 mL of a 0.1578 M NaOH solution to neutralize the acid. Calculate the molar mass of the acid.

4.106 Acetic acid (CH_3COOH) is an important ingredient of vinegar. A sample of 50.0 mL of a commercial vinegar is titrated against a 1.00 M NaOH solution. What is the concentration (in M) of acetic acid present in the vinegar if 5.75 mL of the base are needed for the titration?

4.107 A 15.00-mL solution of potassium nitrate (KNO_3) was diluted to 125.0 mL, and 25.00 mL of this solution were then diluted to 1.000×10^3 mL. The concentration of the final solution is 0.00383 M. Calculate the concentration of the original solution.

4.108 When 2.50 g of a zinc strip were placed in a $AgNO_3$ solution, silver metal formed on the surface of the strip. After some time had passed, the strip was removed from the solution, dried, and weighed. If the mass of the strip was 3.37 g, calculate the mass of Ag and Zn metals present.

4.109 Calculate the mass of the precipitate formed when 2.27 L of 0.0820 M Ba(OH)$_2$ are mixed with 3.06 L of 0.0664 M Na$_2$SO$_4$.

4.110 Calculate the concentration of the acid (or base) remaining in solution when 10.7 mL of 0.211 M HNO$_3$ are added to 16.3 mL of 0.258 M NaOH.

4.111 (a) Describe a preparation for magnesium hydroxide [Mg(OH)$_2$] and predict its solubility. (b) Milk of magnesia contains mostly Mg(OH)$_2$ and is effective in treating acid (mostly hydrochloric acid) indigestion. Calculate the volume of a 0.035 M HCl solution (a typical acid concentration in an upset stomach) needed to react with two spoonfuls (approximately 10 mL) of milk of magnesia [at 0.080 g Mg(OH)$_2$/mL].

4.112 A 1.00-g sample of a metal X (that is known to form X^{2+} ions) was added to 0.100 L of 0.500 M H$_2$SO$_4$. After all the metal had reacted, the remaining acid required 0.0334 L of 0.500 M NaOH solution for neutralization. Calculate the molar mass of the metal and identify the element.

4.113 A quantitative definition of solubility is the number of grams of a solute that will dissolve in a given volume of water at a particular temperature. Describe an experiment that would enable you to determine the solubility of a soluble compound.

4.114 A 60.0-mL 0.513 M glucose (C$_6$H$_{12}$O$_6$) solution is mixed with 120.0 mL of 2.33 M glucose solution. What is the concentration of the final solution? Assume the volumes are additive.

4.115 An ionic compound X is only slightly soluble in water. What test would you employ to show that the compound does indeed dissolve in water to a certain extent?

4.116 A student is given an unknown that is either iron(II) sulfate or iron(III) sulfate. Suggest a chemical procedure for determining its identity. (Both iron compounds are water soluble.)

4.117 You are given a colorless liquid. Describe three chemical tests you would perform on the liquid to show that it is water.

4.118 Using the apparatus shown in Figure 4.1, a student found that a sulfuric acid solution caused the lightbulb to glow brightly. However, after the addition of a certain amount of a barium hydroxide [Ba(OH)$_2$] solution, the light began to dim even though Ba(OH)$_2$ is also a strong electrolyte. Explain.

4.119 You are given a soluble compound of unknown molecular formula. (a) Describe three tests that would show that the compound is an acid. (b) Once you have established that the compour.d is an acid, describe how you would determine its molar mass using a NaOH solution of known concentration. (Assume the acid is monoprotic.) (c) How would you find out

whether the acid is weak or strong? You are provided with a sample of NaCl and an apparatus like that shown in Figure 4.1 for comparison.

4.120 You are given two colorless solutions, one containing NaCl and the other sucrose (C$_{12}$H$_{22}$O$_{11}$). Suggest a chemical and a physical test that would allow you to distinguish between these two solutions.

4.121 The concentration of lead ions (Pb^{2+}) in a sample of polluted water that also contains nitrate ions (NO$_3^-$) is determined by adding solid sodium sulfate (Na$_2$SO$_4$) to exactly 500 mL of the water. (a) Write the molecular and net ionic equations for the reaction. (b) Calculate the molar concentration of Pb^{2+} if 0.00450 g of Na$_2$SO$_4$ was needed for the complete precipitation of Pb^{2+} ions as PbSO$_4$.

4.122 Hydrochloric acid is not an oxidizing agent in the sense that sulfuric acid and nitric acid are. Explain why the chloride ion is not a strong oxidizing agent like SO$_4^{2-}$ and NO$_3^-$.

4.123 Explain how you would prepare potassium iodide (KI) by means of (a) an acid-base reaction and (b) a reaction between an acid and a carbonate compound.

4.124 Sodium reacts with water to yield hydrogen gas. Why is this reaction not used in the laboratory preparation of hydrogen?

4.125 Describe how you would prepare the following compounds: (a) Mg(OH)$_2$, (b) AgI, (c) Ba$_3$(PO$_4$)$_2$.

4.126 Someone spilled concentrated sulfuric acid on the floor of a chemistry laboratory. To neutralize the acid, would it be preferrable to pour concentrated sodium hydroxide solution or spray solid sodium bicarbonate over the acid? Explain your choice and the chemical basis for the action.

4.127 Describe in each case how you would separate the cations or anions in an aqueous solution of: (a) NaNO$_3$ and Ba(NO$_3$)$_2$, (b) Mg(NO$_3$)$_2$ and KNO$_3$, (c) KBr and KNO$_3$, (d) K$_3$PO$_4$ and KNO$_3$, (e) Na$_2$CO$_3$ and NaNO$_3$.

4.128 The following are common household compounds: table salt (NaCl), table sugar (sucrose), vinegar (contains acetic acid), baking soda (NaHCO$_3$), washing soda (Na$_2$CO$_3$ · 10H$_2$O), boric acid (H$_3$BO$_3$, used in eyewash), epsom salt (MgSO$_4$ · 7H$_2$O), sodium hydroxide (used in drain openers), ammonia, milk of magnesia [Mg(OH)$_2$], and calcium carbonate. Based on what you have learned in this chapter, describe test(s) that would enable you to identify each of these compounds.

4.129 Sulfites (compounds containing the SO$_3^{2-}$ ions) are used as preservatives in dried fruit and vegetables and in wine making. In an experiment to test the presence of sulfite in fruit, a student first soaked several dried apricots in water overnight and then filtered the solution to remove all solid particles. She then treated the solution with hydrogen peroxide (H_2O_2) to oxidize the sulfite ions to sulfate ions. Finally, the sulfate ions were precipitated by treating the solution with a few drops of a barium chloride ($BaCl_2$) solution. Write a balanced equation for each of the preceding steps.

4.130 A 0.8870-g sample of a mixture of NaCl and KCl is dissolved in water, and the solution is then treated with an excess of $AgNO_3$ to yield 1.913 g of AgCl. Calculate the percent by mass of each compound in the mixture.

4.131 Chlorine forms a number of oxides with the following oxidation numbers: +1, +3, +4, +6, and +7. Write a formula for each of these compounds.

4.132 A useful application of oxalic acid is the removal of rust (Fe_2O_3) from, say, bathtub rings according to the reaction

$$Fe_2O_3(s) + 6H_2C_2O_4(aq) \longrightarrow$$
$$2Fe(C_2O_4)_3^{3-}(aq) + 3H_2O + 6H^+(aq)$$

Calculate the number of grams of rust that can be removed by 5.00×10^2 mL of a 0.100 M solution of oxalic acid.

4.133 Acetylsalicylic acid ($C_9H_8O_4$) is a monoprotic acid commonly known as "aspirin." A typical aspirin tablet, however, contains only a small amount of the acid. In an experiment to determine its composition, an aspirin tablet was crushed and dissolved in water. It took 12.25 mL of 0.1466 M NaOH to neutralize the solution. Calculate the number of grains of aspirin in the tablet. (One grain = 0.0648 g.)

4.134 A 0.9157-g mixture of $CaBr_2$ and NaBr is dissolved in water, and $AgNO_3$ is added to the solution to form AgBr precipitate. If the mass of the precipitate is 1.6930 g, what is the percent by mass of NaBr in the original mixture?

4.135 Hydrogen halides (HF, HCl, HBr, HI) are highly reactive compounds that have many industrial and laboratory uses. (a) In the laboratory, HF and HCl can be generated by reacting CaF_2 and NaCl with concentrated sulfuric acid. Write appropriate equations for the reactions. (*Hint:* These are not redox reactions.) (b) Why is it that HBr and HI cannot be prepared similarly, that is, by reacting NaBr and NaI with concentrated sulfuric acid? (*Hint:* H_2SO_4 is a stronger oxidizing agent than both Br_2 and I_2.) (c) HBr can be prepared by reacting phosphorus tribromide (PBr_3) with water. Write an equation for this reaction.

4.136 A 325-mL sample of solution contains 25.3 g of $CaCl_2$. (a) Calculate the molar concentration of Cl^- in this solution. (b) How many grams of Cl^- are in 0.100 L of this solution?

4.137 Phosphoric acid (H_3PO_4) is an important industrial chemical used in fertilizers, in detergents, and in the food industry. It is produced by two different methods. In the *electric furnace method,* elemental phosphorus (P_4) is burned in air to form P_4O_{10}, which is then reacted with water to give H_3PO_4. In the *wet process,* the mineral phosphate rock [$Ca_5(PO_4)_3F$] is reacted with sulfuric acid to give H_3PO_4 (and HF and $CaSO_4$). Write equations for these processes and classify each step as precipitation, acid-base, or redox reaction.

4.138 Ammonium nitrate (NH_4NO_3) is one of the most important nitrogen-containing fertilizers. Its purity can be analyzed by titrating a solution of NH_4NO_3 with a standard NaOH solution. In one experiment a 0.2041-g sample of industrially prepared NH_4NO_3 required 24.42 mL of 0.1023 M NaOH for neutralization.

(a) Write a net ionic equation for the reaction.

(b) What is the percent purity of the sample?

4.139 Is the following reaction a redox reaction? Explain.

$$3O_2(g) \longrightarrow 2O_3(g)$$

4.140 What is the oxidation number of O in HFO?

4.141 Use molecular models like those in Figures 4.7 and 4.8 to represent the following acid-base reactions:

(a) $OH^- + H_3O^+ \longrightarrow 2H_2O$

(b) $NH_4^+ + NH_2^- \longrightarrow 2NH_3$

Identify the Brønsted acid and base in each case.

4.142 The alcohol content in a 10.0-g sample of blood from a driver required 4.23 mL of 0.07654 M $K_2Cr_2O_7$ for titration. Should the police prosecute the individual for drunken driving? (*Hint:* See Chemistry in Action essay on p. 143.)

4.143 On standing, a concentrated nitric acid gradually turns yellow in color. Explain. (*Hint:* Nitric acid slowly decomposes. Nitrogen dioxide is a colored gas.)

4.144 Describe the laboratory preparation for the following gases: (a) hydrogen, (b) oxygen, (c) carbon dioxide, and (d) nitrogen. Indicate the physical states of the reactants and products in each case. [*Hint:* Nitrogen can be obtained by heating ammonium nitrite (NH_4NO_2).]

4.145 Referring to Figure 4.18, explain why one must first dissolve the solid completely before making up the solution to the correct volume.

4.146 Can the following decomposition reaction be characterized as an acid-base reaction? Explain.

$$NH_4Cl(s) \longrightarrow NH_3(g) + HCl(g)$$

Special Problems

4.147 Give a chemical explanation for each of the following: (a) When calcium metal is added to a sulfuric acid solution, hydrogen gas is generated. After a few minutes, the reaction slows down and eventually stops even though none of the reactants is used up. Explain. (b) In the activity series, aluminum is above hydrogen, yet the metal appears to be unreactive toward steam and hydrochloric acid. Why? (c) Sodium and potassium lie above copper in the activity series. Explain why Cu^{2+} ions in a $CuSO_4$ solution are not converted to metallic copper upon the addition of these metals. (d) A metal M reacts slowly with steam. There is no visible change when it is placed in a pale green iron(II) sulfate solution. Where should we place M in the activity series? (e) Before aluminum metal was obtained by electrolysis, it was produced by reducing its chloride ($AlCl_3$) with an active metal. What metals would you use to produce aluminum in that way?

4.148 The recommended procedure for preparing a very dilute solution is not to weigh out a very small mass or measure a very small volume of a stock solution. Instead, it is done by a series of dilutions. A sample of 0.8214 g of $KMnO_4$ was dissolved in water and made up to the volume in a 500-mL volumetric flask. A 2.000-mL sample of this solution was transferred to a 1000-mL volumetric flask and diluted to the mark with water. Next, 10.00 mL of the diluted solution were transferred to a 250-mL flask and diluted to the mark with water. (a) Calculate the concentration (in molarity) of the final solution. (b) Calculate the mass of $KMnO_4$ needed to directly prepare the final solution.

4.149 The following "cycle of copper" experiment is performed in some general chemistry laboratories. The series of reactions starts with copper and ends with metallic copper. The steps are as follows: (1) A piece of copper wire of known mass is allowed to react with concentrated nitric acid [the products are copper(II) nitrate, nitrogen dioxide, and water]. (2) The copper(II) nitrate is treated with a sodium hydroxide solution to form copper(II) hydroxide precipitate. (3) On heating, copper(II) hydroxide decomposes to yield copper(II) oxide. (4) The copper(II) oxide is reacted with concentrated sulfuric acid to yield copper(II) sulfate. (5) Copper(II) sulfate is treated with an excess of zinc metal to form metallic copper. (6) The remaining zinc metal is removed by treatment with hydrochloric acid, and metallic copper is filtered, dried, and weighed. (a) Write a balanced equation for each step and classify the reactions. (b) Assuming that a student started

with 65.6 g of copper, calculate the theoretical yield at each step. (c) Considering the nature of the steps, comment on why it is possible to recover most of the copper used at the start.

4.150 A quantity of 25.0 mL of a solution containing both Fe^{2+} and Fe^{3+} ions is titrated with 23.0 mL of 0.0200 M $KMnO_4$ (in dilute sulfuric acid). As a result, all of the Fe^{2+} ions are oxidized to Fe^{3+} ions. Next, the solution is treated with Zn metal to convert all of the Fe^{3+} ions to Fe^{2+} ions. Finally, the solution containing only the Fe^{2+} ions requires 40.0 mL of the same $KMnO_4$ solution for oxidation to Fe^{3+}. Calculate the molar concentrations of Fe^{2+} and Fe^{3+} in the original solution. The net ionic equation is

$$MnO_4^- + 5Fe^{2+} + 8H^+ \longrightarrow Mn^{2+} + 5Fe^{3+} + 4H_2O$$

4.151 Use the periodic table framework shown to show the names and positions of two metals that can (a) displace hydrogen from cold water, (b) displace hydrogen from steam, and (c) displace hydrogen from acid. Also show two metals that can react neither with water nor acid.

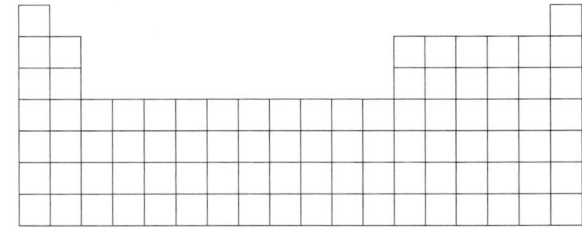

4.152 Referring to the Chemistry in Action essay on page 155, answer the following questions: (a) Identify the precipitation, acid-base, and redox processes. (b) Instead of calcium oxide, why don't we simply add sodium hydroxide to seawater to precipitate magnesium hydroxide? (c) Sometimes a mineral called dolomite (a mixture of $CaCO_3$ and $MgCO_3$) is substituted for limestone to bring about the precipitation of magnesium hydroxide. What is the advantage of using dolomite?

4.153 A 22.02-mL solution containing 1.615 g $Mg(NO_3)_2$ is mixed with a 28.64-mL solution containing 1.073 g NaOH. Calculate the concentrations of the ions remaining in solution after the reaction is complete. Assume volumes are additive.

4.154 Because acid-base and precipitation reactions discussed in this chapter all involve ionic species, their progress can be monitored by measuring the electrical conductance of the solution. Match the following reactions with the diagrams shown here. The electrical conductance is shown in arbitrary units.

(1) A 1.0 M KOH solution is added to 1.0 L of 1.0 M CH_3COOH.

(2) A 1.0 M NaOH solution is added to 1.0 L of 1.0 M HCl.

(3) A 1.0 M $BaCl_2$ solution is added to 1.0 L of 1.0 M K_2SO_4.

(4) A 1.0 M NaCl solution is added to 1.0 L of 1.0 M $AgNO_3$.

(5) A 1.0 M CH_3COOH solution is added to 1.0 L of 1.0 M NH_3.

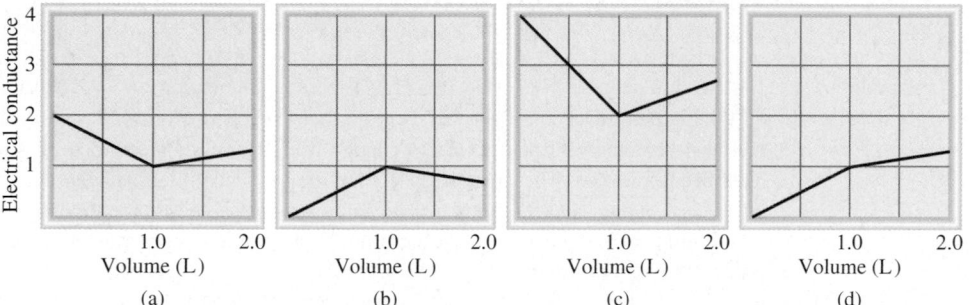

(a)   (b)   (c)   (d)

Answers to Practice Exercises

4.1 (a) Insoluble, (b) insoluble, (c) soluble. **4.2** $Al^{3+}(aq) + 3OH^-(aq) \longrightarrow Al(OH)_3(s)$. **4.3** (a) Brønsted base, (b) Brønsted acid. **4.4** (a) P: $+3$, F: -1; (b) Mn: $+7$, O: -2. **4.5** (a) Hydrogen displacement reaction, (b) combination reaction, (c) disproportionation reaction, (d) metal displacement reaction. **4.6** 0.452 M. **4.7** 494 mL. **4.8** Dilute 34.2 mL of the stock solution to 200 mL. **4.9** 92.02%. **4.10** 0.3822 g. **4.11** 10.1 mL. **4.12** 204 mL.

Who Killed Napoleon?

After his defeat at Waterloo in 1815, Napoleon was exiled to St. Helena, a small island in the Atlantic Ocean, where he spent the last six years of his life. In the 1960s, samples of his hair were analyzed and found to contain a high level of arsenic, suggesting that he might have been poisoned. The prime suspects are the governor of St. Helena, with whom Napoleon did not get along, and the French royal family, who wanted to prevent his return to France.

Elemental arsenic is not that harmful. The commonly used poison is actually arsenic(III) oxide, As_2O_3, a white compound that dissolves in water, is tasteless, and if administered over a period of time, is hard to detect. It was once known as the "inheritance powder" because it could be added to grandfather's wine to hasten his demise so that his grandson could inherit the estate!

In 1832 the English chemist James Marsh devised a procedure for detecting arsenic. This test, which now bears Marsh's name, combines hydrogen formed by the reaction between zinc and sulfuric acid with a sample of the suspected poison. If As_2O_3 is present, it reacts with hydrogen to form a toxic gas, arsine (AsH_3). When arsine gas is heated, it decomposes to form arsenic, which is recognized by its metallic luster. The Marsh test is an effective deterrent to

Apparatus for Marsh's test. Sulfuric acid is added to zinc metal and a solution containing arsenic(III) oxide. The hydrogen produced reacts with As_2O_3 to yield arsine (AsH_3). On heating, arsine decomposes to elemental arsenic, which has a metallic appearance, and hydrogen gas.

H₂SO₄

Hydrogen flame

Shiny metallic ring

As_2O_3 solution

Zinc granules

murder by As_2O_3, but it was invented too late to do Napoleon any good, if, in fact, he was a victim of deliberate arsenic poisoning.

Doubts about the conspiracy theory of Napoleon's death developed in the early 1990s, when a sample of the wallpaper from his drawing room was found to contain copper arsenate ($CuHAsO_4$), a green pigment that was commonly used at the time Napoleon lived. It has been suggested that the damp climate on St. Helena promoted the growth of molds on the wallpaper. To rid themselves of arsenic, the molds could have converted it to trimethyl arsine [$(CH_3)_3As$], which is a volatile and highly poisonous compound. Prolonged exposure to these vapors would have ruined Napoleon's health and would also account for the presence of arsenic in his body, though it may not have been the primary cause of his death. This provocative theory is supported by the fact that Napoleon's regular guests suffered from gastrointestinal disturbances and other symptoms of arsenic poisoning and that their health all seemed to improve whenever they spent hours working outdoors in the garden, their main hobby on the island.

We will probably never know whether Napoleon died from arsenic poisoning, intentional or accidental, but this exercise in historical sleuthing provides a fascinating example of the use of chemical analysis. Not only is chemical analysis used in forensic science, but it also plays an essential part in endeavors ranging from pure research to practical applications, such as quality control of commercial products and medical diagnosis.

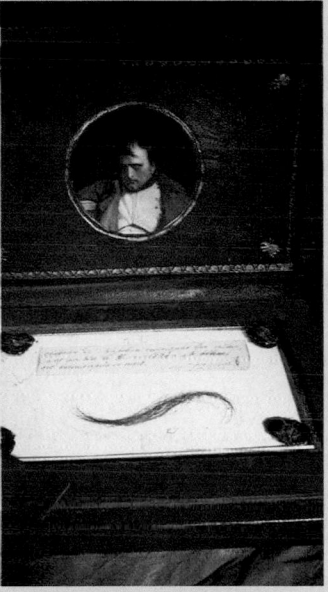

A lock of Napoleon's hair.

Chemical Clues

1. The arsenic in Napoleon's hair was detected using a technique called *neutron activation.* When As-75 is bombarded with high-energy neutrons, it is converted to the radioactive As-76 isotope. The energy of the γ rays emitted by the radioactive isotope is characteristic of arsenic, and the intensity of the rays establishes how much arsenic is present in a sample. With this technique, as little as 5 ng (5×10^{-9} g) of arsenic can be detected in 1 g of material. (a) Write symbols for the two isotopes of As, showing mass number and atomic number. (b) Name two advantages of analyzing the arsenic content by neutron activation instead of a chemical analysis.

2. Arsenic is not an essential element for the human body. (a) Based on its position in the periodic table, suggest a reason for its toxicity. (b) In addition to hair, where else might one look for the accumulation of the element if arsenic poisoning is suspected?

3. The Marsh test for arsenic involves the following steps: (a) The generation of hydrogen gas when sulfuric acid is added to zinc. (b) The reaction of hydrogen with As(III) oxide to produce arsine. (c) Conversion of arsine to arsenic by heating. Write equations representing these steps and identify the type of the reaction in each step.

5

A tornado is a violently rotating column of air extending from a thunderstorm to the ground. The models show the major constituents in a tornado: nitrogen, oxygen, water, and carbon dioxide molecules and an argon atom.

Gases

A LOOK AHEAD

- We begin by examining the substances that exist as gases and their general properties. (5.1)

- We learn units for expressing gas pressure and the characteristics of atmospheric pressure. (5.2)

- Next, we study the relationship among pressure, volume, temperature, and amount of a gas in terms of various gas laws. We will see that these laws can be summarized by the ideal gas equation, which can be used to calculate the density or molar mass of a gas. (5.3 and 5.4)

- We will see that the ideal gas equation can be used to study the stoichiometry involving gases. (5.5)

- We learn that the behavior of a mixture of gases can be understood by Dalton's law of partial pressures, which is an extension of the ideal gas equation. (5.6)

- We will see how the kinetic molecular theory of gases, which is based on the properties of individual molecules, can be used to describe macroscopic properties such as the pressure and temperature of a gas. We learn that this theory enables us to obtain an expression for the speed of molecules at a given temperature, and understand phenomena such as gas diffusion and effusion. (5.7)

- The chapter ends with a discussion of the correction for the nonideal behavior of gases using the van der Waals equation. (5.8)

Interactive Activity Summary

1. Animation: Gas Laws (5.3)
2. Interactivity: Boyle's Law (5.3)
3. Interactivity: Volume in Gas Laws (5.3)
4. Interactivity: Dalton's Law (5.6)
5. Animation: Collecting a Gas over Water (5.6)
6. Animation: Diffusion of Gases (5.7)

Under certain conditions of pressure and temperature, most substances can exist in any one of the three states of matter: solid, liquid, or gas. Water, for example, can be solid ice, liquid water, or steam or water vapor. The physical properties of a substance often depend on its state.

Gases, the subject of this chapter, are simpler than liquids or solids in many ways. Molecular motion in gases is totally random, and the forces of attraction between gas molecules are so small that each molecule moves freely and essentially independently of other molecules. Subjected to changes in temperature and pressure, it is easier to predict the behavior of gases. The laws that govern this behavior have played an important role in the development of the atomic theory of matter and the kinetic molecular theory of gases.

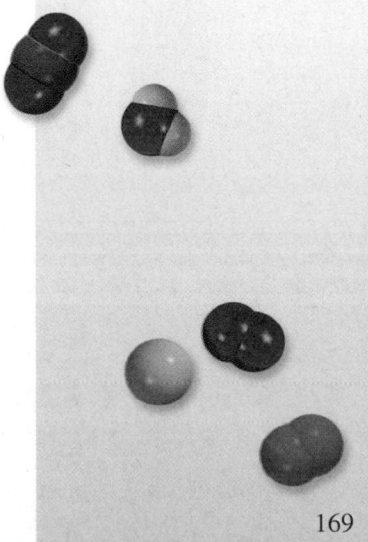

5.1 Substances That Exist as Gases

We live at the bottom of an ocean of air whose composition by volume is roughly 78 percent N_2, 21 percent O_2, and 1 percent other gases, including CO_2. Today, the chemistry of this vital mixture of gases has become a source of great interest because of the detrimental effects of environmental pollution. The chemistry of the atmosphere and polluting gases is discussed in Chapter 17. Here we will focus generally on the behavior of substances that exist as gases under normal atmospheric conditions, which are defined as 25°C and 1 atmosphere (atm) pressure.

Figure 5.1 shows the elements that are gases under normal atmospheric conditions. Note that hydrogen, nitrogen, oxygen, fluorine, and chlorine exist as gaseous diatomic molecules: H_2, N_2, O_2, F_2, and Cl_2. An allotrope of oxygen, ozone (O_3), is also a gas at room temperature. All the elements in Group 8A, the noble gases, are monatomic gases: He, Ne, Ar, Kr, Xe, and Rn.

Ionic compounds do not exist as gases at 25°C and 1 atm, because cations and anions in an ionic solid are held together by very strong electrostatic forces; that is, forces between positive and negative charges. To overcome these attractions we must apply a large amount of energy, which in practice means strongly heating the solid. Under normal conditions, all we can do is melt the solid; for example, NaCl melts at the rather high temperature of 801°C. In order to boil it, we would have to raise the temperature to well above 1000°C.

The behavior of molecular compounds is more varied. Some—for example, CO, CO_2, HCl, NH_3, and CH_4 (methane)—are gases, but the majority of molecular compounds are liquids or solids at room temperature. However, on heating they are converted to gases much more easily than ionic compounds. In other words, molecular compounds usually boil at much lower temperatures than ionic compounds do. There is no simple rule to help us determine whether a certain molecular compound is a gas under normal atmospheric conditions. To make such a determination we need to understand the nature and magnitude of the attractive forces among the molecules, called *intermolecular forces* (discussed in Chapter 11). In general, the stronger these attractions, the less likely a compound can exist as a gas at ordinary temperatures.

Figure 5.1 *Elements (in blue) that exist as gases at 25°C and 1 atm. The noble gases (the Group 8A elements) are monatomic species; the other elements exist as diatomic molecules. Ozone (O_3) is also a gas.*

TABLE 5.1	Some Substances Found as Gases at 1 atm and 25°C	

Elements	Compounds
H$_2$ (molecular hydrogen)	HF (hydrogen fluoride)
N$_2$ (molecular nitrogen)	HCl (hydrogen chloride)
O$_2$ (molecular oxygen)	HBr (hydrogen bromide)
O$_3$ (ozone)	HI (hydrogen iodide)
F$_2$ (molecular fluorine)	CO (carbon monoxide)
Cl$_2$ (molecular chlorine)	CO$_2$ (carbon dioxide)
He (helium)	NH$_3$ (ammonia)
Ne (neon)	NO (nitric oxide)
Ar (argon)	NO$_2$ (nitrogen dioxide)
Kr (krypton)	N$_2$O (nitrous oxide)
Xe (xenon)	SO$_2$ (sulfur dioxide)
Rn (radon)	H$_2$S (hydrogen sulfide)
	HCN (hydrogen cyanide)*

*The boiling point of HCN is 26°C, but it is close enough to qualify as a gas at ordinary atmospheric conditions.

A gas is a substance that is normally in the gaseous state at ordinary temperatures and pressures; a vapor is the gaseous form of any substance that is a liquid or a solid at normal temperatures and pressures. Thus, at 25°C and 1 atm pressure, we speak of water vapor and oxygen gas.

Of the gases listed in Table 5.1, only O$_2$ is essential for our survival. Hydrogen sulfide (H$_2$S) and hydrogen cyanide (HCN) are deadly poisons. Several others, such as CO, NO$_2$, O$_3$, and SO$_2$, are somewhat less toxic. The gases He, Ne, and Ar are chemically inert; that is, they do not react with any other substance. Most gases are colorless. Exceptions are F$_2$, Cl$_2$, and NO$_2$. The dark-brown color of NO$_2$ is sometimes visible in polluted air. All gases have the following physical characteristics:

• Gases assume the volume and shape of their containers.

• Gases are the most compressible of the states of matter.

• Gases will mix evenly and completely when confined to the same container.

• Gases have much lower densities than liquids and solids.

NO$_2$ gas.

5.2 Pressure of a Gas

Gases exert pressure on any surface with which they come in contact, because gas molecules are constantly in motion. We humans have adapted so well physiologically to the pressure of the air around us that we are usually unaware of it, perhaps as fish are not conscious of the water's pressure on them.

It is easy to demonstrate atmospheric pressure. One everyday example is the ability to drink a liquid through a straw. Sucking air out of the straw reduces the pressure inside the straw. The greater atmospheric pressure on the liquid pushes it up into the straw to replace the air that has been sucked out.

SI Units of Pressure

Pressure is one of the most readily measurable properties of a gas. In order to understand how we measure the pressure of a gas, it is helpful to know how the units of measurement are derived. We begin with velocity and acceleration.

Velocity is defined as the change in distance with elapsed time; that is,

$$\text{velocity} = \frac{\text{distance moved}}{\text{elapsed time}}$$

The SI unit for velocity is m/s, although we also use cm/s.

Acceleration is the change in velocity with time, or

$$\text{acceleration} = \frac{\text{change in velocity}}{\text{elapsed time}}$$

Acceleration is measured in m/s^2 (or cm/s^2).

The second law of motion, formulated by Sir Isaac Newton[†] in the late seventeenth century, defines another term, from which the units of pressure are derived, namely, *force*. According to this law,

$$\text{force} = \text{mass} \times \text{acceleration}$$

1 N is roughly equivalent to the force exerted by Earth's gravity on an apple.

In this context, the *SI unit of force* is the **newton (N),** where

$$1 \text{ N} = 1 \text{ kg m/s}^2$$

Finally, we define **pressure** as *force applied per unit area:*

$$\text{pressure} = \frac{\text{force}}{\text{area}}$$

The SI unit of pressure is the **pascal (Pa),**[‡] defined as *one newton per square meter:*

$$1 \text{ Pa} = 1 \text{ N/m}^2$$

Atmospheric Pressure

The atoms and molecules of the gases in the atmosphere, like those of all other matter, are subject to Earth's gravitational pull. As a consequence, the atmosphere is much denser near the surface of Earth than at high altitudes. (The air outside the pressurized cabin of an airplane at 9 km is too thin to breathe.) In fact, the density of air decreases very rapidly with increasing distance from Earth. Measurements show that about 50 percent of the atmosphere lies within 6.4 km of Earth's surface, 90 percent within 16 km, and 99 percent within 32 km. Not surprisingly, the denser the air is, the greater the pressure it exerts. The force experienced by any area exposed to Earth's atmosphere is equal to *the weight of the column of air above it.* **Atmospheric pressure** is *the pressure exerted by Earth's atmosphere* (Figure 5.2). The actual value of atmospheric pressure depends on location, temperature, and weather conditions.

Does atmospheric pressure act only downward, as you might infer from its definition? Imagine what would happen, then, if you were to hold a piece of paper tight (with both hands) above your head. You might expect the paper to bend due to the pressure

Figure 5.2 *A column of air extending from sea level to the upper atmosphere.*

[†]Sir Issac Newton (1642–1726). English mathematician, physicist, and astronomer. Newton is regarded by many as one of the two greatest physicists the world has known (the other is Albert Einstein). There was hardly a branch of physics to which Newton did not make a significant contribution. His book *Principia,* published in 1687, marks a milestone in the history of science.

[‡]Blaise Pascal (1623–1662). French mathematician and physicist. Pascal's work ranged widely in mathematics and physics, but his specialty was in the area of hydrodynamics (the study of the motion of fluids). He also invented a calculating machine.

of air acting on it, but this does not happen. The reason is that air, like water, is a fluid. The pressure exerted on an object in a fluid comes from all directions—downward and upward, as well as from the left and from the right. At the molecular level, air pressure results from collisions between the air molecules and any surface with which they come in contact. The magnitude of pressure depends on how often and how strongly the molecules impact the surface. It turns out that there are just as many molecules hitting the paper from the top as there are from underneath, so the paper stays flat.

How is atmospheric pressure measured? The **barometer** is probably the most familiar *instrument for measuring atmospheric pressure.* A simple barometer consists of a long glass tube, closed at one end and filled with mercury. If the tube is carefully inverted in a dish of mercury so that no air enters the tube, some mercury will flow out of the tube into the dish, creating a vacuum at the top (Figure 5.3). The weight of the mercury remaining in the tube is supported by atmospheric pressure acting on the surface of the mercury in the dish. *Standard atmospheric pressure (1 atm)* is equal to *the pressure that supports a column of mercury exactly 760 mm (or 76 cm) high at 0°C at sea level.* In other words, the standard atmosphere equals a pressure of 760 mmHg, where mmHg represents the pressure exerted by a column of mercury 1 mm high. The mmHg unit is also called the *torr,* after the Italian scientist Evangelista Torricelli,[†] who invented the barometer. Thus

Figure 5.3 *A barometer for measuring atmospheric pressure. Above the mercury in the tube is a vacuum. The column of mercury is supported by the atmospheric pressure.*

$$1 \text{ torr} = 1 \text{ mmHg}$$

and

$$1 \text{ atm} = 760 \text{ mmHg} \qquad \text{(exactly)}$$

The relation between atmospheres and pascals (see Appendix 2) is

$$1 \text{ atm} = 101,325 \text{ Pa}$$
$$= 1.01325 \times 10^5 \text{ Pa}$$

and because 1000 Pa = 1 kPa (kilopascal)

$$1 \text{ atm} = 1.01325 \times 10^2 \text{ kPa}$$

Examples 5.1 and 5.2 show the conversion from mmHg to atm and kPa.

Example 5.1

The pressure outside a jet plane flying at high altitude falls considerably below standard atmospheric pressure. Therefore, the air inside the cabin must be pressurized to protect the passengers. What is the pressure in atmospheres in the cabin if the barometer reading is 688 mmHg?

Strategy Because 1 atm = 760 mmHg, the following conversion factor is needed to obtain the pressure in atmospheres

$$\frac{1 \text{ atm}}{760 \text{ mmHg}}$$

(Continued)

[†]Evangelista Torricelli (1608–1674). Italian mathematician. Torricelli was supposedly the first person to recognize the existence of atmospheric pressure.

Solution The pressure in the cabin is given by

$$\text{pressure} = 688 \text{ mmHg} \times \frac{1 \text{ atm}}{760 \text{ mmHg}}$$

$$= 0.905 \text{ atm}$$

Similar problem: 5.13.

Practice Exercise Convert 749 mmHg to atmospheres.

Example 5.2

The atmospheric pressure in San Francisco on a certain day was 732 mmHg. What was the pressure in kPa?

Strategy Here we are asked to convert mmHg to kPa. Because

$$1 \text{ atm} = 1.01325 \times 10^5 \text{ Pa} = 760 \text{ mmHg}$$

the conversion factor we need is

$$\frac{1.01325 \times 10^5 \text{ Pa}}{760 \text{ mmHg}}$$

Solution The pressure in kPa is

$$\text{pressure} = 732 \text{ mmHg} \times \frac{1.01325 \times 10^5 \text{ Pa}}{760 \text{ mmHg}}$$

$$= 9.76 \times 10^4 \text{ Pa}$$

$$= 97.6 \text{ kPa}$$

Similar problem: 5.14.

Practice Exercise Convert 295 mmHg to kilopascals.

A **manometer** is *a device used to measure the pressure of gases other than the atmosphere*. The principle of operation of a manometer is similar to that of a barometer. There are two types of manometers, shown in Figure 5.4. The *closed-tube*

Figure 5.4 *Two types of manometers used to measure gas pressures. (a) Gas pressure is less than atmospheric pressure. (b) Gas pressure is greater than atmospheric pressure.*

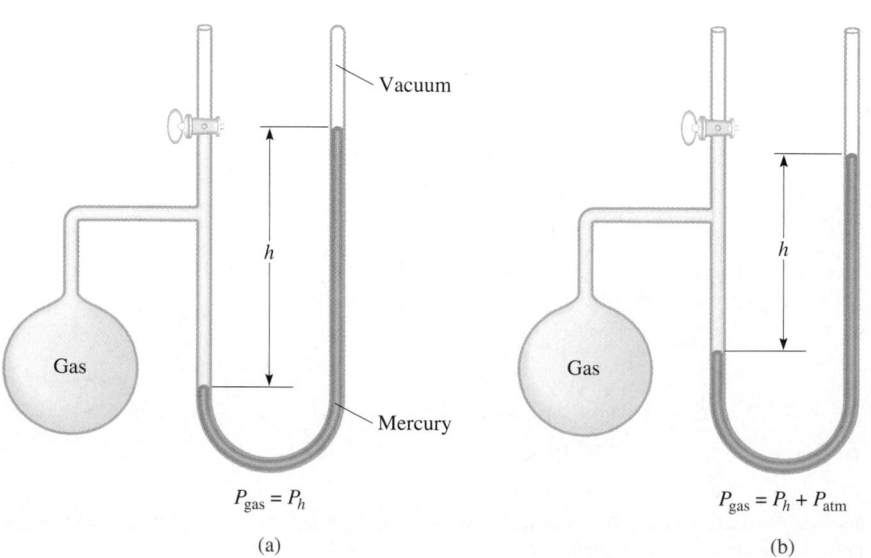

$P_{gas} = P_h$

(a)

$P_{gas} = P_h + P_{atm}$

(b)

manometer is normally used to measure pressures below atmospheric pressure [Figure 5.4(a)], whereas the *open-tube manometer* is better suited for measuring pressures equal to or greater than atmospheric pressure [Figure 5.4(b)].

Nearly all barometers and many manometers use mercury as the working fluid, despite the fact that it is a toxic substance with a harmful vapor. The reason is that mercury has a very high density (13.6 g/mL) compared with most other liquids. Because the height of the liquid in a column is inversely proportional to the liquid's density, this property enables the construction of manageably small barometers and manometers.

5.3 The Gas Laws

The gas laws we will study in this chapter are the product of countless experiments on the physical properties of gases that were carried out over several centuries. Each of these generalizations regarding the macroscopic behavior of gaseous substances represents a milestone in the history of science. Together they have played a major role in the development of many ideas in chemistry.

Animation:
The Gas Laws
ARIS, Animations

The Pressure-Volume Relationship: Boyle's Law

In the seventeenth century, Robert Boyle[†] studied the behavior of gases systematically and quantitatively. In one series of studies, Boyle investigated the pressure-volume relationship of a gas sample. Typical data collected by Boyle are shown in Table 5.2. Note that as the pressure (P) is increased at constant temperature, the volume (V) occupied by a given amount of gas decreases. Compare the first data point with a pressure of 724 mmHg and a volume of 1.50 (in arbitrary unit) to the last data point with a pressure of 2250 mmHg and a volume of 0.58. Clearly there is an inverse relationship between pressure and volume of a gas at constant temperature. As the pressure is increased, the volume occupied by the gas decreases. Conversely, if the applied pressure is decreased, the volume the gas occupies increases. This relationship is now known as **Boyle's law,** which states that *the pressure of a fixed amount of gas at a constant temperature is inversely proportional to the volume of the gas.*

Interactivity:
Boyle's Law
ARIS, Interactives

The pressure applied to a gas is equal to the gas pressure.

The apparatus used by Boyle in this experiment was very simple (Figure 5.5). In Figure 5.5(a), the pressure exerted on the gas is equal to atmospheric pressure and the volume of the gas is 100 mL. (Note that the tube is open at the top and is therefore exposed to atmospheric pressure.) In Figure 5.5(b), more mercury has been added to double the pressure on the gas, and the gas volume decreases to 50 mL. Tripling the pressure on the gas decreases its volume to a third of the original value [Figure 5.5(c)].

[†]Robert Boyle (1627–1691). British chemist and natural philosopher. Although Boyle is commonly associated with the gas law that bears his name, he made many other significant contributions in chemistry and physics. Despite the fact that Boyle was often at odds with scientists of his generation, his book *The Skeptical Chymist* (1661) influenced generations of chemists.

TABLE 5.2	Typical Pressure-Volume Relationship Obtained by Boyle						
P (mmHg)	724	869	951	998	1230	1893	2250
V (arbitrary units)	1.50	1.33	1.22	1.18	0.94	0.61	0.58
PV	1.09×10^3	1.16×10^3	1.16×10^3	1.18×10^3	1.2×10^3	1.2×10^3	1.3×10^3

Figure 5.5 *Apparatus for studying the relationship between pressure and volume of a gas. (a) The levels of mercury are equal and the pressure of the gas is equal to the atmospheric pressure (760 mmHg). The gas volume is 100 mL. (b) Doubling the pressure by adding more mercury reduces the gas volume to 50 mL. (c) Tripling the pressure decreases the gas volume to one-third of the original value. The temperature and amount of gas are kept constant.*

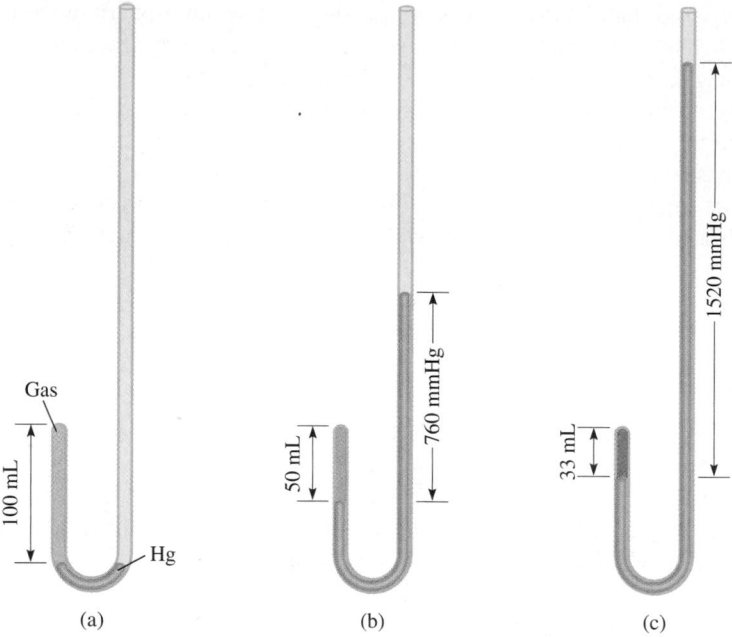

We can write a mathematical expression showing the inverse relationship between pressure and volume:

$$P \propto \frac{1}{V}$$

where the symbol $\propto$ means *proportional to*. We can change $\propto$ to an equals sign and write

$$P = k_1 \times \frac{1}{V} \tag{5.1a}$$

where k_1 is a constant called the *proportionality constant*. Equation (5.1a) is the mathematical expression of Boyle's law. We can rearrange Equation (5.1a) and obtain

$$PV = k_1 \tag{5.1b}$$

This form of Boyle's law says that the product of the pressure and volume of a gas at constant temperature and amount of gas is a constant. The top diagram in Figure 5.6 is a schematic representation of Boyle's law. The quantity n is the number of moles of the gas and R is a constant to be defined in Section 5.4. We will see in Section 5.4 that the proportionality constant k_1 in Equations (5.1) is equal to nRT.

The concept of one quantity being proportional to another and the use of a proportionality constant can be clarified through the following analogy. The daily income of a movie theater depends on both the price of the tickets (in dollars per ticket) and the number of tickets sold. Assuming that the theater charges one price for all tickets, we write

$$\text{income} = (\text{dollar/ticket}) \times \text{number of tickets sold}$$

Because the number of tickets sold varies from day to day, the income on a given day is said to be proportional to the number of tickets sold:

$$\text{income} \propto \text{number of tickets sold}$$
$$= C \times \text{number of tickets sold}$$

where C, the proportionality constant, is the price per ticket.

Increasing or decreasing the volume of a gas
at a constant temperature

Volume decreases
(Pressure increases)

Volume increases
(Pressure decreases)

Boyle's Law

Boyle's Law
$$P = (nRT)\frac{1}{V} \quad nRT \text{ is constant}$$

Heating or cooling a gas at constant pressure

Lower temperature
(Volume decreases)

Higher temperature
(Volume increases)

Charles's Law
$$V = \left(\frac{nR}{P}\right) T \quad \frac{nR}{P} \text{ is constant}$$

Charles's Law

Heating or cooling a gas at constant volume

Lower temperature
(Pressure decreases)

Higher temperature
(Pressure increases)

Charles's Law
$$P = \left(\frac{nR}{V}\right) T \quad \frac{nR}{V} \text{ is constant}$$

Dependence of volume on amount
of gas at constant temperature and pressure

Gas cylinder

Remove gas
(Volume decreases)

Add gas molecules
(Volume increases)

Valve

Avogadro's Law
$$V = \left(\frac{RT}{P}\right) n \quad \frac{RT}{P} \text{ is constant}$$

Figure 5.6 *Schematic illustrations of Boyle's law, Charles's law, and Avogadro's law.*

Figure 5.7 *Graphs showing variation of the volume of a gas with the pressure exerted on the gas, at constant temperature. (a) P versus V. Note that the volume of the gas doubles as the pressure is halved. (b) P versus 1/V. The slope of the line is equal to k_1.*

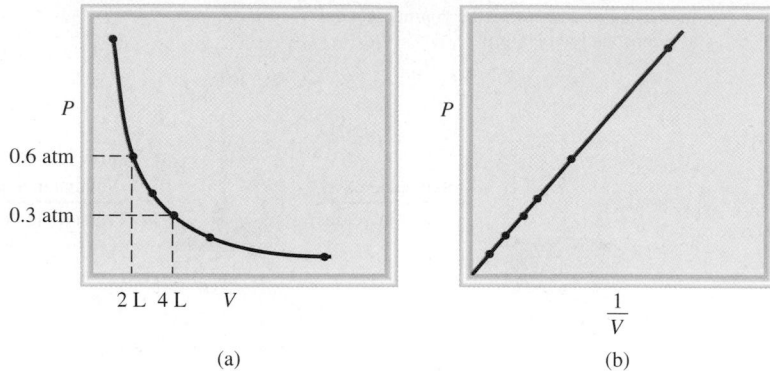

(a)   (b)

Figure 5.7 shows two conventional ways of expressing Boyle's findings graphically. Figure 5.7(a) is a graph of the equation $PV = k_1$; Figure 5.7(b) is a graph of the equivalent equation $P = k_1 \times 1/V$. Note that the latter is a linear equation of the form $y = mx + b$, where $b = 0$.

Although the individual values of pressure and volume can vary greatly for a given sample of gas, as long as the temperature is held constant and the amount of the gas does not change, P times V is always equal to the same constant. Therefore, for a given sample of gas under two different sets of conditions at constant temperature, we have

$$P_1V_1 = k_1 = P_2V_2$$

or

$$P_1V_1 = P_2V_2 \tag{5.2}$$

where V_1 and V_2 are the volumes at pressures P_1 and P_2, respectively.

The Temperature-Volume Relationship: Charles's and Gay-Lussac's Law

Boyle's law depends on the temperature of the system remaining constant. But suppose the temperature changes: How does a change in temperature affect the volume and pressure of a gas? Let us first look at the effect of temperature on the volume of a gas. The earliest investigators of this relationship were French scientists, Jacques Charles[†] and Joseph Gay-Lussac.[‡] Their studies showed that, at constant pressure, the volume of a gas sample expands when heated and contracts when cooled (Figure 5.8). The quantitative relations involved in changes in gas temperature and volume turn out to be remarkably consistent. For example, we observe an interesting phenomenon when we study the temperature-volume relationship at various pressures. At any given pressure, the plot of volume versus temperature yields a straight line. By extending the line to zero volume, we find the intercept on the temperature axis to be −273.15°C. At any other pressure, we obtain a different

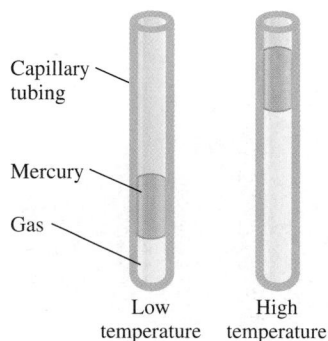

Figure 5.8 *Variation of the volume of a gas sample with temperature, at constant pressure. The pressure exerted on the gas is the sum of the atmospheric pressure and the pressure due to the weight of the mercury.*

[†]Jacques Alexandre Cesar Charles (1746–1823). French physicist. He was a gifted lecturer, an inventor of scientific apparatus, and the first person to use hydrogen to inflate balloons.

[‡]Joseph Louis Gay-Lussac (1778–1850). French chemist and physicist. Like Charles, Gay-Lussac was a balloon enthusiast. Once he ascended to an altitude of 20,000 ft to collect air samples for analysis.

Figure 5.9 *Variation of the volume of a gas sample with temperature, at constant pressure. Each line represents the variation at a certain pressure. The pressures increase from P_1 to P_4. All gases ultimately condense (become liquids) if they are cooled to sufficiently low temperatures; the solid portions of the lines represent the temperature region above the condensation point. When these lines are extrapolated, or extended (the dashed portions), they all intersect at the point representing zero volume and a temperature of −273.15°C.*

straight line for the volume-temperature plot, but we get the *same* zero-volume temperature intercept at −273.15°C (Figure 5.9). (In practice, we can measure the volume of a gas over only a limited temperature range, because all gases condense at low temperatures to form liquids.)

In 1848 Lord Kelvin[§] realized the significance of this phenomenon. He identified −273.15°C as *absolute zero, theoretically the lowest attainable temperature.* Then he set up an *absolute temperature scale,* now called the *Kelvin temperature scale,* with *absolute zero as the starting point.* (see Section 1.7). On the Kelvin scale, one kelvin (K) is equal *in magnitude* to one degree Celsius. The only difference between the absolute temperature scale and the Celsius scale is that the zero position is shifted. Important points on the two scales match up as follows:

	Kelvin Scale	Celsius Scale
Absolute zero	0 K	−273.15°C
Freezing point of water	273.15 K	0°C
Boiling point of water	373.15 K	100°C

Under special experimental conditions, scientists have succeeded in approaching absolute zero to within a small fraction of a kelvin.

The conversion between °C and K is given on p. 20. In most calculations we will use 273 instead of 273.15 as the term relating K and °C. By convention, we use T to denote absolute (kelvin) temperature and t to indicate temperature on the Celsius scale.

The dependence of the volume of a gas on temperature is given by

$$V \propto T$$
$$V = k_2 T$$

or
$$\frac{V}{T} = k_2 \qquad\qquad (5.3)$$

where k_2 is the proportionality constant. Equation (5.3) is known as *Charles's and Gay-Lussac's law,* or simply *Charles's law,* which states that *the volume of a fixed amount of gas maintained at constant pressure is directly proportional to the absolute temperature of the gas.* Charles's law is also illustrated in Figure 5.6. We see that the proportionality constant k_2 in Equation (5.3) is equal to nR/P.

[§]William Thomson, Lord Kelvin (1824–1907). Scottish mathematician and physicist. Kelvin did important work in many branches of physics.

Just as we did for pressure-volume relationships at constant temperature, we can compare two sets of volume-temperature conditions for a given sample of gas at constant pressure. From Equation (5.3) we can write

$$\frac{V_1}{T_1} = k_2 = \frac{V_2}{T_2}$$

or

$$\frac{V_1}{T_1} = \frac{V_2}{T_2} \tag{5.4}$$

where V_1 and V_2 are the volumes of the gas at temperatures T_1 and T_2 (both in kelvins), respectively.

Another form of Charles's law shows that at constant amount of gas and volume, the pressure of a gas is proportional to temperature

$$P \propto T$$
$$P = k_3T$$

or

$$\frac{P}{T} = k_3 \tag{5.5}$$

From Figure 5.6 we see that $k_3 = nR/V$. Starting with Equation (5.5), we have

$$\frac{P_1}{T_1} = k_3 = \frac{P_2}{T_2}$$

or

$$\frac{P_1}{T_1} = \frac{P_2}{T_2} \tag{5.6}$$

where P_1 and P_2 are the pressures of the gas at temperatures T_1 and T_2, respectively.

The Volume-Amount Relationship: Avogadro's Law

Avogadro's name first appeared in Section 3.2.

The work of the Italian scientist Amedeo Avogadro complemented the studies of Boyle, Charles, and Gay-Lussac. In 1811 he published a hypothesis stating that at the same temperature and pressure, equal volumes of different gases contain the same number of molecules (or atoms if the gas is monatomic). It follows that the volume of any given gas must be proportional to the number of moles of molecules present; that is,

$$V \propto n$$
$$V = k_4n \tag{5.7}$$

where n represents the number of moles and k_4 is the proportionality constant. Equation (5.7) is the mathematical expression of *Avogadro's law,* which states that *at constant pressure and temperature, the volume of a gas is directly proportional to the number of moles of the gas present.* From Figure 5.6 we see that $k_4 = RT/P$.

According to Avogadro's law we see that when two gases react with each other, their reacting volumes have a simple ratio to each other. If the product is a gas, its volume is related to the volume of the reactants by a simple ratio (a fact demonstrated earlier by Gay-Lussac). For example, consider the synthesis of ammonia from molecular hydrogen and molecular nitrogen:

$$3H_2(g) + N_2(g) \longrightarrow 2NH_3(g)$$

3 mol   1 mol   2 mol

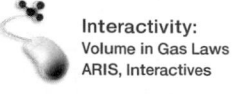
Interactivity:
Volume in Gas Laws
ARIS, Interactives

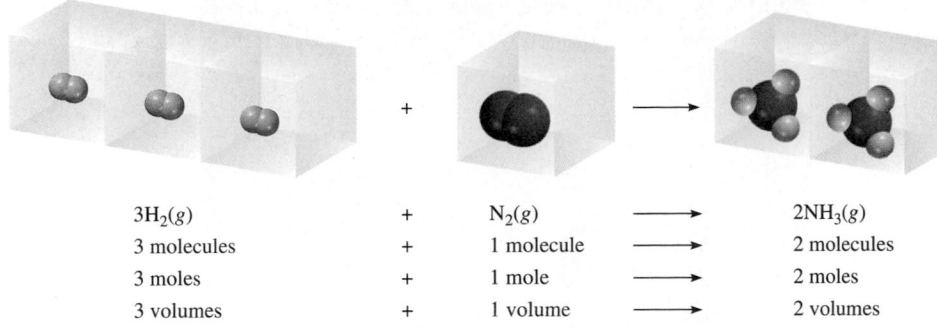

$3H_2(g)$	+	$N_2(g)$	$\longrightarrow$	$2NH_3(g)$
3 molecules	+	1 molecule	$\longrightarrow$	2 molecules
3 moles	+	1 mole	$\longrightarrow$	2 moles
3 volumes	+	1 volume	$\longrightarrow$	2 volumes

Because, at the same temperature and pressure, the volumes of gases are directly proportional to the number of moles of the gases present, we can now write

$$3H_2(g) + N_2(g) \longrightarrow 2NH_3(g)$$

3 volumes   1 volume   2 volumes

The volume ratio of molecular hydrogen to molecular nitrogen is 3:1, and that of ammonia (the product) to molecular hydrogen and molecular nitrogen (the reactants) combined is 2:4, or 1:2 (Figure 5.10).

Worked examples illustrating the gas laws are presented in Section 5.4.

5.4 The Ideal Gas Equation

Let us summarize the gas laws we have discussed so far:

$$\text{Boyle's law: } V \propto \frac{1}{P} \quad \text{(at constant } n \text{ and } T)$$

$$\text{Charles's law: } V \propto T \quad \text{(at constant } n \text{ and } P)$$

$$\text{Avogadro's law: } V \propto n \quad \text{(at constant } P \text{ and } T)$$

We can combine all three expressions to form a single master equation for the behavior of gases:

$$V \propto \frac{nT}{P}$$

$$V = R\frac{nT}{P}$$

or

$$PV = nRT \tag{5.8}$$

where **R,** *the proportionality constant,* is called the **gas constant.** Equation (5.8), which is called the **ideal gas equation,** *describes the relationship among the four variables P, V, T, and n.* An **ideal gas** is *a hypothetical gas whose pressure-volume-temperature behavior can be completely accounted for by the ideal gas equation.* The molecules of an ideal gas do not attract or repel one another, and their volume is negligible compared with the volume of the container. Although there is no such thing in nature as an ideal gas, the ideal gas approximation works rather well for most reasonable temperature and pressure ranges. Thus, we can safely use the ideal gas equation to solve many gas problems.

Keep in mind that the ideal gas equation, unlike the gas laws discussed in Section 5.3, applies to systems that do not undergo changes in pressure, volume, temperature, and amount of a gas.

Figure 5.11 *A comparison of the molar volume at STP (which is approximately 22.4 L) with a basketball.*

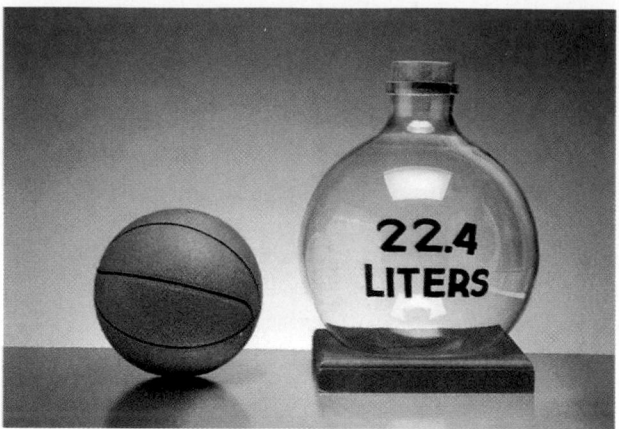

Before we can apply the ideal gas equation to a real system, we must evaluate the gas constant R. At 0°C (273.15 K) and 1 atm pressure, many real gases behave like an ideal gas. Experiments show that under these conditions, 1 mole of an ideal gas occupies 22.414 L, which is somewhat greater than the volume of a basketball, as shown in Figure 5.11. *The conditions 0°C and 1 atm are called **standard temperature and pressure,** often abbreviated **STP.*** From Equation (5.8) we can write

The gas constant can be expressed in different units (see Appendix 2).

$$
\begin{aligned}
R &= \frac{PV}{nT} \\
&= \frac{(1\ \text{atm})(22.414\ \text{L})}{(1\ \text{mol})(273.15\ \text{K})} \\
&= 0.082057\ \frac{\text{L} \cdot \text{atm}}{\text{K} \cdot \text{mol}} \\
&= 0.082057\ \text{L} \cdot \text{atm/K} \cdot \text{mol}
\end{aligned}
$$

The dots between L and atm and between K and mol remind us that both L and atm are in the numerator and both K and mol are in the denominator. For most calculations, we will round off the value of R to three significant figures (0.0821 L · atm/K · mol) and use 22.41 L for the molar volume of a gas at STP.

Example 5.3 shows that if we know the quantity, volume, and temperature of a gas, we can calculate its pressure using the ideal gas equation. Unless otherwise stated, we assume that the temperatures given in °C in calculations are exact so that they do not affect the number of significant figures.

SF_6

Example 5.3

Sulfur hexafluoride (SF_6) is a colorless, odorless, very unreactive gas. Calculate the pressure (in atm) exerted by 1.82 moles of the gas in a steel vessel of volume 5.43 L at 69.5°C.

Strategy The problem gives the amount of the gas and its volume and temperature. Is the gas undergoing a change in any of its properties? What equation should we use to solve for the pressure? What temperature unit should we use?

Solution Because no changes in gas properties occur, we can use the ideal gas equation to calculate the pressure. Rearranging Equation (5.8), we write

(Continued)

$$P = \frac{nRT}{V}$$

$$= \frac{(1.82 \text{ mol})(0.0821 \text{ L} \cdot \text{atm/K} \cdot \text{mol})(69.5 + 273) \text{ K}}{5.43 \text{ L}}$$

$$= 9.42 \text{ atm}$$

Similar problem: 5.32.

Practice Exercise Calculate the volume (in liters) occupied by 2.12 moles of nitric oxide (NO) at 6.54 atm and 76°C.

By using the fact that the molar volume of a gas occupies 22.41 L at STP, we can calculate the volume of a gas at STP without using the ideal gas equation.

Example 5.4

Calculate the volume (in liters) occupied by 7.40 g of NH_3 at STP.

Strategy What is the volume of one mole of an ideal gas at STP? How many moles are there in 7.40 g of NH_3?

Solution Recognizing that 1 mole of an ideal gas occupies 22.41 L at STP and using the molar mass of NH_3 (17.03 g), we write the sequence of conversions as

NH_3

$$\text{grams of } NH_3 \longrightarrow \text{moles of } NH_3 \longrightarrow \text{liters of } NH_3 \text{ at STP}$$

so the volume of NH_3 is given by

$$V = 7.40 \text{ g } NH_3 \times \frac{1 \text{ mol } NH_3}{17.03 \text{ g } NH_3} \times \frac{22.41 \text{ L}}{1 \text{ mol } NH_3}$$

$$= 9.74 \text{ L}$$

It is often true in chemistry, particularly in gas-law calculations, that a problem can be solved in more than one way. Here the problem can also be solved by first converting 7.40 g of NH_3 to number of moles of NH_3, and then applying the ideal gas equation $(V = nRT/P)$. Try it.

Check Because 7.40 g of NH_3 is smaller than its molar mass, its volume at STP should be smaller than 22.41 L. Therefore, the answer is reasonable.

Similar problem: 5.40.

Practice Exercise What is the volume (in liters) occupied by 49.8 g of HCl at STP?

The ideal gas equation is useful for problems that do not involve changes in P, V, T, and n for a gas sample. Thus, if we know any three of the variables we can calculate the fourth one using the equation. At times, however, we need to deal with changes in pressure, volume, and temperature, or even in the amount of gas. When conditions change, we must employ a modified form of the ideal gas equation that takes into account the initial and final conditions. We derive the modified equation as follows. From Equation (5.8),

$$R = \frac{P_1 V_1}{n_1 T_1} \text{ (before change)} \quad \text{and} \quad R = \frac{P_2 V_2}{n_2 T_2} \text{ (after change)}$$

The subscripts 1 and 2 denote the initial and final states of the gas, respectively.

Therefore,

$$\frac{P_1 V_1}{n_1 T_1} = \frac{P_2 V_2}{n_2 T_2} \qquad (5.9)$$

It is interesting to note that all the gas laws discussed in Section 5.3 can be derived from Equation (5.9). If $n_1 = n_2$, as is usually the case because the amount of gas normally does not change, the equation then becomes

$$\frac{P_1V_1}{T_1} = \frac{P_2V_2}{T_2} \tag{5.10}$$

Applications of Equation (5.9) are shown in Examples 5.5, 5.6, and 5.7.

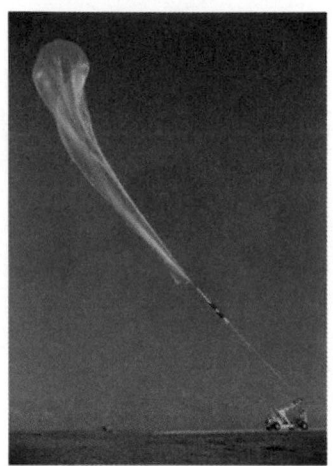

A scientific research helium balloon.

Example 5.5

An inflated helium balloon with a volume of 0.55 L at sea level (1.0 atm) is allowed to rise to a height of 6.5 km, where the pressure is about 0.40 atm. Assuming that the temperature remains constant, what is the final volume of the balloon?

Strategy The amount of gas inside the balloon and its temperature remain constant, but both the pressure and the volume change. What gas law do you need?

Solution We start with Equation (5.9)

$$\frac{P_1V_1}{n_1T_1} = \frac{P_2V_2}{n_2T_2}$$

Because $n_1 = n_2$ and $T_1 = T_2$,

$$P_1V_1 = P_2V_2$$

which is Boyle's law [see Equation (5.2)]. The given information is tabulated:

Initial Conditions	Final Conditions
$P_1 = 1.0$ atm	$P_2 = 0.40$ atm
$V_1 = 0.55$ L	$V_2 = ?$

Therefore,

$$V_2 = V_1 \times \frac{P_1}{P_2}$$
$$= 0.55 \text{ L} \times \frac{1.0 \text{ atm}}{0.40 \text{ atm}}$$
$$= 1.4 \text{ L}$$

Similar problem: 5.19.

Check When pressure applied on the balloon is reduced (at constant temperature), the helium gas expands and the balloon's volume increases. The final volume is greater than the initial volume, so the answer is reasonable.

Practice Exercise A sample of chlorine gas occupies a volume of 946 mL at a pressure of 726 mmHg. Calculate the pressure of the gas (in mmHg) if the volume is reduced at constant temperature to 154 mL.

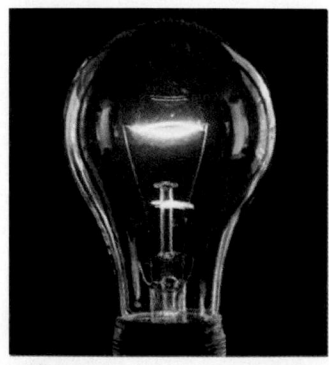

Electric lightbulbs are usually filled with argon.

Example 5.6

Argon is an inert gas used in lightbulbs to retard the vaporization of the tungsten filament. A certain lightbulb containing argon at 1.20 atm and 18°C is heated to 85°C at constant volume. Calculate its final pressure (in atm).

(Continued)

Strategy The temperature and pressure of argon change but the amount and volume of gas remain the same. What equation would you use to solve for the final pressure? What temperature unit should you use?

Solution Because $n_1 = n_2$ and $V_1 = V_2$, Equation (5.9) becomes

$$\frac{P_1}{T_1} = \frac{P_2}{T_2}$$

which is Charles's law [see Equation (5.6)]. Next we write

Initial Conditions	Final Conditions
$P_1 = 1.20$ atm	$P_2 = ?$
$T_1 = (18 + 273)$ K $= 291$ K	$T_2 = (85 + 273)$ K $= 358$ K

Remember to convert °C to K when solving gas-law problems.

The final pressure is given by

$$P_2 = P_1 \times \frac{T_2}{T_1}$$

$$= 1.20 \text{ atm} \times \frac{358 \text{ K}}{291 \text{ K}}$$

$$= 1.48 \text{ atm}$$

One practical consequence of this relationship is that automobile tire pressures should be checked only when the tires are at normal temperatures. After a long drive (especially in the summer), tires become quite hot, and the air pressure inside them rises.

Check At constant volume, the pressure of a given amount of gas is directly proportional to its absolute temperature. Therefore the increase in pressure is reasonable.

Similar problem: 5.36.

Practice Exercise A sample of oxygen gas initially at 0.97 atm is cooled from 21°C to −68°C at constant volume. What is its final pressure (in atm)?

Example 5.7

A small bubble rises from the bottom of a lake, where the temperature and pressure are 8°C and 6.4 atm, to the water's surface, where the temperature is 25°C and the pressure is 1.0 atm. Calculate the final volume (in mL) of the bubble if its initial volume was 2.1 mL.

Strategy In solving this kind of problem, where a lot of information is given, it is sometimes helpful to make a sketch of the situation, as shown here:

What temperature unit should be used in the calculation?

Solution According to Equation (5.9)

$$\frac{P_1 V_1}{n_1 T_1} = \frac{P_2 V_2}{n_2 T_2}$$

(Continued)

We can use any appropriate units for volume (or pressure) as long as we use the same units on both sides of the equation.

We assume that the amount of air in the bubble remains constant, that is, $n_1 = n_2$ so that

$$\frac{P_1 V_1}{T_1} = \frac{P_2 V_2}{T_2}$$

which is Equation (5.10). The given information is summarized:

Initial Conditions	Final Conditions
$P_1 = 6.4$ atm	$P_2 = 1.0$ atm
$V_1 = 2.1$ mL	$V_2 = ?$
$T_1 = (8 + 273)$ K $= 281$ K	$T_2 = (25 + 273)$ K $= 298$ K

Rearranging Equation (5.10) gives

$$V_2 = V_1 \times \frac{P_1}{P_2} \times \frac{T_2}{T_1}$$

$$= 2.1 \text{ mL} \times \frac{6.4 \text{ atm}}{1.0 \text{ atm}} \times \frac{298 \text{ K}}{281 \text{ K}}$$

$$= 14 \text{ mL}$$

Check We see that the final volume involves multiplying the initial volume by a ratio of pressures (P_1/P_2) and a ratio of temperatures (T_2/T_1). Recall that volume is inversely proportional to pressure, and volume is directly proportional to temperature. Because the pressure decreases and temperature increases as the bubble rises, we expect the bubble's volume to increase. In fact, here the change in pressure plays a greater role in the volume change.

Practice Exercise A gas initially at 4.0 L, 1.2 atm, and 66°C undergoes a change so that its final volume and temperature are 1.7 L and 42°C. What is its final pressure? Assume the number of moles remains unchanged.

Similar problem: 5.35.

Density Calculations

If we rearrange the ideal gas equation, we can calculate the density of a gas:

$$\frac{n}{V} = \frac{P}{RT}$$

The number of moles of the gas, n, is given by

$$n = \frac{m}{\mathcal{M}}$$

where m is the mass of the gas in grams and $\mathcal{M}$ is its molar mass. Therefore

$$\frac{m}{\mathcal{M}V} = \frac{P}{RT}$$

Because density, d, is mass per unit volume, we can write

$$d = \frac{m}{V} = \frac{P\mathcal{M}}{RT} \tag{5.11}$$

Unlike molecules in condensed matter (that is, in liquids and solids), gaseous molecules are separated by distances that are large compared with their size. Consequently, the density of gases is very low under atmospheric conditions. For this reason, gas densities are usually expressed in grams per liter (g/L) rather than grams per milliliter (g/mL), as Example 5.8 shows.

CO_2

Example 5.8

Calculate the density of carbon dioxide (CO_2) in grams per liter (g/L) at 0.990 atm and 55°C.

Strategy We need Equation (5.11) to calculate gas density. Is sufficient information provided in the problem? What temperature unit should be used?

Solution To use Equation (5.11), we convert temperature to kelvins ($T = 273 + 55 = 328$ K) and use 44.01 g for the molar mass of CO_2:

$$d = \frac{P\mathcal{M}}{RT}$$

$$= \frac{(0.990 \text{ atm})(44.01 \text{ g/mol})}{(0.0821 \text{ L} \cdot \text{atm/K} \cdot \text{mol})(328 \text{ K})} = 1.62 \text{ g/L}$$

Alternatively, we can solve for the density by writing

$$\text{density} = \frac{\text{mass}}{\text{volume}}$$

Assuming that we have 1 mole of CO_2, the mass is 44.01 g. The volume of the gas can be obtained from the ideal gas equation

$$V = \frac{nRT}{P}$$

$$= \frac{(1 \text{ mol})(0.0821 \text{ L} \cdot \text{atm/K} \cdot \text{mol})(328 \text{ K})}{0.990 \text{ atm}}$$

$$= 27.2 \text{ L}$$

Therefore, the density of CO_2 is given by

$$d = \frac{44.01 \text{ g}}{27.2 \text{ L}} = 1.62 \text{ g/L}$$

Being an intensive property, density is independent of the amount of substance. Therefore, we can use any convenient amount to help us solve the problem.

Comment In units of grams per milliliter, the gas density is 1.62×10^{-3} g/mL, which is a very small number. In comparison, the density of water is 1.0 g/mL and that of gold is 19.3 g/cm^3.

Similar problem: 5.48.

Practice Exercise What is the density (in g/L) of uranium hexafluoride (UF_6) at 779 mmHg and 62°C?

The Molar Mass of a Gaseous Substance

From what we have said so far, you may have the impression that the molar mass of a substance is found by examining its formula and summing the molar masses of its component atoms. However, this procedure works only if the actual formula of the substance is known. In practice, chemists often deal with substances of unknown or only partially defined composition. If the unknown substance is gaseous, its molar mass can nevertheless be found thanks to the ideal gas equation. All that is needed is an experimentally determined density value (or mass and volume data) for the gas at a known temperature and pressure. By rearranging Equation (5.11) we get

$$\mathcal{M} = \frac{dRT}{P} \qquad\qquad (5.12)$$

Figure 5.12 *An apparatus for measuring the density of a gas. A bulb of known volume is filled with the gas under study at a certain temperature and pressure. First the bulb is weighed, and then it is emptied (evacuated) and weighed again. The difference in masses gives the mass of the gas. Knowing the volume of the bulb, we can calculate the density of the gas. Under atmospheric conditions, 100 mL of air weigh about 0.12 g, an easily measured quantity.*

In a typical experiment, a bulb of known volume is filled with the gaseous substance under study. The temperature and pressure of the gas sample are recorded, and the total mass of the bulb plus gas sample is determined (Figure 5.12). The bulb is then evacuated (emptied) and weighed again. The difference in mass is the mass of the gas. The density of the gas is equal to its mass divided by the volume of the bulb. Once we know the density of a gas, we can calculate the molar mass of the substance using Equation (5.12). Of course, a mass spectrometer would be the ideal instrument to determine the molar mass, but not every chemist can afford one.

Example 5.9 shows the density method for molar mass determination.

Example 5.9

A chemist has synthesized a greenish-yellow gaseous compound of chlorine and oxygen and finds that its density is 7.71 g/L at 36°C and 2.88 atm. Calculate the molar mass of the compound and determine its molecular formula.

Strategy Because Equations (5.11) and (5.12) are rearrangements of each other, we can calculate the molar mass of a gas if we know its density, temperature, and pressure. The molecular formula of the compound must be consistent with its molar mass. What temperature unit should we use?

Solution From Equation (5.12)

$$\mathcal{M} = \frac{dRT}{P}$$

$$= \frac{(7.71 \text{ g/L})(0.0821 \text{ L} \cdot \text{atm/K} \cdot \text{mol})(36 + 273) \text{ K}}{2.88 \text{ atm}}$$

$$= 67.9 \text{ g/mol}$$

Alternatively, we can solve for the molar mass by writing

$$\text{molar mass of compound} = \frac{\text{mass of compound}}{\text{moles of compound}}$$

From the given density we know there are 7.71 g of the gas in 1 L. The number of moles of the gas in this volume can be obtained from the ideal gas equation

$$n = \frac{PV}{RT}$$

$$= \frac{(2.88 \text{ atm})(1.00 \text{ L})}{(0.0821 \text{ L} \cdot \text{atm/K} \cdot \text{mol})(309 \text{ K})}$$

$$= 0.1135 \text{ mol}$$

Therefore, the molar mass is given by

$$\mathcal{M} = \frac{7.71 \text{ g}}{0.1135 \text{ mol}} = 67.9 \text{ g/mol}$$

We can determine the molecular formula of the compound by trial and error, using only the knowledge of the molar masses of chlorine (35.45 g) and oxygen (16.00 g). We know that a compound containing one Cl atom and one O atom would have a molar mass of 51.45 g, which is too low, while the molar mass of a compound made up of two Cl

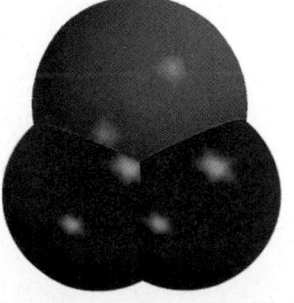

ClO₂

(Continued)

atoms and one O atom is 86.90 g, which is too high. Thus, the compound must contain one Cl atom and two O atoms and have the formula ClO_2 , which has a molar mass of 67.45 g.

Similar problems: 5.43, 5.47.

Practice Exercise The density of a gaseous organic compound is 3.38 g/L at 40°C and 1.97 atm. What is its molar mass?

Because Equation (5.12) is derived from the ideal gas equation, we can also calculate the molar mass of a gaseous substance using the ideal gas equation, as shown in Example 5.10.

Example 5.10

Chemical analysis of a gaseous compound showed that it contained 33.0 percent silicon (Si) and 67.0 percent fluorine (F) by mass. At 35°C, 0.210 L of the compound exerted a pressure of 1.70 atm. If the mass of 0.210 L of the compound was 2.38 g, calculate the molecular formula of the compound.

Strategy This problem can be divided into two parts. First, it asks for the empirical formula of the compound from the percent by mass of Si and F. Second, the information provided enables us to calculate the molar mass of the compound and hence determine its molecular formula. What is the relationship between empirical molar mass and molar mass calculated from the molecular formula?

Si_2F_6

Solution We follow the procedure in Example 3.9 (p. 88) to calculate the empirical formula by assuming that we have 100 g of the compound, so the percentages are converted to grams. The number of moles of Si and F are given by

$$n_{Si} = 33.0 \text{ g Si} \times \frac{1 \text{ mol Si}}{28.09 \text{ g Si}} = 1.17 \text{ mol Si}$$

$$n_F = 67.0 \text{ g F} \times \frac{1 \text{ mol F}}{19.00 \text{ g F}} = 3.53 \text{ mol F}$$

Therefore, the empirical formula is $Si_{1.17}F_{3.53}$, or, dividing by the smaller subscript (1.17), we obtain SiF_3.

To calculate the molar mass of the compound, we need first to calculate the number of moles contained in 2.38 g of the compound. From the ideal gas equation

$$n = \frac{PV}{RT}$$

$$= \frac{(1.70 \text{ atm})(0.210 \text{ L})}{(0.0821 \text{ L} \cdot \text{atm/K} \cdot \text{mol})(308 \text{ K})} = 0.0141 \text{ mol}$$

Because there are 2.38 g in 0.0141 mole of the compound, the mass in 1 mole, or the molar mass, is given by

$$\mathcal{M} = \frac{2.38 \text{ g}}{0.0141 \text{ mol}} = 169 \text{ g/mol}$$

The molar mass of the empirical formula SiF_3 is 85.09 g. Recall that the ratio (molar mass/empirical molar mass) is always an integer ($169/85.09 \approx 2$). Therefore, the molecular formula of the compound must be $(SiF_3)_2$ or Si_2F_6 .

Similar problem: 5.49.

Practice Exercise A gaseous compound is 78.14 percent boron and 21.86 percent hydrogen. At 27°C, 74.3 mL of the gas exerted a pressure of 1.12 atm. If the mass of the gas was 0.0934 g, what is its molecular formula?

5.5 Gas Stoichiometry

In Chapter 3 we used relationships between amounts (in moles) and masses (in grams) of reactants and products to solve stoichiometry problems. When the reactants and/or products are gases, we can also use the relationships between amounts (moles, n) and volume (V) to solve such problems (Figure 5.13). Examples 5.11, 5.12, and 5.13 show how the gas laws are used in these calculations.

Figure 5.13 *Stoichiometric calculations involving gases.*

The reaction of calcium carbide (CaC₂) with water produces acetylene, a flammable gas.

Similar problem: 5.26.

Example 5.11

Calculate the volume of O_2 (in liters) required for the complete combustion of 7.64 L of acetylene (C_2H_2) measured at the same temperature and pressure.

$$2C_2H_2(g) + 5O_2(g) \longrightarrow 4CO_2(g) + 2H_2O(l)$$

Strategy Note that the temperature and pressure of O_2 and C_2H_2 are the same. Which gas law do we need to relate the volume of the gases to the moles of gases?

Solution According to Avogadro's law, at the same temperature and pressure, the number of moles of gases are directly related to their volumes. From the equation, we have 5 mol $O_2 \simeq 2$ mol C_2H_2; therefore, we can also write 5 L $O_2 \simeq 2$ L C_2H_2. The volume of O_2 that will react with 7.64 L C_2H_2 is given by

$$\text{volume of } O_2 = 7.64 \text{ L } C_2H_2 \times \frac{5 \text{ L } O_2}{2 \text{ L } C_2H_2}$$

$$= 19.1 \text{ L}$$

Practice Exercise Assuming no change in temperature and pressure, calculate the volume of O_2 (in liters) required for the complete combustion of 14.9 L of butane (C_4H_{10}):

$$2C_4H_{10}(g) + 13O_2(g) \longrightarrow 8CO_2(g) + 10H_2O(l)$$

Example 5.12

Sodium azide (NaN_3) is used in some automobile air bags. The impact of a collision triggers the decomposition of NaN_3 as follows:

$$2NaN_3(s) \longrightarrow 2Na(s) + 3N_2(g)$$

The nitrogen gas produced quickly inflates the bag between the driver and the windshield and dashboard. Calculate the volume of N_2 generated at 80°C and 823 mmHg by the decomposition of 60.0 g of NaN_3.

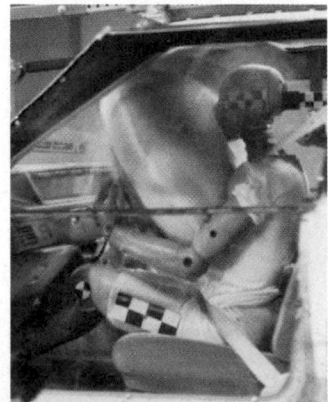

An air bag can protect the driver in an automobile collision.

(Continued)

Strategy From the balanced equation we see that 2 mol NaN_3 ≏ 3 mol N_2 so the conversion factor between NaN_3 and N_2 is

$$\frac{3 \text{ mol } N_2}{2 \text{ mol } NaN_3}$$

Because the mass of NaN_3 is given, we can calculate the number of moles of NaN_3 and hence the number of moles of N_2 produced. Finally, we can calculate the volume of N_2 using the ideal gas equation.

Solution First we calculate number of moles of N_2 produced by 60.0 g NaN_3 using the following sequence of conversions

$$\text{grams of } NaN_3 \longrightarrow \text{moles of } NaN_3 \longrightarrow \text{moles of } N_2$$

so that

$$\text{moles of } N_2 = 60.0 \text{ g } NaN_3 \times \frac{1 \text{ mol } NaN_3}{65.02 \text{ g } NaN_3} \times \frac{3 \text{ mol } N_2}{2 \text{ mol } NaN_3}$$

$$= 1.38 \text{ mol } N_2$$

The volume of 1.38 moles of N_2 can be obtained by using the ideal gas equation:

$$V = \frac{nRT}{P} = \frac{(1.38 \text{ mol})(0.0821 \text{ L} \cdot \text{atm/K} \cdot \text{mol})(80 + 273 \text{ K})}{(823/760) \text{ atm}}$$

$$= 36.9 \text{ L}$$

Similar problem: 5.60.

Practice Exercise The equation for the metabolic breakdown of glucose ($C_6H_{12}O_6$) is the same as the equation for the combustion of glucose in air:

$$C_6H_{12}O_6(s) + 6O_2(g) \longrightarrow 6CO_2(g) + 6H_2O(l)$$

Calculate the volume of CO_2 produced at 37°C and 1.00 atm when 5.60 g of glucose is used up in the reaction.

Example 5.13

Aqueous lithium hydroxide solution is used to purify air in spacecrafts and submarines because it absorbs carbon dioxide, which is an end product of metabolism, according to the equation

$$2LiOH(aq) + CO_2(g) \longrightarrow Li_2CO_3(aq) + H_2O(l)$$

The pressure of carbon dioxide inside the cabin of a submarine having a volume of 2.4×10^5 L is 7.9×10^{-3} atm at 312 K. A solution of lithium hydroxide (LiOH) of negligible volume is introduced into the cabin. Eventually the pressure of CO_2 falls to 1.2×10^{-4} atm. How many grams of lithium carbonate are formed by this process?

Strategy How do we calculate the number of moles of CO_2 reacted from the drop in CO_2 pressure? What is the conversion factor between CO_2 and Li_2CO_3?

Solution First we calculate the number of moles of CO_2 consumed in the reaction. The drop in CO_2 pressure, which is $(7.9 \times 10^{-3}$ atm$) - (1.2 \times 10^{-4}$ atm$)$, or

The air in submerged submarines and space vehicles needs to be purified continuously.

(Continued)

7.8×10^{-3} atm, corresponds to the consumption of CO_2. Using the ideal gas equation, we write

$$n = \frac{PV}{RT}$$

$$= \frac{(7.8 \times 10^{-3} \text{ atm})(2.4 \times 10^5 \text{ L})}{(0.0821 \text{ L} \cdot \text{atm/K} \cdot \text{mol})(312 \text{ K})} = 73 \text{ mol}$$

From the chemical equation we see that 1 mol $CO_2 \triangleq 1$ mol Li_2CO_3, so the amount of Li_2CO_3 formed is also 73 moles. Then, with the molar mass of Li_2CO_3 (73.89 g), we calculate its mass:

$$\text{mass of } Li_2CO_3 \text{ formed} = 73 \text{ mol } \cancel{Li_2CO_3} \times \frac{73.89 \text{ g } Li_2CO_3}{1 \text{ mol } \cancel{Li_2CO_3}}$$

$$= 5.4 \times 10^3 \text{ g } Li_2CO_3$$

Similar problem: 5.99.

Practice Exercise A 2.14-L sample of hydrogen chloride (HCl) gas at 2.61 atm and 28°C is completely dissolved in 668 mL of water to form hydrochloric acid solution. Calculate the molarity of the acid solution. Assume no change in volume.

5.6 Dalton's Law of Partial Pressures

Thus far we have concentrated on the behavior of pure gaseous substances, but experimental studies very often involve mixtures of gases. For example, for a study of air pollution, we may be interested in the pressure-volume-temperature relationship of a sample of air, which contains several gases. In this case, and all cases involving mixtures of gases, the total gas pressure is related to *partial pressures,* that is, *the pressures of individual gas components in the mixture.* In 1801 Dalton formulated a law, now known as ***Dalton's law of partial pressures,*** which states that *the total pressure of a mixture of gases is just the sum of the pressures that each gas would exert if it were present alone.* Figure 5.14 illustrates Dalton's law.

Interactivity:
Dalton's Law
ARIS, Interactives

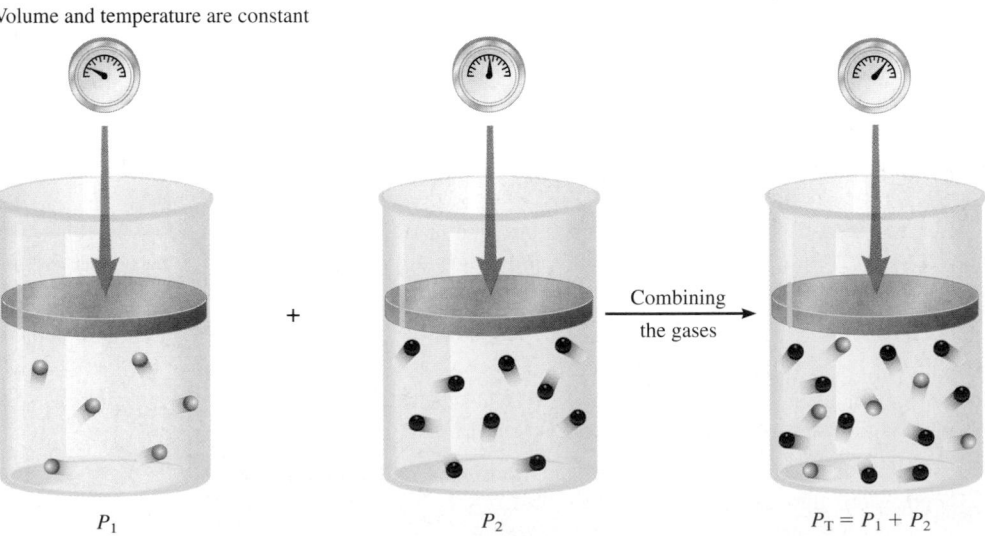

Volume and temperature are constant

P_1 P_2 Combining the gases $P_T = P_1 + P_2$

Figure 5.14 *Schematic illustration of Dalton's law of partial pressures.*

Consider a case in which two gases, A and B, are in a container of volume V. The pressure exerted by gas A, according to the ideal gas equation, is

$$P_A = \frac{n_A RT}{V}$$

where n_A is the number of moles of A present. Similarly, the pressure exerted by gas B is

$$P_B = \frac{n_B RT}{V}$$

In a mixture of gases A and B, the total pressure P_T is the result of the collisions of both types of molecules, A and B, with the walls of the container. Thus, according to Dalton's law,

$$
\begin{aligned}
P_T &= P_A + P_B \\
&= \frac{n_A RT}{V} + \frac{n_B RT}{V} \\
&= \frac{RT}{V}(n_A + n_B) \\
&- \frac{nRT}{V}
\end{aligned}
$$

where n, the total number of moles of gases present, is given by $n = n_A + n_B$, and P_A and P_B are the partial pressures of gases A and B, respectively. For a mixture of gases, then, P_T depends only on the total number of moles of gas present, not on the nature of the gas molecules.

In general, the total pressure of a mixture of gases is given by

$$P_T = P_1 + P_2 + P_3 + \cdots$$

where P_1, P_2, P_3, . . . are the partial pressures of components 1, 2, 3, ... To see how each partial pressure is related to the total pressure, consider again the case of a mixture of two gases A and B. Dividing P_A by P_T, we obtain

$$
\begin{aligned}
\frac{P_A}{P_T} &= \frac{n_A RT/V}{(n_A + n_B)RT/V} \\
&= \frac{n_A}{n_A + n_B} \\
&= X_A
\end{aligned}
$$

where X_A is called the mole fraction of A. The **mole fraction** is *a dimensionless quantity that expresses the ratio of the number of moles of one component to the number of moles of all components present.* In general, the mole fraction of component i in a mixture is given by

$$X_i = \frac{n_i}{n_T} \tag{5.13}$$

where n_i and n_T are the number of moles of component i and the total number of moles present, respectively. The mole fraction is always smaller than 1. We can now express the partial pressure of A as

$$P_A = X_A P_T$$

Similarly,

$$P_B = X_B P_T$$

Note that the sum of the mole fractions for a mixture of gases must be unity. If only two components are present, then

$$X_A + X_B = \frac{n_A}{n_A + n_B} + \frac{n_B}{n_A + n_B} = 1$$

If a system contains more than two gases, then the partial pressure of the ith component is related to the total pressure by

$$P_i = X_i P_T \qquad (5.14)$$

How are partial pressures determined? A manometer can measure only the total pressure of a gaseous mixture. To obtain the partial pressures, we need to know the mole fractions of the components, which would involve elaborate chemical analyses. The most direct method of measuring partial pressures is using a mass spectrometer. The relative intensities of the peaks in a mass spectrum are directly proportional to the amounts, and hence to the mole fractions, of the gases present.

From mole fractions and total pressure, we can calculate the partial pressures of individual components, as Example 5.14 shows. A direct application of Dalton's law of partial pressures to scuba diving is discussed in the Chemistry in Action essay on p. 198.

Example 5.14

A mixture of gases contains 4.46 moles of neon (Ne), 0.74 mole of argon (Ar), and 2.15 moles of xenon (Xe). Calculate the partial pressures of the gases if the total pressure is 2.00 atm at a certain temperature.

Strategy What is the relationship between the partial pressure of a gas and the total gas pressure? How do we calculate the mole fraction of a gas?

Solution According to Equation (5.14), the partial pressure of Ne (P_{Ne}) is equal to the product of its mole fraction (X_{Ne}) and the total pressure (P_T)

$$\overset{\text{need to find}}{\underset{\underset{\text{want to calculate}}{}}{P_{Ne}}} = X_{Ne} \underset{\text{given}}{P_T}$$

Using Equation (5.13), we calculate the mole fraction of Ne as follows:

$$X_{Ne} = \frac{n_{Ne}}{n_{Ne} + n_{Ar} + n_{Xe}} = \frac{4.46\ \text{mol}}{4.46\ \text{mol} + 0.74\ \text{mol} + 2.15\ \text{mol}}$$
$$= 0.607$$

Therefore

$$P_{Ne} = X_{Ne} P_T$$
$$= 0.607 \times 2.00\ \text{atm}$$
$$= 1.21\ \text{atm}$$

(Continued)

Similarly,

$$P_{Ar} = X_{Ar}P_T$$
$$= 0.10 \times 2.00 \text{ atm}$$
$$= 0.20 \text{ atm}$$

and

$$P_{Xe} = X_{Xe}P_T$$
$$= 0.293 \times 2.00 \text{ atm}$$
$$= 0.586 \text{ atm}$$

Check Make sure that the sum of the partial pressures is equal to the given total pressure; that is, (1.21 + 0.20 + 0.586) atm = 2.00 atm.

Similar problem: 5.63.

Practice Exercise A sample of natural gas contains 8.24 moles of methane (CH_4), 0.421 mole of ethane (C_2H_6), and 0.116 mole of propane (C_3H_8). If the total pressure of the gases is 1.37 atm, what are the partial pressures of the gases?

Dalton's law of partial pressures is useful for calculating volumes of gases collected over water. For example, when potassium chlorate ($KClO_3$) is heated, it decomposes to KCl and O_2:

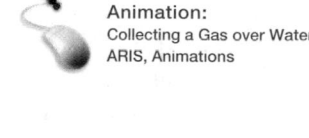

Animation:
Collecting a Gas over Water
ARIS, Animations

$$2KClO_3(s) \longrightarrow 2KCl(s) + 3O_2(g)$$

The oxygen gas can be collected over water, as shown in Figure 5.15. Initially, the inverted bottle is completely filled with water. As oxygen gas is generated, the gas bubbles rise to the top and displace water from the bottle. This method of collecting a gas is based on the assumptions that the gas does not react with water and that it

Bottle being filled with oxygen gas

$KClO_3$ and MnO_2

Bottle filled with water
ready to be placed in
the plastic basin

Bottle full of oxygen gas
plus water vapor

Figure 5.15 *An apparatus for collecting gas over water. The oxygen generated by heating potassium chlorate ($KClO_3$) in the presence of a small amount of manganese dioxide (MnO_2), which speeds up the reaction, is bubbled through water and collected in a bottle as shown. Water originally present in the bottle is pushed into the trough by the oxygen gas.*

196   Gases

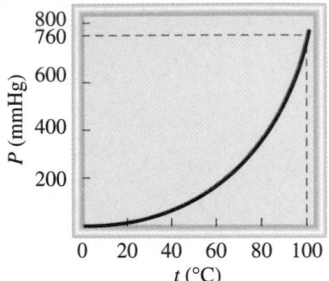

Figure 5.16 *The pressure of water vapor as a function of temperature. Note that at the boiling point of water (100°C) the pressure is 760 mmHg, which is exactly equal to 1 atm.*

is not appreciably soluble in it. These assumptions are valid for oxygen gas, but not for gases such as NH_3, which dissolves readily in water. The oxygen gas collected in this way is not pure, however, because water vapor is also present in the bottle. The total gas pressure is equal to the sum of the pressures exerted by the oxygen gas and the water vapor:

$$P_T = P_{O_2} + P_{H_2O}$$

Consequently, we must allow for the pressure caused by the presence of water vapor when we calculate the amount of O_2 generated. Table 5.3 shows the pressure of water vapor at various temperatures. These data are plotted in Figure 5.16.

Example 5.15 shows how to use Dalton's law to calculate the amount of a gas collected over water.

TABLE 5.3

Pressure of Water Vapor at Various Temperatures

Temperature (°C)	Water Vapor Pressure (mmHg)
0	4.58
5	6.54
10	9.21
15	12.79
20	17.54
25	23.76
30	31.82
35	42.18
40	55.32
45	71.88
50	92.51
55	118.04
60	149.38
65	187.54
70	233.7
75	289.1
80	355.1
85	433.6
90	525.76
95	633.90
100	760.00

Similar problem: 5.68.

Example 5.15

Oxygen gas generated by the decomposition of potassium chlorate is collected as shown in Figure 5.15. The volume of oxygen collected at 24°C and atmospheric pressure of 762 mmHg is 128 mL. Calculate the mass (in grams) of oxygen gas obtained. The pressure of the water vapor at 24°C is 22.4 mmHg.

Strategy To solve for the mass of O_2 generated, we must first calculate the partial pressure of O_2 in the mixture. What gas law do we need? How do we convert pressure of O_2 gas to mass of O_2 in grams?

Solution From Dalton's law of partial pressures we know that

$$P_T = P_{O_2} + P_{H_2O}$$

Therefore

$$P_{O_2} = P_T - P_{H_2O}$$
$$= 762 \text{ mmHg} - 22.4 \text{ mmHg}$$
$$= 740 \text{ mmHg}$$

From the ideal gas equation we write

$$PV = nRT = \frac{m}{\mathcal{M}}RT$$

where m and $\mathcal{M}$ are the mass of O_2 collected and the molar mass of O_2, respectively. Rearranging the equation we obtain

$$m = \frac{PV\mathcal{M}}{RT} = \frac{(740/760)\text{atm}(0.128 \text{ L})(32.00 \text{ g/mol})}{(0.0821 \text{ L} \cdot \text{atm/K} \cdot \text{mol})(273 + 24) \text{ K}}$$
$$= 0.164 \text{ g}$$

Check The density of the oxygen gas is (0.164 g/0.128 L), or 1.28 g/L, which is a reasonable value for gases under atmospheric conditions (see Example 5.8).

Practice Exercise Hydrogen gas generated when calcium metal reacts with water is collected as shown in Figure 5.15. The volume of gas collected at 30°C and pressure of 988 mmHg is 641 mL. What is the mass (in grams) of the hydrogen gas obtained? The pressure of water vapor at 30°C is 31.82 mmHg.

5.7 The Kinetic Molecular Theory of Gases

The gas laws help us to predict the behavior of gases, but they do not explain what happens at the molecular level to cause the changes we observe in the macroscopic world. For example, why does a gas expand on heating?

In the nineteenth century, a number of physicists, notably Ludwig Boltzmann[†] and James Clerk Maxwell,[‡] found that the physical properties of gases can be explained in terms of the motion of individual molecules. This molecular movement is a form of *energy,* which we define as the capacity to do work or to produce change. In mechanics, *work* is defined as force times distance. Because energy can be measured as work, we can write

energy = work done
= force × distance

The *joule (J)*[§] is *the SI unit of energy*

$$1 \text{ J} = 1 \text{ kg m}^2/\text{s}^2$$
$$= 1 \text{ N m}$$

Alternatively, energy can be expressed in kilojoules (kJ):

$$1 \text{ kJ} = 1000 \text{ J}$$

As we will see in Chapter 6, there are many different kinds of energy. **Kinetic energy (KE)** is the type of energy expended by a moving object, or *energy of motion.*

The findings of Maxwell, Boltzmann, and others resulted in *a number of generalizations about gas behavior* that have since been known as the **kinetic molecular theory of gases,** or simply the *kinetic theory of gases.* Central to the kinetic theory are the following assumptions:

1. A gas is composed of molecules that are separated from each other by distances far greater than their own dimensions. The molecules can be considered to be "points"; that is, they possess mass but have negligible volume.

2. Gas molecules are in constant motion in random directions, and they frequently collide with one another. Collisions among molecules are perfectly elastic. In other words, energy can be transferred from one molecule to another as a result of a collision. Nevertheless, the total energy of all the molecules in a system remains the same.

3. Gas molecules exert neither attractive nor repulsive forces on one another.

4. The average kinetic energy of the molecules is proportional to the temperature of the gas in kelvins. Any two gases at the same temperature will have the same average kinetic energy. The average kinetic energy of a molecule is given by

$$\overline{\text{KE}} = \tfrac{1}{2}m\overline{u^2}$$

The kinetic theory of gases treats molecules as hard spheres without internal structure.

[†]Ludwig Eduard Boltzmann (1844–1906). Austrian physicist. Although Boltzmann was one of the greatest theoretical physicists of all time, his work was not recognized by other scientists in his own lifetime. Suffering from poor health and great depression, he committed suicide in 1906.

[‡]James Clerk Maxwell (1831–1879). Scottish physicist. Maxwell was one of the great theoretical physicists of the nineteenth century; his work covered many areas in physics, including kinetic theory of gases, thermodynamics, and electricity and magnetism.

[§]James Prescott Joule (1818–1889). English physicist. As a young man, Joule was tutored by John Dalton. He is most famous for determining the mechanical equivalent of heat, the conversion between mechanical energy and thermal energy.

CHEMISTRY
in Action

Scuba Diving and the Gas Laws

Scuba diving is an exhilarating sport, and, thanks in part to the gas laws, it is also a safe activity for trained individuals who are in good health. ("Scuba" is an acronym for self-contained underwater breathing apparatus.) Two applications of the gas laws to this popular pastime are the development of guidelines for returning safely to the surface after a dive and the determination of the proper mix of gases to prevent a potentially fatal condition during a dive.

A typical dive might be 40 to 65 ft, but dives to 90 ft are not uncommon. Because seawater has a slightly higher density than fresh water—about 1.03 g/mL, compared with 1.00 g/mL—the pressure exerted by a column of 33 ft of seawater is equivalent to 1 atm pressure. Pressure increases with increasing depth, so at a depth of 66 ft the pressure of the water will be 2 atm, and so on.

What would happen if a diver rose to the surface from a depth of, say, 20 ft rather quickly without breathing? The total decrease in pressure for this change in depth would be (20 ft/33 ft) × 1 atm, or 0.6 atm. When the diver reached the surface, the volume of air trapped in the lungs would have increased by a factor of (1 + 0.6) atm/l atm, or 1.6 times. This sudden expansion of air can fatally rupture the membranes of the lungs. Another serious possibility is that an *air embolism* might develop. As air expands in the lungs, it is forced into tiny blood vessels called capillaries. The presence

of air bubbles in these vessels can block normal blood flow to the brain. As a result, the diver might lose consciousness before reaching the surface. The only cure for an air embolism is recompression. For this painful process, the victim is placed in a chamber filled with compressed air. Here bubbles in the blood are slowly squeezed down to harmless size over the course of several hours to a day. To avoid these unpleasant complications, divers know they must ascend slowly, pausing at certain points to give their bodies time to adjust to the falling pressure.

Our second example is a direct application of Dalton's law. Oxygen gas is essential for our survival, so it is hard to believe that an excess of oxygen could be harmful. Nevertheless, the toxicity of too much oxygen is well established. For example, newborn infants placed in oxygen tents often sustain damage to the retinal tissue, which can cause partial or total blindness.

Our bodies function best when oxygen gas has a partial pressure of about 0.20 atm, as it does in the air we breathe. The oxygen partial pressure is given by

$$P_{O_2} = X_{O_2} P_T = \frac{n_{O_2}}{n_{O_2} + n_{N_2}} P_T$$

where P_T is the total pressure. However, because volume is directly proportional to the number of moles of gas present (at

where m is the mass of the molecule and u is its speed. The horizontal bar denotes an average value. The quantity $\overline{u^2}$ is called mean square speed; it is the average of the square of the speeds of all the molecules:

$$\overline{u^2} = \frac{u_1^2 + u_2^2 + \cdots + u_N^2}{N}$$

where N is the number of molecules.

Assumption 4 enables us to write

$$\overline{KE} \propto T$$
$$\tfrac{1}{2}m\overline{u^2} \propto T$$
$$\tfrac{1}{2}m\overline{u^2} = CT \tag{5.15}$$

where C is the proportionality constant and T is the absolute temperature.

According to the kinetic molecular theory, gas pressure is the result of collisions between molecules and the walls of their container. It depends on the frequency of collision per unit area and on how "hard" the molecules strike the constant temperature and pressure), we can now write

$$P_{O_2} = \frac{V_{O_2}}{V_{O_2} + V_{N_2}} P_T$$

Thus, the composition of air is 20 percent oxygen gas and 80 percent nitrogen gas by volume. When a diver is submerged, the pressure of the water on the diver is greater than atmospheric pressure. The air pressure inside the body cavities (for example, lungs, sinuses) must be the same as the pressure of the surrounding water; otherwise they would collapse. A special valve automatically adjusts the pressure of the air breathed from a scuba tank to ensure that the air pressure equals the water pressure at all times. For example, at a depth where the total pressure is 2.0 atm, the oxygen content in air should be reduced to 10 percent by volume to maintain the same partial pressure of 0.20 atm; that is,

$$P_{O_2} = 0.20 \text{ atm} = \frac{V_{O_2}}{V_{O_2} + V_{N_2}} \times 2.0 \text{ atm}$$

$$\frac{V_{O_2}}{V_{O_2} + V_{N_2}} = \frac{0.20 \text{ atm}}{2.0 \text{ atm}} = 0.10 \text{ or } 10\%$$

A scuba diver.

Although nitrogen gas may seem to be the obvious choice to mix with oxygen gas, there is a serious problem with it. When the partial pressure of nitrogen gas exceeds 1 atm, enough of the gas dissolves in the blood to cause a condition known as *nitrogen narcosis*. The effects on the diver resemble those associated with alcohol intoxication. Divers suffering from nitrogen narcosis have been known to do strange things, such as dancing on the seafloor and chasing sharks. For this reason, helium is often used to dilute oxygen gas. An inert gas, helium is much less soluble in blood than nitrogen and produces no narcotic effects.

wall. The theory also provides a molecular interpretation of temperature. According to Equation (5.15), the absolute temperature of a gas is a measure of the average kinetic energy of the molecules. In other words, the absolute temperature is an indication of the random motion of the molecules—the higher the temperature, the more energetic the molecules. Because it is related to the temperature of the gas sample, random molecular motion is sometimes referred to as thermal motion.

Application to the Gas Laws

Although the kinetic theory of gases is based on a rather simple model, the mathematical details involved are very complex. However, on a qualitative basis, it is possible to use the theory to account for the general properties of substances in the gaseous state. The following examples illustrate the range of its utility.

- **Compressibility of Gases.** Because molecules in the gas phase are separated by large distances (assumption 1), gases can be compressed easily to occupy less volume.

- **Boyle's Law.** The pressure exerted by a gas results from the impact of its molecules on the walls of the container. The collision rate, or the number of molecular collisions with the walls per second, is proportional to the number density (that is, number of molecules per unit volume) of the gas. Decreasing the volume of a given amount of gas increases its number density and hence its collision rate. For this reason, the pressure of a gas is inversely proportional to the volume it occupies; as volume decreases, pressure increases and vice versa.

- **Charles's Law.** Because the average kinetic energy of gas molecules is proportional to the sample's absolute temperature (assumption 4), raising the temperature increases the average kinetic energy. Consequently, molecules will collide with the walls of the container more frequently and with greater impact if the gas is heated, and thus the pressure increases. The volume of gas will expand until the gas pressure is balanced by the constant external pressure (see Figure 5.8).

- **Avogadro's Law.** We have shown that the pressure of a gas is directly proportional to both the density and the temperature of the gas. Because the mass of the gas is directly proportional to the number of moles (n) of the gas, we can represent density by n/V. Therefore

Another way of stating Avogadro's law is that at the same pressure and temperature, equal volumes of gases, whether they are the same or different gases, contain equal numbers of molecules.

$$P \propto \frac{n}{V} T$$

For two gases, 1 and 2, we write

$$P_1 \propto \frac{n_1 T_1}{V_1} = C \frac{n_1 T_1}{V_1}$$
$$P_2 \propto \frac{n_2 T_2}{V_2} = C \frac{n_2 T_2}{V_2}$$

where C is the proportionality constant. Thus, for two gases under the same conditions of pressure, volume, and temperature (that is, when $P_1 = P_2$, $T_1 = T_2$, and $V_1 = V_2$), it follows that $n_1 = n_2$, which is a mathematical expression of Avogadro's law.

- **Dalton's Law of Partial Pressures.** If molecules do not attract or repel one another (assumption 3), then the pressure exerted by one type of molecule is unaffected by the presence of another gas. Consequently, the total pressure is given by the sum of individual gas pressures.

Distribution of Molecular Speeds

The kinetic theory of gases enables us to investigate molecular motion in more detail. Suppose we have a large number of gas molecules, say, 1 mole, in a container. As long as we hold the temperature constant, the average kinetic energy and the mean-square speed will remain unchanged as time passes. As you might expect, the motion of the molecules is totally random and unpredictable. At a given instant, how many molecules are moving at a particular speed? To answer this question Maxwell analyzed the behavior of gas molecules at different temperatures.

Figure 5.17(a) shows typical *Maxwell speed distribution curves* for nitrogen gas at three different temperatures. At a given temperature, the distribution curve tells us the number of molecules moving at a certain speed. The peak of each curve represents the *most probable speed,* that is, the speed of the largest number of molecules. Note

Figure 5.17 *(a) The distribution of speeds for nitrogen gas at three different temperatures. At the higher temperatures, more molecules are moving at faster speeds. (b) The distribution of speeds for three gases at 300 K. At a given temperature, the lighter molecules are moving faster, on the average.*

that the most probable speed increases as temperature increases (the peak shifts toward the right). Furthermore, the curve also begins to flatten out with increasing temperature, indicating that larger numbers of molecules are moving at greater speed. Figure 5.17(b) shows the speed distributions of three gases at the *same* temperature. The difference in the curves can be explained by noting that lighter molecules move faster, on average, than heavier ones.

The distribution of molecular speeds can be demonstrated with the apparatus shown in Figure 5.18. A beam of atoms (or molecules) exits from an oven at a known temperature and passes through a pinhole (to collimate the beam). Two circular plates mounted on the same shaft are rotated by a motor. The first plate is called the "chopper" and the second is the detector. The purpose of the chopper is to allow small bursts of atoms (or molecules) to pass through it whenever the slit is aligned with the beam. Within each burst, the faster-moving molecules will reach the detector earlier than the slower-moving ones. Eventually, a layer of deposit will accumulate on the

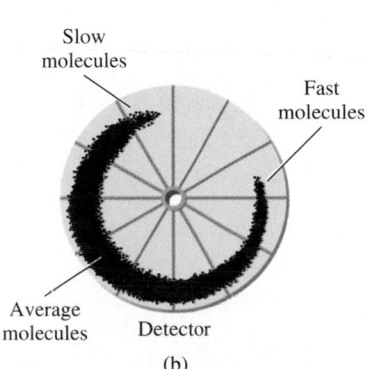

Figure 5.18 *(a) Apparatus for studying molecular speed distribution at a certain temperature. The vacuum pump causes the molecules to travel from left to right as shown. (b) The spread of the deposit on the detector gives the range of molecular speeds, and the density of the deposit is proportional to the fraction of molecules moving at different speeds.*

detector. Because the two plates are rotating at the same speed, molecules in the next burst will hit the detector plate at approximately the same place as molecules from the previous burst having the same speed. In time, the molecular deposition will become visible. The density of the deposition indicates the distribution of molecular speeds at that particular temperature.

Root-Mean-Square Speed

How fast does a molecule move, on the average, at any temperature T? One way to estimate molecular speed is to calculate the **root-mean-square (rms) speed (u_{rms})**, which is *an average molecular speed.* One of the results of the kinetic theory of gases is that the total kinetic energy of a mole of any gas equals $\frac{3}{2}RT$. Earlier we saw that the average kinetic energy of one molecule is $\frac{1}{2}m\overline{u^2}$ and so we can write

$$N_A(\tfrac{1}{2}m\overline{u^2}) = \tfrac{3}{2}RT$$

where N_A is Avogadro's number. Because $N_A m = \mathcal{M}$, the above equation can be rearranged to give

$$\overline{u^2} = \frac{3RT}{\mathcal{M}}$$

Taking the square root of both sides gives

$$\sqrt{\overline{u^2}} = u_{rms} = \sqrt{\frac{3RT}{\mathcal{M}}} \tag{5.16}$$

Equation (5.16) shows that the root-mean-square speed of a gas increases with the square root of its temperature (in kelvins). Because $\mathcal{M}$ appears in the denominator, it follows that the heavier the gas, the more slowly its molecules move. If we substitute 8.314 J/K · mol for R (see Appendix 2) and convert the molar mass to kg/mol, then u_{rms} will be calculated in meters per second (m/s). This procedure is illustrated in Example 5.16.

Example 5.16

Calculate the root-mean-square speeds of helium atoms and nitrogen molecules in m/s at 25°C.

Strategy To calculate the root-mean-square speed we need Equation (5.16). What units should we use for R and $\mathcal{M}$ so that u_{rms} will be expressed in m/s?

Solution To calculate u_{rms}, the units of R should be 8.314 J/K · mol and, because 1 J = 1 kg m²/s², the molar mass must be in kg/mol. The molar mass of He is 4.003 g/mol, or 4.003×10^{-3} kg/mol. From Equation (5.16),

$$u_{rms} = \sqrt{\frac{3RT}{\mathcal{M}}}$$
$$= \sqrt{\frac{3(8.314 \text{ J/K} \cdot \text{mol})(298 \text{ K})}{4.003 \times 10^{-3} \text{ kg/mol}}}$$
$$= \sqrt{1.86 \times 10^6 \text{ J/kg}}$$

(Continued)

Using the conversion factor $1 \text{ J} = 1 \text{ kg m}^2/\text{s}^2$ we get

$$u_{rms} = \sqrt{1.86 \times 10^6 \text{ kg m}^2/\text{kg} \cdot \text{s}^2}$$
$$= \sqrt{1.86 \times 10^6 \text{ m}^2/\text{s}^2}$$
$$= 1.36 \times 10^3 \text{ m/s}$$

The procedure is the same for N_2, the molar mass of which is 28.02 g/mol, or 2.802×10^{-2} kg/mol so that we write

$$u_{rms} = \sqrt{\frac{3(8.314 \text{ J/K} \cdot \text{mole})(298 \text{ K})}{2.802 \times 10^{-2} \text{ kg/mol}}}$$
$$= \sqrt{2.65 \times 10^5 \text{ m}^2/\text{s}^2}$$
$$= 515 \text{ m/s}$$

Check Because He is a lighter gas, we expect it to move faster, on average, than N_2. A quick way to check the answers is to note that the ratio of the two u_{rms} values $(1.36 \times 10^3/515 \approx 2.6)$ should be equal to the square root of the ratios of the molar masses of N_2 to He, that is, $\sqrt{28/4} \approx 2.6$.

Similar problems: 5.77, 5.78.

Practice Exercise Calculate the root-mean-square speed of molecular chlorine in m/s at 20°C.

The calculation in Example 5.16 has an interesting relationship to the composition of Earth's atmosphere. Unlike Jupiter, Earth does not have appreciable amounts of hydrogen or helium in its atmosphere. Why is this the case? A smaller planet than Jupiter, Earth has a weaker gravitational attraction for these lighter molecules. A fairly straightforward calculation shows that to escape Earth's gravitational field, a molecule must possess an escape velocity equal to or greater than 1.1×10^4 m/s. Because the average speed of helium is considerably greater than that of molecular nitrogen or molecular oxygen, more helium atoms escape from Earth's atmosphere into outer space. Consequently, only a trace amount of helium is present in our atmosphere. On the other hand, Jupiter, with a mass about 320 times greater than that of Earth, retains both heavy and light gases in its atmosphere.

The Chemistry in Action essay on p. 205 describes a fascinating phenomenon involving gases at extremely low temperatures.

Jupiter. The interior of this massive planet consists mainly of hydrogen.

Gas Diffusion and Effusion

We will now discuss two phenomena based on gaseous motion.

Gas Diffusion

A direct demonstration of gaseous random motion is provided by *diffusion, the gradual mixing of molecules of one gas with molecules of another by virtue of their kinetic properties.* Despite the fact that molecular speeds are very great, the diffusion process takes a relatively long time to complete. For example, when a bottle of concentrated ammonia solution is opened at one end of a lab bench, it takes some time before a person at the other end of the bench can smell it. The reason is that a molecule experiences numerous collisions while moving from one end of the bench to the other, as shown in Figure 5.19. Thus, diffusion of gases always happens gradually, and not instantly as molecular speeds seem to suggest. Furthermore, because the root-mean-square speed of a light gas is greater than that of a heavier gas (see Example 5.16), a lighter gas will diffuse through a certain space more quickly than will a heavier gas. Figure 5.20 illustrates gaseous diffusion.

Diffusion always proceeds from a region of higher concentration to one where the concentration is lower.

Figure 5.19 *The path traveled by a single gas molecule. Each change in direction represents a collision with another molecule.*

Figure 5.20 *A demonstration of gas diffusion. NH$_3$ gas (from a bottle containing aqueous ammonia) combines with HCl gas (from a bottle containing hydrochloric acid) to form solid NH$_4$Cl. Because NH$_3$ is lighter and therefore diffuses faster, solid NH$_4$Cl first appears nearer the HCl bottle (on the right).*

In 1832 the Scottish chemist Thomas Graham[†] found that *under the same conditions of temperature and pressure, rates of diffusion for gases are inversely proportional to the square roots of their molar masses.* This statement, now known as **Graham's law of diffusion,** is expressed mathematically as

$$\frac{r_1}{r_2} = \sqrt{\frac{\mathcal{M}_2}{\mathcal{M}_1}} \qquad (5.17)$$

where r_1 and r_2 are the diffusion rates of gases 1 and 2, and $\mathcal{M}_1$ and $\mathcal{M}_2$ are their molar masses, respectively.

Animation:
Diffusion of Gases
ARIS, Animations

Gas Effusion

Whereas diffusion is a process by which one gas gradually mixes with another, *effusion* is *the process by which a gas under pressure escapes from one compartment of a container to another by passing through a small opening.* Figure 5.21 shows the effusion of a gas into a vacuum. Although effusion differs from diffusion in nature, the rate of effusion of a gas has the same form as Graham's law of diffusion [see Equation (5.17)]. A helium-filled rubber balloon deflates faster than an air-filled one because the rate of effusion through the pores of the rubber is faster for the lighter helium atoms than for the air molecules. Industrially, gas effusion is used to separate uranium isotopes in the forms of gaseous ^{235}UF$_6$ and ^{238}UF$_6$. By subjecting the gases to many stages of effusion, scientists were able to obtain highly enriched ^{235}U isotope, which was used in the construction of atomic bombs during World War II.

Example 5.17 shows an application of Graham's law.

Gas   Vacuum

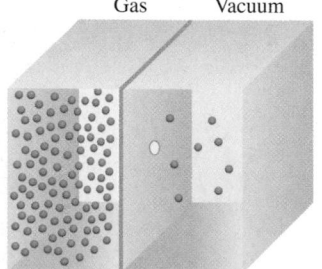

Example 5.17

A flammable gas made up only of carbon and hydrogen is found to effuse through a porous barrier in 1.50 min. Under the same conditions of temperature and pressure, it takes an equal volume of bromine vapor 4.73 min to effuse through the same barrier. Calculate the molar mass of the unknown gas, and suggest what this gas might be.

(Continued)

Figure 5.21 *Gas effusion. Gas molecules move from a high-pressure region (left) to a low-pressure one through a pinhole.*

[†]Thomas Graham (1805–1869). Scottish chemist. Graham did important work on osmosis and characterized a number of phosphoric acids.

CHEMISTRY
in Action

Super Cold Atoms

What happens to a gas when cooled to nearly absolute zero? More than 70 years ago, Albert Einstein, extending work by the Indian physicist Satyendra Nath Bose, predicted that at extremely low temperatures gaseous atoms of certain elements would "merge" or "condense" to form a single entity and a new form of matter. Unlike ordinary gases, liquids, and solids, this supercooled substance, which was named the *Bose-Einstein condensate (BEC)*, would contain no individual atoms because the original atoms would overlap one another, leaving no space in between.

Einstein's hypothesis inspired an international effort to produce the BEC. But, as sometimes happens in science, the necessary technology was not available until fairly recently, and so early investigations were fruitless. Lasers, which use a process based on another of Einstein's ideas, were not designed specifically for BEC research, but they became a critical tool for this work.

Finally, in 1995, physicists found the evidence they had sought for so long. A team at the University of Colorado was the first to report success. They created a BEC by cooling a sample of gaseous rubidium (Rb) atoms to about 1.7×10^{-7} K using a technique called "laser cooling," a process in which a laser light is directed at a beam of atoms, hitting them head on and dramatically slowing them down. The Rb atoms were further cooled in an "optical molasses" produced by the intersection of six lasers. The slowest, coolest atoms were trapped in a magnetic field while the faster-moving, "hotter" atoms escaped, thereby removing more energy from the gas. Under these conditions, the kinetic energy of the trapped atoms was virtually zero, which accounts for the extremely low temperature of the gas. At this point the Rb atoms formed the condensate, just as Einstein had predicted. Although this BEC was invisible to the naked eye (it measured only 5×10^{-3} cm across), the scientists were able to capture its image on a computer screen by focusing another laser beam on it. The laser caused the BEC to break up after about 15 seconds, but that was long enough to record its existence.

The figure shows the Maxwell velocity distribution[†] of the Rb atoms at this temperature. The colors indicate the number of atoms having velocity specified by the two horizontal axes. The blue and white portions represent atoms that have merged to form the BEC.

Within weeks of the Colorado team's discovery, a group of scientists at Rice University, using similar techniques, succeeded in producing a BEC with lithium atoms and in 1998

scientists at the Massachusetts Institute of Technology were able to produce a BEC with hydrogen atoms. Since then, many advances have been made in understanding the properties of the BEC in general and experiments are being extended to molecular systems. It is expected that studies of the BEC will shed light on atomic properties that are still not fully understood (see Chapter 7) and on the mechanism of superconductivity (see the Chemistry in Action essay on this topic in Chapter 11). An additional benefit might be the development of better lasers. Other applications will depend on further study of the BEC itself. Nevertheless, the discovery of a new form of matter has to be one of the foremost scientific achievements of the twentieth century.

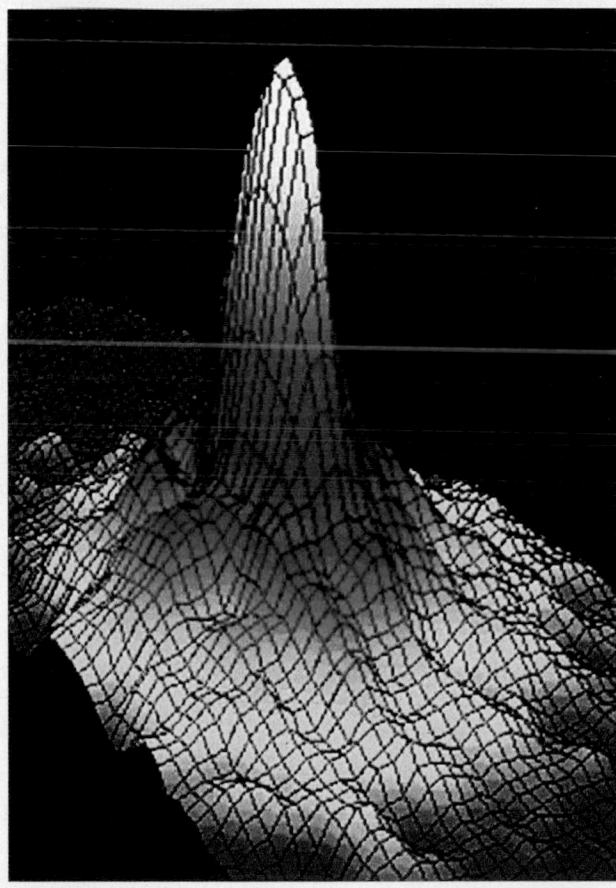

Maxwell velocity distribution of Rb atoms at about 1.7×10^{-7} K. The velocity increases from the center (zero) outward along the two axes. The red color represents the lowest number of Rb atoms and the white color the highest. The average speed in the white region is about 0.5 mm/s.

[†]Velocity distribution differs from speed distribution in that velocity has both magnitude and direction. Thus, velocity can have both positive and negative values but speed can have only zero or positive values.

Strategy The rate of effusion is the number of molecules passing through a porous hole in a given time. The longer the time it takes, the slower is the rate of effusion. Therefore, Equation (5.17) can be written as $r_1/r_2 = t_2/t_1 = \sqrt{M_2/M_1}$, where t_1 and t_2 are the times for effusion for gases 1 and 2, respectively.

Solution From the molar mass of Br_2, we write

$$\frac{1.50\ \text{min}}{4.73\ \text{min}} = \sqrt{\frac{M}{159.8\ \text{g/mol}}}$$

where M is the molar mass of the unknown gas. Solving for M, we obtain

$$M = \left(\frac{1.50\ \text{min}}{4.73\ \text{min}}\right)^2 \times 159.8\ \text{g/mol}$$
$$= \boxed{16.1\ \text{g/mol}}$$

Because the molar mass of carbon is 12.01 g and that of hydrogen is 1.008 g, the gas is methane (CH_4).

Practice Exercise It takes 192 s for an unknown gas to effuse through a porous wall and 84 s for the same volume of N_2 gas to effuse at the same temperature and pressure. What is the molar mass of the unknown gas?

Similar problems: 5.83, 5.84.

5.8 Deviation from Ideal Behavior

The gas laws and the kinetic molecular theory assume that molecules in the gaseous state do not exert any force, either attractive or repulsive, on one another. The other assumption is that the volume of the molecules is negligibly small compared with that of the container. A gas that satisfies these two conditions is said to exhibit *ideal behavior.*

Although we can assume that real gases behave like an ideal gas, we cannot expect them to do so under all conditions. For example, without intermolecular forces, gases could not condense to form liquids. The important question is: Under what conditions will gases most likely exhibit nonideal behavior?

Figure 5.22 shows PV/RT plotted against P for three real gases and an ideal gas at a given temperature. This graph provides a test of ideal gas behavior. According to the ideal gas equation (for 1 mole of gas), PV/RT equals 1, regardless of the actual gas pressure. (When $n = 1$, $PV = nRT$ becomes $PV = RT$, or $PV/RT = 1$.) For real gases, this is true only at moderately low pressures (≤ 5 atm); significant deviations occur as

Figure 5.22 *Plot of PV/RT versus P of 1 mole of a gas at 0°C. For 1 mole of an ideal gas, PV/RT is equal to 1, no matter what the pressure of the gas is. For real gases, we observe various deviations from ideality at high pressures. At very low pressures, all gases exhibit ideal behavior; that is, their PV/RT values all converge to 1 as P approaches zero.*

pressure increases. Attractive forces operate among molecules at relatively short distances. At atmospheric pressure, the molecules in a gas are far apart and the attractive forces are negligible. At high pressures, the density of the gas increases; the molecules are much closer to one another. Intermolecular forces can then be significant enough to affect the motion of the molecules, and the gas will not behave ideally.

Another way to observe the nonideal behavior of gases is to lower the temperature. Cooling a gas decreases the molecules' average kinetic energy, which in a sense deprives molecules of the drive they need to break from their mutual attraction.

To study real gases accurately, then, we need to modify the ideal gas equation, taking into account intermolecular forces and finite molecular volumes. Such an analysis was first made by the Dutch physicist J. D. van der Waals[†] in 1873. Besides being mathematically simple, van der Waals' treatment provides us with an interpretation of real gas behavior at the molecular level.

Consider the approach of a particular molecule toward the wall of a container (Figure 5.23). The intermolecular attractions exerted by its neighbors tend to soften the impact made by this molecule against the wall. The overall effect is a lower gas pressure than we would expect for an ideal gas. Van der Waals suggested that the pressure exerted by an ideal gas, P_{ideal}, is related to the experimentally measured pressure, P_{real}, by the equation

$$P_{ideal} = P_{real} + \frac{an^2}{V^2}$$

$$\uparrow \qquad\qquad \uparrow$$

observed   correction
pressure   term

where a is a constant and n and V are the number of moles and volume of the container, respectively. The correction term for pressure (an^2/V^2) can be understood as follows. The intermolecular interaction that gives rise to nonideal behavior depends on how frequently any two molecules approach each other closely. The frequency of such "encounters" increases with the square of the number of molecules per unit volume (n^2/V^2), because the probability of finding each of the two molecules in a particular region is proportional to n/V. Thus, a is just a proportionality constant.

Another correction concerns the volume occupied by the gas molecules. In the ideal gas equation, V represents the volume of the container. However, each molecule does occupy a finite, although small, intrinsic volume, so the effective volume of the gas becomes ($V - nb$), where n is the number of moles of the gas and b is a constant. The term nb represents the volume occupied by n moles of the gas.

Having taken into account the corrections for pressure and volume, we can rewrite the ideal gas equation as follows:

$$\left(P + \frac{an^2}{V^2} \right)(V - nb) = nRT \qquad\qquad (5.18)$$

corrected   corrected
pressure   volume

Equation (5.18), *relating P, V, T, and n for a nonideal gas,* is known as the **van der Waals equation.** The van der Waals constants a and b are selected to give the best possible agreement between Equation (5.18) and observed behavior of a particular gas.

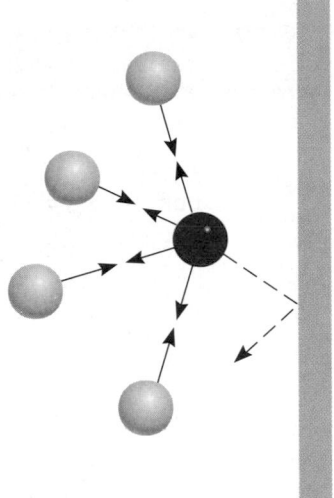

Figure 5.23 *Effect of intermolecular forces on the pressure exerted by a gas. The speed of a molecule that is moving toward the container wall (red sphere) is reduced by the attractive forces exerted by its neighbors (gray spheres). Consequently, the impact this molecule makes with the wall is not as great as it would be if no intermolecular forces were present. In general, the measured gas pressure is lower than the pressure the gas would exert if it behaved ideally.*

[†]Johannes Diderck van der Waals (1837–1923). Dutch physicist. Van der Waals received the Nobel Prize in Physics in 1910 for his work on the properties of gases and liquids.

TABLE 5.4

van der Waals Constants of Some Common Gases

Gas	a $\left(\dfrac{\text{atm} \cdot \text{L}^2}{\text{mol}^2}\right)$	b $\left(\dfrac{\text{L}}{\text{mol}}\right)$
He	0.034	0.0237
Ne	0.211	0.0171
Ar	1.34	0.0322
Kr	2.32	0.0398
Xe	4.19	0.0266
H_2	0.244	0.0266
N_2	1.39	0.0391
O_2	1.36	0.0318
Cl_2	6.49	0.0562
CO_2	3.59	0.0427
CH_4	2.25	0.0428
CCl_4	20.4	0.138
NH_3	4.17	0.0371
H_2O	5.46	0.0305

Table 5.4 lists the values of a and b for a number of gases. The value of a indicates how strongly molecules of a given type of gas attract one another. We see that helium atoms have the weakest attraction for one another, because helium has the smallest a value. There is also a rough correlation between molecular size and b. Generally, the larger the molecule (or atom), the greater b is, but the relationship between b and molecular (or atomic) size is not a simple one.

Example 5.18 compares the pressure of a gas calculated using the ideal gas equation and the van der Waals equation.

Example 5.18

Given that 3.50 moles of NH_3 occupy 5.20 L at 47°C, calculate the pressure of the gas (in atm) using (a) the ideal gas equation and (b) the van der Waals equation.

Strategy To calculate the pressure of NH_3 using the ideal gas equation, we proceed as in Example 5.3. What corrections are made to the pressure and volume terms in the van der Waals equation?

Solution (a) We have the following data:

$$V = 5.20\,\text{L}$$
$$T = (47 + 273)\,\text{K} = 320\,\text{K}$$
$$n = 3.50\,\text{mol}$$
$$R = 0.0821\,\text{L} \cdot \text{atm/K} \cdot \text{mol}$$

Substituting these values in the ideal gas equation, we write

$$P = \frac{nRT}{V}$$
$$= \frac{(3.50\,\text{mol})(0.0821\,\text{L} \cdot \text{atm/K} \cdot \text{mol})(320\,\text{K})}{5.20\,\text{L}}$$
$$= 17.7\,\text{atm}$$

(b) We need Equation (5.18). It is convenient to first calculate the correction terms in Equation (5.18) separately. From Table 5.4, we have

$$a = 4.17\,\text{atm} \cdot \text{L}^2/\text{mol}^2$$
$$b = 0.0371\,\text{L/mol}$$

so that the correction terms for pressure and volume are

$$\frac{an^2}{V^2} = \frac{(4.17\,\text{atm} \cdot \text{L}^2/\text{mol}^2)(3.50\,\text{mol})^2}{(5.20\,\text{L})^2} = 1.89\,\text{atm}$$
$$nb = (3.50\,\text{mol})(0.0371\,\text{L/mol}) = 0.130\,\text{L}$$

Finally, substituting these values in the van der Waals equation, we have

$$(P + 1.89\,\text{atm})(5.20\,\text{L} - 0.130\,\text{L}) = (3.50\,\text{mol})(0.0821\,\text{L} \cdot \text{atm/K} \cdot \text{mol})(320\,\text{K})$$
$$P = 16.2\,\text{atm}$$

Check Based on your understanding of nonideal gas behavior, is it reasonable that the pressure calculated using the van der Waals equation should be smaller than that using the ideal gas equation? Why?

Practice Exercise Using the data shown in Table 5.4, calculate the pressure exerted by 4.37 moles of molecular chlorine confined in a volume of 2.45 L at 38°C. Compare the pressure with that calculated using the ideal gas equation.

Similar problem: 5.89.

Summary of Facts and Concepts

1. At 25°C and 1 atm, a number of elements and molecular compounds exist as gases. Ionic compounds are solids rather than gases under atmospheric conditions.

2. Gases exert pressure because their molecules move freely and collide with any surface with which they make contact. Units of gas pressure include millimeters of mercury (mmHg), torr, pascals, and atmospheres. One atmosphere equals 760 mmHg, or 760 torr.

3. The pressure-volume relationships of ideal gases are governed by Boyle's law: Volume is inversely proportional to pressure (at constant T and n).

4. The temperature-volume relationships of ideal gases are described by Charles's and Gay-Lussac's law: Volume is directly proportional to temperature (at constant P and n).

5. Absolute zero ($-273.15°C$) is the lowest theoretically attainable temperature. The Kelvin temperature scale takes 0 K as absolute zero. In all gas law calculations, temperature must be expressed in kelvins.

6. The amount-volume relationships of ideal gases are described by Avogadro's law: Equal volumes of gases contain equal numbers of molecules (at the same T and P).

7. The ideal gas equation, $PV = nRT$, combines the laws of Boyle, Charles, and Avogadro. This equation describes the behavior of an ideal gas.

8. Dalton's law of partial pressures states that each gas in a mixture of gases exerts the same pressure that it would if it were alone and occupied the same volume.

9. The kinetic molecular theory, a mathematical way of describing the behavior of gas molecules, is based on the following assumptions: Gas molecules are separated by distances far greater than their own dimensions, they possess mass but have negligible volume, they are in constant motion, and they frequently collide with one another. The molecules neither attract nor repel one another.

10. A Maxwell speed distribution curve shows how many gas molecules are moving at various speeds at a given temperature. As temperature increases, more molecules move at greater speeds.

11. In diffusion, two gases gradually mix with each other. In effusion, gas molecules move through a small opening under pressure. Both processes are governed by the same mathematical law—Graham's law of diffusion and effusion.

12. The van der Waals equation is a modification of the ideal gas equation that takes into account the nonideal behavior of real gases. It corrects for the fact that real gas molecules do exert forces on each other and that they do have volume. The van der Waals constants are determined experimentally for each gas.

Key Words

Absolute temperature
 scale, p. 179
Absolute zero, p. 179
Atmospheric pressure, p. 172
Avogadro's law, p. 180
Barometer, p. 173
Boyle's law, p. 175
Charles's and Gay-Lussac's
 law, p. 179
Charles's law, p. 179

Dalton's law of partial
 pressures, p. 192
Diffusion, p. 203
Effusion, p. 204
Gas constant (R), p. 181
Graham's law of
 diffusion, p. 204
Ideal gas, p. 181
Ideal gas equation, p. 181
Joule (J), p. 197

Kelvin temperature
 scale, p. 179
Kinetic energy (KE), p. 197
Kinetic molecular theory
 of gases, p. 197
Manometer, p. 174
Mole fraction, p. 193
Newton (N), p. 172
Partial pressure, p. 192
Pascal (Pa), p. 172

Pressure, p. 172
Root-mean-square (rms) speed
 (u_{rms}), p. 202
Standard atmospheric pressure
 (1 atm), p. 173
Standard temperature and
 pressure (STP), p. 182
van der Waals equation, p. 207

Questions and Problems

Substances That Exist as Gases
Review Questions

5.1 Name five elements and five compounds that exist as gases at room temperature.

5.2 List the physical characteristics of gases.

Pressure of a Gas
Review Questions

5.3 Define pressure and give the common units for pressure.

5.4 Describe how a barometer and a manometer are used to measure gas pressure.

5.5   Why is mercury a more suitable substance to use in a barometer than water?

5.6   Explain why the height of mercury in a barometer is independent of the cross-sectional area of the tube. Would the barometer still work if the tubing were tilted at an angle, say 15° (see Figure 5.3)?

5.7   Would it be easier to drink water with a straw on top of Mt. Everest or at the foot? Explain.

5.8   Is the atmospheric pressure in a mine that is 500 m below sea level greater or less than 1 atm?

5.9   What is the difference between a gas and a vapor? At 25°C, which of the following substances in the gas phase should be properly called a gas and which should be called a vapor: molecular nitrogen (N_2), mercury?

5.10   If the maximum distance that water may be brought up a well by a suction pump is 34 ft (10.3 m), how is it possible to obtain water and oil from hundreds of feet below the surface of Earth?

5.11   Why is it that if the barometer reading falls in one part of the world, it must rise somewhere else?

5.12   Why do astronauts have to wear protective suits when they are on the surface of the moon?

Problems

5.13   Convert 562 mmHg to atm.

5.14   The atmospheric pressure at the summit of Mt. McKinley is 606 mmHg on a certain day. What is the pressure in atm and in kPa?

The Gas Laws
Review Questions

5.15   State the following gas laws in words and also in the form of an equation: Boyle's law, Charles's law, Avogadro's law. In each case, indicate the conditions under which the law is applicable, and give the units for each quantity in the equation.

5.16   Explain why a helium weather balloon expands as it rises in the air. Assume that the temperature remains constant.

Problems

5.17   A gaseous sample of a substance is cooled at constant pressure. Which of the following diagrams best represents the situation if the final temperature is (a) above the boiling point of the substance and (b) below the boiling point but above the freezing point of the substance?

   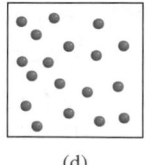

(a)   (b)   (c)   (d)

5.18   Consider the following gaseous sample in a cylinder fitted with a movable piston. Initially there are n moles of the gas at temperature T, pressure P, and volume V.

Choose the cylinder that correctly represents the gas after each of the following changes. (1) The pressure on the piston is tripled at constant n and T. (2) The temperature is doubled at constant n and P. (3) n moles of another gas are added at constant T and P. (4) T is halved and pressure on the piston is reduced to a quarter of its original value.

(a)   (b)   (c)

5.19   A gas occupying a volume of 725 mL at a pressure of 0.970 atm is allowed to expand at constant temperature until its pressure reaches 0.541 atm. What is its final volume?

5.20   At 46°C a sample of ammonia gas exerts a pressure of 5.3 atm. What is the pressure when the volume of the gas is reduced to one-tenth (0.10) of the original value at the same temperature?

5.21   The volume of a gas is 5.80 L, measured at 1.00 atm. What is the pressure of the gas in mmHg if the volume is changed to 9.65 L? (The temperature remains constant.)

5.22   A sample of air occupies 3.8 L when the pressure is 1.2 atm. (a) What volume does it occupy at 6.6 atm? (b) What pressure is required in order to compress it to 0.075 L? (The temperature is kept constant.)

5.23   A 36.4-L volume of methane gas is heated from 25°C to 88°C at constant pressure. What is the final volume of the gas?

5.24   Under constant-pressure conditions a sample of hydrogen gas initially at 88°C and 9.6 L is cooled until its final volume is 3.4 L. What is its final temperature?

5.25   Ammonia burns in oxygen gas to form nitric oxide (NO) and water vapor. How many volumes of NO are obtained from one volume of ammonia at the same temperature and pressure?

5.26 Molecular chlorine and molecular fluorine combine to form a gaseous product. Under the same conditions of temperature and pressure it is found that one volume of Cl_2 reacts with three volumes of F_2 to yield two volumes of the product. What is the formula of the product?

The Ideal Gas Equation
Review Questions

5.27 List the characteristics of an ideal gas. Write the ideal gas equation and also state it in words. Give the units for each term in the equation.

5.28 Use Equation (5.9) to derive all the gas laws.

5.29 What are standard temperature and pressure (STP)? What is the significance of STP in relation to the volume of 1 mole of an ideal gas?

5.30 Why is the density of a gas much lower than that of a liquid or solid under atmospheric conditions? What units are normally used to express the density of gases?

Problems

5.31 A sample of nitrogen gas kept in a container of volume 2.3 L and at a temperature of 32°C exerts a pressure of 4.7 atm. Calculate the number of moles of gas present.

5.32 Given that 6.9 moles of carbon monoxide gas are present in a container of volume 30.4 L, what is the pressure of the gas (in atm) if the temperature is 62°C?

5.33 What volume will 5.6 moles of sulfur hexafluoride (SF_6) gas occupy if the temperature and pressure of the gas are 128°C and 9.4 atm?

5.34 A certain amount of gas at 25°C and at a pressure of 0.800 atm is contained in a glass vessel. Suppose that the vessel can withstand a pressure of 2.00 atm. How high can you raise the temperature of the gas without bursting the vessel?

5.35 A gas-filled balloon having a volume of 2.50 L at 1.2 atm and 25°C is allowed to rise to the stratosphere (about 30 km above the surface of Earth), where the temperature and pressure are -23°C and 3.00×10^{-3} atm, respectively. Calculate the final volume of the balloon.

5.36 The temperature of 2.5 L of a gas initially at STP is raised to 250°C at constant volume. Calculate the final pressure of the gas in atm.

5.37 The pressure of 6.0 L of an ideal gas in a flexible container is decreased to one-third of its original pressure, and its absolute temperature is decreased by one-half. What is the final volume of the gas?

5.38 A gas evolved during the fermentation of glucose (wine making) has a volume of 0.78 L at 20.1°C and 1.00 atm. What was the volume of this gas at the fermentation temperature of 36.5°C and 1.00 atm pressure?

5.39 An ideal gas originally at 0.85 atm and 66°C was allowed to expand until its final volume, pressure, and temperature were 94 mL, 0.60 atm, and 45°C, respectively. What was its initial volume?

5.40 Calculate its volume (in liters) of 88.4 g of CO_2 at STP.

5.41 A gas at 772 mmHg and 35.0°C occupies a volume of 6.85 L. Calculate its volume at STP.

5.42 Dry ice is solid carbon dioxide. A 0.050-g sample of dry ice is placed in an evacuated 4.6-L vessel at 30°C. Calculate the pressure inside the vessel after all the dry ice has been converted to CO_2 gas.

5.43 At STP, 0.280 L of a gas weighs 0.400 g. Calculate the molar mass of the gas.

5.44 At 741 torr and 44°C, 7.10 g of a gas occupy a volume of 5.40 L. What is the molar mass of the gas?

5.45 Ozone molecules in the stratosphere absorb much of the harmful radiation from the sun. Typically, the temperature and pressure of ozone in the stratosphere are 250 K and 1.0×10^{-3} atm, respectively. How many ozone molecules are present in 1.0 L of air under these conditions?

5.46 Assuming that air contains 78 percent N_2, 21 percent O_2, and 1 percent Ar, all by volume, how many molecules of each type of gas are present in 1.0 L of air at STP?

5.47 A 2.10-L vessel contains 4.65 g of a gas at 1.00 atm and 27.0°C. (a) Calculate the density of the gas in grams per liter. (b) What is the molar mass of the gas?

5.48 Calculate the density of hydrogen bromide (HBr) gas in grams per liter at 733 mmHg and 46°C.

5.49 A certain anesthetic contains 64.9 percent C, 13.5 percent H, and 21.6 percent O by mass. At 120°C and 750 mmHg, 1.00 L of the gaseous compound weighs 2.30 g. What is the molecular formula of the compound?

5.50 A compound has the empirical formula SF_4. At 20°C, 0.100 g of the gaseous compound occupies a volume of 22.1 mL and exerts a pressure of 1.02 atm. What is the molecular formula of the gas?

Gas Stoichiometry
Problems

5.51 Consider the formation of nitrogen dioxide from nitric oxide and oxygen:

$$2NO(g) + O_2(g) \longrightarrow 2NO_2(g)$$

If 9.0 L of NO are reacted with excess O_2 at STP, what is the volume in liters of the NO_2 produced?

5.52 Methane, the principal component of natural gas, is used for heating and cooking. The combustion process is

$$CH_4(g) + 2O_2(g) \longrightarrow CO_2(g) + 2H_2O(l)$$

If 15.0 moles of CH_4 are reacted, what is the volume of CO_2 (in liters) produced at 23.0°C and 0.985 atm?

5.53 When coal is burned, the sulfur present in coal is converted to sulfur dioxide (SO_2), which is responsible for the acid rain phenomenon.

$$S(s) + O_2(g) \longrightarrow SO_2(g)$$

If 2.54 kg of S are reacted with oxygen, calculate the volume of SO_2 gas (in mL) formed at 30.5°C and 1.12 atm.

5.54 In alcohol fermentation, yeast converts glucose to ethanol and carbon dioxide:

$$C_6H_{12}O_6(s) \longrightarrow 2C_2H_5OH(l) + 2CO_2(g)$$

If 5.97 g of glucose are reacted and 1.44 L of CO_2 gas are collected at 293 K and 0.984 atm, what is the percent yield of the reaction?

5.55 A compound of P and F was analyzed as follows: Heating 0.2324 g of the compound in a 378-cm³ container turned all of it to gas, which had a pressure of 97.3 mmHg at 77°C. Then the gas was mixed with calcium chloride solution, which turned all of the F to 0.2631 g of CaF_2. Determine the molecular formula of the compound.

5.56 A quantity of 0.225 g of a metal M (molar mass = 27.0 g/mol) liberated 0.303 L of molecular hydrogen (measured at 17°C and 741 mmHg) from an excess of hydrochloric acid. Deduce from these data the corresponding equation and write formulas for the oxide and sulfate of M.

5.57 What is the mass of the solid NH_4Cl formed when 73.0 g of NH_3 are mixed with an equal mass of HCl? What is the volume of the gas remaining, measured at 14.0°C and 752 mmHg? What gas is it?

5.58 Dissolving 3.00 g of an impure sample of calcium carbonate in hydrochloric acid produced 0.656 L of carbon dioxide (measured at 20.0°C and 792 mmHg). Calculate the percent by mass of calcium carbonate in the sample. State any assumptions.

5.59 Calculate the mass in grams of hydrogen chloride produced when 5.6 L of molecular hydrogen measured at STP react with an excess of molecular chlorine gas.

5.60 Ethanol (C_2H_5OH) burns in air:

$$C_2H_5OH(l) + O_2(g) \longrightarrow CO_2(g) + H_2O(l)$$

Balance the equation and determine the volume of air in liters at 35.0°C and 790 mmHg required to burn 227 g of ethanol. Assume that air is 21.0 percent O_2 by volume.

Dalton's Law of Partial Pressures

Review Questions

5.61 State Dalton's law of partial pressures and explain what mole fraction is. Does mole fraction have units?

5.62 A sample of air contains only nitrogen and oxygen gases whose partial pressures are 0.80 atm and 0.20 atm,

respectively. Calculate the total pressure and the mole fractions of the gases.

Problems

5.63 A mixture of gases contains 0.31 mol CH_4, 0.25 mol C_2H_6, and 0.29 mol C_3H_8. The total pressure is 1.50 atm. Calculate the partial pressures of the gases.

5.64 A 2.5-L flask at 15°C contains a mixture of N_2, He, and Ne at partial pressures of 0.32 atm for N_2, 0.15 atm for He, and 0.42 atm for Ne. (a) Calculate the total pressure of the mixture. (b) Calculate the volume in liters at STP occupied by He and Ne if the N_2 is removed selectively.

5.65 Dry air near sea level has the following composition by volume: N_2, 78.08 percent; O_2, 20.94 percent; Ar, 0.93 percent; CO_2, 0.05 percent. The atmospheric pressure is 1.00 atm. Calculate (a) the partial pressure of each gas in atm and (b) the concentration of each gas in moles per liter at 0°C. (*Hint:* Because volume is proportional to the number of moles present, mole fractions of gases can be expressed as ratios of volumes at the same temperature and pressure.)

5.66 A mixture of helium and neon gases is collected over water at 28.0°C and 745 mmHg. If the partial pressure of helium is 368 mmHg, what is the partial pressure of neon? (Vapor pressure of water at 28°C = 28.3 mmHg.)

5.67 A piece of sodium metal reacts completely with water as follows:

$$2Na(s) + 2H_2O(l) \longrightarrow 2NaOH(aq) + H_2(g)$$

The hydrogen gas generated is collected over water at 25.0°C. The volume of the gas is 246 mL measured at 1.00 atm. Calculate the number of grams of sodium used in the reaction. (Vapor pressure of water at 25°C = 0.0313 atm.)

5.68 A sample of zinc metal reacts completely with an excess of hydrochloric acid:

$$Zn(s) + 2HCl(aq) \longrightarrow ZnCl_2(aq) + H_2(g)$$

The hydrogen gas produced is collected over water at 25.0°C using an arrangement similar to that shown in Figure 5.15. The volume of the gas is 7.80 L, and the pressure is 0.980 atm. Calculate the amount of zinc metal in grams consumed in the reaction. (Vapor pressure of water at 25°C = 23.8 mmHg.)

5.69 Helium is mixed with oxygen gas for deep-sea divers. Calculate the percent by volume of oxygen gas in the mixture if the diver has to submerge to a depth where the total pressure is 4.2 atm. The partial pressure of oxygen is maintained at 0.20 atm at this depth.

5.70 A sample of ammonia (NH_3) gas is completely decomposed to nitrogen and hydrogen gases over heated iron wool. If the total pressure is 866 mmHg, calculate the partial pressures of N_2 and H_2.

Kinetic Molecular Theory of Gases
Review Questions

5.71 What are the basic assumptions of the kinetic molecular theory of gases?

5.72 How does the kinetic molecular theory explain Boyle's law, Charles's law, Avogadro's law, and Dalton's law of partial pressures?

5.73 What does the Maxwell speed distribution curve tell us? Does Maxwell's theory work for a sample of 200 molecules? Explain.

5.74 Which of the following statements is correct? (a) Heat is produced by the collision of gas molecules against one another. (b) When a gas is heated, the molecules collide with one another more often.

5.75 Uranium hexafluoride (UF_6) is a much heavier gas than helium, yet at a given temperature, the average kinetic energies of the samples of the two gases are the same. Explain.

5.76 What is the difference between gas diffusion and effusion? State Graham's law and define the terms in Equation (5.17).

Problems

5.77 Compare the root-mean-square speeds of O_2 and UF_6 at 65°C.

5.78 The temperature in the stratosphere is −23°C. Calculate the root-mean-square speeds of N_2, O_2, and O_3 molecules in this region.

5.79 The average distance traveled by a molecule between successive collisions is called *mean free path*. For a given amount of a gas, how does the mean free path of a gas depend on (a) density, (b) temperature at constant volume, (c) pressure at constant temperature, (d) volume at constant temperature, and (e) size of the atoms?

5.80 At a certain temperature the speeds of six gaseous molecules in a container are 2.0 m/s, 2.2 m/s, 2.6 m/s, 2.7 m/s, 3.3 m/s, and 3.5 m/s. Calculate the root-mean-square speed and the average speed of the molecules. These two average values are close to each other, but the root-mean-square value is always the larger of the two. Why?

5.81 Based on your knowledge of the kinetic theory of gases, derive Graham's law [Equation (5.17)].

5.82 The ^{235}U isotope undergoes fission when bombarded with neutrons. However, its natural abundance is only 0.72 percent. To separate it from the more abundant ^{238}U isotope, uranium is first converted to UF_6, which is easily vaporized above room temperature. The mixture of the $^{235}UF_6$ and $^{238}UF_6$ gases is then subjected to many stages of effusion. Calculate the separation factor, that is, the enrichment of ^{235}U relative to ^{238}U after one stage of effusion.

5.83 A gas evolved from the fermentation of glucose is found to effuse through a porous barrier in 15.0 min. Under the same conditions of temperature and pressure, it takes an equal volume of N_2 12.0 min to effuse through the same barrier. Calculate the molar mass of the gas and suggest what the gas might be.

5.84 Nickel forms a gaseous compound of the formula $Ni(CO)_x$. What is the value of x given the fact that under the same conditions of temperature and pressure, methane (CH_4) effuses 3.3 times faster than the compound?

Deviation from Ideal Behavior
Review Questions

5.85 Cite two pieces of evidence to show that gases do not behave ideally under all conditions.

5.86 Under what set of conditions would a gas be expected to behave most ideally? (a) High temperature and low pressure, (b) high temperature and high pressure, (c) low temperature and high pressure, (d) low temperature and low pressure.

5.87 Write the van der Waals equation for a real gas. Explain the corrective terms for pressure and volume.

5.88 (a) A real gas is introduced into a flask of volume V. Is the corrected volume of the gas greater or less than V? (b) Ammonia has a larger *a* value than neon does (see Table 5.4). What can you conclude about the relative strength of the attractive forces between molecules of ammonia and between atoms of neon?

Problems

5.89 Using the data shown in Table 5.4, calculate the pressure exerted by 2.50 moles of CO_2 confined in a volume of 5.00 L at 450 K. Compare the pressure with that predicted by the ideal gas equation.

5.90 At 27°C, 10.0 moles of a gas in a 1.50-L container exert a pressure of 130 atm. Is this an ideal gas?

Additional Problems

5.91 Discuss the following phenomena in terms of the gas laws: (a) the pressure increase in an automobile tire on a hot day, (b) the "popping" of a paper bag, (c) the expansion of a weather balloon as it rises in the air, (d) the loud noise heard when a lightbulb shatters.

5.92 Under the same conditions of temperature and pressure, which of the following gases would behave most ideally: Ne, N_2, or CH_4? Explain.

5.93 Nitroglycerin, an explosive compound, decomposes according to the equation

$$4C_3H_5(NO_3)_3(s) \longrightarrow$$
$$12CO_2(g) + 10H_2O(g) + 6N_2(g) + O_2(g)$$

Calculate the total volume of gases when collected at 1.2 atm and 25°C from 2.6×10^2 g of nitroglycerin.

What are the partial pressures of the gases under these conditions?

5.94 The empirical formula of a compound is CH. At 200°C, 0.145 g of this compound occupies 97.2 mL at a pressure of 0.74 atm. What is the molecular formula of the compound?

5.95 When ammonium nitrite (NH_4NO_2) is heated, it decomposes to give nitrogen gas. This property is used to inflate some tennis balls. (a) Write a balanced equation for the reaction. (b) Calculate the quantity (in grams) of NH_4NO_2 needed to inflate a tennis ball to a volume of 86.2 mL at 1.20 atm and 22°C.

5.96 The percent by mass of bicarbonate (HCO_3^-) in a certain Alka-Seltzer product is 32.5 percent. Calculate the volume of CO_2 generated (in mL) at 37°C and 1.00 atm when a person ingests a 3.29-g tablet. (*Hint:* The reaction is between HCO_3^- and HCl acid in the stomach.)

5.97 The boiling point of liquid nitrogen is −196°C. On the basis of this information alone, do you think nitrogen is an ideal gas?

5.98 In the metallurgical process of refining nickel, the metal is first combined with carbon monoxide to form tetracarbonylnickel, which is a gas at 43°C:

$$Ni(s) + 4CO(g) \longrightarrow Ni(CO)_4(g)$$

This reaction separates nickel from other solid impurities. (a) Starting with 86.4 g of Ni, calculate the pressure of $Ni(CO)_4$ in a container of volume 4.00 L. (Assume the above reaction goes to completion.) (b) At temperatures above 43°C, the pressure of the gas is observed to increase much more rapidly than predicted by the ideal gas equation. Explain.

5.99 The partial pressure of carbon dioxide varies with seasons. Would you expect the partial pressure in the Northern Hemisphere to be higher in the summer or winter? Explain.

5.100 A healthy adult exhales about 5.0×10^2 mL of a gaseous mixture with each breath. Calculate the number of molecules present in this volume at 37°C and 1.1 atm. List the major components of this gaseous mixture.

5.101 Sodium bicarbonate ($NaHCO_3$) is called baking soda because when heated, it releases carbon dioxide gas, which is responsible for the rising of cookies, doughnuts, and bread. (a) Calculate the volume (in liters) of CO_2 produced by heating 5.0 g of $NaHCO_3$ at 180°C and 1.3 atm. (b) Ammonium bicarbonate (NH_4HCO_3) has also been used for the same purpose. Suggest one advantage and one disadvantage of using NH_4HCO_3 instead of $NaHCO_3$ for baking.

5.102 A barometer having a cross-sectional area of 1.00 cm^2 at sea level measures a pressure of 76.0 cm of mercury. The pressure exerted by this column of mercury is equal to the pressure exerted by all the air on 1 cm^2

of Earth's surface. Given that the density of mercury is 13.6 g/mL and the average radius of Earth is 6371 km, calculate the total mass of Earth's atmosphere in kilograms. (*Hint:* The surface area of a sphere is $4\pi r^2$ where r is the radius of the sphere.)

5.103 Some commercial drain cleaners contain a mixture of sodium hydroxide and aluminum powder. When the mixture is poured down a clogged drain, the following reaction occurs:

$$2NaOH(aq) + 2Al(s) + 6H_2O(l) \longrightarrow$$
$$2NaAl(OH)_4(aq) + 3H_2(g)$$

The heat generated in this reaction helps melt away obstructions such as grease, and the hydrogen gas released stirs up the solids clogging the drain. Calculate the volume of H_2 formed at 23°C and 1.00 atm if 3.12 g of Al are treated with an excess of NaOH.

5.104 The volume of a sample of pure HCl gas was 189 mL at 25°C and 108 mmHg. It was completely dissolved in about 60 mL of water and titrated with an NaOH solution; 15.7 mL of the NaOH solution were required to neutralize the HCl. Calculate the molarity of the NaOH solution.

5.105 Propane (C_3H_8) burns in oxygen to produce carbon dioxide gas and water vapor. (a) Write a balanced equation for this reaction. (b) Calculate the number of liters of carbon dioxide measured at STP that could be produced from 7.45 g of propane.

5.106 Consider the following apparatus. Calculate the partial pressures of helium and neon after the stopcock is open. The temperature remains constant at 16°C.

1.2 L   3.4 L
0.63 atm   2.8 atm

5.107 Nitric oxide (NO) reacts with molecular oxygen as follows:

$$2NO(g) + O_2(g) \longrightarrow 2NO_2(g)$$

Initially NO and O_2 are separated as shown here. When the valve is opened, the reaction quickly goes to completion. Determine what gases remain at the end and calculate their partial pressures. Assume that the temperature remains constant at 25°C.

4.00 L at   2.00 L at
0.500 atm   1.00 atm

5.108 Consider the apparatus shown here. When a small amount of water is introduced into the flask by squeezing the bulb of the medicine dropper, water is squirted upward out of the long glass tubing. Explain this observation. (*Hint:* Hydrogen chloride gas is soluble in water.)

5.109 Describe how you would measure, by either chemical or physical means, the partial pressures of a mixture of gases of the following composition: (a) CO_2 and H_2, (b) He and N_2.

5.110 A certain hydrate has the formula $MgSO_4 \cdot xH_2O$. A quantity of 54.2 g of the compound is heated in an oven to drive off the water. If the steam generated exerts a pressure of 24.8 atm in a 2.00-L container at 120°C, calculate x.

5.111 A mixture of Na_2CO_3 and $MgCO_3$ of mass 7.63 g is reacted with an excess of hydrochloric acid. The CO_2 gas generated occupies a volume of 1.67 L at 1.24 atm and 26°C. From these data, calculate the percent composition by mass of Na_2CO_3 in the mixture.

5.112 The following apparatus can be used to measure atomic and molecular speed. Suppose that a beam of metal atoms is directed at a rotating cylinder in a vacuum. A small opening in the cylinder allows the atoms to strike a target area. Because the cylinder is rotating, atoms traveling at different speeds will strike the target at different positions. In time, a layer of the metal will deposit on the target area, and the variation in its thickness is found to correspond to Maxwell's speed distribution. In one experiment it is found that at 850°C some bismuth (Bi) atoms struck the target at a point 2.80 cm from the spot directly opposite the slit. The diameter of the cylinder is 15.0 cm and it is rotating at 130 revolutions per second. (a) Calculate the speed (m/s) at which the target is moving. (*Hint:* The circumference of a circle is given by $2\pi r$, where r is the radius.) (b) Calculate the time (in seconds) it takes for the target to travel 2.80 cm. (c) Determine the speed of the Bi atoms. Compare your result in (c) with the u_{rms} of Bi at 850°C. Comment on the difference.

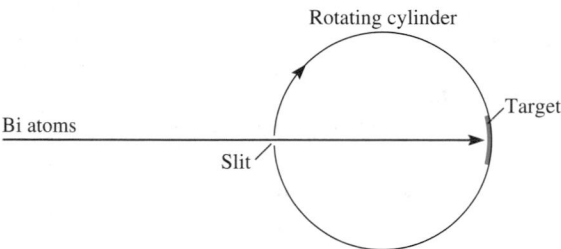

5.113 If 10.00 g of water are introduced into an evacuated flask of volume 2.500 L at 65°C, calculate the mass of water vaporized. (*Hint:* Assume that the volume of the remaining liquid water is negligible; the vapor pressure of water at 65°C is 187.5 mmHg.)

5.114 Commercially, compressed oxygen is sold in metal cylinders. If a 120-L cylinder is filled with oxygen to a pressure of 132 atm at 22°C, what is the mass (in grams) of O_2 present? How many liters of O_2 gas at 1.00 atm and 22°C could the cylinder produce? (Assume ideal behavior.)

5.115 The shells of hard-boiled eggs sometimes crack due to the rapid thermal expansion of the shells at high temperatures. Suggest another reason why the shells may crack.

5.116 Ethylene gas (C_2H_4) is emitted by fruits and is known to be responsible for their ripening. Based on this information, explain why a bunch of bananas ripens faster in a closed paper bag than in a bowl.

5.117 About 8.0×10^6 tons of urea $[(NH_2)_2CO]$ are used annually as a fertilizer. The urea is prepared at 200°C and under high-pressure conditions from carbon dioxide and ammonia (the products are urea and steam). Calculate the volume of ammonia (in liters) measured at 150 atm needed to prepare 1.0 ton of urea.

5.118 Some ballpoint pens have a small hole in the main body of the pen. What is the purpose of this hole?

5.119 The gas laws are vitally important to scuba divers. The pressure exerted by 33 ft of seawater is equivalent to 1 atm pressure. (a) A diver ascends quickly to the surface of the water from a depth of 36 ft without exhaling gas from his lungs. By what factor will the volume of his lungs increase by the time he reaches the surface? Assume that the temperature is constant. (b) The partial pressure of oxygen in air is about 0.20 atm. (Air is 20 percent oxygen by volume.) In deep-sea diving, the composition of air the diver breathes must be changed to maintain this partial pressure. What must the oxygen content (in percent by volume) be when the total pressure exerted on the diver is 4.0 atm? (At constant temperature and pressure, the volume of a gas is directly proportional to the number of moles of gases.) (*Hint:* See Chemistry in Action essay on p. 198.)

5.120 Nitrous oxide (N_2O) can be obtained by the thermal decomposition of ammonium nitrate (NH_4NO_3). (a) Write a balanced equation for the reaction. (b) In a certain experiment, a student obtains 0.340 L of the gas at 718 mmHg and 24°C. If the gas weighs 0.580 g, calculate the value of the gas constant.

5.121 Two vessels are labeled A and B. Vessel A contains NH_3 gas at 70°C, and vessel B contains Ne gas at the same temperature. If the average kinetic energy of NH_3 is 7.1×10^{-21} J/molecule, calculate the mean-square speed of Ne atoms in m^2/s^2.

5.122 Which of the following molecules has the largest *a* value: CH_4, F_2, C_6H_6, Ne?

5.123 The following procedure is a simple though somewhat crude way to measure the molar mass of a gas. A liquid of mass 0.0184 g is introduced into a syringe like the one shown here by injection through the rubber tip using a hypodermic needle. The syringe is then transferred to a temperature bath heated to 45°C, and the liquid vaporizes. The final volume of the vapor (measured by the outward movement of the plunger) is 5.58 mL and the atmospheric pressure is 760 mmHg. Given that the compound's empirical formula is CH_2, determine the molar mass of the compound.

Rubber tip

5.124 In 1995 a man suffocated as he walked by an abandoned mine in England. At that moment there was a sharp drop in atmospheric pressure due to a change in the weather. Suggest what might have caused the man's death.

5.125 Acidic oxides such as carbon dioxide react with basic oxides like calcium oxide (CaO) and barium oxide (BaO) to form salts (metal carbonates). (a) Write equations representing these two reactions. (b) A student placed a mixture of BaO and CaO of combined mass 4.88 g in a 1.46-L flask containing carbon dioxide gas at 35°C and 746 mmHg. After the reactions were complete, she found that the CO_2 pressure had dropped to 252 mmHg. Calculate the percent composition by mass of the mixture. Assume volumes of the solids are negligible.

5.126 (a) What volume of air at 1.0 atm and 22°C is needed to fill a 0.98-L bicycle tire to a pressure of 5.0 atm at the same temperature? (Note that the 5.0 atm is the gauge pressure, which is the difference between the pressure in the tire and atmospheric pressure. Before

filling, the pressure in the tire was 1.0 atm.) (b) What is the total pressure in the tire when the gauge pressure reads 5.0 atm? (c) The tire is pumped by filling the cylinder of a hand pump with air at 1.0 atm and then, by compressing the gas in the cylinder, adding all the air in the pump to the air in the tire. If the volume of the pump is 33 percent of the tire's volume, what is the gauge pressure in the tire after three full strokes of the pump? Assume constant temperature.

5.127 The running engine of an automobile produces carbon monoxide (CO), a toxic gas, at the rate of about 188 g CO per hour. A car is left idling in a poorly ventilated garage that is 6.0 m long, 4.0 m wide, and 2.2 m high at 20°C. (a) Calculate the rate of CO production in moles per minute. (b) How long would it take to build up a lethal concentration of CO of 1000 ppmv (parts per million by volume)?

5.128 Interstellar space contains mostly hydrogen atoms at a concentration of about 1 atom/cm^3. (a) Calculate the pressure of the H atoms. (b) Calculate the volume (in liters) that contains 1.0 g of H atoms. The temperature is 3 K.

5.129 Atop Mt. Everest, the atmospheric pressure is 210 mmHg and the air density is 0.426 kg/m^3. (a) Calculate the air temperature, given that the molar mass of air is 29.0 g/mol. (b) Assuming no change in air composition, calculate the percent decrease in oxygen gas from sea level to the top of Mt. Everest.

5.130 Relative humidity is defined as the ratio (expressed as a percentage) of the partial pressure of water vapor in the air to the equilibrium vapor pressure (see Table 5.3) at a given temperature. On a certain summer day in North Carolina the partial pressure of water vapor in the air is 3.9×10^3 Pa at 30°C. Calculate the relative humidity.

5.131 Under the same conditions of temperature and pressure, why does one liter of moist air weigh less than one liter of dry air? In weather forecasts, an oncoming low-pressure front usually means imminent rainfall. Explain.

5.132 Air entering the lungs ends up in tiny sacs called alveoli. It is from the alveoli that oxygen diffuses into the blood. The average radius of the alveoli is 0.0050 cm and the air inside contains 14 percent oxygen. Assuming that the pressure in the alveoli is 1.0 atm and the temperature is 37°C, calculate the number of oxygen molecules in one of the alveoli. (*Hint:* The volume of a sphere of radius *r* is $\frac{4}{3}\pi r^3$.)

5.133 A student breaks a thermometer and spills most of the mercury (Hg) onto the floor of a laboratory that measures 15.2 m long, 6.6 m wide, and 2.4 m high. (a) Calculate the mass of mercury vapor (in grams) in the room at 20°C. The vapor pressure of mercury at 20°C is 1.7×10^{-6} atm. (b) Does the concentration of mercury vapor exceed the air quality regulation of

0.050 mg Hg/m^3 of air? (c) One way to treat small quantities of spilled mercury is to spray sulfur powder over the metal. Suggest a physical and a chemical reason for this action.

5.134 Nitrogen forms several gaseous oxides. One of them has a density of 1.33 g/L measured at 764 mmHg and 150°C. Write the formula of the compound.

5.135 Nitrogen dioxide (NO_2) cannot be obtained in a pure form in the gas phase because it exists as a mixture of NO_2 and N_2O_4. At 25°C and 0.98 atm, the density of this gas mixture is 2.7 g/L. What is the partial pressure of each gas?

5.136 The Chemistry in Action essay on p. 205 describes the cooling of rubidium vapor to 1.7×10^{-7} K. Calculate the root-mean-square speed and average kinetic energy of a Rb atom at this temperature.

5.137 Lithium hydride reacts with water as follows:

$$LiH(s) + H_2O(l) \longrightarrow LiOH(aq) + H_2(g)$$

During World War II, U.S. pilots carried LiH tablets. In the event of a crash landing at sea, the LiH would react with the seawater and fill their life belts and lifeboats with hydrogen gas. How many grams of LiH are needed to fill a 4.1-L life belt at 0.97 atm and 12°C?

5.138 The atmosphere on Mars is composed mainly of carbon dioxide. The surface temperature is 220 K and the atmospheric pressure is about 6.0 mmHg. Taking these values as Martian "STP," calculate the molar volume in liters of an ideal gas on Mars.

5.139 Venus's atmosphere is composed of 96.5 percent CO_2, 3.5 percent N_2, and 0.015 percent SO_2 by volume. Its standard atmospheric pressure is 9.0×10^6 Pa. Calculate the partial pressures of the gases in pascals.

5.140 A student tries to determine the volume of a bulb like the one shown on p. 188. These are her results: Mass of the bulb filled with dry air at 23°C and 744 mmHg = 91.6843 g; mass of evacuated bulb = 91.4715 g. Assume the composition of air is 78 percent N_2, 21 percent O_2, and 1 percent argon. What is the volume (in milliliters) of the bulb? (*Hint:* First calculate the average molar mass of air, as shown in Problem 3.140.)

5.141 Apply your knowledge of the kinetic theory of gases to the following situations. (a) Two flasks of volumes V_1 and V_2 ($V_2 > V_1$) contain the same number of helium atoms at the same temperature. (i) Compare the root-mean-square (rms) speeds and average kinetic energies of the helium (He) atoms in the flasks. (ii) Compare the frequency and the force with which the He atoms collide with the walls of their containers. (b) Equal numbers of He atoms are placed in two flasks of the same volume at temperatures T_1 and T_2 ($T_2 > T_1$). (i) Compare the rms speeds of the atoms in the two flasks. (ii) Compare the frequency and the force with which the He atoms collide with the walls of their containers. (c) Equal numbers of He and neon

(Ne) atoms are placed in two flasks of the same volume, and the temperature of both gases is 74°C. Comment on the validity of the following statements: (i) The rms speed of He is equal to that of Ne. (ii) The average kinetic energies of the two gases are equal. (iii) The rms speed of each He atom is 1.47×10^3 m/s.

5.142 It has been said that every breath we take, on average, contains molecules that were once exhaled by Wolfgang Amadeus Mozart (1756–1791). The following calculations demonstrate the validity of this statement. (a) Calculate the total number of molecules in the atmosphere. (*Hint:* Use the result in Problem 5.102 and 29.0 g/mol as the molar mass of air.) (b) Assuming the volume of every breath (inhale or exhale) is 500 mL, calculate the number of molecules exhaled in each breath at 37°C, which is the body temperature. (c) If Mozart's lifespan was exactly 35 years, what is the number of molecules he exhaled in that period? (Given that an average person breathes 12 times per minute.) (d) Calculate the fraction of molecules in the atmosphere that was exhaled by Mozart. How many of Mozart's molecules do we breathe in with every inhale of air? Round off your answer to one significant figure. (e) List three important assumptions in these calculations.

5.143 At what temperature will He atoms have the same u_{rms} value as N_2 molecules at 25°C?

5.144 Estimate the distance (in nanometers) between molecules of water vapor at 100°C and 1.0 atm. Assume ideal behavior. Repeat the calculation for liquid water at 100°C, given that the density of water is 0.96 g/cm^3 at that temperature. Comment on your results. (Assume water molecule to be a sphere with a diameter of 0.3 nm.) (*Hint:* First calculate the number density of water molecules. Next, convert the number density to linear density, that is, number of molecules in one direction.)

5.145 Which of the noble gases would not behave ideally under any circumstance? Why?

5.146 A relation known as the barometric formula is useful for estimating the change in atmospheric pressure with altitude. The formula is given by $P = P_0 e^{-g\mathcal{M}h/RT}$, where P and P_0 are the pressures at height h and sea level, respectively, g is the acceleration due to gravity (9.8 m/s^2), $\mathcal{M}$ is the average molar mass of air (29.0 g/mol), and R is the gas constant. Calculate the atmospheric pressure in atm at a height of 5.0 km, assuming the temperature is constant at 5°C and $P_0 = 1.0$ atm.

5.147 A 5.72-g sample of graphite was heated with 68.4 g of O_2 in a 8.00-L flask. The reaction that took place was

$$C(graphite) + O_2(g) \longrightarrow CO_2(g)$$

After the reaction was complete, the temperature in the flask was 182°C. What was the total pressure inside the flask?

5.148 A 6.11-g sample of a Cu-Zn alloy reacts with HCl acid to produce hydrogen gas. If the hydrogen gas has a volume of 1.26 L at 22°C and 728 mmHg, what is the percent of Zn in the alloy? (*Hint:* Cu does not react with HCl.)

5.149 A stockroom supervisor measured the contents of a partially filled 25.0-gallon acetone drum on a day when the temperature was 18.0°C and atmospheric pressure was 750 mmHg, and found that 15.4 gallons of the solvent remained. After tightly sealing the drum, an assistant dropped the drum while carrying it upstairs to the organic laboratory. The drum was dented and its internal volume was decreased to 20.4 gallons. What is the total pressure inside the drum after the accident? The vapor pressure of acetone at 18.0°C is 400 mmHg. (*Hint:* At the time the drum was sealed, the pressure inside the drum, which is equal to the sum of the pressures of air and acetone, was equal to the atmospheric pressure.)

Special Problems

5.150 In 2.00 min, 29.7 mL of He effuse through a small hole. Under the same conditions of pressure and temperature, 10.0 mL of a mixture of CO and CO_2 effuse through the hole in the same amount of time. Calculate the percent composition by volume of the mixture.

5.151 Referring to Figure 5.22, explain the following: (a) Why do the curves dip below the horizontal line labeled ideal gas at low pressures and then why do they arise above the horizontal line at high pressures? (b) Why do the curves all converge to 1 at very low pressures? (c) Each curve intercepts the horizontal line labeled ideal gas. Does it mean that at that point the gas behaves ideally?

5.152 A mixture of methane (CH_4) and ethane (C_2H_6) is stored in a container at 294 mmHg. The gases are burned in air to form CO_2 and H_2O. If the pressure of CO_2 is 356 mmHg measured at the same temperature and volume as the original mixture, calculate the mole fractions of the gases.

5.153 Use the kinetic theory of gases to explain why hot air rises.

5.154 One way to gain a physical understanding of *b* in the van der Waals equation is to calculate the "excluded volume." Assume that the distance of closest approach between two similar atoms is the sum of their radii (2*r*). (a) Calculate the volume around each atom into which the center of another atom cannot penetrate. (b) From your result in (a), calculate the excluded volume for 1 mole of the atoms, which is the constant *b*. How does this volume compare with the sum of the volumes of 1 mole of the atoms?

5.155 A 5.00-mole sample of NH_3 gas is kept in a 1.92 L container at 300 K. If the van der Waals equation is assumed to give the correct answer for the pressure of the gas, calculate the percent error made in using the ideal gas equation to calculate the pressure.

5.156 The root-mean-square speed of a certain gaseous oxide is 493 m/s at 20°C. What is the molecular formula of the compound?

5.157 Referring to Figure 5.17, we see that the maximum of each speed distribution plot is called the most proba-ble speed (u_{mp}) because it is the speed possessed by the largest number of molecules. It is given by $u_{mp} = \sqrt{2RT/\mathcal{M}}$. (a) Compare u_{mp} with u_{rms} for nitrogen at 25°C. (b) The following diagram shows the Maxwell speed distribution curves for an ideal gas at two different temperatures T_1 and T_2. Calculate the value of T_2.

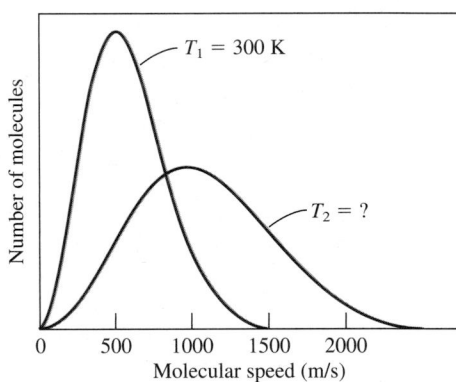

5.158 A gaseous reaction takes place at constant volume and constant pressure in a cylinder shown here. Which of the following equations best describes the reaction? The initial temperature (T_1) is twice that of the final temperature (T_2).

(a) $A + B \longrightarrow C$
(b) $AB \longrightarrow C + D$
(c) $A + B \longrightarrow C + D$
(d) $A + B \longrightarrow 2C + D$

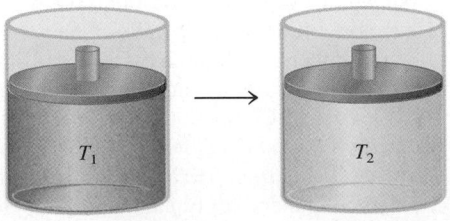

Answers to Practice Exercises

5.1 0.986 atm. **5.2** 39.3 kPa. **5.3** 9.29 L. **5.4** 30.6 L.
5.5 4.46×10^3 mmHg. **5.6** 0.68 atm. **5.7** 2.6 atm.
5.8 13.1 g/L. **5.9** 44.1 g/mol. **5.10** B_2H_6. **5.11** 96.9 L.
5.12 4.75 L. **5.13** 0.338 M. **5.14** CH_4: 1.29 atm; C_2H_6:
0.0657 atm; C_3H_8: 0.0181 atm. **5.15** 0.0653 g.
5.16 321 m/s. **5.17** 146 g/mol. **5.18** 30.0 atm; 45.5 atm
using the ideal gas equation.

Out of Oxygen†

In September 1991 four men and four women entered the world's largest glass bubble, known as Biosphere II, to test the idea that humans could design and build a totally self-contained ecosystem, a model for some future colony on another planet. Biosphere II (Earth is considered Biosphere I) was a 3-acre mini-world, complete with a tropical rain forest, savanna, marsh, desert, and working farm that was intended to be fully self-sufficient. This unique experiment was to continue for 2 to 3 years, but almost immediately there were signs that the project could be in jeopardy.

Soon after the bubble had been sealed, sensors inside the facility showed that the concentration of oxygen in Biosphere II's atmosphere had fallen from its initial level of 21 percent (by volume), while the amount of carbon dioxide had risen from a level of 0.035 percent (by volume), or 350 ppm (parts per million). Alarmingly, the oxygen level continued to fall at a rate of about 0.5 percent a month and the level of carbon dioxide kept rising, forcing the crew to turn on electrically powered chemical scrubbers, similar to those on submarines, to remove some of the excess CO_2. Gradually the CO_2 level stabilized around 4000 ppm, which is high but not dangerous. The loss of oxygen did not stop, though. By January 1993—16 months into the experiment—the oxygen concentration had dropped to 14 percent, which is equivalent to the O_2 concentration in air at an elevation of 4360 m (14,300 ft). The crew began having trouble performing normal tasks. For their safety it was necessary to pump pure oxygen into Biosphere II.

With all the plants present in Biosphere II, the production of oxygen should have been greater as a consequence of photosynthesis. Why had the oxygen concentration declined to such a low level? A small part of the loss was blamed on unusually cloudy weather, which had slowed down plant growth. The possibility that iron in the soil was reacting with oxygen to form iron(III) oxide or rust was ruled out along with several other explanations for lack of evidence. The most plausible hypothesis was that microbes (microorganisms) were using oxygen to metabolize the excess organic matter that had been added to the soils to promote plant growth. This turned out to be the case.

Identifying the cause of oxygen depiction raised another question. Metabolism produces carbon dioxide. Based on the amount of oxygen consumed by the microbes, the CO_2 level should have been at 40,000 ppm, 10 times what was measured. What happened to the excess gas? After ruling out leakage to the outside world and reactions between CO_2 with compounds in the soils and in water, scientists found that the concrete inside Biosphere II was consuming large amounts of CO_2!

Concrete is a mixture of sand and gravel held together by a binding agent that is a mixture of calcium silicate hydrates and calcium hydroxide. The calcium hydroxide is the key ingredient in the CO_2 mystery. Carbon dioxide diffuses into the porous structure of concrete, then reacts with calcium hydroxide to form calcium carbonate and water:

$$Ca(OH)_2(s) + CO_2(g) \longrightarrow CaCO_3(s) + H_2O(l)$$

Under normal conditions, this reaction goes on slowly. But CO_2 concentrations in Biosphere II were much higher than normal, so the reaction proceeded much faster. In fact, in just over 2 years,

---

†Adapted with permission from "Biosphere II: Out of Oxygen," by Joe Alper, CHEM MATTERS, February, 1995, p. 8. Copyright 1995 American Chemical Society.

$CaCO_3$ had accumulated to a depth of more than 2 cm in Biosphere II's concrete. Some 10,000 m^2 of exposed concrete was hiding 500,000 to 1,500,000 moles of CO_2.

The water produced in the reaction between $Ca(OH)_2$ and CO_2 created another problem: CO_2 also reacts with water to form carbonic acid (H_2CO_3), and hydrogen ions produced by the acid promote the corrosion of the reinforcing iron bars in the concrete, thereby weakening its structure. This situation was dealt with effectively by painting all concrete surfaces with an impermeable coating.

In the meantime, the decline in oxygen (and hence also the rise in carbon dioxide) slowed, perhaps because there was now less organic matter in the soils and also because new lights in the agricultural areas may have boosted photosynthesis. The project was terminated prematurely and in 1996, the facility was transformed into a science education and research center. As of 2005, the Biosphere is up for sale.

The Biosphere II experiment is an interesting project from which we can learn a lot about Earth and its inhabitants. If nothing else, it has shown us how complex Earth's ecosystems are and how difficult it is to mimic nature, even on a small scale.

Chemical Clues

1. What solution would you use in a chemical scrubber to remove carbon dioxide?

2. Photosynthesis converts carbon dioxide and water to carbohydrates and oxygen gas, while metabolism is the process by which carbohydrates react with oxygen to form carbon dioxide and water. Using glucose ($C_6H_{12}O_6$) to represent carbohydrates, write equations for these two processes.

3. Why was diffusion of O_2 from Biosphere II to the outside world not considered a possible cause for the depletion in oxygen?

4. Carbonic acid is a diprotic acid. Write equations for the stepwise ionization of the acid in water.

5. What are the factors to consider in choosing a planet on which to build a structure like Biosphere II?

6

The analysis of particles formed from burning methane in a flame is performed with a visible laser. The models show methane and oxygen molecules and the combustion products carbon dioxide and water molecules.

Thermochemistry

A LOOK AHEAD

- We begin by studying the nature and different types of energy, which, in principle, are interconvertible. (6.1)

- Next, we build up our vocabulary in learning thermochemistry, which is the study of heat change in chemical reactions. We see that the vast majority of reactions are either endothermic (absorbing heat) or exothermic (releasing heat). (6.2)

- We learn that thermochemistry is part of a broader subject called the first law of thermodynamics, which is based on the law of conservation of energy. We see that the change in internal energy can be expressed in terms of the changes in heat and work done of a system. (6.3)

- We then become acquainted with a new term for energy, called enthalpy, whose change applies to processes carried out under constant-pressure conditions. (6.4)

- We learn ways to measure the heats of reaction or calorimetry under constant-volume and constant-pressure conditions, and the meaning of specific heat and heat capacity, quantities used in experimental work. (6.5)

- Knowing the standard enthalpies of formation of reactants and products enables us to calculate the enthalpy of a reaction. We will discuss ways to determine these quantities either by the direct method from the elements or by the indirect method, which is based on Hess's law of heat summation. (6.6)

- Finally, we will study the heat changes when a solute dissolves in a solvent (heat of solution) and when a solution is diluted (heat of dilution). (6.7)

Interactive Activity Summary

1. Interactivity: Conservation of Energy (6.3)
2. Animation: Heat Flow (6.4)

Every chemical reaction obeys two fundamental laws: the law of conservation of mass and the law of conservation of energy. We discussed the mass relationships between reactants and products in Chapter 3; here we will look at the energy changes that accompany chemical reactions.

6.1 The Nature of Energy and Types of Energy

"Energy" is a much-used term that represents a rather abstract concept. For instance, when we feel tired, we might say we haven't any *energy;* and we read about the need to find alternatives to nonrenewable *energy* sources. Unlike matter, energy is known and recognized by its effects. It cannot be seen, touched, smelled, or weighed.

Energy is usually defined as *the capacity to do work.* In Chapter 5 we defined work as "force × distance," but we will soon see that there are other kinds of work. All forms of energy are capable of doing work (that is, of exerting a force over a distance), but not all of them are equally relevant to chemistry. The energy contained in tidal waves, for example, can be harnessed to perform useful work, but the relationship between tidal waves and chemistry is minimal. Chemists define **work** as *directed energy change resulting from a process.* Kinetic energy—the energy produced by a moving object—is one form of energy that is of particular interest to chemists. Others include radiant energy, thermal energy, chemical energy, and potential energy.

Radiant energy, or *solar energy, comes from the sun* and is Earth's primary energy source. Solar energy heats the atmosphere and Earth's surface, stimulates the growth of vegetation through the process known as photosynthesis, and influences global climate patterns.

Thermal energy is *the energy associated with the random motion of atoms and molecules.* In general, thermal energy can be calculated from temperature measurements. The more vigorous the motion of the atoms and molecules in a sample of matter, the hotter the sample is and the greater its thermal energy. However, we need to distinguish carefully between thermal energy and temperature. A cup of coffee at 70°C has a higher temperature than a bathtub filled with warm water at 40°C, but much more thermal energy is stored in the bathtub water because it has a much larger volume and greater mass than the coffee and therefore more water molecules and more molecular motion.

Chemical energy is *stored within the structural units of chemical substances;* its quantity is determined by the type and arrangement of constituent atoms. When substances participate in chemical reactions, chemical energy is released, stored, or converted to other forms of energy.

Potential energy is *energy available by virtue of an object's position.* For instance, because of its altitude, a rock at the top of a cliff has more potential energy and will make a bigger splash if it falls into the water below than a similar rock located partway down the cliff. Chemical energy can be considered a form of potential energy because it is associated with the relative positions and arrangements of atoms within a given substance.

All forms of energy can be converted (at least in principle) from one form to another. We feel warm when we stand in sunlight because radiant energy is converted to thermal energy on our skin. When we exercise, chemical energy stored in our bodies is used to produce kinetic energy. When a ball starts to roll downhill, its potential energy is converted to kinetic energy. You can undoubtedly think of many other examples. Although energy can assume many different forms that are interconvertible, scientists have concluded that energy can be neither destroyed nor created. When one form of energy disappears, some other form of energy (of equal magnitude) must appear, and vice versa. This principle is summarized by the ***law of conservation of energy:*** *the total quantity of energy in the universe is assumed constant.*

Kinetic energy was introduced in Chapter 5 (p. 197).

As the water falls over the dam, its potential energy is converted to kinetic energy. Use of this energy to generate electricity is called hydroelectric power.

6.2 Energy Changes in Chemical Reactions

Often the energy changes that take place during chemical reactions are of as much practical interest as the mass relationships we discussed in Chapter 3. For example, combustion reactions involving fuels such as natural gas and oil are carried out in daily life more for the thermal energy they release than for their products, which are water and carbon dioxide.

This infrared photo shows where energy (heat) leaks through the house. The more red the color, the more energy is lost to the outside.

Almost all chemical reactions absorb or produce (release) energy, generally in the form of heat. It is important to understand the distinction between thermal energy and heat. **Heat** is *the transfer of thermal energy between two bodies that are at different temperatures.* Thus, we often speak of the "heat flow" from a hot object to a cold one. Although the term "heat" by itself implies the transfer of energy, we customarily talk of "heat absorbed" or "heat released" when describing the energy changes that occur during a process. **Thermochemistry** is *the study of heat change in chemical reactions.*

To analyze energy changes associated with chemical reactions we must first define the **system,** or *the specific part of the universe that is of interest to us.* For chemists, systems usually include substances involved in chemical and physical changes. For example, in an acid-base neutralization experiment, the system may be a beaker containing 50 mL of HCl to which 50 mL of NaOH is added. The **surroundings** are *the rest of the universe outside the system.*

There are three types of systems. An **open system** *can exchange mass and energy, usually in the form of heat with its surroundings.* For example, an open system may consist of a quantity of water in an open container, as shown in Figure 6.1(a). If we close the flask, as in Figure 6.1(b), so that no water vapor can escape from or condense into the container, we create a **closed system,** which *allows the transfer of energy (heat) but not mass.* By placing the water in a totally insulated container, we can construct an **isolated system,** which *does not allow the transfer of either mass or energy,* as shown in Figure 6.1(c).

The combustion of hydrogen gas in oxygen is one of many chemical reactions that release considerable quantities of energy (Figure 6.2):

$$2H_2(g) + O_2(g) \longrightarrow 2H_2O(l) + \text{energy}$$

In this case, we label the reacting mixture (hydrogen, oxygen, and water molecules) the *system* and the rest of the universe the *surroundings.* Because energy cannot be

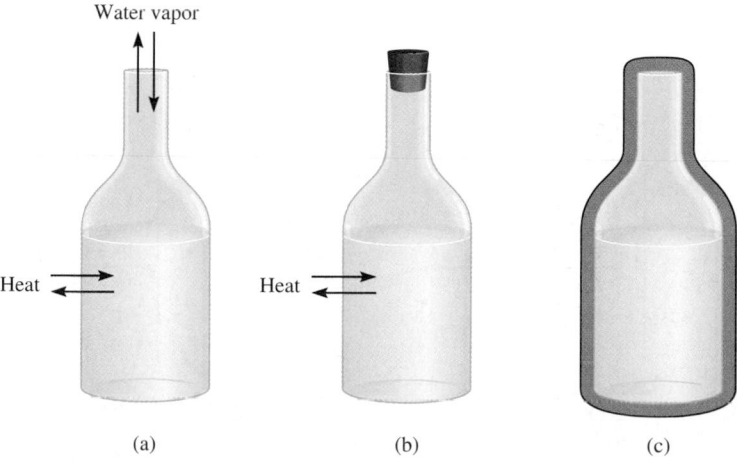

Water vapor

Heat

Heat

(a)   (b)   (c)

Figure 6.1 *Three systems represented by water in a flask: (a) an open system, which allows the exchange of both energy and mass with surroundings; (b) a closed system, which allows the exchange of energy but not mass; and (c) an isolated system, which allows neither energy nor mass to be exchanged (here the flask is enclosed by a vacuum jacket).*

Figure 6.2 *The Hindenburg disaster. The Hindenburg, a German airship filled with hydrogen gas, was destroyed in a spectacular fire at Lakehurst, New Jersey, in 1937.*

Exo- comes from the Greek word meaning "outside"; endo- means "within."

On heating, HgO decomposes to give Hg and O$_2$.

created or destroyed, any energy lost by the system must be gained by the surroundings. Thus, the heat generated by the combustion process is transferred from the system to its surroundings. This reaction is an example of an ***exothermic process,*** which is *any process that gives off heat—that is, transfers thermal energy to the surroundings.* Figure 6.3(a) shows the energy change for the combustion of hydrogen gas.

Now consider another reaction, the decomposition of mercury(II) oxide (HgO) at high temperatures:

$$\text{energy} + 2\text{HgO}(s) \longrightarrow 2\text{Hg}(l) + \text{O}_2(g)$$

This reaction is an ***endothermic process,*** *in which heat has to be supplied to the system* (that is, to HgO) *by the surroundings* [Figure 6.3(b)].

From Figure 6.3 you can see that in exothermic reactions, the total energy of the products is less than the total energy of the reactants. The difference is the heat supplied by the system to the surroundings. Just the opposite happens in endothermic reactions. Here, the difference between the energy of the products and the energy of the reactants is equal to the heat supplied to the system by the surroundings.

Figure 6.3 *(a) An exothermic process. (b) An endothermic process. Parts (a) and (b) are not drawn to the same scale; that is, the heat released in the formation of H$_2$O from H$_2$ and O$_2$ is not equal to the heat absorbed in the decomposition of HgO.*

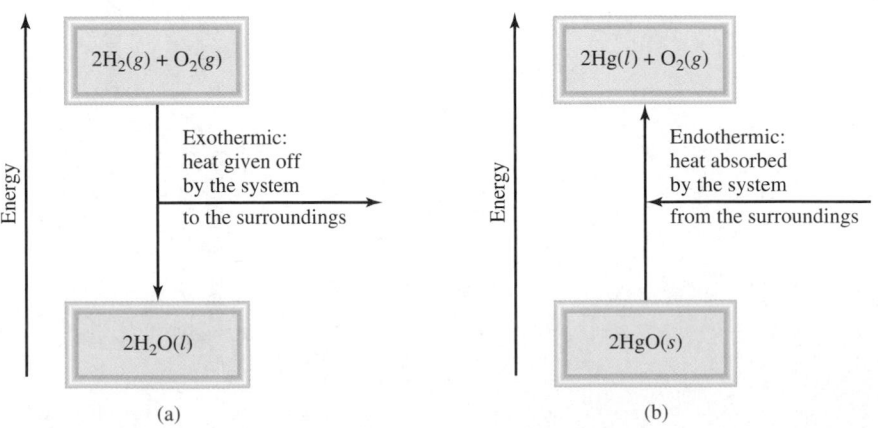

6.3 Introduction to Thermodynamics

Thermochemistry is part of a broader subject called ***thermodynamics,*** which is *the scientific study of the interconversion of heat and other kinds of energy.* The laws of thermodynamics provide useful guidelines for understanding the energetics and directions of processes. In this section we will concentrate on the first law of thermodynamics, which is particularly relevant to the study of thermochemistry. We will continue our discussion of thermodynamics in Chapter 18.

In thermodynamics, we study changes in the ***state of a system,*** which is defined by *the values of all relevant macroscopic properties, for example, composition, energy, temperature, pressure, and volume.* Energy, pressure, volume, and temperature are said to be ***state functions***—*properties that are determined by the state of the system, regardless of how that condition was achieved.* In other words, when the state of a system changes, the magnitude of change in any state function depends only on the initial and final states of the system and not on how the change is accomplished.

The state of a given amount of a gas is specified by its volume, pressure, and temperature. Consider a gas at 2 atm, 300 K, and 1 L (the initial state). Suppose a process is carried out at constant temperature such that the gas pressure decreases to 1 atm. According to Boyle's law, its volume must increase to 2 L. The final state then corresponds to 1 atm, 300 K, and 2 L. The change in volume (ΔV) is

$$\begin{aligned} \Delta V &= V_\text{f} - V_\text{i} \\ &= 2\,\text{L} - 1\,\text{L} \\ &= 1\,\text{L} \end{aligned}$$

The Greek letter *delta*, Δ, symbolizes change. We use Δ in this text to mean final − initial.

where V_i and V_f denote the initial and final volume, respectively. No matter how we arrive at the final state (for example, the pressure of the gas can be increased first and then decreased to 1 atm), the change in volume is always 1 L. Thus, the volume of a gas is a state function. In a similar manner, we can show that pressure and temperature are also state functions.

Energy is another state function. Using potential energy as an example, we find that the net increase in gravitational potential energy when we go from the same starting point to the top of a mountain is always the same, regardless of how we get there (Figure 6.4).

Recall that an object possesses potential energy by virtue of its position or chemical composition.

The First Law of Thermodynamics

The ***first law of thermodynamics,*** which is based on the law of conservation of energy, states that *energy can be converted from one form to another, but cannot be created or destroyed.*[†] How do we know this is so? It would be impossible to prove the validity of the first law of thermodynamics if we had to determine the total energy content

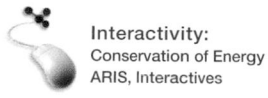

Interactivity:
Conservation of Energy
ARIS, Interactives

[†]See footnote on p. 43 (Chapter 2) for a discussion of mass and energy relationship in chemical reactions.

Figure 6.4 *The gain in gravitational potential energy that occurs when a person climbs from the base to the top of a mountain is independent of the path taken.*

of the universe. Even determining the total energy content of 1 g of iron, say, would be extremely difficult. Fortunately, we can test the validity of the first law by measuring only the *change* in the internal energy of a system between its *initial state* and its *final state* in a process. The change in internal energy ΔE is given by

$$\Delta E = E_f - E_i$$

where E_i and E_f are the internal energies of the system in the initial and final states, respectively.

The internal energy of a system has two components: kinetic energy and potential energy. The kinetic energy component consists of various types of molecular motion and the movement of electrons within molecules. Potential energy is determined by the attractive interactions between electrons and nuclei and by repulsive interactions between electrons and between nuclei in individual molecules, as well as by interaction between molecules. It is impossible to measure all these contributions accurately, so we cannot calculate the total energy of a system with any certainty. Changes in energy, on the other hand, can be determined experimentally.

Consider the reaction between 1 mole of sulfur and 1 mole of oxygen gas to produce 1 mole of sulfur dioxide:

$$S(s) + O_2(g) \longrightarrow SO_2(g)$$

In this case, our system is composed of the reactant molecules S and O_2 and the product molecules SO_2. We do not know the internal energy content of either the reactant molecules or the product molecules, but we can accurately measure the *change* in energy content, ΔE, given by

$\Delta E = E(\text{product}) - E(\text{reactants})$
$\quad\quad = \text{energy content of 1 mol } SO_2(g) - \text{energy content of } [1 \text{ mol } S(s) + 1 \text{ mol } O_2(g)]$

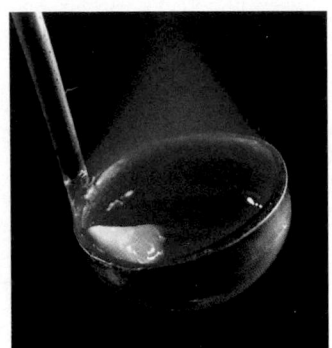

Sulfur burning in air to form SO_2.

We find that this reaction gives off heat. Therefore, the energy of the product is less than that of the reactants, and ΔE is negative.

Interpreting the release of heat in this reaction to mean that some of the chemical energy contained in the molecules has been converted to thermal energy, we conclude that the transfer of energy from the system to the surroundings does not change the total energy of the universe. That is, the sum of the energy changes must be zero:

$$\Delta E_{sys} + \Delta E_{surr} = 0$$

or
$$\Delta E_{sys} = -\Delta E_{surr}$$

where the subscripts "sys" and "surr" denote system and surroundings, respectively. Thus, if one system undergoes an energy change ΔE_{sys}, the rest of the universe, or the surroundings, must undergo a change in energy that is equal in magnitude but opposite in sign ($-\Delta E_{surr}$); energy gained in one place must have been lost somewhere else. Furthermore, because energy can be changed from one form to another, the energy lost by one system can be gained by another system in a different form. For example, the energy lost by burning oil in a power plant may ultimately turn up in our homes as electrical energy, heat, light, and so on.

In chemistry, we are normally interested in the energy changes associated with the system (which may be a flask containing reactants and products), not with its surroundings. Therefore, a more useful form of the first law is

We use lowercase letters (such as w and q) to represent thermodynamic quantities that are not state functions.

$$\Delta E = q + w \tag{6.1}$$

TABLE 6.1	Sign Conventions for Work and Heat	
Process		**Sign**
Work done by the system on the surroundings		−
Work done on the system by the surroundings		+
Heat absorbed by the system from the surroundings (endothermic process)		+
Heat absorbed by the surroundings from the system (exothermic process)		−

(We drop the subscript "sys" for simplicity.) Equation (6.1) says that the change in the internal energy ΔE of a system is the sum of the heat exchange q between the system and the surroundings and the work done w on (or by) the system. The sign conventions for q and w are as follows: q is positive for an endothermic process and negative for an exothermic process and w is positive for work done on the system by the surroundings and negative for work done by the system on the surroundings. We can think of the first law of thermodynamics as an energy balance sheet, much like a money balance sheet kept in a bank that does currency exchange. You can withdraw or deposit money in either of two different currencies (like energy change due to heat exchange and work done). However, the value of your bank account depends only on the net amount of money left in it after these transactions, not on which currency you used.

For convenience, we sometimes omit the word "internal" when discussing the energy of a system.

Equation (6.1) may seem abstract, but it is actually quite logical. If a system loses heat to the surroundings or does work on the surroundings, we would expect its internal energy to decrease because they are energy-depleting processes. For this reason, both q and w are negative. Conversely, if heat is added to the system or if work is done on the system, then the internal energy of the system would increase. In this case, both q and w are positive. Table 6.1 summarizes the sign conventions for q and w.

Work and Heat

We will now look at the nature of work and heat in more detail.

Work

We have seen that work can be defined as force F multiplied by distance d:

$$w = Fd \tag{6.2}$$

In thermodynamics, work has a broader meaning that includes mechanical work (for example, a crane lifting a steel beam), electrical work (a battery supplying electrons to light the bulb of a flashlight), and surface work (blowing up a soap bubble). In this section we will concentrate on mechanical work; in Chapter 19 we will discuss the nature of electrical work.

One way to illustrate mechanical work is to study the expansion or compression of a gas. Many chemical and biological processes involve gas volume changes. Breathing and exhaling air involves the expansion and contraction of the tiny sacs called alveoli in the lungs. Another example is the internal combustion engine of the automobile. The successive expansion and compression of the cylinders due to the combustion of the gasoline-air mixture provide power to the vehicle. Figure 6.5 shows a

Figure 6.5 *The expansion of a gas against a constant external pressure (such as atmospheric pressure). The gas is in a cylinder fitted with a weightless movable piston. The work done is given by* $-P\Delta V$. *Because* $\Delta V > 0$, *the work done is a negative quantity.*

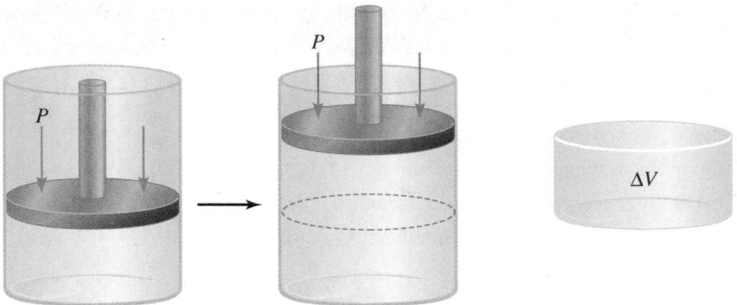

gas in a cylinder fitted with a weightless, frictionless movable piston at a certain temperature, pressure, and volume. As it expands, the gas pushes the piston upward against a constant opposing external atmospheric pressure P. The work done by the gas on the surroundings is

$$w = -P\Delta V \tag{6.3}$$

where ΔV, the change in volume, is given by $V_f - V_i$. The minus sign in Equation (6.3) takes care of the convention for w. For gas expansion, $\Delta V > 0$, so $-P\Delta V$ is a negative quantity. For gas compression (work done on the system), $\Delta V < 0$, and $-P\Delta V$ is a positive quantity.

Equation (6.3) derives from the fact that pressure $\times$ volume can be expressed as (force/area) $\times$ volume; that is,

$$P \times V = \underset{\text{pressure}}{\frac{F}{d^2}} \times \underset{\text{volume}}{d^3} = Fd = w$$

where F is the opposing force and d has the dimension of length, d^2 has the dimensions of area, and d^3 has the dimensions of volume. Thus, the product of pressure and volume is equal to force times distance, or work. You can see that for a given increase in volume (that is, for a certain value of ΔV), the work done depends on the magnitude of the external, opposing pressure P. If P is zero (that is, if the gas is expanding against a vacuum), the work done must also be zero. If P is some positive, nonzero value, then the work done is given by $-P\Delta V$.

According to Equation (6.3), the units for work done by or on a gas are liters atmospheres. To express the work done in the more familiar unit of joules, we use the conversion factor (see Appendix 2).

$$1 \text{ L} \cdot \text{atm} = 101.3 \text{ J}$$

Example 6.1

A certain gas expands in volume from 2.0 L to 6.0 L at constant temperature. Calculate the work done by the gas if it expands (a) against a vacuum and (b) against a constant pressure of 1.2 atm.

(Continued)

Strategy A simple sketch of the situation is helpful here:

Opposing pressure
P

Initial volume	Final volume
2.0 L	6.0 L

Gas

(a) $P = 0$

(b) $P = 1.2\ atm$

$\Delta V = (6.0 - 2.0)\,L$
$= 4.0\,L$

The work done in gas expansion is equal to the product of the external, opposing pressure and the change in volume. What is the conversion factor between L · atm and J?

Solution

(a) Because the external pressure is zero, no work is done in the expansion.

$$w = -P\Delta V$$
$$= -(0)(6.0 - 2.0)\,L$$
$$= 0$$

(b) The external, opposing pressure is 1.2 atm, so

$$w = -P\Delta V$$
$$= -(1.2\ atm)(6.0 - 2.0)\,L$$
$$= -4.8\ L \cdot atm$$

To convert the answer to joules, we write

$$w = -4.8\ L \cdot atm \times \frac{101.3\ J}{1\ L \cdot atm}$$
$$= -4.9 \times 10^2\ J$$

Check Because this is gas expansion (work is done by the system on the surroundings), the work done has a negative sign.

Similar problems: 6.15, 6.16.

Practice Exercise A gas expands from 264 mL to 971 mL at constant temperature. Calculate the work done (in joules) by the gas if it expands (a) against a vacuum and (b) against a constant pressure of 4.00 atm.

Example 6.1 shows that work is not a state function. Although the initial and final states are the same in (a) and (b), the amount of work done is different because the external, opposing pressures are different. We *cannot* write $\Delta w = w_f - w_i$ for a change. Work done depends not only on the initial state and final state, but also on how the process is carried out, that is, on the path.

> Because temperature is kept constant, you can use Boyle's law to show that the final pressure is the same in (a) and (b).

Heat

The other component of internal energy is q, heat. Like work, heat is not a state function. Suppose that we raise the temperature of 100.0 g of water initially at 20.0°C and 1 atm to 30.0°C and 1 atm. What is the heat transferred to the water for this process? We do not know the answer because the process is not specified. One way to raise the temperature is to heat the water using a Bunsen burner or electrically using an immersion heater. In either case, we can calculate the heat transferred to be 4184 J.[†]

Alternatively, we can bring about the temperature increase by stirring the water with a magnetic stirring bar until the desired temperature is reached as a result of friction. The heat transferred in this case is zero. Or we could first raise the temperature of water from 20°C to 25°C by direct heating, and then stir the bar to bring it up to 30°C. In each case, q is somewhere between zero and 4184 J. This simple example shows that heat associated with a given process, like work, depends on how the process is carried out; that is, we *cannot* write $\Delta q = q_f - q_i$. It is important to note that although neither heat nor work is a state function, their sum ($q + w$) is equal to ΔE and, as we saw earlier, E is a state function. Thus, if changing the path from the initial state to the final state increases the value of q, it will decrease the value of w by the same amount and vice versa.

In summary, heat and work are not state functions because they are not properties of a system. They manifest themselves only during a process (during a change). Thus, their values depend on the path of the process and vary accordingly.

Example 6.2

The work done when a gas is compressed in a cylinder like that shown in Figure 6.5 is 462 J. During this process, there is a heat transfer of 128 J from the gas to the surroundings. Calculate the energy change for this process.

Strategy Compression is work done on the gas, so what is the sign for w? Heat is released by the gas to the surroundings. Is this an endothermic or exothermic process? What is the sign for q?

Solution To calculate the energy change of the gas, we need Equation (6.1). Work of compression is positive and because heat is released by the gas, q is negative. Therefore, we have

$$\Delta E = q + w$$
$$= -128\ J + 462\ J$$
$$= \boxed{334\ J}$$

As a result, the energy of the gas increases by 334 J.

Practice Exercise A gas expands and does *P-V* work on the surroundings equal to 279 J. At the same time, it absorbs 216 J of heat from the surroundings. What is the change in energy of the system?

Similar problems: 6.17, 6.18.

6.4 Enthalpy of Chemical Reactions

Our next step is to see how the first law of thermodynamics can be applied to processes carried out under different conditions. Specifically, we will consider two situations most commonly encountered in the laboratory; one in which the volume of the system is kept constant and one in which the pressure applied on the system is kept constant.

[†]The heat transferred to water is $q = ms\Delta t$, where m is the mass of water in grams, s is the specific heat of water (4.184 J/g · °C), and Δt is the temperature change. Thus, $q = (100.0\ g)(4.184\ J/g · °C)(10°C)$ = 4184 J. Specific heat will be discussed in Section 6.5.

CHEMISTRY
in Action

Making Snow and Inflating a Bicycle Tire

Many phenomena in everyday life can be explained by the first law of thermodynamics. Here we will discuss two examples of interest to lovers of the outdoors.

Making Snow

If you are an avid downhill skier, you have probably skied on artificial snow. How is this stuff made in quantities large enough to meet the needs of skiers on snowless days? The secret of snowmaking is in the equation $\Delta E = q + w$. A snowmaking machine contains a mixture of compressed air and water vapor at about 20 atm. Because of the large difference in pressure between the tank and the outside atmosphere, when the mixture is sprayed into the atmosphere it expands so rapidly that, as a good approximation, no heat exchange occurs between the system (air and water) and its surroundings; that is, $q = 0$. (In thermodynamics, such a process is called an *adiabatic process.*) Thus, we write

$$\Delta E = q + w = w$$

Because the system does work on the surroundings, w is a negative quantity, and there is a decrease in the system's energy.

Kinetic energy is part of the total energy of the system. In Section 5.7 we saw that the average kinetic energy of a gas is directly proportional to the absolute temperature [Equation (5.15)]. It follows, therefore, that the change in energy ΔE is given by

$$\Delta E = C\Delta T$$

where C is the proportionality constant. Because ΔE is negative, ΔT must also be negative, and it is this cooling effect (or the decrease in the kinetic energy of the water molecules) that is responsible for the formation of snow. Although we need only water to form snow, the presence of air, which also cools on expansion, helps to lower the temperature of the water vapor.

Inflating a Bicycle Tire

If you have ever pumped air into a bicycle tire, you probably noticed a warming effect at the valve stem. This phenomenon, too,

can be explained by the first law of thermodynamics. The action of the pump compresses the air inside the pump and the tire. The process is rapid enough to be treated as approximately adiabatic, so that $q = 0$ and $\Delta E = w$. Because work is done on the gas in this case (it is being compressed), w is positive, and there is an increase in energy. Hence, the temperature of the system increases also, according to the equation

$$\Delta E = C\Delta T$$

A snowmaking machine in operation.

If a chemical reaction is run at constant volume, then $\Delta V = 0$ and no P-V work will result from this change. From Equation (6.1) it follows that

$$\Delta E = q - P\Delta V$$
$$= q_v \qquad (6.4)$$

We add the subscript "v" to remind us that this is a constant-volume process. This equality may seem strange at first, for we showed earlier that q is not a state function.

The process is carried out under constant-volume conditions, however, so that the heat change can have only a specific value, which is equal to ΔE.

Enthalpy

Constant-volume conditions are often inconvenient and sometimes impossible to achieve. Most reactions occur under conditions of constant pressure (usually atmospheric pressure). If such a reaction results in a net increase in the number of moles of a gas, then the system does work on the surroundings (expansion). This follows from the fact that for the gas formed to enter the atmosphere, it must push the surrounding air back. Conversely, if more gas molecules are consumed than are produced, work is done on the system by the surroundings (compression). Finally, no work is done if there is no net change in the number of moles of gases from reactants to products.

In general, for a constant-pressure process we write

$$\Delta E = q + w$$
$$= q_p - P\Delta V$$

or
$$q_p = \Delta E + P\Delta V \tag{6.5}$$

where the subscript "p" denotes constant-pressure condition.

We now introduce a new thermodynamic function of a system called ***enthalpy*** (**H**), which is defined by the equation

$$H = E + PV \tag{6.6}$$

where E is the internal energy of the system and P and V are the pressure and volume of the system, respectively. Because E and PV have energy units, enthalpy also has energy units. Furthermore, E, P, and V are all state functions, that is, the changes in $(E + PV)$ depend only on the initial and final states. It follows, therefore, that the change in H, or ΔH, also depends only on the initial and final states. Thus, H is a state function.

For any process, the change in enthalpy according to Equation (6.6) is given by

$$\Delta H = \Delta E + \Delta(PV) \tag{6.7}$$

If the pressure is held constant, then

$$\Delta H = \Delta E + P\Delta V \tag{6.8}$$

Comparing Equation (6.8) with Equation (6.5), we see that for a constant-pressure process, $q_p = \Delta H$. Again, although q is not a state function, the heat change at constant pressure is equal to ΔH because the "path" is defined and therefore it can have only a specific value.

We now have two quantities—ΔE and ΔH—that can be associated with a reaction. If the reaction occurs under constant-volume conditions, then the heat change, q_v, is equal to ΔE. On the other hand, when the reaction is carried out at constant pressure, the heat change, q_p, is equal to ΔH.

In Section 6.5 we will discuss ways to measure heat changes at constant volume and constant pressure.

Enthalpy of Reactions

Because most reactions are constant-pressure processes, we can equate the heat change in these cases to the change in enthalpy. For any reaction of the type

$$\text{reactants} \longrightarrow \text{products}$$

we define the change in enthalpy, called the ***enthalpy of reaction, ΔH,*** as *the differ-ence between the enthalpies of the products and the enthalpies of the reactants:*

$$\Delta H = H(\text{products}) - H(\text{reactants}) \tag{6.9}$$

The enthalpy of reaction can be positive or negative, depending on the process. For an endothermic process (heat absorbed by the system from the surroundings), ΔH is positive (that is, $\Delta H > 0$). For an exothermic process (heat released by the system to the surroundings), ΔH is negative (that is, $\Delta H < 0$).

An analogy for enthalpy change is a change in the balance in your bank account. Suppose your initial balance is \$100. After a transaction (deposit or withdrawal), the change in your bank balance, ΔX, is given by

$$\Delta X = X_{\text{final}} - X_{\text{initial}}$$

where X represents the bank balance. If you deposit \$80 into your account, then $\Delta X = \$180 - \$100 = \$80$. This corresponds to an endothermic reaction. (The balance increases and so does the enthalpy of the system.) On the other hand, a withdrawal of \$60 means $\Delta X = \$40 - \$100 = -\$60$. The negative sign of ΔX means your balance has decreased. Similarly, a negative value of ΔH reflects a decrease in enthalpy of the system as a result of an exothermic process. The difference between this analogy and Equation (6.9) is that while you always know your exact bank balance, there is no way to know the enthalpies of individual products and reactants. In practice, we can only measure the *difference* in their values.

Now let us apply the idea of enthalpy changes to two common processes, the first involving a physical change, the second a chemical change.

> This analogy assumes that you will not overdraw your bank account. The enthalpy of a substance *cannot* be negative.

Thermochemical Equations

At 0°C and a pressure of 1 atm, ice melts to form liquid water. Measurements show that for every mole of ice converted to liquid water under these conditions, 6.01 kilojoules (kJ) of heat energy are absorbed by the system (ice). Because the pressure is constant, the heat change is equal to the enthalpy change, ΔH. Furthermore, this is an endothermic process, as expected for the energy-absorbing change of melting ice [Figure 6.6(a)]. Therefore, ΔH is a positive quantity. The equation for this physical change is

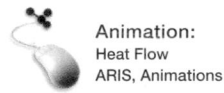

Animation:
Heat Flow
ARIS, Animations

$$H_2O(s) \longrightarrow H_2O(l) \qquad\qquad \Delta H = 6.01 \text{ kJ/mol}$$

(a)

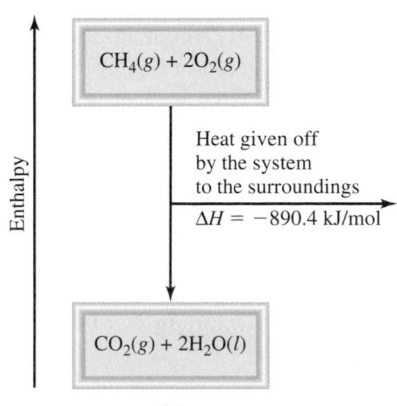

(b)

Figure 6.6 *(a) Melting 1 mole of ice at 0°C (an endothermic process) results in an enthalpy increase in the system of 6.01 kJ. (b) Burning 1 mole of methane in oxygen gas (an exothermic process) results in an enthalpy decrease in the system of 890.4 kJ.*

Methane gas burning from a Bunsen burner.

Keep in mind that H is an extensive property.

The "per mole" in the unit for ΔH means that this is the enthalpy change *per mole of the reaction (or process) as it is written,* that is, when 1 mole of ice is converted to 1 mole of liquid water.

As another example, consider the combustion of methane (CH_4), the principal component of natural gas:

$$CH_4(g) + 2O_2(g) \longrightarrow CO_2(g) + 2H_2O(l) \quad \Delta H = -890.4 \text{ kJ/mol}$$

From experience we know that burning natural gas releases heat to the surroundings, so it is an exothermic process. Under constant-pressure condition this heat change is equal to enthalpy change and ΔH must have a negative sign [Figure 6.6(b)]. Again, the per mole of reaction unit for ΔH means that when 1 mole of CH_4 reacts with 2 moles of O_2 to yield 1 mole of CO_2 and 2 moles of liquid H_2O, 890.4 kJ of heat are released to the surroundings. It is important to keep in mind that each ΔH value relates to the reaction as written in the chemical equation.

The equations for the melting of ice and the combustion of methane are examples of **thermochemical equations,** which *show the enthalpy changes as well as the mass relationships.* It is essential to specify a balanced equation when quoting the enthalpy change of a reaction. The following guidelines are helpful in writing and interpreting thermochemical equations.

1. When writing thermochemical equations, we must always specify the physical states of all reactants and products, because they help determine the actual enthalpy changes. For example, in the equation for the combustion of methane, if we show water vapor rather than liquid water as a product,

$$CH_4(g) + 2O_2(g) \longrightarrow CO_2(g) + 2H_2O(g) \qquad \Delta H = -802.4 \text{ kJ/mol}$$

the enthalpy change is -802.4 kJ rather than -890.4 kJ because 88.0 kJ are needed to convert 2 moles of liquid water to water vapor; that is,

$$2H_2O(l) \longrightarrow 2H_2O(g) \qquad \Delta H = 88.0 \text{ kJ/mol}$$

2. If we multiply both sides of a thermochemical equation by a factor n, then ΔH must also change by the same factor. Thus, for the melting of ice, if $n = 2$, we have

$$2H_2O(s) \longrightarrow 2H_2O(l) \quad \Delta H = 2(6.01 \text{ kJ/mol}) = 12.0 \text{ kJ/mol}$$

3. When we reverse an equation, we change the roles of reactants and products. Consequently, the magnitude of ΔH for the equation remains the same, but its sign changes. For example, if a reaction consumes thermal energy from its surroundings (that is, if it is endothermic), then the reverse reaction must release thermal energy back to its surroundings (that is, it must be exothermic) and the enthalpy change expression must also change its sign. Thus, reversing the melting of ice and the combustion of methane, the thermochemical equations become

$$H_2O(l) \longrightarrow H_2O(s) \qquad \Delta H = -6.01 \text{ kJ/mol}$$
$$CO_2(g) + 2H_2O(l) \longrightarrow CH_4(g) + 2O_2(g) \qquad \Delta H = 890.4 \text{ kJ/mol}$$

and what was an endothermic process becomes exothermic, and vice versa.

Example 6.3

Given the thermochemical equation

$$SO_2(g) + \tfrac{1}{2}O_2(g) \longrightarrow SO_3(g) \qquad \Delta H = -99.1 \text{ kJ/mol}$$

calculate the heat evolved when 74.6 g of SO_2 (molar mass = 64.07 g/mol) is converted to SO_3.

Strategy The thermochemical equation shows that for every mole of SO_2 burned, 99.1 kJ of heat are given off (note the negative sign). Therefore, the conversion factor is

$$\frac{-99.1 \text{ kJ}}{1 \text{ mol } SO_2}$$

How many moles of SO_2 are in 74.6 g of SO_2? What is the conversion factor between grams and moles?

Solution We need to first calculate the number of moles of SO_2 in 74.6 g of the compound and then find the number of kilojoules produced from the exothermic reaction. The sequence of conversions is as follows:

$$\text{grams of } SO_2 \longrightarrow \text{moles of } SO_2 \longrightarrow \text{kilojoules of heat generated}$$

Therefore, the heat produced is given by

$$74.6 \text{ g } SO_2 \times \frac{1 \text{ mol } SO_2}{64.07 \text{ g } SO_2} \times \frac{-99.1 \text{ kJ}}{1 \text{ mol } SO_2} = \boxed{-115 \text{ kJ}}$$

Check Because 74.6 g is greater than the molar mass of SO_2, we expect the heat released to be larger than −99.1 kJ. The negative sign indicates that this is an exothermic reaction.

Similar problem: 6.26.

Practice Exercise Calculate the heat evolved when 266 g of white phosphorus (P_4) burns in air according to the equation

$$P_4(s) + 5O_2(g) \longrightarrow P_4O_{10}(s) \qquad \Delta H = -3013 \text{ kJ/mol}$$

A Comparison of ΔH and ΔE

What is the relationship between ΔH and ΔE for a process? To find out, let us consider the reaction between sodium metal and water:

$$2Na(s) + 2H_2O(l) \longrightarrow 2NaOH(aq) + H_2(g) \quad \Delta H = -367.5 \text{ kJ/mol}$$

This thermochemical equation says that when two moles of sodium react with an excess of water, 367.5 kJ of heat are given off. Note that one of the products is hydrogen gas, which must push back air to enter the atmosphere. Consequently, some of the energy produced by the reaction is used to do work of pushing back a volume of air (ΔV) against atmospheric pressure (P) (Figure 6.7). To calculate the change in internal energy, we rearrange Equation (6.8) as follows:

$$\Delta E = \Delta H - P\Delta V$$

Sodium reacting with water to form hydrogen gas.

Figure 6.7 *(a) A beaker of water inside a cylinder fitted with a movable piston. The pressure inside is equal to the atmospheric pressure. (b) As the sodium metal reacts with water, the hydrogen gas generated pushes the piston upward (doing work on the surroundings) until the pressure inside is again equal to that of outside.*

(a)   (b)

If we assume the temperature to be 25°C and ignore the small change in the volume of the solution, we can show that the volume of 1 mole of H_2 gas at 1.0 atm and 298 K is 24.5 L, so that $-P\Delta V = -24.5$ L · atm or -2.5 kJ. Finally,

$$\Delta E = -367.5 \text{ kJ/mol} - 2.5 \text{ kJ/mol}$$
$$= -370.0 \text{ kJ/mol}$$

For reactions that do not result in a change in the number of moles of gases from reactants to products [for example, $H_2(g) + F_2(g) \longrightarrow 2HF(g)$], $\Delta E = \Delta H$.

This calculation shows that ΔE and ΔH are approximately the same. The reason ΔH is smaller than ΔE in magnitude is that some of the internal energy released is used to do gas expansion work, so less heat is evolved. For reactions that do not involve gases, ΔV is usually very small and so ΔE is practically the same as ΔH.

Another way to calculate the internal energy change of a gaseous reaction is to assume ideal gas behavior and constant temperature. In this case,

$$\Delta E = \Delta H - \Delta(PV)$$
$$= \Delta H - \Delta(nRT)$$
$$= \Delta H - RT\Delta n \qquad (6.10)$$

where Δn is defined as

$$\Delta n = \text{number of moles of product gases} - \text{number of moles of reactant gases}$$

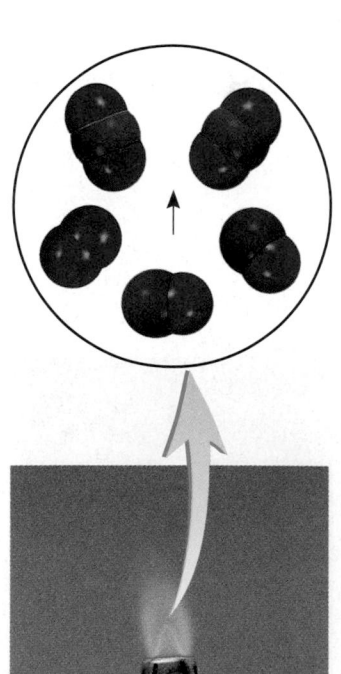

Carbon monoxide burns in air to form carbon dioxide.

Example 6.4

Calculate the change in internal energy when 2 moles of CO are converted to 2 moles of CO_2 at 1 atm and 25°C:

$$2CO(g) + O_2(g) \longrightarrow 2CO_2(g) \qquad \Delta H = -566.0 \text{ kJ/mol}$$

Strategy We are given the enthalpy change, ΔH, for the reaction and are asked to calculate the change in internal energy, ΔE. Therefore, we need Equation (6.10). What is the change in the number of moles of gases? ΔH is given in kilojoules, so what units should we use for R?

Solution From the chemical equation we see that 3 moles of gases are converted to 2 moles of gases so that

$$\Delta n = \text{number of moles of product gas} - \text{number of moles of reactant gases}$$
$$= 2 - 3$$
$$= -1$$

(Continued)

Using 8.314 J/K · mol for R and $T = 298$ K in Equation (6.10), we write

$$\Delta E = \Delta H - RT\Delta n$$

$$= -566.0 \text{ kJ/mol} - (8.314 \text{ J/K} \cdot \text{mol})\left(\frac{1 \text{ kJ}}{1000 \text{ J}}\right)(298 \text{ K})(-1)$$

$$= -563.5 \text{ kJ/mol}$$

Check Knowing that the reacting gaseous system undergoes a compression (3 moles to 2 moles), is it reasonable to have $\Delta H > \Delta E$ in magnitude?

Practice Exercise What is ΔE for the formation of 1 mole of CO at 1 atm and 25°C?

$$C(\text{graphite}) + \tfrac{1}{2}O_2(g) \longrightarrow CO(g) \qquad \Delta H = -110.5 \text{ kJ/mol}$$

Similar problem: 6.27.

6.5 Calorimetry

In the laboratory, heat changes in physical and chemical processes are measured with a *calorimeter*, a closed container designed specifically for this purpose. Our discussion of **calorimetry**, *the measurement of heat changes*, will depend on an understanding of specific heat and heat capacity, so let us consider them first.

Specific Heat and Heat Capacity

The **specific heat** (*s*) of a substance is *the amount of heat required to raise the temperature of one gram of the substance by one degree Celsius*. It has the units J/g · °C. The **heat capacity** (*C*) of a substance is *the amount of heat required to raise the temperature of a given quantity of the substance by one degree Celsius*. Its units are J/°C. Specific heat is an intensive property whereas heat capacity is an extensive property. The relationship between the heat capacity and specific heat of a substance is

$$C = ms \tag{6.11}$$

where m is the mass of the substance in grams. For example, the specific heat of water is 4.184 J/g · °C, and the heat capacity of 60.0 g of water is

$$(60.0 \text{ g})(4.184 \text{ J/g} \cdot °C) = 251 \text{ J/°C}$$

Table 6.2 shows the specific heat of some common substances.

If we know the specific heat and the amount of a substance, then the change in the sample's temperature (Δt) will tell us the amount of heat (q) that has been absorbed or released in a particular process. The equations for calculating the heat change are given by

$$q = ms\Delta t \tag{6.12}$$

$$q = C\Delta t \tag{6.13}$$

where Δt is the temperature change:

$$\Delta t = t_{\text{final}} - t_{\text{initial}}$$

TABLE 6.2

The Specific Heats of Some Common Substances

Substance	Specific Heat (J/g · °C)
Al	0.900
Au	0.129
C (graphite)	0.720
C (diamond)	0.502
Cu	0.385
Fe	0.444
Hg	0.139
H_2O	4.184
C_2H_5OH (ethanol)	2.46

The sign convention for q is the same as that for enthalpy change; q is positive for endothermic processes and negative for exothermic processes.

Example 6.5

A 466-g sample of water is heated from 8.50°C to 74.60°C. Calculate the amount of heat absorbed (in kilojoules) by the water.

Strategy We know the quantity of water and the specific heat of water. With this information and the temperature rise, we can calculate the amount of heat absorbed (q).

Solution Using Equation (6.12), we write

$$q = ms\Delta t$$
$$= (466 \text{ g})(4.184 \text{ J/g} \cdot °\text{C})(74.60°\text{C} - 8.50°\text{C})$$
$$= 1.29 \times 10^5 \text{ J} \times \frac{1 \text{ kJ}}{1000 \text{ J}}$$
$$= 129 \text{ kJ}$$

Similar problem: 6.34.

Check The units g and °C cancel, and we are left with the desired unit kJ. Because heat is absorbed by the water from the surroundings, it has a positive sign.

Practice Exercise An iron bar of mass 869 g cools from 94°C to 5°C. Calculate the heat released (in kilojoules) by the metal.

Constant-Volume Calorimetry

"Constant volume" refers to the volume of the container, which does not change during the reaction. Note that the container remains intact after the measurement. The term "bomb calorimeter" connotes the explosive nature of the reaction (on a small scale) in the presence of excess oxygen gas.

Heat of combustion is usually measured by placing a known mass of a compound in a steel container called a *constant-volume bomb calorimeter,* which is filled with oxygen at about 30 atm of pressure. The closed bomb is immersed in a known amount of water, as shown in Figure 6.8. The sample is ignited electrically, and the heat produced by the combustion reaction can be calculated accurately by recording the rise in temperature of the water. The heat given off by the sample is absorbed by the water and the bomb. The special design of the calorimeter enables us to assume that no heat (or mass) is lost to the surroundings during the time it takes to make measurements. Therefore, we can call the bomb and the water in which it is submerged an isolated system. Because no heat enters or leaves the system throughout the process, the heat change of the system (q_{system}) must be zero and we can write

$$q_{\text{system}} = q_{\text{cal}} + q_{\text{rxn}}$$
$$= 0 \tag{6.14}$$

where q_{cal} and q_{rxn} are the heat changes for the calorimeter and the reaction, respectively. Thus,

$$q_{\text{rxn}} = -q_{\text{cal}} \tag{6.15}$$

Note that C_{cal} comprises both the bomb and the surrounding water.

To calculate q_{cal}, we need to know the heat capacity of the calorimeter (C_{cal}) and the temperature rise, that is

$$q_{\text{cal}} = C_{\text{cal}}\Delta t \tag{6.16}$$

The quantity C_{cal} is calibrated by burning a substance with an accurately known heat of combustion. For example, it is known that the combustion of 1 g of benzoic acid

Figure 6.8 *A constant-volume bomb calorimeter. The calorimeter is filled with oxygen gas before it is placed in the bucket. The sample is ignited electrically, and the heat produced by the reaction can be accurately determined by measuring the temperature increase in the known amount of surrounding water.*

(C_6H_5COOH) releases 26.42 kJ of heat. If the temperature rise is 4.673°C, then the heat capacity of the calorimeter is given by

$$C_{cal} = \frac{q_{cal}}{\Delta t}$$
$$= \frac{26.42 \text{ kJ}}{4.673°C} = 5.654 \text{ kJ/°C}$$

Once C_{cal} has been determined, the calorimeter can be used to measure the heat of combustion of other substances.

Note that because reactions in a bomb calorimeter occur under constant-volume rather than constant-pressure conditions, the heat changes *do not* correspond to the enthalpy change ΔH (see Section 6.4). It is possible to correct the measured heat changes so that they correspond to ΔH values, but the corrections usually are quite small so we will not concern ourselves with the details here. Finally, it is interesting to note that the energy contents of food and fuel (usually expressed in calories where 1 cal = 4.184 J) are measured with constant-volume calorimeters.

Example 6.6

A quantity of 1.435 g of naphthalene ($C_{10}H_8$), a pungent-smelling substance used in moth repellents, was burned in a constant-volume bomb calorimeter. Consequently, the temperature of the water rose from 20.28°C to 25.95°C. If the heat capacity of the

(Continued)

$C_{10}H_8$

bomb plus water was 10.17 kJ/°C, calculate the heat of combustion of naphthalene on a molar basis; that is, find the molar heat of combustion.

Strategy Knowing the heat capacity and the temperature rise, how do we calculate the heat absorbed by the calorimeter? What is the heat generated by the combustion of 1.435 g of naphthalene? What is the conversion factor between grams and moles of naphthalene?

Solution The heat absorbed by the bomb and water is equal to the product of the heat capacity and the temperature change. From Equation (6.16), assuming no heat is lost to the surroundings, we write

$$q_{cal} = C_{cal}\Delta t$$
$$= (10.17 \text{ kJ/°C})(25.95°C - 20.28°C)$$
$$= 57.66 \text{ kJ}$$

Because $q_{sys} = q_{cal} + q_{rxn} = 0$, $q_{cal} = -q_{rxn}$. The heat change of the reaction is -57.66 kJ. This is the heat released by the combustion of 1.435 g of $C_{10}H_8$; therefore, we can write the conversion factor as

$$\frac{-57.66 \text{ kJ}}{1.435 \text{ g } C_{10}H_8}$$

The molar mass of naphthalene is 128.2 g, so the heat of combustion of 1 mole of naphthalene is

$$\text{molar heat of combustion} = \frac{-57.66 \text{ kJ}}{1.435 \text{ g } C_{10}H_8} \times \frac{128.2 \text{ g } C_{10}H_8}{1 \text{ mol } C_{10}H_8}$$
$$= -5.151 \times 10^3 \text{ kJ/mol}$$

Check Knowing that the combustion reaction is exothermic and that the molar mass of naphthalene is much greater than 1.4 g, is the answer reasonable? Under the reaction conditions, can the heat change (-57.66 kJ) be equated to the enthalpy change of the reaction?

Practice Exercise A quantity of 1.922 g of methanol (CH_3OH) was burned in a constant-volume bomb calorimeter. Consequently, the temperature of the water rose by 4.20°C. If the heat capacity of the bomb plus water was 10.4 kJ/°C, calculate the molar heat of combustion of methanol.

Similar problem: 6.37.

Figure 6.9 *A constant-pressure calorimeter made of two Styrofoam coffee cups. The outer cup helps to insulate the reacting mixture from the surroundings. Two solutions of known volume containing the reactants at the same temperature are carefully mixed in the calorimeter. The heat produced or absorbed by the reaction can be determined by measuring the temperature change.*

Constant-Pressure Calorimetry

A simpler device than the constant-volume calorimeter is the constant-pressure calorimeter, which is used to determine the heat changes for noncombustion reactions. A crude constant-pressure calorimeter can be constructed from two Styrofoam coffee cups, as shown in Figure 6.9. This device measures the heat effects of a variety of reactions, such as acid-base neutralization, as well as the heat of solution and heat of dilution. Because the pressure is constant, the heat change for the process (q_{rxn}) is equal to the enthalpy change (ΔH). As in the case of a constant-volume calorimeter, we treat the calorimeter as an isolated system. Furthermore, we neglect the small heat capacity of the coffee cups in our calculations. Table 6.3 lists some reactions that have been studied with the constant-pressure calorimeter.

TABLE 6.3	Heats of Some Typical Reactions Measured at Constant Pressure	
Type of Reaction	**Example**	**ΔH (kJ/mol)**
Heat of neutralization	$HCl(aq) + NaOH(aq) \longrightarrow NaCl(aq) + H_2O(l)$	−56.2
Heat of ionization	$H_2O(l) \longrightarrow H^+(aq) + OH^-(aq)$	56.2
Heat of fusion	$H_2O(s) \longrightarrow H_2O(l)$	6.01
Heat of vaporization	$H_2O(l) \longrightarrow H_2O(g)$	44.0*
Heat of reaction	$MgCl_2(s) + 2Na(l) \longrightarrow 2NaCl(s) + Mg(s)$	−180.2

*Measured at 25°C. At 100°C, the value is 40.79 kJ.

Example 6.7

A lead (Pb) pellet having a mass of 26.47 g at 89.98°C was placed in a constant-pressure calorimeter of negligible heat capacity containing 100.0 mL of water. The water temperature rose from 22.50°C to 23.17°C. What is the specific heat of the lead pellet?

Strategy A sketch of the initial and final situation is as follows:

We know the masses of water and the lead pellet as well as the initial and final temperatures. Assuming no heat is lost to the surroundings, we can equate the heat lost by the lead pellet to the heat gained by the water. Knowing the specific heat of water, we can then calculate the specific heat of lead.

Solution Treating the calorimeter as an isolated system (no heat lost to the surroundings), we write

$$q_{Pb} + q_{H_2O} = 0$$

or

$$q_{Pb} = -q_{H_2O}$$

The heat gained by the water is given by

$$q_{H_2O} = ms\Delta t$$

where m and s are the mass and specific heat and $\Delta t = t_{final} - t_{initial}$. Therefore,

$$q_{H_2O} = (100.0 \text{ g})(4.184 \text{ J/g} \cdot {}^\circ\text{C})(23.17^\circ\text{C} - 22.50^\circ\text{C})$$
$$= 280.3 \text{ J}$$

(Continued)

Because the heat lost by the lead pellet is equal to the heat gained by the water, so $q_{Pb} = -280.3$ J. Solving for the specific heat of Pb, we write

$$q_{Pb} = ms\Delta t$$
$$-280.3 \text{ J} = (26.47 \text{ g})(s)(23.17°C - 89.98°C)$$
$$s = 0.158 \text{ J/g} \cdot °C$$

Similar problem: 6.82.

Check The specific heat falls within the metals shown in Table 6.2.

Practice Exercise A 30.14-g stainless steel ball bearing at 117.82°C is placed in a constant-pressure calorimeter containing 120.0 mL of water at 18.44°C. If the specific heat of the ball bearing is 0.474 J/g · °C, calculate the final temperature of the water. Assume the calorimeter to have negligible heat capacity.

Example 6.8

A quantity of 1.00×10^2 mL of 0.500 M HCl was mixed with 1.00×10^2 mL of 0.500 M NaOH in a constant-pressure calorimeter of negligible heat capacity. The initial temperature of the HCl and NaOH solutions was the same, 22.50°C, and the final temperature of the mixed solution was 25.86°C. Calculate the heat change for the neutralization reaction on a molar basis

$$\text{NaOH}(aq) + \text{HCl}(aq) \longrightarrow \text{NaCl}(aq) + \text{H}_2\text{O}(l)$$

Assume that the densities and specific heats of the solutions are the same as for water (1.00 g/mL and 4.184 J/g · °C, respectively).

Strategy Because the temperature rose, the neutralization reaction is exothermic. How do we calculate the heat absorbed by the combined solution? What is the heat of the reaction? What is the conversion factor for expressing the heat of reaction on a molar basis?

Solution Assuming no heat is lost to the surroundings, $q_{sys} = q_{soln} + q_{rxn} = 0$, so $q_{rxn} = -q_{soln}$, where q_{soln} is the heat absorbed by the combined solution. Because the density of the solution is 1.00 g/mL, the mass of a 100-mL solution is 100 g. Thus,

$$q_{soln} = ms\Delta t$$
$$= (1.00 \times 10^2 \text{ g} + 1.00 \times 10^2 \text{ g})(4.184 \text{ J/g} \cdot °C)(25.86°C - 22.50°C)$$
$$= 2.81 \times 10^3 \text{ J}$$
$$= 2.81 \text{ kJ}$$

Because $q_{rxn} = -q_{soln}$, $q_{rxn} = -2.81$ kJ.

From the molarities given, the number of moles of both HCl and NaOH in 1.00×10^2 mL solution is

$$\frac{0.500 \text{ mol}}{1 \text{ L}} \times 0.100 \text{ L} = 0.0500 \text{ mol}$$

Therefore, the heat of neutralization when 1.00 mole of HCl reacts with 1.00 mole of NaOH is

$$\text{heat of neutralization} = \frac{-2.81 \text{ kJ}}{0.0500 \text{ mol}} = -56.2 \text{ kJ/mol}$$

Similar problem: 6.38.

Check Is the sign consistent with the nature of the reaction? Under the reaction condition, can the heat change be equated to the enthalpy change?

(Continued)

CHEMISTRY
in Action

Fuel Values of Foods and Other Substances

The food we eat is broken down, or metabolized, in stages by a group of complex biological molecules called enzymes. Most of the energy released at each stage is captured for function and growth. One interesting aspect of metabolism is that the overall change in energy is the same as it is in combustion. For example, the total enthalpy change for the conversion of glucose ($C_6H_{12}O_6$) to carbon dioxide and water is the same whether we burn the substance in air or digest it in our bodies:

$$C_6H_{12}O_6(s) + 6O_2(g) \longrightarrow 6CO_2(g) + 6H_2O(l)$$
$$\Delta H = -2801 \text{ kJ/mol}$$

The important difference between metabolism and combustion is that the latter is usually a one-step, high-temperature process. Consequently, much of the energy released by combustion is lost to the surroundings.

Various foods have different compositions and hence different energy contents. The energy content of food is generally measured in calories. The *calorie* (*cal*) is a non-SI unit of energy that is equivalent to 4.184 J:

$$1 \text{ cal} = 4.184 \text{ J}$$

In the context of nutrition, however, the calorie we speak of (sometimes called a "big calorie") is actually equal to a *kilocalorie*; that is,

$$1 \text{ Cal} = 1000 \text{ cal} = 4184 \text{ J}$$

Note the use of a capital "C" to represent the "big calorie."

The bomb calorimeter described in Section 6.5 is ideally suited for measuring the energy content, or "fuel value," of foods. Fuel values are just the enthalpies of combustion (see table). In order to be analyzed in a bomb calorimeter, food must be dried first because most foods contain a considerable amount of water. Because the composition of particular foods is often not known, fuel values are expressed in terms of kJ/g rather than kJ/mol.

Fuel Values of Foods and Some Common Fuels

Substance	$\Delta H_{combustion}$ (kJ/g)
Apple	−2
Beef	−8
Beer	−1.5
Bread	−11
Butter	−34
Cheese	−18
Eggs	−6
Milk	−3
Potatoes	−3
Charcoal	−35
Coal	−30
Gasoline	−34
Kerosene	−37
Natural gas	−50
Wood	−20

Nutrition Facts
Serving Size 6 cookies (28g)
Servings Per Container about 11

Amount Per Serving

Calories 120   Calories from Fat 30

	% Daily Value*
Total Fat 4g	6%
Saturated Fat 0.5g	4%
Polyunsaturated Fat 0g	
Monounsaturated Fat 1g	
Cholesterol 5mg	2%
Sodium 105mg	4%
Total Carbohydrate 20g	7%
Dietary Fiber Less than 1gram	2%
Sugars 7g	
Protein 2g	

The labels on food packages reveal the calorie content of the food inside.

Practice Exercise A quantity of 4.00×10^2 mL of 0.600 M HNO_3 is mixed with 4.00×10^2 mL of 0.300 M $Ba(OH)_2$ in a constant-pressure calorimeter of negligible heat capacity. The initial temperature of both solutions is the same at 18.46°C. What is the final temperature of the solution? (Use the result in Example 6.8 for your calculation.)

6.6 Standard Enthalpy of Formation and Reaction

So far we have learned that we can determine the enthalpy change that accompanies a reaction by measuring the heat absorbed or released (at constant pressure). From Equation (6.9) we see that ΔH can also be calculated if we know the actual enthalpies of all reactants and products. However, as mentioned earlier, there is no way to measure the *absolute* value of the enthalpy of a substance. Only values *relative* to an arbitrary reference can be determined. This problem is similar to the one geographers face in expressing the elevations of specific mountains or valleys. Rather than trying to devise some type of "absolute" elevation scale (perhaps based on distance from the center of Earth?), by common agreement all geographic heights and depths are expressed relative to sea level, an arbitrary reference with a defined elevation of "zero" meters or feet. Similarly, chemists have agreed on an arbitrary reference point for enthalpy.

The "sea level" reference point for all enthalpy expressions is called the ***standard enthalpy of formation*** (ΔH_f°). Substances are said to be in the ***standard state*** at 1 atm,[†] hence the term "standard enthalpy." The superscript "°" represents standard-state conditions (1 atm), and the subscript "f" stands for formation. By convention, *the standard enthalpy of formation of any element in its most stable form is zero.* Take the element oxygen as an example. Molecular oxygen (O_2) is more stable than the other allotropic form of oxygen, ozone (O_3), at 1 atm and 25°C. Thus, we can write $\Delta H_f^\circ(O_2) = 0$, but $\Delta H_f^\circ(O_3) \neq 0$. Similarly, graphite is a more stable allotropic form of carbon than diamond at 1 atm and 25°C, so we have ΔH_f°(C, graphite) = 0 and ΔH_f°(C, diamond) $\neq$ 0. Based on this reference for elements, we can now define the standard enthalpy of formation of a compound as *the heat change that results when 1 mole of the compound is formed from its elements at a pressure of 1 atm.* Table 6.4 lists the standard enthalpies of formation for a number of elements and compounds. (For a more complete list of ΔH_f° values, see Appendix 2.) Note that although the standard state does not specify a temperature, we will always use ΔH_f° values measured at 25°C for our discussion because most of the thermodynamic data are collected at this temperature.

The importance of the standard enthalpies of formation is that once we know their values, we can readily calculate the ***standard enthalpy of reaction,*** ΔH_{rxn}° defined as *the enthalpy of a reaction carried out at 1 atm.* For example, consider the hypothetical reaction

$$a\text{A} + b\text{B} \longrightarrow c\text{C} + d\text{D}$$

where *a, b, c,* and *d* are stoichiometric coefficients. For this reaction ΔH_{rxn}° is given by

$$\Delta H_{rxn}^\circ = [c\Delta H_f^\circ(\text{C}) + d\Delta H_f^\circ(\text{D})] - [a\Delta H_f^\circ(\text{A}) + b\Delta H_f^\circ(\text{B})] \qquad (6.17)$$

We can generalize Equation (6.17) as

$$\Delta H_{rxn}^\circ = \Sigma n\Delta H_f^\circ(\text{products}) - \Sigma m\Delta H_f^\circ(\text{reactants}) \qquad (6.18)$$

where *m* and *n* denote the stoichiometric coefficients for the reactants and products, and Σ (sigma) means "the sum of." Note that in calculations, the stoichiometric coefficients are just numbers without units.

Graphite (top) and diamond (bottom).

[†]In thermodynamics, the standard pressure is defined as 1 bar, where 1 bar = 10^5 Pa = 0.987 atm. Because 1 bar differs from 1 atm by only 1.3 percent, we will continue to use 1 atm as the standard pressure. Note that the normal melting point and boiling point of a substance are defined in terms of 1 atm.

TABLE 6.4	Standard Enthalpies of Formation of Some Inorganic Substances at 25°C		
Substance	**ΔH_f° (kJ/mol)**	**Substance**	**ΔH_f° (kJ/mol)**
$Ag(s)$	0	$H_2O_2(l)$	−187.6
$AgCl(s)$	−127.0	$Hg(l)$	0
$Al(s)$	0	$I_2(s)$	0
$Al_2O_3(s)$	−1669.8	$HI(g)$	25.9
$Br_2(l)$	0	$Mg(s)$	0
$HBr(g)$	−36.2	$MgO(s)$	−601.8
$C(graphite)$	0	$MgCO_3(s)$	−1112.9
$C(diamond)$	1.90	$N_2(g)$	0
$CO(g)$	−110.5	$NH_3(g)$	−46.3
$CO_2(g)$	−393.5	$NO(g)$	90.4
$Ca(s)$	0	$NO_2(g)$	33.85
$CaO(s)$	−635.6	$N_2O(g)$	81.56
$CaCO_3(s)$	−1206.9	$N_2O_4(g)$	9.66
$Cl_2(g)$	0	$O(g)$	249.4
$HCl(g)$	−92.3	$O_2(g)$	0
$Cu(s)$	0	$O_3(g)$	142.2
$CuO(s)$	−155.2	$S(rhombic)$	0
$F_2(g)$	0	$S(monoclinic)$	0.30
$HF(g)$	−271.6	$SO_2(g)$	−296.1
$H(g)$	218.2	$SO_3(g)$	−395.2
$H_2(g)$	0	$H_2S(g)$	−20.15
$H_2O(g)$	−241.8	$ZnO(s)$	−348.0
$H_2O(l)$	−285.8		

To use Equation (6.18) to calculate ΔH_{rxn}°, we must know the ΔH_f° values of the compounds that take part in the reaction. These values can be determined by applying the direct method or the indirect method.

The Direct Method

This method of measuring ΔH_f° works for compounds that can be readily synthesized from their elements. Suppose we want to know the enthalpy of formation of carbon dioxide. We must measure the enthalpy of the reaction when carbon (graphite) and molecular oxygen in their standard states are converted to carbon dioxide in its standard state:

$$C(graphite) + O_2(g) \longrightarrow CO_2(g) \quad \Delta H_{rxn}^\circ = -393.5 \text{ kJ/mol}$$

We know from experience that this combustion easily goes to completion. Thus, from Equation (6.18) we can write

$$\Delta H_{rxn}^\circ = \Delta H_f^\circ(CO_2, g) - [\Delta H_f^\circ(C, \text{graphite}) + \Delta H_f^\circ(O_2, g)]$$
$$= -393.5 \text{ kJ/mol}$$

Because both graphite and O_2 are stable allotropic forms of the elements, it follows that $\Delta H_f^\circ(C, \text{graphite})$ and $\Delta H_f^\circ(O_2, g)$ are zero. Therefore,

$$\Delta H_{rxn}^\circ = \Delta H_f^\circ(CO_2, g) = -393.5 \text{ kJ/mol}$$

or
$$\Delta H_f^\circ(CO_2, g) = -393.5 \text{ kJ/mol}$$

Note that arbitrarily assigning zero ΔH_f° for each element in its most stable form at the standard state does not affect our calculations in any way. Remember, in thermochemistry we are interested only in enthalpy *changes* because they can be determined experimentally whereas the absolute enthalpy values cannot. The choice of a zero "reference level" for enthalpy makes calculations easier to handle. Again referring to the terrestrial altitude analogy, we find that Mt. Everest is 8708 ft higher than Mt. McKinley. This difference in altitude is unaffected by the decision to set sea level at 0 ft or at 1000 ft.

Other compounds that can be studied by the direct method are SF_6, P_4O_{10}, and CS_2. The equations representing their syntheses are

$$S(\text{rhombic}) + 3F_2(g) \longrightarrow SF_6(g)$$
$$P_4(\text{white}) + 5O_2(g) \longrightarrow P_4O_{10}(s)$$
$$C(\text{graphite}) + 2S(\text{rhombic}) \longrightarrow CS_2(l)$$

Note that S(rhombic) and P(white) are the most stable allotropes of sulfur and phosphorus, respectively, at 1 atm and 25°C, so their ΔH_f° values are zero.

P_4

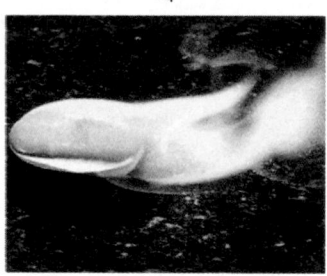

White phosphorus burns in air to form P_4O_{10}.

The Indirect Method

Many compounds cannot be directly synthesized from their elements. In some cases, the reaction proceeds too slowly, or side reactions produce substances other than the desired compound. In these cases, ΔH_f° can be determined by an indirect approach, which is based on Hess's law of heat summation, or simply Hess's law, named after the Swiss chemist Germain Hess.[†] **Hess's law** can be stated as follows: *When reactants are converted to products, the change in enthalpy is the same whether the reaction takes place in one step or in a series of steps.* In other words, if we can break down the reaction of interest into a series of reactions for which ΔH_{rxn}° can be measured, we can calculate ΔH_{rxn}° for the overall reaction. Hess's law is based on the fact that because H is a state function, ΔH depends only on the initial and final state (that is, only on the nature of reactants and products). The enthalpy change would be the same whether the overall reaction takes place in one step or many steps.

An analogy for Hess's law is as follows. Suppose you go from the first floor to the sixth floor of a building by elevator. The gain in your gravitational potential energy (which corresponds to the enthalpy change for the overall process) is the same whether you go directly there or stop at each floor on your way up (breaking the trip into a series of steps).

Let's say we are interested in the standard enthalpy of formation of carbon monoxide (CO). We might represent the reaction as

$$C(\text{graphite}) + \tfrac{1}{2}O_2(g) \longrightarrow CO(g)$$

However, burning graphite also produces some carbon dioxide (CO_2), so we cannot measure the enthalpy change for CO directly as shown. Instead, we must employ an

[†]Germain Henri Hess (1802–1850). Swiss chemist. Hess was born in Switzerland but spent most of his life in Russia. For formulating Hess's law, he is called the father of thermochemistry.

indirect route, based on Hess's law. It is possible to carry out the following two separate reactions, which do go to completion:

(a) $\qquad$ C(graphite) + $O_2(g) \longrightarrow CO_2(g)$ $\quad \Delta H°_{rxn} = -393.5$ kJ/mol
(b) $\qquad$ CO(g) + $\frac{1}{2}O_2(g) \longrightarrow CO_2(g)$ $\quad \Delta H°_{rxn} = -283.0$ kJ/mol

First, we reverse Equation (b) to get

(c) $\qquad$ $CO_2(g) \longrightarrow CO(g) + \frac{1}{2}O_2(g)$ $\quad \Delta H°_{rxn} = +283.0$ kJ/mol

Because chemical equations can be added and subtracted just like algebraic equations, we carry out the operation (a) + (c) and obtain

(a) $\qquad$ C(graphite) + $O_2(g) \longrightarrow CO_2(g)$ $\qquad \Delta H°_{rxn} = -393.5$ kJ/mol
(c) $\qquad$ $CO_2(g) \longrightarrow CO(g) + \frac{1}{2}O_2(g)$ $\qquad \Delta H°_{rxn} = +283.0$ kJ/mol
───
(d) $\qquad$ C(graphite) + $\frac{1}{2}O_2(g) \longrightarrow CO(g)$ $\qquad \Delta H°_{rxn} = -110.5$ kJ/mol

Thus, $\Delta H°_f(CO) = -110.5$ kJ/mol. Looking back, we see that the overall reaction is the formation of CO_2 [Equation (a)], which can be broken down into two parts [Equations (d) and (b)]. Figure 6.10 shows the overall scheme of our procedure.

The general rule in applying Hess's law is to arrange a series of chemical equations (corresponding to a series of steps) in such a way that, when added together, all species will cancel except for the reactants and products that appear in the overall reaction. This means that we want the elements on the left and the compound of interest on the right of the arrow. Further, we often need to multiply some or all of the equations representing the individual steps by the appropriate coefficients.

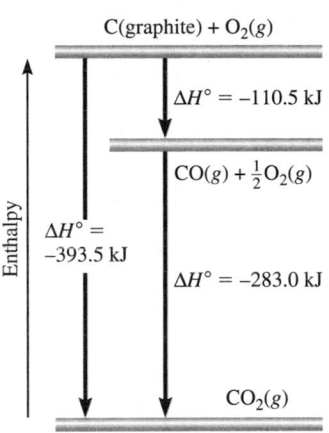

Figure 6.10 *The enthalpy change for the formation of 1 mole of CO_2 from graphite and O_2 can be broken down into two steps according to Hess's law.*

Remember to reverse the sign of ΔH when you reverse an equation.

Example 6.9

Calculate the standard enthalpy of formation of acetylene (C_2H_2) from its elements:

$$2C(graphite) + H_2(g) \longrightarrow C_2H_2(g)$$

The equations for each step and the corresponding enthalpy changes are

(a) $\qquad$ C(graphite) + $O_2(g) \longrightarrow CO_2(g)$ $\qquad \Delta H°_{rxn} = -393.5$ kJ/mol
(b) $\qquad$ $H_2(g) + \frac{1}{2}O_2(g) \longrightarrow H_2O(l)$ $\qquad \Delta H°_{rxn} = -285.8$ kJ/mol
(c) $\qquad$ $2C_2H_2(g) + 5O_2(g) \longrightarrow 4CO_2(g) + 2H_2O(l)$ $\quad \Delta H°_{rxn} = -2598.8$ kJ/mol

Strategy Our goal here is to calculate the enthalpy change for the formation of C_2H_2 from its elements C and H_2. The reaction does not occur directly, however, so we must use an indirect route using the information given by Equations (a), (b), and (c).

Solution Looking at the synthesis of C_2H_2, we need 2 moles of graphite as reactant. So we multiply Equation (a) by 2 to get

(d) $\qquad$ 2C(graphite) + $2O_2(g) \longrightarrow 2CO_2(g)$ $\quad \Delta H°_{rxn} = 2(-393.5$ kJ/mol$)$
$\qquad\qquad\qquad\qquad\qquad\qquad\qquad\qquad\qquad\qquad\qquad\quad = -787.0$ kJ/mol

Next, we need 1 mole of H_2 as a reactant and this is provided by Equation (b). Last, we need 1 mole of C_2H_2 as a product. Equation (c) has 2 moles of C_2H_2 as a reactant so we need to reverse the equation and divide it by 2:

(e) $\qquad$ $2CO_2(g) + H_2O(l) \longrightarrow C_2H_2(g) + \frac{5}{2}O_2(g)$ $\quad \Delta H°_{rxn} = \frac{1}{2}(2598.8$ kJ/mol$)$
$\qquad\qquad\qquad\qquad\qquad\qquad\qquad\qquad\qquad\qquad\qquad\qquad = 1299.4$ kJ/mol

(Continued)

C_2H_2

An oxyacetylene torch has a high flame temperature (3000°C) and is used to weld metals.

Adding Equations (d), (b), and (e) together, we get

$$2C(\text{graphite}) + 2O_2(g) \longrightarrow 2CO_2(g) \qquad \Delta H^\circ_{\text{rxn}} = -787.0 \text{ kJ/mol}$$
$$H_2(g) + \tfrac{1}{2}O_2(g) \longrightarrow H_2O(l) \qquad \Delta H^\circ_{\text{rxn}} = -285.8 \text{ kJ/mol}$$
$$\underline{2CO_2(g) + H_2O(l) \longrightarrow C_2H_2(g) + \tfrac{5}{2}O_2(g) \quad \Delta H^\circ_{\text{rxn}} = 1299.4 \text{ kJ/mol}}$$
$$2C(\text{graphite}) + H_2(g) \longrightarrow C_2H_2(g) \qquad \Delta H^\circ_{\text{rxn}} = 226.6 \text{ kJ/mol}$$

Therefore, $\Delta H^\circ_f = \Delta H^\circ_{\text{rxn}} = 226.6$ kJ/mol. The ΔH°_f value means that when 1 mole of C_2H_2 is synthesized from 2 moles of C(graphite) and 1 mole of H_2, 226.6 kJ of heat are absorbed by the reacting system from the surroundings. Thus, this is an endothermic process.

Practice Exercise Calculate the standard enthalpy of formation of carbon disulfide (CS_2) from its elements, given that

$$C(\text{graphite}) + O_2(g) \longrightarrow CO_2(g) \qquad \Delta H^\circ_{\text{rxn}} = -393.5 \text{ kJ/mol}$$
$$S(\text{rhombic}) + O_2(g) \longrightarrow SO_2(g) \qquad \Delta H^\circ_{\text{rxn}} = -296.4 \text{ kJ/mol}$$
$$CS_2(l) + 3O_2(g) \longrightarrow CO_2(g) + 2SO_2(g) \quad \Delta H^\circ_{\text{rxn}} = -1073.6 \text{ kJ/mol}$$

Similar problems: 6.62, 6.63.

We can calculate the enthalpy of reactions from the values of ΔH°_f, as shown in Example 6.10

The molten iron formed in a thermite reaction is run down into a mold between the ends of two railroad rails. On cooling, the rails are welded together.

Example 6.10

The thermite reaction involves aluminum and iron(III) oxide

$$2Al(s) + Fe_2O_3(s) \longrightarrow Al_2O_3(s) + 2Fe(l)$$

This reaction is highly exothermic and the liquid iron formed is used to weld metals. Calculate the heat released in kilojoules per gram of Al reacted with Fe_2O_3. The ΔH°_f for Fe(l) is 12.40 kJ/mol.

Strategy The enthalpy of a reaction is the difference between the sum of the enthalpies of the products and the sum of the enthalpies of the reactants. The enthalpy of each species (reactant or product) is given by the product of the stoichiometric coefficient and the standard enthalpy of formation of the species.

Solution Using the given ΔH°_f value for Fe(l) and other ΔH°_f values in Appendix 3 and Equation (6.18), we write

$$\Delta H^\circ_{\text{rxn}} = \left[\Delta H^\circ_f(Al_2O_3) + 2\Delta H^\circ_f(Fe)\right] - \left[2\Delta H^\circ_f(Al) + \Delta H^\circ_f(Fe_2O_3)\right]$$
$$= \left[(-1669.8 \text{ kJ/mol}) + 2(12.40 \text{ kJ/mol})\right] - \left[2(0) + (-822.2 \text{ kJ/mol})\right]$$
$$= -822.8 \text{ kJ/mol}$$

This is the amount of heat released for two moles of Al reacted. We use the following ratio

$$\frac{-822.8 \text{ kJ}}{2 \text{ mol Al}}$$

to convert to kJ/g Al. The molar mass of Al is 26.98 g, so

$$\text{heat released per gram of Al} = \frac{-822.8 \text{ kJ}}{2 \text{ mol Al}} \times \frac{1 \text{ mol Al}}{26.98 \text{ g Al}}$$
$$= -15.25 \text{ kJ/g}$$

(Continued)

CHEMISTRY
in Action

How a Bombardier Beetle Defends Itself

$\mathbf{S}$urvival techniques of insects and small animals in a fiercely competitive environment take many forms. For example, chameleons have developed the ability to change color to match their surroundings and the butterfly *Limenitis* has evolved into a form that mimics the poisonous and unpleasant-tasting monarch butterfly (*Danaus*). A less passive defense mechanism is employed by bombardier beetles (*Brachinus*), which repel predators with a "chemical spray."

The bombardier beetle has a pair of glands at the tip of its abdomen. Each gland consists of two compartments. The inner compartment contains an aqueous solution of hydroquinone and hydrogen peroxide, and the outer compartment holds a mixture of enzymes. (Enzymes are biological molecules that can speed up a reaction.) When threatened, the beetle squeezes some fluid from the inner compartment into the outer compartment, where, in the presence of the enzymes, an exothermic reaction takes place:

(a) $C_6H_4(OH)_2(aq) + H_2O_2(aq) \longrightarrow$
    hydroquinone

$$C_6H_4O_2(aq) + 2H_2O(l)$$
            quinone

To estimate the heat of reaction, let us consider the following steps:

(b) $C_6H_4(OH)_2(aq) \longrightarrow C_6H_4O_2(aq) + H_2(g)$
                             $\Delta H^\circ = 177 \text{ kJ/mol}$
(c) $H_2O_2(aq) \longrightarrow H_2O(l) + \frac{1}{2}O_2(g)$ $\Delta H^\circ = -94.6 \text{ kJ/mol}$
(d) $H_2(g) + \frac{1}{2}O_2(g) \longrightarrow H_2O(l)$ $\Delta H^\circ = -286 \text{ kJ/mol}$

Recalling Hess's law, we find that the heat of reaction for (a) is simply the *sum* of those for (b), (c), and (d).

A bombardier beetle discharging a chemical spray.

Therefore, we write

$$\Delta H_a^\circ = \Delta H_b^\circ + \Delta H_c^\circ + \Delta H_d^\circ$$
$$= (177 - 94.6 - 286) \text{ kJ/mol}$$
$$= -204 \text{ kJ/mol}$$

The large amount of heat generated is sufficient to bring the mixture to its boiling point. By rotating the tip of its abdomen, the beetle can quickly discharge the vapor in the form of a fine mist toward an unsuspecting predator. In addition to the thermal effect, the quinones also act as a repellent to other insects and animals. One bombardier beetle carries enough reagents to produce 20 to 30 discharges in quick succession, each with an audible detonation.

Check Is the negative sign consistent with the exothermic nature of the reaction? As a quick check, we see that 2 moles of Al weigh about 54 g and give off about 823 kJ of heat when reacted with Fe_2O_3. Therefore, the heat given off per gram of Al reacted is approximately $-830 \text{ kJ}/54 \text{ g}$ or -15.4 kJ/g.

Similar problems: 6.54, 6.57.

Practice Exercise Benzene (C_6H_6) burns in air to produce carbon dioxide and liquid water. Calculate the heat released (in kilojoules) per gram of the compound reacted with oxygen. The standard enthalpy of formation of benzene is 49.04 kJ/mol.

In general, the more negative the standard enthalpy of formation of a compound the more stable is the compound. Thus, in the thermite reaction the less stable Fe_2O_3 is converted to the more stable Al_2O_3 and we expect the reaction to release a large amount of heat.

6.7 Heat of Solution and Dilution

Although we have focused so far on the thermal energy effects resulting from chemical reactions, many physical processes, such as the melting of ice or the condensation of a vapor, also involve the absorption or release of heat. Enthalpy changes occur as well when a solute dissolves in a solvent or when a solution is diluted. Let us look at these two related physical processes, involving heat of solution and heat of dilution.

Heat of Solution

In the vast majority of cases, dissolving a solute in a solvent produces measurable heat change. At constant pressure, the heat change is equal to the enthalpy change. The **heat of solution,** or **enthalpy of solution, ΔH_{soln},** is *the heat generated or absorbed when a certain amount of solute dissolves in a certain amount of solvent.* The quantity ΔH_{soln} represents the difference between the enthalpy of the final solution and the enthalpies of its original components (that is, solute and solvent) before they are mixed. Thus,

$$\Delta H_{soln} = H_{soln} - H_{components} \qquad (6.19)$$

Neither H_{soln} nor $H_{components}$ can be measured, but their difference, ΔH_{soln}, can be readily determined in a constant-pressure calorimeter. Like other enthalpy changes, ΔH_{soln} is positive for endothermic (heat-absorbing) processes and negative for exothermic (heat-generating) processes.

Consider the heat of solution of a process in which an ionic compound is the solute and water is the solvent. For example, what happens when solid NaCl dissolves in water? In solid NaCl, the Na^+ and Cl^- ions are held together by strong positive-negative (electrostatic) forces, but when a small crystal of NaCl dissolves in water, the three-dimensional network of ions breaks into its individual units. (The structure of solid NaCl is shown in Figure 2.13.) The separated Na^+ and Cl^- ions are stabilized in solution by their interaction with water molecules (see Figure 4.2). These ions are said to be *hydrated.* In this case water plays a role similar to that of a good electrical insulator. Water molecules shield the ions (Na^+ and Cl^-) from each other and effectively reduce the electrostatic attraction that held them together in the solid state. The heat of solution is defined by the following process:

$$NaCl(s) \xrightarrow{H_2O} Na^+(aq) + Cl^-(aq) \qquad \Delta H_{soln} = ?$$

Dissolving an ionic compound such as NaCl in water involves complex interactions among the solute and solvent species. However, for the sake of analysis we can imagine that the solution process takes place in two separate steps, illustrated in Figure 6.11. First, the Na^+ and Cl^- ions in the solid crystal are separated from each other and converted to the gaseous state:

$$energy + NaCl(s) \longrightarrow Na^+(g) + Cl^-(g)$$

The word "lattice" describes arrangement in space of isolated points (occupied by ions) in a regular pattern. Lattice energy is a positive quantity.

The energy required to completely separate one mole of a solid ionic compound into gaseous ions is called **lattice energy (U).** The lattice energy of NaCl is 788 kJ/mol. In other words, we would need to supply 788 kJ of energy to break 1 mole of solid NaCl into 1 mole of Na^+ ions and 1 mole of Cl^- ions.

Next, the "gaseous" Na^+ and Cl^- ions enter the water and become hydrated:

$$Na^+(g) + Cl^-(g) \xrightarrow{H_2O} Na^+(aq) + Cl^-(aq) + energy$$

The enthalpy change associated with the hydration process is called the **heat of hydration, ΔH_{hydr}** (heat of hydration is a negative quantity for cations and anions).

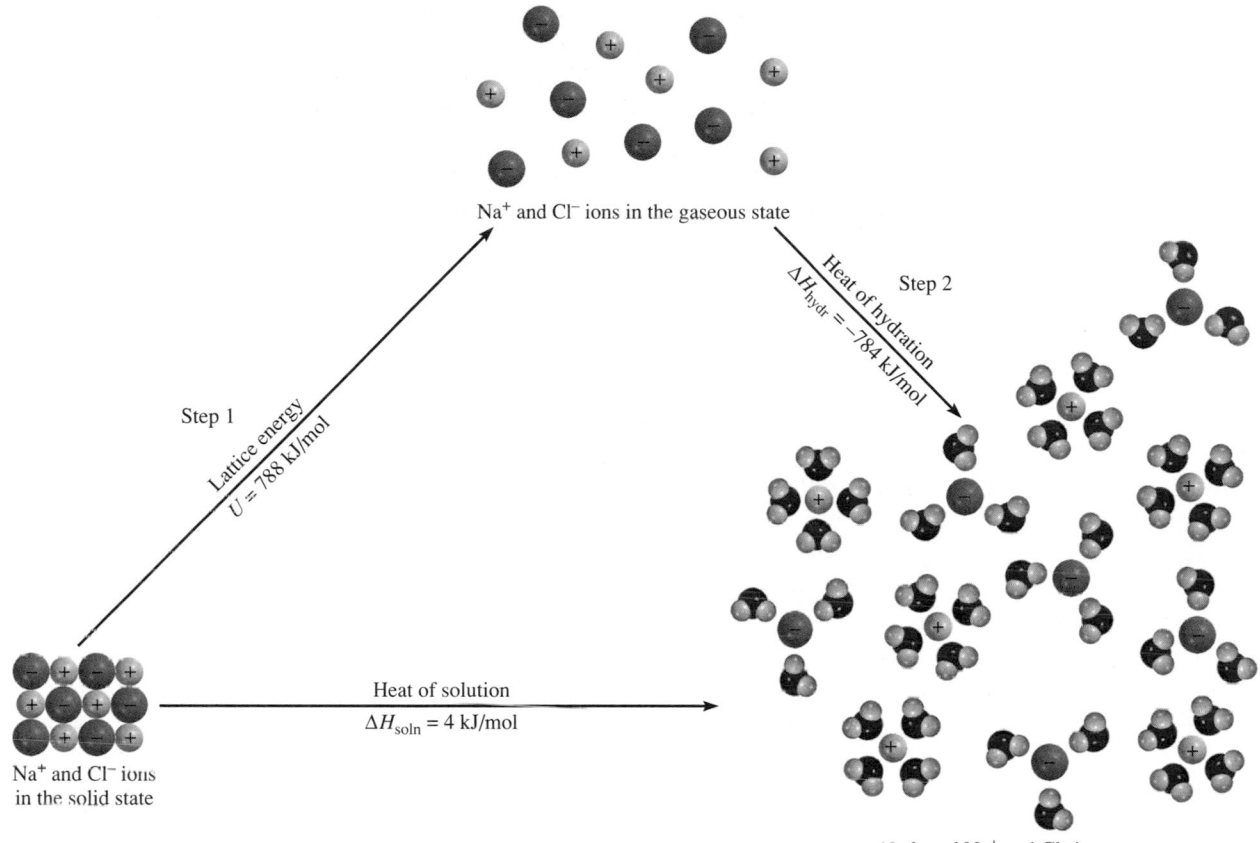

Na$^+$ and Cl$^-$ ions in the gaseous state

Step 2

Heat of hydration
$\Delta H_{hydr} = -784$ kJ/mol

Step 1

Lattice energy
$U = 788$ kJ/mol

Heat of solution
$\Delta H_{soln} = 4$ kJ/mol

Na$^+$ and Cl$^-$ ions
in the solid state

Hydrated Na$^+$ and Cl$^-$ ions

Figure 6.11 *The solution process for NaCl. The process can be considered to occur in two separate steps: (1) separation of ions from the crystal state to the gaseous state and (2) hydration of the gaseous ions. The heat of solution is equal to the energy changes for these two steps, $\Delta H_{soln} = U + \Delta H_{hydr}$.*

Applying Hess's law, it is possible to consider ΔH_{soln} as the sum of two related quantities, lattice energy (U) and heat of hydration (ΔH_{hydr}), as shown in Figure 6.11:

$$\Delta H_{soln} = U + \Delta H_{hydr} \qquad (6.20)$$

Therefore,

$$\begin{array}{ll} NaCl(s) \longrightarrow Na^+(g) + Cl^-(g) & U = 788 \text{ kJ/mol} \\ Na^+(g) + Cl^-(g) \xrightarrow{H_2O} Na^+(aq) + Cl^-(aq) & \Delta H_{hydr} = -784 \text{ kJ/mol} \\ \hline NaCl(s) \xrightarrow{H_2O} Na^+(aq) + Cl^-(aq) & \Delta H_{soln} = 4 \text{ kJ/mol} \end{array}$$

Thus, when 1 mole of NaCl dissolves in water, 4 kJ of heat will be absorbed from the surroundings. We would observe this effect by noting that the beaker containing the solution becomes slightly colder. Table 6.5 lists the ΔH_{soln} of several ionic compounds. Depending on the nature of the cation and anion involved, ΔH_{soln} for an ionic compound may be either negative (exothermic) or positive (endothermic).

Heat of Dilution

When a previously prepared solution is *diluted,* that is, when more solvent is added to lower the overall concentration of the solute, additional heat is usually given off or absorbed. The **heat of dilution** is *the heat change associated with the dilution process.*

TABLE 6.5

Heats of Solution of Some Ionic Compounds

Compound	ΔH_{soln} (kJ/mol)
LiCl	−37.1
CaCl$_2$	−82.8
NaCl	4.0
KCl	17.2
NH$_4$Cl	15.2
NH$_4$NO$_3$	26.2

If a certain solution process is endothermic and the solution is subsequently diluted, *more* heat will be absorbed by the same solution from the surroundings. The converse holds true for an exothermic solution process—more heat will be liberated if additional solvent is added to dilute the solution. Therefore, always be cautious when working on a dilution procedure in the laboratory. Because of its highly exothermic heat of dilution, concentrated sulfuric acid (H_2SO_4) poses a particularly hazardous problem if its concentration must be reduced by mixing it with additional water. Concentrated H_2SO_4 is composed of 98 percent acid and 2 percent water by mass. Diluting it with water releases considerable amount of heat to the surroundings. This process is so exothermic that you must *never* attempt to dilute the concentrated acid by adding water to it. The heat generated could cause the acid solution to boil and splatter. The recommended procedure is to add the concentrated acid slowly to the water (while constantly stirring).

Generations of chemistry students have been reminded of the safe procedure for diluting acids by the venerable saying, "Do as you oughter, add acid to water."

Summary of Facts and Concepts

1. Energy is the capacity to do work. There are many forms of energy and they are interconvertible. The law of conservation of energy states that the total amount of energy in the universe is constant.

2. A process that gives off heat to the surroundings is exothermic; a process that absorbs heat from the surroundings is endothermic.

3. The state of a system is defined by properties such as composition, volume, temperature, and pressure. These properties are called state functions.

4. The change in a state function for a system depends only on the initial and final states of the system, and not on the path by which the change is accomplished. Energy is a state function; work and heat are not.

5. Energy can be converted from one form to another, but it cannot be created or destroyed (first law of thermodynamics). In chemistry we are concerned mainly with thermal energy, electrical energy, and mechanical energy, which is usually associated with pressure-volume work.

6. Enthalpy is a state function. A change in enthalpy ΔH is equal to $\Delta E + P\Delta V$ for a constant-pressure process.

7. The change in enthalpy (ΔH, usually given in kilojoules) is a measure of the heat of reaction (or any other process) at constant pressure.

8. Constant-volume and constant-pressure calorimeters are used to measure heat changes that occur in physical and chemical processes.

9. Hess's law states that the overall enthalpy change in a reaction is equal to the sum of enthalpy changes for individual steps in the overall reaction.

10. The standard enthalpy of a reaction can be calculated from the standard enthalpies of formation of reactants and products.

11. The heat of solution of an ionic compound in water is the sum of the lattice energy of the compound and the heat of hydration. The relative magnitudes of these two quantities determine whether the solution process is endothermic or exothermic. The heat of dilution is the heat absorbed or evolved when a solution is diluted.

Key Words

Calorimetry, p. 239
Chemical energy, p. 224
Closed system, p. 225
Endothermic process, p. 226
Energy, p. 224
Enthalpy (H), p. 234
Enthalpy of reaction (ΔH_{rxn}), p. 235
Enthalpy of solution (ΔH_{soln}), p. 252
Exothermic process, p. 226

First law of thermodynamics, p. 227
Heat, p. 225
Heat capacity (C), p. 239
Heat of dilution, p. 253
Heat of hydration (ΔH_{hydr}), p. 252
Heat of solution (ΔH_{soln}), p. 252
Hess's law, p. 248
Isolated system, p. 225

Lattice energy (U), p. 252
Law of conservation of energy, p. 224
Open system, p. 225
Potential energy, p. 224
Radiant energy, p. 224
Specific heat (s), p. 239
Standard enthalpy of formation (ΔH_f°), p. 246
Standard enthalpy of reaction (ΔH_{rxn}°), p. 246

Standard state, p. 246
State function, p. 227
State of a system, p. 227
Surroundings, p. 225
System, p. 225
Thermal energy, p. 224
Thermochemical equation, p. 236
Thermochemistry, p. 225
Thermodynamics, p. 227
Work, p. 224

Questions and Problems

Definitions

Review Questions

6.1 Define these terms: system, surroundings, open system, closed system, isolated system, thermal energy, chemical energy, potential energy, kinetic energy, law of conservation of energy.

6.2 What is heat? How does heat differ from thermal energy? Under what condition is heat transferred from one system to another?

6.3 What are the units for energy commonly employed in chemistry?

6.4 A truck initially traveling at 60 km per hour is brought to a complete stop at a traffic light. Does this change violate the law of conservation of energy? Explain.

6.5 These are various forms of energy: chemical, heat, light, mechanical, and electrical. Suggest ways of interconverting these forms of energy.

6.6 Describe the interconversions of forms of energy occurring in these processes: (a) You throw a softball up into the air and catch it. (b) You switch on a flashlight. (c) You ride the ski lift to the top of the hill and then ski down. (d) You strike a match and let it burn down.

Energy Changes in Chemical Reactions

Review Questions

6.7 Define these terms: thermochemistry, exothermic process, endothermic process.

6.8 Stoichiometry is based on the law of conservation of mass. On what law is thermochemistry based?

6.9 Describe two exothermic processes and two endothermic processes.

6.10 Decomposition reactions are usually endothermic, whereas combination reactions are usually exothermic. Give a qualitative explanation for these trends.

First Law of Thermodynamics

Review Questions

6.11 On what law is the first law of thermodynamics based? Explain the sign conventions in the equation $\Delta E = q + w$.

6.12 Explain what is meant by a state function. Give two examples of quantities that are state functions and two that are not.

6.13 The internal energy of an ideal gas depends only on its temperature. Do a first-law analysis of this process. A sample of an ideal gas is allowed to expand at constant temperature against atmospheric pressure. (a) Does

the gas do work on its surroundings? (b) Is there heat exchange between the system and the surroundings? If so, in which direction? (c) What is ΔE for the gas for this process?

6.14 Consider these changes.

(a) $Hg(l) \longrightarrow Hg(g)$

(b) $3O_2(g) \longrightarrow 2O_3(g)$

(c) $CuSO_4 \cdot 5H_2O(s) \longrightarrow CuSO_4(s) + 5H_2O(g)$

(d) $H_2(g) + F_2(g) \longrightarrow 2HF(g)$

At constant pressure, in which of the reactions is work done by the system on the surroundings? By the surroundings on the system? In which of them is no work done?

Problems

6.15 A sample of nitrogen gas expands in volume from 1.6 L to 5.4 L at constant temperature. Calculate the work done in joules if the gas expands (a) against a vacuum, (b) against a constant pressure of 0.80 atm, and (c) against a constant pressure of 3.7 atm.

6.16 A gas expands in volume from 26.7 mL to 89.3 mL at constant temperature. Calculate the work done (in joules) if the gas expands (a) against a vacuum, (b) against a constant pressure of 1.5 atm, and (c) against a constant pressure of 2.8 atm.

6.17 A gas expands and does P-V work on the surroundings equal to 325 J. At the same time, it absorbs 127 J of heat from the surroundings. Calculate the change in energy of the gas.

6.18 The work done to compress a gas is 74 J. As a result, 26 J of heat is given off to the surroundings. Calculate the change in energy of the gas.

6.19 Calculate the work done when 50.0 g of tin dissolves in excess acid at 1.00 atm and 25°C:

$$Sn(s) + 2H^+(aq) \longrightarrow Sn^{2+}(aq) + H_2(g)$$

Assume ideal gas behavior.

6.20 Calculate the work done in joules when 1.0 mole of water vaporizes at 1.0 atm and 100°C. Assume that the volume of liquid water is negligible compared with that of steam at 100°C, and ideal gas behavior.

Enthalpy of Chemical Reactions

Review Questions

6.21 Define these terms: enthalpy, enthalpy of reaction. Under what condition is the heat of a reaction equal to the enthalpy change of the same reaction?

6.22 In writing thermochemical equations, why is it important to indicate the physical state (that is, gaseous, liquid, solid, or aqueous) of each substance?

256   Thermochemistry

6.23 Explain the meaning of this thermochemical equation:

$$4NH_3(g) + 5O_2(g) \longrightarrow 4NO(g) + 6H_2O(g)$$
$$\Delta H = -904 \text{ kJ/mol}$$

6.24 Consider this reaction:

$$2CH_3OH(l) + 3O_2(g) \longrightarrow 4H_2O(l) + 2CO_2(g)$$
$$\Delta H = -1452.8 \text{ kJ/mol}$$

What is the value of ΔH if (a) the equation is multiplied throughout by 2, (b) the direction of the reaction is reversed so that the products become the reactants and vice versa, (c) water vapor instead of liquid water is formed as the product?

Problems

6.25 The first step in the industrial recovery of zinc from the zinc sulfide ore is roasting, that is, the conversion of ZnS to ZnO by heating:

$$2ZnS(s) + 3O_2(g) \longrightarrow 2ZnO(s) + 2SO_2(g)$$
$$\Delta H = -879 \text{ kJ/mol}$$

Calculate the heat evolved (in kJ) per gram of ZnS roasted.

6.26 Determine the amount of heat (in kJ) given off when 1.26×10^4 g of NO_2 are produced according to the equation

$$2NO(g) + O_2(g) \longrightarrow 2NO_2(g)$$
$$\Delta H = -114.6 \text{ kJ/mol}$$

6.27 Consider the reaction

$$2H_2O(g) \longrightarrow 2H_2(g) + O_2(g)$$
$$\Delta H = 483.6 \text{ kJ/mol}$$

If 2.0 moles of $H_2O(g)$ are converted to $H_2(g)$ and $O_2(g)$ against a pressure of 1.0 atm at 125°C, what is ΔE for this reaction?

6.28 Consider the reaction

$$H_2(g) + Cl_2(g) \longrightarrow 2HCl(g)$$
$$\Delta H = -184.6 \text{ kJ/mol}$$

If 3 moles of H_2 react with 3 moles of Cl_2 to form HCl, calculate the work done (in joules) against a pressure of 1.0 atm at 25°C. What is ΔE for this reaction? Assume the reaction goes to completion.

Calorimetry
Review Questions

6.29 What is the difference between specific heat and heat capacity? What are the units for these two quantities? Which is the intensive property and which is the extensive property?

6.30 Consider two metals A and B, each having a mass of 100 g and an initial temperature of 20°C. The specific heat of A is larger than that of B. Under the same

heating conditions, which metal would take longer to reach a temperature of 21°C?

6.31 Define calorimetry and describe two commonly used calorimeters. In a calorimetric measurement, why is it important that we know the heat capacity of the calorimeter? How is this value determined?

6.32 Consider the following data:

Metal	Al	Cu
Mass (g)	10	30
Specific heat (J/g · °C)	0.900	0.385
Temperature (°C)	40	60

When these two metals are placed in contact, which of the following will take place?
(a) Heat will flow from Al to Cu because Al has a larger specific heat.
(b) Heat will flow from Cu to Al because Cu has a larger mass.
(c) Heat will flow from Cu to Al because Cu has a larger heat capacity.
(d) Heat will flow from Cu to Al because Cu is at a higher temperature.
(e) No heat will flow in either direction.

Problems

6.33 A piece of silver of mass 362 g has a heat capacity of 85.7 J/°C. What is the specific heat of silver?

6.34 A 6.22-kg piece of copper metal is heated from 20.5°C to 324.3°C. Calculate the heat absorbed (in kJ) by the metal.

6.35 Calculate the amount of heat liberated (in kJ) from 366 g of mercury when it cools from 77.0°C to 12.0°C.

6.36 A sheet of gold weighing 10.0 g and at a temperature of 18.0°C is placed flat on a sheet of iron weighing 20.0 g and at a temperature of 55.6°C. What is the final temperature of the combined metals? Assume that no heat is lost to the surroundings. (*Hint:* The heat gained by the gold must be equal to the heat lost by the iron. The specific heats of the metals are given in Table 6.2.)

6.37 A 0.1375-g sample of solid magnesium is burned in a constant-volume bomb calorimeter that has a heat capacity of 3024 J/°C. The temperature increases by 1.126°C. Calculate the heat given off by the burning Mg, in kJ/g and in kJ/mol.

6.38 A quantity of 2.00×10^2 mL of 0.862 M HCl is mixed with 2.00×10^2 mL of 0.431 M Ba(OH)$_2$ in a constant-pressure calorimeter of negligible heat capacity. The initial temperature of the HCl and Ba(OH)$_2$ solutions is the same at 20.48°C. For the process

$$H^+(aq) + OH^-(aq) \longrightarrow H_2O(l)$$

the heat of neutralization is -56.2 kJ/mol. What is the final temperature of the mixed solution?

Standard Enthalpy of Formation and Reaction

Review Questions

6.39 What is meant by the standard-state condition?

6.40 How are the standard enthalpies of an element and of a compound determined?

6.41 What is meant by the standard enthalpy of a reaction?

6.42 Write the equation for calculating the enthalpy of a reaction. Define all the terms.

6.43 State Hess's law. Explain, with one example, the usefulness of Hess's law in thermochemistry.

6.44 Describe how chemists use Hess's law to determine the ΔH_f° of a compound by measuring its heat (enthalpy) of combustion.

Problems

6.45 Which of the following standard enthalpy of formation values is not zero at 25°C? $Na(s)$, $Ne(g)$, $CH_4(g)$, $S_8(s)$, $Hg(l)$, $H(g)$.

6.46 The ΔH_f° values of the two allotropes of oxygen, O_2 and O_3, are 0 and 142.2 kJ/mol, respectively, at 25°C. Which is the more stable form at this temperature?

6.47 Which is the more negative quantity at 25°C: ΔH_f° for $H_2O(l)$ or ΔH_f° for $H_2O(g)$?

6.48 Predict the value of ΔH_f° (greater than, less than, or equal to zero) for these elements at 25°C: (a) $Br_2(g)$; $Br_2(l)$, (b) $I_2(g)$; $I_2(s)$.

6.49 In general, compounds with negative ΔH_f° values are more stable than those with positive ΔH_f° values. $H_2O_2(l)$ has a negative ΔH_f° (see Table 6.4). Why, then, does $H_2O_2(l)$ have a tendency to decompose to $H_2O(l)$ and $O_2(g)$?

6.50 Suggest ways (with appropriate equations) that would enable you to measure the ΔH_f° values of $Ag_2O(s)$ and $CaCl_2(s)$ from their elements. No calculations are necessary.

6.51 Calculate the heat of decomposition for this process at constant pressure and 25°C:

$$CaCO_3(s) \longrightarrow CaO(s) + CO_2(g)$$

(Look up the standard enthalpy of formation of the reactant and products in Table 6.4.)

6.52 The standard enthalpies of formation of ions in aqueous solutions are obtained by arbitrarily assigning a value of zero to H^+ ions; that is, $\Delta H_f^\circ[H^+(aq)] = 0$.

(a) For the following reaction

$$HCl(g) \xrightarrow{H_2O} H^+(aq) + Cl^-(aq)$$
$$\Delta H^\circ = -74.9 \text{ kJ/mol}$$

calculate ΔH_f° for the Cl^- ions.

(b) Given that ΔH_f° for OH^- ions is -229.6 kJ/mol, calculate the enthalpy of neutralization when 1 mole of a strong monoprotic acid (such as HCl) is titrated by 1 mole of a strong base (such as KOH) at 25°C.

6.53 Calculate the heats of combustion for the following reactions from the standard enthalpies of formation listed in Appendix 3:

(a) $2H_2(g) + O_2(g) \longrightarrow 2H_2O(l)$

(b) $2C_2H_2(g) + 5O_2(g) \longrightarrow 4CO_2(g) + 2H_2O(l)$

6.54 Calculate the heats of combustion for the following reactions from the standard enthalpies of formation listed in Appendix 3:

(a) $C_2H_4(g) + 3O_2(g) \longrightarrow 2CO_2(g) + 2H_2O(l)$

(b) $2H_2S(g) + 3O_2(g) \longrightarrow 2H_2O(l) + 2SO_2(g)$

6.55 Methanol, ethanol, and n-propanol are three common alcohols. When 1.00 g of each of these alcohols is burned in air, heat is liberated as shown by the following data: (a) methanol (CH_3OH), -22.6 kJ; (b) ethanol (C_2H_5OH), -29.7 kJ; (c) n-propanol (C_3H_7OH), -33.4 kJ. Calculate the heats of combustion of these alcohols in kJ/mol.

6.56 The standard enthalpy change for the following reaction is 436.4 kJ/mol:

$$H_2(g) \longrightarrow H(g) + H(g)$$

Calculate the standard enthalpy of formation of atomic hydrogen (H).

6.57 From the standard enthalpies of formation, calculate ΔH_{rxn}° for the reaction

$$C_6H_{12}(l) + 9O_2(g) \longrightarrow 6CO_2(g) + 6H_2O(l)$$

For $C_6H_{12}(l)$, $\Delta H_f^\circ = -151.9$ kJ/mol.

6.58 Pentaborane-9, B_5H_9, is a colorless, highly reactive liquid that will burst into flame when exposed to oxygen. The reaction is

$$2B_5H_9(l) + 12O_2(g) \longrightarrow 5B_2O_3(s) + 9H_2O(l)$$

Calculate the kilojoules of heat released per gram of the compound reacted with oxygen. The standard enthalpy of formation of B_5H_9 is 73.2 kJ/mol.

6.59 Determine the amount of heat (in kJ) given off when 1.26×10^4 g of ammonia are produced according to the equation

$$N_2(g) + 3H_2(g) \longrightarrow 2NH_3(g)$$
$$\Delta H_{rxn}^\circ = -92.6 \text{ kJ/mol}$$

Assume that the reaction takes place under standard-state conditions at 25°C.

6.60 At 850°C, $CaCO_3$ undergoes substantial decomposition to yield CaO and CO_2. Assuming that the ΔH_f° values of the reactant and products are the same at 850°C as they are at 25°C, calculate the enthalpy change (in kJ) if 66.8 g of CO_2 are produced in one reaction.

6.61 From these data,

$$S(\text{rhombic}) + O_2(g) \longrightarrow SO_2(g)$$
$$\Delta H^\circ_{\text{rxn}} = -296.06 \text{ kJ/mol}$$
$$S(\text{monoclinic}) + O_2(g) \longrightarrow SO_2(g)$$
$$\Delta H^\circ_{\text{rxn}} = -296.36 \text{ kJ/mol}$$

calculate the enthalpy change for the transformation

$$S(\text{rhombic}) \longrightarrow S(\text{monoclinic})$$

(Monoclinic and rhombic are different allotropic forms of elemental sulfur.)

6.62 From the following data,

$$C(\text{graphite}) + O_2(g) \longrightarrow CO_2(g)$$
$$\Delta H^\circ_{\text{rxn}} = -393.5 \text{ kJ/mol}$$
$$H_2(g) + \tfrac{1}{2}O_2(g) \longrightarrow H_2O(l)$$
$$\Delta H^\circ_{\text{rxn}} = -285.8 \text{ kJ/mol}$$
$$2C_2H_6(g) + 7O_2(g) \longrightarrow 4CO_2(g) + 6H_2O(l)$$
$$\Delta H^\circ_{\text{rxn}} = -3119.6 \text{ kJ/mol}$$

calculate the enthalpy change for the reaction

$$2C(\text{graphite}) + 3H_2(g) \longrightarrow C_2H_6(g)$$

6.63 From the following heats of combustion,

$$CH_3OH(l) + \tfrac{3}{2}O_2(g) \longrightarrow CO_2(g) + 2H_2O(l)$$
$$\Delta H^\circ_{\text{rxn}} = -726.4 \text{ kJ/mol}$$
$$C(\text{graphite}) + O_2(g) \longrightarrow CO_2(g)$$
$$\Delta H^\circ_{\text{rxn}} = -393.5 \text{ kJ/mol}$$
$$H_2(g) + \tfrac{1}{2}O_2(g) \longrightarrow H_2O(l)$$
$$\Delta H^\circ_{\text{rxn}} = -285.8 \text{ kJ/mol}$$

calculate the enthalpy of formation of methanol (CH_3OH) from its elements:

$$C(\text{graphite}) + 2H_2(g) + \tfrac{1}{2}O_2(g) \longrightarrow CH_3OH(l)$$

6.64 Calculate the standard enthalpy change for the reaction

$$2Al(s) + Fe_2O_3(s) \longrightarrow 2Fe(s) + Al_2O_3(s)$$

given that

$$2Al(s) + \tfrac{3}{2}O_2(g) \longrightarrow Al_2O_3(s)$$
$$\Delta H^\circ_{\text{rxn}} = -1669.8 \text{ kJ/mol}$$
$$2Fe(s) + \tfrac{3}{2}O_2(g) \longrightarrow Fe_2O_3(s)$$
$$\Delta H^\circ_{\text{rxn}} = -822.2 \text{ kJ/mol}$$

Heat of Solution and Dilution

Review Questions

6.65 Define the following terms: enthalpy of solution, hydration, heat of hydration, lattice energy, heat of dilution.

6.66 Why is the lattice of a solid always a positive quantity? Why is the hydration of ions always a negative quantity?

6.67 Consider two ionic compounds A and B. A has a larger lattice energy than B. Which of the two compounds is more stable?

6.68 Mg^{2+} is a smaller cation than Na^+ and also carries more positive charge. Which of the two species has a larger hydration energy (in kJ/mol)? Explain.

6.69 Consider the dissolution of an ionic compound such as potassium fluoride in water. Break the process into the following steps: separation of the cations and anions in the vapor phase and the hydration of the ions in the aqueous medium. Discuss the energy changes associated with each step. How does the heat of solution of KF depend on the relative magnitudes of these two quantities? On what law is the relationship based?

6.70 Why is it dangerous to add water to a concentrated acid such as sulfuric acid in a dilution process?

Additional Problems

6.71 The convention of arbitrarily assigning a zero enthalpy value for the most stable form of each element in the standard state at 25°C is a convenient way of dealing with enthalpies of reactions. Explain why this convention cannot be applied to nuclear reactions.

6.72 Consider the following two reactions:

$$A \longrightarrow 2B \qquad \Delta H^\circ_{\text{rxn}} = \Delta H_1$$
$$A \longrightarrow C \qquad \Delta H^\circ_{\text{rxn}} = \Delta H_2$$

Determine the enthalpy change for the process

$$2B \longrightarrow C$$

6.73 The standard enthalpy change ΔH° for the thermal decomposition of silver nitrate according to the following equation is +78.67 kJ:

$$AgNO_3(s) \longrightarrow AgNO_2(s) + \tfrac{1}{2}O_2(g)$$

The standard enthalpy of formation of $AgNO_3(s)$ is −123.02 kJ/mol. Calculate the standard enthalpy of formation of $AgNO_2(s)$.

6.74 Hydrazine, N_2H_4, decomposes according to the following reaction:

$$3N_2H_4(l) \longrightarrow 4NH_3(g) + N_2(g)$$

(a) Given that the standard enthalpy of formation of hydrazine is 50.42 kJ/mol, calculate ΔH° for its decomposition. (b) Both hydrazine and ammonia burn in oxygen to produce $H_2O(l)$ and $N_2(g)$. Write balanced equations for each of these processes and calculate ΔH° for each of them. On a mass basis (per kg), would hydrazine or ammonia be the better fuel?

6.75 Consider the reaction

$$N_2(g) + 3H_2(g) \longrightarrow 2NH_3(g)$$
$$\Delta H^\circ_{\text{rxn}} = -92.6 \text{ kJ/mol}$$

If 2.0 moles of N_2 react with 6.0 moles of H_2 to form NH_3, calculate the work done (in joules) against a pressure of 1.0 atm at 25°C. What is ΔE for this reaction? Assume the reaction goes to completion.

6.76 Calculate the heat released when 2.00 L of $Cl_2(g)$ with a density of 1.88 g/L react with an excess of sodium metal at 25°C and 1 atm to form sodium chloride.

6.77 Photosynthesis produces glucose, $C_6H_{12}O_6$, and oxygen from carbon dioxide and water:

$$6CO_2 + 6H_2O \longrightarrow C_6H_{12}O_6 + 6O_2$$

(a) How would you determine experimentally the $\Delta H°_{rxn}$ value for this reaction? (b) Solar radiation produces about 7.0×10^{14} kg glucose a year on Earth. What is the corresponding $\Delta H°$ change?

6.78 A 2.10-mole sample of crystalline acetic acid, initially at 17.0°C, is allowed to melt at 17.0°C and is then heated to 118.1°C (its normal boiling point) at 1.00 atm. The sample is allowed to vaporize at 118.1°C and is then rapidly quenched to 17.0°C, so that it recrystallizes. Calculate $\Delta H°$ for the total process as described.

6.79 Calculate the work done in joules by the reaction

$$2Na(s) + 2H_2O(l) \longrightarrow 2NaOH(aq) + H_2(g)$$

when 0.34 g of Na reacts with water to form hydrogen gas at 0°C and 1.0 atm.

6.80 You are given the following data:

$$H_2(g) \longrightarrow 2H(g) \quad \Delta H° = 436.4 \text{ kJ/mol}$$
$$Br_2(g) \longrightarrow 2Br(g) \quad \Delta H° = 192.5 \text{ kJ/mol}$$
$$H_2(g) + Br_2(g) \longrightarrow 2HBr(g)$$
$$\Delta H° = -72.4 \text{ kJ/mol}$$

Calculate $\Delta H°$ for the reaction

$$H(g) + Br(g) \longrightarrow HBr(g)$$

6.81 Methanol (CH_3OH) is an organic solvent and is also used as a fuel in some automobile engines. From the following data, calculate the standard enthalpy of formation of methanol:

$$2CH_3OH(l) + 3O_2(g) \longrightarrow 2CO_2(g) + 4H_2O(l)$$
$$\Delta H°_{rxn} = -1452.8 \text{ kJ/mol}$$

6.82 A 44.0-g sample of an unknown metal at 99.0°C was placed in a constant-pressure calorimeter containing 80.0 g of water at 24.0°C. The final temperature of the system was found to be 28.4°C. Calculate the specific heat of the metal. (The heat capacity of the calorimeter is 12.4 J/°C.)

6.83 A 1.00-mole sample of ammonia at 14.0 atm and 25°C in a cylinder fitted with a movable piston expands against a constant external pressure of 1.00 atm. At equilibrium, the pressure and volume of the gas are 1.00 atm and 23.5 L, respectively. (a) Calculate the final temperature of the sample. (b) Calculate q, w, and ΔE for the process. The specific heat of ammonia is 0.0258 J/g · °C.

6.84 Producer gas (carbon monoxide) is prepared by passing air over red-hot coke:

$$C(s) + \tfrac{1}{2}O_2(g) \longrightarrow CO(g)$$

Water gas (mixture of carbon monoxide and hydrogen) is prepared by passing steam over red-hot coke:

$$C(s) + H_2O(g) \longrightarrow CO(g) + H_2(g)$$

For many years, both producer gas and water gas were used as fuels in industry and for domestic cooking. The large-scale preparation of these gases was carried out alternately, that is, first producer gas, then water gas, and so on. Using thermochemical reasoning, explain why this procedure was chosen.

6.85 Compare the heat produced by the complete combustion of 1 mole of methane (CH_4) with a mole of water gas (0.50 mole H_2 and 0.50 mole CO) under the same conditions. On the basis of your answer, would you prefer methane over water gas as a fuel? Can you suggest two other reasons why methane is preferable to water gas as a fuel?

6.86 The so-called hydrogen economy is based on hydrogen produced from water using solar energy. The gas is then burned as a fuel:

$$2H_2(g) + O_2(g) \longrightarrow 2H_2O(l)$$

A primary advantage of hydrogen as a fuel is that it is nonpolluting. A major disadvantage is that it is a gas and therefore is harder to store than liquids or solids. Calculate the volume of hydrogen gas at 25°C and 1.00 atm required to produce an amount of energy equivalent to that produced by the combustion of a gallon of octane (C_8H_{18}). The density of octane is 2.66 kg/gal, and its standard enthalpy of formation is −249.9 kJ/mol.

6.87 Ethanol (C_2H_5OH) and gasoline (assumed to be all octane, C_8H_{18}) are both used as automobile fuel. If gasoline is selling for $2.50/gal, what would the price of ethanol have to be in order to provide the same amount of heat per dollar? The density and $\Delta H°_f$ of octane are 0.7025 g/mL and −249.9 kJ/mol and of ethanol are 0.7894 g/mL and −277.0 kJ/mol, respectively. 1 gal = 3.785 L.

6.88 The combustion of what volume of ethane (C_2H_6), measured at 23.0°C and 752 mmHg, would be required to heat 855 g of water from 25.0°C to 98.0°C?

6.89 If energy is conserved, how can there be an energy crisis?

6.90 The heat of vaporization of a liquid (ΔH_{vap}) is the energy required to vaporize 1.00 g of the liquid at its boiling point. In one experiment, 60.0 g of liquid nitrogen (boiling point −196°C) are poured into a Styrofoam cup containing 2.00×10^2 g of water at 55.3°C. Calculate the molar heat of vaporization of liquid nitrogen if the final temperature of the water is 41.0°C.

6.91 Explain the cooling effect experienced when ethanol is rubbed on your skin, given that

$$C_2H_5OH(l) \longrightarrow C_2H_5OH(g) \quad \Delta H° = 42.2 \text{ kJ/mol}$$

6.92 For which of the following reactions does $\Delta H^\circ_{rxn} = \Delta H^\circ_f$?

(a) $H_2(g) + S(\text{rhombic}) \longrightarrow H_2S(g)$

(b) $C(\text{diamond}) + O_2(g) \longrightarrow CO_2(g)$

(c) $H_2(g) + CuO(s) \longrightarrow H_2O(l) + Cu(s)$

(d) $O(g) + O_2(g) \longrightarrow O_3(g)$

6.93 Calculate the work done (in joules) when 1.0 mole of water is frozen at 0°C and 1.0 atm. The volumes of one mole of water and ice at 0°C are 0.0180 L and 0.0196 L, respectively.

6.94 A quantity of 0.020 mole of a gas initially at 0.050 L and 20°C undergoes a constant-temperature expansion until its volume is 0.50 L. Calculate the work done (in joules) by the gas if it expands (a) against a vacuum and (b) against a constant pressure of 0.20 atm. (c) If the gas in (b) is allowed to expand unchecked until its pressure is equal to the external pressure, what would its final volume be before it stopped expanding, and what would be the work done?

6.95 Calculate the standard enthalpy of formation for diamond, given that

$$C(\text{graphite}) + O_2(g) \longrightarrow CO_2(g)$$
$$\Delta H^\circ = -393.5 \text{ kJ/mol}$$
$$C(\text{diamond}) + O_2(g) \longrightarrow CO_2(g)$$
$$\Delta H^\circ = -395.4 \text{ kJ/mol}$$

6.96 (a) For most efficient use, refrigerator freezer compartments should be fully packed with food. What is the thermochemical basis for this recommendation? (b) Starting at the same temperature, tea and coffee remain hot longer in a thermal flask than chicken noodle soup. Explain.

6.97 Calculate the standard enthalpy change for the fermentation process. (See Problem 3.72.)

6.98 Portable hot packs are available for skiers and people engaged in other outdoor activities in a cold climate. The air-permeable paper packet contains a mixture of powdered iron, sodium chloride, and other components, all moistened by a little water. The exothermic reaction that produces the heat is a very common one—the rusting of iron:

$$4Fe(s) + 3O_2(g) \longrightarrow 2Fe_2O_3(s)$$

When the outside plastic envelope is removed, O_2 molecules penetrate the paper, causing the reaction to begin. A typical packet contains 250 g of iron to warm your hands or feet for up to 4 hours. How much heat (in kJ) is produced by this reaction? (*Hint:* See Appendix 3 for ΔH°_f values.)

6.99 A person ate 0.50 pound of cheese (an energy intake of 4000 kJ). Suppose that none of the energy was stored in his body. What mass (in grams) of water would he need to perspire in order to maintain his original temperature? (It takes 44.0 kJ to vaporize 1 mole of water.)

6.100 The total volume of the Pacific Ocean is estimated to be 7.2×10^8 km^3. A medium-sized atomic bomb produces 1.0×10^{15} J of energy upon explosion. Calculate the number of atomic bombs needed to release enough energy to raise the temperature of the water in the Pacific Ocean by 1°C.

6.101 A 19.2-g quantity of dry ice (solid carbon dioxide) is allowed to sublime (evaporate) in an apparatus like the one shown in Figure 6.5. Calculate the expansion work done against a constant external pressure of 0.995 atm and at a constant temperature of 22°C. Assume that the initial volume of dry ice is negligible and that CO_2 behaves like an ideal gas.

6.102 The enthalpy of combustion of benzoic acid (C_6H_5COOH) is commonly used as the standard for calibrating constant-volume bomb calorimeters; its value has been accurately determined to be −3226.7 kJ/mol. When 1.9862 g of benzoic acid are burned in a calorimeter, the temperature rises from 21.84°C to 25.67°C. What is the heat capacity of the bomb? (Assume that the quantity of water surrounding the bomb is exactly 2000 g.)

6.103 The combustion of a 25.0-g gaseous mixture of H_2 and CH_4 releases 2354 kJ of heat. Calculate the amounts of the gases in grams.

6.104 Calcium oxide (CaO) is used to remove sulfur dioxide generated by coal-burning power stations:

$$2CaO(s) + 2SO_2(g) + O_2(g) \longrightarrow 2CaSO_4(s)$$

Calculate the enthalpy change for this process if 6.6×10^5 g of SO_2 are removed by this process every day.

6.105 Glauber's salt, sodium sulfate decahydrate ($Na_2SO_4 \cdot 10H_2O$), undergoes a phase transition (that is, melting or freezing) at a convenient temperature of about 32°C:

$$Na_2SO_4 \cdot 10H_2O(s) \longrightarrow Na_2SO_4 \cdot 10H_2O(l)$$
$$\Delta H^\circ = 74.4 \text{ kJ/mol}$$

As a result, this compound is used to regulate the temperature in homes. It is placed in plastic bags in the ceiling of a room. During the day, the endothermic melting process absorbs heat from the surroundings, cooling the room. At night, it gives off heat as it freezes. Calculate the mass of Glauber's salt in kilograms needed to lower the temperature of air in a room by 8.2°C at 1.0 atm. The dimensions of the room are 2.80 m × 10.6 m × 17.2 m, the specific heat of air is 1.2 J/g · °C, and the molar mass of air may be taken as 29.0 g/mol.

6.106 A balloon 16 m in diameter is inflated with helium at 18°C. (a) Calculate the mass of He in the balloon, assuming ideal behavior. (b) Calculate the work done (in joules) during the inflation process if the atmospheric pressure is 98.7 kPa.

6.107 An excess of zinc metal is added to 50.0 mL of a 0.100 *M* AgNO$_3$ solution in a constant-pressure calorimeter like the one pictured in Figure 6.9. As a result of the reaction

$$Zn(s) + 2Ag^+(aq) \longrightarrow Zn^{2+}(aq) + 2Ag(s)$$

the temperature rises from 19.25°C to 22.17°C. If the heat capacity of the calorimeter is 98.6 J/°C, calculate the enthalpy change for the above reaction on a molar basis. Assume that the density and specific heat of the solution are the same as those for water, and ignore the specific heats of the metals.

6.108 (a) A person drinks four glasses of cold water (3.0°C) every day. The volume of each glass is 2.5×10^2 mL. How much heat (in kJ) does the body have to supply to raise the temperature of the water to 37°C, the body temperature? (b) How much heat would your body lose if you were to ingest 8.0×10^2 g of snow at 0°C to quench thirst? (The amount of heat necessary to melt snow is 6.01 kJ/mol.)

6.109 A driver's manual states that the stopping distance quadruples as the speed doubles; that is, if it takes 30 ft to stop a car moving at 25 mph then it would take 120 ft to stop a car moving at 50 mph. Justify this statement by using mechanics and the first law of thermodynamics. [Assume that when a car is stopped, its kinetic energy ($\frac{1}{2}mu^2$) is totally converted to heat.]

6.110 At 25°C, the standard enthalpy of formation of HF(*aq*) is given by −320.1 kJ/mol; of OH⁻(*aq*), it is −229.6 kJ/mol; of F⁻(*aq*), it is −329.1 kJ/mol; and of H$_2$O(*l*), it is −285.8 kJ/mol.

(a) Calculate the standard enthalpy of neutralization of HF(*aq*):

$$HF(aq) + OH^-(aq) \longrightarrow F^-(aq) + H_2O(l)$$

(b) Using the value of −56.2 kJ as the standard enthalpy change for the reaction

$$H^+(aq) + OH^-(aq) \longrightarrow H_2O(l)$$

calculate the standard enthalpy change for the reaction

$$HF(aq) \longrightarrow H^+(aq) + F^-(aq)$$

6.111 Why are cold, damp air and hot, humid air more uncomfortable than dry air at the same temperatures? (The specific heats of water vapor and air are approximately 1.9 J/g · °C and 1.0 J/g · °C, respectively.)

6.112 From the enthalpy of formation for CO$_2$ and the following information, calculate the standard enthalpy of formation for carbon monoxide (CO).

$$CO(g) + \tfrac{1}{2}O_2(g) \longrightarrow CO_2(g)$$
$$\Delta H° = -283.0 \text{ kJ/mol}$$

Why can't we obtain it directly by measuring the enthalpy of the following reaction?

$$C(graphite) + \tfrac{1}{2}O_2(g) \longrightarrow CO(g)$$

6.113 A 46-kg person drinks 500 g of milk, which has a "caloric" value of approximately 3.0 kJ/g. If only 17 percent of the energy in milk is converted to mechanical work, how high (in meters) can the person climb based on this energy intake? [*Hint:* The work done in ascending is given by *mgh*, where *m* is the mass (in kilograms), *g* the gravitational acceleration (9.8 m/s²), and *h* the height (in meters).]

6.114 The height of Niagara Falls on the American side is 51 m. (a) Calculate the potential energy of 1.0 g of water at the top of the falls relative to the ground level. (b) What is the speed of the falling water if all of the potential energy is converted to kinetic energy? (c) What would be the increase in temperature of the water if all the kinetic energy were converted to heat? (See Problem 6.113 for suggestions.)

6.115 In the nineteenth century two scientists named Dulong and Petit noticed that for a solid element, the product of its molar mass and its specific heat is approximately 25 J/°C. This observation, now called Dulong and Petit's law, was used to estimate the specific heat of metals. Verify the law for the metals listed in Table 6.2. The law does not apply to one of the metals. Which one is it? Why?

6.116 Determine the standard enthalpy of formation of ethanol (C$_2$H$_5$OH) from its standard enthalpy of combustion (−1367.4 kJ/mol).

6.117 Acetylene (C$_2$H$_2$) and benzene (C$_6$H$_6$) have the same empirical formula. In fact, benzene can be made from acetylene as follows:

$$3C_2H_2(g) \longrightarrow C_6H_6(l)$$

The enthalpies of combustion for C$_2$H$_2$ and C$_6$H$_6$ are −1299.4 kJ/mol and −3267.4 kJ/mol, respectively. Calculate the standard enthalpies of formation of C$_2$H$_2$ and C$_6$H$_6$ and hence the enthalpy change for the formation of C$_6$H$_6$ from C$_2$H$_2$.

6.118 Ice at 0°C is placed in a Styrofoam cup containing 361 g of a soft drink at 23°C. The specific heat of the drink is about the same as that of water. Some ice remains after the ice and soft drink reach an equilibrium temperature of 0°C. Determine the mass of ice that has melted. Ignore the heat capacity of the cup. (*Hint:* It takes 334 J to melt 1 g of ice at 0°C.)

6.119 A gas company in Massachusetts charges $1.30 for 15 ft³ of natural gas (CH$_4$) measured at 20°C and 1.0 atm. Calculate the cost of heating 200 mL of water (enough to make a cup of coffee or tea) from 20°C to 100°C. Assume that only 50 percent of the heat generated by the combustion is used to heat the water; the rest of the heat is lost to the surroundings.

6.120 Calculate the internal energy of a Goodyear blimp filled with helium gas at 1.2×10^5 Pa. The volume of the blimp is 5.5×10^3 m³. If all the energy were used to heat 10.0 tons of copper at 21°C, calculate the final temperature of the metal. (*Hint:* See Section 5.7 for help in calculating the internal energy of a gas. 1 ton = 9.072×10^5 g.)

6.121 Decomposition reactions are usually endothermic, whereas combination reactions are usually exothermic. Give a qualitative explanation for these trends.

6.122 Acetylene (C_2H_2) can be made by reacting calcium carbide (CaC_2) with water. (a) Write an equation for the reaction. (b) What is the maximum amount of heat (in joules) that can be obtained from the combustion of acetylene, starting with 74.6 g of CaC_2?

6.123 The average temperature in deserts is high during the day but quite cool at night, whereas that in regions along the coastline is more moderate. Explain.

6.124 When 1.034 g of naphthalene ($C_{10}H_8$) are burned in a constant-volume bomb calorimeter at 298 K, 41.56 kJ of heat are evolved. Calculate ΔE and ΔH for the reaction on a molar basis.

6.125 From a thermochemical point of view, explain why a carbon dioxide fire extinguisher or water should not be used on a magnesium fire.

Special Problems

6.126 Calculate the ΔE for the following reaction at 298 K

$$2H_2(g) + O_2(g) \longrightarrow 2H_2O(l)$$

6.127 Lime is a term that includes calcium oxide (CaO, also called quicklime) and calcium hydroxide [$Ca(OH)_2$, also called slaked lime]. It is used in the steel industry to remove acidic impurities, in air-pollution control to remove acidic oxides such as SO_2, and in water treatment. Quicklime is made industrially by heating limestone ($CaCO_3$) above 2000°C:

$$CaCO_3(s) \longrightarrow CaO(s) + CO_2(g)$$
$$\Delta H° = 177.8 \text{ kJ/mol}$$

Slaked lime is produced by treating quicklime with water:

$$CaO(s) + H_2O(l) \longrightarrow Ca(OH)_2(s)$$
$$\Delta H° = -65.2 \text{ kJ/mol}$$

The exothermic reaction of quicklime with water and the rather small specific heats of both quicklime (0.946 J/g · °C) and slaked lime (1.20 J/g · °C) make it hazardous to store and transport lime in vessels made of wood. Wooden sailing ships carrying lime would occasionally catch fire when water leaked into the hold. (a) If a 500-g sample of water reacts with an equimolar amount of CaO (both at an initial temperature of 25°C), what is the final temperature of the product, $Ca(OH)_2$? Assume that the product absorbs all of the heat released in the reaction. (b) Given that the standard enthalpies of formation of CaO and H_2O are -635.6 kJ/mol and -285.8 kJ/mol, respectively, calculate the standard enthalpy of formation of $Ca(OH)_2$.

6.128 A 4.117-g impure sample of glucose ($C_6H_{12}O_6$) was burned in a constant-volume calorimeter having a heat capacity of 19.65 kJ/°C. If the rise in temperature is

3.134°C, calculate the percent by mass of the glucose in the sample. Assume that the impurities are unaffected by the combustion process. See Appendix 3 for thermodynamic data.

6.129 Construct a table with the headings q, w, ΔE, and ΔH. For each of the following processes, deduce whether each of the quantities listed is positive (+), negative ($-$), or zero (0). (a) Freezing of benzene. (b) Compression of an ideal gas at constant temperature. (c) Reaction of sodium with water. (d) Boiling liquid ammonia, (e) Heating a gas at constant volume. (f) Melting of ice.

6.130 The combustion of 0.4196 g of a hydrocarbon releases 17.55 kJ of heat. The masses of the products are $CO_2 = 1.419$ g and $H_2O = 0.290$ g. (a) What is the empirical formula of the compound? (b) If the approximate molar mass of the compound is 76 g, calculate its standard enthalpy of formation.

6.131 Metabolic activity in the human body releases approximately 1.0×10^4 kJ of heat per day. Assuming the body is 50 kg of water, how much would the body temperature rise if it were an isolated system? How much water must the body eliminate as perspiration to maintain the normal body temperature (98.6°F)? Comment on your results. The heat of vaporization of water may be taken as 2.41 kJ/g.

6.132 From the following data, calculate the heat of solution for KI:

	NaCl	NaI	KCl	KI
Lattice energy (kJ/mol)	788	686	699	632
Heat of solution (kJ/mol)	4.0	-5.1	17.2	?

6.133 Starting at A, an ideal gas undergoes a cyclic process involving expansion and compression at constant temperature, as shown here. Calculate the total work done. Does your result support the notion that work is not a state function?

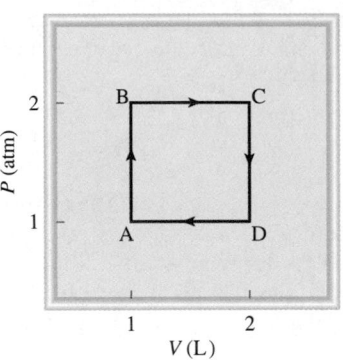

Answers to Practice Exercises

6.1 (a) 0, (b) -286 J. **6.2** -63 J. **6.3** -6.47×10^3 kJ.
6.4 -111.7 kJ/mol. **6.5** -34.3 kJ. **6.6** -728 kJ/mol.
6.7 $21.19°C$. **6.8** $22.49°C$. **6.9** 87.3 kJ/mol.
6.10 -41.83 kJ/g.

CHEMICAL
Mystery

The Exploding Tire†

It was supposed to be a routine job: Fix the flat tire on Harvey Smith's car. The owner of Tom's Garage, Tom Lee, gave the tire to Jerry to work on, while he went outside to pump gas. A few minutes later, Tom heard a loud bang. He rushed inside to find the tire blown to pieces, a wall collapsed, equipment damaged, and Jerry lying on the floor, unconscious and bleeding. Luckily Jerry's injury was not serious. As he lay in the hospital recovering, the mystery of the exploding tire unfolded.

The tire had gone flat when Harvey drove over a nail. Being a cautious driver, Harvey carried a can of instant tire repair in the car, so he was able to reinflate the tire and drive safely home. The can of tire repair Harvey used contained latex (natural rubber) dissolved in a liquid propellant, which is a mixture of propane (C_3H_8) and butane (C_4H_{10}). Propane and butane are gases under atmospheric conditions but exist as liquids under compression in the can. When the valve on the top of the can is pressed, it opens, releasing the pressure inside. The mixture boils, forming a latex foam which is propelled by the gases into the tire to seal the puncture while the gas reinflates the tire.

The pressure in a flat tire is approximately one atmosphere, or roughly 15 pounds per square inch (psi). Using the aerosol tire repair, Harvey reinflated his damaged tire to a pressure of 35 psi. This is called the gauge pressure, which is the pressure of the tire *above* the atmospheric pressure. Thus, the total pressure in the tire was actually (15 + 35) psi, or 50 psi. One problem with using natural gases like propane and butane as propellants is that they are highly flammable. In fact, these gases can react explosively when mixed with air at a concentration of 2 percent to 9 percent by volume. Jerry was aware of the hazards of repairing Harvey's tire and look precautions to avoid an accident. First he let out the excess gas in the tire. Next he reinflated the tire to 35 psi with air. And he repeated the procedure once. Clearly, this is a dilution process intended to gradually decrease the concentrations of propane and butane. The fact that the tire exploded means that Jerry had not diluted the gases enough. But what was the source of ignition?

When Jerry found the nail hole in the tire, he used a tire reamer, a metal file-like instrument, to clean dirt and loose rubber from the hole before applying a rubber plug and liquid sealant. The last thing Jerry remembered was pulling the reamer out of the hole. The next thing he knew he was lying in the hospital, hurting all over. To solve this mystery, make use of the following clues.

---

†Adapted with permission from "The Exploding Tire," by Jay A. Young, CHEM MATTERS, April, 1988, p. 12. Copyright 1995 American Chemical Society.

Chemical Clues

1. Write balanced equations for the combustion of propane and butane. The products are carbon dioxide and water.

2. When Harvey inflated his flat tire to 35 psi, the composition by volume of the propane and butane gases is given by (35 psi/50 psi) × 100%, or 70 percent. When Jerry deflated the tire the first time, the pressure fell to 15 psi but the composition remained at 70 percent. Based on these facts, calculate the percent composition of propane and butane at the end of two deflation-inflation steps. Does it fall within the explosive range?

3. Given that Harvey's flat tire is a steel-belted tire, explain how the ignition of the gas mixture might have been triggered. (A steel-belted tire has two belts of steel wire for outer reinforcement and two belts of polyester cord for inner reinforcement.)

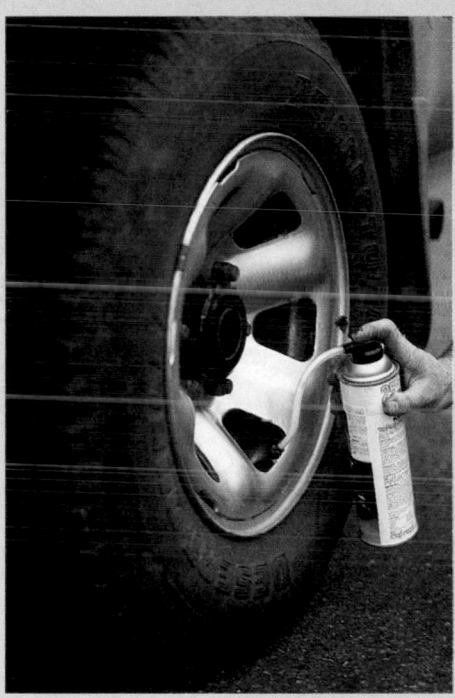

Instant flat tire repair.

7

Quantum Theory and the Electronic Structure of Atoms

A LOOK AHEAD

- We begin by discussing the transition from classical physics to quantum theory. In particular, we become familiar with properties of waves and electromagnetic radiation and Planck's formulation of the quantum theory. (7.1)

- Einstein's explanation of the photoelectric effect is another step toward the development of the quantum theory. To explain experimental observations, Einstein suggested that light behaves like a bundle of particles called photons. (7.2)

- We then study Bohr's theory for the emission spectrum of the hydrogen atom. In particular, Bohr postulated that the energies of an electron in the atom are quantized and transitions from higher levels to lower ones account for the emission lines. (7.3)

- Some of the mysteries of Bohr's theory are explained by de Broglie, who suggested that electrons can behave like waves. (7.4)

- We see that the early ideas of quantum theory led to a new era in physics called quantum mechanics. The Heisenberg uncertainty principle sets the limits for measurement of quantum mechanical systems. The Schrödinger wave equation describes the behavior of electrons in atoms and molecules. (7.5)

- We learn that there are four quantum numbers to describe an electron in an atom and the characteristics of orbitals in which the electrons reside. (7.6 and 7.7)

- Electron configuration enables us to keep track of the distribution of electrons in an atom and understand its magnetic properties. (7.8)

- Finally, we apply the rules in writing electron configurations to the entire periodic table. In particular, we group elements according to their outer electron configurations. (7.9)

Interactive Activity Summary

1. Interactivity: Wavelength, Frequency, Amplitude (7.1)
2. Animation: Emission Spectra (7.3)
3. Interactivity: Orbital Shapes and Energy (7.7)
4. Animation: Electron Configurations (7.8)
5. Interactivity: Pauli Exclusion Principle (7.8)
6. Interactivity: Orbital Filling Rules (7.8)

Quantum theory enables us to predict and understand the critical role that electrons play in chemistry. In one sense, studying atoms amounts to asking the following questions:

1. How many electrons are present in a particular atom?
2. What energies do individual electrons possess?
3. Where in the atom can electrons be found?

The answers to these questions have a direct relationship to the behavior of all substances in chemical reactions, and the story of the search for answers provides a fascinating backdrop for our discussion.

7.1 From Classical Physics to Quantum Theory

Early attempts by nineteenth-century physicists to understand atoms and molecules met with only limited success. By assuming that molecules behave like rebounding balls, physicists were able to predict and explain some macroscopic phenomena, such as the pressure exerted by a gas. However, this model did not account for the stability of molecules; that is, it could not explain the forces that hold atoms together. It took a long time to realize—and an even longer time to accept—that the properties of atoms and molecules are *not* governed by the same physical laws as larger objects.

The new era in physics started in 1900 with a young German physicist named Max Planck.[†] While analyzing the data on radiation emitted by solids heated to various temperatures, Planck discovered that atoms and molecules emit energy only in certain discrete quantities, or *quanta*. Physicists had always assumed that energy is continuous and that any amount of energy could be released in a radiation process. Planck's *quantum theory* turned physics upside down. Indeed, the flurry of research that ensued altered our concept of nature forever.

Figure 7.1 *Ocean water waves.*

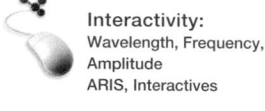

Interactivity:
Wavelength, Frequency,
Amplitude
ARIS, Interactives

Properties of Waves

To understand Planck's quantum theory, we must know something about the nature of waves. A **wave** can be thought of as *a vibrating disturbance by which energy is transmitted*. The fundamental properties of a wave are illustrated by a familiar type—water waves. (Figure 7.1). The regular variation of the peaks and troughs enable us to sense the propagation of the waves.

Waves are characterized by their length and height and by the number of waves that pass through a certain point in one second (Figure 7.2). **Wavelength λ** (lambda) is *the distance between identical points on successive waves*. The **frequency ν** (nu) is *the number of waves that pass through a particular point in 1 second*. **Amplitude** is *the vertical distance from the midline of a wave to the peak or trough*.

[†]Max Karl Ernst Ludwig Planck (1858–1947). German physicist. Planck received the Nobel Prize in Physics in 1918 for his quantum theory. He also made significant contributions in thermodynamics and other areas of physics.

(a)

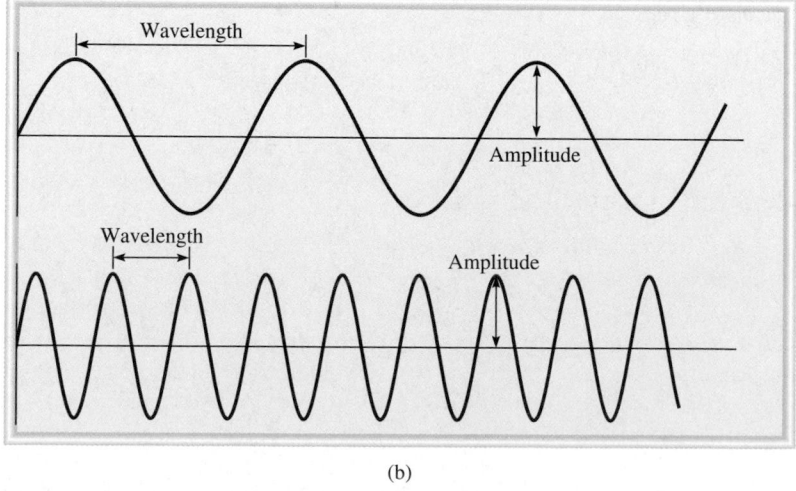

(b)

Figure 7.2 *(a) Wavelength and amplitude. (b) Two waves having different wavelengths and frequencies. The wavelength of the top wave is three times that of the lower wave, but its frequency is only one-third that of the lower wave. Both waves have the same speed and amplitude.*

Another important property of waves is their speed, which depends on the type of wave and the nature of the medium through which the wave is traveling (for example, air, water, or a vacuum). The speed (u) of a wave is the product of its wavelength and its frequency:

$$u = \lambda \nu \tag{7.1}$$

The inherent "sensibility" of Equation (7.1) becomes apparent if we analyze the physical dimensions involved in the three terms. The wavelength (λ) expresses the length of a wave, or distance/wave. The frequency (ν) indicates the number of these waves that pass any reference point per unit of time, or waves/time. Thus, the product of these terms results in dimensions of distance/time, which is speed:

$$\frac{\text{distance}}{\text{time}} = \frac{\text{distance}}{\cancel{\text{wave}}} \times \frac{\cancel{\text{waves}}}{\text{time}}$$

Wavelength is usually expressed in units of meters, centimeters, or nanometers, and frequency is measured in hertz (Hz), where

$$1 \text{ Hz} = 1 \text{ cycle/s}$$

The word "cycle" may be left out and the frequency expressed as, for example, 25/s or 25 s^{-1} (read as "25 per second").

Example 7.1

Calculate the speed of a wave whose wavelength and frequency are 17.4 cm and 87.4 Hz, respectively.

Solution Recall that 87.4 Hz is the same as 87.4/s. From Equation (7.1),

$$
\begin{aligned}
u &= \lambda \nu \\
&= 17.4 \text{ cm} \times 87.4 \text{ Hz} \\
&= 17.4 \text{ cm} \times 87.4/\text{s} \\
&= 1.52 \times 10^3 \text{ cm/s}
\end{aligned}
$$

Similar problem: 7.8.

Practice Exercise Calculate the frequency (in Hz) of a wave whose speed and wavelength are 713 m/s and 1.14 m, respectively.

Electromagnetic Radiation

There are many kinds of waves, such as water waves, sound waves, and light waves. In 1873 James Clerk Maxwell proposed that visible light consists of electromagnetic waves. According to Maxwell's theory, an ***electromagnetic wave** has an electric field component and a magnetic field component.* These two components have the same wavelength and frequency, and hence the same speed, but they travel in mutually perpendicular planes (Figure 7.3). The significance of Maxwell's theory is that it provides a mathematical description of the general behavior of light. In particular, his model accurately describes how energy in the form of radiation can be propagated through space as vibrating electric and magnetic fields. ***Electromagnetic radiation** is the emission and transmission of energy in the form of electromagnetic waves.*

Sound waves and water waves are not electromagnetic waves, but X rays and radio waves are.

Figure 7.3 *The electric field and magnetic field components of an electromagnetic wave. These two components have the same wavelength, frequency, and amplitude, but they vibrate in two mutually perpendicular planes.*

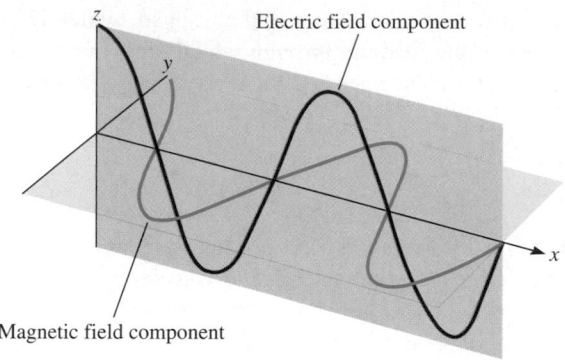

Electric field component

Magnetic field component

A more accurate value for the speed of light is given on the inside back cover of the book.

Electromagnetic waves travel 3.00×10^8 meters per second (rounded off), or 186,000 miles per second in a vacuum. This speed does differ from one medium to another, but not enough to distort our calculations significantly. By convention, we use the symbol c for the speed of electromagnetic waves, or as it is more commonly called, the *speed of light*. The wavelength of electromagnetic waves is usually given in nanometers (nm).

Example 7.2

The wavelength of the green light from a traffic signal is centered at 522 nm. What is the frequency of this radiation?

Strategy We are given the wavelength of an electromagnetic wave and asked to calculate its frequency. Rearranging Equation (7.1) and replacing u with c (the speed of light) gives

$$\nu = \frac{c}{\lambda}$$

Solution Because the speed of light is given in meters per second, it is convenient to first convert wavelength to meters. Recall that $1 \text{ nm} = 1 \times 10^{-9}$ m (see Table 1.3). We write

$$\lambda = 522 \text{ nm} \times \frac{1 \times 10^{-9} \text{ m}}{1 \text{ nm}} = 522 \times 10^{-9} \text{ m}$$

$$= 5.22 \times 10^{-7} \text{ m}$$

Substituting in the wavelength and the speed of light (3.00×10^8 m/s), the frequency is

$$\nu = \frac{3.00 \times 10^8 \text{ m/s}}{5.22 \times 10^{-7} \text{ m}}$$

$$= 5.75 \times 10^{14}/\text{s, or } 5.75 \times 10^{14} \text{ Hz}$$

Check The answer shows that 5.75×10^{14} waves pass a fixed point every second. This very high frequency is in accordance with the very high speed of light.

Similar problem: 7.7.

Practice Exercise What is the wavelength (in meters) of an electromagnetic wave whose frequency is 3.64×10^7 Hz?

Figure 7.4 shows various types of electromagnetic radiation, which differ from one another in wavelength and frequency. The long radio waves are emitted by large antennas, such as those used by broadcasting stations. The shorter, visible light waves

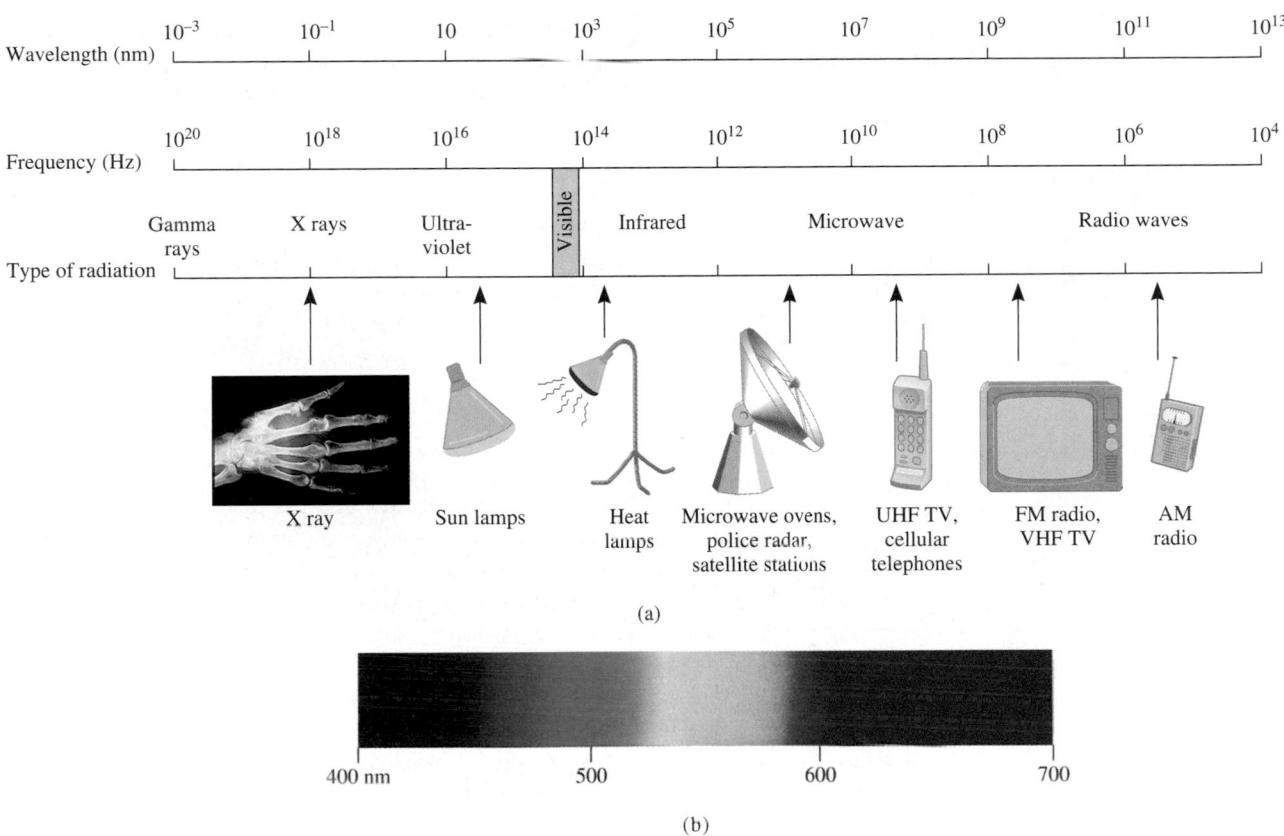

Figure 7.4 *(a) Types of electromagnetic radiation. Gamma rays have the shortest wavelength and highest frequency; radio waves have the longest wavelength and the lowest frequency. Each type of radiation is spread over a specific range of wavelengths (and frequencies). (b) Visible light ranges from a wavelength of 400 nm (violet) to 700 nm (red).*

are produced by the motions of electrons within atoms and molecules. The shortest waves, which also have the highest frequency, are associated with γ (gamma) rays, which result from changes within the nucleus of the atom (see Chapter 2). As we will see shortly, the higher the frequency, the more energetic the radiation. Thus, ultraviolet radiation, X rays, and γ rays are high-energy radiation.

Planck's Quantum Theory

When solids are heated, they emit electromagnetic radiation over a wide range of wavelengths. The dull red glow of an electric heater and the bright white light of a tungsten lightbulb are examples of radiation from heated solids.

Measurements taken in the latter part of the nineteenth century showed that the amount of radiation energy emitted by an object at a certain temperature depends on its wavelength. Attempts to account for this dependence in terms of established wave theory and thermodynamic laws were only partially successful. One theory explained short-wavelength dependence but failed to account for the longer wavelengths. Another theory accounted for the longer wavelengths but failed for short wavelengths. It seemed that something fundamental was missing from the laws of classical physics.

Planck solved the problem with an assumption that departed drastically from accepted concepts. Classical physics assumed that atoms and molecules could emit (or absorb) any arbitrary amount of radiant energy. Planck said that atoms and molecules

Incident
light

Metal

+   −

Voltage
source

Meter

Figure 7.5 *An apparatus for studying the photoelectric effect. Light of a certain frequency falls on a clean metal surface. Ejected electrons are attracted toward the positive electrode. The flow of electrons is registered by a detecting meter. Light meters used in cameras are based on photoelectric effect.*

could emit (or absorb) energy only in discrete quantities, like small packages or bundles. Planck gave the name ***quantum*** to *the smallest quantity of energy that can be emitted (or absorbed) in the form of electromagnetic radiation.* The energy E of a single quantum of energy is given by

$$E = h\nu \tag{7.2}$$

where h is called *Planck's constant* and ν is the frequency of radiation. The value of Planck's constant is 6.63×10^{-34} J · s. Because $\nu = c/\lambda$, Equation (7.2) can also be expressed as

$$E = h\frac{c}{\lambda} \tag{7.3}$$

According to quantum theory, energy is always emitted in multiples of $h\nu$; for example, $h\nu$, $2\,h\nu$, $3\,h\nu$, . . . , but never, for example, $1.67\,h\nu$ or $4.98\,h\nu$. At the time Planck presented his theory, he could not explain why energies should be fixed or quantized in this manner. Starting with this hypothesis, however, he had no trouble correlating the experimental data for emission by solids over the *entire* range of wavelengths; they all supported the quantum theory.

The idea that energy should be quantized or "bundled" may seem strange, but the concept of quantization has many analogies. For example, an electric charge is also quantized; there can be only whole-number multiples of e, the charge of one electron. Matter itself is quantized, for the numbers of electrons, protons, and neutrons and the numbers of atoms in a sample of matter must also be integers. Our money system is based on a "quantum" of value called a penny. Even processes in living systems involve quantized phenomena. The eggs laid by hens are quantized, and a pregnant cat gives birth to an integral number of kittens, not to one-half or three-quarters of a kitten.

7.2 The Photoelectric Effect

In 1905, only five years after Planck presented his quantum theory, Albert Einstein[†] used the theory to solve another mystery in physics, the ***photoelectric effect,*** a phenomenon in which *electrons are ejected from the surface of certain metals exposed to light of at least a certain minimum frequency,* called *the threshold frequency* (Figure 7.5). The number of electrons ejected was proportional to the intensity (or brightness) of the light, but the energies of the ejected electrons were not. Below the threshold frequency no electrons were ejected no matter how intense the light.

The photoelectric effect could not be explained by the wave theory of light. Einstein, however, made an extraordinary assumption. He suggested that a beam of light is really a stream of particles. These *particles of light* are now called ***photons.*** Using Planck's quantum theory of radiation as a starting point, Einstein deduced that each photon must possess energy E, given by the equation

$$E = h\nu$$

This equation has the same form as Equation (7.2) because, as we will see shortly, electromagnetic radiation is emitted as well as absorbed in the form of photons.

[†]Albert Einstein (1879–1955). German-born American physicist. Regarded by many as one of the two greatest physicists the world has known (the other is Isaac Newton). The three papers (on special relativity, Brownian motion, and the photoelectric effect) that he published in 1905 while employed as a technical assistant in the Swiss patent office in Berne have profoundly influenced the development of physics. He received the Nobel Prize in Physics in 1921 for his explanation of the photoelectric effect.

where ν is the frequency of light. Electrons are held in a metal by attractive forces, and so removing them from the metal requires light of a sufficiently high frequency (which corresponds to sufficiently high energy) to break them free. Shining a beam of light onto a metal surface can be thought of as shooting a beam of particles—photons—at the metal atoms. If the frequency of photons is such that $h\nu$ is exactly equal to the energy that binds the electrons in the metal, then the light will have just enough energy to knock the electrons loose. If we use light of a higher frequency, then not only will the electrons be knocked loose, but they will also acquire some kinetic energy. This situation is summarized by the equation

$$h\nu = \text{KE} + \text{BE} \qquad (7.4)$$

where KE is the kinetic energy of the ejected electron and BE is the binding energy of the electron in the metal. Rewriting Equation (7.4) as

$$\text{KE} = h\nu - \text{BE}$$

shows that the more energetic the photon (that is, the higher its frequency), the greater the kinetic energy of the ejected electron.

Now consider two beams of light having the same frequency (which is greater than the threshold frequency) but different intensities. The more intense beam of light consists of a larger number of photons; consequently, it ejects more electrons from the metal's surface than the weaker beam of light. Thus, the more intense the light, the greater the number of electrons emitted by the target metal; the higher the frequency of the light, the greater the kinetic energy of the ejected electrons.

Example 7.3

Calculate the energy (in joules) of (a) a photon with a wavelength of 5.00×10^4 nm (infrared region) and (b) a photon with a wavelength of 5.00×10^{-2} nm (X ray region).

Strategy In both (a) and (b) we are given the wavelength of a photon and asked to calculate its energy. We need to use Equation (7.3) to calculate the energy. Planck's constant is given in the text and also on the back inside cover.

Solution (a) From Equation (7.3),

$$E = h\frac{c}{\lambda}$$
$$= \frac{(6.63 \times 10^{-34}\,\text{J} \cdot \text{s})(3.00 \times 10^8\,\text{m/s})}{(5.00 \times 10^4\,\text{nm})\dfrac{1 \times 10^{-9}\,\text{m}}{1\,\text{nm}}}$$
$$= 3.98 \times 10^{-21}\,\text{J}$$

This is the energy of a single photon with a 5.00×10^4 nm wavelength.

(b) Following the same procedure as in (a), we can show that the energy of the photon that has a wavelength of 5.00×10^{-2} nm is 3.98×10^{-15} J .

Check Because the energy of a photon increases with decreasing wavelength, we see that an "X-ray" photon is 1×10^6, or a million times, more energetic than an "infrared" photon.

Similar problem: 7.15.

Practice Exercise The energy of a photon is 5.87×10^{-20} J. What is its wavelength (in nanometers)?

Einstein's theory of light posed a dilemma for scientists. On the one hand, it explains the photoelectric effect satisfactorily. On the other hand, the particle theory of light is not consistent with the known wave behavior of light. The only way to resolve the dilemma is to accept the idea that light possesses *both* particlelike and wavelike properties. Depending on the experiment, light behaves either as a wave or as a stream of particles. This concept, called particle-wave duality, was totally alien to the way physicists had thought about matter and radiation, and it took a long time for them to accept it. We will see in Section 7.4 that a dual nature (particles and waves) is not unique to light but is characteristic of all matter, including electrons.

7.3 Bohr's Theory of the Hydrogen Atom

Einstein's work paved the way for the solution of yet another nineteenth-century "mystery" in physics: the emission spectra of atoms.

Emission Spectra

Animation:
Emission Spectra
ARIS, Animations

Ever since the seventeenth century, when Newton showed that sunlight is composed of various color components that can be recombined to produce white light, chemists and physicists have studied the characteristics of **emission spectra,** that is, *either continuous or line spectra of radiation emitted by substances.* The emission spectrum of a substance can be seen by energizing a sample of material either with thermal energy or with some other form of energy (such as a high-voltage electrical discharge). A "red-hot" or "white-hot" iron bar freshly removed from a high-temperature source produces a characteristic glow. This visible glow is the portion of its emission spectrum that is sensed by eye. The warmth of the same iron bar represents another portion of its emission spectrum—the infrared region. A feature common to the emission spectra of the sun and of a heated solid is that both are continuous; that is, all wavelengths of visible light are represented in the spectra (see the visible region in Figure 7.4).

The emission spectra of atoms in the gas phase, on the other hand, do not show a continuous spread of wavelengths from red to violet; rather, the atoms produce bright lines in different parts of the visible spectrum. These **line spectra** are *the light emission only at specific wavelengths.* Figure 7.6 is a schematic diagram of a discharge tube that is used to study emission spectra, and Figure 7.7 shows the color emitted by hydrogen atoms in a discharge tube.

Every element has a unique emission spectrum. The characteristic lines in atomic spectra can be used in chemical analysis to identify unknown atoms, much as fingerprints are used to identify people. When the lines of the emission spectrum of a known element exactly match the lines of the emission spectrum of an unknown sample, the identity of the sample is established. Although the utility of this procedure was recognized some time ago in chemical analysis, the origin of these lines was unknown until early in the twentieth century. Figure 7.8 on p. 276 shows the emission spectra of several elements.

Emission Spectrum of the Hydrogen Atom

In 1913, not too long after Planck's and Einstein's discoveries, a theoretical explanation of the emission spectrum of the hydrogen atom was presented by the Danish physicist Niels Bohr.[†] Bohr's treatment is very complex and is no longer considered

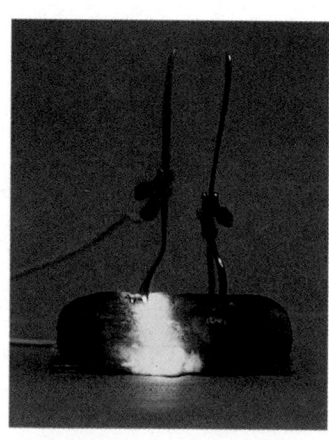

When a high voltage is applied between the forks, some of the sodium ions in the pickle are converted to sodium atoms in an excited state. These atoms emit the characteristic yellow light as they relax to the ground state.

[†]Niels Henrik David Bohr (1885–1962). Danish physicist. One of the founders of modern physics, he received the Nobel Prize in Physics in 1922 for his theory explaining the spectrum of the hydrogen atom.

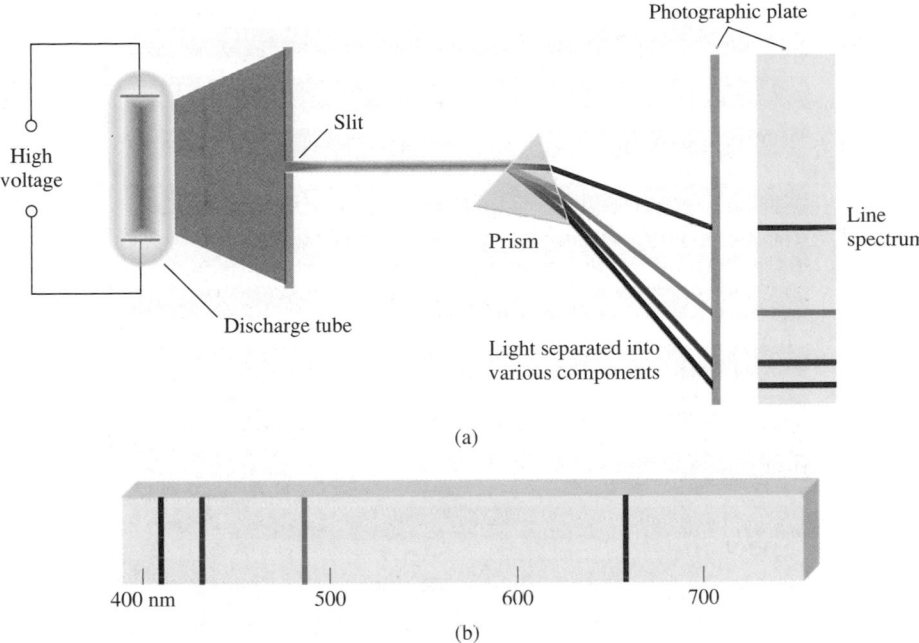

(a)

(b)

400 nm   500   600   700

Figure 7.6 *(a) An experimental arrangement for studying the emission spectra of atoms and molecules. The gas under study is in a discharge tube containing two electrodes. As electrons flow from the negative electrode to the positive electrode, they collide with the gas. This collision process eventually leads to the emission of light by the atoms (or molecules). The emitted light is separated into its components by a prism. Each component color is focused at a definite position, according to its wavelength, and forms a colored image of the slit on the photographic plate. The colored images are called spectral lines. (b) The line emission spectrum of hydrogen atoms.*

to be correct in all its details. Thus, we will concentrate only on his important assumptions and final results, which do account for the spectral lines.

When Bohr first tackled this problem, physicists already knew that the atom contains electrons and protons. They thought of an atom as an entity in which electrons whirled around the nucleus in circular orbits at high velocities. This was an appealing model because it resembled the motions of the planets around the sun. In the hydrogen atom, it was believed that the electrostatic attraction between the positive "solar" proton and the negative "planetary" electron pulls the electron inward and that this force is balanced exactly by the outward acceleration due to the circular motion of the electron.

Bohr's model of the atom included the idea of electrons moving in circular orbits, but he imposed a rather severe restriction: The single electron in the hydrogen atom could be located only in certain orbits. Because each orbit has a particular energy associated with it, the energies associated with electron motion in the permitted orbits must be fixed in value, or *quantized*. Bohr attributed the emission of radiation by an energized hydrogen atom to the electron dropping from a higher-energy orbit to a lower one and giving up a quantum of energy (a photon) in the form of light (Figure 7.9). Using arguments based on electrostatic interaction and Newton's laws of motion, Bohr showed that the energies that the electron in the hydrogen atom can possess are given by

$$E_n = -R_\mathrm{H}\left(\frac{1}{n^2}\right) \tag{7.5}$$

where R_H, the Rydberg[†] constant, has the value 2.18×10^{-18} J. The number n is an integer called the principal quantum number; it has the values $n = 1, 2, 3, \ldots$.

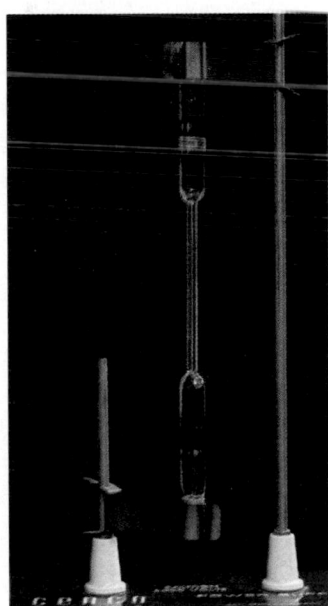

Figure 7.7 *Color emitted by hydrogen atoms in a discharge tube. The color observed results from the combination of the colors emitted in the visible spectrum.*

[†]Johannes Robert Rydberg (1854–1919). Swedish physicist. Rydberg's major contribution to physics was his study of the line spectra of many elements.

Figure 7.8 *The emission spectra of various elements.*

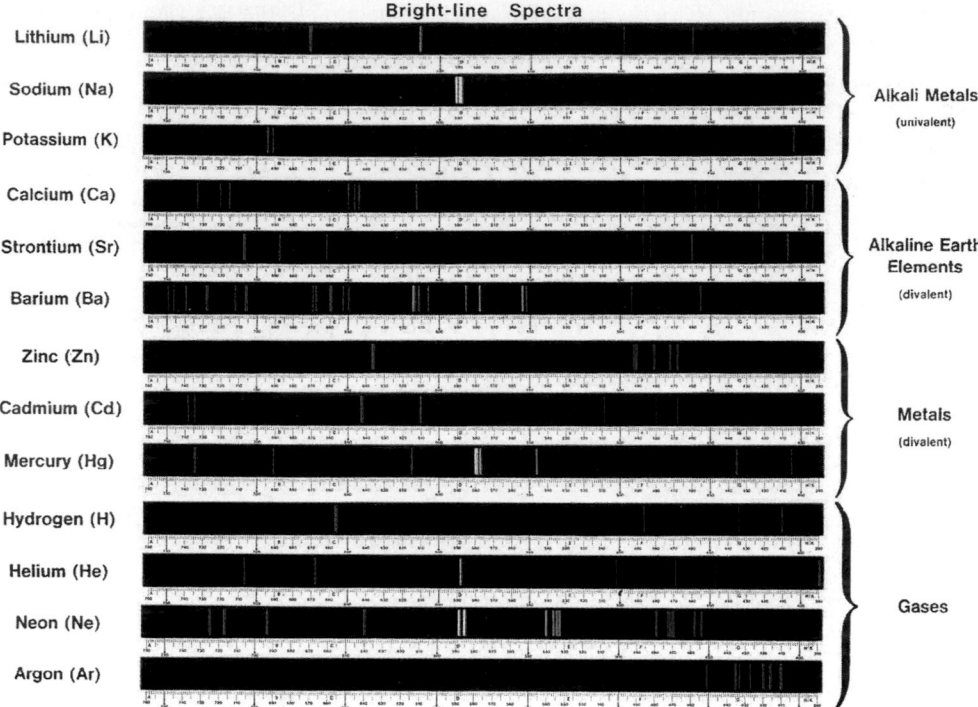

Bright-line Spectra

Lithium (Li)
Sodium (Na)
Potassium (K)
} Alkali Metals (univalent)

Calcium (Ca)
Strontium (Sr)
Barium (Ba)
} Alkaline Earth Elements (divalent)

Zinc (Zn)
Cadmium (Cd)
Mercury (Hg)
} Metals (divalent)

Hydrogen (H)
Helium (He)
Neon (Ne)
Argon (Ar)
} Gases

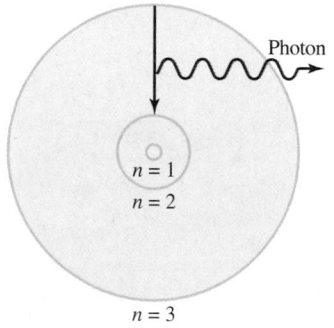

Figure 7.9 *The emission process in an excited hydrogen atom, according to Bohr's theory. An electron originally in a higher-energy orbit (n = 3) falls back to a lower-energy orbit (n = 2). As a result, a photon with energy hν is given off. The value of hν is equal to the difference in energies of the two orbits occupied by the electron in the emission process. For simplicity, only three orbits are shown.*

The negative sign in Equation (7.5) is an arbitrary convention, signifying that the energy of the electron in the atom is *lower* than the energy of a *free electron*, which is an electron that is infinitely far from the nucleus. The energy of a free electron is arbitrarily assigned a value of zero. Mathematically, this corresponds to setting n equal to infinity in Equation (7.5), so that $E_\infty = 0$. As the electron gets closer to the nucleus (as n decreases), E_n becomes larger in absolute value, but also more negative. The most negative value, then, is reached when $n = 1$, which corresponds to the most stable energy state. We call this the **ground state,** or the **ground level,** which refers to *the lowest energy state of a system* (which is an atom in our discussion). The stability of the electron diminishes for $n = 2, 3, \ldots$. Each of these levels is called an **excited state,** or **excited level,** which is *higher in energy than the ground state.* A hydrogen electron for which n is greater than 1 is said to be in an excited state. The radius of each circular orbit in Bohr's model depends on n^2. Thus, as n increases from 1 to 2 to 3, the orbit radius increases very rapidly. The higher the excited state, the farther away the electron is from the nucleus (and the less tightly it is held by the nucleus).

Bohr's theory enables us to explain the line spectrum of the hydrogen atom. Radiant energy absorbed by the atom causes the electron to move from a lower-energy state (characterized by a smaller n value) to a higher-energy state (characterized by a larger n value). Conversely, radiant energy (in the form of a photon) is emitted when the electron moves from a higher-energy state to a lower-energy state. The quantized movement of the electron from one energy state to another is analogous to the movement of a tennis ball either up or down a set of stairs (Figure 7.10). The ball can be on any of several steps but never between steps. The journey from a lower step to a higher one is an energy-requiring process, whereas movement from a higher step to a lower step is an energy-releasing process. The quantity of energy involved in either type of change is determined by the distance between the beginning and ending steps.

7.3 Bohr's Theory of the Hydrogen Atom 277

Similarly, the amount of energy needed to move an electron in the Bohr atom depends on the difference in energy levels between the initial and final states.

To apply Equation (7.5) to the emission process in a hydrogen atom, let us suppose that the electron is initially in an excited state characterized by the principal quantum number n_i. During emission, the electron drops to a lower energy state characterized by the principal quantum number n_f (the subscripts i and f denote the initial and final states, respectively). This lower energy state may be either a less excited state or the ground state. The difference between the energies of the initial and final states is

$$\Delta E = E_f - E_i$$

From Equation (7.5),

$$E_f = -R_H\left(\frac{1}{n_f^2}\right)$$

and

$$E_i = -R_H\left(\frac{1}{n_i^2}\right)$$

Therefore,

$$\Delta E = \left(\frac{-R_H}{n_f^2}\right) - \left(\frac{-R_H}{n_i^2}\right)$$

$$= R_H\left(\frac{1}{n_i^2} - \frac{1}{n_f^2}\right)$$

Figure 7.10 *A mechanical analogy for the emission processes. The ball can rest on any step but not between steps.*

Because this transition results in the emission of a photon of frequency ν and energy $h\nu$, we can write

$$\Delta E = h\nu = R_H\left(\frac{1}{n_i^2} - \frac{1}{n_f^2}\right) \tag{7.6}$$

When a photon is emitted, $n_i > n_f$. Consequently the term in parentheses is negative and ΔE is negative (energy is lost to the surroundings). When energy is absorbed, $n_i < n_f$ and the term in parentheses is positive, so ΔE is positive. Each spectral line in the emission spectrum corresponds to a particular transition in a hydrogen atom. When we study a large number of hydrogen atoms, we observe all possible transitions and hence the corresponding spectral lines. The brightness of a spectral line depends on how many photons of the same wavelength are emitted.

The emission spectrum of hydrogen includes a wide range of wavelengths from the infrared to the ultraviolet. Table 7.1 lists the series of transitions in the hydrogen

TABLE 7.1	The Various Series in Atomic Hydrogen Emission Spectrum		
Series	n_f	n_i	**Spectrum Region**
Lyman	1	2, 3, 4, ...	Ultraviolet
Balmer	2	3, 4, 5, ...	Visible and ultraviolet
Paschen	3	4, 5, 6, ...	Infrared
Brackett	4	5, 6, 7, ...	Infrared

Figure 7.11 *The energy levels in the hydrogen atom and the various emission series. Each energy level corresponds to the energy associated with an allowed energy state for an orbit, as postulated by Bohr and shown in Figure 7.9. The emission lines are labeled according to the scheme in Table 7.1.*

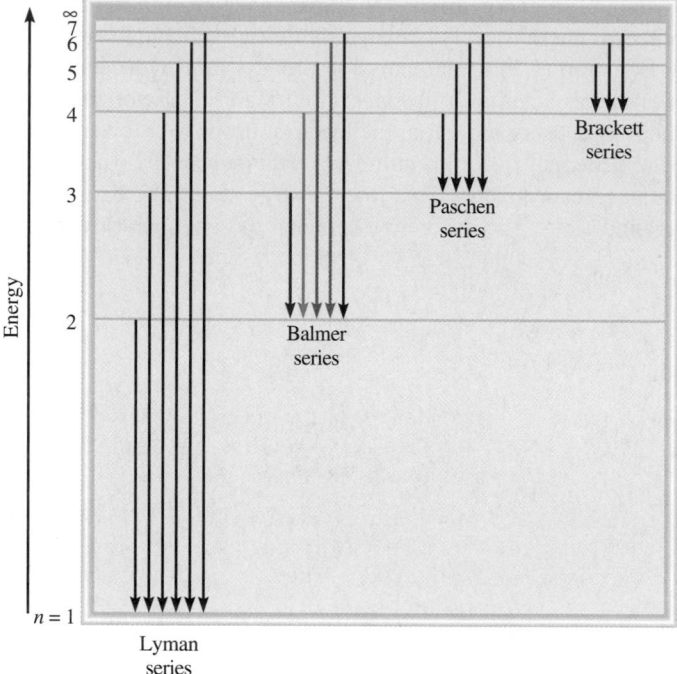

spectrum; they are named after their discoverers. The Balmer series was particularly easy to study because a number of its lines fall in the visible range.

Figure 7.9 shows a single transition. However, it is more informative to express transitions as shown in Figure 7.11. Each horizontal line represents an allowed energy level for the electron in a hydrogen atom. The energy levels are labeled with their principal quantum numbers.

Example 7.4 illustrates the use of Equation (7.6).

Example 7.4

What is the wavelength of a photon (in nanometers) emitted during a transition from the $n_i = 5$ state to the $n_f = 2$ state in the hydrogen atom?

Strategy We are given the initial and final states in the emission process. We can calculate the energy of the emitted photon using Equation (7.6). Then from Equations (7.2) and (7.1) we can solve for the wavelength of the photon. The value of Rydberg's constant is given in the text.

Solution From Equation (7.6) we write

$$\Delta E = R_H \left(\frac{1}{n_i^2} - \frac{1}{n_f^2} \right)$$

$$= 2.18 \times 10^{-18} \, J \left(\frac{1}{5^2} - \frac{1}{2^2} \right)$$

$$= -4.58 \times 10^{-19} \, J$$

The negative sign is in accord with our convention that energy is given off to the surroundings.

The negative sign indicates that this is energy associated with an emission process. To calculate the wavelength, we will omit the minus sign for ΔE because the wavelength of

(Continued)

the photon must be positive. Because $\Delta E = h\nu$ or $\nu = \Delta E/h$, we can calculate the wavelength of the photon by writing

$$\lambda = \frac{c}{\nu}$$

$$= \frac{ch}{\Delta E}$$

$$= \frac{(3.00 \times 10^8 \text{ m/s})(6.63 \times 10^{-34} \text{ J} \cdot \text{s})}{4.58 \times 10^{-19} \text{ J}}$$

$$= 4.34 \times 10^{-7} \text{ m}$$

$$= 4.34 \times 10^{-7} \text{ m} \times \left(\frac{1 \text{ nm}}{1 \times 10^{-9} \text{ m}}\right) = 434 \text{ nm}$$

Check The wavelength is in the visible region of the electromagnetic region (see Figure 7.4). This is consistent with the fact that because $n_f = 2$, this transition gives rise to a spectral line in the Balmer series (see Figure 7.6).

Similar problems: 7.31, 7.32.

Practice Exercise What is the wavelength (in nanometers) of a photon emitted during a transition from $n_i = 6$ to $n_f = 4$ state in the H atom?

The Chemistry in Action essay on p. 280 discusses a special type of atomic emission—lasers.

7.4 The Dual Nature of the Electron

Physicists were both mystified and intrigued by Bohr's theory. They questioned why the energies of the hydrogen electron are quantized. Or, phrasing the question in a more concrete way, Why is the electron in a Bohr atom restricted to orbiting the nucleus at certain fixed distances? For a decade no one, not even Bohr himself, had a logical explanation. In 1924 Louis de Broglie[†] provided a solution to this puzzle. De Broglie reasoned that if light waves can behave like a stream of particles (photons), then perhaps particles such as electrons can possess wave properties. According to de Broglie, an electron bound to the nucleus behaves like a *standing wave*. Standing waves can be generated by plucking, say, a guitar string (Figure 7.12). The waves are described as standing, or stationary, because they do not travel along the string. Some points on the string, called **nodes,** do not move at all; that is, *the amplitude of the wave at these points is zero.* There is a node at each end, and there may be nodes between the ends. The greater the frequency of vibration, the shorter the wavelength of the standing wave and the greater the number of nodes. As Figure 7.12 shows, there can be only certain wavelengths in any of the allowed motions of the string.

[†]Louis Victor Pierre Raymond Duc de Broglie (1892–1977). French physicist. Member of an old and noble family in France, he held the title of a prince. In his doctoral dissertation, he proposed that matter and radiation have the properties of both wave and particle. For this work, de Broglie was awarded the Nobel Prize in Physics in 1929.

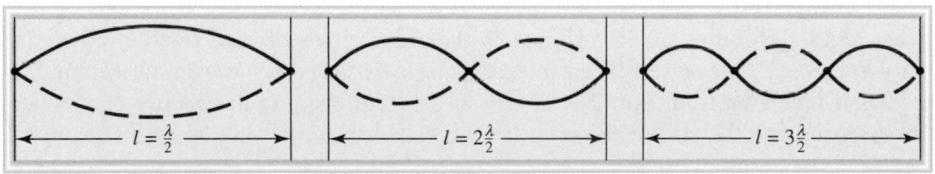

Figure 7.12 *The standing waves generated by plucking a guitar string. Each dot represents a node. The length of the string (l) must be equal to a whole number times one-half the wavelength (λ/2).*

CHEMISTRY
in Action

Laser—The Splendid Light

Laser is an acronym for light amplification by stimulated emission of radiation. It is a special type of emission that involves either atoms or molecules. Since the discovery of laser in 1960, it has been used in numerous systems designed to operate in the gas, liquid, and solid states. These systems emit radiation with wavelengths ranging from infrared through visible and ultraviolet. The advent of laser has truly revolutionized science, medicine, and technology.

Ruby laser was the first known laser. Ruby is a deep-red mineral containing corundum, Al_2O_3, in which some of the Al^{3+}

The emission of laser light from a ruby laser.

Totally reflecting mirror   Flash lamp

Laser beam

Ruby rod   Partially reflecting mirror

$\lambda = 694.3$ nm

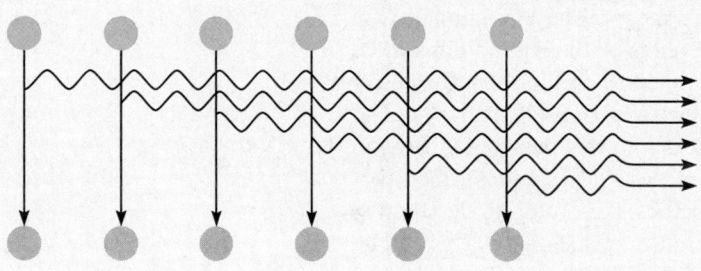

The stimulated emission of one photon by another photon in a cascade event that leads to the emission of laser light. The synchronization of the light waves produces an intensely penetrating laser beam.

De Broglie argued that if an electron does behave like a standing wave in the hydrogen atom, the length of the wave must fit the circumference of the orbit exactly (Figure 7.13). Otherwise the wave would partially cancel itself on each successive orbit. Eventually the amplitude of the wave would be reduced to zero, and the wave would not exist.

The relation between the circumference of an allowed orbit ($2\pi r$) and the wavelength (λ) of the electron is given by

$$2\pi r = n\lambda \tag{7.7}$$

where r is the radius of the orbit, λ is the wavelength of the electron wave, and $n = 1, 2, 3, \ldots$. Because n is an integer, it follows that r can have only certain values as n increases from 1 to 2 to 3 and so on. And because the energy of the electron depends on the size of the orbit (or the value of r), its value must be quantized.

ions have been replaced by Cr^{3+} ions. A flashlamp is used to excite the chromium atoms to a higher energy level. The excited atoms are unstable, so at a given instant some of them will return to the ground state by emitting a photon in the red region of the spectrum. The photon bounces back and forth many times between mirrors at opposite ends of the laser tube. This photon can stimulate the emission of photons of exactly the same wavelength from other excited chromium atoms; these photons in turn can stimulate the emission of more photons, and so on. Because the light waves are *in phase*—that is, their maxima and minima coincide—the photons enhance one another, increasing their power with each passage between the mirrors. One of the mirrors is only partially reflecting, so that when the light reaches a certain intensity it emerges from the mirror as a laser beam. Depending on the mode of operation, the laser light may be emitted in pulses (as in the ruby laser case) or in continuous waves.

Laser light is characterized by three properties: It is intense, it has precisely known wavelength and hence energy, and it is coherent. By *coherent* we mean that the light waves are all in phase. The applications of lasers are quite numerous. Their high intensity and ease of focus make them suitable for doing eye surgery, for drilling holes in metals and welding, and for carrying out nuclear fusion. The fact that they are highly directional and have precisely known wavelengths makes them very useful for telecommunications. Lasers are also used in isotope separation, in holography (three-dimensional photography), in compact disc players, and in supermarket scanners. Lasers have played an important role in the spectroscopic investigation of molecular properties and of many chemical and biological processes. Laser lights are increasingly being used to probe the details of chemical reactions (see Chapter 13).

State-of-the-art lasers used in the research laboratory of Dr. A. H. Zewail at the California Institute of Technology.

De Broglie's reasoning led to the conclusion that waves can behave like particles and particles can exhibit wavelike properties. De Broglie deduced that the particle and wave properties are related by the expression

$$\lambda = \frac{h}{mu} \tag{7.8}$$

where λ, m, and u are the wavelengths associated with a moving particle, its mass, and its velocity, respectively. Equation (7.8) implies that a particle in motion can be treated as a wave, and a wave can exhibit the properties of a particle. Note that the left side of Equation (7.8) involves the wavelike property of wavelength, whereas the right side makes references to mass, a distinctly particlelike property.

(a)

(b)

Figure 7.13 *(a) The circumference of the orbit is equal to an integral number of wavelengths. This is an allowed orbit. (b) The circumference of the orbit is not equal to an integral number of wavelengths. As a result, the electron wave does not close in on itself. This is a nonallowed orbit.*

Similar problems: 7.40, 7.41.

Example 7.5

Calculate the wavelength of the "particle" in the following two cases: (a) The fastest serve in tennis is about 150 miles per hour, or 68 m/s. Calculate the wavelength associated with a 6.0×10^{-2}-kg tennis ball traveling at this speed. (b) Calculate the wavelength associated with an electron (9.1094×10^{-31} kg) moving at 68 m/s.

Strategy We are given the mass and the speed of the particle in (a) and (b) and asked to calculate the wavelength so we need Equation (7.8). Note that because the units of Planck's constants are J·s, m and u must be in kg and m/s (1 J = 1 kg m^2/s^2), respectively.

Solution (a) Using Equation (7.8) we write

$$\lambda = \frac{h}{mu}$$
$$= \frac{6.63 \times 10^{-34} \text{ J} \cdot \text{s}}{(6.0 \times 10^{-2} \text{ kg}) \times 68 \text{ m/s}}$$
$$= 1.6 \times 10^{-34} \text{ m}$$

Comment This is an exceedingly small wavelength considering that the size of an atom itself is on the order of 1×10^{-10} m. For this reason, the wave properties of a tennis ball cannot be detected by any existing measuring device.

(b) In this case,

$$\lambda = \frac{h}{mu}$$
$$= \frac{6.63 \times 10^{-34} \text{ J} \cdot \text{s}}{(9.1094 \times 10^{-31} \text{ kg}) \times 68 \text{ m/s}}$$
$$= 1.1 \times 10^{-5} \text{ m}$$

Comment This wavelength (1.1×10^{-5} m or 1.1×10^4 nm) is in the infrared region. This calculation shows that only electrons (and other submicroscopic particles) have measurable wavelengths.

Practice Exercise Calculate the wavelength (in nanometers) of a H atom (mass = 1.674×10^{-27} kg) moving at 7.00×10^2 cm/s.

Example 7.5 shows that although de Broglie's equation can be applied to diverse systems, the wave properties become observable only for submicroscopic objects. This distinction is due to the smallness of Planck's constant, h, which appears in the numerator in Equation (7.8).

Shortly after de Broglie introduced his equation, Clinton Davisson[†] and Lester Germer[‡] in the United States and G. P. Thomson[§] in England demonstrated that electrons do indeed possess wavelike properties. By directing a beam of electrons through a thin piece of gold foil, Thomson obtained a set of concentric rings on a screen,

---

[†]Clinton Joseph Davisson (1881–1958). American physicist. He and G. P. Thomson shared the Nobel Prize in Physics in 1937 for demonstrating wave properties of electrons.

[‡]Lester Halbert Germer (1896–1972). American physicist. Discoverer (with Davisson) of the wave properties of electrons.

[§]George Paget Thomson (1892–1975). English physicist. Son of J. J. Thomson, he received the Nobel Prize in Physics in 1937, along with Clinton Davisson, for demonstrating wave properties of electrons.

(a)   (b)

Figure 7.14 *(a) X-ray diffraction pattern of aluminum foil. (b) Electron diffraction of aluminum foil. The similarity of these two patterns shows that electrons can behave like X rays and display wave properties.*

similar to the pattern observed when X rays (which are waves) were used. Figure 7.14 shows such a pattern for aluminum.

The Chemistry in Action essay on p. 284 describes electron microscopy.

7.5 Quantum Mechanics

The spectacular success of Bohr's theory was followed by a series of disappointments. Bohr's approach did not account for the emission spectra of atoms containing more than one electron, such as atoms of helium and lithium. Nor did it explain why extra lines appear in the hydrogen emission spectrum when a magnetic field is applied. Another problem arose with the discovery that electrons are wavelike: How can the "position" of a wave be specified? We cannot define the precise location of a wave because a wave extends in space.

To describe the problem of trying to locate a subatomic particle that behaves like a wave, Werner Heisenberg[†] formulated what is now known as the ***Heisenberg uncertainty principle:*** *it is impossible to know simultaneously both the momentum p* (defined as mass times velocity) *and the position of a particle with certainty.* Stated mathematically,

$$\Delta x \Delta p \geq \frac{h}{4\pi} \qquad (7.9)$$

where Δx and Δp are the uncertainties in measuring the position and momentum, respectively. Equation (7.9) says that if we make the measurement of the momentum of a particle more precise (that is, if we make Δp a small quantity), our knowledge of the position will become correspondingly less precise (that is, Δx will become larger). Similarly, if the position of the particle is known more precisely, then its momentum measurement must be less precise. Applying the Heisenberg uncertainty principle to the hydrogen atom, we see that in reality the electron does not orbit the nucleus in a

In reality, Bohr's theory accounted for the observed emission spectra of He[+] and Li[2+] ions, as well as that of hydrogen. However, all three systems have one feature in common—each contains a single electron. Thus, the Bohr model worked successfully only for the hydrogen atom and for "hydrogenlike ions."

The $\geq$ sign means that the product $\Delta x \Delta p$ can be greater than or equal to $h/4\pi$, but it can never be smaller than $h/4\pi$.

[†]Werner Karl Heisenberg (1901–1976). German physicist. One of the founders of modern quantum theory, Heisenberg received the Nobel Prize in Physics in 1932.

Electron Microscopy

The electron microscope is an extremely valuable application of the wavelike properties of electrons because it produces images of objects that cannot be seen with the naked eye or with light microscopes. According to the laws of optics, it is impossible to form an image of an object that is smaller than half the wavelength of the light used for the observation. Because the range of visible light wavelengths starts at around 400 nm, or 4×10^{-5} cm, we cannot see anything smaller than 2×10^{-5} cm. In principle, we can see objects on the atomic and molecular scale by using X rays, whose wavelengths range from about 0.01 nm to 10 nm. However, X rays cannot be focused, so they do not produce well-formed images. Electrons, on the other hand, are charged particles, which can be focused in the same way the image on a TV screen is focused, that is, by applying an electric field or a magnetic field. According to Equation (7.8), the wavelength of an electron is inversely proportional to its velocity. By accelerating electrons to very high velocities, we can obtain wavelengths as short as 0.004 nm.

A different type of electron microscope, called the *scanning tunneling microscope (STM)*, makes use of another quantum mechanical property of the electron to produce an image of the atoms on the surface of a sample. Because of its extremely small mass, an electron is able to move or "tunnel" through an energy barrier (instead of going over it). The STM consists of a tungsten metal needle with a very fine point, the source of the tunneling electrons. A voltage is maintained between the needle and the surface of the sample to induce electrons to tunnel through space to the sample. As the needle moves over the sample, at a distance of a few atomic diameters from the surface, the tunneling current is measured. This current decreases with increasing distance from the sample. By using a feedback loop, the vertical position of the tip can be adjusted to a constant distance from the surface. The extent of these adjustments, which profile the sample, is recorded and displayed as a three-dimensional false-colored image.

Both the electron microscope and the STM are among the most powerful tools in chemical and biological research.

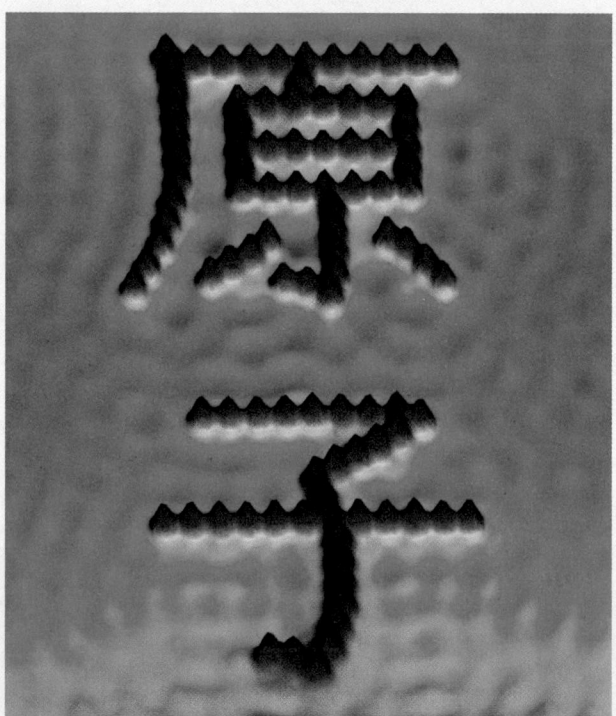

STM image of iron atoms arranged to display the Chinese characters for atom on a copper surface.

An electron micrograph showing a normal red blood cell and a sickled red blood cell from the same person.

well-defined path, as Bohr thought. If it did, we could determine precisely both the position of the electron (from its location on a particular orbit) and its momentum (from its kinetic energy) at the same time, a violation of the uncertainty principle.

To be sure, Bohr made a significant contribution to our understanding of atoms, and his suggestion that the energy of an electron in an atom is quantized remains unchallenged. But his theory did not provide a complete description of electronic behavior in atoms. In 1926 the Austrian physicist Erwin Schrödinger,[†] using a complicated mathematical technique, formulated an equation that describes the behavior and energies of submicroscopic particles in general, an equation analogous to Newton's laws of motion for macroscopic objects. The *Schrödinger equation* requires advanced calculus to solve, and we will not discuss it here. It is important to know, however, that the equation incorporates both particle behavior, in terms of mass m, and wave behavior, in terms of a *wave function* ψ (psi), which depends on the location in space of the system (such as an electron in an atom).

The wave function itself has no direct physical meaning. However, the probability of finding the electron in a certain region in space is proportional to the square of the wave function, ψ^2. The idea of relating ψ^2 to probability stemmed from a wave theory analogy. According to wave theory, the intensity of light is proportional to the square of the amplitude of the wave, or ψ^2. The most likely place to find a photon is where the intensity is greatest, that is, where the value of ψ^2 is greatest. A similar argument associates ψ^2 with the likelihood of finding an electron in regions surrounding the nucleus.

Schrödinger's equation began a new era in physics and chemistry, for it launched a new field, *quantum mechanics* (also called *wave mechanics*). We now refer to the developments in quantum theory from 1913—the time Bohr presented his analysis for the hydrogen atom—to 1926 as "old quantum theory."

The Quantum Mechanical Description of the Hydrogen Atom

The Schrödinger equation specifies the possible energy states the electron can occupy in a hydrogen atom and identifies the corresponding wave functions (ψ^2). These energy states and wave functions are characterized by a set of quantum numbers (to be discussed shortly), with which we can construct a comprehensive model of the hydrogen atom.

Although quantum mechanics tells us that we cannot pinpoint an electron in an atom, it does define the region where the electron might be at a given time. The concept of **electron density** *gives the probability that an electron will be found in a particular region of an atom.* The square of the wave function, ψ^2, defines the distribution of electron density in three-dimensional space around the nucleus. Regions of high electron density represent a high probability of locating the electron, whereas the opposite holds for regions of low electron density (Figure 7.15).

To distinguish the quantum mechanical description of an atom from Bohr's model, we speak of an atomic orbital, rather than an orbit. An **atomic orbital** can be thought of as *the wave function of an electron in an atom.* When we say that an electron is in a certain orbital, we mean that the distribution of the electron density or the probability of locating the electron in space is described by the square of the wave function associated with that orbital. An atomic orbital, therefore, has a characteristic energy, as well as a characteristic distribution of electron density.

The Schrödinger equation works nicely for the simple hydrogen atom with its one proton and one electron, but it turns out that it cannot be solved exactly for any

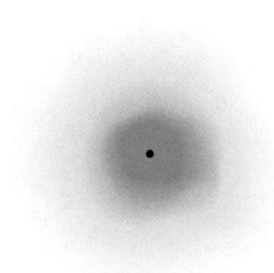

Figure 7.15 *A representation of the electron density distribution surrounding the nucleus in the hydrogen atom. It shows a high probability of finding the electron closer to the nucleus.*

[†]Erwin Schrödinger (1887–1961). Austrian physicist. Schrödinger formulated wave mechanics, which laid the foundation for modern quantum theory. He received the Nobel Prize in Physics in 1933.

atom containing more than one electron! Fortunately, chemists and physicists have learned to get around this kind of difficulty by approximation. For example, although the behavior of electrons in ***many-electron atoms*** (that is, *atoms containing two or more electrons*) is not the same as in the hydrogen atom, we assume that the difference is probably not too great. Thus we can use the energies and wave functions obtained from the hydrogen atom as good approximations of the behavior of electrons in more complex atoms. In fact, this approach provides fairly reliable descriptions of electronic behavior in many-electron atoms.

7.6 Quantum Numbers

In quantum mechanics, three ***quantum numbers*** are required to *describe the distribution of electrons in hydrogen and other atoms.* These numbers are derived from the mathematical solution of the Schrödinger equation for the hydrogen atom. They are called the *principal quantum number,* the *angular momentum quantum number,* and the *magnetic quantum number.* These quantum numbers will be used to describe atomic orbitals and to label electrons that reside in them. A fourth quantum number— the *spin quantum number*—describes the behavior of a specific electron and completes the description of electrons in atoms.

The Principal Quantum Number (n)

The principal quantum number (n) can have integral values 1, 2, 3, and so forth; it corresponds to the quantum number in Equation (7.5). In a hydrogen atom, the value of n determines the energy of an orbital. As we will see shortly, this is not the case for a many-electron atom. The principal quantum number also relates to the average distance of the electron from the nucleus in a particular orbital. The larger n is, the greater the average distance of an electron in the orbital from the nucleus and therefore the larger the orbital.

The Angular Momentum Quantum Number (ℓ)

The angular momentum quantum number (ℓ) tells us the "shape" of the orbitals (see Section 7.7). The values of ℓ depend on the value of the principal quantum number, n. For a given value of n, ℓ has possible integral values from 0 to $(n - 1)$. If $n = 1$, there is only one possible value of ℓ; that is, $\ell = n - 1 = 1 - 1 = 0$. If $n = 2$, there are two values of ℓ, given by 0 and 1. If $n = 3$, there are three values of ℓ, given by 0, 1, and 2. The value of ℓ is generally designated by the letters $s, p, d, \ldots$ as follows:

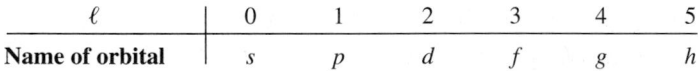

ℓ	0	1	2	3	4	5
Name of orbital	s	p	d	f	g	h

Thus if $\ell = 0$, we have an s orbital; if $\ell = 1$, we have a p orbital; and so on.

The unusual sequence of letters ($s, p,$ and d) has a historical origin. Physicists who studied atomic emission spectra tried to correlate the observed spectral lines with the particular energy states involved in the transitions. They noted that some of the lines were *s*harp; some were rather spread out, or *d*iffuse; and some were very strong and hence referred to as *p*rincipal lines. Subsequently, the initial letters of each adjective were assigned to those energy states. However, after the letter d and starting with the letter f (for *f*undamental), the orbital designations follow alphabetical order.

A collection of orbitals with the same value of n is frequently called a shell. One or more orbitals with the same n and ℓ values are referred to as a subshell. For

Although the helium atom has only two electrons, in quantum mechanics it is regarded as a many-electron atom.

Equation (7.5) holds only for the hydrogen atom.

example, the shell with $n = 2$ is composed of two subshells, $\ell = 0$ and 1 (the allowed values for $n = 2$). These subshells are called the $2s$ and $2p$ subshells where 2 denotes the value of n, and s and p denote the values of ℓ.

Remember that the "2" in 2s refers to the value of n and the "s" symbolizes the value of ℓ.

The Magnetic Quantum Number (m_ℓ)

The magnetic quantum number (m_ℓ) describes the orientation of the orbital in space (to be discussed in Section 7.7). Within a subshell, the value of m_ℓ depends on the value of the angular momentum quantum number, ℓ. For a certain value of ℓ, there are $(2\ell + 1)$ integral values of m_ℓ as follows:

$$-\ell, (-\ell + 1), \ldots 0, \ldots (+\ell - 1), +\ell$$

If $\ell = 0$, then $m_\ell = 0$. If $\ell = 1$, then there are $[(2 \times 1) + 1]$, or three values of m_ℓ, namely, -1, 0, and 1. If $\ell = 2$, there are $[(2 \times 2) + 1]$, or five values of m_ℓ, namely, $-2, -1, 0, 1$, and 2. The number of m_ℓ values indicates the number of orbitals in a subshell with a particular ℓ value.

To conclude our discussion of these three quantum numbers, let us consider a situation in which $n = 2$ and $\ell = 1$. The values of n and ℓ indicate that we have a $2p$ subshell, and in this subshell we have *three* $2p$ orbitals (because there are three values of m_ℓ, given by -1, 0, and 1).

The Electron Spin Quantum Number (m_s)

Experiments on the emission spectra of hydrogen and sodium atoms indicated that lines in the emission spectra could be split by the application of an external magnetic field. The only way physicists could explain these results was to assume that electrons act like tiny magnets. If electrons are thought of as spinning on their own axes, as Earth does, their magnetic properties can be accounted for. According to electromagnetic theory, a spinning charge generates a magnetic field, and it is this motion that causes an electron to behave like a magnet. Figure 7.16 shows the two possible spinning motions of an electron, one clockwise and the other counterclockwise. To take the electron spin into account, it is necessary to introduce a fourth quantum number, called the electron spin quantum number (m_s), which has a value of $+\frac{1}{2}$ or $-\frac{1}{2}$.

Conclusive proof of electron spin was provided by Otto Stern[†] and Walther Gerlach[‡] in 1924. Figure 7.17 shows the basic experimental arrangement. A beam of

Figure 7.16 *The (a) clockwise and (b) counterclockwise spins of an electron. The magnetic fields generated by these two spinning motions are analogous to those from the two magnets. The upward and downward arrows are used to denote the direction of spin.*

In their experiment, Stern and Gerlach used silver atoms, which contain just one unpaired electron. To illustrate the principle, we can assume that hydrogen atoms are used in the study.

[†]Otto Stern (1888–1969). German physicist. He made important contributions to the study of magnetic properties of atoms and the kinetic theory of gases. Stern was awarded the Nobel Prize in Physics in 1943.

[‡]Walther Gerlach (1889–1979). German physicist. Gerlach's main area of research was in quantum theory.

Figure 7.17 *Experimental arrangement for demonstrating the spinning motion of electrons. A beam of atoms is directed through a magnetic field. For example, when a hydrogen atom with a single electron passes through the field, it is deflected in one direction or the other, depending on the direction of the spin. In a stream consisting of many atoms, there will be equal distributions of the two kinds of spins, so that two spots of equal intensity are detected on the screen.*

gaseous atoms generated in a hot furnace passes through a nonhomogeneous magnetic field. The interaction between an electron and the magnetic field causes the atom to be deflected from its straight-line path. Because the spinning motion is completely random, the electrons in half of the atoms will be spinning in one direction, and those atoms will be deflected in one way; the electrons in the other half of the atoms will be spinning in the opposite direction, and those atoms will be deflected in the other direction. Thus, two spots of equal intensity are observed on the detecting screen.

7.7 Atomic Orbitals

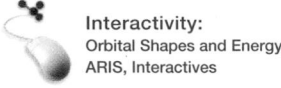

Interactivity:
Orbital Shapes and Energy
ARIS, Interactives

That the wave function for an orbital theoretically has no outer limit as one moves outward from the nucleus raises interesting philosophical questions regarding the sizes of atoms. Chemists have agreed on an operational definition of atomic size, as we will see in later chapters.

Table 7.2 shows the relation between quantum numbers and atomic orbitals. We see that when $\ell = 0$, $(2\ell + 1) = 1$ and there is only one value of m_ℓ, thus we have an s orbital. When $\ell = 1$, $(2\ell + 1) = 3$, so there are three values of m_ℓ or three p orbitals, labeled p_x, p_y, and p_z. When $\ell = 2$, $(2\ell + 1) = 5$ and there are five values of m_ℓ, and the corresponding five d orbitals are labeled with more elaborate subscripts. In the following sections we will consider the s, p, and d orbitals separately.

s **Orbitals.** One of the important questions we ask when studying the properties of atomic orbitals is, What are the shapes of the orbitals? Strictly speaking, an orbital does not have a well-defined shape because the wave function characterizing the orbital extends from the nucleus to infinity. In that sense, it is difficult to say what an orbital looks like. On the other hand, it is certainly convenient to think of orbitals as having specific shapes, particularly in discussing the formation of chemical bonds between atoms, as we will do in Chapters 9 and 10.

Although in principle an electron can be found anywhere, we know that most of the time it is quite close to the nucleus. Figure 7.18(a) shows the distribution of electron density in a hydrogen 1s orbital moving outward from the nucleus. As you can see, the electron density falls off rapidly as the distance from the nucleus increases. Roughly speaking, there is about a 90 percent probability of finding the electron within a sphere of radius 100 pm (1 pm = 1×10^{-12} m) surrounding the nucleus. Thus, we can represent the 1s orbital by drawing a ***boundary surface diagram*** that *encloses about 90 percent of the total electron density in an orbital,* as shown in Figure 7.18(b). A 1s orbital represented in this manner is merely a sphere.

An s subshell has one orbital, a p subshell has three orbitals, and a d subshell has five orbitals.

			Number	Atomic
TABLE 7.2		**Relation Between Quantum Numbers and Atomic Orbitals**		
n	ℓ	m_ℓ	Number of Orbitals	Atomic Orbital Designations
1	0	0	1	1s
2	0	0	1	2s
	1	$-1, 0, 1$	3	$2p_x$, $2p_y$, $2p_z$
3	0	0	1	3s
	1	$-1, 0, 1$	3	$3p_x$, $3p_y$, $3p_z$
	2	$-2, -1, 0, 1, 2$	5	$3d_{xy}$, $3d_{yz}$, $3d_{xz}$, $3d_{x^2-y^2}$, $3d_{z^2}$
$\vdots$	$\vdots$	$\vdots$	$\vdots$	$\vdots$

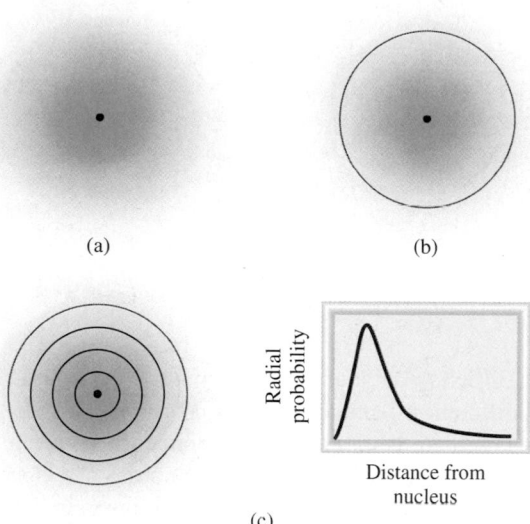

(a)

(b)

(c)

Radial probability

Distance from nucleus

Figure 7.18 *(a) Plot of electron density in the hydrogen 1s orbital as a function of the distance from the nucleus. The electron density falls off rapidly as the distance from the nucleus increases. (b) Boundary surface diagram of the hydrogen 1s orbital. (c) A more realistic way of viewing electron density distribution is to divide the 1s orbital into successive spherical thin shells. A plot of the probability of finding the electron in each shell, called radial probability, as a function of distance shows a maximum at 52.9 pm from the nucleus. Interestingly, this is equal to the radius of the innermost orbit in the Bohr model.*

Figure 7.19 shows boundary surface diagrams for the 1s, 2s, and 3s hydrogen atomic orbitals. All s orbitals are spherical in shape but differ in size, which increases as the principal quantum number increases. Although the details of electron density variation within each boundary surface are lost, there is no serious disadvantage. For us the most important features of atomic orbitals are their shapes and *relative* sizes, which are adequately represented by boundary surface diagrams.

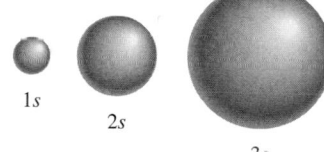

1s 2s 3s

Figure 7.19 *Boundary surface diagrams of the hydrogen 1s, 2s, and 3s orbitals. Each sphere contains about 90 percent of the total electron density. All s orbitals are spherical. Roughly speaking, the size of an orbital is proportional to n^2, where n is the principal quantum number.*

***p* Orbitals.** It should be clear that the p orbitals start with the principal quantum number $n = 2$. If $n = 1$, then the angular momentum quantum number ℓ can assume only the value of zero; therefore, there is only a 1s orbital. As we saw earlier, when $\ell = 1$, the magnetic quantum number m_ℓ can have values of $-1, 0, 1$. Starting with $n = 2$ and $\ell = 1$, we therefore have three 2p orbitals: $2p_x$, $2p_y$, and $2p_z$ (Figure 7.20). The letter subscripts indicate the axes along which the orbitals are oriented. These three p orbitals are identical in size, shape, and energy; they differ from one another only in orientation. Note, however, that there is no simple relation between the values of m_ℓ and the x, y, and z directions. For our purpose, you need only remember that because there are three possible values of m_ℓ, there are three p orbitals with different orientations.

The boundary surface diagrams of p orbitals in Figure 7.20 show that each p orbital can be thought of as two lobes on opposite sides of the nucleus. Like s orbitals, p orbitals increase in size from 2p to 3p to 4p orbital and so on.

***d* Orbitals and Other Higher-Energy Orbitals.** When $\ell = 2$, there are five values of m_ℓ, which correspond to five d orbitals. The lowest value of n for a d orbital is 3. Because ℓ can never be greater than $n - 1$, when $n = 3$ and $\ell = 2$, we have five 3d

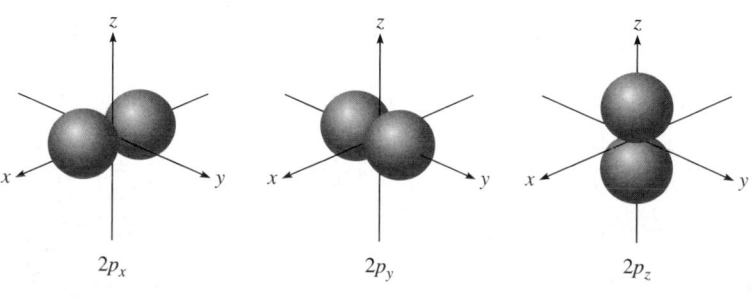

$2p_x$ $2p_y$ $2p_z$

Figure 7.20 *The boundary surface diagrams of the three 2p orbitals. These orbitals are identical in shape and energy, but their orientations are different. The p orbitals of higher principal quantum numbers have a similar shape.*

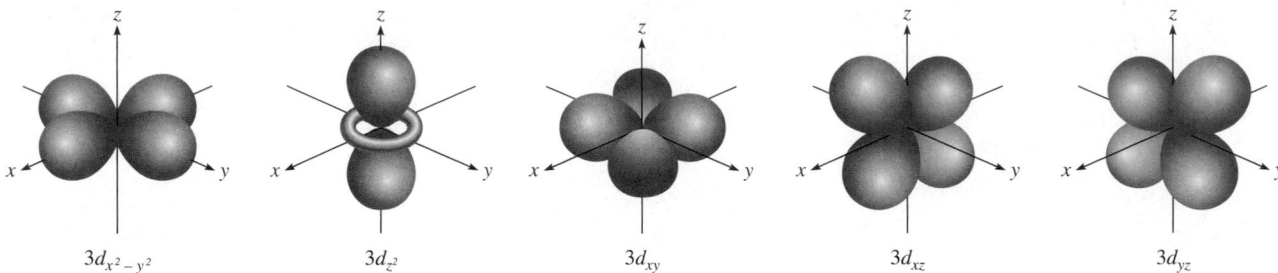

$3d_{x^2-y^2}$ $3d_{z^2}$ $3d_{xy}$ $3d_{xz}$ $3d_{yz}$

Figure 7.21 *Boundary surface diagrams of the five 3d orbitals. Although the 3d$_{z^2}$ orbital looks different, it is equivalent to the other four orbitals in all other respects. The d orbitals of higher principal quantum numbers have similar shapes.*

orbitals ($3d_{xy}$, $3d_{yz}$, $3d_{xz}$, $3d_{x^2-y^2}$, and $3d_{z^2}$), shown in Figure 7.21. As in the case of the p orbitals, the different orientations of the d orbitals correspond to the different values of m_ℓ, but again there is no direct correspondence between a given orientation and a particular m_ℓ value. All the $3d$ orbitals in an atom are identical in energy. The d orbitals for which n is greater than 3 ($4d$, $5d$, . . .) have similar shapes.

Orbitals having higher energy than d orbitals are labeled f, g, . . . and so on. The f orbitals are important in accounting for the behavior of elements with atomic numbers greater than 57, but their shapes are difficult to represent. In general chemistry, we are not concerned with orbitals having ℓ values greater than 3 (the g orbitals and beyond).

Examples 7.6 and 7.7 illustrate the labeling of orbitals with quantum numbers and the calculation of total number of orbitals associated with a given principal quantum number.

Example 7.6

List the values of n, ℓ, and m_ℓ for orbitals in the $4d$ subshell.

Strategy What are the relationships among n, ℓ, and m_ℓ? What do "4" and "d" represent in $4d$?

Solution As we saw earlier, the number given in the designation of the subshell is the principal quantum number, so in this case $n = 4$. The letter designates the type of orbital. Because we are dealing with d orbitals, $\ell = 2$. The values of m_ℓ can vary from $-\ell$ to ℓ. Therefore, m_ℓ can be -2, -1, 0, 1, or 2.

Check The values of n and ℓ are fixed for $4d$, but m_ℓ can have any one of the five values, which correspond to the five d orbitals.

Similar problem: 7.57.

Practice Exercise Give the values of the quantum numbers associated with the orbitals in the $3p$ subshell.

Example 7.7

What is the total number of orbitals associated with the principal quantum number $n = 3$?

Strategy To calculate the total number of orbitals for a given n value, we need to first write the possible values of ℓ. We then determine how many m_ℓ values are

(Continued)

associated with each value of ℓ. The total number of orbitals is equal to the sum of all the m_ℓ values.

Solution For $n = 3$, the possible values of ℓ are 0, 1, and 2. Thus, there is one $3s$ orbital ($n = 3$, $\ell = 0$, and $m_\ell = 0$); there are three $3p$ orbitals ($n = 3$, $\ell = 1$, and $m_\ell = -1, 0, 1$); there are five $3d$ orbitals ($n = 3$, $\ell = 2$, and $m_\ell = -2, -1, 0, 1, 2$). The total number of orbitals is $1 + 3 + 5 = 9$.

Check The total number of orbitals for a given value of n is n^2. So here we have $3^2 = 9$. Can you prove the validity of this relationship?

Similar problem: 7.62.

Practice Exercise What is the total number of orbitals associated with the principal quantum number $n = 4$?

The Energies of Orbitals

Now that we have some understanding of the shapes and sizes of atomic orbitals, we are ready to inquire into their relative energies and look at how energy levels affect the actual arrangement of electrons in atoms.

According to Equation (7.5), the energy of an electron in a hydrogen atom is determined solely by its principal quantum number. Thus, the energies of hydrogen orbitals increase as follows (Figure 7.22):

$$1s < 2s = 2p < 3s = 3p = 3d < 4s = 4p = 4d = 4f < \cdots$$

Although the electron density distributions are different in the $2s$ and $2p$ orbitals, hydrogen's electron has the same energy whether it is in the $2s$ orbital or a $2p$ orbital. The $1s$ orbital in a hydrogen atom corresponds to the most stable condition, the ground state. An electron residing in this orbital is most strongly held by the nucleus because it is closest to the nucleus. An electron in the $2s$, $2p$, or higher orbitals in a hydrogen atom is in an excited state.

The energy picture is more complex for many-electron atoms than for hydrogen. The energy of an electron in such an atom depends on its angular momentum quantum number as well as on its principal quantum number (Figure 7.23). For many-electron atoms, the $3d$ energy level is very close to the $4s$ energy level. The total energy of an

Figure 7.22 *Orbital energy levels in the hydrogen atom. Each short horizontal line represents one orbital. Orbitals with the same principal quantum number (n) all have the same energy.*

Figure 7.23 *Orbital energy levels in a many-electron atom. Note that the energy level depends on both n and ℓ values.*

Figure 7.24 *The order in which atomic subshells are filled in a many-electron atom. Start with the 1s orbital and move downward, following the direction of the arrows. Thus, the order goes as follows: 1s < 2s < 2p < 3s < 3p < 4s < 3d < . . . .*

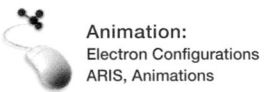

Animation:
Electron Configurations
ARIS, Animations

atom, however, depends not only on the sum of the orbital energies but also on the energy of repulsion between the electrons in these orbitals (each orbital can accommodate up to two electrons, as we will see in Section 7.8). It turns out that the total energy of an atom is lower when the 4s subshell is filled before a 3d subshell. Figure 7.24 depicts the order in which atomic orbitals are filled in a many-electron atom. We will consider specific examples in Section 7.8.

7.8 Electron Configuration

The four quantum numbers n, ℓ, m_ℓ, and m_s enable us to label completely an electron in any orbital in any atom. In a sense, we can regard the set of four quantum numbers as the "address" of an electron in an atom, somewhat in the same way that a street address, city, state, and postal ZIP code specify the address of an individual. For example, the four quantum numbers for a $2s$ orbital electron are $n = 2$, $\ell = 0$, $m_\ell = 0$, and $m_s = +\frac{1}{2}$ or $-\frac{1}{2}$. It is inconvenient to write out all the individual quantum numbers, and so we use the simplified notation (n, ℓ, m_ℓ, m_s). For the preceding example, the quantum numbers are either $(2, 0, 0, +\frac{1}{2})$ or $(2, 0, 0, -\frac{1}{2})$. The value of m_s has no effect on the energy, size, shape, or orientation of an orbital, but it determines how electrons are arranged in an orbital.

Example 7.8 shows how quantum numbers of an electron in an orbital are assigned.

Example 7.8

Write the four quantum numbers for an electron in a $3p$ orbital.

Strategy What do the "3" and "p" designate in $3p$? How many orbitals (values of m_ℓ) are there in a $3p$ subshell? What are the possible values of electron spin quantum number?

Solution To start with, we know that the principal quantum number n is 3 and the angular momentum quantum number ℓ must be 1 (because we are dealing with a p orbital).

(Continued)

For $\ell = 1$, there are three values of m_ℓ given by -1, 0, and 1. Because the electron spin quantum number m_s can be either $+\frac{1}{2}$ or $-\frac{1}{2}$, we conclude that there are six possible ways to designate the electron using the (n, ℓ, m_ℓ, m_s) notation:

$$(3, 1, -1, +\tfrac{1}{2}) \qquad (3, 1, -1, -\tfrac{1}{2})$$
$$(3, 1, 0, +\tfrac{1}{2}) \qquad (3, 1, 0, -\tfrac{1}{2})$$
$$(3, 1, 1, +\tfrac{1}{2}) \qquad (3, 1, 1, -\tfrac{1}{2})$$

Check In these six designations we see that the values of n and ℓ are constant, but the values of m_ℓ and m_s can vary.

Similar problem: 7.58.

Practice Exercise Write the four quantum numbers for an electron in a $5p$ orbital.

The hydrogen atom is a particularly simple system because it contains only one electron. The electron may reside in the $1s$ orbital (the ground state), or it may be found in some higher-energy orbital (an excited state). For many-electron atoms, however, we must know the ***electron configuration*** of the atom, that is, *how the electrons are distributed among the various atomic orbitals,* in order to understand electronic behavior. We will use the first 10 elements (hydrogen to neon) to illustrate the rules for writing electron configurations for atoms in the *ground state.* (Section 7.9 will describe how these rules can be applied to the remainder of the elements in the periodic table.) For this discussion, recall that the number of electrons in an atom is equal to its atomic number Z.

Figure 7.22 indicates that the electron in a ground-state hydrogen atom must be in the $1s$ orbital, so its electron configuration is $1s^1$:

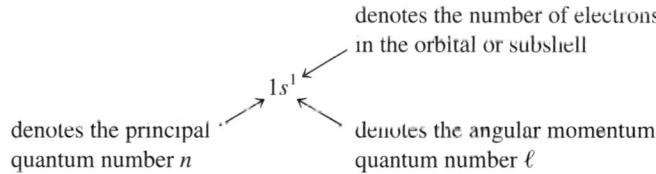

The electron configuration can also be represented by an *orbital diagram* that shows the spin of the electron (see Figure 7.16):

$$\text{H} \quad \boxed{\uparrow}$$
$$1s^1$$

The upward arrow denotes one of the two possible spinning motions of the electron. (Alternatively, we could have represented the electron with a downward arrow.) The box represents an atomic orbital.

Remember that the direction of electron spin has no effect on the energy of the electron.

The Pauli Exclusion Principle

For many-electron atoms we use the ***Pauli***[†] ***exclusion principle*** to determine electron configurations. This principle states that *no two electrons in an atom can have the same four quantum numbers.* If two electrons in an atom should have the same n, ℓ, and m_ℓ values (that is, these two electrons are in the *same* atomic orbital), then they

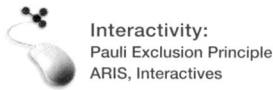

Interactivity:
Pauli Exclusion Principle
ARIS, Interactives

[†]Wolfgang Pauli (1900–1958). Austrian physicist. One of the founders of quantum mechanics, Pauli was awarded the Nobel Prize in Physics in 1945.

must have different values of m_s. In other words, only two electrons may occupy the same atomic orbital, and these electrons must have opposite spins. Consider the helium atom, which has two electrons. The three possible ways of placing two electrons in the $1s$ orbital are as follows:

$$\text{He} \quad \boxed{\uparrow\uparrow} \quad \boxed{\downarrow\downarrow} \quad \boxed{\uparrow\downarrow}$$
$$\qquad\quad 1s^2 \qquad 1s^2 \qquad 1s^2$$
$$\qquad\quad\ (a) \qquad\ (b) \qquad\ (c)$$

Diagrams (a) and (b) are ruled out by the Pauli exclusion principle. In (a), both electrons have the same upward spin and would have the quantum numbers $(1, 0, 0, +\frac{1}{2})$; in (b), both electrons have downward spins and would have the quantum numbers $(1, 0, 0, -\frac{1}{2})$. Only the configuration in (c) is physically acceptable, because one electron has the quantum numbers $(1, 0, 0, +\frac{1}{2})$ and the other has $(1, 0, 0, -\frac{1}{2})$. Thus, the helium atom has the following configuration:

$$\text{He} \quad \boxed{\uparrow\downarrow}$$
$$\qquad\quad 1s^2$$

Note that $1s^2$ is read "one s two," not "one s squared."

Electrons that have opposite spins are said to be paired. In helium, $m_s = +\frac{1}{2}$ for one electron; $m_s = -\frac{1}{2}$ for the other.

Diamagnetism and Paramagnetism

The Pauli exclusion principle is one of the fundamental principles of quantum mechanics. It can be tested by a simple observation. If the two electrons in the $1s$ orbital of a helium atom had the same, or parallel, spins ($\uparrow\uparrow$ or $\downarrow\downarrow$), their net magnetic fields would reinforce each other [Figure 7.25(a)]. Such an arrangement would make the helium gas paramagnetic. *Paramagnetic* substances are those that *contain net unpaired spins and are attracted by a magnet.* On the other hand, if the electron spins are paired, or antiparallel to each other ($\uparrow\downarrow$ or $\downarrow\uparrow$), the magnetic effects cancel out [Figure 7.25(b)]. *Diamagnetic* substances *do not contain net unpaired spins and are slightly repelled by a magnet.*

Measurements of magnetic properties provide the most direct evidence for specific electron configurations of elements. Advances in instrument design during the last 30 years or so enable us to determine the number of unpaired electrons in an atom (Figure 7.26). By experiment we find that the helium atom in its ground state has no net magnetic field. Therefore, the two electrons in the $1s$ orbital must be paired in accord with the Pauli exclusion principle and the helium gas is diamagnetic. A useful rule to keep in mind is that any atom with an *odd* number of electrons will always

Figure 7.25 *The (a) parallel and (b) antiparallel spins of two electrons. In (a) the two magnetic fields reinforce each other. In (b) the two magnetic fields cancel each other.*

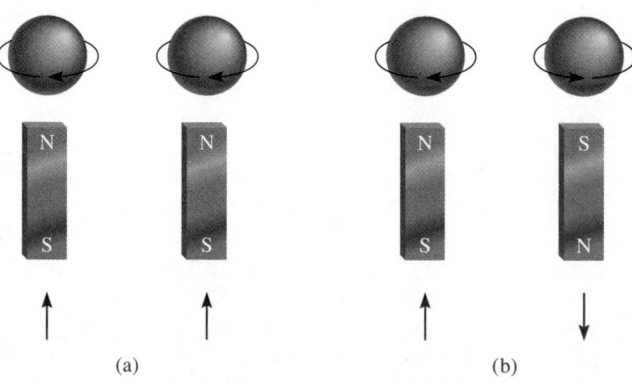

contain one or more unpaired spins because we need an even number of electrons for complete pairing. On the other hand, atoms containing an even number of electrons may or may not contain unpaired spins. We will see the reason for this behavior shortly.

As another example, consider the lithium atom ($Z = 3$) which has three electrons. The third electron cannot go into the $1s$ orbital because it would inevitably have the same four quantum numbers as one of the first two electrons. Therefore, this electron "enters" the next (energetically) higher orbital, which is the $2s$ orbital (see Figure 7.23). The electron configuration of lithium is $1s^2 2s^1$, and its orbital diagram is

Li   ⊣↑↓⊢   ⊣↑⊢
     $1s^2$ $2s^1$

The lithium atom contains one unpaired electron and the lithium metal is therefore paramagnetic.

The Shielding Effect in Many-Electron Atoms

Experimentally we find that the $2s$ orbital lies at a lower energy level than the $2p$ orbital in a many-electron atom. Why? In comparing the electron configurations of $1s^2 2s^1$ and $1s^2 2p^1$, we note that, in both cases, the $1s$ orbital is filled with two electrons. Figure 7.27 shows the radial probability plots for the $1s$, $2s$, and $2p$ orbitals. Because the $2s$ and $2p$ orbitals are larger than the $1s$ orbital, an electron in either of these orbitals will spend more time away from the nucleus than an electron in the $1s$ orbital. Thus, we can speak of a $2s$ or $2p$ electron being partly "shielded" from the attractive force of the nucleus by the $1s$ electrons. The important consequence of the shielding effect is that it *reduces* the electrostatic attraction between the protons in the nucleus and the electron in the $2s$ or $2p$ orbital.

The manner in which the electron density varies as we move from the nucleus outward depends on the type of orbital. Although a $2s$ electron spends most of its time (on average) slightly farther from the nucleus than a $2p$ electron, the electron density near the nucleus is actually greater for the $2s$ electron (see the small maximum for the $2s$ orbital in Figure 7.27). For this reason, the $2s$ orbital is said to be more "penetrating" than the $2p$ orbital. Therefore, a $2s$ electron is less shielded by the $1s$ electrons and is more strongly held by the nucleus. In fact, for the same principal quantum number n, the penetrating power decreases as the angular momentum quantum number ℓ increases, or

$$s > p > d > f > \cdots$$

Because the stability of an electron is determined by the strength of its attraction to the nucleus, it follows that a $2s$ electron will be lower in energy than a $2p$ electron. To put it another way, less energy is required to remove a $2p$ electron than a $2s$ electron because a $2p$ electron is not held quite as strongly by the nucleus. The hydrogen atom has only one electron and, therefore, is without such a shielding effect.

Continuing our discussion of atoms of the first 10 elements, we go next to beryllium ($Z = 4$). The ground-state electron configuration of beryllium is $1s^2 2s^2$, or

Be   ⊣↑↓⊢   ⊣↑↓⊢
     $1s^2$ $2s^2$

Beryllium is diamagnetic, as we would expect.

Figure 7.26 *Initially the paramagnetic substance was weighed on a balance. When the electromagnet is turned on, the balance is offset because the sample tube is drawn into the magnetic field. Knowing the concentration and the additional mass needed to reestablish balance, it is possible to calculate the number of unpaired electrons in the substance.*

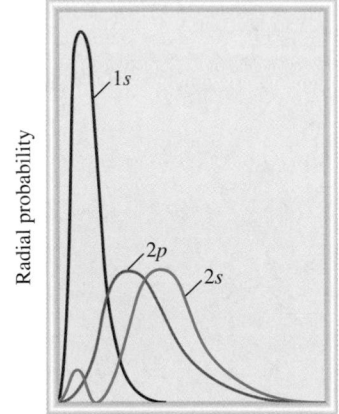

Distance from nucleus

Figure 7.27 *Radial probability plots (see Figure 7.18) for the 1s, 2s, and 2p orbitals. The 1s electrons effectively shield both the 2s and 2p electrons from the nucleus. The 2s orbital is more penetrating than the 2p orbital.*

The electron configuration of boron ($Z = 5$) is $1s^2 2s^2 2p^1$, or

B   [↑↓]   [↑↓]   [↑][ ][ ]
    $1s^2$ $2s^2$ $2p^1$

Note that the unpaired electron can be in the $2p_x$, $2p_y$, or $2p_z$ orbital. The choice is completely arbitrary because the three p orbitals are equivalent in energy. As the diagram shows, boron is paramagnetic.

Hund's Rule

The electron configuration of carbon ($Z = 6$) is $1s^2 2s^2 2p^2$. The following are different ways of distributing two electrons among three p orbitals:

   $2p_x \ 2p_y \ 2p_z$ $2p_x \ 2p_y \ 2p_z$ $2p_x \ 2p_y \ 2p_z$
       (a)   (b)   (c)

None of the three arrangements violates the Pauli exclusion principle, so we must determine which one will give the greatest stability. The answer is provided by ***Hund's rule,***[†] which states that *the most stable arrangement of electrons in subshells is the one with the greatest number of parallel spins.* The arrangement shown in (c) satisfies this condition. In both (a) and (b) the two spins cancel each other. Thus, the orbital diagram for carbon is

C   [↑↓]   [↑↓]   [↑][↑][ ]
    $1s^2$ $2s^2$ $2p^2$

Qualitatively, we can understand why (c) is preferred to (a). In (a), the two electrons are in the same $2p_x$ orbital, and their proximity results in a greater mutual repulsion than when they occupy two separate orbitals, say $2p_x$ and $2p_y$. The choice of (c) over (b) is more subtle but can be justified on theoretical grounds. The fact that carbon atoms contain two unpaired electrons is in accord with Hund's rule.

The electron configuration of nitrogen ($Z = 7$) is $1s^2 2s^2 2p^3$:

N   [↑↓]   [↑↓]   [↑][↑][↑]
    $1s^2$ $2s^2$ $2p^3$

Again, Hund's rule dictates that all three $2p$ electrons have spins parallel to one another; the nitrogen atom contains three unpaired electrons.

The electron configuration of oxygen ($Z = 8$) is $1s^2 2s^2 2p^4$. An oxygen atom has two unpaired electrons:

O   [↑↓]   [↑↓]   [↑↓][↑][↑]
    $1s^2$ $2s^2$ $2p^4$

[†]Frederick Hund (1896–1997). German physicist. Hund's work was mainly in quantum mechanics. He also helped to develop the molecular orbital theory of chemical bonding.

The electron configuration of fluorine $(Z = 9)$ is $1s^2 2s^2 2p^5$. The nine electrons are arranged as follows:

$$F \quad \boxed{\uparrow\downarrow} \quad \boxed{\uparrow\downarrow} \quad \boxed{\uparrow\downarrow}\,\boxed{\uparrow\downarrow}\,\boxed{\uparrow}$$
$$\quad 1s^2 \qquad 2s^2 \qquad 2p^5$$

The fluorine atom has one unpaired electron.

In neon $(Z = 10)$, the $2p$ subshell is completely filled. The electron configuration of neon is $1s^2 2s^2 2p^6$, and *all* the electrons are paired, as follows:

$$Ne \quad \boxed{\uparrow\downarrow} \quad \boxed{\uparrow\downarrow} \quad \boxed{\uparrow\downarrow}\,\boxed{\uparrow\downarrow}\,\boxed{\uparrow\downarrow}$$
$$\quad 1s^2 \qquad 2s^2 \qquad 2p^6$$

The neon gas should be diamagnetic, and experimental observation bears out this prediction.

General Rules for Assigning Electrons to Atomic Orbitals

Based on the preceding examples we can formulate some general rules for determining the maximum number of electrons that can be assigned to the various subshells and orbitals for a given value of n:

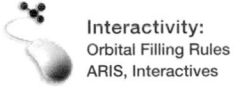

Interactivity:
Orbital Filling Rules
ARIS, Interactives

1. Each shell or principal level of quantum number n contains n subshells. For example, if $n = 2$, then there are two subshells (two values of ℓ) of angular momentum quantum numbers 0 and 1.

2. Each subshell of quantum number ℓ contains $(2\ell + 1)$ orbitals. For example, if $\ell = 1$, then there are three p orbitals.

3. No more than two electrons can be placed in each orbital. Therefore, the maximum number of electrons is simply twice the number of orbitals that are employed.

4. A quick way to determine the maximum number of electrons that an atom can have in a principal level n is to use the formula $2n^2$.

Examples 7.9 and 7.10 illustrate the procedure for calculating the number of electrons in orbitals and labeling electrons with the four quantum numbers.

Example 7.9

What is the maximum number of electrons that can be present in the principal level for which $n = 3$?

Strategy We are given the principal quantum number (n) so we can determine all the possible values of the angular momentum quantum number (ℓ). The preceding rule shows that the number of orbitals for each value of ℓ is $(2\ell + 1)$. Thus, we can determine the total number of orbitals. How many electrons can each orbital accommodate?

Solution When $n = 3$, $\ell = 0$, 1, and 2. The number of orbitals for each value of ℓ is given by

Value of ℓ	Number of Orbitals $(2\ell + 1)$
0	1
1	3
2	5

(Continued)

The total number of orbitals is nine. Because each orbital can accommodate two electrons, the maximum number of electrons that can reside in the orbitals is 2×9, or 18.

Check If we use the formula (n^2) in Example 7.7, we find that the total number of orbitals is 3^2 and the total number of electrons is $2(3^2)$ or 18. In general, the number of electrons in a given principal energy level n is $2n^2$.

Similar problems: 7.64, 7.65.

Practice Exercise Calculate the total number of electrons that can be present in the principal level for which $n = 4$.

Example 7.10

An oxygen atom has a total of eight electrons. Write the four quantum numbers for each of the eight electrons in the ground state.

Strategy We start with $n = 1$ and proceed to fill orbitals in the order shown in Figure 7.24. For each value of n we determine the possible values of ℓ. For each value of ℓ, we assign the possible values of m_ℓ. We can place electrons in the orbitals according to the Pauli exclusion principle and Hund's rule.

Solution We start with $n = 1$, so $\ell = 0$, a subshell corresponding to the $1s$ orbital. This orbital can accommodate a total of two electrons. Next, $n = 2$, and ℓ may be either 0 or 1. The $\ell = 0$ subshell contains one $2s$ orbital, which can accommodate two electrons. The remaining four electrons are placed in the $\ell = 1$ subshell, which contains three $2p$ orbitals. The orbital diagram is

$$\text{O} \quad \boxed{\uparrow\downarrow} \quad \boxed{\uparrow\downarrow} \quad \boxed{\uparrow\downarrow \,|\, \uparrow \,|\, \uparrow}$$
$$\quad\quad 1s^2 \quad\quad 2s^2 \quad\quad 2p^4$$

The results are summarized in the following table:

Electron	n	ℓ	m_ℓ	m_s	Orbital
1	1	0	0	$+\frac{1}{2}$	$1s$
2	1	0	0	$-\frac{1}{2}$	
3	2	0	0	$+\frac{1}{2}$	$2s$
4	2	0	0	$-\frac{1}{2}$	
5	2	1	-1	$+\frac{1}{2}$	
6	2	1	0	$+\frac{1}{2}$	$2p_x, 2p_y, 2p_z$
7	2	1	1	$+\frac{1}{2}$	
8	2	1	1	$-\frac{1}{2}$	

Similar problem: 7.91.

Of course, the placement of the eighth electron in the orbital labeled $m_\ell = 1$ is completely arbitrary. It would be equally correct to assign it to $m_\ell = 0$ or $m_\ell = -1$.

Practice Exercise Write a complete set of quantum numbers for each of the electrons in boron (B).

7.9 The Building-Up Principle

Here we will extend the rules used in writing electron configurations for the first 10 elements to the rest of the elements. This process is based on the Aufbau principle. The ***Aufbau principle*** dictates that *as protons are added one by one to the nucleus*

The German word "Aufbau" means "building up."

to build up the elements, electrons are similarly added to the atomic orbitals. Through this process we gain a detailed knowledge of the ground-state electron configurations of the elements. As we will see later, knowledge of electron configurations helps us to understand and predict the properties of the elements; it also explains why the periodic table works so well.

Table 7.3 gives the ground-state electron configurations of elements from H ($Z = 1$) through Rg ($Z = 111$). The electron configurations of all elements except hydrogen and helium are represented by a ***noble gas core,*** which *shows in brackets the noble gas element that most nearly precedes the element being considered,* followed by the symbol for the highest filled subshells in the outermost shells. Notice that the electron configurations of the highest filled subshells in the outermost shells for the elements sodium ($Z = 11$) through argon ($Z = 18$) follow a pattern similar to those of lithium ($Z = 3$) through neon ($Z = 10$).

The noble gases.

As mentioned in Section 7.7, the $4s$ subshell is filled before the $3d$ subshell in a many-electron atom (see Figure 7.24). Thus, the electron configuration of potassium ($Z = 19$) is $1s^2 2s^2 2p^6 3s^2 3p^6 4s^1$. Because $1s^2 2s^2 2p^6 3s^2 3p^6$ is the electron configuration of argon, we can simplify the electron configuration of potassium by writing [Ar]$4s^1$, where [Ar] denotes the "argon core." Similarly, we can write the electron configuration of calcium ($Z = 20$) as [Ar]$4s^2$. The placement of the outermost electron in the $4s$ orbital (rather than in the $3d$ orbital) of potassium is strongly supported by experimental evidence. The following comparison also suggests that this is the correct configuration. The chemistry of potassium is very similar to that of lithium and sodium, the first two alkali metals. The outermost electron of both lithium and sodium is in an s orbital (there is no ambiguity in assigning their electron configurations); therefore, we expect the last electron in potassium to occupy the $4s$ rather than the $3d$ orbital.

The elements from scandium ($Z = 21$) to copper ($Z = 29$) are transition metals. *Transition metals* either have incompletely filled d subshells or readily give rise to cations that have incompletely filled d subshells. Consider the first transition metal series, from scandium through copper. In this series additional electrons are placed in the $3d$ orbitals, according to Hund's rule. However, there are two irregularities. The electron configuration of chromium ($Z = 24$) is [Ar]$4s^1 3d^5$ and not [Ar]$4s^2 3d^4$, as we might expect. A similar break in the pattern is observed for copper, whose electron configuration is [Ar]$4s^1 3d^{10}$ rather than [Ar]$4s^2 3d^9$. The reason for these irregularities is that a slightly greater stability is associated with the half-filled ($3d^5$) and completely filled ($3d^{10}$) subshells. Electrons in the same subshell (in this case, the d orbitals) have equal energy but different spatial distributions. Consequently, their shielding of one another is relatively small, and the electrons are more strongly attracted by the nucleus when they have the $3d^5$ configuration. According to Hund's rule, the orbital diagram for Cr is

The transition metals.

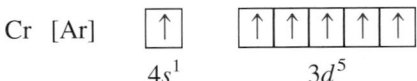

Thus, Cr has a total of six unpaired electrons. The orbital diagram for copper is

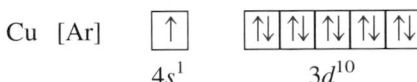

Again, extra stability is gained in this case by having the $3d$ subshell completely filled.

For elements Zn ($Z = 30$) through Kr ($Z = 36$), the $4s$ and $4p$ subshells fill in a straightforward manner. With rubidium ($Z = 37$), electrons begin to enter the $n = 5$ energy level.

TABLE 7.3   The Ground-State Electron Configurations of the Elements*

Atomic Number	Symbol	Electron Configuration	Atomic Number	Symbol	Electron Configuration	Atomic Number	Symbol	Electron Configuration
1	H	$1s^1$	38	Sr	$[Kr]5s^2$	75	Re	$[Xe]6s^24f^{14}5d^5$
2	He	$1s^2$	39	Y	$[Kr]5s^24d^1$	76	Os	$[Xe]6s^24f^{14}5d^6$
3	Li	$[He]2s^1$	40	Zr	$[Kr]5s^24d^2$	77	Ir	$[Xe]6s^24f^{14}5d^7$
4	Be	$[He]2s^2$	41	Nb	$[Kr]5s^14d^4$	78	Pt	$[Xe]6s^14f^{14}5d^9$
5	B	$[He]2s^22p^1$	42	Mo	$[Kr]5s^14d^5$	79	Au	$[Xe]6s^14f^{14}5d^{10}$
6	C	$[He]2s^22p^2$	43	Tc	$[Kr]5s^24d^5$	80	Hg	$[Xe]6s^24f^{14}5d^{10}$
7	N	$[He]2s^22p^3$	44	Ru	$[Kr]5s^14d^7$	81	Tl	$[Xe]6s^24f^{14}5d^{10}6p^1$
8	O	$[He]2s^22p^4$	45	Rh	$[Kr]5s^14d^8$	82	Pb	$[Xe]6s^24f^{14}5d^{10}6p^2$
9	F	$[He]2s^22p^5$	46	Pd	$[Kr]4d^{10}$	83	Bi	$[Xe]6s^24f^{14}5d^{10}6p^3$
10	Ne	$[He]2s^22p^6$	47	Ag	$[Kr]5s^14d^{10}$	84	Po	$[Xe]6s^24f^{14}5d^{10}6p^4$
11	Na	$[Ne]3s^1$	48	Cd	$[Kr]5s^24d^{10}$	85	At	$[Xe]6s^24f^{14}5d^{10}6p^5$
12	Mg	$[Ne]3s^2$	49	In	$[Kr]5s^24d^{10}5p^1$	86	Rn	$[Xe]6s^24f^{14}5d^{10}6p^6$
13	Al	$[Ne]3s^23p^1$	50	Sn	$[Kr]5s^24d^{10}5p^2$	87	Fr	$[Rn]7s^1$
14	Si	$[Ne]3s^23p^2$	51	Sb	$[Kr]5s^24d^{10}5p^3$	88	Ra	$[Rn]7s^2$
15	P	$[Ne]3s^23p^3$	52	Te	$[Kr]5s^24d^{10}5p^4$	89	Ac	$[Rn]7s^26d^1$
16	S	$[Ne]3s^23p^4$	53	I	$[Kr]5s^24d^{10}5p^5$	90	Th	$[Rn]7s^26d^2$
17	Cl	$[Ne]3s^23p^5$	54	Xe	$[Kr]5s^24d^{10}5p^6$	91	Pa	$[Rn]7s^25f^26d^1$
18	Ar	$[Ne]3s^23p^6$	55	Cs	$[Xe]6s^1$	92	U	$[Rn]7s^25f^36d^1$
19	K	$[Ar]4s^1$	56	Ba	$[Xe]6s^2$	93	Np	$[Rn]7s^25f^46d^1$
20	Ca	$[Ar]4s^2$	57	La	$[Xe]6s^25d^1$	94	Pu	$[Rn]7s^25f^6$
21	Sc	$[Ar]4s^23d^1$	58	Ce	$[Xe]6s^24f^15d^1$	95	Am	$[Rn]7s^25f^7$
22	Ti	$[Ar]4s^23d^2$	59	Pr	$[Xe]6s^24f^3$	96	Cm	$[Rn]7s^25f^76d^1$
23	V	$[Ar]4s^23d^3$	60	Nd	$[Xe]6s^24f^4$	97	Bk	$[Rn]7s^25f^9$
24	Cr	$[Ar]4s^13d^5$	61	Pm	$[Xe]6s^24f^5$	98	Cf	$[Rn]7s^25f^{10}$
25	Mn	$[Ar]4s^23d^5$	62	Sm	$[Xe]6s^24f^6$	99	Es	$[Rn]7s^25f^{11}$
26	Fe	$[Ar]4s^23d^6$	63	Eu	$[Xe]6s^24f^7$	100	Fm	$[Rn]7s^25f^{12}$
27	Co	$[Ar]4s^23d^7$	64	Gd	$[Xe]6s^24f^75d^1$	101	Md	$[Rn]7s^25f^{13}$
28	Ni	$[Ar]4s^23d^8$	65	Tb	$[Xe]6s^24f^9$	102	No	$[Rn]7s^25f^{14}$
29	Cu	$[Ar]4s^13d^{10}$	66	Dy	$[Xe]6s^24f^{10}$	103	Lr	$[Rn]7s^25f^{14}6d^1$
30	Zn	$[Ar]4s^23d^{10}$	67	Ho	$[Xe]6s^24f^{11}$	104	Rf	$[Rn]7s^25f^{14}6d^2$
31	Ga	$[Ar]4s^23d^{10}4p^1$	68	Er	$[Xe]6s^24f^{12}$	105	Db	$[Rn]7s^25f^{14}6d^3$
32	Ge	$[Ar]4s^23d^{10}4p^2$	69	Tm	$[Xe]6s^24f^{13}$	106	Sg	$[Rn]7s^25f^{14}6d^4$
33	As	$[Ar]4s^23d^{10}4p^3$	70	Yb	$[Xe]6s^24f^{14}$	107	Bh	$[Rn]7s^25f^{14}6d^5$
34	Se	$[Ar]4s^23d^{10}4p^4$	71	Lu	$[Xe]6s^24f^{14}5d^1$	108	Hs	$[Rn]7s^25f^{14}6d^6$
35	Br	$[Ar]4s^23d^{10}4p^5$	72	Hf	$[Xe]6s^24f^{14}5d^2$	109	Mt	$[Rn]7s^25f^{14}6d^7$
36	Kr	$[Ar]4s^23d^{10}4p^6$	73	Ta	$[Xe]6s^24f^{14}5d^3$	110	Ds	$[Rn]7s^25f^{14}6d^8$
37	Rb	$[Kr]5s^1$	74	W	$[Xe]6s^24f^{14}5d^4$	111	Rg	$[Rn]7s^25f^{14}6d^9$

*The symbol [He] is called the helium core and represents $1s^2$. [Ne] is called the neon core and represents $1s^22s^22p^6$. [Ar] is called the argon core and represents $[Ne]3s^23p^6$. [Kr] is called the krypton core and represents $[Ar]4s^23d^{10}4p^6$. [Xe] is called the xenon core and represents $[Kr]5s^24d^{10}5p^6$. [Rn] is called the radon core and represents $[Xe]6s^24f^{14}5d^{10}6p^6$.

1s						1s
2s						2p
3s						3p
4s	3d					4p
5s	4d					5p
6s	5d					6p
7s	6d					7p

4f
5f

Figure 7.28 *Classification of groups of elements in the periodic table according to the type of subshell being filled with electrons.*

The electron configurations in the second transition metal series [yttrium ($Z = 39$) to silver ($Z = 47$)] are also irregular, but we will not be concerned with the details here.

The sixth period of the periodic table begins with cesium ($Z = 55$) and barium ($Z = 56$), whose electron configurations are [Xe]$6s^1$ and [Xe]$6s^2$, respectively. Next we come to lanthanum ($Z = 57$). From Figure 7.24 we would expect that after filling the $6s$ orbital we would place the additional electrons in $4f$ orbitals. In reality, the energies of the $5d$ and $4f$ orbitals are very close; in fact, for lanthanum $4f$ is slightly higher in energy than $5d$. Thus, lanthanum's electron configuration is [Xe]$6s^2 5d^1$ and not [Xe]$6s^2 4f^1$.

Following lanthanum are the 14 elements known as the ***lanthanides,*** or ***rare earth series*** [cerium ($Z = 58$) to lutetium ($Z = 71$)]. The rare earth metals *have incompletely filled $4f$ subshells or readily give rise to cations that have incompletely filled $4f$ subshells.* In this series, the added electrons are placed in $4f$ orbitals. After the $4f$ subshell is completely filled, the next electron enters the $5d$ subshell of lutetium. Note that the electron configuration of gadolinium ($Z = 64$) is [Xe]$6s^2 4f^7 5d^1$ rather than [Xe]$6s^2 4f^8$. Like chromium, gadolinium gains extra stability by having a half-filled subshell ($4f^7$).

The third transition metal series, including lanthanum and hafnium ($Z = 72$) and extending through gold ($Z = 79$), is characterized by the filling of the $5d$ subshell. The $6s$ and $6p$ subshells are filled next, which takes us to radon ($Z = 86$).

The *last row of elements* is the ***actinide series,*** which starts at thorium ($Z = 90$). *Most of these elements are not found in nature but have been synthesized.*

With few exceptions, you should be able to write the electron configuration of any element, using Figure 7.24 as a guide. Elements that require particular care are the transition metals, the lanthanides, and the actinides. As we noted earlier, at larger values of the principal quantum number n, the order of subshell filling may reverse from one element to the next. Figure 7.28 groups the elements according to the type of subshell in which the outermost electrons are placed.

Example 7.11

Write the ground-state electron configurations for (a) sulfur (S) and (b) palladium (Pd), which is diamagnetic.

(Continued)

(a) Strategy How many electrons are in the S ($Z = 16$) atom? We start with $n = 1$ and proceed to fill orbitals in the order shown in Figure 7.24. For each value of ℓ, we assign the possible values of m_ℓ. We can place electrons in the orbitals according to the Pauli exclusion principle and Hund's rule and then write the electron configuration. The task is simplified if we use the noble-gas core preceding S for the inner electrons.

Solution Sulfur has 16 electrons. The noble gas core in this case is [Ne]. (Ne is the noble gas in the period preceding sulfur.) [Ne] represents $1s^2 2s^2 2p^6$. This leaves us 6 electrons to fill the $3s$ subshell and partially fill the $3p$ subshell. Thus, the electron configuration of S is $1s^2 2s^2 2p^6 3s^2 3p^4$ or $[Ne]3s^2 3p^4$.

(b) Strategy We use the same approach as that in (a). What does it mean to say that Pd is a diamagnetic element?

Solution Palladium has 46 electrons. The noble-gas core in this case is [Kr]. (Kr is the noble gas in the period preceding palladium.) [Kr] represents

$$1s^2 2s^2 2p^6 3s^2 3p^6 4s^2 3d^{10} 4p^6$$

The remaining 10 electrons are distributed among the $4d$ and $5s$ orbitals. The three choices are (1) $4d^{10}$, (2) $4d^9 5s^1$, and (3) $4d^8 5s^2$. Because palladium is diamagnetic, all the electrons are paired and its electron configuration must be

$$1s^2 2s^2 2p^6 3s^2 3p^6 4s^2 3d^{10} 4p^6 4d^{10}$$

or simply $[Kr]4d^{10}$. The configurations in (2) and (3) both represent paramagnetic elements.

Check To confirm the answer, write the orbital diagrams for (1), (2), and (3).

Practice Exercise Write the ground-state electron configuration for phosphorus (P).

Similar problems: 7.87, 7.88.

Summary of Facts and Concepts

1. The quantum theory developed by Planck successfully explains the emission of radiation by heated solids. The quantum theory states that radiant energy is emitted by atoms and molecules in small discrete amounts (quanta), rather than over a continuous range. This behavior is governed by the relationship $E = h\nu$, where E is the energy of the radiation, h is Planck's constant, and ν is the frequency of the radiation. Energy is always emitted in whole-number multiples of $h\nu$ (1 $h\nu$, 2 $h\nu$, 3 $h\nu$, . . .).

2. Using quantum theory, Einstein solved another mystery of physics—the photoelectric effect. Einstein proposed that light can behave like a stream of particles (photons).

3. The line spectrum of hydrogen, yet another mystery to nineteenth-century physicists, was also explained by applying the quantum theory. Bohr developed a model of the hydrogen atom in which the energy of its single electron is quantized—limited to certain energy values determined by an integer, the principal quantum number.

4. An electron in its most stable energy state is said to be in the ground state, and an electron at an energy level higher than its most stable state is said to be in an excited state. In the Bohr model, an electron emits a photon when it drops from a higher-energy state (an excited state) to a lower-energy state (the ground state or another, less excited state). The release of specific amounts of energy in the form of photons accounts for the lines in the hydrogen emission spectrum.

5. De Broglie extended Einstein's wave-particle description of light to all matter in motion. The wavelength of a moving particle of mass m and velocity u is given by the de Broglie equation $\lambda = h/mu$.

6. The Schrödinger equation describes the motions and energies of submicroscopic particles. This equation launched quantum mechanics and a new era in physics.

7. The Schrödinger equation tells us the possible energy states of the electron in a hydrogen atom and the probability of its location in a particular region surrounding the nucleus. These results can be applied with reasonable accuracy to many-electron atoms.

8. An atomic orbital is a function (ψ) that defines the distribution of electron density (ψ^2) in space. Orbitals are represented by electron density diagrams or boundary surface diagrams.

9. Four quantum numbers characterize each electron in an atom: the principal quantum number n identifies the main energy level, or shell, of the orbital; the angular momentum quantum number ℓ indicates the shape of the orbital; the magnetic quantum number m_ℓ specifies the orientation of the orbital in space; and the electron spin quantum number m_s indicates the direction of the electron's spin on its own axis.

10. The single s orbital for each energy level is spherical and centered on the nucleus. The three p orbitals present at $n = 2$ and higher; each has two lobes, and the pairs of lobes are arranged at right angles to one another. Starting with $n = 3$, there are five d orbitals, with more complex shapes and orientations.

11. The energy of the electron in a hydrogen atom is determined solely by its principal quantum number. In many-electron atoms, the principal quantum number and the angular momentum quantum number together determine the energy of an electron.

12. No two electrons in the same atom can have the same four quantum numbers (the Pauli exclusion principle).

13. The most stable arrangement of electrons in a subshell is the one that has the greatest number of parallel spins (Hund's rule). Atoms with one or more unpaired electron spins are paramagnetic. Atoms in which all electrons are paired are diamagnetic.

14. The Aufbau principle provides the guideline for building up the elements. The periodic table classifies the elements according to their atomic numbers and thus also by the electronic configurations of their atoms.

Key Words

Actinide series, p. 301
Amplitude, p. 268
Atomic orbital, p. 285
Aufbau principle, p. 298
Boundary surface diagram, p. 288
Diamagnetic, p. 294
Electromagnetic radiation, p. 269
Electromagnetic wave, p. 269

Electron configuration, p. 293
Electron density, p. 285
Emission spectra, p. 274
Excited level (or state), p. 276
Frequency (ν), p. 268
Ground level (or state), p. 276
Ground state, p. 276

Heisenberg uncertainty principle, p. 284
Hund's rule, p. 296
Lanthanide (rare earth) series, p. 301
Line spectra, p. 274
Many-electron atom, p. 286
Noble gas core, p. 299
Node, p. 279
Paramagnetic, p. 294

Pauli exclusion principle, p. 293
Photoelectric effect, p. 272
Photon, p. 272
Quantum, p. 272
Quantum numbers, p. 286
Rare earth series, p. 301
Transition metals, p. 299
Wave, p. 268
Wavelength (λ), p. 268

Questions and Problems

Quantum Theory and Electromagnetic Radiation

Review Questions

7.1 What is a wave? Explain the following terms associated with waves: wavelength, frequency, amplitude.

7.2 What are the units for wavelength and frequency of electromagnetic waves? What is the speed of light in meters per second and miles per hour?

7.3 List the types of electromagnetic radiation, starting with the radiation having the longest wavelength and ending with the radiation having the shortest wavelength.

7.4 Give the high and low wavelength values that define the visible region of the electromagnetic spectrum.

7.5 Briefly explain Planck's quantum theory and explain what a quantum is. What are the units for Planck's constant?

7.6 Give two everyday examples that illustrate the concept of quantization.

Problems

7.7 (a) What is the wavelength (in nanometers) of light having a frequency of 8.6×10^{13} Hz? (b) What is the frequency (in Hz) of light having a wavelength of 566 nm?

7.8 (a) What is the frequency of light having a wavelength of 456 nm? (b) What is the wavelength (in nanometers) of radiation having a frequency of 2.45×10^9 Hz? (This is the type of radiation used in microwave ovens.)

7.9 The average distance between Mars and Earth is about 1.3×10^8 miles. How long would it take TV pictures transmitted from the *Viking* space vehicle on Mars' surface to reach Earth? (1 mile = 1.61 km.)

7.10 How many minutes would it take a radio wave to travel from the planet Venus to Earth? (Average distance from Venus to Earth = 28 million miles.)

7.11 The SI unit of time is the second, which is defined as 9,192,631,770 cycles of radiation associated with a certain emission process in the cesium atom. Calculate the wavelength of this radiation (to three significant figures). In which region of the electromagnetic spectrum is this wavelength found?

7.12 The SI unit of length is the meter, which is defined as the length equal to 1,650,763.73 wavelengths of the light emitted by a particular energy transition in krypton atoms. Calculate the frequency of the light to three significant figures.

The Photoelectric Effect
Review Questions

7.13 Explain what is meant by the photoelectric effect.

7.14 What are photons? What role did Einstein's explanation of the photoelectric effect play in the development of the particle-wave interpretation of the nature of electromagnetic radiation?

Problems

7.15 A photon has a wavelength of 624 nm. Calculate the energy of the photon in joules.

7.16 The blue color of the sky results from the scattering of sunlight by air molecules. The blue light has a frequency of about 7.5×10^{14} Hz. (a) Calculate the wavelength, in nm, associated with this radiation, and (b) calculate the energy, in joules, of a single photon associated with this frequency.

7.17 A photon has a frequency of 6.0×10^4 Hz. (a) Convert this frequency into wavelength (nm). Does this frequency fall in the visible region? (b) Calculate the energy (in joules) of this photon. (c) Calculate the energy (in joules) of 1 mole of photons all with this frequency.

7.18 What is the wavelength, in nm, of radiation that has an energy content of 1.0×10^3 kJ/mol? In which region of the electromagnetic spectrum is this radiation found?

7.19 When copper is bombarded with high-energy electrons, X rays are emitted. Calculate the energy (in joules) associated with the photons if the wavelength of the X rays is 0.154 nm.

7.20 A particular form of electromagnetic radiation has a frequency of 8.11×10^{14} Hz. (a) What is its wavelength in nanometers? In meters? (b) To what region of the electromagnetic spectrum would you assign it?

(c) What is the energy (in joules) of one quantum of this radiation?

Bohr's Theory of the Hydrogen Atom
Review Questions

7.21 What are emission spectra? How do line spectra differ from continuous spectra?

7.22 What is an energy level? Explain the difference between ground state and excited state.

7.23 Briefly describe Bohr's theory of the hydrogen atom and how it explains the appearance of an emission spectrum. How does Bohr's theory differ from concepts of classical physics?

7.24 Explain the meaning of the negative sign in Equation (7.5).

Problems

7.25 Explain why elements produce their own characteristic colors when they emit photons?

7.26 Some copper compounds emit green light when they are heated in a flame. How would you determine whether the light is of one wavelength or a mixture of two or more wavelengths?

7.27 Is it possible for a fluorescent material to emit radiation in the ultraviolet region after absorbing visible light? Explain your answer.

7.28 Explain how astronomers are able to tell which elements are present in distant stars by analyzing the electromagnetic radiation emitted by the stars.

7.29 Consider the following energy levels of a hypothetical atom:

$$E_4 \text{_____} -1.0 \times 10^{-19} \text{ J}$$
$$E_3 \text{_____} -5.0 \times 10^{-19} \text{ J}$$
$$E_2 \text{_____} -10 \times 10^{-19} \text{ J}$$
$$E_1 \text{_____} -15 \times 10^{-19} \text{ J}$$

(a) What is the wavelength of the photon needed to excite an electron from E_1 to E_4? (b) What is the energy (in joules) a photon must have in order to excite an electron from E_2 to E_3? (c) When an electron drops from the E_3 level to the E_1 level, the atom is said to undergo emission. Calculate the wavelength of the photon emitted in this process.

7.30 The first line of the Balmer series occurs at a wavelength of 656.3 nm. What is the energy difference between the two energy levels involved in the emission that results in this spectral line?

7.31 Calculate the wavelength (in nanometers) of a photon emitted by a hydrogen atom when its electron drops from the $n = 5$ state to the $n = 3$ state.

7.32 Calculate the frequency (Hz) and wavelength (nm) of the emitted photon when an electron drops from the $n = 4$ to the $n = 2$ level in a hydrogen atom.

7.33 Careful spectral analysis shows that the familiar yellow light of sodium lamps (such as street lamps) is made up of photons of two wavelengths, 589.0 nm and 589.6 nm. What is the difference in energy (in joules) between photons with these wavelengths?

7.34 An electron in the hydrogen atom makes a transition from an energy state of principal quantum numbers n_i to the $n = 2$ state. If the photon emitted has a wavelength of 434 nm, what is the value of n_i?

Particle-Wave Duality

Review Questions

7.35 Explain the statement, Matter and radiation have a "dual nature."

7.36 How does de Broglie's hypothesis account for the fact that the energies of the electron in a hydrogen atom are quantized?

7.37 Why is Equation (7.8) meaningful only for submicroscopic particles, such as electrons and atoms, and not for macroscopic objects?

7.38 Does a baseball in flight possess wave properties? If so, why can we not determine its wave properties?

Problems

7.39 Thermal neutrons are neutrons that move at speeds comparable to those of air molecules at room temperature. These neutrons are most effective in initiating a nuclear chain reaction among ^{235}U isotopes. Calculate the wavelength (in nm) associated with a beam of neutrons moving at 7.00×10^2 m/s. (Mass of a neutron = 1.675×10^{-27} kg.)

7.40 Protons can be accelerated to speeds near that of light in particle accelerators. Estimate the wavelength (in nm) of such a proton moving at 2.90×10^8 m/s. (Mass of a proton = 1.673×10^{-27} kg.)

7.41 What is the de Broglie wavelength, in cm, of a 12.4-g hummingbird flying at 1.20×10^2 mph? (1 mile = 1.61 km.)

7.42 What is the de Broglie wavelength (in nm) associated with a 2.5-g Ping-Pong ball traveling 35 mph?

Quantum Mechanics

Review Questions

7.43 What are the inadequacies of Bohr's theory?

7.44 What is the Heisenberg uncertainty principle? What is the Schrödinger equation?

7.45 What is the physical significance of the wave function?

7.46 How is the concept of electron density used to describe the position of an electron in the quantum mechanical treatment of an atom?

7.47 What is an atomic orbital? How does an atomic orbital differ from an orbit?

Atomic Orbitals

Review Questions

7.48 Describe the shapes of s, p, and d orbitals. How are these orbitals related to the quantum numbers n, ℓ, and m_ℓ?

7.49 List the hydrogen orbitals in increasing order of energy.

7.50 Describe the characteristics of an s orbital, a p orbital, and a d orbital. Which of the following orbitals do not exist: $1p$, $2s$, $2d$, $3p$, $3d$, $3f$, $4g$?

7.51 Why is a boundary surface diagram useful in representing an atomic orbital?

7.52 Describe the four quantum numbers used to characterize an electron in an atom.

7.53 Which quantum number defines a shell? Which quantum numbers define a subshell?

7.54 Which of the four quantum numbers (n, ℓ, m_ℓ, m_s) determine (a) the energy of an electron in a hydrogen atom and in a many-electron atom, (b) the size of an orbital, (c) the shape of an orbital, (d) the orientation of an orbital in space?

Problems

7.55 An electron in a certain atom is in the $n = 2$ quantum level. List the possible values of ℓ and m_ℓ that it can have.

7.56 An electron in an atom is in the $n = 3$ quantum level. List the possible values of ℓ and m_ℓ that it can have.

7.57 Give the values of the quantum numbers associated with the following orbitals. (a) $2p$, (b) $3s$, (c) $5d$.

7.58 Give the values of the four quantum numbers of an electron in the following orbitals: (a) $3s$, (b) $4p$, (c) $3d$.

7.59 Discuss the similarities and differences between a $1s$ and a $2s$ orbital.

7.60 What is the difference between a $2p_x$ and a $2p_y$ orbital?

7.61 List all the possible subshells and orbitals associated with the principal quantum number n, if $n = 5$.

7.62 List all the possible subshells and orbitals associated with the principal quantum number n, if $n = 6$.

7.63 Calculate the total number of electrons that can occupy (a) one s orbital, (b) three p orbitals, (c) five d orbitals, (d) seven f orbitals.

7.64 What is the total number of electrons that can be held in all orbitals having the same principal quantum number n?

7.65 Determine the maximum number of electrons that can be found in each of the following subshells: $3s$, $3d$, $4p$, $4f$, $5f$.

7.66 Indicate the total number of (a) p electrons in N ($Z = 7$); (b) s electrons in Si ($Z = 14$); and (c) $3d$ electrons in S ($Z = 16$).

7.67 Make a chart of all allowable orbitals in the first four principal energy levels of the hydrogen atom. Designate each by type (for example, s, p) and indicate how many orbitals of each type there are.

7.68 Why do the $3s$, $3p$, and $3d$ orbitals have the same energy in a hydrogen atom but different energies in a many-electron atom?

7.69 For each of the following pairs of hydrogen orbitals, indicate which is higher in energy: (a) $1s$, $2s$; (b) $2p$, $3p$; (c) $3d_{xy}$, $3d_{yz}$; (d) $3s$, $3d$; (e) $4f$, $5s$.

7.70 Which orbital in each of the following pairs is lower in energy in a many-electron atom? (a) $2s$, $2p$; (b) $3p$, $3d$; (c) $3s$, $4s$; (d) $4d$, $5f$.

Electron Configuration

Review Questions

7.71 What is electron configuration? Describe the roles that the Pauli exclusion principle and Hund's rule play in writing the electron configuration of elements.

7.72 Explain the meaning of the symbol $4d^6$.

7.73 Explain the meaning of diamagnetic and paramagnetic. Give an example of an element that is diamagnetic and one that is paramagnetic. What does it mean when we say that electrons are paired?

7.74 What is meant by the term "shielding of electrons" in an atom? Using the Li atom as an example, describe the effect of shielding on the energy of electrons in an atom.

Problems

7.75 Indicate which of the following sets of quantum numbers in an atom are unacceptable and explain why: (a) $(1, 0, \frac{1}{2}, \frac{1}{2})$, (b) $(3, 0, 0, +\frac{1}{2})$, (c) $(2, 2, 1, +\frac{1}{2})$, (d) $(4, 3, -2, +\frac{1}{2})$, (e) $(3, 2, 1, 1)$.

7.76 The ground-state electron configurations listed here are incorrect. Explain what mistakes have been made in each and write the correct electron configurations.
Al: $1s^2 2s^2 2p^4 3s^2 3p^3$
B: $1s^2 2s^2 2p^5$
F: $1s^2 2s^2 2p^6$

7.77 The atomic number of an element is 73. Is this element diamagnetic or paramagnetic?

7.78 Indicate the number of unpaired electrons present in each of the following atoms: B, Ne, P, Sc, Mn, Se, Kr, Fe, Cd, I, Pb.

The Building-Up Principle

Review Questions

7.79 State the Aufbau principle and explain the role it plays in classifying the elements in the periodic table.

7.80 Describe the characteristics of the following groups of elements: transition metals, lanthanides, actinides.

7.81 What is the noble gas core? How does it simplify the writing of electron configurations?

7.82 What are the group and period of the element osmium?

7.83 Define the following terms and give an example of each: transition metals, lanthanides, actinides.

7.84 Explain why the ground-state electron configurations of Cr and Cu are different from what we might expect.

7.85 Explain what is meant by a noble gas core. Write the electron configuration of a xenon core.

7.86 Comment on the correctness of the following statement: The probability of finding two electrons with the same four quantum numbers in an atom is zero.

Problems

7.87 Use the Aufbau principle to obtain the ground-state electron configuration of selenium.

7.88 Use the Aufbau principle to obtain the ground-state electron configuration of technetium.

7.89 Write the ground-state electron configurations for the following elements: B, V, Ni, As, I, Au.

7.90 Write the ground-state electron configurations for the following elements: Ge, Fe, Zn, Ni, W, Tl.

7.91 The electron configuration of a neutral atom is $1s^2 2s^2 2p^6 3s^2$. Write a complete set of quantum numbers for each of the electrons. Name the element.

7.92 Which of the following species has the most unpaired electrons? S^+, S, or S^-. Explain how you arrive at your answer.

Additional Problems

7.93 When a compound containing cesium ion is heated in a Bunsen burner flame, photons with an energy of 4.30×10^{-19} J are emitted. What color is the cesium flame?

7.94 Discuss the current view of the correctness of the following statements. (a) The electron in the hydrogen atom is in an orbit that never brings it closer than 100 pm to the nucleus. (b) Atomic absorption spectra result from transitions of electrons from lower to higher energy levels. (c) A many-electron atom behaves somewhat like a solar system that has a number of planets.

7.95 Distinguish carefully between the following terms: (a) wavelength and frequency, (b) wave properties and particle properties, (c) quantization of energy and continuous variation in energy.

7.96 What is the maximum number of electrons in an atom that can have the following quantum numbers? Specify the orbitals in which the electrons would be found. (a) $n = 2$, $m_s = +\frac{1}{2}$; (b) $n = 4$, $m_\ell = +1$; (c) $n = 3$, $\ell = 2$; (d) $n = 2$, $\ell = 0$, $m_s = -\frac{1}{2}$; (e) $n = 4$, $\ell = 3$, $m_\ell = -2$.

7.97 Identify the following individuals and their contributions to the development of quantum theory: Bohr, de Broglie, Einstein, Planck, Heisenberg, Schrödinger.

7.98 What properties of electrons are used in the operation of an electron microscope?

7.99 In a photoelectric experiment a student uses a light source whose frequency is greater than that needed to eject electrons from a certain metal. However, after continuously shining the light on the same area of the metal for a long period of time the student notices that the maximum kinetic energy of ejected electrons begins to decrease, even though the frequency of the light is held constant. How would you account for this behavior?

7.100 A certain pitcher's fastballs have been clocked at about 100 mph. (a) Calculate the wavelength of a 0.141-kg baseball (in nm) at this speed. (b) What is the wavelength of a hydrogen atom at the same speed? (1 mile = 1609 m.)

7.101 Considering only the ground-state electron configuration, are there more diamagnetic or paramagnetic elements? Explain.

7.102 A ruby laser produces radiation of wavelength 633 nm in pulses whose duration is 1.00×10^{-9} s. (a) If the laser produces 0.376 J of energy per pulse, how many photons are produced in each pulse? (b) Calculate the power (in watts) delivered by the laser per pulse. (1 W = 1 J/s.)

7.103 A 368-g sample of water absorbs infrared radiation at 1.06×10^4 nm from a carbon dioxide laser. Suppose all the absorbed radiation is converted to heat. Calculate the number of photons at this wavelength required to raise the temperature of the water by 5.00°C.

7.104 Photodissociation of water

$$H_2O(l) + h\nu \longrightarrow H_2(g) + \tfrac{1}{2}O_2(g)$$

has been suggested as a source of hydrogen. The ΔH°_{rxn} for the reaction, calculated from thermochemical data, is 285.8 kJ per mole of water decomposed. Calculate the maximum wavelength (in nm) that would provide the necessary energy. In principle, is it feasible to use sunlight as a source of energy for this process?

7.105 Spectral lines of the Lyman and Balmer series do not overlap. Verify this statement by calculating the longest wavelength associated with the Lyman series and the shortest wavelength associated with the Balmer series (in nm).

7.106 Only a fraction of the electrical energy supplied to a tungsten lightbulb is converted to visible light. The rest of the energy shows up as infrared radiation (that is, heat). A 75-W lightbulb converts 15.0 percent of the energy supplied to it into visible light (assume the wavelength to be 550 nm). How many photons are emitted by the lightbulb per second? (1 W = 1 J/s.)

7.107 Certain sunglasses have small crystals of silver chloride (AgCl) incorporated in the lenses. When the lenses are exposed to light of the appropriate wavelength, the following reaction occurs:

$$AgCl \longrightarrow Ag + Cl$$

The Ag atoms formed produce a uniform gray color that reduces the glare. If ΔH for the preceding reaction is 248 kJ/mol, calculate the maximum wavelength of light that can induce this process.

7.108 The He^+ ion contains only one electron and is therefore a hydrogenlike ion. Calculate the wavelengths, in increasing order, of the first four transitions in the Balmer series of the He^+ ion. Compare these wavelengths with the same transitions in a H atom. Comment on the differences. (The Rydberg constant for He^+ is 8.72×10^{-18} J.)

7.109 Ozone (O_3) in the stratosphere absorbs the harmful radiation from the sun by undergoing decomposition: $O_3 \longrightarrow O + O_2$. (a) Referring to Table 6.3, calculate the ΔH° for this process. (b) Calculate the maximum wavelength of photons (in nm) that possess this energy to cause the decomposition of ozone photochemically.

7.110 The retina of a human eye can detect light when radiant energy incident on it is at least 4.0×10^{-17} J. For light of 600-nm wavelength, how many photons does this correspond to?

7.111 An electron in an excited state in a hydrogen atom can return to the ground state in two different ways: (a) via a direct transition in which a photon of wavelength λ_1 is emitted and (b) via an intermediate excited state reached by the emission of a photon of wavelength λ_2. This intermediate excited state then decays to the ground state by emitting another photon of wavelength λ_3. Derive an equation that relates λ_1 to λ_2 and λ_3.

7.112 A photoelectric experiment was performed by separately shining a laser at 450 nm (blue light) and a laser at 560 nm (yellow light) on a clean metal surface and measuring the number and kinetic energy of the ejected electrons. Which light would generate more electrons? Which light would eject electrons with greater kinetic energy? Assume that the same amount of energy is delivered to the metal surface by each laser and that the frequencies of the laser lights exceed the threshold frequency.

7.113 Draw the shapes (boundary surfaces) of the following orbitals: (a) $2p_y$, (b) $3d_{z^2}$, (c) $3d_{x^2-y^2}$. (Show coordinate axes in your sketches.)

7.114 The electron configurations described in this chapter all refer to gaseous atoms in their ground states. An atom may absorb a quantum of energy and promote one of its electrons to a higher-energy orbital. When this happens, we say that the atom is in an excited state. The electron configurations of some excited atoms are given. Identify these atoms and write their ground-state configurations:

(a) $1s^1 2s^1$
(b) $1s^2 2s^2 2p^2 3d^1$
(c) $1s^2 2s^2 2p^6 4s^1$
(d) $[Ar]4s^1 3d^{10} 4p^4$
(e) $[Ne]3s^2 3p^4 3d^1$

7.115 Draw orbital diagrams for atoms with the following electron configurations:
(a) $1s^2 2s^2 2p^5$
(b) $1s^2 2s^2 2p^6 3s^2 3p^3$
(c) $1s^2 2s^2 2p^6 3s^2 3p^6 4s^2 3d^7$

7.116 If Rutherford and his coworkers had used electrons instead of alpha particles to probe the structure of the nucleus as described in Section 2.2, what might they have discovered?

7.117 Scientists have found interstellar hydrogen atoms with quantum number n in the hundreds. Calculate the wavelength of light emitted when a hydrogen atom undergoes a transition from $n = 236$ to $n = 235$. In what region of the electromagnetic spectrum does this wavelength fall?

7.118 Calculate the wavelength of a helium atom whose speed is equal to the root-mean-square speed at 20°C.

7.119 Ionization energy is the minimum energy required to remove an electron from an atom. It is usually expressed in units of kJ/mol, that is, the energy in kilojoules required to remove one mole of electrons from one mole of atoms. (a) Calculate the ionization energy for the hydrogen atom. (b) Repeat the calculation, assuming in this second case that the electrons are removed from the $n = 2$ state.

7.120 An electron in a hydrogen atom is excited from the ground state to the $n = 4$ state. Comment on the correctness of the following statements (true or false).
(a) $n = 4$ is the first excited state.
(b) It takes more energy to ionize (remove) the electron from $n = 4$ than from the ground state.
(c) The electron is farther from the nucleus (on average) in $n = 4$ than in the ground state.
(d) The wavelength of light emitted when the electron drops from $n = 4$ to $n = 1$ is longer than that from $n = 4$ to $n = 2$.
(e) The wavelength the atom absorbs in going from $n = 1$ to $n = 4$ is the same as that emitted as it goes from $n = 4$ to $n = 1$.

7.121 The ionization energy of a certain element is 412 kJ/mol (see Problem 7.119). However, when the atoms of this element are in the first excited state, the ionization energy is only 126 kJ/mol. Based on this information, calculate the wavelength of light emitted in a transition from the first excited state to the ground state.

7.122 Alveoli are the tiny sacs of air in the lungs (see Problem 5.132) whose average diameter is 5.0×10^{-5} m. Consider an oxygen molecule (5.3×10^{-26} kg) trapped within a sac. Calculate the uncertainty in the velocity of the oxygen molecule. (*Hint:* The maximum uncertainty in the position of the molecule is given by the diameter of the sac.)

7.123 How many photons at 660 nm must be absorbed to melt 5.0×10^2 g of ice? On average, how many H_2O molecules does one photon convert from ice to water? (*Hint:* It takes 334 J to melt 1 g of ice at 0°C.)

7.124 Shown below are portions of orbital diagrams representing the ground-state electron configurations of certain elements. Which of them violate the Pauli exclusion principle? Hund's rule?

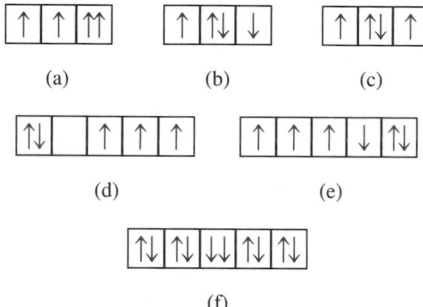

7.125 The UV light that is responsible for tanning the skin falls in the 320- to 400-nm region. Calculate the total energy (in joules) absorbed by a person exposed to this radiation for 2.0 h, given that there are 2.0×10^{16} photons hitting Earth's surface per square centimeter per second over a 80-nm (320 nm to 400 nm) range and that the exposed body area is 0.45 m^2. Assume that only half of the radiation is absorbed and the other half is reflected by the body. (*Hint:* Use an average wavelength of 360 nm in calculating the energy of a photon.)

7.126 The sun is surrounded by a white circle of gaseous material called the corona, which becomes visible during a total eclipse of the sun. The temperature of the corona is in the millions of degrees Celsius, which is high enough to break up molecules and remove some or all of the electrons from atoms. One way astronomers have been able to estimate the temperature of the corona is by studying the emission lines of ions of certain elements. For example, the emission spectrum of Fe^{14+} ions has been recorded and analyzed. Knowing that it takes 3.5×10^4 kJ/mol to convert Fe^{13+} to Fe^{14+}, estimate the temperature of the sun's corona. (*Hint:* The average kinetic energy of one mole of a gas is $\frac{3}{2}RT$.)

7.127 In 1996 physicists created an anti-atom of hydrogen. In such an atom, which is the antimatter equivalent of an ordinary atom, the electrical charges of all the component particles are reversed. Thus, the nucleus of an anti-atom is made of an anti-proton, which has the same mass as a proton but bears a negative charge, while the electron is replaced by an anti-electron (also called positron) with the same mass as an electron, but bearing a positive charge. Would you expect the energy levels, emission spectra, and atomic orbitals of an antihydrogen atom to be different from those of a hydrogen atom? What would happen if an anti-atom of hydrogen collided with a hydrogen atom?

7.128 Use Equation (5.16) to calculate the de Broglie wavelength of a N_2 molecule at 300 K.

7.129 When an electron makes a transition between energy levels of a hydrogen atom, there are no restrictions on the initial and final values of the principal quantum number n. However, there is a quantum mechanical rule that restricts the initial and final values of the orbital angular momentum ℓ. This is the *selection rule,* which states that $\Delta\ell = \pm 1$, that is, in a transition, the value of ℓ can only increase or decrease by one. According to this rule, which of the following transitions are allowed: (a) $1s \rightarrow 2s$, (b) $2p \rightarrow 1s$, (c) $1s \rightarrow 3d$, (d) $3d \rightarrow 4f$, (e) $4d \rightarrow 3s$?

7.130 In an electron microscope, electrons are accelerated by passing them through a voltage difference. The kinetic energy thus acquired by the electrons is equal to the voltage times the charge on the electron. Thus, a voltage difference of 1 volt imparts a kinetic energy of 1.602×10^{-19} volt-coulomb or 1.602×10^{-19} J. Calculate the wavelength associated with electrons accelerated by 5.00×10^3 volts.

7.131 A microwave oven operating at 1.22×10^8 nm is used to heat 150 mL of water (roughly the volume of a tea cup) from 20°C to 100°C. Calculate the number of photons needed if 92.0 percent of microwave energy is converted to the thermal energy of water.

7.132 The radioactive Co-60 isotope is used in nuclear medicine to treat certain types of cancer. Calculate the wavelength and frequency of an emitted gamma particle having the energy of 1.29×10^{11} J/mol.

7.133 (a) An electron in the ground state of the hydrogen atom moves at an average speed of 5×10^6 m/s. If the speed is known to an uncertainty of 1 percent, what is the uncertainty in knowing its position? Given that the radius of the hydrogen atom in the ground state is 5.29×10^{-11} m, comment on your result. The mass of an electron is 9.1094×10^{-31} kg. (b) A 0.15-kg baseball thrown at 100 mph has a momentum of 6.7 kg·m/s. If the uncertainty in measuring the momentum is 1.0×10^{-7} of the momentum, calculate the uncertainty in the baseball's position.

Special Problems

7.134 For hydrogenlike ions, that is, ions containing only one electron, Equation (7.5) is modified as follows: $E_n = -R_H Z^2(1/n^2)$, where Z is the atomic number of the parent atom. The figure here represents the emission spectrum of such a hydrogenlike ion in the gas phase. All the lines result from the electronic transitions from the excited states to the $n = 2$ state. (a) What electronic transitions correspond to lines B and C? (b) If the wavelength of line C is 27.1 nm, calculate the wavelengths of lines A and B. (c) Calculate the energy needed to remove the electron from the ion in the $n = 4$ state. (d) What is the physical significance of the continuum?

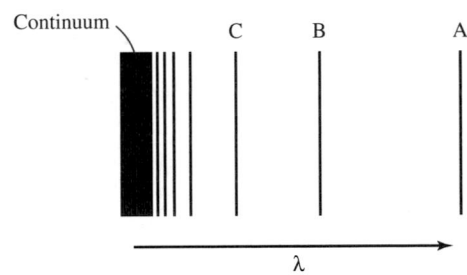

7.135 When two atoms collide, some of their kinetic energy may be converted into electronic energy in one or both atoms. If the average kinetic energy is about equal to the energy for some allowed electronic transition, an appreciable number of atoms can absorb enough energy through an inelastic collision to be raised to an excited electronic state. (a) Calculate the average kinetic energy per atom in a gas sample at 298 K. (b) Calculate the energy difference between the $n = 1$ and $n = 2$ levels in hydrogen. (c) At what temperature is it possible to excite a hydrogen atom from the $n = 1$ level to $n = 2$ level by collision? [The average kinetic energy of 1 mole of an ideal gas is $(\frac{3}{2})RT$].

7.136 Calculate the energies needed to remove an electron from the $n = 1$ state and the $n = 5$ state in the Li^{2+} ion. What is the wavelength (in nm) of the emitted photon in a transition from $n = 5$ to $n = 1$? The Rydberg constant for hydrogen-like ions is $(2.18 \times 10^{-18} J)Z^2$, where Z is the atomic number.

7.137 According to Einstein's special theory of relativity, the mass of a moving particle, m_{moving}, is related to its mass at rest, m_{rest}, by the following equation

$$m_{moving} = \frac{m_{rest}}{\sqrt{1 - \left(\frac{u}{c}\right)^2}}$$

where u and c are the speeds of the particle and light, respectively. (a) In particle accelerators, protons, electrons, and other charged particles are often accelerated to speeds close to the speed of light. Calculate the wavelength (in nm) of a proton moving at 50.0 percent the speed of light. The mass of a proton is 1.673×10^{-27} kg. (b) Calculate the mass of a 6.0×10^{-2} kg tennis ball moving at 63 m/s. Comment on your results.

7.138 The mathematical equation for studying the photoelectric effect is

$$h\nu = W + \tfrac{1}{2}m_e u^2$$

where ν is the frequency of light shining on the metal, W is the energy needed to remove an electron from the metal [same as BE in Equation (7.4)], m_e and u are the mass and speed of the ejected electron. In an experiment, a student found that a maximum wavelength of 351 nm is needed to just dislodge electrons from a zinc metal surface. Calculate the velocity (in m/s) of an ejected electron when she employed light with a wavelength of 313 nm.

7.139 In the beginning of the twentieth century, some scientists thought that a nucleus may contain both electrons and protons. Use the Heisenberg uncertainty principle to show that an electron cannot be confined within a nucleus. Repeat the calculation for a proton. Comment on your results. Assume the radius of a nucleus to be 1.0×10^{-15} m. The masses of an electron and a proton are 9.109×10^{-31} kg and 1.673×10^{-27} kg, respectively. (*Hint*: Treat the radius of the nucleus as the uncertainty in position.)

7.140 Blackbody radiation is the term used to describe the dependence of the radiation energy emitted by an object on wavelength at a certain temperature. Planck proposed the quantum theory to account for this dependence. Shown in the figure is a plot of the radiation energy emitted by our sun versus wavelength. This curve is characteristic of objects at about 6000 K, which is the temperature at the surface of the sun. At a higher temperature, the curve has a similar shape but the maximum will shift to a shorter wavelength. (a) What does this curve reveal about two consequences of great biological significance on Earth? (b) How are astronomers able to determine the temperature at the surface of stars in general?

Answers to Practice Exercises

7.1 625 Hz. **7.2** 8.24 m. **7.3** 3.39×10^3 nm. **7.4** 2.63×10^3 nm. **7.5** 56.6 nm. **7.6** $n = 3$, $\ell = 1$, $m_\ell = -1, 0, 1$. **7.7** 16. **7.8** $(5, 1, -1, +\tfrac{1}{2})$, $(5, 1, 0, +\tfrac{1}{2})$, $(5, 1, 1, +\tfrac{1}{2})$, $(5, 1, -1, -\tfrac{1}{2})$, $(5, 1, 0, -\tfrac{1}{2})$, $(5, 1, 1, -\tfrac{1}{2})$. **7.9** 32. **7.10** $(1, 0, 0, +\tfrac{1}{2})$, $(1, 0, 0, -\tfrac{1}{2})$, $(2, 0, 0, +\tfrac{1}{2})$, $(2, 0, 0, -\tfrac{1}{2})$, $(2, 1, -1, -\tfrac{1}{2})$. There are 5 other acceptable ways to write the quantum numbers for the last electron. **7.11** $[Ne]3s^2 3p^3$.

CHEMICAL
Mystery

Discovery of Helium and the Rise and Fall of Coronium

Scientists know that our sun and other stars contain certain elements. How was this information obtained?

In the early nineteenth century, the German physicist Josef Fraunhofer studied the emission spectrum of the sun and noticed certain dark lines at specific wavelengths. We interpret the appearance of these lines by supposing that originally a continuous band of color was radiated and that, as the emitted light moves outward from the sun, some of the radiation is reabsorbed at those wavelengths by the atoms in space. These dark lines are therefore absorption lines. For atoms, the emission and absorption of light occur at the same wavelengths. By matching the absorption lines in the emission spectra of a star with the emission spectra of known elements in the laboratory, scientists have been able to deduce the types of elements present in the star.

Another way to study the sun spectroscopically is during its eclipse. In 1868 the French physicist Pierre Janssen observed a bright yellow line (see Figure 7.8) in the emission spectrum of the sun's corona during the totality of the eclipse. (The corona is the pearly white crown of light visible around the sun during a total eclipse.) This line did not match the emission lines of known elements, but did match one of the dark lines in the spectrum sketched by Fraunhofer. The name helium (from Helios, the sun god in Greek mythology) was given to the element responsible for the emission line. Twenty-seven years later, helium was discovered on Earth by the British chemist William Ramsay in a mineral of uranium. On Earth, the only source of helium is through radioactive decay processes—α particles emitted during nuclear decay are eventually converted to helium atoms.

Fraunhofer's original drawing, in 1814, showing the dark absorption lines in the sun's emission spectrum. The top of the diagram shows the overall brightness of the sun at different colors.

The search for new elements from the sun did not end with helium. Around the time of Janssen's work, scientists also detected a bright green line in the spectrum from the corona. They did not know the identity of the element giving rise to the line, so they called it coronium because it was only found in the corona. Over the following years, additional mystery coronal emission lines were found. The coronium problem proved much harder to solve than the helium case because no matchings were found with the emission lines of known elements. It was not until the late 1930s that the Swedish physicist Bengt Edlén identified these lines as coming from partially ionized atoms of iron, calcium, and nickel. At very high temperatures (over a million degrees Celsius), many atoms become ionized by losing one or more electrons. Therefore, the mystery emission lines come from the resulting ions of the metals and not from a new element. So, after some 70 years the coronium problem was finally solved. There is no such element as coronium after all!

During the total eclipse of the sun, which lasts for only a few minutes, the corona becomes visible.

Chemical Clues

1. Sketch a two-energy-level system (E_1 and E_2) to illustrate the absorption and emission processes.

2. Explain why the sun's spectrum provides only absorption lines (the dark lines), whereas the corona spectrum provides only emission lines.

3. Why is it difficult to detect helium on Earth?

4. How are scientists able to determine the abundances of elements in stars?

5. Knowing the identity of an ion of an element giving rise to a coronal emission line, describe in qualitative terms how you can estimate the temperature of the corona.

8

The periodic table places the most reactive metals in Group 1A and the most reactive nonmetals in Group 7A. When these elements are mixed, we predict a vigorous reaction to ensue, as evidenced by the formation of sodium chloride from sodium and chlorine. The models show Na metal, Cl_2 molecules, and NaCl.

Periodic Relationships Among the Elements

A LOOK AHEAD

- We start with the development of the periodic table and the contributions made by nineteenth-century scientists, in particular Mendeleev. (8.1)

- We see that electron configuration is the logical way to build up the periodic table, which explains some of the early anomalies. We also learn the rules for writing the electron configurations of cations and anions. (8.2)

- Next, we examine the periodic trends in physical properties, such as the size of atoms and ions in terms of effective nuclear charge. (8.3)

- We continue our study of periodic trends by examining chemical properties like ionization energy and electron affinity. (8.4 and 8.5)

- We then apply the knowledge acquired in the chapter to systematically study the properties of the representative elements as individual groups and also across a given period. (8.6)

Interactive Activity Summary

1. Interactivity: Attraction of Nucleus (8.3)
2. Animation: Atomic and Ionic Radius (8.3)
3. Interactivity: Atomic Radii (8.3)
4. Interactivity: Ionic Radii (8.3)
5. Interactivity: Ionization Energy (8.4)

Many of the chemical properties of the elements can be understood in terms of their electron configurations. Because electrons fill atomic orbitals in a fairly regular fashion, it is not surprising that elements with similar electron configurations, such as sodium and potassium, behave similarly in many respects and that, in general, the properties of the elements exhibit observable trends. Chemists in the nineteenth century recognized periodic trends in the physical and chemical properties of elements, long before quantum theory came onto the scene. Although these chemists were not aware of the existence of electrons and protons, their efforts to systematize the chemistry of the elements were remarkably successful. Their main sources of information were the atomic masses of the elements and other known physical and chemical properties.

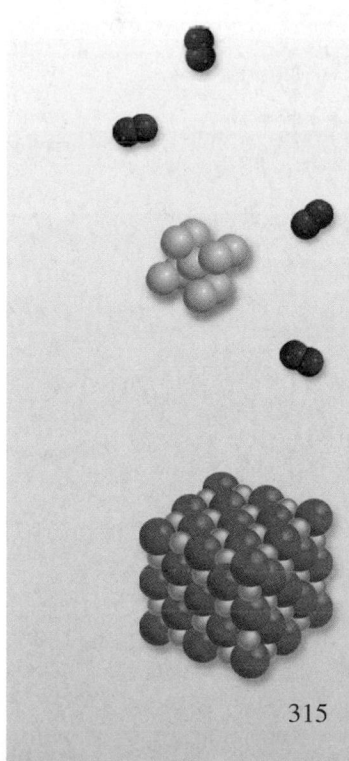

8.1 Development of the Periodic Table

In the nineteenth century, when chemists had only a vague idea of atoms and molecules and did not know of the existence of electrons and protons, they devised the periodic table using their knowledge of atomic masses. Accurate measurements of the atomic masses of many elements had already been made. Arranging elements according to their atomic masses in a periodic table seemed logical to those chemists, who felt that chemical behavior should somehow be related to atomic mass.

In 1864 the English chemist John Newlands[†] noticed that when the elements were arranged in order of atomic mass, every eighth element had similar properties. Newlands referred to this peculiar relationship as the *law of octaves*. However, this "law" turned out to be inadequate for elements beyond calcium, and Newlands's work was not accepted by the scientific community.

In 1869 the Russian chemist Dmitri Mendeleev[‡] and the German chemist Lothar Meyer[§] independently proposed a much more extensive tabulation of the elements based on the regular, periodic recurrence of properties. Mendeleev's classification system was a great improvement over Newlands's for two reasons. First, it grouped the elements together more accurately, according to their properties. Equally important, it made possible the prediction of the properties of several elements that had not yet been discovered. For example, Mendeleev proposed the existence of an unknown element that he called eka-aluminum and predicted a number of its properties. (*Eka* is a Sanskrit word meaning "first"; thus eka-aluminum would be the first element under aluminum in the same group.) When gallium was discovered four years later, its properties matched the predicted properties of eka-aluminum remarkably well:

Gallium melts in a person's hand (body temperature is about 37°C).

Appendix 1 explains the names and symbols of the elements.

	Eka-Aluminum (Ea)	Gallium (Ga)
Atomic mass	68 amu	69.9 amu
Melting point	Low	29.78°C
Density	5.9 g/cm^3	5.94 g/cm^3
Formula of oxide	Ea_2O_3	Ga_2O_3

Mendeleev's periodic table included 66 known elements. By 1900, some 30 more had been added to the list, filling in some of the empty spaces. Figure 8.1 charts the discovery of the elements chronologically.

Although this periodic table was a celebrated success, the early versions had some glaring inconsistencies. For example, the atomic mass of argon (39.95 amu) is greater than that of potassium (39.10 amu). If elements were arranged solely according to increasing atomic mass, argon would appear in the position occupied by potassium in our modern periodic table (see the inside front cover). But no chemist would place argon, an inert gas, in the same group as lithium and sodium, two very reactive metals. This and other discrepancies suggested that some fundamental property other than atomic mass must be the basis of periodicity. This property turned out to be associated with atomic number, a concept unknown to Mendeleev and his contemporaries.

[†]John Alexander Reina Newlands (1838–1898). English chemist. Newlands's work was a step in the right direction in the classification of the elements. Unfortunately, because of its shortcomings, he was subjected to much criticism, and even ridicule. At one meeting he was asked if he had ever examined the elements according to the order of their initial letters! Nevertheless, in 1887 Newlands was honored by the Royal Society of London for his contribution.

[‡]Dmitri Ivanovich Mendeleev (1836–1907). Russian chemist. His work on the periodic classification of elements is regarded by many as the most significant achievement in chemistry in the nineteenth century.

[§]Julius Lothar Meyer (1830–1895). German chemist. In addition to his contribution to the periodic table, Meyer also discovered the chemical affinity of hemoglobin for oxygen.

Figure 8.1 *A chronological chart of the discovery of the elements. To date, 114 elements have been identified.*

Using data from α-scattering experiments (see Section 2.2), Rutherford estimated the number of positive charges in the nucleus of a few elements, but the significance of these numbers was overlooked for several more years. In 1913 a young English physicist, Henry Moseley,[†] discovered a correlation between what he called *atomic number* and the frequency of X rays generated by bombarding an element with high-energy electrons. Moseley noticed that the frequencies of X rays emitted from the elements could be correlated by the equation

$$\sqrt{v} = a(Z - b)$$

where v is the frequency of the emitted X rays and a and b are constants that are the same for all the elements. Thus, from the square root of the measured frequency of the X rays emitted, we can determine the atomic number of the element.

With a few exceptions, Moseley found that atomic number increases in the same order as atomic mass. For example, calcium is the twentieth element in order of increasing atomic mass, and it has an atomic number of 20. The discrepancies that

---

[†]Henry Gwyn-Jeffreys Moseley (1887–1915). English physicist. Moseley discovered the relationship between X-ray spectra and atomic number. A lieutenant in the Royal Engineers, he was killed in action at the age of 28 during the British campaign in Gallipoli, Turkey.

had puzzled earlier scientists now made sense. The atomic number of argon is 18 and that of potassium is 19, so potassium should follow argon in the periodic table.

A modern periodic table usually shows the atomic number along with the element symbol. As you already know, the atomic number also indicates the number of electrons in the atoms of an element. Electron configurations of elements help to explain the recurrence of physical and chemical properties. The importance and usefulness of the periodic table lie in the fact that we can use our understanding of the general properties and trends within a group or a period to predict with considerable accuracy the properties of any element, even though that element may be unfamiliar to us.

8.2 Periodic Classification of the Elements

Figure 8.2 shows the periodic table together with the outermost ground-state electron configurations of the elements. (The electron configurations of the elements are also given in Table 7.3.) Starting with hydrogen, we see that subshells are filled in the order shown in Figure 7.24. According to the type of subshell being filled, the elements can be divided into categories—the representative elements, the noble gases, the transition elements (or transition metals), the lanthanides, and the actinides. The *representative elements* (also called *main group elements*) are *the elements in Groups 1A through 7A, all of which have incompletely filled s or p subshells of the highest principal quantum number*. With the exception of helium, the *noble gases* (the Group 8A elements) all have a completely filled p subshell. (The electron configurations are $1s^2$ for helium and ns^2np^6 for the other noble gases, where n is the principal quantum number for the outermost shell.)

Figure 8.2 *The ground-state electron configurations of the elements. For simplicity, only the configurations of the outer electrons are shown.*

The transition metals are the elements in Groups 1B and 3B through 8B, which have incompletely filled d subshells, or readily produce cations with incompletely filled d subshells. (These metals are sometimes referred to as the d-block transition elements.) The nonsequential numbering of the transition metals in the periodic table (that is, 3B–8B, followed by 1B–2B) acknowledges a correspondence between the outer electron configurations of these elements and those of the representative elements. For example, scandium and gallium both have three outer electrons. However, because they are in different types of atomic orbitals, they are placed in different groups (3B and 3A). The metals iron (Fe), cobalt (Co), and nickel (Ni) do not fit this classification and are all placed in Group 8B. The Group 2B elements, Zn, Cd, and Hg, are neither representative elements nor transition metals. There is no special name for this group of metals. It should be noted that the designation of A and B groups is not universal. In Europe the practice is to use B for representative elements and A for transition metals, which is just the opposite of the American convention. The International Union of Pure and Applied Chemistry (IUPAC) has recommended numbering the columns sequentially with Arabic numerals 1 through 18 (see Figure 8.2). The proposal has sparked much controversy in the international chemistry community, and its merits and drawbacks will be deliberated for some time to come. In this text we will adhere to the American designation.

The lanthanides and actinides are sometimes called f-block transition elements because they have incompletely filled f subshells. Figure 8.3 distinguishes the groups of elements discussed here.

A clear pattern emerges when we examine the electron configurations of the elements in a particular group. The electron configurations for Groups 1A and 2A are shown in Table 8.1. All members of the Group 1A alkali metals have similar outer

TABLE 8.1

Electron Configurations of Group 1A and Group 2A Elements

Group 1A	Group 2A
Li [He]$2s^1$	Be [He]$2s^2$
Na [Ne]$3s^1$	Mg [Ne]$3s^2$
K [Ar]$4s^1$	Ca [Ar]$4s^2$
Rb [Kr]$5s^1$	Sr [Kr]$5s^2$
Cs [Xe]$6s^1$	Ba [Xe]$6s^2$
Fr [Rn]$7s^1$	Ra [Rn]$7s^2$

Figure 8.3 *Classification of the elements. Note that the Group 2B elements are often classified as transition metals even though they do not exhibit the characteristics of the transition metals.*

electron configurations; each has a noble gas core and an ns^1 outer electron. Similarly, the Group 2A alkaline earth metals have a noble gas core and an outer electron configuration of ns^2. *The outer electrons of an atom, which are the ones involved in chemical bonding,* are often called **valence electrons.** The similarity of the outer electron configurations (that is, they have the same number and type of valence electrons) is what makes the elements in the same group resemble one another in chemical behavior. This observation holds true for the other representative elements. Thus, for instance, the halogens (the Group 7A elements) all have outer electron configurations of ns^2np^5, and they have very similar properties. We must be careful, however, in predicting properties for Groups 3A through 7A. For example, the elements in Group 4A all have the same outer electron configuration, ns^2np^2, but there is some variation in chemical properties among these elements: Carbon is a nonmetal, silicon and germanium are metalloids, and tin and lead are metals.

As a group, the noble gases behave very similarly. With the exception of krypton and xenon, the rest of these elements are totally inert chemically. The reason is that these elements all have completely filled outer ns and np subshells, a condition that represents great stability. Although the outer electron configuration of the transition metals is not always the same within a group and there is no regular pattern in the change of the electron configuration from one metal to the next in the same period, all transition metals share many characteristics that set them apart from other elements. The reason is that these metals all have an incompletely filled d subshell. Likewise, the lanthanide (and the actinide) elements resemble one another because they have incompletely filled f subshells.

Example 8.1

An atom of a certain element has 15 electrons. Without consulting a periodic table, answer the following questions: (a) What is the ground-state electron configuration of the element? (b) How should the element be classified? (c) Is the element diamagnetic or paramagnetic?

Strategy (a) We refer to the building-up principle discussed in Section 7.9 and start writing the electron configuration with principal quantum number $n = 1$ and continuing upward until all the electrons are accounted for. (b) What are the electron configuration characteristics of representative elements? transition elements? noble gases? (c) Examine the pairing scheme of the electrons in the outermost shell. What determines whether an element is diamagnetic or paramagnetic?

Solution (a) We know that for $n = 1$ we have a $1s$ orbital (2 electrons); for $n = 2$ we have a $2s$ orbital (2 electrons) and three $2p$ orbitals (6 electrons); for $n = 3$ we have a $3s$ orbital (2 electrons). The number of electrons left is $15 - 12 = 3$ and these three electrons are placed in the $3p$ orbitals. The electron configuration is $1s^22s^22p^63s^23p^3$.

(b) Because the $3p$ subshell is not completely filled, this is a representative element. Based on the information given, we cannot say whether it is a metal, a nonmetal, or a metalloid.

(c) According to Hund's rule, the three electrons in the $3p$ orbitals have parallel spins (three unpaired electrons). Therefore, the element is paramagnetic.

Check For (b), note that a transition metal possesses an incompletely filled d subshell and a noble gas has a completely filled outer shell. For (c), recall that if the atoms of an element contain an odd number of electrons, then the element must be paramagnetic.

Similar problem: 8.20.

Practice Exercise An atom of a certain element has 20 electrons. (a) Write the ground-state electron configuration of the element, (b) classify the element, (c) determine whether the element is diamagnetic or paramagnetic.

Representing Free Elements in Chemical Equations

Having classified the elements according to their ground-state electron configurations, we can now look at the way chemists represent metals, metalloids, and nonmetals as free elements in chemical equations. Because metals do not exist in discrete molecular units, we always use their empirical formulas in chemical equations. The empirical formulas are the same as the symbols that represent the elements. For example, the empirical formula for iron is Fe, the same as the symbol for the element.

For nonmetals there is no single rule. Carbon, for example, exists as an extensive three-dimensional network of atoms, and so we use its empirical formula (C) to represent elemental carbon in chemical equations. But hydrogen, nitrogen, oxygen, and the halogens exist as diatomic molecules, and so we use their molecular formulas (H_2, N_2, O_2, F_2, Cl_2, Br_2, I_2) in equations. The stable form of phosphorus is molecular (P_4), and so we use P_4. For sulfur, chemists often use the empirical formula (S) in chemical equations, rather than S_8, which is the stable form. Thus, instead of writing the equation for the combustion of sulfur as

$$S_8(s) + 8O_2(g) \longrightarrow 8SO_2(g)$$

we usually write

$$S(s) + O_2(g) \longrightarrow SO_2(g)$$

All the noble gases are monatomic species; thus we use their symbols: He, Ne, Ar, Kr, Xe, and Rn. The metalloids, like the metals, all have complex three-dimensional networks, and we represent them, too, with their empirical formulas, that is, their symbols: B, Si, Ge, and so on.

Note that these two equations for the combustion of sulfur have identical stoichiometry. This correspondence should not be surprising, because both equations describe the same chemical system. In both cases, a number of sulfur atoms react with twice as many oxygen atoms.

Electron Configurations of Cations and Anions

Because many ionic compounds are made up of monatomic anions and cations, it is helpful to know how to write the electron configurations of these ionic species. Just as for neutral atoms, we use the Pauli exclusion principle and Hund's rule in writing the ground-state electron configurations of cations and anions. We will group the ions in two categories for discussion.

Ions Derived from Representative Elements

Ions formed from atoms of most representative elements have the noble-gas outer-electron configuration of ns^2np^6. In the formation of a cation from the atom of a representative element, one or more electrons are removed from the highest occupied n shell. Following are the electron configurations of some atoms and their corresponding cations:

$$\text{Na: } [\text{Ne}]3s^1 \qquad \text{Na}^+\text{: } [\text{Ne}]$$
$$\text{Ca: } [\text{Ar}]4s^2 \qquad \text{Ca}^{2+}\text{: } [\text{Ar}]$$
$$\text{Al: } [\text{Ne}]3s^23p^1 \quad \text{Al}^{3+}\text{: } [\text{Ne}]$$

Note that each ion has a stable noble gas configuration.

In the formation of an anion, one or more electrons are added to the highest partially filled n shell. Consider the following examples:

$$\text{H: } 1s^1 \qquad\qquad \text{H}^-\text{: } 1s^2 \text{ or } [\text{He}]$$
$$\text{F: } 1s^22s^22p^5 \qquad \text{F}^-\text{: } 1s^22s^22p^6 \text{ or } [\text{Ne}]$$
$$\text{O: } 1s^22s^22p^4 \qquad \text{O}^{2-}\text{: } 1s^22s^22p^6 \text{ or } [\text{Ne}]$$
$$\text{N: } 1s^22s^22p^3 \qquad \text{N}^{3-}\text{: } 1s^22s^22p^6 \text{ or } [\text{Ne}]$$

All of these anions also have stable noble gas configurations. Notice that F^-, Na^+, and Ne (and Al^{3+}, O^{2-}, and N^{3-}) have the same electron configuration. They are said to be ***isoelectronic*** because they *have the same number of electrons, and hence the same ground-state electron configuration.* Thus, H^- and He are also isoelectronic.

Cations Derived from Transition Metals

In Section 7.9 we saw that in the first-row transition metals (Sc to Cu), the $4s$ orbital is always filled before the $3d$ orbitals. Consider manganese, whose electron configuration is $[Ar]4s^23d^5$. When the Mn^{2+} ion is formed, we might expect the two electrons to be removed from the $3d$ orbitals to yield $[Ar]4s^23d^3$. In fact, the electron configuration of Mn^{2+} is $[Ar]3d^5$! The reason is that the electron-electron and electron-nucleus interactions in a neutral atom can be quite different from those in its ion. Thus, whereas the $4s$ orbital is always filled before the $3d$ orbital in Mn, electrons are removed from the $4s$ orbital in forming Mn^{2+} because the $3d$ orbital is more stable than the $4s$ orbital in transition metal ions. Therefore, when a cation is formed from an atom of a transition metal, electrons are always removed first from the ns orbital and then from the $(n - 1)d$ orbitals.

Keep in mind that most transition metals can form more than one cation and that frequently the cations are not isoelectronic with the preceding noble gases.

Bear in mind that the order of electron filling does not determine or predict the order of electron removal for transition metals.

8.3 Periodic Variation in Physical Properties

As we have seen, the electron configurations of the elements show a periodic variation with increasing atomic number. Consequently, there are also periodic variations in physical and chemical behavior. In this section and the next two, we will examine some physical properties of elements that are in the same group or period and additional properties that influence the chemical behavior of the elements. First, let's look at the concept of effective nuclear charge, which has a direct bearing on atomic size and on the tendency for ionization.

Effective Nuclear Charge

In Chapter 7, we discussed the shielding effect that electrons close to the nucleus have on outer-shell electrons in many-electron atoms. The presence of shielding electrons reduces the electrostatic attraction between the positively charged protons in the nucleus and the outer electrons. Moreover, the repulsive forces between electrons in a many-electron atom further offset the attractive force exerted by the nucleus. The concept of effective nuclear charge enables us to account for the effects of shielding on periodic properties.

Consider, for example, the helium atom, which has the ground-state electron configuration $1s^2$. Helium's two protons give the nucleus a charge of $+2$, but the full attractive force of this charge on the two $1s$ electrons is partially offset by electron-electron repulsion. Consequently, we say that the $1s$ electrons shield each other from the nucleus. The effective nuclear charge (Z_{eff}), which is the charge felt by an electron, is given by

$$Z_{eff} = Z - \sigma \tag{8.1}$$

The increase in effective nuclear charge from left to right across a period and from bottom to top in a group for representative elements.

where Z is the actual nuclear charge (that is, the atomic number of the element) and σ (sigma) is called the *shielding constant* (also called the *screening constant*). The shielding constant is greater than zero but smaller than Z.

One way to illustrate electron shielding is to consider the amounts of energy required to remove the two electrons from a helium atom. Measurements show that it takes 2373 kJ of energy to remove the first electron from 1 mole of He atoms and 5251 kJ of energy to remove the remaining electron from 1 mole of He$^+$ ions. The reason it takes so much more energy to remove the second electron is that with only one electron present, there is no shielding, and the electron feels the full effect of the $+2$ nuclear charge.

For atoms with three or more electrons, the electrons in a given shell are shielded by electrons in inner shells (that is, shells closer to the nucleus) but not by electrons in outer shells. Thus, in a lithium atom, whose electron configuration is $1s^2 2s^1$, the $2s$ electron is shielded by the two $1s$ electrons, but the $2s$ electron does not have a shielding effect on the $1s$ electrons. In addition, filled inner shells shield outer electrons more effectively than electrons in the same subshell shield each other.

Atomic Radius

A number of physical properties, including density, melting point, and boiling point, are related to the sizes of atoms, but atomic size is difficult to define. As we saw in Chapter 7, the electron density in an atom extends far beyond the nucleus, but we normally think of atomic size as the volume containing about 90 percent of the total electron density around the nucleus. When we must be even more specific, we define the size of an atom in terms of its **atomic radius,** which is *one-half the distance between the two nuclei in two adjacent metal atoms or in a diatomic molecule.*

For atoms linked together to form an extensive three-dimensional network, atomic radius is simply one-half the distance between the nuclei in two neighboring atoms [Figure 8.4(a)]. For elements that exist as simple diatomic molecules, the atomic radius is one-half the distance between the nuclei of the two atoms in a particular molecule [Figure 8.4(b)].

Figure 8.5 shows the atomic radii of many elements according to their positions in the periodic table, and Figure 8.6 plots the atomic radii of these elements against their atomic numbers. Periodic trends are clearly evident. In studying the trends, bear in mind that the atomic radius is determined to a large extent by the strength of the attraction between the nucleus and the outer-shell electrons. The larger the effective nuclear charge, the stronger the hold of the nucleus on these electrons, and the smaller the atomic radius. Consider the second-period elements from Li to F, for example. Moving from left to right, we find that the number of electrons in the inner shell ($1s^2$) remains constant while the nuclear charge increases. The electrons that are added to counterbalance the increasing nuclear charge are ineffective in shielding one another. Consequently, the effective nuclear charge increases steadily while the principal quantum number remains constant ($n = 2$). For example, the outer $2s$ electron in lithium is shielded from the nucleus (which has three protons) by the two $1s$ electrons. As an approximation, we assume that the shielding effect of the two $1s$ electrons is to cancel two positive charges in the nucleus. Thus, the $2s$ electron only feels the attraction of one proton in the nucleus; the effective nuclear charge is $+1$. In beryllium ($1s^2 2s^2$), each of the $2s$ electrons is shielded by the inner two $1s$ electrons, which cancel two of the four positive charges in the nucleus. Because the $2s$ electrons do not shield each other as effectively, the net result is that the effective nuclear charge of each $2s$ electron

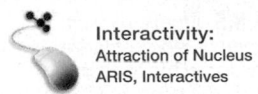
Interactivity:
Attraction of Nucleus
ARIS, Interactives

See Figure 7.27 for radial probability plots of 1s and 2s orbitals.

Animation:
Atomic and Ionic Radius
ARIS, Animations

Interactivity:
Atomic Radii
ARIS, Interactives

(a)

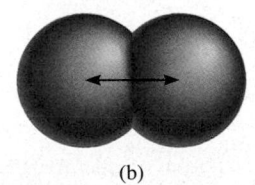

(b)

Figure 8.4 *(a) In metals such as beryllium, the atomic radius is defined as one-half the distance between the centers of two adjacent atoms. (b) For elements that exist as diatomic molecules, such as iodine, the radius of the atom is defined as one-half the distance between the centers of the atoms in the molecule.*

Figure 8.5 *Atomic radii (in picometers) of representative elements according to their positions in the periodic table. Note that there is no general agreement on the size of atomic radii. We focus only on the trends in atomic radii, not on their precise values.*

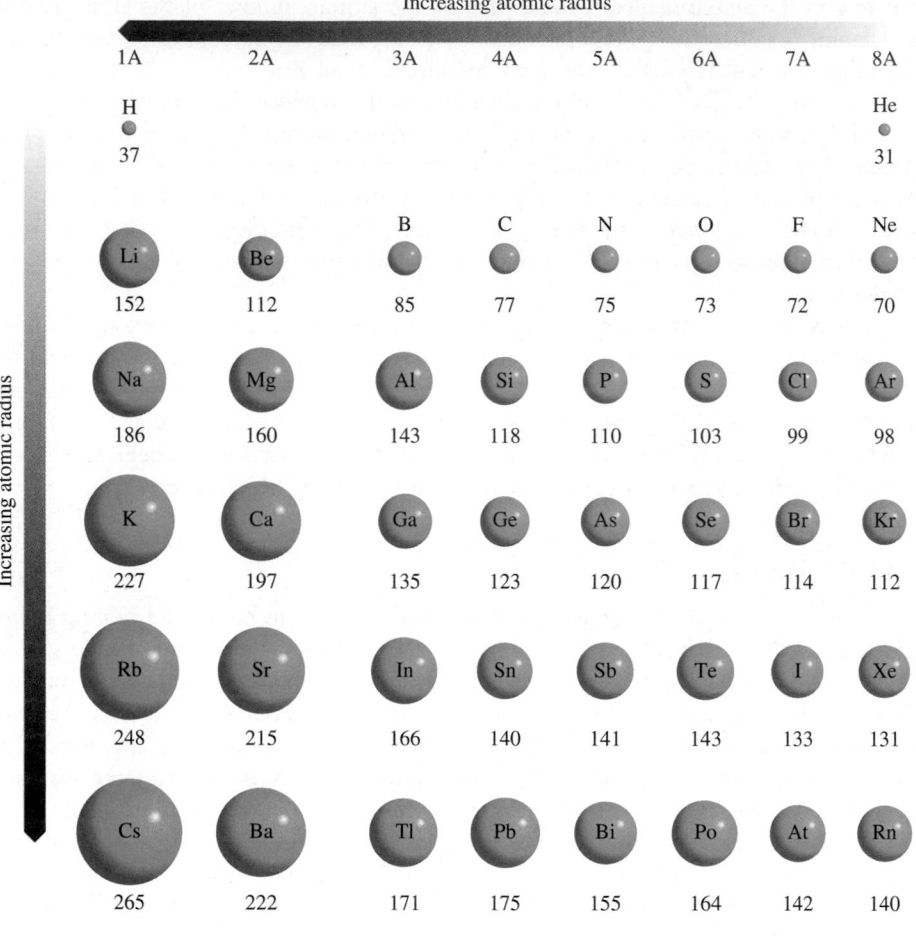

is greater than +1. Thus, as the effective nuclear charge increases, the atomic radius decreases steadily from lithium to fluorine.

Within a group of elements we find that atomic radius increases with increasing atomic number. For the alkali metals in Group 1A, the outermost electron resides in the *ns* orbital. Because orbital size increases with the increasing principal quantum number *n*, the size of the metal atoms increases from Li to Cs. We can apply the same reasoning to the elements in other groups.

Example 8.2

Referring to a periodic table, arrange the following atoms in order of increasing atomic radius: P, Si, N.

Strategy What are the trends in atomic radii in a periodic group and in a particular period? Which of the preceding elements are in the same group? in the same period?

(Continued)

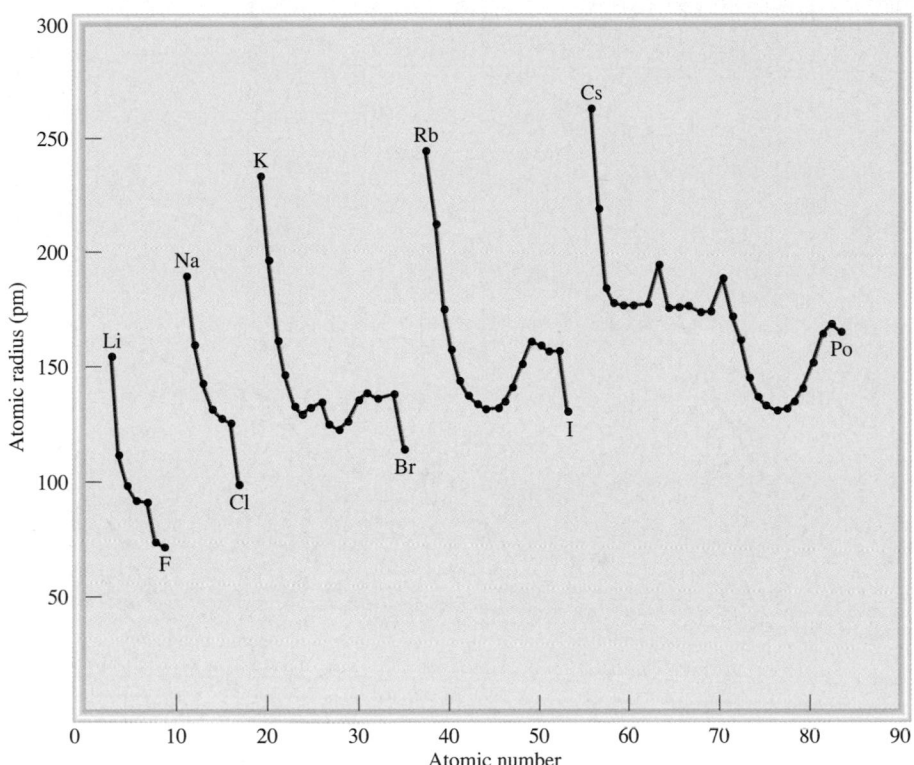

Figure 8.6 *Plot of atomic radii (in picometers) of elements against their atomic numbers.*

Solution From Figure 8.1 we see that N and P are in the same group (Group 5A). Therefore, the radius of N is smaller than that of P (atomic radius increases as we go down a group). Both Si and P are in the third period, and Si is to the left of P. Therefore, the radius of P is smaller than that of Si (atomic radius decreases as we move from left to right across a period). Thus, the order of increasing radius is
N < P < Si .

Similar problems: 8.37, 8.38.

Practice Exercise Arrange the following atoms in order of decreasing radius: C, Li, Be.

Ionic Radius

Ionic radius is *the radius of a cation or an anion*. It can be measured by X-ray diffraction (see Chapter 11). Ionic radius affects the physical and chemical properties of an ionic compound. For example, the three-dimensional structure of an ionic compound depends on the relative sizes of its cations and anions.

When a neutral atom is converted to an ion, we expect a change in size. If the atom forms an anion, its size (or radius) increases, because the nuclear charge remains the same but the repulsion resulting from the additional electron(s) enlarges the domain of the electron cloud. On the other hand, removing one or more electrons from an atom reduces electron-electron repulsion but the nuclear charge remains the same, so the electron cloud shrinks, and the cation is smaller than the atom. Figure 8.7 shows the changes in size that result when alkali metals are converted to cations and halogens are converted to anions; Figure 8.8 shows

Interactivity:
Ionic Radii
ARIS, Interactives

Figure 8.7 *Comparison of atomic radii with ionic radii. (a) Alkali metals and alkali metal cations. (b) Halogens and halide ions.*

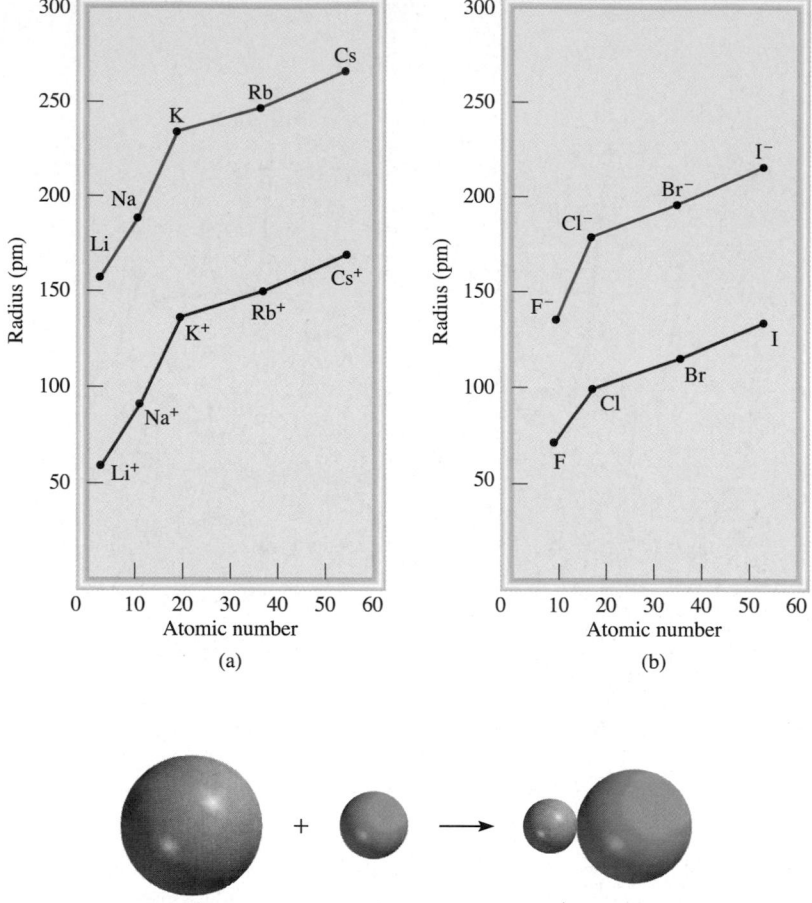

(a)

(b)

Figure 8.8 *Changes in the sizes of Li and F when they react to form LiF.*

the changes in size that occur when a lithium atom reacts with a fluorine atom to form a LiF unit.

Figure 8.9 shows the radii of ions derived from the familiar elements, arranged according to elements' positions in the periodic table. We can see parallel trends between atomic radii and ionic radii. For example, from top to bottom both the atomic radius and the ionic radius increase within a group. For ions derived from elements in different groups, a size comparison is meaningful only if the ions are isoelectronic. If we examine isoelectronic ions, we find that cations are smaller than anions. For example, Na^+ is smaller than F^-. Both ions have the same number of electrons, but Na ($Z = 11$) has more protons than F ($Z = 9$). The larger effective nuclear charge of Na^+ results in a smaller radius.

Focusing on isoelectronic cations, we see that the radii of *tripositive ions* (ions that bear three positive charges) are smaller than those of *dipositive ions* (ions that bear two positive charges), which in turn are smaller than *unipositive ions* (ions that bear one positive charge). This trend is nicely illustrated by the sizes of three isoelectronic ions in the third period: Al^{3+}, Mg^{2+}, and Na^+ (see Figure 8.9). The Al^{3+} ion has the same number of electrons as Mg^{2+}, but it has one more proton. Thus, the electron cloud in Al^{3+} is pulled inward more than that in Mg^{2+}. The smaller radius of Mg^{2+} compared with that of Na^+ can be similarly explained. Turning to isoelectronic anions, we find that the radius increases as we go from ions with uninegative

Figure 8.9 *The radii (in picometers) of ions of familiar elements arranged according to the elements' positions in the periodic table.*

charge ($-$) to those with dinegative charge ($2-$), and so on. Thus, the oxide ion is larger than the fluoride ion because oxygen has one fewer proton than fluorine; the electron cloud is spread out more in O^{2-}.

Example 8.3

For each of the following pairs, indicate which one of the two species is larger: (a) N^{3-} or F^-; (b) Mg^{2+} or Ca^{2+}; (c) Fe^{2+} or Fe^{3+}.

Strategy In comparing ionic radii, it is useful to classify the ions into three categories: (1) isoelectronic ions, (2) ions that carry the same charges and are generated from atoms of the same periodic group, and (3) ions carry different charges but are generated from the same atom. In case (1), ions carrying a greater negative charge are always larger; in case (2), ions from atoms having a greater atomic number are always larger; in case (3), ions having a smaller positive charge are always larger.

Solution (a) N^{3-} and F^- are isoelectronic anions, both containing 10 electrons. Because N^{3-} has only seven protons and F^- has nine, the smaller attraction exerted by the nucleus on the electrons results in a larger N^{3-} ion.

(b) Both Mg and Ca belong to Group 2A (the alkaline earth metals). Thus, Ca^{2+} ion is larger than Mg^{2+} because Ca's valence electrons are in a larger shell ($n = 4$) than are Mg's ($n = 3$).

(c) Both ions have the same nuclear charge, but Fe^{2+} has one more electron (24 electrons compared to 23 electrons for Fe^{3+}) and hence greater electron-electron repulsion. The radius of Fe^{2+} is larger.

Similar problems: 8.43, 8.45.

Practice Exercise Select the smaller ion in each of the following pairs: (a) K^+, Li^+; (b) Au^+, Au^{3+}; (c) P^{3-}, N^{3-}.

Figure 8.10 *The third-period elements. The photograph of argon, which is a colorless, odorless gas, shows the color emitted by the gas from a discharge tube.*

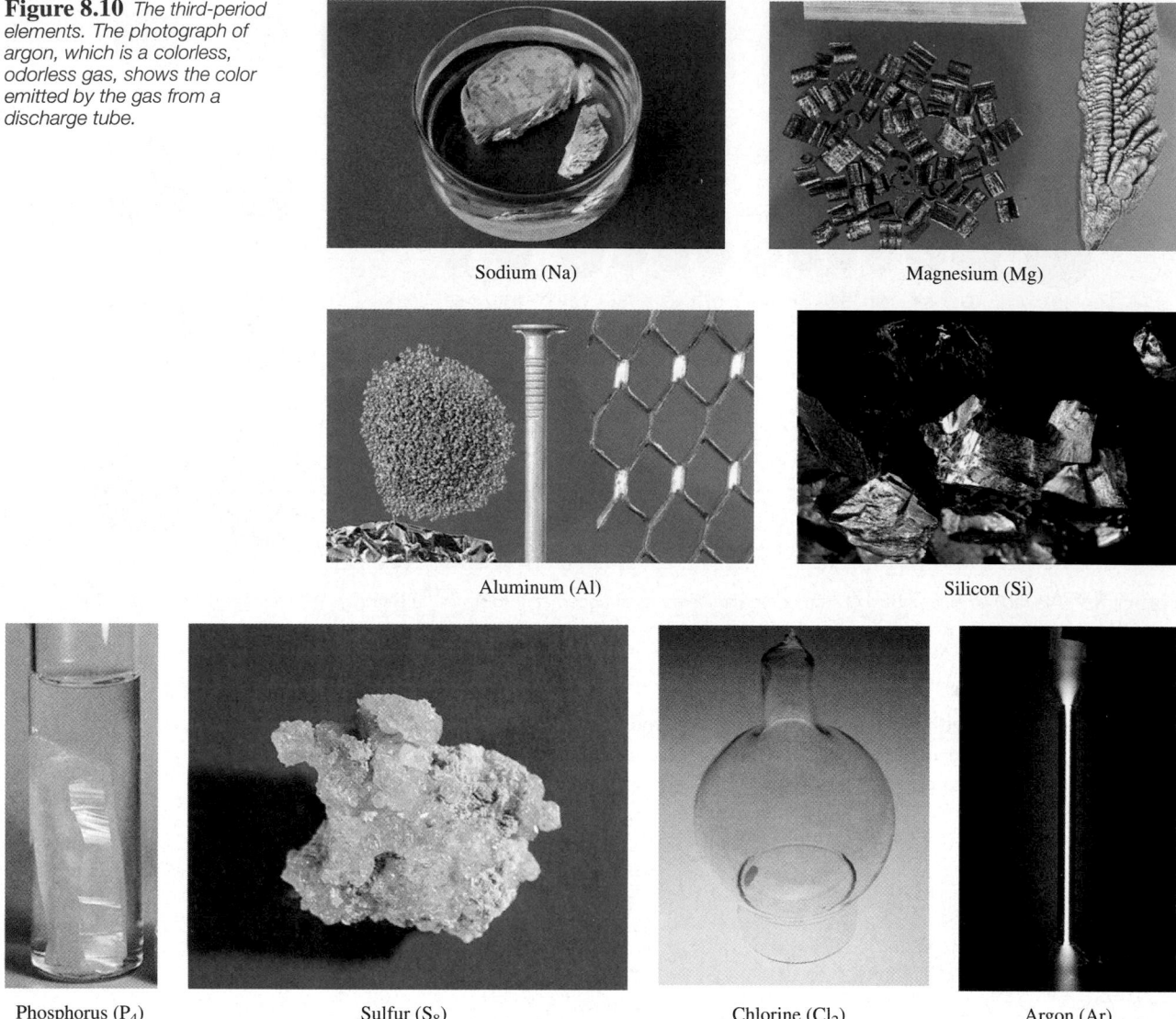

Sodium (Na)

Magnesium (Mg)

Aluminum (Al)

Silicon (Si)

Phosphorus (P_4)

Sulfur (S_8)

Chlorine (Cl_2)

Argon (Ar)

Variation of Physical Properties Across a Period and Within a Group

From left to right across a period there is a transition from metals to metalloids to nonmetals. Consider the third-period elements from sodium to argon (Figure 8.10). Sodium, the first element in the third period, is a very reactive metal, whereas chlorine, the second-to-last element of that period, is a very reactive nonmetal. In between, the elements show a gradual transition from metallic properties to nonmetallic properties. Sodium, magnesium, and aluminum all have extensive three-dimensional atomic networks, which are held together by forces characteristic of the metallic state. Silicon is a metalloid; it has a giant three-dimensional structure in which the Si atoms are held together very strongly. Starting with phosphorus, the elements exist in simple, discrete molecular units (P_4, S_8, Cl_2, and Ar) that have low melting points and boiling points.

Within a periodic group the physical properties vary more predictably, especially if the elements are in the same physical state. For example, the melting points of argon and xenon are $-189.2°C$ and $-111.9°C$, respectively. We can estimate the melting

CHEMISTRY
in Action

The Third Liquid Element?

Of the 114 known elements, 11 are gases under atmospheric conditions. Six of these are the Group 8A elements (the noble gases He, Ne, Ar, Kr, Xe, and Rn), and the other five are hydrogen (H_2), nitrogen (N_2), oxygen (O_2), fluorine (F_2), and chlorine (Cl_2). Curiously, only two elements are liquids at 25°C: mercury (Hg) and bromine (Br_2).

We do not know the properties of all the known elements because some of them have never been prepared in quantities large enough for investigation. In these cases, we must rely on periodic trends to predict their properties. What are the chances, then, of discovering a third liquid element?

Let us look at francium (Fr), the last member of Group 1A, to see if it might be a liquid at 25°C. All of francium's isotopes are radioactive. The most stable isotope is francium-223, which has a half-life of 21 minutes. (*Half-life* is the time it takes for one-half of the nuclei in any given amount of a radioactive substance to disintegrate.) This short half-life means that only very small traces of francium could possibly exist on Earth. And although it is feasible to prepare francium in the laboratory, no weighable quantity of the element has been prepared or isolated. Thus, we know very little about francium's physical and chemical properties. Yet we can use the group periodic trends to predict some of those properties.

Take francium's melting point as an example. The plot shows how the melting points of the alkali metals vary with atomic number. From lithium to sodium, the melting point

drops 81.4°; from sodium to potassium, 34.6°; from potassium to rubidium, 24°; from rubidium to cesium, 11°. On the basis of this trend, we can predict that the change from cesium to francium would be about 5°. If so, the melting point of francium would be about 23°C, which would make it a liquid under atmospheric conditions.

A plot of the melting points of the alkali metals versus their atomic numbers. By extrapolation, the melting point of francium should be 23°C.

point of the intermediate element krypton by taking the average of these two values as follows:

$$\text{melting point of Kr} = \frac{[(-189.2°C) + (-111.9°C)]}{2} = -150.6°C$$

This value is quite close to the actual melting point of −156.6°C.

The Chemistry in Action essay above illustrates one interesting application of periodic group properties.

8.4 Ionization Energy

Not only is there a correlation between electron configuration and physical properties, but a close correlation also exists between electron configuration (a microscopic property) and chemical behavior (a macroscopic property). As we will see throughout this book, the chemical properties of any atom are determined by the configuration of the atom's valence electrons. The stability of these outermost electrons is reflected directly in the atom's ionization energies. *Ionization energy* is *the minimum*

Interactivity:
Ionization Energy
ARIS, Interactives

energy *(in kJ/mol) required to remove an electron from a gaseous atom in its ground state.* In other words, ionization energy is the amount of energy in kilojoules needed to strip 1 mole of electrons from 1 mole of gaseous atoms. Gaseous atoms are specified in this definition because an atom in the gas phase is virtually uninfluenced by its neighbors and so there are no intermolecular forces (that is, forces between molecules) to take into account when measuring ionization energy.

The magnitude of ionization energy is a measure of how "tightly" the electron is held in the atom. The higher the ionization energy, the more difficult it is to remove the electron. For a many-electron atom, the amount of energy required to remove the first electron from the atom in its ground state,

$$\text{energy} + X(g) \longrightarrow X^+(g) + e^- \tag{8.2}$$

is called the *first ionization energy* (I_1). In Equation (8.2), X represents an atom of any element and e^- is an electron. The second ionization energy (I_2) and the third ionization energy (I_3) are shown in the following equations:

$$\text{energy} + X^+(g) \longrightarrow X^{2+}(g) + e^- \qquad \text{second ionization}$$
$$\text{energy} + X^{2+}(g) \longrightarrow X^{3+}(g) + e^- \qquad \text{third ionization}$$

The pattern continues for the removal of subsequent electrons.

When an electron is removed from an atom, the repulsion among the remaining electrons decreases. Because the nuclear charge remains constant, more energy is needed to remove another electron from the positively charged ion. Thus, ionization energies always increase in the following order:

$$I_1 < I_2 < I_3 < \cdots$$

Table 8.2 lists the ionization energies of the first 20 elements. Ionization is always an endothermic process. By convention, energy absorbed by atoms (or ions) in the ionization process has a positive value. Thus, ionization energies are all positive quantities. Figure 8.11 shows the variation of the first ionization energy with atomic number. The plot clearly exhibits the periodicity in the stability of the most loosely held electron. Note that, apart from small irregularities, the first ionization energies of

The increase in first ionization energy from left to right across a period and from bottom to top in a group for representative elements.

Figure 8.11 *Variation of the first ionization energy with atomic number. Note that the noble gases have high ionization energies, whereas the alkali metals and alkaline earth metals have low ionization energies.*

TABLE 8.2 The Ionization Energies (kJ/mol) of the First 20 Elements

Z	Element	First	Second	Third	Fourth	Fifth	Sixth
1	H	1,312					
2	He	2,373	5,251				
3	Li	520	7,300	11,815			
4	Be	899	1,757	14,850	21,005		
5	B	801	2,430	3,660	25,000	32,820	
6	C	1,086	2,350	4,620	6,220	38,000	47,261
7	N	1,400	2,860	4,580	7,500	9,400	53,000
8	O	1,314	3,390	5,300	7,470	11,000	13,000
9	F	1,680	3,370	6,050	8,400	11,000	15,200
10	Ne	2,080	3,950	6,120	9,370	12,200	15,000
11	Na	495.9	4,560	6,900	9,540	13,400	16,600
12	Mg	738.1	1,450	7,730	10,500	13,600	18,000
13	Al	577.9	1,820	2,750	11,600	14,800	18,400
14	Si	786.3	1,580	3,230	4,360	16,000	20,000
15	P	1,012	1,904	2,910	4,960	6,240	21,000
16	S	999.5	2,250	3,360	4,660	6,990	8,500
17	Cl	1,251	2,297	3,820	5,160	6,540	9,300
18	Ar	1,521	2,666	3,900	5,770	7,240	8,800
19	K	418.7	3,052	4,410	5,900	8,000	9,600
20	Ca	589.5	1,145	4,900	6,500	8,100	11,000

elements in a period increase with increasing atomic number. This trend is due to the increase in effective nuclear charge from left to right (as in the case of atomic radii variation). A larger effective nuclear charge means a more tightly held outer electron, and hence a higher first ionization energy. A notable feature of Figure 8.11 is the peaks, which correspond to the noble gases. The high ionization energies of the noble gases, stemming from their stable ground-state electron configurations, account for the fact that most of them are chemically unreactive. In fact, helium ($1s^2$) has the highest first ionization energy of all the elements.

At the bottom of the graph in Figure 8.11 are the Group 1A elements (the alkali metals) which have the lowest first ionization energies. Each of these metals has one valence electron (the outermost electron configuration is ns^1), which is effectively shielded by the completely filled inner shells. Consequently, it is energetically easy to remove an electron from the atom of an alkali metal to form a unipositive ion (Li^+, Na^+, K^+, . . .). Significantly, the electron configurations of these cations are isoelectronic with those noble gases just preceding them in the periodic table.

The Group 2A elements (the alkaline earth metals) have higher first ionization energies than the alkali metals do. The alkaline earth metals have two valence electrons (the outermost electron configuration is ns^2). Because these two s electrons do not shield each other well, the effective nuclear charge for an alkaline earth metal atom is larger than that for the preceding alkali metal. Most alkaline earth compounds contain dipositive ions (Mg^{2+}, Ca^{2+}, Sr^{2+}, Ba^{2+}). The Be^{2+} ion is isoelectronic with Li^+ and with He, Mg^{2+} is isoelectronic with Na^+ and with Ne, and so on.

As Figure 8.11 shows, metals have relatively low ionization energies compared to nonmetals. The ionization energies of the metalloids generally fall between those of metals and nonmetals. The difference in ionization energies suggests why metals

always form cations and nonmetals form anions in ionic compounds. (The only important nonmetallic cation is the ammonium ion, NH_4^+.) For a given group, ionization
energy decreases with increasing atomic number (that is, as we move down the group).
Elements in the same group have similar outer electron configurations. However, as
the principal quantum number n increases, so does the average distance of a valence
electron from the nucleus. A greater separation between the electron and the nucleus
means a weaker attraction, so that it becomes increasingly easier to remove the first
electron as we go from element to element down a group. Thus, the metallic character of the elements within a group increases from top to bottom. This trend is particularly noticeable for elements in Groups 3A to 7A. For example, in Group 4A, carbon is a nonmetal, silicon and germanium are metalloids, and tin and lead are metals.

Although the general trend in the periodic table is for first ionization energies to
increase from left to right, some irregularities do exist. The first exception occurs
between Group 2A and 3A elements in the same period (for example, between Be and
B and between Mg and Al). The Group 3A elements have lower first ionization energies than 2A elements because they all have a single electron in the outermost p subshell (ns^2np^1), which is well shielded by the inner electrons and the ns^2 electrons. Therefore, less energy is needed to remove a single p electron than to remove a paired s
electron from the same principal energy level. The second irregularity occurs between
Groups 5A and 6A (for example, between N and O and between P and S). In the Group
5A elements (ns^2np^3), the p electrons are in three separate orbitals according to Hund's
rule. In Group 6A (ns^2np^4), the additional electron must be paired with one of the three
p electrons. The proximity of two electrons in the same orbital results in greater electrostatic repulsion, which makes it easier to ionize an atom of the Group 6A element,
even though the nuclear charge has increased by one unit. Thus, the ionization energies
for Group 6A elements are lower than those for Group 5A elements in the same period.

Example 8.4 compares the ionization energies of some elements.

Example 8.4

(a) Which atom should have a smaller first ionization energy: oxygen or sulfur? (b) Which
atom should have a higher second ionization energy: lithium or beryllium?

Strategy (a) First ionization energy decreases as we go down a group because the
outermost electron is farther away from the nucleus and feels less attraction. (b) Removal
of the outermost electron requires less energy if it is shielded by a filled inner shell.

Solution (a) Oxygen and sulfur are members of Group 6A. They have the same
valence electron configuration (ns^2np^4), but the $3p$ electron in sulfur is farther from
the nucleus and experiences less nuclear attraction than the $2p$ electron in oxygen.
Thus, we predict that sulfur should have a smaller first ionization energy.

(b) The electron configurations of Li and Be are $1s^22s^1$ and $1s^22s^2$, respectively. The
second ionization energy is the minimum energy required to remove an electron from a
gaseous unipositive ion in its ground state. For the second ionization process, we write

$$Li^+(g) \longrightarrow Li^{2+}(g) + e^-$$
$$\;\;1s^2 \qquad\qquad 1s^1$$
$$Be^+(g) \longrightarrow Be^{2+}(g) + e^-$$
$$\;1s^22s^1 \qquad\qquad 1s^2$$

Because $1s$ electrons shield $2s$ electrons much more effectively than they shield
each other, we predict that it should be easier to remove a $2s$ electron from Be^+
than to remove a $1s$ electron from Li^+.

(Continued)

Check Compare your result with the data shown in Table 8.2. In (a), is your prediction consistent with the fact that the metallic character of the elements increases as we move down a periodic group? In (b), does your prediction account for the fact that alkali metals form +1 ions while alkaline earth metals form +2 ions?

Similar problem: 8.55.

Practice Exercise (a) Which of the following atoms should have a larger first ionization energy: N or P? (b) Which of the following atoms should have a smaller second ionization energy: Na or Mg?

8.5 Electron Affinity

Another property that greatly influences the chemical behavior of atoms is their ability to accept one or more electrons. This property is called *electron affinity*, which is *the negative of the energy change that occurs when an electron is accepted by an atom in the gaseous state to form an anion.*

$$X(g) + e^- \longrightarrow X^-(g) \tag{8.3}$$

Consider the process in which a gaseous fluorine atom accepts an electron:

$$F(g) + e^- \longrightarrow F^-(g) \qquad \Delta H = -328 \text{ kJ/mol}$$

The electron affinity of fluorine is therefore assigned a value of +328 kJ/mol. The more positive is the electron affinity of an element, the greater is the affinity of an atom of the element to accept an electron. Another way of viewing electron affinity is to think of it as the energy that must be supplied to remove an electron from the anion. For fluorine, we write

Electron affinity is positive if the reaction is exothermic and negative if the reaction is endothermic.

$$F^-(g) \longrightarrow F(g) + e^- \qquad \Delta H = +328 \text{ kJ/mol}$$

Thus, a large positive electron affinity means that the negative ion is very stable (that is, the atom has a great tendency to accept an electron), just as a high ionization energy of an atom means that the electron in the atom is very stable.

Experimentally, electron affinity is determined by removing the additional electron from an anion. In contrast to ionization energies, however, electron affinities are difficult to measure because the anions of many elements are unstable. Table 8.3 shows the electron affinities of some representative elements and the noble gases, and Figure 8.12 plots the electron affinities of the first 56 elements versus atomic number. The overall trend is an increase in the tendency to accept electrons (electron affinity values become more positive) from left to right across a period. The electron affinities of metals are generally lower than those of nonmetals. The values vary little within a given group. The halogens (Group 7A) have the highest electron affinity values. This is not surprising when we realize that by accepting an electron, each halogen atom assumes the stable electron configuration of the noble gas immediately to its right. For example, the electron configuration of F^- is $1s^2 2s^2 2p^6$, or [Ne]; for Cl^- it is $[Ne]3s^2 3p^6$ or [Ar]; and so on. Calculations show that the noble gases all have electron affinities of less than zero. Thus, the anions of these gases, if formed, would be inherently unstable.

The electron affinity of oxygen has a positive value (141 kJ/mol), which means that the process

$$O(g) + e^- \longrightarrow O^-(g) \qquad \Delta H = -141 \text{ kJ/mol}$$

TABLE 8.3	Electron Affinities (kJ/mol) of Some Representative Elements and the Noble Gases*						
1A	2A	3A	4A	5A	6A	7A	8A
H 73							He <0
Li 60	Be ≤ 0	B 27	C 122	N 0	O 141	F 328	Ne <0
Na 53	Mg ≤ 0	Al 44	Si 134	P 72	S 200	Cl 349	Ar <0
K 48	Ca 2.4	Ga 29	Ge 118	As 77	Se 195	Br 325	Kr <0
Rb 47	Sr 4.7	In 29	Sn 121	Sb 101	Te 190	I 295	Xe <0
Cs 45	Ba 14	Tl 30	Pb 110	Bi 110	Po ?	At ?	Rn <0

*The electron affinities of the noble gases, Be, and Mg have not been determined experimentally, but are believed to be close to zero or negative.

is favorable (exothermic). On the other hand, the electron affinity of the O^- ion is highly negative (-780 kJ/mol), which means the process

$$O^-(g) + e^- \longrightarrow O^{2-}(g) \qquad \Delta H = 780 \text{ kJ/mol}$$

is endothermic even though the O^{2-} ion is isoelectronic with the noble gas Ne. This process is unfavorable in the gas phase because the resulting increase in electron-electron

Figure 8.12 *A plot of electron affinity against atomic number from hydrogen to barium.*

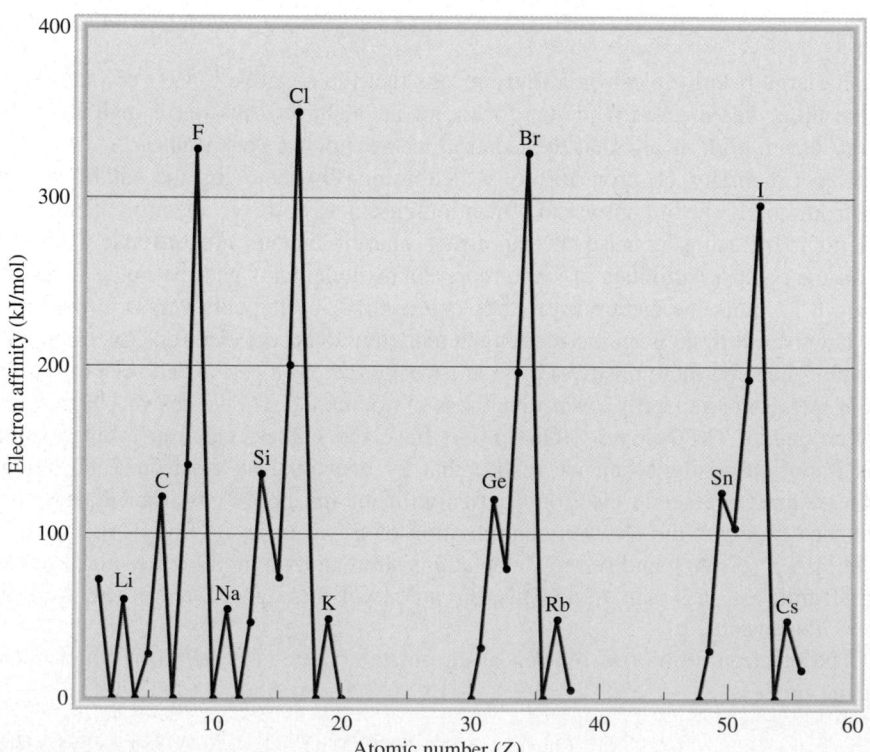

repulsion outweighs the stability gained by achieving a noble gas configuration. However, note that O^{2-} is common in ionic compounds (for example, Li_2O and MgO); in solids, the O^{2-} ion is stabilized by the neighboring cations. We will study the stability of ionic compounds in Chapter 9.

Example 8.5 shows why the alkaline earth metals do not have a great tendency to accept electrons.

Example 8.5

Why are the electron affinities of the alkaline earth metals, shown in Table 8.3, either negative or small positive values?

Strategy What are the electron configurations of alkaline earth metals? Would the added electron to such an atom be held strongly by the nucleus?

Solution The valence electron configuration of the alkaline earth metals is ns^2, where n is the highest principal quantum number. For the process

$$M(g) + e^- \longrightarrow M^-(g)$$
$$ns^2 \qquad\qquad ns^2np^1$$

where M denotes a member of the Group 2A family, the extra electron must enter the np subshell, which is effectively shielded by the two ns electrons (the ns electrons are more penetrating than the np electrons) and the inner electrons. Consequently, alkaline earth metals have little tendency to pick up an extra electron.

Practice Exercise Is it likely that Ar will form the anion Ar^-?

Similar problem: 8.63.

8.6 Variation in Chemical Properties of the Representative Elements

Ionization energy and electron affinity help chemists understand the types of reactions that elements undergo and the nature of the elements' compounds. On a conceptual level, these two measures are related in a simple way: Ionization energy measures the attraction of an atom for its own electrons, whereas electron affinity expresses the attraction of an atom for an additional electron from some other source. Together they give us insight into the general attraction of an atom for electrons. With these concepts we can survey the chemical behavior of the elements systematically, paying particular attention to the relationship between their chemical properties and their electron configurations.

We have seen that the metallic character of the elements *decreases* from left to right across a period and *increases* from top to bottom within a group. On the basis of these trends and the knowledge that metals usually have low ionization energies while nonmetals usually have high electron affinities, we can frequently predict the outcome of a reaction involving some of these elements.

General Trends in Chemical Properties

Before we study the elements in individual groups, let us look at some overall trends. We have said that elements in the same group resemble one another in chemical behavior because they have similar outer electron configurations. This statement, although correct in the general sense, must be applied with caution. Chemists have

Figure 8.13 *Diagonal relationships in the periodic table.*

long known that the first member of each group (the element in the second period from lithium to fluorine) differs from the rest of the members of the same group. Lithium, for example, exhibits many, but not all, of the properties characteristic of the alkali metals. Similarly, beryllium is a somewhat atypical member of Group 2A, and so on. The difference can be attributed to the unusually small size of the first element in each group (see Figure 8.5).

Another trend in the chemical behavior of the representative elements is the diagonal relationship. ***Diagonal relationships*** are *similarities between pairs of elements in different groups and periods of the periodic table.* Specifically, the first three members of the second period (Li, Be, and B) exhibit many similarities to those elements located diagonally below them in the periodic table (Figure 8.13). The reason for this phenomenon is the closeness of the charge densities of their cations. (*Charge density* is the charge of an ion divided by its volume.) Cations with comparable charge densities react similarly with anions and therefore form the same type of compounds. Thus, the chemistry of lithium resembles that of magnesium in some ways; the same holds for beryllium and aluminum and for boron and silicon. Each of these pairs is said to exhibit a diagonal relationship. We will see a number of examples of this relationship later.

Bear in mind that a comparison of the properties of elements in the same group is most valid if we are dealing with elements of the same type with respect to their metallic character. This guideline applies to the elements in Groups 1A and 2A, which are all metals, and to the elements in Groups 7A and 8A, which are all nonmetals. In Groups 3A through 6A, where the elements change either from nonmetals to metals or from nonmetals to metalloids, it is natural to expect greater variation in chemical properties even though the members of the same group have similar outer electron configurations.

Now let us take a closer look at the chemical properties of the representative elements and the noble gases. (We will consider the chemistry of the transition metals in Chapter 22.)

Hydrogen ($1s^1$)

There is no totally suitable position for hydrogen in the periodic table. Traditionally hydrogen is shown in Group 1A, but it really could be a class by itself. Like the alkali metals, it has a single *s* valence electron and forms a unipositive ion (H^+), which is hydrated in solution. On the other hand, hydrogen also forms the hydride ion (H^-) in ionic compounds such as NaH and CaH_2. In this respect, hydrogen resembles the halogens, all of which form uninegative ions (F^-, Cl^-, Br^-, and I^-) in ionic compounds. Ionic hydrides react with water to produce hydrogen gas and the corresponding metal hydroxides:

$$2NaH(s) + 2H_2O(l) \longrightarrow 2NaOH(aq) + H_2(g)$$
$$CaH_2(s) + 2H_2O(l) \longrightarrow Ca(OH)_2(s) + 2H_2(g)$$

Of course, the most important compound of hydrogen is water, which forms when hydrogen burns in air:

$$2H_2(g) + O_2(g) \longrightarrow 2H_2O(l)$$

Group 1A Elements (ns^1, $n \geq 2$)

Figure 8.14 shows the Group 1A elements, the alkali metals. All of these elements have low ionization energies and therefore a great tendency to lose the single valence electron. In fact, in the vast majority of their compounds they are unipositive ions.

Figure 8.14 *The Group 1A elements: the alkali metals. Francium (not shown) is radioactive.*

Lithium (Li)   Sodium (Na)

Potassium (K)   Rubidium (Rb)   Cesium (Cs)

These metals are so reactive that they are never found in the pure state in nature. They react with water to produce hydrogen gas and the corresponding metal hydroxide:

$$2M(s) + 2H_2O(l) \longrightarrow 2MOH(aq) + H_2(g)$$

where M denotes an alkali metal. When exposed to air, they gradually lose their shiny appearance as they combine with oxygen gas to form oxides. Lithium forms lithium oxide (containing the O^{2-} ion):

$$4Li(s) + O_2(g) \longrightarrow 2Li_2O(s)$$

The other alkali metals all form oxides and *peroxides* (containing the O_2^{2-} ion). For example,

$$2Na(s) + O_2(g) \longrightarrow Na_2O_2(s)$$

Potassium, rubidium, and cesium also form *superoxides* (containing the O_2^{-} ion):

$$K(s) + O_2(g) \longrightarrow KO_2(s)$$

The reason that different types of oxides are formed when alkali metals react with oxygen has to do with the stability of the oxides in the solid state. Because these oxides are all ionic compounds, their stability depends on how strongly the cations and anions attract one another. Lithium tends to form predominantly lithium oxide because this compound is more stable than lithium peroxide. The formation of other alkali metal oxides can be explained similarly.

Group 2A Elements (ns^2, $n \geq 2$)

Figure 8.15 shows the Group 2A elements. As a group, the alkaline earth metals are somewhat less reactive than the alkali metals. Both the first and the second ionization

Beryllium (Be)   Magnesium (Mg)   Calcium (Ca)

Strontium (Sr)   Barium (Ba)   Radium (Ra)

Figure 8.15 *The Group 2A elements: the alkaline earth metals. Radium is radioactive.*

energies decrease from beryllium to barium. Thus, the tendency is to form M^{2+} ions (where M denotes an alkaline earth metal atom), and hence the metallic character increases from top to bottom. Most beryllium compounds (BeH_2 and beryllium halides, such as $BeCl_2$) and some magnesium compounds (MgH_2, for example) are molecular rather than ionic in nature.

The reactivities of alkaline earth metals with water vary quite markedly. Beryllium does not react with water; magnesium reacts slowly with steam; calcium, strontium, and barium are reactive enough to attack cold water:

$$Ba(s) + 2H_2O(l) \longrightarrow Ba(OH)_2(aq) + H_2(g)$$

The reactivities of the alkaline earth metals toward oxygen also increase from Be to Ba. Beryllium and magnesium form oxides (BeO and MgO) only at elevated temperatures, whereas CaO, SrO, and BaO form at room temperature.

Magnesium reacts with acids in aqueous solution, liberating hydrogen gas:

$$Mg(s) + 2H^+(aq) \longrightarrow Mg^{2+}(aq) + H_2(g)$$

Calcium, strontium, and barium also react with aqueous acid solutions to produce hydrogen gas. However, because these metals also attack water, two different reactions will occur simultaneously.

The chemical properties of calcium and strontium provide an interesting example of periodic group similarity. Strontium-90, a radioactive isotope, is a major product of an atomic bomb explosion. If an atomic bomb is exploded in the atmosphere, the strontium-90 formed will eventually settle on land and water, and it will reach our bodies via a relatively short food chain. For example, if cows eat contaminated grass and drink contaminated water, they will pass along strontium-90 in their milk. Because calcium and strontium are chemically similar, Sr^{2+} ions can replace Ca^{2+} ions in our bones. Constant exposure of the body to the high-energy radiation emitted by the strontium-90 isotopes can lead to anemia, leukemia, and other chronic illnesses.

Boron (B)   Aluminum (Al)

Gallium (Ga)   Indium (In)

Figure 8.16 *The Group 3A elements. The low melting point of gallium (29.8°C) causes it to melt when held in hand.*

Group 3A Elements (ns^2np^1, $n \geq 2$)

The first member of Group 3A, boron, is a metalloid; the rest are metals (Figure 8.16). Boron does not form binary ionic compounds and is unreactive toward oxygen gas and water. The next element, aluminum, readily forms aluminum oxide when exposed to air:

$$4Al(s) + 3O_2(g) \longrightarrow 2Al_2O_3(s)$$

Aluminum that has a protective coating of aluminum oxide is less reactive than elemental aluminum. Aluminum forms only tripositive ions. It reacts with hydrochloric acid as follows:

$$2Al(s) + 6H^+(aq) \longrightarrow 2Al^{3+}(aq) + 3H_2(g)$$

The other Group 3A metallic elements form both unipositive and tripositive ions. Moving down the group, we find that the unipositive ion becomes more stable than the tripositive ion.

The metallic elements in Group 3A also form many molecular compounds. For example, aluminum reacts with hydrogen to form AlH_3, which resembles BeH_2 in its properties. (Here is an example of the diagonal relationship.) Thus, from left to right across the periodic table, we are seeing a gradual shift from metallic to nonmetallic character in the representative elements.

Group 4A Elements (ns^2np^2, $n \geq 2$)

The first member of Group 4A, carbon, is a nonmetal, and the next two members, silicon and germanium, are metalloids (Figure 8.17). The metallic elements of this group, tin and lead, do not react with water, but they do react with acids (hydrochloric acid, for example) to liberate hydrogen gas:

$$Sn(s) + 2H^+(aq) \longrightarrow Sn^{2+}(aq) + H_2(g)$$
$$Pb(s) + 2H^+(aq) \longrightarrow Pb^{2+}(aq) + H_2(g)$$

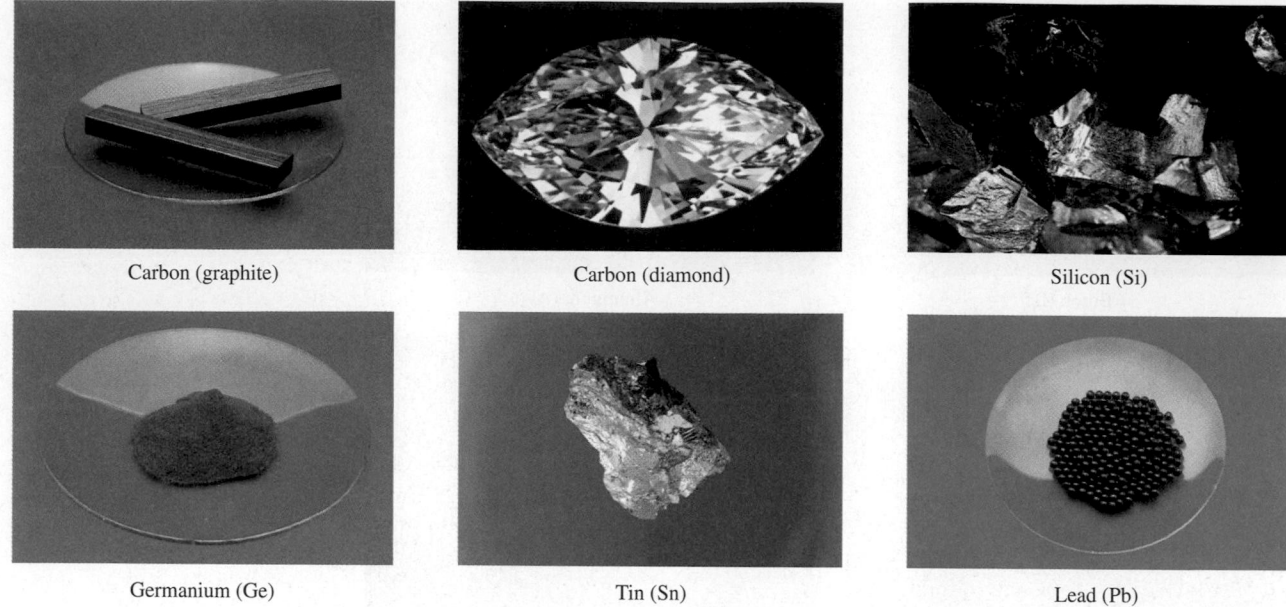

Carbon (graphite)   Carbon (diamond)   Silicon (Si)

Germanium (Ge)   Tin (Sn)   Lead (Pb)

Figure 8.17 *The Group 4A elements.*

The Group 4A elements form compounds in both the +2 and +4 oxidation states. For carbon and silicon, the +4 oxidation state is the more stable one. For example, CO_2 is more stable than CO, and SiO_2 is a stable compound, but SiO does not exist under normal conditions. As we move down the group, however, the trend in stability is reversed. In tin compounds the +4 oxidation state is only slightly more stable than the +2 oxidation state. In lead compounds the +2 oxidation state is unquestionably the more stable one. The outer electron configuration of lead is $6s^2 6p^2$, and lead tends to lose only the $6p$ electrons (to form Pb^{2+}) rather than both the $6p$ and $6s$ electrons (to form Pb^{4+}).

Group 5A Elements ($ns^2 np^3$, $n \geq 2$)

In Group 5A, nitrogen and phosphorus are nonmetals, arsenic and antimony are metalloids, and bismuth is a metal (Figure 8.18). Thus, we expect a greater variation in properties within the group.

Elemental nitrogen is a diatomic gas (N_2). It forms a number of oxides (NO, N_2O, NO_2, N_2O_4, and N_2O_5), of which only N_2O_5 is a solid; the others are gases. Nitrogen has a tendency to accept three electrons to form the nitride ion, N^{3-} (thus achieving the electron configuration $1s^2 2s^2 2p^6$, which is isoelectronic with neon). Most metallic nitrides (Li_3N and Mg_3N_2, for example) are ionic compounds. Phosphorus exists as P_4 molecules. It forms two solid oxides with the formulas P_4O_6 and P_4O_{10}. The important oxoacids HNO_3 and H_3PO_4 are formed when the following oxides react with water:

$$N_2O_5(s) + H_2O(l) \longrightarrow 2HNO_3(aq)$$
$$P_4O_{10}(s) + 6H_2O(l) \longrightarrow 4H_3PO_4(aq)$$

Arsenic, antimony, and bismuth have extensive three-dimensional structures. Bismuth is a far less reactive metal than those in the preceding groups.

Figure 8.18 *The Group 5A elements. Molecular nitrogen is a colorless, odorless gas.*

Nitrogen (N_2)

White and red phosphorus (P)

Arsenic (As)

Antimony (Sb)

Bismuth (Bi)

Group 6A Elements (ns^2np^4, $n \geq 2$)

The first three members of Group 6A (oxygen, sulfur, and selenium) are nonmetals, and the last two (tellurium and polonium) are metalloids (Figure 8.19). Oxygen is a diatomic gas; elemental sulfur and selenium have the molecular formulas S_8 and Se_8, respectively; tellurium and polonium have more extensive three-dimensional structures. (Polonium, the last member, is a radioactive element that is difficult to study in the laboratory.) Oxygen has a tendency to accept two electrons to form the oxide ion (O^{2-}) in many ionic compounds. Sulfur, selenium, and tellurium also form dinegative anions (S^{2-}, Se^{2-}, and Te^{2-}). The elements in this group (especially oxygen) form a large number of molecular compounds with nonmetals. The important compounds of sulfur are SO_2, SO_3, and H_2S. Sulfuric acid is formed when sulfur trioxide reacts with water:

$$SO_3(g) + H_2O(l) \longrightarrow H_2SO_4(aq)$$

Sulfur (S_8)   Selenium (Se_8)   Tellurium (Te)

Figure 8.19 *The Group 6A elements sulfur, selenium, and tellurium. Molecular oxygen is a colorless, odorless gas. Polonium (not shown) is radioactive.*

Group 7A Elements (ns^2np^5, $n \geq 2$)

All the halogens are nonmetals with the general formula X_2, where X denotes a halogen element (Figure 8.20). Because of their great reactivity, the halogens are never found in the elemental form in nature. (The last member of Group 7A, astatine, is a radioactive element. Little is known about its properties.) Fluorine is so reactive that it attacks water to generate oxygen:

$$2F_2(g) + 2H_2O(l) \longrightarrow 4HF(aq) + O_2(g)$$

Actually the reaction between molecular fluorine and water is quite complex; the products formed depend on reaction conditions. The reaction shown above is one of several possible changes.

The halogens have high ionization energies and large positive electron affinities. Anions derived from the halogens (F^-, Cl^-, Br^-, and I^-) are called *halides*. They are isoelectronic with the noble gases immediately to their right in the periodic table. For example, F^- is isoelectronic with Ne, Cl^- with Ar, and so on. The vast majority of the alkali metal halides and alkaline earth metal halides are ionic compounds. The halogens also form many molecular compounds among themselves (such as ICl and BrF_3) and with nonmetallic elements in other groups (such as NF_3, PCl_5, and SF_6). The halogens react with hydrogen to form hydrogen halides:

$$H_2(g) + X_2(g) \longrightarrow 2HX(g)$$

When this reaction involves fluorine, it is explosive, but it becomes less and less violent as we substitute chlorine, bromine, and iodine. The hydrogen halides dissolve in

Figure 8.20 *The Group 7A elements chlorine, bromine, and iodine. Fluorine is a greenish-yellow gas that attacks ordinary glassware. Astatine is radioactive.*

Figure 8.21 *All noble gases are colorless and odorless. These pictures show the colors emitted by the gases from a discharge tube.*

water to form hydrohalic acids. Hydrofluoric acid (HF) is a weak acid (that is, it is a weak electrolyte), but the other hydrohalic acids (HCl, HBr, and HI) are all strong acids (strong electrolytes).

Group 8A Elements (ns^2np^6, $n \geq 2$)

All noble gases exist as monatomic species (Figure 8.21). Their atoms have completely filled outer ns and np subshells, which give them great stability. (Helium is $1s^2$.) The Group 8A ionization energies are among the highest of all elements, and these gases have no tendency to accept extra electrons. For years these elements were called inert gases, and rightly so. Until 1963 no one had been able to prepare a compound containing any of these elements. The British chemist Neil Bartlett[†] shattered chemists' long-held views of these elements when he exposed xenon to platinum hexafluoride, a strong oxidizing agent, and brought about the following reaction (Figure 8.22):

$$Xe(g) + 2PtF_6(g) \longrightarrow XeF^+Pt_2F_{11}^-(s)$$

Since then, a number of xenon compounds (XeF_4, XeO_3, XeO_4, $XeOF_4$) and a few krypton compounds (KrF_2, for example) have been prepared (Figure 8.23). Despite the immense interest in the chemistry of the noble gases, however, their compounds do not have any major commercial applications, and they are not involved in natural biological processes. No compounds of helium and neon are known.

In 2000, chemists prepared a compound containing argon (HArF), which is stable only at very low temperatures.

Comparison of Group 1A and Group 1B Elements

When we compare the Group 1A elements (alkali metals) and the Group 1B elements (copper, silver, and gold), we arrive at an interesting conclusion. Although the metals

[†]Neil Bartlett (1932–). English chemist. Bartlett's work is mainly in the preparation and study of compounds with unusual oxidation states and in solid-state chemistry.

Figure 8.22 *(a) Xenon gas (colorless) and PtF₆ (red gas) separated from each other. (b) When the two gases are allowed to mix, a yellow-orange solid compound is formed. Note that the product was initially given the incorrect formula XePtF₆.*

(a)   (b)

Figure 8.23 *Crystals of xenon tetrafluoride (XeF_4).*

in these two groups have similar outer electron configurations, with one electron in the outermost s orbital, their chemical properties are quite different.

The first ionization energies of Cu, Ag, and Au are 745 kJ/mol, 731 kJ/mol, and 890 kJ/mol, respectively. Because these values are considerably larger than those of the alkali metals (see Table 8.2), the Group 1B elements are much less reactive. The higher ionization energies of the Group 1B elements result from incomplete shielding of the nucleus by the inner d electrons (compared with the more effective shielding of the completely filled noble gas cores). Consequently the outer s electrons of these elements are more strongly attracted by the nucleus. In fact, copper, silver, and gold are so unreactive that they are usually found in the uncombined state in nature. The inertness and rarity of these metals make them valuable in the manufacture of coins and in jewelry. For this reason, these metals are also called "coinage metals." The difference in chemical properties between the Group 2A elements (the alkaline earth metals) and the Group 2B metals (zinc, cadmium, and mercury) can be explained in a similar way.

Properties of Oxides Across a Period

One way to compare the properties of the representative elements across a period is to examine the properties of a series of similar compounds. Because oxygen combines with almost all elements, we will compare the properties of oxides of the third-period elements to see how metals differ from metalloids and nonmetals. Some elements in the third period (P, S, and Cl) form several types of oxides, but for simplicity we will consider only those oxides in which the elements have the highest oxidation number. Table 8.4 lists a few general characteristics of these oxides. We observed earlier that oxygen has a tendency to form the oxide ion. This tendency is greatly favored when oxygen combines with metals that have low ionization energies, namely, those in Groups 1A and 2A, plus aluminum. Thus, Na_2O, MgO, and Al_2O_3 are ionic compounds, as indicated by their high melting points and boiling points. They have extensive three-dimensional structures in which each cation is surrounded by a specific number of anions, and vice versa. As the ionization energies of the elements increase from left to right, so does the molecular nature of the oxides that are formed. Silicon is a metalloid; its oxide (SiO_2) also has a huge three-dimensional network, although no ions are present. The oxides of phosphorus, sulfur, and chlorine are molecular compounds composed of small discrete units. The weak attractions among these molecules result in relatively low melting points and boiling points.

TABLE 8.4	Some Properties of Oxides of the Third-Period Elements						
	Na_2O	MgO	Al_2O_3	SiO_2	P_4O_{10}	SO_3	Cl_2O_7
Type of compound	←	Ionic	→	←	Molecular	→	
Structure	← Extensive three-dimensional →			← Discrete → molecular units			
Melting point (°C)	1275	2800	2045	1610	580	16.8	−91.5
Boiling point (°C)	?	3600	2980	2230	?	44.8	82
Acid-base nature	Basic	Basic	Amphoteric	←	Acidic	→	

Most oxides can be classified as acidic or basic depending on whether they produce acids or bases when dissolved in water or react as acids or bases in certain processes. Some oxides are **amphoteric,** which means that they *display both acidic and basic properties.* The first two oxides of the third period, Na_2O and MgO, are basic oxides. For example, Na_2O reacts with water to form the base sodium hydroxide:

$$Na_2O(s) + H_2O(l) \longrightarrow 2NaOH(aq)$$

Magnesium oxide is quite insoluble; it does not react with water to any appreciable extent. However, it does react with acids in a manner that resembles an acid-base reaction:

$$MgO(s) + 2HCl(aq) \longrightarrow MgCl_2(aq) + H_2O(l)$$

Note that the products of this reaction are a salt ($MgCl_2$) and water, the usual products of an acid-base neutralization.

Aluminum oxide is even less soluble than magnesium oxide; it too does not react with water. However, it shows basic properties by reacting with acids:

$$Al_2O_3(s) + 6HCl(aq) \longrightarrow 2AlCl_3(aq) + 3H_2O(l)$$

It also exhibits acidic properties by reacting with bases:

$$Al_2O_3(s) + 2NaOH(aq) + 3H_2O(l) \longrightarrow 2NaAl(OH)_4(aq)$$

Note that this acid-base neutralization produces a salt but no water.

Thus, Al_2O_3 is classified as an amphoteric oxide because it has properties of both acids and bases. Other amphoteric oxides are ZnO, BeO, and Bi_2O_3.

Silicon dioxide is insoluble and does not react with water. It has acidic properties, however, because it reacts with very concentrated bases:

$$SiO_2(s) + 2NaOH(aq) \longrightarrow Na_2SiO_3(aq) + H_2O(l)$$

For this reason, concentrated aqueous, strong bases such as NaOH(aq) should not be stored in Pyrex glassware, which is made of SiO_2.

The remaining third-period oxides are acidic. They react with water to form phosphoric acid (H_3PO_4), sulfuric acid (H_2SO_4), and perchloric acid ($HClO_4$):

$$P_4O_{10}(s) + 6H_2O(l) \longrightarrow 4H_3PO_4(aq)$$
$$SO_3(g) + H_2O(l) \longrightarrow H_2SO_4(aq)$$
$$Cl_2O_7(l) + H_2O(l) \longrightarrow 2HClO_4(aq)$$

Certain oxides such as CO and NO are neutral; that is, they do not react with water to produce an acidic or basic solution. In general, oxides containing nonmetallic elements are not basic.

CHEMISTRY
in Action

Discovery of the Noble Gases

In the late 1800s John William Strutt, Third Baron of Rayleigh, who was a professor of physics at the Cavendish Laboratory in Cambridge, England, accurately determined the atomic masses of a number of elements, but he obtained a puzzling result with nitrogen. One of his methods of preparing nitrogen was by the thermal decomposition of ammonia:

$$2NH_3(g) \longrightarrow N_2(g) + 3H_2(g)$$

Another method was to start with air and remove from it oxygen, carbon dioxide, and water vapor. Invariably, the nitrogen from air was a little denser (by about 0.5 percent) than the nitrogen from ammonia.

Lord Rayleigh's work caught the attention of Sir William Ramsay, a professor of chemistry at the University College, London. In 1898 Ramsay passed nitrogen, which he had obtained from air by Rayleigh's procedure, over red-hot magnesium to convert it to magnesium nitride:

$$3Mg(s) + N_2(g) \longrightarrow Mg_3N_2(s)$$

After all of the nitrogen had reacted with magnesium, Ramsay was left with an unknown gas that would not combine with anything.

With the help of Sir William Crookes, the inventor of the discharge tube, Ramsay and Lord Rayleigh found that the emission spectrum of the gas did not match any of the known elements. The gas was a new element! They determined its atomic mass to be 39.95 amu and called it argon, which means "the lazy one" in Greek.

Once argon had been discovered, other noble gases were quickly identified. Also in 1898 Ramsay isolated helium from uranium ores (see Chemical Mystery essay on p. 311). From the atomic masses of helium and argon, their lack of chemical reactivity, and what was then known about the periodic table, Ramsay was convinced that there were other unreactive gases and that they were all members of one periodic group. He and his student Morris Travers set out to find the unknown gases. They used a refrigeration machine to first produce liquid air. Applying a technique called *fractional distillation,* they then allowed the liquid air to warm up gradually and collected components that boiled off at different temperatures. In this manner, they analyzed and identified three new elements—neon, krypton, and xenon—in only three months. Three new elements in three months is a record that may never be broken!

The discovery of the noble gases helped to complete the periodic table. Their atomic masses suggested that these ele-ments should be placed to the right of the halogens. The apparent discrepancy with the position of argon was resolved by Moseley, as discussed in the chapter.

Finally, the last member of the noble gases, radon, was discovered by the German chemist Frederick Dorn in 1900. A radioactive element and the heaviest elemental gas known, radon's discovery not only completed the Group 8A elements, but also advanced our understanding about the nature of radioactive decay and transmutation of elements.

Lord Rayleigh and Ramsay both won Nobel Prizes in 1904 for the discovery of argon. Lord Rayleigh received the prize in physics and Ramsay's award was in chemistry.

Sir William Ramsay (1852–1916).

This brief examination of oxides of the third-period elements shows that as the metallic character of the elements decreases from left to right across the period, their oxides change from basic to amphoteric to acidic. Metallic oxides are usually basic, and most oxides of nonmetals are acidic. The intermediate properties of the oxides (as shown by the amphoteric oxides) are exhibited by elements whose positions are intermediate within the period. Note also that because the metallic character of the elements increases from top to bottom within a group of representative elements, we would expect oxides of elements with higher atomic numbers to be more basic than the lighter elements. This is indeed the case.

Example 8.6

Classify the following oxides as acidic, basic, or amphoteric: (a) Rb_2O, (b) BeO, (c) As_2O_5.

Strategy What type of elements form acidic oxides? basic oxides? amphoteric oxides?

Solution (a) Because rubidium is an alkali metal, we would expect Rb_2O to be a basic oxide.

(b) Beryllium is an alkaline earth metal. However, because it is the first member of Group 2A, we expect that it may differ somewhat from the other members of the group. In the text we saw that Al_2O_3 is amphoteric. Because beryllium and aluminum exhibit a diagonal relationship, BeO may resemble Al_2O_3 in properties. It turns out that BeO is also an amphoteric oxide.

(c) Because arsenic is a nonmetal, we expect As_2O_5 to be an acidic oxide.

Practice Exercise Classify the following oxides as acidic, basic, or amphoteric: (a) ZnO, (b) P_4O_{10}, (c) CaO

Similar problem: 8.72.

Summary of Facts and Concepts

1. Nineteenth-century chemists developed the periodic table by arranging elements in the increasing order of their atomic masses. Discrepancies in early versions of the periodic table were resolved by arranging the elements in order of their atomic numbers.

2. Electron configuration determines the properties of an element. The modern periodic table classifies the elements according to their atomic numbers, and thus also by their electron configurations. The configuration of the valence electrons directly affects the properties of the atoms of the representative elements.

3. Periodic variations in the physical properties of the elements reflect differences in atomic structure. The metallic character of elements decreases across a period from metals through the metalloids to nonmetals and increases from top to bottom within a particular group of representative elements.

4. Atomic radius varies periodically with the arrangement of the elements in the periodic table. It decreases from left to right and increases from top to bottom.

5. Ionization energy is a measure of the tendency of an atom to resist the loss of an electron. The higher the ionization energy, the stronger the attraction between the nucleus and an electron. Electron affinity is a measure of the tendency of an atom to gain an electron. The more positive the electron affinity, the greater the tendency for the atom to gain an electron. Metals usually have low ionization energies, and nonmetals usually have high electron affinities.

6. Noble gases are very stable because their outer ns and np subshells are completely filled. The metals among the representative elements (in Groups 1A, 2A, and 3A) tend to lose electrons until their cations become isoelectronic with the noble gases that precede them in the periodic table. The nonmetals in Groups 5A, 6A, and 7A tend to accept electrons until their anions become isoelectronic with the noble gases that follow them in the periodic table.

Key Words

Amphoteric oxide, p. 345
Atomic radius, p. 323
Diagonal relationship, p. 336

Electron affinity, p. 333
Ionic radius, p. 325
Ionization energy, p. 329

Isoelectronic, p. 322
Representative
  elements, p. 318

Valence electrons, p. 320

Questions and Problems

Development of the Periodic Table
Review Questions

8.1   Briefly describe the significance of Mendeleev's periodic table.

8.2   What is Moseley's contribution to the modern periodic table?

8.3   Describe the general layout of a modern periodic table.

8.4   What is the most important relationship among elements in the same group in the periodic table?

Periodic Classification of the Elements
Review Questions

8.5   Which of the following elements are metals, nonmetals, or metalloids? As, Xe, Fe, Li, B, Cl, Ba, P, I, Si.

8.6   Compare the physical and chemical properties of metals and nonmetals.

8.7   Draw a rough sketch of a periodic table (no details are required). Indicate regions where metals, nonmetals, and metalloids are located.

8.8   What is a representative element? Give names and symbols of four representative elements.

8.9   Without referring to a periodic table, write the name and give the symbol for an element in each of the following groups: 1A, 2A, 3A, 4A, 5A, 6A, 7A, 8A, transition metals.

8.10   Indicate whether the following elements exist as atomic species, molecular species, or extensive three-dimensional structures in their most stable states at 25°C and 1 atm and write the molecular or empirical formula for each one: phosphorus, iodine, magnesium, neon, carbon, sulfur, cesium, and oxygen.

8.11   You are given a dark shiny solid and asked to determine whether it is iodine or a metallic element. Suggest a nondestructive test that would enable you to arrive at the correct answer.

8.12   What are valence electrons? For representative elements, the number of valence electrons of an element is equal to its group number. Show that this is true for the following elements: Al, Sr, K, Br, P, S, C.

8.13   Write the outer electron configurations for the (a) alkali metals, (b) alkaline earth metals, (c) halogens, (d) noble gases.

8.14   Use the first-row transition metals (Sc to Cu) as an example to illustrate the characteristics of the electron configurations of transition metals.

8.15   How does the electron configuration of ions derived from representative elements give them stability?

8.16   What do we mean when we say that two ions or an atom and an ion are isoelectronic?

8.17   What is wrong with the statement "The atoms of element X are isoelectronic with the atoms of element Y"?

8.18   Give three examples of first-row transition metal (Sc to Cu) ions whose electron configurations are represented by the argon core.

Problems

8.19   In the periodic table, the element hydrogen is sometimes grouped with the alkali metals (as in this book) and sometimes with the halogens. Explain why hydrogen can resemble the Group 1A and the Group 7A elements.

8.20   A neutral atom of a certain element has 17 electrons. Without consulting a periodic table, (a) write the ground-state electron configuration of the element, (b) classify the element, (c) determine whether this element is diamagnetic or paramagnetic.

8.21   Group the following electron configurations in pairs that would represent similar chemical properties of their atoms:
(a) $1s^2 2s^2 2p^6 3s^2$
(b) $1s^2 2s^2 2p^3$
(c) $1s^2 2s^2 2p^6 3s^2 3p^6 4s^2 3d^{10} 4p^6$
(d) $1s^2 2s^2$
(e) $1s^2 2s^2 2p^6$
(f) $1s^2 2s^2 2p^6 3s^2 3p^3$

8.22   Group the following electron configurations in pairs that would represent similar chemical properties of their atoms:
(a) $1s^2 2s^2 2p^5$
(b) $1s^2 2s^1$

(c) $1s^2 2s^2 2p^6$

(d) $1s^2 2s^2 2p^6 3s^2 3p^5$

(e) $1s^2 2s^2 2p^6 3s^2 3p^6 4s^1$

(f) $1s^2 2s^2 2p^6 3s^2 3p^6 4s^2 3d^{10} 4p^6$.

8.23 Without referring to a periodic table, write the electron configuration of elements with the following atomic numbers: (a) 9, (b) 20, (c) 26, (d) 33. Classify the elements.

8.24 Specify the group of the periodic table in which each of the following elements is found: (a) $[Ne]3s^1$, (b) $[Ne]3s^2 3p^3$, (c) $[Ne]3s^2 3p^6$, (d) $[Ar]4s^2 3d^8$.

8.25 A M^{2+} ion derived from a metal in the first transition metal series has four electrons in the $3d$ subshell. What element might M be?

8.26 A metal ion with a net $+3$ charge has five electrons in the $3d$ subshell. Identify the metal.

8.27 Write the ground-state electron configurations of the following ions: (a) Li^+, (b) H^-, (c) N^{3-}, (d) F^-, (e) S^{2-}, (f) Al^{3+}, (g) Se^{2-}, (h) Br^-, (i) Rb^+, (j) Sr^{2+}, (k) Sn^{2+}, (l) Te^{2-}, (m) Ba^{2+}, (n) Pb^{2+}, (o) In^{3+}, (p) Tl^+, (q) Tl^{3+}.

8.28 Write the ground-state electron configurations of the following ions, which play important roles in biochemical processes in our bodies: (a) Na^+, (b) Mg^{2+}, (c) Cl^-, (d) K^+, (e) Ca^{2+}, (f) Fe^{2+}, (g) Cu^{2+}, (h) Zn^{2+}.

8.29 Write the ground-state electron configurations of the following transition metal ions: (a) Sc^{3+}, (b) Ti^{4+}, (c) V^{5+}, (d) Cr^{3+}, (e) Mn^{2+}, (f) Fe^{2+}, (g) Fe^{3+}, (h) Co^{2+}, (i) Ni^{2+}, (j) Cu^+, (k) Cu^{2+}, (l) Ag^+, (m) Au^+, (n) Au^{3+}, (o) Pt^{2+}.

8.30 Name the ions with $+3$ charges that have the following electron configurations: (a) $[Ar]3d^3$, (b) $[Ar]$, (c) $[Kr]4d^6$, (d) $[Xe]4f^{14}5d^6$.

8.31 Which of the following species are isoelectronic with each other? C, Cl^-, Mn^{2+}, B^-, Ar, Zn, Fe^{3+}, Ge^{2+}.

8.32 Group the species that are isoelectronic: Be^{2+}, F^-, Fe^{2+}, N^{3-}, He, S^{2-}, Co^{3+}, Ar.

Periodic Variation in Physical Properties
Review Questions

8.33 Define atomic radius. Does the size of an atom have a precise meaning?

8.34 How does atomic radius change (a) from left to right across a period and (b) from top to bottom in a group?

8.35 Define ionic radius. How does the size of an atom change when it is converted to (a) an anion and (b) a cation?

8.36 Explain why, for isoelectronic ions, the anions are larger than the cations.

Problems

8.37 On the basis of their positions in the periodic table, select the atom with the larger atomic radius in each of the following pairs: (a) Na, Cs; (b) Be, Ba; (c) N, Sb; (d) F, Br; (e) Ne, Xe.

8.38 Arrange the following atoms in order of decreasing atomic radius: Na, Al, P, Cl, Mg.

8.39 Which is the largest atom in Group 4A?

8.40 Which is the smallest atom in Group 7A?

8.41 Why is the radius of the lithium atom considerably larger than the radius of the hydrogen atom?

8.42 Use the second period of the periodic table as an example to show that the size of atoms decreases as we move from left to right. Explain the trend.

8.43 Indicate which one of the two species in each of the following pairs is smaller: (a) Cl or Cl^-; (b) Na or Na^+; (c) O^{2-} or S^{2-}; (d) Mg^{2+} or Al^{3+}; (e) Au^+ or Au^{3+}.

8.44 List the following ions in order of increasing ionic radius: N^{3-}, Na^+, F^-, Mg^{2+}, O^{2-}.

8.45 Explain which of the following cations is larger, and why: Cu^+ or Cu^{2+}.

8.46 Explain which of the following anions is larger, and why: Se^{2-} or Te^{2-}.

8.47 Give the physical states (gas, liquid, or solid) of the representative elements in the fourth period (K, Ca, Ga, Ge, As, Se, Br) at 1 atm and 25°C.

8.48 The boiling points of neon and krypton are -245.9°C and -152.9°C, respectively. Using these data, estimate the boiling point of argon.

Ionization Energy
Review Questions

8.49 Define ionization energy. Ionization energy measurements are usually made when atoms are in the gaseous state. Why? Why is the second ionization energy always greater than the first ionization energy for any element?

8.50 Sketch the outline of the periodic table and show group and period trends in the first ionization energy of the elements. What types of elements have the highest ionization energies and what types the lowest ionization energies?

Problems

8.51 Arrange the following in order of increasing first ionization energy: Na, Cl, Al, S, and Cs.

8.52 Arrange the following in order of increasing first ionization energy: F, K, P, Ca, and Ne.

8.53 Use the third period of the periodic table as an example to illustrate the change in first ionization energies of the elements as we move from left to right. Explain the trend.

8.54 In general, ionization energy increases from left to right across a given period. Aluminum, however, has a lower ionization energy than magnesium. Explain.

8.55 The first and second ionization energies of K are 419 kJ/mol and 3052 kJ/mol, and those of Ca are 590 kJ/mol and 1145 kJ/mol, respectively. Compare their values and comment on the differences.

8.56 Two atoms have the electron configurations $1s^2 2s^2 2p^6$ and $1s^2 2s^2 2p^6 3s^1$. The first ionization energy of one is 2080 kJ/mol, and that of the other is 496 kJ/mol. Match each ionization energy with one of the given electron configurations. Justify your choice.

8.57 A hydrogenlike ion is an ion containing only one electron. The energies of the electron in a hydrogenlike ion are given by

$$E_n = -(2.18 \times 10^{-18}\ \text{J})Z^2\left(\frac{1}{n^2}\right)$$

where n is the principal quantum number and Z is the atomic number of the element. Calculate the ionization energy (in kJ/mol) of the He^+ ion.

8.58 Plasma is a state of matter consisting of positive gaseous ions and electrons. In the plasma state, a mercury atom could be stripped of its 80 electrons and therefore would exist as Hg^{80+}. Use the equation in Problem 8.57 to calculate the energy required for the last ionization step, that is,

$$Hg^{79+}(g) \longrightarrow Hg^{80+}(g) + e^-$$

Electron Affinity
Review Questions

8.59 (a) Define electron affinity. (b) Electron affinity measurements are made with gaseous atoms. Why? (c) Ionization energy is always a positive quantity, whereas electron affinity may be either positive or negative. Explain.

8.60 Explain the trends in electron affinity from aluminum to chlorine (see Table 8.3).

Problems

8.61 Arrange the elements in each of the following groups in increasing order of the most positive electron affinity: (a) Li, Na, K; (b) F, Cl, Br, I.

8.62 Specify which of the following elements you would expect to have the greatest electron affinity: He, K, Co, S, Cl.

8.63 Considering their electron affinities, do you think it is possible for the alkali metals to form an anion like M^-, where M represents an alkali metal?

8.64 Explain why alkali metals have a greater affinity for electrons than alkaline earth metals.

Variation in Chemical Properties of the Representative Elements
Review Questions

8.65 What is meant by the diagonal relationship? Name two pairs of elements that show this relationship.

8.66 Which elements are more likely to form acidic oxides? Basic oxides? Amphoteric oxides?

Problems

8.67 Use the alkali metals and alkaline earth metals as examples to show how we can predict the chemical properties of elements simply from their electron configurations.

8.68 Based on your knowledge of the chemistry of the alkali metals, predict some of the chemical properties of francium, the last member of the group.

8.69 As a group, the noble gases are very stable chemically (only Kr and Xe are known to form compounds). Why?

8.70 Why are Group 1B elements more stable than Group 1A elements even though they seem to have the same outer electron configuration, ns^1, where n is the principal quantum number of the outermost shell?

8.71 How do the chemical properties of oxides change from left to right across a period? From top to bottom within a particular group?

8.72 Write balanced equations for the reactions between each of the following oxides and water: (a) Li_2O, (b) CaO, (c) SO_3.

8.73 Write formulas for and name the binary hydrogen compounds of the second-period elements (Li to F). Describe how the physical and chemical properties of these compounds change from left to right across the period.

8.74 Which oxide is more basic, MgO or BaO? Why?

Additional Problems

8.75 State whether each of the following properties of the representative elements generally increases or decreases (a) from left to right across a period and (b) from top to bottom within a group: metallic character, atomic size, ionization energy, acidity of oxides.

8.76 With reference to the periodic table, name (a) a halogen element in the fourth period, (b) an element similar to phosphorus in chemical properties, (c) the most reactive metal in the fifth period, (d) an element that has an atomic number smaller than 20 and is similar to strontium.

8.77 Write equations representing the following processes:
(a) The electron affinity of S^-.
(b) The third ionization energy of titanium.
(c) The electron affinity of Mg^{2+}.
(d) The ionization energy of O^{2-}.

8.78 Arrange the following isoelectronic species in order of (a) increasing ionic radius and (b) increasing ionization energy: O^{2-}, F^-, Na^+, Mg^{2+}.

8.79 Write the empirical (or molecular) formulas of compounds that the elements in the third period (sodium to chlorine) should form with (a) molecular oxygen and (b) molecular chlorine. In each case indicate whether you would expect the compound to be ionic or molecular in character.

8.80 Element M is a shiny and highly reactive metal (melting point 63°C), and element X is a highly reactive nonmetal (melting point −7.2°C). They react to form a compound with the empirical formula MX, a colorless, brittle white solid that melts at 734°C. When dissolved in water or when in the molten state, the substance conducts electricity. When chlorine gas is bubbled through an aqueous solution containing MX, a reddish-brown liquid appears and Cl^- ions are formed. From these observations, identify M and X. (You may need to consult a handbook of chemistry for the melting-point values.)

8.81 Match each of the elements on the right with its description on the left:

(a) A dark-red liquid   Calcium (Ca)
(b) A colorless gas that burns   Gold (Au)
    in oxygen gas   Hydrogen (H_2)
(c) A reactive metal that attacks   Argon (Ar)
    water   Bromine (Br_2)
(d) A shiny metal that is used in
    jewelry
(e) An inert gas

8.82 Arrange the following species in isoelectronic pairs: O^+, Ar, S^{2-}, Ne, Zn, Cs^+, N^{3-}, As^{3+}, N, Xe.

8.83 In which of the following are the species written in decreasing order by size of radius? (a) Be, Mg, Ba, (b) N^{3-}, O^{2-}, F^-, (c) Tl^{3+}, Tl^{2+}, Tl^+.

8.84 Which of the following properties show a clear periodic variation? (a) first ionization energy, (b) molar mass of the elements, (c) number of isotopes of an element, (d) atomic radius.

8.85 When carbon dioxide is bubbled through a clear calcium hydroxide solution, the solution appears milky. Write an equation for the reaction and explain how this reaction illustrates that CO_2 is an acidic oxide.

8.86 You are given four substances: a fuming red liquid, a dark metallic-looking solid, a pale-yellow gas, and a yellow-green gas that attacks glass. You are told that these substances are the first four members of Group 7A, the halogens. Name each one.

8.87 For each pair of elements listed below, give three properties that show their chemical similarity: (a) sodium and potassium and (b) chlorine and bromine.

8.88 Name the element that forms compounds, under appropriate conditions, with every other element in the periodic table except He, Ne, and Ar.

8.89 Explain why the first electron affinity of sulfur is 200 kJ/mol but the second electron affinity is −649 kJ/mol.

8.90 The H^- ion and the He atom have two $1s$ electrons each. Which of the two species is larger? Explain.

8.91 Predict the products of the following oxides with water: Na_2O, BaO, CO_2, N_2O_5, P_4O_{10}, SO_3. Write an equation for each of the reactions. Specify whether the oxides are acidic, basic, or amphoteric.

8.92 Write the formulas and names of the oxides of the second-period elements (Li to N). Identify the oxides as acidic, basic, or amphoteric.

8.93 State whether each of the following elements is a gas, a liquid, or a solid under atmospheric conditions. Also state whether it exists in the elemental form as atoms, as molecules, or as a three-dimensional network: Mg, Cl, Si, Kr, O, I, Hg, Br.

8.94 What factors account for the unique nature of hydrogen?

8.95 The air in a manned spacecraft or submarine needs to be purified of exhaled carbon dioxide. Write equations for the reactions between carbon dioxide and (a) lithium oxide (Li_2O), (b) sodium peroxide (Na_2O_2), and (c) potassium superoxide (KO_2).

8.96 The formula for calculating the energies of an electron in a hydrogenlike ion is given in Problem 8.57. This equation cannot be applied to many-electron atoms. One way to modify it for the more complex atoms is to replace Z with $(Z − \sigma)$, where Z is the atomic number and σ is a positive dimensionless quantity called the shielding constant. Consider the helium atom as an example. The physical significance of σ is that it represents the extent of shielding that the two $1s$ electrons exert on each other. Thus, the quantity $(Z − \sigma)$ is appropriately called the "effective nuclear charge." Calculate the value of σ if the first ionization energy of helium is 3.94×10^{-18} J per atom. (Ignore the minus sign in the given equation in your calculation.)

8.97 Why do noble gases have negative electron affinity values?

8.98 The atomic radius of K is 216 pm and that of K^+ is 133 pm. Calculate the percent decrease in volume that occurs when K(g) is converted to K^+(g). [The volume of a sphere is $(\frac{4}{3})\pi r^3$, where r is the radius of the sphere.]

8.99 The atomic radius of F is 72 pm and that of F^- is 136 pm. Calculate the percent increase in volume that occurs when F(g) is converted to F^-(g). (See Problem 8.98 for the volume of a sphere.)

8.100 A technique called photoelectron spectroscopy is used to measure the ionization energy of atoms. A sample is irradiated with UV light, and electrons are ejected from the valence shell. The kinetic energies of the ejected electrons are measured. Because the energy of the UV photon and the kinetic energy of the ejected electron are known, we can write

$$h\nu = \text{IE} + \tfrac{1}{2}mu^2$$

where v is the frequency of the UV light, and m and u are the mass and velocity of the electron, respectively. In one experiment the kinetic energy of the ejected electron from potassium is found to be 5.34×10^{-19} J using a UV source of wavelength 162 nm. Calculate the ionization energy of potassium. How can you be sure that this ionization energy corresponds to the electron in the valence shell (that is, the most loosely held electron)?

8.101 Referring to the Chemistry in Action essay on p. 346, answer the following questions. (a) Why did it take so long to discover the first noble gas (argon) on Earth? (b) Once argon had been discovered, why did it take relatively little time to discover the rest of the noble gases? (c) Why was helium not isolated by the fractional distillation of liquid air?

8.102 The energy needed for the following process is 1.96×10^4 kJ/mol:

$$Li(g) \longrightarrow Li^{3+}(g) + 3e^-$$

If the first ionization energy of lithium is 520 kJ/mol, calculate the second ionization energy of lithium, that is, the energy required for the process

$$Li^+(g) \longrightarrow Li^{2+}(g) + e^-$$

(*Hint:* You need the equation in Problem 8.57.)

8.103 An element X reacts with hydrogen gas at 200°C to form compound Y. When Y is heated to a higher temperature, it decomposes to the element X and hydrogen gas in the ratio of 559 mL of H_2 (measured at STP) for 1.00 g of X reacted. X also combines with chlorine to form a compound Z, which contains 63.89 percent by mass of chlorine. Deduce the identity of X.

8.104 A student is given samples of three elements, X, Y, and Z, which could be an alkali metal, a member of Group 4A, and a member of Group 5A. She makes the following observations: Element X has a metallic luster and conducts electricity. It reacts slowly with hydrochloric acid to produce hydrogen gas. Element Y is a light-yellow solid that does not conduct electricity. Element Z has a metallic luster and conducts electricity. When exposed to air, it slowly forms a white powder. A solution of the white powder in water is basic. What can you conclude about the elements from these observations?

8.105 Using the following boiling-point data and the procedure in the Chemistry in Action essay on p. 329, estimate the boiling point of francium:

metal	Li	Na	K	Rb	Cs
boiling point (°C)	1347	882.9	774	688	678.4

8.106 What is the electron affinity of the Na^+ ion?

8.107 The ionization energies of sodium (in kJ/mol), starting with the first and ending with the eleventh, are 495.9, 4560, 6900, 9540, 13,400, 16,600, 20,120, 25,490, 28,930, 141,360, 170,000. Plot the log of ionization energy (y axis) versus the number of ionization (x axis); for example, log 495.9 is plotted versus 1 (labeled I_1, the first ionization energy), log 4560 is plotted versus 2 (labeled I_2, the second ionization energy), and so on. (a) Label I_1 through I_{11} with the electrons in orbitals such as 1s, 2s, 2p, and 3s. (b) What can you deduce about electron shells from the breaks in the curve?

8.108 Experimentally, the electron affinity of an element can be determined by using a laser light to ionize the anion of the element in the gas phase:

$$X^-(g) + hv \longrightarrow X(g) + e^-$$

Referring to Table 8.3, calculate the photon wavelength (in nanometers) corresponding to the electron affinity for chlorine. In what region of the electromagnetic spectrum does this wavelength fall?

8.109 Explain, in terms of their electron configurations, why Fe^{2+} is more easily oxidized to Fe^{3+} than Mn^{2+} to Mn^{3+}.

8.110 The standard enthalpy of atomization of an element is the energy required to convert one mole of an element in its most stable form at 25°C to one mole of monatomic gas. Given that the standard enthalpy of atomization for sodium is 108.4 kJ/mol, calculate the energy in kilojoules required to convert one mole of sodium metal at 25°C to one mole of gaseous Na^+ ions.

8.111 Write the formulas and names of the hydrides of the following second-period elements: Li, C, N, O, F. Predict their reactions with water.

8.112 Based on knowledge of the electronic configuration of titanium, state which of the following compounds of titanium is unlikely to exist: K_3TiF_6, $K_2Ti_2O_5$, $TiCl_3$, K_2TiO_4, K_2TiF_6.

8.113 Name an element in Group 1A or Group 2A that is an important constituent of each of the following substances: (a) remedy for acid indigestion, (b) coolant in nuclear reactors, (c) Epsom salt, (d) baking powder, (e) gunpowder, (f) a light alloy, (g) fertilizer that also neutralizes acid rain, (h) cement, and (i) grit for icy roads. You may need to ask your instructor about some of the items.

8.114 In halogen displacement reactions a halogen element can be generated by oxidizing its anions with a halogen element that lies above it in the periodic table. This means that there is no way to prepare elemental fluorine, because it is the first member of Group 7A. Indeed, for years the only way to prepare elemental fluorine was to oxidize F^- ions by electrolytic means. Then, in 1986, a chemist reported that by reacting potassium hexafluoromanganate(IV) (K_2MnF_6) with antimony pentafluoride (SbF_5) at 150°C, he had generated elemental fluorine. Balance the following equation representing the reaction:

$$K_2MnF_6 + SbF_5 \longrightarrow KSbF_6 + MnF_3 + F_2$$

8.115 Write a balanced equation for the preparation of (a) molecular oxygen, (b) ammonia, (c) carbon dioxide, (d) molecular hydrogen, (e) calcium oxide. Indicate the physical state of the reactants and products in each equation.

8.116 Write chemical formulas for oxides of nitrogen with the following oxidation numbers: $+1$, $+2$, $+3$, $+4$, $+5$. (*Hint:* There are *two* oxides of nitrogen with $+4$ oxidation number.)

8.117 Most transition metal ions are colored. For example, a solution of $CuSO_4$ is blue. How would you show that the blue color is due to the hydrated Cu^{2+} ions and not the SO_4^{2-} ions?

8.118 In general, atomic radius and ionization energy have opposite periodic trends. Why?

8.119 Explain why the electron affinity of nitrogen is approximately zero, while the elements on either side, carbon and oxygen, have substantial positive electron affinities.

8.120 Consider the halogens chlorine, bromine, and iodine. The melting point and boiling point of chlorine are $-101.0°C$ and $-34.6°C$ while those of iodine are $113.5°C$ and $184.4°C$, respectively. Thus, chlorine is a gas and iodine is a solid under room conditions. Estimate the melting point and boiling point of bromine. Compare your values with those from a handbook of chemistry.

8.121 While it is possible to determine the second, third, and higher ionization energies of an element, the same cannot usually be done with the electron affinities of an element. Explain.

8.122 The only confirmed compound of radon is radon fluoride, RnF. One reason that it is difficult to study the chemistry of radon is that all isotopes of radon are radioactive so it is dangerous to handle the substance. Can you suggest another reason why there are so few known radon compounds? (*Hint:* Radioactive decays are exothermic processes.)

8.123 Little is known of the chemistry of astatine, the last member of Group 7A. Describe the physical characteristics that you would expect this halogen to have. Predict the products of the reaction between sodium astatide (NaAt) and sulfuric acid. (*Hint:* Sulfuric acid is an oxidizing agent.)

8.124 As discussed in the chapter, the atomic mass of argon is greater than that of potassium. This observation created a problem in the early development of the periodic table because it meant that argon should be placed after potassium. (a) How was this difficulty resolved? (b) From the following data, calculate the average atomic masses of argon and potassium: Ar-36 (35.9675 amu;

0.337 percent), Ar-38 (37.9627 amu; 0.063 percent), Ar-40 (39.9624 amu; 99.60 percent); K-39 (38.9637 amu; 93.258 percent), K-40 (39.9640 amu; 0.0117 percent), K-41 (40.9618 amu; 6.730 percent).

8.125 Calculate the maximum wavelength of light (in nanometers) required to ionize a single sodium atom.

8.126 Predict the atomic number and ground-state electron configuration of the next member of the alkali metals after francium.

8.127 Why do elements that have high ionization energies also have more positive electron affinities? Which group of elements would be an exception to this generalization?

8.128 The first four ionization energies of an element are approximately 738 kJ/mol, 1450 kJ/mol, 7.7×10^3 kJ/mol, and 1.1×10^4 kJ/mol. To which periodic group does this element belong? Why?

8.129 Some chemists think that helium should properly be called "helon." Why? What does the ending in helium (-ium) suggest?

8.130 (a) The formula of the simplest hydrocarbon is CH_4 (methane). Predict the formulas of the simplest compounds formed between hydrogen and the following elements: silicon, germanium, tin, and lead. (b) Sodium hydride (NaH) is an ionic compound. Would you expect rubidium hydride (RbH) to be more or less ionic than NaH? (c) Predict the reaction between radium (Ra) and water. (d) When exposed to air, aluminum forms a tenacious oxide (Al_2O_3) coating that protects the metal from corrosion. Which metal in Group 2A would you expect to exhibit similar properties? Why?

8.131 Match each of the elements on the right with its description on the left:

(a) A pale yellow gas that reacts with water.

(b) A soft metal that reacts with water to produce hydrogen.

(c) A metalloid that is hard and has a high melting point.

(d) A colorless, odorless gas.

(e) A metal that is more reactive than iron, but does not corrode in air.

Nitrogen (N_2)
Boron (B)
Aluminum (Al)
Fluorine (F_2)
Sodium (Na)

8.132 Write an account on the importance of the periodic table. Pay particular attention to the significance of the position of an element in the table and how the position relates to the chemical and physical properties of the element.

8.133 On the same graph, plot the effective nuclear charge (shown in parentheses) and atomic radius (see Figure 8.5) versus atomic number for the second-period elements: Li(1.30), Be(1.95), B(2.60), C(3.25), N(3.90), O(4.55), F(5.20), Ne(5.85). Comment on the trends.

8.134 One allotropic form of an element X is a colorless crystalline solid. The reaction of X with an excess amount of oxygen produces a colorless gas. This gas dissolves in water to yield an acidic solution. Choose one of the following elements that matches X: (a) sulfur, (b) phosphorus, (c) carbon, (d) boron, and (e) silicon.

8.135 When magnesium metal is burned in air, it forms two products A and B. A reacts with water to form a basic solution. B reacts with water to form a similar solution as that of A plus a gas with a pungent odor. Identify A and B and write equations for the reactions. (*Hint:* See Chemistry in Action on p. 346.)

Special Problems

8.136 The ionization energy of a certain element is 412 kJ/mol. When the atoms of this element are in the first excited state, however, the ionization energy is only 126 kJ/mol. Based on this information, calculate the wavelength of light emitted in a transition from the first excited state to the ground state.

8.137 Potassium superoxide (see p. 337) is used in breathing equipment because it produces oxygen when reacted with water vapor and carbon dioxide in exhaled air. (a) Write equations for the reactions. (b) Calculate the pressure (in atm) at which oxygen gas stored at 20°C would have the same density as the oxygen gas provided by KO_2. The density of KO_2 at 20°C is 2.15 g/cm^3.

8.138 Referring to Table 8.2, explain why the first ionization energy of helium is less than twice the ionization energy of hydrogen, but the second ionization energy of helium is greater than twice the ionization energy of

hydrogen. [*Hint:* According to Coulomb's law, the energy between two charges Q_1 and Q_2 separated by distance r is proportional to (Q_1Q_2/r).]

8.139 As mentioned in Chapter 3 (p. 104), ammonium nitrate (NH_4NO_3) is the most important nitrogen-containing fertilizer in the world. Describe how you would prepare this compound, given only air and water as the starting materials. You may have any device at your disposal for this task.

8.140 One way to estimate the effective charge (Z_{eff}) of a many-electron atom is to use the equation $I_1 = (1312 \text{ kJ/mol})(Z_{eff}^2/n^2)$, where I_1 is the first ionization energy and n is the principal quantum number of the shell in which the electron resides. Use this equation to calculate the effective charges of Li, Na, and K. Also calculate Z_{eff}/n for each metal. Comment on your results.

Answers to Practice Exercises

8.1 (a) $1s^22s^22p^63s^23p^64s^2$, (b) it is a representative element, (c) diamagnetic. **8.2** Li > Be > C.
8.3 (a) Li^+, (b) Au^{3+}, (c) N^{3-}. **8.4** (a) N, (b) Mg.
8.5 No. **8.6** (a) amphoteric, (b) acidic, (c) basic.

9

Lewis first sketched his idea about the octet rule on the back of an envelope. The models show water, ammonia, methane, ethylene, and acetylene molecules.

Chemical Bonding I
Basic Concepts

A LOOK AHEAD

- Our study of chemical bonds begins with an introduction to Lewis dot symbols, which shows the valence electrons on an atom. (9.1)

- We then study the formation of ionic bonds and learn the determination of lattice energy, which is a measure of the stability of ionic compounds. (9.2 and 9.3)

- Next, we turn our attention to the formation of covalent bonds. We learn to write Lewis structures, which are governed by the octet rule. (9.4)

- We see that electronegativity is an important concept in understanding the properties of molecules. (9.5)

- We continue to practice writing Lewis structures for molecules and ions and use formal charges to study the distribution of electrons in these species. (9.6 and 9.7)

- We learn further aspects of writing Lewis structures in terms of resonance structures, which are alternate Lewis structures to represent a molecule. We also see that there are important exceptions to the octet rule. (9.8 and 9.9)

- The chapter ends with an examination of the strength of covalent bonds, which leads to the use of bond enthalpies to determine the enthalpy of a reaction. (9.10)

Interactive Activity Summary

1. Interactivity: Ionic Bonds (9.2)
2. Interactivity: Born-Haber Cycle for Lithium Fluoride (9.3)
3. Animation: Ionic vs. Covalent Bonding (9.4)
4. Interactivity: Covalent Bonds (9.4)
5. Interactivity: Lewis Dot Structure (9.6)
6. Interactivity: Resonance (9.8)
7. Animation: Resonance (9.8)
8. Interactivity: Octet Rule Exceptions (9.9)

Why do atoms of different elements react? What are the forces that hold atoms together in molecules and ions in ionic compounds? What shapes do they assume? These are some of the questions addressed in this chapter and in Chapter 10. We begin by looking at the two types of bonds—ionic and covalent—and the forces that stabilize them.

9.1 Lewis Dot Symbols

The development of the periodic table and concept of electron configuration gave chemists a rationale for molecule and compound formation. This explanation, formulated by Gilbert Lewis,[†] is that atoms combine in order to achieve a more stable electron configuration. Maximum stability results when an atom is isoelectronic with a noble gas.

When atoms interact to form a chemical bond, only their outer regions are in contact. For this reason, when we study chemical bonding, we are concerned primarily with the valence electrons of the atoms. To keep track of valence electrons in a chemical reaction, and to make sure that the total number of electrons does not change, chemists use a system of dots devised by Lewis and called Lewis dot symbols. A *Lewis dot symbol* **consists of the symbol of an element and one dot for each valence electron in an atom of the element.** Figure 9.1 shows the Lewis dot symbols for the representative elements and the noble gases. Note that, except for helium, the number of valence electrons each atom has is the same as the group number of the element. For example, Li is a Group 1A element and has one dot for one valence electron; Be, a Group 2A element, has two valence electrons (two dots); and so on. Elements in the same group have similar outer electron configurations and hence similar Lewis dot symbols. The transition metals, lanthanides, and actinides all have incompletely filled inner shells, and in general, we cannot write simple Lewis dot symbols for them.

In this chapter we will learn to use electron configurations and the periodic table to predict the type of bond atoms will form, as well as the number of bonds an atom of a particular element can form and the stability of the product.

[†]Gilbert Newton Lewis (1875–1946). American chemist. Lewis made many important contributions in the areas of chemical bonding, thermodynamics, acids and bases, and spectroscopy. Despite the significance of Lewis's work, he was never awarded a Nobel Prize.

Figure 9.1 *Lewis dot symbols for the representative elements and the noble gases. The number of unpaired dots corresponds to the number of bonds an atom of the element can form in a compound.*

9.2 The Ionic Bond

In Chapter 8 we saw that atoms of elements with low ionization energies tend to form cations, while those with high electron affinities tend to form anions. As a rule, the elements most likely to form cations in ionic compounds are the alkali metals and alkaline earth metals, and the elements most likely to form anions are the halogens and oxygen. Consequently, a wide variety of ionic compounds combine a Group 1A or Group 2A metal with a halogen or oxygen. An **ionic bond** is *the electrostatic force that holds ions together in an ionic compound.* Consider, for example, the reaction between lithium and fluorine to form lithium fluoride, a poisonous white powder used in lowering the melting point of solders and in manufacturing ceramics. The electron configuration of lithium is $1s^2 2s^1$, and that of fluorine is $1s^2 2s^2 2p^5$. When lithium and fluorine atoms come in contact with each other, the outer $2s^1$ valence electron of lithium is transferred to the fluorine atom. Using Lewis dot symbols, we represent the reaction like this:

$$\cdot \text{Li} \;+\; :\!\ddot{\text{F}}\!\cdot \;\longrightarrow\; \text{Li}^+ \quad :\!\ddot{\text{F}}\!:^- \quad (\text{or LiF})$$
$$1s^2 2s^1 \qquad 1s^2 2s^2 2p^5 \qquad 1s^2 \;\; 1s^2 2s^2 2p^6$$

(9.1)

Interactivity:
Ionic Bonds
ARIS, Interactives

For convenience, imagine that this reaction occurs in separate steps—first the ionization of Li:

$$\cdot \text{Li} \longrightarrow \text{Li}^+ + e^-$$

and then the acceptance of an electron by F:

$$:\!\ddot{\text{F}}\!\cdot \;+\; e \longrightarrow \;:\!\ddot{\text{F}}\!:$$

Next, imagine the two separate ions joining to form a LiF unit:

$$\text{Li}^+ + :\!\ddot{\text{F}}\!:^- \longrightarrow \text{Li}^+ :\!\ddot{\text{F}}\!:^-$$

Note that the sum of these three equations is

$$\cdot \text{Li} + \cdot \ddot{\text{F}} \cdot \longrightarrow \text{Li}^+ \cdot \ddot{\text{F}} \cdot {}^-$$

which is the same as Equation (9.1). The ionic bond in LiF is the electrostatic attraction between the positively charged lithium ion and the negatively charged fluoride ion. The compound itself is electrically neutral.

Many other common reactions lead to the formation of ionic bonds. For instance, calcium burns in oxygen to form calcium oxide:

$$2\text{Ca}(s) + \text{O}_2(g) \longrightarrow 2\text{CaO}(s)$$

Assuming that the diatomic O_2 molecule first splits into separate oxygen atoms (we will look at the energetics of this step later), we can represent the reaction with Lewis symbols:

$$\cdot \text{Ca} \cdot \;+\; \cdot \ddot{\text{O}} \cdot \;\longrightarrow\; \text{Ca}^{2+} \quad :\!\ddot{\text{O}}\!:^{2-}$$
$$[\text{Ar}]4s^2 \qquad 1s^2 2s^2 2p^4 \qquad [\text{Ar}] \qquad [\text{Ne}]$$

There is a transfer of two electrons from the calcium atom to the oxygen atom. Note that the resulting calcium ion (Ca^{2+}) has the argon electron configuration, the oxide ion (O^{2-}) is isoelectronic with neon, and the compound (CaO) is electrically neutral.

Lithium fluoride. Industrially, LiF (like most other ionic compounds) is obtained by purifying minerals containing the compound.

We normally write the empirical formulas of ionic compounds without showing the charges. The + and − are shown here to emphasize the transfer of electrons.

In many cases, the cation and the anion in a compound do not carry the same charges. For instance, when lithium burns in air to form lithium oxide (Li_2O), the balanced equation is

$$4Li(s) + O_2(g) \longrightarrow 2Li_2O(s)$$

Using Lewis dot symbols, we write

$$2 \cdot Li + \cdot \overset{\cdot\cdot}{\underset{\cdot\cdot}{O}} \cdot \longrightarrow 2Li^+ \quad :\overset{\cdot\cdot}{\underset{\cdot\cdot}{O}}:^{2-} \text{ (or } Li_2O)$$
$$1s^2 2s^1 \quad 1s^2 2s^2 2p^4 \qquad \text{[He]} \quad \text{[Ne]}$$

In this process, the oxygen atom receives two electrons (one from each of the two lithium atoms) to form the oxide ion. The Li^+ ion is isoelectronic with helium.

When magnesium reacts with nitrogen at elevated temperatures, a white solid compound, magnesium nitride (Mg_3N_2), forms:

$$3Mg(s) + N_2(g) \longrightarrow Mg_3N_2(s)$$

or

$$3 \cdot Mg \cdot + 2 \cdot \overset{\cdot\cdot}{N} \cdot \longrightarrow 3Mg^{2+} \quad 2 :\overset{\cdot\cdot}{N}:^{3-} \text{ (or } Mg_3N_2)$$
$$\text{[Ne]}3s^2 \quad 1s^2 2s^2 2p^3 \qquad \text{[Ne]} \qquad \text{[Ne]}$$

The reaction involves the transfer of six electrons (two from each Mg atom) to two nitrogen atoms. The resulting magnesium ion (Mg^{2+}) and the nitride ion (N^{3-}) are both isoelectronic with neon. Because there are three +2 ions and two −3 ions, the charges balance and the compound is electrically neutral.

In Example 9.1, we apply the Lewis dot symbols to study the formation of an ionic compound.

The mineral corundum (Al_2O_3).

Example 9.1

Use Lewis dot symbols to show the formation of aluminum oxide (Al_2O_3).

Strategy We use electroneutrality as our guide in writing formulas for ionic compounds, that is, the total positive charges on the cations must be equal to the total negative charges on the anions.

Solution According to Figure 9.1, the Lewis dot symbols of Al and O are

$$\cdot \overset{\cdot}{Al} \cdot \qquad \cdot \overset{\cdot\cdot}{\underset{\cdot\cdot}{O}} \cdot$$

Because aluminum tends to form the cation (Al^{3+}) and oxygen the anion (O^{2-}) in ionic compounds, the transfer of electrons is from Al to O. There are three valence electrons in each Al atom; each O atom needs two electrons to form the O^{2-} ion, which is isoelectronic with neon. Thus, the simplest neutralizing ratio of Al^{3+} to O^{2-} is 2:3; two Al^{3+} ions have a total charge of +6, and three O^{2-} ions have a total charge of −6. So the empirical formula of aluminum oxide is Al_2O_3, and the reaction is

$$2 \cdot \overset{\cdot}{Al} \cdot + 3 \cdot \overset{\cdot\cdot}{\underset{\cdot\cdot}{O}} \cdot \longrightarrow 2Al^{3+} \quad 3 :\overset{\cdot\cdot}{\underset{\cdot\cdot}{O}}:^{2-} \text{ (or } Al_2O_3)$$
$$\text{[Ne]}3s^2 3p^1 \quad 1s^2 2s^2 2p^4 \qquad \text{[Ne]} \qquad \text{[Ne]}$$

(Continued)

Check Make sure that the number of valence electrons (24) is the same on both sides of the equation. Are the subscripts in Al_2O_3 reduced to the smallest possible whole numbers?

Similar problems: 9.17, 9.18.

Practice Exercise Use Lewis dot symbols to represent the formation of barium hydride.

9.3 Lattice Energy of Ionic Compounds

We can predict which elements are likely to form ionic compounds based on ionization energy and electron affinity, but how do we evaluate the stability of an ionic compound? Ionization energy and electron affinity are defined for processes occurring in the gas phase, but at 1 atm and 25°C all ionic compounds are solids. The solid state is a very different environment because each cation in a solid is surrounded by a specific number of anions, and vice versa. Thus, the overall stability of a solid ionic compound depends on the interactions of all these ions and not merely on the interaction of a single cation with a single anion. A quantitative measure of the stability of any ionic solid is its *lattice energy,* defined as *the energy required to completely separate one mole of a solid ionic compound into gaseous ions.*

The Born-Haber Cycle for Determining Lattice Energies

Lattice energy cannot be measured directly. However, if we know the structure and composition of an ionic compound, we can calculate the compound's lattice energy by using *Coulomb's[†] law,* which states that *the potential energy (E) between two ions is directly proportional to the product of their charges and inversely proportional to the distance of separation between them.* For a single Li^+ ion and a single F^- ion separated by distance r, the potential energy of the system is given by

$$E \propto \frac{Q_{Li^+}Q_{F^-}}{r}$$

$$= k\frac{Q_{Li^+}Q_{F^-}}{r} \tag{9.2}$$

Because energy = force × distance, Coulomb's law can also be stated as

$$F = k\frac{Q_{Li^+}Q_{F^-}}{r^2}$$

where F is the force between the ions.

where Q_{Li^+} and Q_{F^-} are the charges on the Li^+ and F^- ions and k is the proportionality constant. Because Q_{Li^+} is positive and Q_{F^-} is negative, E is a negative quantity, and the formation of an ionic bond from Li^+ and F^- is an exothermic process. Consequently, energy must be supplied to reverse the process (in other words, the lattice energy of LiF is positive), and so a bonded pair of Li^+ and F^- ions is more stable than separate Li^+ and F^- ions.

We can also determine lattice energy indirectly, by assuming that the formation of an ionic compound takes place in a series of steps. This procedure, known as the *Born-Haber cycle, relates lattice energies of ionic compounds to ionization energies, electron affinities, and other atomic and molecular properties.* It is based on Hess's

[†]Charles Augustin de Coulomb (1736–1806). French physicist. Coulomb did research in electricity and magnetism and applied Newton's inverse square law to electricity. He also invented a torsion balance.

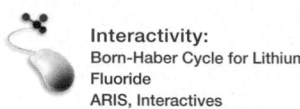

Interactivity:
Born-Haber Cycle for Lithium
Fluoride
ARIS, Interactives

law (see Section 6.6). Developed by Max Born[‡] and Fritz Haber,[§] the Born-Haber cycle defines the various steps that precede the formation of an ionic solid. We will illustrate its use to find the lattice energy of lithium fluoride.

Consider the reaction between lithium and fluorine:

$$Li(s) + \tfrac{1}{2}F_2(g) \longrightarrow LiF(s)$$

The standard enthalpy change for this reaction is -594.1 kJ/mol. (Because the reactants and product are in their standard states, that is, at 1 atm, the enthalpy change is also the standard enthalpy of formation for LiF.) Keeping in mind that the sum of enthalpy changes for the steps is equal to the enthalpy change for the overall reaction (-594.1 kJ/mol), we can trace the formation of LiF from its elements through five separate steps. The process may not occur exactly this way, but this pathway enables us to analyze the energy changes of ionic compound formation, with the application of Hess's law.

1. Convert solid lithium to lithium vapor (the direct conversion of a solid to a gas is called sublimation):

$$Li(s) \longrightarrow Li(g) \qquad\qquad \Delta H_1^\circ = 155.2 \text{ kJ/mol}$$

    The energy of sublimation for lithium is 155.2 kJ/mol.

2. Dissociate $\tfrac{1}{2}$ mole of F_2 gas into separate gaseous F atoms:

$$\tfrac{1}{2}F_2(g) \longrightarrow F(g) \qquad\qquad \Delta H_2^\circ = 75.3 \text{ kJ/mol}$$

    The F atoms in a F_2 molecule are held together by a covalent bond. The energy required to break this bond is called the bond enthalpy (Section 9.10).

    The energy needed to break the bonds in 1 mole of F_2 molecules is 150.6 kJ. Here we are breaking the bonds in half a mole of F_2, so the enthalpy change is 150.6/2, or 75.3, kJ.

3. Ionize 1 mole of gaseous Li atoms (see Table 8.3):

$$Li(g) \longrightarrow Li^+(g) + e^- \qquad\qquad \Delta H_3^\circ = 520 \text{ kJ/mol}$$

    This process corresponds to the first ionization of lithium.

4. Add 1 mole of electrons to 1 mole of gaseous F atoms. As discussed on page 333, the energy change for this process is just the opposite of electron affinity (see Table 8.3):

$$F(g) + e^- \longrightarrow F^-(g) \qquad\qquad \Delta H_4^\circ = -328 \text{ kJ/mol}$$

5. Combine 1 mole of gaseous Li^+ and 1 mole of F^- to form 1 mole of solid LiF:

$$Li^+(g) + F^-(g) \longrightarrow LiF(s) \qquad\qquad \Delta H_5^\circ = ?$$

The reverse of step 5,

$$energy + LiF(s) \longrightarrow Li^+(g) + F^-(g)$$

[‡]Max Born (1882–1970). German physicist. Born was one of the founders of modern physics. His work covered a wide range of topics. He received the Nobel Prize in Physics in 1954 for his interpretation of the wave function for particles.

[§]Fritz Haber (1868–1934). German chemist. Haber's process for synthesizing ammonia from atmospheric nitrogen kept Germany supplied with nitrates for explosives during World War I. He also did work on gas warfare. In 1918 Haber received the Nobel Prize in Chemistry.

defines the lattice energy of LiF. Thus, the lattice energy must have the same magnitude as ΔH_5° but an opposite sign. Although we cannot determine ΔH_5° directly, we can calculate its value by the following procedure.

1.	$Li(s) \longrightarrow Li(g)$	$\Delta H_1^\circ = 155.2$ kJ/mol
2.	$\frac{1}{2}F_2(g) \longrightarrow F(g)$	$\Delta H_2^\circ = 75.3$ kJ/mol
3.	$Li(g) \longrightarrow Li^+(g) + e^-$	$\Delta H_3^\circ = 520$ kJ/mol
4.	$F(g) + e^- \longrightarrow F^-(g)$	$\Delta H_4^\circ = -328$ kJ/mol
5.	$Li^+(g) + F^-(g) \longrightarrow LiF(s)$	$\Delta H_5^\circ = ?$

$$Li(s) + \tfrac{1}{2}F_2(g) \longrightarrow LiF(s) \qquad \Delta H_{overall}^\circ = -594.1 \text{ kJ/mol}$$

According to Hess's law, we can write

$$\Delta H_{overall}^\circ = \Delta H_1^\circ + \Delta H_2^\circ + \Delta H_3^\circ + \Delta H_4^\circ + \Delta H_5^\circ$$

or

$$-594.1 \text{ kJ/mol} = 155.2 \text{ kJ/mol} + 75.3 \text{ kJ/mol} + 520 \text{ kJ/mol} - 328 \text{ kJ/mol} + \Delta H_5^\circ$$

Hence

$$\Delta H_5^\circ = -1017 \text{ kJ/mol}$$

and the lattice energy of LiF is +1017 kJ/mol.

Figure 9.2 summarizes the Born-Haber cycle for LiF. Steps 1, 2, and 3 all require the input of energy. On the other hand, steps 4 and 5 release energy. Because ΔH_5° is a large negative quantity, the lattice energy of LiF is a large positive quantity, which accounts for the stability of solid LiF. The greater the lattice energy, the more stable the ionic compound. Keep in mind that lattice energy is *always* a positive quantity because the separation of ions in a solid into ions in the gas phase is, by Coulomb's law, an endothermic process.

Table 9.1 lists the lattice energies and the melting points of several common ionic compounds. There is a rough correlation between lattice energy and melting point. The larger the lattice energy, the more stable the solid and the more tightly held the ions. It takes more energy to melt such a solid, and so the solid has a higher melting point than one with a smaller lattice energy. Note that $MgCl_2$, Na_2O, and MgO have

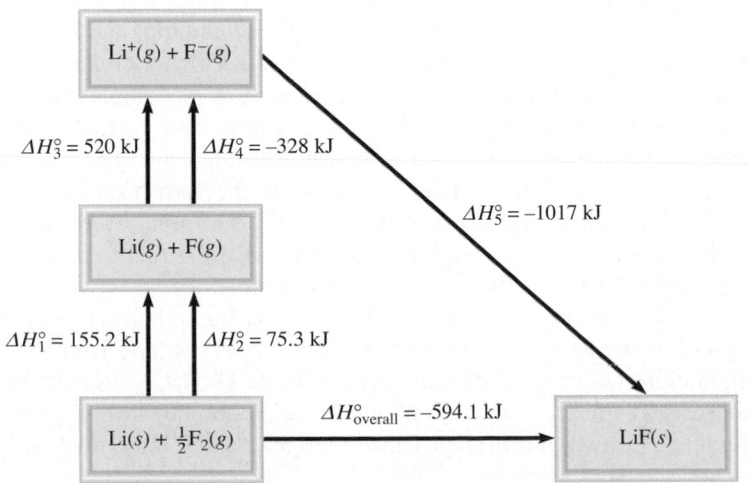

Figure 9.2 *The Born-Haber cycle for the formation of 1 mole of solid LiF.*

TABLE 9.1	Lattice Energies and Melting Points of Some Alkali Metal and Alkaline Earth Metal Halides and Oxides	
Compound	Lattice Energy (kJ/mol)	Melting Point (°C)
LiF	1017	845
LiCl	828	610
LiBr	787	550
LiI	732	450
NaCl	788	801
NaBr	736	750
NaI	686	662
KCl	699	772
KBr	689	735
KI	632	680
$MgCl_2$	2527	714
Na_2O	2570	Sub*
MgO	3890	2800

*Na_2O sublimes at 1275°C.

unusually high lattice energies. The first of these ionic compounds has a doubly charged cation (Mg^{2+}) and the second a doubly charged anion (O^{2-}); in the third compound there is an interaction between two doubly charged species (Mg^{2+} and O^{2-}). The coulombic attractions between two doubly charged species, or between a doubly charged ion and a singly charged ion, are much stronger than those between singly charged anions and cations.

Lattice Energy and the Formulas of Ionic Compounds

Because lattice energy is a measure of the stability of ionic compounds, its value can help us explain the formulas of these compounds. Consider magnesium chloride as an example. We have seen that the ionization energy of an element increases rapidly as successive electrons are removed from its atom. For example, the first ionization energy of magnesium is 738 kJ/mol, and the second ionization energy is 1450 kJ/mol, almost twice the first. We might ask why, from the standpoint of energy, magnesium does not prefer to form unipositive ions in its compounds. Why doesn't magnesium chloride have the formula MgCl (containing the Mg^+ ion) rather than $MgCl_2$ (containing the Mg^{2+} ion)? Admittedly, the Mg^{2+} ion has the noble gas configuration [Ne], which represents stability because of its completely filled shells. But the stability gained through the filled shells does not, in fact, outweigh the energy input needed to remove an electron from the Mg^+ ion. The reason the formula is $MgCl_2$ lies in the extra stability gained by the formation of solid magnesium chloride. The lattice energy of $MgCl_2$ is 2527 kJ/mol, which is more than enough to compensate for the energy needed to remove the first two electrons from a Mg atom (738 kJ/mol + 1450 kJ/mol = 2188 kJ/mol).

What about sodium chloride? Why is the formula for sodium chloride NaCl and not $NaCl_2$ (containing the Na^{2+} ion)? Although Na^{2+} does not have the noble gas electron configuration, we might expect the compound to be $NaCl_2$ because Na^{2+} has a higher charge and therefore the hypothetical $NaCl_2$ should have a greater lattice energy. Again the answer lies in the balance between energy input (that is, ionization

Sodium Chloride—A Common and Important Ionic Compound

We are all familiar with sodium chloride as table salt. It is a typical ionic compound, a brittle solid with a high melting point (801°C) that conducts electricity in the molten state and in aqueous solution. The structure of solid NaCl is shown in Figure 2.13.

One source of sodium chloride is rock salt, which is found in subterranean deposits often hundreds of meters thick. It is also obtained from seawater or brine (a concentrated NaCl solution) by solar evaporation. Sodium chloride also occurs in nature as the mineral *halite*.

Sodium chloride is used more often than any other material in the manufacture of inorganic chemicals. World consumption of this substance is about 150 million tons per year. The major use of sodium chloride is in the production of other essential inorganic chemicals such as chlorine gas, sodium hydroxide, sodium metal, hydrogen gas, and sodium carbonate. It is also used to melt ice and snow on highways and roads. However, because sodium chloride is harmful to plant life and promotes corrosion of cars, its use for this purpose is of considerable environmental concern.

Solar evaporation process for obtaining sodium chloride.

Underground rock salt mining.

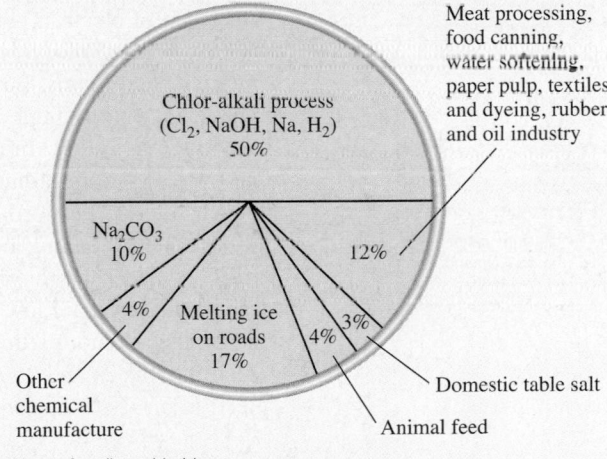

Uses of sodium chloride.

energies) and the stability gained from the formation of the solid. The sum of the first two ionization energies of sodium is

$$496 \text{ kJ/mol} + 4560 \text{ kJ/mol} = 5056 \text{ kJ/mol}$$

The compound $NaCl_2$ does not exist, but if we assume a value of 2527 kJ/mol as its lattice energy (same as that for $MgCl_2$), we see that the energy yield would be far too small to compensate for the energy required to produce the Na^{2+} ion.

What has been said about the cations applies also to the anions. In Section 8.5 we observed that the electron affinity of oxygen is 141 kJ/mol, meaning that the following process releases energy (and is therefore favorable):

$$O(g) + e^- \longrightarrow O^-(g)$$

As we would expect, adding another electron to the O^- ion

$$O^-(g) + e^- \longrightarrow O^{2-}(g)$$

would be unfavorable because of the increase in electrostatic repulsion. Indeed, the electron affinity of O^- is negative. Yet compounds containing the oxide ion (O^{2-}) do exist and are very stable, whereas compounds containing the O^- ion are not known. Again, the high lattice energy resulting from the presence of O^{2-} ions in compounds such as Na_2O or MgO far outweighs the energy needed to produce the O^{2-} ion.

9.4 The Covalent Bond

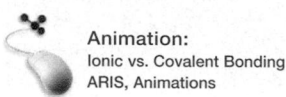

Animation:
Ionic vs. Covalent Bonding
ARIS, Animations

Although the concept of molecules goes back to the seventeenth century, it was not until early in the twentieth century that chemists began to understand how and why molecules form. The first major breakthrough was Gilbert Lewis's suggestion that a chemical bond involves electron sharing by atoms. He depicted the formation of a chemical bond in H_2 as

$$H\cdot \; + \; \cdot H \longrightarrow H:H$$

This type of electron pairing is an example of a ***covalent bond,*** *a bond in which two electrons are shared by two atoms.* ***Covalent compounds*** *are compounds that contain only covalent bonds.* For the sake of simplicity, the shared pair of electrons is often represented by a single line. Thus, the covalent bond in the hydrogen molecule can be written as H—H. In a covalent bond, each electron in a shared pair is attracted to the nuclei of both atoms. This attraction holds the two atoms in H_2 together and is responsible for the formation of covalent bonds in other molecules.

This discussion applies only to representative elements. Remember that for these elements, the number of valence electrons is equal to the group number (Groups 1A–7A).

Covalent bonding between many-electron atoms involves only the valence electrons. Consider the fluorine molecule, F_2. The electron configuration of F is $1s^2 2s^2 2p^5$. The $1s$ electrons are low in energy and stay near the nucleus most of the time. For this reason they do not participate in bond formation. Thus, each F atom has seven valence electrons (the $2s$ and $2p$ electrons). According to Figure 9.1, there is only one unpaired electron on F, so the formation of the F_2 molecule can be represented as follows:

$$:\!\ddot{F}\!\cdot \; + \; \cdot\ddot{F}\!: \longrightarrow :\!\ddot{F}\!:\!\ddot{F}\!: \quad \text{or} \quad :\!\ddot{F}\!-\!\ddot{F}\!:$$

Note that only two valence electrons participate in the formation of F_2. The other, nonbonding electrons, are called ***lone pairs***—*pairs of valence electrons that are not involved in covalent bond formation.* Thus, each F in F_2 has three lone pairs of electrons:

lone pairs $\longrightarrow :\!\ddot{F}\!-\!\ddot{F}\!: \longleftarrow$ lone pairs

The structures we use to represent covalent compounds, such as H_2 and F_2, are called Lewis structures. A ***Lewis structure*** is *a representation of covalent bonding in* *which shared electron pairs are shown either as lines or as pairs of dots between two atoms, and lone pairs are shown as pairs of dots on individual atoms.* Only valence electrons are shown in a Lewis structure.

Let us consider the Lewis structure of the water molecule. Figure 9.1 shows the Lewis dot symbol for oxygen with two unpaired dots or two unpaired electrons, so we expect that O might form two covalent bonds. Because hydrogen has only one electron, it can form only one covalent bond. Thus, the Lewis structure for water is

$$\text{H}\!:\!\overset{\displaystyle ..}{\underset{\displaystyle ..}{\text{O}}}\!:\!\text{H} \qquad \text{or} \qquad \text{H}\!-\!\overset{\displaystyle ..}{\underset{\displaystyle ..}{\text{O}}}\!-\!\text{H}$$

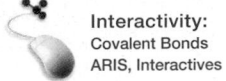

Interactivity:
Covalent Bonds
ARIS, Interactives

In this case, the O atom has two lone pairs. The hydrogen atom has no lone pairs because its only electron is used to form a covalent bond.

In the F_2 and H_2O molecules, the F and O atoms achieve the stable noble gas configuration by sharing electrons:

$$\left(\overset{..}{\underset{..}{:\text{F}}}\,\overset{..}{\underset{..}{\text{F}:}}\right) \qquad \left(\text{H}\,\overset{..}{\underset{..}{\text{O}}}\,\text{H}\right)$$

$$8e^- \quad 8e^- \qquad\qquad 2e^- \quad 8e^- \quad 2e^-$$

The formation of these molecules illustrates the **octet rule,** formulated by Lewis: *An atom other than hydrogen tends to form bonds until it is surrounded by eight valence electrons.* In other words, a covalent bond forms when there are not enough electrons for each individual atom to have a complete octet. By sharing electrons in a covalent bond, the individual atoms can complete their octets. The requirement for hydrogen is that it attain the electron configuration of helium, or a total of two electrons.

The octet rule works mainly for elements in the second period of the periodic table. These elements have only $2s$ and $2p$ subshells, which can hold a total of eight electrons. When an atom of one of these elements forms a covalent compound, it can attain the noble gas electron configuration [Ne] by sharing electrons with other atoms in the same compound. Later, we will discuss a number of important exceptions to the octet rule that give us further insight into the nature of chemical bonding.

Atoms can form different types of covalent bonds. In a **single bond,** *two atoms are held together by one electron pair.* Many compounds are held together by **multiple bonds,** that is, bonds formed when *two atoms share two or more pairs of electrons.* If *two atoms share two pairs of electrons,* the covalent bond is called a **double bond.** Double bonds are found in molecules of carbon dioxide (CO_2) and ethylene (C_2H_4):

$$\left(\overset{..}{\underset{..}{\text{O}}}\,\text{C}\,\overset{..}{\underset{..}{\text{O}}}\right) \quad \text{or} \quad \overset{..}{\underset{..}{\text{O}}}\!=\!\text{C}\!=\!\overset{..}{\underset{..}{\text{O}}}$$

$$8e^- \;\; 8e^- \;\; 8e^-$$

$$\begin{array}{cc} \text{H} & \text{H} \\ \left(\text{C}\,\,\text{C}\right) \\ \text{H} & \text{H} \end{array} \quad \text{or} \quad \begin{array}{cc} \text{H} & \text{H} \\ \diagdown\!\!\diagup \\ \text{C}\!=\!\text{C} \\ \diagup\!\!\diagdown \\ \text{H} & \text{H} \end{array}$$

$$8e^- \;\; 8e^-$$

Shortly, you will be introduced to the rules for writing proper Lewis structures. Here we simply want to become familiar with the language associated with them.

A **triple bond** arises when *two atoms share three pairs of electrons,* as in the nitrogen molecule (N_2):

$$\left(:\text{N}\,\,\text{N}:\right) \qquad \text{or} \qquad :\text{N}\!\equiv\!\text{N}:$$

$$8e^- \;\; 8e^-$$

Figure 9.3 *Bond length (in pm) in H_2 and HI.*

The acetylene molecule (C_2H_2) also contains a triple bond, in this case between two carbon atoms:

$$H : C :: C : H \qquad \text{or} \qquad H—C≡C—H$$
$$8e^- \quad 8e^-$$

Note that in ethylene and acetylene all the valence electrons are used in bonding; there are no lone pairs on the carbon atoms. In fact, with the exception of carbon monoxide, stable molecules containing carbon do not have lone pairs on the carbon atoms.

Multiple bonds are shorter than single covalent bonds. *Bond length* is defined as the *distance between the nuclei of two covalently bonded atoms in a molecule* (Figure 9.3). Table 9.2 shows some experimentally determined bond lengths. For a given pair of atoms, such as carbon and nitrogen, triple bonds are shorter than double bonds, which, in turn, are shorter than single bonds. The shorter multiple bonds are also more stable than single bonds, as we will see later.

Comparison of the Properties of Covalent and Ionic Compounds

Ionic and covalent compounds differ markedly in their general physical properties because of differences in the nature of their bonds. There are two types of attractive forces in covalent compounds. The first type is the force that holds the atoms together in a molecule. A quantitative measure of this attraction is given by bond enthalpy, to be discussed in Section 9.10. The second type of attractive force operates *between* molecules and is called an *intermolecular force*. Because intermolecular forces are usually quite weak compared with the forces holding atoms together within a molecule, molecules of a covalent compound are not held together tightly. Consequently covalent compounds are usually gases, liquids, or low-melting solids. On the other hand, the electrostatic forces holding ions together in an ionic compound are usually very strong, so ionic compounds are solids at room temperature and have high melting points. Many ionic compounds are soluble in water, and the resulting aqueous solutions conduct electricity, because the compounds are strong electrolytes. Most

If intermolecular forces are weak, it is relatively easy to break up aggregates of molecules to form liquids (from solids) and gases (from liquids).

TABLE 9.2

Average Bond Lengths of Some Common Single, Double, and Triple Bonds

Bond Type	Bond Length (pm)
C—H	107
C—O	143
C=O	121
C—C	154
C=C	133
C≡C	120
C—N	143
C=N	138
C≡N	116
N—O	136
N=O	122
O—H	96

TABLE 9.3 — **Comparison of Some General Properties of an Ionic Compound and a Covalent Compound**

Property	NaCl	CCl_4
Appearance	White solid	Colorless liquid
Melting point (°C)	801	−23
Molar heat of fusion* (kJ/mol)	30.2	2.5
Boiling point (°C)	1413	76.5
Molar heat of vaporization* (kJ/mol)	600	30
Density (g/cm³)	2.17	1.59
Solubility in water	High	Very low
Electrical conductivity		
Solid	Poor	Poor
Liquid	Good	Poor

*Molar heat of fusion and molar heat of vaporization are the amounts of heat needed to melt 1 mole of the solid and to vaporize 1 mole of the liquid, respectively.

covalent compounds are insoluble in water, or if they do dissolve, their aqueous solutions generally do not conduct electricity, because the compounds are nonelectrolytes. Molten ionic compounds conduct electricity because they contain mobile cations and anions; liquid or molten covalent compounds do not conduct electricity because no ions are present. Table 9.3 compares some of the general properties of a typical ionic compound, sodium chloride, with those of a covalent compound, carbon tetrachloride (CCl_4).

Figure 9.4 *Electrostatic potential map of the HF molecule. The distribution varies according to the colors of the rainbow. The most electron-rich region is red; the most electron-poor region is blue.*

9.5 Electronegativity

A covalent bond, as we have said, is the sharing of an electron pair by two atoms. In a molecule like H_2, in which the atoms are identical, we expect the electrons to be equally shared—that is, the electrons spend the same amount of time in the vicinity of each atom. However, in the covalently bonded HF molecule, the H and F atoms do not share the bonding electrons equally because H and F are different atoms:

Hydrogen fluoride is a clear, fuming liquid that boils at 19.8°C. It is used to make refrigerants and to prepare hydrofluoric acid.

$$H—\overset{..}{\underset{..}{F}}:$$

The bond in HF is called a ***polar covalent bond,*** or simply a *polar bond,* because *the electrons spend more time in the vicinity of one atom than the other.* Experimental evidence indicates that in the HF molecule the electrons spend more time near the F atom. We can think of this unequal sharing of electrons as a partial electron transfer or a shift in electron density, as it is more commonly described, from H to F (Figure 9.4). This "unequal sharing" of the bonding electron pair results in a relatively greater electron density near the fluorine atom and a correspondingly lower electron density near hydrogen. The HF bond and other polar bonds can be thought of as being intermediate between a (nonpolar) covalent bond, in which the sharing of electrons is exactly equal, and an ionic bond, in which the *transfer of the electron(s) is nearly complete.*

A property that helps us distinguish a nonpolar covalent bond from a polar covalent bond is ***electronegativity,*** *the ability of an atom to attract toward itself the electrons in a chemical bond.* Elements with high electronegativity have a greater tendency to attract electrons than do elements with low electronegativity. As we might expect, electronegativity is related to electron affinity and ionization energy. Thus, an atom such as fluorine, which has a high electron affinity (tends to pick up electrons easily) and a high ionization energy (does not lose electrons easily), has a high electronegativity. On the other hand, sodium has a low electron affinity, a low ionization energy, and a low electronegativity.

Electronegativity is a relative concept, meaning that an element's electronegativity can be measured only in relation to the electronegativity of other elements. Linus Pauling[†] devised a method for calculating *relative* electronegativities of most elements. These values are shown in Figure 9.5. A careful examination of this chart reveals trends and relationships among electronegativity values of different elements. In general, electronegativity increases from left to right across a period in the periodic table, as the metallic character of the elements decreases. Within each group,

Electronegativity values have no units.

[†]Linus Carl Pauling (1901–1994). American chemist. Regarded by many as the most influential chemist of the twentieth century, Pauling did research in a remarkably broad range of subjects, from chemical physics to molecular biology. Pauling received the Nobel Prize in Chemistry in 1954 for his work on protein structure, and the Nobel Peace Prize in 1962. He is the only person to be the sole recipient of two Nobel Prizes.

Increasing electronegativity

1A																	8A
H 2.1	2A											3A	4A	5A	6A	7A	
Li 1.0	**Be** 1.5											**B** 2.0	**C** 2.5	**N** 3.0	**O** 3.5	**F** 4.0	
Na 0.9	**Mg** 1.2	3B	4B	5B	6B	7B		8B		1B	2B	**Al** 1.5	**Si** 1.8	**P** 2.1	**S** 2.5	**Cl** 3.0	
K 0.8	**Ca** 1.0	**Sc** 1.3	**Ti** 1.5	**V** 1.6	**Cr** 1.6	**Mn** 1.5	**Fe** 1.8	**Co** 1.9	**Ni** 1.9	**Cu** 1.9	**Zn** 1.6	**Ga** 1.6	**Ge** 1.8	**As** 2.0	**Se** 2.4	**Br** 2.8	**Kr** 3.0
Rb 0.8	**Sr** 1.0	**Y** 1.2	**Zr** 1.4	**Nb** 1.6	**Mo** 1.8	**Tc** 1.9	**Ru** 2.2	**Rh** 2.2	**Pd** 2.2	**Ag** 1.9	**Cd** 1.7	**In** 1.7	**Sn** 1.8	**Sb** 1.9	**Te** 2.1	**I** 2.5	**Xe** 2.6
Cs 0.7	**Ba** 0.9	**La-Lu** 1.0-1.2	**Hf** 1.3	**Ta** 1.5	**W** 1.7	**Re** 1.9	**Os** 2.2	**Ir** 2.2	**Pt** 2.2	**Au** 2.4	**Hg** 1.9	**Tl** 1.8	**Pb** 1.9	**Bi** 1.9	**Po** 2.0	**At** 2.2	
Fr 0.7	**Ra** 0.9																

Increasing electronegativity

Figure 9.5 *The electronegativities of common elements.*

electronegativity decreases with increasing atomic number, and increasing metallic character. Note that the transition metals do not follow these trends. The most electronegative elements—the halogens, oxygen, nitrogen, and sulfur—are found in the upper right-hand corner of the periodic table, and the least electronegative elements (the alkali and alkaline earth metals) are clustered near the lower left-hand corner. These trends are readily apparent on a graph, as shown in Figure 9.6.

Atoms of elements with widely different electronegativities tend to form ionic bonds (such as those that exist in NaCl and CaO compounds) with each other because the atom of the less electronegative element gives up its electron(s) to the atom of the more electronegative element. An ionic bond generally joins an atom of a metallic element and an atom of a nonmetallic element. Atoms of elements with comparable electronegativities tend to form polar covalent bonds with each other because

Figure 9.6 *Variation of electronegativity with atomic number. The halogens have the highest electronegativities, and the alkali metals the lowest.*

the shift in electron density is usually small. Most covalent bonds involve atoms of nonmetallic elements. Only atoms of the same element, which have the same electronegativity, can be joined by a pure covalent bond. These trends and characteristics are what we would expect, given our knowledge of ionization energies and electron affinities.

There is no sharp distinction between a polar bond and an ionic bond, but the following general rule is helpful in distinguishing between them. An ionic bond forms when the electronegativity difference between the two bonding atoms is 2.0 or more. This rule applies to most but not all ionic compounds. Sometimes chemists use the quantity *percent ionic character* to describe the nature of a bond. A purely ionic bond would have 100 percent ionic character, although no such bond is known, whereas a nonpolar or purely covalent bond has 0 percent ionic character. As Figure 9.7 shows, there is a correlation between the percent ionic character of a bond and the electronegativity difference between the bonding atoms.

Electronegativity and electron affinity are related but different concepts. Both indicate the tendency of an atom to attract electrons. However, electron affinity refers to an isolated atom's attraction for an additional electron, whereas electronegativity signifies the ability of an atom in a chemical bond (with another atom) to attract the shared electrons. Furthermore, electron affinity is an experimentally measurable quantity, whereas electronegativity is an estimated number that cannot be measured.

Example 9.2 shows how a knowledge of electronegativity can help us determine whether a chemical bond is covalent or ionic.

Figure 9.7 *Relation between percent ionic character and electronegativity difference.*

Example 9.2

Classify the following bonds as ionic, polar covalent, or covalent: (a) the bond in HCl, (b) the bond in KF, and (c) the CC bond in H_3CCH_3.

Strategy We follow the 2.0 rule of electronegativity difference and look up the values in Figure 9.5.

Solution (a) The electronegativity difference between H and Cl is 0.9, which is appreciable but not large enough (by the 2.0 rule) to qualify HCl as an ionic compound. Therefore, the bond between H and Cl is polar covalent.

(b) The electronegativity difference between K and F is 3.2, which is well above the 2.0 mark; therefore, the bond between K and F is ionic.

(c) The two C atoms are identical in every respect—they are bonded to each other and each is bonded to three other H atoms. Therefore, the bond between them is purely covalent.

Practice Exercise Which of the following bonds is covalent, which is polar covalent, and which is ionic? (a) the bond in CsCl, (b) the bond in H_2S, (c) the NN bond in H_2NNH_2.

The most electronegative elements are the nonmetals (Groups 5A–7A) and the least electronegative elements are the alkali and alkaline earth metals (Groups 1A–2A) and aluminum. Beryllium, the first member of Group 2A, forms mostly covalent compounds.

Similar problems: 9.39, 9.40.

Electronegativity and Oxidation Number

In Chapter 4 we introduced the rules for assigning oxidation numbers of elements in their compounds. The concept of electronegativity is the basis for these rules. In essence, oxidation number refers to the number of charges an atom would have if electrons were transferred completely to the more electronegative of the bonded atoms in a molecule.

Consider the NH_3 molecule, in which the N atom forms three single bonds with the H atoms. Because N is more electronegative than H, electron density will be shifted from H to N. If the transfer were complete, each H would donate an electron to N, which would have a total charge of -3 while each H would have a charge of $+1$. Thus, we assign an oxidation number of -3 to N and an oxidation number of $+1$ to H in NH_3.

Oxygen usually has an oxidation number of -2 in its compounds, except in hydrogen peroxide (H_2O_2), whose Lewis structure is

$$H—\overset{..}{\underset{..}{O}}—\overset{..}{\underset{..}{O}}—H$$

A bond between identical atoms makes no contribution to the oxidation number of those atoms because the electron pair of that bond is *equally* shared. Because H has an oxidation number of $+1$, each O atom has an oxidation number of -1.

Can you see now why fluorine always has an oxidation number of -1? It is the most electronegative element known, and it *always* forms a single bond in its compounds. Therefore, it would bear a -1 charge if electron transfer were complete.

9.6 Writing Lewis Structures

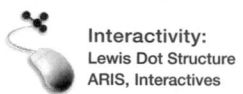

Interactivity:
Lewis Dot Structure
ARIS, Interactives

Although the octet rule and Lewis structures do not present a complete picture of covalent bonding, they do help to explain the bonding scheme in many compounds and account for the properties and reactions of molecules. For this reason, you should practice writing Lewis structures of compounds. The basic steps are as follows:

1. Write the skeletal structure of the compound, using chemical symbols and placing bonded atoms next to one another. For simple compounds, this task is fairly easy. For more complex compounds, we must either be given the information or make an intelligent guess about it. In general, the least electronegative atom occupies the central position. Hydrogen and fluorine usually occupy the terminal (end) positions in the Lewis structure.

2. Count the total number of valence electrons present, referring, if necessary, to Figure 9.1. For polyatomic anions, add the number of negative charges to that total. (For example, for the CO_3^{2-} ion we add two electrons because the $2-$ charge indicates that there are two more electrons than are provided by the atoms.) For polyatomic cations, we subtract the number of positive charges from this total. (Thus, for NH_4^+ we subtract one electron because the $1+$ charge indicates a loss of one electron from the group of atoms.)

3. Draw a single covalent bond between the central atom and each of the surrounding atoms. Complete the octets of the atoms bonded to the central atom. (Remember that the valence shell of a hydrogen atom is complete with only two electrons.) Electrons belonging to the central or surrounding atoms must be shown as lone pairs if they are not involved in bonding. The total number of electrons to be used is that determined in step 2.

4. After completing steps 1–3, if the central atom has fewer than eight electrons, try adding double or triple bonds between the surrounding atoms and the central atom, using lone pairs from the surrounding atoms to complete the octet of the central atom.

Examples 9.3, 9.4, and 9.5 illustrate the four-step procedure for writing Lewis structures of compounds and an ion.

Example 9.3

Write the Lewis structure for nitrogen trifluoride (NF_3) in which all three F atoms are bonded to the N atom.

Solution We follow the preceding procedure for writing Lewis structures.

Step 1: The N atom is less electronegative than F, so the skeletal structure of NF_3 is

$$F \quad N \quad F$$

$$F$$

Step 2: The outer-shell electron configurations of N and F are $2s^2 2p^3$ and $2s^2 2p^5$, respectively. Thus, there are $5 + (3 \times 7)$, or 26, valence electrons to account for in NF_3.

Step 3: We draw a single covalent bond between N and each F, and complete the octets for the F atoms. We place the remaining two electrons on N:

$$:\ddot{F}—\ddot{N}—\ddot{F}:$$
$$|$$
$$:\ddot{F}:$$

Because this structure satisfies the octet rule for all the atoms, step 4 is not required.

Check Count the valence electrons in NF_3 (in bonds and in lone pairs). The result is 26, the same as the total number of valence electrons on three F atoms ($3 \times 7 = 21$) and one N atom (5).

Practice Exercise Write the Lewis structure for carbon disulfide (CS_2).

NF_3 is a colorless, odorless, unreactive gas.

Similar problem: 9.45.

Example 9.4

Write the Lewis structure for nitric acid (HNO_3) in which the three O atoms are bonded to the central N atom and the ionizable H atom is bonded to one of the O atoms.

Solution We follow the procedure already outlined for writing Lewis structures.

Step 1: The skeletal structure of HNO_3 is

$$O \quad N \quad O \quad H$$

$$O$$

Step 2: The outer-shell electron configurations of N, O, and H are $2s^2 2p^3$, $2s^2 2p^4$, and $1s^1$, respectively. Thus, there are $5 + (3 \times 6) + 1$, or 24, valence electrons to account for in HNO_3.

Step 3: We draw a single covalent bond between N and each of the three O atoms and between one O atom and the H atom. Then we fill in electrons to comply with the octet rule for the O atoms:

$$:\ddot{O}—N—\ddot{O}—H$$
$$|$$
$$:\ddot{O}:$$

HNO_3 is a strong electrolyte.

(Continued)

Step 4: We see that this structure satisfies the octet rule for all the O atoms but not for the N atom. The N atom has only six electrons. Therefore, we move a lone pair from one of the end O atoms to form another bond with N. Now the octet rule is also satisfied for the N atom:

$$\overset{..}{\underset{..}{O}}=N-\overset{..}{\underset{..}{O}}-H$$
$$|$$
$$:\overset{..}{\underset{..}{O}}:$$

Check Make sure that all the atoms (except H) satisfy the octet rule. Count the valence electrons in HNO_3 (in bonds and in lone pairs). The result is 24, the same as the total number of valence electrons on three O atoms ($3 \times 6 = 18$), one N atom (5), and one H atom (1).

Similar problem: 9.45.

Practice Exercise Write the Lewis structure for formic acid (HCOOH).

CO_3^{2-}

Example 9.5

Write the Lewis structure for the carbonate ion (CO_3^{2-}).

Solution We follow the preceding procedure for writing Lewis structures and note that this is an anion with two negative charges.

Step 1: We can deduce the skeletal structure of the carbonate ion by recognizing that C is less electronegative than O. Therefore, it is most likely to occupy a central position as follows:

$$O$$
$$O \quad C \quad O$$

Step 2: The outer-shell electron configurations of C and O are $2s^2 2p^2$ and $2s^2 2p^4$, respectively, and the ion itself has two negative charges. Thus, the total number of electrons is $4 + (3 \times 6) + 2$, or 24.

Step 3: We draw a single covalent bond between C and each O and comply with the octet rule for the O atoms:

$$:\overset{..}{\underset{..}{O}}:$$
$$|$$
$$:\overset{..}{\underset{..}{O}}-C-\overset{..}{\underset{..}{O}}:$$

This structure shows all 24 electrons.

Step 4: Although the octet rule is satisfied for the O atoms, it is not for the C atom. Therefore, we move a lone pair from one of the O atoms to form another bond with C. Now the octet rule is also satisfied for the C atom:

$$\left[\begin{array}{c} :\overset{..}{O}: \\ \| \\ :\overset{..}{\underset{..}{O}}-C-\overset{..}{\underset{..}{O}}: \end{array} \right]^{2-}$$

We use the brackets to indicate that the −2 charge is on the whole molecule.

Check Make sure that all the atoms satisfy the octet rule. Count the valence electrons in CO_3^{2-} (in chemical bonds and in lone pairs). The result is 24, the same as the total number of valence electrons on three O atoms ($3 \times 6 = 18$), one C atom (4), and two negative charges (2).

Similar problem: 9.44.

Practice Exercise Write the Lewis structure for the nitrite ion (NO_2^-).

9.7 Formal Charge and Lewis Structure

By comparing the number of electrons in an isolated atom with the number of electrons that are associated with the same atom in a Lewis structure, we can determine the distribution of electrons in the molecule and draw the most plausible Lewis structure. The bookkeeping procedure is as follows: In an isolated atom, the number of electrons associated with the atom is simply the number of valence electrons. (As usual, we need not be concerned with the inner electrons.) In a molecule, electrons associated with the atom are the nonbonding electrons plus the electrons in the bonding pair(s) between the atom and other atom(s). However, because electrons are shared in a bond, we must divide the electrons in a bonding pair equally between the atoms forming the bond. An atom's *formal charge* is *the electrical charge difference between the valence electrons in an isolated atom and the number of electrons assigned to that atom in a Lewis structure.*

To assign the number of electrons on an atom in a Lewis structure, we proceed as follows:

- All the atom's nonbonding electrons are assigned to the atom.
- We break the bond(s) between the atom and other atom(s) and assign half of the bonding electrons to the atom.

Let us illustrate the concept of formal charge using the ozone molecule (O_3). Proceeding by steps, as we did in Examples 9.3 and 9.4, we draw the skeletal structure of O_3 and then add bonds and electrons to satisfy the octet rule for the two end atoms:

$$:\ddot{O}-\ddot{O}-\ddot{O}:$$

You can see that although all available electrons are used, the octet rule is not satisfied for the central atom. To remedy this, we convert a lone pair on one of the end atoms to a second bond between that end atom and the central atom, as follows:

$$\ddot{O}=\ddot{O}-\ddot{O}:$$

The formal charge on each atom in O_3 can now be calculated according to the following scheme:

$$\ddot{O}\lessgtr\ddot{O}\lessgtr\ddot{O}:$$

Valence e^-	6 6 6
e^- assigned to atom	6 5 7
Difference (formal charge)	0 +1 −1

where the wavy red lines denote the breaking of the bonds. Note that the breaking of a single bond results in the transfer of an electron, the breaking of a double bond results in a transfer of two electrons to each of the bonding atoms, and so on. Thus, the formal charges of the atoms in O_3 are

$$\ddot{O}=\overset{+}{\ddot{O}}-\ddot{O}:^-$$

For single positive and negative charges, we normally omit the numeral 1.

Liquid ozone below its boiling point (−111.3°C). Ozone is a toxic, light-blue gas with a pungent odor.

Assign half of the bonding electrons to each atom.

When you write formal charges, these rules are helpful:

1. For molecules, the sum of the formal charges must add up to zero because molecules are electrically neutral species. (This rule applies, for example, to the O_3 molecule.)

2. For cations, the sum of the formal charges must equal the positive charge.

3. For anions, the sum of the formal charges must equal the negative charge.

Keep in mind that formal charges do not represent actual charge separation within the molecule. In the O_3 molecule, for example, there is no evidence that the central atom bears a net $+1$ charge or that one of the end atoms bears a -1 charge. Writing these charges on the atoms in the Lewis structure merely helps us keep track of the valence electrons in the molecule.

Example 9.6

Write formal charges for the carbonate ion.

Strategy The Lewis structure for the carbonate ion was developed in Example 9.5:

The formal charges on the atoms can be calculated using the given procedure.

Solution We subtract the number of nonbonding electrons and half of the bonding electrons from the valence electrons of each atom.

The C atom: The C atom has four valence electrons and there are no nonbonding electrons on the atom in the Lewis structure. The breaking of the double bond and two single bonds results in the transfer of four electrons to the C atom. Therefore, the formal charge is $4 - 4 = 0$.

The O atom in C=O: The O atom has six valence electrons and there are four nonbonding electrons on the atom. The breaking of the double bond results in the transfer of two electrons to the O atom. Here the formal charge is $6 - 4 - 2 = 0$.

The O atom in C—O: This atom has six nonbonding electrons and the breaking of the single bond transfers another electron to it. Therefore, the formal charge is $6 - 6 - 1 = -1$.

Thus, the Lewis structure for CO_3^{2-} with formal charges is

Check Note that the sum of the formal charges is -2, the same as the charge on the carbonate ion.

Similar problem: 9.46.

Practice Exercise Write formal charges for the nitrite ion (NO_2^-).

Sometimes there is more than one acceptable Lewis structure for a given species. In such cases, we can often select the most plausible Lewis structure by using formal charges and the following guidelines:

• For molecules, a Lewis structure in which there are no formal charges is preferable to one in which formal charges are present.

- Lewis structures with large formal charges ($+2$, $+3$, and/or -2, -3, and so on) are less plausible than those with small formal charges.

- Among Lewis structures having similar distributions of formal charges, the most plausible structure is the one in which negative formal charges are placed on the more electronegative atoms.

Example 9.7 shows how formal charges facilitate the choice of the correct Lewis structure for a molecule.

Example 9.7

Formaldehyde (CH_2O), a liquid with a disagreeable odor, traditionally has been used to preserve laboratory specimens. Draw the most likely Lewis structure for the compound.

Strategy A plausible Lewis structure should satisfy the octet rule for all the elements, except H, and have the formal charges (if any) distributed according to electronegativity guidelines.

Solution The two possible skeletal structures are

CH_2O

H   C   O   H

H
 C   O
H

(a)   (b)

First we draw the Lewis structures for each of these possibilities

$$H-\overset{..}{\underset{..}{C}}=\overset{+}{\underset{}{O}}-H$$

$$\overset{H}{\underset{H}{>}}C=\overset{..}{\underset{..}{O}}$$

(a)   (b)

To show the formal charges, we follow the procedure given in Example 9.6. In (a) the C atom has a total of five electrons (one lone pair plus three electrons from the breaking of a single and a double bond). Because C has four valence electrons, the formal charge on the atom is $4 - 5 = -1$. The O atom has a total of five electrons (one lone pair and three electrons from the breaking of a single and a double bond). Because O has six valence electrons, the formal charge on the atom is $6 - 5 = +1$. In (b) the C atom has a total of four electrons from the breaking of two single bonds and a double bond, so its formal charge is $4 - 4 = 0$. The O atom has a total of six electrons (two lone pairs and two electrons from the breaking of the double bond). Therefore, the formal charge on the atom is $6 - 6 = 0$. Although both structures satisfy the octet rule, (b) is the more likely structure because it carries no formal charges.

Check In each case make sure that the total number of valence electrons is 12. Can you suggest two other reasons why (a) is less plausible?

Similar problem: 9.47.

Practice Exercise Draw the most reasonable Lewis structure of a molecule that contains a N atom, a C atom, and an H atom.

9.8 The Concept of Resonance

Our drawing of the Lewis structure for ozone (O_3) satisfied the octet rule for the central atom because we placed a double bond between it and one of the two end O

Electrostatic potential map of O_3. The electron density is evenly distributed between the two end O atoms.

Interactivity:
Resonance
ARIS, Interactives

Animation:
Resonance
ARIS, Animations

atoms. In fact, we can put the double bond at either end of the molecule, as shown by these two equivalent Lewis structures:

$$\ddot{O}=\overset{+}{\ddot{O}}-\ddot{\underset{..}{O}}:^{-} \qquad ^{-}:\ddot{\underset{..}{O}}-\overset{+}{\ddot{O}}=\ddot{O}$$

However, neither one of these two Lewis structures accounts for the known bond lengths in O_3.

We would expect the O—O bond in O_3 to be longer than the O=O bond because double bonds are known to be shorter than single bonds. Yet experimental evidence shows that both oxygen-to-oxygen bonds are equal in length (128 pm). We resolve this discrepancy by using *both* Lewis structures to represent the ozone molecule:

$$\ddot{O}=\overset{+}{\ddot{O}}-\ddot{\underset{..}{O}}:^{-} \longleftrightarrow ^{-}:\ddot{\underset{..}{O}}-\overset{+}{\ddot{O}}=\ddot{\underset{..}{O}}$$

Each of these structures is called a resonance structure. A **resonance structure,** then, is *one of two or more Lewis structures for a single molecule that cannot be represented accurately by only one Lewis structure.* The double-headed arrow indicates that the structures shown are resonance structures.

The term **resonance** itself means *the use of two or more Lewis structures to represent a particular molecule.* Like the medieval European traveler to Africa who described a rhinoceros as a cross between a griffin and a unicorn, two familiar but imaginary animals, we describe ozone, a real molecule, in terms of two familiar but nonexistent structures.

A common misconception about resonance is the notion that a molecule such as ozone somehow shifts quickly back and forth from one resonance structure to the other. Keep in mind that *neither* resonance structure adequately represents the actual molecule, which has its own unique, stable structure. "Resonance" is a human invention, designed to address the limitations in these simple bonding models. To extend the animal analogy, a rhinoceros is a distinct creature, not some oscillation between mythical griffin and unicorn!

The carbonate ion provides another example of resonance:

$$^{-}:\ddot{\underset{..}{O}}-\overset{\displaystyle :O:}{\overset{\displaystyle \|}{C}}-\ddot{\underset{..}{O}}:^{-} \longleftrightarrow \overset{\displaystyle :\ddot{O}:^{-}}{\underset{\displaystyle :\ddot{\underset{..}{O}}:^{-}}{\ddot{O}=C}} \longleftrightarrow ^{-}:\ddot{\underset{..}{O}}-\overset{\displaystyle :\ddot{O}:^{-}}{C}=\ddot{O}$$

According to experimental evidence, all carbon-to-oxygen bonds in CO_3^{2-} are equivalent. Therefore, the properties of the carbonate ion are best explained by considering its resonance structures together.

The concept of resonance applies equally well to organic systems. A good example is the benzene molecule (C_6H_6):

The hexagonal structure of benzene was first proposed by the German chemist August Kekulé (1829–1896).

If one of these resonance structures corresponded to the actual structure of benzene, there would be two different bond lengths between adjacent C atoms, one characteristic of the single bond and the other of the double bond. In fact, the distance between all adjacent C atoms in benzene is 140 pm, which is shorter than a C—C bond (154 pm) and longer than a C=C bond (133 pm).

A simpler way of drawing the structure of the benzene molecule and other compounds containing the "benzene ring" is to show only the skeleton and not the carbon and hydrogen atoms. By this convention the resonance structures are represented by

Note that the C atoms at the corners of the hexagon and the H atoms are all omitted, although they are understood to exist. Only the bonds between the C atoms are shown.

Remember this important rule for drawing resonance structures: The positions of electrons, but not those of atoms, can be rearranged in different resonance structures. In other words, the same atoms must be bonded to one another in all the resonance structures for a given species.

Example 9.8 illustrates the procedure for drawing resonance structures of a molecule.

Example 9.8

Draw resonance structures (including formal charges) for the nitrate ion, NO_3^-, which has the following skeletal arrangement:

$$O$$
$$O \quad N \quad O$$

Strategy We follow the procedure used for drawing Lewis structures and calculating formal charges in Examples 9.5 and 9.6.

Solution Just as in the case of the carbonate ion, we can draw three equivalent resonance structures for the nitrate ion:

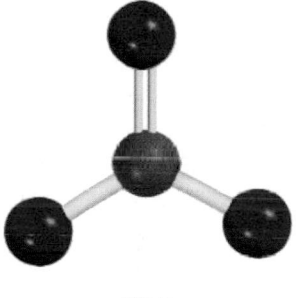

NO_3^-

Check Because N has five valence electrons and each O has six valence electrons and there is a net negative charge, the total number of valence electrons is $5 + (3 \times 6) + 1 = 24$, the same as the number of valence electrons in the NO_3^- ion.

Similar problems: 9.51, 9.56.

Practice Exercise Draw resonance structures for the nitrite ion (NO_2^-).

9.9 Exceptions to the Octet Rule

As mentioned earlier, the octet rule applies mainly to the second-period elements. Exceptions to the octet rule fall into three categories characterized by an incomplete octet, an odd number of electrons, or more than eight valence electrons around the central atom.

Interactivity:
Octet Rule Exceptions
ARIS, Interactives

Beryllium, unlike the other Group 2A elements, forms mostly covalent compounds of which BeH_2 is an example.

The Incomplete Octet

In some compounds the number of electrons surrounding the central atom in a stable molecule is fewer than eight. Consider, for example, beryllium, which is a Group 2A (and a second-period) element. The electron configuration of beryllium is $1s^2 2s^2$; it has two valence electrons in the $2s$ orbital. In the gas phase, beryllium hydride (BeH_2) exists as discrete molecules. The Lewis structure of BeH_2 is

$$H — Be — H$$

As you can see, only four electrons surround the Be atom, and there is no way to satisfy the octet rule for beryllium in this molecule.

Elements in Group 3A, particularly boron and aluminum, also tend to form compounds in which they are surrounded by fewer than eight electrons. Take boron as an example. Because its electron configuration is $1s^2 2s^2 2p^1$, it has a total of three valence electrons. Boron reacts with the halogens to form a class of compounds having the general formula BX_3, where X is a halogen atom. Thus, in boron trifluoride there are only six electrons around the boron atom:

$$\begin{array}{c} : \ddot{F} : \\ | \\ : \ddot{F} - B \\ | \\ : \ddot{F} : \end{array}$$

The following resonance structures all contain a double bond between B and F and satisfy the octet rule for boron:

$$\begin{array}{ccccc} & : \ddot{F} : & & : \ddot{F} :^+ & & : \ddot{F} : \\ & | & & || & & | \\ {}^+\ddot{F} = B^- & & : \ddot{F} - B^- & & : \ddot{F} - B^- \\ & | & & | & & || \\ & : \ddot{F} : & & : \ddot{F} : & & : \ddot{F} :^+ \end{array}$$

The fact that the B—F bond length in BF_3 (130.9 pm) is shorter than a single bond (137.3 pm) lends support to the resonance structures even though in each case the negative formal charge is placed on the B atom and the positive formal charge on the more electronegative F atom.

Although boron trifluoride is stable, it readily reacts with ammonia. This reaction is better represented by using the Lewis structure in which boron has only six valence electrons around it:

$$\begin{array}{ccccc} : \ddot{F} : & H & & : \ddot{F} : & H \\ | & | & & | & | \\ : \ddot{F} - B & + & : N - H \longrightarrow & : \ddot{F} - B^- - N^+ - H \\ | & | & & | & | \\ : \ddot{F} : & H & & : \ddot{F} : & H \end{array}$$

It seems that the properties of BF_3 are best explained by all four resonance structures.

The B—N bond in the above compound is different from the covalent bonds discussed so far in the sense that both electrons are contributed by the N atom. This type of bond is called a ***coordinate covalent bond*** (also referred to as a *dative bond*), defined as *a covalent bond in which one of the atoms donates both electrons.* Although the properties of a coordinate covalent bond do not differ from

$$NH_3 + BF_3 \longrightarrow H_3N — BF_3$$

those of a normal covalent bond (because all electrons are alike no matter what their source), the distinction is useful for keeping track of valence electrons and assigning formal charges.

Odd-Electron Molecules

Some molecules contain an *odd* number of electrons. Among them are nitric oxide (NO) and nitrogen dioxide (NO_2):

$$\ddot{N}=\ddot{O} \qquad \ddot{O}=\overset{+}{N}-\ddot{O}:^-$$

Because we need an even number of electrons for complete pairing (to reach eight), the octet rule clearly cannot be satisfied for all the atoms in any of these molecules.

Odd-electron molecules are sometimes called *radicals*. Many radicals are highly reactive. The reason is that there is a tendency for the unpaired electron to form a covalent bond with an unpaired electron on another molecule. For example, when two nitrogen dioxide molecules collide, they form dinitrogen tetroxide in which the octet rule is satisfied for both the N and O atoms:

$$\ddot{O}{\diagdown}N\cdot\diagup_{\ddot{O}} + \cdot N\diagup^{\ddot{O}}_{\diagdown\ddot{O}} \longrightarrow \ddot{O}{\diagdown}N-N\diagup^{\ddot{O}}_{\diagdown\ddot{O}}\diagup_{\ddot{O}}$$

The Expanded Octet

Atoms of the second-period elements cannot have more than eight valence electrons around the central atom, but atoms of elements in and beyond the third period of the periodic table form some compounds in which more than eight electrons surround the central atom. In addition to the 3s and 3p orbitals, elements in the third period also have 3d orbitals that can be used in bonding. These orbitals allow an atom to form an *expanded octet*. One compound in which there is an expanded octet is sulfur hexafluoride, a very stable compound. The electron configuration of sulfur is $[Ne]3s^2 3p^4$. In SF_6, each of sulfur's six valence electrons forms a covalent bond with a fluorine atom, so there are 12 electrons around the central sulfur atom:

Yellow: second-period elements cannot have an expanded octet. Blue: third-period elements and beyond can have an expanded octet. Green: the noble gases usually only have an expanded octet.

$$:\ddot{F}{\diagdown}\overset{\displaystyle :\ddot{F}:}{\underset{\displaystyle :\ddot{F}:}{\overset{|}{\underset{|}{S}}}}\diagup\ddot{F}:$$

In Chapter 10 we will see that these 12 electrons, or six bonding pairs, are accommodated in six orbitals that originate from the one 3s, the three 3p, and two of the five 3d orbitals. Sulfur also forms many compounds in which it obeys the octet rule. In sulfur dichloride, for instance, S is surrounded by only eight electrons:

$$:\ddot{Cl}-\ddot{S}-\ddot{Cl}:$$

Sulfur dichloride is a toxic, foul-smelling cherry-red liquid (boiling point: 59°C).

Examples 9.9–9.11 concern compounds that do not obey the octet rule.

AlI$_3$ has a tendency to dimerize or form two units as Al$_2$I$_6$.

Similar problem: 9.62.

Example 9.9

Draw the Lewis structure for aluminum triiodide (AlI$_3$).

Strategy We follow the procedures used in Examples 9.5 and 9.6 to draw the Lewis structure and calculate formal charges.

Solution The outer-shell electron configurations of Al and I are $3s^23p^1$ and $5s^25p^5$, respectively. The total number of valence electrons is $3 + 3 \times 7$ or 24. Because Al is less electronegative than I, it occupies a central position and forms three bonds with the I atoms:

Note that there are no formal charges on the Al and I atoms.

Check Although the octet rule is satisfied for the I atoms, there are only six valence electrons around the Al atom. Thus, AlI$_3$ is an example of the incomplete octet.

Practice Exercise Draw the Lewis structure for BeF$_2$.

Example 9.10

Draw the Lewis structure for phosphorus pentafluoride (PF$_5$), in which all five F atoms are bonded to the central P atom.

Strategy Note that P is a third-period element. We follow the procedures given in Examples 9.5 and 9.6 to draw the Lewis structure and calculate formal charges.

Solution The outer-shell electron configurations for P and F are $3s^23p^3$ and $2s^22p^5$, respectively, and so the total number of valence electrons is $5 + (5 \times 7)$, or 40. Phosphorus, like sulfur, is a third-period element, and therefore it can have an expanded octet. The Lewis structure of PF$_5$ is

PF$_5$ is a reactive gaseous compound.

Note that there are no formal charges on the P and F atoms.

Check Although the octet rule is satisfied for the F atoms, there are 10 valence electrons around the P atom, giving it an expanded octet.

Similar problem: 9.64.

Practice Exercise Draw the Lewis structure for arsenic pentafluoride (AsF$_5$).

Example 9.11

Draw a Lewis structure for the sulfate ion (SO$_4^{2-}$) in which all four O atoms are bonded to the central S atom.

(Continued)

Strategy Note that S is a third-period element. We follow the procedures given in Examples 9.5 and 9.6 to draw the Lewis structure and calculate formal charges.

Solution The outer-shell electron configurations of S and O are $3s^2 3p^4$ and $2s^2 2p^4$, respectively.

Step 1: The skeletal structure of (SO_4^{2-}) is

$$
\begin{array}{c}
\text{O} \\
\text{O S O} \\
\text{O}
\end{array}
$$

Step 2: Both O and S are Group 6A elements and so have six valence electrons each. Including the two negative charges, we must therefore account for a total of $6 + (4 \times 6) + 2$, or 32, valence electrons in SO_4^{2-}.

Step 3: We draw a single covalent bond between all the bonding atoms:

$$
\begin{array}{c}
: \ddot{\text{O}} : \\
| \\
: \ddot{\text{O}} - \text{S} - \ddot{\text{O}} : \\
| \\
: \ddot{\text{O}} :
\end{array}
$$

Next we show formal charges on the S and O atoms:

$$
\begin{array}{c}
: \ddot{\text{O}} :^{-} \\
| \\
^{-} : \ddot{\text{O}} - \overset{2+}{\text{S}} - \ddot{\text{O}} :^{-} \\
| \\
: \ddot{\text{O}} : \\
\;^{-}
\end{array}
$$

Check One of six other equivalent structures for SO_4^{2-} is as follows:

$$
\begin{array}{c}
: \text{O} : \\
\| \\
^{-} : \ddot{\text{O}} - \text{S} - \ddot{\text{O}} :^{-} \\
\| \\
: \text{O} :
\end{array}
$$

This structure involves an expanded octet on S but may be considered more plausible because it bears fewer formal charges. However, detailed theoretical calculation shows that the most likely structure is the one that satisfies the octet rule, even though it has greater formal charge separations. The general rule for elements in the third period and beyond is that a resonance structure that obeys the octet rule is preferred over one that involves an expanded octet but bears fewer formal charges.

Practice Exercise Draw the Lewis structure of sulfuric acid (H_2SO_4).

SO_4^{2-}

Similar problem: 9.85.

A final note about the expanded octet: In drawing Lewis structures of compounds containing a central atom from the third period and beyond, sometimes we find that the octet rule is satisfied for all the atoms but there are still valence electrons left to place. In such cases, the extra electrons should be placed as lone pairs on the central atom. Example 9.12 shows this approach.

Just Say NO

Nitric oxide (NO), the simplest nitrogen oxide, is an odd-electron molecule, and therefore it is paramagnetic. A colorless gas (boiling point: $-152°C$), NO can be prepared in the laboratory by reacting sodium nitrite ($NaNO_2$) with a reducing agent such as Fe^{2+} in an acidic medium.

$$NO_2^-(aq) + Fe^{2+}(aq) + 2H^+(aq) \longrightarrow \\ NO(g) + Fe^{3+}(aq) + H_2O(l)$$

Environmental sources of nitric oxide include the burning of fossil fuels containing nitrogen compounds and the reaction between nitrogen and oxygen inside the automobile engine at high temperatures

$$N_2(g) + O_2(g) \longrightarrow 2NO(g)$$

Lightning also contributes to the atmospheric concentration of NO. Exposed to air, nitric oxide quickly forms brown nitrogen dioxide gas:

$$2NO(g) + O_2(g) \longrightarrow 2NO_2(g)$$

Nitrogen dioxide is a major component of smog.

About 24 years ago scientists studying muscle relaxation discovered that our bodies produce nitric oxide for use as a neurotransmitter. (A *neurotransmitter* is a small molecule that serves to facilitate cell-to-cell communications.) Since then, it has been detected in at least a dozen cell types in various parts of the body. Cells in the brain, the liver, the pancreas, the gastrointestinal tract, and the blood vessels can synthesize nitric oxide. This molecule also functions as a cellular toxin to kill harmful bacteria. And that's not all: In 1996 it was reported that NO binds to hemoglobin, the oxygen-carrying protein in the blood. No doubt it helps to regulate blood pressure.

The discovery of the biological role of nitric oxide has shed light on how nitroglycerin ($C_3H_5N_3O_9$) works as a drug. For many years, nitroglycerin tablets have been prescribed for heart patients to relieve pain (*angina pectoris*) caused by a brief interference in the flow of blood to the heart, although how it worked was not understood. We now know that nitroglycerin produces nitric oxide, which causes muscles to relax and allows the arteries to dilate. In this respect, it is interesting to note that Alfred Nobel, the inventor of dynamite (a mixture of nitroglycerin and clay that stabilizes the explosive before use), who established the prizes bearing his name, had heart trouble. But he refused his doctor's recommendation to ingest a small amount of nitroglycerin to ease the pain.

That NO evolved as a messenger molecule is entirely appropriate. Nitric oxide is small and so can diffuse quickly from cell to cell. It is a stable molecule, but under certain circumstances it is highly reactive, which accounts for its protective function. The enzyme that brings about muscle relaxation contains iron for which nitric oxide has a high affinity. It is the binding of NO to the iron that activates the enzyme. Nevertheless, in the cell, where biological effectors are typically very large molecules, the pervasive effects of one of the smallest known molecules are unprecedented.

Colorless nitric oxide gas is produced by the action of Fe^{2+} on an acidic sodium nitrite solution. The gas is bubbled through water and immediately reacts with oxygen to form the brown NO_2 gas when exposed to air.

Example 9.12

Draw a Lewis structure of the noble gas compound xenon tetrafluoride (XeF_4) in which all F atoms are bonded to the central Xe atom.

(Continued)

Strategy Note that Xe is a fifth-period element. We follow the procedures in Examples 9.5 and 9.6 for drawing the Lewis structure and calculating formal charges.

Solution *Step 1:* The skeletal structure of XeF_4 is

$$
\begin{array}{ccc}
F & & F \\
 & Xe & \\
F & & F
\end{array}
$$

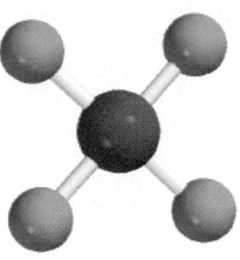

XeF_4

Step 2: The outer-shell electron configurations of Xe and F are $5s^2 5p^6$ and $2s^2 2p^5$, respectively, and so the total number of valence electrons is $8 + (4 \times 7)$ or 36.

Step 3: We draw a single covalent bond between all the bonding atoms. The octet rule is satisfied for the F atoms, each of which has three lone pairs. The sum of the lone pair electrons on the four F atoms (4×6) and the four bonding pairs (4×2) is 32. Therefore, the remaining four electrons are shown as two lone pairs on the Xe atom:

$$
\begin{array}{ccc}
:\ddot{F} & & \ddot{F}: \\
 & \ddot{Xe} & \\
:\ddot{F} & & \ddot{F}:
\end{array}
$$

We see that the Xe atom has an expanded octet. There are no formal charges on the Xe and F atoms.

Similar problem: 9.63.

Practice Exercise Write the Lewis structure of sulfur tetrafluoride (SF_4).

9.10 Bond Enthalpy

A measure of the stability of a molecule is its **bond enthalpy**, which is *the enthalpy change required to break a particular bond in 1 mole of gaseous molecules.* (Bond enthalpies in solids and liquids are affected by neighboring molecules.) The experimentally determined bond enthalpy of the diatomic hydrogen molecule, for example, is

$$H_2(g) \longrightarrow H(g) + H(g) \qquad \Delta H^\circ = 436.4 \text{ kJ/mol}$$

This equation tells us that breaking the covalent bonds in 1 mole of gaseous H_2 molecules requires 436.4 kJ of energy. For the less stable chlorine molecule,

$$Cl_2(g) \longrightarrow Cl(g) + Cl(g) \qquad \Delta H^\circ = 242.7 \text{ kJ/mol}$$

Bond enthalpies can also be directly measured for diatomic molecules containing unlike elements, such as HCl,

$$HCl(g) \longrightarrow H(g) + Cl(g) \qquad \Delta H^\circ = 431.9 \text{ kJ/mol}$$

as well as for molecules containing double and triple bonds:

$$O_2(g) \longrightarrow O(g) + O(g) \qquad \Delta H^\circ = 498.7 \text{ kJ/mol}$$
$$N_2(g) \longrightarrow N(g) + N(g) \qquad \Delta H^\circ = 941.4 \text{ kJ/mol}$$

The Lewis structure of O_2 is $\ddot{O}=\ddot{O}$.

Measuring the strength of covalent bonds in polyatomic molecules is more complicated. For example, measurements show that the energy needed to break the first O—H bond in H_2O is different from that needed to break the second O—H bond:

$$H_2O(g) \longrightarrow H(g) + OH(g) \qquad \Delta H^\circ = 502 \text{ kJ/mol}$$
$$OH(g) \longrightarrow H(g) + O(g) \qquad \Delta H^\circ = 427 \text{ kJ/mol}$$

TABLE 9.4	Some Bond Enthalpies of Diatomic Molecules* and Average Bond Enthalpies for Bonds in Polyatomic Molecules		
Bond	**Bond Enthalpy (kJ/mol)**	**Bond**	**Bond Enthalpy (kJ/mol)**
H—H	436.4	C—S	255
H—N	393	C=S	477
H—O	460	N—N	193
H—S	368	N=N	418
H—P	326	N≡N	941.4
H—F	568.2	N—O	176
H—Cl	431.9	N=O	607
H—Br	366.1	O—O	142
H—I	298.3	O=O	498.7
C—H	414	O—P	502
C—C	347	O=S	469
C=C	620	P—P	197
C≡C	812	P=P	489
C—N	276	S—S	268
C=N	615	S=S	352
C≡N	891	F—F	156.9
C—O	351	Cl—Cl	242.7
C=O†	745	Br—Br	192.5
C—P	263	I—I	151.0

*Bond enthalpies for diatomic molecules (in color) have more significant figures than bond enthalpies for bonds in polyatomic molecules because the bond enthalpies of diatomic molecules are directly measurable quantities and not averaged over many compounds.
†The C=O bond enthalpy in CO_2 is 799 kJ/mol.

In each case, an O—H bond is broken, but the first step is more endothermic than the second. The difference between the two $\Delta H°$ values suggests that the second O—H bond itself has undergone change, because of the changes in the chemical environment.

Now we can understand why the bond enthalpy of the same O—H bond in two different molecules such as methanol (CH_3OH) and water (H_2O) will not be the same: their environments are different. Thus, for polyatomic molecules we speak of the *average* bond enthalpy of a particular bond. For example, we can measure the energy of the O—H bond in 10 different polyatomic molecules and obtain the average O—H bond enthalpy by dividing the sum of the bond enthalpies by 10. Table 9.4 lists the average bond enthalpies of a number of diatomic and polyatomic molecules. As stated earlier, triple bonds are stronger than double bonds, which, in turn, are stronger than single bonds.

Use of Bond Enthalpies in Thermochemistry

A comparison of the thermochemical changes that take place during a number of reactions (Chapter 6) reveals a strikingly wide variation in the enthalpies of different reactions. For example, the combustion of hydrogen gas in oxygen gas is fairly exothermic:

$$H_2(g) + \tfrac{1}{2}O_2(g) \longrightarrow H_2O(l) \qquad \Delta H° = -285.8 \text{ kJ/mol}$$

On the other hand, the formation of glucose ($C_6H_{12}O_6$) from water and carbon dioxide, best achieved by photosynthesis, is highly endothermic:

$$6CO_2(g) + 6H_2O(l) \longrightarrow C_6H_{12}O_6(s) + 6O_2(g) \quad \Delta H° = 2801 \text{ kJ/mol}$$

We can account for such variations by looking at the stability of individual reactant and product molecules. After all, most chemical reactions involve the making and breaking of bonds. Therefore, knowing the bond enthalpies and hence the stability of molecules tells us something about the thermochemical nature of reactions that molecules undergo.

In many cases, it is possible to predict the approximate enthalpy of reaction by using the average bond enthalpies. Because energy is always required to break chemical bonds and chemical bond formation is always accompanied by a release of energy, we can estimate the enthalpy of a reaction by counting the total number of bonds broken and formed in the reaction and recording all the corresponding energy changes. The enthalpy of reaction in the *gas phase* is given by

$$\Delta H° = \Sigma BE(\text{reactants}) - \Sigma BE(\text{products})$$
$$= \text{total energy input} - \text{total energy released} \qquad (9.3)$$

where BE stands for average bond enthalpy and Σ is the summation sign. As written, Equation (9.3) takes care of the sign convention for $\Delta H°$. Thus, if the total energy input is greater than the total energy released, $\Delta H°$ is positive and the reaction is endothermic. On the other hand, if more energy is released than absorbed, $\Delta H°$ is negative and the reaction is exothermic (Figure 9.8). If reactants and products are all diatomic molecules, then Equation (9.3) will yield accurate results because the bond enthalpies of diatomic molecules are accurately known. If some or all of the reactants and products are polyatomic molecules, Equation (9.3)

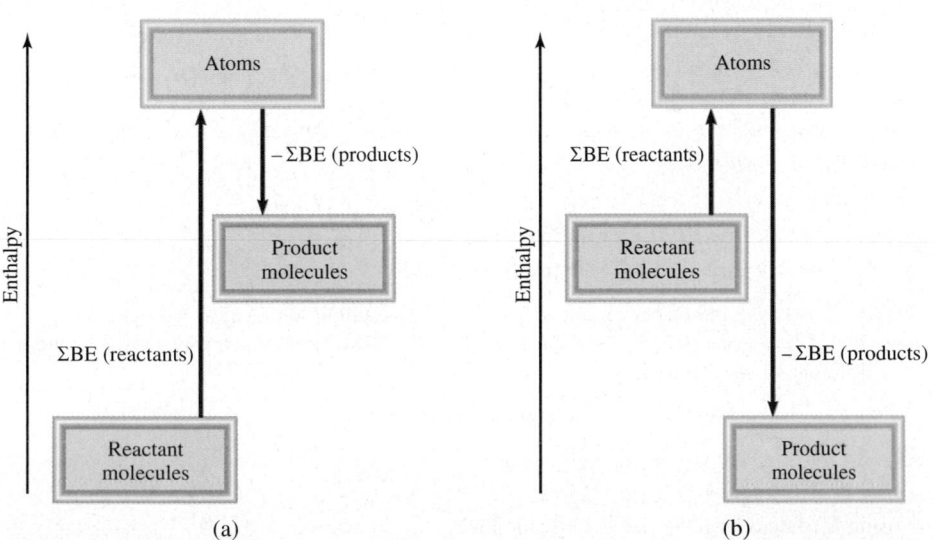

(a)   (b)

Figure 9.8 *Bond enthalpy changes in (a) an endothermic reaction and (b) an exothermic reaction.*

will yield only approximate results because the bond enthalpies used will be averages.

For diatomic molecules, Equation (9.3) is equivalent to Equation (6.18), so the results obtained from these two equations should correspond, as Example 9.13 illustrates.

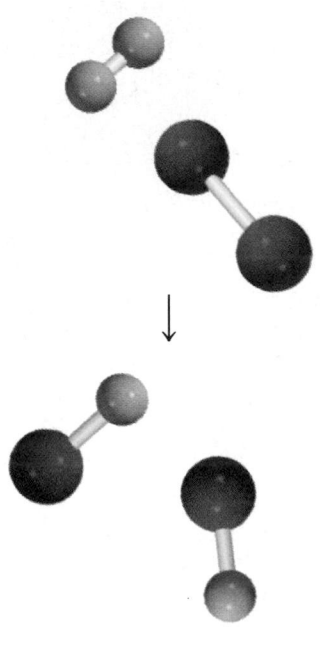

Refer to Table 9.4 for bond enthalpies of these diatomic molecules.

Similar problem: 9.104.

Example 9.13

Use Equation (9.3) to calculate the enthalpy of reaction for the process

$$H_2(g) + Cl_2(g) \longrightarrow 2HCl(g)$$

Compare your result with that obtained using Equation (6.18).

Strategy Keep in mind that bond breaking is an energy absorbing (endothermic) process and bond making is an energy releasing (exothermic) process. Therefore, the overall energy change is the difference between these two opposing processes, as described by Equation (9.3).

Solution We start by counting the number of bonds broken and the number of bonds formed and the corresponding energy changes. This is best done by creating a table:

Type of bonds broken	Number of bonds broken	Bond enthalpy (kJ/mol)	Energy change (kJ/mol)
H—H (H_2)	1	436.4	436.4
Cl—Cl (Cl_2)	1	242.7	242.7

Type of bonds formed	Number of bonds formed	Bond enthalpy (kJ/mol)	Energy change (kJ/mol)
H—Cl (HCl)	2	431.9	863.8

Next, we obtain the total energy input and total energy released:

total energy input = 436.4 kJ/mol + 242.7 kJ/mol = 679.1 kJ/mol
total energy released = 863.8 kJ/mol

Using Equation (9.3), we write

$$\Delta H° = 679.1 \text{ kJ/mol} - 863.8 \text{ kJ/mol} = -184.7 \text{ kJ/mol}$$

Alternatively, we can use Equation (6.18) and the data in Appendix 3 to calculate the enthalpy of reaction:

$$\Delta H° = 2\Delta H_f°(HCl) - [\Delta H_f°(H_2) + \Delta H_f°(Cl_2)]$$
$$= (2)(-92.3 \text{ kJ/mol}) - 0 - 0$$
$$= -184.6 \text{ kJ/mol}$$

Check Because the reactants and products are all diatomic molecules, we expect the results of Equations (9.3) and (6.18) to be the same. The small discrepancy here is due to different ways of rounding off.

Practice Exercise Calculate the enthalpy of the reaction

$$H_2(g) + F_2(g) \longrightarrow 2HF(g)$$

using (a) Equation (9.3) and (b) Equation (6.18).

Example 9.14 uses Equation (9.3) to estimate the enthalpy of a reaction involving a polyatomic molecule.

Example 9.14

Estimate the enthalpy change for the combustion of hydrogen gas:

$$2H_2(g) + O_2(g) \longrightarrow 2H_2O(g)$$

Strategy We basically follow the same procedure as that in Example 9.13. Note, however, that H_2O is a polyatomic molecule, and so we need to use the average bond enthalpy value for the O—H bond.

Solution We construct the following table:

Type of bonds broken	Number of bonds broken	Bond enthalpy (kJ/mol)	Energy change (kJ/mol)
H—H (H_2)	2	436.4	872.8
O=O (O_2)	2	498.7	498.7
Type of bonds formed	Number of bonds formed	Bond enthalpy (kJ/mol)	Energy change (kJ/mol)
O—H (H_2O)	4	460	1840

Next, we obtain the total energy input and total energy released:

$$\text{total energy input} = 872.8 \text{ kJ/mol} + 498.7 \text{ kJ/mol} = 1371.5 \text{ kJ/mol}$$
$$\text{total energy released} = 1840 \text{ kJ/mol}$$

Using Equation (9.3), we write

$$\Delta H° = 1371.5 \text{ kJ/mol} - 1840 \text{ kJ/mol} = -469 \text{ kJ/mol}$$

This result is only an estimate because the bond enthalpy of O—H is an average quantity. Alternatively, we can use Equation (6.18) and the data in Appendix 3 to calculate the enthalpy of reaction:

$$\Delta H° = 2\Delta H_f°(H_2O) - [2\Delta H_f°(H_2) + \Delta H_f°(O_2)]$$
$$= 2(-241.8 \text{ kJ/mol}) - 0 - 0$$
$$= -483.6 \text{ kJ/mol}$$

Check Note that the estimated value based on average bond enthalpies is quite close to the value calculated using $\Delta H_f°$ data. In general, Equation (9.3) works best for reactions that are either quite endothermic or quite exothermic, that is, reactions for which $\Delta H_{rxn}° > 100 \text{ kJ/mol}$ or for which $\Delta H_{rxn}° < -100 \text{ kJ/mol}$.

Similar problem: 9.72.

Practice Exercise For the reaction

$$H_2(g) + C_2H_4(g) \longrightarrow C_2H_6(g)$$

(a) Estimate the enthalpy of reaction, using the bond enthalpy values in Table 9.4.
(b) Calculate the enthalpy of reaction, using standard enthalpies of formation. ($\Delta H_f°$ for H_2, C_2H_4, and C_2H_6 are 0, 52.3 kJ/mol, and −84.7 kJ/mol, respectively.)

Summary of Facts and Concepts

1. A Lewis dot symbol shows the number of valence electrons possessed by an atom of a given element. Lewis dot symbols are useful mainly for the representative elements.

2. The elements most likely to form ionic compounds have low ionization energies (such as the alkali metals and the alkaline earth metals, which form cations) or high electron affinities (such as the halogens and oxygen, which form anions).

3. An ionic bond is the product of the electrostatic forces of attraction between positive and negative ions. An ionic compound consists of a large network of ions in which positive and negative charges are balanced. The structure of a solid ionic compound maximizes the net attractive forces among the ions.

4. Lattice energy is a measure of the stability of an ionic solid. It can be calculated by means of the Born-Haber cycle, which is based on Hess's law.

5. In a covalent bond, two electrons (one pair) are shared by two atoms. In multiple covalent bonds, two or three pairs of electrons are shared by two atoms. Some covalently bonded atoms also have lone pairs, that is, pairs of valence electrons that are not involved in bonding. The arrangement of bonding electrons and lone pairs in a molecule is represented by a Lewis structure.

6. The octet rule predicts that atoms form enough covalent bonds to surround themselves with eight electrons each. When one atom in a covalently bonded pair donates two electrons to the bond, the Lewis structure can include the formal charge on each atom as a means of keeping track of the valence electrons. There are exceptions to the octet rule, particularly for covalent beryllium compounds, elements in Group 3A, odd–electron molecules, and elements in the third period and beyond in the periodic table.

7. Electronegativity is a measure of an atom's ability to attract electrons in a chemical bond.

8. For some molecules or polyatomic ions, two or more Lewis structures based on the same skeletal structure satisfy the octet rule and appear chemically reasonable. Taken together, such resonance structures represent the molecule or ion more accurately than any single Lewis structure does.

9. The strength of a covalent bond is measured in terms of its bond enthalpy. Bond enthalpies can be used to estimate the enthalpy of reactions.

Key Words

Bond enthalpy, p. 385
Bond length, p. 368
Born-Haber cycle, p. 361
Coordinate covalent
    bond, p. 380
Coulomb's law, p. 361

Covalent bond, p. 366
Covalent compound, p. 366
Double bond, p. 367
Electronegativity, p. 369
Formal charge, p. 375
Ionic bond, p. 359

Lattice energy, p. 361
Lewis dot symbol, p. 358
Lewis structure, p. 366
Lone pair, p. 366
Multiple bond, p. 367
Octet rule, p. 367

Polar covalent bond, p. 369
Resonance, p. 378
Resonance structure, p. 378
Single bond, p. 367
Triple bond, p. 367

Questions and Problems

Lewis Dot Symbols

Review Questions

9.1 What is a Lewis dot symbol? To what elements does the symbol mainly apply?

9.2 Use the second member of each group from Group 1A to Group 7A to show that the number of valence electrons on an atom of the element is the same as its group number.

9.3 Without referring to Figure 9.1, write Lewis dot symbols for atoms of the following elements: (a) Be, (b) K, (c) Ca, (d) Ga, (e) O, (f) Br, (g) N, (h) I, (i) As, (j) F.

9.4 Write Lewis dot symbols for the following ions: (a) Li^+, (b) Cl^-, (c) S^{2-}, (d) Sr^{2+}, (e) N^{3-}.

9.5 Write Lewis dot symbols for the following atoms and ions: (a) I, (b) I^-, (c) S, (d) S^{2-}, (e) P, (f) P^{3-}, (g) Na, (h) Na^+, (i) Mg, (j) Mg^{2+}, (k) Al, (l) Al^{3+}, (m) Pb, (n) Pb^{2+}.

The Ionic Bond
Review Questions

9.6 Explain what an ionic bond is.

9.7 Explain how ionization energy and electron affinity determine whether atoms of elements will combine to form ionic compounds.

9.8 Name five metals and five nonmetals that are very likely to form ionic compounds. Write formulas for compounds that might result from the combination of these metals and nonmetals. Name these compounds.

9.9 Name one ionic compound that contains only non-metallic elements.

9.10 Name one ionic compound that contains a polyatomic cation and a polyatomic anion (see Table 2.3).

9.11 Explain why ions with charges greater than 3 are seldom found in ionic compounds.

9.12 The term "molar mass" was introduced in Chapter 3. What is the advantage of using the term "molar mass" when we discuss ionic compounds?

9.13 In which of the following states would NaCl be electrically conducting? (a) solid, (b) molten (that is, melted), (c) dissolved in water. Explain your answers.

9.14 Beryllium forms a compound with chlorine that has the empirical formula $BeCl_2$. How would you determine whether it is an ionic compound? (The compound is not soluble in water.)

Problems

9.15 An ionic bond is formed between a cation A^+ and an anion B^-. How would the energy of the ionic bond [see Equation (9.2)] be affected by the following changes? (a) doubling the radius of A^+, (b) tripling the charge on A^+, (c) doubling the charges on A^+ and B^-, (d) decreasing the radii of A^+ and B^- to half their original values.

9.16 Give the empirical formulas and names of the compounds formed from the following pairs of ions: (a) Rb^+ and I^-, (b) Cs^+ and SO_4^{2-}, (c) Sr^{2+} and N^{3-}, (d) Al^{3+} and S^{2-}.

9.17 Use Lewis dot symbols to show the transfer of electrons between the following atoms to form cations and anions: (a) Na and F, (b) K and S, (c) Ba and O, (d) Al and N.

9.18 Write the Lewis dot symbols of the reactants and products in the following reactions. (First balance the equations.)
(a) $Sr + Se \longrightarrow SrSe$
(b) $Ca + H_2 \longrightarrow CaH_2$
(c) $Li + N_2 \longrightarrow Li_3N$
(d) $Al + S \longrightarrow Al_2S_3$

9.19 For each of the following pairs of elements, state whether the binary compound they form is likely to be ionic or covalent. Write the empirical formula and name of the compound: (a) I and Cl, (b) Mg and F.

9.20 For each of the following pairs of elements, state whether the binary compound they form is likely to be ionic or covalent. Write the empirical formula and name of the compound: (a) B and F, (b) K and Br.

Lattice Energy of Ionic Compounds
Review Questions

9.21 What is lattice energy and what role does it play in the stability of ionic compounds?

9.22 Explain how the lattice energy of an ionic compound such as KCl can be determined using the Born-Haber cycle. On what law is this procedure based?

9.23 Specify which compound in the following pairs of ionic compounds has the higher lattice energy: (a) KCl or MgO, (b) LiF or LiBr, (c) Mg_3N_2 or NaCl. Explain your choice.

9.24 Compare the stability (in the solid state) of the following pairs of compounds: (a) LiF and LiF_2 (containing the Li^{2+} ion), (b) Cs_2O and CsO (containing the O^- ion), (c) $CaBr_2$ and $CaBr_3$ (containing the Ca^{3+} ion).

Problems

9.25 Use the Born-Haber cycle outlined in Section 9.3 for LiF to calculate the lattice energy of NaCl. [The heat of sublimation of Na is 108 kJ/mol and $\Delta H_f^\circ(NaCl) = -411$ kJ/mol. Energy needed to dissociate $\frac{1}{2}$ mole of Cl_2 into Cl atoms = 121.4 kJ.]

9.26 Calculate the lattice energy of calcium chloride given that the heat of sublimation of Ca is 121 kJ/mol and $\Delta H_f^\circ(CaCl_2) = -795$ kJ/mol. (See Tables 8.2 and 8.3 for other data.)

The Covalent Bond
Review Questions

9.27 What is Lewis's contribution to our understanding of the covalent bond?

9.28 Use an example to illustrate each of the following terms: lone pairs, Lewis structure, the octet rule, bond length.

9.29 What is the difference between a Lewis dot symbol and a Lewis structure?

9.30 How many lone pairs are on the underlined atoms in these compounds? H$\underline{Br}$, H$_2\underline{S}$, $\underline{C}H_4$

9.31 Compare single, double, and triple bonds in a molecule, and give an example of each. For the same bonding atoms, how does the bond length change from single bond to triple bond?

9.32 Compare the properties of ionic compounds and covalent compounds.

Electronegativity and Bond Type

Review Questions

9.33 Define electronegativity, and explain the difference between electronegativity and electron affinity. Describe in general how the electronegativities of the elements change according to position in the periodic table.

9.34 What is a polar covalent bond? Name two compounds that contain one or more polar covalent bonds.

Problems

9.35 List the following bonds in order of increasing ionic character: the lithium-to-fluorine bond in LiF, the potassium-to-oxygen bond in K_2O, the nitrogen-to-nitrogen bond in N_2, the sulfur-to-oxygen bond in SO_2, the chlorine-to-fluorine bond in ClF_3.

9.36 Arrange the following bonds in order of increasing ionic character: carbon to hydrogen, fluorine to hydrogen, bromine to hydrogen, sodium to chlorine, potassium to fluorine, lithium to chlorine.

9.37 Four atoms are arbitrarily labeled D, E, F, and G. Their electronegativities are as follows: D = 3.8, E = 3.3, F = 2.8, and G = 1.3. If the atoms of these elements form the molecules DE, DG, EG, and DF, how would you arrange these molecules in order of increasing covalent bond character?

9.38 List the following bonds in order of increasing ionic character: cesium to fluorine, chlorine to chlorine, bromine to chlorine, silicon to carbon.

9.39 Classify the following bonds as ionic, polar covalent, or covalent, and give your reasons: (a) the CC bond in H_3CCH_3, (b) the KI bond in KI, (c) the NB bond in H_3NBCl_3, (d) the CF bond in CF_4.

9.40 Classify the following bonds as ionic, polar covalent, or covalent, and give your reasons: (a) the SiSi bond in $Cl_3SiSiCl_3$, (b) the SiCl bond in $Cl_3SiSiCl_3$, (c) the CaF bond in CaF_2, (d) the NH bond in NH_3.

Lewis Structure and the Octet Rule

Review Questions

9.41 Summarize the essential features of the Lewis octet rule. The octet rule applies mainly to the second-period elements. Explain.

9.42 Explain the concept of formal charge. Do formal charges represent actual separation of charges?

Problems

9.43 Write Lewis structures for the following molecules and ions: (a) NCl_3, (b) OCS, (c) H_2O_2, (d) CH_3COO^-, (e) CN^-, (f) $CH_3CH_2NH_3^+$.

9.44 Write Lewis structures for the following molecules and ions: (a) OF_2, (b) N_2F_2, (c) Si_2H_6, (d) OH^-, (e) CH_2ClCOO^-, (f) $CH_3NH_3^+$.

9.45 Write Lewis structures for the following molecules: (a) ICl, (b) PH_3, (c) P_4 (each P is bonded to three other P atoms), (d) H_2S, (e) N_2H_4, (f) $HClO_3$, (g) $COBr_2$ (C is bonded to O and Br atoms).

9.46 Write Lewis structures for the following ions: (a) O_2^{2-}, (b) C_2^{2-}, (c) NO^+, (d) NH_4^+. Show formal charges.

9.47 The following Lewis structures are incorrect. Explain what is wrong with each one and give a correct Lewis structure for the molecule. (Relative positions of atoms are shown correctly.)

(a) $H-\ddot{C}=\ddot{N}$

(b) $H=C=C=H$

(c) $\ddot{O}-Sn-\ddot{O}$

(d) structure with B, F atoms

(e) $H-\ddot{O}=\ddot{F}$

(f) structure with H, C, F, O atoms

(g) structure with F, N, F atoms

9.48 The skeletal structure of acetic acid shown below is correct, but some of the bonds are wrong. (a) Identify the incorrect bonds and explain what is wrong with them. (b) Write the correct Lewis structure for acetic acid.

The Concept of Resonance

Review Questions

9.49 Define bond length, resonance, and resonance structure. What are the rules for writing resonance structures?

9.50 Is it possible to "trap" a resonance structure of a compound for study? Explain.

Problems

9.51 Write Lewis structures for the following species, including all resonance forms, and show formal charges: (a) HCO_2^-, (b) $CH_2NO_2^-$. Relative positions of the atoms are as follows:

$$\begin{array}{cccc} & O & H & O \\ H & C & & C \quad N \\ & O & H & O \end{array}$$

9.52 Draw three resonance structures for the chlorate ion, ClO_3^-. Show formal charges.

9.53 Write three resonance structures for hydrazoic acid, HN_3. The atomic arrangement is HNNN. Show formal charges.

9.54 Draw two resonance structures for diazomethane, CH_2N_2. Show formal charges. The skeletal structure of the molecule is

$$\begin{array}{c} H \\ \quad\quad C\;\; N\;\; N \\ H \end{array}$$

9.55 Draw three reasonable resonance structures for the OCN^- ion. Show formal charges.

9.56 Draw three resonance structures for the molecule N_2O in which the atoms are arranged in the order NNO. Indicate formal charges.

Exceptions to the Octet Rule
Review Questions

9.57 Why does the octet rule not hold for many compounds containing elements in the third period of the periodic table and beyond?

9.58 Give three examples of compounds that do not satisfy the octet rule. Write a Lewis structure for each.

9.59 Because fluorine has seven valence electrons $(2s^2 2p^5)$, seven covalent bonds in principle could form around the atom. Such a compound might be FH_7 or FCl_7. These compounds have never been prepared. Why?

9.60 What is a coordinate covalent bond? Is it different from a normal covalent bond?

Problems

9.61 The AlI_3 molecule has an incomplete octet around Al. Draw three resonance structures of the molecule in which the octet rule is satisfied for both the Al and the I atoms. Show formal charges.

9.62 In the vapor phase, beryllium chloride consists of discrete $BeCl_2$ molecules. Is the octet rule satisfied for Be in this compound? If not, can you form an octet around Be by drawing another resonance structure? How plausible is this structure?

9.63 Of the noble gases, only Kr, Xe, and Rn are known to form a few compounds with O and/or F. Write Lewis structures for the following molecules: (a) XeF_2, (b) XeF_4, (c) XeF_6, (d) $XeOF_4$, (e) XeO_2F_2. In each case Xe is the central atom.

9.64 Write a Lewis structure for $SbCl_5$. Does this molecule obey the octet rule?

9.65 Write Lewis structures for SeF_4 and SeF_6. Is the octet rule satisfied for Se?

9.66 Write Lewis structures for the reaction

$$AlCl_3 + Cl^- \longrightarrow AlCl_4^-$$

What kind of bond joins Al and Cl in the product?

Bond Enthalpy
Review Questions

9.67 What is bond enthalpy? Bond enthalpies of polyatomic molecules are average values, whereas those of diatomic molecules can be accurately determined. Why?

9.68 Explain why the bond enthalpy of a molecule is usually defined in terms of a gas-phase reaction. Why are bond-breaking processes always endothermic and bond-forming processes always exothermic?

Problems

9.69 From the following data, calculate the average bond enthalpy for the N—H bond:

$$\begin{array}{ll} NH_3(g) \longrightarrow NH_2(g) + H(g) & \Delta H^\circ = 435 \text{ kJ/mol} \\ NH_2(g) \longrightarrow NH(g) + H(g) & \Delta H^\circ = 381 \text{ kJ/mol} \\ NH(g) \longrightarrow N(g) + H(g) & \Delta H^\circ = 360 \text{ kJ/mol} \end{array}$$

9.70 For the reaction

$$O(g) + O_2(g) \longrightarrow O_3(g) \quad \Delta H^\circ = -107.2 \text{ kJ/mol}$$

Calculate the average bond enthalpy in O_3.

9.71 The bond enthalpy of $F_2(g)$ is 156.9 kJ/mol. Calculate ΔH_f° for F(g).

9.72 For the reaction

$$2C_2H_6(g) + 7O_2(g) \longrightarrow 4CO_2(g) + 6H_2O(g)$$

(a) Predict the enthalpy of reaction from the average bond enthalpies in Table 9.4.

(b) Calculate the enthalpy of reaction from the standard enthalpies of formation (see Appendix 3) of the reactant and product molecules, and compare the result with your answer for part (a).

Additional Problems

9.73 Classify the following substances as ionic compounds or covalent compounds containing discrete molecules: CH_4, KF, CO, $SiCl_4$, $BaCl_2$.

9.74 Which of the following are ionic compounds? Which are covalent compounds? RbCl, PF_5, BrF_3, KO_2, CI_4

9.75 Match each of the following energy changes with one of the processes given: ionization energy, electron affinity, bond enthalpy, and standard enthalpy of formation.

(a) $F(g) + e^- \longrightarrow F^-(g)$
(b) $F_2(g) \longrightarrow 2F(g)$
(c) $Na(g) \longrightarrow Na^+(g) + e^-$
(d) $Na(s) + \frac{1}{2}F_2(g) \longrightarrow NaF(s)$

9.76 The formulas for the fluorides of the third-period elements are NaF, MgF_2, AlF_3, SiF_4, PF_5, SF_6, and ClF_3. Classify these compounds as covalent or ionic.

9.77 Use ionization energy (see Table 8.2) and electron affinity values (see Table 8.3) to calculate the energy change (in kJ/mol) for the following reactions:

(a) $Li(g) + I(g) \longrightarrow Li^+(g) + I^-(g)$
(b) $Na(g) + F(g) \longrightarrow Na^+(g) + F^-(g)$
(c) $K(g) + Cl(g) \longrightarrow K^+(g) + Cl^-(g)$

9.78 Describe some characteristics of an ionic compound such as KF that would distinguish it from a covalent compound such as benzene (C_6H_6).

9.79 Write Lewis structures for BrF_3, ClF_5, and IF_7. Identify those in which the octet rule is not obeyed.

9.80 Write three reasonable resonance structures for the azide ion N_3^- in which the atoms are arranged as NNN. Show formal charges.

9.81 The amide group plays an important role in determining the structure of proteins:

$$\begin{array}{c} :O: \\ \| \\ -N-C- \\ | \\ H \end{array}$$

Draw another resonance structure for this group. Show formal charges.

9.82 Give an example of an ion or molecule containing Al that (a) obeys the octet rule, (b) has an expanded octet, and (c) has an incomplete octet.

9.83 Draw four reasonable resonance structures for the PO_3F^{2-} ion. The central P atom is bonded to the three O atoms and to the F atom. Show formal charges.

9.84 Attempts to prepare the compounds listed here as stable species under atmospheric conditions have failed. Suggest possible reasons for the failure. CF_2, LiO_2, $CsCl_2$, PI_5

9.85 Draw reasonable resonance structures for the following ions: (a) HSO_4^-, (b) PO_4^{3-}, (c) HSO_3^-, (d) SO_3^{2-}. (Hint: See comment on p. 383.)

9.86 Are the following statements true or false? (a) Formal charges represent actual separation of charges. (b) ΔH_{rxn}° can be estimated from the bond enthalpies of reactants and products. (c) All second-period elements obey the octet rule in their compounds. (d) The resonance structures of a molecule can be separated from one another.

9.87 A rule for drawing plausible Lewis structures is that the central atom is invariably less electronegative than the surrounding atoms. Explain why this is so.

9.88 Using the following information and the fact that the average C—H bond enthalpy is 414 kJ/mol, estimate the standard enthalpy of formation of methane (CH_4).

$$C(s) \longrightarrow C(g) \quad \Delta H_{rxn}^\circ = 716 \text{ kJ/mol}$$
$$2H_2(g) \longrightarrow 4H(g) \quad \Delta H_{rxn}^\circ = 872.8 \text{ kJ/mol}$$

9.89 Based on energy considerations, which of the following reactions will occur more readily?

(a) $Cl(g) + CH_4(g) \longrightarrow CH_3Cl(g) + H(g)$
(b) $Cl(g) + CH_4(g) \longrightarrow CH_3(g) + HCl(g)$

(Hint: Refer to Table 9.4, and assume that the average bond enthalpy of the C—Cl bond is 338 kJ/mol.)

9.90 Which of the following molecules has the shortest nitrogen-to-nitrogen bond? Explain. N_2H_4, N_2O, N_2, N_2O_4

9.91 Most organic acids can be represented as RCOOH, where COOH is the carboxyl group and R is the rest of the molecule. (For example, R is CH_3 in acetic acid, CH_3COOH). (a) Draw a Lewis structure for the carboxyl group. (b) Upon ionization, the carboxyl group is converted to the carboxylate group, COO^-. Draw resonance structures for the carboxylate group.

9.92 Which of the following species are isoelectronic? NH_4^+, C_6H_6, CO, CH_4, N_2, $B_3N_3H_6$

9.93 The following species have been detected in interstellar space: (a) CH, (b) OH, (c) C_2, (d) HNC, (e) HCO. Draw Lewis structures for these species and indicate whether they are diamagnetic or paramagnetic.

9.94 The amide ion, NH_2^-, is a Brønsted base. Represent the reaction between the amide ion and water.

9.95 Draw Lewis structures for the following organic molecules: (a) tetrafluoroethylene (C_2F_4), (b) propane (C_3H_8), (c) butadiene ($CH_2CHCHCH_2$), (d) propyne (CH_3CCH), (e) benzoic acid (C_6H_5COOH). (To draw C_6H_5COOH, replace a H atom in benzene with a COOH group.)

9.96 The triiodide ion (I_3^-) in which the I atoms are arranged in a straight line is stable, but the corresponding F_3^- ion does not exist. Explain.

9.97 Compare the bond enthalpy of F_2 with the energy change for the following process:

$$F_2(g) \longrightarrow F^+(g) + F^-(g)$$

Which is the preferred dissociation for F_2, energetically speaking?

9.98 Methyl isocyanate (CH_3NCO) is used to make certain pesticides. In December 1984, water leaked into a tank containing this substance at a chemical plant, producing a toxic cloud that killed thousands of people in Bhopal, India. Draw Lewis structures for CH_3NCO, showing formal charges.

9.99 The chlorine nitrate molecule ($ClONO_2$) is believed to be involved in the destruction of ozone in the Antarctic stratosphere. Draw a plausible Lewis structure for this molecule.

9.100 Several resonance structures for the molecule CO_2 are shown next. Explain why some of them are likely to be of little importance in describing the bonding in this molecule.

(a) $\ddot{O}=C=\ddot{O}$

(c) $:\overset{+}{\ddot{O}}\equiv C \;\;\ddot{\ddot{O}}:$

(b) $:\overset{+}{O}\equiv C-\overset{..}{\underset{..}{O}}:^{-}$

(d) $:\overset{-}{\underset{..}{O}}-\overset{2+}{C}-\overset{-}{\underset{..}{O}}:$

9.101 For each of the following organic molecules draw a Lewis structure in which the carbon atoms are bonded to each other by single bonds: (a) C_2H_6, (b) C_4H_{10}, (c) C_5H_{12}. For (b) and (c), show only structures in which each C atom is bonded to no more than two other C atoms.

9.102 Draw Lewis structures for the following chlorofluorocarbons (CFCs), which are partly responsible for the depletion of ozone in the stratosphere: (a) $CFCl_3$, (b) CF_2Cl_2, (c) CHF_2Cl, (d) CF_3CHF_2.

9.103 Draw Lewis structures for the following organic molecules. In each there is one $C=C$ bond, and the rest of the carbon atoms are joined by $C-C$ bonds. C_2H_3F, C_3H_6, C_4H_8.

9.104 Calculate ΔH° for the reaction

$$H_2(g) + I_2(g) \longrightarrow 2HI(g)$$

using (a) Equation (9.3) and (b) Equation (6.18), given that ΔH_f° for $I_2(g)$ is 61.0 kJ/mol.

9.105 Draw Lewis structures for the following organic molecules: (a) methanol (CH_3OH); (b) ethanol (CH_3CH_2OH); (c) tetraethyllead [$Pb(CH_2CH_3)_4$], which is used in "leaded gasoline"; (d) methylamine (CH_3NH_2), which is used in tanning; (e) mustard gas ($ClCH_2CH_2SCH_2CH_2Cl$), a poisonous gas used in World War I; (f) urea [$(NH_2)_2CO$], a fertilizer; and (g) glycine (NH_2CH_2COOH), an amino acid.

9.106 Write Lewis structures for the following four isoelectronic species: (a) CO, (b) NO^+, (c) CN^-, (d) N_2. Show formal charges.

9.107 Oxygen forms three types of ionic compounds in which the anions are oxide (O^{2-}), peroxide (O_2^{2-}), and superoxide (O_2^-). Draw Lewis structures of these ions.

9.108 Comment on the correctness of the statement, "All compounds containing a noble gas atom violate the octet rule."

9.109 Write three resonance structures for (a) the cyanate ion (NCO^-) and (b) the isocyanate ion (CNO^-). In each case, rank the resonance structures in order of increasing importance.

9.110 (a) From the following data calculate the bond enthalpy of the F_2^- ion.

$F_2(g) \longrightarrow 2F(g)$	$\Delta H_{rxn}^{\circ} = 156.9$ kJ/mol
$F^-(g) \longrightarrow F(g) + e^-$	$\Delta H_{rxn}^{\circ} = 333$ kJ/mol
$F_2^-(g) \longrightarrow F_2(g) + e^-$	$\Delta H_{rxn}^{\circ} = 290$ kJ/mol

(b) Explain the difference between the bond enthalpies of F_2 and F_2^-.

9.111 The resonance concept is sometimes described by analogy to a mule, which is a cross between a horse and a donkey. Compare this analogy with the one used in this chapter, that is, the description of a rhinoceros as a cross between a griffin and a unicorn. Which description is more appropriate? Why?

9.112 What are the other two reasons for choosing (b) in Example 9.7?

9.113 In the Chemistry in Action essay on p. 384, nitric oxide is said to be one of about 10 of the smallest stable molecules known. Based on what you have learned in the course so far, write all the diatomic molecules you know, give their names, and show their Lewis structures.

9.114 The $N-O$ bond distance in nitric oxide is 115 pm, which is intermediate between a triple bond (106 pm) and a double bond (120 pm). (a) Draw two resonance structures for NO and comment on their relative importance. (b) Is it possible to draw a resonance structure having a triple bond between the atoms?

9.115 Although nitrogen dioxide (NO_2) is a stable compound, there is a tendency for two such molecules to combine to form dinitrogen tetroxide (N_2O_4). Why? Draw four resonance structures of N_2O_4, showing formal charges.

9.116 Another possible skeletal structure for the CO_3^{2-} (carbonate) ion besides the one presented in Example 9.5 is O C O O. Why would we not use this structure to represent CO_3^{2-}?

9.117 Draw a Lewis structure for nitrogen pentoxide (N_2O_5) in which each N is bonded to three O atoms.

9.118 In the gas phase, aluminum chloride exists as a dimer (a unit of two) with the formula Al_2Cl_6. Its skeletal structure is given by

Complete the Lewis structure and indicate the coordinate covalent bonds in the molecule.

9.119 The hydroxyl radical (OH) plays an important role in atmospheric chemistry. It is highly reactive and has a tendency to combine with a H atom from other compounds, causing them to break up. Thus, OH is sometimes called a "detergent" radical because it helps to clean up the atmosphere. (a) Write the Lewis structure for the radical. (b) Refer to Table 9.4 and explain why the radical has a high affinity for H atoms. (c) Estimate the enthalpy change for the following reaction:

$$OH(g) + CH_4(g) \longrightarrow CH_3(g) + H_2O(g)$$

(d) The radical is generated when sunlight hits water vapor. Calculate the maximum wavelength (in nanometers) required to break an $O-H$ bond in H_2O.

9.120 Experiments show that it takes 1656 kJ/mol to break all the bonds in methane (CH_4) and 4006 kJ/mol to break all the bonds in propane (C_3H_8). Based on these data, calculate the average bond enthalpy of the C—C bond.

9.121 Draw three resonance structures of sulfur dioxide (SO_2). Indicate the most plausible structure(s). (*Hint:* See Example 9.11.)

9.122 Vinyl chloride (C_2H_3Cl) differs from ethylene (C_2H_4) in that one of the H atoms is replaced with a Cl atom. Vinyl chloride is used to prepare poly(vinyl chloride), which is an important polymer used in pipes. (a) Draw the Lewis structure of vinyl chloride. (b) The repeating unit in poly(vinyl chloride) is —CH_2—CHCl—. Draw a portion of the molecule showing three such repeating units. (c) Calculate the enthalpy change when 1.0×10^3 kg of vinyl chloride forms poly(vinyl chloride).

9.123 In 1998 scientists using a special type of electron microscope were able to measure the force needed to break a *single* chemical bond. If 2.0×10^{-9} N was needed to break a C—Si bond, estimate the bond enthalpy in kJ/mol. Assume that the bond had to be stretched by a distance of 2 Å (2×10^{-10} m) before it is broken.

9.124 The American chemist Robert S. Mulliken suggested a different definition for the electronegativity (EN) of an element, given by

$$EN = \frac{IE + EA}{2}$$

where IE is the first ionization energy and EA the electron affinity of the element. Calculate the electronegativities of O, F, and Cl using the above equation. Compare the electronegativities of these elements on the Mulliken and Pauling scale. (To convert to the Pauling scale, divide each EN value by 230 kJ/mol.)

9.125 Among the common inhaled anesthetics are:

halothane: $CF_3CHClBr$
enflurane: $CHFClCF_2OCHF_2$
isoflurane: $CF_3CHClOCHF_2$
methoxyflurane: $CHCl_2CF_2OCH_3$

Draw Lewis structures of these molecules.

9.126 A student in your class claims that magnesium oxide actually consists of Mg^+ and O^- ions, not Mg^{2+} and O^{2-} ions. Suggest some experiments one could do to show that your classmate is wrong.

Special Problems

9.127 Sulfuric acid (H_2SO_4), the most important industrial chemical in the world, is prepared by oxidizing sulfur to sulfur dioxide and then to sulfur trioxide. Although sulfur trioxide reacts with water to form sulfuric acid, it forms a mist of fine droplets of H_2SO_4 with water vapor that is hard to condense. Instead, sulfur trioxide is first dissolved in 98 percent sulfuric acid to form oleum ($H_2S_2O_7$). On treatment with water, concentrated sulfuric acid can be generated. Write equations for all the steps and draw Lewis structures of oleum based on the discussion in Example 9.11.

9.128 From the lattice energy of KCl in Table 9.1 and the ionization energy of K and electron affinity of Cl in Tables 8.2 and 8.3, calculate the $\Delta H°$ for the reaction

$$K(g) + Cl(g) \longrightarrow KCl(s)$$

9.129 The species H_3^+ is the simplest polyatomic ion. The geometry of the ion is that of an equilateral triangle. (a) Draw three resonance structures to represent the ion. (b) Given the following information

$$2H + H^+ \longrightarrow H_3^+ \quad \Delta H° = -849 \text{ kJ/mol}$$

and

$$H_2 \longrightarrow 2H \quad \Delta H° = 436.4 \text{ kJ/mol}$$

calculate $\Delta H°$ for the reaction

$$H^+ + H_2 \longrightarrow H_3^+$$

9.130 The bond enthalpy of the C—N bond in the amide group of proteins (see Problem 9.81) can be treated as an average of C—N and C=N bonds. Calculate the maximum wavelength of light needed to break the bond.

9.131 In 1999 an unusual cation containing only nitrogen (N_5^+) was prepared. Draw three resonance structures of the ion, showing formal charges. (*Hint:* The N atoms are joined in a linear fashion.)

9.132 Nitroglycerin, one of the most commonly used explosives, has the following structure

$$
\begin{array}{l}
CH_2ONO_2 \\
| \\
CHONO_2 \\
| \\
CH_2ONO_2
\end{array}
$$

The decomposition reaction is

$$4C_3H_5N_3O_9(l) \longrightarrow$$
$$12CO_2(g) + 10H_2O(g) + 6N_2(g) + O_2(g)$$

The explosive action is the result of the heat released and the large increase in gaseous volume. (a) Calculate the $\Delta H°$ for the decomposition of one mole of nitroglycerin using both standard enthalpy of formation values and bond enthalpies. Assume that the two O atoms in the NO_2 groups are attached to N with one single bond and one double bond. (b) Calculate the combined volume of the gases at STP. (c) Assuming an initial explosion temperature of 3000 K, estimate the pressure exerted by the gases using the result from (b). (The standard enthalpy of formation of nitroglycerin is -371.1 kJ/mol.)

Answers to Practice Exercises

9.1 $\cdot Ba \cdot + 2 \cdot H \longrightarrow Ba^{2+} \ 2H:^-$ (or BaH_2)
   [Xe]$6s^2$ $1s^1$ [Xe] [He]

9.2 (a) Ionic, (b) polar covalent, (c) covalent.

9.3 $\ddot{S}{=}C{=}\ddot{S}$ **9.4** $H{-}\overset{\displaystyle \overset{..}{O}\!\!:}{\overset{\|}{C}}{-}\ddot{O}{-}H$ **9.5** $\left[\ddot{O}{=}\overset{..}{N}{-}\ddot{O}:\right]^-$

9.6 $\ddot{O}{=}\overset{..}{N}{-}\ddot{O}:$ **9.7** $H{-}C{\equiv}N:$

9.8 $\ddot{O}{=}\overset{..}{N}{-}\ddot{O}:^- \longleftrightarrow {}^-:\ddot{O}{-}\overset{..}{N}{=}\ddot{O}$

9.9 $:\!\ddot{F}{-}Be{-}\ddot{F}\!:$

9.10 $:\!\underset{\displaystyle :\ddot{F}:}{\overset{\displaystyle :\ddot{F}:}{F}}{-}As\!\!\begin{smallmatrix} \ddot{F}: \\[2pt] \ddot{F}: \end{smallmatrix}$ **9.11** $H{-}\ddot{O}{-}\overset{\displaystyle \overset{:O:}{\|}}{\underset{\displaystyle \underset{:O:}{\|}}{S}}{-}\ddot{O}{-}H$

9.12 $\begin{smallmatrix} :\ddot{F} \\ \end{smallmatrix}\!\!\diagdown\!\!\begin{smallmatrix} \ddot{F}: \\ \end{smallmatrix} \\ \quad S \\ :\ddot{F}\!\!\diagup\!\!\diagdown\!\!\ddot{F}:$

9.13 (a) -543.1 kJ/mol, (b) -543.2 kJ/mol.

9.14 (a) -119 kJ/mol, (b) -137.0 kJ/mol.

10

Electrostatic potential map showing the buildup of electron density (red color) between the nuclei as two hydrogen atoms approach each other to form a hydrogen molecule. The models show hydrogen atoms and hydrogen molecules.

Chemical Bonding II
Molecular Geometry and Hybridization of Atomic Orbitals

A LOOK AHEAD

- We first examine the role of chemical bonds and lone pairs on the geometry of a molecule in terms of a simple approach called the VSEPR model (10.1)

- We then learn the factors that determine whether a molecule possesses a dipole moment and how its measurement can help us in the study of molecular geometry. (10.2)

- Next, we learn a quantum mechanical approach, called the valence bond (VB) theory, in the study of chemical bonds. The VB theory explains why and how chemical bonds form in terms of atomic orbital overlaps. (10.3)

- We see that the VB approach, in terms of the concept of mixing or hybridization of atomic orbitals, accounts for both chemical bond formation and molecular geometry. (10.4 and 10.5)

- We then examine another quantum mechanical treatment of the chemical bond, called the molecular orbital (MO) theory. The MO theory considers the formation of molecular orbitals as a result of the overlap of atomic orbitals, and is able to explain the paramagnetism of the oxygen molecule. (10.6)

- We see that writing molecular orbital configuration is analogous to writing electron configuration for atoms in that both the Pauli exclusion principle and Hund's rule apply. Using homonuclear diatomic molecules as examples, we can learn about the strength of a bond as well as general magnetic properties from the molecular orbital configurations. (10.7)

- Finally, the concept of molecular orbital formation is extended to delocalized molecular orbitals, which cover three or more atoms. We see that these delocalized orbitals impart extra stability to molecules like benzene. (10.8)

In Chapter 9 we discussed bonding in terms of the Lewis theory. Here we will study the shape, or geometry, of molecules. Geometry has an important influence on the physical and chemical properties of molecules, such as melting point, boiling point, and reactivity. We will see that we can predict the shapes of molecules with considerable accuracy using a simple method based on Lewis structures.

The Lewis theory of chemical bonding, although useful and easy to apply, does not tell us how and why bonds form. A proper understanding of bonding comes from quantum mechanics. Therefore, in the second part of this chapter, we will apply quantum mechanics to the study of the geometry and stability of molecules.

10.1 Molecular Geometry

Molecular geometry is the three-dimensional arrangement of atoms in a molecule. A molecule's geometry affects its physical and chemical properties, such as melting point, boiling point, density, and the types of reactions it undergoes. In general, bond lengths and bond angles must be determined by experiment. However, there is a simple procedure that enables us to predict with considerable success the overall geometry of a molecule or ion if we know the number of electrons surrounding a central atom in its Lewis structure. The basis of this approach is the assumption that electron pairs in the valence shell of an atom repel one another. The *valence shell* is *the outermost electron-occupied shell of an atom; it holds the electrons that are usually involved in bonding.* In a covalent bond, a pair of electrons, often called the *bonding pair,* is responsible for holding two atoms together. However, in a polyatomic molecule, where there are two or more bonds between the central atom and the surrounding atoms, the repulsion between electrons in different bonding pairs causes them to remain as far apart as possible. The geometry that the molecule ultimately assumes (as defined by the positions of all the atoms) minimizes the repulsion. This approach to the study of molecular geometry is called the *valence-shell electron-pair repulsion (VSEPR) model,* because *it accounts for the geometric arrangements of electron pairs around a central atom in terms of the electrostatic repulsion between electron pairs.*

Two general rules govern the use of the VSEPR model:

1. As far as electron-pair repulsion is concerned, double bonds and triple bonds can be treated like single bonds. This approximation is good for qualitative purposes. However, you should realize that in reality multiple bonds are "larger" than single bonds; that is, because there are two or three bonds between two atoms, the electron density occupies more space.

2. If a molecule has two or more resonance structures, we can apply the VSEPR model to any one of them. Formal charges are usually not shown.

With this model in mind, we can predict the geometry of molecules (and ions) in a systematic way. For this purpose, it is convenient to divide molecules into two categories, according to whether or not the central atom has lone pairs.

Molecules in Which the Central Atom Has No Lone Pairs

For simplicity we will consider molecules that contain atoms of only two elements, A and B, of which A is the central atom. These molecules have the general formula AB_x, where x is an integer 2, 3, ... (If $x = 1$, we have the diatomic molecule AB, which is linear by definition.) In the vast majority of cases, x is between 2 and 6.

Table 10.1 shows five possible arrangements of electron pairs around the central atom A. As a result of mutual repulsion, the electron pairs stay as far from one another as possible. Note that the table shows arrangements of the electron pairs but not the positions of the atoms that surround the central atom. Molecules in which the central atom has no lone pairs have one of these five arrangements of bonding pairs. Using Table 10.1 as a reference, let us take a close look at the geometry of molecules with the formulas AB_2, AB_3, AB_4, AB_5, and AB_6.

AB_2: Beryllium Chloride ($BeCl_2$)

The Lewis structure of beryllium chloride in the gaseous state is

$$:\!\ddot{C}l\!-\!Be\!-\!\ddot{C}l\!:$$

The term "central atom" means an atom that is not a terminal atom in a polyatomic molecule.

VSEPR is pronounced "vesper."

Animation:
VSEPR
ARIS, Animations

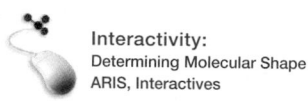
Interactivity:
Determining Molecular Shape
ARIS, Interactives

| TABLE 10.1 | Arrangement of Electron Pairs About a Central Atom (A) in a Molecule and Geometry of Some Simple Molecules and Ions in Which the Central Atom Has No Lone Pairs | | |

Number of Electron Pairs	Arrangement of Electron Pairs*	Molecular Geometry*	Examples
2	180° :⎯A⎯: Linear	B⎯A⎯B Linear	$BeCl_2$, $HgCl_2$
3	120° Trigonal planar	Trigonal planar	BF_3
4	109.5° Tetrahedral	Tetrahedral	CH_4, NH_4^+
5	90° 120° Trigonal bipyramidal	Trigonal bipyramidal	PCl_5
6	90° 90° Octahedral	Octahedral	SF_6

*The colored lines are used only to show the overall shapes; they do not represent bonds.

Because the bonding pairs repel each other, they must be at opposite ends of a straight line in order for them to be as far apart as possible. Thus, the ClBeCl angle is predicted to be 180°, and the molecule is linear (see Table 10.1). The "ball-and-stick" model of $BeCl_2$ is

180°

The blue and yellow spheres are for atoms in general.

AB₃: Boron Trifluoride (BF₃)

Boron trifluoride contains three covalent bonds, or bonding pairs. In the most stable arrangement, the three BF bonds point to the corners of an equilateral triangle with B in the center of the triangle:

$$
\begin{array}{c}
:\ddot{F}: \\
| \\
B \\
:\ddot{F} \qquad \ddot{F}:
\end{array}
$$

According to Table 10.1, the geometry of BF₃ is *trigonal planar* because the three end atoms are at the corners of an equilateral triangle which is planar:

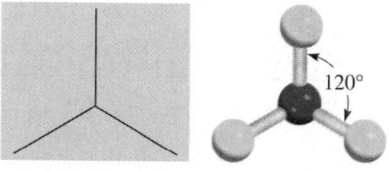

Planar

Thus, each of the three FBF angles is 120°, and all four atoms lie in the same plane.

AB₄: Methane (CH₄)

The Lewis structure of methane is

$$
\begin{array}{c}
H \\
| \\
H-C-H \\
| \\
H
\end{array}
$$

Because there are four bonding pairs, the geometry of CH₄ is tetrahedral (see Table 10.1). A *tetrahedron* has four sides (the prefix *tetra* means "four"), or faces, all of which are equilateral triangles. In a tetrahedral molecule, the central atom (C in this case) is located at the center of the tetrahedron and the other four atoms are at the corners. The bond angles are all 109.5°.

Tetrahedral

AB₅: Phosphorus Pentachloride (PCl₅)

The Lewis structure of phosphorus pentachloride (in the gas phase) is

$$
\begin{array}{c}
:\ddot{C}l \quad :\ddot{C}l: \\
\diagdown \quad | \\
P-\ddot{C}l: \\
\diagup \quad | \\
:\ddot{C}l \quad :\ddot{C}l:
\end{array}
$$

The only way to minimize the repulsive forces among the five bonding pairs is to arrange the PCl bonds in the form of a trigonal bipyramid (see Table 10.1). A trigonal bipyramid can be generated by joining two tetrahedrons along a common triangular base:

Trigonal
bipyramidal

The central atom (P in this case) is at the center of the common triangle with the surrounding atoms positioned at the five corners of the trigonal bipyramid. The atoms that are above and below the triangular plane are said to occupy *axial* positions, and those that are in the triangular plane are said to occupy *equatorial* positions. The angle between any two equatorial bonds is 120°; that between an axial bond and an equatorial bond is 90°, and that between the two axial bonds is 180°.

AB_6: Sulfur Hexafluoride (SF_6)

The Lewis structure of sulfur hexafluoride is

$$\begin{array}{ccc}
 & :\overset{\cdot\cdot}{F}: & \\
:\overset{\cdot\cdot}{F} & | & \overset{\cdot\cdot}{F}: \\
 & \diagdown S \diagup & \\
:\overset{\cdot\cdot}{F} & | & \overset{\cdot\cdot}{F}: \\
 & :\overset{\cdot\cdot}{F}: &
\end{array}$$

The most stable arrangement of the six SF bonding pairs is in the shape of an octahedron, shown in Table 10.1. An octahedron has eight sides (the prefix *octa* means "eight"). It can be generated by joining two square pyramids on a common base. The central atom (S in this case) is at the center of the square base and the surrounding atoms are at the six corners. All bond angles are 90° except the one made by the bonds between the central atom and the pairs of atoms that are diametrically opposite each other. That angle is 180°. Because the six bonds are equivalent in an octahedral molecule, we cannot use the terms "axial" and "equatorial" as in a trigonal bipyramidal molecule.

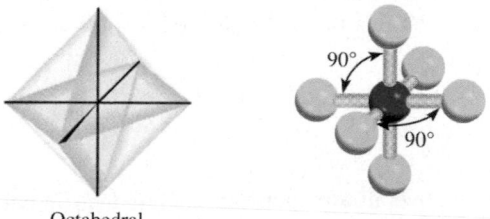

Octahedral

Molecules in Which the Central Atom Has One or More Lone Pairs

Determining the geometry of a molecule is more complicated if the central atom has both lone pairs and bonding pairs. In such molecules there are three types of repulsive forces—those between bonding pairs, those between lone pairs, and those between a bonding pair and a lone pair. In general, according to the VSEPR model, the repulsive forces decrease in the following order:

lone-pair vs. lone-pair > lone-pair vs. bonding- > bonding-pair vs. bonding-
      repulsion   pair repulsion   pair repulsion

Electrons in a bond are held by the attractive forces exerted by the nuclei of the two bonded atoms. These electrons have less "spatial distribution" than lone pairs; that is, they take up less space than lone-pair electrons, which are associated with only one particular atom. Because lone-pair electrons in a molecule occupy more space, they experience greater repulsion from neighboring lone pairs and bonding pairs. To keep track of the total number of bonding pairs and lone pairs, we designate molecules with lone pairs as AB_xE_y, where A is the central atom, B is a surrounding atom, and E is a lone pair on A. Both x and y are integers; $x = 2, 3, \ldots$, and $y = 1, 2, \ldots$. Thus, the values of x and y indicate the number of surrounding atoms and number of lone pairs on the central atom, respectively. The simplest such molecule would be a triatomic molecule with one lone pair on the central atom and the formula is AB_2E.

For $x = 1$ we have a diatomic molecule, which by definition has a linear geometry.

As the following examples show, in most cases the presence of lone pairs on the central atom makes it difficult to predict the bond angles accurately.

AB_2E: Sulfur Dioxide (SO_2)

The Lewis structure of sulfur dioxide is

$$\ddot{\text{O}}=\ddot{\text{S}}=\ddot{\text{O}}$$

Because VSEPR treats double bonds as though they were single, the SO_2 molecule can be viewed as consisting of three electron pairs on the central S atom. Of these, two are bonding pairs and one is a lone pair. In Table 10.1 we see that the overall arrangement of three electron pairs is trigonal planar. But because one of the electron pairs is a lone pair, the SO_2 molecule has a "bent" shape.

$$\ddot{\text{O}}\diagdown\overset{\textstyle\ddot{\text{S}}}{}\diagup\ddot{\text{O}}$$

SO₂

Because the lone-pair versus bonding-pair repulsion is greater than the bonding-pair versus bonding-pair repulsion, the two sulfur-to-oxygen bonds are pushed together slightly and the OSO angle is less than 120°.

AB_3E: Ammonia (NH_3)

The ammonia molecule contains three bonding pairs and one lone pair:

$$\text{H}-\overset{\displaystyle ..}{\underset{\displaystyle |}{\text{N}}}-\text{H}$$
$$\text{H}$$

As Table 10.1 shows, the overall arrangement of four electron pairs is tetrahedral. But in NH_3 one of the electron pairs is a lone pair, so the geometry of NH_3 is trigonal pyramidal (so called because it looks like a pyramid, with the N atom at the apex). Because the lone pair repels the bonding pairs more strongly, the three NH bonding pairs are pushed closer together:

$$\overset{\displaystyle ..}{\text{N}}$$
$$\text{H}\underset{\displaystyle \text{H}}{\diagup|\diagdown}\text{H}$$

Thus, the HNH angle in ammonia is smaller than the ideal tetrahedral angle of 109.5° (Figure 10.1).

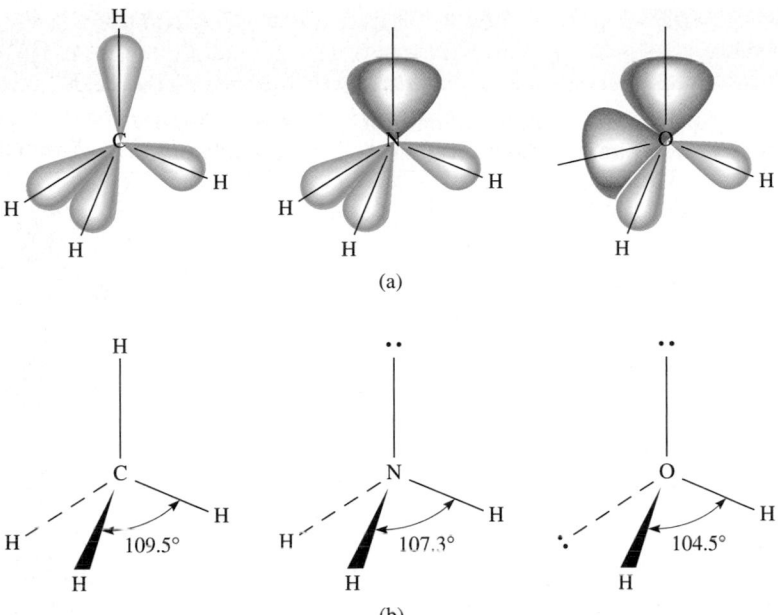

Figure 10.1 *(a) The relative sizes of bonding pairs and lone pairs in CH_4, NH_3, and H_2O. (b) The bond angles in CH_4, NH_3, and H_2O. Note that the dashed lines represent bond axes behind the plane of the paper, the wedged lines represent bond axes in front of the plane of the paper, and the thin solid lines represent bonds in the plane of the paper.*

AB_2E_2: Water (H_2O)

A water molecule contains two bonding pairs and two lone pairs:

$$H-\ddot{O}-H$$

The overall arrangement of the four electron pairs in water is tetrahedral, the same as in ammonia. However, unlike ammonia, water has two lone pairs on the central O atom. These lone pairs tend to be as far from each other as possible. Consequently, the two OH bonding pairs are pushed toward each other, and we predict an even greater deviation from the tetrahedral angle than in NH_3. As Figure 10.1 shows, the HOH angle is 104.5°. The geometry of H_2O is bent:

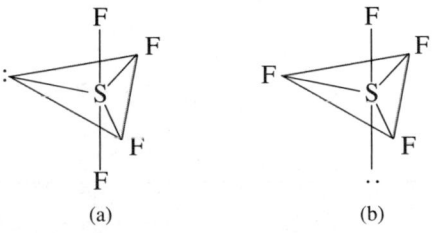

AB_4E: Sulfur Tetrafluoride (SF_4)

The Lewis structure of SF_4 is

The central sulfur atom has five electron pairs whose arrangement, according to Table 10.1, is trigonal bipyramidal. In the SF_4 molecule, however, one of the electron pairs is a lone pair, so the molecule must have one of the following geometries:

SF_4

| TABLE 10.2 | Geometry of Simple Molecules and Ions in Which the Central Atom Has One or More Lone Pairs | | | | | |

Class of Molecule	Total Number of Electron Pairs	Number of Bonding Pairs	Number of Lone Pairs	Arrangement of Electron Pairs*	Geometry of Molecule or Ion	Examples
AB_2E	3	2	1	Trigonal planar	Bent	SO_2
AB_3E	4	3	1	Tetrahedral	Trigonal pyramidal	NH_3
AB_2E_2	4	2	2	Tetrahedral	Bent	H_2O
AB_4E	5	4	1	Trigonal bipyramidal	Distorted tetrahedron (or seesaw)	SF_4
AB_3E_2	5	3	2	Trigonal bipyramidal	T-shaped	ClF_3
AB_2E_3	5	2	3	Trigonal bipyramidal	Linear	I_3^-
AB_5E	6	5	1	Octahedral	Square pyramidal	BrF_5
AB_4E_2	6	4	2	Octahedral	Square planar	XeF_4

*The colored lines are used to show the overall shape, not bonds.

In (a) the lone pair occupies an equatorial position, and in (b) it occupies an axial position. The axial position has three neighboring pairs at 90° and one at 180°, while the equatorial position has two neighboring pairs at 90° and two more at 120°. The repulsion is smaller for (a), and indeed (a) is the structure observed experimentally. This shape is sometimes described as a distorted tetrahedron (or seesaw if you turn the structure 90° to the right to view it). The angle between the axial F atoms and S is 173°, and that between the equatorial F atoms and S is 102°.

Table 10.2 shows the geometries of simple molecules in which the central atom has one or more lone pairs, including some that we have not discussed.

Geometry of Molecules with More Than One Central Atom

So far we have discussed the geometry of molecules having only one central atom. The overall geometry of molecules with more than one central atom is difficult to define in most cases. Often we can only describe the shape around each of the central atoms. For example, consider methanol, CH_3OH, whose Lewis structure is shown below:

$$H-\overset{\overset{\displaystyle H}{|}}{\underset{\underset{\displaystyle H}{|}}{C}}-\overset{..}{\underset{..}{O}}-H$$

The two central (nonterminal) atoms in methanol are C and O. We can say that the three CH and the CO bonding pairs are tetrahedrally arranged about the C atom. The HCH and OCH bond angles are approximately 109°. The O atom here is like the one in water in that it has two lone pairs and two bonding pairs. Therefore, the HOC portion of the molecule is bent, and the angle HOC is approximately equal to 105° (Figure 10.2).

Figure 10.2 *The geometry of CH_3OH.*

Guidelines for Applying the VSEPR Model

Having studied the geometries of molecules in two categories (central atoms with and without lone pairs), let us consider some rules for applying the VSEPR model to all types of molecules:

1. Write the Lewis structure of the molecule, considering only the electron pairs around the central atom (that is, the atom that is bonded to more than one other atom).

2. Count the number of electron pairs around the central atom (bonding pairs and lone pairs). Treat double and triple bonds as though they were single bonds. Refer to Table 10.1 to predict the overall arrangement of the electron pairs.

3. Use Tables 10.1 and 10.2 to predict the geometry of the molecule.

4. In predicting bond angles, note that a lone pair repels another lone pair or a bonding pair more strongly than a bonding pair repels another bonding pair. Remember that in general there is no easy way to predict bond angles accurately when the central atom possesses one or more lone pairs.

The VSEPR model generates reliable predictions of the geometries of a variety of molecular structures. Chemists use the VSEPR approach because of its simplicity. Although there are some theoretical concerns about whether "electron-pair repulsion" actually determines molecular shapes, the assumption that it does leads to useful (and generally reliable) predictions. We need not ask more of any model at this stage in the study of chemistry. Example 10.1 illustrates the application of VSEPR.

Example 10.1

Use the VSEPR model to predict the geometry of the following molecules and ions: (a) AsH_3, (b) OF_2, (c) $AlCl_4^-$, (d) I_3^-, (e) C_2H_4.

Strategy The sequence of steps in determining molecular geometry is as follows:

draw Lewis $\longrightarrow$ find arrangement of $\longrightarrow$ find arrangement $\longrightarrow$ determine geometry
   structure   electron pairs   of bonding pairs   based on bonding pairs

Solution (a) The Lewis structure of AsH_3 is

$$H\!-\!\overset{..}{As}\!-\!H$$
$$\underset{\displaystyle H}{|}$$

AsH_3

There are four electron pairs around the central atom; therefore, the electron pair arrangement is tetrahedral (see Table 10.1). Recall that the geometry of a molecule is determined only by the arrangement of atoms (in this case the As and H atoms). Thus, removing the lone pair leaves us with three bonding pairs and a trigonal pyramidal geometry, like NH_3. We cannot predict the HAsH angle accurately, but we know that it is less than 109.5° because the repulsion of the bonding electron pairs in the As—H bonds by the lone pair on As is greater than the repulsion between the bonding pairs.

(b) The Lewis structure of OF_2 is

$$:\!\overset{..}{\underset{..}{F}}\!-\!\overset{..}{\underset{..}{O}}\!-\!\overset{..}{\underset{..}{F}}\!:$$

OF_2

There are four electron pairs around the central atom; therefore, the electron pair arrangement is tetrahedral (see Table 10.1). Recall that the geometry of a molecule is determined only by the arrangement of atoms (in this case the O and F atoms). Thus, removing the two lone pairs leaves us with two bonding pairs and a bent geometry, like H_2O. We cannot predict the FOF angle accurately, but we know that it must be less than 109.5° because the repulsion of the bonding electron pairs in the O—F bonds by the lone pairs on O is greater than the repulsion between the bonding pairs.

(c) The Lewis structure of $AlCl_4^-$ is

$$\left[\begin{array}{c} :\overset{..}{Cl}: \\ | \\ :\overset{..}{\underset{..}{Cl}}\!-\!Al\!-\!\overset{..}{\underset{..}{Cl}}: \\ | \\ :\overset{..}{\underset{..}{Cl}}: \end{array}\right]^-$$

$AlCl_4^-$

There are four electron pairs around the central atom; therefore, the electron pair arrangement is tetrahedral. Because there are no lone pairs present, the arrangement of the bonding pairs is the same as the electron pair arrangement. Therefore, $AlCl_4^-$ has a tetrahedral geometry and the ClAlCl angles are all 109.5°.

(d) The Lewis structure of I_3^- is

$$\left[:\overset{..}{\underset{..}{I}}\!-\!\overset{..}{\underset{..}{I}}\!-\!\overset{..}{\underset{..}{I}}:\right]^-$$

I_3^-

(Continued)

There are five electron pairs around the central I atom; therefore, the electron pair arrangement is trigonal bipyramidal. Of the five electron pairs, three are lone pairs and two are bonding pairs. Recall that the lone pairs preferentially occupy the equatorial positions in a trigonal bipyramid (see Table 10.2). Thus, removing the lone pairs leaves us with a linear geometry for I_3^-, that is, all three I atoms lie in a straight line.

(e) The Lewis structure of C_2H_4 is

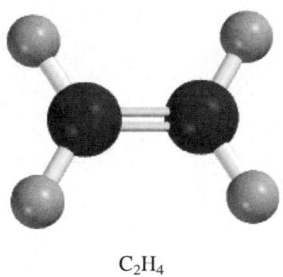

C_2H_4

The C=C bond is treated as though it were a single bond in the VSEPR model. Because there are three electron pairs around each C atom and there are no lone pairs present, the arrangement around each C atom has a trigonal planar shape like BF_3, discussed earlier. Thus, the predicted bond angles in C_2H_4 are all 120°.

Comment (1) The I_3^- ion is one of the few structures for which the bond angle (180°) can be predicted accurately even though the central atom contains lone pairs. (2) In C_2H_4, all six atoms lie in the same plane. The overall planar geometry is not predicted by the VSEPR model, but we will see why the molecule prefers to be planar later. In reality, the angles are close, but not equal, to 120° because the bonds are not all equivalent.

Similar problems: 10.7, 10.8, 10.9.

Practice Exercise Use the VSEPR model to predict the geometry of (a) $SiBr_4$, (b) CS_2, and (c) NO_3^-.

10.2 Dipole Moments

In Section 9.4 we learned that hydrogen fluoride is a covalent compound with a polar bond. There is a shift of electron density from H to F because the F atom is more electronegative than the H atom (see Figure 9.4). The shift of electron density is symbolized by placing a crossed arrow (+—→) above the Lewis structure to indicate the direction of the shift. For example,

The consequent charge separation can be represented as

where δ (delta) denotes a partial charge. This separation of charges can be confirmed in an electric field (Figure 10.3). When the field is turned on, HF molecules orient their negative ends toward the positive plate and their positive ends toward the negative plate. This alignment of molecules can be detected experimentally.

A quantitative measure of the polarity of a bond is its **dipole moment (μ),** which is *the product of the charge Q and the distance r between the charges:*

$$\mu = Q \times r \tag{10.1}$$

Figure 10.3 *Behavior of polar molecules (a) in the absence of an external electric field and (b) when the electric field is turned on. Nonpolar molecules are not affected by an electric field.*

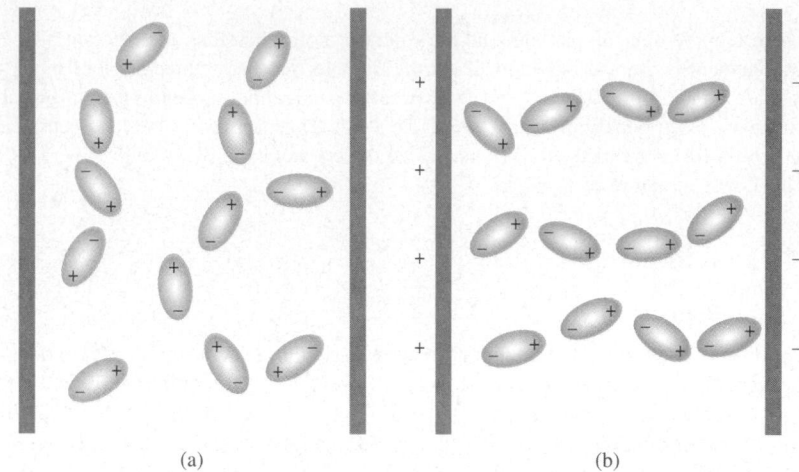

(a)   (b)

In a diatomic molecule like HF, the charge Q is equal to $\delta+$ and $\delta-$.

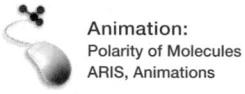

Animation:
Polarity of Molecules
ARIS, Animations

Each carbon-to-oxygen bond is polar, with the electron density shifted toward the more electronegative oxygen atom. However, the linear geometry of the molecule results in the cancellation of the two bond moments.

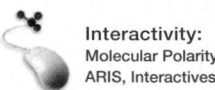

Interactivity:
Molecular Polarity
ARIS, Interactives

To maintain electrical neutrality, the charges on both ends of an electrically neutral diatomic molecule must be equal in magnitude and opposite in sign. However, in Equation (10.1), Q refers only to the magnitude of the charge and not to its sign, so μ is always positive. Dipole moments are usually expressed in debye units (D), named for Peter Debye.[†] The conversion factor is

$$1\,D = 3.336 \times 10^{-30}\,C\,m$$

where C is coulomb and m is meter.

Diatomic molecules containing atoms of *different* elements (for example, HCl, CO, and NO) *have dipole moments* and are called **polar molecules.** Diatomic molecules containing atoms of the *same* element (for example, H_2, O_2, and F_2) are examples of **nonpolar molecules** because they *do not have dipole moments.* For a molecule made up of three or more atoms both the polarity of the bonds and the molecular geometry determine whether there is a dipole moment. Even if polar bonds are present, the molecule will not necessarily have a dipole moment. Carbon dioxide (CO_2), for example, is a triatomic molecule, so its geometry is either linear or bent:

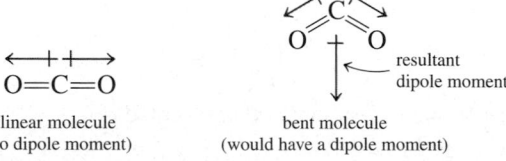

resultant
dipole moment

O=C=O

linear molecule
(no dipole moment)

bent molecule
(would have a dipole moment)

The arrows show the shift of electron density from the less electronegative carbon atom to the more electronegative oxygen atom. In each case, the dipole moment of the entire molecule is made up of two *bond moments,* that is, individual dipole moments in the polar C=O bonds. The bond moment is a *vector quantity,* which means that it has both magnitude and direction. The measured dipole moment is equal to the vector sum of the bond moments. The two bond moments in CO_2 are equal in magnitude. Because they point in opposite directions in a linear CO_2 molecule, the

---

[†]Peter Joseph William Debye (1884–1966). American chemist and physicist of Dutch origin. Debye made many significant contributions in the study of molecular structure, polymer chemistry, X-ray analysis, and electrolyte solution. He was awarded the Nobel Prize in Chemistry in 1936.

sum or resultant dipole moment would be zero. On the other hand, if the CO_2 molecule were bent, the two bond moments would partially reinforce each other, so that the molecule would have a dipole moment. Experimentally it is found that carbon dioxide has no dipole moment. Therefore, we conclude that the carbon dioxide molecule is linear. The linear nature of carbon dioxide has been confirmed through other experimental measurements.

The VSEPR model predicts that CO_2 is a linear molecule.

Next let us consider the NH_3 and NF_3 molecules shown in Figure 10.4. In both cases, the central N atom has a lone pair, whose charge density is away from the N atom. From Figure 9.5 we know that N is more electronegative than H, and F is more electronegative than N. For this reason, the shift of electron density in NH_3 is toward N and so contributes a larger dipole moment, whereas the NF bond moments are directed away from the N atom and so together they offset the contribution of the lone pair to the dipole moment. Thus, the resultant dipole moment in NH_3 is larger than that in NF_3.

Dipole moments can be used to distinguish between molecules that have the same formula but different structures. For example, the following molecules both exist; they have the same molecular formula ($C_2H_2Cl_2$), the same number and type of bonds, but different molecular structures:

cis-dichloroethylene
$\mu = 1.89$ D

trans-dichloroethylene
$\mu = 0$

Because *cis*-dichloroethylene is a polar molecule but *trans*-dichloroethylene is not, they can readily be distinguished by a dipole moment measurement. Additionally, as

cis-dichloroethylene

trans-dichloroethylene

Microwave Ovens—Dipole Moments at Work

In the last 20 years the microwave oven has become a ubiquitous appliance. Microwave technology enables us to thaw and cook food much more rapidly than conventional appliances do. How do microwaves heat food so quickly?

In Chapter 7 we saw that microwaves are a form of electromagnetic radiation (see Figure 7.3). Microwaves are generated by a magnetron, which was invented during World War II when radar technology was being developed. The magnetron is a hollow cylinder encased in a horseshoe-shaped magnet. In the center of the cylinder is a cathode rod. The walls of the cylinder act as an anode. When heated, the cathode emits electrons that travel toward the anode. The magnetic field forces

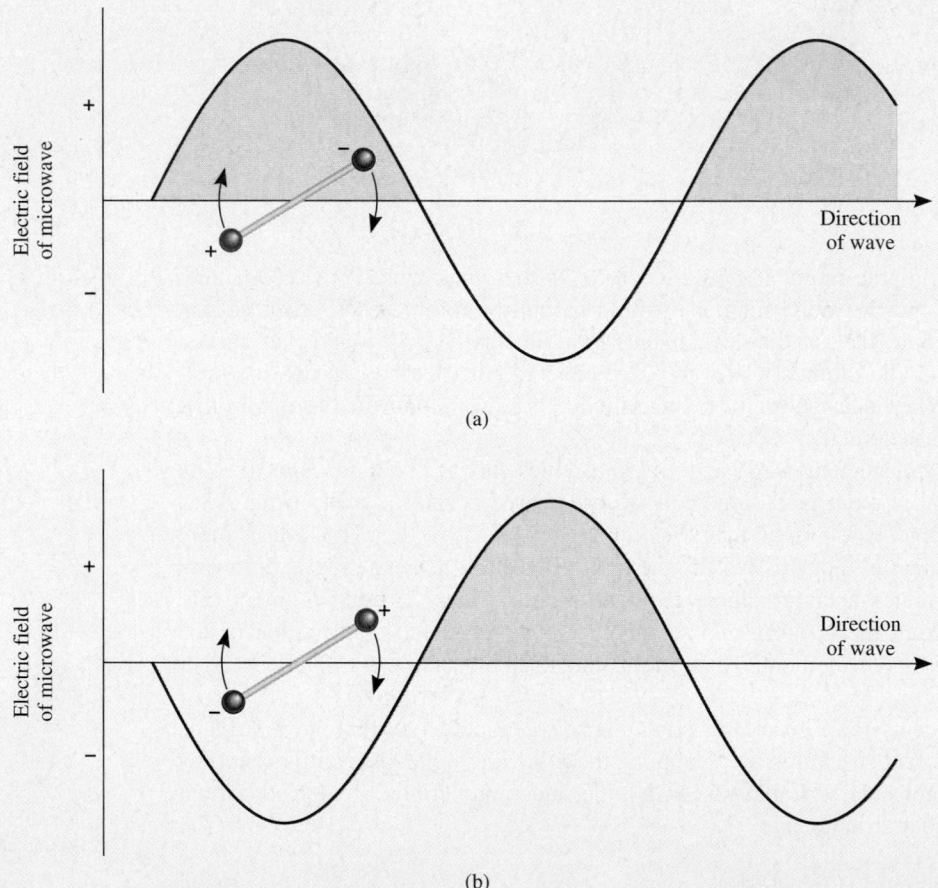

(a)

(b)

Interaction between the electric field component of the microwave and a polar molecule. (a) The negative end of the dipole follows the propagation of the wave (the positive region) and rotates in a clockwise direction. (b) If, after the molecule has rotated to the new position the radiation has also moved along to its next cycle, the positive end of the dipole will move into the negative region of the wave while the negative end will be pushed up. Thus, the molecule will rotate faster. No such interaction can occur with nonpolar molecules.

the electrons to move in a circular path. This motion of charged particles generates microwaves, which are adjusted to a frequency of 2.45 GHz (2.45×10^9 Hz) for cooking. A "waveguide" directs the microwaves into the cooking compartment. Rotating fan blades reflect the microwaves to all parts of the oven.

The cooking action in a microwave oven results from the interaction between the electric field component of the radiation with the polar molecules—mostly water—in food. All molecules rotate at room temperature. If the frequency of the radiation and that of the molecular rotation are equal, energy can be transferred from microwave to the polar molecule. As a result, the molecule will rotate faster. This is what happens in a gas. In the condensed state (for example, in food), a molecule cannot execute the free rotation. Nevertheless, it still experiences a torque (a force that causes rotation) that tends to align its dipole moment with the oscillating field of the microwave. Consequently, there is friction between the molecules, which appears as heat in the food.

The reason that a microwave oven can cook food so fast is that the radiation is not absorbed by nonpolar molecules and can therefore reach different parts of food at the same time.

(Depending on the amount of water present, microwaves can penetrate food to a depth of several inches.) In a conventional oven, heat can affect the center of foods only by conduction (that is, by transfer of heat from hot air molecules to cooler molecules in food in a layer-by-layer fashion), which is a very slow process.

The following points are relevant to the operation of a microwave oven. Plastics and Pyrex glasswares do not contain polar molecules and are therefore not affected by microwave radiation. (Styrofoam and certain plastics cannot be used in microwaves because they melt from the heat of the food.) Metals, however, reflect microwaves, thereby shielding the food and possibly returning enough energy to the microwave emitter to overload it. Because microwaves can induce a current in the metal, this action can lead to sparks jumping between the container and the bottom or walls of the oven. Finally, although water molecules in ice are locked in position and therefore cannot rotate, we routinely thaw food in a microwave oven. The reason is that at room temperature a thin film of liquid water quickly forms on the surface of frozen food and the mobile molecules in that film can absorb the radiation to start the thawing process.

A microwave oven. The microwaves generated by the magnetron are reflected to all parts of the oven by the rotating fan blades.

TABLE 10.3	Dipole Moments of Some Polar Molecules	
Molecule	**Geometry**	**Dipole Moment (D)**
HF	Linear	1.92
HCl	Linear	1.08
HBr	Linear	0.78
HI	Linear	0.38
H_2O	Bent	1.87
H_2S	Bent	1.10
NH_3	Trigonal pyramidal	1.46
SO_2	Bent	1.60

we will see in Chapter 11, the strength of intermolecular forces is partially determined by whether molecules possess a dipole moment. Table 10.3 lists the dipole moments of several polar molecules.

Example 10.2 shows how we can predict whether a molecule possesses a dipole moment if we know its molecular geometry.

Example 10.2

Predict whether each of the following molecules has a dipole moment: (a) IBr, (b) BF_3 (trigonal planar), (c) CH_2Cl_2 (tetrahedral).

Strategy Keep in mind that the dipole moment of a molecule depends on both the difference in electronegativities of the elements present and its geometry. A molecule can have polar bonds (if the bonded atoms have different electronegativities), but it may not possess a dipole moment if it has a highly symmetrical geometry.

Solution (a) Because IBr (iodine bromide) is diatomic, it has a linear geometry. Bromine is more electronegative than iodine (see Figure 9.5), so IBr is polar with bromine at the negative end.

$$\overset{\longmapsto}{\text{I}-\text{Br}}$$

Thus, the molecule does have a dipole moment.

(b) Because fluorine is more electronegative than boron, each B—F bond in BF_3 (boron trifluoride) is polar and the three bond moments are equal. However, the symmetry of a trigonal planar shape means that the three bond moments exactly cancel one another:

An analogy is an object that is pulled in the directions shown by the three bond moments. If the forces are equal, the object will not move. Consequently, BF_3 has no dipole moment; it is a nonpolar molecule.

(Continued)

All diatomic molecules containing different elements possess a dipole moment.

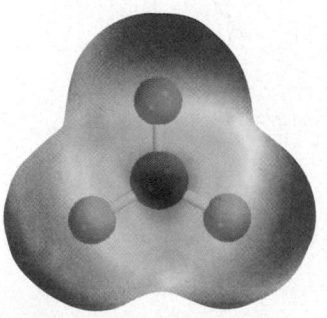

Electrostatic potential map shows that the electron density is symmetrically distributed in the BF_3 molecule.

(c) The Lewis structure of CH_2Cl_2 (methylene chloride) is

$$
\begin{array}{c}
\text{Cl} \\
| \\
\text{H—C—H} \\
| \\
\text{Cl}
\end{array}
$$

This molecule is similar to CH_4 in that it has an overall tetrahedral shape. However, because not all the bonds are identical, there are three different bond angles: HCH, HCCl, and ClCCl. These bond angles are close to, but not equal to, 109.5°. Because chlorine is more electronegative than carbon, which is more electronegative than hydrogen, the bond moments do not cancel and the molecule possesses a dipole moment:

resultant dipole moment

Thus, CH_2Cl_2 is a polar molecule.

Practice Exercise Does the $AlCl_3$ molecule have a dipole moment?

Electrostatic potential map of CH_2Cl_2. The electron density is shifted toward the electronegative Cl atoms.

Similar problems: 10.21, 10.22, 10.23.

10.3 Valence Bond Theory

The VSEPR model, based largely on Lewis structures, provides a relatively simple and straightforward method for predicting the geometry of molecules. But as we noted earlier, the Lewis theory of chemical bonding does not clearly explain why chemical bonds exist. Relating the formation of a covalent bond to the pairing of electrons was a step in the right direction, but it did not go far enough. For example, the Lewis theory describes the single bond between the H atoms in H_2 and that between the F atoms in F_2 in essentially the same way—as the pairing of two electrons. Yet these two molecules have quite different bond enthalpies and bond lengths (436.4 kJ/mol and 74 pm for H_2 and 150.6 kJ/mol and 142 pm for F_2). These and many other facts cannot be explained by the Lewis theory. For a more complete explanation of chemical bond formation we look to quantum mechanics. In fact, the quantum mechanical study of chemical bonding also provides a means for understanding molecular geometry.

At present, two quantum mechanical theories are used to describe covalent bond formation and the electronic structure of molecules. *Valence bond (VB) theory* assumes that the electrons in a molecule occupy atomic orbitals of the individual atoms. It enables us to retain a picture of individual atoms taking part in the bond formation. The second theory, called *molecular orbital (MO) theory,* assumes the formation of molecular orbitals from the atomic orbitals. Neither theory perfectly explains all aspects of bonding, but each has contributed something to our understanding of many observed molecular properties.

Let us start our discussion of valence bond theory by considering the formation of a H_2 molecule from two H atoms. The Lewis theory describes the H—H bond in terms of the pairing of the two electrons on the H atoms. In the framework of valence bond theory, the covalent H—H bond is formed by the *overlap* of the two 1s orbitals in the H atoms. By overlap, we mean that the two orbitals share a common region in space.

Figure 10.5 *Change in potential energy of two H atoms with their distance of separation. At the point of minimum potential energy, the H_2 molecule is in its most stable state and the bond length is 74 pm. The spheres represent the 1s orbitals.*

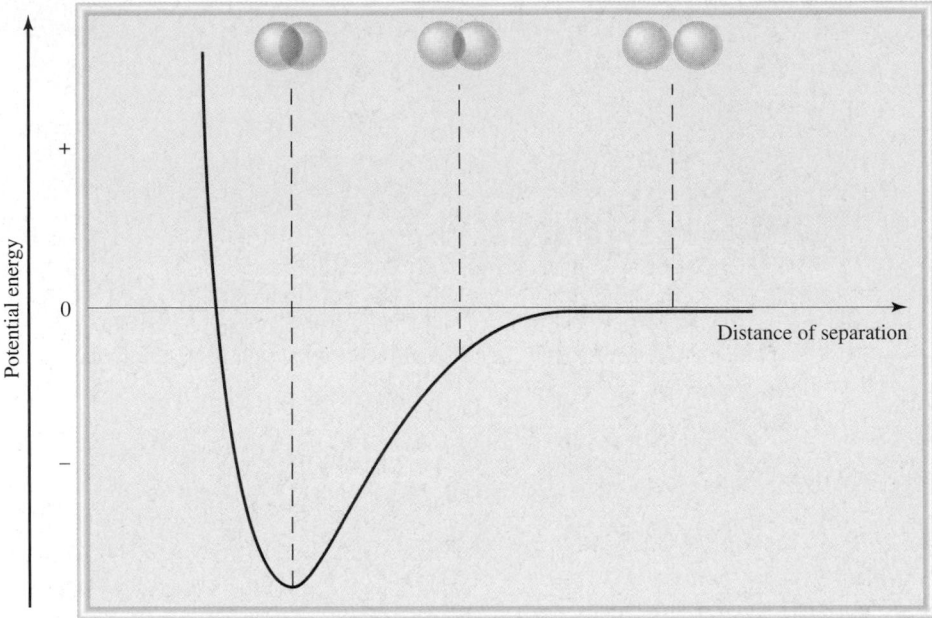

Recall that an object has potential energy by virtue of its position.

What happens to two H atoms as they move toward each other and form a bond? Initially, when the two atoms are far apart, there is no interaction. We say that the potential energy of this system (that is, the two H atoms) is zero. As the atoms approach each other, each electron is attracted by the nucleus of the other atom; at the same time, the electrons repel each other, as do the nuclei. While the atoms are still separated, attraction is stronger than repulsion, so that the potential energy of the system *decreases* (that is, it becomes negative) as the atoms approach each other (Figure 10.5). This trend continues until the potential energy reaches a minimum value. At this point, when the system has the lowest potential energy, it is most stable. This condition corresponds to substantial overlap of the 1s orbitals and the formation of a stable H_2 molecule. If the distance between nuclei were to decrease further, the potential energy would rise steeply and finally become positive as a result of the increased electron-electron and nuclear-nuclear repulsions. In accord with the law of conservation of energy, the decrease in potential energy as a result of H_2 formation must be accompanied by a release of energy. Experiments show that as a H_2 molecule is formed from two H atoms, heat is given off. The converse is also true. To break a H—H bond, energy must be supplied to the molecule. Figure 10.6 is another way of viewing the formation of an H_2 molecule.

Thus, valence bond theory gives a clearer picture of chemical bond formation than the Lewis theory does. Valence bond theory states that a stable molecule forms from reacting atoms when the potential energy of the system has decreased to a minimum; the Lewis theory ignores energy changes in chemical bond formation.

The orbital diagram of the F atom is shown on p. 297.

The concept of overlapping atomic orbitals applies equally well to diatomic molecules other than H_2. Thus, a stable F_2 molecule forms when the $2p$ orbitals (containing the unpaired electrons) in the two F atoms overlap to form a covalent bond. Similarly, the formation of the HF molecule can be explained by the overlap of the 1s orbital in H with the $2p$ orbital in F. In each case, VB theory accounts for the changes in potential energy as the distance between the reacting atoms changes. Because the orbitals involved are not the same kind in all cases, we can see why the bond enthalpies and bond lengths in H_2, F_2, and HF might be different. As we stated earlier, Lewis theory treats *all* covalent bonds the same way and offers no explanation for the differences among covalent bonds.

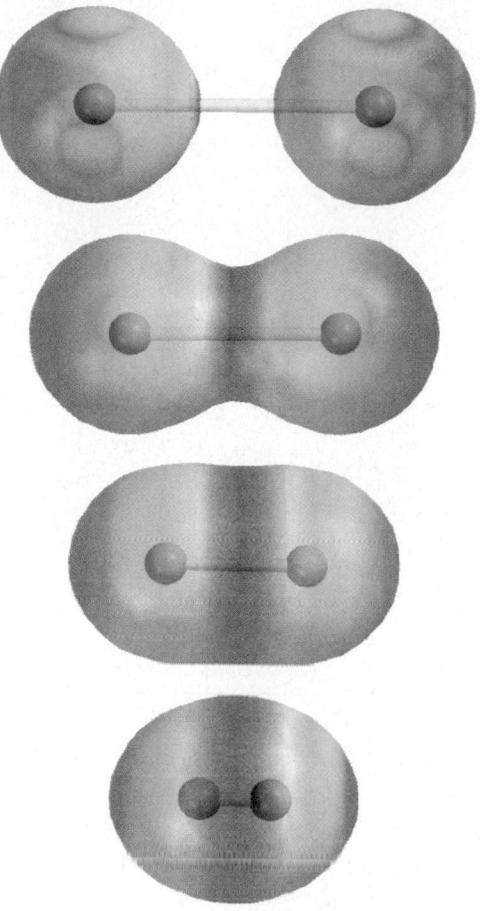

Figure 10.6 *Top to bottom: As two H atoms approach each other, their 1s orbitals begin to interact and each electron begins to feel the attraction of the other proton. Gradually, the electron density builds up in the region between the two nuclei (red color). Eventually, a stable H$_2$ molecule is formed when the internuclear distance is 74 pm.*

10.4 Hybridization of Atomic Orbitals

The concept of atomic orbital overlap should apply also to polyatomic molecules. However, a satisfactory bonding scheme must account for molecular geometry. We will discuss three examples of VB treatment of bonding in polyatomic molecules.

sp^3 Hybridization

Consider the CH$_4$ molecule. Focusing only on the valence electrons, we can represent the orbital diagram of C as

Because the carbon atom has two unpaired electrons (one in each of the two 2p orbitals), it can form only two bonds with hydrogen in its ground state. Although the species CH$_2$ is known, it is very unstable. To account for the four C—H bonds in methane, we can try to promote (that is, energetically excite) an electron from the 2s orbital to the 2p orbital:

Animation:
Hybridization
ARIS, Animations

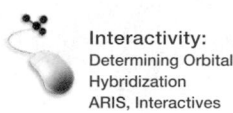
Interactivity:
Determining Orbital
Hybridization
ARIS, Interactives

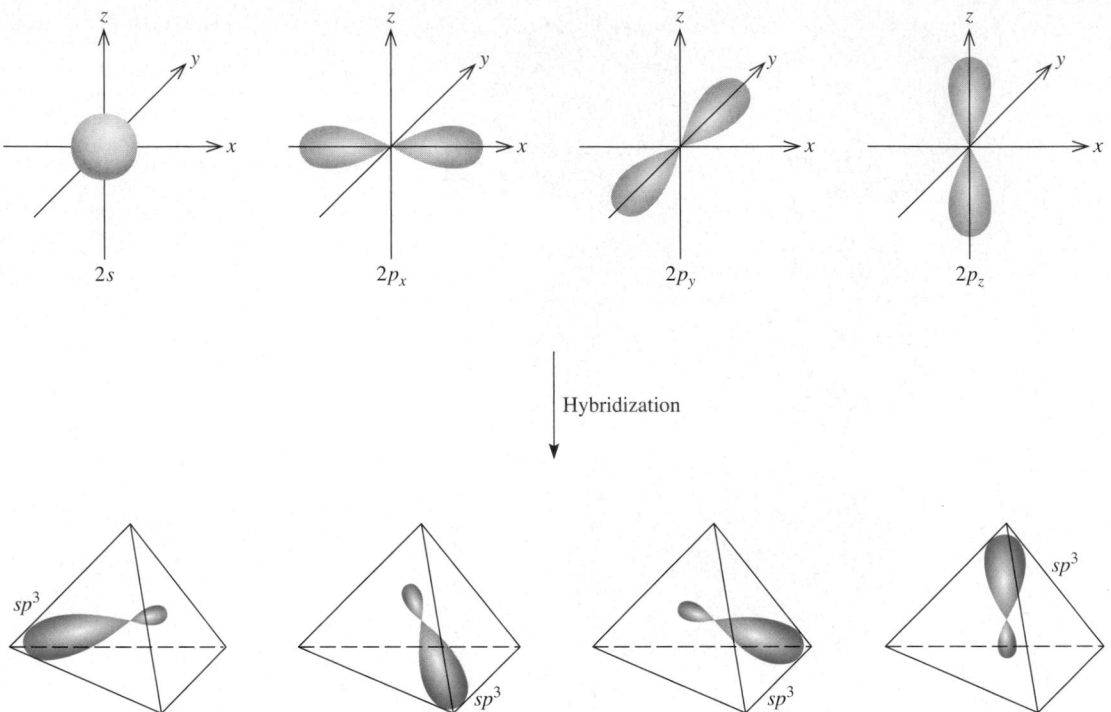

Figure 10.7 *Formation of four sp³ hybrid orbitals from one 2s and three 2p orbitals. The sp³ orbitals point to the corners of a tetrahedron.*

Now there are four unpaired electrons on C that could form four C—H bonds. However, the geometry is wrong, because three of the HCH bond angles would have to be 90° (remember that the three $2p$ orbitals on carbon are mutually perpendicular), and yet *all* HCH angles are 109.5°.

To explain the bonding in methane, VB theory uses hypothetical **hybrid orbitals,** which are *atomic orbitals obtained when two or more nonequivalent orbitals of the same atom combine in preparation for covalent bond formation.* **Hybridization** is the term applied to *the mixing of atomic orbitals in an atom (usually a central atom) to generate a set of hybrid orbitals.* We can generate four equivalent hybrid orbitals for carbon by mixing the $2s$ orbital and the three $2p$ orbitals:

sp^3 is pronounced "s-p three."

sp^3 orbitals

Because the new orbitals are formed from one s and three p orbitals, they are called sp^3 hybrid orbitals. Figure 10.7 shows the shape and orientations of the sp^3 orbitals. These four hybrid orbitals are directed toward the four corners of a regular tetrahedron. Figure 10.8 shows the formation of four covalent bonds between the carbon sp^3 hybrid orbitals and the hydrogen $1s$ orbitals in CH₄. Thus CH₄ has a tetrahedral shape, and all the HCH angles are 109.5°. Note that although energy is required to bring about hybridization, this input is more than compensated for by the energy released upon the formation of C—H bonds. (Recall that bond formation is an exothermic process.)

The following analogy is useful for understanding hybridization. Suppose that we have a beaker of a red solution and three beakers of blue solutions and that the volume of each is 50 mL. The red solution corresponds to one $2s$ orbital, the blue solutions rep-

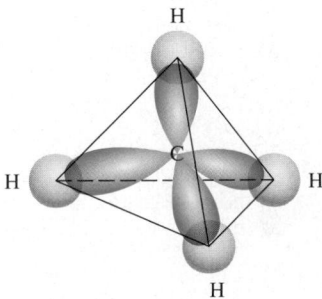

Figure 10.8 *Formation of four bonds between the carbon sp³ hybrid orbitals and the hydrogen 1s orbitals in CH₄. The smaller lobes are not shown.*

resent three $2p$ orbitals, and the four equal volumes symbolize four separate orbitals. By mixing the solutions we obtain 200 mL of a purple solution, which can be divided into four 50-mL portions (that is, the hybridization process generates four sp^3 orbitals). Just as the purple color is made up of the red and blue components of the original solutions, the sp^3 hybrid orbitals possess both s and p orbital characteristics.

Another example of sp^3 hybridization is ammonia (NH_3). Table 10.1 shows that the arrangement of four electron pairs is tetrahedral, so that the bonding in NH_3 can be explained by assuming that N, like C in CH_4, is sp^3-hybridized. The ground-state electron configuration of N is $1s^2 2s^2 2p^3$, so that the orbital diagram for the sp^3 hybridized N atom is

sp^3 orbitals

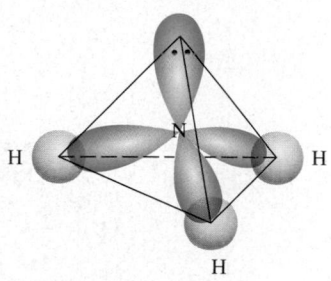

Figure 10.9 *The sp^3-hybridized N atom in NH_3. Three sp^3 hybrid orbitals form bonds with the H atoms. The fourth is occupied by nitrogen's lone pair.*

Three of the four hybrid orbitals form covalent N—H bonds, and the fourth hybrid orbital accommodates the lone pair on nitrogen (Figure 10.9). Repulsion between the lone-pair electrons and electrons in the bonding orbitals decreases the HNH bond angles from 109.5° to 107.3°.

It is important to understand the relationship between hybridization and the VSEPR model. We use hybridization to describe the bonding scheme only when the arrangement of electron pairs has been predicted using VSEPR. If the VSEPR model predicts a tetrahedral arrangement of electron pairs, then we assume that one s and three p orbitals are hybridized to form four sp^3 hybrid orbitals. The following are examples of other types of hybridization.

sp Hybridization

The beryllium chloride ($BeCl_2$) molecule is predicted to be linear by VSEPR. The orbital diagram for the valence electrons in Be is

$2s$ $2p$

We know that in its ground state, Be does not form covalent bonds with Cl because its electrons are paired in the $2s$ orbital. So we turn to hybridization for an explanation of Be's bonding behavior. First, we promote a $2s$ electron to a $2p$ orbital, resulting in

$2s$ $2p$

Now there are two Be orbitals available for bonding, the $2s$ and $2p$. However, if two Cl atoms were to combine with Be in this excited state, one Cl atom would share a $2s$ electron and the other Cl would share a $2p$ electron, making two nonequivalent BeCl bonds. This scheme contradicts experimental evidence. In the actual $BeCl_2$ molecule, the two BeCl bonds are identical in every respect. Thus, the $2s$ and $2p$ orbitals must be mixed, or hybridized, to form two equivalent sp hybrid orbitals:

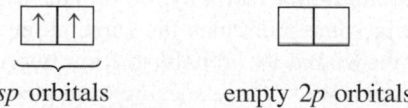

sp orbitals   empty $2p$ orbitals

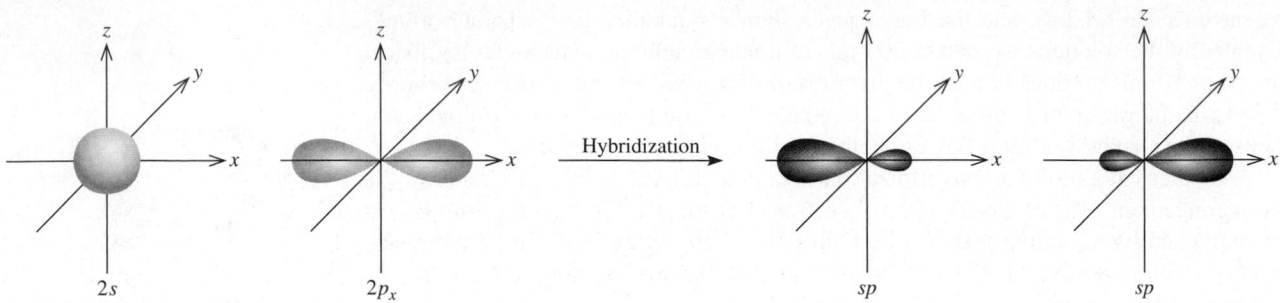

Figure 10.10 *Formation of sp hybrid orbitals.*

Figure 10.10 shows the shape and orientation of the sp orbitals. These two hybrid orbitals lie on the same line, the x-axis, so that the angle between them is 180°. Each of the BeCl bonds is then formed by the overlap of a Be sp hybrid orbital and a Cl $3p$ orbital, and the resulting $BeCl_2$ molecule has a linear geometry (Figure 10.11).

sp^2 Hybridization

Next we will look at the BF_3 (boron trifluoride) molecule, known to have a planar geometry. Considering only the valence electrons, the orbital diagram of B is

$$\boxed{\uparrow\downarrow}\qquad\boxed{\uparrow}\ \boxed{\ }\ \boxed{\ }$$
$$2s\qquad\qquad 2p$$

First, we promote a $2s$ electron to an empty $2p$ orbital:

$$\boxed{\uparrow}\qquad\boxed{\uparrow}\ \boxed{\uparrow}\ \boxed{\ }$$
$$2s\qquad\qquad 2p$$

sp^2 is pronounced "s-p two."

Mixing the $2s$ orbital with the two $2p$ orbitals generates three sp^2 hybrid orbitals:

$$\underbrace{\boxed{\uparrow\ |\ \uparrow\ |\ \uparrow}}_{sp^2 \text{ orbitals}}\qquad\qquad\boxed{\ }$$
$$\text{empty } 2p \text{ orbital}$$

These three sp^2 orbitals lie in the same plane, and the angle between any two of them is 120° (Figure 10.12). Each of the BF bonds is formed by the overlap of a boron sp^2 hybrid orbital and a fluorine $2p$ orbital (Figure 10.13). The BF_3 molecule is planar with all the FBF angles equal to 120°. This result conforms to experimental findings and also to VSEPR predictions.

You may have noticed an interesting connection between hybridization and the octet rule. Regardless of the type of hybridization, an atom starting with one s and three p orbitals would still possess four orbitals, enough to accommodate a total of eight electrons in a compound. For elements in the second period of the periodic table, eight is the maximum number of electrons that an atom of any of these elements can accommodate in the valence shell. This is the reason that the octet rule is usually obeyed by the second-period elements.

Figure 10.11 *The linear geometry of BeCl₂ can be explained by assuming that Be is sp-hybridized. The two sp hybrid orbitals overlap with the two chlorine 3p orbitals to form two covalent bonds.*

The situation is different for an atom of a third-period element. If we use only the $3s$ and $3p$ orbitals of the atom to form hybrid orbitals in a molecule, then the octet rule applies. However, in some molecules the same atom may use one or more $3d$ orbitals, in addition to the $3s$ and $3p$ orbitals, to form hybrid orbitals. In these cases, the octet rule does not hold. We will see specific examples of the participation of the $3d$ orbital in hybridization shortly.

Figure 10.12 *Formation of sp² hybrid orbitals from one 2s and two 2p orbitals. The sp² orbitals point to the corners of an equilateral triangle.*

To summarize our discussion of hybridization, we note that

- The concept of hybridization is not applied to isolated atoms. It is a theoretical model used only to explain covalent bonding.

- Hybridization is the mixing of at least two nonequivalent atomic orbitals, for example, *s* and *p* orbitals. Therefore, a hybrid orbital is not a pure atomic orbital. Hybrid orbitals and pure atomic orbitals have very different shapes.

- The number of hybrid orbitals generated is equal to the number of pure atomic orbitals that participate in the hybridization process.

- Hybridization requires an input of energy; however, the system more than recovers this energy during bond formation.

- Covalent bonds in polyatomic molecules and ions are formed by the overlap of hybrid orbitals, or of hybrid orbitals with unhybridized ones. Therefore, the hybridization bonding scheme is still within the framework of valence bond theory; electrons in a molecule are assumed to occupy hybrid orbitals of the individual atoms.

Table 10.4 summarizes *sp*, *sp²*, and *sp³* hybridization (as well as other types that we will discuss shortly).

Procedure for Hybridizing Atomic Orbitals

Before going on to discuss the hybridization of *d* orbitals, let us specify what we need to know in order to apply hybridization to bonding in polyatomic molecules in general. In essence, hybridization simply extends Lewis theory and the VSEPR model. To assign a suitable state of hybridization to the central atom in a molecule, we must have some idea about the geometry of the molecule. The steps are as follows:

1. Draw the Lewis structure of the molecule.

2. Predict the overall arrangement of the electron pairs (both bonding pairs and lone pairs) using the VSEPR model (see Table 10.1).

3. Deduce the hybridization of the central atom by matching the arrangement of the electron pairs with those of the hybrid orbitals shown in Table 10.4.

Example 10.3 illustrates this procedure.

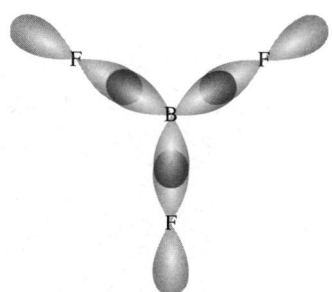

Figure 10.13 *The sp² hybrid orbitals of boron overlap with the 2p orbitals of fluorine. The BF₃ molecule is planar, and all the FBF angles are 120°.*

TABLE 10.4   Important Hybrid Orbitals and Their Shapes

Pure Atomic Orbitals of the Central Atom	Hybridization of the Central Atom	Number of Hybrid Orbitals	Shape of Hybrid Orbitals	Examples
s, p	sp	2	Linear	$BeCl_2$
s, p, p	sp^2	3	Trigonal planar	BF_3
s, p, p, p	sp^3	4	Tetrahedral	CH_4, NH_4^+
s, p, p, p, d	sp^3d	5	Trigonal bipyramidal	PCl_5
s, p, p, p, d, d	sp^3d^2	6	Octahedral	SF_6

Example 10.3

Determine the hybridization state of the central (underlined) atom in each of the following molecules: (a) $\underline{Be}H_2$, (b) $\underline{Al}I_3$, and (c) $\underline{P}F_3$. Describe the hybridization process and determine the molecular geometry in each case.

Strategy The steps for determining the hybridization of the central atom in a molecule are:

draw Lewis structure of the molecule $\longrightarrow$ use VSEPR to determine the electron pair arrangement surrounding the central atom (Table 10.1) $\longrightarrow$ use Table 10.4 to determine the hybridization state of the central atom

Solution (a) The ground-state electron configuration of Be is $1s^2 2s^2$ and the Be atom has two valence electrons. The Lewis structure of BeH_2 is

$$H—Be—H$$

There are two bonding pairs around Be; therefore, the electron pair arrangement is linear. We conclude that Be uses sp hybrid orbitals in bonding with H, because sp orbitals have a linear arrangement (see Table 10.4). The hybridization process can be imagined as follows. First, we draw the orbital diagram for the ground state of Be:

2s   2p

By promoting a 2s electron to the 2p orbital, we get the excited state:

2s   2p

The 2s and 2p orbitals then mix to form two hybrid orbitals:

sp orbitals   empty 2p
orbitals

The two Be—H bonds are formed by the overlap of the Be sp orbitals with the 1s orbitals of the H atoms. Thus, BeH_2 is a linear molecule.

(b) The ground-state electron configuration of Al is $[Ne]3s^2 3p^1$. Therefore, the Al atom has three valence electrons. The Lewis structure of AlI_3 is

$$\ddot{:}\ddot{I}\ddot{:}$$
$$|$$
$$\ddot{:}\ddot{I}—Al—\ddot{I}\ddot{:}$$

There are three pairs of electrons around Al; therefore, the electron pair arrangement is trigonal planar. We conclude that Al uses sp^2 hybrid orbitals in bonding with I because sp^2 orbitals have a trigonal planar arrangement (see Table 10.4). The orbital diagram of the ground-state Al atom is

(Continued)

BeH₂

AlI₃

By promoting a 3s electron into the 3p orbital we obtain the following excited state:

The 3s and two 3p orbitals then mix to form three sp^2 hybrid orbitals:

The sp^2 hybrid orbitals overlap with the 5p orbitals of I to form three covalent Al—I bonds. We predict that the AlI_3 molecule is trigonal planar and all the IAlI angles are 120°.

(c) The ground-state electron configuration of P is $[Ne]3s^23p^3$. Therefore, P atom has five valence electrons. The Lewis structure of PF_3 is

There are four pairs of electrons around P; therefore, the electron pair arrangement is tetrahedral. We conclude that P uses sp^3 hybrid orbitals in bonding to F, because sp^3 orbitals have a tetrahedral arrangement (see Table 10.4). The hybridization process can be imagined to take place as follows. The orbital diagram of the ground-state P atom is

By mixing the 3s and 3p orbitals, we obtain four sp^3 hybrid orbitals.

As in the case of NH_3, one of the sp^3 hybrid orbitals is used to accommodate the lone pair on P. The other three sp^3 hybrid orbitals form covalent P—F bonds with the 2p orbitals of F. We predict the geometry of the molecule to be trigonal pyramidal; the FPF angle should be somewhat less than 109.5°.

Practice Exercise Determine the hybridization state of the underlined atoms in the following compounds: (a) $\underline{Si}Br_4$ and (b) $\underline{B}Cl_3$.

PF₃

Similar problems: 10.33, 10.34.

Hybridization of *s*, *p*, and *d* Orbitals

We have seen that hybridization neatly explains bonding that involves *s* and *p* orbitals. For elements in the third period and beyond, however, we cannot always account for molecular geometry by assuming that only *s* and *p* orbitals hybridize. To understand the formation of molecules with trigonal bipyramidal and octahedral geometries, for instance, we must include *d* orbitals in the hybridization concept.

Consider the SF_6 molecule as an example. In Section 10.1 we saw that this molecule has octahedral geometry, which is also the arrangement of the six electron pairs. Table 10.4 shows that the S atom is sp^3d^2-hybridized in SF_6. The ground-state electron configuration of S is $[Ne]3s^23p^4$:

Because the 3*d* level is quite close in energy to the 3*s* and 3*p* levels, we can promote 3*s* and 3*p* electrons to two of the 3*d* orbitals:

Mixing the 3*s*, three 3*p*, and two 3*d* orbitals generates six sp^3d^2 hybrid orbitals:

sp^3d^2 orbitals   empty 3*d* orbitals

The six S—F bonds are formed by the overlap of the hybrid orbitals of the S atom with the 2*p* orbitals of the F atoms. Because there are 12 electrons around the S atom, the octet rule is violated. The use of *d* orbitals in addition to *s* and *p* orbitals to form an expanded octet (see Section 9.9) is an example of *valence-shell expansion*. Second-period elements, unlike third-period elements, do not have 2*d* energy levels, so they can never expand their valence shells. (Recall that when *n* = 2, *l* = 0 and 1. Thus, we can only have 2*s* and 2*p* orbitals.) Hence atoms of second-period elements can never be surrounded by more than eight electrons in any of their compounds.

Example 10.4 deals with valence-shell expansion in a third-period element.

SF_6

sp^3d^2 is pronounced "s-p three d two."

Example 10.4

Describe the hybridization state of phosphorus in phosphorus pentabromide (PBr_5).

Strategy Follow the same procedure shown in Example 10.3.

Solution The ground-state electron configuration of P is $[Ne]3s^23p^3$. Therefore, the P atom has five valence electrons. The Lewis structure of PBr_5 is

There are five pairs of electrons around P; therefore, the electron pair arrangement is trigonal bipyramidal. We conclude that P uses sp^3d hybrid orbitals in bonding to Br, because sp^3d hybrid orbitals have a trigonal bipyramidal arrangement (see Table 10.4). The hybridization process can be imagined as follows. The orbital diagram of the ground-state P atom is

(Continued)

PBr_5

Ground
state

Promotion
of electron

sp^2-
Hybridized
state

Figure 10.14 *The sp^2 hybrid-ization of a carbon atom. The 2s orbital is mixed with only two 2p orbitals to form three equivalent sp^2 hybrid orbitals. This process leaves an electron in the unhybridized orbital, the $2p_z$ orbital.*

Similar problem: 10.42.

Promoting a 3s electron into a 3d orbital results in the following excited state:

Mixing the one 3s, three 3p, and one 3d orbitals generates five sp^3d hybrid orbitals:

sp^3d orbitals   empty 3d orbitals

These hybrid orbitals overlap the 4p orbitals of Br to form five covalent P—Br bonds. Because there are no lone pairs on the P atom, the geometry of PBr_5 is trigonal bipyramidal.

Practice Exercise Describe the hybridization state of Se in SeF_6.

10.5 Hybridization in Molecules Containing Double and Triple Bonds

The concept of hybridization is useful also for molecules with double and triple bonds. Consider the ethylene molecule, C_2H_4, as an example. In Example 10.1 we saw that C_2H_4 contains a carbon-carbon double bond and has planar geometry. Both the geometry and the bonding can be understood if we assume that each carbon atom is sp^2-hybridized. Figure 10.14 shows orbital diagrams of this hybridization process. We assume that only the $2p_x$ and $2p_y$ orbitals combine with the 2s orbital, and that the $2p_z$ orbital remains unchanged. Figure 10.15 shows that the $2p_z$ orbital is perpendicular to the plane of the hybrid orbitals. Now how do we account for the bonding of the C atoms? As Figure 10.16(a) shows, each carbon atom uses the three sp^2 hybrid orbitals to form two bonds with the two hydrogen 1s orbitals and one bond with the sp^2 hybrid orbital of the adjacent C atom. In addition, the two unhybridized $2p_z$ orbitals of the C atoms form another bond by overlapping sideways [Figure 10.16(b)].

A distinction is made between the two types of covalent bonds in C_2H_4. The three bonds formed by each C atom in Figure 10.16(a) are all *sigma bonds (σ bonds)*, *covalent bonds formed by orbitals overlapping end-to-end, with the electron density concentrated between the nuclei of the bonding atoms.* The second type is called a *pi bond (π bond)*, which is defined as *a covalent bond formed by sideways overlapping orbitals with electron density concentrated above and below the plane of the nuclei of the bonding atoms.* The two C atoms form a pi bond as shown in Figure 10.16(b). It is this pi bond formation that gives ethylene its planar geometry. Figure 10.16(c) shows the orientation of the sigma and pi bonds. Figure 10.17 is yet another way of looking at the planar C_2H_4 molecule and the formation of the pi bond. Although we normally represent the carbon-carbon double bond as C=C (as in a Lewis structure), it is important to keep in mind that the two bonds are different types: One is a sigma bond and the other is a pi bond. In fact, the bond enthalpies of the carbon-carbon pi and sigma bonds are about 270 kJ/mol and 350 kJ/mol, respectively.

The acetylene molecule (C_2H_2) contains a carbon-carbon triple bond. Because the molecule is linear, we can explain its geometry and bonding by assuming that each C atom is sp-hybridized by mixing the 2s with the $2p_x$ orbital (Figure 10.18). As

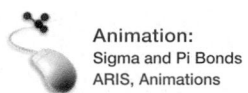

Animation:
Sigma and Pi Bonds
ARIS, Animations

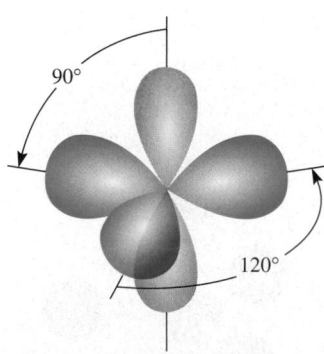

90°

120°

Figure 10.15 *Each carbon atom in the C_2H_4 molecule has three sp^2 hybrid orbitals (green) and one unhybridized $2p_z$ orbital (gray), which is perpendicular to the plane of the hybrid orbitals.*

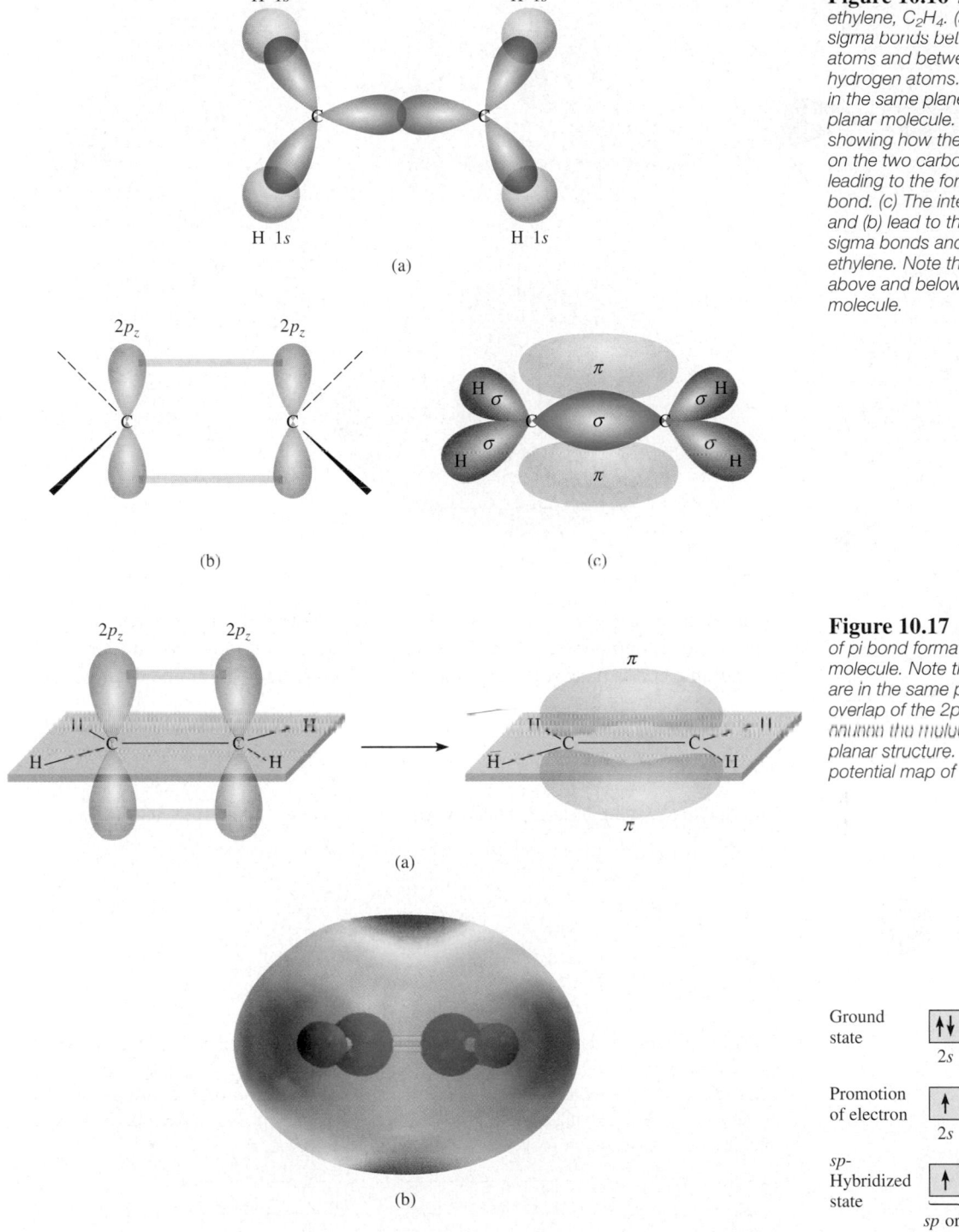

H 1s   H 1s

C   C

H 1s   H 1s

(a)

Figure 10.16 *Bonding in ethylene, C_2H_4. (a) Top view of the sigma bonds between carbon atoms and between carbon and hydrogen atoms. All the atoms lie in the same plane, making C_2H_4 a planar molecule. (b) Side view showing how the two $2p_z$ orbitals on the two carbon atoms overlap, leading to the formation of a pi bond. (c) The interactions in (a) and (b) lead to the formation of the sigma bonds and the pi bond in ethylene. Note that the pi bond lies above and below the plane of the molecule.*

$2p_z$ $2p_z$

C   C

(b)

π

H   H

σ σ

C σ C

σ σ

H   H

π

(c)

$2p_z$ $2p_z$

H   H

C   C

H   H

π

H   H

C   C

H   H

π

(a)

Figure 10.17 *(a) Another view of pi bond formation in the C_2H_4 molecule. Note that all six atoms are in the same plane. It is the overlap of the $2p_z$ orbitals that causes the molecule to assume a planar structure. (b) Electrostatic potential map of C_2H_4.*

(b)

	2s		2p		
Ground state	↑↓		↑	↑	
Promotion of electron	↑		↑	↑	↑

sp-Hybridized state

↑	↑		↑	↑

sp orbitals $2p_y$ $2p_z$

Figure 10.18 *The sp hybridization of a carbon atom. The 2s orbital is mixed with only one 2p orbital to form two sp hybrid orbitals. This process leaves an electron in each of the two unhybridized 2p orbitals, namely, the $2p_y$ and $2p_z$ orbitals.*

Figure 10.19 shows, the two *sp* hybrid orbitals of each C atom form one sigma bond with a hydrogen 1s orbital and another sigma bond with the other C atom. In addition, two pi bonds are formed by the sideways overlap of the unhybridized $2p_y$ and $2p_z$ orbitals. Thus, the C≡C bond is made up of one sigma bond and two pi bonds.

The following rule helps us predict hybridization in molecules containing multiple bonds: If the central atom forms a double bond, it is sp^2-hybridized; if it forms two

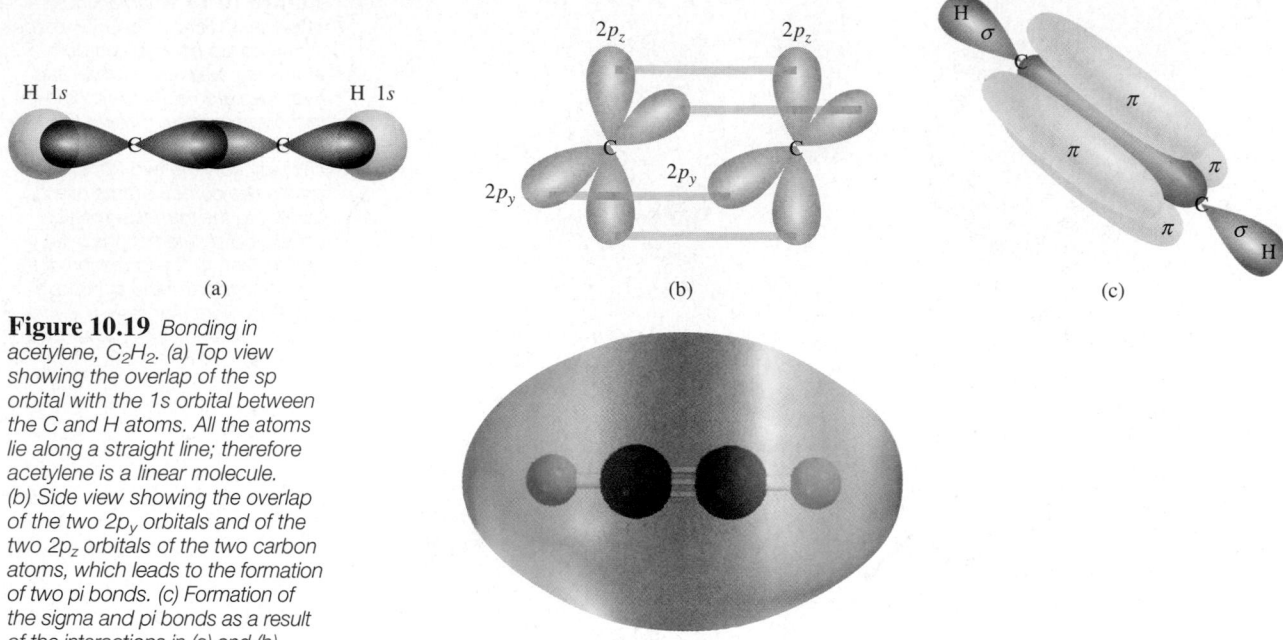

Figure 10.19 *Bonding in acetylene, C₂H₂. (a) Top view showing the overlap of the sp orbital with the 1s orbital between the C and H atoms. All the atoms lie along a straight line; therefore acetylene is a linear molecule. (b) Side view showing the overlap of the two 2pᵧ orbitals and of the two 2pₓ orbitals of the two carbon atoms, which leads to the formation of two pi bonds. (c) Formation of the sigma and pi bonds as a result of the interactions in (a) and (b). (d) Electrostatic potential map of C₂H₂.*

double bonds or a triple bond, it is *sp*-hybridized. Note that this rule applies only to atoms of the second-period elements. Atoms of third-period elements and beyond that form multiple bonds present a more complicated picture and will not be dealt with here.

Example 10.5

Describe the bonding in the formaldehyde molecule whose Lewis structure is

$$\begin{array}{c} H \\ \\ H \end{array}\!\!\!\!> C = \overset{\displaystyle\cdot\cdot}{\underset{\displaystyle\cdot\cdot}{O}}$$

Assume that the O atom is *sp²*-hybridized.

Strategy Follow the procedure shown in Example 10.3.

Solution There are three pairs of electrons around the C atom; therefore, the electron pair arrangement is trigonal planar. (Recall that a double bond is treated as a single bond in the VSEPR model.) We conclude that C uses *sp²* hybrid orbitals in bonding, because *sp²* hybrid orbitals have a trigonal planar arrangement (see Table 10.4). We can imagine the hybridization processes for C and O as follows:

CH₂O

(Continued)

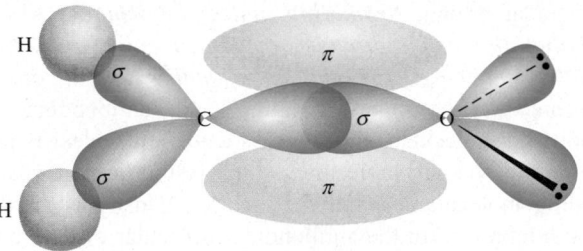

Figure 10.20 *Bonding in the formaldehyde molecule. A sigma bond is formed by the overlap of the sp^2 hybrid orbital of carbon and the sp^2 hybrid orbital of oxygen; a pi bond is formed by the overlap of the $2p_z$ orbitals of the carbon and oxygen atoms. The two lone pairs on oxygen are placed in the other two sp^2 orbitals of oxygen.*

Carbon has one electron in each of the three sp^2 orbitals, which are used to form sigma bonds with the H atoms and the O atom. There is also an electron in the $2p_z$ orbital, which forms a pi bond with oxygen. Oxygen has two electrons in two of its sp^2 hybrid orbitals. These are the lone pairs on oxygen. Its third sp^2 hybrid orbital with one electron is used to form a sigma bond with carbon. The $2p_z$ orbital (with one electron) overlaps with the $2p_z$ orbital of C to form a pi bond (Figure 10.20).

Practice Exercise Describe the bonding in the hydrogen cyanide molecule, HCN. Assume that N is *sp*-hybridized.

Similar problems: 10.38, 10.39, 10.41.

10.6 Molecular Orbital Theory

Valence bond theory is one of the two quantum mechanical approaches that explain bonding in molecules. It accounts, at least qualitatively, for the stability of the covalent bond in terms of overlapping atomic orbitals. Using the concept of hybridization, valence bond theory can explain molecular geometries predicted by the VSEPR model. However, the assumption that electrons in a molecule occupy atomic orbitals of the individual atoms can only be an approximation, because each bonding electron in a molecule must be in an orbital that is characteristic of the molecule as a whole.

In some cases, valence bond theory cannot satisfactorily account for observed properties of molecules. Consider the oxygen molecule, whose Lewis structure is

$$\ddot{O}=\ddot{O}$$

According to this description, all the electrons in O_2 are paired and oxygen should therefore be diamagnetic. But experiments have shown that the oxygen molecule has two unpaired electrons (Figure 10.21). This finding suggests a fundamental deficiency in valence bond theory, one that justifies searching for an alternative bonding approach that accounts for the properties of O_2 and other molecules that do not match the predictions of valence bond theory.

Magnetic and other properties of molecules are sometimes better explained by another quantum mechanical approach called *molecular orbital (MO) theory.* Molecular orbital theory describes covalent bonds in terms of ***molecular orbitals,*** which *result from interaction of the atomic orbitals of the bonding atoms and are associated with the entire molecule.* The difference between a molecular orbital and an atomic orbital is that an atomic orbital is associated with only one atom.

Bonding and Antibonding Molecular Orbitals

According to MO theory, the overlap of the $1s$ orbitals of two hydrogen atoms leads to the formation of two molecular orbitals: one bonding molecular orbital and one

Figure 10.21 *Liquid oxygen caught between the poles of a magnet, because the O_2 molecules are paramagnetic, having two parallel spins.*

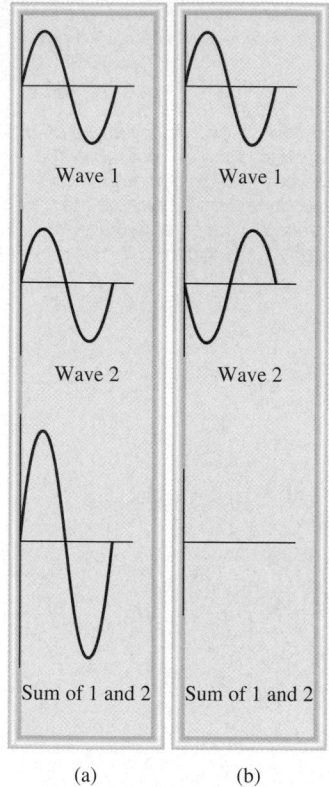

Figure 10.22 *Constructive interference (a) and destructive interference (b) of two waves of the same wavelength and amplitude.*

The two electrons in the sigma molecular orbital are paired. The Pauli exclusion principle applies to molecules as well as to atoms.

Figure 10.23 *(a) Energy levels of bonding and antibonding molecular orbitals in the H₂ molecule. Note that the two electrons in the σ₁ₛ orbital must have opposite spins in accord with the Pauli exclusion principle. Keep in mind that the higher the energy of the molecular orbital, the less stable the electrons in that molecular orbital. (b) Constructive and destructive interferences between the two hydrogen 1s orbitals lead to the formation of a bonding and an antibonding molecular orbital. In the bonding molecular orbital, there is a buildup between the nuclei of electron density, which acts as a negatively charged "glue" to hold the positively charged nuclei together. In the antibonding molecular orbital, there is a nodal plane between the nuclei, where the electron density is zero.*

antibonding molecular orbital. A **bonding molecular orbital** has *lower energy and greater stability than the atomic orbitals from which it was formed.* An **antibonding molecular orbital** has *higher energy and lower stability than the atomic orbitals from which it was formed.* As the names "bonding" and "antibonding" suggest, placing electrons in a bonding molecular orbital yields a stable covalent bond, whereas placing electrons in an antibonding molecular orbital results in an unstable bond.

In the bonding molecular orbital, the electron density is greatest between the nuclei of the bonding atoms. In the antibonding molecular orbital, on the other hand, the electron density decreases to zero between the nuclei. We can understand this distinction if we recall that electrons in orbitals have wave characteristics. A property unique to waves enables waves of the same type to interact in such a way that the resultant wave has either an enhanced amplitude or a diminished amplitude. In the former case, we call the interaction *constructive interference;* in the latter case, it is *destructive interference* (Figure 10.22).

The formation of bonding molecular orbitals corresponds to constructive interference (the increase in amplitude is analogous to the buildup of electron density between the two nuclei). The formation of antibonding molecular orbitals corresponds to destructive interference (the decrease in amplitude is analogous to the decrease in electron density between the two nuclei). The constructive and destructive interactions between the two 1s orbitals in the H₂ molecule, then, lead to the formation of a sigma bonding molecular orbital σ_{1s} and a sigma antibonding molecular orbital $\sigma_{1s}^{\star}$:

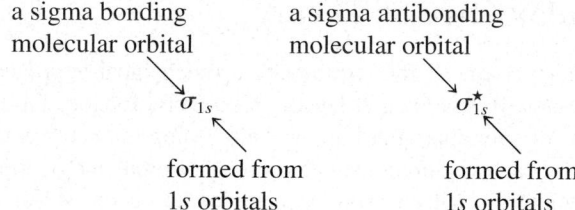

where the star denotes an antibonding molecular orbital.

In a **sigma molecular orbital** (bonding or antibonding) *the electron density is concentrated symmetrically around a line between the two nuclei of the bonding atoms.* Two electrons in a sigma molecular orbital form a sigma bond (see Section 10.5). Remember that a single covalent bond (such as H—H or F—F) is almost always a sigma bond.

Figure 10.23 shows the *molecular orbital energy level diagram*—that is, the relative energy levels of the orbitals produced in the formation of the H₂ molecule—and the constructive and destructive interferences between the two 1s orbitals. Notice that in the antibonding molecular orbital there is a *nodal plane* between the nuclei that signifies zero electron density. The nuclei are repelled by each other's positive charges, rather than held together. Electrons in the antibonding molecular orbital have higher

Figure 10.24 *Two possible interactions between two equivalent p orbitals and the corresponding molecular orbitals. (a) When the p orbitals overlap end-to-end, a sigma bonding and a sigma antibonding molecular orbital form. (b) When the p orbitals overlap side-to-side, a pi bonding and a pi antibonding molecular orbital form. Normally, a sigma bonding molecular orbital is more stable than a pi bonding molecular orbital, because side-to-side interaction leads to a smaller overlap of the p orbitals than does end-to-end interaction. We assume that the $2p_x$ orbitals take part in the sigma molecular orbital formation. The $2p_y$ and $2p_z$ orbitals can interact to form only π molecular orbitals. The behavior shown in (b) represents the interaction between the $2p_y$ orbitals or the $2p_z$ orbitals. In both cases, the dash line represents a nodal plane between the nuclei, where the electron density is zero.*

energy (and less stability) than they would have in the isolated atoms. On the other hand, electrons in the bonding molecular orbital have less energy (and hence greater stability) than they would have in the isolated atoms.

Although we have used the hydrogen molecule to illustrate molecular orbital formation, the concept is equally applicable to other molecules. In the H_2 molecule, we consider only the interaction between $1s$ orbitals; with more complex molecules we need to consider additional atomic orbitals as well. Nevertheless, for all s orbitals, the process is the same as for $1s$ orbitals. Thus, the interaction between two $2s$ or $3s$ orbitals can be understood in terms of the molecular orbital energy level diagram and the formation of bonding and antibonding molecular orbitals shown in Figure 10.23.

For p orbitals, the process is more complex because they can interact with each other in two different ways. For example, two $2p$ orbitals can approach each other end-to-end to produce a sigma bonding and a sigma antibonding molecular orbital, as shown in Figure 10.24(a). Alternatively, the two p orbitals can overlap sideways to generate a bonding and an antibonding pi molecular orbital [Figure 10.24(b)].

In a **pi molecular orbital** (bonding or antibonding), *the electron density is concentrated above and below a line joining the two nuclei of the bonding atoms.* Two electrons in a pi molecular orbital form a pi bond (see Section 10.5). A double bond is almost always composed of a sigma bond and a pi bond; a triple bond is always a sigma bond plus two pi bonds.

10.7 Molecular Orbital Configurations

To understand properties of molecules, we must know how electrons are distributed among molecular orbitals. The procedure for determining the electron configuration of a molecule is analogous to the one we use to determine the electron configurations of atoms (see Section 7.8).

Rules Governing Molecular Electron Configuration and Stability

In order to write the electron configuration of a molecule, we must first arrange the molecular orbitals in order of increasing energy. Then we can use the following guidelines to fill the molecular orbitals with electrons. The rules also help us understand the stabilities of the molecular orbitals.

1. The number of molecular orbitals formed is always equal to the number of atomic orbitals combined.

2. The more stable the bonding molecular orbital, the less stable the corresponding antibonding molecular orbital.

3. The filling of molecular orbitals proceeds from low to high energies. In a stable molecule, the number of electrons in bonding molecular orbitals is always greater than that in antibonding molecular orbitals because we place electrons first in the lower-energy bonding molecular orbitals.

4. Like an atomic orbital, each molecular orbital can accommodate up to two electrons with opposite spins in accordance with the Pauli exclusion principle.

5. When electrons are added to molecular orbitals of the same energy, the most stable arrangement is predicted by Hund's rule; that is, electrons enter these molecular orbitals with parallel spins.

6. The number of electrons in the molecular orbitals is equal to the sum of all the electrons on the bonding atoms.

Hydrogen and Helium Molecules

Later in this section we will study molecules formed by atoms of the second-period elements. Before we do, it will be instructive to predict the relative stabilities of the simple species H_2^+, H_2, He_2^+, and He_2, using the energy-level diagrams shown in Figure 10.25. The σ_{1s} and $\sigma_{1s}^\star$ orbitals can accommodate a maximum of four electrons.

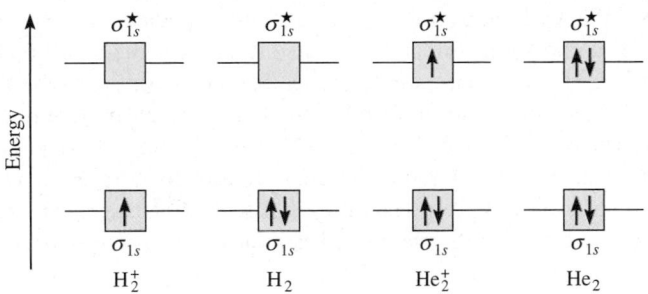

The total number of electrons increases from one for H_2^+ to four for He_2. The Pauli exclusion principle stipulates that each molecular orbital can accommodate a maximum of two electrons with opposite spins. We are concerned only with the ground-state electron configurations in these cases.

To evaluate the stabilities of these species we determine their **bond order,** defined as

$$\text{bond order} = \frac{1}{2}\left(\begin{array}{c}\text{number of electrons}\\ \text{in bonding MOs}\end{array} - \begin{array}{c}\text{number of electrons}\\ \text{in antibonding MOs}\end{array}\right) \qquad (10.2)$$

The bond order indicates the strength of a bond. For example, if there are two electrons in the bonding molecular orbital and none in the antibonding molecular orbital, the bond order is one, which means that there is one covalent bond and that the molecule is stable. Note that the bond order can be a fraction, but a bond order of zero (or a negative value) means the bond has no stability and the molecule cannot exist. Bond order can be used only qualitatively for purposes of comparison. For example, a bonding sigma molecular orbital with two electrons and a bonding pi molecular orbital with two electrons would each have a bond order of one. Yet, these two bonds must differ in bond strength (and bond length) because of the differences in the extent of atomic orbital overlap.

The quantitative measure of the strength of a bond is bond enthalpy (Section 9.10).

We are ready now to make predictions about the stability of H_2^+, H_2, He_2^+, and He_2 (see Figure 10.25). The H_2^+ molecular ion has only one electron in the σ_{1s} orbital. Because a covalent bond consists of two electrons in a bonding molecular orbital, H_2^+ has only half of one bond, or a bond order of $\frac{1}{2}$. Thus, we predict that the H_2^+ molecule may be a stable species. The electron configuration of H_2^+ is written as $(\sigma_{1s})^1$.

The superscript in $(\sigma_{1s})^1$ indicates that there is one electron in the sigma bonding molecular orbital.

The H_2 molecule has two electrons, both of which are in the σ_{1s} orbital. According to our scheme, two electrons equal one full bond; therefore, the H_2 molecule has a bond order of one, or one full covalent bond. The electron configuration of H_2 is $(\sigma_{1s})^2$.

As for the He_2^+ molecular ion, we place the first two electrons in the σ_{1s} orbital and the third electron in the $\sigma_{1s}^\star$ orbital. Because the antibonding molecular orbital is destabilizing, we expect He_2^+ to be less stable than H_2. Roughly speaking, the instability resulting from the electron in the $\sigma_{1s}^\star$ orbital is balanced by one of the σ_{1s} electrons. The bond order is $\frac{1}{2}(2-1) = \frac{1}{2}$ and the overall stability of He_2^+ is similar to that of the H_2^+ molecule. The electron configuration of He_2^+ is $(\sigma_{1s})^2(\sigma_{1s}^\star)^1$.

In He_2 there would be two electrons in the σ_{1s} orbital and two electrons in the $\sigma_{1s}^\star$ orbital, so the molecule would have a bond order of zero and no net stability. The electron configuration of He_2 would be $(\sigma_{1s})^2(\sigma_{1s}^\star)^2$.

To summarize, we can arrange our examples in order of decreasing stability:

$$H_2 > H_2^+, He_2^+ > He_2$$

We know that the hydrogen molecule is a stable species. Our simple molecular orbital method predicts that H_2^+ and He_2^+ also possess some stability, because both have bond orders of $\frac{1}{2}$. Indeed, their existence has been confirmed by experiment. It turns out that H_2^+ is somewhat more stable than He_2^+, because there is only one electron in the hydrogen molecular ion and therefore it has no electron-electron repulsion. Furthermore, H_2^+ also has less nuclear repulsion than He_2^+. Our prediction about He_2 is that it would have no stability, but in 1993 He_2 gas was found to exist. The "molecule" is extremely unstable and has only a transient existence under specially created conditions.

Homonuclear Diatomic Molecules of Second-Period Elements

We are now ready to study the ground-state electron configuration of molecules containing second-period elements. We will consider only the simplest case, that of **homonuclear diatomic molecules,** or *diatomic molecules containing atoms of the same elements.*

Figure 10.26 shows the molecular orbital energy level diagram for the first member of the second period, Li_2. These molecular orbitals are formed by the overlap of $1s$ and $2s$ orbitals. We will use this diagram to build up all the diatomic molecules, as we will see shortly.

The situation is more complex when the bonding also involves p orbitals. Two p orbitals can form either a sigma bond or a pi bond. Because there are three p orbitals for each atom of a second-period element, we know that one sigma and two pi molecular orbitals will result from the constructive interaction. The sigma molecular orbital is formed by the overlap of the $2p_x$ orbitals along the internuclear axis, that is, the x-axis. The $2p_y$ and $2p_z$ orbitals are perpendicular to the x-axis, and they will overlap sideways to give two pi molecular orbitals. The molecular orbitals are called σ_{2p_x}, π_{2p_y},

Figure 10.26 *Molecular orbital energy level diagram for the Li_2 molecule. The six electrons in Li_2 (Li's electron configuration is $1s^2 2s^1$) are in the σ_{1s}, $\sigma_{1s}^\star$, and σ_{2s} orbitals. Because there are two electrons each in σ_{1s} and $\sigma_{1s}^\star$ (just as in He_2), there is no net bonding or antibonding effect. Therefore, the single covalent bond in Li_2 is formed by the two electrons in the bonding molecular orbital σ_{2s}. Note that although the antibonding orbital ($\sigma_{1s}^\star$) has higher energy and is thus less stable than the bonding orbital (σ_{1s}), this antibonding orbital has less energy and greater stability than the σ_{2s} bonding orbital.*

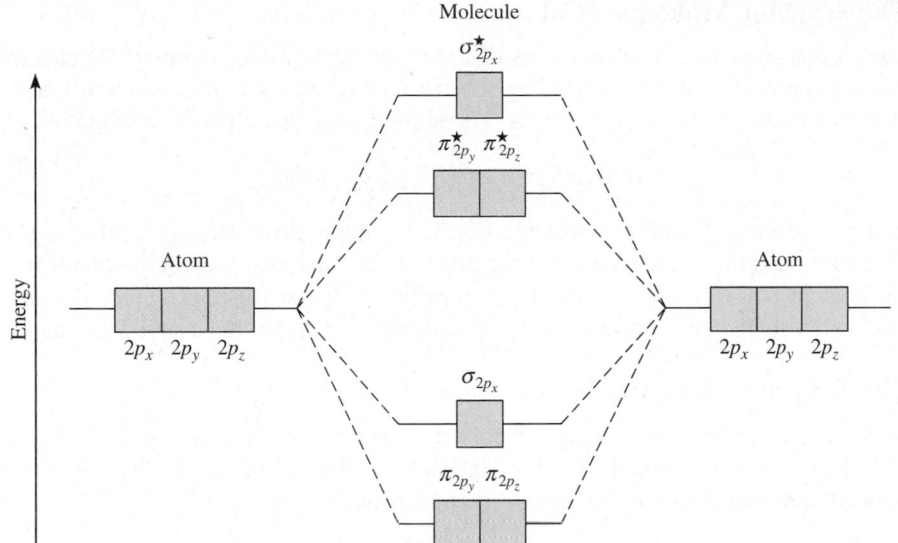

Figure 10.27 *General molecular orbital energy level diagram for the second-period homonuclear diatomic molecules Li$_2$, Be$_2$, B$_2$, C$_2$, and N$_2$. For simplicity, the σ_{1s} and σ_{2s} orbitals have been omitted. Note that in these molecules the σ_{2p_x} orbital is higher in energy than either the π_{2p_y} or the π_{2p_z} orbitals. This means that electrons in the σ_{2p_x} orbitals are less stable than those in π_{2p_y} and π_{2p_z}. For O$_2$ and F$_2$, the σ_{2p_x} orbital is lower in energy than π_{2p_y} and π_{2p_z}.*

and π_{2p_z} orbitals, where the subscripts indicate which atomic orbitals take part in forming the molecular orbitals. As shown in Figure 10.24, overlap of the two p orbitals is normally greater in a σ molecular orbital than in a π molecular orbital, so we would expect the former to be lower in energy. However, the energies of molecular orbitals actually increase as follows:

$$\sigma_{1s} < \sigma_{1s}^{\star} < \sigma_{2s} < \sigma_{2s}^{\star} < \pi_{2p_y} = \pi_{2p_z} < \sigma_{2p_x} < \pi_{2p_y}^{\star} = \pi_{2p_z}^{\star} < \sigma_{2p_x}^{\star}$$

The inversion of the σ_{2p_x} orbital and the π_{2p_y} and π_{2p_z} orbitals is due to the interaction between the 2s orbital on one atom with the 2p orbital on the other. In MO terminology, we say there is mixing between these orbitals. The condition for mixing is that the 2s and 2p orbitals must be close in energy. This condition is met for the lighter molecules B$_2$, C$_2$, and N$_2$ with the result that the σ_{2p_x} orbital is raised in energy relative to the π_{2p_y} and π_{2p_z} orbitals as already shown. The mixing is less pronounced for O$_2$ and F$_2$ so the σ_{2p_x} orbital lies lower in energy than the π_{2p_y} and π_{2p_z} orbitals in these molecules.

With these concepts and Figure 10.27, which shows the order of increasing energies for 2p molecular orbitals, we can write the electron configurations and predict the magnetic properties and bond orders of second-period homonuclear diatomic molecules. We will consider a few examples.

The Lithium Molecule (Li$_2$)

The electron configuration of Li is $1s^2 2s^1$, so Li$_2$ has a total of six electrons. According to Figure 10.26, these electrons are placed (two each) in the σ_{1s}, $\sigma_{1s}^{\star}$, and σ_{2s} molecular orbitals. The electrons of σ_{1s} and $\sigma_{1s}^{\star}$ make no net contribution to the bonding in Li$_2$. Thus, the electron configuration of the molecular orbitals in Li$_2$ is $(\sigma_{1s})^2(\sigma_{1s}^{\star})^2(\sigma_{2s})^2$. Since there are two more electrons in the bonding molecular orbitals than in antibonding orbitals, the bond order is 1 [see Equation (10.2)]. We conclude that the Li$_2$ molecule is stable, and because it has no unpaired electron spins, it should be diamagnetic. Indeed, diamagnetic Li$_2$ molecules are known to exist in the vapor phase.

The Carbon Molecule (C_2)

The carbon atom has the electron configuration $1s^2 2s^2 2p^2$; thus, there are 12 electrons in the C_2 molecule. From the bonding scheme for Li_2, we place four additional carbon electrons in the π_{2p_y} and π_{2p_z} orbitals. Therefore, C_2 has the electron configuration

$$(\sigma_{1s})^2(\sigma_{1s}^{\star})^2(\sigma_{2s})^2(\sigma_{2s}^{\star})^2(\pi_{2p_y})^2(\pi_{2p_z})^2$$

Its bond order is 2, and the molecule has no unpaired electrons. Again, diamagnetic C_2 molecules have been detected in the vapor state. Note that the double bonds in C_2 are both pi bonds because of the four electrons in the two pi molecular orbitals. In most other molecules, a double bond is made up of a sigma bond and a pi bond.

The Oxygen Molecule (O_2)

As we stated earlier, valence bond theory does not account for the magnetic properties of the oxygen molecule. To show the two unpaired electrons on O_2, we need to draw an alternative to the resonance structure present on p. 429:

$$\cdot \ddot{O}\!-\!\ddot{O} \cdot$$

This structure is unsatisfactory on at least two counts. First, it implies the presence of a single covalent bond, but experimental evidence strongly suggests that there is a double bond in this molecule. Second, it places seven valence electrons around each oxygen atom, a violation of the octet rule.

The ground-state electron configuration of O is $1s^2 2s^2 2p^4$; thus, there are 16 electrons in O_2. Using the order of increasing energies of the molecular orbitals discussed above, we write the ground-state electron configuration of O_2 as

$$(\sigma_{1s})^2(\sigma_{1s}^{\star})^2(\sigma_{2s})^2(\sigma_{2s}^{\star})^2(\sigma_{2p_x})^2(\pi_{2p_y})^2(\pi_{2p_z})^2(\pi_{2p_y}^{\star})^1(\pi_{2p_z}^{\star})^1$$

TABLE 10.5   Properties of Homonuclear Diatomic Molecules of the Second-Period Elements*

	Li_2	B_2	C_2	N_2	O_2	F_2	
$\sigma_{2p_x}^{\star}$	☐	☐	☐	☐	☐	☐	$\sigma_{2p_x}^{\star}$
$\pi_{2p_y}^{\star}, \pi_{2p_z}^{\star}$	☐☐	☐☐	☐☐	☐☐	↑ ↑	�↑↓ ↑↓	$\pi_{2p_y}^{\star}, \pi_{2p_z}^{\star}$
σ_{2p_x}	☐	☐	☐	↑↓	↑↓ ↑↓	↑↓ ↑↓	π_{2p_y}, π_{2p_z}
π_{2p_y}, π_{2p_z}	☐☐	↑ ↑	↑↓ ↑↓	↑↓ ↑↓	↑↓	↑↓	σ_{2p_x}
$\sigma_{2s}^{\star}$	☐	↑↓	↑↓	↑↓	↑↓	↑↓	$\sigma_{2s}^{\star}$
σ_{2s}	↑↓	↑↓	↑↓	↑↓	↑↓	↑↓	σ_{2s}
Bond order	1	1	2	3	2	1	
Bond length (pm)	267	159	131	110	121	142	
Bond enthalpy (kJ/mol)	104.6	288.7	627.6	941.4	498.7	156.9	
Magnetic properties	Diamagnetic	Paramagnetic	Diamagnetic	Diamagnetic	Paramagnetic	Diamagnetic	

*For simplicity the σ_{1s} and $\sigma_{1s}^{\star}$ orbitals are omitted. These two orbitals hold a total of four electrons. Remember that for O_2 and F_2, σ_{2p_x} is lower in energy than π_{2p_y} and π_{2p_z}.

According to Hund's rule, the last two electrons enter the $\pi_{2p_y}^{\star}$ and $\pi_{2p_z}^{\star}$ orbitals with parallel spins. Ignoring the σ_{1s} and σ_{2s} orbitals (because their net effects on bonding are zero), we calculate the bond order of O_2 using Equation (10.2):

$$\text{bond order} = \tfrac{1}{2}(6 - 2) = 2$$

Therefore, the O_2 molecule has a bond order of 2 and oxygen is paramagnetic, a prediction that corresponds to experimental observations.

Table 10.5 summarizes the general properties of the stable diatomic molecules of the second period.

Example 10.6 shows how MO theory can help predict molecular properties of ions.

Example 10.6

The N_2^+ ion can be prepared by bombarding the N_2 molecule with fast-moving electrons. Predict the following properties of N_2^+: (a) electron configuration, (b) bond order, (c) magnetic properties, and (d) bond length relative to the bond length of N_2 (is it longer or shorter?).

Strategy From Table 10.5 we can deduce the properties of ions generated from the homonuclear molecules. How does the stability of a molecule depend on the number of electrons in bonding and antibonding molecular orbitals? From what molecular orbital is an electron removed to form the N_2^+ ion from N_2? What properties determine whether a species is diamagnetic or paramagnetic?

Solution From Table 10.5 we can deduce the properties of ions generated from the homonuclear diatomic molecules.

(a) Because N_2^+ has one fewer electron than N_2, its electron configuration is

$$(\sigma_{1s})^2(\sigma_{1s}^{\star})^2(\sigma_{2s})^2(\sigma_{2s}^{\star})^2(\pi_{2p_y})^2(\pi_{2p_z})^2(\sigma_{2p_x})^1$$

(b) The bond order of N_2^+ is found by using Equation (10.2):

$$\text{bond order} = \tfrac{1}{2}(9 - 4) = 2.5$$

(c) N_2^+ has one unpaired electron, so it is paramagnetic.

(d) Because the electrons in the bonding molecular orbitals are responsible for holding the atoms together, N_2^+ should have a weaker and, therefore, longer bond than N_2. (In fact, the bond length of N_2^+ is 112 pm, compared with 110 pm for N_2.)

Check Because an electron is removed from a bonding molecular orbital, we expect the bond order to decrease. The N_2^+ ion has an odd number of electrons (13), so it should be paramagnetic.

Similar problems: 10.57, 10.58.

Practice Exercise Which of the following species has a longer bond length: F_2 or F_2^-?

10.8 Delocalized Molecular Orbitals

So far we have discussed chemical bonding only in terms of electron pairs. However, the properties of a molecule cannot always be explained accurately by a single structure. A case in point is the O_3 molecule, discussed in Section 9.8. There we overcame the dilemma by introducing the concept of resonance. In this section we will tackle the problem in another way—by applying the molecular orbital approach. As in

Figure 10.28 *The sigma bond framework in the benzene molecule. Each carbon atom is sp^2-hybridized and forms sigma bonds with two adjacent carbon atoms and another sigma bond with a hydrogen atom.*

Electrostatic potential map of benzene shows the electron density (red color) above and below the plane of the molecule. For simplicity, only the framework of the molecule is shown.

Section 9.8, we will use the benzene molecule and the carbonate ion as examples. Note that in discussing the bonding of polyatomic molecules or ions, it is convenient to determine first the hybridization state of the atoms present (a valence bond approach), followed by the formation of appropriate molecular orbitals.

The Benzene Molecule

Benzene (C_6H_6) is a planar hexagonal molecule with carbon atoms situated at the six corners. All carbon-carbon bonds are equal in length and strength, as are all carbon-hydrogen bonds, and the CCC and HCC angles are all 120°. Therefore, each carbon atom is sp^2-hybridized; it forms three sigma bonds with two adjacent carbon atoms and a hydrogen atom (Figure 10.28). This arrangement leaves an unhybridized $2p_z$ orbital on each carbon atom, perpendicular to the plane of the benzene molecule, or *benzene ring*, as it is often called. So far the description resembles the configuration of ethylene (C_2H_4), discussed in Section 10.5, except that in this case there are six unhybridized $2p_z$ orbitals in a cyclic arrangement.

Because of their similar shape and orientation, each $2p_z$ orbital overlaps two others, one on each adjacent carbon atom. According to the rules listed on p. 432, the interaction of six $2p_z$ orbitals leads to the formation of six pi molecular orbitals, of which three are bonding and three antibonding. A benzene molecule in the ground state therefore has six electrons in the three pi bonding molecular orbitals, two electrons with paired spins in each orbital (Figure 10.29).

Unlike the pi bonding molecular orbitals in ethylene, those in benzene form **delocalized molecular orbitals,** which *are not confined between two adjacent bonding atoms, but actually extend over three or more atoms.* Therefore, electrons residing in any of these orbitals are free to move around the benzene ring. For this reason, the structure of benzene is sometimes represented as

in which the circle indicates that the pi bonds between carbon atoms are not confined to individual pairs of atoms; rather, the pi electron densities are evenly distributed throughout the benzene molecule. The carbon and hydrogen atoms are not shown in the simplified diagram.

We can now state that each carbon-to-carbon linkage in benzene contains a sigma bond and a "partial" pi bond. The bond order between any two adjacent carbon atoms is therefore between 1 and 2. Thus, molecular orbital theory offers an alternative to the resonance approach, which is based on valence bond theory. (The resonance structures of benzene are shown on p. 379.)

Figure 10.29 *(a) The six $2p_z$ orbitals on the carbon atoms in benzene. (b) The delocalized molecular orbital formed by the overlap of the $2p_z$ orbitals. The delocalized molecular orbital possesses pi symmetry and lies above and below the plane of the benzene ring. Actually, these $2p_z$ orbitals can combine in six different ways to yield three bonding molecular orbitals and three antibonding molecular orbitals. The one shown here is the most stable.*

(a)   (b)

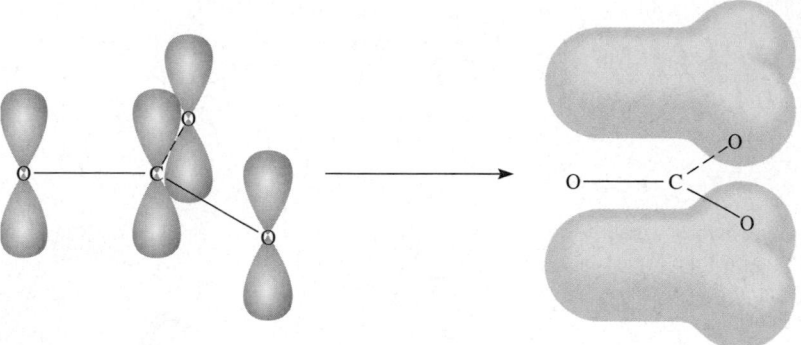

Figure 10.30 *Bonding in the carbonate ion. The carbon atom forms three sigma bonds with the three oxygen atoms. In addition, the $2p_z$ orbitals of the carbon and oxygen atoms overlap to form delocalized molecular orbitals, so that there is also a partial pi bond between the carbon atom and each of the three oxygen atoms.*

The Carbonate Ion

Cyclic compounds like benzene are not the only ones with delocalized molecular orbitals. Let's look at bonding in the carbonate ion (CO_3^{2-}). VSEPR predicts a trigonal planar geometry for the carbonate ion, like that for BF_3. The planar structure of the carbonate ion can be explained by assuming that the carbon atom is sp^2-hybridized. The C atom forms sigma bonds with three O atoms. Thus, the unhybridized $2p_z$ orbital of the C atom can simultaneously overlap the $2p_z$ orbitals of all three O atoms (Figure 10.30). The result is a delocalized molecular orbital that extends over all four nuclei in such a way that the electron densities (and hence the bond orders) in the carbon-to-oxygen bonds are all the same. Molecular orbital theory therefore provides an acceptable alternative explanation of the properties of the carbonate ion as compared with the resonance structures of the ion shown on p. 378.

We should note that molecules with delocalized molecular orbitals are generally more stable than those containing molecular orbitals extending over only two atoms. For example, the benzene molecule, which contains delocalized molecular orbitals, is chemically less reactive (and hence more stable) than molecules containing "localized" C=C bonds, such as ethylene.

Summary of Facts and Concepts

1. The VSEPR model for predicting molecular geometry is based on the assumption that valence-shell electron pairs repel one another and tend to stay as far apart as possible.
2. According to the VSEPR model, molecular geometry can be predicted from the number of bonding electron pairs and lone pairs. Lone pairs repel other pairs more forcefully than bonding pairs do and thus distort bond angles from the ideal geometry.
3. Dipole moment is a measure of the charge separation in molecules containing atoms of different electronegativities. The dipole moment of a molecule is the resultant of whatever bond moments are present. Information about molecular geometry can be obtained from dipole moment measurements.
4. There are two quantum mechanical explanations for covalent bond formation: valence bond theory and molecular orbital theory. In valence bond theory, hybridized atomic orbitals are formed by the combination and rearrangement of orbitals from the same atom. The hybridized orbitals are all of equal energy and electron density, and the number of hybridized orbitals is equal to the number of pure atomic orbitals that combine.
5. Valence-shell expansion can be explained by assuming hybridization of s, p, and d orbitals.
6. In sp hybridization, the two hybrid orbitals lie in a straight line; in sp^2 hybridization, the three hybrid orbitals are directed toward the corners of an equilateral triangle; in sp^3 hybridization, the four hybrid orbitals are directed toward the corners of a tetrahedron; in sp^3d hybridization, the five hybrid orbitals are directed toward the corners of a trigonal bipyramid; in sp^3d^2 hybridization, the six hybrid orbitals are directed toward the corners of an octahedron.

CHEMISTRY
in Action

Buckyball, Anyone?

In 1985 chemists at Rice University in Texas used a high-powered laser to vaporize graphite in an effort to create unusual molecules believed to exist in interstellar space. Mass spectrometry revealed that one of the products was an unknown species with the formula C_{60}. Because of its size and the fact that it is pure carbon, this molecule has an exotic shape, which the researchers worked out using paper, scissors, and tape. Subsequent spectroscopic and X-ray measurements confirmed that C_{60} is shaped like a hollow sphere with a carbon atom at each of the 60 vertices. Geometrically, buckyball (short for "buckminsterfullerene") is the most symmetrical molecule known. In spite of its unique features, however, its bonding scheme is straightforward. Each carbon is sp^2-hybridized, and there are extensive delocalized molecular orbitals over the entire structure.

The discovery of buckyball generated tremendous interest within the scientific community. Here was a new allotrope of carbon with an intriguing geometry and unknown properties to investigate. Since 1985 chemists have created a whole class of *fullerenes*, with 70, 76, and even larger numbers of carbon atoms. Moreover, buckyball has been found to be a natural component of soot.

Buckyball and its heavier members represent a whole new concept in molecular architecture with far-reaching implications. For example, buckyball has been prepared with a helium atom trapped in its cage. Buckyball also reacts with potassium to give K_3C_{60}, which acts as a superconductor at 18 K. It is also possible to attach transition metals to buckyball. These derivatives show promise as catalysts. Because of its unique shape, buckyball can be used as a lubricant.

One fascinating discovery, made in 1991 by Japanese scientists, was the identification of structural relatives of buckyball. These molecules are hundreds of nanometers long with a tubular shape and an internal cavity about 15 nanometers in diameter. Dubbed "buckytubes" or "nanotubes" (because of their size), these molecules have two distinctly different structures.

The geometry of a buckyball C_{60} (left) resembles a soccer ball (right). Scientists arrived at this structure by fitting together paper cutouts of enough hexagons and pentagons to accommodate 60 carbon atoms at the points where they intersect.

One is a single sheet of graphite that is capped at both ends with a kind of truncated buckyball. The other is a scroll-like tube having anywhere from 2 to 30 graphitelike layers. Nanotubes are many times stronger than steel wires of similar dimensions. Numerous potential applications have been proposed for them, including conducting and high-strength materials, hydrogen storage media, molecular sensors, semiconductor devices, and molecular probes. The study of these materials has created a new field called *nanotechnology*, so called because scientists can manipulate materials on a molecular scale to create useful devices.

In the first biological application of buckyball, chemists at the University of California at San Francisco and Santa Barbara made a discovery in 1993 that could help in designing drugs to treat AIDS. The human immunodeficiency virus (HIV) that causes AIDS reproduces by synthesizing a long protein chain, which is cut into smaller segments by an enzyme called HIV-protease. One way to stop AIDS, then, might

7. In an sp^2-hybridized atom (for example, carbon), the one unhybridized *p* orbital can form a pi bond with another *p* orbital. A carbon-carbon double bond consists of a sigma bond and a pi bond. In an *sp*-hybridized carbon atom, the two unhybridized *p* orbitals can form two pi bonds with two *p* orbitals on another atom (or atoms). A carbon-carbon triple bond consists of one sigma bond and two pi bonds.

8. Molecular orbital theory describes bonding in terms of the combination and rearrangement of atomic orbitals to form orbitals that are associated with the molecule as a whole.

9. Bonding molecular orbitals increase electron density between the nuclei and are lower in energy than individual atomic orbitals. Antibonding molecular orbitals have a region of zero electron density between the

Graphite is made up of layers of six-membered rings of carbon.

335 pm

Computer-generated model of the binding of a buckyball derivative to the site of HIV-protease that normally attaches to a protein needed for the reproduction of HIV. The buckyball structure (purple color) fits tightly into the active site, thus preventing the enzyme from carrying out its function.

The structure of a buckytube that consists of a single layer of carbon atoms. Note that the truncated buckyball "cap," which has been separated from the rest of the buckytube in this view, has a different structure than the graphitelike cylindrical portion of the tube. Chemists have devised ways to open the cap in order to place other molecules inside the tube.

be to inactivate the enzyme. When the chemists reacted a water-soluble derivative of buckyball with HIV-protease, they found that it binds to the portion of the enzyme that would ordinarily cleave the reproductive protein, thereby preventing the HIV virus from reproducing. Consequently the virus could no longer infect the human cells they had grown in the laboratory. The buckyball compound itself is not a suitable drug for use against AIDS because of potential side effects and delivery difficulties, but it does provide a model for the development of such drugs.

nuclei, and an energy level higher than that of the individual atomic orbitals.

10. We write electron configurations for molecular orbitals as we do for atomic orbitals, filling in electrons in the order of increasing energy levels. The number of molecular orbitals always equals the number of atomic orbitals that were combined. The Pauli exclusion principle and Hund's rule govern the filling of molecular orbitals.

11. Molecules are stable if the number of electrons in bonding molecular orbitals is greater than that in antibonding molecular orbitals.

12. Delocalized molecular orbitals, in which electrons are free to move around a whole molecule or group of atoms, are formed by electrons in p orbitals of adjacent atoms. Delocalized molecular orbitals are an alternative to resonance structures in explaining observed molecular properties.

Key Words

Antibonding molecular
  orbital, p. 430
Bond order, p. 433
Bonding molecular
  orbital, p. 430
Delocalized molecular
  orbital, p. 438

Dipole moment (μ), p. 409
Homonuclear diatomic
  molecule, p. 434
Hybrid orbital, p. 418
Hybridization, p. 418
Molecular orbital, p. 429
Nonpolar molecule, p. 410

Pi bond (π bond), p. 426
Pi molecular orbital, p. 432
Polar molecule, p. 410
Sigma bond (σ bond), p. 426
Sigma molecular
  orbital, p. 430
Valence shell, p. 400

Valence-shell electron-pair
  repulsion (VSEPR)
  model, p. 400

Questions and Problems

Molecular Geometry
Review Questions

10.1   How is the geometry of a molecule defined and why is the study of molecular geometry important?

10.2   Sketch the shape of a linear triatomic molecule, a trigonal planar molecule containing four atoms, a tetrahedral molecule, a trigonal bipyramidal molecule, and an octahedral molecule. Give the bond angles in each case.

10.3   How many atoms are directly bonded to the central atom in a tetrahedral molecule, a trigonal bipyramidal molecule, and an octahedral molecule?

10.4   Discuss the basic features of the VSEPR model. Explain why the magnitude of repulsion decreases in the following order: lone pair-lone pair > lone pair-bonding pair > bonding pair-bonding pair.

10.5   In the trigonal bipyramidal arrangement, why does a lone pair occupy an equatorial position rather than an axial position?

10.6   The geometry of CH_4 could be square planar, with the four H atoms at the corners of a square and the C atom at the center of the square. Sketch this geometry and compare its stability with that of a tetrahedral CH_4 molecule.

Problems

10.7   Predict the geometries of the following species using the VSEPR method: (a) PCl_3, (b) $CHCl_3$, (c) SiH_4, (d) $TeCl_4$.

10.8   Predict the geometries of the following species: (a) $AlCl_3$, (b) $ZnCl_2$, (c) $ZnCl_4^{2-}$.

10.9   Predict the geometry of the following molecules and ion using the VSEPR model: (a) CBr_4, (b) BCl_3, (c) NF_3, (d) H_2Se, (e) NO_2^-.

10.10 Predict the geometry of the following molecules and ion using the VSEPR model: (a) CH_3I, (b) ClF_3, (c) H_2S, (d) SO_3, (e) SO_4^{2-}.

10.11 Predict the geometry of the following molecules using the VSEPR method: (a) $HgBr_2$, (b) N_2O (arrangement of atoms is NNO), (c) SCN^- (arrangement of atoms is SCN).

10.12 Predict the geometries of the following ions: (a) NH_4^+, (b) NH_2^-, (c) CO_3^{2-}, (d) ICl_2^-, (e) ICl_4^-, (f) AlH_4^-, (g) $SnCl_5^-$, (h) H_3O^+, (i) BeF_4^{2-}.

10.13 Describe the geometry around each of the three central atoms in the CH_3COOH molecule.

10.14 Which of the following species are tetrahedral? $SiCl_4$, SeF_4, XeF_4, CI_4, $CdCl_4^{2-}$

Dipole Moments
Review Questions

10.15 Define dipole moment. What are the units and symbol for dipole moment?

10.16 What is the relationship between the dipole moment and the bond moment? How is it possible for a molecule to have bond moments and yet be nonpolar?

10.17 Explain why an atom cannot have a permanent dipole moment.

10.18 The bonds in beryllium hydride (BeH_2) molecules are polar, and yet the dipole moment of the molecule is zero. Explain.

Problems

10.19 Referring to Table 10.3, arrange the following molecules in order of increasing dipole moment: H_2O, H_2S, H_2Te, H_2Se.

10.20 The dipole moments of the hydrogen halides decrease from HF to HI (see Table 10.3). Explain this trend.

10.21 List the following molecules in order of increasing dipole moment: H_2O, CBr_4, H_2S, HF, NH_3, CO_2.

10.22 Does the molecule OCS have a higher or lower dipole moment than CS_2?

10.23 Which of the following molecules has a higher dipole moment?

(a)   (b)

10.24 Arrange the following compounds in order of increasing dipole moment:

(a)   (b)   (c)   (d)

Valence Bond Theory
Review Questions

10.25 What is valence bond theory? How does it differ from the Lewis concept of chemical bonding?

10.26 Use valence bond theory to explain the bonding in Cl_2 and HCl. Show how the atomic orbitals overlap when a bond is formed.

10.27 Draw a potential energy curve for the bond formation in F_2.

Hybridization
Review Questions

10.28 What is the hybridization of atomic orbitals? Why is it impossible for an isolated atom to exist in the hybridized state?

10.29 How does a hybrid orbital differ from a pure atomic orbital? Can two $2p$ orbitals of an atom hybridize to give two hybridized orbitals?

10.30 What is the angle between the following two hybrid orbitals on the same atom? (a) sp and sp hybrid orbitals, (b) sp^2 and sp^2 hybrid orbitals, (c) sp^3 and sp^3 hybrid orbitals

10.31 How would you distinguish between a sigma bond and a pi bond?

10.32 Which of the following pairs of atomic orbitals of adjacent nuclei can overlap to form a sigma bond? Which overlap to form a pi bond? Which cannot overlap (no bond)? Consider the x-axis to be the internuclear axis, that is, the line joining the nuclei of the two atoms. (a) $1s$ and $1s$, (b) $1s$ and $2p_x$, (c) $2p_x$ and $2p_y$, (d) $3p_y$ and $3p_y$, (e) $2p_x$ and $2p_x$, (f) $1s$ and $2s$

Problems

10.33 Describe the bonding scheme of the AsH_3 molecule in terms of hybridization.

10.34 What is the hybridization state of Si in SiH_4 and in $H_3Si—SiH_3$?

10.35 Describe the change in hybridization (if any) of the Al atom in the following reaction:

$$AlCl_3 + Cl^- \longrightarrow AlCl_4^-$$

10.36 Consider the reaction

$$BF_3 + NH_3 \longrightarrow F_3B—NH_3$$

Describe the changes in hybridization (if any) of the B and N atoms as a result of this reaction.

10.37 What hybrid orbitals are used by nitrogen atoms in the following species? (a) NH_3, (b) $H_2N—NH_2$, (c) NO_3^-

10.38 What are the hybrid orbitals of the carbon atoms in the following molecules?
(a) $H_3C—CH_3$
(b) $H_3C—CH=CH_2$
(c) $CH_3—C≡C—CH_2OH$
(d) $CH_3CH=O$
(e) CH_3COOH

10.39 Specify which hybrid orbitals are used by carbon atoms in the following species: (a) CO, (b) CO_2, (c) CN^-.

10.40 What is the hybridization state of the central N atom in the azide ion, N_3^-? (Arrangement of atoms: NNN.)

10.41 The allene molecule $H_2C=C=CH_2$ is linear (the three C atoms lie on a straight line). What are the hybridization states of the carbon atoms? Draw diagrams to show the formation of sigma bonds and pi bonds in allene.

10.42 Describe the hybridization of phosphorus in PF_5.

10.43 How many sigma bonds and pi bonds are there in each of the following molecules?

(a)   (b)   (c)

10.44 How many pi bonds and sigma bonds are there in the tetracyanoethylene molecule?

Molecular Orbital Theory
Review Questions

10.45 What is molecular orbital theory? How does it differ from valence bond theory?

10.46 Define the following terms: bonding molecular orbital, antibonding molecular orbital, pi molecular orbital, sigma molecular orbital.

10.47 Sketch the shapes of the following molecular orbitals: σ_{1s}, $\sigma_{1s}^{\star}$, π_{2p}, and $\pi_{2p}^{\star}$. How do their energies compare?

10.48 Explain the significance of bond order. Can bond order be used for quantitative comparisons of the strengths of chemical bonds?

Problems

10.49 Explain in molecular orbital terms the changes in H—H internuclear distance that occur as the molecular H_2 is ionized first to H_2^+ and then to H_2^{2+}.

10.50 The formation of H_2 from two H atoms is an energetically favorable process. Yet statistically there is less than a 100 percent chance that any two H atoms will undergo the reaction. Apart from energy considerations, how would you account for this observation based on the electron spins in the two H atoms?

10.51 Draw a molecular orbital energy level diagram for each of the following species: He_2, HHe, He_2^+. Compare their relative stabilities in terms of bond orders. (Treat HHe as a diatomic molecule with three electrons.)

10.52 Arrange the following species in order of increasing stability: Li_2, Li_2^+, Li_2^-. Justify your choice with a molecular orbital energy level diagram.

10.53 Use molecular orbital theory to explain why the Be_2 molecule does not exist.

10.54 Which of these species has a longer bond, B_2 or B_2^+? Explain in terms of molecular orbital theory.

10.55 Acetylene (C_2H_2) has a tendency to lose two protons (H^+) and form the carbide ion (C_2^{2-}), which is present in a number of ionic compounds, such as CaC_2 and MgC_2. Describe the bonding scheme in the C_2^{2-} ion in terms of molecular orbital theory. Compare the bond order in C_2^{2-} with that in C_2.

10.56 Compare the Lewis and molecular orbital treatments of the oxygen molecule.

10.57 Explain why the bond order of N_2 is greater than that of N_2^+, but the bond order of O_2 is less than that of O_2^+.

10.58 Compare the relative stability of the following species and indicate their magnetic properties (that is, diamagnetic or paramagnetic): O_2, O_2^+, O_2^- (superoxide ion), O_2^{2-} (peroxide ion).

10.59 Use molecular orbital theory to compare the relative stabilities of F_2 and F_2^+.

10.60 A single bond is almost always a sigma bond, and a double bond is almost always made up of a sigma bond and a pi bond. There are very few exceptions to this rule. Show that the B_2 and C_2 molecules are examples of the exceptions.

Delocalized Molecular Orbitals
Review Questions

10.61 How does a delocalized molecular orbital differ from a molecular orbital such as that found in H_2 or C_2H_4? What do you think are the minimum conditions (for example, number of atoms and types of orbitals) for forming a delocalized molecular orbital?

10.62 In Chapter 9 we saw that the resonance concept is useful for dealing with species such as the benzene molecule and the carbonate ion. How does molecular orbital theory deal with these species?

Problems

10.63 Both ethylene (C_2H_4) and benzene (C_6H_6) contain the C=C bond. The reactivity of ethylene is greater than that of benzene. For example, ethylene readily reacts with molecular bromine, whereas benzene is normally quite inert toward molecular bromine and many other compounds. Explain this difference in reactivity.

10.64 Explain why the symbol on the left is a better representation of benzene molecules than that on the right.

10.65 Determine which of these molecules has a more delocalized orbital and justify your choice.

(*Hint:* Both molecules contain two benzene rings. In naphthalene, the two rings are fused together. In biphenyl, the two rings are joined by a single bond, around which the two rings can rotate.)

10.66 Nitryl fluoride (FNO_2) is very reactive chemically. The fluorine and oxygen atoms are bonded to the nitrogen atom. (a) Write a Lewis structure for FNO_2. (b) Indicate the hybridization of the nitrogen atom. (c) Describe the bonding in terms of molecular orbital theory. Where would you expect delocalized molecular orbitals to form?

10.67 Describe the bonding in the nitrate ion NO_3^- in terms of delocalized molecular orbitals.

10.68 What is the state of hybridization of the central O atom in O_3? Describe the bonding in O_3 in terms of delocalized molecular orbitals.

Additional Problems

10.69 Which of the following species is not likely to have a tetrahedral shape? (a) $SiBr_4$, (b) NF_4^+, (c) SF_4, (d) $BeCl_4^{2-}$, (e) BF_4^-, (f) $AlCl_4^-$

10.70 Draw the Lewis structure of mercury(II) bromide. Is this molecule linear or bent? How would you establish its geometry?

10.71 Sketch the bond moments and resultant dipole moments for the following molecules: H_2O, PCl_3, XeF_4, PCl_5, SF_6.

10.72 Although both carbon and silicon are in Group 4A, very few $Si=Si$ bonds are known. Account for the instability of silicon-to-silicon double bonds in general. (*Hint:* Compare the atomic radii of C and Si in Figure 8.5. What effect would the larger size have on pi bond formation?)

10.73 Predict the geometry of sulfur dichloride (SCl_2) and the hybridization of the sulfur atom.

10.74 Antimony pentafluoride, SbF_5, reacts with XeF_4 and XeF_6 to form ionic compounds, $XeF_3^+SbF_6^-$ and $XeF_5^+SbF_6^-$. Describe the geometries of the cations and anion in these two compounds.

10.75 Draw Lewis structures and give the other information requested for the following molecules: (a) PF_3. Shape: planar or nonplanar? (b) ClO_3^-. Shape: planar or nonplanar? (c) H_2O. Show the direction of the resultant dipole moment. (d) OF_2. Polar or nonpolar molecule? (e) NO_2. Estimate the ONO bond angle.

10.76 Predict the bond angles for the following molecules: (a) $BeCl_2$, (b) BCl_3, (c) CCl_4, (d) CH_3Cl, (e) Hg_2Cl_2 (arrangement of atoms: ClHgHgCl), (f) $SnCl_2$, (g) H_2O_2, (h) SnH_4.

10.77 Briefly compare the VSEPR and hybridization approaches to the study of molecular geometry.

10.78 Describe the hybridization state of arsenic in arsenic pentafluoride (AsF_5).

10.79 Draw Lewis structures and give the other information requested for the following: (a) SO_3. Polar or nonpolar molecule? (b) PF_3. Polar or nonpolar molecule? (c) F_3SiH. Show the direction of the resultant dipole moment. (d) SiH_3^-. Planar or pyramidal shape? (e) Br_2CH_2. Polar or nonpolar molecule?

10.80 Which of the following molecules are linear? ICl_2^-, IF_2^+, OF_2, SnI_2, $CdBr_2$

10.81 Draw the Lewis structure for the $BeCl_4^{2-}$ ion. Predict its geometry and describe the hybridization state of the Be atom.

10.82 The N_2F_2 molecule can exist in either of the following two forms:

(a) What is the hybridization of N in the molecule?

(b) Which structure has a dipole moment?

10.83 Cyclopropane (C_3H_6) has the shape of a triangle in which a C atom is bonded to two H atoms and two other C atoms at each corner. Cubane (C_8H_8) has the shape of a cube in which a C atom is bonded to one H atom and three other C atoms at each corner. (a) Draw Lewis structures of these molecules. (b) Compare the CCC angles in these molecules with those predicted for an sp^3-hybridized C atom. (c) Would you expect these molecules to be easy to make?

10.84 The compound 1,2-dichloroethane ($C_2H_4Cl_2$) is nonpolar, while *cis*-dichloroethylene ($C_2H_2Cl_2$) has a dipole moment:

1,2-dichloroethane   *cis*-dichloroethylene

The reason for the difference is that groups connected by a single bond can rotate with respect to each other, but no rotation occurs when a double bond connects the groups. On the basis of bonding considerations, explain why rotation occurs in 1,2-dichloroethane but not in *cis*-dichloroethylene.

10.85 Does the following molecule have a dipole moment?

(*Hint:* See the answer to Problem 10.41.)

10.86 So-called greenhouse gases, which contribute to global warming, have a dipole moment or can be bent or distorted into shapes that have a dipole moment. Which of the following gases are greenhouse gases? N_2, O_2, O_3, CO, CO_2, NO_2, N_2O, CH_4, $CFCl_3$

10.87 The bond angle of SO_2 is very close to $120°$, even though there is a lone pair on S. Explain.

10.88 3'-azido-3'-deoxythymidine, shown on p. 446, commonly known as AZT, is one of the drugs used to treat acquired immune deficiency syndrome (AIDS). What are the hybridization states of the C and N atoms in this molecule?

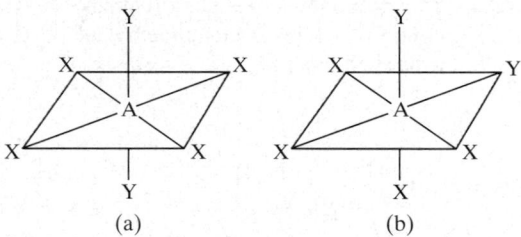

10.89 The following molecules (AX_4Y_2) all have octahedral geometry. Group the molecules that are equivalent to each other.

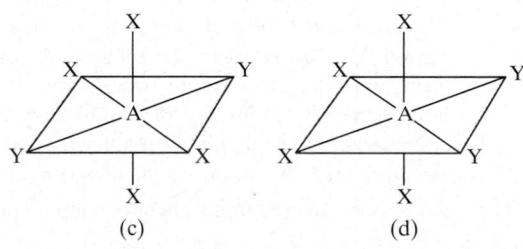

(a)   (b)

(c)   (d)

10.90 The compounds carbon tetrachloride (CCl_4) and silicon tetrachloride ($SiCl_4$) are similar in geometry and hybridization. However, CCl_4 does not react with water but $SiCl_4$ does. Explain the difference in their chemical reactivities. (*Hint:* The first step of the reaction is believed to be the addition of a water molecule to the Si atom in $SiCl_4$.)

10.91 Write the ground-state electron configuration for B_2. Is the molecule diamagnetic or paramagnetic?

10.92 What are the hybridization states of the C and N atoms in this molecule?

10.93 Use molecular orbital theory to explain the difference between the bond enthalpies of F_2 and F_2^- (see Problem 9.110).

10.94 Referring to the Chemistry in Action on p. 412, answer the following questions: (a) If you wanted to cook a roast (beef or lamb), would you use a microwave oven or a conventional oven? (b) Radar is a means of locating an object by measuring the time for the echo of a microwave from the object to return to the source and the direction from which it returns. Would radar work if oxygen, nitrogen, and carbon dioxide were polar molecules? (c) In early tests of radar at the English Channel during World War II, the results were inconclusive even though there was no equipment malfunction. Why? (*Hint:* The weather is often foggy in the region.)

10.95 The stable allotropic form of phosphorus is P_4, in which each P atom is bonded to three other P atoms. Draw a Lewis structure of this molecule and describe its geometry. At high temperatures, P_4 dissociates to form P_2 molecules containing a P=P bond. Explain why P_4 is more stable than P_2.

10.96 Referring to Table 9.4, explain why the bond enthalpy for Cl_2 is greater than that for F_2. (*Hint:* The bond lengths of F_2 and Cl_2 are 142 pm and 199 pm, respectively.)

10.97 Use molecular orbital theory to explain the bonding in the azide ion (N_3^-). (Arrangement of atoms is NNN.)

10.98 The ionic character of the bond in a diatomic molecule can be estimated by the formula

$$\frac{\mu}{ed} \times 100\%$$

where μ is the experimentally measured dipole moment (in C m), e the electronic charge, and d the bond length in meters. (The quantity ed is the hypothetical dipole moment for the case in which the transfer of an electron from the less electronegative to the more electronegative atom is complete.) Given that the dipole moment and bond length of HF are 1.92 D and 91.7 pm, respectively, calculate the percent ionic character of the molecule.

10.99 Draw three Lewis structures for compounds with the formula $C_2H_2F_2$. Indicate which of the compound(s) are polar.

10.100 Greenhouse gases absorb (and trap) outgoing infared radiation (heat) from Earth and contribute to global warming. The molecule of a greenhouse gas either possesses a permanent dipole moment or has a changing dipole moment during its vibrational motions. Consider three of the vibrational modes of carbon dioxide where the arrows indicate the movement of the atoms. (During a complete cycle of vibration, the atoms move toward one extreme position and then reverse their direction to the other extreme position.) Which of the preceding vibrations are responsible for CO_2 to behave as a greenhouse gas? Which of the following molecules can act as a greenhouse gas: N_2, O_2, CO, NO_2, and N_2O?

10.101 Aluminum trichloride ($AlCl_3$) is an electron-deficient molecule. It has a tendency to form a dimer (a molecule made of two $AlCl_3$ units):

$$AlCl_3 + AlCl_3 \longrightarrow Al_2Cl_6$$

(a) Draw a Lewis structure for the dimer. (b) Describe the hybridization state of Al in $AlCl_3$ and Al_2Cl_6. (c) Sketch the geometry of the dimer. (d) Do these molecules possess a dipole moment?

10.102 The molecules *cis*-dichloroethylene and *trans*-dichloroethylene shown on p. 411 can be interconverted by heating or irradiation. (a) Starting with *cis*-dichloroethylene, show that rotating the C=C bond by 180° will break only the pi bond but will leave the sigma bond intact. Explain the formation of *trans*-dichloroethylene from this process. (Treat the rotation as two stepwise 90° rotations.) (b) Account for the difference in the bond enthalpies for the pi bond (about 270 kJ/mol) and the sigma bond (about 350 kJ/mol). (c) Calculate the longest wavelength of light needed to bring about this conversion.

10.103 Progesterone is a hormone responsible for female sex characteristics. In the usual shorthand structure, each point where lines meet represent a C atom, and most H atoms are not shown. Draw the complete structure of the molecule, showing all C and H atoms. Indicate which C atoms are sp^2- and sp^3-hybridized.

Special Problems

10.104 For each pair listed here, state which one has a higher first ionization energy and explain your choice: (a) H or H_2, (b) N or N_2, (c) O or O_2, (d) F or F_2.

10.105 The molecule benzyne (C_6H_4) is a very reactive species. It resembles benzene in that it has a six-membered ring of carbon atoms. Draw a Lewis structure of the molecule and account for the molecule's high reactivity.

10.106 Assume that the third-period element phosphorus forms a diatomic molecule, P_2, in an analogous way as nitrogen does to form N_2. (a) Write the electronic configuration for P_2. Use [Ne_2] to represent the electron configuration for the first two periods. (b) Calculate its bond order. (c) What are its magnetic properties (diamagnetic or paramagnetic)?

10.107 Consider a N_2 molecule in its first excited electronic state; that is, when an electron in the highest occupied molecular orbital is promoted to the lowest empty molecular obital. (a) Identify the molecular orbitals involved and sketch a diagram to show the transition. (b) Compare the bond order and bond length of N_2^* with N_2, where the asterisk denotes the excited molecule. (c) Is N_2^* diamagnetic or paramagnetic? (d) When N_2^* loses its excess energy and converts to the ground state N_2, it emits a photon of wavelength 470 nm, which makes up part of the auroras lights. Calculate the energy difference between these levels.

10.108 As mentioned in the chapter, the Lewis structure for O_2 is

$$\ddot{O}=\ddot{O}$$

Use the molecular orbital theory to show that the structure actually corresponds to an excited state of the oxygen molecule.

10.109 Draw the Lewis structure of ketene (C_2H_2O) and describe the hybridization states of the C atoms. The molecule does not contain O—H bonds. On separate diagrams, sketch the formation of sigma and pi bonds.

10.110 TCDD, or 2,3,7,8-tetrachlorodibenzo-p-dioxin, is a highly toxic compound

It gained considerable notoriety in 2004 when it was implicated in the murder plot of a Ukrainian politician. (a) Describe its geometry and state whether the molecule has a dipole moment. (b) How many pi bonds and sigma bonds are there in the molecule?

10.111 Write the electron configuration of the cyanide ion (CN^-). Name a stable molecule that is isoelectronic with the ion.

10.112 Carbon monoxide (CO) is a poisonous compound due to its ability to bind strongly to Fe^{2+} in the hemoglobin molecule. The molecular orbitals of CO have the same energy order as those of the N_2 molecule, (a) Draw a Lewis structure of CO and assign formal charges. Explain why CO has a rather small dipole moment of 0.12 D. (b) Compare the bond order of CO with that from the molecular orbital theory.

(c) Which of the atoms (C or O) is more likely to form bonds with the Fe^{2+} ion in hemoglobin?

10.113 The geometries discussed in this chapter all lend themselves to fairly straightforward elucidation of bond angles. The exception is the tetrahedron, because its bond angles are hard to visualize. Consider the CCl_4 molecule, which has a tetrahedral geometry and is nonpolar. By equating the bond moment of a particular C—Cl bond to the resultant bond moments of the other three C—Cl bonds in opposite directions, show that the bond angles are all equal to 109.5°.

Answers to Practice Exercises

10.1 (a) Tetrahedral, (b) linear, (c) trigonal planar. **10.2** No. **10.3** (a) sp^3, (b) sp^2. **10.4** sp^3d^2. **10.5** The C atom is sp-hybridized. It forms a sigma bond with the H atom and another sigma bond with the N atom. The two unhybridized p orbitals on the C atom are used to form two pi bonds with the N atom. The lone pair on the N atom is placed in the sp orbital. **10.6** F_2^-.

11

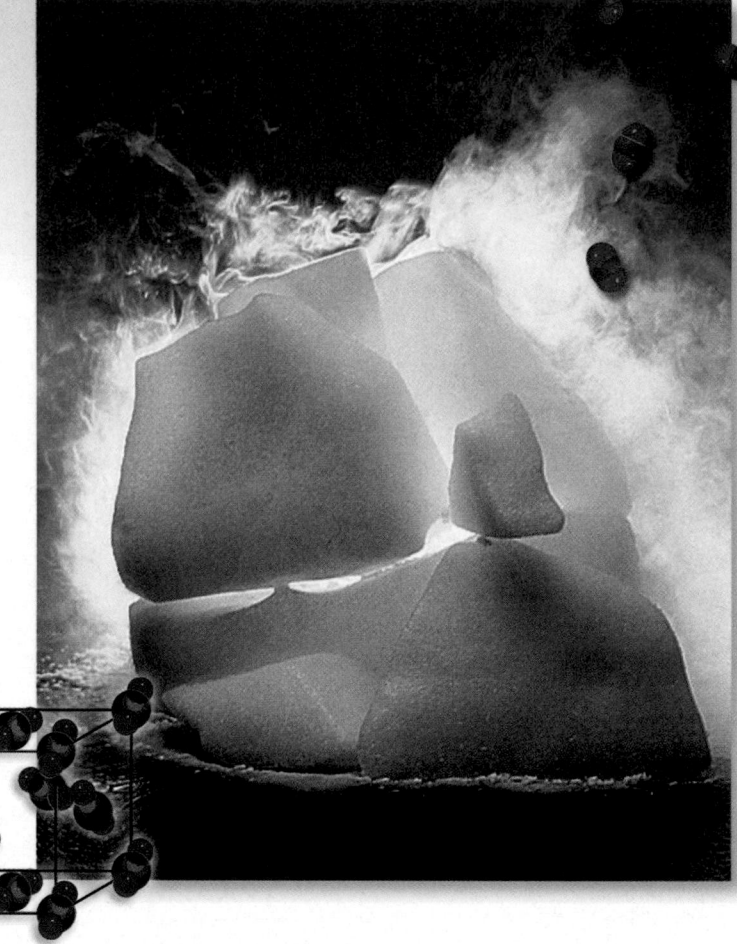

Under atmospheric conditions, solid carbon dioxide (dry ice) does not melt; it only sublimes. The models show a unit cell of carbon dioxide (face-centered cubic cell) and gaseous carbon dioxide molecules.

Intermolecular Forces and Liquids and Solids

A LOOK AHEAD

- We begin by applying the kinetic molecular theory to liquids and solids and compare their properties with those of gases. (11.1)

- Next, we examine the different types of intermolecular forces between molecules and between ions and molecules. We also study a special type of intermolecular interaction called hydrogen bonding that involves hydrogen and electronegative elements nitrogen, oxygen, and fluorine. (11.2)

- We see that two important properties of liquids—surface tension and viscosity—can be understood in terms of intermolecular forces. (11.3)

- We then move on to the world of solids and learn about the nature of crystals and ways of packing spheres to form different unit cells. (11.4)

- We see that the best way to determine the dimensions of a crystal structure is by X-ray diffraction, which is based on the scattering of X rays by the atoms or molecules in a crystal. (11.5)

- The major types of crystals are ionic, covalent, molecular, and metallic. Intermolecular forces help us understand their structure and physical properties such as density, melting point, and electrical conductivity. (11.6)

- We learn that solids can also exist in the amorphous form, which lacks orderly three-dimensional arrangement. A well-known example of a amorphous solid is glass. (11.7)

- We next study phase changes, or transitions among gas, liquids, and solids. We see that the dynamic equilibrium between liquid and vapor gives rise to equilibrium vapor pressure. The energy required for vaporization depends on the strength of intermolecular forces. We also learn that every substance has a critical temperature above which its vapor form cannot be liquefied. We then examine liquid-solid and solid-vapor transitions. (11.8)

- The various types of phase transitions are summarized in a phase diagram, which helps us understand conditions under which a phase is stable and changes in pressure and/or temperature needed to bring about a phase transition. (11.9)

Although we live immersed in a mixture of gases that make up Earth's atmosphere, we are more familiar with the behavior of liquids and solids because they are more visible. Every day we use water and other liquids for drinking, bathing, cleaning, and cooking, and we handle, sit upon, and wear solids.

Molecular motion is more restricted in liquids than in gases; and in solids, the atoms and molecules are packed even more tightly together. In fact, in a solid they are held in well-defined positions and are capable of little free motion relative to one another. In this chapter we will examine the structure of liquids and solids and discuss some of the fundamental properties of these two states of matter.

11.1 The Kinetic Molecular Theory of Liquids and Solids

In Chapter 5 we used the kinetic molecular theory to explain the behavior of gases in terms of the constant, random motion of gas molecules. In gases, the distances between molecules are so great (compared with their diameters) that at ordinary temperatures and pressures (say, 25°C and 1 atm), there is no appreciable interaction between the molecules. Because there is a great deal of empty space in a gas—that is, space that is not occupied by molecules—gases can be readily compressed. The lack of strong forces between molecules also allows a gas to expand to fill the volume of its container. Furthermore, the large amount of empty space explains why gases have very low densities under normal conditions.

Liquids and solids are quite a different story. The principal difference between the condensed states (liquids and solids) and the gaseous state is the distance between molecules. In a liquid, the molecules are so close together that there is very little empty space. Thus, liquids are much more difficult to compress than gases, and they are also much denser under normal conditions. Molecules in a liquid are held together by one or more types of attractive forces, which will be discussed in Section 11.2. A liquid also has a definite volume, because molecules in a liquid do not break away from the attractive forces. The molecules can, however, move past one another freely, and so a liquid can flow, can be poured, and assumes the shape of its container.

In a solid, molecules are held rigidly in position with virtually no freedom of motion. Many solids are characterized by long-range order; that is, the molecules are arranged in regular configurations in three dimensions. There is even less empty space in a solid than in a liquid. Thus, solids are almost incompressible and possess definite shape and volume. With very few exceptions (water being the most important), the density of the solid form is higher than that of the liquid form for a given substance. It is not uncommon for two states of a substance to coexist. An ice cube (solid) floating in a glass of water (liquid) is a familiar example. Chemists refer to the different states of a substance that are present in a system as phases. A *phase* is *a homogeneous part of the system in contact with other parts of the system but separated from them by a well-defined boundary.* Thus, our glass of ice water contains both the solid phase and the liquid phase of water. In this chapter we will use the term "phase" when talking about changes of state involving one substance, as well as systems containing more than one phase of a substance. Table 11.1 summarizes some of the characteristic properties of the three phases of matter.

TABLE 11.1	Characteristic Properties of Gases, Liquids, and Solids			
State of Matter	Volume/Shape	Density	Compressibility	Motion of Molecules
Gas	Assumes the volume and shape of its container	Low	Very compressible	Very free motion
Liquid	Has a definite volume but assumes the shape of its container	High	Only slightly compressible	Slide past one another freely
Solid	Has a definite volume and shape	High	Virtually incompressible	Vibrate about fixed positions

11.2 Intermolecular Forces

Figure 11.1 *Molecules that have a permanent dipole moment tend to align with opposite polarities in the solid phase for maximum attractive interaction.*

Intermolecular forces are *attractive forces between molecules.* Intermolecular forces are responsible for the nonideal behavior of gases described in Chapter 5. They exert even more influence in the condensed phases of matter—liquids and solids. As the temperature of a gas drops, the average kinetic energy of its molecules decreases. Eventually, at a sufficiently low temperature, the molecules no longer have enough energy to break away from the attraction of neighboring molecules. At this point, the molecules aggregate to form small drops of liquid. This transition from the gaseous to the liquid phase is known as *condensation.*

In contrast to intermolecular forces, **intramolecular forces** *hold atoms together in a molecule.* (Chemical bonding, discussed in Chapters 9 and 10, involves intramolecular forces.) Intramolecular forces stabilize individual molecules, whereas intermolecular forces are primarily responsible for the bulk properties of matter (for example, melting point and boiling point).

Generally, intermolecular forces are much weaker than intramolecular forces. It usually requires much less energy to evaporate a liquid than to break the bonds in the molecules of the liquid. For example, it takes about 41 kJ of energy to vaporize 1 mole of water at its boiling point; but about 930 kJ of energy are necessary to break the two O—H bonds in 1 mole of water molecules. The boiling points of substances often reflect the strength of the intermolecular forces operating among the molecules. At the boiling point, enough energy must be supplied to overcome the attractive forces among molecules before they can enter the vapor phase. If it takes more energy to separate molecules of substance A than of substance B because A molecules are held together by stronger intermolecular forces, then the boiling point of A is higher than that of B. The same principle applies also to the melting points of the substances. In general, the melting points of substances increase with the strength of the intermolecular forces.

To discuss the properties of condensed matter, we must understand the different types of intermolecular forces. *Dipole-dipole, dipole-induced dipole,* and *dispersion forces* make up what chemists commonly refer to as **van der Waals forces,** after the Dutch physicist Johannes van der Waals (see Section 5.8). Ions and dipoles are attracted to one another by electrostatic forces called *ion-dipole forces,* which are *not* van der Waals forces. *Hydrogen bonding* is a particularly strong type of dipole-dipole interaction. Because only a few elements can participate in hydrogen bond formation, it is treated as a separate category. Depending on the phase of a substance, the nature of chemical bonds, and the types of elements present, more than one type of interaction may contribute to the total attraction between molecules, as we will see below.

Dipole-Dipole Forces

Dipole-dipole forces are *attractive forces between polar molecules,* that is, between molecules that possess dipole moments (see Section 10.2). Their origin is electrostatic, and they can be understood in terms of Coulomb's law. The larger the dipole moment, the greater the force. Figure 11.1 shows the orientation of polar molecules in a solid. In liquids, polar molecules are not held as rigidly as in a solid, but they tend to align in a way that, on average, maximizes the attractive interaction.

Ion-Dipole Forces

Coulomb's law also explains **ion-dipole forces,** which *attract an ion (either a cation or an anion) and a polar molecule to each other* (Figure 11.2). The strength of this

Figure 11.2 *Two types of ion-dipole interaction.*

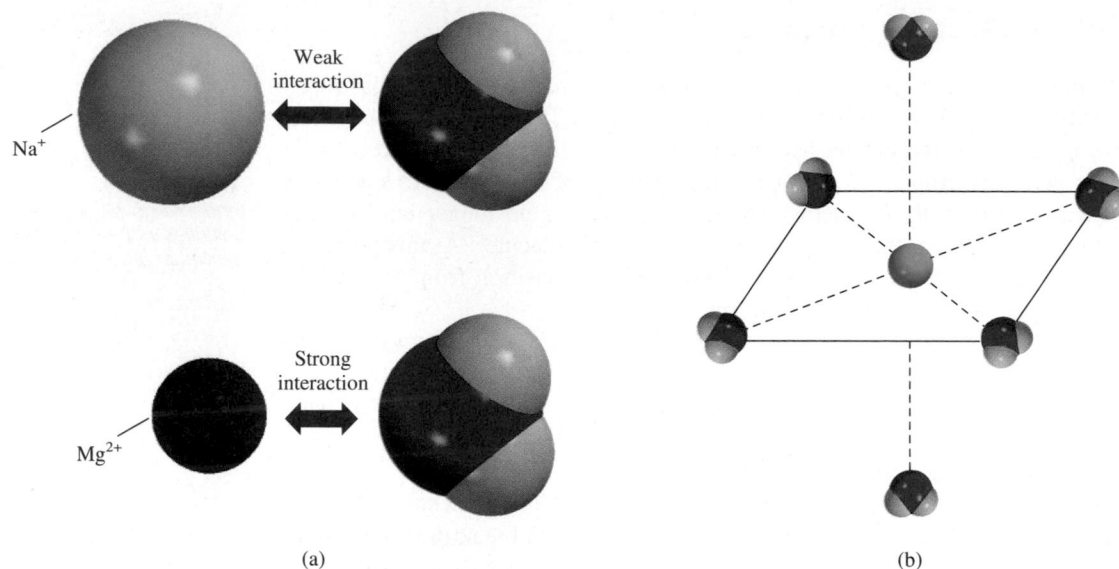

(a)   (b)

Figure 11.3 *(a) Interaction of a water molecule with a Na⁺ ion and a Mg²⁺ ion. (b) In aqueous solutions, metal ions are usually surrounded by six water molecules in an octahedral arrangement.*

interaction depends on the charge and size of the ion and on the magnitude of the dipole moment and size of the molecule. The charges on cations are generally more concentrated, because cations are usually smaller than anions. Therefore, a cation interacts more strongly with dipoles than does an anion having a charge of the same magnitude.

Hydration, discussed in Section 4.1, is one example of ion-dipole interaction. Heat of hydration (see p. 252) is the result of the favorable interaction between the cations and anions of an ionic compound with water. Figure 11.3 shows the ion-dipole interaction between the Na⁺ and Mg²⁺ ions with a water molecule, which has a large dipole moment (1.87 D). Because the Mg²⁺ ion has a higher charge and a smaller ionic radius (78 pm) than that of the Na⁺ ion (98 pm), it interacts more strongly with water molecules. (In reality, each ion is surrounded by a number of water molecules in solution.) Consequently, the heats of hydration for the Na⁺ and Mg²⁺ ions are −405 kJ/mol and −1926 kJ/mol, respectively.[†] Similar differences exist for anions of different charges and sizes.

Dispersion Forces

(a)

Cation   Induced dipole

(b)

Dipole   Induced dipole

(c)

Figure 11.4 *(a) Spherical charge distribution in a helium atom. (b) Distortion caused by the approach of a cation. (c) Distortion caused by the approach of a dipole.*

What attractive interaction occurs in nonpolar substances? To learn the answer to this question, consider the arrangement shown in Figure 11.4. If we place an ion or a polar molecule near an atom (or a nonpolar molecule), the electron distribution of the atom (or molecule) is distorted by the force exerted by the ion or the polar molecule, resulting in a kind of dipole. The dipole in the atom (or nonpolar molecule) is said to be an ***induced dipole*** because *the separation of positive and negative charges in the atom (or nonpolar molecule) is due to the proximity of an ion or a polar molecule.* The attractive interaction between an ion and the induced dipole is called *ion-induced dipole interaction,* and the attractive interaction between a polar molecule and the induced dipole is called *dipole-induced dipole interaction.*

The likelihood of a dipole moment being induced depends not only on the charge on the ion or the strength of the dipole but also on the *polarizability* of the atom or molecule—that is, the ease with which the electron distribution in the atom (or molecule) can be distorted. Generally, the larger the number of electrons and the more

---

[†]Heats of hydration of individual ions cannot be measured directly, but they can be reliably estimated.

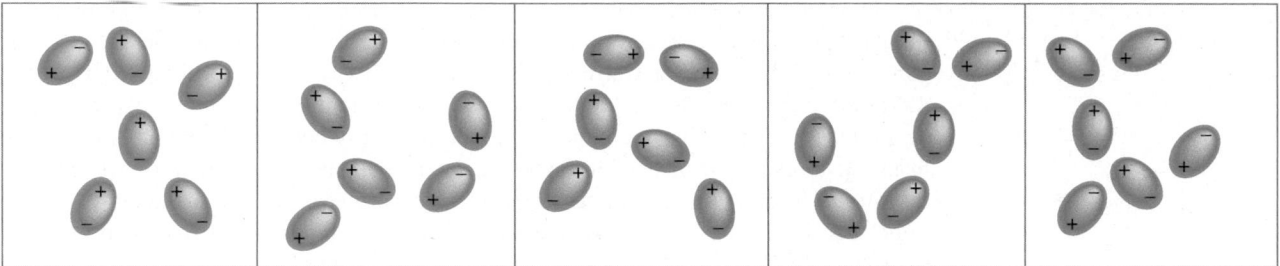

Figure 11.5 *Induced dipoles interacting with each other. Such patterns exist only momentarily; new arrangements are formed in the next instant. This type of interaction is responsible for the condensation of nonpolar gases.*

diffuse the electron cloud in the atom or molecule, the greater its polarizability. By *diffuse cloud* we mean an electron cloud that is spread over an appreciable volume, so that the electrons are not held tightly by the nucleus.

Polarizability allows gases containing atoms or nonpolar molecules (for example, He and N_2) to condense. In a helium atom the electrons are moving at some distance from the nucleus. At any instant it is likely that the atom has a dipole moment created by the specific positions of the electrons. This dipole moment is called an *instantaneous dipole* because it lasts for just a tiny fraction of a second. In the next instant the electrons are in different locations and the atom has a new instantaneous dipole, and so on. Averaged over time (that is, the time it takes to make a dipole moment measurement), however, the atom has no dipole moment because the instantaneous dipoles all cancel one another. In a collection of He atoms, an instantaneous dipole of one He atom can induce a dipole in each of its nearest neighbors (Figure 11.5). At the next moment, a different instantaneous dipole can create temporary dipoles in the surrounding He atoms. The important point is that this kind of interaction produces **dispersion forces,** *attractive forces that arise as a result of temporary dipoles induced in atoms or molecules.* At very low temperatures (and reduced atomic speeds), dispersion forces are strong enough to hold He atoms together, causing the gas to condense. The attraction between nonpolar molecules can be explained similarly.

A quantum mechanical interpretation of temporary dipoles was provided by Fritz London[†] in 1930. London showed that the magnitude of this attractive interaction is directly proportional to the polarizability of the atom or molecule. As we might expect, dispersion forces may be quite weak. This is certainly true for helium, which has a boiling point of only 4.2 K, or −269°C. (Note that helium has only two electrons, which are tightly held in the 1s orbital. Therefore, the helium atom has a low polarizability.)

Dispersion forces, which are also called London forces, usually increase with molar mass because molecules with larger molar mass tend to have more electrons, and dispersion forces increase in strength with the number of electrons. Furthermore, larger molar mass often means a bigger atom whose electron distribution is more easily disturbed because the outer electrons are less tightly held by the nuclei. Table 11.2 compares the melting points of similar substances that consist of nonpolar molecules. As expected, the melting point increases as the number of electrons in the molecule increases. Because these are all nonpolar molecules, the only attractive intermolecular forces present are the dispersion forces.

For simplicity we use the term "intermolecular forces" for both atoms and molecules.

TABLE 11.2

Melting Points of Similar Nonpolar Compounds

Compound	Melting Point (°C)
CH_4	−182.5
CF_4	−150.0
CCl_4	−23.0
CBr_4	90.0
CI_4	171.0

[†]Fritz London (1900–1954). German physicist. London was a theoretical physicist whose major work was on superconductivity in liquid helium.

In many cases, dispersion forces are comparable to or even greater than the dipole-dipole forces between polar molecules. For a dramatic illustration, let us compare the boiling points of CH_3F ($-78.4°C$) and CCl_4 (76.5°C). Although CH_3F has a dipole moment of 1.8 D, it boils at a much lower temperature than CCl_4, a nonpolar molecule. CCl_4 boils at a higher temperature simply because it contains more electrons. As a result, the dispersion forces between CCl_4 molecules are stronger than the dispersion forces plus the dipole-dipole forces between CH_3F molecules. (Keep in mind that dispersion forces exist among species of all types, whether they are neutral or bear a net charge and whether they are polar or nonpolar.)

Example 11.1 shows that if we know the kind of species present, we can readily determine the types of intermolecular forces that exist between the species.

Example 11.1

What type(s) of intermolecular forces exist between the following pairs: (a) HBr and H_2S, (b) Cl_2 and CBr_4, (c) I_2 and NO_3^-, (d) NH_3 and C_6H_6?

Strategy Classify the species into three categories: ionic, polar (possessing a dipole moment), and nonpolar. Keep in mind that dispersion forces exist between *all* species.

Solution (a) Both HBr and H_2S are polar molecules

Therefore, the intermolecular forces present are dipole-dipole forces, as well as dispersion forces.

(b) Both Cl_2 and CBr_4 are nonpolar, so there are only dispersion forces between these molecules.

(c) I_2 is a homonuclear diatomic molecule and therefore nonpolar, so the forces between it and the ion NO_3^- are ion-induced dipole forces and dispersion forces.

(d) NH_3 is polar, and C_6H_6 is nonpolar. The forces are dipole-induced dipole forces and dispersion forces.

Similar problem: 11.10.

Practice Exercise Name the type(s) of intermolecular forces that exists between molecules (or basic units) in each of the following species: (a) LiF, (b) CH_4, (c) SO_2.

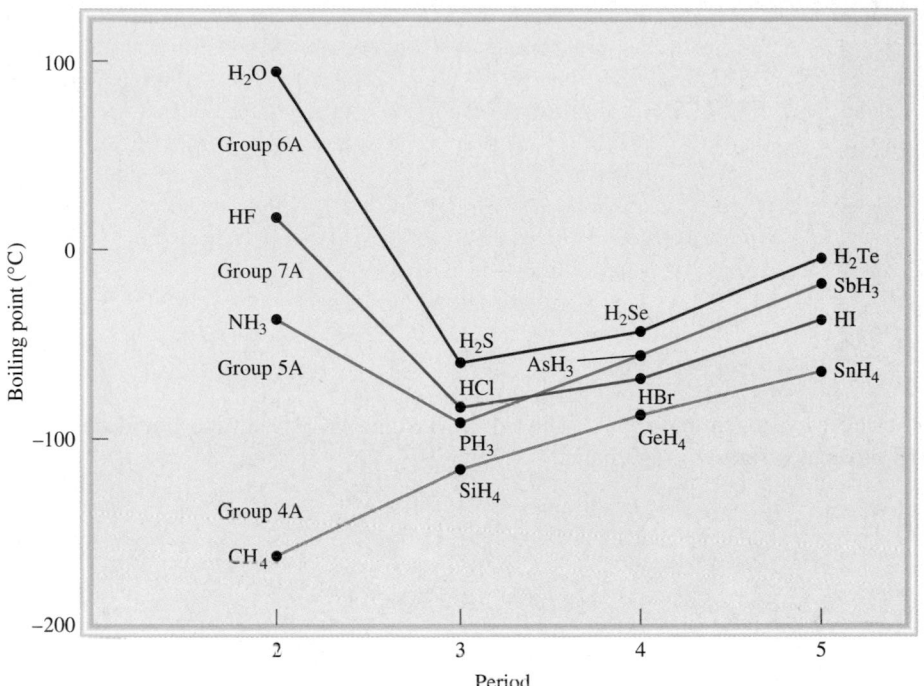

Figure 11.6 *Boiling points of the hydrogen compounds of Groups 4A, 5A, 6A, and 7A elements. Although normally we expect the boiling point to increase as we move down a group, we see that three compounds (NH_3, H_2O, and HF) behave differently. The anomaly can be explained in terms of intermolecular hydrogen bonding.*

The Hydrogen Bond

Normally, the boiling points of a series of similar compounds containing elements in the same periodic group increase with increasing molar mass. This increase in boiling point is due to the increase in dispersion forces for molecules with more electrons. Hydrogen compounds of Group 4A follow this trend, as Figure 11.6 shows. The lightest compound, CH_4, has the lowest boiling point, and the heaviest compound, SnH_4, has the highest boiling point. However, hydrogen compounds of the elements in Groups 5A, 6A, and 7A do not follow this trend. In each of these series, the lightest compound (NH_3, H_2O, and HF) has the highest boiling point, contrary to our expectations based on molar mass. This observation must mean that there are stronger intermolecular attractions in NH_3, H_2O, and HF, compared to other molecules in the same groups. In fact, this particularly strong type of intermolecular attraction is called the ***hydrogen bond,*** which is *a special type of dipole-dipole interaction between the hydrogen atom in a polar bond, such as N—H, O—H, or F—H, and an electronegative O, N, or F atom.* The interaction is written

$$A—H \cdots B \quad \text{or} \quad A—H \cdots A$$

A and B represent O, N, or F; A—H is one molecule or part of a molecule and B is a part of another molecule; and the dotted line represents the hydrogen bond. The three atoms usually lie in a straight line, but the angle AHB (or AHA) can deviate as much as 30° from linearity. Note that the O, N, and F atoms all possess at least one lone pair that can interact with the hydrogen atom in hydrogen bonding.

The average strength of a hydrogen bond is quite large for a dipole-dipole interaction (up to 40 kJ/mol). Thus, hydrogen bonds have a powerful effect on the structures and properties of many compounds. Figure 11.7 shows several examples of hydrogen bonding.

The strength of a hydrogen bond is determined by the coulombic interaction between the lone-pair electrons of the electronegative atom and the hydrogen nucleus. For example, fluorine is more electronegative than oxygen, and so we would expect

The three most electronegative elements that take part in hydrogen bonding.

Figure 11.7 *Hydrogen bonding in water, ammonia, and hydrogen fluoride. Solid lines represent covalent bonds, and dotted lines represent hydrogen bonds.*

a stronger hydrogen bond to exist in liquid HF than in H_2O. In the liquid phase, the HF molecules form zigzag chains:

The boiling point of HF is lower than that of water because each H_2O takes part in *four* intermolecular hydrogen bonds. Therefore, the forces holding the molecules together are stronger in H_2O than in HF. We will return to this very important property of water in Section 11.3. Example 11.2 shows the type of species that can form hydrogen bonds with water.

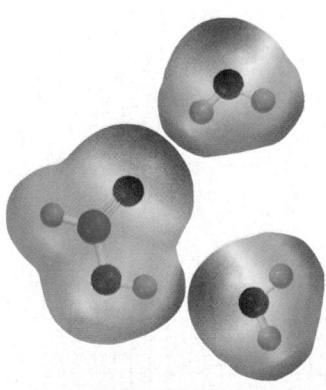

HCOOH forms hydrogen bonds with two H_2O molecules.

Example 11.2

Which of the following can form hydrogen bonds with water? CH_3OCH_3, CH_4, F^-, HCOOH, Na^+.

Strategy A species can form hydrogen bonds with water if it contains one of the three electronegative elements (F, O, or N) or it has an H atom bonded to one of these three elements.

Solution There are no electronegative elements (F, O, or N) in either CH_4 or Na^+. Therefore, only CH_3OCH_3, F^-, and HCOOH can form hydrogen bonds with water.

Check Note that HCOOH (formic acid) can form hydrogen bonds with water in two different ways.

Practice Exercise Which of the following species are capable of hydrogen bonding among themselves? (a) H_2S, (b) C_6H_6, (c) CH_3OH.

Similar problem: 11.12.

The intermolecular forces discussed so far are all attractive in nature. Keep in mind, though, that molecules also exert repulsive forces on one another. Thus, when two molecules approach each other, the repulsion between the electrons and between the nuclei in the molecules comes into play. The magnitude of the repulsive force rises very steeply as the distance separating the molecules in a condensed phase decreases. This is the reason that liquids and solids are so hard to compress. In these phases, the molecules are already in close contact with one another, and so they greatly resist being compressed further.

11.3 Properties of Liquids

Intermolecular forces give rise to a number of structural features and properties of liquids. In this section we will look at two such phenomena associated with liquids in general: surface tension and viscosity. Then we will discuss the structure and properties of water.

Figure 11.8 *Intermolecular forces acting on a molecule in the surface layer of a liquid and in the interior region of the liquid.*

Surface Tension

Molecules within a liquid are pulled in all directions by intermolecular forces; there is no tendency for them to be pulled in any one way. However, molecules at the surface are pulled downward and sideways by other molecules, but not upward away from the surface (Figure 11.8). These intermolecular attractions thus tend to pull the molecules into the liquid and cause the surface to tighten like an elastic film. Because there is little or no attraction between polar water molecules and, say, the nonpolar wax molecules on a freshly waxed car, a drop of water assumes the shape of a small round bead, because a sphere minimizes the surface area of a liquid. The waxy surface of a wet apple also produces this effect (Figure 11.9).

A measure of the elastic force in the surface of a liquid is surface tension. The **surface tension** is *the amount of energy required to stretch or increase the surface of a liquid by a unit area* (for example, by 1 cm^2). Liquids that have strong intermolecular forces also have high surface tensions. Thus, because of hydrogen bonding, water has a considerably greater surface tension than most other liquids.

Another example of surface tension is *capillary action*. Figure 11.10(a) shows water rising spontaneously in a capillary tube. A thin film of water adheres to the wall of the glass tube. The surface tension of water causes this film to contract, and as it does, it pulls the water up the tube. Two types of forces bring about capillary action. One is **cohesion,** which is *the intermolecular attraction between like molecules* (in this case, the water molecules). The second force, called **adhesion,** is *an attraction between unlike molecules,* such as those in water and in the sides of a glass tube. If adhesion is stronger than cohesion, as it is in Figure 11.10(a), the contents of the tube will be pulled upward. This process continues until the adhesive force is balanced by the weight of the water in the tube. This action is by no means universal among liquids, as Figure 11.10(b) shows. In mercury, cohesion is greater than the adhesion between mercury and glass, so that when a capillary tube is dipped in mercury, the result is a depression or lowering, at the mercury level—that is, the height of the liquid in the capillary tube is below the surface of the mercury.

Surface tension enables the water strider to "walk" on water.

Viscosity

The expression "slow as molasses in January" owes its truth to another physical property of liquids called viscosity. **Viscosity** is *a measure of a fluid's resistance to flow.* The greater the viscosity, the more slowly the liquid flows. The viscosity of a liquid

Figure 11.9 *Water beads on an apple which has a waxy surface.*

Figure 11.10 *(a) When adhesion is greater than cohesion, the liquid (for example, water) rises in the capillary tube. (b) When cohesion is greater than adhesion, as it is for mercury, a depression of the liquid in the capillary tube results. Note that the meniscus in the tube of water is concave, or rounded downward, whereas that in the tube of mercury is convex, or rounded upward.*

(a)   (b)

usually decreases as temperature increases; thus, hot molasses flows much faster than cold molasses.

Liquids that have strong intermolecular forces have higher viscosities than those that have weak intermolecular forces (Table 11.3). Water has a higher viscosity than many other liquids because of its ability to form hydrogen bonds. Interestingly, the viscosity of glycerol is significantly higher than that of all the other liquids listed in Table 11.3. Glycerol has the structure

$$CH_2-OH$$
$$CH-OH$$
$$CH_2-OH$$

Like water, glycerol can form hydrogen bonds. Each glycerol molecule has three —OH groups that can participate in hydrogen bonding with other glycerol molecules.

Glycerol is a clear, odorless, syrupy liquid used to make explosives, ink, and lubricants.

TABLE 11.3	Viscosity of Some Common Liquids at 20°C
Liquid	**Viscosity (N s/m^2)***
Acetone (C_3H_6O)	3.16×10^{-4}
Benzene (C_6H_6)	6.25×10^{-4}
Blood	4×10^{-3}
Carbon tetrachloride (CCl_4)	9.69×10^{-4}
Ethanol (C_2H_5OH)	1.20×10^{-3}
Diethyl ether ($C_2H_5OC_2H_5$)	2.33×10^{-4}
Glycerol ($C_3H_8O_3$)	1.49
Mercury (Hg)	1.55×10^{-3}
Water (H_2O)	1.01×10^{-3}

*The SI units of viscosity are newton-second per meter squared.

Furthermore, because of their shape, the molecules have a great tendency to become entangled rather than to slip past one another as the molecules of less viscous liquids do. These interactions contribute to its high viscosity.

The Structure and Properties of Water

Water is so common a substance on Earth that we often overlook its unique nature. All life processes involve water. Water is an excellent solvent for many ionic compounds, as well as for other substances capable of forming hydrogen bonds with water.

As Table 6.2 shows, water has a high specific heat. The reason is that to raise the temperature of water (that is, to increase the average kinetic energy of water molecules), we must first break the many intermolecular hydrogen bonds. Thus, water can absorb a substantial amount of heat while its temperature rises only slightly. The converse is also true: Water can give off much heat with only a slight decrease in its temperature. For this reason, the huge quantities of water that are present in our lakes and oceans can effectively moderate the climate of adjacent land areas by absorbing heat in the summer and giving off heat in the winter, with only small changes in the temperature of the body of water.

The most striking property of water is that its solid form is less dense than its liquid form: ice floats at the surface of liquid water. The density of almost all other substances is greater in the solid state than in the liquid state (Figure 11.11).

To understand why water is different, we have to examine the electronic structure of the H_2O molecule. As we saw in Chapter 9, there are two pairs of nonbonding electrons, or two lone pairs, on the oxygen atom:

Although many compounds can form intermolecular hydrogen bonds, the difference between H_2O and other polar molecules, such as NH_3 and HF, is that each oxygen atom can form *two* hydrogen bonds, the same as the number of lone electron pairs on the oxygen atom. Thus, water molecules are joined together in an extensive three-dimensional network in which each oxygen atom is approximately tetrahedrally bonded to four hydrogen atoms, two by covalent bonds and two by hydrogen bonds. This equality in the number of hydrogen atoms and lone pairs is not characteristic of NH_3 or HF or, for that matter, of any other molecule capable of forming hydrogen

If water did not have the ability to form hydrogen bonds, it would be a gas at room temperature.

Electrostatic potential map of water.

Figure 11.11 *Left: Ice cubes float on water. Right: Solid benzene sinks to the bottom of liquid benzene.*

$= O$
$= H$

Figure 11.12 *The three-dimensional structure of ice. Each O atom is bonded to four H atoms. The covalent bonds are shown by short solid lines and the weaker hydrogen bonds by long dotted lines between O and H. The empty space in the structure accounts for the low density of ice.*

Figure 11.13 *Plot of density versus temperature for liquid water. The maximum density of water is reached at 4°C. The density of ice at 0°C is about 0.92 g/cm³.*

bonds. Consequently, these other molecules can form rings or chains, but not three-dimensional structures.

The highly ordered three-dimensional structure of ice (Figure 11.12) prevents the molecules from getting too close to one another. But consider what happens when ice melts. At the melting point, a number of water molecules have enough kinetic energy to break free of the intermolecular hydrogen bonds. These molecules become trapped in the cavities of the three-dimensional structure, which is broken down into smaller clusters. As a result, there are more molecules per unit volume in liquid water than in ice. Thus, because density = mass/volume, the density of water is greater than that of ice. With further heating, more water molecules are released from intermolecular hydrogen bonding, so that the density of water tends to increase with rising temperature just above the melting point. Of course, at the same time, water expands as it is being heated so that its density is decreased. These two processes—the trapping of free water molecules in cavities and thermal expansion—act in opposite directions. From 0°C to 4°C, the trapping prevails and water becomes progressively denser. Beyond 4°C, however, thermal expansion predominates and the density of water decreases with increasing temperature (Figure 11.13).

11.4 Crystal Structure

Solids can be divided into two categories: crystalline and amorphous. Ice is a ***crystalline solid,*** which *possesses rigid and long-range order; its atoms, molecules, or ions occupy specific positions.* The arrangement of such particles in a crystalline solid is such that the net attractive intermolecular forces are at their maximum. The forces responsible for

CHEMISTRY *in Action*

Why Do Lakes Freeze from the Top Down?

The fact that ice is less dense than water has a profound ecological significance. Consider, for example, the temperature changes in the fresh water of a lake in a cold climate. As the temperature of the water near the surface drops, the density of this water increases. The colder water then sinks toward the bottom, while warmer water, which is less dense, rises to the top. This normal convection motion continues until the temperature throughout the water reaches 4°C. Below this temperature, the density of water begins to decrease with decreasing temperature (see Figure 11.13), so that it no longer sinks. On further cooling, the water begins to freeze at the surface. The ice layer formed does not sink because it is less dense than the liquid; it even acts as a thermal insulator for the water below it. Were ice heavier, it would sink to the bottom of the lake and eventually the water would freeze upward. Most living organisms in the body of water could not survive being frozen in ice. Fortunately, lake water does not freeze upward from the bottom. This unusual property of water makes the sport of ice fishing possible.

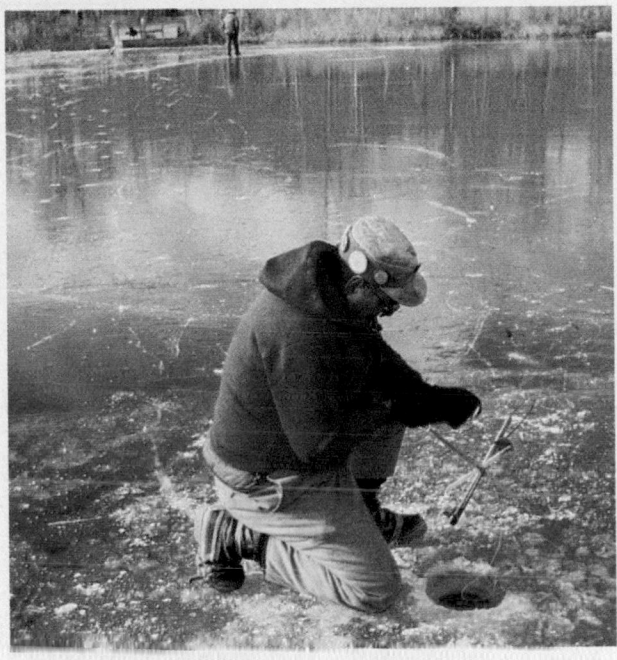

Ice fishing. The ice layer that forms on the surface of a lake insulates the water beneath and maintains a high enough temperature to sustain aquatic life.

the stability of a crystal can be ionic forces, covalent bonds, van der Waals forces, hydrogen bonds, or a combination of these forces. *Amorphous solids* such as glass lack a well-defined arrangement and long-range molecular order. We will discuss them in Section 11.7. In this section we will concentrate on the structure of crystalline solids.

A **unit cell** is *the basic repeating structural unit of a crystalline solid*. Figure 11.14 shows a unit cell and its extension in three dimensions. Each sphere represents an atom, ion, or molecule and is called a *lattice point*. In many crystals, the lattice point does not actually contain such a particle. Rather, there may be several atoms, ions, or molecules identically arranged about each lattice point. For simplicity, however, we can assume that each lattice point is occupied by an atom. This is certainly the case with most metals. Every crystalline solid can be described in terms of one of the seven types of unit cells shown in Figure 11.15. The geometry of the cubic unit cell is particularly simple because all sides and all angles are equal. Any of the unit cells, when repeated in space in all three dimensions, forms the lattice structure characteristic of a crystalline solid.

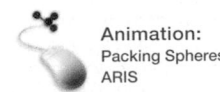

Animation:
Packing Spheres
ARIS

Packing Spheres

We can understand the general geometric requirements for crystal formation by considering the different ways of packing a number of identical spheres (Ping-Pong balls,

Figure 11.14 *(a) A unit cell and (b) its extension in three dimensions. The black spheres represent either atoms or molecules.*

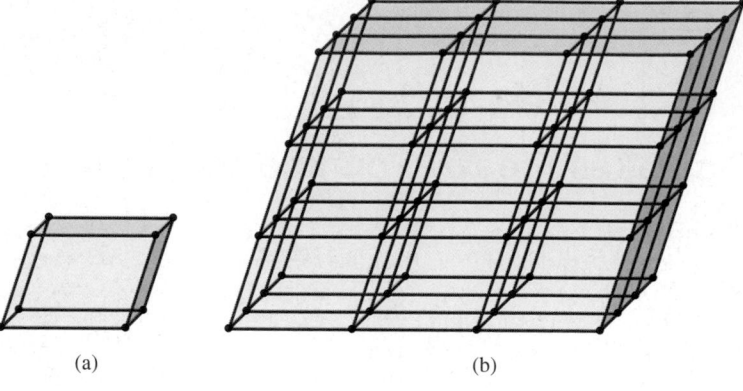

(a)   (b)

Figure 11.15 *The seven types of unit cells. Angle α is defined by edges b and c, angle β by edges a and c, and angle γ by edges a and b.*

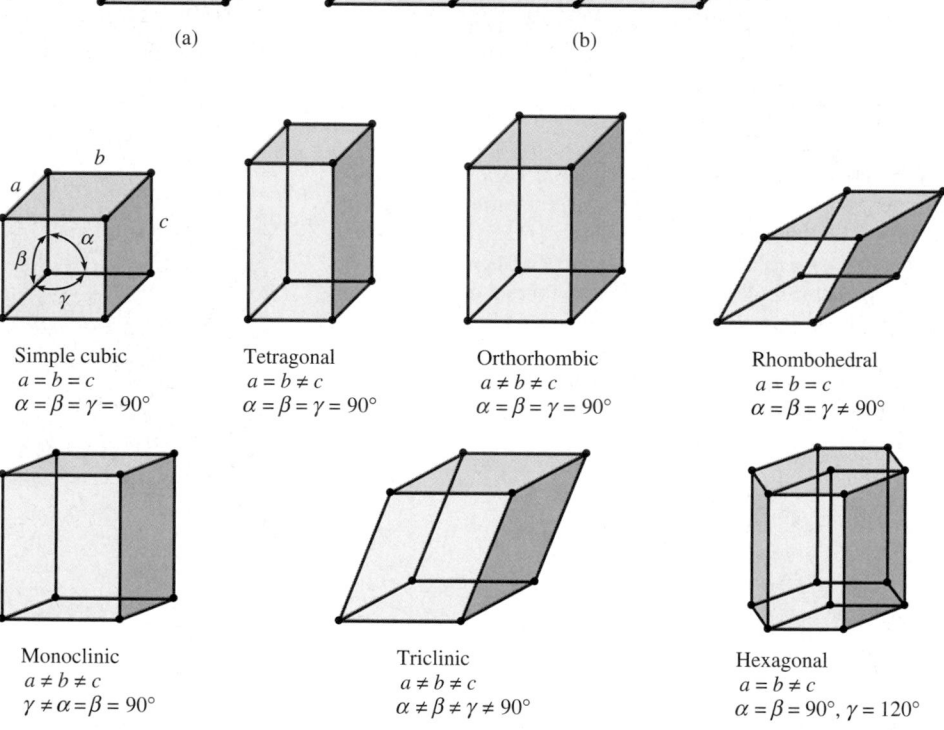

Simple cubic
$a = b = c$
$\alpha = \beta = \gamma = 90°$

Tetragonal
$a = b \neq c$
$\alpha = \beta = \gamma = 90°$

Orthorhombic
$a \neq b \neq c$
$\alpha = \beta = \gamma = 90°$

Rhombohedral
$a = b = c$
$\alpha = \beta = \gamma \neq 90°$

Monoclinic
$a \neq b \neq c$
$\gamma \neq \alpha = \beta = 90°$

Triclinic
$a \neq b \neq c$
$\alpha \neq \beta \neq \gamma \neq 90°$

Hexagonal
$a = b \neq c$
$\alpha = \beta = 90°, \gamma = 120°$

for example) to form an ordered three-dimensional structure. The way the spheres are arranged in layers determines what type of unit cell we have.

In the simplest case, a layer of spheres can be arranged as shown in Figure 11.16(a). The three-dimensional structure can be generated by placing a layer above and below this layer in such a way that spheres in one layer are directly over the spheres in the layer below it. This procedure can be extended to generate many, many layers, as in the case of a crystal. Focusing on the sphere labeled with an "*x*," we see that it is in

Figure 11.16 *Arrangement of identical spheres in a simple cubic cell. (a) Top view of one layer of spheres. (b) Definition of a simple cubic cell. (c) Since each sphere is shared by eight unit cells and there are eight corners in a cube, there is the equivalent of one complete sphere inside a simple cubic unit cell.*

(a)   (b)   (c)

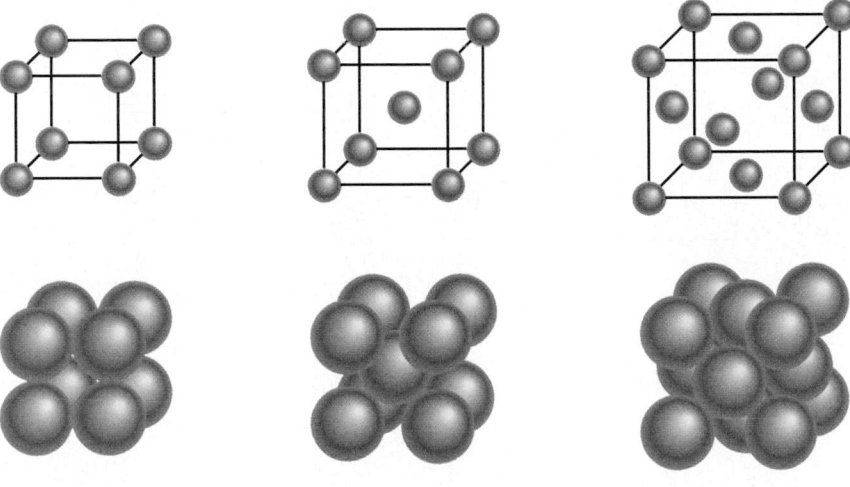

Figure 11.17 *Three types of cubic cells. In reality, the spheres representing atoms, molecules, or ions are in contact with one another in these cubic cells.*

Simple cubic   Body-centered cubic   Face-centered cubic

contact with four spheres in its own layer, one sphere in the layer above, and one sphere in the layer below. Each sphere in this arrangement is said to have a *coordination number* of 6 because it has six immediate neighbors. The **coordination number** is defined as *the number of atoms (or ions) surrounding an atom (or ion) in a crystal lattice.* Its value gives us a measure of how tightly the spheres are packed together—the larger the coordination number, the closer the spheres are to each other. The basic, repeating unit in the array of spheres is called a *simple cubic cell* (scc) [Figure 11.16(b)].

The other types of cubic cells are the *body-centered cubic cell* (bcc) and the *face-centered cubic cell* (fcc) (Figure 11.17). A body-centered cubic arrangement differs from a simple cube in that the second layer of spheres fits into the depressions of the first layer and the third layer into the depressions of the second layer (Figure 11.18). The coordination number of each sphere in this structure is 8 (each sphere is in contact with four spheres in the layer above and four spheres in the layer below). In the face-centered cubic cell, there are spheres at the center of each of the six faces of the cube, in addition to the eight corner spheres.

Because every unit cell in a crystalline solid is adjacent to other unit cells, most of a cell's atoms are shared by neighboring cells. For example, in all types of cubic cells, each corner atom belongs to eight unit cells [Figure 11.19(a)]; an edge atom is shared by four unit cells [Figure 11.19(b)], and a face-centered atom is shared by two unit cells [Figure 11.19(c)]. Because each corner sphere is shared by eight unit cells and there are eight corners in a cube, there will be the equivalent of only one complete sphere inside a simple cubic unit cell (see Figure 11.17). A body-centered cubic cell contains the equivalent of two complete spheres, one in the center and eight shared corner spheres. A face-centered cubic cell contains four

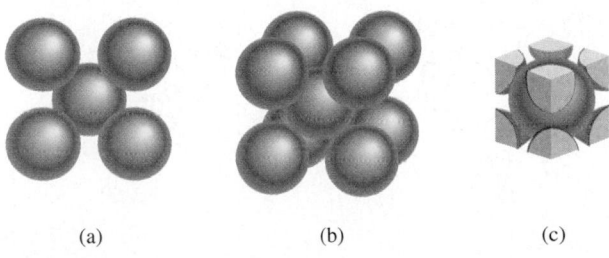

(a)   (b)   (c)

Figure 11.18 *Arrangement of identical spheres in a body-centered cube. (a) Top view. (b) Definition of a body-centered cubic unit cell. (c) There is the equivalent of two complete spheres inside a body-centered cubic unit cell.*

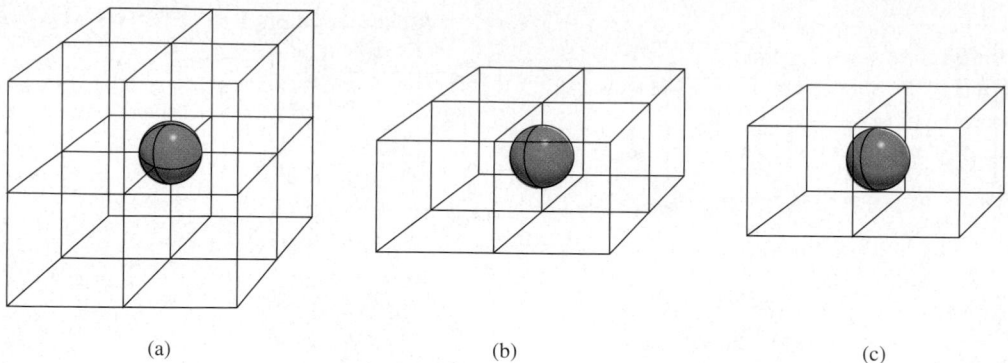

(a)   (b)   (c)

Figure 11.19 *(a) A corner atom in any cell is shared by eight unit cells. (b) An edge atom is shared by four unit cells. (c) A face-centered atom in a cubic cell is shared by two unit cells.*

complete spheres—three from the six face-centered atoms and one from the eight shared corner spheres.

Closest Packing

Clearly there is more empty space in the simple cubic and body-centered cubic cells than in the face-centered cubic cell. ***Closest packing,*** *the most efficient arrangement of spheres,* starts with the structure shown in Figure 11.20(a), which we call layer A.

Figure 11.20 *(a) In a close-packed layer, each sphere is in contact with six others. (b) Spheres in the second layer fit into the depressions between the first-layer spheres. (c) In the hexagonal close-packed structure, each third-layer sphere is directly over a first-layer sphere. (d) In the cubic close-packed structure, each third-layer sphere fits into a depression that is directly over a depression in the first layer.*

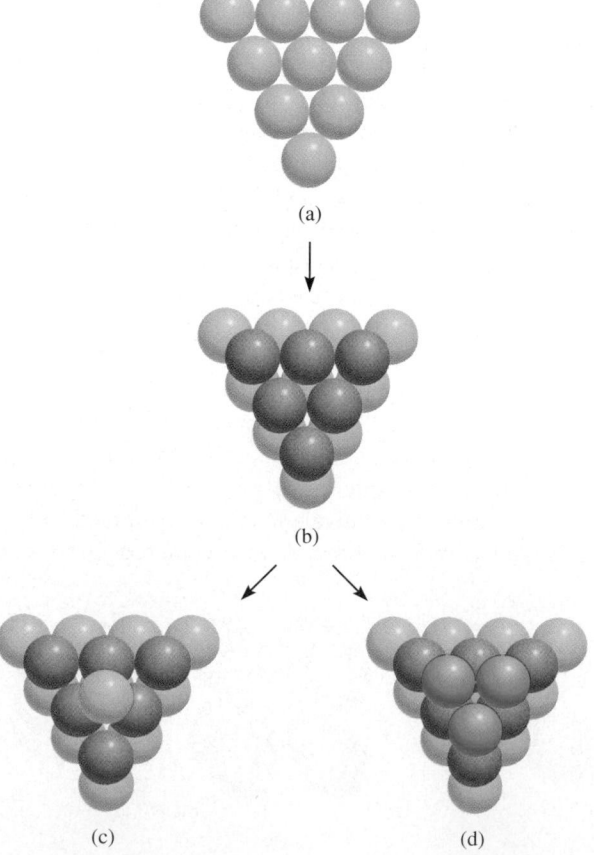

(a)

(b)

(c)   (d)

Focusing on the only enclosed sphere, we see that it has six immediate neighbors in that layer. In the second layer (which we call layer B), spheres are packed into the depressions between the spheres in the first layer so that all the spheres are as close together as possible [Figure 11.20(b)].

There are two ways that a third-layer sphere may cover the second layer to achieve closest packing. The spheres may fit into the depressions so that each third-layer sphere is directly over a first-layer sphere [Figure 11.20(c)]. Because there is no difference between the arrangement of the first and third layers, we also call the third layer layer A. Alternatively, the third-layer spheres may fit into the depressions that lie directly over the depressions in the first layer [Figure 11.20(d)]. In this case, we call the third layer layer C. Figure 11.21 shows the "exploded views" and the structures resulting from these two arrangements. The ABA arrangement is known as the *hexagonal close-packed (hcp) structure,* and the ABC arrangement is the *cubic close-packed (ccp) structure,* which corresponds to the face-centered cube already described. Note that in the hcp structure, the spheres in every other layer occupy the same vertical position (ABABAB. . .), while in the ccp structure, the spheres in every fourth layer occupy the same vertical position (ABCABCA. . .). In both structures, each sphere has a coordination number of 12 (each sphere is in contact with six spheres in its own layer, three spheres in the layer above, and three spheres in the layer below). Both the hcp and ccp structures represent the most efficient way of packing identical spheres in a unit cell, and there is no way to increase the coordination number to beyond 12.

These oranges are in a closest packed arrangement, as shown in Figure 11.20(a).

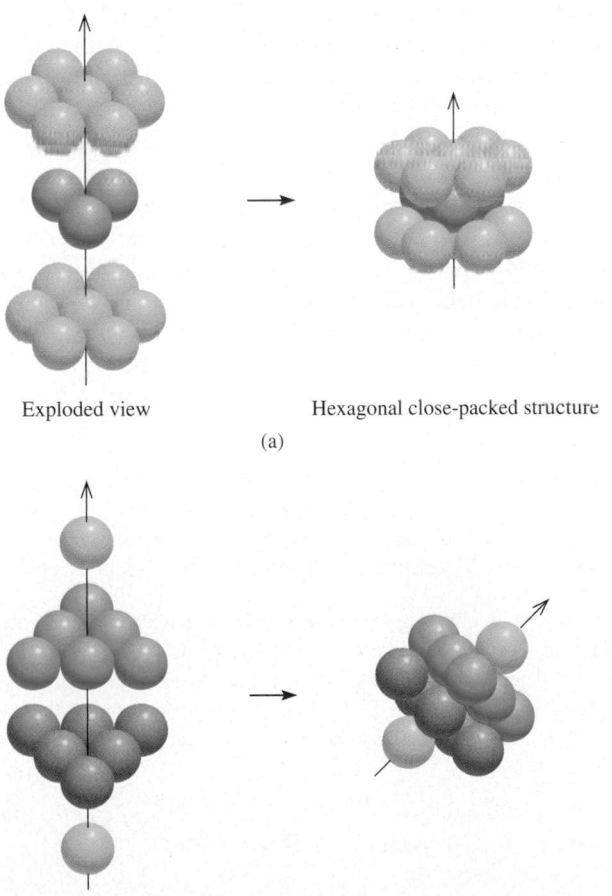

Exploded view   Hexagonal close-packed structure

(a)

Exploded view   Cubic close-packed structure

(b)

Figure 11.21 *Exploded views of (a) a hexagonal close-packed structure and (b) a cubic close-packed structure. The arrow is tilted to show the face-centered cubic unit cell more clearly. Note that this arrangement is the same as the face-centered unit cell.*

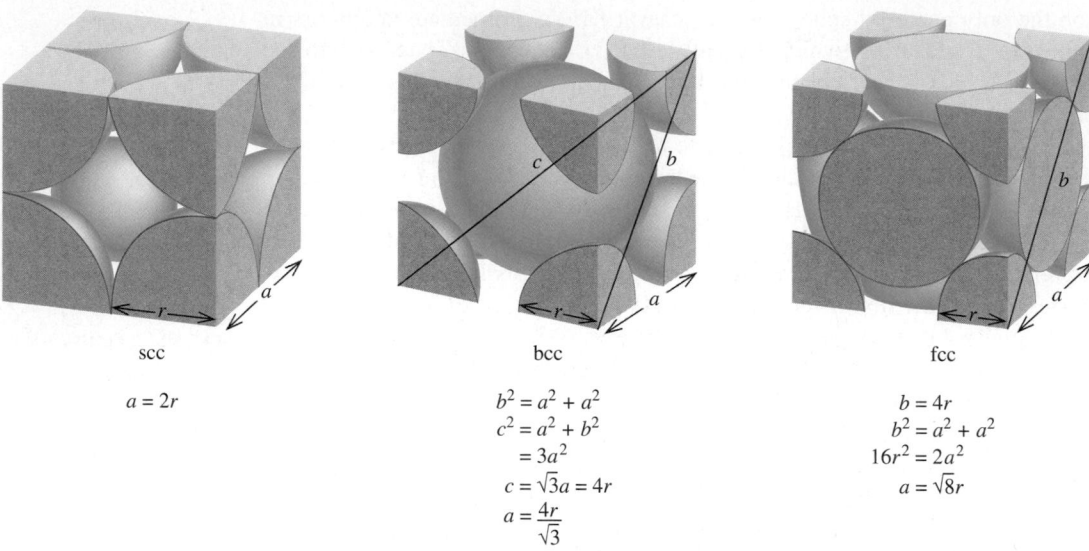

Figure 11.22 *The relationship between the edge length (a) and radius (r) of atoms in the simple cubic cell, body-centered cubic cell, and face-centered cubic cell.*

Many metals and noble gases, which are monatomic, form crystals with hcp or ccp structures. For example, magnesium, titanium, and zinc crystallize with their atoms in a hcp array, while aluminum, nickel, and silver crystallize in the ccp arrangement. All solid noble gases have the ccp structure except helium, which crystallizes in the hcp structure. It is natural to ask why a series of related substances, such as the transition metals or the noble gases, would form different crystal structures. The answer lies in the relative stability of a particular crystal structure, which is governed by intermolecular forces. Thus, magnesium metal has the hcp structure because this arrangement of Mg atoms results in the greatest stability of the solid.

Figure 11.22 summarizes the relationship between the atomic radius r and the edge length a of a simple cubic cell, a body-centered cubic cell, and a face-centered cubic cell. This relationship can be used to determine the atomic radius of a sphere if the density of the crystal is known, as Example 11.3 shows.

Example 11.3

Gold (Au) crystallizes in a cubic close-packed structure (the face-centered cubic unit cell) and has a density of 19.3 g/cm³. Calculate the atomic radius of gold in picometers.

Strategy We want to calculate the radius of a gold atom. For a face-centered cubic unit cell, the relationship between radius (r) and edge length (a), according to Figure 11.22, is $a = \sqrt{8}r$. Therefore, to determine r of a Au atom, we need to find a. The volume of a cube is $V = a^3$ or $a = \sqrt[3]{V}$. Thus, if we can determine the volume of the unit cell, we can calculate a. We are given the density in the problem.

$$\text{density} = \frac{\text{mass}}{\text{volume}}$$

given ↗   ↖ need to find
↘ want to calculate

(Continued)

The sequence of steps is summarized as follows:

$$\begin{array}{ccc} \text{density of} \\ \text{unit cell} \end{array} \longrightarrow \begin{array}{c} \text{volume of} \\ \text{unit cell} \end{array} \longrightarrow \begin{array}{c} \text{edge length} \\ \text{of unit cell} \end{array} \longrightarrow \begin{array}{c} \text{radius of} \\ \text{Au atom} \end{array}$$

Solution

Step 1: We know the density, so in order to determine the volume, we find the mass of the unit cell. Each unit cell has eight corners and six faces. The total number of atoms within such a cell, according to Figure 11.19, is

$$\left(8 \times \frac{1}{8}\right) + \left(6 \times \frac{1}{2}\right) = 4$$

The mass of a unit cell in grams is

$$m = \frac{4 \text{ atoms}}{1 \text{ unit cell}} \times \frac{1 \text{ mol}}{6.022 \times 10^{23} \text{ atoms}} \times \frac{197.0 \text{ g Au}}{1 \text{ mol Au}}$$
$$= 1.31 \times 10^{-21} \text{ g/unit cell}$$

From the definition of density ($d = m/V$), we calculate the volume of the unit cell as follows:

$$V = \frac{m}{d} = \frac{1.31 \times 10^{-21} \text{ g}}{19.3 \text{ g/cm}^3} = 6.79 \times 10^{-23} \text{ cm}^3$$

Remember that density is an intensive property, so that it is the same for one unit cell and 1 cm^3 of the substance.

Step 2: Because volume is length cubed, we take the cubic root of the volume of the unit cell to obtain the edge length (a) of the cell

$$a = \sqrt[3]{V}$$
$$= \sqrt[3]{6.79 \times 10^{-23} \text{ cm}^3}$$
$$= 4.08 \times 10^{-8} \text{ cm}$$

Step 3: From Figure 11.22 we see that the radius of an Au sphere (r) is related to the edge length by

$$a = \sqrt{8}\, r$$

Therefore,

$$r = \frac{a}{\sqrt{8}} = \frac{4.08 \times 10^{-8} \text{ cm}}{\sqrt{8}}$$
$$= 1.44 \times 10^{-8} \text{ cm}$$
$$= 1.44 \times 10^{-8} \text{ cm} \times \frac{1 \times 10^{-2} \text{ m}}{1 \text{ cm}} \times \frac{1 \text{ pm}}{1 \times 10^{-12} \text{ m}}$$
$$= 144 \text{ pm}$$

Similar problem: 11.39.

Practice Exercise When silver crystallizes, it forms face-centered cubic cells. The unit cell edge length is 408.7 pm. Calculate the density of silver.

11.5 X-Ray Diffraction by Crystals

Virtually all we know about crystal structure has been learned from X-ray diffraction studies. *X-ray diffraction* refers to *the scattering of X rays by the units of a crystalline solid.* The scattering, or diffraction, patterns produced are used to deduce the arrangement of particles in the solid lattice.

Figure 11.23 *An arrangement for obtaining the X-ray diffraction pattern of a crystal. The shield prevents the strong undiffracted X rays from damaging the photographic plate.*

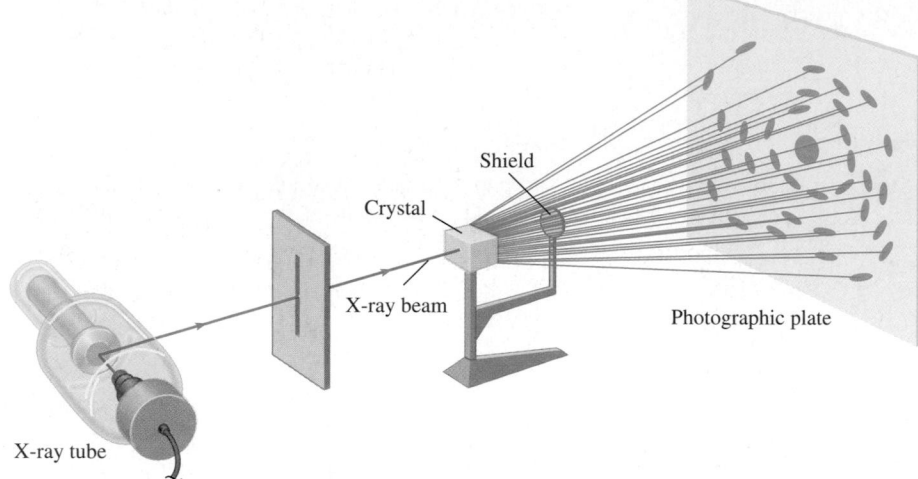

In Section 10.6 we discussed the interference phenomenon associated with waves (see Figure 10.21). Because X rays are one form of electromagnetic radiation, and therefore waves, we would expect them to exhibit such behavior under suitable conditions. In 1912 the German physicist Max von Laue[†] correctly suggested that, because the wavelength of X rays is comparable in magnitude to the distances between lattice points in a crystal, the lattice should be able to *diffract* X rays. An X-ray diffraction pattern is the result of interference in the waves associated with X rays.

Figure 11.23 shows a typical X-ray diffraction setup. A beam of X rays is directed at a mounted crystal. Atoms in the crystal absorb some of the incoming radiation and then reemit it; the process is called the *scattering of X rays.*

To understand how a diffraction pattern may be generated, consider the scattering of X rays by atoms in two parallel planes (Figure 11.24). Initially, the two incident rays are *in phase* with each other (their maxima and minima occur at the same positions). The upper wave is scattered, or reflected, by an atom in the first layer, while the lower wave is scattered by an atom in the second layer. In order for these

---

[†]Max Theodor Felix von Laue (1879–1960). German physicist. Von Laue received the Nobel Prize in Physics in 1914 for his discovery of X-ray diffraction.

Figure 11.24 *Reflection of X rays from two layers of atoms. The lower wave travels a distance 2d sin θ longer than the upper wave does. For the two waves to be in phase again after reflection, it must be true that 2d sin θ = nλ, where λ is the wavelength of the X ray and n = 1, 2, 3, . . . The sharply defined spots in Figure 11.23 are observed only if the crystal is large enough to consist of hundreds of parallel layers.*

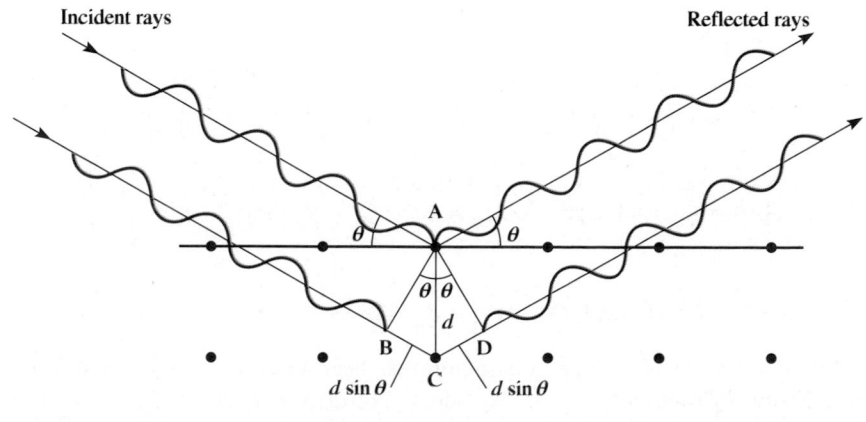

two scattered waves to be in phase again, the extra distance traveled by the lower wave must be an integral multiple of the wavelength (λ) of the X ray; that is,

$$BC + CD = 2d\sin\theta = n\lambda \qquad n = 1, 2, 3, \ldots$$

or

$$2d\sin\theta = n\lambda \qquad (11.1)$$

where θ is the angle between the X rays and the plane of the crystal and d is the distance between adjacent planes. Equation (11.1) is known as the Bragg equation after William H. Bragg[‡] and Sir William L. Bragg.[§] The reinforced waves produce a dark spot on a photographic film for each value of θ that satisfies the Bragg equation.

Reinforced waves are waves that have interacted constructively (see Figure 10.21).

Example 11.4 illustrates the use of Equation (11.1).

Example 11.4

X rays of wavelength 0.154 nm strike an aluminum crystal; the rays are reflected at an angle of 19.3°. Assuming that $n = 1$, calculate the spacing between the planes of aluminum atoms (in pm) that is responsible for this angle of reflection. The conversion factor is obtained from 1 nm = 1000 pm.

Strategy This is an application of Equation (11.1).

Solution Converting the wavelength to picometers and using the angle of reflection (19.3°), we write

$$d = \frac{n\lambda}{2\sin\theta} = \frac{\lambda}{2\sin\theta}$$

$$= \frac{0.154 \text{ nm} \times \dfrac{1000 \text{ pm}}{1 \text{ nm}}}{2\sin 19.3°}$$

$$= 233 \text{ pm}$$

Similar problems: 11.47, 11.48.

Practice Exercise X rays of wavelength 0.154 nm are diffracted from a crystal at an angle of 14.17°. Assuming that $n = 1$, calculate the distance (in pm) between layers in the crystal.

The X-ray diffraction technique offers the most accurate method for determining bond lengths and bond angles in molecules in the solid state. Because X rays are scattered by electrons, chemists can construct an electron-density contour map from the diffraction patterns by using a complex mathematical procedure. Basically, an *electron-density contour map* tells us the relative electron densities at various locations in a molecule. The densities reach a maximum near the center of each atom. In this manner, we can determine the positions of the nuclei and hence the geometric parameters of the molecule.

11.6 Types of Crystals

The structures and properties of crystals, such as melting point, density, and hardness, are determined by the kinds of forces that hold the particles together. We can classify any crystal as one of four types: ionic, covalent, molecular, or metallic.

[‡]William Henry Bragg (1862–1942). English physicist. Bragg's work was mainly in X-ray crystallography. He shared the Nobel Prize in Physics with his son Sir William Bragg in 1915.

[§]Sir William Lawrence Bragg (1890–1972). English physicist. Bragg formulated the fundamental equation for X-ray diffraction and shared the Nobel Prize in Physics with his father in 1915.

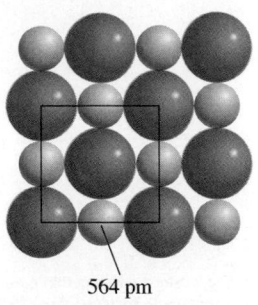

564 pm

Figure 11.25 *Relation between the radii of Na⁺ and Cl⁻ ions and the unit cell dimensions. Here the cell edge length is equal to twice the sum of the two ionic radii.*

These giant potassium dihydrogen phosphate crystals were grown in the laboratory. The largest one weighs 701 lb!

Ionic Crystals

Ionic crystals have two important characteristics: (1) They are composed of charged species and (2) anions and cations are generally quite different in size. Knowing the radii of the ions is helpful in understanding the structure and stability of these compounds. There is no way to measure the radius of an individual ion, but sometimes it is possible to come up with a reasonable estimate. For example, if we know the radius of I^- in KI is about 216 pm, we can determine the radius of K^+ ion in KI, and from that, the radius of Cl^- in KCl, and so on. The ionic radii in Figure 8.9 are average values derived from many different compounds. Let us consider the NaCl crystal, which has a face-centered cubic lattice (see Figure 2.13). Figure 11.25 shows that the edge length of the unit cell of NaCl is twice the sum of the ionic radii of Na^+ and Cl^-. Using the values given in Figure 8.9, we calculate the edge length to be 2(95 + 181) pm, or 552 pm. But the edge length shown in Figure 11.25 was determined by X-ray diffraction to be 564 pm. The discrepancy between these two values tells us that the radius of an ion actually varies slightly from one compound to another.

Figure 11.26 shows the crystal structures of three ionic compounds: CsCl, ZnS, and CaF_2. Because Cs^+ is considerably larger than Na^+, CsCl has the simple cubic lattice. ZnS has the *zincblende* structure, which is based on the face-centered cubic lattice. If the S^{2-} ions occupy the lattice points, the Zn^{2+} ions are located one-fourth of the distance along each body diagonal. Other ionic compounds that have the zincblende structure include CuCl, BeS, CdS, and HgS. CaF_2 has the *fluorite* structure. The Ca^{2+} ions occupy the lattice points, and each F^- ion is tetrahedrally surrounded by four Ca^{2+} ions. The compounds SrF_2, BaF_2, $BaCl_2$, and PbF_2 also have the fluorite structure.

Examples 11.5 and 11.6 show how to calculate the number of ions in and the density of a unit cell.

Example 11.5

How many Na^+ and Cl^- ions are in each NaCl unit cell?

Solution NaCl has a structure based on a face-centered cubic lattice. As Figure 2.13 shows, one whole Na^+ ion is at the center of the unit cell, and there are twelve Na^+ ions at the edges. Because each edge Na^+ ion is shared by four unit cells [see Figure 11.19(b)],

(Continued)

(a)

(b)

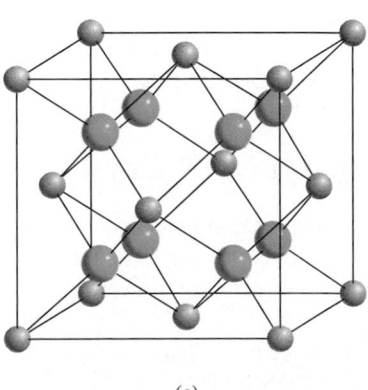

(c)

Figure 11.26 *Crystal structures of (a) CsCl, (b) ZnS, and (c) CaF₂. In each case, the cation is the smaller sphere.*

the total number of Na^+ ions is $1 + (12 \times \frac{1}{4}) = 4$. Similarly, there are six Cl^- ions at the face centers and eight Cl^- ions at the corners. Each face-centered ion is shared by two unit cells, and each corner ion is shared by eight unit cells [see Figures 11.19(a) and (c)], so the total number of Cl^- ions is $(6 \times \frac{1}{2}) + (8 \times \frac{1}{8}) = 4$. Thus, there are four Na^+ ions and four Cl^- ions in each NaCl unit cell. Figure 11.27 shows the portions of the Na^+ and Cl^- ions *within* a unit cell.

Check This result agrees with sodium chloride's empirical formula.

Practice Exercise How many atoms are in a body-centered cube, assuming that all atoms occupy lattice points?

Similar problem: 11.41.

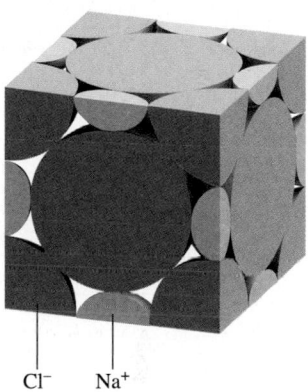

Cl^- Na^+

Figure 11.27 *Portions of Na^+ and Cl^- ions within a face-centered cubic unit cell.*

Example 11.6

The edge length of the NaCl unit cell is 564 pm. What is the density of NaCl in g/cm^3?

Strategy To calculate the density, we need to know the mass of the unit cell. The volume can be calculated from the given edge length because $V = a^3$. How many Na^+ and Cl^- ions are in a unit cell? What is the total mass in amu? What are the conversion factors between amu and g and between pm and cm?

Solution From Example 11.5 we see that there are four Na^+ ions and four Cl^- ions in each unit cell. So the total mass (in amu) of a unit cell is

$$\text{mass} = 4(22.99 \text{ amu} + 35.45 \text{ amu}) = 233.8 \text{ amu}$$

Converting amu to grams, we write

$$233.8 \text{ amu} \times \frac{1 \text{ g}}{6.022 \times 10^{23} \text{ amu}} = 3.882 \times 10^{-22} \text{ g}$$

The volume of the unit cell is $V = a^3 = (564 \text{ pm})^3$. Converting pm^3 to cm^3, the volume is given by

$$V = (564 \text{ pm})^3 \times \left(\frac{1 \times 10^{-12} \text{ m}}{1 \text{ pm}}\right)^3 \times \left(\frac{1 \text{ cm}}{1 \times 10^{-2} \text{ m}}\right)^3 = 1.794 \times 10^{-22} \text{ cm}^3$$

Finally, from the definition of density

$$\text{density} = \frac{\text{mass}}{\text{volume}} = \frac{3.882 \times 10^{-22} \text{ g}}{1.794 \times 10^{-22} \text{ cm}^3}$$
$$= 2.16 \text{ g/cm}^3$$

Similar problem: 11.42.

Practice Exercise Copper crystallizes in a face-centered cubic lattice (the Cu atoms are at the lattice points only). If the density of the metal is 8.96 g/cm^3, what is the unit cell edge length in pm?

Most ionic crystals have high melting points, an indication of the strong cohesive forces holding the ions together. A measure of the stability of ionic crystals is the lattice energy (see Section 9.3); the higher the lattice energy, the more stable the compound. These solids do not conduct electricity because the ions are fixed in position. However, in the molten state (that is, when melted) or dissolved in water, the ions are free to move and the resulting liquid is electrically conducting.

Figure 11.28 *(a) The structure of diamond. Each carbon is tetrahedrally bonded to four other carbon atoms. (b) The structure of graphite. The distance between successive layers is 335 pm.*

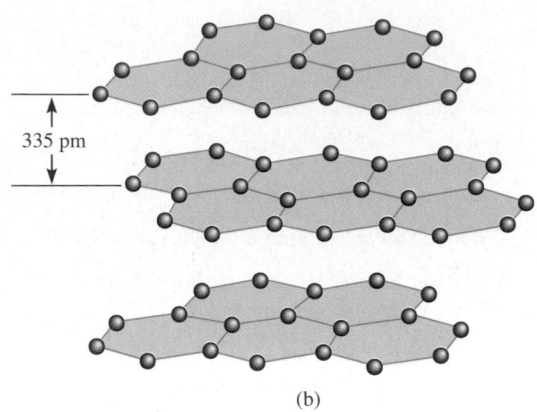

335 pm

(a)   (b)

Covalent Crystals

In covalent crystals, atoms are held together in an extensive three-dimensional network entirely by covalent bonds. Well-known examples are the two allotropes of carbon: diamond and graphite (see Figure 8.17). In diamond, each carbon atom is sp^3-hybridized; it is bonded to four other atoms (Figure 11.28). The strong covalent bonds in three dimensions contribute to diamond's unusual hardness (it is the hardest material known) and very high melting point (3550°C). In graphite, carbon atoms are arranged in six-membered rings. The atoms are all sp^2-hybridized; each atom is covalently bonded to three other atoms. The remaining unhybridized $2p$ orbital is used in pi bonding. In fact, each layer of graphite has the kind of delocalized molecular orbital that is present in benzene (see Section 10.8). Because electrons are free to move around in this extensively delocalized molecular orbital, graphite is a good conductor of electricity in directions along the planes of carbon atoms. The layers are held together by weak van der Waals forces. The covalent bonds in graphite account for its hardness; however, because the layers can slide over one another, graphite is slippery to the touch and is effective as a lubricant. It is also used in pencils and in ribbons made for computer printers and typewriters.

The central electrode in flashlight batteries is made of graphite.

Another covalent crystal is quartz (SiO_2). The arrangement of silicon atoms in quartz is similar to that of carbon in diamond, but in quartz there is an oxygen atom between each pair of Si atoms. Because Si and O have different electronegativities, the Si—O bond is polar. Nevertheless, SiO_2 is similar to diamond in many respects, such as hardness and high melting point (1610°C).

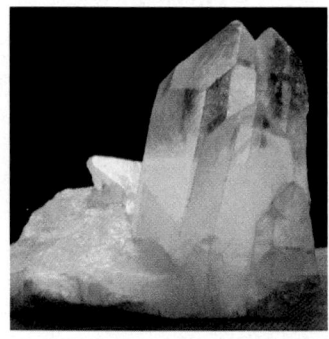

Quartz.

Molecular Crystals

In a molecular crystal, the lattice points are occupied by molecules, and the attractive forces between them are van der Waals forces and/or hydrogen bonding. An example of a molecular crystal is solid sulfur dioxide (SO_2), in which the predominant attractive force is a dipole-dipole interaction. Intermolecular hydrogen bonding is mainly responsible for maintaining the three-dimensional lattice of ice (see Figure 11.12). Other examples of molecular crystals are I_2, P_4, and S_8.

In general, except in ice, molecules in molecular crystals are packed together as closely as their size and shape allow. Because van der Waals forces and hydrogen bonding are generally quite weak compared with covalent and ionic bonds, molecular crystals are more easily broken apart than ionic and covalent crystals. Indeed, most molecular crystals melt at temperatures below 100°C.

Sulfur.

																		18 8A
1 1A																		

Figure 11.29 *Crystal structures of metals. The metals are shown in their positions in the periodic table. Mn has a cubic structure, Ga an orthorhombic structure, In and Sn a tetragonal structure, and Hg a rhombohedral structure (see Figure 11.15).*

Metallic Crystals

In a sense, the structure of metallic crystals is the simplest because every lattice point in a crystal is occupied by an atom of the same metal. Metallic crystals are generally body-centered cubic, face-centered cubic, or hexagonal close-packed (Figure 11.29). Consequently, metallic elements are usually very dense.

The bonding in metals is quite different from that in other types of crystals. In a metal, the bonding electrons are delocalized over the entire crystal. In fact, metal atoms in a crystal can be imagined as an array of positive ions immersed in a sea of delocalized valence electrons (Figure 11.30). The great cohesive force resulting from delocalization is responsible for a metal's strength. The mobility of the delocalized electrons makes metals good conductors of heat and electricity.

Table 11.4 summarizes the properties of the four different types of crystals discussed.

Figure 11.30 *A cross section of a metallic crystal. Each circled positive charge represents the nucleus and inner electrons of a metal atom. The gray area surrounding the positive metal ions indicates the mobile sea of electrons.*

TABLE 11.4	Types of Crystals and General Properties		
Type of Crystal	**Force(s) Holding the Units Together**	**General Properties**	**Examples**
Ionic	Electrostatic attraction	Hard, brittle, high melting point, poor conductor of heat and electricity	NaCl, LiF, MgO, CaCO$_3$
Covalent	Covalent bond	Hard, high melting point, poor conductor of heat and electricity	C (diamond),[†] SiO$_2$ (quartz)
Molecular*	Dispersion forces, dipole-dipole forces, hydrogen bonds	Soft, low melting point, poor conductor of heat and electricity	Ar, CO$_2$, I$_2$, H$_2$O, C$_{12}$H$_{22}$O$_{11}$ (sucrose)
Metallic	Metallic bond	Soft to hard, low to high melting point, good conductor of heat and electricity	All metallic elements; for example, Na, Mg, Fe, Cu

*Included in this category are crystals made up of individual atoms.
[†]Diamond is a good thermal conductor.

High-Temperature Superconductors

Metals such as copper and aluminum are good conductors of electricity, but they do possess some electrical resistance. In fact, up to about 20 percent of electrical energy may be lost in the form of heat when cables made of these metals are used to transmit electricity. Wouldn't it be marvelous if we could produce cables that possessed no electrical resistance?

Actually it has been known for over 90 years that certain metals and alloys, when cooled to very low temperatures (around the boiling point of liquid helium, or 4 K), lose their resistance totally. However, it is not practical to use these sub-

stances, called superconductors, for transmission of electric power because the cost of maintaining electrical cables at such low temperatures is prohibitive and would far exceed the savings from more efficient electricity transmission.

In 1986 two physicists in Switzerland discovered a new class of materials that are superconducting at around 30 K. Although 30 K is still a very low temperature, the improvement over the 4 K range was so dramatic that their work generated immense interest and triggered a flurry of research activity. Within months, scientists synthesized compounds that are superconducting

Crystal structure of $YBa_2Cu_3O_x$ (x = 6 or 7). Because some of the O atom sites are vacant, the formula is not constant.

Cu
O
Y
Ba

The levitation of a magnet above a high-temperature superconductor immersed in liquid nitrogen.

11.7 Amorphous Solids

Solids are most stable in crystalline form. However, if a solid is formed rapidly (for example, when a liquid is cooled quickly), its atoms or molecules do not have time to align themselves and may become locked in positions other than those of a regular crystal. The resulting solid is said to be *amorphous*. **Amorphous solids,** such as glass, *lack a regular three-dimensional arrangement of atoms.* In this section, we will discuss briefly the properties of glass.

Glass is one of civilization's most valuable and versatile materials. It is also one of the oldest—glass articles date back as far as 1000 B.C. **Glass** commonly refers to around 95 K, which is well above the boiling point of liquid nitrogen (77 K). The figure on p. 476 shows the crystal structure of one of these compounds, a mixed oxide of yttrium, barium, and copper with the formula $YBa_2Cu_3O_x$ (where $x = 6$ or 7). The accompanying figure shows a magnet being levitated above such a superconductor, which is immersed in liquid nitrogen.

Despite the initial excitement, this class of high-temperature superconductors has not fully lived up to its promise. After almost 20 years of intense research and development, scientists still puzzle over how and why these compounds superconduct. It has also proved difficult to make wires of these compounds, and other technical problems have limited their large-scale commercial applications thus far.

In another encouraging development, in 2001 scientists in Japan discovered that magnesium diboride (MgB_2) becomes superconducting at about 40 K. Although liquid neon (b.p. 27 K) must be used as coolant instead of liquid nitrogen, it is still much cheaper than using liquid helium. Magnesium diboride has several advantages as a high-temperature superconductor. First, it is an inexpensive compound (about $2 per gram) so large quantities are available for testing. Second, the mechanism of super-

conductivity in MgB_2 is similar to the well-understood metal alloy superconductors at 4 K. Third, it is much easier to fabricate this compound; that is, to make it into wires or thin films. With further research effort, it is hoped that someday soon different types of high-temperature superconductors will be used to build supercomputers, whose speeds are limited by how fast electric current flows, more powerful particle accelerators, efficient devices for nuclear fusion, and more accurate magnetic resonance imaging (MRI) machines for medical use. The progress in high-temperature superconductors is just warming up!

An experimental levitation train that operates on superconducting material at temperature of liquid helium.

Crystal structure of MgB_2. The Mg atoms (blue) form a hexagonal layer, while the B atoms (gold) form a graphitelike honeycomb layer.

an optically transparent fusion product of inorganic materials that has cooled to a rigid state without crystallizing. By fusion product we mean that the glass is formed by mixing molten silicon dioxide (SiO_2), its chief component, with compounds such as sodium oxide (Na_2O), boron oxide (B_2O_3), and certain transition metal oxides for color and other properties. In some respects glass behaves more like a liquid than a solid. X-ray diffraction studies show that glass lacks long-range periodic order.

There are about 800 different types of glass in common use today. Figure 11.31 shows two-dimensional schematic representations of crystalline quartz and amorphous quartz glass. Table 11.5 shows the composition and properties of quartz, Pyrex, and soda-lime glass.

CHEMISTRY
in Action

And All for the Want of a Button

In June 1812, Napoleon's mighty army, some 600,000 strong, marched into Russia. By early December, however, his forces were reduced to fewer than 10,000 men. An intriguing theory for Napoleon's defeat has to do with the tin buttons on his soldiers' coats! Tin has two allotropic forms called α (gray tin) and β (white tin). White tin, which has a cubic structure and a shiny metallic appearance, is stable at room temperature and above. Below 13°C, it slowly changes into gray tin. The random growth of the microcrystals of gray tin, which has a tetragonal structure, weakens the metal and makes it crumble. Thus, in the severe Russian winter, the soldiers were probably more busy holding their coats together with their hands than carrying weapons.

Actually, the so-called "tin disease" has been known for centuries. In the unheated cathedrals of medieval Europe, organ pipes made of tin were found to crumble as a result of the allotropic transition from white tin to gray tin. It is puzzling, therefore, that Napoleon, a great believer in keeping his troops fit for battle, would permit the use of tin for buttons. The tin story, if true, could be paraphrased in the old English Nursery Rhyme: "And all for the want of a button."

Is Napoleon trying to instruct his soldiers how to keep their coats tight?

The color of glass is due largely to the presence of metal ions (as oxides). For example, green glass contains iron(III) oxide, Fe_2O_3, or copper(II) oxide, CuO; yellow glass contains uranium(IV) oxide, UO_2; blue glass contains cobalt(II) and copper(II) oxides, CoO and CuO; and red glass contains small particles of gold and copper. Note that most of the ions mentioned here are derived from the transition metals.

Figure 11.31 *Two-dimensional representation of (a) crystalline quartz and (b) noncrystalline quartz glass. The small spheres represent silicon. In reality, the structure of quartz is three-dimensional. Each Si atom is tetrahedrally bonded to four O atoms.*

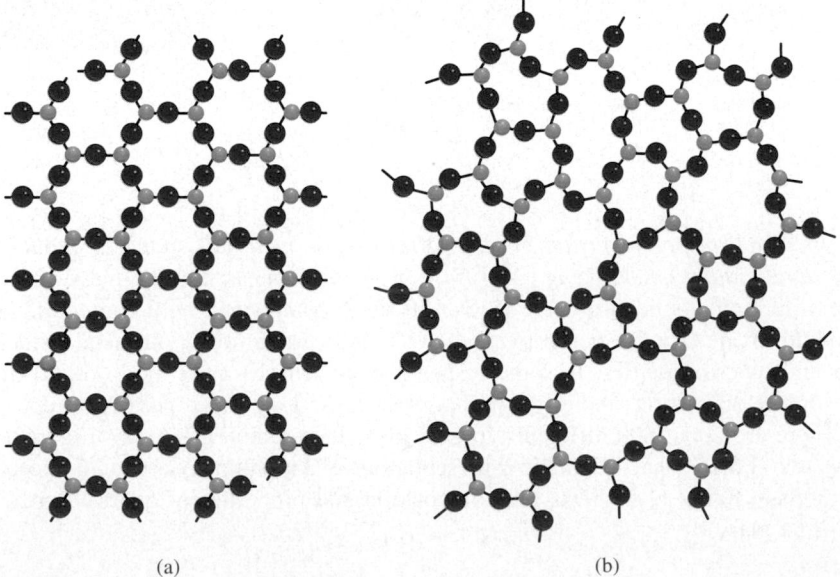

(a)   (b)

TABLE 11.5	Composition and Properties of Three Types of Glass	
Name	**Composition**	**Properties and Uses**
Pure quartz glass	100% SiO_2	Low thermal expansion, transparent to wide range of wavelengths. Used in optical research.
Pyrex glass	SiO_2, 60–80% B_2O_3, 10–25% Al_2O_3, small amount	Low thermal expansion; transparent to visible and infrared, but not to UV, radiation. Used mainly in laboratory and household cooking glassware.
Soda-lime glass	SiO_2, 75% Na_2O, 15% CaO, 10%	Easily attacked by chemicals and sensitive to thermal shocks. Transmits visible light, but absorbs UV radiation. Used mainly in windows and bottles.

11.8 Phase Changes

The discussions in Chapter 5 and in this chapter have given us an overview of the properties of the three phases of matter: gas, liquid, and solid. ***Phase changes, transformations from one phase to another,*** occur when energy (usually in the form of heat) is added or removed. Phase changes are physical changes characterized by changes in molecular order; molecules in the solid phase have the greatest order, and those in the gas phase have the greatest randomness. Keeping in mind the relationship between energy change and the increase or decrease in molecular order will help us understand the nature of these physical changes.

Liquid-Vapor Equilibrium

Molecules in a liquid are not fixed in a rigid lattice. Although they lack the total freedom of gaseous molecules, these molecules are in constant motion. Because liquids are denser than gases, the collision rate among molecules is much higher in the liquid phase than in the gas phase. When the molecules in a liquid have sufficient energy to escape from the surface a phase change occurs. ***Evaporation,*** or ***vaporization,*** is *the process in which a liquid is transformed into a gas.*

How does evaporation depend on temperature? Figure 11.32 shows the kinetic energy distribution of molecules in a liquid at two different temperatures. As we can see, the higher the temperature, the greater the kinetic energy, and hence more molecules are leaving the liquid.

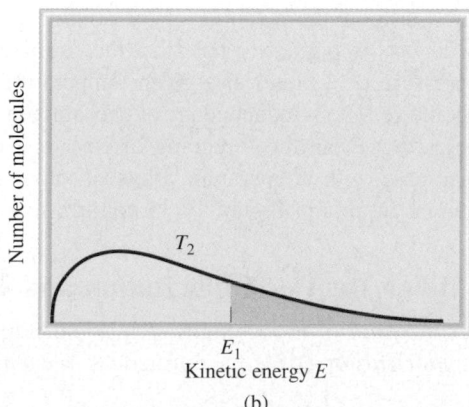

Figure 11.32 *Kinetic energy distribution curves for molecules in a liquid (a) at a temperature T_1 and (b) at a higher temperature T_2. Note that at the higher temperature, the curve flattens out. The shaded areas represent the number of molecules possessing kinetic energy equal to or greater than a certain kinetic energy E_1. The higher the temperature, the greater the number of molecules with high kinetic energy.*

Figure 11.33 *Apparatus for measuring the vapor pressure of a liquid (a) before the evaporation begins and (b) at equilibrium, when no further change is evident. In (b) the number of molecules leaving the liquid is equal to the number of molecules returning to the liquid. The difference in the mercury levels (h) gives the equilibrium vapor pressure of the liquid at the specified temperature.*

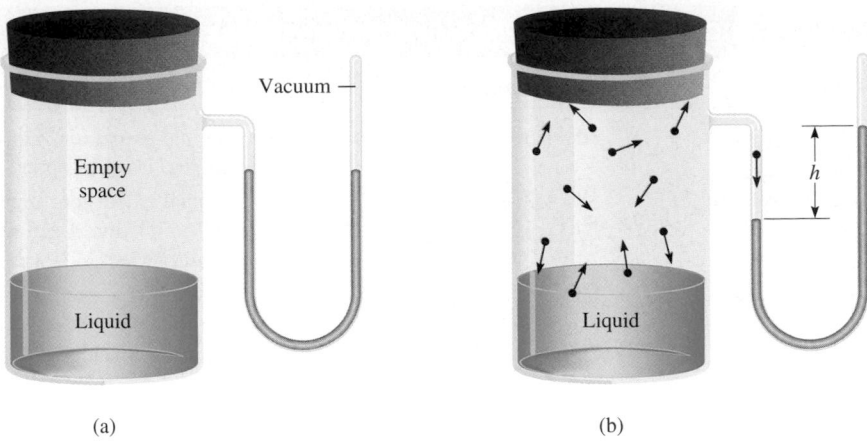

(a)   (b)

Vapor Pressure

The difference between a gas and a vapor is explained on p. 171.

Animation:
Equilibrium Vapor Pressure
ARIS

When a liquid evaporates, its gaseous molecules exert a vapor pressure. Consider the apparatus shown in Figure 11.33. Before the evaporation process starts, the mercury levels in the U-shaped manometer tube are equal. As soon as some molecules leave the liquid, a vapor phase is established. The vapor pressure is measurable only when a fair amount of vapor is present. The process of evaporation does not continue indefinitely, however. Eventually, the mercury levels stabilize and no further changes are seen.

What happens at the molecular level during evaporation? In the beginning, the traffic is only one way: Molecules are moving from the liquid to the empty space. Soon the molecules in the space above the liquid establish a vapor phase. As the concentration of molecules in the vapor phase increases, some molecules *condense,* that is, they return to the liquid phase. **Condensation,** *the change from the gas phase to the liquid phase,* occurs because a molecule strikes the liquid surface and becomes trapped by intermolecular forces in the liquid.

The rate of evaporation is constant at any given temperature, and the rate of condensation increases with the increasing concentration of molecules in the vapor phase. A state of **dynamic equilibrium,** in which *the rate of a forward process is exactly balanced by the rate of the reverse process,* is reached when the rates of condensation and evaporation become equal (Figure 11.34). The **equilibrium vapor pressure** is *the vapor pressure measured when a dynamic equilibrium exists between condensation and evaporation.* We often use the simpler term "vapor pressure" when we talk about the equilibrium vapor pressure of a liquid. This practice is acceptable as long as we know the meaning of the abbreviated term.

It is important to note that the equilibrium vapor pressure is the *maximum* vapor pressure of a liquid at a given temperature and that it is constant at a constant temperature. (It is independent of the amount of liquid as long as there is some liquid present.) From the foregoing discussion we expect the vapor pressure of a liquid to increase with temperature. Plots of vapor pressure versus temperature for three different liquids in Figure 11.35 confirm this expectation.

Equilibrium vapor pressure is independent of the amount of liquid as long as there is some liquid present.

Figure 11.34 *Comparison of the rates of evaporation and condensation at constant temperature.*

Molar Heat of Vaporization and Boiling Point

A measure of the strength of intermolecular forces in a liquid is the **molar heat of vaporization (ΔH_{vap}),** defined as *the energy* (usually in kilojoules) *required to*

Figure 11.35 *The increase in vapor pressure with temperature for three liquids. The normal boiling points of the liquids (at 1 atm) are shown on the horizontal axis. The strong metallic bonding in mercury results in a much lower vapor pressure of the liquid at room temperature.*

vaporize 1 mole of a liquid. The molar heat of vaporization is directly related to the strength of intermolecular forces that exist in the liquid. If the intermolecular attraction is strong, it takes a lot of energy to free the molecules from the liquid phase. Consequently, the liquid has a relatively low vapor pressure and a high molar heat of vaporization.

The quantitative relationship between the vapor pressure P of a liquid and the absolute temperature T is given by the Clausius[†]-Clapeyron[‡] equation

$$\ln P = -\frac{\Delta H_{vap}}{RT} + C \qquad (11.2)$$

where ln is the natural logarithm, R is the gas constant (8.314 J/K · mol), and C is a constant. The Clausius-Clapeyron equation has the form of the linear equation $y = mx + b$:

$$\ln P = \left(-\frac{\Delta H_{vap}}{R}\right)\left(\frac{1}{T}\right) + C$$

$$\updownarrow \qquad \updownarrow \quad \updownarrow \quad \updownarrow$$

$$y = \qquad m \quad x \ + \ b$$

By measuring the vapor pressure of a liquid at different temperatures (see Figure 11.35) and plotting ln P versus $1/T$, we determine the slope, which is equal to $-\Delta H_{vap}/R$. (ΔH_{vap} is assumed to be independent of temperature.) This is the method used to determine heats of vaporization (Table 11.6). Figure 11.36 shows plots of ln P versus $1/T$ for water and diethylether. Note that the straight line for water has a steeper slope because water has a larger ΔH_{vap}.

If we know the values of ΔH_{vap} and P of a liquid at one temperature, we can use the Clausius-Clapeyron equation to calculate the vapor pressure of the liquid at a

Figure 11.36 *Plots of ln P versus 1/T for water and diethyl ether. The slope in each case is equal to $-\Delta H_{vap}/R$.*

[†]Rudolf Julius Emanuel Clausius (1822–1888). German physicist. Clausius's work was mainly in electricity, kinetic theory of gases, and thermodynamics.

[‡]Benoit Paul Emile Clapeyron (1799–1864). French engineer. Clapeyron made contributions to the thermodynamic aspects of steam engines.

TABLE 11.6	Molar Heats of Vaporization for Selected Liquids	
Substance	**Boiling Point* (°C)**	**ΔH_{vap} (kJ/mol)**
Argon (Ar)	−186	6.3
Benzene (C_6H_6)	80.1	31.0
Ethanol (C_2H_5OH)	78.3	39.3
Diethyl ether ($C_2H_5OC_2H_5$)	34.6	26.0
Mercury (Hg)	357	59.0
Methane (CH_4)	−164	9.2
Water (H_2O)	100	40.79

* Measured at 1 atm.

different temperature. At temperatures T_1 and T_2, the vapor pressures are P_1 and P_2. From Equation (11.2) we can write

$$\ln P_1 = -\frac{\Delta H_{vap}}{RT_1} + C \tag{11.3}$$

$$\ln P_2 = -\frac{\Delta H_{vap}}{RT_2} + C \tag{11.4}$$

Subtracting Equation (11.4) from Equation (11.3) we obtain

$$\ln P_1 - \ln P_2 = -\frac{\Delta H_{vap}}{RT_1} - \left(-\frac{\Delta H_{vap}}{RT_2}\right)$$
$$= \frac{\Delta H_{vap}}{R}\left(\frac{1}{T_2} - \frac{1}{T_1}\right)$$

Hence

$$\ln \frac{P_1}{P_2} = \frac{\Delta H_{vap}}{R}\left(\frac{1}{T_2} - \frac{1}{T_1}\right)$$

or

$$\ln \frac{P_1}{P_2} = \frac{\Delta H_{vap}}{R}\left(\frac{T_1 - T_2}{T_1 T_2}\right) \tag{11.5}$$

Example 11.7 illustrates the use of Equation (11.5).

$C_2H_5OC_2H_5$

Example 11.7

Diethyl ether is a volatile, highly flammable organic liquid that is used mainly as a solvent. The vapor pressure of diethyl ether is 401 mmHg at 18°C. Calculate its vapor pressure at 32°C.

Strategy We are given the vapor pressure of diethyl ether at one temperature and asked to find the pressure at another temperature. Therefore, we need Equation (11.5).

(Continued)

Solution Table 11.6 tells us that $\Delta H_{vap} = 26.0$ kJ/mol. The data are

$$P_1 = 401 \text{ mmHg} \qquad P_2 = ?$$
$$T_1 = 18°C = 291 \text{ K} \qquad T_2 = 32°C = 305 \text{ K}$$

From Equation (11.5) we have

$$\ln \frac{401}{P_2} = \frac{26{,}000 \text{ J/mol}}{8.314 \text{ J/K} \cdot \text{mol}} \left[\frac{291 \text{ K} - 305 \text{ K}}{(291 \text{ K})(305 \text{ K})} \right]$$
$$= -0.493$$

Taking the antilog of both sides (see Appendix 4), we obtain

$$\frac{401}{P_2} = e^{-0.493} = 0.611$$

Hence

$$P_2 = 656 \text{ mmHg}$$

Check We expect the vapor pressure to be greater at the higher temperature. Therefore, the answer is reasonable.

Similar problem: 11.86.

Practice Exercise The vapor pressure of ethanol is 100 mmHg at 34.9°C. What is its vapor pressure at 63.5°C? (ΔH_{vap} for ethanol is 39.3 kJ/mol.)

A practical way to demonstrate the molar heat of vaporization is by rubbing an alcohol such as ethanol (C_2H_5OH) or isopropanol (C_3H_7OH), or rubbing alcohol, on your hands. These alcohols have a lower ΔH_{vap} than water, so that the heat from your hands is enough to increase the kinetic energy of the alcohol molecules and evaporate them. As a result of the loss of heat, your hands feel cool. This process is similar to perspiration, which is one of the means by which the human body maintains a constant temperature. Because of the strong intermolecular hydrogen bonding that exists in water, a considerable amount of energy is needed to vaporize the water in perspiration from the body's surface. This energy is supplied by the heat generated in various metabolic processes.

You have already seen that the vapor pressure of a liquid increases with temperature. Every liquid has a temperature at which it begins to boil. The **boiling point** is *the temperature at which the vapor pressure of a liquid is equal to the external pressure.* The *normal* boiling point of a liquid is the temperature at which it boils when the external pressure is 1 atm.

At the boiling point, bubbles form within the liquid. When a bubble forms, the liquid originally occupying that space is pushed aside, and the level of the liquid in the container is forced to rise. The pressure exerted *on* the bubble is largely atmospheric pressure, plus some *hydrostatic pressure* (that is, pressure due to the presence of liquid). The pressure *inside* the bubble is due solely to the vapor pressure of the liquid. When the vapor pressure becomes equal to the external pressure, the bubble rises to the surface of the liquid and bursts. If the vapor pressure in the bubble were lower than the external pressure, the bubble would collapse before it could rise. We can thus conclude that the boiling point of a liquid depends on the external pressure. (We usually ignore the small contribution due to the hydrostatic pressure.) For example, at 1 atm, water boils at 100°C, but if the pressure is reduced to 0.5 atm, water boils at only 82°C.

Because the boiling point is defined in terms of the vapor pressure of the liquid, we expect the boiling point to be related to the molar heat of vaporization: The higher ΔH_{vap}, the higher the boiling point. The data in Table 11.6 roughly confirm our prediction. Ultimately, both the boiling point and ΔH_{vap} are determined by the strength of intermolecular forces. For example, argon (Ar) and methane (CH_4), which have weak dispersion forces, have low boiling points and small molar heats of vaporization. Diethyl ether ($C_2H_5OC_2H_5$) has a dipole moment, and the dipole-dipole forces account for its moderately high boiling point and ΔH_{vap}. Both ethanol (C_2H_5OH) and water have strong hydrogen bonding, which accounts for their high boiling points and large ΔH_{vap} values. Strong metallic bonding causes mercury to have the highest boiling point and ΔH_{vap} of this group of liquids. Interestingly, the boiling point of benzene, which is nonpolar, is comparable to that of ethanol. Benzene has a high polarizability due to the distribution of its electrons in the delocalized pi molecular orbitals, and the dispersion forces among benzene molecules can be as strong as or even stronger than dipole-dipole forces and/or hydrogen bonds.

Critical Temperature and Pressure

The opposite of evaporation is condensation. In principle, a gas can be made to liquefy by either one of two techniques. By cooling a sample of gas we decrease the kinetic energy of its molecules, so that eventually molecules aggregate to form small drops of liquid. Alternatively, we can apply pressure to the gas. Compression reduces the average distance between molecules so that they are held together by mutual attraction. Industrial liquefaction processes combine these two methods.

Every substance has a ***critical temperature (T_c), above which its gas phase cannot be made to liquefy, no matter how great the applied pressure.*** This is also *the highest temperature at which a substance can exist as a liquid.* Putting it another way, above the critical temperature there is no fundamental distinction between a liquid and a gas—we simply have a fluid. ***Critical pressure (P_c)*** is *the minimum pressure that must be applied to bring about liquefaction at the critical temperature.* The existence of the critical temperature can be qualitatively explained as follows. Intermolecular attraction is a finite quantity for any given substance and it is independent of temperature. Below T_c, this force is sufficiently strong to hold the molecules together (under some appropriate pressure) in a liquid. Above T_c, molecular motion becomes so energetic that the molecules can break away from this attraction. Figure 11.37 shows what happens when sulfur hexafluoride is heated above its critical temperature (45.5°C) and then cooled down to below 45.5°C.

Table 11.7 lists the critical temperatures and critical pressures of a number of common substances. The critical temperature of a substance reflects the strength of its intermolecular forces. Benzene, ethanol, mercury, and water, which have strong intermolecular forces, also have high critical temperatures compared with the other substances listed in the table.

Liquid-Solid Equilibrium

The transformation of liquid to solid is called *freezing,* and the reverse process is called *melting,* or *fusion.* The ***melting point*** of a solid or the ***freezing point*** of a liquid is *the temperature at which solid and liquid phases coexist in equilibrium.* The *normal* melting (or freezing) point of a substance is the temperature at which a substance melts (or freezes) at 1 atm pressure. We generally omit the word "normal" when the pressure is at 1 atm.

Intermolecular forces are independent of temperature; the kinetic energy of molecules increases with temperature.

"Fusion" refers to the process of melting. Thus, a "fuse" breaks an electrical circuit when a metallic strip melts due to the heat generated by excessively high electrical current.

Figure 11.37 *The critical phenomenon of sulfur hexafluoride. (a) Below the critical temperature the clear liquid phase is visible. (b) Above the critical temperature the liquid phase has disappeared. (c) The substance is cooled just below its critical temperature. The fog represents the condensation of vapor. (d) Finally, the liquid phase reappears.*

The most familiar liquid-solid equilibrium is that of water and ice. At 0°C and 1 atm, the dynamic equilibrium is represented by

$$\text{ice} \rightleftharpoons \text{water}$$

A practical illustration of this dynamic equilibrium is provided by a glass of ice water. As the ice cubes melt to form water, some of the water between ice cubes

TABLE 11.7	Critical Temperatures and Critical Pressures of Selected Substances	
Substance	**T_c (°C)**	**P_c (atm)**
Ammonia (NH_3)	132.4	111.5
Argon (Ar)	−186	6.3
Benzene (C_6H_6)	288.9	47.9
Carbon dioxide (CO_2)	31.0	73.0
Ethanol (C_2H_5OH)	243	63.0
Diethyl ether ($C_2H_5OC_2H_5$)	192.6	35.6
Mercury (Hg)	1462	1036
Methane (CH_4)	−83.0	45.6
Molecular hydrogen (H_2)	−239.9	12.8
Molecular nitrogen (N_2)	−147.1	33.5
Molecular oxygen (O_2)	−118.8	49.7
Sulfur hexafluoride (SF_6)	45.5	37.6
Water (H_2O)	374.4	219.5

Figure 11.38 *A typical heating curve, from the solid phase through the liquid phase to the gas phase of a substance. Because ΔH_{fus} is smaller than ΔH_{vap}, a substance melts in less time than it takes to boil. This explains why AB is shorter than CD. The steepness of the solid, liquid, and vapor heating lines is determined by the specific heat of the substance in each state.*

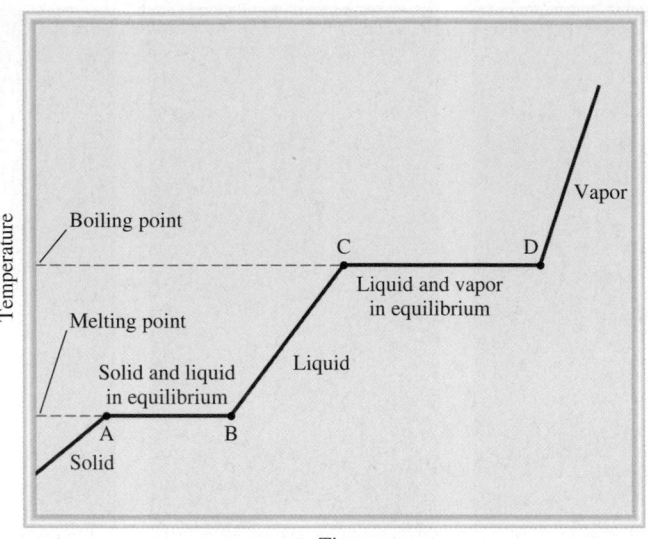

may freeze, thus joining the cubes together. This is not a true dynamic equilibrium; because the glass is not kept at 0°C, all the ice cubes will eventually melt away.

Because molecules are more strongly held in the solid phase than in the liquid phase, heat is required to bring about the solid-liquid phase transition. Looking at the heating curve shown in Figure 11.38, we see that when a solid is heated, its temperature increases gradually until point A is reached. At this point, the solid begins to melt. During the melting period (A ⟶ B), the first flat portion of the curve in Figure 11.38, heat is being absorbed by the system, yet its temperature remains constant. The heat helps the molecules to overcome the attractive forces in the solid. Once the sample has melted completely (point B), the heat absorbed increases the average kinetic energy of the liquid molecules, and the liquid temperature rises (B ⟶ C). The vaporization process (C ⟶ D) can be explained similarly. The temperature remains constant during the period when the increased kinetic energy is used to overcome the cohesive forces in the liquid. When all molecules are in the gas phase, the temperature rises again.

Molar heat of fusion (ΔH_{fus}) is *the energy* (usually in kilojoules) *required to melt 1 mole of a solid.* Table 11.8 shows the molar heats of fusion for the substances listed in Table 11.6. A comparison of the data in the two tables shows that for each substance ΔH_{fus} is smaller than ΔH_{vap}. This is consistent with the fact that molecules in a liquid are still fairly closely packed together, so that some energy is needed to bring about the rearrangement from solid to liquid. On the other hand, when a liquid evaporates, its molecules become completely separated from one another and considerably more energy is required to overcome the attractive force.

As we would expect, *cooling* a substance has the opposite effect of heating it. If we remove heat from a gas sample at a steady rate, its temperature decreases. As the liquid is being formed, heat is given off by the system, because its potential energy is decreasing. For this reason, the temperature of the system remains constant over the condensation period (D ⟶ C). After all the vapor has condensed, the temperature of the liquid begins to drop. Continued cooling of the liquid finally leads to freezing (B ⟶ A).

TABLE 11.8	Molar Heats of Fusion for Selected Substances	
Substance	Melting Point* (°C)	ΔH_{fus} (kJ/mol)
Argon (Ar)	−190	1.3
Benzene (C_6H_6)	5.5	10.9
Ethanol (C_2H_5OH)	−117.3	7.61
Diethyl ether ($C_2H_5OC_2H_5$)	−116.2	6.90
Mercury (Hg)	−39	23.4
Methane (CH_4)	−183	0.84
Water (H_2O)	0	6.01

*Measured at 1 atm.

The phenomenon known as **supercooling** refers to the situation in which *a liquid can be temporarily cooled to below its freezing point.* Supercooling occurs when heat is removed from a liquid so rapidly that the molecules literally have no time to assume the ordered structure of a solid. A supercooled liquid is unstable; gentle stirring or the addition to it of a small "seed" crystal of the same substance will cause it to solidify quickly.

Solid-Vapor Equilibrium

Solids, too, undergo evaporation and, therefore, possess a vapor pressure. Consider the following dynamic equilibrium:

$$\text{solid} \rightleftharpoons \text{vapor}$$

Sublimation is *the process in which molecules go directly from the solid into the vapor phase.* **Deposition** is the reverse process, that is, *molecules make the transition from vapor to solid directly.* Naphthalene, which is the substance used to make mothballs, has a fairly high (equilibrium) vapor pressure for a solid (1 mmHg at 53°C); thus, its pungent vapor quickly permeates an enclosed space. Iodine also sublimes. At room temperature, the violet color of iodine vapor is easily visible in a closed container.

Because molecules are more tightly held in a solid, the vapor pressure of a solid is generally much less than that of the corresponding liquid. **Molar heat of sublimation (ΔH_{sub})** of a substance is *the energy* (usually in kilojoules) *required to sublime 1 mole of a solid.* It is equal to the sum of the molar heats of fusion and vaporization:

Solid iodine in equilibrium with its vapor.

$$\Delta H_{sub} = \Delta H_{fus} + \Delta H_{vap} \tag{11.6}$$

Equation (11.6) is an illustration of Hess's law (see Section 6.6). The enthalpy, or heat change, for the overall process is the same whether the substance changes directly from the solid to the vapor form or from the solid to the liquid and then to the vapor. Note that Equation (11.6) holds only if all the phase changes occur at the *same* temperature. If not, the equation can be used only as an approximation.

Figure 11.39 summarizes the types of phase changes discussed in this section.

When a substance is heated, its temperature will rise and eventually it will undergo a phase transition. To calculate the total energy change for such a process we must include all of the steps, shown in Example 11.8.

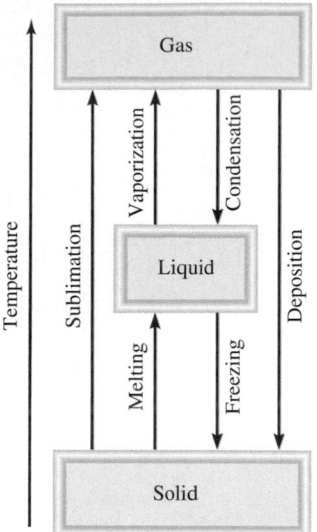

Figure 11.39 *The various phase changes that a substance can undergo.*

Example 11.8

Calculate the amount of energy (in kilojoules) needed to heat 346 g of liquid water from 0°C to 182°C. Assume that the specific heat of water is 4.184 J/g · °C over the entire liquid range and that the specific heat of steam is 1.99 J/g · °C.

Strategy The heat change (q) at each stage is given by $q = ms\Delta t$, where m is the mass of water, s is the specific heat, and Δt is the temperature change. If there is a phase change, such as vaporization, then q is given by $n\Delta H_{vap}$, where n is the number of moles of water.

Solution The calculation can be broken down in three steps.

Step 1: Heating water from 0°C to 100°C
     Using Equation (6.12) we write

$$q_1 = ms\Delta t$$
$$= (346 \text{ g})(4.184 \text{ J/g} \cdot °C)(100°C - 0°C)$$
$$= 1.45 \times 10^5 \text{ J}$$
$$= 145 \text{ kJ}$$

Step 2: Evaporating 346 g of water at 100°C (a phase change)
     In Table 11.6 we see $\Delta H_{vap} = 40.79$ kJ/mol for water, so

$$q_2 = 346 \text{ g H}_2\text{O} \times \frac{1 \text{ mol H}_2\text{O}}{18.02 \text{ g H}_2\text{O}} \times \frac{40.79 \text{ kJ}}{1 \text{ mol H}_2\text{O}}$$
$$= 783 \text{ kJ}$$

Step 3: Heating steam from 100°C to 182°C

$$q_3 = ms\Delta t$$
$$= (346 \text{ g})(1.99 \text{ J/g} \cdot °C)(182°C - 100°C)$$
$$= 5.65 \times 10^4 \text{ J}$$
$$= 56.5 \text{ kJ}$$

The overall energy required is given by

$$q_{overall} = q_1 + q_2 + q_3$$
$$= 145 \text{ kJ} + 783 \text{ kJ} + 56.5 \text{ kJ}$$
$$= 985 \text{ kJ}$$

Check All the qs have a positive sign, which is consistent with the fact that heat is absorbed to raise the temperature from 0°C to 182°C. Also, as expected, much more heat is absorbed during phase transition.

Practice Exercise Calculate the heat released when 68.0 g of steam at 124°C is converted to water at 45°C.

Similar problem: 11.78.

11.9 Phase Diagrams

The overall relationships among the solid, liquid, and vapor phases are best represented in a single graph known as a phase diagram. A ***phase diagram*** summarizes *the conditions at which a substance exists as a solid, liquid, or gas.* In this section we will briefly discuss the phase diagrams of water and carbon dioxide.

Water

Figure 11.40(a) shows the phase diagram of water. The graph is divided into three regions, each of which represents a pure phase. The line separating any two regions

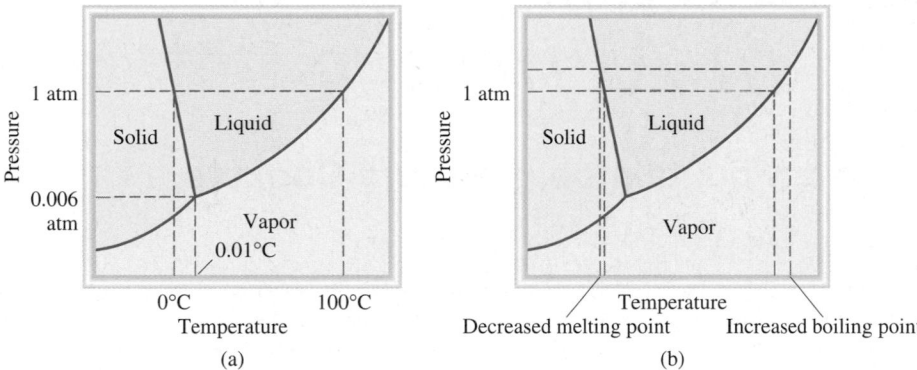

Figure 11.40 *(a) The phase diagram of water. Each solid line between two phases specifies the conditions of pressure and temperature under which the two phases can exist in equilibrium. The point at which all three phases can exist in equilibrium (0.006 atm and 0.01°C) is called the triple point. (b) This phase diagram tells us that increasing the pressure on ice lowers its melting point and that increasing the pressure of liquid water raises its boiling point.*

indicates conditions under which these two phases can exist in equilibrium. For example, the curve between the liquid and vapor phases shows the variation of vapor pressure with temperature. (Compare this curve with Figure 11.35.) The other two curves similarly indicate conditions for equilibrium between ice and liquid water and between ice and water vapor. (Note that the solid-liquid boundary line has a negative slope.) The point at which all three curves meet is called the ***triple point,*** which is *the only condition under which all three phases can be in equilibrium with one another.* For water, this point is at 0.01°C and 0.006 atm.

Phase diagrams enable us to predict changes in the melting point and boiling point of a substance as a result of changes in the external pressure; we can also anticipate directions of phase transitions brought about by changes in temperature and pressure. The normal melting point and boiling point of water at 1 atm are 0°C and 100°C, respectively. What would happen if melting and boiling were carried out at some other pressure? Figure 11.40(b) shows that increasing the pressure above 1 atm will raise the boiling point and lower the melting point. A decrease in pressure will lower the boiling point and raise the melting point.

Figure 11.41 *The phase diagram of carbon dioxide. Note that the solid-liquid boundary line has a positive slope. The liquid phase is not stable below 5.2 atm, so that only the solid and vapor phases can exist under atmospheric conditions.*

Carbon Dioxide

The phase diagram of carbon dioxide (Figure 11.41) is generally similar to that of water, with one important exception—the slope of the curve between solid and liquid is positive. In fact, this holds true for almost all other substances. Water behaves differently because ice is *less* dense than liquid water. The triple point of carbon dioxide is at 5.2 atm and −57°C.

An interesting observation can be made about the phase diagram in Figure 11.41. As you can see, the entire liquid phase lies well above atmospheric pressure; therefore, it is impossible for solid carbon dioxide to melt at 1 atm. Instead, when solid CO_2 is heated to −78°C at 1 atm, it sublimes. In fact, solid carbon dioxide is called dry ice because it looks like ice and *does not melt* (Figure 11.42). Because of this property, dry ice is useful as a refrigerant.

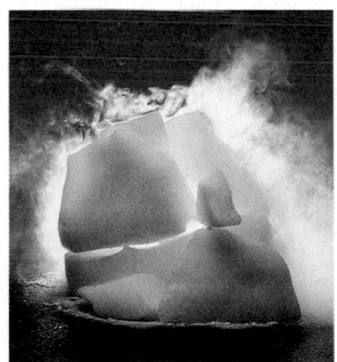

Figure 11.42 *Under atmospheric conditions, solid carbon dioxide does not melt; it can only sublime. The cold carbon dioxide gas causes nearby water vapor to condense and form a fog.*

CHEMISTRY
in Action

Hard-Boiling an Egg on a Mountaintop, Pressure Cookers, and Ice Skating

Phase equilibria are affected by external pressure. Depending on atmospheric conditions, the boiling point and freezing point of water may deviate appreciably from 100°C and 0°C, respectively, as we see below.

Hard-Boiling an Egg on a Mountaintop

Suppose you have just scaled Pike's Peak in Colorado. To help regain your strength following the strenuous work, you decide to hard-boil an egg and eat it. To your surprise, water seems to boil more quickly than usual, but after 10 min in boiling water, the egg is still not cooked. A little knowledge of phase equilibria could have saved you the disappointment of cracking open an uncooked egg (especially if it is the only egg you brought with you). The summit of Pike's Peak is 14,000 ft above sea level. At this altitude, the atmospheric pressure is only about 0.6 atm. From Figure 11.40(b), we see that the boiling point of water decreases with decreasing pressure, so at the lower pressure water will boil at about 86°C. However, it is not the boiling action but the amount of heat delivered to the egg that does the actual cooking, and the amount of heat delivered is proportional to the temperature of the water. For this reason, it would take considerably longer, perhaps 30 min, to hard-cook your egg.

Pressure Cookers

The effect of pressure on boiling point also explains why pressure cookers save time in the kitchen. A pressure cooker is a sealed container that allows steam to escape only when it exceeds a certain pressure. The pressure above the water in the cooker is the sum of the atmospheric pressure and the pressure of the steam. Consequently, the water in the pressure cooker will boil at a higher temperature than 100°C and the food in it will be hotter and cook faster.

Ice Skating

Let us now turn to the ice-water equilibrium. The negative slope of the solid-liquid curve means that the melting point of ice decreases with increasing external pressure, as shown in Figure 11.40(b). This phenomenon helps to make ice skating possible. Because skates have very thin runners, a 130-lb person can exert a pressure equivalent to 500 atm on the ice. (Remember that pressure is defined as force per unit area.) Consequently, at a temperature lower than 0°C, the ice under the skates melts and the film of water formed under the runner facilitates the movement of the skater over ice. Calculations show that the melting point of ice decreases by 7.4×10^{-3} °C when the pressure increases by 1 atm. Thus, when the pressure exerted on the ice by the skater is 500 atm, the melting point falls to $-(500 \times 7.4 \times 10^{-3})$, or -3.7°C. Actually, it turns out that friction between the blades and the ice is the major cause for melting the ice. This explains why it is possible to skate outdoors even when the temperature drops below -20°C.

The pressure exerted by the skater on ice lowers its melting point, and the film of water formed under the blades acts as a lubricant between the skate and the ice.

CHEMISTRY
in Action

Liquid Crystals

Ordinarily, there is a sharp distinction between the highly ordered state of a crystalline solid and the more random molecular arrangement of liquids. Crystalline ice and liquid water, for example, differ from each other in this respect. One class of substances, however, tends so greatly toward an ordered arrangement that a melting crystal first forms a milky liquid, called the *paracrystalline state,* with characteristically crystalline properties. At higher temperatures, this milky fluid changes sharply into a clear liquid that behaves like an ordinary liquid. Such substances are known as *liquid crystals.*

Molecules that exhibit liquid crystallinity are usually long and rodlike. An important class of liquid crystals is called thermotropic liquid crystals, which form when the solid is heated. The two common structures of thermotropic liquid crystals are nematic and smectic. In smectic liquid crystals, the long axes of the molecules are perpendicular to the plane of the layers. The layers are free to slide over one another so that the substance has the mechanical properties of a two-dimensional solid. Nematic liquid crystals are less ordered. Although the molecules in nematic liquid crystals are aligned with their long axes parallel to one another, they are not separated into layers.

Thermotropic liquid crystals have many applications in science, technology, and medicine. The familiar black-and-white displays in timepieces and calculators are based on the properties of these substances. Transparent aligning agents made of tin oxide (SnO_2) applied to the lower and upper inside surfaces of the liquid crystal cell preferentially orient the molecules in the nematic phase by 90° relative to each other. In this way, the molecules become "twisted" through the liquid crystal phase. When properly adjusted, this twist rotates the plane of polarization by 90°

A liquid crystal display (LCD) using nematic liquid crystals. Molecules in contact with the bottom and top cell surfaces are aligned at right angles to one another. (a) The extent of twist in the molecular orientation between the surfaces is adjusted so as to rotate the plane of polarized light by 90°, allowing it to pass through the top polarizer. Consequently, the cell appears clear. (b) When the electric field is on, molecules orient along the direction of the field, the plane of polarized light can no longer pass through the top polarizer, and the cell appears black. (c) A cross section of a LCD such as that used in watches and calculators.

(Continued)

and allows the light to pass through the two polarizers (arranged at 90° to each other). When an electric field is applied, the nematic molecules experience a torque (a torsion or rotation) that forces them to align along the direction of the field. Now the incident polarized light cannot pass through the top polarizer. In watches and calculators, a mirror is placed under the bottom polarizer. In the absence of an electric field, the reflected light goes through both polarizers and the cell looks clear from the top. When the electric field is turned on, the incident light from the top cannot pass through the bottom polarizer to reach the reflector and the cell becomes dark. Typically a few volts are applied across a nematic layer about 10 μm thick (1μm $= 10^{-6}$ m). The response time for molecules to align and relax when the electric field is turned on and off is in the ms range (1 ms $= 10^{-3}$ s).

Another type of thermotropic liquid crystals is called cholesteric liquid crystals. The color of cholesteric liquid crystals changes with temperature and therefore they are suitable for use as sensitive thermometers. In metallurgy, for example, they are used to detect metal stress, heat sources, and conduction paths. Medically, the temperature of the body at specific sites can be determined with the aid of liquid crystals. This technique has become an important diagnostic tool in treating infection and tumor growth (for example, breast tumors). Because localized infections and tumors increase metabolic rate and hence temperature in the affected tissues, a thin film of liquid crystal can help a physician see whether an infection or tumor is present by responding to a temperature difference with a change of color.

Nematic

Smectic

The alignment of molecules in two types of liquid crystals. Nematic liquid crystals behave like a one-dimensional solid and smectic liquid crystals behave like a two-dimensional solid.

A liquid crystal thermogram. The red color represents the highest temperature and the blue color the lowest temperature.

Summary of Facts and Concepts

1. All substances exist in one of three states: gas, liquid, or solid. The major difference between the condensed state and the gaseous state is the distance separating molecules.

2. Intermolecular forces act between molecules or between molecules and ions. Generally, these attractive forces are much weaker than bonding forces.

3. Dipole-dipole forces and ion-dipole forces attract molecules with dipole moments to other polar molecules or ions.

4. Dispersion forces are the result of temporary dipole moments induced in ordinarily nonpolar molecules. The extent to which a dipole moment can be induced in a molecule is called its polarizability. The term "van der Waals forces" refers to dipole-dipole, dipole-induced dipole, and dispersion forces.

5. Hydrogen bonding is a relatively strong dipole-dipole interaction between a polar bond containing a hydrogen atom and an electronegative O, N, or F atom. Hydrogen bonds between water molecules are particularly strong.

6. Liquids tend to assume a geometry that minimizes surface area. Surface tension is the energy needed to expand a liquid surface area; strong intermolecular forces lead to greater surface tension.

7. Viscosity is a measure of the resistance of a liquid to flow; it decreases with increasing temperature.

8. Water molecules in the solid state form a three-dimensional network in which each oxygen atom is covalently bonded to two hydrogen atoms and is hydrogen-bonded to two hydrogen atoms. This unique structure accounts for the fact that ice is less dense than liquid water, a property that allows life to survive under the ice in ponds and lakes in cold climates.

9. Water is also ideally suited for its ecological role by its high specific heat, another property imparted by its strong hydrogen bonding. Large bodies of water are able to moderate Earth's climate by giving off and absorbing substantial amounts of heat with only small changes in the water temperature.

10. All solids are either crystalline (with a regular structure of atoms, ions, or molecules) or amorphous (without a regular structure). Glass is an example of an amorphous solid.

11. The basic structural unit of a crystalline solid is the unit cell, which is repeated to form a three-dimensional crystal lattice. X-ray diffraction has provided much of our knowledge about crystal structure.

12. The four types of crystals and the forces that hold their particles together are ionic crystals, held together by ionic bonding; covalent crystals, covalent bonding; molecular crystals, van der Waals forces and/or hydrogen bonding; and metallic crystals, metallic bonding.

13. A liquid in a closed vessel eventually establishes a dynamic equilibrium between evaporation and condensation. The vapor pressure over the liquid under these conditions is the equilibrium vapor pressure, which is often referred to simply as "vapor pressure."

14. At the boiling point, the vapor pressure of a liquid equals the external pressure. The molar heat of vaporization of a liquid is the energy required to vaporize one mole of the liquid. It can be determined by measuring the vapor pressure of the liquid as a function of temperature and using the Clausius-Clapeyron equation [Equation (11.2)]. The molar heat of fusion of a solid is the energy required to melt one mole of the solid.

15. For every substance there is a temperature, called the critical temperature, above which its gas phase cannot be made to liquefy.

16. The relationships among the phases of a single substance are illustrated by a phase diagram, in which each region represents a pure phase and the boundaries between the regions show the temperatures and pressures at which the two phases are in equilibrium. At the triple point, all three phases are in equilibrium.

Key Words

Adhesion, p. 459
Amorphous solid, p. 476
Boiling point, p. 483
Closest packing, p. 466
Cohesion, p. 459
Condensation, p. 480
Coordination number, p. 465
Critical pressure (P_c), p. 484

Critical temperature (T_c), p. 484
Crystalline solid, p. 463
Deposition, p. 487
Dipole-dipole forces, p. 453
Dispersion forces, p. 455
Dynamic equilibrium, p. 480

Equilibrium vapor pressure, p. 480
Evaporation, p. 479
Freezing point, p. 484
Glass, p. 476
Hydrogen bond, p. 457
Induced dipole, p. 454
Intermolecular forces, p. 453

Intramolecular forces, p. 453
Ion-dipole forces, p. 453
Melting point, p. 484
Molar heat of fusion (ΔH_{fus}), p. 487
Molar heat of sublimation (ΔH_{sub}), p. 487

Molar heat of vaporization
   (ΔH_{vap}), p. 480
Phase, p. 452
Phase changes, p. 479

Phase diagram, p. 488
Sublimation, p. 487
Supercooling, p. 487
Surface tension, p. 459

Triple point, p. 489
Unit cell, p. 463
van der Waals
   forces, p. 453

Vaporization, p. 479
Viscosity, p. 459
X-ray diffraction, p. 469

Questions and Problems

Intermolecular Forces
Review Questions

11.1 Give an example for each type of intermolecular forces. (a) dipole-dipole interaction, (b) dipole-induced dipole interaction, (c) ion-dipole interaction, (d) dispersion forces, (e) van der Waals forces

11.2 Explain the term "polarizability." What kind of molecules tend to have high polarizabilities? What is the relationship between polarizability and intermolecular forces?

11.3 Explain the difference between a temporary dipole moment and the permanent dipole moment.

11.4 Give some evidence that all atoms and molecules exert attractive forces on one another.

11.5 What physical properties should you consider in comparing the strength of intermolecular forces in solids and in liquids?

11.6 Which elements can take part in hydrogen bonding? Why is hydrogen unique in this kind of interaction?

Problems

11.7 The compounds Br_2 and ICl have the same number of electrons, yet Br_2 melts at $-7.2°C$ and ICl melts at $27.2°C$. Explain.

11.8 If you lived in Alaska, which of the following natural gases would you keep in an outdoor storage tank in winter? Explain why. methane (CH_4), propane (C_3H_8), or butane (C_4H_{10})

11.9 The binary hydrogen compounds of the Group 4A elements and their boiling points are: CH_4, $-162°C$; SiH_4, $-112°C$; GeH_4, $-88°C$; and SnH_4, $-52°C$. Explain the increase in boiling points from CH_4 to SnH_4.

11.10 List the types of intermolecular forces that exist between molecules (or basic units) in each of the following species: (a) benzene (C_6H_6), (b) CH_3Cl, (c) PF_3, (d) $NaCl$, (e) CS_2.

11.11 Ammonia is both a donor and an acceptor of hydrogen in hydrogen-bond formation. Draw a diagram showing the hydrogen bonding of an ammonia molecule with two other ammonia molecules.

11.12 Which of the following species are capable of hydrogen-bonding among themselves? (a) C_2H_6, (b) HI, (c) KF, (d) BeH_2, (e) CH_3COOH

11.13 Arrange the following in order of increasing boiling point: RbF, CO_2, CH_3OH, CH_3Br. Explain your reasoning.

11.14 Diethyl ether has a boiling point of $34.5°C$, and 1-butanol has a boiling point of $117°C$:

H H   H H   H H H H
| | | | | | | |
H—C—C—O—C—C—H H—C—C—C—C—OH
| | | | | | | |
H H   H H   H H H H

diethyl ether   1-butanol

Both of these compounds have the same numbers and types of atoms. Explain the difference in their boiling points.

11.15 Which member of each of the following pairs of substances would you expect to have a higher boiling point? (a) O_2 and Cl_2, (b) SO_2 and CO_2, (c) HF and HI

11.16 Which substance in each of the following pairs would you expect to have the higher boiling point? Explain why. (a) Ne or Xe, (b) CO_2 or CS_2, (c) CH_4 or Cl_2, (d) F_2 or LiF, (e) NH_3 or PH_3

11.17 Explain in terms of intermolecular forces why (a) NH_3 has a higher boiling point than CH_4 and (b) KCl has a higher melting point than I_2.

11.18 What kind of attractive forces must be overcome in order to (a) melt ice, (b) boil molecular bromine, (c) melt solid iodine, and (d) dissociate F_2 into F atoms?

11.19 The following compounds have the same molecular formulas (C_4H_{10}). Which one would you expect to have a higher boiling point?

11.20 Explain the difference in the melting points of the following compounds:

m.p. 45°C   m.p. 115°C

(*Hint:* Only one of the two can form intramolecular hydrogen bonds.)

Properties of Liquids
Review Questions

11.21 Explain why liquids, unlike gases, are virtually incompressible.

11.22 What is surface tension? What is the relationship between intermolecular forces and surface tension? How does surface tension change with temperature?

11.23 Despite the fact that stainless steel is much denser than water, a stainless-steel razor blade can be made to float on water. Why?

11.24 Use water and mercury as examples to explain adhesion and cohesion.

11.25 A glass can be filled slightly above the rim with water. Explain why the water does not overflow.

11.26 Draw diagrams showing the capillary action of (a) water and (b) mercury in three tubes of different radii.

11.27 What is viscosity? What is the relationship between intermolecular forces and viscosity?

11.28 Why does the viscosity of a liquid decrease with increasing temperature?

11.29 Why is ice less dense than water?

11.30 Outdoor water pipes have to be drained or insulated in winter in a cold climate. Why?

Problems

11.31 Predict which of the following liquids has greater surface tension: ethanol (C_2H_5OH) or dimethyl ether (CH_3OCH_3).

11.32 Predict the viscosity of ethylene glycol relative to that of ethanol and glycerol (see Table 11.3).

$$CH_2\!-\!OH$$
$$|$$
$$CH_2\!-\!OH$$
ethylene glycol

Crystal Structure
Review Questions

11.33 Define the following terms: crystalline solid, lattice point, unit cell, coordination number, closest packing.

11.34 Describe the geometries of the following cubic cells: simple cubic, body-centered cubic, face-centered cubic. Which of these structures would give the highest density for the same type of atoms? Which the lowest?

11.35 Classify the solid states in terms of crystal types of the elements in the third period of the periodic table. Predict the trends in their melting points and boiling points.

11.36 The melting points of the oxides of the third-period elements are given in parentheses: Na_2O (1275°C), MgO (2800°C), Al_2O_3 (2045°C), SiO_2 (1610°C), P_4O_{10} (580°C), SO_3 (16.8°C), Cl_2O_7 (−91.5°C). Classify these solids in terms of crystal types.

Problems

11.37 What is the coordination number of each sphere in (a) a simple cubic cell, (b) a body-centered cubic cell, and (c) a face-centered cubic cell? Assume the spheres are all the same.

11.38 Calculate the number of spheres that would be found within a simple cubic, a body-centered cubic, and a face-centered cubic cell. Assume that the spheres are the same.

11.39 Metallic iron crystallizes in a cubic lattice. The unit cell edge length is 287 pm. The density of iron is 7.87 g/cm^3. How many iron atoms are within a unit cell?

11.40 Barium metal crystallizes in a body-centered cubic lattice (the Ba atoms are at the lattice points only). The unit cell edge length is 502 pm, and the density of the metal is 3.50 g/cm^3. Using this information, calculate Avogadro's number. [*Hint:* First calculate the volume (in cm^3) occupied by 1 mole of Ba atoms in the unit cells. Next calculate the volume (in cm^3) occupied by one Ba atom in the unit cell. Assume that 68% of the unit cell is occupied by Ba atoms.]

11.41 Vanadium crystallizes in a body-centered cubic lattice (the V atoms occupy only the lattice points). How many V atoms are present in a unit cell?

11.42 Europium crystallizes in a body-centered cubic lattice (the Eu atoms occupy only the lattice points). The density of Eu is 5.26 g/cm^3. Calculate the unit cell edge length in pm.

11.43 Crystalline silicon has a cubic structure. The unit cell edge length is 543 pm. The density of the solid is 2.33 g/cm^3. Calculate the number of Si atoms in one unit cell.

11.44   A face-centered cubic cell contains 8 X atoms at the corners of the cell and 6 Y atoms at the faces. What is the empirical formula of the solid?

X-Ray Diffraction of Crystals

Review Questions

11.45   Define X-ray diffraction. What are the typical wavelengths (in nanometers) of X rays (see Figure 7.4).

11.46   Write the Bragg equation. Define every term and describe how this equation can be used to measure interatomic distances.

Problems

11.47   When X rays of wavelength 0.090 nm are diffracted by a metallic crystal, the angle of first-order diffraction ($n = 1$) is measured to be 15.2°. What is the distance (in pm) between the layers of atoms responsible for the diffraction?

11.48   The distance between layers in a NaCl crystal is 282 pm. X rays are diffracted from these layers at an angle of 23.0°. Assuming that $n = 1$, calculate the wavelength of the X rays in nm.

Types of Crystals

Review Questions

11.49   Describe and give examples of the following types of crystals: (a) ionic crystals, (b) covalent crystals, (c) molecular crystals, (d) metallic crystals.

11.50   Why are metals good conductors of heat and electricity? Why does the ability of a metal to conduct electricity decrease with increasing temperature?

Problems

11.51   A solid is hard, brittle, and electrically nonconducting. Its melt (the liquid form of the substance) and an aqueous solution containing the substance conduct electricity. Classify the solid.

11.52   A solid is soft and has a low melting point (below 100°C). The solid, its melt, and an aqueous solution containing the substance are all nonconductors of electricity. Classify the solid.

11.53   A solid is very hard and has a high melting point. Neither the solid nor its melt conducts electricity. Classify the solid.

11.54   Which of the following are molecular solids and which are covalent solids? Se_8, HBr, Si, CO_2, C, P_4O_6, SiH_4

11.55   Classify the solid state of the following substances as ionic crystals, covalent crystals, molecular crystals, or metallic crystals: (a) CO_2, (b) B_{12}, (c) S_8, (d) KBr, (e) Mg, (f) SiO_2, (g) LiCl, (h) Cr.

11.56   Explain why diamond is harder than graphite. Why is graphite an electrical conductor but diamond is not?

Amorphous Solids

Review Questions

11.57   What is an amorphous solid? How does it differ from crystalline solid?

11.58   Define glass. What is the chief component of glass? Name three types of glass.

Phase Changes

Review Questions

11.59   What is a phase change? Name all possible changes that can occur among the vapor, liquid, and solid phases of a substance.

11.60   What is the equilibrium vapor pressure of a liquid? How is it measured and how does it change with temperature?

11.61   Use any one of the phase changes to explain what is meant by dynamic equilibrium.

11.62   Define the following terms: (a) molar heat of vaporization, (b) molar heat of fusion, (c) molar heat of sublimation. What are their units?

11.63   How is the molar heat of sublimation related to the molar heats of vaporization and fusion? On what law are these relationships based?

11.64   What can we learn about the intermolecular forces in a liquid from the molar heat of vaporization?

11.65   The greater the molar heat of vaporization of a liquid, the greater its vapor pressure. True or false?

11.66   Define boiling point. How does the boiling point of a liquid depend on external pressure? Referring to Table 5.3, what is the boiling point of water when the external pressure is 187.5 mmHg?

11.67   As a liquid is heated at constant pressure, its temperature rises. This trend continues until the boiling point of the liquid is reached. No further rise in temperature of the liquid can be induced by heating. Explain.

11.68   What is critical temperature? What is the significance of critical temperature in liquefaction of gases?

11.69   What is the relationship between intermolecular forces in a liquid and the liquid's boiling point and critical temperature? Why is the critical temperature of water greater than that of most other substances?

11.70   How do the boiling points and melting points of water and carbon tetrachloride vary with pressure? Explain any difference in behavior of these two substances.

11.71   Why is solid carbon dioxide called dry ice?

11.72   The vapor pressure of a liquid in a closed container depends on which of the following? (a) the volume above the liquid, (b) the amount of liquid present, (c) temperature, (d) intermolecular forces between the molecules in the liquid

11.73 Referring to Figure 11.35, estimate the boiling points of diethyl ether, water, and mercury at 0.5 atm.

11.74 Wet clothes dry more quickly on a hot, dry day than on a hot, humid day. Explain.

11.75 Which of the following phase transitions gives off more heat? (a) 1 mole of steam to 1 mole of water at 100°C, or (b) 1 mole of water to 1 mole of ice at 0°C.

11.76 A beaker of water is heated to boiling by a Bunsen burner. Would adding another burner raise the boiling point of water? Explain.

Problems

11.77 Calculate the amount of heat (in kJ) required to convert 74.6 g of water to steam at 100°C.

11.78 How much heat (in kJ) is needed to convert 866 g of ice at −10°C to steam at 126°C? (The specific heats of ice and steam are 2.03 J/g · °C and 1.99 J/g · °C, respectively.)

11.79 How is the rate of evaporation of a liquid affected by (a) temperature, (b) the surface area of a liquid exposed to air, (c) intermolecular forces?

11.80 The molar heats of fusion and sublimation of molecular iodine are 15.27 kJ/mol and 62.30 kJ/mol, respectively. Estimate the molar heat of vaporization of liquid iodine.

11.81 The following compounds, listed with their boiling points, are liquid at −10°C: butane, 0.5°C; ethanol, 78.3°C; toluene, 110.6°C. At −10°C, which of these liquids would you expect to have the highest vapor pressure? Which the lowest? Explain.

11.82 Freeze-dried coffee is prepared by freezing brewed coffee and then removing the ice component with a vacuum pump. Describe the phase changes taking place during these processes.

11.83 A student hangs wet clothes outdoors on a winter day when the temperature is −15°C. After a few hours, the clothes are found to be fairly dry. Describe the phase changes in this drying process.

11.84 Steam at 100°C causes more serious burns than water at 100°C. Why?

11.85 Vapor pressure measurements at several different temperatures are shown below for mercury. Determine graphically the molar heat of vaporization for mercury.

t (°C)	200	250	300	320	340
P (mmHg)	17.3	74.4	246.8	376.3	557.9

11.86 The vapor pressure of benzene, C_6H_6, is 40.1 mmHg at 7.6°C. What is its vapor pressure at 60.6°C? The molar heat of vaporization of benzene is 31.0 kJ/mol.

11.87 The vapor pressure of liquid X is lower than that of liquid Y at 20°C, but higher at 60°C. What can you

deduce about the relative magnitude of the molar heats of vaporization of X and Y?

11.88 Estimate the molar heat of vaporization of a liquid whose vapor pressure doubles when the temperature is raised from 85°C to 95°C.

Phase Diagrams
Review Questions

11.89 What is a phase diagram? What useful information can be obtained from study of a phase diagram?

11.90 Explain how water's phase diagram differs from those of most substances. What property of water causes the difference?

Problems

11.91 The blades of ice skates are quite thin, so that the pressure exerted on ice by a skater can be substantial. Explain how this fact enables a person to skate on ice.

11.92 A length of wire is placed on top of a block of ice. The ends of the wire extend over the edges of the ice, and a heavy weight is attached to each end. It is found that the ice under the wire gradually melts, so that the wire slowly moves through the ice block. At the same time, the water above the wire refreezes. Explain the phase changes that accompany this phenomenon.

11.93 The boiling point and freezing point of sulfur dioxide are −10°C and −72.7°C (at 1 atm), respectively. The triple point is −75.5°C and 1.65 × 10⁻³ atm, and its critical point is at 157°C and 78 atm. On the basis of this information, draw a rough sketch of the phase diagram of SO_2.

11.94 A phase diagram of water is shown at the end of this problem. Label the regions. Predict what would happen as a result of the following changes: (a) Starting at A, we raise the temperature at constant pressure. (b) Starting at C, we lower the temperature at constant pressure. (c) Starting at B, we lower the pressure at constant temperature.

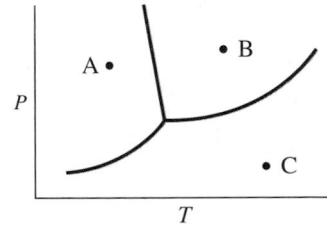

Additional Problems

11.95 Name the kinds of attractive forces that must be overcome in order to (a) boil liquid ammonia, (b) melt solid phosphorus (P_4), (c) dissolve CsI in liquid HF, (d) melt potassium metal.

11.96 Which of the following properties indicates very strong intermolecular forces in a liquid? (a) very low surface tension, (b) very low critical temperature, (c) very low boiling point, (d) very low vapor pressure

11.97 At $-35°C$, liquid HI has a higher vapor pressure than liquid HF. Explain.

11.98 Based on the following properties of elemental boron, classify it as one of the crystalline solids discussed in Section 11.6: high melting point $(2300°C)$, poor conductor of heat and electricity, insoluble in water, very hard substance.

11.99 Referring to Figure 11.41, determine the stable phase of CO_2 at (a) 4 atm and $-60°C$ and (b) 0.5 atm and $-20°C$.

11.100 Which of the following substances has the highest polarizability? CH_4, H_2, CCl_4, SF_6, H_2S

11.101 A CO_2 fire extinguisher is located on the outside of a building in Massachusetts. During the winter months, one can hear a sloshing sound when the extinguisher is gently shaken. In the summertime there is often no sound when it is shaken. Explain. Assume that the extinguisher has no leaks and that it has not been used.

11.102 What is the vapor pressure of mercury at its normal boiling point $(357°C)$?

11.103 A flask of water is connected to a powerful vacuum pump. When the pump is turned on, the water begins to boil. After a few minutes, the same water begins to freeze. Eventually, the ice disappears. Explain what happens at each step.

11.104 The liquid-vapor boundary line in the phase diagram of any substance always stops abruptly at a certain point. Why?

11.105 The interionic distance of several alkali halide crystals are:

NaCl   NaBr   NaI   KCl   KBr   KI
282 pm 299 pm 324 pm 315 pm 330 pm 353 pm

Plot lattice energy versus the reciprocal interionic distance. How would you explain the plot in terms of the dependence of lattice energy on distance of separation between ions? What law governs this interaction? (For lattice energies, see Table 9.1.)

11.106 Which has a greater density, crystalline SiO_2 or amorphous SiO_2? Why?

11.107 A student is given four solid samples labeled W, X, Y, and Z. All except Z have a metallic luster. She is told that the solids could be gold, lead sulfide, quartz (SiO_2), and iodine. The results of her investigations are: (a) W is a good electrical conductor; X, Y, and Z are poor electrical conductors. (b) When the solids are hit with a hammer, W flattens out, X shatters into many pieces, Y is smashed into a powder, and Z is cracked. (c) When the solids are heated with a Bunsen burner, Y melts with some sublima-

tion, but X, W, and Z do not melt. (d) In treatment with 6 M HNO_3, X dissolves; there is no effect on W, Y, or Z. On the basis of these test results, identify the solids.

11.108 Which of the following statements are false? (a) Dipole-dipole interactions between molecules are greatest if the molecules possess only temporary dipole moments. (b) All compounds containing hydrogen atoms can participate in hydrogen-bond formation. (c) Dispersion forces exist between all atoms, molecules, and ions. (d) The extent of ion-induced dipole interaction depends only on the charge on the ion.

11.109 The diagram below shows a kettle of boiling water on a stove. Identify the phases in regions A and B.

11.110 The south pole of Mars is covered with dry ice, which partly sublimes during the summer. The CO_2 vapor recondenses in the winter when the temperature drops to 150 K. Given that the heat of sublimation of CO_2 is 25.9 kJ/mol, calculate the atmospheric pressure on the surface of Mars. [*Hint:* Use Figure 11.41 to determine the normal sublimation temperature of dry ice and Equation (11.5), which also applies to sublimations.]

11.111 The properties of gases, liquids, and solids differ in a number of respects. How would you use the kinetic molecular theory (see Section 5.7) to explain the following observations? (a) Ease of compressibility decreases from gas to liquid to solid. (b) Solids retain a definite shape, but gases and liquids do not. (c) For most substances, the volume of a given amount of material increases as it changes from solid to liquid to gas.

11.112 Select the substance in each pair that should have the higher boiling point. In each case identify the principal intermolecular forces involved and account briefly for your choice. (a) K_2S or $(CH_3)_3N$, (b) Br_2 or $CH_3CH_2CH_2CH_3$

11.113 A small drop of oil in water assumes a spherical shape. Explain. (*Hint:* Oil is made up of nonpolar molecules, which tend to avoid contact with water.)

11.114 Under the same conditions of temperature and density, which of the following gases would you expect to behave less ideally: CH_4, SO_2? Explain.

11.115 The fluorides of the second-period elements and their melting points are: LiF, 845°C; BeF_2, 800°C; BF_3, −126.7°C; CF_4, −184°C; NF_3, −206.6°C; OF_2, −223.8°C; F_2, −219.6°C. Classify the type(s) of intermolecular forces present in each compound.

11.116 The standard enthalpy of formation of gaseous molecular iodine is 62.4 kJ/mol. Use this information to calculate the molar heat of sublimation of molecular iodine at 25°C.

11.117 The distance between Li^+ and Cl^- is 257 pm in solid LiCl and 203 pm in a LiCl unit in the gas phase. Explain the difference in the bond lengths.

11.118 Heat of hydration, that is, the heat change that occurs when ions become hydrated in solution, is largely due to ion-dipole interactions. The heats of hydration for the alkali metal ions are Li^+, −520 kJ/mol; Na^+, −405 kJ/mol; K^+, −321 kJ/mol. Account for the trend in these values.

11.119 If water were a linear molecule, (a) would it still be polar, and (b) would the water molecules still be able to form hydrogen bonds with one another?

11.120 Calculate the $\Delta H°$ for the following processes at 25°C: (a) $Br_2(l) \longrightarrow Br_2(g)$ and (b) $Br_2(g) \longrightarrow 2Br(g)$. Comment on the relative magnitudes of these $\Delta H°$ values in terms of the forces involved in each case. {*Hint:* See Table 9.4, and given that $\Delta H_f°[Br_2(g)] = 30.7$ kJ/mol.}

11.121 Which liquid would you expect to have a greater viscosity, water or diethyl ether? The structure of diethyl ether is shown in Problem 11.14.

11.122 A beaker of water is placed in a closed container. Predict the effect on the vapor pressure of the water when (a) its temperature is lowered, (b) the volume of the container is doubled, (c) more water is added to the beaker.

11.123 Ozone (O_3) is a strong oxidizing agent that can oxidize all the common metals except gold and platinum. A convenient test for ozone is based on its action on mercury. When exposed to ozone, mercury becomes dull looking and sticks to glass tubing (instead of flowing freely through it). Write a balanced equation for the reaction. What property of mercury is altered by its interaction with ozone?

11.124 A sample of limestone ($CaCO_3$) is heated in a closed vessel until it is partially decomposed. Write an equation for the reaction and state how many phases are present.

11.125 Silicon used in computer chips must have an impurity level below 10^{-9} (that is, fewer than one impurity atom for every 10^9 Si atoms). Silicon is prepared by the reduction of quartz (SiO_2) with coke (a form of carbon made by the destructive distillation of coal) at about 2000°C:

$$SiO_2(s) + 2C(s) \longrightarrow Si(l) + 2CO(g)$$

Next, solid silicon is separated from other solid impurities by treatment with hydrogen chloride at 350°C to form gaseous trichlorosilane ($SiCl_3H$):

$$Si(s) + 3HCl(g) \longrightarrow SiCl_3H(g) + H_2(g)$$

Finally, ultrapure Si can be obtained by reversing the above reaction at 1000°C:

$$SiCl_3H(g) + H_2(g) \longrightarrow Si(s) + 3HCl(g)$$

(a) Trichlorosilane has a vapor pressure of 0.258 atm at −2°C. What is its normal boiling point? Is trichlorosilane's boiling point consistent with the type of intermolecular forces that exist among its molecules? (The molar heat of vaporization of trichlorosilane is 28.8 kJ/mol.) (b) What types of crystals do Si and SiO_2 form? (c) Silicon has a diamond crystal structure (see Figure 11.28). Each cubic unit cell (edge length $a = 543$ pm) contains eight Si atoms. If there are 1.0×10^{13} boron atoms per cubic centimeter in a sample of pure silicon, how many Si atoms are there for every B atom in the sample? Does this sample satisfy the 10^{-9} purity requirement for the electronic grade silicon?

11.126 Carbon and silicon belong to Group 4A of the periodic table and have the same valence electron configuration (ns^2np^2). Why does silicon dioxide (SiO_2) have a much higher melting point than carbon dioxide (CO_2)?

11.127 A pressure cooker is a sealed container that allows steam to escape when it exceeds a predetermined pressure. How does this device reduce the time needed for cooking?

11.128 A 1.20-g sample of water is injected into an evacuated 5.00-L flask at 65°C. What percentage of the water will be vapor when the system reaches equilibrium? Assume ideal behavior of water vapor and that the volume of liquid water is negligible. The vapor pressure of water at 65°C is 187.5 mmHg.

11.129 What are the advantages of cooking the vegetable broccoli with steam instead of boiling it in water?

11.130 A quantitative measure of how efficiently spheres pack into unit cells is called *packing efficiency*, which is the percentage of the cell space occupied by the spheres. Calculate the packing efficiencies of a simple cubic cell, a body-centered cubic cell, and a face-centered cubic cell. (*Hint:* Refer to Figure 11.22 and use the relationship that the volume of a sphere is $\frac{4}{3}\pi r^3$, where r is the radius of the sphere.)

11.131 Provide an explanation for each of the following phenomena: (a) Solid argon (m.p. −189.2°C; b.p. −185.7°C) can be prepared by immersing a flask containing argon gas in liquid nitrogen (b.p. −195.8°C) until it liquefies and then connecting the flask to a vacuum pump. (b) The melting point of cyclohexane (C_6H_{12}) increases with increasing pressure exerted on the solid cyclohexane. (c) Certain high-altitude clouds contain water droplets at $-10°C$. (d) When a piece of dry ice is added to a beaker of water, fog forms above the water.

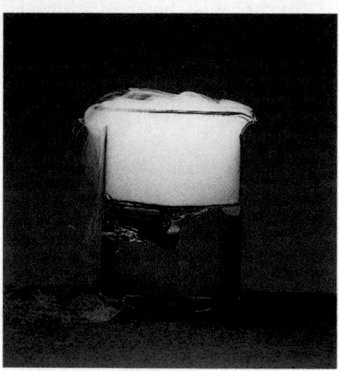

11.132 Argon crystallizes in the face-centered cubic arrangement at 40 K. Given that the atomic radius of argon is 191 pm, calculate the density of solid argon.

11.133 A chemistry instructor performed the following mystery demonstration. Just before the students arrived in class, she heated some water to boiling in an Erlenmeyer flask. She then removed the flask from the flame and closed the flask with a rubber stopper. After the class commenced, she held the flask in front of the students and announced that she could make the water boil simply by rubbing an ice cube on the outside walls of the flask. To the amazement of everyone, it worked. Give an explanation for this phenomenon.

11.134 Given the phase diagram of carbon shown, answer the following questions: (a) How many triple points are there and what are the phases that can coexist at each triple point? (b) Which has a higher density, graphite or diamond? (c) Synthetic diamond can be made from graphite. Using the phase diagram, how would you go about making diamond?

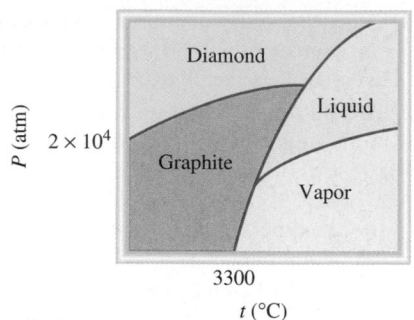

11.135 Swimming coaches sometimes suggest that a drop of alcohol (ethanol) placed in an ear plugged with water "draws out the water." Explain this action from a molecular point of view.

11.136 Use the concept of intermolecular forces to explain why the far end of a walking cane rises when one raises the handle.

11.137 Why do citrus growers spray their trees with water to protect them from freezing?

11.138 What is the origin of dark spots on the inner glass walls of an old tungsten lightbulb? What is the purpose of filling these lightbulbs with argon gas?

11.139 The compound dichlorodifluoromethane (CCl_2F_2) has a normal boiling point of $-30°C$, a critical temperature of $112°C$, and a corresponding critical pressure of 40 atm. If the gas is compressed to 18 atm at $20°C$, will the gas condense? Your answer should be based on a graphical interpretation.

11.140 A student heated a beaker of cold water (on a tripod) with a Bunsen burner. When the gas is ignited, she noticed that there was water condensed on the outside of the beaker. Explain what happened.

Special Problems

11.141 Sketch the cooling curves of water from about $110°C$ to about $-10°C$. How would you also show the formation of supercooled liquid below $0°C$ which then freezes to ice? The pressure is at 1 atm throughout the process. The curves need not be drawn quantitatively.

11.142 Iron crystallizes in a body-centered cubic lattice. The cell length as determined by X-ray diffraction is 286.7 pm. Given that the density of iron is 7.874 g/cm³, calculate Avogadro's number.

11.143 The boiling point of methanol is $65.0°C$ and the standard enthalpy of formation of methanol vapor is

−201.2 kJ/mol. Calculate the vapor pressure of methanol (in mmHg) at 25°C. (*Hint:* See Appendix 3 for other thermodynamic data of methanol.)

11.144 An alkali metal in the form of a cube of edge length 0.171 cm is vaporized in a 0.843-L container at 1235 K. The vapor pressure is 19.2 mmHg. Identify the metal by calculating the atomic radius in picometers and the density. (*Hint:* You need to consult Figures 8.5, 11.22, 11.29, and a chemistry handbook.)

11.145 A closed vessel of volume 9.6 L contains 2.0 g of water. Calculate the temperature (in °C) at which only half of the water remains in the liquid phase. (See Table 5.3 for vapor pressures of water at different temperatures.)

11.146 A sample of water shows the following behavior as it is heated at a constant rate:

If twice the mass of water has the same amount of heat transferred to it, which of the following graphs best describes the temperature variation? Note that the scales for all the graphs are the same.

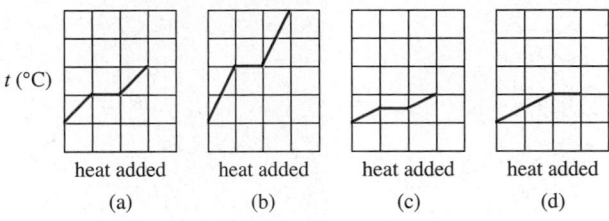

(Used with permission from the *Journal of Chemical Education,* Vol. 79, No. 7, 2002, pp. 889–895; © 2002, Division of Chemical Education, Inc.)

Answers to Practice Exercises

11.1 (a) Ionic and dispersion forces, (b) dispersion forces, (c) dipole-dipole and dispersion forces. **11.2** Only (c). **11.3** 10.50 g/cm^3. **11.4** 315 pm. **11.5** Two. **11.6** 361 pm. **11.7** 369 mmHg. **11.8** 173 kJ.

12

A sugar cube dissolving in water. The properties of a solution are markedly different from those of its solvent. The solubility of sugar molecules in water is mainly due to hydrogen bond formation between the solute and the solvent. The models show glucose and water molecules.

Physical Properties
of Solutions

A LOOK AHEAD

- We begin by examining different types of solutions that can be formed from the three states of matter: solid, liquid, and gas. We also characterize a solution by the amount of solute present as unsaturated, saturated, and supersaturated. (12.1)

- Next we study the formation of solutions at the molecular level and see how intermolecular forces affect the energetics of the solution process and solubility. (12.2)

- We study the four major types of concentration units—percent by mass, mole fraction, molarity, and molality—and their interconversions. (12.3)

- Temperature in general has a marked effect on the solubility of gases as well as liquids and solids. (12.4)

- We see that pressure has no influence on the solubility of liquids and solids, but greatly affects the solubility of gases. The quantitative relationship between gas solubility and pressure is given by Henry's law. (12.5)

- We learn that physical properties such as the vapor pressure, melting point, boiling point, and osmotic pressure of a solution depend only on the concentration and not on the identity of the solute present. We first study these *colligative properties* and their applications for nonelectrolyte solutions. (12.6)

- We then extend our study of colligative properties to electrolyte solutions and learn about the influence of ion pair formation on the colligative properties. (12.7)

- The chapter ends with a brief examination of colloids, which are particles larger than individual molecules that are dispersed in another medium. (12.8)

Interactive Activity Summary

1. Animation: Dissolution of an Ionic and a Covalent Compound (12.2)

2. Animation: Osmosis (12.6)

3. Interactivity: Test Solution with Electrolytes (12.7)

Most chemical reactions take place, not between pure solids, liquids, or gases, but among ions and molecules dissolved in water or other solvents. In Chapters 5 and 11, we looked at the properties of gases, liquids, and solids. In this chapter we examine the properties of solutions, concentrating mainly on the role of intermolecular forces in solubility and other physical properties of solutions.

12.1 Types of Solutions

In Section 4.1 we noted that a solution is a homogeneous mixture of two or more substances. Because this definition places no restriction on the nature of the substances involved, we can distinguish six types of solutions, depending on the original states (solid, liquid, or gas) of the solution components. Table 12.1 gives examples of each type.

Our focus in this chapter will be on solutions involving at least one liquid component—that is, gas-liquid, liquid-liquid, and solid-liquid solutions. And, perhaps not too surprisingly, the liquid solvent in most of the solutions we will study is water.

Chemists also characterize solutions by their capacity to dissolve a solute. A *saturated solution* contains the maximum amount of a solute that will dissolve in a given solvent at a specific temperature. An **unsaturated solution** contains less solute than it has the capacity to dissolve. A third type, a **supersaturated solution,** contains more solute than is present in a saturated solution. Supersaturated solutions are not very stable. In time, some of the solute will come out of a supersaturated solution as crystals. *Crystallization* is *the process in which dissolved solute comes out of solution and forms crystals* (Figure 12.1). Note that both precipitation and crystallization describe the

TABLE 12.1	Types of Solutions		
Component 1	Component 2	State of Resulting Solution	Examples
Gas	Gas	Gas	Air
Gas	Liquid	Liquid	Soda water (CO$_2$ in water)
Gas	Solid	Solid	H$_2$ gas in palladium
Liquid	Liquid	Liquid	Ethanol in water
Solid	Liquid	Liquid	NaCl in water
Solid	Solid	Solid	Brass (Cu/Zn), solder (Sn/Pb)

Figure 12.1 *In a supersaturated sodium acetate solution (left), sodium acetate crystals rapidly form when a small seed crystal is added.*

separation of excess solid substance from a supersaturated solution. However, solids formed by the two processes differ in appearance. We normally think of precipitates as being made up of small particles, whereas crystals may be large and well formed.

12.2 A Molecular View of the Solution Process

The intermolecular attractions that hold molecules together in liquids and solids also play a central role in the formation of solutions. When one substance (the solute) dissolves in another (the solvent), particles of the solute disperse throughout the solvent. The solute particles occupy positions that are normally taken by solvent molecules. The ease with which a solute particle replaces a solvent molecule depends on the relative strengths of three types of interactions:

In Section 6.6 we discussed the solution process from a macroscopic point of view.

- solvent-solvent interaction
- solute-solute interaction
- solvent-solute interaction

For simplicity, we can imagine the solution process taking place in three distinct steps (Figure 12.2). Step 1 is the separation of solvent molecules, and step 2 entails the separation of solute molecules. These steps require energy input to break attractive intermolecular forces, therefore, they are endothermic. In step 3 the solvent and solute molecules mix. This process can be exothermic or endothermic. The heat of solution ΔH_{soln} is given by

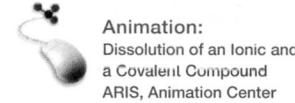

Animation:
Dissolution of an Ionic and a Covalent Compound
ARIS, Animation Center

$$\Delta H_{soln} = \Delta H_1 + \Delta H_2 + \Delta H_3$$

This equation is an application of Hess's law.

If the solute-solvent attraction is stronger than the solvent-solvent attraction and solute-solute attraction, the solution process is favorable, or exothermic ($\Delta H_{soln} < 0$). If the solute-solvent interaction is weaker than the solvent-solvent and solute-solute interactions, then the solution process is endothermic ($\Delta H_{soln} > 0$).

You may wonder why a solute dissolves in a solvent at all if the attraction for its own molecules is stronger than the solute-solvent attraction. The solution process, like all physical and chemical processes, is governed by two factors. One is energy, which determines whether a solution process is exothermic or endothermic. The second factor is an inherent tendency toward disorder in all natural events. In much the same way that a deck of new playing cards becomes mixed up after it has been

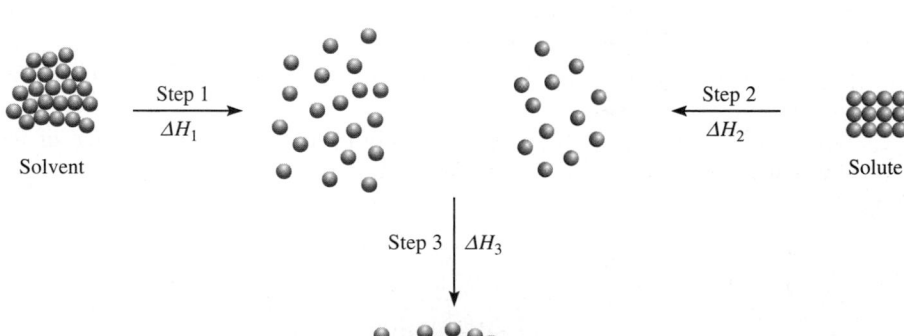

Solvent

Step 1
ΔH_1

Step 2
ΔH_2

Solute

Step 3 ΔH_3

Solution

Figure 12.2 *A molecular view of the solution process portrayed as taking place in three steps: First the solvent and solute molecules are separated (steps 1 and 2). Then the solvent and solute molecules mix (step 3).*

shuffled a few times, when solute and solvent molecules mix to form a solution, there is an increase in randomness, or disorder. In the pure state, the solvent and solute possess a fair degree of order, characterized by the more or less regular arrangement of atoms, molecules, or ions in three-dimensional space. Much of this order is destroyed when the solute dissolves in the solvent (see Figure 12.2). Therefore, the solution process is accompanied by an increase in disorder. It is the increase in disorder of the system that favors the solubility of any substance, even if the solution process is endothermic.

Solubility is a measure of how much solute will dissolve in a solvent at a specific temperature. The saying "like dissolves like" is helpful in predicting the solubility of a substance in a given solvent. What this expression means is that two substances with intermolecular forces of similar type and magnitude are likely to be soluble in each other. For example, both carbon tetrachloride (CCl_4) and benzene (C_6H_6) are nonpolar liquids. The only intermolecular forces present in these substances are dispersion forces (see Section 11.2). When these two liquids are mixed, they readily dissolve in each other, because the attraction between CCl_4 and C_6H_6 molecules is comparable in magnitude to the forces between CCl_4 molecules and between C_6H_6 molecules. Two liquids are said to be ***miscible*** if *they are completely soluble in each other in all proportions.* Alcohols such as methanol, ethanol, and 1,2-ethylene glycol are miscible with water because they can form hydrogen bonds with water molecules:

CH_3OH

C_2H_5OH

methanol   ethanol   1,2-ethylene glycol

The rules given in Table 4.2 (p. 123) enable us to predict the solubility of a particular ionic compound in water. When sodium chloride dissolves in water, the ions are stabilized in solution by hydration, which involves ion-dipole interaction. In general, we predict that ionic compounds should be much more soluble in polar solvents, such as water, liquid ammonia, and liquid hydrogen fluoride, than in nonpolar solvents, such as benzene and carbon tetrachloride. Because the molecules of nonpolar solvents lack a dipole moment, they cannot effectively solvate the Na^+ and Cl^- ions. (***Solvation*** is *the process in which an ion or a molecule is surrounded by solvent molecules arranged in a specific manner.* The process is called *hydration* when the solvent is water.) The predominant intermolecular interaction between ions and nonpolar compounds is ion-induced dipole interaction, which is much weaker than ion-dipole interaction. Consequently, ionic compounds usually have extremely low solubility in nonpolar solvents.

Example 12.1 illustrates how to predict solubility based on a knowledge of the intermolecular forces in the solute and the solvent.

$CH_2(OH)CH_2(OH)$

Example 12.1

Predict the relative solubilities in the following cases: (a) Bromine (Br_2) in benzene (C_6H_6, $\mu = 0$ D) and in water ($\mu = 1.87$ D), (b) KCl in carbon tetrachloride (CCl_4, $\mu = 0$ D) and in liquid ammonia (NH_3, $\mu = 1.46$ D), (c) formaldehyde (CH_2O) in carbon disulfide (CS_2, $\mu = 0$) and in water.

(Continued)

Strategy In predicting solubility, remember the saying: Like dissolves like. A nonpolar solute will dissolve in a nonpolar solvent; ionic compounds will generally dissolve in polar solvents due to favorable ion-dipole interaction; solutes that can form hydrogen bonds with the solvent will have high solubility in the solvent.

Solution (a) Br_2 is a nonpolar molecule and therefore should be more soluble in C_6H_6, which is also nonpolar, than in water. The only intermolecular forces between Br_2 and C_6H_6 are dispersion forces.

(b) KCl is an ionic compound. For it to dissolve, the individual K^+ and Cl^- ions must be stabilized by ion-dipole interaction. Because CCl_4 has no dipole moment, KCl should be more soluble in liquid NH_3, a polar molecule with a large dipole moment.

(c) Because CH_2O is a polar molecule and CS_2 (a linear molecule) is nonpolar,

the forces between molecules of CH_2O and CS_2 are dipole-induced dipole and dispersion. On the other hand, CH_2O can form hydrogen bonds with water, so it should be more soluble in that solvent.

Practice Exercise Is iodine (I_2) more soluble in water or in carbon disulfide (CS_2)?

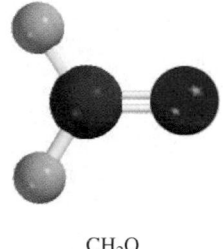

CH_2O

Similar problem: 12.11.

12.3 Concentration Units

Quantitative study of a solution requires knowing its *concentration*, that is, the amount of solute present in a given amount of solution. Chemists use several different concentration units, each of which has advantages as well as limitations. Let us examine the four most common units of concentration: percent by mass, mole fraction, molarity, and molality.

Types of Concentration Units

Percent by Mass

The **percent by mass** (also called *percent by weight* or *weight percent*) is *the ratio of the mass of a solute to the mass of the solution, multiplied by 100 percent:*

$$\text{percent by mass} = \frac{\text{mass of solute}}{\text{mass of solute} + \text{mass of solvent}} \times 100\%$$

or
$$\text{percent by mass} = \frac{\text{mass of solute}}{\text{mass of soln}} \times 100\% \qquad (12.1)$$

The percent by mass has no units because it is a ratio of two similar quantities.

Example 12.2

A sample of 0.892 g of potassium chloride (KCl) is dissolved in 54.6 g of water. What is the percent by mass of KCl in the solution?

(Continued)

Strategy We are given the mass of a solute dissolved in a certain amount of solvent. Therefore, we can calculate the mass percent of KCl using Equation (12.1).

Solution We write

$$\text{percent by mass of KCl} = \frac{\text{mass of solute}}{\text{mass of soln}} \times 100\%$$

$$= \frac{0.892 \text{ g}}{0.892 \text{ g} + 54.6 \text{ g}} \times 100\%$$

$$= 1.61\%$$

Similar problem: 12.15.

Practice Exercise A sample of 6.44 g of naphthalene ($C_{10}H_8$) is dissolved in 80.1 g of benzene (C_6H_6). Calculate the percent by mass of naphthalene in this solution.

Mole Fraction (X)

The mole fraction was introduced in Section 5.6. The mole fraction of a component of a solution, say, component A, is written X_A and is defined as

$$\text{mole fraction of component A} = X_A = \frac{\text{moles of A}}{\text{sum of moles of all components}}$$

The mole fraction has no units, because it too is a ratio of two similar quantities.

Molarity (M)

For calculations involving molarity, see Examples 4.6 and 4.7 on p. 144.

In Section 4.5 molarity was defined as the number of moles of solute in 1 L of solution; that is,

$$\text{molarity} = \frac{\text{moles of solute}}{\text{liters of soln}}$$

Thus, the units of molarity are mol/L.

Molality (m)

Molality is *the number of moles of solute dissolved in 1 kg (1000 g) of solvent*—that is,

$$\text{molality} = \frac{\text{moles of solute}}{\text{mass of solvent (kg)}} \tag{12.2}$$

For example, to prepare a 1 molal, or 1 *m*, sodium sulfate (Na_2SO_4) aqueous solution, we need to dissolve 1 mole (142.0 g) of the substance in 1000 g (1 kg) of water. Depending on the nature of the solute-solvent interaction, the final volume of the solution will be either greater or less than 1000 mL. It is also possible, though very unlikely, that the final volume could be equal to 1000 mL.

Example 12.3 shows how to calculate the molality of a solution.

Example 12.3

Calculate the molality of a sulfuric acid solution containing 24.4 g of sulfuric acid in 198 g of water. The molar mass of sulfuric acid is 98.08 g.

(Continued)

H_2SO_4

Strategy To calculate the molality of a solution, we need to know the number of moles of solute and the mass of the solvent in kilograms.

Solution The definition of molality (m) is

$$m = \frac{\text{moles of solute}}{\text{mass of solvent (kg)}}$$

First, we find the number of moles of sulfuric acid in 24.4 g of the acid, using its molar mass as the conversion factor.

$$\text{moles of } H_2SO_4 = 24.4 \text{ g } H_2SO_4 \times \frac{1 \text{ mol } H_2SO_4}{98.09 \text{ g } H_2SO_4}$$

$$= 0.249 \text{ mol } H_2SO_4$$

The mass of water is 198 g, or 0.198 kg. Therefore,

$$m = \frac{0.249 \text{ mol } H_2SO_4}{0.198 \text{ kg } H_2O}$$

$$= 1.26 \ m$$

Similar problem: 12.17.

Practice Exercise What is the molality of a solution containing 7.78 g of urea $[(NH_2)_2CO]$ in 203 g of water?

Comparison of Concentration Units

The choice of a concentration unit is based on the purpose of the experiment. For instance, the mole fraction is not used to express the concentrations of solutions for titrations and gravimetric analyses, but it is appropriate for calculating partial pressures of gases (see Section 5.6) and for dealing with vapor pressures of solutions (to be discussed later in this chapter).

The advantage of molarity is that it is generally easier to measure the volume of a solution, using precisely calibrated volumetric flasks, than to weigh the solvent, as we saw in Section 4.5. For this reason, molarity is often preferred over molality. On the other hand, molality is independent of temperature, because the concentration is expressed in number of moles of solute and mass of solvent. The volume of a solution typically increases with increasing temperature, so that a solution that is 1.0 M at 25°C may become 0.97 M at 45°C because of the increase in volume. This concentration dependence on temperature can significantly affect the accuracy of an experiment. Therefore, it is sometimes preferable to use molality instead of molarity.

Percent by mass is similar to molality in that it is independent of temperature. Furthermore, because it is defined in terms of ratio of mass of solute to mass of solution, we do not need to know the molar mass of the solute in order to calculate the percent by mass.

Sometimes it is desirable to convert one concentration unit of a solution to another; for example, the same solution may be employed for different experiments that require different concentration units for calculations. Suppose we want to express the concentration of a 0.396 m glucose ($C_6H_{12}O_6$) solution in molarity. We know there is 0.396 mole of glucose in 1000 g of the solvent and we need to determine the volume of this solution to calculate molarity. First, we calculate the mass of the solution from the molar mass of glucose:

$$\left(0.396 \text{ mol } C_6H_{12}O_6 \times \frac{180.2 \text{ g}}{1 \text{ mol } C_6H_{12}O_6} \right) + 1000 \text{ g } H_2O \text{ soln} = 1071 \text{ g}$$

The next step is to experimentally determine the density of the solution, which is found to be 1.16 g/mL. We can now calculate the volume of the solution in liters by writing

$$\text{volume} = \frac{\text{mass}}{\text{density}}$$

$$= \frac{1071\ \text{g}}{1.16\ \text{g/mL}} \times \frac{1\ \text{L}}{1000\ \text{mL}}$$

$$= 0.923\ \text{L}$$

Finally, the molarity of the solution is given by

$$\text{molarity} = \frac{\text{moles of solute}}{\text{liters of soln}}$$

$$= \frac{0.396\ \text{mol}}{0.923\ \text{L}}$$

$$= 0.429\ \text{mol/L} = 0.429\ M$$

As you can see, the density of the solution serves as a conversion factor between molality and molarity.

Examples 12.4 and 12.5 show concentration unit conversions.

CH₃OH

Example 12.4

The density of a 2.45 M aqueous solution of methanol (CH_3OH) is 0.976 g/mL. What is the molality of the solution? The molar mass of methanol is 32.04 g.

Strategy To calculate the molality, we need to know the number of moles of methanol and the mass of solvent in kilograms. We assume 1 L of solution, so the number of moles of methanol is 2.45 mol.

$$m = \frac{\overset{\text{given}}{\text{moles of solute}}}{\underset{\text{need to find}}{\text{mass of solvent (kg)}}}$$

want to calculate

Solution Our first step is to calculate the mass of water in one liter of the solution, using density as a conversion factor. The total mass of 1 L of a 2.45 M solution of methanol is

$$1\ \text{L soln} \times \frac{1000\ \text{mL soln}}{1\ \text{L soln}} \times \frac{0.976\ \text{g}}{1\ \text{mL soln}} = 976\ \text{g}$$

Because this solution contains 2.45 moles of methanol, the amount of water (solvent) in the solution is

$$\text{mass of } H_2O = \text{mass of soln} - \text{mass of solute}$$

$$= 976\ \text{g} - \left(2.45\ \text{mol CH}_3\text{OH} \times \frac{32.04\ \text{g CH}_3\text{OH}}{1\ \text{mol CH}_3\text{OH}} \right)$$

$$= 898\ \text{g}$$

(Continued)

The molality of the solution can be calculated by converting 898 g to 0.898 kg:

$$\text{molality} = \frac{2.45 \text{ mol CH}_3\text{OH}}{0.898 \text{ kg H}_2\text{O}}$$

$$= 2.73 \; m$$

Similar problems: 12.18(a), 12.19.

Practice Exercise Calculate the molality of a 5.86 M ethanol (C$_2$H$_5$OH) solution whose density is 0.927 g/mL.

Example 12.5

Calculate the molality of a 35.4 percent (by mass) aqueous solution of phosphoric acid (H$_3$PO$_4$). The molar mass of phosphoric acid is 98.00 g.

Strategy In solving this type of problem, it is convenient to assume that we start with a 100.0 g of the solution. If the mass of phosphoric acid is 35.4 percent, or 35.4 g, the percent by mass and mass of water must be 100.0% − 35.4% = 64.6% and 64.6 g.

Solution From the known molar mass of phosphoric acid, we can calculate the molality in two steps, as shown in Example 12.3. First we calculate the number of moles of phosphoric acid in 35.4 g of the acid

H$_3$PO$_4$

$$\text{moles of H}_3\text{PO}_4 = 35.4 \text{ g H}_3\text{PO}_4 \times \frac{1 \text{ mol H}_3\text{PO}_4}{97.99 \text{ g H}_3\text{PO}_4}$$

$$= 0.361 \text{ mol H}_3\text{PO}_4$$

The mass of water is 64.6 g, or 0.0646 kg. Therefore, the molality is given by

$$\text{molality} = \frac{0.361 \text{ mol H}_3\text{PO}_4}{0.0646 \text{ kg H}_2\text{O}}$$

$$= 5.59 \; m$$

Similar problem: 12.18(b).

Practice Exercise Calculate the molality of a 44.6 percent (by mass) aqueous solution of sodium chloride.

12.4 The Effect of Temperature on Solubility

Recall that solubility is defined as the maximum amount of a solute that will dissolve in a given quantity of solvent *at a specific temperature*. Temperature affects the solubility of most substances. In this section we will consider the effects of temperature on the solubility of solids and gases.

Solid Solubility and Temperature

Figure 12.3 shows the temperature dependence of the solubility of some ionic compounds in water. In most but certainly not all cases, the solubility of a solid substance increases with temperature. However, there is no clear correlation between the sign of ΔH_{soln} and the variation of solubility with temperature. For example, the solution process of CaCl$_2$ is exothermic, and that of NH$_4$NO$_3$ is endothermic. But the solubility of both compounds increases with increasing temperature. In general, the effect of temperature on solubility is best determined experimentally.

Figure 12.3 *Temperature dependence of the solubility of some ionic compounds in water.*

Fractional Crystallization

The dependence of the solubility of a solid on temperature varies considerably, as Figure 12.3 shows. The solubility of $NaNO_3$, for example, increases sharply with temperature, while that of NaCl changes very little. This wide variation provides a means of obtaining pure substances from mixtures. ***Fractional crystallization*** is *the separation of a mixture of substances into pure components on the basis of their differing solubilities.*

Suppose we have a sample of 90 g of KNO_3 that is contaminated with 10 g of NaCl. To purify the KNO_3 sample, we dissolve the mixture in 100 mL of water at 60°C and then gradually cool the solution to 0°C. At this temperature, the solubilities of KNO_3 and NaCl are 12.1 g/100 g H_2O and 34.2 g/100 g H_2O, respectively. Thus, (90−12) g, or 78 g, of KNO_3 will crystallize out of the solution, but all of the NaCl will remain dissolved (Figure 12.4). In this manner, we can obtain about 90 percent of the original amount of KNO_3 in pure form. The KNO_3 crystals can be separated from the solution by filtration.

Many of the solid inorganic and organic compounds that are used in the laboratory were purified by fractional crystallization. Generally, the method works best if the compound to be purified has a steep solubility curve, that is, if it is considerably more soluble at high temperatures than at low temperatures. Otherwise, much of it will remain dissolved as the solution is cooled. Fractional crystallization also works well if the amount of impurity in the solution is relatively small.

Gas Solubility and Temperature

The solubility of gases in water usually decreases with increasing temperature (Figure 12.5). When water is heated in a beaker, you can see bubbles of air forming on the side of the glass before the water boils. As the temperature rises, the dissolved air molecules begin to "boil out" of the solution long before the water itself boils.

The reduced solubility of molecular oxygen in hot water has a direct bearing on *thermal pollution*—that is, the heating of the environment (usually waterways) to temperatures that are harmful to its living inhabitants. It is estimated that every year in the United States some 100,000 billion gallons of water are used for industrial cooling, mostly in electric power and nuclear power production. This process heats the

Figure 12.4 *The solubilities of KNO_3 and NaCl at 0°C and 60°C. The difference in temperature dependence enables us to isolate one of these compounds from a solution containing both of them, through fractional crystallization.*

water, which is then returned to the rivers and lakes from which it was taken. Ecologists have become increasingly concerned about the effect of thermal pollution on aquatic life. Fish, like all other cold-blooded animals, have much more difficulty coping with rapid temperature fluctuation in the environment than humans do. An increase in water temperature accelerates their rate of metabolism, which generally doubles with each 10°C rise. The speedup of metabolism increases the fish's need for oxygen at the same time that the supply of oxygen decreases because of its lower solubility in heated water. Effective ways to cool power plants while doing only minimal damage to the biological environment are being sought.

On the lighter side, a knowledge of the variation of gas solubility with temperature can improve one's performance in a popular recreational sport—fishing. On a hot summer day, an experienced fisherman usually picks a deep spot in the river or lake to cast the bait. Because the oxygen content is greater in the deeper, cooler region, most fish will be found there.

Figure 12.5 *Dependence on temperature of the solubility of O_2 gas in water. Note that the solubility decreases as temperature increases. The pressure of the gas over the solution is 1 atm.*

12.5 The Effect of Pressure on the Solubility of Gases

For all practical purposes, external pressure has no influence on the solubilities of liquids and solids, but it does greatly affect the solubility of gases. The quantitative relationship between gas solubility and pressure is given by **Henry's**[†] **law,** which states that *the solubility of a gas in a liquid is proportional to the pressure of the gas over the solution:*

$$c \propto P$$
$$c = kP \tag{12.3}$$

[†]William Henry (1775–1836). English chemist. Henry's major contribution to science was his discovery of the law describing the solubility of gases, which now bears his name.

Figure 12.6 *A molecular interpretation of Henry's law. When the partial pressure of the gas over the solution increases from (a) to (b), the concentration of the dissolved gas also increases according to Equation (12.2).*

(a)   (b)

Each gas has a different k value at a given temperature.

Here c is the molar concentration (mol/L) of the dissolved gas; P is the pressure (in atm) of the gas over the solution; and, for a given gas, k is a constant that depends only on temperature. The constant k has the units mol/L · atm. You can see that when the pressure of the gas is 1 atm, c is *numerically* equal to k. If several gases are present, P is the partial pressure.

Henry's law can be understood qualitatively in terms of the kinetic molecular theory. The amount of gas that will dissolve in a solvent depends on how frequently the gas molecules collide with the liquid surface and become trapped by the condensed phase. Suppose we have a gas in dynamic equilibrium with a solution [Figure 12.6(a)]. At every instant, the number of gas molecules entering the solution is equal to the number of dissolved molecules moving into the gas phase. If the partial pressure of the gas is greater [Figure 12.6(b)], more molecules dissolve in the liquid because more molecules are striking the surface of the liquid. This process continues until the concentration of the solution is again such that the number of molecules leaving the solution per second equals the number entering the solution. Because of the higher concentration of molecules in both the gas and solution phases, this number is greater in (b) than in (a), where the partial pressure is lower.

A practical demonstration of Henry's law is the effervescence of a soft drink when the cap of the bottle is removed. Before the beverage bottle is sealed, it is pressurized with a mixture of air and CO_2 saturated with water vapor. Because of the high partial pressure of CO_2 in the pressurizing gas mixture, the amount dissolved in the soft drink is many times the amount that would dissolve under normal atmospheric conditions. When the cap is removed, the pressurized gases escape, eventually the pressure in the bottle falls to atmospheric pressure, and the amount of CO_2 remaining in the beverage is determined only by the normal atmospheric partial pressure of CO_2, 0.0003 atm. The excess dissolved CO_2 comes out of solution, causing the effervescence.

Example 12.6 applies Henry's law to nitrogen gas.

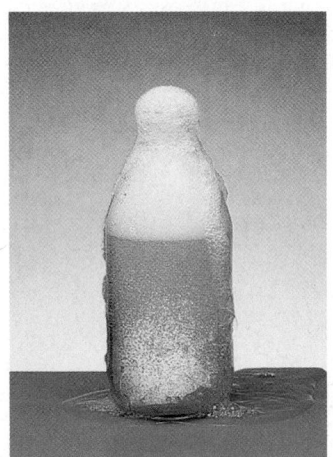

The effervescence of a soft drink. The bottle was shaken before being opened to dramatize the escape of CO_2.

Example 12.6

The solubility of nitrogen gas at 25°C and 1 atm is 6.8×10^{-4} mol/L. What is the concentration (in molarity) of nitrogen dissolved in water under atmospheric conditions? The partial pressure of nitrogen gas in the atmosphere is 0.78 atm.

Strategy The given solubility enables us to calculate Henry's law constant (k), which can then be used to determine the concentration of the solution.

(Continued)

Solution The first step is to calculate the quantity k in Equation (12.3):

$$c = kP$$
$$6.8 \times 10^{-4} \text{ mol/L} = k \, (1 \text{ atm})$$
$$k = 6.8 \times 10^{-4} \text{ mol/L} \cdot \text{atm}$$

Therefore, the solubility of nitrogen gas in water is

$$c = (6.8 \times 10^{-4} \text{ mol/L} \cdot \text{atm})(0.78 \text{ atm})$$
$$= 5.3 \times 10^{-4} \text{ mol/L}$$
$$= 5.3 \times 10^{-4} \, M$$

The decrease in solubility is the result of lowering the pressure from 1 atm to 0.78 atm.

Check The ratio of the concentrations $[(5.3 \times 10^{-4} \, M/6.8 \times 10^{-4} \, M) = 0.78]$ should be equal to the ratio of the pressures (0.78 atm/1.0 atm = 0.78).

Similar problem: 12.37.

Practice Exercise Calculate the molar concentration of oxygen in water at 25°C for a partial pressure of 0.22 atm. The Henry's law constant for oxygen is 1.3×10^{-3} mol/L · atm.

Most gases obey Henry's law, but there are some important exceptions. For example, if the dissolved gas *reacts* with water, higher solubilities can result. The solubility of ammonia is much higher than expected because of the reaction

$$NH_3 + H_2O \rightleftharpoons NH_4^+ + OH^-$$

Carbon dioxide also reacts with water, as follows:

$$CO_2 + H_2O \rightleftharpoons H_2CO_3$$

Another interesting example is the dissolution of molecular oxygen in blood. Normally, oxygen gas is only sparingly soluble in water (see Practice Exercise in Example 12.6). However, its solubility in blood is dramatically greater because of the high content of hemoglobin (Hb) molecules. Each hemoglobin molecule can bind up to four oxygen molecules, which are eventually delivered to the tissues for use in metabolism:

$$Hb + 4O_2 \rightleftharpoons Hb(O_2)_4$$

It is this process that accounts for the high solubility of molecular oxygen in blood.

The Chemistry in Action essay on p. 516 explains a natural disaster with Henry's law.

12.6 Colligative Properties of Nonelectrolyte Solutions

Colligative properties (or collective properties) are *properties that depend only on the number of solute particles in solution and not on the nature of the solute particles.* These properties are bound together by a common origin—they all depend on the number of solute particles present, regardless of whether they are atoms, ions, or molecules. The colligative properties are vapor-pressure lowering, boiling-point elevation, freezing-point depression, and osmotic pressure. For our discussion of colligative properties of nonelectrolyte solutions it is important to keep in mind that we are talking about relatively dilute solutions, that is, solutions whose concentrations are $\leq 0.2 \, M$.

CHEMISTRY
in Action

The Killer Lake

Disaster struck swiftly and without warning. On August 21, 1986, Lake Nyos in Cameroon, a small nation on the west coast of Africa, suddenly belched a dense cloud of carbon dioxide. Speeding down a river valley, the cloud asphyxiated over 1700 people and many livestock.

How did this tragedy happen? Lake Nyos is stratified into layers that do not mix. A boundary separates the freshwater at the surface from the deeper, denser solution containing dissolved minerals and gases, including CO_2. The CO_2 gas comes from springs of carbonated groundwater that percolate upward into the bottom of the volcanically formed lake. Given the high water pressure at the bottom of the lake, the concentration of CO_2 gradually accumulated to a dangerously high level, in accordance with Henry's law. What triggered the release of CO_2 is not known for certain. It is believed that an earthquake, landslide, or even strong winds may have upset the delicate balance within the lake, creating waves that overturned the water layers. When the deep water rose, dissolved CO_2 came out of solution, just as a soft drink fizzes when the bottle is uncapped. Being heavier than air, the CO_2 traveled close to the ground and literally smothered an entire village 15 miles away.

Now, more than 20 years after the incident, scientists are concerned that the CO_2 concentration at the bottom of Lake Nyos is again reaching saturation level. To prevent a recurrence of the earlier tragedy, an attempt has been made to pump up the deep water, thus releasing the dissolved CO_2. In addition to being costly, this approach is controversial because it might disturb the waters near the bottom of the lake, leading to an uncontrollable release of CO_2 to the surface. In the meantime, a natural time bomb is ticking away.

Deep waters in Lake Nyos are pumped to the surface to remove dissolved CO_2 gas.

Vapor-Pressure Lowering

To review the concept of equilibrium vapor pressure as it applies to pure liquids, see Section 11.8.

If a solute is ***nonvolatile*** (that is, it *does not have a measurable vapor pressure*), the vapor pressure of its solution is always less than that of the pure solvent. Thus, the relationship between solution vapor pressure and solvent vapor pressure depends on the concentration of the solute in the solution. This relationship is expressed by ***Raoult's*[†] *law,*** which states that *the partial pressure of a solvent over a solution, P_1, is given by the vapor pressure of the pure solvent, P_1°, times the mole fraction of the solvent in the solution, X_1:*

$$P_1 = X_1 P_1^\circ \tag{12.4}$$

[†]François Marie Raoult (1830–1901). French chemist. Raoult's work was mainly in solution properties and electrochemistry.

In a solution containing only one solute, $X_1 = 1 - X_2$, where X_2 is the mole fraction of the solute. Equation (12.4) can therefore be rewritten as

$$P_1 = (1 - X_2)P_1^\circ$$

or

$$P_1 = P_1^\circ - X_2 P_1^\circ$$

so that

$$P_1^\circ - P_1 = \Delta P = X_2 P_1^\circ \qquad (12.5)$$

We see that the *decrease* in vapor pressure, ΔP, is directly proportional to the solute concentration (measured in mole fraction).

Example 12.7 illustrates the use of Raoult's law [Equation (12.5)].

Example 12.7

Calculate the vapor pressure of a solution made by dissolving 218 g of glucose (molar mass = 180.2 g/mol) in 460 mL of water at 30°C. What is the vapor-pressure lowering? The vapor pressure of pure water at 30°C is given in Table 5.3 (p. 196). Assume the density of the solution is 1.00 g/mL.

Strategy We need Raoult's law [Equation (12.4)] to determine the vapor pressure of a solution. Note that glucose is a nonvolatile solute.

Solution The vapor pressure of a solution (P_1) is

$C_6H_{12}O_6$

First we calculate the number of moles of glucose and water in the solution:

$$n_1(\text{water}) = 460 \; \text{mL} \times \frac{1.00 \; g}{1 \; \text{mL}} \times \frac{1 \; \text{mol}}{18.02 \; g} = 25.5 \; \text{mol}$$

$$n_2(\text{glucose}) = 218 \; g \times \frac{1 \; \text{mol}}{180.2 \; g} = 1.21 \; \text{mol}$$

The mole fraction of water, X_1, is given by

$$X_1 = \frac{n_1}{n_1 + n_2}$$

$$= \frac{25.5 \; \text{mol}}{25.5 \; \text{mol} + 1.21 \; \text{mol}} = 0.955$$

From Table 5.3, we find the vapor pressure of water at 30°C to be 31.82 mmHg. Therefore, the vapor pressure of the glucose solution is

$$P_1 = 0.955 \times 31.82 \; \text{mmHg}$$
$$= 30.4 \; \text{mmHg}$$

Finally, the vapor-pressure lowering is (31.82 − 30.4) mmHg, or 1.4 mmHg.

(Continued)

Similar problems: 12.51, 12.52.

Check We can also calculate the vapor pressure lowering by using Equation (12.5). Because the mole fraction of glucose is $(1 - 0.955)$, or 0.045, the vapor pressure lowering is given by $(0.045)(31.82 \text{ mmHg})$ or 1.4 mmHg.

Practice Exercise Calculate the vapor pressure of a solution made by dissolving 82.4 g of urea (molar mass = 60.06 g/mol) in 212 mL of water at 35°C. What is the vapor-pressure lowering?

Why is the vapor pressure of a solution less than that of the pure solvent? As was mentioned in Section 12.2, one driving force in physical and chemical processes is an increase in disorder—the greater the disorder, the more favorable the process. Vaporization increases the disorder of a system because molecules in a vapor have less order than those in a liquid. Because a solution is more disordered than a pure solvent, the difference in disorder between a solution and a vapor is less than that between a pure solvent and a vapor. Thus, solvent molecules have less of a tendency to leave a solution than to leave the pure solvent to become vapor, and the vapor pressure of a solution is less than that of the solvent.

If both components of a solution are *volatile* (that is, *have measurable vapor pressure*), the vapor pressure of the solution is the sum of the individual partial pressures. Raoult's law holds equally well in this case:

$$P_A = X_A P_A^\circ$$
$$P_B = X_B P_B^\circ$$

where P_A and P_B are the partial pressures over the solution for components A and B; P_A° and P_B° are the vapor pressures of the pure substances; and X_A and X_B are their mole fractions. The total pressure is given by Dalton's law of partial pressure (see Section 5.6):

$$P_T = P_A + P_B$$

or

$$P_T = X_A P_A^\circ + X_B P_B^\circ$$

For example, benzene and toluene are volatile components that have similar structures and therefore similar intermolecular forces:

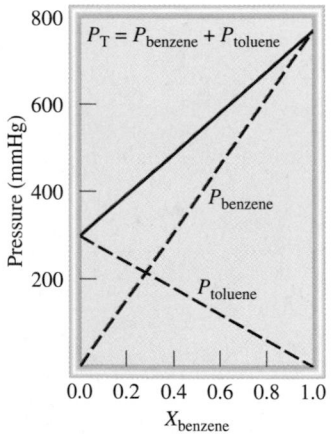

Figure 12.7 *The dependence of the partial pressures of benzene and toluene on their mole fractions in a benzene-toluene solution $(X_{toluene} = 1 - X_{benzene})$ at 80°C. This solution is said to be ideal because the vapor pressures obey Raoult's law.*

CH₃

benzene   toluene

In a solution of benzene and toluene, the vapor pressure of each component obeys Raoult's law. Figure 12.7 shows the dependence of the total vapor pressure (P_T) in a benzene-toluene solution on the composition of the solution. Note that we need only express the composition of the solution in terms of the mole fraction of one component. For every value of $X_{benzene}$, the mole fraction of toluene, $X_{toluene}$, is given by $(1 - X_{benzene})$. The benzene-toluene solution is one of the few examples of an ***ideal solution,*** which is *any solution that obeys Raoult's law.* One characteristic of an ideal solution is that the heat of solution, ΔH_{soln}, is zero.

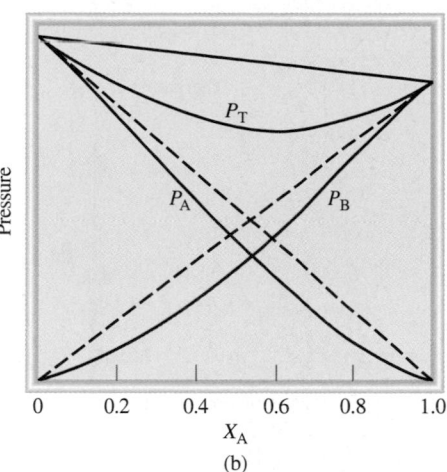

Figure 12.8 *Nonideal solutions. (a) Positive deviation occurs when P_T is greater than that predicted by Raoult's law (the solid black line). (b) Negative deviation. Here, P_T is less than that predicted by Raoult's law (the solid black line).*

Most solutions do not behave ideally in this respect. Designating two volatile substances as A and B, we can consider the following two cases:

Case 1: If the intermolecular forces between A and B molecules are weaker than those between A molecules and between B molecules, then there is a greater tendency for these molecules to leave the solution than in the case of an ideal solution. Consequently, the vapor pressure of the solution is greater than the sum of the vapor pressures as predicted by Raoult's law for the same concentration. This behavior gives rise to the *positive deviation* [Figure 12.8(a)]. In this case, the heat of solution is positive (that is, mixing is an endothermic process).

Case 2: If A molecules attract B molecules more strongly than they do their own kind, the vapor pressure of the solution is less than the sum of the vapor pressures as predicted by Raoult's law. Here we have a *negative deviation* [Figure 12.8(b)]. In this case, the heat of solution is negative (that is, mixing is an exothermic process).

Fractional Distillation

Solution vapor pressure has a direct bearing on ***fractional distillation,*** *a procedure for separating liquid components of a solution based on their different boiling points.* Fractional distillation is somewhat analogous to fractional crystallization. Suppose we want to separate a *binary system* (a system with two components), say, benzene-toluene. Both benzene and toluene are relatively volatile, yet their boiling points are appreciably different (80.1°C and 110.6°C, respectively). When we boil a solution containing these two substances, the vapor formed is somewhat richer in the more volatile component, benzene. If the vapor is condensed in a separate container and that liquid is boiled again, a still higher concentration of benzene will be obtained in the vapor phase. By repeating this process many times, it is possible to separate benzene completely from toluene.

In practice, chemists use an apparatus like that shown in Figure 12.9 to separate volatile liquids. The round-bottomed flask containing the benzene-toluene solution is fitted with a long column packed with small glass beads. When the solution boils, the vapor condenses on the beads in the lower portion of the column, and the liquid falls back into the distilling flask. As time goes on, the beads gradually heat up, allowing the vapor to move upward slowly. In essence, the packing material causes the benzene-toluene mixture to be subjected continuously to numerous vaporization-condensation steps. At each step the composition of the vapor in the column will be richer in the more volatile, or lower boiling-point, component (in this case, benzene). The vapor that rises to the top of the column is essentially pure benzene, which is then condensed and collected in a receiving flask.

Figure 12.9 *An apparatus for small-scale fractional distillation. The fractionating column is packed with tiny glass beads. The longer the fractionating column, the more complete the separation of the volatile liquids.*

Fractional distillation is as important in industry as it is in the laboratory. The petroleum industry employs fractional distillation on a large scale to separate the components of crude oil. More will be said of this process in Chapter 24.

Boiling-Point Elevation

The boiling point of a solution is the temperature at which its vapor pressure equals the external atmospheric pressure (see Section 11.8). Because the presence of a non-volatile solute lowers the vapor pressure of a solution, it must also affect the boiling point of the solution. Figure 12.10 shows the phase diagram of water and the changes that occur in an aqueous solution. Because at any temperature the vapor pressure of the solution is lower than that of the pure solvent regardless of temperature, the liquid-vapor curve for the solution lies below that for the pure solvent. Consequently, the dashed solution curve intersects the horizontal line that marks $P = 1$ atm at a *higher* temperature than the normal boiling point of the pure solvent. This graphical analysis shows that the boiling point of the solution is higher than that of water. The **boiling-point elevation (ΔT_b)** is defined as *the boiling point of the solution (T_b) minus the boiling point of the pure solvent (T_b°):*

$$\Delta T_b = T_b - T_b^\circ$$

Because $T_b > T_b^\circ$, ΔT_b is a positive quantity.

The value of ΔT_b is proportional to the vapor-pressure lowering, and so it is also proportional to the concentration (molality) of the solution. That is,

$$\Delta T_b \propto m$$

$$\Delta T_b = K_b m \qquad (12.6)$$

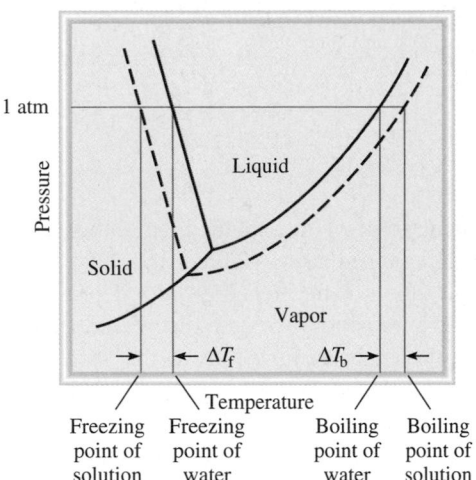

Figure 12.10 *Phase diagram illustrating the boiling-point elevation and freezing-point depression of aqueous solutions. The dashed curves pertain to the solution, and the solid curves to the pure solvent. As you can see, the boiling point of the solution is higher than that of water, and the freezing point of the solution is lower than that of water.*

where m is the molality of the solution and K_b is the *molal boiling-point elevation constant*. The units of K_b are °C/m. It is important to understand the choice of concentration unit here. We are dealing with a system (the solution) whose temperature is *not* constant, so we cannot express the concentration units in molarity because molarity changes with temperature.

Table 12.2 lists values of K_b for several common solvents. Using the boiling-point elevation constant for water and Equation (12.6), you can see that if the molality of an aqueous solution is 1.00 m, the boiling point will be 100.52°C.

Freezing-Point Depression

A nonscientist may remain forever unaware of the boiling-point elevation phenomenon, but a careful observer living in a cold climate is familiar with freezing-point depression. Ice on frozen roads and sidewalks melts when sprinkled with salts such as NaCl or $CaCl_2$. This method of thawing succeeds because it depresses the freezing point of water.

Figure 12.10 shows that lowering the vapor pressure of the solution shifts the solid-liquid curve to the left. Consequently, this line intersects the horizontal line at a temperature *lower* than the freezing point of water. The *freezing point depression (ΔT_f)* is defined as *the freezing point of the pure solvent (T_f°) minus the freezing point of the solution (T_f):*

$$\Delta T_f = T_f^\circ - T_f$$

De-icing of airplanes is based on freezing-point depression.

	Molal Boiling-Point Elevation and Freezing-Point Depression			
TABLE 12.2	**Constants of Several Common Liquids**			
Solvent	**Normal Freezing Point (°C)***	**K_f (°C/m)**	**Normal Boiling Point (°C)***	**K_b (°C/m)**
Water	0	1.86	100	0.52
Benzene	5.5	5.12	80.1	2.53
Ethanol	−117.3	1.99	78.4	1.22
Acetic acid	16.6	3.90	117.9	2.93
Cyclohexane	6.6	20.0	80.7	2.79

*Measured at 1 atm.

Because $T_f^\circ > T_f$, ΔT_f is a positive quantity. Again, ΔT_f is proportional to the concentration of the solution:

$$\Delta T_f \propto m$$

$$\Delta T_f = K_f m \qquad (12.7)$$

where m is the concentration of the solute in molality units, and K_f is the *molal freezing-point depression constant* (see Table 12.2). Like K_b, K_f has the units °C/m.

A qualitative explanation of the freezing-point depression phenomenon is as follows. Freezing involves a transition from the disordered state to the ordered state. For this to happen, energy must be removed from the system. Because a solution has greater disorder than the solvent, more energy needs to be removed from it to create order than in the case of a pure solvent. Therefore, the solution has a lower freezing point than its solvent. Note that when a solution freezes, the solid that separates is the pure solvent component.

In order for boiling-point elevation to occur, the solute must be nonvolatile, but no such restriction applies to freezing-point depression. For example, methanol (CH_3OH), a fairly volatile liquid that boils at only 65°C, has sometimes been used as an antifreeze in automobile radiators.

A practical application of the freezing-point depression is described in Example 12.8.

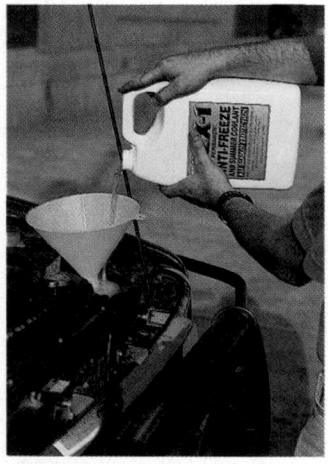

In cold climate regions, antifreeze must be used in car radiators in winter.

Example 12.8

Ethylene glycol (EG), $CH_2(OH)CH_2(OH)$, is a common automobile antifreeze. It is water soluble and fairly nonvolatile (b.p. 197°C). Calculate the freezing point of a solution containing 651 g of this substance in 2505 g of water. Would you keep this substance in your car radiator during the summer? The molar mass of ethylene glycol is 62.01 g.

Strategy This question asks for the depression in freezing point of the solution.

$$\underset{\text{want to calculate}}{\Delta T_f} = K_f \underset{\text{need to find}}{m} \overset{\text{constant}}{}$$

The information given enables us to calculate the molality of the solution and we refer to Table 12.2 for the K_f of water.

Solution To solve for the molality of the solution, we need to know the number of moles of EG and the mass of the solvent in kilograms. We find the molar mass of EG, and convert the mass of the solvent to 2.505 kg, and calculate the molality as follows:

$$651 \text{ g EG} \times \frac{1 \text{ mol EG}}{62.07 \text{ g EG}} = 10.5 \text{ mol EG}$$

$$m = \frac{\text{moles of solute}}{\text{mass of solvent (kg)}}$$

$$= \frac{10.5 \text{ mol EG}}{2.505 \text{ kg } H_2O} = 4.19 \text{ mol EG/kg } H_2O$$

$$= 4.19 \ m$$

(Continued)

From Equation (12.7) and Table 12.2 we write

$$\Delta T_f = K_f m$$
$$= (1.86°C/m)(4.19\ m)$$
$$= 7.79°C$$

Because pure water freezes at 0°C, the solution will freeze at −7.79°C. We can calculate boiling-point elevation in the same way as follows:

$$\Delta T_b = K_b m$$
$$= (0.52°C/m)(4.19\ m)$$
$$= 2.2°C$$

Because the solution will boil at $(100 + 2.2)°C$, or 102.2°C, it would be preferable to leave the antifreeze in your car radiator in summer to prevent the solution from boiling.

Similar problems: 12.58, 12.61.

Practice Exercise Calculate the boiling point and freezing point of a solution containing 478 g of ethylene glycol in 3202 g of water.

Osmotic Pressure

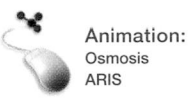

Animation:
Osmosis
ARIS

Many chemical and biological processes depend on **osmosis,** *the selective passage of solvent molecules through a porous membrane from a dilute solution to a more concentrated one.* Figure 12.11 illustrates this phenomenon. The left compartment of the apparatus contains pure solvent; the right compartment contains a solution. The two compartments are separated by a **semipermeable membrane,** which *allows the passage of solvent molecules but blocks the passage of solute molecules.* At the start, the water levels in the two tubes are equal [see Figure 12.11(a)]. After some time, the level in the right tube begins to rise and continues to go up until equilibrium is reached, that is, until no further change can be observed. The **osmotic pressure (π)** of a solution is *the pressure required to stop osmosis.* As shown in Figure 12.11(b), this pressure can be measured directly from the difference in the final fluid levels.

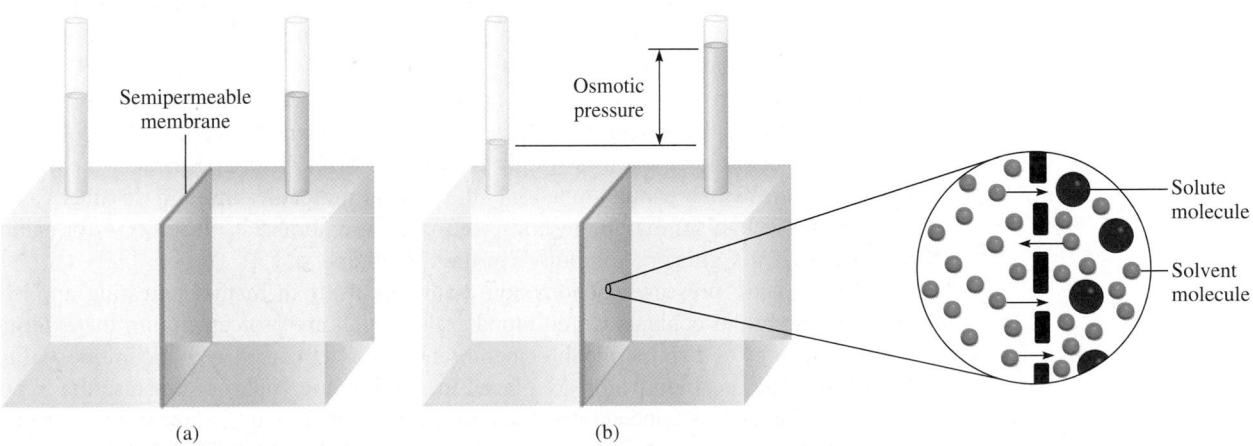

Figure 12.11 *Osmotic pressure. (a) The levels of the pure solvent (left) and of the solution (right) are equal at the start. (b) During osmosis, the level on the solution side rises as a result of the net flow of solvent from left to right. The osmotic pressure is equal to the hydrostatic pressure exerted by the column of fluid in the right tube at equilibrium. Basically the same effect occurs when the pure solvent is replaced by a more dilute solution than that on the right.*

Figure 12.12 *(a) Unequal vapor pressures inside the container lead to a net transfer of water from the left beaker (which contains pure water) to the right one (which contains a solution). (b) At equilibrium, all the water in the left beaker has been transferred to the right beaker. This driving force for solvent transfer is analogous to the osmotic phenomenon that is shown in Figure 12.11.*

Net transfer of solvent

(a)   (b)

What causes water to move spontaneously from left to right in this case? The situation depicted in Figure 12.12 helps us understand the driving force behind osmosis. Because the vapor pressure of pure water is higher than the vapor pressure of the solution, there is a net transfer of water from the left beaker to the right one. Given enough time, the transfer will continue until no more water remains in the left beaker. A similar driving force causes water to move from the pure solvent into the solution during osmosis.

The osmotic pressure of a solution is given by

$$\pi = MRT \tag{12.8}$$

where M is the molarity of solution, R is the gas constant ($0.0821 \text{ L} \cdot \text{atm/K} \cdot \text{mol}$), and T is the absolute temperature. The osmotic pressure, π, is expressed in atm. Because osmotic pressure measurements are carried out at constant temperature, we express the concentration in terms of the more convenient units of molarity rather than molality.

Like boiling-point elevation and freezing-point depression, osmotic pressure is directly proportional to the concentration of solution. This is what we would expect, because all colligative properties depend only on the number of solute particles in solution. If two solutions are of equal concentration and, hence, have the same osmotic pressure, they are said to be *isotonic*. If two solutions are of unequal osmotic pressures, the more concentrated solution is said to be *hypertonic* and the more dilute solution is described as *hypotonic* (Figure 12.13).

Although osmosis is a common and well-studied phenomenon, relatively little is known about how the semipermeable membrane stops some molecules yet allows others to pass. In some cases, it is simply a matter of size. A semipermeable membrane may have pores small enough to let only the solvent molecules through. In other cases, a different mechanism may be responsible for the membrane's selectivity—for example, the solvent's greater "solubility" in the membrane.

The osmotic pressure phenomenon manifests itself in many interesting applications. To study the contents of red blood cells, which are protected from the external environment by a semipermeable membrane, biochemists use a technique called hemolysis. The red blood cells are placed in a hypotonic solution. Because the hypotonic solution is less concentrated than the interior of the cell, water moves into the cells, as shown in the middle photo of Figure 12.13(d). The cells swell and eventually burst, releasing hemoglobin and other molecules.

Home preserving of jam and jelly provides another example of the use of osmotic pressure. A large quantity of sugar is actually essential to the preservation process

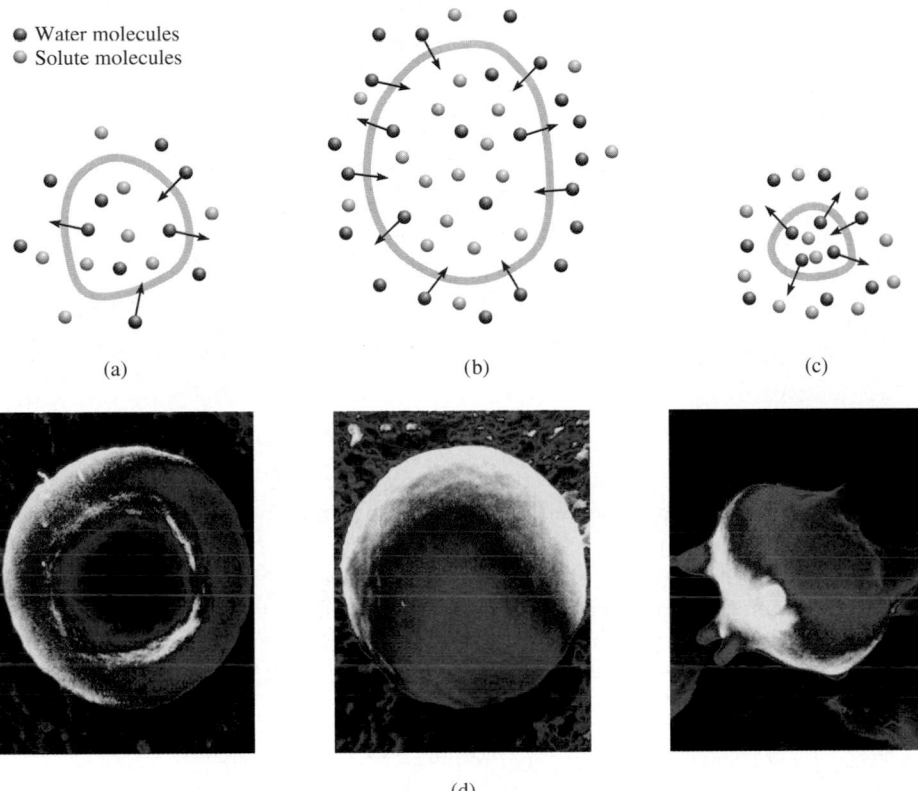

● Water molecules
● Solute molecules

(a)   (b)   (c)

(d)

Figure 12.13 *A cell in (a) an isotonic solution, (b) a hypotonic solution, and (c) a hypertonic solution. The cell remains unchanged in (a), swells in (b), and shrinks in (c). (d) From left to right: a red blood cell in an isotonic solution, in a hypotonic solution, and in a hypertonic solution.*

because the sugar helps to kill bacteria that may cause botulism. As Figure 12.13(c) shows, when a bacterial cell is in a hypertonic (high-concentration) sugar solution, the intracellular water tends to move out of the bacterial cell to the more concentrated solution by osmosis. This process, known as *crenation*, causes the cell to shrink and, eventually, to cease functioning. The natural acidity of fruits also inhibits bacteria growth.

Osmotic pressure also is the major mechanism for transporting water upward in plants. Because leaves constantly lose water to the air, in a process called *transpiration*, the solute concentrations in leaf fluids increase. Water is pulled up through the trunk, branches, and stems of trees by osmotic pressure. Up to 10 to 15 atm pressure is necessary to transport water to the leaves at the tops of California's redwoods, which reach about 120 m in height. (The capillary action discussed in Section 11.3 is responsible for the rise of water only up to a few centimeters.)

Example 12.9 shows that an osmotic pressure measurement can be used to find the concentration of a solution.

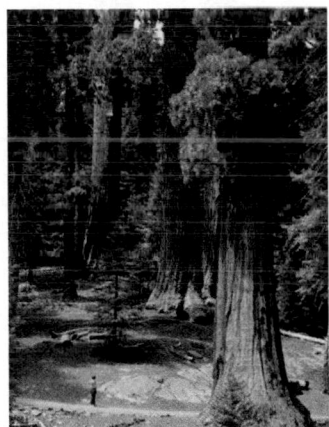

California redwoods.

Example 12.9

The average osmotic pressure of seawater, measured in the kind of apparatus shown in Figure 12.11, is about 30.0 atm at 25°C. Calculate the molar concentration of an aqueous solution of sucrose ($C_{12}H_{22}O_{11}$) that is isotonic with seawater.

Strategy When we say the sucrose solution is isotonic with seawater, what can we conclude about the osmotic pressures of these two solutions?

(Continued)

Solution A solution of sucrose that is isotonic with seawater must have the same osmotic pressure, 30.0 atm. Using Equation (12.8).

$$\pi = MRT$$

$$M = \frac{\pi}{RT} = \frac{30.0 \text{ atm}}{(0.0821 \text{ L} \cdot \text{atm/K} \cdot \text{mol})(298 \text{ K})}$$

$$= 1.23 \text{ mol/L}$$

$$= 1.23 \ M$$

Similar problem: 12.65.

Practice Exercise What is the osmotic pressure (in atm) of a 0.884 M urea solution at 16°C?

Using Colligative Properties to Determine Molar Mass

The colligative properties of nonelectrolyte solutions provide a means of determining the molar mass of a solute. Theoretically, any of the four colligative properties is suitable for this purpose. In practice, however, only freezing-point depression and osmotic pressure are used because they show the most pronounced changes. The procedure is as follows. From the experimentally determined freezing-point depression or osmotic pressure, we can calculate the molality or molarity of the solution. Knowing the mass of the solute, we can readily determine its molar mass, as Examples 12.10 and 12.11 demonstrate.

$C_{10}H_8$

Example 12.10

A 7.85-g sample of a compound with the empirical formula C_5H_4 is dissolved in 301 g of benzene. The freezing point of the solution is 1.05°C below that of pure benzene. What are the molar mass and molecular formula of this compound?

Strategy Solving this problem requires three steps. First, we calculate the molality of the solution from the depression in freezing point. Next, from the molality we determine the number of moles in 7.85 g of the compound and hence its molar mass. Finally, comparing the experimental molar mass with the empirical molar mass enables us to write the molecular formula.

Solution The sequence of conversions for calculating the molar mass of the compound is

$$\text{freezing-point} \longrightarrow \text{molality} \longrightarrow \text{number of} \longrightarrow \text{molar mass}$$
$$\text{depression} \qquad\qquad\qquad\qquad \text{moles}$$

Our first step is to calculate the molality of the solution. From Equation (12.7) and Table 12.2 we write

$$\text{molality} = \frac{\Delta T_f}{K_f} = \frac{1.05°C}{5.12°C/m} = 0.205 \ m$$

Because there is 0.205 mole of the solute in 1 kg of solvent, the number of moles of solute in 301 g, or 0.301 kg, of solvent is

$$0.301 \text{ kg} \times \frac{0.205 \text{ mol}}{1 \text{ kg}} = 0.0617 \text{ mol}$$

(Continued)

Thus, the molar mass of the solute is

$$\text{molar mass} = \frac{\text{grams of compound}}{\text{moles of compound}}$$
$$= \frac{7.85 \text{ g}}{0.0617 \text{ mol}} = 127 \text{ g/mol}$$

Now we can determine the ratio

$$\frac{\text{molar mass}}{\text{empirical molar mass}} = \frac{127 \text{ g/mol}}{64 \text{ g/mol}} \approx 2$$

Therefore, the molecular formula is $(C_5H_4)_2$ or $C_{10}H_8$ (naphthalene).

Similar problem: 12.59.

Practice Exercise A solution of 0.85 g of an organic compound in 100.0 g of benzene has a freezing point of 5.16°C. What are the molality of the solution and the molar mass of the solute?

Example 12.11

A solution is prepared by dissolving 35.0 g of hemoglobin (Hb) in enough water to make up 1 L in volume. If the osmotic pressure of the solution is found to be 10.0 mmHg at 25°C, calculate the molar mass of hemoglobin.

Strategy We are asked to calculate the molar mass of Hb. The steps are similar to those outlined in Example 12.10. From the osmotic pressure of the solution, we calculate the molarity of the solution. Then, from the molarity, we determine the number of moles in 35.0 g of Hb and hence its molar mass. What units should we use for π and temperature?

Solution The sequence of conversions is as follows:

$$\text{osmotic pressure} \longrightarrow \text{molarity} \longrightarrow \text{number of moles} \longrightarrow \text{molar mass}$$

First we calculate the molarity using Equation (12.8)

$$\pi = MRT$$
$$M = \frac{\pi}{RT}$$
$$= \frac{10.0 \text{ mmHg} \times \dfrac{1 \text{ atm}}{760 \text{ mmHg}}}{(0.0821 \text{ L} \cdot \text{atm/K} \cdot \text{mol})(298 \text{ K})}$$
$$= 5.38 \times 10^{-4} \, M$$

The volume of the solution is 1 L, so it must contain 5.38×10^{-4} mol of Hb. We use this quantity to calculate the molar mass:

$$\text{moles of Hb} = \frac{\text{mass of Hb}}{\text{molar mass of Hb}}$$
$$\text{molar mass of Hb} = \frac{\text{mass of Hb}}{\text{moles of Hb}}$$
$$= \frac{35.0 \text{ g}}{5.38 \times 10^{-4} \text{ mol}}$$
$$= 6.51 \times 10^4 \text{ g/mol}$$

Similar problems: 12.66, 12.68.

Practice Exercise A 202-mL benzene solution containing 2.47 g of an organic polymer has an osmotic pressure of 8.63 mmHg at 21°C. Calculate the molar mass of the polymer.

A pressure of 10.0 mmHg, as in Example 12.11, can be measured easily and accurately. For this reason, osmotic pressure measurements are very useful for determining the molar masses of large molecules, such as proteins. To see how much more practical the osmotic pressure technique is than freezing-point depression would be, let us estimate the change in freezing point of the same hemoglobin solution. If an aqueous solution is quite dilute, we can assume that molarity is roughly equal to molality. (Molarity would be equal to molality if the density of the aqueous solution were 1 g/mL.) Hence, from Equation (12.7) we write

$$\Delta T_f = (1.86°C/m)(5.38 \times 10^{-4}\ m)$$
$$= 1.00 \times 10^{-3}°C$$

The freezing-point depression of one-thousandth of a degree is too small a temperature change to measure accurately. For this reason, the freezing-point depression technique is more suitable for determining the molar mass of smaller and more soluble molecules, those having molar masses of 500 g or less, because the freezing-point depressions of their solutions are much greater.

12.7 Colligative Properties of Electrolyte Solutions

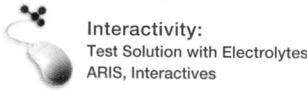

The study of colligative properties of electrolytes requires a slightly different approach than the one used for the colligative properties of nonelectrolytes. The reason is that electrolytes dissociate into ions in solution, and so one unit of an electrolyte compound separates into two or more particles when it dissolves. (Remember, it is the number of solute particles that determines the colligative properties of a solution.) For example, each unit of NaCl dissociates into two ions—Na^+ and Cl^-. Thus, the colligative properties of a 0.1 m NaCl solution should be twice as great as those of a 0.1 m solution containing a nonelectrolyte, such as sucrose. Similarly, we would expect a 0.1 m $CaCl_2$ solution to depress the freezing point by three times as much as a 0.1 m sucrose solution because each $CaCl_2$ produces three ions. To account for this effect we define a quantity called the ***van't Hoff*[†] *factor,*** given by

$$i = \frac{\text{actual number of particles in soln after dissociation}}{\text{number of formula units initially dissolved in soln}} \qquad (12.9)$$

Thus, i should be 1 for all nonelectrolytes. For strong electrolytes such as NaCl and KNO_3, i should be 2, and for strong electrolytes such as Na_2SO_4 and $CaCl_2$, i should be 3. Consequently, the equations for colligative properties must be modified as

$$\Delta T_b = iK_b m \qquad (12.10)$$

$$\Delta T_f = iK_f m \qquad (12.11)$$

$$\pi = iMRT \qquad (12.12)$$

In reality, the colligative properties of electrolyte solutions are usually smaller than anticipated because at higher concentrations, electrostatic forces come into play

---

[†]Jacobus Hendricus van't Hoff (1852–1911). Dutch chemist. One of the most prominent chemists of his time, van't Hoff did significant work in thermodynamics, molecular structure and optical activity, and solution chemistry. In 1901 he received the first Nobel Prize in Chemistry.

TABLE 12.3	The van't Hoff Factor of 0.0500 M Electrolyte Solutions at 25°C	
Electrolyte	**i (Measured)**	**i (Calculated)**
Sucrose*	1.0	1.0
HCl	1.9	2.0
NaCl	1.9	2.0
MgSO₄	1.3	2.0
MgCl₂	2.7	3.0
FeCl₃	3.4	4.0

*Sucrose is a nonelectrolyte. It is listed here for comparison only.

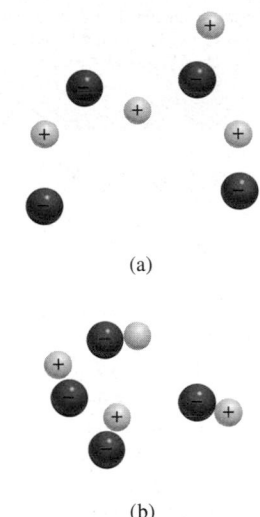

(a)

(b)

Figure 12.14 *(a) Free ions and (b) ion pairs in solution. Such an ion pair bears no net charge and therefore cannot conduct electricity in solution.*

and bring about the formation of ion pairs. An ***ion pair*** is made up of *one or more cations and one or more anions held together by electrostatic forces.* The presence of an ion pair reduces the number of particles in solution, causing a reduction in the colligative properties (Figure 12.14). Electrolytes containing multicharged ions such as Mg^{2+}, Al^{3+}, SO_4^{2-}, and PO_4^{3-} have a greater tendency to form ion pairs than electrolytes such as NaCl and KNO_3, which are made up of singly charged ions.

Table 12.3 shows the experimentally measured values of i and those calculated assuming complete dissociation. As you can see, the agreement is close but not perfect, indicating that the extent of ion-pair formation in these solutions at that concentration is appreciable.

As Example 12.12 shows, the van't Hoff factor can be determined from colligative properties measurements.

Example 12.12

The osmotic pressure of a 0.010 M potassium iodide (KI) solution at 25°C is 0.465 atm. Calculate the van't Hoff factor for KI at this concentration.

Strategy Note that KI is a strong electrolyte, so we expect it to dissociate completely in solution. If so, its osmotic pressure would be

$$2(0.010\ M)(0.0821\ \text{L}\cdot\text{atm/K}\cdot\text{mol})(298\ \text{K}) = 0.489\ \text{atm}$$

However, the measured osmotic pressure is only 0.465 atm. The smaller than predicted osmotic pressure means that there is ion-pair formation, which reduces the number of solute particles (K^+ and I^- ions) in solution.

Solution From Equation (12.12) we have

$$i = \frac{\pi}{MRT}$$

$$= \frac{0.465\ \text{atm}}{(0.010\ M)(0.0821\ \text{L}\cdot\text{atm/K}\cdot\text{mol})(298\ \text{K})}$$

$$= 1.90$$

Similar problem: 12.81.

Practice Exercise The freezing-point depression of a 0.100 m MgSO₄ solution is 0.225°C. Calculate the van't Hoff factor of MgSO₄ at this concentration.

The Chemistry in Action essay on p. 530 describes three physical techniques for obtaining the pure solvent (water) from a solution (seawater).

CHEMISTRY
in Action

Desalination

Over the centuries, scientists have sought ways of removing salts from seawater, a process called *desalination*, to augment the supply of fresh water. The ocean is an enormous and extremely complex aqueous solution. There are about 1.5×10^{21} L of seawater in the ocean, of which 3.5 percent (by mass) is dissolved material. The accompanying table lists the concentrations of seven substances that together comprise more than 99 percent of the dissolved constituents of ocean water. In an age when astronauts have landed on the moon and spectacular advances in science and medicine have been made, desalination may seem a simple enough objective. However, the technology is very costly. It is an interesting paradox that in our technological society, accomplishing something simple like desalination at a socially acceptable cost is often as difficult as achieving something complex, such as sending an astronaut to the moon.

Composition of Seawater

Ions	g/kg of Seawater
Chloride (Cl^-)	19.35
Sodium (Na^+)	10.76
Sulfate (SO_4^{2-})	2.71
Magnesium (Mg^{2+})	1.29
Calcium (Ca^{2+})	0.41
Potassium (K^+)	0.39
Bicarbonate (HCO_3^-)	0.14

Distillation

The oldest method of desalination, distillation, accounts for more than 90 percent of the approximately 500 million gallons per day capacity of the desalination systems currently in operation worldwide. The process involves vaporizing seawater and then condensing the pure water vapor. Most distillation systems use heat energy to do this. Attempts to reduce the cost of distillation include the use of solar radiation as the energy source.

A solar still for desalinating seawater.

This approach is attractive because sunshine is normally more intense in arid lands, where the need for water is also greatest. However, despite intensive research and development efforts, several engineering problems persist, and "solar stills" do not yet operate on a large scale.

Freezing

Desalination by freezing has also been under development for a number of years, but it has not yet become commercially feasible. This method is based on the fact that when an aqueous solution (in this case, seawater) freezes, the solid that separates from solution is almost pure water. Thus, ice crystals from frozen seawater at desalination plants could be rinsed off and thawed to provide usable water. The main advantage of freezing is its low energy consumption, as compared with distillation. The heat of vaporization of water is 40.79 kJ/mol, whereas that of fusion is only 6.01 kJ/mol. Some scientists have even suggested that a partial solution to the water shortage in California would be to tow icebergs from the Arctic down to the West Coast. The major disadvantages of freezing are

12.8 Colloids

The solutions discussed so far are true homogeneous mixtures. Now consider what happens if we add fine sand to a beaker of water and stir. The sand particles are suspended at first but then gradually settle to the bottom. This is an example of a heterogeneous mixture. Between these two extremes is an intermediate state called a colloidal suspension, or simply, a colloid. A **colloid** is *a dispersion of particles of one substance (the dispersed phase) throughout a dispersing medium made of another substance.* Colloidal particles are much larger than the normal solute

Pressure

Semipermeable membrane

Freshwater

Seawater

Reverse osmosis. By applying enough pressure on the solution side, freshwater can be made to flow from right to left. The semipermeable membrane allows the passage of water molecules but not of dissolved ions.

associated with the slow growth of ice crystals and with washing the salt deposits off the crystals.

Reverse Osmosis

Both distillation and freezing involve phase changes that require considerable energy. On the other hand, desalination by reverse osmosis does not involve a phase change and is economically more desirable. *Reverse osmosis* uses high pressure to force water from a more concentrated solution to a less concentrated one through a semipermeable membrane. The osmotic pressure of seawater is about 30 atm—this is the pressure that must be applied to the saline solution in order to stop the flow of water from left to right. If the pressure on the salt solution were increased beyond 30 atm, the osmotic flow would be reversed, and freshwater would actually pass from the solution through the membrane into the left compartment. Desalination by reverse osmosis is considerably cheaper than distillation and it avoids the technical difficulties associated with freezing. The main obstacle to this method is the development of a membrane that is permeable to water but not to

other dissolved substances and that can be used on a large scale for prolonged periods under high-pressure conditions. Once this problem has been solved, and present signs are encouraging, reverse osmosis could become a major desalination technique.

A small reverse-osmosis apparatus enables a person to obtain drinkable freshwater from seawater.

molecules; they range from 1×10^3 pm to 1×10^6 pm. Also, a colloidal suspension lacks the homogeneity of an ordinary solution. The dispersed phase and the dispersing medium can be gases, liquids, solids, or a combination of different phases, as shown in Table 12.4.

A number of colloids are familiar to us. An *aerosol* consists of liquid droplets or solid particles dispersed in a gas. Examples are fog and smoke. Mayonnaise, which is made by breaking oil into small droplets in water, is an example of *emulsion,* which consists of liquid droplets dispersed in another liquid. Milk of magnesia is an example of *sol,* a suspension of solid particles in a liquid.

Figure 12.15 *Three beams of white light, passing through a colloid of sulfur particles in water, change to orange, pink, and bluish-green. The colors produced depend on the size of the particles and also on the position of the viewer. The smaller the dispersed particles, the shorter (and bluer) the wavelengths.*

TABLE 12.4	Types of Colloids		
Dispersing Medium	**Dispersed Phase**	**Name**	**Example**
Gas	Liquid	Aerosol	Fog, mist
Gas	Solid	Aerosol	Smoke
Liquid	Gas	Foam	Whipped cream
Liquid	Liquid	Emulsion	Mayonnaise
Liquid	Solid	Sol	Milk of magnesia
Solid	Gas	Foam	Plastic foams
Solid	Liquid	Gel	Jelly, butter
Solid	Solid	Solid sol	Certain alloys (steel), gemstones (glass with dispersed metal)

One way to distinguish a solution from a colloid is by the *Tyndall*[†] *effect.* When a beam of light passes through a colloid, it is scattered by the dispersed phase (Figure 12.15). No such scattering is observed with ordinary solutions because the solute molecules are too small to interact with visible light. Another demonstration of the Tyndall effect is the scattering of sunlight by dust or smoke in the air (Figure 12.16).

Hydrophilic and Hydrophobic Colloids

Among the most important colloids are those in which the dispersing medium is water. Such colloids are divided into two categories called **hydrophilic,** or *water-loving,* and **hydrophobic,** or *water-fearing.* Hydrophilic colloids are usually solutions containing extremely large molecules such as proteins. In the aqueous phase, a protein like hemoglobin folds in such a way that the hydrophilic parts of the molecule, the parts that can interact favorably with water molecules by ion-dipole forces or hydrogen-bond formation, are on the outside surface (Figure 12.17).

A hydrophobic colloid normally would not be stable in water, and the particles would clump together, like droplets of oil in water merging to form a film of oil at water's surface. They can be stabilized, however, by *adsorption* of ions on their surface (Figure 12.18). (Adsorption refers to adherence onto a surface. It differs from absorption in that the latter means passage to the interior of the medium.) These adsorbed ions can interact

Figure 12.16 *Sunlight scattered by dust particles in the air.*

[†]John Tyndall (1820–1893). Irish physicist. Tyndall did important work in magnetism, and explained glacier motion.

Figure 12.17 *Hydrophilic groups on the surface of a large molecule such as protein stabilize the molecule in water. Note that all these groups can form hydrogen bonds with water.*

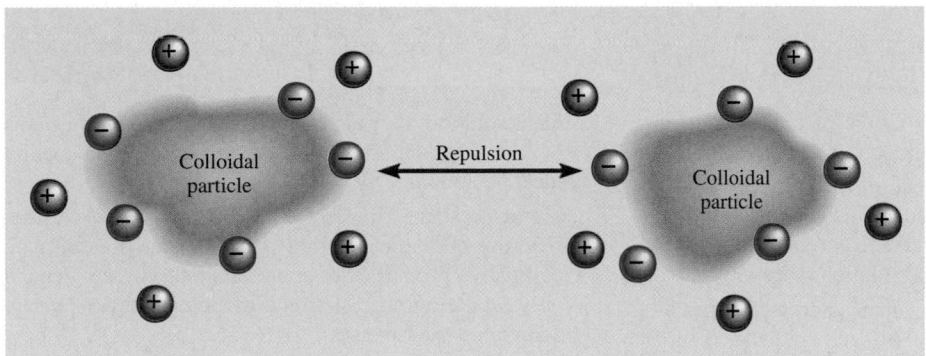

Figure 12.18 *Diagram showing the stabilization of hydrophobic colloids. Negative ions are adsorbed onto the surface and the repulsion between like charges prevents the clumping of the particles.*

with water, thus stabilizing the colloid. At the same time, the electrostatic repulsion between the particles prevents them from clumping together. Soil particles in rivers and streams are hydrophobic particles stabilized this way. When the fresh water enters the sea, the charges on the particles are neutralized by the high-salt medium, and the particles clump together to form the silt that is seen at the mouth of the river.

Another way hydrophobic colloids can be stabilized is by the presence of other hydrophilic groups on their surfaces. Consider sodium stearate, a soap molecule that has a polar head and a long hydrocarbon tail that is nonpolar (Figure 12.19). The cleansing action of soap is the result of the dual nature of the hydrophobic tail and the hydrophilic end group. The hydrocarbon tail is readily soluble in oily substances, which are also nonpolar, while the ionic—COO$^-$ group remains outside the oily surface. When enough soap molecules have surrounded an oil droplet, as shown in Figure 12.20, the entire system becomes stabilized in water because the exterior portion is now largely hydrophilic. This is how greasy substances are removed by the action of soap.

Figure 12.19 *(a) A sodium stearate molecule. (b) The simplified representation of the molecule that shows a hydrophilic head and a hydrophobic tail.*

Sodium stearate (C$_{17}$H$_{35}$COO$^-$Na$^+$)

(a)

Hydrophilic head

Hydrophobic tail

(b)

Grease

(a)

(b)

(c)

Figure 12.20 *The cleansing action of soap. (a) Grease (oily substance) is not soluble in water. (b) When soap is added to water, the nonpolar tails of soap molecules dissolve in grease. (c) Finally, the grease is removed in the form of an emulsion. Note that each oily droplet now has an ionic exterior that is hydrophilic.*

Summary of Facts and Concepts

1. Solutions are homogeneous mixtures of two or more substances, which may be solids, liquids, or gases.
2. The ease of dissolving a solute in a solvent is governed by intermolecular forces. Energy and the disorder that results when molecules of the solute and solvent mix to form a solution are the forces driving the solution process.
3. The concentration of a solution can be expressed as percent by mass, mole fraction, molarity, and molality. The choice of units depends on the circumstances.
4. Increasing temperature usually increases the solubility of solid and liquid substances and usually decreases the solubility of gases in water.
5. According to Henry's law, the solubility of a gas in a liquid is directly proportional to the partial pressure of the gas over the solution.
6. Raoult's law states that the partial pressure of a substance A over a solution is equal to the mole fraction (X_A) of A times the vapor pressure (P_A°) of pure A. An ideal solution obeys Raoult's law over the entire range of concentration. In practice, very few solutions exhibit ideal behavior.
7. Vapor-pressure lowering, boiling-point elevation, freezing-point depression, and osmotic pressure are colligative properties of solutions; that is, they depend only on the number of solute particles that are present and not on their nature.
8. In electrolyte solutions, the interaction between ions leads to the formation of ion pairs. The van't Hoff factor provides a measure of the extent of dissociation of electrolytes in solution.
9. A colloid is a dispersion of particles (about 1×10^3 pm to 1×10^6 pm) of one substance in another substance. A colloid is distinguished from a regular solution by the Tyndall effect, which is the scattering of visible light by colloidal particles. Colloids in water are classified as hydrophilic colloids and hydrophobic colloids.

Key Words

Boiling-point elevation (ΔT_b), p. 520
Colligative properties, p. 515
Colloid, p. 530
Crystallization, p. 504
Fractional crystallization, p. 512
Fractional distillation, p. 519

Freezing-point depression (ΔT_f), p. 521
Henry's law, p. 513
Hydrophilic, p. 532
Hydrophobic, p. 532
Ideal solution, p. 518
Ion pair, p. 529
Miscible, p. 506

Molality, p. 508
Nonvolatile, p. 516
Osmosis, p. 523
Osmotic pressure (π), p. 523
Percent by mass, p. 507
Raoult's law, p. 516
Saturated solution, p. 504

Semipermeable membrane, p. 523
Solvation, p. 506
Supersaturated solution, p. 504
Unsaturated solution, p. 504
van't Hoff factor (i), p. 528
Volatile, p. 518

Questions and Problems

Types of Solutions
Review Questions

12.1 Distinguish between an unsaturated solution, a saturated solution, and a supersaturated solution.

12.2 From which type of solution listed in Question 12.1 does crystallization or precipitation occur? How does a crystal differ from a precipitate?

A Molecular View of the Solution Process
Review Questions

12.3 Briefly describe the solution process at the molecular level. Use the dissolution of a solid in a liquid as an example.

12.4 Basing your answer on intermolecular force considerations, explain what "like dissolves like" means.

12.5 What is solvation? What factors influence the extent to which solvation occurs? Give two examples of solvation; include one that involves ion-dipole interaction and one in which dispersion forces come into play.

12.6 As you know, some solution processes are endothermic and others are exothermic. Provide a molecular interpretation for the difference.

12.7 Explain why the solution process invariably leads to an increase in disorder.

12.8 Describe the factors that affect the solubility of a solid in a liquid. What does it mean to say that two liquids are miscible?

Problems

12.9 Why is naphthalene ($C_{10}H_8$) more soluble than CsF in benzene?

12.10 Explain why ethanol (C_2H_5OH) is not soluble in cyclohexane (C_6H_{12}).

12.11 Arrange the following compounds in order of increasing solubility in water: O_2, LiCl, Br_2, methanol (CH_3OH).

12.12 Explain the variations in solubility in water of the alcohols listed here:

Compound	Solubility in Water (g/100 g) at 20°C
CH_3OH	∞
CH_3CH_2OH	∞
$CH_3CH_2CH_2OH$	∞
$CH_3CH_2CH_2CH_2OH$	9
$CH_3CH_2CH_2CH_2CH_2OH$	2.7

(*Note:* ∞ means that the alcohol and water are completely miscible in all proportions.)

Concentration Units

Review Questions

12.13 Define the following concentration terms and give their units: percent by mass, mole fraction, molarity, molality. Compare their advantages and disadvantages.

12.14 Outline the steps required for conversion between molarity, molality, and percent by mass.

Problems

12.15 Calculate the percent by mass of the solute in each of the following aqueous solutions: (a) 5.50 g of NaBr in 78.2 g of solution, (b) 31.0 g of KCl in 152 g of water, (c) 4.5 g of toluene in 29 g of benzene.

12.16 Calculate the amount of water (in grams) that must be added to (a) 5.00 g of urea ($(NH_2)_2CO$) in the preparation of a 16.2 percent by mass solution, and (b) 26.2 g of $MgCl_2$ in the preparation of a 1.5 percent by mass solution.

12.17 Calculate the molality of each of the following solutions: (a) 14.3 g of sucrose ($C_{12}H_{22}O_{11}$) in 676 g of water, (b) 7.20 moles of ethylene glycol ($C_2H_6O_2$) in 3546 g of water.

12.18 Calculate the molality of each of the following aqueous solutions: (a) 2.50 *M* NaCl solution (density of solution = 1.08 g/mL), (b) 48.2 percent by mass KBr solution.

12.19 Calculate the molalities of the following aqueous solutions: (a) 1.22 *M* sugar ($C_{12}H_{22}O_{11}$) solution (density of solution = 1.12 g/mL), (b) 0.87 *M* NaOH solution (density of solution = 1.04 g/mL), (c) 5.24 *M* $NaHCO_3$ solution (density of solution = 1.19 g/mL).

12.20 For dilute aqueous solutions in which the density of the solution is roughly equal to that of the pure solvent, the molarity of the solution is equal to its molality. Show that this statement is correct for a 0.010 *M* aqueous urea ($(NH_2)_2CO$) solution.

12.21 The alcohol content of hard liquor is normally given in terms of the "proof," which is defined as twice the percentage by volume of ethanol (C_2H_5OH) present. Calculate the number of grams of alcohol present in 1.00 L of 75-proof gin. The density of ethanol is 0.798 g/mL.

12.22 The concentrated sulfuric acid we use in the laboratory is 98.0 percent H_2SO_4 by mass. Calculate the molality and molarity of the acid solution. The density of the solution is 1.83 g/mL.

12.23 Calculate the molarity and the molality of an NH_3 solution made up of 30.0 g of NH_3 in 70.0 g of water. The density of the solution is 0.982 g/mL.

12.24 The density of an aqueous solution containing 10.0 percent of ethanol (C_2H_5OH) by mass is 0.984 g/mL. (a) Calculate the molality of this solution. (b) Calculate its molarity. (c) What volume of the solution would contain 0.125 mole of ethanol?

The Effect of Temperature on Solubility

Review Questions

12.25 How do the solubilities of most ionic compounds in water change with temperature? With pressure?

12.26 Describe the fractional crystallization process and its application.

Problems

12.27 A 3.20-g sample of a salt dissolves in 9.10 g of water to give a saturated solution at 25°C. What is the solubility (in g salt/100 g of H_2O) of the salt?

12.28 The solubility of KNO_3 is 155 g per 100 g of water at 75°C and 38.0 g at 25°C. What mass (in grams) of KNO_3 will crystallize out of solution if exactly 100 g of its saturated solution at 75°C is cooled to 25°C?

12.29 A 50-g sample of impure $KClO_3$ (solubility = 7.1 g per 100 g H_2O at 20°C) is contaminated with 10 percent of KCl (solubility = 25.5 g per 100 g of H_2O at 20°C). Calculate the minimum quantity of 20°C water needed to dissolve all the KCl from the sample. How much $KClO_3$ will be left after this treatment? (Assume that the solubilities are unaffected by the presence of the other compound.)

Gas Solubility

Review Questions

12.30 Discuss the factors that influence the solubility of a gas in a liquid.

12.31 What is thermal pollution? Why is it harmful to aquatic life?

12.32 What is Henry's law? Define each term in the equation, and give its units. How would you account for the law in terms of the kinetic molecular theory of gases? Give two exceptions to Henry's law.

12.33 A student is observing two beakers of water. One beaker is heated to 30°C, and the other is heated to 100°C. In each case, bubbles form in the water. Are these bubbles of the same origin? Explain.

12.34 A man bought a goldfish in a pet shop. Upon returning home, he put the goldfish in a bowl of recently boiled water that had been cooled quickly. A few minutes later the fish was found dead. Explain what happened to the fish.

Problems

12.35 A beaker of water is initially saturated with dissolved air. Explain what happens when He gas at 1 atm is bubbled through the solution for a long time.

12.36 A miner working 260 m below sea level opened a carbonated soft drink during a lunch break. To his surprise, the soft drink tasted rather "flat." Shortly afterward, the miner took an elevator to the surface. During the trip up, he could not stop belching. Why?

12.37 The solubility of CO_2 in water at 25°C and 1 atm is 0.034 mol/L. What is its solubility under atmospheric conditions? (The partial pressure of CO_2 in air is 0.0003 atm.) Assume that CO_2 obeys Henry's law.

12.38 The solubility of N_2 in blood at 37°C and at a partial pressure of 0.80 atm is 5.6×10^{-4} mol/L. A deep-sea diver breathes compressed air with the partial pressure of N_2 equal to 4.0 atm. Assume that the total volume of blood in the body is 5.0 L. Calculate the amount of N_2 gas released (in liters at 37°C and 1 atm) when the diver returns to the surface of the water, where the partial pressure of N_2 is 0.80 atm.

Colligative Properties of Nonelectrolyte Solutions
Review Questions

12.39 What are colligative properties? What is the meaning of the word "colligative" in this context?

12.40 Give two examples of (a) a volatile liquid and (b) a nonvolatile liquid.

12.41 Write the equation representing Raoult's law, and express it in words.

12.42 Use a solution of benzene in toluene to explain what is meant by an ideal solution.

12.43 Write the equations relating boiling-point elevation and freezing-point depression to the concentration of the solution. Define all the terms, and give their units.

12.44 How is vapor-pressure lowering related to a rise in the boiling point of a solution?

12.45 Use a phase diagram to show the difference in freezing points and boiling points between an aqueous urea solution and pure water.

12.46 What is osmosis? What is a semipermeable membrane?

12.47 Write the equation relating osmotic pressure to the concentration of a solution. Define all the terms and specify their units.

12.48 What does it mean when we say that the osmotic pressure of a sample of seawater is 25 atm at a certain temperature?

12.49 Explain why molality is used for boiling-point elevation and freezing-point depression calculations and molarity is used in osmotic pressure calculations.

12.50 Describe how you would use freezing-point depression and osmotic pressure measurements to determine the molar mass of a compound. Why are boiling-point elevation and vapor-pressure lowering normally not used for this purpose?

Problems

12.51 A solution is prepared by dissolving 396 g of sucrose ($C_{12}H_{22}O_{11}$) in 624 g of water. What is the vapor pressure of this solution at 30°C? (The vapor pressure of water is 31.8 mmHg at 30°C.)

12.52 How many grams of sucrose ($C_{12}H_{22}O_{11}$) must be added to 552 g of water to give a solution with a vapor pressure 2.0 mmHg less than that of pure water at 20°C? (The vapor pressure of water at 20°C is 17.5 mmHg.)

12.53 The vapor pressure of benzene is 100.0 mmHg at 26.1°C. Calculate the vapor pressure of a solution containing 24.6 g of camphor ($C_{10}H_{16}O$) dissolved in 98.5 g of benzene. (Camphor is a low-volatility solid.)

12.54 The vapor pressures of ethanol (C_2H_5OH) and 1-propanol (C_3H_7OH) at 35°C are 100 mmHg and 37.6 mmHg, respectively. Assume ideal behavior and calculate the partial pressures of ethanol and 1-propanol at 35°C over a solution of ethanol in 1-propanol, in which the mole fraction of ethanol is 0.300.

12.55 The vapor pressure of ethanol (C_2H_5OH) at 20°C is 44 mmHg, and the vapor pressure of methanol (CH_3OH) at the same temperature is 94 mmHg. A mixture of 30.0 g of methanol and 45.0 g of ethanol is prepared (and can be assumed to behave as an ideal solution). (a) Calculate the vapor pressure of methanol and ethanol above this solution at 20°C. (b) Calculate the mole fraction of methanol and ethanol in the vapor above this solution at 20°C. (c) Suggest a method for separating the two components of the solution.

12.56 How many grams of urea [$(NH_2)_2CO$] must be added to 450 g of water to give a solution with a vapor pressure 2.50 mmHg less than that of pure water at 30°C? (The vapor pressure of water at 30°C is 31.8 mmHg.)

12.57 What are the boiling point and freezing point of a 2.47 m solution of naphthalene in benzene? (The boiling point and freezing point of benzene are 80.1°C and 5.5°C, respectively.)

12.58 An aqueous solution contains the amino acid glycine (NH_2CH_2COOH). Assuming that the acid does not ionize in water, calculate the molality of the solution if it freezes at $-1.1°C$.

12.59 Pheromones are compounds secreted by the females of many insect species to attract males. One of these compounds contains 80.78 percent C, 13.56 percent H, and 5.66 percent O. A solution of 1.00 g of this pheromone in 8.50 g of benzene freezes at 3.37°C. What are the molecular formula and molar mass of the compound? (The normal freezing point of pure benzene is 5.50°C.)

12.60 The elemental analysis of an organic solid extracted from gum arabic (a gummy substance used in adhesives, inks, and pharmaceuticals) showed that it contained 40.0 percent C, 6.7 percent H, and 53.3 percent O. A solution of 0.650 g of the solid in 27.8 g of the solvent diphenyl gave a freezing-point depression of 1.56°C. Calculate the molar mass and molecular formula of the solid. (K_f for diphenyl is 8.00°C/m.)

12.61 How many liters of the antifreeze ethylene glycol [$CH_2(OH)CH_2(OH)$] would you add to a car radiator containing 6.50 L of water if the coldest winter temperature in your area is $-20°C$? Calculate the boiling point of this water-ethylene glycol mixture. (The density of ethylene glycol is 1.11 g/mL.)

12.62 A solution is prepared by condensing 4.00 L of a gas, measured at 27°C and 748 mmHg pressure, into 58.0 g of benzene. Calculate the freezing point of this solution.

12.63 The molar mass of benzoic acid (C_6H_5COOH) determined by measuring the freezing-point depression in benzene is twice what we would expect for the molecular formula, $C_7H_6O_2$. Explain this apparent anomaly.

12.64 A solution of 2.50 g of a compound having the empirical formula C_6H_5P in 25.0 g of benzene is observed to freeze at 4.3°C. Calculate the molar mass of the solute and its molecular formula.

12.65 What is the osmotic pressure (in atm) of a 1.36 M aqueous solution of urea [$(NH_2)_2CO$] at 22.0°C?

12.66 A solution containing 0.8330 g of a polymer of unknown structure in 170.0 mL of an organic solvent was found to have an osmotic pressure of 5.20 mmHg at 25°C. Determine the molar mass of the polymer.

12.67 A quantity of 7.480 g of an organic compound is dissolved in water to make 300.0 mL of solution. The solution has an osmotic pressure of 1.43 atm at 27°C. The analysis of this compound shows that it contains 41.8 percent C, 4.7 percent H, 37.3 percent O, and 16.3 percent N. Calculate the molecular formula of the compound.

12.68 A solution of 6.85 g of a carbohydrate in 100.0 g of water has a density of 1.024 g/mL and an osmotic pressure of 4.61 atm at 20.0°C. Calculate the molar mass of the carbohydrate.

Colligative Properties of Electrolyte Solutions
Review Questions

12.69 Why is the discussion of the colligative properties of electrolyte solutions more involved than that of nonelectrolyte solutions?

12.70 What are ion pairs? What effect does ion-pair formation have on the colligative properties of a solution? How does the ease of ion-pair formation depend on (a) charges on the ions, (b) size of the ions, (c) nature of the solvent (polar versus nonpolar), (d) concentration?

12.71 Indicate which compound in each of the following pairs is more likely to form ion pairs in water: (a) NaCl or Na_2SO_4, (b) $MgCl_2$ or $MgSO_4$, (c) LiBr or KBr.

12.72 What is the van't Hoff factor? What information does it provide?

Problems

12.73 Which of the following aqueous solutions has (a) the higher boiling point, (b) the higher freezing point, and (c) the lower vapor pressure: 0.35 m $CaCl_2$ or 0.90 m urea? Explain. Assume $CaCl_2$ to undergo complete dissociation.

12.74 Consider two aqueous solutions, one of sucrose ($C_{12}H_{22}O_{11}$) and the other of nitric acid (HNO_3). Both solutions freeze at $-1.5°C$. What other properties do these solutions have in common?

12.75 Arrange the following solutions in order of decreasing freezing point: 0.10 m Na_3PO_4, 0.35 m NaCl, 0.20 m $MgCl_2$, 0.15 m $C_6H_{12}O_6$, 0.15 m CH_3COOH.

12.76 Arrange the following aqueous solutions in order of decreasing freezing point, and explain your reasoning: 0.50 m HCl, 0.50 m glucose, 0.50 m acetic acid.

12.77 What are the normal freezing points and boiling points of the following solutions? (a) 21.2 g NaCl in 135 mL of water and (b) 15.4 g of urea in 66.7 mL of water

12.78 At 25°C the vapor pressure of pure water is 23.76 mmHg and that of seawater is 22.98 mmHg. Assuming that seawater contains only NaCl, estimate its molal concentration.

12.79 Both NaCl and $CaCl_2$ are used to melt ice on roads and sidewalks in winter. What advantages do these substances have over sucrose or urea in lowering the freezing point of water?

12.80 A 0.86 percent by mass solution of NaCl is called "physiological saline" because its osmotic pressure is equal to that of the solution in blood cells. Calculate the osmotic pressure of this solution at normal body temperature (37°C). Note that the density of the saline solution is 1.005 g/mL.

12.81 The osmotic pressure of 0.010 M solutions of $CaCl_2$ and urea at 25°C are 0.605 atm and 0.245 atm, respectively. Calculate the van't Hoff factor for the $CaCl_2$ solution.

12.82 Calculate the osmotic pressure of a 0.0500 M $MgSO_4$ solution at 25°C. (*Hint:* See Table 12.3.)

Colloids

Review Questions

12.83 What are colloids? Referring to Table 12.4, why is there no colloid in which both the dispersed phase and the dispersing medium are gases?

12.84 Describe how hydrophilic and hydrophobic colloids are stabilized in water.

Additional Problems

12.85 Lysozyme is an enzyme that cleaves bacterial cell walls. A sample of lysozyme extracted from egg white has a molar mass of 13,930 g. A quantity of 0.100 g of this enzyme is dissolved in 150 g of water at 25°C. Calculate the vapor-pressure lowering, the depression in freezing point, the elevation in boiling point, and the osmotic pressure of this solution. (The vapor pressure of water at 25°C is 23.76 mmHg.)

12.86 Solutions A and B have osmotic pressures of 2.4 atm and 4.6 atm, respectively, at a certain temperature. What is the osmotic pressure of a solution prepared by mixing equal volumes of A and B at the same temperature?

12.87 A cucumber placed in concentrated brine (salt water) shrivels into a pickle. Explain.

12.88 Two liquids A and B have vapor pressures of 76 mmHg and 132 mmHg, respectively, at 25°C. What is the total vapor pressure of the ideal solution made up of (a) 1.00 mole of A and 1.00 mole of B and (b) 2.00 moles of A and 5.00 moles of B?

12.89 Calculate the van't Hoff factor of Na_3PO_4 in a 0.40 m solution whose freezing point is −2.6°C.

12.90 A 262-mL sample of a sugar solution containing 1.22 g of the sugar has an osmotic pressure of 30.3 mmHg at 35°C. What is the molar mass of the sugar?

12.91 Consider the three mercury manometers shown in the top right column. One of them has 1 mL of water on top of the mercury, another has 1 mL of a

1 m urea solution on top of the mercury, and the third one has 1 mL of a 1 m NaCl solution placed on top of the mercury. Which of these solutions is in the tube labeled X, which is in Y, and which is in Z?

12.92 A forensic chemist is given a white powder for analysis. She dissolves 0.50 g of the substance in 8.0 g of benzene. The solution freezes at 3.9°C. Can the chemist conclude that the compound is cocaine ($C_{17}H_{21}NO_4$)? What assumptions are made in the analysis?

12.93 "Time-release" drugs have the advantage of releasing the drug to the body at a constant rate so that the drug concentration at any time is not too high as to have harmful side effects or too low as to be ineffective. A schematic diagram of a pill that works on this basis is shown below. Explain how it works.

12.94 A solution of 1.00 g of anhydrous aluminum chloride, $AlCl_3$, in 50.0 g of water freezes at −1.11°C. Does the molar mass determined from this freezing point agree with that calculated from the formula? Why?

12.95 Explain why reverse osmosis is (theoretically) more desirable as a desalination method than distillation or freezing. What minimum pressure must be applied to seawater at 25°C in order for reverse osmosis to occur? (Treat seawater as a 0.70 M NaCl solution.)

12.96 What masses of sodium chloride, magnesium chloride, sodium sulfate, calcium chloride, potassium chloride, and sodium bicarbonate are needed to produce 1 L of artificial seawater for an aquarium? The required ionic concentrations are $[Na^+] = 2.56\ M$, $[K^+] = 0.0090\ M$, $[Mg^{2+}] = 0.054\ M$, $[Ca^{2+}] = 0.010\ M$, $[HCO_3^-] = 0.0020\ M$, $[Cl^-] = 2.60\ M$, $[SO_4^{2-}] = 0.051\ M$.

12.97 A protein has been isolated as a salt with the formula $Na_{20}P$ (this notation means that there are 20 Na^+ ions associated with a negatively charged protein P^{20-}). The osmotic pressure of a 10.0-mL solution containing 0.225 g of the protein is 0.257 atm at 25.0°C. (a) Calculate the molar mass of the protein from these data. (b) Calculate the actual molar mass of the protein.

12.98 A nonvolatile organic compound Z was used to make up two solutions. Solution A contains 5.00 g of Z dissolved in 100 g of water, and solution B contains 2.31 g of Z dissolved in 100 g of benzene. Solution A has a vapor pressure of 754.5 mmHg at the normal boiling point of water, and solution B has the same vapor pressure at the normal boiling point of benzene. Calculate the molar mass of Z in solutions A and B and account for the difference.

12.99 Hydrogen peroxide with a concentration of 3.0 percent (3.0 g of H_2O_2 in 100 mL of solution) is sold in drugstores for use as an antiseptic. For a 10.0-mL 3.0 percent H_2O_2 solution, calculate (a) the oxygen gas produced (in liters) at STP when the compound undergoes complete decomposition and (b) the ratio of the volume of O_2 collected to the initial volume of the H_2O_2 solution.

12.100 State which of the alcohols listed in Problem 12.12 you would expect to be the best solvent for each of the following substances, and explain why: (a) I_2, (b) KBr, (c) $CH_3CH_2CH_2CH_2CH_3$.

12.101 Before a carbonated beverage bottle is sealed, it is pressurized with a mixture of air and carbon dioxide. (a) Explain the effervescence that occurs when the cap of the bottle is removed. (b) What causes the fog to form near the mouth of the bottle right after the cap is removed?

12.102 Iodine (I_2) is only sparingly soluble in water (top left photo). Yet upon the addition of iodide ions (for example, from KI), iodine is converted to the triiodide ion, which readily dissolves (top right photo):

$$I_2(s) + I^-(aq) \rightleftharpoons I_3^-(aq)$$

Describe the change in solubility of I_2 in terms of the change in intermolecular forces.

12.103 Two beakers, one containing a 50-mL aqueous 1.0 M glucose solution and the other a 50-mL aqueous 2.0 M glucose solution, are placed under a tightly sealed bell jar at room temperature. What are the volumes in these two beakers at equilibrium?

12.104 In the apparatus shown below, what will happen if the membrane is (a) permeable to both water and the Na^+ and Cl^- ions, (b) permeable to water and Na^+ ions but not to Cl^- ions, (c) permeable to water but not to Na^+ and Cl^- ions?

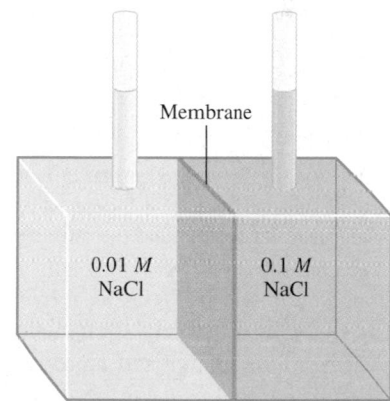

Membrane

0.01 M NaCl   0.1 M NaCl

12.105 Explain why it is essential that fluids used in intravenous injections have approximately the same osmotic pressure as blood.

12.106 Concentrated hydrochloric acid is usually available at a concentration of 37.7 percent by mass. What is its molar concentration? (The density of the solution is 1.19 g/mL.)

12.107 Explain each of the following statements: (a) The boiling point of seawater is higher than that of pure water. (b) Carbon dioxide escapes from the solution when the cap is removed from a carbonated soft-drink bottle. (c) Molal and molar concentrations of dilute aqueous solutions are approximately equal. (d) In discussing the colligative properties of a solution (other than osmotic pressure), it is preferable to express the concentration in units of molality rather than in molarity. (e) Methanol (b.p. 65°C) is useful as an antifreeze, but it should be removed from the car radiator during the summer season.

12.108 A mixture of NaCl and sucrose ($C_{12}H_{22}O_{11}$) of combined mass 10.2 g is dissolved in enough water to make up a 250 mL solution. The osmotic pressure of the solution is 7.32 atm at 23°C. Calculate the mass percent of NaCl in the mixture.

12.109 A 1.32-g sample of a mixture of cyclohexane (C_6H_{12}) and naphthalene ($C_{10}H_8$) is dissolved in 18.9 g of benzene (C_6H_6). The freezing point of the solution is 2.2°C. Calculate the mass percent of the mixture. (See Table 12.2 for constants.)

12.110 How does each of the following affect the solubility of an ionic compound? (a) lattice energy, (b) solvent (polar versus nonpolar), (c) enthalpies of hydration of cation and anion

12.111 A solution contains two volatile liquids A and B. Complete the following table, in which the symbol $\longleftrightarrow$ indicates attractive intermolecular forces.

Attractive Forces	Deviation from Raoult's Law	ΔH_{soln}
A $\longleftrightarrow$ A, B $\longleftrightarrow$ B > A $\longleftrightarrow$ B		
	Negative	
		Zero

12.112 The concentration of commercially available concentrated sulfuric acid is 98.0 percent by mass, or 18 *M*. Calculate the density and the molality of the solution.

12.113 The concentration of commercially available concentrated nitric acid is 70.0 percent by mass, or 15.9 *M*. Calculate the density and the molality of the solution.

12.114 A mixture of ethanol and 1-propanol behaves ideally at 36°C and is in equilibrium with its vapor. If the mole fraction of ethanol in the solution is 0.62, calculate its mole fraction in the vapor phase at this temperature. (The vapor pressures of pure ethanol and 1-propanol at 36°C are 108 mmHg and 40.0 mmHg, respectively.)

12.115 For ideal solutions, the volumes are additive. This means that if 5 mL of A and 5 mL of B form an ideal solution, the volume of the solution is 10 mL. Provide a molecular interpretation for this observation. When 500 mL of ethanol (C_2H_5OH) are mixed with 500 mL of water, the final volume is less than 1000 mL. Why?

12.116 Ammonia (NH_3) is very soluble in water, but nitrogen trichloride (NCl_3) is not. Explain.

12.117 Aluminum sulfate [$Al_2(SO_4)_3$] is sometimes used in municipal water treatment plants to remove undesirable particles. Explain how this process works.

12.118 Acetic acid is a weak acid that ionizes in solution as follows:

$$CH_3COOH(aq) \rightleftharpoons CH_3COO^-(aq) + H^+(aq)$$

If the freezing point of a 0.106 *m* CH_3COOH solution is −0.203°C, calculate the percent of the acid that has undergone ionization.

12.119 Making mayonnaise involves beating oil into small droplets in water, in the presence of egg yolk. What is the purpose of the egg yolk? (*Hint:* Egg yolk contains lecithins, which are molecules with a polar head and a long nonpolar hydrocarbon tail.)

12.120 Acetic acid is a polar molecule and can form hydrogen bonds with water molecules. Therefore, it has a high solubility in water. Yet acetic acid is also soluble in benzene (C_6H_6), a nonpolar solvent that lacks the ability to form hydrogen bonds. A solution of 3.8 g of CH_3COOH in 80 g C_6H_6 has a freezing point of 3.5°C. Calculate the molar mass of the solute and suggest what its structure might be. (*Hint:* Acetic acid molecules can form hydrogen bonds between themselves.)

12.121 A 2.6-L sample of water contains 192 μg of lead. Does this concentration of lead exceed the safety limit of 0.050 ppm of lead per liter of drinking water? [*Hint:* 1 μg = 1×10^{-6} g. Parts per million (ppm) is defined as (mass of component/mass of solution) $\times 10^6$.]

12.122 Fishes in the Antarctic Ocean swim in water at about −2°C. (a) To prevent their blood from freezing, what must be the concentration (in molality) of the blood? Is this a reasonable physiological concentration? (b) In recent years scientists have discovered a special type of protein in these fishes' blood which, although present in quite low concentrations (≤ 0.001 *m*), has the ability to prevent the blood from freezing. Suggest a mechanism for its action.

12.123 As we know, if a soft drink can is shaken and then opened, the drink escapes violently. However, if after shaking the can we tap it several times with a metal spoon, no such "explosion" of the drink occurs. Why?

12.124 Why are ice cubes (for example, those you see in the trays in the freezer of a refrigerator) cloudy inside?

12.125 Two beakers are placed in a closed container. Beaker A initially contains 0.15 mole of naphthalene ($C_{10}H_8$) in 100 g of benzene (C_6H_6) and beaker B initially contains 31 g of an unknown compound dissolved in 100 g of benzene. At equilibrium, beaker A is found to have lost 7.0 g of benzene.

Assuming ideal behavior, calculate the molar mass of the unknown compound. State any assumptions made.

12.126 At 27°C, the vapor pressure of pure water is 23.76 mmHg and that of an urea solution is 22.98 mmHg. Calculate the molality of solution.

12.127 An example of the positive deviation shown in Figure 12.8(a) is a solution made of acetone (CH_3COCH_3) and carbon disulfide (CS_2). (a) Draw Lewis structures of these molecules. Explain the deviation from ideal behavior in terms of intermolecular forces. (b) A solution composed of 0.60 mole of acetone and 0.40 mole of carbon disulfide has a vapor pressure of 615 mmHg at 35.2°C. What would be the vapor pressure if the solution behaved ideally? The vapor pressure of the pure solvents at the same temperature are: acetone: 349 mmHg; carbon disulfide: 501 mmHg. (c) Predict the sign of ΔH_{soln}.

12.128 Liquids A (molar mass 100 g/mol) and B (molar mass 110 g/mol) form an ideal solution. At 55°C, A has a vapor pressure of 95 mmHg and B has a vapor pressure of 42 mmHg. A solution is prepared by mixing equal masses of A and B. (a) Calculate the mole fraction of each component in the solution. (b) Calculate the partial pressures of A and B over the solution at 55°C. (c) Suppose that some of the vapor described in (b) is condensed to a liquid. Calculate the mole fraction of each component in this liquid and the vapor pressure of each component above this liquid at 55°C.

Special Problems

12.129 A very long pipe is capped at one end with a semipermeable membrane. How deep (in meters) must the pipe be immersed into the sea for fresh water to begin to pass through the membrane? Assume the water to be at 20°C and treat it as a 0.70 *M* NaCl solution. The density of seawater is 1.03 g/cm³ and the acceleration due to gravity is 9.81 m/s².

12.130 Two beakers, 1 and 2, containing 50 mL of 0.10 *M* urea and 50 mL of 0.20 *M* urea, respectively, are placed under a tightly sealed container (see Figure 12.12) at 298 K. Calculate the mole fraction of urea in the solutions at equilibrium. Assume ideal behavior.

12.131 A mixture of liquids A and B exhibits ideal behavior. At 84°C, the total vapor pressure of a solution containing 1.2 moles of A and 2.3 moles of B is 331 mmHg. Upon the addition of another mole of B to the solution, the vapor pressure increases to 347 mmHg. Calculate the vapor pressures of pure A and B at 84°C.

12.132 Using Henry's law and the ideal gas equation to prove the statement that the volume of a gas that dissolves in a given amount of solvent is *independent* of the pressure of the gas. (*Hint:* Henry's law can be modified as $n = kP$, where n is the number of moles of the gas dissolved in the solvent.)

12.133 (a) Derive the equation relating the molality (*m*) of a solution to its molarity (*M*)

$$m = \frac{M}{d - \frac{M\mathcal{M}}{1000}}$$

where *d* is the density of the solution (g/mL) and $\mathcal{M}$ is the molar mass of the solute (g/mol). (*Hint:* Start by expressing the solvent in kilograms in terms of the difference between the mass of the solution and the mass of the solute.) (b) Show that, for dilute aqueous solutions, *m* is approximately equal to *M*.

12.134 At 298 K, the osmotic pressure of a glucose solution is 10.50 atm. Calculate the freezing point of the solution. The density of the solution is 1.16 g/mL.

Answers to Practice Exercises

12.1 Carbon disulfide. **12.2** 7.44 percent. **12.3** 0.638 *m*. **12.4** 8.92 *m*. **12.5** 13.8 *m*. **12.6** 2.9×10^{-4} *M*. **12.7** 37.8 mmHg; 4.4 mmHg. **12.8** T_b: 101.3°C; T_f: −4.48°C. **12.9** 21.0 atm. **12.10** 0.066 *m* and 1.3×10^2 g/mol. **12.11** 2.60×10^4 g. **12.12** 1.21.

CHEMICAL
Mystery

The Wrong Knife[†]

Dr. Thomas Noguchi, the renowned Los Angeles coroner, was performing an autopsy on a young man in his twenties who had been stabbed to death. A Los Angeles Police Department homicide detective entered the room, carrying a brown bag that held the fatal weapon. "Do you want to take a look at it?" he asked.

"No," Dr. Noguchi said. "I'll tell *you* exactly what it looks like."

Dr. Noguchi wasn't showing off. He wanted to demonstrate an important forensic technique to the pathology residents who were observing the autopsy. The traditional method of measuring a knife was to pour barium sulfate ($BaSO_4$) solution into the wound and X ray it. Dr. Noguchi thought he had found a better way.

He lit a little Bunsen burner and melted some Wood's metal over it while the detective and the residents watched. (Wood's metal is an alloy of bismuth, lead, tin, and cadmium that has a low melting point of 71°C.) Then he selected a wound in the victim's chest above the location of the liver and poured the liquid metal into it. The metal slid down through the wound into the punctured liver. When it was cool he removed an exact mold of the tip of the murder weapon. He added the length of this tip to the distance between the liver and the skin surface of the chest. Then he said to the homicide detective, "It's a knife five and a half inches long, one inch wide and one sixteenth of an inch thick."

The detective smiled and reached into his bag. "Sorry, Dr. Noguchi." He pulled out a much smaller pocketknife, only about three inches in length.

"That's the wrong knife," Dr. Noguchi said at once.

"Oh, now, come on," the detective said. "We found the knife that killed him right at the scene."

"You don't have the murder weapon," Dr. Noguchi insisted.

The detective didn't believe him. But two days later police found a blood-stained knife in a trash can two blocks from the crime scene. That weapon was exactly five and a half inches long, one inch wide, and one sixteenth of an inch thick. And the blood on its blade matched the victim's.

It turned out to be the murder weapon. The pocketknife the police discovered at the scene had been used by the victim in self-defense. And two knives indicated a knife fight. Was it part of a gang war? The police investigated and found out that the victim was a member of a gang that was at war with another gang. By interrogating members of the rival gang, they eventually identified the murderer.

[†]Adapted with the permission of Simon & Schuster from "Coroner," by Thomas T. Noguchi, M.D., Copyright 1984 by Thomas Noguchi and Joseph DiMona.

Composition of Wood's Metal*	
Component	Melting Point (°C)
Bismuth (50%)	271
Cadmium (12.5%)	321
Lead (25%)	328
Tin (12.5%)	232

*The components are shown in percent by mass, and the melting point is that of the pure metal.

Chemical Clues

1. What is the function of the $BaSO_4$ solution as a traditional method for measuring a knife wound in a homicide victim's body? Describe a medical application of $BaSO_4$.

2. As the table shows, the melting points of the pure metals are much higher than that of Wood's metal. What phenomenon accounts for its low melting point?

3. Wood's metal is used in automatic sprinklers in the ceilings of hotels and stores. Explain how such a sprinkling system works.

4. The melting point of an alloy can be altered by changing the composition. Certain organic materials have also been developed for the same purpose. Shown below is a simplified diagram of the pop-up thermometer used in cooking turkeys. Describe how this thermometer works.

A pop-up thermometer used for cooking turkeys.

13

A hot platinum wire glows when held over a concentrated ammonia solution. The oxidation of ammonia to produce nitric oxide and water, catalyzed by platinum, is highly exothermic. This reaction is the first step toward the synthesis of nitric acid. The models show ammonia, oxygen, nitric oxide, and water molecules.

Chemical Kinetics

A LOOK AHEAD

- We begin by studying the rate of a reaction expressed in terms of the concentrations of reactants and products and how the rate is related to the stoichiometry of a reaction. (13.1)

- We then see how the rate law of a reaction is defined in terms of the rate constant and reaction order. (13.2)

- Next, we examine the relationship between reaction concentration and time for three types of reactions: zero order, first order, and second order. The half-life, which is the time required for the concentration of a reaction to decrease to half of its initial value, is useful for distinguishing between reactions of different orders. (13.3)

- We see that the rate of a reaction always increases with temperature. Activation energy, which is the minimum amount of energy required to initiate a chemical reaction, also influences the rate. (13.4)

- We examine the mechanism of a reaction in terms of the elementary steps and see that we can determine the rate law from the slowest or rate-determining step. We learn how chemists verify mechanisms by experiments. (13.5)

- Finally, we study the effect of catalyst on the rate of a reaction. We learn the characteristics of heterogeneous catalysis, homogeneous catalysis, and enzyme catalysis. (13.6)

Interactive Activity Summary

1. Interactivity: Rate Laws (13.2)
2. Animation: Activation Energy (13.4)
3. Animation: Orientation of Collision (13.4)
4. Interactivity: Mechanisms and Rates (13.5)
5. Animation: Catalysis (13.6)

In previous chapters we studied basic definitions in chemistry, and we examined the properties of gases, liquids, solids, and solutions. We have discussed molecular properties and looked at several types of reactions in some detail. In this chapter and in subsequent chapters, we will look more closely at the relationships and the laws that govern chemical reactions.

How can we predict whether or not a reaction will take place? Once started, how fast does the reaction proceed? How far will the reaction go before it stops? The laws of thermodynamics (to be discussed in Chapter 18) help us answer the first question. Chemical kinetics, the subject of this chapter, provides answers to the question about the speed of a reaction. The last question is one of many answered by the study of chemical equilibrium, which we will consider in Chapters 14, 15, 16, and 18.

13.1 The Rate of a Reaction

Chemical kinetics is *the area of chemistry concerned with the speeds, or rates, at which a chemical reaction occurs.* The word "kinetic" suggests movement or change; in Chapter 5 we defined kinetic energy as the energy available because of the motion of an object. Here kinetics refers to the rate of a reaction, or the ***reaction rate,*** which is *the change in the concentration of a reactant or a product with time (M/s).*

There are many reasons for studying the rate of a reaction. To begin with, there is intrinsic curiosity about why reactions have such vastly different rates. Some processes, such as the initial steps in vision and photosynthesis and nuclear chain reactions, take place on a time scale as short as 10^{-12} s to 10^{-6} s. Others, like the curing of cement and the conversion of graphite to diamond, take years or millions of years to complete. On a practical level, a knowledge of reaction rates is useful in drug design, in pollution control, and in food processing. Industrial chemists often place more emphasis on speeding up the rate of a reaction rather than on maximizing its yield.

We know that any reaction can be represented by the general equation

$$\text{reactants} \longrightarrow \text{products}$$

This equation tells us that during the course of a reaction, reactants are consumed while products are formed. As a result, we can follow the progress of a reaction by monitoring either the decrease in concentration of the reactants or the increase in concentration of the products.

Figure 13.1 shows the progress of a simple reaction in which A molecules are converted to B molecules:

$$A \longrightarrow B$$

The decrease in the number of A molecules and the increase in the number of B molecules with time are shown in Figure 13.2. In general, it is more convenient to express the reaction rate in terms of the change in concentration with time. Thus, for the reaction $A \longrightarrow B$ we can express the rate as

Recall that Δ denotes the difference between the final and initial state.

$$\text{rate} = -\frac{\Delta[A]}{\Delta t} \qquad \text{or} \qquad \text{rate} = \frac{\Delta[B]}{\Delta t}$$

where $\Delta[A]$ and $\Delta[B]$ are the changes in concentration (molarity) over a time period Δt. Because the concentration of A *decreases* during the time interval, $\Delta[A]$ is a negative quantity. The rate of a reaction is a positive quantity, so a minus sign is needed in the rate expression to make the rate positive. On the other hand, the rate of product

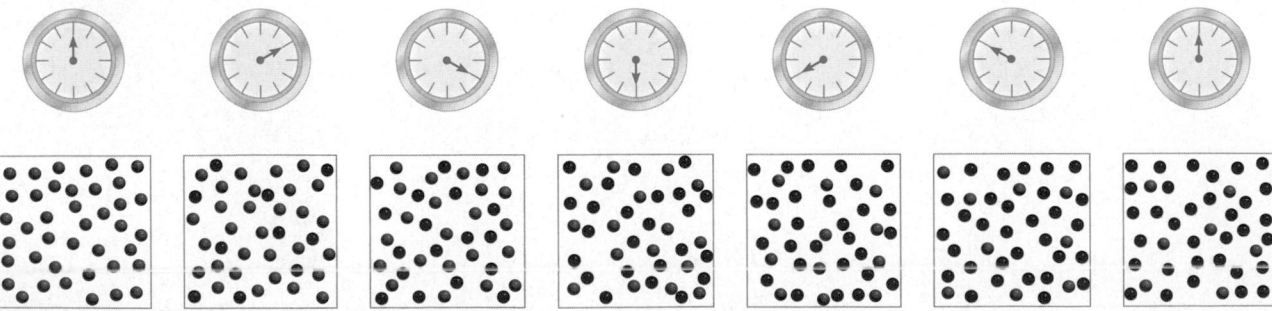

Figure 13.1 *The progress of reaction A ⟶ B at 10-s intervals over a period of 60 s. Initially, only A molecules (gray spheres) are present. As time progresses, B molecules (red spheres) are formed.*

Figure 13.2 *The rate of reaction A ⟶ B, represented as the decrease of A molecules with time and as the increase of B molecules with time.*

formation does not require a minus sign because $\Delta[B]$ is a positive quantity (the concentration of B *increases* with time). These rates are *average rates* because they are averaged over a certain time period Δt.

Our next step is to see how the rate of a reaction is obtained experimentally. By definition, we know that to determine the rate of a reaction we have to monitor the concentration of the reactant (or product) as a function of time. For reactions in solution, the concentration of a species can often be measured by spectroscopic means. If ions are involved, the change in concentration can also be detected by an electrical conductance measurement. Reactions involving gases are most conveniently followed by pressure measurements. We will consider two specific reactions for which different methods are used to measure the reaction rates.

Reaction of Molecular Bromine and Formic Acid

In aqueous solutions, molecular bromine reacts with formic acid (HCOOH) as follows:

$$Br_2(aq) + HCOOH(aq) \longrightarrow 2Br^-(aq) + 2H^+(aq) + CO_2(g)$$

Molecular bromine is reddish-brown in color. All the other species in the reaction are colorless. As the reaction progresses, the concentration of Br_2 steadily decreases and its color fades (Figure 13.3). This loss of color and hence concentration can be monitored easily with a spectrometer, which registers the amount of visible light absorbed by bromine (Figure 13.4).

Figure 13.3 *From left to right: The decrease in bromine concentration as time elapses shows up as a loss of color.*

Figure 13.4 *Plot of absorption of bromine versus wavelength. The maximum absorption of visible light by bromine occurs at 393 nm. As the reaction progresses, the absorption, which is proportional to [Br₂], decreases with time, indicating a depletion in bromine.*

Measuring the change (decrease) in bromine concentration at some initial time and then at some final time enables us to determine the average rate of the reaction during that interval:

$$\text{average rate} = -\frac{\Delta[\text{Br}_2]}{\Delta t}$$

$$= -\frac{[\text{Br}_2]_{\text{final}} - [\text{Br}_2]_{\text{initial}}}{t_{\text{final}} - t_{\text{initial}}}$$

Using the data provided in Table 13.1 we can calculate the average rate over the first 50-s time interval as follows:

$$\text{average rate} = -\frac{(0.0101 - 0.0120)\ M}{50.0\ \text{s}} = 3.80 \times 10^{-5}\ M/\text{s}$$

If we had chosen the first 100 s as our time interval, the average rate would then be given by:

$$\text{average rate} = -\frac{(0.00846 - 0.0120)\ M}{100.0\ \text{s}} = 3.54 \times 10^{-5}\ M/\text{s}$$

These calculations demonstrate that the average rate of the reaction depends on the time interval we choose.

By calculating the average reaction rate over shorter and shorter intervals, we can obtain the rate for a specific instant in time, which gives us the *instantaneous rate* of the reaction at that time. Figure 13.5 shows the plot of [Br$_2$] versus time, based on the data shown in Table 13.1. Graphically, the instantaneous rate at 100 s after the start of the reaction, say, is given by the slope of the tangent to the curve at that instant. The instantaneous rate at any other time can be determined in a similar manner. Note that the instantaneous rate determined in this way will always have the same value for the same concentrations of reactants, as long as the temperature is kept constant. We do not need to be concerned with what time interval to use. Unless otherwise stated, we will refer to the instantaneous rate merely as "the rate."

The following travel analogy helps to distinguish between average rate and instantaneous rate. The distance by car from San Francisco to Los Angeles is 512 miles along

Figure 13.5 *The instantaneous rates of the reaction between molecular bromine and formic acid at t = 100 s, 200 s, and 300 s are given by the slopes of the tangents at these times.*

TABLE 13.1	Rates of the Reaction Between Molecular Bromine and Formic Acid at 25°C		
Time (s)	[Br$_2$] (M)	Rate (M/s)	$k = \dfrac{\text{rate}}{[\text{Br}_2]}$ (s^{-1})
0.0	0.0120	4.20×10^{-5}	3.50×10^{-3}
50.0	0.0101	3.52×10^{-5}	3.49×10^{-3}
100.0	0.00846	2.96×10^{-5}	3.50×10^{-3}
150.0	0.00710	2.49×10^{-5}	3.51×10^{-3}
200.0	0.00596	2.09×10^{-5}	3.51×10^{-3}
250.0	0.00500	1.75×10^{-5}	3.50×10^{-3}
300.0	0.00420	1.48×10^{-5}	3.52×10^{-3}
350.0	0.00353	1.23×10^{-5}	3.48×10^{-3}
400.0	0.00296	1.04×10^{-5}	3.51×10^{-3}

a certain route. If it takes a person 11.4 hours to go from one city to the other, the average speed is 512 miles/11.4 hours or 44.9 mph. But if the car is traveling at 55.3 mph 3 hours and 26 minutes after departure, then the instantaneous speed of the car is 55.3 mph. Note that the speed of the car in our example can increase or decrease during the trip, but the instantaneous rate of a reaction must always decrease with time.

The rate of the bromine-formic acid reaction also depends on the concentration of formic acid. However, by adding a large excess of formic acid to the reaction mixture we can ensure that the concentration of formic acid remains virtually constant throughout the course of the reaction. Under this condition the change in the amount of formic acid present in solution has no effect on the measured rate.

Let's consider the effect that the bromine concentration has on the rate of reaction. Look at the data in Table 13.1. Compare the concentration of Br$_2$ and the reaction rate at $t = 50$ s and $t = 250$ s. At $t = 50$ s, the bromine concentration is 0.0101 M and the rate of reaction is 3.52×10^{-5} M/s. At $t = 250$ s, the bromine concentration is 0.00500 M and the rate of reaction is 1.75×10^{-5} M/s. The concentration at $t = 50$ s is double the concentration at $t = 250$ s (0.0101 M versus 0.00500 M), and the rate of reaction at $t = 50$ s is double the rate at $t = 250$ s (3.52×10^{-5} M/s versus 1.75×10^{-5} M/s). We see that as the concentration of bromine is doubled, the rate of reaction also doubles. Thus, the rate is directly proportional to the Br$_2$ concentration, that is

$$\text{rate} \propto [\text{Br}_2]$$
$$= k[\text{Br}_2]$$

where the term k is known as the **rate constant,** *a constant of proportionality between the reaction rate and the concentration of reactant.* This direct proportionality between Br$_2$ concentration and rate is also supported by plotting the data.

Figure 13.6 is a plot of the rate versus Br$_2$ concentration. The fact that this graph is a straight line shows that the rate is directly proportional to the concentration; the higher the concentration, the higher the rate. Rearranging the last equation gives

$$k = \frac{\text{rate}}{[\text{Br}_2]}$$

Because reaction rate has the units M/s, and [Br$_2$] is in M, the unit of k is 1/s, or s^{-1} in this case. It is important to understand that k is *not* affected by the concentration

As we will see, for a given reaction, k is affected only by a change in temperature.

Figure 13.6 *Plot of rate versus molecular bromine concentration for the reaction between molecular bromine and formic acid. The straight-line relationship shows that the rate of reaction is directly proportional to the molecular bromine concentration.*

Figure 13.7 *The rate of hydrogen peroxide decomposition can be measured with a manometer, which shows the increase in the oxygen gas pressure with time. The arrows show the mercury levels in the U tube.*

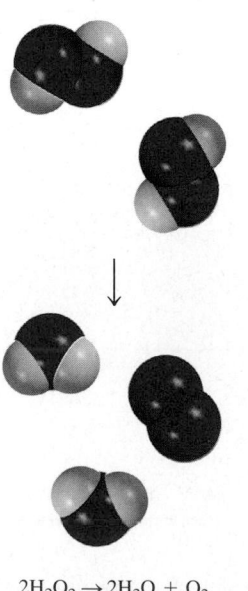

$2H_2O_2 \rightarrow 2H_2O + O_2$

of Br_2. To be sure, the rate is greater at a higher concentration and smaller at a lower concentration of Br_2, but the *ratio* of rate/$[Br_2]$ remains the same provided the temperature does not change.

From Table 13.1 we can calculate the rate constant for the reaction. Taking the data for $t = 50$ s, we write

$$k = \frac{\text{rate}}{[Br_2]}$$
$$= \frac{3.52 \times 10^{-5}\ M/s}{0.0101\ M} = 3.49 \times 10^{-3}\ s^{-1}$$

We can use the data for any t to calculate k. The slight variations in the values of k listed in Table 13.1 are due to experimental deviations in rate measurements.

Decomposition of Hydrogen Peroxide

If one of the products or reactants is a gas, we can use a manometer to find the reaction rate. Consider the decomposition of hydrogen peroxide at 20°C:

$$2H_2O_2(aq) \longrightarrow 2H_2O(l) + O_2(g)$$

In this case, the rate of decomposition can be determined by monitoring the rate of oxygen evolution with a manometer (Figure 13.7). The oxygen pressure can be readily converted to concentration by using the ideal gas equation:

$$PV = nRT$$

or

$$P = \frac{n}{V}RT = [O_2]RT$$

where n/V gives the molarity of oxygen gas. Rearranging the equation, we get

$$[O_2] = \frac{1}{RT}P$$

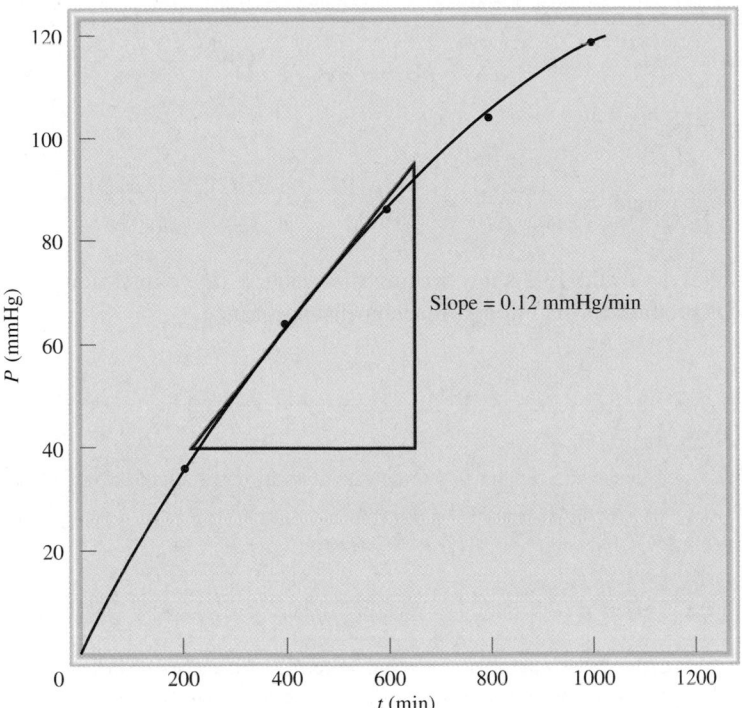

Figure 13.8 *The instantaneous rate for the decomposition of hydrogen peroxide at 400 min is given by the slope of the tangent multiplied by 1/RT.*

The reaction rate, which is given by the rate of oxygen production, can now be written as

$$\text{rate} = \frac{\Delta[O_2]}{\Delta t} = \frac{1}{RT}\frac{\Delta P}{\Delta t}$$

Figure 13.8 shows the increase in oxygen pressure with time and the determination of an instantaneous rate at 400 min. To express the rate in the normal units of *M*/s, we convert mmHg/min to atm/s, then multiply the slope of the tangent ($\Delta P/\Delta t$) by 1/*RT*, as shown in the above equation.

Reaction Rates and Stoichiometry

We have seen that for stoichiometrically simple reactions of the type A ⟶ B, the rate can be either expressed in terms of the decrease in reactant concentration with time, $-\Delta[A]/\Delta t$, or the increase in product concentration with time, $\Delta[B]/\Delta t$. For more complex reactions, we must be careful in writing the rate expressions. Consider, for example, the reaction

$$2A \longrightarrow B$$

Two moles of A disappear for each mole of B that forms—that is, the rate of disappearance of A is twice as fast as the rate of appearance of B. We write the rate as either

$$\text{rate} = -\frac{1}{2}\frac{\Delta[A]}{\Delta t} \qquad \text{or} \qquad \text{rate} = \frac{\Delta[B]}{\Delta t}$$

In general, for the reaction

$$aA + bB \longrightarrow cC + dD$$

the rate is given by

$$\text{rate} = -\frac{1}{a}\frac{\Delta[A]}{\Delta t} = -\frac{1}{b}\frac{\Delta[B]}{\Delta t} = \frac{1}{c}\frac{\Delta[C]}{\Delta t} = \frac{1}{d}\frac{\Delta[D]}{\Delta t}$$

Examples 13.1 and 13.2 show writing the reaction rate expressions and calculating rates of product formation and reactant disappearance.

Example 13.1

Write the rate expressions for the following reactions in terms of the disappearance of the reactants and the appearance of the products:

(a) $I^-(aq) + OCl^-(aq) \longrightarrow Cl^-(aq) + OI^-(aq)$

(b) $3O_2(g) \longrightarrow 2O_3(g)$

(c) $4NH_3(g) + 5O_2(g) \longrightarrow 4NO(g) + 6H_2O(g)$

Strategy To express the rate of the reaction in terms of the change in concentration of a reactant or product with time, we need to use the proper sign (minus or plus) and the reciprocal of the stoichiometric coefficient.

Solution (a) Because each of the stoichiometric coefficients equals 1,

$$\text{rate} = -\frac{\Delta[I^-]}{\Delta t} = -\frac{\Delta[OCl^-]}{\Delta t} = \frac{\Delta[Cl^-]}{\Delta t} = \frac{\Delta[OI^-]}{\Delta t}$$

(b) Here the coefficients are 3 and 2, so

$$\text{rate} = -\frac{1}{3}\frac{\Delta[O_2]}{\Delta t} = \frac{1}{2}\frac{\Delta[O_3]}{\Delta t}$$

(c) In this reaction

$$\text{rate} = -\frac{1}{4}\frac{\Delta[NH_3]}{\Delta t} = -\frac{1}{5}\frac{\Delta[O_2]}{\Delta t} = \frac{1}{4}\frac{\Delta[NO]}{\Delta t} = \frac{1}{6}\frac{\Delta[H_2O]}{\Delta t}$$

Similar problems: 13.5, 13.6.

Practice Exercise Write the rate expression for the following reaction:

$$CH_4(g) + 2O_2(g) \longrightarrow CO_2(g) + 2H_2O(g)$$

Example 13.2

Consider the reaction

$$4NO_2(g) + O_2(g) \longrightarrow 2N_2O_5(g)$$

Suppose that, at a particular moment during the reaction, molecular oxygen is reacting at the rate of 0.024 M/s. (a) At what rate is N_2O_5 being formed? (b) At what rate is NO_2 reacting?

(Continued)

Strategy To calculate the rate of formation of N_2O_5 and disappearance of NO_2, we need to express the rate of the reaction in terms of the stoichiometric coefficients as in Example 13.1:

$$\text{rate} = -\frac{1}{4}\frac{\Delta[NO_2]}{\Delta t} = -\frac{\Delta[O_2]}{\Delta t} = \frac{1}{2}\frac{\Delta[N_2O_5]}{\Delta t}$$

We are given

$$\frac{\Delta[O_2]}{\Delta t} = -0.024 \; M/s$$

where the minus sign shows that the concentration of O_2 is decreasing with time.

Solution (a) From the preceding rate expression we have

$$-\frac{\Delta[O_2]}{\Delta t} = \frac{1}{2}\frac{\Delta[N_2O_5]}{\Delta t}$$

Therefore,

$$\frac{\Delta[N_2O_5]}{\Delta t} = -2(-0.024 \; M/s) = 0.048 \; M/s$$

(b) Here we have

$$-\frac{1}{4}\frac{\Delta[NO_2]}{\Delta t} = -\frac{\Delta[O_2]}{\Delta t}$$

so

$$\frac{\Delta[NO_2]}{\Delta t} = 4(-0.024 \; M/s) = -0.096 \; M/s$$

Similar problems: 13.7, 13.8.

Practice Exercise Consider the reaction

$$4PH_3(g) \longrightarrow P_4(g) + 6H_2(g)$$

Suppose that, at a particular moment during the reaction, molecular hydrogen is being formed at the rate of 0.078 M/s. (a) At what rate is P_4 being formed? (b) At what rate is PH_3 reacting?

13.2 The Rate Law

So far we have learned that the rate of a reaction is proportional to the concentration of reactants and that the proportionality constant k is called the rate constant. The ***rate law*** *expresses the relationship of the rate of a reaction to the rate constant and the concentrations of the reactants raised to some powers.* For the general reaction

$$aA + bB \longrightarrow cC + dD$$

the rate law takes the form

$$\text{rate} = k[A]^x[B]^y \tag{13.1}$$

where x and y are numbers that must be determined experimentally. Note that, in general, x and y are *not* equal to the stoichiometric coefficients a and b. When we know

Interactivity:
Rate Laws
ARIS, Interactives

the values of x, y, and k, we can use Equation (13.1) to calculate the rate of the reaction, given the concentrations of A and B.

The exponents x and y specify the relationships between the concentrations of reactants A and B and the reaction rate. Added together, they give us the overall **reaction order,** defined as *the sum of the powers to which all reactant concentrations appearing in the rate law are raised.* For Equation (13.1) the overall reaction order is $x + y$. Alternatively, we can say that the reaction is xth order in A, yth order in B, and $(x + y)$th order overall.

To see how to determine the rate law of a reaction, let us consider the reaction between fluorine and chlorine dioxide:

$$F_2(g) + 2ClO_2(g) \longrightarrow 2FClO_2(g)$$

One way to study the effect of reactant concentration on reaction rate is to determine how the *initial rate* depends on the starting concentrations. It is preferable to measure the initial rates because as the reaction proceeds, the concentrations of the reactants decrease and it may become difficult to measure the changes accurately. Also, there may be a reverse reaction of the type

$$\text{products} \longrightarrow \text{reactants}$$

which would introduce error into the rate measurement. Both of these complications are virtually absent during the early stages of the reaction.

Table 13.2 shows three rate measurements for the formation of $FClO_2$. Looking at entries 1 and 3, we see that as we double $[F_2]$ while holding $[ClO_2]$ constant, the reaction rate doubles. Thus, the rate is directly proportional to $[F_2]$. Similarly, the data in entries 1 and 2 show that as we quadruple $[ClO_2]$ at constant $[F_2]$, the rate increases by four times, so that the rate is also directly proportional to $[ClO_2]$. We can summarize our observations by writing the rate law as

$$\text{rate} = k[F_2][ClO_2]$$

Because both $[F_2]$ and $[ClO_2]$ are raised to the first power, the reaction is first order in F_2, first order in ClO_2, and $(1 + 1)$ or second order overall. Note that $[ClO_2]$ is raised to the power of 1 whereas its stoichiometric coefficient in the overall equation is 2. The equality of reaction order (first) and stoichiometric coefficient (1) for F_2 is coincidental in this case.

From the reactant concentrations and the initial rate, we can also calculate the rate constant. Using the first entry of data in Table 13.2, we can write

$$\begin{aligned} k &= \frac{\text{rate}}{[F_2][ClO_2]} \\ &= \frac{1.2 \times 10^{-3}\,M/s}{(0.10\,M)(0.010\,M)} \\ &= 1.2/M \cdot s \end{aligned}$$

$F_2 + 2ClO_2 \rightarrow 2FClO_2$

TABLE 13.2	Rate Data for the Reaction Between F_2 and ClO_2	
$[F_2]$ (M)	$[ClO_2]$ (M)	Initial Rate (M/s)
1. 0.10	0.010	1.2×10^{-3}
2. 0.10	0.040	4.8×10^{-3}
3. 0.20	0.010	2.4×10^{-3}

Reaction order enables us to understand how the reaction depends on reactant concentrations. Suppose, for example, that for the general reaction $a\text{A} + b\text{B} \longrightarrow c\text{C} + d\text{D}$ we have $x = 1$ and $y = 2$. The rate law for the reaction is [see Equation (13.1)]

$$\text{rate} = k[\text{A}][\text{B}]^2$$

This reaction is first order in A, second order in B, and third order overall ($1 + 2 = 3$). Let us assume that initially $[\text{A}] = 1.0\ M$ and $[\text{B}] = 1.0\ M$. The rate law tells us that if we double the concentration of A from $1.0\ M$ to $2.0\ M$ at constant $[\text{B}]$, we also double the reaction rate:

for $[\text{A}] = 1.0\ M$ $\qquad\qquad$ $\text{rate}_1 = k(1.0\ M)(1.0\ M)^2$
$\qquad\qquad\qquad\qquad\qquad\qquad\ = k(1.0\ M^3)$

for $[\text{A}] = 2.0\ M$ $\qquad\qquad$ $\text{rate}_2 = k(2.0\ M)(1.0\ M)^2$
$\qquad\qquad\qquad\qquad\qquad\qquad\ = k(2.0\ M^3)$

Hence, $\qquad\qquad\qquad\qquad$ $\text{rate}_2 = 2(\text{rate}_1)$

On the other hand, if we double the concentration of B from $1.0\ M$ to $2.0\ M$ at constant $[\text{A}] = 1\ M$, the rate will increase by a factor of 4 because of the power 2 in the exponent:

for $[\text{B}] = 1.0\ M$ $\qquad\qquad$ $\text{rate}_1 = k(1.0\ M)(1.0\ M)^2$
$\qquad\qquad\qquad\qquad\qquad\qquad\ = k(1.0\ M^3)$

for $[\text{B}] = 2.0\ M$ $\qquad\qquad$ $\text{rate}_2 = k(1.0\ M)(2.0\ M)^2$
$\qquad\qquad\qquad\qquad\qquad\qquad\ = k(4.0\ M^3)$

Hence, $\qquad\qquad\qquad\qquad$ $\text{rate}_2 = 4(\text{rate}_1)$

If, for a certain reaction, $x = 0$ and $y = 1$, then the rate law is

$$\text{rate} = k[\text{A}]^0[\text{B}]$$
$$= k[\text{B}]$$

This reaction is zero order in A, first order in B, and first order overall. The exponent zero tells us that the rate of this reaction is *independent* of the concentration of A. Note that reaction order can also be a fraction.

The following points summarize our discussion of the rate law:

1. Rate laws are always determined experimentally. From the concentrations of reactants and the initial reaction rates we can determine the reaction order and then the rate constant of the reaction.

2. Reaction order is always defined in terms of reactant (not product) concentrations.

3. The order of a reactant is not related to the stoichiometric coefficient of the reactant in the overall balanced equation.

Example 13.3 illustrates the procedure for determining the rate law of a reaction.

Example 13.3

The reaction of nitric oxide with hydrogen at 1280°C is

$$2\text{NO}(g) + 2\text{H}_2(g) \longrightarrow \text{N}_2(g) + 2\text{H}_2\text{O}(g)$$

(Continued)

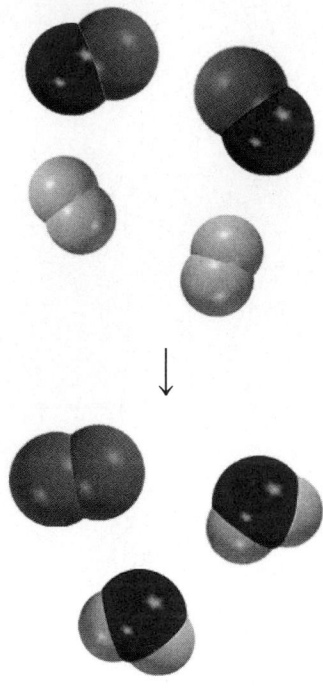

$$2NO + 2H_2 \longrightarrow N_2 + 2H_2O$$

From the following data collected at this temperature, determine (a) the rate law, (b) the rate constant, and (c) the rate of the reaction when $[NO] = 12.0 \times 10^{-3}\ M$ and $[H_2] = 6.0 \times 10^{-3}\ M$.

Experiment	[NO] (M)	[H₂] (M)	Initial Rate (M/s)
1	5.0×10^{-3}	2.0×10^{-3}	1.3×10^{-5}
2	10.0×10^{-3}	2.0×10^{-3}	5.0×10^{-5}
3	10.0×10^{-3}	4.0×10^{-3}	10.0×10^{-5}

Strategy We are given a set of concentration and reaction rate data and asked to determine the rate law and the rate constant. We assume that the rate law takes the form

$$rate = k[NO]^x[H_2]^y$$

How do we use the data to determine x and y? Once the orders of the reactants are known, we can calculate k from any set of rate and concentrations. Finally, the rate law enables us to calculate the rate at any concentrations of NO and H_2.

Solution (a) Experiments 1 and 2 show that when we double the concentration of NO at constant concentration of H_2, the rate quadruples. Taking the ratio of the rates from these two experiments

$$\frac{rate_2}{rate_1} = \frac{5.0 \times 10^{-5}\ M/s}{1.3 \times 10^{-5}\ M/s} \approx 4 = \frac{k(10.0 \times 10^{-3}\ M)^x(2.0 \times 10^{-3}\ M)^y}{k(5.0 \times 10^{-3}\ M)^x(2.0 \times 10^{-3}\ M)^y}$$

Therefore,

$$\frac{(10.0 \times 10^{-3}\ M)^x}{(5.0 \times 10^{-3}\ M)^x} = 2^x = 4$$

or $x = 2$, that is, the reaction is second order in NO. Experiments 2 and 3 indicate that doubling $[H_2]$ at constant [NO] doubles the rate. Here we write the ratio as

$$\frac{rate_3}{rate_2} = \frac{10.0 \times 10^{-5}\ M/s}{5.0 \times 10^{-5}\ M/s} = 2 = \frac{k(10.0 \times 10^{-3}\ M)^x(4.0 \times 10^{-3}\ M)^y}{k(10.0 \times 10^{-3}\ M)^x(2.0 \times 10^{-3}\ M)^y}$$

Therefore,

$$\frac{(4.0 \times 10^{-3}\ M)^y}{(2.0 \times 10^{-3}\ M)^y} = 2^y = 2$$

or $y = 1$, that is, the reaction is first order in H_2. Hence the rate law is given by

$$rate = k[NO]^2[H_2]$$

which shows that it is a $(2 + 1)$ or third-order reaction overall.

(b) The rate constant k can be calculated using the data from any one of the experiments. Rearranging the rate law, we get

$$k = \frac{rate}{[NO]^2[H_2]}$$

(Continued)

The data from experiment 2 give us

$$k = \frac{5.0 \times 10^{-5}\,M/s}{(10.0 \times 10^{-3}\,M)^2(2.0 \times 10^{-3}\,M)}$$
$$= 2.5 \times 10^{2}/M^2 \cdot s$$

(c) Using the known rate constant and concentrations of NO and H_2, we write

$$\text{rate} = (2.5 \times 10^{2}/M^2 \cdot s)(12.0 \times 10^{-3}\,M)^2(6.0 \times 10^{-3}\,M)$$
$$= 2.2 \times 10^{-4}\,M/s$$

Comment Note that the reaction is first order in H_2, whereas the stoichiometric coefficient for H_2 in the balanced equation is 2. The order of a reactant is not related to the stoichiometric coefficient of the reactant in the overall balanced equation.

Similar problem: 13.17.

Practice Exercise The reaction of peroxydisulfate ion ($S_2O_8^{2-}$) with iodide ion (I^-) is

$$S_2O_8^{2-}(aq) + 3I^-(aq) \longrightarrow 2SO_4^{2-}(aq) + I_3^-(aq)$$

From the following data collected at a certain temperature, determine the rate law and calculate the rate constant.

Experiment	$[S_2O_8^{2-}]$ (M)	$[I^-]$ (M)	Initial Rate (M/s)
1	0.080	0.034	2.2×10^{-4}
2	0.080	0.017	1.1×10^{-4}
3	0.16	0.017	2.2×10^{-4}

13.3 The Relation Between Reactant Concentration and Time

Rate law expressions enable us to calculate the rate of a reaction from the rate constant and reactant concentrations. The rate laws can also be used to determine the concentrations of reactants at any time during the course of a reaction. We will illustrate this application by first considering two of the most common rate laws—those applying to reactions that are first order overall and those applying to reactions that are second order overall.

First-Order Reactions

A *first-order reaction* is *a reaction whose rate depends on the reactant concentration raised to the first power.* In a first-order reaction of the type

$$A \longrightarrow \text{product}$$

the rate is

$$\text{rate} = -\frac{\Delta[A]}{\Delta t}$$

From the rate law we also know that

$$\text{rate} = k[A]$$

To obtain the units of k for this rate law, we write

$$k = \frac{\text{rate}}{[\text{A}]} = \frac{M/\text{s}}{M} = 1/\text{s or s}^{-1}$$

Combining the first two equations for the rate we get

$$-\frac{\Delta[\text{A}]}{\Delta t} = k[\text{A}] \tag{13.2}$$

Using calculus, we can show from Equation (13.2) that

$$\ln \frac{[\text{A}]_t}{[\text{A}]_0} = -kt \tag{13.3}$$

In differential form, Equation (13.2) becomes

$$-\frac{d[\text{A}]}{dt} = k[\text{A}]$$

Rearranging, we get

$$-\frac{d[\text{A}]}{[\text{A}]} = -k\,dt$$

Integrating between $t = 0$ and $t = t$ gives

$$\int_{[\text{A}]_0}^{[\text{A}]_t} \frac{d[\text{A}]}{[\text{A}]} = -k \int_0^t dt$$

$$\ln [\text{A}]_t - \ln [\text{A}]_0 = -kt$$

or

$$\ln \frac{[\text{A}]_t}{[\text{A}]_0} = -kt$$

where ln is the natural logarithm, and $[\text{A}]_0$ and $[\text{A}]_t$ are the concentrations of A at times $t = 0$ and $t = t$, respectively. It should be understood that $t = 0$ need not correspond to the beginning of the experiment; it can be any time when we choose to start monitoring the change in the concentration of A.

Equation (13.3) can be rearranged as follows:

$$\ln [\text{A}]_t = -kt + \ln [\text{A}]_0 \tag{13.4}$$

Equation (13.4) has the form of the linear equation $y = mx + b$, in which m is the slope of the line that is the graph of the equation:

$$
\begin{array}{ccccc}
\ln [\text{A}]_t & = & (-k)(t) & + & \ln [\text{A}]_0 \\
\updownarrow & & \updownarrow \quad \updownarrow & & \updownarrow \\
y & = & m \quad x & + & b
\end{array}
$$

Consider Figure 13.9. As we would expect during the course of a reaction, the concentration of the reactant A decreases with time [Figure 13.9(a)]. For a first-order reaction, if we plot $\ln [\text{A}]_t$ versus time (y versus x), we obtain a straight line with a slope equal to $-k$ and a y intercept equal to $\ln [\text{A}]_0$ [Figure 13.9(b)]. Thus, we can calculate the rate constant from the slope of this plot.

There are many first-order reactions. An example is the decomposition of ethane (C_2H_6) into highly reactive fragments called methyl radicals (CH_3):

$$C_2H_6 \longrightarrow 2CH_3$$

Figure 13.9 *First-order reaction characteristics: (a) Decrease of reactant concentration with time; (b) A plot of ln $[\text{A}]_t$ versus t. The slope of the line is equal to $-k$.*

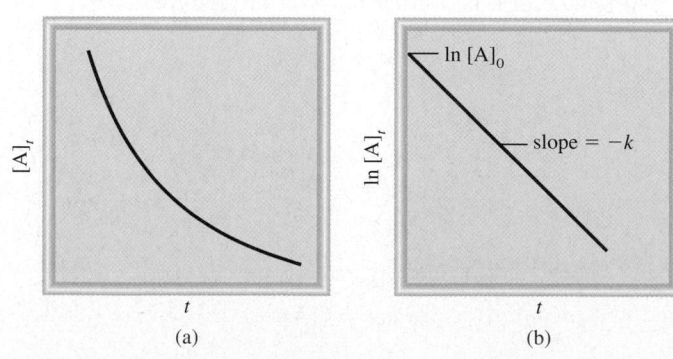

The decomposition of N_2O_5 is also a first-order reaction

$$2N_2O_5(g) \longrightarrow 4NO_2(g) + O_2(g)$$

In Example 13.4 we apply Equation (13.3) to an organic reaction.

Example 13.4

The conversion of cyclopropane to propene in the gas phase is a first-order reaction with a rate constant of 6.7×10^{-4} s^{-1} at 500°C.

$$
\begin{array}{c}
\quad CH_2 \\
\diagup \quad \diagdown \\
CH_2{-}CH_2 \quad \longrightarrow \quad CH_3{-}CH{=}CH_2 \\
\text{cyclopropane} \qquad\qquad \text{propene}
\end{array}
$$

(a) If the initial concentration of cyclopropane was 0.25 M, what is the concentration after 8.8 min? (b) How long (in minutes) will it take for the concentration of cyclopropane to decrease from 0.25 M to 0.15 M? (c) How long (in minutes) will it take to convert 74 percent of the starting material?

Strategy The relationship between the concentrations of a reactant at different times in a first-order reaction is given by Equation (13.3) or (13.4). In (a) we are given $[A]_0 =$ 0.25 M and asked for $[A]_t$ after 8.8 min. In (b) we are asked to calculate the time it takes for cyclopropane to decrease in concentration from 0.25 M to 0.15 M. No concentration values are given for (c). However, if initially we have 100 percent of the compound and 74 percent has reacted, then what is left must be $(100\% - 74\%)$, or 26%. Thus, the ratio of the percentages will be equal to the ratio of the actual concentrations; that is, $[A]_t/[A]_0 = 26\%/100\%$, or 0.26/1.00.

Solution (a) In applying Equation (13.4), we note that because k is given in units of s^{-1}, we must first convert 8.8 min to seconds:

$$8.8 \text{ min} \times \frac{60 \text{ s}}{1 \text{ min}} = 528 \text{ s}$$

We write

$$
\begin{aligned}
\ln [A]_t &= -kt + \ln [A]_0 \\
&= -(6.7 \times 10^{-4} \text{ s}^{-1})(528 \text{ s}) + \ln (0.25) \\
&= -1.74
\end{aligned}
$$

Hence, $[A]_t = e^{-1.74} = \boxed{0.18 \ M}$

Note that in the $\ln [A]_0$ term, $[A]_0$ is expressed as a dimensionless quantity (0.25) because we cannot take the logarithm of units.

(b) Using Equation (13.3),

$$\ln \frac{0.15 \ M}{0.25 \ M} = -(6.7 \times 10^{-4} \text{ s}^{-1})t$$

$$t = 7.6 \times 10^2 \text{ s} \times \frac{1 \text{ min}}{60 \text{ s}}$$

$$= \boxed{13 \text{ min}}$$

(Continued)

(c) From Equation (13.3),

$$\ln \frac{0.26}{1.00} = -(6.7 \times 10^{-4} \, \text{s}^{-1})t$$

$$t = 2.0 \times 10^3 \, \text{s} \times \frac{1 \, \text{min}}{60 \, \text{s}} = 33 \, \text{min}$$

Similar problem: 13.86.

Practice Exercise The reaction $2A \longrightarrow B$ is first order in A with a rate constant of $2.8 \times 10^{-2} \, \text{s}^{-1}$ at 80°C. How long (in seconds) will it take for A to decrease from 0.88 M to 0.14 M?

N_2O_5

N$_2$O$_5$ decomposes to give NO$_2$ (brown color).

Now let us determine graphically the order and rate constant of the decomposition of nitrogen pentoxide in carbon tetrachloride (CCl$_4$) solvent at 45°C:

$$2N_2O_5(CCl_4) \longrightarrow 4NO_2(g) + O_2(g)$$

The following table shows the variation of N$_2$O$_5$ concentration with time, and the corresponding ln [N$_2$O$_5$] values

t (s)	[N$_2$O$_5$] (M)	ln [N$_2$O$_5$]
0	0.91	−0.094
300	0.75	−0.29
600	0.64	−0.45
1200	0.44	−0.82
3000	0.16	−1.83

Applying Equation (13.4) we plot ln [N$_2$O$_5$] versus t, as shown in Figure 13.10. The fact that the points lie on a straight line shows that the rate law is first order. Next, we determine the rate constant from the slope. We select two points far apart on the line and subtract their y and x values as follows:

$$\text{slope } (m) = \frac{\Delta y}{\Delta x}$$

$$= \frac{-1.50 - (-0.34)}{(2430 - 400) \, \text{s}}$$

$$= -5.7 \times 10^{-4} \, \text{s}^{-1}$$

Because $m = -k$, we get $k = 5.7 \times 10^{-4} \, \text{s}^{-1}$.

For gas-phase reactions we can replace the concentration terms in Equation (13.3) with the pressures of the gaseous reactant. Consider the first-order reaction

$$A(g) \longrightarrow \text{product}$$

Using the ideal gas equation we write

$$PV = n_A RT$$

or

$$\frac{n_A}{V} = [A] = \frac{P}{RT}$$

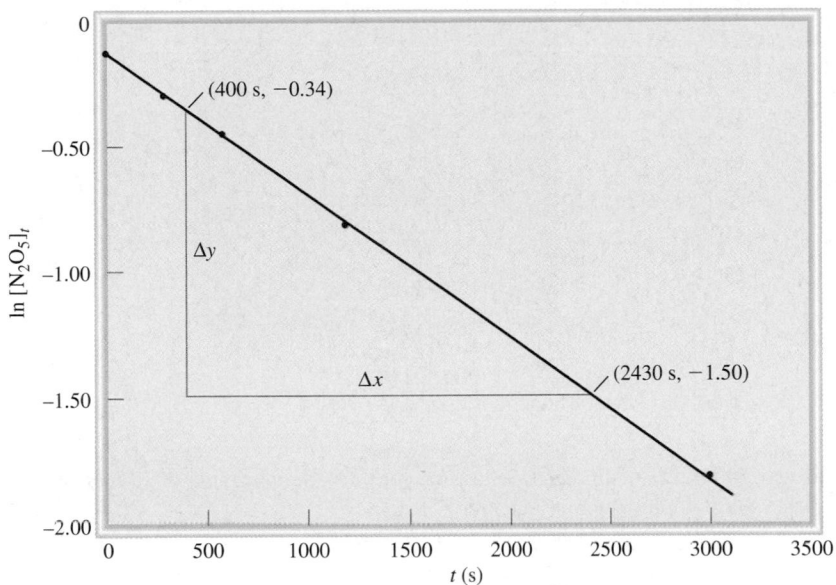

Figure 13.10 *Plot of ln [N₂O₅]ₜ versus time. The rate constant can be determined from the slope of the straight line.*

Substituting $[A] = P/RT$ in Equation (13.3), we get

$$\ln \frac{[A]_t}{[A]_0} = \ln \frac{P_t/RT}{P_0/RT} = \ln \frac{P_t}{P_0} = -kt$$

The equation corresponding to Equation (13.4) now becomes

$$\ln P_t = -kt + \ln P_0 \qquad (13.5)$$

Example 13.5 shows the use of pressure measurements to study the kinetics of a first-order reaction.

Example 13.5

The rate of decomposition of azomethane is studied by monitoring the partial pressure of the reactant as a function of time:

$$CH_3—N{=}N—CH_3(g) \longrightarrow N_2(g) + C_2H_6(g)$$

The data obtained at 300°C are shown in the following table:

Time (s)	Partial Pressure of Azomethane (mmHg)
0	284
100	220
150	193
200	170
250	150
300	132

Are these values consistent with first-order kinetics? If so, determine the rate constant.

(Continued)

Figure 13.11 *Plot of ln P_t versus time for the decomposition of azomethane.*

Strategy To test for first-order kinetics, we consider the integrated first-order rate law that has a linear form, which is Equation (13.4)

$$\ln [A]_t = -kt + \ln [A]_0$$

If the reaction is first order, then a plot of ln $[A]_t$ versus t (y versus x) will produce a straight line with a slope equal to $-k$. Note that the partial pressure of azomethane at any time is directly proportional to its concentration in moles per liter ($PV = nRT$, so $P \propto n/V$). Therefore, we substitute partial pressure for concentration [Equation (13.5)]:

$$\ln P_t = -kt + \ln P_0$$

where P_0 and P_t are the partial pressures of azomethane at $t = 0$ and $t = t$, respectively.

Solution First we construct the following table of t versus ln P_t.

t (s)	ln P_t
0	5.649
100	5.394
150	5.263
200	5.136
250	5.011
300	4.883

Figure 13.11, which is based on the data given in the table, shows that a plot of ln P_t versus t yields a straight line, so the reaction is indeed first order. The slope of the line is given by

$$\text{slope} = \frac{5.05 - 5.56}{(233 - 33)\ \text{s}} = -2.55 \times 10^{-3}\ \text{s}^{-1}$$

According to Equation (13.4), the slope is equal to $-k$, so $k = 2.55 \times 10^{-3}\ \text{s}^{-1}$.

Practice Exercise Ethyl iodide (C_2H_5I) decomposes at a certain temperature in the gas phase as follows:

$$C_2H_5I(g) \longrightarrow C_2H_4(g) + HI(g)$$

From the following data determine the order of the reaction and the rate constant.

Time (min)	$[C_2H_5I]$ (M)
0	0.36
15	0.30
30	0.25
48	0.19
75	0.13

Similar problems: 13.21, 13.22.

Reaction Half-life

As a reaction proceeds, the concentration of the reactant(s) decreases. Another measure of the rate of a reaction, relating concentration to time, is the **half-life,** $t_{\frac{1}{2}}$, which is *the time required for the concentration of a reactant to decrease to half of its initial concentration.* We can obtain an expression for $t_{\frac{1}{2}}$ for a first-order reaction as follows. Equation (13.3) can be rearranged to give

$$t = \frac{1}{k} \ln \frac{[A]_0}{[A]_t}$$

By the definition of half-life, when $t = t_{\frac{1}{2}}$, $[A]_t = [A]_0/2$, so

$$t_{\frac{1}{2}} = \frac{1}{k} \ln \frac{[A]_0}{[A]_0/2}$$

or

$$t_{\frac{1}{2}} = \frac{1}{k} \ln 2 = \frac{0.693}{k} \qquad (13.6)$$

Equation (13.6) tells us that the half-life of a first-order reaction is *independent* of the initial concentration of the reactant. Thus, it takes the same time for the concentration of the reactant to decrease from 1.0 M to 0.50 M, say, as it does for a decrease in concentration from 0.10 M to 0.050 M (Figure 13.12). Measuring the half-life of a reaction is one way to determine the rate constant of a first-order reaction.

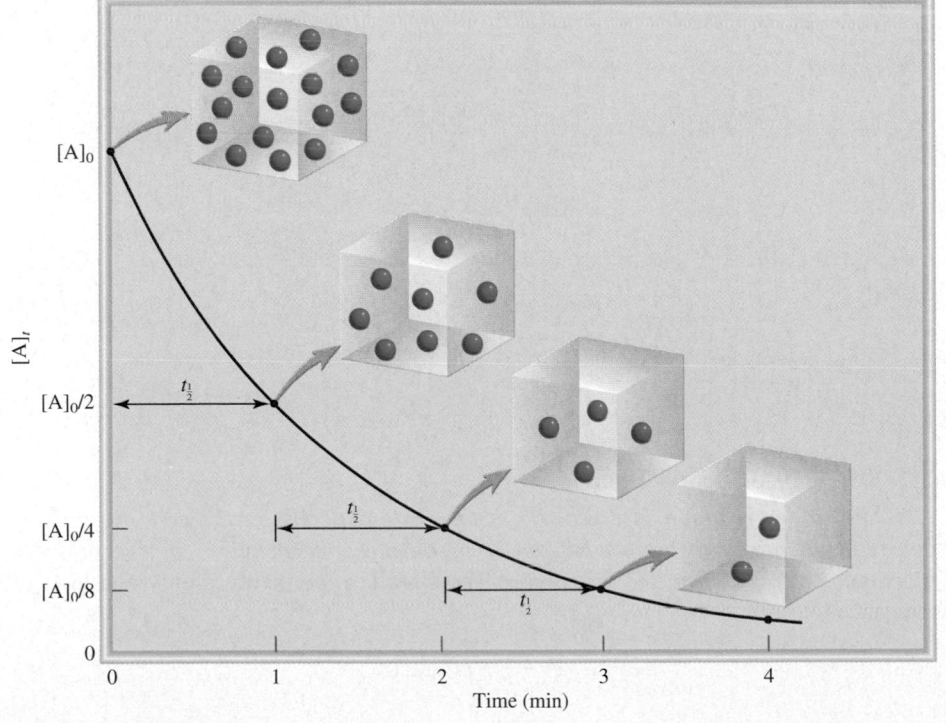

Figure 13.12 *A plot of [A] versus time for the first-order reaction A → products. The half-life of the reaction is 1 min. After the elapse of each half-life, the concentration of A is halved.*

The following analogy may be helpful for understanding Equation (13.6). The duration of a college undergraduate's career, assuming the student does not take any time off, is four years. Thus, the half-life of his or her stay at the college is two years. This half-life is not affected by how many other students are present. Similarly, the half-life of a first-order reaction is concentration independent.

The usefulness of $t_{\frac{1}{2}}$ is that it gives us an estimate of the magnitude of the rate constant—the shorter the half-life, the larger the k. Consider, for example, two radioactive isotopes used in nuclear medicine: ^{24}Na ($t_{\frac{1}{2}} = 14.7$ h) and ^{60}Co ($t_{\frac{1}{2}} = 5.3$ yr). It is obvious that the ^{24}Na isotope decays faster because it has a shorter half-life. If we started with 1 mole each of the isotopes, most of the ^{24}Na would be gone in a week while the ^{60}Co sample would be mostly intact.

In Example 13.6 we calculate the half-life of a first-order reaction.

Similar problem: 13.28.

Example 13.6

The decomposition of ethane (C_2H_6) to methyl radicals is a first-order reaction with a rate constant of 5.36×10^{-4} s^{-1} at 700°C:

$$C_2H_6(g) \longrightarrow 2CH_3(g)$$

Calculate the half-life of the reaction in minutes.

Strategy To calculate the half-life of a first-order reaction, we use Equation (13.6). A conversion is needed to express the half-life in minutes.

Solution For a first-order reaction, we only need the rate constant to calculate the half-life of the reaction. From Equation (13.6)

$$t_{\frac{1}{2}} = \frac{0.693}{k}$$
$$= \frac{0.693}{5.36 \times 10^{-4} \text{ s}^{-1}}$$
$$= 1.29 \times 10^3 \text{ s} \times \frac{1 \text{ min}}{60 \text{ s}}$$
$$= 21.5 \text{ min}$$

Practice Exercise Calculate the half-life of the decomposition of N_2O_5, discussed on p. 560.

Second-Order Reactions

A **second-order reaction** is *a reaction whose rate depends on the concentration of one reactant raised to the second power or on the concentrations of two different reactants, each raised to the first power.* The simpler type involves only one kind of reactant molecule:

$$A \longrightarrow product$$

where

$$\text{rate} = -\frac{\Delta[A]}{\Delta t}$$

From the rate law,

$$\text{rate} = k[A]^2$$

As before, we can determine the units of k by writing

$$k = \frac{\text{rate}}{[A]^2} = \frac{M/s}{M^2} = 1/M \cdot s$$

Another type of second-order reaction is

$$A + B \longrightarrow \text{product}$$

and the rate law is given by

$$\text{rate} = k[A][B]$$

The reaction is first order in A and first order in B, so it has an overall reaction order of 2.

Using calculus, we can obtain the following expressions for "A $\longrightarrow$ product" second-order reactions:

$$\frac{1}{[A]_t} = kt + \frac{1}{[A]_0} \qquad (13.7)$$

Equation (13.7) has the form of a linear equation. As Figure 13.13 shows, a plot of $1/[A]_t$ versus t gives a straight line with slope $= k$ and y intercept $= 1/[A]_0$. (The corresponding equation for "A + B $\longrightarrow$ product" reactions is too complex for our discussion.)

We can obtain an equation for the half-life of a second-order reaction by setting $[A]_t = [A]_0/2$ in Equation (13.7).

$$\frac{1}{[A]_0/2} = kt_{\frac{1}{2}} + \frac{1}{[A]_0}$$

Solving for $t_{\frac{1}{2}}$ we obtain

$$t_{\frac{1}{2}} = \frac{1}{k[A]_0} \qquad (13.8)$$

Note that the half-life of a second-order reaction is inversely proportional to the initial reactant concentration. This result makes sense because the half-life should be shorter in the early stage of the reaction when more reactant molecules are present to collide with each other. Measuring the half-lives at different initial concentrations is one way to distinguish between a first-order and a second-order reaction.

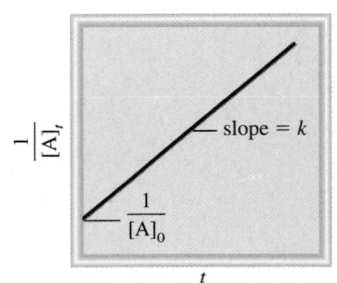

Figure 13.13 *A plot of $1/[A]_t$ versus t for a second-order reaction. The slope of the line is equal to k.*

The kinetic analysis of a second-order reaction is shown in Example 13.7.

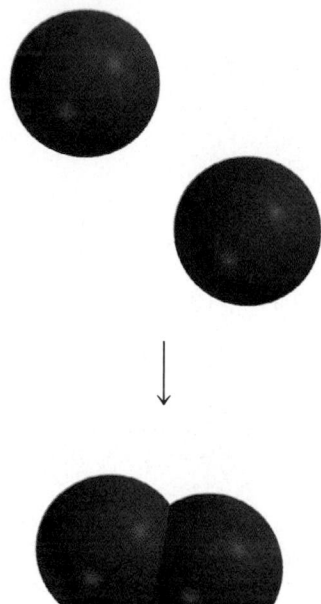

Example 13.7

Iodine atoms combine to form molecular iodine in the gas phase

$$I(g) + I(g) \longrightarrow I_2(g)$$

This reaction follows second-order kinetics and has the high rate constant $7.0 \times 10^9/M \cdot s$ at 23°C. (a) If the initial concentration of I was 0.086 M, calculate the concentration after 2.0 min. (b) Calculate the half-life of the reaction if the initial concentration of I is 0.60 M and if it is 0.42 M.

Strategy (a) The relationship between the concentrations of a reactant at different times is given by the integrated rate law. Because this is a second-order reaction, we use Equation (13.7). (b) We are asked to calculate the half-life. The half-life for a second-order reaction is given by Equation (13.8).

Solution (a) To calculate the concentration of a species at a later time of a second-order reaction, we need the initial concentration and the rate constant. Applying Equation (13.7)

$$\frac{1}{[A]_t} = kt + \frac{1}{[A]_0}$$

$$\frac{1}{[A]_t} = (7.0 \times 10^9/M \cdot s)\left(2.0 \text{ min} \times \frac{60 \text{ s}}{1 \text{ min}}\right) + \frac{1}{0.086 \ M}$$

where $[A]_t$ is the concentration at t = 2.0 min. Solving the equation, we get

$$[A]_t = 1.2 \times 10^{-12} \ M$$

This is such a low concentration that it is virtually undetectable. The very large rate constant for the reaction means that practically all the I atoms combine after only 2.0 min of reaction time.

(b) We need Equation (13.8) for this part.
For $[I]_0$ = 0.60 M

$$t_{\frac{1}{2}} = \frac{1}{k[A]_0}$$

$$= \frac{1}{(7.0 \times 10^9/M \cdot s)(0.60 \ M)}$$

$$= 2.4 \times 10^{-10} \text{ s}$$

For $[I]_0$ = 0.42 M

$$t_{\frac{1}{2}} = \frac{1}{(7.0 \times 10^9/M \cdot s)(0.42 \ M)}$$

$$= 3.4 \times 10^{-10} \text{ s}$$

Check These results confirm that the half-life of a second-order reaction, unlike that of a first-order reaction, is not a constant but depends on the initial concentration of the reactant(s).

Similar problems: 13.29, 13.30.

Practice Exercise The reaction 2A $\longrightarrow$ B is second order with a rate constant of 51/M · min at 24°C. (a) Starting with $[A]_0$ = 0.0092 M, how long will it take for $[A]_t$ = 3.7×10^{-3} M? (b) Calculate the half-life of the reaction.

Zero-Order Reactions

First- and second-order reactions are the most common reaction types. Reactions whose order is zero are rare. For a zero-order reaction

$$A \longrightarrow \text{product}$$

the rate law is given by

$$\text{rate} = k[A]^0$$
$$= k$$

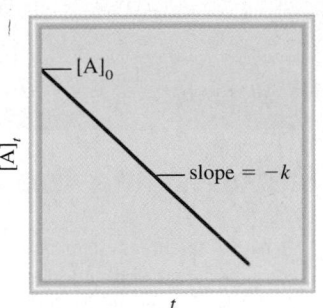

Figure 13.14 *A plot of $[A]_t$ versus t for a zero-order reaction. The slope of the line is equal to $-k$.*

Thus, the rate of a zero-order reaction is a *constant*, independent of reactant concentration. Using calculus, we can show that

$$[A]_t = -kt + [A]_0 \qquad (13.9)$$

Equation (13.9) has the form of a linear equation. As Figure 13.14 shows, a plot of $[A]_t$ versus t gives a straight line with slope $= -k$ and y intercept $= [A]_0$. To calculate the half-life of a zero-order reaction, we set $[A]_t = [A]_0/2$ in Equation (13.9) and obtain

$$t_{\frac{1}{2}} = \frac{[A]_0}{2k} \qquad (13.10)$$

Many of the known zero-order reactions take place on a metal surface. An example is the decomposition of nitrous oxide (N_2O) to nitrogen and oxygen in the presence of platinum (Pt):

$$2N_2O(g) \longrightarrow 2N_2(g) + O_2(g)$$

When all the binding sites on Pt are occupied, the rate becomes constant regardless of the amount of N_2O present in the gas phase. As we will see in Section 13.6, another well-studied zero-order reaction occurs in enzyme catalysis.

Third-order and higher order reactions are quite complex; they are not presented in this book. Table 13.3 summarizes the kinetics of zero-order, first-order, and second-order reactions. The Chemistry in Action essay on p. 568 describes the application of chemical kinetics to estimating the ages of objects.

TABLE 13.3	Summary of the Kinetics of Zero-Order, First-Order, and Second-Order Reactions		
Order	**Rate Law**	**Concentration-Time Equation**	**Half-Life**
0	Rate $= k$	$[A]_t = -kt + [A]_0$	$\dfrac{[A]_0}{2k}$
1	Rate $= k[A]$	$\ln \dfrac{[A]_t}{[A]_0} = -kt$	$\dfrac{0.693}{k}$
2	Rate $= k[A]^2$	$\dfrac{1}{[A]_t} = kt + \dfrac{1}{[A]_0}$	$\dfrac{1}{k[A]_0}$

CHEMISTRY
in Action

Determining the Age of the Shroud of Turin

How do scientists determine the ages of artifacts from archaeological excavations? If someone tried to sell you a manuscript supposedly dating from 1000 B.C., how could you be certain of its authenticity? Is a mummy found in an Egyptian pyramid *really* 3000 years old? Is the so-called Shroud of Turin truly the burial cloth of Jesus Christ? The answers to these and other similar questions can usually be found by applying chemical kinetics and the *radiocarbon dating technique.*

Earth's atmosphere is constantly being bombarded by cosmic rays of extremely high penetrating power. These rays, which originate in outer space, consist of electrons, neutrons, and atomic nuclei. One of the important reactions between the atmosphere and cosmic rays is the capture of neutrons by atmospheric nitrogen (nitrogen-14 isotope) to produce the radioactive carbon-14 isotope and hydrogen. The unstable carbon atoms eventually form $^{14}CO_2$, which mixes with the ordinary carbon dioxide ($^{12}CO_2$) in the air. As the carbon-14 isotope decays, it emits β particles (electrons). The rate of decay (as measured by the number of electrons emitted per second) obeys first-order kinetics. It is customary in the study of radioactive decay to write the rate law as

$$\text{rate} = kN$$

where k is the first-order rate constant and N the number of ^{14}C nuclei present. The half-life of the decay, $t_{\frac{1}{2}}$, is 5.73×10^3 yr, so that from Equation (13.6) we write

$$k = \frac{0.693}{5.73 \times 10^3 \text{ yr}} = 1.21 \times 10^{-4} \text{ yr}^{-1}$$

The Shroud of Turin. For generations there was controversy about whether the shroud, a piece of linen bearing the image of a man, was the burial cloth of Jesus Christ. The age of the shroud has been determined by radiocarbon dating.

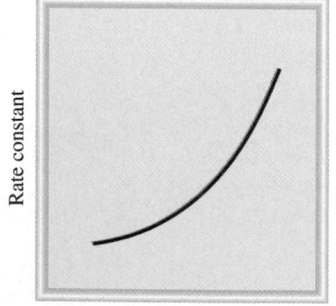

Figure 13.15 *Dependence of rate constant on temperature. The rate constants of most reactions increase with increasing temperature.*

13.4 Activation Energy and Temperature Dependence of Rate Constants

With very few exceptions, reaction rates increase with increasing temperature. For example, the time required to hard-boil an egg in water is much shorter if the "reaction" is carried out at 100°C (about 10 min) than at 80°C (about 30 min). Conversely, an effective way to preserve foods is to store them at subzero temperatures, thereby slowing the rate of bacterial decay. Figure 13.15 shows a typical example of the relationship between the rate constant of a reaction and temperature. In order to explain this behavior, we must ask how reactions get started in the first place.

The Collision Theory of Chemical Kinetics

The kinetic molecular theory of gases (p. 197) postulates that gas molecules frequently collide with one another. Therefore, it seems logical to assume—and it is generally

The carbon-14 isotopes enter the biosphere when carbon dioxide is taken up in plant photosynthesis. Plants are eaten by animals, which exhale carbon-14 in CO_2. Eventually, carbon-14 participates in many aspects of the carbon cycle. The ^{14}C lost by radioactive decay is constantly replenished by the production of new isotopes in the atmosphere. In this decay-replenishment process, a dynamic equilibrium is established whereby the ratio of ^{14}C to ^{12}C remains constant in living matter. But when an individual plant or an animal dies, the carbon-14 isotope in it is no longer replenished, so the ratio decreases as ^{14}C decays. This same change occurs when carbon atoms are trapped in coal, petroleum, or wood preserved underground, and, of course, in Egyptian mummies. After a number of years, there are proportionately fewer ^{14}C nuclei in, say, a mummy than in a living person.

In 1955, Willard F. Libby[†] suggested that this fact could be used to estimate the length of time the carbon-14 isotope in a particular specimen has been decaying without replenishment. Rearranging Equation (13.3), we can write

$$\ln \frac{N_0}{N_t} = kt$$

where N_0 and N_t are the number of ^{14}C nuclei present at $t = 0$ and $t = t$, respectively. Because the rate of decay is directly pro-

portional to the number of ^{14}C nuclei present, the preceding equation can be rewritten as

$$
\begin{aligned}
t &= \frac{1}{k} \ln \frac{N_0}{N_t} \\
&= \frac{1}{1.21 \times 10^{-4}\,\text{yr}^{-1}} \ln \frac{\text{decay rate at } t = 0}{\text{decay rate at } t = t} \\
&= \frac{1}{1.21 \times 10^{-4}\,\text{yr}^{-1}} \ln \frac{\text{decay rate of fresh sample}}{\text{decay rate of old sample}}
\end{aligned}
$$

Knowing k and the decay rates for the fresh sample and the old sample, we can calculate t, which is the age of the old sample. This ingenious technique is based on a remarkably simple idea. Its success depends on how accurately we can measure the rate of decay. In fresh samples, the ratio $^{14}C/^{12}C$ is about $1/10^{12}$, so the equipment used to monitor the radioactive decay must be very sensitive. Precision is more difficult with older samples because they contain even fewer ^{14}C nuclei. Nevertheless, radiocarbon dating has become an extremely valuable tool for estimating the age of archaeological artifacts, paintings, and other objects dating back 1000 to 50,000 years.

A recent major application of radiocarbon dating was the determination of the age of the Shroud of Turin. In 1988 three laboratories in Europe and the United States, working on samples of less than 50 mg of the shroud, independently showed by carbon-14 dating that the shroud dates from between A.D. 1260 and A.D. 1390. Thus, the shroud could not have been the burial cloth of Christ.

[†]Willard Frank Libby (1908–1980). American chemist. Libby received the Nobel Prize in Chemistry in 1960 for his work on radiocarbon dating.

true—that chemical reactions occur as a result of collisions between reacting molecules. In terms of the *collision theory* of chemical kinetics, then, we expect the rate of a reaction to be directly proportional to the number of molecular collisions per second, or to the frequency of molecular collisions:

$$\text{rate} \propto \frac{\text{number of collisions}}{\text{s}}$$

This simple relationship explains the dependence of reaction rate on concentration.

Consider the reaction of A molecules with B molecules to form some product. Suppose that each product molecule is formed by the direct combination of an A molecule and a B molecule. If we doubled the concentration of A, then the number of A-B collisions would also double, because there would be twice as many A molecules that could collide with B molecules in any given volume (Figure 13.16). Consequently, the rate would increase by a factor of 2. Similarly,

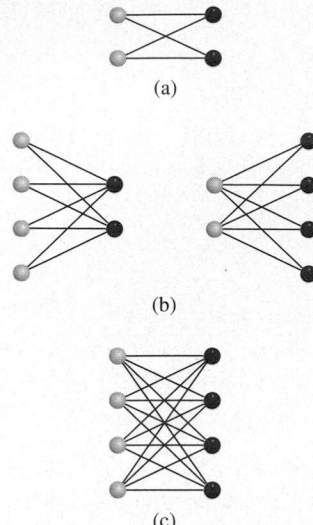

Figure 13.16 *Dependence of number of collisions on concentration. We consider here only A-B collisions, which can lead to formation of products. (a) There are four possible collisions among two A and two B molecules. (b) Doubling the number of either type of molecule (but not both) increases the number of collisions to eight. (c) Doubling both the A and B molecules increases the number of collisions to sixteen. In each case, the collision between a red sphere and a gray sphere can only be counted once.*

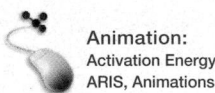

Animation:
Activation Energy
ARIS, Animations

doubling the concentration of B molecules would increase the rate twofold. Thus, we can express the rate law as

$$\text{rate} = k[\text{A}][\text{B}]$$

The reaction is first order in both A and B and obeys second-order kinetics.

The collision theory is intuitively appealing, but the relationship between rate and molecular collisions is more complicated than you might expect. The implication of the collision theory is that a reaction always occurs when an A and a B molecule collide. However, not all collisions lead to reactions. Calculations based on the kinetic molecular theory show that, at ordinary pressures (say, 1 atm) and temperatures (say, 298 K), there are about 1×10^{27} binary collisions (collisions between two molecules) in 1 mL of volume every second in the gas phase. Even more collisions per second occur in liquids. If every binary collision led to a product, then most reactions would be complete almost instantaneously. In practice, we find that the rates of reactions differ greatly. This means that, in many cases, collisions alone do not guarantee that a reaction will take place.

Any molecule in motion possesses kinetic energy; the faster it moves, the greater the kinetic energy. But a fast-moving molecule will not break up into fragments on its own. To react, it must collide with another molecule. When molecules collide, part of their kinetic energy is converted to vibrational energy. If the initial kinetic energies are large, then the colliding molecules will vibrate so strongly as to break some of the chemical bonds. This bond fracture is the first step toward product formation. If the initial kinetic energies are small, the molecules will merely bounce off each other intact. Energetically speaking, there is some minimum collision energy below which no reaction occurs. Lacking this energy, the molecules remain intact, and no change results from the collision.

We postulate that in order to react, the colliding molecules must have a total kinetic energy equal to or greater than the **activation energy (E_a),** which is *the minimum amount of energy required to initiate a chemical reaction.* When molecules collide they form an **activated complex** (also called the **transition state**), *a temporary species formed by the reactant molecules as a result of the collision before they form the product.*

Figure 13.17 shows two different potential energy profiles for the reaction

$$\text{A} + \text{B} \longrightarrow \text{AB}^{\ddagger} \longrightarrow \text{C} + \text{D}$$

where $\text{AB}^{\ddagger}$ denotes an activated complex formed by the collision between A and B. If the products are more stable than the reactants, then the reaction will be accompanied

Figure 13.17 *Potential energy profiles for (a) exothermic and (b) endothermic reactions. These plots show the change in potential energy as reactants A and B are converted to products C and D. The activated complex ($AB^{\ddagger}$) is a highly unstable species with a high potential energy. The activation energy is defined for the forward reaction in both (a) and (b). Note that the products C and D are more stable than the reactants in (a) and less stable than those in (b).*

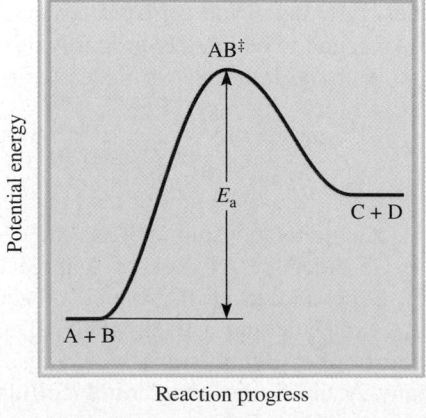

by a release of heat; that is, the reaction is exothermic [Figure 13.17(a)]. On the other hand, if the products are less stable than the reactants, then heat will be absorbed by the reacting mixture from the surroundings and we have an endothermic reaction [Figure 13.17(b)]. In both cases we plot the potential energy of the reacting system versus the progress of the reaction. Qualitatively, these plots show the potential energy changes as reactants are converted to products.

We can think of activation energy as a barrier that prevents less energetic molecules from reacting. Because the number of reactant molecules in an ordinary reaction is very large, the speeds, and hence also the kinetic energies of the molecules, vary greatly. Normally, only a small fraction of the colliding molecules—the fastest-moving ones—have enough kinetic energy to exceed the activation energy. These molecules can therefore take part in the reaction. The increase in the rate (or the rate constant) with temperature can now be explained: The speeds of the molecules obey the Maxwell distributions shown in Figure 5.17. Compare the speed distributions at two different temperatures. Because more high-energy molecules are present at the higher temperature, the rate of product formation is also greater at the higher temperature.

The Arrhenius Equation

The dependence of the rate constant of a reaction on temperature can be expressed by the following equation, known as the *Arrhenius equation:*

$$k = Ae^{-E_a/RT} \tag{13.11}$$

where E_a is the activation energy of the reaction (in kJ/mol), R the gas constant (8.314 J/K · mol), T the absolute temperature, and e the base of the natural logarithm scale (see Appendix 4). The quantity A represents the collision frequency and is called the frequency factor. It can be treated as a constant for a given reacting system over a fairly wide temperature range. Equation (13.11) shows that the rate constant is directly proportional to A and, therefore, to the collision frequency. In addition, because of the minus sign associated with the exponent E_a/RT, the rate constant decreases with increasing activation energy and increases with increasing temperature. This equation can be expressed in a more useful form by taking the natural logarithm of both sides:

$$\ln k = \ln Ae^{-E_a/RT}$$

or

$$\ln k = \ln A - \frac{E_a}{RT} \tag{13.12}$$

Equation (13.12) can be rearranged to a linear equation:

$$\ln k = \left(-\frac{E_a}{R}\right)\left(\frac{1}{T}\right) + \ln A \tag{13.13}$$

$$\updownarrow \qquad \updownarrow \quad \updownarrow \qquad \updownarrow$$
$$y \;\; = \;\; m \;\; x \;\; + \;\; b$$

Thus, a plot of $\ln k$ versus $1/T$ gives a straight line whose slope m is equal to $-E_a/R$ and whose intercept b with the y axis is $\ln A$.

Example 13.8 demonstrates a graphical method for determining the activation energy of a reaction.

Example 13.8

The rate constants for the decomposition of acetaldehyde

$$CH_3CHO(g) \longrightarrow CH_4(g) + CO(g)$$

were measured at five different temperatures. The data are shown in the table. Plot ln k versus $1/T$, and determine the activation energy (in kJ/mol) for the reaction. Note that the reaction is "$\frac{3}{2}$" order in CH_3CHO, so k has the units of $1/M^{\frac{1}{2}} \cdot s$.

k $(1/M^{\frac{1}{2}} \cdot s)$	T (K)
0.011	700
0.035	730
0.105	760
0.343	790
0.789	810

Strategy Consider the Arrhenius equation written as a linear equation

$$\ln k = \left(-\frac{E_a}{R}\right)\left(\frac{1}{T}\right) + \ln A$$

A plot of ln k versus $1/T$ (y versus x) will produce a straight line with a slope equal to $-E_a/R$. Thus, the activation energy can be determined from the slope of the plot.

Solution First we convert the data to the following table

ln k	$1/T$ (K^{-1})
−4.51	1.43×10^{-3}
−3.35	1.37×10^{-3}
−2.254	1.32×10^{-3}
−1.070	1.27×10^{-3}
−0.237	1.23×10^{-3}

A plot of these data yields the graph in Figure 13.18. The slope of the line is calculated from two pairs of coordinates:

$$\text{slope} = \frac{-4.00 - (-0.45)}{(1.41 - 1.24) \times 10^{-3} \text{ K}^{-1}} = -2.09 \times 10^4 \text{ K}$$

Figure 13.18 *Plot of ln k versus 1/T. The slope of the line is equal to* $-E_a/R$.

(Continued)

From the linear form of Equation (13.13)

$$\text{slope} = -\frac{E_a}{R} = -2.09 \times 10^4 \text{ K}$$
$$E_a = (8.314 \text{ J/K} \cdot \text{mol})(2.09 \times 10^4 \text{ K})$$
$$= 1.74 \times 10^5 \text{ J/mol}$$
$$= 1.74 \times 10^2 \text{ kJ/mol}$$

Check It is important to note that although the rate constant itself has the units $1/M^{\frac{1}{2}} \cdot \text{s}$, the quantity ln k has no units (we cannot take the logarithm of a unit).

Similar problem: 13.37.

Practice Exercise The second-order rate constant for the decomposition of nitrous oxide (N_2O) into nitrogen molecule and oxygen atom has been measured at different temperatures:

k (1/M·s)	t (°C)
1.87×10^{-3}	600
0.0113	650
0.0569	700
0.244	750

Determine graphically the activation energy for the reaction.

An equation relating the rate constants k_1 and k_2 at temperatures T_1 and T_2 can be used to calculate the activation energy or to find the rate constant at another temperature if the activation energy is known. To derive such an equation we start with Equation (13.12):

$$\ln k_1 = \ln A - \frac{E_a}{RT_1}$$
$$\ln k_2 = \ln A - \frac{E_a}{RT_2}$$

Subtracting ln k_2 from ln k_1 gives

$$\ln k_1 - \ln k_2 = \frac{E_a}{R}\left(\frac{1}{T_2} - \frac{1}{T_1}\right)$$
$$\ln \frac{k_1}{k_2} = \frac{E_a}{R}\left(\frac{1}{T_2} - \frac{1}{T_1}\right)$$
$$\ln \frac{k_1}{k_2} = \frac{E_a}{R}\left(\frac{T_1 - T_2}{T_1 T_2}\right) \tag{13.14}$$

Example 13.9 illustrates the use of the equation we have just derived.

Example 13.9

The rate constant of a first-order reaction is $3.46 \times 10^{-2} \text{ s}^{-1}$ at 298 K. What is the rate constant at 350 K if the activation energy for the reaction is 50.2 kJ/mol?

Strategy A modified form of the Arrhenius equation relates two rate constants at two different temperatures [see Equation (13.14)]. Make sure the units of R and E_a are consistent.

Solution The data are

$$k_1 = 3.46 \times 10^{-2} \text{ s}^{-1} \qquad k_2 = ?$$
$$T_1 = 298 \text{ K} \qquad\qquad T_2 = 350 \text{ K}$$

(Continued)

Substituting in Equation (13.14),

$$\ln \frac{3.46 \times 10^{-2}\,s^{-1}}{k_2} = \frac{50.2 \times 10^3\,J/mol}{8.314\,J/K \cdot mol} \left[\frac{298\,K - 350\,K}{(298\,K)(350\,K)} \right]$$

We convert E_a to units of J/mol to match the units of R. Solving the equation gives

$$\ln \frac{3.46 \times 10^{-2}\,s^{-1}}{k_2} = -3.01$$

$$\frac{3.46 \times 10^{-2}\,s^{-1}}{k_2} = e^{-3.01} = 0.0493$$

$$k_2 = \boxed{0.702\,s^{-1}}$$

Check The rate constant is expected to be greater at a higher temperature. Therefore, the answer is reasonable.

Practice Exercise The first-order rate constant for the reaction of methyl chloride (CH_3Cl) with water to produce methanol (CH_3OH) and hydrochloric acid (HCl) is $3.32 \times 10^{-10}\,s^{-1}$ at 25°C. Calculate the rate constant at 40°C if the activation energy is 116 kJ/mol.

Similar problem: 13.40.

Animation:
Orientation of Collision
ARIS, Animations

For simple reactions (for example, reactions between atoms), we can equate the frequency factor (A) in the Arrhenius equation with the frequency of collisions between the reacting species. For more complex reactions, we must also consider the "orientation factor," that is, how reacting molecules are oriented relative to each other. The reaction between potassium atoms (K) and methyl iodide (CH_3I) to form potassium iodide (KI) and a methyl radical (CH_3) illustrates this point:

$$K + CH_3I \longrightarrow KI + CH_3$$

This reaction is most favorable when the K atom collides with the I atom in CH_3I head-on (Figure 13.19). Otherwise, few or no products are formed. The nature of the

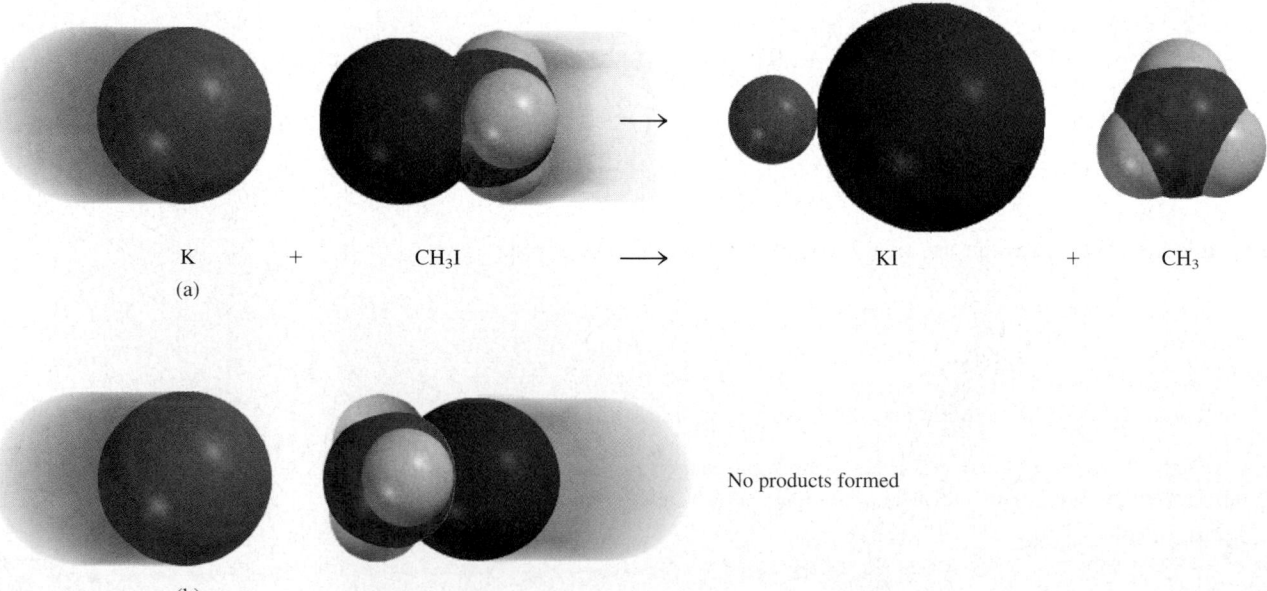

K   + CH_3I $\longrightarrow$ KI   + CH_3
(a)

No products formed

(b)

Figure 13.19 *Relative orientation of reacting molecules. Only when the K atom collides directly with the I atom will the reaction most likely occur.*

orientation factor is satisfactorily dealt with in a more advanced treatment of chemical kinetics.

13.5 Reaction Mechanisms

As we mentioned earlier, an overall balanced chemical equation does not tell us much about how a reaction actually takes place. In many cases, it merely represents the sum of several *elementary steps,* or *elementary reactions, a series of simple reactions that represent the progress of the overall reaction at the molecular level.* The term for *the sequence of elementary steps that leads to product formation* is **reaction mechanism.** The reaction mechanism is comparable to the route of travel followed during a trip; the overall chemical equation specifies only the origin and destination.

As an example of a reaction mechanism, let us consider the reaction between nitric oxide and oxygen:

$$2NO(g) + O_2(g) \longrightarrow 2NO_2(g)$$

We know that the products are not formed directly from the collision of two NO molecules with an O_2 molecule because N_2O_2 is detected during the course of the reaction. Let us assume that the reaction actually takes place via two elementary steps as follows:

$$2NO(g) \longrightarrow N_2O_2(g)$$

$$N_2O_2(g) + O_2(g) \longrightarrow 2NO_2(g)$$

In the first elementary step, two NO molecules collide to form a N_2O_2 molecule. This event is followed by the reaction between N_2O_2 and O_2 to give two molecules of NO_2. The net chemical equation, which represents the overall change, is given by the sum of the elementary steps:

Step 1:	$NO + NO \longrightarrow N_2O_2$
Step 2:	$N_2O_2 + O_2 \longrightarrow 2NO_2$
Overall reaction:	$2NO + \cancel{N_2O_2} + O_2 \longrightarrow \cancel{N_2O_2} + 2NO_2$

The sum of the elementary steps must give the overall balanced equation.

Species such as N_2O_2 are called *intermediates* because they *appear in the mechanism of the reaction (that is, the elementary steps) but not in the overall balanced equation.* Keep in mind that an intermediate is always formed in an early elementary step and consumed in a later elementary step.

The *molecularity of a reaction* is *the number of molecules reacting in an elementary step.* These molecules may be of the same or different types. Each of the elementary steps discussed above is called a *bimolecular reaction, an elementary step that involves two molecules.* An example of a *unimolecular reaction, an elementary step in which only one reacting molecule participates,* is the conversion of cyclopropane to propene discussed in Example 13.4. Very few *termolecular reactions, reactions that involve the participation of three molecules in one elementary step,* are known, because the simultaneous encounter of three molecules is a far less likely event than a bimolecular collision.

Rate Laws and Elementary Steps

Knowing the elementary steps of a reaction enables us to deduce the rate law. Suppose we have the following elementary reaction:

$$A \longrightarrow products$$

Because there is only one molecule present, this is a unimolecular reaction. It follows that the larger the number of A molecules present, the faster the rate of product formation. Thus, the rate of a unimolecular reaction is directly proportional to the concentration of A, or is first order in A:

$$rate = k[A]$$

For a bimolecular elementary reaction involving A and B molecules

$$A + B \longrightarrow product$$

the rate of product formation depends on how frequently A and B collide, which in turn depends on the concentrations of A and B. Thus, we can express the rate as

$$rate = k[A][B]$$

Similarly, for a bimolecular elementary reaction of the type

$$A + A \longrightarrow products$$

or

$$2A \longrightarrow products$$

the rate becomes

$$rate = k[A]^2$$

The preceding examples show that the reaction order for each reactant in an elementary reaction is equal to its stoichiometric coefficient in the chemical equation for that step. In general, we cannot tell by merely looking at the overall balanced equation whether the reaction occurs as shown or in a series of steps. This determination is made in the laboratory.

When we study a reaction that has more than one elementary step, the rate law for the overall process is given by the ***rate-determining step,*** which is *the slowest step in the sequence of steps leading to product formation.*

An analogy for the rate-determining step is the flow of traffic along a narrow road. Assuming the cars cannot pass one another on the road, the rate at which the cars travel is governed by the slowest-moving car.

Experimental studies of reaction mechanisms begin with the collection of data (rate measurements). Next, we analyze the data to determine the rate constant and order of the reaction, and we write the rate law. Finally, we suggest a plausible mechanism for the reaction in terms of elementary steps (Figure 13.20). The elementary steps must satisfy two requirements:

Figure 13.20 *Sequence of steps in the study of a reaction mechanism.*

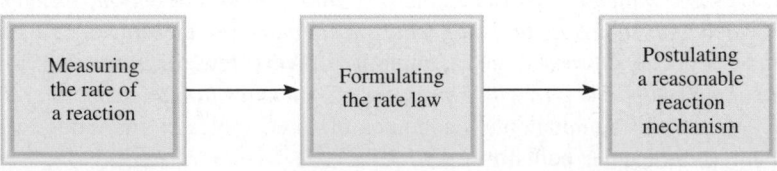

- The sum of the elementary steps must give the overall balanced equation for the reaction.
- The rate-determining step should predict the same rate law as is determined experimentally.

Remember that for a proposed reaction scheme, we must be able to detect the presence of any intermediate(s) formed in one or more elementary steps.

The decomposition of hydrogen peroxide and the formation of hydrogen iodide from molecular hydrogen and molecular iodine illustrate the elucidation of reaction mechanisms by experimental studies.

Hydrogen Peroxide Decomposition

The decomposition of hydrogen peroxide is facilitated by iodide ions (Figure 13.21). The overall reaction is

$$2H_2O_2(aq) \longrightarrow 2H_2O(l) + O_2(g)$$

By experiment, the rate law is found to be

$$\text{rate} = k[H_2O_2][I^-]$$

Thus, the reaction is first order with respect to both H_2O_2 and I^-.

You can see that H_2O_2 decomposition does not occur in a single elementary step corresponding to the overall balanced equation. If it did, the reaction would be second order in H_2O_2 (as a result of the collision of two H_2O_2 molecules). What's more, the I^- ion, which is not even part of the overall equation, appears in the rate law expression. How can we reconcile these facts? First, we can account for the observed rate law by assuming that the reaction takes place in two separate elementary steps, each of which is bimolecular:

Figure 13.21 *The decomposition of hydrogen peroxide is catalyzed by the iodide ion. A few drops of liquid soap have been added to the solution to dramatize the evolution of oxygen gas. (Some of the iodide ions are oxidized to molecular iodine, which then reacts with iodide ions to form the brown triiodide ion, I_3^-).*

$$\text{Step 1:} \qquad H_2O_2 + I^- \xrightarrow{k_1} H_2O + IO^-$$
$$\text{Step 2:} \qquad H_2O_2 + IO^- \xrightarrow{k_2} H_2O + O_2 + I^-$$

If we further assume that step 1 is the rate-determining step, then the rate of the reaction can be determined from the first step alone:

$$\text{rate} = k_1[H_2O_2][I^-]$$

where $k_1 = k$. Note that the IO^- ion is an intermediate because it does not appear in the overall balanced equation. Although the I^- ion also does not appear in the overall equation, I^- differs from IO^- in that the former is present at the start of the reaction and at its completion. The function of I^- is to speed up the reaction—that is, it is a *catalyst*. We will discuss catalysis in Section 13.6. Figure 13.22 shows the potential energy profile for a reaction like the decomposition of H_2O_2. We see that the first step, which is rate determining, has a larger activation energy than the second step. The intermediate, although stable enough to be observed, reacts quickly to form the products.

The Hydrogen Iodide Reaction

A common reaction mechanism is one that involves at least two elementary steps, the first of which is very rapid in both the forward and reverse directions compared with the second step. An example is the reaction between molecular hydrogen and molecular iodine to produce hydrogen iodide:

$$H_2(g) + I_2(g) \longrightarrow 2HI(g)$$

Reaction progress

Figure 13.22 *Potential energy profile for a two-step reaction in which the first step is rate-determining. R and P represent reactants and products, respectively.*

$H_2 + I_2 \longrightarrow 2HI$

Experimentally, the rate law is found to be

$$\text{rate} = k[H_2][I_2]$$

For many years it was thought that the reaction occurred just as written; that is, it is a bimolecular reaction involving a hydrogen molecule and an iodine molecule, as shown on p. 577. However, in the 1960s chemists found that the actual mechanism is more complicated. A two-step mechanism was proposed:

Step 1: $I_2 \underset{k_{-1}}{\overset{k_1}{\rightleftharpoons}} 2I$

Step 2: $H_2 + 2I \xrightarrow{k_2} 2HI$

where k_1, k_{-1}, and k_2 are the rate constants for the reactions. The I atoms are the intermediate in this reaction.

When the reaction begins, there are very few I atoms present. But as I_2 dissociates, the concentration of I_2 decreases while that of I increases. Therefore, the forward rate of step 1 decreases and the reverse rate increases. Soon the two rates become equal, and a chemical equilibrium is established. Because the elementary reactions in step 1 are much faster than the one in step 2, equilibrium is reached before any significant reaction with hydrogen occurs, and it persists throughout the reaction.

In the equilibrium condition of step 1 the forward rate is equal to the reverse rate; that is,

$$k_1[I_2] = k_{-1}[I]^2$$

or

$$[I]^2 = \frac{k_1}{k_{-1}}[I_2]$$

The rate of the reaction is given by the slow, rate-determining step, which is step 2:

$$\text{rate} = k_2[H_2][I]^2$$

Substituting the expression for $[I]^2$ into this rate law, we obtain

$$\text{rate} = \frac{k_1 k_2}{k_{-1}}[H_2][I_2]$$
$$= k[H_2][I_2]$$

where $k = k_1 k_2 / k_{-1}$. As you can see, this two-step mechanism also gives the correct rate law for the reaction. This agreement along with the observation of intermediate I atoms provides strong evidence that the mechanism is correct.

Finally we note that not all reactions have a single rate-determining step. A reaction may have two or more comparably slow steps. The kinetic analysis of such reactions is generally more involved.

Example 13.10 concerns the mechanistic study of a relatively simple reaction.

Example 13.10

The gas-phase decomposition of nitrous oxide (N_2O) is believed to occur via two elementary steps:

Step 1: $N_2O \xrightarrow{k_1} N_2 + O$

Step 2: $N_2O + O \xrightarrow{k_2} N_2 + O_2$

(Continued)

Experimentally the rate law is found to be rate = $k[N_2O]$. (a) Write the equation for the overall reaction. (b) Identify the intermediates. (c) What can you say about the relative rates of steps 1 and 2?

Strategy (a) Because the overall reaction can be broken down into elementary steps, knowing the elementary steps would enable us to write the overall reaction. (b) What are the characteristics of an intermediate? Does it appear in the overall reaction? (c) What determines which elementary step is rate determining? How does a knowledge of the rate-determining step help us write the rate law of a reaction?

Solution (a) Adding the equations for steps 1 and 2 gives the overall reaction

$$2N_2O \longrightarrow 2N_2 + O_2$$

(b) Because the O atom is produced in the first elementary step and it does not appear in the overall balanced equation, it is an intermediate.

(c) If we assume that step 1 is the rate-determining step (that is, if $k_2 \gg k_1$), then the rate of the overall reaction is given by

$$\text{rate} = k_1[N_2O]$$

and $k = k_1$.

Check Step 1 must be the rate-determining step because the rate law written from this step matches the experimentally determined rate law, that is, rate = $k[N_2O]$.

Practice Exercise The reaction between NO_2 and CO to produce NO and CO_2 is believed to occur via two steps:

Step 1: $NO_2 + NO_2 \longrightarrow NO + NO_3$
Step 2: $NO_3 + CO \longrightarrow NO_2 + CO_2$

The experimental rate law is rate = $k[NO_2]^2$. (a) Write the equation for the overall reaction. (b) Identify the intermediate. (c) What can you say about the relative rates of steps 1 and 2?

$2N_2O \longrightarrow 2N_2 + O_2$

Similar problem: 13.51.

Experimental Support for Reaction Mechanisms

How can we find out whether the proposed mechanism for a particular reaction is correct? In the case of hydrogen peroxide decomposition we might try to detect the presence of the IO^- ions by spectroscopic means. Evidence of their presence would support the reaction scheme. Similarly, for the hydrogen iodide reaction, detection of iodine atoms would lend support to the two-step mechanism. For example, I_2 dissociates into atoms when it is irradiated with visible light. Thus, we might predict that the formation of HI from H_2 and I_2 would speed up as the intensity of light is increased because that should increase the concentration of I atoms. Indeed, this is just what is observed.

In one case, chemists wanted to know which C—O bond is broken in the reaction between methyl acetate and water in order to better understand the reaction mechanism

$$CH_3-\overset{O}{\overset{\|}{C}}-O-CH_3 + H_2O \longrightarrow CH_3-\overset{O}{\overset{\|}{C}}-OH + CH_3OH$$

methyl acetate   acetic acid   methanol

CHEMISTRY
in Action

Femtochemistry

The ability to follow chemical reactions at the molecular level has been one of the most relentlessly pursued goals in chemistry. Accomplishing this goal means chemists will be able to understand when a certain reaction occurs and the dependence of its rate on temperature and other parameters. On the practical side, this information will help chemists control reaction rates and increase reaction yields. A complete understanding of reaction mechanism requires a detailed knowledge of the activated complex (also called the transition state). However, the transition state is a highly energetic species that could not be isolated because of its extremely short lifetime.

The situation changed in the 1980s when chemists at the California Institute of Technology began to use very short laser pulses to probe chemical reactions. Because transition states last only 10 to 1000 femtoseconds, the laser pulses needed to probe them must be extraordinarily short. (1 femtosecond, or 1 fs, is 1×10^{-15} s. To appreciate how short this time duration is, note that there are as many femtoseconds in one second as there are seconds in about 32 million years!) One of the reactions studied was the decomposition of cyclobutane (C_4H_8) to ethylene (C_2H_4). There are two possible mechanisms. The first is a single step process in which two carbon-carbon bonds break simultaneously to form the product.

$$\begin{array}{c} CH_2{-}CH_2 \\ |\qquad| \\ CH_2{-}CH_2 \end{array} \longrightarrow 2CH_2{=}CH_2$$

The second mechanism has two steps, with an intermediate

$$\begin{array}{c} CH_2{-}CH_2 \\ |\qquad| \\ CH_2{-}CH_2 \end{array} \longrightarrow \begin{array}{c} \overset{\bullet}{C}H_2\ \ \overset{\bullet}{C}H_2 \\ |\qquad| \\ CH_2{-}CH_2 \end{array} \longrightarrow 2CH_2{=}CH_2$$

where the dot represents an unpaired electron.

The Cal Tech chemists initiated the reaction with a pump laser pulse, which energized the reactant. The first probe pulse hits the molecules a few femtoseconds later and is followed by many thousands more, every 10 fs or so, for the duration of the reaction. Each probe pulse results in an absorption spectrum and changes in the spectrum reveal the motion of the molecule and the state of the chemical bonds. In this way, the chemists were effectively equipped with a camera having different shutter speeds to capture the progress of the reaction. The results show that the second mechanism is what happens. The lifetime of the intermediate is about 700 fs.

The femtosecond laser technique has been applied to unravel the mechanisms of many chemical reactions and biological processes such as photosynthesis and vision. It has created a new area in chemical kinetics that has become known as femtochemistry.

(a)

(b)

The decomposition of cyclobutane to form two ethylene molecules can take place in one of two ways. (a) The reaction proceeds via a single step, which involves the breaking of two C — C bonds simultaneously. (b) The reaction proceeds in two steps, with the formation of a short-lived intermediate in which just one bond is broken. There is only a small energy barrier for the intermediate to proceed to the final products. The correct mechanism is (b).

The two possibilities are

$$CH_3-\overset{\overset{\displaystyle O}{\|}}{C}+O-CH_3 \quad CH_3-\overset{\overset{\displaystyle O}{\|}}{C}-O+CH_3$$
$$\text{(a)} \qquad\qquad\qquad \text{(b)}$$

To distinguish between schemes (a) and (b), chemists used water containing the oxygen-18 isotope instead of ordinary water (which contains the oxygen-16 isotope). When the oxygen-18 water was used, only the acetic acid formed contained oxygen-18:

$$CH_3-\overset{\overset{\displaystyle O}{\|}}{C}-{}^{18}O-H$$

Thus, the reaction must have occurred via bond-breaking scheme (a), because the product formed via scheme (b) would retain both of its original oxygen atoms.

Another example is photosynthesis, the process by which green plants produce glucose from carbon dioxide and water

$$6CO_2 + 6H_2O \longrightarrow C_6H_{12}O_6 + 6O_2$$

A question that arose early in studies of photosynthesis was whether the molecular oxygen was derived from water, from carbon dioxide, or from both. By using water containing the oxygen-18 isotope, it was demonstrated that the evolved oxygen came from water, and none came from carbon dioxide, because the O_2 contained only the ^{18}O isotopes. This result supported the mechanism in which water molecules are "split" by light:

$$2H_2O + h\nu \longrightarrow O_2 + 4H^+ + 4e^-$$

where $h\nu$ represents the energy of a photon. The protons and electrons are used to drive energetically unfavorable reactions that are necessary for plant growth and function.

These examples give some idea of how inventive chemists must be in studying reaction mechanisms. For complex reactions, however, it is virtually impossible to prove the uniqueness of any particular mechanism.

13.6 Catalysis

For the decomposition of hydrogen peroxide we saw that the reaction rate depends on the concentration of iodide ions even though I^- does not appear in the overall equation. We noted that I^- acts as a catalyst for that reaction. A **catalyst** is *a substance that increases the rate of a chemical reaction without itself being consumed.* The catalyst may react to form an intermediate, but it is regenerated in a subsequent step of the reaction.

In the laboratory preparation of molecular oxygen, a sample of potassium chlorate is heated, as shown in Figure 4.12(b). The reaction is

$$2KClO_3(s) \longrightarrow 2KCl(s) + 3O_2(g)$$

However, this thermal decomposition process is very slow in the absence of a catalyst. The rate of decomposition can be increased dramatically by adding a small amount of the catalyst manganese(IV) dioxide (MnO_2), a black powdery substance.

A rise in temperature also increases the rate of a reaction. However, at high temperatures the products formed may undergo other reactions, thereby reducing the yield.

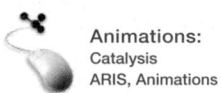

Animations:
Catalysis
ARIS, Animations

All of the MnO_2 can be recovered at the end of the reaction, just as all the I^- ions remain following H_2O_2 decomposition.

To extend the traffic analogy, adding a catalyst can be compared with building a tunnel through a mountain to connect two towns that were previously linked by a winding road over the mountain.

A catalyst speeds up a reaction by providing a set of elementary steps with more favorable kinetics than those that exist in its absence. From Equation (13.11) we know that the rate constant k (and hence the rate) of a reaction depends on the frequency factor A and the activation energy E_a—the larger A or the smaller E_a, the greater the rate. In many cases, a catalyst increases the rate by lowering the activation energy for the reaction.

Let us assume that the following reaction has a certain rate constant k and an activation energy E_a.

$$A + B \xrightarrow{k} C + D$$

In the presence of a catalyst, however, the rate constant is k_c (called the *catalytic rate constant*):

$$A + B \xrightarrow{k_c} C + D$$

By the definition of a catalyst,

$$\text{rate}_{\text{catalyzed}} > \text{rate}_{\text{uncatalyzed}}$$

A catalyst lowers the activation energy for both the forward and reverse reactions.

Figure 13.23 shows the potential energy profiles for both reactions. Note that the total energies of the reactants (A and B) and those of the products (C and D) are unaffected by the catalyst; the only difference between the two is a lowering of the activation energy from E_a to E_a'. Because the activation energy for the reverse reaction is also lowered, a catalyst enhances the rates of the reverse and forward reactions equally.

There are three general types of catalysis, depending on the nature of the rate-increasing substance: heterogeneous catalysis, homogeneous catalysis, and enzyme catalysis.

Heterogeneous Catalysis

Metals and compounds of metals that are most frequently used in heterogeneous catalysis.

In *heterogeneous catalysis*, the reactants and the catalyst are in different phases. Usually the catalyst is a solid and the reactants are either gases or liquids. Heterogeneous catalysis is by far the most important type of catalysis in industrial chemistry, especially

Figure 13.23 *Comparison of the activation energy barriers of an uncatalyzed reaction and the same reaction with a catalyst. The catalyst lowers the energy barrier but does not affect the actual energies of the reactants or products. Although the reactants and products are the same in both cases, the reaction mechanisms and rate laws are different in (a) and (b).*

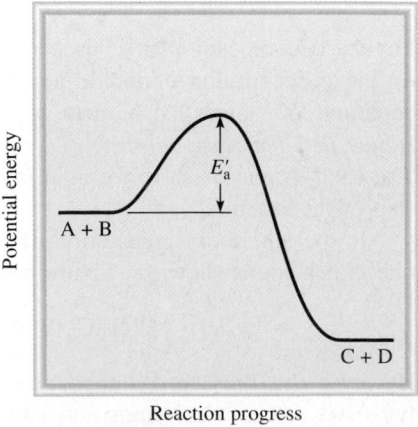

in the synthesis of many key chemicals. Here we describe three specific examples of heterogeneous catalysis that account for millions of tons of chemicals produced annually on an industrial scale.

The Haber Synthesis of Ammonia

Ammonia is an extremely valuable inorganic substance used in the fertilizer industry, the manufacture of explosives, and many other applications. Around the turn of the century, many chemists strove to synthesize ammonia from nitrogen and hydrogen. The supply of atmospheric nitrogen is virtually inexhaustible, and hydrogen gas can be produced readily by passing steam over heated coal:

$$H_2O(g) + C(s) \longrightarrow CO(g) + H_2(g)$$

Hydrogen is also a by-product of petroleum refining.

The formation of NH_3 from N_2 and H_2 is exothermic:

$$N_2(g) + 3H_2(g) \longrightarrow 2NH_3(g) \qquad \Delta H° = -92.6 \text{ kJ/mol}$$

But the reaction rate is extremely slow at room temperature. To be practical on a large scale, a reaction must occur at an appreciable rate *and* it must have a high yield of the desired product. Raising the temperature does accelerate the above reaction, but at the same time it promotes the decomposition of NH_3 molecules into N_2 and H_2, thus lowering the yield of NH_3.

In 1905, after testing literally hundreds of compounds at various temperatures and pressures, Fritz Haber discovered that iron plus a few percent of oxides of potassium and aluminum catalyze the reaction of hydrogen with nitrogen to yield ammonia at about 500°C. This procedure is known as the *Haber process*.

In heterogeneous catalysis, the surface of the solid catalyst is usually the site of the reaction. The initial step in the Haber process involves the dissociation of N_2 and H_2 on the metal surface (Figure 13.24). Although the dissociated species are not truly free atoms because they are bonded to the metal surface, they are highly reactive. The two reactant molecules behave very differently on the catalyst surface. Studies show that H_2 dissociates into atomic hydrogen at temperatures as low as −196°C (the boiling point of liquid nitrogen). Nitrogen molecules, on the other hand, dissociate at about 500°C. The highly reactive N and H atoms combine rapidly at high temperatures to produce the desired NH_3 molecules:

$$N + 3H \longrightarrow NH_3$$

Figure 13.24 *The catalytic action in the synthesis of ammonia. First the H_2 and N_2 molecules bind to the surface of the catalyst. This interaction weakens the covalent bonds within the molecules and eventually causes the molecules to dissociate. The highly reactive H and N atoms combine to form NH_3 molecules, which then leave the surface.*

Figure 13.25 *Platinum-rhodium catalyst used in the Ostwald process.*

The Manufacture of Nitric Acid

Nitric acid is one of the most important inorganic acids. It is used in the production of fertilizers, dyes, drugs, and explosives. The major industrial method of producing nitric acid is the *Ostwald*[†] *process*. The starting materials, ammonia and molecular oxygen, are heated in the presence of a platinum-rhodium catalyst (Figure 13.25) to about 800°C:

$$4NH_3(g) + 5O_2(g) \longrightarrow 4NO(g) + 6H_2O(g)$$

The nitric oxide readily oxidizes (without catalysis) to nitrogen dioxide:

$$2NO(g) + O_2(g) \longrightarrow 2NO_2(g)$$

When dissolved in water, NO_2 forms both nitrous acid and nitric acid:

$$2NO_2(g) + H_2O(l) \longrightarrow HNO_2(aq) + HNO_3(aq)$$

On heating, nitrous acid is converted to nitric acid as follows:

$$3HNO_2(aq) \longrightarrow HNO_3(aq) + H_2O(l) + 2NO(g)$$

The NO generated can be recycled to produce NO_2 in the second step.

Catalytic Converters

At high temperatures inside a running car's engine, nitrogen and oxygen gases react to form nitric oxide:

$$N_2(g) + O_2(g) \longrightarrow 2NO(g)$$

When released into the atmosphere, NO rapidly combines with O_2 to form NO_2. Nitrogen dioxide and other gases emitted by an automobile, such as carbon monoxide (CO) and various unburned hydrocarbons, make automobile exhaust a major source of air pollution.

[†]Wilhelm Ostwald (1853–1932). German chemist. Ostwald made important contributions to chemical kinetics, thermodynamics, and electrochemistry. He developed the industrial process for preparing nitric acid that now bears his name. He received the Nobel Prize in Chemistry in 1909.

Figure 13.26 *A two-stage catalytic converter for an automobile.*

Exhaust manifold

Exhaust pipe

Tail pipe

Air compressor: source of secondary air

Catalytic converters

Most new cars are equipped with catalytic converters (Figure 13.26). An efficient catalytic converter serves two purposes: It oxidizes CO and unburned hydrocarbons to CO_2 and H_2O, and it reduces NO and NO_2 to N_2 and O_2. Hot exhaust gases into which air has been injected are passed through the first chamber of one converter to accelerate the complete burning of hydrocarbons and to decrease CO emission. (A cross section of the catalytic converter is shown in Figure 13.27.) However, because high temperatures increase NO production, a second chamber containing a different catalyst (a transition metal or a transition metal oxide such as CuO or Cr_2O_3) and operating at a lower temperature are required to dissociate NO into N_2 and O_2 before the exhaust is discharged through the tailpipe.

Homogeneous Catalysis

In *homogeneous catalysis* the reactants and catalyst are dispersed in a single phase, usually liquid. Acid and base catalyses are the most important types of homogeneous catalysis in liquid solution. For example, the reaction of ethyl acetate with water to form acetic acid and ethanol normally occurs too slowly to be measured.

$$CH_3-\overset{\overset{\displaystyle O}{\|}}{C}-O-C_2H_5 + H_2O \longrightarrow CH_3-\overset{\overset{\displaystyle O}{\|}}{C}-OH + C_2H_5OH$$
$$\text{ethyl acetate} \qquad\qquad\qquad \text{acetic acid} \quad\quad \text{ethanol}$$

In the absence of the catalyst, the rate law is given by

$$\text{rate} = k[CH_3COOC_2H_5]$$

Figure 13.27 *A cross-sectional view of a catalytic converter. The beads contain platinum, palladium, and rhodium, which catalyze the conversion of CO and hydrocarbons to carbon dioxide and water.*

However, the reaction can be catalyzed by an acid. In the presence of hydrochloric acid, the rate is faster and the rate law is given by

$$\text{rate} = k_c[\text{CH}_3\text{COOC}_2\text{H}_5][\text{H}^+]$$

Note that because $k_c > k$, the rate is determined solely by the catalyzed portion of the reaction.

Homogeneous catalysis can also take place in the gas phase. A well-known example of catalyzed gas-phase reactions is the lead chamber process, which for many years was the primary method of manufacturing sulfuric acid. Starting with sulfur, we would expect the production of sulfuric acid to occur in the following steps:

$$\text{S}(s) + \text{O}_2(g) \longrightarrow \text{SO}_2(g)$$
$$2\text{SO}_2(g) + \text{O}_2(g) \longrightarrow 2\text{SO}_3(g)$$
$$\text{H}_2\text{O}(l) + \text{SO}_3(g) \longrightarrow \text{H}_2\text{SO}_4(aq)$$

In reality, however, sulfur dioxide is not converted directly to sulfur trioxide; rather, the oxidation is more efficiently carried out in the presence of the catalyst nitrogen dioxide:

$$2\text{SO}_2(g) + 2\text{NO}_2(g) \longrightarrow 2\text{SO}_3(g) + 2\text{NO}(g)$$
$$2\text{NO}(g) + \text{O}_2(g) \longrightarrow 2\text{NO}_2(g)$$

Overall reaction: $\quad 2\text{SO}_2(g) + \text{O}_2(g) \longrightarrow 2\text{SO}_3(g)$

Note that there is no net loss of NO_2 in the overall reaction, so that NO_2 meets the criteria for a catalyst.

In recent years, chemists have devoted much effort to developing a class of metallic compounds to serve as homogeneous catalysts. These compounds are soluble in various organic solvents and therefore can catalyze reactions in the same phase as the dissolved reactants. Many of the processes they catalyze are organic. For example, a red-violet compound of rhodium, $[(\text{C}_6\text{H}_5)_3\text{P}]_3\text{RhCl}$, catalyzes the conversion of a carbon-carbon double bond to a carbon-carbon single bond as follows:

This reaction is important in the food industry. It converts "unsaturated fats" (compounds containing many C=C bonds) to "saturated fats" (compounds containing few or no C=C bonds).

$$\overset{|}{\underset{|}{\text{C}}}=\overset{|}{\underset{|}{\text{C}}} + \text{H}_2 \longrightarrow -\overset{|}{\underset{|}{\text{C}}}-\overset{|}{\underset{|}{\text{C}}}- \\ \qquad\qquad\qquad \text{H} \quad\ \text{H}$$

Homogeneous catalysis has several advantages over heterogeneous catalysis. For one thing, the reactions can often be carried out under atmospheric conditions, thus reducing production costs and minimizing the decomposition of products at high temperatures. In addition, homogeneous catalysts can be designed to function selectively for a particular type of reaction, and homogeneous catalysts cost less than the precious metals (for example, platinum and gold) used in heterogeneous catalysis.

Enzyme Catalysis

Of all the intricate processes that have evolved in living systems, none is more striking or more essential than enzyme catalysis. **Enzymes** are *biological catalysts*. The amazing fact about enzymes is that not only can they increase the rate of biochemical reactions by factors ranging from 10^6 to 10^{18}, but they are also highly specific. An enzyme acts only on certain molecules, called *substrates* (that is, reactants), while leaving the rest of the system unaffected. It has been estimated that an average living

Figure 13.28 *The lock-and-key model of an enzyme's specificity for substrate molecules.*

Substrate + Enzyme → Enzyme-substrate complex → Products + Enzyme

cell may contain some 3000 different enzymes, each of them catalyzing a specific reaction in which a substrate is converted into the appropriate products. Enzyme catalysis is usually homogeneous because the substrate and enzyme are present in aqueous solution.

An enzyme is typically a large protein molecule that contains one or more *active sites* where interactions with substrates take place. These sites are structurally compatible with specific substrate molecules, in much the same way as a key fits a particular lock. In fact, the notion of a rigid enzyme structure that binds only to molecules whose shape exactly matches that of the active site was the basis of an early theory of enzyme catalysis, the so-called lock-and-key theory developed by the German chemist Emil Fischer[†] in 1894 (Figure 13.28). Fischer's hypothesis accounts for the specificity of enzymes, but it contradicts research evidence that a single enzyme binds to substrates of different sizes and shapes. Chemists now know that an enzyme molecule (or at least its active site) has a fair amount of structural flexibility and can modify its shape to accommodate more than one type of substrate. Figure 13.29 shows a molecular model of an enzyme in action.

[†]Emil Fischer (1852–1919). German chemist. Regarded by many as the greatest organic chemist of the nineteenth century, Fischer made many significant contributions in the synthesis of sugars and other important molecules. He was awarded the Nobel Prize in Chemistry in 1902.

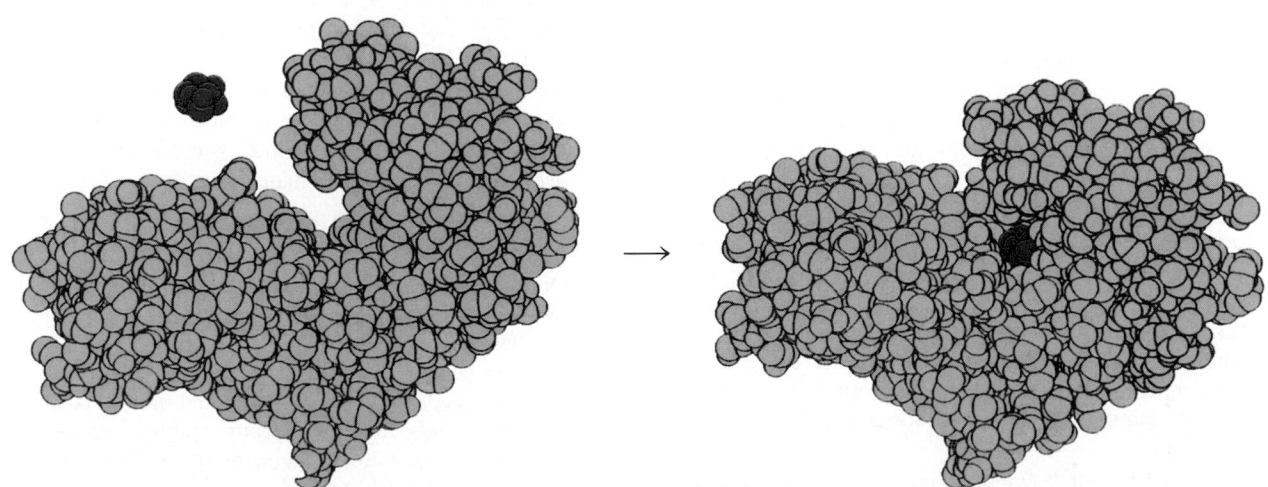

Figure 13.29 *Left to right: The binding of glucose molecule (red) to hexokinase (an enzyme in the metabolic pathway). Note how the region at the active site closes around glucose after binding. Frequently, the geometries of both the substrate and the active site are altered to fit each other.*

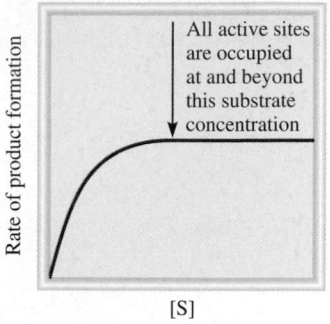

Rate of product formation

All active sites are occupied at and beyond this substrate concentration

[S]

Figure 13.30 *Plot of the rate of product formation versus substrate concentration in an enzyme-catalyzed reaction.*

This scheme is similar to the formation of HI from H_2 and I_2 discussed on p. 578.

The mathematical treatment of enzyme kinetics is quite complex, even when we know the basic steps involved in the reaction. A simplified scheme is given by the following elementary steps:

$$E + S \underset{k_{-1}}{\overset{k_1}{\rightleftharpoons}} ES$$

$$ES \xrightarrow{k_2} E + P$$

where E, S, and P represent enzyme, substrate, and product, and ES is the enzyme-substrate intermediate. It is often assumed that the formation of ES and its decomposition back to enzyme and substrate molecules occur rapidly and that the rate-determining step is the formation of product.

In general, the rate of such a reaction is given by the equation

$$\text{rate} = \frac{\Delta[P]}{\Delta t}$$
$$= k_2[ES]$$

The concentration of the ES intermediate is itself proportional to the amount of the substrate present, and a plot of the rate versus concentration of substrate typically yields a curve like that shown in Figure 13.30. Initially the rate rises rapidly with increasing substrate concentration. However, above a certain concentration all the active sites are occupied, and the reaction becomes zero order in the substrate. In other words, the rate remains the same even though the substrate concentration increases. At and beyond this point, the rate of formation of product depends only on how fast the ES intermediate breaks down, not on the number of substrate molecules present.

Summary of Facts and Concepts

1. The rate of a chemical reaction is the change in the concentration of reactants or products over time. The rate is not constant, but varies continuously as concentrations change.

2. The rate law expresses the relationship of the rate of a reaction to the rate constant and the concentrations of the reactants raised to appropriate powers. The rate constant k for a given reaction changes only with temperature.

3. Reaction order is the power to which the concentration of a given reactant is raised in the rate law. Overall reaction order is the sum of the powers to which reactant concentrations are raised in the rate law. The rate law and the reaction order cannot be determined from the stoichiometry of the overall equation for a reaction; they must be determined by experiment. For a zero-order reaction, the reaction rate is equal to the rate constant.

4. The half-life of a reaction (the time it takes for the concentration of a reactant to decrease by one-half) can be used to determine the rate constant of a first-order reaction.

5. In terms of collision theory, a reaction occurs when molecules collide with sufficient energy, called the activation energy, to break the bonds and initiate the reaction. The rate constant and the activation energy are related by the Arrhenius equation.

6. The overall balanced equation for a reaction may be the sum of a series of simple reactions, called elementary steps. The complete series of elementary steps for a reaction is the reaction mechanism.

7. If one step in a reaction mechanism is much slower than all other steps, it is the rate-determining step.

8. A catalyst speeds up a reaction usually by lowering the value of E_a. A catalyst can be recovered unchanged at the end of a reaction.

9. In heterogeneous catalysis, which is of great industrial importance, the catalyst is a solid and the reactants are gases or liquids. In homogeneous catalysis, the catalyst and the reactants are in the same phase. Enzymes are catalysts in living systems.

Key Words

Questions and Problems

The Rate of a Reaction

Review Questions

13.1 What is meant by the rate of a chemical reaction? What are the units of the rate of a reaction?

13.2 Distinguish between average rate and instantaneous rate. Which of the two rates gives us an unambiguous measurement of reaction rate? Why?

13.3 What are the advantages of measuring the initial rate of a reaction?

13.4 Can you suggest two reactions that are very slow (take days or longer to complete) and two reactions that are very fast (reactions that are over in minutes or seconds)?

Problems

13.5 Write the reaction rate expressions for the following reactions in terms of the disappearance of the reactants and the appearance of products:
(a) $H_2(g) + I_2(g) \longrightarrow 2HI(g)$
(b) $5Br^-(aq) + BrO_3^-(aq) + 6H^+(aq) \longrightarrow$
$\qquad\qquad\qquad 3Br_2(aq) + 3H_2O(l)$

13.6 Write the reaction rate expressions for the following reactions in terms of the disappearance of the reactants and the appearance of products:
(a) $2H_2(g) + O_2(g) \longrightarrow 2H_2O(g)$
(b) $4NH_3(g) + 5O_2(g) \longrightarrow 4NO(g) + 6H_2O(g)$

13.7 Consider the reaction

$$2NO(g) + O_2(g) \longrightarrow 2NO_2(g)$$

Suppose that at a particular moment during the reaction nitric oxide (NO) is reacting at the rate of 0.066 M/s. (a) At what rate is NO_2 being formed? (b) At what rate is molecular oxygen reacting?

13.8 Consider the reaction

$$N_2(g) + 3H_2(g) \longrightarrow 2NH_3(g)$$

Suppose that at a particular moment during the reaction molecular hydrogen is reacting at the rate of 0.074 M/s. (a) At what rate is ammonia being formed? (b) At what rate is molecular nitrogen reacting?

The Rate Law

Review Questions

13.9 Explain what is meant by the rate law of a reaction.

13.10 What is meant by the order of a reaction?

13.11 What are the units for the rate constants of zero-order, first-order, and second-order reactions?

13.12 Consider the zero-order reaction: A $\longrightarrow$ product. (a) Write the rate law for the reaction. (b) What are the units for the rate constant? (c) Plot the rate of the reaction versus [A].

13.13 The rate constant of a first-order reaction is 66 s^{-1}. What is the rate constant in units of minutes?

13.14 On which of the following properties does the rate constant of a reaction depend? (a) reactant concentrations, (b) nature of reactants, (c) temperature.

Problems

13.15 The rate law for the reaction

$$NH_4^+(aq) + NO_2^-(aq) \longrightarrow N_2(g) + 2H_2O(l)$$

is given by rate $= k[NH_4^+][NO_2^-]$. At 25°C, the rate constant is $3.0 \times 10^{-4}/M \cdot$ s. Calculate the rate of the reaction at this temperature if [NH_4^+] = 0.26 M and [NO_2^-] = 0.080 M.

13.16 Use the data in Table 13.2 to calculate the rate of the reaction at the time when [F_2] = 0.010 M and [ClO_2] = 0.020 M.

13.17 Consider the reaction

$$A + B \longrightarrow products$$

From the following data obtained at a certain temperature, determine the order of the reaction and calculate the rate constant:

[A] (M)	[B] (M)	Rate (M/s)
1.50	1.50	3.20×10^{-1}
1.50	2.50	3.20×10^{-1}
3.00	1.50	6.40×10^{-1}

13.18 Consider the reaction

$$X + Y \longrightarrow Z$$

From the following data, obtained at 360 K, (a) determine the order of the reaction, and (b) determine the initial rate of disappearance of X when the concentration of X is 0.30 M and that of Y is 0.40 M.

Initial Rate of Disappearance of X (M/s)	[X] (M)	[Y] (M)
0.053	0.10	0.50
0.127	0.20	0.30
1.02	0.40	0.60
0.254	0.20	0.60
0.509	0.40	0.30

13.19 Determine the overall orders of the reactions to which the following rate laws apply: (a) rate = $k[NO_2]^2$, (b) rate = k, (c) rate = $k[H_2][Br_2]^{\frac{1}{2}}$, (d) rate = $k[NO]^2[O_2]$.

13.20 Consider the reaction

$$A \longrightarrow B$$

The rate of the reaction is 1.6×10^{-2} M/s when the concentration of A is 0.35 M. Calculate the rate constant if the reaction is (a) first order in A and (b) second order in A.

13.21 Cyclobutane decomposes to ethylene according to the equation

$$C_4H_8(g) \longrightarrow 2C_2H_4(g)$$

Determine the order of the reaction and the rate constant based on the following pressures, which were recorded when the reaction was carried out at 430°C in a constant-volume vessel.

Time (s)	$P_{C_4H_8}$ (mmHg)
0	400
2,000	316
4,000	248
6,000	196
8,000	155
10,000	122

13.22 The following gas-phase reaction was studied at 290°C by observing the change in pressure as a function of time in a constant-volume vessel:

$$ClCO_2CCl_3(g) \longrightarrow 2COCl_2(g)$$

Determine the order of the reaction and the rate constant based on the following data:

Time (s)	P (mmHg)
0	15.76
181	18.88
513	22.79
1164	27.08

where P is the total pressure.

The Relation Between Reactant Concentration and Time
Review Questions

13.23 Write an equation relating the concentration of a reactant A at $t = 0$ to that at $t = t$ for a first-order reaction. Define all the terms and give their units. Do the same for a second-order reaction.

13.24 Define half-life. Write the equation relating the half-life of a first-order reaction to the rate constant.

13.25 Write the equations relating the half-life of a second-order reaction to the rate constant. How does it differ from the equation for a first-order reaction?

13.26 For a first-order reaction, how long will it take for the concentration of reactant to fall to one-eighth its original value? Express your answer in terms of the half-life ($t_{\frac{1}{2}}$) and in terms of the rate constant k.

Problems

13.27 What is the half-life of a compound if 75 percent of a given sample of the compound decomposes in 60 min? Assume first-order kinetics.

13.28 The thermal decomposition of phosphine (PH_3) into phosphorus and molecular hydrogen is a first-order reaction:

$$4PH_3(g) \longrightarrow P_4(g) + 6H_2(g)$$

The half-life of the reaction is 35.0 s at 680°C. Calculate (a) the first-order rate constant for the reaction and (b) the time required for 95 percent of the phosphine to decompose.

13.29 The rate constant for the second-order reaction

$$2NOBr(g) \longrightarrow 2NO(g) + Br_2(g)$$

is $0.80/M \cdot$ s at 10°C. (a) Starting with a concentration of 0.086 M, calculate the concentration of NOBr after 22 s. (b) Calculate the half-lives when $[NOBr]_0 = 0.072$ M and $[NOBr]_0 = 0.054$ M.

13.30 The rate constant for the second-order reaction

$$2NO_2(g) \longrightarrow 2NO(g) + O_2(g)$$

is $0.54/M \cdot s$ at $300°C$. How long (in seconds) would it take for the concentration of NO_2 to decrease from $0.62\ M$ to $0.28\ M$?

Activation Energy

Review Questions

13.31 Define activation energy. What role does activation energy play in chemical kinetics?

13.32 Write the Arrhenius equation and define all terms.

13.33 Use the Arrhenius equation to show why the rate constant of a reaction (a) decreases with increasing activation energy and (b) increases with increasing temperature.

13.34 The burning of methane in oxygen is a highly exothermic reaction. Yet a mixture of methane and oxygen gas can be kept indefinitely without any apparent change. Explain.

13.35 Sketch a potential energy versus reaction progress plot for the following reactions:
(a) $S(s) + O_2(g) \longrightarrow SO_2(g)\quad \Delta H° = -296\text{ kJ/mol}$
(b) $Cl_2(g) \longrightarrow Cl(g) + Cl(g)\quad \Delta H° = 243\text{ kJ/mol}$

13.36 The reaction $H + H_2 \longrightarrow H_2 + H$ has been studied for many years. Sketch a potential energy versus reaction progress diagram for this reaction.

Problems

13.37 Variation of the rate constant with temperature for the first-order reaction

$$2N_2O_5(g) \longrightarrow 2N_2O_4(g) + O_2(g)$$

is given in the following table. Determine graphically the activation energy for the reaction.

T (K)	k (s^{-1})
298	1.74×10^{-5}
308	6.61×10^{-5}
318	2.51×10^{-4}
328	7.59×10^{-4}
338	2.40×10^{-3}

13.38 Given the same reactant concentrations, the reaction

$$CO(g) + Cl_2(g) \longrightarrow COCl_2(g)$$

at $250°C$ is 1.50×10^3 times as fast as the same reaction at $150°C$. Calculate the activation energy for this reaction. Assume that the frequency factor is constant.

13.39 For the reaction

$$NO(g) + O_3(g) \longrightarrow NO_2(g) + O_2(g)$$

the frequency factor A is $8.7 \times 10^{12}\ s^{-1}$ and the activation energy is 63 kJ/mol. What is the rate constant for the reaction at $75°C$?

13.40 The rate constant of a first-order reaction is $4.60 \times 10^{-4}\ s^{-1}$ at $350°C$. If the activation energy is 104 kJ/mol, calculate the temperature at which its rate constant is $8.80 \times 10^{-4}\ s^{-1}$.

13.41 The rate constants of some reactions double with every 10-degree rise in temperature. Assume that a reaction takes place at 295 K and 305 K. What must the activation energy be for the rate constant to double as described?

13.42 The rate at which tree crickets chirp is 2.0×10^2 per minute at $27°C$ but only 39.6 per minute at $5°C$. From these data, calculate the "activation energy" for the chirping process. (*Hint:* The ratio of rates is equal to the ratio of rate constants.)

Reaction Mechanisms

Review Questions

13.43 What do we mean by the mechanism of a reaction?

13.44 What is an elementary step? What is the molecularity of a reaction?

13.45 Classify the following elementary reactions as unimolecular, bimolecular, and termolecular:
(a) $2NO + Br_2 \longrightarrow 2NOBr$
(b) $CH_3NC \longrightarrow CH_3CN$
(c) $SO + O_2 \longrightarrow SO_2 + O$

13.46 Reactions can be classified as unimolecular, bimolecular, and so on. Why are there no zero-molecular reactions? Explain why termolecular reactions are rare.

13.47 Determine the molecularity and write the rate law for each of the following elementary steps:
(a) $X \longrightarrow$ products
(b) $X + Y \longrightarrow$ products
(c) $X + Y + Z \longrightarrow$ products
(d) $X + X \longrightarrow$ products
(e) $X + 2Y \longrightarrow$ products

13.48 What is the rate-determining step of a reaction? Give an everyday analogy to illustrate the meaning of "rate determining."

13.49 The equation for the combustion of ethane (C_2H_6) is

$$2C_2H_6(g) + 7O_2(g) \longrightarrow 4CO_2(g) + 6H_2O(l)$$

Explain why it is unlikely that this equation also represents the elementary step for the reaction.

13.50 Specify which of the following species cannot be isolated in a reaction: activated complex, product, intermediate.

Problems

13.51 The rate law for the reaction

$$2NO(g) + Cl_2(g) \longrightarrow 2NOCl(g)$$

is given by rate = $k[NO][Cl_2]$. (a) What is the order of the reaction? (b) A mechanism involving the following steps has been proposed for the reaction:

$$NO(g) + Cl_2(g) \longrightarrow NOCl_2(g)$$
$$NOCl_2(g) + NO(g) \longrightarrow 2NOCl(g)$$

If this mechanism is correct, what does it imply about the relative rates of these two steps?

13.52 For the reaction $X_2 + Y + Z \longrightarrow XY + XZ$ it is found that doubling the concentration of X_2 doubles the reaction rate, tripling the concentration of Y triples the rate, and doubling the concentration of Z has no effect. (a) What is the rate law for this reaction? (b) Why is it that the change in the concentration of Z has no effect on the rate? (c) Suggest a mechanism for the reaction that is consistent with the rate law.

13.53 The rate law for the decomposition of ozone to molecular oxygen

$$2O_3(g) \longrightarrow 3O_2(g)$$

is

$$rate = k\frac{[O_3]^2}{[O_2]}$$

The mechanism proposed for this process is

$$O_3 \underset{k_{-1}}{\overset{k_1}{\rightleftharpoons}} O + O_2$$

$$O + O_3 \overset{k_2}{\longrightarrow} 2O_2$$

Derive the rate law from these elementary steps. Clearly state the assumptions you use in the derivation. Explain why the rate decreases with increasing O_2 concentration.

13.54 The rate law for the reaction

$$2H_2(g) + 2NO(g) \longrightarrow N_2(g) + 2H_2O(g)$$

is rate = $k[H_2][NO]^2$. Which of the following mechanisms can be ruled out on the basis of the observed rate expression?

Mechanism I
$$\begin{array}{ll} H_2 + NO \longrightarrow H_2O + N & \text{(slow)} \\ N + NO \longrightarrow N_2 + O & \text{(fast)} \\ O + H_2 \longrightarrow H_2O & \text{(fast)} \end{array}$$

Mechanism II
$$\begin{array}{ll} H_2 + 2NO \longrightarrow N_2O + H_2O & \text{(slow)} \\ N_2O + H_2 \longrightarrow N_2 + H_2O & \text{(fast)} \end{array}$$

Mechanism III
$$\begin{array}{ll} 2NO \rightleftharpoons N_2O_2 & \text{(fast equilibrium)} \\ N_2O_2 + H_2 \longrightarrow N_2O + H_2O & \text{(slow)} \\ N_2O + H_2 \longrightarrow N_2 + H_2O & \text{(fast)} \end{array}$$

Catalysis
Review Questions

13.55 How does a catalyst increase the rate of a reaction?

13.56 What are the characteristics of a catalyst?

13.57 A certain reaction is known to proceed slowly at room temperature. Is it possible to make the reaction proceed at a faster rate without changing the temperature?

13.58 Distinguish between homogeneous catalysis and heterogeneous catalysis. Describe three important industrial processes that utilize heterogeneous catalysis.

13.59 Are enzyme-catalyzed reactions examples of homogeneous or heterogeneous catalysis? Explain.

13.60 The concentrations of enzymes in cells are usually quite small. What is the biological significance of this fact?

Problems

13.61 Most reactions, including enzyme-catalyzed reactions, proceed faster at higher temperatures. However, for a given enzyme, the rate drops off abruptly at a certain temperature. Account for this behavior.

13.62 Consider the following mechanism for the enzyme-catalyzed reaction:

$$E + S \underset{k_{-1}}{\overset{k_1}{\rightleftharpoons}} ES \qquad \text{(fast equilibrium)}$$
$$ES \overset{k_2}{\longrightarrow} E + P \qquad \text{(slow)}$$

Derive an expression for the rate law of the reaction in terms of the concentrations of E and S. (*Hint:* To solve for [ES], make use of the fact that, at equilibrium, the rate of forward reaction is equal to the rate of the reverse reaction.)

Additional Problems

13.63 Suggest experimental means by which the rates of the following reactions could be followed:
(a) $CaCO_3(s) \longrightarrow CaO(s) + CO_2(g)$
(b) $Cl_2(g) + 2Br^-(aq) \longrightarrow Br_2(aq) + 2Cl^-(aq)$
(c) $C_2H_6(g) \longrightarrow C_2H_4(g) + H_2(g)$
(d) $C_2H_5I(g) + H_2O(l) \longrightarrow$
$$C_2H_5OH(aq) + H^+(aq) + I^-(aq)$$

13.64 List four factors that influence the rate of a reaction.

13.65 "The rate constant for the reaction

$$NO_2(g) + CO(g) \longrightarrow NO(g) + CO_2(g)$$

is $1.64 \times 10^{-6}/M \cdot s$." What is incomplete about this statement?

13.66 In a certain industrial process involving a heterogeneous catalyst, the volume of the catalyst (in the shape of a sphere) is 10.0 cm³. Calculate the surface area of the catalyst. If the sphere is broken down into eight spheres, each having a volume of 1.25 cm^3, what is the total surface area of the spheres? Which of the two geometric configurations of the catalyst is more effective? (The surface area of a sphere is $4\pi r^2$, where r is the radius of the sphere.) Based on your analysis here, explain why it is sometimes dangerous to work in grain elevators.

13.67 Use the data in Example 13.5 to determine graphically the half-life of the reaction.

13.68 The following data were collected for the reaction between hydrogen and nitric oxide at 700°C:

$$2H_2(g) + 2NO(g) \longrightarrow 2H_2O(g) + N_2(g)$$

Experiment	[H$_2$]	[NO]	Initial Rate (M/s)
1	0.010	0.025	2.4×10^{-6}
2	0.0050	0.025	1.2×10^{-6}
3	0.010	0.0125	0.60×10^{-6}

(a) Determine the order of the reaction. (b) Calculate the rate constant. (c) Suggest a plausible mechanism that is consistent with the rate law. (*Hint:* Assume that the oxygen atom is the intermediate.)

13.69 When methyl phosphate is heated in acid solution, it reacts with water:

$$CH_3OPO_3H_2 + H_2O \longrightarrow CH_3OH + H_3PO_4$$

If the reaction is carried out in water enriched with ^{18}O, the oxygen 18 isotope is found in the phosphoric acid product but not in the methanol. What does this tell us about the mechanism of the reaction?

13.70 The rate of the reaction

$$CH_3COOC_2H_5(aq) + H_2O(l) \longrightarrow$$
$$CH_3COOH(aq) + C_2H_5OH(aq)$$

shows first-order characteristics—that is, rate = $k[CH_3COOC_2H_5]$—even though this is a second-order reaction (first order in $CH_3COOC_2H_5$ and first order in H_2O). Explain.

13.71 Explain why most metals used in catalysis are transition metals.

13.72 The reaction 2A + 3B $\longrightarrow$ C is first order with respect to A and B. When the initial concentrations are [A] = 1.6×10^{-2} M and [B] = 2.4×10^{-3} M, the rate is 4.1×10^{-4} M/s. Calculate the rate constant of the reaction.

13.73 The bromination of acetone is acid-catalyzed:

$$CH_3COCH_3 + Br_2 \xrightarrow[\text{catalyst}]{H^+} CH_3COCH_2Br + H^+ + Br^-$$

The rate of disappearance of bromine was measured for several different concentrations of acetone, bromine, and H$^+$ ions at a certain temperature:

	[CH$_3$COCH$_3$]	[Br$_2$]	[H$^+$]	Rate of Disappearance of Br$_2$ (M/s)
(1)	0.30	0.050	0.050	5.7×10^{-5}
(2)	0.30	0.10	0.050	5.7×10^{-5}
(3)	0.30	0.050	0.10	1.2×10^{-4}
(4)	0.40	0.050	0.20	3.1×10^{-4}
(5)	0.40	0.050	0.050	7.6×10^{-5}

(a) What is the rate law for the reaction? (b) Determine the rate constant. (c) The following mechanism has been proposed for the reaction:

$$CH_3\!-\!\overset{\displaystyle O}{\overset{\|}{C}}\!-\!CH_3 + H_3O^+ \rightleftharpoons CH_3\!-\!\overset{\displaystyle ^+OH}{\overset{\|}{C}}\!-\!CH_3 + H_2O$$
(fast equilibrium)

$$CH_3\!-\!\overset{\displaystyle ^+OH}{\overset{\|}{C}}\!-\!CH_3 + H_2O \longrightarrow CH_3\!-\!\overset{\displaystyle OH}{\overset{|}{C}}\!=\!CH_2 + H_3O^+ \; \text{(slow)}$$

$$CH_3\!-\!\overset{\displaystyle OH}{\overset{|}{C}}\!-\!CH_2 + Br_2 \longrightarrow CH_3\!-\!\overset{\displaystyle O}{\overset{\|}{C}}\; CH_2Br + HBr \; \text{(fast)}$$

Show that the rate law deduced from the mechanism is consistent with that shown in (a).

13.74 The decomposition of N$_2$O to N$_2$ and O$_2$ is a first-order reaction. At 730°C the half-life of the reaction is 3.58×10^3 min. If the initial pressure of N$_2$O is 2.10 atm at 730°C, calculate the total gas pressure after one half-life. Assume that the volume remains constant.

13.75 The reaction $S_2O_8^{2-} + 2I^- \longrightarrow 2SO_4^{2-} + I_2$ proceeds slowly in aqueous solution, but it can be catalyzed by the Fe^{3+} ion. Given that Fe^{3+} can oxidize I$^-$ and Fe^{2+} can reduce $S_2O_8^{2-}$, write a plausible two-step mechanism for this reaction. Explain why the uncatalyzed reaction is slow.

13.76 What are the units of the rate constant for a third-order reaction?

13.77 The integrated rate law for the zero-order reaction A $\longrightarrow$ B is [A]$_t$ = [A]$_0$ $- kt$. (a) Sketch the following plots: (i) rate versus [A]$_t$ and (ii) [A]$_t$ versus t. (b) Derive an expression for the half-life of the reaction. (c) Calculate the time in half-lives when the integrated rate law is no longer valid, that is, when [A]$_t = 0$.

13.78 A flask contains a mixture of compounds A and B. Both compounds decompose by first-order kinetics. The half-lives are 50.0 min for A and 18.0 min for B. If the concentrations of A and B are equal initially, how long will it take for the concentration of A to be four times that of B?

13.79 Referring to Example 13.5, explain how you would measure the partial pressure of azomethane experimentally as a function of time.

13.80 The rate law for the reaction $2NO_2(g) \longrightarrow N_2O_4(g)$ is rate $= k[NO_2]^2$. Which of the following changes will change the value of k? (a) The pressure of NO_2 is doubled. (b) The reaction is run in an organic solvent. (c) The volume of the container is doubled. (d) The temperature is decreased. (e) A catalyst is added to the container.

13.81 The reaction of G_2 with E_2 to form 2EG is exothermic, and the reaction of G_2 with X_2 to form 2XG is endothermic. The activation energy of the exothermic reaction is greater than that of the endothermic reaction. Sketch the potential energy profile diagrams for these two reactions on the same graph.

13.82 In the nuclear industry, workers use a rule of thumb that the radioactivity from any sample will be relatively harmless after ten half-lives. Calculate the fraction of a radioactive sample that remains after this time period. (*Hint:* Radioactive decays obey first-order kinetics.)

13.83 Briefly comment on the effect of a catalyst on each of the following: (a) activation energy, (b) reaction mechanism, (c) enthalpy of reaction, (d) rate of forward step, (e) rate of reverse step.

13.84 When 6 g of granulated Zn is added to a solution of 2 *M* HCl in a beaker at room temperature, hydrogen gas is generated. For each of the following changes (at constant volume of the acid) state whether the rate of hydrogen gas evolution will be increased, decreased, or unchanged: (a) 6 g of powdered Zn is used; (b) 4 g of granulated Zn is used; (c) 2 *M* acetic acid is used instead of 2 *M* HCl; (d) temperature is raised to 40°C.

13.85 Strictly speaking, the rate law derived for the reaction in Problem 13.68 applies only to certain concentrations of H_2. The general rate law for the reaction takes the form

$$\text{rate} = \frac{k_1[NO]^2[H_2]}{1 + k_2[H_2]}$$

where k_1 and k_2 are constants. Derive rate law expressions under the conditions of very high and very low hydrogen concentrations. Does the result from Problem 13.68 agree with one of the rate expressions here?

13.86 A certain first-order reaction is 35.5 percent complete in 4.90 min at 25°C. What is its rate constant?

13.87 The decomposition of dinitrogen pentoxide has been studied in carbon tetrachloride solvent (CCl_4) at a certain temperature:

$$2N_2O_5 \longrightarrow 4NO_2 + O_2$$

$[N_2O_5]$	Initial Rate (*M*/s)
0.92	0.95×10^{-5}
1.23	1.20×10^{-5}
1.79	1.93×10^{-5}
2.00	2.10×10^{-5}
2.21	2.26×10^{-5}

Determine graphically the rate law for the reaction and calculate the rate constant.

13.88 The thermal decomposition of N_2O_5 obeys first-order kinetics. At 45°C, a plot of ln $[N_2O_5]$ versus t gives a slope of -6.18×10^{-4} min^{-1}. What is the half-life of the reaction?

13.89 When a mixture of methane and bromine is exposed to visible light, the following reaction occurs slowly:

$$CH_4(g) + Br_2(g) \longrightarrow CH_3Br(g) + HBr(g)$$

Suggest a reasonable mechanism for this reaction. (*Hint:* Bromine vapor is deep red; methane is colorless.)

13.90 The rate of the reaction between H_2 and I_2 to form HI (discussed on p. 577) increases with the intensity of visible light. (a) Explain why this fact supports the two-step mechanism given. (The color of I_2 vapor is shown on p. 487.) (b) Explain why the visible light has no effect on the formation of H atoms.

13.91 The carbon-14 decay rate of a sample obtained from a young tree is 0.260 disintegration per second per gram of the sample. Another wood sample prepared from an object recovered at an archaeological excavation gives a decay rate of 0.186 disintegration per second per gram of the sample. What is the age of the object? (*Hint:* See Chemistry in Action essay on p. 568.)

13.92 Consider the following elementary step:

$$X + 2Y \longrightarrow XY_2$$

(a) Write a rate law for this reaction. (b) If the initial rate of formation of XY_2 is 3.8×10^{-3} *M*/s and the initial concentrations of X and Y are 0.26 *M* and 0.88 *M*, what is the rate constant of the reaction?

13.93 In recent years ozone in the stratosphere has been depleted at an alarmingly fast rate by chlorofluorocarbons (CFCs). A CFC molecule such as $CFCl_3$ is first decomposed by UV radiation:

$$CFCl_3 \longrightarrow CFCl_2 + Cl$$

The chlorine radical then reacts with ozone as follows:

$$Cl + O_3 \longrightarrow ClO + O_2$$
$$ClO + O \longrightarrow Cl + O_2$$

The O atom is from the photochemical decomposition of O_2 molecules.

(a) Write the overall reaction for the last two steps. (b) What are the roles of Cl and ClO? (c) Why is the fluorine radical not important in this mechanism? (d) One suggestion to reduce the concentration of chlorine radicals is to add hydrocarbons such as ethane (C_2H_6) to the stratosphere. How will this work? (e) Draw potential energy versus reaction progress diagrams for the uncatalyzed and catalyzed (by Cl) destruction of ozone: $O_3 + O \longrightarrow 2O_2$. Use the thermodynamic data in Appendix 3 to determine whether the reaction is exothermic or endothermic.

13.94 Chlorine oxide (ClO), which plays an important role in the depletion of ozone (see Problem 13.93), decays rapidly at room temperature according to the equation

$$2ClO(g) \longrightarrow Cl_2(g) + O_2(g)$$

From the following data, determine the reaction order and calculate the rate constant of the reaction

Time (s)	[ClO] (M)
0.12×10^{-3}	8.49×10^{-6}
0.96×10^{-3}	7.10×10^{-6}
2.24×10^{-3}	5.79×10^{-6}
3.20×10^{-3}	5.20×10^{-6}
4.00×10^{-3}	4.77×10^{-6}

13.95 A compound X undergoes two *simultaneous* first-order reactions as follows: X $\longrightarrow$ Y with rate constant k_1 and X $\longrightarrow$ Z with rate constant k_2. The ratio of k_1/k_2 at 40°C is 8.0. What is the ratio at 300°C? Assume that the frequency factors of the two reactions are the same.

13.96 Consider a car fitted with a catalytic converter. The first five minutes or so after it is started are the most polluting. Why?

13.97 The following scheme in which A is converted to B, which is then converted to C is known as a consecutive reaction.

$$A \longrightarrow B \longrightarrow C$$

Assuming that both steps are first-order, sketch on the same graph the variations of [A], [B], and [C] with time.

13.98 (a) What can you deduce about the activation energy of a reaction if its rate constant changes significantly with a small change in temperature? (b) If a bimolecular reaction occurs every time an A and a B molecule collide, what can you say about the orientation factor and activation energy of the reaction?

13.99 The rate law for the following reaction

$$CO(g) + NO_2(g) \longrightarrow CO_2(g) + NO(g)$$

is rate = $k[NO_2]^2$. Suggest a plausible mechanism for the reaction, given that the unstable species NO_3 is an intermediate.

13.100 Radioactive plutonium-239 ($t_{\frac{1}{2}} = 2.44 \times 10^5$ yr) is used in nuclear reactors and atomic bombs. If there are 5.0×10^2 g of the isotope in a small atomic bomb, how long will it take for the substance to decay to 1.0×10^2 g, too small an amount for an effective bomb?

13.101 Many reactions involving heterogeneous catalysts are zero order; that is, rate = k. An example is the decomposition of phosphine (PH_3) over tungsten (W):

$$4PH_3(g) \longrightarrow P_4(g) + 6H_2(g)$$

It is found that the reaction is independent of [PH_3] as long as phosphine's pressure is sufficiently high (≥ 1 atm). Explain.

13.102 Thallium(I) is oxidized by cerium(IV) as follows:

$$Tl^+ + 2Ce^{4+} \longrightarrow Tl^{3+} + 2Ce^{3+}$$

The elementary steps, in the presence of Mn(II), are as follows:

$$Ce^{4+} + Mn^{2+} \longrightarrow Ce^{3+} + Mn^{3+}$$
$$Ce^{4+} + Mn^{3+} \longrightarrow Ce^{3+} + Mn^{4+}$$
$$Tl^+ + Mn^{4+} \longrightarrow Tl^{3+} + Mn^{2+}$$

(a) Identify the catalyst, intermediates, and the rate-determining step if the rate law is rate = $k[Ce^{4+}][Mn^{2+}]$. (b) Explain why the reaction is slow without the catalyst. (c) Classify the type of catalysis (homogeneous or heterogeneous).

13.103 Sucrose ($C_{12}H_{22}O_{11}$), commonly called table sugar, undergoes hydrolysis (reaction with water) to produce fructose ($C_6H_{12}O_6$) and glucose ($C_6H_{12}O_6$):

$$C_{12}H_{22}O_{11} + H_2O \longrightarrow \underset{\text{fructose}}{C_6H_{12}O_6} + \underset{\text{glucose}}{C_6H_{12}O_6}$$

This reaction is of considerable importance in the candy industry. First, fructose is sweeter than sucrose. Second, a mixture of fructose and glucose, called *invert sugar*, does not crystallize, so the candy containing this sugar would be chewy rather than brittle as candy containing sucrose crystals would be. (a) From the following data determine the order of the reaction. (b) How long does it take to hydrolyze 95 percent of sucrose? (c) Explain why the rate law does not include [H_2O] even though water is a reactant.

Time (min)	[$C_{12}H_{22}O_{11}$]
0	0.500
60.0	0.400
96.4	0.350
157.5	0.280

13.104 The first-order rate constant for the decomposition of dimethyl ether

$$(CH_3)_2O(g) \longrightarrow CH_4(g) + H_2(g) + CO(g)$$

is $3.2 \times 10^{-4} \, s^{-1}$ at 450°C. The reaction is carried out in a constant-volume flask. Initially only dimethyl ether is present and the pressure is 0.350 atm. What is the pressure of the system after 8.0 min? Assume ideal behavior.

13.105 At 25°C, the rate constant for the ozone-depleting reaction $O(g) + O_3(g) \longrightarrow 2O_2(g)$ is 7.9×10^{-15} cm^3/molecule · s. Express the rate constant in units of $1/M \cdot s$.

13.106 Consider the following elementary steps for a consecutive reaction:

$$A \xrightarrow{k_1} B \xrightarrow{k_2} C$$

(a) Write an expression for the rate of change of B. (b) Derive an expression for the concentration of B under steady-state conditions; that is, when B is decomposing to C at the same rate as it is formed from A.

13.107 Ethanol is a toxic substance that, when consumed in excess, can impair respiratory and cardiac functions by interference with the neurotransmitters of the nervous system. In the human body, ethanol is metabolized by the enzyme alcohol dehydrogenase to acetaldehyde, which causes "hangovers." (a) Based on your knowledge of enzyme kinetics, explain why binge drinking (that is, consuming too much alcohol too fast) can prove fatal. (b) Methanol is even more toxic than ethanol. It is also metabolized by alcohol dehydrogenase, and the product, formaldehyde, can cause blindness or death. An antidote to methanol poisoning is ethanol. Explain how this procedure works.

13.108 Strontium-90, a radioactive isotope, is a major product of an atomic bomb explosion. It has a half-life of 28.1 yr. (a) Calculate the first-order rate constant for the nuclear decay. (b) Calculate the fraction of ^{90}Sr that remains after 10 half-lives. (c) Calculate the number of years required for 99.0 percent of ^{90}Sr to disappear.

13.109 Consider the potential energy profiles for the following three reactions (from left to right). (1) Rank the rates (slowest to fastest) of the reactions. (2) Calculate ΔH for each reaction and determine which reaction(s) are exothermic and which reaction(s) are endothermic. Assume the reactions have roughly the same frequency factors.

(a)   (b)   (c)

13.110 Consider the following potential energy profile for the A $\longrightarrow$ D reaction. (a) How many elementary

steps are there? (b) How many intermediates are formed? (c) Which step is rate determining? (d) Is the overall reaction exothermic or endothermic?

Reaction progress

13.111 A factory that specializes in the refinement of transition metals such as titanium was on fire. The firefighters were advised not to douse the fire with water. Why?

13.112 The activation energy for the decomposition of hydrogen peroxide

$$2H_2O_2(aq) \longrightarrow 2H_2O_2(l) + O_2(g)$$

is 42 kJ/mol, whereas when the reaction is catalyzed by the enzyme catalase, it is 7.0 kJ/mol. Calculate the temperature that would cause the nonenzymatic catalysis to proceed as rapidly as the enzyme-catalyzed decomposition at 20°C. Assume the frequency factor A to be the same in both cases.

13.113 The *activity* of a radioactive sample is the number of nuclear disintegrations per second, which is equal to the first-order rate constant times the number of radioactive nuclei present. The fundamental unit of radioactivity is the *curie* (Ci), where 1 Ci corresponds to exactly 3.70×10^{10} disintegrations per second. This decay rate is equivalent to that of 1 g of radium-226. Calculate the rate constant and half-life for the radium decay. Starting with 1.0 g of the radium sample, what is the activity after 500 yr? The molar mass of Ra-226 is 226.03 g/mol.

13.114 To carry out metabolism, oxygen is taken up by hemoglobin (Hb) to form oxyhemoglobin (HbO$_2$) according to the simplified equation

$$Hb(aq) + O_2(aq) \xrightarrow{k} HbO_2(aq)$$

where the second-order rate constant is $2.1 \times 10^6/M \cdot s$ at 37°C. For an average adult, the concentrations of Hb and O$_2$ in the blood at the lungs are $8.0 \times 10^{-6} \, M$ and $1.5 \times 10^{-6} \, M$, respectively. (a) Calculate the rate of formation of HbO$_2$. (b) Calculate the rate of consumption of O$_2$. (c) The rate of formation of HbO$_2$ increases to $1.4 \times 10^{-4} \, M/s$ during exercise to meet the demand of increased metabolism rate. Assuming the Hb concentration to remain the same, what must be the oxygen concentration to sustain this rate of HbO$_2$ formation?

13.115 At a certain elevated temperature, ammonia decomposes on the surface of tungsten metal as follows:

$$2NH_3 \longrightarrow N_2 + 3H_2$$

From the following plot of the rate of the reaction versus the pressure of NH_3, describe the mechanism of the reaction.

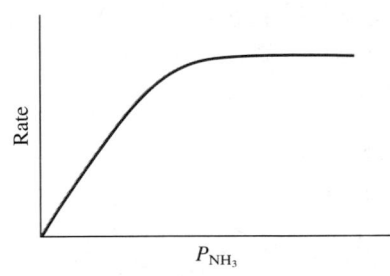

13.116 The following expression shows the dependence of the half-life of a reaction ($t_{\frac{1}{2}}$) on the initial reactant concentration $[A]_0$:

$$t_{\frac{1}{2}} \propto \frac{1}{[A]_0^{n-1}}$$

where n is the order of the reaction. Verify this dependence for zero-, first-, and second-order reactions.

Special Problems

13.117 Polyethylene is used in many items, including water pipes, bottles, electrical insulation, toys, and mailer envelopes. It is a *polymer,* a molecule with a very high molar mass made by joining many ethylene molecules together. (Ethylene is the basic unit, or monomer for polyethylene.) The initiation step is

$$R_2 \xrightarrow{k_i} 2R \cdot \qquad \text{initiation}$$

The R · species (called a radical) reacts with an ethylene molecule (M) to generate another radical

$$R \cdot + M \longrightarrow M_1 \cdot$$

Reaction of M_1 · with another monomer leads to the growth or propagation of the polymer chain:

$$M_1 \cdot + M \xrightarrow{k_p} M_2 \cdot \qquad \text{propagation}$$

This step can be repeated with hundreds of monomer units. The propagation terminates when two radicals combine

$$M' \cdot + M'' \cdot \xrightarrow{k_t} M' - M'' \qquad \text{termination}$$

The initiator frequently used in the polymerization of ethylene is benzoyl peroxide $[(C_6H_5COO)_2]$:

$$[(C_6H_5COO)_2] \longrightarrow 2C_6H_5COO \cdot$$

This is a first-order reaction. The half-life of benzoyl peroxide at 100°C is 19.8 min. (a) Calculate the rate constant (in min^{-1}) of the reaction. (b) If the half-life of benzoyl peroxide is 7.30 h, or 438 min, at 70°C, what is the activation energy (in kJ/mol) for the decomposition of benzoyl peroxide? (c) Write the rate laws for the elementary steps in the above polymerization process, and identify the reactant, product, and intermediates. (d) What condition would favor the growth of long, high-molar-mass polyethylenes?

13.118 The rate constant for the gaseous reaction

$$H_2(g) + I_2(g) \longrightarrow 2HI(g)$$

is $2.42 \times 10^{-2}/M \cdot s$ at 400°C. Initially an equimolar sample of H_2 and I_2 is placed in a vessel at 400°C and the total pressure is 1658 mmHg. (a) What is the initial rate (M/min) of formation of HI? (b) What are the rate of formation of HI and the concentration of HI (in molarity) after 10.0 min?

13.119 A protein molecule, P, of molar mass $\mathcal{M}$ dimerizes when it is allowed to stand in solution at room temperature. A plausible mechanism is that the protein molecule is first denatured (that is, loses its activity due to a change in overall structure) before it dimerizes:

$$
\begin{aligned}
P &\xrightarrow{k} P^* \text{ (denatured)} & \text{slow} \\
2P^* &\longrightarrow P_2 & \text{fast}
\end{aligned}
$$

where the asterisk denotes a denatured protein molecule. Derive an expression for the average molar mass (of P and P_2), $\overline{\mathcal{M}}$, in terms of the initial protein concentration $[P]_0$ and the concentration at time t, $[P]_t$, and $\mathcal{M}$. Describe how you would determine k from molar mass measurements.

13.120 When the concentration of A in the reaction A → B was changed from 1.20 M to 0.60 M, the half-life increased from 2.0 min to 4.0 min at 25°C. Calculate the order of the reaction and the rate constant. (*Hint:* Use the equation in Problem 13.116.)

13.121 At a certain elevated temperature, ammonia decomposes on the surface of tungsten metal as follows:

$$NH_3 \longrightarrow \tfrac{1}{2}N_2 + \tfrac{3}{2}H_2$$

The kinetic data are expressed as the variation of the half-life with the initial pressure of NH_3:

P (mmHg)	264	130	59	16
$t_{\frac{1}{2}}$ (s)	456	228	102	60

(a) Determine the order of the reaction. (b) How does the order depend on the initial pressure? (c) How does the mechanism of the reaction vary with pressure? (*Hint:* You need to use the equation in Problem 13.116 and plot log $t_{\frac{1}{2}}$ versus log P.)

13.122 The activation energy for the reaction

$$N_2O(g) \longrightarrow N_2(g) + O(g)$$

is 2.4×10^2 kJ/mol at 600 K. Calculate the percentage of the increase in rate from 600 K to 606 K. Comment on your results.

13.123 The rate of a reaction was followed by the absorption of light by the reactants and products as a function of wavelengths $(\lambda_1, \lambda_2, \lambda_3)$ as time progresses. Which of the following mechanisms is consistent with the experimental data?

(a) A $\longrightarrow$ B, A $\longrightarrow$ C
(b) A $\longrightarrow$ B + C
(c) A $\longrightarrow$ B, B $\longrightarrow$ C + D
(d) A $\longrightarrow$ B, B $\longrightarrow$ C

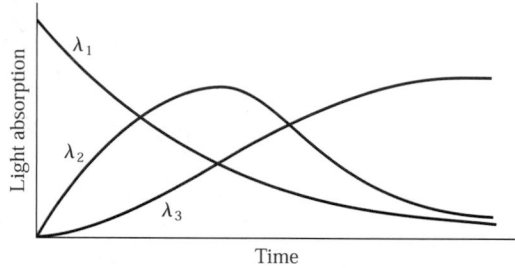

Answers to Practice Exercises

13.1

$$\text{rate} = -\frac{\Delta[CH_4]}{\Delta t} = -\frac{1}{2}\frac{\Delta[O_2]}{\Delta t} = \frac{\Delta[CO_2]}{\Delta t} = \frac{1}{2}\frac{\Delta[H_2O]}{\Delta t}.$$

13.2 (a) 0.013 M/s. (b) -0.052 M/s.
13.3 rate $= k[S_2O_8^{2-}][I^-]$; $k = 8.1 \times 10^{-2}/M \cdot s$.
13.4 66 s. **13.5** First order. 1.4×10^{-2} min^{-1}.
13.6 1.2×10^3 s. **13.7** (a) 3.2 min. (b) 2.1 min.
13.8 240 kJ/mol. **13.9** 3.13×10^{-9} s^{-1}.
13.10 (a) $NO_2 + CO \longrightarrow NO + CO_2$. (b) NO_3.
(c) The first step is rate-determining.

14

The equilibrium between dinitrogen tetroxide (colorless) and nitrogen dioxide (brown color) gases favor the formation of the latter as temperature increases (from bottom to top). The models show dinitrogen tetroxide and nitrogen dioxide molecules.

Chemical Equilibrium

A LOOK AHEAD

- We begin by discussing the nature of equilibrium and the difference between chemical and physical equilibrium. We define the equilibrium constant in terms of the law of mass action. (14.1)

- We then learn to write the equilibrium constant expression for homogeneous and heterogeneous equilibria. We see how to express equilibrium constants for multiple equilibria. (14.2)

- Next, we examine the relationship between the rate constants and equilibrium constant of a reaction. This exercise shows why the equilibrium constant is a constant and why it varies with temperature. (14.3)

- We see that knowing the equilibrium constant enables us to predict the direction of a net reaction toward equilibrium and to calculate equilibrium concentrations. (14.4)

- The chapter concludes with a discussion of the four factors that might affect the position of an equilibrium: concentration, volume or pressure, temperature, and catalyst. We learn to use Le Châtelier's principle to predict the changes. (14.5)

Interactive Activity Summary

1. Animation: Chemical Equilibrium (14.1)
2. Interactivity: Determining Extent—Equilibrium Constant (14.4)
3. Interactivity: Determining Extent—Concentration from Equilibrium Expression (14.4)
4. Animation: Le Châtelier's Principle (14.5)

Equilibrium is a state in which there are no observable changes as time goes by. When a chemical reaction has reached the equilibrium state, the concentrations of reactants and products remain constant over time, and there are no visible changes in the system. However, there is much activity at the molecular level because reactant molecules continue to form product molecules while product molecules react to yield reactant molecules. This dynamic situation is the subject of this chapter. Here we will discuss different types of equilibrium reactions, the meaning of the equilibrium constant and its relationship to the rate constant, and factors that can disrupt a system at equilibrium.

14.1 The Concept of Equilibrium and the Equilibrium Constant

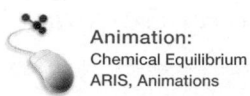

Animation:
Chemical Equilibrium
ARIS, Animations

Liquid water in equilibrium with its vapor in a closed system at room temperature.

NO$_2$ and N$_2$O$_4$ gases at equilibrium.

Figure 14.1 *A reversible reaction between N$_2$O$_4$ and NO$_2$ molecules.*

Few chemical reactions proceed in only one direction. Most are reversible, at least to some extent. At the start of a reversible process, the reaction proceeds toward the formation of products. As soon as some product molecules are formed, the reverse process begins to take place and reactant molecules are formed from product molecules. **Chemical equilibrium** is achieved when *the rates of the forward and reverse reactions are equal and the concentrations of the reactants and products remain constant.*

Chemical equilibrium is a dynamic process. As such, it can be likened to the movement of skiers at a busy ski resort, where the number of skiers carried up the mountain on the chair lift is equal to the number coming down the slopes. Although there is a constant transfer of skiers, the number of people at the top and the number at the bottom of the slope do not change.

Note that chemical equilibrium involves different substances as reactants and products. Equilibrium between two phases of the same substance is called **physical equilibrium** because *the changes that occur are physical processes.* The vaporization of water in a closed container at a given temperature is an example of physical equilibrium. In this instance, the number of H$_2$O molecules leaving and the number returning to the liquid phase are equal:

$$H_2O(l) \rightleftharpoons H_2O(g)$$

(Recall from Chapter 4 that the double arrow means that the reaction is reversible.)

The study of physical equilibrium yields useful information, such as the equilibrium vapor pressure (see Section 11.8). However, chemists are particularly interested in chemical equilibrium processes, such as the reversible reaction involving nitrogen dioxide (NO$_2$) and dinitrogen tetroxide (N$_2$O$_4$) (Figure 14.1). The progress of the reaction

$$N_2O_4(g) \rightleftharpoons 2NO_2(g)$$

can be monitored easily because N$_2$O$_4$ is a colorless gas, whereas NO$_2$ has a dark-brown color that makes it sometimes visible in polluted air. Suppose that N$_2$O$_4$ is injected into an evacuated flask. Some brown color appears immediately, indicating the formation of NO$_2$ molecules. The color intensifies as the dissociation of N$_2$O$_4$ continues until eventually equilibrium is reached. Beyond that point, no further change in color is evident because the concentrations of both N$_2$O$_4$ and NO$_2$ remain constant. We can also bring about an equilibrium state by starting with pure NO$_2$. As some of the NO$_2$ molecules combine to form N$_2$O$_4$, the color fades. Yet another way to create an equilibrium state is to start with a mixture of NO$_2$ and N$_2$O$_4$ and monitor the system until the color stops changing. These studies demonstrate that the preceding

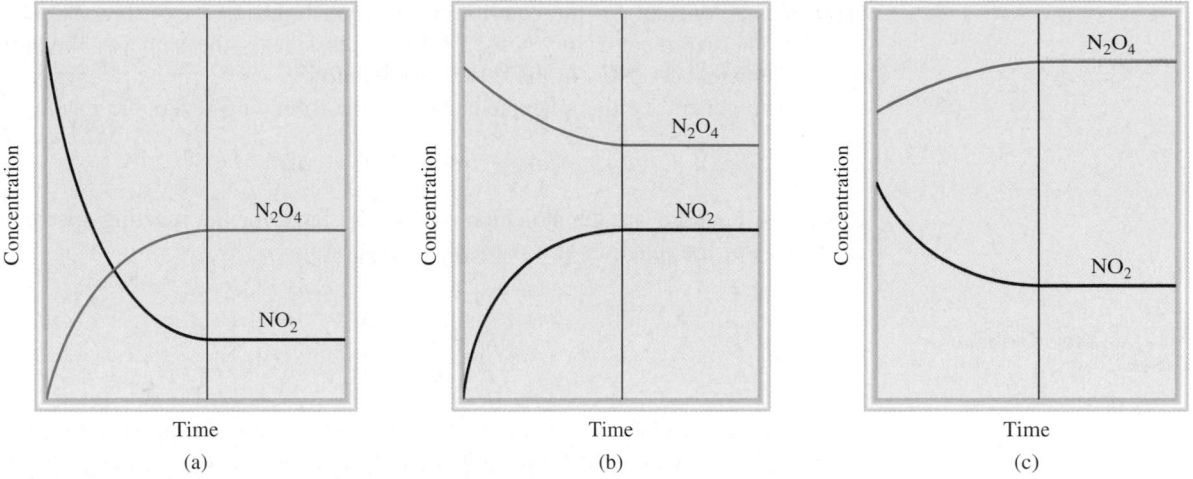

Figure 14.2 *Change in the concentrations of NO_2 and N_2O_4 with time, in three situations. (a) Initially only NO_2 is present. (b) Initially only N_2O_4 is present. (c) Initially a mixture of NO_2 and N_2O_4 is present. In each case, equilibrium is established to the right of the vertical line.*

reaction is indeed reversible, because a pure component (N_2O_4 or NO_2) reacts to give the other gas. The important thing to keep in mind is that at equilibrium, the conversions of N_2O_4 to NO_2 and of NO_2 to N_2O_4 are still going on. We do not see a color change because the two rates are equal—the removal of NO_2 molecules takes place as fast as the production of NO_2 molecules, and N_2O_4 molecules are formed as quickly as they dissociate. Figure 14.2 summarizes these three situations.

The Equilibrium Constant

Table 14.1 shows some experimental data for the NO_2–N_2O_4 system at 25°C. The gas concentrations are expressed in molarity, which can be calculated from the number of moles of the gases present initially and at equilibrium and the volume of the flask in liters. Analysis of the equilibrium data shows that although the ratio $[NO_2]/[N_2O_4]$ gives scattered values, the ratio $[NO_2]^2/[N_2O_4]$ gives a nearly constant value that averages 4.63×10^{-3}:

$$K = \frac{[NO_2]^2}{[N_2O_4]} = 4.63 \times 10^{-3} \qquad (14.1)$$

TABLE 14.1	The NO₂–N₂O₄ System at 25°C				
Initial Concentrations (*M*)		Equilibrium Concentrations (*M*)		Ratio of Concentrations at Equilibrium	
[NO₂]	**[N₂O₄]**	**[NO₂]**	**[N₂O₄]**	$\dfrac{[NO_2]}{[N_2O_4]}$	$\dfrac{[NO_2]^2}{[N_2O_4]}$
0.000	0.670	0.0547	0.643	0.0851	4.65×10^{-3}
0.0500	0.446	0.0457	0.448	0.102	4.66×10^{-3}
0.0300	0.500	0.0475	0.491	0.0967	4.60×10^{-3}
0.0400	0.600	0.0523	0.594	0.0880	4.60×10^{-3}
0.200	0.000	0.0204	0.0898	0.227	4.63×10^{-3}

where K is a constant for the equilibrium reaction $N_2O_4(g) \rightleftharpoons 2NO_2(g)$ at 25°C. Note that the exponent 2 for $[NO_2]$ in this expression is the same as the stoichiometric coefficient for NO_2 in the reversible reaction.

We can generalize this phenomenon with the following reversible reaction:

$$a\text{A} + b\text{B} \rightleftharpoons c\text{C} + d\text{D}$$

where a, b, c, and d are the stoichiometric coefficients for the reacting species A, B, C, and D. For the reaction at a particular temperature

Equilibrium concentrations must be used in this equation.

$$K = \frac{[\text{C}]^c[\text{D}]^d}{[\text{A}]^a[\text{B}]^b} \qquad (14.2)$$

where K is the **equilibrium constant.** Equation (14.2) was formulated by two Norwegian chemists, Cato Guldberg[†] and Peter Waage,[‡] in 1864. It is the mathematical expression of their **law of mass action,** which holds that *for a reversible reaction at equilibrium and a constant temperature, a certain ratio of reactant and product concentrations has a constant value, K (the equilibrium constant).* Note that although the concentrations may vary, as long as a given reaction is at equilibrium and the temperature does not change, according to the law of mass action, the value of K remains constant. The validity of Equation (14.2) and the law of mass action has been established by studying many reversible reactions.

The equilibrium constant, then, is defined by a *quotient,* the numerator of which is obtained by multiplying together the equilibrium concentrations of the *products,* each raised to a power equal to its stoichiometric coefficient in the balanced equation. Applying the same procedure to the equilibrium concentrations of *reactants* gives the denominator. The magnitude of the equilibrium constant tells us whether an equilibrium reaction favors the products or reactants. If K is much greater than 1 (that is, $K \gg 1$), the equilibrium will lie to the right and favors the products. Conversely, if the equilibrium constant is much smaller than 1 (that is, $K \ll 1$), the equilibrium will lie to the left and favor the reactants (Figure 14.3). In this context, any number greater than 10 is considered to be much greater than 1, and any number less than 0.1 is much less than 1.

The signs ≫ and ≪ mean "much greater than" and "much smaller than," respectively.

Although the use of the words "reactants" and "products" may seem confusing because any substance serving as a reactant in the forward reaction also is a product of the reverse reaction, it is in keeping with the convention of referring to substances on the left of the equilibrium arrows as "reactants" and those on the right as "products."

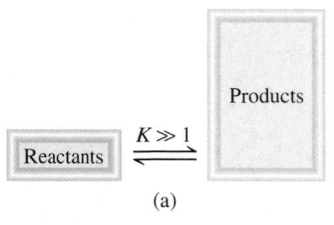

14.2 Writing Equilibrium Constant Expressions

The concept of equilibrium constants is extremely important in chemistry. As you will soon see, equilibrium constants are the key to solving a wide variety of stoichiometry problems involving equilibrium systems. For example, an industrial chemist who wants to maximize the yield of sulfuric acid, say, must have a clear understanding of the equilibrium constants for all the steps in the process, starting from the oxidation

Figure 14.3 *(a) At equilibrium, there are more products than reactants, and the equilibrium is said to lie to the right. (b) In the opposite situation, when there are more reactants than products, the equilibrium is said to lie to the left.*

[†]Cato Maximilian Guldberg (1836–1902). Norwegian chemist and mathematician. Guldberg's research was mainly in thermodynamics.

[‡]Peter Waage (1833–1900). Norwegian chemist. Like that of his coworker, Guldberg, Waage's research was primarily in thermodynamics.

of sulfur and ending with the formation of the final product. A physician specializing in clinical cases of acid-base imbalance needs to know the equilibrium constants of weak acids and bases. And a knowledge of equilibrium constants of pertinent gas-phase reactions will help an atmospheric chemist better understand the process of ozone destruction in the stratosphere.

To use equilibrium constants, we must express them in terms of the reactant and product concentrations. Our only guide is the law of mass action [Equation (14.2)], which is the general formula for finding equilibrium concentrations. However, because the concentrations of the reactants and products can be expressed in different units and because the reacting species are not always in the same phase, there may be more than one way to express the equilibrium constant for the *same* reaction. To begin with, we will consider reactions in which the reactants and products are in the same phase.

Homogeneous Equilibria

The term ***homogeneous equilibrium*** applies to reactions in which *all reacting species are in the same phase*. An example of homogeneous gas-phase equilibrium is the dissociation of N_2O_4. The equilibrium constant, as given in Equation (14.1), is

$$K_c = \frac{[NO_2]^2}{[N_2O_4]}$$

Note that the subscript in K_c indicates that the concentrations of the reacting species are expressed in molarity or moles per liter. The concentrations of reactants and products in gaseous reactions can also be expressed in terms of their partial pressures. From Equation (5.8) we see that at constant temperature the pressure P of a gas is directly related to the concentration in mol/L of the gas, that is, $P = (n/V)RT$. Thus, for the equilibrium process

$$N_2O_4(g) \rightleftharpoons 2NO_2(g)$$

we can write

$$K_P = \frac{P_{NO_2}^2}{P_{N_2O_4}} \tag{14.3}$$

where P_{NO_2} and $P_{N_2O_4}$ are the equilibrium partial pressures (in atm) of NO_2 and N_2O_4, respectively. The subscript in K_P tells us that equilibrium concentrations are expressed in terms of pressure.

In general, K_c is not equal to K_P, because the partial pressures of reactants and products are not equal to their concentrations expressed in moles per liter. A simple relationship between K_P and K_c can be derived as follows. Let us consider the following equilibrium in the gas phase:

$$aA(g) \rightleftharpoons bB(g)$$

where a and b are stoichiometric coefficients. The equilibrium constant K_c is given by

$$K_c = \frac{[B]^b}{[A]^a}$$

and the expression for K_P is

$$K_P = \frac{P_B^b}{P_A^a}$$

where P_A and P_B are the partial pressures of A and B. Assuming ideal gas behavior,

$$P_A V = n_A RT$$
$$P_A = \frac{n_A RT}{V}$$

where V is the volume of the container in liters. Also

$$P_B V = n_B RT$$
$$P_B = \frac{n_B RT}{V}$$

Substituting these relations into the expression for K_P, we obtain

$$K_P = \frac{\left(\dfrac{n_B RT}{V}\right)^b}{\left(\dfrac{n_A RT}{V}\right)^a} = \frac{\left(\dfrac{n_B}{V}\right)^b}{\left(\dfrac{n_A}{V}\right)^a}(RT)^{b-a}$$

Now both n_A/V and n_B/V have units of mol/L and can be replaced by [A] and [B], so that

$$K_P = \frac{[B]^b}{[A]^a}(RT)^{\Delta n}$$
$$= K_c(RT)^{\Delta n} \tag{14.4}$$

where

$$\Delta n = b - a$$
$$= \text{moles of gaseous products} - \text{moles of gaseous reactants}$$

Because pressures are usually expressed in atm, the gas constant R is given by 0.0821 L · atm/K · mol, and we can write the relationship between K_P and K_c as

$$K_P = K_c(0.0821T)^{\Delta n} \tag{14.5}$$

To use this equation, the pressures in K_P must be in atm.

In general, $K_P \neq K_c$ except in the special case in which $\Delta n = 0$ as in the equilibrium mixture of molecular hydrogen, molecular bromine, and hydrogen bromide:

$$H_2(g) + Br_2(g) \rightleftharpoons 2HBr(g)$$

In this case, Equation (14.5) can be written as

$$K_P = K_c(0.0821T)^0$$
$$= K_c$$

Any number raised to the zero power is equal to 1.

As another example of homogeneous equilibrium, let us consider the ionization of acetic acid (CH_3COOH) in water:

$$CH_3COOH(aq) + H_2O(l) \rightleftharpoons CH_3COO^-(aq) + H_3O^+(aq)$$

The equilibrium constant is

$$K_c' = \frac{[CH_3COO^-][H_3O^+]}{[CH_3COOH][H_2O]}$$

(We use the prime for K_c here to distinguish it from the final form of equilibrium constant to be derived below.) In 1 L, or 1000 g, of water, there are 1000 g/(18.02 g/mol), or 55.5 moles, of water. Therefore, the "concentration" of water, or $[H_2O]$, is 55.5 mol/L, or 55.5 M. This is a large quantity compared to the concentrations of other species in solution (usually 1 M or smaller), and we can assume that it does not change appreciably during the course of a reaction. Thus, we can treat $[H_2O]$ as a constant and rewrite the equilibrium constant as

$$K_c = \frac{[CH_3COO^-][H_3O^+]}{[CH_3COOH]}$$

where

$$K_c = K_c'[H_2O]$$

Equilibrium Constant and Units

Note that it is general practice not to include units for the equilibrium constant. In thermodynamics, the equilibrium constant is defined in terms of *activities* rather than concentrations. For an ideal system, the activity of a substance is the ratio of its concentration (or partial pressure) to a standard value, which is 1 M (or 1 atm). This procedure eliminates all units but does not alter the numerical parts of the concentration or pressure. Consequently, K has no units. We will extend this practice to acid-base equilibria and solubility equilibria in Chapters 15 and 16.

For nonideal systems, the activities are not exactly numerically equal to concentrations. In some cases, the differences can be appreciable. Unless otherwise noted, we will treat all systems as ideal.

Examples 14.1 through 14.3 illustrate the procedure for writing equilibrium constant expressions and calculating equilibrium constants and equilibrium concentrations.

Example 14.1

Write expressions for K_c, and K_P if applicable, for the following reversible reactions at equilibrium:

(a) $HF(aq) + H_2O(l) \rightleftharpoons H_3O^+(aq) + F^-(aq)$
(b) $2NO(g) + O_2(g) \rightleftharpoons 2NO_2(g)$
(c) $CH_3COOH(aq) + C_2H_5OH(aq) \rightleftharpoons CH_3COOC_2H_5(aq) + H_2O(l)$

Strategy Keep in mind the following facts: (1) the K_P expression applies only to gaseous reactions and (2) the concentration of solvent (usually water) does not appear in the equilibrium constant expression.

Solution (a) Because there are no gases present, K_P does not apply and we have only K_c.

$$K_c' = \frac{[H_3O^+][F^-]}{[HF][H_2O]}$$

HF is a weak acid, so that the amount of water consumed in acid ionizations is negligible compared with the total amount of water present as solvent. Thus, we can rewrite the equilibrium constant as

$$K_c = \frac{[H_3O^+][F^-]}{[HF]}$$

(b)

$$K_c = \frac{[NO_2]^2}{[NO]^2[O_2]} \qquad K_P = \frac{P_{NO_2}^2}{P_{NO}^2 \, P_{O_2}}$$

(Continued)

(c) The equilibrium constant K_c' is given by

$$K_c' = \frac{[CH_3COOC_2H_5][H_2O]}{[CH_3COOH][C_2H_5OH]}$$

Because the water produced in the reaction is negligible compared with the water solvent, the concentration of water does not change. Thus, we can write the new equilibrium constant as

$$K_c = \frac{[CH_3COOC_2H_5]}{[CH_3COOH][C_2H_5OH]}$$

Similar problems: 14.7, 14.8.

Practice Exercise Write K_c and K_P for the decomposition of nitrogen pentoxide:

$$2N_2O_5(g) \rightleftharpoons 4NO_2(g) + O_2(g)$$

Example 14.2

The following equilibrium process has been studied at 230°C:

$$2NO(g) + O_2(g) \rightleftharpoons 2NO_2(g)$$

In one experiment, the concentrations of the reacting species at equilibrium are found to be [NO] = 0.0542 M, [O$_2$] = 0.127 M, and [NO$_2$] = 15.5 M. Calculate the equilibrium constant (K_c) of the reaction at this temperature.

Strategy The concentrations given are equilibrium concentrations. They have units of mol/L, so we can calculate the equilibrium constant (K_c) using the law of mass action [Equation (14.2)].

Solution The equilibrium constant is given by

$$K_c = \frac{[NO_2]^2}{[NO]^2[O_2]}$$

Substituting the concentrations, we find that

$$K_c = \frac{(15.5)^2}{(0.0542)^2(0.127)} = 6.44 \times 10^5$$

Check Note that K_c is given without units. Also, the large magnitude of K_c is consistent with the high product (NO$_2$) concentration relative to the concentrations of the reactants (NO and O$_2$).

Similar problem: 14.16.

Practice Exercise Carbonyl chloride (COCl$_2$), also called phosgene, was used in World War I as a poisonous gas. The equilibrium concentrations for the reaction between carbon monoxide and molecular chlorine to form carbonyl chloride

$$CO(g) + Cl_2(g) \rightleftharpoons COCl_2(g)$$

at 74°C are [CO] = 1.2 × 10^{-2} M, [Cl$_2$] = 0.054 M, and [COCl$_2$] = 0.14 M. Calculate the equilibrium constant (K_c).

Example 14.3

The equilibrium constant K_P for the decomposition of phosphorus pentachloride to phosphorus trichloride and molecular chlorine

$$PCl_5(g) \rightleftharpoons PCl_3(g) + Cl_2(g)$$

is found to be 1.05 at 250°C. If the equilibrium partial pressures of PCl_5 and PCl_3 are 0.875 atm and 0.463 atm, respectively, what is the equilibrium partial pressure of Cl_2 at 250°C?

Strategy The concentrations of the reacting gases are given in atm, so we can express the equilibrium constant in K_P. From the known K_P value and the equilibrium pressures of PCl_3 and PCl_5, we can solve for P_{Cl_2}.

Solution First, we write K_P in terms of the partial pressures of the reacting species

$$K_P = \frac{P_{PCl_3} P_{Cl_2}}{P_{PCl_5}}$$

Knowing the partial pressures, we write

$$1.05 = \frac{(0.463)(P_{Cl_2})}{(0.875)}$$

or

$$P_{Cl_2} = \frac{(1.05)(0.875)}{(0.463)} = 1.98 \text{ atm}$$

Check Note that we have added atm as the unit for P_{Cl_2}.

Practice Exercise The equilibrium constant K_P for the reaction

$$2NO_2(g) \rightleftharpoons 2NO(g) + O_2(g)$$

is 158 at 1000 K. Calculate P_{O_2} if $P_{NO_2} = 0.400$ atm and $P_{NO} = 0.270$ atm.

Similar problem: 14.19.

Example 14.4

Methanol (CH_3OH) is manufactured industrially by the reaction

$$CO(g) + 2H_2(g) \rightleftharpoons CH_3OH(g)$$

The equilibrium constant (K_c) for the reaction is 10.5 at 220°C. What is the value of K_P at this temperature?

Strategy The relationship between K_c and K_P is given by Equation (14.5). What is the change in the number of moles of gases from reactants to product? Recall that

$$\Delta n = \text{moles of gaseous products} - \text{moles of gaseous reactants}$$

What unit of temperature should we use?

Solution The relationship between K_c and K_P is

$$K_P = K_c(0.0821T)^{\Delta n}$$

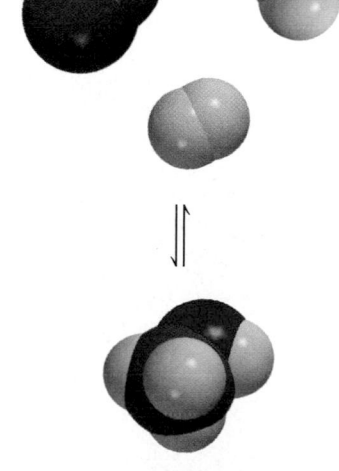

(Continued)

Because $T = 273 + 220 = 493$ K and $\Delta n = 1 - 3 = -2$, we have

$$K_P = (10.5)(0.0821 \times 493)^{-2}$$
$$= 6.41 \times 10^{-3}$$

Check Note that K_P, like K_c, is a dimensionless quantity. This example shows that we can get a quite different value for the equilibrium constant for the same reaction, depending on whether we express the concentrations in moles per liter or in atmospheres.

Similar problems: 14.17, 14.21.

Practice Exercise For the reaction

$$N_2(g) + 3H_2(g) \rightleftharpoons 2NH_3(g)$$

K_P is 4.3×10^{-4} at 375°C. Calculate K_c for the reaction.

Heterogeneous Equilibria

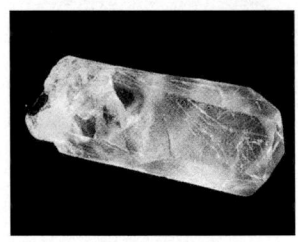

The mineral calcite is made of calcium carbonate, as are chalk and marble.

As you might expect, a **heterogeneous equilibrium** results from *a reversible reaction involving reactants and products that are in different phases*. For example, when calcium carbonate is heated in a closed vessel, the following equilibrium is attained:

$$CaCO_3(s) \rightleftharpoons CaO(s) + CO_2(g)$$

The two solids and one gas constitute three separate phases. At equilibrium, we might write the equilibrium constant as

$$K_c' = \frac{[CaO][CO_2]}{[CaCO_3]} \tag{14.6}$$

(Again, the prime for K_c here is to distinguish it from the final form of equilibrium constant to be derived shortly.) However, the "concentration" of a solid, like its density, is an intensive property and does not depend on how much of the substance is present. For example, the "molar concentration" of copper (density: 8.96 g/cm³) at 20°C is the same, whether we have 1 gram or 1 ton of the metal:

$$[Cu] = \frac{8.96 \text{ g}}{1 \text{ cm}^3} \times \frac{1 \text{ mol}}{63.55 \text{ g}} = 0.141 \text{ mol/cm}^3 = 141 \text{ mol/L}$$

For this reason, the terms $[CaCO_3]$ and $[CaO]$ are themselves constants and can be combined with the equilibrium constant. We can simplify Equation (14.6) by writing

$$\frac{[CaCO_3]}{[CaO]}K_c' = K_c = [CO_2] \tag{14.7}$$

where K_c, the "new" equilibrium constant, is conveniently expressed in terms of a single concentration, that of CO_2. Note that the value of K_c does not depend on how much $CaCO_3$ and CaO are present, as long as some of each is present at equilibrium (Figure 14.4).

The situation becomes simpler if we replace concentrations with activities. In thermodynamics, the activity of a pure solid is 1. Thus, the concentration terms for $CaCO_3$ and CaO are both unity, and from the preceding equilibrium equation, we can immediately write $K_c = [CO_2]$. Similarly, the activity of a pure liquid is also 1. Thus, if a reactant or a product is a liquid, we can omit it in the equilibrium constant expression.

Figure 14.4 In (a) and (b) the equilibrium pressure of CO_2 is the same at the same temperature, despite the presence of different amounts of $CaCO_3$ and CaO.

Alternatively, we can express the equilibrium constant as

$$K_P = P_{CO_2} \qquad (14.8)$$

The equilibrium constant in this case is numerically equal to the pressure of CO_2 gas, an easily measurable quantity.

Example 14.5

Write the equilibrium constant expression K_c, and K_P if applicable, for each of the following heterogeneous systems:

(a) $(NH_4)_2Se(s) \rightleftharpoons 2NH_3(g) + H_2Se(g)$
(b) $AgCl(s) \rightleftharpoons Ag^+(aq) + Cl^-(aq)$
(c) $P_4(s) + 6Cl_2(g) \rightleftharpoons 4PCl_3(l)$

Strategy We omit any pure solids or pure liquids in the equilibrium constant expression because their activities are unity.

Solution (a) Because $(NH_4)_2Se$ is a solid, the equilibrium constant K_c is given by

$$K_c = [NH_3]^2[H_2Se]$$

Alternatively, we can express the equilibrium constant K_P in terms of the partial pressures of NH_3 and H_2Se:

$$K_P = P_{NH_3}^2 P_{H_2Se}$$

(b) Here $AgCl$ is a solid so the equilibrium constant is given by

$$K_c = [Ag^+][Cl^-]$$

Because no gases are present, there is no K_P expression.

(c) We note that P_4 is a solid and PCl_3 is a liquid, so they do not appear in the equilibrium constant expression. Thus, K_c is given by

$$K_c = \frac{1}{[Cl_2]^6}$$

(Continued)

Similar problem: 14.8.

Alternatively, we can express the equilibrium constant in terms of the pressure of Cl_2:

$$K_P = \frac{1}{P_{Cl_2}^6}$$

Practice Exercise Write equilibrium constant expressions for K_c and K_P for the formation of nickel tetracarbonyl, which is used to separate nickel from other impurities:

$$Ni(s) + 4CO(g) \rightleftharpoons Ni(CO)_4(g)$$

Example 14.6

Consider the following heterogeneous equilibrium:

$$CaCO_3(s) \rightleftharpoons CaO(s) + CO_2(g)$$

At 800°C, the pressure of CO_2 is 0.236 atm. Calculate (a) K_P and (b) K_c for the reaction at this temperature.

Strategy Remember that pure solids do not appear in the equilibrium constant expression. The relationship between K_P and K_c is given by Equation (14.5).

Solution (a) Using Equation (14.8) we write

$$K_P = P_{CO_2}$$
$$= 0.236$$

(b) From Equation (14.5), we know

$$K_P = K_c(0.0821T)^{\Delta n}$$

In this case, $T = 800 + 273 = 1073$ K and $\Delta n = 1$, so we substitute these values in the equation and obtain

$$0.236 = K_c(0.0821 \times 1073)$$
$$K_c = 2.68 \times 10^{-3}$$

Similar problem: 14.22.

Practice Exercise Consider the following equilibrium at 395 K:

$$NH_4HS(s) \rightleftharpoons NH_3(g) + H_2S(g)$$

The partial pressure of each gas is 0.265 atm. Calculate K_P and K_c for the reaction.

Multiple Equilibria

The reactions we have considered so far are all relatively simple. A more complicated situation is one in which the product molecules in one equilibrium system are involved in a second equilibrium process:

$$A + B \rightleftharpoons C + D$$
$$C + D \rightleftharpoons E + F$$

The products formed in the first reaction, C and D, react further to form products E and F. At equilibrium we can write two separate equilibrium constants:

$$K_c' = \frac{[C][D]}{[A][B]}$$

and

$$K_c'' = \frac{[E][F]}{[C][D]}$$

The overall reaction is given by the sum of the two reactions

$$
\begin{array}{ll}
A + B \rightleftharpoons C + D & K_c' \\
C + D \rightleftharpoons E + F & K_c'' \\
\hline
\text{Overall reaction:} \quad A + B \rightleftharpoons E + F & K_c
\end{array}
$$

and the equilibrium constant K_c for the overall reaction is

$$K_c = \frac{[E][F]}{[A][B]}$$

We obtain the same expression if we take the product of the expressions for K_c' and K_c'':

$$K_c'K_c'' = \frac{[C][D]}{[A][B]} \times \frac{[E][F]}{[C][D]} = \frac{[E][F]}{[A][B]}$$

Therefore,

$$K_c = K_c'K_c'' \tag{14.9}$$

We can now make an important statement about multiple equilibria: *If a reaction can be expressed as the sum of two or more reactions, the equilibrium constant for the overall reaction is given by the product of the equilibrium constants of the individual reactions.*

Among the many known examples of multiple equilibria is the ionization of diprotic acids in aqueous solution. The following equilibrium constants have been determined for carbonic acid (H_2CO_3) at 25°C:

$$H_2CO_3(aq) \rightleftharpoons H^+(aq) + HCO_3^-(aq) \qquad K_c' = \frac{[H^+][HCO_3^-]}{[H_2CO_3]} = 4.2 \times 10^{-7}$$

$$HCO_3^-(aq) \rightleftharpoons H^+(aq) + CO_3^{2-}(aq) \qquad K_c'' = \frac{[H^+][CO_3^{2-}]}{[HCO_3^-]} = 4.8 \times 10^{-11}$$

The overall reaction is the sum of these two reactions

$$H_2CO_3(aq) \rightleftharpoons 2H^+(aq) + CO_3^{2-}(aq)$$

and the corresponding equilibrium constant is given by

$$K_c = \frac{[H^+]^2[CO_3^{2-}]}{[H_2CO_3]}$$

Using Equation (14.9) we arrive at

$$\begin{aligned} K_c &= K_c' K_c'' \\ &= (4.2 \times 10^{-7})(4.8 \times 10^{-11}) \\ &= 2.0 \times 10^{-17} \end{aligned}$$

The Form of K and the Equilibrium Equation

Before concluding this section, let us look at two important rules for writing equilibrium constants:

The reciprocal of x is $1/x$.

1. When the equation for a reversible reaction is written in the opposite direction, the equilibrium constant becomes the reciprocal of the original equilibrium constant. Thus, if we write the NO_2–N_2O_4 equilibrium as

$$N_2O_4(g) \rightleftharpoons 2NO_2(g)$$

then at 25°C,

$$K_c = \frac{[NO_2]^2}{[N_2O_4]} = 4.63 \times 10^{-3}$$

However, we can represent the equilibrium equally well as

$$2NO_2(g) \rightleftharpoons N_2O_4(g)$$

and the equilibrium constant is now given by

$$K_c' = \frac{[N_2O_4]}{[NO_2]^2} = \frac{1}{K_c} = \frac{1}{4.63 \times 10^{-3}} = 216$$

You can see that $K_c = 1/K_c'$ or $K_c K_c' = 1.00$. Either K_c or K_c' is a valid equilibrium constant, but it is meaningless to say that the equilibrium constant for the NO_2–N_2O_4 system is 4.63×10^{-3}, or 216, unless we also specify how the equilibrium equation is written.

2. The value of K also depends on how the equilibrium equation is balanced. Consider the following ways of describing the same equilibrium:

$$\tfrac{1}{2}N_2O_4(g) \rightleftharpoons NO_2(g) \qquad K_c' = \frac{[NO_2]}{[N_2O_4]^{\frac{1}{2}}}$$

$$N_2O_4(g) \rightleftharpoons 2NO_2(g) \qquad K_c = \frac{[NO_2]^2}{[N_2O_4]}$$

Looking at the exponents we see that $K_c' = \sqrt{K_c}$. In Table 14.1 we find $K_c = 4.63 \times 10^{-3}$; therefore $K_c' = 0.0680$.

According to the law of mass action, each concentration term in the equilibrium constant expression is raised to a power equal to its stoichiometric coefficient. Thus, if you double a chemical equation throughout, the corresponding equilibrium constant will be the square of the original value; if you triple the equation, the equilibrium constant will be the cube of the original value, and so on. The NO_2–N_2O_4 example illustrates once again the need to write the chemical equation when quoting the numerical value of an equilibrium constant.

Example 14.7 deals with the relationship between the equilibrium constants for differently balanced equations describing the same reaction.

Example 14.7

The reaction for the production of ammonia can be written in a number of ways:

(a) $N_2(g) + 3H_2(g) \rightleftharpoons 2NH_3(g)$

(b) $\frac{1}{2}N_2(g) + \frac{3}{2}H_2(g) \rightleftharpoons NH_3(g)$

(c) $\frac{1}{3}N_2(g) + H_2(g) \rightleftharpoons \frac{2}{3}NH_3(g)$

Write the equilibrium constant expression for each formulation. (Express the concentrations of the reacting species in mol/L.)

(d) How are the equilibrium constants related to one another?

Strategy We are given three different expressions for the same reacting system. Remember that the equilibrium constant expression depends on how the equation is balanced, that is, on the stoichiometric coefficients used in the equation.

Solution

(a)
$$K_a = \frac{[NH_3]^2}{[N_2][H_2]^3}$$

(b)
$$K_b = \frac{[NH_3]}{[N_2]^{\frac{1}{2}}[H_2]^{\frac{3}{2}}}$$

(c)
$$K_c = \frac{[NH_3]^{\frac{2}{3}}}{[N_2]^{\frac{1}{3}}[H_2]}$$

(d)
$$K_a = K_b^2$$
$$K_a = K_c^3$$
$$K_b^2 = K_c^3 \quad \text{or} \quad K_b = K_c^{\frac{3}{2}}$$

Similar problem: 14.20.

Practice Exercise Write the equilibrium expression (K_c) for each of the following reactions and show how they are related to each other: (a) $3O_2(g) \rightleftharpoons 2O_3(g)$, (b) $O_2(g) \rightleftharpoons \frac{2}{3}O_3(g)$.

Summary of Guidelines for Writing Equilibrium Constant Expressions

1. The concentrations of the reacting species in the condensed phase are expressed in mol/L; in the gaseous phase, the concentrations can be expressed in mol/L or in atm. K_c is related to K_P by a simple equation [Equation (14.5)].

2. The concentrations of pure solids, pure liquids (in heterogeneous equilibria), and solvents (in homogeneous equilibria) do not appear in the equilibrium constant expressions.

3. The equilibrium constant (K_c or K_P) is a dimensionless quantity.

4. In quoting a value for the equilibrium constant, we must specify the balanced equation and the temperature.

5. If a reaction can be expressed as the sum of two or more reactions, the equilibrium constant for the overall reaction is given by the product of the equilibrium constants of the individual reactions.

14.3 The Relationship Between Chemical Kinetics and Chemical Equilibrium

We have seen that K, defined in Equation (14.2), is constant at a given temperature regardless of variations in individual equilibrium concentrations (review Table 14.1). We can find out why this is so and at the same time gain insight into the equilibrium process by considering the kinetics of chemical reactions.

To review reaction mechanisms, see Section 13.5.

Let us suppose that the following reversible reaction occurs via a mechanism consisting of a single *elementary step* in both the forward and reverse directions:

$$A + 2B \underset{k_r}{\overset{k_f}{\rightleftarrows}} AB_2$$

The forward rate is given by

$$\text{rate}_f = k_f[A][B]^2$$

and the reverse rate is given by

$$\text{rate}_r = k_r[AB_2]$$

where k_f and k_r are the rate constants for the forward and reverse directions. At equilibrium, when no net changes occur, the two rates must be equal:

$$\text{rate}_f = \text{rate}_r$$

or

$$k_f[A][B]^2 = k_r[AB_2]$$
$$\frac{k_f}{k_r} = \frac{[AB_2]}{[A][B]^2}$$

Because both k_f and k_r are constants at a given temperature, their ratio is also a constant, which is equal to the equilibrium constant K_c.

$$\frac{k_f}{k_r} = K_c = \frac{[AB_2]}{[A][B]^2}$$

So K_c is always a constant regardless of the equilibrium concentrations of the reacting species because it is always equal to k_f/k_r, the quotient of two quantities that are themselves constant at a given temperature. Because rate constants are temperature-dependent [see Equation (13.11)], it follows that the equilibrium constant must also change with temperature.

Now suppose the same reaction has a mechanism with more than one elementary step. Suppose it occurs via a two-step mechanism as follows:

$$\textit{Step 1:} \qquad 2B \underset{k_r'}{\overset{k_f'}{\rightleftarrows}} B_2$$

$$\textit{Step 2:} \quad A + B_2 \underset{k_r''}{\overset{k_f''}{\rightleftarrows}} AB_2$$

$$\textit{Overall reaction:} \quad A + 2B \rightleftharpoons AB_2$$

This is an example of multiple equilibria, discussed in Section 14.2. We write the expressions for the equilibrium constants:

$$K' = \frac{k_f'}{k_r'} = \frac{[B_2]}{[B]^2} \qquad\qquad (14.10)$$

$$K'' = \frac{k_f''}{k_r''} = \frac{[AB_2]}{[A][B_2]} \qquad (14.11)$$

Multiplying Equation (14.10) by Equation (14.11), we get

$$K'K'' = \frac{[B_2][AB_2]}{[B]^2[A][B_2]} = \frac{[AB_2]}{[A][B]^2}$$

For the overall reaction, we can write

$$K_c = \frac{[AB_2]}{[A][B]^2} = K'K''$$

Because both K' and K'' are constants, K_c is also a constant. This result lets us generalize our treatment of the reaction

$$aA + bB \rightleftharpoons cC + dD$$

Regardless of whether this reaction occurs via a single-step or a multistep mechanism, we can write the equilibrium constant expression according to the law of mass action shown in Equation (14.2):

$$K = \frac{[C]^c[D]^d}{[A]^a[B]^b}$$

In summary, we see that in terms of chemical kinetics, the equilibrium constant of a reaction can be expressed as a ratio of the rate constants of the forward and reverse reactions. This analysis explains why the equilibrium constant is a constant and why its value changes with temperature.

14.4 What Does the Equilibrium Constant Tell Us?

We have seen that the equilibrium constant for a given reaction can be calculated from known equilibrium concentrations. Once we know the value of the equilibrium constant, we can use Equation (14.2) to calculate unknown equilibrium concentrations remembering, of course, that the equilibrium constant has a constant value only if the temperature does not change. In general, the equilibrium constant helps us to predict the direction in which a reaction mixture will proceed to achieve equilibrium and to calculate the concentrations of reactants and products once equilibrium has been reached. These uses of the equilibrium constant will be explored in this section.

Predicting the Direction of a Reaction

The equilibrium constant K_c for the formation of hydrogen iodide from molecular hydrogen and molecular iodine in the gas phase

$$H_2(g) + I_2(g) \rightleftharpoons 2HI(g)$$

is 54.3 at 430°C. Suppose that in a certain experiment we place 0.243 mole of H_2, 0.146 mole of I_2, and 1.98 moles of HI all in a 1.00-L container at 430°C. Will there be a net reaction to form more H_2 and I_2 or more HI? Inserting the starting concentrations in the equilibrium constant expression, we write

$$\frac{[HI]_0^2}{[H_2]_0[I_2]_0} = \frac{(1.98)^2}{(0.243)(0.146)} = 111$$

$H_2 + I_2 \rightleftharpoons 2HI$

where the subscript 0 indicates initial concentrations (before equilibrium is reached). Because the quotient $[HI]_0^2/[H_2]_0[I_2]_0$ is greater than K_c, this system is not at equilibrium. Consequently, some of the HI will react to form more H_2 and I_2 (decreasing the value of the quotient). Thus, the net reaction proceeds from right to left to reach equilibrium.

For reactions that have not reached equilibrium, such as the formation of HI considered above, we obtain the ***reaction quotient (Q_c),*** instead of the equilibrium constant *by substituting the initial concentrations into the equilibrium constant expression.* To determine the direction in which the net reaction will proceed to achieve equilibrium, we compare the values of Q_c and K_c. The three possible cases are as follows:

- $Q_c < K_c$ The ratio of initial concentrations of products to reactants is too small. To reach equilibrium, reactants must be converted to products. The system proceeds from left to right (consuming reactants, forming products) to reach equilibrium.

- $Q_c = K_c$ The initial concentrations are equilibrium concentrations. The system is at equilibrium.

- $Q_c > K_c$ The ratio of initial concentrations of products to reactants is too large. To reach equilibrium, products must be converted to reactants. The system proceeds from right to left (consuming products, forming reactants) to reach equilibrium.

Figure 14.5 shows a comparison of K_c with Q_c.

Example 14.8 shows how the value of Q_c can help us determine the direction of net reaction toward equilibrium.

$N_2 + 3H_2 \rightleftharpoons 2NH_3$

Example 14.8

At the start of a reaction, there are 0.249 mol N_2, 3.21×10^{-2} mol H_2, and 6.42×10^{-4} mol NH_3 in a 3.50-L reaction vessel at 375°C. If the equilibrium constant (K_c) for the reaction

$$N_2(g) + 3H_2(g) \rightleftharpoons 2NH_3(g)$$

is 1.2 at this temperature, decide whether the system is at equilibrium. If it is not, predict which way the net reaction will proceed.

Strategy We are given the initial amounts of the gases (in moles) in a vessel of known volume (in liters), so we can calculate their molar concentrations and hence the reaction quotient (Q_c). How does a comparison of Q_c with K_c enable us to determine if the system is at equilibrium or, if not, in which the direction the net reaction will proceed to reach equilibrium?

Solution The initial concentrations of the reacting species are

$$[N_2]_0 = \frac{0.249 \text{ mol}}{3.50 \text{ L}} = 0.0711 \, M$$

$$[H_2]_0 = \frac{3.21 \times 10^{-2} \text{ mol}}{3.50 \text{ L}} = 9.17 \times 10^{-3} \, M$$

$$[NH_3]_0 = \frac{6.42 \times 10^{-4} \text{ mol}}{3.50 \text{ L}} = 1.83 \times 10^{-4} \, M$$

(Continued)

Reactants → Products　　　Equilibrium : no net change　　　Reactants ← Products

Figure 14.5 *The direction of a reversible reaction to reach equilibrium depends on the relative magnitudes of Q_c and K_c. Note that K_c is a constant at a given temperature, but Q_c varies according to the relative amounts of reactants and products present.*

Next we write

$$Q_c = \frac{[NH_3]_0^2}{[N_2]_0[H_2]_0^3} = \frac{(1.83 \times 10^{-4})^2}{(0.0711)(9.17 \times 10^{-3})^3} = 0.611$$

Because Q_c is smaller than K_c (1.2), the system is not at equilibrium. The net result will be an increase in the concentration of NH_3 and a decrease in the concentrations of N_2 and H_2. That is, the net reaction will proceed from left to right until equilibrium is reached.

Practice Exercise The equilibrium constant (K_c) for the formation of nitrosyl chloride, an orange-yellow compound, from nitric oxide and molecular chlorine

$$2NO(g) + Cl_2(g) \rightleftharpoons 2NOCl(g)$$

is 6.5×10^4 at 35°C. In a certain experiment, 2.0×10^{-2} mole of NO, 8.3×10^{-3} mole of Cl_2, and 6.8 moles of NOCl are mixed in a 2.0-L flask. In which direction will the system proceed to reach equilibrium?

Similar problems: 14.39, 14.40.

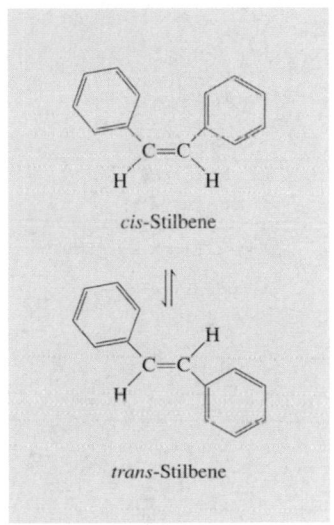

cis-Stilbene

trans-Stilbene

Figure 14.6 *The equilibrium between cis-stilbene and trans-stilbene. Note that both molecules have the same molecular formula ($C_{14}H_{12}$) and also the same type of bonds. However, in cis-stilbene, the benzene rings are on one side of the C=C bond and the H atoms are on the other side whereas in trans-stilbene the benzene rings (and the H atoms) are across from the C=C bond. These compounds have different melting points and dipole moments.*

Calculating Equilibrium Concentrations

If we know the equilibrium constant for a particular reaction, we can calculate the concentrations in the equilibrium mixture from the initial concentrations. Commonly, only the initial reactant concentrations are given. Let us consider the following system involving two organic compounds, *cis*-stilbene and *trans*-stilbene, in a nonpolar hydrocarbon solvent (Figure 14.6):

$$cis\text{-stilbene} \rightleftharpoons trans\text{-stilbene}$$

The equilibrium constant (K_c) for this system is 24.0 at 200°C. Suppose that initially only *cis*-stilbene is present at a concentration of 0.850 mol/L. How do we calculate the concentrations of *cis*- and *trans*-stilbene at equilibrium? From the stoichiometry of the reaction we see that for every mole of *cis*-stilbene converted, 1 mole of *trans*-stilbene is formed. Let x be the equilibrium concentration of *trans*-stilbene in mol/L; therefore, the equilibrium concentration of *cis*-stilbene must be $(0.850 - x)$ mol/L. It is useful to summarize the changes in concentration as follows:

	cis-stilbene $\rightleftharpoons$	*trans*-stilbene
Initial (M):	0.850	0
Change (M):	$-x$	$+x$
Equilibrium (M):	$(0.850 - x)$	x

This procedure of solving equilibrium concentrations is sometimes referred to as the ICE method, where the acronym stands for Initial, Change, and Equilibrium.

A positive (+) change represents an increase and a negative (−) change a decrease in concentration at equilibrium. Next, we set up the equilibrium constant expression

$$K_c = \frac{[\textit{trans}\text{-stilbene}]}{[\textit{cis}\text{-stilbene}]}$$

$$24.0 = \frac{x}{0.850 - x}$$

$$x = 0.816 \ M$$

Having solved for x, we calculate the equilibrium concentrations of *cis*-stilbene and *trans*-stilbene as follows:

$$[\textit{cis}\text{-stilbene}] = (0.850 - 0.816) \ M = 0.034 \ M$$
$$[\textit{trans}\text{-stilbene}] = 0.816 \ M$$

To check the results we could use the equilibrium concentrations to calculate K_c.

We summarize our approach to solving equilibrium constant problems as follows:

Interactivity:
Determining Extent—
Equilibrium Constant
ARIS, Interactives

1. Express the equilibrium concentrations of all species in terms of the initial concentrations and a single unknown x, which represents the change in concentration.

2. Write the equilibrium constant expression in terms of the equilibrium concentrations. Knowing the value of the equilibrium constant, solve for x.

Interactivity:
Determining Extent—
Concentration from Equilibrium
Expression
ARIS, Interactives

3. Having solved for x, calculate the equilibrium concentrations of all species.

Examples 14.9 and 14.10 illustrate the application of this three-step procedure.

Example 14.9

A mixture of 0.500 mol H_2 and 0.500 mol I_2 was placed in a 1.00-L stainless-steel flask at 430°C. The equilibrium constant K_c for the reaction $H_2(g) + I_2(g) \rightleftharpoons 2HI(g)$ is 54.3 at this temperature. Calculate the concentrations of H_2, I_2, and HI at equilibrium.

Strategy We are given the initial amounts of the gases (in moles) in a vessel of known volume (in liters), so we can calculate their molar concentrations. Because initially no HI was present, the system could not be at equilibrium. Therefore, some H_2 would react with the same amount of I_2 (why?) to form HI until equilibrium was established.

Solution We follow the preceding procedure to calculate the equilibrium concentrations.

Step 1: The stoichiometry of the reaction is 1 mol H_2 reacting with 1 mol I_2 to yield 2 mol HI. Let x be the depletion in concentration (mol/L) of H_2 and I_2 at equilibrium. It follows that the equilibrium concentration of HI must be $2x$. We summarize the changes in concentrations as follows:

	H_2	+	I_2	$\rightleftharpoons$	2HI
Initial (*M*):	0.500		0.500		0.000
Change (*M*):	$-x$		$-x$		$+2x$
Equilibrium (*M*):	$(0.500 - x)$		$(0.500 - x)$		$2x$

Step 2: The equilibrium constant is given by

$$K_c = \frac{[HI]^2}{[H_2][I_2]}$$

(Continued)

Substituting, we get

$$54.3 = \frac{(2x)^2}{(0.500 - x)(0.500 - x)}$$

Taking the square root of both sides, we get

$$7.37 = \frac{2x}{0.500 - x}$$
$$x = 0.393 \, M$$

Step 3: At equilibrium, the concentrations are

$$[H_2] = (0.500 - 0.393) \, M = 0.107 \, M$$
$$[I_2] = (0.500 - 0.393) \, M = 0.107 \, M$$
$$[HI] = 2 \times 0.393 \, M = 0.786 \, M$$

Check You can check your answers by calculating K_c using the equilibrium concentrations. Remember that K_c is a constant for a particular reaction at a given temperature.

Similar problem: 14.48.

Practice Exercise Consider the reaction in Example 14.9. Starting with a concentration of 0.040 M for HI, calculate the concentrations of HI, H_2, and I_2 at equilibrium.

Example 14.10

For the same reaction and temperature as in Example 14.9, suppose that the initial concentrations of H_2, I_2, and HI are 0.00623 M, 0.00414 M, and 0.0224 M, respectively. Calculate the concentrations of these species at equilibrium.

Strategy From the initial concentrations we can calculate the reaction quotient (Q_c) to see if the system is at equilibrium or, if not, in which direction the net reaction will proceed to reach equilibrium. A comparison of Q_c with K_c also enables us to determine if there will be a depletion in H_2 and I_2 or HI as equilibrium is established.

Solution First we calculate Q_c as follows:

$$Q_c = \frac{[HI]_0^2}{[H_2]_0[I_2]_0} = \frac{(0.0224)^2}{(0.00623)(0.00414)} = 19.5$$

Because Q_c (19.5) is smaller than K_c (54.3), we conclude that the net reaction will proceed from left to right until equilibrium is reached (see Figure 14.4); that is, there will be a depletion of H_2 and I_2 and a gain in HI.

Step 1: Let x be the depletion in concentration (mol/L) of H_2 and I_2 at equilibrium. From the stoichiometry of the reaction it follows that the increase in concentration for HI must be $2x$. Next we write

	H_2	+	I_2	$\rightleftharpoons$	2HI
Initial (M):	0.00623		0.00414		0.0224
Change (M):	$-x$		$-x$		$+2x$
Equilibrium (M):	$(0.00623 - x)$		$(0.00414 - x)$		$(0.0224 + 2x)$

(Continued)

Step 2: The equilibrium constant is

$$K_c = \frac{[HI]^2}{[H_2][I_2]}$$

Substituting, we get

$$54.3 = \frac{(0.0224 + 2x)^2}{(0.00623 - x)(0.00414 - x)}$$

It is not possible to solve this equation by the square root shortcut, as the starting concentrations $[H_2]$ and $[I_2]$ are unequal. Instead, we must first carry out the multiplications

$$54.3(2.58 \times 10^{-5} - 0.0104x + x^2) = 5.02 \times 10^{-4} + 0.0896x + 4x^2$$

Collecting terms, we get

$$50.3x^2 - 0.654x + 8.98 \times 10^{-4} = 0$$

This is a quadratic equation of the form $ax^2 + bx + c = 0$. The solution for a quadratic equation (see Appendix 4) is

$$x = \frac{-b \pm \sqrt{b^2 - 4ac}}{2a}$$

Here we have $a = 50.3$, $b = -0.654$, and $c = 8.98 \times 10^{-4}$, so that

$$x = \frac{0.654 \pm \sqrt{(-0.654)^2 - 4(50.3)(8.98 \times 10^{-4})}}{2 \times 50.3}$$

$$x = 0.0114\, M \qquad \text{or} \qquad x = 0.00156\, M$$

The first solution is physically impossible because the amounts of H_2 and I_2 reacted would be more than those originally present. The second solution gives the correct answer. Note that in solving quadratic equations of this type, one answer is always physically impossible, so choosing a value for x is easy.

Step 3: At equilibrium, the concentrations are

$$[H_2] = (0.00623 - 0.00156)\, M = 0.00467\, M$$
$$[I_2] = (0.00414 - 0.00156)\, M = 0.00258\, M$$
$$[HI] = (0.0224 + 2 \times 0.00156)\, M = 0.0255\, M$$

Check You can check the answers by calculating K_c using the equilibrium concentrations. Remember that K_c is a constant for a particular reaction at a given temperature.

Similar problem: 14.88.

Practice Exercise At 1280°C the equilibrium constant (K_c) for the reaction

$$Br_2(g) \rightleftharpoons 2Br(g)$$

is 1.1×10^{-3}. If the initial concentrations are $[Br_2] = 6.3 \times 10^{-2}\, M$ and $[Br] = 1.2 \times 10^{-2}\, M$, calculate the concentrations of these species at equilibrium.

Examples 14.9 and 14.10 show that we can calculate the concentrations of all the reacting species at equilibrium if we know the equilibrium constant and the initial concentrations. This information is valuable if we need to estimate the yield of a reaction. For example, if the reaction between H_2 and I_2 to form HI were to go to completion, the number of moles of HI formed in Example 14.9 would be 2×0.500 mol, or 1.00 mol. However, because of the equilibrium process, the actual amount of HI formed can be no more than 2×0.393 mol, or 0.786 mol, a 78.6 percent yield.

14.5 Factors That Affect Chemical Equilibrium

Chemical equilibrium represents a balance between forward and reverse reactions. In most cases, this balance is quite delicate. Changes in experimental conditions may disturb the balance and shift the equilibrium position so that more or less of the desired product is formed. When we say that an equilibrium position shifts to the right, for example, we mean that the net reaction is now from left to right. Variables that can be controlled experimentally are concentration, pressure, volume, and temperature. Here we will examine how each of these variables affects a reacting system at equilibrium. In addition, we will examine the effect of a catalyst on equilibrium.

Le Châtelier's Principle

There is a general rule that helps us to predict the direction in which an equilibrium reaction will move when a change in concentration, pressure, volume, or temperature occurs. The rule, known as *Le Châtelier's[†] principle,* states that *if an external stress is applied to a system at equilibrium, the system adjusts in such a way that the stress is partially offset as the system reaches a new equilibrium position.* The word "stress" here means a change in concentration, pressure, volume, or temperature that removes the system from the equilibrium state. We will use Le Châtelier's principle to assess the effects of such changes.

Animation:
Le Châtelier's Principle
ARIS, Animations

Changes in Concentration

Iron(III) thiocyanate [$Fe(SCN)_3$] dissolves readily in water to give a red solution. The red color is due to the presence of hydrated $FeSCN^{2+}$ ion. The equilibrium between undissociated $FeSCN^{2+}$ and the Fe^{3+} and SCN^- ions is given by

$$FeSCN^{2+}(aq) \rightleftharpoons Fe^{3+}(aq) + SCN^-(aq)$$
$$\text{red} \qquad\qquad \text{pale yellow} \quad \text{colorless}$$

What happens if we add some sodium thiocyanate (NaSCN) to this solution? In this case, the stress applied to the equilibrium system is an increase in the concentration of SCN^- (from the dissociation of NaSCN). To offset this stress, some Fe^{3+} ions react with the added SCN^- ions, and the equilibrium shifts from right to left:

$$FeSCN^{2+}(aq) \longleftarrow Fe^{3+}(aq) + SCN^-(aq)$$

Consequently, the red color of the solution deepens (Figure 14.7). Similarly, if we added iron(III) nitrate [$Fe(NO_3)_3$] to the original solution, the red color would also deepen because the additional Fe^{3+} ions [from $Fe(NO_3)_3$] would shift the equilibrium from right to left.

Both Na^+ and NO_3^- are colorless spectator ions.

[†]Henri Louis Le Châtelier (1850–1936). French chemist. Le Châtelier did work on metallurgy, cements, glasses, fuels, and explosives. He was also noted for his skills in industrial management.

Figure 14.7 *Effect of concentration change on the position of equilibrium. (a) An aqueous Fe(SCN)$_3$ solution. The color of the solution is due to both the red FeSCN^{2+} and the yellow Fe^{3+} species. (b) After the addition of some NaSCN to the solution in (a), the equilibrium shifts to the left. (c) After the addition of some Fe(NO$_3$)$_3$ to the solution in (a), the equilibrium shifts to the left. (d) After the addition of some H$_2$C$_2$O$_4$ to the solution in (a), the equilibrium shifts to the right. The yellow color is due to the Fe(C$_2$O$_4$)$_3^{3-}$ ions.*

(a)   (b)   (c)   (d)

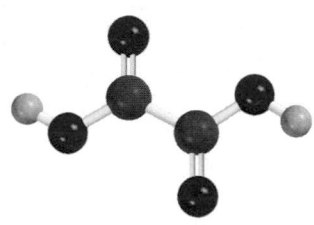

Oxalic acid is sometimes used to remove bathtub rings that consist of rust, or Fe$_2$O$_3$.

Le Châtelier's principle simply summarizes the observed behavior of equilibrium systems; therefore, it is incorrect to say that a given equilibrium shift occurs "because of" Le Châtelier's principle.

Now suppose we add some oxalic acid (H$_2$C$_2$O$_4$) to the original solution. Oxalic acid ionizes in water to form the oxalate ion, C$_2$O$_4^{2-}$, which binds strongly to the Fe^{3+} ions. The formation of the stable yellow ion Fe(C$_2$O$_4$)$_3^{3-}$ removes free Fe^{3+} ions in solution. Consequently, more FeSCN^{2+} units dissociate and the equilibrium shifts from left to right:

$$\text{FeSCN}^{2+}(aq) \longrightarrow \text{Fe}^{3+}(aq) + \text{SCN}^{-}(aq)$$

The red solution will turn yellow due to the formation of Fe(C$_2$O$_4$)$_3^{3-}$ ions.

This experiment demonstrates that all reactants and products are present in the reacting system at equilibrium. Second, increasing the concentrations of the products (Fe^{3+} or SCN^{-}) shifts the equilibrium to the left, and decreasing the concentration of the product Fe^{3+} shifts the equilibrium to the right. These results are just as predicted by Le Châtelier's principle.

The effect of a change in concentration on the equilibrium position is shown in Example 14.11.

Example 14.11

At 720°C, the equilibrium constant K_c for the reaction

$$\text{N}_2(g) + 3\text{H}_2(g) \rightleftharpoons 2\text{NH}_3(g)$$

is 2.37×10^{-3}. In a certain experiment, the equilibrium concentrations are [N$_2$] = 0.683 M, [H$_2$] = 8.80 M, and [NH$_3$] = 1.05 M. Suppose some NH$_3$ is added to the mixture so that its concentration is increased to 3.65 M. (a) Use Le Châtelier's principle to predict the shift in direction of the net reaction to reach a new equilibrium. (b) Confirm your prediction by calculating the reaction quotient Q_c and comparing its value with K_c.

Strategy (a) What is the stress applied to the system? How does the system adjust to offset the stress? (b) At the instant when some NH$_3$ is added, the system is no longer at equilibrium. How do we calculate the Q_c for the reaction at this point? How does a comparison of Q_c with K_c tell us the direction of the net reaction to reach equilibrium.

Solution (a) The stress applied to the system is the addition of NH$_3$. To offset this stress, some NH$_3$ reacts to produce N$_2$ and H$_2$ until a new equilibrium is established. The net reaction therefore shifts from right to left; that is,

$$\text{N}_2(g) + 3\text{H}_2(g) \longleftarrow 2\text{NH}_3(g)$$

(Continued)

(b) At the instant when some of the NH$_3$ is added, the system is no longer at equilibrium. The reaction quotient is given by

$$Q_c = \frac{[NH_3]_0^2}{[N_2]_0[H_2]_0^3}$$
$$= \frac{(3.65)^2}{(0.683)(8.80)^3}$$
$$= 2.86 \times 10^{-2}$$

Because this value is greater than 2.37×10^{-3}, the net reaction shifts from right to left until Q_c equals K_c.

Figure 14.8 shows qualitatively the changes in concentrations of the reacting species.

Similar problem: 14.46.

Practice Exercise At 430°C, the equilibrium constant (K_P) for the reaction

$$2NO(g) + O_2(g) \rightleftharpoons 2NO_2(g)$$

is 1.5×10^5. In one experiment, the initial pressures of NO, O$_2$, and NO$_2$ are 2.1×10^{-3} atm, 1.1×10^{-2} atm, and 0.14 atm, respectively. Calculate Q_P and predict the direction that the net reaction will shift to reach equilibrium.

Changes in Volume and Pressure

Changes in pressure ordinarily do not affect the concentrations of reacting species in condensed phases (say, in an aqueous solution) because liquids and solids are virtually incompressible. On the other hand, concentrations of gases are greatly affected by changes in pressure. Let us look again at Equation (5.8):

$$PV = nRT$$
$$P = \left(\frac{n}{V}\right)RT$$

Note that P and V are related to each other inversely: The greater the pressure, the smaller the volume, and vice versa. Note, too, that the term (n/V) is the concentration of the gas in mol/L, and it varies directly with pressure.

Suppose that the equilibrium system

$$N_2O_4(g) \rightleftharpoons 2NO_2(g)$$

is in a cylinder fitted with a movable piston. What happens if we increase the pressure on the gases by pushing down on the piston at constant temperature? Because the volume decreases, the concentration (n/V) of both NO$_2$ and N$_2$O$_4$ increases. Note that the concentration of NO$_2$ is squared in the equilibrium constant expression, so the increase in pressure increases the numerator more than the denominator. The system is no longer at equilibrium and we write

$$Q_c = \frac{[NO_2]_0^2}{[N_2O_4]_0}$$

Thus, $Q_c > K_c$ and the net reaction will shift to the left until $Q_c = K_c$ (Figure 14.9). Conversely, a decrease in pressure (increase in volume) would result in $Q_c < K_c$, and the net reaction would shift to the right until $Q_c = K_c$. (This conclusion is also predicted by Le Châtelier's principle.)

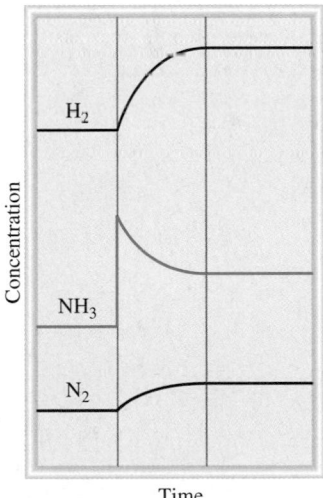

Figure 14.8 *Changes in concentration of H$_2$, N$_2$, and NH$_3$ after the addition of NH$_3$ to the equilibrium mixture. When the new equilibrium is established, all the concentrations are changed but K_c remains the same because temperature remains constant.*

Figure 14.9 *The effect of an increase in pressure on the $N_2O_4(g) \rightleftharpoons 2NO_2(g)$ equilibrium.*

In general, an increase in pressure (decrease in volume) favors the net reaction that decreases the total number of moles of gases (the reverse reaction, in this case), and a decrease in pressure (increase in volume) favors the net reaction that increases the total number of moles of gases (here, the forward reaction). For reactions in which there is no change in the number of moles of gases, a pressure (or volume) change has no effect on the position of equilibrium.

It is possible to change the pressure of a system without changing its volume. Suppose the NO_2–N_2O_4 system is contained in a stainless-steel vessel whose volume is constant. We can increase the total pressure in the vessel by adding an inert gas (helium, for example) to the equilibrium system. Adding helium to the equilibrium mixture at constant volume increases the total gas pressure and decreases the mole fractions of both NO_2 and N_2O_4; but the partial pressure of each gas, given by the product of its mole fraction and total pressure (see Section 5.6), does not change. Thus, the presence of an inert gas in such a case does not affect the equilibrium.

Example 14.12 illustrates the effect of a pressure change on the equilibrium position.

Example 14.12

Consider the following equilibrium systems:

(a) $2PbS(s) + 3O_2(g) \rightleftharpoons 2PbO(s) + 2SO_2(g)$

(b) $PCl_5(g) \rightleftharpoons PCl_3(g) + Cl_2(g)$

(c) $H_2(g) + CO_2(g) \rightleftharpoons H_2O(g) + CO(g)$

Predict the direction of the net reaction in each case as a result of increasing the pressure (decreasing the volume) on the system at constant temperature.

Strategy A change in pressure can affect only the volume of a gas, but not that of a solid because solids (and liquids) are much less compressible. The stress applied is an increase in pressure. According to Le Châtelier's principle, the system will adjust to partially offset this stress. In other words, the system will adjust to decrease the pressure. This can be achieved by shifting to the side of the equation that has fewer moles of gas. Recall that pressure is directly proportional to moles of gas: $PV = nRT$ so $P \propto n$.

Solution (a) Consider only the gaseous molecules. In the balanced equation, there are 3 moles of gaseous reactants and 2 moles of gaseous products. Therefore, the net reaction will shift toward the products (to the right) when the pressure is increased.

(b) The number of moles of products is 2 and that of reactants is 1; therefore, the net reaction will shift to the left, toward the reactant.

(c) The number of moles of products is equal to the number of moles of reactants, so a change in pressure has no effect on the equilibrium.

Check In each case, the prediction is consistent with Le Châtelier's principle.

Practice Exercise Consider the equilibrium reaction involving nitrosyl chloride, nitric oxide, and molecular chlorine

$$2NOCl(g) \rightleftharpoons 2NO(g) + Cl_2(g)$$

Predict the direction of the net reaction as a result of decreasing the pressure (increasing the volume) on the system at constant temperature.

Similar problem: 14.56.

Changes in Temperature

A change in concentration, pressure, or volume may alter the equilibrium position, that is, the relative amounts of reactants and products, but it does not change the value of the equilibrium constant. Only a change in temperature can alter the equilibrium constant. To see why, let us consider the reaction

$$N_2O_4(g) \rightleftharpoons 2NO_2(g)$$

The forward reaction is endothermic (absorbs heat, $\Delta H° > 0$):

$$\text{heat} + N_2O_4(g) \longrightarrow 2NO_2(g) \qquad \Delta H° = 58.0 \text{ kJ/mol}$$

so the reverse reaction is exothermic (releases heat, $\Delta H° < 0$):

$$2NO_2(g) \longrightarrow N_2O_4(g) + \text{heat} \qquad \Delta H° = -58.0 \text{ kJ/mol}$$

At equilibrium at a certain temperature, the heat effect is zero because there is no net reaction. If we treat heat as though it were a chemical reagent, then a rise in temperature "adds" heat to the system and a drop in temperature "removes" heat from the system. As with a change in any other parameter (concentration, pressure, or volume), the system shifts to reduce the effect of the change. Therefore, a temperature increase favors the endothermic direction (from left to right of the equilibrium equation) and a temperature decrease favors the exothermic direction (from right to left of the equilibrium equation). Consequently, the equilibrium constant, given by

$$K_c = \frac{[NO_2]^2}{[N_2O_4]}$$

increases when the system is heated and decreases when the system is cooled (Figure 14.10).

As another example, consider the equilibrium between the following ions:

$$\underset{\text{blue}}{CoCl_4^{2-}} + 6H_2O \rightleftharpoons \underset{\text{pink}}{Co(H_2O)_6^{2+}} + 4Cl^-$$

The formation of $CoCl_4^{2-}$ is endothermic. On heating, the equilibrium shifts to the left and the solution turns blue. Cooling favors the exothermic reaction [the formation of $Co(H_2O)_6^{2+}$] and the solution turns pink (Figure 14.11).

(a)   (b)

Figure 14.10 *(a) Two bulbs containing a mixture of NO_2 and N_2O_4 gases at equilibrium. (b) When one bulb is immersed in ice water (left), its color becomes lighter, indicating the formation of colorless N_2O_4 gas. When the other bulb is immersed in hot water, its color darkens, indicating an increase in NO_2.*

Figure 14.11 *(Left) Heating favors the formation of the blue CoCl$_4^{2-}$ ion. (Right) Cooling favors the formation of the pink Co(H$_2$O)$_6^{2+}$ ion.*

In summary, *a temperature increase favors an endothermic reaction, and a temperature decrease favors an exothermic reaction.*

The Effect of a Catalyst

We know that a catalyst enhances the rate of a reaction by lowering the reaction's activation energy (Section 13.6). However, as Figure 13.21 shows, a catalyst lowers the activation energy of the forward reaction and the reverse reaction to the same extent. We can therefore conclude that the presence of a catalyst does not alter the equilibrium constant, nor does it shift the position of an equilibrium system. Adding a catalyst to a reaction mixture that is not at equilibrium will simply cause the mixture to reach equilibrium sooner. The same equilibrium mixture could be obtained without the catalyst, but we might have to wait much longer for it to happen.

Summary of Factors That May Affect the Equilibrium Position

We have considered four ways to affect a reacting system at equilibrium. It is important to remember that, of the four, *only a change in temperature changes the value of the equilibrium constant.* Changes in concentration, pressure, and volume can alter the equilibrium concentrations of the reacting mixture, but they cannot change the equilibrium constant as long as the temperature does not change. A catalyst can speed up the process, but it has no effect on the equilibrium constant or on the equilibrium concentrations of the reacting species. Two processes that illustrate the effects of changed conditions on equilibrium processes are discussed in Chemistry in Action essays on pp. 630 and 631.

The effects of temperature, concentration, and pressure change, as well as the addition of an inert gas, on an equilibrium system are treated in Example 14.13.

Example 14.13

Consider the following equilibrium process between dinitrogen tetrafluoride (N$_2$F$_4$) and nitrogen difluoride (NF$_2$):

$$N_2F_4(g) \rightleftharpoons 2NF_2(g) \qquad\qquad \Delta H^\circ = 38.5 \text{ kJ/mol}$$

(Continued)

$N_2F_4 \rightleftharpoons 2NF_2$

Predict the changes in the equilibrium if (a) the reacting mixture is heated at constant volume; (b) some N_2F_4 gas is removed from the reacting mixture at constant temperature and volume; (c) the pressure on the reacting mixture is decreased at constant temperature; and (d) a catalyst is added to the reacting mixture.

Strategy (a) What does the sign of $\Delta H°$ indicate about the heat change (endothermic or exothermic) for the forward reaction? (b) Would the removal of some N_2F_4 increase or decrease the Q_c of the reaction? (c) How would the decrease in pressure change the volume of the system? (d) What is the function of a catalyst? How does it affect a reacting system not at equilibrium? at equilibrium?

Solution (a) The stress applied is the heat added to the system. Note that the $N_2F_4 \longrightarrow 2NF_2$ reaction is an endothermic process ($\Delta H° > 0$), which absorbs heat from the surroundings. Therefore, we can think of heat as a reactant

$$\text{heat} + N_2F_4(g) \rightleftharpoons 2NF_2(g)$$

The system will adjust to remove some of the added heat by undergoing a decomposition reaction (from left to right). The equilibrium constant

$$K_c = \frac{[NF_2]^2}{[N_2F_4]}$$

will therefore increase with increasing temperature because the concentration of NF_2 has increased and that of N_2F_4 has decreased. Recall that the equilibrium constant is a constant only at a particular temperature. If the temperature is changed, then the equilibrium constant will also change.

(b) The stress here is the removal of N_2F_4 gas. The system will shift to replace some of the N_2F_4 removed. Therefore, the system shifts from right to left until equilibrium is reestablished. As a result, some NF_2 combines to form N_2F_4.

Comment The equilibrium constant remains unchanged in this case because temperature is held constant. It might seem that K_c should change because NF_2 combines to produce N_2F_4. Remember, however, that initially some N_2F_4 was removed. The system adjusts to replace only some of the N_2F_4 that was removed, so that overall the amount of N_2F_4 has decreased. In fact, by the time the equilibrium is reestablished, the amounts of both NF_2 and N_2F_4 have decreased. Looking at the equilibrium constant expression, we see that dividing a smaller numerator by a smaller denominator gives the same value of K_c.

(c) The stress applied is a decrease in pressure (which is accompanied by an increase in gas volume). The system will adjust to remove the stress by increasing the pressure. Recall that pressure is directly proportional to the number of moles of a gas. In the balanced equation we see that the formation of NF_2 from N_2F_4 will increase the total number of moles of gases and hence the pressure. Therefore, the system will shift from left to right to reestablish equilibrium. The equilibrium constant will remain unchanged because temperature is held constant.

(d) The function of a catalyst is to increase the rate of a reaction. If a catalyst is added to a reacting system not at equilibrium, the system will reach equilibrium faster than if left undisturbed. If a system is already at equilibrium, as in this case, the addition of a catalyst will not affect either the concentrations of NF_2 and N_2F_4 or the equilibrium constant.

Similar problems: 14.57, 14.58.

(Continued)

CHEMISTRY
in Action

Life at High Altitudes and Hemoglobin Production

In the human body, countless chemical equilibria must be maintained to ensure physiological well-being. If environmental conditions change, the body must adapt to keep functioning. The consequences of a sudden change in altitude dramatize this fact. Flying from San Francisco, which is at sea level, to Mexico City, where the elevation is 2.3 km (1.4 mi), or scaling a 3-km mountain in two days can cause headache, nausea, extreme fatigue, and other discomforts. These conditions are all symptoms of hypoxia, a deficiency in the amount of oxygen reaching body tissues. In serious cases, the victim may slip into a coma and die if not treated quickly. And yet a person living at a high altitude for weeks or months gradually recovers from altitude sickness and adjusts to the low oxygen content in the atmosphere, so that he or she can function normally.

The combination of oxygen with the hemoglobin (Hb) molecule, which carries oxygen through the blood, is a complex reaction, but for our purposes it can be represented by a simplified equation:

$$Hb(aq) + O_2(aq) \rightleftharpoons HbO_2(aq)$$

where HbO_2 is oxyhemoglobin, the hemoglobin-oxygen complex that actually transports oxygen to tissues. The equilibrium constant is

$$K_c = \frac{[HbO_2]}{[Hb][O_2]}$$

At an altitude of 3 km the partial pressure of oxygen is only about 0.14 atm, compared with 0.2 atm at sea level. According to Le Châtelier's principle, a decrease in oxygen concentration will shift the equilibrium shown in the equation above from right to left. This change depletes the supply of oxyhemoglobin, causing hypoxia. Given enough time, the body copes with this problem by producing more hemoglobin molecules. The equilibrium will then gradually shift back toward the formation of oxyhemoglobin. It takes two to three weeks for the increase in hemoglobin production to meet the body's basic needs adequately. A return to full capacity may require several years to occur. Studies show that long-time residents of high-altitude areas have high hemoglobin levels in their blood—sometimes as much as 50 percent more than individuals living at sea level!

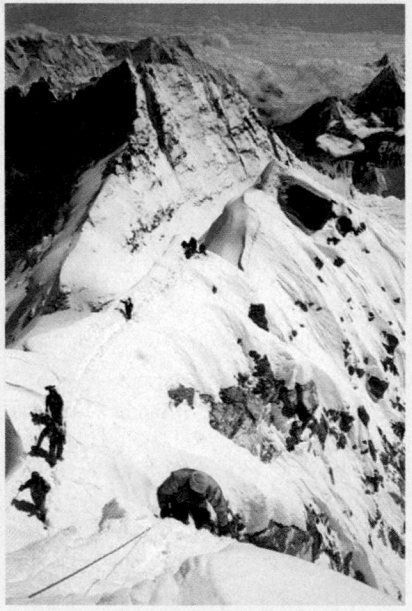

Mountaineers need weeks or even months to become acclimatized before scaling summits such as Mount Everest.

Practice Exercise Consider the equilibrium between molecular oxygen and ozone

$$3O_2(g) \rightleftharpoons 2O_3(g) \qquad\qquad \Delta H° = 284 \text{ kJ/mol}$$

What would be the effect of (a) increasing the pressure on the system by decreasing the volume, (b) adding O_2 to the system at constant volume, (c) decreasing the temperature, and (d) adding a catalyst?

CHEMISTRY
in Action

The Haber Process

Knowing the factors that affect chemical equilibrium has great practical value for industrial applications, such as the synthesis of ammonia. The Haber process for synthesizing ammonia from molecular hydrogen and nitrogen uses a heterogeneous catalyst to speed up the reaction (see p. 583). Let us look at the equilibrium reaction for ammonia synthesis to determine whether there are factors that could be manipulated to enhance the yield.

Suppose, as a prominent industrial chemist at the turn of the twentieth century, you are asked to design an efficient procedure for synthesizing ammonia from hydrogen and nitrogen. Your main objective is to obtain a high yield of the product while keeping the production costs down. Your first step is to take a careful look at the balanced equation for the production of ammonia:

$$N_2(g) + 3H_2(g) \rightleftharpoons 2NH_3(g) \quad \Delta H° = -92.6 \text{ kJ/mol}$$

Two ideas strike you: *First*, because 1 mole of N_2 reacts with 3 moles of H_2 to produce 2 moles of NH_3, a higher yield of NH_3 can be obtained at equilibrium if the reaction is carried out under high pressures. This is indeed the case, as shown by the plot of mole percent of NH_3 versus the total pressure of the reacting system. *Second*, the exothermic nature of the forward reaction tells you that the equilibrium constant for the reaction will decrease with increasing temperature. Thus, for maximum yield of NH_3, the reaction should be run at the lowest possible temperature. The graph (above right) shows that the yield of ammonia increases with decreasing temperature. A low-temperature operation (say,

The composition (mole percent) of $H_2 + N_2$ and NH_3 at equilibrium (for a certain starting mixture) as a function of temperature.

220 K or −53°C) is desirable in other respects too. The boiling point of NH_3 is −33.5°C, so as it formed it would quickly condense to a liquid, which could be conveniently removed from the reacting system. (Both H_2 and N_2 are still gases at this temperature.) Consequently, the net reaction would shift from left to right, just as desired.

On paper, then, these are your conclusions. Let us compare your recommendations with the actual conditions in an industrial plant. Typically, the operating pressures are between

Mole percent of NH_3 as a function of the total pressures of the gases at 425°C.

Schematic diagram of the Haber process for ammonia synthesis. The heat generated from the reaction is used to heat the incoming gases.

(Continued)

500 atm and 1000 atm, so you are right to advocate high pressure. Furthermore, in the industrial process the NH_3 never reaches its equilibrium value but is constantly removed from the reaction mixture in a continuous process operation. This design makes sense, too, as you had anticipated. The only discrepancy is that the operation is usually carried out at about 500°C. This high-temperature operation is costly and the yield of NH_3 is low.

The justification for this choice is that the *rate* of NH_3 production increases with increasing temperature. Commercially, faster production of NH_3 is preferable even if it means a lower yield and higher operating cost. For this reason, the combination of high-pressure, high-temperature conditions and the proper catalyst is the most efficient way to produce ammonia on a large scale.

Summary of Facts and Concepts

1. Dynamic equilibria between phases are called physical equilibria. Chemical equilibrium is a reversible process in which the rates of the forward and reverse reactions are equal and the concentrations of reactants and products do not change with time.

2. For the general chemical reaction

$$aA + bB \rightleftharpoons cC + dD$$

the concentrations of reactants and products at equilibrium (in moles per liter) are related by the equilibrium constant expression [Equation (14.2)].

3. The equilibrium constant for gases, K_P, expresses the relationship of the equilibrium partial pressures (in atm) of reactants and products.

4. A chemical equilibrium process in which all reactants and products are in the same phase is homogeneous. If the reactants and products are not all in the same phase, the equilibrium is heterogeneous. The concentrations of pure solids, pure liquids, and solvents are constant and do not appear in the equilibrium constant expression of a reaction.

5. If a reaction can be expressed as the sum of two or more reactions, the equilibrium constant for the overall reaction is given by the product of the equilibrium constants of the individual reactions.

6. The value of K depends on how the chemical equation is balanced, and the equilibrium constant for the reverse of a particular reaction is the reciprocal of the equilibrium constant of that reaction.

7. The equilibrium constant is the ratio of the rate constant for the forward reaction to that for the reverse reaction.

8. The reaction quotient Q has the same form as the equilibrium constant, but it applies to a reaction that may not be at equilibrium. If $Q > K$, the reaction will proceed from right to left to achieve equilibrium. If $Q < K$, the reaction will proceed from left to right to achieve equilibrium.

9. Le Châtelier's principle states that if an external stress is applied to a system at chemical equilibrium, the system will adjust to partially offset the stress.

10. Only a change in temperature changes the value of the equilibrium constant for a particular reaction. Changes in concentration, pressure, or volume may change the equilibrium concentrations of reactants and products. The addition of a catalyst hastens the attainment of equilibrium but does not affect the equilibrium concentrations of reactants and products.

Key Words

Chemical equilibrium, p. 602
Equilibrium constant
  (K), p. 604

Heterogeneous
  equilibrium, p. 610
Homogeneous
  equilibrium, p. 605

Law of mass action, p. 604
Le Châtelier's
  principle, p. 623

Physical equilibrium, p. 602
Reaction quotient
  (Q), p. 618

Questions and Problems

The Concept of Equilibrium and the Equilibrium Constant

Review Questions

14.1   Define equilibrium. Give two examples of a dynamic equilibrium.

14.2   Explain the difference between physical equilibrium and chemical equilibrium. Give two examples of each.

14.3   What is the law of mass action?

14.4   Briefly describe the importance of equilibrium in the study of chemical reactions.

Equilibrium Constant Expressions

Review Questions

14.5   Define homogeneous equilibrium and heterogeneous equilibrium. Give two examples of each.

14.6   What do the symbols K_c and K_P represent?

14.7   Write the expressions for the equilibrium constants K_P of the thermal decomposition reactions:
(a) $2NaHCO_3(s) \rightleftharpoons$
$$Na_2CO_3(s) + CO_2(g) + H_2O(g)$$
(b) $2CaSO_4(s) \rightleftharpoons 2CaO(s) + 2SO_2(g) + O_2(g)$

14.8   Write equilibrium constant expressions for K_c, and for K_P, if applicable, for the following processes:
(a) $2CO_2(g) \rightleftharpoons 2CO(g) + O_2(g)$
(b) $3O_2(g) \rightleftharpoons 2O_3(g)$
(c) $CO(g) + Cl_2(g) \rightleftharpoons COCl_2(g)$
(d) $H_2O(g) + C(s) \rightleftharpoons CO(g) + H_2(g)$
(e) $HCOOH(aq) \rightleftharpoons H^+(aq) + HCOO^-(aq)$
(f) $2HgO(s) \rightleftharpoons 2Hg(l) + O_2(g)$

14.9   Write the equilibrium constant expressions for K_c and K_P, if applicable, for the following reactions:
(a) $2NO_2(g) + 7H_2(g) \rightleftharpoons 2NH_3(g) + 4H_2O(l)$
(b) $2ZnS(s) + 3O_2(g) \rightleftharpoons 2ZnO(s) + 2SO_2(g)$
(c) $C(s) + CO_2(g) \rightleftharpoons 2CO(g)$
(d) $C_6H_5COOH(aq) \rightleftharpoons$
$$C_6H_5COO^-(aq) + H^+(aq)$$

14.10 Write the equation relating K_c to K_P, and define all the terms.

14.11 What is the rule for writing the equilibrium constant for the overall reaction involving two or more reactions?

14.12 Give an example of a multiple equilibria reaction.

Problems

14.13 The equilibrium constant for the reaction $A \rightleftharpoons B$ is $K_c = 10$ at a certain temperature. (1) Starting with only reactant A, which of the diagrams shown here best represents the system at equilibrium? (2) Which of the diagrams best represents the system at equilibrium if $K_c = 0.10$? Explain why you can calculate K_c in each case without knowing the volume of the container. The gray spheres represent the A molecules and the green spheres represent the B molecules.

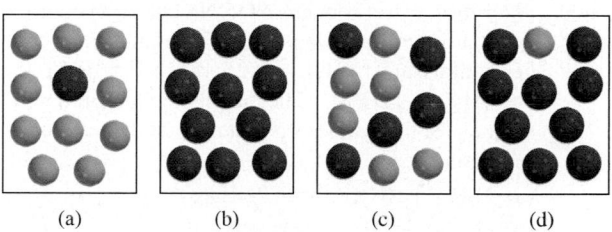

(a)   (b)   (c)   (d)

14.14 The following diagrams represent the equilibrium state for three different reactions of the type $A + X \rightleftharpoons AX$ (X = B, C, or D):

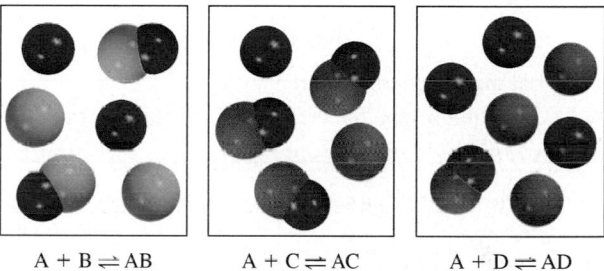

$A + B \rightleftharpoons AB$ $A + C \rightleftharpoons AC$ $A + D \rightleftharpoons AD$

(a) Which reaction has the largest equilibrium constant? (b) Which reaction has the smallest equilibrium constant?

14.15 The equilibrium constant (K_c) for the reaction
$$2HCl(g) \rightleftharpoons H_2(g) + Cl_2(g)$$
is 4.17×10^{-34} at 25°C. What is the equilibrium constant for the reaction
$$H_2(g) + Cl_2(g) \rightleftharpoons 2HCl(g)$$
at the same temperature?

14.16 Consider the following equilibrium process at 700°C:
$$2H_2(g) + S_2(g) \rightleftharpoons 2H_2S(g)$$
Analysis shows that there are 2.50 moles of H_2, 1.35×10^{-5} mole of S_2, and 8.70 moles of H_2S present in a 12.0-L flask. Calculate the equilibrium constant K_c for the reaction.

14.17 What is K_P at 1273°C for the reaction
$$2CO(g) + O_2(g) \rightleftharpoons 2CO_2(g)$$
if K_c is 2.24×10^{22} at the same temperature?

14.18 The equilibrium constant K_P for the reaction

$$2SO_3(g) \rightleftharpoons 2SO_2(g) + O_2(g)$$

is 1.8×10^{-5} at 350°C. What is K_c for this reaction?

14.19 Consider the following reaction:

$$N_2(g) + O_2(g) \rightleftharpoons 2NO(g)$$

If the equilibrium partial pressures of N_2, O_2, and NO are 0.15 atm, 0.33 atm, and 0.050 atm, respectively, at 2200°C, what is K_P?

14.20 A reaction vessel contains NH_3, N_2, and H_2 at equilibrium at a certain temperature. The equilibrium concentrations are $[NH_3] = 0.25\ M$, $[N_2] = 0.11\ M$, and $[H_2] = 1.91\ M$. Calculate the equilibrium constant K_c for the synthesis of ammonia if the reaction is represented as

(a) $N_2(g) + 3H_2(g) \rightleftharpoons 2NH_3(g)$

(b) $\frac{1}{2}N_2(g) + \frac{3}{2}H_2(g) \rightleftharpoons NH_3(g)$

14.21 The equilibrium constant K_c for the reaction

$$I_2(g) \rightleftharpoons 2I(g)$$

is 3.8×10^{-5} at 727°C. Calculate K_c and K_P for the equilibrium

$$2I(g) \rightleftharpoons I_2(g)$$

at the same temperature.

14.22 At equilibrium, the pressure of the reacting mixture

$$CaCO_3(s) \rightleftharpoons CaO(s) + CO_2(g)$$

is 0.105 atm at 350°C. Calculate K_P and K_c for this reaction.

14.23 The equilibrium constant K_P for the reaction

$$PCl_5(g) \rightleftharpoons PCl_3(g) + Cl_2(g)$$

is 1.05 at 250°C. The reaction starts with a mixture of PCl_5, PCl_3, and Cl_2 at pressures 0.177 atm, 0.223 atm, and 0.111 atm, respectively, at 250°C. When the mixture comes to equilibrium at that temperature, which pressures will have decreased and which will have increased? Explain why.

14.24 Ammonium carbamate, $NH_4CO_2NH_2$, decomposes as follows:

$$NH_4CO_2NH_2(s) \rightleftharpoons 2NH_3(g) + CO_2(g)$$

Starting with only the solid, it is found that at 40°C the total gas pressure (NH_3 and CO_2) is 0.363 atm. Calculate the equilibrium constant K_P.

14.25 Consider the following reaction at 1600°C:

$$Br_2(g) \rightleftharpoons 2Br(g)$$

When 1.05 moles of Br_2 are put in a 0.980-L flask, 1.20 percent of the Br_2 undergoes dissociation. Calculate the equilibrium constant K_c for the reaction.

14.26 Pure phosgene gas ($COCl_2$), 3.00×10^{-2} mol, was placed in a 1.50-L container. It was heated to 800 K, and at equilibrium the pressure of CO was found to be 0.497 atm. Calculate the equilibrium constant K_P for the reaction

$$CO(g) + Cl_2(g) \rightleftharpoons COCl_2(g)$$

14.27 Consider the equilibrium

$$2NOBr(g) \rightleftharpoons 2NO(g) + Br_2(g)$$

If nitrosyl bromide, NOBr, is 34 percent dissociated at 25°C and the total pressure is 0.25 atm, calculate K_P and K_c for the dissociation at this temperature.

14.28 A 2.50-mole quantity of NOCl was initially in a 1.50-L reaction chamber at 400°C. After equilibrium was established, it was found that 28.0 percent of the NOCl had dissociated:

$$2NOCl(g) \rightleftharpoons 2NO(g) + Cl_2(g)$$

Calculate the equilibrium constant K_c for the reaction.

14.29 The following equilibrium constants have been determined for hydrosulfuric acid at 25°C:

$$H_2S(aq) \rightleftharpoons H^+(aq) + HS^-(aq)$$
$$K_c' = 9.5 \times 10^{-8}$$
$$HS^-(aq) \rightleftharpoons H^+(aq) + S^{2-}(aq)$$
$$K_c'' = 1.0 \times 10^{-19}$$

Calculate the equilibrium constant for the following reaction at the same temperature:

$$H_2S(aq) \rightleftharpoons 2H^+(aq) + S^{2-}(aq)$$

14.30 The following equilibrium constants have been determined for oxalic acid at 25°C:

$$C_2H_2O_4(aq) \rightleftharpoons H^+(aq) + C_2HO_4^-(aq)$$
$$K_c' = 6.5 \times 10^{-2}$$
$$C_2HO_4^-(aq) \rightleftharpoons H^+(aq) + C_2O_4^{2-}(aq)$$
$$K_c'' = 6.1 \times 10^{-5}$$

Calculate the equilibrium constant for the following reaction at the same temperature:

$$C_2H_2O_4(aq) \rightleftharpoons 2H^+(aq) + C_2O_4^{2-}(aq)$$

14.31 The following equilibrium constants were determined at 1123 K:

$$C(s) + CO_2(g) \rightleftharpoons 2CO(g) \quad K_P' = 1.3 \times 10^{14}$$
$$CO(g) + Cl_2(g) \rightleftharpoons COCl_2(g) \quad K_P'' = 6.0 \times 10^{-3}$$

Write the equilibrium constant expression K_P, and calculate the equilibrium constant at 1123 K for

$$C(s) + CO_2(g) + 2Cl_2(g) \rightleftharpoons 2COCl_2(g)$$

14.32 At a certain temperature the following reactions have the constants shown:

$$S(s) + O_2(g) \rightleftharpoons SO_2(g) \quad K_c' = 4.2 \times 10^{52}$$
$$2S(s) + 3O_2(g) \rightleftharpoons 2SO_3(g) \quad K_c'' = 9.8 \times 10^{128}$$

Calculate the equilibrium constant K_c for the following reaction at that temperature:

$$2SO_2(g) + O_2(g) \rightleftharpoons 2SO_3(g)$$

The Relationship Between Chemical Kinetics and Chemical Equilibrium
Review Questions

14.33 Based on rate constant considerations, explain why the equilibrium constant depends on temperature.

14.34 Explain why reactions with large equilibrium constants, such as the formation of rust (Fe_2O_3), may have very slow rates.

Problems

14.35 Water is a very weak electrolyte that undergoes the following ionization (called autoionization):

$$H_2O(l) \underset{k_{-1}}{\overset{k_1}{\rightleftharpoons}} H^+(aq) + OH^-(aq)$$

(a) If $k_1 = 2.4 \times 10^{-5} s^{-1}$ and $k_{-1} = 1.3 \times 10^{11}/M \cdot s$, calculate the equilibrium constant K where $K = [H^+][OH^-]/[H_2O]$. (b) Calculate the product $[H^+][OH^-]$ and $[H^+]$ and $[OH^-]$.

14.36 Consider the following reaction, which takes place in a single elementary step:

$$2A + B \underset{k_{-1}}{\overset{k_1}{\rightleftharpoons}} A_2B$$

If the equilibrium constant K_c is 12.6 at a certain temperature and if $k_r = 5.1 \times 10^{-2} s^{-1}$, calculate the value of k_f.

What Does the Equilibrium Constant Tell Us?
Review Questions

14.37 Define reaction quotient. How does it differ from equilibrium constant?

14.38 Outline the steps for calculating the concentrations of reacting species in an equilibrium reaction.

Problems

14.39 The equilibrium constant K_P for the reaction

$$2SO_2(g) + O_2(g) \rightleftharpoons 2SO_3(g)$$

is 5.60×10^4 at 350°C. The initial pressures of SO_2 and O_2 in a mixture are 0.350 atm and 0.762 atm, respectively, at 350°C. When the mixture equilibrates, is the total pressure less than or greater than the sum of the initial pressures (1.112 atm)?

14.40 For the synthesis of ammonia

$$N_2(g) + 3H_2(g) \rightleftharpoons 2NH_3(g)$$

the equilibrium constant K_c at 375°C is 1.2. Starting with $[H_2]_0 = 0.76 M$, $[N_2]_0 = 0.60 M$, and $[NH_3]_0 = 0.48 M$, which gases will have increased in concentration and which will have decreased in concentration when the mixture comes to equilibrium?

14.41 For the reaction

$$H_2(g) + CO_2(g) \rightleftharpoons H_2O(g) + CO(g)$$

at 700°C, $K_c = 0.534$. Calculate the number of moles of H_2 that are present at equilibrium if a mixture of 0.300 mole of CO and 0.300 mole of H_2O is heated to 700°C in a 10.0-L container.

14.42 At 1000 K, a sample of pure NO_2 gas decomposes:

$$2NO_2(g) \rightleftharpoons 2NO(g) + O_2(g)$$

The equilibrium constant K_P is 158. Analysis shows that the partial pressure of O_2 is 0.25 atm at equilibrium. Calculate the pressure of NO and NO_2 in the mixture.

14.43 The equilibrium constant K_c for the reaction

$$H_2(g) + Br_2(g) \rightleftharpoons 2HBr(g)$$

is 2.18×10^6 at 730°C. Starting with 3.20 moles of HBr in a 12.0-L reaction vessel, calculate the concentrations of H_2, Br_2, and HBr at equilibrium.

14.44 The dissociation of molecular iodine into iodine atoms is represented as

$$I_2(g) \rightleftharpoons 2I(g)$$

At 1000 K, the equilibrium constant K_c for the reaction is 3.80×10^{-5}. Suppose you start with 0.0456 mole of I_2 in a 2.30-L flask at 1000 K. What are the concentrations of the gases at equilibrium?

14.45 The equilibrium constant K_c for the decomposition of phosgene, $COCl_2$, is 4.63×10^{-3} at 527°C:

$$COCl_2(g) \rightleftharpoons CO(g) + Cl_2(g)$$

Calculate the equilibrium partial pressure of all the components, starting with pure phosgene at 0.760 atm.

14.46 Consider the following equilibrium process at 686°C:

$$CO_2(g) + H_2(g) \rightleftharpoons CO(g) + H_2O(g)$$

The equilibrium concentrations of the reacting species are $[CO] = 0.050 M$, $[H_2] = 0.045 M$, $[CO_2] = 0.086 M$, and $[H_2O] = 0.040 M$. (a) Calculate K_c for the reaction at 686°C. (b) If we add CO_2 to increase its concentration to 0.50 mol/L, what will the concentrations of all the gases be when equilibrium is reestablished?

14.47 Consider the heterogeneous equilibrium process:

$$C(s) + CO_2(g) \rightleftharpoons 2CO(g)$$

At 700°C, the total pressure of the system is found to be 4.50 atm. If the equilibrium constant K_P is 1.52, calculate the equilibrium partial pressures of CO_2 and CO.

14.48 The equilibrium constant K_c for the reaction

$$H_2(g) + CO_2(g) \rightleftharpoons H_2O(g) + CO(g)$$

is 4.2 at 1650°C. Initially 0.80 mol H_2 and 0.80 mol CO_2 are injected into a 5.0-L flask. Calculate the concentration of each species at equilibrium.

Factors That Affect Chemical Equilibrium

Review Questions

14.49 Explain Le Châtelier's principle. How can this principle help us maximize the yields of reactions?

14.50 Use Le Châtelier's principle to explain why the equilibrium vapor pressure of a liquid increases with increasing temperature.

14.51 List four factors that can shift the position of an equilibrium. Only one of these factors can alter the value of the equilibrium constant. Which one is it?

14.52 Does the addition of a catalyst have any effects on the position of an equilibrium?

Problems

14.53 Consider the following equilibrium system involving SO_2, Cl_2, and SO_2Cl_2 (sulfuryl dichloride):

$$SO_2(g) + Cl_2(g) \rightleftharpoons SO_2Cl_2(g)$$

Predict how the equilibrium position would change if (a) Cl_2 gas were added to the system; (b) SO_2Cl_2 were removed from the system; (c) SO_2 were removed from the system. The temperature remains constant.

14.54 Heating solid sodium bicarbonate in a closed vessel establishes the following equilibrium:

$$2NaHCO_3(s) \rightleftharpoons Na_2CO_3(s) + H_2O(g) + CO_2(g)$$

What would happen to the equilibrium position if (a) some of the CO_2 were removed from the system; (b) some solid Na_2CO_3 were added to the system; (c) some of the solid $NaHCO_3$ were removed from the system? The temperature remains constant.

14.55 Consider the following equilibrium systems:

(a) $A \rightleftharpoons 2B$ $\qquad \Delta H° = 20.0$ kJ/mol
(b) $A + B \rightleftharpoons C$ $\qquad \Delta H° = -5.4$ kJ/mol
(c) $A \rightleftharpoons B$ $\qquad \Delta H° = 0.0$ kJ/mol

Predict the change in the equilibrium constant K_c that would occur in each case if the temperature of the reacting system were raised.

14.56 What effect does an increase in pressure have on each of the following systems at equilibrium? The temperature is kept constant and, in each case, the reactants are in a cylinder fitted with a movable piston.

(a) $A(s) \rightleftharpoons 2B(s)$
(b) $2A(l) \rightleftharpoons B(l)$
(c) $A(s) \rightleftharpoons B(g)$

(d) $A(g) \rightleftharpoons B(g)$
(e) $A(g) \rightleftharpoons 2B(g)$

14.57 Consider the equilibrium

$$2I(g) \rightleftharpoons I_2(g)$$

What would be the effect on the position of equilibrium of (a) increasing the total pressure on the system by decreasing its volume; (b) adding I_2 to the reaction mixture; and (c) decreasing the temperature?

14.58 Consider the following equilibrium process:

$$PCl_5(g) \rightleftharpoons PCl_3(g) + Cl_2(g) \quad \Delta H° = 92.5 \text{ kJ/mol}$$

Predict the direction of the shift in equilibrium when (a) the temperature is raised; (b) more chlorine gas is added to the reaction mixture; (c) some PCl_3 is removed from the mixture; (d) the pressure on the gases is increased; (e) a catalyst is added to the reaction mixture.

14.59 Consider the reaction

$$2SO_2(g) + O_2(g) \rightleftharpoons 2SO_3(g) \quad \Delta H° = -198.2 \text{ kJ/mol}$$

Comment on the changes in the concentrations of SO_2, O_2, and SO_3 at equilibrium if we were to (a) increase the temperature; (b) increase the pressure; (c) increase SO_2; (d) add a catalyst; (e) add helium at constant volume.

14.60 In the uncatalyzed reaction

$$N_2O_4(g) \rightleftharpoons 2NO_2(g)$$

the pressure of the gases at equilibrium are $P_{N_2O_4} = 0.377$ atm and $P_{NO_2} = 1.56$ atm at 100°C. What would happen to these pressures if a catalyst were added to the mixture?

14.61 Consider the gas-phase reaction

$$2CO(g) + O_2(g) \rightleftharpoons 2CO_2(g)$$

Predict the shift in the equilibrium position when helium gas is added to the equilibrium mixture (a) at constant pressure and (b) at constant volume.

14.62 Consider the following equilibrium reaction in a closed container:

$$CaCO_3(s) \rightleftharpoons CaO(s) + CO_2(g)$$

What will happen if (a) the volume is increased; (b) some CaO is added to the mixture; (c) some $CaCO_3$ is removed; (d) some CO_2 is added to the mixture; (e) a few drops of a NaOH solution are added to the mixture; (f) a few drops of a HCl solution are added to the mixture (ignore the reaction between CO_2 and water); (g) temperature is increased?

Additional Problems

14.63 Consider the statement: "The equilibrium constant of a reacting mixture of solid NH_4Cl and gaseous

NH$_3$ and HCl is 0.316." List three important pieces of information that are missing from this statement.

14.64 Pure nitrosyl chloride (NOCl) gas was heated to 240°C in a 1.00-L container. At equilibrium the total pressure was 1.00 atm and the NOCl pressure was 0.64 atm.

$$2NOCl(g) \rightleftharpoons 2NO(g) + Cl_2(g)$$

(a) Calculate the partial pressures of NO and Cl$_2$ in the system. (b) Calculate the equilibrium constant K_P.

14.65 The equilibrium constant (K_P) for the formation of the air pollutant nitric oxide (NO) in an automobile engine at 530°C is 2.9×10^{-11}:

$$N_2(g) + O_2(g) \rightleftharpoons 2NO(g)$$

(a) Calculate the partial pressure of NO under these conditions if the partial pressures of nitrogen and oxygen are 3.0 atm and 0.012 atm, respectively. (b) Repeat the calculation for atmospheric conditions where the partial pressures of nitrogen and oxygen are 0.78 atm and 0.21 atm and the temperature is 25°C. (The K_P for the reaction is 4.0×10^{-31} at this temperature.) (c) Is the formation of NO endothermic or exothermic? (d) What natural phenomenon promotes the formation of NO? Why?

14.66 Baking soda (sodium bicarbonate) undergoes thermal decomposition as follows:

$$2NaHCO_3(s) \rightleftharpoons Na_2CO_3(s) + CO_2(g) + H_2O(g)$$

Would we obtain more CO$_2$ and H$_2$O by adding extra baking soda to the reaction mixture in (a) a closed vessel or (b) an open vessel?

14.67 Consider the following reaction at equilibrium:

$$A(g) \rightleftharpoons 2B(g)$$

From the data shown here, calculate the equilibrium constant (both K_P and K_c) at each temperature. Is the reaction endothermic or exothermic?

Temperature (°C)	[A] (M)	[B] (M)
200	0.0125	0.843
300	0.171	0.764
400	0.250	0.724

14.68 The equilibrium constant K_P for the reaction

$$2H_2O(g) \rightleftharpoons 2H_2(g) + O_2(g)$$

is 2×10^{-42} at 25°C. (a) What is K_c for the reaction at the same temperature? (b) The very small value of K_P (and K_c) indicates that the reaction overwhelmingly favors the formation of water molecules. Explain why, despite this fact, a mixture of hydrogen and oxygen gases can be kept at room temperature without any change.

14.69 Consider the following reacting system:

$$2NO(g) + Cl_2(g) \rightleftharpoons 2NOCl(g)$$

What combination of temperature and pressure would maximize the yield of nitrosyl chloride (NOCl)? [*Hint:* ΔH_f°(NOCl) = 51.7 kJ/mol. You will also need to consult Appendix 3.]

14.70 At a certain temperature and a total pressure of 1.2 atm, the partial pressures of an equilibrium mixture

$$2A(g) \rightleftharpoons B(g)$$

are P_A = 0.60 atm and P_B = 0.60 atm. (a) Calculate the K_P for the reaction at this temperature. (b) If the total pressure were increased to 1.5 atm, what would be the partial pressures of A and B at equilibrium?

14.71 The decomposition of ammonium hydrogen sulfide

$$NH_4HS(s) \rightleftharpoons NH_3(g) + H_2S(g)$$

is an endothermic process. A 6.1589-g sample of the solid is placed in an evacuated 4.000-L vessel at exactly 24°C. After equilibrium has been established, the total pressure inside is 0.709 atm. Some solid NH$_4$HS remains in the vessel. (a) What is the K_P for the reaction? (b) What percentage of the solid has decomposed? (c) If the volume of the vessel were doubled at constant temperature, what would happen to the amount of solid in the vessel?

14.72 Consider the reaction

$$2NO(g) + O_2(g) \rightleftharpoons 2NO_2(g)$$

At 430°C, an equilibrium mixture consists of 0.020 mole of O$_2$, 0.040 mole of NO, and 0.96 mole of NO$_2$. Calculate K_P for the reaction, given that the total pressure is 0.20 atm.

14.73 When heated, ammonium carbamate decomposes as follows:

$$NH_4CO_2NH_2(s) \rightleftharpoons 2NH_3(g) + CO_2(g)$$

At a certain temperature the equilibrium pressure of the system is 0.318 atm. Calculate K_P for the reaction.

14.74 A mixture of 0.47 mole of H$_2$ and 3.59 moles of HCl is heated to 2800°C. Calculate the equilibrium partial pressures of H$_2$, Cl$_2$, and HCl if the total pressure is 2.00 atm. For the reaction

$$H_2(g) + Cl_2(g) \rightleftharpoons 2HCl(g)$$

K_P is 193 at 2800°C.

14.75 When heated at high temperatures, iodine vapor dissociates as follows:

$$I_2(g) \rightleftharpoons 2I(g)$$

In one experiment, a chemist finds that when 0.054 mole of I$_2$ was placed in a flask of volume 0.48 L at

587 K, the degree of dissociation (that is, the fraction of I_2 dissociated) was 0.0252. Calculate K_c and K_P for the reaction at this temperature.

14.76 One mole of N_2 and three moles of H_2 are placed in a flask at 375°C. Calculate the total pressure of the system at equilibrium if the mole fraction of NH_3 is 0.21. The K_P for the reaction is 4.31×10^{-4}.

14.77 At 1130°C the equilibrium constant (K_c) for the reaction

$$2H_2S(g) \rightleftharpoons 2H_2(g) + S_2(g)$$

is 2.25×10^{-4}. If $[H_2S] = 4.84 \times 10^{-3}$ M and $[H_2] = 1.50 \times 10^{-3}$ M, calculate $[S_2]$.

14.78 A quantity of 6.75 g of SO_2Cl_2 was placed in a 2.00-L flask. At 648 K, there is 0.0345 mole of SO_2 present. Calculate K_c for the reaction

$$SO_2Cl_2(g) \rightleftharpoons SO_2(g) + Cl_2(g)$$

14.79 The formation of SO_3 from SO_2 and O_2 is an intermediate step in the manufacture of sulfuric acid, and it is also responsible for the acid rain phenomenon. The equilibrium constant K_P for the reaction

$$2SO_2(g) + O_2(g) \rightleftharpoons 2SO_3(g)$$

is 0.13 at 830°C. In one experiment 2.00 mol SO_2 and 2.00 mol O_2 were initially present in a flask. What must the total pressure at equilibrium be in order to have an 80.0 percent yield of SO_3?

14.80 Consider the dissociation of iodine:

$$I_2(g) \rightleftharpoons 2I(g)$$

A 1.00-g sample of I_2 is heated to 1200°C in a 500-mL flask. At equilibrium the total pressure is 1.51 atm. Calculate K_P for the reaction. [*Hint:* Use the result in 14.109(a). The degree of dissociation α can be obtained by first calculating the ratio of observed pressure over calculated pressure, assuming no dissociation.]

14.81 Eggshells are composed mostly of calcium carbonate ($CaCO_3$) formed by the reaction

$$Ca^{2+}(aq) + CO_3^{2-}(aq) \rightleftharpoons CaCO_3(s)$$

The carbonate ions are supplied by carbon dioxide produced as a result of metabolism. Explain why eggshells are thinner in the summer when the rate of panting by chickens is greater. Suggest a remedy for this situation.

14.82 The equilibrium constant K_P for the following reaction is 4.31×10^{-4} at 375°C:

$$N_2(g) + 3H_2(g) \rightleftharpoons 2NH_3(g)$$

In a certain experiment a student starts with 0.862 atm of N_2 and 0.373 atm of H_2 in a constant-volume vessel at 375°C. Calculate the partial pressures of all species when equilibrium is reached.

14.83 A quantity of 0.20 mole of carbon dioxide was heated to a certain temperature with an excess of graphite in a closed container until the following equilibrium was reached:

$$C(s) + CO_2(g) \rightleftharpoons 2CO(g)$$

Under these conditions, the average molar mass of the gases was 35 g/mol. (a) Calculate the mole fractions of CO and CO_2. (b) What is K_P if the total pressure is 11 atm? (*Hint:* The average molar mass is the sum of the products of the mole fraction of each gas and its molar mass.)

14.84 When dissolved in water, glucose (corn sugar) and fructose (fruit sugar) exist in equilibrium as follows:

$$\text{fructose} \rightleftharpoons \text{glucose}$$

A chemist prepared a 0.244 M fructose solution at 25°C. At equilibrium, it was found that its concentration had decreased to 0.113 M. (a) Calculate the equilibrium constant for the reaction. (b) At equilibrium, what percentage of fructose was converted to glucose?

14.85 At room temperature, solid iodine is in equilibrium with its vapor through sublimation and deposition (see p. 487). Describe how you would use radioactive iodine, in either solid or vapor form, to show that there is a dynamic equilibrium between these two phases.

14.86 At 1024°C, the pressure of oxygen gas from the decomposition of copper(II) oxide (CuO) is 0.49 atm:

$$4CuO(s) \rightleftharpoons 2Cu_2O(s) + O_2(g)$$

(a) What is K_P for the reaction? (b) Calculate the fraction of CuO that will decompose if 0.16 mole of it is placed in a 2.0-L flask at 1024°C. (c) What would the fraction be if a 1.0 mole sample of CuO were used? (d) What is the smallest amount of CuO (in moles) that would establish the equilibrium?

14.87 A mixture containing 3.9 moles of NO and 0.88 mole of CO_2 was allowed to react in a flask at a certain temperature according to the equation

$$NO(g) + CO_2(g) \rightleftharpoons NO_2(g) + CO(g)$$

At equilibrium, 0.11 mole of CO_2 was present. Calculate the equilibrium constant K_c of this reaction.

14.88 The equilibrium constant K_c for the reaction

$$H_2(g) + I_2(g) \rightleftharpoons 2HI(g)$$

is 54.3 at 430°C. At the start of the reaction there are 0.714 mole of H_2, 0.984 mole of I_2, and 0.886 mole of HI in a 2.40-L reaction chamber. Calculate the concentrations of the gases at equilibrium.

14.89 When heated, a gaseous compound A dissociates as follows:

$$A(g) \rightleftharpoons B(g) + C(g)$$

In an experiment, A was heated at a certain temperature until its equilibrium pressure reached $0.14P$, where P is the total pressure. Calculate the equilibrium constant K_P of this reaction.

14.90 When a gas was heated under atmospheric conditions, its color deepened. Heating above 150°C caused the color to fade, and at 550°C the color was barely detectable. However, at 550°C, the color was partially restored by increasing the pressure of the system. Which of the following best fits the above description? Justify your choice. (a) A mixture of hydrogen and bromine, (b) pure bromine, (c) a mixture of nitrogen dioxide and dinitrogen tetroxide. (*Hint:* Bromine has a reddish color and nitrogen dioxide is a brown gas. The other gases are colorless.)

14.91 In this chapter we learned that a catalyst has no effect on the position of an equilibrium because it speeds up both the forward and reverse rates to the same extent. To test this statement, consider a situation in which an equilibrium of the type

$$2A(g) \rightleftharpoons B(g)$$

is established inside a cylinder fitted with a weightless piston. The piston is attached by a string to the cover of a box containing a catalyst. When the piston moves upward (expanding against atmospheric pressure), the cover is lifted and the catalyst is exposed to the gases. When the piston moves downward, the box is closed. Assume that the catalyst speeds up the forward reaction ($2A \longrightarrow B$) but does not affect the reverse process ($B \longrightarrow 2A$). Suppose the catalyst is suddenly exposed to the equilibrium system as shown here. Describe what would happen subsequently. How does this "thought" experiment convince you that no such catalyst can exist?

14.92 The equilibrium constant K_c for the following reaction is 1.2 at 375°C.

$$N_2(g) + 3H_2(g) \rightleftharpoons 2NH_3(g)$$

(a) What is the value of K_P for this reaction?

(b) What is the value of the equilibrium constant K_c for $2NH_3(g) \rightleftharpoons N_2(g) + 3H_2(g)$?

(c) What is the value of K_c for $\frac{1}{2}N_2(g) + \frac{3}{2}H_2(g) \rightleftharpoons NH_3(g)$?

(d) What are the values of K_P for the reactions described in (b) and (c)?

14.93 A sealed glass bulb contains a mixture of NO_2 and N_2O_4 gases. Describe what happens to the following properties of the gases when the bulb is heated from 20°C to 40°C: (a) color, (b) pressure, (c) average molar mass, (d) degree of dissociation (from N_2O_4 to NO_2), (e) density. Assume that volume remains constant. (*Hint:* NO_2 is a brown gas; N_2O_4 is colorless.)

14.94 At 20°C, the vapor pressure of water is 0.0231 atm. Calculate K_P and K_c for the process

$$H_2O(l) \rightleftharpoons H_2O(g)$$

14.95 Industrially, sodium metal is obtained by electrolyzing molten sodium chloride. The reaction at the cathode is $Na^+ + e^- \longrightarrow Na$. We might expect that potassium metal would also be prepared by electrolyzing molten potassium chloride. However, potassium metal is soluble in molten potassium chloride and therefore is hard to recover. Furthermore, potassium vaporizes readily at the operating temperature, creating hazardous conditions. Instead, potassium is prepared by the distillation of molten potassium chloride in the presence of sodium vapor at 892°C:

$$Na(g) + KCl(l) \rightleftharpoons NaCl(l) + K(g)$$

In view of the fact that potassium is a stronger reducing agent than sodium, explain why this approach works. (The boiling points of sodium and potassium are 892°C and 770°C, respectively.)

14.96 In the gas phase, nitrogen dioxide is actually a mixture of nitrogen dioxide (NO_2) and dinitrogen tetroxide (N_2O_4). If the density of such a mixture is 2.3 g/L at 74°C and 1.3 atm, calculate the partial pressures of the gases and K_P for the dissociation of N_2O_4.

14.97 About 75 percent of hydrogen for industrial use is produced by the *steam-reforming* process. This process is carried out in two stages called primary and secondary reforming. In the primary stage, a mixture of steam and methane at about 30 atm is heated over a nickel catalyst at 800°C to give hydrogen and carbon monoxide:

$$CH_4(g) + H_2O(g) \rightleftharpoons CO(g) + 3H_2(g)$$
$$\Delta H° = 206 \text{ kJ/mol}$$

The secondary stage is carried out at about 1000°C, in the presence of air, to convert the remaining methane to hydrogen:

$$CH_4(g) + \tfrac{1}{2}O_2(g) \rightleftharpoons CO(g) + 2H_2(g)$$
$$\Delta H° = 35.7 \text{ kJ/mol}$$

(a) What conditions of temperature and pressure would favor the formation of products in both the primary and secondary stage? (b) The equilibrium constant K_c for the primary stage is 18 at 800°C. (i) Calculate K_P for the reaction. (ii) If the partial pressures of methane and steam were both 15 atm at the start, what are the pressures of all the gases at equilibrium?

14.98 Photosynthesis can be represented by

$$6CO_2(g) + 6H_2O(l) \rightleftharpoons C_6H_{12}O_6(s) + 6O_2(g)$$
$$\Delta H° = 2801 \text{ kJ/mol}$$

Explain how the equilibrium would be affected by the following changes: (a) partial pressure of CO_2 is increased, (b) O_2 is removed from the mixture, (c) $C_6H_{12}O_6$ (glucose) is removed from the mixture, (d) more water is added, (e) a catalyst is added, (f) temperature is decreased.

14.99 Consider the decomposition of ammonium chloride at a certain temperature:

$$NH_4Cl(s) \rightleftharpoons NH_3(g) + HCl(g)$$

Calculate the equilibrium constant K_P if the total pressure is 2.2 atm at that temperature.

14.100 At 25°C, the equilibrium partial pressures of NO_2 and N_2O_4 are 0.15 atm and 0.20 atm, respectively. If the volume is doubled at constant temperature, calculate the partial pressures of the gases when a new equilibrium is established.

14.101 In 1899 the German chemist Ludwig Mond developed a process for purifying nickel by converting it to the volatile nickel tetracarbonyl [Ni(CO)$_4$] (b.p. = 42.2°C):

$$Ni(s) + 4CO(g) \rightleftharpoons Ni(CO)_4(g)$$

(a) Describe how you can separate nickel and its solid impurities. (b) How would you recover nickel? [$\Delta H_f°$ for Ni(CO)$_4$ is -602.9 kJ/mol.]

14.102 Consider the equilibrium reaction described in Problem 14.23. A quantity of 2.50 g of PCl$_5$ is placed in an evacuated 0.500-L flask and heated to 250°C. (a) Calculate the pressure of PCl$_5$, assuming it does not dissociate. (b) Calculate the partial pressure of PCl$_5$ at equilibrium. (c) What is the total pressure at equilibrium? (d) What is the degree of dissociation of PCl$_5$? (The degree of dissociation is given by the fraction of PCl$_5$ that has undergone dissociation.)

14.103 Consider the equilibrium system 3A $\rightleftharpoons$ B. Sketch the changes in the concentrations of A and B over time for the following situations: (a) initially only A is present; (b) initially only B is present; (c) initially both A and B are present (with A in higher concentration). In each case, assume that the concentration of B is higher than that of A at equilibrium.

14.104 The vapor pressure of mercury is 0.0020 mmHg at 26°C. (a) Calculate K_c and K_P for the process Hg(l) $\rightleftharpoons$ Hg(g). (b) A chemist breaks a thermometer and spills mercury onto the floor of a laboratory measuring 6.1 m long, 5.3 m wide, and 3.1 m high. Calculate the mass of mercury (in grams) vaporized at equilibrium and the concentration of mercury vapor in mg/m^3. Does this concentration exceed the safety limit of 0.05 mg/m^3? (Ignore the volume of furniture and other objects in the laboratory.)

14.105 At 25°C, a mixture of NO_2 and N_2O_4 gases are in equilibrium in a cylinder fitted with a movable piston. The concentrations are [NO_2] = 0.0475 M and [N_2O_4] = 0.487 M. The volume of the gas mixture is halved by pushing down on the piston at constant temperature. Calculate the concentrations of the gases when equilibrium is re-established. Will the color become darker or lighter after the change? [*Hint:* K_c for the dissociation of N_2O_4 to NO_2 is 4.63×10^{-3}. $N_2O_4(g)$ is colorless and $NO_2(g)$ has a brown color.]

14.106 A student placed a few ice cubes in a drinking glass with water. A few minutes later she noticed that some of the ice cubes were fused together. Explain what happened.

14.107 Consider the potential energy diagrams for two types of reactions A $\rightleftharpoons$ B. In each case, answer the following questions for the system at equilibrium. (a) How would a catalyst affect the forward and reverse rates of the reaction? (b) How would a catalyst affect the energies of the reactant and product? (c) How would an increase in temperature affect the equilibrium constant? (d) If the only effect of a catalyst is to lower the activation energies for the forward and reverse reactions, show that the equilibrium constant remains unchanged if a catalyst is added to the reacting mixture.

14.108 The equilibrium constant K_c for the reaction $2NH_3(g) \rightleftharpoons N_2(g) + 3H_2(g)$ is 0.83 at 375°C. A 14.6-g sample of ammonia is placed in a 4.00-L flask and heated to 375°C. Calculate the concentrations of all the gases when equilibrium is reached.

Special Problems

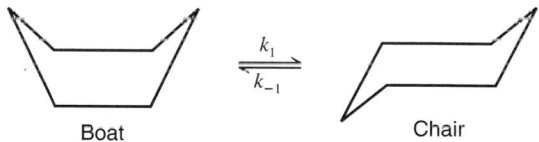

14.109 Consider the reaction between NO_2 and N_2O_4 in a closed container:

$$N_2O_4(g) \rightleftharpoons 2NO_2(g)$$

Initially, 1 mole of N_2O_4 is present. At equilibrium, α mole of N_2O_4 has dissociated to form NO_2. (a) Derive an expression for K_P in terms of α and P, the total pressure. (b) How does the expression in (a) help you predict the shift in equilibrium due to an increase in P? Does your prediction agree with Le Châtelier's principle?

14.110 The dependence of the equilibrium constant of a reaction on temperature is given by the van't Hoff equation:

$$\ln K = -\frac{\Delta H°}{RT} + C$$

where C is a constant. The following table gives the equilibrium constant (K_P) for the reaction at various temperatures

$$2NO(g) + O_2(g) \rightleftharpoons 2NO_2(g)$$

K_P	138	5.12	0.436	0.0626	0.0130
$T(K)$	600	700	800	900	1000

Determine graphically the $\Delta H°$ for the reaction.

14.111 (a) Use the van't Hoff equation in Problem 14.110 to derive the following expression, which relates the equilibrium constants at two different temperatures

$$\ln \frac{K_1}{K_2} = \frac{\Delta H°}{R}\left(\frac{1}{T_2} - \frac{1}{T_1}\right)$$

How does this equation support the prediction based on Le Châtelier's principle about the shift in equilibrium with temperature? (b) The vapor pressures of water are 31.82 mmHg at 30°C and 92.51 mmHg at 50°C. Calculate the molar heat of vaporization of water.

14.112 The K_P for the reaction

$$SO_2Cl_2(g) \rightleftharpoons SO_2(g) + Cl_2(g)$$

is 2.05 at 648 K. A sample of SO_2Cl_2 is placed in a container and heated to 648 K while the total pressure is kept constant at 9.00 atm. Calculate the partial pressures of the gases at equilibrium.

14.113 The "boat" form and "chair" form of cyclohexane (C_6H_{12}) interconverts as shown here:

Boat   Chair

In this representation, the H atoms are omitted and a C atom is assumed to be at each intersection of two lines (bonds). The conversion is first order in each direction. The activation energy for the chair → boat conversion is 41 kJ/mol. If the frequency factor is 1.0×10^{12} s^{-1}, what is k_1 at 298 K? The equilibrium constant K_c for the reaction is 9.83×10^3 at 298 K.

14.114 Consider the following reaction at a certain temperature

$$A_2 + B_2 \rightleftharpoons 2AB$$

The mixing of 1 mole of A_2 with 3 moles of B_2 gives rise to x mole of AB at equilibrium. The addition of 2 more moles of A_2 produces another x mole of AB. What is the equilibrium constant for the reaction?

14.115 Iodine is sparingly soluble in water but much more so in carbon tetrachloride (CCl_4). The equilibrium constant, also called the partition coefficient, for the distribution of I_2 between these two phases

$$I_2(aq) \rightleftharpoons I_2(CCl_4)$$

is 83 at 20°C. (a) A student adds 0.030 L of CCl_4 to 0.200 L of an aqueous solution containing 0.032 g I_2. The mixture is shaken and the two phases are then allowed to separate. Calculate the fraction of I_2 remaining in the aqueous phase. (b) The student now repeats the extraction of I_2 with another 0.030 L of CCl_4. Calculate the fraction of the I_2 from the original solution that remains in the aqueous phase. (c) Compare the result in (b) with a single extraction using 0.060 L of CCl_4. Comment on the difference.

Answers to Practice Exercises

14.1 $K_c = \dfrac{[NO_2]^4[O_2]}{[N_2O_5]^2}$; $K_P = \dfrac{P_{NO_2}^4 P_{O_2}}{P_{N_2O_5}^2}$ **14.2** 2.2×10^2

14.3 347 atm **14.4** 1.2

14.5 $K_c = \dfrac{[Ni(CO)_4]}{[CO]^4}$; $K_P = \dfrac{P_{Ni(CO)_4}}{P_{CO}^4}$

14.6 $K_P = 0.0702$; $K_c = 6.68 \times 10^{-5}$

14.7 (a) $K_a = \dfrac{[O_3]^2}{[O_2]^3}$ (b) $K_b = \dfrac{[O_3]^{\frac{2}{3}}}{[O_2]}$; $K_a = K_b^3$

14.8 From right to left. **14.9** [HI] = 0.031 M, [H$_2$] = 4.3 × 10^{-3} M, [I$_2$] = 4.3 × 10^{-3} M **14.10** [Br$_2$] = 0.065 M, [Br] = 8.4 × 10^{-3} M **14.11** $Q_P = 4.0 \times 10^5$; the net reaction will shift from right to left. **14.12** Left to right.
14.13 The equilibrium will shift from (a) left to right, (b) left to right, and (c) right to left. (d) A catalyst has no effect on the equilibrium.

15

Many organic acids occur in the vegetable kingdom. The molecular models show ascorbic acid, also known as vitamin C ($C_6H_8O_6$), citric acid ($C_6H_8O_7$) (from lemons, oranges, and tomatoes), and oxalic acid ($C_2H_2O_4$) (from rhubarbs and spinach).

Acids and Bases

A LOOK AHEAD

- We start by reviewing and extending Brønsted's definitions of acids and bases (in Chapter 4) in terms of acid-base conjugate pairs. (15.1)

- Next, we examine the acid-base properties of water and define the ion-product constant for the autoionization of water to give H^+ and OH^- ions. (15.2)

- We define pH as a measure of acidity and also introduce the pOH scale. We see that the acidity of a solution depends on the relative concentrations of H^+ and OH^- ions. (15.3)

- Acids and bases can be classified as strong or weak, depending on the extent of their ionization in solution. (15.4)

- We learn to calculate the pH of a weak acid solution from its concentration and ionization constant and to perform similar calculations for weak bases. (15.5 and 15.6)

- We derive an important relationship between the acid and base ionization constants of a conjugate pair. (15.7)

- We then study diprotic and polyprotic acids. (15.8)

- We continue by exploring the relationship between acid strength and molecular structure. (15.9)

- The reactions between salts and water can be studied in terms of acid and base ionizations of the individual cations and anions making up the salt. (15.10)

- Oxides and hydroxides can be classified as acidic, basic, and amphoteric. (15.11)

- The chapter concludes with a discussion of Lewis acids and Lewis bases. A Lewis acid is an electron acceptor and a Lewis base is an electron donor. (15.12)

Interactive Activity Summary

1. Animation: Acid Ionization (15.5)

2. Interactivity: Calculating pH of Acid Solution—Steps 1–4 (15.5)

3. Animation: Base Ionization (15.6)

4. Interactivity: Calculating pH of Base Solution—Steps 1–4 (15.6)

5. Interactivity: Molecular Structure and Acid Strength (15.9)

6. Interactivity: Acid-Base Properties of Salts (15.10)

Some of the most important processes in chemical and biological systems are acid-base reactions in aqueous solutions. In this first of two chapters on the properties of acids and bases, we will study the definitions of acids and bases, the pH scale, the ionization of weak acids and weak bases, and the relationship between acid strength and molecular structure. We will also look at oxides that can act as acids and bases.

15.1 Brønsted Acids and Bases

In Chapter 4 we defined a Brønsted acid as a substance capable of donating a proton, and a Brønsted base as a substance that can accept a proton. These definitions are generally suitable for a discussion of the properties and reactions of acids and bases.

An extension of the Brønsted definition of acids and bases is the concept of the **_conjugate acid-base pair_**, which can be defined as _an acid and its conjugate base or a base and its conjugate acid_. The conjugate base of a Brønsted acid is the species that remains when one proton has been removed from the acid. Conversely, a conjugate acid results from the addition of a proton to a Brønsted base.

Every Brønsted acid has a conjugate base, and every Brønsted base has a conjugate acid. For example, the chloride ion (Cl^-) is the conjugate base formed from the acid HCl, and H_2O is the conjugate base of the acid H_3O^+ (hydronium ion). Similarly, the ionization of acetic acid can be represented as

$$CH_3COOH(aq) + H_2O(l) \rightleftharpoons CH_3COO^-(aq) + H_3O^+(aq)$$
$$\text{acid}_1 \qquad\qquad \text{base}_2 \qquad\qquad \text{base}_1 \qquad\qquad \text{acid}_2$$

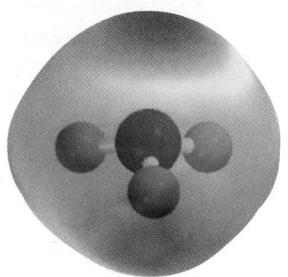

Conjugate means "joined together."

The proton is always associated with water molecules in aqueous solution. The H_3O^+ ion is the simplest formula of a hydrated proton.

The subscripts 1 and 2 designate the two conjugate acid-base pairs. Thus, the acetate ion (CH_3COO^-) is the conjugate base of CH_3COOH. Both the ionization of HCl (see Section 4.3) and the ionization of CH_3COOH are examples of Brønsted acid-base reactions.

The Brønsted definition also enables us to classify ammonia as a base because of its ability to accept a proton:

$$NH_3(aq) + H_2O(l) \rightleftharpoons NH_4^+(aq) + OH^-(aq)$$
$$\text{base}_1 \qquad\qquad \text{acid}_2 \qquad\qquad \text{acid}_1 \qquad\qquad \text{base}_2$$

In this case, NH_4^+ is the conjugate acid of the base NH_3, and the hydroxide ion OH^- is the conjugate base of the acid H_2O. Note that the atom in the Brønsted base that accepts a H^+ ion must have a lone pair.

In Example 15.1, we identify the conjugate pairs in an acid-base reaction.

Example 15.1

Identify the conjugate acid-base pairs in the reaction between ammonia and hydrofluoric acid in aqueous solution

$$NH_3(aq) + HF(aq) \rightleftharpoons NH_4^+(aq) + F^-(aq)$$

(Continued)

Strategy Remember that a conjugate base always has one fewer H atom and one more negative charge (or one fewer positive charge) than the formula of the corresponding acid.

Solution NH_3 has one fewer H atom and one fewer positive charge than NH_4^+. F^- has one fewer H atom and one more negative charge than HF. Therefore, the conjugate acid-base pairs are (1) NH_4^+ and NH_3 and (2) HF and F^-.

Similar problem: 15.5.

Practice Exercise Identify the conjugate acid-base pairs for the reaction

$$CN^- + H_2O \rightleftharpoons HCN + OH^-$$

It is acceptable to represent the proton in aqueous solution either as H^+ or as H_3O^+. The formula H^+ is less cumbersome in calculations involving hydrogen ion concentrations and in calculations involving equilibrium constants, whereas H_3O^+ is more useful in a discussion of Brønsted acid-base properties.

15.2 The Acid-Base Properties of Water

Water, as we know, is a unique solvent. One of its special properties is its ability to act either as an acid or as a base. Water functions as a base in reactions with acids such as HCl and CH_3COOH, and it functions as an acid in reactions with bases such as NH_3. Water is a very weak electrolyte and therefore a poor conductor of electricity, but it does undergo ionization to a small extent:

$$H_2O(l) \rightleftharpoons H^+(aq) + OH^-(aq)$$

Tap water and water from underground sources do conduct electricity because they contain many dissolved ions.

This reaction is sometimes called the *autoionization* of water. To describe the acid-base properties of water in the Brønsted framework, we express its autoionization as follows (also shown in Figure 15.1):

$$
\begin{array}{ccc}
H\;\;O: & +\;\; H\;\;O: & \rightleftharpoons \left[H\;\;O\;\;H \right]^+ + H\;\;\ddot{O}:^- \\
\;\;\;\; | & \;\;\;\; | & \;\;\;\;\;\;\;\;\; | \\
\;\;\;\; H & \;\;\;\; H & \;\;\;\;\;\;\;\;\; H
\end{array}
$$

or

$$\underset{acid_1}{H_2O} + \underset{base_2}{H_2O} \rightleftharpoons \underset{acid_2}{H_3O^+} + \underset{base_1}{OH^-} \qquad (15.1)$$

The acid-base conjugate pairs are (1) H_2O (acid) and OH^- (base) and (2) H_3O^+ (acid) and H_2O (base).

The Ion Product of Water

In the study of acid-base reactions, the hydrogen ion concentration is key; its value indicates the acidity or basicity of the solution. Because only a very small fraction of water molecules are ionized, the concentration of water, $[H_2O]$, remains virtually

Recall that in pure water, $[H_2O] = 55.5\ M$ (see p. 607).

Figure 15.1 *Reaction between two water molecules to form hydronium and hydroxide ions.*

unchanged. Therefore, the equilibrium constant for the autoionization of water, according to Equation (15.1), is

$$K_c = [H_3O^+][OH^-]$$

Because we use $H^+(aq)$ and $H_3O^+(aq)$ interchangeably to represent the hydrated proton, the equilibrium constant can also be expressed as

$$K_c = [H^+][OH^-]$$

To indicate that the equilibrium constant refers to the autoionization of water, we replace K_c by K_w

$$K_w = [H_3O^+][OH^-] = [H^+][OH^-] \qquad (15.2)$$

where K_w is called the **ion-product constant,** which is *the product of the molar concentrations of H^+ and OH^- ions at a particular temperature.*

If you could randomly remove and examine 10 particles (H_2O, H^+, or OH^-) per second from a liter of water, it would take you 2 years, working nonstop, to find one H^+ ion!

In pure water at 25°C, the concentrations of H^+ and OH^- ions are equal and found to be $[H^+] = 1.0 \times 10^{-7}\ M$ and $[OH^-] = 1.0 \times 10^{-7}M$. Thus, from Equation (15.2), at 25°C

$$K_w = (1.0 \times 10^{-7})(1.0 \times 10^{-7}) = 1.0 \times 10^{-14}$$

Whether we have pure water or an aqueous solution of dissolved species, the following relation *always* holds at 25°C:

$$K_w = [H^+][OH^-] = 1.0 \times 10^{-14} \qquad (15.3)$$

Whenever $[H^+] = [OH^-]$, the aqueous solution is said to be neutral. In an acidic solution there is an excess of H^+ ions and $[H^+] > [OH^-]$. In a basic solution there is an excess of hydroxide ions, so $[H^+] < [OH^-]$. In practice we can change the concentration of either H^+ or OH^- ions in solution, but we cannot vary both of them independently. If we adjust the solution so that $[H^+] = 1.0 \times 10^{-6}\ M$, the OH^- concentration *must* change to

$$[OH^-] = \frac{K_w}{[H^+]} = \frac{1.0 \times 10^{-14}}{1.0 \times 10^{-6}} = 1.0 \times 10^{-8}\ M$$

An application of Equation (15.3) is given in Example 15.2.

Example 15.2

The concentration of OH^- ions in a certain household ammonia cleaning solution is 0.0025 M. Calculate the concentration of H^+ ions.

Strategy We are given the concentration of the OH^- ions and asked to calculate $[H^+]$. The relationship between $[H^+]$ and $[OH^-]$ in water or an aqueous solution is given by the ion-product of water, K_w [Equation (15.3)].

Solution Rearranging Equation (15.3), we write

$$[H^+] = \frac{K_w}{[OH^-]} = \frac{1.0 \times 10^{-14}}{0.0025} = 4.0 \times 10^{-12}\ M$$

(Continued)

Check Because [H$^+$] < [OH$^-$], the solution is basic, as we would expect from the earlier discussion of the reaction of ammonia with water.

Similar problems: 15.15, 15.16.

Practice Exercise Calculate the concentration of OH$^-$ ions in a HCl solution whose hydrogen ion concentration is 1.3 M.

15.3 pH—A Measure of Acidity

Because the concentrations of H$^+$ and OH$^-$ ions in aqueous solutions are frequently very small numbers and therefore inconvenient to work with, Soren Sorensen[†] in 1909 proposed a more practical measure called pH. The **pH** of a solution is defined as *the negative logarithm of the hydrogen ion concentration (in mol/L):*

$$pH = -\log [H_3O^+] \quad \text{or} \quad pH = -\log [H^+] \tag{15.4}$$

Keep in mind that Equation (15.4) is simply a definition designed to give us convenient numbers to work with. The negative logarithm gives us a positive number for pH, which otherwise would be negative due to the small value of [H$^+$]. Furthermore, the term [H$^+$] in Equation (15.4) pertains only to the *numerical part* of the expression for hydrogen ion concentration, for we cannot take the logarithm of units. Thus, like the equilibrium constant, the pH of a solution is a dimensionless quantity.

The pH of concentrated acid solutions can be negative. For example, the pH of a 2.0 M HCl solution is −0.30.

Because pH is simply a way to express hydrogen ion concentration, acidic and basic solutions at 25°C can be distinguished by their pH values, as follows:

Acidic solutions: [H$^+$] > 1.0×10^{-7} M, pH < 7.00
Basic solutions: [H$^+$] < 1.0×10^{-7} M, pH > 7.00
Neutral solutions: [H$^+$] = 1.0×10^{-7} M, pH = 7.00

Notice that pH increases as [H$^+$] decreases.

Sometimes we may be given the pH value of a solution and asked to calculate the H$^+$ ion concentration. In that case, we need to take the antilog of Equation (15.4) as follows:

$$[H^+] = 10^{-pH} \tag{15.5}$$

Be aware that the definition of pH just shown, and indeed all the calculations involving solution concentrations (expressed either as molarity or molality) discussed in previous chapters, are subject to error because we have implicitly assumed ideal behavior. In reality, ion-pair formation and other types of intermolecular interactions may affect the actual concentrations of species in solution. The situation is analogous to the relationships between ideal gas behavior and the behavior of real gases discussed in Chapter 5. Depending on temperature, volume, and amount and type of gas present, the measured gas pressure may differ from that calculated using the ideal gas equation. Similarly, the actual or "effective" concentration of a solute may not be what we think it is, knowing the amount of substance originally dissolved in solution. Just as we have the van der Waals and other equations to reconcile discrepancies between the ideal gas and nonideal gas behavior, we can account for nonideal behavior in solution.

[†]Soren Peer Lauritz Sorensen (1868–1939). Danish biochemist. Sorensen originally wrote the symbol as p$_H$ and called p the "hydrogen ion exponent" (*Wasserstoffionexponent*); it is the initial letter of *Potenz* (German), *puissance* (French), and *power* (English). It is now customary to write the symbol as pH.

Figure 15.2 *A pH meter is commonly used in the laboratory to determine the pH of a solution. Although many pH meters have scales marked with values from 1 to 14, pH values can, in fact, be less than 1 and greater than 14.*

TABLE 15.1

The pHs of Some Common Fluids

Sample	pH Value
Gastric juice in the stomach	1.0–2.0
Lemon juice	2.4
Vinegar	3.0
Grapefruit juice	3.2
Orange juice	3.5
Urine	4.8–7.5
Water exposed to air*	5.5
Saliva	6.4–6.9
Milk	6.5
Pure water	7.0
Blood	7.35–7.45
Tears	7.4
Milk of magnesia	10.6
Household ammonia	11.5

*Water exposed to air for a long period of time absorbs atmospheric CO_2 to form carbonic acid, H_2CO_3.

One way is to replace the concentration term with *activity,* which is the effective concentration. Strictly speaking, then, the pH of solution should be defined as

$$pH = -\log a_{H^+} \tag{15.6}$$

where a_{H^+} is the activity of the H^+ ion. As mentioned in Chapter 14 (see p. 607), for an ideal solution activity is numerically equal to concentration. For real solutions, activity usually differs from concentration, sometimes appreciably. Knowing the solute concentration, there are reliable ways based on thermodynamics for estimating its activity, but the details are beyond the scope of this text. Keep in mind, therefore, that the measured pH of a solution is usually not the same as that calculated from Equation (15.4) because the concentration of the H^+ ion in molarity is not numerically equal to its activity value. Although we will continue to use concentration in our discussion, it is important to know that this approach will give us only an approximation of the chemical processes that actually take place in the solution phase.

In the laboratory, the pH of a solution is measured with a pH meter (Figure 15.2). Table 15.1 lists the pHs of a number of common fluids. As you can see, the pH of body fluids varies greatly, depending on location and function. The low pH (high acidity) of gastric juices facilitates digestion whereas a higher pH of blood is necessary for the transport of oxygen. These pH-dependent actions will be illustrated in Chemistry in Action essays in this chapter and Chapter 16.

A pOH scale analogous to the pH scale can be devised using the negative logarithm of the hydroxide ion concentration of a solution. Thus, we define pOH as

$$pOH = -\log [OH^-] \tag{15.7}$$

Now consider again the ion-product constant for water at 25°C:

$$[H^+][OH^-] = K_w = 1.0 \times 10^{-14}$$

Taking the negative logarithm of both sides, we obtain

$$-(\log [H^+] + \log [OH^-]) = -\log (1.0 \times 10^{-14})$$
$$-\log [H^+] - \log [OH^-] = 14.00$$

From the definitions of pH and pOH we obtain

$$pH + pOH = 14.00 \tag{15.8}$$

Equation (15.8) provides us with another way to express the relationship between the H^+ ion concentration and the OH^- ion concentration.

Examples 15.3, 15.4, and 15.5 illustrate calculations involving pH.

Example 15.3

The concentration of H^+ ions in a bottle of table wine was 3.2×10^{-4} M right after the cork was removed. Only half of the wine was consumed. The other half, after it had been standing open to the air for a month, was found to have a hydrogen ion concentration equal to 1.0×10^{-3} M. Calculate the pH of the wine on these two occasions.

Strategy We are given the H^+ ion concentration and asked to calculate the pH of the solution. What is the definition of pH?

Solution According to Equation (15.4), pH $= -\log [H^+]$. When the bottle was first opened, $[H^+] = 3.2 \times 10^{-4}$ M, which we substitute in Equation (15.4)

$$\text{pH} = -\log [H^+]$$
$$= -\log (3.2 \times 10^{-4}) = 3.49$$

On the second occasion, $[H^+] = 1.0 \times 10^{-3}$ M, so that

$$\text{pH} = -\log (1.0 \times 10^{-3}) = 3.00$$

In each case, the pH has only two significant figures. The two digits to the right of the decimal in 3.49 tell us that there are two significant figures in the original number (see Appendix 4).

Comment The increase in hydrogen ion concentration (or decrease in pH) is largely the result of the conversion of some of the alcohol (ethanol) to acetic acid, a reaction that takes place in the presence of molecular oxygen.

Similar problems: 15.17, 15.18.

Practice Exercise Nitric acid (HNO_3) is used in the production of fertilizer, dyes, drugs, and explosives. Calculate the pH of a HNO_3 solution having a hydrogen ion concentration of 0.76 M.

Example 15.4

The pH of rainwater collected in a certain region of the northeastern United States on a particular day was 4.82. Calculate the H^+ ion concentration of the rainwater.

Strategy Here we are given the pH of a solution and asked to calculate $[H^+]$. Because pH is defined as pH $= -\log [H^+]$, we can solve for $[H^+]$ by taking the antilog of the pH; that is, $[H^+] = 10^{-\text{pH}}$, as shown in Equation (15.5).

Solution From Equation (15.4)

$$\text{pH} = -\log [H^+] = 4.82$$

Therefore,

$$\log [H^+] = -4.82$$

To calculate $[H^+]$, we need to take the antilog of -4.82

$$[H^+] = 10^{-4.82} = 1.5 \times 10^{-5} \ M$$

Scientific calculators have an antilog function that is sometimes labeled INV log or 10^x.

Check Because the pH is between 4 and 5, we can expect $[H^+]$ to be between 1×10^{-4} M and 1×10^{-5} M. Therefore, the answer is reasonable.

Similar problem: 15.19.

Practice Exercise The pH of a certain orange juice is 3.33. Calculate the H^+ ion concentration.

Example 15.5

In a NaOH solution $[OH^-]$ is $2.9 \times 10^{-4}\ M$. Calculate the pH of the solution.

Strategy Solving this problem takes two steps. First, we need to calculate pOH using Equation (15.7). Next, we use Equation (15.8) to calculate the pH of the solution.

Solution We use Equation (15.7):

$$\begin{aligned} pOH &= -\log\,[OH^-] \\ &= -\log\,(2.9 \times 10^{-4}) \\ &= 3.54 \end{aligned}$$

Now we use Equation (15.8):

$$\begin{aligned} pH + pOH &= 14.00 \\ pH &= 14.00 - pOH \\ &= 14.00 - 3.54 = \boxed{10.46} \end{aligned}$$

Alternatively, we can use the ion-product constant of water, $K_w = [H^+][OH^-]$ to calculate $[H^+]$, and then we can calculate the pH from the $[H^+]$. Try it.

Check The answer shows that the solution is basic (pH > 7), which is consistent with a NaOH solution.

Practice Exercise The OH^- ion concentration of a blood sample is $2.5 \times 10^{-7}\ M$. What is the pH of the blood?

Similar problem: 15.18.

15.4 Strength of Acids and Bases

In reality, no acids are known to ionize completely in water.

Strong acids are strong electrolytes that, for practical purposes, *are assumed to ionize completely in water* (Figure 15.3). Most of the strong acids are inorganic acids: hydrochloric acid (HCl), nitric acid (HNO_3), perchloric acid ($HClO_4$), and sulfuric acid (H_2SO_4):

$$\begin{aligned} HCl(aq) + H_2O(l) &\longrightarrow H_3O^+(aq) + Cl^-(aq) \\ HNO_3(aq) + H_2O(l) &\longrightarrow H_3O^+(aq) + NO_3^-(aq) \\ HClO_4(aq) + H_2O(l) &\longrightarrow H_3O^+(aq) + ClO_4^-(aq) \\ H_2SO_4(aq) + H_2O(l) &\longrightarrow H_3O^+(aq) + HSO_4^-(aq) \end{aligned}$$

Note that H_2SO_4 is a diprotic acid; we show only the first stage of ionization here. At equilibrium, solutions of strong acids will not contain any nonionized acid molecules.

Most acids are **weak acids,** which *ionize only to a limited extent in water.* At equilibrium, aqueous solutions of weak acids contain a mixture of nonionized acid molecules, H_3O^+ ions, and the conjugate base. Examples of weak acids are hydrofluoric acid (HF), acetic acid (CH_3COOH), and the ammonium ion (NH_4^+). The limited ionization of weak acids is related to the equilibrium constant for ionization, which we will study in the next section.

Like strong acids, **strong bases** *are all strong electrolytes that ionize completely in water.* Hydroxides of alkali metals and certain alkaline earth metals are strong bases. [All alkali metal hydroxides are soluble. Of the alkaline earth hydroxides, $Be(OH)_2$ and $Mg(OH)_2$ are insoluble; $Ca(OH)_2$ and $Sr(OH)_2$ are slightly soluble; and $Ba(OH)_2$ is soluble.] Some examples of strong bases are

$$\begin{aligned} NaOH(s) &\xrightarrow{\ H_2O\ } Na^+(aq) + OH^-(aq) \\ KOH(s) &\xrightarrow{\ H_2O\ } K^+(aq) + OH^-(aq) \\ Ba(OH)_2(s) &\xrightarrow{\ H_2O\ } Ba^{2+}(aq) + 2OH^-(aq) \end{aligned}$$

Zn reacts more vigorously with a strong acid like HCl (left) than with a weak acid like CH_3COOH (right) of the same concentration because there are more H^+ ions in the former solution.

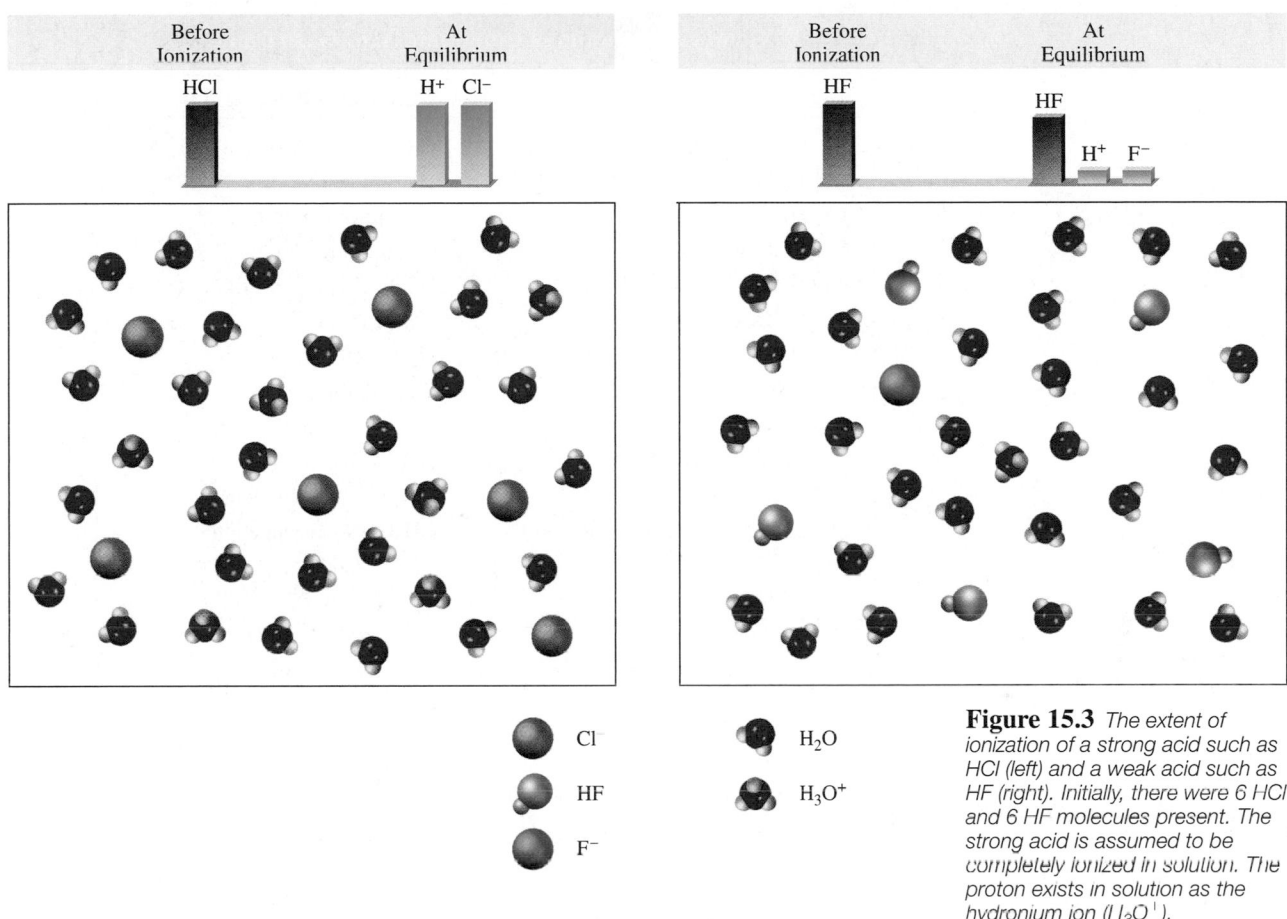

	Before Ionization	At Equilibrium				Before Ionization	At Equilibrium	

Cl	H_2O
HF	H_3O^+
F^-	

Figure 15.3 *The extent of ionization of a strong acid such as HCl (left) and a weak acid such as HF (right). Initially, there were 6 HCl and 6 HF molecules present. The strong acid is assumed to be completely ionized in solution. The proton exists in solution as the hydronium ion (H_3O^+).*

Strictly speaking, these metal hydroxides are not Brønsted bases because they cannot accept a proton. However, the hydroxide ion (OH^-) formed when they ionize *is* a Brønsted base because it can accept a proton:

$$H_3O^+(aq) + OH^-(aq) \longrightarrow 2H_2O(l)$$

Thus, when we call NaOH or any other metal hydroxide a base, we are actually referring to the OH^- species derived from the hydroxide.

Weak bases, like weak acids, *are weak electrolytes.* Ammonia is a weak base. It ionizes to a very limited extent in water:

$$NH_3(aq) + H_2O(l) \rightleftharpoons NH_4^+(aq) + OH^-(aq)$$

Note that NH_3 does not ionize like an acid because it does not split up to form ions the way, say, HCl does.

Table 15.2 lists some important conjugate acid-base pairs, in order of their relative strengths. Conjugate acid-base pairs have the following properties:

1. If an acid is strong, its conjugate base has no measurable strength. Thus, the Cl^- ion, which is the conjugate base of the strong acid HCl, is an extremely weak base.

2. H_3O^+ is the strongest acid that can exist in aqueous solution. Acids stronger than H_3O^+ react with water to produce H_3O^+ and their conjugate bases. Thus, HCl, which is a stronger acid than H_3O^+, reacts with water completely to form H_3O^+ and Cl^-:

$$HCl(aq) + H_2O(l) \longrightarrow H_3O^+(aq) + Cl^-(aq)$$

TABLE 15.2   Relative Strengths of Conjugate Acid-Base Pairs

Acid	Conjugate Base
$HClO_4$ (perchloric acid)	ClO_4^- (perchlorate ion)
HI (hydroiodic acid)	I^- (iodide ion)
HBr (hydrobromic acid)	Br^- (bromide ion)
HCl (hydrochloric acid)	Cl^- (chloride ion)
H_2SO_4 (sulfuric acid)	HSO_4^- (hydrogen sulfate ion)
HNO_3 (nitric acid)	NO_3^- (nitrate ion)
H_3O^+ (hydronium ion)	H_2O (water)
HSO_4^- (hydrogen sulfate ion)	SO_4^{2-} (sulfate ion)
HF (hydrofluoric acid)	F^- (fluoride ion)
HNO_2 (nitrous acid)	NO_2^- (nitrite ion)
HCOOH (formic acid)	$HCOO^-$ (formate ion)
CH_3COOH (acetic acid)	CH_3COO^- (acetate ion)
NH_4^+ (ammonium ion)	NH_3 (ammonia)
HCN (hydrocyanic acid)	CN^- (cyanide ion)
H_2O (water)	OH^- (hydroxide ion)
NH_3 (ammonia)	NH_2^- (amide ion)

Left side: Strong acids, Weak acids; Acid strength increases. Right side: Base strength increases.

Acids weaker than H_3O^+ react with water to a much smaller extent, producing H_3O^+ and their conjugate bases. For example, the following equilibrium lies primarily to the left:

$$HF(aq) + H_2O(l) \rightleftharpoons H_3O^+(aq) + F^-(aq)$$

3. The OH^- ion is the strongest base that can exist in aqueous solution. Bases stronger than OH^- react with water to produce OH^- and their conjugate acids. For example, the oxide ion (O^{2-}) is a stronger base than OH^-, so it reacts with water completely as follows:

$$O^{2-}(aq) + H_2O(l) \longrightarrow 2OH^-(aq)$$

For this reason the oxide ion does not exist in aqueous solutions.

Example 15.6 shows calculations of pH for a solution containing a strong acid and a solution of a strong base.

Example 15.6

Calculate the pH of (a) a 1.0×10^{-3} M HCl solution and (b) a 0.020 M $Ba(OH)_2$ solution.

Strategy Keep in mind that HCl is a strong acid and $Ba(OH)_2$ is a strong base. Thus, these species are completely ionized and no HCl or $Ba(OH)_2$ will be left in solution.

Solution (a) The ionization of HCl is

$$HCl(aq) \longrightarrow H^+(aq) + Cl^-(aq)$$

(Continued)

The concentrations of all the species (HCl, H^+, and Cl^-) before and after ionization can be represented as follows:

	$HCl(aq)$	$\longrightarrow$	$H^+(aq)$	$+$	$Cl^-(aq)$
Initial (M):	1.0×10^{-3}		0.0		0.0
Change (M):	-1.0×10^{-3}		$+1.0 \times 10^{-3}$		$+1.0 \times 10^{-3}$
Final (M):	0.0		1.0×10^{-3}		1.0×10^{-3}

A positive ($+$) change represents an increase and a negative ($-$) change indicates a decrease in concentration. Thus,

$$[H^+] = 1.0 \times 10^{-3}\ M$$
$$pH = -\log(1.0 \times 10^{-3})$$
$$= 3.00$$

(b) $Ba(OH)_2$ is a strong base; each $Ba(OH)_2$ unit produces two OH^- ions:

$$Ba(OH)_2(aq) \longrightarrow Ba^{2+}(aq) + 2OH^-(aq)$$

The changes in the concentrations of all the species can be represented as follows:

	$Ba(OH)_2(aq)$	$\longrightarrow$	$Ba^{2+}(aq)$	$+$	$2OH^-(aq)$
Initial (M):	0.020		0.00		0.00
Change (M):	-0.020		$+0.020$		$+2(0.020)$
Final (M):	0.00		0.020		0.040

Thus,

$$[OH^-] = 0.040\ M$$
$$pOH = -\log 0.040 = 1.40$$

Therefore, from Equation (15.8),

$$pH = 14.00 - pOH$$
$$= 14.00 - 1.40$$
$$= 12.60$$

Check Note that in both (a) and (b) we have neglected the contribution of the autoionization of water to $[H^+]$ and $[OH^-]$ because $1.0 \times 10^{-7}\ M$ is so small compared with $1.0 \times 10^{-3}\ M$ and $0.040\ M$.

Practice Exercise Calculate the pH of a $1.8 \times 10^{-2}\ M$ $Ba(OH)_2$ solution.

Similar problem: 15.18.

If we know the relative strengths of two acids, we can predict the position of equilibrium between one of the acids and the conjugate base of the other, as illustrated in Example 15.7.

Example 15.7

Predict the direction of the following reaction in aqueous solution:

$$HNO_2(aq) + CN^-(aq) \rightleftharpoons HCN(aq) + NO_2^-(aq)$$

Strategy The problem is to determine whether, at equilibrium, the reaction will be shifted to the right, favoring HCN and NO_2^-, or to the left, favoring HNO_2 and CN^-. Which of the

(Continued)

two is a stronger acid and hence a stronger proton donor: HNO_2 or HCN? Which of the two is a stronger base and hence a stronger proton acceptor: CN^- or NO_2^-? Remember that the stronger the acid, the weaker its conjugate base.

Solution In Table 15.2 we see that HNO_2 is a stronger acid than HCN. Thus, CN^- is a stronger base than NO_2^-. The net reaction will proceed from left to right as written because HNO_2 is a better proton donor than HCN (and CN^- is a better proton acceptor than NO_2^-).

Practice Exercise Predict whether the equilibrium constant for the following reaction is greater than or smaller than 1:

$$CH_3COOH(aq) + HCOO^-(aq) \rightleftharpoons CH_3COO^-(aq) + HCOOH(aq)$$

Similar problem: 15.37.

15.5 Weak Acids and Acid Ionization Constants

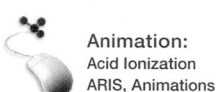

Animation:
Acid Ionization
ARIS, Animations

As we have seen, there are relatively few strong acids. The vast majority of acids are weak acids. Consider a weak monoprotic acid, HA. Its ionization in water is represented by

$$HA(aq) + H_2O(l) \rightleftharpoons H_3O^+(aq) + A^-(aq)$$

or simply

$$HA(aq) \rightleftharpoons H^+(aq) + A^-(aq)$$

The equilibrium expression for this ionization is

All concentrations in this equation are equilibrium concentrations.

$$K_a = \frac{[H_3O^+][A^-]}{[HA]} \quad \text{or} \quad K_a = \frac{[H^+][A^-]}{[HA]} \quad (15.9)$$

where K_a, the **acid ionization constant,** is the *equilibrium constant for the ionization of an acid.* At a given temperature, the strength of the acid HA is measured quantitatively by the magnitude of K_a. The larger K_a, the stronger the acid—that is, the greater the concentration of H^+ ions at equilibrium due to its ionization. Keep in mind, however, that only weak acids have K_a values associated with them.

The back endpaper gives an index to all the useful tables and figures in this text.

Table 15.3 lists a number of weak acids and their K_a values at 25°C in order of decreasing acid strength. Although all these acids are weak, within the group there is great variation in their strengths. For example, K_a for HF (7.1×10^{-4}) is about 1.5 million times that for HCN (4.9×10^{-10}).

Generally, we can calculate the hydrogen ion concentration or pH of an acid solution at equilibrium, given the initial concentration of the acid and its K_a value. Alternatively, if we know the pH of a weak acid solution and its initial concentration, we can determine its K_a. The basic approach for solving these problems, which deal with equilibrium concentrations, is the same one outlined in Chapter 14. However, because acid ionization represents a major category of chemical equilibrium in aqueous solution, we will develop a systematic procedure for solving this type of problem that will also help us to understand the chemistry involved.

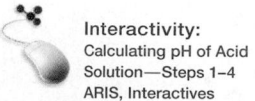

Interactivity:
Calculating pH of Acid
Solution—Steps 1–4
ARIS, Interactives

Suppose we are asked to calculate the pH of a 0.50 *M* HF solution at 25°C. The ionization of HF is given by

$$HF(aq) \rightleftharpoons H^+(aq) + F^-(aq)$$

TABLE 15.3   Ionization Constants of Some Weak Acids and Their Conjugate Bases at 25°C

Name of Acid	Formula	Structure	K_a	Conjugate Base	K_b
Hydrofluoric acid	HF	H—F	7.1×10^{-4}	F^-	1.4×10^{-11}
Nitrous acid	HNO_2	O=N—O—H	4.5×10^{-4}	NO_2^-	2.2×10^{-11}
Acetylsalicylic acid (aspirin)	$C_9H_8O_4$		3.0×10^{-4}	$C_9H_7O_4^-$	3.3×10^{-11}
Formic acid	HCOOH		1.7×10^{-4}	$HCOO^-$	5.9×10^{-11}
Ascorbic acid*	$C_6H_8O_6$		8.0×10^{-5}	$C_6H_7O_6^-$	1.3×10^{-10}
Benzoic acid	C_6H_5COOH		6.5×10^{-5}	$C_6H_5COO^-$	1.5×10^{-10}
Acetic acid	CH_3COOH		1.8×10^{-5}	CH_3COO^-	5.6×10^{-10}
Hydrocyanic acid	HCN	H—C≡N	4.9×10^{-10}	CN^-	2.0×10^5
Phenol	C_6H_5OH		1.3×10^{-10}	$C_6H_5O^-$	7.7×10^{-5}

*For ascorbic acid it is the upper left hydroxyl group that is associated with this ionization constant.

From Table 15.3 we write

$$K_a = \frac{[H^+][F^-]}{[HF]} = 7.1 \times 10^{-4}$$

The first step is to identify all the species present in solution that may affect its pH. Because weak acids ionize to a small extent, at equilibrium the major species present are nonionized HF and some H^+ and F^- ions. Another major species is H_2O, but its very small K_w (1.0×10^{-14}) means that water is not a significant contributor to the H^+ ion concentration. Therefore, unless otherwise stated, we will always ignore the H^+ ions produced by the autoionization of water. Note that we need not be concerned with the OH^- ions that are also present in solution. The OH^- concentration can be determined from Equation (15.3) after we have calculated $[H^+]$.

We can summarize the changes in the concentrations of HF, H^+, and F^- according to the steps shown on p. 620 as follows:

	HF(aq) $\rightleftharpoons$ $H^+(aq)$ + $F^-(aq)$		
Initial (M):	0.50	0.00	0.00
Change (M):	$-x$	$+x$	$+x$
Equilibrium (M):	$0.50 - x$	x	x

The equilibrium concentrations of HF, H^+, and F^-, expressed in terms of the unknown x, are substituted into the ionization constant expression to give

$$K_a = \frac{(x)(x)}{0.50 - x} = 7.1 \times 10^{-4}$$

Rearranging this expression, we write

$$x^2 + 7.1 \times 10^{-4}x - 3.6 \times 10^{-4} = 0$$

This is a quadratic equation which can be solved using the quadratic formula (see Appendix 4). Or we can try using a shortcut to solve for x. Because HF is a weak acid and weak acids ionize only to a slight extent, we reason that x must be small compared to 0.50. Therefore, we can make the approximation

$$0.50 - x \approx 0.50$$

The sign $\approx$ means "approximately equal to." An analogy of the approximation is a truck loaded with coal. Losing a few lumps of coal on a delivery trip will not appreciably change the overall mass of the load.

Now the ionization constant expression becomes

$$\frac{x^2}{0.50 - x} \approx \frac{x^2}{0.50} = 7.1 \times 10^{-4}$$

Rearranging, we get

$$x^2 = (0.50)(7.1 \times 10^{-4}) = 3.55 \times 10^{-4}$$
$$x = \sqrt{3.55 \times 10^{-4}} = 0.019 \, M$$

Thus, we have solved for x without having to use the quadratic equation. At equilibrium, we have

$$[HF] = (0.50 - 0.019) \, M = 0.48 \, M$$
$$[H^+] = 0.019 \, M$$
$$[F^-] = 0.019 \, M$$

and the pH of the solution is

$$pH = -\log (0.019) = 1.72$$

How good is this approximation? Because K_a values for weak acids are generally known to an accuracy of only $\pm 5\%$, it is reasonable to require x to be less than 5% of 0.50, the number from which it is subtracted. In other words, the approximation is valid if the following expression is equal to or less than 5%:

$$\frac{0.019 \, M}{0.50 \, M} \times 100\% = 3.8\%$$

Thus, the approximation we made is acceptable.

Now consider a different situation. If the initial concentration of HF is 0.050 M, and we use the above procedure to solve for x, we would get $6.0 \times 10^{-3}\ M$. However, the following test shows that this answer is not a valid approximation because it is greater than 5% of 0.050 M:

$$\frac{6.0 \times 10^{-3}\ M}{0.050\ M} \times 100\% = 12\%$$

In this case, we can get an accurate value for x by solving the quadratic equation.

The Quadratic Equation

We start by writing the ionization expression in terms of the unknown x:

$$\frac{x^2}{0.050 - x} = 7.1 \times 10^{-4}$$
$$x^2 + 7.1 \times 10^{-4}x - 3.6 \times 10^{-5} = 0$$

This expression fits the quadratic equation $ax^2 + bx + c = 0$. Using the quadratic formula, we write

$$x = \frac{-b \pm \sqrt{b^2 - 4ac}}{2a}$$
$$= \frac{-7.1 \times 10^{-4} \pm \sqrt{(7.1 \times 10^{-4})^2 - 4(1)(-3.6 \times 10^{-5})}}{2(1)}$$
$$= \frac{-7.1 \times 10^{-4} \pm 0.012}{2}$$
$$= 5.6 \times 10^{-3}\ M \quad \text{or} \quad -6.4 \times 10^{-3}\ M$$

The second solution ($x = -6.4 \times 10^{-3}\ M$) is physically impossible because the concentration of ions produced as a result of ionization cannot be negative. Choosing $x = 5.6 \times 10^{-3}\ M$, we can solve for [HF], [H$^+$], and [F$^-$] as follows:

$$[\text{HF}] = (0.050 - 5.6 \times 10^{-3})\ M = 0.044\ M$$
$$[\text{H}^+] = 5.6 \times 10^{-3}\ M$$
$$[\text{F}^-] = 5.6 \times 10^{-3}\ M$$

The pH of the solution, then, is

$$\text{pH} = -\log (5.6 \times 10^{-3}) = 2.25$$

In summary, the main steps for solving weak acid ionization problems are:

1. Identify the major species that can affect the pH of the solution. In most cases we can ignore the ionization of water. We omit the hydroxide ion because its concentration is determined by that of the H$^+$ ion.

2. Express the equilibrium concentrations of these species in terms of the initial concentration of the acid and a single unknown x, which represents the change in concentration.

3. Write the weak acid ionization and express the ionization constant K_a in terms of the equilibrium concentrations of H$^+$, the conjugate base, and the unionized acid. First solve for x by the approximate method. If the approximate method is not valid, use the quadratic equation to solve for x.

4. Having solved for x, calculate the equilibrium concentrations of all species and/or the pH of the solution.

Example 15.8 provides another illustration of this procedure.

HNO$_2$

Example 15.8

Calculate the pH of a 0.036 M nitrous acid (HNO$_2$) solution:

$$HNO_2(aq) \rightleftharpoons H^+(aq) + NO_2^-(aq)$$

Strategy Recall that a weak acid only partially ionizes in water. We are given the initial concentration of a weak acid and asked to calculate the pH of the solution at equilibrium. It is helpful to make a sketch to keep track of the pertinent species.

Major species at equilibrium

$[HNO_2]_0 = 0.036\,M$

$HNO_2 \rightleftharpoons H^+ + NO_2^-$

$H^+ \quad NO_2^-$
HNO_2

Ignore

$H_2O \rightleftharpoons H^+ + OH^-$

As in Example 15.6, we ignore the ionization of H$_2$O so the major source of H$^+$ ions is the acid. The concentration of OH$^-$ ions is very small as we would expect from an acidic solution so it is present as a minor species.

Solution We follow the procedure already outlined.

Step 1: The species that can affect the pH of the solution are HNO$_2$, H$^+$, and the conjugate base NO$_2^-$. We ignore water's contribution to [H$^+$].

Step 2: Letting x be the equilibrium concentration of H$^+$ and NO$_2^-$ ions in mol/L, we summarize:

	HNO$_2$(aq) $\rightleftharpoons$	H$^+$(aq) +	NO$_2^-$(aq)
Initial (*M*):	0.036	0.00	0.00
Change (*M*):	$-x$	$+x$	$+x$
Equilibrium (*M*):	$0.036 - x$	x	x

Step 3: From Table 15.3 we write

$$K_a = \frac{[H^+][NO_2^-]}{[HNO_2]}$$

$$4.5 \times 10^{-4} = \frac{x^2}{0.036 - x}$$

Applying the approximation $0.036 - x \approx 0.036$, we obtain

$$4.5 \times 10^{-4} = \frac{x^2}{0.036 - x} \approx \frac{x^2}{0.036}$$
$$x^2 = 1.62 \times 10^{-5}$$
$$x = 4.0 \times 10^{-3}\,M$$

To test the approximation,

$$\frac{4.0 \times 10^{-3}\,M}{0.036\,M} \times 100\% = 11\%$$

(Continued)

Because this is greater than 5%, our approximation is not valid and we must solve the quadratic equation, as follows:

$$x^2 + 4.5 \times 10^{-4}x - 1.62 \times 10^{-5} = 0$$

$$x = \frac{-4.5 \times 10^{-4} \pm \sqrt{(4.5 \times 10^{-4})^2 - 4(1)(-1.62 \times 10^{-5})}}{2(1)}$$

$$= 3.8 \times 10^{-3}\,M \quad \text{or} \quad -4.3 \times 10^{-3}\,M$$

The second solution is physically impossible, because the concentration of ions produced as a result of ionization cannot be negative. Therefore, the solution is given by the positive root, $x = 3.8 \times 10^{-3}$ M.

Step 4: At equilibrium

$$[H^+] = 3.8 \times 10^{-3}\,M$$
$$pH = -\log(3.8 \times 10^{-3})$$
$$= 2.42$$

Check Note that the calculated pH indicates that the solution is acidic, which is what we would expect for a weak acid solution. Compare the calculated pH with that of a 0.036 M strong acid solution such as HCl to convince yourself of the difference between a strong acid and a weak acid.

Similar problem: 15.43.

Practice Exercise What is the pH of a 0.122 M monoprotic acid whose K_a is 5.7×10^{-4}?

One way to determine K_a of an acid is to measure the pH of the acid solution of known concentration at equilibrium. Example 15.9 shows this approach.

Example 15.9

The pH of a 0.10 M solution of formic acid (HCOOH) is 2.39. What is the K_a of the acid?

Strategy Formic acid is a weak acid. It only partially ionizes in water. Note that the concentration of formic acid refers to the initial concentration, before ionization has started. The pH of the solution, on the other hand, refers to the equilibrium state. To calculate K_a, then, we need to know the concentrations of all three species: $[H^+]$, $[HCOO^-]$, and $[HCOOH]$ at equilibrium. As usual, we ignore the ionization of water. The following sketch summarizes the situation.

HCOOH

Solution We proceed as follows.

Step 1: The major species in solution are HCOOH, H^+, and the conjugate base HCOO$^-$.

Step 2: First we need to calculate the hydrogen ion concentration from the pH value

$$pH = -\log[H^+]$$
$$2.39 = -\log[H^+]$$

(Continued)

Taking the antilog of both sides, we get

$$[H^+] = 10^{-2.39} = 4.1 \times 10^{-3} \, M$$

Next we summarize the changes:

	$HCOOH(aq)$	$\rightleftharpoons$	$H^+(aq)$	$+$	$HCOO^-(aq)$
Initial (M):	0.10		0.00		0.00
Change (M):	-4.1×10^{-3}		$+4.1 \times 10^{-3}$		$+4.1 \times 10^{-3}$
Equilibrium (M):	$(0.10 - 4.1 \times 10^{-3})$		4.1×10^{-3}		4.1×10^{-3}

Note that because the pH and hence the H^+ ion concentration is known, it follows that we also know the concentrations of HCOOH and $HCOO^-$ at equilibrium.

Step 3: The ionization constant of formic acid is given by

$$
\begin{aligned}
K_a &= \frac{[H^+][HCOO^-]}{[HCOOH]} \\
&= \frac{(4.1 \times 10^{-3})(4.1 \times 10^{-3})}{(0.10 - 4.1 \times 10^{-3})} \\
&= 1.8 \times 10^{-4}
\end{aligned}
$$

Check The K_a value differs slightly from the one listed in Table 15.3 because of the rounding-off procedure we used in the calculation.

Practice Exercise The pH of a 0.060 M weak monoprotic acid is 3.44. Calculate the K_a of the acid.

Similar problem: 15.45.

Percent Ionization

We have seen that the magnitude of K_a indicates the strength of an acid. Another measure of the strength of an acid is its ***percent ionization,*** which is defined as

We can compare the strengths of acids in terms of percent ionization only if concentrations of the acids are the same.

$$\text{percent ionization} = \frac{\text{ionized acid concentration at equilibrium}}{\text{initial concentration of acid}} \times 100\% \quad (15.10)$$

The stronger the acid, the greater the percent ionization. For a monoprotic acid HA, the concentration of the acid that undergoes ionization is equal to the concentration of the H^+ ions or the concentration of the A^- ions at equilibrium. Therefore, we can write the percent ionization as

$$\text{percent ionization} = \frac{[H^+]}{[HA]_0} \times 100\%$$

where $[H^+]$ is the concentration at equilibrium and $[HA]_0$ is the initial concentration.

Referring to Example 15.8, we see that the percent ionization of a 0.036 M HNO_2 solution is

$$\text{percent ionization} = \frac{3.8 \times 10^{-3} \, M}{0.036 \, M} \times 100\% = 11\%$$

Thus, only about one out of every 9 HNO_2 molecules has ionized. This is consistent with the fact that HNO_2 is a weak acid.

The extent to which a weak acid ionizes depends on the initial concentration of the acid. The more dilute the solution, the greater the percent ionization (Figure 15.4).

In qualitative terms, when an acid is diluted, the number of particles (nonionized acid molecules plus ions) per unit volume is reduced. According to Le Châtelier's principle (see Section 14.5), to counteract this "stress" (that is, the dilution), the equilibrium shifts from nonionized acid to H^+ and its conjugate base to produce more particles (ions). The dependence of percent ionization on initial concentration can be illustrated by the HF case discussed on page 656:

0.50 *M* HF

$$\text{percent ionization} = \frac{0.019\ M}{0.50\ M} \times 100\% = 3.8\%$$

0.050 *M* HF

$$\text{percent ionization} = \frac{5.6 \times 10^{-3}\ M}{0.050\ M} \times 100\% = 11\%$$

We see that, as expected, a more dilute HF solution has a greater percent ionization of the acid.

Figure 15.4 *Dependence of percent ionization on initial concentration of acid. Note that at very low concentrations, all acids (weak and strong) are almost completely ionized.*

15.6 Weak Bases and Base Ionization Constants

The ionization of weak bases is treated in the same way as the ionization of weak acids. When ammonia dissolves in water, it undergoes the reaction

$$NH_3(aq) + H_2O(l) \rightleftharpoons NH_4^+(aq) + OH^-(aq)$$

The equilibrium constant is given by

$$K = \frac{[NH_4^+][OH^-]}{[NH_3][H_2O]}$$

The lone pair (red color) on the N atom accounts for ammonia's basicity.

Compared with the total concentration of water, very few water molecules are consumed by this reaction, so we can treat $[H_2O]$ as a constant. Thus, we can write the ***base ionization constant*** (***K_b***), which is *the equilibrium constant for the ionization reaction*, as

$$K_b = K[H_2O] = \frac{[NH_4^+][OH^-]}{[NH_3]}$$
$$= 1.8 \times 10^{-5}$$

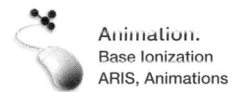

Animation:
Base Ionization
ARIS, Animations

Table 15.4 lists a number of common weak bases and their ionization constants. Note that the basicity of all these compounds is attributable to the lone pair of electrons on the nitrogen atom. The ability of the lone pair to accept a H^+ ion makes these substances Brønsted bases.

In solving problems involving weak bases, we follow the same procedure we used for weak acids. The main difference is that we calculate $[OH^-]$ first, rather than $[H^+]$. Example 15.10 shows this approach.

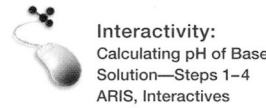

Interactivity:
Calculating pH of Base
Solution—Steps 1–4
ARIS, Interactives

Example 15.10

What is the pH of a 0.40 *M* ammonia solution?

Strategy The procedure here is similar to the one used for a weak acid (see Example 15.8). From the ionization of ammonia, we see that the major species in solution at equilibrium are

(Continued)

TABLE 15.4   Ionization Constants of Some Weak Bases and Their Conjugate Acids at 25°C

Name of Base	Formula	Structure	K_b*	Conjugate Acid	K_a
Ethylamine	$C_2H_5NH_2$	$CH_3\!-\!CH_2\!-\!\overset{..}{\underset{H}{N}}\!-\!H$	5.6×10^{-4}	$C_2H_5\overset{+}{N}H_3$	1.8×10^{-11}
Methylamine	CH_3NH_2	$CH_3\!-\!\overset{..}{\underset{H}{N}}\!-\!H$	4.4×10^{-4}	$CH_3\overset{+}{N}H_3$	2.3×10^{-11}
Ammonia	NH_3	$H\!-\!\overset{..}{\underset{H}{N}}\!-\!H$	1.8×10^{-5}	NH_4^+	5.6×10^{-10}
Pyridine	C_5H_5N	(ring structure) $N:$	1.7×10^{-9}	$C_5H_5\overset{+}{N}H$	5.9×10^{-6}
Aniline	$C_6H_5NH_2$	(ring structure) $\overset{..}{\underset{H}{N}}\!-\!H$	3.8×10^{-10}	$C_6H_5\overset{+}{N}H_3$	2.6×10^{-5}
Caffeine	$C_8H_{10}N_4O_2$	(structure)	5.3×10^{-14}	$C_8H_{11}\overset{+}{N}_4O_2$	0.19
Urea	$(NH_2)_2CO$	(structure)	1.5×10^{-14}	$H_2NCO\overset{+}{N}H_3$	0.67

*The nitrogen atom with the lone pair accounts for each compound's basicity. In the case of urea, K_b can be associated with either nitrogen atom.

NH_3, NH_4^+, and OH^-. The hydrogen ion concentration is very small as we would expect from a basic solution, so it is present as a minor species. As before, we ignore the ionization of water. We make a sketch to keep track of the pertinent species as follows:

(Continued)

Solution We proceed according to the following steps.

Step 1: The major species in an ammonia solution are NH_3, NH_4^+, and OH^-. We ignore the very small contribution to OH^- concentration by water.

Step 2: Letting x be the equilibrium concentration of NH_4^+ and OH^- ions in mol/L, we summarize:

	$NH_3(aq) + H_2O(l) \rightleftharpoons NH_4^+(aq) + OH^-(aq)$		
Initial (*M*):	0.40	0.00	0.00
Change (*M*):	$-x$	$+x$	$+x$
Equilibrium (*M*):	$0.40 - x$	x	x

Step 3: Table 15.4 gives us K_b:

$$K_b = \frac{[NH_4^+][OH^-]}{[NH_3]}$$

$$1.8 \times 10^{-5} = \frac{x^2}{0.40 - x}$$

Applying the approximation $0.40 - x \approx 0.40$, we obtain

$$1.8 \times 10^{-5} = \frac{x^2}{0.40 - x} \approx \frac{x^2}{0.40}$$
$$x^2 = 7.2 \times 10^{-6}$$
$$x = 2.7 \times 10^{-3} \, M$$

To test the approximation, we write

$$\frac{2.7 \times 10^{-3} \, M}{0.40 \, M} \times 100\% = 0.68\%$$

The 5 percent rule (p. 658) also applies to bases.

Therefore, the approximation is valid.

Step 4: At equilibrium, $[OH^-] = 2.7 \times 10^{-3} \, M$. Thus,

$$pOH = -\log (2.7 \times 10^{-3})$$
$$= 2.57$$
$$pH = 14.00 - 2.57$$
$$= 11.43$$

Check Note that the pH calculated is basic, which is what we would expect from a weak base solution. Compare the calculated pH with that of a 0.40 *M* strong base solution, such as KOH, to convince yourself of the difference between a strong base and a weak base.

Similar problem: 15.53.

Practice Exercise Calculate the pH of a 0.26 *M* methylamine solution (see Table 15.4).

15.7 The Relationship Between the Ionization Constants of Acids and Their Conjugate Bases

An important relationship between the acid ionization constant and the ionization constant of its conjugate base can be derived as follows, using acetic acid as an example:

$$CH_3COOH(aq) \rightleftharpoons H^+(aq) + CH_3COO^-(aq)$$

$$K_a = \frac{[H^+][CH_3COO^-]}{[CH_3COOH]}$$

The conjugate base, CH_3COO^-, supplied by a sodium acetate (CH_3COONa) solution, reacts with water according to the equation

$$CH_3COO^-(aq) + H_2O(l) \rightleftharpoons CH_3COOH(aq) + OH^-(aq)$$

and we can write the base ionization constant as

$$K_b = \frac{[CH_3COOH][OH^-]}{[CH_3COO^-]}$$

The product of these two ionization constants is given by

$$K_aK_b = \frac{[H^+][\cancel{CH_3COO^-}]}{[\cancel{CH_3COOH}]} \times \frac{[\cancel{CH_3COOH}][OH^-]}{[\cancel{CH_3COO^-}]}$$
$$= [H^+][OH^-]$$
$$= K_w$$

This result may seem strange at first, but if we add the two equations we see that the sum is simply the autoionization of water.

$$
\begin{array}{cll}
(1) & CH_3COOH(aq) \rightleftharpoons H^+(aq) + CH_3COO^-(aq) & K_a \\
(2) & CH_3COO^-(aq) + H_2O(l) \rightleftharpoons CH_3COOH(aq) + OH^-(aq) & K_b \\
\hline
(3) & H_2O(l) \rightleftharpoons H^+(aq) + OH^-(aq) & K_w
\end{array}
$$

This example illustrates one of the rules for chemical equilibria: When two reactions are added to give a third reaction, the equilibrium constant for the third reaction is the product of the equilibrium constants for the two added reactions (see Section 14.2). Thus, for any conjugate acid-base pair it is always true that

$$K_aK_b = K_w \tag{15.11}$$

Expressing Equation (15.11) as

$$K_a = \frac{K_w}{K_b} \qquad K_b = \frac{K_w}{K_a}$$

enables us to draw an important conclusion: The stronger the acid (the larger K_a), the weaker its conjugate base (the smaller K_b), and vice versa (see Tables 15.3 and 15.4).

We can use Equation (15.11) to calculate the K_b of the conjugate base (CH_3COO^-) of CH_3COOH as follows. We find the K_a value of CH_3COOH in Table 15.3 and write

$$
\begin{aligned}
K_b &= \frac{K_w}{K_a} \\
&= \frac{1.0 \times 10^{-14}}{1.8 \times 10^{-5}} \\
&= 5.6 \times 10^{-10}
\end{aligned}
$$

15.8 Diprotic and Polyprotic Acids

The treatment of diprotic and polyprotic acids is more involved than that of monoprotic acids because these substances may yield more than one hydrogen ion per molecule. These acids ionize in a stepwise manner; that is, they lose one proton at a time.

An ionization constant expression can be written for each ionization stage. Consequently, two or more equilibrium constant expressions must often be used to calculate the concentrations of species in the acid solution. For example, for carbonic acid, H_2CO_3, we write

$$H_2CO_3(aq) \rightleftharpoons H^+(aq) + HCO_3^-(aq) \qquad K_{a_1} = \frac{[H^+][HCO_3^-]}{[H_2CO_3]}$$

$$HCO_3^-(aq) \rightleftharpoons H^+(aq) + CO_3^{2-}(aq) \qquad K_{a_2} = \frac{[H^+][CO_3^{2-}]}{[HCO_3^-]}$$

Note that the conjugate base in the first ionization stage becomes the acid in the second ionization stage.

Table 15.5 on p. 668 shows the ionization constants of several diprotic acids and one polyprotic acid. For a given acid, the first ionization constant is much larger than the second ionization constant, and so on. This trend is reasonable because it is easier to remove a H^+ ion from a neutral molecule than to remove another H^+ ion from a negatively charged ion derived from the molecule.

In Example 15.11 we calculate the equilibrium concentrations of all the species of a diprotic acid in aqueous solution.

Top to bottom: H_2CO_3, HCO_3^-, and CO_3^{2-}.

Example 15.11

Oxalic acid ($C_2H_2O_4$) is a poisonous substance used chiefly as a bleaching and cleansing agent (for example, to remove bathtub rings). Calculate the concentrations of all the species present at equilibrium in a 0.10 M solution.

Strategy Determining the equilibrium concentrations of the species of a diprotic acid in aqueous solution is more involved than for a monoprotic acid. We follow the same procedure as that used for a monoprotic acid for each stage, as in Example 15.8. Note that the conjugate base from the first stage of ionization becomes the acid for the second stage ionization.

Solution We proceed according to the following steps.

Step 1: The major species in solution at this stage are the nonionized acid, H^+ ions, and the conjugate base, $C_2HO_4^-$.

Step 2: Letting x be the equilibrium concentration of H^+ and $C_2HO_4^-$ ions in mol/L, we summarize:

	$C_2H_2O_4(aq)$	$\rightleftharpoons$	$H^+(aq)$	$+$	$C_2HO_4^-(aq)$
Initial (M):	0.10		0.00		0.00
Change (M):	$-x$		$+x$		$+x$
Equilibrium (M):	$0.10 - x$		x		x

Step 3: Table 15.5 gives us

$$K_a = \frac{[H^+][C_2HO_4^-]}{[C_2H_2O_4]}$$

$$6.5 \times 10^{-2} = \frac{x^2}{0.10 - x}$$

$C_2H_2O_4$

(Continued)

TABLE 15.5 Ionization Constants of Some Diprotic Acids and a Polyprotic Acid and Their Conjugate Bases at 25°C

Name of Acid	Formula	Structure	K_a	Conjugate Base	K_b
Sulfuric acid	H_2SO_4	H—O—S—O—H (with O double bonds top and bottom)	very large	HSO_4^-	very small
Hydrogen sulfate ion	HSO_4^-	H—O—S—O$^-$ (with O double bonds top and bottom)	1.3×10^{-2}	SO_4^{2-}	7.7×10^{-13}
Oxalic acid	$C_2H_2O_4$	H—O—C—C—O—H (with two O double bonds)	6.5×10^{-2}	$C_2HO_4^-$	1.5×10^{-13}
Hydrogen oxalate ion	$C_2HO_4^-$	H—O—C—C—O$^-$ (with two O double bonds)	6.1×10^{-5}	$C_2O_4^{2-}$	1.6×10^{-10}
Sulfurous acid*	H_2SO_3	H—O—S—O—H (with O double bond top)	1.3×10^{-2}	HSO_3^-	7.7×10^{-13}
Hydrogen sulfite ion	HSO_3^-	H—O—S—O$^-$ (with O double bond top)	6.3×10^{-8}	SO_3^{2-}	1.6×10^{-7}
Carbonic acid	H_2CO_3	H—O—C—O—H (with O double bond top)	4.2×10^{-7}	HCO_3^-	2.4×10^{-8}
Hydrogen carbonate ion	HCO_3^-	H—O—C—O$^-$ (with O double bond top)	4.8×10^{-11}	CO_3^{2-}	2.1×10^{-4}
Hydrosulfuric acid	H_2S	H—S—H	9.5×10^{-8}	HS^-	1.1×10^{-7}
Hydrogen sulfide ion†	HS^-	H—S$^-$	1×10^{-19}	S^{2-}	1×10^{5}
Phosphoric acid	H_3PO_4	H—O—P—O—H (with O double bond top, O—H below)	7.5×10^{-3}	$H_2PO_4^-$	1.3×10^{-12}
Dihydrogen phosphate ion	$H_2PO_4^-$	H—O—P—O$^-$ (with O double bond top, O—H below)	6.2×10^{-8}	HPO_4^{2-}	1.6×10^{-7}
Hydrogen phosphate ion	HPO_4^{2-}	H—O—P—O$^-$ (with O double bond top, O$^-$ below)	4.8×10^{-13}	PO_4^{3-}	2.1×10^{-2}

*H_2SO_3 has never been isolated and exists in only minute concentration in aqueous solution of SO_2. The K_a value here refers to the process $SO_2(g) + H_2O(l) \rightleftharpoons H^+(aq) + HSO_3^-(aq)$.

†The ionization constant of HS^- is very low and difficult to measure. The value listed here is only an estimate.

Applying the approximation $0.10 - x \approx 0.10$, we obtain

$$6.5 \times 10^{-2} = \frac{x^2}{0.10 - x} \approx \frac{x^2}{0.10}$$
$$x^2 = 6.5 \times 10^{-3}$$
$$x = 8.1 \times 10^{-2}\,M$$

To test the approximation,

$$\frac{8.1 \times 10^{-2}\,M}{0.10\,M} \times 100\% = 81\%$$

Clearly the approximation is not valid. Therefore, we must solve the quadratic equation

$$x^2 + 6.5 \times 10^{-2}x - 6.5 \times 10^{-3} = 0$$

The result is $x = 0.054\,M$.

Step 4: When the equilibrium for the first stage of ionization is reached, the concentrations are

$$[\text{H}^+] = 0.054\,M$$
$$[\text{C}_2\text{HO}_4^-] = 0.054\,M$$
$$[\text{C}_2\text{H}_2\text{O}_4] = (0.10 - 0.054)\,M = 0.046\,M$$

Next we consider the second stage of ionization.

Step 1: At this stage, the major species are C_2HO_4^-, which acts as the acid in the second stage of ionization, H^+, and the conjugate base $\text{C}_2\text{O}_4^{2-}$.

Step 2: Letting y be the equilibrium concentration of H^+ and $\text{C}_2\text{O}_4^{2-}$ ions in mol/L, we summarize:

	$\text{C}_2\text{HO}_4^-(aq)$	$\rightleftharpoons$	$\text{H}^+(aq)$	$+$	$\text{C}_2\text{O}_4^{2-}(aq)$
Initial (*M*):	0.054		0.054		0.00
Change (*M*):	$-y$		$+y$		$+y$
Equilibrium (*M*):	$0.054 - y$		$0.054 + y$		y

Step 3: Table 15.5 gives us

$$K_a = \frac{[\text{H}^+][\text{C}_2\text{O}_4^{2-}]}{[\text{C}_2\text{HO}_4^-]}$$
$$6.1 \times 10^{-5} = \frac{(0.054 + y)(y)}{(0.054 - y)}$$

Applying the approximation $0.054 + y \approx 0.054$ and $0.054 - y \approx 0.054$, we obtain

$$\frac{(0.054)(y)}{(0.054)} = y = 6.1 \times 10^{-5}\,M$$

and we test the approximation,

$$\frac{6.1 \times 10^{-5}\,M}{0.054\,M} \times 100\% = 0.11\%$$

The approximation is valid.

(Continued)

Step 4: At equilibrium,

$$[C_2H_2O_4] = 0.046\ M$$
$$[C_2HO_4^-] = (0.054 - 6.1 \times 10^{-5})\ M = 0.054\ M$$
$$[H^+] = (0.054 + 6.1 \times 10^{-5})\ M = 0.054\ M$$
$$[C_2O_4^{2-}] = 6.1 \times 10^{-5}\ M$$
$$[OH^-] = 1.0 \times 10^{-14}/0.054 = 1.9 \times 10^{-13}\ M$$

Similar problem: 15.64.

Practice Exercise Calculate the concentrations of $C_2H_2O_4$, $C_2HO_4^-$, $C_2O_4^{2-}$, and H^+ ions in a 0.20 M oxalic acid solution.

Example 15.11 shows that for diprotic acids, if $K_{a_1} \gg K_{a_2}$, then we can assume that the concentration of H^+ ions is the product of only the first stage of ionization. Furthermore, the concentration of the conjugate base for the second-stage ionization is *numerically* equal to K_{a_2}.

Phosphoric acid (H_3PO_4) is a polyprotic acid with three ionizable hydrogen atoms:

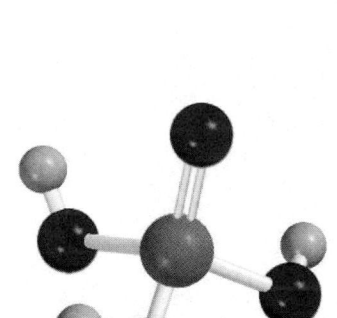

H_3PO_4

$$H_3PO_4(aq) \rightleftharpoons H^+(aq) + H_2PO_4^-(aq) \quad K_{a_1} = \frac{[H^+][H_2PO_4^-]}{[H_3PO_4]} = 7.5 \times 10^{-3}$$

$$H_2PO_4^-(aq) \rightleftharpoons H^+(aq) + HPO_4^{2-}(aq) \quad K_{a_2} = \frac{[H^+][HPO_4^{2-}]}{[H_2PO_4^-]} = 6.2 \times 10^{-8}$$

$$HPO_4^{2-}(aq) \rightleftharpoons H^+(aq) + PO_4^{3-}(aq) \quad K_{a_3} = \frac{[H^+][PO_4^{3-}]}{[HPO_4^{2-}]} = 4.8 \times 10^{-13}$$

We see that phosphoric acid is a weak polyprotic acid and that its ionization constants decrease markedly for the second and third stages. Thus, we can predict that, in a solution containing phosphoric acid, the concentration of the nonionized acid is the highest, and the only other species present in significant concentrations are H^+ and $H_2PO_4^-$ ions.

15.9 Molecular Structure and the Strength of Acids

The strength of an acid depends on a number of factors, such as the properties of the solvent, the temperature, and, of course, the molecular structure of the acid. When we compare the strengths of two acids, we can eliminate some variables by considering their properties in the same solvent and at the same temperature and concentration. Then we can focus on the structure of the acids.

Let us consider a certain acid HX. The strength of the acid is measured by its tendency to ionize:

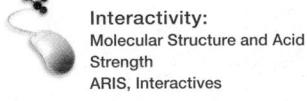

Interactivity:
Molecular Structure and Acid
Strength
ARIS, Interactives

$$HX \longrightarrow H^+ + X^-$$

Two factors influence the extent to which the acid undergoes ionization. One is the strength of the H—X bond—the stronger the bond, the more difficult it is for the HX molecule to break up and hence the *weaker* the acid. The other factor is the polarity of the H—X bond. The difference in the electronegativities between H and X results in a polar bond like

$$\overset{\delta+}{H}\!-\!\overset{\delta-}{X}$$

TABLE 15.6	Bond Enthalpies for Hydrogen Halides and Acid Strengths for Hydrohalic Acids		
Bond	Bond Enthalpy (kJ/mol)		Acid Strength
H—F	568.2		weak
H—Cl	431.9		strong
H—Br	366.1		strong
H—I	298.3		strong

If the bond is highly polarized, that is, if there is a large accumulation of positive and negative charges on the H and X atoms, HX will tend to break up into H^+ and X^- ions. So a high degree of polarity characterizes a *stronger* acid. Below we will consider some examples in which either bond strength or bond polarity plays a prominent role in determining acid strength.

Hydrohalic Acids

The halogens form a series of binary acids called the hydrohalic acids (HF, HCl, HBr, and HI). Of this series, which factor (bond strength or bond polarity) is the predominant factor in determining the strength of the binary acids? Consider first the strength of the H—X bond in each of these acids. Table 15.6 shows that HF has the highest bond enthalpy of the four hydrogen halides, and HI has the lowest bond enthalpy. It takes 568.2 kJ/mol to break the H—F bond and only 298.3 kJ/mol to break the H—I bond. Based on bond enthalpy, HI should be the strongest acid because it is easiest to break the bond and form the H^+ and I^- ions. Second, consider the polarity of the H—X bond. In this series of acids, the polarity of the bond decreases from HF to HI because F is the most electronegative of the halogens (see Figure 9.5). Based on bond polarity, then, HF should be the strongest acid because of the largest accumulation of positive and negative charges on the H and F atoms. Thus, we have two competing factors to consider in determining the strength of binary acids. The fact that HI is a strong acid and that HF is a weak acid indicates that bond enthalpy is the predominant factor in determining the acid strength of binary acids. In this series of binary acids, the weaker the bond, the stronger the acid so that the strength of the acids increases as follows:

$$HF \ll HCl < HBr < HI$$

Strength of hydrohalic acids increases from HF to HI.

Oxoacids

Now let us consider the oxoacids. Oxoacids, as we learned in Chapter 2, contain hydrogen, oxygen, and one other element Z, which occupies a central position. Figure 15.5 shows the Lewis structures of several common oxoacids. As you can see, these acids are characterized by the presence of one or more O—H bonds. The central atom Z might also have other groups attached to it:

$$\overset{\displaystyle\diagdown}{\underset{\displaystyle\diagup}{}}Z{-}O{-}H$$

To review the nomenclature of inorganic acids, see Section 2.8.

If Z is an electronegative element, or is in a high oxidation state, it will attract electrons, thus making the Z—O bond more covalent and the O—H bond more

As the oxidation number of an atom becomes larger, its ability to draw electrons in a bond toward itself increases.

Figure 15.5 *Lewis structures of some common oxoacids. For simplicity, the formal charges have been omitted.*

polar. Consequently, the tendency for the hydrogen to be donated as a H^+ ion increases:

$$\overset{|}{\underset{|}{Z}}-\overset{\delta-}{O}-\overset{\delta+}{H} \longrightarrow \overset{|}{\underset{|}{Z}}-O^- + H^+$$

To compare their strengths, it is convenient to divide the oxoacids into two groups.

1. *Oxoacids Having Different Central Atoms That Are from the Same Group of the Periodic Table and That Have the Same Oxidation Number.* Within this group, acid strength increases with increasing electronegativity of the central atom, as $HClO_3$ and $HBrO_3$ illustrate:

Strength of halogen-containing oxoacids having the same number of O atoms increases from bottom to top.

Cl and Br have the same oxidation number, $+5$. However, because Cl is more electronegative than Br, it attracts the electron pair it shares with oxygen (in the Cl—O—H group) to a greater extent than Br does. Consequently, the O—H bond is more polar in chloric acid than in bromic acid and ionizes more readily. Thus, the relative acid strengths are

$$HClO_3 > HBrO_3$$

2. *Oxoacids Having the Same Central Atom but Different Numbers of Attached Groups.* Within this group, acid strength increases as the oxidation number of the

Figure 15.6 *Lewis structures of the oxoacids of chlorine. The oxidation number of the Cl atom is shown in parentheses. For simplicity, the formal charges have been omitted. Note that although hypochlorous acid is written as HClO, the H atom is bonded to the O atom.*

central atom increases. Consider the oxoacids of chlorine shown in Figure 15.6. In this series the ability of chlorine to draw electrons away from the OH group (thus making the O—H bond more polar) increases with the number of electronegative O atoms attached to Cl. Thus, $HClO_4$ is the strongest acid because it has the largest number of O atoms attached to Cl, and the acid strength decreases as follows:

$$HClO_4 > HClO_3 > HClO_2 > HClO$$

Example 15.12 compares the strengths of acids based on their molecular structures.

Example 15.12

Predict the relative strengths of the oxoacids in each of the following groups: (a) HClO, HBrO, and HIO; (b) HNO_3 and HNO_2.

Strategy Examine the molecular structure. In (a) the two acids have similar structure but differ only in the central atom (Cl, Br, and I). Which central atom is the most electronegative? In (b) the acids have the same central atom (N) but differ in the number of O atoms. What is the oxidation number of N in each of these two acids?

Solution (a) These acids all have the same structure, and the halogens all have the same oxidation number $(+1)$. Because the electronegativity decreases from Cl to I, the polarity of the X—O bond (where X denotes a halogen atom) increases from HClO to HIO, and the polarity of the O—H bond decreases from HClO to HIO. Thus, the acid strength decreases as follows:

$$HClO > HBrO > HIO$$

(b) The structures of HNO_3 and HNO_2 are shown in Figure 15.5. Because the oxidation number of N is $+5$ in HNO_3 and $+3$ in HNO_2, HNO_3 is a stronger acid than HNO_2.

Similar problem: 15.68.

Practice Exercise Which of the following acids is weaker: $HClO_2$ or $HClO_3$?

Carboxylic Acids

So far the discussion has focused on inorganic acids. A group of organic acids that also deserves attention is the carboxylic acids, whose Lewis structures can be represented by

where R is part of the acid molecule and the shaded portion represents the *carboxyl* group, —COOH. The strength of carboxylic acids depends on the nature of the R group. Consider, for example, acetic acid and chloroacetic acid:

acetic acid ($K_a = 1.8 \times 10^{-5}$)   chloroacetic acid ($K_a = 1.4 \times 10^{-3}$)

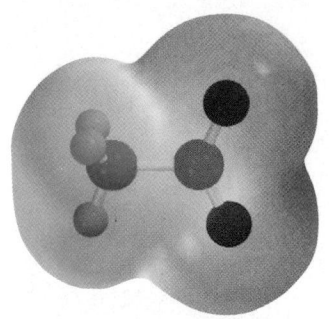

Electrostatic potential map of the acetate ion. The electron density is evenly distributed between the two O atoms.

The presence of the electronegative Cl atom in chloroacetic acid shifts electron density toward the R group, thereby making the O—H bond more polar. Consequently, there is a greater tendency for the acid to ionize:

$$CH_2ClCOOH(aq) \rightleftharpoons CH_2ClCOO^-(aq) + H^+(aq)$$

The conjugate base of the carboxylic acid, called the carboxylate anion ($RCOO^-$), can exhibit resonance:

$$
\overset{\displaystyle :\overset{..}{O}:}{\underset{\displaystyle }{R-C-\overset{..}{\underset{..}{O}}:^-}} \longleftrightarrow \overset{\displaystyle :\overset{..}{O}:^-}{\underset{\displaystyle }{R-C=\overset{..}{\underset{..}{O}}}}
$$

In the language of molecular orbital theory, we attribute the stability of the anion to its ability to spread or delocalize the electron density over several atoms. The greater the extent of electron delocalization, the more stable the anion and the greater the tendency for the acid to undergo ionization. Thus, benzoic acid (C_6H_5COOH, $K_a = 6.5 \times 10^{-5}$) is a stronger acid than acetic acid because the benzene ring (see p. 438) facilitates electron delocalization, so that the benzoate anion ($C_6H_5COO^-$) is more stable than the acetate anion (CH_3COO^-).

15.10 Acid-Base Properties of Salts

As defined in Section 4.3, a salt is an ionic compound formed by the reaction between an acid and a base. Salts are strong electrolytes that completely dissociate into ions in water. The term **salt hydrolysis** describes *the reaction of an anion or a cation of a salt, or both, with water.* Salt hydrolysis usually affects the pH of a solution.

The word "hydrolysis" is derived from the Greek words *hydro*, meaning "water," and *lysis*, meaning "to split apart."

Salts That Produce Neutral Solutions

In reality, all positive ions give acid solutions in water.

It is generally true that salts containing an alkali metal ion or alkaline earth metal ion (except Be^{2+}) and the conjugate base of a strong acid (for example, Cl^-, Br^-, and NO_3^-) do not undergo hydrolysis to an appreciable extent, and their solutions are assumed to be neutral. For instance, when $NaNO_3$, a salt formed by the reaction of NaOH with HNO_3, dissolves in water, it dissociates completely as follows:

$$NaNO_3(s) \xrightarrow{H_2O} Na^+(aq) + NO_3^-(aq)$$

The hydrated Na^+ ion neither donates nor accepts H^+ ions. The NO_3^- ion is the conjugate base of the strong acid HNO_3, and it has no affinity for H^+ ions. Consequently, a solution containing Na^+ and NO_3^- ions is neutral, with a pH of about 7.

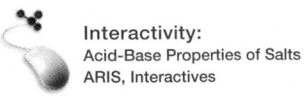

Interactivity:
Acid-Base Properties of Salts
ARIS, Interactives

Salts That Produce Basic Solutions

The solution of a salt derived from a strong base and a weak acid is basic. For example, the dissociation of sodium acetate (CH_3COONa) in water is given by

$$CH_3COONa(s) \xrightarrow{H_2O} Na^+(aq) + CH_3COO^-(aq)$$

The mechanism by which metal ions produce acid solutions is discussed on p. 677.

The hydrated Na^+ ion has no acidic or basic properties. The acetate ion CH_3COO^-, however, is the conjugate base of the weak acid CH_3COOH and therefore has an affinity for H^+ ions. The hydrolysis reaction is given by

$$CH_3COO^-(aq) + H_2O(l) \rightleftharpoons CH_3COOH(aq) + OH^-(aq)$$

Because this reaction produces OH^- ions, the sodium acetate solution will be basic. The equilibrium constant for this hydrolysis reaction is the same as the base ionization constant expression for CH_3COO^-, so we write (see p. 666)

$$K_b = \frac{[CH_3COOH][OH^-]}{[CH_3COO^-]} = 5.6 \times 10^{-10}$$

Because each CH_3COO^- ion that hydrolyzes produces one OH^- ion, the concentration of OH^- at equilibrium is the same as the concentration of CH_3COO^- that hydrolyzed. We can define the *percent hydrolysis* as

$$\% \text{ hydrolysis} = \frac{[CH_3COO^-]_{\text{hydrolyzed}}}{[CH_3COO^-]_{\text{initial}}} \times 100\%$$

$$= \frac{[OH^-]_{\text{equilibrium}}}{[CH_3COO^-]_{\text{initial}}} \times 100\%$$

A calculation based on the hydrolysis of CH_3COONa is illustrated in Example 15.13. In solving salt hydrolysis problems, we follow the same procedure we used for weak acids and weak bases.

Example 15.13

Calculate the pH of a 0.15 M solution of sodium acetate (CH_3COONa). What is the percent hydrolysis?

Strategy What is a salt? In solution, CH_3COONa dissociates completely into Na^+ and CH_3COO^- ions. The Na^+ ion, as we saw earlier, does not react with water and has no effect on the pH of the solution. The CH_3COO^- ion is the conjugate base of the weak acid CH_3COOH. Therefore, we expect that it will react to a certain extent with water to produce CH_3COOH and OH^-, and the solution will be basic.

Solution

Step 1: Because we started with a 0.15 M sodium acetate solution, the concentrations of the ions are also equal to 0.15 M after dissociation:

	$CH_3COONa(aq) \longrightarrow$	$Na^+(aq) +$	$CH_3COO^-(aq)$
Initial (M):	0.15	0	0
Change (M):	−0.15	+0.15	+0.15
Final (M):	0	0.15	0.15

Of these ions, only the acetate ion will react with water

$$CH_3COO^-(aq) + H_2O(l) \rightleftharpoons CH_3COOH(aq) + OH^-(aq)$$

At equilibrium, the major species in solution are CH_3COOH, CH_3COO^-, and OH^-. The concentration of the H^+ ion is very small as we would expect for a basic solution, so it is treated as a minor species. We ignore the ionization of water.

Step 2: Let x be the equilibrium concentration of CH_3COOH and OH^- ions in mol/L, we summarize:

	$CH_3COO^-(aq) + H_2O(l) \rightleftharpoons$	$CH_3COOH(aq) +$	$OH^-(aq)$
Initial (M):	0.15	0.00	0.00
Change (M):	−x	+x	+x
Equilibrium (M):	0.15 − x	x	x

(Continued)

Step 3: From the preceding discussion and Table 15.3 we write the equilibrium constant of hydrolysis, or the base ionization constant, as

$$K_b = \frac{[CH_3COOH][OH^-]}{[CH_3COO^-]}$$

$$5.6 \times 10^{-10} = \frac{x^2}{0.15 - x}$$

Because K_b is very small and the initial concentration of the base is large, we can apply the approximation $0.15 - x \approx 0.15$:

$$5.6 \times 10^{-10} = \frac{x^2}{0.15 - x} \approx \frac{x^2}{0.15}$$

$$x = 9.2 \times 10^{-6}\, M$$

Step 4: At equilibrium:

$$[OH^-] = 9.2 \times 10^{-6}\, M$$
$$pOH = -\log\,(9.2 \times 10^{-6})$$
$$= 5.04$$
$$pH = 14.00 - 5.04$$
$$= 8.96$$

Thus the solution is basic, as we would expect. The percent hydrolysis is given by

$$\% \text{ hydrolysis} = \frac{9.2 \times 10^{-6}\, M}{0.15\, M} \times 100\%$$
$$= 0.0061\%$$

Check The result shows that only a very small amount of the anion undergoes hydrolysis. Note that the calculation of percent hydrolysis takes the same form as the test for the approximation, which is valid in this case.

Practice Exercise Calculate the pH of a 0.24 M sodium formate solution (HCOONa).

Similar problem: 15.79.

Salts That Produce Acidic Solutions

When a salt derived from a strong acid such as HCl and a weak base such as NH_3 dissolves in water, the solution becomes acidic. For example, consider the process

$$NH_4Cl(s) \xrightarrow{H_2O} NH_4^+(aq) + Cl^-(aq)$$

The Cl^- ion, being the conjugate base of a strong acid, has no affinity for H^+ and no tendency to hydrolyze. The ammonium ion NH_4^+ is the weak conjugate acid of the weak base NH_3 and ionizes as follows:

$$NH_4^+(aq) + H_2O(l) \rightleftharpoons NH_3(aq) + H_3O^+(aq)$$

or simply

$$NH_4^+(aq) \rightleftharpoons NH_3(aq) + H^+(aq)$$

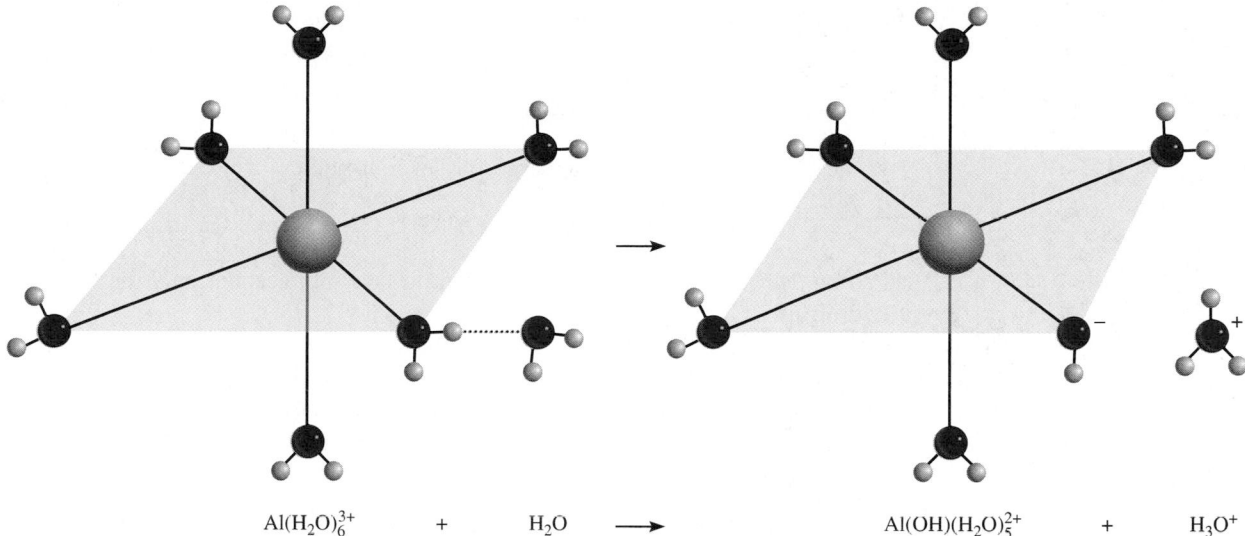

$$\text{Al(H}_2\text{O)}_6^{3+} \quad + \quad \text{H}_2\text{O} \quad \longrightarrow \quad \text{Al(OH)(H}_2\text{O)}_5^{2+} \quad + \quad \text{H}_3\text{O}^+$$

Figure 15.7 *The six H_2O molecules surround the Al^{3+} ion octahedrally. The attraction of the small Al^{3+} ion for the lone pairs on the oxygen atoms is so great that the O—H bonds in a H_2O molecule attached to the metal cation are weakened, allowing the loss of a proton (H^+) to an incoming H_2O molecule. This hydrolysis of the metal cation makes the solution acidic.*

Note that this reaction also represents the hydrolysis of the NH_4^+ ion. Because H^+ ions are produced, the pH of the solution decreases. The equilibrium constant (or ionization constant) for this process is given by

$$K_a = \frac{[\text{NH}_3][\text{H}^+]}{[\text{NH}_4^+]} = \frac{K_w}{K_b} = \frac{1.0 \times 10^{-14}}{1.8 \times 10^{-5}} = 5.6 \times 10^{-10}$$

By coincidence, K_a of NH_4^+ has the same numerical value as K_b of CH_3COO^-.

and we can calculate the pH of an ammonium chloride solution following the same procedure used in Example 15.13.

In principle, *all* metal ions react with water to produce an acidic solution. However, because the extent of hydrolysis is most pronounced for the small and highly charged metal cations such as Al^{3+}, Cr^{3+}, Fe^{3+}, Bi^{3+}, and Be^{2+}, we generally neglect the relatively small interaction of alkali metal ions and most alkaline earth metal ions with water. When aluminum chloride ($AlCl_3$) dissolves in water, the Al^{3+} ions take the hydrated form $Al(H_2O)_6^{3+}$ (Figure 15.7). Let us consider one bond between the metal ion and an oxygen atom from one of the six water molecules in $Al(H_2O)_6^{3+}$:

$$\text{Al} \Longleftarrow \overset{+}{\text{O}} \underset{\text{H}}{\overset{\text{H}}{\Big\langle}}$$

The positively charged Al^{3+} ion draws electron density toward itself, increasing the polarity of the O—H bonds. Consequently, the H atoms have a greater tendency to ionize than those in water molecules not involved in hydration. The resulting ionization process can be written as

$$\text{Al(H}_2\text{O)}_6^{3+}(aq) + \text{H}_2\text{O}(l) \rightleftharpoons \text{Al(OH)(H}_2\text{O)}_5^{2+}(aq) + \text{H}_3\text{O}^+(aq)$$

or simply

$$\text{Al(H}_2\text{O)}_6^{3+}(aq) \rightleftharpoons \text{Al(OH)(H}_2\text{O)}_5^{2+}(aq) + \text{H}^+(aq)$$

The hydrated Al^{3+} qualifies as a proton donor and thus a Brønsted acid in this reaction.

The equilibrium constant for the metal cation hydrolysis is given by

Note that Al(H₂O)₆³⁺ is roughly as strong an acid as CH₃COOH.

$$K_a = \frac{[Al(OH)(H_2O)_5^{2+}][H^+]}{[Al(H_2O)_6^{3+}]} = 1.3 \times 10^{-5}$$

Note that $Al(OH)(H_2O)_5^{2+}$ can undergo further ionization

$$Al(OH)(H_2O)_5^{2+}(aq) \rightleftharpoons Al(OH)_2(H_2O)_4^+(aq) + H^+(aq)$$

and so on. However, it is generally sufficient to take into account only the first stage of hydrolysis.

The extent of hydrolysis is greatest for the smallest and most highly charged ions because a "compact" highly charged ion is more effective in polarizing the O—H bond and facilitating ionization. This is why relatively large ions of low charge such as Na^+ and K^+ do not undergo appreciable hydrolysis.

Salts in Which Both the Cation and the Anion Hydrolyze

So far we have considered salts in which only one ion undergoes hydrolysis. For salts derived from a weak acid and a weak base, both the cation and the anion hydrolyze. However, whether a solution containing such a salt is acidic, basic, or neutral depends on the relative strengths of the weak acid and the weak base. Because the mathematics associated with this type of system is rather involved, we will focus on making qualitative predictions about these solutions based on the following guidelines:

- **$K_b > K_a$.** If K_b for the anion is greater than K_a for the cation, then the solution must be basic because the anion will hydrolyze to a greater extent than the cation. At equilibrium, there will be more OH^- ions than H^+ ions.

- **$K_b < K_a$.** Conversely, if K_b for the anion is smaller than K_a for the cation, the solution will be acidic because cation hydrolysis will be more extensive than anion hydrolysis.

- **$K_b \approx K_a$.** If K_a is approximately equal to K_b, the solution will be nearly neutral.

Table 15.7 summarizes the behavior in aqueous solution of the salts discussed in this section.

Example 15.14 illustrates how to predict the acid-base properties of salt solutions.

TABLE 15.7	Acid-Base Properties of Salts		
Type of Salt	**Examples**	**Ions That Undergo Hydrolysis**	**pH of Solution**
Cation from strong base; anion from strong acid	NaCl, KI, KNO₃, RbBr, BaCl₂	None	≈ 7
Cation from strong base; anion from weak acid	CH₃COONa, KNO₂	Anion	> 7
Cation from weak base; anion from strong acid	NH₄Cl, NH₄NO₃	Cation	< 7
Cation from weak base; anion from weak acid	NH₄NO₂, CH₃COONH₄, NH₄CN	Anion and cation	< 7 if $K_b < K_a$
			≈ 7 if $K_b \approx K_a$
			> 7 if $K_b > K_a$
Small, highly charged cation; anion from strong acid	AlCl₃, Fe(NO₃)₃	Hydrated cation	< 7

Example 15.14

Predict whether the following solutions will be acidic, basic, or nearly neutral: (a) NH_4I, (b) $NaNO_2$, (c) $FeCl_3$, (d) NH_4F.

Strategy In deciding whether a salt will undergo hydrolysis, ask yourself the following questions: Is the cation a highly charged metal ion or an ammonium ion? Is the anion the conjugate base of a weak acid? If yes to either question, then hydrolysis will occur. In cases where both the cation and the anion react with water, the pH of the solution will depend on the relative magnitudes of K_a for the cation and K_b for the anion (see Table 15.7).

Solution We first break up the salt into its cation and anion components and then examine the possible reaction of each ion with water.

(a) The cation is NH_4^+, which will hydrolyze to produce NH_3 and H^+. The I^- anion is the conjugate base of the strong acid HI. Therefore, I^- will not hydrolyze and the solution is acidic.

(b) The Na^+ cation does not hydrolyze. The NO_2^- is the conjugate base of the weak acid HNO_2 and will hydrolyze to give HNO_2 and OH^-. The solution will be basic.

(c) Fe^{3+} is a small metal ion with a high charge and hydrolyzes to produce H^+ ions. The Cl^- does not hydrolyze. Consequently, the solution will be acidic.

(d) Both the NH_4^+ and F^- ions will hydrolyze. From Tables 15.3 and 15.4 we see that the K_a of NH_4^+ (5.6×10^{-10}) is greater than the K_b for F^- (1.4×10^{-11}). Therefore, the solution will be acidic.

Similar problems: 15.75, 15.76.

Practice Exercise Predict whether the following solutions will be acidic, basic, or nearly neutral: (a) $LiClO_4$, (b) Na_3PO_4, (c) $Bi(NO_3)_3$, (d) NH_4CN.

Finally we note that some anions can act either as an acid or as a base. For example, the bicarbonate ion (HCO_3^-) can ionize or undergo hydrolysis as follows (see Table 15.5):

$$HCO_3^-(aq) + H_2O(l) \rightleftharpoons H_3O^+(aq) + CO_3^{2-}(aq) \qquad K_a = 4.8 \times 10^{-11}$$
$$HCO_3^-(aq) + H_2O(l) \rightleftharpoons H_2CO_3(aq) + OH^-(aq) \qquad K_b = 2.4 \times 10^{-8}$$

Because $K_b > K_a$, we predict that the hydrolysis reaction will outweigh the ionization process. Thus, a solution of sodium bicarbonate ($NaHCO_3$) will be basic.

15.11 Acid-Base Properties of Oxides and Hydroxides

As we saw in Chapter 8, oxides can be classified as acidic, basic, or amphoteric. Our discussion of acid-base reactions would be incomplete if we did not examine the properties of these compounds.

Figure 15.8 shows the formulas of a number of oxides of the representative elements in their highest oxidation states. Note that all alkali metal oxides and all alkaline earth metal oxides except BeO are basic. Beryllium oxide and several metallic oxides in Groups 3A and 4A are amphoteric. Nonmetallic oxides in which the oxidation number of the representative element is high are acidic (for example, N_2O_5, SO_3, and Cl_2O_7), but those in which the oxidation number of the representative element is low (for example, CO and NO) show no measurable acidic properties. No nonmetallic oxides are known to have basic properties.

Figure 15.8 *Oxides of the representative elements in their highest oxidation states.*

The basic metallic oxides react with water to form metal hydroxides:

$$Na_2O(s) \xrightarrow{H_2O} 2NaOH(aq)$$
$$BaO(s) \xrightarrow{H_2O} Ba(OH)_2(aq)$$

The reactions between acidic oxides and water are as follows:

$$CO_2(g) + H_2O(l) \rightleftharpoons H_2CO_3(aq)$$
$$SO_3(g) + H_2O(l) \rightleftharpoons H_2SO_4(aq)$$
$$N_2O_5(g) + H_2O(l) \rightleftharpoons 2HNO_3(aq)$$
$$P_4O_{10}(s) + 6H_2O(l) \rightleftharpoons 4H_3PO_4(aq)$$
$$Cl_2O_7(l) + H_2O(l) \rightleftharpoons 2HClO_4(aq)$$

The reaction between CO_2 and H_2O explains why when pure water is exposed to air (which contains CO_2) it gradually reaches a pH of about 5.5 (Figure 15.9). The reaction between SO_3 and H_2O is largely responsible for acid rain (Figure 15.10).

We will look at the causes and effects of acid rain in Chapter 17.

Reactions between acidic oxides and bases and those between basic oxides and acids resemble normal acid-base reactions in that the products are a salt and water:

$$\underset{\text{acidic oxide}}{CO_2(g)} + \underset{\text{base}}{2NaOH(aq)} \longrightarrow \underset{\text{salt}}{Na_2CO_3(aq)} + \underset{\text{water}}{H_2O(l)}$$

$$\underset{\text{basic oxide}}{BaO(s)} + \underset{\text{acid}}{2HNO_3(aq)} \longrightarrow \underset{\text{salt}}{Ba(NO_3)_2(aq)} + \underset{\text{water}}{H_2O(l)}$$

As Figure 15.8 shows, aluminum oxide (Al_2O_3) is amphoteric. Depending on the reaction conditions, it can behave either as an acidic oxide or as a basic oxide. For example, Al_2O_3 acts as a base with hydrochloric acid to produce a salt ($AlCl_3$) and water:

$$Al_2O_3(s) + 6HCl(aq) \longrightarrow 2AlCl_3(aq) + 3H_2O(l)$$

Figure 15.9 *(Left) A beaker of water to which a few drops of bromothymol blue indicator have been added. (Right) As dry ice is added to the water, the CO_2 reacts to form carbonic acid, which turns the solution acidic and changes the color from blue to yellow.*

and acts as an acid with sodium hydroxide:

$$Al_2O_3(s) + 2NaOH(aq) \longrightarrow 2NaAlO_2(aq) + H_2O(l)$$

Some transition metal oxides in which the metal has a high oxidation number act as acidic oxides. Two familiar examples are manganese(VII) oxide (Mn_2O_7) and chromium(VI) oxide (CrO_3), both of which react with water to produce acids:

$$Mn_2O_7(l) + H_2O(l) \longrightarrow \underset{\text{permanganic acid}}{2HMnO_4(aq)}$$

$$CrO_3(s) + H_2O(l) \longrightarrow \underset{\text{chromic acid}}{H_2CrO_4(aq)}$$

Figure 15.10 *A forest damaged by acid rain.*

The higher the oxidation number of the metal, the more covalent the compound; the lower the oxidation number, the more ionic the compound.

Basic and Amphoteric Hydroxides

We have seen that the alkali and alkaline earth metal hydroxides [except $Be(OH)_2$] are basic in properties. The following hydroxides are amphoteric: $Be(OH)_2$, $Al(OH)_3$, $Sn(OH)_2$, $Pb(OH)_2$, $Cr(OH)_3$, $Cu(OH)_2$, $Zn(OH)_2$, and $Cd(OH)_2$. For example, aluminum hydroxide reacts with both acids and bases:

$$Al(OH)_3(s) + 3H^+(aq) \longrightarrow Al^{3+}(aq) + 3H_2O(l)$$
$$Al(OH)_3(s) + OH^-(aq) \rightleftharpoons Al(OH)_4^-(aq)$$

All amphoteric hydroxides are insoluble.

It is interesting that beryllium hydroxide, like aluminum hydroxide, exhibits amphoterism:

$$Be(OH)_2(s) + 2H^+(aq) \longrightarrow Be^{2+}(aq) + 2H_2O(l)$$
$$Be(OH)_2(s) + 2OH^-(aq) \rightleftharpoons Be(OH)_4^{2-}(aq)$$

This is another example of the diagonal relationship between beryllium and aluminum (see p. 336).

15.12 Lewis Acids and Bases

Figure 15.11 *A Lewis acid-base reaction involving BF_3 and NH_3.*

So far we have discussed acid-base properties in terms of the Brønsted theory. To behave as a Brønsted base, for example, a substance must be able to accept protons. By this definition both the hydroxide ion and ammonia are bases:

$$H^+ + {}^-:\ddot{O}-H \longrightarrow H-\ddot{O}-H$$

$$H^+ + :\overset{\displaystyle H}{\underset{\displaystyle H}{N}}-H \longrightarrow \left[H-\overset{\displaystyle H}{\underset{\displaystyle H}{N}}-H \right]^+$$

In each case, the atom to which the proton becomes attached possesses at least one unshared pair of electrons. This characteristic property of OH^-, NH_3, and other Brønsted bases suggests a more general definition of acids and bases.

In 1932 the American chemist G. N. Lewis formulated such a definition. He defined what we now call a ***Lewis base*** as *a substance that can donate a pair of electrons*. A ***Lewis acid*** is *a substance that can accept a pair of electrons*. For example, in the protonation of ammonia, NH_3 acts as a Lewis base because it donates a pair of electrons to the proton H^+, which acts as a Lewis acid by accepting the pair of electrons. A Lewis acid-base reaction, therefore, is one that involves the donation of a pair of electrons from one species to another. Such a reaction does not produce a salt and water.

> Lewis acids are either deficient in electrons (cations) or the central atom has a vacant valence orbital.

The significance of the Lewis concept is that it is more general than other definitions. Lewis acid-base reactions include many reactions that do not involve Brønsted acids. Consider, for example, the reaction between boron trifluoride (BF_3) and ammonia to form an adduct compound (Figure 15.11):

$$\underset{\text{acid}}{\overset{\displaystyle F}{\underset{\displaystyle F}{F-B}}} + \underset{\text{base}}{:\overset{\displaystyle H}{\underset{\displaystyle H}{N}}-H} \longrightarrow \overset{\displaystyle F\;\;H}{\underset{\displaystyle F\;\;H}{F-B-N-H}}$$

> A coordinate covalent bond (see p. 380) is always formed in a Lewis acid-base reaction.

In Section 10.4 we saw that the B atom in BF_3 is sp^2-hybridized. The vacant, unhybridized $2p_z$ orbital accepts the pair of electrons from NH_3. So BF_3 functions as an acid according to the Lewis definition, even though it does not contain an ionizable proton. Note that a coordinate covalent bond is formed between the B and N atoms, as is the case in all Lewis acid-base reactions.

Another Lewis acid containing boron is boric acid. Boric acid (a weak acid used in eyewash) is an oxoacid with the following structure:

$$H-\ddot{O}-\overset{\displaystyle \overset{\displaystyle H}{|}}{\underset{}{B}}-\ddot{O}-H$$
$$\phantom{H-\ddot{O}-}{:}\ddot{O}{:}$$

H_3BO_3

Boric acid does not ionize in water to produce a H^+ ion. Its reaction with water is

$$B(OH)_3(aq) + H_2O(l) \rightleftharpoons B(OH)_4^-(aq) + H^+(aq)$$

In this Lewis acid-base reaction, boric acid accepts a pair of electrons from the hydroxide ion that is derived from the H_2O molecule.

The hydration of carbon dioxide to produce carbonic acid

$$CO_2(g) + H_2O(l) \rightleftharpoons H_2CO_3(aq)$$

can be understood in the Lewis framework as follows: The first step involves donation of a lone pair on the oxygen atom in H_2O to the carbon atom in CO_2. An orbital is vacated on the C atom to accommodate the lone pair by removal of the electron pair in the C—O pi bond. These shifts of electrons are indicated by the curved arrows.

Therefore, H_2O is a Lewis base and CO_2 is a Lewis acid. Next, a proton is transferred onto the O atom bearing a negative charge to form H_2CO_3.

Other examples of Lewis acid-base reactions are

$$\underset{\text{acid}}{Ag^+(aq)} + \underset{\text{base}}{2NH_3(aq)} \rightleftharpoons Ag(NH_3)_2^+(aq)$$

$$\underset{\text{acid}}{Cd^{2+}(aq)} + \underset{\text{base}}{4I^-(aq)} \rightleftharpoons CdI_4^{2-}(aq)$$

$$\underset{\text{acid}}{Ni(s)} + \underset{\text{base}}{4CO(g)} \rightleftharpoons Ni(CO)_4(g)$$

It is important to note that the hydration of metal ions in solution is in itself a Lewis acid base reaction (see Figure 15.7). Thus, when copper(II) sulfate ($CuSO_4$) dissolves in water, each Cu^{2+} ion is associated with six water molecules as $Cu(H_2O)_6^{2+}$. In this case, the Cu^{2+} ion acts as the acid and the H_2O molecules act as the base.

Although the Lewis definition of acids and bases has greater significance because of its generality, we normally speak of "an acid" and "a base" in terms of the Brønsted definition. The term "Lewis acid" usually is reserved for substances that can accept a pair of electrons but do not contain ionizable hydrogen atoms.

Example 15.15 classifies Lewis acids and Lewis bases.

Example 15.15

Identify the Lewis acid and Lewis base in each of the following reactions:

(a) $C_2H_5OC_2H_5 + AlCl_3 \rightleftharpoons (C_2H_5)_2OAlCl_3$

(b) $Hg^{2+}(aq) + 4CN^-(aq) \rightleftharpoons Hg(CN)_4^{2-}(aq)$

(Continued)

CHEMISTRY
in Action

Antacids and the pH Balance in Your Stomach

An average adult produces between 2 and 3 L of gastric juice daily. Gastric juice is a thin, acidic digestive fluid secreted by glands in the mucous membrane that lines the stomach. It contains, among other substances, hydrochloric acid. The pH of gastric juice is about 1.5, which corresponds to a hydrochloric acid concentration of 0.03 M—a concentration strong enough to dissolve zinc metal! What is the purpose of this highly acidic medium? Where do the H^+ ions come from? What happens when there is an excess of H^+ ions present in the stomach?

A simplified diagram of the stomach is shown on the right. The inside lining is made up of parietal cells, which are fused together to form tight junctions. The interiors of the cells are protected from the surroundings by cell membranes. These membranes allow water and neutral molecules to pass in and out of the stomach, but they usually block the movement of ions such as H^+, Na^+, K^+, and Cl^-. The H^+ ions come from carbonic acid (H_2CO_3) formed as a result of the hydration of CO_2, an end product of metabolism:

$$CO_2(g) + H_2O(l) \rightleftharpoons H_2CO_3(aq)$$
$$H_2CO_2(aq) \rightleftharpoons H^+(aq) + HCO_3^-(aq)$$

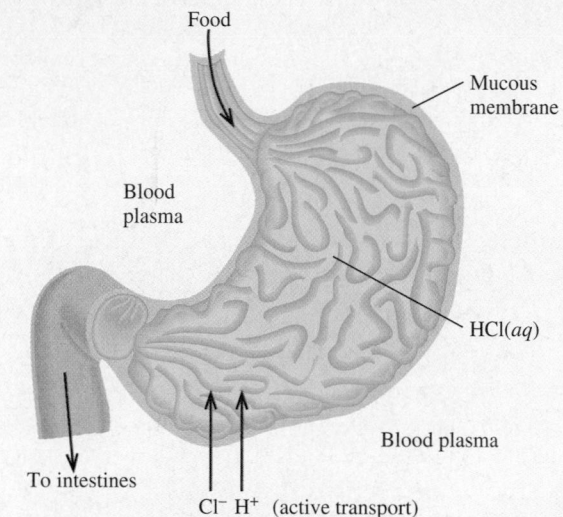

A simplified diagram of the human stomach.

These reactions take place in the blood plasma bathing the cells in the mucosa. By a process known as *active transport,* H^+ ions move across the membrane into the stomach interior. (Active transport processes are aided by enzymes.) To maintain electrical balance, an equal number of Cl^- ions also move from the blood plasma into the stomach. Once in the stomach, most of these ions are prevented from diffusing back into the blood plasma by cell membranes.

The purpose of the highly acidic medium within the stomach is to digest food and to activate certain digestive enzymes. Eating stimulates H^+ ion secretion. A small fraction of these ions normally are reabsorbed by the mucosa, causing many tiny hemorrhages. About half a million cells are shed by the lining every minute, and a healthy stomach is completely relined every three days or so. However, if the acid content is excessively high, the constant influx of H^+ ions through the membrane back to the blood plasma can cause muscle contraction, pain, swelling, inflammation, and bleeding.

One way to temporarily reduce the H^+ ion concentration in the stomach is to take an antacid. The major function of antacids is to neutralize excess HCl in gastric juice. The table on p. 685 lists the active ingredients of some popular antacids. The reactions by which these antacids neutralize stomach acid are as follows:

$$NaHCO_3(aq) + HCl(aq) \longrightarrow$$
$$NaCl(aq) + H_2O(l) + CO_2(g)$$
$$CaCO_3(s) + 2HCl(aq) \longrightarrow CaCl_2(aq) + H_2O(l) + CO_2(g)$$
$$MgCO_3(s) + 2HCl(aq) \longrightarrow$$
$$MgCl_2(aq) + H_2O(l) + CO_2(g)$$

Strategy In Lewis acid-base reactions, the acid is usually a cation or an electron-deficient molecule, whereas the base is an anion or a molecule containing an atom with lone pairs. (a) Draw the molecular structure for $C_2H_5OC_2H_5$. What is the hybridization state of Al in $AlCl_3$? (b) Which ion is likely to be an electron acceptor? An electron donor?

Solution (a) The Al is sp^2-hybridized in $AlCl_3$ with an empty $2p_z$ orbital. It is electron-deficient, sharing only six electrons. Therefore, the Al atom has a tendency to gain two electrons to complete its octet. This property makes $AlCl_3$ a Lewis acid.

(Continued)

When an Alka-Seltzer tablet dissolves in water, the bicarbonate ions in it react with the acid component in the tablet to produce carbon dioxide gas.

$$Mg(OH)_2(s) + 2HCl(aq) \longrightarrow MgCl_2(aq) + 2H_2O(l)$$
$$Al(OH)_2NaCO_3(s) + 4HCl(aq) \longrightarrow$$
$$AlCl_3(aq) + NaCl(aq) + 3H_2O(l) + CO_2(g)$$

Some Common Commercial Antacid Preparations

Commercial Name	Active Ingredients
Alka-2	Calcium carbonate
Alka-Seltzer	Aspirin, sodium bicarbonate, citric acid
Bufferin	Aspirin, magnesium carbonate, aluminum glycinate
Buffered aspirin	Aspirin, magnesium carbonate, aluminum hydroxide-glycine
Milk of magnesia	Magnesium hydroxide
Rolaids	Dihydroxy aluminum sodium carbonate
Tums	Calcium carbonate

The CO_2 released by most of these reactions increases gas pressure in the stomach, causing the person to belch. The fizzing that takes place when an Alka-Seltzer tablet dissolves in water is caused by carbon dioxide, which is released by the reaction between citric acid and sodium bicarbonate:

$$C_4H_7O_5(COOH)(aq) + NaHCO_3(aq) \longrightarrow$$
citric acid
$$C_4H_7O_5COONa(aq) + H_2O(l) + CO_2(g)$$
sodium citrate

This action helps to disperse the ingredients and even enhances the taste of the solution.

The mucosa of the stomach is also damaged by the action of aspirin, the chemical name of which is acetylsalicylic acid. Aspirin is itself a moderately weak acid:

acetylsalicylic acid   acetylsalicylate ion

In the presence of the high concentration of H^+ ions in the stomach, this acid remains largely nonionized. A relatively non-polar molecule, acetylsalicylic acid has the ability to penetrate membrane barriers that are also made up of nonpolar molecules. However, inside the membrane are many small water pockets, and when an acetylsalicylic acid molecule enters such a pocket, it ionizes into H^+ and acetylsalicylate ions. These ionic species become trapped in the interior regions of the membrane. The continued buildup of ions in this fashion weakens the structure of the membrane and eventually causes bleeding. Approximately 2 mL of blood are usually lost for every aspirin tablet taken, an amount not generally considered harmful. However, the action of aspirin can result in severe bleeding in some individuals. It is interesting to note that the presence of alcohol makes acetylsalicylic acid even more soluble in the membrane, and so further promotes the bleeding.

On the other hand, the lone pairs on the oxygen atom in $C_2H_5OC_2H_5$ make the compound a Lewis base:

(Continued)

685

Similar problem: 15.92.

(b) Here the Hg^{2+} ion accepts four pairs of electrons from the CN^- ions. Therefore, Hg^{2+} is the Lewis acid and CN^- is the Lewis base.

Practice Exercise Identify the Lewis acid and Lewis base in the reaction

$$Co^{3+}(aq) + 6NH_3(aq) \rightleftharpoons Co(NH_3)_6^{3+}(aq)$$

Summary of Facts and Concepts

1. Brønsted acids donate protons, and Brønsted bases accept protons. These are the definitions that normally underlie the use of the terms "acid" and "base."

2. The acidity of an aqueous solution is expressed as its pH, which is defined as the negative logarithm of the hydrogen ion concentration (in mol/L).

3. At 25°C, an acidic solution has pH < 7, a basic solution has pH > 7, and a neutral solution has pH = 7.

4. In aqueous solution, the following are classified as strong acids: $HClO_4$, HI, HBr, HCl, H_2SO_4 (first stage of ionization), and HNO_3. Strong bases in aqueous solution include hydroxides of alkali metals and of alkaline earth metals (except beryllium).

5. The acid ionization constant K_a increases with acid strength. K_b similarly expresses the strengths of bases.

6. Percent ionization is another measure of the strength of acids. The more dilute a solution of a weak acid, the greater the percent ionization of the acid.

7. The product of the ionization constant of an acid and the ionization constant of its conjugate base is equal to the ion-product constant of water.

8. The relative strengths of acids can be explained qualitatively in terms of their molecular structures.

9. Most salts are strong electrolytes that dissociate completely into ions in solution. The reaction of these ions with water, called salt hydrolysis, can produce acidic or basic solutions. In salt hydrolysis, the conjugate bases of weak acids yield basic solutions, and the conjugate acids of weak bases yield acidic solutions.

10. Small, highly charged metal ions, such as Al^{3+} and Fe^{3+}, hydrolyze to yield acidic solutions.

11. Most oxides can be classified as acidic, basic, or amphoteric. Metal hydroxides are either basic or amphoteric.

12. Lewis acids accept pairs of electrons and Lewis bases donate pairs of electrons. The term "Lewis acid" is generally reserved for substances that can accept electron pairs but do not contain ionizable hydrogen atoms.

Key Words

Acid ionization constant (K_a), p. 656	Conjugate acid-base pair, p. 646	Lewis base, p. 682	Strong acid, p. 652
Base ionization constant (K_b), p. 663	Ion-product constant, p. 648	Percent ionization, p. 662	Strong base, p. 652
	Lewis acid, p. 682	pH, p. 649	Weak acid, p. 652
		Salt hydrolysis, p. 674	Weak base, p. 653

Questions and Problems[†]

Brønsted Acids and Bases

Review Questions

15.1 Define Brønsted acids and bases. Give an example of a conjugate pair in an acid-base reaction.

15.2 In order for a species to act as a Brønsted base, an atom in the species must possess a lone pair of electrons. Explain why this is so.

Problems

15.3 Classify each of the following species as a Brønsted acid or base, or both: (a) H_2O, (b) OH^-, (c) H_3O^+, (d) NH_3, (e) NH_4^+, (f) NH_2^-, (g) NO_3^-, (h) CO_3^{2-}, (i) HBr, (j) HCN.

15.4 Write the formulas of the conjugate bases of the following acids: (a) HNO_2, (b) H_2SO_4, (c) H_2S, (d) HCN, (e) $HCOOH$ (formic acid).

[†]Unless otherwise stated, the temperature is assumed to be 25°C.

15.5 Identify the acid-base conjugate pairs in each of the following reactions:

(a) $CH_3COO^- + HCN \rightleftharpoons CH_3COOH + CN^-$
(b) $HCO_3^- + HCO_3^- \rightleftharpoons H_2CO_3 + CO_3^{2-}$
(c) $H_2PO_4^- + NH_3 \rightleftharpoons HPO_4^{2-} + NH_4^+$
(d) $HClO + CH_3NH_2 \rightleftharpoons CH_3NH_3^+ + ClO^-$
(e) $CO_3^{2-} + H_2O \rightleftharpoons HCO_3^- + OH^-$

15.6 Write the formula for the conjugate acid of each of the following bases: (a) HS^-, (b) HCO_3^-, (c) CO_3^{2-}, (d) $H_2PO_4^-$, (e) HPO_4^{2-}, (f) PO_4^{3-}, (g) HSO_4^-, (h) SO_4^{2-}, (i) SO_3^{2-}.

15.7 Oxalic acid ($C_2H_2O_4$) has the following structure:

$$O{=}C{-}OH$$
$$|$$
$$O{=}C{-}OH$$

An oxalic acid solution contains the following species in varying concentrations: $C_2H_2O_4$, $C_2HO_4^-$, $C_2O_4^{2-}$, and H^+. (a) Draw Lewis structures of $C_2HO_4^-$ and $C_2O_4^{2-}$. (b) Which of the above four species can act only as acids, which can act only as bases, and which can act as both acids and bases?

15.8 Write the formula for the conjugate base of each of the following acids: (a) $CH_2ClCOOH$, (b) HIO_4, (c) H_3PO_4, (d) $H_2PO_4^-$, (e) HPO_4^{2-}, (f) H_2SO_4, (g) HSO_4^-, (h) HIO_3, (i) HSO_3^-, (j) NH_4^+, (k) H_2S, (l) HS^-, (m) $HClO$.

The Acid-Base Properties of Water
Review Questions

15.9 What is the ion-product constant for water?

15.10 Write an equation relating $[H^+]$ and $[OH^-]$ in solution at 25°C.

15.11 The ion-product constant for water is 1.0×10^{-14} at 25°C and 3.8×10^{-14} at 40°C. Is the forward process

$$H_2O(l) \rightleftharpoons H^+(aq) + OH^-(aq)$$

endothermic or exothermic?

pH—A Measure of Acidity
Review Questions

15.12 Define pH. Why do chemists normally choose to discuss the acidity of a solution in terms of pH rather than hydrogen ion concentration, $[H^+]$?

15.13 The pH of a solution is 6.7. From this statement alone, can you conclude that the solution is acidic? If not, what additional information would you need? Can the pH of a solution be zero or negative? If so, give examples to illustrate these values.

15.14 Define pOH. Write the equation relating pH and pOH.

Problems

15.15 Calculate the concentration of OH^- ions in a 1.4×10^{-3} *M* HCl solution.

15.16 Calculate the concentration of H^+ ions in a 0.62 *M* NaOH solution.

15.17 Calculate the pH of each of the following solutions: (a) 0.0010 *M* HCl, (b) 0.76 *M* KOH.

15.18 Calculate the pH of each of the following solutions: (a) 2.8×10^{-4} *M* $Ba(OH)_2$, (b) 5.2×10^{-4} *M* HNO_3.

15.19 Calculate the hydrogen ion concentration in mol/L for solutions with the following pH values: (a) 2.42, (b) 11.21, (c) 6.96, (d) 15.00.

15.20 Calculate the hydrogen ion concentration in mol/L for each of the following solutions: (a) a solution whose pH is 5.20, (b) a solution whose pH is 16.00, (c) a solution whose hydroxide concentration is 3.7×10^{-9} *M*.

15.21 Complete the following table for a solution:

pH	$[H^+]$	Solution is
<7		
	$<1.0 \times 10^{-7}$ *M*	
		Neutral

15.22 Fill in the word *acidic, basic,* or *neutral* for the following solutions:

(a) pOH > 7; solution is
(b) pOH = 7; solution is
(c) pOH < 7; solution is

15.23 The pOH of a solution is 9.40. Calculate the hydrogen ion concentration of the solution.

15.24 Calculate the number of moles of KOH in 5.50 mL of a 0.360 *M* KOH solution. What is the pOH of the solution?

15.25 How much NaOH (in grams) is needed to prepare 546 mL of solution with a pH of 10.00?

15.26 A solution is made by dissolving 18.4 g of HCl in 662 mL of water. Calculate the pH of the solution. (Assume that the volume remains constant.)

Strength of Acids and Bases
Review Questions

15.27 Explain what is meant by the strength of an acid.

15.28 Without referring to the text, write the formulas of four strong acids and four weak acids.

15.29 What are the strongest acid and strongest base that can exist in water?

15.30 H_2SO_4 is a strong acid, but HSO_4^- is a weak acid. Account for the difference in strength of these two related species.

Problems

15.31 Which of the following diagrams best represents a strong acid, such as HCl, dissolved in water? Which represents a weak acid? Which represents a very weak acid? (The hydrated proton is shown as a hydronium ion. Water molecules are omitted for clarity.)

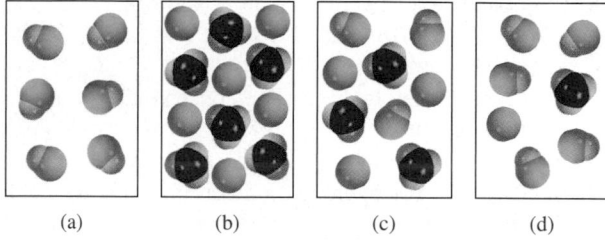

| (a) | (b) | (c) | (d) |

15.32 (1) Which of the following diagrams represents a solution of a weak diprotic acid? (2) Which diagrams represent chemically implausible situations? (The hydrated proton is shown as a hydronium ion. Water molecules are omitted for clarity.)

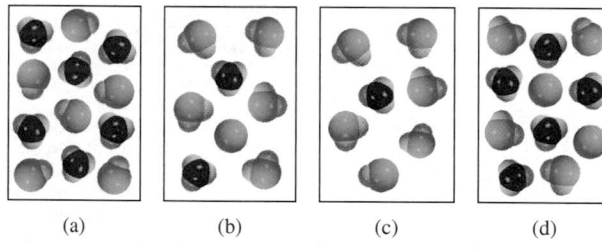

| (a) | (b) | (c) | (d) |

15.33 Classify each of the following species as a weak or strong acid: (a) HNO_3, (b) HF, (c) H_2SO_4, (d) HSO_4^-, (e) H_2CO_3, (f) HCO_3^-, (g) HCl, (h) HCN, (i) HNO_2.

15.34 Classify each of the following species as a weak or strong base: (a) LiOH, (b) CN^-, (c) H_2O, (d) ClO_4^-, (e) NH_2^-.

15.35 Which of the following statements is/are true for a 0.10 M solution of a weak acid HA?

(a) The pH is 1.00.
(b) $[H^+] \gg [A^-]$
(c) $[H^+] = [A^-]$
(d) The pH is less than 1.

15.36 Which of the following statements is/are true regarding a 1.0 M solution of a strong acid HA?

(a) $[A^-] > [H^+]$
(b) The pH is 0.00.
(c) $[H^+] = 1.0\ M$
(d) $[HA] = 1.0\ M$

15.37 Predict the direction that predominates in this reaction:

$$F^-(aq) + H_2O(l) \rightleftharpoons HF(aq) + OH^-(aq)$$

15.38 Predict whether the following reaction will proceed from left to right to any measurable extent:

$$CH_3COOH(aq) + Cl^-(aq) \longrightarrow$$

Weak Acids and Acid Ionization Constants
Review Questions

15.39 What does the ionization constant tell us about the strength of an acid?

15.40 List the factors on which the K_a of a weak acid depends.

15.41 Why do we normally not quote K_a values for strong acids such as HCl and HNO_3? Why is it necessary to specify temperature when giving K_a values?

15.42 Which of the following solutions has the highest pH? (a) 0.40 M HCOOH, (b) 0.40 M $HClO_4$, (c) 0.40 M CH_3COOH.

Problems

15.43 The K_a for benzoic acid is 6.5×10^{-5}. Calculate the pH of a 0.10 M benzoic acid solution.

15.44 A 0.0560-g quantity of acetic acid is dissolved in enough water to make 50.0 mL of solution. Calculate the concentrations of H^+, CH_3COO^-, and CH_3COOH at equilibrium. (K_a for acetic acid = 1.8×10^{-5}.)

15.45 The pH of an acid solution is 6.20. Calculate the K_a for the acid. The initial acid concentration is 0.010 M.

15.46 What is the original molarity of a solution of formic acid (HCOOH) whose pH is 3.26 at equilibrium?

15.47 Calculate the percent ionization of benzoic acid having the following concentrations: (a) 0.20 M, (b) 0.00020 M.

15.48 Calculate the percent ionization of hydrofluoric acid at the following concentrations: (a) 0.60 M, (b) 0.0046 M, (c) 0.00028 M. Comment on the trends.

15.49 A 0.040 M solution of a monoprotic acid is 14 percent ionized. Calculate the ionization constant of the acid.

15.50 (a) Calculate the percent ionization of a 0.20 M solution of the monoprotic acetylsalicylic acid (aspirin) for which $K_a = 3.0 \times 10^{-4}$. (b) The pH of gastric juice in the stomach of a certain individual is 1.00. After a few aspirin tablets have been swallowed, the concentration of acetylsalicylic acid in the stomach is 0.20 M. Calculate the percent ionization of the acid under these conditions. What effect does the nonionized acid have on the membranes lining the stomach? (*Hint:* See the Chemistry in Action essay on p. 684.)

Weak Bases and Base Ionization Constants
Review Questions

15.51 Use NH_3 to illustrate what we mean by the strength of a base.

15.52 Which of the following has a higher pH? (a) 0.20 M NH_3, (b) 0.20 M NaOH

Problems

15.53 Calculate the pH for each of the following solutions: (a) 0.10 M NH_3, (b) 0.050 M C_5H_5N (pyridine).

15.54 The pH of a 0.30 M solution of a weak base is 10.66. What is the K_b of the base?

15.55 What is the original molarity of a solution of ammonia whose pH is 11.22?

15.56 In a 0.080 M NH_3 solution, what percent of the NH_3 is present as NH_4^+?

The Relationship Between the Ionization Constants of Acids and Their Conjugate Bases
Review Questions

15.57 Write the equation relating K_a for a weak acid and K_b for its conjugate base. Use NH_3 and its conjugate acid NH_4^+ to derive the relationship between K_a and K_b.

15.58 From the relationship $K_aK_b = K_w$, what can you deduce about the relative strengths of a weak acid and its conjugate base?

Diprotic and Polyprotic Acids
Review Questions

15.59 Carbonic acid is a diprotic acid. Explain what that means.

15.60 Write all the species (except water) that are present in a phosphoric acid solution. Indicate which species can act as a Brønsted acid, which as a Brønsted base, and which as both a Brønsted acid and a Brønsted base.

Problems

15.61 The first and second ionization constants of a diprotic acid H_2A are K_{a_1} and K_{a_2} at a certain temperature. Under what conditions will $[A^{2-}] = K_{a_2}$?

15.62 Compare the pH of a 0.040 M HCl solution with that of a 0.040 M H_2SO_4 solution.

15.63 What are the concentrations of HSO_4^-, SO_4^{2-}, and H^+ in a 0.20 M $KHSO_4$ solution? (*Hint:* H_2SO_4 is a strong acid; K_a for $HSO_4^- = 1.3 \times 10^{-2}$.)

15.64 Calculate the concentrations of H^+, HCO_3^-, and CO_3^{2-} in a 0.025 M H_2CO_3 solution.

Molecular Structure and the Strength of Acids
Review Questions

15.65 List four factors that affect the strength of an acid.

15.66 How does the strength of an oxoacid depend on the electronegativity and oxidation number of the central atom?

Problems

15.67 Predict the acid strengths of the following compounds: H_2O, H_2S, and H_2Se.

15.68 Compare the strengths of the following pairs of acids: (a) H_2SO_4 and H_2SeO_4, (b) H_3PO_4 and H_3AsO_4.

15.69 Which of the following is the stronger acid: $CH_2ClCOOH$ or $CHCl_2COOH$? Explain your choice.

15.70 Consider the following compounds:

phenol   methanol

Experimentally, phenol is found to be a stronger acid than methanol. Explain this difference in terms of the structures of the conjugate bases. (*Hint:* A more stable conjugate base favors ionization. Only one of the conjugate bases can be stabilized by resonance.)

Acid-Base Properties of Salts
Review Questions

15.71 Define salt hydrolysis. Categorize salts according to how they affect the pH of a solution.

15.72 Explain why small, highly charged metal ions are able to undergo hydrolysis.

15.73 Al^{3+} is not a Brønsted acid but $Al(H_2O)_6^{3+}$ is. Explain.

15.74 Specify which of the following salts will undergo hydrolysis: KF, $NaNO_3$, NH_4NO_2, $MgSO_4$, KCN, C_6H_5COONa, RbI, Na_2CO_3, $CaCl_2$, HCOOK.

Problems

15.75 Predict the pH (> 7, < 7, or ≈ 7) of aqueous solutions containing the following salts. (a) KBr, (b) $Al(NO_3)_3$, (c) $BaCl_2$, (d) $Bi(NO_3)_3$.

15.76 Predict whether the following solutions are acidic, basic, or nearly neutral: (a) NaBr, (b) K_2SO_3, (c) NH_4NO_2, (d) $Cr(NO_3)_3$.

15.77 A certain salt, MX (containing the M^+ and X^- ions), is dissolved in water, and the pH of the resulting solution is 7.0. Can you say anything about the strengths of the acid and the base from which the salt is derived?

15.78 In a certain experiment a student finds that the pHs of 0.10 M solutions of three potassium salts KX, KY, and KZ are 7.0, 9.0, and 11.0, respectively. Arrange the acids HX, HY, and HZ in the order of increasing acid strength.

15.79 Calculate the pH of a 0.36 M CH_3COONa solution.

15.80 Calculate the pH of a 0.42 M NH_4Cl solution.

15.81 Predict the pH (> 7, < 7, ≈ 7) of a $NaHCO_3$ solution.

15.82 Predict whether a solution containing the salt K_2HPO_4 will be acidic, neutral, or basic.

Acidic and Basic Oxides and Hydroxides

Review Questions

15.83 Classify the following oxides as acidic, basic, amphoteric, or neutral: (a) CO_2, (b) K_2O, (c) CaO, (d) N_2O_5, (e) CO, (f) NO, (g) SnO_2, (h) SO_3, (i) Al_2O_3, (j) BaO.

15.84 Write equations for the reactions between (a) CO_2 and NaOH(aq), (b) Na_2O and HNO_3(aq).

Problems

15.85 Explain why metal oxides tend to be basic if the oxidation number of the metal is low and acidic if the oxidation number of the metal is high. (*Hint:* Metallic compounds in which the oxidation numbers of the metals are low are more ionic than those in which the oxidation numbers of the metals are high.)

15.86 Arrange the oxides in each of the following groups in order of increasing basicity: (a) K_2O, Al_2O_3, BaO, (b) CrO_3, CrO, Cr_2O_3.

15.87 $Zn(OH)_2$ is an amphoteric hydroxide. Write balanced ionic equations to show its reaction with (a) HCl, (b) NaOH [the product is $Zn(OH)_4^{2-}$].

15.88 $Al(OH)_3$ is an insoluble compound. It dissolves in excess NaOH in solution. Write a balanced ionic equation for this reaction. What type of reaction is this?

Lewis Acids and Bases

Review Questions

15.89 What are the Lewis definitions of an acid and a base? In what way are they more general than the Brønsted definitions?

15.90 In terms of orbitals and electron arrangements, what must be present for a molecule or an ion to act as a Lewis acid (use H^+ and BF_3 as examples)? What must be present for a molecule or ion to act as a Lewis base (use OH^- and NH_3 as examples)?

Problems

15.91 Classify each of the following species as a Lewis acid or a Lewis base: (a) CO_2, (b) H_2O, (c) I^-, (d) SO_2, (e) NH_3, (f) OH^-, (g) H^+, (h) BCl_3.

15.92 Describe the following reaction in terms of the Lewis theory of acids and bases:

$$AlCl_3(s) + Cl^-(aq) \longrightarrow AlCl_4^-(aq)$$

15.93 Which would be considered a stronger Lewis acid: (a) BF_3 or BCl_3, (b) Fe^{2+} or Fe^{3+}? Explain.

15.94 All Brønsted acids are Lewis acids, but the reverse is not true. Give two examples of Lewis acids that are not Brønsted acids.

Additional Problems

15.95 The K_a of formic acid is 1.7×10^{-4} at 25°C. Will the acid become stronger or weaker at 40°C? Explain.

15.96 A typical reaction between an antacid and the hydrochloric acid in gastric juice is

$$NaHCO_3(s) + HCl(aq) \rightleftharpoons$$
$$NaCl(aq) + H_2O(l) + CO_2(g)$$

Calculate the volume (in L) of CO_2 generated from 0.350 g of $NaHCO_3$ and excess gastric juice at 1.00 atm and 37.0°C.

15.97 To which of the following would the addition of an equal volume of 0.60 M NaOH lead to a solution having a lower pH? (a) water, (b) 0.30 M HCl, (c) 0.70 M KOH, (d) 0.40 M $NaNO_3$.

15.98 The pH of a 0.0642 M solution of a monoprotic acid is 3.86. Is this a strong acid?

15.99 Like water, liquid ammonia undergoes autoionization:

$$NH_3 + NH_3 \rightleftharpoons NH_4^+ + NH_2^-$$

(a) Identify the Brønsted acids and Brønsted bases in this reaction. (b) What species correspond to H^+ and OH^- and what is the condition for a neutral solution?

15.100 HA and HB are both weak acids although HB is the stronger of the two. Will it take a larger volume of a 0.10 M NaOH solution to neutralize 50.0 mL of 0.10 M HB than would be needed to neutralize 50.0 mL of 0.10 M HA?

15.101 A solution contains a weak monoprotic acid HA and its sodium salt NaA both at 0.1 M concentration. Show that $[OH^-] = K_w/K_a$.

15.102 The three common chromium oxides are CrO, Cr_2O_3, and CrO_3. If Cr_2O_3 is amphoteric, what can you say about the acid-base properties of CrO and CrO_3?

15.103 Use the data in Table 15.3 to calculate the equilibrium constant for the following reaction:

$$HCOOH(aq) + OH^-(aq) \rightleftharpoons$$
$$HCOO^-(aq) + H_2O(l)$$

15.104 Use the data in Table 15.3 to calculate the equilibrium constant for the following reaction:

$$CH_3COOH(aq) + NO_2^-(aq) \rightleftharpoons$$
$$CH_3COO^-(aq) + HNO_2(aq)$$

15.105 Most of the hydrides of Group 1A and Group 2A metals are ionic (the exceptions are BeH_2 and MgH_2, which are covalent compounds). (a) Describe the reaction between the hydride ion (H^-) and water in terms of a Brønsted acid-base reaction. (b) The same reaction can also be classified as a redox reaction. Identify the oxidizing and reducing agents.

15.106 Calculate the pH of a 0.20 M ammonium acetate (CH_3COONH_4) solution.

15.107 Novocaine, used as a local anesthetic by dentists, is a weak base ($K_b = 8.91 \times 10^{-6}$). What is the ratio of the concentration of the base to that of its acid in the blood plasma (pH = 7.40) of a patient?

15.108 Which of the following is the stronger base: NF_3 or NH_3? (*Hint:* F is more electronegative than H.)

15.109 Which of the following is a stronger base: NH_3 or PH_3? (*Hint:* The N—H bond is stronger than the P—H bond.)

15.110 The ion product of D_2O is 1.35×10^{-15} at 25°C. (a) Calculate pD where pD = $-\log [D^+]$. (b) For what values of pD will a solution be acidic in D_2O? (c) Derive a relation between pD and pOD.

15.111 Give an example of (a) a weak acid that contains oxygen atoms, (b) a weak acid that does not contain oxygen atoms, (c) a neutral molecule that acts as a Lewis acid, (d) a neutral molecule that acts as a Lewis base, (e) a weak acid that contains two ionizable H atoms, (f) a conjugate acid-base pair, both of which react with HCl to give carbon dioxide gas.

15.112 What is the pH of 250.0 mL of an aqueous solution containing 0.616 g of the strong acid trifluoromethane sulfonic acid (CF_3SO_3H)?

15.113 (a) Use VSEPR to predict the geometry of the hydronium ion, H_3O^+. (b) The O atom in H_2O has two lone pairs and in principle can accept two H^+ ions. Explain why the species H_4O^{2+} does not exist. What would be its geometry if it did exist?

15.114 HF is a weak acid, but its strength increases with concentration. Explain. (*Hint:* F^- reacts with HF to form HF_2^-. The equilibrium constant for this reaction is 5.2 at 25°C.)

15.115 When chlorine reacts with water, the resulting solution is weakly acidic and reacts with $AgNO_3$ to give a white precipitate. Write balanced equations to represent these reactions. Explain why manufacturers of household bleaches add bases such as NaOH to their products to increase their effectiveness.

15.116 When the concentration of a strong acid is not substantially higher than $1.0 \times 10^{-7} M$, the ionization of water must be taken into account in the calculation of the solution's pH. (a) Derive an expression for the pH of a strong acid solution, including the contribution to $[H^+]$ from H_2O. (b) Calculate the pH of a $1.0 \times 10^{-7} M$ HCl solution.

15.117 Calculate the pH of a 2.00 M NH_4CN solution.

15.118 Calculate the concentrations of all species in a 0.100 M H_3PO_4 solution.

15.119 In the vapor phase, acetic acid molecules associate to a certain extent to form dimers:

$$2CH_3COOH(g) \rightleftharpoons (CH_3COOH)_2(g)$$

At 51°C the pressure of a certain acetic acid vapor system is 0.0342 atm in a 360-mL flask. The vapor is condensed and neutralized with 13.8 mL of 0.0568 M NaOH. (a) Calculate the degree of dissociation (α) of the dimer under these conditions:

$$(CH_3COOH)_2 \rightleftharpoons 2CH_3COOH$$

(*Hint:* See Problem 14.109 for general procedure.) (b) Calculate the equilibrium constant K_P for the reaction in (a).

15.120 Calculate the concentrations of all the species in a 0.100 M Na_2CO_3 solution.

15.121 Henry's law constant for CO_2 at 38°C is 2.28×10^{-3} mol/L·atm. Calculate the pH of a solution of CO_2 at 38°C in equilibrium with the gas at a partial pressure of 3.20 atm.

15.122 Hydrocyanic acid (HCN) is a weak acid and a deadly poisonous compound—in the gaseous form (hydrogen cyanide) it is used in gas chambers. Why is it dangerous to treat sodium cyanide with acids (such as HCl) without proper ventilation?

15.123 How many grams of NaCN would you need to dissolve in enough water to make exactly 250 mL of solution with a pH of 10.00?

15.124 A solution of formic acid (HCOOH) has a pH of 2.53. How many grams of formic acid are there in 100.0 mL of the solution?

15.125 Calculate the pH of a 1-L solution containing 0.150 mole of CH_3COOH and 0.100 mole of HCl.

15.126 A 1.87-g sample of Mg reacts with 80.0 mL of a HCl solution whose pH is -0.544. What is the pH of the solution after all the Mg has reacted? Assume constant volume.

15.127 You are given two beakers, one containing an aqueous solution of strong acid (HA) and the other an aqueous solution of weak acid (HB) of the same concentration. Describe how you would compare the strengths of these two acids by (a) measuring the pH, (b) measuring electrical conductance, (c) studying the rate of hydrogen gas evolution when these solutions are reacted with an active metal such as Mg or Zn.

15.128 Use Le Châtelier's principle to predict the effect of the following changes on the extent of hydrolysis of sodium nitrite ($NaNO_2$) solution: (a) HCl is added, (b) NaOH is added, (c) NaCl is added, (d) the solution is diluted.

15.129 Describe the hydration of SO_2 as a Lewis acid-base reaction. (*Hint:* Refer to the discussion of the hydration of CO_2 on p. 683.)

15.130 The disagreeable odor of fish is mainly due to organic compounds (RNH_2) containing an amino group, —NH_2, where R is the rest of the molecule. Amines are bases just like ammonia. Explain why putting some lemon juice on fish can greatly reduce the odor.

15.131 A solution of methylamine (CH_3NH_2) has a pH of 10.64. How many grams of methylamine are there in 100.0 mL of the solution?

15.132 A 0.400 M formic acid (HCOOH) solution freezes at $-0.758°C$. Calculate the K_a of the acid at that temperature. (*Hint:* Assume that molarity is equal to molality. Carry your calculations to three significant figures and round off to two for K_a.)

15.133 Both the amide ion (NH_2^-) and the nitride ion (N^{3-}) are stronger bases than the hydroxide ion and hence do not exist in aqueous solutions. (a) Write equations showing the reactions of these ions with water, and identify the Brønsted acid and base in each case. (b) Which of the two is the stronger base?

15.134 The atmospheric sulfur dioxide (SO_2) concentration over a certain region is 0.12 ppm by volume. Calculate the pH of the rainwater due to this pollutant. Assume that the dissolution of SO_2 does not affect its pressure.

15.135 Calcium hypochlorite [$Ca(OCl)_2$] is used as a disinfectant for swimming pools. When dissolved in water it produces hypochlorous acid

$$Ca(OCl)_2(s) + 2H_2O(l) \rightleftharpoons$$
$$2HClO(aq) + Ca(OH)_2(s)$$

which ionizes as follows:

$$HClO(aq) \rightleftharpoons H^+(aq) + ClO^-(aq)$$
$$K_a = 3.0 \times 10^{-8}$$

As strong oxidizing agents, both HClO and ClO^- can kill bacteria by destroying their cellular components. However, too high a HClO concentration is irritating to the eyes of swimmers and too high a concentration of ClO^- will cause the ions to decompose in sunlight. The recommended pH for pool water is 7.8. Calculate the percent of these species present at this pH.

15.136 Explain the action of smelling salt, which is ammonium carbonate [$(NH_4)_2CO_3$]. (*Hint:* The thin film of aqueous solution that lines the nasal passage is slightly basic.)

15.137 About half of the hydrochloric acid produced annually in the United States (3.0 billion pounds) is used in metal pickling. This process involves the removal of metal oxide layers from metal surfaces to prepare them for coating. (a) Write the overall and net ionic equations for the reaction between iron(III) oxide, which represents the rust layer over iron, and HCl. Identify the Brønsted acid and base. (b) Hydrochloric acid is also used to remove scale (which is mostly $CaCO_3$) from water pipes (see p. 126). Hydrochloric acid reacts with calcium carbonate in two stages; the first stage forms the bicarbonate ion, which then reacts further to form carbon dioxide. Write equations for these two stages and for the overall reaction. (c) Hydrochloric acid is used to recover oil from the ground. It dissolves rocks (often $CaCO_3$) so that the oil can flow more easily. In one process, a 15 percent (by mass) HCl solution is injected into an oil well to dissolve the rocks. If the density of the acid solution is 1.073 g/mL, what is the pH of the solution?

15.138 Which of the following does not represent a Lewis acid-base reaction?

(a) $H_2O + H^+ \longrightarrow H_3O^+$
(b) $NH_3 + BF_3 \longrightarrow H_3NBF_3$
(c) $PF_3 + F_2 \longrightarrow PF_5$
(d) $Al(OH)_3 + OH^- \longrightarrow Al(OH)_4^-$

15.139 True or false? If false, explain why the statement is wrong. (a) All Lewis acids are Brønsted acids, (b) the conjugate base of an acid always carries a negative charge, (c) the percent ionization of a base increases with its concentration in solution, (d) a solution of barium fluoride is acidic.

15.140 How many milliliters of a strong monoprotic acid solution at pH = 4.12 must be added to 528 mL of the same acid solution at pH = 5.76 to change its pH to 5.34? Assume that the volumes are additive.

Special Problems

15.141 Hemoglobin (Hb) is a blood protein that is responsible for transporting oxygen. It can exist in the protonated form as HbH^+. The binding of oxygen can be represented by the simplified equation

$$HbH^+ + O_2 \rightleftharpoons HbO_2 + H^+$$

(a) What form of hemoglobin is favored in the lungs where oxygen concentration is highest? (b) In body tissues, where the cells release carbon dioxide produced by metabolism, the blood is more acidic due to the formation of carbonic acid. What form of hemoglobin is favored under this condition? (c) When a person hyperventilates, the concentration of CO_2 in his or her blood decreases. How does this action affect the above equilibrium? Frequently a person who is hyperventilating is advised to breathe into a paper bag. Why does this action help the individual?

15.142 A 1.294-g sample of a metal carbonate (MCO_3) is reacted with 500 mL of a 0.100 M HCl solution. The excess HCl acid is then neutralized by 32.80 mL of 0.588 M NaOH. Identify M.

15.143 Prove the statement that when the concentration of a weak acid HA decreases by a factor of 10, its percent ionization increases by a factor of $\sqrt{10}$. State any assumptions.

15.144 Calculate the pH of a solution that is 1.00 M HCN and 1.00 M HF. Compare the concentration (in molarity) of the CN^- ion in this solution with that in a 1.00 M HCN solution. Comment on the difference.

15.145 Teeth enamel is largely hydroxyapatite [$Ca_3(PO_4)_3OH$]. When it dissolves in water (a process called *demineralization*), it dissociates as follows:

$$Ca_5(PO_4)_3OH \longrightarrow 5Ca^{2+} + 3PO_4^{3-} + OH^-$$

The reverse process, called *remineralization*, is the body's natural defense against tooth decay. Acids produced from food remove the OH^- ions and thereby weaken the enamel layer. Most toothpastes contain a flouride compound such as NaF or SnF_2. What is the function of these compounds in preventing tooth decay?

15.146 Use the van't Hoff equation (see Problem 14.111) and the data in Appendix 3 to calculate the pH of water at its normal boiling point.

Answers to Practice Exercises

15.1 (1) H_2O (acid) and OH^- (base); (2) HCN (acid) and CN^- (base). **15.2** 7.7×10^{-15} M. **15.3** 0.12. **15.4** 4.7×10^{-4} M. **15.5** 7.40. **15.6** 12.56. **15.7** Smaller than 1. **15.8** 2.09. **15.9** 2.2×10^{-6}. **15.10** 12.03. **15.11** $[C_2H_2O_4] = 0.11$ M, $[C_2HO_4^-] = 0.086$ M, $[C_2O_4^{2-}] = 6.1 \times 10^{-5}$ M, $[H^+] = 0.086$ M. **15.12** $HClO_2$. **15.13** 8.58. **15.14** (a) pH $\approx$ 7, (b) pH $>$ 7, (c) pH $<$ 7, (d) pH $>$ 7. **15.15** Lewis acid: Co^{3+}; Lewis base: NH_3.

C H E M I C A L
Mystery

Decaying Papers

Librarians are worried about their books. Many of the old books in their collections are crumbling. The situation is so bad, in fact, that about one-third of the books in the U.S. Library of Congress cannot be circulated because the pages are too brittle. Why are the books deteriorating?

Until the latter part of the eighteenth century, practically all paper produced in the western hemisphere was made from rags of linen or cotton, which is mostly cellulose. Cellulose is a polymer comprised of glucose ($C_6H_{12}O_6$) units joined together in a specific fashion:

Glucose

A portion of cellulose

As the demand for paper grew, wood pulp was substituted for rags as a source of cellulose. Wood pulp also contains lignin, an organic polymer that imparts rigidity to the paper, but lignin oxidizes easily, causing the paper to discolor. Paper made from wood pulp that has not been treated to remove the lignin is used for books and newspapers for which a long life is not an important consideration.

Another problem with paper made from wood pulp is that it is porous. Tiny holes in the surface of the paper soak up ink from a printing press, spreading it over a larger area than is intended. To prevent ink creep, a coating of aluminum sulfate [$Al_2(SO_4)_3$] and rosin is applied to some paper to seal the holes. This process, called sizing, results in a smooth surface. You can readily tell the difference between papers with and without sizing by feeling the surface of a newspaper and this page. (Or try to write on them with a felt-tip pen.) Aluminum sulfate was chosen for the treatment because it is colorless and cheap. Because paper without sizing does not crumble, aluminum sulfate must be responsible for the slow decay. But how?

Chemical Clues

1. When books containing "sized" paper are stored in a high-humidity environment, $Al_2(SO_4)_3$ absorbs moisture, which eventually leads to the production of H^+ ions. The H^+ ions catalyze the hydrolysis of cellulose by attaching to the shaded O atoms in cellulose. The long chain unit of glucose units breaks apart, resulting in the crumbling of the paper. Write equations for the production of H^+ ions from $Al_2(SO_4)_3$.

2. To prevent papers from decaying, the obvious solution is to treat them with a base. However, both NaOH (a strong base) and NH_3 (a weak base) are unsatisfactory choices. Suggest how you could use these substances to neutralize the acid in the paper and describe their drawbacks.

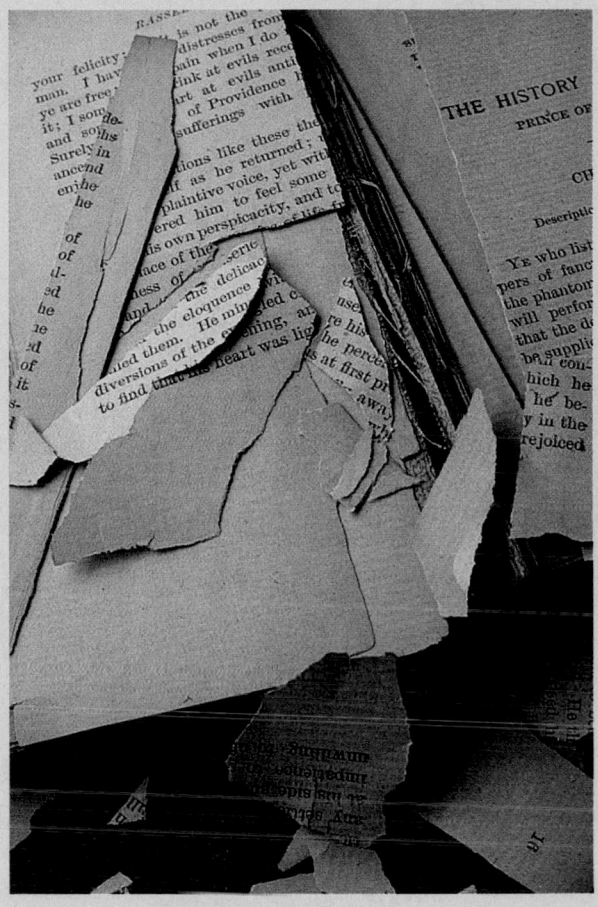
Acid-damaged paper.

3. After much testing, chemists developed a compound that stabilizes paper: diethylzinc [$Zn(C_2H_5)_2$]. Diethylzinc is volatile so it can be sprayed onto books. It reacts with water to form zinc oxide (ZnO) and gaseous ethane (C_2H_6). (a) Write an equation for this reaction. (b) ZnO is an amphoteric oxide. What is its reaction with H^+ ions?

4. One disadvantage of diethylzinc is that it is extremely flammable in air. Therefore, oxygen must not be present when this compound is applied. How would you remove oxygen from a room before spraying diethylzinc onto stacks of books in a library?

5. Nowadays papers are sized with titanium dioxide (TiO_2), which, like ZnO, is a nontoxic white compound that will prevent the hydrolysis of cellulose. What advantage does TiO_2 have over ZnO?

16

Downward-growing, icicle-like stalactites and upward growing, columnar stalagmites. It may take thousands of years for these structures, which are mostly calcium carbonate, to form. The models show calcium and carbonate ions and calcium carbonate.

Acid-Base Equilibria and Solubility Equilibria

A LOOK AHEAD

- We continue our study of acid-base properties and reactions from Chapter 15 by considering the effect of common ions on the extent of acid ionization and hence the pH of the solution. (16.2)

- We then extend our discussion to buffer solutions, whose pH remains largely unchanged upon the addition of small amounts of acids and bases. (16.3)

- We conclude our study of acid-base chemistry by examining acid-base titration in more detail. We learn to calculate the pH during any stage of titration involving strong and/or weak acids and bases. In addition, we see how acid-base indicators are used to determine the end point of a titration. (16.4 and 16.5)

- Next, we explore a type of heterogeneous equilibrium, which deals with the solubility of sparingly soluble substances. We learn to express the solubility of these substances in terms of solubility product. We see that different types of metal ions can be effectively separated by adding a suitable anion depending on their differing solubility products. (16.6 and 16.7)

- We then see how Le Châtelier's principle helps us explain the effects of common ions and pH on solubility. (16.8 and 16.9)

- We learn how complex-ion formation, which is a type of Lewis acid-base reaction, can enhance the solubility of an insoluble compound. (16.10)

- Finally, we apply the solubility product principle to qualitative analysis, which is the identification of ions in solution. (16.11)

Interactive Activity Summary

1. Animation: Buffer Solutions (16.3)

2. Animation: Acid-Base Titrations (16.4)

3. Interactivity: Neutralization Reactions I and II (16.4)

In this chapter we will continue the study of acid-base reactions with a discussion of buffer action and titrations. We will also look at another type of aqueous equilibrium—that between slightly soluble compounds and their ions in solution.

16.1 Homogeneous Versus Heterogeneous Solution Equilibria

In Chapter 15 we saw that weak acids and weak bases never ionize completely in water. Thus, at equilibrium a weak acid solution, for example, contains nonionized acid as well as H^+ ions and the conjugate base. Nevertheless, all of these species are dissolved so the system is an example of homogeneous equilibrium (see Chapter 14).

Another type of equilibrium, which we will consider in the second half of this chapter, involves the dissolution and precipitation of slightly soluble substances. These processes are examples of heterogeneous equilibria—that is, they pertain to reactions in which the components are in more than one phase.

16.2 The Common Ion Effect

Our discussion of acid-base ionization and salt hydrolysis in Chapter 15 was limited to solutions containing a single solute. In this section we will consider the acid-base properties of a solution with two dissolved solutes that contain the same ion (cation or anion), called the *common ion.*

The presence of a common ion suppresses the ionization of a weak acid or a weak base. If sodium acetate and acetic acid are dissolved in the same solution, for example, they both dissociate and ionize to produce CH_3COO^- ions:

$$CH_3COONa(s) \xrightarrow{H_2O} CH_3COO^-(aq) + Na^+(aq)$$
$$CH_3COOH(aq) \rightleftharpoons CH_3COO^-(aq) + H^+(aq)$$

CH_3COONa is a strong electrolyte, so it dissociates completely in solution, but CH_3COOH, a weak acid, ionizes only slightly. According to Le Châtelier's principle, the addition of CH_3COO^- ions from CH_3COONa to a solution of CH_3COOH will suppress the ionization of CH_3COOH (that is, shift the equilibrium from right to left), thereby decreasing the hydrogen ion concentration. Thus, a solution containing both CH_3COOH and CH_3COONa will be *less* acidic than a solution containing only CH_3COOH at the same concentration. The shift in equilibrium of the acetic acid ionization is caused by the acetate ions from the salt. CH_3COO^- is the common ion because it is supplied by both CH_3COOH and CH_3COONa.

The ***common ion effect*** is *the shift in equilibrium caused by the addition of a compound having an ion in common with the dissolved substance.* The common ion effect plays an important role in determining the pH of a solution and the solubility of a slightly soluble salt (to be discussed later in this chapter). Here we will study the common ion effect as it relates to the pH of a solution. Keep in mind that despite its distinctive name, the common ion effect is simply a special case of Le Châtelier's principle.

Let us consider the pH of a solution containing a weak acid, HA, and a soluble salt of the weak acid, such as NaA. We start by writing

$$HA(aq) + H_2O(l) \rightleftharpoons H_3O^+(aq) + A^-(aq)$$

or simply

$$HA(aq) \rightleftharpoons H^+(aq) + A^-(aq)$$

The ionization constant K_a is given by

$$K_a = \frac{[H^+][A^-]}{[HA]} \tag{16.1}$$

Rearranging Equation (16.1) gives

$$[H^+] = \frac{K_a[HA]}{[A^-]}$$

Taking the negative logarithm of both sides, we obtain

$$-\log[H^+] = -\log K_a - \log \frac{[HA]}{[A^-]}$$

or

$$-\log[H^+] = -\log K_a + \log \frac{[A^-]}{[HA]}$$

So

$$pH = pK_a + \log \frac{[A^-]}{[HA]} \tag{16.2}$$

where

$$pK_a = -\log K_a \tag{16.3}$$

pK_a is related to K_a as pH is related to [H$^+$]. Remember that the stronger the acid (that is, the larger the K_a), the smaller the pK_a.

Equation (16.2) is called the *Henderson-Hasselbalch equation.* A more general form of this expression is

$$pH = pK_a + \log \frac{[\text{conjugate base}]}{[\text{acid}]} \tag{16.4}$$

Keep in mind that pK_a is a constant, but the ratio of the two concentration terms in Equation (16.4) depends on a particular solution.

In our example, HA is the acid and A^- is the conjugate base. Thus, if we know K_a and the concentrations of the acid and the salt of the acid, we can calculate the pH of the solution.

It is important to remember that the Henderson-Hasselbalch equation is derived from the equilibrium constant expression. It is valid regardless of the source of the conjugate base (that is, whether it comes from the acid alone or is supplied by both the acid and its salt).

In problems that involve the common ion effect, we are usually given the starting concentrations of a weak acid HA and its salt, such as NaA. As long as the concentrations of these species are reasonably high ($\geq 0.1\ M$), we can neglect the ionization of the acid and the hydrolysis of the salt. This is a valid approximation because HA is a weak acid and the extent of the hydrolysis of the A^- ion is generally very small. Moreover, the presence of A^- (from NaA) further suppresses the ionization of HA and the presence of HA further suppresses the hydrolysis of A^-. Thus, we can use the *starting* concentrations as the equilibrium concentrations in Equation (16.1) or Equation (16.4).

In Example 16.1 we calculate the pH of a solution containing a common ion.

Example 16.1

(a) Calculate the pH of a 0.20 M CH_3COOH solution. (b) What is the pH of a solution containing both 0.20 M CH_3COOH and 0.30 M CH_3COONa? The K_a of CH_3COOH is 1.8×10^{-5}.

Strategy (a) We calculate $[H^+]$ and hence the pH of the solution by following the procedure in Example 15.8 (p. 660). (b) CH_3COOH is a weak acid ($CH_3COOH \rightleftharpoons CH_3COO^- + H^+$), and CH_3COONa is a soluble salt that is completely dissociated in solution ($CH_3COONa \longrightarrow Na^+ + CH_3COO^-$). The common ion here is the acetate ion, CH_3COO^-. At equilibrium, the major species in solution are CH_3COOH, CH_3COO^-, Na^+, H^+, and H_2O. The Na^+ ion has no acid or base properties and we ignore the ionization of water. Because K_a is an equilibrium constant, its value is the same whether we have just the acid or a mixture of the acid and its salt in solution. Therefore, we can calculate $[H^+]$ at equilibrium and hence pH if we know both $[CH_3COOH]$ and $[CH_3COO^-]$ at equilibrium.

Solution (a) In this case, the changes are

$$CH_3COOH(aq) \rightleftharpoons H^+(aq) + CH_3COO^-(aq)$$

Initial (M):	0.20	0	0
Change (M):	$-x$	$+x$	$+x$
Equilibrium (M):	$0.20 - x$	x	x

$$K_a = \frac{[H^+][CH_3COO^-]}{[CH_3COOH]}$$

$$1.8 \times 10^{-5} = \frac{x^2}{0.20 - x}$$

Assuming $0.20 - x \approx 0.20$, we obtain

$$1.8 \times 10^{-5} = \frac{x^2}{0.20 - x} \approx \frac{x^2}{0.20}$$

or

$$x = [H^+] = 1.9 \times 10^{-3} \, M$$

Thus,

$$pH = -\log (1.9 \times 10^{-3}) = 2.72$$

(b) Sodium acetate is a strong electrolyte, so it dissociates completely in solution:

$$CH_3COONa(aq) \longrightarrow Na^+(aq) + CH_3COO^-(aq)$$
$$0.30 \, M \qquad\qquad 0.30 \, M$$

The initial concentrations, changes, and final concentrations of the species involved in the equilibrium are

$$CH_3COOH(aq) \rightleftharpoons H^+(aq) + CH_3COO^-(aq)$$

Initial (M):	0.20	0	0.30
Change (M):	$-x$	$+x$	$+x$
Equilibrium (M):	$0.20 - x$	x	$0.30 + x$

From Equation (16.1),

$$K_a = \frac{[H^+][CH_3COO^-]}{[CH_3COOH]}$$

$$1.8 \times 10^{-5} = \frac{(x)(0.30 + x)}{0.20 - x}$$

(Continued)

Assuming that $0.30 + x \approx 0.30$ and $0.20 - x \approx 0.20$, we obtain

$$1.8 \times 10^{-5} = \frac{(x)(0.30 + x)}{0.20 - x} \approx \frac{(x)(0.30)}{0.20}$$

or

$$x = [H^+] = 1.2 \times 10^{-5} \, M$$

Thus,

$$pH = -\log [H^+]$$
$$= -\log (1.2 \times 10^{-5}) = 4.92$$

Check Comparing the results in (a) and (b), we see that when the common ion (CH_3COO^-) is present, according to Le Châtelier's principle, the equilibrium shifts from right to left. This action decreases the extent of ionization of the weak acid. Consequently, fewer H^+ ions are produced in (b) and the pH of the solution is higher than that in (a). As always, you should check the validity of the assumptions.

Practice Exercise What is the pH of a solution containing 0.30 M HCOOH and 0.52 M HCOOK? Compare your result with the pH of a 0.30 M HCOOH solution.

Similar problem: 16.5.

The common ion effect also operates in a solution containing a weak base, such as NH_3, and a salt of the base, say NH_4Cl. At equilibrium,

$$NH_4^+(aq) \rightleftharpoons NH_3(aq) + H^+(aq)$$
$$K_a = \frac{[NH_3][H^+]}{[NH_4^+]}$$

We can derive the Henderson-Hasselbalch equation for this system as follows. Rearranging the above equation we obtain

$$[H^+] = \frac{K_a[NH_4^+]}{[NH_3]}$$

Taking the negative logarithm of both sides gives

$$-\log [H^+] = -\log K_a - \log \frac{[NH_4^+]}{[NH_3]}$$
$$-\log [H^+] = -\log K_a + \log \frac{[NH_3]}{[NH_4^+]}$$

or

$$pH = pK_a + \log \frac{[NH_3]}{[NH_4^+]}$$

A solution containing both NH_3 and its salt NH_4Cl is *less* basic than a solution containing only NH_3 at the same concentration. The common ion NH_4^+ suppresses the ionization of NH_3 in the solution containing both the base and the salt.

Fluids for intravenous injection must include buffer systems to maintain the proper blood pH.

16.3 Buffer Solutions

A **buffer solution** is *a solution of (1) a weak acid or a weak base and (2) its salt; both components must be present. The solution has the ability to resist changes in pH upon the addition of small amounts of either acid or base.* Buffers are very important to

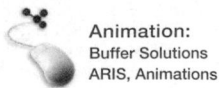

Animation:
Buffer Solutions
ARIS, Animations

chemical and biological systems. The pH in the human body varies greatly from one fluid to another; for example, the pH of blood is about 7.4, whereas the gastric juice in our stomachs has a pH of about 1.5. These pH values, which are crucial for proper enzyme function and the balance of osmotic pressure, are maintained by buffers in most cases.

A buffer solution must contain a relatively large concentration of acid to react with any OH^- ions that are added to it, and it must contain a similar concentration of base to react with any added H^+ ions. Furthermore, the acid and the base components of the buffer must not consume each other in a neutralization reaction. These requirements are satisfied by an acid-base conjugate pair, for example, a weak acid and its conjugate base (supplied by a salt) or a weak base and its conjugate acid (supplied by a salt).

A simple buffer solution can be prepared by adding comparable molar amounts of acetic acid (CH_3COOH) and its salt sodium acetate (CH_3COONa) to water. The equilibrium concentrations of both the acid and the conjugate base (from CH_3COONa) are assumed to be the same as the starting concentrations (see p. 699). A solution containing these two substances has the ability to neutralize either added acid or added base. Sodium acetate, a strong electrolyte, dissociates completely in water:

$$CH_3COONa(s) \xrightarrow{H_2O} CH_3COO^-(aq) + Na^+(aq)$$

If an acid is added, the H^+ ions will be consumed by the conjugate base in the buffer, CH_3COO^-, according to the equation

$$CH_3COO^-(aq) + H^+(aq) \longrightarrow CH_3COOH(aq)$$

If a base is added to the buffer system, the OH^- ions will be neutralized by the acid in the buffer:

$$CH_3COOH(aq) + OH^-(aq) \longrightarrow CH_3COO^-(aq) + H_2O(l)$$

As you can see, the two reactions that characterize this buffer system are identical to those for the common ion effect described in Example 16.1. The *buffering capacity,* that is, the effectiveness of the buffer solution, depends on the amount of acid and conjugate base from which the buffer is made. The larger the amount, the greater the buffering capacity.

In general, a buffer system can be represented as salt-acid or conjugate base–acid. Thus, the sodium acetate–acetic acid buffer system discussed above can be written as CH_3COONa/CH_3COOH or simply CH_3COO^-/CH_3COOH. Figure 16.1 shows this buffer system in action.

Example 16.2 distinguishes buffer systems from acid-salt combinations that do not function as buffers.

Figure 16.1 *The acid-base indicator bromophenol blue (added to all solutions shown) is used to illustrate buffer action. The indicator's color is blue-purple above pH 4.6 and yellow below pH 3.0. (a) A buffer solution made up of 50 mL of 0.1 M CH₃COOH and 50 mL of 0.1 M CH₃COONa. The solution has a pH of 4.7 and turns the indicator blue-purple. (b) After the addition of 40 mL of 0.1 M HCl solution to the solution in (a), the color remains blue-purple. (c) A 100-mL CH₃COOH solution whose pH is 4.7. (d) After the addition of 6 drops (about 0.3 mL) of 0.1 M HCl solution, the color turns yellow. Without buffer action, the pH of the solution decreases rapidly to less than 3.0 upon the addition of 0.1 M HCl.*

(a)   (b)   (c)   (d)

Example 16.2

Which of the following solutions can be classified as buffer systems? (a) KH_2PO_4/H_3PO_4, (b) $NaClO_4/HClO_4$, (c) C_5H_5N/C_5H_5NHCl (C_5H_5N is pyridine; its K_b is given in Table 15.4). Explain your answer.

Strategy What constitutes a buffer system? Which of the preceding solutions contains a weak acid and its salt (containing the weak conjugate base)? Which of the preceding solutions contains a weak base and its salt (containing the weak conjugate acid)? Why is the conjugate base of a strong acid not able to neutralize an added acid?

Solution The criteria for a buffer system is that we must have a weak acid and its salt (containing the weak conjugate base) or a weak base and its salt (containing the weak conjugate acid).

(a) H_3PO_4 is a weak acid, and its conjugate base, $H_2PO_4^-$, is a weak base (see Table 15.5). Therefore, this is a buffer system.

(b) Because $HClO_4$ is a strong acid, its conjugate base, ClO_4^-, is an extremely weak base. This means that the ClO_4^- ion will not combine with a H^+ ion in solution to form $HClO_4$. Thus, the system cannot act as a buffer system.

(c) As Table 15.4 shows, C_5H_5N is a weak base and its conjugate acid, $C_5H_5\overset{+}{N}H$ (the cation of the salt C_5H_5NHCl), is a weak acid. Therefore, this is a buffer system.

Similar problems: 16.9, 16.10.

Practice Exercise Which of the following couples are buffer systems? (a) KF/HF, (b) KBr/HBr, (c) $Na_2CO_3/NaHCO_3$.

The effect of a buffer solution on pH is illustrated by Example 16.3.

Example 16.3

(a) Calculate the pH of a buffer system containing 1.0 M CH_3COOH and 1.0 M CH_3COONa. (b) What is the pH of the buffer system after the addition of 0.10 mole of gaseous HCl to 1.0 L of the solution? Assume that the volume of the solution does not change when the HCl is added.

Strategy (a) The pH of the buffer system before the addition of HCl can be calculated with the procedure described in Example 16.1, because it is similar to the common-ion problem. The K_a of CH_3COOH is 1.8×10^{-5} (see Table 15.3). (b) It is helpful to make a sketch of the changes that occur in this case.

HCl

Buffer soln
$[CH_3COOH] = 1.0 M$
$[CH_3COO^-] = 1.0 M$

H^+ Cl^-

Buffer action in (b)
$CH_3COO^- + H^+ \rightarrow CH_3COOH$

Solution (a) We summarize the concentrations of the species at equilibrium as follows:

	$CH_3COOH(aq) \rightleftharpoons$	$H^+(aq) +$	$CH_3COO^-(aq)$
Initial (*M*):	1.0	0	1.0
Change (*M*):	$-x$	$+x$	$+x$
Equilibrium (*M*):	$1.0 - x$	x	$1.0 + x$

(Continued)

$$K_a = \frac{[H^+][CH_3COO^-]}{[CH_3COOH]}$$

$$1.8 \times 10^{-5} = \frac{(x)(1.0 + x)}{(1.0 - x)}$$

Assuming $1.0 + x \approx 1.0$ and $1.0 - x \approx 1.0$, we obtain

$$1.8 \times 10^{-5} = \frac{(x)(1.0 + x)}{(1.0 - x)} \approx \frac{x(1.0)}{1.0}$$

or $\qquad\qquad x = [H^+] = 1.8 \times 10^{-5}\,M$

Thus, $\qquad\qquad pH = -\log(1.8 \times 10^{-5}) = 4.74$

When the concentrations of the acid and the conjugate base are the same, the pH of the buffer is equal to the pK_a of the acid.

(b) When HCl is added to the solution, the initial changes are

	HCl(aq) $\longrightarrow$	H$^+$(aq) +	Cl$^-$(aq)
Initial (mol):	0.10	0	0
Change (mol):	−0.10	+0.10	+0.10
Final (mol):	0	0.10	0.10

The Cl$^-$ ion is a spectator ion in solution because it is the conjugate base of a strong acid.

The H$^+$ ions provided by the strong acid HCl react completely with the conjugate base of the buffer, which is CH$_3$COO$^-$. At this point it is more convenient to work with moles rather than molarity. The reason is that in some cases the volume of the solution may change when a substance is added. A change in volume will change the molarity, but not the number of moles. The neutralization reaction is summarized next:

	CH$_3$COO$^-$(aq) +	H$^+$(aq) $\longrightarrow$	CH$_3$COOH(aq)
Initial (mol):	1.0	0.10	1.0
Change (mol):	−0.10	−0.10	+0.10
Final (mol):	0.90	0	1.1

Finally, to calculate the pH of the buffer after neutralization of the acid, we convert back to molarity by dividing moles by 1.0 L of solution.

	CH$_3$COOH(aq) $\rightleftharpoons$	H$^+$(aq) +	CH$_3$COO$^-$(aq)
Initial (M):	1.1	0	0.90
Change (M):	−x	+x	+x
Equilibrium (M):	1.1 − x	x	0.90 + x

$$K_a = \frac{[H^+][CH_3COO^-]}{[CH_3COOH]}$$

$$1.8 \times 10^{-5} = \frac{(x)(0.90 + x)}{1.1 - x}$$

Assuming $0.90 + x \approx 0.90$ and $1.1 - x \approx 1.1$, we obtain

$$1.8 \times 10^{-5} = \frac{(x)(0.90 + x)}{1.1 - x} \approx \frac{x(0.90)}{1.1}$$

or $\qquad\qquad x = [H^+] = 2.2 \times 10^{-5}\,M$

Thus, $\qquad\qquad pH = -\log(2.2 \times 10^{-5}) = 4.66$

Check The pH decreases by only a small amount upon the addition of HCl. This is consistent with the action of a buffer solution.

Practice Exercise Calculate the pH of the 0.30 M NH$_3$/0.36 M NH$_4$Cl buffer system. What is the pH after the addition of 20.0 mL of 0.050 M NaOH to 80.0 mL of the buffer solution?

Similar problem: 16.17.

In the buffer solution examined in Example 16.3, there is a decrease in pH (the solution becomes more acidic) as a result of added HCl. We can also compare the changes in H^+ ion concentration as follows:

Before addition of HCl: $[H^+] = 1.8 \times 10^{-5} M$
After addition of HCl: $[H^+] = 2.2 \times 10^{-5} M$

Thus, the H^+ ion concentration increases by a factor of

$$\frac{2.2 \times 10^{-5} M}{1.8 \times 10^{-5} M} = 1.2$$

To appreciate the effectiveness of the CH_3COONa/CH_3COOH buffer, let us find out what would happen if 0.10 mol HCl were added to 1 L of water, and compare the increase in H^+ ion concentration.

Before addition of HCl: $[H^+] = 1.0 \times 10^{-7} M$
After addition of HCl: $[H^+] = 0.10 M$

As a result of the addition of HCl, the H^+ ion concentration increases by a factor of

$$\frac{0.10 M}{1.0 \times 10^{-7} M} = 1.0 \times 10^6$$

amounting to a millionfold increase! This comparison shows that a properly chosen buffer solution can maintain a fairly constant H^+ ion concentration, or pH (Figure 16.2).

Figure 16.2 *A comparison of the change in pH when 0.10 mol HCl is added to pure water and to an acetate buffer solution as described in Example 16.3.*

Preparing a Buffer Solution with a Specific pH

Now suppose we want to prepare a buffer solution with a specific pH. How do we go about it? Equation (16.4) indicates that if the molar concentrations of the acid and its conjugate base are approximately equal, that is, if [acid] $\approx$ [conjugate base], then

$$\log \frac{[conjugate\ base]}{[acid]} \approx 0$$

or

$$pH \approx pK_a$$

Thus, to prepare a buffer solution, we work backwards. First we choose a weak acid whose pK_a is close to the desired pH. Next, we substitute the pH and pK_a values in Equation (16.4) to obtain the ratio [conjugate base]/[acid]. This ratio can then be converted to molar quantities for the preparation of the buffer solution. Example 16.4 shows this approach.

Example 16.4

Describe how you would prepare a "phosphate buffer" with a pH of about 7.40.

Strategy For a buffer to function effectively, the concentrations of the acid component must be roughly equal to the conjugate base component. According to Equation (16.4), when the desired pH is close to the pK_a of the acid, that is, when pH $\approx pK_a$,

(Continued)

Maintaining the pH of Blood

All higher animals need a circulatory system to carry fuel and oxygen for their life processes and to remove wastes. In the human body this vital exchange takes place in the versatile fluid known as blood, of which there are about 5 L (10.6 pints) in an average adult. Blood circulating deep in the tissues carries oxygen and nutrients to keep cells alive, and removes carbon dioxide and other waste materials. Using several buffer systems, nature has provided an extremely efficient method for the delivery of oxygen and the removal of carbon dioxide.

Blood is an enormously complex system, but for our purposes we need look at only two essential components: blood plasma and red blood cells, or *erythrocytes*. Blood plasma contains many compounds, including proteins, metal ions, and inorganic phosphates. The erythrocytes contain hemoglobin molecules, as well as the enzyme *carbonic anhydrase,* which catalyzes both the formation of carbonic acid (H_2CO_3) and its decomposition:

$$CO_2(aq) + H_2O(l) \rightleftharpoons H_2CO_3(aq)$$

The substances inside the erythrocyte are protected from extracellular fluid (blood plasma) by a cell membrane that allows only certain molecules to diffuse through it.

The pH of blood plasma is maintained at about 7.40 by several buffer systems, the most important of which is the HCO_3^-/H_2CO_3 system. In the erythrocyte, where the pH is 7.25, the principal buffer systems are HCO_3^-/H_2CO_3 and hemoglobin. The hemoglobin molecule is a complex protein molecule (molar mass 65,000 g) that contains a number of ionizable protons. As a very rough approximation, we can treat it as a monoprotic acid of the form HHb:

$$HHb(aq) \rightleftharpoons H^+(aq) + Hb^-(aq)$$

where HHb represents the hemoglobin molecule and Hb^- the conjugate base of HHb. Oxyhemoglobin ($HHbO_2$), formed by the combination of oxygen with hemoglobin, is a stronger acid than HHb:

$$HHbO_2(aq) \rightleftharpoons H^+(aq) + HbO_2^-(aq)$$

As the figure on p. 707 shows, carbon dioxide produced by metabolic processes diffuses into the erythrocyte, where it is rapidly converted to H_2CO_3 by carbonic anhydrase:

Electron micrograph of red blood cells in a small branch of an artery.

$$CO_2(aq) + H_2O(l) \rightleftharpoons H_2CO_3(aq)$$

The ionization of the carbonic acid

$$H_2CO_3(aq) \rightleftharpoons H^+(aq) + HCO_3^-(aq)$$

has two important consequences. First, the bicarbonate ion diffuses out of the erythrocyte and is carried by the blood plasma to the lungs. This is the major mechanism for removing carbon dioxide. Second, the H^+ ions shift the equilibrium in favor of the nonionized oxyhemoglobin molecule:

$$H^+(aq) + HbO_2^-(aq) \rightleftharpoons HHbO_2(aq)$$

Because $HHbO_2$ releases oxygen more readily than does its conjugate base (HbO_2^-), the formation of the acid promotes the following reaction from left to right:

$$HHbO_2(aq) \rightleftharpoons HHb(aq) + O_2(aq)$$

The O_2 molecules diffuse out of the erythrocyte and are taken up by other cells to carry out metabolism.

When the venous blood returns to the lungs, the above processes are reversed. The bicarbonate ions now diffuse into

Oxygen–carbon dioxide transport and release by blood. (a) The partial pressure of CO_2 is higher in the metabolizing tissues than in the plasma. Thus, it diffuses into the blood capillaries and then into erythrocytes. There it is converted to carbonic acid by the enzyme carbonic anhydrase (CA). The protons provided by the carbonic acid then combine with the HbO_2^- anions to form $HHbO_2$, which eventually dissociates into HHb and O_2. Because the partial pressure of O_2 is higher in the erythrocytes than in the tissues, oxygen molecules diffuse out of the erythrocytes and then into the tissues. The bicarbonate ions also diffuse out of the erythrocytes and are carried by the plasma to the lungs. (b) In the lungs, the processes are exactly reversed. Oxygen molecules diffuse from the lungs, where they have a higher partial pressure, into the erythrocytes. There they combine with HHb to form $HHbO_2$. The protons provided by $HHbO_2$ combine with the bicarbonate ions diffused into the erythrocytes from the plasma to form carbonic acid. In the presence of carbonic anhydrase, carbonic acid is converted to H_2O and CO_2. The CO_2 then diffuses out of the erythrocytes and into the lungs, where it is exhaled.

the erythrocyte, where they react with hemoglobin to form carbonic acid:

$$HHb(aq) + HCO_3^-(aq) \rightleftharpoons Hb^-(aq) + H_2CO_3(aq)$$

Most of the acid is then converted to CO_2 by carbonic anhydrase:

$$H_2CO_3(aq) \rightleftharpoons H_2O(l) + CO_2(aq)$$

The carbon dioxide diffuses to the lungs and is eventually exhaled. The formation of the Hb^- ions (due to the reaction between HHb and HCO_3^- shown in the left column) also favors the uptake of oxygen at the lungs

$$Hb^-(aq) + O_2(aq) \rightleftharpoons HbO_2^-(aq)$$

because Hb^- has a greater affinity for oxygen than does HHb.

When the arterial blood flows back to the body tissues, the entire cycle is repeated.

$$\log \frac{[\text{conjugate base}]}{[\text{acid}]} \approx 0$$

or

$$\frac{[\text{conjugate base}]}{[\text{acid}]} \approx 1$$

Solution Because phosphoric acid is a triprotic acid, we write the three stages of ionization as follows. The K_a values are obtained from Table 15.5 and the pK_a values are found by applying Equation (16.3).

$$H_3PO_4(aq) \rightleftharpoons H^+(aq) + H_2PO_4^-(aq) \quad K_{a_1} = 7.5 \times 10^{-3}; \ pK_{a_1} = 2.12$$
$$H_2PO_4^-(aq) \rightleftharpoons H^+(aq) + HPO_4^{2-}(aq) \quad K_{a_2} = 6.2 \times 10^{-8}; \ pK_{a_2} = 7.21$$
$$HPO_4^{2-}(aq) \rightleftharpoons H^+(aq) + PO_4^{3-}(aq) \quad K_{a_3} = 4.8 \times 10^{-13}; \ pK_{a_3} = 12.32$$

The most suitable of the three buffer systems is $HPO_4^{2-}/H_2PO_4^-$, because the pK_a of the acid $H_2PO_4^-$ is closest to the desired pH. From the Henderson-Hasselbalch equation we write

$$pH = pK_a + \log \frac{[\text{conjugate base}]}{[\text{acid}]}$$

$$7.40 = 7.21 + \log \frac{[HPO_4^{2-}]}{[H_2PO_4^-]}$$

$$\log \frac{[HPO_4^{2-}]}{[H_2PO_4^-]} = 0.19$$

Taking the antilog, we obtain

$$\frac{[HPO_4^{2-}]}{[H_2PO_4^-]} = 10^{0.19} = 1.5$$

Thus, one way to prepare a phosphate buffer with a pH of 7.40 is to dissolve disodium hydrogen phosphate (Na_2HPO_4) and sodium dihydrogen phosphate (NaH_2PO_4) in a mole ratio of 1.5:1.0 in water. For example, we could dissolve 1.5 moles of Na_2HPO_4 and 1.0 mole of NaH_2PO_4 in enough water to make up a 1-L solution.

Practice Exercise How would you prepare a liter of "carbonate buffer" at a pH of 10.10? You are provided with carbonic acid (H_2CO_3), sodium hydrogen carbonate ($NaHCO_3$), and sodium carbonate (Na_2CO_3). See Table 15.5 for K_a values.

Similar problems: 16.19, 16.20.

The Chemistry in Action essay on p. 706 illustrates the importance of buffer systems in the human body.

16.4 Acid-Base Titrations

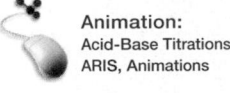

Animation:
Acid-Base Titrations
ARIS, Animations

Having discussed buffer solutions, we can now look in more detail at the quantitative aspects of acid-base titrations (see Section 4.6). We will consider three types of reactions: (1) titrations involving a strong acid and a strong base, (2) titrations involving a weak acid and a strong base, and (3) titrations involving a strong acid and a weak base. Titrations involving a weak acid and a weak base are complicated by the hydrolysis of both the cation and the anion of the salt formed. It is difficult to determine the equivalence point in these cases. Therefore, these titrations will not be dealt with here. Figure 16.3 shows the arrangement for monitoring the pH during the course of a titration.

Figure 16.3 *A pH meter is used to monitor an acid-base titration.*

Strong Acid–Strong Base Titrations

The reaction between a strong acid (say, HCl) and a strong base (say, NaOH) can be represented by

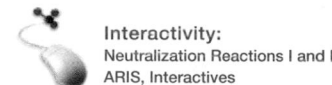

Interactivity:
Neutralization Reactions I and II
ARIS, Interactives

$$NaOH(aq) + HCl(aq) \longrightarrow NaCl(aq) + H_2O(l)$$

or in terms of the net ionic equation

$$H^+(aq) + OH^-(aq) \longrightarrow H_2O(l)$$

Consider the addition of a 0.100 *M* NaOH solution (from a buret) to an Erlenmeyer flask containing 25.0 mL of 0.100 *M* HCl. For convenience, we will use only three significant figures for volume and concentration and two significant figures for pH. Figure 16.4 shows the pH profile of the titration (also known as the titration curve). Before the addition of NaOH, the pH of the acid is given by $-\log(0.100)$, or 1.00. When NaOH is added, the pH of the solution increases slowly at first. Near the equivalence point the pH begins to rise steeply, and at the equivalence point (that is, the point at which equimolar amounts of acid and base have reacted) the curve rises almost vertically. In a strong acid–strong base titration both the hydrogen ion and hydroxide ion concentrations are very small at the equivalence point (approximately 1×10^{-7} *M*); consequently, the addition of a single drop of the base can cause a large increase in [OH$^-$] and in the pH of the solution. Beyond the equivalence point, the pH again increases slowly with the addition of NaOH.

It is possible to calculate the pH of the solution at every stage of titration. Here are three sample calculations.

1. *After the addition of 10.0 mL of 0.100 M NaOH to 25.0 mL of 0.100 M HCl.* The total volume of the solution is 35.0 mL. The number of moles of NaOH in 10.0 mL is

$$10.0 \text{ mL} \times \frac{0.100 \text{ mol NaOH}}{1 \text{ L NaOH}} \times \frac{1 \text{ L}}{1000 \text{ mL}} = 1.00 \times 10^{-3} \text{ mol}$$

The number of moles of HCl originally present in 25.0 mL of solution is

$$25.0 \text{ mL} \times \frac{0.100 \text{ mol HCl}}{1 \text{ L HCl}} \times \frac{1 \text{ L}}{1000 \text{ mL}} = 2.50 \times 10^{-3} \text{ mol}$$

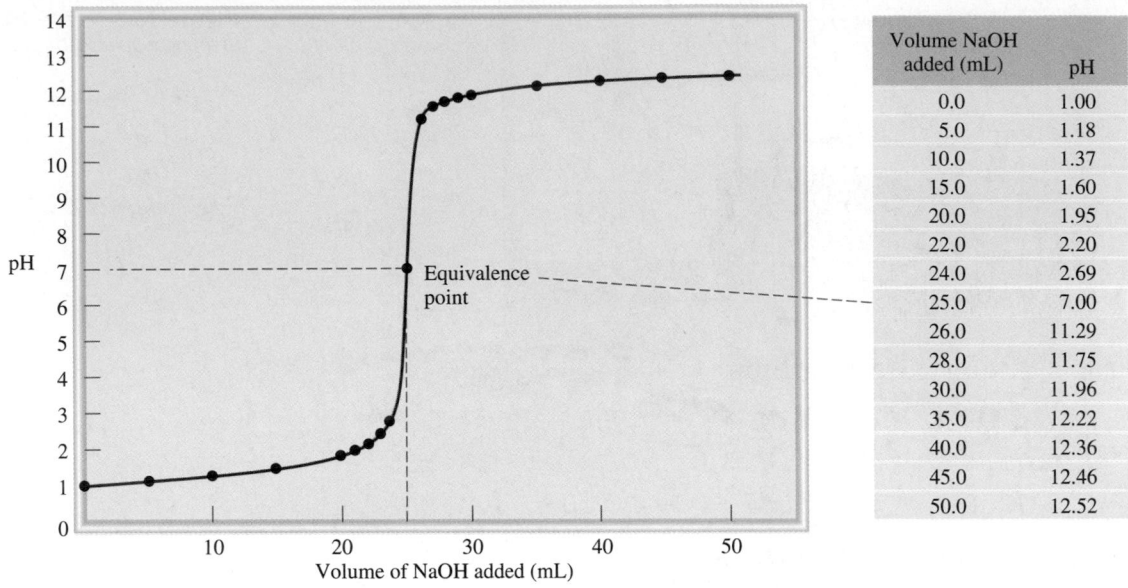

Figure 16.4 *pH profile of a strong acid–strong base titration. A 0.100 M NaOH solution is added from a buret to 25.0 mL of a 0.100 M HCl solution in an Erlenmeyer flask (see Figure 4.21). This curve is sometimes referred to as a titration curve.*

Volume NaOH added (mL)	pH
0.0	1.00
5.0	1.18
10.0	1.37
15.0	1.60
20.0	1.95
22.0	2.20
24.0	2.69
25.0	7.00
26.0	11.29
28.0	11.75
30.0	11.96
35.0	12.22
40.0	12.36
45.0	12.46
50.0	12.52

Keep in mind that 1 mol NaOH ≏ 1 mol HCl.

Thus, the amount of HCl left after partial neutralization is $(2.50 \times 10^{-3}) - (1.00 \times 10^{-3})$, or 1.50×10^{-3} mol. Next, the concentration of H^+ ions in 35.0 mL of solution is found as follows:

$$\frac{1.50 \times 10^{-3} \text{ mol HCl}}{35.0 \text{ mL}} \times \frac{1000 \text{ mL}}{1 \text{ L}} = 0.0429 \text{ mol HCl/L}$$
$$= 0.0429 \, M \text{ HCl}$$

Thus, $[H^+] = 0.0429 \, M$, and the pH of the solution is

$$pH = -\log 0.0429 = 1.37$$

2. *After the addition of 25.0 mL of 0.100 M NaOH to 25.0 mL of 0.100 M HCl.* This is a simple calculation, because it involves a complete neutralization reaction and the salt (NaCl) does not undergo hydrolysis. At the equivalence point, $[H^+] = [OH^-] = 1.00 \times 10^{-7} \, M$ and the pH of the solution is 7.00.

Neither Na$^+$ nor Cl$^-$ undergoes hydrolysis.

3. *After the addition of 35.0 mL of 0.100 M NaOH to 25.0 mL of 0.100 M HCl.* The total volume of the solution is now 60.0 mL. The number of moles of NaOH added is

$$35.0 \text{ mL} \times \frac{0.100 \text{ mol NaOH}}{1 \text{ L NaOH}} \times \frac{1 \text{ L}}{1000 \text{ mL}} = 3.50 \times 10^{-3} \text{ mol}$$

The number of moles of HCl in 25.0 mL solution is 2.50×10^{-3} mol. After complete neutralization of HCl, the number of moles of NaOH left is $(3.50 \times 10^{-3}) - (2.50 \times 10^{-3})$, or 1.00×10^{-3} mol. The concentration of NaOH in 60.0 mL of solution is

$$\frac{1.00 \times 10^{-3} \text{ mol NaOH}}{60.0 \text{ mL}} \times \frac{1000 \text{ mL}}{1 \text{ L}} = 0.0167 \text{ mol NaOH/L}$$

$$= 0.0167 \, M \text{ NaOH}$$

Thus, $[OH^-] = 0.0167 \, M$ and $pOH = -\log 0.0167 = 1.78$. Hence, the pH of the solution is

$$pH = 14.00 - pOH$$
$$= 14.00 - 1.78$$
$$= 12.22$$

Weak Acid–Strong Base Titrations

Consider the neutralization reaction between acetic acid (a weak acid) and sodium hydroxide (a strong base):

$$CH_3COOH(aq) + NaOH(aq) \longrightarrow CH_3COONa(aq) + H_2O(l)$$

This equation can be simplified to

$$CH_3COOH(aq) + OH^-(aq) \longrightarrow CH_3COO^-(aq) + H_2O(l)$$

The acetate ion undergoes hydrolysis as follows:

$$CH_3COO^-(aq) + H_2O(l) \rightleftharpoons CH_3COOH(aq) + OH^-(aq)$$

Therefore, at the equivalence point, when we only have sodium acetate present, the pH will be *greater than* 7 as a result of the excess OH^- ions formed (Figure 16.5).

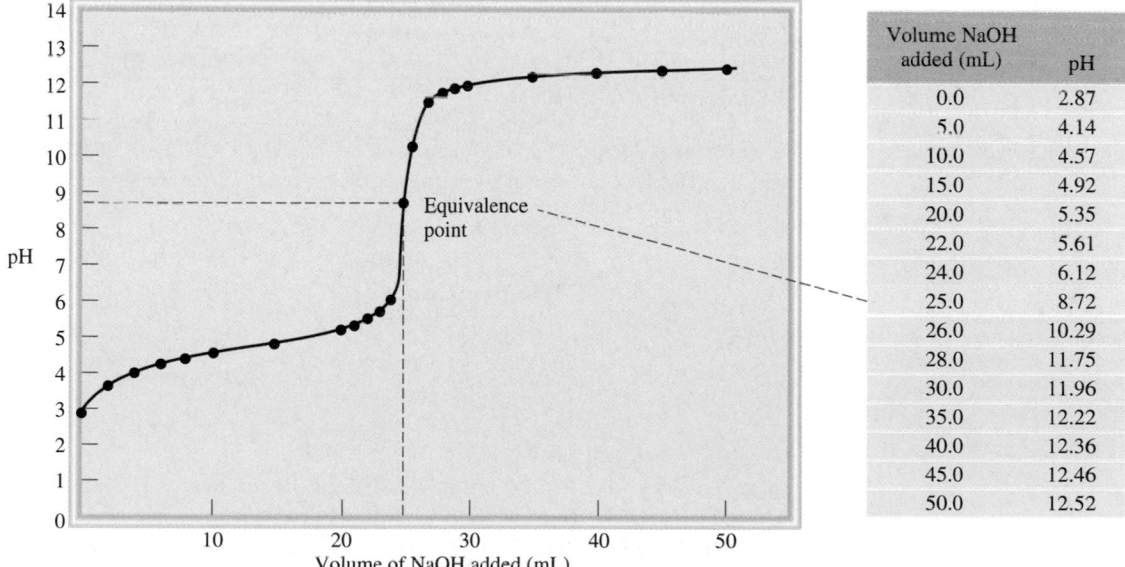

Volume NaOH added (mL)	pH
0.0	2.87
5.0	4.14
10.0	4.57
15.0	4.92
20.0	5.35
22.0	5.61
24.0	6.12
25.0	8.72
26.0	10.29
28.0	11.75
30.0	11.96
35.0	12.22
40.0	12.36
45.0	12.46
50.0	12.52

Figure 16.5 *pH profile of a weak acid–strong base titration. A 0.100 M NaOH solution is added from a buret to 25.0 mL of a 0.100 M CH₃COOH solution in an Erlenmeyer flask. Due to the hydrolysis of the salt formed, the pH at the equivalence point is greater than 7.*

Note that this situation is analogous to the hydrolysis of sodium acetate (CH_3COONa) (see p. 674).

Example 16.5 deals with the titration of a weak acid with a strong base.

Example 16.5

Calculate the pH in the titration of 25.0 mL of 0.100 M acetic acid by sodium hydroxide after the addition to the acid solution of (a) 10.0 mL of 0.100 M NaOH, (b) 25.0 mL of 0.100 M NaOH, (c) 35.0 mL of 0.100 M NaOH.

Strategy The reaction between CH_3COOH and NaOH is

$$CH_3COOH(aq) + NaOH(aq) \longrightarrow CH_3COONa(aq) + H_2O(l)$$

We see that 1 mol $CH_3COOH \rightleftharpoons$ 1 mol NaOH. Therefore, at every stage of the titration we can calculate the number of moles of base reacting with the acid, and the pH of the solution is determined by the excess acid or base left over. At the equivalence point, however, the neutralization is complete and the pH of the solution will depend on the extent of the hydrolysis of the salt formed, which is CH_3COONa.

Solution (a) The number of moles of NaOH in 10.0 mL is

$$10.0 \text{ mL} \times \frac{0.100 \text{ mol NaOH}}{1 \text{ L NaOH soln}} \times \frac{1 \text{ L}}{1000 \text{ mL}} = 1.00 \times 10^{-3} \text{ mol}$$

The number of moles of CH_3COOH originally present in 25.0 mL of solution is

$$25.0 \text{ mL} \times \frac{0.100 \text{ mol } CH_3COOH}{1 \text{ L } CH_3COOH \text{ soln}} \times \frac{1 \text{ L}}{1000 \text{ mL}} = 2.50 \times 10^{-3} \text{ mol}$$

We work with moles at this point because when two solutions are mixed, the solution volume increases. As the volume increases, molarity will change but the number of moles will remain the same. The changes in number of moles are summarized next:

	$CH_3COOH(aq)$	+ NaOH(aq)	$\longrightarrow CH_3COONa(aq)$	+ $H_2O(l)$
Initial (mol):	2.50×10^{-3}	1.00×10^{-3}	0	
Change (mol):	-1.00×10^{-3}	-1.00×10^{-3}	$+1.00 \times 10^{-3}$	
Final (mol):	1.50×10^{-3}	0	1.00×10^{-3}	

At this stage we have a buffer system made up of CH_3COOH and CH_3COO^- (from the salt, CH_3COONa). To calculate the pH of the solution, we write

$$K_a = \frac{[H^+][CH_3COO^-]}{[CH_3COOH]}$$

$$[H^+] = \frac{[CH_3COOH]K_a}{[CH_3COO^-]}$$

$$= \frac{(1.50 \times 10^{-3})(1.8 \times 10^{-5})}{1.00 \times 10^{-3}} = 2.7 \times 10^{-5} M$$

Because the volume of the solution is the same for CH_3COOH and CH_3COO^- (35 mL), the ratio of the number of moles present is equal to the ratio of their molar concentrations.

Therefore, $pH = -\log (2.7 \times 10^{-5}) = 4.57$

(b) These quantities (that is, 25.0 mL of 0.100 M NaOH reacting with 25.0 mL of 0.100 M CH_3COOH) correspond to the equivalence point. The number of moles of NaOH in 25.0 mL of the solution is

$$25.0 \text{ mL} \times \frac{0.100 \text{ mol NaOH}}{1 \text{ L NaOH soln}} \times \frac{1 \text{ L}}{1000 \text{ mL}} = 2.50 \times 10^{-3} \text{ mol}$$

(Continued)

The changes in number of moles are summarized next:

$$CH_3COOH(aq) + NaOH(aq) \longrightarrow CH_3COONa(aq) + H_2O(l)$$

Initial (mol):	2.50×10^{-3}	2.50×10^{-3}	0
Change (mol):	-2.50×10^{-3}	-2.50×10^{-3}	$+2.50 \times 10^{-3}$
Final (mol):	0	0	2.50×10^{-3}

At the equivalence point, the concentrations of both the acid and the base are zero. The total volume is $(25.0 + 25.0)$ mL or 50.0 mL, so the concentration of the salt is

$$[CH_3COONa] = \frac{2.50 \times 10^{-3} \text{ mol}}{50.0 \text{ mL}} \times \frac{1000 \text{ mL}}{1 \text{ L}}$$
$$= 0.0500 \text{ mol/L} = 0.0500 \; M$$

The next step is to calculate the pH of the solution that results from the hydrolysis of the CH_3COO^- ions. Following the procedure described in Example 15.13 and looking up the base ionization constant (K_b) for CH_3COO^- in Table 15.3, we write

$$K_b = 5.6 \times 10^{-10} = \frac{[CH_3COOH][OH^-]}{[CH_3COO^-]} = \frac{x^2}{0.0500 - x}$$
$$x = [OH^-] = 5.3 \times 10^{-6} \; M, \text{pH} = 8.72$$

(c) After the addition of 35.0 mL of NaOH, the solution is well past the equivalence point. The number of moles of NaOH originally present is

$$35.0 \text{ mL} \times \frac{0.100 \text{ mol NaOH}}{1 \text{ L NaOH soln}} \times \frac{1 \text{ L}}{1000 \text{ mL}} = 3.50 \times 10^{-3} \text{ mol}$$

The changes in number of moles are summarized next:

$$CH_3COOH(aq) + NaOH(aq) \longrightarrow CH_3COONa(aq) + H_2O(l)$$

Initial (mol):	2.50×10^{-3}	3.50×10^{-3}	0
Change (mol):	-2.50×10^{-3}	-2.50×10^{-3}	$+2.50 \times 10^{-3}$
Final (mol):	0	1.00×10^{-3}	2.50×10^{-3}

At this stage we have two species in solution that are responsible for making the solution basic: OH^- and CH_3COO^- (from CH_3COONa). However, because OH^- is a much stronger base than CH_3COO^-, we can safely neglect the hydrolysis of the CH_3COO^- ions and calculate the pH of the solution using only the concentration of the OH^- ions. The total volume of the combined solutions is $(25.0 + 35.0)$ mL or 60.0 mL, so we calculate OH^- concentration as follows:

$$[OH^-] = \frac{1.00 \times 10^{-3} \text{ mol}}{60.0 \text{ mL}} \times \frac{1000 \text{ mL}}{1 \text{ L}}$$
$$= 0.0167 \text{ mol/L} = 0.0167 \; M$$
$$\text{pOH} = -\log [OH^-] = -\log 0.0167 = 1.78$$
$$\text{pH} = 14.00 - 1.78 = 12.22$$

Similar problem: 16.96.

Practice Exercise Exactly 100 mL of 0.10 M nitrous acid (HNO_2) are titrated with a 0.10 M NaOH solution. Calculate the pH for (a) the initial solution, (b) the point at which 80 mL of the base has been added, (c) the equivalence point, (d) the point at which 105 mL of the base has been added.

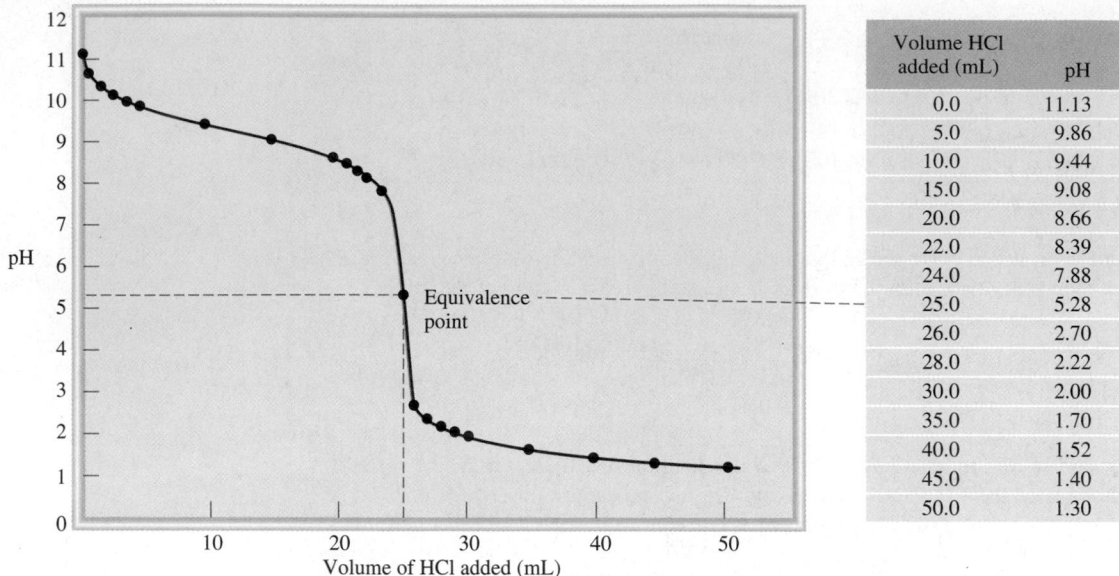

Volume HCl added (mL)	pH
0.0	11.13
5.0	9.86
10.0	9.44
15.0	9.08
20.0	8.66
22.0	8.39
24.0	7.88
25.0	5.28
26.0	2.70
28.0	2.22
30.0	2.00
35.0	1.70
40.0	1.52
45.0	1.40
50.0	1.30

Figure 16.6 *pH profile of a strong acid–weak base titration. A 0.100 M HCl solution is added from a buret to 25.0 mL of a 0.100 M NH$_3$ solution in an Erlenmeyer flask. As a result of salt hydrolysis, the pH at the equivalence point is lower than 7.*

Strong Acid–Weak Base Titrations

Consider the titration of HCl, a strong acid, with NH$_3$, a weak base:

$$HCl(aq) + NH_3(aq) \longrightarrow NH_4Cl(aq)$$

or simply

$$H^+(aq) + NH_3(aq) \longrightarrow NH_4^+(aq)$$

The pH at the equivalence point is *less than* 7 due to the hydrolysis of the NH$_4^+$ ion:

$$NH_4^+(aq) + H_2O(l) \rightleftharpoons NH_3(aq) + H_3O^+(aq)$$

or simply

$$NH_4^+(aq) \rightleftharpoons NH_3(aq) + H^+(aq)$$

Because of the volatility of an aqueous ammonia solution, it is more convenient to add hydrochloric acid from a buret to the ammonia solution. Figure 16.6 shows the titration curve for this experiment.

Example 16.6

Calculate the pH at the equivalence point when 25.0 mL of 0.100 *M* NH$_3$ is titrated by a 0.100 *M* HCl solution.

Strategy The reaction between NH$_3$ and HCl is

$$NH_3(aq) + HCl(aq) \longrightarrow NH_4Cl(aq)$$

(Continued)

We see that 1 mol $NH_3 \simeq$ 1 mol HCl. At the equivalence point, the major species in solution are the salt NH_4Cl (dissociated into NH_4^+ and Cl^- ions) and H_2O. First, we determine the concentration of NH_4Cl formed. Then we calculate the pH as a result of the NH_4^+ ion hydrolysis. The Cl^- ion, being the conjugate base of a strong acid HCl, does not react with water. As usual, we ignore the ionization of water.

Solution The number of moles of NH_3 in 25.0 mL of 0.100 M solution is

$$25.0 \text{ mL} \times \frac{0.100 \text{ mol } NH_3}{1 \text{ L } NH_3} \times \frac{1 \text{ L}}{1000 \text{ mL}} = 2.50 \times 10^{-3} \text{ mol}$$

At the equivalence point the number of moles of HCl added equals the number of moles of NH_3. The changes in number of moles are summarized below:

	$NH_3(aq)$	$+$	$HCl(aq)$	$\longrightarrow$	$NH_4Cl(aq)$
Initial (mol):	2.50×10^{-3}		2.50×10^{-3}		0
Change (mol):	-2.50×10^{-3}		-2.50×10^{-3}		$+2.50 \times 10^{-3}$
Final (mol):	0		0		2.50×10^{-3}

At the equivalence point, the concentrations of both the acid and the base are zero. The total volume is (25.0 + 25.0) mL, or 50.0 mL, so the concentration of the salt is

$$[NH_4Cl] = \frac{2.50 \times 10^{-3} \text{ mol}}{50.0 \text{ mL}} \times \frac{1000 \text{ mL}}{1 \text{ L}}$$
$$= 0.0500 \text{ mol/L} = 0.0500 \text{ } M$$

The pH of the solution at the equivalence point is determined by the hydrolysis of NH_4^+ ions. We follow the procedure on p. 675.

Step 1: We represent the hydrolysis of the cation NH_4^+, and let x be the equilibrium concentration of NH_3 and H^+ ions in mol/L:

	$NH_4^+(aq)$	$\rightleftharpoons$	$NH_3(aq) + H^+(aq)$	
Initial (M):	0.0500		0.000	0.000
Change (M):	$-x$		$+x$	$+x$
Equilibrium (M):	$(0.0500 - x)$		x	x

Step 2: From Table 15.4 we obtain the K_a for NH_4^+:

$$K_a = \frac{[NH_3][H^+]}{[NH_4^+]}$$

$$5.6 \times 10^{-10} = \frac{x^2}{0.0500 - x}$$

Applying the approximation $0.0500 - x \approx 0.0500$, we get

Always check the validity of the approximation.

$$5.6 \times 10^{-10} = \frac{x^2}{0.0500 - x} \approx \frac{x^2}{0.0500}$$
$$x = 5.3 \times 10^{-6} \text{ } M$$

Thus, the pH is given by

$$pH = -\log (5.3 \times 10^{-6})$$
$$= 5.28$$

(Continued)

Similar problem: 16.29.

Check Note that the pH of the solution is acidic. This is what we would expect from the hydrolysis of the ammonium ion.

Practice Exercise Calculate the pH at the equivalence point in the titration of 50 mL of 0.10 M methylamine (see Table 15.4) with a 0.20 M HCl solution.

16.5 Acid-Base Indicators

The equivalence point, as we have seen, is the point at which the number of moles of OH^- ions added to a solution is equal to the number of moles of H^+ ions originally present. To determine the equivalence point in a titration, then, we must know exactly how much volume of a base to add from a buret to an acid in a flask. One way to achieve this goal is to add a few drops of an acid-base indicator to the acid solution at the start of the titration. You will recall from Chapter 4 that an indicator is usually a weak organic acid or base that has distinctly different colors in its nonionized and ionized forms. These two forms are related to the pH of the solution in which the indicator is dissolved. The ***end point*** of a titration *occurs when the indicator changes color.* However, not all indicators change color at the same pH, so the choice of indicator for a particular titration depends on the nature of the acid and base used in the titration (that is, whether they are strong or weak). By choosing the proper indicator for a titration, we can use the end point to determine the equivalence point, as we will see below.

Let us consider a weak monoprotic acid that we will call HIn. To be an effective indicator, HIn and its conjugate base, In^-, must have distinctly different colors. In solution, the acid ionizes to a small extent:

$$HIn(aq) \rightleftharpoons H^+(aq) + In^-(aq)$$

If the indicator is in a sufficiently acidic medium, the equilibrium, according to Le Châtelier's principle, shifts to the left and the predominant color of the indicator is that of the nonionized form (HIn). On the other hand, in a basic medium the equilibrium shifts to the right and the color of the solution will be due mainly to that of the conjugate base (In^-). Roughly speaking, we can use the following concentration ratios to predict the perceived color of the indicator:

$$\frac{[HIn]}{[In^-]} \geq 10 \qquad \text{color of acid (HIn) predominates}$$

$$\frac{[HIn]}{[In^-]} \leq 0.1 \qquad \text{color of conjugate base (}In^-\text{) predominates}$$

If $[HIn] \approx [In^-]$, then the indicator color is a combination of the colors of HIn and In^-.

The end point of an indicator does not occur at a specific pH; rather, there is a range of pH within which the end point will occur. In practice, we choose an indicator whose end point lies on the steep part of the titration curve. Because the equivalence point also lies on the steep part of the curve, this choice ensures that the pH at the equivalence point will fall within the range over which the indicator changes color. In Section 4.6 we mentioned that phenolphthalein is a suitable indicator for the titration of NaOH and HCl. Phenolphthalein is colorless in acidic and neutral solutions, but reddish pink in basic solutions. Measurements show that at pH < 8.3 the indicator is colorless but that it begins to turn reddish pink when the pH exceeds 8.3. As shown in Figure 16.4, the steepness of the pH curve near the equivalence point means that the addition of a very small quantity of NaOH (say, 0.05 mL, which is about the volume of a drop from the buret) brings about a large rise in the pH of the solution. What is important, however, is the fact that

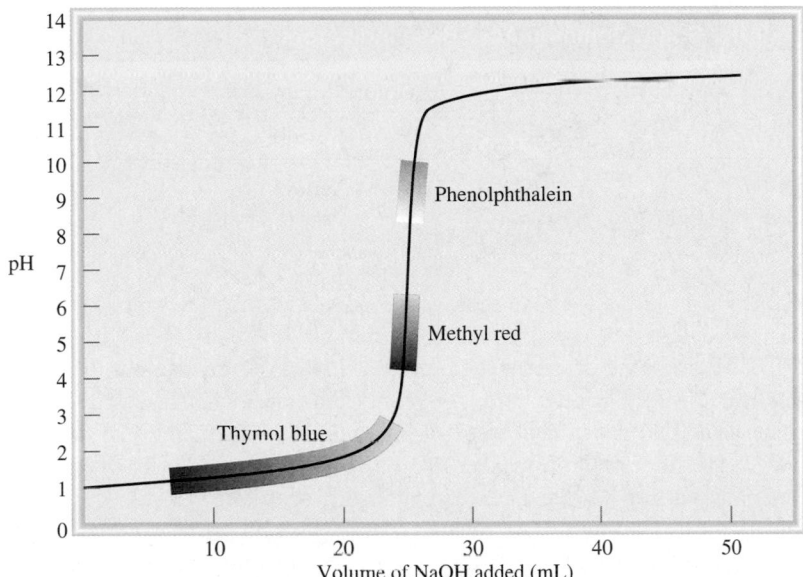

Figure 16.7 *The titration curve of a strong acid with a strong base. Because the regions over which the indicators methyl red and phenolphthalein change color along the steep portion of the curve, they can be used to monitor the equivalence point of the titration. Thymol blue, on the other hand, cannot be used for the same purpose (see Table 16.1).*

Figure 16.8 *Solutions containing extracts of red cabbage (obtained by boiling the cabbage in water) produce different colors when treated with an acid and a base. The pH of the solutions increases from left to right.*

the steep portion of the pH profile includes the range over which phenolphthalein changes from colorless to reddish pink. Whenever such a correspondence occurs, the indicator can be used to locate the equivalence point of the titration (Figure 16.7).

Many acid-base indicators are plant pigments. For example, by boiling chopped red cabbage in water we can extract pigments that exhibit many different colors at various pHs (Figure 16.8). Table 16.1 lists a number of indicators commonly used in acid-base titrations. The choice of a particular indicator depends on the strength of the acid and base to be titrated. Example 16.7 illustrates this point.

Example 16.7

Which indicator or indicators listed in Table 16.1 would you use for the acid-base titrations shown in (a) Figure 16.4, (b) Figure 16.5, and (c) Figure 16.6?

(Continued)

TABLE 16.1	Some Common Acid-Base Indicators		
		Color	
Indicator	In Acid	In Base	pH Range*
Thymol blue	Red	Yellow	1.2–2.8
Bromophenol blue	Yellow	Bluish purple	3.0–4.6
Methyl orange	Orange	Yellow	3.1–4.4
Methyl red	Red	Yellow	4.2–6.3
Chlorophenol blue	Yellow	Red	4.8–6.4
Bromothymol blue	Yellow	Blue	6.0–7.6
Cresol red	Yellow	Red	7.2–8.8
Phenolphthalein	Colorless	Reddish pink	8.3–10.0

*The pH range is defined as the range over which the indicator changes from the acid color to the base color.

Strategy The choice of an indicator for a particular titration is based on the fact that its pH range for color change must overlap the steep portion of the titration curve. Otherwise we cannot use the color change to locate the equivalence point.

Solution (a) Near the equivalence point, the pH of the solution changes abruptly from 4 to 10. Therefore, all the indicators except thymol blue, bromophenol blue, and methyl orange are suitable for use in the titration.

(b) Here the steep portion covers the pH range between 7 and 10; therefore, the suitable indicators are cresol red and phenolphthalein.

(c) Here the steep portion of the pH curve covers the pH range between 3 and 7; therefore, the suitable indicators are bromophenol blue, methyl orange, methyl red, and chlorophenol blue.

Practice Exercise Referring to Table 16.1, specify which indicator or indicators you would use for the following titrations: (a) HBr versus CH_3NH_2, (b) HNO_3 versus NaOH, (c) HNO_2 versus KOH.

Similar problem: 16.35.

16.6 Solubility Equilibria

Precipitation reactions are important in industry, medicine, and everyday life. For example, the preparation of many essential industrial chemicals such as sodium carbonate (Na_2CO_3) is based on precipitation reactions. The dissolving of tooth enamel, which is mainly made of hydroxyapatite [$Ca_5(PO_4)_3OH$], in an acidic medium leads to tooth decay. Barium sulfate ($BaSO_4$), an insoluble compound that is opaque to X rays, is used to diagnose ailments of the digestive tract. Stalactites and stalagmites, which consist of calcium carbonate ($CaCO_3$), are produced by a precipitation reaction, and so are many foods, such as fudge.

The general rules for predicting the solubility of ionic compounds in water were introduced in Section 4.2. Although useful, these solubility rules do not enable us to make quantitative predictions about how much of a given ionic compound will dissolve in water. To develop a quantitative approach, we start with what we already know about chemical equilibrium. Unless otherwise stated, in the following discussion the solvent is water and the temperature is 25°C.

$BaSO_4$ imaging of human large intestine.

Solubility Product

Consider a saturated solution of silver chloride that is in contact with solid silver chloride. The solubility equilibrium can be represented as

$$AgCl(s) \rightleftharpoons Ag^+(aq) + Cl^-(aq)$$

Because salts such as AgCl are considered as strong electrolytes, all the AgCl that dissolves in water is assumed to dissociate completely into Ag^+ and Cl^- ions. We know from Chapter 14 that for heterogeneous reactions the concentration of the solid is a constant. Thus, we can write the equilibrium constant for the dissolution of AgCl (see Example 14.5) as

$$K_{sp} = [Ag^+][Cl^-]$$

where K_{sp} is called the solubility product constant or simply *the solubility product*. In general, the **solubility product** of a compound is *the product of the molar concentrations of the constituent ions, each raised to the power of its stoichiometric coefficient in the equilibrium equation.*

Because each AgCl unit contains only one Ag^+ ion and one Cl^- ion, its solubility product expression is particularly simple to write. The following cases are more complex:

- MgF_2

$$MgF_2(s) \rightleftharpoons Mg^{2+}(aq) + 2F^-(aq) \qquad K_{sp} = [Mg^{2+}][F^-]^2$$

- Ag_2CO_3

$$Ag_2CO_3(s) \rightleftharpoons 2Ag^+(aq) + CO_3^{2-}(aq) \qquad K_{sp} = [Ag^+]^2[CO_3^{2-}]$$

- $Ca_3(PO_4)_2$

$$Ca_3(PO_4)_2(s) \rightleftharpoons 3Ca^{2+}(aq) + 2PO_4^{3-}(aq) \qquad K_{sp} = [Ca^{2+}]^3[PO_4^{3-}]^2$$

Table 16.2 lists the solubility products for a number of salts of low solubility. Soluble salts such as NaCl and KNO_3, which have very large K_{sp} values, are not listed in the table for essentially the same reason that we did not include K_a values for strong acids in Table 15.3. The value of K_{sp} indicates the solubility of an ionic compound— the smaller the value, the less soluble the compound in water. However, in using K_{sp} values to compare solubilities, you should choose compounds that have similar formulas, such as AgCl and ZnS, or CaF_2 and $Fe(OH)_2$.

A cautionary note: In Chapter 15 (p. 649) we assumed that dissolved substances exhibit ideal behavior for our calculations involving solution concentrations, but this assumption is not always valid. For example, a solution of barium fluoride (BaF_2) may contain both neutral and charged ion pairs, such as BaF_2 and BaF^+, in addition to free Ba^{2+} and F^- ions. Furthermore, many anions in the ionic compounds listed in Table 16.2 are conjugate bases of weak acids. Consider copper sulfide (CuS). The S^{2-} ion can hydrolyze as follows

$$S^{2-}(aq) + H_2O(l) \rightleftharpoons HS^-(aq) + OH^-(aq)$$
$$HS^-(aq) + H_2O(l) \rightleftharpoons H_2S(aq) + OH^-(aq)$$

And highly charged small metal ions such as Al^{3+} and Bi^{3+} will undergo hydrolysis as discussed in Section 15.10. Both ion-pair formation and salt hydrolysis decrease the concentrations of the ions that appear in the K_{sp} expression, but we need not be concerned with the deviations from ideal behavior here.

TABLE 16.2	Solubility Products of Some Slightly Soluble Ionic Compounds at 25°C		
Compound	K_{sp}	**Compound**	K_{sp}
Aluminum hydroxide [Al(OH)$_3$]	1.8×10^{-33}	Lead(II) chromate (PbCrO$_4$)	2.0×10^{-14}
Barium carbonate (BaCO$_3$)	8.1×10^{-9}	Lead(II) fluoride (PbF$_2$)	4.1×10^{-8}
Barium fluoride (BaF$_2$)	1.7×10^{-6}	Lead(II) iodide (PbI$_2$)	1.4×10^{-8}
Barium sulfate (BaSO$_4$)	1.1×10^{-10}	Lead(II) sulfide (PbS)	3.4×10^{-28}
Bismuth sulfide (Bi$_2$S$_3$)	1.6×10^{-72}	Magnesium carbonate (MgCO$_3$)	4.0×10^{-5}
Cadmium sulfide (CdS)	8.0×10^{-28}	Magnesium hydroxide [Mg(OH)$_2$]	1.2×10^{-11}
Calcium carbonate (CaCO$_3$)	8.7×10^{-9}	Manganese(II) sulfide (MnS)	3.0×10^{-14}
Calcium fluoride (CaF$_2$)	4.0×10^{-11}	Mercury(I) chloride (Hg$_2$Cl$_2$)	3.5×10^{-18}
Calcium hydroxide [Ca(OH)$_2$]	8.0×10^{-6}	Mercury(II) sulfide (HgS)	4.0×10^{-54}
Calcium phosphate [Ca$_3$(PO$_4$)$_2$]	1.2×10^{-26}	Nickel(II) sulfide (NiS)	1.4×10^{-24}
Chromium(III) hydroxide [Cr(OH)$_3$]	3.0×10^{-29}	Silver bromide (AgBr)	7.7×10^{-13}
Cobalt(II) sulfide (CoS)	4.0×10^{-21}	Silver carbonate (Ag$_2$CO$_3$)	8.1×10^{-12}
Copper(I) bromide (CuBr)	4.2×10^{-8}	Silver chloride (AgCl)	1.6×10^{-10}
Copper(I) iodide (CuI)	5.1×10^{-12}	Silver iodide (AgI)	8.3×10^{-17}
Copper(II) hydroxide [Cu(OH)$_2$]	2.2×10^{-20}	Silver sulfate (Ag$_2$SO$_4$)	1.4×10^{-5}
Copper(II) sulfide (CuS)	6.0×10^{-37}	Silver sulfide (Ag$_2$S)	6.0×10^{-51}
Iron(II) hydroxide [Fe(OH)$_2$]	1.6×10^{-14}	Strontium carbonate (SrCO$_3$)	1.6×10^{-9}
Iron(III) hydroxide [Fe(OH)$_3$]	1.1×10^{-36}	Strontium sulfate (SrSO$_4$)	3.8×10^{-7}
Iron(II) sulfide (FeS)	6.0×10^{-19}	Tin(II) sulfide (SnS)	1.0×10^{-26}
Lead(II) carbonate (PbCO$_3$)	3.3×10^{-14}	Zinc hydroxide [Zn(OH)$_2$]	1.8×10^{-14}
Lead(II) chloride (PbCl$_2$)	2.4×10^{-4}	Zinc sulfide (ZnS)	3.0×10^{-23}

For the dissolution of an ionic solid in aqueous solution, any one of the following conditions may exist: (1) the solution is unsaturated, (2) the solution is saturated, or (3) the solution is supersaturated. For concentrations of ions that do not correspond to equilibrium conditions we use the reaction quotient (see Section 14.4), which in this case is called the *ion product (Q)*, to predict whether a precipitate will form. Note that Q has the same form as K_{sp} except that the concentrations of ions are *not* equilibrium concentrations. For example, if we mix a solution containing Ag$^+$ ions with one containing Cl$^-$ ions, then the ion product is given by

$$Q = [\text{Ag}^+]_0[\text{Cl}^-]_0$$

The subscript 0 reminds us that these are initial concentrations and do not necessarily correspond to those at equilibrium. The possible relationships between Q and K_{sp} are

$$Q < K_{sp}$$
$$[\text{Ag}^+]_0[\text{Cl}^-]_0 < 1.6 \times 10^{-10}$$
Unsaturated solution (no precipitation)

$$Q = K_{sp}$$
$$[\text{Ag}^+][\text{Cl}^-] = 1.6 \times 10^{-10}$$
Saturated solution (no precipitation)

$$Q > K_{sp}$$
$$[\text{Ag}^+]_0[\text{Cl}^-]_0 > 1.6 \times 10^{-10}$$
Supersaturated solution; AgCl will precipitate out until the product of the ionic concentrations is equal to 1.6×10^{-10}

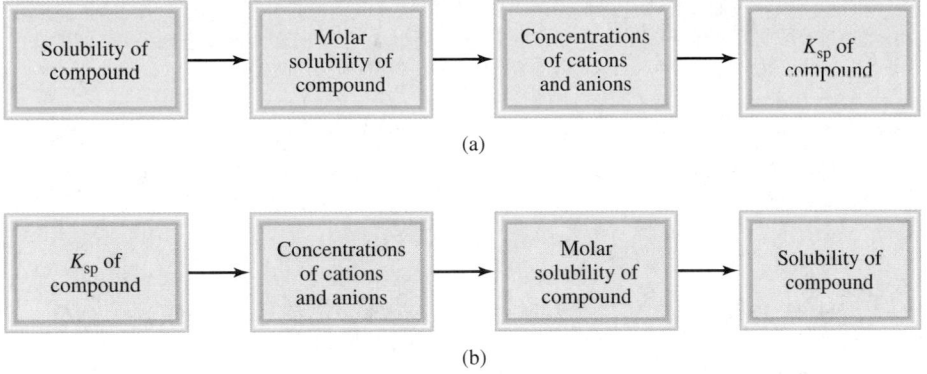

Figure 16.9 *Sequence of steps (a) for calculating K_{sp} from solubility data and (b) for calculating solubility from K_{sp} data.*

Molar Solubility and Solubility

There are two other ways to express a substance's solubility: ***molar solubility,*** which is *the number of moles of solute in 1 L of a saturated solution (mol/L),* and ***solubility,*** which is *the number of grams of solute in 1 L of a saturated solution (g/L).* Note that both these expressions refer to the concentration of saturated solutions at some given temperature (usually 25°C).

Both molar solubility and solubility are convenient to use in the laboratory. We can use them to determine K_{sp} by following the steps outlined in Figure 16.9(a). Example 16.8 illustrates this procedure.

Example 16.8

The solubility of calcium sulfate ($CaSO_4$) is found to be 0.67 g/L. Calculate the value of K_{sp} for calcium sulfate.

Strategy We are given the solubility of $CaSO_4$ and asked to calculate its K_{sp}. The sequence of conversion steps, according to Figure 16.9(a), is

$$\text{solubility of } CaSO_4 \text{ in g/L} \longrightarrow \text{molar solubility of } CaSO_4 \longrightarrow [Ca^{2+}] \text{ and } [SO_4^{2-}] \longrightarrow K_{sp} \text{ of } CaSO_4$$

Solution Consider the dissociation of $CaSO_4$ in water. Let s be the molar solubility (in mol/L) of $CaSO_4$.

Calcium sulfate is used as a drying agent and in the manufacture of paints, ceramics, and paper. A hydrated form of calcium sulfate, called plaster of Paris, is used to make casts for broken bones.

	$CaSO_4(s) \rightleftharpoons$	$Ca^{2+}(aq)$ +	$SO_4^{2-}(aq)$
Initial (*M*):		0	0
Change (*M*):	$-s$	$+s$	$+s$
Equilibrium (*M*):		s	s

The solubility product for $CaSO_4$ is

$$K_{sp} = [Ca^{2+}][SO_4^{2-}] = s^2$$

First, we calculate the number of moles of $CaSO_4$ dissolved in 1 L of solution:

$$\frac{0.67 \text{ g } CaSO_4}{1 \text{ L soln}} \times \frac{1 \text{ mol } CaSO_4}{136.2 \text{ g } CaSO_4} = 4.9 \times 10^{-3} \text{ mol/L} = s$$

(Continued)

From the solubility equilibrium we see that for every mole of $CaSO_4$ that dissolves, 1 mole of Ca^{2+} and 1 mole of SO_4^{2-} are produced. Thus, at equilibrium,

$$[Ca^{2+}] = 4.9 \times 10^{-3}\,M \quad \text{and} \quad [SO_4^{2-}] = 4.9 \times 10^{-3}\,M$$

Now we can calculate K_{sp}:

$$\begin{aligned}
K_{sp} &= [Ca^{2+}][SO_4^{2-}] \\
&= (4.9 \times 10^{-3})(4.9 \times 10^{-3}) \\
&= 2.4 \times 10^{-5}
\end{aligned}$$

Similar problem: 16.48.

Practice Exercise The solubility of lead chromate ($PbCrO_4$) is 4.5×10^{-5} g/L. Calculate the solubility product of this compound.

Sometimes we are given the value of K_{sp} for a compound and asked to calculate the compound's molar solubility. For example, the K_{sp} of silver bromide (AgBr) is 7.7×10^{-13}. We can calculate its molar solubility by the same procedure as that for acid ionization constants. First we identify the species present at equilibrium. Here we have Ag^+ and Br^- ions. Let s be the molar solubility (in mol/L) of AgBr. Because one unit of AgBr yields one Ag^+ and one Br^- ion, at equilibrium both $[Ag^+]$ and $[Br^-]$ are equal to s. We summarize the changes in concentrations as follows:

	AgBr(s) $\rightleftharpoons$ Ag$^+$(aq) +		Br$^-$(aq)
Initial (M):		0.00	0.00
Change (M):	$-s$	$+s$	$+s$
Equilibrium (M):		s	s

From Table 16.2 we write

$$\begin{aligned}
K_{sp} &= [Ag^+][Br^-] \\
7.7 \times 10^{-13} &= (s)(s) \\
s &= \sqrt{7.7 \times 10^{-13}} = 8.8 \times 10^{-7}\,M
\end{aligned}$$

Therefore, at equilibrium

$$[Ag^+] = 8.8 \times 10^{-7}\,M$$
$$[Br^-] = 8.8 \times 10^{-7}\,M$$

Thus, the molar solubility of AgBr also is $8.8 \times 10^{-7}\,M$.

Example 16.9 makes use of this approach.

Example 16.9

Using the data in Table 16.2, calculate the solubility of copper(II) hydroxide, $Cu(OH)_2$, in g/L.

Strategy We are given the K_{sp} of $Cu(OH)_2$ and asked to calculate its solubility in g/L. The sequence of conversion steps, according to Figure 16.9(b), is

$$\begin{array}{ccccc}
K_{sp}\ \text{of} & \longrightarrow & [Cu^{2+}]\ \text{and} & \longrightarrow & \text{molar solubility} & \longrightarrow & \text{solubility of} \\
Cu(OH)_2 & & [OH^-] & & \text{of } Cu(OH)_2 & & Cu(OH)_2 \text{ in g/L}
\end{array}$$

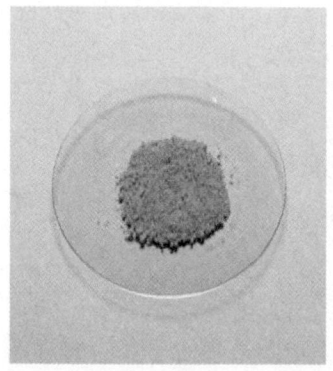

Silver bromide is used in photographic emulsions.

Copper(II) hydroxide is used as a pesticide and to treat seeds.

(Continued)

Solution Consider the dissociation of $Cu(OH)_2$ in water:

$$Cu(OH)_2(s) \rightleftharpoons Cu^{2+}(aq) + 2OH^-(aq)$$

Initial (*M*):		0	0
Change (*M*):	$-s$	$+s$	$+2s$
Equilibrium (*M*):		s	$2s$

Note that the molar concentration of OH^- is twice that of Cu^{2+}. The solubility product of $Cu(OH)_2$ is

$$K_{sp} = [Cu^{2+}][OH^-]^2$$
$$= (s)(2s)^2 = 4s^3$$

From the K_{sp} value in Table 16.2, we solve for the molar solubility of $Cu(OH)_2$ as follows:

$$2.2 \times 10^{-20} = 4s^3$$
$$s^3 = \frac{2.2 \times 10^{-20}}{4} = 5.5 \times 10^{-21}$$

Hence
$$s = 1.8 \times 10^{-7} \, M$$

Finally, from the molar mass of $Cu(OH)_2$ and its molar solubility, we calculate the solubility in g/L:

$$\text{solubility of } Cu(OH)_2 = \frac{1.8 \times 10^{-7} \text{ mol } Cu(OH)_2}{1 \text{ L soln}} \times \frac{97.57 \text{ g } Cu(OH)_2}{1 \text{ mol } Cu(OH)_2}$$
$$= 1.8 \times 10^{-5} \text{ g/L}$$

Similar problem: 16.50.

Practice Exercise Calculate the solubility of silver chloride (AgCl) in g/L.

As Examples 16.8 and 16.9 show, solubility and solubility product are related. If we know one, we can calculate the other, but each quantity provides different information. Table 16.3 shows the relationship between molar solubility and solubility product for a number of ionic compounds.

When carrying out solubility and/or solubility product calculations, keep in mind the following important points:

1. Solubility is the quantity of a substance that dissolves in a certain quantity of water. In solubility equilibria calculations, it is usually expressed as *grams* of

TABLE 16.3 Relationship Between K_{sp} and Molar Solubility (s)

Compound	K_{sp} Expression	Cation	Anion	Relation Between K_{sp} and s
AgCl	$[Ag^+][Cl^-]$	s	s	$K_{sp} = s^2; s = (K_{sp})^{\frac{1}{2}}$
BaSO₄	$[Ba^{2+}][SO_4^{2-}]$	s	s	$K_{sp} = s^2; s = (K_{sp})^{\frac{1}{2}}$
Ag₂CO₃	$[Ag^+]^2[CO_3^{2-}]$	$2s$	s	$K_{sp} = 4s^3; s = \left(\frac{K_{sp}}{4}\right)^{\frac{1}{3}}$
PbF₂	$[Pb^{2+}][F^-]^2$	s	$2s$	$K_{sp} = 4s^3; s = \left(\frac{K_{sp}}{4}\right)^{\frac{1}{3}}$
Al(OH)₃	$[Al^{3+}][OH^-]^3$	s	$3s$	$K_{sp} = 27s^4; s = \left(\frac{K_{sp}}{27}\right)^{\frac{1}{4}}$
Ca₃(PO₄)₂	$[Ca^{2+}]^3[PO_4^{3-}]^2$	$3s$	$2s$	$K_{sp} = 108s^5; s = \left(\frac{K_{sp}}{108}\right)^{\frac{1}{5}}$

solute per liter of solution. Molar solubility is the number of *moles* of solute per liter of solution.

2. Solubility product is an equilibrium constant.

3. Molar solubility, solubility, and solubility product all refer to a *saturated solution*.

Predicting Precipitation Reactions

A kidney stone.

From a knowledge of the solubility rules (see Section 4.2) and the solubility products listed in Table 16.2, we can predict whether a precipitate will form when we mix two solutions or add a soluble compound to a solution. This ability often has practical value. In industrial and laboratory preparations, we can adjust the concentrations of ions until the ion product exceeds K_{sp} in order to obtain a given compound (in the form of a precipitate). The ability to predict precipitation reactions is also useful in medicine. For example, kidney stones, which can be extremely painful, consist largely of calcium oxalate, CaC_2O_4 ($K_{sp} = 2.3 \times 10^{-9}$). The normal physiological concentration of calcium ions in blood plasma is about 5 mM (1 mM = 1×10^{-3} M). Oxalate ions ($C_2O_4^{2-}$), derived from oxalic acid present in many vegetables such as rhubarb and spinach, react with the calcium ions to form insoluble calcium oxalate, which can gradually build up in the kidneys. Proper adjustment of a patient's diet can help to reduce precipitate formation. Example 16.10 illustrates the steps involved in predicting precipitation reactions.

Example 16.10

Exactly 200 mL of 0.0040 M $BaCl_2$ are mixed with exactly 600 mL of 0.0080 M K_2SO_4. Will a precipitate form?

Strategy Under what condition will an ionic compound precipitate from solution? The ions in solution are Ba^{2+}, Cl^-, K^+, and SO_4^{2-}. According to the solubility rules listed in Table 4.2 (p. 123), the only precipitate that can form is $BaSO_4$. From the information given, we can calculate $[Ba^{2+}]$ and $[SO_4^{2-}]$ because we know the number of moles of the ions in the original solutions and the volume of the combined solution. Next, we calculate the reaction quotient Q ($Q = [Ba^{2+}]_0[SO_4^{2-}]_0$) and compare the value of Q with K_{sp} of $BaSO_4$ to see if a precipitate will form, that is, if the solution is supersaturated. It is helpful to make a sketch of the situation.

Solution The number of moles of Ba^{2+} present in the original 200 mL of solution is

$$200 \text{ mL} \times \frac{0.0040 \text{ mol } Ba^{2+}}{1 \text{ L soln}} \times \frac{1 \text{ L}}{1000 \text{ mL}} = 8.0 \times 10^{-4} \text{ mol } Ba^{2+}$$

(Continued)

The total volume after combining the two solutions is 800 mL. The concentration of Ba^{2+} in the 800 mL volume is

$$[Ba^{2+}] = \frac{8.0 \times 10^{-4} \text{ mol}}{800 \text{ mL}} \times \frac{1000 \text{ mL}}{1 \text{ L soln}}$$
$$= 1.0 \times 10^{-3} M$$

We assume that the volumes are additive.

The number of moles of SO_4^{2-} in the original 600 mL solution is

$$600 \text{ mL} \times \frac{0.0080 \text{ mol } SO_4^{2-}}{1 \text{ L soln}} \times \frac{1 \text{ L}}{1000 \text{ mL}} = 4.8 \times 10^{-3} \text{ mol } SO_4^{2-}$$

The concentration of SO_4^{2-} in the 800 mL of the combined solution is

$$[SO_4^{2-}] = \frac{4.8 \times 10^{-3} \text{ mol}}{800 \text{ mL}} \times \frac{1000 \text{ mL}}{1 \text{ L soln}}$$
$$= 6.0 \times 10^{-3} M$$

Now we must compare Q and K_{sp}. From Table 16.2,

$$BaSO_4(s) \rightleftharpoons Ba^{2+}(aq) + SO_4^{2}(aq) \qquad K_{sp} = 1.1 \times 10^{-10}$$

As for Q,

$$Q = [Ba^{2+}]_0[SO_4^{2-}]_0 = (1.0 \times 10^{-3})(6.0 \times 10^{-3})$$
$$= 6.0 \times 10^{-6}$$

Therefore,

$$Q > K_{sp}$$

The solution is supersaturated because the value of Q indicates that the concentrations of the ions are too large. Thus, some of the $BaSO_4$ will precipitate out of solution until

$$[Ba^{2+}][SO_4^{2-}] = 1.1 \times 10^{-10}$$

Similar problem: 16.53.

Practice Exercise If 2.00 mL of 0.200 M NaOH are added to 1.00 L of 0.100 M $CaCl_2$, will precipitation occur?

16.7 Separation of Ions by Fractional Precipitation

In chemical analysis, it is sometimes desirable to remove one type of ion from solution by precipitation while leaving other ions in solution. For instance, the addition of sulfate ions to a solution containing both potassium and barium ions causes $BaSO_4$ to precipitate out, thereby removing most of the Ba^{2+} ions from the solution. The other "product," K_2SO_4, is soluble and will remain in solution. The $BaSO_4$ precipitate can be separated from the solution by filtration.

Even when *both* products are insoluble, we can still achieve some degree of separation by choosing the proper reagent to bring about precipitation. Consider a solution that contains Cl^-, Br^-, and I^- ions. One way to separate these ions is to convert them to insoluble silver halides. As the K_{sp} values in the margin show, the solubility of the halides decreases from AgCl to AgI. Thus, when a soluble compound such as silver nitrate is slowly added to this solution, AgI begins to precipitate first, followed by AgBr and then AgCl.

Compound	K_{sp}
AgCl	1.6×10^{-10}
AgBr	7.7×10^{-13}
AgI	8.3×10^{-17}

Example 16.11 describes the separation of only two ions (Cl^- and Br^-), but the procedure can be applied to a solution containing more than two different types of ions if precipitates of differing solubility can be formed.

AgCl (left) and AgBr (right).

Similar problems: 16.55, 16.56.

Example 16.11

A solution contains 0.020 M Cl$^-$ ions and 0.020 M Br$^-$ ions. To separate the Cl$^-$ ions from the Br$^-$ ions, solid AgNO$_3$ is slowly added to the solution without changing the volume. What concentration of Ag$^+$ ions (in mol/L) is needed to precipitate as much AgBr as possible without precipitating AgCl?

Strategy In solution, AgNO$_3$ dissociates into Ag$^+$ and NO$_3^-$ ions. The Ag$^+$ ions then combine with the Cl$^-$ and Br$^-$ ions to form AgCl and AgBr precipitates. Because AgBr is less soluble (it has a smaller K_{sp} than that of AgCl), it will precipitate first. Therefore, this is a fractional precipitation problem. Knowing the concentrations of Cl$^-$ and Br$^-$ ions, we can calculate [Ag$^+$] from the K_{sp} values. Keep in mind that K_{sp} refers to a saturated solution. To initiate precipitation, [Ag$^+$] must exceed the concentration in the saturated solution in each case.

Solution The solubility equilibrium for AgBr is

$$AgBr(s) \rightleftharpoons Ag^+(aq) + Br^-(aq) \qquad K_{sp} = [Ag^+][Br^-]$$

Because [Br$^-$] = 0.020 M, the concentration of Ag$^+$ that must be exceeded to initiate the precipitation of AgBr is

$$[Ag^+] = \frac{K_{sp}}{[Br^-]} = \frac{7.7 \times 10^{-13}}{0.020}$$
$$= 3.9 \times 10^{-11} \, M$$

Thus, [Ag$^+$] > $3.9 \times 10^{-11} \, M$ is required to start the precipitation of AgBr. The solubility equilibrium for AgCl is

$$AgCl(s) \rightleftharpoons Ag^+(aq) + Cl^-(aq) \qquad K_{sp} = [Ag^+][Cl^-]$$

so that

$$[Ag^+] = \frac{K_{sp}}{[Cl^-]} = \frac{1.6 \times 10^{-10}}{0.020}$$
$$= 8.0 \times 10^{-9} \, M$$

Therefore, [Ag$^+$] > $8.0 \times 10^{-9} \, M$ is needed to initiate the precipitation of AgCl.

To precipitate the Br$^-$ ions as AgBr without precipitating the Cl$^-$ ions as AgCl, then, [Ag$^+$] must be greater than $3.9 \times 10^{-11} \, M$ and lower than $8.0 \times 10^{-9} \, M$.

Practice Exercise The solubility products of AgCl and Ag$_3$PO$_4$ are 1.6×10^{-10} and 1.8×10^{-18}, respectively. If Ag$^+$ is added (without changing the volume) to 1.00 L of a solution containing 0.10 mol Cl$^-$ and 0.10 mol PO$_4^{3-}$, calculate the concentration of Ag$^+$ ions (in mol/L) required to initiate (a) the precipitation of AgCl and (b) the precipitation of Ag$_3$PO$_4$.

Example 16.11 raises the question, What is the concentration of Br$^-$ ions remaining in solution just before AgCl begins to precipitate? To answer this question we let [Ag$^+$] = $8.0 \times 10^{-9} \, M$. Then

$$[Br^-] = \frac{K_{sp}}{[Ag^+]}$$
$$= \frac{7.7 \times 10^{-13}}{8.0 \times 10^{-9}}$$
$$= 9.6 \times 10^{-5} \, M$$

The percent of Br^- remaining in solution (the *unprecipitated* Br^-) at the critical concentration of Ag^+ is

$$
\begin{aligned}
\% \ Br^- &= \frac{[Br^-]_{unppt'd}}{[Br^-]_{original}} \times 100\% \\
&= \frac{9.6 \times 10^{-5} \, M}{0.020 \, M} \times 100\% \\
&= 0.48\% \ \text{unprecipitated}
\end{aligned}
$$

Thus, $(100 - 0.48)$ percent, or 99.52 percent, of Br^- will have precipitated as AgBr just before AgCl begins to precipitate. By this procedure, the Br^- ions can be quantitatively separated from the Cl^- ions.

16.8 The Common Ion Effect and Solubility

In Section 16.2 we discussed the effect of a common ion on acid and base ionizations. Here we will examine the relationship between the common ion effect and solubility.

As we have noted, the solubility product is an equilibrium constant; precipitation of an ionic compound from solution occurs whenever the ion product exceeds K_{sp} for that substance. In a saturated solution of AgCl, for example, the ion product $[Ag^+][Cl^-]$ is, of course, equal to K_{sp}. Furthermore, simple stoichiometry tells us that $[Ag^+] = [Cl^-]$. But this equality does not hold in all situations.

Suppose we study a solution containing two dissolved substances that share a common ion, say, AgCl and $AgNO_3$. In addition to the dissociation of AgCl, the following process also contributes to the total concentration of the common silver ions in solution:

$$AgNO_3(s) \xrightarrow{H_2O} Ag^+(aq) + NO_3^-(aq)$$

The solubility equilibrium of AgCl is

$$AgCl(s) \rightleftharpoons Ag^+(aq) + Cl^-(aq)$$

If $AgNO_3$ is added to a saturated AgCl solution, the increase in $[Ag^+]$ will make the ion product greater than the solubility product:

$$Q = [Ag^+]_0[Cl^-]_0 > K_{sp}$$

To reestablish equilibrium, some AgCl will precipitate out of the solution, as Le Châtelier's principle would predict, until the ion product is once again equal to K_{sp}. The effect of adding a common ion, then, is a *decrease* in the solubility of the salt (AgCl) in solution. Note that in this case $[Ag^+]$ is no longer equal to $[Cl^-]$ at equilibrium; rather, $[Ag^+] > [Cl^-]$.

Example 16.12 shows the common ion effect on solubility.

At a given temperature, only the solubility of a compound is altered (decreased) by the common ion effect. Its solubility product, which is an equilibrium constant, remains the same whether or not other substances are present in the solution.

Example 16.12

Calculate the solubility of silver chloride (in g/L) in a $6.5 \times 10^{-3} \, M$ silver nitrate solution.

Strategy This is a common-ion problem. The common ion here is Ag^+, which is supplied by both AgCl and $AgNO_3$. Remember that the presence of the common ion will affect only the solubility of AgCl (in g/L), but not the K_{sp} value because it is an equilibrium constant.

(Continued)

Solution *Step 1:* The relevant species in solution are Ag^+ ions (from both AgCl and $AgNO_3$) and Cl^- ions. The NO_3^- ions are spectator ions.

Step 2: Because $AgNO_3$ is a soluble strong electrolyte, it dissociates completely:

$$AgNO_3(s) \xrightarrow{H_2O} Ag^+(aq) + NO_3^-(aq)$$
$$6.5 \times 10^{-3}\,M \quad 6.5 \times 10^{-3}\,M$$

Let s be the molar solubility of AgCl in $AgNO_3$ solution. We summarize the changes in concentrations as follows:

	AgCl(s) $\rightleftharpoons$	$Ag^+(aq)$	+ $Cl^-(aq)$
Initial (*M*):		6.5×10^{-3}	0.00
Change (*M*):	$-s$	$+s$	$+s$
Equilibrium (*M*):		$(6.5 \times 10^{-3} + s)$	s

Step 3:
$$K_{sp} = [Ag^+][Cl^-]$$
$$1.6 \times 10^{-10} = (6.5 \times 10^{-3} + s)(s)$$

Because AgCl is quite insoluble and the presence of Ag^+ ions from $AgNO_3$ further lowers the solubility of AgCl, s must be very small compared with 6.5×10^{-3}. Therefore, applying the approximation $6.5 \times 10^{-3} + s \approx 6.5 \times 10^{-3}$, we obtain

$$1.6 \times 10^{-10} = (6.5 \times 10^{-3})s$$
$$s = 2.5 \times 10^{-8}\,M$$

Step 4: At equilibrium

$$[Ag^+] = (6.5 \times 10^{-3} + 2.5 \times 10^{-8})\,M \approx 6.5 \times 10^{-3}\,M$$
$$[Cl^-] = 2.5 \times 10^{-8}\,M$$

and so our approximation was justified in step 3. Because all the Cl^- ions must come from AgCl, the amount of AgCl dissolved in $AgNO_3$ solution also is $2.5 \times 10^{-8}\,M$. Then, knowing the molar mass of AgCl (143.4 g), we can calculate the solubility of AgCl as follows:

$$\text{solubility of AgCl in } AgNO_3 \text{ solution} = \frac{2.5 \times 10^{-8}\text{ mol AgCl}}{1\text{ L soln}} \times \frac{143.4\text{ g AgCl}}{1\text{ mol AgCl}}$$
$$= 3.6 \times 10^{-6}\text{ g/L}$$

Check The solubility of AgCl in pure water is 1.9×10^{-3} g/L (see the Practice Exercise in Example 16.9). Therefore, the lower solubility (3.6×10^{-6} g/L) in the presence of $AgNO_3$ is reasonable. You should also be able to predict the lower solubility using Le Châtelier's principle. Adding Ag^+ ions shifts the equilibrium to the left, thus decreasing the solubility of AgCl.

Similar problem: 16.60.

Practice Exercise Calculate the solubility in g/L of AgBr in (a) pure water and (b) 0.0010 *M* NaBr.

16.9 pH and Solubility

The solubilities of many substances also depend on the pH of the solution. Consider the solubility equilibrium of magnesium hydroxide:

$$Mg(OH)_2(s) \rightleftharpoons Mg^{2+}(aq) + 2OH^-(aq)$$

Adding OH^- ions (increasing the pH) shifts the equilibrium from right to left, thereby decreasing the solubility of $Mg(OH)_2$. (This is another example of the common ion effect.) On the other hand, adding H^+ ions (decreasing the pH) shifts the equilibrium from left to right, and the solubility of $Mg(OH)_2$ increases. Thus, insoluble bases tend to dissolve in acidic solutions. Similarly, insoluble acids dissolve in basic solutions.

To explore the quantitative effect of pH on the solubility of $Mg(OH)_2$, let us first calculate the pH of a saturated $Mg(OH)_2$ solution. We write

$$K_{sp} = [Mg^{2+}][OH^-]^2 = 1.2 \times 10^{-11}$$

Let s be the molar solubility of $Mg(OH)_2$. Proceeding as in Example 16.9,

$$K_{sp} = (s)(2s)^2 = 4s^3$$
$$4s^3 = 1.2 \times 10^{-11}$$
$$s^3 = 3.0 \times 10^{-12}$$
$$s = 1.4 \times 10^{-4}\,M$$

At equilibrium, therefore,

$$[OH^-] = 2 \times 1.4 \times 10^{-4}\,M = 2.8 \times 10^{-4}\,M$$
$$pOH = -\log(2.8 \times 10^{-4}) = 3.55$$
$$pH = 14.00 - 3.55 = 10.45$$

In a medium with a pH of less than 10.45, the solubility of $Mg(OH)_2$ would increase. This follows from the fact that a lower pH indicates a higher $[H^+]$ and thus a lower $[OH^-]$, as we would expect from $K_w = [H^+][OH^-]$. Consequently, $[Mg^{2+}]$ rises to maintain the equilibrium condition, and more $Mg(OH)_2$ dissolves. The dissolution process and the effect of extra H^+ ions can be summarized as follows:

$$Mg(OH)_2(s) \rightleftharpoons Mg^{2+}(aq) + 2OH^-(aq)$$
$$2H^+(aq) + 2OH^-(aq) \rightleftharpoons 2H_2O(l)$$

Overall: $Mg(OH)_2(s) + 2H^+(aq) \rightleftharpoons Mg^{2+}(aq) + 2H_2O(l)$

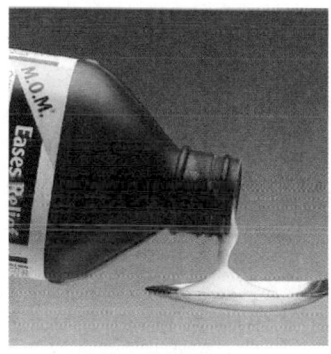

Milk of magnesia, which contains $Mg(OH)_2$, is used to treat acid indigestion.

If the pH of the medium were higher than 10.45, $[OH^-]$ would be higher and the solubility of $Mg(OH)_2$ would decrease because of the common ion (OH^-) effect.

The pH also influences the solubility of salts that contain a basic anion. For example, the solubility equilibrium for BaF_2 is

$$BaF_2(s) \rightleftharpoons Ba^{2+}(aq) + 2F^-(aq)$$

and

$$K_{sp} = [Ba^{2+}][F^-]^2$$

In an acidic medium, the high $[H^+]$ will shift the following equilibrium from left to right:

$$H^+(aq) + F^-(aq) \rightleftharpoons HF(aq)$$

Because HF is a weak acid, its conjugate base, F^-, has an affinity for H^+.

As $[F^-]$ decreases, $[Ba^{2+}]$ must increase to maintain the equilibrium condition. Thus, more BaF_2 dissolves. The dissolution process and the effect of pH on the solubility of BaF_2 can be summarized as follows:

$$BaF_2(s) \rightleftharpoons Ba^{2+}(aq) + 2F^-(aq)$$
$$2H^+(aq) + 2F^-(aq) \rightleftharpoons 2HF(aq)$$

Overall: $BaF_2(s) + 2H^+(aq) \rightleftharpoons Ba^{2+}(aq) + 2HF(aq)$

The solubilities of salts containing anions that do not hydrolyze are unaffected by pH. Examples of such anions are Cl^-, Br^-, and I^-.

Examples 16.13 and 16.14 deal with the effect of pH on solubility.

Example 16.13

Which of the following compounds will be more soluble in acidic solution than in water: (a) CuS, (b) AgCl, (c) $PbSO_4$?

Strategy In each case write the dissociation reaction of the salt into its cation and anion. The cation will not interact with the H^+ ion because they both bear positive charges. The anion will act as a proton acceptor only if it is the conjugate base of a weak acid. How would the removal of the anion affect the solubility of the salt?

Solution (a) The solubility equilibrium for CuS is

$$CuS(s) \rightleftharpoons Cu^{2+}(aq) + S^{2-}(aq)$$

The sulfide ion is a weak base because it is the conjugate base of the weak acid HS^-. Therefore, the S^{2-} ion reacts with the H^+ ion as follows:

$$S^{2-}(aq) + H^+(aq) \longrightarrow HS^-(aq)$$

This reaction removes the S^{2-} ions from solution. According to Le Châtelier's principle, the equilibrium will shift to the right to replace some of the S^{2-} ions that were removed, thereby increasing the solubility of CuS.

(b) The solubility equilibrium is

$$AgCl(s) \rightleftharpoons Ag^+(aq) + Cl^-(aq)$$

Because Cl^- is the conjugate base of a strong acid (HCl), the solubility of AgCl is not affected by an acid solution.

(c) The solubility equilibrium for $PbSO_4$ is

$$PbSO_4(s) \rightleftharpoons Pb^{2+}(aq) + SO_4^{2-}(aq)$$

The sulfate ion is a weak base because it is the conjugate base of the weak acid HSO_4^-. Therefore, the SO_4^{2-} ion reacts with the H^+ ion as follows:

$$SO_4^{2-}(aq) + H^+(aq) \longrightarrow HSO_4^-(aq)$$

Similar problem: 16.64.

This reaction removes the SO_4^{2-} ions from solution. According to Le Châtelier's principle, the equilibrium will shift to the right to replace some of the SO_4^{2-} ions that were removed, thereby increasing the solubility of $PbSO_4$.

Practice Exercise Are the following compounds more soluble in water or in an acidic solution: (a) $Ca(OH)_2$, (b) $Mg_3(PO_4)_2$, (c) $PbBr_2$?

Example 16.14

Calculate the concentration of aqueous ammonia necessary to initiate the precipitation of iron(II) hydroxide from a 0.0030 M solution of $FeCl_2$.

(Continued)

Strategy For iron(II) hydroxide to precipitate from solution, the product $[Fe^{2+}][OH^-]^2$ must be greater than its K_{sp}. First, we calculate $[OH^-]$ from the known $[Fe^{2+}]$ and the K_{sp} value listed in Table 16.2. This is the concentration of OH^- in a saturated solution of $Fe(OH)_2$. Next, we calculate the concentration of NH_3 that will supply this concentration of OH^- ions. Finally, any NH_3 concentration greater than the calculated value will initiate the precipitation of $Fe(OH)_2$ because the solution will become supersaturated.

Solution Ammonia reacts with water to produce OH^- ions, which then react with Fe^{2+} to form $Fe(OH)_2$. The equilibria of interest are

$$NH_3(aq) + H_2O(l) \rightleftharpoons NH_4^+(aq) + OH^-(aq)$$
$$Fe^{2+}(aq) + 2OH^-(aq) \rightleftharpoons Fe(OH)_2(s)$$

First we find the OH^- concentration above which $Fe(OH)_2$ begins to precipitate. We write

$$K_{sp} = [Fe^{2+}][OH^-]^2 = 1.6 \times 10^{-14}$$

Because $FeCl_2$ is a strong electrolyte, $[Fe^{2+}] = 0.0030\ M$ and

$$[OH^-]^2 = \frac{1.6 \times 10^{-14}}{0.0030} = 5.3 \times 10^{-12}$$
$$[OH^-] = 2.3 \times 10^{-6}\ M$$

Next, we calculate the concentration of NH_3 that will supply $2.3 \times 10^{-6}\ M\ OH^-$ ions. Let x be the initial concentration of NH_3 in mol/L. We summarize the changes in concentrations resulting from the ionization of NH_3 as follows.

	$NH_3(aq)$	$+ H_2O(l) \rightleftharpoons$	$NH_4^+(aq)$	$+$	$OH^-(aq)$
Initial (M):	x		0.00		0.00
Change (M):	-2.3×10^{-6}		$+2.3 \times 10^{-6}$		$+2.3 \times 10^{-6}$
Equilibrium (M):	$(x - 2.3 \times 10^{-6})$		2.3×10^{-6}		2.3×10^{-6}

Substituting the equilibrium concentrations in the expression for the ionization constant (see Table 15.4),

$$K_b = \frac{[NH_4^+][OH^-]}{[NH_3]}$$
$$1.8 \times 10^{-5} = \frac{(2.3 \times 10^{-6})(2.3 \times 10^{-6})}{(x - 2.3 \times 10^{-6})}$$

Solving for x, we obtain

$$x = 2.6 \times 10^{-6}\ M$$

Therefore, the concentration of NH_3 must be slightly greater than $2.6 \times 10^{-6}\ M$ to initiate the precipitation of $Fe(OH)_2$.

Similar problem: 16.68.

Practice Exercise Calculate whether or not a precipitate will form if 2.0 mL of 0.60 M NH_3 are added to 1.0 L of $1.0 \times 10^{-3}\ M$ $ZnSO_4$.

16.10 Complex Ion Equilibria and Solubility

Lewis acid-base reactions in which a metal cation combines with a Lewis base result in the formation of complex ions. Thus, we can define a ***complex ion*** as *an ion containing a central metal cation bonded to one or more molecules or ions.* Complex ions are crucial to many chemical and biological processes. Here we will consider the

Lewis acids and bases are discussed in Section 15.12.

Figure 16.10 *(Left) An aqueous cobalt(II) chloride solution. The pink color is due to the presence of Co(H₂O)₆²⁺ ions. (Right) After the addition of HCl solution, the solution turns blue because of the formation of the complex CoCl₄²⁻ ions.*

According to our definition, Co(₂O)₆²⁺ itself is a complex ion. When we write Co(H₂O)₆²⁺, we mean the hydrated Co²⁺ ion.

effect of complex ion formation on solubility. In Chapter 22 we will discuss the chemistry of complex ions in more detail.

Transition metals have a particular tendency to form complex ions because they have more than one oxidation state. This property allows them to act effectively as Lewis acids in reactions with many molecules or ions that serve as electron donors, or as Lewis bases. For example, a solution of cobalt(II) chloride is pink because of the presence of the $Co(H_2O)_6^{2+}$ ions (Figure 16.10). When HCl is added, the solution turns blue as a result of the formation of the complex ion $CoCl_4^{2-}$:

$$Co^{2+}(aq) + 4Cl^-(aq) \rightleftharpoons CoCl_4^{2-}(aq)$$

Copper(II) sulfate ($CuSO_4$) dissolves in water to produce a blue solution. The hydrated copper(II) ions are responsible for this color; many other sulfates (Na_2SO_4, for example) are colorless. Adding a *few drops* of concentrated ammonia solution to a $CuSO_4$ solution causes the formation of a light-blue precipitate, copper(II) hydroxide:

$$Cu^{2+}(aq) + 2OH^-(aq) \longrightarrow Cu(OH)_2(s)$$

The OH^- ions are supplied by the ammonia solution. If more NH_3 is added, the blue precipitate redissolves to produce a beautiful dark-blue solution, this time due to the formation of the complex ion $Cu(NH_3)_4^{2+}$ (Figure 16.11):

$$Cu(OH)_2(s) + 4NH_3(aq) \rightleftharpoons Cu(NH_3)_4^{2+}(aq) + 2OH^-(aq)$$

Thus, the formation of the complex ion $Cu(NH_3)_4^{2+}$ increases the solubility of $Cu(OH)_2$.

Figure 16.11 *Left: An aqueous solution of copper(II) sulfate. Center: After the addition of a few drops of a concentrated aqueous ammonia solution, a light-blue precipitate of Cu(OH)₂ is formed. Right: When more concentrated aqueous ammonia solution is added, the Cu(OH)₂ precipitate dissolves to form the dark-blue complex ion Cu(NH₃)₄²⁺.*

TABLE 16.4 Formation Constants of Selected Complex Ions in Water at 25°C

Complex Ion	Equilibrium Expression	Formation Constant (K_f)
$Ag(NH_3)_2^+$	$Ag^+ + 2NH_3 \rightleftharpoons Ag(NH_3)_2^+$	1.5×10^7
$Ag(CN)_2^-$	$Ag^+ + 2CN^- \rightleftharpoons Ag(CN)_2^-$	1.0×10^{21}
$Cu(CN)_4^{2-}$	$Cu^{2+} + 4CN^- \rightleftharpoons Cu(CN)_4^{2-}$	1.0×10^{25}
$Cu(NH_3)_4^{2+}$	$Cu^{2+} + 4NH_3 \rightleftharpoons Cu(NH_3)_4^{2+}$	5.0×10^{13}
$Cd(CN)_4^{2-}$	$Cd^{2+} + 4CN^- \rightleftharpoons Cd(CN)_4^{2-}$	7.1×10^{16}
CdI_4^{2-}	$Cd^{2+} + 4I^- \rightleftharpoons CdI_4^{2-}$	2.0×10^6
$HgCl_4^{2-}$	$Hg^{2+} + 4Cl^- \rightleftharpoons HgCl_4^{2-}$	1.7×10^{16}
HgI_4^{2-}	$Hg^{2+} + 4I^- \rightleftharpoons HgI_4^{2-}$	2.0×10^{30}
$Hg(CN)_4^{2-}$	$Hg^{2+} + 4CN^- \rightleftharpoons Hg(CN)_4^{2-}$	2.5×10^{41}
$Co(NH_3)_6^{3+}$	$Co^{3+} + 6NH_3 \rightleftharpoons Co(NH_3)_6^{3+}$	5.0×10^{31}
$Zn(NH_3)_4^{2+}$	$Zn^{2+} + 4NH_3 \rightleftharpoons Zn(NH_3)_4^{2+}$	2.9×10^9

A measure of the tendency of a metal ion to form a particular complex ion is given by the **formation constant K_f** (also called the *stability constant*), which is *the equilibrium constant for the complex ion formation*. The larger K_f is, the more stable the complex ion is. Table 16.4 lists the formation constants of a number of complex ions.

The formation of the $Cu(NH_3)_4^{2+}$ ion can be expressed as

$$Cu^{2+}(aq) + 4NH_3(aq) \rightleftharpoons Cu(NH_3)_4^{2+}(aq)$$

for which the formation constant is

$$K_f = \frac{[Cu(NH_3)_4^{2+}]}{[Cu^{2+}][NH_3]^4}$$
$$= 5.0 \times 10^{13}$$

The very large value of K_f in this case indicates that the complex ion is quite stable in solution and accounts for the very low concentration of copper(II) ions at equilibrium.

Example 16.15

A 0.20-mole quantity of $CuSO_4$ is added to a liter of 1.20 M NH_3 solution. What is the concentration of Cu^{2+} ions at equilibrium?

Strategy The addition of $CuSO_4$ to the NH_3 solution results in complex ion formation

$$Cu^{2+}(aq) + 4NH_3(aq) \rightleftharpoons Cu(NH_3)_4^{2+}(aq)$$

From Table 16.4 we see that the formation constant (K_f) for this reaction is very large; therefore, the reaction lies mostly to the right. At equilibrium, the concentration of Cu^{2+} will be very small. As a good approximation, we can assume that essentially all the dissolved Cu^{2+} ions end up as $Cu(NH_3)_4^{2+}$ ions. How many moles of NH_3 will react with 0.20 mole of Cu^{2+}? How many moles of $Cu(NH_3)_4^{2+}$ will be produced? A very small amount of Cu^{2+} will be present at equilibrium. Set up the K_f expression for the preceding equilibrium to solve for $[Cu^{2+}]$.

(Continued)

Solution The amount of NH_3 consumed in forming the complex ion is 4×0.20 mol, or 0.80 mol. (Note that 0.20 mol Cu^{2+} is initially present in solution and four NH_3 molecules are needed to form a complex ion with one Cu^{2+} ion.) The concentration of NH_3 at equilibrium is therefore $(1.20 - 0.80)$ mol/L soln or 0.40 M, and that of $Cu(NH_3)_4^{2+}$ is 0.20 mol/L soln or 0.20 M, the same as the initial concentration of Cu^{2+}. [There is a 1:1 mole ratio between Cu^{2+} and $Cu(NH_3)_4^{2+}$.] Because $Cu(NH_3)_4^{2+}$ does dissociate to a slight extent, we call the concentration of Cu^{2+} at equilibrium x and write

$$K_f = \frac{[Cu(NH_3)_4^{2+}]}{[Cu^{2+}][NH_3]^4}$$

$$5.0 \times 10^{13} = \frac{0.20}{x(0.40)^4}$$

Solving for x and keeping in mind that the volume of the solution is 1 L, we obtain

$$x = [Cu^{2+}] = 1.6 \times 10^{-13} \, M$$

Check The small value of $[Cu^{2+}]$ at equilibrium, compared with 0.20 M, certainly justifies our approximation.

Similar problem: 16.71.

Practice Exercise If 2.50 g of $CuSO_4$ are dissolved in 9.0×10^2 mL of 0.30 M NH_3, what are the concentrations of Cu^{2+}, $Cu(NH_3)_4^{2+}$, and NH_3 at equilibrium?

The effect of complex ion formation generally is to *increase* the solubility of a substance, as Example 16.16 shows.

Example 16.16

Calculate the molar solubility of AgCl in a 1.0 M NH_3 solution.

Strategy AgCl is only slightly soluble in water

$$AgCl(s) \rightleftharpoons Ag^+(aq) + Cl^-(aq)$$

The Ag^+ ions form a complex ion with NH_3 (see Table 16.4)

$$Ag^+(aq) + 2NH_3(aq) \rightleftharpoons Ag(NH_3)_2^+$$

Combining these two equilibria will give the overall equilibrium for the process.

Solution *Step 1:* Initially, the species in solution are Ag^+ and Cl^- ions and NH_3. The reaction between Ag^+ and NH_3 produces the complex ion $Ag(NH_3)_2^+$.

Step 2: The equilibrium reactions are

$$AgCl(s) \rightleftharpoons Ag^+(aq) + Cl^-(aq)$$
$$K_{sp} = [Ag^+][Cl^-] = 1.6 \times 10^{-10}$$
$$Ag^+(aq) + 2NH_3(aq) \rightleftharpoons Ag(NH_3)_2^+(aq)$$
$$K_f = \frac{[Ag(NH_3)_2^+]}{[Ag^+][NH_3]^2} = 1.5 \times 10^7$$

Overall: $AgCl(s) + 2NH_3(aq) \rightleftharpoons Ag(NH_3)_2^+(aq) + Cl^-(aq)$

(Continued)

The equilibrium constant K for the overall reaction is the product of the equilibrium constants of the individual reactions (see Section 14.2):

$$K = K_{sp}K_f = \frac{[Ag(NH_3)_2^+][Cl^-]}{[NH_3]^2}$$
$$= (1.6 \times 10^{-10})(1.5 \times 10^7)$$
$$= 2.4 \times 10^{-3}$$

Let s be the molar solubility of AgCl (mol/L). We summarize the changes in concentrations that result from formation of the complex ion as follows:

	AgCl(s) + 2NH$_3$(aq) $\rightleftharpoons$	Ag(NH$_3$)$_2^+$(aq) +	Cl$^-$(aq)
Initial (M):	1.0	0.0	0.0
Change (M):	$-s$	$-2s$	$+s$	$+s$
Equilibrium (M):	(1.0 − 2s)	s	s

The formation constant for Ag(NH$_3$)$_2^+$ is quite large, so most of the silver ions exist in the complexed form. In the absence of ammonia we have, at equilibrium, [Ag$^+$] = [Cl$^-$]. As a result of complex ion formation, however, we can write [Ag(NH$_3$)$_2^+$] = [Cl$^-$].

Step 3:
$$K = \frac{(s)(s)}{(1.0 - 2s)^2}$$
$$2.4 \times 10^{-3} = \frac{s^2}{(1.0 - 2s)^2}$$

Taking the square root of both sides, we obtain

$$0.049 = \frac{s}{1.0 - 2s}$$
$$s = 0.045\ M$$

Step 4: At equilibrium, 0.045 mole of AgCl dissolves in 1 L of 1.0 M NH$_3$ solution.

Check The molar solubility of AgCl in pure water is $1.3 \times 10^{-5}\ M$. Thus, the formation of the complex ion Ag(NH$_3$)$_2^+$ enhances the solubility of AgCl (Figure 16.12).

Practice Exercise Calculate the molar solubility of AgBr in a 1.0 M NH$_3$ solution.

Similar problem: 16.74.

Figure 16.12 *From left to right: Formation of AgCl precipitate when AgNO$_3$ solution is added to NaCl solution. With the addition of NH$_3$ solution, the AgCl precipitate dissolves as the soluble Ag(NH$_3$)$_2^+$ forms.*

CHEMISTRY
in Action

How an Eggshell Is Formed

The formation of the shell of a hen's egg is a fascinating example of a natural precipitation process.

An average eggshell weighs about 5 g and is 40 percent calcium. Most of the calcium in an eggshell is laid down within a 16-h period. This means that it is deposited at a rate of about 125 mg per hour. No hen can consume calcium fast enough to meet this demand. Instead, it is supplied by special bony masses in the hen's long bones, which accumulate large reserves of calcium for eggshell formation. [The inorganic calcium component of the bone is calcium phosphate, $Ca_3(PO_4)_2$, an insoluble compound.] If a hen is fed a low-calcium diet, her eggshells become progressively thinner; she might have to mobilize 10 percent of the total amount of calcium in her bones just to lay one egg! When the food supply is consistently low in calcium, egg production eventually stops.

The eggshell is largely composed of calcite, a crystalline form of calcium carbonate ($CaCO_3$). Normally, the raw materials, Ca^{2+} and CO_3^{2-}, are carried by the blood to the shell gland. The calcification process is a precipitation reaction:

$$Ca^{2+}(aq) + CO_3^{2-}(aq) \rightleftharpoons CaCO_3(s)$$

In the blood, free Ca^{2+} ions are in equilibrium with calcium ions bound to proteins. As the free ions are taken up by the shell gland, more are provided by the dissociation of the protein-bound calcium.

The carbonate ions necessary for eggshell formation are a metabolic byproduct. Carbon dioxide produced during metabolism is converted to carbonic acid (H_2CO_3) by the enzyme carbonic anhydrase (CA):

$$CO_2(g) + H_2O(l) \xrightarrow{\text{CA}} H_2CO_3(aq)$$

Chicken eggs.

X-ray micrograph of an eggshell, showing columns of calcite.

Carbonic acid ionizes stepwise to produce carbonate ions:

$$H_2CO_3(aq) \rightleftharpoons H^+(aq) + HCO_3^-(aq)$$
$$HCO_3^-(aq) \rightleftharpoons H^+(aq) + CO_3^{2-}(aq)$$

Chickens do not perspire and so must pant to cool themselves. Panting expels more CO_2 from the chicken's body than normal respiration does. According to Le Châtelier's principle, panting will shift the CO_2–H_2CO_3 equilibrium shown above from right to left, thereby lowering the concentration of the CO_3^{2-} ions in solution and resulting in thin eggshells. One remedy for this problem is to give chickens carbonated water to drink in hot weather. The CO_2 dissolved in the water adds CO_2 to the chicken's body fluids and shifts the CO_2–H_2CO_3 equilibrium to the right.

All amphoteric hydroxides are insoluble compounds.

Finally, we note that there is a class of hydroxides, called *amphoteric hydroxides,* which can react with both acids and bases. Examples are $Al(OH)_3$, $Pb(OH)_2$, $Cr(OH)_3$, $Zn(OH)_2$, and $Cd(OH)_2$. Thus, $Al(OH)_3$ reacts with acids and bases as follows:

$$Al(OH)_3(s) + 3H^+(aq) \longrightarrow Al^{3+}(aq) + 3H_2O(l)$$
$$Al(OH)_3(s) + OH^-(aq) \rightleftharpoons Al(OH)_4^-(aq)$$

The increase in solubility of $Al(OH)_3$ in a basic medium is the result of the formation of the complex ion $Al(OH)_4^-$ in which $Al(OH)_3$ acts as the Lewis acid and OH^- acts as the Lewis base. Other amphoteric hydroxides behave in a similar manner.

16.11 Application of the Solubility Product Principle to Qualitative Analysis

In Section 4.6, we discussed the principle of gravimetric analysis, by which we measure the amount of an ion in an unknown sample. Here we will briefly discuss *qualitative analysis, the determination of the types of ions present in a solution.* We will focus on the cations.

There are some 20 common cations that can be analyzed readily in aqueous solution. These cations can be divided into five groups according to the solubility products of their insoluble salts (Table 16.5). Because an unknown solution may contain from one to all 20 ions, any analysis must be carried out systematically from group 1 through group 5. Let us consider the general procedure for separating these 20 ions by adding precipitating reagents to an unknown solution.

Do not confuse the groups in Table 16.5, which are based on solubility products, with those in the periodic table, which are based on the electron configurations of the elements.

- **Group 1 Cations.** When dilute HCl is added to the unknown solution, only the Ag^+, Hg_2^{2+}, and Pb^{2+} ions precipitate as insoluble chlorides. The other ions, whose chlorides are soluble, remain in solution.

- **Group 2 Cations.** After the chloride precipitates have been removed by filtration, hydrogen sulfide is reacted with the unknown acidic solution. Under this condition, the concentration of the S^{2-} ion in solution is negligible. Therefore, the precipitation of metal sulfides is best represented as

$$M^{2+}(aq) + H_2S(aq) \rightleftharpoons MS(s) + 2H^+(aq)$$

TABLE 16.5 Separation of Cations into Groups According to Their Precipitation Reactions with Various Reagents

Group	Cation	Precipitating Reagents	Insoluble Compound	K_{sp}
1	Ag^+	HCl	AgCl	1.6×10^{-10}
	Hg_2^{2+}	↓	Hg_2Cl_2	3.5×10^{-18}
	Pb^{2+}		$PbCl_2$	2.4×10^{-4}
2	Bi^{3+}	H_2S	Bi_2S_3	1.6×10^{-72}
	Cd^{2+}	in acidic	CdS	8.0×10^{-28}
	Cu^{2+}	solutions	CuS	6.0×10^{-37}
	Hg^{2+}		HgS	4.0×10^{-54}
	Sn^{2+}	↓	SnS	1.0×10^{-26}
3	Al^{3+}	H_2S	$Al(OH)_3$	1.8×10^{-33}
	Co^{2+}	in basic	CoS	4.0×10^{-21}
	Cr^{3+}	solutions	$Cr(OH)_3$	3.0×10^{-29}
	Fe^{2+}		FeS	6.0×10^{-19}
	Mn^{2+}		MnS	3.0×10^{-14}
	Ni^{2+}		NiS	1.4×10^{-24}
	Zn^{2+}	↓	ZnS	3.0×10^{-23}
4	Ba^{2+}	Na_2CO_3	$BaCO_3$	8.1×10^{-9}
	Ca^{2+}		$CaCO_3$	8.7×10^{-9}
	Sr^{2+}	↓	$SrCO_3$	1.6×10^{-9}
5	K^+	No precipitating	None	
	Na^+	reagent	None	
	NH_4^+		None	

Figure 16.13 *Left to right: Flame colors of lithium, sodium, potassium, and copper.*

Adding acid to the solution shifts this equilibrium to the left so that only the least soluble metal sulfides, that is, those with the smallest K_{sp} values, will precipitate out of solution. These are Bi_2S_3, CdS, CuS, HgS, and SnS (see Table 16.5).

- **Group 3 Cations.** At this stage, sodium hydroxide is added to the solution to make it basic. In a basic solution, the above equilibrium shifts to the right. Therefore, the more soluble sulfides (CoS, FeS, MnS, NiS, ZnS) now precipitate out of solution. Note that the Al^{3+} and Cr^{3+} ions actually precipitate as the hydroxides $Al(OH)_3$ and $Cr(OH)_3$, rather than as the sulfides, because the hydroxides are less soluble. The solution is then filtered to remove the insoluble sulfides and hydroxides.

- **Group 4 Cations.** After all the group 1, 2, and 3 cations have been removed from solution, sodium carbonate is added to the basic solution to precipitate Ba^{2+}, Ca^{2+}, and Sr^{2+} ions as $BaCO_3$, $CaCO_3$, and $SrCO_3$. These precipitates too are removed from solution by filtration.

- **Group 5 Cations.** At this stage, the only cations possibly remaining in solution are Na^+, K^+, and NH_4^+. The presence of NH_4^+ can be determined by adding sodium hydroxide:

$$NaOH(aq) + NH_4^+(aq) \longrightarrow Na^+(aq) + H_2O(l) + NH_3(g)$$

The ammonia gas is detected either by noting its characteristic odor or by observing a piece of wet red litmus paper turning blue when placed above (not in contact with) the solution. To confirm the presence of Na^+ and K^+ ions, we usually use a flame test, as follows: A piece of platinum wire (chosen because platinum is inert) is moistened with the solution and is then held over a Bunsen burner flame. Each type of metal ion gives a characteristic color when heated in this manner. For example, the color emitted by Na^+ ions is yellow, that of K^+ ions is violet, and that of Cu^{2+} ions is green (Figure 16.13).

Because NaOH is added in group 3 and Na_2CO_3 is added in group 4, the flame test for Na^+ ions is carried out using the original solution.

Figure 16.14 summarizes this scheme for separating metal ions.

Two points regarding qualitative analysis must be mentioned. First, the separation of the cations into groups is made as selective as possible; that is, the anions that are added as reagents must be such that they will precipitate the fewest types of cations. For example, all the cations in group 1 also form insoluble sulfides. Thus, if H_2S were reacted with the solution at the start, as many as seven different sulfides might precipitate out of solution (group 1 *and* group 2 sulfides), an undesirable outcome. Second, the removal of cations at each step must be carried out as completely as possible. For example, if we do not add enough HCl to the unknown solution to remove all the group 1 cations, they will precipitate with the group 2 cations as insoluble sulfides, interfering with further chemical analysis and leading to erroneous conclusions.

Summary of Facts and Concepts

1. The common ion effect tends to suppress the ionization of a weak acid or a weak base. This action can be explained by Le Châtelier's principle.

2. A buffer solution is a combination of either a weak acid and its weak conjugate base (supplied by a salt) or a weak base and its weak conjugate acid (supplied by a salt); the solution reacts with small amounts of added acid or base in such a way that the pH of the solution remains nearly constant. Buffer systems play a vital role in maintaining the pH of body fluids.

3. The pH at the equivalence point of an acid-base titration depends on hydrolysis of the salt formed in the neutralization reaction. For strong acid–strong base titrations, the pH at the equivalence point is 7; for weak acid–strong base titrations, the pH at the equivalence point is greater than 7; for strong acid–weak base titrations, the pH at the equivalence point is less than 7.

4. Acid-base indicators are weak organic acids or bases that change color near the equivalence point in an acid-base neutralization reaction.

5. The solubility product K_{sp} expresses the equilibrium between a solid and its ions in solution. Solubility can be found from K_{sp} and vice versa.

6. The presence of a common ion decreases the solubility of a slightly soluble salt.

7. The solubility of slightly soluble salts containing basic anions increases as the hydrogen ion concentration increases. The solubility of salts with anions derived from strong acids is unaffected by pH.

8. Complex ions are formed in solution by the combination of a metal cation with a Lewis base. The formation constant K_f measures the tendency toward the formation of a specific complex ion. Complex ion formation can increase the solubility of an insoluble substance.

9. Qualitative analysis is the identification of cations and anions in solution.

Key Words

Questions and Problems[†]

The Common Ion Effect

Review Questions

16.1   Use Le Châtelier's principle to explain how the common ion effect affects the pH of a solution.

16.2   Describe the effect on pH (increase, decrease, or no change) that results from each of the following additions: (a) potassium acetate to an acetic acid solution; (b) ammonium nitrate to an ammonia solution; (c) sodium formate (HCOONa) to a formic acid (HCOOH) solution; (d) potassium chloride to a hydrochloric acid solution; (e) barium iodide to a hydroiodic acid solution.

16.3   Define pK_a for a weak acid. What is the relationship between the value of the pK_a and the strength of the acid? Do the same for a weak base.

16.4   The pK_as of two monoprotic acids HA and HB are 5.9 and 8.1, respectively. Which of the two is the stronger acid?

Problems

16.5   Determine the pH of (a) a 0.40 M CH$_3$COOH solution, (b) a solution that is 0.40 M CH$_3$COOH and 0.20 M CH$_3$COONa.

16.6   Determine the pH of (a) a 0.20 M NH$_3$ solution, (b) a solution that is 0.20 M in NH$_3$ and 0.30 M NH$_4$Cl.

Buffer Solutions

Review Questions

16.7   What is a buffer solution? What constitutes a buffer solution?

16.8   How would you distinguish between an acid solution from a buffer solution at the same pH? You are provided with only a pH meter, water, and a measuring cylinder.

Problems

16.9   Which of the following solutions can act as a buffer? (a) KCl/HCl, (b) KHSO$_4$/H$_2$SO$_4$, (c) Na$_2$HPO$_4$/NaH$_2$PO$_4$, (d) KNO$_2$/HNO$_2$.

16.10   Which of the following solutions can act as a buffer? (a) KCN/HCN, (b) Na$_2$SO$_4$/NaHSO$_4$, (c) NH$_3$/NH$_4$NO$_3$, (d) NaI/HI.

16.11   Calculate the pH of the buffer system made up of 0.15 M NH$_3$/0.35 M NH$_4$Cl.

16.12   Calculate the pH of the following two buffer solutions: (a) 2.0 M CH$_3$COONa/2.0 M CH$_3$COOH, (b) 0.20 M CH$_3$COONa/0.20 M CH$_3$COOH. Which is the more effective buffer? Why?

16.13   The pH of a bicarbonate-carbonic acid buffer is 8.00. Calculate the ratio of the concentration of carbonic acid (H$_2$CO$_3$) to that of the bicarbonate ion (HCO$_3^-$).

16.14   What is the pH of the buffer 0.10 M Na$_2$HPO$_4$/0.15 M KH$_2$PO$_4$?

16.15   The pH of a sodium acetate–acetic acid buffer is 4.50. Calculate the ratio [CH$_3$COO$^-$]/[CH$_3$COOH].

16.16   The pH of blood plasma is 7.40. Assuming the principal buffer system is HCO$_3^-$/H$_2$CO$_3$, calculate the ratio [HCO$_3^-$]/[H$_2$CO$_3$]. Is this buffer more effective against an added acid or an added base?

16.17   Calculate the pH of the 0.20 M NH$_3$/0.20 M NH$_4$Cl buffer. What is the pH of the buffer after the addition of 10.0 mL of 0.10 M HCl to 65.0 mL of the buffer?

16.18   Calculate the pH of 1.00 L of the buffer 1.00 M CH$_3$COONa/1.00 M CH$_3$COOH before and after the addition of (a) 0.080 mol NaOH, (b) 0.12 mol HCl. (Assume that there is no change in volume.)

16.19   A diprotic acid, H$_2$A, has the following ionization constants: $K_{a_1} = 1.1 \times 10^{-3}$ and $K_{a_2} = 2.5 \times 10^{-6}$. In order to make up a buffer solution of pH 5.80, which combination would you choose? NaHA/H$_2$A or Na$_2$A/NaHA.

16.20   A student is asked to prepare a buffer solution at pH = 8.60, using one of the following weak acids: HA ($K_a = 2.7 \times 10^{-3}$), HB ($K_a = 4.4 \times 10^{-6}$), HC ($K_a = 2.6 \times 10^{-9}$). Which acid should she choose? Why?

Acid-Base Titrations

Review Questions

16.21   Briefly describe what happens in an acid-base titration.

[†]The temperature is assumed to be 25°C for all the problems.

16.22 Sketch titration curves for the following acid-base titrations: (a) HCl versus NaOH, (b) HCl versus CH_3NH_2, (c) CH_3COOH versus NaOH. In each case, the base is added to the acid in an Erlenmeyer flask. Your graphs should show pH on the *y*-axis and volume of base added on the *x*-axis.

Problems

16.23 A 0.2688-g sample of a monoprotic acid neutralizes 16.4 mL of 0.08133 *M* KOH solution. Calculate the molar mass of the acid.

16.24 A 5.00-g quantity of a diprotic acid was dissolved in water and made up to exactly 250 mL. Calculate the molar mass of the acid if 25.0 mL of this solution required 11.1 mL of 1.00 *M* KOH for neutralization. Assume that both protons of the acid were titrated.

16.25 In a titration experiment, 12.5 mL of 0.500 *M* H_2SO_4 neutralize 50.0 mL of NaOH. What is the concentration of the NaOH solution?

16.26 In a titration experiment, 20.4 mL of 0.883 *M* HCOOH neutralize 19.3 mL of $Ba(OH)_2$. What is the concentration of the $Ba(OH)_2$ solution?

16.27 A 0.1276-g sample of an unknown monoprotic acid was dissolved in 25.0 mL of water and titrated with 0.0633 *M* NaOH solution. The volume of base required to bring the solution to the equivalence point was 18.4 mL. (a) Calculate the molar mass of the acid. (b) After 10.0 mL of base had been added during the titration, the pH was determined to be 5.87. What is the K_a of the unknown acid?

16.28 A solution is made by mixing 5.00×10^2 mL of 0.167 *M* NaOH with 5.00×10^2 mL of 0.100 *M* CH_3COOH. Calculate the equilibrium concentrations of H^+, CH_3COOH, CH_3COO^-, OH^-, and Na^+.

16.29 Calculate the pH at the equivalence point for the following titration: 0.20 *M* HCl versus 0.20 *M* methylamine (CH_3NH_2).

16.30 Calculate the pH at the equivalence point for the following titration: 0.10 *M* HCOOH versus 0.10 *M* NaOH.

16.31 A 25.0-mL solution of 0.100 *M* CH_3COOH is titrated with a 0.200 *M* KOH solution. Calculate the pH after the following additions of the KOH solution: (a) 0.0 mL, (b) 5.0 mL, (c) 10.0 mL, (d) 12.5 mL, (e) 15.0 mL.

16.32 A 10.0-mL solution of 0.300 *M* NH_3 is titrated with a 0.100 *M* HCl solution. Calculate the pH after the following additions of the HCl solution: (a) 0.0 mL, (b) 10.0 mL, (c) 20.0 mL, (d) 30.0 mL, (e) 40.0 mL.

Acid-Base Indicators
Review Questions

16.33 Explain how an acid-base indicator works in a titration. What are the criteria for choosing an indicator for a particular acid-base titration?

16.34 The amount of indicator used in an acid-base titration must be small. Why?

Problems

16.35 Referring to Table 16.1, specify which indicator or indicators you would use for the following titrations: (a) HCOOH versus NaOH, (b) HCl versus KOH, (c) HNO_3 versus CH_3NH_2.

16.36 A student carried out an acid-base titration by adding NaOH solution from a buret to an Erlenmeyer flask containing HCl solution and using phenolphthalein as indicator. At the equivalence point, she observed a faint reddish-pink color. However, after a few minutes, the solution gradually turned colorless. What do you suppose happened?

16.37 The ionization constant K_a of an indicator HIn is 1.0×10^{-6}. The color of the nonionized form is red and that of the ionized form is yellow. What is the color of this indicator in a solution whose pH is 4.00?

16.38 The K_a of a certain indicator is 2.0×10^{-6}. The color of HIn is green and that of In^- is red. A few drops of the indicator are added to a HCl solution, which is then titrated against a NaOH solution. At what pH will the indicator change color?

Solubility Equilibria
Review Questions

16.39 Use $BaSO_4$ to distinguish between solubility, molar solubility, and solubility product.

16.40 Why do we usually not quote the K_{sp} values for soluble ionic compounds?

16.41 Write balanced equations and solubility product expressions for the solubility equilibria of the following compounds: (a) CuBr, (b) ZnC_2O_4, (c) Ag_2CrO_4, (d) Hg_2Cl_2, (e) $AuCl_3$, (f) $Mn_3(PO_4)_2$.

16.42 Write the solubility product expression for the ionic compound A_xB_y.

16.43 How can we predict whether a precipitate will form when two solutions are mixed?

16.44 Silver chloride has a larger K_{sp} than silver carbonate (see Table 16.2). Does this mean that AgCl also has a larger molar solubility than Ag_2CO_3?

Problems

16.45 Calculate the concentration of ions in the following saturated solutions: (a) $[I^-]$ in AgI solution with $[Ag^+] = 9.1 \times 10^{-9}$ *M*, (b) $[Al^{3+}]$ in $Al(OH)_3$ solution with $[OH^-] = 2.9 \times 10^{-9}$ *M*.

16.46 From the solubility data given, calculate the solubility products for the following compounds: (a) SrF_2, 7.3×10^{-2} g/L, (b) Ag_3PO_4, 6.7×10^{-3} g/L.

16.47 The molar solubility of $MnCO_3$ is 4.2×10^{-6} *M*. What is K_{sp} for this compound?

16.48 The solubility of an ionic compound MX (molar mass = 346 g) is 4.63×10^{-3} g/L. What is K_{sp} for the compound?

16.49 The solubility of an ionic compound M_2X_3 (molar mass = 288 g) is 3.6×10^{-17} g/L. What is K_{sp} for the compound?

16.50 Using data from Table 16.2, calculate the molar solubility of CaF_2.

16.51 What is the pH of a saturated zinc hydroxide solution?

16.52 The pH of a saturated solution of a metal hydroxide MOH is 9.68. Calculate the K_{sp} for the compound.

16.53 If 20.0 mL of 0.10 M $Ba(NO_3)_2$ are added to 50.0 mL of 0.10 M Na_2CO_3, will $BaCO_3$ precipitate?

16.54 A volume of 75 mL of 0.060 M NaF is mixed with 25 mL of 0.15 M $Sr(NO_3)_2$. Calculate the concentrations in the final solution of NO_3^-, Na^+, Sr^{2+}, and F^-. (K_{sp} for $SrF_2 = 2.0 \times 10^{-10}$.)

Fractional Precipitation

Problems

16.55 Solid NaI is slowly added to a solution that is 0.010 M in Cu^+ and 0.010 M in Ag^+. (a) Which compound will begin to precipitate first? (b) Calculate $[Ag^+]$ when CuI just begins to precipitate. (c) What percent of Ag^+ remains in solution at this point?

16.56 Find the approximate pH range suitable for the separation of Fe^{3+} and Zn^{2+} ions by precipitation of $Fe(OH)_3$ from a solution that is initially 0.010 M in both Fe^{3+} and Zn^{2+}.

The Common Ion Effect and Solubility

Review Questions

16.57 How does the common ion effect influence solubility equilibria? Use Le Châtelier's principle to explain the decrease in solubility of $CaCO_3$ in a Na_2CO_3 solution.

16.58 The molar solubility of AgCl in 6.5×10^{-3} M $AgNO_3$ is 2.5×10^{-8} M. In deriving K_{sp} from these data, which of the following assumptions are reasonable?
   (a) K_{sp} is the same as solubility.
   (b) K_{sp} of AgCl is the same in 6.5×10^{-3} M $AgNO_3$ as in pure water.
   (c) Solubility of AgCl is independent of the concentration of $AgNO_3$.
   (d) $[Ag^+]$ in solution does not change significantly upon the addition of AgCl to 6.5×10^{-3} M $AgNO_3$.
   (e) $[Ag^+]$ in solution after the addition of AgCl to 6.5×10^{-3} M $AgNO_3$ is the same as it would be in pure water.

Problems

16.59 How many grams of $CaCO_3$ will dissolve in 3.0×10^2 mL of 0.050 M $Ca(NO_3)_2$?

16.60 The solubility product of $PbBr_2$ is 8.9×10^{-6}. Determine the molar solubility (a) in pure water, (b) in 0.20 M KBr solution, (c) in 0.20 M $Pb(NO_3)_2$ solution.

16.61 Calculate the molar solubility of AgCl in a 1.00-L solution containing 10.0 g of dissolved $CaCl_2$.

16.62 Calculate the molar solubility of $BaSO_4$ (a) in water, (b) in a solution containing 1.0 M SO_4^{2-} ions.

pH and Solubility

Problems

16.63 Which of the following ionic compounds will be more soluble in acid solution than in water? (a) $BaSO_4$, (b) $PbCl_2$, (c) $Fe(OH)_3$, (d) $CaCO_3$

16.64 Which of the following will be more soluble in acid solution than in pure water? (a) CuI, (b) Ag_2SO_4, (c) $Zn(OH)_2$, (d) BaC_2O_4, (e) $Ca_3(PO_4)_2$

16.65 Compare the molar solubility of $Mg(OH)_2$ in water and in a solution buffered at a pH of 9.0.

16.66 Calculate the molar solubility of $Fe(OH)_2$ in a solution buffered at (a) pH 8.00, (b) pH 10.00.

16.67 The solubility product of $Mg(OH)_2$ is 1.2×10^{-11}. What minimum OH^- concentration must be attained (for example, by adding NaOH) to decrease the Mg^{2+} concentration in a solution of $Mg(NO_3)_2$ to less than 1.0×10^{-10} M?

16.68 Calculate whether or not a precipitate will form if 2.00 mL of 0.60 M NH_3 are added to 1.0 L of 1.0×10^{-3} M $FeSO_4$.

Complex Ion Equilibria and Solubility

Review Questions

16.69 Explain the formation of complexes in Table 16.4 in terms of Lewis acid-base theory.

16.70 Give an example to illustrate the general effect of complex ion formation on solubility.

Problems

16.71 If 2.50 g of $CuSO_4$ are dissolved in 9.0×10^2 mL of 0.30 M NH_3, what are the concentrations of Cu^{2+}, $Cu(NH_3)_4^{2+}$, and NH_3 at equilibrium?

16.72 Calculate the concentrations of Cd^{2+}, $Cd(CN)_4^{2-}$, and CN^- at equilibrium when 0.50 g of $Cd(NO_3)_2$ dissolves in 5.0×10^2 mL of 0.50 M NaCN.

16.73 If NaOH is added to 0.010 M Al^{3+}, which will be the predominant species at equilibrium: $Al(OH)_3$ or $Al(OH)_4^-$? The pH of the solution is 14.00. [K_f for $Al(OH)_4^- = 2.0 \times 10^{33}$.]

16.74 Calculate the molar solubility of AgI in a 1.0 M NH_3 solution.

16.75 Both Ag^+ and Zn^{2+} form complex ions with NH_3. Write balanced equations for the reactions. However, $Zn(OH)_2$ is soluble in 6 M NaOH, and AgOH is not. Explain.

16.76 Explain, with balanced ionic equations, why (a) CuI_2 dissolves in ammonia solution, (b) AgBr dissolves in NaCN solution, (c) $HgCl_2$ dissolves in KCl solution.

Qualitative Analysis

Review Questions

16.77 Outline the general procedure of qualitative analysis.

16.78 Give two examples of metal ions in each group (1 through 5) in the qualitative analysis scheme.

Problems

16.79 In a group 1 analysis, a student obtained a precipitate containing both AgCl and $PbCl_2$. Suggest one reagent that would enable her to separate $AgCl(s)$ from $PbCl_2(s)$.

16.80 In a group 1 analysis, a student adds HCl acid to the unknown solution to make $[Cl^-] = 0.15$ M. Some $PbCl_2$ precipitates. Calculate the concentration of Pb^{2+} remaining in solution.

16.81 Both KCl and NH_4Cl are white solids. Suggest one reagent that would enable you to distinguish between these two compounds.

16.82 Describe a simple test that would allow you to distinguish between $AgNO_3(s)$ and $Cu(NO_3)_2(s)$.

Additional Problems

16.83 The buffer range is defined by the equation $pH = pK_a \pm 1$. Calculate the range of the ratio [conjugate base]/[acid] that corresponds to this equation.

16.84 The pK_a of the indicator methyl orange is 3.46. Over what pH range does this indicator change from 90 percent HIn to 90 percent In^-?

16.85 Sketch the titration curve of a weak acid versus a strong base like the one shown in Figure 16.5. On your graph indicate the volume of base used at the equivalence point and also at the half-equivalence point, that is, the point at which half of the acid has been neutralized. Show how you can measure the pH of the solution at the half-equivalence point. Using Equation (16.4), explain how you can determine the pK_a of the acid by this procedure.

16.86 A 200-mL volume of NaOH solution was added to 400 mL of a 2.00 M HNO_2 solution. The pH of the mixed solution was 1.50 units greater than that of the original acid solution. Calculate the molarity of the NaOH solution.

16.87 The pK_a of butyric acid (HBut) is 4.7. Calculate K_b for the butyrate ion (But^-).

16.88 A solution is made by mixing 5.00×10^2 mL of 0.167 M NaOH with 5.00×10^2 mL 0.100 M HCOOH. Calculate the equilibrium concentrations of H^+, HCOOH, $HCOO^-$, OH^-, and Na^+.

16.89 $Cd(OH)_2$ is an insoluble compound. It dissolves in excess NaOH in solution. Write a balanced ionic equation for this reaction. What type of reaction is this?

16.90 A student mixes 50.0 mL of 1.00 M $Ba(OH)_2$ with 86.4 mL of 0.494 M H_2SO_4. Calculate the mass of $BaSO_4$ formed and the pH of the mixed solution.

16.91 For which of the following reactions is the equilibrium constant called a solubility product?
(a) $Zn(OH)_2(s) + 2OH^-(aq) \rightleftharpoons Zn(OH)_4^{2-}(aq)$
(b) $3Ca^{2+}(aq) + 2PO_4^{3-}(aq) \rightleftharpoons Ca_3(PO_4)_2(s)$
(c) $CaCO_3(s) + 2H^+(aq) \rightleftharpoons$
$\qquad Ca^{2+}(aq) + H_2O(l) + CO_2(g)$
(d) $PbI_2(s) \rightleftharpoons Pb^{2+}(aq) + 2I^-(aq)$

16.92 A 2.0-L kettle contains 116 g of boiler scale ($CaCO_3$). How many times would the kettle have to be completely filled with distilled water to remove all of the deposit at 25°C?

16.93 Equal volumes of 0.12 M $AgNO_3$ and 0.14 M $ZnCl_2$ solution are mixed. Calculate the equilibrium concentrations of Ag^+, Cl^-, Zn^{2+}, and NO_3^-.

16.94 Calculate the solubility (in g/L) of Ag_2CO_3.

16.95 Find the approximate pH range suitable for separating Mg^{2+} and Zn^{2+} by the precipitation of $Zn(OH)_2$ from a solution that is initially 0.010 M in Mg^{2+} and Zn^{2+}.

16.96 A volume of 25.0 mL of 0.100 M HCl is titrated against a 0.100 M CH_3NH_2 solution added to it from a buret. Calculate the pH values of the solution (a) after 10.0 mL of CH_3NH_2 solution have been added, (b) after 25.0 mL of CH_3NH_2 solution have been added, (c) after 35.0 mL of CH_3NH_2 solution have been added.

16.97 The molar solubility of $Pb(IO_3)_2$ in a 0.10 M $NaIO_3$ solution is 2.4×10^{-11} mol/L. What is K_{sp} for $Pb(IO_3)_2$?

16.98 When a KI solution was added to a solution of mercury(II) chloride, a precipitate [mercury(II) iodide] formed. A student plotted the mass of the precipitate versus the volume of the KI solution added and obtained the following graph. Explain the appearance of the graph.

16.99 Barium is a toxic substance that can seriously impair heart function. For an X ray of the gastrointestinal tract, a patient drinks an aqueous suspension of 20 g $BaSO_4$. If this substance were to equilibrate with the 5.0 L of the blood in the patient's body, what would be $[Ba^{2+}]$? For a good estimate, we may assume that the temperature is at 25°C. Why is $Ba(NO_3)_2$ not chosen for this procedure?

16.100 The pK_a of phenolphthalein is 9.10. Over what pH range does this indicator change from 95 percent HIn to 95 percent In$^-$?

16.101 Solid NaBr is slowly added to a solution that is 0.010 M in Cu^+ and 0.010 M in Ag^+. (a) Which compound will begin to precipitate first? (b) Calculate $[Ag^+]$ when CuBr just begins to precipitate. (c) What percent of Ag^+ remains in solution at this point?

16.102 Cacodylic acid is $(CH_3)_2AsO_2H$. Its ionization constant is 6.4×10^{-7}. (a) Calculate the pH of 50.0 mL of a 0.10 M solution of the acid. (b) Calculate the pH of 25.0 mL of 0.15 M $(CH_3)_2AsO_2Na$. (c) Mix the solutions in part (a) and part (b). Calculate the pH of the resulting solution.

16.103 Radiochemical techniques are useful in estimating the solubility product of many compounds. In one experiment, 50.0 mL of a 0.010 M $AgNO_3$ solution containing a silver isotope with a radioactivity of 74,025 counts per min per mL were mixed with 100 mL of a 0.030 M $NaIO_3$ solution. The mixed solution was diluted to 500 mL and filtered to remove all of the $AgIO_3$ precipitate. The remaining solution was found to have a radioactivity of 44.4 counts per min per mL. What is the K_{sp} of $AgIO_3$?

16.104 The molar mass of a certain metal carbonate, MCO_3, can be determined by adding an excess of HCl acid to react with all the carbonate and then "back-titrating" the remaining acid with NaOH. (a) Write an equation for these reactions. (b) In a certain experiment, 20.00 mL of 0.0800 M HCl were added to a 0.1022-g sample of MCO_3. The excess HCl required 5.64 mL of 0.1000 M NaOH for neutralization. Calculate the molar mass of the carbonate and identify M.

16.105 Acid-base reactions usually go to completion. Confirm this statement by calculating the equilibrium constant for each of the following cases: (a) A strong acid reacting with a strong base. (b) A strong acid reacting with a weak base (NH_3). (c) A weak acid (CH_3COOH) reacting with a strong base. (d) A weak acid (CH_3COOH) reacting with a weak base (NH_3). (*Hint:* Strong acids exist as H^+ ions and strong bases exist as OH^- ions in solution. You need to look up K_a, K_b, and K_w.)

16.106 Calculate x, the number of molecules of water in oxalic acid hydrate, $H_2C_2O_4 \cdot xH_2O$, from the following data: 5.00 g of the compound is made up to exactly 250 mL solution, and 25.0 mL of this solution requires 15.9 mL of 0.500 M NaOH solution for neutralization.

16.107 Describe how you would prepare a 1-L 0.20 M CH_3COONa/0.20 M CH_3COOH buffer system by (a) mixing a solution of CH_3COOH with a solution of CH_3COONa, (b) reacting a solution of CH_3COOH with a solution of NaOH, and (c) reacting a solution of CH_3COONa with a solution of HCl.

16.108 Phenolphthalein is the common indicator for the titration of a strong acid with a strong base. (a) If the pK_a of phenolphthalein is 9.10, what is the ratio of the nonionized form of the indicator (colorless) to the ionized form (reddish pink) at pH 8.00? (b) If 2 drops of 0.060 M phenolphthalein are used in a titration involving a 50.0-mL volume, what is the concentration of the ionized form at pH 8.00? (Assume that 1 drop = 0.050 mL.)

16.109 Oil paintings containing lead(II) compounds as constituents of their pigments darken over the years. Suggest a chemical reason for the color change.

16.110 What reagents would you employ to separate the following pairs of ions in solution? (a) Na^+ and Ba^{2+}, (b) K^+ and Pb^{2+}, (c) Zn^{2+} and Hg^{2+}.

16.111 Look up the K_{sp} values for $BaSO_4$ and $SrSO_4$ in Table 16.2. Calculate the concentrations of Ba^{2+}, Sr^{2+}, and SO_4^{2-} in a solution that is saturated with both compounds.

16.112 In principle, amphoteric oxides, such as Al_2O_3 and BeO can be used to prepare buffer solutions because they possess both acidic and basic properties (see Section 15.11). Explain why these compounds are of little practical use as buffer components.

16.113 $CaSO_4$ ($K_{sp} = 2.4 \times 10^{-5}$) has a larger K_{sp} value than that of Ag_2SO_4 ($K_{sp} = 1.4 \times 10^{-5}$). Does it follow that $CaSO_4$ also has greater solubility (g/L)?

16.114 When lemon juice is squirted into tea, the color becomes lighter. In part, the color change is due to dilution, but the main reason for the change is an acid-base reaction. What is the reaction? (*Hint:* Tea contains "polyphenols" which are weak acids and lemon juice contains citric acid.)

16.115 How many milliliters of 1.0 M NaOH must be added to a 200 mL of 0.10 M NaH_2PO_4 to make a buffer solution with a pH of 7.50?

16.116 The maximum allowable concentration of Pb^{2+} ions in drinking water is 0.05 ppm (that is, 0.05 g of Pb^{2+} in one million grams of water). Is this guideline exceeded if an underground water supply is at equilibrium with the mineral anglesite, $PbSO_4$ ($K_{sp} = 1.6 \times 10^{-8}$)?

16.117 One of the most common antibiotics is penicillin G (benzylpenicillinic acid), which has the structure shown next:

It is a weak monoprotic acid:

$$HP \rightleftharpoons H^+ + P^- \qquad K_a = 1.64 \times 10^{-3}$$

where HP denotes the parent acid and P^- the conjugate base. Penicillin G is produced by growing molds in fermentation tanks at 25°C and a pH range of 4.5 to 5.0. The crude form of this antibiotic is obtained by extracting the fermentation broth with an organic solvent in which the acid is soluble. (a) Identify the acidic hydrogen atom. (b) In one stage of purification, the organic extract of the crude penicillin G is treated with a buffer solution at pH = 6.50. What is the ratio of the conjugate base of penicillin G to the acid at this pH? Would you expect the conjugate base to be more soluble in water than the acid? (c) Penicillin G is not suitable for oral administration, but the sodium salt (NaP) is because it is soluble. Calculate the pH of a 0.12 M NaP solution formed when a tablet containing the salt is dissolved in a glass of water.

16.118 Which of the following solutions has the highest $[H^+]$? (a) 0.10 M HF, (b) 0.10 M HF in 0.10 M NaF, (c) 0.10 M HF in 0.10 M SbF$_5$. (*Hint:* SbF$_5$ reacts with F^- to form the complex ion SbF_6^-.)

16.119 Distribution curves show how the fractions of non-ionized acid and its conjugate base vary as a function of pH of the medium. Plot distribution curves for CH_3COOH and its conjugate base CH_3COO^- in solution. Your graph should show fraction as the y axis and pH as the x axis. What are the fractions and pH at the point where these two curves intersect?

16.120 Water containing Ca^{2+} and Mg^{2+} ions is called *hard water* and is unsuitable for some household and industrial use because these ions react with soap to form insoluble salts, or curds. One way to remove the Ca^{2+} ions from hard water is by adding washing soda ($Na_2CO_3 \cdot 10H_2O$). (a) The molar solubility of $CaCO_3$ is 9.3×10^{-5} M. What is its molar solubility in a 0.050 M Na_2CO_3 solution? (b) Why are Mg^{2+} ions not removed by this procedure? (c) The Mg^{2+} ions are removed as $Mg(OH)_2$ by adding slaked lime [$Ca(OH)_2$] to the water to produce a saturated solution. Calculate the pH of a saturated $Ca(OH)_2$ solution. (d) What is the concentration of Mg^{2+} ions at this pH? (e) In general, which ion (Ca^{2+} or Mg^{2+}) would you remove first? Why?

16.121 Consider the ionization of the following acid-base indicator:

$$HIn(aq) \rightleftharpoons H^+(aq) + In^-(aq)$$

The indicator changes color according to the ratios of the concentrations of the acid to its conjugate base as described on p. 716. Show that the pH range over which the indicator changes from the acid color to the base color is pH = $pK_a \pm 1$, where K_a is the ionization constant of the acid.

16.122 Amino acids are building blocks of proteins. These compounds contain at least one amino group (—NH$_2$) and one carboxyl group (—COOH). Consider glycine (NH_2CH_2COOH). Depending on the pH of the solution, glycine can exist in one of three possible forms:

Fully protonated: $\overset{+}{N}H_3$—CH$_2$—COOH

Dipolar ion: $\overset{+}{N}H_3$—CH$_2$—COO$^-$

Fully ionized: NH$_2$—CH$_2$—COO$^-$

Predict the predominant form of glycine at pH 1.0, 7.0, and 12.0. The pK_a of the carboxyl group is 2.3 and that of the ammonium group (—NH$_3^+$) is 9.6.

16.123 (a) Referring to Figure 16.6, describe how you would determine the pK_b of the base. (b) Derive an analogous Henderson-Hasselbalch equation relating pOH to pK_b of a weak base B and its conjugate acid HB$^+$. Sketch a titration curve showing the variation of the pOH of the base solution versus the volume of a strong acid added from a buret. Describe how you would determine the pK_b from this curve.

Special Problems

16.124 One way to distinguish a buffer solution with an acid solution is by dilution. (a) Consider a buffer solution made of 0.500 M CH_3COOH and 0.500 M CH_3COONa. Calculate its pH and the pH after it has been diluted 10-fold. (b) Compare the result in (a) with the pHs of a 0.500 M CH_3COOH solution before and after it has been diluted 10-fold.

16.125 Draw distribution curves for an aqueous carbonic acid solution. Your graph should show fraction of species present as the y axis and pH as the x axis. Note that at any pH, only two of the three species (H_2CO_3, HCO_3^-, and CO_3^{2-}) are present in appreciable concentrations. Use the pK_a values in Table 15.5.

16.126 A sample of 0.96 L of HCl at 372 mmHg and 22°C is bubbled into 0.034 L of 0.57 M NH_3. What is the pH of the resulting solution? Assume the volume of solution remains constant and that the HCl is totally dissolved in the solution.

16.127 Histidine is one of the 20 amino acids found in proteins. Shown here is a fully protonated histidine molecule where the numbers denote the pK_a values of the acidic groups.

(a) Show stepwise ionization of histidine in solution (*Hint:* The H^+ ion will first come off from the strongest acid group followed by the next strongest acid group and so on.) (b) A dipolar ion is one in which the species has an equal number of positive and negative charges. Identify the dipolar ion in (a). (c) The pH at which the dipolar ion predominates is called the isoelectric point, denoted by pI. The isoelectric point is the average of the pK_a values leading to and following the formation of the dipolar ion. Calculate the pI of histidine. (d) The histidine group plays an important role in buffering blood (see Chemistry in Action on p. 706). Which conjugate acid-base pair shown in (a) is responsible for this action?

16.128 A 1.0-L saturated silver carbonate solution at 5°C is treated with enough hydrochloric acid to decompose the compound. The carbon dioxide generated is collected in a 19-mL vial and exerts a pressure of 114 mmHg at 25°C. What is the K_{sp} of Ag_2CO_3 at 5°C?

Answers to Practice Exercises

16.1 4.01; 2.15. **16.2** (a) and (c). **16.3** 9.17; 9.20. **16.4** Weigh out Na_2CO_3 and $NaHCO_3$ in mole ratio of 0.60 to 1.0. Dissolve in enough water to make up a 1-L solution. **16.5** (a) 2.19, (b) 3.95, (c) 8.02, (d) 11.39. **16.6** 5.92. **16.7** (a) Bromophenol blue, methyl orange, methyl red, and chlorophenol blue; (b) all except thymol blue, bromophenol blue, and methyl orange; (c) cresol red and phenolphthalein. **16.8** 2.0×10^{-14}. **16.9** 1.9×10^{-3} g/L. **16.10** No. **16.11** (a) $> 1.6 \times 10^{-9}\,M$, (b) $> 2.6 \times 10^{-6}\,M$. **16.12** (a) 1.7×10^{-4} g/L, (b) 1.4×10^{-7} g/L. **16.13** (a) More soluble in acid solution, (b) more soluble in acid solution, (c) about the same. **16.14** $Zn(OH)_2$ precipitate will form. **16.15** $[Cu^{2+}] = 1.2 \times 10^{-13}\,M$, $[Cu(NH_3)_4^{2+}]$ = 0.017 M, $[NH_3]$ = 0.23 M. **16.16** 3.5×10^{-3} mol/L.

CHEMICAL
Mystery

A Hard-Boiled Snack

Most of us have eaten hard-boiled eggs. They are easy to cook and nutritious. But when was the last time you thought about the process of boiling an egg or looked carefully at a hard-boiled egg? A lot of interesting chemical and physical changes occur while an egg cooks.

A hen's egg is a complicated biochemical system, but here we will focus on the three major parts that we see when we crack open an egg: the shell, the egg white or *albumen*, and the yolk. The shell protects the inner components from the outside environment, but it has many microscopic pores through which air can pass. The albumen is about 88 percent water and 12 percent protein. The yolk contains 50 percent water, 34 percent fat, 16 percent protein, and a small amount of iron in the form of Fe^{2+} ions.

Proteins are polymers made up of amino acids. In solution, each long chain of a protein molecule folds in such a way that the hydrophobic parts of the molecule are buried inside and the hydrophilic parts are on the exterior, in contact with the solution. This is the stable or *native* state of a protein which allows it to perform normal physiological functions. Heat causes protein molecules to unfold, or denature. Chemicals such as acids and salt (NaCl) can also denature proteins. To avoid contact with water, the hydrophobic parts of denatured proteins will clump together, or coagulate to form a semirigid opaque white solid. Heating also decomposes some proteins so that the sulfur in them combines with hydrogen to form hydrogen sulfide (H_2S), an unpleasant smelling gas that can sometimes be detected when the shell of a boiled egg is cracked.

The accompanying photo of hard-boiled eggs shows an egg that has been boiled for about 12 minutes and one that has been overcooked. Note that the outside of the overcooked yolk is green.

What is the chemical basis for the changes brought about by boiling an egg?

Chemical Clues

1. One frequently encountered problem with hard-boiled eggs is that their shells crack in water. The recommended procedure for hard boiling eggs is to place the eggs in cold water

Schematic diagram of an egg. The chalazae are the cords that anchor the yolk to the shell and keep it centered.

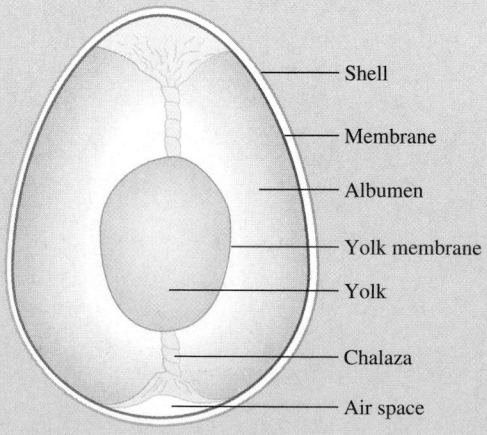

Shell

Membrane

Albumen

Yolk membrane

Yolk

Chalaza

Air space

and then bring the water to a boil. What causes the shells to crack in this case? How does pin holing, that is, piercing the shell with a needle, prevent the shells from cracking? A less satisfactory way of hard boiling eggs is to place room-temperature eggs or cold eggs from the refrigerator in boiling water. What additional mechanism might cause the shells to crack?

2.   When an eggshell cracks during cooking, some of the egg white leaks into the hot water to form unsightly "streamers." An experienced cook adds salt or vinegar to the water prior to heating eggs to minimize the formation of streamers. Explain the chemical basis for this action.

3.   Identify the green substance on the outer layer of the yolk of an overcooked egg and write an equation representing its formation. The unsightly "green yolk" can be eliminated or minimized if the overcooked egg is rinsed with cold water immediately after it has been removed from the boiling water. How does this action remove the green substance?

4.   The way to distinguish a raw egg from a hard-boiled egg, without cracking the shells, is to spin the eggs. How does this method work?

A 12-minute egg (left) and an overcooked hardboiled egg (right).

Iron(II) sulfide.

17

Lightning causes atmospheric nitrogen and oxygen to form nitric oxide, which is eventually converted to nitrates. The models show nitrogen, oxygen, and nitric oxide molecules.

Chemistry in the Atmosphere

A LOOK AHEAD

- We begin by examining the regions and composition of Earth's atmosphere. (17.1)

- We then study a natural phenomenon—aurora borealis—and a human-made phenomenon—the glow of space shuttles—in the outer layers of the atmosphere. (17.2)

- Next, we study the depletion of ozone in the stratosphere and its detrimental effects and ways to slow the progress. (17.3)

- Focusing on events in the troposphere, we first examine volcanic eruptions. (17.4)

- We study the cause and effect of greenhouse gases and ways to curtail the emission of carbon dioxide and other harmful gases. (17.5)

- We see that acid rain is largely caused by human activities such as the burning of fossil fuels and roasting of metal sulfides. We discuss ways to minimize production of sulfur dioxide and nitrogen oxides. (17.6)

- Another human-made pollution is smog formation, which is the result of the heavy use of automobiles. We examine mechanisms of smog formation and ways to reduce the pollution. (17.7)

- The chapter ends with a discussion of indoor pollutants such as radon, carbon dioxide and carbon monoxide, and formaldehyde. (17.8)

Interactive Activity Summary

1. Interactivity: Protecting the Ozone Layer (17.3)
2. Interactivity: Global Warming: The Greenhouse Effect (17.5)

We have studied basic definitions in chemistry, and we have examined the properties of gases, liquid, solids, and solutions. We have discussed chemical bonding and intermolecular forces and seen how chemical kinetics and chemical equilibrium concepts help us understand the nature of chemical reactions. It is appropriate at this stage to apply our knowledge to the study of one extremely important system: the atmosphere. Although Earth's atmosphere is fairly simple in composition, its chemistry is very complex and not fully understood. The chemical processes that take place in our atmosphere are induced by solar radiation, but they are inextricably connected to natural events and human activities on Earth's surface.

In this chapter we will discuss the structure and composition of the atmosphere, together with some of the chemical processes that occur there. In addition, we will take a look at the major sources of air pollution and prospects for controlling them.

TABLE 17.1	
Composition of Dry Air at Sea Level	
Gas	**Composition (% by Volume)**
N_2	78.03
O_2	20.99
Ar	0.94
CO_2	0.033
Ne	0.0015
He	0.000524
Kr	0.00014
Xe	0.000006

17.1 Earth's Atmosphere

Earth is unique among the planets of our solar system in having an atmosphere that is chemically active and rich in oxygen. Mars, for example, has a much thinner atmosphere that is about 90 percent carbon dioxide. Jupiter, on the other hand, has no solid surface; it is made up of 90 percent hydrogen, 9 percent helium, and 1 percent other substances.

It is generally believed that three billion or four billion years ago, Earth's atmosphere consisted mainly of ammonia, methane, and water. There was little, if any, free oxygen present. Ultraviolet (UV) radiation from the sun probably penetrated the atmosphere, rendering the surface of Earth sterile. However, the same UV radiation may have triggered the chemical reactions (perhaps beneath the surface) that eventually led to life on Earth. Primitive organisms used energy from the sun to break down carbon dioxide (produced by volcanic activity) to obtain carbon, which they incorporated in their own cells. The major by-product of this process, called *photosynthesis,* is oxygen. Another important source of oxygen is the *photodecomposition* of water vapor by UV light. Over time, the more reactive gases such as ammonia and methane have largely disappeared, and today our atmosphere consists mainly of oxygen and nitrogen gases. Biological processes determine to a great extent the atmospheric concentrations of these gases, one of which is reactive (oxygen) and the other unreactive (nitrogen).

Table 17.1 shows the composition of dry air at sea level. The total mass of the atmosphere is about 5.3×10^{18} kg. Water is excluded from this table because its concentration in air can vary drastically from location to location.

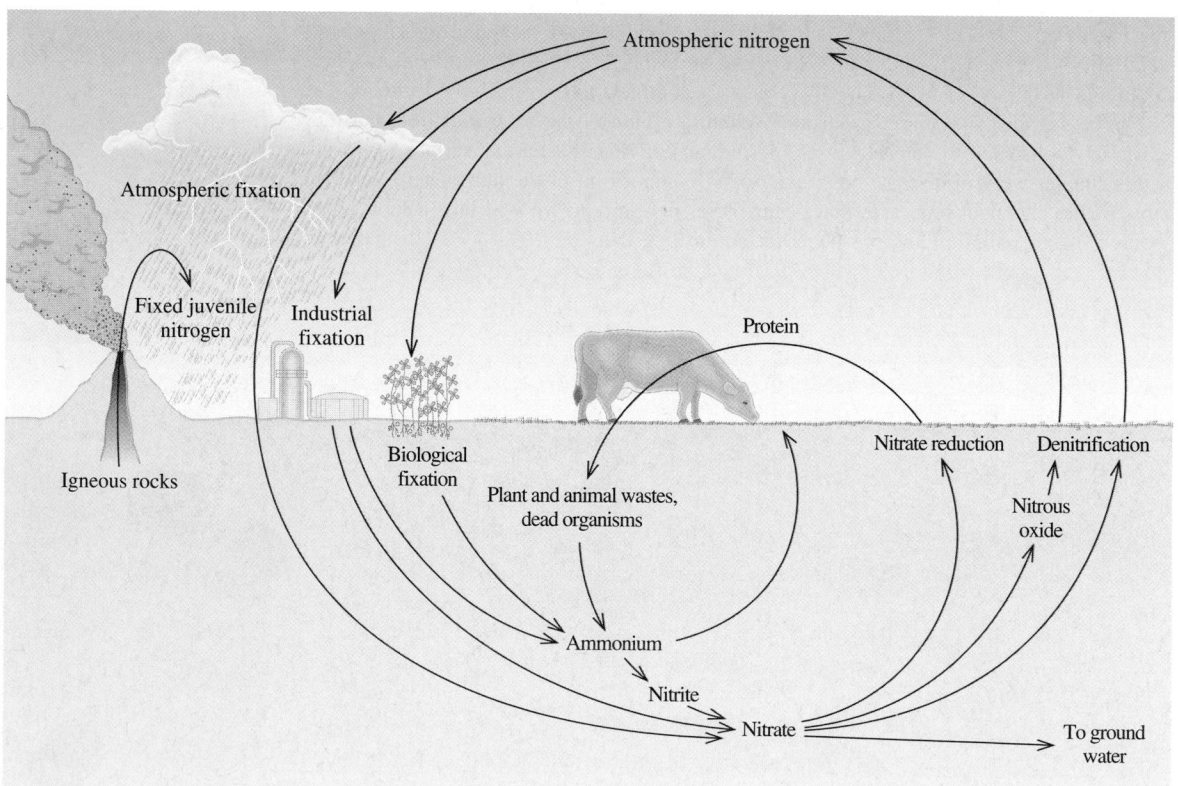

Figure 17.1 *The nitrogen cycle. Although the supply of nitrogen in the atmosphere is virtually inexhaustible, it must be combined with hydrogen or oxygen before it can be assimilated by higher plants, which in turn are consumed by animals. Juvenile nitrogen is nitrogen that has not previously participated in the nitrogen cycle.*

Figure 17.1 shows the major processes involved in the cycle of nitrogen in nature. Molecular nitrogen, with its triple bond, is a very stable molecule. However, through biological and industrial **nitrogen fixation,** *the conversion of molecular nitrogen into nitrogen compounds,* atmospheric nitrogen gas is converted into nitrates and other compounds suitable for assimilation by algae and plants. Another important mechanism for producing nitrates from nitrogen gas is lightning. The steps are

$$N_2(g) + O_2(g) \xrightarrow[\text{energy}]{\text{electrical}} 2NO(g)$$
$$2NO(g) + O_2(g) \longrightarrow 2NO_2(g)$$
$$2NO_2(g) + H_2O(l) \longrightarrow HNO_2(aq) + HNO_3(aq)$$

About 30 million tons of HNO_3 are produced this way annually. Nitric acid is converted to nitrate salts in the soil. These nutrients are taken up by plants, which in turn are ingested by animals. Animals use the nutrients from plants to make proteins and other essential biomolecules. Denitrification reverses nitrogen fixation to complete the cycle. For example, certain anaerobic organisms decompose animal wastes as well as dead plants and animals to produce free molecular nitrogen from nitrates.

The main processes of the global oxygen cycle are shown in Figure 17.2. This cycle is complicated by the fact that oxygen takes so many different chemical forms. Atmospheric oxygen is removed through respiration and various industrial processes (mostly combustion), which produce carbon dioxide. Photosynthesis is the major mechanism by which molecular oxygen is regenerated from carbon dioxide and water.

Scientists divide the atmosphere into several different layers according to temperature variation and composition (Figure 17.3). As far as visible events are concerned, the most active region is the **troposphere,** *the layer of the atmosphere that*

Figure 17.2 *The oxygen cycle. The cycle is complicated because oxygen appears in so many chemical forms and combinations, primarily as molecular oxygen, in water, and in organic and inorganic compounds.*

Figure 17.3 *Regions of Earth's atmosphere. Notice the variation of temperature with altitude. Most of the phenomena shown here are discussed in the chapter.*

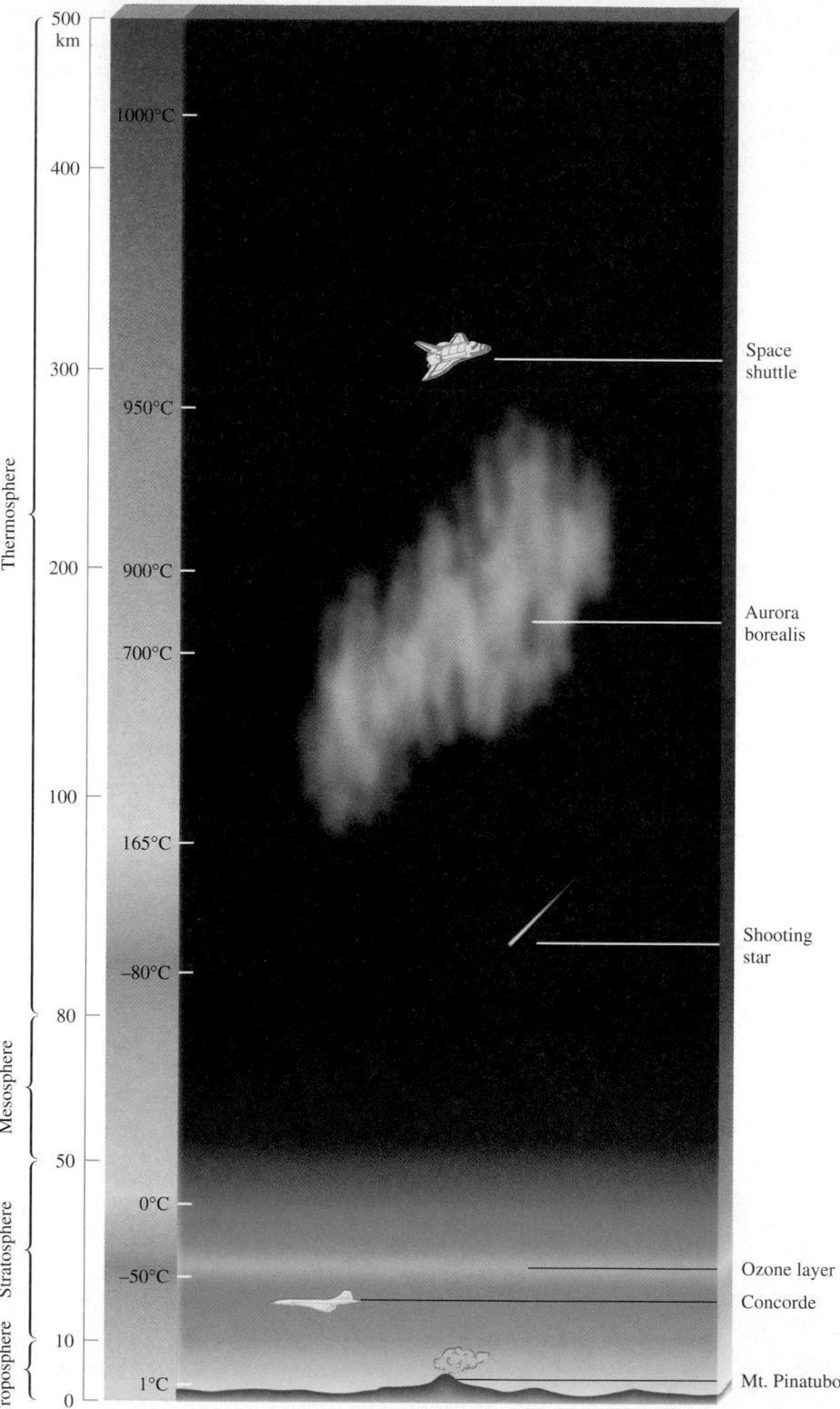

contains about 80 percent of the total mass of air and practically all of the atmosphere's water vapor. The troposphere is the thinnest layer of the atmosphere (10 km), but it is where all the dramatic events of weather—rain, lightning, hurricanes—occur. Temperature decreases almost linearly with increasing altitude in this region.

Above the troposphere is the **stratosphere,** *which consists of nitrogen, oxygen, and ozone.* In the stratosphere, the air temperature *rises* with altitude. This warming effect is the result of exothermic reactions triggered by UV radiation from the sun (to be discussed in Section 17.3). One of the products of this reaction sequence is ozone (O_3), which, as we will see shortly, serves to prevent harmful UV rays from reaching Earth's surface.

In the **mesosphere,** which is *above the stratosphere,* the concentration of ozone and other gases is low, and the temperature decreases with increasing altitude. The **thermosphere,** or **ionosphere,** is *the uppermost layer of the atmosphere.* The rise in temperature in this region is the result of the bombardment of molecular oxygen and nitrogen and atomic species by energetic particles, such as electrons and protons, from the sun. Typical reactions are

$$N_2 \longrightarrow 2N \qquad \Delta H° = 941.4 \text{ kJ/mol}$$
$$N \longrightarrow N^+ + e^- \qquad \Delta H° = 1400 \text{ kJ/mol}$$
$$O_2 \longrightarrow O_2^+ + e^- \qquad \Delta H° = 1176 \text{ kJ/mol}$$

In reverse, these processes liberate the equivalent amount of energy, mostly as heat. Ionized particles are responsible for the reflection of radio waves back toward Earth.

17.2 Phenomena in the Outer Layers of the Atmosphere

In this section we will discuss two dazzling phenomena that occur in the outer regions of the atmosphere. One is a natural event. The other is a curious by-product of human space travel.

Aurora Borealis and Aurora Australis

Violent eruptions on the surface of the sun, called *solar flares,* result in the ejection of myriad electrons and protons into space, where they disrupt radio transmission and provide us with spectacular celestial light shows known as *auroras* (Figure 17.4). These electrons and protons collide with the molecules and atoms in Earth's upper atmosphere, causing them to become ionized and electronically excited. Eventually, the excited molecules and ions return to the ground state with the emission of light. For example, an excited oxygen atom emits photons at wavelengths of 558 nm (green) and between 630 nm and 636 nm (red):

$$O^* \longrightarrow O + hv$$

where the asterisk denotes an electronically excited species and hv the emitted photon (see Section 7.2). Similarly, the blue and violet colors often observed in auroras result from the transition in the ionized nitrogen molecule:

$$N_2^+{}^* \longrightarrow N_2^+ + hv$$

The wavelengths for this transition fall between 391 and 470 nm.

The incoming streams of solar protons and electrons are oriented by Earth's magnetic field so that most auroral displays occur in doughnut-shaped zones about 2000 km in diameter centered on the North and South Poles. *Aurora borealis* is the name given to this phenomenon in the Northern Hemisphere. In the Southern Hemisphere, it is

Figure 17.4 *Aurora borealis, commonly referred to as the northern lights.*

called *aurora australis.* Sometimes, the number of solar particles is so immense that auroras are also visible from other locations on Earth.

Example 17.1

The bond enthalpy of O_2 is 498.7 kJ/mol. Calculate the maximum wavelength (nm) of a photon that can cause the dissociation of an O_2 molecule.

Strategy We want to calculate the wavelength of a photon that will break an O=O bond. Therefore, we need the amount of energy in one bond. The bond enthalpy of O_2 is given in units of kJ/mol. The units needed for the energy of one bond are J/molecule. Once we know the energy in one bond, we can calculate the minimum frequency and maximum wavelength needed to dissociate one O_2 molecule. The conversion steps are

$$\text{kJ/mol} \longrightarrow \text{J/molecule} \longrightarrow \text{frequency of photon} \longrightarrow \text{wavelength of photon}$$

Solution First we calculate the energy required to break one O=O bond:

$$\frac{498.7 \times 10^3 \, \text{J}}{1 \, \text{mol}} \times \frac{1 \, \text{mol}}{6.022 \times 10^{23} \, \text{molecules}} = 8.281 \times 10^{-19} \, \frac{\text{J}}{\text{molecule}}$$

The energy of the photon is given by $E = h\nu$ [Equation (7.2)]. Therefore,

$$\nu = \frac{E}{h} = \frac{8.281 \times 10^{-19} \, \text{J}}{6.63 \times 10^{-34} \, \text{J} \cdot \text{s}}$$
$$= 1.25 \times 10^{15} \, \text{s}^{-1}$$

Finally, we calculate the wavelength of the photon, given by $\lambda = c/\nu$ [see Equation (7.1)], as follows:

$$\lambda = \frac{3.00 \times 10^8 \, \text{m/s}}{1.25 \times 10^{15} \, \text{s}^{-1}}$$
$$= 2.40 \times 10^{-7} \, \text{m} = 240 \, \text{nm}$$

(Continued)

Comment In principle, any photon with a wavelength of 240 nm or *shorter* can dissociate an O_2 molecule.

Similar problem: 17.11.

Practice Exercise Calculate the wavelength (in nm) of a photon needed to dissociate an O_3 molecule:

$$O_3 \longrightarrow O + O_2 \qquad \Delta H° = 107.2 \text{ kJ/mol}$$

The Mystery Glow of Space Shuttles

A human-made light show that baffled scientists for several years is produced by space shuttles orbiting Earth. In 1983, astronauts first noticed an eerie orange glow on the outside surface of their spacecraft at an altitude about 300 km above Earth (Figure 17.5). The light, which usually extends about 10 cm away from the protective silica heat tiles and other surface materials, is most pronounced on the parts of the shuttle facing its direction of travel. This fact led scientists to postulate that collision between oxygen atoms in the atmosphere and the fast-moving shuttle somehow produced the orange light. Spectroscopic measurements of the glow, as well as laboratory tests, strongly suggested that nitric oxide (NO) and nitrogen dioxide (NO_2) also played a part. It is believed that oxygen atoms interact with nitric oxide adsorbed on (that is, bound to) the shuttle's surface to form electronically excited nitrogen dioxide:

$$O + NO \longrightarrow NO_2{}^*$$

As the $NO_2{}^*$ leaves the shell of the spacecraft, it emits photons at a wavelength of 680 nm (orange).

$$NO_2{}^* \longrightarrow NO_2 + h\nu$$

Support for this explanation came inadvertently in 1991, when astronauts aboard *Discovery* released various gases, including carbon dioxide, neon, xenon, and nitric oxide, from the cargo bay in the course of an unrelated experiment. Expelled one at a time, these gases scattered onto the surface of the shuttle's tail. The nitric oxide caused the normal shuttle glow to intensify markedly, but the other gases had no effect on it.

What is the source of the nitric oxide on the outside of the spacecraft? Scientists believe that some of it may come from the exhaust gases emitted by the shuttle's rockets and that some of it is present in the surrounding atmosphere. The shuttle glow does not harm the vehicle, but it does interfere with spectroscopic measurements on distant objects made from the spacecraft.

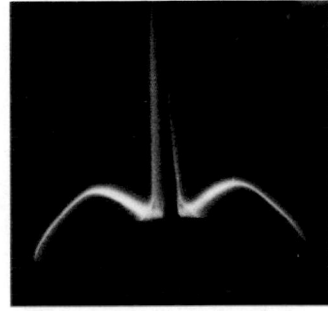

Figure 17.5 *The glowing tail section of the space shuttle viewed from inside the vehicle.*

17.3 Depletion of Ozone in the Stratosphere

As mentioned earlier, ozone in the stratosphere prevents UV radiation emitted by the sun from reaching Earth's surface. The formation of ozone in this region begins with the *photodissociation* of oxygen molecules by solar radiation at wavelengths below 240 nm:

Photodissociation is the breaking of chemical bonds by radiant energy.

$$O_2 \xrightarrow[< 240 \text{ nm}]{\text{UV}} O + O \qquad (17.1)$$

The highly reactive O atoms combine with oxygen molecules to form ozone as follows:

$$O + O_2 + M \longrightarrow O_3 + M \qquad (17.2)$$

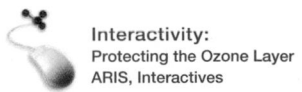

Interactivity:
Protecting the Ozone Layer
ARIS, Interactives

758   Chemistry in the Atmosphere

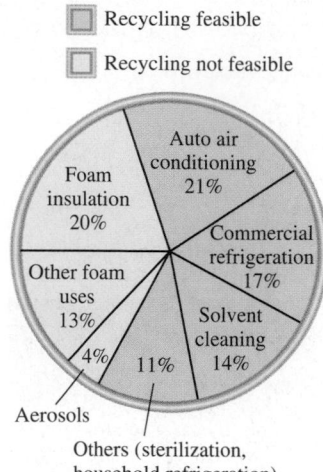

Recycling feasible

Recycling not feasible

Auto air conditioning 21%
Foam insulation 20%
Commercial refrigeration 17%
Other foam uses 13%
Solvent cleaning 14%
4%
11%
Aerosols
Others (sterilization, household refrigeration)

Figure 17.6 *Uses of CFCs. Since 1978, the use of aerosol propellants has been banned in the United States.*

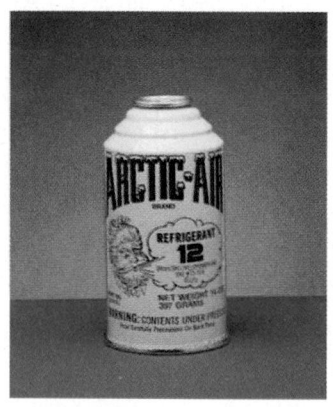

A can of CFC used in an air conditioner.

It can take years for CFCs to reach the stratosphere.

Cl is a homogeneous catalyst.

where M is some inert substance such as N_2. The role of M in this exothermic reaction is to absorb some of the excess energy released and prevent the spontaneous decomposition of the O_3 molecule. The energy that is not absorbed by M is given off as heat. (As the M molecules themselves become de-excited, they release more heat to the surroundings.) In addition, ozone itself absorbs UV light between 200 and 300 nm:

$$O_3 \xrightarrow{\text{UV}} O + O_2 \tag{17.3}$$

The process continues when O and O_2 recombine to form O_3 as shown in Equation (17.2), further warming the stratosphere.

If all the stratospheric ozone were compressed into a single layer at STP on Earth, that layer would be only about 3 mm thick! Although the concentration of ozone in the stratosphere is very low, it is sufficient to filter out (that is, absorb) solar radiation in the 200- to 300-nm range [see Equation (17.3)]. In the stratosphere, it acts as our protective shield against UV radiation, which can induce skin cancer, cause genetic mutations, and destroy crops and other forms of vegetation.

The formation and destruction of ozone by natural processes is a dynamic equilibrium that maintains a constant concentration of ozone in the stratosphere. Since the mid-1970s scientists have been concerned about the harmful effects of certain chlorofluorocarbons (CFCs) on the ozone layer. The CFCs, which are generally known by the trade name Freons, were first synthesized in the 1930s. Some of the common ones are $CFCl_3$ (Freon 11), CF_2Cl_2 (Freon 12), $C_2F_3Cl_3$ (Freon 113), and $C_2F_4Cl_2$ (Freon 114). Because these compounds are readily liquefied, relatively inert, nontoxic, noncombustible, and volatile, they have been used as coolants in refrigerators and air conditioners, in place of highly toxic liquid sulfur dioxide (SO_2) and ammonia (NH_3). Large quantities of CFCs are also used in the manufacture of disposable foam products such as cups and plates, as aerosol propellants in spray cans, and as solvents to clean newly soldered electronic circuit boards (Figure 17.6). In 1977, the peak year of production, nearly 1.5×10^6 tons of CFCs were produced in the United States. Most of the CFCs produced for commercial and industrial use are eventually discharged into the atmosphere.

Because of their relative inertness, the CFCs slowly diffuse unchanged up to the stratosphere, where UV radiation of wavelengths between 175 nm and 220 nm causes them to decompose:

$$CFCl_3 \longrightarrow CFCl_2 + Cl$$
$$CF_2Cl_2 \longrightarrow CF_2Cl + Cl$$

The reactive chlorine atoms then undergo the following reactions:

$$Cl + O_3 \longrightarrow ClO + O_2 \tag{17.4}$$

$$ClO + O \longrightarrow Cl + O_2 \tag{17.5}$$

The overall result [sum of Equations (17.4) and (17.5)] is the net removal of an O_3 molecule from the stratosphere:

$$O_3 + O \longrightarrow 2O_2 \tag{17.6}$$

The oxygen atoms in Equation (17.5) are supplied by the photochemical decomposition of molecular oxygen and ozone described earlier. Note that the Cl atom plays the role of a catalyst in the reaction mechanism scheme represented by Equations (17.4) and (17.5) because it is not used up and therefore can take part in many such reactions.

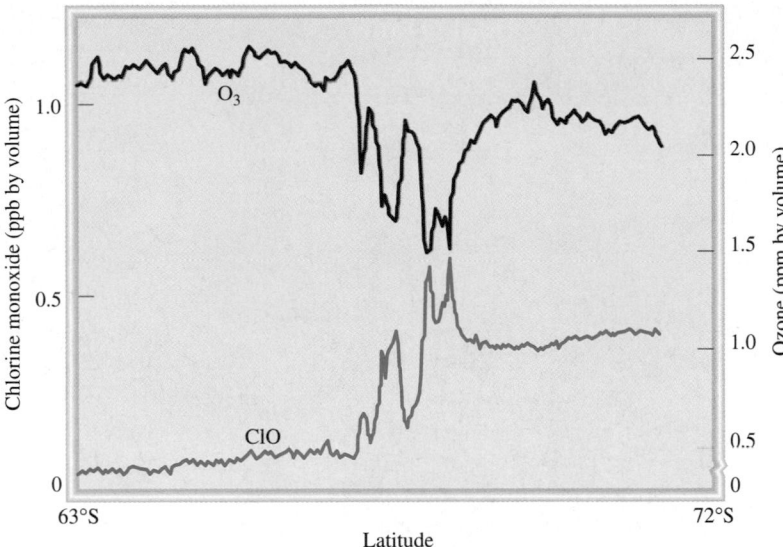

Figure 17.7 *The variations in the concentrations of ClO and O_3 with latitude.*

One Cl atom can destroy up to 100,000 O_3 molecules before it is removed by some other reaction. The ClO (chlorine monoxide) species is an intermediate because it is produced in the first elementary step [Equation (17.4)] and consumed in the second step [Equation (17.5)]. The preceding mechanism for the destruction of ozone has been supported by the detection of ClO in the stratosphere in recent years (Figure 17.7). As can be seen, the concentration of O_3 decreases in regions that have high amounts of ClO.

Another group of compounds that can destroy stratospheric ozone are the nitrogen oxides, generally denoted as NO_x. (Examples of NO_x are NO and NO_2.) These compounds come from the exhausts of high-altitude supersonic aircraft and from human and natural activities on Earth. Solar radiation decomposes a substantial amount of the other nitrogen oxides to nitric oxide (NO), which participates in the destruction of ozone as follows:

$$O_3 \longrightarrow O_2 + O$$
$$NO + O_3 \longrightarrow NO_2 + O_2$$
$$\underline{NO_2 + O \longrightarrow NO + O_2}$$
$$\text{Overall:} \qquad 2O_3 \longrightarrow 3O_2$$

In this case, NO is the catalyst and NO_2 is the intermediate. Nitrogen dioxide also reacts with chlorine monoxide to form chlorine nitrate:

$$ClO + NO_2 \longrightarrow ClONO_2$$

Chlorine nitrate is relatively stable and serves as a "chlorine reservoir," which plays a role in the depletion of the stratospheric ozone over the North and South Poles.

Polar Ozone Holes

In the mid-1980s, evidence began to accumulate that an "Antarctic ozone hole" developed in late winter, depleting the stratospheric ozone over Antarctica by as much as 50 percent (Figure 17.8). In the stratosphere, a stream of air known as the "polar vortex" circles Antarctica in winter. Air trapped within this vortex becomes extremely

Figure 17.8 *In recent years, scientists have found that the ozone layer in the stratosphere over the South Pole has become thinner. This map, based on data collected over a number of years, shows the depletion of ozone in purple (Source: NASA/Goddard Space Flight Center).*

cold during the polar night. This condition leads to the formation of ice particles known as polar stratospheric clouds (PSCs) (Figure 17.9). Acting as a heterogeneous catalyst, these PSCs provide a surface for reactions converting HCl (emitted from Earth) and chlorine nitrate to more reactive chlorine molecules:

$$HCl + ClONO_2 \longrightarrow Cl_2 + HNO_3$$

By early spring, the sunlight splits molecular chlorine into chlorine atoms

$$Cl_2 + h\nu \longrightarrow 2Cl$$

which then attack ozone as shown earlier.

The situation is not as severe in the warmer Arctic region, where the vortex does not persist quite as long. Studies have shown that ozone levels in this region have declined between 4 and 8 percent in the past decade. Volcanic eruptions, such as that

Figure 17.9 *Polar stratospheric clouds containing ice particles can catalyze the formation of Cl atoms and lead to the destruction of ozone.*

of Mount Pinatubo in the Philippines in 1991, inject large quantities of dust-sized particles and sulfuric acid aerosols (see p. 531) into the atmosphere. These particles can perform the same catalytic function as the ice crystals at the South Pole. As a result, the Arctic hole is expected to grow larger during the next few years.

Recognizing the serious implications of the loss of ozone in the stratosphere, nations throughout the world have acknowledged the need to drastically curtail or totally stop the production of CFCs. In 1978 the United States was one of the few countries to ban the use of CFCs in hair sprays and other aerosols. An international treaty—the Montreal protocol—was signed by most industrialized nations in 1987, setting targets for cutbacks in CFC production and the complete elimination of these substances by the year 2000. While some progress has been made in this respect, many nations have not been able to abide by the treaty because of the importance of CFCs to their economies. Recycling could play a significant supplementary role in preventing CFCs already in appliances from escaping into the atmosphere. As Figure 17.6 shows, more than half of the CFCs in use are recoverable.

An intense effort is under way to find CFC substitutes that are effective refrigerants but not harmful to the ozone layer. One of the promising candidates is hydrochlorofluorocarbon 134a, or HCFC-134a (CH_2FCF_3). The presence of the hydrogen atoms makes the compound more susceptible to oxidation in the lower atmosphere, so that it never reaches the stratosphere. Specifically, it is attacked by the hydroxyl radical in the troposphere:

$$CH_2FCF_3 + OH \longrightarrow CHFCF_3 + H_2O$$

The OH radical is formed by a series of complex reactions in the troposphere that are driven by sunlight.

The $CHFCF_3$ fragments react with oxygen, eventually decomposing to CO_2, water, and hydrogen fluoride that are removed by rainwater.

Although it is not clear whether the CFCs already released to the atmosphere will eventually result in catastrophic damage to life on Earth, it is conceivable that the depletion of ozone can be slowed by reducing the availability of Cl atoms. Indeed, some chemists have suggested sending a fleet of planes to spray 50,000 tons of ethane (C_2H_6) or propane (C_3H_8) high over the South Pole in an attempt to heal the hole in the ozone layer. Being a reactive species, the chlorine atom would react with the hydrocarbons as follows:

$$Cl + C_2H_6 \longrightarrow HCl + C_2H_5$$
$$Cl + C_3H_8 \longrightarrow HCl + C_3H_7$$

The products of these reactions would not affect the ozone concentration. A less realistic plan is to rejuvenate the ozone layer by producing large quantities of ozone and releasing it into the stratosphere from airplanes. Technically this solution is feasible, but it would be enormously costly and it would require the collaboration of many nations.

Having discussed the chemistry in the outer regions of Earth's atmosphere, we will focus in Sections 17.4 through 17.8 on events closer to us, that is, in the troposphere.

17.4 Volcanoes

Volcanic eruptions, Earth's most spectacular natural displays of energy, are instrumental in forming large parts of Earth's crust. The upper mantle, immediately under the crust, is nearly molten. A slight increase in heat, such as that generated by the movement of one crustal plate under another, melts the rock. The molten rock, called *magma,* rises to the surface and generates some types of volcanic eruptions (Figure 17.10).

An active volcano emits gases, liquids, and solids. The gases spewed into the atmosphere include primarily N_2, CO_2, HCl, HF, H_2S, and water vapor. It is estimated that volcanoes are the source of about two-thirds of the sulfur in the air. On the slopes of Mount St. Helens, which last erupted in 1980, deposits of elemental sulfur are visible near the eruption site. At high temperatures, the hydrogen sulfide gas given off by a volcano is oxidized by air:

$$2H_2S(g) + 3O_2(g) \longrightarrow 2SO_2(g) + 2H_2O(g)$$

Some of the SO_2 is reduced by more H_2S from the volcano to elemental sulfur and water:

$$2H_2S(g) + SO_2(g) \longrightarrow 3S(s) + 2H_2O(g)$$

The rest of the SO_2 is released into the atmosphere, where it reacts with water to form acid rain (see Section 17.6).

The tremendous force of a volcanic eruption carries a sizable amount of gas into the stratosphere. There SO_2 is oxidized to SO_3, which is eventually converted to sulfuric acid aerosols in a series of complex mechanisms. In addition to destroying ozone in the stratosphere (see p. 761), these aerosols can also affect climate. Because the

Sulfur deposits at a volcanic site.

Figure 17.10 *A volcanic eruption on the island of Hawaii.*

stratosphere is above the atmospheric weather patterns, the aerosol clouds often persist for more than a year. They absorb solar radiation and thereby cause a drop in temperature at Earth's surface. However, this cooling effect is local rather than global, because it depends on the site and frequency of volcanic eruptions.

17.5 The Greenhouse Effect

Although carbon dioxide is only a trace gas in Earth's atmosphere, with a concentration of about 0.033 percent by volume (see Table 17.1), it plays a critical role in controlling our climate. The so-called *greenhouse effect* describes *the trapping of heat near Earth's surface by gases in the atmosphere, particularly carbon dioxide.* The glass roof of a greenhouse transmits visible sunlight and absorbs some of the outgoing infrared (IR) radiation, thereby trapping the heat. Carbon dioxide acts somewhat like a glass roof, except that the temperature rise in the greenhouse is due mainly to the restricted air circulation inside. Calculations show that if the atmosphere did not contain carbon dioxide, Earth would be 30°C cooler!

Figure 17.11 shows the carbon cycle in our global ecosystem. The transfer of carbon dioxide to and from the atmosphere is an essential part of the carbon cycle. Carbon dioxide is produced when any form of carbon or a carbon-containing compound is burned in an excess of oxygen. Many carbonates give off CO_2 when heated, and all give off CO_2 when treated with acid:

$$CaCO_3(s) \longrightarrow CaO(s) + CO_2(g)$$
$$CaCO_3(s) + 2HCl(aq) \longrightarrow CaCl_2(aq) + H_2O(l) + CO_2(g)$$

A dramatic illustration of the greenhouse effect is found on Venus, where the atmosphere is 97 percent CO_2 and the atmospheric pressure is 9×10^6 Pa (equivalent to 89 atm). The surface temperature of Venus is about 730 K!

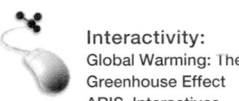

Interactivity:
Global Warming: The
Greenhouse Effect
ARIS, Interactives

Figure 17.11 *The carbon cycle.*

Figure 17.12 *The incoming radiation from the sun and the outgoing radiation from Earth's surface.*

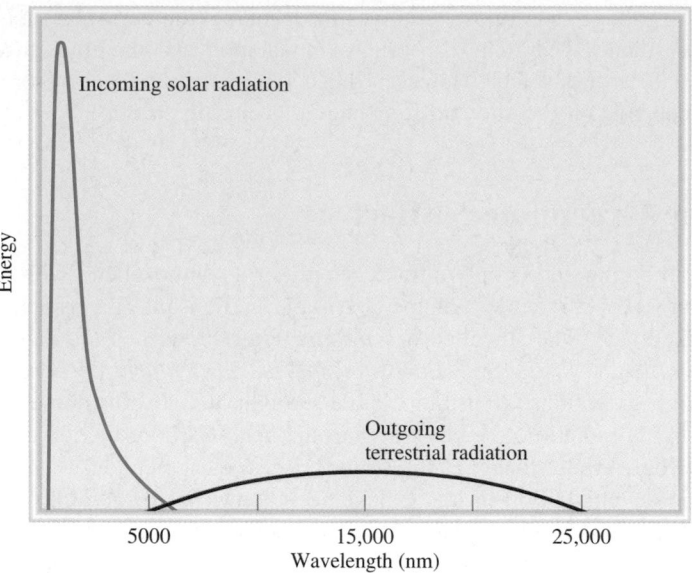

Carbon dioxide is also a by-product of the fermentation of sugar:

$$C_6H_{12}O_6(aq) \xrightarrow{\text{yeast}} 2C_2H_5OH(aq) + 2CO_2(g)$$
$$\text{glucose} \qquad\qquad \text{ethanol}$$

Carbohydrates and other complex carbon-containing molecules are consumed by animals, which respire and release CO_2 as an end product of metabolism:

$$C_6H_{12}O_6(aq) + 6O_2(g) \longrightarrow 6CO_2(g) + 6H_2O(l)$$

As mentioned earlier, another major source of CO_2 is volcanic activity.

Carbon dioxide is removed from the atmosphere by photosynthetic plants and certain microorganisms:

This reaction requires radiant energy (visible light).

$$6CO_2(g) + 6H_2O(l) \longrightarrow C_6H_{12}O_6(aq) + 6O_2(g)$$

After plants and animals die, the carbon in their tissues is oxidized to CO_2 and returns to the atmosphere. In addition, there is a dynamic equilibrium between atmospheric CO_2 and carbonates in the oceans and lakes.

The solar radiant energy received by Earth is distributed over a band of wavelengths between 100 and 5000 nm, but much of it is concentrated in the 400- to 700-nm range, which is the visible region of the spectrum (Figure 17.12). By contrast, the thermal radiation emitted by Earth's surface is characterized by wavelengths longer than 4000 nm (IR region) because of the much lower average surface temperature compared to that of the sun. The outgoing IR radiation can be absorbed by water and carbon dioxide, but not by nitrogen and oxygen.

All molecules vibrate, even at the lowest temperatures. The energy associated with molecular vibration is quantized, much like the electronic energies of atoms and molecules. To vibrate more energetically, a molecule must absorb a photon of a specific wavelength in the IR region. First, however, its dipole moment *must* change during the course of a vibration. [Recall that the dipole moment of a molecule is the product of the charge and the distance between charges (see p. 409).] Figure 17.13

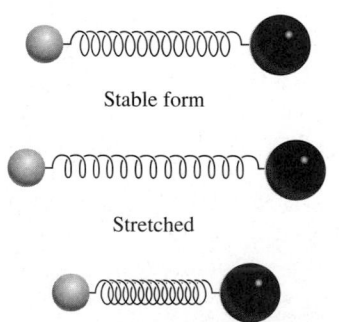

Stable form

Stretched

Compressed

Figure 17.13 *Vibrational motion of a diatomic molecule. Chemical bonds can be stretched and compressed like a spring.*

shows how a diatomic molecule can vibrate. If the molecule is homonuclear like N_2 and O_2, there can be no change in the dipole moment; the molecule has a zero dipole moment no matter how far apart or close together the two atoms are. We call such molecules IR-inactive because they *cannot* absorb IR radiation. On the other hand, all heteronuclear diatomic molecules are IR-active; that is, they all can absorb IR radiation because their dipole moments constantly change as the bond lengths change.

A *polyatomic* molecule can vibrate in more than one way. Water, for example, can vibrate in three different ways, as shown in Figure 17.14. Because water is a polar molecule, it is easy to see that any of these vibrations results in a change in dipole moment because there is a change in bond length. Therefore, a H_2O molecule is IR-active. Carbon dioxide has a linear geometry and is nonpolar. Figure 17.15 shows two of the four ways a CO_2 molecule can vibrate. One of them [Figure 17.15(a)] symmetrically displaces atoms from the center of gravity and will not create a dipole moment, but the other vibration [Figure 17.15(b)] is IR-active because the dipole moment changes from zero to a maximum value in one direction and then reaches the same maximum value when it changes to the other extreme position.

Upon receiving a photon in the IR region, a molecule of H_2O or CO_2 is promoted to a higher vibrational energy level:

$$H_2O + h\nu \longrightarrow H_2O^*$$
$$CO_2 + h\nu \longrightarrow CO_2^*$$

Figure 17.14 *The three different modes of vibration of a water molecule. Each mode of vibration can be imagined by moving the atoms along the arrows and then reversing their directions.*

(the asterisk denotes a vibrationally excited molecule). These energetically excited molecules soon lose their excess energy either by collision with other molecules or by spontaneous emission of radiation. Part of this radiation is emitted to outer space and part returns to Earth's surface.

Although the total amount of water vapor in our atmosphere has not altered noticeably over the years, the concentration of CO_2 has been rising steadily since the turn of the twentieth century as a result of the burning of fossil fuels (petroleum, natural gas, and coal). Figure 17.16 shows the percentages of CO_2 emitted due to human activities in the United States in 1998, and Figure 17.17 shows the variation of carbon dioxide concentration over a period of years, as measured in Hawaii. In the Northern Hemisphere, the seasonal oscillations are caused by removal of carbon dioxide by photosynthesis during the growing season and its buildup during the fall and winter months. Clearly, the trend is toward an increase in CO_2. The current rate of increase is about 1 ppm (1 part CO_2 per million parts air) by volume per year, which is equivalent to 9×10^9 tons of CO_2! Scientists have estimated that by the year 2010 the CO_2 concentration will exceed preindustrial levels by about 25 percent.

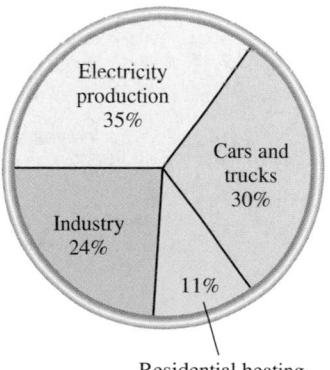

Figure 17.16 *Sources of carbon dioxide emission in the United States. Note that not all of the emitted CO_2 enters the atmosphere. Some of it is taken up by carbon dioxide "sinks," such as the ocean.*

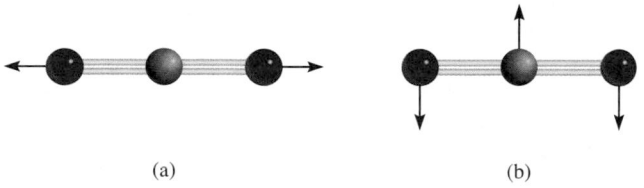

(a)   (b)

Figure 17.15 *Two of the four ways a carbon dioxide molecule can vibrate. The vibration in (a) does not result in a change in dipole moment, but the vibration in (b) renders the molecule IR active.*

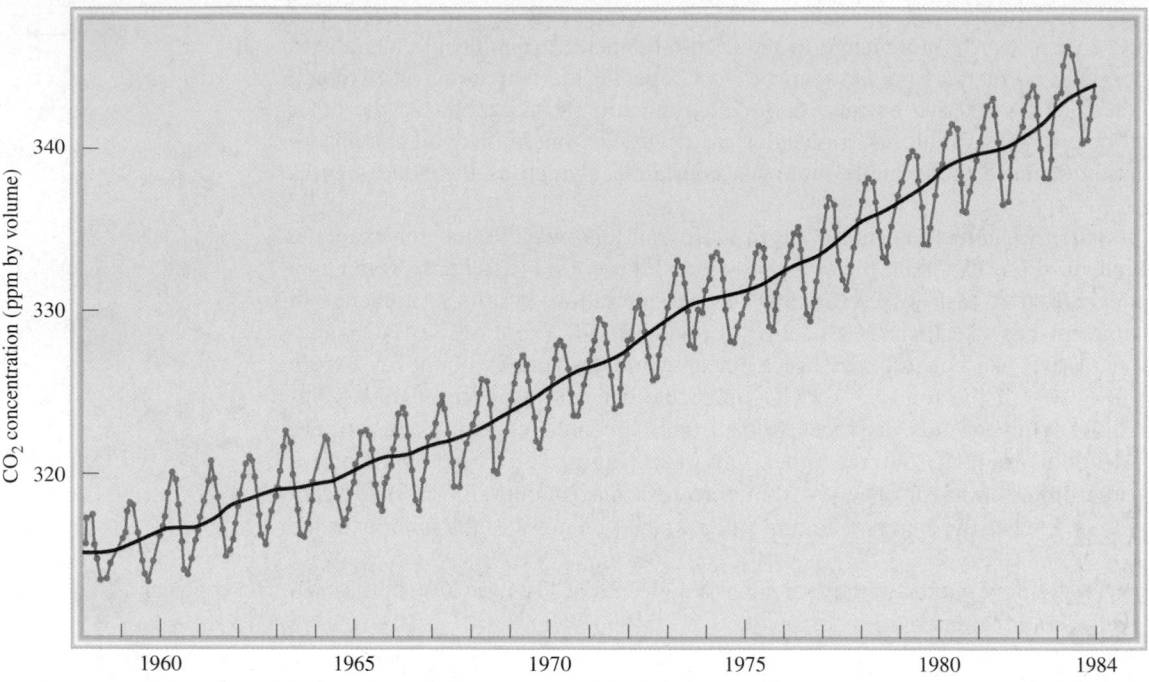

Figure 17.17 *Yearly variation of carbon dioxide concentration at Mauna Loa, Hawaii. The general trend clearly points to an increase of carbon dioxide in the atmosphere. This trend has continued: in 2004 the CO_2 concentration reached 377 ppm.*

In addition to CO_2 and H_2O, other greenhouse gases, such as the CFCs, CH_4, NO_x, and N_2O also contribute appreciably to the warming of the atmosphere. Figure 17.18 shows the gradual increase in temperature over the years and Figure 17.19 shows the relative contributions of the greenhouse gases to global warming.

It is predicted by some meteorologists that should the buildup of greenhouse gases continue at its current rate, Earth's average temperature will increase by about 1° to 3°C in this century. Although a temperature increase of a few degrees may seem

The difference in global temperatures between today and the last ice age is only 4° to 5°C.

Figure 17.18 *Temperature rise on Earth's surface from 1880 to 1996. Zero represents the average temperature for the years 1951–1980. (Source: NASA Goddard Institute for Space Studies.)*

insignificant, it is actually large enough to disrupt the delicate thermal balance on Earth and could cause glaciers and icecaps to melt. Consequently, the sea level would rise and coastal areas would be flooded. Of course, predicting weather trends is extremely difficult, and there are other potentially moderating factors to take into account that may affect the global weather pattern. For example, the ash from volcanic eruptions diffuses upward and can stay in the atmosphere for years. By reflecting incoming sunlight, volcanic ash can cause a cooling effect. Furthermore, the warming effect of CFCs in the troposphere is offset by its action in the stratosphere. Because ozone is a polar polyatomic molecule, it is also an effective greenhouse gas. A decrease in ozone brought about by CFCs actually produces a noticeable drop in temperature.

To combat the greenhouse effect, we must lower carbon dioxide emission. This can be done by improving energy efficiency in automobiles and in household heating and lighting, and by developing nonfossil fuel energy sources, such as photovoltaic cells. Nuclear energy is a viable alternative, but its use is highly controversial due to the difficulty of disposing of radioactive waste and the fact that nuclear power stations are more prone to accidents than conventional power stations (see Chapter 23). The proposed phasing out of CFCs, the most potent greenhouse gas, will help to slow down the warming trend. The recovery of methane gas generated at landfills and the reduction of natural gas leakages are other steps we could take to control CO_2 emission. Finally, the preservation of the Amazon jungle, tropical forests in Southeast Asia, and other large forests is vital to maintaining the steady-state concentration of CO_2 in the atmosphere. Converting forests to farmland for crops and grassland for cattle may do irreparable damage to the delicate ecosystem and permanently alter the climate pattern on Earth.

As more nations industrialize, the production of CO_2 will increase appreciably.

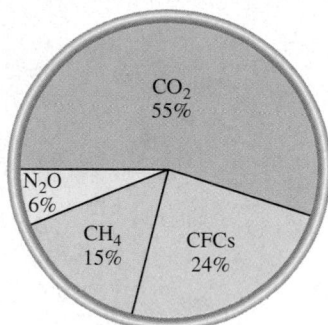

Figure 17.19 *Contribution to global warming by various greenhouse gases. The concentrations of CFCs and methane are much lower than that of carbon dioxide. However, because they can absorb IR radiation much more effectively than CO_2, they make an appreciable contribution to the overall warming effect.*

Example 17.2

Which of the following gases qualify as a greenhouse gas: CO, NO, NO_2, Cl_2, H_2, Ne?

Strategy To behave as a greenhouse gas, either the molecule must possess a dipole moment or some of its vibrational motions must generate a temporary dipole moment. These conditions immediately rule out homonuclear diatomic molecules and atomic species.

Solution Only CO, NO, and NO_2, which are all polar molecules, qualify as greenhouse gases. Both Cl_2 and H_2 are homonuclear diatomic molecules, and Ne is atomic. These three species are all IR-inactive.

Practice Exercise Which of the following is a more effective greenhouse gas: CO or H_2O?

Similar problem: 17.36.

17.6 Acid Rain

Every year acid rain causes hundreds of millions of dollars' worth of damage to stone buildings and statues throughout the world. The term "stone leprosy" is used by some environmental chemists to describe the corrosion of stone by acid rain (Figure 17.20). Acid rain is also toxic to vegetation and aquatic life. Many well-documented cases show dramatically how acid rain has destroyed agricultural and forest lands and killed aquatic organisms (see Figure 15.10).

Precipitation in the northeastern United States has an average pH of about 4.3 (Figure 17.21). Because atmospheric CO_2 in equilibrium with rainwater would not be

Scientists have known about acid rain since the late nineteenth century, but it has been a public issue for only about 30 yr.

Figure 17.20 *The effect of acid rain on the marble statue of George Washington in Washington Square, New York City. The photos were taken 50 years apart (1944–1994).*

Figure 17.21 *Mean precipitation pH in the United States in 1994. Most SO$_2$ comes from the midwestern states. Prevailing winds carry the acid droplets formed over the Northeast. Nitrogen oxides also contribute to the acid rain formation.*

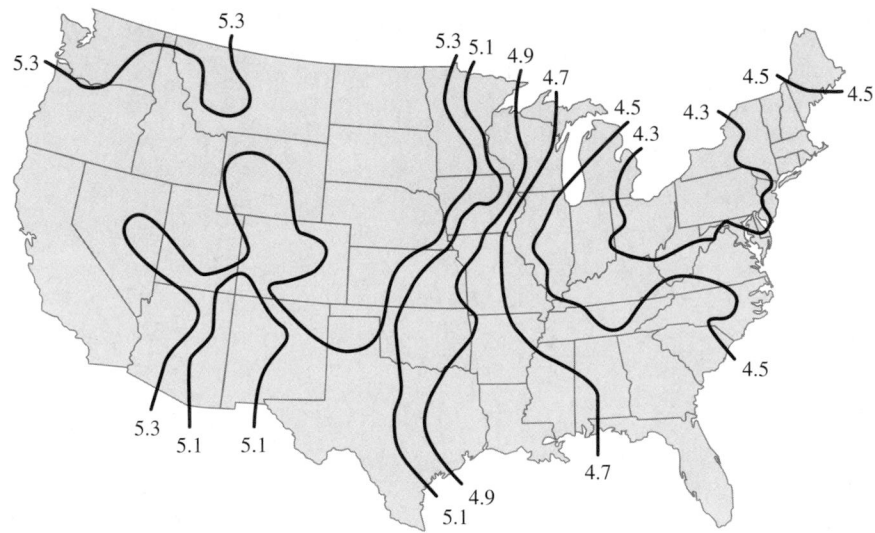

expected to result in a pH less than 5.5, sulfur dioxide (SO$_2$) and, to a lesser extent, nitrogen oxides from auto emissions are believed to be responsible for the high acidity of rainwater. Acidic oxides, such as SO$_2$, react with water to give the corresponding acids. There are several sources of atmospheric SO$_2$. Nature itself contributes much SO$_2$ in the form of volcanic eruptions. Also, many metals exist combined with sulfur in nature. Extracting the metals often entails *smelting,* or *roasting,* the ores—that is, heating the metal sulfide in air to form the metal oxide and SO$_2$. For example,

$$2ZnS(s) + 3O_2(g) \longrightarrow 2ZnO(s) + 2SO_2(g)$$

The metal oxide can be reduced more easily than the sulfide (by a more reactive metal or in some cases by carbon) to the free metal.

Although smelting is a major source of SO$_2$, the burning of fossil fuels in industry, in power plants, and in homes accounts for most of the SO$_2$ emitted to the atmosphere

Figure 17.22 *Sulfur dioxide and other air pollutants being released into the atmosphere from a coal-burning power plant.*

(Figure 17.22). The sulfur content of coal ranges from 0.5 to 5 percent by mass, depending on the source of the coal. The sulfur content of other fossil fuels is similarly variable. Oil from the Middle East, for instance, is low in sulfur, while that from Venezuela has a high sulfur content. To a lesser extent, the nitrogen-containing compounds in oil and coal are converted to nitrogen oxides, which can also acidify rainwater.

All in all, some 50 million to 60 million tons of SO_2 are released into the atmosphere each year! In the troposphere, SO_2 is almost all oxidized to H_2SO_4 in the form of aerosol, which ends up in wet precipitation or acid rain. The mechanism for the conversion of SO_2 to H_2SO_4 is quite complex and not fully understood. The reaction is believed to be initiated by the hydroxyl radical (OH):

$$OH + SO_2 \longrightarrow HOSO_2$$

The $HOSO_2$ radical is further oxidized to SO_3:

$$HOSO_2 + O_2 \longrightarrow HO_2 + SO_3$$

The sulfur trioxide formed would then rapidly react with water to form sulfuric acid:

$$SO_3 + H_2O \longrightarrow H_2SO_4$$

SO_2 can also be oxidized to SO_3 and then converted to H_2SO_4 on particles by heterogeneous catalysis. Eventually, the acid rain can corrode limestone and marble ($CaCO_3$). A typical reaction is

$$CaCO_3(s) + H_2SO_4(aq) \longrightarrow CaSO_4(s) + H_2O(l) + CO_2(g)$$

Sulfur dioxide can also attack calcium carbonate directly:

$$2CaCO_3(s) + 2SO_2(g) + O_2(g) \longrightarrow 2CaSO_4(s) + 2CO_2(g)$$

There are two ways to minimize the effects of SO_2 pollution. The most direct approach is to remove sulfur from fossil fuels before combustion, but this is technologically difficult to accomplish. A cheaper but less efficient way is to remove SO_2

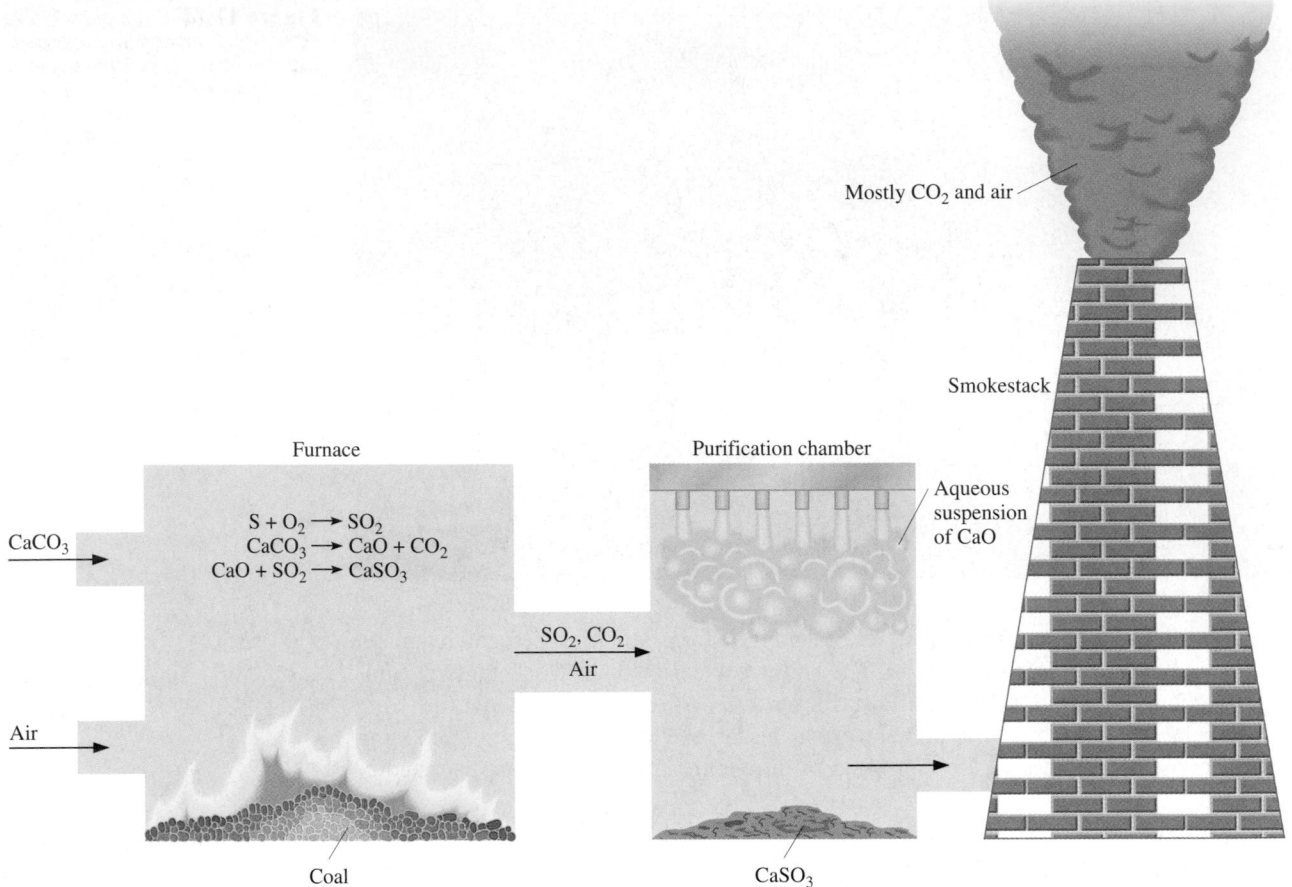

Figure 17.23 *Common procedure for removing SO_2 from burning fossil fuel. Powdered limestone decomposes into CaO, which reacts with SO_2 to form $CaSO_3$. The remaining SO_2 is reacted with an aqueous suspension of CaO to form $CaSO_3$.*

as it is formed. For example, in one process powdered limestone is injected into the power plant boiler or furnace along with coal (Figure 17.23). At high temperatures the following decomposition occurs:

$$\underset{\text{limestone}}{CaCO_3(s)} \longrightarrow \underset{\text{quicklime}}{CaO(s)} + CO_2(g)$$

The quicklime reacts with SO_2 to form calcium sulfite and some calcium sulfate:

$$CaO(s) + SO_2(g) \longrightarrow CaSO_3(s)$$
$$2CaO(s) + 2SO_2(g) + O_2(g) \longrightarrow 2CaSO_4(s)$$

To remove any remaining SO_2, an aqueous suspension of quicklime is injected into a purification chamber prior to the gases' escape through the smokestack. Quicklime is also added to lakes and soils in a process called *liming* to reduce their acidity (Figure 17.24).

Installing a sulfuric acid plant near a metal ore refining site is also an effective way to cut SO_2 emission because the SO_2 produced by roasting metal sulfides can be captured for use in the synthesis of sulfuric acid. This is a very sensible way to turn what is a pollutant in one process into a starting material for another process!

Figure 17.24 *Spreading calcium oxide (CaO) over acidified soil. This process is called liming.*

17.7 Photochemical Smog

The word "smog" was coined to describe the combination of smoke and fog that shrouded London during the 1950s. The primary cause of this noxious cloud was sulfur dioxide. Today, however, we are more familiar with *photochemical smog,* which *is formed by the reactions of automobile exhaust in the presence of sunlight.*

Automobile exhaust consists mainly of NO, CO, and various unburned hydrocarbons. These gases are called *primary pollutants* because they set in motion a series of photochemical reactions that produce *secondary pollutants.* It is the secondary pollutants—chiefly NO_2 and O_3—that are responsible for the buildup of smog.

Nitric oxide is the product of the reaction between atmospheric nitrogen and oxygen at high temperatures inside an automobile engine:

$$N_2(g) + O_2(g) \longrightarrow 2NO(g)$$

Once released into the atmosphere, nitric oxide is oxidized to nitrogen dioxide:

$$2NO(g) + O_2(g) \longrightarrow 2NO_2(g)$$

Sunlight causes the photochemical decomposition of NO_2 (at a wavelength shorter than 400 nm) into NO and O:

$$NO_2(g) + h\nu \longrightarrow NO(g) + O(g)$$

Atomic oxygen is a highly reactive species that can initiate a number of important reactions, one of which is the formation of ozone:

$$O(g) + O_2(g) + M \longrightarrow O_3(g) + M$$

where M is some inert substance such as N_2. Ozone attacks the C=C linkage in rubber:

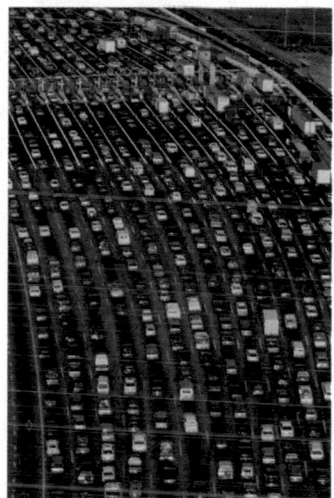

The heavy use of automobiles is the cause of photochemical smog formation.

Ozone plays a dual role in the atmosphere: It is Dr. Jekyll in the stratosphere and Mr. Hyde in the troposphere.

$$\underset{R}{\overset{R}{>}}C=C\underset{R}{\overset{R}{<}} + O_3 \longrightarrow \underset{R}{\overset{R}{>}}C\underset{O-O}{\overset{O}{<}}C\underset{R}{\overset{R}{<}} \overset{H_2O}{\longrightarrow} \underset{R}{\overset{R}{>}}C=O + O=C\underset{R}{\overset{R}{<}} + H_2O_2$$

Figure 17.25 *Typical variations with time in concentration of air pollutants on a smoggy day.*

PAN

where R represents groups of C and H atoms. In smog-ridden areas, this reaction can cause automobile tires to crack. Similar reactions are also damaging to lung tissues and other biological substances.

Ozone can be formed also by a series of very complex reactions involving unburned hydrocarbons, nitrogen oxides, and oxygen. One of the products of these reactions is peroxyacetyl nitrate, PAN:

$$CH_3—\underset{\underset{O}{\|}}{C}—O—O—NO_2$$

PAN is a powerful lachrymator, or tear producer, and causes breathing difficulties.

Figure 17.25 shows typical variations with time of primary and secondary pollutants. Initially, the concentration of NO_2 is quite low. As soon as solar radiation penetrates the atmosphere, more NO_2 is formed from NO and O_2. Note that the concentration of ozone remains fairly constant at a low level in the early morning hours. As the concentration of unburned hydrocarbons and aldehydes increases in the air, the concentrations of NO_2 and O_3 also rise rapidly. The actual amounts, of course, depend on the location, traffic, and weather conditions, but their presence is always accompanied by haze (Figure 17.26). The oxidation of hydrocarbons produces various organic intermediates, such as alcohols and carboxylic acids, which are all less volatile than the hydrocarbons themselves. These substances eventually condense into small droplets of liquid. The dispersion of these droplets in air, called *aerosol,* scatters sunlight and reduces visibility. This interaction also makes the air look hazy.

Figure 17.26 *A smoggy day in New York City.*

As the mechanism of photochemical smog formation has become better understood, major efforts have been made to reduce the buildup of primary pollutants. Most automobiles now are equipped with catalytic converters designed to oxidize CO and unburned hydrocarbons to CO_2 and H_2O and to reduce NO and NO_2 to N_2 and O_2 (see Section 13.6). More efficient automobile engines and better public transportation systems would also help to decrease air pollution in urban areas. A recent technological innovation to combat photochemical smog is to coat automobile radiators and air conditioner compressors with a platinum catalyst. So equipped, a running car can purify the air that flows under the hood by converting ozone and carbon monoxide to oxygen and carbon dioxide:

$$O_3(g) + CO(g) \xrightarrow{\text{Pt}} O_2(g) + CO_2(g)$$

In a city like Los Angeles, where the number of miles driven in one day equals nearly 300 million, this approach would significantly improve the air quality and reduce the "high-ozone level" warnings frequently issued to its residents. In fact, a drive on the freeway would help to clean up the air!

The haze over the Smoky Mountains is caused by aerosols produced by the oxidation of hydrocarbons emitted by pine trees.

17.8 Indoor Pollution

Difficult as it is to avoid air pollution outdoors, it is no easier to avoid indoor pollution. The air quality in homes and in the workplace is affected by human activities, by construction materials, and by other factors in our immediate environment. The common indoor pollutants are radon, carbon monoxide and carbon dioxide, and formaldehyde.

The Risk from Radon

In a highly publicized case in the mid-1980s, an employee reporting for work at the Limerick Nuclear Power Plant in Pennsylvania set off the plant's radiation monitor. Astonishingly, the source of his contamination turned out not to be the plant, but radon in his home!

A lot has been said and written about the potential dangers of radon as an air pollutant. Just what is radon? Where does it come from? And how does it affect our health?

Radon is a member of Group 8A (the noble gases). It is an intermediate product of the radioactive decay of uranium 238. All isotopes of radon are radioactive, but radon-222 is the most hazardous because it has the longest half-life—3.8 days. Radon, which accounts for slightly over half the background radioactivity on Earth, is generated mostly from the phosphate minerals of uranium (Figure 17.27).

The uranium decay series is discussed in Chapter 23.

Since the 1970s, high levels of radon have been detected in homes built on reclaimed land above uranium mill tailing deposits. The colorless, odorless, and

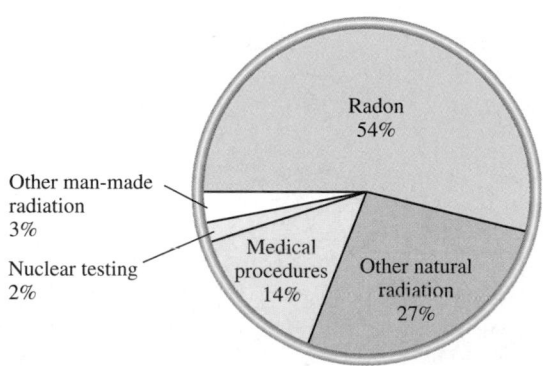

Figure 17.27 *Sources of background radiation.*

Radon
54%

Other man-made radiation
3%

Nuclear testing
2%

Medical procedures
14%

Other natural radiation
27%

After cigarette smoking, radon is the leading cause of lung cancer in the United States. It is responsible for perhaps 20,000 deaths per year.

Basement

Radon

Uranium $\longrightarrow$ Radium

Figure 17.28 *Radon usually enters houses through the foundation or basement walls.*

tasteless radon gas enters a building through tiny cracks in the basement floor (Figure 17.28). It is slightly soluble in water, so it can be spread in different media. Radon-222 is an α-emitter. When it decays, it produces radioactive polonium-214 and polonium-218, which can build up to high levels in an enclosed space. These solid radioactive particles can adhere to airborne dust and smoke, which are inhaled into the lungs and deposited in the respiratory tract. Over a long period of time, the α particles emitted by polonium and its decay products, which are also radioactive, can cause lung cancer.

What can be done to combat radon pollution indoors? The first step is to measure the radon level in the basement with a reliable test kit. Short-term and long-term kits are available (Figure 17.29). The short-term tests use activated charcoal (that is, heat-treated charcoal) to collect the decay products of radon over a period of several days. The container is sent to a laboratory where a technician measures the radioactivity (γ rays) from radon-decay products lead-214 and bismuth-214. Knowing the length of exposure, the lab technician back-calculates to determine radon concentration. The long-term test kits use a piece of special polymer film on which an α particle will leave a "track." After several months' exposure, the film is etched with a sodium hydroxide solution and the number of tracks counted. Knowing the length of exposure enables the technician to calculate the radon concentration. If the radon level is unacceptably high, then the house must be regularly ventilated. This precaution is particularly important in recently built houses, which are well insulated. A more effective way to prevent radon pollution is to reroute the gas before it gets into the house, for example, by installing a ventilation duct to draw air from beneath the basement floor to the outside.

Currently there is considerable controversy regarding the health effects of radon. The first detailed studies of the effects of radon on human health were carried out in the 1950s when it was recognized that uranium miners suffered from an abnormally high incidence of lung cancer. Some scientists have challenged the validity of these studies because the miners were also smokers. It seems quite likely that there is a synergistic effect between radon and smoking on the development of lung cancer. Radon-decay products will adhere not only to tobacco tar deposits in the lungs, but also to the solid particles in cigarette smoke, which can be inhaled by smokers and nonsmokers. More systematic studies are needed to evaluate the environmental impact of radon. In the meantime, the Environmental Protection Agency (EPA) has recommended remedial action where the radioactivity level due to radon exceeds 4 picocuries (pCi) per liter of air. (A curie corresponds to 3.70×10^{10} disintegrations of radioactive nuclei per second; a picocurie is a trillionth of a curie, or 3.70×10^{-2} disintegrations per second.)

Figure 17.29 *Home radon detectors: Long-term track etch (left) and short-term charcoal canister (right).*

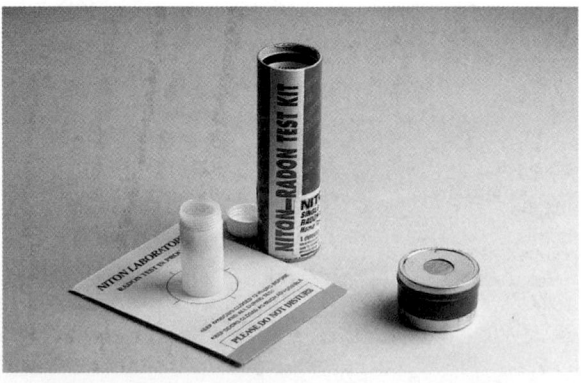

Example 17.3

The half-life of Rn-222 is 3.8 days. Starting with 1.0 g of Rn-222, how much will be left after 10 half-lives? Recall that radioactive decays obey first-order kinetics.

Strategy All radioactive decays obey first-order kinetics. Therefore, its half-life is independent of the initial concentration.

Solution After one half-life, the amount of Rn left is 0.5×1.0 g, or 0.5 g. After two half-lives, only 0.25 g of Rn remains. Generalizing the fraction of the isotope left after n half lives as $(1/2)^n$, where $n = 10$, we write

$$\text{quantity of Rn-222 left} = 1.0 \text{ g} \times \left(\frac{1}{2}\right)^{10}$$
$$= 9.8 \times 10^{-4} \text{ g}$$

An alternative solution is to calculate the first-order rate constant from the half-life. Next, use Equation (13.3) to calculate the concentration of radon after 10 half-lives. Try it.

Similar problem: 17.73.

Practice Exercise The concentration of Rn-222 in the basement of a house is 1.8×10^{-6} mol/L. Assume the air remains static and calculate the concentration of the radon after 2.4 days.

Carbon Dioxide and Carbon Monoxide

Both carbon dioxide (CO_2) and carbon monoxide (CO) are products of combustion. In the presence of an abundant supply of oxygen, CO_2 is formed; in a limited supply of oxygen, both CO and CO_2 are formed. The indoor sources of these gases are gas cooking ranges, woodstoves, space heaters, tobacco smoke, human respiration, and exhaust fumes from cars (in garages). Carbon dioxide is not a toxic gas, but it does have an asphyxiating effect (see Chemistry in Action on p. 516). In airtight buildings, the concentration of CO_2 can reach as high as 2000 ppm by volume (compared with 3 ppm outdoors). Workers exposed to high concentrations of CO_2 in skyscrapers and other sealed environments become fatigued more easily and have difficulty concentrating. Adequate ventilation is the solution to CO_2 pollution.

Like CO_2, CO is a colorless and odorless gas, but it differs from CO_2 in that it is highly poisonous. The toxicity of CO lies in its unusual ability to bind very strongly to hemoglobin, the oxygen carrier in blood. Both O_2 and CO bind to the Fe(II) ion in hemoglobin, but the affinity of hemoglobin for CO is about 200 times greater than that for O_2 (see Chapter 25). Hemoglobin molecules with tightly bound CO (called carboxyhemoglobin) cannot carry the oxygen needed for metabolic processes. A small amount of CO intake can cause drowsiness and headache; death may result when about half the hemoglobin molecules are complexed with CO. The best first-aid response to CO poisoning is to remove the victim immediately to an area with a plentiful oxygen supply or to give mouth-to-mouth resuscitation.

The concentration of carboxyhemoglobin in the blood of regular smokers is two to five times higher than that in nonsmokers.

Formaldehyde

Formaldehyde (CH_2O) is a rather disagreeable-smelling liquid used as a preservative for laboratory specimens. Industrially, formaldehyde resins are used as bonding agents in building and furniture construction materials such as plywood and particle board. In addition, urea-formaldehyde insulation foams are used to fill wall cavities. The resins and foams slowly break down to release free formaldehyde, especially under

CH_2O

acid and humid conditions. Low concentrations of formaldehyde in the air can cause drowsiness, nausea, headaches, and other respiratory ailments. Laboratory tests show that breathing high concentrations of formaldehyde can induce cancers in animals, but whether it has a similar effect in humans is unclear. The safe standard of formaldehyde in indoor air has been set at 0.1 ppm by volume.

Because formaldehyde is a reducing agent, devices have been constructed to remove it by means of a redox reaction. Indoor air is circulated through an air purifier containing an oxidant such as $Al_2O_3/KMnO_4$, which converts formaldehyde to the less harmful and less volatile formic acid (HCOOH). Proper ventilation is the best way to remove formaldehyde. However, care should be taken not to remove the air from a room too quickly without replenishment, because a reduced pressure would cause the formaldehyde resins to decompose faster, resulting in the release of *more* formaldehyde.

Summary of Facts and Concepts

1. Earth's atmosphere is made up mainly of nitrogen and oxygen, plus a number of other trace gases. The chemical processes that go on in the atmosphere are influenced by solar radiation, volcanic eruption, and human activities.
2. In the outer regions of the atmosphere the bombardment of molecules and atoms by solar particles gives rise to auroras. The glow on space shuttles is caused by excitation of molecules adsorbed on the shuttles' surface.
3. Ozone in the stratosphere absorbs harmful UV radiation in the 200- to 300-nm range and protects life underneath. For many years, chlorofluorocarbons have been destroying the ozone layer.
4. Volcanic eruptions can lead to air pollution, deplete ozone in the stratosphere, and affect climate.
5. Carbon dioxide's ability to absorb infrared radiation enables it to trap some of the outgoing heat from Earth, warming its surface. Other gases such as the CFCs and methane also contribute to global warming.
6. Sulfur dioxide, and to a lesser extent nitrogen oxides, generated mainly from the burning of fossil fuels and from the roasting of metal sulfides, causes acid rain.
7. Photochemical smog is formed by the photochemical reaction of automobile exhaust in the presence of sunlight. It is a complex reaction involving nitrogen oxides, ozone, and hydrocarbons.
8. Indoor air pollution is caused by radon, a radioactive gas formed during uranium decay; carbon monoxide and carbon dioxide, products of combustion; and formaldehyde, a volatile organic substance released from resins used in construction materials.

Key Words

Greenhouse effect, p. 763
Ionosphere, p. 755
Mesosphere, p. 755
Nitrogen fixation, p. 753
Photochemical smog, p. 771
Stratosphere, p. 755
Thermosphere, p. 755
Troposphere, p. 753

Questions and Problems

Earth's Atmosphere
Review Questions

17.1 Describe the regions of Earth's atmosphere.
17.2 Briefly outline the main processes of the nitrogen and oxygen cycles.
17.3 Explain why, for maximum performance, supersonic airplanes need to fly at a high altitude (in the stratosphere).

17.4 Jupiter's atmosphere consists mainly of hydrogen (90 percent) and helium (9 percent). How does this mixture of gases contrast with the composition of Earth's atmosphere? Why does the composition differ?

Problems

17.5 Referring to Table 17.1, calculate the mole fraction of CO_2 and its concentration in parts per million by volume.

17.6 Calculate the partial pressure of CO_2 (in atm) in dry air when the atmospheric pressure is 754 mmHg.

17.7 Describe the processes that result in the warming of the stratosphere.

17.8 Calculate the total mass (in kilograms) of nitrogen, oxygen, and carbon dioxide gases in the atmosphere. (*Hint:* See Problem 5.102 and Table 17.1. Use 29.0 g/mol for the molar mass of air.)

Phenomena in the Outer Layers of the Atmosphere

Review Questions

17.9 What process gives rise to aurora borealis and aurora australis?

17.10 Why can astronauts not release oxygen atoms to test the mechanism of shuttle glow?

Problems

17.11 The highly reactive OH radical (a species with an unpaired electron) is believed to be involved in some atmospheric processes. Table 9.4 lists the bond enthalpy for the oxygen-to-hydrogen bond in OH as 460 kJ/mol. What is the longest wavelength (in nm) of radiation that can bring about the reaction

$$OH(g) \longrightarrow O(g) + H(g)$$

17.12 The green color observed in aurora borealis is produced by the emission of a photon by an electronically excited oxygen atom at 558 nm. Calculate the energy difference between the two levels involved in the emission process.

Depletion of Ozone in the Stratosphere

Review Questions

17.13 Briefly describe the absorption of solar radiation in the stratosphere by O_2 and O_3 molecules.

17.14 Explain the processes that have a warming effect on the stratosphere.

17.15 List the properties of CFCs, and name four major uses of these compounds.

17.16 How do CFCs and nitrogen oxides destroy ozone in the stratosphere?

17.17 What causes the polar ozone holes?

17.18 How do volcanic eruptions contribute to ozone destruction?

17.19 Describe ways to curb the destruction of ozone in the stratosphere.

17.20 Discuss the effectiveness of some of the CFC substitutes.

Problems

17.21 Given that the quantity of ozone in the stratosphere is equivalent to a 3.0-mm-thick layer of ozone on Earth at STP, calculate the number of ozone molecules in the stratosphere and their mass in kilograms. (*Hint:* The radius of Earth is 6371 km and the surface area of a sphere is $4\pi r^2$, where r is the radius.)

17.22 Referring to the answer in Problem 17.21, and assuming that the level of ozone in the stratosphere has already fallen 6.0 percent, calculate the number of kilograms of ozone that would have to be manufactured on a daily basis so that we could restore the ozone to the original level in 100 years. If ozone is made according to the process $3O_2(g) \longrightarrow 2O_3(g)$, how many kilojoules of energy would be required?

17.23 Both Freon-11 and Freon-12 are made by the reaction of carbon tetrachloride (CCl_4) with hydrogen fluoride. Write equations for these reactions.

17.24 Why are CFCs not decomposed by UV radiation in the troposphere?

17.25 The average bond enthalpies of the C—Cl and C—F bonds are 340 kJ/mol and 485 kJ/mol, respectively. Based on this information, explain why the C—Cl bond in a CFC molecule is preferentially broken by solar radiation at 250 nm.

17.26 Like CFCs, certain bromine-containing compounds such as CF_3Br can also participate in the destruction of ozone by a similar mechanism starting with the Br atom:

$$CF_3Br \longrightarrow CF_3 + Br$$

Given that the average C—Br bond enthalpy is 276 kJ/mol, estimate the longest wavelength required to break this bond. Will this compound be decomposed in the troposphere only or in both the troposphere and stratosphere?

17.27 Draw Lewis structures for chlorine nitrate ($ClONO_2$) and chlorine monoxide (ClO).

17.28 Draw Lewis structures for HCFC-123 (CF_3CHCl_2) and CF_3CFH_2.

Volcanoes

Review Questions

17.29 What are the effects of volcanic eruptions on climate?

17.30 Classify the reaction between H_2S and SO_2 that leads to the formation of sulfur at the site of a volcanic eruption.

The Greenhouse Effect

Review Questions

17.31 What is the greenhouse effect? What is the criterion for classifying a gas as a greenhouse gas?

17.32 Why is more emphasis placed on the role of carbon dioxide in the greenhouse effect than on that of water?

17.33 Describe three human activities that generate carbon dioxide. List two major mechanisms for the uptake of carbon dioxide.

17.34 Deforestation contributes to the greenhouse effect in two ways. What are they?

17.35 How does an increase in world population enhance the greenhouse effect?

17.36 Is ozone a greenhouse gas? If so, sketch three ways an ozone molecule can vibrate.

17.37 What effects do CFCs and their substitutes have on Earth's temperature?

17.38 Why are CFCs more effective greenhouse gases than methane and carbon dioxide?

Problems

17.39 The annual production of zinc sulfide (ZnS) is 4.0×10^4 tons. Estimate the number of tons of SO_2 produced by roasting it to extract zinc metal.

17.40 Calcium oxide or quicklime (CaO) is used in steel-making, cement manufacture, and pollution control. It is prepared by the thermal decomposition of calcium carbonate:

$$CaCO_3(s) \longrightarrow CaO(s) + CO_2(g)$$

Calculate the yearly release of CO_2 (in kilograms) to the atmosphere if the annual production of CaO in the United States is 1.7×10^{10} kg.

17.41 The molar heat capacity of a diatomic molecule is 29.1 J/K · mol. Assuming the atmosphere contains only nitrogen gas and there is no heat loss, calculate the total heat intake (in kilojoules) if the atmosphere warms up by 3°C during the next 50 years. Given that there are 1.8×10^{20} moles of diatomic molecules present, how many kilograms of ice (at the North and South Poles) will this quantity of heat melt at 0°C? (The molar heat of fusion of ice is 6.01 kJ/mol.)

17.42 As mentioned in the chapter, spraying the stratosphere with hydrocarbons such as ethane and propane should eliminate Cl atoms. What is the drawback of this procedure if used on a large scale for an extended period of time?

Acid Rain
Review Questions

17.43 Name the gas that is largely responsible for the acid rain phenomenon.

17.44 List three detrimental effects of acid rain.

17.45 Briefly discuss two industrial processes that lead to acid rain.

17.46 Discuss ways to curb acid rain.

17.47 Water and sulfur dioxide are both polar molecules and their geometry is similar. Why is SO_2 not considered a major greenhouse gas?

17.48 Describe the removal of SO_2 by CaO (to form $CaSO_3$) in terms of a Lewis acid-base reaction.

Problems

17.49 An electric power station annually burns 3.1×10^7 kg of coal containing 2.4 percent sulfur by mass. Calculate the volume of SO_2 emitted at STP.

17.50 The concentration of SO_2 in the troposphere over a certain region is 0.16 ppm by volume. The gas dissolves in rainwater as follows:

$$SO_2(g) + H_2O(l) \rightleftharpoons H^+(aq) + HSO_3^-(aq)$$

Given that the equilibrium constant for the preceding reaction is 1.3×10^{-2}, calculate the pH of the rainwater. Assume that the reaction does not affect the partial pressure of SO_2.

Photochemical Smog
Review Questions

17.51 What is photochemical smog? List the factors that favor the formation of photochemical smog.

17.52 What are primary and secondary pollutants?

17.53 Identify the gas that is responsible for the brown color of photochemical smog.

17.54 The safety limits of ozone and carbon monoxide are 120 ppb by volume and 9 ppm by volume, respectively. Why does ozone have a lower limit?

17.55 Suggest ways to minimize the formation of photochemical smog.

17.56 In which region of the atmosphere is ozone beneficial? In which region is it detrimental?

Problems

17.57 Assume that the formation of nitrogen dioxide:

$$2NO(g) + O_2(g) \longrightarrow 2NO_2(g)$$

is an elementary reaction. (a) Write the rate law for this reaction. (b) A sample of air at a certain temperature is contaminated with 2.0 ppm of NO by volume. Under these conditions, can the rate law be simplified? If so, write the simplified rate law. (c) Under the conditions described in (b), the half-life of the reaction has been estimated to be 6.4×10^3 min. What would the half-life be if the initial concentration of NO were 10 ppm?

17.58 The gas-phase decomposition of peroxyacetyl nitrate (PAN) obeys first-order kinetics:

$$CH_3COOONO_2 \longrightarrow CH_3COOO + NO_2$$

with a rate constant of $4.9 \times 10^{-4}\,s^{-1}$. Calculate the rate of decomposition in M/s if the concentration of PAN is 0.55 ppm by volume. Assume STP conditions.

17.59 On a smoggy day in a certain city the ozone concentration was 0.42 ppm by volume. Calculate the partial pressure of ozone (in atm) and the number of ozone molecules per liter of air if the temperature and pressure were 20.0°C and 748 mmHg, respectively.

17.60 Which of the following settings is the most suitable for photochemical smog formation? (a) Gobi desert at noon in June, (b) New York City at 1 P.M. in July, (c) Boston at noon in January. Explain your choice.

Indoor Pollution

Review Questions

17.61 List the major indoor pollutants and their sources.

17.62 What is the best way to deal with indoor pollution?

17.63 Why is it dangerous to idle a car's engine in a poorly ventilated place, such as the garage?

17.64 Describe the properties that make radon an indoor pollutant. Would radon be more hazardous if ^{222}Rn had a longer half-life?

Problems

17.65 A concentration of 8.00×10^2 ppm by volume of CO is considered lethal to humans. Calculate the minimum mass of CO in grams that would become a lethal concentration in a closed room 17.6 m long, 8.80 m wide, and 2.64 m high. The temperature and pressure are 20.0°C and 756 mmHg, respectively.

17.66 A volume of 5.0 L of polluted air at 18.0°C and 747 mmHg is passed through lime water [an aqueous suspension of $Ca(OH)_2$], so that all the carbon dioxide present is precipitated as $CaCO_3$. If the mass of the $CaCO_3$ precipitate is 0.026 g, calculate the percentage by volume of CO_2 in the air sample.

Additional Problems

17.67 Briefly describe the harmful effects of the following substances: O_3, SO_2, NO_2, CO, $CH_3COOONO_2$ (PAN), Rn.

17.68 The equilibrium constant (K_P) for the reaction

$$N_2(g) + O_2(g) \rightleftharpoons 2NO(g)$$

is 4.0×10^{-31} at 25°C and 2.6×10^{-6} at 1100°C, the temperature of a running car's engine. Is this an endothermic or exothermic reaction?

17.69 As stated in the chapter, carbon monoxide has a much higher affinity for hemoglobin than oxygen does. (a) Write the equilibrium constant expression (K_c) for the following process:

$$CO(g) + HbO_2(aq) \rightleftharpoons O_2(g) + HbCO(aq)$$

where HbO_2 and $HbCO$ are oxygenated hemoglobin and carboxyhemoglobin, respectively. (b) The composition of a breath of air inhaled by a person smoking a

cigarette is 1.9×10^{-6} mol/L CO and 8.6×10^{-3} mol/L O_2. Calculate the ratio of [HbCO] to [HbO_2], given that K_c is 212 at 37°C.

17.70 Instead of monitoring carbon dioxide, suggest another gas that scientists could study to substantiate the fact that CO_2 concentration is steadily increasing in the atmosphere.

17.71 In 1991 it was discovered that nitrous oxide (N_2O) is produced in the synthesis of nylon. This compound, which is released into the atmosphere, contributes *both* to the depletion of ozone in the stratosphere and to the greenhouse effect. (a) Write equations representing the reactions between N_2O and oxygen atoms in the stratosphere to produce nitric oxide (NO), which is then oxidized by ozone to form nitrogen dioxide. (b) Is N_2O a more effective greenhouse gas than carbon dioxide? Explain. (c) One of the intermediates in nylon manufacture is adipic acid [$HOOC(CH_2)_4COOH$]. About 2.2×10^9 kg of adipic acid are consumed every year. It is estimated that for every mole of adipic acid produced, 1 mole of N_2O is generated. What is the maximum number of moles of O_3 that can be destroyed as a result of this process per year?

17.72 A glass of water initially at pH 7.0 is exposed to dry air at sea level at 20°C. Calculate the pH of the water when equilibrium is reached between atmospheric CO_2 and CO_2 dissolved in the water, given that Henry's law constant for CO_2 at 20°C is 0.032 mol/L · atm. (*Hint:* Assume no loss of water due to evaporation and use Table 17.1 to calculate the partial pressure of CO_2. Your answer should correspond roughly to the pH of rainwater.)

17.73 A 14-m by 10-m by 3.0-m basement had a high radon content. On the day the basement was sealed off from its surroundings so that no exchange of air could take place, the partial pressure of ^{222}Rn was 1.2×10^{-6} mmHg. Calculate the number of ^{222}Rn isotopes ($t_{\frac{1}{2}} = 3.8$ d) at the beginning and end of 31 days. Assume STP conditions.

17.74 Ozone in the troposphere is formed by the following steps:

$$NO_2 \longrightarrow NO + O \qquad (1)$$
$$O + O_2 \longrightarrow O_3 \qquad (2)$$

The first step is initiated by the absorption of visible light (NO_2 is a brown gas). Calculate the longest wavelength required for step (1) at 25°C. [*Hint:* You need to first calculate ΔH and hence ΔE for (1). Next, determine the wavelength for decomposing NO_2 from ΔE.]

17.75 Although the hydroxyl radical (OH) is present only in a trace amount in the troposphere, it plays a central role in its chemistry because it is a strong oxidizing agent and can react with many pollutants as well as some CFC substitutes (see p. 761). The hydroxyl radical is formed by the following reactions:

$$O_3 \xrightarrow{\lambda < 320 \text{ nm}} O^* + O_2$$
$$O + H_2O \longrightarrow 2OH$$

where O^* denotes an electronically excited atom. (a) Explain why the concentration of OH is so small even though the concentrations of O_3 and H_2O are quite large in the troposphere. (b) What property makes OH a strong oxidizing agent? (c) The reaction between OH and NO_2 contributes to acid rain. Write an equation for this process. (d) The hydroxyl radical can oxidize SO_2 to H_2SO_4. The first step is the formation of a neutral HSO_3 species, followed by its reaction with O_2 and H_2O to form H_2SO_4 and the hydroperoxyl radical (HO_2). Write equations for these processes.

17.76   The equilibrium constant (K_P) for the reaction

$$2CO(g) + O_2(g) \rightleftharpoons 2CO_2(g)$$

is 1.4×10^{90} at 25°C. Given this enormous value, why doesn't CO convert totally to CO_2 in the troposphere?

17.77   A person was found dead of carbon monoxide poisoning in a well-insulated cabin. Investigation showed that he had used a blackened bucket to heat water on a butane burner. The burner was found to function properly with no leakage. Explain, with an appropriate equation, the cause of his death.

17.78   The carbon dioxide level in the atmosphere today is often compared with that in preindustrial days. Explain how scientists use tree rings and air trapped in polar ice to arrive at the comparison.

17.79   What is funny about the following cartoon?

17.80   Calculate the standard enthalpy of formation (ΔH_f°) of ClO from the following bond enthalpies: Cl_2: 242.7 kJ/mol; O_2: 498.7 kJ/mol; ClO: 206 kJ/mol.

Special Problems

17.81   Methyl bromide (CH_3Br, b.pt. 3.6°C) is used as a soil fumigant to control insects and weeds. It is also a marine by-product. Photodissociation of the C—Br bond produces Br atoms that can react with ozone similar to Cl, except more effectively. Do you expect CH_3Br to be photolyzed in the troposphere? The bond enthalpy of the C—Br bond is about 293 kJ/mol.

17.82   The effective incoming solar radiation per unit area on Earth is 342 W/m². Of this radiation, 6.7 W/m² is absorbed by CO_2 at 14,993 nm in the atmosphere. How many photons at this wavelength are absorbed per second in 1 m² by CO_2? (1 W = 1 J/s)

17.83   As stated in the chapter, about 50 million tons of sulfur dioxide are released into the atmosphere every year. (a) If 20 percent of the SO_2 is eventually converted to H_2SO_4, calculate the number of 1000 lb marble statues the resulting acid rain can damage. As an estimate, assume that the acid rain only destroys the surface layer of each statue, which is made up of 5 percent of its total mass.

(b) What is the other undesirable result of the acid rain damage?

17.84   Peroxyacetyl nitrate (PAN) undergoes thermal decomposition as follows:

$$CH_3(CO)OONO_2 \longrightarrow CH_3(CO)OO + NO_2$$

The rate constant is 3.0×10^{-4} s⁻¹ at 25°C. At the boundary between the troposphere and stratosphere, where the temperature is about −40°C, the rate constant is reduced to 2.6×10^{-7} s⁻¹. (a) Calculate the activation energy for the decomposition of PAN. (b) What is the half-life of the reaction (in minutes) at 25°C?

17.85   How are past temperatures determined from ice cores obtained from the Artic or Antarctica? (*Hint:* Look up the stable isotopes of hydrogen and oxygen. How does energy required for vaporization depend on the masses of H_2O molecules containing different isotopes? How would you determine the age of an ice core?)

17.86 The balance between SO_2 and SO_3 is important in understanding acid rain formation in the troposphere. From the following information at 25°C

$$S(s) + O_2(g) \rightleftharpoons SO_2(g) \qquad K_1 = 4.2 \times 10^{52}$$

$$2S(s) + 3O_2(g) \rightleftharpoons 2SO_3(g) \qquad K_2 = 9.8 \times 10^{128}$$

calculate the equilibrium constant for the reaction

$$2SO_2(g) + O_2(g) \rightleftharpoons 2SO_3(g)$$

Answers to Practice Exercises

17.1 1.12×10^3 nm. **17.2** H_2O. **17.3** 1.2×10^{-6} mol/L.

18

The production of quicklime (CaO) from limestone (CaCO₃) in a rotary kiln. The models show structures of CaCO₃ and CaO and carbon dioxide molecules.

Entropy, Free Energy, and Equilibrium

A LOOK AHEAD

● This chapter begins with a discussion of the three laws of thermodynamics and the nature of spontaneous processes. (18.1 and 18.2)

● We then see that entropy is the thermodynamic function for predicting the spontaneity of a reaction. Entropy is related to probability, and on a molecular level, the entropy of a system can in principle be calculated from the number of microstates associated with the system. We learn that, in practice, entropy is determined by calorimetric methods and standard entropy values are known for many substances. (18.3)

● The second law of thermodynamics states that the entropy of the universe increases in a spontaneous process and remains unchanged in an equilibrium process. We learn ways to calculate the entropy change of a system and of its surroundings, which together make up for the change in the entropy of the universe. We also discuss the third law of thermodynamics, which enables us to determine the absolute value of entropy of a substance. (18.4)

● We see that a new thermodynamic function called Gibbs free energy is needed to focus on the system. The change in Gibbs free energy at constant temperature and pressure can be used to predict spontaneity and equilibrium. For changes carried out under standard-state conditions, the change in Gibbs free energy is related to the equilibrium constant of a reaction. (18.5 and 18.6)

● The chapter concludes with a discussion of how thermodynamics is applied to living systems. We see that coupled reactions, usually aided by enzymes, play a crucial role in many biological processes. (18.7)

Thermodynamics is an extensive and far-reaching scientific discipline that deals with the interconversion of heat and other forms of energy. Thermodynamics enables us to use information gained from experiments on a system to draw conclusions about other aspects of the same system without further experimentation. For example, we saw in Chapter 6 that it is possible to calculate the heat of reaction from the standard enthalpies of formation of the reactant and product molecules. This chapter introduces the second law of thermodynamics and the Gibbs free-energy function. It also discusses the relationship between Gibbs free energy and chemical equilibrium.

18.1 The Three Laws of Thermodynamics

In Chapter 6 we encountered the first of three laws of thermodynamics, which says that energy can be converted from one form to another, but it cannot be created or destroyed. One measure of these changes is the amount of heat given off or absorbed by a system during a constant-pressure process, which chemists define as a change in enthalpy (ΔH).

The second law of thermodynamics explains why chemical processes tend to favor one direction. The third law is an extension of the second law and will be examined briefly in Section 18.4.

18.2 Spontaneous Processes

One of the main objectives in studying thermodynamics, as far as chemists are concerned, is to be able to predict whether or not a reaction will occur when reactants are brought together under a specific set of conditions (for example, at a certain temperature, pressure, and concentration). This knowledge is important whether one is synthesizing compounds in a research laboratory, manufacturing chemicals on an industrial scale, or trying to understand the intricate biological processes in a cell. A reaction that *does* occur under the given set of conditions is called a *spontaneous reaction*. If a reaction does not occur under specified conditions, it is said to be nonspontaneous. We observe spontaneous physical and chemical processes every day, including many of the following examples:

- A waterfall runs downhill, but never up, spontaneously.

- A lump of sugar spontaneously dissolves in a cup of coffee, but dissolved sugar does not spontaneously reappear in its original form.

- Water freezes spontaneously below 0°C, and ice melts spontaneously above 0°C (at 1 atm).

- Heat flows from a hotter object to a colder one, but the reverse never happens spontaneously.

- The expansion of a gas into an evacuated bulb is a spontaneous process [Figure 18.1(a)]. The reverse process, that is, the gathering of all the molecules into one bulb, is not spontaneous [Figure 18.1(b)].

- A piece of sodium metal reacts violently with water to form sodium hydroxide and hydrogen gas. However, hydrogen gas does not react with sodium hydroxide to form water and sodium.

- Iron exposed to water and oxygen forms rust, but rust does not spontaneously change back to iron.

These examples show that processes that occur spontaneously in one direction cannot, under the same conditions, also take place spontaneously in the opposite direction.

If we assume that spontaneous processes occur so as to decrease the energy of a system, we can explain why a ball rolls downhill and why springs in a clock unwind. Similarly, a large number of exothermic reactions are spontaneous. An example is the combustion of methane:

$$CH_4(g) + 2O_2(g) \longrightarrow CO_2(g) + 2H_2O(l) \quad \Delta H° = -890.4 \text{ kJ/mol}$$

Another example is the acid-base neutralization reaction:

$$H^+(aq) + OH^-(aq) \longrightarrow H_2O(l) \quad \Delta H° = -56.2 \text{ kJ/mol}$$

A spontaneous reaction does not necessarily mean an instantaneous reaction.

A spontaneous and a nonspontaneous process.

© Harry Bliss. Originally published in the *New Yorker Magazine*.

Because of the activation energy barrier, an input of energy is needed to get this reaction going at an observable rate.

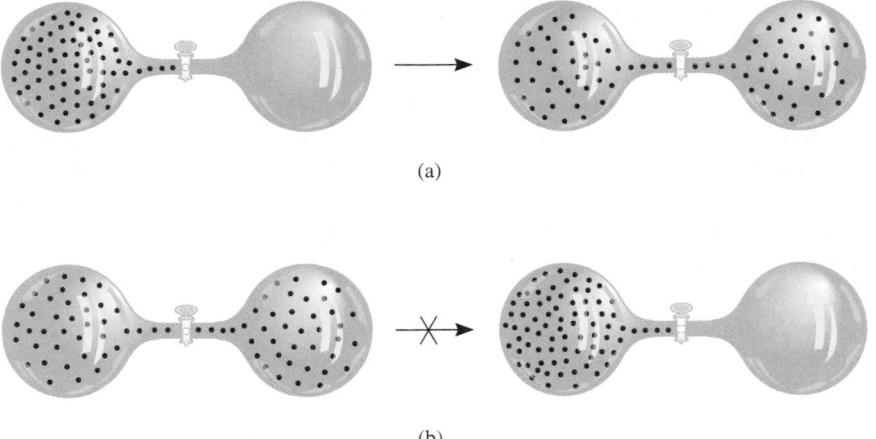

Figure 18.1 *(a) A spontaneous process. (b) A nonspontaneous process.*

(a)

(b)

But consider a solid-to-liquid phase transition such as

$$H_2O(s) \longrightarrow H_2O(l) \qquad \Delta H° = 6.01 \text{ kJ/mol}$$

In this case, the assumption that spontaneous processes always decrease a system's energy fails. Experience tells us that ice melts spontaneously above 0°C even though the process is endothermic. Another example that contradicts our assumption is the dissolution of ammonium nitrate in water:

$$NH_4NO_3(s) \xrightarrow{H_2O} NH_4^+(aq) + NO_3^-(aq) \qquad \Delta H° = 25 \text{ kJ/mol}$$

This process is spontaneous, and yet it is also endothermic. The decomposition of mercury(II) oxide is an endothermic reaction that is nonspontaneous at room temperature, but it becomes spontaneous when the temperature is raised:

$$2HgO(s) \longrightarrow 2Hg(l) + O_2(g) \qquad \Delta H° = 90.7 \text{ kJ/mol}$$

From a study of the examples mentioned and many more cases, we come to the following conclusion: Exothermicity favors the spontaneity of a reaction but does not guarantee it. Just as it is possible for an endothermic reaction to be spontaneous, it is possible for an exothermic reaction to be nonspontaneous. In other words, we cannot decide whether or not a chemical reaction will occur spontaneously solely on the basis of energy changes in the system. To make this kind of prediction we need another thermodynamic quantity, which turns out to be *entropy*.

When heated, HgO decomposes to give Hg and O_2.

18.3 Entropy

In order to predict the spontaneity of a process, we need to know two things about the system. One is the change in enthalpy. The other is the change in entropy. *Entropy (S)* is often described as *a measure of the randomness or disorder of a system.* The greater the disorder of a system, the greater its entropy. Conversely, the more ordered a system, the smaller its entropy. One way to illustrate order and disorder is with a deck of playing cards. A new deck of cards is arranged in an ordered fashion (the cards are from ace to king and the suits are in the order of spades to hearts to diamonds to clubs). Once the deck has been shuffled, the cards are no longer in sequence by number or by suit. It is possible, but extremely unlikely, that by reshuffling the cards we can restore the original order. There are many ways for the cards to be out of sequence but only one way for them to be ordered according to our definition.

A quantitative way to conceptualize order and disorder is in terms of probability. A probable event is one that can happen in many ways, and an improbable event is one that can happen in only one or a few ways. For example, referring to Figure 18.1(a), suppose there is only one molecule present initially. Because the two bulbs have equal volume, the probability of finding the molecule in either bulb after the stopcock is opened is $\frac{1}{2}$. If two molecules are present to start with, the probability of finding both molecules in the *same* bulb (say the left bulb) after we open the stopcock becomes $\frac{1}{2} \times \frac{1}{2}$, or $\frac{1}{4}$. Now $\frac{1}{4}$ is a high ratio, and so it would not be surprising to find both molecules in the left bulb after the stopcock has been opened. However, it is not difficult to see that as the number of molecules increases, the probability (P) of finding all the molecules in the left bulb becomes progressively smaller:

$$P = \left(\tfrac{1}{2}\right) \times \left(\tfrac{1}{2}\right) \times \left(\tfrac{1}{2}\right) \times \cdots$$
$$= \left(\tfrac{1}{2}\right)^N$$

where N is the total number of molecules present. If $N = 100$, we have

$$P = \left(\tfrac{1}{2}\right)^{100} = 8 \times 10^{-31}$$

If N is of the order of 6×10^{23}, the number of molecules in 1 mole of a gas, the probability becomes $\left(\tfrac{1}{2}\right)^{6 \times 10^{23}}$, which is such a small number that, for all practical purposes, it can be regarded as zero. On the basis of probability considerations, we would expect the gas to fill both bulbs spontaneously and evenly. By the same token, we now understand that the situation depicted in Figure 18.1(b) is not spontaneous because it represents a highly improbable event. To summarize our discussion: An ordered state has a low probability of occurring and a small entropy, while a disordered state has a high probability of occurring and a large entropy.

Microstates and Entropy

The concept of probability is useful for predicting the direction of spontaneous processes. Our next step is to provide a proper definition of entropy. To do so let us consider a simple system of four molecules distributed between two equal compartments, as shown in Figure 18.2. There is only one way to arrange all the molecules in the left compartment, four ways to have three molecules in the left compartment and one in the right compartment, and six ways to have two molecules in each of the two compartments. The eleven possible ways of distributing the molecules are called microscopic states or microstates and each set of similar microstates is called a distribution.[†] As you can see, distribution III is the most probable because there are six microstates or six ways to achieve it and distribution I is the least probable because it has one microstate and therefore there is only one way to achieve it. Based on this analysis, we conclude that the probability of occurrence of a particular distribution (state) depends on the number of ways (microstates) in which

---

[†]Actually there are still other possible ways to distribute the four molecules between the two compartments. We can have all four molecules in the right compartment (one way) and three molecules in the right compartment and one molecule in the left compartment (four ways). However, the distributions shown in Figure 18.2 are sufficient for our discussion.

Distribution   Microstates

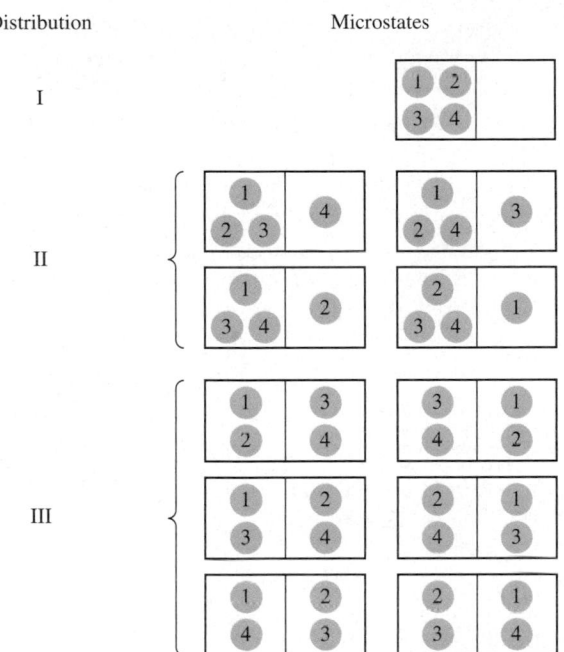

Figure 18.2 *Some possible ways of distributing four molecules between two equal compartments. Distribution I can be achieved in only one way (all four molecules in the left compartment) and has one microstate. Distribution II can be achieved in four ways and has four microstates. Distribution III can be achieved in six ways and has six microstates.*

the distribution can be achieved. As the number of molecules approaches macroscopic scale, it is not difficult to see that they will be evenly distributed between the two compartments because this distribution has many, many more microstates than all other distributions.

In 1868 Boltzmann showed that the entropy of a system is related to the natural log of the number of microstates (W):

$$S = k \ln W \tag{18.1}$$

where k is called the Boltzmann constant (1.38×10^{-23} J/K). Thus, the larger the W, the greater is the entropy of the system. Like enthalpy, entropy is a state function (see Section 6.3). Consider a certain process in a system. The entropy change for the process, ΔS, is

$$\Delta S = S_f - S_i \tag{18.2}$$

where S_i and S_f are the entropies of the system in the initial and final states, respectively. From Equation (18.1) we can write

$$\begin{aligned} \Delta S &= k \ln W_f - k \ln W_i \\ &= k \ln \frac{W_f}{W_i} \end{aligned} \tag{18.3}$$

where W_i and W_f are the corresponding numbers of microstates in the initial and final state. Thus, if $W_f > W_i$, $\Delta S > 0$ and the entropy of the system increases.

Engraved on Ludwig Boltzmann's tombstone in Vienna is his famous equation. The "log" stands for "$\log_e$," which is the natural logarithm or ln.

Entropy and Disorder

As stated earlier, entropy is often described as a measure of disorder or randomness. While useful, these terms must be used with caution because they are subjective

Figure 18.3 *Processes that lead to an increase in entropy of the system: (a) melting: $S_{liquid} > S_{solid}$; (b) vaporization: $S_{vapor} > S_{liquid}$; (c) dissolving; (d) heating: $S_{T_2} > S_{T_1}$.*

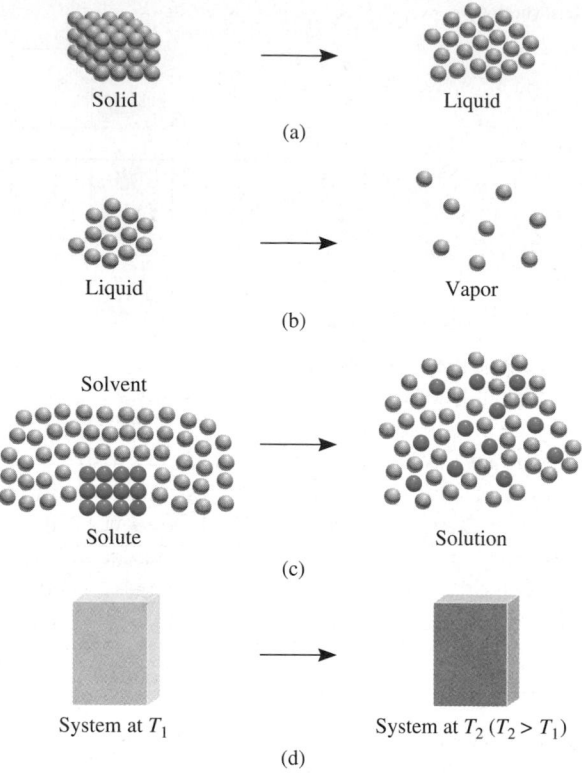

concepts. In general, however, it is preferrable to view the change in entropy of a system in terms of the change in the number of microstates of the system.

Consider the situations shown in Figure 18.3. In a solid, the atoms or molecules are confined to fixed positions and the number of microstates is small. Upon melting, these atoms or molecules can occupy many more positions as they move away from the lattice points. Consequently, the number of microstates increases because there are now many more ways to arrange the particles. Therefore, we predict this "order $\longrightarrow$ disorder" phase transition to result in an increase in entropy because the number of microstates has increased. Similarly, we predict the vaporization process will also lead to an increase in the entropy of the system. The increase will be considerably greater than that for melting, however, because molecules in the gas phase occupy much more space and therefore there are far more microstates than in the liquid phase. The solution process usually leads to an increase in entropy. When a sugar crystal dissolves in water, the highly ordered structure of the solid and part of the ordered structure of water break down. Thus, the solution has a greater number of microstates than the pure solute and pure solvent combined. When an ionic solid such as NaCl dissolves in water, there are two contributions to entropy increase: the solution process (mixing of solute with solvent) and the dissociation of the compound into ions:

$$NaCl(s) \xrightarrow{\text{H}_2\text{O}} Na^+(aq) + Cl^-(aq)$$

More particles lead to a greater number of microstates. However, we must also consider hydration, which causes water molecules to become more ordered around the ions. This process decreases entropy because it reduces the number of microstates of the solvent molecules. For small, highly charged ions such as Al^{3+}

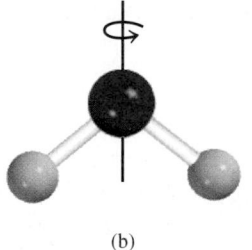

(a)   (b)

Figure 18.4 *(a) A vibrational motion in a water molecule. The atoms are displaced, as shown by the arrows, and then reverse their directions to complete a cycle of vibration. (b) A rotational motion of a water molecule about an axis through the oxygen atom. The molecule can also vibrate and rotate in other ways.*

and Fe^{3+}, the decrease in entropy due to hydration can outweigh the increase in entropy due to mixing and dissociation so that the entropy change for the overall process can actually be negative. Heating also increases the entropy of a system. In addition to translational motion (that is, motion through space of the whole molecule), molecules can also execute rotational and vibrational motions (Figure 18.4). As the temperature is increased, the energies associated with all types of molecular motion increase. This increase in energy is distributed or dispersed among the quantized energy levels. Consequently, more microstates become available at a higher temperature; therefore, the entropy of a system always increases with increasing temperature.

Standard Entropy

Equation (18.1) provides a useful molecular interpretation of entropy, but is normally not used to calculate the entropy of a system because it is difficult to determine the number of microstates for a macroscopic system containing many molecules. Instead, entropy is obtained by calorimetric methods. In fact, as we will see shortly, it is possible to determine the absolute value of entropy of a substance, called absolute entropy, something we cannot do for energy or enthalpy. *Standard entropy* is the absolute entropy of a substance at 1 atm and 25°C. (Recall that the standard state refers only to 1 atm. The reason for specifying 25°C is that many processes are carried out at room temperature.) Table 18.1 lists standard entropies of a few elements and compounds; Appendix 3 provides a more extensive listing. The units of entropy are J/K or J/K · mol for 1 mole of the substance. We use joules rather than kilojoules because entropy values are typically quite small. Entropies of elements and compounds are all positive (that is, $S° > 0$). By contrast, the standard enthalpy of formation ($\Delta H_f°$) for elements in their stable form is arbitrarily set equal to zero, and for compounds, it may be positive or negative.

Referring to Table 18.1, we see that the standard entropy of water vapor is greater than that of liquid water. Similarly, bromine vapor has a higher standard entropy than liquid bromine, and iodine vapor has a greater standard entropy than solid iodine. For different substances in the same phase, molecular complexity determines which ones have higher entropies. Both diamond and graphite are solids, but diamond has a more ordered structure and hence a smaller number of microstates (see Figure 11.28). Therefore, diamond has a smaller standard entropy than graphite. Consider the natural gases methane and ethane. Ethane has a more complex structure and hence more ways to execute molecular motions, which also increase its microstates. Therefore, ethane has a greater standard entropy than methane. Both helium and neon are monatomic gases, which cannot execute rotational or vibrational motions, but neon has a greater standard entropy than helium because its molar mass is greater. Heavier atoms have more closely spaced energy levels so there is a greater distribution of the

TABLE 18.1

Standard Entropy Values ($S°$) for Some Substances at 25°C

Substance	$S°$ (J/K · mol)
$H_2O(l)$	69.9
$H_2O(g)$	188.7
$Br_2(l)$	152.3
$Br_2(g)$	245.3
$I_2(s)$	116.7
$I_2(g)$	260.6
C (diamond)	2.4
C (graphite)	5.69
CH_4 (methane)	186.2
C_2H_6 (ethane)	229.5
He(g)	126.1
Ne(g)	146.2

atoms' energy among the levels. Consequently, there are more microstates associated with these atoms.

Example 18.1

Predict whether the entropy change is greater or less than zero for each of the following processes: (a) freezing ethanol, (b) evaporating a beaker of liquid bromine at room temperature, (c) dissolving glucose in water, (d) cooling nitrogen gas from 80°C to 20°C.

Strategy To determine the entropy change in each case, we examine whether the number of microstates of the system increases or decreases. The sign of ΔS will be positive if there is an increase in the number of microstates and negative if the number of microstates decreases.

Solution (a) Upon freezing, the ethanol molecules are held rigid in position. This phase transition reduces the number of microstates and therefore the entropy decreases; that is, $\Delta S < 0$.

(b) Evaporating bromine increases the number of microstates because the Br_2 molecules can occupy many more positions in nearly empty space. Therefore, $\Delta S > 0$.

(c) Glucose is a nonelectrolyte. The solution process leads to a greater dispersal of matter due to the mixing of glucose and water molecules so we expect $\Delta S > 0$.

(d) The cooling process decreases various molecular motions. This leads to a decrease in microstates and so $\Delta S < 0$.

Practice Exercise How does the entropy of a system change for each of the following processes? (a) condensing water vapor, (b) forming sucrose crystals from a supersaturated solution, (c) heating hydrogen gas from 60°C to 80°C, and (d) subliming dry ice.

Bromine is a fuming liquid at room temperature.

Similar problem: 18.5.

18.4 The Second Law of Thermodynamics

Just talking about entropy increases its value in the universe.

The connection between entropy and the spontaneity of a reaction is expressed by the *second law of thermodynamics: The entropy of the universe increases in a spontaneous process and remains unchanged in an equilibrium process.* Because the universe is made up of the system and the surroundings, the entropy change in the universe (ΔS_{univ}) for any process is the *sum* of the entropy changes in the system (ΔS_{sys}) and in the surroundings (ΔS_{surr}). Mathematically, we can express the second law of thermodynamics as follows:

For a spontaneous process:

$$\Delta S_{univ} = \Delta S_{sys} + \Delta S_{surr} > 0 \qquad (18.4)$$

For an equilibrium process:

$$\Delta S_{univ} = \Delta S_{sys} + \Delta S_{surr} = 0 \qquad (18.5)$$

For a spontaneous process, the second law says that ΔS_{univ} must be greater than zero, but it does not place a restriction on either ΔS_{sys} or ΔS_{surr}. Thus, it is possible for either ΔS_{sys} or ΔS_{surr} to be negative, as long as the sum of these two quantities is greater than zero. For an equilibrium process, ΔS_{univ} is zero. In this case, ΔS_{sys} and ΔS_{surr} must be equal in magnitude, but opposite in sign. What if for some hypothetical process we find that ΔS_{univ} is negative? What this means is that the process is not spontaneous in the direction described. Rather, it is spontaneous in the *opposite* direction.

Entropy Changes in the System

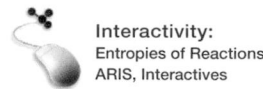

Interactivity:
Entropies of Reactions
ARIS, Interactives

To calculate ΔS_{univ}, we need to know both ΔS_{sys} and ΔS_{surr}. Let us focus first on ΔS_{sys}. Suppose that the system is represented by the following reaction:

$$a\text{A} + b\text{B} \longrightarrow c\text{C} + d\text{D}$$

As is the case for the enthalpy of a reaction [see Equation (6.18)], the **standard entropy of reaction** ΔS°_{rxn} is given by *the difference in standard entropies between products and reactants:*

$$\Delta S^\circ_{rxn} = [cS^\circ(\text{C}) + dS^\circ(\text{D})] - [aS^\circ(\text{A}) + bS^\circ(\text{B})] \qquad (18.6)$$

or, in general, using Σ to represent summation and m and n for the stoichiometric coefficients in the reaction,

$$\Delta S^\circ_{rxn} = \Sigma nS^\circ(\text{products}) - \Sigma mS^\circ(\text{reactants}) \qquad (18.7)$$

The standard entropy values of a large number of compounds have been measured in $J/K \cdot mol$. To calculate ΔS°_{rxn} (which is ΔS_{sys}), we look up their values in Appendix 3 and proceed according to Example 18.2.

Example 18.2

From the standard entropy values in Appendix 3, calculate the standard entropy changes for the following reactions at 25°C.

(a) $\text{CaCO}_3(s) \longrightarrow \text{CaO}(s) + \text{CO}_2(g)$

(b) $\text{N}_2(g) + 3\text{H}_2(g) \longrightarrow 2\text{NH}_3(g)$

(c) $\text{H}_2(g) + \text{Cl}_2(g) \longrightarrow 2\text{HCl}(g)$

Strategy To calculate the standard entropy of a reaction, we look up the standard entropies of reactants and products in Appendix 3 and apply Equation (18.7). As in the calculation of enthalpy of reaction [see Equation (6.18)], the stoichiometric coefficients have no units, so ΔS°_{rxn} is expressed in units of $J/K \cdot mol$.

Solution

(a) $\Delta S^\circ_{rxn} = [S^\circ(\text{CaO}) + S^\circ(\text{CO}_2)] - [S^\circ(\text{CaCO}_3)]$

$= [(39.8 \ J/K \cdot mol) + (213.6 \ J/K \cdot mol)] - (92.9 \ J/K \cdot mol)$

$= 160.5 \ J/K \cdot mol$

Thus, when 1 mole of CaCO_3 decomposes to form 1 mole of CaO and 1 mole of gaseous CO_2, there is an increase in entropy equal to $160.5 \ J/K \cdot mol$.

(b) $\Delta S^\circ_{rxn} = [2S^\circ(\text{NH}_3)] - [S^\circ(\text{N}_2) + 3S^\circ(\text{H}_2)]$

$= (2)(193 \ J/K \cdot mol) - [(192 \ J/K \cdot mol) + (3)(131 \ J/K \cdot mol)]$

$= -199 \ J/K \cdot mol$

This result shows that when 1 mole of gaseous nitrogen reacts with 3 moles of gaseous hydrogen to form 2 moles of gaseous ammonia, there is a decrease in entropy equal to $-199 \ J/K \cdot mol$.

(c) $\Delta S^\circ_{rxn} = [2S^\circ(\text{HCl})] - [S^\circ(\text{H}_2) + S^\circ(\text{Cl}_2)]$

$= (2)(187 \ J/K \cdot mol) - [(131 \ J/K \cdot mol) + (223 \ J/K \cdot mol)]$

$= 20 \ J/K \cdot mol$

(Continued)

Similar problems: 18.11 and 18.12.

Thus, the formation of 2 moles of gaseous HCl from 1 mole of gaseous H_2 and 1 mole of gaseous Cl_2 results in a small increase in entropy equal to 20 J/K · mol.

Comment The ΔS°_{rxn} values all apply to the system.

Practice Exercise Calculate the standard entropy change for the following reactions at 25°C:

(a) $2CO(g) + O_2(g) \longrightarrow 2CO_2(g)$

(b) $3O_2(g) \longrightarrow 2O_3(g)$

(c) $2NaHCO_3(s) \longrightarrow Na_2CO_3(s) + H_2O(l) + CO_2(g)$

We omit the subscript rxn for simplicity.

The results of Example 18.2 are consistent with those observed for many other reactions. Taken together, they support the following general rules:

- If a reaction produces more gas molecules than it consumes [Example 18.2(a)], ΔS° is positive.

- If the total number of gas molecules diminishes [Example 18.2(b)], ΔS° is negative.

- If there is no net change in the total number of gas molecules [Example 18.2(c)], then ΔS° may be positive or negative, but will be relatively small numerically.

These conclusions make sense, given that gases invariably have greater entropy than liquids and solids. For reactions involving only liquids and solids, predicting the sign of ΔS° is more difficult, but in many such cases an increase in the total number of molecules and/or ions is accompanied by an increase in entropy.

Example 18.3 shows how knowing the nature of reactants and products makes it possible to predict entropy changes.

Example 18.3

Predict whether the entropy change of the system in each of the following reactions is positive or negative.

(a) $2H_2(g) + O_2(g) \longrightarrow 2H_2O(l)$

(b) $NH_4Cl(s) \longrightarrow NH_3(g) + HCl(g)$

(c) $H_2(g) + Br_2(g) \longrightarrow 2HBr(g)$

Strategy We are asked to predict, not calculate, the sign of entropy change in the reactions. The factors that lead to an increase in entropy are: (1) a transition from a condensed phase to the vapor phase and (2) a reaction that produces more product molecules than reactant molecules in the same phase. It is also important to compare the relative complexity of the product and reactant molecules. In general, the more complex the molecular structure, the greater the entropy of the compound.

Solution (a) Two reactant molecules combine to form one product molecule. Even though H_2O is a more complex molecule than either H_2 and O_2, the fact that there is a net decrease of one molecule and gases are converted to liquid ensures that the number of microstates will be diminished and hence ΔS° is negative.

(b) A solid is converted to two gaseous products. Therefore, ΔS° is positive.

(c) The same number of molecules is involved in the reactants as in the product. Furthermore, all molecules are diatomic and therefore of similar complexity. As a result, we cannot predict the sign of ΔS°, but we know that the change must be quite small in magnitude.

Similar problems: 18.13 and 18.14.

(Continued)

Practice Exercise Discuss qualitatively the sign of the entropy change expected for each of the following processes:

(a) $I_2(s) \longrightarrow 2I(g)$

(b) $2Zn(s) + O_2(g) \longrightarrow 2ZnO(s)$

(c) $N_2(g) + O_2(g) \longrightarrow 2NO(g)$

Entropy Changes in the Surroundings

Next we see how ΔS_{surr} is calculated. When an exothermic process takes place in the system, the heat transferred to the surroundings enhances motion of the molecules in the surroundings. Consequently, there is an increase in the number of microstates and the entropy of the surroundings increases. Conversely, an endothermic process in the system absorbs heat from the surroundings and so decreases the entropy of the surroundings because molecular motion decreases (Figure 18.5). For constant-pressure processes the heat change is equal to the enthalpy change of the system, ΔH_{sys}. Therefore, the change in entropy of the surroundings, ΔS_{surr}, is proportional to ΔH_{sys}:

$$\Delta S_{surr} \propto -\Delta H_{sys}$$

The minus sign is used because if the process is exothermic, ΔH_{sys} is negative and ΔS_{surr} is a positive quantity, indicating an increase in entropy. On the other hand, for an endothermic process, ΔH_{sys} is positive and the negative sign ensures that the entropy of the surroundings decreases.

The change in entropy for a given amount of heat absorbed also depends on the temperature. If the temperature of the surroundings is high, the molecules are already quite energetic. Therefore, the absorption of heat from an exothermic process in the system will have relatively little impact on molecular motion and the resulting increase in entropy of the surroundings will be small. However, if the temperature of the surroundings is low, then the addition of the same amount of heat will cause a more drastic increase in molecular motion and hence a larger increase

(a)

(b)

Figure 18.5 *(a) An exothermic process transfers heat from the system to the surroundings and results in an increase in the entropy of the surroundings. (b) An endothermic process absorbs heat from the surroundings and thereby decreases the entropy of the surroundings.*

in entropy. By analogy, someone coughing in a crowded restaurant will not disturb too many people, but someone coughing in a library definitely will. From the inverse relationship between ΔS_{surr} and temperature T (in kelvins)—that is, the higher the temperature, the smaller the ΔS_{surr} and vice versa—we can rewrite the above relationship as

This equation, which can be derived from the laws of thermodynamics, assumes that both the system and the surroundings are at temperature T.

$$\Delta S_{surr} = \frac{-\Delta H_{sys}}{T} \qquad (18.8)$$

Let us now apply the procedure for calculating ΔS_{sys} and ΔS_{surr} to the synthesis of ammonia and ask whether the reaction is spontaneous at 25°C:

$$N_2(g) + 3H_2(g) \longrightarrow 2NH_3(g) \qquad \Delta H^{\circ}_{rxn} = -92.6 \text{ kJ/mol}$$

From Example 18.2(b) we have $\Delta S_{sys} = -199 \text{ J/K} \cdot \text{mol}$, and substituting ΔH_{sys} (-92.6 kJ/mol) in Equation (18.8), we obtain

$$\Delta S_{surr} = \frac{-(-92.6 \times 1000) \text{ J/mol}}{298 \text{ K}} = 311 \text{ J/K} \cdot \text{mol}$$

The change in entropy of the universe is

$$\begin{aligned} \Delta S_{univ} &= \Delta S_{sys} + \Delta S_{surr} \\ &= -199 \text{ J/K} \cdot \text{mol} + 311 \text{ J/K} \cdot \text{mol} \\ &= 112 \text{ J/K} \cdot \text{mol} \end{aligned}$$

Because ΔS_{univ} is positive, we predict that the reaction is spontaneous at 25°C. It is important to keep in mind that just because a reaction is spontaneous does not mean that it will occur at an observable rate. The synthesis of ammonia is, in fact, extremely slow at room temperature. Thermodynamics can tell us whether a reaction will occur spontaneously under specific conditions, but it does not say how fast it will occur. Reaction rates are the subject of chemical kinetics (see Chapter 13).

The Third Law of Thermodynamics and Absolute Entropy

Finally, it is appropriate to consider the *third law of thermodynamics* briefly in connection with the determination of entropy values. So far we have related entropy to microstates—the greater the number of microstates a system possesses, the larger is the entropy of the system. Consider a perfect crystalline substance at absolute zero (0 K). Under these conditions, molecular motions are kept at a minimum and the number of microstates (W) is one (there is only one way to arrange the atoms or molecules to form a perfect crystal). From Equation (18.1) we write

$$\begin{aligned} S &= k \ln W \\ &= k \ln 1 = 0 \end{aligned}$$

According to the ***third law of thermodynamics,*** *the entropy of a perfect crystalline substance is zero at the absolute zero of temperature.* As the temperature increases, the freedom of motion increases and hence also the number of microstates. Thus, the entropy of any substance at a temperature above 0 K is greater than zero. Note also that if the crystal is impure or if it has defects, then its entropy is greater than zero even at 0 K, because it would not be perfectly ordered and the number of microstates would be greater than one.

The important point about the third law of thermodynamics is that it enables us to determine the *absolute* entropies of substances. Starting with the knowledge that the entropy of a pure crystalline substance is zero at absolute zero, we can measure the increase in entropy of the substance when it is heated from 0 K to, say, 298 K. The change in entropy, ΔS, is given by

$$\Delta S = S_f - S_i$$
$$= S_f$$

because S_i is zero. The entropy of the substance at 298 K, then, is given by ΔS or S_f, which is called the absolute entropy because this is the *true* value and not a value derived using some arbitrary reference as in the case of standard enthalpy of formation. Thus, the entropy values quoted so far and those listed in Appendix 3 are all absolute entropies. Because measurements are carried out at 1 atm, we usually refer to absolute entropies as standard entropies. In contrast, we cannot have the absolute energy or enthalpy of a substance because the zero of energy or enthalpy is undefined. Figure 18.6 shows the change (increase) in entropy of a substance with temperature. At absolute zero, it has a zero entropy value (assuming that it is a perfect crystalline substance). As it is heated, its entropy increases gradually because of greater molecular motion. At the melting point, there is a sizable increase in entropy as the liquid state is formed. Further heating increases the entropy of the liquid again due to enhanced molecular motion. At the boiling point there is a large increase in entropy as a result of the liquid-to-vapor transition. Beyond that temperature, the entropy of the gas continues to rise with increasing temperature.

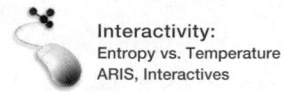

Interactivity:
Entropy vs. Temperature
ARIS, Interactives

The entropy increase can be calculated from the temperature change and heat capacity of the substance, plus any phase changes.

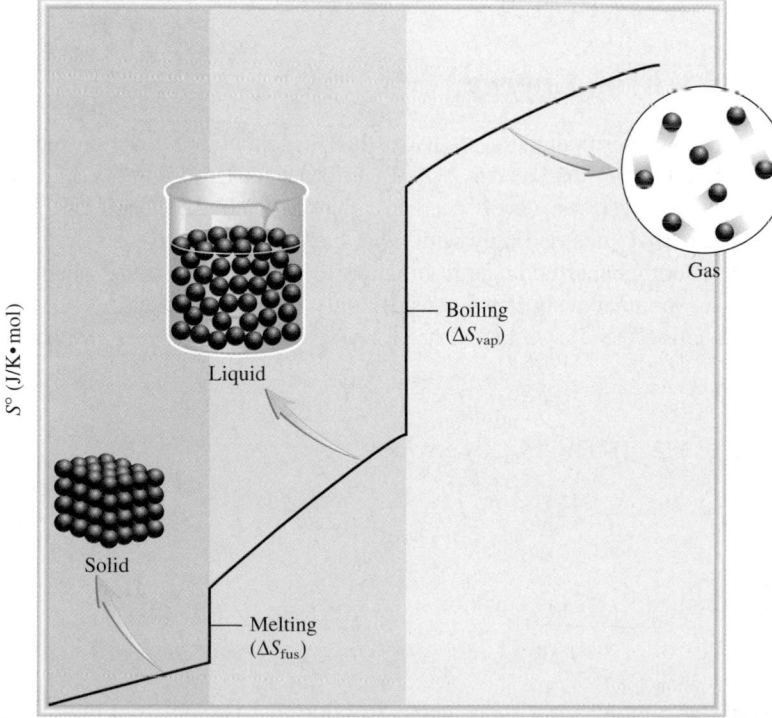

Figure 18.6 *Entropy increase of a substance as the temperature rises from absolute zero.*

CHEMISTRY
in Action

The Efficiency of Heat Engines

An engine is a machine that converts energy to work; a *heat engine* is a machine that converts *thermal energy* to work. Heat engines play an essential role in our technological society; they range from automobile engines to the giant steam turbines that run generators to produce electricity. Regardless of the type of heat engine, its efficiency level is of great importance; that is, for a given amount of heat input, how much useful work can we get out of the engine? The second law of thermodynamics helps us answer this question.

The figure shows a simple form of a heat engine. A cylinder fitted with a weightless piston is initially at temperature T_1. Next, the cylinder is heated to a higher temperature T_2. The gas in the cylinder expands and pushes up the piston. Finally the cylinder is cooled down to T_1 and the apparatus returns to its original state. By repeating this cycle, the up-and-down movement of the piston can be made to do mechanical work.

A unique feature of heat engines is that some heat must be given off to the surroundings when they do work. With the piston in the up position, no further work can be done if we do not cool the cylinder back to T_1. The cooling process removes some of the thermal energy that could otherwise be converted to work and thereby places a limit on the efficiency of heat engines.

The figure on p. 797 shows the heat transfer processes in a heat engine. Initially, a certain amount of heat flows from the heat reservoir (at temperature T_h) into the engine. As the engine does work, some of the heat is given off to the surroundings, or

T_1 T_2 T_1

(a)   (b)   (c)

A simple heat engine. (a) The engine is initially at T_1. (b) When heated to T_2, the piston is pushed up due to gas expansion. (c) When cooled to T_1, the piston returns to the original position.

18.5 Gibbs Free Energy

The second law of thermodynamics tells us that a spontaneous reaction increases the entropy of the universe; that is, $\Delta S_{univ} > 0$. In order to determine the sign of ΔS_{univ} for a reaction, however, we would need to calculate both ΔS_{sys} and ΔS_{surr}. In general, we are usually concerned only with what happens in a particular system. Therefore, we need another thermodynamic function to help us determine whether a reaction will occur spontaneously if we consider only the system itself.

From Equation (18.4), we know that for a spontaneous process, we have

$$\Delta S_{univ} = \Delta S_{sys} + \Delta S_{surr} > 0$$

Substituting $-\Delta H_{sys}/T$ for ΔS_{surr}, we write

$$\Delta S_{univ} = \Delta S_{sys} - \frac{\Delta H_{sys}}{T} > 0$$

Multiplying both sides of the equation by T gives

$$T\Delta S_{univ} = -\Delta H_{sys} + T\Delta S_{sys} > 0$$

Now we have a criterion for a spontaneous reaction that is expressed only in terms of the properties of the system (ΔH_{sys} and ΔS_{sys}) and we can ignore the surroundings.

Heat transfers during the operation of a heat engine.

the heat sink (at temperature T_c). By definition, the efficiency of a heat engine is

$$\text{efficiency} = \frac{\text{useful work output}}{\text{energy input}} \times 100\%$$

Analysis based on the second law shows that efficiency can also be expressed as

$$\text{efficiency} = \left(1 - \frac{T_c}{T_h}\right) \times 100\%$$

$$= \frac{T_h - T_c}{T_h} \times 100\%$$

Thus, the efficiency of a heat engine is given by the difference in temperatures between the heat reservoir and the heat sink (both in kelvins), divided by the temperature of the heat reservoir. In practice, we can make $(T_h - T_c)$ as large as possible, but because T_c cannot be zero and T_h cannot be infinite, the efficiency of a heat engine can therefore never be 100 percent.

At a power plant, superheated steam at about 560°C (833 K) is used to drive a turbine for electricity generation. The temperature of the heat sink is about 38°C (or 311 K). The efficiency is given by

$$\text{efficiency} = \frac{833 \text{ K} - 311 \text{ K}}{833 \text{ K}} \times 100\%$$

$$= 63\%$$

In practice, because of friction, heat loss, and other complications, the maximum efficiency of a steam turbine is only about 40 percent. Therefore, for every ton of coal used at a power plant, 0.40 ton generates electricity while the rest of it ends up warming the surroundings!

For convenience, we can change the preceding equation by multiplying it throughout by -1 and replacing the $>$ sign with $<$:

$$-T\Delta S_{\text{univ}} = \Delta H_{\text{sys}} - T\Delta S_{\text{sys}} < 0$$

The change in unequal sign when we multiply the equation by -1 follows from the fact that $1 > 0$ and $-1 < 0$.

This equation says that for a process carried out at constant pressure and temperature T, if the changes in enthalpy and entropy of the system are such that $\Delta H_{\text{sys}} - T\Delta S_{\text{sys}}$ is less than zero, the process must be spontaneous.

In order to express the spontaneity of a reaction more directly, we introduce another thermodynamic function called **Gibbs**[†] ***free energy (G),*** or simply ***free energy:***

$$G = H - TS \qquad (18.9)$$

A 2005 commemorative stamp honoring Gibbs.

All quantities in Equation (18.9) pertain to the system, and T is the temperature of the system. You can see that G has units of energy (both H and TS are in energy units). Like H and S, G is a state function.

[†]Josiah Willard Gibbs (1839–1903). American physicist. One of the founders of thermodynamics, Gibbs was a modest and private individual who spent almost all of his professional life at Yale University. Because he published most of his works in obscure journals, Gibbs never gained the eminence that his contemporary and admirer James Maxwell did. Even today, very few people outside of chemistry and physics have ever heard of Gibbs.

The change in free energy (ΔG) of a system for a *constant-temperature* process is

$$\Delta G = \Delta H - T\Delta S \qquad (18.10)$$

The word "free" in the term "free energy" does not mean without cost.

In this context, free energy is *the energy available to do work*. Thus, if a particular reaction is accompanied by a release of usable energy (that is, if ΔG is negative), this fact alone guarantees that it is spontaneous, and there is no need to worry about what happens to the rest of the universe.

Note that we have merely organized the expression for the entropy change of the universe and equating the free-energy change of the system (ΔG) with $-T\Delta S_{univ}$, so that we can focus on changes in the system. We can now summarize the conditions for spontaneity and equilibrium at constant temperature and pressure in terms of ΔG as follows:

$\Delta G < 0$ The reaction is spontaneous in the forward direction.
$\Delta G > 0$ The reaction is nonspontaneous. The reaction is spontaneous in the opposite direction.
$\Delta G = 0$ The system is at equilibrium. There is no net change.

TABLE 18.2

Conventions for Standard States

State of Matter	Standard State
Gas	1 atm pressure
Liquid	Pure liquid
Solid	Pure solid
Elements*	$\Delta G_f^\circ = 0$
Solution	1 molar concentration

*The most stable allotropic form at 25°C and 1 atm.

Standard Free-Energy Changes

The **standard free-energy of reaction** (ΔG_{rxn}°) is *the free-energy change for a reaction when it occurs under standard-state conditions, when reactants in their standard states are converted to products in their standard states*. Table 18.2 summarizes the conventions used by chemists to define the standard states of pure substances as well as solutions. To calculate ΔG_{rxn}° we start with the equation

$$a\text{A} + b\text{B} \longrightarrow c\text{C} + d\text{D}$$

The standard free-energy change for this reaction is given by

$$\Delta G_{rxn}^\circ = [c\Delta G_f^\circ(\text{C}) + d\Delta G_f^\circ(\text{D})] - [a\Delta G_f^\circ(\text{A}) + b\Delta G_f^\circ(\text{B})] \qquad (18.11)$$

or, in general,

$$\Delta G_{rxn}^\circ = \Sigma n\Delta G_f^\circ(\text{products}) - \Sigma m\Delta G_f^\circ(\text{reactants}) \qquad (18.12)$$

where m and n are stoichiometric coefficients. The term ΔG_f° is the **standard free energy of formation** of a compound, that is, *the free-energy change that occurs when 1 mole of the compound is synthesized from its elements in their standard states*. For the combustion of graphite:

$$\text{C(graphite)} + \text{O}_2(g) \longrightarrow \text{CO}_2(g)$$

the standard free-energy change [from Equation (18.12)] is

$$\Delta G_{rxn}^\circ = \Delta G_f^\circ(\text{CO}_2) - [\Delta G_f^\circ(\text{C, graphite}) + \Delta G_f^\circ(\text{O}_2)]$$

As in the case of the standard enthalpy of formation (p. 246), we define the standard free energy of formation of any element in its stable allotropic form at 1 atm and 25°C as zero. Thus,

$$\Delta G_f^\circ(\text{C, graphite}) = 0 \qquad \text{and} \qquad \Delta G_f^\circ(\text{O}_2) = 0$$

Therefore, the standard free-energy change for the reaction in this case is equal to the standard free energy of formation of CO_2:

$$\Delta G^\circ_{rxn} = \Delta G^\circ_f(CO_2)$$

Appendix 3 lists the values of ΔG°_f for a number of compounds.

Calculations of standard free-energy changes are handled as shown in Example 18.4.

Example 18.4

Calculate the standard free-energy changes for the following reactions at 25°C.

(a) $CH_4(g) + 2O_2(g) \longrightarrow CO_2(g) + 2H_2O(l)$
(b) $2MgO(s) \longrightarrow 2Mg(s) + O_2(g)$

Strategy To calculate the standard free-energy change of a reaction, we look up the standard free energies of formation of reactants and products in Appendix 3 and apply Equation (18.12). Note that all the stoichiometric coefficients have no units so ΔG°_{rxn} is expressed in units of kJ/mol, and ΔG°_f for O_2 is zero because it is the stable allotropic element at 1 atm and 25°C.

Solution (a) According to Equation (18.12), we write

$$\Delta G^\circ_{rxn} = [\Delta G^\circ_f(CO_2) + 2\Delta G^\circ_f(H_2O)] - [\Delta G^\circ_f(CH_4) + 2\Delta G^\circ_f(O_2)]$$

We insert the appropriate values from Appendix 3:

$$\Delta G^\circ_{rxn} = [(-394.4 \text{ kJ/mol}) + (2)(-237.2 \text{ kJ/mol})] -$$
$$[(-50.8 \text{ kJ/mol}) + (2)(0 \text{ kJ/mol})]$$
$$= -818.0 \text{ kJ/mol}$$

(b) The equation is

$$\Delta G^\circ_{rxn} = [2\Delta G^\circ_f(Mg) + \Delta G^\circ_f(O_2)] - [2\Delta G^\circ_f(MgO)]$$

From data in Appendix 3 we write

$$\Delta G^\circ_{rxn} = [(2)(0 \text{ kJ/mol}) + (0 \text{ kJ/mol})] - [(2)(-569.6 \text{ kJ/mol})]$$
$$= 1139 \text{ kJ/mol}$$

Similar problems: 18.17 and 18.18.

Practice Exercise Calculate the standard free-energy changes for the following reactions at 25°C:

(a) $H_2(g) + Br_2(l) \longrightarrow 2HBr(g)$
(b) $2C_2H_6(g) + 7O_2(g) \longrightarrow 4CO_2(g) + 6H_2O(l)$

Applications of Equation (18.10)

In order to predict the sign of ΔG, according to Equation (18.10), we need to know both ΔH and ΔS. A negative ΔH (an exothermic reaction) and a positive ΔS (a reaction that results in an increase in the microstates of the system) tend to make ΔG negative, although temperature may also influence the *direction* of a spontaneous reaction. The four possible outcomes of this relationship are

• If both ΔH and ΔS are positive, then ΔG will be negative only when the $T\Delta S$ term is greater in magnitude than ΔH. This condition is met when T is large.

• If ΔH is positive and ΔS is negative, ΔG will always be positive, regardless of temperature.

TABLE 18.3		Factors Affecting the Sign of ΔG in the Relationship $\Delta G = \Delta H - T\Delta S$	
ΔH	ΔS	ΔG	Example
+	+	Reaction proceeds spontaneously at high temperatures. At low temperatures, reaction is spontaneous in the reverse direction.	$2HgO(s) \longrightarrow 2Hg(l) + O_2(g)$
+	−	ΔG is always positive. Reaction is spontaneous in the reverse direction at all temperatures.	$3O_2(g) \longrightarrow 2O_3(g)$
−	+	ΔG is always negative. Reaction proceeds spontaneously at all temperatures.	$2H_2O_2(aq) \longrightarrow 2H_2O(l) + O_2(g)$
−	−	Reaction proceeds spontaneously at low temperatures. At high temperatures, the reverse reaction becomes spontaneous.	$NH_3(g) + HCl(g) \longrightarrow NH_4Cl(s)$

- If ΔH is negative and ΔS is positive, then ΔG will always be negative regardless of temperature.

- If ΔH is negative and ΔS is negative, then ΔG will be negative only when $T\Delta S$ is smaller in magnitude than ΔH. This condition is met when T is small.

The temperatures that will cause ΔG to be negative for the first and last cases depend on the actual values of ΔH and ΔS of the system. Table 18.3 summarizes the effects of the possibilities just described.

Before we apply the change in free energy to predict reaction spontaneity, it is useful to distinguish between ΔG and $\Delta G°$. Suppose we carry out a reaction in solution with all the reactants in their standard states (that is, all at 1 M concentration). As soon as the reaction starts, the standard-state condition no longer exists for the reactants or the products because their concentrations are different from 1 M. Under nonstandard state conditions, we must use the sign of ΔG rather than that of $\Delta G°$ to predict the direction of the reaction. The sign of $\Delta G°$, on the other hand, tells us whether the products or the reactants are favored when the reacting system reaches equilibrium. Thus, a negative value of $\Delta G°$ indicates that the reaction favors product formation whereas a positive value of $\Delta G°$ indicates that there will be more reactants than products at equilibrium.

We will now consider two specific applications of Equation (18.10).

In Section 18.6 we will see an equation relating $\Delta G°$ to the equilibrium constant K.

Temperature and Chemical Reactions

Calcium oxide (CaO), also called quicklime, is an extremely valuable inorganic substance used in steelmaking, production of calcium metal, the paper industry, water treatment, and pollution control. It is prepared by decomposing limestone ($CaCO_3$) in a kiln at a high temperature (see p. 782):

$$CaCO_3(s) \rightleftharpoons CaO(s) + CO_2(g)$$

Le Châtelier's principle predicts that the forward, endothermic reaction is favored by heating.

The reaction is reversible, and CaO readily combines with CO_2 to form $CaCO_3$. The pressure of CO_2 in equilibrium with $CaCO_3$ and CaO increases with temperature. In the industrial preparation of quicklime, the system is never maintained at equilibrium; rather, CO_2 is constantly removed from the kiln to shift the equilibrium from left to right, promoting the formation of calcium oxide.

The important information for the practical chemist is the temperature at which the decomposition of $CaCO_3$ becomes appreciable (that is, the temperature at which the reaction begins to favor products). We can make a reliable estimate of that temperature as follows. First we calculate ΔH° and ΔS° for the reaction at 25°C, using the data in Appendix 3. To determine ΔH° we apply Equation (6.18):

$$\begin{aligned}\Delta H^\circ &= [\Delta H_f^\circ(CaO) + \Delta H_f^\circ(CO_2)] - [\Delta H_f^\circ(CaCO_3)] \\ &= [(-635.6 \text{ kJ/mol}) + (-393.5 \text{ kJ/mol})] - (-1206.9 \text{ kJ/mol}) \\ &= 177.8 \text{ kJ/mol}\end{aligned}$$

Next we apply Equation (18.6) to find ΔS°:

$$\begin{aligned}\Delta S^\circ &= [S^\circ(CaO) + S^\circ(CO_2)] - S^\circ(CaCO_3) \\ &= [(39.8 \text{ J/K}\cdot\text{mol}) + (213.6 \text{ J/K}\cdot\text{mol})] - (92.9 \text{ J/K}\cdot\text{mol}) \\ &= 160.5 \text{ J/K}\cdot\text{mol}\end{aligned}$$

From Equation (18.10),

$$\Delta G^\circ = \Delta H^\circ - T\Delta S^\circ$$

we obtain

$$\begin{aligned}\Delta G^\circ &= 177.8 \text{ kJ/mol} - (298 \text{ K})(160.5 \text{ J/K}\cdot\text{mol})\left(\frac{1 \text{ kJ}}{1000 \text{ J}}\right) \\ &= 130.0 \text{ kJ/mol}\end{aligned}$$

Because ΔG° is a large positive quantity, we conclude that the reaction is not favored for product formation at 25°C (or 298 K). Indeed, the pressure of CO_2 is so low at room temperature that it cannot be measured. In order to make ΔG° negative, we first have to find the temperature at which ΔG° is zero; that is,

$$0 = \Delta H^\circ - T\Delta S^\circ$$

or

$$\begin{aligned}T &= \frac{\Delta H^\circ}{\Delta S^\circ} \\ &= \frac{(177.8 \text{ kJ/mol})(1000 \text{ J }/1 \text{ kJ})}{160.5 \text{ J/K}\cdot\text{mol}} \\ &= 1108 \text{ K or } 835°C\end{aligned}$$

At a temperature higher than 835°C, ΔG° becomes negative, indicating that the reaction now favors the formation of CaO and CO_2. For example, at 840°C, or 1113 K,

$$\begin{aligned}\Delta G^\circ &= \Delta H^\circ - T\Delta S^\circ \\ &= 177.8 \text{ kJ/mol} - (1113 \text{ K})(160.5 \text{ J/K}\cdot\text{mol})\left(\frac{1 \text{ kJ}}{1000 \text{ J}}\right) \\ &= -0.8 \text{ kJ/mol}\end{aligned}$$

Figure 18.7 *Equilibrium pressure of CO_2 from the decomposition of $CaCO_3$, as a function of temperature. This curve is calculated by assuming that ΔH° and ΔS° of the reaction do not change with temperature.*

Two points are worth making about such a calculation. First, we used the ΔH° and ΔS° values at 25°C to calculate changes that occur at a much higher temperature. Because both ΔH° and ΔS° change with temperature, this approach will not give us an accurate value of ΔG°, but it is good enough for "ballpark" estimates. Second, we should not be misled into thinking that nothing happens below 835°C and that at 835°C $CaCO_3$ suddenly begins to decompose. Far from it. The fact that ΔG° is a positive value at some temperature below 835°C does not mean that no CO_2 is produced, but rather that the pressure of the CO_2 gas formed at that temperature will be below 1 atm (its standard-state value; see Table 18.2). As Figure 18.7 shows, the pressure of CO_2 at first increases very slowly with temperature; it becomes easily measurable

The equilibrium constant of this reaction is $K_P = P_{CO_2}$.

above 700°C. The significance of 835°C is that this is the temperature at which the equilibrium pressure of CO_2 reaches 1 atm. Above 835°C, the equilibrium pressure of CO_2 exceeds 1 atm.

Phase Transitions

At the temperature at which a phase transition occurs (that is, at the melting point or boiling point) the system is at equilibrium ($\Delta G = 0$), so Equation (18.10) becomes

$$\Delta G = \Delta H - T\Delta S$$
$$0 = \Delta H - T\Delta S$$

or

$$\Delta S = \frac{\Delta H}{T}$$

Let us first consider the ice-water equilibrium. For the ice → water transition, ΔH is the molar heat of fusion (see Table 11.8), and T is the melting point. The entropy change is therefore

The melting of ice is an endothermic process (ΔH is positive), and the freezing of water is exothermic (ΔH is negative).

$$\Delta S_{ice \to water} = \frac{6010 \text{ J/mol}}{273 \text{ K}}$$
$$= 22.0 \text{ J/K} \cdot \text{mol}$$

Thus, when 1 mole of ice melts at 0°C, there is an increase in entropy of 22.0 J/K · mol. The increase in entropy is consistent with the increase in microstates from solid to liquid. Conversely, for the water → ice transition, the decrease in entropy is given by

$$\Delta S_{water \to ice} = \frac{-6010 \text{ J/mol}}{273 \text{ K}}$$
$$= -22.0 \text{ J/K} \cdot \text{mol}$$

In the laboratory we normally carry out unidirectional changes, that is, either ice to water or water to ice transition. We can calculate entropy change in each case using the equation $\Delta S = \Delta H/T$ as long as the temperature remains at 0°C. The same procedure can be applied to the water → steam transition. In this case ΔH is the heat of vaporization and T is the boiling point of water. Example 18.5 examines the phase transitions in benzene.

Liquid and solid benzene in equilibrium at 5.5°C.

Example 18.5

The molar heats of fusion and vaporization of benzene are 10.9 kJ/mol and 31.0 kJ/mol, respectively. Calculate the entropy changes for the solid → liquid and liquid → vapor transitions for benzene. At 1 atm pressure, benzene melts at 5.5°C and boils at 80.1°C.

Strategy At the melting point, liquid and solid benzene are at equilibrium, so $\Delta G = 0$. From Equation (18.10) we have $\Delta G = 0 = \Delta H - T\Delta S$ or $\Delta S = \Delta H/T$. To calculate the entropy change for the solid benzene → liquid benzene transition, we write $\Delta S_{fus} = \Delta H_{fus}/T_f$. Here ΔH_{fus} is positive for an endothermic process, so ΔS_{fus} is also positive, as expected for a solid to liquid transition. The same procedure applies to the liquid benzene → vapor benzene transition. What temperature unit should be used?

(Continued)

Solution The entropy change for melting 1 mole of benzene at 5.5°C is

$$\Delta S_{\text{fus}} = \frac{\Delta H_{\text{fus}}}{T_f}$$

$$= \frac{(10.9 \text{ kJ/mol})(1000 \text{ J/1 kJ})}{(5.5 + 273) \text{ K}}$$

$$= 39.1 \text{ J/K} \cdot \text{mol}$$

Similarly, the entropy change for boiling 1 mole of benzene at 80.1°C is

$$\Delta S_{\text{vap}} = \frac{\Delta H_{\text{vap}}}{T_{\text{bp}}}$$

$$= \frac{(31.0 \text{ kJ/mol})(1000 \text{ J/1 kJ})}{(80.1 + 273) \text{ K}}$$

$$= 87.8 \text{ J/K} \cdot \text{mol}$$

Check Because vaporization creates more microstates than the melting process, $\Delta S_{\text{vap}} > \Delta S_{\text{fus}}$.

Similar problem: 18.60.

Practice Exercise The molar heats of fusion and vaporization of argon are 1.3 kJ/mol and 6.3 kJ/mol, and argon's melting point and boiling point are −190°C and −186°C, respectively. Calculate the entropy changes for fusion and vaporization.

18.6 Free Energy and Chemical Equilibrium

As mentioned earlier, during the course of a chemical reaction not all the reactants and products will be at their standard states. Under this condition, the relationship between ΔG and $\Delta G°$, which can be derived from thermodynamics, is

$$\Delta G = \Delta G° + RT \ln Q \tag{18.13}$$

where R is the gas constant (8.314 J/K · mol), T is the absolute temperature of the reaction, and Q is the reaction quotient (see p. 618). We see that ΔG depends on two quantities: $\Delta G°$ and $RT \ln Q$. For a given reaction at temperature T the value of $\Delta G°$ is fixed but that of $RT \ln Q$ is not, because Q varies according to the composition of the reaction mixture. Let us consider two special cases:

Case 1: A large negative value of $\Delta G°$ will tend to make ΔG also negative. Thus, the net reaction will proceed from left to right until a significant amount of product has been formed. At that point, the $RT \ln Q$ term will become positive enough to match the negative $\Delta G°$ term in magnitude.

Case 2: A large positive $\Delta G°$ term will tend to make ΔG also positive. Thus, the net reaction will proceed from right to left until a significant amount of reactant has been formed. At that point the $RT \ln Q$ term will become negative enough to match the positive $\Delta G°$ term in magnitude.

At equilibrium, by definition, $\Delta G = 0$ and $Q = K$, where K is the equilibrium constant. Thus,

$$0 = \Delta G° + RT \ln K$$

Sooner or later a reversible reaction will reach equilibrium.

or
$$\Delta G^\circ = -RT \ln K \qquad (18.14)$$

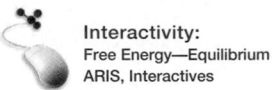

Interactivity:
Free Energy—Equilibrium
ARIS, Interactives

In this equation, K_P is used for gases and K_c for reactions in solution. Note that the larger the K is, the more negative ΔG° is. For chemists, Equation (18.14) is one of the most important equations in thermodynamics because it enables us to find the equilibrium constant of a reaction if we know the change in standard free energy and vice versa.

It is significant that Equation (18.14) relates the equilibrium constant to the *standard* free-energy change ΔG° rather than to the *actual* free-energy change ΔG. The actual free-energy change of the system varies as the reaction progresses and becomes zero at equilibrium. On the other hand, ΔG° is a constant for a particular reaction at a given temperature. Figure 18.8 shows plots of the free energy of a reacting system versus the extent of the reaction for two types of reactions. As you can see, if $\Delta G^\circ < 0$, the products are favored over reactants at equilibrium. Conversely, if $\Delta G^\circ > 0$, there will be more reactants than products at equilibrium. Table 18.4 summarizes the three possible relations between ΔG° and K, as predicted by Equation (18.14). Remember this important distinction: It is the sign of ΔG and not that of ΔG° that determines the direction of reaction spontaneity. The sign of ΔG° only tells us the relative amounts of products and reactants when equilibrium is reached, not the direction of the net reaction.

For reactions having very large or very small equilibrium constants, it is generally very difficult, if not impossible, to measure the K values by monitoring the concentrations of all the reacting species. Consider, for example, the formation of nitric oxide from molecular nitrogen and molecular oxygen:

$$N_2(g) + O_2(g) \rightleftharpoons 2NO(g)$$

At 25°C, the equilibrium constant K_P is

$$K_P = \frac{P_{NO}^2}{P_{N_2}P_{O_2}} = 4.0 \times 10^{-31}$$

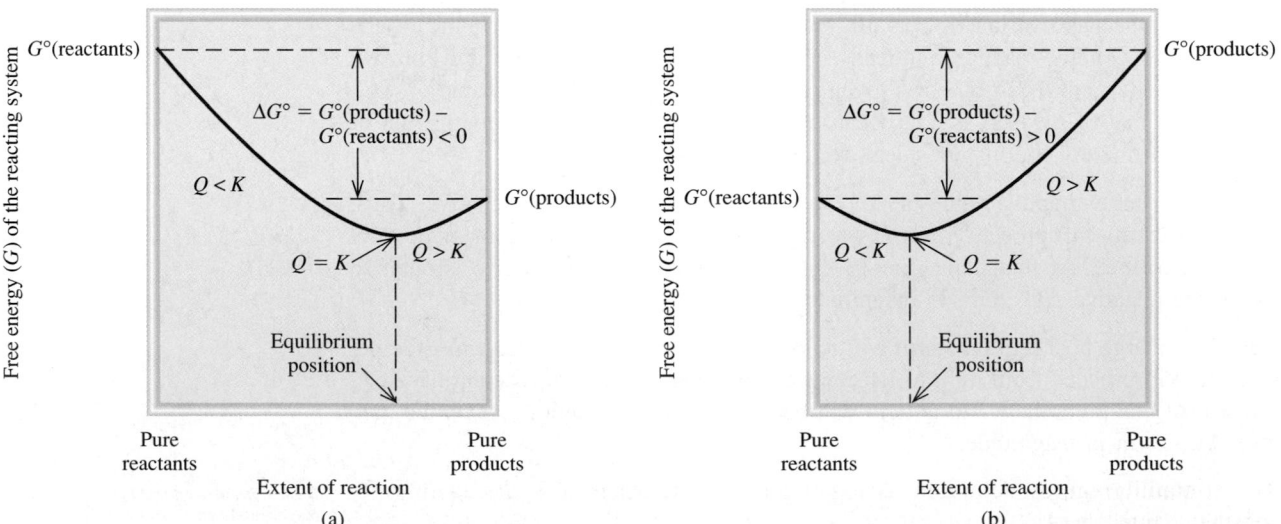

Figure 18.8 *(a) $\Delta G^\circ < 0$. At equilibrium, there is a significant conversion of reactants to products. (b) $\Delta G^\circ > 0$. At equilibrium, reactants are favored over products. In both cases, the net reaction toward equilibrium is from left to right (reactants to products) if $Q < K$ and right to left (products to reactants) if $Q > K$. At equilibrium, $Q = K$.*

K	ln K	$\Delta G°$	Comments
> 1	Positive	Negative	Products are favored over reactants at equilibrium.
= 1	0	0	Products and reactants are equally favored at equilibrium.
< 1	Negative	Positive	Reactants are favored over products at equilibrium.

TABLE 18.4 Relation Between $\Delta G°$ and K as Predicted by the Equation $\Delta G° = -RT \ln K$

The very small value of K_P means that the concentration of NO at equilibrium will be exceedingly low. In such a case the equilibrium constant is more conveniently obtained from $\Delta G°$. (As we have seen, $\Delta G°$ can be calculated from $\Delta H°$ and $\Delta S°$.) On the other hand, the equilibrium constant for the formation of hydrogen iodide from molecular hydrogen and molecular iodine is near unity at room temperature:

$$H_2(g) + I_2(g) \rightleftharpoons 2HI(g)$$

For this reaction, it is easier to measure K_P and then calculate $\Delta G°$ using Equation (18.14) than to measure $\Delta H°$ and $\Delta S°$ and use Equation (18.10).

Examples 18.6–18.8 illustrate the use of Equations (18.13) and (18.14).

Example 18.6

Using data listed in Appendix 3, calculate the equilibrium constant (K_P) for the following reaction at 25°C:

$$2H_2O(l) \rightleftharpoons 2H_2(g) + O_2(g)$$

Strategy According to Equation (18.14), the equilibrium constant for the reaction is related to the standard free-energy change; that is, $\Delta G° = -RT \ln K$. Therefore, we first need to calculate $\Delta G°$ by following the procedure in Example 18.4. Then we can calculate K_P. What temperature unit should be used?

Solution According to Equation (18.12),

$$\Delta G°_{rxn} = [2\Delta G°_f(H_2) + \Delta G°_f(O_2)] - [2\Delta G°_f(H_2O)]$$
$$= [(2)(0 \text{ kJ/mol}) + (0 \text{ kJ/mol})] - [(2)(-237.2 \text{ kJ/mol})]$$
$$= 474.4 \text{ kJ/mol}$$

Using Equation (18.14)

$$\Delta G°_{rxn} = -RT \ln K_P$$

$$474.4 \text{ kJ/mol} \times \frac{1000 \text{ J}}{1 \text{ kJ}} = -(8.314 \text{ J/K} \cdot \text{mol})(298 \text{ K}) \ln K_P$$

$$\ln K_P = -191.5$$
$$K_P = e^{-191.5} = 7 \times 10^{-84}$$

To calculate K_P, enter −191.5 on your calculator and then press the key labeled "e" or "inv(erse) ln x."

Comment This extremely small equilibrium constant is consistent with the fact that water does not spontaneously decompose into hydrogen and oxygen gases at 25°C. Thus, a large positive $\Delta G°$ favors reactants over products at equilibrium.

Similar problems: 18.23 and 18.26.

(Continued)

Practice Exercise Calculate the equilibrium constant (K_P) for the reaction

$$2O_3(g) \longrightarrow 3O_2(g)$$

at 25°C.

Example 18.7

In Chapter 16 we discussed the solubility product of slightly soluble substances. Using the solubility product of silver chloride at 25°C (1.6×10^{-10}), calculate $\Delta G°$ for the process

$$AgCl(s) \rightleftharpoons Ag^+(aq) + Cl^-(aq)$$

Strategy According to Equation (18.14), the equilibrium constant for the reaction is related to standard free-energy change; that is, $\Delta G° = -RT \ln K$. Because this is a heterogeneous equilibrium, the solubility product (K_{sp}) is the equilibrium constant. We calculate the standard free-energy change from the K_{sp} value of AgCl. What temperature unit should be used?

Solution The solubility equilibrium for AgCl is

$$AgCl(s) \rightleftharpoons Ag^+(aq) + Cl^-(aq)$$
$$K_{sp} = [Ag^+][Cl^-] = 1.6 \times 10^{-10}$$

Using Equation (18.14) we obtain

$$\begin{aligned} \Delta G° &= -(8.314 \text{ J/K} \cdot \text{mol})(298 \text{ K}) \ln (1.6 \times 10^{-10}) \\ &= 5.6 \times 10^4 \text{ J/mol} \\ &= 56 \text{ kJ/mol} \end{aligned}$$

Check The large, positive $\Delta G°$ indicates that AgCl is slightly soluble and that the equilibrium lies mostly to the left.

Similar problem: 18.25.

Practice Exercise Calculate $\Delta G°$ for the following process at 25°C:

$$BaF_2(s) \rightleftharpoons Ba^{2+}(aq) + 2F^-(aq)$$

The K_{sp} of BaF_2 is 1.7×10^{-6}.

Example 18.8

The equilibrium constant (K_P) for the reaction

$$N_2O_4(g) \rightleftharpoons 2NO_2(g)$$

is 0.113 at 298 K, which corresponds to a standard free-energy change of 5.40 kJ/mol. In a certain experiment, the initial pressures are $P_{NO_2} = 0.122$ atm and $P_{N_2O_4} = 0.453$ atm. Calculate ΔG for the reaction at these pressures and predict the direction of the net reaction toward equilibrium.

Strategy From the information given we see that neither the reactant nor the product is at its standard state of 1 atm. To determine the direction of the net reaction, we need to calculate the free-energy change under nonstandard-state conditions (ΔG) using Equation (18.13) and the given $\Delta G°$ value. Note that the partial pressures are expressed as dimensionless quantities in the reaction quotient Q_P because they are divided by the standard-state value of 1 atm (see p. 607 and Table 18.2).

(Continued)

The Thermodynamics of a Rubber Band

We all know how useful a rubber band can be. But not everyone is aware that a rubber band has some very interesting thermodynamic properties based on its structure.

You can easily perform the following experiments with a rubber band that is at least 0.5 cm wide. Quickly stretch the rubber band and then press it against your lips. You will feel a slight warming effect. Next, reverse the process. Stretch a rubber band and hold it in position for a few seconds. Then quickly release the tension and press the rubber band against your lips. This time you will feel a slight cooling effect. A thermodynamic analysis of these two experiments can tell us something about the molecular structure of rubber.

Rearranging Equation (18.10) ($\Delta G = \Delta H - T\Delta S$) gives

$$T\Delta S = \Delta H - \Delta G$$

The warming effect (an exothermic process) due to stretching means that $\Delta H < 0$, and since stretching is nonspontaneous (that is, $\Delta G > 0$ and $-\Delta G < 0$) $T\Delta S$ must be negative. Because T, the absolute temperature, is always positive, we conclude that ΔS due to stretching must be negative, and therefore

(a) Rubber molecules in their normal state. Note the high degree of disorder (high entropy). (b) Under tension, the molecules line up and the arrangement becomes much more ordered (low entropy).

rubber in its natural state is more entangled (has more microstates) than when it is under tension.

When the tension is removed, the stretched rubber band spontaneously snaps back to its original shape; that is, ΔG is negative and $-\Delta G$ is positive. The cooling effect means that it is an endothermic process ($\Delta H > 0$), so that $T\Delta S$ is positive. Thus, the entropy of the rubber band increases when it goes from the stretched state to the natural state.

Solution Equation (18.13) can be written as

$$\Delta G = \Delta G^\circ + RT \ln Q_P$$
$$= \Delta G^\circ + RT \ln \frac{P_{NO_2}^2}{P_{N_2O_4}}$$
$$= 5.40 \times 10^3 \text{ J/mol} + (8.314 \text{ J/K} \cdot \text{mol})(298 \text{ K}) \times \ln \frac{(0.122)^2}{0.453}$$
$$= 5.40 \times 10^3 \text{ J/mol} - 8.46 \times 10^3 \text{ J/mol}$$
$$= -3.06 \times 10^3 \text{ J/mol} = -3.06 \text{ kJ/mol}$$

Because $\Delta G < 0$, the net reaction proceeds from left to right to reach equilibrium.

Check Note that although $\Delta G^\circ > 0$, the reaction can be made to favor product formation initially by having a small concentration (pressure) of the product compared to that of the reactant. Confirm the prediction by showing that $Q_P < K_P$.

Similar problems: 18.27 and 18.28.

Practice Exercise The ΔG° for the reaction

$$H_2(g) + I_2(g) \rightleftharpoons 2HI(g)$$

is 2.60 kJ/mol at 25°C. In one experiment, the initial pressures are $P_{H_2} = 4.26$ atm, $P_{I_2} = 0.024$ atm, and $P_{HI} = 0.23$ atm. Calculate ΔG for the reaction and predict the direction of the net reaction.

A mechanical analog for coupled reactions. We can make the smaller weight move upward (a nonspontaneous process) by coupling it with the falling of a larger weight.

The price we pay for this procedure is acid rain.

18.7 Thermodynamics in Living Systems

Many biochemical reactions have a positive ΔG° value, yet they are essential to the maintenance of life. In living systems these reactions are coupled to an energetically favorable process, one that has a negative ΔG° value. The principle of *coupled reactions* is based on a simple concept: we can use a thermodynamically favorable reaction to drive an unfavorable one. Consider an industrial process. Suppose we wish to extract zinc from the ore sphalerite (ZnS). The following reaction will not work because it has a large positive ΔG° value:

$$\text{ZnS}(s) \longrightarrow \text{Zn}(s) + \text{S}(s) \qquad \Delta G^\circ = 198.3 \text{ kJ/mol}$$

On the other hand, the combustion of sulfur to form sulfur dioxide is favored because of its large negative ΔG° value:

$$\text{S}(s) + \text{O}_2(g) \longrightarrow \text{SO}_2(g) \qquad \Delta G^\circ = -300.1 \text{ kJ/mol}$$

By coupling the two processes we can bring about the separation of zinc from zinc sulfide. In practice, this means heating ZnS in air so that the tendency of S to form SO_2 will promote the decomposition of ZnS:

$$
\begin{aligned}
\text{ZnS}(s) &\longrightarrow \text{Zn}(s) + \text{S}(s) & \Delta G^\circ &= 198.3 \text{ kJ/mol} \\
\text{S}(s) + \text{O}_2(g) &\longrightarrow \text{SO}_2(g) & \Delta G^\circ &= -300.1 \text{ kJ/mol} \\
\hline
\text{ZnS}(s) + \text{O}_2(g) &\longrightarrow \text{Zn}(s) + \text{SO}_2(g) & \Delta G^\circ &= -101.8 \text{ kJ/mol}
\end{aligned}
$$

Coupled reactions play a crucial role in our survival. In biological systems, enzymes facilitate a wide variety of nonspontaneous reactions. For example, in the human body, food molecules, represented by glucose ($C_6H_{12}O_6$), are converted to carbon dioxide and water during metabolism with a substantial release of free energy:

$$\text{C}_6\text{H}_{12}\text{O}_6(s) + 6\text{O}_2(g) \longrightarrow 6\text{CO}_2(g) + 6\text{H}_2\text{O}(l) \qquad \Delta G^\circ = -2880 \text{ kJ/mol}$$

In a living cell, this reaction does not take place in a single step (as burning glucose in a flame would); rather, the glucose molecule is broken down with the aid of enzymes in a series of steps. Much of the free energy released along the way is used to synthesize adenosine triphosphate (ATP) from adenosine diphosphate (ADP) and phosphoric acid (Figure 18.9):

$$\text{ADP} + \text{H}_3\text{PO}_4 \longrightarrow \text{ATP} + \text{H}_2\text{O} \qquad \Delta G^\circ = +31 \text{ kJ/mol}$$

The function of ATP is to store free energy until it is needed by cells. Under appropriate conditions, ATP undergoes hydrolysis to give ADP and phosphoric acid, with

Figure 18.9 *Structure of ATP and ADP in ionized forms. The adenine group is in blue, the ribose group in black, and the phosphate group in red. Note that ADP has one fewer phosphate group than ATP.*

Adenosine triphosphate
(ATP)

Adenosine diphosphate
(ADP)

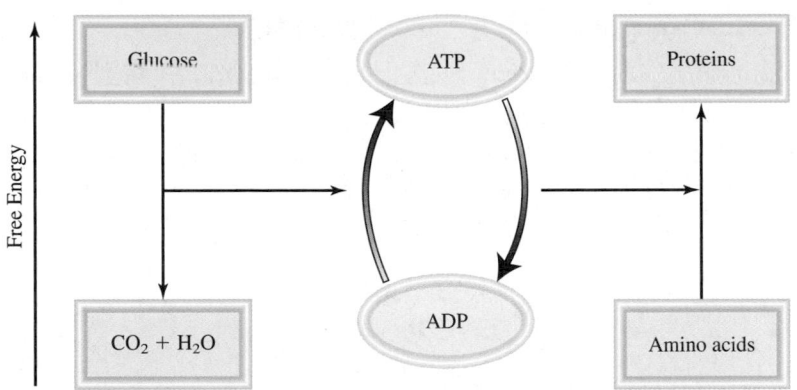

Figure 18.10 *Schematic representation of ATP synthesis and coupled reactions in living systems. The conversion of glucose to carbon dioxide and water during metabolism releases free energy. The released free energy is used to convert ADP into ATP. The ATP molecules are then used as an energy source to drive unfavorable reactions, such as protein synthesis from amino acids.*

a release of 31 kJ/mol of free energy, which can be used to drive energetically unfavorable reactions, such as protein synthesis.

Proteins are polymers made of amino acids. The stepwise synthesis of a protein molecule involves the joining of individual amino acids. Consider the formation of the dipeptide (a two-amino-acid unit) alanylglycine from alanine and glycine. This reaction represents the first step in the synthesis of a protein molecule:

$$\text{Alanine} + \text{Glycine} \longrightarrow \text{Alanylglycine} \quad \Delta G^\circ = +29 \text{ kJ/mol}$$

As you can see, this reaction does not favor the formation of product, and so only a little of the dipeptide would be formed at equilibrium. However, with the aid of an enzyme, the reaction is coupled to the hydrolysis of ATP as follows:

$$\text{ATP} + \text{H}_2\text{O} + \text{Alanine} + \text{Glycine} \longrightarrow \text{ADP} + \text{H}_3\text{PO}_4 + \text{Alanylglycine}$$

The overall free-energy change is given by $\Delta G^\circ = -31$ kJ/mol + 29 kJ/mol = -2 kJ/mol, which means that the coupled reaction now favors the formation of product, and an appreciable amount of alanylglycine will be formed under this condition. Figure 18.10 shows the ATP-ADP interconversions that act as energy storage (from metabolism) and free-energy release (from ATP hydrolysis) to drive essential reactions.

Summary of Facts and Concepts

1. Entropy is usually described as a measure of the disorder of a system. Any spontaneous process must lead to a net increase in entropy in the universe (second law of thermodynamics).

2. The standard entropy of a chemical reaction can be calculated from the absolute entropies of reactants and products.

3. The third law of thermodynamics states that the entropy of a perfect crystalline substance is zero at 0 K. This law enables us to measure the absolute entropies of substances.

4. Under conditions of constant temperature and pressure, the free-energy change ΔG is less than zero for a spontaneous process and greater than zero for a nonspontaneous process. For an equilibrium process, $\Delta G = 0$.

5. For a chemical or physical process at constant temperature and pressure, $\Delta G = \Delta H - T\Delta S$. This equation can be used to predict the spontaneity of a process.

6. The standard free-energy change for a reaction, ΔG°, can be calculated from the standard free energies of formation of reactants and products.

7. The equilibrium constant of a reaction and the standard free-energy change of the reaction are related by the equation $\Delta G^\circ = -RT \ln K$.

8. Many biological reactions are nonspontaneous. They are driven by the hydrolysis of ATP, for which ΔG° is negative.

Key Words

Entropy (S), p. 785
Free energy (G), p. 797
Gibbs free energy
  (G), p. 797

Second law of
  thermodynamics, p. 790
Standard entropy of reaction
  (ΔS_{rxn}°), p. 791

Standard free energy of
  formation (ΔG_f°), p. 798
Standard free energy of
  reaction (ΔG_{rxn}°), p. 798

Third law of
  thermodynamics, p. 794

Questions and Problems

Spontaneous Processes and Entropy

Review Questions

18.1   Explain what is meant by a spontaneous process. Give two examples each of spontaneous and nonspontaneous processes.

18.2   Which of the following processes are spontaneous and which are nonspontaneous? (a) dissolving table salt (NaCl) in hot soup; (b) climbing Mt. Everest; (c) spreading fragrance in a room by removing the cap from a perfume bottle; (d) separating helium and neon from a mixture of the gases

18.3   Which of the following processes are spontaneous and which are nonspontaneous at a given temperature?
(a) $NaNO_3(s) \xrightarrow{H_2O} NaNO_3(aq)$ saturated soln
(b) $NaNO_3(s) \xrightarrow{H_2O} NaNO_3(aq)$ unsaturated soln
(c) $NaNO_3(s) \xrightarrow{H_2O} NaNO_3(aq)$ supersaturated soln

18.4   Define entropy. What are the units of entropy?

18.5   How does the entropy of a system change for each of the following processes?
(a) A solid melts.
(b) A liquid freezes.
(c) A liquid boils.
(d) A vapor is converted to a solid.
(e) A vapor condenses to a liquid.
(f) A solid sublimes.
(g) Urea dissolves in water.

Problems

18.6   Referring to the setup in Figure 18.1(a), calculate the probability of all the molecules ending up in the same flask if the number is (a) 6, (b) 60, (c) 600.

The Second Law of Thermodynamics

Review Questions

18.7   State the second law of thermodynamics in words and express it mathematically.

18.8   State the third law of thermodynamics and explain its usefulness in calculating entropy values.

Problems

18.9   For each pair of substances listed here, choose the one having the larger standard entropy value at 25°C. The same molar amount is used in the comparison. Explain the basis for your choice. (a) Li(s) or Li(l); (b) $C_2H_5OH(l)$ or $CH_3OCH_3(l)$ (Hint: Which molecule can hydrogen-bond?); (c) Ar(g) or Xe(g); (d) CO(g) or $CO_2(g)$; (e) $O_2(g)$ or $O_3(g)$; (f) $NO_2(g)$ or $N_2O_4(g)$

18.10 Arrange the following substances (1 mole each) in order of increasing entropy at 25°C: (a) Ne(g), (b) $SO_2(g)$, (c) Na(s), (d) NaCl(s), (e) $H_2(g)$. Give the reasons for your arrangement.

18.11 Using the data in Appendix 3, calculate the standard entropy changes for the following reactions at 25°C:
(a) $S(s) + O_2(g) \longrightarrow SO_2(g)$
(b) $MgCO_3(s) \longrightarrow MgO(s) + CO_2(g)$

18.12 Using the data in Appendix 3, calculate the standard entropy changes for the following reactions at 25°C:
(a) $H_2(g) + CuO(s) \longrightarrow Cu(s) + H_2O(g)$
(b) $2Al(s) + 3ZnO(s) \longrightarrow Al_2O_3(s) + 3Zn(s)$
(c) $CH_4(g) + 2O_2(g) \longrightarrow CO_2(g) + 2H_2O(l)$

18.13 Without consulting Appendix 3, predict whether the entropy change is positive or negative for each of the following reactions. Give reasons for your predictions.
(a) $2KClO_4(s) \longrightarrow 2KClO_3(s) + O_2(g)$
(b) $H_2O(g) \longrightarrow H_2O(l)$
(c) $2Na(s) + 2H_2O(l) \longrightarrow 2NaOH(aq) + H_2(g)$
(d) $N_2(g) \longrightarrow 2N(g)$

18.14 State whether the sign of the entropy change expected for each of the following processes will be positive or negative, and explain your predictions.
(a) $PCl_3(l) + Cl_2(g) \longrightarrow PCl_5(s)$
(b) $2HgO(s) \longrightarrow 2Hg(l) + O_2(g)$
(c) $H_2(g) \longrightarrow 2H(g)$
(d) $U(s) + 3F_2(g) \longrightarrow UF_6(s)$

Gibbs Free Energy
Review Questions

18.15 Define free energy. What are its units?

18.16 Why is it more convenient to predict the direction of a reaction in terms of ΔG_{sys} instead of ΔS_{univ}? Under what conditions can ΔG_{sys} be used to predict the spontaneity of a reaction?

Problems

18.17 Calculate $\Delta G°$ for the following reactions at 25°C:
(a) $N_2(g) + O_2(g) \longrightarrow 2NO(g)$
(b) $H_2O(l) \longrightarrow H_2O(g)$
(c) $2C_2H_2(g) + 5O_2(g) \longrightarrow 4CO_2(g) + 2H_2O(l)$
(*Hint:* Look up the standard free energies of formation of the reactants and products in Appendix 3.)

18.18 Calculate $\Delta G°$ for the following reactions at 25°C:
(a) $2Mg(s) + O_2(g) \longrightarrow 2MgO(s)$
(b) $2SO_2(g) + O_2(g) \longrightarrow 2SO_3(g)$
(c) $2C_2H_6(g) + 7O_2(g) \longrightarrow 4CO_2(g) + 6H_2O(l)$
See Appendix 3 for thermodynamic data.

18.19 From the values of ΔH and ΔS, predict which of the following reactions would be spontaneous at 25°C: Reaction A: $\Delta H = 10.5$ kJ/mol, $\Delta S = 30$ J/K · mol; reaction B: $\Delta H = 1.8$ kJ/mol, $\Delta S = -113$ J/K · mol. If either of the reactions is nonspontaneous at 25°C, at what temperature might it become spontaneous?

18.20 Find the temperatures at which reactions with the following ΔH and ΔS values would become spontaneous: (a) $\Delta H = -126$ kJ/mol, $\Delta S = 84$ J/K · mol; (b) $\Delta H = -11.7$ kJ/mol, $\Delta S = -105$ J/K · mol.

Free Energy and Chemical Equilibrium
Review Questions

18.21 Explain the difference between ΔG and $\Delta G°$.

18.22 Explain why Equation (18.14) is of great importance in chemistry.

Problems

18.23 Calculate K_P for the following reaction at 25°C:
$$H_2(g) + I_2(g) \rightleftharpoons 2HI(g) \quad \Delta G° = 2.60 \text{ kJ/mol}$$

18.24 For the autoionization of water at 25°C,
$$H_2O(l) \rightleftharpoons H^+(aq) + OH^-(aq)$$
K_w is 1.0×10^{-14}. What is $\Delta G°$ for the process?

18.25 Consider the following reaction at 25°C:
$$Fe(OH)_2(s) \rightleftharpoons Fe^{2+}(aq) + 2OH^-(aq)$$
Calculate $\Delta G°$ for the reaction. K_{sp} for $Fe(OH)_2$ is 1.6×10^{-14}.

18.26 Calculate $\Delta G°$ and K_P for the following equilibrium reaction at 25°C.
$$2H_2O(g) \rightleftharpoons 2H_2(g) + O_2(g)$$

18.27 (a) Calculate $\Delta G°$ and K_P for the following equilibrium reaction at 25°C. The $\Delta G_f°$ values are 0 for $Cl_2(g)$, -286 kJ/mol for $PCl_3(g)$, and -325 kJ/mol for $PCl_5(g)$.
$$PCl_5(g) \rightleftharpoons PCl_3(g) + Cl_2(g)$$
(b) Calculate ΔG for the reaction if the partial pressures of the initial mixture are $P_{PCl_5} = 0.0029$ atm, $P_{PCl_3} = 0.27$ atm, and $P_{Cl_2} = 0.40$ atm.

18.28 The equilibrium constant (K_P) for the reaction
$$H_2(g) + CO_2(g) \rightleftharpoons H_2O(g) + CO(g)$$
is 4.40 at 2000 K. (a) Calculate $\Delta G°$ for the reaction. (b) Calculate ΔG for the reaction when the partial pressures are $P_{H_2} = 0.25$ atm, $P_{CO_2} = 0.78$ atm, $P_{H_2O} = 0.66$ atm, and $P_{CO} = 1.20$ atm.

18.29 Consider the decomposition of calcium carbonate:
$$CaCO_3(s) \rightleftharpoons CaO(s) + CO_2(g)$$
Calculate the pressure in atm of CO_2 in an equilibrium process (a) at 25°C and (b) at 800°C. Assume that $\Delta H° = 177.8$ kJ/mol and $\Delta S° = 160.5$ J/K · mol for the temperature range.

18.30 The equilibrium constant K_P for the reaction
$$CO(g) + Cl_2(g) \rightleftharpoons COCl_2(g)$$
is 5.62×10^{35} at 25°C. Calculate $\Delta G_f°$ for $COCl_2$ at 25°C.

18.31 At 25°C, $\Delta G°$ for the process
$$H_2O(l) \rightleftharpoons H_2O(g)$$
is 8.6 kJ/mol. Calculate the vapor pressure of water at this temperature.

18.32 Calculate $\Delta G°$ for the process
$$C(\text{diamond}) \longrightarrow C(\text{graphite})$$
Is the formation of graphite from diamond favored at 25°C? If so, why is it that diamonds do not become graphite on standing?

Thermodynamics in Living Systems
Review Questions

18.33 What is a coupled reaction? What is its importance in biological reactions?

18.34 What is the role of ATP in biological reactions?

Problems

18.35 Referring to the metabolic process involving glucose on p. 808, calculate the maximum number of moles of ATP that can be synthesized from ADP from the breakdown of one mole of glucose.

18.36 In the metabolism of glucose, the first step is the conversion of glucose to glucose 6-phosphate:

glucose + $H_3PO_4 \longrightarrow$ glucose 6-phosphate + H_2O
$$\Delta G° = 13.4 \text{ kJ/mol}$$

Because $\Delta G°$ is positive, this reaction does not favor the formation of products. Show how this reaction can be made to proceed by coupling it with the hydrolysis of ATP. Write an equation for the coupled reaction and estimate the equilibrium constant for the coupled process.

Additional Problems

18.37 Explain the following nursery rhyme in terms of the second law of thermodynamics.

Humpty Dumpty sat on a wall;

Humpty Dumpty had a great fall.

All the King's horses and all the King's men

Couldn't put Humpty together again.

18.38 Calculate ΔG for the reaction

$$H_2O(l) \rightleftharpoons H^+(aq) + OH^-(aq)$$

at 25°C for the following conditions:
(a) $[H^+] = 1.0 \times 10^{-7} M$, $[OH^-] = 1.0 \times 10^{-7} M$
(b) $[H^+] = 1.0 \times 10^{-3} M$, $[OH^-] = 1.0 \times 10^{-4} M$
(c) $[H^+] = 1.0 \times 10^{-12} M$, $[OH^-] = 2.0 \times 10^{-8} M$
(d) $[H^+] = 3.5 M$, $[OH^-] = 4.8 \times 10^{-4} M$

18.39 Which of the following thermodynamic functions are associated only with the first law of thermodynamics: S, E, G, and H?

18.40 A student placed 1 g of each of three compounds A, B, and C in a container and found that after 1 week no change had occurred. Offer some possible explanations for the fact that no reactions took place. Assume that A, B, and C are totally miscible liquids.

18.41 Use the data in Appendix 3 to calculate the equilibrium constant for the reaction $AgI(s) \rightleftharpoons Ag^+(aq) + I^-(aq)$ at 25°C. Compare your result with the K_{sp} value in Table 16.2.

18.42 Predict the signs of ΔH, ΔS, and ΔG of the system for the following processes at 1 atm: (a) ammonia melts at $-60°C$, (b) ammonia melts at $-77.7°C$, (c) ammonia melts at $-100°C$. (The normal melting point of ammonia is $-77.7°C$.)

18.43 Consider the following facts: Water freezes spontaneously at $-5°C$ and 1 atm, and ice has a more ordered structure than liquid water. Explain how a spontaneous process can lead to a decrease in entropy.

18.44 Ammonium nitrate (NH_4NO_3) dissolves spontaneously and endothermically in water. What can you deduce about the sign of ΔS for the solution process?

18.45 Calculate the equilibrium pressure of CO_2 due to the decomposition of barium carbonate ($BaCO_3$) at 25°C.

18.46 (a) Trouton's rule states that the ratio of the molar heat of vaporization of a liquid (ΔH_{vap}) to its boiling point in kelvins is approximately 90 J/K · mol. Use the following data to show that this is the case and explain why Trouton's rule holds true:

	$t_{bp}(°C)$	$\Delta H_{vap}(\text{kJ/mol})$
Benzene	80.1	31.0
Hexane	68.7	30.8
Mercury	357	59.0
Toluene	110.6	35.2

(b) Use the values in Table 11.6 to calculate the same ratio for ethanol and water. Explain why Trouton's rule does not apply to these two substances as well as it does to other liquids.

18.47 Referring to Problem 18.46, explain why the ratio is considerably smaller than 90 J/K · mol for liquid HF.

18.48 Carbon monoxide (CO) and nitric oxide (NO) are polluting gases contained in automobile exhaust. Under suitable conditions, these gases can be made to react to form nitrogen (N_2) and the less harmful carbon dioxide (CO_2). (a) Write an equation for this reaction. (b) Identify the oxidizing and reducing agents. (c) Calculate the K_P for the reaction at 25°C. (d) Under normal atmospheric conditions, the partial pressures are $P_{N_2} = 0.80$ atm, $P_{CO_2} = 3.0 \times 10^{-4}$ atm, $P_{CO} = 5.0 \times 10^{-5}$ atm, and $P_{NO} = 5.0 \times 10^{-7}$ atm. Calculate Q_P and predict the direction toward which the reaction will proceed. (e) Will raising the temperature favor the formation of N_2 and CO_2?

18.49 For reactions carried out under standard-state conditions, Equation (18.10) takes the form $\Delta G° = \Delta H° - T\Delta S°$. (a) Assuming $\Delta H°$ and $\Delta S°$ are independent of temperature, derive the equation

$$\ln \frac{K_2}{K_1} = \frac{\Delta H°}{R}\left(\frac{T_2 - T_1}{T_1 T_2}\right)$$

where K_1 and K_2 are the equilibrium constants at T_1 and T_2, respectively. (b) Given that at 25°C K_c is 4.63×10^{-3} for the reaction

$$N_2O_4(g) \rightleftharpoons 2NO_2(g) \quad \Delta H° = 58.0 \text{ kJ/mol}$$

calculate the equilibrium constant at 65°C.

18.50 The K_{sp} of AgCl is given in Table 16.2. What is its value at 60°C? [*Hint:* You need the result of Problem 18.49(a) and the data in Appendix 3 to calculate $\Delta H°$.]

18.51 Under what conditions does a substance have a standard entropy of zero? Can a substance ever have a negative standard entropy?

18.52 Water gas, a mixture of H_2 and CO, is a fuel made by reacting steam with red-hot coke (a by-product of coal distillation):

$$H_2O(g) + C(s) \rightleftharpoons CO(g) + H_2(g)$$

From the data in Appendix 3, estimate the temperature at which the reaction begins to favor the formation of products.

18.53 Consider the following Brønstead acid-base reaction at 25°C:

$$HF(aq) + Cl^-(aq) \rightleftharpoons HCl(aq) + F^-(aq)$$

(a) Predict whether K will be greater or smaller than unity. (b) Does $\Delta S°$ or $\Delta H°$ make a greater contribution to $\Delta G°$? (c) Is $\Delta H°$ likely to be positive or negative?

18.54 Crystallization of sodium acetate from a supersaturated solution occurs spontaneously (see p. 504). What can you deduce about the signs of ΔS and ΔH?

18.55 Consider the thermal decomposition of $CaCO_3$:

$$CaCO_3(s) \rightleftharpoons CaO(s) + CO_2(g)$$

The equilibrium vapor pressures of CO_2 are 22.6 mmHg at 700°C and 1829 mmHg at 950°C. Calculate the standard enthalpy of the reaction. [*Hint:* See Problem 18.49(a).]

18.56 A certain reaction is spontaneous at 72°C. If the enthalpy change for the reaction is 19 kJ/mol, what is the *minimum* value of ΔS (in J/K · mol) for the reaction?

18.57 Predict whether the entropy change is positive or negative for each of these reactions:
(a) $Zn(s) + 2HCl(aq) \longrightarrow ZnCl_2(aq) + H_2(g)$
(b) $O(g) + O(g) \longrightarrow O_2(g)$
(c) $NH_4NO_3(s) \longrightarrow N_2O(g) + 2H_2O(g)$
(d) $2H_2O_2(l) \longrightarrow 2H_2O(l) + O_2(g)$

18.58 The reaction $NH_3(g) + HCl(g) \longrightarrow NH_4Cl(s)$ proceeds spontaneously at 25°C even though there is a decrease in disorder in the system (gases are converted to a solid). Explain.

18.59 Use the following data to determine the normal boiling point, in kelvins, of mercury. What assumptions must you make in order to do the calculation?

Hg(l):	$\Delta H_f° = 0$ (by definition)
	$S° = 77.4$ J/K · mol
Hg(g):	$\Delta H_f° = 60.78$ kJ/mol
	$S° = 174.7$ J/K · mol

18.60 The molar heat of vaporization of ethanol is 39.3 kJ/mol and the boiling point of ethanol is 78.3°C. Calculate ΔS for the vaporization of 0.50 mol ethanol.

18.61 A certain reaction is known to have a $\Delta G°$ value of −122 kJ/mol. Will the reaction necessarily occur if the reactants are mixed together?

18.62 In the Mond process for the purification of nickel, carbon monoxide is reacted with heated nickel to produce $Ni(CO)_4$, which is a gas and can therefore be separated from solid impurities:

$$Ni(s) + 4CO(g) \rightleftharpoons Ni(CO)_4(g)$$

Given that the standard free energies of formation of CO(g) and $Ni(CO)_4(g)$ are −137.3 kJ/mol and −587.4 kJ/mol, respectively, calculate the equilibrium constant of the reaction at 80°C. Assume that $\Delta G_f°$ is temperature independent.

18.63 Calculate $\Delta G°$ and K_P for the following processes at 25°C:
(a) $H_2(g) + Br_2(l) \rightleftharpoons 2HBr(g)$
(b) $\frac{1}{2}H_2(g) + \frac{1}{2}Br_2(l) \rightleftharpoons HBr(g)$
Account for the differences in $\Delta G°$ and K_P obtained for (a) and (b).

18.64 Calculate the pressure of O_2 (in atm) over a sample of NiO at 25°C if $\Delta G° = 212$ kJ/mol for the reaction

$$NiO(s) \rightleftharpoons Ni(s) + \frac{1}{2}O_2(g)$$

18.65 Comment on the statement: "Just talking about entropy increases its value in the universe."

18.66 For a reaction with a negative $\Delta G°$ value, which of the following statements is false? (a) The equilibrium constant K is greater than one, (b) the reaction is spontaneous when all the reactants and products are in their standard states, and (c) the reaction is always exothermic.

18.67 Consider the reaction

$$N_2(g) + O_2(g) \rightleftharpoons 2NO(g)$$

Given that $\Delta G°$ for the reaction at 25°C is 173.4 kJ/mol, (a) calculate the standard free energy of formation of NO, and (b) calculate K_P of the reaction. (c) One of the starting substances in smog formation is NO. Assuming that the temperature in a running automobile engine is 1100°C, estimate K_P for the above reaction. (d) As farmers know, lightning helps to produce a better crop. Why?

18.68 Heating copper(II) oxide at 400°C does not produce any appreciable amount of Cu:

$$CuO(s) \rightleftharpoons Cu(s) + \frac{1}{2}O_2(g) \qquad \Delta G° = 127.2 \text{ kJ/mol}$$

However, if this reaction is coupled to the conversion of graphite to carbon monoxide, it becomes spontaneous. Write an equation for the coupled process and calculate the equilibrium constant for the coupled reaction.

18.69 The internal engine of a 1200-kg car is designed to run on octane (C_8H_{18}), whose enthalpy of combustion is 5510 kJ/mol. If the car is moving up a slope, calculate the maximum height (in meters) to which the car can be driven on 1.0 gallon of the fuel. Assume that the engine cylinder temperature is 2200°C and the exit temperature is 760°C, and neglect all forms of friction. The mass of 1 gallon of fuel is 3.1 kg. [*Hint:* See the Chemistry in Action essay on p. 796. The work done in moving the car over a vertical distance is *mgh,* where *m* is the mass of the car in kg, *g* the acceleration due to gravity (9.81 m/s^2), and *h* the height in meters.]

18.70 Consider the decomposition of magnesium carbonate:

$$MgCO_3(s) \rightleftharpoons MgO(s) + CO_2(g)$$

Calculate the temperature at which the decomposition begins to favor products. Assume that both $\Delta H°$ and $\Delta S°$ are independent of temperature.

18.71 (a) Over the years there have been numerous claims about "perpetual motion machines," machines that will produce useful work with no input of energy. Explain why the first law of thermodynamics prohibits the possibility of such a machine existing. (b) Another kind of machine, sometimes called a "perpetual motion of the second kind," operates as follows. Suppose an ocean liner sails by scooping up water from the ocean and then extracting heat from the water, converting the heat to electric power to run the ship, and dumping the water back into the ocean. This process does not violate the first law of thermodynamics, for no energy is created—energy from the ocean is just converted to electrical energy. Show that the second law of thermodynamics prohibits the existence of such a machine.

18.72 The activity series in Section 4.4 shows that reaction (a) is spontaneous while reaction (b) is nonspontaneous at 25°C:

(a) $Fe(s) + 2H^+ \longrightarrow Fe^{2+}(aq) + H_2(g)$
(b) $Cu(s) + 2H^+ \longrightarrow Cu^{2+}(aq) + H_2(g)$

Use the data in Appendix 3 to calculate the equilibrium constant for these reactions and hence confirm that the activity series is correct.

18.73 The rate constant for the elementary reaction

$$2NO(g) + O_2(g) \longrightarrow 2NO_2(g)$$

is $7.1 \times 10^9/M^2 \cdot s$ at 25°C. What is the rate constant for the reverse reaction at the same temperature?

18.74 The following reaction was described as the cause of sulfur deposits formed at volcanic sites (see p. 762):

$$2H_2S(g) + SO_2(g) \rightleftharpoons 3S(s) + 2H_2O(g)$$

It may also be used to remove SO_2 from powerplant stack gases. (a) Identify the type of redox reaction it is. (b) Calculate the equilibrium constant (K_P) at 25°C and comment on whether this method is feasible for removing SO_2. (c) Would this procedure become more or less effective at a higher temperature?

18.75 Describe two ways that you could measure $\Delta G°$ of a reaction.

18.76 The following reaction represents the removal of ozone in the stratosphere:

$$2O_3(g) \rightleftharpoons 3O_2(g)$$

Calculate the equilibrium constant (K_P) for the reaction. In view of the magnitude of the equilibrium constant, explain why this reaction is not considered a major cause of ozone depletion in the absence of man-made pollutants such as the nitrogen oxides and CFCs? Assume the temperature of the stratosphere to be $-30°C$ and $\Delta G_f°$ to be temperature independent.

18.77 A 74.6-g ice cube floats in the Arctic Sea. The temperature and pressure of the system and surroundings are at 1 atm and 0°C. Calculate ΔS_{sys}, ΔS_{surr}, and ΔS_{univ} for the melting of the ice cube. What can you conclude about the nature of the process from the value of ΔS_{univ}? (The molar heat of fusion of water is 6.01 kJ/mol.)

18.78 Comment on the feasibility of extracting copper from its ore chalcocite (Cu_2S) by heating:

$$Cu_2S(s) \longrightarrow 2Cu(s) + S(s)$$

Calculate the $\Delta G°$ for the overall reaction if the above process is coupled to the conversion of sulfur to sulfur dioxide. Given that $\Delta G_f°(Cu_2S) = -86.1$ kJ/mol.

18.79 Active transport is the process in which a substance is transferred from a region of lower concentration to one of higher concentration. This is a nonspontaneous process and must be coupled to a spontaneous process, such as the hydrolysis of ATP. The concentrations of K^+ ions in the blood plasma and in nerve cells are 15 mM and 400 mM, respectively (1 m$M = 1 \times 10^{-3}$ M). Use Equation (18.13) to calculate ΔG for the process at the physiological temperature of 37°C:

$$K^+(15\ mM) \longrightarrow K^+(400\ mM)$$

In this calculation, the $\Delta G°$ term can be set to zero. What is the justification for this step?

18.80 Large quantities of hydrogen are needed for the synthesis of ammonia. One preparation of hydrogen involves the reaction between carbon monoxide and steam at 300°C in the presence of a copper-zinc catalyst:

$$CO(g) + H_2O(g) \rightleftharpoons CO_2(g) + H_2(g)$$

Calculate the equilibrium constant (K_P) for the reaction and the temperature at which the reaction favors the formation of CO and H_2O. Will a larger K_P be attained at the same temperature if a more efficient catalyst is used?

18.81 Consider two carboxylic acids (acids that contain the —COOH group): CH_3COOH (acetic acid, $K_a = 1.8 \times 10^{-5}$) and $CH_2ClCOOH$ (chloroacetic acid, $K_a = 1.4 \times 10^{-3}$). (a) Calculate $\Delta G°$ for the ionization of these acids at 25°C. (b) From the equation $\Delta G° = \Delta H° - T\Delta S°$, we see that the contributions to the $\Delta G°$ term are an enthalpy term ($\Delta H°$) and a temperature times entropy term ($T\Delta S°$).

These contributions are listed below for the two acids:

	$\Delta H°$(kJ/mol)	$T\Delta S°$(kJ/mol)
CH_3COOH	−0.57	−27.6
$CH_2ClCOOH$	−4.7	−21.1

Which is the dominant term in determining the value of $\Delta G°$ (and hence K_a of the acid)? (c) What processes contribute to $\Delta H°$? (Consider the ionization of the acids as a Brønsted acid-base reaction.) (d) Explain why the $T\Delta S°$ term is more negative for CH_3COOH.

18.82 Many hydrocarbons exist as structural isomers, which are compounds that have the same molecular formula but different structures. For example, both butane and isobutane have the same molecular formula of C_4H_{10} (see Problem 11.19 on p. 494). Calculate the mole percent of these molecules in an equilibrium mixture at 25°C, given that the standard free energy of formation of butane is −15.9 kJ/mol and that of isobutane is −18.0 kJ/mol. Does your result support the notion that straight-chain hydrocarbons (that is, hydrocarbons in which the C atoms are joined along a line) are less stable than branch-chain hydrocarbons?

18.83 A rubber band is stretched vertically by attaching a weight to one end and holding the other end by hand. On heating the rubber band with a hot-air blower, it is observed to shrink slightly in length. Give a thermodynamic analysis for this behavior. (*Hint:* See the Chemistry in Action essay on p. 807.)

18.84 One of the steps in the extraction of iron from its ore (FeO) is the reduction of iron(II) oxide by carbon monoxide at 900°C:

$$FeO(s) + CO(g) \rightleftharpoons Fe(s) + CO_2(g)$$

If CO is allowed to react with an excess of FeO, calculate the mole fractions of CO and CO_2 at equilibrium. State any assumptions.

18.85 Derive the following equation

$$\Delta G = RT \ln (Q/K)$$

where Q is the reaction quotient and describe how you would use it to predict the spontaneity of a reaction.

18.86 The sublimation of carbon dioxide at −78°C is

$$CO_2(s) \longrightarrow CO_2(g) \quad \Delta H_{sub} = 25.2 \text{ kJ/mol}$$

Calculate ΔS_{sub} when 84.8 g of CO_2 sublimes at this temperature.

18.87 Entropy has sometimes been described as "time's arrow" because it is the property that determines the forward direction of time. Explain.

18.88 Referring to Figure 18.1, we see that the probability of finding all 100 molecules in the same flask is 8×10^{-31}. Assuming that the age of the universe is 13 billion years, calculate the time in seconds during which this event can be observed.

18.89 A student looked up the $\Delta G_f°$, $\Delta H_f°$, and $S°$ values for CO_2 in Appendix 3. Plugging these values into Equation (18.10), he found that $\Delta G_f° \neq \Delta H_f° - TS°$ at 298 K. What is wrong with his approach?

18.90 Consider the following reaction at 298 K:

$$2H_2(g) + O_2(g) \longrightarrow 2H_2O(l) \quad \Delta H° = -571.6 \text{ kJ/mol}$$

Calculate ΔS_{sys}, ΔS_{surr}, and ΔS_{univ} for the reaction.

18.91 As an approximation, we can assume that proteins exist either in the native (or physiologically functioning) state and the denatured state

$$\text{native} \rightleftharpoons \text{denatured}$$

The standard molar enthalpy and entropy of the denaturation of a certain protein are 512 kJ/mol and 1.60 kJ/K · mol, respectively. Comment on the signs and magnitudes of these quantities, and calculate the temperature at which the process favors the denatured state.

18.92 Which of the following are not state functions: S, H, q, w, T?

18.93 Which of the following is not accompanied by an increase in the entropy of the system? (a) mixing of two gases at the same temperature and pressure, (b) mixing of ethanol and water, (c) discharging a battery, (d) expansion of a gas followed by compression to its original temperature, pressure, and volume.

18.94 Hydrogenation reactions (for example, the process of converting C=C bonds to C—C bonds in food industry) are facilitated by the use of a transition metal catalyst, such as Ni or Pt. The initial step is the adsorption, or binding, of hydrogen gas onto the metal surface. Predict the signs of ΔH, ΔS, and ΔG when hydrogen gas is adsorbed onto the surface of Ni metal.

Special Problems

18.95 Give a detailed example of each of the following, with an explanation: (a) a thermodynamically spontaneous process; (b) a process that would violate the first law of thermodynamics; (c) a process that would violate the second law of thermodynamics; (d) an irreversible process; (e) an equilibrium process.

18.96 At 0 K, the entropy of carbon monoxide crystal is not zero but has a value of 4.2 J/K · mol, called the residual entropy. According to the third law of thermodynamics, this means that the crystal does not have a perfect arrangement of the CO molecules. (a) What would be the residual entropy if the arrangement were totally random? (b) Comment on the difference between the result in (a) and 4.2 J/K · mol. [*Hint:* Assume that each CO molecule has two choices for orientation and use Equation (18.1) to calculate the residual entropy.]

18.97 Comment on the correctness of the analogy sometimes used to relate a student's dormitory room becoming untidy to an increase in entropy.

18.98 The standard enthalpy of formation and the standard entropy of gaseous benzene are 82.93 kJ/mol and 269.2 J/K · mol, respectively. Calculate $\Delta H°$, $\Delta S°$, and $\Delta G°$ for the process at 25°C. Comment on your answers.

$$C_6H_6(l) \longrightarrow C_6H_6(g)$$

18.99 In chemistry, the standard state for a solution is 1 M (see Table 18.2). This means that each solute concentration expressed in molarity is divided by 1 M. In biological systems, however, we define the standard state for the H^+ ions to be 1×10^{-7} M because the physiological pH is about 7. Consequently, the change in the standard Gibbs free energy according to these two conventions will be different involving uptake or release of H^+ ions, depending on which convention is used. We will therefore replace $\Delta G°$ with $\Delta G°'$, where the prime denotes that it is the standard Gibbs free-energy change for a biological process. (a) Consider the reaction

$$A + B \longrightarrow C + xH^+$$

where x is a stoichiometric coefficient. Use Equation (18.13) to derive a relation between $\Delta G°$ and $\Delta G°'$, keeping in mind that ΔG is the same for a process regardless of which convention is used. Repeat the derivation for the reverse process:

$$C + xH^+ \longrightarrow A + B$$

(b) NAD^+ and NADH are the oxidized and reduced forms of nicotinamide adenine dinucleotide, two key compounds in the metabolic pathways. For the oxidation of NADH

$$NADH + H^+ \longrightarrow NAD^+ + H_2$$

$\Delta G°$ is -21.8 kJ/mol at 298 K. Calculate $\Delta G°'$. Also calculate ΔG using both the chemical and biological conventions when [NADH] = 1.5×10^{-2} M, $[H^+]$ = 3.0×10^{-5} M, [NAD] = 4.6×10^{-3} M, and P_{H_2} = 0.010 atm.

18.100 The following diagram shows the variation of the equilibrium constant with temperature for the reaction

$$I_2(g) \rightleftharpoons 2I(g)$$

Calculate $\Delta G°$, $\Delta H°$, and $\Delta S°$ for the reaction at 872 K. (*Hint:* See Problem 18.49.)

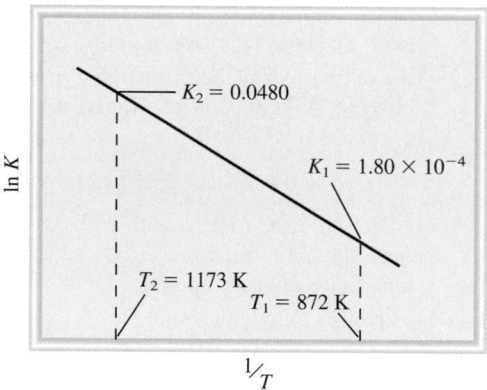

Answers to Practice Exercises

18.1 (a) Entropy decreases, (b) entropy decreases, (c) entropy increases, (d) entropy increases. **18.2** (a) -173.6 J/K · mol, (b) -139.8 J/K · mol, (c) 215.3 J/K · mol.
18.3 (a) $\Delta S > 0$, (b) $\Delta S < 0$, (c) $\Delta S \approx 0$.
18.4 (a) -106.4 kJ/mol, (b) -2935.0 kJ/mol.
18.5 $\Delta S_{\text{fus}} = 16$ J/K · mol; $\Delta S_{\text{vap}} = 72$ J/K · mol.
18.6 2×10^{57}. **18.7** 33 kJ/mol. **18.8** $\Delta G = 0.97$ kJ/mol; direction is from right to left.

19

Hydrogen gas generated from an illuminated photoelectrode. Using light energy to produce hydrogen from water can play an important role in the development of fuel cells. The models show water, hydrogen, and oxygen molecules.

Electrochemistry

A LOOK AHEAD

- We begin with a review of redox reactions and learn how to balance equations describing these processes. (19.1)

- Next, we examine the essentials of galvanic cells. (19.2)

- We learn to determine the standard reduction potentials based on the standard hydrogen electrode reference and use them to calculate the emf of a cell and hence the spontaneity of a cell reaction. A relationship exists between a cell's emf, the change in the standard Gibbs energy, and the equilibrium constant for the cell reaction. (19.3 and 19.4)

- We see that the emf of a cell under nonstandard state conditions can be calculated using the Nernst equation. (19.5)

- We examine several common types of batteries and the operation of fuel cells. (19.6)

- We then study a spontaneous electrochemical process—corrosion—and learn ways to prevent it. (19.7)

- Finally, we explore nonspontaneous electrochemical reactions or electrolysis and learn the quantitative aspects of electrolytic processes. (19.8)

Interactive Activity Summary

1. Interactivity: Redox Reactions—Oxidation States for Nitrogen (19.1)

2. Interactivity: Redox Reactions—Oxidized or Reduced? (19.1)

3. Animation: Galvanic Cells (19.2)

One form of energy that has tremendous practical significance is electrical energy. A day without electricity from either the power company or batteries is unimaginable in our technological society. The area of chemistry that deals with the interconversion of electrical energy and chemical energy is electrochemistry.

Electrochemical processes are redox reactions in which the energy released by a spontaneous reaction is converted to electricity or in which electricity is used to drive a nonspontaneous chemical reaction. The latter type is called electrolysis.

This chapter explains the fundamental principles and applications of galvanic cells, the thermodynamics of electrochemical reactions, and the cause and prevention of corrosion by electrochemical means. Some simple electrolytic processes and the quantitative aspects of electrolysis are also discussed.

19.1 Redox Reactions

Electrochemistry is the branch of chemistry that deals with the interconversion of electrical energy and chemical energy. Electrochemical processes are redox (oxidation-reduction) reactions in which the energy released by a spontaneous reaction is converted to electricity or in which electrical energy is used to cause a nonspontaneous reaction to occur. Although redox reactions were discussed in Chapter 4, it is helpful to review some of the basic concepts that will come up again in this chapter.

In redox reactions electrons are transferred from one substance to another. The reaction between magnesium metal and hydrochloric acid is an example of a redox reaction:

$$\overset{0}{Mg}(s) + 2\overset{+1}{HCl}(aq) \longrightarrow \overset{+2}{MgCl_2}(aq) + \overset{0}{H_2}(g)$$

Recall that the numbers above the elements are the oxidation numbers of the elements. The loss of electrons by an element during oxidation is marked by an increase in the element's oxidation number. In reduction, there is a decrease in oxidation number resulting from a gain of electrons by an element. In the preceding reaction Mg metal is oxidized and H^+ ions are reduced; the Cl^- ions are spectator ions.

Balancing Redox Equations

Interactivity:
Redox Reactions—Oxidation
States for Nitrogen
ARIS, Interactives

Interactivity:
Redox Reactions—Oxidized
or Reduced?
ARIS, Interactives

Equations for redox reactions like the preceding one are relatively easy to balance. However, in the laboratory we often encounter more complex redox reactions involving oxoanions such as chromate (CrO_4^{2-}), dichromate ($Cr_2O_7^{2-}$), permanganate (MnO_4^-), nitrate (NO_3^-), and sulfate (SO_4^{2-}). In principle, we can balance any redox equation using the procedure outlined in Section 3.7, but there are some special techniques for handling redox reactions, techniques that also give us insight into electron transfer processes. Here we will discuss one such procedure, called the *ion-electron method*. In this approach, the overall reaction is divided into two half-reactions, one for oxidation and one for reduction. The equations for the two half-reactions are balanced separately and then added together to give the overall balanced equation.

Suppose we are asked to balance the equation showing the oxidation of Fe^{2+} ions to Fe^{3+} ions by dichromate ions ($Cr_2O_7^{2-}$) in an acidic medium. As a result, the $Cr_2O_7^{2-}$ ions are reduced to Cr^{3+} ions. The following steps will help us balance the equation.

Step 1: Write the unbalanced equation for the reaction in ionic form.

$$Fe^{2+} + Cr_2O_7^{2-} \longrightarrow Fe^{3+} + Cr^{3+}$$

Step 2: Separate the equation into two half-reactions.

$$\text{Oxidation:} \quad \overset{+2}{Fe^{2+}} \longrightarrow \overset{+3}{Fe^{3+}}$$

$$\text{Reduction:} \ \overset{+6}{Cr_2O_7^{2-}} \longrightarrow \overset{+3}{Cr^{3+}}$$

Step 3: Balance each half-reaction for number and type of atoms and charges. For reactions in an acidic medium, add H_2O to balance the O atoms and H^+ to balance the H atoms.

Oxidation half-reaction: The atoms are already balanced. To balance the charge, we add an electron to the right-hand side of the arrow:

In an oxidation half-reaction, electrons appear as a product; in a reduction half-reaction, electrons appear as a reactant.

$$Fe^{2+} \longrightarrow Fe^{3+} + e^-$$

Reduction half-reaction: Because the reaction takes place in an acidic medium, we add seven H_2O molecules to the right-hand side of the arrow to balance the O atoms:

$$Cr_2O_7^{2-} \longrightarrow 2Cr^{3+} + 7H_2O$$

To balance the H atoms, we add 14 H^+ ions on the left-hand side:

$$14H^+ + Cr_2O_7^{2-} \longrightarrow 2Cr^{3+} + 7H_2O$$

There are now 12 positive charges on the left-hand side and only six positive charges on the right-hand side. Therefore, we add six electrons on the left

$$14H^+ + Cr_2O_7^{2-} + 6e^- \longrightarrow 2Cr^{3+} + 7H_2O$$

Step 4: Add the two half-equations together and balance the final equation by inspection. The electrons on both sides must cancel. If the oxidation and reduction half-reactions contain different numbers of electrons, we need to multiply one or both half-reactions to equalize the number of electrons.

Here we have only one electron for the oxidation half-reaction and six electrons for the reduction half-reaction, so we need to multiply the oxidation half-reaction by 6 and write

$$6(Fe^{2+} \longrightarrow Fe^{3+} + e^-)$$
$$14H^+ + Cr_2O_7^{2-} + 6e^- \longrightarrow 2Cr^{3+} + 7H_2O$$
$$\overline{6Fe^{2+} + 14H^+ + Cr_2O_7^{2-} + 6e^- \longrightarrow 6Fe^{3+} + 2Cr^{3+} + 7H_2O + 6e^-}$$

The electrons on both sides cancel, and we are left with the balanced net ionic equation:

$$6Fe^{2+} + 14H^+ + Cr_2O_7^{2-} \longrightarrow 6Fe^{3+} + 2Cr^{3+} + 7H_2O$$

Step 5: Verify that the equation contains the same type and numbers of atoms and the same charges on both sides of the equation.

A final check shows that the resulting equation is "atomically" and "electrically" balanced.

For reactions in a basic medium, we proceed through step 4 as if the reaction were carried out in a acidic medium. Then, for every H^+ ion we add an equal number of OH^- ions to *both* sides of the equation. Where H^+ and OH^- ions appear on the same side of the equation, we combine the ions to give H_2O. Example 19.1 illustrates this procedure.

Example 19.1

Write a balanced ionic equation to represent the oxidation of iodide ion (I^-) by permanganate ion (MnO_4^-) in basic solution to yield molecular iodine (I_2) and manganese(IV) oxide (MnO_2).

Strategy We follow the preceding procedure for balancing redox equations. Note that the reaction takes place in a basic medium.

Solution *Step 1:* The unbalanced equation is

$$MnO_4^- + I^- \longrightarrow MnO_2 + I_2$$

(Continued)

Step 2: The two half-reactions are

$$\text{Oxidation:} \quad \overset{-1}{I^-} \longrightarrow \overset{0}{I_2}$$

$$\text{Reduction:} \quad \overset{+7}{MnO_4^-} \longrightarrow \overset{+4}{MnO_2}$$

Step 3: We balance each half-reaction for number and type of atoms and charges. Oxidation half-reaction: We first balance the I atoms:

$$2I^- \longrightarrow I_2$$

To balance charges, we add two electrons to the right-hand side of the equation:

$$2I^- \longrightarrow I_2 + 2e^-$$

Reduction half-reaction: To balance the O atoms, we add two H_2O molecules on the right:

$$MnO_4^- \longrightarrow MnO_2 + 2H_2O$$

To balance the H atoms, we add four H^+ ions on the left:

$$MnO_4^- + 4H^+ \longrightarrow MnO_2 + 2H_2O$$

There are three net positive charges on the left, so we add three electrons to the same side to balance the charges:

$$MnO_4^- + 4H^+ + 3e^- \longrightarrow MnO_2 + 2H_2O$$

Step 4: We now add the oxidation and reduction half reactions to give the overall reaction. In order to equalize the number of electrons, we need to multiply the oxidation half-reaction by 3 and the reduction half-reaction by 2 as follows:

$$3(2I^- \longrightarrow I_2 + 2e^-)$$
$$\underline{2(MnO_4^- + 4H^+ + 3e^- \longrightarrow MnO_2 + 2H_2O)}$$
$$6I^- + 2MnO_4^- + 8H^+ + \cancel{6e^-} \longrightarrow 3I_2 + 2MnO_2 + 4H_2O + \cancel{6e^-}$$

The electrons on both sides cancel, and we are left with the balanced net ionic equation:

$$6I^- + 2MnO_4^- + 8H^+ \longrightarrow 3I_2 + 2MnO_2 + 4H_2O$$

This is the balanced equation in an acidic medium. However, because the reaction is carried out in a basic medium, for every H^+ ion we need to add equal number of OH^- ions to both sides of the equation:

$$6I^- + 2MnO_4^- + 8H^+ + 8OH^- \longrightarrow 3I_2 + 2MnO_2 + 4H_2O + 8OH^-$$

Finally, combining the H^+ and OH^- ions to form water, we obtain

$$6I^- + 2MnO_4^- + 4H_2O \longrightarrow 3I_2 + 2MnO_2 + 8OH^-$$

Step 5: A final check shows that the equation is balanced in terms of both atoms and charges.

Similar problems: 19.1, 19.2.

Practice Exercise   Balance the following equation for the reaction in an acidic medium by the ion-electron method:

$$Fe^{2+} + MnO_4^- \longrightarrow Fe^{3+} + Mn^{2+}$$

19.2 Galvanic Cells

In Section 4.4 we saw that when a piece of zinc metal is placed in a $CuSO_4$ solution, Zn is oxidized to Zn^{2+} ions while Cu^{2+} ions are reduced to metallic copper (see Figure 4.10):

$$Zn(s) + Cu^{2+}(aq) \longrightarrow Zn^{2+}(aq) + Cu(s)$$

The electrons are transferred directly from the reducing agent (Zn) to the oxidizing agent (Cu^{2+}) in solution. However, if we physically separate the oxidizing agent from the reducing agent, the transfer of electrons can take place via an external conducting medium (a metal wire). As the reaction progresses, it sets up a constant flow of electrons and hence generates electricity (that is, it produces electrical work such as driving an electric motor).

The experimental apparatus for generating electricity through the use of a spontaneous reaction is called a **galvanic cell** or *voltaic cell,* after the Italian scientists Luigi Galvani and Alessandro Volta, who constructed early versions of the device. Figure 19.1 shows the essential components of a galvanic cell. A zinc bar is immersed in a $ZnSO_4$ solution, and a copper bar is immersed in a $CuSO_4$ solution. The cell

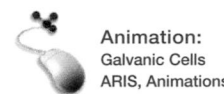

Animation:
Galvanic Cells
ARIS, Animations

Voltmeter

e^- e^-

Zinc anode $\leftarrow$ Cl$^-$ K$^+$ $\rightarrow$ Copper cathode

Salt bridge

Cotton plugs

Cu^{2+}

Zn^{2+} SO_4^{2-}

ZnSO$_4$ solution   CuSO$_4$ solution

$2e^-$

Zn Zn^{2+}

Cu^{2+}

$2e^-$

Cu

Zn is oxidized
to Zn^{2+} at anode.

$$Zn(s) \longrightarrow Zn^{2+}(aq) + 2e^-$$

Cu^{2+} is reduced
to Cu at cathode.

$$2e^- + Cu^{2+}(aq) \longrightarrow Cu(s)$$

Net reaction

$$Zn(s) + Cu^{2+}(aq) \longrightarrow Zn^{2+}(aq) + Cu(s)$$

Figure 19.1 *A galvanic cell. The salt bridge (an inverted U tube) containing a KCl solution provides an electrically conducting medium between two solutions. The openings of the U tube are loosely plugged with cotton balls to prevent the KCl solution from flowing into the containers while allowing the anions and cations to move across. Electrons flow externally from the Zn electrode (anode) to the Cu electrode (cathode).*

operates on the principle that the oxidation of Zn to Zn^{2+} and the reduction of Cu^{2+} to Cu can be made to take place simultaneously in separate locations with the transfer of electrons between them occurring through an external wire. The zinc and copper bars are called *electrodes*. This particular arrangement of electrodes (Zn and Cu) and solutions ($ZnSO_4$ and $CuSO_4$) is called the Daniell cell. By definition, the **anode** in a galvanic cell is *the electrode at which oxidation occurs* and the **cathode** is *the electrode at which reduction occurs.*

For the Daniell cell, the **half-cell reactions,** that is, *the oxidation and reduction reactions at the electrodes,* are

Zn electrode (anode): $\quad Zn(s) \longrightarrow Zn^{2+}(aq) + 2e^-$
Cu electrode (cathode): $\quad Cu^{2+}(aq) + 2e^- \longrightarrow Cu(s)$

Note that unless the two solutions are separated from each other, the Cu^{2+} ions will react directly with the zinc bar:

$$Cu^{2+}(aq) + Zn(s) \longrightarrow Cu(s) + Zn^{2+}(aq)$$

and no useful electrical work will be obtained.

To complete the electrical circuit, the solutions must be connected by a conducting medium through which the cations and anions can move from one electrode compartment to the other. This requirement is satisfied by a *salt bridge,* which, in its simplest form, is an inverted U tube containing an inert electrolyte solution, such as KCl or NH_4NO_3, whose ions will not react with other ions in solution or with the electrodes (see Figure 19.1). During the course of the overall redox reaction, electrons flow externally from the anode (Zn electrode) through the wire and voltmeter to the cathode (Cu electrode). In the solution, the cations (Zn^{2+}, Cu^{2+}, and K^+) move toward the cathode, while the anions (SO_4^{2-} and Cl^-) move toward the anode. Without the salt bridge connecting the two solutions, the buildup of positive charge in the anode compartment (due to the formation of Zn^{2+} ions) and negative charge in the cathode compartment (created when some of the Cu^{2+} ions are reduced to Cu) would quickly prevent the cell from operating.

An electric current flows from the anode to the cathode because there is a difference in electrical potential energy between the electrodes. This flow of electric current is analogous to that of water down a waterfall, which occurs because there is a difference in gravitational potential energy, or the flow of gas from a high-pressure region to a low-pressure region. Experimentally the *difference in electrical potential between the anode and the cathode* is measured by a voltmeter (Figure 19.2) and the reading (in volts) is called **cell voltage.** However, two other terms, **electromotive force** or **emf (E)** and *cell potential* are also used to denote cell voltage. We will see that the voltage of a cell depends not only on the nature of the electrodes and the ions, but also on the concentrations of the ions and the temperature at which the cell is operated.

The conventional notation for representing galvanic cells is the *cell diagram.* For the Daniell cell shown in Figure 19.1, if we assume that the concentrations of Zn^{2+} and Cu^{2+} ions are 1 M, the cell diagram is

$$Zn(s)|Zn^{2+}(1\ M)\|Cu^{2+}(1\ M)|Cu(s)$$

The single vertical line represents a phase boundary. For example, the zinc electrode is a solid and the Zn^{2+} ions (from $ZnSO_4$) are in solution. Thus, we draw a line between Zn and Zn^{2+} to show the phase boundary. The double vertical lines denote the salt bridge. By convention, the anode is written first, to the left of the double lines

Figure 19.2 *Practical setup of the galvanic cell described in Figure 19.1. Note the U tube (salt bridge) connecting the two beakers. When the concentrations of ZnSO$_4$ and CuSO$_4$ are 1 molar (1 M) at 25°C, the cell voltage is 1.10 V.*

and the other components appear in the order in which we would encounter them in moving from the anode to the cathode.

19.3 Standard Reduction Potentials

When the concentrations of the Cu^{2+} and Zn^{2+} ions are both 1.0 M, we find that the voltage or emf of the Daniell cell is 1.10 V at 25°C (see Figure 19.2). This voltage must be related directly to the redox reactions, but how? Just as the overall cell reaction can be thought of as the sum of two half-cell reactions, the measured emf of the cell can be treated as the sum of the electrical potentials at the Zn and Cu electrodes. Knowing one of these electrode potentials, we could obtain the other by subtraction (from 1.10 V). It is impossible to measure the potential of just a single electrode, but if we arbitrarily set the potential value of a particular electrode at zero, we can use it to determine the relative potentials of other electrodes. The hydrogen electrode, shown in Figure 19.3, serves as the reference for this purpose. Hydrogen gas is bubbled into a hydrochloric acid solution at 25°C. The platinum electrode has two functions. First, it provides a surface on which the dissociation of hydrogen molecules can take place:

$$H_2 \longrightarrow 2H^+ + 2e^-$$

Second, it serves as an electrical conductor to the external circuit.

Under standard-state conditions (when the pressure of H_2 is 1 atm and the concentration of the HCl solution is 1 M; see Table 18.2), the potential for the reduction of H^+ at 25°C is taken to be *exactly* zero:

$$2H^+(1\ M) + 2e^- \longrightarrow H_2(1\ \text{atm}) \qquad\qquad E° = 0\ V$$

The superscript "°" denotes standard-state conditions, and $E°$ is the ***standard reduction potential,*** or *the voltage associated with a reduction reaction at an electrode when all solutes are 1 M and all gases are at 1 atm.* Thus, the standard reduction potential of the hydrogen electrode is defined as zero. The hydrogen electrode is called the *standard hydrogen electrode (SHE).*

We can use the SHE to measure the potentials of other kinds of electrodes. For example, Figure 19.4(a) shows a galvanic cell with a zinc electrode and a SHE. In this case the zinc electrode is the anode and the SHE is the cathode. We deduce this fact

The choice of an arbitrary reference for measuring electrode potential is analogous to choosing the surface of the ocean as the reference for altitude, calling it 0 m, and then referring to any terrestrial altitude as being a certain number of meters above or below sea level.

Standard states are defined in Table 18.2.

H$_2$ gas at 1 atm

Pt electrode

1 M HCl

Figure 19.3 *A hydrogen electrode operating under standard-state conditions. Hydrogen gas at 1 atm is bubbled through a 1 M HCl solution. The platinum electrode is part of the hydrogen electrode.*

Figure 19.4 *(a) A cell consisting of a zinc electrode and a hydrogen electrode. (b) A cell consisting of a copper electrode and a hydrogen electrode. Both cells are operating under standard-state conditions. Note that in (a) the SHE acts as the cathode, but in (b) it is the anode.*

from the decrease in mass of the zinc electrode during the operation of the cell, which is consistent with the loss of zinc to the solution caused by the oxidation reaction:

$$Zn(s) \longrightarrow Zn^{2+}(aq) + 2e^-$$

The cell diagram is

$$Zn(s)\,|\,Zn^{2+}(1\ M)\,\|\,H^+(1\ M)\,|\,H_2(1\ atm)\,|\,Pt(s)$$

As mentioned earlier, the Pt electrode provides the surface on which the reduction takes place. When all the reactants are in their standard states (that is, H_2 at 1 atm, H^+ and Zn^{2+} ions at 1 M), the emf of the cell is 0.76 V at 25°C. We can write the half-cell reactions as follows:

Anode (oxidation): $Zn(s) \longrightarrow Zn^{2+}(1\ M) + 2e^-$
Cathode (reduction): $\underline{2H^+(1\ M) + 2e^- \longrightarrow H_2(1\ atm)}$
Overall: $Zn(s) + 2H^+(1\ M) \longrightarrow Zn^{2+}(1\ M) + H_2(1\ atm)$

By convention, the ***standard emf*** of the cell, E°_{cell}, which is composed of a contribution from the anode and a contribution from the cathode, is given by

$$E^\circ_{cell} = E^\circ_{cathode} - E^\circ_{anode} \qquad (19.1)$$

where *both* $E^\circ_{cathode}$ and E°_{anode} are the standard reduction potentials of the electrodes. For the Zn-SHE cell, we write

$$E^\circ_{cell} = E^\circ_{H^+/H_2} - E^\circ_{Zn^{2+}/Zn}$$
$$0.76\ V = 0 - E^\circ_{Zn^{2+}/Zn}$$

where the subscript H^+/H_2 means $2H^+ + 2e^- \rightarrow H_2$ and the subscript Zn^{2+}/Zn means $Zn^{2+} + 2e^- \rightarrow Zn$. Thus, the standard reduction potential of zinc, $E^\circ_{Zn^{2+}/Zn}$, is -0.76 V.

The standard electrode potential of copper can be obtained in a similar fashion, by using a cell with a copper electrode and a SHE [Figure 19.4(b)]. In this case, the copper electrode is the cathode because its mass increases during the operation of the cell, as is consistent with the reduction reaction:

$$Cu^{2+}(aq) + 2e^- \longrightarrow Cu(s)$$

The cell diagram is

$$Pt(s)|H_2(1\ atm)|H^+(1\ M)\|Cu^{2+}(1\ M)|Cu(s)$$

and the half-cell reactions are

Anode (oxidation):	$H_2(1\ atm) \longrightarrow 2H^+(1\ M) + 2e^-$
Cathode (reduction):	$Cu^{2+}(1\ M) + 2e^- \longrightarrow Cu(s)$
Overall:	$H_2(1\ atm) + Cu^{2+}(1\ M) \longrightarrow 2H^+(1\ M) + Cu(s)$

Under standard-state conditions and at 25°C, the emf of the cell is 0.34 V, so we write

$$E_{cell}^{\circ} = E_{cathode}^{\circ} - E_{anode}^{\circ}$$
$$0.34\ V = E_{Cu^{2+}/Cu}^{\circ} - E_{H^+/H_2}^{\circ}$$
$$= E_{Cu^{2+}/Cu}^{\circ} - 0$$

In this case the standard reduction potential of copper, $E_{Cu^{2+}/Cu}^{\circ}$, is 0.34 V, where the subscript means $Cu^{2+} + 2e^- \rightarrow Cu$.

For the Daniell cell shown in Figure 19.1, we can now write

Anode (oxidation):	$Zn(s) \longrightarrow Zn^{2+}(1\ M) + 2e^-$
Cathode (reduction):	$Cu^{2+}(1\ M) + 2e^- \longrightarrow Cu(s)$
Overall:	$Zn(s) + Cu^{2+}(1\ M) \longrightarrow Zn^{2+}(1\ M) + Cu(s)$

The emf of the cell is

$$E_{cell}^{\circ} = E_{cathode}^{\circ} - E_{anode}^{\circ}$$
$$= E_{Cu^{2+}/Cu}^{\circ} - E_{Zn^{2+}/Zn}^{\circ}$$
$$= 0.34\ V - (-0.76\ V)$$
$$= 1.10\ V$$

As in the case of ΔG° (p. 800), we can use the sign of E° to predict the extent of a redox reaction. A positive E° means the redox reaction will favor the formation of products at equilibrium. Conversely, a negative E° means that more reactants than products will be formed at equilibrium. We will examine the relationships among E_{cell}°, ΔG°, and K later in this chapter.

Table 19.1 lists standard reduction potentials for a number of half-cell reactions. By definition, the SHE has an E° value of 0.00 V. Below the SHE the negative standard reduction potentials increase, and above it the positive standard reduction potentials increase. It is important to know the following points about the table in calculations:

1. The E° values apply to the half-cell reactions as read in the forward (left to right) direction.

2. The more positive E° is, the greater the tendency for the substance to be reduced. For example, the half-cell reaction

$$F_2(1\ atm) + 2e^- \longrightarrow 2F^-(1\ M) \qquad E^{\circ} = 2.87\ V$$

has the highest positive E° value among all the half-cell reactions. Thus, F_2 is the *strongest* oxidizing agent because it has the greatest tendency to be reduced. At the other extreme is the reaction

$$Li^+(1\ M) + e^- \longrightarrow Li(s) \qquad E^{\circ} = -3.05\ V$$

The activity series in Figure 4.16 is based on data given in Table 19.1.

TABLE 19.1	Standard Reduction Potentials at 25°C*

Half-Reaction	$E°$(V)
$F_2(g) + 2e^- \longrightarrow 2F^-(aq)$	+2.87
$O_3(g) + 2H^+(aq) + 2e^- \longrightarrow O_2(g) + H_2O$	+2.07
$Co^{3+}(aq) + e^- \longrightarrow Co^{2+}(aq)$	+1.82
$H_2O_2(aq) + 2H^+(aq) + 2e^- \longrightarrow 2H_2O$	+1.77
$PbO_2(s) + 4H^+(aq) + SO_4^{2-}(aq) + 2e^- \longrightarrow PbSO_4(s) + 2H_2O$	+1.70
$Ce^{4+}(aq) + e^- \longrightarrow Ce^{3+}(aq)$	+1.61
$MnO_4^-(aq) + 8H^+(aq) + 5e^- \longrightarrow Mn^{2+}(aq) + 4H_2O$	+1.51
$Au^{3+}(aq) + 3e^- \longrightarrow Au(s)$	+1.50
$Cl_2(g) + 2e^- \longrightarrow 2Cl^-(aq)$	+1.36
$Cr_2O_7^{2-}(aq) + 14H^+(aq) + 6e^- \longrightarrow 2Cr^{3+}(aq) + 7H_2O$	+1.33
$MnO_2(s) + 4H^+(aq) + 2e^- \longrightarrow Mn^{2+}(aq) + 2H_2O$	+1.23
$O_2(g) + 4H^+(aq) + 4e^- \longrightarrow 2H_2O$	+1.23
$Br_2(l) + 2e^- \longrightarrow 2Br^-(aq)$	+1.07
$NO_3^-(aq) + 4H^+(aq) + 3e^- \longrightarrow NO(g) + 2H_2O$	+0.96
$2Hg^{2+}(aq) + 2e^- \longrightarrow Hg_2^{2+}(aq)$	+0.92
$Hg_2^{2+}(aq) + 2e^- \longrightarrow 2Hg(l)$	+0.85
$Ag^+(aq) + e^- \longrightarrow Ag(s)$	+0.80
$Fe^{3+}(aq) + e^- \longrightarrow Fe^{2+}(aq)$	+0.77
$O_2(g) + 2H^+(aq) + 2e^- \longrightarrow H_2O_2(aq)$	+0.68
$MnO_4^-(aq) + 2H_2O + 3e^- \longrightarrow MnO_2(s) + 4OH^-(aq)$	+0.59
$I_2(s) + 2e^- \longrightarrow 2I^-(aq)$	+0.53
$O_2(g) + 2H_2O + 4e^- \longrightarrow 4OH^-(aq)$	+0.40
$Cu^{2+}(aq) + 2e^- \longrightarrow Cu(s)$	+0.34
$AgCl(s) + e^- \longrightarrow Ag(s) + Cl^-(aq)$	+0.22
$SO_4^{2-}(aq) + 4H^+(aq) + 2e^- \longrightarrow SO_2(g) + 2H_2O$	+0.20
$Cu^{2+}(aq) + e^- \longrightarrow Cu^+(aq)$	+0.15
$Sn^{4+}(aq) + 2e^- \longrightarrow Sn^{2+}(aq)$	+0.13
$2H^+(aq) + 2e^- \longrightarrow H_2(g)$	0.00
$Pb^{2+}(aq) + 2e^- \longrightarrow Pb(s)$	−0.13
$Sn^{2+}(aq) + 2e^- \longrightarrow Sn(s)$	−0.14
$Ni^{2+}(aq) + 2e^- \longrightarrow Ni(s)$	−0.25
$Co^{2+}(aq) + 2e^- \longrightarrow Co(s)$	−0.28
$PbSO_4(s) + 2e^- \longrightarrow Pb(s) + SO_4^{2-}(aq)$	−0.31
$Cd^{2+}(aq) + 2e^- \longrightarrow Cd(s)$	−0.40
$Fe^{2+}(aq) + 2e^- \longrightarrow Fe(s)$	−0.44
$Cr^{3+}(aq) + 3e^- \longrightarrow Cr(s)$	−0.74
$Zn^{2+}(aq) + 2e^- \longrightarrow Zn(s)$	−0.76
$2H_2O + 2e^- \longrightarrow H_2(g) + 2OH^-(aq)$	−0.83
$Mn^{2+}(aq) + 2e^- \longrightarrow Mn(s)$	−1.18
$Al^{3+}(aq) + 3e^- \longrightarrow Al(s)$	−1.66
$Be^{2+}(aq) + 2e^- \longrightarrow Be(s)$	−1.85
$Mg^{2+}(aq) + 2e^- \longrightarrow Mg(s)$	−2.37
$Na^+(aq) + e^- \longrightarrow Na(s)$	−2.71
$Ca^{2+}(aq) + 2e^- \longrightarrow Ca(s)$	−2.87
$Sr^{2+}(aq) + 2e^- \longrightarrow Sr(s)$	−2.89
$Ba^{2+}(aq) + 2e^- \longrightarrow Ba(s)$	−2.90
$K^+(aq) + e^- \longrightarrow K(s)$	−2.93
$Li^+(aq) + e^- \longrightarrow Li(s)$	−3.05

Increasing strength as oxidizing agent (left margin, arrow pointing up)

Increasing strength as reducing agent (right margin, arrow pointing down)

*For all half-reactions the concentration is 1 M for dissolved species and the pressure is 1 atm for gases. These are the standard-state values.

which has the most negative $E°$ value. Thus, Li^+ is the *weakest* oxidizing agent because it is the most difficult species to reduce. Conversely, we say that F^- is the weakest reducing agent and Li metal is the strongest reducing agent. Under standard-state conditions, the oxidizing agents (the species on the left-hand side of the half-reactions in Table 19.1) increase in strength from bottom to top and the reducing agents (the species on the right-hand side of the half-reactions) increase in strength from top to bottom.

3. The half-cell reactions are reversible. Depending on the conditions, any electrode can act either as an anode or as a cathode. Earlier we saw that the SHE is the cathode (H^+ is reduced to H_2) when coupled with zinc in a cell and that it becomes the anode (H_2 is oxidized to H^+) when used in a cell with copper.

4. Under standard-state conditions, any species on the left of a given half-cell reaction will react spontaneously with a species that appears on the right of any half-cell reaction located *below* it in Table 19.1. This principle is sometimes called the *diagonal rule.* In the case of the Daniell cell

$$Cu^{2+}(1\,M) + 2e^- \longrightarrow Cu(s) \qquad E° = 0.34\text{ V}$$
$$Zn^{2+}(1\,M) + 2e^- \longrightarrow Zn(s) \qquad E° = -0.76\text{ V}$$

We see that the substance on the left of the first half-cell reaction is Cu^{2+} and the substance on the right in the second half-cell reaction is Zn. Therefore, as we saw earlier, Zn spontaneously reduces Cu^{2+} to form Zn^{2+} and Cu.

5. Changing the stoichiometric coefficients of a half-cell reaction *does not* affect the value of $E°$ because electrode potentials are intensive properties. This means that the value of $E°$ is unaffected by the size of the electrodes or the amount of solutions present. For example,

$$I_2(s) + 2e^- \longrightarrow 2I^-(1\,M) \qquad E° = 0.53\text{ V}$$

but $E°$ does not change if we multiply the half-reaction by 2:

$$2I_2(s) + 4e^- \longrightarrow 4I^-(1\,M) \qquad E° = 0.53\text{ V}$$

6. Like ΔH, ΔG, and ΔS, the sign of $E°$ changes but its magnitude remains the same when we reverse a reaction.

As Examples 19.2 and 19.3 show, Table 19.1 enables us to predict the outcome of redox reactions under standard-state conditions, whether they take place in a galvanic cell, where the reducing agent and oxidizing agent are physically separated from each other, or in a beaker, where the reactants are all mixed together.

Example 19.2

Predict what will happen if molecular bromine (Br_2) is added to a solution containing NaCl and NaI at 25°C. Assume all species are in their standard states.

Strategy To predict what redox reaction(s) will take place, we need to compare the standard reduction potentials of Cl_2, Br_2, and I_2 and apply the diagonal rule.

(Continued)

Solution From Table 19.1, we write the standard reduction potentials as follows:

$$\text{Cl}_2(1 \text{ atm}) + 2e^- \longrightarrow 2\text{Cl}^-(1 \text{ } M) \qquad E° = 1.36 \text{ V}$$
$$\text{Br}_2(l) + 2e^- \longrightarrow 2\text{Br}^-(1 \text{ } M) \qquad E° = 1.07 \text{ V}$$
$$\text{I}_2(s) + 2e^- \longrightarrow 2\text{I}^-(1 \text{ } M) \qquad E° = 0.53 \text{ V}$$

Applying the diagonal rule we see that Br_2 will oxidize I^- but will not oxidize Cl^-. Therefore, the only redox reaction that will occur appreciably under standard-state conditions is

Oxidation: $2\text{I}^-(1 \text{ } M) \longrightarrow \text{I}_2(s) + 2e^-$
Reduction: $\underline{\text{Br}_2(l) + 2e^- \longrightarrow 2\text{Br}^-(1 \text{ } M)}$

Overall: $2\text{I}^-(1 \text{ } M) + \text{Br}_2(l) \longrightarrow \text{I}_2(s) + 2\text{Br}^-(1 \text{ } M)$

Check We can confirm our conclusion by calculating $E°_{\text{cell}}$. Try it. Note that the Na^+ ions are inert and do not enter into the redox reaction.

Similar problems: 19.14, 19.17.

Practice Exercise Can Sn reduce $\text{Zn}^{2+}(aq)$ under standard-state conditions?

Example 19.3

A galvanic cell consists of a Mg electrode in a 1.0 M $\text{Mg(NO}_3)_2$ solution and a Ag electrode in a 1.0 M AgNO_3 solution. Calculate the standard emf of this cell at 25°C.

Strategy At first it may not be clear how to assign the electrodes in the galvanic cell. From Table 19.1 we write the standard reduction potentials of Ag and Mg and apply the diagonal rule to determine which is the anode and which is the cathode.

Solution The standard reduction potentials are

$$\text{Ag}^+(1.0 \text{ } M) + e^- \longrightarrow \text{Ag}(s) \qquad E° = 0.80 \text{ V}$$
$$\text{Mg}^{2+}(1.0 \text{ } M) + 2e^- \longrightarrow \text{Mg}(s) \qquad E° = -2.37 \text{ V}$$

Applying the diagonal rule, we see that Ag^+ will oxidize Mg:

Anode (oxidation): $\text{Mg}(s) \longrightarrow \text{Mg}^{2+}(1.0 \text{ } M) + 2e^-$
Cathode (reduction): $\underline{2\text{Ag}^+(1.0 \text{ } M) + 2e^- \longrightarrow 2\text{Ag}(s)}$

Overall: $\text{Mg}(s) + 2\text{Ag}^+(1.0 \text{ } M) \longrightarrow \text{Mg}^{2+}(1.0 \text{ } M) + 2\text{Ag}(s)$

Note that in order to balance the overall equation we multiplied the reduction of Ag^+ by 2. We can do so because, as an intensive property, $E°$ is not affected by this procedure. We find the emf of the cell by using Equation (19.1) and Table 19.1:

$$E°_{\text{cell}} = E°_{\text{cathode}} - E°_{\text{anode}}$$
$$= E°_{\text{Ag}^+/\text{Ag}} - E°_{\text{Mg}^{2+}/\text{Mg}}$$
$$= 0.80 \text{ V} - (-2.37 \text{ V})$$
$$= \boxed{3.17 \text{ V}}$$

Similar problems: 19.11, 19.12.

Check The positive value of $E°$ shows that the forward reaction is favored.

Practice Exercise What is the standard emf of a galvanic cell made of a Cd electrode in a 1.0 M $\text{Cd(NO}_3)_2$ solution and a Cr electrode in a 1.0 M $\text{Cr(NO}_3)_3$ solution at 25°C?

19.4 Spontaneity of Redox Reactions

Our next step is to see how $E°_{cell}$ is related to thermodynamic quantities such as $\Delta G°$ and K. In a galvanic cell, chemical energy is converted to electrical energy. Electrical energy in this case is the product of the emf of the cell and the total electrical charge (in coulombs) that passes through the cell:

$$\text{electrical energy} = \text{volts} \times \text{coulombs}$$
$$= \text{joules}$$

The total charge is determined by the number of moles of electrons (n) that pass through the circuit. By definition

$$\text{total charge} = nF$$

where F, the Faraday[†] constant, is the electrical charge contained in 1 mole of electrons. Experiments have shown that *1 faraday* is *equivalent to 96,485.3 coulombs,* or 96,500 coulombs, rounded off to three significant figures. Thus,

$$1\ F = 96,500\ \text{C/mol}\ e^-$$

Because

$$1\ \text{J} = 1\ \text{C} \times 1\ \text{V}$$

we can also express the units of faraday as

$$1\ F = 96,500\ \text{J/V} \cdot \text{mol}\ e^-$$

The measured emf is the *maximum* voltage that the cell can achieve. This value is used to calculate the maximum amount of electrical energy that can be obtained from the chemical reaction. This energy is used to do electrical work (w_{ele}), so

$$w_{max} = w_{ele}$$
$$= -nFE_{cell}$$

where w_{max} is the maximum amount of work that can be done. The negative sign on the right-hand side indicates that the electrical work is done by the system on the surroundings. In Chapter 18 we defined free energy as the energy available to do work. Specifically, the change in free energy (ΔG) represents the maximum amount of useful work that can be obtained from a reaction:

$$\Delta G = w_{max}$$

Therefore, we can write

$$\Delta G = -nFE_{cell} \tag{19.2}$$

n is the number of moles of electrons exchanged between the reducing agent and the oxidizing agent in the overall redox equation.

The sign convention for electrical work is the same as that for *P-V* work, discussed in Section 6.3.

[†]Michael Faraday (1791–1867). English chemist and physicist. Faraday is regarded by many as the greatest experimental scientist of the nineteenth century. He started as an apprentice to a bookbinder at the age of 13, but became interested in science after reading a book on chemistry. Faraday invented the electric motor and was the first person to demonstrate the principle governing electrical generators. Besides making notable contributions to the fields of electricity and magnetism, Faraday also worked on optical activity, and discovered and named benzene.

Both n and F are positive quantities and ΔG is negative for a spontaneous process, so E_{cell} must be positive. For reactions in which reactants and products are in their standard states, Equation (19.2) becomes

$$\Delta G^\circ = -nFE^\circ_{\text{cell}} \qquad (19.3)$$

Now we can relate E°_{cell} to the equilibrium constant (K) of a redox reaction. In Section 18.5 we saw that the standard free-energy change ΔG° for a reaction is related to its equilibrium constant as follows [see Equation (18.14)]:

$$\Delta G^\circ = -RT \ln K$$

Therefore, if we combine Equations (18.14) and (19.3) we obtain

$$-nFE^\circ_{\text{cell}} = -RT \ln K$$

Solving for E°_{cell}

$$E^\circ_{\text{cell}} = \frac{RT}{nF} \ln K \qquad (19.4)$$

When $T = 298$ K, Equation (19.4) can be simplified by substituting for R and F:

In calculations involving F, we sometimes omit the symbol e^-.

$$E^\circ_{\text{cell}} = \frac{(8.314 \text{ J/K} \cdot \text{mol})(298 \text{ K})}{n(96{,}500 \text{ J/V} \cdot \text{mol})} \ln K$$

or

$$E^\circ_{\text{cell}} = \frac{0.0257 \text{ V}}{n} \ln K \qquad (19.5)$$

Alternatively, Equation (19.5) can be written using the base-10 logarithm of K:

$$E^\circ_{\text{cell}} = \frac{0.0592 \text{ V}}{n} \log K \qquad (19.6)$$

Thus, if any one of the three quantities ΔG°, K, or E°_{cell} is known, the other two can be calculated using Equation (18.14), Equation (19.3), or Equation (19.4) (Figure 19.5). We summarize the relationships among ΔG°, K, and E°_{cell} and characterize the spontaneity of a redox reaction in Table 19.2. For simplicity, we sometimes omit the subscript "cell" in E° and E.

Examples 19.4 and 19.5 apply Equations (19.3) and (19.5).

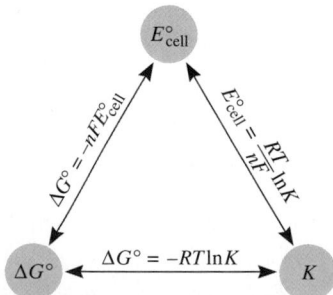

Figure 19.5 *Relationships among E°_{cell}, K, and ΔG°.*

Example 19.4

Calculate the equilibrium constant for the following reaction at 25°C:

$$\text{Sn}(s) + 2\text{Cu}^{2+}(aq) \rightleftharpoons \text{Sn}^{2+}(aq) + 2\text{Cu}^{+}(aq)$$

Strategy The relationship between the equilibrium constant K and the standard emf is given by Equation (19.5): $E^\circ_{\text{cell}} = (0.0257 \text{ V}/n)\ln K$. Thus, if we can determine the

(Continued)

$\Delta G°$	K	$E°_{cell}$	Reaction Under Standard-State Conditions
Negative	>1	Positive	Favors formation of products.
0	=1	0	Reactants and products are equally favored.
Positive	<1	Negative	Favors formation of reactants.

TABLE 19.2 Relationships Among $\Delta G°$, K, and $E°_{cell}$

standard emf, we can calculate the equilibrium constant. We can determine the $E°_{cell}$ of a hypothetical galvanic cell made up of two couples (Sn^{2+}/Sn and Cu^{2+}/Cu^+) from the standard reduction potentials in Table 19.1.

Solution The half-cell reactions are

Anode (oxidation): $Sn(s) \longrightarrow Sn^{2+}(aq) + 2e^-$
Cathode (reduction): $2Cu^{2+}(aq) + 2e^- \longrightarrow 2Cu^+(aq)$

$$E°_{cell} = E°_{cathode} - E°_{anode}$$
$$= E°_{Cu^{2+}/Cu^+} - E°_{Sn^{2+}/Sn}$$
$$= 0.15\ V - (-0.14\ V)$$
$$= 0.29\ V$$

Equation (19.5) can be written

$$\ln K = \frac{nE°}{0.0257\ V}$$

In the overall reaction we find $n = 2$. Therefore,

$$\ln K = \frac{(2)(0.29\ V)}{0.0257\ V} = 22.6$$
$$K = e^{22.6} = 7 \times 10^9$$

Similar problems: 19.21, 19.22.

Practice Exercise Calculate the equilibrium constant for the following reaction at 25°C:

$$Fe^{2+}(aq) + 2Ag(s) \rightleftharpoons Fe(s) + 2Ag^+(aq)$$

Example 19.5

Calculate the standard free-energy change for the following reaction at 25°C:

$$2Au(s) + 3Ca^{2+}(1.0\ M) \longrightarrow 2Au^{3+}(1.0\ M) + 3Ca(s)$$

Strategy The relationship between the standard free energy change and the standard emf of the cell is given by Equation (19.3): $\Delta G° = -nFE°_{cell}$. Thus, if we can determine $E°_{cell}$, we can calculate $\Delta G°$. We can determine the $E°_{cell}$ of a hypothetical galvanic cell made up of two couples (Au^{3+}/Au and Ca^{2+}/Ca) from the standard reduction potentials in Table 19.1.

(Continued)

Solution The half-cell reactions are

Anode (oxidation): $\qquad 2Au(s) \longrightarrow 2Au^{3+}(1.0\,M) + 6e^-$
Cathode (reduction): $\quad 3Ca^{2+}(1.0\,M) + 6e^- \longrightarrow 3Ca(s)$

$$
\begin{aligned}
E^\circ_{cell} &= E^\circ_{cathode} - E^\circ_{anode} \\
&= E^\circ_{Ca^{2+}/Ca} - E^\circ_{Au^{3+}/Au} \\
&= -2.87\,V - 1.50\,V \\
&= -4.37\,V
\end{aligned}
$$

Now we use Equation (19.3):

$$\Delta G^\circ = -nFE^\circ$$

The overall reaction shows that $n = 6$, so

$$
\begin{aligned}
\Delta G^\circ &= -(6)(96{,}500\,J/V \cdot mol)(-4.37\,V) \\
&= 2.53 \times 10^6\,J/mol \\
&= 2.53 \times 10^3\,kJ/mol
\end{aligned}
$$

Check The large positive value of ΔG° tells us that the reaction favors the reactants at equilibrium. The result is consistent with the fact that E° for the galvanic cell is negative.

Similar problem: 19.24.

Practice Exercise Calculate ΔG° for the following reaction at 25°C:

$$2Al^{3+}(aq) + 3Mg(s) \rightleftharpoons 2Al(s) + 3Mg^{2+}(aq)$$

19.5 The Effect of Concentration on Cell Emf

So far we have focused on redox reactions in which reactants and products are in their standard states, but standard-state conditions are often difficult, and sometimes impossible, to maintain. Nevertheless, there is a mathematical relationship between the emf of a galvanic cell and the concentration of reactants and products in a redox reaction under nonstandard-state conditions. This equation is derived next.

The Nernst Equation

Consider a redox reaction of the type

$$a\mathrm{A} + b\mathrm{B} \longrightarrow c\mathrm{C} + d\mathrm{D}$$

From Equation (18.13),

$$\Delta G = \Delta G^\circ + RT \ln Q$$

Because $\Delta G = -nFE$ and $\Delta G^\circ = -nFE^\circ$, the equation can be expressed as

$$-nFE = -nFE^\circ + RT \ln Q$$

Dividing the equation through by $-nF$, we get

$$E = E^\circ - \frac{RT}{nF} \ln Q \tag{19.7}$$

where Q is the reaction quotient (see Section 14.4). Equation (19.7) is known as the *Nernst[†] equation*. At 298 K, Equation (19.7) can be rewritten as

$$E = E^\circ - \frac{0.0257 \text{ V}}{n} \ln Q \qquad (19.8)$$

or, expressing Equation (19.8) using the base-10 logarithm of Q:

$$E = E^\circ - \frac{0.0592 \text{ V}}{n} \log Q \qquad (19.9)$$

During the operation of a galvanic cell, electrons flow from the anode to the cathode, resulting in product formation and a decrease in reactant concentration. Thus, Q increases, which means that E decreases. Eventually, the cell reaches equilibrium. At equilibrium, there is no net transfer of electrons, so $E = 0$ and $Q = K$, where K is the equilibrium constant.

The Nernst equation enables us to calculate E as a function of reactant and product concentrations in a redox reaction. For example, for the Daniell cell in Figure 19.1

$$Zn(s) + Cu^{2+}(aq) \longrightarrow Zn^{2+}(aq) + Cu(s)$$

The Nernst equation for this cell at 25°C can be written as

$$E = 1.10 \text{ V} - \frac{0.0257 \text{ V}}{2} \ln \frac{[Zn^{2+}]}{[Cu^{2+}]}$$

Remember that concentrations of pure solids (and pure liquids) do not appear in the expression for Q.

If the ratio $[Zn^{2+}]/[Cu^{2+}]$ is less than 1, $\ln([Zn^{2+}]/[Cu^{2+}])$ is a negative number, so that the second term on the right-hand side of the preceding equation is positive. Under this condition E is greater than the standard emf E°. If the ratio is greater than 1, E is smaller than E°.

Example 19.6 illustrates the use of the Nernst equation.

Example 19.6

Predict whether the following reaction would proceed spontaneously as written at 298 K:

$$Co(s) + Fe^{2+}(aq) \longrightarrow Co^{2+}(aq) + Fe(s)$$

given that $[Co^{2+}] = 0.15 \, M$ and $[Fe^{2+}] = 0.68 \, M$.

Strategy Because the reaction is not run under standard-state conditions (concentrations are not 1 M), we need Nernst's equation [Equation (19.8)] to calculate the emf (E) of a hypothetical galvanic cell and determine the spontaneity of the reaction. The standard emf (E°) can be calculated using the standard reduction potentials in Table 19.1. Remember that solids do not appear in the reaction quotient (Q) term in the Nernst equation. Note that 2 moles of electrons are transferred per mole of reaction, that is, $n = 2$.

(Continued)

[†]Walter Hermann Nernst (1864–1941). German chemist and physicist. Nernst's work was mainly on electrolyte solution and thermodynamics. He also invented an electric piano. Nernst was awarded the Nobel Prize in Chemistry in 1920 for his contribution to thermodynamics.

Solution The half-cell reactions are

Anode (oxidation): $Co(s) \longrightarrow Co^{2+}(aq) + 2e^-$
Cathode (reduction): $Fe^{2+}(aq) + 2e^- \longrightarrow Fe(s)$

$$E^\circ_{cell} = E^\circ_{cathode} - E^\circ_{anode}$$
$$= E^\circ_{Fe^{2+}/Fe} - E^\circ_{Co^{2+}/Co}$$
$$= -0.44 \text{ V} - (-0.28 \text{ V})$$
$$= -0.16 \text{ V}$$

From Equation (19.8) we write

$$E = E^\circ - \frac{0.0257 \text{ V}}{n} \ln Q$$
$$= E^\circ - \frac{0.0257 \text{ V}}{n} \ln \frac{[Co^{2+}]}{[Fe^{2+}]}$$
$$= -0.16 \text{ V} - \frac{0.0257 \text{ V}}{2} \ln \frac{0.15}{0.68}$$
$$= -0.16 \text{ V} + 0.019 \text{ V}$$
$$= -0.14 \text{ V}$$

Similar problems: 19.29, 19.30.

Because E is negative, the reaction is not spontaneous in the direction written.

Practice Exercise Will the following reaction occur spontaneously at 25°C, given that $[Fe^{2+}] = 0.60 \, M$ and $[Cd^{2+}] = 0.010 \, M$?

$$Cd(s) + Fe^{2+}(aq) \longrightarrow Cd^{2+}(aq) + Fe(s)$$

Now suppose we want to determine at what ratio of $[Co^{2+}]$ to $[Fe^{2+}]$ the reaction in Example 19.6 would become spontaneous. We can use Equation (19.8) as follows:

$$E = E^\circ - \frac{0.0257 \text{ V}}{n} \ln Q$$

When $E = 0$, $Q = K$.

We first set E equal to zero, which corresponds to the equilibrium situation.

$$0 = -0.16 \text{ V} - \frac{0.0257 \text{ V}}{2} \ln \frac{[Co^{2+}]}{[Fe^{2+}]}$$
$$\ln \frac{[Co^{2+}]}{[Fe^{2+}]} = -12.5$$
$$\frac{[Co^{2+}]}{[Fe^{2+}]} = e^{-12.5} = K$$

or $K = 4 \times 10^{-6}$

Thus, for the reaction to be spontaneous, the ratio $[Co^{2+}]/[Fe^{2+}]$ must be smaller than 4×10^{-6} so that E would become positive.

As Example 19.7 shows, if gases are involved in the cell reaction, their concentrations should be expressed in atm.

Example 19.7

Consider the galvanic cell shown in Figure 19.4(a). In a certain experiment, the emf (E) of the cell is found to be 0.54 V at 25°C. Suppose that $[Zn^{2+}] = 1.0 \, M$ and $P_{H_2} = 1.0$ atm. Calculate the molar concentration of H^+.

(Continued)

Strategy The equation that relates standard emf and nonstandard emf is the Nernst equation. The overall cell reaction is

$$Zn(s) + 2H^+(? \, M) \longrightarrow Zn^{2+}(1.0 \, M) + H_2(1.0 \text{ atm})$$

Given the emf of the cell (E), we apply the Nernst equation to solve for [H^+]. Note that 2 moles of electrons are transferred per mole of reaction; that is, $n = 2$.

Solution As we saw earlier (p. 826), the standard emf ($E°$) for the cell is 0.76 V. From Equation (19.8) we write

$$E = E° - \frac{0.0257 \text{ V}}{n} \ln Q$$

$$= E° - \frac{0.0257 \text{ V}}{n} \ln \frac{[Zn^{2+}]P_{H_2}}{[H^+]^2}$$

$$0.54 \text{ V} = 0.76 \text{ V} - \frac{0.0257 \text{ V}}{2} \ln \frac{(1.0)(1.0)}{[H^+]^2}$$

$$-0.22 \text{ V} = -\frac{0.0257 \text{ V}}{2} \ln \frac{1}{[H^+]^2}$$

$$17.1 = \ln \frac{1}{[H^+]^2}$$

$$e^{17.1} = \frac{1}{[H^+]^2}$$

$$[H^+] = \sqrt{\frac{1}{3 \times 10^7}} = 2 \times 10^{-4} \, M$$

The concentrations in Q are divided by their standard-state value of 1 M and pressures are divided by 1 atm.

Check The fact that the nonstandard-state emf (E) is given in the problem means that not all the reacting species are in their standard-state concentrations. Thus, because both Zn^{2+} ions and H_2 gas are in their standard states, [H^+] is not 1 M.

Similar problem: 19.32.

Practice Exercise What is the emf of a galvanic cell consisting of a Cd^{2+}/Cd half-cell and a $Pt/H^+/H_2$ half-cell if [Cd^{2+}] = 0.20 M, [H^+] = 0.16 M, and P_{H_2} = 0.80 atm?

Example 19.7 shows that a galvanic cell whose cell reaction involves H^+ ions can be used to measure [H^+] or pH. The pH meter described in Section 15.3 is based on this principle. However, the hydrogen electrode (see Figure 19.3) is normally not employed in laboratory work because it is awkward to use. Instead, it is replaced by a *glass electrode,* shown in Figure 19.6. The electrode consists of a very thin glass membrane that is permeable to H^+ ions. A silver wire coated with silver chloride is immersed in a dilute hydrochloric acid solution. When the electrode is placed in a solution whose pH is different from that of the inner solution, the potential difference that develops between the two sides of the membrane can be monitored using a reference electrode. The emf of the cell made up of the glass electrode and the reference electrode is measured with a voltmeter that is calibrated in pH units.

Concentration Cells

Because electrode potential depends on ion concentrations, it is possible to construct a galvanic cell from two half-cells composed of the *same* material but differing in ion concentrations. Such a cell is called a *concentration cell.*

Consider a situation in which zinc electrodes are put into two aqueous solutions of zinc sulfate at 0.10 M and 1.0 M concentrations. The two solutions are connected

Ag—AgCl electrode

Thin-walled glass membrane

HCl solution

Figure 19.6 *A glass electrode that is used in conjunction with a reference electrode in a pH meter.*

by a salt bridge, and the electrodes are joined by a piece of wire in an arrangement like that shown in Figure 19.1. According to Le Châtelier's principle, the tendency for the reduction

$$Zn^{2+}(aq) + 2e^- \longrightarrow Zn(s)$$

increases with increasing concentration of Zn^{2+} ions. Therefore, reduction should occur in the more concentrated compartment and oxidation should take place on the more dilute side. The cell diagram is

$$Zn(s)\,|\,Zn^{2+}(0.10\ M)\,\|\,Zn^{2+}(1.0\ M)\,|\,Zn(s)$$

and the half-reactions are

Oxidation: $Zn(s) \longrightarrow Zn^{2+}(0.10\ M) + 2e^-$
Reduction: $Zn^{2+}(1.0\ M) + 2e^- \longrightarrow Zn(s)$
Overall: $Zn^{2+}(1.0\ M) \longrightarrow Zn^{2+}(0.10\ M)$

The emf of the cell is

$$E = E° - \frac{0.0257\ V}{2} \ln \frac{[Zn^{2+}]_{dil}}{[Zn^{2+}]_{conc}}$$

where the subscripts "dil" and "conc" refer to the 0.10 M and 1.0 M concentrations, respectively. The $E°$ for this cell is zero (the same electrode and the same type of ions are involved), so

$$E = 0 - \frac{0.0257\ V}{2} \ln \frac{0.10}{1.0}$$
$$= 0.0296\ V$$

The emf of concentration cells is usually small and decreases continually during the operation of the cell as the concentrations in the two compartments approach each other. When the concentrations of the ions in the two compartments are the same, E becomes zero, and no further change occurs.

A biological cell can be compared to a concentration cell for the purpose of calculating its *membrane potential*. Membrane potential is the electrical potential that exists across the membrane of various kinds of cells, including muscle cells and nerve cells. It is responsible for the propagation of nerve impulses and heartbeat. A membrane potential is established whenever there are unequal concentrations of the same type of ion in the interior and exterior of a cell. For example, the concentrations of K^+ ions in the interior and exterior of a nerve cell are 400 mM and 15 mM, respectively. Treating the situation as a concentration cell and applying the Nernst equation for just one kind of ions, we can write

1 mM = 1 × 10^{-3} M.

$$E = E° - \frac{0.0257\ V}{1} \ln \frac{[K^+]_{ex}}{[K^+]_{in}}$$
$$= -(0.0257\ V) \ln \frac{15}{400}$$
$$= 0.084\ V\ or\ 84\ mV$$

where "ex" and "in" denote exterior and interior. Note that we have set $E° = 0$ because the same type of ion is involved. Thus, an electrical potential of 84 mV exists across the membrane due to the unequal concentrations of K^+ ions.

19.6 Batteries

A **battery** is *a galvanic cell, or a series of combined galvanic cells, that can be used as a source of direct electric current at a constant voltage.* Although the operation of a battery is similar in principle to that of the galvanic cells described in Section 19.2, a battery has the advantage of being completely self-contained and requiring no auxiliary components such as salt bridges. Here we will discuss several types of batteries that are in widespread use.

Figure 19.7 *Interior section of a dry cell of the kind used in flashlights and transistor radios. Actually, the cell is not completely dry, as it contains a moist electrolyte paste.*

The Dry Cell Battery

The most common dry cell, that is, a cell without a fluid component, is the *Leclanché cell* used in flashlights and transistor radios. The anode of the cell consists of a zinc can or container that is in contact with manganese dioxide (MnO_2) and an electrolyte. The electrolyte consists of ammonium chloride and zinc chloride in water, to which starch is added to thicken the solution to a pastelike consistency so that it is less likely to leak (Figure 19.7). A carbon rod serves as the cathode, which is immersed in the electrolyte in the center of the cell. The cell reactions are

Anode: $$Zn(s) \longrightarrow Zn^{2+}(aq) + 2e^-$$
Cathode: $$2NH_4^+(aq) + 2MnO_2(s) + 2e^- \longrightarrow Mn_2O_3(s) + 2NH_3(aq) + H_2O(l)$$
Overall: $$Zn(s) + 2NH_4^+(aq) + 2MnO_2(s) \longrightarrow Zn^{2+}(aq) + 2NH_3(aq) + H_2O(l) + Mn_2O_3(s)$$

Actually, this equation is an oversimplification of a complex process. The voltage produced by a dry cell is about 1.5 V.

The Mercury Battery

The mercury battery is used extensively in medicine and electronic industries and is more expensive than the common dry cell. Contained in a stainless steel cylinder, the mercury battery consists of a zinc anode (amalgamated with mercury) in contact with a strongly alkaline electrolyte containing zinc oxide and mercury(II) oxide (Figure 19.8). The cell reactions are

Anode: $$Zn(Hg) + 2OH^-(aq) \longrightarrow ZnO(s) + H_2O(l) + 2e^-$$
Cathode: $$HgO(s) + H_2O(l) + 2e^- \longrightarrow Hg(l) + 2OH^-(aq)$$
Overall: $$Zn(Hg) + HgO(s) \longrightarrow ZnO(s) + Hg(l)$$

Because there is no change in electrolyte composition during operation—the overall cell reaction involves only solid substances—the mercury battery provides a more constant voltage (1.35 V) than the Leclanché cell. It also has a considerably higher capacity and longer life. These qualities make the mercury battery ideal for use in pacemakers, hearing aids, electric watches, and light meters.

The Lead Storage Battery

The lead storage battery commonly used in automobiles consists of six identical cells joined together in series. Each cell has a lead anode and a cathode made of lead dioxide (PbO_2) packed on a metal plate (Figure 19.9). Both the cathode and the anode are

Electrolyte solution containing KOH and paste of $Zn(OH)_2$ and HgO

Figure 19.8 *Interior section of a mercury battery.*

immersed in an aqueous solution of sulfuric acid, which acts as the electrolyte. The cell reactions are

$$\text{Anode:} \quad \text{Pb}(s) + \text{SO}_4^{2-}(aq) \longrightarrow \text{PbSO}_4(s) + 2e^-$$
$$\text{Cathode:} \quad \text{PbO}_2(s) + 4\text{H}^+(aq) + \text{SO}_4^{2-}(aq) + 2e^- \longrightarrow \text{PbSO}_4(s) + 2\text{H}_2\text{O}(l)$$
$$\overline{\text{Overall:} \ \text{Pb}(s) + \text{PbO}_2(s) + 4\text{H}^+(aq) + 2\text{SO}_4^{2-}(aq) \longrightarrow 2\text{PbSO}_4(s) + 2\text{H}_2\text{O}(l)}$$

Under normal operating conditions, each cell produces 2 V; a total of 12 V from the six cells is used to power the ignition circuit of the automobile and its other electrical systems. The lead storage battery can deliver large amounts of current for a short time, such as the time it takes to start up the engine.

Unlike the Leclanché cell and the mercury battery, the lead storage battery is rechargeable. Recharging the battery means reversing the normal electrochemical reaction by applying an external voltage at the cathode and the anode. (This kind of process is called *electrolysis,* see p. 848.) The reactions that replenish the original materials are

$$\text{PbSO}_4(s) + 2e^- \longrightarrow \text{Pb}(s) + \text{SO}_4^{2-}(aq)$$
$$\text{PbSO}_4(s) + 2\text{H}_2\text{O}(l) \longrightarrow \text{PbO}_2(s) + 4\text{H}^+(aq) + \text{SO}_4^{2-}(aq) + 2e^-$$
$$\overline{\text{Overall:} \ 2\text{PbSO}_4(s) + 2\text{H}_2\text{O}(l) \longrightarrow \text{Pb}(s) + \text{PbO}_2(s) + 4\text{H}^+(aq) + 2\text{SO}_4^{2-}(aq)}$$

The overall reaction is exactly the opposite of the normal cell reaction.

Two aspects of the operation of a lead storage battery are worth noting. First, because the electrochemical reaction consumes sulfuric acid, the degree to which the battery has been discharged can be checked by measuring the density of the electrolyte with a hydrometer, as is usually done at gas stations. The density of the fluid in a "healthy," fully charged battery should be equal to or greater than 1.2 g/mL. Second, people living in cold climates sometimes have trouble starting their cars because the battery has "gone dead." Thermodynamic calculations show that the emf of many galvanic cells decreases with decreasing temperature. However, for a lead storage battery, the temperature coefficient is about 1.5×10^{-4} V/°C; that is, there is a decrease in voltage of 1.5×10^{-4} V for every degree drop in temperature. Thus, even allowing for a 40°C change in temperature, the decrease in voltage amounts to only 6×10^{-3} V, which is about

$$\frac{6 \times 10^{-3} \text{ V}}{12 \text{ V}} \times 100\% = 0.05\%$$

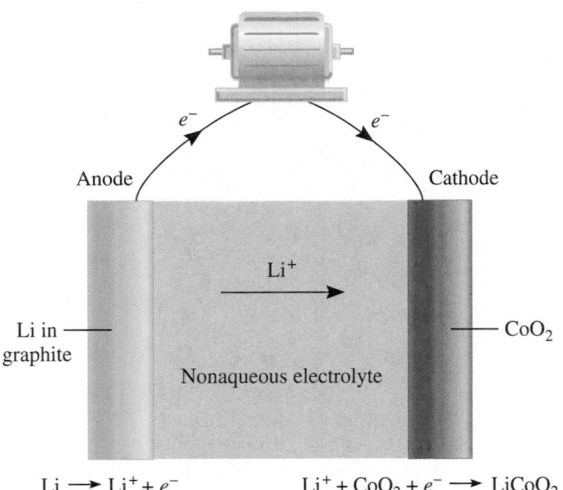

Figure 19.10 *A lithium-ion battery. Lithium atoms are embedded in the graphite, which serves as the anode and CoO_2 is the cathode. During operation, Li^+ ions migrate through the nonaqueous electrolyte from the anode to the cathode while electrons flow externally from the anode to the cathode to complete the circuit.*

of the operating voltage, an insignificant change. The real cause of a battery's apparent breakdown is an increase in the viscosity of the electrolyte as the temperature decreases. For the battery to function properly, the electrolyte must be fully conducting. However, the ions move much more slowly in a viscous medium, so the resistance of the fluid increases, leading to a decrease in the power output of the battery. If an apparently "dead battery" is warmed to near room temperature on a frigid day, it recovers its ability to deliver normal power.

The Lithium-Ion Battery

Figure 19.10 shows a schematic diagram of a lithium-ion battery. The anode is made of a conducting carbonaceous material, usually graphite, which has tiny spaces in its structure that can hold both Li atoms and Li^+ ions. The cathode is made of a transition metal oxide such as CoO_2, which can also hold Li^+ ions. Because of the high reactivity of the metal, nonaqueous electrolyte (organic solvent plus dissolved salt) must be used. During the discharge of the battery, the half-cell reactions are

$$\begin{aligned} \text{Anode (oxidation):} &\quad Li(s) \longrightarrow Li^+ + e^- \\ \text{Cathode (reduction):} &\quad Li^+ + CoO_2 + e^- \longrightarrow LiCoO_2(s) \\ \hline \text{Overall:} &\quad Li(s) + CoO_2 \longrightarrow LiCoO_2(s) \qquad E_{\text{cell}} = 3.4\ V \end{aligned}$$

The advantage of the battery is that lithium has the most negative standard reduction potential (see Table 19.1) and hence the greatest reducing strength. Furthermore, lithium is the lightest metal so that only 6.941 g of Li (its molar mass) are needed to produce 1 mole of electrons. A lithium-ion battery can be recharged literally hundreds of times without deterioration. These desirable characteristics make it suitable for use in cellular telephones, digital cameras, and laptop computers.

Fuel Cells

Fossil fuels are a major source of energy, but conversion of fossil fuel into electrical energy is a highly inefficient process. Consider the combustion of methane:

$$CH_4(g) + 2O_2(g) \longrightarrow CO_2(g) + 2H_2O(l) + \text{energy}$$

Figure 19.11 *A hydrogen-oxygen fuel cell. The Ni and NiO embedded in the porous carbon electrodes are electrocatalysts.*

Porous carbon electrode containing Ni

Porous carbon electrode containing Ni and NiO

Hot KOH solution

Oxidation
$$2H_2(g) + 4OH^-(aq) \longrightarrow 4H_2O(l) + 4e^-$$

Reduction
$$O_2(g) + 2H_2O(l) + 4e^- \longrightarrow 4OH^-(aq)$$

To generate electricity, heat produced by the reaction is first used to convert water to steam, which then drives a turbine that drives a generator. An appreciable fraction of the energy released in the form of heat is lost to the surroundings at each step; even the most efficient power plant converts only about 40 percent of the original chemical energy into electricity. Because combustion reactions are redox reactions, it is more desirable to carry them out directly by electrochemical means, thereby greatly increasing the efficiency of power production. This objective can be accomplished by a device known as a ***fuel cell,*** *a galvanic cell that requires a continuous supply of reactants to keep functioning.*

In its simplest form, a hydrogen-oxygen fuel cell consists of an electrolyte solution, such as potassium hydroxide solution, and two inert electrodes. Hydrogen and oxygen gases are bubbled through the anode and cathode compartments (Figure 19.11), where the following reactions take place:

Anode: $\quad 2H_2(g) + 4OH^-(aq) \longrightarrow 4H_2O(l) + 4e^-$

Cathode: $\quad O_2(g) + 2H_2O(l) + 4e^- \longrightarrow 4OH^-(aq)$

Overall: $\qquad\qquad 2H_2(g) + O_2(g) \longrightarrow 2H_2O(l)$

The standard emf of the cell can be calculated as follows, with data from Table 19.1:

$$
\begin{aligned}
E^\circ_{cell} &= E^\circ_{cathode} - E^\circ_{anode} \\
&= 0.40 \text{ V} - (-0.83 \text{ V}) \\
&= 1.23 \text{ V}
\end{aligned}
$$

Thus, the cell reaction is spontaneous under standard-state conditions. Note that the reaction is the same as the hydrogen combustion reaction, but the oxidation and reduction are carried out separately at the anode and the cathode. Like platinum in the standard hydrogen electrode, the electrodes have a twofold function. They serve as electrical conductors, and they provide the necessary surfaces for the initial decomposition of the molecules into atomic species, prior to electron transfer. They are *electrocatalysts.* Metals such as platinum, nickel, and rhodium are good electrocatalysts.

CHEMISTRY
in Action

Bacteria Power

U sable electricity generated from bacteria? Yes, it is possible. Since 1987, scientists at the University of Massachusetts at Amherst have discovered an organism known as the *Geobacter* species that do exactly that. The ubiquitous *Geobacter* bacteria normally grow at the bottom of rivers or lakes. They get their energy by oxidizing the decaying organic matter to produce carbon dioxide. The bacteria possess tentacles 10 times the length of their own size to reach the electron acceptors [mostly iron(III) oxide] in the overall anaerobic redox process.

The Massachusetts scientists constructed a bacterial fuel cell using graphite electrodes. The *Geobacter* grow naturally on the surface of the electrode, forming a stable "biofilm." The overall reaction is

$$CH_3COO^- + 2O_2 + H^+ \longrightarrow 2CO_2 + 2H_2O$$

where the acetate ion represents organic matter. The electrons are transferred directly from *Geobacter* to the graphite anode and then flow externally to the graphite cathode. Here, the electron acceptor is oxygen.

So far, the current generated by such a fuel cell is small. With proper development, however, it can someday be used to generate electricity for cooking, lighting, and powering electrical appliances and computers in homes, and in remote sensing devices. This is also a desirable way to clean the environment. Although the end product in the redox process is carbon dioxide, a greenhouse gas, the same product would be formed from the normal decay of the organic wastes.

The oxidizing action of *Geobacter* has another beneficial effect. Tests show that uranium salts can replace iron(III) oxide as the electron acceptor. Thus, by adding acetate ions and the bacteria to the groundwater contaminated with uranium, it is possible to reduce the soluble uranium(VI) salts to the insoluble uranium(IV) salts, which can be readily removed before the water ends up in households and farmlands.

A bacterial fuel cell. The blowup shows the scanning electron micrograph of the bacteria growing on a graphite anode. The fritted disc allows the ions to pass between the compartments.

In addition to the H_2-O_2 system, a number of other fuel cells have been developed. Among these is the propane-oxygen fuel cell. The half-cell reactions are

Anode:	$C_3H_8(g) + 6H_2O(l) \longrightarrow 3CO_2(g) + 20H^+(aq) + 20e^-$
Cathode:	$5O_2(g) + 20H^+(aq) + 20e^- \longrightarrow 10H_2O(l)$
Overall:	$C_3H_8(g) + 5O_2(g) \longrightarrow 3CO_2(g) + 4H_2O(l)$

The overall reaction is identical to the burning of propane in oxygen.

Figure 19.12 *A hydrogen-oxygen fuel cell used in the space program. The pure water produced by the cell is consumed by the astronauts.*

A car powered by hydrogen fuel cells manufactured by General Motors.

Unlike batteries, fuel cells do not store chemical energy. Reactants must be constantly resupplied, and products must be constantly removed from a fuel cell. In this respect, a fuel cell resembles an engine more than it does a battery. However, the fuel cell does not operate like a heat engine and therefore is not subject to the same kind of thermodynamic limitations in energy conversion (see the Chemistry in Action essay on p. 796).

Properly designed fuel cells may be as much as 70 percent efficient, about twice as efficient as an internal combustion engine. In addition, fuel-cell generators are free of the noise, vibration, heat transfer, thermal pollution, and other problems normally associated with conventional power plants. Nevertheless, fuel cells are not yet in widespread use. A major problem lies in the lack of cheap electrocatalysts able to function efficiently for long periods of time without contamination. The most successful application of fuel cells to date has been in space vehicles (Figure 19.12).

19.7 Corrosion

Corrosion is the term usually applied to *the deterioration of metals by an electrochemical process*. We see many examples of corrosion around us. Rust on iron, tarnish on silver, and the green patina formed on copper and brass are a few of them (Figure 19.13). Corrosion causes enormous damage to buildings, bridges, ships, and cars. The cost of metallic corrosion to the U.S. economy has been estimated to be well over 100 billion dollars a year! This section discusses some of the fundamental processes that occur in corrosion and methods used to protect metals against it.

By far the most familiar example of corrosion is the formation of rust on iron. Oxygen gas and water must be present for iron to rust. Although the reactions involved are quite complex and not completely understood, the main steps are believed to be as follows. A region of the metal's surface serves as the anode, where oxidation occurs:

$$\text{Fe}(s) \longrightarrow \text{Fe}^{2+}(aq) + 2e^-$$

The electrons given up by iron reduce atmospheric oxygen to water at the cathode, which is another region of the same metal's surface:

$$\text{O}_2(g) + 4\text{H}^+(aq) + 4e^- \longrightarrow 2\text{H}_2\text{O}(l)$$

(a)

(b)

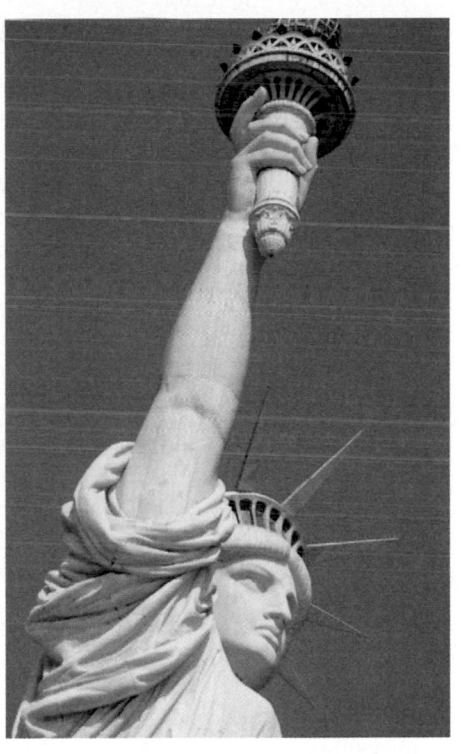

(c)

The overall redox reaction is

$$2\text{Fe}(s) + \text{O}_2(g) + 4\text{H}^+(aq) \longrightarrow 2\text{Fe}^{2+}(aq) + 2\text{H}_2\text{O}(l)$$

With data from Table 19.1, we find the standard emf for this process:

$$
\begin{aligned}
E^\circ_{\text{cell}} &= E^\circ_{\text{cathode}} - E^\circ_{\text{anode}} \\
&= 1.23\ \text{V} - (-0.44\ \text{V}) \\
&= 1.67\ \text{V}
\end{aligned}
$$

The positive standard emf means that the process will favor rust formation.

Figure 19.14 *The electro-chemical process involved in rust formation. The H^+ ions are supplied by H_2CO_3, which forms when CO_2 dissolves in water.*

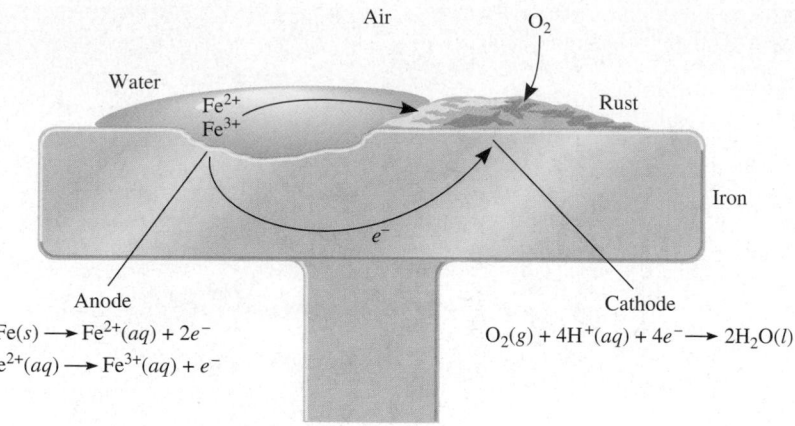

Note that this reaction occurs in an acidic medium; the H^+ ions are supplied in part by the reaction of atmospheric carbon dioxide with water to form H_2CO_3.

The Fe^{2+} ions formed at the anode are further oxidized by oxygen:

$$4Fe^{2+}(aq) + O_2(g) + (4 + 2x)H_2O(l) \longrightarrow 2Fe_2O_3 \cdot xH_2O(s) + 8H^+(aq)$$

This hydrated form of iron(III) oxide is known as rust. The amount of water associated with the iron oxide varies, so we represent the formula as $Fe_2O_3 \cdot xH_2O$.

Figure 19.14 shows the mechanism of rust formation. The electrical circuit is completed by the migration of electrons and ions; this is why rusting occurs so rapidly in salt water. In cold climates, salts (NaCl or $CaCl_2$) spread on roadways to melt ice and snow are a major cause of rust formation on automobiles.

Metallic corrosion is not limited to iron. Consider aluminum, a metal used to make many useful things, including airplanes and beverage cans. Aluminum has a much greater tendency to oxidize than iron does; in Table 19.1 we see that Al has a more negative standard reduction potential than Fe. Based on this fact alone, we might expect to see airplanes slowly corrode away in rainstorms, and soda cans transformed into piles of corroded aluminum. These processes do not occur because the layer of insoluble aluminum oxide (Al_2O_3) that forms on its surface when the metal is exposed to air serves to protect the aluminum underneath from further corrosion. The rust that forms on the surface of iron, however, is too porous to protect the underlying metal.

Coinage metals such as copper and silver also corrode, but much more slowly.

$$Cu(s) \longrightarrow Cu^{2+}(aq) + 2e^-$$
$$Ag(s) \longrightarrow Ag^+(aq) + e^-$$

In normal atmospheric exposure, copper forms a layer of copper carbonate ($CuCO_3$), a green substance also called patina, that protects the metal underneath from further corrosion. Likewise, silverware that comes into contact with foodstuffs develops a layer of silver sulfide (Ag_2S).

A number of methods have been devised to protect metals from corrosion. Most of these methods are aimed at preventing rust formation. The most obvious approach is to coat the metal surface with paint. However, if the paint is scratched, pitted, or dented to expose even the smallest area of bare metal, rust will form under the paint layer. The surface of iron metal can be made inactive by a process called *passivation*. A thin oxide layer is formed when the metal is treated with a strong oxidizing agent such as concentrated nitric acid. A solution of sodium chromate is often added to cooling systems and radiators to prevent rust formation.

Figure 19.15 *An iron nail that is cathodically protected by a piece of zinc strip does not rust in water, while an iron nail without such protection rusts readily.*

The tendency for iron to oxidize is greatly reduced when it is alloyed with certain other metals. For example, in stainless steel, an alloy of iron and chromium, a layer of chromium oxide forms that protects the iron from corrosion.

An iron container can be covered with a layer of another metal such as tin or zinc. A "tin" can is made by applying a thin layer of tin over iron. Rust formation is prevented as long as the tin layer remains intact. However, once the surface has been scratched, rusting occurs rapidly. If we look up the standard reduction potentials, according to the diagonal rule, we find that iron acts as the anode and tin as the cathode in the corrosion process:

$$\text{Sn}^{2+}(aq) + 2e^- \longrightarrow \text{Sn}(s) \qquad E° = -0.14 \text{ V}$$
$$\text{Fe}^{2+}(aq) + 2e^- \longrightarrow \text{Fe}(s) \qquad E° = -0.44 \text{ V}$$

The protective process is different for zinc-plated, or *galvanized,* iron. Zinc is more easily oxidized than iron (see Table 19.1):

$$\text{Zn}^{2+}(aq) + 2e^- \longrightarrow \text{Zn}(s) \qquad E° = -0.76 \text{ V}$$

So even if a scratch exposes the iron, the zinc is still attacked. In this case, the zinc metal serves as the anode and the iron is the cathode.

Cathodic protection is a process in which the metal that is to be protected from corrosion is made the cathode in what amounts to a galvanic cell. Figure 19.15 shows how an iron nail can be protected from rusting by connecting the nail to a piece of zinc. Without such protection, an iron nail quickly rusts in water. Rusting of underground iron pipes and iron storage tanks can be prevented or greatly reduced by connecting them to metals such as zinc and magnesium, which oxidize more readily than iron (Figure 19.16).

Oxidation: $\text{Mg}(s) \longrightarrow \text{Mg}^{2+}(aq) + 2e^-$ Reduction: $\text{O}_2(g) + 4\text{H}^+(aq) + 4e^- \longrightarrow 2\text{H}_2\text{O}(l)$

Figure 19.16 *Cathodic protection of an iron storage tank (cathode) by magnesium, a more electropositive metal (anode). Since only the magnesium is depleted in the electrochemical process, it is sometimes called the sacrificial anode.*

The Chemistry in Action essay on p. 853 shows that dental filling discomfort can result from an electrochemical phenomenon.

19.8 Electrolysis

In contrast to spontaneous redox reactions, which result in the conversion of chemical energy into electrical energy, *electrolysis* is the process in which *electrical energy is used to cause a nonspontaneous chemical reaction to occur*. An *electrolytic cell* is *an apparatus for carrying out electrolysis*. The same principles underlie electrolysis and the processes that take place in galvanic cells. Here we will discuss three examples of electrolysis based on those principles. Then we will look at the quantitative aspects of electrolysis.

Electrolysis of Molten Sodium Chloride

In its molten state, sodium chloride, an ionic compound, can be electrolyzed to form sodium metal and chlorine. Figure 19.17(a) is a diagram of a *Downs cell,* which is used for large-scale electrolysis of NaCl. In molten NaCl, the cations and anions are the Na^+ and Cl^- ions, respectively. Figure 19.17(b) is a simplified diagram showing the reactions that occur at the electrodes. The electrolytic cell contains a pair of electrodes connected to the battery. The battery serves as an "electron pump," driving electrons to the cathode, where reduction occurs, and withdrawing electrons from the anode, where oxidation occurs. The reactions at the electrodes are

$$
\begin{aligned}
\text{Anode (oxidation):} \quad & 2Cl^-(l) \longrightarrow Cl_2(g) + 2e^- \\
\text{Cathode (reduction):} \quad & \underline{2Na^+(l) + 2e^- \longrightarrow 2Na(l)} \\
\text{Overall:} \quad & 2Na^+(l) + 2Cl^-(l) \longrightarrow 2Na(l) + Cl_2(g)
\end{aligned}
$$

This process is a major source of pure sodium metal and chlorine gas.

Theoretical estimates show that the $E°$ value for the overall process is about -4 V, which means that this is a nonspontaneous process. Therefore, a *minimum* of 4 V must be supplied by the battery to carry out the reaction. In practice, a higher voltage is necessary because of inefficiencies in the electrolytic process and because of overvoltage, to be discussed shortly.

Figure 19.17 *(a) A practical arrangement called a Downs cell for the electrolysis of molten NaCl (m.p. = 801°C). The sodium metal formed at the cathodes is in the liquid state. Since liquid sodium metal is lighter than molten NaCl, the sodium floats to the surface, as shown, and is collected. Chlorine gas forms at the anode and is collected at the top. (b) A simplified diagram showing the electrode reactions during the electrolysis of molten NaCl. The battery is needed to drive the nonspontaneous reactions.*

(a)   (b)

Electrolysis of Water

Water in a beaker under atmospheric conditions (1 atm and 25°C) will not sponta-neously decompose to form hydrogen and oxygen gas because the standard free-energy change for the reaction is a large positive quantity:

$$2H_2O(l) \longrightarrow 2H_2(g) + O_2(g) \qquad \Delta G° = 474.4 \text{ kJ/mol}$$

However, this reaction can be induced in a cell like the one shown in Figure 19.18. This electrolytic cell consists of a pair of electrodes made of a nonreactive metal, such as platinum, immersed in water. When the electrodes are connected to the battery, nothing happens because there are not enough ions in pure water to carry much of an electric current. (Remember that at 25°C, pure water has only 1×10^{-7} M H^+ ions and 1×10^{-7} M OH^- ions.) On the other hand, the reaction occurs readily in a 0.1 M H_2SO_4 solution because there are a sufficient number of ions to conduct electricity. Immediately, gas bubbles begin to appear at both electrodes.

Figure 19.19 shows the electrode reactions. The process at the anode is

$$2H_2O(l) \longrightarrow O_2(g) + 4H^+(aq) + 4e^-$$

while at the cathode we have

$$H^+(aq) + e^- \longrightarrow \tfrac{1}{2}H_2(g)$$

The overall reaction is given by

Anode (oxidation):	$2H_2O(l) \longrightarrow O_2(g) + 4H^+(aq) + 4e^-$
Cathode (reduction):	$4[H^+(aq) + e^- \longrightarrow \tfrac{1}{2}H_2(g)]$
Overall:	$2H_2O(l) \longrightarrow 2H_2(g) + O_2(g)$

Note that no net H_2SO_4 is consumed.

Electrolysis of an Aqueous Sodium Chloride Solution

This is the most complicated of the three examples of electrolysis considered here because aqueous sodium chloride solution contains several species that could be oxi-dized and reduced. The oxidation reactions that might occur at the anode are

(1) $2Cl^-(aq) \longrightarrow Cl_2(g) + 2e^-$
(2) $2H_2O(l) \longrightarrow O_2(g) + 4H^+(aq) + 4e^-$

Figure 19.18 *Apparatus for small-scale electrolysis of water. The volume of hydrogen gas generated at the cathode is twice that of oxygen gas generated at the anode.*

What is the minimum voltage needed for this electrolytic process?

Battery

e^- e^-

Anode   Cathode

Dilute H_2SO_4 solution

Oxidation   Reduction

$2H_2O(l) \longrightarrow O_2(g) + 4H^+(aq) + 4e^-$ $4H^+(aq) + 4e^- \longrightarrow 2H_2(g)$

Figure 19.19 *A diagram showing the electrode reactions during the electrolysis of water.*

Referring to Table 19.1, we find

$$Cl_2(g) + 2e^- \longrightarrow 2Cl^-(aq) \qquad E° = 1.36 \text{ V}$$
$$O_2(g) + 4H^+(aq) + 4e^- \longrightarrow 2H_2O(l) \qquad E° = 1.23 \text{ V}$$

Because Cl_2 is more easily reduced than O_2, it follows that it would be more difficult to oxidize Cl^- than H_2O at the anode.

The standard reduction potentials of (1) and (2) are not very different, but the values do suggest that H_2O should be preferentially oxidized at the anode. However, by experiment we find that the gas liberated at the anode is Cl_2, not O_2! In studying electrolytic processes, we sometimes find that the voltage required for a reaction is considerably higher than the electrode potential indicates. The **overvoltage** is *the difference between the electrode potential and the actual voltage required to cause electrolysis*. The overvoltage for O_2 formation is quite high. Therefore, under normal operating conditions Cl_2 gas is actually formed at the anode instead of O_2.

The reductions that might occur at the cathode are

$$(3) \quad 2H^+(aq) + 2e^- \longrightarrow H_2(g) \qquad E° = 0.00 \text{ V}$$
$$(4) \quad 2H_2O(l) + 2e^- \longrightarrow H_2(g) + 2OH^-(aq) \qquad E° = -0.83 \text{ V}$$
$$(5) \quad Na^+(aq) + e^- \longrightarrow Na(s) \qquad E° = -2.71 \text{ V}$$

Reaction (5) is ruled out because it has a very negative standard reduction potential. Reaction (3) is preferred over (4) under standard-state conditions. At a pH of 7 (as is the case for a NaCl solution), however, they are equally probable. We generally use (4) to describe the cathode reaction because the concentration of H^+ ions is too low (about $1 \times 10^{-7} M$) to make (3) a reasonable choice.

Thus, the half-cell reactions in the electrolysis of aqueous sodium chloride are

Anode (oxidation): $\qquad 2Cl^-(aq) \longrightarrow Cl_2(g) + 2e^-$
Cathode (reduction): $\qquad \underline{2H_2O(l) + 2e^- \longrightarrow H_2(g) + 2OH^-(aq)}$

Overall: $\quad 2H_2O(l) + 2Cl^-(aq) \longrightarrow H_2(g) + Cl_2(g) + 2OH^-(aq)$

As the overall reaction shows, the concentration of the Cl^- ions decreases during electrolysis and that of the OH^- ions increases. Therefore, in addition to H_2 and Cl_2, the useful by-product NaOH can be obtained by evaporating the aqueous solution at the end of the electrolysis.

Keep in mind the following from our analysis of electrolysis: cations are likely to be reduced at the cathode and anions are likely to be oxidized at the anode, and in aqueous solutions water itself may be oxidized and/or reduced. The outcome depends on the nature of other species present.

Example 19.8 deals with the electrolysis of an aqueous solution of sodium sulfate (Na_2SO_4).

Example 19.8

An aqueous Na_2SO_4 solution is electrolyzed, using the apparatus shown in Figure 19.18. If the products formed at the anode and cathode are oxygen gas and hydrogen gas, respectively, describe the electrolysis in terms of the reactions at the electrodes.

The SO_4^{2-} ion is the conjugate base of the weak acid HSO_4^- ($K_a = 1.3 \times 10^{-2}$). However, the extent to which SO_4^{2-} hydrolyzes is negligible. Also, the SO_4^{2-} ion is not oxidized at the anode.

Strategy Before we look at the electrode reactions, we should consider the following facts: (1) Because Na_2SO_4 does not hydrolyze, the pH of the solution is close to 7. (2) The Na^+ ions are not reduced at the cathode and the SO_4^{2-} ions are not oxidized at the anode. These conclusions are drawn from the electrolysis of water in the presence of sulfuric acid and in aqueous sodium chloride solution, as discussed earlier. Therefore, both the oxidation and reduction reactions involve only water molecules.

(Continued)

Solution The electrode reactions are

Anode: $2H_2O(l) \longrightarrow O_2(g) + 4H^+(aq) + 4e^-$
Cathode: $2H_2O(l) + 2e^- \longrightarrow H_2(g) + 2OH^-(aq)$

The overall reaction, obtained by doubling the cathode reaction coefficients and adding the result to the anode reaction, is

$$6H_2O(l) \longrightarrow 2H_2(g) + O_2(g) + 4H^+(aq) + 4OH^-(aq)$$

If the H^+ and OH^- ions are allowed to mix, then

$$4H^+(aq) + 4OH^-(aq) \longrightarrow 4H_2O(l)$$

and the overall reaction becomes

$$2H_2O(l) \longrightarrow 2H_2(g) + O_2(g)$$

Similar problem: 19.92.

Practice Exercise An aqueous solution of $Mg(NO_3)_2$ is electrolyzed. What are the gaseous products at the anode and cathode?

Electrolysis has many important applications in industry, mainly in the extraction and purification of metals. We will discuss some of these applications in Chapter 20.

Quantitative Aspects of Electrolysis

The quantitative treatment of electrolysis was developed primarily by Faraday. He observed that the mass of product formed (or reactant consumed) at an electrode is proportional to both the amount of electricity transferred at the electrode and the molar mass of the substance in question. For example, in the electrolysis of molten NaCl, the cathode reaction tells us that one Na atom is produced when one Na^+ ion accepts an electron from the electrode. To reduce 1 mole of Na^+ ions, we must supply Avogadro's number (6.02×10^{23}) of electrons to the cathode. On the other hand, the stoichiometry of the anode reaction shows that oxidation of two Cl^- ions yields one chlorine molecule. Therefore, the formation of 1 mole of Cl_2 results in the transfer of 2 moles of electrons from the Cl^- ions to the anode. Similarly, it takes 2 moles of electrons to reduce 1 mole of Mg^{2+} ions and 3 moles of electrons to reduce 1 mole of Al^{3+} ions:

$$Mg^{2+} + 2e^- \longrightarrow Mg$$
$$Al^{3+} + 3e^- \longrightarrow Al$$

In an electrolysis experiment, we generally measure the current (in amperes, A) that passes through an electrolytic cell in a given period of time. The relationship between charge (in coulombs, C) and current is

$$1 \text{ C} = 1 \text{ A} \times 1 \text{ s}$$

that is, a coulomb is the quantity of electrical charge passing any point in the circuit in 1 second when the current is 1 ampere.

Figure 19.20 shows the steps involved in calculating the quantities of substances produced in electrolysis. Let us illustrate the approach by considering molten $CaCl_2$ in an electrolytic cell. Suppose a current of 0.452 A is passed through the cell for 1.50 h. How much product will be formed at the anode and at the cathode? In solving

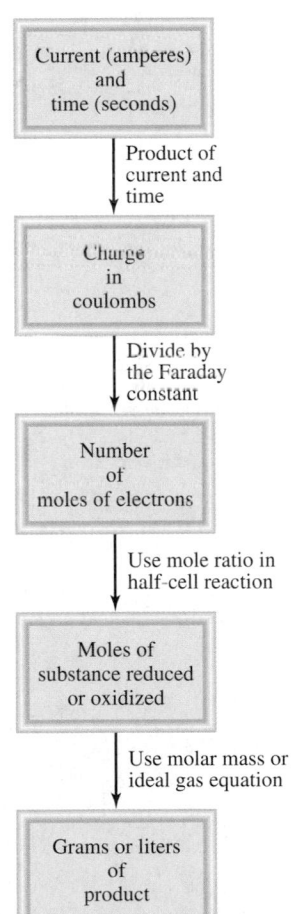

Figure 19.20 *Steps involved in calculating amounts of substances reduced or oxidized in electrolysis.*

electrolysis problems of this type, the first step is to determine which species will be oxidized at the anode and which species will be reduced at the cathode. Here the choice is straightforward because we only have Ca^{2+} and Cl^- ions in molten $CaCl_2$. Thus, we write the half- and overall cell reactions as

Anode (oxidation): $2Cl^-(l) \longrightarrow Cl_2(g) + 2e^-$
Cathode (reduction): $Ca^{2+}(l) + 2e^- \longrightarrow Ca(l)$
Overall: $Ca^{2+}(l) + 2Cl^-(l) \longrightarrow Ca(l) + Cl_2(g)$

The quantities of calcium metal and chlorine gas formed depend on the number of electrons that pass through the electrolytic cell, which in turn depends on current $\times$ time, or charge:

$$? \, C = 0.452 \, A \times 1.50 \, h \times \frac{3600 \, s}{1 \, h} \times \frac{1 \, C}{1 \, A \cdot s} = 2.44 \times 10^3 \, C$$

Because 1 mol $e^- = 96{,}500$ C and 2 mol e^- are required to reduce 1 mole of Ca^{2+} ions, the mass of Ca metal formed at the cathode is calculated as follows:

$$? \, g \, Ca = 2.44 \times 10^3 \, C \times \frac{1 \, mol \, e^-}{96{,}500 \, C} \times \frac{1 \, mol \, Ca}{2 \, mol \, e^-} \times \frac{40.08 \, g \, Ca}{1 \, mol \, Ca} = 0.507 \, g \, Ca$$

The anode reaction indicates that 1 mole of chlorine is produced per 2 mol e^- of electricity. Hence the mass of chlorine gas formed is

$$? \, g \, Cl_2 = 2.44 \times 10^3 \, C \times \frac{1 \, mol \, e^-}{96{,}500 \, C} \times \frac{1 \, mol \, Cl_2}{2 \, mol \, e^-} \times \frac{70.90 \, g \, Cl_2}{1 \, mol \, Cl_2} = 0.896 \, g \, Cl_2$$

Example 19.9 applies this approach to the electrolysis in an aqueous solution.

Example 19.9

A current of 1.26 A is passed through an electrolytic cell containing a dilute sulfuric acid solution for 7.44 h. Write the half-cell reactions and calculate the volume of gases generated at STP.

Strategy Earlier (see p. 849) we saw that the half-cell reactions for the process are

Anode (oxidation): $2H_2O(l) \longrightarrow O_2(g) + 4H^+(aq) + 4e^-$
Cathode (reduction): $4[H^+(aq) + e^- \longrightarrow \frac{1}{2}H_2(g)]$
Overall: $2H_2O(l) \longrightarrow 2H_2(g) + O_2(g)$

According to Figure 19.20, we carry out the following conversion steps to calculate the quantity of O_2 in moles:

current $\times$ time $\rightarrow$ coulombs $\rightarrow$ moles of $e^- \rightarrow$ moles of O_2

Then, using the ideal gas equation we can calculate the volume of O_2 in liters at STP. A similar procedure can be used for H_2.

Solution First we calculate the number of coulombs of electricity that pass through the cell:

$$? \, C = 1.26 \, A \times 7.44 \, h \times \frac{3600 \, s}{1 \, h} \times \frac{1 \, C}{1 \, A \cdot s} = 3.37 \times 10^4 \, C$$

(Continued)

Dental Filling Discomfort

In modern dentistry the material most commonly used to fill decaying teeth is known as *dental amalgam.* (An amalgam is a substance made by combining mercury with another metal or metals.) Dental amalgam actually consists of three solid phases having stoichiometries approximately corresponding to Ag_2Hg_3, Ag_3Sn, and Sn_8Hg. The standard reduction potentials for these solid phases are: Hg_2^{2+}/Ag_2Hg_3, 0.85 V; Sn^{2+}/Ag_3Sn, -0.05 V; and Sn^{2+}/Sn_8Hg, -0.13 V.

Anyone who bites a piece of aluminum foil (such as that used for wrapping candies) in such a way that the foil presses against a dental filling will probably experience a momentary sharp pain. In effect, an electrochemical cell has been created in the mouth, with aluminum ($E° = -1.66$ V) as the anode, the filling as the cathode, and saliva as the electrolyte. Contact between the aluminum foil and the filling short-circuits the cell, causing a weak current to flow between the electrodes. This current stimulates the sensitive nerve of the tooth, causing an unpleasant sensation.

Another type of discomfort results when a less electropositive metal touches a dental filling. For example, if a filling makes contact with a gold inlay in a nearby tooth, corrosion of the filling will occur. In this case, the dental filling acts as the anode and the gold inlay as the cathode. Referring to the $E°$ values for the three phases, we see that the Sn_8Hg phase is most likely to corrode.

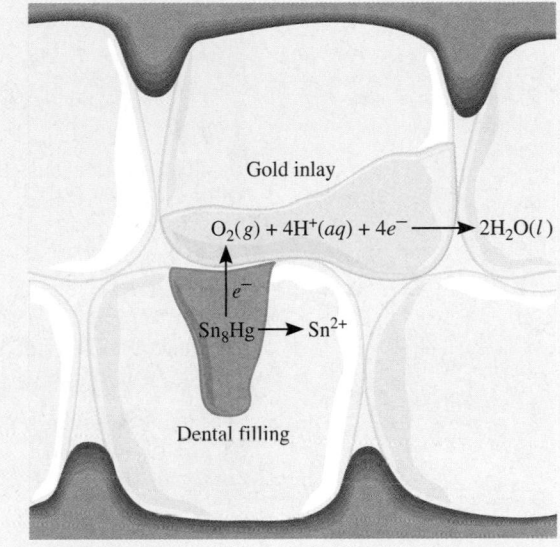

Corrosion of a dental filling brought about by contact with a gold inlay.

When that happens, release of Sn(II) ions in the mouth produces an unpleasant metallic taste. Prolonged corrosion will eventually result in another visit to the dentist for a replacement filling.

Next, we convert number of coulombs to number of moles of electrons

$$3.37 \times 10^4 \, \text{C} \times \frac{1 \, \text{mol} \, e^-}{96,500 \, \text{C}} = 0.349 \, \text{mol} \, e^-$$

From the oxidation half-reaction we see that 1 mol $O_2 \simeq 4$ mol e^-. Therefore, the number of moles of O_2 generated is

$$0.349 \, \text{mol} \, e^- \times \frac{1 \, \text{mol} \, O_2}{4 \, \text{mol} \, e^-} = 0.0873 \, \text{mol} \, O_2$$

The volume of 0.0873 mol O_2 at STP is given by

$$V = \frac{nRT}{P}$$
$$= \frac{(0.0873 \, \text{mol})(0.0821 \, \text{L} \cdot \text{atm/K} \cdot \text{mol})(273 \, \text{K})}{1 \, \text{atm}} = 1.96 \, \text{L}$$

(Continued)

The procedure for hydrogen is similar. To simplify, we combine the first two steps to calculate the number of moles of H_2 generated:

$$3.37 \times 10^4 \ \cancel{C} \times \frac{1 \ \cancel{mol \ e^-}}{96{,}500 \ \cancel{C}} \times \frac{1 \ mol \ H_2}{2 \ \cancel{mol \ e^-}} = 0.175 \ mol \ H_2$$

The volume of 0.175 mol H_2 at STP is given by

$$
\begin{aligned}
V &= \frac{nRT}{P} \\
&= \frac{(0.175 \ mol)(0.0821 \ L \cdot atm/K \cdot mol)(273 \ K)}{1 \ atm} \\
&= \boxed{3.92 \ L}
\end{aligned}
$$

Check Note that the volume of H_2 is twice that of O_2 (see Figure 19.18), which is what we would expect based on Avogadro's law (at the same temperature and pressure, volume is directly proportional to the number of moles of gases).

Similar problem: 19.49.

Practice Exercise A constant current is passed through an electrolytic cell containing molten $MgCl_2$ for 18 h. If 4.8×10^5 g of Cl_2 are obtained, what is the current in amperes?

Summary of Facts and Concepts

1. Redox reactions involve the transfer of electrons. Equations representing redox processes can be balanced using the ion-electron method.

2. All electrochemical reactions involve the transfer of electrons and therefore are redox reactions.

3. In a galvanic cell, electricity is produced by a spontaneous chemical reaction. Oxidation and reduction take place separately at the anode and cathode, respectively, and the electrons flow through an external circuit.

4. The two parts of a galvanic cell are the half-cells, and the reactions at the electrodes are the half-cell reactions. A salt bridge allows ions to flow between the half-cells.

5. The electromotive force (emf) of a cell is the voltage difference between the two electrodes. In the external circuit, electrons flow from the anode to the cathode in a galvanic cell. In solution, the anions move toward the anode and the cations move toward the cathode.

6. The quantity of electricity carried by 1 mole of electrons is called a faraday, which is equal to 96,500 C.

7. Standard reduction potentials show the relative likelihood of half-cell reduction reactions and can be used to predict the products, direction, and spontaneity of redox reactions between various substances.

8. The decrease in free energy of the system in a spontaneous redox reaction is equal to the electrical work done by the system on the surroundings, or $\Delta G = -nFE$.

9. The equilibrium constant for a redox reaction can be found from the standard electromotive force of a cell.

10. The Nernst equation gives the relationship between the cell emf and the concentrations of the reactants and products under non-standard-state conditions.

11. Batteries, which consist of one or more galvanic cells, are used widely as self-contained power sources. Some of the better-known batteries are the dry cell, such as the Leclanché cell, the mercury battery, and the lead storage battery used in automobiles. Fuel cells produce electrical energy from a continuous supply of reactants.

12. The corrosion of metals, such as the rusting of iron, is an electrochemical phenomenon.

13. Electric current from an external source is used to drive a nonspontaneous chemical reaction in an electrolytic cell. The amount of product formed or reactant consumed depends on the quantity of electricity transferred at the electrode.

Key Words

Questions and Problems

Balancing Redox Equations

Problems

19.1 Balance the following redox equations by the ion-electron method:

(a) $H_2O_2 + Fe^{2+} \longrightarrow Fe^{3+} + H_2O$ (in acidic solution)

(b) $Cu + HNO_3 \longrightarrow Cu^{2+} + NO + H_2O$ (in acidic solution)

(c) $CN^- + MnO_4^- \longrightarrow CNO^- + MnO_2$ (in basic solution)

(d) $Br_2 \longrightarrow BrO_3^- + Br^-$ (in basic solution)

(e) $S_2O_3^{2-} + I_2 \longrightarrow I^- + S_4O_6^{2-}$ (in acidic solution)

19.2 Balance the following redox equations by the ion-electron method:

(a) $Mn^{2+} + H_2O_2 \longrightarrow MnO_2 + H_2O$ (in basic solution)

(b) $Bi(OH)_3 + SnO_2^{2-} \longrightarrow SnO_3^{2-} + Bi$ (in basic solution)

(c) $Cr_2O_7^{2-} + C_2O_4^{2-} \longrightarrow Cr^{3+} + CO_2$ (in acidic solution)

(d) $ClO_3^- + Cl^- \longrightarrow Cl_2 + ClO_2$ (in acidic solution)

Galvanic Cells and Standard Emfs

Review Questions

19.3 Define the following terms: anode, cathode, cell voltage, electromotive force, standard reduction potential.

19.4 Describe the basic features of a galvanic cell. Why are the two components of the cell separated from each other?

19.5 What is the function of a salt bridge? What kind of electrolyte should be used in a salt bridge?

19.6 What is a cell diagram? Write the cell diagram for a galvanic cell consisting of an Al electrode placed in a 1 M $Al(NO_3)_3$ solution and a Ag electrode placed in a 1 M $AgNO_3$ solution.

19.7 What is the difference between the half-reactions discussed in redox processes in Chapter 4 and the half-cell reactions discussed in Section 19.2?

19.8 After operating a Daniell cell (see Figure 19.1) for a few minutes, a student notices that the cell emf begins to drop. Why?

19.9 Use the information in Table 2.1, and calculate the Faraday constant.

19.10 Discuss the spontaneity of an electrochemical reaction in terms of its standard emf (E_{cell}°).

Problems

19.11 Calculate the standard emf of a cell that uses the Mg/Mg^{2+} and Cu/Cu^{2+} half-cell reactions at 25°C. Write the equation for the cell reaction that occurs under standard-state conditions.

19.12 Calculate the standard emf of a cell that uses Ag/Ag^+ and Al/Al^{3+} half-cell reactions. Write the cell reaction that occurs under standard-state conditions.

19.13 Predict whether Fe^{3+} can oxidize I^- to I_2 under standard-state conditions.

19.14 Which of the following reagents can oxidize H_2O to $O_2(g)$ under standard-state conditions? $H^+(aq)$, $Cl^-(aq)$, $Cl_2(g)$, $Cu^{2+}(aq)$, $Pb^{2+}(aq)$, $MnO_4^-(aq)$ (in acid).

19.15 Consider the following half-reactions:

$$MnO_4^-(aq) + 8H^+(aq) + 5e^- \longrightarrow Mn^{2+}(aq) + 4H_2O(l)$$
$$NO_3^-(aq) + 4H^+(aq) + 3e^- \longrightarrow NO(g) + 2H_2O(l)$$

Predict whether NO_3^- ions will oxidize Mn^{2+} to MnO_4^- under standard-state conditions.

19.16 Predict whether the following reactions would occur spontaneously in aqueous solution at 25°C. Assume that the initial concentrations of dissolved species are all 1.0 M.

(a) $Ca(s) + Cd^{2+}(aq) \longrightarrow Ca^{2+}(aq) + Cd(s)$

(b) $2Br^-(aq) + Sn^{2+}(aq) \longrightarrow Br_2(l) + Sn(s)$

(c) $2Ag(s) + Ni^{2+}(aq) \longrightarrow 2Ag^+(aq) + Ni(s)$

(d) $Cu^+(aq) + Fe^{3+}(aq) \longrightarrow$
$$Cu^{2+}(aq) + Fe^{2+}(aq)$$

19.17 Which species in each pair is a better oxidizing agent under standard-state conditions? (a) Br_2 or Au^{3+}, (b) H_2 or Ag^+, (c) Cd^{2+} or Cr^{3+}, (d) O_2 in acidic media or O_2 in basic media.

19.18 Which species in each pair is a better reducing agent under standard-state conditions? (a) Na or Li, (b) H_2 or I_2, (c) Fe^{2+} or Ag, (d) Br^- or Co^{2+}.

Spontaneity of Redox Reactions
Review Questions

19.19 Write the equations relating $\Delta G°$ and K to the standard emf of a cell. Define all the terms.

19.20 Compare the ease of measuring the equilibrium constant electrochemically with that by chemical means [see Equation (18.14)].

Problems

19.21 What is the equilibrium constant for the following reaction at 25°C?
$$Mg(s) + Zn^{2+}(aq) \rightleftharpoons Mg^{2+}(aq) + Zn(s)$$

19.22 The equilibrium constant for the reaction
$$Sr(s) + Mg^{2+}(aq) \rightleftharpoons Sr^{2+}(aq) + Mg(s)$$
is 2.69×10^{12} at 25°C. Calculate $E°$ for a cell made up of Sr/Sr^{2+} and Mg/Mg^{2+} half-cells.

19.23 Use the standard reduction potentials to find the equilibrium constant for each of the following reactions at 25°C:
(a) $Br_2(l) + 2I^-(aq) \rightleftharpoons 2Br^-(aq) + I_2(s)$
(b) $2Ce^{4+}(aq) + 2Cl^-(aq) \rightleftharpoons$
$$Cl_2(g) + 2Ce^{3+}(aq)$$
(c) $5Fe^{2+}(aq) + MnO_4^-(aq) + 8H^+(aq) \rightleftharpoons$
$$Mn^{2+}(aq) + 4H_2O(l) + 5Fe^{3+}(aq)$$

19.24 Calculate $\Delta G°$ and K_c for the following reactions at 25°C:
(a) $Mg(s) + Pb^{2+}(aq) \rightleftharpoons Mg^{2+}(aq) + Pb(s)$
(b) $Br_2(l) + 2I^-(aq) \rightleftharpoons 2Br^-(aq) + I_2(s)$
(c) $O_2(g) + 4H^+(aq) + 4Fe^{2+}(aq) \rightleftharpoons$
$$2H_2O(l) + 4Fe^{3+}(aq)$$
(d) $2Al(s) + 3I_2(s) \rightleftharpoons 2Al^{3+}(aq) + 6I^-(aq)$

19.25 Under standard-state conditions, what spontaneous reaction will occur in aqueous solution among the ions Ce^{4+}, Ce^{3+}, Fe^{3+}, and Fe^{2+}? Calculate $\Delta G°$ and K_c for the reaction.

19.26 Given that $E° = 0.52$ V for the reduction $Cu^+(aq) + e^- \rightarrow Cu(s)$, calculate $E°$, $\Delta G°$, and K for the following reaction at 25°C:
$$2Cu^+(aq) \longrightarrow Cu^{2+}(aq) + Cu(s)$$

The Effect of Concentration on Cell Emf
Review Questions

19.27 Write the Nernst equation and explain all the terms.

19.28 Write the Nernst equation for the following processes at some temperature T:
(a) $Mg(s) + Sn^{2+}(aq) \longrightarrow Mg^{2+}(aq) + Sn(s)$
(b) $2Cr(s) + 3Pb^{2+}(aq) \longrightarrow 2Cr^{3+}(aq) + 3Pb(s)$

Problems

19.29 What is the potential of a cell made up of Zn/Zn^{2+} and Cu/Cu^{2+} half-cells at 25°C if $[Zn^{2+}] = 0.25 M$ and $[Cu^{2+}] = 0.15 M$?

19.30 Calculate $E°$, E, and ΔG for the following cell reactions.
(a) $Mg(s) + Sn^{2+}(aq) \longrightarrow Mg^{2+}(aq) + Sn(s)$
$[Mg^{2+}] = 0.045 M$, $[Sn^{2+}] = 0.035 M$
(b) $3Zn(s) + 2Cr^{3+}(aq) \longrightarrow 3Zn^{2+}(aq) + 2Cr(s)$
$[Cr^{3+}] = 0.010 M$, $[Zn^{2+}] = 0.0085 M$

19.31 Calculate the standard potential of the cell consisting of the Zn/Zn^{2+} half-cell and the SHE. What will the emf of the cell be if $[Zn^{2+}] = 0.45 M$, $P_{H_2} = 2.0$ atm, and $[H^+] = 1.8 M$?

19.32 What is the emf of a cell consisting of a Pb^{2+}/Pb half-cell and a $Pt/H^+/H_2$ half-cell if $[Pb^{2+}] = 0.10 M$, $[H^+] = 0.050 M$, and $P_{H_2} = 1.0$ atm?

19.33 Referring to the arrangement in Figure 19.1, calculate the $[Cu^{2+}]/[Zn^{2+}]$ ratio at which the following reaction is spontaneous at 25°C:
$$Cu(s) + Zn^{2+}(aq) \longrightarrow Cu^{2+}(aq) + Zn(s)$$

19.34 Calculate the emf of the following concentration cell:
$$Mg(s)|Mg^{2+}(0.24\ M)\|Mg^{2+}(0.53\ M)|Mg(s)$$

Batteries and Fuel Cells
Review Questions

19.35 Explain the differences between a primary galvanic cell—one that is not rechargeable—and a storage cell (for example, the lead storage battery), which is rechargeable.

19.36 Discuss the advantages and disadvantages of fuel cells over conventional power plants in producing electricity.

Problems

19.37 The hydrogen-oxygen fuel cell is described in Section 19.6. (a) What volume of $H_2(g)$, stored at 25°C at a pressure of 155 atm, would be needed to run an electric motor drawing a current of 8.5 A for 3.0 h? (b) What volume (liters) of air at 25°C and 1.00 atm will have to pass into the cell per minute to run the motor? Assume that air is 20 percent O_2 by volume and that all the O_2 is consumed in the cell. The other components of air do not affect the fuel-cell reactions. Assume ideal gas behavior.

19.38 Calculate the standard emf of the propane fuel cell discussed on p. 843 at 25°C, given that ΔG_f° for propane is -23.5 kJ/mol.

Corrosion

Review Questions

19.39 Steel hardware, including nuts and bolts, is often coated with a thin plating of cadmium. Explain the function of the cadmium layer.

19.40 "Galvanized iron" is steel sheet that has been coated with zinc; "tin" cans are made of steel sheet coated with tin. Discuss the functions of these coatings and the electrochemistry of the corrosion reactions that occur if an electrolyte contacts the scratched surface of a galvanized iron sheet or a tin can.

19.41 Tarnished silver contains Ag_2S. The tarnish can be removed by placing silverware in an aluminum pan containing an inert electrolyte solution, such as NaCl. Explain the electrochemical principle for this procedure. [The standard reduction potential for the half-cell reaction $Ag_2S(s) + 2e^- \rightarrow 2Ag(s) + S^{2-}(aq)$ is -0.71 V.]

19.42 How does the tendency of iron to rust depend on the pH of solution?

Electrolysis

Review Questions

19.43 What is the difference between a galvanic cell (such as a Daniell cell) and an electrolytic cell?

19.44 What is Faraday's contribution to quantitative electrolysis?

Problems

19.45 The half-reaction at an electrode is

$$Mg^{2+}(\text{molten}) + 2e^- \longrightarrow Mg(s)$$

Calculate the number of grams of magnesium that can be produced by supplying 1.00 F to the electrode.

19.46 Consider the electrolysis of molten barium chloride, $BaCl_2$. (a) Write the half-reactions. (b) How many grams of barium metal can be produced by supplying 0.50 A for 30 min?

19.47 Considering only the cost of electricity, would it be cheaper to produce a ton of sodium or a ton of aluminum by electrolysis?

19.48 If the cost of electricity to produce magnesium by the electrolysis of molten magnesium chloride is $155 per ton of metal, what is the cost (in dollars) of the electricity necessary to produce (a) 10.0 tons of

aluminum, (b) 30.0 tons of sodium, (c) 50.0 tons of calcium?

19.49 One of the half-reactions for the electrolysis of water is

$$2H_2O(l) \longrightarrow O_2(g) + 4H^+(aq) + 4e^-$$

If 0.076 L of O_2 is collected at 25°C and 755 mmHg, how many faradays of electricity had to pass through the solution?

19.50 How many faradays of electricity are required to produce (a) 0.84 L of O_2 at exactly 1 atm and 25°C from aqueous H_2SO_4 solution; (b) 1.50 L of Cl_2 at 750 mmHg and 20°C from molten NaCl; (c) 6.0 g of Sn from molten $SnCl_2$?

19.51 Calculate the amounts of Cu and Br_2 produced in 1.0 h at inert electrodes in a solution of $CuBr_2$ by a current of 4.50 A.

19.52 In the electrolysis of an aqueous $AgNO_3$ solution, 0.67 g of Ag is deposited after a certain period of time. (a) Write the half-reaction for the reduction of Ag^+. (b) What is the probable oxidation half-reaction? (c) Calculate the quantity of electricity used, in coulombs.

19.53 A steady current was passed through molten $CoSO_4$ until 2.35 g of metallic cobalt was produced. Calculate the number of coulombs of electricity used.

19.54 A constant electric current flows for 3.75 h through two electrolytic cells connected in series. One contains a solution of $AgNO_3$ and the second a solution of $CuCl_2$. During this time 2.00 g of silver are deposited in the first cell. (a) How many grams of copper are deposited in the second cell? (b) What is the current flowing, in amperes?

19.55 What is the hourly production rate of chlorine gas (in kg) from an electrolytic cell using aqueous NaCl electrolyte and carrying a current of 1.500×10^3 A? The anode efficiency for the oxidation of Cl is 93.0 percent.

19.56 Chromium plating is applied by electrolysis to objects suspended in a dichromate solution, according to the following (unbalanced) half-reaction:

$$Cr_2O_7^{2-}(aq) + e^- + H^+(aq) \longrightarrow Cr(s) + H_2O(l)$$

How long (in hours) would it take to apply a chromium plating 1.0×10^{-2} mm thick to a car bumper with a surface area of 0.25 m^2 in an electrolytic cell carrying a current of 25.0 A? (The density of chromium is 7.19 g/cm^3.)

19.57 The passage of a current of 0.750 A for 25.0 min deposited 0.369 g of copper from a $CuSO_4$ solution. From this information, calculate the molar mass of copper.

19.58 A quantity of 0.300 g of copper was deposited from a $CuSO_4$ solution by passing a current of 3.00 A through the solution for 304 s. Calculate the value of the faraday constant.

19.59 In a certain electrolysis experiment, 1.44 g of Ag were deposited in one cell (containing an aqueous $AgNO_3$ solution), while 0.120 g of an unknown metal X was deposited in another cell (containing an aqueous XCl_3 solution) in series with the $AgNO_3$ cell. Calculate the molar mass of X.

19.60 One of the half-reactions for the electrolysis of water is

$$2H^+(aq) + 2e^- \longrightarrow H_2(g)$$

If 0.845 L of H_2 is collected at 25°C and 782 mmHg, how many faradays of electricity had to pass through the solution?

Additional Problems

19.61 For each of the following redox reactions, (i) write the half-reactions; (ii) write a balanced equation for the whole reaction, (iii) determine in which direction the reaction will proceed spontaneously under standard-state conditions:

(a) $H_2(g) + Ni^{2+}(aq) \longrightarrow H^+(aq) + Ni(s)$
(b) $MnO_4^-(aq) + Cl^-(aq) \longrightarrow$
    $\qquad Mn^{2+}(aq) + Cl_2(g)$ (in acid solution)
(c) $Cr(s) + Zn^{2+}(aq) \longrightarrow Cr^{3+}(aq) + Zn(s)$

19.62 The oxidation of 25.0 mL of a solution containing Fe^{2+} requires 26.0 mL of 0.0250 M $K_2Cr_2O_7$ in acidic solution. Balance the following equation and calculate the molar concentration of Fe^{2+}:

$$Cr_2O_7^{2-} + Fe^{2+} + H^+ \longrightarrow Cr^{3+} + Fe^{3+}$$

19.63 The SO_2 present in air is mainly responsible for the phenomenon of acid rain. The concentration of SO_2 can be determined by titrating against a standard permanganate solution as follows:

$$5SO_2 + 2MnO_4^- + 2H_2O \longrightarrow$$
$$5SO_4^{2-} + 2Mn^{2+} + 4H^+$$

Calculate the number of grams of SO_2 in a sample of air if 7.37 mL of 0.00800 M $KMnO_4$ solution are required for the titration.

19.64 A sample of iron ore weighing 0.2792 g was dissolved in an excess of a dilute acid solution. All the iron was first converted to Fe(II) ions. The solution then required 23.30 mL of 0.0194 M $KMnO_4$ for oxidation to Fe(III) ions. Calculate the percent by mass of iron in the ore.

19.65 The concentration of a hydrogen peroxide solution can be conveniently determined by titration against a standardized potassium permanganate solution in an acidic medium according to the following unbalanced equation:

$$MnO_4^- + H_2O_2 \longrightarrow O_2 + Mn^{2+}$$

(a) Balance the above equation. (b) If 36.44 mL of a 0.01652 M $KMnO_4$ solution are required to

completely oxidize 25.00 mL of a H_2O_2 solution, calculate the molarity of the H_2O_2 solution.

19.66 Oxalic acid ($H_2C_2O_4$) is present in many plants and vegetables. (a) Balance the following equation in acid solution:

$$MnO_4^- + C_2O_4^{2-} \longrightarrow Mn^{2+} + CO_2$$

(b) If a 1.00-g sample of $H_2C_2O_4$ requires 24.0 mL of 0.0100 M $KMnO_4$ solution to reach the equivalence point, what is the percent by mass of $H_2C_2O_4$ in the sample?

19.67 Complete the following table. State whether the cell reaction is spontaneous, nonspontaneous, or at equilibrium.

E	ΔG	Cell Reaction
> 0		
	> 0	
$= 0$		

19.68 Calcium oxalate (CaC_2O_4) is insoluble in water. This property has been used to determine the amount of Ca^{2+} ions in blood. The calcium oxalate isolated from blood is dissolved in acid and titrated against a standardized $KMnO_4$ solution as described in Problem 19.66. In one test it is found that the calcium oxalate isolated from a 10.0-mL sample of blood requires 24.2 mL of 9.56×10^{-4} M $KMnO_4$ for titration. Calculate the number of milligrams of calcium per milliliter of blood.

19.69 From the following information, calculate the solubility product of AgBr:

$Ag^+(aq) + e^- \longrightarrow Ag(s)$ $E° = 0.80$ V
$AgBr(s) + e^- \longrightarrow Ag(s) + Br^-(aq)$ $E° = 0.07$ V

19.70 Consider a galvanic cell composed of the SHE and a half-cell using the reaction $Ag^+(aq) + e^- \rightarrow Ag(s)$. (a) Calculate the standard cell potential. (b) What is the spontaneous cell reaction under standard-state conditions? (c) Calculate the cell potential when $[H^+]$ in the hydrogen electrode is changed to (i) 1.0×10^{-2} M and (ii) 1.0×10^{-5} M, all other reagents being held at standard-state conditions. (d) Based on this cell arrangement, suggest a design for a pH meter.

19.71 A galvanic cell consists of a silver electrode in contact with 346 mL of 0.100 M $AgNO_3$ solution and a magnesium electrode in contact with 288 mL of 0.100 M $Mg(NO_3)_2$ solution. (a) Calculate E for the cell at 25°C. (b) A current is drawn from the cell until 1.20 g of silver have been deposited at the silver electrode. Calculate E for the cell at this stage of operation.

19.72 Explain why chlorine gas can be prepared by electrolyzing an aqueous solution of NaCl but fluorine gas cannot be prepared by electrolyzing an aqueous solution of NaF.

19.73 Calculate the emf of the following concentration cell at 25°C:

$$Cu(s)\,|\,Cu^{2+}(0.080\,M)\,\|\,Cu^{2+}(1.2\,M)\,|\,Cu(s)$$

19.74 The cathode reaction in the Leclanché cell is given by

$$2MnO_2(s) + Zn^{2+}(aq) + 2e^- \longrightarrow ZnMn_2O_4(s)$$

If a Leclanché cell produces a current of 0.0050 A, calculate how many hours this current supply will last if there are initially 4.0 g of MnO_2 present in the cell. Assume that there is an excess of Zn^{2+} ions.

19.75 Suppose you are asked to verify experimentally the electrode reactions shown in Example 19.8. In addition to the apparatus and the solution, you are also given two pieces of litmus paper, one blue and the other red. Describe what steps you would take in this experiment.

19.76 For a number of years it was not clear whether mercury(I) ions existed in solution as Hg^+ or as Hg_2^{2+}. To distinguish between these two possibilities, we could set up the following system:

$$Hg(l)\,|\,soln\ A\,\|\,soln\ B\,|\,Hg(l)$$

where soln A contained 0.263 g mercury(I) nitrate per liter and soln B contained 2.63 g mercury(I) nitrate per liter. If the measured emf of such a cell is 0.0289 V at 18°C, what can you deduce about the nature of the mercury(I) ions?

19.77 An aqueous KI solution to which a few drops of phenolphthalein have been added is electrolyzed using an apparatus like the one shown here:

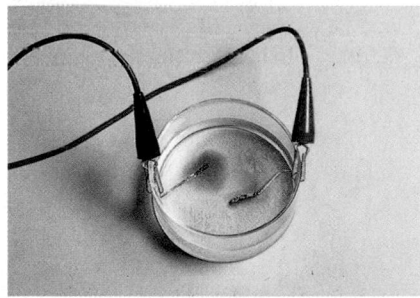

Describe what you would observe at the anode and the cathode. (*Hint:* Molecular iodine is only slightly soluble in water, but in the presence of I^- ions, it forms the brown color of I_3^- ions. See Problem 12.102.)

19.78 A piece of magnesium metal weighing 1.56 g is placed in 100.0 mL of 0.100 M $AgNO_3$ at 25°C. Calculate $[Mg^{2+}]$ and $[Ag^+]$ in solution at equilibrium. What is the mass of the magnesium left? The volume remains constant.

19.79 Describe an experiment that would enable you to determine which is the cathode and which is the anode in a galvanic cell using copper and zinc electrodes.

19.80 An acidified solution was electrolyzed using copper electrodes. A constant current of 1.18 A caused the anode to lose 0.584 g after 1.52×10^3 s. (a) What is the gas produced at the cathode and what is its volume at STP? (b) Given that the charge of an electron is 1.6022×10^{-19} C, calculate Avogadro's number. Assume that copper is oxidized to Cu^{2+} ions.

19.81 In a certain electrolysis experiment involving Al^{3+} ions, 60.2 g of Al is recovered when a current of 0.352 A is used. How many minutes did the electrolysis last?

19.82 Consider the oxidation of ammonia:

$$4NH_3(g) + 3O_2(g) \longrightarrow 2N_2(g) + 6H_2O(l)$$

(a) Calculate the $\Delta G°$ for the reaction. (b) If this reaction were used in a fuel cell, what would the standard cell potential be?

19.83 When an aqueous solution containing gold(III) salt is electrolyzed, metallic gold is deposited at the cathode and oxygen gas is generated at the anode. (a) If 9.26 g of Au is deposited at the cathode, calculate the volume (in liters) of O_2 generated at 23°C and 747 mmHg. (b) What is the current used if the electrolytic process took 2.00 h?

19.84 In an electrolysis experiment, a student passes the same quantity of electricity through two electrolytic cells, one containing a silver salt and the other a gold salt. Over a certain period of time, she finds that 2.64 g of Ag and 1.61 g of Au are deposited at the cathodes. What is the oxidation state of gold in the gold salt?

19.85 People living in cold-climate countries where there is plenty of snow are advised not to heat their garages in the winter. What is the electrochemical basis for this recommendation?

19.86 Given that

$$2Hg^{2+}(aq) + 2e^- \longrightarrow Hg_2^{2+}(aq) \qquad E° = 0.92\ V$$
$$Hg_2^{2+}(aq) + 2e^- \longrightarrow 2Hg(l) \qquad E° = 0.85\ V$$

calculate $\Delta G°$ and K for the following process at 25°C:

$$Hg_2^{2+}(aq) \longrightarrow Hg^{2+}(aq) + Hg(l)$$

(The preceding reaction is an example of a *disproportionation reaction* in which an element in one oxidation state is both oxidized and reduced.)

19.87 Fluorine (F_2) is obtained by the electrolysis of liquid hydrogen fluoride (HF) containing potassium fluoride (KF). (a) Write the half-cell reactions and the overall reaction for the process. (b) What is the purpose of KF? (c) Calculate the volume of F_2 (in liters) collected at 24.0°C and 1.2 atm after electrolyzing the solution for 15 h at a current of 502 A.

19.88 A 300-mL solution of NaCl was electrolyzed for 6.00 min. If the pH of the final solution was 12.24, calculate the average current used.

19.89 Industrially, copper is purified by electrolysis. The impure copper acts as the anode, and the cathode is made of pure copper. The electrodes are immersed in a $CuSO_4$ solution. During electrolysis, copper at the anode enters the solution as Cu^{2+} while Cu^{2+} ions are reduced at the cathode. (a) Write half-cell reactions and the overall reaction for the electrolytic process. (b) Suppose the anode was contaminated with Zn and Ag. Explain what happens to these impurities during electrolysis. (c) How many hours will it take to obtain 1.00 kg of Cu at a current of 18.9 A?

19.90 An aqueous solution of a platinum salt is electrolyzed at a current of 2.50 A for 2.00 h. As a result, 9.09 g of metallic Pt are formed at the cathode. Calculate the charge on the Pt ions in this solution.

19.91 Consider a galvanic cell consisting of a magnesium electrode in contact with $1.0\ M$ $Mg(NO_3)_2$ and a cadmium electrode in contact with $1.0\ M$ $Cd(NO_3)_2$. Calculate $E°$ for the cell, and draw a diagram showing the cathode, anode, and direction of electron flow.

19.92 A current of 6.00 A passes through an electrolytic cell containing dilute sulfuric acid for 3.40 h. If the volume of O_2 gas generated at the anode is 4.26 L (at STP), calculate the charge (in coulombs) on an electron.

19.93 Gold will not dissolve in either concentrated nitric acid or concentrated hydrochloric acid. However, the metal does dissolve in a mixture of the acids (one part HNO_3 and three parts HCl by volume), called *aqua regia*. (a) Write a balanced equation for this reaction. (*Hint:* Among the products are $HAuCl_4$ and NO_2.) (b) What is the function of HCl?

19.94 Explain why most useful galvanic cells give voltages of no more than 1.5 to 2.5 V. What are the prospects for developing practical galvanic cells with voltages of 5 V or more?

19.95 A silver rod and a SHE are dipped into a saturated aqueous solution of silver oxalate, $Ag_2C_2O_4$, at 25°C. The measured potential difference between the rod and the SHE is 0.589 V, the rod being positive. Calculate the solubility product constant for silver oxalate.

19.96 Zinc is an amphoteric metal; that is, it reacts with both acids and bases. The standard reduction potential is -1.36 V for the reaction

$$Zn(OH)_4^{2-}(aq) + 2e^- \longrightarrow Zn(s) + 4OH^-(aq)$$

Calculate the formation constant (K_f) for the reaction

$$Zn^{2+}(aq) + 4OH^-(aq) \rightleftharpoons Zn(OH)_4^{2-}(aq)$$

19.97 Use the data in Table 19.1 to determine whether or not hydrogen peroxide will undergo disproportionation in an acid medium: $2H_2O_2 \rightarrow 2H_2O + O_2$.

19.98 The magnitudes (but *not* the signs) of the standard reduction potentials of two metals X and Y are

$$Y^{2+} + 2e^- \longrightarrow Y \quad |E°| = 0.34\ V$$
$$X^{2+} + 2e^- \longrightarrow X \quad |E°| = 0.25\ V$$

where the $|\ |$ notation denotes that only the magnitude (but not the sign) of the $E°$ value is shown. When the half-cells of X and Y are connected, electrons flow from X to Y. When X is connected to a SHE, electrons flow from X to SHE. (a) Are the $E°$ values of the half-reactions positive or negative? (b) What is the standard emf of a cell made up of X and Y?

19.99 A galvanic cell is constructed as follows. One half-cell consists of a platinum wire immersed in a solution containing $1.0\ M$ Sn^{2+} and $1.0\ M$ Sn^{4+}; the other half-cell has a thallium rod immersed in a solution of $1.0\ M$ Tl^+. (a) Write the half-cell reactions and the overall reaction. (b) What is the equilibrium constant at 25°C? (c) What is the cell voltage if the Tl^+ concentration is increased tenfold? ($E°_{Tl^+/Tl} = -0.34\ V$.)

19.100 Given the standard reduction potential for Au^{3+} in Table 19.1 and

$$Au^+(aq) + e^- \longrightarrow Au(s) \quad E° = 1.69\ V$$

answer the following questions. (a) Why does gold not tarnish in air? (b) Will the following disproportionation occur spontaneously?

$$3Au^+(aq) \longrightarrow Au^{3+}(aq) + 2Au(s)$$

(c) Predict the reaction between gold and fluorine gas.

19.101 The ingestion of a very small quantity of mercury is not considered too harmful. Would this statement still hold if the gastric juice in your stomach were mostly nitric acid instead of hydrochloric acid?

19.102 When 25.0 mL of a solution containing both Fe^{2+} and Fe^{3+} ions is titrated with 23.0 mL of 0.0200 M $KMnO_4$ (in dilute sulfuric acid), all of the Fe^{2+} ions are oxidized to Fe^{3+} ions. Next, the solution is treated with Zn metal to convert all of the Fe^{3+} ions to Fe^{2+} ions. Finally, 40.0 mL of the same $KMnO_4$ solution are added to the solution in order to oxidize the Fe^{2+} ions to Fe^{3+}. Calculate the molar concentrations of Fe^{2+} and Fe^{3+} in the original solution.

19.103 Consider the Daniell cell in Figure 19.1. When viewed externally, the anode appears negative and the cathode positive (electrons are flowing from the anode to the cathode). Yet in solution anions are moving toward the anode, which means that it must appear positive to the anions. Because the anode cannot simultaneously be negative and positive, give an explanation for this apparently contradictory situation.

19.104 Use the data in Table 19.1 to show that the decomposition of H_2O_2 (a disproportionation reaction) is spontaneous at 25°C:

$$2H_2O_2(aq) \longrightarrow 2H_2O(l) + O_2(g)$$

19.105 The concentration of sulfuric acid in the lead-storage battery of an automobile over a period of time has decreased from 38.0 percent by mass (density = 1.29 g/mL) to 26.0 percent by mass (1.19 g/mL). Assume the volume of the acid remains constant at 724 mL. (a) Calculate the total charge in coulombs supplied by the battery. (b) How long (in hours) will it take to recharge the battery back to the original sulfuric acid concentration using a current of 22.4 amperes?

19.106 Consider a Daniell cell operating under nonstandard-state conditions. Suppose that the cell's reaction is multiplied by 2. What effect does this have on each of the following quantities in the Nernst equation? (a) E, (b) $E°$, (c) Q, (d) $\ln Q$, and (e) n?

19.107 A spoon was silver-plated electrolytically in a $AgNO_3$ solution. (a) Sketch a diagram for the process. (b) If 0.884 g of Ag was deposited on the spoon at a constant current of 18.5 mA, how long (in minutes) did the electrolysis take?

19.108 Comment on whether F_2 will become a stronger oxidizing agent with increasing H^+ concentration.

19.109 In recent years there has been much interest in electric cars. List some advantages and disadvantages of electric cars compared to automobiles with internal combustion engines.

19.110 Calculate the pressure of H_2 (in atm) required to maintain equilibrium with respect to the following reaction at 25°C:

$$Pb(s) + 2H^+(aq) \rightleftharpoons Pb^{2+}(aq) + H_2(g)$$

Given that $[Pb^{2+}] = 0.035\ M$ and the solution is buffered at pH 1.60.

19.111 A piece of magnesium ribbon and a copper wire are partially immersed in a 0.1 M HCl solution in a beaker. The metals are joined externally by another piece of metal wire. Bubbles are seen to evolve at both the Mg and Cu surfaces. (a) Write equations representing the reactions occurring at the metals. (b) What visual evidence would you seek to show that Cu is not oxidized to Cu^{2+}? (c) At some stage, NaOH solution is added to the beaker to neutralize the HCl acid. Upon further addition of NaOH, a white precipitate forms. What is it?

19.112 The zinc-air battery shows much promise for electric cars because it is lightweight and rechargeable:

The net transformation is $Zn(s) + \frac{1}{2}O_2(g) \rightarrow ZnO(s)$. (a) Write the half-reactions at the zinc-air electrodes and calculate the standard emf of the battery at 25°C. (b) Calculate the emf under actual operating conditions when the partial pressure of oxygen is 0.21 atm. (c) What is the energy density (measured as the energy in kilojoules that can be obtained from 1 kg of the metal) of the zinc electrode? (d) If a current of 2.1×10^5 A is to be drawn from a zinc-air battery system, what volume of air (in liters) would need to be supplied to the battery every second? Assume that the temperature is 25°C and the partial pressure of oxygen is 0.21 atm.

19.113 Calculate $E°$ for the reactions of mercury with (a) 1 M HCl and (b) 1 M HNO_3. Which acid will oxidize Hg to Hg_2^{2+} under standard-state conditions? Can you identify which test tube below contains HNO_3 and Hg and which contains HCl and Hg?

19.114 Because all alkali metals react with water, it is not possible to measure the standard reduction potentials of these metals directly as in the case of, say, zinc. An indirect method is to consider the following hypothetical reaction

$$Li^+(aq) + \frac{1}{2}H_2(g) \longrightarrow Li(s) + H^+(aq)$$

Use the appropriate equation presented in this chapter and the thermodynamic data in Appendix 3, calculate $E°$ for $Li^+(aq) + e^- \rightarrow Li(s)$ at 298 K. Compare your result with that listed in Table 19.1. (See back endpaper for the Faraday constant.)

19.115 A galvanic cell using Mg/Mg^{2+} and Cu/Cu^{2+} half-cells operates under standard-state conditions at 25°C and each compartment has a volume of 218 mL. The cell delivers 0.22 A for 31.6 h. (a) How many grams of Cu are deposited? (b) What is the $[Cu^{2+}]$ remaining?

19.116 Given the following standard reduction potentials, calculate the ion-product, K_w, for water at 25°C:

$$2H^+(aq) + 2e^- \longrightarrow H_2(g) \qquad E° = 0.00\ V$$
$$2H_2O(l) + 2e^- \longrightarrow H_2(g) + 2OH^-(aq)$$
$$E° = -0.83\ V$$

Special Problems

19.117 Compare the pros and cons of a fuel cell, such as the hydrogen-oxygen fuel cell, and a coal-fired power station for generating electricity.

19.118 Lead storage batteries are rated by ampere hours, that is, the number of amperes they can deliver in an hour. (a) Show that $1 \text{ A} \cdot \text{h} = 3600 \text{ C}$. (b) The lead anodes of a certain lead-storage battery have a total mass of 406 g. Calculate the maximum theoretical capacity of the battery in ampere hours. Explain why in practice we can never extract this much energy from the battery. (*Hint:* Assume all of the lead will be used up in the electrochemical reaction and refer to the electrode reactions on p. 840.) (c) Calculate E_{cell}° and ΔG° for the battery.

19.119 Use Equations (18.10) and (19.3) to calculate the emf values of the Daniell cell at 25°C and 80°C. Comment on your results. What assumptions are used in the derivation? (*Hint:* You need the thermodynamic data in Appendix 3.)

19.120 A construction company is installing an iron culvert (a long cylindrical tube) that is 40.0 m long with a radius of 0.900 m. To prevent corrosion, the culvert must be galvanized. This process is carried out by first passing an iron sheet of appropriate dimensions through an electrolytic cell containing Zn^{2+} ions, using graphite as the anode and the iron sheet as the cathode. If the voltage is 3.26 V, what is the cost of electricity for depositing a layer 0.200 mm thick if the efficiency of the process is 95 percent? The electricity rate is $0.12 per kilowatt hour (kWh), where $1 \text{ W} = 1 \text{ J/s}$ and the density of Zn is 7.14 g/cm^3.

19.121 A 9.00×10^2-mL 0.200 M MgI_2 was electrolyzed. As a result, hydrogen gas was generated at the cathode and iodine was formed at the anode. The volume of hydrogen collected at 26°C and 779 mmHg was 1.22×10^3 mL. (a) Calculate the charge in coulombs consumed in the process. (b) How long (in min) did the electrolysis last if a current of 7.55 A was used? (c) A white precipitate was formed in the process. What was it and what was its mass in grams? Assume the volume of the solution was constant.

19.122 Based on the following standard reduction potentials:

$$Fe^{2+}(aq) + 2e^- \longrightarrow Fe(s) \qquad E_1^\circ = -0.44 \text{ V}$$
$$Fe^{3+}(aq) + e^- \longrightarrow Fe^{2+}(aq) \qquad E_2^\circ = 0.77 \text{ V}$$

calculate the standard reduction potential for the half-reaction

$$Fe^{3+}(aq) + 3e^- \longrightarrow Fe(s) \qquad E_3^\circ = ?$$

19.123 A galvanic cell is constructed by immersing a piece of copper wire in 25.0 mL of a 0.20 M $CuSO_4$ solution and a zinc strip in 25.0 mL of a 0.20 M $ZnSO_4$ solution. (a) Calculate the emf of the cell at 25°C and predict what would happen if a small amount of concentrated NH_3 solution were added to (i) the $CuSO_4$ solution and (ii) the $ZnSO_4$ solution. Assume that the volume in each compartment remains constant at 25.0 mL. (b) In a separate experiment, 25.0 mL of 3.00 M NH_3 are added to the $CuSO_4$ solution. If the emf of the cell is 0.68 V, calculate the formation constant (K_f) of $Cu(NH_3)_4^{2+}$.

19.124 Calculate the equilibrium constant for the following reaction at 298 K:

$$Zn(s) + Cu^{2+}(aq) \longrightarrow Zn^{2+}(aq) + Cu(s)$$

19.125 To remove the tarnish (Ag_2S) on a silver spoon, a student carried out the following steps. First, she placed the spoon in a large pan filled with water so the spoon was totally immersed. Next, she added a few tablespoonful of baking soda (sodium bicarbonate), which readily dissolved. Finally, she placed some aluminum foil at the bottom of the pan in contact with the spoon and then heated the solution to about 80°C. After a few minutes, the spoon was removed and rinsed with cold water. The tarnish was gone and the spoon regained its original shiny appearance. (a) Describe with equations the electrochemical basis for the procedure. (b) Adding NaCl instead of $NaHCO_3$ would also work because both compounds are strong electrolytes. What is the added advantage of using $NaHCO_3$? (*Hint:* Consider the pH of the solution.) (c) What is the purpose of heating the solution? (d) Some commercial tarnish removers containing a fluid (or paste) that is a dilute HCl solution. Rubbing the spoon with the fluid will also remove the tarnish. Name two disadvantages of using this procedure compared to the one described above.

Answers to Practice Exercises

19.1 $5Fe^{2+} + MnO_4^- + 8H^+ \rightarrow 5Fe^{3+} + Mn^{2+} + 4H_2O$.
19.2 No. **19.3** 0.34 V. **19.4** 1×10^{-42}.
19.5 $\Delta G° = -4.1 \times 10^2$ kJ/mol. **19.6** Yes, $E = +0.01$ V.
19.7 0.38 V. **19.8** Anode, O_2; cathode, H_2.
19.9 2.0×10^4 A.

CHEMICAL
Mystery

Tainted Water†

The salesman was persuasive and persistent.
"Do you realize what's in your drinking water?" he asked Tom.

Before Tom could answer, he continued: "Let me demonstrate." First he filled a glass of water from the kitchen faucet, then he produced an electrical device that had a pair of probes and a lightbulb. It resembled a standard conductivity tester. He inserted the probes into the water and the bulb immediately beamed brightly. Next the salesman poured some water from a jar labeled "distilled water" into another glass. This time when he inserted the probes into the water, the bulb did not light.

"Okay, can you explain the difference?" the salesman looked at Tom with a triumphant smile. "Sure," Tom began to recall an experiment he did in high school long ago, "The tap water contains minerals that caused. . . ."

---

†Adapted with permission from "Tainted Water," by Joseph J. Hesse, CHEM MATTERS, February, 1988, p. 13. Copyright 1988 American Chemical Society.

The precipitator with its electrodes immersed in tap water. Left: Before electrolysis has started. Right: 15 minutes after electrolysis commenced.

"Right on!" the salesman interrupted. "But I'm not sure if you realize how harmful the nation's drinking water has become." He handed Tom a booklet entitled *The Miracle of Distilled Water*. "Read the section called 'Heart Conditions Can Result from Mineral Deposits,'" he told Tom.

"The tap water may look clear, although we know it contains dissolved minerals. What most people don't realize is that it also contains other invisible substances that are harmful to our health. Let me show you." The salesman proceeded to do another demonstration. This time he produced a device that he called a "precipitator," which had two large electrodes attached to a black box. "Just look what's in our tap water," he said, while filling another large glassful from the faucet. The tap water appeared clean and pure. The salesman plugged the precipitator into the ac (alternating current) outlet. Within seconds, bubbles rose from both electrodes. The tap water took on a yellow hue. In a few minutes a brownish scum covered the surface of the water. After 15 minutes the glass of water was filled with a black-brown precipitate. When he repeated the experiment with distilled water, nothing happened.

Tom was incredulous. "You mean all this gunk came from the water I drink?"

"Where else?" beamed the salesman. "What the precipitator did was to bring out all the heavy metals and other undesirable substances. Now don't worry. There is a remedy for this problem. My company makes a distiller that will convert tap water to distilled water, which is the only safe water to drink. For a price of $600 you will be able to produce distilled water for pennies with the distiller instead of paying 80 cents for a gallon of water from the supermarket."

Tom was tempted but decided to wait. After all, $600 is a lot to pay for a gadget that he only saw briefly. He decided to consult his friend Sarah, the chemistry teacher at the local high school, before making the investment. The salesman promised to return in a few days and left the precipitator with Tom so that he could do further testing.

Chemical Clues

1. After Sarah examined the precipitator, she concluded that it was an electrolytic device consisting of what seemed like an aluminum electrode and an iron electrode. Because electrolysis cannot take place with ac (why not?), the precipitator must contain a rectifier, a device that converts ac to dc (direct current). Why does the water heat up so quickly during electrolysis?

2. From the brown color of the electrolysis product(s), deduce which metal acts as the cathode and which electrode acts as the anode.

3. Write all possible reactions at the anode and the cathode. Explain why there might be more than one type of reaction occurring at an electrode.

4. In analyzing the solution, Sarah detected aluminum. Suggest a plausible structure for the aluminum-containing ion. What property of aluminum causes it to dissolve in the solution?

5. Suggest two tests that would confirm Sarah's conclusion that the precipitate originated from the electrodes and not from the tap water.

20

Crystals of salt composed of sodium anion and a complex sodium cation. The molecular models show the complex of an alkali metal cation (Na^+ or K^+) with an organic compound called crown ether. The large green sphere is the alkali metal anion.

Metallurgy
and the Chemistry of Metals

A LOOK AHEAD

- We first survey the occurrence of ores containing various metals. (20.1)

- We then study the sequence of steps from the preparation of the ores to the production of metals. We focus mainly on the metallurgy of iron and the making of steel. We also examine several methods of metal purification. (20.2)

- Next, we study the properties of solids and see how the band theory explains the difference between conductors (metals) and insulators. We learn the special properties of semiconductors. (20.3)

- We briefly examine the periodic trends in metallic properties. (20.4)

- For alkali metals, we discuss sodium and potassium and focus on their preparations, properties, compounds, and uses. (20.5)

- For alkaline earth metals, we discuss magnesium and calcium and focus on their preparations, properties, compounds, and uses. (20.6)

- Finally, we study the preparation, properties, compounds and uses of a Group 3A metal—aluminum. (20.7).

Interactive Activity Summary

1. Movie: Aluminum Production (20.7)

U p to this point we have concentrated mainly on fundamental principles: theories of chemical bonding, intermolecular forces, rates and mechanisms of chemical reactions, equilibrium, the laws of thermodynamics, and electrochemistry. An understanding of these topics is necessary for the study of the properties of representative metallic elements and their compounds.

The use and refinement of metals date back to early human history. For example, archeologists have found evidence that in the first millennium A.D. inhabitants of Sri Lanka used monsoon winds to run iron-smelting furnaces to produce high-carbon steel. Through the years, these furnaces could have been sources of steel for the legendary Damascus swords, known for their sharpness and durability.

In this chapter we will study the methods for extracting, refining, and purifying metals and examine the properties of metals that belong to the representative elements. We will emphasize (1) the occurrence and preparation of metals, (2) the physical and chemical properties of some of their compounds, and (3) their uses in modern society and their roles in biological systems.

20.1 Occurrence of Metals

Most metals come from minerals. A *mineral* is *a naturally occurring substance with a range of chemical composition. A mineral deposit concentrated enough to allow economical recovery of a desired metal* is known as *ore.* Table 20.1 lists the principal types of minerals, and Figure 20.1 shows a classification of metals according to their minerals.

The most abundant metals, which exist as minerals in Earth's crust, are aluminum, iron, calcium, magnesium, sodium, potassium, titanium, and manganese (see p. 52). Seawater is a rich source of some metal ions, including Na^+, Mg^{2+}, and Ca^{2+}. Furthermore, vast areas of the ocean floor are covered with *manganese nodules,* which are made up mostly of manganese, along with iron, nickel, copper, and cobalt in a chemically combined state (Figure 20.2).

20.2 Metallurgical Processes

Metallurgy is *the science and technology of separating metals from their ores and of compounding alloys.* An *alloy* is *a solid solution either of two or more metals, or of a metal or metals with one or more nonmetals.*

The three principal steps in the recovery of a metal from its ore are (1) preparation of the ore, (2) production of the metal, and (3) purification of the metal.

Preparation of the Ore

In the preliminary treatment of an ore, the desired mineral is separated from waste materials—usually clay and silicate minerals—which are collectively called the *gangue.* One very useful method for carrying out such a separation is called *flotation.* In this process, the ore is finely ground and added to water containing oil and detergent. The liquid mixture is then beaten or blown to form a froth. The oil preferentially

TABLE 20.1	Principal Types of Minerals
Type	**Minerals**
Uncombined metals	Ag, Au, Bi, Cu, Pd, Pt
Carbonates	$BaCO_3$ (witherite), $CaCO_3$ (calcite, limestone), $MgCO_3$ (magnesite), $CaCO_3 \cdot MgCO_3$ (dolomite), $PbCO_3$ (cerussite), $ZnCO_3$ (smithsonite)
Halides	CaF_2 (fluorite), $NaCl$ (halite), KCl (sylvite), Na_3AlF_6 (cryolite)
Oxides	$Al_2O_3 \cdot 2H_2O$ (bauxite), Al_2O_3 (corundum), Fe_2O_3 (hematite), Fe_3O_4 (magnetite), Cu_2O (cuprite), MnO_2 (pyrolusite), SnO_2 (cassiterite), TiO_2 (rutile), ZnO (zincite)
Phosphates	$Ca_3(PO_4)_2$ (phosphate rock), $Ca_5(PO_4)_3OH$ (hydroxyapatite)
Silicates	$Be_3Al_2Si_6O_{18}$ (beryl), $ZrSiO_4$ (zircon), $NaAlSi_3O_8$ (albite), $Mg_3(Si_4O_{10})(OH)_2$ (talc)
Sulfides	Ag_2S (argentite), CdS (greenockite), Cu_2S (chalcocite), FeS_2 (pyrite), HgS (cinnabar), PbS (galena), ZnS (sphalerite)
Sulfates	$BaSO_4$ (barite), $CaSO_4$ (anhydrite), $PbSO_4$ (anglesite), $SrSO_4$ (celestite), $MgSO_4 \cdot 7H_2O$ (epsomite)

Figure 20.1 *Metals and their best-known minerals. Lithium is found in spodumene (LiAlSi$_2$O$_6$), and beryllium in beryl (see Table 20.1). The rest of the alkaline earth metals are found in minerals that are carbonates and sulfates. The minerals for Sc, Y, and La are the phosphates. Some metals have more than one type of important mineral. For example, in addition to the sulfide, iron is found as the oxides hematite (Fe$_2$O$_3$) and magnetite (Fe$_3$O$_4$); and aluminum, in addition to the oxide, is found in beryl (Be$_3$Al$_2$Si$_6$O$_{18}$). Technetium (Tc) is a synthetic element.*

wets the mineral particles, which are then carried to the top in the froth, while the gangue settles to the bottom. The froth is skimmed off, allowed to collapse, and dried to recover the mineral particles.

Another physical separation process makes use of the magnetic properties of certain minerals. **Ferromagnetic** *metals are strongly attracted to magnets.* The mineral magnetite (Fe$_3$O$_4$), in particular, can be separated from the gangue by using a strong electromagnet. Cobalt is another ferromagnetic metal.

Mercury forms amalgams with a number of metals. An **amalgam** is *an alloy of mercury with another metal or metals.* Mercury can therefore be used to extract metal from ore. Mercury dissolves the silver and gold in an ore to form a liquid amalgam, which is easily separated from the remaining ore. The gold or silver is recovered by distilling off mercury.

> Unreactive metals such as gold and silver can be leached from the ores using the cyanide ions (see Section 21.3).

Production of Metals

Because metals in their combined forms always have positive oxidation numbers, the production of a free metal is a reduction process. Preliminary operations may be necessary to convert the ore to a chemical state more suitable for reduction. For example, an ore may be *roasted* to drive off volatile impurities and at the same time to convert the carbonates and sulfides to the corresponding oxides, which can be reduced more conveniently to yield the pure metals:

$$CaCO_3(s) \longrightarrow CaO(s) + CO_2(g)$$
$$2PbS(s) + 3O_2(g) \longrightarrow 2PbO(s) + 2SO_2(g)$$

This last equation points out the fact that the conversion of sulfides to oxides is a major source of sulfur dioxide, a notorious air pollutant (p. 768).

Figure 20.2 *Manganese nodules on the ocean floor.*

TABLE 20.2	Reduction Processes for Some Common Metals
Metal	**Reduction Process**
Lithium, sodium, magnesium, calcium	Electrolytic reduction of the molten chloride
Aluminum	Electrolytic reduction of anhydrous oxide (in molten cryolite)
Chromium, manganese, titanium, vanadium, iron, zinc	Reduction of the metal oxide with a more electropositive metal, or reduction with coke and carbon monoxide
Mercury, silver, platinum, copper, gold	These metals occur in the free (uncombined) state or can be obtained by roasting their sulfides

(left margin, vertical: Decreasing activity of metals ↓)

How a pure metal is obtained by reduction from its combined form depends on the standard reduction potential of the metal (see Table 19.1). Table 20.2 outlines the reduction processes for several metals. Most major metallurgical processes now in use involve **pyrometallurgy,** *procedures carried out at high temperatures.* The reduction in these procedures may be accomplished either chemically or electrolytically.

Chemical Reduction

A more electropositive metal has a more negative standard reduction potential (see Table 19.1).

We can use a more electropositive metal as a reducing agent to separate a less electropositive metal from its compound at high temperatures:

$$V_2O_5(s) + 5Ca(l) \longrightarrow 2V(l) + 5CaO(s)$$
$$TiCl_4(g) + 2Mg(l) \longrightarrow Ti(s) + 2MgCl_2(l)$$
$$Cr_2O_3(s) + 2Al(s) \longrightarrow 2Cr(l) + Al_2O_3(s)$$
$$3Mn_3O_4(s) + 8Al(s) \longrightarrow 9Mn(l) + 4Al_2O_3(s)$$

In some cases, even molecular hydrogen can be used as a reducing agent, as in the preparation of tungsten (used as filaments in lightbulbs) from tungsten(VI) oxide:

$$WO_3(s) + 3H_2(g) \longrightarrow W(s) + 3H_2O(g)$$

Electrolytic Reduction

Electrolytic reduction is suitable for very electropositive metals, such as sodium, magnesium, and aluminum. The process is usually carried out on the anhydrous molten oxide or halide of the metal:

$$2MO(l) \longrightarrow 2M \text{ (at cathode)} + O_2 \text{ (at anode)}$$
$$2MCl(l) \longrightarrow 2M \text{ (at cathode)} + Cl_2 \text{ (at anode)}$$

We will describe the specific procedures later in this chapter.

The Metallurgy of Iron

The extraction of iron from FeS_2 leads to SO_2 production and acid rain (see Section 17.6).

Iron exists in Earth's crust in many different minerals, such as iron pyrite (FeS_2), siderite ($FeCO_3$), hematite (Fe_2O_3), and magnetite (Fe_3O_4, often represented as $FeO \cdot Fe_2O_3$). Of these, hematite and magnetite are particularly suitable for the extraction of iron. The metallurgical processing of iron involves the chemical reduction of the minerals by carbon (in the form of coke) in a blast furnace (Figure 20.3). The concentrated iron ore, limestone ($CaCO_3$), and coke are introduced into the furnace from the top. A blast of hot air is forced up the furnace from the bottom—hence the name *blast furnace.* The oxygen gas reacts with the carbon in the coke to form mostly carbon monoxide and some carbon dioxide. These reactions are highly exothermic, and as the hot CO and CO_2 gases rise, they react with the iron oxides in different temperature zones as shown in Figure 20.3. The key steps in the extraction of iron are

$$3Fe_2O_3(s) + CO(g) \longrightarrow 2Fe_3O_4(s) + CO_2(g)$$
$$Fe_3O_4(s) + CO(g) \longrightarrow 3FeO(s) + CO_2(g)$$
$$FeO(s) + CO(g) \longrightarrow Fe(l) + CO_2(g)$$

The limestone decomposes in the furnace as follows:

$$CaCO_3(s) \longrightarrow CaO(s) + CO_2(g)$$

The calcium oxide then reacts with the impurities in the iron, which are mostly sand (SiO_2) and aluminum oxide (Al_2O_3):

$$CaO(s) + SiO_2(s) \longrightarrow CaSiO_3(l)$$
$$CaO(s) + Al_2O_3(s) \longrightarrow Ca(AlO_2)_2(l)$$

The mixture of calcium silicate and calcium aluminate that remains molten at the furnace temperature is known as *slag*.

By the time the ore works its way down to the bottom of the furnace, most of it has already been reduced to iron. The temperature of the lower part of the furnace is above the melting point of impure iron, and so the molten iron at the lower level can be run off to a receiver. The slag, because it is less dense, forms the top layer above the molten iron and can be run off at that level, as shown in Figure 20.3.

$CaCO_3$ and other compounds that are used to form a molten mixture with the impurities in the ore for easy removal are called *flux*.

Figure 20.3 *A blast furnace. Iron ore, limestone, and coke are introduced at the top of the furnace. Iron is obtained from the ore by reduction with carbon.*

Iron extracted in this way contains many impurities and is called *pig iron;* it may contain up to 5 percent carbon and some silicon, phosphorus, manganese, and sulfur. Some of the impurities stem from the silicate and phosphate minerals, while carbon and sulfur come from coke. Pig iron is granular and brittle. It has a relatively low melting point (about 1180°C), so it can be cast in various forms; for this reason it is also called *cast iron.*

Steelmaking

Steel manufacturing is one of the most important metal industries. In the United States, the annual consumption of steel is well above 100 million tons. Steel is an iron alloy that contains from 0.03 to 1.4 percent carbon plus various amounts of other elements. The wide range of useful mechanical properties associated with steel is primarily a function of chemical composition and heat treatment of a particular type of steel.

Whereas the production of iron is basically a reduction process (converting iron oxides to metallic iron), the conversion of iron to steel is essentially an oxidation process in which the unwanted impurities are removed from the iron by reaction with oxygen gas. One of several methods used in steelmaking is the *basic oxygen process.* Because of its ease of operation and the relatively short time (about 20 minutes) required for each large-scale (hundreds of tons) conversion, the basic oxygen process is by far the most common means of producing steel today.

Figure 20.4 shows the basic oxygen process. Molten iron from the blast furnace is poured into an upright cylindrical vessel. Pressurized oxygen gas is introduced via a water-cooled tube above the molten metal. Under these conditions, manganese, phosphorus, and silicon, as well as excess carbon, react with oxygen to form oxides. These oxides are then reacted with the appropriate fluxes (for example, CaO or SiO_2) to form slag. The type of flux chosen depends on the composition of the

Figure 20.4 *The basic oxygen process of steelmaking. The capacity of a typical vessel is 100 tons of cast iron.*

Figure 20.5 *Steelmaking.*

iron. If the main impurities are silicon and phosphorus, a basic flux such as CaO is added to the iron:

$$SiO_2(s) + CaO(s) \longrightarrow CaSiO_3(l)$$
$$P_4O_{10}(l) + 6CaO(s) \longrightarrow 2Ca_3(PO_4)_2(l)$$

On the other hand, if manganese is the main impurity, then an acidic flux such as SiO_2 is needed to form the slag:

$$MnO(s) + SiO_2(s) \longrightarrow MnSiO_3(l)$$

The molten steel is sampled at intervals. When the desired blend of carbon and other impurities has been reached, the vessel is rotated to a horizontal position so that the molten steel can be tapped off (Figure 20.5).

The properties of steel depend not only on its chemical composition but also on the heat treatment. At high temperatures, iron and carbon in steel combine to form iron carbide, Fe_3C, called *cementite:*

$$3Fe(s) + C(s) \rightleftharpoons Fe_3C(s)$$

The forward reaction is endothermic, so that the formation of cementite is favored at high temperatures. When steel containing cementite is cooled slowly, the preceding equilibrium shifts to the left, and the carbon separates as small particles of graphite, which give the steel a gray color. (Very slow decomposition of cementite also takes place at room temperature.) If the steel is cooled rapidly, equilibrium is not attained and the carbon remains largely in the form of cementite, Fe_3C. Steel containing cementite is light in color, and it is harder and more brittle than that containing graphite.

Heating the steel to some appropriate temperature for a short time and then cooling it rapidly in order to give it the desired mechanical properties is known as "tempering." In this way, the ratio of carbon present as graphite and as cementite can be varied within rather wide limits. Table 20.3 shows the composition, properties, and uses of various types of steel.

TABLE 20.3	Types of Steel								
	Composition (Percent by Mass)*								
Type	**C**	**Mn**	**P**	**S**	**Si**	**Ni**	**Cr**	**Others**	**Uses**
Plain	1.35	1.65	0.04	0.05	0.06	—	—	Cu (0.2–0.6)	Sheet products, tools
High-strength	0.25	1.65	0.04	0.05	0.15–0.9	0.4–1.0	0.3–1.3	Cu (0.01–0.08)	Construction, steam turbines
Stainless	0.03–1.2	1.0–10	0.04–0.06	0.03	1–3	1–22	4.0–27	—	Kitchen utensils, razor blades

*A single number indicates the maximum amount of the substance present.

Purification of Metals

Metals prepared by reduction usually need further treatment to remove impurities. The extent of purification, of course, depends on how the metal will be used. Three common purification procedures are distillation, electrolysis, and zone refining.

Distillation

Metals that have low boiling points, such as mercury, magnesium, and zinc, can be separated from other metals by fractional distillation. One well-known method of fractional distillation is the *Mond*[†] *process* for the purification of nickel. Carbon monoxide gas is passed over the impure nickel metal at about 70°C to form the volatile tetracarbonylnickel (b.p. 43°C), a highly toxic substance, which is separated from the less volatile impurities by distillation:

$$Ni(s) + 4CO(g) \longrightarrow Ni(CO)_4(g)$$

Pure metallic nickel is recovered from $Ni(CO)_4$ by heating the gas at 200°C:

$$Ni(CO)_4(g) \longrightarrow Ni(s) + 4CO(g)$$

The carbon monoxide that is released is recycled back into the process.

Electrolysis

Electrolysis is another important purification technique. The copper metal obtained by roasting copper sulfide usually contains impurities such as zinc, iron, silver, and gold. The more electropositive metals are removed by an electrolysis process in which the impure copper acts as the anode and *pure* copper acts as the cathode in a sulfuric acid solution containing Cu^{2+} ions (Figure 20.6). The reactions are

Anode (oxidation): $Cu(s) \longrightarrow Cu^{2+}(aq) + 2e^-$
Cathode (reduction): $Cu^{2+}(aq) + 2e^- \longrightarrow Cu(s)$

Reactive metals in the copper anode, such as iron and zinc, are also oxidized at the anode and enter the solution as Fe^{2+} and Zn^{2+} ions. They are not reduced at the

Figure 20.6 *Electrolytic purification of copper.*

[†]Ludwig Mond (1839–1909). British chemist of German origin. Mond made many important contributions to industrial chemistry. His method for purifying nickel by converting it to the volatile $Ni(CO)_4$ compound has been described as having given "wings" to the metal.

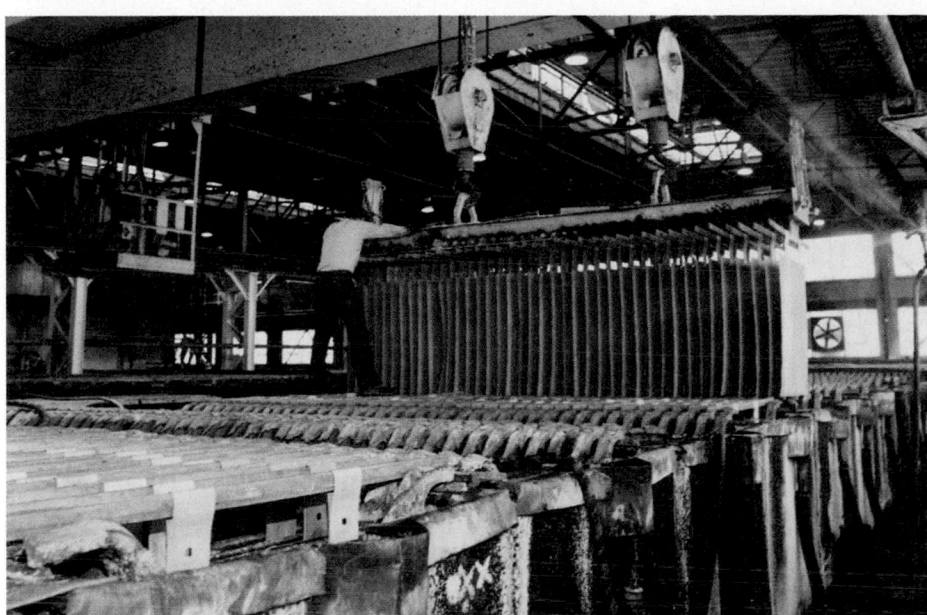

Figure 20.7 *Copper cathodes used in the electrorefining process.*

cathode, however. The less electropositive metals, such as gold and silver, are not oxidized at the anode. Eventually, as the copper anode dissolves, these metals fall to the bottom of the cell. Thus, the net result of this electrolysis process is the transfer of copper from the anode to the cathode. Copper prepared this way has a purity greater than 99.5 percent (Figure 20.7).

The metal impurities separated from the copper anode are valuable by-products, the sale of which often pays for the electricity needed to drive the electrolysis.

Zone Refining

Another often-used method of obtaining extremely pure metals is zone refining. In this process, a metal rod containing a few impurities is drawn through an electrical heating coil that melts the metal (Figure 20.8). Most impurities dissolve in the molten metal. As the metal rod emerges from the heating coil, it cools and the pure metal crystallizes, leaving the impurities in the molten metal portion that is still in the heating coil. (This is analogous to the freezing of seawater, in which the solid that separates

Heating coil   Metal rod

Figure 20.8 *Zone-refining technique for purifying metals. Top to bottom: An impure metal rod is moved slowly through a heating coil. As the metal rod moves forward, the impurities dissolve in the molten portion of the metal while pure metal crystallizes out in front of the molten zone.*

is mostly pure solvent—water. In zone refining, the liquid metal acts as the solvent and the impurities as the solutes.) When the molten zone carrying the impurities, now at increased concentration, reaches the end of the rod, it is allowed to cool and is then cut off. Repeating this procedure a number of times results in metal with a purity greater than 99.99 percent.

20.3 Band Theory of Conductivity

In Section 11.6 we saw that the ability of metals to conduct heat and electricity can be explained with molecular orbital theory. To gain a better understanding of the conductivity properties of metals we must also apply our knowledge of quantum mechanics. The model we will use to study metallic bonding is **band theory,** so called because it states that *delocalized electrons move freely through "bands" formed by overlapping molecular orbitals.* We will also apply band theory to certain elements that are semiconductors.

Conductors

Metals are characterized by high electrical conductivity. Consider magnesium, for example. The electron configuration of Mg is $[Ne]3s^2$, so each atom has two valence electrons in the $3s$ orbital. In a metallic crystal, the atoms are packed closely together, so the energy levels of each magnesium atom are affected by the immediate neighbors of the atom as a result of orbital overlaps. In Chapter 10 we saw that, in terms of molecular orbital theory, the interaction between two atomic orbitals leads to the formation of a bonding and an antibonding molecular orbital. Because the number of atoms in even a small piece of magnesium is enormously large (on the order of 10^{20} atoms), the number of molecular orbitals they form is also very large. These molecular orbitals are so closely spaced on the energy scale that they are more appropriately described as a "band" (Figure 20.9). The closely spaced *filled* energy levels make up the *valence band.* The upper half of the energy levels corresponds to the empty, delocalized molecular orbitals formed by the overlap of the $3p$ orbitals. This set of closely spaced *empty* levels is called the *conduction band.*

We can imagine a metallic crystal as an array of positive ions immersed in a sea of delocalized valence electrons (see Figure 11.30). The great cohesive force resulting from the delocalization is partly responsible for the strength noted in most metals. Because the valence band and the conduction band are adjacent to each other, the amount of energy needed to promote a valence electron to the conduction band is negligible. There, the

Figure 20.9 *Formation of conduction bands in magnesium. The electrons in the 1s, 2s, and 2p orbitals are localized on each Mg atom. However, the 3s and 3p orbitals overlap to form delocalized molecular orbitals. Electrons in these orbitals can travel throughout the metal, and this accounts for the electrical conductivity of the metal.*

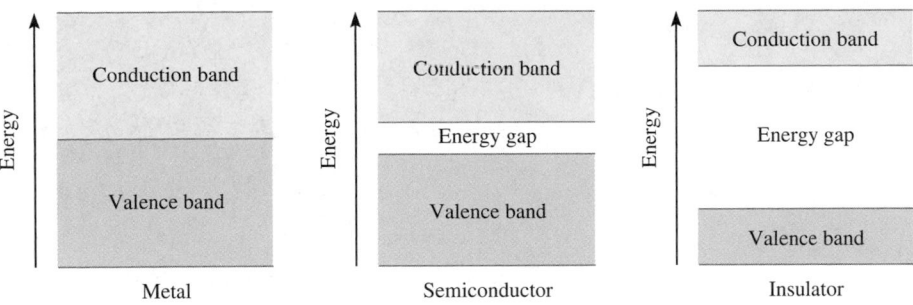

Figure 20.10 *Comparison of the energy gaps between the valence band and the conduction band in a metal, a semiconductor, and an insulator. In a metal the energy gap is virtually nonexistent; in a semiconductor the energy gap is small; and in an insulator the energy gap is very large, thus making the promotion of an electron from the valence band to the conduction band difficult.*

electron can travel freely through the metal, because the conduction band is void of electrons. This freedom of movement accounts for the fact that metals are good *conductors,* that is, they are *capable of conducting electric current.*

Why don't substances like wood and glass conduct electricity as metals do? Figure 20.10 provides an answer to this question. Basically, the electrical conductivity of a solid depends on the spacing and the state of occupancy of the energy bands. In magnesium and other metals the valence bands are adjacent to the conduction bands, and, therefore, these metals readily act as conductors. In wood and glass, on the other hand, the gap between the valence band and the conduction band is considerably greater than that in a metal. Consequently, much more energy is needed to excite an electron into the conduction band. Lacking this energy, electrons cannot move freely. Therefore, glass and wood are **insulators,** *ineffective conductors of electricity.*

Semiconductors

A number of elements are **semiconductors,** that is, they *normally are not conductors, but will conduct electricity at elevated temperatures or when combined with a small amount of certain other elements.* The Group 4A elements silicon and germanium are especially suited for this purpose. The use of semiconductors in transistors and solar cells, to name two applications, has revolutionized the electronic industry in recent decades, leading to increased miniaturization of electronic equipment.

The energy gap between the filled and empty bands of these solids is much smaller than that for insulators (see Figure 20.10). If the energy needed to excite electrons from the valence band into the conduction band is provided, the solid becomes a conductor. Note that this behavior is opposite that of the metals. A metal's ability to conduct electricity *decreases* with increasing temperature, because the enhanced vibration of atoms at higher temperatures tends to disrupt the flow of electrons.

The ability of a semiconductor to conduct electricity can also be enhanced by adding small amounts of certain impurities to the element, a process called *doping.* Let us consider what happens when a trace amount of boron or phosphorus is added to solid silicon. (Only about five out of every million Si atoms are replaced by B or P atoms.) The structure of solid silicon is similar to that of diamond; each Si atom is covalently bonded to four other Si atoms. Phosphorus ($[Ne]3s^23p^3$) has one more valence electron than silicon ($[Ne]3s^23p^2$), so there is a valence electron left over after four of them are used to form covalent bonds with silicon (Figure 20.11). This extra electron can be removed from the phosphorus atom by applying a voltage across the solid. The free electron can move through the structure and function as a conduction electron. Impurities of this type are known as **donor impurities,** because they *provide conduction electrons. Solids containing donor impurities* are called **n-type semiconductors,** where *n* stands for negative (the charge of the "extra" electron).

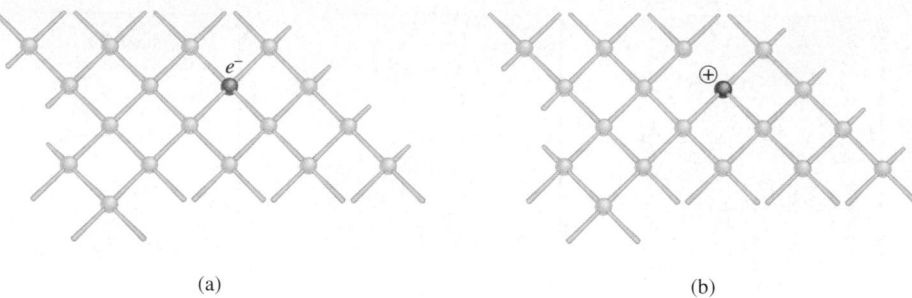

(a)   (b)

The opposite effect occurs if boron is added to silicon. A boron atom has three valence electrons $(1s^2 2s^2 2p^1)$. Thus, for every boron atom in the silicon crystal there is a single *vacancy* in a bonding orbital. It is possible to excite a valence electron from a nearby Si into this vacant orbital. A vacancy created at that Si atom can then be filled by an electron from a neighboring Si atom, and so on. In this manner, electrons can move through the crystal in one direction while the vacancies, or "positive holes," move in the opposite direction, and the solid becomes an electrical conductor. *Impurities that are electron deficient* are called **acceptor impurities.** Semiconductors that *contain acceptor impurities* are called **p-type semiconductors,** where *p* stands for positive.

In both the *p*-type and *n*-type semiconductors, the energy gap between the valence band and the conduction band is effectively reduced, so that only a small amount of energy is needed to excite the electrons. Typically, the conductivity of a semiconductor is increased by a factor of 100,000 or so by the presence of impurity atoms.

The growth of the semiconductor industry since the early 1960s has been truly remarkable. Today semiconductors are essential components of nearly all electronic equipment, ranging from radios and television sets to pocket calculators and computers. One of the main advantages of solid-state devices over vacuum-tube electronics is that the former can be made on a single "chip" of silicon no larger than the cross section of a pencil eraser. Consequently, much more equipment can be packed into a small volume—a point of particular importance in space travel, as well as in hand-held calculators and microprocessors (computers-on-a-chip).

20.4 Periodic Trends in Metallic Properties

Metals are lustrous in appearance, solid at room temperature (with the exception of mercury), good conductors of heat and electricity, malleable (can be hammered flat), and ductile (can be drawn into wire). Figure 20.12 shows the positions of the representative metals and the Group 2B metals in the periodic table. (The transition metals are discussed in Chapter 22.) As we saw in Figure 9.5, the electronegativity of elements increases from left to right across a period and from bottom to top in a group. The metallic character of metals increases in just the opposite directions, that is, from right to left across a period and from top to bottom in a group. Because metals generally have low electronegativities, they tend to form cations and almost always have positive oxidation numbers in their compounds. However, beryllium and magnesium in Group 2A and metals in Group 3A and beyond also form covalent compounds.

In Sections 20.5, 20.6, and 20.7 we will study the chemistry of selected metals from Group 1A (the alkali metals), Group 2A (the alkaline earth metals), and Group 3A (aluminum).

Figure 20.12 *Representative metals (green) and Group 2B metals (blue) according to their positions in the periodic table.*

20.5 The Alkali Metals

As a group, the alkali metals (the Group 1A elements) are the most electropositive (or the least electronegative) elements known. They exhibit many similar properties, some of which are listed in Table 20.4. From their electron configurations we expect the oxidation number of these elements in their compounds to be +1 because the cations would be isoelectronic with the noble gases. This is indeed the case.

The alkali metals have low melting points and are soft enough to be sliced with a knife (see Figure 8.14). These metals all possess a body-centered crystal structure (see Figure 11.29) with low packing efficiency. This accounts for their low densities among metals. In fact, lithium is the lightest metal known. Because of their great chemical reactivity, the alkali metals never occur naturally in elemental form; they are found combined with halide, sulfate, carbonate, and silicate ions. In this section we will describe the chemistry of two members of Group 1A—sodium and potassium.

TABLE 20.4   Properties of Alkali Metals

	Li	Na	K	Rb	Cs
Valence electron configuration	$2s^1$	$3s^1$	$4s^1$	$5s^1$	$6s^1$
Density (g/cm^3)	0.534	0.97	0.86	1.53	1.87
Melting point (°C)	179	97.6	63	39	28
Boiling point (°C)	1317	892	770	688	678
Atomic radius (pm)	155	190	235	248	267
Ionic radius (pm)*	60	95	133	148	169
Ionization energy (kJ/mol)	520	496	419	403	375
Electronegativity	1.0	0.9	0.8	0.8	0.7
Standard reduction potential (V)[†]	−3.05	−2.71	−2.93	−2.93	−2.92

*Refers to the cation M$^+$, where M denotes an alkali metal atom.
[†]The half-reaction M$^+$(aq) + e$^-$ $\longrightarrow$ M(s).

Figure 20.13 *Halite (NaCl).*

Remember that Ca^{2+} is harder to reduce than Na^+.

Note that this is a chemical rather than electrolytic reduction.

The chemistry of lithium, rubidium, and cesium is less important; all isotopes of francium, the last member of the group, are radioactive.

Sodium and potassium are about equally abundant in nature. They occur in silicate minerals such as albite ($NaAlSi_3O_8$) and orthoclase ($KAlSi_3O_8$). Over long periods of time (on a geologic scale), silicate minerals are slowly decomposed by wind and rain, and their sodium and potassium ions are converted to more soluble compounds. Eventually rain leaches these compounds out of the soil and carries them to the sea. Yet when we look at the composition of seawater, we find that the concentration ratio of sodium to potassium is about 28 to 1. The reason for this uneven distribution is that potassium is essential to plant growth, while sodium is not. Plants take up many of the potassium ions along the way, while sodium ions are free to move on to the sea. Other minerals that contain sodium or potassium are halite ($NaCl$), shown in Figure 20.13, Chile saltpeter ($NaNO_3$), and sylvite (KCl). Sodium chloride is also obtained from rock salt (see p. 365).

Metallic sodium is most conveniently obtained from molten sodium chloride by electrolysis in the Downs cell (see Section 19.8). The melting point of sodium chloride is rather high (801°C), and much energy is needed to keep large amounts of the substance molten. Adding a suitable substance, such as $CaCl_2$, lowers the melting point to about 600°C—a more convenient temperature for the electrolysis process.

Metallic potassium cannot be easily prepared by the electrolysis of molten KCl because it is too soluble in the molten KCl to float to the top of the cell for collection. Moreover, it vaporizes readily at the operating temperatures, creating hazardous conditions. Instead, it is usually obtained by the distillation of molten KCl in the presence of sodium vapor at 892°C. The reaction that takes place at this temperature is

$$Na(g) + KCl(l) \rightleftharpoons NaCl(l) + K(g)$$

This reaction may seem strange given that potassium is a stronger reducing agent than sodium (see Table 20.4). However, potassium has a lower boiling point (770°C) than sodium (892°C), so it is more volatile at 892°C and distills off more easily. According to Le Châtelier's principle, constant removal of potassium vapor shifts the above equilibrium from left to right, assuring recovery of metallic potassium.

Sodium and potassium are both extremely reactive, but potassium is the more reactive of the two. Both react with water to form the corresponding hydroxides. In a limited supply of oxygen, sodium burns to form sodium oxide (Na_2O). However, in the presence of excess oxygen, sodium forms the pale-yellow peroxide:

$$2Na(s) + O_2(g) \longrightarrow Na_2O_2(s)$$

Sodium peroxide reacts with water to give an alkaline solution and hydrogen peroxide:

$$Na_2O_2(s) + 2H_2O(l) \longrightarrow 2NaOH(aq) + H_2O_2(aq)$$

Like sodium, potassium forms the peroxide. In addition, potassium also forms the superoxide when it burns in air:

$$K(s) + O_2(g) \longrightarrow KO_2(s)$$

When potassium superoxide reacts with water, oxygen gas is evolved:

$$2KO_2(s) + 2H_2O(l) \longrightarrow 2KOH(aq) + O_2(g) + H_2O_2(aq)$$

This reaction is utilized in breathing equipment (Figure 20.14). Exhaled air contains both moisture and carbon dioxide. The moisture reacts with KO_2 in the apparatus to

Figure 20.14 *Self-contained breathing apparatus.*

generate oxygen gas as shown in the preceding equation. Furthermore, KO_2 also reacts with exhaled CO_2, which produces more oxygen gas:

$$4KO_2(s) + 2CO_2(g) \longrightarrow 2K_2CO_3(s) + 3O_2(g)$$

Thus, a person using the apparatus can continue to breathe oxygen without being exposed to toxic fumes outside.

Sodium and potassium metals dissolve in liquid ammonia to produce a beautiful blue solution:

$$Na \xrightarrow{\text{NH}_3} Na^+ + e^-$$
$$K \xrightarrow{\text{NH}_3} K^+ + e^-$$

Both the cation and the electron exist in the solvated form; the solvated electrons are responsible for the characteristic blue color of such solutions. Metal-ammonia solutions are powerful reducing agents (because they contain free electrons); they are useful in synthesizing both organic and inorganic compounds. It was discovered that the hitherto unknown alkali metal anions, M^-, are also formed in such solutions. This means that an ammonia solution of an alkali metal contains ion pairs such as Na^+Na^- and K^+K^-! (Keep in mind that in each case the metal cation exists as a complex ion with *crown ether*, an organic compound with a high affinity for cations.) In fact, these "salts" are so stable that they can be isolated in crystalline form (see p. 866). This finding is of considerable theoretical interest, for it shows clearly that the alkali metals can have an oxidation number of -1, although -1 is not found in ordinary compounds.

Sodium and potassium are essential elements of living matter. Sodium ions and potassium ions are present in intracellular and extracellular fluids, and they are essential for osmotic balance and enzyme functions. We now describe the preparations and uses of several of the important compounds of sodium and potassium.

Sodium Chloride

The source, properties, and uses of sodium chloride were discussed in Chapter 9 (see p. 365).

Sodium Carbonate

Sodium carbonate (called soda ash) is used in all kinds of industrial processes, including water treatment and the manufacture of soaps, detergents, medicines, and food additives. Today about half of all Na_2CO_3 produced is used in the glass industry (in soda-lime glass; see Section 11.7). Sodium carbonate ranks eleventh among the chemicals produced in the United States (11 million tons in 2004). For many years Na_2CO_3 was produced by the Solvay[†] process, in which ammonia is first dissolved in a saturated solution of sodium chloride. Bubbling carbon dioxide into the solution results in the precipitation of sodium bicarbonate as follows:

$$NH_3(aq) + NaCl(aq) + H_2CO_3(aq) \longrightarrow NaHCO_3(s) + NH_4Cl(aq)$$

Sodium bicarbonate is then separated from the solution and heated to give sodium carbonate:

$$2NaHCO_3(s) \longrightarrow Na_2CO_3(s) + CO_2(g) + H_2O(g)$$

The last plant using the Solvay process in the United States closed in 1986.

However, the rising cost of ammonia and the pollution problem resulting from by-products have prompted chemists to look for other sources of sodium carbonate. One is the mineral *trona* $[Na_5(CO_3)_2(HCO_3) \cdot 2H_2O]$, large deposits of which have been found in Wyoming. When trona is crushed and heated, it decomposes as follows:

$$2Na_5(CO_3)_2(HCO_3) \cdot 2H_2O(s) \longrightarrow 5Na_2CO_3(s) + CO_2(g) + 3H_2O(g)$$

The sodium carbonate obtained this way is dissolved in water, the solution is filtered to remove the insoluble impurities, and the sodium carbonate is crystallized as $Na_2CO_3 \cdot 10H_2O$. Finally, the hydrate is heated to give pure, anhydrous sodium carbonate.

Sodium Hydroxide and Potassium Hydroxide

The properties of sodium hydroxide and potassium hydroxide are very similar. These hydroxides are prepared by the electrolysis of aqueous NaCl and KCl solutions (see Section 19.8); both hydroxides are strong bases and very soluble in water. Sodium hydroxide is used in the manufacture of soap and many organic and inorganic compounds. Potassium hydroxide is used as an electrolyte in some storage batteries, and aqueous potassium hydroxide is used to remove carbon dioxide and sulfur dioxide from air.

Sodium Nitrate and Potassium Nitrate

Large deposits of sodium nitrate (*chile saltpeter*) are found in Chile. It decomposes with the evolution of oxygen at about 500°C:

$$2NaNO_3(s) \longrightarrow 2NaNO_2(s) + O_2(g)$$

Potassium nitrate (*saltpeter*) is prepared beginning with the "reaction"

$$KCl(aq) + NaNO_3(aq) \longrightarrow KNO_3(aq) + NaCl(aq)$$

[†]Ernest Solvay (1838–1922). Belgian chemist. Solvay's main contribution to industrial chemistry was the development of the process for the production of sodium carbonate that now bears his name.

This process is carried out just below 100°C. Because KNO_3 is the least soluble salt at room temperature, it is separated from the solution by fractional crystallization. Like $NaNO_3$, KNO_3 decomposes when heated.

Gunpowder consists of potassium nitrate, wood charcoal, and sulfur in the approximate proportions of 6:1:1 by mass. When gunpowder is heated, the reaction is

$$2KNO_3(s) + S(l) + 3C(s) \longrightarrow K_2S(s) + N_2(g) + 3CO_2(g)$$

The sudden formation of hot expanding gases causes an explosion.

Figure 20.15 *Dolomite* *($CaCO_3 \cdot MgCO_3$).*

20.6 The Alkaline Earth Metals

The alkaline earth metals are somewhat less electropositive and less reactive than the alkali metals. Except for the first member of the family, beryllium, which resembles aluminum (a Group 3A metal) in some respects, the alkaline earth metals have similar chemical properties. Because their M^{2+} ions attain the stable electron configuration of the preceding noble gas, the oxidation number of alkaline earth metals in the combined form is almost always +2. Table 20.5 lists some common properties of these metals. Radium is not included in the table because all radium isotopes are radioactive and it is difficult and expensive to study the chemistry of this Group 2A element.

Magnesium

Magnesium (see Figure 8.15) is the sixth most plentiful element in Earth's crust (about 2.5 percent by mass). Among the principal magnesium ores are brucite, $Mg(OH)_2$; dolomite, $CaCO_3 \cdot MgCO_3$ (Figure 20.15); and epsomite, $MgSO_4 \cdot 7H_2O$. Seawater is a good source of magnesium; there are about 1.3 g of magnesium in each kilogram of seawater. As is the case with most alkali and alkaline earth metals, metallic magnesium is obtained by electrolysis, in this case from its molten chloride, $MgCl_2$ (obtained from seawater, see p. 155).

TABLE 20.5	Properties of Alkaline Earth Metals				
	Be	**Mg**	**Ca**	**Sr**	**Ba**
Valence electron configuration	$2s^2$	$3s^2$	$4s^2$	$5s^2$	$6s^2$
Density (g/cm³)	1.86	1.74	1.55	2.6	3.5
Melting point (°C)	1280	650	838	770	714
Boiling point (°C)	2770	1107	1484	1380	1640
Atomic radius (pm)	112	160	197	215	222
Ionic radius (pm)*	31	65	99	113	135
First and second ionization	899	738	590	548	502
energies (kJ/mol)	1757	1450	1145	1058	958
Electronegativity	1.5	1.2	1.0	1.0	0.9
Standard reduction potential (V)†	−1.85	−2.37	−2.87	−2.89	−2.90

*Refers to the cation M^{2+}, where M denotes an alkali earth metal atom.
†The half-reaction is $M^{2+}(aq) + 2e^- \longrightarrow M(s)$.

The chemistry of magnesium is intermediate between that of beryllium and the heavier Group 2A elements. Magnesium does not react with cold water but does react slowly with steam:

$$Mg(s) + H_2O(g) \longrightarrow MgO(s) + H_2(g)$$

It burns brilliantly in air to produce magnesium oxide and magnesium nitride (see Figure 4.9):

$$2Mg(s) + O_2(g) \longrightarrow 2MgO(s)$$
$$3Mg(s) + N_2(g) \longrightarrow Mg_3N_2(s)$$

This property makes magnesium (in the form of thin ribbons or fibers) useful in flash photography and flares.

Magnesium oxide reacts very slowly with water to form magnesium hydroxide, a white solid suspension called *milk of magnesia* (see p. 729), which is used to treat acid indigestion:

$$MgO(s) + H_2O(l) \longrightarrow Mg(OH)_2(s)$$

Magnesium is a typical alkaline earth metal in that its hydroxide is a strong base. [The only alkaline earth hydroxide that is not a strong base is $Be(OH)_2$, which is amphoteric.]

The major uses of magnesium are in lightweight structural alloys, for cathodic protection (see Section 19.7), in organic synthesis, and in batteries. Magnesium is essential to plant and animal life, and Mg^{2+} ions are not toxic. It is estimated that the average adult ingests about 0.3 g of magnesium ions daily. Magnesium plays several important biological roles. It is present in intracellular and extracellular fluids. Magnesium ions are essential for the proper functioning of a number of enzymes. Magnesium is also present in the green plant pigment chlorophyll, which plays an important part in photosynthesis.

Calcium

Earth's crust contains about 3.4 percent calcium (see Figure 8.15) by mass. Calcium occurs in limestone, calcite, chalk, and marble as $CaCO_3$; in dolomite as $CaCO_3 \cdot MgCO_3$ (see Figure 20.15); in gypsum as $CaSO_4 \cdot 2H_2O$; and in fluorite as CaF_2 (Figure 20.16). Metallic calcium is best prepared by the electrolysis of molten calcium chloride ($CaCl_2$).

As we read down Group 2A from beryllium to barium, we note an increase in metallic properties. Unlike beryllium and magnesium, calcium (like strontium and barium) reacts with cold water to yield the corresponding hydroxide, although the rate of reaction is much slower than those involving the alkali metals (see Figure 4.14):

$$Ca(s) + 2H_2O(l) \longrightarrow Ca(OH)_2(aq) + H_2(g)$$

Calcium hydroxide [$Ca(OH)_2$] is commonly known as slaked lime or hydrated lime.

Lime (CaO), which is also referred to as quicklime, is one of the oldest materials known to mankind. Quicklime is produced by the thermal decomposition of calcium carbonate (see Section 18.3):

$$CaCO_3(s) \longrightarrow CaO(s) + CO_2(g)$$

Figure 20.16 *Fluorite (CaF_2).*

while slaked lime is produced by the reaction between quicklime and water:

$$CaO(s) + H_2O(l) \longrightarrow Ca(OH)_2(aq)$$

Quicklime is used in metallurgy (see Section 20.2) and the removal of SO_2 when fossil fuel is burned (see p. 770). Slaked lime is used in water treatment.

For many years, farmers have used lime to lower the acidity of soil for their crops (a process called *liming*). Nowadays lime is also applied to lakes affected by acid rain (see Section 17.6).

Metallic calcium has rather limited uses. It serves mainly as an alloying agent for metals like aluminum and copper and in the preparation of beryllium metal from its compounds. It is also used as a dehydrating agent for organic solvents.

Calcium is an essential element in living matter. It is the major component of bones and teeth; the calcium ion is present in a complex phosphate salt, hydroxyapatite, $Ca_5(PO_4)_3OH$. A characteristic function of Ca^{2+} ions in living systems is the activation of a variety of metabolic processes. Calcium plays a vital role in heart action, blood clotting, muscle contraction, and nerve impulse transmission.

Figure 20.17 *Corundum (Al_2O_3).*

20.7 Aluminum

Aluminum (see Figure 8.16) is the most abundant metal and the third most plentiful element in Earth's crust (7.5 percent by mass). The elemental form does not occur in nature; its principal ore is bauxite ($Al_2O_3 \cdot 2H_2O$). Other minerals containing aluminum are orthoclase ($KAlSi_3O_8$), beryl ($Be_3Al_2Si_6O_{18}$), cryolite (Na_3AlF_6), and corundum (Al_2O_3) (Figure 20.17).

Aluminum is usually prepared from bauxite, which is frequently contaminated with silica (SiO_2), iron oxides, and titanium(IV) oxide. The ore is first heated in sodium hydroxide solution to convert the silica into soluble silicates:

$$SiO_2(s) + 2OH^-(aq) \longrightarrow SiO_3^{2-}(aq) + H_2O(l)$$

At the same time, aluminum oxide is converted to the aluminate ion (AlO_2^-):

$$Al_2O_3(s) + 2OH^-(aq) \longrightarrow 2AlO_2^-(aq) + H_2O(l)$$

Iron oxide and titanium oxide are unaffected by this treatment and are filtered off. Next, the solution is treated with acid to precipitate the insoluble aluminum hydroxide:

$$AlO_2^-(aq) + H_3O^+(aq) \longrightarrow Al(OH)_3(s)$$

After filtration, the aluminum hydroxide is heated to obtain aluminum oxide:

$$2Al(OH)_3(s) \longrightarrow Al_2O_3(s) + 3H_2O(g)$$

Anhydrous aluminum oxide, or *corundum,* is reduced to aluminum by the *Hall*[†] *process.* Figure 20.18 shows a Hall electrolytic cell, which contains a series of carbon anodes. The cathode is also made of carbon and constitutes the lining inside the

Movie:
Aluminum Production
ARIS, Animations

Carbon anodes

Carbon cathode

Molten aluminum

Al_2O_3 in molten cryolite

Figure 20.18 *Electrolytic production of aluminum based on the Hall process.*

[†]Charles Martin Hall (1863–1914). American inventor. While Hall was an undergraduate at Oberlin College, he became interested in finding an inexpensive way to extract aluminum. Shortly after graduation, when he was only 22 years old, Hall succeeded in obtaining aluminum from aluminum oxide in a backyard woodshed. Amazingly, the same discovery was made at almost the same moment in France, by Paul Héroult, another 22-year-old inventor working in a similar makeshift laboratory.

cell. The key to the Hall process is the use of cryolite, or Na_3AlF_6 (m.p. 1000°C), as the solvent for aluminum oxide (m.p. 2045°C). The mixture is electrolyzed to produce aluminum and oxygen gas:

$$
\begin{aligned}
\text{Anode (oxidation):} \quad & 3[2O^{2-} \longrightarrow O_2(g) + 4e^-] \\
\text{Cathode (reduction):} \quad & 4[Al^{3+} + 3e^- \longrightarrow Al(l)] \\
\hline
\text{Overall:} \quad & 2Al_2O_3 \longrightarrow 4Al(l) + 3O_2(g)
\end{aligned}
$$

Oxygen gas reacts with the carbon anodes (at elevated temperatures) to form carbon monoxide, which escapes as a gas. The liquid aluminum metal (m.p. 660.2°C) sinks to the bottom of the vessel, from which it can be drained from time to time during the procedure.

Aluminum is one of the most versatile metals known. It has a low density (2.7 g/cm^3) and high tensile strength (that is, it can be stretched or drawn out). Aluminum is malleable, it can be rolled into thin foils, and it is an excellent electrical conductor. Its conductivity is about 65 percent that of copper. However, because aluminum is cheaper and lighter than copper, it is widely used in high-voltage transmission lines. Although aluminum's chief use is in aircraft construction, the pure metal itself is too soft and weak to withstand much strain. Its mechanical properties are greatly improved by alloying it with small amounts of metals such as copper, magnesium, and manganese, as well as silicon. Aluminum is not used by living systems and is generally considered to be nontoxic.

As we read across the periodic table from left to right in a given period, we note a gradual decrease in metallic properties. Thus, although aluminum is considered an active metal, it does not react with water as do sodium and calcium. Aluminum reacts with hydrochloric acid and with strong bases as follows:

$$2Al(s) + 6HCl(aq) \longrightarrow 2AlCl_3(aq) + 3H_2(g)$$
$$2Al(s) + 2NaOH(aq) + 2H_2O(l) \longrightarrow 2NaAlO_2(aq) + 3H_2(g)$$

Aluminum readily forms the oxide Al_2O_3 when exposed to air:

$$4Al(s) + 3O_2(g) \longrightarrow 2Al_2O_3(s)$$

A tenacious film of this oxide protects metallic aluminum from further corrosion and accounts for some of the unexpected inertness of aluminum.

Aluminum oxide has a very large exothermic enthalpy of formation ($\Delta H_f^\circ = -1670$ kJ/mol). This property makes aluminum suitable for use in solid propellants for rockets such as those used for some space shuttles. When a mixture of aluminum and ammonium perchlorate (NH_4ClO_4) is ignited, aluminum is oxidized to Al_2O_3, and the heat liberated in the reaction causes the gases that are formed to expand with great force. This action lifts the rocket.

The great affinity of aluminum for oxygen is illustrated nicely by the reaction of aluminum powder with a variety of metal oxides, particularly the transition metal oxides, to produce the corresponding metals. A typical reaction is

$$2Al(s) + Fe_2O_3(s) \longrightarrow Al_2O_3(s) + 2Fe(l) \qquad \Delta H^\circ = -822.8 \text{ kJ/mol}$$

which can result in temperatures approaching 3000°C. This reaction, which is used in the welding of steel and iron, is called the *thermite reaction* (Figure 20.19).

Aluminum chloride exists as a dimer:

Figure 20.19 *The temperature of a thermite reaction can reach 3000°C.*

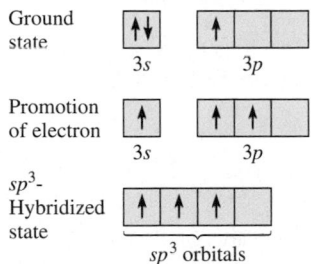

Figure 20.20 *The sp^3 hybridization of an Al atom in Al_2Cl_6. Each Al atom has one vacant sp^3 hybrid orbital that can accept a lone pair from the bridging Cl atom.*

Each of the bridging chlorine atoms forms a normal covalent bond and a coordinate covalent bond (indicated by →) with two aluminum atoms. Each aluminum atom is assumed to be sp^3-hybridized, so the vacant sp^3 hybrid orbital can accept a lone pair from the chlorine atom (Figure 20.20). Aluminum chloride undergoes hydrolysis as follows:

$$AlCl_3(s) + 3H_2O(l) \longrightarrow Al(OH)_3(s) + 3HCl(aq)$$

Aluminum hydroxide, like $Be(OH)_2$, is amphoteric:

$$Al(OH)_3(s) + 3H^+(aq) \longrightarrow Al^{3+}(aq) + 3H_2O(l)$$
$$Al(OH)_3(s) + OH^-(aq) \longrightarrow Al(OH)_4^-(aq)$$

In contrast to the boron hydrides, which are a well-defined series of compounds, aluminum hydride is a polymer in which each aluminum atom is surrounded octahedrally by bridging hydrogen atoms (Figure 20.21).

In 2002 chemists prepared the first member of aluminum hydride (Al_2H_6), which possesses bridging H atoms like diborane, B_2H_6.

When an aqueous mixture of aluminum sulfate and potassium sulfate is evaporated slowly, crystals of $KAl(SO_4)_2 \cdot 12H_2O$ are formed. Similar crystals can be formed by substituting Na^+ or NH_4^+ for K^+, and Cr^{3+} or Fe^{3+} for Al^{3+}. These compounds are called *alums,* and they have the general formula

$$M^+M^{3+}(SO_4)_2 \cdot 12H_2O \qquad \begin{array}{l} M^+: K^+, Na^+, NH_4^+ \\ M^{3+}: Al^{3+}, Cr^{3+}, Fe^{3+} \end{array}$$

Alums are examples of double salts, that is, salts that contain two different cations.

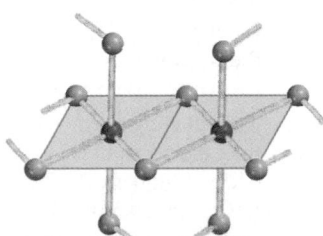

Figure 20.21 *Structure of aluminum hydride. Note that this compound is a polymer. Each Al atom is surrounded octahedrally by six bridging H atoms.*

CHEMISTRY
in Action

Recycling Aluminum

Aluminum beverage cans were virtually unknown in 1960; yet by the early 1970s over 1.3 billion pounds of aluminum had been used for these containers. The reasons for aluminum's popularity in the beverage industry are that it is nontoxic, odorless, tasteless, and lightweight. Furthermore, it is thermally conducting, so the fluid inside the container can be chilled rapidly.

Left: Collecting aluminum cans for recycling.
Right: Melting and purifying recycled aluminum.

Summary of Facts and Concepts

1. Depending on their reactivities, metals exist in nature in either the free or combined state.

2. Recovering a metal from its ore is a three-stage process. First, the ore must be prepared. The metal is then separated, usually by a reduction process, and finally, it is purified.

3. The methods commonly used for purifying metals are distillation, electrolysis, and zone refining.

4. Metallic bonds can be thought of as the force between positive ions immersed in a sea of electrons. In terms of band theory, the atomic orbitals merge to form energy bands. A substance is a conductor when electrons can be readily promoted to the conduction band, where they are free to move through the substance.

5. In insulators, the energy gap between the valence band and the conduction band is so large that electrons cannot be promoted into the conduction band. In semiconductors, electrons can cross the energy gap at higher temperatures, and therefore conductivity increases with increasing temperature as more electrons are able to reach the conduction band.

6. n-Type semiconductors contain donor impurities and extra electrons. p-Type semiconductors contain acceptor impurities and "positive holes."

7. The alkali metals are the most reactive of all the metallic elements. They have an oxidation number of $+1$ in their compounds. Under special conditions, some of them also form uninegative ions.

8. The alkaline earth metals are somewhat less reactive than the alkali metals. They almost always have an oxidation number of $+2$ in their compounds. The properties of the alkaline earth elements become increasingly metallic from top to bottom in their periodic group.

9. Aluminum does not react with water due to the formation of a protective oxide; its hydroxide is amphoteric.

The tremendous increase in the demand for aluminum does have a definite drawback, however. More than 3 billion pounds of the metal cans and foils are discarded in the United States annually. They litter the countryside and clog landfills. The best solution to this environmental problem, and the way to prevent the rapid depletion of a finite resource, is recycling.

What are the economic benefits of recycling aluminum? Let us compare the energy consumed in the production of aluminum from bauxite with that consumed when aluminum is recycled. The overall reaction for the Hall process can be represented as

$$Al_2O_3 \text{ (in molten cryolite)} + 3C(s) \longrightarrow 2Al(l) + 3CO(g)$$

for which $\Delta H^\circ = 1340$ kJ/mol and $\Delta S^\circ = 586$ J/K · mol. At 1000°C, which is the temperature of the process, the standard free-energy change for the reaction is given by

$$\Delta G^\circ = \Delta H^\circ - T\Delta S^\circ$$
$$= 1340 \text{ kJ/mol} - (1273 \text{ K})\left(\frac{586 \text{ J}}{K \cdot mol}\right)\left(\frac{1 \text{ kJ}}{1000 \text{ J}}\right)$$
$$= 594 \text{ kJ/mol}$$

Equation (19.3) states that $\Delta G^\circ = -nFE^\circ$; therefore, the amount of electrical energy needed to produce 1 mole of Al from bauxite is 594 kJ/2, or 297 kJ.

Recycling aluminum requires only enough energy to heat the metal to its melting point (660°C) plus the heat of fusion

(10.7 kJ/mol). The heat change where 1 mole of aluminum is heated from 25°C to 660°C is

$$\text{heat input} = Ms\Delta t$$
$$= (27.0 \text{ g})(0.900 \text{ J/g} \cdot {}^\circ\text{C})(660 - 25){}^\circ\text{C}$$
$$= 15.4 \text{ kJ}$$

where M is the molar mass, s is the specific heat of Al, and Δt is the temperature change. Thus, the total energy needed to recycle 1 mole of Al is given by

$$\text{total energy} = 15.4 \text{ kJ} + 10.7 \text{ kJ}$$
$$= 26.1 \text{ kJ}$$

To compare the energy requirements of the two methods we write

$$\frac{\text{energy needed to recycle 1 mol Al}}{\text{energy needed to produce 1 mol Al by electrolysis}}$$
$$= \frac{26.1 \text{ kJ}}{297 \text{ kJ}} \times 100\%$$
$$= 8.8\%$$

Thus, by recycling aluminum cans we can save about 91 percent of the energy required to extract the metal from bauxite. Recycling most of the aluminum cans thrown away each year saves 20 billion kilowatt-hours of electricity—about 1 percent of the electric power used in the United States annually. (Watt is the unit for power, 1 watt = 1 joule per second.)

Key Words

Acceptor impurity, p. 878
Alloy, p. 868
Amalgam, p. 869
Band theory, p. 876

Conductor, p. 877
Donor impurity, p. 877
Ferromagnetic, p. 869
Insulator, p. 877

Metallurgy, p. 868
Mineral, p. 868
n-Type semiconductor, p. 877
Ore, p. 868

p-Type semiconductor, p. 878
Pyrometallurgy, p. 870
Semiconductors, p. 877

Questions and Problems

Occurrence of Metals
Review Questions

20.1 Define mineral, ore, and metallurgy.

20.2 List three metals that are usually found in an uncombined state in nature and three metals that are always found in a combined state in nature.

20.3 Write chemical formulas for the following minerals: (a) calcite, (b) dolomite, (c) fluorite, (d) halite, (e) corundum, (f) magnetite, (g) beryl, (h) galena, (i) epsomite, (j) anhydrite.

20.4 Name the following minerals: (a) $MgCO_3$, (b) Na_3AlF_6, (c) Al_2O_3, (d) Ag_2S, (e) HgS, (f) ZnS, (g) $SrSO_4$, (h) $PbCO_3$, (i) MnO_2, (j) TiO_2.

Metallurgical Processes

Review Questions

20.5   Describe the main steps involved in the preparation of an ore.

20.6   What does roasting mean in metallurgy? Why is roasting a major source of air pollution and acid rain?

20.7   Describe with examples the chemical and electrolytic reduction processes used in the production of metals.

20.8   Describe the main steps used to purify metals.

20.9   Describe the extraction of iron in a blast furnace.

20.10 Briefly discuss the steelmaking process.

Problems

20.11 In the Mond process for the purification of nickel, CO is passed over metallic nickel to give $Ni(CO)_4$:

$$Ni(s) + 4CO(g) \rightleftharpoons Ni(CO)_4(g)$$

Given that the standard free energies of formation of $CO(g)$ and $Ni(CO)_4(g)$ are -137.3 kJ/mol and -587.4 kJ/mol, respectively, calculate the equilibrium constant of the reaction at 80°C. (Assume ΔG_f° to be independent of temperature.)

20.12 Copper is purified by electrolysis (see Figure 20.6). A 5.00-kg anode is used in a cell where the current is 37.8 A. How long (in hours) must the current run to dissolve this anode and electroplate it onto the cathode?

20.13 Consider the electrolytic procedure for purifying copper described in Figure 20.6. Suppose that a sample of copper contains the following impurities: Fe, Ag, Zn, Au, Co, Pt, and Pb. Which of the metals will be oxidized and dissolved in solution and which will be unaffected and simply form the sludge that accumulates at the bottom of the cell?

20.14 How would you obtain zinc from sphalerite (ZnS)?

20.15 Starting with rutile (TiO_2), explain how you would obtain pure titanium metal. (*Hint:* First convert TiO_2 to $TiCl_4$. Next, reduce $TiCl_4$ with Mg. Look up physical properties of $TiCl_4$, Mg, and $MgCl_2$ in a chemistry handbook.)

20.16 A certain mine produces 2.0×10^8 kg of copper from chalcopyrite ($CuFeS_2$) each year. The ore contains only 0.80 percent Cu by mass. (a) If the density of the ore is 2.8 g/cm^3, calculate the volume (in cm^3) of ore removed each year. (b) Calculate the mass (in kg) of SO_2 produced by roasting (assume chalcopyrite to be the only source of sulfur).

20.17 Which of the following compounds would require electrolysis to yield the free metals? Ag_2S, $CaCl_2$, NaCl, Fe_2O_3, Al_2O_3, $TiCl_4$.

20.18 Although iron is only about two-thirds as abundant as aluminum in Earth's crust, mass for mass it costs only about one-quarter as much to produce. Why?

Band Theory of Conductivity

Review Questions

20.19 Define the following terms: conductor, insulator, semiconducting elements, donor impurities, acceptor impurities, n-type semiconductors, p-type semiconductors.

20.20 Briefly discuss the nature of bonding in metals, insulators, and semiconducting elements.

20.21 Describe the general characteristics of n-type and p-type semiconductors.

20.22 State whether silicon would form n-type or p-type semiconductors with the following elements: Ga, Sb, Al, As.

Alkali Metals

Review Questions

20.23 How is sodium prepared commercially?

20.24 Why is potassium usually not prepared electrolytically from one of its salts?

20.25 Describe the uses of the following compounds: NaCl, Na_2CO_3, NaOH, KOH, KO_2.

20.26 Under what conditions do sodium and potassium form Na^- and K^- ions?

Problems

20.27 Complete and balance the following equations:
(a) $K(s) + H_2O(l) \longrightarrow$
(b) $NaH(s) + H_2O(l) \longrightarrow$
(c) $Na(s) + O_2(g) \longrightarrow$
(d) $K(s) + O_2(g) \longrightarrow$

20.28 Write a balanced equation for each of the following reactions: (a) sodium reacts with water; (b) an aqueous solution of NaOH reacts with CO_2; (c) solid Na_2CO_3 reacts with a HCl solution; (d) solid $NaHCO_3$ reacts with a HCl solution; (e) solid $NaHCO_3$ is heated; (f) solid Na_2CO_3 is heated.

20.29 Sodium hydride (NaH) can be used as a drying agent for many organic solvents. Explain how it works.

20.30 Calculate the volume of CO_2 at 10.0°C and 746 mmHg pressure obtained by treating 25.0 g of Na_2CO_3 with an excess of hydrochloric acid.

Alkaline Earth Metals

Review Questions

20.31 List the common ores of magnesium and calcium.

20.32 How are the metals magnesium and calcium obtained commercially?

Problems

20.33 From the thermodynamic data in Appendix 3, calculate the ΔH° values for the following decompositions:

(a) $MgCO_3(s) \longrightarrow MgO(s) + CO_2(g)$

(b) $CaCO_3(s) \longrightarrow CaO(s) + CO_2(g)$

Which of the two compounds is more easily decomposed by heat?

20.34 Starting with magnesium and concentrated nitric acid, describe how you would prepare magnesium oxide. [*Hint:* First convert Mg to $Mg(NO_3)_2$. Next, MgO can be obtained by heating $Mg(NO_3)_2$.]

20.35 Describe two ways of preparing magnesium chloride.

20.36 The second ionization energy of magnesium is only about twice as great as the first, but the third ionization energy is 10 times as great. Why does it take so much more energy to remove the third electron?

20.37 List the sulfates of the Group 2A metals in order of increasing solubility in water. Explain the trend. (*Hint:* You need to consult a chemistry handbook.)

20.38 Helium contains the same number of electrons in its outer shell as do the alkaline earth metals. Explain why helium is inert whereas the Group 2A metals are not.

20.39 When exposed to air, calcium first forms calcium oxide, which is then converted to calcium hydroxide, and finally to calcium carbonate. Write a balanced equation for each step.

20.40 Write chemical formulas for (a) quicklime, (b) slaked lime, (c) limewater.

Aluminum

Review Questions

20.41 Describe the Hall process for preparing aluminum.

20.42 What action renders aluminum inert?

Problems

20.43 Before Hall invented his electrolytic process, aluminum was produced by the reduction of its chloride with an active metal. Which metals would you use for the production of aluminum in that way?

20.44 With the Hall process, how many hours will it take to deposit 664 g of Al at a current of 32.6 A?

20.45 Aluminum forms the complex ions $AlCl_4^-$ and AlF_6^{3-}. Describe the shapes of these ions. $AlCl_6^{3-}$ does not form. Why? (*Hint:* Consider the relative sizes of Al^{3+}, F^-, and Cl^- ions.)

20.46 The overall reaction for the electrolytic production of aluminum by means of the Hall process may be represented as

$$Al_2O_3(s) + 3C(s) \longrightarrow 2Al(l) + 3CO(g)$$

At 1000°C, the standard free-energy change for this process is 594 kJ/mol. (a) Calculate the minimum voltage required to produce 1 mole of aluminum at this temperature. (b) If the actual voltage applied is exactly three times the ideal value, calculate the energy required to produce 1.00 kg of the metal.

20.47 In basic solution, aluminum metal is a strong reducing agent and is oxidized to AlO_2^-. Give balanced equations for the reaction of Al in basic solution with the following: (a) $NaNO_3$, to give ammonia; (b) water, to give hydrogen; (c) Na_2SnO_3, to give metallic tin.

20.48 Write a balanced equation for the thermal decomposition of aluminum nitrate to form aluminum oxide, nitrogen dioxide, and oxygen gas.

20.49 Describe some of the properties of aluminum that make it one of the most versatile metals known.

20.50 The pressure of gaseous Al_2Cl_6 increases more rapidly with temperature than predicted by the ideal gas equation even though Al_2Cl_6 behaves like an ideal gas. Explain.

20.51 Starting with aluminum, describe with balanced equations how you would prepare (a) Al_2Cl_6, (b) Al_2O_3, (c) $Al_2(SO_4)_3$, (d) $NH_4Al(SO_4)_2 \cdot 12H_2O$.

20.52 Explain the change in bonding when Al_2Cl_6 dissociates to form $AlCl_3$ in the gas phase.

Additional Problems

20.53 In steelmaking, nonmetallic impurities such as P, S, and Si are removed as the corresponding oxides. The inside of the furnace is usually lined with $CaCO_3$ and $MgCO_3$, which decompose at high temperatures to yield CaO and MgO. How do CaO and MgO help in the removal of the nonmetallic oxides?

20.54 When 1.164 g of a certain metal sulfide was roasted in air, 0.972 g of the metal oxide was formed. If the oxidation number of the metal is $+2$, calculate the molar mass of the metal.

20.55 An early view of metallic bonding assumed that bonding in metals consisted of localized, shared electron-pair bonds between metal atoms. What evidence would help you to argue against this viewpoint?

20.56 Referring to Figure 20.6, would you expect H_2O and H^+ to be reduced at the cathode and H_2O oxidized at the anode?

20.57 A 0.450-g sample of steel contains manganese as an impurity. The sample is dissolved in acidic solution and the manganese is oxidized to the permanganate ion MnO_4^-. The MnO_4^- ion is reduced to Mn^{2+} by reacting with 50.0 mL of 0.0800 M $FeSO_4$ solution. The excess Fe^{2+} ions are then oxidized to Fe^{3+} by 22.4 mL of 0.0100 M $K_2Cr_2O_7$. Calculate the percent by mass of manganese in the sample.

20.58 Given that $\Delta G_f^\circ(Fe_2O_3) = -741.0$ kJ/mol and that $\Delta G_f^\circ(Al_2O_3) = -1576.4$ kJ/mol, calculate ΔG° for the following reactions at 25°C:

(a) $2Fe_2O_3(s) \longrightarrow 4Fe(s) + 3O_2(g)$

(b) $2Al_2O_3(s) \longrightarrow 4Al(s) + 3O_2(g)$

20.59 Use compounds of aluminum as an example to explain what is meant by amphoterism.

20.60 When an inert atmosphere is needed for a metallurgical process, nitrogen is frequently used. However, in the reduction of $TiCl_4$ by magnesium, helium is used. Explain why nitrogen is not suitable for this process.

20.61 It has been shown that Na_2 species form in the vapor phase. Describe the formation of the "disodium molecule" in terms of a molecular orbital energy-level diagram. Would you expect the alkaline earth metals to exhibit a similar property?

20.62 Explain each of the following statements: (a) An aqueous solution of $AlCl_3$ is acidic. (b) $Al(OH)_3$ is soluble in NaOH solutions but not in NH_3 solution.

20.63 Write balanced equations for the following reactions: (a) the heating of aluminum carbonate; (b) the reaction between $AlCl_3$ and K; (c) the reaction between solutions of Na_2CO_3 and $Ca(OH)_2$.

20.64 Write a balanced equation for the reaction between calcium oxide and dilute HCl solution.

20.65 What is wrong with the following procedure for obtaining magnesium?

$$MgCO_3 \longrightarrow MgO(s) + CO_2(g)$$
$$MgO(s) + CO(g) \longrightarrow Mg(s) + CO_2(g)$$

20.66 Explain why most metals have a flickering appearance.

20.67 Predict the chemical properties of francium, the last member of Group 1A.

20.68 Describe a medicinal or health-related application for each of the following compounds: NaF, Li_2CO_3, $Mg(OH)_2$, $CaCO_3$, $BaSO_4$, $Al(OH)_2NaCO_3$ (see p. 684).

20.69 The following are two reaction schemes involving magnesium. *Scheme I:* When magnesium burns in oxygen, a white solid (A) is formed. A dissolves in 1 *M* HCl to give a colorless solution (B). Upon addition of Na_2CO_3 to B, a white precipitate is formed (C). On heating, C decomposes to D and a colorless gas is generated (E). When E is passed through limewater [an aqueous suspension of $Ca(OH)_2$], a white precipitate appears (F). *Scheme II:* Magnesium reacts with 1 *M* H_2SO_4 to produce a colorless solution (G). Treating G with an excess of NaOH produces a white precipitate (H). H dissolves in 1 *M* HNO_3 to form a colorless solution. When the solution is slowly evaporated, a white solid (I) appears. On heating I, a brown gas is given off. Identify A–I and write equations representing the reactions involved.

20.70 Lithium and magnesium exhibit a diagonal relationship in some chemical properties. How does lithium resemble magnesium in its reaction with oxygen and nitrogen? Consult a handbook of chemistry and compare the solubilities of carbonates, fluorides, and phosphates of these metals.

20.71 To prevent the formation of oxides, peroxides and superoxides, alkali metals are sometimes stored in an inert atmosphere. Which of the following gases should not be used for lithium? Why? Ne, Ar, N_2, Kr.

20.72 Which of the following metals is not found in the free state in nature: Ag, Cu, Zn, Au, Pt?

Special Problems

20.73 After heating, a metal surface (such as that of a cooking pan or skillet) develops a color pattern like an oil slick on water. Explain.

20.74 Chemical tests of four metals A, B, C, and D show the following results.

(a) Only B and C react with 0.5 M HCl to give H_2 gas.

(b) When B is added to a solution containing the ions of the other metals, metallic A, C, and D are formed.

(c) A reacts with 6 M HNO$_3$ but D does not.

Arrange the metals in the increasing order as reducing agents. Suggest four metals that fit these descriptions.

20.75 The electrical conductance of copper metal decreases with temperature, but that of a CuSO$_4$ solution increases with temperature. Explain.

20.76 As stated in the chapter, potassium superoxide (KO$_2$) is a useful source of oxygen employed in breathing equipment. Calculate the pressure at which oxygen gas stored at 20°C would have the same density as the oxygen gas provided by KO$_2$. The density of KO$_2$ at 20°C is 2.15 g/cm^3.

20.77 A sample of 10.00 g of sodium reacts with oxygen to form 13.83 g of sodium oxide (Na$_2$O) and sodium peroxide (Na$_2$O$_2$). Calculate the percent composition of the mixture.

21

The nose cone of the space shuttle is made of graphite and silicon carbide and can withstand the tremendous heat generated when the vehicle enters Earth's atmosphere. The models show graphite and silicon carbide, which has a diamond structure.

Nonmetallic Elements and Their Compounds

A LOOK AHEAD

- This chapter starts by examining the general properties of the nonmetals. (21.1)

- We see that hydrogen does not have a unique position in the periodic table. We learn the preparation of hydrogen and study several different types of compounds containing hydrogen. We also discuss the hydrogenation reaction and the role hydrogen plays in energy production. (21.2)

- Next, we consider the inorganic world of carbon in terms of carbides, cyanides, and carbon monoxide and carbon dioxide. (21.3)

- Nitrogen is the most abundant element in the atmosphere. Its major compounds are ammonia, hydrazine, and several oxides. Nitric acid, a strong oxidizing agent, is a major industrial chemical. Phosphorus is the other important element in Group 5A. It is a major component of teeth and bones and in genetic materials like deoxyribonucleic acid (DNA) and ribonucleic acid (RNA). Phosphorus compounds include hydride and oxides. Phosphoric acid has many commercial applications. (21.4)

- Oxygen is the most abundant element in Earth's crust. It forms compounds with most other elements as oxides, peroxides, and superoxides. Its allotropic form, ozone, is a strong oxidizing agent. Sulfur, the second member of Group 6A, also forms many compounds with metals and nonmetals. Sulfuric acid is the most important industrial chemical in the world. (21.5)

- The halogens are the most electronegative and most reactive of the nonmetals. We study their preparations, properties, and reactions and applications of their compounds. (21.6)

Interactive Activity Summary

1. Interactivity: Properties of Nonmetals (21.1)
2. Interactivity: Nonmetal Elements (21.1)
3. Interactivity: Halogens (21.6)

Of the 114 known elements, only 25 are nonmetallic elements. Unlike the metals, the chemistry of these elements is diverse. Despite their relatively small number, most of the essential elements in biological systems are nonmetals (O, C, H, N, P, and S). This group also includes the most unreactive of the elements—the noble gases. The unique properties of hydrogen set it aside from the rest of the elements in the periodic table. A whole branch of chemistry—organic chemistry—is based on carbon compounds.

In this chapter we continue our survey of the elements by concentrating on the nonmetals. The emphasis will be on important chemical properties and on the roles of nonmetals and their compounds in industrial, chemical, and biological processes.

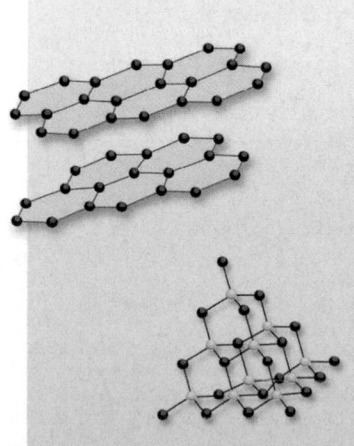

21.1 General Properties of Nonmetals

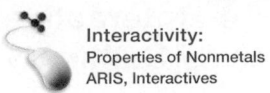

Interactivity:
Properties of Nonmetals
ARIS, Interactives

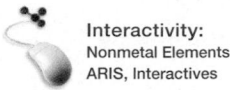

Interactivity:
Nonmetal Elements
ARIS, Interactives

Recall that there is no totally suitable position for hydrogen in the periodic table.

Properties of nonmetals are more varied than those of metals. A number of nonmetals are gases in the elemental state: hydrogen, oxygen, nitrogen, fluorine, chlorine, and the noble gases. Only one, bromine, is a liquid. All the remaining nonmetals are solids at room temperature. Unlike metals, nonmetallic elements are poor conductors of heat and electricity; they exhibit both positive and negative oxidation numbers.

A small group of elements, called metalloids, have properties characteristic of both metals and nonmetals. The metalloids boron, silicon, germanium, and arsenic are semiconducting elements (see Section 20.3).

Nonmetals are more electronegative than metals. The electronegativity of elements increases from left to right across any period and from bottom to top in any group in the periodic table (see Figure 9.5). With the exception of hydrogen, the nonmetals are concentrated in the upper right-hand corner of the periodic table (Figure 21.1). Compounds formed by a combination of metals and nonmetals tend to be ionic, having a metallic cation and a nonmetallic anion.

In this chapter we will discuss the chemistry of a number of common and important nonmetallic elements: hydrogen; carbon (Group 4A); nitrogen and phosphorus (Group 5A); oxygen and sulfur (Group 6A); and fluorine, chlorine, bromine, and iodine (Group 7A).

21.2 Hydrogen

Hydrogen is the simplest element known—its most common atomic form contains only one proton and one electron. The atomic form of hydrogen exists only at very high temperatures, however. Normally, elemental hydrogen is a diatomic molecule, the product of an exothermic reaction between H atoms:

$$H(g) + H(g) \longrightarrow H_2(g) \qquad \Delta H° = -436.4 \text{ kJ/mol}$$

Molecular hydrogen is a colorless, odorless, and nonpoisonous gas. At 1 atm, liquid hydrogen has a boiling point of $-252.9°C$ (20.3 K).

1 1A																	18 8A
1 H	2 2A											13 3A	14 4A	15 5A	16 6A	17 7A	2 He
3 Li	4 Be											5 B	6 C	7 N	8 O	9 F	10 Ne
11 Na	12 Mg	3 3B	4 4B	5 5B	6 6B	7 7B	8	9 8B	10	11 1B	12 2B	13 Al	14 Si	15 P	16 S	17 Cl	18 Ar
19 K	20 Ca	21 Sc	22 Ti	23 V	24 Cr	25 Mn	26 Fe	27 Co	28 Ni	29 Cu	30 Zn	31 Ga	32 Ge	33 As	34 Se	35 Br	36 Kr
37 Rb	38 Sr	39 Y	40 Zr	41 Nb	42 Mo	43 Tc	44 Ru	45 Rh	46 Pd	47 Ag	48 Cd	49 In	50 Sn	51 Sb	52 Te	53 I	54 Xe
55 Cs	56 Ba	57 La	72 Hf	73 Ta	74 W	75 Re	76 Os	77 Ir	78 Pt	79 Au	80 Hg	81 Tl	82 Pb	83 Bi	84 Po	85 At	86 Rn
87 Fr	88 Ra	89 Ac	104 Rf	105 Db	106 Sg	107 Bh	108 Hs	109 Mt	110 Ds	111 Rg	112	(113)	114	(115)	116	(117)	(118)

Figure 21.1 *Representative nonmetallic elements (in blue) and metalloids (gray).*

Hydrogen is the most abundant element in the universe, accounting for about 70 percent of the universe's total mass. It is the tenth most abundant element in Earth's crust, where it is found in combination with other elements. Unlike Jupiter and Saturn, Earth does not have a strong enough gravitational pull to retain the lightweight H_2 molecules, so hydrogen is not found in our atmosphere.

The ground-state electron configuration of H is $1s^1$. It resembles the alkali metals in that it can be oxidized to the H^+ ion, which exists in aqueous solutions in the hydrated form. On the other hand, hydrogen resembles the halogens in that it forms the uninegative hydride ion (H^-), which is isoelectronic with helium ($1s^2$). Hydrogen is found in a large number of covalent compounds. It also has the unique capacity for hydrogen-bond formation (see Section 11.2).

Hydrogen gas plays an important role in industrial processes. About 95 percent of the hydrogen produced is used captively; that is, it is produced at or near the plant where it is used for industrial processes, such as the synthesis of ammonia. The large-scale industrial preparation is the reaction between propane (from natural gas and also as a product of oil refineries) and steam in the presence of a catalyst at 900°C:

$$C_3H_8(g) + 3H_2O(g) \longrightarrow 3CO(g) + 7H_2(g)$$

In another process, steam is passed over a bed of red-hot coke:

$$C(s) + H_2O(g) \longrightarrow CO(g) + H_2(g)$$

The mixture of carbon monoxide and hydrogen gas produced in this reaction is commonly known as *water gas*. Because both CO and H_2 burn in air, water gas was used as a fuel for many years. But because CO is poisonous, water gas has been replaced by natural gases, such as methane and propane.

Small quantities of hydrogen gas can be prepared conveniently in the laboratory by reacting zinc with dilute hydrochloric acid (Figure 21.2):

$$Zn(s) + 2HCl(aq) \longrightarrow ZnCl_2(aq) + H_2(g)$$

Hydrogen gas can also be produced by the reaction between an alkali metal or an alkaline earth metal (Ca or Ba) and water (see Section 4.4), but these reactions are

Figure 21.2 *Apparatus for the laboratory preparation of hydrogen gas. The gas is collected over water, as is also the case of oxygen gas (see Figure 5.12).*

too violent to be suitable for the laboratory preparation of hydrogen gas. Very pure hydrogen gas can be obtained by the electrolysis of water, but this method consumes too much energy to be practical on a large scale.

Binary Hydrides

Binary hydrides are compounds containing hydrogen and another element, either a metal or a nonmetal. Depending on structure and properties, these hydrides are broadly divided into three types: (1) ionic hydrides, (2) covalent hydrides, and (3) interstitial hydrides.

Ionic Hydrides

Ionic hydrides are formed when molecular hydrogen combines directly with any alkali metal or with the alkaline earth metals Ca, Sr, or Ba:

$$2Li(s) + H_2(g) \longrightarrow 2LiH(s)$$
$$Ca(s) + H_2(g) \longrightarrow CaH_2(s)$$

All ionic hydrides are solids that have the high melting points characteristic of ionic compounds. The anion in these compounds is the hydride ion, H^-, which is a very strong Brønsted base. It readily accepts a proton from a proton donor such as water:

$$H^-(aq) + H_2O(l) \longrightarrow OH^-(aq) + H_2(g)$$

Due to their high reactivity with water, ionic hydrides are frequently used to remove traces of water from organic solvents.

Covalent Hydrides

This is an example of the diagonal relationship between Be and Al (see p. 336).

In *covalent hydrides,* the hydrogen atom is covalently bonded to the atom of another element. There are two types of covalent hydrides—those containing discrete molecular units, such as CH_4 and NH_3, and those having complex polymeric structures, such as $(BeH_2)_x$ and $(AlH_3)_x$, where x is a very large number.

Figure 21.3 shows the binary ionic and covalent hydrides of the representative elements. The physical and chemical properties of these compounds change from ionic to covalent across a given period. Consider, for example, the hydrides of the second-period elements: LiH, BeH_2, B_2H_6, CH_4, NH_3, H_2O, and HF. LiH is an ionic compound with a high melting point (680°C). The structure of BeH_2 (in the solid state) is polymeric; it is a covalent compound. The molecules B_2H_6 and CH_4 are nonpolar. In contrast, NH_3, H_2O, and HF are all polar molecules in which the hydrogen atom is the *positive* end of the polar bond. Of this group of hydrides (NH_3, H_2O, and HF), only HF is acidic in water.

As we move down any group in Figure 21.3, the compounds change from covalent to ionic. In Group 2A, for example, BeH_2 and MgH_2 are covalent, but CaH_2, SrH_2, and BaH_2 are ionic.

Interstitial Hydrides

Interstitial compounds are sometimes called nonstoichiometric compounds. Note that they do not obey the law of definite proportions (see Section 2.1).

Molecular hydrogen forms a number of hydrides with transition metals. In some of these compounds, the ratio of hydrogen atoms to metal atoms is *not* a constant. Such compounds are called *interstitial hydrides.* For example, depending on conditions, the formula for titanium hydride can vary between $TiH_{1.8}$ and TiH_2.

Many of the interstitial hydrides have metallic properties such as electrical conductivity. Yet it is known that hydrogen is definitely bonded to the metal in these compounds, although the exact nature of the bonding is often not clear.

1 1A	2 2A	3 3B	4 4B	5 5B	6 6B	7 7B	8	9 8B	10	11 1B	12 2B	13 3A	14 4A	15 5A	16 6A	17 7A	18 8A
LiH	BeH_2											B_2H_6	CH_4	NH_3	H_2O	HF	
NaH	MgH_2											AlH_3	SiH_4	PH_3	H_2S	HCl	
KH	CaH_2											GaH_3	GeH_4	AsH_3	H_2Se	HBr	
RbH	SrH_2											InH_3	SnH_4	SbH_3	H_2Te	HI	
CsH	BaH_2											TlH_3	PbH_4	BiH_3			

Legend: Discrete molecular units · Polymeric structure; covalent compound · Ionic compound

Figure 21.3 *Binary hydrides of the representative elements. In cases in which hydrogen forms more than one compound with the same element, only the formula of the simplest hydride is shown. The properties of many of the transition metal hydrides are not well characterized.*

Molecular hydrogen interacts in a unique way with palladium (Pd). Hydrogen gas is readily adsorbed onto the surface of the palladium metal, where it dissociates into atomic hydrogen. The H atoms then "dissolve" into the metal. On heating and under the pressure of H_2 gas on one side of the metal, these atoms diffuse through the metal and recombine to form molecular hydrogen, which emerges as the gas from the other side. Because no other gas behaves in this way with palladium, this process has been used to separate hydrogen gas from other gases on a small scale.

Isotopes of Hydrogen

Hydrogen has three isotopes: $_1^1H$ (hydrogen), $_1^2H$ (deuterium, symbol D), and $_1^3H$ (tritium, symbol T). The natural abundances of the stable hydrogen isotopes are hydrogen, 99.985 percent; and deuterium, 0.015 percent. Tritium is a radioactive isotope with a half-life of about 12.5 years.

The $_1^1H$ isotope is also called protium. Hydrogen is the only element whose isotopes are given different names.

Table 21.1 compares some of the common properties of H_2O with those of D_2O. Deuterium oxide, or heavy water as it is commonly called, is used in some nuclear reactors as a coolant and a moderator of nuclear reactions (see Chapter 23). D_2O can be separated from H_2O by fractional distillation because H_2O boils at a lower

TABLE 21.1	Properties of H_2O and D_2O	
Property	**H_2O**	**D_2O**
Molar mass (g/mol)	18.02	20.03
Melting point (°C)	0	3.8
Boiling point (°C)	100	101.4
Density at 4°C (g/cm³)	1.000	1.108

temperature, as Table 21.1 shows. Another technique for its separation is electrolysis of water. Because H_2 gas is formed about eight times as fast as D_2 during electrolysis, the water remaining in the electrolytic cell becomes progressively enriched with D_2O. Interestingly, the Dead Sea, which for thousands of years has entrapped water that has no outlet other than through evaporation, has a higher $[D_2O]/[H_2O]$ ratio than water found elsewhere.

Although D_2O chemically resembles H_2O in most respects, it is a toxic substance. The reason is that deuterium is heavier than hydrogen; thus, its compounds often react more slowly than those of the lighter isotope. Regular drinking of D_2O instead of H_2O could prove fatal because of the slower rate of transfer of D^+ compared with that of H^+ in the acid-base reactions involved in enzyme catalysis. This *kinetic isotope effect* is also manifest in acid ionization constants. For example, the ionization constant of acetic acid

$$CH_3COOH(aq) \rightleftharpoons CH_3COO^-(aq) + H^+(aq) \quad K_a = 1.8 \times 10^{-5}$$

is about three times as large as that of deuterated acetic acid:

$$CH_3COOD(aq) \rightleftharpoons CH_3COO^-(aq) + D^+(aq) \quad K_a = 6 \times 10^{-6}$$

Hydrogenation

Hydrogenation is *the addition of hydrogen to compounds containing multiple bonds, especially C=C and C≡C bonds.* A simple hydrogenation reaction is the conversion of ethylene to ethane:

Platinum catalyst on alumina (Al_2O_3) used in hydrogenation.

This reaction is quite slow under normal conditions, but the rate can be greatly increased by the presence of a catalyst such as nickel or platinum. As in the Haber synthesis of ammonia (see Section 13.6), the main function of the catalyst is to weaken the H—H bond and facilitate the reaction.

Hydrogenation is an important process in the food industry. Vegetable oils have considerable nutritional value, but some oils must be hydrogenated before we can use them because of their unsavory flavor and their inappropriate molecular structures (that is, there are too many C=C bonds present). Upon exposure to air, these *polyunsaturated* molecules (that is, molecules with many C=C bonds) undergo oxidation to yield unpleasant-tasting products (oil that has oxidized is said to be rancid). In the hydrogenation process, a small amount of nickel (about 0.1 percent by mass) is added to the oil and the mixture is exposed to hydrogen gas at high temperature and pressure. Afterward, the nickel is removed by filtration. Hydrogenation reduces the number of double bonds in the molecule but does not completely eliminate them. If all the double bonds are eliminated, the oil becomes hard and brittle. Under controlled conditions, suitable cooking oils and margarine may be prepared by hydrogenation from vegetable oils extracted from cottonseed, corn, and soybeans.

The Hydrogen Economy

The world's fossil fuel reserves are being depleted at an alarmingly fast rate. Faced with this dilemma, scientists have made intensive efforts in recent years to develop a

CHEMISTRY
in Action

Metallic Hydrogen

Scientists have long been interested in how nonmetallic substances, including hydrogen, behave under exceedingly high pressure. It was predicted that when atoms or molecules are compressed, their bonding electrons might be delocalized, producing a metallic state. In 1996, physicists at the Lawrence Livermore Laboratory used a 60-foot-long gun to generate a shock compression onto a thin (0.5-mm) layer of liquid hydrogen. For an instant, at pressures between 0.9 and 1.4 million atm, they were able to measure the electrical conductivity of the hydrogen sample and found that it was comparable to that of cesium metal at 2000 K. (The temperature of the hydrogen sample rose as a result of compression, although it remained in the molecular form.) As the pressure fell rapidly, the metallic state of hydrogen disappeared.

The Livermore experiment suggested that metallic hydrogen, if it can be kept in a stable state, may act as a room-temperature superconductor. The fact that hydrogen becomes metallic at pressures lower than previously thought possible also has provided new insight into planetary science. For many years scientists were puzzled by Jupiter's strong magnetic field, which is 20 times greater than that of Earth. A planet's magnetic field results from the convection motion of electrically conductive fluid in its interior. (For example, Earth's magnetic field is due to the heat-driven motion of liquid iron within its core.)

Jupiter is composed of an outer layer of nonmetallic molecular hydrogen that continuously transforms hydrogen within the core to metallic fluid hydrogen. It is now believed that this metallic layer is much closer to the surface (because the pressure needed to convert molecular hydrogen to metallic hydrogen is not as high as previously thought), which would account for Jupiter's unusually strong magnetic field.

— Insulating molecular hydrogen
— Metallic molecular hydrogen
— Metallic atomic hydrogen
— Rock core

Interior composition of Jupiter.

method of obtaining hydrogen gas as an alternative energy source. Hydrogen gas could replace gasoline to power automobiles (after considerable modification of the engine, of course) or be used with oxygen gas in fuel cells to generate electricity (see p. 842). One major advantage of using hydrogen gas in these ways is that the reactions are essentially free of pollutants; the end product formed in a hydrogen-powered engine or in a fuel cell would be water, just as in the burning of hydrogen gas in air:

$$2H_2(g) + O_2(g) \longrightarrow 2H_2O(l)$$

Of course, success of a hydrogen economy would depend on how cheaply we could produce hydrogen gas and how easily we could store it.

Although electrolysis of water consumes too much energy for large-scale application, if scientists can devise a more practical method of "splitting" water molecules, we could obtain vast amounts of hydrogen from seawater. One approach that is currently in the early stages of development would use solar energy. In this scheme, a catalyst (a complex molecule containing one or more transition metal atoms, such as ruthenium) absorbs a photon from solar radiation and becomes energetically excited. In its excited state, the catalyst is capable of reducing water to molecular hydrogen.

The total volume of ocean water is about 1×10^{21} L. Thus, the ocean contains an almost inexhaustible supply of hydrogen.

Some of the interstitial hydrides we have discussed would make suitable storage compounds for hydrogen. The reactions that form these hydrides are usually reversible, so hydrogen gas can be obtained simply by reducing the pressure of the hydrogen gas above the metal. The advantages of using interstitial hydrides are as follows: (1) many metals have a high capacity to take up hydrogen gas—sometimes up to three times as many hydrogen atoms as there are metal atoms; and (2) because these hydrides are solids, they can be stored and transported more easily than gases or liquids.

The Chemistry in Action essay on p. 901 describes what happens to hydrogen under pressure.

21.3 Carbon

The carbon cycle is discussed on p. 763.

Although it constitutes only about 0.09 percent by mass of Earth's crust, carbon is an essential element of living matter. It is found free in the form of diamond and graphite (see Figure 8.17), and it is also a component of natural gas, petroleum, and coal. (Coal is a natural dark-brown to black solid used as a fuel; it is formed from fossilized plants and consists of amorphous carbon with various organic and some inorganic compounds.) Carbon combines with oxygen to form carbon dioxide in the atmosphere and occurs as carbonate in limestone and chalk.

Diamond and graphite are allotropes of carbon. Figure 21.4 shows the phase diagram of carbon. Although graphite is the stable form of carbon at 1 atm and 25°C, owners of diamond jewelry need not be alarmed, for the rate of the spontaneous process

$$\text{C(diamond)} \longrightarrow \text{C(graphite)} \qquad \Delta G° = -2.87 \text{ kJ/mol}$$

is extremely slow. Millions of years may pass before a diamond turns to graphite.

Synthetic diamond can be prepared from graphite by applying very high pressures and temperatures. Figure 21.5 shows a synthetic diamond and its starting material, graphite. Synthetic diamonds generally lack the optical properties of natural diamonds. They are useful, however, as abrasives and in cutting concrete and many other hard substances, including metals and alloys. The uses of graphite are described on p. 474.

Carbon has the unique ability to form long chains (consisting of more than 50 C atoms) and stable rings with five or six members. This phenomenon is called *catenation, the linking of like atoms.* Carbon's versatility is responsible for the millions of organic compounds (made up of carbon and hydrogen and other elements such as oxygen, nitrogen, and halogens) found on Earth. The chemistry of organic compounds is discussed in Chapter 24.

Figure 21.4 *Phase diagram of carbon. Note that under atmospheric conditions, graphite is the stable form of carbon.*

Figure 21.5 *A synthetic diamond and the starting material—graphite.*

Carbides and Cyanides

Carbon combines with metals to form ionic compounds called **carbides,** such as CaC_2 and Be_2C, in which carbon is in the form of C_2^{2-} or C^{4-} ions. These ions are strong Brønsted bases and react with water as follows:

$$C_2^{2-}(aq) + 2H_2O(l) \longrightarrow 2OH^-(aq) + C_2H_2(g)$$
$$C^{4-}(aq) + 4H_2O(l) \longrightarrow 4OH^-(aq) + CH_4(g)$$

Carbon also forms a covalent compound with silicon. Silicon carbide, SiC, is called *carborundum* and is prepared as follows:

$$SiO_2(s) + 3C(s) \longrightarrow SiC(s) + 2CO(g)$$

Carborundum is also formed by heating silicon with carbon at 1500°C. Carborundum is almost as hard as diamond and it has the diamond structure; each carbon atom is tetrahedrally bonded to four Si atoms, and vice versa. It is used mainly for cutting, grinding, and polishing metals and glasses.

Another important class of carbon compounds, the **cyanides,** *contain the anion group* $:C \equiv N:^-$. Cyanide ions are extremely toxic because they bind almost irreversibly to the Fe(III) ion in cytochrome oxidase, a key enzyme in metabolic processes. Hydrogen cyanide, which has the aroma of bitter almonds, is even more dangerous because of its volatility (b.p. 26°C). A few tenths of 1 percent by volume of HCN in air can cause death within minutes. Hydrogen cyanide can be prepared by treating sodium cyanide or potassium cyanide with acid:

HCN is the gas used in gas execution chambers.

$$NaCN(s) + HCl(aq) \longrightarrow NaCl(aq) + HCN(aq)$$

Because HCN (in solution, called hydrocyanic acid) is a very weak acid ($K_a = 4.9 \times 10^{-10}$), most of the HCN produced in this reaction is in the nonionized form and leaves the solution as hydrogen cyanide gas. For this reason, acids should never be mixed with metal cyanides in the laboratory without proper ventilation.

Cyanide ions are used to extract gold and silver. Although these metals are usually found in the uncombined state in nature, in other metal ores they may be present in relatively small concentrations and are more difficult to extract. In a typical

Figure 21.6 *A cyanide pond for extracting gold from metal ore.*

process, the crushed ore is treated with an aqueous cyanide solution in the presence of air to dissolve the gold by forming the soluble complex ion $[Au(CN)_2]^-$:

$$4Au(s) + 8CN^-(aq) + O_2(g) + 2H_2O(l) \longrightarrow 4[Au(CN)_2]^-(aq) + 4OH^-(aq)$$

The complex ion $[Au(CN)_2]^-$ (along with some cation, such as Na^+) is separated from other insoluble materials by filtration and treated with an electropositive metal such as zinc to recover the gold:

$$Zn(s) + 2[Au(CN)_2]^-(aq) \longrightarrow [Zn(CN)_4]^{2-}(aq) + 2Au(s)$$

Figure 21.6 shows an aerial view of a "cyanide pond" used for the extraction of gold.

Oxides of Carbon

Of the several oxides of carbon, the most important are carbon monoxide, CO, and carbon dioxide, CO_2. Carbon monoxide is a colorless, odorless gas formed by the incomplete combustion of carbon or carbon-containing compounds:

$$2C(s) + O_2(g) \longrightarrow 2CO(g)$$

The role of CO as an indoor air pollutant is discussed on p. 775.

Carbon monoxide is used in metallurgical process for extracting nickel (see p. 874), in organic synthesis, and in the production of hydrocarbon fuels with hydrogen. Industrially, it is prepared by passing steam over heated coke. Carbon monoxide burns readily in oxygen to form carbon dioxide:

$$2CO(g) + O_2(g) \longrightarrow 2CO_2(g) \qquad \Delta H° = -566 \text{ kJ/mol}$$

Carbon monoxide is not an acidic oxide (it differs from carbon dioxide in that regard), and it is only slightly soluble in water.

Carbon dioxide is the primary greenhouse gas (see p. 763).

Carbon dioxide is a colorless and odorless gas. Unlike carbon monoxide, CO_2 is nontoxic. It is an acidic oxide (see p. 680). Carbon dioxide is used in beverages, in fire

CHEMISTRY
in Action

Synthetic Gas from Coal

The very existence of our technological society depends on an abundant supply of energy. Although the United States has only 5 percent of the world's population, we consume about 20 percent of the world's energy! At present, the two major sources of energy are nuclear fission and fossil fuels (discussed in Chapters 23 and 24, respectively). Coal, oil (which is also known as petroleum), and natural gas (mostly methane) are collectively called fossil fuels because they are the end result of the decomposition of plants and animals over tens or hundreds of millions of years. Oil and natural gas are cleaner-burning and more efficient fuels than coal, so they are preferred for most purposes. However, supplies of oil and natural gas are being depleted at an alarming rate, and research is under way to make coal a more versatile source of energy.

Coal consists of many high-molar-mass carbon compounds that also contain oxygen, hydrogen, and small amounts of nitrogen and sulfur. Coal constitutes about 90 percent of the world's fossil fuel reserves. For centuries coal has been used as a fuel both in homes and in industry. However, underground coal mining is expensive and dangerous, and strip mining (that is, mining in an open pit after removal of the overlaying earth and rock) is tremendously harmful to the environment. Another problem, this one associated with the burning of coal, is the formation of sulfur dioxide (SO_2) from the sulfur-containing compounds. This process leads to the formation of "acid rain," discussed on p. 767.

One of the most promising methods for making coal a more efficient and cleaner fuel involves the conversion of coal to a gaseous form, called *syngas* for "synthetic gas." This process is called *coal gasification*. In the presence of very hot steam and air, coal decomposes and reacts according to the following simplified scheme:

$$C(s) + H_2O(g) \longrightarrow CO(g) + H_2(g)$$
$$C(s) + 2H_2(g) \longrightarrow CH_4(g)$$

The main component of syngas is methane. In addition, the first reaction yields hydrogen and carbon monoxide gases and other useful by-products. Under suitable conditions, CO and H_2 combine to form methanol:

$$CO(g) + 2H_2(g) \longrightarrow CH_3OH(l)$$

Methanol has many uses, for example, as a solvent and a starting material for plastics. Syngas is easier than coal to store and transport. What's more, it is not a major source of air pollution because sulfur is removed in the gasification process.

Underground coal mining.

extinguishers, and in the manufacture of baking soda, $NaHCO_3$, and soda ash, Na_2CO_3. Solid carbon dioxide, called *dry ice,* is used as a refrigerant (see Figure 11.42).

21.4 Nitrogen and Phosphorus

Nitrogen

The nitrogen cycle is discussed on p. 752.

About 78 percent of air by volume is nitrogen. The most important mineral sources of nitrogen are saltpeter (KNO_3) and Chile saltpeter ($NaNO_3$). Nitrogen is an essential element of life; it is a component of proteins and nucleic acids.

Molecular nitrogen will boil off before molecular oxygen does during the fractional distillation of liquid air.

Molecular nitrogen is obtained by fractional distillation of air (the boiling points of liquid nitrogen and liquid oxygen are $-196°C$ and $-183°C$, respectively). In the laboratory, very pure nitrogen gas can be prepared by the thermal decomposition of ammonium nitrite:

$$NH_4NO_2(s) \longrightarrow 2H_2O(g) + N_2(g)$$

The N_2 molecule contains a triple bond and is very stable with respect to dissociation into atomic species. However, nitrogen forms a large number of compounds with hydrogen and oxygen in which the oxidation number of nitrogen varies from -3 to $+5$ (Table 21.2). Most nitrogen compounds are covalent; however, when heated with certain metals, nitrogen forms ionic nitrides containing the N^{3-} ion:

$$6Li(s) + N_2(g) \longrightarrow 2Li_3N(s)$$

TABLE 21.2	Common Compounds of Nitrogen		
Oxidation Number	**Compound**	**Formula**	**Structure**
-3	Ammonia	NH_3	H—N—H with H below
-2	Hydrazine	N_2H_4	H—N—N—H with H below each N
-1	Hydroxylamine	NH_2OH	H—N—O—H with H below N
0	Nitrogen* (dinitrogen)	N_2	:N≡N:
$+1$	Nitrous oxide (dinitrogen monoxide)	N_2O	:N≡N—O:
$+2$	Nitric oxide (nitrogen monoxide)	NO	:N=O
$+3$	Nitrous acid	HNO_2	O=N—O—H
$+4$	Nitrogen dioxide	NO_2	:O—N=O
$+5$	Nitric acid	HNO_3	O=N—O—H with O below

*We list the element here as a reference.

The nitride ion is a strong Brønsted base and reacts with water to produce ammonia and hydroxide ions:

$$N^{3-}(aq) + 3H_2O(l) \longrightarrow NH_3(g) + 3OH^-(aq)$$

Ammonia

Ammonia is one of the best-known nitrogen compounds. It is prepared industrially from nitrogen and hydrogen by the Haber process (see Section 13.6 and p. 630). It can be prepared in the laboratory by treating ammonium chloride with sodium hydroxide:

$$NH_4Cl(aq) + NaOH(aq) \longrightarrow NaCl(aq) + H_2O(l) + NH_3(g)$$

Ammonia is a colorless gas (b.p. $-33.4°C$) with an irritating odor. About three-quarters of the ammonia produced annually in the United States (about 18 million tons in 2005) is used in fertilizers.

Liquid ammonia, like water, undergoes autoionization:

$$2NH_3(l) \rightleftharpoons NH_4^+ + NH_2^-$$

or simply

$$NH_3(l) \rightleftharpoons H^+ + NH_2^-$$

where NH_2^- is called the *amide ion*. Note that both H^+ and NH_2^- are solvated with the NH_3 molecules. (Here is an example of ion-dipole interaction.) At $-50°C$, the ion product $[H^+][NH_2^-]$ is about 1×10^{-33}, considerably smaller than 1×10^{-14} for water at $25°C$. Nevertheless, liquid ammonia is a suitable solvent for many electrolytes, especially when a more basic medium is required or if the solutes react with water. The ability of liquid ammonia to dissolve alkali metals was discussed in Section 20.5.

The amide ion is a strong Brønsted base and does not exist in water.

Hydrazine

Another important hydride of nitrogen is hydrazine:

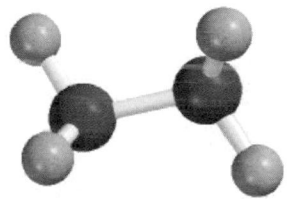

N_2H_4

Each N atom is sp^3-hybridized. Hydrazine is a colorless liquid that smells like ammonia. It melts at $2°C$ and boils at $114°C$.

Hydrazine is a base that can be protonated to give the $N_2H_5^+$ and $N_2H_6^{2+}$ ions. As a reducing agent, it can reduce Fe^{3+} to Fe^{2+}, MnO_4^- to Mn^{2+}, and I_2 to I^-. Its reaction with oxygen is highly exothermic:

$$N_2H_4(l) + O_2(g) \longrightarrow N_2(g) + 2H_2O(l) \quad \Delta H° = -666.6 \text{ kJ/mol}$$

Hydrazine and its derivative methylhydrazine, $N_2H_3(CH_3)$, together with the oxidizer dinitrogen tetroxide (N_2O_4), are used as rocket fuels. Hydrazine also plays a role in polymer synthesis and in the manufacture of pesticides.

Oxides and Oxoacids of Nitrogen

There are many nitrogen oxides, but the three particularly important ones are: nitrous oxide, nitric oxide, and nitrogen dioxide.

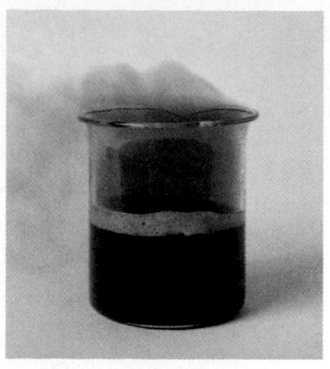

Figure 21.7 *The production of NO$_2$ gas when copper reacts with concentrated nitric acid.*

Nitrous oxide, N$_2$O, is a colorless gas with a pleasing odor and sweet taste. It is prepared by heating ammonium nitrate to about 270°C:

$$NH_4NO_3(s) \longrightarrow N_2O(g) + 2H_2O(g)$$

Nitrous oxide resembles molecular oxygen in that it supports combustion. It does so because it decomposes when heated to form molecular nitrogen and molecular oxygen:

$$2N_2O(g) \longrightarrow 2N_2(g) + O_2(g)$$

It is chiefly used as an anesthetic in dental procedures and other minor surgery. Nitrous oxide is also called "laughing gas" because a person inhaling the gas becomes somewhat giddy. No satisfactory explanation has yet been proposed for this unusual physiological response. Nitrous oxide is also used as the propellant in cans of whipped cream due to its high solubility in the whipped cream mixture.

Nitric oxide, NO, is a colorless gas. The reaction of N$_2$ and O$_2$ in the atmosphere

$$N_2(g) + O_2(g) \rightleftharpoons 2NO(g) \qquad \Delta G° = 173.4 \text{ kJ/mol}$$

is a form of nitrogen fixation (see p. 753). The equilibrium constant for the above reaction is very small at room temperature: K_P is only 4.0×10^{-31} at 25°C, so very little NO will form at that temperature. However, the equilibrium constant increases rapidly with temperature, for example, in a running auto engine. An appreciable amount of nitric oxide is formed in the atmosphere by the action of lightning. In the laboratory the gas can be prepared by the reduction of dilute nitric acid with copper:

$$3Cu(s) + 8HNO_3(aq) \longrightarrow 3Cu(NO_3)_2(aq) + 4H_2O(l) + 2NO(g)$$

The nitric oxide molecule is paramagnetic, containing one unpaired electron. It can be represented by the following resonance structures:

$$\dot{N}=\ddot{O} \longleftrightarrow {}^{-}\ddot{N}=\ddot{O}^{+}$$

As we noted in Chapter 9, this molecule does not obey the octet rule. The properties of nitric oxide are discussed on p. 384.

Unlike nitrous oxide and nitric oxide, nitrogen dioxide is a highly toxic yellow-brown gas with a choking odor. In the laboratory nitrogen dioxide is prepared by the action of concentrated nitric acid on copper (Figure 21.7):

$$Cu(s) + 4HNO_3(aq) \longrightarrow Cu(NO_3)_2(aq) + 2H_2O(l) + 2NO_2(g)$$

Nitrogen dioxide is paramagnetic. It has a strong tendency to dimerize to dinitrogen tetroxide, which is a diamagnetic molecule:

$$2NO_2 \rightleftharpoons N_2O_4$$

This reaction occurs in both the gas phase and the liquid phase.

Nitrogen dioxide is an acidic oxide; it reacts rapidly with cold water to form both nitrous acid, HNO$_2$, and nitric acid:

$$2NO_2(g) + H_2O(l) \longrightarrow HNO_2(aq) + HNO_3(aq)$$

This is a disproportionation reaction (see p. 141) in which the oxidation number of nitrogen changes from +4 (in NO$_2$) to +3 (in HNO$_2$) and +5 (in HNO$_3$). Note that

According to Le Châtelier's principle, the forward endothermic reaction is favored by heating.

The role of NO$_2$ in smog formation is discussed on p. 771.

Neither N$_2$O nor NO reacts with water.

this reaction is quite different from that between CO_2 and H_2O, in which only one acid (carbonic acid) is formed.

Nitric acid is one of the most important inorganic acids. It is a liquid (b.p. 82.6°C), but it does not exist as a pure liquid because it decomposes spontaneously to some extent as follows:

$$4HNO_3(l) \longrightarrow 4NO_2(g) + 2H_2O(l) + O_2(g)$$

On standing, a concentrated nitric acid solution turns slightly yellow as a result of NO_2 formation.

The major industrial method of producing nitric acid is the Ostwald process, discussed in Section 13.6. The concentrated nitric acid used in the laboratory is 68 percent HNO_3 by mass (density 1.42 g/cm^3), which corresponds to 15.7 M.

Nitric acid is a powerful oxidizing agent. The oxidation number of N in HNO_3 is +5. The most common reduction products of nitric acid are NO_2 (oxidation number of N = +4), NO (oxidation number of N = +2), and NH_4^+ (oxidation number of N = −3). Nitric acid can oxidize metals both below and above hydrogen in the activity series (see Figure 4.16). For example, copper is oxidized by concentrated nitric acid, as discussed earlier.

In the presence of a strong reducing agent, such as zinc metal, nitric acid can be reduced all the way to the ammonium ion:

$$4Zn(s) + 10H^+(aq) + NO_3^-(aq) \longrightarrow 4Zn^{2+}(aq) + NH_4^+(aq) + 3H_2O(l)$$

Concentrated nitric acid does not oxidize gold. However, when the acid is added to concentrated hydrochloric acid in a 1:3 ratio by volume (one part HNO_3 to three parts HCl), the resulting solution, called *aqua regia,* can oxidize gold, as follows:

$$Au(s) + 3HNO_3(aq) + 4HCl(aq) \longrightarrow HAuCl_4(aq) + 3H_2O(l) + 3NO_2(g)$$

The oxidation of Au is promoted by the complexing ability of the Cl^- ion (to form the $AuCl_4^-$ ion).

Concentrated nitric acid also oxidizes a number of nonmetals to their corresponding oxoacids:

$$P_4(s) + 20HNO_3(aq) \longrightarrow 4H_3PO_4(aq) + 20NO_2(g) + 4H_2O(l)$$
$$S(s) + 6HNO_3(aq) \longrightarrow H_2SO_4(aq) + 6NO_2(g) + 2H_2O(l)$$

Nitric acid is used in the manufacture of fertilizers, dyes, drugs, and explosives. The Chemistry in Action essay on p. 913 describes a nitrogen-containing fertilizer that can be highly explosive.

Phosphorus

Like nitrogen, phosphorus is a member of the Group 5A family; in some respects the chemistry of phosphorus resembles that of nitrogen. Phosphorus occurs most commonly in nature as *phosphate rocks,* which are mostly calcium phosphate, $Ca_3(PO_4)_2$, and fluoroapatite, $Ca_5(PO_4)_3F$ (Figure 21.8). Elemental phosphorus can be obtained by heating calcium phosphate with coke and silica sand:

$$2Ca_3(PO_4)_2(s) + 10C(s) + 6SiO_2(s) \longrightarrow 6CaSiO_3(s) + 10CO(g) + P_4(s)$$

There are several allotropic forms of phosphorus, but only white phosphorus and red phosphorus (see Figure 8.18) are of importance. White phosphorus consists of discrete tetrahedral P_4 molecules (Figure 21.9). A solid (m.p. 44.2°C), white phosphorus is insoluble in water but quite soluble in carbon disulfide (CS_2) and in organic solvents such as chloroform ($CHCl_3$). White phosphorus is a highly toxic substance.

Figure 21.8 *Phosphate mining.*

It bursts into flames spontaneously when exposed to air; hence it is used in incendiary bombs and grenades:

$$P_4(s) + 5O_2(g) \longrightarrow P_4O_{10}(s)$$

The high reactivity of white phosphorus is attributed to structural strain: The P—P bonds are compressed in the tetrahedral P_4 molecule. White phosphorus was once used in matches, but because of its toxicity it has been replaced by tetraphosphorus trisulfide, P_4S_3.

When heated in the absence of air, white phosphorus is slowly converted to red phosphorus at about 300°C:

$$nP_4(\text{white phosphorus}) \longrightarrow (P_4)_n(\text{red phosphorus})$$

Red phosphorus has a polymeric structure (see Figure 21.9) and is more stable and less volatile than white phosphorus.

Hydride of Phosphorus

The most important hydride of phosphorus is phosphine, PH_3, a colorless, very poisonous gas formed by heating white phosphorus in concentrated sodium hydroxide:

$$P_4(s) + 3NaOH(aq) + 3H_2O(l) \longrightarrow 3NaH_2PO_2(aq) + PH_3(g)$$

Figure 21.9 *The structures of white and red phosphorus. Red phosphorus is believed to have a chain structure, as shown.*

White phosphorus

Red phosphorus

Phosphine is moderately soluble in water and more soluble in carbon disulfide and organic solvents. Its aqueous solution is neutral, unlike that of ammonia. In liquid ammonia, phosphine dissolves to give $NH_4^+PH_2^-$. Phosphine is a strong reducing agent; it reduces many metal salts to the corresponding metal. The gas burns in air:

$$PH_3(g) + 2O_2(g) \longrightarrow H_3PO_4(s)$$

Halides of Phosphorus

Phosphorus forms binary compounds with halogens: the trihalides, PX_3, and the pentahalides, PX_5, where X denotes a halogen atom. In contrast, nitrogen can form only trihalides (NX_3). Unlike nitrogen, phosphorus has a $3d$ subshell, which can be used for valence-shell expansion. We can explain the bonding in PCl_5 by assuming that phosphorus undergoes sp^3d hybridization of its $3s$, $3p$, and $3d$ orbitals (see Example 10.4). The five sp^3d hybrid orbitals also account for the trigonal bipyramidal geometry of the PCl_5 molecule (see Table 10.4).

Phosphorus trichloride is prepared by heating white phosphorus in chlorine:

$$P_4(l) + 6Cl_2(g) \longrightarrow 4PCl_3(g)$$

A colorless liquid (b.p. 76°C), PCl_3 is hydrolyzed according to the equation:

$$PCl_3(l) + 3H_2O(l) \longrightarrow H_3PO_3(aq) + 3HCl(g)$$

In the presence of an excess of chlorine gas, PCl_3 is converted to phosphorus pentachloride, which is a light-yellow solid:

$$PCl_3(l) + Cl_2(g) \longrightarrow PCl_5(s)$$

X-ray studies have shown that solid phosphorus pentachloride exists as $[PCl_4^+][PCl_6^-]$, in which the PCl_4^+ ion has a tetrahedral geometry and the PCl_6^- ion has an octahedral geometry. In the gas phase, PCl_5 (which has trigonal bipyramidal geometry) is in equilibrium with PCl_3 and Cl_2:

$$PCl_5(g) \rightleftharpoons PCl_3(g) + Cl_2(g)$$

Phosphorus pentachloride reacts with water as follows:

$$PCl_5(s) + 4H_2O(l) \longrightarrow H_3PO_4(aq) + 5HCl(aq)$$

Oxides and Oxoacids of Phosphorus

The two important oxides of phosphorus are tetraphosphorus hexaoxide, P_4O_6, and tetraphosphorus decaoxide, P_4O_{10} (Figure 21.10). The oxides are obtained by burning white phosphorus in limited and excess amounts of oxygen gas, respectively:

$$P_4(s) + 3O_2(s) \longrightarrow P_4O_6(s)$$
$$P_4(s) + 5O_2(g) \longrightarrow P_4O_{10}(s)$$

Both oxides are acidic; that is, they are converted to acids in water. The compound P_4O_{10} is a white flocculent powder (m.p. 420°C) that has a great affinity for water:

$$P_4O_{10}(s) + 6H_2O(l) \longrightarrow 4H_3PO_4(aq)$$

For this reason, it is often used for drying gases and for removing water from solvents.

Figure 21.10 *The structures of P$_4$O$_6$ and P$_4$O$_{10}$. Note the tetrahedral arrangement of the P atoms in P$_4$O$_{10}$.*

P$_4$O$_6$ P$_4$O$_{10}$

Phosphoric acid is the most important phosphorus-containing oxoacid.

There are many oxoacids containing phosphorus. Some examples are phosphorous acid, H$_3$PO$_3$; phosphoric acid, H$_3$PO$_4$; hypophosphorous acid, H$_3$PO$_2$; and triphosphoric acid, H$_5$P$_3$O$_{10}$ (Figure 21.11). Phosphoric acid, also called orthophosphoric acid, is a weak triprotic acid (see p. 670). It is prepared industrially by the reaction of calcium phosphate with sulfuric acid:

$$Ca_3(PO_4)_2(s) + 3H_2SO_4(aq) \longrightarrow 2H_3PO_4(aq) + 3CaSO_4(s)$$

In the pure form phosphoric acid is a colorless solid (m.p. 42.2°C). The phosphoric acid we use in the laboratory is usually an 82 percent H$_3$PO$_4$ solution (by mass). Phosphoric acid and phosphates have many commercial applications in detergents, fertilizers, flame retardants, and toothpastes, and as buffers in carbonated beverages.

Like nitrogen, phosphorus is an element that is essential to life. It constitutes only about 1 percent by mass of the human body, but it is a very important 1 percent. About 23 percent of the human skeleton is mineral matter. The phosphorus content of this mineral matter, calcium phosphate, Ca$_3$(PO$_4$)$_2$, is 20 percent. Our teeth are basically Ca$_3$(PO$_4$)$_2$ and Ca$_5$(PO$_4$)$_3$OH. Phosphates are also important components of the genetic materials deoxyribonucleic acid (DNA) and ribonucleic acid (RNA).

Figure 21.11 *Structures of some common phosphorus-containing oxoacids.*

Phosphorous acid (H$_3$PO$_3$)

Hypophosphorous acid (H$_3$PO$_2$)

Phosphoric acid (H$_3$PO$_4$)

Triphosphoric acid (H$_5$P$_3$O$_{10}$)

CHEMISTRY
in Action

Ammonium Nitrate—The Explosive Fertilizer

Ammonium nitrate is the most important fertilizer in the world (see p. 104). It ranked fifteenth among the industrial chemicals produced in the United States in 2005 (8 million tons). Unfortunately, it is also a powerful explosive. In 1947 an explosion occurred aboard a ship being loaded with the fertilizer in Texas. The fertilizer was in paper bags and apparently blew up after sailors tried to stop a fire in the ship's hold by closing a hatch, thereby creating the compression and heat necessary for an explosion. More than six hundred people died as a result of the accident. More recent disasters involving ammonium nitrate took place at the World Trade Center in New York City in 1993 and at the Alfred P. Murrah Federal Building in Oklahoma City in 1995.

A strong oxidizer, ammonium nitrate is stable at room temperature. At 250°C, it begins to decompose as follows:

$$NH_4NO_3(g) \longrightarrow N_2O(g) + 2H_2O(g)$$

At 300°C, different gaseous products and more heat are produced:

$$2NH_4NO_3(g) \longrightarrow 2N_2(g) + 4H_2O(g) + O_2(g)$$

About 1.46 kJ of heat are generated per gram of the compound decomposed. When it is combined with a combustible material, such as fuel oil, the energy released increases almost threefold.

Ammonium nitrate can also be mixed with charcoal, flour, sugar, sulfur, rosin, and paraffin to form an explosive. Intense heat from the explosion causes the gases to expand rapidly, generating shock waves that destroy most objects in their path.

Federal law regulates the sale of explosive-grade ammonium nitrate, which is used for 95 percent of all commercial blasting in road construction and mining. However, the wide availability of large quantities of ammonium nitrate and other substances that enhance its explosive power make it possible for anyone who is so inclined to construct a bomb. The bomb that destroyed the federal building in Oklahoma City is estimated to have contained 4000 pounds of ammonium nitrate and fuel oil, which was set off by another small explosive device.

How can the use of ammonium nitrate by terrorists be prevented? The most logical approach is to desensitize or neutralize the compound's ability to act as an explosive, but to date no satisfactory way has been found to do so without diminishing its value as a fertilizer. A more passive method is to add to the fertilizer an agent known as a *taggant,* which would allow law enforcement to trace the source of an ammonium nitrate explosive. A number of European countries now forbid the sale of ammonium nitrate without taggants, although the U.S. Congress has yet to pass such a law.

The Alfred P. Murrah building after a deadly explosion caused by an ammonium nitrate bomb.

A bag of ammonium nitrate fertilizer, which is labeled as an explosive.

21.5 Oxygen and Sulfur

Oxygen

The oxygen cycle is discussed on p. 753.

Oxygen is by far the most abundant element in Earth's crust, constituting about 46 percent of its mass. In addition, the atmosphere contains about 21 percent molecular oxygen by volume (23 percent by mass). Like nitrogen, oxygen in the free state is a diatomic molecule (O_2). In the laboratory, oxygen gas can be obtained by heating potassium chlorate (see Figure 5.15):

$$2KClO_3(s) \longrightarrow 2KCl(s) + 3O_2(g)$$

The reaction is usually catalyzed by manganese(IV) dioxide, MnO_2. Pure oxygen gas can be prepared by electrolyzing water (p. 849). Industrially, oxygen gas is prepared by the fractional distillation of liquefied air (p. 906). Oxygen gas is colorless and odorless.

Oxygen is a building block of practically all biomolecules, accounting for about a fourth of the atoms in living matter. Molecular oxygen is the essential oxidant in the metabolic breakdown of food molecules. Without it, a human being cannot survive for more than a few minutes.

Properties of Diatomic Oxygen

Although oxygen has two allotropes, O_2 and O_3, when we speak of molecular oxygen, we normally mean O_2. Ozone, O_3, is less stable than O_2. The O_2 molecule is paramagnetic because it contains two unpaired electrons (see Section 10.7).

A strong oxidizing agent, molecular oxygen is one of the most widely used industrial chemicals. Its main uses are in the steel industry (see Section 20.2) and in sewage treatment. Oxygen is also used as a bleaching agent for pulp and paper, in medicine to ease breathing difficulties, in oxyacetylene torches, and as an oxidizing agent in many inorganic and organic reactions.

Oxides, Peroxides, and Superoxides

Oxygen forms three types of oxides: the normal oxide (or simply the oxide), which contains the O^{2-} ion; the peroxide, which contains the O_2^{2-} ion; and the superoxide, which contains the O_2^- ion:

$$:\overset{..}{\underset{..}{O}}:^{2-} \qquad :\overset{..}{\underset{..}{O}}:\overset{..}{\underset{..}{O}}:^{2-} \qquad :\overset{..}{\underset{..}{O}}:\overset{.}{\underset{..}{O}}:^{-}$$

oxide   peroxide   superoxide

The ions are all strong Brønsted bases and react with water as follows:

$$\begin{aligned}
\text{Oxide:} \quad & O^{2-}(aq) + H_2O(l) \longrightarrow 2OH^-(aq) \\
\text{Peroxide:} \quad & 2O_2^{2-}(aq) + 2H_2O(l) \longrightarrow O_2(g) + 4OH^-(aq) \\
\text{Superoxide:} \quad & 4O_2^-(aq) + 2H_2O(l) \longrightarrow 3O_2(g) + 4OH^-(aq)
\end{aligned}$$

Note that the reaction of O^{2-} with water is a hydrolysis reaction, but those involving O_2^{2-} and O_2^- are redox processes.

The nature of bonding in oxides changes across any period in the periodic table (see Figure 15.8). Oxides of elements on the left side of the periodic table, such as those of the alkali metals and alkaline earth metals, are generally ionic solids with high melting points. Oxides of the metalloids and of the metallic elements toward the middle of the periodic table are also solids, but they have much less ionic character. Oxides of nonmetals are covalent compounds that generally exist as liquids or gases at room temperature. The acidic character of the oxides increases from left to right.

Consider the oxides of the third-period elements (see Table 8.4):

$$\underbrace{Na_2O \quad MgO}_{basic} \quad \underbrace{Al_2O_3}_{amphoteric} \quad \underbrace{SiO_2 \quad P_4O_{10} \quad SO_3 \quad Cl_2O_7}_{acidic}$$

The basicity of the oxides increases as we move down a particular group. MgO does not react with water but reacts with acid as follows:

$$MgO(s) + 2H^+(aq) \longrightarrow Mg^{2+}(aq) + H_2O(l)$$

On the other hand, BaO, which is more basic, undergoes hydrolysis to yield the corresponding hydroxide:

$$BaO(s) + H_2O(l) \longrightarrow Ba(OH)_2(aq)$$

The best-known peroxide is hydrogen peroxide (H_2O_2). It is a colorless, syrupy liquid (m.p. $-0.9°C$), prepared in the laboratory by the action of cold dilute sulfuric acid on barium peroxide octahydrate:

$$BaO_2 \cdot 8H_2O(s) + H_2SO_4(aq) \longrightarrow BaSO_4(s) + H_2O_2(aq) + 8H_2O(l)$$

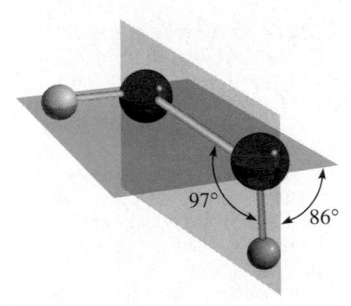

Figure 21.12 *The structure of H_2O_2.*

The structure of hydrogen peroxide is shown in Figure 21.12. Using the VSEPR method we see that the H—O and O—O bonds are bent around each oxygen atom in a configuration similar to the structure of water. The lone-pair–bonding-pair repulsion is greater in H_2O_2 than in H_2O, so that the HOO angle is only $97°$ (compared with $104.5°$ for HOH in H_2O). Hydrogen peroxide is a polar molecule ($\mu = 2.16$ D).

Hydrogen peroxide readily decomposes when heated or exposed to sunlight or even in the presence of dust particles or certain metals, including iron and copper:

$$2H_2O_2(l) \longrightarrow 2H_2O(l) + O_2(g) \quad \Delta H° = -196.4 \text{ kJ/mol}$$

Note that this is a disproportionation reaction. The oxidation number of oxygen changes from -1 to -2 and 0.

Hydrogen peroxide is miscible with water in all proportions due to its ability to hydrogen-bond with water. Dilute hydrogen peroxide solutions (3 percent by mass), available in drugstores, are used as mild antiseptics; more concentrated H_2O_2 solutions are employed as bleaching agents for textiles, fur, and hair. The high heat of decomposition of hydrogen peroxide also makes it a suitable component in rocket fuel.

Hydrogen peroxide is a strong oxidizing agent; it can oxidize Fe^{2+} ions to Fe^{3+} ions in an acidic solution:

$$H_2O_2(aq) + 2Fe^{2+}(aq) + 2H^+(aq) \longrightarrow 2Fe^{3+}(aq) + 2H_2O(l)$$

It also oxidizes SO_3^{2-} ions to SO_4^{2-} ions:

$$H_2O_2(aq) + SO_3^{2-}(aq) \longrightarrow SO_4^{2-}(aq) + H_2O(l)$$

In addition, hydrogen peroxide can act as a reducing agent toward substances that are stronger oxidizing agents than itself. For example, hydrogen peroxide reduces silver oxide to metallic silver:

$$H_2O_2(aq) + Ag_2O(s) \longrightarrow 2Ag(s) + H_2O(l) + O_2(g)$$

and permanganate, MnO_4^-, to manganese(II) in an acidic solution:

$$5H_2O_2(aq) + 2MnO_4^-(aq) + 6H^+(aq) \longrightarrow 2Mn^{2+}(aq) + 5O_2(g) + 8H_2O(l)$$

Figure 21.13 *The preparation of O₃ from O₂ by electrical discharge. The outside of the outer tube and the inside of the inner tube are coated with metal foils that are connected to a high-voltage source. (The metal foil on the inside of the inner tube is not shown.) During the electrical discharge, O₂ gas is passed through the tube. The O₃ gas formed exits from the upper right-hand tube, along with some unreacted O₂ gas.*

Liquid ozone.

If we want to determine hydrogen peroxide concentration, this reaction can be carried out as a redox titration, using a standard permanganate solution.

There are relatively few known superoxides, that is, compounds containing the O_2^- ion. In general, only the most reactive alkali metals (K, Rb, and Cs) form superoxides.

We should take note of the fact that both the peroxide ion and the superoxide ion are by-products of metabolism. Because these ions are highly reactive, they can inflict great damage on living cells. Fortunately, our bodies are equipped with the enzymes catalase, peroxidase, and superoxide dismutase which convert these toxic substances to water and molecular oxygen.

Ozone

Ozone is a rather toxic, light-blue gas (b.p. $-111.3°C$). Its pungent odor is noticeable around sources of significant electrical discharges (such as a subway train). Ozone can be prepared from molecular oxygen, either photochemically or by subjecting O_2 to an electrical discharge (Figure 21.13):

$$3O_2(g) \longrightarrow 2O_3(g) \qquad \Delta G° = 326.8 \text{ kJ/mol}$$

Because the standard free energy of formation of ozone is a large positive quantity [$\Delta G_f° = (326.8/2)$ kJ/mol or 163.4 kJ/mol], ozone is less stable than molecular oxygen. The ozone molecule has a bent structure in which the bond angle is 116.5°:

Ozone is mainly used to purify drinking water, to deodorize air and sewage gases, and to bleach waxes, oils, and textiles.

Ozone is a very powerful oxidizing agent—its oxidizing power is exceeded only by that of molecular fluorine (see Table 19.1). For example, ozone can oxidize sulfides of many metals to the corresponding sulfates:

$$4O_3(g) + PbS(s) \longrightarrow PbSO_4(s) + 4O_2(g)$$

Ozone oxidizes all the common metals except gold and platinum. In fact, a convenient test for ozone is based on its action on mercury. When exposed to ozone, mercury loses its metallic luster and sticks to glass tubing (instead of flowing freely through it). This behavior is attributed to the change in surface tension caused by the formation of mercury(II) oxide:

$$O_3(g) + 3Hg(l) \longrightarrow 3HgO(s)$$

The beneficial effect of ozone in the stratosphere and its undesirable action in smog formation were discussed in Chapter 17.

Sulfur

Although sulfur is not a very abundant element (it constitutes only about 0.06 percent of Earth's crust by mass), it is readily available because it occurs commonly in nature in the elemental form. The largest known reserves of sulfur are found in sedimentary deposits. In addition, sulfur occurs widely in gypsum ($CaSO_4 \cdot 2H_2O$) and various sulfide minerals such as pyrite (FeS_2) (Figure 21.14). Sulfur is also present in natural gas as H_2S, SO_2, and other sulfur-containing compounds.

Sulfur is extracted from underground deposits by the *Frasch*[†] *process,* shown in Figure 21.15. In this process, superheated water (liquid water heated to about 160°C under high pressure to prevent it from boiling) is pumped down the outermost pipe to melt the sulfur (Figure 21.16). Next, compressed air is forced down the innermost pipe. Liquid sulfur mixed with air forms an emulsion that is less dense than water and therefore rises to the surface as it is forced up the middle pipe. Sulfur produced in this manner, which amounts to about 10 million tons per year, has a purity of about 99.5 percent.

[†]Herman Frasch (1851–1914). German chemical engineer. Besides inventing the process for obtaining pure sulfur, Frasch developed methods for refining petroleum.

Figure 21.14 *Pyrite (FeS₂), commonly called "fool's gold" because of its gold luster.*

Compressed air

Sulfur

Superheated water

Molten sulfur

Figure 21.15 *The Frasch process. Three concentric pipes are inserted into a hole drilled down to the sulfur deposit. Superheated water is forced down the outer pipe into the sulfur, causing it to melt. Molten sulfur is then forced up the middle pipe by compressed air.*

Figure 21.16 *Steam injection in the Frasch process.*

There are several allotropic forms of sulfur, the most important being the rhombic and monoclinic forms. Rhombic sulfur is thermodynamically the most stable form; it has a puckered S_8 ring structure:

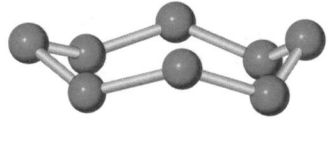

S_8

It is a yellow, tasteless, and odorless solid (m.p. 112°C) (see Figure 8.19) that is insoluble in water but soluble in carbon disulfide. When heated, it is slowly converted to monoclinic sulfur (m.p. 119°C), which also consists of the S_8 units. When liquid sulfur is heated above 150°C, the rings begin to break up, and the entangling of the sulfur chains results in a sharp increase in the liquid's viscosity. Further heating tends to rupture the chains, and the viscosity decreases.

Like nitrogen, sulfur shows a wide variety of oxidation numbers in its compounds (Table 21.3). The best-known hydrogen compound of sulfur is hydrogen sulfide, which is prepared by the action of an acid on a sulfide; for example,

$$FeS(s) + H_2SO_4(aq) \longrightarrow FeSO_4(aq) + H_2S(g)$$

Nowadays, hydrogen sulfide used in qualitative analysis (see Section 16.11) is prepared by the hydrolysis of thioacetamide:

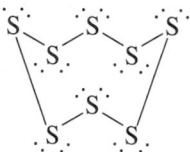

thioacetamide   acetic acid

Hydrogen sulfide is a colorless gas (b.p. −60.2°C) that smells like rotten eggs. (The odor of rotten eggs actually does come from hydrogen sulfide, which is formed by the bacterial decomposition of sulfur-containing proteins.) Hydrogen sulfide is a highly toxic substance that, like hydrogen cyanide, attacks respiratory enzymes. It is a very weak diprotic acid (see Table 15.5). In basic solution, H_2S is a reducing agent. For example, it is oxidized by permanganate to elemental sulfur:

$$3H_2S(aq) + 2MnO_4^-(aq) \longrightarrow 3S(s) + 2MnO_2(s) + 2H_2O(l) + 2OH^-(aq)$$

TABLE 21.3	Common Compounds of Sulfur		
Oxidation Number	Compound	Formula	Structure
−2	Hydrogen sulfide	H_2S	
0	Sulfur*	S_8	
+1	Disulfur dichloride	S_2Cl_2	
+2	Sulfur dichloride	SCl_2	
+4	Sulfur dioxide	SO_2	
+6	Sulfur trioxide	SO_3	

*We list the element here as a reference.

Oxides of Sulfur

Sulfur has two important oxides: sulfur dioxide, SO_2; and sulfur trioxide, SO_3. Sulfur dioxide is formed when sulfur burns in air:

$$S(s) + O_2(g) \longrightarrow SO_2(g)$$

In the laboratory, it can be prepared by the action of an acid on a sulfite; for example,

$$2HCl(aq) + Na_2SO_3(aq) \longrightarrow 2NaCl(aq) + H_2O(l) + SO_2(g)$$

or by the action of concentrated sulfuric acid on copper:

$$Cu(s) + 2H_2SO_4(aq) \longrightarrow CuSO_4(aq) + 2H_2O(l) + SO_2(g)$$

Sulfur dioxide (b.p. −10°C) is a pungent, colorless gas that is quite toxic. As an acidic oxide, it reacts with water as follows:

$$SO_2(g) + H_2O(l) \rightleftharpoons H^+(aq) + HSO_3^-(aq)$$

There is no evidence for the formation of sulfurous acid, H_2SO_3, in water.

Sulfur dioxide is slowly oxidized to sulfur trioxide, but the reaction rate can be greatly enhanced by a platinum or vanadium oxide catalyst (see Section 13.6):

$$2SO_2(g) + O_2(g) \longrightarrow 2SO_3(g)$$

Sulfur trioxide dissolves in water to form sulfuric acid:

$$SO_3(g) + H_2O(l) \longrightarrow H_2SO_4(aq)$$

The contributing role of sulfur dioxide to acid rain is discussed on p. 767.

Sulfuric Acid

Sulfuric acid is the world's most important industrial chemical. It is prepared industrially by first burning sulfur in air:

$$S(s) + O_2(g) \longrightarrow SO_2(g)$$

Next is the key step of converting sulfur dioxide to sulfur trioxide:

$$2SO_2(g) + O_2(g) \longrightarrow 2SO_3(g)$$

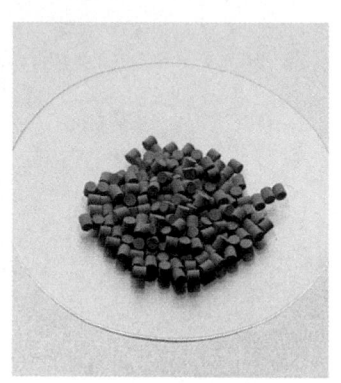

Vanadium oxide on alumina (Al₂O₃).

Vanadium(V) oxide (V_2O_5) is the catalyst used for the second step. Because the sulfur dioxide and oxygen molecules react in contact with the surface of solid V_2O_5, the process is referred to as the *contact process*.

Although sulfur trioxide reacts with water to produce sulfuric acid, it forms a mist of fine droplets of H_2SO_4 with water vapor that is hard to condense. Instead, sulfur trioxide is first dissolved in 98 percent sulfuric acid to form *oleum* ($H_2S_2O_7$):

$$SO_3(g) + H_2SO_4(aq) \longrightarrow H_2S_2O_7(aq)$$

On treatment with water, concentrated sulfuric acid can be generated:

$$H_2S_2O_7(aq) + H_2O(l) \longrightarrow 2H_2SO_4(aq)$$

Sulfuric acid is a diprotic acid (see Table 15.5). It is a colorless, viscous liquid (m.p. 10.4°C). The concentrated sulfuric acid we use in the laboratory is 98 percent H_2SO_4 by mass (density: 1.84 g/cm³), which corresponds to a concentration of 18 M. The oxidizing strength of sulfuric acid depends on its temperature and concentration. A cold, dilute sulfuric acid solution reacts with metals above hydrogen in the activity series (see Figure 4.15), thereby liberating molecular hydrogen in a displacement reaction:

$$Mg(s) + H_2SO_4(aq) \longrightarrow MgSO_4(aq) + H_2(g)$$

This is a typical reaction of an active metal with an acid. The strength of sulfuric acid as an oxidizing agent is greatly enhanced when it is both hot and concentrated. In such a solution, the oxidizing agent is actually the sulfate ion rather than the hydrated proton, $H^+(aq)$. Thus, copper reacts with concentrated sulfuric acid as follows:

$$Cu(s) + 2H_2SO_4(aq) \longrightarrow CuSO_4(aq) + SO_2(g) + 2H_2O(l)$$

Depending on the nature of the reducing agents, the sulfate ion may be further reduced to elemental sulfur or the sulfide ion. For example, reduction of H_2SO_4 by HI yields H_2S and I_2:

$$8HI(aq) + H_2SO_4(aq) \longrightarrow H_2S(aq) + 4I_2(s) + 4H_2O(l)$$

Concentrated sulfuric acid oxidizes nonmetals. For example, it oxidizes carbon to carbon dioxide and sulfur to sulfur dioxide:

$$C(s) + 2H_2SO_4(aq) \longrightarrow CO_2(g) + 2SO_2(g) + 2H_2O(l)$$
$$S(s) + 2H_2SO_4(aq) \longrightarrow 3SO_2(g) + 2H_2O(l)$$

Other Compounds of Sulfur

Carbon disulfide, a colorless, flammable liquid (b.p. 46°C), is formed by heating carbon and sulfur to a high temperature:

$$C(s) + 2S(l) \longrightarrow CS_2(l)$$

It is only slightly soluble in water. Carbon disulfide is a good solvent for sulfur, phosphorus, iodine, and nonpolar substances such as waxes and rubber.

Another interesting compound of sulfur is sulfur hexafluoride, SF_6, which is prepared by heating sulfur in an atmosphere of fluorine:

$$S(l) + 3F_2(g) \longrightarrow SF_6(g)$$

Sulfur hexafluoride is a nontoxic, colorless gas (b.p. $-63.8°C$). It is the most inert of all sulfur compounds; it resists attack even by molten KOH. The structure and bonding of SF_6 were discussed in Chapters 9 and 10 and its critical phenomenon illustrated in Chapter 11 (see Figure 11.37).

21.6 The Halogens

The halogens—fluorine, chlorine, bromine, and iodine—are reactive nonmetals (see Figure 8.20). Table 21.4 lists some of the properties of these elements. Although all halogens are highly reactive and toxic, the magnitude of reactivity and toxicity generally decreases from fluorine to iodine. The chemistry of fluorine differs from that of the rest of the halogens in the following ways:

1. Fluorine is the most reactive of all the halogens. The difference in reactivity between fluorine and chlorine is greater than that between chlorine and bromine. Table 21.4 shows that the F—F bond is considerably weaker than the

Interactivity:
Halogens
ARIS, Interactives

Recall that the first member of a group usually differs in properties from the rest of the members of the group (see p. 336).

TABLE 21.4	Properties of the Halogens			
Property	**F**	**Cl**	**Br**	**I**
Valence electron configuration	$2s^2 2p^5$	$3s^2 3p^5$	$4s^2 4p^5$	$5s^2 5p^5$
Melting point (°C)	-223	-102	-7	114
Boiling point (°C)	-187	-35	59	183
Appearance*	Pale-yellow gas	Yellow-green gas	Red-brown liquid	Dark-violet vapor Dark metallic-looking solid
Atomic radius (pm)	72	99	114	133
Ionic radius (pm)[†]	136	181	195	216
Ionization energy (kJ/mol)	1680	1251	1139	1003
Electronegativity	4.0	3.0	2.8	2.5
Standard reduction potential (V)*	2.87	1.36	1.07	0.53
Bond enthalpy (kJ/mol)*	150.6	242.7	192.5	151.0

*These values and descriptions apply to the diatomic species X_2, where X represents a halogen atom. The half-reaction is $X_2(g) + 2e^- \longrightarrow 2X^-(aq)$.
[†]Refers to the anion X^-.

Cl—Cl bond. The weak bond in F_2 can be explained in terms of the lone pairs on the F atoms:

$$: \ddot{F} - \ddot{F} :$$

The small size of the F atoms (see Table 21.4) allows a close approach of the three lone pairs on each of the F atoms, resulting in a greater repulsion than that found in Cl_2, which consists of larger atoms.

2. Hydrogen fluoride, HF, has a high boiling point (19.5°C) as a result of strong intermolecular hydrogen bonding, whereas all other hydrogen halides have much lower boiling points (see Figure 11.6).

3. Hydrofluoric acid is a weak acid, whereas all other hydrohalic acids (HCl, HBr, and HI) are strong acids.

4. Fluorine reacts with cold sodium hydroxide solution to produce oxygen difluoride as follows:

$$2F_2(g) + 2NaOH(aq) \longrightarrow 2NaF(aq) + H_2O(l) + OF_2(g)$$

The same reaction with chlorine or bromine, on the other hand, produces a halide and a hypohalite:

$$X_2(g) + 2NaOH(aq) \longrightarrow NaX(aq) + NaXO(aq) + H_2O(l)$$

where X stands for Cl or Br. Iodine does not react under the same conditions.

5. Silver fluoride, AgF, is soluble. All other silver halides (AgCl, AgBr, and AgI) are insoluble (see Table 4.2).

The element astatine also belongs to the Group 7A family. However, all isotopes of astatine are radioactive; its longest-lived isotope is astatine-210, which has a half-life of 8.3 h. Therefore it is both difficult and expensive to study astatine in the laboratory.

The halogens form a very large number of compounds. In the elemental state they form diatomic molecules, X_2. In nature, however, because of their high reactivity, halogens are always found combined with other elements. Chlorine, bromine, and iodine occur as halides in seawater, and fluorine occurs in the minerals fluorite (CaF_2) (see Figure 20.17) and cryolite (Na_3AlF_6).

Preparation and General Properties of the Halogens

Because fluorine and chlorine are strong oxidizing agents, they must be prepared by electrolysis rather than by chemical oxidation of the fluoride and chloride ions. Electrolysis does not work for aqueous solutions of fluorides, however, because fluorine is a stronger oxidizing agent than oxygen. From Table 19.1 we find that

$$F_2(g) + 2e^- \longrightarrow 2F^-(aq) \qquad E° = 2.87 \text{ V}$$
$$O_2(g) + 4H^+(aq) + 4e^- \longrightarrow 2H_2O(l) \qquad E° = 1.23 \text{ V}$$

If F_2 were formed by the electrolysis of an aqueous fluoride solution, it would immediately oxidize water to oxygen. For this reason, fluorine is prepared by electrolyzing liquid hydrogen fluoride containing potassium fluoride to increase its conductivity, at about 70°C (Figure 21.17):

Anode (oxidation):	$2F^- \longrightarrow F_2(g) + 2e^-$
Cathode (reduction):	$2H^+ + 2e^- \longrightarrow H_2(g)$
Overall reaction:	$2HF(l) \longrightarrow H_2(g) + F_2(g)$

Figure 21.17 *Electrolytic cell for the preparation of fluorine gas. Note that because H_2 and F_2 form an explosive mixture, these gases must be separated from each other.*

Chlorine gas, Cl_2, is prepared industrially by the electrolysis of molten NaCl (see Section 19.8) or by the ***chlor-alkali process,*** *the electrolysis of a concentrated aqueous NaCl solution* (called brine). (*Chlor* denotes chlorine and *alkali* denotes an alkali metal, such as sodium.) Two of the common cells used in the chlor-alkali process are the mercury cell and the diaphragm cell. In both cells the overall reaction is

$$2NaCl(aq) + 2H_2O(l) \xrightarrow{\text{electrolysis}} 2NaOH(aq) + H_2(g) + Cl_2(g)$$

As you can see, this reaction yields two useful by-products, NaOH and H_2. The cells are designed to separate the molecular chlorine from the sodium hydroxide solution and the molecular hydrogen to prevent side reactions such as

$$2NaOH(aq) + Cl_2(g) \longrightarrow NaOCl(aq) + NaCl(aq) + H_2O(l)$$
$$H_2(g) + Cl_2(g) \longrightarrow 2HCl(g)$$

These reactions consume the desired products and can be dangerous because a mixture of H_2 and Cl_2 is explosive.

Figure 21.18 shows the mercury cell used in the chlor-alkali process. The cathode is a liquid mercury pool at the bottom of the cell, and the anode is made of either graphite or titanium coated with platinum. Brine is continuously passed through the cell as shown in the diagram. The electrode reactions are

Anode (oxidation): $2Cl^-(aq) \longrightarrow Cl_2(g) + 2e^-$

Cathode (reduction): $2Na^+(aq) + 2e^- \xrightarrow{Hg(l)} 2Na/Hg$

Overall reaction: $2NaCl(aq) \longrightarrow 2Na/Hg + Cl_2(g)$

Figure 21.18 *Mercury cell used in the chlor-alkali process. The cathode contains mercury. The sodium-mercury amalgam is treated with water outside the cell to produce sodium hydroxide and hydrogen gas.*

Figure 21.19 *The industrial manufacture of chlorine gas.*

where Na/Hg denotes the formation of sodium amalgam. The chlorine gas generated this way is very pure. The sodium amalgam does not react with the brine solution but decomposes as follows when treated with pure water outside the cell:

$$2Na/Hg + 2H_2O(l) \longrightarrow 2NaOH(aq) + H_2(g) + 2Hg(l)$$

the by-products are sodium hydroxide and hydrogen gas. Although the mercury is cycled back into the cell for reuse, some of it is always discharged with waste solutions into the environment, resulting in mercury pollution. This is a major drawback of the mercury cell. Figure 21.19 shows the industrial manufacture of chlorine gas.

The half-cell reactions in a diaphragm cell are shown in Figure 21.20. The asbestos diaphragm is permeable to the ions but not to the hydrogen and chlorine gases and so prevents the gases from mixing. During electrolysis a positive pressure is applied on the anode side of the compartment to prevent the migration of the OH^- ions from the cathode compartment. Periodically, fresh brine solution is added to the cell and the sodium hydroxide solution is run off as shown. The diaphragm cell presents no pollution problems. Its main disadvantage is that the sodium hydroxide solution is contaminated with unreacted sodium chloride.

From Table 19.1 we see that the oxidizing strength decreases from Cl_2 to Br_2 to I_2.

The preparation of molecular bromine and iodine from seawater by oxidation with chlorine was discussed in Section 4.4. In the laboratory, chlorine, bromine, and iodine can be prepared by heating the alkali halides (NaCl, KBr, or KI) in concentrated sulfuric acid in the presence of manganese(IV) oxide. A representative reaction is

$$MnO_2(s) + 2H_2SO_4(aq) + 2NaCl(aq) \longrightarrow$$
$$MnSO_4(aq) + Na_2SO_4(aq) + 2H_2O(l) + Cl_2(g)$$

Figure 21.20 *Diaphragm cell used in the chlor-alkali process.*

Battery

e^- e^-

Anode   Asbestos diaphragm   Cathode

Brine

NaOH solution

Oxidation   Reduction
$2Cl^-(aq) \longrightarrow Cl_2(g) + 2e^-$ $2H_2O(l) + 2e^- \longrightarrow H_2(g) + 2OH^-(aq)$

Compounds of the Halogens

Most of the halides can be classified into two categories. The fluorides and chlorides of many metallic elements, especially those belonging to the alkali metal and alkaline earth metal (except beryllium) families, are ionic compounds. Most of the halides of nonmetals such as sulfur and phosphorus are covalent compounds. As Figure 4.10 shows, the oxidation numbers of the halogens can vary from -1 to $+7$. The only exception is fluorine. Because it is the most electronegative element, fluorine can have only two oxidation numbers, 0 (as in F_2) and -1, in its compounds.

The Hydrogen Halides

The hydrogen halides, an important class of halogen compounds, can be formed by the direct combination of the elements:

$$H_2(g) + X_2(g) \rightleftharpoons 2HX(g)$$

where X denotes a halogen atom. These reactions (especially the ones involving F_2 and Cl_2) can occur with explosive violence. Industrially, hydrogen chloride is produced as a by-product in the manufacture of chlorinated hydrocarbons:

$$C_2H_6(g) + Cl_2(g) \longrightarrow C_2H_5Cl(g) + HCl(g)$$

In the laboratory, hydrogen fluoride and hydrogen chloride can be prepared by reacting the metal halides with concentrated sulfuric acid:

$$CaF_2(s) + H_2SO_4(aq) \longrightarrow 2HF(g) + CaSO_4(s)$$
$$2NaCl(s) + H_2SO_4(aq) \longrightarrow 2HCl(g) + Na_2SO_4(aq)$$

Hydrogen bromide and hydrogen iodide cannot be prepared this way because they are oxidized to elemental bromine and iodine. For example, the reaction between NaBr and H_2SO_4 is

$$2NaBr(s) + 2H_2SO_4(aq) \longrightarrow Br_2(l) + SO_2(g) + Na_2SO_4(aq) + 2H_2O(l)$$

Instead, hydrogen bromide is prepared by first reacting bromine with phosphorus to form phosphorus tribromide:

$$P_4(s) + 6Br_2(l) \longrightarrow 4PBr_3(l)$$

Next, PBr_3 is treated with water to yield HBr:

$$PBr_3(l) + 3H_2O(l) \longrightarrow 3HBr(g) + H_3PO_3(aq)$$

Hydrogen iodide can be prepared in a similar manner.

The high reactivity of HF is demonstrated by the fact that it attacks silica and silicates:

$$6HF(aq) + SiO_2(s) \longrightarrow H_2SiF_6(aq) + 2H_2O(l)$$

This property makes HF suitable for etching glass and is the reason that hydrogen fluoride must be kept in plastic or inert metal (for example, Pt) containers. Hydrogen fluoride is used in the manufacture of Freons (see Chapter 17); for example,

$$CCl_4(l) + HF(g) \longrightarrow CFCl_3(g) + HCl(g)$$
$$CFCl_3(g) + HF(g) \longrightarrow CF_2Cl_2(g) + HCl(g)$$

It is also important in the production of aluminum (see Section 20.7). Hydrogen chloride is used in the preparation of hydrochloric acid, inorganic chlorides, and in various metallurgical processes. Hydrogen bromide and hydrogen iodide do not have any major industrial uses.

Aqueous solutions of hydrogen halides are acidic. The strength of the acids increases as follows:

$$HF \ll HCl < HBr < HI$$

Oxoacids of the Halogens

The halogens also form a series of oxoacids with the following general formulas:

HXO	HXO$_2$	HXO$_3$	HXO$_4$
hypohalous acid	halous acid	halic acid	perhalic acid

Chlorous acid, $HClO_2$, is the only known halous acid. All the halogens except fluorine form halic and perhalic acids. The Lewis structures of the chlorine oxoacids are

$$H:\overset{..}{\underset{..}{O}}:\overset{..}{\underset{..}{Cl}}: \qquad H:\overset{..}{\underset{..}{O}}:\overset{..}{\underset{..}{Cl}}:\overset{..}{\underset{..}{O}}: \qquad H:\overset{..}{\underset{..}{O}}:\overset{..}{Cl}:\overset{..}{\underset{..}{O}}: \qquad H:\overset{..}{\underset{..}{O}}:\overset{..}{Cl}:\overset{..}{\underset{..}{O}}:$$

hypochlorous acid   chlorous acid   chloric acid   perchloric acid

For a given halogen, the acid strength decreases from perhalic acid to hypohalous acid; the explanation of this trend is discussed in Section 15.9.

Table 21.5 lists some of the halogen compounds. Periodic acid, HIO_4, does not appear because this compound cannot be isolated in the pure form. Instead the formula H_5IO_6 is often used to represent periodic acid.

Uses of the Halogens

Fluorine

Applications of the halogens and their compounds are widespread in industry, health care, and other areas. One is fluoridation, the practice of adding small quantities of fluorides (about 1 ppm by mass) such as NaF to drinking water to reduce dental caries.

TABLE 21.5	Common Compounds of Halogens*			
Compound	**F**	**Cl**	**Br**	**I**
Hydrogen halide	HF (-1)	HCl (-1)	HBr (-1)	HI (-1)
Oxides	OF$_2$ (-1)	Cl$_2$O $(+1)$	Br$_2$O $(+1)$	I$_2$O$_5$ $(+5)$
		ClO$_2$ $(+4)$	BrO$_2$ $(+4)$	
		Cl$_2$O$_7$ $(+7)$		
Oxoacids	HFO (-1)	HClO $(+1)$	HBrO $(+1)$	HIO $(+1)$
		HClO$_2$ $(+3)$		
		HClO$_3$ $(+5)$	HBrO$_3$ $(+5)$	HIO$_3$ $(+5)$
		HClO$_4$ $(+7)$	HBrO$_4$ $(+7)$	H$_5$IO$_6$ $(+7)$

*The number in parentheses indicates the oxidation number of the halogen.

One of the most important inorganic fluorides is uranium hexafluoride, UF_6, which is essential to the gaseous diffusion process for separating isotopes of uranium (U-235 and U-238). Industrially, fluorine is used to produce polytetrafluoroethylene, a polymer better known as Teflon:

$$-(CF_2-CF_2)_n$$

where n is a large number. Teflon is used in electrical insulators, high-temperature plastics, cooking utensils, and so on.

Chlorine

Chlorine plays an important biological role in the human body, where the chloride ion is the principal anion in intracellular and extracellular fluids. Chlorine is widely used as an industrial bleaching agent for paper and textiles. Ordinary household laundry bleach contains the active ingredient sodium hypochlorite (about 5 percent by mass), which is prepared by reacting chlorine gas with a cold solution of sodium hydroxide:

$$Cl_2(g) + 2NaOH(aq) \longrightarrow NaCl(aq) + NaClO(aq) + H_2O(l)$$

Chlorine is also used to purify water and disinfect swimming pools. When chlorine dissolves in water, it undergoes the following reaction:

$$Cl_2(g) + H_2O(l) \longrightarrow HCl(aq) + HClO(aq)$$

It is thought that the ClO^- ions destroy bacteria by oxidizing life-sustaining compounds within them.

Chlorinated methanes, such as carbon tetrachloride and chloroform, are useful organic solvents. Large quantities of chlorine are used to produce insecticides, such as DDT. However, in view of the damage they inflict on the environment, the use of many of these compounds is either totally banned or greatly restricted in the United States. Chlorine is also used to produce polymers such as poly(vinyl chloride).

Bromine

So far as we know, bromine compounds occur naturally only in some marine organisms. Seawater is about $1 \times 10^{-3}\,M\,Br^-$; therefore, it is the main source of bromine. Bromine is used to prepare ethylene dibromide ($BrCH_2CH_2Br$), which is used as an insecticide and as a scavenger for lead (that is, to combine with lead) in gasoline to keep lead deposits from clogging engines. Studies have shown that ethylene dibromide is a very potent carcinogen.

Bromine combines directly with silver to form silver bromide (AgBr), which is used in photographic films.

Iodine

Iodine is not used as widely as the other halogens. A 50 percent (by mass) alcohol solution of iodine, known as *tincture of iodine,* is used medicinally as an antiseptic. Iodine is an essential constituent of the thyroid hormone thyroxine:

Figure 21.21 *Cloud seeding using AgI particles.*

Iodine deficiency in the diet may result in enlargement of the thyroid gland (known as goiter). Iodized table salt sold in the United States usually contains 0.01 percent KI or NaI, which is more than sufficient to satisfy the 1 mg of iodine per week required for the formation of thyroxine in the human body.

A compound of iodine that deserves mention is silver iodide, AgI. It is a pale-yellow solid that darkens when exposed to light. In this respect it is similar to silver bromide. Silver iodide is sometimes used in cloud seeding, a process for inducing rainfall on a small scale (Figure 21.21). The advantage of using silver iodide is that enormous numbers of nuclei (that is, small particles of silver iodide on which ice crystals can form) become available. About 10^{15} nuclei are produced from 1 g of AgI by vaporizing an acetone solution of silver iodide in a hot flame. The nuclei are then dispersed into the clouds from an airplane.

Summary of Facts and Concepts

1. Hydrogen atoms contain one proton and one electron. They are the simplest atoms. Hydrogen combines with many metals and nonmetals to form hydrides; some hydrides are ionic and some are covalent.

2. There are three isotopes of hydrogen: $_1^1H$, $_1^2H$ (deuterium), and $_1^3H$ (tritium). Heavy water contains deuterium.

3. The important inorganic compounds of carbon are the carbides; the cyanides, most of which are extremely toxic; carbon monoxide, also toxic and a major air pollutant; the carbonates and bicarbonates; and carbon dioxide, an end product of metabolism and a component of the global carbon cycle.

4. Elemental nitrogen, N_2, contains a triple bond and is very stable. Compounds in which nitrogen has oxidation numbers from -3 to $+5$ are formed between nitrogen and hydrogen and/or oxygen atoms. Ammonia, NH_3, is widely used in fertilizers.

5. White phosphorus, P_4, is highly toxic, very reactive, and flammable; the polymeric red phosphorus, $(P_4)_n$, is more stable. Phosphorus forms oxides and halides with oxidation numbers of $+3$ and $+5$ and several oxoacids. The phosphates are the most important phosphorus compounds.

6. Elemental oxygen, O_2, is paramagnetic and contains two unpaired electrons. Oxygen forms ozone (O_3), oxides (O^{2-}), peroxides (O_2^{2-}), and superoxides (O_2^-). The most abundant element in Earth's crust, oxygen is essential for life on Earth.

7. Sulfur is taken from Earth's crust by the Frasch process as a molten liquid. Sulfur exists in a number of allotropic forms and has a variety of oxidation numbers in its compounds.

8. Sulfuric acid is the cornerstone of the chemical industry. It is produced from sulfur via sulfur dioxide and sulfur trioxide by means of the contact process.

9. The halogens are toxic and reactive elements that are found only in compounds with other elements. Fluorine and chlorine are strong oxidizing agents and are prepared by electrolysis.

10. The reactivity, toxicity, and oxidizing ability of the halogens decrease from fluorine to iodine. The halogens all form binary acids (HX) and a series of oxoacids.

Key Words

Carbide, p. 903
Catenation, p. 902

Chlor-alkali process, p. 923
Cyanide, p. 903

Hydrogenation, p. 900

Questions and Problems

General Properties of Nonmetals
Review Questions

21.1 Without referring to Figure 21.1, state whether each of the following elements are metals, metalloids, or nonmetals: (a) Cs, (b) Ge, (c) I, (d) Kr, (e) W, (f) Ga, (g) Te, (h) Bi.

21.2 List two chemical and two physical properties that distinguish a metal from a nonmetal.

21.3 Make a list of physical and chemical properties of chlorine (Cl_2) and magnesium. Comment on their differences with reference to the fact that one is a metal and the other is a nonmetal.

21.4 Carbon is usually classified as a nonmetal. However, the graphite used in "lead" pencils conducts electricity. Look at a pencil and list two nonmetallic properties of graphite.

Hydrogen
Review Questions

21.5 Explain why hydrogen has a unique position in the periodic table.

21.6 Describe two laboratory and two industrial preparations for hydrogen.

21.7 Hydrogen exhibits three types of bonding in its compounds. Describe each type of bonding with an example.

21.8 What are interstitial hydrides?

21.9 Give the name of (a) an ionic hydride and (b) a covalent hydride. In each case describe the preparation and give the structure of the compound.

21.10 Describe what is meant by the "hydrogen economy."

Problems

21.11 Elements number 17 and 20 form compounds with hydrogen. Write the formulas for these two compounds and compare their chemical behavior in water.

21.12 Give an example of hydrogen as (a) an oxidizing agent and (b) a reducing agent.

21.13 Compare the physical and chemical properties of the hydrides of each of the following elements: Na, Ca, C, N, O, Cl.

21.14 Suggest a physical method that would enable you to separate hydrogen gas from neon gas.

21.15 Write a balanced equation to show the reaction between CaH_2 and H_2O. How many grams of CaH_2 are needed to produce 26.4 L of H_2 gas at 20°C and 746 mmHg?

21.16 How many kilograms of water must be processed to obtain 2.0 L of D_2 at 25°C and 0.90 atm pressure? Assume that deuterium abundance is 0.015 percent and that recovery is 80 percent.

21.17 Predict the outcome of the following reactions:
(a) $CuO(s) + H_2(g) \longrightarrow$
(b) $Na_2O(s) + H_2(g) \longrightarrow$

21.18 Starting with H_2, describe how you would prepare (a) HCl, (b) NH_3, (c) LiOH.

Carbon
Review Questions

21.19 Give an example of a carbide and a cyanide.

21.20 How are cyanide ions used in metallurgy?

21.21 Briefly discuss the preparation and properties of carbon monoxide and carbon dioxide.

21.22 What is coal?

21.23 Explain what is meant by coal gasification.

21.24 Describe two chemical differences between CO and CO_2.

Problems

21.25 Describe the reaction between CO_2 and OH^- in terms of a Lewis acid-base reaction such as that shown on p. 683.

21.26 Draw a Lewis structure for the C_2^{2-} ion.

21.27 Balance the following equations:

(a) $Be_2C(s) + H_2O(l) \longrightarrow$

(b) $CaC_2(s) + H_2O(l) \longrightarrow$

21.28 Unlike $CaCO_3$, Na_2CO_3 does not readily yield CO_2 when heated. On the other hand, $NaHCO_3$ undergoes thermal decomposition to produce CO_2 and Na_2CO_3. (a) Write a balanced equation for the reaction. (b) How would you test for the CO_2 evolved? [*Hint:* Treat the gas with limewater, an aqueous solution of $Ca(OH)_2$.]

21.29 Two solutions are labeled A and B. Solution A contains Na_2CO_3 and solution B contains $NaHCO_3$. Describe how you would distinguish between the two solutions if you were provided with a $MgCl_2$ solution. (*Hint:* You need to know the solubilities of $MgCO_3$ and $MgHCO_3$.)

21.30 Magnesium chloride is dissolved in a solution containing sodium bicarbonate. On heating, a white precipitate is formed. Explain what causes the precipitation.

21.31 A few drops of concentrated ammonia solution added to a calcium bicarbonate solution cause a white precipitate to form. Write a balanced equation for the reaction.

21.32 Sodium hydroxide is hygroscopic—that is, it absorbs moisture when exposed to the atmosphere. A student placed a pellet of NaOH on a watch glass. A few days later, she noticed that the pellet was covered with a white solid. What is the identity of this solid? (*Hint:* Air contains CO_2.)

21.33 A piece of red-hot magnesium ribbon will continue to burn in an atmosphere of CO_2 even though CO_2 does not support combustion. Explain.

21.34 Is carbon monoxide isoelectronic with nitrogen (N_2)?

Nitrogen and Phosphorus

Review Questions

21.35 Describe a laboratory and an industrial preparation of nitrogen gas.

21.36 What is meant by nitrogen fixation? Describe a process for fixation of nitrogen on an industrial scale.

21.37 Describe an industrial preparation of phosphorus.

21.38 Why is the P_4 molecule unstable?

Problems

21.39 Nitrogen can be obtained by (a) passing ammonia over red-hot copper(II) oxide and (b) heating ammonium dichromate [one of the products is Cr(III) oxide]. Write a balanced equation for each preparation.

21.40 Write balanced equations for the preparation of sodium nitrite by (a) heating sodium nitrate and (b) heating sodium nitrate with carbon.

21.41 Sodium amide ($NaNH_2$) reacts with water to produce sodium hydroxide and ammonia. Describe this reaction as a Brønsted acid-base reaction.

21.42 Write a balanced equation for the formation of urea, $(NH_2)_2CO$, from carbon dioxide and ammonia. Should the reaction be run at a high or low pressure to maximize the yield?

21.43 Some farmers feel that lightning helps produce a better crop. What is the scientific basis for this belief?

21.44 At 620 K the vapor density of ammonium chloride relative to hydrogen (H_2) under the same conditions of temperature and pressure is 14.5, although, according to its formula mass, it should have a vapor density of 26.8. How would you account for this discrepancy?

21.45 Explain, giving one example in each case, why nitrous acid can act both as a reducing agent and as an oxidizing agent.

21.46 Explain why nitric acid can be reduced but not oxidized.

21.47 Write a balanced equation for each of the following processes: (a) On heating, ammonium nitrate produces nitrous oxide. (b) On heating, potassium nitrate produces potassium nitrite and oxygen gas. (c) On heating, lead nitrate produces lead(II) oxide, nitrogen dioxide (NO_2), and oxygen gas.

21.48 Explain why, under normal conditions, the reaction of zinc with nitric acid does not produce hydrogen.

21.49 Potassium nitrite can be produced by heating a mixture of potassium nitrate and carbon. Write a balanced equation for this reaction. Calculate the theoretical yield of KNO_2 produced by heating 57.0 g of KNO_3 with an excess of carbon.

21.50 Predict the geometry of nitrous oxide, N_2O, by the VSEPR method and draw resonance structures for the molecule. (*Hint:* The atoms are arranged as NNO.)

21.51 Consider the reaction

$$N_2(g) + O_2(g) \rightleftharpoons 2NO(g)$$

Given that the $\Delta G°$ for the reaction at 298 K is 173.4 kJ/mol, calculate (a) the standard free energy of formation of NO, (b) K_P for the reaction, and (c) K_c for the reaction.

21.52 From the data in Appendix 3, calculate $\Delta H°$ for the synthesis of NO (which is the first step in the manufacture of nitric acid) at 25°C:

$$4NH_3(g) + 5O_2(g) \longrightarrow 4NO(g) + 6H_2O(l)$$

21.53 Explain why two N atoms can form a double bond or a triple bond, whereas two P atoms normally can form only a single bond.

21.54 When 1.645 g of white phosphorus are dissolved in 75.5 g of CS_2, the solution boils at 46.709°C, whereas pure CS_2 boils at 46.300°C. The molal boiling-point elevation constant for CS_2 is 2.34°C/m. Calculate the molar mass of white phosphorus and give the molecular formula.

21.55 Starting with elemental phosphorus, P_4, show how you would prepare phosphoric acid.

21.56 Dinitrogen pentoxide is a product of the reaction between P_4O_{10} and HNO_3. Write a balanced equation for this reaction. Calculate the theoretical yield of N_2O_5 if 79.4 g of P_4O_{10} are reacted with an excess of HNO_3. (*Hint:* One of the products is HPO_3.)

21.57 Explain why (a) NH_3 is more basic than PH_3, (b) NH_3 has a higher boiling point than PH_3, (c) PCl_5 exists but NCl_5 does not, (d) N_2 is more inert than P_4.

21.58 What is the hybridization of phosphorus in the phosphonium ion, PH_4^+?

Oxygen and Sulfur
Review Questions

21.59 Describe one industrial and one laboratory preparation of O_2.

21.60 Give an account of the various kinds of oxides that exist and illustrate each type by two examples.

21.61 Hydrogen peroxide can be prepared by treating barium peroxide with sulfuric acid. Write a balanced equation for this reaction.

21.62 Describe the Frasch process for obtaining sulfur.

21.63 Describe the contact process for the production of sulfuric acid.

21.64 How is hydrogen sulfide generated in the laboratory?

Problems

21.65 Draw molecular orbital energy level diagrams for O_2, O_2^-, and O_2^{2-}.

21.66 One of the steps involved in the depletion of ozone in the stratosphere by nitric oxide may be represented as

$$NO(g) + O_3(g) \longrightarrow NO_2(g) + O_2(g)$$

From the data in Appendix 3 calculate $\Delta G°$, K_P, and K_c for the reaction at 25°C.

21.67 Hydrogen peroxide is unstable and decomposes readily:

$$2H_2O_2(aq) \longrightarrow 2H_2O(l) + O_2(g)$$

This reaction is accelerated by light, heat, or a catalyst. (a) Explain why hydrogen peroxide sold in drugstores comes in dark bottles. (b) The concentrations of aqueous hydrogen peroxide solutions are normally expressed as percent by mass. In the decomposition of hydrogen peroxide, how many liters of oxygen gas can be produced at STP from 15.0 g of a 7.50 percent hydrogen peroxide solution?

21.68 What are the oxidation numbers of O and F in HFO?

21.69 Oxygen forms double bonds in O_2, but sulfur forms single bonds in S_8. Explain.

21.70 In 2004, about 48 million tons of sulfuric acid were produced in the United States. Calculate the amount of sulfur (in grams and moles) used to produce that amount of sulfuric acid.

21.71 Sulfuric acid is a dehydrating agent. Write balanced equations for the reactions between sulfuric acid and the following substances: (a) HCOOH, (b) H_3PO_4, (c) HNO_3, (d) $HClO_3$. (*Hint:* Sulfuric acid is not decomposed by the dehydrating action.)

21.72 Calculate the amount of $CaCO_3$ (in grams) that would be required to react with 50.6 g of SO_2 emitted by a power plant.

21.73 SF_6 exists but OF_6 does not. Explain.

21.74 Explain why SCl_6, SBr_6, and SI_6 cannot be prepared.

21.75 Compare the physical and chemical properties of H_2O and H_2S.

21.76 The bad smell of water containing hydrogen sulfide can be removed by the action of chlorine. The reaction is

$$H_2S(aq) + Cl_2(aq) \longrightarrow 2HCl(aq) + S(s)$$

If the hydrogen sulfide content of contaminated water is 22 ppm by mass, calculate the amount of Cl_2 (in grams) required to remove all the H_2S from 2.0×10^2 gallons of water. (1 gallon = 3.785 L.)

21.77 Describe two reactions in which sulfuric acid acts as an oxidizing agent.

21.78 Concentrated sulfuric acid reacts with sodium iodide to produce molecular iodine, hydrogen sulfide, and sodium hydrogen sulfate. Write a balanced equation for the reaction.

The Halogens
Review Questions

21.79 Describe an industrial method for preparing each of the halogens.

21.80 Name the major uses of the halogens.

Problems

21.81 Metal chlorides can be prepared in a number of ways: (a) direct combination of metal and molecular chlorine, (b) reaction between metal and hydrochloric acid, (c) acid-base neutralization, (d) metal carbonate treated with hydrochloric acid, (e) precipitation reaction. Give an example for each type of preparation.

21.82 Sulfuric acid is a weaker acid than hydrochloric acid. Yet hydrogen chloride is evolved when concentrated sulfuric acid is added to sodium chloride. Explain.

21.83 Show that chlorine, bromine, and iodine are very much alike by giving an account of their behavior (a) with hydrogen, (b) in producing silver salts, (c) as oxidizing agents, and (d) with sodium hydroxide. (e) In what respects is fluorine not a typical halogen element?

21.84 A 375-gallon tank is filled with water containing 167 g of bromine in the form of Br^- ions. How many liters of Cl_2 gas at 1.00 atm and 20°C will be required to oxidize all the bromide to molecular bromine?

21.85 Draw structures for (a) $(HF)_2$ and (b) HF_2^-.

21.86 Hydrogen fluoride can be prepared by the action of sulfuric acid on sodium fluoride. Explain why hydrogen bromide cannot be prepared by the action of the same acid on sodium bromide.

21.87 Aqueous copper(II) sulfate solution is blue. When aqueous potassium fluoride is added to the $CuSO_4$ solution, a green precipitate is formed. If aqueous potassium chloride is added instead, a bright-green solution is formed. Explain what happens in each case.

21.88 What volume of bromine (Br_2) vapor measured at 100°C and 700 mmHg pressure would be obtained if 2.00 L of dry chlorine (Cl_2), measured at 15°C and 760 mmHg, were absorbed by a potassium bromide solution?

21.89 Use the VSEPR method to predict the geometries of the following species: (a) I_3^-, (b) $SiCl_4$, (c) PF_5, (d) SF_4.

21.90 Iodine pentoxide, I_2O_5, is sometimes used to remove carbon monoxide from the air by forming carbon dioxide and iodine. Write a balanced equation for this reaction and identify species that are oxidized and reduced.

Additional Problems

21.91 Write a balanced equation for each of the following reactions: (a) Heating phosphorous acid yields phosphoric acid and phosphine (PH_3). (b) Lithium carbide reacts with hydrochloric acid to give lithium chloride and methane. (c) Bubbling HI gas through an aqueous solution of HNO_2 yields molecular iodine and nitric oxide. (d) Hydrogen sulfide is oxidized by chlorine to give HCl and SCl_2.

21.92 (a) Which of the following compounds has the greatest ionic character? PCl_5, $SiCl_4$, CCl_4, BCl_3 (b) Which of the following ions has the smallest ionic radius? F^-, C^{4-}, N^{3-}, O^{2-} (c) Which of the following atoms has the highest ionization energy? F, Cl, Br, I (d) Which of the following oxides is most acidic? H_2O, SiO_2, CO_2

21.93 Both N_2O and O_2 support combustion. Suggest one physical and one chemical test to distinguish between the two gases.

21.94 What is the change in oxidation number for the following reaction?

$$3O_2 \longrightarrow 2O_3$$

21.95 Describe the bonding in the C_2^{2-} ion in terms of the molecular orbital theory.

21.96 Starting with deuterium oxide (D_2O), describe how you would prepare (a) NaOD, (b) DCl, (c) ND_3, (d) C_2D_2, (e) CD_4, (f) D_2SO_4.

21.97 Solid PCl_5 exists as $[PCl_4^+][PCl_6^-]$. Draw Lewis structures for these ions. Describe the hybridization state of the P atoms.

21.98 Consider the Frasch process. (a) How is it possible to heat water well above 100°C without turning it into steam? (b) Why is water sent down the outermost pipe? (c) Why would excavating a mine and digging for sulfur be a dangerous procedure for obtaining the element?

21.99 Predict the physical and chemical properties of astatine, a radioactive element and the last member of Group 7A.

21.100 Lubricants used in watches usually consist of long-chain hydrocarbons. Oxidation by air forms solid polymers that eventually destroy the effectiveness of the lubricants. It is believed that one of the initial steps in the oxidation is removal of a hydrogen atom (hydrogen abstraction). By replacing the hydrogen atoms at reactive sites with deuterium atoms, it is possible to substantially slow down the overall oxidation rate. Why? (*Hint:* Consider the kinetic isotope effect.)

21.101 How are lightbulbs frosted? (*Hint:* Consider the action of hydrofluoric acid on glass, which is made of silicon dioxide.)

Special Problems

21.102 Life evolves to adapt to its environment. In this respect, explain why life most frequently needs oxygen for survival, rather than the more abundant nitrogen.

21.103 As mentioned in Chapter 3, ammonium nitrate is the most important nitrogen-containing fertilizer in the world. Given only air and water as starting materials and any equipment and catalyst at your disposal, describe how you would prepare ammonium nitrate. State conditions under which you can increase the yield in each step.

21.104 As we saw in Section 20.2, the reduction of iron oxides is accomplished by using carbon monoxide as a reducing agent. Starting with coke in a blast furnace, the following equilibrium plays a key role in the extraction of iron:

$$C(s) + CO_2(g) \rightleftharpoons 2CO(g)$$

Use the data in Appendix 3 to calculate the equilibrium constant at 25°C and 1000°C. Assume $\Delta H°$ and $\Delta S°$ to be independent of temperature.

21.105 Assuming ideal behavior, calculate the density of gaseous HF at its normal boiling point (19.5°C). The experimentally measured density under the same conditions is 3.10 g/L. Account for the discrepancy between your calculated value and the experimental result.

21.106 A 10.0-g sample of white phosphorus was burned in an excess of oxygen. The product was dissolved in enough water to make 500 mL of solution. Calculate the pH of the solution at 25°C.

22

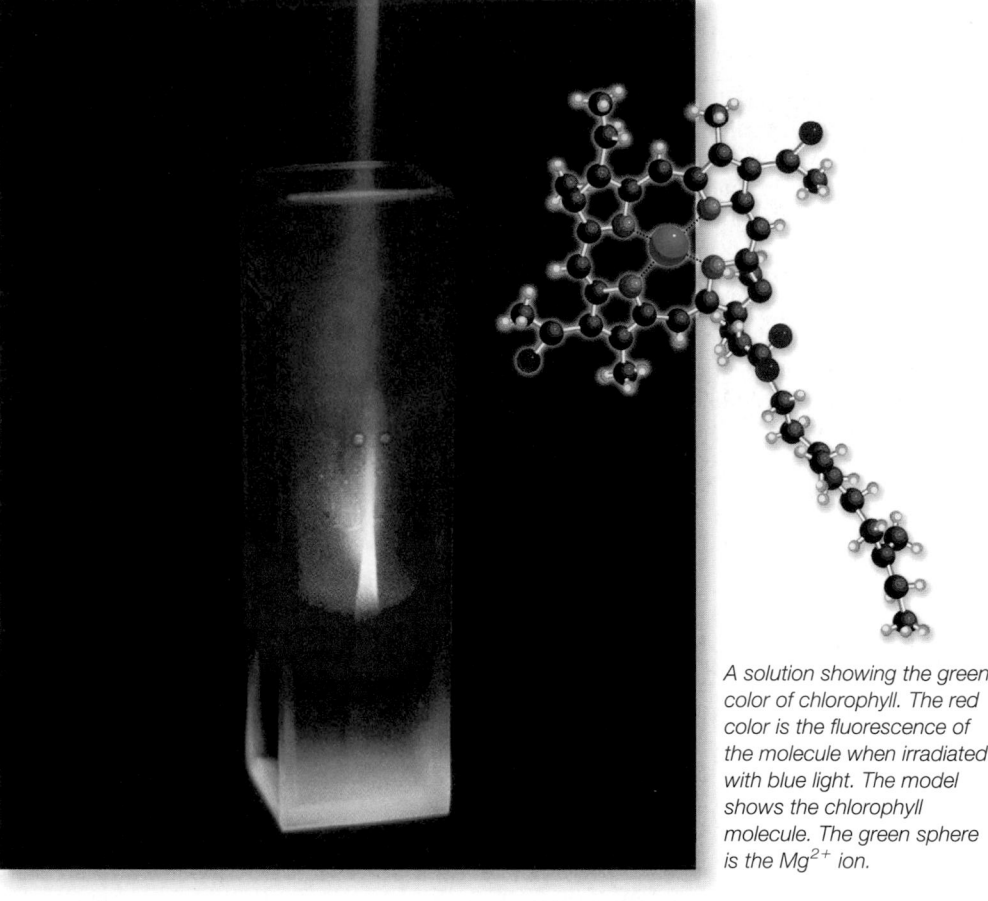

A solution showing the green color of chlorophyll. The red color is the fluorescence of the molecule when irradiated with blue light. The model shows the chlorophyll molecule. The green sphere is the Mg^{2+} ion.

Transition Metal Chemistry and Coordination Compounds

A LOOK AHEAD

- We first survey the general properties of transition metals, focusing on their electron configurations and oxidation states. (22.1)

- Next, we study the chemistry of two representative transition metals—iron and copper. (22.2)

- We then consider the general characteristics of coordination compounds in terms of the nature of ligands and also study the nomenclature of these compounds. (22.3)

- We see that the structure of coordination compounds can give rise to geometric and/or optical isomers. We become acquainted with the use of a polarimeter in studying optical isomers. (22.4)

- Crystal field theory can satisfactorily explain the origin of color in and magnetic properties of octahedral, tetrahedral, and square-planar complexes. (22.5)

- We examine the reactivity of coordination compounds and learn that they can be classified as labile or inert with regard to ligand exchange reactions. (22.6)

- This chapter concludes with a discussion of several applications of coordination compounds. (22.7)

Interactive Activity Summary

The series of elements in the periodic table in which the d and f subshells are gradually filled are called the transition elements. There are about 50 transition elements, and they have widely varying and fascinating properties. To present even one interesting feature of each transition element is beyond the scope of this book. We will therefore limit our discussion to the transition elements that have incompletely filled d subshells and to their most commonly encountered property—the tendency to form complex ions.

22.1 Properties of the Transition Metals

Transition metals typically have incompletely filled d subshells or readily give rise to ions with incompletely filled d subshells (Figure 22.1). (The Group 2B metals—Zn, Cd, and Hg—do not have this characteristic electron configuration and so, although they are sometimes called transition metals, they really do not belong in this category.) This attribute is responsible for several notable properties, including distinctive coloring, formation of paramagnetic compounds, catalytic activity, and especially a great tendency to form complex ions. In this chapter we focus on the first-row elements from scandium to copper, the most common transition metals. Table 22.1 lists some of their properties.

As we read across any period from left to right, atomic numbers increase, electrons are added to the outer shell, and the nuclear charge increases by the addition of protons. In the third-period elements—sodium to argon—the outer electrons weakly shield one another from the extra nuclear charge. Consequently, atomic radii decrease rapidly from sodium to argon, and the electronegativities and ionization energies increase steadily (see Figures 8.5, 8.11, and 9.5).

For the transition metals, the trends are different. Looking at Table 22.1 we see that the nuclear charge, of course, increases from scandium to copper, but electrons are being added to the inner $3d$ subshell. These $3d$ electrons shield the $4s$ electrons from the increasing nuclear charge somewhat more effectively than outer-shell electrons can shield one another, so the atomic radii decrease less rapidly. For the same reason, electronegativities and ionization energies increase only slightly from scandium across to copper compared with the increases from sodium to argon.

Although the transition metals are less electropositive (or more electronegative) than the alkali and alkaline earth metals, their standard reduction potentials suggest that all of them except copper should react with strong acids such as hydrochloric acid to produce hydrogen gas. However, most transition metals are inert toward acids or react slowly with them because of a protective layer of oxide. A case in point is

Figure 22.1 *The transition metals (blue squares). Note that although the Group 2B elements (Zn, Cd, Hg) are described as transition metals by some chemists, neither the metals nor their ions possess incompletely filled d subshells.*

TABLE 22.1	Electron Configurations and Other Properties of the First-Row Transition Metals								
	Sc	**Ti**	**V**	**Cr**	**Mn**	**Fe**	**Co**	**Ni**	**Cu**
Electron configuration									
M	$4s^23d^1$	$4s^23d^2$	$4s^23d^3$	$4s^13d^5$	$4s^23d^5$	$4s^23d^6$	$4s^23d^7$	$4s^23d^8$	$4s^13d^{10}$
M^{2+}	—	$3d^2$	$3d^3$	$3d^4$	$3d^5$	$3d^6$	$3d^7$	$3d^8$	$3d^9$
M^{3+}	[Ar]	$3d^1$	$3d^2$	$3d^3$	$3d^4$	$3d^5$	$3d^6$	$3d^7$	$3d^8$
Electronegativity	1.3	1.5	1.6	1.6	1.5	1.8	1.9	1.9	1.9
Ionization energy (kJ/mol)									
First	631	658	650	652	717	759	760	736	745
Second	1235	1309	1413	1591	1509	1561	1645	1751	1958
Third	2389	2650	2828	2986	3250	2956	3231	3393	3578
Radius (pm)									
M	162	147	134	130	135	126	125	124	128
M^{2+}	—	90	88	85	80	77	75	69	72
M^{3+}	81	77	74	64	66	60	64	—	—
Standard reduction potential (V)*	−2.08	−1.63	−1.2	−0.74	−1.18	−0.44	−0.28	−0.25	0.34

*The half-reaction is $M^{2+}(aq) + 2e^- \longrightarrow M(s)$ (except for Sc and Cr, where the ions are Sc^{3+} and Cr^{3+}, respectively).

chromium: Despite a rather negative standard reduction potential, it is quite inert chemically because of the formation on its surfaces of chromium(III) oxide, Cr_2O_3. Consequently, chromium is commonly used as a protective and noncorrosive plating on other metals. On automobile bumpers and trim, chromium plating serves a decorative as well as a functional purpose.

General Physical Properties

Most of the transition metals have a close-packed structure (see Figure 11.29) in which each atom has a coordination number of 12. Furthermore, these elements have relatively small atomic radii. The combined effect of closest packing and small atomic size results in strong metallic bonds. Therefore, transition metals have higher densities, higher melting points and boiling points, and higher heats of fusion and vaporization than the Group 1A, 2A, and 2B metals (Table 22.2).

TABLE 22.2	Physical Properties of Elements K to Zn										
	1A	**2A**	**Transition Metals**								**2B**
	K	**Ca**	**Sc**	**Ti**	**V**	**Cr**	**Mn**	**Fe**	**Co**	**Ni**	**Cu**	**Zn**
Atomic radius (pm)	235	197	162	147	134	130	135	126	125	124	128	138
Melting point (°C)	63.7	838	1539	1668	1900	1875	1245	1536	1495	1453	1083	419.5
Boiling point (°C)	760	1440	2730	3260	3450	2665	2150	3000	2900	2730	2595	906
Density (g/cm³)	0.86	1.54	3.0	4.51	6.1	7.19	7.43	7.86	8.9	8.9	8.96	7.14

Electron Configurations

The electron configurations of the first-row transition metals were discussed in Section 7.9. Calcium has the electron configuration $[Ar]4s^2$. From scandium across to copper, electrons are added to the $3d$ orbitals. Thus, the outer electron configuration of scandium is $4s^23d^1$, that of titanium is $4s^23d^2$, and so on. The two exceptions are chromium and copper, whose outer electron configurations are $4s^13d^5$ and $4s^13d^{10}$, respectively. These irregularities are the result of the extra stability associated with half-filled and completely filled $3d$ subshells.

When the first-row transition metals form cations, electrons are removed first from the $4s$ orbitals and then from the $3d$ orbitals. (This is the opposite of the order in which orbitals are filled in atoms.) For example, the outer electron configuration of Fe^{2+} is $3d^6$, not $4s^23d^4$.

Oxidation States

Transition metals exhibit variable oxidation states in their compounds. Figure 22.2 shows the oxidation states from scandium to copper. Note that the common oxidation states for each element include $+2$, $+3$, or both. The $+3$ oxidation states are more stable at the beginning of the series, whereas toward the end the $+2$ oxidation states are more stable. The reason for this trend can be understood by examining the ionization energy plots in Figure 22.3. In general, the ionization energies increase gradually from left to right. However, the third ionization energy (when an electron is removed from the $3d$ orbital) increases more rapidly than the first and second ionization energies. Because it takes more energy to remove the third electron from the metals near the end of the row than from those near the beginning, the metals near the end tend to form M^{2+} ions rather than M^{3+} ions.

The highest oxidation state for a transition metal is $+7$, for manganese ($4s^23d^5$). For elements to the right of Mn (Fe to Cu), oxidation numbers are lower. Transition metals usually exhibit their highest oxidation states in compounds with very electronegative elements such as oxygen and fluorine—for example, V_2O_5, CrO_3, and Mn_2O_7.

Recall that oxides in which the metal has a high oxidation number are covalent and acidic, whereas those in which the metal has a low oxidation number are ionic and basic (see Section 15.11).

Figure 22.2 *Oxidation states of the first-row transition metals. The most stable oxidation numbers are shown in color. The zero oxidation state is encountered in some compounds, such as Ni(CO)$_4$ and Fe(CO)$_5$.*

Sc	Ti	V	Cr	Mn	Fe	Co	Ni	Cu
				+7				
			+6	+6	+6			
		+5	+5	+5	+5			
	+4	+4	+4	+4	+4	+4		
+3	+3	+3	+3	+3	+3	+3	+3	+3
	+2	+2	+2	+2	+2	+2	+2	+2
								+1

Figure 22.3 *Variation of the first, second, and third ionization energies for the first-row transition metals.*

22.2 Chemistry of Iron and Copper

Figure 22.4 on p. 940 shows the first-row transition metals. In this section we will briefly survey the chemistry of two of these elements—iron and copper—paying particular attention to their occurrence, preparation, uses, and important compounds.

Iron

After aluminum, iron is the most abundant metal in Earth's crust (6.2 percent by mass). It is found in many ores; some of the important ones are *hematite,* Fe_2O_3; *siderite,* $FeCO_3$; and *magnetite,* Fe_3O_4 (Figure 22.5).

The preparation of iron in a blast furnace and steelmaking were discussed in Section 20.2. Pure iron is a gray metal and is not particularly hard. It is an essential element in living systems.

Iron reacts with hydrochloric acid to give hydrogen gas:

$$Fe(s) + 2H^+(aq) \longrightarrow Fe^{2+}(aq) + H_2(g)$$

Concentrated sulfuric acid oxidizes the metal to Fe^{3+}, but concentrated nitric acid renders the metal "passive" by forming a thin layer of Fe_3O_4 over the surface. One of the best-known reactions of iron is rust formation (see Section 19.7). The two oxidation states of iron are +2 and +3. Iron(II) compounds include FeO (black), $FeSO_4 \cdot 7H_2O$ (green), $FeCl_2$ (yellow), and FeS (black). In the presence of oxygen, Fe^{2+} ions in solution are readily oxidized to Fe^{3+} ions. Iron(III) oxide is reddish brown, and iron(III) chloride is brownish black.

Copper

Copper, a rare element (6.8×10^{-3} percent of Earth's crust by mass), is found in nature in the uncombined state as well as in ores such as chalcopyrite, $CuFeS_2$ (Figure 22.6). The reddish-brown metal is obtained by roasting the ore to give Cu_2S and then metallic copper:

$$2CuFeS_2(s) + 4O_2(g) \longrightarrow Cu_2S(s) + 2FeO(s) + 3SO_2(g)$$
$$Cu_2S(s) + O_2(g) \longrightarrow 2Cu(l) + SO_2(g)$$

Impure copper can be purified by electrolysis (see Section 20.2). After silver, which is too expensive for large-scale use, copper has the highest electrical conductivity. It

Scandium (Sc)   **Titanium (Ti)**   **Vanadium (V)**

Chromium (Cr)   **Manganese (Mn)**   **Iron (Fe)**

Cobalt (Co)   **Nickel (Ni)**   **Copper (Cu)**

Figure 22.4 *The first-row transition metals.*

Figure 22.5 *The iron ore magnetite, Fe_3O_4.*

Figure 22.6 *Chalcopyrite, $CuFeS_2$.*

is also a good thermal conductor. Copper is used in alloys, electrical cables, plumbing (pipes), and coins.

Copper reacts only with hot concentrated sulfuric acid and nitric acid (see Figure 21.7). Its two important oxidation states are +1 and +2. The +1 state is less stable and disproportionates in solution:

$$2Cu^+(aq) \longrightarrow Cu(s) + Cu^{2+}(aq)$$

All compounds of Cu(I) are diamagnetic and colorless except for Cu_2O, which is red. The Cu(II) compounds are all paramagnetic and colored. The hydrated Cu^{2+} ion is blue. Some important Cu(II) compounds are CuO (black), $CuSO_4 \cdot 5H_2O$ (blue), and CuS (black).

22.3 Coordination Compounds

Transition metals have a distinct tendency to form complex ions (see p. 731). A ***coordination compound*** *typically consists of a complex ion and counter ion.* [Note that some coordination compounds such as $Fe(CO)_5$ do not contain complex ions.] Our understanding of the nature of coordination compounds stems from the classic work of Alfred Werner,[†] who prepared and characterized many coordination compounds. In 1893, at the age of 26, Werner proposed what is now commonly referred to as *Werner's coordination theory*.

Recall that a complex ion contains a central metal ion bonded to one or more ions or molecules (see Section 16.10).

Nineteenth-century chemists were puzzled by a certain class of reactions that seemed to violate valence theory. For example, the valences of the elements in cobalt(III) chloride and in ammonia seem to be completely satisfied, and yet these two substances react to form a stable compound having the formula $CoCl_3 \cdot 6NH_3$. To explain this behavior, Werner postulated that most elements exhibit two types of valence: *primary valence and secondary valence*. In modern terminology, primary valence corresponds to the oxidation number and secondary valence to the coordination number of the element. In $CoCl_3 \cdot 6NH_3$, according to Werner, cobalt has a primary valence of 3 and a secondary valence of 6.

Today we use the formula $[Co(NH_3)_6]Cl_3$ to indicate that the ammonia molecules and the cobalt atom form a complex ion; the chloride ions are not part of the complex but are held to it by ionic forces. Most, but not all, of the metals in coordination compounds are transition metals.

The molecules or ions that surround the metal in a complex ion are called **ligands** (Table 22.3). The interactions between a metal atom and the ligands can be thought of as Lewis acid-base reactions. As we saw in Section 15.12, a Lewis base is a substance capable of donating one or more electron pairs. Every ligand has at least one unshared pair of valence electrons, as these examples show:

$$\overset{\cdot\cdot}{\underset{H \qquad H}{O}} \qquad \overset{\cdot\cdot}{\underset{H \ H \ H}{N}} \qquad :\overset{\cdot\cdot}{\underset{\cdot\cdot}{Cl}}:^{-} \qquad :C\equiv O:$$

Therefore, ligands play the role of Lewis bases. On the other hand, a transition metal atom (in either its neutral or positively charged state) acts as a Lewis acid, accepting (and sharing) pairs of electrons from the Lewis bases. Thus, the metal-ligand bonds are usually coordinate covalent bonds (see Section 9.9).

The atom in a ligand that is bound directly to the metal atom is known as the **donor atom.** For example, nitrogen is the donor atom in the $[Cu(NH_3)_4]^{2+}$ complex ion. The **coordination number** in coordination compounds is defined as *the number of donor atoms surrounding the central metal atom in a complex ion*. For example, the coordination number of Ag^+ in $[Ag(NH_3)_2]^+$ is 2, that of Cu^{2+} in $[Cu(NH_3)_4]^{2+}$ is 4, and that of Fe^{3+} in $[Fe(CN)_6]^{3-}$ is 6. The most common coordination numbers are 4 and 6, but coordination numbers such as 2 and 5 are also known.

In a crystal lattice the coordination number of an atom (or ion) is defined as the number of atoms (or ions) surrounding the atom (or ion).

Depending on the number of donor atoms present, ligands are classified as *monodentate, bidentate,* or *polydentate* (see Table 22.3). H_2O and NH_3 are monodentate ligands with only one donor atom each. One bidentate ligand is ethylenediamine (sometimes abbreviated "en"):

$$H_2\overset{\cdot\cdot}{N}—CH_2—CH_2—\overset{\cdot\cdot}{N}H_2$$

The two nitrogen atoms can coordinate with a metal atom as shown in Figure 22.7.

Bidentate and polydentate ligands are also called **chelating agents** because of *their ability to hold the metal atom like a claw* (from the Greek *chele*, meaning

---

[†]Alfred Werner (1866–1919). Swiss chemist. Werner started as an organic chemist but became interested in coordination chemistry. For his theory of coordination compounds, Werner was awarded the Nobel Prize in Chemistry in 1913.

TABLE 22.3	Some Common Ligands
Name	**Structure**

Monodentate ligands

Ammonia

$$H\!-\!\overset{\cdot\cdot}{N}\!-\!H$$
$$\underset{H}{|}$$

Carbon monoxide

$$:C\!\equiv\!O:$$

Chloride ion

$$:\overset{\cdot\cdot}{\underset{\cdot\cdot}{Cl}}:^{-}$$

Cyanide ion

$$[:C\!\equiv\!N:]^{-}$$

Thiocyanate ion

$$[:\overset{\cdot\cdot}{\underset{\cdot\cdot}{S}}\!-\!C\!\equiv\!N:]^{-}$$

Water

$$H\!-\!\overset{\cdot\cdot}{O}\!-\!H$$

Bidentate ligands

Ethylenediamine

$$H_2\overset{\cdot\cdot}{N}\!-\!CH_2\!-\!CH_2\!-\!\overset{\cdot\cdot}{N}H_2$$

Oxalate ion

$$\left[\begin{array}{c}\underset{}{\overset{:O:\qquad\qquad :O:}{\underset{:O:\qquad\qquad :O:}{C\!-\!C}}}\end{array}\right]^{2-}$$

Polydentate ligand

Ethylenediaminetetraacetate ion (EDTA)

$$\left[\begin{array}{c} \text{EDTA structure} \end{array}\right]^{4-}$$

"claw"). One example is ethylenediaminetetraacetate ion (EDTA), a polydentate ligand used to treat metal poisoning (Figure 22.8). Six donor atoms enable EDTA to form a very stable complex ion with lead. In this form, it is removed from the blood and tissues and excreted from the body. EDTA is also used to clean up spills of radioactive metals.

Figure 22.7 *(a) Structure of a metal-ethylenediamine complex cation, such as [Co(en)$_3$]$^{2+}$. Each ethylenediamine molecule provides two N donor atoms and is therefore a bidentate ligand. (b) Simplified structure of the same complex cation.*

(a)

(b)

Figure 22.8 *(a) EDTA complex of lead. The complex bears a net charge of −2 because each O donor atom has one negative charge and the lead ion carries two positive charges. Only the lone pairs that participate in bonding are shown. Note the octahedral geometry around the Pb^{2+} ion. (b) Molecular model of the Pb^{2+}-EDTA complex. The yellow sphere is the Pb^{2+} ion.*

(a)   (b)

Oxidation Numbers of Metals in Coordination Compounds

Another important property of coordination compounds is the oxidation number of the central metal atom. The net charge of a complex ion is the sum of the charges on the central metal atom and its surrounding ligands. In the $[PtCl_6]^{2-}$ ion, for example, each chloride ion has an oxidation number of −1, so the oxidation number of Pt must be +4. If the ligands do not bear net charges, the oxidation number of the metal is equal to the charge of the complex ion. Thus, in $[Cu(NH_3)_4]^{2+}$ each NH_3 is neutral, so the oxidation number of Cu is +2.

Example 22.1 deals with oxidation numbers of metals in coordination compounds.

Example 22.1

Specify the oxidation number of the central metal atom in each of the following compounds: (a) $[Ru(NH_3)_5(H_2O)]Cl_2$, (b) $[Cr(NH_3)_6](NO_3)_3$, (c) $[Fe(CO)_5]$, and (d) $K_4[Fe(CN)_6]$.

Strategy The oxidation number of the metal atom is equal to its charge. First we examine the anion or the cation that electrically balances the complex ion. This step gives us the net charge of the complex ion. Next, from the nature of the ligands (charged or neutral species) we can deduce the net charge of the metal and hence its oxidation number.

Solution (a) Both NH_3 and H_2O are neutral species. Because each chloride ion carries a −1 charge, and there are two Cl^- ions, the oxidation number of Ru must be +2.

(b) Each nitrate ion has a charge of −1; therefore, the cation must be $[Cr(NH_3)_6]^{3+}$. NH_3 is neutral, so the oxidation number of Cr is +3.

(c) Because the CO species are neutral, the oxidation number of Fe is zero.

(d) Each potassium ion has a charge of +1; therefore, the anion is $[Fe(CN)_6]^{4-}$. Next, we know that each cyanide group bears a charge of −1, so Fe must have an oxidation number of +2.

Similar problems: 22.13, 22.14.

Practice Exercise Write the oxidation numbers of the metals in the compound $K[Au(OH)_4]$.

TABLE 22.4	Names of Common Ligands in Coordination Compounds
Ligand	**Name of Ligand in Coordination Compound**
Bromide, Br^-	Bromo
Chloride, Cl^-	Chloro
Cyanide, CN^-	Cyano
Hydroxide, OH^-	Hydroxo
Oxide, O^{2-}	Oxo
Carbonate, CO_3^{2-}	Carbonato
Nitrite, NO_2^-	Nitro
Oxalate, $C_2O_4^{2-}$	Oxalato
Ammonia, NH_3	Ammine
Carbon monoxide, CO	Carbonyl
Water, H_2O	Aqua
Ethylenediamine	Ethylenediamine
Ethylenediaminetetraacetate	Ethylenediaminetetraacetato

Naming Coordination Compounds

Now that we have discussed the various types of ligands and the oxidation numbers of metals, our next step is to learn what to call these coordination compounds. The rules for naming coordination compounds are as follows:

1. The cation is named before the anion, as in other ionic compounds. The rule holds regardless of whether the complex ion bears a net positive or a negative charge. For example, in $K_3[Fe(CN)_6]$ and $[Co(NH_3)_4Cl_2]Cl$ compound, we name the K^+ and $[Co(NH_3)_4Cl_2]^+$ cations first, respectively.

2. Within a complex ion the ligands are named first, in alphabetical order, and the metal ion is named last.

3. The names of anionic ligands end with the letter *o*, whereas a neutral ligand is usually called by the name of the molecule. The exceptions are H_2O (aqua), CO (carbonyl), and NH_3 (ammine). Table 22.4 lists some common ligands.

4. When several ligands of a particular kind are present, we use the Greek prefixes *di-, tri-, tetra-, penta-,* and *hexa-* to name them. Thus, the ligands in the cation $[Co(NH_3)_4Cl_2]^+$ are "tetraamminedichloro." (Note that prefixes are ignored when alphabetizing ligands.) If the ligand itself contains a Greek prefix, we use the prefixes *bis* (2), *tris* (3), and *tetrakis* (4) to indicate the number of ligands present. For example, the ligand ethylenediamine already contains *di*; therefore, if two such ligands are present the name is *bis(ethylenediamine)*.

5. The oxidation number of the metal is written in Roman numerals following the name of the metal. For example, the Roman numeral III is used to indicate the +3 oxidation state of chromium in $[Cr(NH_3)_4Cl_2]^+$, which is called tetraamminedichlorochromium(III) ion.

6. If the complex is an anion, its name ends in *-ate*. For example, in $K_4[Fe(CN)_6]$ the anion $[Fe(CN)_6]^{4-}$ is called hexacyanoferrate(II) ion. Note that the Roman numeral II indicates the oxidation state of iron. Table 22.5 gives the names of anions containing metal atoms.

Examples 22.2 and 22.3 deal with the nomenclature of coordination compounds.

TABLE 22.5	
Names of Anions Containing Metal Atoms	
Metal	**Name of Metal in Anionic Complex**
Aluminum	Aluminate
Chromium	Chromate
Cobalt	Cobaltate
Copper	Cuprate
Gold	Aurate
Iron	Ferrate
Lead	Plumbate
Manganese	Manganate
Molybdenum	Molybdate
Nickel	Nickelate
Silver	Argentate
Tin	Stannate
Tungsten	Tungstate
Zinc	Zincate

Example 22.2

Write the systematic names of the following coordination compounds: (a) $Ni(CO)_4$, (b) $NaAuF_4$, (c) $K_3[Fe(CN)_6]$, (d) $[Cr(en)_3]Cl_3$.

Strategy We follow the preceding procedure for naming coordination compounds and refer to Tables 22.4 and 22.5 for names of ligands and anions containing metal atoms.

Solution (a) The CO ligands are neutral species and therefore the Ni atom bears no net charge. The compound is called tetracarbonylnickel(0), or more commonly, nickel tetracarbonyl.

(b) The sodium cation has a positive charge; therefore, the complex anion has a negative charge (AuF_4^-). Each fluoride ion has a negative charge so the oxidation number of gold must be +3 (to give a net negative charge). The compound is called sodium tetrafluoroaurate(III).

(c) The complex ion is the anion and it bears three negative charges because each potassium ion bears a +1 charge. Looking at $[Fe(CN)_6]^{3-}$, we see that the oxidation number of Fe must be +3 because each cyanide ion bears a −1 charge (−6 total). The compund is potassium hexacyanoferrate(III). This compound is commonly called potassium ferricyanide.

(d) As we noted earlier, *en* is the abbreviation for the ligand ethylenediamine. Because there are three chloride ions each with a −1 charge, the cation is $[Cr(en)_3]^{3+}$. The *en* ligands are neutral so the oxidation number of Cr must be +3. Because there are three *en* groups present and the name of the ligand already contains *di* (rule 4), the compound is called *tris*(ethylenediamine)chromium(III) chloride.

Similar problems: 22.15, 22.16.

Practice Exercise What is the systematic name of $[Cr(H_2O)_4Cl_2]Cl$?

Example 22.3

Write the formulas for the following compounds: (a) pentaamminechlorocobalt(III) chloride, (b) dichlorobis(ethylenediamine)platinum(IV) nitrate, (c) sodium hexanitrocobaltate(III).

Strategy We follow the preceding procedure and refer to Tables 22.4 and 22.5 for names of ligands and anions containing metal atoms.

Solution (a) The complex cation contains five NH_3 groups, a Cl ion, and a Co ion having a +3 oxidation number. The net charge of the cation must be +2, $[Co(NH_3)_5Cl]^{2+}$. Two chloride anions are needed to balance the positive charges. Therefore, the formula of the compound is $[Co(NH_3)_5Cl]Cl_2$.

(b) There are two chloride ions (−1 each), two *en* groups (neutral), and a Pt ion with an oxidation number of +4. The net charge on the cation must be +2, $[Pt(en)_2Cl_2]^{2+}$. Two nitrate ions are needed to balance the +2 charge of the complex cation. Therefore, the formula of the compound is $[Pt(en)_2Cl_2](NO_3)_2$.

(c) The complex anion contains six nitro groups (−1 each) and a cobalt ion with an oxidation number of +3. The net charge on the complex anion must be −3, $[Co(NO_2)_6]^{3-}$. Three sodium cations are needed to balance the −3 charge of the complex anion. Therefore, the formula of the compound is $Na_3[Co(NO_2)_6]$.

Similar problems: 22.17, 22.18.

Practice Exercise Write the formula for the following compound: *tris*(ethylenediamine)cobalt(III) sulfate.

Figure 22.9 *Common geometries of complex ions. In each case M is a metal and L is a monodentate ligand.*

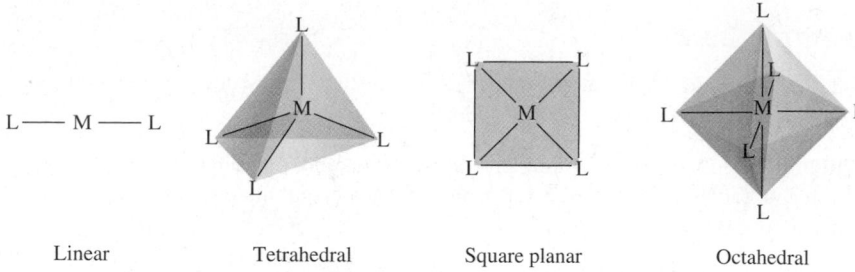

Linear   Tetrahedral   Square planar   Octahedral

22.4 Structure of Coordination Compounds

In studying the geometry of coordination compounds, we often find that there is more than one way to arrange ligands around the central atom. Compounds rearranged in this fashion have distinctly different physical and chemical properties. Figure 22.9 shows four different geometric arrangements for metal atoms with monodentate ligands. In these diagrams, we see that structure and coordination number of the metal atom relate to each other as follows:

Coordination number	Structure
2	Linear
4	Tetrahedral or square planar
6	Octahedral

Stereoisomers are *compounds that are made up of the same types and numbers of atoms bonded together in the same sequence but with different spatial arrangements.* There are two types of stereoisomers: geometric isomers and optical isomers. Coordination compounds may exhibit one or both types of isomerism. Note, however, that many coordination compounds do not have stereoisomers.

Geometric Isomers

Geometric isomers are *stereoisomers that cannot be interconverted without breaking a chemical bond.* Geometric isomers usually come in pairs. We use the terms "*cis*" and "*trans*" to distinguish one geometric isomer of a compound from the other. *Cis* means that two particular atoms (or groups of atoms) are adjacent to each other, and *trans* means that the atoms (or groups of atoms) are on opposite sides in the structural formula. The *cis* and *trans* isomers of coordination compounds generally have quite different colors, melting points, dipole moments, and chemical reactivities. Figure 22.10 shows the *cis* and *trans* isomers of diamminedichloroplatinum(II). Note that although the types of bonds are the same in both isomers (two Pt—N and two Pt—Cl bonds), the spatial arrangements are different. Another example is tetraamminedichlorocobalt(III) ion, shown in Figure 22.11.

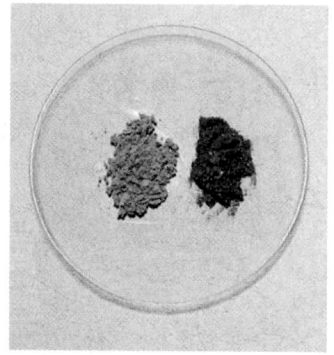

cis-tetraamminedichlorocobalt(III) chloride (left) and *trans*-tetraamminedichlorocobalt(III) chloride (right).

Figure 22.10 *The (a) cis and (b) trans isomers of diamminedichloroplatinum(II). Note that the two Cl atoms are adjacent to each other in the cis isomer and diagonally across from each other in the trans isomer.*

(a)   (b)

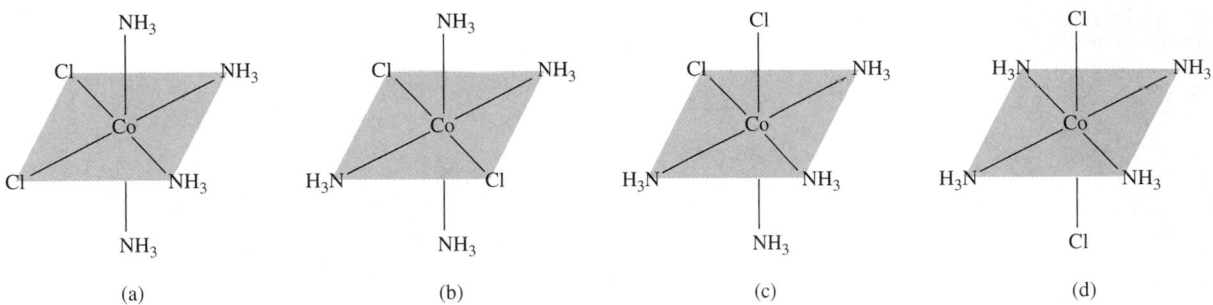

Figure 22.11 *The (a) cis and (b) trans isomers of tetraamminedichlorocobalt(III) ion, [Co(NH₃)₄Cl₂]⁺. The structure shown in (c) can be generated by rotating that in (a), and the structure shown in (d) can be generated by rotating that in (b). The ion has only two geometric isomers, (a) [or (c)] and (b) [or (d)].*

Optical Isomers

Optical isomers *are nonsuperimposable mirror images.* ("Superimposable" means that if one structure is laid over the other, the positions of all the atoms will match.) Like geometric isomers, optical isomers come in pairs. However, the optical isomers of a compound have *identical* physical and chemical properties, such as melting point, boiling point, dipole moment, and chemical reactivity toward molecules that are not optical isomers themselves. Optical isomers differ from each other in their interactions with plane-polarized light, as we will see.

The structural relationship between two optical isomers is analogous to the relationship between your left and right hands. If you place your left hand in front of a mirror, the image you see will look like your right hand (Figure 22.12). We say that your left hand and right hand are mirror images of each other. However, they are nonsuperimposable, because when you place your left hand over your right hand (with both palms facing down), they do not match.

Figure 22.13 shows the *cis* and *trans* isomers of dichlorobis(ethylenediamine)-cobalt(III) ion and their images. Careful examination reveals that the *trans* isomer and its mirror image are superimposable, but the *cis* isomer and its mirror image are not. Therefore, the *cis* isomer and its mirror image are optical isomers.

Optical isomers are described as ***chiral*** (from the Greek word for "hand") because, like your left and right hands, chiral molecules are nonsuperimposable. Isomers that are superimposable with their mirror images are said to be *achiral*. Chiral molecules play a vital role in enzyme reactions in biological systems. Many drug molecules are chiral. It is interesting to note that frequently only one of a pair of chiral isomers is biologically effective.

Figure 22.12 *A left hand and its mirror image, which looks the same as the right hand.*

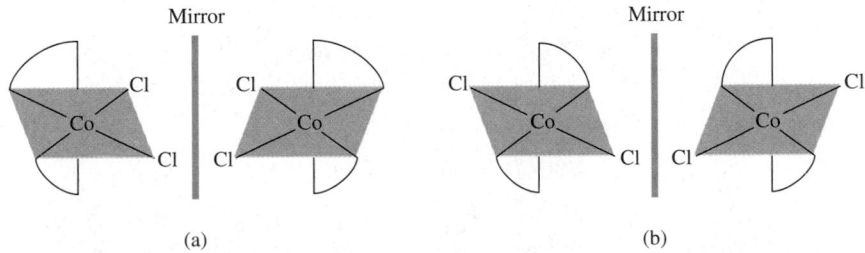

Figure 22.13 *The (a) cis and (b) trans isomers of dichlorobis(ethylenediamine)cobalt(III) ion and their mirror images. If you could rotate the mirror image in (b) 90° clockwise about the vertical position and place the ion over the trans isomer, you would find that the two are superimposable. No matter how you rotated the cis isomer and its mirror image in (a), however, you could not superimpose one on the other.*

Figure 22.14 *Operation of a polarimeter. Initially, the tube is filled with an achiral compound. The analyzer is rotated so that its plane of polarization is perpendicular to that of the polarizer. Under this condition, no light reaches the observer. Next, a chiral compound is placed in the tube as shown. The plane of polarization of the polarized light is rotated as it travels through the tube so that some light reaches the observer. Rotating the analyzer (either to the left or to the right) until no light reaches the observer again allows the angle of optical rotation to be measured.*

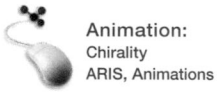

Animation:
Chirality
ARIS, Animations

Polaroid sheets are used to make Polaroid glasses.

Chiral molecules are said to be optically active because of their ability to rotate the plane of polarization of polarized light as it passes through them. Unlike ordinary light, which vibrates in all directions, *plane-polarized light* vibrates only in a single plane. We use a ***polarimeter*** to *measure the rotation of polarized light by optical isomers* (Figure 22.14). A beam of unpolarized light first passes through a Polaroid sheet, called the polarizer, and then through a sample tube containing a solution of an optically active, chiral compound. As the polarized light passes through the sample tube, its plane of polarization is rotated either to the right or to the left. This rotation can be measured directly by turning the analyzer in the appropriate direction until minimal light transmission is achieved (Figure 22.15). If the plane of polarization is rotated

Figure 22.15 *With one Polaroid sheet over a picture, light passes through. With a second sheet of Polaroid placed over the first so that the axes of polarization of the sheets are perpendicular, little or no light passes through. If the axes of polarization of the two sheets were parallel, light would pass through.*

to the right, the isomer is said to be *dextrorotatory (d)*; it is *levorotatory (l)* if the rotation is to the left. *The d and l isomers of a chiral substance,* called **enantiomers,** always rotate the light by the same amount, but in opposite directions. Thus, in *an equimolar mixture of two enantiomers,* called a **racemic mixture,** the net rotation is zero.

22.5 Bonding in Coordination Compounds: Crystal Field Theory

A satisfactory theory of bonding in coordination compounds must account for properties such as color and magnetism, as well as stereochemistry and bond strength. No single theory as yet does all this for us. Rather, several different approaches have been applied to transition metal complexes. We will consider only one of them here—crystal field theory—because it accounts for both the color and magnetic properties of many coordination compounds.

We will begin our discussion of crystal field theory with the most straightforward case, namely, complex ions with octahedral geometry. Then we will see how it is applied to tetrahedral and square-planar complexes.

Crystal Field Splitting in Octahedral Complexes

Crystal field theory explains the bonding in complex ions purely in terms of electrostatic forces. In a complex ion, two types of electrostatic interaction come into play. One is the attraction between the positive metal ion and the negatively charged ligand or the negatively charged end of a polar ligand. This is the force that binds the ligands to the metal. The second type of interaction is electrostatic repulsion between the lone pairs on the ligands and the electrons in the d orbitals of the metals.

As we saw in Chapter 7, d orbitals have different orientations, but in the absence of external disturbance they all have the same energy. In an octahedral complex, a central metal atom is surrounded by six lone pairs of electrons (on the six ligands), so all five d orbitals experience electrostatic repulsion. The magnitude of this repulsion depends on the orientation of the d orbital that is involved. Take the $d_{x^2-y^2}$ orbital as an example. In Figure 22.16, we see that the lobes of this orbital point toward corners

The name "crystal field" is associated with the theory used to explain the properties of solid, crystalline materials. The same theory is used to study coordination compounds.

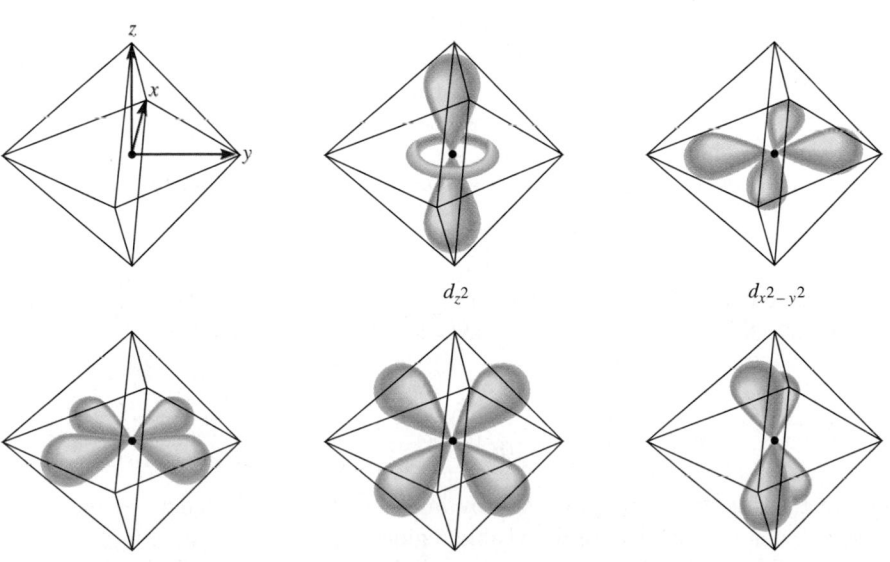

Figure 22.16 *The five d orbitals in an octahedral environment. The metal atom (or ion) is at the center of the octahedron, and the six lone pairs on the donor atoms of the ligands are at the corners.*

d_{z^2}

$d_{x^2-y^2}$

d_{xy}

d_{yz}

d_{xz}

Figure 22.17 *Crystal field splitting between d orbitals in an octahedral complex.*

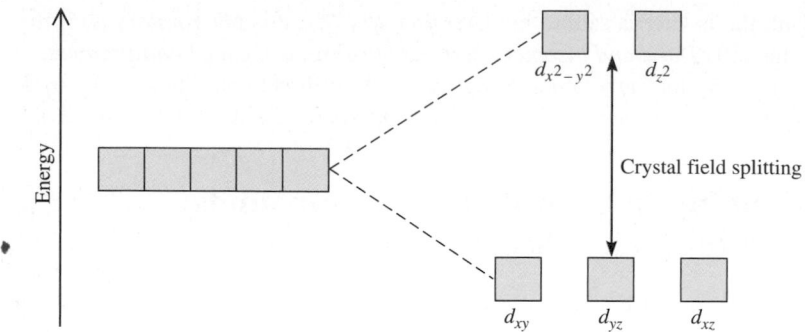

of the octahedron along the x and y axes, where the lone-pair electrons are positioned. Thus, an electron residing in this orbital would experience a greater repulsion from the ligands than an electron would in, say, the d_{xy} orbital. For this reason, the energy of the $d_{x^2-y^2}$ orbital is increased relative to the d_{xy}, d_{yz}, and d_{xz} orbitals. The d_{z^2} orbital's energy is also greater, because its lobes are pointed at the ligands along the z-axis.

As a result of these metal-ligand interactions, the five d orbitals in an octahedral complex are split between two sets of energy levels: a higher level with two orbitals ($d_{x^2-y^2}$ and d_{z^2}) having the same energy and a lower level with three equal-energy orbitals (d_{xy}, d_{yz}, and d_{xz}), as shown in Figure 22.17. The ***crystal field splitting (Δ)*** is *the energy difference between two sets of d orbitals in a metal atom when ligands are present*. The magnitude of Δ depends on the metal and the nature of the ligands; it has a direct effect on the color and magnetic properties of complex ions.

Color

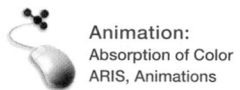

Animation:
Absorption of Color
ARIS, Animations

In Chapter 7 we learned that white light, such as sunlight, is a combination of all colors. A substance appears black if it absorbs all the visible light that strikes it. If it absorbs no visible light, it is white or colorless. An object appears green if it absorbs all light but reflects the green component. An object also looks green if it reflects all colors except red, the *complementary* color of green (Figure 22.18).

What has been said of reflected light also applies to transmitted light (that is, the light that passes through the medium, for example, a solution). Consider the hydrated cupric ion, $[Cu(H_2O)_6]^{2+}$, which absorbs light in the orange region of the spectrum so that a solution of $CuSO_4$ appears blue to us. Recall from Chapter 7 that when the energy of a photon is equal to the difference between the ground state and an excited state, absorption occurs as the photon strikes the atom (or ion or compound), and an electron is promoted to a higher level. This knowledge enables us to calculate the energy change involved in the electron transition. The energy of a photon, given by Equation (7.2), is

$$E = h\nu$$

Figure 22.18 *A color wheel with appropriate wavelengths. Complementary colors, such as red and green, are on opposite sides of the wheel.*

where h represents Planck's constant (6.63×10^{-34} J · s) and ν is the frequency of the radiation, which is 5.00×10^{14}/s for a wavelength of 600 nm. Here $E = \Delta$, so we have

$$\begin{aligned}\Delta &= h\nu \\ &= (6.63 \times 10^{-34} \text{ J} \cdot \text{s})(5.00 \times 10^{14}\text{/s}) \\ &= 3.32 \times 10^{-19} \text{ J}\end{aligned}$$

(Note that this is the energy absorbed by *one* ion.) If the wavelength of the photon absorbed by an ion lies outside the visible region, then the transmitted light looks the same (to us) as the incident light—white—and the ion appears colorless.

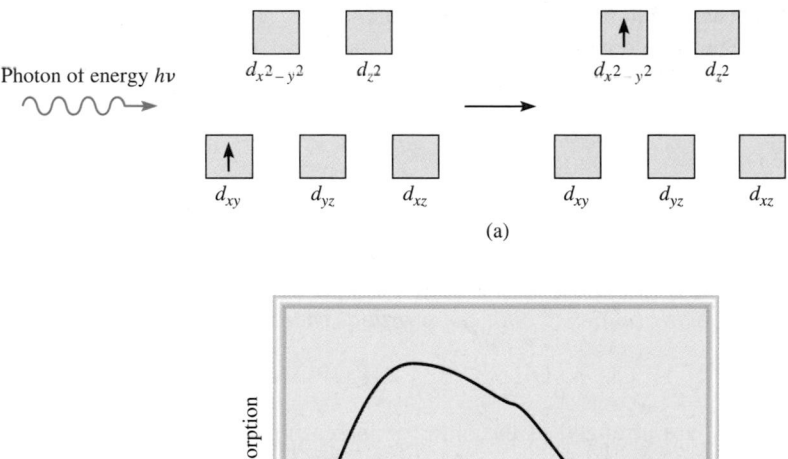

(a)

(b)

Figure 22.19 *(a) The process of photon absorption and (b) a graph of the absorption spectrum of $[Ti(H_2O)_6]^{3+}$. The energy of the incoming photon is equal to the crystal field splitting. The maximum absorption peak in the visible region occurs at 498 nm.*

The best way to measure crystal field splitting is to use spectroscopy to determine the wavelength at which light is absorbed. The $[Ti(H_2O)_6]^{3+}$ ion provides a straightforward example, because Ti^{3+} has only one $3d$ electron (Figure 22.19). The $[Ti(H_2O)_6]^{3+}$ ion absorbs light in the visible region of the spectrum (Figure 22.20). The wavelength corresponding to maximum absorption is 498 nm [Figure 22.19(b)]. This information enables us to calculate the crystal field splitting as follows. We start by writing

$$\Delta = h\nu \qquad (22.1)$$

Also

$$\nu = \frac{c}{\lambda}$$

where c is the speed of light and λ is the wavelength. Therefore,

$$\Delta = \frac{hc}{\lambda} = \frac{(6.63 \times 10^{-34}\,\text{J} \cdot \text{s})(3.00 \times 10^{8}\,\text{m/s})}{(498\,\text{nm})(1 \times 10^{-9}\,\text{m/1 nm})}$$
$$= 3.99 \times 10^{-19}\,\text{J}$$

Equation (7.3) shows that $E = hc/\lambda$.

Figure 22.20 *Colors of some of the first-row transition metal ions in solution. From left to right: Ti^{3+}, Cr^{3+}, Mn^{2+}, Fe^{3+}, Co^{2+}, Ni^{2+}, Cu^{2+}. The Sc^{3+} and V^{5+} ions are colorless.*

This is the energy required to excite *one* $[Ti(H_2O)_6]^{3+}$ ion. To express this energy difference in the more convenient units of kilojoules per mole, we write

$$\Delta = (3.99 \times 10^{-19} \text{ J/ion})(6.02 \times 10^{23} \text{ ions/mol})$$
$$= 240,000 \text{ J/mol}$$
$$= 240 \text{ kJ/mol}$$

Aided by spectroscopic data for a number of complexes, all having the same metal ion but different ligands, chemists calculated the crystal splitting for each ligand and established a ***spectrochemical series,*** which is *a list of ligands arranged in increasing order of their abilities to split the d orbital energy levels:*

$$I^- < Br^- < Cl^- < OH^- < F^- < H_2O < NH_3 < en < CN^- < CO$$

The order in the spectrochemical series is the same no matter which metal atom (or ion) is present.

These ligands are arranged in the order of increasing value of Δ. CO and CN^- are called *strong-field ligands,* because they cause a large splitting of the *d* orbital energy levels. The halide ions and hydroxide ion are *weak-field ligands,* because they split the *d* orbitals to a lesser extent.

Magnetic Properties

The magnitude of the crystal field splitting also determines the magnetic properties of a complex ion. The $[Ti(H_2O)_6]^{3+}$ ion, having only one *d* electron, is always paramagnetic. However, for an ion with several *d* electrons, the situation is less clearcut. Consider, for example, the octahedral complexes $[FeF_6]^{3-}$ and $[Fe(CN)_6]^{3-}$ (Figure 22.21). The electron configuration of Fe^{3+} is $[Ar]3d^5$, and there are two possible ways to distribute the five *d* electrons among the *d* orbitals. According to Hund's rule (see Section 7.8), maximum stability is reached when the electrons are placed in five separate orbitals with parallel spins. But this arrangement can be achieved only at a cost; two of the five electrons must be promoted to the higher-energy $d_{x^2-y^2}$ and d_{z^2} orbitals. No such energy investment is needed if all five electrons enter the d_{xy}, d_{yz}, and d_{xz} orbitals. According to Pauli's exclusion principle (p. 293), there will be only one unpaired electron present in this case.

Figure 22.22 shows the distribution of electrons among *d* orbitals that results in low- and high-spin complexes. The actual arrangement of the electrons is determined by the amount of stability gained by having maximum parallel spins versus the investment in energy required to promote electrons to higher *d* orbitals. Because F^- is a weak-field ligand, the five *d* electrons enter five separate *d* orbitals with parallel spins to create a high-spin complex (see Figure 22.21). On the other hand, the cyanide ion is a strong-field ligand, so it is energetically preferable for all five electrons to be in

Figure 22.21 *Energy-level diagrams for the Fe^{3+} ion and for the $[FeF_6]^{3-}$ and $[Fe(CN)_6]^{3-}$ complex ions.*

High spin   Low spin

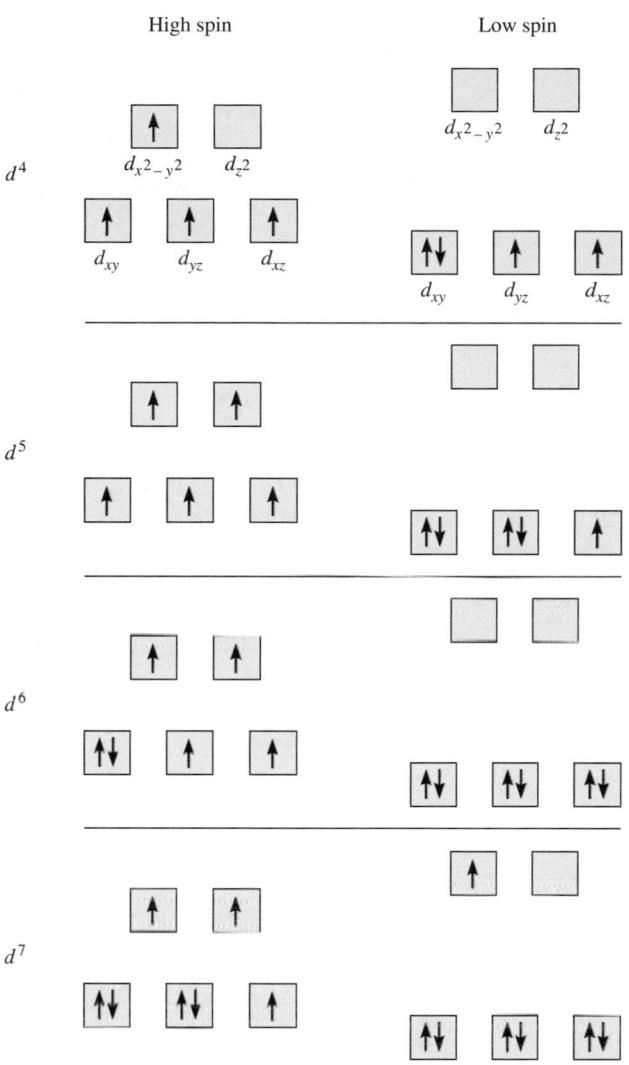

Figure 22.22 *Orbital diagrams for the high-spin and low-spin octahedral complexes corresponding to the electron configurations d^4, d^5, d^6, and d^7. No such distinctions can be made for d^1, d^2, d^3, d^8, d^9, and d^{10}.*

the lower orbitals and therefore a low-spin complex is formed. High-spin complexes are more paramagnetic than low-spin complexes.

The actual number of unpaired electrons (or spins) in a complex ion can be found by magnetic measurements, and in general, experimental findings support predictions based on crystal field splitting. However, a distinction between low- and high-spin complexes can be made only if the metal ion contains more than three and fewer than eight d electrons, as shown in Figure 22.22.

The magnetic properties of a complex ion depend on the number of unpaired electrons present.

Example 22.4

Predict the number of unpaired spins in the $[Cr(en)_3]^{2+}$ ion.

Strategy The magnetic properties of a complex ion depend on the strength of the ligands. Strong-field ligands, which cause a high degree of splitting among the d orbital energy levels, result in low-spin complexes. Weak-field ligands, which cause a small degree of splitting among the d orbital energy levels, result in high-spin complexes.

(Continued)

Similar problem: 22.35.

Solution The electron configuration of Cr^{2+} is $[Ar]3d^4$. Because en is a strong-field ligand, we expect $[Cr(en)_3]^{2+}$ to be a low-spin complex. According to Figure 22.22, all four electrons will be placed in the lower-energy d orbitals (d_{xy}, d_{yz}, and d_{xz}) and there will be a total of two unpaired spins.

Practice Exercise How many unpaired spins are in $[Mn(H_2O)_6]^{2+}$? (H_2O is a weak-field ligand.)

Tetrahedral and Square-Planar Complexes

So far we have concentrated on octahedral complexes. The splitting of the d orbital energy levels in two other types of complexes—tetrahedral and square-planar—can also be accounted for satisfactorily by the crystal field theory. In fact, the splitting pattern for a tetrahedral ion is just the reverse of that for octahedral complexes. In this case, the d_{xy}, d_{yz}, and d_{xz} orbitals are more closely directed at the ligands and therefore have more energy than the $d_{x^2-y^2}$ and d_{z^2} orbitals (Figure 22.23). Most tetrahedral complexes are high-spin complexes. Presumably, the tetrahedral arrangement reduces the magnitude of metal-ligand interactions, resulting in a smaller Δ value compared to the octahedral case. This is a reasonable assumption because the number of ligands is smaller in a tetrahedral complex.

As Figure 22.24 shows, the splitting pattern for square-planar complexes is the most complicated of the three cases. Clearly, the $d_{x^2-y^2}$ orbital possesses the highest

Figure 22.23 *Crystal field splitting between d orbitals in a tetrahedral complex.*

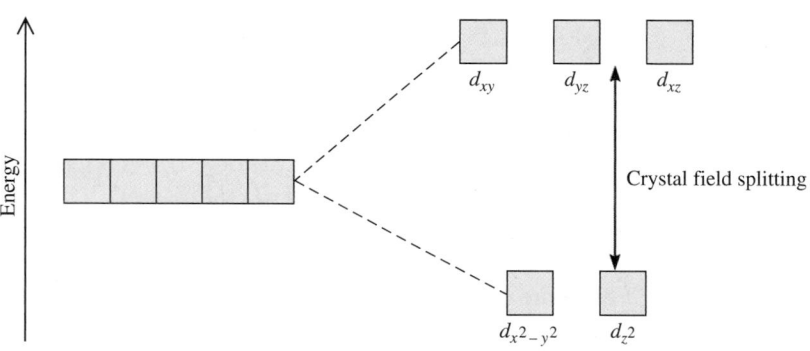

Figure 22.24 *Energy-level diagram for a square-planar complex. Because there are more than two energy levels, we cannot define crystal field splitting as we can for octahedral and tetrahedral complexes.*

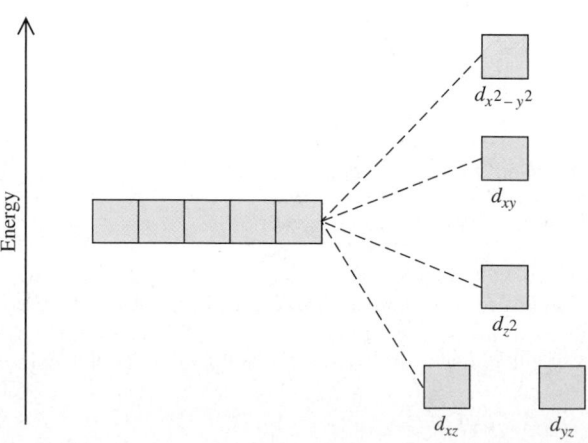

energy (as in the octahedral case), and the d_{xy} orbital the next highest. However, the relative placement of the d_{z^2} and the d_{xz} and d_{yz} orbitals cannot be determined simply by inspection and must be calculated.

22.6 Reactions of Coordination Compounds

Complex ions undergo ligand exchange (or substitution) reactions in solution. The rates of these reactions vary widely, depending on the nature of the metal ion and the ligands.

In studying ligand exchange reactions, it is often useful to distinguish between the stability of a complex ion and its tendency to react, which we call *kinetic lability*. Stability in this context is a thermodynamic property, which is measured in terms of the species' formation constant K_f (see p. 733). For example, we say that the complex ion tetracyanonickelate(II) is stable because it has a large formation constant ($K_f \approx 1 \times 10^{30}$)

$$Ni^{2+} + 4CN^- \rightleftharpoons [Ni(CN)_4]^{2-}$$

By using cyanide ions labeled with the radioactive isotope carbon-14, chemists have shown that $[Ni(CN)_4]^{2-}$ undergoes ligand exchange very rapidly in solution. The following equilibrium is established almost as soon as the species are mixed:

$$[Ni(CN)_4]^{2-} + 4{*}CN^- \rightleftharpoons [Ni({*}CN)_4]^{2-} + 4CN^-$$

At equilibrium, there is a distribution of *CN$^-$ ions in the complex ion.

where the asterisk denotes a ^{14}C atom. Complexes like the tetracyanonickelate(II) ion are termed **labile complexes** because they *undergo rapid ligand exchange reactions.* Thus, a thermodynamically stable species (that is, one that has a large formation constant) is not necessarily unreactive. (In Section 13.4 we saw that the smaller the activation energy, the larger the rate constant, and hence the greater the rate.)

A complex that is thermodynamically *unstable* in acidic solution is $[Co(NH_3)_6]^{3+}$. The equilibrium constant for the following reaction is about 1×10^{20}:

$$[Co(NH_3)_6]^{3+} + 6H^+ + 6H_2O \rightleftharpoons [Co(H_2O)_6]^{3+} + 6NH_4^+$$

When equilibrium is reached, the concentration of the $[Co(NH_3)_6]^{3+}$ ion is very low. However, this reaction requires several days to complete because of the inertness of the $[Co(NH_3)_6]^{3+}$ ion. This is an example of an **inert complex,** *a complex ion that undergoes very slow exchange reactions* (on the order of hours or even days). It shows that a thermodynamically unstable species is not necessarily chemically reactive. The rate of reaction is determined by the energy of activation, which is high in this case.

Most complex ions containing Co^{3+}, Cr^{3+}, and Pt^{2+} are kinetically inert. Because they exchange ligands very slowly, they are easy to study in solution. As a result, our knowledge of the bonding, structure, and isomerism of coordination compounds has come largely from studies of these compounds.

22.7 Applications of Coordination Compounds

Coordination compounds are found in living systems and have many uses in the home, in industry, and in medicine. We describe a few examples here and in the Chemistry in Action essay on p. 956.

Coordination Compounds in Living Systems

Coordination compounds play many important roles in animals and plants. They are essential in the storage and transport of oxygen, as electron transfer agents, as catalysts, and in photosynthesis. Here we focus on coordination compounds containing iron and magnesium.

Because of its central function as an oxygen carrier for metabolic processes, hemoglobin is probably the most studied of all the proteins. The molecule contains four folded long chains called *subunits*. Hemoglobin carries oxygen in the blood from the lungs to the tissues, where it delivers the oxygen molecules to myoglobin. Myoglobin, which is made up of only one subunit, stores oxygen for metabolic processes in muscle.

The porphine molecule forms an important part of the hemoglobin structure. Upon coordination to a metal, the H^+ ions that are bonded to two of the four nitrogen atoms in porphine are displaced. Complexes derived from porphine are

The heme group in hemoglobin. The Fe^{2+} ion is coordinated with the nitrogen atoms of the heme group. The ligand below the porphyrin is the histidine group, which is attached to the protein. The sixth ligand is a water molecule.

Porphine   Fe²⁺-porphyrin

Simplified structures of the porphine molecule and the Fe^{2+}-porphyrin complex. The dashed lines represent coordinate covalent bonds.

(a)   (b)   (c)

Three possible ways for molecular oxygen to bind to the heme group in hemoglobin. The structure shown in (a) would have a coordination number of 7, which is considered unlikely for Fe(II) complexes. Although the end-on arrangement in (b) seems the most reasonable, evidence points to structure in (c) as the correct one. The structure shown in (c) is the most plausible.

Metallurgy

The extraction of silver and gold by the formation of cyanide complexes (p. 903) and the purification of nickel (p. 874) by converting the metal to the gaseous compound $Ni(CO)_4$ are typical examples of the use of coordination compounds in metallurgical processes.

Therapeutic Chelating Agents

Earlier we mentioned that the chelating agent EDTA is used in the treatment of lead poisoning. Certain platinum-containing compounds can effectively inhibit the growth of cancerous cells. A specific case is discussed on p. 958.

called *porphyrins*, and the iron-porphyrin combination is called the *heme* group. The iron in the heme group has an oxidation number of +2; it is coordinated to the four nitrogen atoms in the porphine group and also to a nitrogen donor atom in a ligand that is attached to the protein. The sixth ligand is a water molecule, which binds to the Fe^{2+} ion on the other side of the ring to complete the octahedral complex. This hemoglobin molecule is called *deoxyhemoglobin* and imparts a bluish tinge to venous blood. The water ligand can be replaced readily by molecular oxygen to form red oxyhemoglobin found in arterial blood. Each subunit contains a heme group, so each hemoglobin molecule can bind up to four O_2 molecules.

There are three possible structures for oxyhemoglobin. For a number of years, the exact arrangement of the oxygen molecule relative to the porphyrin group was not clear. Most experimental evidence suggests that the bond between O and Fe is bent relative to the heme group.

The porphyrin group is a very effective chelating agent, and not surprisingly, we find it in a number of biological systems. The iron-heme complex is present in another class of proteins, called the *cytochromes*. The iron forms an octahedral complex in these proteins, but because both the histidine and the methionine groups are firmly bound to the metal ion, they cannot be displaced by oxygen or other ligands. Instead, the cytochromes act as electron carriers, which are essential to metabolic processes. In cytochromes, iron undergoes rapid reversible redox reactions:

$$Fe^{3+} + e^- \rightleftharpoons Fe^{2+}$$

which are coupled to the oxidation of organic molecules such as the carbohydrates.

The chlorophyll molecule, which is necessary for plant photosynthesis, also contains the porphyrin ring, but in this case the metal ion is Mg^{2+} rather than Fe^{2+}.

The heme group in cytochrome c. The ligands above and below the porphyrin are the methionine group and histidine group of the protein, respectively.

The porphyrin structure in chlorophyll. The dotted lines indicate the coordinate covalent bonds. The electron-delocalized portion of the molecule is shown in color.

Chemical Analysis

Although EDTA has a great affinity for a large number of metal ions (especially 2+ and 3+ ions), other chelates are more selective in binding. For example, dimethylglyoxime,

$$\begin{array}{c} H_3C \\ \\ H_3C \end{array} \begin{array}{c} C=N-OH \\ | \\ C=N-OH \end{array}$$

forms an insoluble brick-red solid with Ni^{2+} and an insoluble bright-yellow solid with Pd^{2+}. These characteristic colors are used in qualitative analysis to identify nickel and

An aqueous suspension of *bis*(dimethylglyoximato)nickel(II).

CHEMISTRY
in Action

Cisplatin—The Anticancer Drug

Luck often plays a role in major scientific breakthroughs, but it takes an alert and well-trained person to recognize the significance of an accidental discovery and to take full advantage of it. Such was the case when, in 1964, the biophysicist Barnett Rosenberg and his research group at Michigan State University were studying the effect of an electric field on the growth of bacteria. They suspended a bacterial culture between two platinum

electrodes and passed an electric current through it. To their surprise, they found that after an hour or so the bacteria cells ceased dividing. It did not take long for the group to determine that a platinum-containing substance extracted from the bacterial culture inhibited cell division.

Rosenberg reasoned that the platinum compound might be useful as an anticancer agent, because cancer involves uncontrolled division of affected cells, so he set out to identify the substance. Given the presence of ammonia and chloride ions in solution during electrolysis, Rosenberg synthesized a number of platinum compounds containing ammonia and chlorine. The one that proved most effective at inhibiting cell division was *cis*-diamminedichloroplatinum(II) [Pt(NH$_3$)$_2$Cl$_2$], also called cisplatin.

The mechanism for the action of cisplatin is the chelation of DNA (deoxyribonucleic acid), the molecule that contains the genetic code. During cell division, the double-stranded DNA splits into two single strands, which must be accurately copied in order for the new cells to be identical to their parent cell. X-ray studies show that cisplatin binds to DNA by forming cross-links in which the two chlorides on cisplatin are replaced by nitrogen atoms in the adjacent guanine bases on the *same* strand of the DNA. (Guanine is one of the four bases in DNA. See Figure 25.17.) Consequently, the double-stranded structure assumes a bent configuration at the binding site. Scientists believe that this structural distortion is a

Cisplatin, a bright yellow compound, is administered intravenously to cancer patients.

palladium. Further, the quantities of ions present can be determined by gravimetric analysis (see Section 4.6) as follows: To a solution containing Ni^{2+} ions, say, we add an excess of dimethylglyoxime reagent, and a brick-red precipitate forms. The precipitate is then filtered, dried, and weighed. Knowing the formula of the complex (Figure 22.25), we can readily calculate the amount of nickel present in the original solution.

Figure 22.25 *Structure of nickel dimethylglyoxime. Note that the overall structure is stabilized by hydrogen bonds.*

958

key factor in inhibiting replication. The damaged cell is then destroyed by the body's immune system. Because the binding of cisplatin to DNA requires both Cl atoms to be on the same side of the complex, the *trans* isomer of the compound is totally ineffective as an anticancer drug. Unfortunately, cisplatin can cause serious side effects, including severe kidney damage. Therefore, ongoing research efforts are directed toward finding related complexes that destroy cancer cells with less harm to healthy tissues.

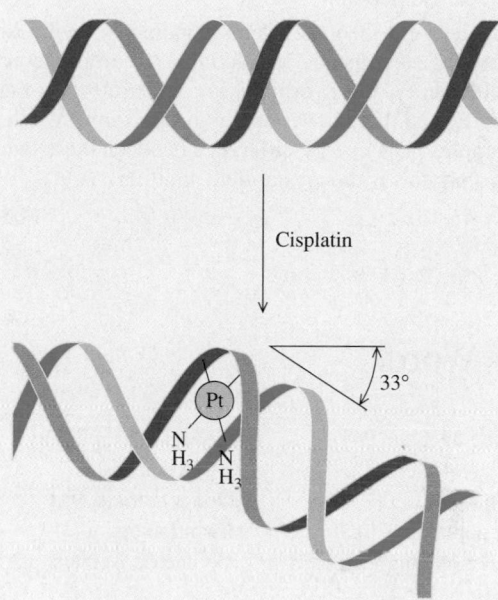

Cisplatin

33°

Cisplatin destroys the cancer cells' ability to reproduce by changing the configuration of their DNA. It binds to two sites on a strand of DNA, causing it to bend about 33° away from the rest of the strand. The structure of this DNA adduct was elucidated by Professor Stephen Lippard's group at MIT.

cis-Pt(NH₃)₂Cl₂

Detergents

The cleansing action of soap in hard water is hampered by the reaction of the Ca^{2+} ions in the water with the soap molecules to form insoluble salts or curds. In the late 1940s the detergent industry introduced a "builder," usually sodium tripolyphosphate, to circumvent this problem. The tripolyphosphate ion is an effective chelating agent that forms stable, soluble complexes with Ca^{2+} ions. Sodium tripolyphosphate revolutionized the detergent industry. However, because phosphates are plant nutrients, waste waters containing phosphates discharged into rivers and lakes cause algae to grow, resulting in oxygen depletion. Under these conditions most or all aquatic life eventually succumbs. This process is called *eutrophication*. Consequently, many states have banned phosphate detergents since the 1970s, and manufacturers have reformulated their products to eliminate phosphates.

Tripolyphosphate ion.

Summary of Facts and Concepts

1. Transition metals usually have incompletely filled *d* subshells and a pronounced tendency to form complexes. Compounds that contain complex ions are called coordination compounds.

2. The first-row transition metals (scandium to copper) are the most common of all the transition metals; their chemistry is characteristic, in many ways, of the entire group.

3. Complex ions consist of a metal ion surrounded by ligands. The donor atoms in the ligands each contribute an electron pair to the central metal ion in a complex.

4. Coordination compounds may display geometric and/or optical isomerism.

5. Crystal field theory explains bonding in complexes in terms of electrostatic interactions. According to crystal field theory, the d orbitals are split into two higher-energy and three lower-energy orbitals in an octahedral complex. The energy difference between these two sets of d orbitals is the crystal field splitting.

6. Strong-field ligands cause a large crystal field splitting, and weak-field ligands cause a small splitting. Electron spins tend to be parallel with weak-field ligands and paired with strong-field ligands, where a greater investment of energy is required to promote electrons into the high-lying d orbitals.

7. Complex ions undergo ligand exchange reactions in solution.

8. Coordination compounds find application in many different areas, for example, as antidotes for metal poisoning and in chemical analysis.

Key Words

Chelating agent, p. 941
Chiral, p. 947
Coordination compound, p. 940
Coordination number, p. 941
Crystal field splitting (Δ), p. 950
Donor atom, p. 941
Enantiomers, p. 949
Geometric isomers, p. 946
Inert complex, p. 955
Labile complex, p. 955
Ligand, p. 941
Optical isomers, p. 947
Polarimeter, p. 948
Racemic mixture, p. 949
Spectrochemical series, p. 952
Stereoisomers, p. 946

Questions and Problems

Properties of the Transition Metals
Review Questions

22.1 What distinguishes a transition metal from a representative metal?

22.2 Why is zinc not considered a transition metal?

22.3 Explain why atomic radii decrease very gradually from scandium to copper.

22.4 Without referring to the text, write the ground-state electron configurations of the first-row transition metals. Explain any irregularities.

22.5 Write the electron configurations of the following ions: V^{5+}, Cr^{3+}, Mn^{2+}, Fe^{3+}, Cu^{2+}, Sc^{3+}, Ti^{4+}.

22.6 Why do transition metals have more oxidation states than other elements?

22.7 Give the highest oxidation states for scandium to copper.

22.8 Why does chromium seem to be less reactive than its standard reduction potential suggests?

Coordination Compounds
Review Questions

22.9 Define the following terms: coordination compound, ligand, donor atom, coordination number, chelating agent.

22.10 Describe the interaction between a donor atom and a metal atom in terms of a Lewis acid-base reaction.

Problems

22.11 Complete the following statements for the complex ion $[Co(en)_2(H_2O)CN]^{2+}$. (a) en is the abbreviation for _____. (b) The oxidation number of Co is _____. (c) The coordination number of Co is _____. (d) _____ is a bidentate ligand.

22.12 Complete the following statements for the complex ion $[Cr(C_2O_4)_2(H_2O)_2]^-$. (a) The oxidation number of Cr is _____. (b) The coordination number of Cr is _____. (c) _____ is a bidentate ligand.

22.13 Give the oxidation numbers of the metals in the following species: (a) $K_3[Fe(CN)_6]$, (b) $K_3[Cr(C_2O_4)_3]$, (c) $[Ni(CN)_4]^{2-}$.

22.14 Give the oxidation numbers of the metals in the following species: (a) Na_2MoO_4, (b) $MgWO_4$, (c) $Fe(CO)_5$.

22.15 What are the systematic names for the following ions and compounds?
(a) $[Co(NH_3)_4Cl_2]^+$
(b) $Cr(NH_3)_3Cl_3$
(c) $[Co(en)_2Br_2]^+$
(d) $[Co(NH_3)_6]Cl_3$

22.16 What are the systematic names for the following ions and compounds?

(a) $[cis\text{-}Co(en)_2Cl_2]^+$

(b) $[Pt(NH_3)_5Cl]Cl_3$

(c) $[Co(NH_3)_5Cl]Cl_2$

22.17 Write the formulas for each of the following ions and compounds: (a) tetrahydroxozincate(II), (b) pentaaquochlorochromium(III) chloride, (c) tetrabromocuprate(II), (d) ethylenediaminetetraacetatoferrate(II).

22.18 Write the formulas for each of the following ions and compounds: (a) bis(ethylenediamine)dichlorochromium(III), (b) pentacarbonyliron(0), (c) potassium tetracyanocuprate(II), (d) tetraammineaquochlorocobalt(III) chloride.

Structure of Coordination Compounds
Review Questions

22.19 Define the following terms: stereoisomers, geometric isomers, optical isomers, plane-polarized light.

22.20 Specify which of the following structures can exhibit geometric isomerism: (a) linear, (b) square-planar, (c) tetrahedral, (d) octahedral.

22.21 What determines whether a molecule is chiral? How does a polarimeter measure the chirality of a molecule?

22.22 Explain the following terms: (a) enantiomers, (b) racemic mixtures.

Problems

22.23 The complex ion $[Ni(CN)_2Br_2]^{2-}$ has a square-planar geometry. Draw the structures of the geometric isomers of this complex.

22.24 How many geometric isomers are in the following species? (a) $[Co(NH_3)_2Cl_4]^-$, (b) $[Co(NH_3)_3Cl_3]$

22.25 Draw structures of all the geometric and optical isomers of each of the following cobalt complexes:

(a) $[Co(NH_3)_6]^{3+}$

(b) $[Co(NH_3)_5Cl]^{2+}$

(c) $[Co(C_2O_4)_3]^{3-}$

22.26 Draw structures of all the geometric and optical isomers of each of the following cobalt complexes: (a) $[Co(NH_3)_4Cl_2]^+$, (b) $[Co(en)_3]^{3+}$.

Bonding in Coordination Compounds
Review Questions

22.27 Briefly describe crystal field theory.

22.28 Define the following terms: crystal field splitting, high-spin complex, low-spin complex, spectrochemical series.

22.29 What is the origin of color in a coordination compound?

22.30 Compounds containing the Sc^{3+} ion are colorless, whereas those containing the Ti^{3+} ion are colored. Explain.

22.31 What factors determine whether a given complex will be diamagnetic or paramagnetic?

22.32 For the same type of ligands, explain why the crystal field splitting for an octahedral complex is always greater than that for a tetrahedral complex.

Problems

22.33 The $[Ni(CN)_4]^{2-}$ ion, which has a square-planar geometry, is diamagnetic, whereas the $[NiCl_4]^{2-}$ ion, which has a tetrahedral geometry, is paramagnetic. Show the crystal field splitting diagrams for those two complexes.

22.34 Transition metal complexes containing CN^- ligands are often yellow in color, whereas those containing H_2O ligands are often green or blue. Explain.

22.35 Predict the number of unpaired electrons in the following complex ions: (a) $[Cr(CN)_6]^{4-}$, (b) $[Cr(H_2O)_6]^{2+}$.

22.36 The absorption maximum for the complex ion $[Co(NH_3)_6]^{3+}$ occurs at 470 nm. (a) Predict the color of the complex and (b) calculate the crystal field splitting in kJ/mol.

22.37 From each of the following pairs, choose the complex that absorbs light at a longer wavelength: (a) $[Co(NH_3)_6]^{2+}$, $[Co(H_2O)_6]^{2+}$; (b) $[FeF_6]^{3-}$, $[Fe(CN)_6]^{3-}$; (c) $[Cu(NH_3)_4]^{2+}$, $[CuCl_4]^{2-}$.

22.38 A solution made by dissolving 0.875 g of $Co(NH_3)_4Cl_3$ in 25.0 g of water freezes at $-0.56°C$. Calculate the number of moles of ions produced when 1 mole of $Co(NH_3)_4Cl_3$ is dissolved in water and suggest a structure for the complex ion present in this compound.

Reactions of Coordination Compounds
Review Questions

22.39 Define the terms (a) labile complex, (b) inert complex.

22.40 Explain why a thermodynamically stable species may be chemically reactive and a thermodynamically unstable species may be unreactive.

Problems

22.41 Oxalic acid, $H_2C_2O_4$, is sometimes used to clean rust stains from sinks and bathtubs. Explain the chemistry underlying this cleaning action.

22.42 The $[Fe(CN)_6]^{3-}$ complex is more labile than the $[Fe(CN)_6]^{4-}$ complex. Suggest an experiment that would prove that $[Fe(CN)_6]^{3-}$ is a labile complex.

22.43 Aqueous copper(II) sulfate solution is blue in color. When aqueous potassium fluoride is added, a green precipitate is formed. When aqueous potassium chloride is added instead, a bright-green solution is formed. Explain what is happening in these two cases.

22.44 When aqueous potassium cyanide is added to a solution of copper(II) sulfate, a white precipitate, soluble in an excess of potassium cyanide, is formed. No precipitate is formed when hydrogen sulfide is bubbled through the solution at this point. Explain.

22.45 A concentrated aqueous copper(II) chloride solution is bright green in color. When diluted with water, the solution becomes light blue. Explain.

22.46 In a dilute nitric acid solution, Fe^{3+} reacts with thiocyanate ion (SCN^-) to form a dark-red complex:

$$[Fe(H_2O)_6]^{3+} + SCN^- \rightleftharpoons$$
$$H_2O + [Fe(H_2O)_5NCS]^{2+}$$

The equilibrium concentration of $[Fe(H_2O)_5NCS]^{2+}$ may be determined by how darkly colored the solution is (measured by a spectrometer). In one such experiment, 1.0 mL of 0.20 M $Fe(NO_3)_3$ was mixed with 1.0 mL of 1.0×10^{-3} M KSCN and 8.0 mL of dilute HNO_3. The color of the solution quantitatively indicated that the $[Fe(H_2O)_5NCS]^{2+}$ concentration was 7.3×10^{-5} M. Calculate the formation constant for $[Fe(H_2O)_5NCS]^{2+}$.

Additional Problems

22.47 As we read across the first-row transition metals from left to right, the +2 oxidation state becomes more stable in comparison with the +3 state. Why is this so?

22.48 Which is a stronger oxidizing agent in aqueous solution, Mn^{3+} or Cr^{3+}? Explain your choice.

22.49 Carbon monoxide binds to Fe in hemoglobin some 200 times more strongly than oxygen. This is the reason why CO is a toxic substance. The metal-to-ligand sigma bond is formed by donating a lone pair from the donor atom to an empty sp^3d^2 orbital on Fe. (a) On the basis of electronegativities, would you expect the C or O atom to form the bond to Fe? (b) Draw a diagram illustrating the overlap of the orbitals involved in the bonding.

22.50 What are the oxidation states of Fe and Ti in the ore ilmenite, $FeTiO_3$? (*Hint:* Look up the ionization energies of Fe and Ti in Table 22.1; the fourth ionization energy of Ti is 4180 kJ/mol.)

22.51 A student has prepared a cobalt complex that has one of the following three structures: $[Co(NH_3)_6]Cl_3$, $[Co(NH_3)_5Cl]Cl_2$, or $[Co(NH_3)_4Cl_2]Cl$. Explain how the student would distinguish between these possibilities by an electrical conductance experiment. At the student's disposal are three strong electrolytes—NaCl, $MgCl_2$, and $FeCl_3$—which may be used for comparison purposes.

22.52 Chemical analysis shows that hemoglobin contains 0.34 percent of Fe by mass. What is the minimum possible molar mass of hemoglobin? The actual molar mass of hemoglobin is about 65,000 g. How do you account for the discrepancy between your minimum value and the actual value?

22.53 Explain the following facts: (a) Copper and iron have several oxidation states, whereas zinc has only one. (b) Copper and iron form colored ions, whereas zinc does not.

22.54 A student in 1895 prepared three coordination compounds containing chromium, with the following properties:

Formula	Color	Cl^- Ions in Solution per Formula Unit
(a) $CrCl_3 \cdot 6H_2O$	Violet	3
(b) $CrCl_3 \cdot 6H_2O$	Light green	2
(c) $CrCl_3 \cdot 6H_2O$	Dark green	1

Write modern formulas for these compounds and suggest a method for confirming the number of Cl^- ions present in solution in each case. (*Hint:* Some of the compounds may exist as hydrates.)

22.55 The formation constant for the reaction $Ag^+ + 2NH_3 \rightleftharpoons [Ag(NH_3)_2]^+$ is 1.5×10^7 and that for the reaction $Ag^+ + 2CN^- \rightleftharpoons [Ag(CN)_2]^-$ is 1.0×10^{21} at 25°C (see Table 16.3). Calculate the equilibrium constant and $\Delta G°$ at 25°C for the reaction

$$[Ag(NH_3)_2]^+ + 2CN^- \rightleftharpoons [Ag(CN)_2]^- + 2NH_3$$

22.56 From the standard reduction potentials listed in Table 19.1 for Zn/Zn^{2+} and Cu^+/Cu^{2+}, calculate $\Delta G°$ and the equilibrium constant for the reaction

$$Zn(s) + 2Cu^{2+}(aq) \longrightarrow Zn^{2+}(aq) + 2Cu^+(aq)$$

22.57 Using the standard reduction potentials listed in Table 19.1 and the *Handbook of Chemistry and Physics*, show that the following reaction is favorable under standard-state conditions:

$$2Ag(s) + Pt^{2+}(aq) \longrightarrow 2Ag^+(aq) + Pt(s)$$

What is the equilibrium constant of this reaction at 25°C?

22.58 The Co^{2+}-porphyrin complex is more stable than the Fe^{2+}-porphyrin complex. Why, then, is iron the metal ion in hemoglobin (and other heme-containing proteins)?

22.59 What are the differences between geometric isomers and optical isomers?

22.60 Oxyhemoglobin is bright red, whereas deoxyhemoglobin is purple. Show that the difference in color can be accounted for qualitatively on the basis of high-spin and low-spin complexes. (*Hint:* O_2 is a strong-field ligand; see Chemistry in Action essay on p. 956.)

22.61 Hydrated Mn^{2+} ions are practically colorless (see Figure 22.20) even though they possess five $3d$ electrons. Explain. (*Hint:* Electronic transitions in which there is a change in the number of unpaired electrons do not occur readily.)

22.62 Which of the following hydrated cations are colorless: $Fe^{2+}(aq)$, $Zn^{2+}(aq)$, $Cu^{+}(aq)$, $Cu^{2+}(aq)$, $V^{5+}(aq)$, $Ca^{2+}(aq)$, $Co^{2+}(aq)$, $Sc^{3+}(aq)$, $Pb^{2+}(aq)$? Explain your choice.

22.63 Aqueous solutions of $CoCl_2$ are generally either light pink or blue. Low concentrations and low temperatures favor the pink form while high concentrations and high temperatures favor the blue form. Adding hydrochloric acid to a pink solution of $CoCl_2$ causes the solution to turn blue; the pink color is restored by the addition of $HgCl_2$. Account for these observations.

22.64 Suggest a method that would allow you to distinguish between *cis*-$Pt(NH_3)_2Cl_2$ and *trans*-$Pt(NH_3)_2Cl_2$.

22.65 You are given two solutions containing $FeCl_2$ and $FeCl_3$ at the same concentration. One solution is light yellow and the other one is brown. Identify these solutions based only on color.

22.66 The label of a certain brand of mayonnaise lists EDTA as a food preservative. How does EDTA prevent the spoilage of mayonnaise?

22.67 The compound 1,1,1-trifluoroacetylacetone (tfa) is a bidentate ligand:

$$CF_3CCH_2CCH_3$$

It forms a tetrahedral complex with Be^{2+} and a square planar complex with Cu^{2+}. Draw structures of these complex ions and identify the type of isomerism exhibited by these ions.

22.68 How many geometric isomers can the following square planar complex have?

22.69 $[Pt(NH_3)_2Cl_2]$ is found to exist in two geometric isomers designated I and II, which react with oxalic acid as follows:

$$I + H_2C_2O_4 \longrightarrow [Pt(NH_3)_2C_2O_4]$$
$$II + H_2C_2O_4 \longrightarrow [Pt(NH_3)_2(HC_2O_4)_2]$$

Comment on the structures of I and II.

Special Problems

22.70 Commercial silver-plating operations frequently use a solution containing the complex $Ag(CN)_2^-$ ion. Because the formation constant (K_f) is quite large, this procedure ensures that the free Ag^+ concentration in solution is low for uniform electrodeposition. In one process, a chemist added 9.0 L of 5.0 M NaCN to 90.0 L of 0.20 M $AgNO_3$. Calculate the concentration of free Ag^+ ions at equilibrium. See Table 16.4 for K_f value.

22.71 Draw qualitative diagrams for the crystal-field splittings in (a) a linear complex ion ML_2, (b) a trigonal-planar complex ion ML_3, and (c) a trigonal-bipyramidal complex ion ML_5.

22.72 (a) The free Cu(I) ion is unstable in solution and has a tendency to disproportionate:

$$2Cu^+(aq) \rightleftharpoons Cu^{2+}(aq) + Cu(s)$$

Use the information in Table 19.1 (p. 828) to calculate the equilibrium constant for the reaction. (b) Based on your result in (a), explain why most Cu(I) compounds are insoluble.

22.73 Consider the following two ligand exchange reactions:

$$[Co(H_2O)_6]^{3+} + 6NH_3 \rightleftharpoons [Co(NH_3)_6]^{3+} + 6H_2O$$
$$[Co(H_2O)_6]^{3+} + 3en \rightleftharpoons [Co(en)_3]^{3+} + 6H_2O$$

(a) Which of the reactions should have a larger $\Delta S°$? (b) Given that the Co—N bond strength is approximately the same in both complexes, which reaction will have a larger equilibrium constant? Explain your choices.

22.74 Copper is also known to exist in +3 oxidation state, which is believed to be involved in some biological electron transfer reactions. (a) Would you expect this oxidation state of copper to be stable? Explain. (b) Name the compound K_3CuF_6 and predict the geometry of the complex ion and its magnetic properties. (c) Most of the known Cu(III) compounds have square planar geometry. Are these compounds diamagnetic or paramagnetic?

Answers to Practice Exercises

22.1 K: $+1$; Au: $+3$. **22.2** Tetraaquadichlorochromium(III) chloride. **22.3** $[Co(en)_3]_2(SO_4)_3$. **22.4** 5.

Dating Paintings with Prussian Blue

In 1995 a painting entitled *Portrait of a Noblewoman* was given to the Mead Art Museum in Amherst, Massachusetts, by an anonymous donor. The small bust-length portrait on wood panel depicts an unidentified adolescent girl of noble birth. The background, blue "wallpaper" with a gold *fleur-de-lys* pattern above a wood-paneled wainscot, is characteristic of settings seen in full-length Renaissance portraits. The rich dress and French royal heraldic device suggest that the subject is a member of the royal court, if not the royal family itself. The painting was attributed to the school of the court painter, François Clouet (1522–1572).

While in the donor's possession, the painting was scratched by a cat. An art conservator who was asked to repair the damage became suspicious about the blue paint used to render the girl's hat and the wallpaper. Subsequent analysis of microscopic samples of the paint revealed that the pigment was Prussian blue (ferric ferrocyanide, $Fe_4[Fe(CN)_6]_3$), a coordination compound discovered by a German dyemaker between 1704 and 1707.

Prior to the discovery of Prussian blue, there were three blue pigments available to painters: azurite $[Cu_3(OH)_2(CO_3)_2]$, smalt (a complex cobalt and arsenic compound), and ultramarine blue, which has the complex formula of $CaNa_7Al_6Si_6O_{24}SO_4$. Prussian blue quickly came to be valued by painters for the intensity and transparency of its color, and it is commonly found in works painted after the early 1700s.

In Prussian blue, the Fe^{2+} ion is bonded to the carbon atom of the cyanide group in an octahedral arrangement, and each Fe^{3+} ion is bonded through the nitrogen atom of the cyanide

Portrait of a Noblewoman.

group with a similar octahedral symmetry. Thus, the cyanide group acts as a bidentate ligand as shown on p. 964.

The blue color arises from the so-called *intervalence charge transfer* between the metal ions. If we designate these two sites of iron as Fe_A^{2+} and Fe_B^{3+}, where A and B denote different sites defined by the ligands, we can represent the transfer of an electron from Fe^{2+} to Fe^{3+} as follows:

$$Fe_A^{2+}, Fe_B^{3+} \xrightarrow{\ h\nu\ } Fe_A^{3+}, Fe_B^{2+}$$

The right-hand side of the preceding equation has more energy than the left-hand side, and the result is an energy level and a light-absorbing scheme similar to that shown in Figure 22.19.

It was Prussian blue's unique color that drew the conservator's suspicion and prompted an analysis that dated the painting at sometime after 1704. Additional analysis of the green pigment used for the jewels showed a mixture of Prussian blue and lemon yellow (zinc chromate, $ZnCrO_4$), a pigment produced commercially beginning around 1850. Thus, *Portrait of a Noblewoman* is no longer ascribed to any sixteenth-century painter, but it is now used by the museum to teach art historians about fakes, forgeries, and mistaken attributions.

Prussian blue can be prepared by mixing a $FeCl_3$ solution with a $K_4Fe(CN)_6$ solution.

Chemical Clues

1. Give the systematic name of Prussian blue. In what region of the visible spectrum does the intervalence charge transfer absorb light?

2. How can you show that the color of Prussian blue arises from intervalence charge transfer and not from a transition within a single ion such as $Fe(CN)_6^{3-}$ or $Fe(CN)_6^{4-}$?

3. Write the formulas and give the systematic names for ferrous ferrocyanide and ferric ferricyanide. Will intervalence charge transfer occur in these two compounds?

4. Kinetically, the $Fe(CN)_6^{4-}$ ion is inert while the $Fe(CN)_6^{3-}$ ion is labile. Based on this knowledge, would you expect Prussian blue to be a poisonous cyanide compound? Explain.

5. When Prussian blue is added to a NaOH solution, an orange-brown precipitate forms. Identify the precipitate.

6. How can the formation of Prussian blue be used to distinguish between Fe^{2+} and Fe^{3+} ions in solution?

23

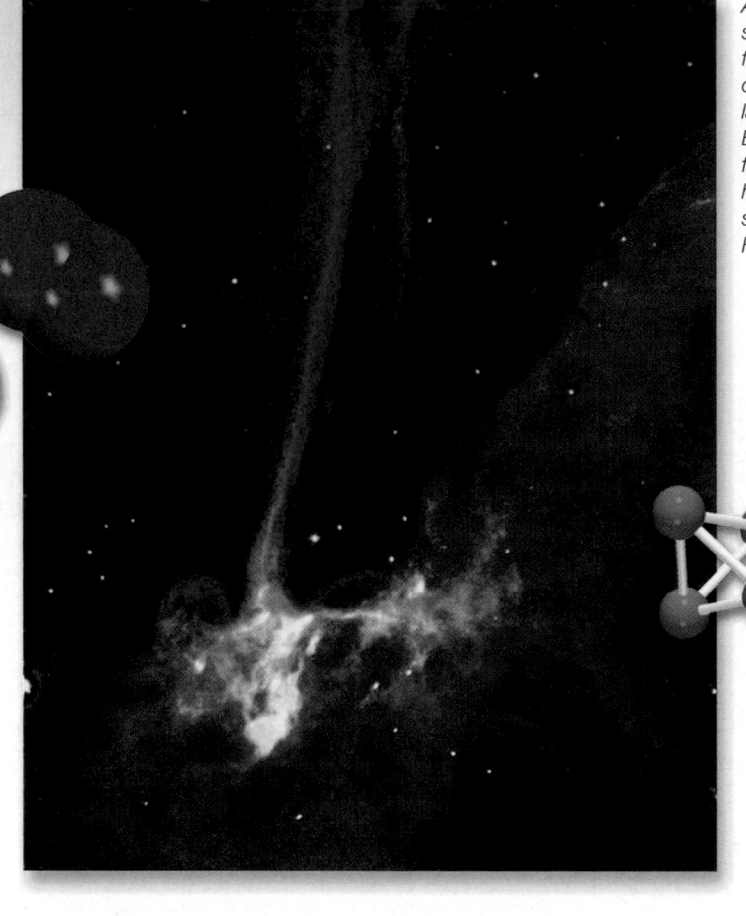

A view of the Cygnus Loop supernova. When most of the fuel in a star is consumed, its core collapses and its outer layer explodes in a supernova. Elements through iron are formed in active stars and heavier elements are formed in supernovas. The models show H_2, He, O_2, P_4, S_8, and Ag.

Nuclear Chemistry

A LOOK AHEAD

- We begin by comparing nuclear reactions with ordinary chemical reactions. We learn to balance nuclear equations in terms of elementary particles like electrons, protons, neutrons, and alpha particles. (23.1)

- Next, we examine the stability of a nucleus in terms of the neutron-to-proton ratio. We use the Einstein mass-energy equation to calculate nuclear binding energy. (23.2)

- We then study the decay of ^{238}U as an example of natural radioactivity. We also see how radioactive decays, which are all first-order rate processes, are used to date objects. (23.3)

- Nuclear transmutations are nuclear reactions induced by the bombardment of a nucleus by particles such as neutrons, alpha particles, or other small nuclei. Transuranium elements are all created this way in a particle accelerator. (23.4)

- In nuclear fission, a heavy nucleus splits into two smaller nuclei when bombarded with a neutron. The process releases large amounts of energy and additional neutrons, which can lead to a chain reaction if a critical mass is present. Nuclear fission reactions are employed in atomic bombs and nuclear reactors. (23.5)

- In nuclear fusion, two small nuclei fuse to yield a larger nucleus with the release of large amounts of energy. Nuclear fusion reactions occur in our sun and other stars and are used in hydrogen or thermonuclear bombs, but nuclear fusion reactors for energy generation are still not commercially available. (23.6)

- Isotopes, especially radioactive isotopes, find many applications in structural determination and mechanistic studies as well as in medicine. (23.7)

- The chapter concludes with a discussion of the biological effects of radiation. (23.8)

Interactive Activity Summary

1. Animation: Radioactive Decay (23.3)

2. Animation: Nuclear Fission (23.5)

Nuclear chemistry is the study of reactions involving changes in atomic nuclei. This branch of chemistry began with the discovery of natural radioactivity by Antoine Becquerel and grew as a result of subsequent investigations by Pierre and Marie Curie and many others. Nuclear chemistry is very much in the news today. In addition to applications in the manufacture of atomic bombs, hydrogen bombs, and neutron bombs, even the peaceful use of nuclear energy has become controversial, in part because of safety concerns about nuclear power plants and also because of problems with radioactive waste disposal. In this chapter we will study nuclear reactions, the stability of the atomic nucleus, radioactivity, and the effects of radiation on biological systems.

23.1 The Nature of Nuclear Reactions

With the exception of hydrogen ($_1^1$H), all nuclei contain two kinds of fundamental particles, called *protons* and *neutrons.* Some nuclei are unstable; they emit particles and/or electromagnetic radiation spontaneously (see Section 2.2). The name for this phenomenon is *radioactivity.* All elements having an atomic number greater than 83 are radioactive. For example, the isotope of polonium, polonium-210 ($_{84}^{210}$Po), decays spontaneously to $_{82}^{206}$Pb by emitting an α particle.

Another type of radioactivity, known as **nuclear transmutation,** *results from the bombardment of nuclei by neutrons, protons, or other nuclei.* An example of a nuclear transmutation is the conversion of atmospheric $_7^{14}$N to $_6^{14}$C and $_1^1$H, which results when the nitrogen isotope captures a neutron (from the sun). In some cases, heavier elements are synthesized from lighter elements. This type of transmutation occurs naturally in outer space, but it can also be achieved artificially, as we will see in Section 23.4.

Radioactive decay and nuclear transmutation are *nuclear reactions,* which differ significantly from ordinary chemical reactions. Table 23.1 summarizes the differences.

Balancing Nuclear Equations

To discuss nuclear reactions in any depth, we need to understand how to write and balance the equations. Writing a nuclear equation differs somewhat from writing equations for chemical reactions. In addition to writing the symbols for various chemical elements, we must also explicitly indicate protons, neutrons, and electrons. In fact, we must show the numbers of protons and neutrons present in *every* species in such an equation.

The symbols for elementary particles are as follows:

$$_1^1\text{p or } _1^1\text{H} \qquad _0^1\text{n} \qquad _{-1}^0e \text{ or } _{-1}^0\beta \qquad _{+1}^0e \text{ or } _{+1}^0\beta \qquad _2^4\text{He or } _2^4\alpha$$
$$\text{proton} \qquad \text{neutron} \qquad \text{electron} \qquad \text{positron} \qquad \alpha \text{ particle}$$

In accordance with the notation used in Section 2.3, the superscript in each case denotes the mass number (the total number of neutrons and protons present) and the subscript is the atomic number (the number of protons). Thus, the "atomic number" of a proton is 1, because there is one proton present, and the "mass number" is also 1, because there is one proton but no neutrons present. On the other hand, the "mass number" of a neutron

---

TABLE 23.1   Comparison of Chemical Reactions and Nuclear Reactions

Chemical Reactions	Nuclear Reactions
1. Atoms are rearranged by the breaking and forming of chemical bonds.	1. Elements (or isotopes of the same elements) are converted from one to another.
2. Only electrons in atomic or molecular orbitals are involved in the breaking and forming of bonds.	2. Protons, neutrons, electrons, and other elementary particles may be involved.
3. Reactions are accompanied by absorption or release of relatively small amounts of energy.	3. Reactions are accompanied by absorption or release of tremendous amounts of energy.
4. Rates of reaction are influenced by temperature, pressure, concentration, and catalysts.	4. Rates of reaction normally are not affected by temperature, pressure, and catalysts.

is 1, but its "atomic number" is zero, because there are no protons present. For the electron, the "mass number" is zero (there are neither protons nor neutrons present), but the "atomic number" is -1, because the electron possesses a unit negative charge.

The symbol $_{-1}^{0}e$ represents an electron in or from an atomic orbital. The symbol $_{-1}^{0}\beta$ represents an electron that, although physically identical to any other electron, comes from a nucleus (in a decay process in which a neutron is converted to a proton and an electron) and not from an atomic orbital. The **positron** *has the same mass as the electron, but bears a +1 charge.* The α particle has two protons and two neutrons, so its atomic number is 2 and its mass number is 4.

In balancing any nuclear equation, we observe the following rules:

- The total number of protons plus neutrons in the products and in the reactants must be the same (conservation of mass number).

- The total number of nuclear charges in the products and in the reactants must be the same (conservation of atomic number).

If we know the atomic numbers and mass numbers of all the species but one in a nuclear equation, we can identify the unknown species by applying these rules, as shown in Example 23.1, which illustrates how to balance nuclear decay equations.

A positron is the antiparticle of the electron. It is produced in some radioactive decays.

Example 23.1

Balance the following nuclear equations (that is, identify the product X):

(a) $_{84}^{212}\text{Po} \longrightarrow \; _{82}^{208}\text{Pb} + X$

(b) $_{55}^{137}\text{Cs} \longrightarrow \; _{56}^{137}\text{Ba} + X$

Strategy In balancing nuclear equations, note that the sum of atomic numbers and that of mass numbers must match on both sides of the equation.

Solution

(a) The mass number and atomic number are 212 and 84, respectively, on the left-hand side and 208 and 82, respectively, on the right-hand side. Thus, X must have a mass number of 4 and an atomic number of 2, which means that it is an α particle. The balanced equation is

$$_{84}^{212}\text{Po} \longrightarrow \; _{82}^{208}\text{Pb} + \; _{2}^{4}\alpha$$

(b) In this case, the mass number is the same on both sides of the equation, but the atomic number of the product is 1 more than that of the reactant. Thus, X must have a mass number of 0 and an atomic number of -1, which means that it is a β particle. The only way this change can come about is to have a neutron in the Cs nucleus transformed into a proton and an electron; that is, $_{0}^{1}\text{n} \longrightarrow \; _{1}^{1}\text{p} + \; _{-1}^{0}\beta$ (note that this process does not alter the mass number). Thus, the balanced equation is

$$_{55}^{137}\text{Cs} \longrightarrow \; _{56}^{137}\text{Ba} + \; _{-1}^{0}\beta$$

We use the $_{-1}^{0}\beta$ notation here because the electron came from the nucleus.

Check Note that the equation in (a) and (b) are balanced for nuclear particles but not for electrical charges. To balance the charges, we would need to add two electrons on the right-hand side of (a) and express barium as a cation (Ba^{+}) in (b).

Similar problems: 23.5, 23.6.

Practice Exercise Identify X in the following nuclear equation:

$$_{33}^{78}\text{As} \longrightarrow \; _{-1}^{0}\beta + X$$

23.2 Nuclear Stability

The nucleus occupies a very small portion of the total volume of an atom, but it contains most of the atom's mass because both the protons and the neutrons reside there. In studying the stability of the atomic nucleus, it is helpful to know something about its density, because it tells us how tightly the particles are packed together. As a sample calculation, let us assume that a nucleus has a radius of 5×10^{-3} pm and a mass of 1×10^{-22} g. These figures correspond roughly to a nucleus containing 30 protons and 30 neutrons. Density is mass/volume, and we can calculate the volume from the known radius (the volume of a sphere is $\frac{4}{3}\pi r^3$, where r is the radius of the sphere). First, we convert the pm units to cm. Then we calculate the density in g/cm³:

$$r = 5 \times 10^{-3} \text{ pm} \times \frac{1 \times 10^{-12} \text{ m}}{1 \text{ pm}} \times \frac{100 \text{ cm}}{1 \text{ m}} = 5 \times 10^{-13} \text{ cm}$$

$$\text{density} = \frac{\text{mass}}{\text{volume}} = \frac{1 \times 10^{-22} \text{ g}}{\frac{4}{3}\pi r^3} = \frac{1 \times 10^{-22} \text{ g}}{\frac{4}{3}\pi (5 \times 10^{-13} \text{ cm})^3}$$

$$= 2 \times 10^{14} \text{ g/cm}^3$$

To dramatize the almost incomprehensibly high density, it has been suggested that it is equivalent to packing the mass of all the world's automobiles into one thimble.

This is an exceedingly high density. The highest density known for an element is 22.6 g/cm³, for osmium (Os). Thus, the average atomic nucleus is roughly 9×10^{12} (or 9 trillion) times more dense than the densest element known!

The enormously high density of the nucleus prompts us to wonder what holds the particles together so tightly. From *Coulomb's law* we know that like charges repel and unlike charges attract one another. We would thus expect the protons to repel one another strongly, particularly when we consider how close they must be to each other. This indeed is so. However, in addition to the repulsion, there are also short-range attractions between proton and proton, proton and neutron, and neutron and neutron. The stability of any nucleus is determined by the difference between coulombic repulsion and the short-range attraction. If repulsion outweighs attraction, the nucleus disintegrates, emitting particles and/or radiation. If attractive forces prevail, the nucleus is stable.

The principal factor that determines whether a nucleus is stable is the *neutron-to-proton ratio (n/p)*. For stable atoms of elements having low atomic number, the n/p value is close to 1. As the atomic number increases, the neutron-to-proton ratios of the stable nuclei become greater than 1. This deviation at higher atomic numbers arises because a larger number of neutrons is needed to counteract the strong repulsion among the protons and stabilize the nucleus. The following rules are useful in predicting nuclear stability:

1. Nuclei that contain 2, 8, 20, 50, 82, or 126 protons or neutrons are generally more stable than nuclei that do not possess these numbers. For example, there are 10 stable isotopes of tin (Sn) with the atomic number 50 and only 2 stable isotopes of antimony (Sb) with the atomic number 51. The numbers 2, 8, 20, 50, 82, and 126 are called *magic numbers*. The significance of these numbers for nuclear stability is similar to the numbers of electrons associated with the very stable noble gases (that is, 2, 10, 18, 36, 54, and 86 electrons).

2. Nuclei with even numbers of both protons and neutrons are generally more stable than those with odd numbers of these particles (Table 23.2).

3. All isotopes of the elements with atomic numbers higher than 83 are radioactive. All isotopes of technetium (Tc, $Z = 43$) and promethium (Pm, $Z = 61$) are radioactive.

Figure 23.1 shows a plot of the number of neutrons versus the number of protons in various isotopes. The stable nuclei are located in an area of the graph known as the *belt of stability*. Most radioactive nuclei lie outside this belt. Above the stability belt,

TABLE 23.2	Number of Stable Isotopes with Even and Odd Numbers of Protons and Neutrons	
Protons	**Neutrons**	**Number of Stable Isotopes**
Odd	Odd	4
Odd	Even	50
Even	Odd	53
Even	Even	164

the nuclei have higher neutron-to-proton ratios than those within the belt (for the same number of protons). To lower this ratio (and hence move down toward the belt of stability), these nuclei undergo the following process, called *β-particle emission*:

$$\ce{_0^1n \longrightarrow _1^1p + _{-1}^0\beta}$$

Beta-particle emission leads to an increase in the number of protons in the nucleus and a simultaneous decrease in the number of neutrons. Some examples are

$$\ce{_6^{14}C \longrightarrow _7^{14}N + _{-1}^0\beta}$$
$$\ce{_{19}^{40}K \longrightarrow _{20}^{40}Ca + _{-1}^0\beta}$$
$$\ce{_{40}^{97}Zr \longrightarrow _{41}^{97}Nb + _{-1}^0\beta}$$

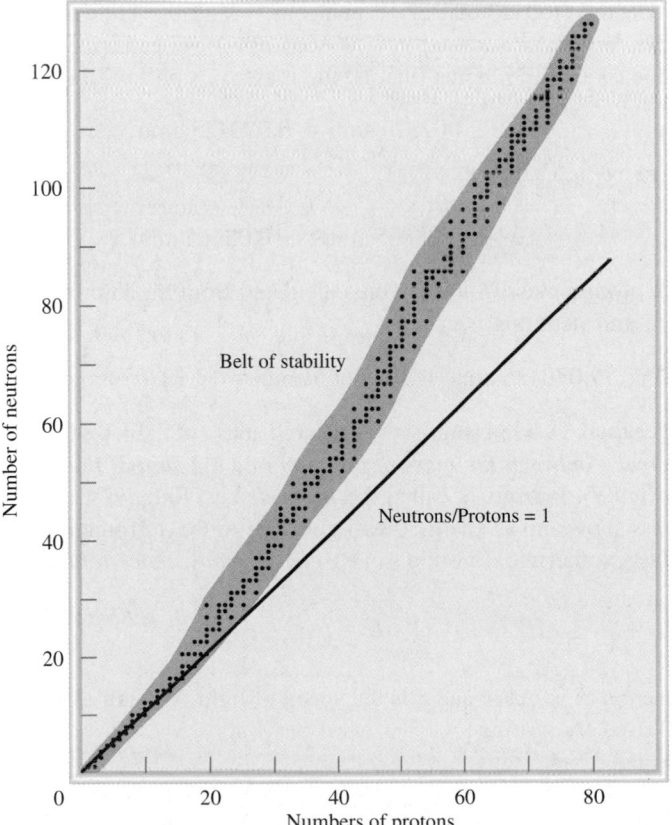

Figure 23.1 *Plot of neutrons versus protons for various stable isotopes, represented by dots. The straight line represents the points at which the neutron-to-proton ratio equals 1. The shaded area represents the belt of stability.*

Below the stability belt the nuclei have lower neutron-to-proton ratios than those in the belt (for the same number of protons). To increase this ratio (and hence move up toward the belt of stability), these nuclei either emit a positron

$$\frac{1}{1}p \longrightarrow \frac{1}{0}n + \frac{0}{+1}\beta$$

or undergo electron capture. An example of positron emission is

$$^{38}_{19}K \longrightarrow {}^{38}_{18}Ar + {}^{0}_{+1}\beta$$

Electron capture is the capture of an electron—usually a 1*s* electron—by the nucleus. The captured electron combines with a proton to form a neutron so that the atomic number decreases by one while the mass number remains the same. This process has the same net effect as positron emission:

$$^{37}_{18}Ar + {}^{0}_{-1}e \longrightarrow {}^{37}_{17}Cl$$
$$^{55}_{26}Fe + {}^{0}_{-1}e \longrightarrow {}^{55}_{25}Mn$$

We use $_{-1}^{0}e$ rather than $_{-1}^{0}\beta$ here because the electron came from an atomic orbital and not from the nucleus.

Nuclear Binding Energy

A quantitative measure of nuclear stability is the **nuclear binding energy,** which is *the energy required to break up a nucleus into its component protons and neutrons.* This quantity represents the conversion of mass to energy that occurs during an exothermic nuclear reaction.

The concept of nuclear binding energy evolved from studies of nuclear properties showing that the masses of nuclei are always less than the sum of the masses of the **nucleons,** which is *a general term for the protons and neutrons in a nucleus.* For example, the $^{19}_{9}F$ isotope has an atomic mass of 18.9984 amu. The nucleus has 9 protons and 10 neutrons and therefore a total of 19 nucleons. Using the known masses of the $^{1}_{1}H$ atom (1.007825 amu) and the neutron (1.008665 amu), we can carry out the following analysis. The mass of 9 $^{1}_{1}H$ atoms (that is, the mass of 9 protons and 9 electrons) is

$$9 \times 1.007825 \text{ amu} = 9.070425 \text{ amu}$$

and the mass of 10 neutrons is

$$10 \times 1.008665 \text{ amu} = 10.08665 \text{ amu}$$

Therefore, the atomic mass of a $^{19}_{9}F$ atom calculated from the known numbers of electrons, protons, and neutrons is

$$9.070425 \text{ amu} + 10.08665 \text{ amu} = 19.15708 \text{ amu}$$

There is no change in the electron's mass because it is not a nucleon.

which is larger than 18.9984 amu (the measured mass of $^{19}_{9}F$) by 0.1587 amu. *The difference between the mass of an atom and the sum of the masses of its protons, neutrons, and electrons* is called the **mass defect.** Relativity theory tells us that the loss in mass shows up as energy (heat) given off to the surroundings. Thus, the formation of $^{19}_{9}F$ is exothermic. Einstein's *mass-energy equivalence relationship* states that

This is the only equation listed in the Bartlett's quotations.

$$E = mc^2 \qquad (23.1)$$

where E is energy, m is mass, and c is the speed of light. We can calculate the amount of energy released by writing

$$\Delta E = (\Delta m)c^2 \qquad (23.2)$$

where ΔE and Δm are defined as follows:

$$\Delta E = \text{energy of product} - \text{energy of reactants}$$
$$\Delta m = \text{mass of product} - \text{mass of reactants}$$

Thus, the change in mass is given by

$$\Delta m = 18.9984 \text{ amu} - 19.15708 \text{ amu}$$
$$= -0.1587 \text{ amu}$$

Because $^{19}_{9}F$ has a mass that is less than the mass calculated from the number of electrons and nucleons present, Δm is a negative quantity. Consequently, ΔE is also a negative quantity; that is, energy is released to the surroundings as a result of the formation of the fluorine-19 nucleus. So we calculate ΔE as follows:

$$\Delta E = (-0.1587 \text{ amu})(3.00 \times 10^8 \text{ m/s})^2$$
$$= -1.43 \times 10^{16} \text{ amu m}^2/\text{s}^2$$

With the conversion factors

$$1 \text{ kg} = 6.022 \times 10^{26} \text{ amu}$$
$$1 \text{ J} = 1 \text{ kg m}^2/\text{s}^2$$

we obtain

$$\Delta E = \left(-1.43 \times 10^{16} \frac{\text{amu} \cdot \text{m}^2}{\text{s}^2}\right) \times \left(\frac{1.00 \text{ kg}}{6.022 \times 10^{26} \text{ amu}}\right) \times \left(\frac{1 \text{ J}}{1 \text{ kg m}^2/\text{s}^2}\right)$$
$$= -2.37 \times 10^{-11} \text{ J}$$

This is the amount of energy released when one fluorine-19 nucleus is formed from 9 protons and 10 neutrons. The nuclear binding energy of the nucleus is 2.37×10^{-11} J, which is the amount of energy needed to decompose the nucleus into separate protons and neutrons. In the formation of 1 mole of fluorine nuclei, for instance, the energy released is

$$\Delta E = (-2.37 \times 10^{-11} \text{ J})(6.022 \times 10^{23}/\text{mol})$$
$$= -1.43 \times 10^{13} \text{ J/mol}$$
$$= -1.43 \times 10^{10} \text{ kJ/mol}$$

The nuclear binding energy, therefore, is 1.43×10^{10} kJ for 1 mole of fluorine-19 nuclei, which is a tremendously large quantity when we consider that the enthalpies of ordinary chemical reactions are of the order of only 200 kJ. The procedure we have followed can be used to calculate the nuclear binding energy of any nucleus.

As we have noted, nuclear binding energy is an indication of the stability of a nucleus. However, in comparing the stability of any two nuclei we must account for the fact that they have different numbers of nucleons. For this reason it is more meaningful to use the *nuclear binding energy per nucleon,* defined as

$$\text{nuclear binding energy per nucleon} = \frac{\text{nuclear binding energy}}{\text{number of nucleons}}$$

For the fluorine-19 nucleus,

$$\text{nuclear binding energy per nucleon} = \frac{2.37 \times 10^{-11} \text{ J}}{19 \text{ nucleons}}$$
$$= 1.25 \times 10^{-12} \text{ J/nucleon}$$

Figure 23.2 *Plot of nuclear binding energy per nucleon versus mass number.*

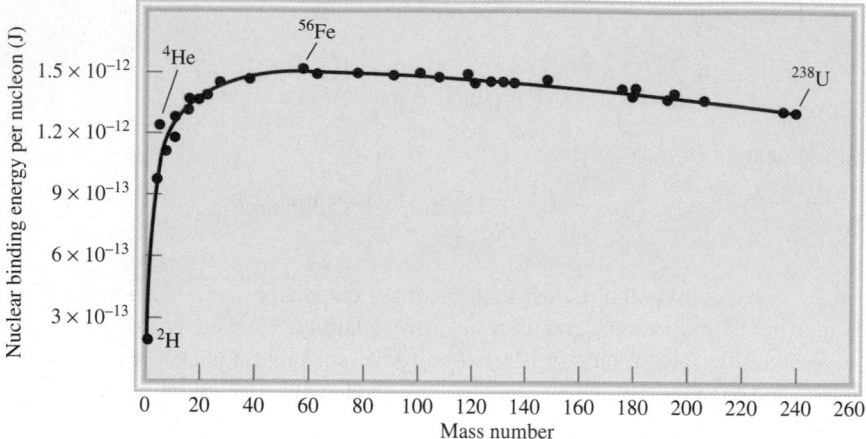

The nuclear binding energy per nucleon enables us to compare the stability of all nuclei on a common basis. Figure 23.2 shows the variation of nuclear binding energy per nucleon plotted against mass number. As you can see, the curve rises rather steeply. The highest binding energies per nucleon belong to elements with intermediate mass numbers—between 40 and 100—and are greatest for elements in the iron, cobalt, and nickel region (the Group 8B elements) of the periodic table. This means that the *net* attractive forces among the particles (protons and neutrons) are greatest for the nuclei of these elements.

Nuclear binding energy and nuclear binding energy per nucleon are calculated for an iodine nucleus in Example 23.2.

Example 23.2

The atomic mass of $^{127}_{53}I$ is 126.9004 amu. Calculate the nuclear binding energy of this nucleus and the corresponding nuclear binding energy per nucleon.

Strategy To calculate the nuclear binding energy, we first determine the difference between the mass of the nucleus and the mass of all the protons and neutrons, which gives us the mass defect. Next, we apply Equation (23.2) [$\Delta E = (\Delta m)c^2$].

Solution There are 53 protons and 74 neutrons in the iodine nucleus. The mass of 53 ^1_1H atom is

$$53 \times 1.007825 \text{ amu} = 53.41473 \text{ amu}$$

and the mass of 74 neutrons is

$$74 \times 1.008665 \text{ amu} = 74.64121 \text{ amu}$$

Therefore, the predicted mass for $^{127}_{53}I$ is 53.41473 + 74.64121 = 128.05594 amu, and the mass defect is

$$\Delta m = 126.9004 \text{ amu} - 128.05594 \text{ amu}$$
$$= -1.1555 \text{ amu}$$

(Continued)

The energy released is

$$\Delta E = (\Delta m)c^2$$
$$= (-1.1555 \text{ amu})(3.00 \times 10^8 \text{ m/s})^2$$
$$= -1.04 \times 10^{17} \text{ amu} \cdot \text{m}^2/\text{s}^2$$

Let's convert to a more familiar energy unit of joules. Recall that $1 \text{ J} = 1 \text{ kg} \cdot \text{m}^2/\text{s}^2$. Therefore, we need to convert amu to kg:

$$\Delta E = -1.04 \times 10^{17} \frac{\text{amu} \cdot \text{m}^2}{\text{s}^2} \times \frac{1.00 \text{ g}}{6.022 \times 10^{23} \text{ amu}} \times \frac{1 \text{ kg}}{1000 \text{ g}}$$
$$= -1.73 \times 10^{-10} \frac{\text{kg} \cdot \text{m}^2}{\text{s}^2} = -1.73 \times 10^{-10} \text{ J}$$

Thus, the nuclear binding energy is $1.73 \times 10^{-10} \text{ J}$. The nuclear binding energy per nucleon is obtained as follows:

The neutron-to-proton ratio is 1.4, which places iodine-127 in the belt of stability.

$$\frac{1.73 \times 10^{-10} \text{ J}}{127 \text{ nucleons}} = 1.36 \times 10^{-12} \text{ J/nucleon}$$

Similar problems: 23.19, 23.20.

Practice Exercise Calculate the nuclear binding energy (in J) and the nuclear binding energy per nucleon of $^{209}_{83}\text{Bi}$ (208.9804 amu).

23.3 Natural Radioactivity

Nuclei outside the belt of stability, as well as nuclei with more than 83 protons, tend to be unstable. The spontaneous emission by unstable nuclei of particles or electromagnetic radiation, or both, is known as radioactivity. The main types of radiation are: α particles (or doubly charged helium nuclei, He^{2+}); β particles (or electrons); γ rays, which are very-short-wavelength (0.1 nm to 10^{-4} nm) electromagnetic waves; positron emission; and electron capture.

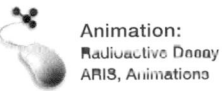

Animation:
Radioactive Decay
ARIS, Animations

The disintegration of a radioactive nucleus is often the beginning of a ***radioactive decay series,*** which is *a sequence of nuclear reactions that ultimately result in the formation of a stable isotope.* Table 23.3 shows the decay series of naturally occurring uranium-238, which involves 14 steps. This decay scheme, known as the *uranium decay series,* also shows the half-lives of all the products.

It is important to be able to balance the nuclear reaction for each of the steps in a radioactive decay series. For example, the first step in the uranium decay series is the decay of uranium-238 to thorium-234, with the emission of an α particle. Hence, the reaction is

$$^{238}_{92}\text{U} \longrightarrow {}^{234}_{90}\text{Th} + {}^{4}_{2}\alpha$$

The next step is represented by

$$^{234}_{90}\text{Th} \longrightarrow {}^{234}_{91}\text{Pa} + {}^{0}_{-1}\beta$$

and so on. In a discussion of radioactive decay steps, the beginning radioactive isotope is called the *parent* and the product, the *daughter.*

TABLE 23.3   The Uranium Decay Series*

$$^{238}_{92}\text{U} \xrightarrow{\quad} \alpha \quad 4.51 \times 10^9 \text{ yr}$$

$$^{234}_{90}\text{Th} \xrightarrow{\quad} \beta \quad 24.1 \text{ days}$$

$$^{234}_{91}\text{Pa} \xrightarrow{\quad} \beta \quad 1.17 \text{ min}$$

$$^{234}_{92}\text{U} \xrightarrow{\quad} \alpha \quad 2.47 \times 10^5 \text{ yr}$$

$$^{230}_{90}\text{Th} \xrightarrow{\quad} \alpha \quad 7.5 \times 10^4 \text{ yr}$$

$$^{226}_{88}\text{Ra} \xrightarrow{\quad} \alpha \quad 1.60 \times 10^3 \text{ yr}$$

$$^{222}_{86}\text{Rn} \xrightarrow{\quad} \alpha \quad 3.82 \text{ days}$$

$$\beta \xleftarrow{\quad} {}^{218}_{84}\text{Po} \xrightarrow{\quad} \alpha$$
$$0.04\% \qquad\qquad 3.05 \text{ min}$$

$$\alpha \xleftarrow{\quad} {}^{218}_{85}\text{At} \qquad {}^{214}_{82}\text{Pb} \xrightarrow{\quad} \beta$$
$$2 \text{ s} \qquad\qquad\qquad 26.8 \text{ min}$$

$$\beta \xleftarrow{\quad} {}^{214}_{83}\text{Bi} \xrightarrow{\quad} \alpha$$
$$99.96\% \qquad\qquad 19.7 \text{ min}$$

$$\alpha \xleftarrow{\quad} {}^{214}_{84}\text{Po} \qquad {}^{210}_{81}\text{Tl} \xrightarrow{\quad} \beta$$
$$1.6 \times 10^{-4} \text{ s} \qquad\qquad 1.32 \text{ min}$$

$$^{210}_{82}\text{Pb} \xrightarrow{\quad} \beta \quad 20.4 \text{ yr}$$

$$\beta \xleftarrow{\quad} {}^{210}_{83}\text{Bi} \xrightarrow{\quad} \alpha$$
$$\sim 100\% \qquad\qquad 5.01 \text{ days}$$

$$\alpha \xleftarrow{\quad} {}^{210}_{84}\text{Po} \qquad {}^{206}_{81}\text{Tl} \xrightarrow{\quad} \beta$$
$$138 \text{ days} \qquad\qquad 4.20 \text{ min}$$

$$^{206}_{82}\text{Pb}$$

*The times denote the half-lives.

Kinetics of Radioactive Decay

All radioactive decays obey first-order kinetics. Therefore, the rate of radioactive decay at any time t is given by

$$\text{rate of decay at time } t = \lambda N$$

where λ is the first-order rate constant and N is the number of radioactive nuclei present at time t. (We use λ instead of k for rate constant in accord with the notation used by nuclear scientists.) According to Equation (13.3), the number of radioactive nuclei at time zero (N_0) and time t (N_t) is

$$\ln \frac{N_t}{N_0} = -\lambda t$$

and the corresponding half-life of the reaction is given by Equation (13.5):

$$t_{\frac{1}{2}} = \frac{0.693}{\lambda}$$

The half-lives (hence the rate constants) of radioactive isotopes vary greatly from nucleus to nucleus. For example, looking at Table 23.3, we find two extreme cases:

$$^{238}_{92}\text{U} \longrightarrow {}^{234}_{90}\text{Th} + {}^{4}_{2}\alpha \qquad t_{\frac{1}{2}} = 4.51 \times 10^9 \text{ yr}$$
$$^{214}_{84}\text{Po} \longrightarrow {}^{210}_{82}\text{Pb} + {}^{4}_{2}\alpha \qquad t_{\frac{1}{2}} = 1.6 \times 10^{-4} \text{ s}$$

We do not have to wait 4.51×10^9 yr to make a half-life measurement of uranium-238. Its value can be calculated from the rate constant using Equation (13.5).

The ratio of these two rate constants after conversion to the same time unit is about 1×10^{21}, an enormously large number. Furthermore, the rate constants are unaffected by changes in environmental conditions such as temperature and pressure. These highly unusual features are not seen in ordinary chemical reactions (see Table 23.1).

Dating Based on Radioactive Decay

The half-lives of radioactive isotopes have been used as "atomic clocks" to determine the ages of certain objects. Some examples of dating by radioactive decay measurements will be described here.

Radiocarbon Dating

The carbon-14 isotope is produced when atmospheric nitrogen is bombarded by cosmic rays:

$$^{14}_{7}\text{N} + {}^{1}_{0}\text{n} \longrightarrow {}^{14}_{6}\text{C} + {}^{1}_{1}\text{H}$$

The radioactive carbon-14 isotope decays according to the equation

$$^{14}_{6}\text{C} \longrightarrow {}^{14}_{7}\text{N} + {}^{0}_{-1}\beta$$

This decay series is the basis of the radiocarbon dating technique described on p. 568.

Dating Using Uranium-238 Isotopes

Because some of the intermediate products in the uranium decay series have very long half-lives (see Table 23.3), this series is particularly suitable for estimating the age of rocks in the earth and of extraterrestrial objects. The half-life for the first step ($^{238}_{92}\text{U}$ to $^{234}_{90}\text{Th}$) is 4.51×10^9 yr. This is about 20,000 times the second largest value (that is, 2.47×10^5 yr), which is the half-life for $^{234}_{92}\text{U}$ to $^{230}_{90}\text{Th}$. Therefore, as a good approximation we can assume that the half-life for the overall process (that is, from $^{238}_{92}\text{U}$ to $^{206}_{82}\text{Pb}$) is governed solely by the first step:

We can think of the first step as the rate-determining step in the overall process.

$$^{238}_{92}\text{U} \longrightarrow {}^{206}_{82}\text{Pb} + 8{}^{4}_{2}\alpha + 6{}^{0}_{-1}\beta \qquad t_{\frac{1}{2}} = 4.51 \times 10^9 \text{ yr}$$

In naturally occurring uranium minerals we should and do find some lead-206 isotopes formed by radioactive decay. Assuming that no lead was present when the mineral was formed and that the mineral has not undergone chemical changes that

Figure 23.3 *After one half-life, half of the original uranium-238 is converted to lead-206.*

would allow the lead-206 isotope to be separated from the parent uranium-238, it is possible to estimate the age of the rocks from the mass ratio of $^{206}_{82}\text{Pb}$ to $^{238}_{92}\text{U}$. The previous equation tells us that for every mole, or 238 g, of uranium that undergoes complete decay, 1 mole, or 206 g, of lead is formed. If only half a mole of uranium-238 has undergone decay, the mass ratio $^{206}\text{Pb}/^{238}\text{U}$ becomes

$$\frac{206 \text{ g}/2}{238 \text{ g}/2} = 0.866$$

and the process would have taken a half-life of 4.51×10^9 yr to complete (Figure 23.3). Ratios lower than 0.866 mean that the rocks are less than 4.51×10^9 yr old, and higher ratios suggest a greater age. Interestingly, studies based on the uranium series as well as other decay series put the age of the oldest rocks and, therefore, probably the age of Earth itself at 4.5×10^9, or 4.5 billion, years.

Dating Using Potassium-40 Isotopes

This is one of the most important techniques in geochemistry. The radioactive potassium-40 isotope decays by several different modes, but the relevant one as far as dating is concerned is that of electron capture:

$$^{40}_{19}\text{K} + {}^{0}_{-1}e \longrightarrow {}^{40}_{18}\text{Ar} \qquad\qquad t_{\frac{1}{2}} = 1.2 \times 10^9 \text{ yr}$$

The accumulation of gaseous argon-40 is used to gauge the age of a specimen. When a potassium-40 atom in a mineral decays, argon-40 is trapped in the lattice of the mineral and can escape only if the material is melted. Melting, therefore, is the procedure for analyzing a mineral sample in the laboratory. The amount of argon-40 present can be conveniently measured with a mass spectrometer (see p. 86). Knowing the ratio of argon-40 to potassium-40 in the mineral and the half-life of decay makes it possible to establish the ages of rocks ranging from millions to billions of years old.

23.4 Nuclear Transmutation

The scope of nuclear chemistry would be rather narrow if study were limited to natural radioactive elements. An experiment performed by Rutherford in 1919, however, suggested the possibility of producing radioactivity artificially. When he bombarded a sample of nitrogen with α particles, the following reaction took place:

$$^{14}_{7}\text{N} + {}^{4}_{2}\alpha \longrightarrow {}^{17}_{8}\text{O} + {}^{1}_{1}\text{p}$$

Note that the ^{17}O isotope is not radioactive.

An oxygen-17 isotope was produced with the emission of a proton. This reaction demonstrated for the first time the feasibility of converting one element into another, by the process of nuclear transmutation. Nuclear transmutation differs from radioactive decay in that the former is brought about by the collision of two particles.

The preceding reaction can be abbreviated as $^{14}_{7}\text{N}(\alpha,\text{p})^{17}_{8}\text{O}$. Note that in the parentheses the bombarding particle is written first, followed by the ejected particle. Example 23.3 illustrates the use of this notation to represent nuclear transmutations.

Example 23.3

Write the balanced equation for the nuclear reaction $^{56}_{26}\text{Fe}(\text{d},\alpha)^{54}_{25}\text{Mn}$, where d represents the deuterium nucleus (that is, $^{2}_{1}\text{H}$).

(Continued)

Strategy To write the balanced nuclear equation, remember that the first isotope $^{56}_{26}Fe$ is the reactant and the second isotope $^{54}_{25}Mn$ is the product. The first symbol in parentheses (d) is the bombarding particle and the second symbol in parentheses (α) is the particle emitted as a result of nuclear transmutation.

Solution The abbreviation tells us that when iron-56 is bombarded with a deuterium nucleus, it produces the manganese-54 nucleus plus an α particle. Thus, the equation for this reaction is

$$^{56}_{26}Fe + ^{2}_{1}H \longrightarrow ^{4}_{2}\alpha + ^{54}_{25}Mn$$

Check Make sure that the sum of mass numbers and the sum of atomic numbers are the same on both sides of the equation.

Similar problems: 23.33, 23.34.

Practice Exercise Write a balanced equation for $^{106}_{46}Pd(\alpha,p)^{109}_{47}Ag$.

The Transuranium Elements

Particle accelerators made it possible to synthesize the so-called *transuranium elements, elements with atomic numbers greater than 92.* Neptunium ($Z = 93$) was first prepared in 1940. Since then, 23 other transuranium elements have been synthesized. All isotopes of these elements are radioactive. Table 23.4 lists the transuranium elements up to $Z = 109$ and the reactions through which they are formed.

Although light elements are generally not radioactive, they can be made so by bombarding their nuclei with appropriate particles. As we saw earlier, the radioactive

TABLE 23.4	**The Transuranium Elements**		

Atomic Number	Name	Symbol	Preparation
93	Neptunium	Np	$^{238}_{92}U + ^{1}_{0}n \longrightarrow ^{239}_{93}Np + ^{0}_{-1}\beta$
94	Plutonium	Pu	$^{239}_{93}Np \longrightarrow ^{239}_{94}Pu + ^{0}_{-1}\beta$
95	Americium	Am	$^{239}_{94}Pu + ^{1}_{0}n \longrightarrow ^{240}_{95}Am + ^{0}_{-1}\beta$
96	Curium	Cm	$^{239}_{94}Pu + ^{4}_{2}\alpha \longrightarrow ^{242}_{96}Cm + ^{1}_{0}n$
97	Berkelium	Bk	$^{241}_{95}Am + ^{4}_{2}\alpha \longrightarrow ^{243}_{97}Bk + 2^{1}_{0}n$
98	Californium	Cf	$^{242}_{96}Cm + ^{4}_{2}\alpha \longrightarrow ^{245}_{98}Cf + ^{1}_{0}n$
99	Einsteinium	Es	$^{238}_{92}U + 15^{1}_{0}n \longrightarrow ^{253}_{99}Es + 7^{0}_{-1}\beta$
100	Fermium	Fm	$^{238}_{92}U + 17^{1}_{0}n \longrightarrow ^{255}_{100}Fm + 8^{0}_{-1}\beta$
101	Mendelevium	Md	$^{253}_{99}Es + ^{4}_{2}\alpha \longrightarrow ^{256}_{101}Md + ^{1}_{0}n$
102	Nobelium	No	$^{246}_{96}Cm + ^{12}_{6}C \longrightarrow ^{254}_{102}No + 4^{1}_{0}n$
103	Lawrencium	Lr	$^{252}_{98}Cf + ^{10}_{5}B \longrightarrow ^{257}_{103}Lr + 5^{1}_{0}n$
104	Rutherfordium	Rf	$^{249}_{98}Cf + ^{12}_{6}C \longrightarrow ^{257}_{104}Rf + 4^{1}_{0}n$
105	Dubnium	Db	$^{249}_{98}Cf + ^{15}_{7}N \longrightarrow ^{260}_{105}Db + 4^{1}_{0}n$
106	Seaborgium	Sg	$^{249}_{98}Cf + ^{18}_{8}O \longrightarrow ^{263}_{106}Sg + 4^{1}_{0}n$
107	Bohrium	Bh	$^{209}_{83}Bi + ^{54}_{24}Cr \longrightarrow ^{262}_{107}Bh + ^{1}_{0}n$
108	Hassium	Hs	$^{208}_{82}Pb + ^{58}_{26}Fe \longrightarrow ^{265}_{108}Hs + ^{1}_{0}n$
109	Meitnerium	Mt	$^{209}_{83}Bi + ^{58}_{26}Fe \longrightarrow ^{266}_{109}Mt + ^{1}_{0}n$

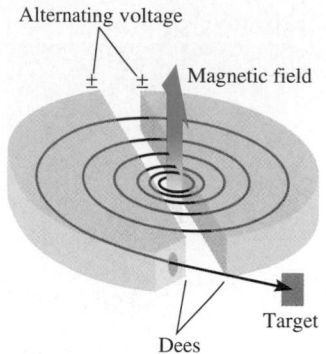

Alternating voltage

Magnetic field

Target

Dees

Figure 23.4 *Schematic diagram of a cyclotron particle accelerator. The particle (an ion) to be accelerated starts at the center and is forced to move in a spiral path through the influence of electric and magnetic fields until it emerges at a high velocity. The magnetic fields are perpendicular to the plane of the dees (so-called because of their shape), which are hollow and serve as electrodes.*

carbon-14 isotope can be prepared by bombarding nitrogen-14 with neutrons. Tritium, ^3_1H, is prepared according to the following bombardment:

$$^6_3\text{Li} + ^1_0\text{n} \longrightarrow ^3_1\text{H} + ^4_2\alpha$$

Tritium decays with the emission of β particles:

$$^3_1\text{H} \longrightarrow ^3_2\text{He} + ^{0}_{-1}\beta \qquad\qquad t_{\frac{1}{2}} = 12.5 \text{ yr}$$

Many synthetic isotopes are prepared by using neutrons as projectiles. This approach is particularly convenient because neutrons carry no charges and therefore are not repelled by the targets—the nuclei. In contrast, when the projectiles are positively charged particles (for example, protons or α particles), they must have considerable kinetic energy to overcome the electrostatic repulsion between themselves and the target nuclei. The synthesis of phosphorus from aluminum is one example:

$$^{27}_{13}\text{Al} + ^4_2\alpha \longrightarrow ^{30}_{15}\text{P} + ^1_0\text{n}$$

A *particle accelerator* uses electric and magnetic fields to increase the kinetic energy of charged species so that a reaction will occur (Figure 23.4). Alternating the polarity (that is, + and −) on specially constructed plates causes the particles to accelerate along a spiral path. When they have the energy necessary to initiate the desired nuclear reaction, they are guided out of the accelerator into a collision with a target substance.

Various designs have been developed for particle accelerators, one of which accelerates particles along a linear path of about 3 km (Figure 23.5). It is now possible to accelerate particles to a speed well above 90 percent of the speed of light. (According to Einstein's theory of relativity, it is impossible for a particle to move *at* the speed of light. The only exception is the photon, which has a zero rest mass.) The extremely energetic particles produced in accelerators are employed by physicists to smash atomic nuclei to fragments. Studying the debris from such disintegrations provides valuable information about nuclear structure and binding forces.

Figure 23.5 *A section of a particle accelerator.*

23.5 Nuclear Fission

Nuclear fission is the process in which *a heavy nucleus (mass number > 200) divides to form smaller nuclei of intermediate mass and one or more neutrons*. Because the heavy nucleus is less stable than its products (see Figure 23.2), this process releases a large amount of energy.

The first nuclear fission reaction to be studied was that of uranium-235 bombarded with slow neutrons, whose speed is comparable to that of air molecules at room temperature. Under these conditions, uranium-235 undergoes fission, as shown in Figure 23.6. Actually, this reaction is very complex: More than 30 different elements have been found among the fission products (Figure 23.7). A representative reaction is

$$^{235}_{92}\text{U} + ^{1}_{0}\text{n} \longrightarrow ^{90}_{38}\text{Sr} + ^{143}_{54}\text{Xe} + 3^{1}_{0}\text{n}$$

Although many heavy nuclei can be made to undergo fission, only the fission of naturally occurring uranium-235 and of the artificial isotope plutonium-239 has any practical importance. Table 23.5 shows the nuclear binding energies of uranium-235 and its fission products. As the table shows, the binding energy per nucleon for uranium-235 is less than the sum of the binding energies for strontium-90 and xenon-143. Therefore, when a uranium-235 nucleus is split into two smaller nuclei, a certain amount of energy is released. Let us estimate the magnitude of this energy. The difference between the binding energies of the reactants and products is $(1.23 \times 10^{-10} + 1.92 \times 10^{-10})$ J $- (2.82 \times 10^{-10})$ J, or 3.3×10^{-11} J per uranium-235 nucleus. For 1 mole of uranium-235, the energy released would be $(3.3 \times 10^{-11}) \times (6.02 \times 10^{23})$, or 2.0×10^{13} J. This is an extremely exothermic reaction, considering that the heat of combustion of 1 ton of coal is only about 5×10^7 J.

The significant feature of uranium-235 fission is not just the enormous amount of energy released, but the fact that more neutrons are produced than are originally captured in the process. This property makes possible a ***nuclear chain reaction,*** which is *a self-sustaining sequence of nuclear fission reactions*. The neutrons generated during the initial stages of fission can induce fission in other uranium-235 nuclei, which in turn produce more neutrons, and so on. In less than a second, the reaction can become uncontrollable, liberating a tremendous amount of heat to the surroundings.

For a chain reaction to occur, enough uranium-235 must be present in the sample to capture the neutrons. Otherwise, many of the neutrons will escape from the

TABLE 23.5	
Nuclear Binding Energies of ^{235}U and Its Fission Products	
	Nuclear Binding Energy
^{235}U	2.82×10^{-10} J
^{90}Sr	1.23×10^{-10} J
^{143}Xe	1.92×10^{-10} J

Animation:
Nuclear Fission
ARIS, Animations

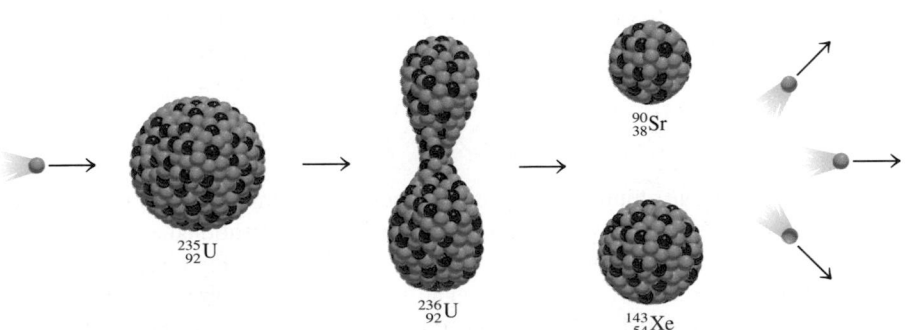

Figure 23.6 *Nuclear fission of ^{235}U. When a ^{235}U nucleus captures a neutron (green sphere), it undergoes fission to yield two smaller nuclei. On the average, 2.4 neutrons are emitted for every ^{235}U nucleus that divides.*

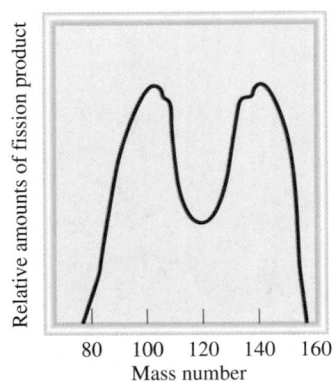

Figure 23.7 *Relative yields of the products resulting from the fission of ^{235}U as a function of mass number.*

Figure 23.8 *If a critical mass is present, many of the neutrons emitted during the fission process will be captured by other ^{235}U nuclei and a chain reaction will occur.*

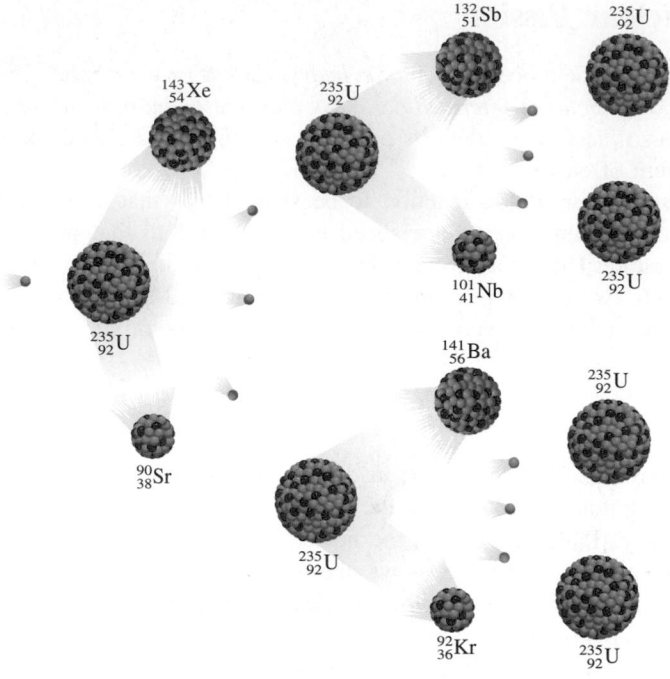

sample and the chain reaction will not occur. In this situation the mass of the sample is said to be *subcritical*. Figure 23.8 shows what happens when the amount of the fissionable material is equal to or greater than the **critical mass,** *the minimum mass of fissionable material required to generate a self-sustaining nuclear chain reaction.* In this case, most of the neutrons will be captured by uranium-235 nuclei, and a chain reaction will occur.

The Atomic Bomb

The first application of nuclear fission was in the development of the atomic bomb. How is such a bomb made and detonated? The crucial factor in the bomb's design is the determination of the critical mass for the bomb. A small atomic bomb is equivalent to 20,000 tons of TNT (trinitrotoluene). Because 1 ton of TNT releases about 4×10^9 J of energy, 20,000 tons would produce 8×10^{13} J. Earlier we saw that 1 mole, or 235 g, of uranium-235 liberates 2.0×10^{13} J of energy when it undergoes fission. Thus, the mass of the isotope present in a small bomb must be at least

$$235 \text{ g} \times \frac{8 \times 10^{13} \text{ J}}{2.0 \times 10^{13} \text{ J}} \approx 1 \text{ kg}$$

For obvious reasons, an atomic bomb is never assembled with the critical mass already present. Instead, the critical mass is formed by using a conventional explosive, such as TNT, to force the fissionable sections together, as shown in Figure 23.9. Neutrons from a source at the center of the device trigger the nuclear chain reaction. Uranium-235 was the fissionable material in the bomb dropped on Hiroshima, Japan, on August 6, 1945. Plutonium-239 was used in the bomb exploded over Nagasaki three days later. The fission reactions generated were similar in these two cases, as was the extent of the destruction.

Subcritical
U-235 mass

Subcritical
U-235 mass

TNT explosive

Figure 23.9 *Schematic diagram of an atomic bomb. The TNT explosives are set off first. The explosion forces the sections of fissionable material together to form an amount considerably larger than the critical mass.*

Shield

Steam

To steam turbine

Shield

Water

Pump

Control rod

Uranium fuel

Figure 23.10 *Schematic diagram of a nuclear fission reactor. The fission process is controlled by cadmium or boron rods. The heat generated by the process is used to produce steam for the generation of electricity via a heat exchange system.*

Nuclear Reactors

A peaceful but controversial application of nuclear fission is the generation of electricity using heat from a controlled chain reaction in a nuclear reactor. Currently, nuclear reactors provide about 20 percent of the electrical energy in the United States. This is a small but by no means negligible contribution to the nation's energy production. Several different types of nuclear reactors are in operation; we will briefly discuss the main features of three of them, along with their advantages and disadvantages.

Light Water Reactors

Most of the nuclear reactors in the United States are *light water reactors.* Figure 23.10 is a schematic diagram of such a reactor, and Figure 23.11 shows the refueling process in the core of a nuclear reactor.

An important aspect of the fission process is the speed of the neutrons. Slow neutrons split uranium-235 nuclei more efficiently than do fast ones. Because fission reactions are highly exothermic, the neutrons produced usually move at high velocities. For greater efficiency they must be slowed down before they can be used to induce nuclear disintegration. To accomplish this goal, scientists use **moderators,** which are *substances that can reduce the kinetic energy of neutrons.* A good moderator must satisfy several requirements: It should be nontoxic and inexpensive (as very large quantities of it are necessary); and it should resist conversion into a radioactive substance by neutron bombardment. Furthermore, it is advantageous for the moderator to be a fluid so that it can also be used as a coolant. No substance fulfills all these requirements, although water comes closer than many others that have been considered. Nuclear reactors that use light water (H_2O) as a moderator are called light water reactors because $_1^1H$ is the lightest isotope of the element hydrogen.

Figure 23.11 *Refueling the core of a nuclear reactor.*

Figure 23.12 *Uranium oxide, U_3O_8.*

The nuclear fuel consists of uranium, usually in the form of its oxide, U_3O_8 (Figure 23.12). Naturally occurring uranium contains about 0.7 percent of the uranium-235 isotope, which is too low a concentration to sustain a small-scale chain reaction. For effective operation of a light water reactor, uranium-235 must be enriched to a concentration of 3 or 4 percent. In principle, the main difference between an atomic bomb and a nuclear reactor is that the chain reaction that takes place in a nuclear reactor is kept under control at all times. The factor limiting the rate of the reaction is the number of neutrons present. This can be controlled by lowering cadmium or boron control rods between the fuel elements. These rods capture neutrons according to the equations

$$^{113}_{48}Cd + ^{1}_{0}n \longrightarrow ^{114}_{48}Cd + \gamma$$
$$^{10}_{5}B + ^{1}_{0}n \longrightarrow ^{7}_{3}Li + ^{4}_{2}\alpha$$

where γ denotes gamma rays. Without the control rods the reactor core would melt from the heat generated and release radioactive materials into the environment.

Nuclear reactors have rather elaborate cooling systems that absorb the heat given off by the nuclear reaction and transfer it outside the reactor core, where it is used to produce enough steam to drive an electric generator. In this respect, a nuclear power plant is similar to a conventional power plant that burns fossil fuel. In both cases, large quantities of cooling water are needed to condense steam for reuse. Thus, most nuclear power plants are built near a river or a lake. Unfortunately this method of cooling causes thermal pollution (see Section 12.4).

Heavy Water Reactors

Another type of nuclear reactor uses D_2O, or heavy water, as the moderator, rather than H_2O. Deuterium absorbs neutrons much less efficiently than does ordinary hydrogen. Because fewer neutrons are absorbed, the reactor is more efficient and does not require enriched uranium. The fact that deuterium is a less efficient moderator has a negative impact on the operation of the reactor, because more neutrons leak out of the reactor. However, this is not a serious disadvantage.

The main advantage of a heavy water reactor is that it eliminates the need for building expensive uranium enrichment facilities. However, D_2O must be prepared by either fractional distillation or electrolysis of ordinary water, which can be very expensive considering the amount of water used in a nuclear reactor. In countries where hydroelectric power is abundant, the cost of producing D_2O by electrolysis can be reasonably low. At present, Canada is the only nation successfully using heavy water nuclear reactors. The fact that no enriched uranium is required in a heavy water reactor enables a country to enjoy the benefits of nuclear power without undertaking work that is closely associated with weapons technology.

Breeder Reactors

A **breeder reactor** uses uranium fuel, but unlike a conventional nuclear reactor, it *produces more fissionable materials than it uses.*

We know that when uranium-238 is bombarded with fast neutrons, the following reactions take place:

Figure 23.13 *The red glow of the radioactive plutonium oxide, PuO_2.*

Plutonium-239 forms plutonium oxide, which can be readily separated from uranium.

$$^{238}_{92}U + ^{1}_{0}n \longrightarrow ^{239}_{92}U$$
$$^{239}_{92}U \longrightarrow ^{239}_{93}Np + ^{0}_{-1}\beta \qquad t_{\frac{1}{2}} = 23.4 \text{ min}$$
$$^{239}_{93}Np \longrightarrow ^{239}_{94}Pu + ^{0}_{-1}\beta \qquad t_{\frac{1}{2}} = 2.35 \text{ days}$$

In this manner the nonfissionable uranium-238 is transmuted into the fissionable isotope plutonium-239 (Figure 23.13).

In a typical breeder reactor, nuclear fuel containing uranium-235 or plutonium-239 is mixed with uranium-238 so that breeding takes place within the core. For every uranium-235 (or plutonium-239) nucleus undergoing fission, more than one neutron is captured by uranium-238 to generate plutonium-239. Thus, the stockpile of fissionable material can be steadily increased as the starting nuclear fuels are consumed. It takes about 7 to 10 yr to regenerate the sizable amount of material needed to refuel the original reactor and to fuel another reactor of comparable size. This interval is called the *doubling time*.

Another fertile isotope is $^{232}_{90}\text{Th}$. Upon capturing slow neutrons, thorium is transmuted to uranium-233, which, like uranium-235, is a fissionable isotope:

$$^{232}_{90}\text{Th} + {}^{1}_{0}\text{n} \longrightarrow {}^{233}_{90}\text{Th}$$
$$^{233}_{90}\text{Th} \longrightarrow {}^{233}_{91}\text{Pa} + {}^{0}_{-1}\beta \qquad\qquad t_{\frac{1}{2}} = 22 \text{ min}$$
$$^{233}_{91}\text{Pa} \longrightarrow {}^{233}_{92}\text{U} + {}^{0}_{-1}\beta \qquad\qquad t_{\frac{1}{2}} = 27.4 \text{ days}$$

Uranium-233 ($t_{\frac{1}{2}} = 1.6 \times 10^5$ yr) is stable enough for long-term storage.

Although the amounts of uranium-238 and thorium-232 in Earth's crust are relatively plentiful (4 ppm and 12 ppm by mass, respectively), the development of breeder reactors has been very slow. To date, the United States does not have a single operating breeder reactor, and only a few have been built in other countries, such as France and Russia. One problem is economics; breeder reactors are more expensive to build than conventional reactors. There are also more technical difficulties associated with the construction of such reactors. As a result, the future of breeder reactors, in the United States at least, is rather uncertain.

Hazards of Nuclear Energy

Many people, including environmentalists, regard nuclear fission as a highly undesirable method of energy production. Many fission products such as strontium-90 are dangerous radioactive isotopes with long half-lives. Plutonium-239, used as a nuclear fuel and produced in breeder reactors, is one of the most toxic substances known. It is an alpha emitter with a half-life of 24,400 yr.

Accidents, too, present many dangers. An accident at the Three Mile Island reactor in Pennsylvania in 1979 first brought the potential hazards of nuclear plants to public attention. In this instance, very little radiation escaped the reactor, but the plant remained closed for more than a decade while repairs were made and safety issues addressed. Only a few years later, on April 26, 1986, a reactor at the Chernobyl nuclear plant in Ukraine surged out of control. The fire and explosion that followed released much radioactive material into the environment. People working near the plant died within weeks as a result of the exposure to the intense radiation. The long-term effect of the radioactive fallout from this incident has not yet been clearly assessed, although agriculture and dairy farming were affected by the fallout. The number of potential cancer deaths attributable to the radiation contamination is estimated to be between a few thousand and more than 100,000.

In addition to the risk of accidents, the problem of radioactive waste disposal has not been satisfactorily resolved even for safely operated nuclear plants. Many suggestions have been made as to where to store or dispose of nuclear waste, including burial underground, burial beneath the ocean floor, and storage in deep geologic formations. But none of these sites has proved absolutely safe in the long run. Leakage of radioactive wastes into underground water, for example, can endanger nearby communities. The ideal disposal site would seem to be the sun, where a bit more radiation would make little difference, but this kind of operation requires 100 percent reliability in space technology.

Molten glass is poured over nuclear waste before burial.

CHEMISTRY
in Action

Nature's Own Fission Reactor

It all started with a routine analysis in May 1972 at the nuclear fuel processing plant in Pierrelatte, France. A staff member was checking the isotope ratio of U-235 to U-238 in a uranium ore and obtained a puzzling result. It had long been known that the relative natural occurrence of U-235 and U-238 is 0.7202 percent and 99.2798 percent, respectively. In this case, however, the amount of U-235 present was only 0.7171 percent. This may seem like a very small deviation, but the measurements were so precise that this difference was considered highly significant. The ore had come from the Oklo mine in the Gabon Republic, a small country on the west coast of Africa. Subsequent analyses of other samples showed that some contained even less U-235, in some cases as little as 0.44 percent.

The logical explanation for the low percentages of U-235 was that a nuclear fission reaction at the mine must have consumed some of the U-235 isotopes. But how did this happen? There are several conditions under which such a nuclear fission reaction could take place. In the presence of heavy water, for example, a chain reaction is possible with unenriched uranium. Without heavy water, such a fission reaction could still occur if the uranium ore and the moderator were arranged according to some specific geometric constraints at the site of the reaction. Both of the possibilities seem rather farfetched. The most plausible explanation is that the uranium ore originally present in the mine was enriched with U-235 and that a nuclear fission reaction took place with light water, as in a conventional nuclear reactor.

As mentioned earlier, the natural abundance of U-235 is 0.7202 percent, but it has not always been that low. The half-lives of U-235 and U-238 are 700 million and 4.51 billion years, respectively. This means that U-235 must have been *more* abundant in the past, because it has a shorter half-life. In fact, at the time Earth was formed, the natural abundance of U-235 was as high as 17 percent! Because the lowest concentration of U-235 required for the operation of a fission reactor is 1 percent, a nuclear chain reaction could have taken place as recently as 400 million years ago. By analyzing the amounts of radioactive fission products left in the ore, scientists concluded that the Gabon "reactor" operated about 2 billion years ago.

Having an enriched uranium sample is only one of the requirements for starting a controlled chain reaction. There must also have been a sufficient amount of the ore and an appropriate moderator present. It appears that as a result of a geological transformation, uranium ore was continually being washed into the Oklo region to yield concentrated deposits. The moderator needed for the fission process was largely water, present as water of crystallization in the sedimentary ore.

Thus, in a series of extraordinary events, a natural nuclear fission reactor operated at the time when the first life forms appeared on Earth. As is often the case in scientific endeavors, humans are not necessarily the innovators but merely the imitators of nature.

Photo showing the natural nuclear reactor site (lower right-hand corner) at Oklo, Gabon Republic.

Because of the hazards, the future of nuclear reactors is clouded. What was once hailed as the ultimate solution to our energy needs in the twenty-first century is now being debated and questioned by both the scientific community and laypeople. It seems likely that the controversy will continue for some time.

23.6 Nuclear Fusion

In contrast to the nuclear fission process, **nuclear fusion,** *the combining of small nuclei into larger ones,* is largely exempt from the waste disposal problem.

Figure 23.2 showed that for the lightest elements, nuclear stability increases with increasing mass number. This behavior suggests that if two light nuclei combine or fuse together to form a larger, more stable nucleus, an appreciable amount of energy will be released in the process. This is the basis for ongoing research into the harnessing of nuclear fusion for the production of energy.

Nuclear fusion occurs constantly in the sun. The sun is made up mostly of hydrogen and helium. In its interior, where temperatures reach about 15 million degrees Celsius, the following fusion reactions are believed to take place:

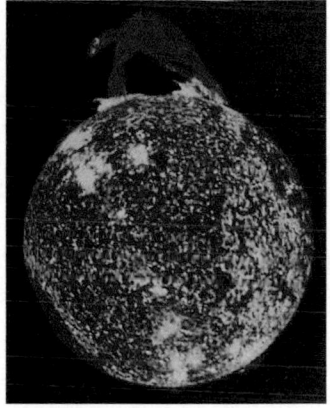

Nuclear fusion keeps the temperature in the interior of the sun at about 15 million °C.

$$\begin{aligned} {}^{1}_{1}\text{H} + {}^{2}_{1}\text{H} &\longrightarrow {}^{3}_{2}\text{He} \\ {}^{3}_{2}\text{He} + {}^{3}_{2}\text{He} &\longrightarrow {}^{4}_{2}\text{He} + 2{}^{1}_{1}\text{H} \\ {}^{1}_{1}\text{H} + {}^{1}_{1}\text{H} &\longrightarrow {}^{2}_{1}\text{H} + {}^{0}_{+1}\beta \end{aligned}$$

Because *fusion reactions take place only at very high temperatures,* they are often called **thermonuclear reactions.**

Fusion Reactors

A major concern in choosing the proper nuclear fusion process for energy production is the temperature necessary to carry out the process. Some promising reactions are

Reaction	Energy Released
${}^{2}_{1}\text{H} + {}^{2}_{1}\text{H} \longrightarrow {}^{3}_{1}\text{H} + {}^{1}_{1}\text{H}$	6.3×10^{-13} J
${}^{2}_{1}\text{H} + {}^{3}_{1}\text{H} \longrightarrow {}^{4}_{2}\text{He} + {}^{1}_{0}\text{n}$	2.8×10^{-12} J
${}^{6}_{3}\text{Li} + {}^{2}_{1}\text{H} \longrightarrow 2{}^{4}_{2}\text{He}$	3.6×10^{-12} J

These reactions take place at extremely high temperatures, on the order of 100 million degrees Celsius, to overcome the repulsive forces between the nuclei. The first reaction is particularly attractive because the world's supply of deuterium is virtually inexhaustible. The total volume of water on Earth is about 1.5×10^{21} L. Because the natural abundance of deuterium is 1.5×10^{-2} percent, the total amount of deuterium present is roughly 4.5×10^{21} g, or 5.0×10^{15} tons. The cost of preparing deuterium is minimal compared with the value of the energy released by the reaction.

In contrast to the fission process, nuclear fusion looks like a very promising energy source, at least "on paper." Although thermal pollution would be a problem, fusion has the following advantages: (1) The fuels are cheap and almost inexhaustible and (2) the process produces little radioactive waste. If a fusion machine were turned off, it would shut down completely and instantly, without any danger of a meltdown.

If nuclear fusion is so great, why isn't there even one fusion reactor producing energy? Although we command the scientific knowledge to design such a reactor, the technical difficulties have not yet been solved. The basic problem is finding a way to hold the nuclei together long enough, and at the appropriate temperature, for fusion to occur. At temperatures of about 100 million degrees Celsius, molecules cannot exist,

Figure 23.14 *A magnetic plasma confinement design called tokamak.*

Plasma   Magnet

and most or all of the atoms are stripped of their electrons. This *state of matter, a gaseous mixture of positive ions and electrons,* is called ***plasma.*** The problem of containing this plasma is a formidable one. What solid container can exist at such temperatures? None, unless the amount of plasma is small; but then the solid surface would immediately cool the sample and quench the fusion reaction. One approach to solving this problem is to use *magnetic confinement.* Because a plasma consists of charged particles moving at high speeds, a magnetic field will exert force on it. As Figure 23.14 shows, the plasma moves through a doughnut-shaped tunnel, confined by a complex magnetic field. Thus, the plasma never comes in contact with the walls of the container.

Another promising design employs high-power lasers to initiate the fusion reaction. In test runs a number of laser beams transfer energy to a small fuel pellet, heating it and causing it to *implode,* that is, to collapse inward from all sides and compress into a small volume (Figure 23.15). Consequently, fusion occurs. Like the magnetic confinement approach, laser fusion presents a number of technical difficulties that still need to be overcome before it can be put to practical use on a large scale.

Figure 23.15 *This small-scale fusion reaction was created at the Lawrence Livermore National Laboratory using the world's most powerful laser, Nova.*

The Hydrogen Bomb

The technical problems inherent in the design of a nuclear fusion reactor do not affect the production of a hydrogen bomb, also called a thermonuclear bomb. In this case, the objective is all power and no control. Hydrogen bombs do not contain gaseous hydrogen or gaseous deuterium; they contain solid lithium deuteride (LiD), which can be packed very tightly. The detonation of a hydrogen bomb occurs in two stages—first a fission reaction and then a fusion reaction. The required temperature for fusion is achieved with an atomic bomb. Immediately after the atomic bomb explodes, the following fusion reactions occur, releasing vast amounts of energy (Figure 23.16):

$$^6_3\text{Li} + ^2_1\text{H} \longrightarrow 2^4_2\alpha$$
$$^2_1\text{H} + ^2_1\text{H} \longrightarrow ^3_1\text{H} + ^1_1\text{H}$$

Figure 23.16 *Explosion of a thermonuclear bomb.*

There is no critical mass in a fusion bomb, and the force of the explosion is limited only by the quantity of reactants present. Thermonuclear bombs are described as being "cleaner" than atomic bombs because the only radioactive isotopes they produce are tritium, which is a weak β-particle emitter ($t_{\frac{1}{2}} = 12.5$ yr), and the products of the fission starter. Their damaging effects on the environment can be aggravated, however, by incorporating in the construction some nonfissionable material such as cobalt. Upon bombardment by neutrons, cobalt-59 is converted to cobalt-60, which is a very strong γ-ray emitter with a half-life of 5.2 yr. The presence of radioactive cobalt isotopes in the debris or fallout from a thermonuclear explosion would be fatal to those who survived the initial blast.

23.7 Uses of Isotopes

Radioactive and stable isotopes alike have many applications in science and medicine. We have previously described the use of isotopes in the study of reaction mechanisms (see Section 13.5) and in dating artifacts (p. 568 and Section 23.3). In this section we will discuss a few more examples.

Structural Determination

The formula of the thiosulfate ion is $S_2O_3^{2-}$. For some years chemists were uncertain as to whether the two sulfur atoms occupied equivalent positions in the ion. The thiosulfate ion is prepared by treatment of the sulfite ion with elemental sulfur:

$$SO_3^{2-}(aq) + S(s) \longrightarrow S_2O_3^{2-}(aq)$$

When thiosulfate is treated with dilute acid, the reaction is reversed. The sulfite ion is reformed and elemental sulfur precipitates:

$$S_2O_3^{2-}(aq) \xrightarrow{\text{H}^+} SO_3^{2-}(aq) + S(s) \tag{23.3}$$

If this sequence is started with elemental sulfur enriched with the radioactive sulfur-35 isotope, the isotope acts as a "label" for S atoms. All the labels are found in the sulfur precipitate in Equation (23.3); none of them appears in the final sulfite ions. Clearly, then, the two atoms of sulfur in $S_2O_3^{2-}$ are not structurally equivalent, as would be the case if the structure were

$$\left[:\overset{..}{\underset{..}{O}} - \overset{..}{\underset{..}{S}} - \overset{..}{\underset{..}{O}} - \overset{..}{\underset{..}{S}} - \overset{..}{\underset{..}{O}}: \right]^{2-}$$

$S_2O_3^{2-}$

Otherwise, the radioactive isotope would be present in both the elemental sulfur precipitate and the sulfite ion. Based on spectroscopic studies, we now know that the structure of the thiosulfate ion is

$$\begin{bmatrix} :\ddot{S}: \\ \| \\ :\ddot{O}-S-\ddot{O}: \\ \| \\ :\ddot{O}: \end{bmatrix}^{2-}$$

Study of Photosynthesis

The study of photosynthesis is also rich with isotope applications. The overall photosynthesis reaction can be represented as

$$6CO_2 + 6H_2O \longrightarrow C_6H_{12}O_6 + 6O_2$$

In Section 13.5 we learned that the ^{18}O isotope was used to determine the source of O_2. The radioactive ^{14}C isotope helped to determine the path of carbon in photosynthesis. Starting with $^{14}CO_2$, it was possible to isolate the intermediate products during photosynthesis and measure the amount of radioactivity of each carbon-containing compound. In this manner the path from CO_2 through various intermediate compounds to carbohydrate could be clearly charted. *Isotopes, especially radioactive isotopes that are used to trace the path of the atoms of an element in a chemical or biological process,* are called **tracers.**

Isotopes in Medicine

Tracers are used also for diagnosis in medicine. Sodium-24 (a β emitter with a half-life of 14.8 h) injected into the bloodstream as a salt solution can be monitored to trace the flow of blood and detect possible constrictions or obstructions in the circulatory system. Iodine-131 (a β emitter with a half-life of 8 days) has been used to test the activity of the thyroid gland. A malfunctioning thyroid can be detected by giving the patient a drink of a solution containing a known amount of $Na^{131}I$ and measuring the radioactivity just above the thyroid to see if the iodine is absorbed at the normal rate. Of course, the amounts of radioisotope used in the human body must always be kept small; otherwise, the patient might suffer permanent damage from the high-energy radiation. Another radioactive isotope of iodine, iodine-123 (a γ-ray emitter), is used to image the thyroid gland (Figure 23.17).

Figure 23.17 *After ingesting $Na^{131}I$, the uptake of the radioactive iodine by the thyroid gland in a patient is monitored with a scanner. The photos show a normal thyroid gland (left) and an enlarged thyroid gland (right).*

Cathode   Anode

Insulator

Window

Amplifier and counter

Argon gas

High voltage

Figure 23.18 *Schematic diagram of a Geiger counter. Radiation (α, β, or γ rays) entering through the window ionized the argon gas to generate a small current flow between the electrodes. This current is amplified and is used to flash a light or operate a counter with a clicking sound.*

Technetium, the first artificially prepared element, is one of the most useful elements in nuclear medicine. Although technetium is a transition metal, all its isotopes are radioactive. In the laboratory it is prepared by the nuclear reactions

$$^{98}_{42}\text{Mo} + {}^{1}_{0}\text{n} \longrightarrow {}^{99}_{42}\text{Mo}$$
$$^{99}_{42}\text{Mo} \longrightarrow {}^{99\text{m}}_{43}\text{Tc} + {}^{0}_{-1}\beta$$

where the superscript m denotes that the technetium-99 isotope is produced in its excited nuclear state. This isotope has a half-life of about 6 h, decaying by γ radiation to technetium-99 in its nuclear ground state. Thus, it is a valuable diagnostic tool. The patient either drinks or is injected with a solution containing $^{99\text{m}}$Tc. By detecting the γ rays emitted by $^{99\text{m}}$Tc, doctors can obtain images of organs such as the heart, liver, and lungs.

A major advantage of using radioactive isotopes as tracers is that they are easy to detect. Their presence even in very small amounts can be detected by photographic techniques or by devices known as counters. Figure 23.18 is a diagram of a Geiger counter, an instrument widely used in scientific work and medical laboratories to detect radiation.

Image of a person's skeleton obtained using $^{99\text{m}}_{43}$Tc.

23.8 Biological Effects of Radiation

In this section we will examine briefly the effects of radiation on biological systems. But first let us define quantitative measures of radiation. The fundamental unit of radioactivity is the *curie* (Ci); 1 Ci corresponds to exactly 3.70×10^{10} nuclear disintegrations per second. This decay rate is equivalent to that of 1 g of radium. A *millicurie* (mCi) is one-thousandth of a curie. Thus, 10 mCi of a carbon-14 sample is the quantity that undergoes

$$(10 \times 10^{-3})(3.70 \times 10^{10}) = 3.70 \times 10^{8}$$

disintegrations per second.

The intensity of radiation depends on the number of disintegrations as well as on the energy and type of radiation emitted. One common unit for the absorbed dose of radiation is the *rad* (radiation *a*bsorbed *d*ose), which is the amount of radiation that results in the absorption of 1×10^{-2} J per kilogram of irradiated material. The biological effect of radiation also depends on the part of the body irradiated and the

TABLE 23.6	Average Yearly Radiation Doses for Americans
Source	**Dose (mrem/yr)***
Cosmic rays	20–50
Ground and surroundings	25
Human body†	26
Medical and dental X rays	50–75
Air travel	5
Fallout from weapons tests	5
Nuclear waste	2
Total	133–188

*1 mrem = 1 millirem = 1×10^{-3} rem.
†The radioactivity in the body comes from food and air.

type of radiation. For this reason, the rad is often multiplied by a factor called *RBE* (*r*elative *b*iological *e*ffectiveness). The RBE is approximately 1 for beta and gamma radiation and about 10 for alpha radiation. To measure the biological damage, which depends on dose rate, total dose, and the type of tissue affected, we introduce another term called a *rem* (*r*oentgen *e*quivalent for *m*an), given by

$$\text{number of rems} = (\text{number of rads})(\text{RBE}) \tag{23.4}$$

Of the three types of nuclear radiation, alpha particles usually have the least penetrating power. Beta particles are more penetrating than alpha particles, but less so than gamma rays. Gamma rays have very short wavelengths and high energies. Furthermore, because they carry no charge, they cannot be stopped by shielding materials as easily as alpha and beta particles. However, if alpha or beta emitters are ingested, their damaging effects are greatly aggravated because the organs will be constantly subject to damaging radiation at close range. For example, strontium-90, a beta emitter, can replace calcium in bones, where it does the greatest damage.

Table 23.6 lists the average amounts of radiation an American receives every year. It should be pointed out that for short-term exposures to radiation, a dosage of 50–200 rem will cause a decrease in white blood cell counts and other complications, while a dosage of 500 rem or greater may result in death within weeks. Current safety standards permit nuclear workers to be exposed to no more than 5 rem per year and specify a maximum of 0.5 rem of human-made radiation per year for the general public.

The chemical basis of radiation damage is that of ionizing radiation. Radiation of either particles or gamma rays can remove electrons from atoms and molecules in its path, leading to the formation of ions and radicals. *Radicals* (also called *free radicals*) are *molecular fragments having one or more unpaired electrons; they are usually short-lived and highly reactive.* For example, when water is irradiated with gamma rays, the following reactions take place:

$$H_2O \xrightarrow{\text{radiation}} H_2O^+ + e^-$$
$$H_2O^+ + H_2O \longrightarrow H_3O^+ + \underset{\text{hydroxyl radical}}{\cdot OH}$$

The electron (in the hydrated form) can subsequently react with water or with a hydrogen ion to form atomic hydrogen, and with oxygen to produce the superoxide ion, O_2^- (a radical):

$$e^- + O_2 \longrightarrow \cdot O_2^-$$

CHEMISTRY
in Action

Food Irradiation

If you eat processed food, you have probably eaten ingredients exposed to radioactive rays. In the United States, up to 10 percent of herbs and spices are irradiated to control mold, zapped with X rays at a dose equal to 60 million chest X rays. Although food irradiation has been used in one way or another for more than 40 yr, it faces an uncertain future in this country.

Back in 1953, the U.S. Army started an experimental program of food irradiation so that deployed troops could have fresh food without refrigeration. The procedure is a simple one. Food is exposed to high levels of radiation to kill insects and harmful bacteria. It is then packaged in airtight containers, in which it can be stored for months without deterioration. The radiation sources for most food preservation are cobalt-60 and cesium-137, both of which are γ emitters, although X rays and electron beams can also be used to irradiate food.

The benefits of food irradiation are obvious—it reduces energy demand by eliminating the need for refrigeration, and it prolongs the shelf life of various foods, which is of vital importance for poor countries. Yet there is considerable opposition to this procedure. First, there is a fear that irradiated food may itself become radioactive. No such evidence has been found. A more serious objection is that irradiation can destroy the nutrients such as vitamins and amino acids. Furthermore, the ionizing radiation produces reactive species, such as the hydroxyl

Strawberries irradiated at 200 kilorads (right) are still fresh after 15 days storage at 4°C; those not irradiated are moldy.

radical, which then react with the organic molecules to produce potentially harmful substances. Interestingly, the same effects are produced when food is cooked by heat.

Food Irradiation Dosages and Their Effects*

Dosage	Effect
Low dose (Up to 100 kilorad)	Inhibits sprouting of potatoes, onions, garlics.
	Inactivates trichinae in pork.
	Kills or prevents insects from reproducing in grains, fruits, and vegetables after harvest.
Medium dose (100 to 1000 kilorads)	Delays spoilage of meat, poultry, and fish by killing spoilage microorganism.
	Reduces salmonella and other food-borne pathogens in meat, fish, and poultry.
	Extends shelf life by delaying mold growth on strawberries and some other fruits.
High dose (1000 to 10,000 kilorads)	Sterilizes meat, poultry, fish, and some other foods.
	Kills microorganisms and insects in spices and seasoning.

*Source: *Chemical & Engineering News,* May 5 (1986).

In the tissues the superoxide ions and other free radicals attack cell membranes and a host of organic compounds, such as enzymes and DNA molecules. Organic compounds can themselves be directly ionized and destroyed by high-energy radiation.

It has long been known that exposure to high-energy radiation can induce cancer in humans and other animals. Cancer is characterized by uncontrolled cellular growth. On the other hand, it is also well established that cancer cells can be destroyed by proper radiation treatment. In radiation therapy, a compromise is sought. The radiation to which the patient is exposed must be sufficient to destroy cancer cells without killing too many normal cells and, it is hoped, without inducing another form of cancer.

Radiation damage to living systems is generally classified as *somatic* or *genetic*. Somatic injuries are those that affect the organism during its own lifetime. Sunburn, skin rash, cancer, and cataracts are examples of somatic damage. Genetic damage means inheritable changes or gene mutations. For example, a person whose chromosomes have been damaged or altered by radiation may have deformed offspring.

Chromosomes are parts of the cell structure that contain the genetic material (DNA).

Summary of Facts and Concepts

1. For stable nuclei of low atomic number, the neutron-to-proton ratio is close to 1. For heavier stable nuclei, the ratio becomes greater than 1. All nuclei with 84 or more protons are unstable and radioactive. Nuclei with even atomic numbers tend to have a greater number of stable isotopes than those with odd atomic numbers.

2. Nuclear binding energy is a quantitative measure of nuclear stability. Nuclear binding energy can be calculated from a knowledge of the mass defect of the nucleus.

3. Radioactive nuclei emit α particles, β particles, positrons, or γ rays. The equation for a nuclear reaction includes the particles emitted, and both the mass numbers and the atomic numbers must balance.

4. Uranium-238 is the parent of a natural radioactive decay series that can be used to determine the ages of rocks.

5. Artificial radioactive elements are created by bombarding other elements with accelerated neutrons, protons, or α particles.

6. Nuclear fission is the splitting of a large nucleus into two smaller nuclei and one or more neutrons. When the free neutrons are captured efficiently by other nuclei, a chain reaction can occur.

7. Nuclear reactors use the heat from a controlled nuclear fission reaction to produce power. The three important types of reactors are light water reactors, heavy water reactors, and breeder reactors.

8. Nuclear fusion, the type of reaction that occurs in the sun, is the combination of two light nuclei to form one heavy nucleus. Fusion takes place only at very high temperatures, so high that controlled large-scale nuclear fusion has so far not been achieved.

9. Radioactive isotopes are easy to detect and thus make excellent tracers in chemical reactions and in medical practice.

10. High-energy radiation damages living systems by causing ionization and the formation of free radicals.

Key Words

Breeder reactor, p. 984
Critical mass, p. 982
Mass defect, p. 972
Moderators, p. 983
Nuclear binding energy, p. 972
Nuclear chain reaction, p. 981
Nuclear fission, p. 981
Nuclear fusion, p. 987
Nuclear transmutation, p. 968
Nucleon, p. 972
Plasma, p. 988
Positron, p. 969
Radical, p. 992
Radioactive decay series, p. 975
Thermonuclear reaction, p. 987
Tracer, p. 990
Transuranium elements, p. 979

Questions and Problems

Nuclear Reactions
Review Questions

23.1 How do nuclear reactions differ from ordinary chemical reactions?

23.2 What are the steps in balancing nuclear equations?

23.3 What is the difference between $_{-1}^{0}e$ and $_{-1}^{0}\beta$?

23.4 What is the difference between an electron and a positron?

Problems

23.5 Complete the following nuclear equations and identify X in each case:

(a) $^{26}_{12}\text{Mg} + ^{1}_{1}\text{p} \longrightarrow ^{4}_{2}\alpha + \text{X}$

(b) $^{59}_{27}\text{Co} + ^{2}_{1}\text{H} \longrightarrow ^{60}_{27}\text{Co} + \text{X}$

(c) $^{235}_{92}\text{U} + ^{1}_{0}\text{n} \longrightarrow ^{94}_{36}\text{Kr} + ^{139}_{56}\text{Ba} + 3\text{X}$

(d) $^{53}_{24}\text{Cr} + ^{4}_{2}\alpha \longrightarrow ^{1}_{0}\text{n} + \text{X}$

(e) $^{20}_{8}\text{O} \longrightarrow ^{20}_{9}\text{F} + \text{X}$

23.6 Complete the following nuclear equations and identify X in each case:

(a) $^{135}_{53}\text{I} \longrightarrow ^{135}_{54}\text{Xe} + \text{X}$

(b) $^{40}_{19}\text{K} \longrightarrow ^{0}_{-1}\beta + \text{X}$

(c) $^{59}_{27}\text{Co} + ^{1}_{0}\text{n} \longrightarrow ^{56}_{25}\text{Mn} + \text{X}$

(d) $^{235}_{92}\text{U} + ^{1}_{0}\text{n} \longrightarrow ^{99}_{40}\text{Zr} + ^{135}_{52}\text{Te} + 2\text{X}$

Nuclear Stability

Review Questions

23.7 State the general rules for predicting nuclear stability.

23.8 What is the belt of stability?

23.9 Why is it impossible for the isotope $^{2}_{2}\text{He}$ to exist?

23.10 Define nuclear binding energy, mass defect, and nucleon.

23.11 How does Einstein's equation, $E = mc^2$, enable us to calculate nuclear binding energy?

23.12 Why is it preferable to use nuclear binding energy per nucleon for a comparison of the stabilities of different nuclei?

Problems

23.13 The radius of a uranium-235 nucleus is about 7.0×10^{-3} pm. Calculate the density of the nucleus in g/cm^3. (Assume the atomic mass is 235 amu.)

23.14 For each pair of isotopes listed, predict which one is less stable: (a) $^{6}_{3}\text{Li}$ or $^{9}_{3}\text{Li}$, (b) $^{23}_{11}\text{Na}$ or $^{25}_{11}\text{Na}$, (c) $^{48}_{20}\text{Ca}$ or $^{48}_{21}\text{Sc}$.

23.15 For each pair of elements listed, predict which one has more stable isotopes: (a) Co or Ni, (b) F or Se, (c) Ag or Cd.

23.16 In each pair of isotopes shown, indicate which one you would expect to be radioactive: (a) $^{20}_{10}\text{Ne}$ and $^{17}_{10}\text{Ne}$, (b) $^{40}_{20}\text{Ca}$ and $^{45}_{20}\text{Ca}$, (c) $^{95}_{42}\text{Mo}$ and $^{92}_{43}\text{Tc}$, (d) $^{195}_{80}\text{Hg}$ and $^{196}_{80}\text{Hg}$, (e) $^{209}_{83}\text{Bi}$ and $^{242}_{96}\text{Cm}$.

23.17 Given that

$$\text{H}(g) + \text{H}(g) \longrightarrow \text{H}_2(g) \quad \Delta H° = -436.4 \text{ kJ/mol}$$

calculate the change in mass (in kg) per mole of H_2 formed.

23.18 Estimates show that the total energy output of the sun is 5×10^{26} J/s. What is the corresponding mass loss in kg/s of the sun?

23.19 Calculate the nuclear binding energy (in J) and the binding energy per nucleon of the following isotopes: (a) $^{7}_{3}\text{Li}$ (7.01600 amu) and (b) $^{35}_{17}\text{Cl}$ (34.95952 amu).

23.20 Calculate the nuclear binding energy (in J) and the binding energy per nucleon of the following isotopes: (a) $^{4}_{2}\text{He}$ (4.0026 amu) and (b) $^{184}_{74}\text{W}$ (183.9510 amu).

Natural Radioactivity

Review Questions

23.21 Discuss factors that lead to nuclear decay.

23.22 Outline the principle for dating materials using radioactive isotopes.

Problems

23.23 Fill in the blanks in the following radioactive decay series:

(a) $^{232}\text{Th} \xrightarrow{\alpha} \underline{\quad} \xrightarrow{\beta} \underline{\quad} \xrightarrow{\beta} {}^{228}\text{Th}$

(b) $^{235}\text{U} \xrightarrow{\alpha} \underline{\quad} \xrightarrow{\beta} \underline{\quad} \xrightarrow{\alpha} {}^{227}\text{Ac}$

(c) $\underline{\quad} \xrightarrow{\alpha} {}^{233}\text{Pa} \xrightarrow{\beta} \underline{\quad} \xrightarrow{\alpha} \underline{\quad}$

23.24 A radioactive substance undergoes decay as follows:

Time (days)	Mass (g)
0	500
1	389
2	303
3	236
4	184
5	143
6	112

Calculate the first-order decay constant and the half-life of the reaction.

23.25 The radioactive decay of Tl-206 to Pb-206 has a half-life of 4.20 min. Starting with 5.00×10^{22} atoms of Tl-206, calculate the number of such atoms left after 42.0 min.

23.26 A freshly isolated sample of ^{90}Y was found to have an activity of 9.8×10^5 disintegrations per minute at 1:00 P.M. on December 3, 2003. At 2:15 P.M. on December 17, 2003, its activity was redetermined and found to be 2.6×10^4 disintegrations per minute. Calculate the half-life of ^{90}Y.

23.27 Why do radioactive decay series obey first-order kinetics?

23.28 In the thorium decay series, thorium-232 loses a total of 6 α particles and 4 β particles in a 10-stage process. What is the final isotope produced?

23.29 Strontium-90 is one of the products of the fission of uranium-235. This strontium isotope is radioactive, with a half-life of 28.1 yr. Calculate how long (in yr) it will take for 1.00 g of the isotope to be reduced to 0.200 g by decay.

23.30 Consider the decay series

$$\text{A} \longrightarrow \text{B} \longrightarrow \text{C} \longrightarrow \text{D}$$

where A, B, and C are radioactive isotopes with half-lives of 4.50 s, 15.0 days, and 1.00 s, respectively, and D is nonradioactive. Starting with 1.00 mole of A, and none of B, C, or D, calculate the number of moles of A, B, C, and D left after 30 days.

Nuclear Transmutation

Review Questions

23.31 What is the difference between radioactive decay and nuclear transmutation?

23.32 How is nuclear transmutation achieved in practice?

Problems

23.33 Write balanced nuclear equations for the following reactions and identify X:
(a) $X(p,\alpha)^{12}_{6}C$, (b) $^{27}_{13}Al(d,\alpha)X$, (c) $^{55}_{25}Mn(n,\gamma)X$

23.34 Write balanced nuclear equations for the following reactions and identify X:
(a) $^{80}_{34}Se(d,p)X$, (b) $X(d,2p)^{9}_{3}Li$, (c) $^{10}_{5}B(n,\alpha)X$

23.35 Describe how you would prepare astatine-211, starting with bismuth-209.

23.36 A long-cherished dream of alchemists was to produce gold from cheaper and more abundant elements. This dream was finally realized when $^{198}_{80}Hg$ was converted into gold by neutron bombardment. Write a balanced equation for this reaction.

Nuclear Fission

Review Questions

23.37 Define nuclear fission, nuclear chain reaction, and critical mass.

23.38 Which isotopes can undergo nuclear fission?

23.39 Explain how an atomic bomb works.

23.40 Explain the functions of a moderator and a control rod in a nuclear reactor.

23.41 Discuss the differences between a light water and a heavy water nuclear fission reactor. What are the advantages of a breeder reactor over a conventional nuclear fission reactor?

23.42 No form of energy production is without risk. Make a list of the risks to society involved in fueling and operating a conventional coal-fired electric power plant, and compare them with the risks of fueling and operating a nuclear fission-powered electric plant.

Nuclear Fusion

Review Questions

23.43 Define nuclear fusion, thermonuclear reaction, and plasma.

23.44 Why do heavy elements such as uranium undergo fission while light elements such as hydrogen and lithium undergo fusion?

23.45 How does a hydrogen bomb work?

23.46 What are the advantages of a fusion reactor over a fission reactor? What are the practical difficulties in operating a large-scale fusion reactor?

Uses of Isotopes

Problems

23.47 Describe how you would use a radioactive iodine isotope to demonstrate that the following process is in dynamic equilibrium:

$$PbI_2(s) \rightleftharpoons Pb^{2+}(aq) + 2I^-(aq)$$

23.48 Consider the following redox reaction:

$$IO_4^-(aq) + 2I^-(aq) + H_2O(l) \longrightarrow$$
$$I_2(s) + IO_3^-(aq) + 2OH^-(aq)$$

When KIO_4 is added to a solution containing iodide ions labeled with radioactive iodine-128, all the radioactivity appears in I_2 and none in the IO_3^- ion. What can you deduce about the mechanism for the redox process?

23.49 Explain how you might use a radioactive tracer to show that ions are not completely motionless in crystals.

23.50 Each molecule of hemoglobin, the oxygen carrier in blood, contains four Fe atoms. Explain how you would use the radioactive $^{59}_{26}Fe$ ($t_{\frac{1}{2}} = 46$ days) to show that the iron in a certain food is converted into hemoglobin.

Additional Problems

23.51 How does a Geiger counter work?

23.52 Nuclei with an even number of protons and an even number of neutrons are more stable than those with an odd number of protons and/or an odd number of neutrons. What is the significance of the even numbers of protons and neutrons in this case?

23.53 Tritium, ^3H, is radioactive and decays by electron emission. Its half-life is 12.5 yr. In ordinary water the ratio of ^1H to ^3H atoms is 1.0×10^{17} to 1. (a) Write a balanced nuclear equation for tritium decay. (b) How many disintegrations will be observed per minute in a 1.00-kg sample of water?

23.54 (a) What is the activity, in millicuries, of a 0.500-g sample of $^{237}_{93}Np$? (This isotope decays by α-particle emission and has a half-life of 2.20×10^6 yr.) (b) Write a balanced nuclear equation for the decay of $^{237}_{93}Np$.

23.55 The following equations are for nuclear reactions that are known to occur in the explosion of an atomic bomb. Identify X.
(a) $^{235}_{92}U + ^1_0n \longrightarrow ^{140}_{56}Ba + 3^1_0n + X$
(b) $^{235}_{92}U + ^1_0n \longrightarrow ^{144}_{55}Cs + ^{90}_{37}Rb + 2X$
(c) $^{235}_{92}U + ^1_0n \longrightarrow ^{87}_{35}Br + 3^1_0n + X$
(d) $^{235}_{92}U + ^1_0n \longrightarrow ^{160}_{62}Sm + ^{72}_{30}Zn + 4X$

23.56 Calculate the nuclear binding energies, in J/nucleon, for the following species: (a) ^{10}B (10.0129 amu), (b) ^{11}B (11.00931 amu), (c) ^{14}N (14.00307 amu), (d) ^{56}Fe (55.9349 amu).

23.57 Write complete nuclear equations for the following processes: (a) tritium, ^{3}H, undergoes β decay; (b) ^{242}Pu undergoes α-particle emission; (c) ^{131}I undergoes β decay; (d) ^{251}Cf emits an α particle.

23.58 The nucleus of nitrogen-18 lies above the stability belt. Write an equation for a nuclear reaction by which nitrogen-18 can achieve stability.

23.59 Why is strontium-90 a particularly dangerous isotope for humans?

23.60 How are scientists able to tell the age of a fossil?

23.61 After the Chernobyl accident, people living close to the nuclear reactor site were urged to take large amounts of potassium iodide as a safety precaution. What is the chemical basis for this action?

23.62 Astatine, the last member of Group 7A, can be prepared by bombarding bismuth-209 with α particles. (a) Write an equation for the reaction. (b) Represent the equation in the abbreviated form, as discussed in Section 23.4.

23.63 To detect bombs that may be smuggled onto airplanes, the Federal Aviation Administration (FAA) will soon require all major airports in the United States to install thermal neutron analyzers. The thermal neutron analyzer will bombard baggage with low-energy neutrons, converting some of the nitrogen-14 nuclei to nitrogen-15, with simultaneous emission of γ rays. Because nitrogen content is usually high in explosives, detection of a high dosage of γ rays will suggest that a bomb may be present. (a) Write an equation for the nuclear process. (b) Compare this technique with the conventional X-ray detection method.

23.64 Explain why achievement of nuclear fusion in the laboratory requires a temperature of about 100 million degrees Celsius, which is much higher than that in the interior of the sun (15 million degrees Celsius).

23.65 Tritium contains one proton and two neutrons. There is no proton-proton repulsion present in the nucleus. Why, then, is tritium radioactive?

23.66 The carbon-14 decay rate of a sample obtained from a young tree is 0.260 disintegration per second per gram of the sample. Another wood sample prepared from an object recovered at an archaeological excavation gives a decay rate of 0.186 disintegration per second per gram of the sample. What is the age of the object?

23.67 The usefulness of radiocarbon dating is limited to objects no older than 50,000 years. What percent of the carbon-14, originally present in the sample, remains after this period of time?

23.68 The radioactive potassium-40 isotope decays to argon-40 with a half-life of 1.2×10^{9} yr. (a) Write a balanced equation for the reaction. (b) A sample of moon rock is found to contain 18 percent potassium-40 and 82 percent argon by mass. Calculate the age of the rock in years.

23.69 Both barium (Ba) and radium (Ra) are members of Group 2A and are expected to exhibit similar chemical properties. However, Ra is not found in barium ores. Instead, it is found in uranium ores. Explain.

23.70 Nuclear waste disposal is one of the major concerns of the nuclear industry. In choosing a safe and stable environment to store nuclear wastes, consideration must be given to the heat released during nuclear decay. As an example, consider the β decay of ^{90}Sr (89.907738 amu):

$$^{90}_{38}\text{Sr} \longrightarrow {}^{90}_{39}\text{Y} + {}^{0}_{-1}\beta \qquad t_{\frac{1}{2}} = 28.1 \text{ yr}$$

The ^{90}Y (89.907152 amu) further decays as follows:

$$^{90}_{39}\text{Y} \longrightarrow {}^{90}_{40}\text{Zr} + {}^{0}_{-1}\beta \qquad t_{\frac{1}{2}} = 64 \text{ h}$$

Zirconium-90 (89.904703 amu) is a stable isotope. (a) Use the mass defect to calculate the energy released (in joules) in each of the above two decays. (The mass of the electron is 5.4857×10^{-4} amu.) (b) Starting with one mole of ^{90}Sr, calculate the number of moles of ^{90}Sr that will decay in a year. (c) Calculate the amount of heat released (in kilojoules) corresponding to the number of moles of ^{90}Sr decayed to ^{90}Zr in (b).

23.71 Which of the following poses a greater health hazard: a radioactive isotope with a short half-life or a radioactive isotope with a long half-life? Explain. [Assume same type of radiation (α or β) and comparable energetics per particle emitted.]

23.72 As a result of being exposed to the radiation released during the Chernobyl nuclear accident, the dose of iodine-131 in a person's body is 7.4 mCi (1 mCi = 1×10^{-3} Ci). Use the relationship rate $= \lambda N$ to calculate the number of atoms of iodine-131 this radioactivity corresponds to. (The half-life of ^{131}I is 8.1 d.)

23.73 Referring to the Chemistry in Action essay on p. 993, why is it highly unlikely that irradiated food would become radioactive?

23.74 From the definition of curie, calculate Avogadro's number. Given that the molar mass of ^{226}Ra is 226.03 g/mol and that it decays with a half-life of 1.6×10^{3} yr.

23.75 Since 1994, elements 110, 111, 112, and 114 have been synthesized. Element 110 was created by bombarding ^{208}Pb with ^{62}Ni; element 111 was created by bombarding ^{209}Bi with ^{64}Ni; element 112 was created by bombarding ^{208}Pb with ^{66}Zn; element 114 was created by bombarding ^{244}Pu with ^{48}Ca. Write an equation for each synthesis. Predict the chemical properties of these elements. Use W for element 110, X for element 111, Y for element 112, and Z for element 114.

23.76 Sources of energy on Earth include fossil fuels, geothermal, gravitational, hydroelectric, nuclear fission, nuclear fusion, solar, wind. Which of these have a "nuclear origin," either directly or indirectly?

23.77 A person received an anonymous gift of a decorative cube, which he placed on his desk. A few months later he became ill and died shortly afterward. After investigation, the cause of his death was linked to the box. The box was air-tight and had no toxic chemicals on it. What might have killed the man?

23.78 Identify two of the most abundant radioactive elements that exist on Earth. Explain why they are still present? (You may need to consult a handbook of chemistry.)

23.79 (a) Calculate the energy released when an U-238 isotope decays to Th-234. The atomic masses are given by: U-238: 238.0508 amu; Th-234: 234.0436 amu; He-4: 4.0026 amu. (b) The energy released in (a) is transformed into the kinetic energy of the recoiling Th-234 nucleus and the α particle. Which of the two will move away faster? Explain.

23.80 Cobalt-60 is an isotope used in diagnostic medicine and cancer treatment. It decays with γ ray emission. Calculate the wavelength of the radiation in nanometers if the energy of the γ ray is 2.4×10^{-13} J/photon.

23.81 Americium-241 is used in smoke detectors because it has a long half-life (458 yr) and its emitted α particles are energetic enough to ionize air molecules. Given the schematic diagram of a smoke detector below, explain how it works.

Current

^{241}Am

Battery

23.82 The constituents of wine contain, among others, carbon, hydrogen, and oxygen atoms. A bottle of wine was sealed about 6 years ago. To confirm its age, which of the isotopes would you choose in a radioactive dating study? The half-lives of the isotopes are: ^{13}C: 5730 yr; ^{15}O: 124 s; ^{3}H: 12.5 yr. Assume that the activities of the isotopes were known at the time the bottle was sealed.

23.83 Name two advantages of a nuclear-powered submarine over a conventional submarine.

23.84 In 1997 a scientist at a nuclear research center in Russia placed a thin shell of copper on a sphere of highly enriched uranium-235. Suddenly, there was a huge burst of radiation, which turned the air blue. Three days later, the scientist died of radiation damage. Explain what caused the accident. (*Hint:* Copper is an effective metal for reflecting neutrons.)

23.85 A radioactive isotope of copper decays as follows:

$$^{64}\text{Cu} \longrightarrow\ ^{64}\text{Zn} +\ _{-1}^{0}\beta \qquad t_{\frac{1}{2}} = 12.8\ \text{h}$$

Starting with 84.0 g of ^{64}Cu, calculate the quantity of ^{64}Zn produced after 18.4 h.

23.86 A 0.0100-g sample of a radioactive isotope with a half-life of 1.3×10^{9} yr decays at the rate of 2.9×10^{4} dpm. Calculate the molar mass of the isotope.

Special Problems

23.87 The half-life of ^{27}Mg is 9.50 min. (a) Initially there were 4.20×10^{12} ^{27}Mg nuclei present. How many ^{27}Mg nuclei are left 30.0 min later? (b) Calculate the ^{27}Mg activities (in Ci) at $t = 0$ and $t = 30.0$ min. (c) What is the probability that any one ^{27}Mg nucleus decays during a 1-s interval? What assumption is made in this calculation?

23.88 The radioactive isotope ^{238}Pu, used in pacemakers, decays by emitting an alpha particle with a half-life of 86 yr. (a) Write an equation for the decay process. (b) The energy of the emitted alpha particle is 9.0×10^{-13} J, which is the energy per decay. Assume that all the alpha particle energy is used to run the pacemaker, calculate the power output at $t = 0$ and $t = 10$ yr. Initially 1.0 mg of ^{238}Pu was present in the pacemaker (*Hint:* After 10 yr, the activity of the isotope decreases by 8.0 percent. Power is measured in watts or J/s.).

23.89 (a) Assume nuclei are spherical in shape, show that its radius (r) is proportional to the cube root of mass number (A). (b) In general, the radius of a nucleus is given by $r = r_0 A^{\frac{1}{3}}$, where r_0, the proportionality constant, is given by 1.2×10^{-15} m. Calculate the volume of the ^{238}U nucleus.

23.90 The quantity of a radioactive material is often measured by its activity (measured in curies or millicuries) rather than by its mass. In a brain scan procedure, a 70-kg patient is injected with 20.0 mCi of ^{99m}Tc, which decays by emitting γ-ray photons with a half-life of 6.0 h. Given that the RBE of these photons is 0.98 and only two-thirds of the photons are absorbed by the body, calculate the rem dose received by the patient. Assume all of the ^{99m}Tc nuclei decay while in the body. The energy of a gamma photon is 2.29×10^{-14} J.

23.91 Describe, with appropriate equations, nuclear processes that lead to the formation of the noble gases He, Ne, Ar, Kr, Xe, and Rn. (*Hint:* Helium is formed from radioactive decay, neon is formed from the positron emission of ^{22}Na, the formation of Ar, Xe, and Rn are discussed in the chapter, and Kr is produced from the fission of ^{235}U.)

23.92 Modern designs of atomic bombs contain, in addition to uranium or plutonium, small amounts of tritium and deuterium to boost the power of explosion. What is the role of tritium and deuterium in these bombs?

Answers to Practice Exercises

23.1 $^{78}_{34}$Se. **23.2** 2.63×10^{-10} J; 1.26×10^{-12} J/nucleon.
23.3 $^{106}_{46}$Pd $+ ^{4}_{2}\alpha \longrightarrow ^{109}_{47}$Ag $+ ^{1}_{1}$p.

The Art Forgery of the Twentieth Century

Han van Meegeren must be one of the few forgers ever to welcome technical analysis of his work. In 1945 he was captured by the Dutch police and accused of selling a painting by the Dutch artist Jan Vermeer (1632–1675) to Nazi Germany. This was a crime punishable by death. Van Meegeren claimed that not only was the painting in question, entitled *The Woman Taken in Adultery,* a forgery, but he had also produced other "Vermeers."

To prove his innocence, van Meegeren created another Vermeer to demonstrate his skill at imitating the Dutch master. He was acquitted of charges of collaboration with the enemy, but was convicted of forgery. He died of a heart attack before he could serve the 1-yr sentence. For 20 yr after van Meegeren's death art scholars debated whether at least one of his alleged works, *Christ and His Disciples at Emmaus,* was a fake or a real Vermeer. The mystery was solved in 1968 using a radiochemical technique.

White lead—lead hydroxy carbonate [$Pb_3(OH)_2(CO_3)_2$]—is a pigment used by artists for centuries. The metal in the compound is extracted from its ore, galena (PbS), which contains uranium and its daughter products in radioactive equilibrium with it. By radioactive equilibrium we mean that a particular isotope along the decay series is formed from its precursor as fast as it breaks down by decay, and so its concentration (and its radioactivity) remains constant with time. This radioactive equilibrium is disturbed in the chemical extraction of lead from its ore. Two isotopes in the uranium decay series are of particular importance in this process: ^{226}Ra ($t_{\frac{1}{2}} = 1600$ yr) and ^{210}Pb ($t_{\frac{1}{2}} = 21$ yr). (See Table 23.3.) Most ^{226}Ra is removed during the extraction of lead from its ore, but ^{210}Pb eventually ends up in the white lead, along with the stable isotope of lead (^{206}Pb). No longer supported by its relatively long-lived ancestor, ^{226}Ra, ^{210}Pb begins to decay without replenishment. This process continues until the ^{210}Pb activity is once more in equilibrium with the much smaller quantity of ^{226}Ra that survived the separation process. Assuming the concentration ratio of ^{210}Pb to ^{226}Ra is 100:1 in the sample after extraction, it would take 270 years to reestablish radioactive equilibrium for ^{210}Pb.

If Vermeer did paint *Emmaus* around the mid-seventeenth century, the radioactive equilibrium would have been restored in the white lead pigment by 1960. But this was not the case. Radiochemical analysis showed that the paint used was less than 100 yr old. Therefore, the painting could not have been the work of Vermeer.

Chemical Clues

1. Write equations for the decay of ^{226}Ra and ^{210}Pb.
2. Consider the following consecutive decay series:

$$A \longrightarrow B \longrightarrow C$$

where A and B are radioactive isotopes and C is a stable isotope. Given that the half-life of A is 100 times that of B, plot the concentrations of all three species versus time on the *same* graph. If only A was present initially, which species would reach radioactive equilibrium?

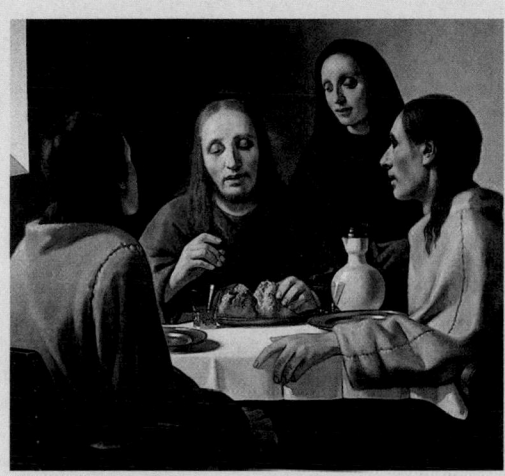

"Christ and His Disciples at Emmaus," a painting attributed to
Han van Meegeren.

3. The radioactive decay rates for ^{210}Pb and ^{226}Ra in white lead paint taken from *Emmaus*
   in 1968 were 8.5 and 0.8 disintegrations per minute per gram of lead (dpm/g), respectively. (a) How many half-lives of ^{210}Pb had elapsed between 1660 and 1968? (b) If
   Vermeer had painted *Emmaus*, what would have been the decay rate of ^{210}Pb in 1660?
   Comment on the reasonableness of this rate value.

4. To make his forgeries look authentic, van Meegeren re-used canvases of old paintings. He
   rolled one of his paintings to create cracks in the paint to resemble old works. X-ray examination of this painting showed not only the underlying painting, but also the cracks in it.
   How did this discovery reveal to the scientists that the painting on top was of a more
   recent origin?

24

A chemical plant. Many small organic compounds form the basis of multibillion dollar pharmaceutical and polymer industries. The molecular models show acetic acid, benzene, ethylene, formaldehyde, and methanol.

Organic Chemistry

A LOOK AHEAD

- We begin by defining the scope and nature of organic chemistry. (24.1)

- Next, we examine aliphatic hydrocarbons. First, we study the nomenclature and reactions of alkanes. We examine the optical isomerism of substituted alkanes and also the properties of cycloalkanes. We then study unsaturated hydrocarbons—alkenes and alkynes—molecules that contain carbon-to-carbon double bonds and triple bonds. We focus on their nomenclature, properties, and geometric isomers. (24.2)

- Aromatic compounds all contain one or more benzene rings. They are, in general, more stable than aliphatic hydrocarbons. (24.3)

- Finally, we see that the reactivity of organic compounds can be largely accounted for by the presence of functional groups. We classify the oxygen- and nitrogen-containing functional groups in alcohols, ethers, aldehydes and ketones, carboxylic acids, esters, and amines. (24.4)

Interactive Activity Summary

Organic chemistry is the study of carbon compounds. The word "organic" was originally used by eighteenth-century chemists to describe substances obtained from living sources—plants and animals. These chemists believed that nature possessed a certain vital force and that only living things could produce organic compounds. This romantic notion was disproved in 1828 by Friedrich Wohler, a German chemist who prepared urea, an organic compound, from the reaction between the inorganic compounds lead cyanate and aqueous ammonia:

$$Pb(OCN)_2 + 2NH_3 + 2H_2O \longrightarrow 2(NH_2)_2CO + Pb(OH)_2$$
$$\text{urea}$$

Today, well over 14 million synthetic and natural organic compounds are known. This number is significantly greater than the 100,000 or so known inorganic compounds.

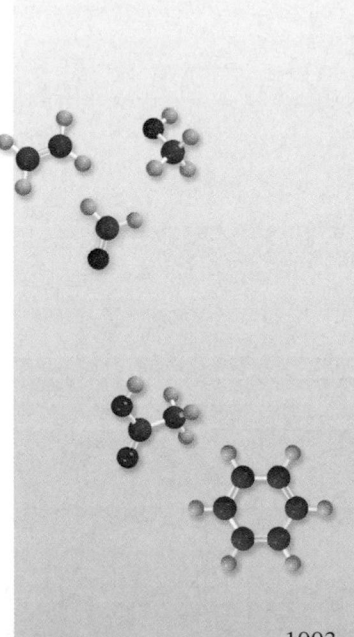

24.1 Classes of Organic Compounds

Recall that the linking of like atoms is called catenation. The ability of carbon to catenate is discussed in Section 21.3.

Common elements in organic compounds.

Carbon can form more compounds than any other element because carbon atoms are able not only to form single, double, and triple carbon-carbon bonds, but also to link up with each other in chains and ring structures. *The branch of chemistry that deals with carbon compounds is* **organic chemistry.**

Classes of organic compounds can be distinguished according to functional groups they contain. A **functional group** is *a group of atoms that is largely responsible for the chemical behavior of the parent molecule.* Different molecules containing the same kind of functional group or groups undergo similar reactions. Thus, by learning the characteristic properties of a few functional groups, we can study and understand the properties of many organic compounds. In the second half of this chapter we will discuss the functional groups known as alcohols, ethers, aldehydes and ketones, carboxylic acids, and amines.

Most organic compounds are derived from a group of compounds known as **hydrocarbons** because they are *made up of only hydrogen and carbon.* On the basis of structure, hydrocarbons are divided into two main classes—aliphatic and aromatic. **Aliphatic hydrocarbons** *do not contain the benzene group, or the benzene ring,* whereas **aromatic hydrocarbons** *contain one or more benzene rings.*

24.2 Aliphatic Hydrocarbons

Aliphatic hydrocarbons are divided into alkanes, alkenes, and alkynes, discussed next (Figure 24.1).

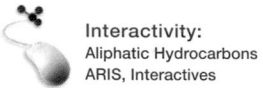

Interactivity:
Aliphatic Hydrocarbons
ARIS, Interactives

Alkanes

Alkanes *have the general formula* C_nH_{2n+2}, *where* $n = 1, 2, \ldots$. The essential characteristic of alkane hydrocarbon molecules is that *only single covalent bonds are present.* The alkanes are known as **saturated hydrocarbons** because they *contain the maximum number of hydrogen atoms that can bond with the number of carbon atoms present.*

The simplest alkane (that is, with $n = 1$) is methane CH_4, which is a natural product of the anaerobic bacterial decomposition of vegetable matter under water. Because it was first collected in marshes, methane became known as "marsh gas." A rather improbable but proven source of methane is termites. When these voracious insects consume wood, the microorganisms that inhabit their digestive system break down cellulose (the major component of wood) into methane, carbon dioxide, and other compounds. An estimated 170 million tons of methane are produced annually by

Figure 24.1 *Classification of hydrocarbons.*

Figure 24.2 *Structures of the first four alkanes. Note that butane can exist in two structurally different forms, called structural isomers.*

termites! It is also produced in some sewage treatment processes. Commercially, methane is obtained from natural gas. The Chemistry in Action essay on p. 1016 describes an interesting compound formed by methane and water molecules.

Figure 24.2 shows the structures of the first four alkanes ($n = 1$ to $n = 4$). Natural gas is a mixture of methane, ethane, and a small amount of propane. We discussed the bonding scheme of methane in Chapter 10. Indeed the carbon atoms in all the alkanes can be assumed to be sp^3-hybridized. The structures of ethane and propane are straightforward, for there is only one way to join the carbon atoms in these molecules. Butane, however, has two possible bonding schemes resulting in the **structural isomers** *n*-butane (*n* stands for normal) and isobutane, *molecules that have the same molecular formula, but different structures*. Alkanes such as the structural isomers of butane are described as having the straight chain or branched chain structures. *n*-Butane is a straight-chain alkane because the carbon atoms are joined along one line. In a branched-chain alkane like isobutane, one or more carbon atoms are bonded to at least three other carbon atoms.

In the alkane series, as the number of carbon atoms increases, the number of structural isomers increases rapidly. For example, butane, C_4H_{10}, has two isomers; decane, $C_{10}H_{22}$, has 75 isomers; and the alkane $C_{30}H_{62}$ has over 400 million, or 4×10^8, possible isomers! Obviously, most of these isomers do not exist in nature nor have they been synthesized. Nevertheless, the numbers help to explain why carbon is found in so many more compounds than any other element.

Example 24.1 deals with the number of structural isomers of an alkane.

Termites are a natural source of methane.

Example 24.1

How many structural isomers can be identified for pentane, C_5H_{12}?

Strategy For small hydrocarbon molecules (eight or fewer C atoms), it is relatively easy to determine the number of structural isomers by trial and error.

Solution The first step is to write the straight-chain structure:

n-pentane
(b.p. 36.1°C)

(Continued)

n-pentane

1006   Organic Chemistry

2-methylbutane

2,2-dimethylpropane

Similar problem: 24.11.

The second structure, by necessity, must be a branched chain:

$$H-\underset{\underset{H}{|}}{\overset{\overset{H}{|}}{C}}-\underset{\underset{H}{|}}{\overset{\overset{CH_3}{|}}{C}}-\underset{\underset{H}{|}}{\overset{\overset{H}{|}}{C}}-\underset{\underset{H}{|}}{\overset{\overset{H}{|}}{C}}-H$$

2-methylbutane
(b.p. 27.9°C)

Yet another branched-chain structure is possible:

$$H-\underset{\underset{H}{|}}{\overset{\overset{H}{|}}{C}}-\underset{\underset{CH_3}{|}}{\overset{\overset{CH_3}{|}}{C}}-\underset{\underset{H}{|}}{\overset{\overset{H}{|}}{C}}-H$$

2,2-dimethylpropane
(b.p. 9.5°C)

We can draw no other structure for an alkane having the molecular formula C_5H_{12}. Thus, pentane has three structural isomers, in which the numbers of carbon and hydrogen atoms remain unchanged despite the differences in structure.

Practice Exercise How many structural isomers are there in the alkane C_6H_{14}?

Table 24.1 shows the melting and boiling points of the straight-chain isomers of the first 10 alkanes. The first four are gases at room temperature; and pentane through decane are liquids. As molecular size increases, so does the boiling point, because of the increasing dispersion forces (see Section 11.2).

Alkane Nomenclature

The nomenclature of alkanes and all other organic compounds is based on the recommendations of the International Union of Pure and Applied Chemistry (IUPAC). The first four alkanes (methane, ethane, propane, and butane) have nonsystematic names. As Table 24.1 shows, the number of carbon atoms is reflected in the Greek

TABLE 24.1	The First 10 Straight-Chain Alkanes			
Name of Hydrocarbon	Molecular Formula	Number of Carbon Atoms	Melting Point (°C)	Boiling Point (°C)
Methane	CH_4	1	−182.5	−161.6
Ethane	CH_3-CH_3	2	−183.3	−88.6
Propane	$CH_3-CH_2-CH_3$	3	−189.7	−42.1
Butane	$CH_3-(CH_2)_2-CH_3$	4	−138.3	−0.5
Pentane	$CH_3-(CH_2)_3-CH_3$	5	−129.8	36.1
Hexane	$CH_3-(CH_2)_4-CH_3$	6	−95.3	68.7
Heptane	$CH_3-(CH_2)_5-CH_3$	7	−90.6	98.4
Octane	$CH_3-(CH_2)_6-CH_3$	8	−56.8	125.7
Nonane	$CH_3-(CH_2)_7-CH_3$	9	−53.5	150.8
Decane	$CH_3-(CH_2)_8-CH_3$	10	−29.7	174.0

prefixes for the alkanes containing five to ten carbons. We now apply the IUPAC rules to the following examples:

1. The parent name of the hydrocarbon is that given to the longest continuous chain of carbon atoms in the molecule. Thus, the parent name of the following compound is heptane because there are seven carbon atoms in the longest chain

$$\overset{1}{C}H_3 - \overset{2}{C}H_2 - \overset{3}{C}H_2 - \overset{4}{C}H - \overset{5}{C}H_2 - \overset{6}{C}H_2 - \overset{7}{C}H_3$$
$$\qquad\qquad\qquad | $$
$$\qquad\qquad\quad CH_3$$

2. An alkane less one hydrogen atom is an *alkyl* group. For example, when a hydrogen atom is removed from methane, we are left with the CH_3 fragment, which is called a *methyl* group. Similarly, removing a hydrogen atom from the ethane molecule gives an *ethyl* group, or C_2H_5. Table 24.2 lists the names of several common alkyl groups. Any chain branching off the longest chain is named as an alkyl group.

3. When one or more hydrogen atoms are replaced by other groups, the name of the compound must indicate the locations of carbon atoms where replacements are made. The procedure is to number each carbon atom on the longest chain in the direction that gives the smaller numbers for the locations of all branches. Consider the two different systems for the *same* compound shown here:

$$\overset{1}{C}H_3 - \overset{2}{C}H - \overset{3}{C}H_2 - \overset{4}{C}H_2 - \overset{5}{C}H_3 \qquad \overset{1}{C}H_3 - \overset{2}{C}H_2 - \overset{3}{C}H_2 - \overset{4}{C}H - \overset{5}{C}H_3$$

2-methylpentane   4-methylpentane

The compound on the left is numbered correctly because the methyl group is located at carbon 2 of the pentane chain; in the compound on the right, the methyl group is located at carbon 4. Thus, the name of the compound is 2-methylpentane, and not 4-methylpentane. Note that the branch name and the parent name are written as a single word, and a hyphen follows the number.

TABLE 24.2	Common Alkyl Groups
Name	**Formula**
Methyl	$-CH_3$
Ethyl	$-CH_2-CH_3$
n-Propyl	$-CH_2-CH_2-CH_3$
n-Butyl	$-CH_2-CH_2-CH_2-CH_3$
Isopropyl	$-\overset{\displaystyle CH_3}{\underset{\displaystyle CH_3}{C}}-H$
t-Butyl*	$-\overset{\displaystyle CH_3}{\underset{\displaystyle CH_3}{C}}-CH_3$

*The letter *t* stands for tertiary.

Organic Chemistry

TABLE 24.3

Names of Common Substituent Groups

Functional Group	Name
—NH$_2$	Amino
—F	Fluoro
—Cl	Chloro
—Br	Bromo
—I	Iodo
—NO$_2$	Nitro
—CH=CH$_2$	Vinyl

4. When there is more than one alkyl branch of the same kind present, we use a prefix such as *di-*, *tri-*, or *tetra-* with the name of the alkyl group. Consider the following examples:

$$\overset{1}{C}H_3 \overset{2}{-}\overset{|}{\underset{}{C}}H \overset{3}{-}\overset{|}{\underset{}{C}}H \overset{4}{-}CH_2 \overset{5}{-}CH_2 \overset{6}{-}CH_3$$

CH$_3$ CH$_3$ above carbons 2 and 3

2,3-dimethylhexane

$$\overset{1}{C}H_3 \overset{2}{-}CH_2 \overset{3}{-}\overset{|}{\underset{|}{C}} \overset{4}{-}CH_2 \overset{5}{-}CH_2 \overset{6}{-}CH_3$$

CH$_3$ above and CH$_3$ below carbon 3

3,3-dimethylhexane

When there are two or more different alkyl groups, the names of the groups are listed alphabetically. For example,

$$\overset{1}{C}H_3 \overset{2}{-}\overset{}{C}H_2 \overset{3}{-}\overset{|}{\underset{}{C}}H \overset{4}{-}\overset{|}{\underset{}{C}}H \overset{5}{-}CH_2 \overset{6}{-}CH_2 \overset{7}{-}CH_3$$

CH$_3$ above carbon 3, C$_2$H$_5$ above carbon 4

4-ethyl-3-methylheptane

5. Of course, alkanes can have many different types of substituents. Table 24.3 lists the names of some substituents, including nitro and bromo. Thus, the compound

$$\overset{1}{C}H_3 \overset{2}{-}\overset{|}{\underset{}{C}}H \overset{3}{-}\overset{|}{\underset{}{C}}H \overset{4}{-}CH_2 \overset{5}{-}CH_2 \overset{6}{-}CH_3$$

NO$_2$ above carbon 2, Br above carbon 3

is called 3-bromo-2-nitrohexane. Note that the substituent groups are listed alphabetically in the name, and the chain is numbered in the direction that gives the lowest number to the first substituted carbon atom.

Example 24.2

Give the IUPAC name of the following compound:

$$CH_3 \overset{|}{\underset{|}{-}} C \overset{}{-} CH_2 \overset{|}{\underset{}{-}} CH \overset{}{-} CH_2 \overset{}{-} CH_3$$

CH$_3$ above and CH$_3$ below the second carbon; CH$_3$ above the fourth carbon

Strategy We follow the IUPAC rules and use the information in Table 24.2 to name the compound. How many C atoms are there in the longest chain?

Solution The longest chain has six C atoms so the parent compound is called hexane. Note that there are two methyl groups attached to carbon number 2 and one methyl group attached to carbon number 4.

$$\overset{1}{C}H_3 \overset{2}{-} \overset{|}{\underset{|}{C}} \overset{3}{-} CH_2 \overset{4}{-} \overset{|}{\underset{}{C}}H \overset{5}{-} CH_2 \overset{6}{-} CH_3$$

CH$_3$ above and CH$_3$ below carbon 2; CH$_3$ above carbon 4

Therefore, we call the compound 2,2,4-trimethylhexane.

Practice Exercise Give the IUPAC name of the following compound:

$$CH_3 \overset{}{-} CH \overset{}{-} CH_2 \overset{}{-} CH \overset{}{-} CH_2 \overset{}{-} CH \overset{}{-} CH_2 \overset{}{-} CH_3$$

CH$_3$ above first CH, C$_2$H$_5$ above second CH, C$_2$H$_5$ above third CH

Similar problem: 24.26.

Example 24.3 shows that prefixes such as di-, tri-, and tetra- are used as needed, but are ignored when alphabetizing.

Example 24.3

Write the structural formula of 3-ethyl-2,2-dimethylpentane.

Strategy We follow the preceding procedure and the information in Table 24.2 to write the structural formula of the compound. How many C atoms are there in the longest chain?

Solution The parent compound is pentane, so the longest chain has five C atoms. There are two methyl groups attached to carbon number 2 and one ethyl group attached to carbon number 3. Therefore, the structure of the compound is

$$
\begin{array}{c}
\overset{\displaystyle CH_3}{}\ \overset{\displaystyle C_2H_5}{} \\
\overset{1}{CH_3}-\overset{2}{\underset{|}{\overset{|}{C}}}-\overset{3}{\underset{}{\overset{|}{CH}}}-\overset{4}{CH_2}-\overset{5}{CH_3} \\
\underset{\displaystyle CH_3}{|}
\end{array}
$$

Similar problem: 24.27.

Practice Exercise Write the structural formula of 5-ethyl-2,4,6-trimethyloctane.

Reactions of Alkanes

Alkanes are generally not considered to be very reactive substances. However, under suitable conditions they do react. For example, natural gas, gasoline, and fuel oil are alkanes that undergo highly exothermic combustion reactions:

$$CH_4(g) + 2O_2(g) \longrightarrow CO_2(g) + 2H_2O(l) \qquad \Delta H° = -890.4 \text{ kJ/mol}$$
$$2C_2H_6(g) + 7O_2(g) \longrightarrow 4CO_2(g) + 6H_2O(l) \qquad \Delta H° = -3119 \text{ kJ/mol}$$

These, and similar combustion reactions, have long been utilized in industrial processes and in domestic heating and cooking.

Halogenation of alkanes—that is, the replacement of one or more hydrogen atoms by halogen atoms—is another type of reaction that alkanes undergo. When a mixture of methane and chlorine is heated above 100°C or irradiated with light of a suitable wavelength, methyl chloride is produced:

$$CH_4(g) + Cl_2(g) \longrightarrow CH_3Cl(g) + HCl(g)$$
$$\text{methyl chloride}$$

The systematic names of methyl chloride, methylene chloride, and chloroform are monochloromethane, dichloromethane, and trichloromethane, respectively.

If an excess of chlorine gas is present, the reaction can proceed further:

$$CH_3Cl(g) + Cl_2(g) \longrightarrow CH_2Cl_2(l) + HCl(g)$$
$$\text{methylene chloride}$$
$$CH_2Cl_2(l) + Cl_2(g) \longrightarrow CHCl_3(l) + HCl(g)$$
$$\text{chloroform}$$
$$CHCl_3(l) + Cl_2(g) \longrightarrow CCl_4(l) + HCl(g)$$
$$\text{carbon tetrachloride}$$

A great deal of experimental evidence suggests that the initial step of the first halogenation reaction occurs as follows:

$$Cl_2 + \text{energy} \longrightarrow Cl\cdot + Cl\cdot$$

Thus, the covalent bond in Cl_2 breaks and two chlorine atoms form. We know it is the Cl—Cl bond that breaks when the mixture is heated or irradiated because the bond enthalpy of Cl_2 is 242.7 kJ/mol, whereas about 414 kJ/mol are needed to break C—H bonds in CH_4.

A chlorine atom is a *radical,* which contains an unpaired electron (shown by a single dot). Chlorine atoms are highly reactive and attack methane molecules according to the equation

$$CH_4 + Cl\cdot \longrightarrow \cdot CH_3 + HCl$$

This reaction produces hydrogen chloride and the methyl radical $\cdot CH_3$. The methyl radical is another reactive species; it combines with molecular chlorine to give methyl chloride and a chlorine atom:

$$\cdot CH_3 + Cl_2 \longrightarrow CH_3Cl + Cl\cdot$$

The production of methylene chloride from methyl chloride and any further reactions can be explained in the same way. The actual mechanism is more complex than the scheme we have shown because "side reactions" that do not lead to the desired products often take place, such as

$$Cl\cdot + Cl\cdot \longrightarrow Cl_2$$
$$\cdot CH_3 + \cdot CH_3 \longrightarrow C_2H_6$$

Alkanes in which one or more hydrogen atoms have been replaced by a halogen atom are called *alkyl halides.* Among the large number of alkyl halides, the best known are chloroform ($CHCl_3$), carbon tetrachloride (CCl_4), methylene chloride (CH_2Cl_2), and the chlorofluorohydrocarbons.

Chloroform is a volatile, sweet-tasting liquid that was used for many years as an anesthetic. However, because of its toxicity (it can severely damage the liver, kidneys, and heart) it has been replaced by other compounds. Carbon tetrachloride, also a toxic substance, serves as a cleaning liquid, for it removes grease stains from clothing. Methylene chloride is used as a solvent to decaffeinate coffee and as a paint remover.

The preparation of chlorofluorocarbons and the effect of these compounds on ozone in the stratosphere were discussed in Chapter 17.

Optical Isomerism of Substituted Alkanes

Optical isomerism was first discussed in Section 22.4.

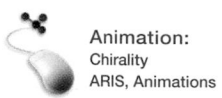

Animation:
Chirality
ARIS, Animations

Optical isomers are compounds that are nonsuperimposable mirror images of each other. Figure 24.3 shows perspective drawings of the substituted methanes CH_2ClBr and CHFClBr and their mirror images. The mirror images of CH_2ClBr are superimposable but those of CHFClBr are not, no matter how we rotate the molecules. Thus, the CHFClBr molecule is chiral. Most simple chiral molecules contain at least one *asymmetric* carbon atom—that is, a carbon atom bonded to four different atoms or groups of atoms.

Example 24.4

Is the following molecule chiral?

$$\underset{\displaystyle CH_3}{\overset{\displaystyle Cl}{H—C—CH_2—CH_3}}$$

(Continued)

Figure 24.3 *(a) The CH$_2$ClBr molecule and its mirror image. Because the molecule and its mirror image are superimposable, the molecule is said to be achiral. (b) The CHFClBr molecule and its mirror image. Since the molecule and its mirror image are not superimposable, no matter how we rotate one with respect to the other, the molecule is said to be chiral.*

(a)   (b)

Strategy Recall the condition for chirality. Is the central C atom asymmetric; that is, does it have four different atoms or different groups attached to it?

Solution We note that the central carbon atom is bonded to a hydrogen atom, a chlorine atom, a — CH$_3$ group, and a —CH$_2$—CH$_3$ group. Therefore, the central carbon atom is asymmetric and the molecule is chiral.

Similar problem: 24.25.

Practice Exercise Is the following molecule chiral?

$$\text{I—C—CH}_2\text{—CH}_3$$
with Br above and Br below the central C.

Cycloalkanes

Alkanes whose carbon atoms are joined in rings are known as **cycloalkanes.** They have the general formula C$_n$H$_{2n}$, where *n* = 3, 4, ... The simplest cycloalkane is cyclopropane, C$_3$H$_6$ (Figure 24.4). Many biologically significant substances such as cholesterol, testosterone, and progesterone contain one or more such ring systems. Theoretical analysis shows that cyclohexane can assume two different geometries that are relatively free of strain (Figure 24.5). By "strain" we mean that bonds are compressed, stretched, or twisted out of normal geometric shapes as predicted by *sp*^{3} hybridization. The most stable geometry is the *chair form*.

Interactivity:
Cyclohexane—Boat and Chair Formations
ARIS, Interactives

Alkenes

The **alkenes** (also called *olefins*) *contain at least one carbon-carbon double bond.* Alkenes have the general formula C$_n$H$_{2n}$, where *n* = 2, 3, ... The simplest alkene

Figure 24.4 *Structures of the first four cycloalkanes and their simplified forms.*

Cyclopropane   Cyclobutane   Cyclopentane   Cyclohexane

Figure 24.5 *The cyclohexane molecule can exist in various shapes. The most stable shape is the chair form and a less stable one is the boat form. Two types of H atoms are labeled axial and equatorial, respectively.*

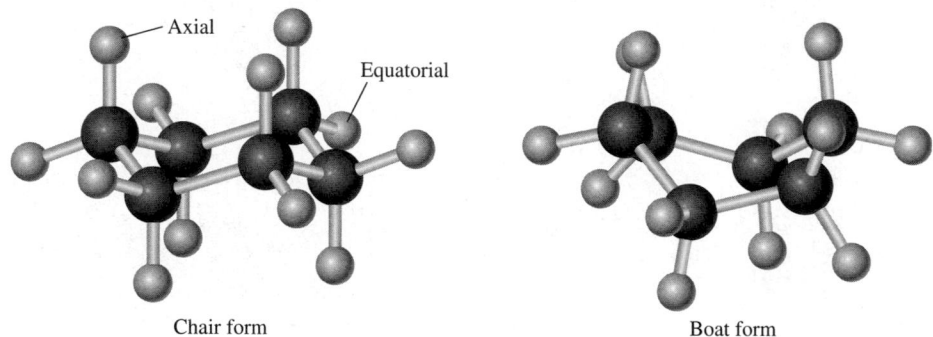

Chair form   Boat form

is C_2H_4, ethylene, in which both carbon atoms are sp^2-hybridized and the double bond is made up of a sigma bond and a pi bond (see Section 10.5).

Alkene Nomenclature

In naming alkenes we indicate the positions of the carbon-carbon double bonds. The names of compounds containing C=C bonds end with *-ene*. As with the alkanes, the name of the parent compound is determined by the number of carbon atoms in the longest chain (see Table 24.1), as shown here:

$$CH_2{=}CH{-}CH_2{-}CH_3 \qquad H_3C{-}CH{=}CH{-}CH_3$$

1-butene   2-butene

The numbers in the names of alkenes refer to the lowest numbered carbon atom in the chain that is part of the C=C bond of the alkene. The name "butene" means that there are four carbon atoms in the longest chain. Alkene nomenclature must specify whether a given molecule is *cis* or *trans* if it is a geometric isomer, such as

In the *cis* isomer, the two H atoms are on the same side of the C=C bond; in the *trans* isomer, the two H atoms are across from each other. Geometric isomerism was introduced in Section 22.4.

4-methyl-*cis*-2-hexene

4-methyl-*trans*-2-hexene

Properties and Reactions of Alkenes

Ethylene is an extremely important substance because it is used in large quantities for the manufacture of organic polymers (to be discussed in Chapter 25) and in the preparation of many other organic chemicals. Ethylene is prepared industrially by the *cracking* process, that is, the thermal decomposition of a large hydrocarbon into smaller molecules. When ethane is heated to about 800°C, it undergoes the following reaction:

$$C_2H_6(g) \xrightarrow{\text{Pt catalyst}} CH_2{=}CH_2(g) \;+\; H_2(g)$$

Other alkenes can be prepared by cracking the higher members of the alkane family.

Alkenes are classified as **unsaturated hydrocarbons,** *compounds with double or triple carbon-carbon bonds that enable them to add hydrogen atoms.* Unsaturated hydrocarbons commonly undergo **addition reactions,** in which *one molecule adds to another to form a single product.* Hydrogenation (see p. 900) is an example of addition reaction. Other addition reactions to the C=C bond include

$$C_2H_4(g) + HX(g) \longrightarrow CH_3{-}CH_2X(g)$$
$$C_2H_4(g) + X_2(g) \longrightarrow CH_2X{-}CH_2X(g)$$

where X represents a halogen (Cl, Br, or I).

The addition of a hydrogen halide to an unsymmetrical alkene such as propene is more complicated because two products are possible:

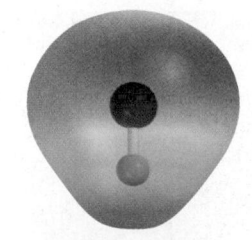

The addition reaction between HCl and ethylene. The initial interaction is between the positive end of HCl (blue) and the electron-rich region of ethylene (red), which is associated with the pi electrons of the C=C bond.

H₃C, H | C=C | H, H + HBr ──→ H₃C—C—C—H (with H and Br substituents) *and/or* H₃C—C—C—H (with Br and H substituents)

propene   1-bromopropane   2-bromopropane

In reality, however, only 2-bromopropane is formed. This phenomenon was observed in all reactions between unsymmetrical reagents and alkenes. In 1871, Vladimir Markovnikov[†] postulated a generalization that enables us to predict the outcome of such an addition reaction. This generalization, now known as *Markovnikov's rule,* states that in the addition of unsymmetrical (that is, polar) reagents to alkenes, the positive portion of the reagent (usually hydrogen) adds to the carbon atom that already has the most hydrogen atoms.

The electron density is higher on the carbon atom in the CH₂ group in propene.

Geometric Isomers of Alkenes

In a compound such as ethane, C_2H_6, the rotation of the two methyl groups about the carbon-carbon single bond (which is a sigma bond) is quite free. The situation is different for molecules that contain carbon-carbon double bonds, such as ethylene, C_2H_4. In addition to the sigma bond, there is a pi bond between the two carbon atoms. Rotation about the carbon-carbon linkage does not affect the sigma bond, but it does move the two $2p_z$ orbitals out of alignment for overlap and, hence, partially or totally destroys the pi bond (see Figure 10.16). This process requires an input of energy on the order of 270 kJ/mol. For this reason, the rotation of a carbon-carbon double bond is considerably restricted, but not impossible. Consequently, molecules containing carbon-carbon double bonds (that is, the alkenes) may have geometric isomers, which cannot be interconverted without breaking a chemical bond.

[†]Vladimir W. Markovnikov (1838–1904). Russian chemist. Markovnikov's observations of the addition reactions to alkenes were published a year after his death.

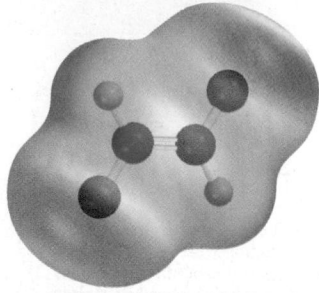

In *cis*-dichloroethylene (top), the bond moments reinforce one another and the molecule is polar. The opposite holds for *trans*-dichloroethylene and the molecule is nonpolar.

The molecule dichloroethylene, ClHC=CHCl, can exist as one of the two geometric isomers called *cis*-dichloroethylene and *trans*-dichloroethylene:

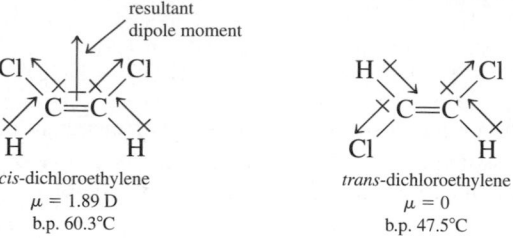

cis-dichloroethylene
$\mu = 1.89$ D
b.p. 60.3°C

trans-dichloroethylene
$\mu = 0$
b.p. 47.5°C

where the term *cis* means that two particular atoms (or groups of atoms) are adjacent to each other, and *trans* means that the two atoms (or groups of atoms) are across from each other. Generally, *cis* and *trans* isomers have distinctly different physical and chemical properties. Heat or irradiation with light is commonly used to bring about the conversion of one geometric isomer to another, a process called *cis-trans isomerization*, or geometric isomerization. As the above data show, dipole moment measurements can be used to distinguish between geometric isomers. In general, *cis* isomers possess a dipole moment, whereas *trans* isomers do not.

Cis-Trans Isomerization in the Vision Process The molecules in the retina that respond to light are rhodopsin, which has two components called 11-*cis* retinal and opsin (Figure 24.6). Retinal is the light-sensitive component and opsin is a protein molecule. Upon receiving a photon in the visible region the 11-*cis* retinal isomerizes to the all-*trans* retinal by breaking a carbon-carbon pi bond. With the pi bond broken, the remaining carbon-carbon sigma bond is free to rotate and transforms into the all-*trans* retinal. At this point an electrical impulse is generated and transmitted to the brain, which forms a visual image. The all-*trans* retinal does not fit into the binding site on opsin and eventually separates from the protein. In time, the *trans* isomer is converted back to 11-*cis* retinal by an enzyme (in the absence of light) and rhodopsin is regenerated by the binding of the *cis* isomer to opsin and the visual cycle can begin again.

An electron micrograph of rod-shaped cells (containing rhodopsins) in the retina.

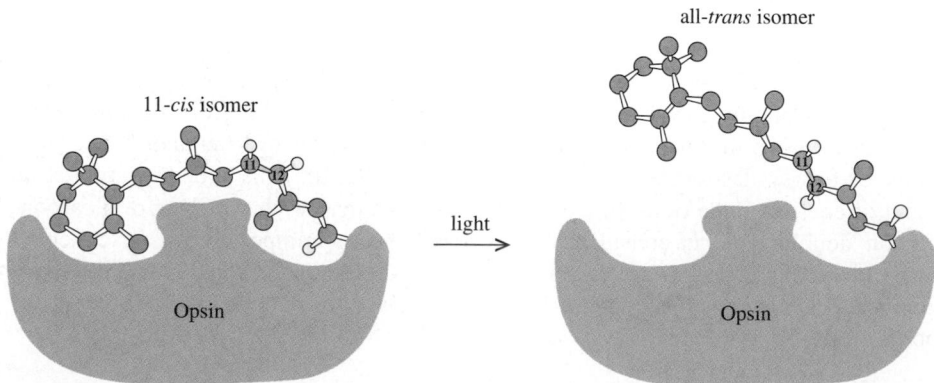

Figure 24.6 *The primary event in the vision process is the conversion of 11-cis retinal to the all-trans isomer on rhodopsin. The double bond at which the isomerization occurs is between carbon-11 and carbon-12. For simplicity, most of the H atoms are omitted. In the absence of light, this transformation takes place about once in a thousand years!*

Alkynes

Alkynes *contain at least one carbon-carbon triple bond.* They have the *general formula* C_nH_{2n-2}*, where n = 2, 3, ...*

Alkyne Nomenclature

Names of compounds containing C≡C bonds end with *-yne*. Again, the name of the parent compound is determined by the number of carbon atoms in the longest chain (see Table 24.1 for names of alkane counterparts). As in the case of alkenes, the names of alkynes indicate the position of the carbon-carbon triple bond, as, for example, in

$$HC≡C—CH_2—CH_3 \qquad H_3C—C≡C—CH_3$$
$$\text{1-butyne} \qquad\qquad\qquad \text{2-butyne}$$

Properties and Reactions of Alkynes

The simplest alkyne is ethyne, better known as acetylene (C_2H_2). The structure and bonding of C_2H_2 were discussed in Section 10.5. Acetylene is a colorless gas (b.p. −84°C) prepared by the reaction between calcium carbide and water:

$$CaC_2(s) + 2H_2O(l) \longrightarrow C_2H_2(g) + Ca(OH)_2(aq)$$

Acetylene has many important uses in industry. Because of its high heat of combustion

$$2C_2H_2(g) + 5O_2(g) \longrightarrow 4CO_2(g) + 2H_2O(l) \quad \Delta H^\circ = -2599.2 \text{ kJ/mol}$$

acetylene burned in an "oxyacetylene torch" gives an extremely hot flame (about 3000°C). Thus, oxyacetylene torches are used to weld metals (see p. 249).

The standard free energy of formation of acetylene is positive ($\Delta G_f^\circ = 209.2$ kJ/mol), unlike that of the alkanes. This means that the molecule is unstable (relative to its elements) and has a tendency to decompose:

$$C_2H_2(g) \longrightarrow 2C(s) + H_2(g)$$

The reaction of calcium carbide with water produces acetylene, a flammable gas.

In the presence of a suitable catalyst or when the gas is kept under pressure, this reaction can occur with explosive violence. To be transported safely, the gas must be dissolved in an organic solvent such as acetone at moderate pressure. In the liquid state, acetylene is very sensitive to shock and is highly explosive.

Acetylene, an unsaturated hydrocarbon, can be hydrogenated to yield ethylene:

$$C_2H_2(g) + H_2(g) \longrightarrow C_2H_4(g)$$

It undergoes the following addition reactions with hydrogen halides and halogens:

$$C_2H_2(g) + HX(g) \longrightarrow CH_2{=}CHX(g)$$
$$C_2H_2(g) + X_2(g) \longrightarrow CHX{=}CHX(g)$$
$$C_2H_2(g) + 2X_2(g) \longrightarrow CHX_2{-}CHX_2(g)$$

Methylacetylene (propyne), $CH_3—C≡C—H$, is the next member in the alkyne family. It undergoes reactions similar to those of acetylene. The addition reactions of propyne also obey Markovnikov's rule:

$$CH_3—C≡C—H + HBr \longrightarrow \begin{matrix} H_3C \\ \\ Br \end{matrix} {\Large{>}}C{=}C{\Large{<}} \begin{matrix} H \\ \\ H \end{matrix}$$

$$\text{propyne} \qquad\qquad\qquad \text{2-bromopropene}$$

Propyne. Can you account for Markovnikov's rule in this molecule?

Ice That Burns

Ice that burns? Yes, there is such a thing. It is called *methane hydrate,* and there is enough of it to meet America's energy needs for years. But scientists have yet to figure out how to mine it without causing an environmental disaster.

Bacteria in the sediments on the ocean floor consume organic material and generate methane gas. Under high-pressure and low-temperature conditions, methane forms methane hydrate, which consists of single molecules of the natural gas trapped within crystalline cages formed by frozen water molecules. A lump of methane hydrate looks like a gray ice cube, but if one puts a lighted match to it, it will burn.

Oil companies have known about methane hydrate since the 1930s, when they began using high-pressure pipelines to transport natural gas in cold climates. Unless water is carefully removed before the gas enters the pipeline, chunks of methane hydrate will impede the flow of gas.

The total reserve of the methane hydrate in the world's oceans is estimated to be 10^{13} tons of carbon content, about twice the amount of carbon in all the coal, oil, and natural gas on land. However, harvesting the energy stored in methane hydrate presents a tremendous engineering challenge. It is believed that methane hydrate acts as a kind of cement to keep the ocean floor sediments together. Tampering with the hydrate deposits could cause underwater landslides, leading to the discharge of methane into the atmosphere. This event could have serious consequences for the environment, because methane is a potent greenhouse gas (see Section 17.5). In fact, scientists have speculated that the abrupt release of methane hydrates may have hastened the end of the last ice age about 10,000 years ago. As the great blanket of continental ice melted, global sea levels swelled by more than 90 m, submerging Arctic regions rich in hydrate deposits. The relatively warm ocean water would have melted the hydrates, unleashing tremendous amounts of methane, which led to global warming.

Methane hydrate. The methane molecule is trapped in a cage of frozen water molecules (blue spheres) held together by hydrogen bonds.

Methane hydrate burning in air.

24.3 Aromatic Hydrocarbons

Benzene, the parent compound of this large family of organic substances, was discovered by Michael Faraday in 1826. Over the next 40 years, chemists were preoccupied with determining its molecular structure. Despite the small number of atoms in the molecule, there are quite a few ways to represent the structure of benzene without violating the tetravalency of carbon. However, most proposed structures were rejected because they did not explain the known properties of benzene. Finally, in 1865, August Kekulé[†] deduced that the benzene molecule could be best represented by a ring structure—a cyclic compound consisting of six carbon atoms:

An electron micrograph of benzene molecules, which shows clearly the ring structure.

As we saw in Section 9.8, the properties of benzene are best represented by both of the above resonance structures. Alternatively, the properties of benzene can be explained in terms of delocalized molecular orbitals (see p. 438):

Nomenclature of Aromatic Compounds

The naming of monosubstituted benzenes, that is, benzenes in which one H atom has been replaced by another atom or a group of atoms, is quite straightforward, as shown here:

CH$_2$CH$_3$ Cl   NH$_2$ NO$_2$

ethylbenzene   chlorobenzene   aminobenzene (aniline)   nitrobenzene

If more than one substituent is present, we must indicate the location of the second group relative to the first. The systematic way to accomplish this is to number the carbon atoms as follows:

[†]August Kekulé (1829–1896). German chemist. Kekulé was a student of architecture before he became interested in chemistry. He supposedly solved the riddle of the structure of the benzene molecule after having a dream in which dancing snakes bit their own tails. Kekulé's work is regarded by many as the crowning achievement of theoretical organic chemistry of the nineteenth century.

Three different dibromobenzenes are possible:

| 1,2-dibromobenzene | 1,3-dibromobenzene | 1,4-dibromobenzene |
| (*o*-dibromobenzene) | (*m*-dibromobenzene) | (*p*-dibromobenzene) |

The prefixes *o*- (*ortho*-), *m*- (*meta*-), and *p*- (*para*-) are also used to denote the relative positions of the two substituted groups, as shown above for the dibromobenzenes. Compounds in which the two substituted groups are different are named accordingly. Thus,

is named 3-bromonitrobenzene, or *m*-bromonitrobenzene.

Finally, we note that the group containing benzene minus a hydrogen atom (C_6H_5) is called the *phenyl* group. Thus, the following molecule is called 2-phenylpropane:

This compound is also called isopropyl benzene (see Table 24.2).

$$CH_3 - CH - CH_3$$

Properties and Reactions of Aromatic Compounds

Benzene is a colorless, flammable liquid obtained chiefly from petroleum and coal tar. Perhaps the most remarkable chemical property of benzene is its relative inertness. Although it has the same empirical formula as acetylene (CH) and a high degree of unsaturation, it is much less reactive than either ethylene or acetylene. The stability of benzene is the result of electron delocalization. In fact, benzene can be hydrogenated, but only with difficulty. The following reaction is carried out at significantly higher temperatures and pressures than are similar reactions for the alkenes:

We saw earlier that alkenes react readily with halogens to form addition products, because the pi bond in C=C can be broken easily. The most common reaction of halogens with benzene is the **substitution reaction,** in which *an atom or* *group of atoms replaces an atom or groups of atoms in another molecule.* For example,

$$\text{benzene} + Br_2 \xrightarrow[\text{catalyst}]{FeBr_3} \text{bromobenzene} + HBr$$

Note that if the reaction were an addition reaction, electron delocalization would be destroyed in the product

and the molecule would not have the aromatic characteristic of chemical unreactivity.

Alkyl groups can be introduced into the ring system by allowing benzene to react with an alkyl halide using $AlCl_3$ as the catalyst:

$$\text{benzene} + CH_3CH_2Cl \xrightarrow[\text{catalyst}]{AlCl_3} \text{ethylbenzene} + HCl$$

ethyl chloride   ethylbenzene

An enormously large number of compounds can be generated from substances in which benzene rings are fused together. Some of these *polycyclic* aromatic hydrocarbons are shown in Figure 24.7. The best known of these compounds is naphthalene, which is used in mothballs. These and many other similar compounds are present in coal tar. Some of the compounds with several rings are powerful carcinogens—they can cause cancer in humans and other animals.

Naphthalene   Anthracene   Phenanthrene   Naphthacene

Benz(*a*)anthracene*   Dibenz(*a,h*)anthracene*   Benzo(*a*)pyrene

Figure 24.7 *Some polycyclic aromatic hydrocarbons. Compounds denoted by * are potent carcinogens. An enormous number of such compounds exist in nature.*

24.4 Chemistry of the Functional Groups

We now examine in greater depth some organic functional groups, groups that are responsible for most of the reactions of the parent compounds. In particular, we focus on oxygen-containing and nitrogen-containing compounds.

Alcohols

C_2H_5OH

All *alcohols* contain *the hydroxyl* functional *group, —OH.* Some common alcohols are shown in Figure 24.8. Ethyl alcohol, or ethanol, is by far the best known. It is produced biologically by the fermentation of sugar or starch. In the absence of oxygen, the enzymes present in bacterial cultures or yeast catalyze the reaction

$$C_6H_{12}O_6(aq) \xrightarrow{\text{enzymes}} 2CH_3CH_2OH(aq) + 2CO_2(g)$$
$$\text{ethanol}$$

This process gives off energy, which microorganisms, in turn, use for growth and other functions.

Commercially, ethanol is prepared by an addition reaction in which water is combined with ethylene at about 280°C and 300 atm:

$$CH_2{=}CH_2(g) + H_2O(g) \xrightarrow{H_2SO_4} CH_3CH_2OH(g)$$

Ethanol has countless applications as a solvent for organic chemicals and as a starting compound for the manufacture of dyes, synthetic drugs, cosmetics, and explosives. It is also a constituent of alcoholic beverages. Ethanol is the only nontoxic (more properly, the least toxic) of the straight-chain alcohols; our bodies produce an enzyme, called *alcohol dehydrogenase,* which helps metabolize ethanol by oxidizing it to acetaldehyde:

$$CH_3CH_2OH \xrightarrow{\text{alcohol dehydrogenase}} CH_3CHO + H_2$$
$$\text{acetaldehyde}$$

This equation is a simplified version of what actually takes place; the H atoms are taken up by other molecules, so that no H_2 gas is evolved.

See Chemistry in Action on p. 143.

Ethanol can also be oxidized by inorganic oxidizing agents, such as acidified dichromate, to acetaldehyde and acetic acid:

$$CH_3CH_2OH \xrightarrow[H^+]{Cr_2O_7^{2-}} CH_3CHO \xrightarrow[H^+]{Cr_2O_7^{2-}} CH_3COOH$$

Figure 24.8 *Common alcohols. Note that all the compounds contain the OH group. The properties of phenol are quite different from those of the aliphatic alcohols.*

Ethanol is called an aliphatic alcohol because it is derived from an alkane (ethane). The simplest aliphatic alcohol is methanol, CH_3OH. Called *wood alcohol,* it was prepared at one time by the dry distillation of wood. It is now synthesized industrially by the reaction of carbon monoxide and molecular hydrogen at high temperatures and pressures:

$$CO(g) + 2H_2(g) \xrightarrow[\text{catalyst}]{Fe_2O_3} CH_3OH(l)$$
$$\text{methanol}$$

Methanol is highly toxic. Ingestion of only a few milliliters can cause nausea and blindness. Ethanol intended for industrial use is often mixed with methanol to prevent people from drinking it. Ethanol containing methanol or other toxic substances is called *denatured alcohol.*

The alcohols are very weakly acidic; they do not react with strong bases, such as NaOH. The alkali metals react with alcohols to produce hydrogen:

$$2CH_3OH + 2Na \longrightarrow 2CH_3ONa + H_2$$
$$\text{sodium methoxide}$$

However, the reaction is much less violent than that between Na and water:

$$2H_2O + 2Na \longrightarrow 2NaOH + H_2$$

Two other familiar aliphatic alcohols are 2-propanol (or isopropanol), commonly known as rubbing alcohol, and ethylene glycol, which is used as an antifreeze. Note that ethylene glycol has two —OH groups and so can form hydrogen bonds with water molecules more effectively than compounds that have only one —OH group (see Figure 24.8). Most alcohols—especially those with low molar masses—are highly flammable.

Alcohols react more slowly with sodium metal than does water.

Ethers

Ethers contain the R—O—R′ linkage, where R and R′ are a hydrocarbon (aliphatic or aromatic) group. They are formed by the reaction between an alkoxide (containing the RO⁻ ion) and an alkyl halide:

$$NaOCH_3 + CH_3Br \longrightarrow CH_3OCH_3 + NaBr$$
$$\text{sodium methoxide}\quad\text{methyl bromide}\quad\quad\text{dimethyl ether}$$

Diethyl ether is prepared on an industrial scale by heating ethanol with sulfuric acid at 140°C

$$C_2H_5OH + C_2H_5OH \longrightarrow C_2H_5OC_2H_5 + H_2O$$

This reaction is an example of a **condensation reaction,** which is characterized by *the joining of two molecules and the elimination of a small molecule, usually water.*

Like alcohols, ethers are extremely flammable. When left standing in air, they have a tendency to slowly form explosive peroxides:

CH_3OCH_3

$$C_2H_5OC_2H_5 + O_2 \longrightarrow C_2H_5O-\underset{\underset{H}{|}}{\overset{\overset{CH_3}{|}}{C}}-O-O-H$$
$$\text{diethyl ether}\quad\quad\quad\quad\text{1-ethyoxyethyl hydroperoxide}$$

Peroxides contain the —O—O— linkage; the simplest peroxide is hydrogen peroxide, H_2O_2. Diethyl ether, commonly known as "ether," was used as an anesthetic for many years. It produces unconsciousness by depressing the activity of the central nervous system. The major disadvantages of diethyl ether are its irritating effects on the respiratory system and the occurrence of postanesthetic nausea and vomiting. "Neothyl," or methyl propyl ether, $CH_3OCH_2CH_2CH_3$, is currently favored as an anesthetic because it is relatively free of side effects.

Aldehydes and Ketones

Under mild oxidation conditions, it is possible to convert alcohols to aldehydes and ketones:

CH₃CHO

The functional group in these compounds is the *carbonyl group,* $\diagdown C{=}O$. In an **aldehyde** *at least one hydrogen atom is bonded to the carbon in the carbonyl group.* In a **ketone,** *the carbon atom in the carbonyl group is bonded to two hydrocarbon groups.*

The simplest aldehyde, formaldehyde ($H_2C{=}O$) has a tendency to *polymerize;* that is, the individual molecules join together to form a compound of high molar mass. This action gives off much heat and is often explosive, so formaldehyde is usually prepared and stored in aqueous solution (to reduce the concentration). This rather disagreeable-smelling liquid is used as a starting material in the polymer industry (see Chapter 25) and in the laboratory as a preservative for animal specimens. Interestingly, the higher molar mass aldehydes, such as cinnamic aldehyde

Cinnamic aldehyde gives cinnamon
its characteristic aroma.

have a pleasant odor and are used in the manufacture of perfumes.

Ketones generally are less reactive than aldehydes. The simplest ketone is acetone, a pleasant-smelling liquid that is used mainly as a solvent for organic compounds and nail polish remover.

Carboxylic Acids

Under appropriate conditions both alcohols and aldehydes can be oxidized to **carboxylic acids,** *acids that contain the carboxyl group,* —COOH:

$$CH_3CH_2OH + O_2 \longrightarrow CH_3COOH + H_2O$$
$$CH_3CHO + \tfrac{1}{2}O_2 \longrightarrow CH_3COOH$$

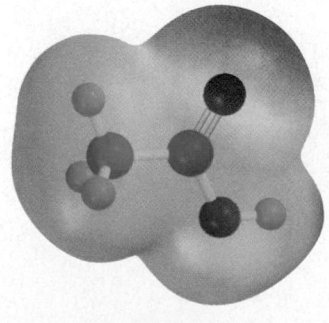

CH₃COOH

Figure 24.9 *Some common carboxylic acids. Note that they all contain the COOH group. (Glycine is one of the amino acids found in proteins.)*

Formic acid   Acetic acid   Butyric acid   Benzoic acid

Glycine   Oxalic acid   Citric acid

These reactions occur so readily, in fact, that wine must be protected from atmospheric oxygen while in storage. Otherwise, it would soon turn to vinegar due to the formation of acetic acid. Figure 24.9 shows the structure of some of the common carboxylic acids.

The oxidization of ethanol to acetic acid in wine is catalyzed by enzymes.

Carboxylic acids are widely distributed in nature; they are found in both the plant and animal kingdoms. All protein molecules are made of amino acids, a special kind of carboxylic acid containing an amino group ($-NH_2$) and a carboxyl group ($-COOH$).

Unlike the inorganic acids HCl, HNO_3, and H_2SO_4, carboxylic acids are usually weak. They react with alcohols to form pleasant-smelling esters:

$$CH_3COOH + HOCH_2CH_3 \longrightarrow CH_3-\overset{\overset{\displaystyle O}{\|}}{C}-O-CH_2CH_3 + H_2O$$

acetic acid   ethanol   ethyl acetate

This is a condensation reaction.

Other common reactions of carboxylic acids are neutralization

$$CH_3COOH + NaOH \longrightarrow CH_3COONa + H_2O$$

and formation of acid halides, such as acetyl chloride

$$CH_3COOH + PCl_5 \longrightarrow CH_3COCl + HCl + POCl_3$$

acetyl chloride   phosphoryl chloride

Acid halides are reactive compounds used as intermediates in the preparation of many other organic compounds. They hydrolyze in much the same way as many nonmetallic halides, such as $SiCl_4$:

$$CH_3COCl(l) + H_2O(l) \longrightarrow CH_3COOH(aq) + HCl(g)$$
$$SiCl_4(l) + 3H_2O(l) \longrightarrow H_2SiO_3(s) + 4HCl(g)$$

silicic acid

Esters

Esters have the general formula R′COOR, where R′ can be H or a hydrocarbon group and R is a hydrocarbon group. Esters are used in the manufacture of perfumes and as flavoring agents in the confectionery and soft-drink industries. Many fruits owe their characteristic smell and flavor to the presence of small quantities of esters. For example, bananas contain 3-methylbutyl acetate [$CH_3COOCH_2CH_2CH(CH_3)_2$], oranges contain octyl acetate ($CH_3COOCHCH_3C_6H_{13}$), and apples contain methyl butyrate ($CH_3CH_2CH_2COOCH_3$).

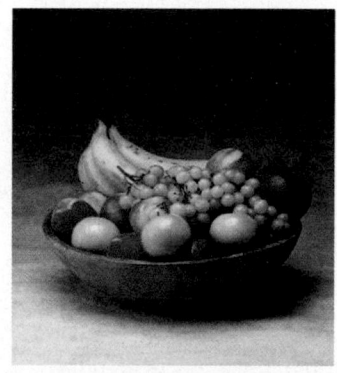

The odor of fruits is mainly due to the ester compounds in them.

The functional group in esters is the —COOR group. In the presence of an acid catalyst, such as HCl, esters undergo hydrolysis to yield a carboxylic acid and an alcohol. For example, in acid solution, ethyl acetate hydrolyzes as follows:

$$CH_3COOC_2H_5 + H_2O \rightleftharpoons CH_3COOH + C_2H_5OH$$

$$\underset{\text{ethyl acetate}}{} \qquad \underset{\text{acetic acid}}{} \qquad \underset{\text{ethanol}}{}$$

However, this reaction does not go to completion because the reverse reaction, that is, the formation of an ester from an alcohol and an acid, also occurs to an appreciable extent. On the other hand, when NaOH solution is used in hydrolysis the sodium acetate does not react with ethanol, so this reaction does go to completion from left to right:

$$CH_3COOC_2H_5 + NaOH \longrightarrow CH_3COO^-Na^+ + C_2H_5OH$$

$$\underset{\text{ethyl acetate}}{} \qquad \underset{\text{sodium acetate}}{} \qquad \underset{\text{ethanol}}{}$$

The action of soap is discussed on p. 533.

For this reason, ester hydrolysis is usually carried out in basic solutions. Note that NaOH does not act as a catalyst; rather, it is consumed by the reaction. The term *saponification* (meaning *soapmaking*) was originally used to describe the alkaline hydrolysis of fatty acid esters to yield soap molecules (sodium stearate):

$$C_{17}H_{35}COOC_2H_5 + NaOH \longrightarrow C_{17}H_{35}COO^-Na^+ + C_2H_5OH$$

$$\underset{\text{ethyl stearate}}{} \qquad \underset{\text{sodium stearate}}{}$$

Saponification has now become *a general term for alkaline hydrolysis of any type of ester.*

Amines

Amines are *organic bases having the general formula R_3N, where R may be H or a hydrocarbon group.* As with ammonia, the reaction of amines with water is

$$RNH_2 + H_2O \longrightarrow RNH_3^+ + OH^-$$

where R represents a hydrocarbon group. Like all bases, the amines form salts when allowed to react with acids:

$$CH_3CH_2NH_2 + HCl \longrightarrow CH_3CH_2NH_3^+Cl^-$$

$$\underset{\text{ethylamine}}{} \qquad \underset{\substack{\text{ethylammonium} \\ \text{chloride}}}{}$$

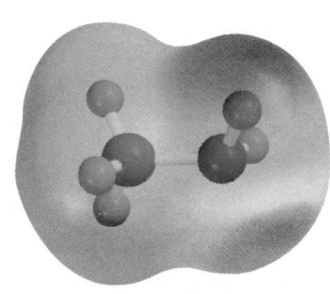

CH_3NH_2

These salts are usually colorless, odorless solids.

Aromatic amines are used mainly in the manufacture of dyes. Aniline, the simplest aromatic amine, itself is a toxic compound; a number of other aromatic amines such as 2-naphthylamine and benzidine are potent carcinogens:

aniline   2-naphthylamine   benzidine

Summary of Functional Groups

Table 24.4 summarizes the common functional groups, including the C=C and C≡C groups. Organic compounds commonly contain more than one functional group. Generally, the reactivity of a compound is determined by the number and types of functional groups in its makeup.

Example 24.5 shows how we can use the functional groups to predict reactions.

TABLE 24.4 Important Functional Groups and Their Reactions

Functional Group	Name	Typical Reactions
$\ce{>C=C<}$	Carbon-carbon double bond	Addition reactions with halogens, hydrogen halides, and water; hydrogenation to yield alkanes
$\ce{-C#C-}$	Carbon-carbon triple bond	Addition reactions with halogens, hydrogen halides; hydrogenation to yield alkenes and alkanes
$-\ddot{\underset{\cdot\cdot}{X}}:$ (X = F, Cl, Br, I)	Halogen	Exchange reactions: $CH_3CH_2Br + KI \longrightarrow CH_3CH_2I + KBr$
$-\ddot{\underset{\cdot\cdot}{O}}-H$	Hydroxyl	Esterification (formation of an ester) with carboxylic acids; oxidation to aldehydes, ketones, and carboxylic acids
$\ce{>C=\ddot{O}}$	Carbonyl	Reduction to yield alcohols; oxidation of aldehydes to yield carboxylic acids
$-\overset{:O:}{\overset{\|}{C}}-\ddot{\underset{\cdot\cdot}{O}}-H$	Carboxyl	Esterification with alcohols; reaction with phosphorus pentachloride to yield acid chlorides
$-\overset{:O:}{\overset{\|}{C}}-\ddot{\underset{\cdot\cdot}{O}}-R$ (R = hydrocarbon)	Ester	Hydrolysis to yield acids and alcohols
$-\ddot{N}\overset{R}{\underset{R}{<}}$ (R = H or hydrocarbon)	Amine	Formation of ammonium salts with acids

Example 24.5

Cholesterol is a major component of gallstones, and it is believed that the cholesterol level in the blood is a contributing factor in certain types of heart disease. From the following structure of the compound, predict its reaction with (a) Br_2, (b) H_2 (in the presence of a Pt catalyst), (c) CH_3COOH.

An artery becoming blocked by cholesterol.

Strategy To predict the type of reactions a molecule may undergo, we must first identify the functional groups present (see Table 24.4).

(Continued on p. 1028)

The Petroleum Industry

In 2005 an estimated 40 percent of the energy needs of the United States were supplied by oil or petroleum. The rest was provided by natural gas (approximately 25 percent), coal (23 percent), hydroelectric power (4 percent), nuclear power (8 percent), and other sources (0.5 percent). In addition to energy, petroleum is the source of numerous organic chemicals used to manufacture drugs, clothing, and many other products.

Unrefined petroleum, a viscous, dark-brown liquid, is often called crude oil. A complex mixture of alkanes, alkenes, cycloalkanes, and aromatic compounds, petroleum was formed in Earth's crust over the course of millions of years by the anaerobic decomposition of animal and vegetable matter by bacteria.

Petroleum deposits are widely distributed throughout the world, but they are found mainly in North America, Mexico, Russia, China, Venezuela, and, of course, the Middle East. The actual composition of petroleum varies with location. In the United States, for example, Pennsylvania crude oils are mostly aliphatic hydrocarbons, whereas the major components of western crude oils are aromatic in nature.

Although petroleum contains literally thousands of hydrocarbon compounds, we can classify its components according to the range of their boiling points. These hydrocarbons can be separated on the basis of molar mass by fractional distillation. Heating crude oil to about 400°C converts the viscous oil into hot vapor and fluid. In this form it enters the fractionating tower. The vapor rises and condenses on various collecting trays according to the temperatures at which the various components of the vapor liquefy. Some gases are drawn off at the top of the column, and the unvaporized residual oil is collected at the bottom.

Gasoline is probably the best-known petroleum product. A mixture of volatile hydrocarbons, gasoline contains mostly alkanes, cycloalkanes, and a few aromatic hydrocarbons. Some of these compounds are far more suitable for fueling an automobile engine than others, and herein lies the problem of the further treatment and refinement of gasoline.

Most automobiles employ the four-stroke operation of the *Otto cycle* engine. A major engineering concern is to control the burning of the gasoline-air mixture inside each cylinder to obtain a smooth expansion of the gas mixture. If the mixture burns too rapidly, the piston receives a hard jerk rather than a smooth, strong push. This action produces a "knocking" or "pinging" sound, as well as a decrease in efficiency in the conversion of combustion energy to mechanical energy. It turns out that straight-chain hydrocarbons have the greatest tendency to produce knocking, whereas the branched-chain and aromatic hydrocarbons give the desired smooth push.

Gasolines are usually rated according to the *octane number,* a measure of their tendency to cause knocking. On this scale, a branched C_8 compound (2,2,4-trimethylpentane, or

Major Fractions of Petroleum

Fraction	Carbon Atoms*	Boiling Point Range (°C)	Uses
Natural gas	C_1-C_4	−161 to 20	Fuel and cooking gas
Petroleum ether	C_5-C_6	30–60	Solvent for organic compounds
Ligroin	C_7	20–135	Solvent for organic compounds
Gasoline	C_6-C_{12}	30–180	Automobile fuels
Kerosene	$C_{11}-C_{16}$	170–290	Rocket and jet engine fuels, domestic heating
Heating fuel oil	$C_{14}-C_{18}$	260–350	Domestic heating and fuel for electricity production
Lubricating oil	$C_{15}-C_{24}$	300–370	Lubricants for automobiles and machines

*The entries in this column indicate the numbers of carbon atoms in the compounds involved. For example, C_1-C_4 tells us that in natural gas the compounds contain 1 to 4 carbon atoms, and so on.

Crude oil.

A fractional distillation column for separating the components of petroleum crude oil. As the hot vapor moves upward, it condenses and the various components of the crude oil are separated according to their boiling points and are drawn off as shown.

Gas

Gasoline
30°C–180°C

Naphtha
110°C–195°C

Kerosene
170°C–290°C

Heating oil
260°C–350°C

Lubricating oil
300°C–370°C

Heated crude oil at 370°C

Residue

isooctane) has been arbitrarily assigned an octane number of 100, and that of *n*-heptane, a straight-chain compound, is zero. The higher the octane number of the hydrocarbon, the better its performance in the internal combustion engine. Aromatic hydrocarbons such as benzene and toluene have high octane numbers (106 and 120, respectively), as do aliphatic hydrocarbons with branched chains.

The octane rating of hydrocarbons can be improved by the addition of small quantities of compounds called *antiknocking agents*. Among the most widely used antiknocking agents are the following:

tetramethyllead

tetraethyllead

The addition of 2 to 4 g of either of these compounds to a gallon of gasoline increases the octane rating by 10 or more. However, lead is a highly toxic metal, and the constant discharge of automobile exhaust into the atmosphere has become a serious environmental problem. Federal regulations require that all automobiles made after 1974 use "unleaded" gasolines. The catalytic converters with which late-model automobiles are equipped can be "poisoned" by lead, another reason for its exclusion from gasoline. To minimize knocking, unleaded gasolines contain methyl *tert*-butyl ether (MTBE), which minimizes knocking and increases the oxygen content of gasoline, making the fuel burn cleaner. Unfortunately, in the late 1990s MTBE was found in drinking water supplies, primarily because of leaking gasoline storage tanks. The substance makes water smell and taste foul and is a possible human carcinogen. At this writing, some states have begun to phase out the use of MTBE in gasoline, although no suitable substitute has been found.

(Continued)

Intake valve open   Spark plug fires   Exhaust valve open

(a)   (b)   (c)   (d)

The four stages of operation of an internal combustion engine. This is the type of engine used in practically all automobiles and is described technically as a four-stroke Otto cycle engine. (a) The intake valve opens to let in a gasoline-air mixture. (b) During the compression stage the two valves are closed. (c) The spark plug fires and the piston is pushed outward. (d) Finally, as the piston is pushed downward, the exhaust valve opens to let out the exhaust gas.

Solution There are two functional groups in cholesterol: the hydroxyl group and the carbon-carbon double bond.

(a) The reaction with bromine results in the addition of bromine to the double-bonded carbons, which become single-bonded.

(b) This is a hydrogenation reaction. Again, the carbon-carbon double bond is converted to a carbon-carbon single bond.

(c) The acid reacts with the hydroxyl group to form an ester and water. Figure 24.10 shows the products of these reactions.

Figure 24.10 *The products formed by the reaction of cholesterol with (a) molecular bromine, (b) molecular hydrogen, and (c) acetic acid.*

Similar problem: 24.41.

(a)   (b)   (c)

(Continued)

1028

Practice Exercise Predict the products of the following reaction:

$$CH_3OH + CH_3CH_2COOH \longrightarrow ?$$

The Chemistry in Action on p. 1026 shows the key organic compounds present in petroleum.

Summary of Facts and Concepts

1. Because carbon atoms can link up with other carbon atoms in straight and branched chains, carbon can form more compounds than any other element.

2. Organic compounds are derived from two types of hydrocarbons: aliphatic hydrocarbons and aromatic hydrocarbons.

3. Methane, CH_4, is the simplest of the alkanes, a family of hydrocarbons with the general formula C_nH_{2n+2}. Cyclopropane, C_3H_6, is the simplest of the cycloalkanes, a family of alkanes whose carbon atoms are joined in a ring. Alkanes and cycloalkanes are saturated hydrocarbons.

4. Ethylene, $CH_2\!=\!CH_2$, is the simplest of the olefins, or alkenes, a class of hydrocarbons containing carbon-

carbon double bonds and having the general formula C_nH_{2n}.

5. Acetylene, $CH\!\equiv\!CH$, is the simplest of the alkynes, which are compounds that have the general formula C_nH_{2n-2} and contain carbon-carbon triple bonds.

6. Compounds that contain one or more benzene rings are called aromatic hydrocarbons. These compounds undergo substitution by halogens and alkyl groups.

7. Functional groups impart specific types of chemical reactivity to molecules. Classes of compounds characterized by their functional groups include alcohols, ethers, aldehydes and ketones, carboxylic acids and esters, and amines.

Key Words

Addition reactions, p. 1013
Alcohol, p. 1020
Aldehyde, p. 1022
Aliphatic hydrocarbon, p. 1004
Alkane, p. 1004
Alkene, p. 1011

Alkyne, p. 1015
Amine, p. 1024
Aromatic hydrocarbon, p. 1004
Carboxylic acid, p. 1022
Condensation reaction, p. 1021
Cycloalkane, p. 1011

Ester, p. 1023
Ether, p. 1021
Functional group, p. 1004
Hydrocarbon, p. 1004
Ketone, p. 1022
Organic chemistry, p. 1004

Saponification, p. 1024
Saturated hydrocarbon, p. 1004
Structural isomer, p. 1005
Substitution reaction, p. 1018
Unsaturated
    hydrocarbon, p. 1013

Questions and Problems

Classes of Organic Compounds
Review Questions

24.1 Explain why carbon is able to form so many more compounds than any other element.

24.2 What is the difference between aliphatic and aromatic hydrocarbons?

Aliphatic Hydrocarbons
Review Questions

24.3 What do "saturated" and "unsaturated" mean when applied to hydrocarbons? Give examples of a saturated hydrocarbon and an unsaturated hydrocarbon.

24.4 Give three sources of methane.

24.5 Alkenes exhibit geometric isomerism because rotation about the C=C bond is restricted. Explain.

24.6 Why is it that alkanes and alkynes, unlike alkenes, have no geometric isomers?

24.7 What is Markovnikov's rule?

24.8 Describe reactions that are characteristic of alkanes, alkenes, and alkynes.

24.9 What factor determines whether a carbon atom in a compound is chiral?

24.10 Give examples of a chiral substituted alkane and an achiral substituted alkane.

Problems

24.11 Draw all possible structural isomers for the following alkane: C_7H_{16}.

24.12 How many distinct chloropentanes, $C_5H_{11}Cl$, could be produced in the direct chlorination of *n*-pentane, $CH_3(CH_2)_3CH_3$? Draw the structure of each molecule.

24.13 Draw all possible isomers for the molecule C_4H_8.

24.14 Draw all possible isomers for the molecule C_3H_5Br.

24.15 The structural isomers of pentane, C_5H_{12}, have quite different boiling points (see Example 24.1). Explain the observed variation in boiling point, in terms of structure.

24.16 Discuss how you can determine which of the following compounds might be alkanes, cycloalkanes, alkenes, or alkynes, without drawing their formulas: (a) C_6H_{12}, (b) C_4H_6, (c) C_5H_{12}, (d) C_7H_{14}, (e) C_3H_4.

24.17 Draw the structures of *cis*-2-butene and *trans*-2-butene. Which of the two compounds would have the higher heat of hydrogenation? Explain.

24.18 Would you expect cyclobutadiene to be a stable molecule? Explain.

24.19 How many different isomers can be derived from ethylene if two hydrogen atoms are replaced by a fluorine atom and a chlorine atom? Draw their structures and name them. Indicate which are structural isomers and which are geometric isomers.

24.20 Suggest two chemical tests that would help you distinguish between these two compounds:

(a) $CH_3CH_2CH_2CH_2CH_3$

(b) $CH_3CH_2CH_2CH=CH_2$

24.21 Sulfuric acid (H_2SO_4) adds to the double bond of alkenes as H^+ and $^-OSO_3H$. Predict the products when sulfuric acid reacts with (a) ethylene and (b) propene.

24.22 Acetylene is an unstable compound. It has a tendency to form benzene as follows:

$$3C_2H_2(g) \longrightarrow C_6H_6(l)$$

Calculate the standard enthalpy change in kilojoules per mole for this reaction at 25°C.

24.23 Predict products when HBr is added to (a) 1-butene and (b) 2-butene.

24.24 Geometric isomers are not restricted to compounds containing the C=C bond. For example, certain disubstituted cycloalkanes can exist in the *cis* and the *trans* forms. Label the following molecules as the *cis* and *trans* isomer, of the same compound:

(a)   (b)

24.25 Which of the following amino acids are chiral: (a) $CH_3CH(NH_2)COOH$, (b) $CH_2(NH_2)COOH$, (c) $CH_2(OH)CH(NH_2)COOH$?

24.26 Name the following compounds:

(a)
$$CH_3-\underset{\underset{CH_3}{|}}{CH}-CH_2-CH_2-CH_3$$

(b)
$$CH_3-\underset{\underset{C_2H_5}{|}}{CH}-\underset{\underset{CH_3}{|}}{CH}-\underset{\underset{CH_3}{|}}{CH}-CH_3$$

(c)
$$CH_3-CH_2-\underset{\underset{CH_2-CH_2-CH_3}{|}}{CH}-CH_2-CH_3$$

(d)
$$CH_2=CH-\underset{\underset{CH_3}{|}}{CH}-CH=CH_2$$

(e) $CH_3-C\equiv C-CH_2-CH_3$

(f) $CH_3-CH_2-CH-CH=CH_2$

24.27 Write structural formulas for the following organic compounds: (a) 3-methylhexane, (b) 1,3,5-trichlorocyclohexane, (c) 2,3-dimethylpentane, (d) 2-bromo-4-phenylpentane, (e) 3,4,5-trimethyloctane.

24.28 Write structural formulas for the following compounds: (a) *trans*-2-pentene, (b) 2-ethyl-1-butene, (c) 4-ethyl-*trans*-2-heptene, (d) 3-phenyl-butyne.

Aromatic Hydrocarbons
Review Questions

24.29 Comment on the extra stability of benzene compared to ethylene. Why does ethylene undergo addition reactions while benzene usually undergoes substitution reactions?

24.30 Benzene and cyclohexane molecules both contain six-membered rings. Benzene is a planar molecule, and cyclohexane is nonplanar. Explain.

Problems

24.31 Write structures for the following compounds: (a) 1-bromo-3-methylbenzene, (b) 1-chloro-2-propyl-benzene, (c) 1,2,4,5-tetramethylbenzene.

24.32 Name the following compounds:

Chemistry of the Functional Groups

Review Questions

24.33 What are functional groups? Why is it logical and useful to classify organic compounds according to their functional groups?

24.34 Draw the Lewis structure for each of the following functional groups: alcohol, ether, aldehyde, ketone, carboxylic acid, ester, amine.

Problems

24.35 Draw structures for molecules with the following formulas: (a) CH_4O, (b) C_2H_6O, (c) $C_3H_6O_2$, (d) C_3H_8O.

24.36 Classify each of the following molecules as alcohol, aldehyde, ketone, carboxylic acid, amine, or ether:

(a) $CH_3-O-CH_2-CH_3$

(b) $CH_3-CH_2-NH_2$

(c) $CH_3-CH_2-C\begin{smallmatrix}O\\\\H\end{smallmatrix}$

(d) $CH_3-C-CH_2-CH_3$ with $\|O$

(e) $H-C-OH$ with O above

(f) $CH_3-CH_2CH_2-OH$

(g)

24.37 Generally aldehydes are more susceptible to oxidation in air than are ketones. Use acetaldehyde and acetone as examples and show why ketones such as acetone are more stable than aldehydes in this respect.

24.38 Complete the following equation and identify the products:

$$HCOOH + CH_3OH \longrightarrow$$

24.39 A compound has the empirical formula $C_5H_{12}O$. Upon controlled oxidation, it is converted into a compound of empirical formula $C_5H_{10}O$, which behaves as a ketone. Draw possible structures for the original compound and the final compound.

24.40 A compound having the molecular formula $C_4H_{10}O$ does not react with sodium metal. In the presence of light, the compound reacts with Cl_2 to form three compounds having the formula C_4H_9OCl. Draw a structure for the original compound that is consistent with this information.

24.41 Predict the product or products of each of the following reactions:

(a) $CH_3CH_2OH + HCOOH \longrightarrow$

(b) $H-C\equiv C-CH_3 + H_2 \longrightarrow$

(c) $\begin{smallmatrix}C_2H_5\\\\H\end{smallmatrix}C=C\begin{smallmatrix}H\\\\H\end{smallmatrix} + HBr \longrightarrow$

24.42 Identify the functional groups in each of the following molecules:

(a) $CH_3CH_2COCH_2CH_2CH_3$

(b) $CH_3COOC_2H_5$

(c) $CH_3CH_2OCH_2CH_2CH_2CH_3$

Additional Problems

24.43 Draw all the possible structural isomers for the molecule having the formula C_7H_7Cl. The molecule contains one benzene ring.

24.44 Given these data

$$C_2H_4(g) + 3O_2(g) \longrightarrow 2CO_2(g) + 2H_2O(l)$$
$$\Delta H° = -1411 \text{ kJ/mol}$$

$$2C_2H_2(g) + 5O_2(g) \longrightarrow 4CO_2(g) + 2H_2O(l)$$
$$\Delta H° = -2599 \text{ kJ/mol}$$

$$H_2(g) + \tfrac{1}{2}O_2(g) \longrightarrow H_2O(l)$$
$$\Delta H° = -285.8 \text{ kJ/mol}$$

calculate the heat of hydrogenation for acetylene:

$$C_2H_2(g) + H_2(g) \longrightarrow C_2H_4(g)$$

24.45 State which member of each of the following pairs of compounds is the more reactive and explain why: (a) propane and cyclopropane, (b) ethylene and methane, (c) acetaldehyde and acetone.

24.46 State which of the following types of compounds can form hydrogen bonds with water molecules: (a) carboxylic acids, (b) alkenes, (c) ethers, (d) aldehydes, (e) alkanes, (f) amines.

24.47 An organic compound is found to contain 37.5 percent carbon, 3.2 percent hydrogen, and 59.3 percent fluorine by mass. The following pressure and volume data were obtained for 1.00 g of this substance at 90°C:

P (atm)	V (L)
2.00	0.332
1.50	0.409
1.00	0.564
0.50	1.028

The molecule is known to have no dipole moment. (a) What is the empirical formula of this substance? (b) Does this substance behave as an ideal gas? (c) What is its molecular formula? (d) Draw the Lewis structure of this molecule and describe its geometry. (e) What is the systematic name of this compound?

24.48 State at least one commercial use for each of the following compounds: (a) 2-propanol (isopropanol), (b) acetic acid, (c) naphthalene, (d) methanol, (e) ethanol, (f) ethylene glycol, (g) methane, (h) ethylene.

24.49 How many liters of air (78 percent N_2, 22 percent O_2 by volume) at 20°C and 1.00 atm are needed for the complete combustion of 1.0 L of octane, C_8H_{18}, a typical gasoline component that has a density of 0.70 g/mL?

24.50 How many carbon-carbon sigma bonds are present in each of the following molecules? (a) 2-butyne, (b) anthracene (see Figure 24.5), (c) 2,3-dimethylpentane

24.51 How many carbon-carbon sigma bonds are present in each of the following molecules? (a) benzene, (b) cyclobutane, (c) 3-ethyl-2-methylpentane

24.52 The combustion of 20.63 mg of compound Y, which contains only C, H, and O, with excess oxygen gave 57.94 mg of CO_2 and 11.85 mg of H_2O. (a) Calculate how many milligrams of C, H, and O were present in the original sample of Y. (b) Derive the empirical formula of Y. (c) Suggest a plausible structure for Y if the empirical formula is the same as the molecular formula.

24.53 Draw all the structural isomers of compounds with the formula $C_4H_8Cl_2$. Indicate which isomers are chiral and give them systematic names.

24.54 The combustion of 3.795 mg of liquid B, which contains only C, H, and O, with excess oxygen gave 9.708 mg of CO_2 and 3.969 mg of H_2O. In a molar mass determination, 0.205 g of B vaporized at 1.00 atm and 200.0°C and occupied a volume of 89.8 mL. Derive the empirical formula, molar mass, and molecular formula of B and draw three plausible structures.

24.55 Beginning with 3-methyl-1-butyne, show how you would prepare the following compounds:

(a) $\text{CH}_2\!=\!\overset{\overset{\displaystyle Br}{|}}{C}\!-\!\overset{\overset{\displaystyle CH_3}{|}}{CH}\!-\!CH_3$

(b) $\text{CH}_2Br\!-\!CBr_2\!-\!\overset{\overset{\displaystyle CH_3}{|}}{CH}\!-\!CH_3$

(c) $\text{CH}_3\!-\!\overset{\overset{\displaystyle Br}{|}}{CH}\!-\!\overset{\overset{\displaystyle CH_3}{|}}{CH}\!-\!CH_3$

24.56 Indicate the asymmetric carbon atoms in the following compounds:

(a) $\text{CH}_3\!-\!CH_2\!-\!\overset{\overset{\displaystyle CH_3}{|}}{CH}\!-\!\underset{\underset{\displaystyle NH_2}{|}}{CH}\!-\!\overset{\overset{\displaystyle O}{\|}}{C}\!-\!NH_2$

(b)
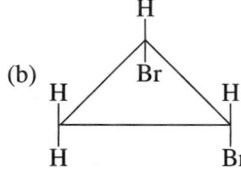

24.57 Suppose benzene contained three distinct single bonds and three distinct double bonds. How many different isomers would there be for dichlorobenzene $(C_6H_4Cl_2)$? Draw all your proposed structures.

24.58 Write the structural formula of an aldehyde that is a structural isomer of acetone.

24.59 Draw structures for the following compounds: (a) cyclopentane, (b) *cis*-2-butene, (c) 2-hexanol, (d) 1,4-dibromobenzene, (e) 2-butyne.

24.60 Name the classes to which the following compounds belong:
(a) C_4H_9OH
(b) $CH_3OC_2H_5$
(c) C_2H_5CHO
(d) C_6H_5COOH
(e) CH_3NH_2

24.61 Ethanol, C_2H_5OH, and dimethyl ether, CH_3OCH_3, are structural isomers. Compare their melting points, boiling points, and solubilities in water.

24.62 Amines are Brønsted bases. The unpleasant smell of fish is due to the presence of certain amines. Explain why cooks often add lemon juice to suppress the odor of fish (in addition to enhancing the flavor).

24.63 You are given two bottles, each containing a colorless liquid. You are told that one liquid is cyclohexane and the other is benzene. Suggest one chemical test that would allow you to distinguish between these two liquids.

24.64 Give the chemical names of the following organic compounds and write their formulas: marsh gas, grain alcohol, wood alcohol, rubbing alcohol, antifreeze, mothballs, chief ingredient of vinegar.

24.65 The compound CH_3—C≡C—CH_3 is hydrogenated to an alkene using platinum as the catalyst. Predict whether the product is the pure *trans* isomer, the pure *cis* isomer, or a mixture of *cis* and *trans* isomers. Based on your prediction, comment on the mechanism of the heterogeneous catalysis.

24.66 How many asymmetric carbon atoms are present in each of the following compounds?

(a)
$$\begin{array}{c} \quad\ \ \text{H}\quad\text{H}\quad\text{H} \\ \quad\ \ |\quad\ |\quad\ | \\ \text{H---C---C---C---Cl} \\ \quad\ \ |\quad\ |\quad\ | \\ \quad\ \ \text{H}\quad\text{Cl}\quad\text{H} \end{array}$$

(b)
$$\begin{array}{c} \quad\quad\ \ \text{OH}\quad\text{CH}_3 \\ \quad\quad\ \ |\quad\quad\ | \\ \text{H}_3\text{C---C------C---CH}_2\text{OH} \\ \quad\quad\ \ |\quad\quad\ | \\ \quad\quad\ \ \text{H}\quad\quad\ \text{H} \end{array}$$

(c)

24.67 Isopropanol is prepared by reacting propylene (CH_3CHCH_2) with sulfuric acid, followed by treatment with water. (a) Show the sequence of steps leading to the product. What is the role of sulfuric acid? (b) Draw the structure of an alcohol that is an isomer of isopropanol. (c) Is isopropanol a chiral molecule? (d) What property of isopropanol makes it useful as a rubbing alcohol?

24.68 When a mixture of methane and bromine vapor is exposed to light, the following reaction occurs slowly:

$$CH_4(g) + Br_2(g) \longrightarrow CH_3Br(g) + HBr(g)$$

Suggest a mechanism for this reaction. (*Hint*: Bromine vapor is deep red; methane is colorless.)

24.69 Under conditions of acid catalysis, alkenes react with water to form alcohols. As in the case with hydrogen halides, the addition reaction in the formation of alcohols is also governed by Markovnikov's rule. An alkene of approximate molar mass of 42 g reacts with water and sulfuric acid to produce a compound that reacts with acidic potassium dichromate solution to produce a ketone. Identify all the compounds in the preceding steps.

Special Problems

24.70 2-Butanone can be reduced to 2-butanol by reagents such as lithium aluminum hydride ($LiAlH_4$). (a) Write the formula of the product. Is it chiral? (b) In reality, the product does not exhibit optical activity. Explain.

24.71 Write the structures of three alkenes that yield 2-methylbutane on hydrogenation.

24.72 An alcohol was converted to a carboxylic acid with acidic potassium dichromate. A 4.46-g sample of the acid was added to 50.0 mL of 2.27 M NaOH and the excess NaOH required 28.7 mL of 1.86 M HCl for neutralization. What is the molecular formula of the alcohol?

24.73 Write the structural formulas of the alcohols with the formula $C_6H_{13}O$ and indicate those that are chiral. Show only the C atoms and the —OH groups.

24.74 Fat and oil are names for the same class of compounds, called triglycerides, which contain three ester groups

$$CH_2-O-\overset{\overset{\textstyle O}{\|}}{C}-R$$
$$CH-O-\overset{\overset{\textstyle O}{\|}}{C}-R'$$
$$CH_2-O-\overset{\overset{\textstyle O}{\|}}{C}-R''$$

A fat or oil

where R, R′, and R″ represent long hydrocarbon chains. (a) Suggest a reaction that leads to the formation of a triglyceride molecule, starting with glycerol and carboxylic acids (see p. 460 for structure of glycerol). (b) In the old days, soaps were made by hydrolyzing animal fat with lye (a sodium hydroxide solution). Write an equation for this reaction. (c) The difference between fats and oils is that at room temperature, the former are solids and the latter are liquids. Fats are usually produced by animals, whereas oils are commonly found in plants. The melting points of these substances are determined by the number of C=C bonds (or the extent of unsaturation) present—the larger the number of C=C bonds, the lower the melting point and the more likely that the substance is a liquid. Explain. (d) One way to convert liquid oil to solid fat is to hydrogenate the oil, a process by which some or all of the C=C bonds are converted to C—C bonds. This procedure prolongs shelf life of the oil by removing the more reactive C=C group and facilitates packaging. How would you carry out such a process (that is, what reagents and catalyst would you employ)? (e) The degree of unsaturation of oil can be determined by reacting the oil with iodine, which reacts with the C=C bond as follows:

$$-\overset{|}{C}-\overset{|}{C}=\overset{|}{C}-\overset{|}{C}- \ + I_2 \longrightarrow -\overset{|}{C}-\overset{\overset{\textstyle I}{|}}{C}-\overset{\overset{\textstyle I}{|}}{C}-\overset{|}{C}-$$

The procedure is to add a known amount of iodine to the oil and allow the reaction to go to completion. The amount of excess (unreacted) iodine is determined by titrating the remaining iodine with a standard sodium thiosulfate ($Na_2S_2O_3$) solution:

$$I_2 + 2Na_2S_2O_3 \longrightarrow Na_2S_4O_6 + 2NaI$$

The number of grams of iodine that react with 100 grams of oil is called the *iodine number*. In one case, 43.8 g of I_2 were treated with 35.3 g of corn oil. The excess iodine required 20.6 mL of a 0.142 M $Na_2S_2O_3$ for neutralization. Calculate the iodine number of the corn oil.

Answers to Practice Exercises

24.1 5.

24.2 4,6-diethyl-2-methyloctane

24.3
$$CH_3-\overset{\overset{\textstyle CH_3}{|}}{CH}-CH_2-\overset{\overset{\textstyle CH_3}{|}}{CH}-\overset{\overset{\textstyle C_2H_5}{|}}{CH}-\overset{\overset{\textstyle CH_3}{|}}{CH}-CH_2-CH_3$$

24.4 No.

24.5 $CH_3CH_2COOCH_3$ and H_2O.

CHEMICAL
Mystery

The Disappearing Fingerprints†

In 1993, a young girl was abducted from her home and taken away in a car. Later she managed to escape from her attacker and was rescued by a local resident and safely returned home unharmed. A few days later the police arrested a suspect and recovered the car. In building the case against the man, the law officers found that they lacked some crucial evidence. The girl's detailed description indicated that she must have been in the car, yet none of her fingerprints could be found. Fortunately, the police were able to link the girl to the car and its owner by matching fibers found in the car with those from the girl's nightgown.

What are fingerprints? Our fingertips are studded with sweat pores. When a finger touches something, the sweat from these pores is deposited on the surface, providing a mirror image of the ridge pattern, called a fingerprint. No two individuals have the same fingerprints. This fact makes fingerprint matching one of the most powerful methods for identifying crime suspects.

Why were the police not able to find the girl's fingerprints in the car? The residue that is deposited by fingerprints is about 99 percent water. The other 1 percent contains oils and fatty acids, esters, amino acids, and salts. Fingerprint samples from adults contain heavy oils and long carbon chains linked together by ester groups, but children's samples contain mostly unesterified and shorter fatty chains that are light and more volatile. (The hydrogen atoms are omitted for clarity.)

$$C-C-C-C-C-C-C-C-C-C-C-C-C-C{\overset{\displaystyle O}{\underset{\displaystyle OH}{}}}$$

from a child's fingerprint

$$C-C-C-C-C-C-C-C-C-C-C-C-C-C-C-C-C-C{\overset{\displaystyle O-C-C-C-C-C-C-C-C-C-C-C-C-C-C-C}{\underset{\displaystyle O}{}}}$$

from an adult's fingerprint

In general, adult fingerprints last at least several days, but children's fingerprints often vanish within 24 hours. For this reason, in cases involving children, crime scene investigation must be done very quickly.

---

†Adapted with permission from "The Disappearing Fingerprints" by Deborah Noble, *CHEM MATTERS*, February, 1997, p. 9. Copyright 1997 American Chemical Society.

Chemical Clues

When a finger touches a surface, it leaves an invisible pattern of oil called a latent fingerprint. Forensic investigators must develop a latent fingerprint into a visible print that can be photographed, then scanned and stored for matching purposes. The following are some of the common methods for developing latent fingerprints.

1. The dusting powder method: This is the traditional method in which fine powder (usually carbon black, which is an amorphous form of carbon obtained by the thermal decomposition of hydrocarbons) is brushed onto nonporous surfaces. The powder sticks to the sweat, making the ridge pattern visible. An improvement on this method is the use of fluorescent powders. What are the advantages of this modification?

2. The iodine method: When heated, iodine sublimes and its vapor reacts with the carbon-carbon double bonds in fats and oils, turning the ridge pattern to a yellow brown color. This method is particularly well suited for fingerprints on porous objects like papers and cardboard. Write an equation showing the reaction of I_2 with fats and oils.

3. The ninhydrin method: This is one of the most popular methods for developing latent fingerprints on porous, absorbent surfaces like paper and wood. This method is based on a complex reaction between ninhydrin and amino acids (see Table 25.2) in the presence of a base to produce a compound, which turns purple when heated. The unbalanced equation is

$$\text{ninhydrin} \quad + \quad H_3\overset{+}{N}CHCOO^- \quad + \quad OH^- \longrightarrow \quad \text{Ruhemann's purple}$$

| ninhydrin | amino acid | | Ruhemann's purple |

where R is a substituent. Because the amino acids in sweat do not interact with the cellulose content of paper or wood, this technique enables prints that may be years old to be developed. Draw resonance structures of Ruhemann's purple, showing the movement of electrons with curved arrows.

25

The strength of one kind of polymer, called Lexan, is so great that it is used to make bullet-proof windows. The models show the starting monomers bisphenol-A ($C_{15}H_{16}O_2$) and phosgene ($COCl_2$) and a repeating unit of Lexan.

Synthetic and Natural Organic Polymers

A LOOK AHEAD

- We begin with a discussion of the general properties of organic polymers. (25.1)

- We then study the synthesis of organic polymers by addition reactions and condensation reactions. We examine both natural and synthetic rubber and other synthetic polymers. (25.2)

- Next, we learn that proteins are polymers of amino acids. We examine the structure of a protein molecule in terms of its primary, secondary, tertiary, and quaternary structures. We also study the stability of a protein molecule, the cooperativity effect, and protein denaturation. (25.3)

- The chapter ends with a brief discussion of the structure and composition of the genetic materials deoxyribonucleic acids (DNA) and ribonucleic acids (RNA). (25.4)

Polymers are very large molecules containing hundreds or thousands of atoms. People have been using polymers since prehistoric time, and chemists have been synthesizing them for the past century. Natural polymers are the basis of all life processes, and our technological society is largely dependent on synthetic polymers.

This chapter discusses some of the preparation and properties of important synthetic organic polymers in addition to two naturally occurring polymers that are vital to living systems—proteins and nucleic acids.

25.1 Properties of Polymers

A *polymer* is *a molecular compound distinguished by a high molar mass, ranging into thousands and millions of grams, and made up of many repeating units.* The physical properties of these so-called macromolecules differ greatly from those of small, ordinary molecules, and special techniques are required to study them.

Naturally occurring polymers include proteins, nucleic acids, cellulose (polysaccharides), and rubber (polyisoprene). Most synthetic polymers are organic compounds. Familiar examples are nylon, poly(hexamethylene adipamide); Dacron, poly(ethylene terephthalate); and Lucite or Plexiglas, poly(methyl methacrylate).

The development of polymer chemistry began in the 1920s with the investigation into a puzzling behavior of certain materials, including wood, gelatin, cotton, and rubber. For example, when rubber, with the known empirical formula of C_5H_8, was dissolved in an organic solvent, the solution displayed several unusual properties—high viscosity, low osmotic pressure, and negligible freezing-point depression. These observations strongly suggested the presence of solutes of very high molar mass, but chemists were not ready at that time to accept the idea that such giant molecules could exist. Instead, they postulated that materials such as rubber consist of aggregates of small molecular units, like C_5H_8 or $C_{10}H_{16}$, held together by intermolecular forces. This misconception persisted for a number of years, until Hermann Staudinger[†] clearly showed that these so-called aggregates are, in fact, enormously large molecules, each of which contains many thousands of atoms held together by covalent bonds.

Once the structures of these macromolecules were understood, the way was open for manufacturing polymers, which now pervade almost every aspect of our daily lives. About 90 percent of today's chemists, including biochemists, work with polymers.

25.2 Synthetic Organic Polymers

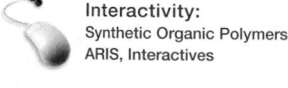

Interactivity:
Synthetic Organic Polymers
ARIS, Interactives

Because of their size, we might expect molecules containing thousands of carbon and hydrogen atoms to form an enormous number of structural and geometric isomers (if C=C bonds are present). However, these molecules are made up of *monomers, simple repeating units,* and this type of composition severely restricts the number of possible isomers. Synthetic polymers are created by joining monomers together, one at a time, by means of addition reactions and condensation reactions.

Addition Reactions

Addition reactions were described on p. 1013.

Addition reactions involve unsaturated compounds containing double or triple bonds, particularly C=C and C≡C. Hydrogenation and reactions of hydrogen halides and halogens with alkenes and alkynes are examples of addition reactions.

Polyethylene, a very stable polymer used in packaging wraps, is made by joining ethylene monomers via an addition-reaction mechanism. First an *initiator* molecule (R_2) is heated to produce two radicals:

$$R_2 \longrightarrow 2R \cdot$$

[†]Hermann Staudinger (1881–1963). German chemist. One of the pioneers in polymer chemistry. Staudinger was awarded the Nobel Prize in Chemistry in 1953.

Figure 25.1 *Structure of polyethylene. Each carbon atom is sp³-hybridized.*

The reactive radical attacks an ethylene molecule to generate a new radical:

$$R\cdot + CH_2{=}CH_2 \longrightarrow R{-}CH_2{-}CH_2\cdot$$

which further reacts with another ethylene molecule, and so on:

$$R{-}CH_2{-}CH_2\cdot + CH_2{=}CH_2 \longrightarrow R{-}CH_2{-}CH_2{-}CH_2{-}CH_2\cdot$$

Very quickly a long chain of CH_2 groups is built. Eventually, this process is terminated by the combination of two long-chain radicals to give the polymer called polyethylene:

$$R{-}(CH_2{-}CH_2)_n CH_2CH_2\cdot + R{-}(CH_2{-}CH_2)_n CH_2CH_2\cdot \longrightarrow$$
$$R\,(\,CH_2{-}CH_2)_n CH_2CH_2{-}CH_2CH_2{-}(CH_2{-}CH_2)_n R$$

where $-(CH_2{-}CH_2)_n$ is a convenient shorthand convention for representing the repeating unit in the polymer. The value of n is understood to be very large, on the order of hundreds.

The individual chains of polyethylene pack together well and so account for the substance's crystalline properties (Figure 25.1). Polyethylene is mainly used in films in frozen food packaging and other product wrappings. A specially treated type of polyethylene called Tyvek is used for home insulation.

Polyethylene is an example of a ***homopolymer,*** which is *a polymer made up of only one type of monomer.* Other homopolymers that are synthesized by the radical mechanism are Teflon, polytetrafluoroethylene (Figure 25.2) and poly(vinyl chloride) (PVC):

$$-(CF_2{-}CF_2)_n \qquad\qquad -(CH_2{-}CH)_n$$
$$\qquad\qquad\qquad\qquad\qquad\qquad |$$
$$\qquad\qquad\qquad\qquad\qquad\qquad Cl$$

$$\text{Teflon} \qquad\qquad\qquad\qquad \text{PVC}$$

The chemistry of polymers is more complex if the starting units are asymmetric:

$$\begin{array}{cc} H_3C & H \\ & \\ C{=}C & \\ & \\ H & H \end{array} \qquad \begin{array}{cc} CH_3 & H \\ | & | \\ -C & C- \\ | & | \\ H & H \end{array}_n$$

$$\text{propene} \qquad\qquad\qquad \text{polypropene}$$

Common mailing envelopes made of Tyvek.

Figure 25.2 *A cooking utensil coated with Silverstone, which contains polytetrafluoroethylene.*

Several geometric isomers can result from an addition reaction of propenes (Figure 25.3). If the additions occur randomly, we obtain *atactic* polypropenes, which do not pack together well. These polymers are rubbery, amorphous, and relatively weak. Two other possibilities are an *isotactic* structure, in which the R groups are all on the same side of the asymmetric carbon atoms, and a *syndiotactic* form, in which the R groups alternate to the left and right of the asymmetric carbons. Of these, the isotactic isomer has the highest melting point and greatest crystallinity and is endowed with superior mechanical properties.

Figure 25.3 *Stereoisomers of polymers. When the R group (green sphere) is CH₃, the polymer is polypropene. (a) When the R groups are all on one side of the chain, the polymer is said to be isotactic. (b) When the R groups alternate from side to side, the polymer is said to be syndiotactic. (c) When the R groups are disposed at random, the polymer is atactic.*

(a)

(b)

(c)

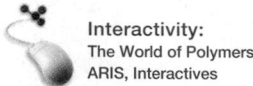

Interactivity:
The World of Polymers
ARIS, Interactives

A major problem that the polymer industry faced in the beginning was how to synthesize either the isotactic or syndiotactic polymer selectively without having it contaminated by other products. The solution came from Giulio Natta[†] and Karl Ziegler,[‡] who demonstrated that certain catalysts, including triethylaluminum $[Al(C_2H_5)_3]$ and titanium trichloride ($TiCl_3$), promote the formation only of specific isomers. Using Natta-Ziegler catalysts, chemists can design polymers to suit any purpose.

Rubber is probably the best known organic polymer and the only true hydrocarbon polymer found in nature. It is formed by the radical addition of the monomer isoprene. Actually, polymerization can result in either poly-*cis*-isoprene or poly-*trans*-isoprene—or a mixture of both, depending on reaction conditions:

$$n\text{CH}_2{=}\overset{\text{CH}_3}{\underset{}{\text{C}}}{-}\text{CH}{=}\text{CH}_2 \longrightarrow \left(\begin{matrix} \text{CH}_3 & & \text{H} \\ & \text{C}{=}\text{C} & \\ \text{CH}_2 & & \text{CH}_2 \end{matrix} \right)_n \quad \text{and/or} \quad \left(\begin{matrix} \text{CH}_2 & & \text{H} \\ & \text{C}{=}\text{C} & \\ \text{CH}_3 & & \text{CH}_2 \end{matrix} \right)_n$$

isoprene   poly-*cis*-isoprene   poly-*trans*-isoprene

Note that in the *cis* isomer the two CH_2 groups are on the same side of the C=C bond, whereas the same groups are across from each other in the *trans* isomer. Natural rubber is poly-*cis*-isoprene, which is extracted from the tree *Hevea brasiliensis* (Figure 25.4).

An unusual and very useful property of rubber is its elasticity. Rubber will stretch up to 10 times its length and, if released, will return to its original size. In contrast, a piece of copper wire can be stretched only a small percentage of its length and still return to its original size. Unstretched rubber has no regular X-ray diffraction pattern and is therefore amorphous. Stretched rubber, however, possesses a fair amount of crystallinity and order.

[†]Giulio Natta (1903–1979). Italian chemist. Natta received the Nobel Prize in Chemistry in 1963 for discovering stereospecific catalysts for polymer synthesis.

[‡]Karl Ziegler (1898–1976). German chemist. Ziegler shared the Nobel Prize in Chemistry in 1963 with Natta for his work in polymer synthesis.

Figure 25.4 *Latex (aqueous suspension of rubber particles) being collected from a rubber tree.*

The elastic property of rubber is due to the flexibility of its long-chain molecules. In the bulk state, however, rubber is a tangle of polymeric chains, and if the external force is strong enough, individual chains slip past one another, thereby causing the rubber to lose most of its elasticity. In 1839, Charles Goodyear[†] discovered that natural rubber could be cross-linked with sulfur (using zinc oxide as the catalyst) to prevent chain slippage (Figure 25.5). His process, known as *vulcanization,* paved the way for many practical and commercial uses of rubber, such as in automobile tires and dentures.

During World War II a shortage of natural rubber in the United States prompted an intensive program to produce synthetic rubber. Most synthetic rubbers (called *elastomers*) are made from petroleum products such as ethylene, propylene, and butadiene. For example, chloroprene molecules polymerize readily to form polychloroprene, commonly known as *neoprene*, which has properties that are comparable or even superior to those of natural rubber:

$$H_2C=CH-CCl=CH_2$$

chloroprene

$$\left(\begin{array}{c} -CH_2 \quad\quad H \\ \quad\ \ C=C \\ Cl \quad\quad CH_2 \end{array} \right)_n$$

polychloroprene

Another important synthetic rubber is formed by the addition of butadiene to styrene in a 3:1 ratio to give styrene-butadiene rubber (SBR). Because styrene and butadiene are different monomers, SBR is called a ***copolymer,*** which is *a polymer containing two or more different monomers.* Table 25.1 shows a number of common and familiar homopolymers and one copolymer produced by addition reactions.

[†]Charles Goodyear (1800–1860). American chemist. Goodyear was the first person to realize the potential of natural rubber. His vulcanization process made rubber usable in countless ways and opened the way for the development of the automobile industry.

(a)

(b)

(c)

Figure 25.5 *Rubber molecules ordinarily are bent and convoluted. Parts (a) and (b) represent the long chains before and after vulcanization, respectively; (c) shows the alignment of molecules when stretched. Without vulcanization these molecules would slip past one another, and rubber's elastic properties would be gone.*

TABLE 25.1   Some Monomers and Their Common Synthetic Polymers

Monomer		Polymer	
Formula	**Name**	**Name and Formula**	**Uses**
$H_2C{=}CH_2$	Ethylene	Polyethylene $\{CH_2{-}CH_2\}_n$	Plastic piping, bottles, electrical insulation, toys
$H_2C{=}\overset{\displaystyle H}{\underset{\displaystyle CH_3}{C}}$	Propene	Polypropene $\left(\overset{\displaystyle}{\underset{\displaystyle CH_3}{CH}}{-}CH_2{-}\overset{\displaystyle}{\underset{\displaystyle CH_3}{CH}}{-}CH_2\right)_n$	Packaging film, carpets, crates for soft-drink bottles, lab wares, toys
$H_2C{=}\overset{\displaystyle H}{\underset{\displaystyle Cl}{C}}$	Vinyl chloride	Poly(vinyl chloride) (PVC) $\{CH_2{-}\underset{\displaystyle Cl}{CH}\}_n$	Piping, siding, gutters, floor tile, clothing, toys
$H_2C{=}\overset{\displaystyle H}{\underset{\displaystyle CN}{C}}$	Acrylonitrile	Polyacrylonitrile (PAN) $\left(CH_2{-}\underset{\displaystyle CN}{CH}\right)_n$	Carpets, knitwear
$F_2C{=}CF_2$	Tetrafluoro-ethylene	Polytetrafluoroethylene (Teflon) $\{CF_2{-}CF_2\}_n$	Coating on cooking utensils, electrical insulation, bearings
$H_2C{=}\overset{\displaystyle COOCH_3}{\underset{\displaystyle CH_3}{C}}$	Methyl methacrylate	Poly(methyl methacrylate) (Plexiglas) $\{CH_2{-}\overset{\displaystyle COOCH_3}{\underset{\displaystyle CH_3}{C}}\}_n$	Optical equipment, home furnishings
$H_2C{=}\overset{\displaystyle H}{C}$ (phenyl)	Styrene	Polystyrene $\{CH_2{-}CH\}_n$ (phenyl)	Containers, thermal insulation (ice buckets, water coolers), toys
$H_2C{=}\overset{\displaystyle H}{C}{-}\overset{\displaystyle H}{C}{=}CH_2$	Butadiene	Polybutadiene $\{CH_2CH{=}CHCH_2\}_n$	Tire tread, coating resin
See above structures	Butadiene and styrene	Styrene-butadiene rubber (SBR) $\{CH{-}CH_2{-}CH_2{-}CH{=}CH{-}CH_2\}_n$ (phenyl)	Synthetic rubber

Bubble gums contain synthetic styrene-butadiene rubber.

$H_2N-(CH_2)_6-NH_2$ + $HOOC-(CH_2)_4-COOH$

Hexamethylenediamine   Adipic acid

↓ Condensation

$H_2N-(CH_2)_6-N-\overset{O}{\overset{\|}{C}}-(CH_2)_4-COOH + H_2O$

|
H

↓ Further condensation reactions

$-(CH_2)_4-\overset{O}{\overset{\|}{C}}-\underset{H}{N}-(CH_2)_6-\underset{H}{N}-\overset{O}{\overset{\|}{C}}-(CH_2)_4-\overset{O}{\overset{\|}{C}}-\underset{H}{N}-(CH_2)_6-$

Figure 25.6 *The formation of nylon by the condensation reaction between hexamethylenediamine and adipic acid.*

Figure 25.7 *The nylon rope trick. Adding a solution of adipoyl chloride (an adipic acid derivative in which the OH groups have been replaced by Cl groups) in cyclohexane to an aqueous solution of hexamethylenediamine causes nylon to form at the interface of the two solutions, which do not mix. It can then be drawn off.*

Condensation reaction was defined on p. 1021.

Condensation Reactions

One of the best-known polymer condensation processes is the reaction between hexamethylenediamine and adipic acid, shown in Figure 25.6. The final product, called nylon 66 (because there are six carbon atoms each in hexamethylenediamine and adipic acid), was first made by Wallace Carothers[‡] at Du Pont in 1931. The versatility of nylons is so great that the annual production of nylons and related substances now amounts to several billion pounds. Figure 25.7 shows how nylon 66 is prepared in the laboratory.

Condensation reactions are also used in the manufacture of Dacron (polyester)

$$n HO-\overset{O}{\overset{\|}{C}}-\bigcirc-\overset{O}{\overset{\|}{C}}-OH + nHO-(CH_2)_2-OH \longrightarrow \left(\overset{O}{\overset{\|}{C}}-\bigcirc-\overset{O}{\overset{\|}{C}}-O-CH_2CH_2-O\right)_n + nH_2O$$

terephthalic acid   1,2-ethylene glycol   Dacron

Polyesters are used in fibers, films, and plastic bottles.

25.3 Proteins

Proteins are *polymers of amino acids;* they play a key role in nearly all biological processes. Enzymes, the catalysts of biochemical reactions, are mostly proteins. Proteins also facilitate a wide range of other functions, such as transport and storage of vital substances, coordinated motion, mechanical support, and protection against diseases. The human body contains an estimated 100,000 different kinds of proteins, each of which has a specific physiological function. As we will see in this section, the chemical composition and structure of these complex natural polymers are the basis of their specificity.

Elements in proteins.

Amino Acids

Proteins have high molar masses, ranging from about 5000 g to 1×10^7 g, and yet the percent composition by mass of the elements in proteins is remarkably constant: carbon, 50 to 55 percent; hydrogen, 7 percent; oxygen, 23 percent; nitrogen, 16 percent; and sulfur, 1 percent.

The basic structural units of proteins are *amino acids*. An **amino acid** is *a compound that contains at least one amino group* ($-NH_2$) *and at least one carboxyl group* ($-COOH$):

amino group   carboxyl group

Twenty different amino acids are the building blocks of all the proteins in the human body. Table 25.2 shows the structures of these vital compounds, along with their three-letter abbreviations.

Amino acids in solution at neutral pH exist as *dipolar ions,* meaning that the proton on the carboxyl group has migrated to the amino group. Consider glycine, the simplest amino acid. The un-ionized form and the dipolar ion of glycine are shown below:

un-ionized form   dipolar ion

The first step in the synthesis of a protein molecule is a condensation reaction between an amino group on one amino acid and a carboxyl group on another amino acid. The molecule formed from the two amino acids is called a *dipeptide,* and the bond joining them together is a *peptide bond:*

It is interesting to compare this reaction with the one shown in Figure 25.6.

peptide bond

where R_1 and R_2 represent a H atom or some other group; $-CO-NH-$ is called the *amide group*. Because the equilibrium of the reaction joining two amino acids lies to the left, the process is coupled to the hydrolysis of ATP (see p. 808).

Either end of a dipeptide can engage in a condensation reaction with another amino acid to form a *tripeptide,* a *tetrapeptide,* and so on. The final product, the protein molecule, is a *polypeptide;* it can also be thought of as a polymer of amino acids.

An amino acid unit in a polypeptide chain is called a *residue*. Typically, a polypeptide chain contains 100 or more amino acid residues. The sequence of amino acids in a polypeptide chain is written conventionally from left to right, starting with the amino-terminal residue and ending with the carboxyl-terminal residue. Let us consider a dipeptide formed from glycine and alanine. Figure 25.8 shows that alanylglycine and glycylalanine are different molecules. With 20 different amino acids to choose from, 20^2, or 400, different dipeptides can be generated. Even for a very small protein such as insulin, which contains only 50 amino acid residues, the number of chemically different

TABLE 25.2	The 20 Amino Acids Essential to Living Organisms*	

Name	Abbreviation	Structure
Alanine	Ala	$H_3C-\overset{\overset{\text{H}}{\vert}}{\underset{\underset{NH_3^+}{\vert}}{C}}-COO^-$
Arginine	Arg	$H_2N-\overset{\overset{\text{H}}{\vert}}{\underset{\underset{NH}{\parallel}}{C}}-N-CH_2-CH_2-CH_2-\overset{\overset{\text{H}}{\vert}}{\underset{\underset{NH_3^+}{\vert}}{C}}-COO^-$
Asparagine	Asn	$H_2N-\overset{\overset{O}{\parallel}}{C}-CH_2-\overset{\overset{\text{H}}{\vert}}{\underset{\underset{NH_3^+}{\vert}}{C}}-COO^-$
Aspartic acid	Asp	$HOOC-CH_2-\overset{\overset{\text{H}}{\vert}}{\underset{\underset{NH_3^+}{\vert}}{C}}-COO^-$
Cysteine	Cys	$HS-CH_2-\overset{\overset{\text{H}}{\vert}}{\underset{\underset{NH_3^+}{\vert}}{C}}-COO^-$
Glutamic acid	Glu	$HOOC-CH_2-CH_2-\overset{\overset{\text{H}}{\vert}}{\underset{\underset{NH_3^+}{\vert}}{C}}-COO^-$
Glutamine	Gln	$H_2N-\overset{\overset{O}{\parallel}}{C}-CH_2-CH_2-\overset{\overset{\text{H}}{\vert}}{\underset{\underset{NH_3^+}{\vert}}{C}}-COO^-$
Glycine	Gly	$H-\overset{\overset{\text{H}}{\vert}}{\underset{\underset{NH_3^+}{\vert}}{C}}-COO^-$
Histidine	His	$\underset{\underset{C}{\underset{\vert}{H}}}{\overset{HC=C-CH_2}{N \diagdown \diagup NH}}-\overset{\overset{\text{H}}{\vert}}{\underset{\underset{NH_3^+}{\vert}}{C}}-COO^-$
Isoleucine	Ile	$H_3C-CH_2-\underset{\underset{H}{\vert}}{\overset{\overset{CH_3}{\vert}}{C}}-\overset{\overset{\text{H}}{\vert}}{\underset{\underset{NH_3^+}{\vert}}{C}}-COO^-$

(Continued)

*The shaded portion is the R group of the amino acid.

TABLE 25.2	The 20 Amino Acids Essential to Living Organisms—Cont.

Name	Abbreviation	Structure
Leucine	Leu	
Lysine	Lys	
Methionine	Met	
Phenylalanine	Phe	
Proline	Pro	
Serine	Ser	
Threonine	Thr	
Tryptophan	Trp	
Tyrosine	Tyr	
Valine	Val	

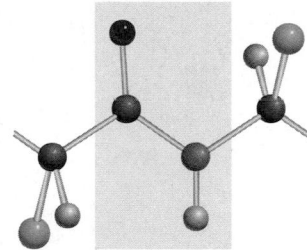

Figure 25.9 *The planar amide group in protein. Rotation about the peptide bond in the amide group is hindered by its double-bond character. The black atoms represent carbon; blue, nitrogen; red, oxygen; green, R group; and gray, hydrogen.*

Figure 25.8 *The formation of two dipeptides from two different amino acids. Alanylglycine is different from glycylalanine in that in alanylglycine the amino and methyl groups are bonded to the same carbon atom.*

structures that is possible is of the order of 20^{50} or 10^{65}! This is an incredibly large number when you consider that the total number of atoms in our galaxy is about 10^{68}. With so many possibilities for protein synthesis, it is remarkable that generation after generation of cells can produce identical proteins for specific physiological functions.

Protein Structure

The type and number of amino acids in a given protein along with the sequence or order in which these amino acids are joined together determine the protein's structure. In the 1930s Linus Pauling and his coworkers conducted a systematic investigation of protein structure. First they studied the geometry of the basic repeating group, that is, the amide group, which is represented by the following resonance structures:

$$\begin{array}{ccc} :\ddot{O} & & :\ddot{O}:^- \\ \| & \longleftrightarrow & | \\ -C-N- & & -C=N^+- \\ | & & | \\ H & & H \end{array}$$

Because it is more difficult (that is, it would take more energy) to twist a double bond than a single bond, the four atoms in the amide group become locked in the same plane (Figure 25.9). Figure 25.10 depicts the repeating amide group in a polypeptide chain.

On the basis of models and X-ray diffraction data, Pauling deduced that there are two common structures for protein molecules, called the *α helix* and the *β-pleated* sheet. The α-helical structure of a polypeptide chain is shown in Figure 25.11. The helix

Figure 25.10 *A polypeptide chain. Note the repeating units of the amide group. The symbol R represents part of the structure characteristic of the individual amino acids. For glycine, R is simply a H atom.*

Figure 25.11 *The α-helical structure of a polypeptide chain. The structure is held in position by intramolecular hydrogen bonds, shown as dotted lines. For color key, see Fig. 25.9.*

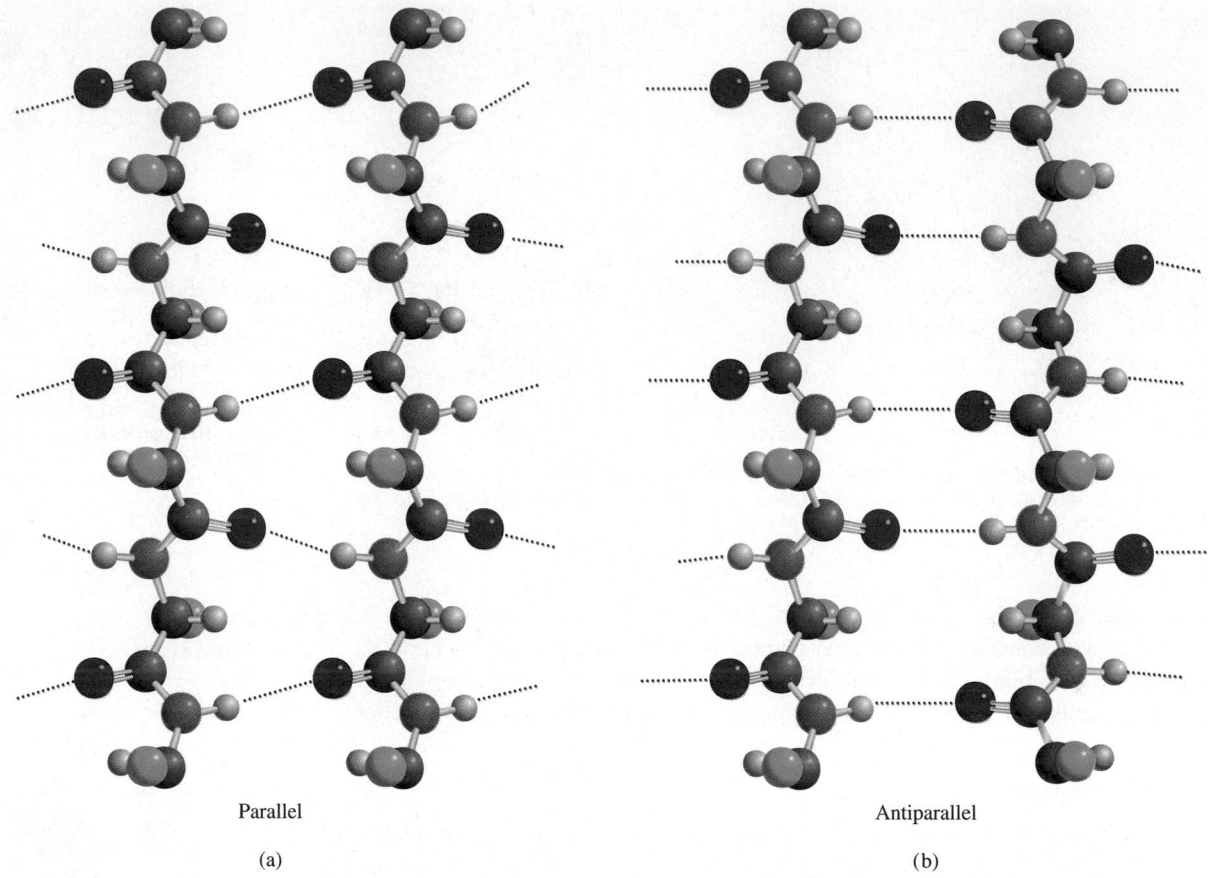

Parallel

(a)

Antiparallel

(b)

Figure 25.12 *Hydrogen bonds (a) in a parallel β-pleated sheet structure, in which all the polypeptide chains are oriented in the same direction, and (b) in an antiparallel β-pleated sheet, in which adjacent polypeptide chains run in opposite directions. For color key, see Fig. 25.9.*

is stabilized by *intramolecular* hydrogen bonds between the NH and CO groups of the main chain, giving rise to an overall rodlike shape. The CO group of each amino acid is hydrogen-bonded to the NH group of the amino acid that is four residues away in the sequence. In this manner all the main-chain CO and NH groups take part in hydrogen bonding. X-ray studies have shown that the structure of a number of proteins, including myoglobin and hemoglobin, is to a great extent α-helical in nature.

The β-pleated structure is markedly different from the α helix in that it is like a sheet rather than a rod. The polypeptide chain is almost fully extended, and each chain forms many *intermolecular* hydrogen bonds with adjacent chains. Figure 25.12 shows the two different types of β-pleated structures, called *parallel* and *antiparallel*. Silk molecules possess the β structure. Because its polypeptide chains are already in extended form, silk lacks elasticity and extensibility, but it is quite strong due to the many intermolecular hydrogen bonds.

It is customary to divide protein structure into four levels of organization. The *primary structure* refers to the unique amino acid sequence of the polypeptide chain. The *secondary structure* includes those parts of the polypeptide chain that are stabilized by a regular pattern of hydrogen bonds between the CO and NH groups of the backbone, for example, the α helix. The term *tertiary structure* applies to the

Primary
structure

Secondary structure

Tertiary structure

Quaternary structure

Figure 25.13 *The primary, secondary, tertiary, and quaternary structure of the hemoglobin molecule.*

three-dimensional structure stabilized by dispersion forces, hydrogen bonding, and other intermolecular forces. It differs from secondary structure in that the amino acids taking part in these interactions may be far apart in the polypeptide chain. A protein molecule may be made up of more than one polypeptide chain. Thus, in addition to the various interactions *within* a chain that give rise to the secondary and tertiary structures, we must also consider the interaction *between* chains. The overall arrangement of the polypeptide chains is called the *quaternary structure*. For example, the hemoglobin molecule consists of four separate polypeptide chains, or *subunits*. These subunits are held together by van der Waals forces and ionic forces (Figure 25.13).

Pauling's work was a great triumph in protein chemistry. It showed for the first time how to predict a protein structure purely from a knowledge of the geometry of its fundamental building blocks—amino acids. However, there are many proteins whose structures do not correspond to the α-helical or β structure. Chemists now know that the three-dimensional structures of these biopolymers are maintained by several types of intermolecular forces in addition to hydrogen bonding (Figure 25.14). The delicate balance of the various interactions can be appreciated by considering an example: When glutamic acid, one of the amino acid residues in two of the four polypeptide chains in hemoglobin, is replaced by valine, another amino acid, the protein molecules aggregate to form insoluble

CHEMISTRY
in Action

Sickle Cell Anemia—A Molecular Disease

Sickle cell anemia is a hereditary disease in which abnormally shaped red blood cells restrict the flow of blood to vital organs in the human body, causing swelling, severe pain, and in many cases a shortened life span. There is currently no cure for this condition, but its painful symptoms are known to be caused by a defect in hemoglobin, the oxygen-carrying protein in red blood cells.

The hemoglobin molecule is a large protein with a molar mass of about 65,000 g. Normal human hemoglobin (HbA) consists of two α chains, each containing 141 amino acids, and two β chains made up of 146 amino acids each. These four polypeptide chains, or subunits, are held together by ionic and van der Waals forces.

There are many mutant hemoglobin molecules—molecules with an amino acid sequence that differs somewhat from the sequence in HbA. Most mutant hemoglobins are harmless, but sickle cell hemoglobin (HbS) and others are known to cause serious diseases. HbS differs from HbA in only one very small detail. A valine molecule replaces a glutamic acid molecule on each of the two β chains:

$$HOOC-CH_2-CH_2-\overset{\overset{\displaystyle H}{|}}{\underset{\underset{\displaystyle NH_3^+}{|}}{C}}-COO^-$$

glutamic acid

$$\overset{\displaystyle H_3C}{\underset{\displaystyle H_3C}{}}CH-\overset{\overset{\displaystyle H}{|}}{\underset{\underset{\displaystyle NH_3^+}{|}}{C}}-COO^-$$

valine

Yet this small change (two amino acids out of 292) has a profound effect on the stability of HbS in solution. The valine groups are located at the bottom outside of the molecule to form a protruding "key" on each of the β chains. The nonpolar portion of valine

$$\overset{\displaystyle H_3C}{\underset{\displaystyle H_3C}{}}CH-$$

can attract another nonpolar group in the α chain of an adjacent HbS molecule through dispersion forces. Biochemists often refer to this kind of attraction between nonpolar groups as *hydrophobic* (see Chapter 12) interaction. Gradually, enough HbS molecules will aggregate to form a "superpolymer."

A general rule about the solubility of a substance is that the larger its molecules, the lower its solubility because the solvation

polymers, causing the disease known as sickle cell anemia (see the above Chemistry in Action essay).

In spite of all the forces that give proteins their structural stability, most proteins have a certain amount of flexibility. Enzymes, for example, are flexible enough to change their geometry to fit substrates of various sizes and shapes. Another interesting

Figure 25.14 *Intermolecular forces in a protein molecule: (a) ionic forces, (b) hydrogen bonding, (c) dispersion forces, and (d) dipole-dipole forces.*

process becomes unfavorable with increasing molecular surface area. For this reason, proteins generally are not very soluble in water. Therefore, the aggregated HbS molecules eventually precipitate out of solution. The precipitate causes normal disk-shaped red blood cells to assume a warped crescent or sickle shape (see figure on p. 284). These deformed cells clog the narrow capillaries, thereby restricting blood flow to organs of the body. It is the reduced blood flow that gives rise to the symptoms of sickle cell anemia. Sickle cell anemia has been termed a molecular disease by Linus Pauling, who did some of the early important chemical research on the nature of the affliction, because the destructive action occurs at the molecular level and the disease is, in effect, due to a molecular defect.

Some substances, such as urea and the cyanate ion,

$$H_2N-\underset{\underset{O}{\|}}{C}-NH_2 \qquad O=C=N^-$$

urea   cyanate ion

The overall structure of hemoglobin. Each hemoglobin molecule contains two α chains and two β chains. Each of the four chains is similar to a myoglobin molecule in structure, and each also contains a heme group for binding oxygen. In sickle cell hemoglobin, the defective regions (the valine groups) are located near the ends of the β chains, as indicated by the dots.

can break up the hydrophobic interaction between HbS molecules and have been applied with some success to reverse the "sickling" of red blood cells. This approach may alleviate the pain and suffering of sickle cell patients, but it does not prevent the body from making more HbS. To cure sickle cell anemia, researchers must find a way to alter the genetic machinery that directs the production of HbS.

example of protein flexibility is found in the binding of hemoglobin to oxygen. Each of the four polypeptide chains in hemoglobin contains a heme group that can bind to an oxygen molecule (see Section 22.7). In deoxyhemoglobin, the affinity of each of the heme groups for oxygen is about the same. However, as soon as one of the heme groups becomes oxygenated, the affinity of the other three hemes for oxygen is greatly enhanced. This phenomenon, called *cooperativity,* makes hemoglobin a particularly suitable substance for the uptake of oxygen in the lungs. By the same token, once a fully oxygenated hemoglobin molecule releases an oxygen molecule (to myoglobin in the tissues), the other three oxygen molecules will depart with increasing ease. The cooperative nature of the binding is such that information about the presence (or absence) of oxygen molecules is transmitted from one subunit to another along the polypeptide chains, a process made possible by the flexibility of the three-dimensional structure (Figure 25.15). It is believed that the Fe^{2+} ion has too large a radius to fit into the porphyrin ring of deoxyhemoglobin. When O_2 binds to Fe^{2+}, however, the ion shrinks somewhat so that it can fit into the plane of the ring. As the ion slips into the ring, it pulls the histidine residue toward the ring and thereby sets off a sequence of structural changes from one subunit to another. Although the details of the changes are not clear, biochemists believe that this is how the binding of an oxygen molecule to one heme group affects another heme group. The structural changes drastically affect the affinity of the remaining heme groups for oxygen molecules.

Figure 25.15 *The structural changes that occur when the heme group in hemoglobin binds to an oxygen molecule. (a) The heme group in deoxyhemoglobin. (b) Oxyhemoglobin.*

Histidine

Porphyrin ring Fe^{2+}

Fe^{2+}

Oxygen molecule

(a)   (b)

Hard-boiling an egg denatures the proteins in the egg white.

When proteins are heated above body temperature or when they are subjected to unusual acid or base conditions or treated with special reagents called *denaturants,* they lose some or all of their tertiary and secondary structure. Called **denatured proteins,** proteins in this state *no longer exhibit normal biological activities.* Figure 25.16 shows the variation of rate with temperature for a typical enzyme-catalyzed reaction. Initially, the rate increases with increasing temperature, as we would expect. Beyond the optimum temperature, however, the enzyme begins to denature and the rate falls rapidly. If a protein is denatured under mild conditions, its original structure can often be regenerated by removing the denaturant or by restoring the temperature to normal conditions. This process is called *reversible denaturation.*

25.4 Nucleic Acids

Nucleic acids are *high molar mass polymers that play an essential role in protein synthesis.* **Deoxyribonucleic acid (DNA)** and **ribonucleic acid (RNA)** are *the two types of nucleic acid.* DNA molecules are among the largest molecules known; they have molar masses of up to tens of billions of grams. On the other hand, RNA molecules vary greatly in size, some having a molar mass of about 25,000 g. Compared with proteins, which are made of up to 20 different amino acids, nucleic acids are fairly simple in composition. A DNA or RNA molecule contains only four types of building blocks: purines, pyrimidines, furanose sugars, and phosphate groups (Figure 25.17). Each purine or pyrimidine is called a *base.*

If the DNA molecules from all the cells in a human were stretched and joined end to end, the length would be about 100 times the distance to the sun!

In the 1940s, Erwin Chargaff[†] studied DNA molecules obtained from various sources and observed certain regularities. *Chargaff's rules,* as his findings are now known, describe these patterns:

1. The amount of adenine (a purine) is equal to that of thymine (a pyrimidine); that is, A = T, or A/T = 1.

2. The amount of cytosine (a pyrimidine) is equal to that of guanine (a purine); that is, C = G, or C/G = 1.

3. The total number of purine bases is equal to the total number of pyrimidine bases; that is, A + G = C + T.

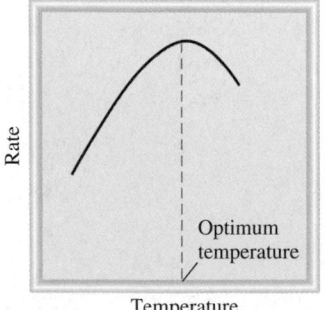

Rate

Optimum temperature

Temperature

Figure 25.16 *Dependence of the rate of an enzyme-catalyzed reaction on temperature. Above the optimum temperature at which an enzyme is most effective, its activity drops off as a consequence of denaturation.*

[†]Erwin Chargaff (1905–2002). American biochemist of Austrian origin. Chargaff was the first to show that different biological species contain different DNA molecules.

Found only in DNA   Found in both DNA and RNA   Found only in RNA

Purines

Adenine   Guanine

Pyrimidines

Thymine   Cytosine   Uracil

Sugars

Deoxyribose   Ribose

Phosphate

$$^-O-P-O^-$$

Phosphate

Figure 25.17 *The components of the nucleic acids DNA and RNA.*

Based on chemical analyses and information obtained from X-ray diffraction measurements, James Watson[‡] and Francis Crick[§] formulated the double-helical structure for the DNA molecule in 1953. Watson and Crick determined that the DNA molecule has two helical strands. Each strand is made up of **nucleotides,** which *consist of a base, a deoxyribose, and a phosphate group linked together* (Figure 25.18).

The key to the double-helical structure of DNA is the formation of hydrogen bonds between bases in the two strands of a molecule. Although hydrogen bonds can form between any two bases, called *base pairs,* Watson and Crick found that the most favorable couplings are between adenine and thymine and between cytosine and guanine (Figure 25.19). Note that this scheme is consistent with Chargaff's rules, because

An electron micrograph of a DNA molecule. The double-helical structure is evident.

[‡]James Dewey Watson (1928–). American biologist. Watson shared the 1962 Nobel Prize in Physiology or Medicine with Crick and Maurice Wilkins for their work on the DNA structure, which is considered by many to be the most significant development in biology in the twentieth century.

[§]Francis Harry Compton Crick (1916–2004). British biologist. Crick started as a physicist but became interested in biology after reading the book *What Is Life?* by Erwin Schrödinger (see Chapter 7). In addition to elucidating the structure of DNA, for which he was a corecipient of the Nobel Prize in Physiology or Medicine in 1962. Crick has made many significant contributions to molecular biology.

Figure 25.18 *Structure of a nucleotide, one of the repeating units in DNA.*

every purine base is hydrogen-bonded to a pyrimidine base, and vice versa (A + G = C + T). Other attractive forces such as dipole-dipole interactions and van der Waals forces between the base pairs also help to stabilize the double helix.

The structure of RNA differs from that of DNA in several respects. First, as shown in Figure 25.17, the four bases found in RNA molecules are adenine, cytosine, guanine, and uracil. Second, RNA contains the sugar ribose rather than the 2-deoxyribose of DNA. Third, chemical analysis shows that the composition of RNA does not obey Chargaff's rules. In other words, the purine-to-pyrimidine ratio is not equal to 1 as in the case of DNA. This and other evidence rule out a double-helical structure. In fact,

(a)

(b)

Figure 25.19 *(a) Base-pair formation by adenine and thymine and by cytosine and guanine. (b) The double-helical strand of a DNA molecule held together by hydrogen bonds (and other intermolecular forces) between base pairs A-T and C-G.*

CHEMISTRY
in Action

DNA Fingerprinting

The human genetic makeup, or *genome,* consists of about 3 billion nucleotides. These 3 billion units compose the 23 pairs of chromosomes, which are continuous strands of DNA ranging in length from 50 million to 500 million nucleotides. Encoded in this DNA and stored in units called *genes* are the instructions for protein synthesis. Each of about 100,000 genes is responsible for the synthesis of a particular protein. In addition to instructions for protein synthesis, each gene contains a sequence of bases, repeated several times, that has no known function. What is interesting about these sequences, called *minisatellites,* is that they appear many times in different locations, not just in a particular gene. Furthermore, each person has a unique number of repeats. Only identical twins have the same number of minisatellite sequences.

In 1985 a British chemist named Alec Jeffreys suggested that minisatellite sequences provide a means of identification, much like fingerprints. *DNA fingerprinting* has since gained prominence with law enforcement officials as a way to identify crime suspects.

To make a DNA fingerprint, a chemist needs a sample of any tissue, such as blood or semen; even hair and saliva contain DNA. The DNA is extracted from cell nuclei and cut into fragments by the addition of so-called restriction enzymes. These fragments, which are negatively charged, are separated by an electric field in gel. The smaller fragments move faster than larger ones, so they eventually separate into bands. The bands of DNA fragments are transferred from the gel to a plastic membrane, and their position is thereby fixed. Then a DNA probe— a DNA fragment that has been tagged with a radioactive label— is added. The probe binds to the fragments that have a complementary DNA sequence. An X-ray film is laid directly over the plastic sheet, and bands appear on the exposed film in the positions corresponding to the fragments recognized by the probe. About four different probes are needed to obtain a profile that is unique to just one individual. It is estimated that the probability of finding identical patterns in the DNA of two randomly selected individuals is on the order of 1 in 10 billion.

The first U.S. case in which a person was convicted of a crime with the help of DNA fingerprints was tried in 1987. Today, DNA fingerprinting has become an indispensable tool of law enforcement.

Bloodstain → DNA is extracted from blood cells → A restriction enzyme cuts DNA into fragments → Fragments are separated into bands by gel electrophoresis → The DNA band pattern in the gel is transferred to a nylon membrane → Radioactive DNA probe binds to specific DNA sequences → X-ray film detects radioactive pattern → Replicate patterns, same person / Pattern from another person

Procedure for obtaining a DNA fingerprint. The developed film shows the DNA fingerprint, which is compared with patterns from known subjects.

In the 1980s chemists discovered that certain RNAs can function as enzymes.

the RNA molecule exists as a single-strand polynucleotide. There are actually three types of RNA molecules—messenger RNA (*m*RNA), ribosomal RNA (*r*RNA), and transfer RNA (*t*RNA). These RNAs have similar nucleotides but differ from one another in molar mass, overall structure, and biological functions.

DNA and RNA molecules direct the synthesis of proteins in the cell, a subject that is beyond the scope of this book. Introductory texts in biochemistry and molecular biology explain this process.

The Chemistry in Action essay on p. 1057 describes a technique in crime investigation that is based on our knowledge of DNA sequence.

Summary of Facts and Concepts

1. Polymers are large molecules made up of small, repeating units called monomers.
2. Proteins, nucleic acids, cellulose, and rubber are natural polymers. Nylon, Dacron, and Lucite are examples of synthetic polymers.
3. Organic polymers can be synthesized via addition reactions or condensation reactions.
4. Stereoisomers of a polymer made up of asymmetric monomers have different properties, depending on how the starting units are joined together.
5. Synthetic rubbers include polychloroprene and styrene-butadiene rubber, which is a copolymer of styrene and butadiene.
6. Structure determines the function and properties of proteins. To a great extent, hydrogen bonding and other intermolecular forces determine the structure of proteins.

7. The primary structure of a protein is its amino acid sequence. Secondary structure is the shape defined by hydrogen bonds joining the CO and NH groups of the amino acid backbone. Tertiary and quaternary structures are the three-dimensional folded arrangements of proteins that are stabilized by hydrogen bonds and other intermolecular forces.
8. Nucleic acids—DNA and RNA—are high-molar-mass polymers that carry genetic instructions for protein synthesis in cells. Nucleotides are the building blocks of DNA and RNA. DNA nucleotides each contain a purine or pyrimidine base, a deoxyribose molecule, and a phosphate group. RNA nucleotides are similar but contain different bases and ribose instead of deoxyribose.

Key Words

Amino acid, p. 1046
Copolymer, p. 1043
Denatured
    protein, p. 1054

Deoxyribonucleic acid
    (DNA), p. 1054
Homopolymer, p. 1041
Monomer, p. 1040

Nucleic acid, p. 1054
Nucleotide, p. 1055
Polymer, p. 1040
Protein, p. 1045

Ribonucleic acid
    (RNA) p. 1054

Questions and Problems

Synthetic Organic Polymers
Review Questions

25.1 Define the following terms: monomer, polymer, homopolymer, copolymer.

25.2 Name 10 objects that contain synthetic organic polymers.

25.3 Calculate the molar mass of a particular polyethylene sample, $+CH_2-CH_2+_n$, where $n = 4600$.

25.4 Describe the two major mechanisms of organic polymer synthesis.

25.5 What are Natta-Ziegler catalysts? What is their role in polymer synthesis?

25.6   In Chapter 12 you learned about the colligative properties of solutions. Which of the colligative properties is suitable for determining the molar mass of a polymer? Why?

Problems

25.7   Teflon is formed by a radical addition reaction involving the monomer tetrafluoroethylene. Show the mechanism for this reaction.

25.8   Vinyl chloride, $H_2C\!=\!CHCl$, undergoes copolymerization with 1,1-dichloroethylene, $H_2C\!=\!CCl_2$, to form a polymer commercially known as Saran. Draw the structure of the polymer, showing the repeating monomer units.

25.9   Kevlar is a copolymer used in bullet-proof vests. It is formed in a condensation reaction between the following two monomers:

Sketch a portion of the polymer chain showing several monomer units. Write the overall equation for the condensation reaction.

25.10   Describe the formation of polystyrene.

25.11   Deduce plausible monomers for polymers with the following repeating units:

(a) $-\!(CH_2\!-\!CF_2)_n$

(b)

25.12   Deduce plausible monomers for polymers with the following repeating units:

(a) $-\!(CH_2\!-\!CH\!=\!CH\!-\!CH_2)_n$

(b) $-\!(CO\!-\!(CH_2)_6\!NH)_n$

Proteins
Review Questions

25.13   Discuss the characteristics of an amide group and its importance in protein structure.

25.14   What is the α-helical structure in proteins?

25.15   Describe the β-pleated structure present in some proteins.

25.16   Discuss the main functions of proteins in living systems.

25.17   Briefly explain the phenomenon of cooperativity exhibited by the hemoglobin molecule in binding oxygen.

25.18   Why is sickle cell anemia called a molecular disease?

Problems

25.19   Draw the structures of the dipeptides that can be formed from the reaction between the amino acids glycine and alanine.

25.20   Draw the structures of the dipeptides that can be formed from the reaction between the amino acids glycine and lysine.

25.21   The amino acid glycine can be condensed to form a polymer called polyglycine. Draw the repeating monomer unit.

25.22   The following are data obtained on the rate of product formation of an enzyme-catalyzed reaction:

Temperature (°C)	Rate of Product Formation (M/s)
10	0.0025
20	0.0048
30	0.0090
35	0.0086
45	0.0012

Comment on the dependence of rate on temperature. (No calculations are required.)

Nucleic Acids
Review Questions

25.23   Describe the structure of a nucleotide.

25.24   What is the difference between ribose and deoxyribose?

25.25   What are Chargaff's rules?

25.26   Describe the role of hydrogen bonding in maintaining the double-helical structure of DNA.

Additional Problems

25.27   Discuss the importance of hydrogen bonding in biological systems. Use proteins and nucleic acids as examples.

25.28   Proteins vary widely in structure, whereas nucleic acids have rather uniform structures. How do you account for this major difference?

25.29   If untreated, fevers of 104°F or higher may lead to brain damage. Why?

25.30   The "melting point" of a DNA molecule is the temperature at which the double-helical strand breaks apart. Suppose you are given two DNA samples. One sample contains 45 percent C-G base pairs while the other contains 64 percent C-G base pairs. The total number of bases is the same in each sample. Which of the two samples has a higher melting point? Why?

25.31   When fruits such as apples and pears are cut, the exposed parts begin to turn brown. This is the result of an oxidation reaction catalyzed by enzymes present in the fruit. Often the browning action can be prevented or slowed by adding a few drops of lemon juice to the exposed areas. What is the chemical basis for this treatment?

25.32 "Dark meat" and "white meat" are one's choices when eating a turkey. Explain what causes the meat to assume different colors. (*Hint:* The more active muscles in a turkey have a higher rate of metabolism and need more oxygen.)

25.33 Nylon can be destroyed easily by strong acids. Explain the chemical basis for the destruction. (*Hint:* The products are the starting materials of the polymerization reaction.)

25.34 Despite what you may have read in science fiction novels or seen in horror movies, it is extremely unlikely that insects can ever grow to human size. Why? (*Hint:* Insects do not have hemoglobin molecules in their blood.)

25.35 How many different tripeptides can be formed by lysine and alanine?

25.36 Chemical analysis shows that hemoglobin contains 0.34 percent Fe by mass. What is the minimum possible molar mass of hemoglobin? The actual molar mass of hemoglobin is four times this minimum value. What conclusion can you draw from these data?

25.37 The folding of a polypeptide chain depends not only on its amino acid sequence but also on the nature of the solvent. Discuss the types of interactions that might occur between water molecules and the amino acid residues of the polypeptide chain. Which groups would be exposed on the exterior of the protein in contact with water and which groups would be buried in the interior of the protein?

25.38 What kind of intermolecular forces are responsible for the aggregation of hemoglobin molecules that leads to sickle cell anemia? (*Hint:* See the Chemistry in Action essay on p. 1052.)

25.39 Draw structures of the nucleotides containing the following components: (a) deoxyribose and cytosine, (b) ribose and uracil.

25.40 When a nonapeptide (containing nine amino acid residues) isolated from rat brains was hydrolyzed, it gave the following smaller peptides as identifiable products: Gly-Ala-Phe, Ala-Leu-Val, Gly-Ala-Leu, Phe-Glu-His, and His-Gly-Ala. Reconstruct the amino acid sequence in the nonapeptide, giving your reasons. (Remember the convention for writing peptides.)

25.41 At neutral pH amino acids exist as dipolar ions. Using glycine as an example, and given that the pK_a of the carboxyl group is 2.3 and that of the ammonium group is 9.6, predict the predominant form of the molecule at pH 1, 7, and 12. Justify your answers using Equation (16.4).

25.42 In Lewis Carroll's tale "Through the Looking Glass," Alice wonders whether "looking-glass milk" on the other side of the mirror would be fit to drink. Based on your knowledge of chirality and enzyme action, comment on the validity of Alice's concern.

25.43 Nylon was designed to be a synthetic silk. (a) The average molar mass of a batch of nylon 66 is 12,000 g/mol. How many monomer units are there in this sample? (b) Which part of nylon's structure is similar to a polypeptide's structure? (c) How many different tripeptides (made up of three amino acids) can be formed from the amino acids alanine (Ala), glycine (Gly), and serine (Ser), which account for most of the amino acids in silk?

25.44 The enthalpy change in the denaturation of a certain protein is 125 kJ/mol. If the entropy change is 397 J/K · mol, calculate the minimum temperature at which the protein would denature spontaneously.

25.45 When deoxyhemoglobin crystals are exposed to oxygen, they shatter. On the other hand, deoxymyoglobin crystals are unaffected by oxygen. Explain. (Myoglobin is made up of only one of the four subunits, or polypeptide chains, in hemoglobin.)

25.46 Draw the structure of the monomer unit shown on p. 1038.

Special Problems

25.47 In protein synthesis, the selection of a particular amino acid is determined by the so-called genetic code, or a sequence of three bases in DNA. Will a sequence of only two bases unambiguously determine the selection of 20 amino acids found in proteins? Explain.

25.48 Consider the fully protonated amino acid valine:

$$\begin{array}{c} \overset{+9.62}{CH_3\ NH_3} \\ | \quad | \\ H-C-C-COOH \\ | \quad | \quad ^{2.32} \\ CH_3\ H \end{array}$$

where the numbers denote the pK_a values. (a) Which of the two groups ($-\overset{+}{N}H_3$ or $-COOH$) is more acidic? (b) Calculate the predominant form of valine at pH 1.0, 7.0, and 12.0. (c) Calculate the isoelectric point of valine. (*Hint:* See Problem 16.127.)

25.49 Consider the formation of a dimeric protein

$$2P \longrightarrow P_2$$

At 25°C, we have $\Delta H° = 17$ kJ/mol and $\Delta S° = 65$ J/K · mol. Is the dimerization favored at this temperature? Comment on the effect of lowering the temperature. Does your result explain why some enzymes lose their activities under cold conditions?

25.50 The diagram (left) below shows the structure of the enzyme ribonuclease in its native form. The three-dimensional protein structure is maintained in part by the disulfide bonds (—S—S—) between the amino acid residues (each color sphere represents an S atom). Using certain denaturants, the compact structure is destroyed and the disulfide bonds are converted to sulfhydryl groups (—SH) shown on the right of the arrow. (a) Describe the bonding scheme in the disulfide bond in terms of hybridization. (b) Which amino acid in Table 22.2 contains the —SH group? (c) Predict the signs of ΔH and ΔS for the denaturation process. If denaturation is induced by a change in temperature, show why a rise in temperature would favor denaturation. (d) The sulfhydryl groups can be oxidized (that is, removing the H atoms) to form the disulfide bonds. If the formation of the disulfide bonds is totally random between any two —SH groups, what is the fraction of the regenerated protein structures that corresponds to the native form? (e) An effective remedy to deodorize a dog that has been sprayed by a skunk is to rub the affected areas with a solution of an oxidizing agent such as hydrogen peroxide. What is the chemical basis for this action? (*Hint:* An odiferous component of a skunk's secretion is 2-butene-1-thiol, $CH_3CH{=}CHCH_2SH$.)

Native form   Denatured form

A Story That Will Curl Your Hair

Since ancient times people have experimented with ways to change their hair. Today, getting a permanent wave is a routine procedure that can be done either in a hairdresser shop or at home. Changing straight hair to curly hair is a practical application of protein denaturation and renaturation.

Hair contains a special class of proteins called *keratins,* which are also present in wool, nails, hoofs, and horns. X-ray studies show that keratins are made of α-helices coiled to form a superhelix. The disulfide bonds (—S—S—) linking the α-helices together are largely responsible for the shape of the hair. The figure on p. 1063 shows the basic steps involved in a permanent wave process. Starting with straight hair, the disulfide bonds are first reduced to the sulfhydryl groups (—SH)

$$2HS—CH_2COO^- + \bullet—S—S—\bullet \longrightarrow {}^-OOCCH_2—S—S—CH_2COO^- + 2\bullet—SH$$

where the red spheres represent different protein molecules joined by the disulfide bonds and thioglycolate ($HS—CH_2COO^-$) is the common reducing agent. The reduced hair is then wrapped around curlers and set in the desired pattern. Next, the hair is treated with an oxidizing agent to reform the disulfide bonds. Because the S—S linkages are now formed between different positions on the polypeptide chains, the result is a new hairdo of wavy hairs.

This process involves the denaturation and renaturation of keratins. Although disulfide bonds are formed at different positions in the renatured proteins, there is no biological consequence because keratins in hair do not have any specific functions. The word "permanent" applies only to the portion of hair treated with the reducing and oxidizing agents, and the wave lasts until new and untreated keratins replace it.

Chemical Clues

1. Describe the bonding in the —S—S— linkage.

2. What are the oxidation numbers of S in the disulfide bond and in the sulfhydryl group?

Straight hair

Wet hair
on curler

Reduced hair
on curler

Oxidized hair
off curler
(permanent wave)

3. In addition to the disulfide bonds, the α helices are joined together by hydrogen bonds. Based on this information, explain why hair swells a bit when it is wet.

4. Hair grows at the approximate rate of 6 in per year. Given that the vertical distance for a complete turn of an α helix is 5.4 Å (1 Å $= 10^{-8}$ cm), how many turns are spun off every second?

5. In the 1980s an English heiress died from a long illness. Autopsy showed that the cause of death was arsenic poisoning. The police suspected that her husband had administered the poison. The year prior to her death the heiress had taken three 1-month trips to America to visit friends on her own. Discuss how forensic analysis eventually helped the law enforcement build their case against her husband. [*Hint:* Arsenic poisoning was discussed in another chemical mystery in Chapter 4 (see p. 167). Studies show that within hours of ingesting as little as 3 mg of arsenic trioxide (As_2O_3), arsenic enters in the blood and becomes trapped and carried up the follicle in the growing hair. At the time of her death, the heiress had shoulder-length hair.]

Appendix 1

Derivation of the Names of Elements*

Element	Symbol	Atomic No.	Atomic Mass†	Date of Discovery	Discoverer and Nationality‡	Derivation
Actinium	Ac	89	(227)	1899	A. Debierne (Fr.)	Gr. *aktis*, beam or ray
Aluminum	Al	13	26.98	1827	F. Woehler (Ge.)	Alum, the aluminum compound in which it was discovered; derived from L. *alumen*, astringent taste
Americium	Am	95	(243)	1944	A. Ghiorso (USA) R. A. James (USA) G. T. Seaborg (USA) S. G. Thompson (USA)	The Americas
Antimony	Sb	51	121.8	Ancient		L. *antimonium* (*anti*, opposite of; *monium*, isolated condition), so named because it is a tangible (metallic) substance which combines readily; symbol L. *stibium*, mark
Argon	Ar	18	39.95	1894	Lord Raleigh (GB) Sir William Ramsay (GB)	Gr. *argos*, inactive
Arsenic	As	33	74.92	1250	Albertus Magnus (Ge.)	Gr. *aksenikon*, yellow pigment; L. *arsenicum*, orpiment; the Greeks once used arsenic trisulfide as a pigment
Astatine	At	85	(210)	1940	D. R. Corson (USA) K. R. MacKenzie (USA) E. Segre (USA)	Gr. *astatos*, unstable
Barium	Ba	56	137.3	1808	Sir Humphry Davy (GB)	barite, a heavy spar, derived from Gr. *barys*, heavy
Berkelium	Bk	97	(247)	1950	G. T. Seaborg (USA) S. G. Thompson (USA) A. Ghiorso (USA)	Berkeley, Calif.
Beryllium	Be	4	9.012	1828	F. Woehler (Ge.) A. A. B. Bussy (Fr.)	Fr. L. *beryl*, sweet

Source: Reprinted with permission from "The Elements and Derivation of Their Names and Symbols," G. P. Dinga, *Chemistry* **41** (2), 20–22 (1968). Copyright by the American Chemical Society.

*At the time this table was drawn up, only 103 elements were known to exist.

†The atomic masses given here correspond to the 1961 values of the Commission on Atomic Weights. Masses in parentheses are those of the most stable or most common isotopes.

‡The abbreviations are (Ar.) Arabic; (Au.) Austrian; (Du.) Dutch; (Fr.) French; (Ge.) German; (GB) British; (Gr.) Greek; (H.) Hungarian; (I.) Italian; (L.) Latin; (P.) Polish; (R.) Russian; (Sp.) Spanish; (Swe.) Swedish; (USA) American.

(Continued)

Element	Symbol	Atomic No.	Atomic Mass[†]	Date of Discovery	Discoverer and Nationality[‡]	Derivation
Bismuth	Bi	83	209.0	1753	Claude Geoffroy (Fr.)	Ge. *bismuth,* probably a distortion of *weisse masse* (white mass) in which it was found
Boron	B	5	10.81	1808	Sir Humphry Davy (GB) J. L. Gay-Lussac (Fr.) L. J. Thenard (Fr.)	The compound borax, derived from Ar. *buraq,* white
Bromine	Br	35	79.90	1826	A. J. Balard (Fr.)	Gr. *bromos,* stench
Cadmium	Cd	48	112.4	1817	Fr. Stromeyer (Ge.)	Gr. *kadmia,* earth; L. *cadmia,* calamine (because it is found along with calamine)
Calcium	Ca	20	40.08	1808	Sir Humphry Davy (GB)	L. *calx,* lime
Californium	Cf	98	(249)	1950	G. T. Seaborg (USA) S. G. Thompson (USA) A. Ghiorso (USA) K. Street, Jr. (USA)	California
Carbon	C	6	12.01	Ancient		L. *carbo,* charcoal
Cerium	Ce	58	140.1	1803	J. J. Berzelius (Swe.) William Hisinger (Swe.) M. H. Klaproth (Ge.)	Asteroid Ceres
Cesium	Cs	55	132.9	1860	R. Bunsen (Ge.) G. R. Kirchhoff (Ge.)	L. *caesium,* blue (cesium was discovered by its spectral lines, which are blue)
Chlorine	Cl	17	35.45	1774	K. W. Scheele (Swe.)	Gr. *chloros,* light green
Chromium	Cr	24	52.00	1797	L. N. Vauquelin (Fr.)	Gr. *chroma,* color (because it is used in pigments)
Cobalt	Co	27	58.93	1735	G. Brandt (Ge.)	Ge. *Kobold,* goblin (because the ore yielded cobalt instead of the expected metal, copper, it was attributed to goblins)
Copper	Cu	29	63.55	Ancient		L. *cuprum,* copper, derived from *cyprium,* Island of Cyprus, the main source of ancient copper
Curium	Cm	96	(247)	1944	G. T. Seaborg (USA) R. A. James (USA) A. Ghiorso (USA)	Pierre and Marie Curie
Dysprosium	Dy	66	162.5	1886	Lecoq de Boisbaudran (Fr.)	Gr. *dysprositos,* hard to get at
Einsteinium	Es	99	(254)	1952	A. Ghiorso (USA)	Albert Einstein
Erbium	Er	68	167.3	1843	C. G. Mosander (Swe.)	Ytterby, Sweden, where many rare earths were discovered
Europium	Eu	63	152.0	1896	E. Demarcay (Fr.)	Europe

(Continued)

Element	Symbol	Atomic No.	Atomic Mass†	Date of Discovery	Discoverer and Nationality‡	Derivation
Fermium	Fm	100	(253)	1953	A. Ghiorso (USA)	Enrico Fermi
Fluorine	F	9	19.00	1886	H. Moissan (Fr.)	Mineral fluorspar, from L. *fluere,* flow (because fluorspar was used as a flux)
Francium	Fr	87	(223)	1939	Marguerite Perey (Fr.)	France
Gadolinium	Gd	64	157.3	1880	J. C. Marignac (Fr.)	Johan Gadolin, Finnish rare earth chemist
Gallium	Ga	31	69.72	1875	Lecoq de Boisbaudran (Fr.)	L. *Gallia,* France
Germanium	Ge	32	72.59	1886	Clemens Winkler (Ge.)	L. *Germania,* Germany
Gold	Au	79	197.0	Ancient		L. *aurum,* shining dawn
Hafnium	Hf	72	178.5	1923	D. Coster (Du.) G. von Hevesey (H.)	L. *Hafnia,* Copenhagen
Helium	He	2	4.003	1868	P. Janssen (spectr) (Fr.) Sir William Ramsay (isolated) (GB)	Gr. *helios,* sun (because it was first discovered in the sun's spectrum)
Holmium	Ho	67	164.9	1879	P. T. Cleve (Swe.)	L. *Holmia,* Stockholm
Hydrogen	H	1	1.008	1766	Sir Henry Cavendish (GB)	Gr. *hydro,* water; *genes,* forming (because it produces water when burned with oxygen)
Indium	In	49	114.8	1863	F. Reich (Ge.) T. Richter (Ge.)	Indigo, because of its indigo blue lines in the spectrum
Iodine	I	53	126.9	1811	B. Courtois (Fr.)	Gr. *iodes,* violet
Iridium	Ir	77	192.2	1803	S. Tennant (GB)	L. *iris,* rainbow
Iron	Fe	26	55.85	Ancient		L. *ferrum,* iron
Krypton	Kr	36	83.80	1898	Sir William Ramsay (GB) M. W. Travers (GB)	Gr. *kryptos,* hidden
Lanthanum	La	57	138.9	1839	C. G. Mosander (Swe.)	Gr. *lanthanein,* concealed
Lawrencium	Lr	103	(257)	1961	A. Ghiorso (USA) T. Sikkeland (USA) A. E. Larsh (USA) R. M. Latimer (USA)	E. O. Lawrence (USA), inventor of the cyclotron
Lead	Pb	82	207.2	Ancient		Symbol, L. *plumbum,* lead, meaning heavy
Lithium	Li	3	6.941	1817	A. Arfvedson (Swe.)	Gr. *lithos,* rock (because it occurs in rocks)
Lutetium	Lu	71	175.0	1907	G. Urbain (Fr.) C. A. von Welsbach (Au.)	*Luteria,* ancient name for Paris
Magnesium	Mg	12	24.31	1808	Sir Humphry Davy (GB)	*Magnesia,* a district in Thessaly; possibly derived from L. *magnesia*
Manganese	Mn	25	54.94	1774	J. G. Gahn (Swe.)	L. *magnes,* magnet

(Continued)

Element	Symbol	Atomic No.	Atomic Mass[†]	Date of Discovery	Discoverer and Nationality[‡]	Derivation
Mendelevium	Md	101	(256)	1955	A. Ghiorso (USA) G. R. Choppin (USA) G. T. Seaborg (USA) B. G. Harvey (USA) S. G. Thompson (USA)	Mendeleev, Russian chemist who prepared the periodic chart and predicted properties of undiscovered elements
Mercury	Hg	80	200.6	Ancient		Symbol, L. *hydrargyrum,* liquid silver
Molybdenum	Mo	42	95.94	1778	G. W. Scheele (Swe.)	Gr. *molybdos,* lead
Neodymium	Nd	60	144.2	1885	C. A. von Welsbach (Au.)	Gr. *neos,* new; *didymos,* twin
Neon	Ne	10	20.18	1898	Sir William Ramsay (GB) M. W. Travers (GB)	Gr. *neos,* new
Neptunium	Np	93	(237)	1940	E. M. McMillan (USA) P. H. Abelson (USA)	Planet Neptune
Nickel	Ni	28	58.69	1751	A. F. Cronstedt (Swe.)	Swe. *kopparnickel,* false copper; also Ge. *nickel,* referring to the devil that prevented copper from being extracted from nickel ores
Niobium	Nb	41	92.91	1801	Charles Hatchett (GB)	Gr. *Niobe,* daughter of Tantalus (niobium was considered identical to tantalum, named after *Tantalus,* until 1884)
Nitrogen	N	7	14.01	1772	Daniel Rutherford (GB)	Fr. *nitrogene,* derived from L. *nitrum,* native soda, or Gr. *nitron,* native soda, and Gr. *genes,* forming
Nobelium	No	102	(253)	1958	A. Ghiorso (USA) T. Sikkeland (USA) J. R. Walton (USA) G. T. Seaborg (USA)	Alfred Nobel
Osmium	Os	76	190.2	1803	S. Tennant (GB)	Gr. *osme,* odor
Oxygen	O	8	16.00	1774	Joseph Priestley (GB) C. W. Scheele (Swe.)	Fr. *oxygene,* generator of acid, derived from Gr. *oxys,* acid, and L. *genes,* forming (because it was once thought to be a part of all acids)
Palladium	Pd	46	106.4	1803	W. H. Wollaston (GB)	Asteroid Pallas
Phosphorus	P	15	30.97	1669	H. Brandt (Ge.)	Gr. *phosphoros,* light bearing
Platinum	Pt	78	195.1	1735 1741	A. de Ulloa (Sp.) Charles Wood (GB)	Sp. *platina,* silver

(Continued)

Element	Symbol	Atomic No.	Atomic Mass[†]	Date of Discovery	Discoverer and Nationality[‡]	Derivation
Plutonium	Pu	94	(242)	1940	G. T. Seaborg (USA) E. M. McMillan (USA) J. W. Kennedy (USA) A. C. Wahl (USA)	Planet Pluto
Polonium	Po	84	(210)	1898	Marie Curie (P.)	Poland
Potassium	K	19	39.10	1807	Sir Humphry Davy (GB)	Symbol, L. *kalium*, potash
Praseodymium	Pr	59	140.9	1885	C. A. von Welsbach (Au.)	Gr. *prasios*, green; *didymos*, twin
Promethium	Pm	61	(147)	1945	J. A. Marinsky (USA) L. E. Glendenin (USA) C. D. Coryell (USA)	Gr. mythology, *Prometheus*, the Greek Titan who stole fire from heaven
Protactinium	Pa	91	(231)	1917	O. Hahn (Ge.) L. Meitner (Au.)	Gr. *protos*, first; *actinium* (because it distintegrates into actinium)
Radium	Ra	88	(226)	1898	Pierre and Marie Curie (Fr., P.)	L. *radius*, ray
Radon	Rn	86	(222)	1900	F. E. Dorn (Ge.)	Derived from radium
Rhenium	Re	75	186.2	1925	W. Noddack (Ge.) I. Tacke (Ge.) Otto Berg (Ge.)	L. *Rhenus*, Rhine
Rhodium	Rh	45	102.9	1804	W. H. Wollaston (GB)	Gr. *rhodon*, rose (because some of its salts are rose-colored)
Rubidium	Rb	37	85.47	1861	R. W. Bunsen (Ge.) G. Kirchhoff (Ge.)	L. *rubidus*, dark red (discovered with the spectroscope, its spectrum shows red lines)
Ruthenium	Ru	44	101.1	1844	K. K. Klaus (R.)	L. *Ruthenia*, Russia
Samarium	Sm	62	150.4	1879	Lecoq de Boisbaudran (Fr.)	Samarskite, after Samarski, a Russian engineer
Scandium	Sc	21	44.96	1879	L. F. Nilson (Swe.)	Scandinavia
Selenium	Se	34	78.96	1817	J. J. Berzelius (Swe.)	Gr. *selene*, moon (because it resembles tellurium, named for the earth)
Silicon	Si	14	28.09	1824	J. J. Berzelius (Swe.)	L. *silex, silicis*, flint
Silver	Ag	47	107.9	Ancient		Symbol, L. *argentum*, silver
Sodium	Na	11	22.99	1807	Sir Humphry Davy (GB)	L. *sodanum*, headache remedy; symbol, L. *natrium*, soda
Strontium	Sr	38	87.62	1808	Sir Humphry Davy (GB)	Strontian, Scotland, derived from mineral strontionite

(Continued)

Element	Symbol	Atomic No.	Atomic Mass[†]	Date of Discovery	Discoverer and Nationality[‡]	Derivation
Sulfur	S	16	32.07	Ancient		L. *sulphurium* (Sanskrit, *sulvere*)
Tantalum	Ta	73	180.9	1802	A. G. Ekeberg (Swe.)	Gr. mythology, *Tantalus,* because of difficulty in isolating it
Technetium	Tc	43	(99)	1937	C. Perrier (I.)	Gr. *technetos,* artificial (because it was the first artificial element)
Tellurium	Te	52	127.6	1782	F. J. Müller (Au.)	L. *tellus,* earth
Terbium	Tb	65	158.9	1843	C. G. Mosander (Swe.)	Ytterby, Sweden
Thallium	Tl	81	204.4	1861	Sir William Crookes (GB)	Gr. *thallos,* a budding twig (because its spectrum shows a bright green line)
Thorium	Th	90	232.0	1828	J. J. Berzelius (Swe.)	Mineral thorite, derived from *Thor,* Norse god of war
Thulium	Tm	69	168.9	1879	P. T. Cleve (Swe.)	*Thule,* early name for Scandinavia
Tin	Sn	50	118.7	Ancient		Symbol, L. *stannum,* tin
Titanium	Ti	22	47.88	1791	W. Gregor (GB)	Gr. giants, the Titans, and L. titans, giant deities
Tungsten	W	74	183.9	1783	J. J. and F. de Elhuyar (Sp.)	Swe. *tung sten,* heavy stone; symbol, wolframite, a mineral
Uranium	U	92	238.0	1789 1841	M. H. Klaproth (Ge.) E. M. Peligot (Fr.)	Planet Uranus
Vanadium	V	23	50.94	1801 1830	A. M. del Rio (Sp.) N. G. Sefstrom (Swe.)	*Vanadis,* Norse goddess of love and beauty
Xenon	Xe	54	131.3	1898	Sir William Ramsay (GB) M. W. Travers (GB)	Gr. *xenos,* stranger
Ytterbium	Yb	70	173.0	1907	G. Urbain (Fr.)	Ytterby, Sweden
Yttrium	Y	39	88.91	1843	C. G. Mosander (Swe.)	Ytterby, Sweden
Zinc	Zn	30	65.39	1746	A. S. Marggraf (Ge.)	Ge. *zink,* of obscure origin
Zirconium	Zr	40	91.22	1789	M. H. Klaproth (Ge.)	Zircon, in which it was found, derived from *Ar. zargum,* gold color

Units for the Gas Constant

In this appendix we will see how the gas constant R can be expressed in units J/K · mol. Our first step is to derive a relationship between atm and pascal. We start with

$$
\begin{aligned}
\text{pressure} &= \frac{\text{force}}{\text{area}} \\
&= \frac{\text{mass} \times \text{acceleration}}{\text{area}} \\
&= \frac{\text{volume} \times \text{density} \times \text{acceleration}}{\text{area}} \\
&= \text{length} \times \text{density} \times \text{acceleration}
\end{aligned}
$$

By definition, the standard atmosphere is the pressure exerted by a column of mercury exactly 76 cm high of density 13.5951 g/cm^3, in a place where acceleration due to gravity is 980.665 cm/s^2. However, to express pressure in N/m^2 it is necessary to write

$$
\begin{aligned}
\text{density of mercury} &= 1.35951 \times 10^4 \, \text{kg/m}^3 \\
\text{acceleration due to gravity} &= 9.80665 \, \text{m/s}^2
\end{aligned}
$$

The standard atmosphere is given by

$$
\begin{aligned}
1 \, \text{atm} &= (0.76 \, \text{m Hg})(1.35951 \times 10^4 \, \text{kg/m}^3)(9.80665 \, \text{m/s}^2) \\
&= 101{,}325 \, \text{kg m/m}^2 \cdot \text{s}^2 \\
&= 101{,}325 \, \text{N/m}^2 \\
&= 101{,}325 \, \text{Pa}
\end{aligned}
$$

From Section 5.4 we see that the gas constant R is given by 0.082057 L · atm/K · mol. Using the conversion factors

$$
\begin{aligned}
1 \, \text{L} &= 1 \times 10^{-3} \, \text{m}^3 \\
1 \, \text{atm} &= 101{,}325 \, \text{N/m}^2
\end{aligned}
$$

we write

$$
\begin{aligned}
R &= \left(0.082057 \, \frac{\text{L atm}}{\text{K mol}}\right)\left(\frac{1 \times 10^{-3} \, \text{m}^3}{1 \, \text{L}}\right)\left(\frac{101{,}325 \, \text{N/m}^2}{1 \, \text{atm}}\right) \\
&= 8.314 \, \frac{\text{N m}}{\text{K mol}} \\
&= 8.314 \, \frac{\text{J}}{\text{K mol}}
\end{aligned}
$$

and

$$
\begin{aligned}
1 \, \text{L} \cdot \text{atm} &= (1 \times 10^{-3} \, \text{m}^3)(101{,}325 \, \text{N/m}^2) \\
&= 101.3 \, \text{N m} \\
&= 101.3 \, \text{J}
\end{aligned}
$$

Appendix 3

Thermodynamic Data at 1 atm and 25°C*

Inorganic Substances

Substance	ΔH_f° (kJ/mol)	ΔG_f° (kJ/mol)	S° (J/K · mol)
$Ag(s)$	0	0	42.7
$Ag^+(aq)$	105.9	77.1	73.9
$AgCl(s)$	−127.0	−109.7	96.1
$AgBr(s)$	−99.5	−95.9	107.1
$AgI(s)$	−62.4	−66.3	114.2
$AgNO_3(s)$	−123.1	−32.2	140.9
$Al(s)$	0	0	28.3
$Al^{3+}(aq)$	−524.7	−481.2	−313.38
$Al_2O_3(s)$	−1669.8	−1576.4	50.99
$As(s)$	0	0	35.15
$AsO_4^{3-}(aq)$	−870.3	−635.97	−144.77
$AsH_3(g)$	171.5		
$H_3AsO_4(s)$	−900.4		
$Au(s)$	0	0	47.7
$Au_2O_3(s)$	80.8	163.2	125.5
$AuCl(s)$	−35.2		
$AuCl_3(s)$	−118.4		
$B(s)$	0	0	6.5
$B_2O_3(s)$	−1263.6	−1184.1	54.0
$H_3BO_3(s)$	−1087.9	−963.16	89.58
$H_3BO_3(aq)$	−1067.8	−963.3	159.8
$Ba(s)$	0	0	66.9
$Ba^{2+}(aq)$	−538.4	−560.66	12.55
$BaO(s)$	−558.2	−528.4	70.3
$BaCl_2(s)$	−860.1	−810.66	125.5
$BaSO_4(s)$	−1464.4	−1353.1	132.2
$BaCO_3(s)$	−1218.8	−1138.9	112.1
$Be(s)$	0	0	9.5
$BeO(s)$	−610.9	−581.58	14.1
$Br_2(l)$	0	0	152.3
$Br^-(aq)$	−120.9	−102.8	80.7
$HBr(g)$	−36.2	−53.2	198.48
$C(graphite)$	0	0	5.69
$C(diamond)$	1.90	2.87	2.4
$CO(g)$	−110.5	−137.3	197.9
$CO_2(g)$	−393.5	−394.4	213.6
$CO_2(aq)$	−412.9	−386.2	121.3
$CO_3^{2-}(aq)$	−676.3	−528.1	−53.1

*The thermodynamic quantities of ions are based on the reference states that $\Delta H_f^\circ[H^+(aq)] = 0$, $\Delta G_f^\circ[H^+(aq)] = 0$, and $S^\circ[H^+(aq)] = 0$.

(Continued)

Substance	ΔH°_f (kJ/mol)	ΔG°_f (kJ/mol)	S° (J/K $\cdot$ mol)
$HCO_3^-(aq)$	−691.1	−587.1	94.98
$H_2CO_3(aq)$	−699.7	−623.2	187.4
$CS_2(g)$	115.3	65.1	237.8
$CS_2(l)$	87.3	63.6	151.0
$HCN(aq)$	105.4	112.1	128.9
$CN^-(aq)$	151.0	165.69	117.99
$(NH_2)_2CO(s)$	−333.19	−197.15	104.6
$(NH_2)_2CO(aq)$	−319.2	−203.84	173.85
$Ca(s)$	0	0	41.6
$Ca^{2+}(aq)$	−542.96	−553.0	−55.2
$CaO(s)$	−635.6	−604.2	39.8
$Ca(OH)_2(s)$	−986.6	−896.8	83.4
$CaF_2(s)$	−1214.6	−1161.9	68.87
$CaCl_2(s)$	−794.96	−750.19	113.8
$CaSO_4(s)$	−1432.69	−1320.3	106.69
$CaCO_3(s)$	−1206.9	−1128.8	92.9
$Cd(s)$	0	0	51.46
$Cd^{2+}(aq)$	−72.38	−77.7	−61.09
$CdO(s)$	−254.6	−225.06	54.8
$CdCl_2(s)$	−389.1	−342.59	118.4
$CdSO_4(s)$	−926.17	−820.2	137.2
$Cl_2(g)$	0	0	223.0
$Cl^-(aq)$	−167.2	−131.2	56.5
$HCl(g)$	−92.3	−95.27	187.0
$Co(s)$	0	0	28.45
$Co^{2+}(aq)$	−67.36	−51.46	155.2
$CoO(s)$	−239.3	−213.38	43.9
$Cr(s)$	0	0	23.77
$Cr^{2+}(aq)$	−138.9		
$Cr_2O_3(s)$	−1128.4	−1046.8	81.17
$CrO_4^{2-}(aq)$	−863.16	−706.26	38.49
$Cr_2O_7^{2-}(aq)$	−1460.6	−1257.29	213.8
$Cs(s)$	0	0	82.8
$Cs^+(aq)$	−247.69	−282.0	133.05
$Cu(s)$	0	0	33.3
$Cu^+(aq)$	51.88	50.2	26.4
$Cu^{2+}(aq)$	64.39	64.98	−99.6
$CuO(s)$	−155.2	−127.2	43.5
$Cu_2O(s)$	−166.69	−146.36	100.8
$CuCl(s)$	−134.7	−118.8	91.6
$CuCl_2(s)$	−205.85	?	?
$CuS(s)$	−48.5	−49.0	66.5
$CuSO_4(s)$	−769.86	−661.9	113.39
$F_2(g)$	0	0	203.34
$F^-(aq)$	−329.1	−276.48	−9.6
$HF(g)$	−271.6	−270.7	173.5
$Fe(s)$	0	0	27.2
$Fe^{2+}(aq)$	−87.86	−84.9	−113.39

Substance	ΔH_f° (kJ/mol)	ΔG_f° (kJ/mol)	S° (J/K · mol)
$Fe^{3+}(aq)$	−47.7	−10.5	−293.3
$FeO(s)$	−272.0	−255.2	60.8
$Fe_2O_3(s)$	−822.2	−741.0	90.0
$Fe(OH)_2(s)$	−568.19	−483.55	79.5
$Fe(OH)_3(s)$	−824.25	?	?
$H(g)$	218.2	203.2	114.6
$H_2(g)$	0	0	131.0
$H^+(aq)$	0	0	0
$OH^-(aq)$	−229.94	−157.30	−10.5
$H_2O(g)$	−241.8	−228.6	188.7
$H_2O(l)$	−285.8	−237.2	69.9
$H_2O_2(l)$	−187.6	−118.1	?
$Hg(l)$	0	0	77.4
$Hg^{2+}(aq)$		−164.38	
$HgO(s)$	−90.7	−58.5	72.0
$HgCl_2(s)$	−230.1		
$Hg_2Cl_2(s)$	−264.9	−210.66	196.2
$HgS(s)$	−58.16	−48.8	77.8
$HgSO_4(s)$	−704.17		
$Hg_2SO_4(s)$	−741.99	−623.92	200.75
$I_2(s)$	0	0	116.7
$I^-(aq)$	−55.9	−51.67	109.37
$HI(g)$	25.9	1.30	206.3
$K(s)$	0	0	63.6
$K^+(aq)$	−251.2	−282.28	102.5
$KOH(s)$	−425.85		
$KCl(s)$	−435.87	−408.3	82.68
$KClO_3(s)$	−391.20	−289.9	142.97
$KClO_4(s)$	−433.46	−304.18	151.0
$KBr(s)$	−392.17	−379.2	96.4
$KI(s)$	−327.65	−322.29	104.35
$KNO_3(s)$	−492.7	−393.1	132.9
$Li(s)$	0	0	28.0
$Li^+(aq)$	−278.46	−293.8	14.2
$Li_2O(s)$	−595.8	?	?
$LiOH(s)$	−487.2	−443.9	50.2
$Mg(s)$	0	0	32.5
$Mg^{2+}(aq)$	−461.96	−456.0	−117.99
$MgO(s)$	−601.8	−569.6	26.78
$Mg(OH)_2(s)$	−924.66	−833.75	63.1
$MgCl_2(s)$	−641.8	−592.3	89.5
$MgSO_4(s)$	−1278.2	−1173.6	91.6
$MgCO_3(s)$	−1112.9	−1029.3	65.69
$Mn(s)$	0	0	31.76
$Mn^{2+}(aq)$	−218.8	−223.4	−83.68
$MnO_2(s)$	−520.9	−466.1	53.1
$N_2(g)$	0	0	191.5
$N_3^-(aq)$	245.18	?	?

(Continued)

Substance	ΔH_f° (kJ/mol)	ΔG_f° (kJ/mol)	S° (J/K · mol)
$NH_3(g)$	−46.3	−16.6	193.0
$NH_4^+(aq)$	−132.80	−79.5	112.8
$NH_4Cl(s)$	−315.39	−203.89	94.56
$NH_3(aq)$	−80.3	−26.5	111.3
$N_2H_4(l)$	50.4		
$NO(g)$	90.4	86.7	210.6
$NO_2(g)$	33.85	51.8	240.46
$N_2O_4(g)$	9.66	98.29	304.3
$N_2O(g)$	81.56	103.6	219.99
$HNO_2(aq)$	−118.8	−53.6	
$HNO_3(l)$	−173.2	−79.9	155.6
$NO_3^-(aq)$	−206.57	−110.5	146.4
$Na(s)$	0	0	51.05
$Na^+(aq)$	−239.66	−261.87	60.25
$Na_2O(s)$	−415.9	−376.56	72.8
$NaCl(s)$	−411.0	−384.0	72.38
$NaI(s)$	−288.0		
$Na_2SO_4(s)$	−1384.49	−1266.8	149.49
$NaNO_3(s)$	−466.68	−365.89	116.3
$Na_2CO_3(s)$	−1130.9	−1047.67	135.98
$NaHCO_3(s)$	−947.68	−851.86	102.09
$Ni(s)$	0	0	30.1
$Ni^{2+}(aq)$	−64.0	−46.4	−159.4
$NiO(s)$	−244.35	−216.3	38.58
$Ni(OH)_2(s)$	−538.06	−453.1	79.5
$O(g)$	249.4	230.1	160.95
$O_2(g)$	0	0	205.0
$O_3(aq)$	−12.09	16.3	110.88
$O_3(g)$	142.2	163.4	237.6
$P(white)$	0	0	44.0
$P(red)$	−18.4	13.8	29.3
$PO_4^{3-}(aq)$	−1284.07	−1025.59	−217.57
$P_4O_{10}(s)$	−3012.48		
$PH_3(g)$	9.25	18.2	210.0
$HPO_4^{2-}(aq)$	−1298.7	−1094.1	−35.98
$H_2PO_4^-(aq)$	−1302.48	−1135.1	89.1
$Pb(s)$	0	0	64.89
$Pb^{2+}(aq)$	1.6	−24.3	21.3
$PbO(s)$	−217.86	−188.49	69.45
$PbO_2(s)$	−276.65	−218.99	76.57
$PbCl_2(s)$	−359.2	−313.97	136.4
$PbS(s)$	−94.3	−92.68	91.2
$PbSO_4(s)$	−918.4	−811.2	147.28
$Pt(s)$	0	0	41.84
$PtCl_4^{2-}(aq)$	−516.3	−384.5	175.7
$Rb(s)$	0	0	69.45
$Rb^+(aq)$	−246.4	−282.2	124.27
$S(rhombic)$	0	0	31.88

Substance	ΔH_f° (kJ/mol)	ΔG_f° (kJ/mol)	S° (J/K · mol)
S(monoclinic)	0.30	0.10	32.55
$SO_2(g)$	−296.4	−300.4	248.5
$SO_3(g)$	−395.2	−370.4	256.2
$SO_3^{2-}(aq)$	−624.25	−497.06	43.5
$SO_4^{2-}(aq)$	−907.5	−741.99	17.15
$H_2S(g)$	−20.15	−33.0	205.64
$HSO_3^-(aq)$	−627.98	−527.3	132.38
$HSO_4^-(aq)$	−885.75	−752.87	126.86
$H_2SO_4(l)$	−811.3	?	?
$SF_6(g)$	−1096.2	?	?
Si(s)	0	0	18.70
$SiO_2(s)$	−859.3	−805.0	41.84
Sr(s)	0	0	54.39
$Sr^{2+}(aq)$	−545.5	−557.3	−39.33
$SrCl_2(s)$	−828.4	−781.15	117.15
$SrSO_4(s)$	−1444.74	−1334.28	121.75
$SrCO_3(s)$	−1218.38	−1137.6	97.07
Zn(s)	0	0	41.6
$Zn^{2+}(aq)$	−152.4	−147.2	−106.48
ZnO(s)	−348.0	−318.2	43.9
$ZnCl_2(s)$	−415.89	−369.26	108.37
ZnS(s)	−202.9	−198.3	57.7
$ZnSO_4(s)$	−978.6	−871.6	124.7

Organic Substances

Substance	Formula	ΔH_f° (kJ/mol)	ΔG_f° (kJ/mol)	S° (J/K · mol)
Acetic acid(l)	CH_3COOH	−484.2	−389.45	159.8
Acetaldehyde(g)	CH_3CHO	−166.35	−139.08	264.2
Acetone(l)	CH_3COCH_3	−246.8	−153.55	198.7
Acetylene(g)	C_2H_2	226.6	209.2	200.8
Benzene(l)	C_6H_6	49.04	124.5	172.8
Butane(g)	C_4H_{10}	−124.7	−15.7	310.0
Ethanol(l)	C_2H_5OH	−276.98	−174.18	161.0
Ethane(g)	C_2H_6	−84.7	−32.89	229.5
Ethylene(g)	C_2H_4	52.3	68.1	219.5
Formic acid(l)	HCOOH	−409.2	−346.0	129.0
Glucose(s)	$C_6H_{12}O_6$	−1274.5	−910.56	212.1
Methane(g)	CH_4	−74.85	−50.8	186.2
Methanol(l)	CH_3OH	−238.7	−166.3	126.8
Propane(g)	C_3H_8	−103.9	−23.5	269.9
Sucrose(s)	$C_{12}H_{22}O_{11}$	−2221.7	−1544.3	360.2

Mathematical Operations

Logarithms

Common Logarithms

The concept of the logarithms is an extension of the concept of exponents, which is discussed in Chapter 1. The *common,* or base-10, logarithm of any number is the power to which 10 must be raised to equal the number. The following examples illustrate this relationship:

Logarithm	Exponent
$\log 1 = 0$	$10^0 = 1$
$\log 10 = 1$	$10^1 = 10$
$\log 100 = 2$	$10^2 = 100$
$\log 10^{-1} = -1$	$10^{-1} = 0.1$
$\log 10^{-2} = -2$	$10^{-2} = 0.01$

In each case the logarithm of the number can be obtained by inspection.

Because the logarithms of numbers are exponents, they have the same properties as exponents. Thus, we have

Logarithm	Exponent
$\log AB = \log A + \log B$	$10^A \times 10^B = 10^{A+B}$
$\log \dfrac{A}{B} = \log A - \log B$	$\dfrac{10^A}{10^B} = 10^{A-B}$

Furthermore, $\log A^n = n \log A$.

Now suppose we want to find the common logarithm of 6.7×10^{-4}. On most electronic calculators, the number is entered first and then the log key is pressed. This operation gives us

$$\log 6.7 \times 10^{-4} = -3.17$$

Note that there are as many digits *after* the decimal point as there are significant figures in the original number. The original number has two significant figures and the "17" in -3.17 tells us that the log has two significant figures. The "3" in -3.17 serves only to locate the decimal point in the number 6.7×10^{-4}. Other examples are

Number	Common Logarithm
62	1.79
0.872	-0.0595
1.0×10^{-7}	-7.00

Sometimes (as in the case of pH calculations) it is necessary to obtain the number whose logarithm is known. This procedure is known as taking the antilogarithm; it is simply the reverse of taking the logarithm of a number. Suppose in a certain calculation we have pH = 1.46 and are asked to calculate $[H^+]$. From the definition of pH (pH $= -\log [H^+]$) we can write

$$[H^+] = 10^{-1.46}$$

Many calculators have a key labeled $\log^{-1}$ or INV log to obtain antilogs. Other calculators have a 10^x or y^x key (where x corresponds to -1.46 in our example and y is 10 for base-10 logarithm). Therefore, we find that $[H^+] = 0.035\ M$.

Natural Logarithms

Logarithms taken to the base e instead of 10 are known as natural logarithms (denoted by ln or $\log_e$); e is equal to 2.7183. The relationship between common logarithms and natural logarithms is as follows:

$$\log 10 = 1 \qquad 10^1 = 10$$
$$\ln 10 = 2.303 \qquad e^{2.303} = 10$$

Thus,

$$\ln x = 2.303 \log x$$

To find the natural logarithm of 2.27, say, we first enter the number on the electronic calculator and then press the ln key to get

$$\ln 2.27 = 0.820$$

If no ln key is provided, we can proceed as follows:

$$2.303 \log 2.27 = 2.303 \times 0.356$$
$$= 0.820$$

Sometimes we may be given the natural logarithm and asked to find the number it represents. For example,

$$\ln x = 59.7$$

On many calculators, we simply enter the number and press the e key:

$$e^{59.7} = 8 \times 10^{25}$$

The Quadratic Equation

A quadratic equation takes the form

$$ax^2 + bx + c = 0$$

If coefficients a, b, and c are known, then x is given by

$$x = \frac{-b \pm \sqrt{b^2 - 4ac}}{2a}$$

Suppose we have the following quadratic equation:

$$2x^2 + 5x - 12 = 0$$

Solving for x, we write

$$x = \frac{-5 \pm \sqrt{(5)^2 - 4(2)(-12)}}{2(2)}$$
$$= \frac{-5 \pm \sqrt{25 + 96}}{4}$$

Therefore,

$$x = \frac{-5 + 11}{4} = \frac{3}{2}$$

and

$$x = \frac{-5 - 11}{4} = -4$$

Glossary

The number in parentheses is the number of the section in which the term first appears.

A

absolute temperature scale. A temperature scale that uses the absolute zero of temperature as the lowest temperature. (5.3)

absolute zero. Theoretically the lowest attainable temperature. (5.3)

acceptor impurities. Impurities that can accept electrons from semiconductors. (20.3)

accuracy. The closeness of a measurement to the true value of the quantity that is measured. (1.8)

acid. A substance that yields hydrogen ions (H^+) when dissolved in water. (2.7)

acid ionization constant (K_a). The equilibrium constant for the acid ionization. (15.5)

actinide series. Elements that have incompletely filled $5f$ subshells or readily give rise to cations that have incompletely filled $5f$ subshells. (7.9)

activated complex. The species temporarily formed by the reactant molecules as a result of the collision before they form the product. (13.4)

activation energy (E_a). The minimum amount of energy required to initiate a chemical reaction. (13.4)

activity series. A summary of the results of many possible displacement reactions. (4.4)

actual yield. The amount of product actually obtained in a reaction. (3.10)

addition reaction. A reaction in which one molecule adds to another. (24.2)

adhesion. Attraction between unlike molecules. (11.3)

alcohol. An organic compound containing the hydroxyl group—OH. (24.4)

aldehydes. Compounds with a carbonyl functional group and the general formula RCHO, where R is an H atom, an alkyl, or an aromatic group. (24.4)

aliphatic hydrocarbons. Hydrocarbons that do not contain the benzene group or the benzene ring. (24.1)

alkali metals. The Group 1A elements (Li, Na, K, Rb, Cs, and Fr). (2.4)

alkaline earth metals. The Group 2A elements (Be, Mg, Ca, Sr, Ba, and Ra). (2.4)

alkanes. Hydrocarbons having the general formula C_nH_{2n+2}, where $n = 1,2, \ldots$ (24.2)

alkenes. Hydrocarbons that contain one or more carbon-carbon double bonds. They have the general formula C_nH_{2n}, where $n = 2,3, \ldots$ (24.2)

alkynes. Hydrocarbons that contain one or more carbon-carbon triple bonds. They have the general formula C_nH_{2n-2}, where $n = 2,3, \ldots$ (24.2)

allotropes. Two or more forms of the same element that differ significantly in chemical and physical properties. (2.6)

alloy. A solid solution composed of two or more metals, or of a metal or metals with one or more nonmetals. (20.2)

alpha particles. See alpha rays.

alpha (α) rays. Helium ions with a positive charge of +2. (2.2)

amalgam. An alloy of mercury with another metal or metals. (20.2)

amines. Organic bases that have the functional group—NR_2, where R may be H, an alkyl group, or an aromatic group. (24.4)

amino acids. A compound that contains at least one amino group and at least one carboxyl group. (25.3)

amorphous solid. A solid that lacks a regular three-dimensional arrangement of atoms or molecules. (11.7)

amphoteric oxide. An oxide that exhibits both acidic and basic properties. (8.6)

amplitude. The vertical distance from the middle of a wave to the peak or trough. (7.1)

anion. An ion with a net negative charge. (2.5)

anode. The electrode at which oxidation occurs. (19.2)

antibonding molecular orbital. A molecular orbital that is of higher energy and lower stability than the atomic orbitals from which it was formed. (10.6)

aqueous solution. A solution in which the solvent is water. (4.1)

aromatic hydrocarbon. A hydrocarbon that contains one or more benzene rings. (24.1)

atmospheric pressure. The pressure exerted by Earth's atmosphere. (5.2)

atom. The basic unit of an element that can enter into chemical combination. (2.2)

atomic mass. The mass of an atom in atomic mass units. (3.1)

atomic mass unit (amu). A mass exactly equal to $\frac{1}{12}$th the mass of one carbon-12 atom. (3.1)

atomic number (Z). The number of protons in the nucleus of an atom. (2.3)

atomic orbital. The wave function (Ψ) of an electron in an atom. (7.5)

atomic radius. One-half the distance between the two nuclei in two adjacent atoms of the same element in a metal. For elements that exist as diatomic units, the atomic radius is one-half the distance between the nuclei of the two atoms in a particular molecule. (8.3)

Aufbau principle. As protons are added one by one to the nucleus to build up the elements, electrons similarly are added to the atomic orbitals. (7.9)

Avogadro's law. At constant pressure and temperature, the volume of a gas is directly proportional to the number of moles of the gas present. (5.3)

Avogadro's number (N_A). 6.022×10^{23}; the number of particles in a mole. (3.2)

B

band theory. Delocalized electrons move freely through "bands" formed by overlapping molecular orbitals. (20.3)

barometer. An instrument that measures atmospheric pressure. (5.2)

base. A substance that yields hydroxide ions (OH^-) when dissolved in water. (2.7)

base ionization constant (K_b). The equilibrium constant for the base ionization. (15.6)

battery. A galvanic cell, or a series of combined galvanic cells, that can be used as a source of direct electric current at a constant voltage. (19.6)

beta particles. See beta rays.

beta (β) rays. Electrons. (2.2)

bimolecular reaction. An elementary step that involves two molecules. (13.5)

binary compounds. Compounds formed from just two elements. (2.7)

boiling point. The temperature at which the vapor pressure of a liquid is equal to the external atmospheric pressure. (11.8)

boiling-point elevation (ΔT_b). The boiling point of the solution (T_b) minus the boiling point of the pure solvent (T_b°). (12.6)

bond enthalpy. The enthalpy change required to break a bond in a mole of gaseous molecules. (9.10)

bond length. The distance between the nuclei of two bonded atoms in a molecule. (9.4)

bond order. The difference between the numbers of electrons in bonding molecular orbitals and antibonding molecular orbitals, divided by two. (10.7)

bonding molecular orbital. A molecular orbital that is of lower energy and greater stability than the atomic orbitals from which it was formed. (10.6)

Born-Haber cycle. The cycle that relates lattice energies of ionic compounds to ionization energies, electron affinities, heats of sublimation and formation, and bond enthalpies. (9.3)

boundary surface diagram. Diagram of the region containing a substantial amount of the electron density (about 90 percent) in an orbital. (7.7)

Boyle's law. The volume of a fixed amount of gas maintained at constant temperature is inversely proportional to the gas pressure. (5.3)

breeder reactor. A nuclear reactor that produces more fissionable materials than it uses. (23.5)

Brønsted acid. A substance capable of donating a proton. (4.3)

Brønsted base. A substance capable of accepting a proton. (4.3)

buffer solution. A solution of (a) a weak acid or base and (b) its salt; both components must be present. The solution has the ability to resist changes in pH upon the addition of small amounts of either acid or base. (16.3)

C

calorimetry. The measurement of heat changes. (6.5)

carbides. Ionic compounds containing the C_2^{2-} or C^{4-} ion. (21.3)

carboxylic acids. Acids that contain the carboxyl group —COOH. (24.4)

catalyst. A substance that increases the rate of a chemical reaction without itself being consumed. (13.6)

catenation. The ability of the atoms of an element to form bonds with one another. (21.3)

cathode. The electrode at which reduction occurs. (19.2)

cation. An ion with a net positive charge. (2.5)

cell voltage. Difference in electrical potential between the anode and the cathode of a galvanic cell. (19.2)

Charles and Gay-Lussac's law. See Charles's law.

Charles's law. The volume of a fixed amount of gas maintained at constant pressure is directly proportional to the absolute temperature of the gas. (5.3)

chelating agent. A substance that forms complex ions with metal ions in solution. (22.3)

chemical energy. Energy stored within the structural units of chemical substances. (6.1)

chemical equation. An equation that uses chemical symbols to show what happens during a chemical reaction. (3.7)

chemical equilibrium. A state in which the rates of the forward and reverse reactions are equal. (14.1)

chemical formula. An expression showing the chemical composition of a compound in terms of the symbols for the atoms of the elements involved. (2.6)

chemical kinetics. The area of chemistry concerned with the speeds, or rates, at which chemical reactions occur. (13.1)

chemical property. Any property of a substance that cannot be studied without converting the substance into some other substance. (1.6)

chemical reaction. A process in which a substance (or substances) is changed into one or more new substances. (3.7)

chemistry. The study of matter and the changes it undergoes. (1.1)

chiral. Compounds or ions that are not superimposable with their mirror images. (22.4)

chlor-alkali process. The production of chlorine gas by the electrolysis of aqueous NaCl solution. (21.6)

closed system. A system that enables the exchange of energy (usually in the form of heat) but not mass with its surroundings. (6.2)

closest packing. The most efficient arrangements for packing atoms, molecules, or ions in a crystal. (11.4)

cohesion. The intermolecular attraction between like molecules. (11.3)

colligative properties. Properties of solutions that depend on the number of solute particles in solution and not on the nature of the solute particles. (12.6)

colloid. A dispersion of particles of one substance (the dispersed phase) throughout a dispersing medium made of another substance. (12.8)

combination reaction. A reaction in which two or more substances combine to form a single product. (4.4)

combustion reaction. A reaction in which a substance reacts with oxygen, usually with the release of heat and light, to produce a flame. (4.4)

common ion effect. The shift in equilibrium caused by the addition of a compound having an ion in common with the dissolved substances. (16.2)

complex ion. An ion containing a central metal cation bonded to one or more molecules or ions. (16.10)

compound. A substance composed of atoms of two or more elements chemically united in fixed proportions. (1.4)

concentration of a solution. The amount of solute present in a given quantity of solvent or solution. (4.5)

condensation. The phenomenon of going from the gaseous state to the liquid state. (11.8)

condensation reaction. A reaction in which two smaller molecules combine to form a larger molecule. Water is invariably one of the products of such a reaction. (24.4)

conductor. Substance capable of conducting electric current. (20.3)

conjugate acid-base pair. An acid and its conjugate base or a base and its conjugate acid. (15.1)

coordinate covalent bond. A bond in which the pair of electrons is supplied by one of the two bonded atoms; also called a dative bond. (9.9)

coordination compound. A neutral species containing one or more complex ions. (22.3)

coordination number. In a crystal lattice it is defined as the number of atoms (or ions) surrounding an atom (or ion) (11.4). In coordination compounds it is defined as the number of donor atoms surrounding the central metal atom in a complex. (22.3)

copolymer. A polymer containing two or more different monomers. (25.2)

corrosion. The deterioration of metals by an electrochemical process. (19.7)

Coulomb's law. The potential energy between two ions is directly proportional to the product of their charges and inversely proportional to the distance between them. (9.3)

covalent bond. A bond in which two electrons are shared by two atoms. (9.4)

covalent compounds. Compounds containing only covalent bonds. (9.4)

critical mass. The minimum mass of fissionable material required to generate a self-sustaining nuclear chain reaction. (23.5)

critical pressure. The minimum pressure necessary to bring about liquefaction at the critical temperature. (11.8)

critical temperature. The temperature above which a gas will not liquefy. (11.8)

crystal field splitting (Δ). The energy difference between two sets of d orbitals in a metal atom when ligands are present. (22.5)

crystalline solid. A solid that possesses rigid and long-range order; its atoms, molecules, or ions occupy specific positions. (11.4)

crystallization. The process in which dissolved solute comes out of solution and forms crystals. (12.1)

cyanides. Compounds containing the CN^- ion. (21.3)

cycloalkanes. Alkanes whose carbon atoms are joined in rings. (24.2)

D

Dalton's law of partial pressures. The total pressure of a mixture of gases is just the sum of the pressures that each gas would exert if it were present alone. (5.6)

decomposition reaction. The breakdown of a compound into two or more components. (4.4)

delocalized molecular orbitals. Molecular orbitals that are not confined between two adjacent bonding atoms but actually extend over three or more atoms. (10.8)

denatured protein. Protein that does not exhibit normal biological activities. (25.3)

density. The mass of a substance divided by its volume. (1.6)

deoxyribonucleic acids (DNA). A type of nucleic acid. (25.4)

deposition. The process in which the molecules go directly from the vapor into the solid phase. (11.8)

diagonal relationship. Similarities between pairs of elements in different groups and periods of the periodic table. (8.6)

diamagnetic. Repelled by a magnet; a diamagnetic substance contains only paired electrons. (7.8)

diatomic molecule. A molecule that consists of two atoms. (2.5)

diffusion. The gradual mixing of molecules of one gas with the molecules of another by virtue of their kinetic properties. (5.7)

dilution. A procedure for preparing a less concentrated solution from a more concentrated solution. (4.5)

dipole moment (μ). The product of charge and the distance between the charges in a molecule. (10.2)

dipole-dipole forces. Forces that act between polar molecules. (11.2)

diprotic acid. Each unit of the acid yields two hydrogen ions upon ionization. (4.3)

dispersion forces. The attractive forces that arise as a result of temporary dipoles induced in the atoms or molecules; also called London forces. (11.2)

displacement reaction. An atom or an ion in a compound is replaced by an atom of another element. (4.4)

disproportionation reaction. A reaction in which an element in one oxidation state is both oxidized and reduced. (4.4)

donor atom. The atom in a ligand that is bonded directly to the metal atom. (22.3)

donor impurities. Impurities that provide conduction electrons to semiconductors. (20.3)

double bond. Two atoms are held together by two pairs of electrons. (9.4)

dynamic equilibrium. The condition in which the rate of a forward process is exactly balanced by the rate of a reverse process. (11.8)

E

effusion. A process by which a gas under pressure escapes from one compartment of a container to another by passing through a small opening. (5.7)

electrochemistry. The branch of chemistry that deals with the interconversion of electrical energy and chemical energy. (19.1)

electrolysis. A process in which electrical energy is used to cause a nonspontaneous chemical reaction to occur. (19.8)

electrolyte. A substance that, when dissolved in water, results in a solution that can conduct electricity. (4.1)

electrolytic cell. An apparatus for carrying out electrolysis. (19.8)

electromagnetic radiation. The emission and transmission of energy in the form of electromagnetic waves. (7.1)

electromagnetic wave. A wave that has an electric field component and a mutually perpendicular magnetic field component. (7.1)

electromotive force (emf) (E). The voltage difference between electrodes. (19.2)

electron. A subatomic particle that has a very low mass and carries a single negative electric charge. (2.2)

electron affinity. The negative of the energy change when an electron is accepted by an atom in the gaseous state to form an anion. (8.5)

electron configuration. The distribution of electrons among the various orbitals in an atom or molecule. (7.8)

electron density. The probability that an electron will be found at a particular region in an atomic orbital. (7.5)

electronegativity. The ability of an atom to attract electrons toward itself in a chemical bond. (9.5)

element. A substance that cannot be separated into simpler substances by chemical means. (1.4)

elementary steps. A series of simple reactions that represent the progress of the overall reaction at the molecular level. (13.5)

emission spectra. Continuous or line spectra emitted by substances. (7.3)

empirical formula. An expression showing the types of elements present and the simplest ratios of the different kinds of atoms. (2.6)

enantiomers. Optical isomers, that is, compounds and their nonsuperimposable mirror images. (22.4)

endothermic processes. Processes that absorb heat from the surroundings. (6.2)

end point. The pH at which the indicator changes color. (16.5)

energy. The capacity to do work or to produce change. (6.1)

enthalpy (H). A thermodynamic quantity used to describe heat changes taking place at constant pressure. (6.4)

enthalpy of reaction (ΔH_{rxn}). The difference between the enthalpies of the products and the enthalpies of the reactants. (6.4)

enthalpy of solution (ΔH_{soln}). The heat generated or absorbed when a certain amount of solute is dissolved in a certain amount of solvent. (6.7)

entropy (S). A direct measure of the randomness or disorder of a system. (18.3)

enzyme. A biological catalyst. (13.6)

equilibrium constant (K). A number equal to the ratio of the equilibrium concentrations of products to the equilibrium concentrations of reactants, each raised to the power of its stoichiometric coefficient. (14.1)

equilibrium vapor pressure. The vapor pressure measured under dynamic equilibrium of condensation and evaporation at some temperature. (11.8)

equivalence point. The point at which the acid has completely reacted with or been neutralized by the base. (4.7)

esters. Compounds that have the general formula R'COOR, where R' can be H or an alkyl group or an aromatic group and R is an alkyl group or an aromatic group. (24.4)

ether. An organic compound containing the R—O—R' linkage, where R and R' are alkyl and/or aromatic groups. (24.4)

evaporation. The process in which a liquid is transformed into a gas; also called vaporization. (11.8)

excess reagents. One or more reactants present in quantities greater than necessary to react with the quantity of the limiting reagent. (3.9)

excited state (or level). A state that has higher energy than the ground state. (7.3)

exothermic processes. Processes that give off heat to the surroundings. (6.2)

extensive property. A property that depends on how much matter is being considered. (1.6)

F

family. The elements in a vertical column of the periodic table. (2.4)

Faraday. Charge contained in 1 mole of electrons, equivalent to 96,485.3 coulombs. (19.4)

ferromagnetic. Attracted by a magnet. The unpaired spins in a ferromagnetic substance are aligned in a common direction. (20.2)

first law of thermodynamics. Energy can be converted from one form to another, but cannot be created or destroyed. (6.3)

first-order reaction. A reaction whose rate depends on reactant concentration raised to the first power. (13.3)

formal charge. The difference between the valence electrons in an isolated atom and the number of electrons assigned to that atom in a Lewis structure. (9.7)

formation constant (K_f). The equilibrium constant for the complex ion formation. (16.10)

fractional crystallization. The separation of a mixture of substances into pure components on the basis of their different solubilities. (12.4)

fractional distillation. A procedure for separating liquid components of a solution that is based on their different boiling points. (12.6)

free energy (*G*). The energy available to do useful work. (18.5)

freezing point. The temperature at which the solid and liquid phases of a substance coexist at equilibrium. (11.8)

freezing point depression (ΔT_f). The freezing point of the pure solvent (T_f°) minus the freezing point of the solution (T_f). (12.6)

frequency (ν). The number of waves that pass through a particular point per unit time. (7.1)

fuel cell. A galvanic cell that requires a continuous supply of reactants to keep functioning. (19.6)

functional group. That part of a molecule characterized by a special arrangement of atoms that is largely responsible for the chemical behavior of the parent molecule. (24.1)

G

galvanic cell. The experimental apparatus for generating electricity through the use of a spontaneous redox reaction. (19.2)

gamma (γ) rays. High-energy radiation. (2.2)

gas constant (*R*). The constant that appears in the ideal gas equation. It is usually expressed as 0.08206 L · atm/K · mol, or 8.314 J/K · mol. (5.4)

geometric isomers. Compounds with the same type and number of atoms and the same chemical bonds but different spatial arrangements; such isomers cannot be interconverted without breaking a chemical bond. (22.4)

Gibbs free energy. See free energy.

glass. The optically transparent fusion product of inorganic materials that has cooled to a rigid state without crystallizing. (11.7)

Graham's law of diffusion. Under the same conditions of temperature and pressure, rates of diffusion for gases are inversely proportional to the square roots of their molar masses. (5.7)

gravimetric analysis. An experimental procedure that involves the measurement of mass. (4.6)

greenhouse effect. Carbon dioxide and other gases' influence on Earth's temperature. (17.5)

ground state (or level). The lowest energy state of a system. (7.3)

group. The elements in a vertical column of the periodic table. (2.4)

H

half-cell reactions. Oxidation and reduction reactions at the electrodes. (19.2)

half-life ($t_\frac{1}{2}$). The time required for the concentration of a reactant to decrease to half of its initial concentration. (13.3)

half-reaction. A reaction that explicitly shows electrons involved in either oxidation or reduction. (4.4)

halogens. The nonmetallic elements in Group 7A (F, Cl, Br, I, and At). (2.4)

heat. Transfer of energy between two bodies that are at different temperatures. (6.2)

heat capacity (*C*). The amount of heat required to raise the temperature of a given quantity of the substance by one degree Celsius. (6.5)

heat of dilution. The heat change associated with the dilution process. (6.7)

heat of hydration (ΔH_{hydr}). The heat change associated with the hydration process. (6.7)

heat of solution. See enthalpy of solution.

Heisenberg uncertainty principle. It is impossible to know simultaneously both the momentum and the position of a particle with certainty. (7.5)

Henry's law. The solubility of a gas in a liquid is proportional to the pressure of the gas over the solution. (12.5)

Hess's law. When reactants are converted to products, the change in enthalpy is the same whether the reaction takes place in one step or in a series of steps. (6.6)

heterogeneous equilibrium. An equilibrium state in which the reacting species are not all in the same phase. (14.2)

heterogeneous mixture. The individual components of a mixture remain physically separated and can be seen as separate components. (1.4)

homogeneous equilibrium. An equilibrium state in which all reacting species are in the same phase. (14.2)

homogeneous mixture. The composition of a mixture, after sufficient stirring, is the same throughout the solution. (1.4)

homonuclear diatomic molecule. A diatomic molecule containing atoms of the same element. (10.7)

homopolymer. A polymer that is made from only one type of monomer. (25.2)

Hund's rule. The most stable arrangement of electrons in subshells is the one with the greatest number of parallel spins. (7.8)

hybrid orbitals. Atomic orbitals obtained when two or more nonequivalent orbitals of the same atom combine. (10.4)

hybridization. The process of mixing the atomic orbitals in an atom (usually the central atom) to generate a set of new atomic orbitals. (10.4)

hydrates. Compounds that have a specific number of water molecules attached to them. (2.7)

hydration. A process in which an ion or a molecule is surrounded by water molecules arranged in a specific manner. (4.1)

hydrocarbons. Compounds made up only of carbon and hydrogen. (24.1)

hydrogen bond. A special type of dipole-dipole interaction between the hydrogen atom bonded to an atom of a very electronegative element (F, N, O) and another atom of one of the three electronegative elements. (11.2)

hydrogenation. The addition of hydrogen, especially to compounds with double and triple carbon-carbon bonds. (21.2)

hydronium ion. The hydrated proton, H_3O^+. (4.3)

hydrophilic. Water-liking. (12.8)

hydrophobic. Water-fearing. (12.8)

hypothesis. A tentative explanation for a set of observations. (1.3)

I

ideal gas. A hypothetical gas whose pressure-volume-temperature behavior can be completely accounted for by the ideal gas equation. (5.4)

ideal gas equation. An equation expressing the relationships among pressure, volume, temperature, and amount of gas ($PV = nRT$, where R is the gas constant). (5.4)

ideal solution. Any solution that obeys Raoult's law. (12.6)

indicators. Substances that have distinctly different colors in acidic and basic media. (4.7)

induced dipole. The separation of positive and negative charges in a neutral atom (or a nonpolar molecule) caused by the proximity of an ion or a polar molecule. (11.2)

inert complex. A complex ion that undergoes very slow ligand exchange reactions. (22.6)

inorganic compounds. Compounds other than organic compounds. (2.7)

insulator. A substance incapable of conducting electricity. (20.3)

intensive property. A property that does not depend on how much matter is being considered. (1.6)

intermediate. A species that appears in the mechanism of the reaction (that is, the elementary steps) but not in the overall balanced equation. (13.5)

intermolecular forces. Attractive forces that exist among molecules. (11.2)

International System of Units (SI). A system of units based on metric units. (1.7)

intramolecular forces. Forces that hold atoms together in a molecule. (11.2)

ion. An atom or a group of atoms that has a net positive or negative charge. (2.5)

ion pair. One or more cations and one or more anions held together by electrostatic forces. (12.7)

ionic bond. The electrostatic force that holds ions together in an ionic compound. (9.2)

ionic compound. Any neutral compound containing cations and anions. (2.5)

ionic equation. An equation that shows dissolved species as free ions. (4.2)

ionic radius. The radius of a cation or an anion as measured in an ionic compound. (8.3)

ionization energy. The minimum energy required to remove an electron from an isolated atom (or an ion) in its ground state. (8.4)

ion pair. A species made up of at least one cation and at least one anion held together by electrostatic forces. (12.7)

ion-dipole forces. Forces that operate between an ion and a dipole. (11.2)

ion-product constant. Product of hydrogen ion concentration and hydroxide ion concentration (both in molarity) at a particular temperature. (15.2)

ionosphere. The uppermost layer of the atmosphere. (17.1)

isoelectronic. Ions, or atoms and ions, that possess the same number of electrons, and hence the same ground-state electron configuration, are said to be isoelectronic. (8.2)

isolated system. A system that does not allow the transfer of either mass or energy to or from its surroundings. (6.2)

isotopes. Atoms having the same atomic number but different mass numbers. (2.3)

J

Joule (J). Unit of energy given by newtons × meters. (5.7)

K

kelvin. The SI base unit of temperature. (1.7)

Kelvin temperature scale. See absolute temperature scale.

ketones. Compounds with a carbonyl functional group and the general formula RR′CO, where R and R′ are alkyl and/or aromatic groups. (24.4)

kinetic energy (KE). Energy available because of the motion of an object. (5.7)

kinetic molecular theory of gases. Treatment of gas behavior in terms of the random motion of molecules. (5.7)

L

labile complex. Complexes that undergo rapid ligand exchange reactions. (22.6)

lanthanide (rare earth) series. Elements that have incompletely filled $4f$ subshells or readily give rise to cations that have incompletely filled $4f$ subshells. (7.9)

lattice energy. The energy required to completely separate one mole of a solid ionic compound into gaseous ions. (6.7)

law. A concise verbal or mathematical statement of a relationship between phenomena that is always the same under the same conditions. (1.3)

law of conservation of energy. The total quantity of energy in the universe is constant. (6.1)

law of conservation of mass. Matter can be neither created nor destroyed. (2.1)

law of definite proportions. Different samples of the same compound always contain its constituent elements in the same proportions by mass. (2.1)

law of mass action. For a reversible reaction at equilibrium and a constant temperature, a certain ratio of reactant and product concentrations has a constant value, K (the equilibrium constant). (14.1)

law of multiple proportions. If two elements can combine to form more than one type of compound, the masses of one element that combine with a fixed mass of the other element are in ratios of small whole numbers. (2.1)

Le Châtelier's principle. If an external stress is applied to a system at equilibrium, the system will adjust itself in such a way as to partially offset the stress as the system reaches a new equilibrium position. (14.5)

Lewis acid. A substance that can accept a pair of electrons. (15.12)

Lewis base. A substance that can donate a pair of electrons. (15.12)

Lewis dot symbol. The symbol of an element with one or more dots that represent the number of valence electrons in an atom of the element. (9.1)

Lewis structure. A representation of covalent bonding using Lewis symbols. Shared electron pairs are shown either as lines or as pairs of dots between two atoms, and lone pairs are shown as pairs of dots on individual atoms. (9.4)

ligand. A molecule or an ion that is bonded to the metal ion in a complex ion. (22.3)

limiting reagent. The reactant used up first in a reaction. (3.9)

line spectra. Spectra produced when radiation is absorbed or emitted by substances only at some wavelengths. (7.3)

liter. The volume occupied by one cubic decimeter. (1.7)

lone pairs. Valence electrons that are not involved in covalent bond formation. (9.4)

M

macroscopic properties. Properties that can be measured directly. (1.7)

manometer. A device used to measure the pressure of gases. (5.2)

many-electron atoms. Atoms that contain two or more electrons. (7.5)

mass. A measure of the quantity of matter contained in an object. (1.6)

mass defect. The difference between the mass of an atom and the sum of the masses of its protons, neutrons, and electrons. (23.2)

mass number (A). The total number of neutrons and protons present in the nucleus of an atom. (2.3)

matter. Anything that occupies space and possesses mass. (1.4)

melting point. The temperature at which solid and liquid phases coexist in equilibrium. (11.8)

mesosphere. A region between the stratosphere and the ionosphere. (17.1)

metalloid. An element with properties intermediate between those of metals and nonmetals. (2.4)

metals. Elements that are good conductors of heat and electricity and have the tendency to form positive ions in ionic compounds. (2.4)

metallurgy. The science and technology of separating metals from their ores and of compounding alloys. (20.2)

metathesis reaction. A reaction that involves the exchange of parts between two compounds. (4.2)

microscopic properties. Properties that cannot be measured directly without the aid of a microscope or other special instrument. (1.7)

mineral. A naturally occurring substance with a range of chemical composition. (20.1)

miscible. Two liquids that are completely soluble in each other in all proportions are said to be miscible. (12.2)

mixture. A combination of two or more substances in which the substances retain their identity. (1.4)

moderator. A substance that can reduce the kinetic energy of neutrons. (23.5)

molality. The number of moles of solute dissolved in one kilogram of solvent. (12.3)

molar concentration. See molarity.

molar heat of fusion (ΔH_{fus}). The energy (in kilojoules) required to melt one mole of a solid. (11.8)

molar heat of sublimation (ΔH_{sub}). The energy (in kilojoules) required to sublime one mole of a solid. (11.8)

molar heat of vaporization (ΔH_{vap}). The energy (in kilojoules) required to vaporize one mole of a liquid. (11.8)

molar mass ($\mathcal{M}$). The mass (in grams or kilograms) of one mole of atoms, molecules, or other particles. (3.2)

molar solubility. The number of moles of solute in one liter of a saturated solution (mol/L). (16.6)

molarity (M). The number of moles of solute in one liter of solution. (4.5)

mole (mol). The amount of substance that contains as many elementary entities (atoms, molecules, or other particles) as there are atoms in exactly 12 grams (or 0.012 kilograms) of the carbon-12 isotope. (3.2)

mole fraction. Ratio of the number of moles of one component of a mixture to the total number of moles of all components in the mixture. (5.6)

mole method. An approach for determining the amount of product formed in a reaction. (3.8)

molecular equations. Equations in which the formulas of the compounds are written as though all species existed as molecules or whole units. (4.2)

molecular formula. An expression showing the exact numbers of atoms of each element in a molecule. (2.6)

molecular mass. The sum of the atomic masses (in amu) present in the molecule. (3.3)

molecular orbital. An orbital that results from the interaction of the atomic orbitals of the bonding atoms. (10.6)

molecularity of a reaction. The number of molecules reacting in an elementary step. (13.5)

molecule. An aggregate of at least two atoms in a definite arrangement held together by special forces. (2.5)

monatomic ion. An ion that contains only one atom. (2.5)

monomer. The single repeating unit of a polymer. (25.2)

monoprotic acid. Each unit of the acid yields one hydrogen ion upon ionization. (4.3)

multiple bonds. Bonds formed when two atoms share two or more pairs of electrons. (9.4)

N

Nernst equation. The relation between the emf of a galvanic cell and the standard emf and the concentrations of the oxidizing and reducing agents. (19.5)

net ionic equation. An equation that indicates only the ionic species that actually take part in the reaction. (4.2)

neutralization reaction. A reaction between an acid and a base. (4.3)

neutron. A subatomic particle that bears no net electric charge. Its mass is slightly greater than a proton's. (2.2)

newton (N). The SI unit for force. (5.2)

nitrogen fixation. The conversion of molecular nitrogen into nitrogen compounds. (17.1)

noble gas core. The electron configuration of the noble gas element that most nearly precedes the element being considered. (7.9)

noble gases. Nonmetallic elements in Group 8A (He, Ne, Ar, Kr, Xe, and Rn). (2.4)

node. The point at which the amplitude of the wave is zero. (7.4)

nonelectrolyte. A substance that, when dissolved in water, gives a solution that is not electrically conducting. (4.1)

nonmetals. Elements that are usually poor conductors of heat and electricity. (2.4)

nonpolar molecule. A molecule that does not possess a dipole moment. (10.2)

nonvolatile. Does not have a measurable vapor pressure. (12.6)

***n*-type semiconductors.** Semiconductors that contain donor impurities. (20.3)

nuclear binding energy. The energy required to break up a nucleus into its protons and neutrons. (23.2)

nuclear chain reaction. A self-sustaining sequence of nuclear fission reactions. (23.5)

nuclear fission. A heavy nucleus (mass number > 200) divides to form smaller nuclei of intermediate mass and one or more neutrons. (23.5)

nuclear fusion. The combining of small nuclei into larger ones. (23.6)

nuclear transmutation. The change undergone by a nucleus as a result of bombardment by neutrons or other particles. (23.1)

nucleic acids. High molar mass polymers that play an essential role in protein synthesis. (25.4)

nucleon. A general term for the protons and neutrons in a nucleus. (23.2)

nucleotide. The repeating unit in each strand of a DNA molecule which consists of a base-deoxyribose-phosphate linkage. (25.4)

nucleus. The central core of an atom. (2.2)

O

octet rule. An atom other than hydrogen tends to form bonds until it is surrounded by eight valence electrons. (9.4)

open system. A system that can exchange mass and energy (usually in the form of heat) with its surroundings. (6.2)

optical isomers. Compounds that are nonsuperimposable mirror images. (22.4)

orbital. See atomic orbital and molecular orbital.

ore. The material of a mineral deposit in a sufficiently concentrated form to allow economical recovery of a desired metal. (20.1)

organic chemistry. The branch of chemistry that deals with carbon compounds. (24.1)

organic compounds. Compounds that contain carbon, usually in combination with elements such as hydrogen, oxygen, nitrogen, and sulfur. (2.7)

osmosis. The net movement of solvent molecules through a semipermeable membrane from a pure solvent or from a dilute solution to a more concentrated solution. (12.6)

osmotic pressure (π). The pressure required to stop osmosis. (12.6)

overvoltage. The difference between the electrode potential and the actual voltage required to cause electrolysis. (19.8)

oxidation number. The number of charges an atom would have in a molecule if electrons were transferred completely in the direction indicated by the difference in electronegativity. (4.4)

oxidation reaction. The half-reaction that involves the loss of electrons. (4.4)

oxidation-reduction reaction. A reaction that involves the transfer of electron(s) or the change in the oxidation state of reactants. (4.4)

oxidation state. See oxidation number.

oxidizing agent. A substance that can accept electrons from another substance or increase the oxidation numbers in another substance. (4.4)

oxoacid. An acid containing hydrogen, oxygen, and another element (the central element). (2.7)

oxoanion. An anion derived from an oxoacid. (2.7)

P

paramagnetic. Attracted by a magnet. A paramagnetic substance contains one or more unpaired electrons. (7.8)

partial pressure. Pressure of one component in a mixture of gases. (5.6)

pascal (Pa). A pressure of one newton per square meter (1 N/m^2). (5.2)

Pauli exclusion principle. No two electrons in an atom can have the same four quantum numbers. (7.8)

percent by mass. The ratio of the mass of a solute to the mass of the solution, multiplied by 100 percent. (12.3)

percent composition by mass. The percent by mass of each element in a compound. (3.5)

percent ionization. Ratio of ionized acid concentration at equilibrium to the initial concentration of acid. (15.5)

percent yield. The ratio of actual yield to theoretical yield, multiplied by 100 percent. (3.10)

period. A horizontal row of the periodic table. (2.4)

periodic table. A tabular arrangement of the elements. (2.4)

pH. The negative logarithm of the hydrogen ion concentration. (15.3)

phase. A homogeneous part of a system in contact with other parts of the system but separated from them by a well-defined boundary. (11.1)

phase change. Transformation from one phase to another. (11.8)

phase diagram. A diagram showing the conditions at which a substance exists as a solid, liquid, or vapor. (11.9)

photochemical smog. Formation of smog by the reactions of automobile exhaust in the presence of sunlight. (17.7)

photoelectric effect. A phenomenon in which electrons are ejected from the surface of certain metals exposed to light of at least a certain minimum frequency. (7.2)

photon. A particle of light. (7.2)

physical equilibrium. An equilibrium in which only physical properties change. (14.1)

physical property. Any property of a substance that can be observed without transforming the substance into some other substance. (1.6)

pi bond (π). A covalent bond formed by sideways overlapping orbitals; its electron density is concentrated above and below the plane of the nuclei of the bonding atoms. (10.5)

pi molecular orbital. A molecular orbital in which the electron density is concentrated above and below the line joining the two nuclei of the bonding atoms. (10.6)

plasma. A gaseous mixture of positive ions and electrons. (23.6)

polar covalent bond. In such a bond, the electrons spend more time in the vicinity of one atom than the other. (9.5)

polar molecule. A molecule that possesses a dipole moment. (10.2)

polarimeter. The instrument for measuring the rotation of polarized light by optical isomers. (22.4)

polyatomic ion. An ion that contains more than one atom. (2.5)

polyatomic molecule. A molecule that consists of more than two atoms. (2.5)

polymer. A compound distinguished by a high molar mass, ranging into thousands and millions of grams, and made up of many repeating units. (25.1)

positron. A particle that has the same mass as the electron, but bears a +1 charge. (23.1)

potential energy. Energy available by virtue of an object's position. (6.1)

precipitate. An insoluble solid that separates from the solution. (4.2)

precipitation reaction. A reaction that results in the formation of a precipitate. (4.2)

precision. The closeness of agreement of two or more measurements of the same quantity. (1.8)

pressure. Force applied per unit area. (5.2)

product. The substance formed as a result of a chemical reaction. (3.7)

protein. Polymers of amino acids. (25.3)

proton. A subatomic particle having a single positive electric charge. The mass of a proton is about 1840 times that of an electron. (2.2)

p-type semiconductors. Semiconductors that contain acceptor impurities. (20.3)

pyrometallurgy. Metallurgical processes that are carried out at high temperatures. (20.2)

Q

qualitative. Consisting of general observations about the system. (1.3)

qualitative analysis. The determination of the types of ions present in a solution. (16.11)

quantitative. Comprising numbers obtained by various measurements of the system. (1.3)

quantitative analysis. The determination of the amount of substances present in a sample. (4.5)

quantum. The smallest quantity of energy that can be emitted (or absorbed) in the form of electromagnetic radiation. (7.1)

quantum numbers. Numbers that describe the distribution of electrons in hydrogen and other atoms. (7.6)

R

racemic mixture. An equimolar mixture of the two enantiomers. (22.4)

radiant energy. Energy transmitted in the form of waves. (6.1)

radiation. The emission and transmission of energy through space in the form of particles and/or waves. (2.2)

radical. Any neutral fragment of a molecule containing an unpaired electron. (23.8)

radioactive decay series. A sequence of nuclear reactions that ultimately result in the formation of a stable isotope. (23.3)

radioactivity. The spontaneous breakdown of an atom by emission of particles and/or radiation. (2.2)

Raoult's law. The partial pressure of the solvent over a solution is given by the product of the vapor pressure of the pure solvent and the mole fraction of the solvent in the solution. (12.6)

rare earth series. See lanthanide series.

rate constant (k). Constant of proportionality between the reaction rate and the concentrations of reactants. (13.1)

rate law. An expression relating the rate of a reaction to the rate constant and the concentrations of the reactants. (13.2)

rate-determining step. The slowest step in the sequence of steps leading to the formation of products. (13.5)

reactants. The starting substances in a chemical reaction. (3.7)

reaction mechanism. The sequence of elementary steps that leads to product formation. (13.5)

reaction order. The sum of the powers to which all reactant concentrations appearing in the rate law are raised. (13.2)

reaction quotient (Q). A number equal to the ratio of product concentrations to reactant concentrations, each raised to the power of its stoichiometric coefficient at some point other than equilibrium. (14.4)

reaction rate. The change in the concentration of reactant or product with time. (13.1)

redox reaction. A reaction in which there is either a transfer of electrons or a change in the oxidation numbers of the substances taking part in the reaction. (4.4)

reducing agent. A substance that can donate electrons to another substance or decrease the oxidation numbers in another substance. (4.4)

reduction reaction. The half-reaction that involves the gain of electrons. (4.4)

representative elements. Elements in Groups 1A through 7A, all of which have incompletely filled s or p subshell of highest principal quantum number. (8.2)

resonance. The use of two or more Lewis structures to represent a particular molecule. (9.8)

resonance structure. One of two or more alternative Lewis structures for a molecule that cannot be described fully with a single Lewis structure. (9.8)

reversible reaction. A reaction that can occur in both directions. (4.1)

ribonucleic acid (RNA). A form of nucleic acid. (25.4)

root-mean-square (rms) speed (u_{rms}). A measure of the average molecular speed at a given temperature. (5.7)

S

salt. An ionic compound made up of a cation other than H^+ and an anion other than OH^- or O^{2-}. (4.3)

salt hydrolysis. The reaction of the anion or cation, or both, of a salt with water. (15.10)

saponification. Soapmaking. (24.4)

saturated hydrocarbons. Hydrocarbons that contain the maximum number of hydrogen atoms that can bond with the number of carbon atoms present. (24.2)

saturated solution. At a given temperature, the solution that results when the maximum amount of a substance has dissolved in a solvent. (12.1)

scientific method. A systematic approach to research. (1.3)

second law of thermodynamics. The entropy of the universe increases in a spontaneous process and remains unchanged in an equilibrium process. (18.4)

second-order reaction. A reaction whose rate depends on reactant concentration raised to the second power or on the concentrations of two different reactants, each raised to the first power. (13.3)

semiconductors. Elements that normally cannot conduct electricity, but can have their conductivity greatly enhanced either by raising the temperature or by adding certain impurities. (20.3)

semipermeable membrane. A membrane that enables solvent molecules to pass through, but blocks the movement of solute molecules. (12.6)

sigma bond (σ). A covalent bond formed by orbitals overlapping end-to-end; its electron density is concentrated between the nuclei of the bonding atoms. (10.5)

sigma molecular orbital. A molecular orbital in which the electron density is concentrated around a line between the two nuclei of the bonding atoms. (10.6)

significant figures. The number of meaningful digits in a measured or calculated quantity. (1.8)

single bond. Two atoms are held together by one electron pair. (9.4)

solubility. The maximum amount of solute that can be dissolved in a given quantity of solvent at a specific temperature. (4.2, 16.6)

solubility product (K_{sp}). The product of the molar concentrations of the constituent ions, each raised to the power of its stoichiometric coefficient in the equilibrium equation. (16.6)

solute. The substance present in smaller amount in a solution. (4.1)

solution. A homogeneous mixture of two or more substances. (4.1)

solvation. The process in which an ion or a molecule is surrounded by solvent molecules arranged in a specific manner. (12.2)

solvent. The substance present in larger amount in a solution. (4.1)

specific heat (s). The amount of heat energy required to raise the temperature of one gram of a substance by one degree Celsius. (6.5)

spectator ions. Ions that are not involved in the overall reaction. (4.2)

spectrochemical series. A list of ligands arranged in increasing order of their abilities to split the d-orbital energy levels. (22.5)

standard atmospheric pressure (1 atm). The pressure that supports a column of mercury exactly 76 cm high at 0°C at sea level. (5.2)

standard emf ($E°$). The difference of the standard reduction potential of the substance that undergoes reduction and the standard reduction potential of the substance that undergoes oxidation. (19.3)

standard enthalpy of formation ($\Delta H_f°$). The heat change that results when one mole of a compound is formed from its elements in their standard states. (6.6)

standard enthalpy of reaction ($\Delta H_{rxn}°$). The enthalpy change when the reaction is carried out under standard-state conditions. (6.6)

standard entropy of reaction ($\Delta S_{rxn}°$). The entropy change when the reaction is carried out under standard-state conditions. (18.4)

standard free-energy of reaction ($\Delta G_{rxn}°$). The free-energy change when the reaction is carried out under standard-state conditions. (18.5)

standard free-energy of formation ($\Delta G_f°$). The free-energy change when 1 mole of a compound is synthesized from its elements in their standard states. (18.5)

standard reduction potential. The voltage measured as a reduction reaction occurs at the electrode when all solutes are 1 M and all gases are at 1 atm. (19.3)

standard solution. A solution of accurately known concentration. (4.7)

standard state. The condition of 1 atm of pressure. (6.6)

standard temperature and pressure (STP). 0°C and 1 atm. (5.4)

state function. A property that is determined by the state of the system. (6.3)

state of a system. The values of all pertinent macroscopic variables (for example, composition, volume, pressure, and temperature) of a system. (6.3)

stereoisomers. Compounds that are made up of the same types and numbers of atoms bonded together in the same sequence but with different spatial arrangements. (22.4)

stoichiometric amounts. The exact molar amounts of reactants and products that appear in the balanced chemical equation. (3.9)

stoichiometry. The quantitative study of reactants and products in a chemical reaction. (3.8)

stratosphere. The region of the atmosphere extending upward from the troposphere to about 50 km from Earth. (17.1)

strong acids. Strong electrolytes which are assumed to ionize completely in water. (15.4)

strong bases. Strong electrolytes which are assumed to ionize completely in water. (15.4)

structural formula. A chemical formula that shows how atoms are bonded to one another in a molecule. (2.6)

structural isomers. Molecules that have the same molecular formula but different structures. (24.2)

sublimation. The process in which molecules go directly from the solid into the vapor phase. (11.8)

substance. A form of matter that has a definite or constant composition (the number and type of basic units present) and distinct properties. (1.4)

substitution reaction. A reaction in which an atom or group of atoms replaces an atom or groups of atoms in another molecule. (24.3)

supercooling. Cooling of a liquid below its freezing point without forming the solid. (11.8)

supersaturated solution. A solution that contains more of the solute than is present in a saturated solution. (12.1)

surface tension. The amount of energy required to stretch or increase the surface of a liquid by a unit area. (11.3)

surroundings. The rest of the universe outside a system. (6.2)

system. Any specific part of the universe that is of interest to us. (6.2)

T

termolecular reaction. An elementary step that involves three molecules. (13.5)

ternary compounds. Compounds consisting of three elements. (2.7)

theoretical yield. The amount of product predicted by the balanced equation when all of the limiting reagent has reacted. (3.10)

theory. A unifying principle that explains a body of facts and the laws that are based on them. (1.3)

thermal energy. Energy associated with the random motion of atoms and molecules. (6.1)

thermochemical equation. An equation that shows both the mass and enthalpy relations. (6.4)

thermochemistry. The study of heat changes in chemical reactions. (6.2)

thermodynamics. The scientific study of the interconversion of heat and other forms of energy. (6.3)

thermonuclear reactions. Nuclear fusion reactions that occur at very high temperatures. (23.6)

thermosphere. The region of the atmosphere in which the temperature increases continuously with altitude. (17.1)

third law of thermodynamics. The entropy of a perfect crystalline substance is zero at the absolute zero of temperature. (18.4)

titration. The gradual addition of a solution of accurately known concentration to another solution of unknown concentration until the chemical reaction between the two solutions is complete. (4.7)

tracers. Isotopes, especially radioactive isotopes, that are used to trace the path of the atoms of an element in a chemical or biological process. (23.7)

transition metals. Elements that have incompletely filled d subshells or readily give rise to cations that have incompletely filled d subshells. (7.9)

transition state. See activated complex.

transuranium elements. Elements with atomic numbers greater than 92. (23.4)

triple bond. Two atoms are held together by three pairs of electrons. (9.4)

triple point. The point at which the vapor, liquid, and solid states of a substance are in equilibrium. (11.9)

triprotic acid. Each unit of the acid yields three protons upon ionization. (4.3)

troposphere. The layer of the atmosphere which contains about 80 percent of the total mass of air and practically all of the atmosphere's water vapor. (17.1)

U

unimolecular reaction. An elementary step in which only one reacting molecule participates. (13.5)

unit cell. The basic repeating unit of the arrangement of atoms, molecules, or ions in a crystalline solid. (11.4)

unsaturated hydrocarbons. Hydrocarbons that contain carbon-carbon double bonds or carbon-carbon triple bonds. (24.2)

unsaturated solution. A solution that contains less solute than it has the capacity to dissolve. (12.1)

V

valence electrons. The outer electrons of an atom, which are those involved in chemical bonding. (8.2)

valence shell. The outermost electron-occupied shell of an atom, which holds the electrons that are usually involved in bonding. (10.1)

valence-shell electron-pair repulsion (VSEPR) model. A model that accounts for the geometrical arrangements of shared and unshared electron pairs around a central atom in terms of the repulsions between electron pairs. (10.1)

van der Waals equation. An equation that describes the P, V, and T of a nonideal gas. (5.8)

van der Waals forces. The dipole-dipole, dipole-induced dipole, and dispersion forces. (11.2)

van't Hoff factor. The ratio of actual number of particles in solution after dissociation to the number of formula units initially dissolved in solution. (12.7)

vaporization. The escape of molecules from the surface of a liquid; also called evaporation. (11.8)

viscosity. A measure of a fluid's resistance to flow. (11.3)

volatile. Has a measurable vapor pressure. (12.6)

volume. It is the length cubed. (1.6)

W

wave. A vibrating disturbance by which energy is transmitted. (7.1)

wavelength (λ). The distance between identical points on successive waves. (7.1)

weak acids. Weak electrolytes that ionize only to a limited extent in water. (15.4)

weak bases. Weak electrolytes that ionize only to a limited extent in water. (15.4)

weight. The force that gravity exerts on an object. (1.7)

work. Directed energy change resulting from a process. (6.1)

X

X-ray diffraction. The scattering of X rays by the units of a regular crystalline solid. (11.5)

Answers

Chapter 1

1.4 (a) Hypothesis. (b) Law. (c) Theory. **1.12** (a) Physical change. (b) Chemical change. (c) Physical change. (d) Chemical change. (e) Physical change. **1.14** (a) K. (b) Sn. (c) Cr. (d) B. (e) Ba. (f) Pu. (g) S. (h) Ar. (i) Hg. **1.16** (a) Homogeneous mixture. (b) Element. (c) Compound. (d) Homogeneous mixture. (e) Heterogeneous mixture. (f) Homogeneous mixture. (g) Heterogeneous mixture. **1.22** 13.9 g. **1.24** (a) 41°C. (b) 11.3°F. (c) 1.1×10^4°F. (d) 233°C. **1.26** (a) -196°C. (b) -269°C. (c) 328°C. **1.30** (a) 0.0152. (b) 0.0000000778. **1.32** (a) 1.8×10^{-2}. (b) 1.14×10^{10}. (c) -5×10^4. (d) 1.3×10^3. **1.34** (a) One. (b) Three. (c) Three. (d) Four. (e) Two or three. (f) One. (g) One or two. **1.36** (a) 1.28. (b) 3.18×10^{-3} mg. (c) 8.14×10^7 dm. **1.38** (a) 1.10×10^8 mg. (b) 6.83×10^{-5} m³. (c) 7.2×10^3 L. (d) 6.24×10^{-8} lb. **1.40** 3.1557×10^7 s. **1.42** (a) 81 in/s. (b) 1.2×10^2 m/min. (c) 7.4 km/h. **1.44** 88 km/h. **1.46** 3.7×10^{-3} g Pb. **1.48** (a) 1.85×10^{-7} m. (b) 1.4×10^{17} s. (c) 7.12×10^{-5} m³. (d) 8.86×10^4 L. **1.50** 6.25×10^{-4} g/cm³. **1.52** (a) Chemical. (b) Chemical. (c) Physical. (d) Physical. (e) Chemical. **1.54** 2.6 g/cm³. **1.56** 0.882 cm. **1.58** 767 mph. **1.60** Liquid must be less dense than ice; temperature below 0°C. **1.62** 2.3×10^3 cm³. **1.64** 6.3¢. **1.66** 73°S. **1.68** (a) 8.6×10^3 L air/day. (b) 0.018 L CO/day. **1.70** 5.5×10^{10} L seawater. **1.72** 7.0×10^{20} L. **1.74** 9.0×10^1 lb; 41 kg. **1.76** O: 4.0×10^4 g; C: 1.1×10^4 g; H: 6.2×10^3 g; N: 2×10^3 g; Ca: 9.9×10^2 g; P: 7.4×10^2 g. **1.78** 4.6×10^2°C; 8.6×10^2°F. **1.80** $\$9.0 \times 10^{11}$. **1.82** 5.4×10^{22} Fe atoms. **1.84** 30 times. **1.86** 1.450×10^{-2} mm. **1.88** 1.3×10^3 mL. **1.90** 2.5 nm. **1.92** (a) $\$3.06 \times 10^{-3}$/L. (b) 5.5¢. **1.94** 1725 sets, 4.576×10^4 g. **1.96** 4.97×10^4 g. The alloy is homogeneous in composition. **1.98** 2.413 g/mL. Yes. The liquids must be totally miscible and their volumes must be additive. **1.100** 0.13 L.

Chapter 2

2.8 0.12 mi. **2.14** 145. **2.16** N(7,8,7); S(16,17,16); Cu(29,34,29); Sr(38,46,38); Ba(56,74,56); W(74,112,74); Hg(80,122,80). **2.18** (a) $^{186}_{74}$W. (b) $^{201}_{80}$Hg. **2.24** (a) Metallic character increases down a group. (b) Metallic character decreases from left to right. **2.26** F and Cl; Na and K; P and N. **2.32** (a) Diatomic molecule and compound. (b) Polyatomic molecule and compound. (c) Polyatomic molecule and element. **2.34** (a) H_2 and F_2. (b) HCl and CO. (c) S_8 and P_4. (d) H_2O and $C_{12}H_{22}O_{11}$ (sucrose). **2.36** (protons, electrons): K^+(19,18); Mg^{2+}(12,10); Fe^{3+}(26,23); Br^-(35,36); Mn^{2+}(25,23); C^{4-}(6,10); Cu^{2+}(29,27). **2.44** (a) CuBr. (b) Mn_2O_3. (c) Hg_2I_2. (d) $Mg_3(PO_4)_2$. **2.46** (a) $AlBr_3$. (b) $NaSO_2$. (c) N_2O_5. (d) $K_2Cr_2O_7$. **2.48** C_2H_6O. **2.50** Ionic: NaBr, BaF_2, CsCl. Molecular: CH_4, CCl_4, ICl, NF_3. **2.58** (a) Potassium hypochlorite. (b) Silver carbonate. (c) Nitrous acid. (d) Potassium permanganate. (e) Cesium chlorate. (f) Potassium ammonium sulfate. (g) Iron(II) oxide. (h) Iron(III) oxide. (i) Titanium(IV) chloride. (j) Sodium hydride. (k) Lithium nitride. (l) Sodium oxide. (m) Sodium peroxide. **2.60** (a) CuCN. (b) $Sr(ClO_2)_2$. (c) $HBrO_4$. (d) HI.

(e) $Na_2(NH_4)PO_4$. (f) $PbCO_3$. (g) SnF_2. (h) P_4S_{10}. (i) HgO. (j) Hg_2I_2. (k) SeF_6. **2.62** C-12 and C-13. **2.64** I^-. **2.66** NaCl is an ionic compound. **2.68** Element: (b), (c), (e), (f), (g), (j), (k). Molecules: (b), (f), (g), (k). Compounds: (i), (l). Compounds and molecules: (a), (d), (h). **2.70** (a) $(NH_4)_2CO_3$. (b) $Ca(OH)_2$. (c) CdS. (d) $ZnCr_2O_7$. **2.72** (a) Ionic compounds formed between metallic and nonmetallic elements. (b) Transition metals. **2.74** ^{23}Na. **2.76** Hg and Br_2. **2.78** H_2, N_2, O_2, F_2, Cl_2, He, Ne, Ar, Kr, Xe, Rn. **2.80** Unreactive. He, Ne, and Ar are chemically inert. **2.82** Ra is a radioactive decay product of U-238. **2.84** Argentina. **2.86** (a) NaH, sodium hydride. (b) B_2O_3, diboron trioxide. (c) Na_2S, sodium sulfide. (d) AlF_3, aluminum fluoride. (e) OF_2, oxygen difluoride. (f) $SrCl_2$, strontium chloride. **2.88** NF_3 (nitrogen trifluoride), PBr_5 (phosphorus pentabromide), SCl_2 (sulfur dichloride), NF_3 (nitrogen trifluoride). **2.90** 1st row: Mg^{2+}, HCO_3^-, $Mg(HCO_3)_2$. 2nd row: Sr^{2+}, Cl^-, strontium chloride. 3rd row: $Fe(NO_3)_3$, Iron(III) nitrite. 4th row: Mn^{2+}, ClO_3^-, $Mn(ClO_3)_2$. 5th row: Sn^{4+}, Br^-, tin(IV) bromide. 6th row: $Co_3(PO_4)_2$, cobalt(II) phosphate. 7th row: Hg_2I_2, mercury(I) iodide. 8th row: Cu^+, CO_3^{2-}, copper(I) carbonate. 9th row: Li^+, N^{3-}, Li_3N. 10th row: Al_2S_3, aluminum sulfide. **2.92** 1.91×10^{-8} g. Mass is too small to be detected. **2.94** (b) Density of nucleus: 3.24×10^{14} g/cm³; density of space occupied by electrons: 3.71×10^{-4} g/cm³. The results support Rutherford's model. **2.96** (a) Yes. (b) Ethane: CH_3 and C_2H_6. Acetylene: CH and C_2H_2. **2.98** Manganese (Mn). **2.100** Chloric acid, nitrous acid, hydrocyanic acid, and sulfuric acid.

Chapter 3

3.6 92.5%. **3.8** 5.1×10^{24} amu. **3.12** 5.8×10^3 light yr. **3.14** 9.96×10^{-15} mol Co. **3.16** 3.01×10^3 g Au. **3.18** (a) 1.244×10^{-22} g/As atom. (b) 9.746×10^{-23} g/Ni atom. **3.20** 2.98×10^{22} Cu atoms. **3.22** Pb. **3.24** (a) 73.89 g. (b) 76.15 g. (c) 119.37 g. (d) 176.12 g. (e) 101.11 g. (f) 100.95 g. **3.26** 6.69×10^{21} C_2H_6 molecules. **3.28** N: 3.37×10^{26} atoms; C: 1.69×10^{26} atoms; O: 1.69×10^{26} atoms; H: 6.74×10^{26} atoms. **3.30** 8.56×10^{22} molecules. **3.34** 7. **3.40** C: 10.06%; H: 0.8442%; Cl: 89.07%. **3.42** NH_3. **3.44** $C_2H_3NO_5$. **3.46** 39.3 g S. **3.48** 5.97 g F. **3.50** (a) CH_2O. (b) KCN. **3.52** C_6H_6. **3.54** $C_5H_8O_4NNa$. **3.60** (a) $2N_2O_5 \longrightarrow 2N_2O_4 + O_2$. (b) $2KNO_3 \longrightarrow 2KNO_2 + O_2$. (c) $NH_4NO_3 \longrightarrow N_2O + 2H_2O$. (d) $NH_4NO_2 \longrightarrow N_2 + 2H_2O$. (e) $2NaHCO_3 \longrightarrow Na_2CO_3 + H_2O + CO_2$. (f) $P_4O_{10} + 6H_2O \longrightarrow 4H_3PO_4$. (g) $2HCl + CaCO_3 \longrightarrow CaCl_2 + H_2O + CO_2$. (h) $2Al + 3H_2SO_4 \longrightarrow Al_2(SO_4)_3 + 3H_2$. (i) $CO_2 + 2KOH \longrightarrow K_2CO_3 + H_2O$. (j) $CH_4 + 2O_2 \longrightarrow CO_2 + 2H_2O$. (k) $Be_2C + 4H_2O \longrightarrow 2Be(OH)_2 + CH_4$. (l) $3Cu + 8HNO_3 \longrightarrow 3Cu(NO_3)_2 + 2NO + 4H_2O$. (m) $S + 6HNO_3 \longrightarrow H_2SO_4 + 6NO_2 + 2H_2O$. (n) $2NH_3 + 3CuO \longrightarrow 3Cu + N_2 + 3H_2O$. **3.64** (d). **3.66** 1.01 mol. **3.68** 20 mol. **3.70** (a) $2NaHCO_3 \longrightarrow Na_2CO_3 + CO_2 + H_2O$. (b) 78.3 g. **3.72** 255.9 g; 0.324 L. **3.74** 0.294 mol. **3.76** (a) $NH_4NO_3 \longrightarrow N_2O + 2H_2O$. (b) 20 g N_2O. **3.78** 18.0 g. **3.82** N_2; 1 H_2 and 6 NH_3. **3.84** O_3; 0.709 g NO_2; 6.9×10^{-3} mol NO. **3.86** HCl; 23.4 g. **3.90** (a) 7.05 g. (b) 92.9%. **3.92** 3.47×10^3 g. **3.94** 8.55 g; 76.6%. **3.96** (b). **3.98** Cl_2O_7. **3.100** (a) 0.212 mol. (b) 0.424 mol. **3.102** 18. **3.104** 2.4×10^{23} atoms. **3.106** 65.4 amu; Zn. **3.108** 89.6%. **3.110** CH_2O; $C_6H_{12}O_6$.

3.112 51.8 g/mol; Cr. **3.114** 1.6×10^4 g/mol. **3.116** NaBr: 24.0%; Na_2SO_4: 76.0%. **3.118** Ca: 38.76%; P: 19.97%; O: 41.26%. **3.120** Yes. **3.122** 2.01×10^{21} molecules. **3.124** 16.00 amu. **3.126** (e). **3.128** $PtCl_2$; $PtCl_4$. **3.130** (a) X: MnO_2; Y: Mn_3O_4. (b) $3MnO_2 \longrightarrow Mn_3O_4 + O_2$. **3.132** 6.1×10^5 tons. **3.134** Mg_3N_2 (magnesium nitride). **3.136** PbC_8H_{20}. **3.138** (a) 4.3×10^{22} atoms. (b) 1.6×10^2 pm. **3.140** 28.97 g/mol. **3.142** 3.1×10^{23} molecules/mol. **3.144** (a) $C_3H_8 + 3H_2O \longrightarrow 3CO + 7H_2$. (b) 9.09×10^2 kg. **3.146** (a) CH_4 (16 amu). NH_3 (17 amu). H_2O (18 amu). SO_2 (64 amu). (b) C_3H_8 because it can give rise to a CH_3 fragment (15 amu). No fragment of CO_2 has a mass of 15 amu. (c) ± 0.030 amu. **3.148** Mg_3N_2: 8.337 g; MgO: 25.66 g. **3.150** Fe_2O_3 formed: 9.6 g; $KClO_3$ decomposed: 7.4 g.

Chapter 4

4.8 (c). **4.10** (a) Strong electrolyte. (b) Nonelectrolyte. (c) Weak electrolyte. (d) Strong electrolyte. **4.12** (b) and (c). **4.14** HCl does not ionize in benzene. **4.18** (b). **4.20** (a) Insoluble. (b) Soluble. (c) Soluble. (d) Insoluble. (e) Soluble. **4.24** (a) Add chloride ions. (b) Add hydroxide ions. (c) Add carbonate ions. (d) Add sulfate ions. **4.32** (a) Brønsted base. (b) Brønsted base. (c) Brønsted acid. (d) Brønsted base and Brønsted acid. **4.34** (a) $CH_3COOH + K^+ + OH^- \longrightarrow K^+ + CH_3COO^- + H_2O$; $CH_3COOH + OH^- \longrightarrow CH_3COO^- + H_2O$. (b) $H_2CO_3 + 2Na^+ + 2OH^- \longrightarrow 2Na^+ + CO_3^{2-} + 2H_2O$; $H_2CO_3 + 2OH^- \longrightarrow CO_3^{2-} + 2H_2O$. (c) $2H^+ + 2NO_3^- + Ba^{2+} + 2OH^- \longrightarrow Ba^{2+} + 2NO_3^- + 2H_2O$; $2H^+ + 2OH^- \longrightarrow 2H_2O$. **4.44** (a) $Fe \longrightarrow Fe^{3+} + 3e^-$; $O_2 + 4e^- \longrightarrow 2O^{2-}$. Oxidizing agent: O_2; reducing agent: Fe. (b) $2Br^- \longrightarrow Br_2 + 2e^-$; $Cl_2 + 2e^- \longrightarrow 2Cl^-$. Oxidizing agent: Cl_2; reducing agent: Br^-. (c) $Si \longrightarrow Si^{4+} + 4e^-$; $F_2 + 2e^- \longrightarrow 2F^-$. Oxidizing agent: F_2; reducing agent: Si. (d) $H_2 \longrightarrow 2H^+ + 2e^-$; $Cl_2 + 2e^- \longrightarrow 2Cl^-$. Oxidizing agent: Cl_2; reducing agent: H_2. **4.46** (a) +5. (b) +1. (c) +3. (d) +5. (e) +5. (f) +5. **4.48** All are zero. **4.50** (a) -3. (b) $-\frac{1}{2}$. (c) -1. (d) +4. (e) +3. (f) -2. (g) +3. (h) +6. **4.52** Li and Ca. **4.54** (a) No reaction. (b) No reaction. (c) $Mg + CuSO_4 \longrightarrow MgSO_4 + Cu$. (d) $Cl_2 + 2KBr \longrightarrow Br_2 + 2KCl$. **4.56** (a) Combination. (b) Decomposition. (c) Displacement. (d) Disproportionation. **4.60** Dissolve 15.0 g $NaNO_3$ in enough water to make up 250 mL. **4.62** 10.8 g. **4.64** (a) 1.37 M. (b) 0.426 M. (c) 0.716 M. **4.66** (a) 6.50 g. (b) 2.45 g. (c) 2.65 g. (d) 7.36 g. (e) 3.95 g. **4.70** 0.0433 M. **4.72** 126 mL. **4.74** 1.09 M. **4.78** 35.72%. **4.80** 2.31×10^{-4} M. **4.86** 0.217 M. **4.88** (a) 6.00 mL. (b) 8.00 mL. **4.92** 9.45×10^{-3} g. **4.94** 0.06020 M. **4.96** 6.16 mL. **4.98** 0.231 mg. **4.100** (i) Only oxygen supports combustion. (ii) Only CO_2 reacts with $Ca(OH)_2$ to form $CaCO_3$ (white precipitate). **4.102** 1.26 M. **4.104** 0.171 M. **4.106** 0.115 M. **4.108** Ag: 1.25 g; Zn: 2.12 g. **4.110** 0.0722 M NaOH. **4.112** 24.0 g/mol; Mg. **4.114** 1.73 M. **4.116** Only Fe(II) is oxidized by $KMnO_4$ solution and can therefore change the purple color to colorless. **4.118** Ions are removed as the $BaSO_4$ precipitate. **4.120** (a) Conductivity test. (b) Only NaCl reacts with $AgNO_3$ to form AgCl precipitate. **4.122** The Cl^- ion cannot accept any electrons. **4.124** Reaction is too violent. **4.126** Use sodium bicarbonate: $HCO_3^- + H^+ \longrightarrow H_2O + CO_2$. NaOH is a caustic substance and unsafe to use in this manner. **4.128** (a) Conductivity. Reaction with $AgNO_3$ to form AgCl. (b) Soluble in water. Nonelectrolyte. (c) Possesses properties of acids. (d) Soluble. Reacts with acids to give CO_2. (e) Soluble, strong electrolyte. Reacts with acids to give CO_2. (f) Weak electrolyte and weak acid. (g) Soluble in water. Reacts with NaOH to produce $Mg(OH)_2$ precipitate. (h) Strong electrolyte and strong base. (i) Characteristic odor. Weak electrolyte and weak base. (j) Insoluble. Reacts with acids. (k) Insoluble. Reacts with acids to produce CO_2.

4.130 NaCl: 44.11%; KCl: 55.89%. **4.132** 1.33 g. **4.134** 56.18%. **4.136** (a) 1.40 M. (b) 4.96 g. **4.138** (a) $NH_4^+ + OH^- \longrightarrow NH_3 + H_2O$. (b) 97.99%. **4.140** Zero. **4.142** 0.224%. **4.144** (a) $Zn + H_2SO_4 \longrightarrow ZnSO_4 + H_2$. (b) $2KClO_3 \longrightarrow 2KCl + 3O_2$. (c) $Na_2CO_3 + 2HCl \longrightarrow 2NaCl + CO_2 + H_2O$. (d) $NH_4NO_2 \longrightarrow N_2 + 2H_2O$. **4.146** Yes. **4.148** (a) $8.316 \times 10^{-7} M$. (b) 3.286×10^{-5} g. **4.150** 0.0680 M. **4.152** (a) Precipitation: $Mg^{2+} + 2OH^- \longrightarrow Mg(OH)_2$; acid-base: $Mg(OH)_2 + 2HCl \longrightarrow MgCl_2 + 2H_2O$; redox: $MgCl_2 \longrightarrow Mg + Cl_2$. (b) NaOH is more expensive than CaO. (c) Dolomite provides additional Mg. **4.154** (a) Reactions (2) and (4). (b) Reaction (5). (c) Reaction (3). (d) Reaction (1).

Chapter 5

5.14 0.797 atm; 80.8 kPa. **5.18** (1) b. (2) a. (3) c. (4) a. **5.20** 53 atm. **5.22** (a) 0.69 L. (b) 61 atm. **5.24** 1.3×10^2 K. **5.26** ClF_3. **5.32** 6.2 atm. **5.34** 745 K. **5.36** 1.9 atm. **5.38** 0.82 L. **5.40** 45.1 L. **5.42** 6.1×10^{-3} atm. **5.44** 35.0 g/mol. **5.46** N_2: 2.1×10^{22}; O_2: 5.7×10^{21}; Ar: 3×10^{20}. **5.48** 2.97 g/L. **5.50** SF_4. **5.52** 370 L. **5.54** 88.9%. **5.56** $M + 3HCl \longrightarrow 1.5H_2 + MCl_3$; M_2O_3, $M_2(SO_4)_3$. **5.58** 2.84×10^{-2} mol CO_2; 94.7%. **5.60** 1.71×10^3 L. **5.64** (a) 0.89 atm. (b) 1.4 L. **5.66** 349 mmHg. **5.68** 19.8 g. **5.70** H_2: 650 mmHg; N_2: 217 mmHg. **5.78** N_2: 472 m/s; O_2: 441 m/s; O_3: 360 m/s. **5.80** 2.8 m/s; 2.7 m/s. Squaring favors the larger values. **5.82** 1.0043. **5.84** 4. **5.90** No. **5.92** Ne. **5.94** C_6H_6. **5.96** 445 mL. **5.98** (a) 9.53 atm. (b) $Ni(CO)_4$ decomposes to give CO, which increases the pressure. **5.100** 1.30×10^{22} molecules; CO_2, O_2, N_2, H_2O. **5.102** 5.25×10^{18} kg. **5.104** 0.0701 M. **5.106** He: 0.16 atm; Ne: 2.0 atm. **5.108** HCl dissolves in the water, creating a partial vacuum. **5.110** 7. **5.112** (a) 61.2 m/s. (b) 4.58×10^{-4} s. (c) 328 m/s; 366 m/s. **5.114** 2.09×10^4 g; 1.58×10^4 L. **5.116** Higher partial pressure inside a paper bag. **5.118** To equalize the pressure as the amount of ink decreases. **5.120** (a) $NH_4NO_3 \longrightarrow N_2O + 2H_2O$. (b) 0.0821 L · atm/K · mol. **5.122** C_6H_6. **5.124** The low atmospheric pressure caused the harmful gases (CO, CO_2, CH_4) to flow out of the mine, and the man suffocated. **5.126** (a) 4.90 L. (b) 6.0 atm. (c) 1 atm. **5.128** (a) 5×10^{-22} atm. (b) 5×10^{20} L. **5.130** 91%. **5.132** 1.7×10^{12} molecules. **5.134** NO_2. **5.136** 7.0×10^{-3} m/s; 3.5×10^{-30} J. **5.138** 2.3×10^3 L. **5.140** 1.8×10^2 mL. **5.142** (a) 1.09×10^{44} molecules. (b) 1.18×10^{22} molecules/breath. (c) 2.60×10^{30} molecules. (d) 2.39×10^{-14}; 3×10^8 molecules. (e) Complete mixing of air; no molecules escaped to the outer atmosphere; no molecules used up during metabolism, nitrogen fixation, etc. **5.144** 3.7 nm; 0.31 nm. **5.146** 0.54 atm. **5.148** 53.4%. **5.150** CO: 54.4%; CO_2: 45.6%. **5.152** CH_4: 0.789; C_2H_6: 0.211. **5.154** (a) $8(4\pi r^3/3)$. (b) $(16/3)N_A \pi r^3$. The excluded volume is 4 times the volumes of the atoms. **5.156** NO. **5.158** (b).

Chapter 6

6.16 (a) 0. (b) -9.5 J. (c) -18 J. **6.18** 48 J. **6.20** -3.1×10^3 J. **6.26** 1.57×10^4 kJ. **6.28** -553.8 kJ/mol. **6.34** 728 kJ. **6.36** 50.7°C. **6.38** 26.3°C. **6.46** O_2. **6.48** (a) $\Delta H_f^\circ[Br_2(l)] = 0$; $\Delta H_f^\circ[Br_2(g)] > 0$. (b) $\Delta H_f^\circ[I_2(s)] = 0$; $\Delta H_f^\circ[I_2(g)] > 0$. **6.50** Measure ΔH° for the formation of Ag_2O from Ag and O_2 and of $CaCl_2$ from Ca and Cl_2. **6.52** (a) -167.2 kJ/mol. (b) -56.2 kJ/mol. **6.54** (a) -1411 kJ/mol. (b) -1124 kJ/mol. **6.56** 218.2 kJ/mol. **6.58** -71.58 kJ/g. **6.60** 2.70×10^2 kJ/mol. **6.62** -84.6 kJ/mol. **6.64** -847.6 kJ/mol. **6.72** $\Delta H_2 - \Delta H_1$. **6.74** (a) -336.5 kJ/mol. (b) NH_3. **6.76** -43.6 kJ. **6.78** 0. **6.80** -350.7 kJ/mol. **6.82** 0.492 J/g · °C. **6.84** The first (exothermic) reaction can be used to promote the second (endothermic) reaction. **6.86** 1.09×10^4 L. **6.88** 4.10 L. **6.90** 5.60 kJ/mol. **6.92** (a). **6.94** (a) 0. (b) -9.1 J. (c) 2.4 L; -48 J. **6.96** (a) A more fully packed freezer has a greater mass and hence a larger heat capacity. (b) Tea or coffee has a greater amount of water, which has a higher specific heat than noodles. **6.98** -1.84×10^3 kJ. **6.100** 3.0×10^9. **6.102** 5.35 kJ/°C. **6.104** -5.2×10^6 kJ. **6.106** (a) 3.4×10^5 g. (b) -2.0×10^8 J. **6.108** (a) 1.4×10^2 kJ. (b) 3.9×10^2 kJ. **6.110** (a) -65.2 kJ/mol. (b) -9.0 kJ/mol. **6.112** -110.5 kJ/mol. It will form both CO and CO_2. **6.114** (a) 0.50 J. (b) 32 m/s. (c) 0.12°C. **6.116** -277.0 kJ/mol. **6.118** 104 g. **6.120** 9.9×10^8 J; 304°C. **6.122** 1.51×10^3 kJ. **6.124** $\Delta E = -5153$ kJ/mol; $\Delta H = -5158$ kJ/mol. **6.126** -564.2 kJ/mol. **6.128** 96.21%. **6.130** (a) CH. (b) 49 kJ/mol. **6.132** 43 kJ/mol.

Chapter 7

7.8 (a) 6.58×10^{14}/s. (b) 1.22×10^8 nm. **7.10** 2.5 min. **7.12** 4.95×10^{14}/s. **7.16** (a) 4.0×10^2 nm. (b) 5.0×10^{-19} J. **7.18** 1.2×10^2 nm (UV). **7.20** (a) 3.70×10^2 nm. (b) UV. (c) 5.38×10^{-19} J. **7.26** Use a prism. **7.28** Compare the emission spectra with those on Earth of known elements. **7.30** 3.027×10^{-19} J. **7.32** 6.17×10^{14}/s. 486 nm. **7.34** 5. **7.40** 1.37×10^{-6} nm. **7.42** 1.7×10^{-23} nm. **7.56** $\ell = 2$: $m_\ell = -2, -1, 0, 1, 2$. $\ell = 1$: $m_\ell = -1, 0, 1$. $\ell = 0$: $m_\ell = 0$. **7.58** (a) $n = 3$, $\ell = 0$, $m_\ell = 0$. (b) $n = 4$, $\ell = 1$, $m_\ell = -1$, 0, 1. (c) $n = 3$, $\ell = 2$, $m_\ell = -2, -1, 0, 1, 2$. In all cases, $m_s = +\frac{1}{2}$ or $-\frac{1}{2}$. **7.60** Differ in orientation only. **7.62** $6s$, $6p$, $6d$, $6f$, $6g$, and $6h$. **7.64** $2n^2$. **7.66** (a) 3. (b) 6. (c) 0. **7.68** There is no shielding in an H atom. **7.70** (a) $2s < 2p$. (b) $3p < 3d$. (c) $3s < 4s$. (d) $4d < 5f$. **7.76** Al: $1s^2 2s^2 2p^6 3s^2 3p^1$. B: $1s^2 2s^2 2p^1$. F: $1s^2 2s^2 2p^5$. **7.78** B(1), Ne(0), P(3), Sc(1), Se(2), Kr(0), Fe(4), Cd(0), I(1), Pb(2). **7.88** $[\text{Kr}]5s^2 4d^5$. **7.90** Ge: $[\text{Ar}]4s^2 3d^{10} 4p^2$. Fe: $[\text{Ar}]4s^2 3d^6$. Zn: $[\text{Ar}]4s^2 3d^{10}$. Ni: $[\text{Ar}]4s^2 3d^8$. W: $[\text{Xe}]6s^2 4f^{14} 5d^4$. Tl: $[\text{Xe}]6s^2 4f^{14} 5d^{10} 6p^1$. **7.92** S^+. **7.94** (a) Incorrect. (b) Correct. (c) Incorrect. **7.96** (a) An e in a $2s$ and an e in each $2p$ orbital. (b) $2e$ each in a $4p$, a $4d$, and a $4f$ orbital. (c) $2e$ in each of the 5 $3d$ orbitals. (d) An e in a $2s$ orbital. (e) $2e$ in a f orbital. **7.98** Wave properties. **7.100** (a) 1.05×10^{-25} nm. (b) 8.86 nm. **7.102** (a) 1.20×10^{18} photons. (b) 3.76×10^8 W. **7.104** 419 nm. In principle, yes; in practice, no. **7.106** 3.0×10^{19} photons. **7.108** He^+: 164 nm, 121 nm, 109 nm, 103 nm (all in the UV region). H: 657 nm, 487 nm, 434 nm, 411 nm (all in the visible region). **7.110** 1.2×10^2 photons. **7.112** Yellow light will generate more electrons; blue light will generate electrons with greater kinetic energy. **7.114** (a) He. (b) N. (c) Na. (d) As. (e) Cl. See Table 7.3 for ground-state electron configurations. **7.116** They might have discovered the wave properties of electrons. **7.118** 7.39×10^{-2} nm. **7.120** (a) False. (b) False. (c) True. (d) False. (e) True. **7.122** 2.0×10^{-5} m/s. **7.124** (a) and (f) violate Pauli exclusion principle; (b), (d), and (e) violate Hund's rule. **7.126** 2.8×10^6 K. **7.128** 2.76×10^{-11} m. **7.130** 17.4 pm. **7.132** 0.929 pm; 3.23×10^{20}/s. **7.134** (a) B: $4 \longrightarrow 2$; C: $5 \longrightarrow 2$. (b) A: 41.1 nm; B: 30.4 nm. (c) 2.18×10^{-18} J. (d) The continuum shows that the electron has been removed from the ion. **7.136** $n = 1$: 1.96×10^{-17} J; $n = 5$: 7.85×10^{-19} J. 10.6 nm. **7.138** 3.87×10^5 m/s. **7.140** (a) Photosynthesis and vision. (b) By comparing the blackbody radiation curve of the star with those obtained from objects at different temperatures in the laboratory.

Chapter 8

8.20 (a) $1s^2 2s^2 2p^6 3s^2 3p^5$. (b) Representative. (c) Paramagnetic. **8.22** (a) and (d); (b) and (e); (c) and (f). **8.24** (a) Group 1A. (b) Group 5A. (c) Group 8A. (d) Group 8B. **8.26** Fe. **8.28** (a) [Ne]. (b) [Ne]. (c) [Ar]. (d) [Ar]. (e) [Ar]. (f) $[\text{Ar}]3d^6$. (g) $[\text{Ar}]3d^9$. (h) $[\text{Ar}]3d^{10}$. **8.30** (a) Cr^{3+}. (b) Sc^{3+}. (c) Rh^{3+}. (d) Ir^{3+}. **8.32** Be^{2+} and He; F^- and N^{3-}; Fe^{2+} and Co^{3+}; S^{2-} and Ar. **8.38** Na > Mg > Al > P > Cl. **8.40** F. **8.42** The effective nuclear charge that the outermost electrons feel increases across the period. **8.44** $Mg^{2+} < Na^+ < F^- < O^{2-} < N^{3-}$. **8.46** Te^{2-}. **8.48** -199.4°C. **8.52** K < Ca < P < F < Ne. **8.54** The single $3p$ electron in Al is well shielded by the $1s$, $2s$, and $3s$ electrons. **8.56** $1s^2 2s^2 2p^6$: 2080 kJ/mol. **8.58** 8.40×10^6 kJ/mol. **8.62** Cl. **8.64** The ns^1 configuration enables them to accept another electron. **8.68** Fr should be the most reactive toward water and oxygen, forming FrOH and Fr_2O_2 and FrO_2. **8.70** The Group 1B elements have higher ionization energies due to the incomplete shielding of the inner d electrons. **8.72** (a) $Li_2O + H_2O \longrightarrow 2LiOH$. (b) $CaO + H_2O \longrightarrow Ca(OH)_2$. (c) $SO_3 + H_2O \longrightarrow H_2SO_4$. **8.74** BaO. **8.76** (a) Bromine. (b) Nitrogen. (c) Rubidium. (d) Magnesium. **8.78** (a) $Mg^{2+} < Na^+ < F^- < O^{2-}$. (b) $O^{2-} < F^- < Na^+ < Mg^{2+}$. **8.80** M is K; X is Br. **8.82** N and O^+; Ne and N^{3-}; Ar and S^{2-}; Zn and As^{3+}; Cs^+ and Xe. **8.84** (a) and (d). **8.86** Yellow-green gas: F_2; yellow gas: Cl_2; red liquid: Br_2; dark solid: I_2. **8.88** Fluorine. **8.90** H^-. **8.92** Li_2O (basic); BeO (amphoteric); B_2O_3 (acidic); CO_2 (acidic); N_2O_5 (acidic). **8.94** It forms both the H^+ and H^- ions; H^+ is a single proton. **8.96** 0.65. **8.98** 76.7%. **8.100** 418 kJ/mol. Use maximum wavelength. **8.102** 7.28×10^3 kJ/mol. **8.104** X: Sn or Pb; Y: P; Z: alkali metal. **8.106** 495.9 kJ/mol. **8.108** 343 nm (UV). **8.110** 604.3 kJ/mol. **8.112** K_2TiO_4. **8.114** $2K_2MnF_6 + 4SbF_5 \longrightarrow 4KSbF_6 + 2MnF_3 + F_2$. **8.116** N_2O (+1), NO (+2), N_2O_3 (+3), NO_2 and N_2O_4 (+4), N_2O_5 (+5). **8.118** The larger the effective nuclear charge, the more tightly held are the electrons. The atomic radius will be small and the ionization energy will be large. **8.120** m.p.: 6.3°C; b.p.: 74.9°C. **8.122** The heat generated from nuclear decay can decompose compounds. **8.124** Ar: 39.95 amu; K: 39.10 amu. **8.126** $Z = 119$; $[\text{Rn}]7s^2 5f^{14} 6d^{10} 7p^6 8s^1$. **8.128** Group 2A. **8.130** (a) SiH_4, GeH_4, SnH_4, PbH_4. (b) RbH more ionic. (c) $Ra + 2H_2O \longrightarrow Ra(OH)_2 + H_2$. (d) Be. **8.132** See chapter. **8.134** Carbon (diamond). **8.136** 419 nm. **8.138** The first ionization energy of He is less than twice the ionization of H because the radius of He is greater than that of H and the shielding in He makes Z_{eff} less than 2. In He^+, there is no shielding and the greater nuclear attraction makes the second ionization of He greater than twice the ionization energy of H. **8.140** Z_{eff}: Li (1.26); Na (1.84); K (2.26). Z_{eff}/n: Li (0.630); Na (0.613); K (0.565). Z_{eff} increases as n increases. Thus, Z_{eff}/n remains fairly constant.

Chapter 9

9.16 (a) RbI, rubidium iodide. (b) Cs_2SO_4, cesium sulfate. (c) Sr_3N_2, strontium nitride. (d) Al_2S_3, aluminum sulfide.

9.18 (a) $\cdot \text{Sr} \cdot + \cdot \ddot{\text{Se}} \cdot \longrightarrow \text{Sr}^{2+} : \ddot{\ddot{\text{Se}}} :^{2-}$

(b) $\cdot \text{Ca} \cdot + 2\text{H} \cdot \longrightarrow \text{Ca}^{2+} \ 2\text{H} :^-$

(c) $3\text{Li} \cdot + \cdot \ddot{\text{N}} \cdot \longrightarrow 3\text{Li}^+ : \ddot{\ddot{\text{N}}} :^{3-}$

(d) $2 \cdot \ddot{\text{Al}} \cdot + 3 \cdot \ddot{\text{S}} \cdot \longrightarrow 2\text{Al}^{3+} \ 3 : \ddot{\ddot{\text{S}}} :^{2-}$

9.20 (a) BF_3, covalent. Boron triflouride. (b) KBr, ionic. Potassium bromide. **9.26** 2195 kJ/mol. **9.36** C—H < Br—H < F—H < Li—Cl < Na—Cl < K—F. **9.38** Cl—Cl < Br—Cl < Si—C < Cs—F. **9.40** (a) Covalent. (b) Polar covalent. (c) Ionic. (d) Polar covalent.

9.44 (a) $: \ddot{\text{F}} - \ddot{\text{O}} - \ddot{\text{F}} :$ (b) $: \ddot{\text{F}} - \ddot{\text{N}} = \ddot{\text{N}} - \ddot{\text{F}} :$

(c) $\text{H} - \underset{\underset{\text{H}}{|}}{\overset{\overset{\text{H}}{|}}{\text{Si}}} - \underset{\underset{\text{H}}{|}}{\overset{\overset{\text{H}}{|}}{\text{Si}}} - \text{H}$ (d) $^- : \ddot{\text{O}} - \text{H}$

(e)
$$H-\overset{\overset{\displaystyle H}{|}}{\underset{\underset{\displaystyle :\ddot{C}l:}{|}}{C}}-\overset{\overset{\displaystyle :\ddot{O}:}{\|}}{C}-\ddot{\underset{..}{O}}:^{-}$$
(f)
$$H-\overset{\overset{\displaystyle H}{|}}{\underset{\underset{\displaystyle H}{|}}{C}}-\overset{\overset{\displaystyle H}{|}}{\underset{\underset{\displaystyle H}{|}}{N}}{}^{+}\!\!-H$$

9.46 (a) $^{-}:\ddot{O}-\ddot{O}:^{-}$ **(b)** $^{-}:C\equiv C:^{-}$ **(c)** $:N\equiv O:^{+}$

9.52
$$\ddot{\underset{..}{O}}=\ddot{\underset{..}{C}l}-\ddot{\underset{..}{O}}:^{-}\;\underset{+}{}\;\longleftrightarrow\;^{-}:\ddot{\underset{..}{O}}-\overset{\overset{\displaystyle :O:}{\|}}{\underset{..}{C}l}-\ddot{\underset{..}{O}}:^{-}\;\underset{+}{}\;\longleftrightarrow\;^{-}:\ddot{\underset{..}{O}}-\overset{\overset{\displaystyle :\ddot{O}:^{-}}{|}}{\underset{..}{C}l}=\ddot{\underset{..}{O}}\;\underset{+}{}$$

9.54
$$H-\overset{\overset{\displaystyle H}{|}}{C}=\overset{+}{\underset{..}{N}}=\ddot{\underset{..}{N}}{}^{-}\;\longleftrightarrow\;H-\overset{\overset{\displaystyle H}{|}}{C}-\overset{+}{\underset{..}{N}}\equiv N:$$

9.56 $^{-}\ddot{\underset{..}{N}}=\overset{+}{N}=\ddot{\underset{..}{O}}\longleftrightarrow:N\equiv \overset{+}{N}-\ddot{\underset{..}{O}}:^{-}\longleftrightarrow{}^{2-}:\ddot{\underset{..}{N}}-\overset{+}{N}\equiv\overset{+}{O}:$

9.62 $^{+}\overset{..}{\underset{..}{C}l}=\overset{2-}{Be}=\overset{..}{\underset{..}{C}l}{}^{+}$ Not plausible.

9.64 $Cl-\overset{\overset{\displaystyle Cl}{|}}{\underset{\underset{\displaystyle Cl}{\diagup\quad}}{Sb}}-Cl$ The octet rule is not obeyed.

9.66 $Cl-\overset{\overset{\displaystyle Cl}{|}}{\underset{\underset{\displaystyle Cl}{|}}{Al}}-Cl$ Coordinate covalent bond.

9.70 303.0 kJ/mol. **9.72 (a)** -2759 kJ/mol. **(b)** -2855 kJ/mol. **9.74** Ionic: $RbCl$, KO_2; covalent: PF_5, BrF_3, CI_4. **9.76** Ionic: NaF, MgF_2, AlF_3; covalent: SiF_4, PF_5, SF_6, ClF_3. **9.78** KF: ionic, high melting point, soluble in water, its melt and solution conduct electricity. C_6H_6: covalent and discrete molecule, low melting point, insoluble in water, does not conduct electricity.

9.80 $^{-}\ddot{\underset{..}{N}}=\overset{+}{N}=\ddot{\underset{..}{N}}{}^{-}\longleftrightarrow:N\equiv\overset{+}{N}-\ddot{\underset{..}{N}}:^{2-}\longleftrightarrow{}^{2-}:\ddot{\underset{..}{N}}-\overset{+}{N}\equiv N:$

9.82 (a) $AlCl_4^{-}$. **(b)** AlF_6^{3-}. **(c)** $AlCl_3$. **9.84** CF_2: violates the octet rule; LiO_2: lattice energy too low; $CsCl_2$: second ionization energy too high to produce Cs^{2+}; PI_5: I atom too bulky to fit around P. **9.86 (a)** False. **(b)** True. **(c)** False. **(d)** False. **9.88** -67 kJ/mol. **9.90** N_2. **9.92** NH_4^{+} and CH_4; CO and N_2; $B_3N_3H_6$ and C_6H_6.

9.94
$$H-\overset{\overset{\displaystyle ..}{\underset{\underset{\displaystyle H}{|}}{N}}}{}:^{-}+H-\ddot{\underset{..}{O}}:\longrightarrow H-\overset{\overset{\displaystyle H}{|}}{\underset{\underset{\displaystyle H}{|}}{N}}-H+{}^{-}:\ddot{\underset{..}{O}}-H$$

9.96 F_3^{-} violates the octet rule.

9.98 $CH_3-\ddot{\underset{..}{N}}=C=\ddot{\underset{..}{O}}\longleftrightarrow CH_3-\overset{+}{\underset{..}{N}}\equiv C-\ddot{\underset{..}{O}}:^{-}$

9.100 (c) No bond between C and O. **(d)** Large formal charges.

9.102 (a) $F-\overset{\overset{\displaystyle Cl}{|}}{\underset{\underset{\displaystyle Cl}{|}}{C}}-Cl$ **(b)** $F-\overset{\overset{\displaystyle Cl}{|}}{\underset{\underset{\displaystyle Cl}{|}}{C}}-F$ **(c)** $H-\overset{\overset{\displaystyle F}{|}}{\underset{\underset{\displaystyle Cl}{|}}{C}}-F$ **(d)** $F-\overset{\overset{\displaystyle F}{|}}{\underset{\underset{\displaystyle F}{|}}{C}}-\overset{\overset{\displaystyle H}{|}}{\underset{\underset{\displaystyle F}{|}}{C}}-F$

9.104 (a) -9.2 kJ/mol. **(b)** -9.2 kJ/mol. **9.106 (a)** $^{-}:C\equiv O:^{+}$ **(b)** $:N\equiv O:^{+}$ **(c)** $^{-}:C\equiv N:$ **(d)** $:N\equiv N:$ **9.108** True. **9.110 (a)** 114 kJ/mol. **(b)** Extra electron increases repulsion between F atoms. **9.112** Lone pair on C and negative formal charge on C.

9.114 (a) $:N=\ddot{\underset{..}{O}}\longleftrightarrow{}^{-}\ddot{\underset{..}{N}}=\ddot{\underset{..}{O}}{}^{+}$ **(b)** No.

9.116 Violates the octet rule.

9.118
$$\overset{\overset{\displaystyle Cl}{}}{\underset{\underset{\displaystyle Cl}{}}{Al}}\diagdown\overset{\overset{\displaystyle Cl}{}}{\diagup}\overset{\overset{\displaystyle Cl}{}}{\underset{\underset{\displaystyle Cl}{}}{Al}}$$
The arrows indicate coordinate covalent bonds.

9.120 347 kJ/mol.

9.122 (a)
$$\overset{\overset{\displaystyle H\quad H}{|\quad\;|}}{\underset{\underset{\displaystyle H\quad Cl}{|\quad\;|}}{C=C}}$$
(b)
$$-\overset{\overset{\displaystyle H\quad H\quad H\quad H}{|\quad\;|\quad\;|\quad\;|}}{\underset{\underset{\displaystyle H\quad Cl\;\,H\;\,Cl}{|\quad\;|\quad\;|\quad\;|}}{C-C-C-C}}-$$
(c) -1.2×10^{6} kJ.

9.124 O: 3.16; F: 4.37; Cl: 3.48. **9.126 (1)** The MgO solid containing Mg^{+} and O^{-} ions would be paramagnetic. **(2)** The lattice energy would be like NaCl (too low). **9.128** -629 kJ/mol. **9.130** 268 nm. **9.132 (a)** -1413.9 kJ/mol and -1937 kJ/mol. **(b)** 162 L. **(c)** 11.0 atm.

Chapter 10

10.8 (a) Trigonal planar. **(b)** Linear. **(c)** Tetrahedral. **10.10 (a)** Tetrahedral. **(b)** T-shaped. **(c)** Bent. **(d)** Trigonal planar. **(e)** Tetrahedral. **10.12 (a)** Tetrahedral. **(b)** Bent. **(c)** Trigonal planar. **(d)** Linear. **(e)** Square planar. **(f)** Tetrahedral. **(g)** Trigonal bipyramidal. **(h)** Trigonal pyramidal. **(i)** Tetrahedral. **10.14** $SiCl_4$, CI_4, $CdCl_4^{2-}$. **10.20** Electronegativity decreases from F to I. **10.22** Higher. **10.24 (b)** $=$ (d) $<$ (c) $<$ (a). **10.34** sp^3 for both. **10.36** B: sp^2 to sp^3; N: remains sp^3. **10.38** From left to right. **(a)** sp^3. **(b)** sp^3, sp^2, sp^3. **(c)** sp^3, sp, sp, sp^3. **(d)** sp^3, sp^2. **(e)** sp^3, sp^2. **10.40** sp. **10.42** sp^3d. **10.44** 9 pi bonds and 9 sigma bonds. **10.50** Electron spins must be paired in H_2. **10.52** $Li_2^{-}=Li_2^{+}<$ Li_2. **10.54** B_2^{+}. **10.56** MO theory predicts O_2 is paramagnetic. **10.58** $O_2^{2-}<O_2^{-}<O_2<O_2^{+}$. **10.60** B_2 contains a pi bond; C_2 contains 2 pi bonds. **10.64** The circle shows electron delocalization.

10.66 (a)
$$\overset{\overset{\displaystyle :\ddot{F}:}{}}{O}=\overset{}{N}-\ddot{\underset{..}{O}}:^{-}\longleftrightarrow{}^{-}:\ddot{\underset{..}{O}}-\overset{\overset{\displaystyle :\ddot{F}:}{}}{N}=\ddot{\underset{..}{O}}$$
(b) sp^2. **(c)** N forms sigma bonds with F and O atoms. There is a pi molecular orbital delocalized over N and O atoms. **10.68** sp^2. **10.70** Linear. Dipole moment measurement. **10.72** The large size of Si results in poor sideways overlap of p orbitals to form pi bonds. **10.74** XeF_3^{+}: T-shaped; XeF_5^{+}: square pyramidal; SbF_6^{-}: octahedral. **10.76 (a)** $180°$. **(b)** $120°$. **(c)** $109.5°$. **(d)** About $109.5°$. **(e)** $180°$. **(f)** About $120°$. **(g)** About $109.5°$. **(h)** $109.5°$. **10.78** sp^3d. **10.80** ICl_2^{-} and $CdBr_2$. **10.82 (a)** sp^2. **(b)** Molecule on the right. **10.84** The pi bond in *cis*-dichloroethylene prevents rotation. **10.86** O_3, CO, CO_2, NO_2, N_2O, CH_4, $CFCl_3$. **10.88** C: all single-bonded C atoms are sp^3, the double-bonded C atoms are sp^2; N: single-bonded N atoms are sp^3, N atoms that form one double bond are sp^2, N atom that forms two double bonds is sp. **10.90** Si has $3d$ orbitals so water can add to Si (valence shell expansion). **10.92** C: sp^2; N: N atom that forms a double bond is sp^2, the others are sp^3. **10.94 (a)** Use a conventional oven. **(b)** No. Polar molecules would absorb microwaves. **(c)** Water molecules absorb part of microwaves. **10.96** The small size of F results in a shorter bond and greater lone pair repulsion. **10.98** 43.6%. **10.100** Second and third vibrations. CO, NO_2, N_2O. **10.102 (a)** The two $90°$ rotations will break and make the pi bond and convert *cis*-dichloroethylene to *trans*-dichloroethylene. **(b)** The pi bond is weaker because of the lesser extent of sideways orbital overlap. **(c)** 444 nm. **10.104 (a)** H_2. The electron is removed from the more stable bonding molecular orbital. **(b)** N_2. Same as (a). **(c)** O. The atomic orbital in O is more stable than the antibonding molecular orbital in O_2. **(d)** The atomic orbital in F is more stable than the antibonding molecular orbital in F_2.

10.106 (a) $[Ne_2](\sigma_{3s})^2(\sigma^{\star}_{3s})^2(\pi_{3p_y})^2(\pi_{3p_z})^2(\sigma_{3p_x})^2$. (b) 3.
(c) Diamagnetic. **10.108** For all the electrons to be paired in O_2 (see Table 10.5), energy is needed to flip the spin of one of the electrons in the antibonding molecular orbitals. This arrangement is less stable according to Hund's rule. **10.110** (a) Planar and no dipole moment. (b) 20 sigma bonds and 6 pi bonds. **10.112** The negative formal charge is placed on the less electronegative carbon, so there is less charge separation and a smaller dipole moment. (b) Both the Lewis structure and the molecular orbital treatment predicts a triple bond. (c) C.

Chapter 11

11.8 Methane. **11.10** (a) Dispersion forces. (b) Dispersion and dipole-dipole forces. (c) Same as (b). (d) Dispersion and ion-ion forces. (e) Same as (a). **11.12** (e). **11.14** Only 1-butanol can form hydrogen bonds. **11.16** (a) Xe. (b) CS_2. (c) Cl_2. (d) LiF. (e) NH_3.
11.18 (a) Hydrogen bond and dispersion forces. (b) Dispersion forces. (c) Dispersion forces. (d) Covalent bond. **11.20** The compound on the left can form intramolecular hydrogen bond.
11.32 Between ethanol and glycerol. **11.38** scc: 1; bcc: 2; fcc: 4.
11.40 6.20×10^{23} Ba atoms/mol. **11.42** 458 pm. **11.44** XY_3.
11.48 0.220 nm. **11.52** Molecular solid. **11.54** Molecular solids: Se_8, HBr, CO_2, P_4O_6, SiH_4. Covalent solids: Si, C. **11.56** Each C atom in diamond is covalently bonded to four other C atoms. Graphite has delocalized electrons in two dimensions. **11.78** 2.67×10^3 kJ.
11.80 47.03 kJ/mol. **11.82** Freezing, sublimation. **11.84** When steam condenses at 100°C, it releases heat equal to heat of vaporization. **11.86** 331 mmHg. **11.88** 75.9 kJ/mol. **11.92** Initially ice melts because of the increase in pressure. As the wire sinks into the ice, the water above it refreezes. In this way, the wire moves through the ice without cutting it in half. **11.94** (a) Ice melts. (b) Water vapor condenses to ice. (c) Water boils. **11.96** (d)
11.98 Covalent crystal. **11.100** CCl_4. **11.102** 760 mmHg.
11.104 It is the critical point. **11.106** Crystalline SiO_2. **11.108** (a), (b), (d). **11.110** 8.3×10^{-3} atm. **11.112** (a) K_2S. (b) Br_2.
11.114 SO_2. It is a polar molecule. **11.116** 62.4 kJ/mol. **11.118** Smaller ions have larger charge densities and a greater extent of hydration. **11.120** (a) 30.7 kJ/mol. (b) 192.5 kJ/mol. **11.122** (a) Decreases. (b) No change. (c) No change. **11.124** $CaCO_3(s) \longrightarrow CaO(s) + CO_2(g)$. Three phases. **11.126** SiO_2 is a covalent crystal. CO_2 exists as discrete molecules. **11.128** 66.8%.
11.130 scc: 52.4%; bcc: 68.0%; fcc: 74.0%. **11.132** 1.69 g/cm³.
11.134 (a) Two (diamond/graphite/liquid and graphite/liquid/vapor). (b) Diamond. (c) Apply high pressure at high temperature.
11.136 Molecules in the cane are held together by intermolecular forces. **11.138** When the tungsten filament is heated to a high temperature (ca. 3000°C), it sublimes and condenses on the inside walls. The inert pressurized Ar gas retards sublimation.
11.140 When methane burns in air, it forms CO_2 and water vapor. The latter condenses on the outside of the cold beaker. **11.142** 6.019×10^{23} Fe atoms/mol. **11.144** Na (186 pm and 0.965 g/cm³).
11.146 (d).

Chapter 12

12.10 Cyclohexane cannot form hydrogen bonds. **12.12** The longer chains become more nonpolar. **12.16** (a) 25.9 g. (b) 1.72×10^3 g.
12.18 (a) 2.68 m. (b) 7.82 m. **12.20** 0.010 m. **12.22** 5.0×10^2 m; 18.3 M. **12.24** (a) 2.41 m. (b) 2.13 M. (c) 0.0587 L. **12.28** 45.9 g.
12.36 CO_2 pressure is greater at the bottom of the mine.
12.38 0.28 L. **12.52** 1.3×10^3 g. **12.54** Ethanol: 30.0 mmHg; 1-propanol: 26.3 mmHg. **12.56** 128 g. **12.58** 0.59 m. **12.60** 120

g/mol. $C_4H_8O_4$. **12.62** −8.6°C. **12.64** 4.3×10^2 g/mol. $C_{24}H_{20}P_4$.
12.66 1.75×10^4 g/mol. **12.68** 343 g/mol. **12.74** Boiling point, vapor-pressure, osmotic pressure. **12.76** 0.50 m glucose > 0.50 m acetic acid > 0.50 m HCl. **12.78** 0.9420 m. **12.80** 7.6 atm. **12.82** 1.6 atm. **12.86** 3.5 atm. **12.88** (a) 104 mmHg. (b) 116 mmHg. **12.90** 2.95×10^3 g/mol. **12.92** No. **12.94** $AlCl_3$ dissociates into Al^{3+} and 3 Cl^- ions. **12.96** NaCl: 143.8 g; $MgCl_2$: 5.14 g; Na_2SO_4: 7.25 g; $CaCl_2$: 1.11 g; KCl: 0.67 g; $NaHCO_3$: 0.17 g. **12.98** The molar mass in B (248 g/mol) is twice as large as that in A (124 g/mol). A dimerization process. **12.100** (a) Last alcohol. (b) Methanol. (c) Last alcohol. **12.102** I_2-water: weak dipole–induced dipole; I_3^--water: favorable ion-dipole interaction. **12.104** (a) Same NaCl solution on both sides. (b) Only water would move from left to right. (c) Normal osmosis. **12.106** 12.3 M. **12.108** 14.2%.
12.110 (a) Decreases with lattice energy. (b) Increases with polarity of solvent. (c) Increases with enthalpy of hydration.
12.112 1.80 g/mL. 5.0×10^2 m. **12.114** 0.815. **12.116** NH_3 can form hydrogen bonds with water. **12.118** 3%. **12.120** 1.2×10^2 g/mol. It forms a dimer in benzene. **12.122** (a) 1.1 m. (b) The protein prevents the formation of ice crystals. **12.124** It is due to the precipitated minerals that refract light and create an opaque appearance. **12.126** 1.9 m. **12.128** (a) $X_A = 0.524$, $X_B = 0.476$.
(b) A: 50 mmHg; B: 20 mmHg. (c) $X_A = 0.71$, $X_B = 0.29$.
$P_A = 67$ mmHg. $P_B = 12$ mmHg. **12.130** 2.7×10^{-3}
12.132 From $n = kP$ and $PV = nRT$, show that $V = kRT$.
12.134 −0.737°C.

Chapter 13

13.6 (a) rate $= -\dfrac{1}{2}\dfrac{\Delta[H_2]}{\Delta t} = -\dfrac{\Delta[O_2]}{\Delta t} = \dfrac{1}{2}\dfrac{\Delta[H_2O]}{\Delta t}$.

(b) rate $= -\dfrac{1}{4}\dfrac{\Delta[NH_3]}{\Delta t} = -\dfrac{1}{5}\dfrac{\Delta[O_2]}{\Delta t} = \dfrac{1}{4}\dfrac{\Delta[NO]}{\Delta t} = \dfrac{1}{6}\dfrac{\Delta[H_2O]}{\Delta t}$.

13.8 (a) 0.049 M/s. (b) −0.025 M/s. **13.16** 2.4×10^{-4} M/s. **13.18** (a) Third order. (b) 0.38 M/s. **13.20** (a) 0.046 s^{-1}. (b) $0.13/M \cdot s$.
13.22 First order. $1.08 \times 10^{-3}\ s^{-1}$. **13.28** (a) 0.0198 s^{-1}. (b) 151 s.
13.30 3.6 s. **13.38** 135 kJ/mol. **13.40** 644 K. **13.42** 51.0 kJ/mol.
13.52 (a) rate $= k[X_2][Y]$. (b) Reaction is zero order in Z. (c) $X_2 + Y \longrightarrow XY + X$ (slow). $X + Z \longrightarrow XZ$ (fast). **13.54** Mechanism I.
13.62 rate $= \dfrac{k_1 k_2}{k_{-1}}[E][S]$. **13.64** Temperature, energy of activation, concentration of reactants, catalyst. **13.66** 22.6 cm²; 44.9 cm². The large surface area of grain dust can result in a violent explosion.
13.68 (a) Third order. (b) $0.38/M^2 \cdot s$. (c) $H_2 + 2NO \longrightarrow N_2 + H_2O + O$ (slow); $O + H_2 \longrightarrow H_2O$ (fast). **13.70** Water is present in excess so its concentration does not change appreciably.
13.72 $10.7/M \cdot s$. **13.74** 2.63 atm. **13.76** $M^{-2} s^{-1}$. **13.78** 56.4 min.
13.80 (b), (d), (e). **13.82** 9.8×10^{-4}. **13.84** (a) Increase.
(b) Decrease. (c) Decrease. (d) Increase. **13.86** 0.0896 min^{-1}.
13.88 1.12×10^3 min. **13.90** (a) I_2 absorbs visible light to form I atoms. (b) UV light is needed to dissociate H_2. **13.92** (a) rate $= k[X][Y]^2$. (b) $1.9 \times 10^{-2}/M^2 \cdot s$. **13.94** Second order. $2.4 \times 10^7/M \cdot s$. **13.96** Because the engine is relatively cold so the exhaust gases will not fully react with the catalytic converter.
13.98 (a) Reaction has a large activation energy. (b) Activation energy is very small and orientation factor not important.
13.100 5.7×10^5 yr. **13.102** (a) Mn^{2+}; Mn^{3+}; first step.
(b) Without the catalyst, reaction would be termolecular.
(c) Homogeneous. **13.104** 0.45 atm. **13.106** (a) $k_1[A] - k_2[B]$.
(b) $[B] = (k_1/k_2)[A]$. **13.108** (a) $2.47 \times 10^{-2}\ yr^{-1}$. (b) 9.8×10^{-4}.
(c) 186 yr. **13.110** (a) 3. (b) 2. (c) $C \longrightarrow D$. (d) Exothermic.
13.112 1.8×10^3 K. **13.114** (a) 2.5×10^{-5} M/s. (b) Same as (a).

(c) 8.3×10^{-6} M. **13.118** (a) 1.13×10^{-3} M/min. (b) 8.8×10^{-3} M.
13.120 Second order. $0.42/M \cdot$ min. **13.122** 60% increase. The
result shows the profound effect of an exponential dependence.

Chapter 14

14.14 (a) $A + C \rightleftharpoons AC$. (b) $A + D \rightleftharpoons AD$. **14.16** 1.08×10^7.
14.18 3.5×10^{-7}. **14.20** (a) 0.082. (b) 0.29. **14.22** 0.105;
2.05×10^{-3}. **14.24** 7.09×10^{-3}. **14.26** 3.3. **14.28** 3.53×10^{-2}.
14.30 4.0×10^{-6}. **14.32** 5.6×10^{23}. **14.36** $0.64/M^2 \cdot$ s.
14.40 $[NH_3]$ will increase and $[N_2]$ and $[H_2]$ will decrease. **14.42**
NO: 0.50 atm; NO_2: 0.020 atm. **14.44** $[I] = 8.58 \times 10^{-4}$ M; $[I_2] =$
0.0194 M. **14.46** (a) 0.52. (b) $[CO_2] = 0.48$ M, $[H_2] = 0.020$ M,
$[CO] = 0.075$ M, $[H_2O] = 0.065$ M. **14.48** $[H_2] = [CO_2] = 0.05$
M, $[H_2O] = [CO] = 0.11$ M. **14.54** (a) Shift position of
equilibrium to the right. (b) No effect. (c) No effect. **14.56** (a) No
effect. (b) No effect. (c) Shift the position of equilibrium to the left.
(d) No effect. (e) To the left. **14.58** (a) To the right. (b) To the left.
(c) To the right. (d) To the left. (e) No effect. **14.60** No change.
14.62 (a) More CO_2 will form. (b) No change. (c) No change.
(d) Some CO_2 will combine with CaO to form $CaCO_3$. (e) Some
CO_2 will react with NaOH so equilibrium will shift to the right.
(f) HCl reacts with $CaCO_3$ to produce CO_2. Equilibrium will shift to
the left. (g) Equilibrium will shift to the right. **14.64** (a) NO: 0.24
atm; Cl_2: 0.12 atm. (b) 0.017. **14.66** (a) No effect. (b) More CO_2
and H_2O will form. **14.68** (a) 8×10^{-44}. (b) The reaction has a
very large activation energy. **14.70** (a) 1.7. (b) A: 0.69 atm, B: 0.81
atm. **14.72** 1.5×10^5. **14.74** H_2: 0.28 atm, Cl_2: 0.049 atm, HCl:
1.67 atm. **14.76** 5.0×10^1 atm. **14.78** 3.84×10^{-2}. **14.80** 3.13.
14.82 N_2: 0.860 atm; H_2: 0.366 atm; NH_3: 4.40×10^{-3} atm.
14.84 (a) 1.16. (b) 53.7%. **14.86** (a) 0.49 atm. (b) 0.23. (c) 0.037.
(d) Greater than 0.037 mol. **14.88** $[H_2] = 0.070$ M, $[I_2] = 0.182$
M, $[HI] = 0.825$ M. **14.90** (c). **14.92** (a) 4.2×10^{-4}. (b) 0.83.
(c) 1.1. (d) In (b): 2.3×10^3; in (c): 0.021. **14.94** 0.0231;
9.60×10^{-4}. **14.96** NO_2: 1.2 atm; N_2O_4: 0.12 atm. $K_P = 12$.
14.98 (a) The equilibrium will shift to the right. (b) To the right.
(c) No change. (d) No change. (e) No change. (f) To the left.
14.100 NO_2: 0.100 atm; N_2O_4: 0.09 atm. **14.102** (a) 1.03 atm.
(b) 0.39 atm. (c) 1.67 atm. (d) 0.620. **14.104** 22 mg/m^3. Yes.
14.106 Temporary dynamic equilibrium between the melting ice
cubes and the freezing of the water between the ice cubes.
14.108 $[NH_3] = 0.042$ M, $[N_2] = 0.086$ M, $[H_2] = 0.26$ M.
14.110 -115 kJ/mol. **14.112** SO_2: 2.71 atm; SO_2Cl_2: 3.58 atm.
14.114 4.0.

Chapter 15

15.4 (a) NO_2^-. (b) HSO_4^-. (c) HS^-. (d) CN^-. (e) $HCOO^-$.
15.6 (a) H_2S. (b) H_2CO_3. (c) HCO_3^-. (d) H_3PO_4. (e) $H_2PO_4^-$.
(f) HPO_4^{2-}. (g) H_2SO_4. (h) HSO_4^-. (i) HSO_3^-. **15.8** (a) CH_2ClCOO^-.
(b) IO_4^-. (c) $H_2PO_4^-$. (d) HPO_4^{2-}. (e) PO_4^{3-}. (f) HSO_4^-. (g) SO_4^{2-}.
(h) IO_3^-. (i) SO_3^{2-}. (j) NH_3. (k) HS^-. (l) S^{2-}. (m) OCl^-. **15.16** 1.6
$\times 10^{-14}$ M. **15.18** (a) 10.74. (b) 3.28. **15.20** (a) 6.3×10^{-6} M.
(b) 1.0×10^{-16} M. (c) 2.7×10^{-6} M. **15.22** (a) Acidic. (b) Neutral.
(c) Basic. **15.24** 1.98×10^{-3} mol. 0.444. **15.26** 0.118. **15.32** (1) c.
(2) b and d. **15.34** (a) Strong. (b) Weak. (c) Weak. (d) Weak.
(e) Strong. **15.36** (b) and (c). **15.38** No. **15.44** $[H^+] = [CH_3COO^-]$
$= 5.8 \times 10^{-4}$ M, $[CH_3COOH] = 0.0181$ M. **15.46** 2.3×10^{-3} M.
15.48 (a) 3.5%. (b) 33%. (c) 79%. Percent ionization increases
with dilution. **15.50** (a) 3.9%. (b) 0.30%. **15.54** 7.1×10^{-7}.
15.56 1.5%. **15.62** HCl: 1.40; H_2SO_4: 1.31. **15.64** $[H^+] = [HCO_3^-]$
$= 1.0 \times 10^{-4}$ M, $[CO_3^{2-}] = 4.8 \times 10^{-11}$ M. **15.68** (a) $H_2SO_4 >$
H_2SeO_4. (b) $H_3PO_4 > H_3AsO_4$. **15.70** The conjugate base of

phenol can be stabilized by resonance. **15.76** (a) Neutral. (b)
Basic. (c) Acidic. (d) Acidic. **15.78** HZ < HY < HX. **15.80** 4.82.
15.82 Basic. **15.86** (a) Al_2O_3 < BaO < K_2O. (b) CrO_3 < Cr_2O_3 <
CrO. **15.88** $Al(OH)_3 + OH^- \longrightarrow Al(OH)_4^-$. Lewis acid-base
reaction. **15.92** $AlCl_3$ is the Lewis acid, Cl^- is the Lewis base.
15.94 CO_2 and BF_3. **15.96** 0.106 L. **15.98** No, volume
is the same. **15.102** CrO is basic and CrO_3 is acidic. **15.104** $4.0 \times$
10^{-2}. **15.106** 7.00. **15.108** NH_3. **15.110** (a) 7.43. (b) pD < 7.43.
(c) pD + pOD = 14.87. **15.112** 1.79. **15.114** F^- reacts with HF to
form HF_2^-, thereby shifting the ionization of HF to the right.
15.116 (b) 6.80. **15.118** $[H^+] = [H_2PO_4^-] = 0.0239$ M, $[H_3PO_4]$
$= 0.076$ M, $[HPO_4^{2-}] = 6.2 \times 10^{-8}$ M, $[PO_4^{3-}] = 1.2 \times 10^{-18}$ M.
15.120 $[Na^+] = 0.200$ M, $[HCO_3^-] = [OH^-] = 4.6 \times 10^{-3}$ M,
$[H_2CO_3] = 2.4 \times 10^{-8}$ M, $[H^+] = 2.2 \times 10^{-12}$ M. **15.122** The H^+
ions convert CN^- to HCN, which escapes as a gas. **15.124** 0.25 g.
15.126 -0.20. **15.128** (a) Equilibrium will shift to the right. (b) To
the left. (c) No effect. (d) To the right. **15.130** The amines are
converted to their salts RNH_3^+. **15.132** 1.4×10^{-4}. **15.134** 4.40.
15.136 In a basic medium, the ammonium salt is converted to the
pungent-smelling ammonia. **15.138** (c). **15.140** 21 mL.
15.142 Mg. **15.144** 1.57. $[CN^-] = 1.8 \times 10^{-8}$ M in 1.00 M HF
and 2.2×10^{-5} M in 1.00 M HCN. HF is a stronger acid than
HCN. **15.146** 6.02.

Chapter 16

16.6 (a) 11.28. (b) 9.08. **16.10** (a), (b), and (c). **16.12** 4.74 for both.
(a) Is more effective because it has a higher concentration. **16.14**
7.03. **16.16** 10. More effective against the acid. **16.18** (a) 4.82.
(b) 4.64. **16.20** HC. **16.24** 90.1 g/mol. **16.26** 0.467 M. **16.28** $[H^+] =$
3.0×10^{-13} M, $[OH^-] = 0.0335$ M, $[Na^+] = 0.0835$ M,
$[CH_3COO^-] = 0.0500$ M, $[CH_3COOH] = 8.4 \times 10^{-10}$ M.
16.30 8.23. **16.32** (a) 11.36. (b) 9.55. (c) 8.95. (d) 5.19. (e) 1.70.
16.36 CO_2 dissolves in water to form H_2CO_3, which neutralizes
NaOH. **16.38** 5.70. **16.46** (a) 7.8×10^{-10}. (b) 1.8×10^{-18}.
16.48 1.80×10^{-10}. **16.50** 2.2×10^{-4} M. **16.52** 2.3×10^{-9}.
16.54 $[Na^+] = 0.045$ M, $[NO_3^-] = 0.076$ M, $[Sr^{2+}] = 0.016$ M,
$[F^-] = 1.1 \times 10^{-4}$ M. **16.56** pH greater than 2.68 and less than
8.11. **16.60** (a) 0.013 M. (b) 2.2×10^{-4} M. (c) 3.3×10^{-3} M.
16.62 (a) 1.0×10^{-5} M. (b) 1.1×10^{-10} M. **16.64** (b), (c), (d),
and (e). **16.66** (a) 0.016 M. (b) 1.6×10^{-6} M. **16.68** Yes.
16.72 $[Cd^{2+}] = 1.1 \times 10^{-18}$ M, $[Cd(CN)_4^{2-}] = 4.2 \times 10^{-3}$ M,
$[CN^-] = 0.48$ M. **16.74** 3.5×10^{-5} M. **16.76** (a) $Cu^{2+} + 4NH_3$
$\rightleftharpoons Cu(NH_3)_4^{2+}$. (b) $Ag^+ + 2CN^- \rightleftharpoons Ag(CN)_2^-$. (c) $Hg^{2+} +$
$4Cl^- \rightleftharpoons HgCl_4^{2-}$. **16.80** 0.011 M. **16.82** Use Cl^- ions or flame
test. **16.84** From 2.51 to 4.41. **16.86** 1.28 M. **16.88** $[H^+] = 3.0 \times$
10^{-13} M, $[OH^-] = 0.0335$ M, $[HCOO^-] = 0.0500$ M, $[HCOOH] =$
8.8×10^{-11} M, $[Na^+] = 0.0835$ M. **16.90** 9.97 g. pH = 13.04.
16.92 6.0×10^3. **16.94** 0.036 g/L. **16.96** (a) 1.37. (b) 5.97.
(c) 10.24. **16.98** Original precipitate was HgI_2. In the presence
of excess KI, it redissolves as HgI_4^{2-}. **16.100** $7.82-10.38$.
16.102 (a) 3.60. (b) 9.69. (c) 6.07. **16.104** (a) $MCO_3 + 2HCl \longrightarrow$
$MCl_2 + H_2O + CO_2$. HCl + NaOH $\longrightarrow$ NaCl + H_2O.
(b) 197 g/mol. Ba. **16.106.** 2. **16.108** (a) 12.6. (b) 8.8×10^{-6} M.
16.110 (a) Sulfate. (b) Sulfide. (c) Iodide. **16.112** They are
insoluble. **16.114** The ionized polyphenols have a dark color. The
H^+ ions from lemon juice shift the equilibrium to the light color
acid. **16.116** Yes. **16.118** (c). **16.120** (a) 1.7×10^{-7} M. (b) $MgCO_3$
is more soluble than $CaCO_3$. (c) 12.40. (d) 1.9×10^{-8} M.
(e) Ca^{2+} because it is present in larger amount. **16.122** pH = 1.0,
fully protonated; pH = 7.0, dipolar ion; pH = 12.0, fully ionized.
16.124 (a) 4.74 before and after dilution. (b) 2.52 before and
3.02 after dilution. **16.126** 4.75. **16.128** 6.2×10^{-12}.

Chapter 17

17.6 3.3×10^{-4} atm. **17.8** N_2: 3.96×10^{18} kg; O_2: 1.22×10^{18} kg; CO_2: 2.63×10^{15} kg. **17.12** 3.57×10^{-19} J. **17.22** 5.2×10^6 kg. 5.6×10^{14} kJ. **17.24** The wavelength is not short enough. **17.26** 434 nm. Both.

17.28 F—C—C—Cl   F—C—C—H **17.40** 1.3×10^{10} kg.

17.42 Ethane and propane are greenhouse gases. **17.50** 4.34. **17.58** 1.2×10^{-11} M/s. **17.60** (b). **17.66** 0.12%. **17.68** Endothermic. **17.70** O_2. **17.72** 5.72. **17.74** 394 nm. **17.76** It has a high activation energy. **17.78** Size of tree rings are related to CO_2 content. Age of CO_2 in ice can be determined by radiocarbon dating. **17.80** 165 kJ/mol. **17.82** 5.1×10^{20} photons. **17.84** (a) 62.6 kJ/mol. (b) 38 min. **17.86** 5.6×10^{23}.

Chapter 18

18.6 (a) 0.02. (b) 9×10^{-19}. (c) 2×10^{-181}. **18.10** (c) < (d) < (e) < (a) < (b). Solids have smaller entropies than gases. More complex structures have higher entropies. **18.12** (a) 47.5 J/K · mol. (b) -12.5 J/K · mol. (c) -242.8 J/K · mol. **18.14** (a) $\Delta S < 0$. (b) $\Delta S > 0$. (c) $\Delta S > 0$. (d) $\Delta S < 0$. **18.18** (a) -1139 kJ/mol. (b) -140.0 kJ/mol. (c) -2935.0 kJ/mol. **18.20** (a) At all temperatures. (b) Below 111 K. **18.24** 8.0×10^1 kJ/mol. **18.26** 4.572×10^2 kJ/mol, 7.2×10^{-81}. **18.28** (a) -24.6 kJ/mol. (b) -1.33 kJ/mol. **18.30** -341 kJ/mol. **18.32** -2.87 kJ/mol. The process has a high activation energy. **18.36** 1×10^3. glucose + ATP $\longrightarrow$ glucose 6-phosphate + ADP. **18.38** (a) 0. (b) 4.0×10^4 J/mol. (c) -3.2×10^4 J/mol. (d) 6.4×10^4 J/mol. **18.40** (a) No reaction is possible because $\Delta G > 0$. (b) The reaction has a very large activation energy. (c) Reactants and products already at their equilibrium concentrations. **18.42** In all cases $\Delta H > 0$ and $\Delta S > 0$. $\Delta G < 0$ for (a), $= 0$ for (b), and > 0 for (c). **18.44** $\Delta S > 0$. **18.46** (a) Most liquids have similar structure so the changes in entropy from liquid to vapor are similar. (b) ΔS_{vap} are larger for ethanol and water because of hydrogen bonding (there are fewer microstates in these liquids). **18.48** (a) $2CO + 2NO \longrightarrow 2CO_2 + N_2$. (b) Oxidizing agent: NO; reducing agent: CO. (c) 3×10^{120}. (d) 1.2×10^{18}. From left to right. (e) No. **18.50** 2.6×10^{-9}. **18.52** 976 K. **18.54** $\Delta S < 0$; $\Delta H < 0$. **18.56** 55 J/K · mol. **18.58** Increase in entropy of the surroundings offsets the decrease in entropy of the system. **18.60** 56 J/K. **18.62** 4.5×10^5. **18.64** 4.8×10^{-75} atm. **18.66** (a) True. (b) True. (c) False. **18.68** $C + CuO \rightleftharpoons CO + Cu$. 6.1. **18.70** 673.2 K. **18.72** (a) 7.6×10^{14}. (b) 4.1×10^{-12}. **18.74** (a) A reverse disproportionation reaction. (b) 8.2×10^{15}. Yes, a large K makes this an efficient process. (c) Less effective. **18.76** 1.8×10^{70}. Reaction has a large activation energy. **18.78** Heating the ore alone is not a feasible process. -214.3 kJ/mol. **18.80** $K_P = 36$. 981 K. No. **18.82** Mole percents: butane = 30%; isobutane = 70%. Yes. **18.84** $X_{CO} = 0.45$; $X_{CO_2} = 0.55$. Use ΔG_f° values at 25°C for 900°C. **18.86** 249 J/K. **18.88** 3×10^{-13} s. **18.90** $\Delta S_{sys} = -327$ J/K · mol, $\Delta S_{surr} = 1918$ J/K · mol, $\Delta S_{univ} = 1591$ J/K · mol. **18.92** q, w. **18.94** $\Delta H < 0$, $\Delta S < 0$, $\Delta G < 0$. **18.96** (a) 5.76 J/K · mol. (b) The orientation is not totally random. **18.98** $\Delta H^{\circ} = 33.89$ kJ/mol; $\Delta S^{\circ} = 96.4$ J/K · mol; $\Delta G^{\circ} = 5.2$ kJ/mol. This is an endothermic liquid to vapor process so both ΔH° and ΔS° are positive. ΔG° is positive because the temperature is below the boiling point of benzene (80.1°C). **18.100** $\Delta G^{\circ} = 62.5$ kJ/mol; $\Delta H^{\circ} = 157.8$ kJ/mol; $\Delta S^{\circ} = 109$ J/K · mol.

Chapter 19

19.2 (a) $Mn^{2+} + H_2O_2 + 2OH^- \longrightarrow MnO_2 + 2H_2O$. (b) $2Bi(OH)_3 + 3SnO_2^{2-} \longrightarrow 2Bi + 3H_2O + 3SnO_3^{2-}$. (c) $Cr_2O_7^{2-} + 14H^+ + 3C_2O_4^{2-} \longrightarrow 2Cr^{3+} + 6CO_2 + 7H_2O$. (d) $2Cl^- + 2ClO_3^- + 4H^+ \longrightarrow Cl_2 + 2ClO_2 + 2H_2O$. **19.12** 2.46 V. $Al + 3Ag^+ \longrightarrow 3Ag + Al^{3+}$. **19.14** $Cl_2(g)$ and $MnO_4^-(aq)$. **19.16** Only (a) and (d) are spontaneous. **19.18** (a) Li. (b) H_2. (c) Fe^{2+}. (d) Br^-. **19.22** 0.368 V. **19.24** (a) -432 kJ/mol, 5×10^{75}. (b) -104 kJ/mol, 2×10^{18}. (c) -178 kJ/mol, 1×10^{31}. (d) -1.27×10^3 kJ/mol, 8×10^{211}. **19.26** 0.37 V, -36 kJ/mol, 2×10^6. **19.30** (a) 2.23 V, 2.23 V, -430 kJ/mol. (b) 0.02 V, 0.04 V, -23 kJ/mol. **19.32** 0.083 V. **19.34** 0.010 V. **19.38** 1.09 V. **19.46** (b) 0.64 g. **19.48** (a) $\$2.10 \times 10^3$. (b) $\$2.46 \times 10^3$. (c) $\$4.70 \times 10^3$. **19.50** (a) 0.14 F. (b) 0.121 F. (c) 0.10 F. **19.52** (a) $Ag^+ + e^- \longrightarrow Ag$. (b) $2H_2O \longrightarrow O_2 + 4H^+ + 4e^-$. (c) 6.0×10^2 C. **19.54** (a) 0.589 Cu. (b) 0.133 A. **19.56** 2.3 h. **19.58** 9.66×10^4 C. **19.60** 0.0710 F. **19.62** 0.156 M. $Cr_2O_7^{2-} + 6Fe^{2+} + 14H^+ \longrightarrow 2Cr^{3+} + 6Fe^{3+} + 7H_2O$. **19.64** 45.1%. **19.66** (a) $2MnO_4^- + 16H^+ + 5C_2O_4^{2-} \longrightarrow 2Mn^{2+} + 10CO_2 + 8H_2O$. (b) 5.40%. **19.68** 0.231 mg Ca^{2+}/mL blood. **19.70** (a) 0.80 V. (b) $2Ag^+ + H_2 \longrightarrow 2Ag + 2H^+$. (c) (i) 0.92 V. (ii) 1.10 V. (d) The cell operates as a pH meter. **19.72** Fluorine gas reacts with water. **19.74** 2.5×10^2 h. **19.76** Hg_2^{2+}. **19.78** $[Mg^{2+}] = 0.0500$ M, $[Ag^+] = 7 \times 10^{-55}$ M, 1.44 g. **19.80** (a) 0.206 L H_2. (b) 6.09×10^{23}/mol e^-. **19.82** (a) -1356.8 kJ/mol. (b) 1.17 V. **19.84** $+3$. **19.86** 6.8 kJ/mol, 0.064. **19.88** 1.4 A. **19.90** $+4$. **19.92** 1.60×10^{-19} C/e^-. **19.94** A cell made of Li^+/Li and F_2/F^- gives the maximum voltage of 5.92 V. Reactive oxidizing and reducing agents are hard to handle. **19.96** 2×10^{20}. **19.98** (a) E° for X is negative; E° for Y is positive. (b) 0.59 V. **19.100** (a) The reduction potential of O_2 is insufficient to oxidize gold. (b) Yes. (c) $2Au + 3F_2 \longrightarrow 2AuF_3$. **19.102** $[Fe^{2+}] = 0.0920$ M, $[Fe^{3+}] = 0.0680$ M. **19.104** $E^{\circ} = 1.09$ V. Spontaneous. **19.106** (a) Unchanged. (b) Unchanged. (c) Squared. (d) Doubled. (e) Doubled. **19.108** Stronger. **19.110** 4.4×10^2 atm. **19.112** (a) $Zn \longrightarrow Zn^{2+} + 2e^-$; $\frac{1}{2}O_2 + 2e^- \longrightarrow O^{2-}$. 1.65 V. (b) 1.63 V. (c) 4.87×10^3 kJ/kg. (d) 62 L. **19.114** -3.05 V. **19.116** 1×10^{-14}. **19.118** (b) 104 A · h The concentration of H_2SO_4 keeps decreasing. (c) 2.01 V; -3.88×10^2 kJ/mol. **19.120** \$217. **19.122** -0.037 V. **19.124** 2×10^{37}.

Chapter 20

20.12 111 h. **20.14** Roast the sulfide followed by reduction of the oxide with coke or carbon monoxide. **20.16** (a) 8.9×10^{12} cm³. (b) 4.0×10^8 kg. **20.18** Iron does not need to be produced electrolytically. **20.28** (a) $2Na + 2H_2O \longrightarrow 2NaOH + H_2$. (b) $2NaOH + CO_2 \longrightarrow Na_2CO_3 + H_2O$. (c) $Na_2CO_3 + 2HCl \longrightarrow 2NaCl + CO_2 + H_2O$. (d) $NaHCO_3 + HCl \longrightarrow NaCl + CO_2 + H_2O$. (e) $2NaHCO_3 \longrightarrow Na_2CO_3 + H_2O$. (f) No reaction. **20.30** 5.59 L. **20.34** First react Mg with HNO_3 to form $Mg(NO_3)_2$. On heating, $2Mg(NO_3)_2 \longrightarrow 2MgO + 4NO_2 + O_2$. **20.36** The third electron is removed from the neon core. **20.38** Helium has a closed-shell noble gas configuration. **20.40** (a) CaO. (b) $Ca(OH)_2$. (c) An aqueous suspension of $Ca(OH)_2$. **20.44** 60.7 h. **20.46** (a) 1.03 V. (b) 3.32×10^4 kJ/mol. **20.48** $4Al(NO_3)_3 \longrightarrow 2Al_2O_3 + 12NO_2 + 3O_2$. **20.50** Because Al_2Cl_6 dissociates to form $AlCl_3$. **20.52** From sp^3 to sp^2. **20.54** 65.4 g/mol. **20.56** No. **20.58** (a) 1482 kJ/mol. (b) 3152.8 kJ/mol. **20.60** Magnesium reacts with nitrogen to form magnesium nitride. **20.62** (a) Al^{3+} hydrolyzes in water to produce H^+ ions. (b) $Al(OH)_3$ dissolves in a strong base to form $Al(OH)_4^-$.

20.64 $CaO + 2HCl \longrightarrow CaCl_2 + H_2O$. **20.66** Electronic transitions (in the visible region) between closely spaced energy levels. **20.68** NaF: toothpaste additive; Li_2CO_3: to treat mental illness; $Mg(OH)_2$: antacid; $CaCO_3$: antacid; $BaSO_4$: for X-ray diagnostic of digestive system; $Al(OH)_2NaCO_3$: antacid. **20.70** (i) Both Li and Mg form oxides. (ii) Like Mg, Li forms nitride. (iii) The carbonates, fluorides, and phosphates of Li and Mg have low solubilities. **20.72** Zn. **20.74** D < A < C < B. **20.76** 727 atm.

Chapter 21

21.12 (a) Hydrogen reacts with alkali metals to form hydrides. (b) Hydrogen reacts with oxygen to form water. **21.14** Use palladium metal to separate hydrogen from other gases. **21.16** 11 kg. **21.18** (a) $H_2 + Cl_2 \longrightarrow 2HCl$. (b) $N_2 + 3H_2 \longrightarrow 2NH_3$. (c) $2Li + H_2 \longrightarrow 2LiH$, $LiH + H_2O \longrightarrow LiOH + H_2$. **21.26** $:C{\equiv}C:^{2-}$. **21.28** (a) $2NaHCO_3 \longrightarrow Na_2CO_3 + H_2O + CO_2$. (b) CO_2 reacts with $Ca(OH)_2$ solution to form a white precipitate ($CaCO_3$). **21.30** On heating, the bicarbonate ion decomposes: $2HCO_3^- \longrightarrow CO_3^{2-} + H_2O + CO_2$. Mg^{2+} ions combines with CO_3^{2-} ions to form $MgCO_3$. **21.32** First, $2NaOH + CO_2 \longrightarrow Na_2CO_3 + H_2O$. Then, $Na_2CO_3 + CO_2 + H_2O \longrightarrow 2NaHCO_3$. **21.34** Yes. **21.40** (a) $2NaNO_3 \longrightarrow 2NaNO_2 + O_2$. (b) $NaNO_3 + C \longrightarrow NaNO_2 + CO$. **21.42** $2NH_3 + CO_2 \longrightarrow (NH_2)_2CO + H_2O$. At high pressures. **21.44** NH_4Cl decomposes to form NH_3 and HCl. **21.46** N is in its highest oxidation state (+5) in HNO_3. **21.48** Favored reaction: $4Zn + NO_3^- + 10H^+ \longrightarrow 4Zn^{2+} + NH_4^+ + 3H_2O$. **21.50** Linear. **21.52** -1168 kJ/mol. **21.54** P_4. 125 g/mol. **21.56** $P_4O_{10} + 4HNO_3 \longrightarrow 2N_2O_5 + 4HPO_3$. 60.4 g. **21.58** sp^3. **21.66** -198.3 kJ/mol, 6×10^{34}, 6×10^{34}. **21.68** 0; -1. **21.70** 4.4×10^{11} mol; 1.4×10^{13} g. **21.72** 79.1 g. **21.74** Cl, Br, and I atoms are too bulky around the S atom. **21.76** 35 g. **21.78** $9H_2SO_4 + 8NaI \longrightarrow H_2S + 4I_2 + 4H_2O + 8NaHSO_4$. **21.82** $H_2SO_4 + NaCl \longrightarrow HCl + NaHSO_4$. The HCl gas escapes, driving the equilibrium to the right. **21.84** 25.3 L. **21.86** Sulfuric acid oxidizes sodium bromide to molecular bromine. **21.88** 2.81 L. **21.90** $I_2O_5 + 5CO \longrightarrow I_2 + 5CO_2$. C is oxidized; I is reduced. **21.92** (a) $SiCl_4$. (b) F^-. (c) F. (d) CO_2. **21.94** No change. **21.96** (a) $2Na + D_2O \longrightarrow 2NaOD + D_2$. (b) $2D_2O \longrightarrow 2D_2 + O_2$ (electrolysis). $D_2 + Cl_2 \longrightarrow 2DCl$. (c) $Mg_3N_2 + 6D_2O \longrightarrow 3Mg(OD)_2 + 2ND_3$. (d) $CaC_2 + 2D_2O \longrightarrow C_2D_2 + Ca(OD)_2$. (e) $Be_2C + 4D_2O \longrightarrow 2Be(OD)_2 + CD_4$. (f) $SO_3 + D_2O \longrightarrow D_2SO_4$. **21.98** (a) At elevated pressure, water boils above 100°C. (b) So the water is able to melt a larger area of sulfur deposit. (c) Sulfur deposits are structurally weak. Conventional mining would be dangerous. **21.100** The C—D bond breaks at a slower rate. **21.102** Molecular oxygen is a powerful oxidizing agent, reacting with substances such as glucose to release energy for growth and function. Molecular nitrogen (containing the nitrogen-to-nitrogen triple bond) is too unreactive at room temperature to be of any practical use. **21.104** 25°C: 9.61×10^{-22}; 1000°C: 138. High temperature favors the formation of CO. **21.106** 1.18.

Chapter 22

22.12 (a) +3. (b) 6. (c) oxalate. **22.14** (a) Na: +1, Mo: +6. (b) Mg: +2, W: +6. (c) Fe: 0. **22.16** (a) cis-dichloro-bis(ethylenediamine)cobalt(III). (b) pentaamminechloro-platinum(IV) chloride. (c) pentaamminechlorocobalt(III) chloride. **22.18** (a) $[Cr(en)_2Cl_2]^+$. (b) $Fe(CO)_5$. (c) $K_2[Cu(CN)_4]$. (d) $[Co(NH_3)_4(H_2O)Cl]Cl_2$. **22.24** (a) 2. (b) 2. **22.26** (a) Two geometric isomers:

trans   cis

(b) Two optical isomers:

22.34 CN^- is a strong-field ligand. Absorbs near UV (blue) so appears yellow. **22.36** (a) Orange. (b) 255 kJ/mol. **22.38** $[Co(NH_3)_4Cl_2]Cl$. 2 moles. **22.42** Use $^{14}CN^-$ label (in NaCN). **22.44** First $Cu(CN)_2$ (white) is formed. It redissolves as $Cu(CN)_4^{2-}$. **22.46** 1.4×10^2. **22.48** Mn^{3+}. $3d^5$ (Cr^{3+}) is a stable electron configuration. **22.50** Ti: +3; Fe: +3. **22.52** Four Fe atoms per hemoglobin molecule. 1.6×10^4 g/mol. **22.54** (a) $[Cr(H_2O)_6]Cl_3$. (b) $[Cr(H_2O)_5Cl]Cl_2 \cdot H_2O$. (c) $[Cr(H_2O)_4Cl_2]Cl \cdot 2H_2O$. Compare electrical conductance with solutions of NaCl, $MgCl_2$, and $FeCl_3$ of the same molar concentration. **22.56** -1.8×10^2 kJ/mol; 6×10^{30}. **22.58** Iron is more abundant. **22.60** Oxyhemoglobin is low spin and therefore absorbs higher energy light. **22.62** All except Fe^{2+}, Cu^{2+}, and Co^{2+}. The colorless ions have electron configurations d^0 and d^{10}. **22.64** Dipole moment measurements. **22.66** EDTA sequesters essential metal ions (Ca^{2+}, Mg^{2+}). **22.68** 3. **22.70** 2.2×10^{-20} M. **22.72** (a) 2.7×10^6. (b) Cu^+ ions are unstable in solution. **22.74** (a) Cu^{3+} is unstable in solution because it can be easily reduced. (b) Potassium hexafluorocuprate(III). Octahedral. Paramagnetic. (c) Diamagnetic.

Chapter 23

23.6 (a) $_{-1}^{0}\beta$. (b) $_{20}^{40}Ca$. (c) $_{2}^{4}\alpha$. (d) $_{0}^{1}n$. **23.14** (a) $_{3}^{9}Li$. (b) $_{11}^{25}Na$. (c) $_{21}^{48}Sc$. **23.16** $_{10}^{17}Ne$. (b) $_{20}^{45}Ca$. (c) $_{43}^{92}Tc$. (d) $_{80}^{195}Hg$. (e) $_{96}^{242}Cm$. **23.18** 6×10^9 kg/s. **23.20** (a) 4.55×10^{-12} J; 1.14×10^{-12} J/nucleon. (b) 2.36×10^{-10} J; 1.28×10^{-12} J/nucleon. **23.24** 0.251 d^{-1}. 2.77 d. **23.26** 2.7 d. **23.28** $_{82}^{208}Pb$. **23.30** A: 0; B: 0.25 mole; C: 0; D: 0.75 mole. **23.34** (a) $_{34}^{80}Se + _{1}^{2}H \longrightarrow _{1}^{1}p + _{34}^{81}Se$. (b) $_{4}^{9}Be + _{1}^{2}H \longrightarrow 2_{1}^{1}p + _{3}^{9}Li$. (c) $_{5}^{10}B + _{0}^{1}n \longrightarrow _{2}^{4}\alpha + _{3}^{7}Li$. **23.36** $_{80}^{198}Hg + _{0}^{1}n \longrightarrow _{79}^{198}Au + _{1}^{1}p$. **23.48** IO_3^- is only formed from IO_4^-. **23.50** Incorporate Fe-59 into a person's body. After a few days isolate red blood cells and monitor radioactivity from the hemoglobin molecules. **23.52** An analogous Pauli exclusion principle for nucleons. **23.54** (a) 0.343 mCi. (b) $_{93}^{237}Np \longrightarrow _{2}^{4}\alpha + _{91}^{233}Pa$. **23.56** (a) 1.040×10^{-12} J/nucleon. (b) 1.111×10^{-12} J/nucleon. (c) 1.199×10^{-12} J/nucleon. (d) 1.410×10^{-12} J/nucleon. **23.58** $_{7}^{18}N \longrightarrow _{8}^{18}O + _{-1}^{0}\beta$. **23.60** Radioactive dating. **23.62** $_{83}^{209}Bi + _{2}^{4}\alpha \longrightarrow _{85}^{211}At + 2_{0}^{1}n$. (b) $_{83}^{209}Bi(\alpha,2n)_{85}^{211}At$. **23.64** The sun exerts a much greater gravity on the particles. **23.66** 2.77×10^3 yr. **23.68** (a) $_{19}^{40}K \longrightarrow _{18}^{40}Ar + _{+1}^{0}\beta$. (b) 3.0×10^9 yr. **23.70** (a) 5.59×10^{-15} J, 2.84×10^{-13} J. (b) 0.024 mole. (c) 4.26×10^6 kJ. **23.72** 2.7×10^{14} I-131 atoms. **23.74** 5.9×10^{23}/mol. **23.76** All except gravitational. **23.78** U-238 and Th-232. Long half-lives. **23.80** 8.3×10^{-4} nm. **23.82** $_{1}^{3}H$. **23.84** The reflected neutrons induced a nuclear chain reaction. **23.86** 2.1×10^2 g/mol. **23.88** (a) $_{94}^{238}Pu \longrightarrow _{2}^{4}\alpha + _{92}^{234}U$. (b) $t = 0$: 0.58 mW; $t = 10$ yr: 0.53 mW. **23.90** 0.49 rem. **23.92** The high temperature attained during the chain reaction causes a small-scale nuclear fusion: $_1^2H + _1^3H \longrightarrow _2^4He + _0^1n$. The additional neutrons will result in a more powerful fission bomb.

Chapter 24

24.12 $CH_3CH_2CH_2CH_2CH_2Cl$. $CH_3CH_2CH_2CHClCH_3$. $CH_3CH_2CHClCH_2CH_3$.

24.14 [structures: $C=C$ with H, CH$_3$, Br, H; $C=C$ with Br, CH$_3$, H, H]

[structures: $C=C$ with H, CH$_2$Br, H, H; cyclopropane ring $C=C$ with H, H, H, Br]

24.16 (a) Alkene or cycloalkane. (b) Alkyne. (c) Alkane. (d) Like (a). (e) Alkyne. **24.18** No, too much strain. **24.20** (a) is alkane and (b) is alkene. Only an alkene reacts with a hydrogen halide and hydrogen. **24.22** -630.8 kJ/mol. **24.24** (a) *cis*-1,2-dichlorocyclopropane. (b) *trans*-1,2-dichlorocyclopropane. **24.26** (a) 2-methylpentane. (b) 2,3,4-trimethylhexane. (c) 3-ethylhexane. (d) 3-methyl-1,4-pentadiene. (e) 2-pentyne. (f) 3-phenyl-1-pentene.

24.28 (a) [$C=C$ with CH$_3$, H, H, C$_2$H$_5$] (b) [$C=C$ with H, C$_2$H$_5$, H, C$_2$H$_5$]

(c) [$C=C$ with CH$_3$, H, H, CH—C$_3$H$_7$ / C$_2$H$_5$] (d) [$H-C\equiv C-CH-CH_3$ with phenyl ring]

24.32 (a) 1,3-dichloro-4-methylbenzene. (b) 2-ethyl-1,4-dinitrobenzene. (c) 1,2,4,5-tetramethylbenzene. **24.36** (a) Ether. (b) Amine. (c) Aldehyde. (d) Ketone. (e) Carboxylic acid. (f) Alcohol. (g) Amino acid. **24.38** $HCOOH + CH_3OH \longrightarrow HCOOCH_3 + H_2O$. Methyl formate. **24.40** $(CH_3)_2CH-O-CH_3$. **24.42** (a) Ketone. (b) Ester. (c) Ether. **24.44** -174 kJ/mol. **24.46** (a), (c), (d), (f). **24.48** (a) Rubbing alcohol. (b) Vinegar. (c) Moth balls. (d) Organic synthesis. (e) Organic synthesis. (f) Antifreeze. (g) Natural gas. (h) Synthetic polymer. **24.50** (a) 3. (b) 16. (c) 6. **24.52** (a) C: 15.81 mg, H: 1.33 mg, O: 3.49 mg. (b) C_6H_6O. (c) Phenol. [phenol ring with OH]

24.54 Empirical and molecular formula: $C_5H_{10}O$. 88.7 g/mol.

[structures: cyclopentane ring with O (oxane/cyclic ether); ring with CH(CH$_3$) and O]

$CH_2=CH-CH_2-O-CH_2-CH_3$. **24.56** (a) The C atoms bonded to the methyl group and the amino group and the H atom. (b) The C atoms bonded to Br. **24.58** CH_3CH_2CHO.

24.60 (a) Alcohol. (b) Ether. (c) Aldehyde. (d) Carboxylic acid. (e) Amine. **24.62** The acids in lemon juice convert the amines to the ammonium salts, which have very low vapor pressures. **24.64** Methane (CH_4), ethanol (C_2H_5OH), methanol (CH_3OH), isopropanol (C_3H_7OH), ethylene glycol (CH_2OHCH_2OH), naphthalene ($C_{10}H_8$), acetic acid (CH_3COOH). **24.66** (a) 1. (b) 2. (c) 5. **24.68** Br_2 dissociates into Br atoms, which react with CH_4 to form CH_3Br and HBr.

24.70 (a) [structure: $CH_3-C(OH)(H)-CH_2-CH_3$]. The compound is chiral. (b) The product is a racemic mixture.

24.72 $CH_3CH_2CH_2OH$ or [structure: $CH_3-CH(OH)-CH_3$]. **24.74** (a) Reaction between glycerol and carboxylic acid (formation of an ester). (b) Fat or oil (shown in problem) + NaOH $\longrightarrow$ Glycerol + $3RCOO^-Na^+$ (soap). (c) Molecules having more C=C bonds are harder to pack tightly. Consequently, they have a lower melting point. (d) H_2 gas with a homogeneous or heterogeneous catalyst. (e) 123.

Chapter 25

25.8 $+CH_2-CHCl-CH_2-CCl_2+$. **25.10** By an addition reaction involving styrene monomers. **25.12** (a) $CH_2=CH-CH=CH_2$. (b) $HO_2C(CH_2)_6NH_2$. **25.22** At 35°C the enzyme begins to denature. **25.28** Proteins are made of 20 amino acids. Nucleic acids are made of four building blocks (purines, pyrimidines, sugar, phosphate group) only. **25.30** C-G base pairs have three hydrogen bonds and higher boiling point; A-T base pairs have two hydrogen bonds. **25.32** Leg muscles are active, have a high metabolic rate and hence a high concentration of myoglobin. The iron content in Mb makes the meat look dark. **25.34** Insects have blood that contains no hemoglobin. It is unlikely that a human-sized insect could obtain sufficient oxygen for metabolism by diffusion. **25.36** There are four Fe atoms per hemoglobin molecule. 1.6×10^4 g/mol. **25.38** Mostly dispersion forces. **25.40** Gly-Ala-Phe-Glu-His-Gly-Ala-Leu-Val. **25.42** No. Enzymes only act on one of the two optical isomers of a compound. **25.44** 315 K.

25.46 [polymer structure: $-C(=O)-O-$ benzene ring $-C(CH_3)_2-$ benzene ring $-O-$]

25.48 (a) The —COOH group. (b) pH = 1.0: The valine is in the fully protonated form. pH = 7.0: Only the —COOH group is ionized. pH = 12.0: Both groups are ionized. **25.50** (a) sp^3. (b) Cysteine. (c) $\Delta H > 0$ and $\Delta S > 0$. The $-T\Delta S$ term will make ΔG negative at high temperature. (d) $\frac{1}{10^5}$. (e) Oxidation leads to formation of disulfide bond and removes odor, which is due to the —SH group.

Credits

Bergman/The Bergman Collection; Figure 8.14 Lithium, Sodium: © McGraw-Hill Higher Education, Inc./Ken Karp, Photographer; Figure 8.14 Potassium: © Albert Fenn/Time Life Science Library/MATTER; Figure 8.15 Barium, Beryllium, Calcium, Magnesium, Strontium: © L.V. Bergman/The Bergman Collection; Figure 8.15 Radium: © Phil Brodatz; Figure 8.16: © McGraw-Hill Higher Education, Inc./Charles D. Winters, Photographer; Figure 8.16 Aluminum, Boron, Indium: L.V. Bergman/The Bergman Collection; Figure 8.17 Carbon, Strontium, Lead: © McGraw-Hill Higher Education, Inc./Ken Karp, Photographer; Figure 8.17 Diamond: © Courtesy Diamond Information Center; Figure 8.17 Silicon: © Frank Wing/Stock Boston; Figure 8.17 Tin: © L.V. Bergman/The Bergman Collection; Figure 8.18 Nitrogen: © Joe McNally; Figure 8.18 Antimony, Arsenic, Bismuth: © L.V. Bergman/The Bergman Collection; Figure 8.18 R&W Phosphorous: © Albert Fenn/Time-Life Science Library/MATTER; Figure 8.19 Selenium, Sulfur: © L.V. Bergman/The Bergman Collection; Figure 8.19 Tellurium: © McGraw-Hill Higher Education, Inc./Ken Karp, Photographer; Figure 8.20: © Joel Gordon 1979; Figure 8.21 (all): © McGraw-Hill Higher Education, Inc./Ken Karp, Photographer; Figure 8.21 Xenon: © McGraw-Hill Higher Education, Inc./Ken Karp, Photographer; Figure 8.22a–b: © Neil Bartlett; Figure 8.23: © McGraw-Hill Higher Education, Inc./Ken Karp, Photographer; Page 346: © Culver Pictures.

Chapter 9

Opener: © G.N. Lewis/Dover Publications; Page 359: © McGraw-Hill Higher Education, Inc./Ken Karp, Photographer; Page 360: © Wards Natural Science Establishment; Page 365: © Courtesy of International Salt Company; Page 365: © Liane Enkelis/Stock Boston; Page 375: © McGraw-Hill Higher Education, Inc./Ken Karp, Photographer; Page 378: © Courtesy of James O. Schreck, Professor of Chemistry/University of Northern Colorado; Page 384: © McGraw-Hill Higher Education, Inc./Ken Karp, Photographer.

Chapter 10

Figure 10.21: © Donald Clegg; Page 440: © F. Stuart Westmorland/Photo Researchers; Page 441: © Riichiro Saito/University of Electro-Communications, Tokyo; Page 514: © McGraw-Hill Higher Education, Inc./Ken Karp, Photographer; Figure 10.14: © Aronson Photo/Stock Boston.

Chapter 11

Opener, Figure 11.9: © McGraw-Hill Higher Education, Inc./Ken Karp, Photographer; Page 459: © Hermann Eisenbeiss/Photo Researchers; Figure 11.11: © McGraw-Hill

Higher Education, Inc./Ken Karp, Photographer; Page 463: © Alan Carey/Image Works; Page 467: © Tony Mendoza/Stock Boston; Page 472: © Byron Quintard/Jacqueline McBride/Lawrence Livermore National Labs; Page 474: © Grant Heilman/Grant Heilman Photography; Page 474: © L.V. Bergman/The Bergman Collection; Page 476: © Courtesy of Edmund Catalogs; Page 477: © Courtesy Railway Technical Research Institute, Tokyo; Page 478: © Christie's Images/Corbis Images; Figure 11.37a–d, Page 487, Figure, 11.42: © McGraw-Hill Higher Education, Inc./Ken Karp, Photographer; Page 490: © David Barnes/Stock Market; Page 492: © Andrew McClenaghan/Science Photo Library/Photo Researchers; Page 492: © E.R. Degginger/Color-Pic; Page 500: © McGraw-Hill Higher Education, Inc./Ken Karp, Photographer; Page 500: © AFP/Corbis.

Chapter 12

Opener: © Richard Megna/Fundamental Photographs; Figure 12.1: © McGraw-Hill Higher Education, Inc./Ken Karp, Photographer; Page 516: Bill Evans, U.S. Geological Survey; Page 521: © Hank Morgan/Photo Researchers; Page 522: © McGraw-Hill Higher Education, Inc./Ken Karp, Photographer; Page 525: © John Mead/Photo Researchers; Page 531: © PUR® Drinking Water Systems, a division of Recovering Engineering, Inc.; Figure 12.13d (all): © David Phillips/Photo Researchers, Inc.; Figure 12.15: © Paul Weller; Figure 12.16: © Anna E. Zuckerman/Tom Stack Associates; Page 539: © McGraw-Hill Higher Education, Inc./Ken Karp, Photographer; Page 540: © George Holton/Photo Researchers, Inc.; Page 542: © Michael Newman/PhotoEdit.

Chapter 13

Opener, Figures 13.3, 13.7, Page 560: © McGraw-Hill Higher Education, Inc./Ken Karp, Photographer; Page 568: © Francois Lochon/Gamma Press; Figure 13.21: © McGraw-Hill Higher Education, Inc./Ken Karp, Photographer; Figure 13.25: © Courtesy of Jason Matthey; Figure 13.27: © General Motors Corp. Used with Permission, GM Media Archives.

Chapter 14

Opener: © Videodiscovery; Page 602: © McGraw-Hill Higher Education, Inc./Ken Karp, Photographer; Page 610: © Collection Varin-Visage/Photo Researchers; Figure 14.7: © McGraw-Hill Higher Education, Inc./Ken Karp, Photographer; Figures 14.10a–b, 14.11: © McGraw-Hill Higher Education, Inc./Ken Karp, Photographer; Page 639: © J.M. Boivin/Gamma Press; Page 640: © McGraw-Hill Higher Education, Inc./Stephen Frisch, Photographer.

Chapter 15

Opener: © McGraw-Hill Higher Education, Inc./Jill Braaten, Photographer; Figure 15.2: © McGraw-Hill Higher Education, Inc./Ken Karp, Photographer; Page 652: © McGraw-Hill Higher Education, Inc./Stephen Frisch, Photographer; Figure 15.10: © Michael Melford/Wheeler Pictures; Figures 15.9 (both), 15.11, Page 685: © McGraw-Hill Higher Education, Inc./Ken Karp, Photographer; Page 695: © Kristen Brochmann/Fundamental Photographs.

Chapter 16

Opener: © Allan Morgan/Peter Arnold; Page 701, Figure 16.1, Page 703: © McGraw-Hill Higher Education, Inc./Ken Karp, Photographer; Page 706: © Professors P.P. Botta and S. Correr/Science Picture Library/Photo Researchers, Inc.; Figure 16.3, Figure 16.8: © McGraw-Hill Higher Education, Inc./Ken Karp, Photographer; Page 718: © CNRI/SPL/Science Source/Photo Researchers, Inc.; Page 722 (both): © McGraw-Hill Higher Education, Inc./Ken Karp, Photographer; Page 724: © Runk/Schoenberger/Grant Heilman Photography; Page 726: © McGraw-Hill Higher Education, Inc./Ken Karp, Photographer; Figures 16.10, 16.11, 16.12a–d: © McGraw-Hill Higher Education, Inc./Ken Karp, Photographer; Page 736 (left): © Jody Dole/Image Bank/Getty Images; Page 736 (right): © Scientific American/A.R. Terepka; Figure 16.13 (all), Page 749: © McGraw-Hill Higher Education, Inc./Stephen Frisch, Photographer; Page 749 (all): © McGraw-Hill Higher Education, Inc./Ken Karp, Photographer.

Chapter 17

Opener: © Corbis/Vol. 188; Figure 17.4: © E.R. Degginger/Color-Pic; Figure 17.5: © NASA; Page 758: © McGraw-Hill Higher Education, Inc./Ken Karp, Photographer; Figure 17.8: National Oceanic and Atmospheric Administration–NOAA; Figure 17.9: © NASA; Page 762: © Roger Ressmeyer/Corbis Images; Figure 17.10: © E.R. Degginger/Color-Pic; Figure 17.20a: © NYC Parks Photo Archive; Figure 17.20b: © Kristen Brochmann/Fundamental Photographs; Figures 17.22, 17.24: © Owen Franken; Page 771: © James A. Sugar/Corbis Images; Figure 17.26: © Stan Ries/Index Stock Imagery; Page 773: © Barth Falkenberg/Stock Boston; Figure 17.29: © McGraw-Hill Higher Education, Inc./Ken Karp, Photographer.

Chapter 18

Opener: © National Lime Association; Page 785: © McGraw-Hill Higher Education, Inc./Charles D. Winters, Photographer;

Index

PORTRAITS

PORTRAITS
5,000 YEARS

JOHN WALKER

HARRY N. ABRAMS, INC.
PUBLISHERS, NEW YORK

CONTENTS

PREFACE

hat is a portrait? Usually it is the representation of an identifiable
individual. But, for example, is a relief or a picture of Christ a
portrait? We do not know what he looked like, yet early representations,
first beardless then bearded, were believed by the devout to represent his
features, and most subsequent representations reflect these models. Usually,
too, the function of a portrait is to show a person as himself, at his most
characteristic. Then, are the many representations of Antinoüs, a humble
Bithynian youth, in the role of one of the gods of the Roman pantheon true
portraits? For the purpose of this book, if a statue or a picture conveys the
sense that a specific person is shown I have considered it a portrait. Many
of the subjects you will find here were not carved or painted from life. A
number died long before their portraits were executed. Whether posing or
shown in action, so long as a man or a woman is portrayed as a recognizable
individual, identifiable or not, I consider his or her likeness a portrait.

I admit that this is an arbitrary approach, but in its generic sense a portrait
is, in the words of the pocket *Oxford Dictionary*, "the likeness of a person or
an animal." I have at least omitted animals! But I have accepted this broad
definition of portraiture as my own, for otherwise much of what our ancestors considered likenesses would have to be excluded. Perhaps the Byzantine emperor Justinian and his empress, Theodora, look quite different on
the walls of S. Vitale than they did in life, but they certainly thought they
were being portrayed by the artist, who added the perhaps equally inaccurate
likenesses of their courtiers on either side of his mosaics (figs. 66, 67). It is
unlikely that anyone posed for the golden statuette shown in figure 69, but
the manikin we see has a face of remarkable individuality and seems to reflect
the features and personality of a specific person. This can be said of many
ancient statues and works of art.

In this book I have endeavored to present a narrative of the history of
Western portraiture from its beginnings in Egypt and Mesopotamia through
the work of contemporary artists in Europe and the United States. Another
volume would be needed to cover adequately portraiture in Asia, Africa,
pre-Columbian America, and the islands of the Pacific, but it may interest
the reader to note the relative quality of Western and Eastern portraiture.
During Egyptian, Mesopotamian, Greek, and Roman times, sculptured and
painted portraits were superior in the West, at least in comparison with
what has been discovered in India, China, and Japan. Between the Early
Christian era and the 13th century, the reverse is true. During this period,
Chinese and Japanese artists created a sophisticated, realistic style, and their
likenesses are far abler than anything done in Europe. These centuries also
produced more interesting portraits in other cultures, especially in those
of the Mayas and the Moche Indians. In the 13th century, there is little to
choose between West and East. But from the Renaissance on, European portraits in numbers, in characterization of sitters, and in psychological penetration far outdistance any work done elsewhere in the world.

What is the test of a great portrait? Is it not empathy, the power of the
artist to enter into the sitter's emotions and then to convey these feelings to
another—to make him also experience empathy? Looking at Verrocchio's
Colleoni (fig. 114), the spectator must feel the impact of an overwhelming
force; or, gazing at a late portrait by Rembrandt, the observer is ineluctably
affected by the profound gravity of the sitter, which creates in him a mood of
solemnity (fig. 182). These are examples of the highest reaches of portraiture.

Queen Nefertiti. *Tell el-Amarna.*
c.1372–1355 B.C. *See figure 12.*

7

ACKNOWLEDGMENTS

An author attempting to write a history of portraiture covering five thousand years must depend on the labors of others. The bibliography I have included indicates my dependence on many scholars. It is invidious, perhaps, to single out particular sources, but I must acknowledge my special debt to a number of people. Roger Hinks was a Keeper of the British Museum whom I have always esteemed. His death has been a great loss to the history of art. *Greek and Roman Portrait Sculpture* helped me through the intricacies of a period I have loved but never especially studied. To his other books mentioned in the bibliography I am also indebted. Similar assistance for the Renaissance chapter, where my studies have been more extensive, has come from the work of a close friend, John Pope-Hennessy. His *The Portraiture in the Renaissance* is a delight and an illumination. I could not have covered the work of the still undervalued but immensely gifted 18th-century British portraitists without David Piper's *The English Face* and without David Mannings's "At the Portrait Painter's."

I frankly admit I know more about painted portraits than I do about sculptured ones; and for sculpture of the postclassical period I turned repeatedly to *A History of European and American Sculpture* written by my old teacher Chandler Post, a work published in 1921 that remains authoritative, whereas most studies in the history of art are shortly outdated.

I was fortunate to enlist the Honorable Mrs. Stephen Hastings, an expert at Christie's, to read over and correct what I had written about Egyptian and Mesopotamian portraiture; and Dr. Susan Walker, Assistant Keeper of Greek and Roman Antiquities at the British Museum, was willing to criticize in the same way my chapters on Greek, Etruscan, and Roman portraits. To both these scholars, my ardent thanks. If there are errors still in these chapters, either of fact or of interpretation, they are mine and in no way the fault of these distinguished ladies.

From the beginning I needed someone to assist me with the appalling amount of research required. For several months I was helped by Nicholas Coulson. He decided, however, that business was more profitable if less attractive than scholarship, and he left me to become a banker. I was most fortunate to find an able successor, James Lambert. For three years he worked with me nearly every day, and I found him indefatigable and wonderfully conscientious. In a close working relationship of the type we developed a sense of humor is vital. James made the preparation of this book a joy from start to finish. It is difficult to express my debt to him.

Lastly, I want to acknowledge the painstaking editorship of Mrs. David Allison. We had previously collaborated on editing the catalogue of the Armand Hammer Collection, and I had come to appreciate her erudition and meticulousness. I was delighted when I was told she would help me with the present book. There is scarcely a page she has not improved, and my gratitude is very great.

It is to these people, and to the books of many others I have read and reread the last several years, that I owe the completion of a task that to the best of my knowledge has never been attempted by anyone else. Now that it is over I understand the reason why!

A dictum we have inherited from Greece is "know thyself," but when commissioning a portrait most human beings require only that the finished image reflect their appearance. The artist's aim is more complex. He strives to obtain a likeness and to have this resemblance reflect the true personality of the sitter, of which he himself may not be aware.

Self-portraits are the artist's endeavor to discover his own character. Though an element of flattery exists in most of them, they are on the whole the artist's search for his own personality. Behind the reflection he sees in the mirror is the spirit informing his every feature, shining through his eyes, curling his lips. Can he catch it, hold it, make it permanently visible? His sitter, too, presents him with an image. If he is a master, every stroke of the brush or cut of the chisel interprets this image, changes it from a facsimile to something new with the distortions of the artist's concept.

The portraitist at his best is looking for the lasting and predominant impression the sitter makes on his mind. This he conveys with a likeness, precise or distorted, yet sufficient for identification. The pre-Assyrian carvers of Mesopotamia admirably balanced the features of their models with a more general appearance. So did the Egyptians. The Greeks, too, sought to harmonize the individual and the ideal. With the Etruscans and the Romans, realism was stressed. In Early Christian and Byzantine times, and in the Middle Ages, stylization increased but much that was specific remained. With the Renaissance, a new and more accurate delineation of the model began and lasted until the advent of Cubism. In the 17th century, certain artists, specifically Velázquez, Hals, and Vermeer, and in the 19th century others like Manet and Degas, carried this search for verisimilitude further and sought to present the true visual effect of the retinal impression, including lighting, amount of detail, and general focus.

Portraits have varied between complete objectivity, as seen, say, in the work of Holbein, and the relative subjectivity brought about by the portraitist's own outlook on life, as we find it in paintings by Rembrandt and Goya. But even the most objective work is affected by the times in which the artist lived, by his relation to his sitter, by his sitter's requirements, and by the technique he employs. These are the elements that make up the history of portraiture.[1]

A likeness is essentially an artist's effort to play the light of his vision on the physiognomy of a sitter, actual or imagined. All portraitists have to work with the same material. Nature has given the human face two eyes, a nose, a mouth. But eyes can be round or almond-shaped, noses snub or aquiline, mouths sensual with thick lips or cruel with thin ones. With the arrangement and representation of these features, the artist must create the individuality that enables us to recognize and differentiate people.

Moreover, there are many more muscles in the human face than there are to be found in that of any other living creature. Consequently, man alone can express emotion through the movement of his eyes, his mouth, and the skin of his forehead. Such emotional reactions on the sitter's part must be taken into consideration by the portraitist.

The infinite variety with which the human face confronts the painter or sculptor can be dealt with in many ways; but except in the case of self-portraits, there must be some give and take between sitter and artist. The patron's taste and requirements vary; so, too, artists have their own preferences, their own ways of seeing. The sitter usually wants considerable objectivity; the artist tends to inject an element of subjectivity. Neither in theory wants a mechanical facsimile; but the model is frequently satisfied with one, and the painter, wearied by his patron's carping about "likeness," sometimes settles for one. Such pictures are not works of art. A good portrait must reflect the artist's predilections, his style.

The sitter should realize that herein lies a dilemma intrinsic to portraiture. Whereas he wants to recognize above all the features he sees in a mirror, the worthwhile painter or sculptor is primarily interested in interpreting these features. Sometimes the two desires coincide. But if one must be sacrificed, the patron should remember that in a short time no one will know whether the likeness is accurate or not; in the long run, only the quality of the portrait matters. Posterity will not care whether the nose is too long or too short, whether the chin is prominent or recessive, whether the eyes are brown or blue. Of course, when the subject is famous, people will continue to be interested in his actual appearance. If the subject was often portrayed, out of the conglomerate of interpretations and images what is relatively true will appear. We have literary descriptions of Alexander the Great, and numerous posthumous portraits. Therefore, we feel, though of course we cannot be certain, that we "know" him better than, say, that other great commander Leonidas, of whom only one assumed likeness exists.

But the sitter clings to his wish for a likeness. He hopes his portrait, which he trusts accurately represents his appearance, will be cherished by his descendants, by the board of his firm, by the trustees of his foundation, or even by his fellow club members. In this regard, a lesson from the Romans might make him more realistic. According to Professor W. H. Flinders Petrie, during the empire many well-to-do Romans had their portraits painted, and these were framed and hung around the atrium of the house, where they gradually suffered damage and became dirty and flyblown. At a later time they were cut down to fit mummy cases. The more expensive mummies were kept in the house as long as any interest in them was felt. Then, when the sitters had passed out of memory and the mummies had become too soiled, they were carted off without ceremony to the cemetery, often as many as a dozen at once, and dumped into a communal pit. All jammed in together, they were left to rot away.

The common sense and practicality of the Romans in disposing of unwanted portraits are exceptional. Few sitters have expected their likenesses to end up as graveyard rubbish. Instead they wish and intend their portraits to endure. While I was director of the National Gallery of Art, the special assistant of the secretary of the treasury called one day. He said that the secretary wanted me urgently and that a Treasury Department car would take me immediately to the Shoreham Hotel. On arrival, I was conducted to a large suite. The sitting room was filled with cigar-smoking businessmen and politicians. They were staring intently at a picture on an easel. This was their first glimpse of the likeness of the secretary, which they had commissioned for his hometown. The leader of the group turned to me and said he and his friends wanted to know what I thought of the portrait; then, before I could speak, presumably wishing a more honest opinion and also to spare the feelings of the artist, who was hovering around, he took me to another room. The picture had rather less artistic merit than a mediocre colored photograph, and I wondered what I could say, for I wanted to be as little derogatory as possible. But my anxiety was unnecessary. The chairman told me why they needed the advice of an expert. There was only one question he and his friends wanted answered, nothing else: "Would the portrait last?" With relief I assured the committee of the portrait's durability. I wanted to add that it would probably outlast the fame of the sitter. Fortunately for me, no inquiry was made about the quality of the painting. Durability was all that mattered.

Permanence has always been of basic importance in portraiture. What patrons have wanted when they commissioned a portrait is something that would last. The physical appearance of human beings is constantly changing; decay is continuous, disappearance ultimate. But in a painted or sculptured likeness, flux can be arrested. That is why portraiture is to be found in all higher civilizations: Chaldean, Assyrian, Egyptian, Chinese, Japanese, Persian, Indian, Greek, Roman, Byzantine, and in the postclassical world on both sides of the Atlantic, from the Middle Ages to the present. It also exists, with a different motivation, in what we consider primitive societies: African, Mexican, Peruvian, North American Indian, Maori, and the aboriginal cultures of the Pacific Islands.

In the higher civilizations, because the intention is to rescue personality from oblivion, an expressionistic portrait from the Secession and the likeness of a well-dressed peer from the Royal Academy, although visually unlike, have much in common. Both are basically perdurable claims on future remembrance. By contrast, a mask from Africa or a portrait skull from the Solomon Islands exists primarily as a channel of supernatural force, a magical aid to human endeavor.

Nothing in the history of portraiture, however, is clear-cut. A desire for the perpetuation of the appearance of the individual and elements of magic appear from time to time in both groups. In Egypt, for example, likenesses of the deceased were also potential homes to which the *ka,* the soul of the departed, might return. In Europe, too, people have believed portraits had miraculous powers. Statues were looked on as capable of prayer. When in 1389 Charles VI of France fell gravely ill, he ordered a wax bust of himself placed beside a statue of Saint Peter of Luxembourg, thus to continue his supplication. There were other religious uses for portraits. They could for instance, be sent on pilgrimages. In 1341 Jeanne de Bretagne and her daughter wishing to benefit by a miracle, shipped silver statues of themselves to the church of St. James of Compostella. Feeling the long journey to Spain would be too risky and too tiring, they were confident Saint James would understand and be satisfied with their surrogate silver representatives.

Portraits have had many functions. They have served to aid or hinder royal matrimonial matches. When Henry VIII of England was thinking of taking a new wife, he dispatched Holbein to paint portraits of contestants for the throne. In Europe dynastic marriages were often arranged on the basis of an exchange of miniatures. Sometimes the royal bridegroom felt cheated by the artist, and considerable contumely might ensue.

At times, portraits have been the symbols of patriotism. In America in the 18th century, for example, Patriots—and also Tories lucky enough to have survived the Revolution—would often hang over the fireplace, if rich, a Gilbert Stuart *Washington,* if poor, a print, usually an engraving after *The Washington Family* by Edward Savage. Such icons conspicuously placed indicated that the owner had supported the winning side. Similarly in Russia, the painting of the Madonna with its vigil lamp has now been generally replaced by an enlarged photograph of Lenin. In this way in different cultures portraits of Washington and Lenin have served as symbols of orthodoxy and of loyalty to the government.

Portraits can be carved or painted. This book deals with both kinds. But the separation between the two was less evident in the past than it is today. In the West until the Renaissance, sculpture was regularly colored. The modern popularity of monochromatic sculpture is largely accidental, a result of the assumptions of early archaeologists. When men in the Renaissance began digging up the treasures of the ancient world, they found them colorless, due to their long burial in the earth, and it did not occur to them that the original paint had been washed away by centuries of rain. Renaissance artists with their deep admiration for Greece and Rome decided that the medieval statues they saw all around them suffered from their coloration. They concluded that sculpture should be for the most part monochromatic. We have inherited their taste, although color is beginning to return in the work of some modern sculptors (fig. 301).

The illustrations in this book allow comparisons between many stylistically different forms of sculptured and painted likenesses. From these reproductions the reader can judge of changing fashions in representing human appearance during fifty centuries, from an Egyptian ivory statuette of the late 4th millennium or early 3d millennium B.C. to the bronze likeness of a contemporary cowboy. During these thousands of years two major incentives for carving or painting portraits recur. In primitive societies portraits are primarily made to induce supernatural power; in higher civilizations they are more often, in Dr. Johnson's words, "a reasonable and natural consequence of affection."

King Tutankhamen and Queen
Ankhensenamen *(detail). Tomb of*
Tutankhamen. c. 1340 B.C. *See figure 14.*

Egyptian portraiture was basically functional, its purpose both religious and magical. During the period of the Old Kingdom (3100–2181 B.C.), and even before, portrait statues of kings were carved specifically for the *serdab*, a small chamber in royal funerary complexes, and also for the courts of the great funerary temples of the Fourth and Fifth dynasties. These effigies not only were a dwelling place for the *ka* and a reassurance of the pharaoh's immortality, should the attempt made to preserve his body fail, but they had a further function: to receive in perpetuity the offerings made for his *ka* by the priests of his funerary cult. Such statues even had a life of their own in the ceremony of the Opening of the Mouth, in which a priest held a ceremonial adze to the lips of each one.

The statues were idealized but they had to be sufficiently individualized to assure recognition by the *ka*. Unimportant details might follow a canon—posture, hands, feet, legs—but the face must have the features of the departed. Consequently, we have a series of relatively accurate portraits of Egyptians executed over a period of 2,600 years.

Among the first individualized portraits carved in Egypt is an ivory figure of a pharaoh (fig. 2). Round-shouldered, he pulls his patterned cape close to his body as he strides forward, his posture skillfully realized. The dating of this tiny figure ranges from 3100 to 2890 B.C., making it approximately contemporary with the statues from the Diyala region of Mesopotamia (figs. 17, 18). Rather unusually, this pharaoh's name is unknown, although statues of the rulers of Egypt are usually identifiable both by inscriptions and through the places where they have been found.

Another very early portrait of a pharaoh is a statue of King Zoser (fig. 1). It shows that the formula of royal portraiture was well established by about 2650 B.C. King Zoser is represented here in a motionless posture, staring straight ahead. Although the features are individualized, there are no indications of the ruler's personality or age. The canon employed was rigid, and it was followed for over a millennium: if the subject is seated, the legs are together, the back upright; if the subject is standing, the left leg is advanced. The arms are held close to the body, and there is often a slab behind the figure against which the deceased is shown sitting or standing.

Zoser was looked upon as both a man and a god. The pharaohs were responsible for order in this world, but they were also man's link between himself and the gods. Alive, the king was identified with Horus, god of light; when deceased, with Osiris, god of the dead. In the royal person, the earthly and the transcendental interpenetrated. The features of Zoser are striking. The stern regularity of the thick lips, the protruding mouth, and the cavernous eyes make his countenance awe-inspiring. Immobile, he sits in judg-

OPPOSITE:

1. King Zoser. Serdab *of the step pyramid at Saqqara. Dynasty III, c. 2650 B.C. Limestone with traces of paint, 55" high. Egyptian Museum, Cairo.*

2. King Wearing the Crown of Upper Egypt. *Temple at Abydos. Dynasty I, 3100–2890 B.C. Ivory, 3 1/4" high. British Museum, London.*

ment, majestically ruling his temporal subjects and prepared to assume cosmic authority.

A statue of this kind was the result of a collaborative effort by a number of craftsmen, as were most Egyptian artifacts. A community of artisans produced specialists to handle certain aspects of the work: to carve the hands, the limbs, the feet, or the face, or to paint the whole. Out of this collaboration it was difficult for an individual artist to emerge, yet in times of artistic decline strong tradition maintained a certain level of quality in the workshop output.

Private portraits were also produced in the royal workshops. During the Old Kingdom, as a token of royal favor, nobles of high rank, who were often related to the king himself, were permitted to use them as tomb statues. Each bears an inscription naming the subject and stating, more or less repeatedly, "A gift that the king gives to Osiris that he may grant bread and beer, flesh and fowl, and every good thing" to the *ka* of the person portrayed. Thus, the portrait was identifiable, not only because it looked like the sitter but because of the inscribed name. Writing the name, "making the name live," is fundamental in Egyptian thought, for while the name lived, the person lived. Each sitter was portrayed as he wished to be—either at the height of his youth and strength; or as a wise man carrying with distinction the dignity

3.   Ka-aper (Sheikh el-Beled). *Saqqara. Dynasty IV, 2613–2494* B.C. *Wood, 43 1/8" high. Egyptian Museum, Cairo.*

4.   Seated Scribe. *Saqqara. Dynasty V, 2494–2345* B.C. *Painted limestone, 23 7/8" high. Louvre, Paris.*

OPPOSITE:
5.   Prince Rahotep and His Wife, Nefert. *Meidum. Dynasty IV, c. 2580* B.C. *Painted limestone, 47 1/4" high. Egyptian Museum, Cairo.*

of age; or as a prosperous figure with the embonpoint of success, like the *Sheikh el-Beled* (fig. 3); or as an alert intellectual, tense and concentrated, holding a papyrus sheet and tremulous with eagerness to transcribe every word, like the figure of a seated scribe in the Louvre (fig. 4).

Among such privileged aristocrats were Prince Rahotep and his wife, Nefert, who lived about 2580 B.C. (fig. 5). Their statues were carved from limestone, then covered with gesso and painted naturalistically. The figures are so lifelike they startle, and one can see similar faces in any street in Egypt today. But the gestures and the poses are conventional, as the position of hands and feet for both sexes was predetermined. Thus, the two young models face eternity in absolute immobility.

In this case, the polychromy has been remarkably preserved, with, as always, the flesh of the man brown, the woman's white. Although all ancient sculpture, as has been said, was colored, the effect is slightly repellent to modern eyes. More attractive are the so-called reserve heads, which have lost their color. They were installed in the tombs (*mastabas*) of private persons in place of a *ka* statue (fig. 6). It was a short-lived fashion of the Old Kingdom but it produced a number of portraits extraordinarily modern in feeling. Each is individualized, yet with the planes of the face simplified and abstracted. Over the lips there usually plays a benign smile.

Dynasties changed during the 3d millennium B.C., but throughout the period of the Old Kingdom, style remained more or less fixed, although there was a tendency toward greater flexibility. We sense this increased freedom in the statue of Ranofer, high priest of Memphis (fig. 7). The static pose, the thick legs with the left one advanced, the body attached to a rectangular slab—all these are traditional elements. But the head, devoid of a protective wig, seems strangely contemporary. The features are noble, with an expression of determination and defiance. The unearthly serenity of earlier portraits has disappeared.

The noblest Egyptian portraits belong to the period of the Old Kingdom. With its end, in 2181 B.C., feudalism, always a disruptive force, began to exact high toll. As local leaders usurped royal prerogatives, poverty increased and the arts declined. This chaotic interval, however, was fortunately short, lasting only about fifty years. After this so-called Intermediate Period, King Mentuhotep, of a Theban princely family, managed to reunite the country and establish a centralized government. With his advent began the Middle Kingdom (2133–1786 B.C.).

The feudalism of the Intermediate Period had altered the nature of pharaonic kingship, a political change that was reflected in portraiture. During the Middle Kingdom the purpose for which royal statues were erected remained the same, but, as the power of a reunited Egypt grew and her dominion extended south into Nubia, it became the custom to erect images of the king not only in his own funerary complex but in every cult temple in the land. This was to reinforce the royal authority—no longer unquestionable—and to make sure that, as high priest of every temple, he was present at the daily ceremonies and could partake in perpetuity of the food offerings made to the statue of the god, gifts which then reverted to local priests, who disposed of them in a more practical fashion.

In the last dynasty of the Middle Kingdom, the Twelfth, royal portraiture, until then idealized, underwent a sudden transformation. For a brief interlude during the reigns of Sesostris III and Amenemhat III, there seems to have

OPPOSITE:

6. "Reserve" Head. *Giza. Dynasty IV, c. 2550 B.C. Limestone, 11 3/4" high. Kunsthistorisches Museum, Vienna.*

7. Ranofer, High Priest of Memphis. *Saqqara. Dynasty V, c. 2560 B.C. Limestone, 73" high. Egyptian Museum, Cairo.*

8. Amenemhat III. *Dynasty XII, 1842–1797 B.C. Obsidian, 4 3/4" high. Calouste Gulbenkian Foundation Museum, Lisbon.*

9. A Nubian Official (?). *Dynasty XII, 1991–1786 B.C. Granite, 5 1/2" high. Calouste Gulbenkian Foundation Museum, Lisbon.*

been a conscious attempt to produce, as it were, an official portrait of the king at different stages of his life—in youth, in full maturity, and in late middle age. In these faces we see both intelligence and restrained power, but the stability and confidence that characterized the rulers of the Old Kingdom have suffered a subtle change. There is a new element, suspicion. Amenemhat I, founder of the dynasty, wrote in his precepts: "Be on thy guard against subordinates . . . approach them not and be not alone. Trust not a brother, know not a friend, and make not for thyself intimates . . . that profiteth nothing. If thou sleepest, guard thine heart, for in the days of adversity a man hath no adherents."[2]

We can see in the portrait head of his descendant Amenemhat III mistrust and foreboding, weariness and disillusionment, joined to uncompromising hauteur and unyielding austerity of character (fig. 8). One feels, looking at his features, the lonely discipline of the absolute ruler who must always be on guard against conspiracy. His disproportionately large ears suggest that he was all-hearing, that he was aware of everything that happened from one end of the country to the other. Yet in the evolution of the human physiognomy as we see it in this book, no more beautiful specimen of the man of intellect is to be found.

Amenemhat's portrait was chiseled from obsidian, a hard and brittle stone. Another head, difficult to date precisely but of about the same time, is of granite, which although less brittle is equally adamantine (fig. 9). Here one sees a different type, the kind of subordinate against whom Amenemhat I warned his descendants to be on guard. It is easy to read into this face, probably of a Nubian official, something of the enmity and resentment of the underling serving an imperious ruler, a monarch like Amenemhat III. The human countenance mirrors an infinite variety of social circumstances and reflects the diversity of character each produces. This is one reason portraiture is so endlessly enthralling.

The complete autocracy of pharaonic kingship required strong rulers. There were stresses to be overcome within Egypt itself and, toward the end of the Middle Kingdom, Asiatics threatened from without. The Nile Delta was lost to the Hyksos, and in Thebes there were only dependent petty kings. The Hyksos contributed nothing to Egyptian art, but they taught the native rulers the use of the horse-drawn chariot, a formidable weapon, which the Egyptians later used against them. Ahmose I, the first ruler of the Eighteenth Dynasty, expelled the invaders and reunited the country. With these victories a period known as the New Kingdom began (1567–1085 B.C.). A policy of expansion followed, under a series of pharaohs who were excellent military leaders and able administrators. These included one woman, Queen Hatshepsut, whose terraced temple remains one of the great sights of Egypt. Along with countless other figures in its colonnade is the portrait of the wife of the ruler of Punt. She is tremendously fat with a swayback and enormous hips. Beside her trots her diminutive and utterly inadequate donkey with a note by the sculptor, "the donkey who carried his wife"—an example of the Egyptian sense of the ridiculous, which we shall meet again.

With Amenhotep II, the policy of expansion ended, and, their boundaries secure, Egyptians became absorbed in outward splendor, in luxury, and in all the delights of this life. The first seeds of decadence had been sown. Egypt was ready for a psychological revolution.

This revolution, entailing a subversion of established religion, of the sublimity of the pharaoh, and of traditional representation in the arts, was brought about by Amenhotep IV (Akhenaten), who reigned from 1379 to 1362 B.C. He rejected the pantheon of Egypt's ancient faith. He worshipped instead a single god, Aten, the round disc of the sun, which he taught was life-giving and life-sustaining. He moved his capital to an uninhabited area on the east bank of the Nile, later known as Tell el-Amarna, where he established his court and erected his temples to the sun. With his wife and children he lived there with a new informality. A true revolutionary, he changed the abstractions of pharaonic art to a novel, vivid realism. We find this most evident in the fragments from the so-called studio of Tuthmosis. These portraits are of actual people, perhaps even their death masks. One of many examples is the portrait of an old woman (fig. 10).

Akhenaten himself has an unforgettable countenance. His face is narrow, his eyes slanting, his nose straight with flaring nostrils. Great intellectual power is evident, but this is accompanied by signs of willfulness and fanaticism. His overall appearance is that of an ascetic; yet the thick lips indicate a strong streak of sensuality. It is a beautiful face, but Akhenaten's body, on the other hand, was distorted, racked by some terrible disease. In his statue in the Cairo museum (fig. 11), his infirmity is evident. He appears deformed, with a swollen abdomen and the large hips of a woman. His effigies show him far removed from the ideal physical specimens inevitably to be found in the portraits of earlier pharaohs. That his artists made no effort to conceal these bodily peculiarities is indicative of the strength of the new realism.

Akhenaten's queen, Nefertiti, by contrast, appears to have been one of the most harmoniously beautiful of women. A bust in Berlin shows the perfection of her features (fig. 12). Her long, slender neck is thrust forward to support the weight of her crown. In grace, refinement, and allure her portrait is unsurpassed. In the same museum there is another statue of the queen, presumably done at a later date. This time she is represented naked. Her features remain beautiful but they have hardened, and her stomach protrudes, as though her body had aged and begun to decay or possibly because she was pregnant. Akhenaten seemingly could not resist revealing, even in his own wife, the cycle of human dissolution or the distortions of pregnancy.

In his tomb there is a relief showing the royal couple with their three children (fig. 13). It is perhaps the first "conversation piece" in art, for the family is shown not quietly posing as in a group portrait, but seemingly engaged in gentle domestic conversation. In no other work of Akhenaten's reign can the radical break with the past be more clearly felt. The silent, almost icy companionship of Rahotep and Nefert (fig. 5) could not be more unlike the charming informality of the pharaoh and his wife playing with their children.

During the 14th century B.C. Egypt still lived on the immense resources of those earlier pharaohs who overran so much of Asia Minor. When it was opened in modern times, the tomb of Tutankhamen, the next pharaoh but one, proved a treasure house beyond belief. The gold-plated mounting from a wooden shrine is an example of the wealth and also of the high degree of craftsmanship among his artists (fig. 14). His portrait and that of his wife are executed in the Amarna style, without idealization, relaxed and informal.

After Tutankhamen's death, internal corruption and the strength of its enemies threatened Egypt with disaster. A great general was needed and he appeared in the person of King Horemheb. Corruption was rooted out, the army was reorganized, and successful campaigns into Syria and Nubia were

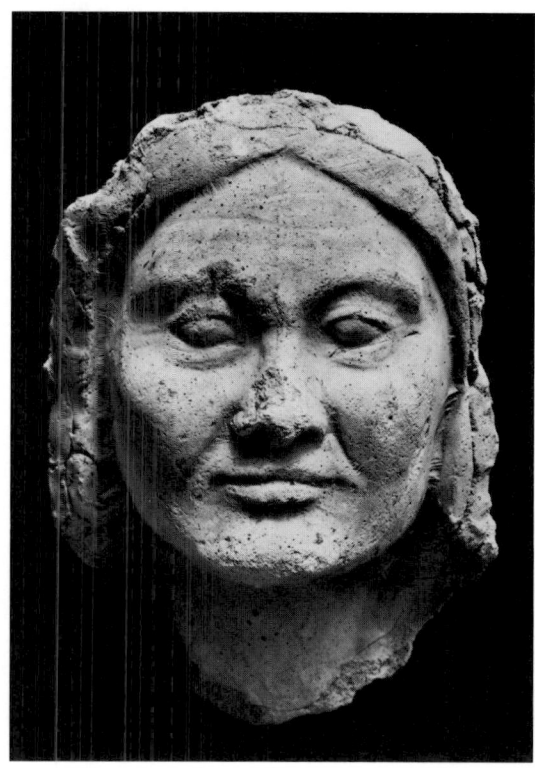

10. An Old Woman. *Tell el-Amarna. Dynasty XVIII, c. 1372–1355* B.C. *Plaster mask, 10 5/8" high. Staatliche Museen, Berlin.*

LEFT:

11. Amenhotep IV (Akhenaten). *Temple of Aten, Karnak. Dynasty XVIII, c. 1360 B.C. Sandstone with traces of color, 157 1/2" high. Egyptian Museum, Cairo.*

OPPOSITE LEFT:

12. Queen Nefertiti. *Tell el-Amarna. Dynasty XVIII, c. 1372–1355 B.C. Painted limestone, 18 7/8" high. Staatliche Museen, Berlin.*

OPPOSITE ABOVE RIGHT:

13. Akhenaten and His Family. *Tell el-Amarna. Dynasty XVIII, c. 1372–1355 B.C. Limestone stele, 12 1/4 × 15 1/8". Staatliche Museen, Berlin.*

OPPOSITE BELOW RIGHT:

14. King Tutankhamen and Queen Ankhesenamen. *Tomb of Tutankhamen. Dynasty XVIII, c. 1340 B.C. Detail of a gold-plated mounting from a wooden shrine. Egyptian Museum, Cairo.*

15. General Horemheb Receiving Foreign Ambassadors. *Saqqara. Dynasty XVIII, c. 1330 B.C. Detail of a limestone relief. Rijksmuseum van Oudheden, Leiden.*

16. Head of a Priest. *Saïte period, 663– 525 B.C. Green schist, 3 5/8" high. Calouste Gulbenkian Foundation Museum, Lisbon.*

launched. Egypt again became a great power. One of the most charming and comic of Egyptian reliefs shows a group of ambassadors of foreign states being received by Horemheb (fig. 15). Again the Egyptian sense of the ridiculous is evident. In their eagerness to get to the throne the ambassadors fall over each other, but even upside down they stretch out their hands in homage. Their clustered profiles form an unintentional group portrait, probably the first in art and certainly one of the funniest ever made.

The Nineteenth and Twentieth dynasties, the Ramessid era, marked a return to tradition. The pharaohs were able to keep the territories recaptured by Horemheb for a time. But troubles were soon to arise. The coastal towns were harassed by the Peoples of the Sea—Tyrenians, Philistines, Achaeans— while the Libyans invaded the Delta. Even a strong ruler like Rameses III was able to stem but not to vanquish the invaders. After his violent death, internal strife and economic difficulties overwhelmed the weakened kingdom. Politically, from the time of Rameses XI at the end of the Twentieth Dynasty until the conquest of Egypt by Alexander the Great in 332 B.C., Egypt declined steadily.

There was, however, a brief renascence between the withdrawal of the Assyrians from the Nile Valley in 664 B.C. and the arrival of the Persians in 525 B.C. This renewal of strength and spirit was brought about by the kings of the city of Saïs. The Saïtes reached one of the summits of realism in sculpture, as figure 16 demonstrates. The subject is a priest, archetype of the sacerdotal bureaucrat who became so important in Egypt. It is interesting to note how different this tight-lipped inquisitor was in character from the exalted and distinguished Amenemhat III (fig. 8) or the Nubian official of the Middle Kingdom (fig. 9). These three heads are a measure of the psychological insight exhibited in Egyptian portraiture during its long history.

The two original centers of Western civilization flourished contemporaneously. One was located along the banks of the Nile and the other between the Tigris and the Euphrates rivers, on a plain generally designated Mesopotamia. It was an area with no natural defense against invaders. The rivers often flooded, sometimes changed their course, and frequently damaged the crops they irrigated. The climate was one of extremes: heat, cold, torrential rains, and thunderstorms. Life in the city states, which rose and fell, although pleasant in times of prosperity, was horrible in times of adversity.

Government was at first theocratic but gradually became monarchical. Religion was always of major importance. Unlike the Egyptians, the Mesopotamians seem to have had little interest in the hereafter, or little confidence in it. Divine assistance was called upon to help in this life, not the next. Ephemeral mortals depended on the gods. They had immense power and strong wills but they were not remote from human beings, who looked at them with love and fear. This closeness between the divine and the human sometimes makes it difficult for archaeologists to tell whether a statue is of a divinity or a mortal. For example, the *Woman Holding a Goblet* (fig. 17) in some recent books has been considered a mother goddess, in others a worshipper, and in still others more specifically the queen of Eshnunna.

Whether of a woman or a goddess, it was carved to be placed in a temple. Its purpose was ritualistic. As in Egypt, portrait statues in Mesopotamia were created for the most part to bring about a symbolic confrontation between a human being and the godhead. The relationship between portrait and divinity is summed up by an Assyrian king who wrote, "I installed my royal statue . . . to appeal for life for myself before the gods in whom I have faith." The suppliant was given individual features to identify him, but the raison d'être of the statue was to aid his supplication, not to immortalize his appearance.

The rise and fall of various Mesopotamian states brought about a diversity of portraiture absent in Egypt where, though dynasties changed, there was a greater political continuity because the pharaoh remained the head of the state. On the other hand, in Mesopotamia new nations conquered those that preceded them and more or less obliterated previous cultures. Also Egyptian portraitists generally observed a prescribed canon, except during the reign of Akhenaten and his immediate successors. And whereas the deification of the pharaoh strongly and continually affected style in the Nile Valley, between the Tigris and the Euphrates, deification of the ruler, which came later than in Egypt, had less effect. For all these reasons, Mesopotamian portraits varied greatly in style and conception—the Diyala figures, the statuettes from Ur, the bronzes from Nineveh, the Gudean statues, and the forbidding reliefs from the palaces of the Assyrian kings. It was a heterogeneous art with no continuing tradition.

Yet in one respect it was homogeneous, and again in this it varied from Egyptian art. It has been said with reason that all Egyptian sculpture in the round is based on a cube. In this sense Mesopotamian statues appear to be

17. Woman Holding a Goblet. *Abu Temple, Eshnunna (Tell Asmar). c. 2700 B.C. Gypsum, shell, limestone, and bitumen, 23 1/4" high. Iraq Museum, Baghdad.*

based instead on a cone or a cylinder. The planes of the body are all subject to this geometric framework. To explain such a basic difference probably requires a Jungian inquiry into the subconscious, beyond the scope of this book.

Most of the portraits from Mesopotamia so far discovered were carved in the round or in low relief; but painted portraits on walls of buildings existed, though it would seem in fewer numbers than in Egypt. As in Egyptian painted portraiture, the subject is shown in profile. The colors are white, black, red, yellow, blue, and brown, painted directly on the thin mud plaster of the wall. But the greatest number of portraits, as far as we can judge, were the work of sculptors, not of painters. Yet the stone from which they were carved was so rare that a single piece was considered a worthy present from one ruler to another. Metal, on the other hand, was used with amazing skill at a very early period, earlier than in Egypt. Few bronzes in antiquity surpass the head of an unknown ruler of Nineveh (fig. 21).

Sumerian portraits are particularly captivating. The earliest, those executed between 4,500 and 5,000 years ago, often seem like cartoons or caricatures of people alive today. The subject of figure 17, for example, whose humanity or divinity archaeologists debate, might have stepped out of the pages of *Vogue*: a supercilious model, complete with sunglasses and wearing a beachcoat over her bathing dress. Since she seems to have held a golden goblet, some scholars believe the statuette was intended to memorialize a ritualistic drinking ceremony unknown to us. Her small hands and naively rendered feet suggest the conventions of a modern sculptress, Marisol. This, too, enhances her contemporary look. Her face with its small lips and haughty expression, her strong, columnar neck, her rounded chin, and her staring eyes lend to the statue an individuality that makes it seem one of the earliest portraits.

Another lady from the Diyala region, of about the same time, has a large nose and enormous eyes (fig. 18). Her personality is irresistible. Although she is supposed to be praying, her slight smile and the wink she seems about to give suggest that though her "words fly up" her "thoughts remain below." Few portraits are more vividly alive.

From the same area are several male busts, likenesses of individuals who look startlingly like urban types one sees constantly. Carved from gypsum or limestone, one resembles a character who might be found at an executive desk in the garment district of New York; another appears to be a retired businessman, an amiable soul such as one might come across at a club listening to a friend telling a story; a third (fig. 19) is the most delightful of all. The sitter is self-satisfaction incarnate! Although he is a priest of Khafaje, he looks more like a fat stockbroker who has just completed a most satisfactory deal. It is astonishing that in the 3d millennium B.C. we should find such telling caricatures of people alive today.

At about the same time that these portraits were being carved, extraordinarily rare and beautiful objects were made, many of them found in the Royal Cemetery at Ur. Judging by these artifacts and the likenesses of their owners, life must have been pleasant. Music and the arts flourished. The statuettes represent friendly, somewhat obese citizens, smiling happily. Typical of these fortunate Sumerians is Ebih-il, superintendent of the temple of Mari (fig. 20). His portrait shows him to have been a corpulent, blue-eyed priest, here half-clad in a tufted skirt, possibly an animal skin. He sits rubbing his

18. Female Worshipper *(detail).*
Khafaje. c. 2600–2500 B.C. *Limestone and shell. Iraq Museum, Baghdad.*

hands with sacerdotal complacency. Doubtless he would have been a jolly companion.

Delightful, too, must have been the singing of Ur-Nina (fig. 22). He or she, for the sex is ambiguous (though a woman is the more likely), was also a dancer and for that reason wears pantaloons. Her strange, twisted smile and her bulging eyes are still hypnotic. Called The Great Singer, she must have enthralled her audiences.

The pleasant Sumerian world, however, was shattered about 2340 B.C. by Sargon of Akkad. The fashionable lady, the cheerful priest, the smiling dancer all vanish. Instead, the stern, ruthless ruler appears. The deification of the king has begun. One of the most majestic examples of portraiture, in spite of its ruined condition, is a bronze head of an Akkadian monarch from ancient Nineveh, dated between 2300 and 2200 B.C. (fig. 21). At some time it was broken and defaced, probably by a conquering enemy, possibly when the empire of Akkad was invaded by the Guti, a barbarous people from the northeast. The inlays of the monarch's eyes were gouged out, the left eye punctured, the lower part of the beard knocked away, and both ears damaged—injuries difficult to explain except as having been purposely inflicted as a symbol of the ruler's overthrow. Yet such was the artistry of the unknown sculptor that the king's effigy, even in its damaged state, remains among the most beautiful artifacts surviving from the remote past. In this battered face, majesty is self-evident, aloof, ironic, disdainful. Such nobility appears in few portraits ancient or modern.

The great promise of Akkadian sculpture was never fulfilled. The grandeur inherent in the bronze head of a king withered away. A century later the likeness of Gudea, Divine Bailiff of Lagash, shows a humbler ruler, who sits on his throne with clasped hands, supplicating his god Ningirsu to pray for his life—a supplication not unanswered since his town, Lagash, survived the doom of most of Mesopotamia (fig. 23). Carved from diorite, an exceptionally hard stone, more than thirty statues from the Gudean period have survived. Many of them bear long inscriptions, and it is significant that they are either petitions similar to the one on the statue of Gudea himself or records of deeds done to glorify the gods. References to victorious wars are scarce, for probably there were few major victories to celebrate. Piety is the keynote of Gudea's dynasty, tranquility the characteristic of his effigies. The "bailiff," as Gudea called himself, refusing for some reason the title of king, is always shown with clasped hands, dressed in a robe that leaves the right shoulder and arm bare. His feet are beautifully carved, his hands superbly articulated. He has high cheekbones, arched eyebrows, and a serene expression. He stares confidently at the spectator. One senses that, though a ruler of limited power, he held autocratic authority in his city state. During his reign of fifteen years, perhaps longer, he made Lagash an unrivalled center of culture. His statues, with their nice relations of volume, their abstractions of form, and their highly polished surfaces, are among the most beautiful examples of purely static sculpture.

During the 18th century B.C., with Hammurabi of Babylon, there was a revival of the majesty of kingship. We have few relics of his reign, but his famous code of laws is engraved on a stele with, at the top, a figure of the monarch confronting a divinity, probably Shamash, Lord of Justice. The god is magisterially instructing the awed and attentive king, whose face is so concealed by his ceremonial beard that it is impossible to discern his features.

19. Sumerian Priest. *Khafaje.*
c. 2500 B.C. Alabaster and inlay, 9″ high.
University Museum, University of
Pennsylvania, Philadelphia.

OPPOSITE:
20. Ebih-il, Superintendent of the
Temple at Mari. *c. 2400* B.C. *Alabaster,*
bitumen, shell, and lapis lazuli, 20 1/2″
high. Louvre, Paris.

RIGHT:
21. Head of an Unknown Ruler.
Nineveh. c. 2300–2200 B.C. *Bronze,*
11 3/4″ high. Iraq Museum, Baghdad.

OVERLEAF LEFT:
22. Ur-Nina, "The Great Singer."
Mari. c. 2400 B.C. *Gypsum, shell, and*
lapis lazuli, 10 1/4″ high. Damascus
Museum, Syria.

OVERLEAF RIGHT:
23. Gudea *(detail). Telloh. c. 2150* B.C.
Diorite. British Museum, London.

24. Hammurabi (?). *Susa. c. 1790–1750 B.C. Diorite, 5 7/8" high. Louvre, Paris.*

OPPOSITE ABOVE:
25. King Idrimi. *Alalakh (Tell Atchana). 16th century B.C. Dolomite and magnesium, inlay, throne of basalt, 41" high. British Museum, London.*

OPPOSITE BELOW:
26. King Ashurnasirpal II at a Ritual Banquet. *Northwest Palace, Nimrud (Kalkhu). 883–859 B.C. Detail of an alabaster relief. British Museum, London.*

There is, however, a head carved from diorite (fig. 24) that may represent Hammurabi toward the end of his life. His face is worn, his cheeks sunken, his features emaciated. But on his lips there is a faint, sardonic smile. The artists working for Hammurabi might have brought a new vitality into an increasingly sterile art, but his dynasty was short-lived. The Kassites, invading from the Kurdish mountains, soon put an end to this nascent Babylonian culture.

After this brief interlude, the decline in artistic ability was resumed. King Idrimi, portrayed in the 16th century B.C., was a ruler with a vapid face and a receding chin, which is only slightly concealed by his beard (fig. 25). The sculptor who carved his portrait was clumsy, and his statue has very little artistic merit. Nevertheless, Idrimi has introduced a novelty in portraiture, an autobiography written all over his effigy, which tells how he was driven by rebels from Aleppo to Emor, the home of his mother, where he was badly received by his brothers and had to flee with his followers to Canaan. There he built ships and sailed back to the land of Mukish, where he became king. Reconciled with his brothers, he then conducted a victorious campaign against the Hittites and returned with sufficient booty to build a palace "worthy of a king." He reigned for thirty years before he had the story of his life engraved on his statue. Looking at his effigy, one can hardly imagine him leading a victorious army. Yet King Idrimi, who seems to stare into space like a half-wit, was, according to his own account, a resolute and successful warrior. Whether true or not, his statue was never defaced. The Akkadian ruler in figure 21, on the other hand, appears to be a formidable person, a born leader; yet the disfigurement of his portrait seems to bear witness to his defeat and overthrow—where or when is unknown. As we shall see repeatedly, the ability of the portraitist affects our idea of the sitter's personality. If he is lucky, the artist he commissions dowers him with a power and a grandeur he may or may not have possessed.

Power and grandeur, however, may be so exaggerated as to destroy all vestiges of personality. The portrait of the 9th-century Assyrian king Ashurnasirpal II seated on his throne at a ritual banquet is an example (fig. 26). The king has been portrayed majestically, but the stylization used to convey his majesty has been carried so far that his individuality has vanished. He has been deified and in the process has become a stereotype. The craftsmanship of the carver is brilliant, but the character of one of the world's great rulers is nonexistent. Here is a monarch who made the kingdom of Assyria a leading power, capable for a time of subduing even Egypt; and yet, although he covered the walls of his palace with scores of pictographs celebrating his victories—all wonderfully rendered and perfectly preserved—one still doesn't know what he really looked like. Assyrian sculpture represents the negation of human portraiture. This was not the fault of the artists but a result of the inhuman and ruthless autocracy of the Assyrian rulers, who wished themselves presented as awe-inspiring tyrants. When their sculptors were carving portraits of animals—horses shot with arrows, a camel falling, a wounded lioness, fleeing gazelles—their observation and skill resulted in moving, as well as technically breathtaking, representations. These animal reliefs are sculpture at its best. Assyrian art never declined from this high level. It reached its peak suddenly, and it ceased abruptly. With its disappearance, after Nineveh fell in 612 B.C., Mesopotamian creativity lapsed for centuries.

Unlike the Egyptians, the Greeks felt no compulsion to individualize their tomb portraits since there was no need for the soul to recognize its former body. It could not return in the Egyptian manner. It was like a breath of air or an insubstantial dream. It existed as a memory of what it had been in life. Thus, Greek funerary art was largely commemorative. The living clasping the hand of the departed, the half-open door leading to the realm of the dead, the unappeased sorrow of those left behind all point to a final separation. Love and companionship were a remembrance, a part of the past. Thus, the grave relief suggested the memory of an ideal person, not the recollection of an individual on whose features are stamped the accidental peculiarities that make for portraiture.

The Greek grave reliefs, which proliferated between the late 5th century and the end of the 4th century B.C., are repetitious; although they show faces of great beauty, these are stereotypes (fig. 27). They are too little individualized to be considered likenesses. The same is true of the *kouroi,* statues of standing youths that were made from the 7th century to the first half of the 5th century B.C., sometimes representing Apollo but more often commemorating mortals—a victorious athlete or a young man who had died before his time. The general posture and structure of the *kouros* figures are derived from Egyptian statues but, although the later *kouroi* achieve an anatomical accuracy beyond the grasp of Egyptian sculptors, they lack the individuality of the Egyptian portraits.

A taboo reinforced this absence of individualization in Hellenic portraiture from 510 to about 390 B.C. With the abolition of the tyranny of the Pisistratids in 510, there was a reaction against what in Communist countries would be called "the cult of personality." Portraits were discouraged or forbidden. For example, in the Athenian marketplace for a long time the only human representations were of Harmodius and Aristogiton, who assassinated the tyrant Hipparchus, and even they were shown as *kouroi*—with only enough of the specific to enable them to be recognized. During the 5th century, the Greeks felt the name inscribed on the base of a statue was of greater importance than the personal features.

Greek statues at the beginning were intended for sanctuaries, tombs, and public places. The Greeks were not like the Romans, who felt it a pious duty to preserve the likenesses of their ancestors. There is nothing in the Hellenic world comparable to the Roman atrium, its cupboards filled with death masks of the progenitors of the owner—a custom that will be described later. Portrait statues were erected either by the state in gratitude for services performed or by individuals to honor a relative or a friend.

Given that they were intended to pay homage to the subject, it is natural that an element of the heroic should appear. Pliny summed up the attitude of the Greek portraitist when he wrote, "In this art, noble men were made to appear still nobler." Consequently, idealization was an inherent part of Hellenic portraiture, and the individual tended to disappear in the type.

A well-known bust of Pericles, who died in 429 B.C., for example, shows a man with a beard who is obviously a warrior (fig. 28). Is he young or middle-aged? It is impossible to say. His face is empty. In it is none of the character

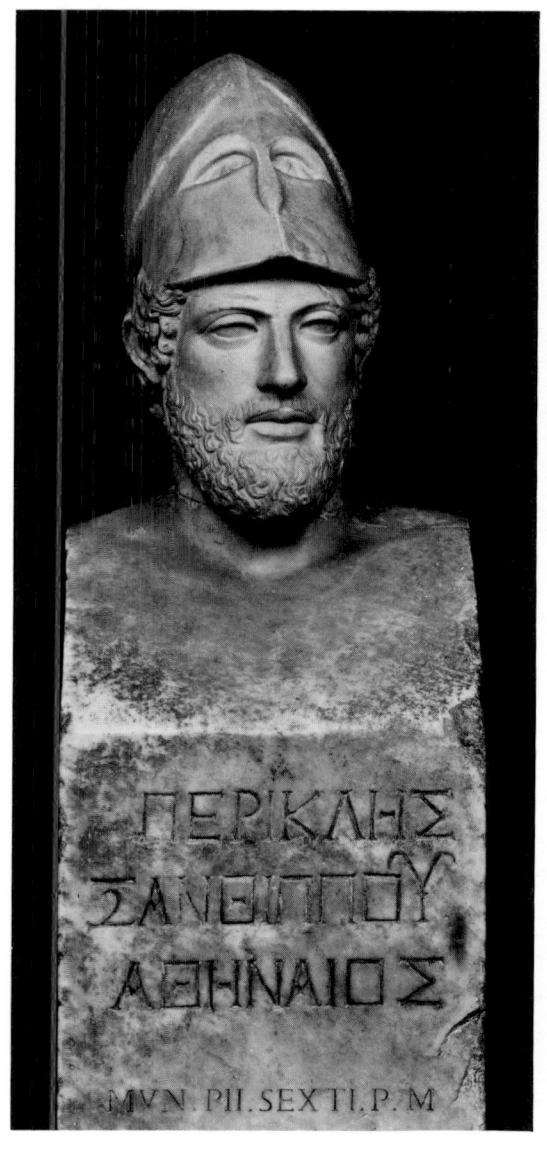

OPPOSITE:

27. Grave Stele of Lysistrate. *c. 400–350 B.C. Pentelic marble, 44 3/4" high. The Metropolitan Museum of Art, New York. Rogers Fund, 1906.*

28. Pericles. *Roman copy of a Greek original of c. 430 B.C. Marble, head 15 1/4" high. Sala delle Muse, Vatican.*

one would expect to find in the face of the leader of the Athenians during the long and fateful years of the Peloponnesian War.

His portrait is typical. During the Golden Age of Greece, the 5th century B.C., likenesses suffer from this tendency to be abstract. There are exceptions. One is a tiny figure adorning the Strangford shield, a reduced copy of the shield of Athena in the Parthenon, a colossal image of the goddess that has vanished. Even in an indifferent copy this manikin in violent action shows such individuality that it is believed to represent Phidias himself, the sculptor of the famous image of the divine protectress of Athens (fig. 29). If so, it is the first known self-portrait in art. And the likelihood that Phidias, the greatest of all Greek sculptors, carved his own likeness is increased by a passage in Plutarch, which says the sculptor was accused of impiety for using the shield of a goddess to immortalize his own features.

Another exception is an amazing 5th-century herm representing Themistocles, found in 1939 at Ostia (fig. 30). His pugnacious face is not a type. It is not idealized. It is the countenance of a tough, sagacious individual, a leader unscrupulous and resolute, one of the greatest geniuses of military history, who defeated the Persian fleet at Salamis. Was Themistocles by some chance portrayed during a moment of realism in 5th-century Greek sculpture? Or was the original of this bust posthumous, as the bust of Pericles certainly was? The question is moot. But if there was a burgeoning realism in the 5th century, collective pressure stifled it.

One reason we know so little about Greek sculptural portraits is that few original examples survive. What we must depend on are Roman copies. Luckily, the Romans, with their deep esteem for the Greeks, commissioned innumerable replicas. But the texture of the Hellenic originals, their nuances of modelling, their subtlety of expression have been lost. Another handicap is that what has survived of Hellenic portrait sculpture consists almost exclusively of the likenesses of famous men. Likenesses of middle-class citizens, such as we find in Roman busts, being of no interest to Roman patrons, were not copied and have disappeared—if they ever existed.

Such subjects would not, in any case, date before the 4th century B.C. It was then that a disparity in Hellenic portraiture began to be resolved. Though the Greeks in the 5th century were perhaps psychologically, probably legally, impelled to generalize and idealize likenesses, they also had an equal desire for truth. They instinctively wanted a veracious record of those peculiarities that differentiate the appearance of human beings, and it was this desire for factual representation that gradually won out. From the 4th century on, portraiture began to be more precise.

There was a deepening sense of individuality, which we find in contemporary philosophy as well as in art. With Plato (c. 427–347 B.C.), the soul took on a new significance and was held to be the vital center of human personality. It had a definite existence, more concrete than in earlier Hellenic belief. Plato argued that there is a personal immortality, that the spiritual side of a human being, which made him a particular entity, continued after his body perished.

A generation earlier, these ideas had influenced the playwrights and increased their interest in problems of the individual. Their characters are carefully delineated and they show a psychological insight not to be equalled until the days of Shakespeare. This intellectual ferment, which appeared as usual first in literature, was bound to influence art. Sculptors of the 4th cen-

29. *After Phidias (born c. 490 B.C.).* Self-Portrait with Raised Battle Axe. *Detail of the Strangford shield (reduced copy of the shield of Athena Parthenos, c. 438 B.C.). Marble. British Museum, London.*

tury began to render emotions stronger than the gentle sorrow of the earlier grave reliefs. Although generalization was not to be discarded at once, it was gradually put aside for a more explicit representation.

Consider, for example, a portrait of Demosthenes, erected about 280 B.C., though the great orator and statesman had died in 322 B.C. It is one of the rare life-size statues to be preserved in a Roman copy (fig. 31). Here, where we see the complete figure, we can appreciate the Greek belief that in portraiture the revelation of personality is not in the face alone but in the entire body. The statue shows in the posture, in the inclination of the head, even in the folds of the garment, the whole human being—a resolute patriot, somber and brooding, whom adversity forced to take his own life. Such psychological penetration would not have been possible before the end of the 4th century or the beginning of the 3d century B.C. Hellenic portraiture has become Hellenistic, bringing transformation from the abstractions of one to the actuality of the other. Demosthenes is not a type but an individual.

An earlier example of this trend toward individualization occurs in one of the most famous monuments of the ancient world, the tomb of Mausolus, satrap of Caria, erected about 350 B.C. at Halicarnassus. The statue in the British Museum long held to be of Mausolus himself (fig. 32) is now thought to be of one of his courtiers, whose colossal effigies were probably set in the intercolumniations of the podium of the tomb. Statues of Mausolus and his wife, Artemisia, may have stood in a chariot on the pyramidal roof, but they have vanished. Regardless of identification, however, the British Museum statue is a portrait. The down-curving moustache, the beard, the long hair falling to the shoulders, the deep-set eyes pensive with a touch of melancholy all combine to form the portrait of an individual.

With the conquests of the Macedonian king Alexander the Great in the second half of the 4th century B.C., a large number of Greek warriors penetrated Asia as far as India. From this contact with the East they brought back new ideas and new forms. Although Hellenic culture proved stronger—the influence flowing in the main from West to East, rather than the reverse—this interfusion had its effect. The Hellenistic age had begun.

Of Alexander himself only unsatisfactory likenesses have been preserved. He is known to have commissioned the painter Apelles, the sculptor Lysippus, and the gem engraver Pyrgoteles to portray him, but their work has vanished. We have literary descriptions of his appearance: his physical beauty, his clean-shaven cheeks, his masses of hair, his melting eyes; but it is tragic that no great portrait remains of a genius whose conquests transformed the world.

Likenesses of Alexander also appear on coins and medallions, but these were done after his death and are unsatisfactory. Hellenistic work of this kind, however, often shows remarkable psychological insight. Working on a small scale and usually limited to representing the face in profile, the artists were able to express an extraordinary range of character: note the truculence—even brutality—apparent in the face of the eunuch Philetaerus of Pergamum (fig. 33), with his small eyes, tight lips, and jutting chin. By contrast, note the friendliness lighting up the face of Antimachus of Bactria (fig. 34), with his humorous look and good-natured smile.

After Alexander the idealization that had characterized work done in the 5th century steadily diminished. With this change, portraiture gradually became the branch of art most in demand, and portrait sculptors were well com-

30. Themistocles. *Ostia. Probably a Roman copy of a Greek original of 465–460 B.C. Marble, head 10 1/4" high. Museo Ostiense, Ostia.*

31. Demosthenes. *Roman copy of a*
Greek original of c. 280 B.C. Marble,
79 1/2″ high, including plinth. Ny
Carlsberg Glyptotek, Copenhagen.

32. Unknown Man *(formerly thought to be Mausolus of Caria). Mausoleum of Halicarnassus. c. 350 B.C. Marble, 118"* high. British Museum, London.

pensated for their likenesses. In the past, as members of the community, they were wage earners; now they began to be paid for individual pieces. Since in Hellenistic and Roman times there was an immense increase in private wealth, portrait sculptors grew rich and, investing their money in property, became members of the landowning class. Overcoming the traditional stigma of manual labor, a few were even accepted in the highest society.

Commissions were abundant. It was as though anyone at the drop of a hat were prepared to put up a statue to someone else. By doing so, patrons both asserted their own personal wealth and indicated a hope for eventual reciprocity, which, if it came about, would provide them with a similar renown. As Demosthenes put it, the honor of a portrait statue was among those things "without which life is not worth living." Such monuments were expensive, costly memorials to egotism: the price for erecting one was the equivalent of ten years' average wages (three thousand drachmas) or roughly eighty thousand dollars today.

Although in Hellenistic portraiture there was a constant trend toward individualization, styles varied. The greatest realism appeared in small-scale bronzes. The statuette in Dumbarton Oaks, Washington, D.C., of an emaciated man (fig. 35), a Roman copy of a Hellenistic work, is an example. The subject's neck, face, and arms are thin, his torso meager, his ribs protruding. He wears but one shoe, and one of his feet seems clubbed. It is difficult to imagine a more graphic portrayal of a man desperately ill, who happens at the same time to be lame. The plethora of Hellenistic statuettes of beggars, hunchbacks, figures with contorted bodies, and old people diseased in various ways makes one acknowledge that realism of this kind is not altogether desirable. In the greatest Hellenistic sculpture, however, the realistic element was kept in balance.

For this reason Hellenistic portraits are superior to Hellenic work that preceded them and to Roman work that followed—a superiority that consists in the sculptor's ability harmoniously to combine idealization and individualization. The Hellenic portraitist overemphasized the first, the Roman portraitist tended too much toward the second. To these generalizations there are many exceptions; but it is in Hellenistic art that we come closest to a perfect equilibrium. Two sculptures in the British Museum illustrate this harmony. In the bronze head of an African (fig. 36) there is idealization, but the portrait is also a recognizable likeness. How skillfully the texture of the moustache, eyebrows, and hair are differentiated without destroying the unity of the overall effect! Here the personality of the model irradiates the whole face.

Equally fine is the head of an Egyptian youth carved from green basalt (fig. 37). The process used to grind the very hard stone resulted in simplified and gradated planes of extraordinary subtlety. Adolescent beauty is perfectly expressed; yet, again, the youth is not a type but an individual. The equal of these two masterpieces of portraiture is difficult to find before the Italian Renaissance. Both heads lack all emotional content—they are, from that point of view, almost too objective.

In the 1st century a gloomy, forbidding expression became common in portrait statuary, especially in those likenesses carved at Athens, when that unlucky city state showed its remarkable genius for backing such losers as Pompey, Brutus, Cassius, and finally Antony. It is something of a relief to see this subjective mood of bleak despair disappear from portraiture after the triumph of Augustus. He chose instead, as the official style of the Principate, an objective and elegant classicism, rigidly formalistic, symbolic of the new order of peace, stability, and centralized government. Under the aegis of Rome, Augustan taste spread throughout the ancient world and left behind innumerable cold but precisely delineated portraits.

36. Male African Head. *Cyrene. Early 3d century* B.C. *Bronze, 11 3/4" high. British Museum, London.*

37. Male Egyptian Head. *Alexandria. c. 100–75* B.C. *Green basalt, 9 × 7 7/8". British Museum, London.*

Etruscan portraiture owes its inspiration to Greek sculpture; however, it developed a character of its own, often harsh and vigorous, occasionally attaining nobility. The art of the Etruscans was to have a strong influence on Roman portraiture of the Republican period.

Everything about the Etruscans, whose language cannot yet be completely deciphered, is mysterious, including their origins. Etruscan cities were well established in western Italy by 800 B.C. These city states reached their maturity about two centuries later, when, through seafaring skill, they began to dominate the western Mediterranean. Allying themselves with the Carthaginians, they won several naval battles against the Greeks. Prosperity followed their successes, and they created loosely federated kingdoms. But decline, first apparent in their ports, soon set in, and gradually their territories withered away. During the 4th century their principal cities succumbed to the Romans, but between 200 and 100 B.C. a number of the inland Etruscan towns—Arezzo, Perugia, and others—revived and in this brief period produced some superb portraits. That was the end, and soon Etruria became a part of Rome and was submerged in the Roman world.

From the period of Etruscan supremacy, the 6th century B.C., only one outstanding portrait group survives, adorning a sarcophagus of a married couple (fig. 39). It is so close to Greek sculpture—the figures having the tight smile we find constantly in Archaic Greek statues—that the artist was in the past believed to be an Ionian Greek working for Etruscan patrons; but more recently the sculptor responsible has been considered a native Etruscan. The couple recline on a couch, and the husband seems to point out to his wife their destination as they apparently float together on their sarcophagus into the next world. They are a touching and charming pair; and, although their features are so abstract that to classify them as portraits is stretching the term considerably, nevertheless the two terra-cotta figures were obviously intended to represent individuals and so deserve inclusion here.

OPPOSITE:

38.   Head of a Man. *Sanctuary of Manganello, Cerveteri. 1st century* B.C. *Painted terra-cotta, 13″ high. Villa Giulia, Rome.*

39.   A Married Couple. *Cerveteri. c. 510–500* B.C. *Terra-cotta sarcophagus lid, 55 1/8 × 78 3/4″. Villa Giulia, Rome.*

The strong Greek influence apparent in this portrait group died away as the Etruscans developed their own idiomatic style. It was marked by a down-to-earth realism, which continued to be the dominant strain in early Roman portraiture. A 4th-century bronze found at Falterona clearly illustrates this naturalism (fig. 40). The subject is a sturdy peasant boy with thick legs and large feet. The beauty of adolescence is entirely lacking. Instead, one sees a country lad, tough and muscular. The portrait has an actuality far greater than any contemporary work done in Greece. Instead of idealization there is a verism, a specific individualization, typically Etruscan.

Characteristically Etruscan too is the head of an old man of the 1st century B.C. (fig. 38). The artist has emphasized the features of a particular individual: his furrowed brow, his crooked nose, his projecting ears, his lips with their suggestion of a sardonic smile.

Occasionally, Etruscan realism approaches caricature. Two terra-cotta portraits of a husband and wife from the end of the 2d century or the beginning of the 1st century B.C. are a study in matrimonial variance (fig. 41). The husband seems a peaceful man joined to a spouse no longer young, whose bitter mouth and spiteful look point to a coming quarrel. The psychological relationship of the pair is effectively stated. This discordant mood, however, seems an odd way to portray the couple on their coffin, as though they intended to fight through all eternity. Who commissioned the portraits is also puzzling. The husband looks as though he were dead, the wife seems still alive. Yet, were she the patron, she would scarcely have had herself portrayed so unattractively. Perhaps the portraits were ordered after both were dead—but the source of the commission will probably always remain a mystery.

More in the spirit of the Renaissance, and most distinguished of all Etruscan funeral monuments, is the lid of a sarcophagus of about the 2d century B.C., found at Tarquinia (fig. 42). On it at full length lies an aged Etruscan. The deceased, a corpulent man, reposes on one arm, seemingly in contemplation. He is relaxed and shows the utmost serenity. There is nobility in his face as he confronts death. This is Etruscan portraiture at its best, realistic in approach but not without powers of generalization and grandeur. No Roman tomb surpasses this sarcophagus in conception and execution.

In Rome the patronage of portraiture came from the aristocracy; the execution largely from Greek artists or artists trained in Greece. A taste for Hellenism goes far back to the early years of the Republic, for the Romans always looked up to Greek culture, although with a guilty conscience. (As early as the 2d century B.C. we find Marcus Porcius Cato inveighing against the admirers of Corinth and Athens.) Statues captured from Greek cities were a regular part of triumphs held by generals who had subjugated Hellas and the Hellenistic East. Toward the end of the Republic there was a mania for collecting—as there is today—and the conquering Roman connoisseurs brought back innumerable masterpieces from Greece and from the Greek colonies. However, they remained uneasy about their treasures. Cicero, denouncing Gaius Verres in 70 B.C., reveals inadvertently a considerable knowledge of Hellenic statues, which he himself collected, but he insists repeatedly that he knows nothing about such objects of luxury. He uses their possession as obvious evidence of villainy and corruption, disregarding at the same time his own knowledge of Greek culture.

40.   Youth. *Falterona. 4th century* B.C. *Bronze, 19 1/2" high. British Museum, London.*

OPPOSITE ABOVE:
41.   A Married Couple. *Volterra. Late 2d century or early 1st century* B.C. *Terracotta sarcophagus lid, 16 1/8" high, 28" wide. Museo Guarnacci, Volterra.*

OPPOSITE BELOW:
42.   An Eminent Etruscan. *Tomb of Partunus, Tarquinia. Probably 2d century* B.C. *Limestone sarcophagus lid, 27 1/8 × 97 5/8 × 25 1/4". Museo Nazionale, Tarquinia.*

43. Unknown Roman. c. 50 B.C. Marble, 13 5/8" high. Staatliche Kunstsammlungen, Skulpturensammlung, Dresden.

Thus, though cosmopolitan Romans admired Greek work, their admiration was somewhat surreptitious. Psychological tensions resulted that affected the development of portraiture, and these complexities can only be understood in relation to Roman history. Chronologically, stylistic changes in Roman sculpture fall into six main periods. The first coincides with the Republican era, those early years when Rome was a republic interspersed with periods of dictatorship. At that time, taste on the whole favored realism. The second period begins in 27 B.C., when Augustus transformed the state into the Principate. Greek artists flocked to Rome. They were imbued with the mixture of idealization and naturalism that characterized Hellenistic art. The harsh, Italic realism the Romans inherited from the Etruscans did not appeal to them. Augustus himself looked to Greece for models for his own portraits, especially to the idealized statues set up in Greek city states. The dynasty he founded, the Julio-Claudian rulers, followed his example and turned to Greek sculptors for their bland imperial portraits. Nero, who reigned from A.D. 54 to 68, was particularly loved by the Greeks, whom he admitted to the Senate and to whom he granted immunity from taxes.

On Nero's death, and the extinction of the "progeny of the Caesars," there ensued a year of internecine struggle. Then the Flavian emperors, Vespasian (r. 69–79) and, in succession, his two sons Titus (r. 79–81) and Domitian (r. 81–96) came to the throne. In their disgust at the excesses of the rulers who followed Augustus, they stressed Republican morality and in art turned back to Italic realism.

During the reigns of Nerva (96–98), Trajan (98–117), Hadrian (117–38), Antoninus Pius (138–61), and Marcus Aurelius (161–80), taste changed again. Once more Greek idealism was in vogue. This fourth shift in fashion continued with Commodus (r. 180–92), the son of Marcus Aurelius, but after his death it gradually came to an end.

A century of war and disorder followed, during which the empire was saved by the stern rule of the soldier-emperors. The first and ablest of these was Septimius Severus (r. 193–211), who founded a short-lived dynasty. This ended with the rule of the virtuous but weak Alexander Severus (r. 222–35), who tried to reinstate the authority of the Senate. A military reaction followed, and the brutal Maximinus Thrax (r. 235–38) came to the throne. Under the soldier-emperors, portraiture swung back to a less idealistic delineation of the features, and a great period of realism took place. This fifth shift in artistic fashion did not endure for long. With Diocletian (r. 285–305) a change began, and when Constantine (r. 306–37) made Christianity the religion of the empire, a distorted, expressionistic style was adopted. Those portrayed have a faraway look as though rapt in the vision of another world. Christianity transformed portraiture, turning it from the realism of the likenesses of the soldier-emperors to the incorporeal images created in the Eastern Empire. In the West, with the exception of the city of Ravenna, the Dark Ages began and portraiture reached a nadir.

Within this historical framework the nature of Roman portraiture becomes clearer. Before discussing it in detail, however, four general observations must be made.

First: Roman portraiture was tied in with the commemoration of ancestors. It was considered pious to preserve in the atrium of a house a collection of family likenesses: death masks, busts, and statues. In the Republican period it was customary immediately after death to cover the face of the deceased with soft wax and to make a mold from the resulting impression. Additional casts could then be made and distributed to other members of the family. For Romans the portrait also had a sociological role. It was a proof of aristocracy and evidence that the descendants of the deceased were of senatorial rank. Some of these death masks have survived, cast in terra-cotta or bronze, others copied in marble. Much of the harsh realism of early Roman sculpture is due to these wax facsimiles of the dead. But they were not always copied exactly; instead, they were used by the portraitist as a photograph might assist an artist today.

Second: Roman busts and statues, like all pre-Renaissance sculpture, were regularly painted.

Third: Most of the illustrations in this chapter are of marbles, but actually bronze portraits were as common as marble ones—and more fashionable. During the Middle Ages, metal was greatly valued, and bronze busts and statues were melted down, whereas carved stone was useful only in lime kilns. Consequently, marbles have survived in their myriads and original bronzes are rare. Nevertheless, the most favored artists were metalworkers, and their style influenced those who carved.

Fourth: Roman portrait busts increased in size during the first two centuries A.D. During the Republic the bust was shown only as far as the bottom of the neck. During the Julio-Claudian period it was increased to take in part of the upper chest. In the Flavian period still more was shown, and the bust spread almost to the shoulders and downward eventually as far as the nipples. In the 2d century, growth continued until the figure became virtually a half-length, resembling many modern busts. Then it began to shrink back to Julio-Claudian proportions.

These four generalizations out of the way, we can now consider in more detail the stylistic discordance already mentioned that affected Roman taste for almost two centuries, from Augustus to the soldier-emperors. It was the inconsonance between Italic realism—a style harsh, veracious, deeply rooted in native tradition—and Hellenism—a style idealistic, subtle, urbane, and cosmopolitan. For the most part, portraiture was an amalgam of both, a commingling of realism and idealistic glorification, until with the soldier-emperors realism obliterated idealism. The differences between the two styles emerge clearly from a comparison of two busts—one a typical Roman portrait, the other a pure Hellenistic likeness, both of Romans, and executed at about the same time, 50 B.C. (figs. 43, 44). The native Roman bust has a dry, uncompromising realism; the Hellenistic sculpture has instead a fluidity of form, a subtlety of modelling, and a smooth, marmoreal texture. The subject of figure 43 is obviously a man of affairs, whose wrinkled face suggests a grim, obdurate personality. The other is seemingly a sophisticated intellectual, whose refined and delicate features appear through a thin envelope of skin. In the face of one is reflected the determination and power of Rome; in the other, the charm and culture of Greece.

The Greek artists who swarmed to Rome under Augustus were confronted with the discordance described above. Portraits were ordered from them and these likenesses had to take their place beside the wax images, the death masks piously treasured by the family. They had to achieve a close resemblance and at the same time maintain a harmonious relationship between the individual parts of the face. Their artistic training opposed the realism of death masks. Yet these masks were offered as a standard of likeness. Eventually, the Greeks

44. Unknown Roman. *Cyprus. c. 50–30* B.C. *Parian marble, 12 1/4" high. British Museum, London.*

hit on a compromise, one that satisfied themselves and their aristocratic patrons. They rendered a facsimile of the sitter but they gave the portrait a pure,
terse elegance, resulting in the cold distinction that characterizes much of
Augustan sculpture.

There were, however, many patrician families who preferred the realistic
style of the Republic. It was connected in their minds with the stricter morality of the earlier period and therefore possessed in itself a certain virtue. They
knew that under Augustus the austerity and simplicity of Republican life were
vanishing, that wealth was rapidly increasing, and that new people who were
not of the aristocracy were in a position to commission portraits. Even slaves
when freed were able to order likenesses for their tombs, though they were
not permitted to include portraits of their ancestors. This privilege continued
to be reserved for the aristocracy.

Slaves were often set up in business by their patrons, who became secret
partners at great profit to themselves. These newly created freemen occasion-

ally made large fortunes, and sometimes on their graves, along with their portraits, one finds carved symbols of their trade. The style of sculpture they invariably chose was the traditional Italic realism rather than the Hellenic grace
and refinement popular at court.

The taste of Augustus and the circle around him for Grecian distinction and
ennoblement is clearly epitomized in one great monument, the *Ara Pacis* (Altar
of Peace), a group portrait in marble (fig. 45). A national portrait gallery in
itself, this monument to Augustus was begun in 13 B.C. and consecrated in 9
B.C. The imperial household and the Roman nobility are shown accompanying
the ruler as he prepares to make his first sacrifice at the Altar of Peace. The two
processions on either side of the monument are made up of priests, dignified
statesmen, young men, beautiful women, and well-mannered children. They
walk behind the emperor or come forward to welcome him. These distinguished Romans have a nobility of deportment and at the same time a courteous informality that is imaginatively conveyed. The Augustan sculptors have

45. Augustus and the Imperial Family
in Procession. *Detail of the south side of
the* Ara Pacis. *Consecrated* 9 B.C. *Marble.
Rome.*

achieved an idealization of form, yet at the same time created resemblances so accurate that many of the figures have been identified. Here are portrayed the people who conquered the world and together are governing it. Their likenesses indicate their consciousness of high worth.

Problems of group portraits—the relationship of the individuals to each other and to the spectator—are brilliantly solved. These impressive personages seem to have a unity new in art. This is accomplished in part by the direction of their vision. The artists of the *Ara Pacis* realized that eyes focus attention. For the first time, as Alois Riegl has noted, the direction of heads and eyes diverge. Few figures gaze straight ahead into the distance. Instead, the participants in the procession look at each other. This innovation, which seems so simple, revolutionized the composition of portraits, especially where a number of people are portrayed in a processional frieze. The *Ara Pacis* is the supreme example of a certain type of Roman portraiture, a portraiture cool, elegant, and of immense dignity. The objectivity so marked in Augustan sculpture was to change, as we shall see, into the subjectivity characteristic of the 3d and 4th centuries A.D. A postclassical analogy might be the change from the style of Raphael to the style of Rembrandt—from the objectivity of one to the subjectivity of the other.

The coolness of the Augustan style was shortly to become frigid. Not only are the portraits of the Julio-Claudian dynasty glacial, they are often mechanical and empty. The so-called *Clytie* in the British Museum, the subject of which has been provisionally identified as Mark Antony's daughter, thus placing her in the Augustan period, foretells a decline in taste. The young lady, rising from the calyx of a flower, suggests Victorian art—or, worse still, Italian cemeteries. Tastelessness also appears in statues made of various marbles—basalt and porphyry in particular—an innovation introduced from Egypt at about this time. The effect of these polychrome pieces, in spite of their richness of appearance, is not without a touch of vulgarity.

It is a relief to turn from the dull, conventional Julio-Claudian sculpture to the portraits of the Flavian emperors. Vespasian, the founder of the dynasty, was a soldier (fig. 46). He despised the decadence of the courtiers who had surrounded his predecessor, Nero. Adulation of Greece found no favor with him. He wished to revive a colloquial, Italic style, and in this he was so successful that portraits done in his reign have been confused with early Republican work. His sculptors, however, possessed a fluency and ease, a feeling for texture and atmosphere, and a self-conscious calculation of effect lacking in earlier Roman portraiture. The precision and linear quality of Augustan and Julio-Claudian statues have given way to a new pictorial technique, with soft transitional planes and rounder modelling.

Flavian naturalism is still compelling, even though statues have lost their original color. With the hair tinted brown or gold and the shiny white marble of the skin covered with translucent washes, these statues must have been extraordinarily lifelike. Whereas in the past, eyes in marble statues or busts had been painted on blank surfaces, Flavian sculptors experimented with incisions to suggest eyeballs, although eyes were not commonly incised until the time of Hadrian. They also treated eyebrows plastically, raising them in relief. These refinements of carving were, of course, learned from portraits in bronze, terra-cotta, and precious stones, where they appeared much earlier.

In Flavian times, women were particularly sensible of their appearance. At court, coiffures became extravagant, ranging from wigs that look like coral

(fig. 47) to turbans of hair with rows of curls that suggest snails. Later, Julia Domna, an economical lady, the wife of Septimius Severus, whom she married in 187, introduced into sculpture hair made of separate and detachable pieces of marble that could be altered when fashion changed.

Roman sculptors, too, were practical. For example, they would carve the figure of a woman and leave slots into which her portrait head could later be fitted (fig. 48). Then, when commissioned to do a likeness, they would portray the lady's features and attach the head to the body, which presumably would first have been shown to the patroness to be sure she found the pose suitable. Sometimes the body—as in figure 48—might be of Pentelic marble and the head of Parian marble; but when the whole was painted no differences were perceptible. A further advantage to the detachable head was that the same statue could be used again. If a husband divorced his wife, or if his wife died and he married again, his second spouse's portrait could be attached to the sculpture of his first wife's body—a somewhat depressing thought for number one!

The economical use of marble was vital. The quarries were often far from the ultimate location of the portrait. Figure 48, for instance, was assembled and displayed in Cyrene, in North Africa, whereas the marbles came from various localities in Greece. Transportation was a serious difficulty and, whenever feasible, both male and female statues were reused. The marble trade in various parts of the empire was an enormous enterprise; but in spite of the almost incredible productivity of Roman quarries—an important factor in the economy of the empire—marble for statues remained expensive and not over-plentiful.

Painted portraits were another matter. The extreme paucity of those that have survived and the excellence of their quality are tantalizing. What we have we owe largely to a catastrophe, the eruption of Vesuvius in A.D. 79. The volcano's lava preserved a number of paintings in Pompeii, Herculaneum, and Stabiae. These include the splendid decoration of the walls of one room in a house in Pompeii known as the Villa of the Mysteries. A lady, presumably the owner of the villa, had herself portrayed observing the initiation of a girl into the orgiastic Bacchic cult (fig. 49). She seems lost in meditation, speculating perhaps on the new mystical religious ceremony being performed in her house. The likeness is idealized, but it is undoubtedly the portrait of an individual.

Portraits were also done in mosaic (fig. 53). Using very small tesserae, the artist has modelled the face with highlights and nuances of shadow, a considerable achievement in this difficult technique. The sitter, like the lady from the Villa of the Mysteries, seems absorbed in her own thoughts. It would seem that Pompeian portraitists liked to give an expression of contemplation to their models. A third portrait (fig. 54) shows a pensive young girl holding a stylus in one hand and writing tablets in the other. She seems preoccupied and puzzled. There is a momentary hesitation; her thoughts remain elusive. The Pompeian painter has caught an instantaneous gesture, an unconscious pose, as skillfully as any modern impressionist.

There are other portraits from the lava-encrusted cities, the most famous of which is known as *The Baker and His Wife,* since the house where it was discovered was next to a shop selling bread (fig. 55). The man has the coarse features of a peasant and the woman the sharp look of a shopkeeper. The fact that he holds a scroll and she a writing tablet does not necessarily mean that they could read and write. Such symbols of culture were popular in portraits

of the middle class. More recent scholars, however, identify the man as a municipal magistrate. This, they think, explains more convincingly the scroll.

These few pictures give a tantalizing glimpse of the work of Roman portrait painters. It is evident that they were capable of vivid, colloquial likenesses, psychologically penetrating. It is frustrating that so little has been preserved. But luckily in Egypt the Roman immigrants, including numerous soldiers rewarded for their bravery with grants of land, as well as prosperous Greeks and Levantines, adopted local customs and had their bodies mummified, with likenesses of themselves inserted. In the dry Egyptian climate a large number of the portraits have survived, some remarkably well preserved.

The excavations of W. M. Flinders Petrie at the Roman cemetery of Hawara in the Faiyum district in Lower Egypt have yielded many of the finest of these portraits. Since the most numerous finds have come from this district, the paintings are usually referred to as Faiyum portraits, although they have been discovered at a number of sites, from Saqqara to Aswan. The earliest date from the Julio-Claudian period, a greater number from the Flavian period and from the 2d and 3d centuries A.D., and about a quarter of the total from the 4th century A.D. With the spread of Christianity, mummification was gradually abandoned. After the 4th century the deceased was buried in his everyday clothes, and the practice of including a likeness in the grave was discontinued.

Flinders Petrie thinks that the portraits were done from life and that for the most part they were originally painted on square pieces of wood, then framed and hung on the wall like modern portraits. His theory is that when the sitter died the picture was taken down and shaped to correspond with the upper section of the deceased's mummy. It was then wrapped in mummy cloth and buried with the embalmed body. Some modern scholars do not agree with Flinders Petrie and believe the portraits to be idealized likenesses; but their realism in many cases supports a belief that some, at least, were painted from life.

The medium generally used was encaustic, or wax emulsion, on either gesso-covered wood or, occasionally, on canvas, though tempera was also employed. On this surface the outline of the sitter was drawn in a thin black line. A gray background was brushed on, up to the edge of the outline. Next the drapery was added in liquid color and with a moderately full brush. Finally the flesh was modelled with rough gradations of shadow. Sometimes the name of the person portrayed has been preserved. The subject of figure 50 is Hermione, the *grammatike,* or teacher of the classics. Although she has something of the pedagogue in her features, she is at the same time the essence of femininity.

Dating these paintings is difficult. Efforts have been made to place them by the jewelry worn and by the coiffures of the women. But in a provincial area like the Faiyum, styles may have persisted long after they had been abandoned in the capital. Men's fashions, however, were more likely to be up to date, for they were based on likenesses of the emperor, which could be seen on coins. Beards, for example, became stylish during Hadrian's reign, close-cropped hair with Alexander Severus. Using these tests, inexact as they are, Flinders Petrie concludes that the best portraits are Flavian and that there was a gradual decline in quality during the Hadrianic, Antonine, Aurelian, and later periods. This is borne out by the modelling of the faces. The early portraits have rough but nevertheless gradual transitions of tone from light to dark. These suggest volume. The late portraits use streaks of black with no modulations of shadow,

a kind of pictographic statement in place of modelling (fig. 51). This is to be expected, for until recently, in the rendering of pictorial form in painting, there seems to be an invariable cycle, a gradual change from a suggestion of relief achieved by gradations of shadow, to a representation limited to line and flat tone, and then back once more to the suggestion of a third dimension. The use of streaks of black in place of shading is a form of symbolic modelling, which is an intermediate step in this stylistic devolution. The late Faiyum portraits are part way to the flatness of medieval painting, which in turn evolves into the representation of relief we find in Giotto. Thus, the transformation from three-dimensional painted portraiture to the beginning of two-dimensional painted portraiture took place in Egypt in just slightly more than three centuries. It can be clearly seen in a comparison between figures 50 and 51.

To return to sculpture, the artists of the Trajanic period continued in much the same style as the artists of the Flavian period. Their portraits, however, are somewhat drier. One feature that appears now and in most portraits hereafter is worth noting. Because artists expected their work to be seen from a single viewpoint—the spectator looking up from below at the bust on its high pedestal—they carved and drilled elaborately the locks just above the forehead, treating the hair covering the rest of the skull, which was less visible, in a summary fashion. This is particularly noticeable toward A.D. 150, when the vogue was for men to have masses of curls.

With Hadrian we find a strong Hellenistic influence and a passionate interest

in classical Greece. In a statue in the British Museum found in Cyrene, the emperor himself wears Greek dress (fig. 52). Perhaps it was this love of Greece that caused Hadrian to grow a beard and thus to resemble bearded Greek intellectuals, philosophers, orators, and rhetoricians. Greek, too, is the most important contribution of Hadrianic sculpture: the creation of a sultry type of beauty based on the features of a Bithynian youth named Antinoüs, with whom the emperor fell passionately in love (fig. 56). This mysterious adolescent, who drowned in the Nile, became, at Hadrian's instigation, a cult figure worshipped throughout the empire in the guise of various gods—Dionysus, Vertumnus, Apollo, Osiris, and Serapis.

Judging by Hadrian's tastes, ladies at his court must have suffered a certain neglect. Nevertheless, many wanted to look like his empress, Sabina, whether-

or not she was cherished by her husband. The lady from Cyrene with a detachable head (fig. 48) has had her hair arranged and herself arrayed to appear as much as possible like the empress. Fashions were as tyrannical in the 2d century as they are today.

Toward 140, portraits of women returned to an earlier simplicity. Men of this period, by contrast, have a mass of curly hair. Originally, this was carved with a chisel, but later drills were employed. The drill, utilized at first only for deeply recessed parts of the hair, came gradually to be used for its own sake. Purely decorative hollows in the curls, for instance, were drilled without regard to texture or growth. This is particularly noticeable in the locks that the viewer would focus on, the ones nearest the forehead (fig. 57).[3]

One work of the Antonine period (138–92) was destined to have a profound effect on Renaissance portrait sculpture: the equestrian statue of Marcus Aurelius (fig. 58), whose influence can be seen in Donatello's *Gattamelata* (fig. 113) and Verrocchio's *Colleoni* (fig. 114). The combination of men and horses has had a long artistic history. The mounted rider appears frequently in Hellenic and Hellenistic sculpture; the Parthenon frieze contains the most beautiful examples. Yet from the ancient world, until a recent discovery, the only well-preserved, freestanding, monumental statue of a horseman is that of the philosopher-emperor, Marcus Aurelius. It owes its preservation to the fact that Christians believed it represented Constantine. So treasured was this example of Roman portrait statuary that in 1538, when it was moved from S. Giovanni in Laterano to the Campidoglio in Rome, Michelangelo was commissioned to design its pedestal.

Philosopher-rulers, even of the ability of Marcus Aurelius, do not often beget philosophical offspring. His son Commodus ranks among the worst of the Roman emperors. But Commodus was fortunate in his portraitist. His bust found in 1874 is among the most fascinating examples of Roman portraiture (fig. 59). The emperor is represented as Hercules, his favorite among the gods. A lion skin covers his head; he holds a club in one hand and the apples of Hesperides in the other. Technically as well as psychologically, the bust is exceptional. Commodus is shown as a beautiful animal. His strong and superbly rendered muscles ripple under a thin covering of skin, calling to mind that he fought often as a gladiator. His hair is chiselled and drilled so that there is an alternation of highlights and deep shadows, which contrast with the ivory smoothness of the flesh. His eyes are spellbinding in their suggestiveness. To the iris are added two dots, indicating the points of reflected light. Thus, the direction of the glance is shown by the position of the pupil, and this gives the countenance a new animation.

Following the death of Commodus there was a struggle for the throne, the winner being the able Septimius Severus. He was followed by Caracalla, who was worse and even more degenerate than Commodus. He started by murdering his brother in his mother's arms and ended by killing thousands of Roman citizens in various parts of his empire. In his bust in the Museo Nazionale in Naples he looks powerful and vigorous, but his face indicates exceptional brutality (fig. 60). The coarse features, the scowling glance, the suggested massiveness of the body, make his portrait one of the most striking, if terrifying, to survive from the ancient world.

Caracalla was murdered by the prefect of the Praetorian Guard, Macrinus (r. 217–18), and the throne was held successively by three emperors, Macrinus, Elagabalus, and Alexander Severus, who together reigned for no more

OPPOSITE:

58. Marcus Aurelius. c. A.D. 165. Gilt bronze, over lifesize. Piazza di Campidoglio, Rome.

59. Commodus As Hercules. c. A.D. 180–92. Marble, 46 1/2" high. Palazzo dei Conservatori, Rome.

ABOVE:
60. Caracalla. *c.* A.D. *215. Marble,*
20 1/8" high. Museo Nazionale, Naples.

RIGHT:
61. Decius. A.D. *249–51. Marble, head*
13" high. Museo Capitolino, Rome.

than eighteen years. These uneasy soldier-emperors who followed one another so quickly have expressions that seem wary and neurotic. The face of Decius (r. 249–51), for example, appears frozen in anxiety (fig. 61). And well it might have been, for while fighting the Goths he led his army into a morass, where his poor generalship caused his legions to be massacred—one of many defeats the Romans at this time suffered from the barbarians.

The intensity of this final outburst of Roman realism requires some explanation. Soldiers rising from the ranks to occupy the imperial throne lacked the sophistication of Nerva, Trajan, Hadrian, and the Antonine rulers and despised the elegance of the age of Augustus. They wanted their rough features to be shown accurately, and their furrowed countenances to reflect their innate mistrust. In Florence in the 15th century, men also rose from humble origins to positions of power and they, too, wished to be portrayed truthfully. Perhaps that is why these busts of late Roman emperors call to mind Donatello. It is no mean compliment to say that Roman artists anticipate and challenge one of the greatest of all Florentine portrait sculptors. The resemblance between the work of the 3d century and that of the 15th is astonishing.

As the barbarians swept across the Roman frontiers a confused and disordered period began. During most of the 3d century the deterioration of the empire continued. The social structure was in chaos, the economy bankrupt, and the enemy—the Alamanni, the Franks, the Goths, and the Persians—at close grips. The transience of human life was all too apparent. The experience of anarchy led to a search for the immutable and numinous, for a faith that would transcend flux and violence. As Ranuccio Bianchi-Bandinelli has written, "The spread of Oriental cults based on 'mysteries' and the concept of *catharsis,* regeneration in a better life, produced an even greater swing away from reality toward the irrational, with particular emphasis on mysticism and magic."4

62. Eutropius. *Ephesus. c.* A.D. *450–500. Marble. 12 5/8" high. Kunsthistorisches Museum, Vienna.*

Portraits changed. From the end of the 3d century, sitters have an otherworldly look. In the deep lines of anxiety that furrow the face, there is anguish, inner torment, and ineffable melancholy. Eyes ceased to glance to the side as they did with the distrustful soldier-emperors, most of whom were destined to rule so briefly; or to look upward as we see them in the portraits of Gallienus (r. 253–68), as though the emperor were imploring heaven for assistance to remain on the throne. Instead, those portrayed gaze fervently ahead. Their sight seems focused on what Saint Augustine later called the City of God, where barbarians were not forever at the gate.

During these dark days of the Roman Empire, artists sacrificed verisimilitude to gain expressiveness. The face no longer has the proportions of classical art. It is elongated, gaunt, attenuated. The corners of the mouth are turned down. The expression is bitter. The eyes are excessively large, staring, almost hypnotic. All these changes and distortions are evident in a head found at Ephesus dating from the second half of the 5th century (fig. 62). The face of this unknown man with sunken cheeks is disproportionately long and cadaverous. The eyes, eyebrows, and eyelids are emphasized, with all the lines converging and the eyeballs riveted on some distant vision. This spiritualization of the portrait has carried artists far from the inspiration of Hellenism. Physical beauty has disappeared from portraiture. Instead, questioning eyes dominate the face. These staring eyes seem to see something other than the pillage and death all around them. Donatello and the Renaissance are far away; the great Romanesque cathedrals are near at hand.

CHAPTER FIVE

250-1400: EARLY CHRISTIAN AND MEDIEVAL EUROPE

Frédéric van der Meer in his enlightening book on Early Christian art has pointed out that "the unique feature of the Christian portrait is the expression of the eyes. The new man, illuminated by faith and born again by the Spirit, is a man of the inner life." This "inner life" was so totally absorbing that in their portraits these Christian converts seem unaware of this world. Whether we see their likenesses in marble, ivory, or mosaic, their gaze is fixed on eternity. Looking straight out at the viewer, they seem to wish to make him cognizant of a soul, which is the true self, and of the insignificance of the body that clothes it. The portrait might bear only a vague relation to the physiognomy of the model but it represented, through those staring eyes, his spirit, his real personality. To express this was the goal of Christian portraiture.

Nevertheless, the early Christians, proud of the historical nature of their revelation, wanted to give their holy men actuality, and this they felt could be accomplished by creating individual likenesses. That authentic portraits, carved or painted, were ever available as models seems quite improbable. We must imagine that the artists were guided by verbal descriptions, but once a type had been established it did not change any more than it would have if the subject had first been painted from life. Thus, Peter has always a round face with a gray beard and thick gray hair; Paul has a furrowed face with piercing eyes, a bald forehead, and a dark beard; Andrew has gray tufts of hair; John is clean-shaven, youthful, with large eyes. From the beginning the Christians looked on these holy representations as true, not symbolic, portraits. Therefore, in accordance with the broad definition I have given to portraiture, these sacred images can be classified as portraits. The resemblances to specific individuals who lived in the early days of the Church may be fanciful; the probably are, but we cannot be certain.

Christ alone appears to have undergone a transformation. In the earliest statues and sarcophagi he is shown as a beardless youth—generally teaching, or carrying a shepherd's crook, or working miracles (fig. 63). Later, in the East, he was shown as a more mature, bearded man, his hair parted in the middle and falling to his shoulders. Again, verbal descriptions of our Lord as he appeared at different periods of his life may explain this anomaly. All this is shrouded in mystery. In any event, the bearded image was eventually adopted in the West and persists to our day.[5]

Among the earliest Christian portraits of private individuals is a small piece of glass, dating probably from the 3d century, with figures painted in gold leaf (fig. 64). To grasp the change from classical to Christian portraiture, compare these likenesses of a mother, her son, and her daughter with the Pompeian painting of a baker and his wife (fig. 55). In both, the people portrayed stare at the spectator. But the man and woman in the fragment from Pompeii seem to be calculating, analyzing the viewer: Will he pay his bill, is he a good risk, will

63. Christ Giving the Law to Saint Peter and Saint Paul. c. 359. Detail of the sarcophagus of Junius Bassus. Marble. Vatican Grottoes.

64. The Family of Vunnerius Keramus. 3d-century miniature set in a 7th-century cross. Gold and glass, 1 7/8" diam. Museo Civico Cristiano, Brescia.

he be a steady customer? The mother and her children in figure 64 are gazing into the distance, their eyes fixed on some eternal vision, some revelation that affords confidence in future happiness. The baker and his wife are concerned with mundane affairs; the family trio are absorbed in thoughts of a transcendent world. There is an immense disparity here. It is the change from paganism to Christianity.

The beauty and simplicity of Early Christian faith was transitory. When in 313 the emperor Constantine made Christianity the established religion of the empire and his capital Byzantium, change inevitably occurred. Church and State gradually merged. The emperor was the source of law and the arbiter between theologians. His authority was absolute. We feel this absolutism in Constantine's colossal portrait head (fig. 65). It is an hieratic image far removed from the likenesses of ordinary men. It performs the function for which it was created: to act as the divine effigy of the imperial cult. This form of symbolism—successor to the naturalism seen in earlier Roman portraits—provided the aesthetic basis of art for a millennium. When symbolism is the objective, the specific peculiarities of the human face, which produce individual likenesses, can be ignored. From this point of view portraiture may be said to have declined; but as works of art many of the portraits done during the Byzantine era and the Middle Ages are treasures of great beauty.

The mosaics of Ravenna, for example, are a glorious witness to this new symbolic style that spread from Constantinople over the Western world. They represent an art more sophisticated, more ostentatious, and more liturgical than the unpretentious images of the early Church. They continue, moreover, the concept of the ruler as remote from the everyday world. Artists increasingly inculcated the commingling of Christianity and the imperium.

Thus, two hundred years after Constantine's death, Church and State were more than ever indissolubly linked. In the mosaics of S. Vitale, beneath the apparition of Christ are the solemn processions of Justinian, ruler of the Eastern Empire from 527 to 565, and his consort, the empress Theodora, probably come to Ravenna for the dedication of the church. The ceremony is imagined as beginning in the narthex. The emperor has not yet entered the sacred precinct, since he still wears his crown, which he would have removed once inside the church itself. He is accompanied by Archbishop Maximianus and is surrounded by officials and guards (fig. 66). Theodora also advances with her courtiers and ladies-in-waiting (fig. 67). Both royal personages carry gifts for the church: the emperor a gold basin, the empress a chalice. Many of the figures in the procession are portraits, for this is the Byzantine equivalent of the *Ara Pacis*. Looking at these stately figures, one would scarcely imagine that the emperor was a barbarian by birth and that the empress, the daughter of a bear-trainer, had once been an actress and a notorious courtesan. In another portrait in S. Appolinare Nuovo, also in Ravenna, Justinian looks jolly if somewhat unreliable. And we know from contemporaries that he was affable and easy of approach. He was also unscrupulous and crafty. His wife by contrast surrounded herself with ceremonious pomp and required all who approached to prostrate themselves before her, something new even in her half-Oriental court. As can be seen in her bejewelled likeness she was small in stature with a graceful figure, beautiful features, and piercing eyes. Even her enemy the historian Procopius had to admit she was "fair of face and generally attractive."

There are many other portraits in S. Vitale. Bishop Ecclesius, who in 522 began building the church, has a typical Italian face: large brown eyes, thick

OPPOSITE:
65. Constantine the Great. 312–15. *Fragment of a colossal marble statue, head and neck 104" high. Palazzo dei Conservatori, Rome.*

OVERLEAF LEFT ABOVE:
66. The Emperor Justinian with Guardsmen, Ecclesiastics, and Court Officials. c. 547. *Detail of a mosaic. S. Vitale, Ravenna.*

OVERLEAF LEFT BELOW:
67. The Empress Theodora with Her Attendants. c. 547. *Detail of a mosaic. S. Vitale, Ravenna.*

OVERLEAF RIGHT:
68. The Emperor Lothair. Mid-9th century. *Illumination from Lothair's gospel-book. Bibliothèque Nationale, Paris.*

black eyebrows, and the blue chin of a man who has shaved a heavy beard; his colleague Maximianus, who dedicated the church after Ecclesius died, has a narrower, more ascetic countenance, heavily lined. All these stern individuals stare at the spectator like frozen, multicolored specters. We have come a long way from the easy informality of the *Ara Pacis*.

Mosaic is a difficult medium for portraiture. It necessarily tends to make likenesses abstract. Compared with the mosaic portrait from Pompeii (fig. 53), a technical decline at Ravenna is evident. The transitions from light to shade are cruder, black lines take the place of modelling, and the tesserae are larger and less systematically arranged. As the S. Vitale figures were to be seen from a distance, however, the overall effect is satisfactory and the glittering color splendid and impressive.

The portraits in S. Vitale are a sample of the best of Byzantine portraiture. Over the centuries there was little change. Byzantine art was chained to a static formula. The theologians, the principal patrons of art, had decreed at the Council of Nicaea that the composition of a subject was dogmatically defined and that the artist was merely the executant of what the Church demanded. All originality was stifled. Since in the Christian East there was only one centralized state, such rigid ecclesiastical conservatism remained unaltered, unaffected by the growth of various nationalities with diverse tastes and demands. Byzantine artists, in the words of Yeats, disdaining "All mere complexities,/ The fury and the mire of human veins," continued in their orthodox and unchanging way to fabricate images bloodless and frozen, devoid of personality.

In the western half of the empire few portraits have survived from what is rightly considered the Dark Ages. Italy lay ravaged by barbarian invaders, who do not appear to have interested themselves in perpetuating their own appearances. But an occasional figure gives us a glimpse of what their vanished portraits, if they existed, may have been like. At Dumbarton Oaks, in Washington, D.C., there is a strange manikin made of solid gold (fig. 69). This baffling object, dating probably from the late 4th century or early 5th century, is a highly individualized portrait. His mouth has the downward, bitter curve of 5th-century Roman busts. His arms are held stiffly at his sides. He wears a tunic decorated with a pattern resembling the cross of Saint Andrew. It is said that he was discovered about 1928 in France, and terra-cotta reliefs found at St.-Bertrand-de-Comminges and a votive figure of a woman uncovered at Caudebec-les-Elbeuf bear some resemblance to him. But nothing really comparable has survived. This lonely figure with his large head and elongated chin opens a window on a culture we know too little about. If only he were not quite so unique!

There are occasional European portraits from this early period in illuminated manuscripts, but until long after Charlemagne they remained merely generalized types. Most are of rulers, and these are patterned to some extent upon the diptychs that late Roman consuls gave out on assuming office, which must have been widely distributed and in Carolingian times were greatly prized.

About the middle of the 9th century the emperor Lothair, grandson of Charlemagne, had himself portrayed in a miniature in his gospel-book (fig. 68). He holds a scepter and sits in the position medieval artists use for ruler-portraits: knees apart, feet together. The painter was as competent as any illu-

69.   An Unknown Man. *Gaul. Late 4th century or early 5th century. Gold, 4 1/2" high. Dumbarton Oaks Collections, Washington, D. C.*

minator of the time, but as a portraitist what a decline from Roman and Hellenistic artists! The Greek sculptors depicted the faces and bodies of their sitters
in such a way as to present individuals and to show their character and psychology; the Romans also analyzed the personality of their models but portrayed
them more realistically. The medieval illuminator did neither. He drew a type,
placed a crown on his head, clothed him in robes of gold and silk, and was satisfied that he had represented the emperor in all his glory.

The long stagnation of portraiture, however, eventually ended. In the 12th
century true likenesses began to appear here and there, on an ornamented
capital, or tucked away among the blessed or the damned on a tympanum.
Sometimes they are identified by a tradition associating them with a saintly
personage or a villainous noble or a bishop well known to the parish or diocese. But more often they portray models the stonecarver found in the people
around him. Thus, the revival of portraiture was first closely connected with
architecture. But it was in the Gothic period rather than the Romanesque
period that it began to appear more abundantly. From architectural decoration, portrait sculptors turned to the next great source of livelihood: grave
monuments.

70. *Master of the Visitation.* The Bamberg
Horseman. *c. 1230. Sandstone, 90 1/2"
high. Bamberg Cathedral.*

71. *Master of Naumburg*. Margrave
Ekkehard and Margravine Uta von
Wettin. *c. 1249. Limestone, 73 1/2" high.
Naumburg Cathedral.*

The dead brought portraiture back to life. The appearance of the deceased
began, in the 13th century, to be perpetuated, especially by effigies placed on
the sepulcher. Such tomb statues in turn stimulated a wish to be portrayed
while still alive. The result has been that, from Gothic times to the present
day, portraiture has steadily increased and has—as we shall see—played a
predominant role in Western art.

Not all 13th-century portraits, however, adorned burial monuments. One
of the first and most beautiful of portrait statues, dating from about 1230, is
the enigmatic mounted knight in the cathedral of Bamberg (fig. 70). Its original significance is uncertain, and where it was originally placed is unknown.
This strange horseman rides on a mysterious mission, unarmed but wearing a
crown. He is sufficiently individualized to be a portrait, but of whom? The
emperor Constantine, who appears in French reliefs, has been suggested. Also

a possibility is Henry II, who established the diocese of Bamberg. But the rider's identity will probably remain as mysterious as his mission. His distant gaze suggests Yeats's epitaph:

> Cast a cold eye
> On life on death.
> Horseman, pass by!

Of almost the same date is a statue of unsurpassed beauty, the portrait of Margravine Uta, the wife of one of the founders of the cathedral of Naumburg. Her husband, Margrave Ekkehard von Wettin, looks heavy and sullen (fig. 71). Both had been dead for two hundred years when their effigies were carved, but the unknown sculptor has brought them to life. With what skill has he differentiated the hands of the two figures: the thick, strong fingers of the man and the sensitive, tapering fingers of the woman. But has the artist also carved, one wonders, a symbol of an unhappy marriage? The lovely margravine seems to shield herself from her husband. She is isolated—a lonely, solitary figure. Here, in this somber lady, who peers coldly into the distance, we see the quintessence of Nordic romanticism. The masculine equivalent of her feminine beauty is the Bamberg knight. Each represents for Germanic taste a canon—an ideal of the beautiful. But mere comeliness is not enough. The hero or heroine must be aloof, inscrutable, and solitary. These two, the horseman and the margravine, fulfill all the demands of romantic art. They are portraits in the generic meaning of the word, a representation of a specific person, in one case unknown, in the other identified.

Expressionism, like romanticism, was a Nordic tendency with its roots deep in the Gothic period. As an illustration, consider the bronze effigy made about 1302 for the tomb of Bishop Wolfhart von Rot of Augsburg (fig. 72). How can arrogance be shown more expressively than in the lines of his face? His stylized nose with nostrils lifted indicates his disdain, his down-curving mouth suggests disgust, his closed eyes imply a repellent sight, his meager countenance and sunken cheeks vaunt his asceticism. This is the portrait of a haughty prelate marked with the sin of pride. It is also the likeness of an old man who has died. But death has erased none of the lines of insolence; the bishop seems unrepentant and scornful as he faces his God.

A contrast in expressionistic portraiture is the statue of another bishop, Friedrich von Hohenlohe of Bamberg (fig. 73). His effigy was carved about 1351, fifty years later than the portrait of Rot. Here the bishop's haggard face has a look of compassion, of gentleness. The eyes are open but fixed on some inward vision. The swaying body, the down-turned posture of the head, the way the book and crosier are held suggest extraordinary delicacy and grace. The bishop of Bamberg seems a saintly priest; the bishop of Augsburg an overweening churchman. But Hohenlohe may simply have been more fortunate in his sculptor. One must always remember that character, personality, and temperament in a portrait are in the eyes of the portraitist as well as in the actual appearance of the sitter.

There is little expressionism in French Gothic sculpture, glorious as it is. French portraitists in the Middle Ages had a great respect for convention, and their work has a certain uniformity, even to the point of monotony. Typical is the tomb in St.-Denis carved by Jean Pépin de Huy for Robert d'Artois, who died in 1317 (fig. 74). The knight has his hands joined in prayer, the usual gesture of French mortuary sculpture of the time. Although the likeness seems

72. Bishop Wolfhart von Rot. c. 1302. *Detail of a bronze effigy, lifesize. Augsburg Cathedral.*

73. Bishop Friedrich von Hohenlohe. *c. 1351. Stone effigy, lifesize. Bamberg Cathedral.*

74. *Jean Pépin de Huy*. Robert d'Artois.
*1317–20. Detail of a marble effigy, lifesize.
Abbey church of St.-Denis, Paris.*

75. Sir John Holcombe. *c. 1270. Stone
effigy, lifesize. Dorchester Abbey, Oxfordshire.*

recognizable, d'Artois's appearance is generalized. The characterization is not incisive.

It is a pleasure to turn from the sameness of these French effigies to the diversity of English tombs. In Dorchester near Oxford there is a recumbent statue of Sir John Holcombe, who was knighted on the field of battle and died of wounds in the Holy Land about 1270 (fig. 75). His family, for some unknown reason, has had him represented as though caught up in a nightmare. His head rests on his pillow, but his body is contorted, his eyes stare, and his tongue protrudes. Grasping his sword, he seems ready to defend himself against an enemy, but perhaps an enemy seen only in his tortured mind. It is as though he had recalled in his dream some terrible attack, one made when he was sleeping in his tent. If he was slain while asleep we have an explanation for this unique effigy. Whatever the reason for Sir John's restless, twisted body he appears a warrior startled but prepared to fight. His portrait is expressionistic realism of a high order. It deeply influenced the wartime drawings of Henry Moore, England's greatest contemporary sculptor.

The tomb effigies in Westminster Abbey are among the finest of all medieval portraits. The tomb of Henry III, who rebuilt the abbey in 1245, was commissioned by his son Edward I. It was designed by Pietro di Oderisio, who came to London from Rome; but the effigy itself, dating from 1291, nineteen years after the king's death, was made by an Englishman, William Torel. The figure of King Henry and that of his daughter-in-law, Queen Eleanor of Castile, also by William Torel (fig. 76), far outshine the statues of the tombs at St. Denis. Eleanor, a remarkable woman, is said to have saved her husband's life at Acre when he was wounded while on a Crusade. The crowns of both figures were originally studded with jewels, but these have been stolen. Each also had a canopy of gilt bronze, which enframed the head and extended down the sides. The one above Henry III has vanished entirely, but the top of Eleanor's remains, and the holes to hold the side portions are visible. This type of terminus at the head of the effigy was included in royal monuments of Westminster Abbey until the early 16th century. The two statues are the first full-length figures in English sculpture to be cast in bronze.

The names of sculptors are rare from the 13th and 14th centuries, but in England a few are known. John Orchard is the putative author of the gilt bronze effigy of Edward III, the founder of the Order of the Garter, whose greatest aim—to win the throne of France—was frustrated. The face was probably based on a wood and plaster funeral effigy still preserved in the museum of Westminster Abbey (fig. 77).

In early times in England, when a ruler died he was carried in the funeral procession with his face exposed, thus proving his death and the right of his successor to reign. So long as the funeral took place immediately after death

Sus in aduito
rium meum in
tende.

Domine ad adiuuandu

and before putrefaction began, there was no difficulty. But as these burial ceremonies grew more complicated, there was a delay for which the primitive
embalmer was unprepared. Consequently, the coffin was closed immediately
and a funeral effigy used in place of the visage of the deceased. Edward's effigy
was made in 1377 by Stephen Hadley, who was paid "for making an image in
the likeness of a king." Carved from wood, the portrait head was covered with
thinly coated wax. The face was fabricated of plaster fixed on linen. When
closely examined, Edward's mouth can be seen to droop to the left, and his left
cheek is flattened. We know that the king, just before he died, was rendered
speechless by a stroke. Since this paralysis is so clearly reflected in figure 77,
one may assume Hadley used an actual death mask for the face. When the effigy
was carried at the funeral, a beard and wig made of human hair would have
been attached. However, the eyebrows, perhaps to make them bristle, seem
to have been fashioned from the hair of a dog, probably a terrier.

Two other Englishmen, Nicholas Broker and Godfrey Prest, were responsible for the bronze figures of the tragic Richard II and his first wife, Anne of
Bohemia, whom he loved so dearly (fig. 81). Richard II ordered the tomb for
himself and Anne at the time of her death in 1394. His own effigy, executed
between 1395 and 1397, was therefore probably done after a drawing from
life. If so, he was the first British monarch to sit for his portrait. It is interesting
to compare the profile of the king as he appears kneeling before the Virgin in
the Wilton diptych (fig. 78) with the effigy on his tomb. His sharp nose is the
same, and his delicate, slightly effeminate features remain; but on the tomb he
has grown a beard and assumed a greater appearance of majesty, which, if Shakespeare is to be believed, awed for a time Bolingbroke and almost brought about
the king's escape from the usurpers.

Portraiture was a genre rapidly evolving after its long dormancy following
the collapse of the Roman Empire, and, toward the end of the 14th century,
likenesses became popular throughout Europe. Especially worth noting are
those of Jean de Berry, the greatest collector of the time and a patron of many
artists, including the Limbourg Brothers. More than fifty likenesses of this
remarkable connoisseur have been preserved, three in marble and most of the
rest in illuminated manuscripts. He was not handsome; and whereas his father,
his brothers, and his nephews all had the long, narrow faces of the Valois, he
had a round head and a pug nose. His passion for jewels was such that in one
manuscript he is shown meeting Saint Peter at the gate of heaven and extending his left hand while with his right he fingers an enormous sapphire (fig. 79).
The adage "You can't take it with you," he seems to have felt did not apply in
his case! He has brought his treasures with him and he looks forward to enjoying them throughout eternity. He was still alive when this illumination was
painted, and in the initial below we see him in prayer, confidently ecstatic at
this vision of his future domicile.

Turning from Burgundy to 14th-century Italy is to enter the purlieus of the
Renaissance. Now we find more painted portraits. According to Giorgio
Vasari, in the chapel of the Palazzo del Podestà in Florence Giotto painted
"Dante Alighieri, a contemporary of his and a very good friend. In the same
chapel are portraits, likewise by Giotto's hand, of Ser Brunetto Latini, the
master of Dante, and of Messer Corso Donati, a great citizen of those times."

Usually portraits were of donors of votive paintings represented smaller in
scale than the sacred personages before whom they kneel. Such pictures,
painted in fulfillment of a vow made in return for a divine favor, often itself a

80. *Simone Martini (c. 1285–1344).*
Guidoriccio da Fogliano. 1328. Fresco.
Palazzo Pubblico, Siena.

miracle, were extremely popular and continue to be offered up by the faithful in Catholic countries today. Sometimes the manikin who donated the picture is superbly characterized. The monk in adoration before our Lady in the 14th-century panel attributed to Lippo Memmi in the National Gallery in Washington, D.C., is a good example (fig. 82). He is an individual whose plump, rubicund face indicates that he drank his Chianti with delight, perhaps taking from time to time a drop too much, but whose fervent gaze reveals a heart brimming over with love for his divine protectress. In this tiny profile, good living and ardent devotion are wonderfully combined. But compared to the lavish output of the 15th century, portraits in the 14th century—apart from those of donors—are relatively few.

Nevertheless, the independent Italian portrait did exist. In 1328 Simone Martini, for example, painted a fresco of Guidoriccio da Fogliano riding forth into battle (fig. 80). He is seen in profile, and his pudgy, extraordinarily unmilitary face is probably a good likeness. He wears a cloak with a diaper pattern, and its undulations are cleverly used by the artist to give him and his horse a remarkable appearance of forward movement.

Simone Martini was one of the most seminal of artists. The pope had left Italy and established himself at Avignon. Thither travelled Simone, the outstanding Sienese painter of his generation. He spent the years 1340 to 1344 at Avignon, bringing to transalpine Europe a knowledge of Italian art. His sojourn at the papal court was a factor in the creation of a fashion in painting marked by sinuous lines, bright colors, and a discursive naturalism, which spread everywhere. In portraiture, one of the most beautiful examples of this so-called International Style is the likeness of Richard II in the Wilton diptych (fig. 78).

81. *Nicholas Broker and Godfrey Prest. Richard II and Anne of Bohemia. 1394–97. Detail of gilt bronze effigies, lifesize. Westminster Abbey, London.*

CHAPTER SIX

1400-1600: RENAISSANCE EUROPE

ITALY

From the earliest recorded time until the Renaissance, the principal medium of portraiture in the West was sculpture. This is true of ancient Mesopotamia and Egypt, classical Greece, Etruria, and Rome, and Europe in the Middle Ages. Other mediums were sometimes chosen, of course—painting in the Faiyum, mosaic in Byzantine times, illumination in the medieval period—but the likenesses depicted in pigment or mosaic appear to have been less numerous and less important (possibly because fewer have been preserved) than those carved in stone or ivory or cast in bronze. With the Renaissance came a change that has lasted till today. Portrait painting became more popular than portrait sculpture.

Painting is a language of expression with its own grammar and vocabulary. Thus, the painted portrait can be executed in various ways, and there are four main stylistic divisions or modes of representation, all determining, singly or in combination, the character of portraiture. From the Middle Ages to modern times, each has had its period of use. First, in medieval illuminations objects were represented in line and flat tone; then in the 13th century and especially in the 14th and 15th centuries, through modelling in light and shade, objects were given the appearance of a third dimension, as though they were actually bas-reliefs. Next, through an arbitrary arrangement of light, shade, and color, artists sought to make three-dimensional objects melt into the ambient atmosphere, to interfuse one with the other until the whole became a single pictorial effect. This was the great innovation of Giovanni Bellini and Giorgione, a mode developed by other Venetians until it was finally taken over by Titian and his contemporaries and handed on to Rubens, Van Dyck, Rembrandt, and their followers.

But note the words "arbitrary arrangement." There is still another way of representing objects, a way that renders a natural, not an arbitrary, visual effect: that is to say, the organization of colors, values, and shapes as the artist has seen them in nature. In this mode of representation, time is a factor. The effect may be as though the object were seen with a careful scrutiny, a quick glance, or a steady gaze. Each of these types of vision determines the amount and the character of the detail to be included. It is a style that reached its peak with Hals and Vermeer in Holland and Velázquez in Spain. In the 19th century it appears in the work of Corot and the impressionists.

During the Renaissance there was an enormous increase in every kind of portraiture: painted and sculptural. Portraits appeared on walls, panels, and canvases; were done in fresco, tempera, or oil; were carved in marble; and were cast in bronze. An upheaval had taken place—spiritual, intellectual, and economic. Men turned back to the thought and values of the ancient world. Their egos were reborn; personality was exalted; and the individual was glorified. Egoism had flourished in classical times, but with the coming of Christianity it had languished. There were always, of course, egoists: rulers, lords, knights, the powerful of the earth. They produced their quota of self-esteem,

82. *Lippo Memmi (active 1317–1347).* Madonna and Child with Donor. *Probably c. 1335. Tempera on panel, 22 1/4 × 9 1/2". National Gallery of Art, Washington, D. C. Andrew W. Mellon Collection.*

as such people had in the ancient world and as they have done ever since. But with the Renaissance there was a wider dissemination of self-assurance in all classes. A sense of individual worth was given a new importance, life in this world a new significance.

The 20th century has been called the age of the common man; the Renaissance was the age of the uncommon man. The individual recognized in himself exceptional capacity. Once liberated from the thrall of theological despotism, he rejoiced in his idiosyncrasies and felt himself reconstituted as a free human being born to express himself in his chosen way. His curiosity was also aroused. He wanted to know all he could about himself and his environment.

This new spirit, reinforced by a revived study of Latin and Greek literature, led to the rejection of the next world as alone significant. Instead, everyday existence became an important reality, and the conviction grew that to mirror man and his activities was the artist's goal. In the visual arts there was a search for the realities of human nature, and this led to an interest in portraits.

Not since Roman times had the human face been observed and analyzed so carefully. The expression of the eyes, the relaxation and contraction of the lips, the light and shade that model jaw and cheekbone, all are carefully noted. The long winter of naturalism during the Early Christian, Byzantine, and medieval periods was ended. Instead, there was a springtime of observation, a renewal of the discernment of actuality. Artists once more transcribed the world about them. This is not to say that with the Renaissance art had improved. Winter and spring both have their beauties. Naturalism is not the only aesthetic goal. But for portraiture a degree of naturalistic representation, some capacity for rendering physical appearance, is beneficial if not essential.

Italy was the first to feel the new spirit, the first to have an unlimited admiration for human achievement and genius. Portraiture, it was felt, could perpetuate the likenesses of those responsible for the government of the state and for great exploits. Consequently, the number of Italian painted portraits is overwhelming, particularly when one realizes that probably five or ten have perished for every one preserved. To organize this vast material, John Pope-Hennessy in his admirable book on Renaissance portraiture has divided 15th-century and 16th-century portraits into categories. The divisions used here are somewhat different, but one hopes they are equally useful: donor portraits; spectator portraits; independent portraits; official portraits; psychological portraits; emblematic portraits; and mannerist portraits.

We have already seen a donor portrait from the 14th century: the tiny figure kneeling before our Lady in figure 82. Though there are some exceptions, the donor figure at that time was minuscule by comparison with the holy figures. In the early 15th century, however, this changed, at least in one case. Tommaso Giovanni di Simone Masaccio, the greatest painter of the period, depicted in the church of S. Maria Novella in Florence a donor and his wife on the same scale as God the Father, the crucified Christ, and the Virgin and Saint John (fig. 83). Moreover, by placing his patrons on the first plane of the picture, Masaccio made them more prominent than the sacred figures. This represented such a tremendous break with iconographic tradition that his innovation was not adopted, and donors were soon relegated to their more usual diminutive scale.

The likeness of Lorenzo Lenzi, the donor of the painting in S. Maria Novella, remains unsurpassed among Renaissance profile portraits. To achieve this masterpiece, Masaccio must have studied diligently classical coins, which

83. *Masaccio (1401–1428)*. The Trinity.
*1427–28. Fresco. S. Maria Novella,
Florence*.

were then being discovered in large quantities. These remnants of antiquity were scrutinized by all Renaissance artists as models for those profile portraits that became so popular in the 15th century and, to a lesser extent, in the 16th century.

In the 14th century the independent portrait was rare, though it existed, as we have seen in Simone Martini's fresco of Guidoriccio da Fogliano, who rides forth to battle in lonely splendor (fig. 80). A century later such individual likenesses had become more common, yet portraiture in the modern sense emerged slowly. At first it is as though the reborn ego were a little diffident, a little shy of being portrayed. It needed some pretext and some accompaniment. As a consequence, the spectator portrait developed. Groups of prominent citizens were shown as participants in significant events.

There is, for example, a fresco by Bicci di Lorenzo of about 1425 showing Florentine nobles watching Pope Martin V consecrating their church of S. Egidio. Or we see, in a painting of the second half of the 15th century by Domenico Ghirlandaio, the humanist Politian walking up the stairs of the Vatican accompanied by the children of Lorenzo de' Medici to attend Pope Honorius III as he confirms the Franciscan order. Sometimes these leading citizens imagine themselves listening to one of the Evangelists preaching, or —in a fresco by Benozzo Gozzoli in the Riccardi Palace, Florence—as part of the Magi's retinue. That distinguished personages wanted to be portrayed as participants in some sacred scene is not surprising. Theirs was the same impulse that causes people in our time to wish to be photographed with the president. They wanted to show that, had they been alive, they would have been on hand at such events as the baptism of Christ, where Pietro Perugino showed the della Rovere family standing around watching the momentous ceremony (Sistine Chapel, Vatican). Likewise Saint Stephen's funeral was assuredly not to be missed, and in 1460 Fra Filippo Lippi depicted Carlo de' Medici and his entourage in attendance there (Cathedral, Florence). Examples of the spectator portrait are exceedingly numerous. It was a genre that persisted throughout the 16th century and sporadically thereafter.

Individuals were also independently portrayed in the 15th century, though they were far outnumbered by sitters in spectator roles. Sometimes independent portraits were actually extracted from spectator portraits. In 1486–90 Giovanna degli Albizzi was depicted by Ghirlandaio in a fresco in S. Maria Novella in Florence looking on at the Visitation. She appears again in the same pose, same dress, and same coiffure in a panel belonging to Baron Thyssen (fig. 84). That the fresco came first is proved by the way the lady's hands in the panel are cut off and by the abbreviated scarf she holds. Giovanna, a great beauty, died young, and her family probably wanted her portrait in their home. Therefore they commissioned Ghirlandaio to do a replica based on his fresco.

Both mural and panel show Giovanna in profile. In the 15th century a majority of portraits of women are thus silhouetted. To follow a fashion is sometimes ill-advised. A profile is not necessarily the most flattering view of a person, and many such portraits make their models look unnecessarily ugly. Sandro Botticelli, Filippino Lippi, Alesso Baldovinetti, and others painted feminine likenesses in profile, whose subjects, one feels, would have shown their unbecoming features less prominently had they been painted full face (fig. 85).

It is psychologically interesting—perhaps sociologically significant—that in 15th-century Italian painting there are very few beautiful women. Most women in their portraits are no more attractive than is Battista Sforza, duchess

84. *Domenico Ghirlandaio (c. 1448–1494). Giovanna degli Albizzi. 1488. Tempera on panel, 30 1/4 × 19 1/4". Thyssen-Bornemisza Collection, Lugano, Switzerland.*

ARS VTINAM MORES
ANIMVMQVE EFFINGERE
POSSES PVLCHRIOR IN TER
RIS NVLLA TABELLA FORET
MCCCCLXXXVIII

85. *Sandro Botticelli (1445–1510).*
Portrait of a Lady. *Tempera (probably)
on panel, 24 × 15 3/4". Palazzo Pitti,
Florence.*

OPPOSITE ABOVE:

86. *Piero della Francesca (c. 1410/20–
1492).* Federigo da Montefeltro, Duke of
Urbino, and His Wife, Battista Sforza.
*c. 1473. Oil on panel, each panel 18 1/2 ×
13". Uffizi, Florence.*

OPPOSITE BELOW:

87. *Giovanni Bellini (c. 1430–1516).*
Portrait of a Condottiere (Giovanni
Emo). *c. 1500. Tempera and oil on panel,
19 1/4 × 13 7/8". National Gallery of Art,
Washington, D. C. Samuel H. Kress
Collection.*

of Urbino, who sits facing her husband in the finest of all double portraits, painted by an artist trained but not born in Florence, Piero della Francesca (fig. 86). Beyond the two is a landscape somewhat resembling the topography of the countryside around Urbino. How impassively and coldly Battista stares at her spouse! He, on the other hand, has a fascinating face, full of a magnetic personality entirely absent from the countenance of his apparently stolid, apathetic wife.

That he should be the more attractive of the two is not surprising, for men, unlike most women in 15th-century Italian portraits, often have definite allure —perhaps a reflection of a social custom of the time. Take, for instance, the mid-century portrait of an unknown man by Andrea del Castagno. He looks nervous, calculating, ruthless—but one feels that he is a person of immense intellectual power, a dynamic human being one would like to know (fig. 89).

Most Florentine artists were not primarily portraitists. The important commissions in the 15th century were for frescos illustrating the Bible and the history of the Church. Botticelli, Domenico Veneziano, Piero di Cosimo, Filippino Lippi, and other Florentines have left us admirable likenesses as have, among Central Italian painters, Luca Signorelli, Perugino, and Pintoricchio, and, among artists difficult to restrict to a single region, Antonello da Messina. But likenesses remained subordinate to church decoration. Sacerdotal patronage—which encouraged the laity to contribute votive panels and frescos— was where painters looked for their money. An exception to this was Venice. There, a vogue for portraiture was stimulated by Giovanni Bellini. Giorgio Vasari said of him, "Since he had the habit of painting portraits from life, he made it the fashion in that city [Venice] for any one of prominence to be portrayed by him or someone else."

Many Venetian likenesses may be designated official portraits since they were commissioned by the government for public display, in contrast to private portraits made for the sitter's family. Gentile Bellini might even be described as a professional portraitist of officials and rulers. When Sultan Mohammed II asked the Signoria, the governing body of Venice, to send him their best portraitist, Gentile was chosen. He gave the sultan reliable service but he was devoid of imagination. His work is boring in its evenness of execution and photographic objectivity.

Giovanni Bellini, on the other hand, was a portraitist both subtle and sophisticated. Furthermore, he was capable of rendering that enlargement of personality desirable in portraying those who govern. In his *Portrait of a Condottiere,* of about 1500, he achieved a likeness of the universal military leader—tough, determined, relentless—while revealing at the same time the character of an individual whose thin, compressed lips suggest a streak of cruelty (fig. 87).

For official portraits, only one other contemporary painter ranked with Giovanni Bellini: his brother-in-law Andrea Mantegna, court painter at Mantua to the Gonzagas. In the Camera degli Sposi of their palace he painted, during the 1470s, the earliest Renaissance group portraits (fig. 88). The term "group portrait," though used before, requires explanation here. It is a painting that represents a number of people portrayed together as a unit without the extraneous interest of the spectator portrait. In executing these group portraits in the Camera degli Sposi, Mantegna ignored two principles of the genre: first, that there should be some contact between the viewer and those portrayed; and second, that the participants should have some contact with each other.[6] Mantegna's individual likenesses are convincing, each modelled

as though carved from stone. They seem to be assembled both inside and outside the room, which permits the spectator to be aware of what is happening in the audience chamber and out-of-doors in the gardens of the palace. But, except for the marquis, who greets an emissary, these courtiers appear unaware that anyone else is there or that anyone is looking on.

In Florence at about the same time, a transformation in portraiture was taking place. It was brought about by that universal and unique genius, Leonardo da Vinci. The contrast between a portrait of a generation earlier—say, Andrea del Castagno's *Portrait of a Man* (fig. 89)—and Leonardo's *Ginevra de' Benci* (fig. 94) irradiates this change. The explanation for it is to be found in Leonardo's notebooks. "Notice," he writes, "in the streets at the fall of the evening when it is bad weather, the faces of the men and women—what grace and softness they display. . . . You should paint at twilight when it is cloudy or misty, for the light is then perfect." Note that Leonardo recommends "grace" and "softness," an illumination "cloudy" and "misty," the type of lighting that leads to an indistinct gradation of modelling. By contrast, Castagno shows his sitter in a hard, clear light and models the separate planes with the sharp clarity of a relief in bronze. The difference between the sculptural mode of Castagno and the pictorial mode of Leonardo marks the boundary between the Early and the High Renaissance. This is one of the most significant stylistic changes in the history of painting. It is a basic transformation from a linear or relief-like style to a more painterly depiction, with light and shade merging imperceptibly and the contours softened to unify the figure and its ambient atmosphere.

A second and even more momentous innovation was introduced at the same time by Leonardo. It is psychological portraiture. To use his own words, he painted "the motions of the mind." This new concept is evident in three portraits of women, each expressing a different mood. Ginevra de' Benci (fig. 94) shows a sullen sadness; Cecilia Gallerani, an appealing wistfulness (National Museum, Krakow); and Lisa di Antonio Maria Gherardini, universally known

88. *Andrea Mantegna (1431–1506).* Ludovico Gonzaga, Marquis of Mantua, with Members of His Family and Court. *1474. Fresco. Camera degli Sposi, Palazzo Ducale, Mantua.*

89. *Andrea del Castagno (c. 1417/19–1457). Portrait of a Man. c. 1450. Oil and tempera on panel, 21 1/4 × 15 3/4". National Gallery of Art, Washington, D. C. Andrew W. Mellon Collection.*

90.   *Leonardo da Vinci (1452–1519).*
Mona Lisa. 1503–5. Oil and tempera on
panel, 38 1/4 × 21″. Louvre, Paris.

ABOVE RIGHT:

91.   *Andrea del Sarto (1486–1531).*
Portrait of an Architect. *c. 1517. Oil on*
canvas, 28 3/8 × 22 1/2″. The National
Gallery, London. Reproduced by courtesy of
the Trustees.

RIGHT:

92.   *Raphael (1483–1520).* Maddalena
Doni. *c. 1506. Oil on panel, 24 3/4 ×*
17 3/4″. Palazzo Pitti, Florence.

as Mona Lisa, a mirthless amusement (fig. 90). The most original of these representations of "the motions of the mind" is the enigmatically melancholy *Ginevra de' Benci*. Sadness is a mood artists have rarely depicted. It is difficult to think of an instance in portraiture before the 17th century and Rembrandt —and even then, the tragic view of life was usually reflected in the faces of men, not of women. To have expressed in the 15th century the psychology of the individual is a stupendous achievement.

After Leonardo, painting was never the same. His influence spread everywhere. The illumination he recommended, for example, a broadly diffused, misty light, falls on Andrea del Sarto's bemused architect (fig. 91). An effort at psychological interpretation is there, too. The sitter is caught in an abstracted, dreamy mood. He looks romantic, for Andrea del Sarto was always sentimental—a sentimentality in this case moderated by the architect's crafty glance, which implies that he may not have been beyond calculating his charges.

To turn from that murky dulcitude which beclouds Andrea del Sarto's otherwise admirable work to the clear, keen perception of one of the greatest of all Italian portraitists, Raphael, is to step from the umbrageous into sunshine. Raphael must have known the *Mona Lisa,* for his portrait of Maddalena Doni (fig. 92) has the same placement of the hands, the same twist of the body, the same direction of the gaze. But the younger artist made less of an attempt to convey the mood of the sitter, to show the motions of her mind. It is an early work, but his maturity was swift. It soon reached a peak in one of the finest of all Italian portraits: the *Cardinal* in the Prado Museum, of 1510 or 1511 (fig. 93). Few paintings so embody pure intelligence. Had there been more churchmen like this, Martin Luther might have remained an obscure monk!

Raphael's psychological characterizations are amazing. Baldassare Castiglione is seen as the insecure courtier he was, nervously clasping his hands (fig. 95). Tommaso Inghirami is a typical functionary surprised at his desk; he quickly looks up at his unexpected visitor with a superbly realized gesture of surprise (fig. 96). Leo X with his crafty nephews (Uffizi, Florence) appears a self-indulgent and self-confident prince of the Church, whose ambitious nepotism helped to bring about the Reformation. All these are distinctive personalities, unforgettably individualized.

To find portraits of equivalent quality one must turn to 16th-century Venice. Work at the beginning of the century was dominated by Giorgione and his followers, who altered the course of painting almost as much as Leonardo da Vinci. The change they brought about consisted principally in the greater degree to which figures blend into the scene. Leonardo made his portraits a part of the air and space forming their background, but the Venetians went further, inseparably fusing figures and their surroundings. Also, the illumination in Giorgionesque paintings is a warm, sunset glow—different from the cold moonlight of Leonardo. However, these stylistic alterations are most apparent in figure subjects and are scarcely evident in portraiture. Giorgione's *Portrait of a Youth* (fig. 97) has a general lighting not greatly different from Leonardo's, but the mood is unlike. There is a poetic sentiment in Giorgione's portraits, which Leonardo would have rejected. It appears clearly in this painting of a pensive young man, so attractive in his melancholy, who touches his breast with his open hand. Is the gesture expressive of unrequited love? Or is it merely a compositional device? (What to do with the hands is always a prob-

93. *Raphael*. Portrait of a Cardinal (*detail*). *1510–11. Oil on panel. Prado, Madrid.*

OVERLEAF LEFT:
94. *Leonardo da Vinci*. Ginevra de' Benci. *c. 1480. Oil (primarily) on panel, 15 1/4 × 14 1/2". National Gallery of Art, Washington, D. C. Ailsa Mellon Bruce Fund.*

OVERLEAF RIGHT:
95. *Raphael*. Baldassare Castiglione. *c. 1515. Oil on canvas, 32 1/4 × 26 3/8". Louvre, Paris.*

96. *Raphael. Tommaso Inghirami.*
1512–14. Oil on panel, 35 3/8 × 23 5/8".
Isabella Stewart Gardner Museum, Boston.

97. *Giorgione (c. 1475–1510). Portrait*
of a Youth. c. 1510. Oil on canvas,
28 1/2 × 21 1/4". Museum of Fine Arts,
Budapest.

lem in a half-length, especially when the subject is posed behind a parapet.) The answer is elusive. Yet instinctively one feels that with Giorgione this was not a device but a true expression of sentiment.

There is a mystery about Giorgione's introspective paintings that we do not find in the work of an extrovert like Titian, whose long life spanned nearly a century, from about 1488 to 1576. His early portraiture, so like Giorgione's in style, is moodless. He is detached, veracious, yet flattering. The unidentified young men in the National Gallery, London, in the Louvre, Paris, in the Pitti Palace, Florence, and in the collection of Lord Halifax need no names to place them among the highest nobility. But Titian could also paint a common, vulgar model like Pietro Aretino and give him such an imposing personality that the viewer is overwhelmed not only by the sitter's bulk but by the intelligence reflected in his gross face (fig. 98). Subtle cruelty was also at Titian's command. The wily Jacopo Strada offering a client a statue of Venus, with its certificate of authenticity lying on the table, and ancient coins conspicuously displayed, is the archetype of the obsequious dealer as he has plied his trade from the days of Pliny to the present (fig. 100). The crafty Paul III, crouching between his nephews—a group portrait now in the Capodimonte Museum, Naples, and for obvious reasons never finished—is the personification of the decadent papacy hated by the Reformers.

But when Titian painted an official portrait of someone he admired, such as Charles V, he dowered his sitter with regal majesty. The most powerful monarch of his time, the emperor sat more than once to Titian. In one painting he is portrayed riding through a twilight world, spear in hand (fig. 99). Here, the painter's sympathy for the beleaguered king, soon to enter a monastery, lends the portrait an ineffable pathos. Titian saw this ruler of a great part of the globe as the last of the questing knights, doomed never to find his grail, the religious unity of Europe.

Jacopo Robusti, called Tintoretto, a contemporary of Titian, did not have such exalted patrons. Nevertheless, he has left us scores of official portraits showing the principal Venetians of his day. He painted with exceptional rapidity, and perhaps for that reason, compared to Titian, his characterizations are apt to be superficial. His renown rests on his religious compositions, whose brilliance has never been surpassed. Yet in a picture in Vienna he achieved one of the most touching portraits of all time (fig. 101). It is a double portrait, a painting of contrasts, of youth and age. The little old man, desiccated, wrinkled, bent, stares into space, absorbed in his memories. The boy beside him, in the first bloom of youth, stands erect, challenging the world. The heartaches of the old man are almost ended, whereas the cares and anxieties of the boy are yet to come; the old man seems wearily falling back into that childhood from which the youth has just emerged.

Titian and Tintoretto toward the end of their lives looked into mirrors and painted themselves. Titian saw a countenance domineering, self-confident, urbane (fig. 102). Tintoretto saw a tragic face with large eyes, sad and searching (fig. 103). Did Tintoretto ever reach the end of his own quest, did he find the grace of faith as he painted his innumerable crucifixions and martyrdoms? Contemporaries tell us of his hours of meditation in the Venetian church of the Madonna dell' Orto. Perhaps in the end there was a reward—a faith denied to Titian.

The emblematic portrait enjoyed considerable popularity in the 16th and 17th centuries. One of the most elaborate examples, painted in 1505

98. *Titian (c. 1488–1576).* Pietro
Aretino. *1548–50. Oil on canvas,
40 1/4 × 33 5/8". Copyright The Frick
Collection, New York.*

LEFT:
99. *Titian.* The Emperor Charles V
at the Battle of Mühlberg. *1548. Oil on
canvas, 130 3/4 × 110". Prado, Madrid.*

OVERLEAF LEFT:
100. *Titian.* Jacopo Strada. *1567–68.
Oil on canvas, 49 1/4 × 37 3/8".
Kunsthistorisches Museum, Vienna.*

OVERLEAF RIGHT ABOVE:
101. *Tintoretto (1518–1594).* Portrait of
an Old Man and a Boy. *c. 1565. Oil on
canvas, 40 1/2 × 32 5/8". Kunsthistorisches
Museum, Vienna.*

OVERLEAF RIGHT BELOW:
102. *Titian.* Self-Portrait. *After 1555.
Oil on canvas, 37 3/4 × 29 1/2". Staatliche
Museen, Berlin.*

103. *Tintoretto. Self-Portrait. 1587. Oil on canvas, 24 × 20". Louvre, Paris.*

104. *Parmigianino (1503–1540). Self-Portrait in a Convex Mirror. 1524. Tempera on panel, diam. 9 5/8". Kunsthistorisches Museum, Vienna.*

OPPOSITE:
105. *Lorenzo Lotto (c. 1480–c. 1556). Allegory. 1505. Oil (primarily) on panel, 22 1/4 × 16 1/2". National Gallery of Art, Washington, D. C. Samuel H. Kress Collection.*

by Lorenzo Lotto, is a portrait of Bernardo de' Rossi di Berceto, bishop of Treviso. On a panel that can be closed over the bishop's likeness is a pictorial description of his life and interests in allegorical terms (fig. 105). Around a shield with his coat-of-arms are grouped a naked child and various instruments that he is picking up—a compass, a carpenter's square, a flute, a scroll. These indicate the bishop's culture. But, as he was human, temptation came his way. On the right, darkness covers the sky, and in this umbrageous gloom a satyr sits among overturned vessels of wine. But Lotto tactfully indicates that the bishop has overcome such vices. His soul is shown in a burst of light mounting to heaven. There are further allegorical references: to death in the Medusa shield and to the renewal of life in the branch growing out of the dead stump. But the main theme is congratulatory: the triumphant virtue of the sitter, Bernardo de' Rossi.

The emblematic portrait flourished throughout the 16th century on both sides of the Alps. Through allegory and symbolism the sitter hoped his way of life would be more clearly manifest, but, though these adjuncts, these emblems, do speak to us, our interest remains basically in the visual aspects of personality, the sitter's physical appearance.

In the second half of the 16th century a new kind of likeness appeared—the mannerist portrait. If art is a moving platform, as Bernard Berenson has said, then novelty is the machinery that keeps it in motion. When the problems of post-medieval painters—perspective, foreshortening, movement, etc.—had all been solved, as they had been during the High Renaissance, something new, it was felt, was needed. Francesco Mazzola, called Parmigianino, who lived from 1503 to 1540, was one of several artists who provided a fresh approach to portraiture. His most unconventional painting, his own self-portrait of 1524, clearly displays a bizarre and untried attitude to likenesses (fig. 104). Artists have, of course, always had to use mirrors for self-portraits. But Parmigianino was the first to use a curved mirror and to note all the distortions that resulted. His picture is a consistent trompe l'oeil, without precedent in portraiture. Here, perspective is no longer simply a means to represent visual depth on a flat surface; it is a plaything to show the painter's virtuosity. This anomalous portrait is not characteristic of his style, but it reflects the boredom beginning to be felt by some artists with the conventions of Renaissance painting. Advanced painters of Parmigianino's generation, loosely grouped as mannerists, were seeking a renewal of the classical likeness through the introduction of distortion. This new attitude was not confined to Italy. The greatest genius in this category of painters was El Greco, whose work will be discussed later.

Only painted likenesses have been mentioned so far in this chapter, but Italian artists were also active carving and casting portraits. One of the earliest and most beautiful is the effigy of Ilaria del Carretto Guinigi, who died young (fig. 106). The work of Jacopo della Quercia, who lived from about 1374 to 1438, it remains a masterpiece of Renaissance funerary art. The great 19th-century critic John Ruskin characterized Ilaria's effigy as "the most beautiful extant marble-work of the Middle Ages." It belongs, however, chronologically to the Renaissance, but Ruskin was correct insofar as the sculpture shows little influence of classical art, at a time when excavations were bringing to light treasures of the ancient world that profoundly affected

106. *Jacopo della Quercia (c. 1374–1438).*
Tomb of Ilaria del Carretto Guinigi.
c. 1406. Marble. Lucca Cathedral.

107. *Leon Battista Alberti (1404–1472).*
Self-Portrait. c. 1435. Bronze, 7 7/8 ×
5 3/8″. National Gallery of Art, Washington,
D. C. Samuel H. Kress Collection.

almost all Renaissance sculptors, among whom one of the most ardent diggers
was Donato di Niccolò Bardi, called Donatello. What he found and what
others excavated deeply impressed him. The uncompromising candor of the
best Roman busts is reflected in his portrait of Niccolò da Uzzano, the implacable opponent of the Medici (fig. 111). Whether Donatello saw traces of
polychromy on ancient statues being uncovered we do not know, but the
realism of Uzzano's likeness (note the ear and the thick throat) is enhanced by
color, although much that we see today is repaint. No Roman sculptor ever
gave such alert vitality to his sitter. Classical art may be more timeless than
Renaissance work, but it lacks the latter's vibrancy, animation, and actuality.

The influence of classical art on Early Renaissance sculpture can be seen
most clearly in medals and plaquettes, which mirror to some extent Roman
coinage. Renaissance medals were cast in large numbers to be sent to friends,
as today photographs are distributed. The finest medallist of the 15th century,
Antonio Pisano, called Pisanello, was also a painter. Born in or near Verona
about 1395, he excelled as a portraitist. The great of Italy were his patrons.
Our concept of the features of many Renaissance leaders would be vague
indeed if it were not for his medallic profiles.

Pisanello was one of many medallists, for whose work there was an increasing demand; but the two greatest masterpieces of Renaissance portraiture in
bronze relief were not by a medallist but by a man of the most varied abilities,
Leon Battista Alberti. So far as we know, he cast only two plaques, both self-
portraits (fig. 107). The exactitude of modelling, boldness of relief, and powerful characterization radiating intellectual strength elevate them to the
highest level of portraiture.

Florentine 15th-century portrait sculpture rivals, and at times surpasses,
any previous work. One of the first notable examples is the self-portrait by
Lorenzo Ghiberti on the east doors of the Baptistery of Florence. He had
portrayed himself on earlier doors, but there his head is generalized and meaningless as a portrait. His second attempt some twenty years later shows an
individual with a high forehead, his brow wrinkled in thought, his eyes
shrewd but kindly, and his mouth on the verge of a smile (fig. 108). Floren-

tine portrait sculpture was launched at a high level of achievement.

Between 1444 and 1447 Bernardo Rossellino executed the effigy of Leonardo Bruni for the famous humanist's bier in S. Croce in Florence (fig. 109). This established the type of burial monument with the portrait of the deceased lying on his sarcophagus, which is placed in an architectural setting. This kind of tomb was chosen repeatedly in the 15th century and with modifications in the 16th century. It is very different from the simpler bier employed by della Quercia for the effigy of Ilaria, a type of grave that has not departed from the style usual in the Middle Ages (fig. 106). Bernardo's brother Antonio carved two of the finest quattrocento busts, one of Giovanni Chellini, a doctor and lecturer on philosophy and logic (fig. 110), and the other of the distinguished ambassador, poet, and scholar Matteo Palmieri. The improvement these represent over earlier work is due partly to the skill of the sculptors but also to the use of life masks. With the aid of these, a subject's features could be reproduced with greater precision.

108. *Lorenzo Ghiberti (1378–1455).* Self-Portrait. 1425–37. *Detail of* The Gates of Paradise *(east doors). Gilt bronze. Baptistery, Florence.*

LEFT:
109. *Bernardo Rossellino (1409–1464).* Tomb of Leonardo Bruni. 1444–47. *Marble, lifesize. S. Croce, Florence.*

110. *Antonio Rossellino (1427–1479).* Giovanni Chellini. *Marble, 20 1/8" high. Victoria and Albert Museum, London.*

The most original quattrocento portraitist of women was not a Florentine. He was Francesco Laurana, born in Dalmatia about 1430, who worked in Naples, Sicily, and France. His busts are more abstract than Florentine work (fig. 112). There is a simplification of planes that anticipates Brancusi. His models are almost invariably women, who with half-closed eyes appear somnolent, dreaming of a love just requited and musing, perhaps, on a sensuality still more exotic. They are like the women in Baudelaire's poems, outrée and subtly wanton.

Two of the greatest masterpieces of 15th-century art are equestrian portraits: Donatello's *Gattamelata* and Verrocchio's *Colleoni* (figs. 113, 114). The *Gattamelata*, finished in 1453, was inspired by the statue of Marcus Aurelius

in the Piazza di Campidoglio, Rome (fig. 58), but it goes beyond its Roman model in the infusion of thought into the stern countenance of the Venetian condottiere Erasmo da Narni. The lineaments of the face so forcefully modelled, the determination in the tight lips, the frowning brows, all point to a leader who will not accept defeat.

The condottiere Bartolommeo Colleoni of Bergamo, subject of Verrocchio's monument of 1481–96, is equally redoubtable as he rides forward scowling at his enemies. But Verrocchio's portrait gains over Donatello's in showing a great general attired, not in classical garb, but as he might have been when leading his troops into battle. The pose of the rider, also, is more vigorous, with the powerful swing of his immense body in concert with the forward stride of his steed, ready for the onslaught. Horse and rider emanate pure energy. Verrocchio's work is undoubtedly the greatest equestrian monument in the world.

Any discussion of portraits in the Renaissance should end with the climactic genius of Michelangelo Buonarroti. Yet in some ways he might also be omitted, since he did not care for portraiture. His statues of Giuliano and Lorenzo de' Medici in S. Lorenzo in Florence are so different from known likenesses of both that it is questionable whether they were intended as portraits at all. But Michelangelo at the end of his life carved one undoubted portrait, his own, in the role of Joseph of Arimathea in the *Pietà* now in the cathedral of Florence

OPPOSITE:
111. Donatello (1386–1466). Niccolò da Uzzano. c. 1460–80. Painted terra-cotta, 18 1/8" high. Bargello, Florence.

LEFT:
112. Francesco Laurana (c. 1430– c. 1502). A Princess of the House of Aragon. 1472–75. Marble, 17 1/2" high. National Gallery of Art, Washington, D. C. Andrew W. Mellon Collection.

OVERLEAF LEFT:
113. Donatello. Gattemelata (Erasmo da Narni). c. 1447–53. Bronze, 132" high. Piazza del Santo, Padua.

OVERLEAF RIGHT:
114. Andrea del Verrocchio (c. 1435– 1488). Bartolommeo Colleoni. c. 1481– 96. Bronze, c. 156" high. Campo SS. Giovanni e Paolo, Venice.

115. *Michelangelo (1475–1564). Self-Portrait As Joseph of Arimathea. Detail of a Pietà left unfinished in 1555. Marble. Florence Cathedral.*

116. *Jan van Eyck (d. 1441). Wedding Portrait. 1434. Oil on panel, 33 × 22 1/2". The National Gallery, London. Reproduced by courtesy of the Trustees.*

(fig. 115). For this identification we have Vasari's word, as well as the similarity of the hooded and bearded figure to contemporary portraits of the sculptor. We know from Michelangelo's poems how passionately he sought atonement, how deeply he prayed for the grace of faith. The tenderness with which Joseph holds up the dead body of Christ and the sorrow in his reverent, devout face are symbolic of the sculptor's own prayer to be worthy of divine love.

BEYOND THE ALPS

Compared to Italian sculpture in the Renaissance, carved portraits north of the Alps are of secondary quality and do not merit inclusion in this brief history. Painted portraits are another matter.

By the 1400s, the Renaissance in the south was in full swing, but northern artists, although in some respects technically in advance of their Italian contemporaries, used little of that classical detail considered the hallmark of Renaissance art. Just as northern architecture in the 15th century appears to be part of a late phase of the Gothic style, so Flemish painting until the beginning of the 16th century might be considered a late, realistic aspect of medieval art. It is difficult, for example, to consider Jan van Eyck as a Renaissance artist, though he was a contemporary of Donatello and Fra Angelico. Yet it was his grasp of reality that destroyed the affectations, the pretty linear patterns, the bright, arbitrary colors of the International Style, the style of Late Gothic painting. The Flemish school, which he established, was a mirror of actuality, a pellucid reflection of the surrounding world. The painter put down on paper or panel, as exactly as possible, what his eye saw. He looked at the sitter microscopically; at the surroundings telescopically; but at both with a prolonged scrutiny.

The school of painting that arose during the 15th century in the Netherlands comprised, besides Van Eyck, a number of distinguished portraitists: Rogier van der Weyden, Dierik Bouts, Petrus Christus, Hugo van der Goes, Joos van Wassenhove (called Justus of Ghent), and Hans Memling. So able were these painters that the 16th century judged all art to be either Flemish or Italian, and Vasari even put the Germans Martin Schöngauer and Albrecht Dürer among the Flemings. In the 15th century, Germany, Austria, France, Spain, and Portugal were completely under the sway of these Flemish painters; until the end of the century the hegemony of Italy and Flanders in transalpine Europe went unchallenged.

On both sides of the Alps there was the same search for individual character, the same scrupulous analysis of the human countenance—more precise in the north, more generalized in the south. Flemish artists, absorbed in what they saw, drew and painted every wrinkle in a face, every hair in a beard, every thread in a mantle; whereas Italian painters sought clear outlines, a mastery of the beauty of the human body, and a knowledge of the laws of perspective and foreshortening.

There was, however, an interpenetration of influences. Italian patrons sat to Flemish painters; works by Jan van Eyck were to be seen in Florence and Urbino; Rogier van der Weyden's portraits were owned in Ferrara and Florence. Italian artists sometimes modelled their paintings on Flemish work: Ghirlandaio's *Saint Jerome* and Botticelli's *Saint Augustine* in the church of the

117. *Jan van Eyck. Nicholas, Cardinal Albergati. c. 1431. Silverpoint. Staatliche Kunstsammlungen, Kupferstichkabinett, Dresden.*

118. *Jan van Eyck. Nicholas, Cardinal Albergati. 1431–32. Oil on panel, 13 3/8 × 10 3/4". Kunsthistorisches Museum, Vienna.*

Ognissanti in Florence, for example, were patterned after a *Saint Jerome* by Van Eyck, then owned by the Medici. But most important of all in this interchange of influences was the Portinari altarpiece, with its beautiful portraits of the donors and their patron saints (fig. 119). It was painted by Hugo van der Goes in Bruges about 1473–75. Installed in S. Maria Novella in Florence, it became an academy attended by every Florentine artist.

Eventually from such studies, as well as from their Flemish-trained compatriot Antonello da Messina, the Italians learned the northern method of painting in oil. But there were also visitors to Italy from the north: Rogier van der Weyden, possibly, and Justus of Ghent, certainly. These were schoolmasters who taught the new technique.

Flemish portraits were nearly all executed in oil. Whether Jan van Eyck was the discoverer of oil painting—a technique in which linseed oil serves as the solvent of pigment rather than egg, which had been employed hitherto—is moot. But he was certainly the first artist to use this technique to depict a sitter in a naturalistically rendered interior space. In his most famous double portrait (fig. 116), the viewer looks at a bedchamber as though he had passed through an open door into the room, an illusion enhanced by the reflection in the mirror on the opposite wall. Although the models are scrupulously observed, Van Eyck's innovation is not their likenesses; it is the reality of the light and air in the room where they stand. Actuality is increased by the conformity of detail. The faces of Arnolfini and his fiancée, though seemingly smooth, are observed with sufficient particularity to be consistent with the recording of the minutiae of the fur, the hat, the coat of the dog. The totality of this uniform rendering gives the scene its reality.

The inscription on the picture, "Johannes de eyck fuit hic" (Jan van Eyck was here), makes the painting a legal document, a record of a betrothal or a marriage. For according to the canon law of the time, marriage was concluded by taking an oath before a witness, joining hands, and by the groom's raising his right arm. Among various functions of portraiture this is a rare example of a likeness replacing a priest or a notary public. Arnolfini confronted with this portrait could be sued for breach of promise or for bigamy if he married again!

Jan van Eyck's procedure in painting a portrait, a method followed by all subsequent Flemish portraitists, was to make a careful drawing of the model, meticulously noting every feature, every furrow, every blemish of the face, and then to execute from this sketch a likeness in oil. In one case, we have such a preliminary drawing and the painting done from it (figs. 117, 118). On the drawing are written comments about Albergati's sanguine nose, the gray stubble of his beard, the tone of his lips. The painting closely follows the drawing done from life. Using oil as a medium—which permitted minute strokes of the brush to build up the image, instead of the broad handling necessitated by the coarser medium of tempera—it was possible to attain a verisimilitude that has never been surpassed.

With the death of Jan van Eyck in 1441, Rogier van der Weyden became the foremost painter in the Netherlands. All the eminent men in Bruges wanted him to perpetuate their appearance. Most, however, were, in the long run, frustrated, for the greater number of Rogier's portraits have been lost. Those that have survived show him to have been a solemn and forceful delineator of character. His male sitters all have the stern look of rectitude.

With women he is more appealing. This is especially true of the *Portrait of a Lady* in the National Gallery of Art, Washington, D.C. (fig. 121). She was

119. *Hugo van der Goes (c. 1440–1482).*
Tommaso, Antonio, and Pigello Portinari
Commended by Saint Thomas and Saint
Anthony. *c. 1473–75. Left wing of the
Portinari altarpiece. Oil on panel, 98 ×
55 1/2". Uffizi, Florence.*

possibly that great heiress Marie de Valengin, the daughter of Philip the Good of Burgundy, whose portrait Rogier also painted. She has a baffling personality. Like many of his sitters she seems withdrawn. Her domed forehead implies intellectuality; her thick underlip and full mouth, sensuality. Taken separately, her features are ugly; combined, they are uniquely fascinating. One is reminded of Francis Bacon's axiom, "There is no excellent beauty that has not some strangeness in the proportion."

Like other portraits of the period, it is painted on wood overlaid with a mixture of glue and chalk known as gesso. On this prepared panel a preliminary drawing was copied in monochrome, and the underpainting was then covered with thin glazes of colored oil. This procedure enabled the artist to render subtle gradations of light, especially noticeable in passages such as the transparent wimple. With age these Flemish paintings, due to the expansion and contraction of the wood, have acquired a web of minute cracks, like the crackle of old porcelain, giving them the same beauty of surface.

With a few exceptions, the independent Flemish portrait, as distinct from the donor portrait, is small and limited to head and shoulders or to a half-length view at most. Often the sitter is posed against a dark background; occasionally the sitter is seen in the corner of a room with a window on one side. A move to increase air and space occurred later, in Hans Memling's portraits, where the model is usually posed near a window through which a cheerful countryside can be seen. At times, under the influence of Italian art, the sitter even appears out-of-doors (fig. 120). The lighting in all these portraits is from the side, and the subject's face is seen in a three-quarter view. Neither frontal nor profile poses were popular in the north.

More than twenty-five portraits by Memling's hand survive; if we multiply this by a factor of at least five, to account for those that have been lost, as suggested by documents and copies, the total comes to more than a hundred. He was the favorite limner of Bruges society, especially the large and rich Italian community. Urbane, flattering, and adaptable, he possessed those specific qualities most helpful to a fashionable portraitist. He had the faculty of giving his sitters dignity and distinction. They all look thoughtful, whether mindless or not, as they peer past the spectator into the distance. Like any popular portraitist, Memling avoided extremes, and his interpretation of character was amiability itself, an attitude his sitters welcomed.

Such moderation was not to be found in the work of a much more tortured individual, Hugo van der Goes. He was a kind of precursor of Van Gogh and like him suffered from "a fever of the brain." At the height of his popularity he retired to a monastery, where he tried to commit suicide. Treated by the monks with great compassion, he recovered but painted very little. In his Portinari altarpiece, the likenesses of the two sons of Tommaso Portinari and his wife, Maria Baroncelli, are enchanting (fig. 119). The elder boy, staring with translucent eyes, his lips on the verge of a smile, the younger, wrapped in dreams of his own, are among the first glimpses in art since Roman times of the beauty of childhood. But an element of irrationality is to be seen in the artist's somewhat later, much-repainted organ shutters in the National Gallery of Scotland, in Edinburgh. On one side are the portraits of James III and Margaret of Scotland, whose heads were added by another hand. On the reverse, which is in better condition, is a portrait of Sir Edward Bonkil, painted from life and entirely by Van der Goes. On this side, the weird perspective of the organ, the contorted body of our Lord, and the bizarre throne of the Trinity foretell the artist's coming dementia.

120. *Hans Memling (1430/35–1494).* Man with a Coin. *Oil on vellum transferred to canvas, 11 × 9″. Musée Royale des Beaux-Arts, Antwerp.*

121. *Rogier van der Weyden (c. 1400–1464).* Portrait of a Lady. *c. 1455. Oil on panel, 14 1/2 × 10 3/4″. National Gallery of Art, Washington, D. C. Andrew W. Mellon Collection.*

122. *Jean Fouquet (c. 1420–c. 1481).*
Etienne Chevalier Commended by Saint
Stephen. c. 1450. Left wing of the Melun
diptych. Tempera on panel, 37 3/4 × 34 5/8".
Staatliche Museen, Gemäldegalerie, Berlin.

123. *Jean Fouquet. Virgin and Child.*
c. 1450. Right wing of the Melun diptych.
Tempera on panel, 35 3/4 × 31 7/8".
Museé Royale des Beaux-Arts, Antwerp.

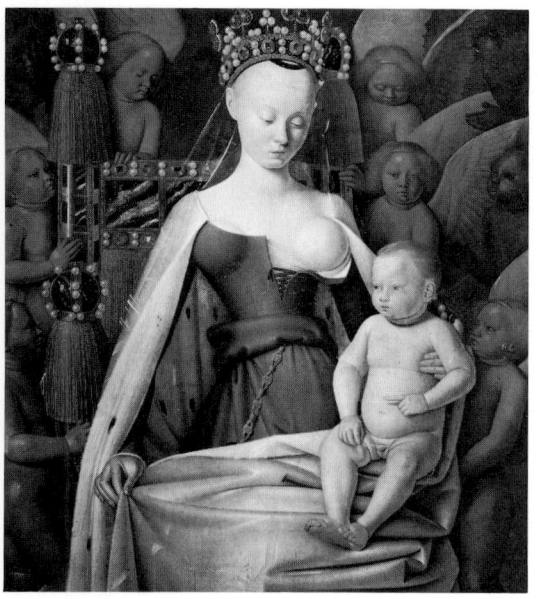

Only one Flemish painter seems to have lost his native character, Joos van Wassenhove (Justus of Ghent). He was summoned about 1476 to Italy by Federigo da Montefeltro because the duke could not "find an Italian portraitist after his heart," although his portrait by Piero della Francesca is a unique masterpiece. Joos portrayed his patron at full-lenth, seated, wearing his armor, and with his son beside him. The portrait (Galleria Nazionale delle Marche, Urbino) is so Italian in feeling, so generalized rather than particularized, that the participation of Melozzo da Forlì has been postulated, probably unnecessarily, for Joos had mastered Italian style.

The two most famous portraits done in France and Portugal during the 15th century show the all-pervasive influence of Flemish painting. About 1450 Jean Fouquet painted a diptych representing on one wing Etienne Chevalier, treasurer of Charles VII of France, with his patron saint, Stephen (fig. 122). Fouquet had been in Italy, where in 1447 the pope had sat to him. From the Italians the Frenchman learned about architectural ornament and how to light his subject; but every detail of Etienne Chevalier's face is scrupulously observed, as it would have been by Jan van Eyck. In this competition of influences, on one side of the diptych the north prevails, for no Italian would have sacrificed ideal harmony to have painted so microscopically; whereas the other wing is more Italian in feeling (fig. 123). On it is portrayed our Lady with the features of Agnès Sorel, the mistress of Charles VII. Her dress, uncorseted to suckle the Child, offered Fouquet an opportunity to show the beauty of her breasts. Here, society portraiture comes close to sacrilege, but this did not trouble the Renaissance patron.

The other masterpiece is the great altarpiece by Nuño Gonçalves in Lisbon (fig. 124). Though showing some Italian influence, it is painted in the Flemish style, which was brought to Portugal by Jan van Eyck, who made two trips to the Iberian peninsula, one to Spain and one to Portugal. While in Lisbon he must have offered Portuguese artists an opportunity to learn the Flemish oil technique. Like other Flemings, Van Eyck painted on panels covered with gesso. But when Nuño Gonçalves, sometime between 1460 and 1470, undertook his one surviving masterpiece, he put his pigment directly on the wood itself, omitting the gesso covering. However, in spite of his unorthodox procedure his altarpiece has lasted flawlessly. His rough technique actually enhances the crude realism with which he portrays the king, Alfonso V, his relations, and retainers. What ferocious character these nobles show as they pray in the presence of Saint Vincent, the patron saint of Portugal! The king, seen in profile, is kneeling. Opposite is Queen Isabella, painted posthumously. Above Alfonso is his son John II, who ruled Portugal from 1481 to 1495. Higher still are Henry the Navigator, one of the greatest of 15th-century explorers, and a self-portrait of the artist himself. At the extreme right is a portrait of a Jew holding the Torah, or Pentateuch, which Hebrews always carried when receiving kings in their villages, an indication of a Semitic tolerance in Portugal much greater than in neighboring Spain. Six large panels by this amazing artist, forming a single picture, represent the total output of any real significance that has survived of Portuguese painting.

A generation later than Nuño Gonçalves, Germany produced her greatest artist, Albrecht Dürer, who lived from 1471 to 1528. He began painting in the Late Gothic tradition and ended by experiencing the full impact of the Italian Renaissance. As a child he learned from his father, a goldsmith, the use of the burin, with which he later created a series of stupendous engravings. As the elder Dürer had been trained in the Netherlands, he taught his son to admire the work of Jan van Eyck and Rogier van der Weyden. This Flemish element was never completely eradicated, even by that canon of ideal beauty which the young Dürer sought in Italy and practiced after his two trips there.

The classical influence of Italian style, however, is scarcely apparent in his portraits. They are thoroughly Teutonic. His portrait engravings and woodcuts are the finest there are in these mediums. As Erasmus remarked in his *De rectalatini*, they reveal "the whole mind of man . . . and almost the voice itself. These things he places before the eye in the most pertinent lines—black ones, yet so that if you spread on pigment you would injure the work."[7] Before Dürer, medals were the portrait photographs of the Renaissance; but the number of replicas that could be cast was limited, whereas prints could be produced in far greater number and at less cost.

Dürer engraved six portraits: two of Cardinal Albrecht of Brandenburg, one each of Frederick the Wise, Philip Melanchthon, Wilibald Pirkheimer, and Erasmus of Rotterdam. The only one not entirely successful is of Erasmus (fig. 125). For once, Dürer did not express "the whole mind of man." Erasmus himself was displeased with the portrait and wrote his friend Boethius: "Dürer has drawn me, but nothing like." Of the great humanist, the engraver wrote in his journal (with apparently some vexation over Erasmus's failure to back the Lutheran cause): "Thou are but an old little man"—and this is the impression the print conveys, not charm, ironic wit, and intellectual force that characterized the sitter and which Holbein had captured so well (fig. 131).

Dürer's portrayals are never subtle. He was most successful with obvious physiognomies like the bulldog face of his lifelong friend Pirkheimer. In this engraving, vast energy seems to flash from the sitter's protruding eyes. Also well characterized is his *Frederick the Wise,* who looks the typical German princeling of the time: fat, complacent, insensitive, but very much alive (fig. 126). Note in his eyes a reflection, perhaps of the window of the room in which he was painted. In many of Dürer's prints and oils, the eyes of the model seem to mirror a window. This trick became almost a signature.

126. *Albrecht Dürer.* Frederick the Wise,
Elector of Saxony. 1524. *Engraving.*
National Gallery of Art, Washington, D. C.
Rosenwald Collection.

RIGHT:

127. *Albrecht Dürer.* Maximilian I.
1518–19. Woodcut. National Gallery of
Art, Washington, D. C. Rosenwald Collection.

OPPOSITE:

128. *Albrecht Dürer.* Self-Portrait at
Twenty-Two. *1493. Tempera and oil on*
vellum transferred to canvas, 22 × 17 1/2."
Louvre, Paris.

The most popular portrait print Dürer executed is of the Holy Roman Emperor Maximilian, whose features live in our memory largely because of this woodcut (fig. 127). The ruler looks weary and disillusioned; and although he appears aloof, Dürer wants us to sense in his stern countenance an underlying benignancy. It is remarkable how few lines the artist needed to create a likeness and to give character to a face.

More than thirty painted portraits are attributed to Dürer, and many more portrait drawings. Space, however, limits us to discussing three self-portraits, but we can see in them a record of much of the artist's life. The first, painted in 1493, shows the painter with a sprig of eryngium, a symbol of luck in love (fig. 128). He could scarcely have been more unlucky. He married that year a girl selected for him by his parents. His wife, in Panofsky's words, "thought the man she had married was a painter in the late-medieval sense, an honest craftsman who produced pictures as a tailor made coats and suits; but to her misfortune her husband discovered that art was both a divine gift and an intellectual achievement, requiring humanistic learning, a knowledge of mathematics and the general attainments of a 'liberal culture.'"[8] They were never on the same intellectual or social level. In this earliest painted self-portrait, the artist looks out of the corner of his eye suspiciously. His youthful face reveals a nervous insecurity.

The next self-portrait, painted seven years later, in 1500, shows that the artist has attained supreme self-confidence (fig. 129). Portraying himself in the conventional likeness of Christ, he also reveals a characteristic insensitivity and egotism. But it is a marvellous portrait! The artist's eyes seem to bore into the spectator as though to X-ray his brain.

Twenty-two years pass and Dürer looks once more in his mirror. This time he draws himself as a sickly old man (fig. 130). It is a weird sketch, a mixture of portraiture and religious imagery. He is nude, and the long, and probably

greasy hair of the earlier self-portrait has grown thin and dishevelled. He holds the instruments of the Passion, the scourge and the whip. His open mouth and tortured face are a cry of pain, and his emaciated body and drooping shoulders show how illness has worn him away. Although he was to live six years longer, he knows his days are numbered. This engraving is surely one of the most tragic of self-portraits.

The two greatest German portraitists of the 16th century were Dürer and Hans Holbein, if the latter may be considered German, for most of his life was spent outside Germany. In 1515, at the age of seventeen or eighteen, Hans Holbein—called the Younger, to distinguish him from his father, a leading painter of Augsburg—left home and traveled to Basel, where he made a name for himself as an illustrator. When Erasmus arrived from Rotterdam to live with his publisher, Johannes Froben, Holbein met the author of *The Praise of Folly* and painted him at least nine times, all superb portraits. What a contrast they make with Dürer's engraving (fig. 125)! This is no "old little man" but a wise, charming humanist, whose smile—sympathetic yet skeptical—implies a profound knowledge of humanity, which he believed should never be allowed to break away from the guiding hands of the Roman Catholic church, for he saw in the coming Reformation the wars and misery Europe was to suffer. The excellence of these likenesses is such that it is difficult to choose among them. One of the earliest and most monumental, however, is privately owned in England (fig. 131). It was sent by Erasmus as a gift to William Warham, archbishop of Canterbury. His Lordship was so delighted that when Holbein arrived in England he asked to have himself painted in the same pose, with a crucifix replacing the column, and with a miter, books, and a wine flask (Lambeth Palace, London). The success of this portrait launched Holbein on his English career.

In artistic matters the British were easily pleased. Since the Middle Ages they had never produced a painter of the first rank. Until the second quarter of the 18th century, those portraitists who have given us our idea of the British face were nearly all foreigners. Among these Holbein was preeminent.

Through Erasmus he came to know Sir Thomas More, who had written *Utopia* as a pendant to *The Praise of Folly*. The painter lived for some time with the Mores and while there painted a life-size group portrait of the family. It has disappeared, but the preliminary drawing remains (fig. 132). According to Paul Ganz, this is the first family group painted north of the Alps. When Erasmus received the drawing he wrote More that he saw the family as clearly as he would have had he been with them.

Holbein's stay in the intellectual and humanistic circle surrounding Sir Thomas doubtless deepened his culture and increased his psychological perceptions. His portrait of More in the Frick Collection, in New York City, reveals an integrity and spirituality in the sitter, from which one might foretell his martyrdom and canonization (fig. 133). In the museum, across from *Thomas More,* hangs a copy of Holbein's portrait of Thomas Cromwell (the original has been lost). He was the king's chamberlain and More's implacable enemy (fig. 134). The two contrasting faces are evidence of how Holbein could represent the outward appearance of a sitter with such perceptiveness that his inner character shines through. For example, consider the eyes in the two portraits. More's seem fixed on some distant vision of another world. He is a contemplative mystic but, which is rare, an urbane and witty one. Cromwell's eyes are shrewd, calculating, and relentless. He is a courtier of boundless ambition—a cold, cruel schemer. Both were close and loyal friends of Henry VIII; yet both were accused of treason. Cromwell laid the trap that led to More's execution; but later, he, too, found his head on the executioner's block. One died generally loved, the other universally hated.

The lives of these three men, More, Holbein, and Cromwell, were destined to be strangely interlocked. More introduced Holbein to many of his early sitters. Cromwell became Holbein's patron at court. It was the success of his protégé that in the end contributed to his own downfall—an example of the truth of the axiom "No good deed goes unpunished." For, as we shall see, the ruin of Cromwell was ironically assisted by Holbein's rare insincerity as a portraitist.

Among the many tasks assigned by Henry VIII to Holbein was the portrayal of bridal candidates. The monarch, a man greatly attracted by the opposite sex, abhorred the idea of an ugly queen; but after the death of Jane Seymour, when he decided to marry again, he was confronted with a problem. Aspirants from the ruling Continental families were not available in England for his inspection. He proposed to have a bevy shipped to his court on approval, but the candidates and their families considered his offer offensive. Consequently, his choice had to be made on the basis of pictures and verbal descriptions. First, he sent as emissaries Holbein and Philip Hoby, a member of the Privy Chamber, to paint in oil and words a likeness of the duchess of Milan, a popular applicant. Portrait and report were both favorable, but negotiations broke down. Next, painter and writer were sent in pursuit of the daughters of the duke of Guise and other candidates, but none proved acceptable, and the king remained a lustful widower.

Cromwell, who determined the king's policies, then took over. He persuaded his master that the balance of power demanded an alliance with the Protestant princes of Germany, who were foes of Charles V and Francis I, the enemies of England. The king's chamberlain chose for an ally the duke of Cleves, who had sisters suitable for marriage. Pourparlers were begun at once with the elector of Saxony, the patron of Lucas Cranach, as intermediary.

OPPOSITE ABOVE:
129. Albrecht Dürer. Self-Portrait at Twenty-Nine. 1500. Oil on panel, 26 3/8 × 19″. Bayerische Staatsgemäldesammlungen, Alte Pinakothek, Munich.

OPPOSITE BELOW:
130. Albrecht Dürer. Self-Portrait As Man of Sorrows. 1522. Drawing. Present whereabouts unknown.

ABOVE:
131. Hans Holbein the Younger (1497–1543). Erasmus of Rotterdam. 1523. Oil and tempera on panel, 29 7/8 × 20 1/8″. Private collection.

LEFT:
132. Hans Holbein the Younger. Sir Thomas More and His Family. 1527. Drawing. Kunstmuseum, Kupferstichkabinett, Basel.

133. *Hans Holbein the Younger*. Sir
Thomas More. *1527. Oil and tempera on
panel, 29 1/8 × 23 1/4". Copyright The
Frick Collection, New York.*

134. *After Hans Holbein the Younger.*
Thomas Cromwell, Master of the Jewel
House. *1533–34. Oil and tempera on panel,
29 1/2 × 24". Copyright The Frick Collection,
New York.*

135. *Hans Holbein the Younger*. Queen
Anne of Cleves. *1539–40. Oil and tempera
on parchment mounted on canvas, 25 5/8 ×
18 7/8". Louvre, Paris.*

Henry as usual requested a portrait. The elector of Saxony said he much regretted "his painter Lucas was sick," and no portraits were available. The last thing the duke wanted was a realistic likeness of his unprepossessing nominee, and this he knew was exactly what Lucas would provide. Henry was not to be put off by a diplomatic illness, and Holbein once more was given the unwelcome task of portraying a potential bride.

On his arrival at Cleves he saw that he was in trouble. His model was far from attractive; but his patron, Cromwell, to whom he owed so much, wanted the marriage. The only solution was to paint a portrait with no individuality whatever. The face of Anne, which he showed the king, was at least not repellent (fig. 135), and the marriage was agreed to. But when Henry met his betrothed he declared, "She is no better than a Flemish mare."

Cromwell was in disgrace; Holbein seemingly escaped censure. He may have painted Anne with some lack of candor. He may tactfully have avoided that acuity Cranach would have applied. But if Holbein was a little less than frank, he did not make Anne a beauty. It is significant that the king complained of verbal descriptions, never of the picture. A less diagrammatic rendering, a bit more accuracy on the part of the painter, might have put the king off, and without the marriage Cromwell might have survived the machinations of his enemies. Instead, the recently created earl of Essex found himself, like More before him, in the Tower with the ax ready to fall.

Shortly before Holbein painted his unlucky likeness of Anne of Cleves, he portrayed the heir to the British throne, Edward VI, not yet two years of age (fig. 139). The future English king wears court attire of gold and velvet; his rattle is held in his left hand as though it were a scepter; and with his right hand he seems to be acknowledging the cheers of his subjects. Thus, the painter has transformed the effigy of a princely infant into a symbol of royalty.

Holbein's portraiture dominated British painting until the arrival of Van Dyck in 1632: his influence is paramount in the likenesses painted by innu-

136. *Nicholas Hilliard (c. 1547–1619).* An Unknown Youth. *c. 1588. Miniature painting, 5 3/8 × 2 3/4". Victoria and Albert Museum, London.*

merable followers that cover the walls of English country houses, but it was less apparent among miniaturists until the next generation. He himself executed a few miniatures, some of them masterpieces. When he died in 1543 there was for a time no miniaturist capable of rivalling him.

Nicholas Hilliard, the first English-born portraitist of real ability, began his career in 1570, almost thirty years after Holbein's death. He soon rose to the top of his profession as a painter of miniatures. In 1600 he published *A Treatise Concerning the Arte of Limning,* a most important exposition of Elizabethan aesthetics and artistic procedures. In it he states categorically, "Holbein's manner of limning I have ever imitated and held for the best." He also discusses chiaroscuro, and his opinion on the matter received the blessing of Queen Elizabeth and became the English fashion. Hilliard says that "a picture a little shadowed may be borne withal for the rounding of it, but so greatly smutted or darkened as some use it disgrace it." From this it is apparent that Hilliard used darker flesh tones to model the face; but, as Graham Reynolds has pointed out, these delicate colors have faded and given the features an unintended flatness (fig. 136).

Hilliard's pupil Isaac Oliver, French by descent, came to England during the Huguenot persecutions of the late 16th century. He surpassed his master in the beauty of his landscape backgrounds. One of the most exquisite shows Lord Herbert of Cherbury reclining under a tree (fig. 137). The verdure stretches into the remote distance and is superbly rendered. As George Montagu, writing Horace Walpole, said, "So sweet a romantic landscape—all Tasso, all Spenser, all truth . . . that I wonder not old Bess [Queen Elizabeth] patted his cheeks. What Ann of Denmark patted he does not tell."

In his autobiography Lord Herbert described how the wife of Sir John Aeres, who had acquired the portrait by "Isaac Oliver, the painter . . . wore

137. *Isaac Oliver (d. 1617).* Edward Herbert, First Baron Herbert of Cherbury. *Miniature painting, 7 1/8 × 9". Trustees, Powis Castle, Wales.*

it about her neck so low that she hid it under her breasts." This aroused the jealousy of her husband, who tried to assassinate his Lordship for "whoring his wife." A horrific fight ensued, in which the wounded Lord Herbert, in spite of having only a fragment of his broken sword, managed to drive off Sir John and his followers. As a consequence, though he was the one attacked, he was summoned by the Lords of the Council to be tried, but the hero of the autobiography was able to produce a letter from Lady Aeres in which she stated that her husband "did lie falsely in saying that [Lord Herbert] had ever whored her." The Council accepted her word and Lord Herbert survived. This shows that having one's portrait painted could be dangerous if an enamored lady chose to have it indiscreetly about her person.

To return to the 16th century, the portraiture of Holbein forms an illuminating contrast with that of Lucas Cranach, a third important German portraitist, who lived from 1472 to 1553. Holbein was a cosmopolitan who served in London one of the most powerful monarchs of Europe. By comparison, Cranach was a provincial who worked most of his life at the unsophisticated court of Wittenberg. When a young prince of Saxony posed for him, the boy wore a jewelled chaplet but was otherwise modestly dressed (fig. 140). There is no indication here of a future ruler, nothing to show exalted station. The youth has on his party clothes; he is not a sovereign in royal regalia. He is painted realistically, with one hand curled as though he had arthritis, a curious mannerism of Cranach's. But in this intimate study, the painter has caught the unembarrassed serenity of his sitter. Whereas Holbein (fig. 139) created a hieratic, formal icon of a prince, Cranach has penetrated to the innocence of boyhood.

The difference between the two painters is clarified by other portraits. When Holbein painted Henry VIII for the Privy Chamber at Whitehall, judging by the cartoon, which is all that remains of the mural, he glorified a vulgar ruffian (fig. 138). The English monarch swaggers, truculent and intimidating. His personality is overwhelming. Cranach's Henry the Pious, on the other hand, does not swagger (fig. 142). He struts. His mannerisms are those of a model advertising gaudy apparel, clothes that are particularly tasteless. Cranach's painting is typical of German art. The German school of portrait painting, except for Dürer, remained rustic and unpolished.

Contemporary French portraiture, on the other hand, is the ultimate in sophistication. The two major French portraitists of the 16th century were Jean Clouet and his son François. Jean worked for Francis I. His famous portrait of the king is majestic but disturbing (fig. 143). The monarch fingers the hilt of his sword and smiles at the spectator, but out of the corner of his eye he looks at him suspiciously and equivocally. Will the beautifully rendered hand draw the weapon? The French king's face is unreliable and cruel. Henry VIII in Holbein's portrait is insolent and menacing, but Francis I in Clouet's is devious and malevolent.

Both Clouets, father and son, were marvellous portrait draftsmen; and, just as Holbein in his drawings has left us an image of the Tudor face, so the Clouets in their sketches from life have recorded the courts of Francis I, Henry II, Francis II, and Charles IX.

François Clouet was more influenced by Italian art than his father, whose style was basically Flemish. Reverberations of Leonardo da Vinci and the Milanese school can be detected in the slight smile of *A Lady in Her Bath* (fig. 141). This signed portrait, once thought to be of Diane de Poitiers, is now regarded

138. *Hans Holbein the Younger. Henry VII and Henry VIII. 1537. Cartoon for a wall painting in the Privy Chamber, Whitehall. Ink on paper. National Portrait Gallery, London.*

OVERLEAF LEFT ABOVE:
139. *Hans Holbein the Younger. Edward VI As a Child. 1538. Oil and tempera on panel, 22 3/8 × 17 3/8". National Gallery of Art, Washington, D. C. Andrew W. Mellon Collection.*

OVERLEAF LEFT BELOW:
140. *Lucas Cranach the Elder (1472–1553). A Prince of Saxony. c. 1517. Oil (primarily) on panel, 17 1/4 × 13 1/2". National Gallery of Art. Washington, D.C. Ralph and Mary Booth Collection.*

OVERLEAF RIGHT:
141. *François Clouet (c. 1510–1572). A Lady in Her Bath. Probably c. 1571. Oil (primarily) on panel, 36 1/4 × 32". National Gallery of Art, Washington, D.C. Samuel H. Kress Collection.*

PARVVLE PATRISSA, PATRIÆ VIRTVTIS ET HÆRES
ESTO, NIHIL MAIVS MAXIMVS ORBIS HABET.
GNATVM VIX POSSVNT COELVM ET NATVRA DEDISSE,
HVIVS QVEM PATRIS, VICTVS HONORET HONOS,
ÆQVATO TANTVM, TANTI TV FACTA PARENTIS,
VOTA HOMINVM, VIX QVO PROGREDIANTVR, HABENT
VINCITO, VICISTI QVOT REGES PRISCVS ADORAT
ORBIS, NEC TE QVI VINCERE POSSIT, ERIT.

142. *Lucas Cranach the Elder*. Henry the
Pious. *1514. Oil on panel transferred to
canvas, 72 5/8 × 32 1/2". Staatliche
Kunstsammlungen, Gemäldegalerie Alte
Meister, Dresden.*

as too late for her to have been the model. Among other identifications, that published in 1966 by Roger Trinquet is the most startling. He believes the sitter to have been Mary, Queen of Scots. His hypothesis, though far from proven, is persuasive. There can be no doubt that the bather's face, although idealized until it has become a beautiful feminine mask, does resemble a drawing by Clouet of the tragic Scottish queen.

This unembarrassed lady, whose maid is warming water for her wicker tub, made bathing-portraits fashionable in France. Trinquet declares that a woman thus portrayed must be of questionable virtue, as Protestants believed Mary, Queen of Scots to be. If this is so, the popularity of portraits of sitters bathing themselves compels one to believe that French ladies of the 16th and 17th centuries were pleased to have their virtue questioned. One must also remember that a bath in the Renaissance was not as private as today. It was often an enjoyable social event. Mary Stuart, if it is she, may have been delighted to reveal her sexual attractions, the magnetism that so often drew her infatuated lovers to death or imprisonment. Is this perhaps the finest portrait in existence of the most fascinating queen in history? The thought is inescapably appealing.

A greater contrast than that between *A Lady in Her Bath* by François Clouet and *Lady in a Fur Wrap* by Domenikos Theotokopoulos, called El Greco, scarcely exists in portraiture (fig. 144). The former arouses thoughts of sensual delight, of the pleasures of the flesh. She looks at the spectator with narrow eyes as though calculating the effect of her beauty. The latter suggests piety, decorum, withdrawal. Her large luminous eyes, her twisted, unhappy smile, lend her a singular beauty, that is complex and far from the frank sensuality of Clouet's model.

The modernity of the appearance of *Lady in a Fur Wrap* is striking, and indeed El Greco, who lived from 1541 to 1614, is the true precursor of modern painters. His style forecasts a change that came three centuries later, a shift from proportions determined by nature to proportions determined by emotion. Academic critics opposed to what they termed "modernism" used to assert that El Greco's eyesight was defective. Astigmatism, however, is not the explanation. His style was formed in Crete from a scrutiny of Byzantine mosaics and icons. It was accepted in the 16th century because paintings by Parmigianino had made slender figures with small heads fashionable. Such exaggerated elongations suited El Greco's impassioned and emotional style. Like Parmigianino he, too, can be classified as a mannerist.

We see these proportions in one of his greatest paintings, *The Burial of Count Orgaz* (fig. 146). Twenty Spanish nobles witness the count's entombment in the presence of the deceased's patron saints, Stephen and Augustine. This mixture of supernatural and natural confronted the artist with complicated problems. He wanted to show a double connection: one with the spectator, which is accomplished by the young page looking out, probably El Greco's son; and the second, a contact with the divine participants above, which is effected by the priest with his back to the viewer and the nobles who gaze upward at the vision in the sky.

Some of the participants are old and gray, some are young, some are bald, some are clean-shaven, though most are bearded; but, apart from these individual differences, they all have long, narrow faces, giving them a general resemblance to one another. This is true of other portraits by El Greco. *Cardinal Don Fernando Niño de Guevara* is typical (fig. 145). His terrifying countenance reflects all the cruelty and intolerance of the Inquisition, and his grim-

143. Jean Clouet (c. 1485–1541). Francis I. 1525–30. Oil on panel, 37 3/4 × 29 1/8". Louvre, Paris.

OVERLEAF LEFT:
144. El Greco (1541–1614). Lady in a Fur Wrap. 1577–79. Oil on canvas, 24 5/8 × 19 1/4". Glasgow Museums and Art Galleries, Stirling Maxwell Collection, Pollok House.

OVERLEAF RIGHT:
145. El Greco. Cardinal Don Fernando Niño de Guevara. c. 1600. Oil on canvas, 67 3/8 × 42 1/2". The Metropolitan Museum of Art, New York. Bequest of Mrs. H. O. Havemeyer, 1929. The H. O. Havemeyer Collection.

ness characterizes most of the artist's portraits of men. Whether nobles, monks, or priests, El Greco's models have the same unsmiling, sometimes bitter look. Their faces are too lacking in distinctiveness, too repetitious psychologically, to place their creator among the greatest portraitists. The Counter-Reformation imposed a common mood in Spain, stamping out humor, caprice, and idiosyncrasy in art—and in literature, too, with the great exception of Cervantes. Certainly those times produced no satisfactory illustrator for *Don Quixote*. Inspired illustrations for that immortal work appeared only in the 19th century with Honoré Daumier.

El Greco's distortions seem particularly eccentric in his likenesses, for in the second half of the 16th century transalpine portraiture was dominated by an international style, modelled not on his proportions, but on the more naturalistic canon of Titian. The work of Antonis Mor, the outstanding painter among many cosmopolitan artists, shows the uniformity of portrait compositions between 1550 and 1580 (fig. 147). Since sitters of various nationalities in the 16th century wore similar clothes, it is difficult to tell from any portrait whether Mor was executing one of his Flemish, Italian, Portuguese, Spanish,

146. *El Greco*. The Burial of Count Orgaz. *1586–88. Oil on canvas. 192 × 142″. S. Tomé, Toledo.*

or English commissions. The model is usually represented at three-quarter length to the mid-thigh. He is erect, turned at a three-quarter angle to right or left and seen from slightly below. His hand often holds a glove or rests on the hilt of a sword. The effect is one of decorous and aloof pride. Mor's color, compared to his exemplar, Titian's, is cold, his surface vitreous. Every detail is carefully recorded: jewels, strands of hair—even eyelashes.

The international school of 16th-century portraiture numbers no geniuses, but these artists, nevertheless, caught in the mirror of art reflections of a now-vanished life. In the work of these second-rate limners we clearly see the face of the century: how men and women looked in France, the Netherlands, Germany, and England, when Europe was being torn apart by dynastic wars, by the Reformation, and by the Counter-Reformation. The fascination of such

portraits is largely the way in which they entrap the past. Rubens, Van Dyck, and Velázquez were giants compared to Antonis Mor, but paintings by Mor and his contemporaries are documents of the human countenance, reliable in their objectivity.

Such portraits do not conceal the fact that from the death of Holbein in 1543 to the maturity of Rubens about 1600 there is a decline in transalpine portraiture. Titian lived to 1576 and Tintoretto to 1594, so Italy continued to produce great portraits. But outside Italy, in the rest of Europe, portraiture in the second half of the 16th century was pedestrian. Artists, with the single exception (in spite of his limitations) of El Greco, were all of minor stature. There is nothing in their work to predict that the golden age of European portraiture was about to begin.

147. *Antonis Mor (c. 1517/20–1576/77). Anton Perrenot-Granvella. 1549. Oil on panel, 42 1/8 × 32 1/4". Kunsthistorisches Museum, Vienna.*

MASTERS OF THE PAINTED PORTRAIT

In the history of European portraiture, the 17th century is the most significant period since Roman times. The seeds of an interest in personality and individuality, which had been sown in the Renaissance and nurtured by many portraitists, especially Raphael and Titian, flowered in the work of five masters: Peter Paul Rubens (1577–1640), Anthony van Dyck (1599–1641), Diego Velázquez (1599–1660), Frans Hals (c. 1580–1666), and Rembrandt (1606–1669). No painter of their generation—Italian, German, French, or English—can be compared to them. They gave the direction to all later portraiture.

Rubens, Van Dyck, and Velázquez established the style of the court portrait that Titian had inaugurated. This was transformed into the type of portrait favored by society in the 18th and 19th centuries. Hals and Velázquez created the portrait of vivid actuality, the likeness true to the total visual effect, which has been the model for impressionistic painting ever since. And Rembrandt, probing deep into the mind, achieved the portrait of profound psychology, which some subsequent artists have emulated but have never equalled.

In the careers of Hals and Rembrandt we also see the effect of a new social force: the middle class. Bourgeois patronage led to new standards of taste, the full impact of which was not felt until the 19th century. Thus, the 17th century was a pivotal age with vast implications for the future.

PETER PAUL RUBENS

Of the five great 17th-century masters, Rubens was the most influential. Born in Siegen, he grew up in Antwerp, where he studied with local painters of indifferent ability. His real training began when he journeyed to Italy at the age of twenty-three. He remained there for eight years, working a large part of the time for Vincenzo I Gonzaga, duke of Mantua. His duties at court did not curtail his travels, and he was able to study and copy the work of Michelangelo, Raphael, Leonardo, Correggio, Titian, and Tintoretto. From them he learned to render form and to compose on a large scale. This training is the strong basis of his decorations, which culminated in the cycle of paintings executed for Marie de' Medici. These huge canvases, combining as they do in a unique way allegorical figures and likenesses of the queen and those who played a part in her life, gave portraiture a new dimension, an amplification never before so gloriously realized.

Portrait painting was not a branch of art that absorbed Rubens as it did Van Dyck, Velázquez, Hals, and Rembrandt. Less than a third of his work can be considered portraiture. Of the five artists, he showed the minimum of psychological perception, and he seems to have felt that to delve into personal character beyond providing a satisfactory likeness was unnecessary. Generalized features were in his opinion sufficient. Between the individual and the universal he leaned strongly toward the latter.

148. Peter Paul Rubens (1577–1640). Helena Fourment in a Fur Coat. 1630–31. Oil on panel, 68 7/8 × 37 3/4". Kunsthistorisches Museum, Vienna.

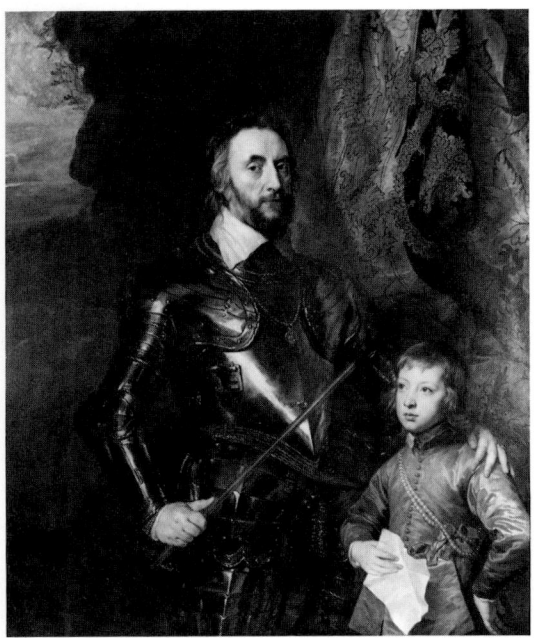

149. *Anthony van Dyck (1599–1641).*
Thomas Howard, Earl of Arundel, and
His Grandson. 1639. Oil on canvas,
55 1/8 × 47 1/4″. Collection His Grace the
Duke of Norfolk.

OPPOSITE ABOVE LEFT:
150. Peter Paul Rubens. Thomas Howard,
Earl of Arundel. *1629–30. Oil on canvas,*
50 × 40 1/8″. Isabella Stewart Gardner
Museum, Boston.

OPPOSITE ABOVE RIGHT:
151. Peter Paul Rubens. Susanna
Fourment (Le Chapeau de Paille). *1620.*
Oil on panel, 31 1/8 × 21 1/2″. National
Gallery, London. Reproduced by courtesy of
the Trustees.

OPPOSITE BELOW:
152. Peter Paul Rubens. Self-Portrait
with Isabella Brant. *1609–10. Oil on*
canvas, 70 1/2 × 53 1/2″. Bayerische
Staatsgemäldesammlungen, Alte Pinakothek,
Munich.

In his portrait in the Gardner Museum in Boston, for example, Thomas Howard, earl of Arundel, is represented as an archetype of the lofty noble, armed and prepared for battle; but in his face there is no sign of the sensibility that made him a fine connoisseur and led him to become one of the world's most ardent collectors (fig. 150). In Van Dyck's portrait of the earl there is more insight into character (fig. 149). The latter showed Arundel not only as a warrior but also as a sensitive human being. Rubens, splendid as he was in so many ways, was not an instinctive portraitist.

Yet the likenesses he painted of himself and his family, amounting to about a quarter of all his portraits, should be exempted from such strictures. These are more perceptive, whether of the ailing Isabella Brant, his first wife, or of the robust Helena Fourment, his second, or of himself, one of the most self-assured of all extroverts.

When he married the second time he was intoxicated by the beauty of his bride. He painted her repeatedly. All the portraits are inspired, but one reveals most clearly the reason for the painter's infatuation. It is the portrait of Helena holding a fur cloak around her naked body (fig. 148). Sexual attraction is clearly and intensely expressed.

Among the other family portraits, probably the most famous, and before cleaning one of the most beautiful, is the *Chapeau de Paille,* as it is popularly, if incorrectly, called (fig. 151). The sitter in this case is Susanna Fourment, Helena's sister, a frequent model and, according to an old engraving, the painter's mistress—an imputation probably fanciful. One cannot any longer judge the radiance this portrait once possessed. It is now cold and harsh. Rubens has suffered more than most painters from injudicious cleaning. The delicate glazes, so essential a part of his work, are vulnerable to solvents; and in recent years many of his paintings have been damaged in the restorer's studio, a list too long to record.

A painting in superb condition, on the other hand, is Rubens's self-portrait with Helena Fourment, now in the Metropolitan Museum, New York (fig. 153). It affords a glimpse of their married life. The aging painter's tenderness as he gazes at his young wife and gently holds her arm, her absorption and wonder as she looks down at their young son, still on leading strings, together make this canvas a touching symbol of family love and unity. Rubens's deepening humanity is evident, and especially so when one places an illustration of this work beside one of another family group representing the painter and his first wife, Isabella Brant, executed just after their marriage, a quarter of a century before (fig. 152). By comparison, how cold and impersonal the earlier painting seems! Age increased the painter's grasp of the values of sympathy and affection.

But age did not diminish his miraculous control of his brush. No other painter has equalled the glorious fluidity of handling, the rhythmic phrasing of brushstrokes so wonderfully visible in that joyous rendering of childhood and maternity, his late portrait of Helena Fourment and her children in the Louvre (fig. 154). Here is a picture by Rubens with all the glazes as yet unruined, and the effect is glorious.

The Metropolitan Museum's painting and the picture in the Louvre are high points of Rubens's work purely as a portraitist. But Rubens's greatness above all consists in his power to orchestrate complex compositions, and this gift he was able to apply to portrait painting in the great cycle of pictures executed

for Marie de' Medici (fig. 155). In these he carried emblematic portraiture to its ultimate expression. Twenty-one huge canvases were ordered to embellish the Luxembourg Palace, built by the queen after she became regent. She selected subjects that would glorify her past, and into these Rubens introduced portraits of his patroness, of her father, of her husband, Henry IV, and of her son, Louis XIII. Following her wishes, he devised as a setting a number of elaborate allegories, which even contemporaries found difficult to interpret. The meaning of the allegories, however, is unimportant. This cycle in scale, complexity of themes, and ingenuity of design is unparalleled.

The work was begun about 1621 and completed in 1625. During those four years Rubens was active as a successful diplomat in the Netherlands, Spain, and England, and as a painter completed numerous other commissions. Such a torrential output would not have been possible without a well-organized studio (one might term it a factory) with a division of labor among the assistants: one man painting hands, another foliage, another drapery, etc. These specializations foreshadow the systematic mass production of modern manufacturing, where, in the automobile industry, for example, a group of men screw on mudguards, others bolt down the engine, still others fasten on the body. Rubens occupied the position of an industrial magnate today and, like many modern industrialists, enjoyed a title and ambassadorial honors. His career represents a complete, if temporary, transformation in the social position of the artist.

Rubens developed a technical procedure suitable for mass production. In small sketches—those for the Medici cycle are preserved in the Hermitage, the Alte Pinakothek in Munich, and the Louvre—he provided his assistants with the equivalent of a contractor's blueprints. Except in a general way it is difficult to judge how much of the painting in the final pictures was executed by the master himself, for in order to maintain a consistent effect he restrained the vivacity of his brushwork, "painted down" to his collaborators, held in check his natural brio, so that he worked at a level neither above nor below his assistants.

To realize his virtuosity one must look at other paintings entirely by his hand. One of his most brilliant portraits is that of Marie de' Medici in the Prado (fig. 156). The amazing rapidity with which it was painted is obvious. The ruff is an example of the infallibility of the artist's brushwork. It is rendered without an alteration, as though with a single stroke.

This painting also displays another characteristic of Rubens's portraiture: his immense tact. Confronted with a stout lady of late middle age, he has managed to give her an attractive appearance; yet he has avoided too evident flattery. Little wonder that his aging patroness was delighted with his work and spent days in her gallery discussing the progress of his paintings.

No painter of the baroque period amplified as did Rubens the simple rhythmic phrase of the High Renaissance, with its emphasized pyramidal forms or its strong horizontals and verticals; nor were any of his contemporaries capable of transforming such static compositions into the complex swirl, the restless agitation, the organic, interwoven unity of his vast designs. That is why the Medici paintings constituted a source of pictorial instruction for artists as late as the 19th century, on a par with the most famous fresco cycles of Renaissance Italy. If Rubens was not the greatest portrait painter who ever lived, he was the greatest virtuoso of design in the history of painting. Considered as portraiture, the Medici cycle is pedestrian, but looked on as a tour de force of pictorial organization it is sublime.

ANTHONY VAN DYCK

Anthony van Dyck, Rubens's protégé, was more strictly a professional portraitist, although he also painted many religious pictures and some mythological ones. Like his master he, too, journeyed to Italy; but whereas Rubens studied not only the Venetian painters but also Michelangelo, Leonardo, and Raphael, Van Dyck's interest was chiefly fixed on Titian and Veronese. This may explain a lack in his work of that structure, that three-dimensional form which Rubens attained.

Form, however, was not Van Dyck's goal. He was supreme among 17th-century painters in other respects. As Raphael created for the 16th century the image of its celestial hierarchy, so Van Dyck created for the 17th century the image of its ruling class. He established the standard type of great gentleman, the ideal aristocrat. Moreover, the impress of his style appears everywhere on the Continent. Fashionable painters in Germany, Holland, Flanders, France, and Italy were influenced by the aristocratic poise of his sitters, by their disdainful expressions, and by their graceful postures. Spain stood apart, because there a master better able to dower his models with nobility was at work. But the 18th-century portrait grew out of Van Dyck, not out of Velázquez, for Van Dyck established an easy formula, while Velázquez's art was too subtle to be imitated.

The finest of Van Dyck's portraits were painted during his long residence in Genoa, where he became the fashionable portraitist of the patrician families. Of these Genoese likenesses, that of Elena Grimaldi is the most spectacular (fig. 158). The marchioness belongs to that imaginary nobility, lofty in stature and aloof in expression, that Van Dyck created. Her majestic bearing as she advances across her terrace and casts at the spectator below an appraising glance is the essence of aristocratic distinction. The parasol held by the blackamoor heightens still further her stature. Although she was merely a Genoese aristocrat, "towering in her pride of place" she seems more royal than any queen or empress. We see again that it is not the model but the artist who fashions our concept of the subject. This enobling power was Van Dyck's great gift, destined to bring him fame and immense wealth.

He was the child of a well-to-do Flemish family, and from the beginning his parents' money seems to have given him self-assurance. The agent of the earl of Arundel, after writing his employer that "Van Dyck's works are beginning to be esteemed almost as highly as those of his master [Rubens]," continued: "He is a young man of about twenty, and the son of wealthy parents in the town [Antwerp], for which reason it will be difficult to induce him to leave his home, especially as he sees what a fortune Rubens is making." The earl, famous as he was, might not have been able to overcome the reluctance of the young painter to leave Antwerp, but a royal summons from James I brought him in 1620 for the first time to England and to a position at court. He stayed only eight months before departing for the Netherlands and then for Italy. He returned to Antwerp in 1627 and from then on travelled back and forth between England and the Continent, passing most of his time at the Court of St. James's, where he became painter to Charles I, who knighted him in 1632.

Even before he settled in England he had come to know many of the most important personages of his day: princes, scholars, collectors, scientists, artists; and, having painted most of their likenesses, he decided to publish what

157. *Anthony van Dyck.* James Stuart,
Duke of Richmond and Lenox. *1632–
40. Oil on canvas, 85 × 50 1/4". The
Metropolitan Museum of Art, New York.
Gift of Henry G. Marquand, 1889.
Marquand Collection.*

OPPOSITE LEFT:
158. *Anthony van Dyck.* Marchesa Elena
Grimaldi, Wife of Marchese Nicola
Cattaneo. *c. 1623. Oil on canvas, 96 7/8
× 68 1/8". National Gallery of Art,
Washington, D. C. Widener Collection.*

OPPOSITE RIGHT:
159. *Anthony van Dyck.* Queen
Henrietta Maria with Her Dwarf.
*Probably c. 1633. Oil on canvas, 86 1/4 ×
53 1/8". National Gallery of Art,
Washington, D. C. Samuel H. Kress
Collection.*

he called an *Iconography,* with one hundred prints executed by the best engravers in Antwerp. For these portraits he provided small grisaille sketches based on his paintings and drawings, and, in addition, he contributed eighteen etchings. In the course of several editions some portraits were replaced and others added until there were 190 engraved or etched likenesses in the *Iconography.* An album of this kind, a Who's Who of celebrities, had never before been issued. It proved to be a remarkably successful venture.

When Van Dyck finally settled in England, his genius was buried to some extent under an avalanche of commissions. We have a description from a contemporary of his studio practice. First he did a quick drawing on gray paper with black and white chalk, giving his sitter a haughty elegance of pose; then he began painting, working on the portrait exactly one hour. He then dismissed his sitter and began with a fresh palette to draw and paint the next person for another hour. This continued all day. Assistants, using the drawing for each portrait as a basis, painted the draperies from the actual clothes, which were left with Van Dyck. The master then went over the portrait himself, concentrating on the likeness, touching up the hands, bringing to the canvas his nervous draftsmanship, his angular lines, and also accentuating the long, slender oval of the face, which became his hallmark. On canvas his sitters found themselves larger than life and much more glamorous.

To what extent did the painter idealize them? Probably a great deal. Young men in his portraits are always attractive. Their expressions are proud, their eyes heavy-lidded, their noses long. Loving horses as they did, it is not surprising that they have a slight equine resemblance (fig. 157). But Van Dyck could paint character when it was there. His portrait of Lord Strafford reveals the fierce and melancholy face of a great leader, who was destined to be betrayed by his king (fig. 160).

Woman in his paintings are always beautiful and never look old. Doubtless he flattered them inordinately. Certainly Charles's queen, Henrietta Maria, "whose teeth stuck out like defense works," was greatly improved in appearance. She is seen in figure 159 with her dwarf, Jeffrey Hudson, whom she first encountered at a state banquet when he emerged from a pie! He was a brave and loyal attendant. On one occasion when insulted by a courtier, he insisted on a duel. Because of their disparity in size, the duelists agreed to fight on horseback. The noble, considering the dwarf's challenge a joke, arrived with a toy pistol. Whereupon, Hudson, deficient in this type of humor, shot his adversary through the heart.

In Van Dyck's paintings we see reflected the face of Cavalier society and above all the features of its doomed leader, Charles I. His portraits of the king are more numerous than the portraits of George Washington by Gilbert Stuart. Our concept of both patrons has been formed by the sheer volume of these likenesses. We see Charles I with his family; we watch him as he rides or as he stands beside his horse (fig. 165). He is depicted in armor, in coronation regalia, as a Knight of the Garter; and, for the bust by Gianlorenzo Bernini, in profile, full face, and three-quarter face. Replicas of these portraits, after the Civil War, were brought out of cupboards and taken from attics, proof during the Restoration that a family had remained faithful to the Stuarts—just as portraits of George Washington, a hundred years later, were used by questionable American patriots to prove they had all along really been loyal Revolutionaries.

Perhaps we read into Van Dyck's portraits the pathos of a society blind to

the possibility of defeat and unconscious of onrushing catastrophe. Only Black Tom, earl of Strafford, with suppressed anger in his face, seems to question the future and the integrity of his royal master (fig. 160). Van Dyck scarcely ever painted the opposite side, the Roundheads. Their final triumph came after his death. But he has left us, as only a great painter can, enduring likenesses of those men and women whose devotion to their king led to ruin, exile, or death; and he has shown them as distinct individuals, with their own personalities enhanced by magnificent pictorial compositions. His designs for three hundred years have been the basis of fashionable portraiture. We see them copied by artists from Thomas Gainsborough to John Singer Sargent, from Peter Lely to Giovanni Boldini. There scarcely exists the likeness of a millionaire or a lady of fashion exhibited at the Royal Academy in London or the Salons in Paris that does not owe something to him.

FRANS HALS

Eugène Fromentin wrote of Van Dyck that he "was admired everywhere, welcomed everywhere . . . the equal of the greatest lords, the favorite and the friend of kings." He died a very rich man. What a contrast with his Dutch contemporary Frans Hals, who died in poverty after a life spent painting the leading citizens of Haarlem!

The two painters are at the antipodes of style. Hals's portraits are matter-of-fact, prosaic, harshly realistic; Van Dyck's are decorative, graceful, with overtones of poetry. They worked in two different modes. Hals was master of a certain type of true visual effect, the impression the eye receives from a quick glance. This, of course, does not mean that the painter looked at his sitter for a moment only; it means merely that the final painting has the immediacy of something glimpsed quickly. Hals does not reinforce this vision with what his mind tells him he is seeing. He puts on canvas nothing over and beyond what first met his eye. Van Dyck delineated his model in the traditional style of the Late Renaissance. He added to what he saw, after looking repeatedly at the sitter, what his imagination told him was there. This is a different approach to portraiture—Van Dyck and Hals exemplify the third and fourth modes of painting discussed at the beginning of Chapter Six.

Snapshots of the veterans of his country's continuing struggle for freedom (fig. 161), Hals's group portraits of Holland's civic guards are like gigantic colored photographs. These volunteers, banqueting or talking together, are painted with their banners, swords, and pikes to show their martial spirit. Hals gave all the officers convincing likenesses, which is what he was paid to do. There was no additional payment for their aggrandizement. Not heroes, they were merely well-to-do burghers organized to defend Haarlem or Amsterdam if either city were attacked. In the 16th century their ancestors had shown great bravery. Now, in the 17th century, they were seldom called out for active duty. Target practice and convivial gathering were their raison d'être.

Hals's group portraits have exceptional verisimilitude. The men appear to be enjoying themselves: some look at the spectator, who seemingly has just entered, some meditate on their exploits in more troubled times, others laugh and smoke. Nevertheless, how flat these military snapshots are compared with Van Dyck's *Charles I,* whose nobility is evident as he rides forth in his

160. *Anthony van Dyck.* Thomas Wentworth, Earl of Strafford. *1636. Oil on canvas, 53 1/2 × 43 3/8". The National Trust, Petworth Park Collection.*

ABOVE:
161. Frans Hals (c. 1581–1666).
Banquet of the Officers of the St.
Hadrian Militia Company. *c. 1627. Oil
on canvas, 72 1/8 × 104 7/8″. Frans Hals
Museum, Haarlem.*

RIGHT:
162. Frans Hals. Portrait of a Man.
*1627. Oil on copper, 7 7/8 × 5 9/16″.
Staatliche Museen, Preussischer Kulturbesitz,
Berlin.*

OPPOSITE:
163. Frans Hals. A Man in a Slouch
Hat. *c. 1660–66. Oil on canvas, 31 1/4 ×
26 1/4″. Staatliche Kunstsammlungen,
Hessisches Landesmuseum, Kassel.*

164. *Frans Hals*. Willem van Heythuyzen. *c. 1625. Oil on canvas, 80 1/2 × 53". Bayerische Staatsgemäldesammlungen, Alte Pinakothek, Munich.*

OPPOSITE:

165. *Anthony van Dyck*. Equestrian Portrait of Charles I. *c. 1632–38. Oil on canvas, 144 1/2 × 115". The National Gallery, London. Reproduced by courtesy of the Trustees.*

armor, prepared for battle (fig. 165); or with Lord Strafford, in whose dark countenance repressed passion seems ready to erupt (fig. 160); or with the men of Rembrandt's so-called *Night Watch,* who march so dramatically forward with drums beating and banners flying (fig. 177).

Which does one prefer in portraiture: like Van Dyck to transmute base metal into golden nobility, or to mirror instead, as Hals has done, the dull reality of middle-aged warriors, whose bravery, if it existed, had been put to the test many years earlier? Preference will always depend on personal taste, but taste, in turn, will be affected by fashion. The artist, too, is influenced not only by his own predilections but also by external factors: his background, the society in which he finds himself, the opportunity for commissions. Van Dyck's venue was the court of Charles I; Hals's, the bourgeois republic of Holland. One worked for the aristocracy, the traditional patrons of artists, the other for the middle class, a new source of commissions. The patronage of court and nobility had behind it centuries of discrimination; the middle class, lacking inherited taste, based its artistic standards on an easily recognized criterion, verisimilitude, or what was considered truth to nature. Ultimately, in the 19th century, aristocratic discernment was to vanish and middle class values were to determine the market in art. In 17th-century Holland we meet these bourgeois standards for the first time. We shall encounter them again when we consider the struggle for recognition of the significant 19th-century French artists.

To realize the enormous disparity of taste between a cosmopolitan like Van Dyck, who was sought after everywhere, and a parochial artist like Hals, who was tied all his life to one town, consider two portraits: Van Dyck's likeness of the duke of Richmond and Lenox (fig. 157) and Hals's of Willem van Heythuyzen (fig. 164). Both depict self-satisfied men. The graceful stance of Van Dyck's young nobleman shows his social distinction. His good manners are effortless, his self-assurance entire. Hals's vulgar warrior boastfully thrusts forward his sword, assumes an assertive truculence, and tries self-consciously to seem impressive. Van Dyck's portrait is artificial. He puts on canvas an ideal aristocrat, the archetype of the gentleman. Hals sees his sitter realistically. He makes no effort to conceal vulgarity; his likeness is truthful but inelegant. These two artists epitomize two different approaches to portraiture: the fashionable and the factual.

The limitation of the forthright portrait is that the artist tends to ignore the mystery that forms part of human personality. One feels in a gallery of Hals's portraits an unsatisfactory familiarity, somewhat the sensation one experiences on an ocean liner surrounded by people about whom one knows everything at first glance and nothing in reality. The facial characteristics of each person Hals portrayed are admirably delineated. No painter was more capable of catching the model's momentary appearance, especially the fugitive expression of the lips. But, having obtained a likeness, Hals stopped. Except in his last two group portraits, he did not create, as Rembrandt did, universal types of human character.

To seize the fleeting look of his subject, Hals used the technique of the oil sketch. It is a method requiring the greatest visual certainty. No touch can be altered without destroying the whole effect. Dispensing in all probability with preliminary drawings, he laid in the lights, half lights, and shadows of the different planes with crisp, incisive strokes, omitting often their transitional tones, so that form in his paintings tends to disintegrate into separate areas

that must be reintegrated by the spectator's eyes. He thus necessarily excluded all detail that cannot be seen from a normal distance with one glance. Such "sketchiness" was curbed in commissioned portraits; its freeest expression occurs in genre figures and in the portraits of his last years, when, through indifference to critical opinion, he gave himself up to unrestrained impressionism.

His works possess a vivid, staccato rhythm. The rapid, angular strokes of the painter's brush are repeated in the angular lines of his compositions, and the assertive virtuosity of his handling is echoed in the aggressive postures of his sitters. The immediacy of these portraits is often increased by the device of a hand or an elbow that breaks the picture plane, so that the spectator feels himself moved close to the figures and made to share their emotional reactions (fig. 162).

Hals could produce a painting as rapidly as anyone else a drawing, and to attain still greater speed, he reduced his palette until eventually he worked almost in monochrome. The light is clear and even, always falling from the left. It defines the shadows and permits their definition into three or four registers. Subtle gradations of tone, either for modelling or to indicate recession, were unsuitable to his style when at its best and most characteristic. Thus, the representation of interior space with luminous shadows and reflected light—the chief interest of Dutch genre painters—is not much in evidence.

Hals's claim to lasting fame is based on his virtuosity with his brush. The pyrotechnics of his handling of paint are unrivalled. He went far beyond his more recent followers, such artists as Sargent, Frank Duveneck, Augustus John, and many others of the 19th and 20th centuries. For connoisseurs who love the swordplay of the brush for its own sake, an arthritic hand, a wrinkled sleeve, or a white collar by Frans Hals is more enjoyable than all the paint-ennobled aristocracy of Sir Anthony van Dyck (fig. 163).

With such talent and with the esteem of the burghers of Haarlem, it is puzzling that Hals died in poverty. He had ample commissions until the 1650s. Yet throughout his life he was unable to earn enough money to keep out of debt. He tried picture dealing, art appraising, restoring—without success. The explanation may be in part his independent spirit. He refused, for instance, to travel twelve miles to Amsterdam to finish a group portrait, thereby probably losing his remuneration. It was once held, through a confusion of identity, that alcohol was the reason for his indigence; but, although an inordinate fondness for drink may account for his penury, there are no documents to prove it. Probably his difficulty was that most portraitists in Holland were poorly paid. The average likeness brought sixty florins. Hals was considered well compensated when he received sixty-six florins for each figure in a group portrait. Yet at that time an ox would bring a minimum of ninety florins. It seems absurd that a portrait by Frans Hals should have been valued less than a bullock.

In any event, Hals experienced such poverty that in 1642 he was unable to pay even half a florin for his membership fee to the guild of painters. But his fellow artists overlooked his impecuniousness and recognized his greatness. In 1664 they made him a member of the board of officers of the guild. The authorities of Haarlem also felt some minimum of respect for their outstanding painter and granted him two hundred florins pension, and at one time when he was too poor to heat his studio, they sent three cartloads of turf for his fire.

The painter rewarded the municipality in return by painting—about two years before his death in 1666—the regents and regentesses of the almshouses,

166.   *Frans Hals*. Regents of the Old Men's Almshouse. *c. 1664. Oil on canvas, 67 1/8 × 98 1/4". Frans Hals Museum, Haarlem.*

in all likelihood his patrons of necessity, though there is no proof that he died in their care. These two group portraits are his supreme masterpieces (fig. 166). The superficiality of his previous work has vanished. The features of these aging guardians of the old—especially the women—are recorded with a new sympathy, a new compassion. The men he paints with a certain acidity. But even here, battered and dishevelled as he portrays them, he shows, as never before, an understanding and an empathy worthy of Rembrandt.

Hals's reputation has fluctuated. In the 18th century he was not greatly admired. In the second half of the 19th century, however, technical virtuosity was once more in fashion, especially with the impressionists, who wished to emulate the way Hals painted directly on the canvas without preliminary studies. In the second half of the 20th century, with the decreasing influence of impressionism, Hals's fame among artists has again declined. With collectors, on the other hand, his popularity has, if anything, increased. His portraits bring immense prices when they come up for auction, as they do on rare occasions; and Haarlem, where his greatest paintings are concentrated, has become a pilgrimage site for art lovers.

JAN VERMEER

This chapter is devoted to the five greatest masters of 17th-century portraiture. But one artist, Jan Vermeer of Delft (1632–1675), who was not primarily a portrait painter, must also be mentioned. Although it is generally held that he portrayed his wife repeatedly, only one likeness is undoubtedly his—a self-portrait, probably with his wife, in which only the artist's back is visible (fig. 167). Like Hals and Velázquez, Vermeer was a master of the total visual effect, which each painter attained in a different way. In *The Artist's Studio,* Vermeer reached the ultimate goal of visualistic painting: the representation of objects in space with a proportional relationship of tones exactly as they are perceived in nature. His achievement is different from that of Hals. Both delineated what could be seen at a normal distance, not by focusing the eyes on different objects but by looking at the subject as a whole. The difference is that Hals depicted only as much as one would see at a quick glance, whereas Vermeer painted what the eye sees with a steady gaze. Hals often omitted transitional tones as he modelled from light to shade. Vermeer included all those tonal relations in a way perfectly consistent with optical truth. No other painter has been able to attain such subtle distinctions of color in different planes of light, nor to maintain this organization of color into such depth of shadow. It is this ability that gives absolute ocular reality to the interior of Vermeer's studio.

In brushstrokes, too, Vermeer differs from Hals. His touch is squarish; Hals's is jagged. This results in a different pictorial rhythm. Vermeer's is legato, Hals's is staccato—to borrow musical terms. But in the compositions of both, the shape of the brushstrokes harmonizes with the whole design and, to some extent, determines its character. Technically, each in his way reached a summit of painting: Vermeer arguably as a portraitist, Hals exclusively as one.

Other Dutch portrait painters were legion; but except for Rembrandt, whom we shall take up shortly, their contribution to the history of portraiture was negligible.

167. *Jan Vermeer (1632–1675). The Artist's Studio. c. 1665. Oil on canvas, 47 1/4 × 39 3/8". Kunsthistorisches Museum, Vienna.*

DIEGO VELÁZQUEZ

A part from Hals and Vermeer, the outstanding master of the true visual effect is Velázquez, a phenomenal figure in 17th-century Spanish painting. His portraits can be fully appreciated only in the Prado. The work of no other major artist is thus limited to a single collection in his own country.

His ablest contemporaries—José Ribera, Bartolomé Esteban Murillo, Francisco de Zurbarán, and Juan de Valdés Leal—were occasional portraitists but seem by comparison provincial. Ribera practiced the Italian painter Caravaggio's strong chiaroscuro and plebian realism with boring monotony. Murillo, by contrast, went in search of ideal beauty and ended in a torrent of sentimentality. Zurbarán painted with rich and sensuous impasto portraits that are often irrationally illuminated and sometimes have bizarre perspective. Valdés Leal, the most eccentric of the four, was so busy prophesying the future of painting that he was never able to achieve a personal style that fulfilled his own prophecies. None of these four had much influence on the development of portraiture.

Velázquez, on the other hand, was not provincial. He left his home at an early age and became the servant of the cosmopolitan court at Madrid. He spent his life at the great capital, where he was encouraged to paint not only the king and the aristocracy but their entourage, their attendant retinue of dwarfs, actors, and artists. In depicting them Velázquez developed a style astoundingly true to the optical impression, a realism that shows the complex organization of form perceived by the eye in the field of vision.

This is what Hals also achieved, but there are differences. The Dutch painter, especially in those canvases that were not commissioned, painted quickly, reducing, in the interest of speed, gradations of tone either in modelling or to indicate recession. Thus, Hals limited shadow to three or four registers. Velázquez's paintings, like Vermeer's, are executed with the subtlest variations of tone from light to dark, and the rendering of deep space, which Hals avoided, presented no problems to him. In brushwork Hals used slashing, angular strokes. Velázquez handled his brush in a more restrained manner, employing at times touches of astounding delicacy. Of the two, Hals was the more innovative, Velázquez the more accomplished.

To Velázquez the physical peculiarities of his models were inapposite. He was a court painter and most of his sitters were either royalty or powerful nobles. Their wrinkles and warts held no interest for him and still less for those he portrayed. Like Van Dyck he overlooked such irregularities, but he lent his subjects actuality, gave a sense of their existence beyond Van Dyck's ability to do so.

Compare, for example, *James Stuart, Duke of Richmond and Lenox* (fig. 157) with *The Infante Don Fernando* (fig. 171). Both are full-length portraits of distinguished noblemen of the highest breeding; but Van Dyck's sitter remains artificial, a model carefully posed, basically a product of the painter's idea of a great gentleman; whereas Velázquez's subject is projected as an actual human being, an individual one might have known, presented without a trace of the artist's own feelings.

Had this most brilliant of all Spanish painters lived in the 20th century, he would probably have been a physicist. The more one studies the art of the

171. *Diego Velázquez.* The Infante Don Fernando. *1632–33. Oil on canvas, 75 1/4 × 42 1/8". Prado, Madrid.*

OPPOSITE ABOVE:

172. *Diego Velázquez.* Equestrian Portrait of Prince Baltasar Carlos. *1634–35. Oil on canvas, 82 1/4 × 68 1/8". Prado, Madrid.*

OPPOSITE BELOW LEFT:

173. *Diego Velázquez.* Innocent X. *1650. Oil on canvas, 55 1/8 × 47 1/4". Galleria Doria-Pamphili, Rome.*

OPPOSITE BELOW RIGHT:

174. *Diego Velázquez.* The Maids of Honor (Las Meninas). *1656. Oil on canvas, 125 7/16 × 108 15/16". Prado, Madrid.*

past, the more apparent it is that today men of the ability of Rubens and Velázquez no longer become painters but instead seek to express themselves in industry or science. Velázquez, for instance, discovered certain facts about optics that were not corroborated until the invention of the camera in the 19th century. His knowledge of the organization of light and form in the retinal impression was certainly as great as that of any 17th-century student of optics, including Galileo. Instead of writing a book on the subject, he tried to summarize his theories in a few great paintings, done in the last years of his life.

There is nothing in his early work to foretell his eventual mastery of the true visual effect. Like many artists at the beginning of the 17th century, he fell under the spell of the Neapolitan Caravaggio, leader of the so-called naturalists. The vogue of Caravaggio's style was prodigious. Velázquez's most famous early work, *The Drinkers,* is as Caravaggesque as a painting by Ribera (fig. 169). It is a perfect example of the style of Neapolitan naturalism. The plebeian types are portrayed realistically, using a limited palette. This was realism of a sort, but it was not the type Velázquez ultimately sought, for it was not the realism of a unified optical impression. His dissatisfaction with *The Drinkers* is proved by his later efforts to change it. Certain sections were repainted and, in these, separate details were blended together as they are in his late paintings. But to gain a true visual effect he must have realized it would be necessary to repaint the picture completely. Otherwise each figure would remain, as it does, an isolated portrait. He must have seen that his partial transformation of *The Drinkers* had proved ineffective.

This and other early naturalistic paintings, tight and harshly realistic, pleased Philip IV, to whom the count of Olivares had introduced Velázquez in 1623. He painted the monarch on several occasions, and in the words of Francisco Pacheco, the painter's father-in-law, "the king had never been properly portrayed before" (fig. 168). Commissions flowed in from the nobility, and Velázquez was admired and praised by everyone. Nevertheless, had he not progressed beyond these early portraits, he would not have ranked much higher than Antonis Mor.

In 1629 Velázquez departed for Italy, perhaps encouraged to do so by Rubens, with whom he had become acquainted during the Flemish master's nine-month stay at the Spanish court. In Italy Velázquez studied the Renaissance painters, especially Titian and Tintoretto, by whose work he remained impressed all his life. They increased his ability as a portraitist, particularly in the use of color and in composition. His great innovations and extraordinary originality, however, came later, after a second Italian journey, from 1649 to 1651.

Velázquez returned to Spain in 1631 under the influence of Tintoretto. In 1634–35 he painted *The Surrender of Breda* (fig. 170), a masterpiece of portraiture in the grand manner. It has the compositional arrangement of many Tintorettos: large figures in the foreground, over which the spectator looks into a declivity and then off to the distance. The two generals in the center express the epitome of military courtesy. The victorious Spanish general, Ambrosio de Spínola, consoles his adversary, Justinus of Nassau, with the words, "The valor of the conquered makes the conqueror famous." The painting was placed in the great hall of a new royal palace in the capital, the Buen Retiro, and surrounded with other works of art, among them the equestrian portrait of Prince Baltasar Carlos, done at about the same time (fig. 172). It is difficult today to judge Velázquez as a decorative painter. His pictures were frequently part of a unified scheme: their hanging, their surroundings, even the way they

175. *Diego Velázquez.* Juan de Calabazas. *c. 1637. Oil on canvas, 41 3/4 × 32 5/8″. Prado, Madrid.*

were lighted, all arranged by the artist himself. Rarely do we see them now in their original settings. For example, the paintings that once hung in the great hall are today in a museum, the Prado, and their removal has adversely affected their appearance. For example, in the portrait of Prince Baltasar Carlos, which was intended to be hung high over a door, the curve of the pony's body is obviously exaggerated when seen from a lower level.

While work continued on the new palace, Philip IV started to refurbish his hunting lodge, the Torre de la Parada, and Velázquez was commissioned to decorate it. In the 18th century, 170 paintings were inventoried as being there, so Velázquez, who was in charge, must have been the curator of a large collection. He himself contributed several pictures with classical subjects and three full-length portraits of the king, the prince, and the Infante Don Fernando (fig. 171), as well as several likenesses of court dwarfs.

But Velázquez was interested in more than decoration in this his decorative period. Already in the equestrian and hunting portraits, the blue of the sky no longer follows the convention of Rubens. It has become the actual dew-washed tone of early morning. For Velázquez was constantly investigating the visual world; yet his scientific interest did not spoil the poetry or diminish the humanity of these great portraits.

In 1649 the king ordered Velázquez to make a second trip to Italy. Philip wanted more Italian paintings for his collection, as well as molds of classical sculpture to be cast for the adornment of his palaces. While in Rome he painted, according to his biographer Palomino, ten portraits and sketched in several others. Of these, five are extant. The greatest is *Innocent X* (fig. 173). Velázquez painted the pope with the detachment of Piero della Francesca. He imposed no mood on his sitter, as El Greco or Rembrandt would have done. He showed him existing in all the complexity of nature, not with the simplicity of a human creation.

To recognize the change in Velázquez's style from his youthful work, look at the hand with the signet ring and note how different it is from the sharply delineated hands (those not repainted by the artist) in *The Drinkers.* The papal fingers seem to twitch with nervous energy. Some critics believe revision or restoration has caused these adumbrated contours, which seem to make the fingers move. But adumbration occurs too often in Velázquez's work for it to be considered a happy accident. We find it, for example, in the hands of the boy with his foot on the dog in *The Maids of Honor* (fig. 174).

When Velázquez returned to Spain in 1651, the goal of his art was already in sight. He painted *The Maids of Honor (Las Meninas)* and achieved such a triumph of observation that Luca Giordano, one of the ablest baroque artists, called it "The Theology of Painting." Looking at this portrait of royalty on a visit to Velázquez's studio, one has the impression of overwhelming truth. The flux of life has stopped, has been made permanent. The artist was apparently struck by some accidental appealing significance in the arrangement of the little Infanta and her companions, as Edgar Degas was often captivated by a pattern in a kaleidoscope of ballerinas. Remembering this fortuitous grouping, Velázquez built his picture around it.

The pervading sense of actuality grows out of the seemingly impromptu placing of the Infanta and her entourage. The design is beautifully balanced, but it is the balance that may occur by chance in the actual world, not the balance that is a pure invention of the mind of the artist. That is why the picture appears casually grouped rather than carefully composed, and why there is not the structural unity that is supremely apparent in the designs of painters like Rubens and Raphael, artists who conceive a rhythmical arrangement and then imaginatively construct from it a composition embodying this rhythm. Velázquez's designs belong to another category. They belong with the pictures of Hals, of Degas, of artists who paint directly on the canvas without preliminary studies, and who group rather than compose their figures. It is significant that we have few drawings by Velázquez and no sketches of whole paintings.

Particularly by contrast with Rubens, Velázquez chose colors that are subdued, a little gray. But in this connection it must be remembered that the chromatic range of nature can only be approximated on canvas and that the artist, if he wishes a true visual effect, must transpose the colors that he sees into a consistent but more limited palette of pigments. The chromatic organization used by Rubens was an arbitrary, decorative scheme—the playing together of warm and cool tones with complete freedom, just as a musician might choose chords for their resonant effect. But Velázquez limited himself largely to the color relations that he actually observed under a cold, diffused morning light. His real interest was not in stimulating effects of color but in their changes in intensity, the gradations of tone as objects recede into the distance or as they approach or recede from the source of light—all the delicate adjustments whereby the eye feels space.

To gain a true optical effect the painter must not only organize values and colors but also determine the amount and character of detail. Long before Velázquez, artists had noticed that objects in the distance should be rendered with less precision than objects in the foreground. But the treatment of detail is determined by two other factors, which earlier artists had ignored: one is focus. In *The Maids of Honor* the focus is in the second plane of the picture. Hence the dog in the foreground is rendered in a blurred, indistinct manner. A camera will corroborate this penetrating discovery of a fact of vision.

The second factor is length of observation. Velázquez most often painted the effect of a rapid impression. But at times—as in his portrait of Juan de Calabazas, he rendered the blurred appearance, the lack of focus that comes from prolonged and fixed staring, when the optical nerve grows tired (fig. 175). It was this out-of-focus effect that Goya used in many of his late portraits.

Velázquez's style had little influence during the 18th century. The painters of the rococo were not interested in the true facts of vision. In the last century there was a gradual change. With Gustave Courbet, the influence of Velázquez is once more apparent, and the flat modelling of Edouard Manet and James Abbott McNeill Whistler certainly derives from him. But again there was a reaction, and with Paul Cézanne the emphasis was placed on volume. After Cézanne the vogue among artists for Velázquez decreased.

REMBRANDT

Rembrandt Harmensz van Rijn was as absorbed in the appearance of things as Velázquez, but he was prepared to subordinate a true visual effect to a plastic ideal. A diffused illumination, such as Velázquez used, is less efficacious in suggesting mass and volume than a concentrated beam of light. This spotlight effect, which Rembrandt learned from Gerard van Honthorst, a pupil of Caravaggio, he employed frequently throughout his life, but espe-

176. *Rembrandt (1606–1669). A Peasant Seated (Self-Portrait). 1630. Etching. British Museum, London.*

177. *Rembrandt*. The Night Watch.
1642. Oil on canvas, 146 × 175".
Rijksmuseum, Amsterdam.

178. *Rembrandt.* The Anatomy Lesson of Dr. Tulp. *1632. Oil on canvas, 64 × 85".* *Mauritshuis, The Hague.*

179. *Rembrandt.* The Shipbuilder and His Wife. *1633. Oil on canvas, 45 × 66 1/2". Collection H. M. The Queen, St. James's Palace, London.*

cially in his early work. Chiaroscuro was popular with the Dutch, and Rembrandt in his youth wanted desperately to be popular.

He began his career in Leiden with the type of portrait admired by his countrymen: a smooth, accurate likeness with every facial peculiarity carefully rendered. Constantin Huygens, a connoisseur and scholar, was the first critic to take a serious interest in the young painter. In 1630 he praised Rembrandt highly; but he linked him with his contemporary Jan Lievens, who, in Huygens's opinion, was abler in invention, boldness, and grandeur—a judgment as wrong as it is possible for even an art critic to make.

For Rembrandt these early years were a period of intensive training. He looked at himself in the mirror, as he was to do throughout his life, and studied the expression of violent emotion. Portraying himself in the role of a beggar, he seems to be snarling at the bourgeois world surrounding him (fig. 176). This truculence and independence noted by his first biographers are the characteristics that eventually pushed him toward ruin. But these traits were subordinate in his early period to a desire for popularity and patronage. In his letters to Huygens in gratitude for a commission from Prince Frederick Henry of Orange, the head of the Dutch state, he expressed the servility of artists of the past, who customarily addressed their benefactors in the submissive language of flunkeys. How so independent a being as Rembrandt must have hated to write in these humble terms! There is no doubt, however, that during his prosperous period he was eager for approbation. He wished to paint to the taste of the Dutch middle class. He might secretly snarl at their stupidity, but he gave them what they wanted. And this acquiescence paid. He was besieged with sitters. He painted his patrons in a style that his pupil in 1628, Gerard Dou, continued to exploit with great financial success. Rembrandt's early portraits have a porcelain-like finish, a clear delineation of features, and a strong side light from the left. There is three-dimensional form but none of the dense massiveness so characteristic of Rembrandt's late work.

One of the most important commissions during this period of prosperity was *The Anatomy Lesson of Dr. Tulp*, painted in 1632 (fig. 178). The portraits are

LEFT:
180. Rembrandt. Rembrandt and Saskia. c. 1635. Oil on canvas, 64 × 51 5/8". Staatliche Kunstsammlungen, Dresden.

181. Rembrandt. Self-Portrait. 1661. Oil on canvas, 35 7/8 × 30 3/8". Rijksmuseum, Amsterdam.

without doubt accurate likenesses. Also the doctors' varied expressions of interest, interrogation, and indifference are superbly conveyed, and the pyramidal composition is skillfully managed. But the picture lacks emotional unity, that unity we find in two 19th-century pictures with a similar subject, *The Gross Clinic* (fig. 269) and *The Agnew Clinic* (University of Pennsylvania, Philadelphia), by Thomas Eakins. It remains an illustration, no more vivid than a *tableau vivant*. It is inferior to Hals's group portraits, even the earliest ones (fig. 161), for it lacks their actuality. The figure of Dr. Tulp, for example, is stiff and unnatural, and the other doctors also seem posed and self-conscious. With Hals, the effect is as though the artist had snapped a photograph when no one was looking. Rembrandt was in the end the greater artist, but in the 1630s his portraiture was inferior to Hals's, and Hals's work, incidentally, Rembrandt seems to have ignored.

But from beginning to end, Rembrandt possessed one talent that the Haarlem artist did not. He was a magnificent illustrator, the most superb of all visual storytellers. He was able to convey narrative in a picture and at the same time to set out all its psychological implications. This quality is, of course, more apparent in Rembrandt's subject pictures than in his portraits, but occasionally one finds it even there. Take, for instance, his double portrait of 1633, *The Shipbuilder and His Wife* (fig. 179). A woman is shown handing her husband a letter, which the ship-designer reaches for, still absorbed in his work. His consort, with one hand on the latch of the door, clearly indicates her eagerness to be about her own business. Building ships, she seems to say, is all very well, but running a house is a more urgent matter and far more exacting. The scene is a brilliant study of the psychology of a husband and wife.

The events of Rembrandt's life were more intimately connected with his work than is the case with most artists. The year after he showed with such insight the relationship of a married couple, Rembrandt himself chose a bride. She was Saskia van Uylenburch, the daughter of a wealthy family and socially above her suitor; but her guardian accepted the betrothal gladly. Rembrandt's fame as an artist seems to have raised his status from that of the son of an obscure miller to the rank of the patrician class. From a worldly point of view it was a highly desirable match. At Saskia's death eight years later the painter estimated that his wife's fortune amounted to 40,750 florins—probably an exaggeration, but there is no doubt that hers was a large estate for the time. Rembrandt, too, was earning a good deal of money. For a portrait he received 500 or 600 florins, compared to an average price of 60 florins for likenesses, and the fashionable world flocked to his studio. Even though he was always improvident, he and his wife had ample means. It was a happy period in his life, a happiness reflected in the portrait of himself with Saskia on his knee (fig. 180). The champagne, the jewels, the rich apparel are signs of extravagance that may explain Saskia's slight look of disapproval. Her relations claimed that her husband had dissipated her patrimony "in dress and ostentation," causing Rembrandt to sue for libel, a suit which was thrown out of court.

His way of life obviously required large earnings. With Saskia's death in 1642, the good times were over. A myth has arisen, supported by earlier art historians, that Rembrandt's gradual ruin can be traced to the general dissatisfaction with *The Night Watch*, which he painted the year his wife died (fig. 177). Recently these theories have been discredited, but it is possible that opinion has swung too far in the opposite direction. *The Night Watch*, which broke with the tradition of the military group portrait, was not well received by all the participants in the scene. Samuel van Hoogstraten, a former pupil of Rembrandt's, wrote in 1678 that it was "so painter-like in thought, so dashing in movement, and so powerful that . . . all the other pieces in the Kloveniersdoelen stand beside it like playing cards." Nevertheless, he added the ominous words, "But in the opinion of many he made the large picture [*The Night Watch*] too much a work executed according to his own wishes than one of individual portraits which he was commissioned to do."⁹

The fact is that without Saskia's restraining influence Rembrandt's spirit of independence gradually took over, and he paid less and less attention to the wishes of his patrons. In *The Night Watch* he had shown that he could paint a heroic work equal in scale and composition to the masterpieces of the Italian Renaissance; yet his patrons complained about the obscurity of their likenesses. This must have been infuriating. He knew himself to be a genius and basically a revolutionary, and as he veered away from the accepted norms of Dutch painting, fashionable taste veered away from him. Artists like Dou, Govaert Flinck, Ferdinand Bol, and others of no greater ability were more sought after than he was, and in 1650 his former patron Huygens omitted Rembrandt's name from a list of artists he submitted to the widow of Prince Frederick Henry, who was engaged in decorating her country home, Huis Ten Bosch. Rembrandt's fame and his talent still attracted sitters, but his commissions were fewer in number and less remunerative.

Two other factors contributed to Rembrandt's financial decline and bankruptcy. First, he was unconventional. He lived for many years with Hendrickje Stoffels, a devoted girl of peasant origin, an admirable stepmother to his son, Titus, without troubling to marry her—a relationship common today but less so in 17th-century Holland. More important, after Saskia's death he made no effort to know the rich and powerful burghers. He preferred to associate with the common people. Thus, he grew more and more isolated from the society that could afford to pay well for pictures.

Second, Rembrandt was financially naive and extravagant. He was an *amateur marchant*, and his picture dealing is an example of his more foolish speculations. His collection of works of art was extensive and his study of the masterpieces in it profoundly influenced his own work. To have to sell his treasures in 1656, when he was declared bankrupt, was a blow made bitterer by the paltry sum he received for them. His self-portrait in the Rijksmuseum of 1661 is a tragic piece of autobiography. His son and his mistress had been made custodians of those pictures still in his studio and even of those he had yet to paint. Again, he turned as he had so often, to a mirror to analyze his features, to try to pierce to the mystery of his personality (fig. 181). He saw reflected a face lined with age and scarred with misfortune. His eyes looked back at him, large, troubled, and questioning. They had seen more profoundly into the human soul than those of any other artist. But he also recorded a mouth and chin weak and infirm of purpose. Here, he may have thought, was a clue to a flaw in his character, which had wrecked his life. He seems to plead for our sympathy as he shows us a ruined man. These likenesses of himself are the most pitiless in their self-analysis and the most pathetic in their self-recrimination to be found in the work of any artist. They are different from Dürer's late self-portrait (fig. 130). The German artist's cry of anguish was caused by his physical suffering; Rembrandt's grief was psychological, provoked by the realization that he had brought destruction on himself through his own folly.

Probing into his own character taught him to understand the character of others. In a unique way he entered into the personality of his sitters, presenting them to us so vividly that we seem to know them better than many people we meet in life (fig. 182). After a long scrutiny of their portraits, they become our friends, but in Rembrandt's later work they are never blithe companions. Instead, there is about them a sadness, a melancholy as intangible as the effect of certain pieces of music. They are not doleful, but rather weighed down with thought, somber rather than morose. Rembrandt has imposed on them something of his own forlornness, but in doing so he has only shaded, not destroyed, their own natural expression. Nevertheless, the mood of his portraits was unsympathetic to bourgeois patrons, who, in the 17th century as in the 18th and 19th centuries, demanded cheerful not tragic portraits. The enlargement of personality, the dramatic power, that gives to Rembrandt's sitters the same majestic personality that one feels before great actors in the traditional roles of high tragedy was of no interest to successful shopkeepers and tradesmen.

Since Holland had never produced a first-rate sculptor, it is not surprising that Rembrandt's style, as it became in the course of many years more plastic, became to the Dutch less comprehensible. This is not to say that no one understood his aims. The stream of commissions that flooded his studio in the 1630s did not dry up entirely but trickled on to the end of his life. But though his fellow citizens seem always to have respected his achievements, and even gave him the commission to paint *The Syndics of the Clothmakers' Guild* (fig. 183) as late as 1662, they did not offer him significant financial support. He stood too far outside the main current of Dutch painting. He takes his place, as does none of the other Dutch artists, in what might be called the plastic tradition of European portraiture.

The abstract words *plastic tradition* require some elucidation. A comparison between the portraits of Rembrandt, Rubens, Velázquez, and Hals will perhaps make their meaning clearer. Rubens and Rembrandt stressed to the utmost the suggestion of density and weight of substance. Velázquez and Hals kept their modelling relatively flat. They made no effort to suggest volume beyond what the eye perceives. They painted figures that always appear to stand on their feet, but those feet do not press into the ground. Their portraits have none of the heavy mass and solid weight of figures by Rubens and Rembrandt. Hals and Velázquez painted only what they saw, whereas Rubens and Rembrandt in some miraculous way seem to transcend vision and to change flesh and blood into a new element that has a specific gravity far weightier than human substance. In the 19th century we find the same effect in Cézanne's *The Artist's Father* (fig. 260).

185.   *Rembrandt*. Self-Portrait Leaning on a Sill   *1639. Etching. The Pierpont Morgan Library, New York.*

186.   *Rembrandt*. Dr. Deyman's Anatomy Lesson *(fragment). 1656. Oil on canvas, 39 3/8 × 52 3/4". Rijksmuseum, Amsterdam.*

In his late portraits Rembrandt's handling of paint also changed. His early enamel-like surfaces suggest three-dimensional form, but later a thick, crumbling paste conveys as well the density of the different volumes. This thick pigmentation, in which the paint surface itself becomes expressive, gives a rough appearance to the flesh, so that, to achieve a harmony of surface, he often dressed his figures in bejewelled and heavily brocaded costumes. By comparison, form in other Dutch pictures seems of an almost egglike fragility. Vermeer, for instance, always creates a three-dimensional effect (fig. 167), but his volumes fail to suggest the tough resistance of compact atoms, the density of substance Rembrandt renders so irresistibly that one's fingers tingle with a tactile impulse.

Rembrandt, however, differs from the great Renaissance masters of the plastic tradition in that he was more attentive to the data of vision, to a remembered optical impression. Earlier artists had concentrated on a general knowledge of form, a synthesis of many visual experiences. The contrast is particularly evident in Rembrandt's drawings and prints. The calligraphic beauty of draftsmanship in earlier artists' work was assisted by their having a mental picture of the appearance of the subject that they had conceived imaginatively. For example, running water does not look like braided hair, as it was often drawn by Leonardo when he was depicting streams and rivers. This is an imaginative concept with no resemblance to actuality, to the appearance of water as we see it in, say, a painting by Monet. A mental image, unaffected by visual data, permitted the Renaissance draftsman to concentrate on linear phrasing, on the rhythmical shape of his strokes, on their organization to suggest volume. But with Rembrandt, as with many 19th-century artists, calligraphic beauty is sacrificed to a recollected actuality. His lines are broken, overlaid, tangled—nothing mattered except that contours should coincide with remembered optical impressions (fig 184). This does not mean that Rembrandt, except when doing portraits, necessarily drew or painted from the model. It does mean, however, that even when he was working purely from imagination, the data bank of images in his memory, on which he depended, was built up of actual observations. It is this visual approach that places Rembrandt closer to Courbet, Degas, and Cézanne than to Leonardo, Raphael, and Titian.

One of the problems of the portrait painter is to devise fresh poses for his sitters, and, despite the limited number of possibilities, Rembrandt was constantly searching for new postures. He ran through the current vocabulary: Van Dyck's elegant hand on breast, Hals's casual bent elbow, Rubens's recessive diagonals, and other ideas of his own. When in 1639 he was in search of further motifs, two Italian masterpieces appeared in Holland, a Raphael and a Titian. From the art market both entered the collection of a Spaniard, Alfonso Lopez. But Rembrandt had an opportunity to study them, even to make a drawing of the Raphael, *Baldassare Castiglione* (figs. 95, 184), on which he noted that it had brought 3,500 guilders. The other painting put up for auction, Titian's *Portrait of a Man* (National Gallery, London), Rembrandt combined with the Raphael for his etched self-portrait of 1639 (fig. 185) and an oil of 1640. Both were done when he was at the peak of his prosperity. What a contrast they make with figure 181, his self-portrait of two decades later!

During those twenty years he had come a long way. A comparison between *The Anatomy Lesson of Dr. Tulp* (fig. 178) and *Dr. Deyman's Anatomy Lesson* (fig. 186) is something of a gauge. In the earlier picture all the actors are frozen in

187. Rembrandt. The Jewish Bride. c. 1665–68. Oil on canvas, 47 × 65 1/2". Rijksmuseum, Amsterdam.

appropriate postures and expressions. They do not, however, move the spectator. The later painting, although only a fragment, casts a spell. As Kenneth Clark has pointed out, the physician at the head of the cadaver, although faceless, seems to offer a solemn benediction. His assistant on the left holds a bowl as an acolyte might approach a priest at Mass. The solemnity of the scene makes one aware that pathology has its own ritual, dignified and humane.

Rembrandt's genius never faltered. When he occasionally received an official commission, he was as ingenious in old age as in youth. *The Syndics of the Clothmakers' Guild* (fig. 183), painted in 1662, represents an innovation in the formula of the group portrait. Instead of relating the participants to each other by gesture and speech and having one or more of them looking out of the picture to form a contact with the spectator, Rembrandt shows all six men staring at an intruder, who has interrupted their meeting and stands just outside the picture. This gives the scene unity and imparts an actuality and a drama absent from Hals's brilliant snapshots.

The most moving of all Rembrandt's late paintings is *The Jewish Bride* (fig. 187), painted between 1665 and 1668. The couple have never been identified. They are simply two human beings who touch each other with an affection without parallel in art. Here, Rembrandt asserts, is the union of husband and wife, or of lovers, and nothing is more sacred. His treatment in its tenderness surpasses even Rubens's painting of himself and Helena Fourment (fig. 153). Rembrandt has shown in this portrait of two unknown people how much we need each other, how love brings a responsibility for mutual support, how bonds of affection bind together individuals and banish the loneliness each person feels and fears. When the painting was done, both his beloved Hendrickje and his son, Titus, were dead. He was absolutely alone in a world that had ceased to care greatly whether he lived or died. In *The Jewish Bride* and in *The Prodigal Son* he painted his valedictory. Its message is eloquent. There are only two things that matter: compassion and love. Both, Rembrandt expressed more profoundly than any other artist.

MASTERS OF THE SCULPTURED PORTRAIT

The great 17th-century portraitists were painters. Among sculptors, the only artist who might be considered a genius was Gianlorenzo Bernini, who was born in 1598 and died in 1680. He came to Rome from Naples at an early age and was immediately launched on a career whose artistic fertility

188. Gianlorenzo Bernini (1598–1680). Costanza Buonarelli. c. 1635. Marble bust, lifesize. Bargello, Florence.

brought him enormous popularity both as an architect and a sculptor. He left Italy only once, for a triumphal sojourn in Paris, where his principal occupation was working on the designs for the Louvre. His portraiture is of the highest order. As Chandler Post has written of his busts, "Not only are they incisive characterizations, but by a selection of the best qualities in his sitters, by stress upon the elements in their personalities common to the constantly recurring types to which they belong, by a slight idealization, and by ingenuity in composition, he has raised them from the sphere of the particular into objects of universal interest and beauty."[10] His magnificent busts of Paul V, Scipione Borghese, Innocent X, Louis XIV, and his mistress Costanza Buonarelli (fig. 188), to mention only a few, show Bernini's dexterity in marble. He could counterfeit skin and flesh with an ease that was the despair of other sculptors, and he was equally adept at modelling and casting vivid, lifelike bronzes.

The sculptured portrait has always been closely associated with grave monuments. The likeness on the tomb is the final effort to rescue the appearance of the individual from oblivion. Mummies, medieval effigies, Renaissance tomb sculptures, all have the same purpose: to give immortality to the features of the deceased. Bernini was the outstanding master of this type of portraiture as well as the supreme designer of its setting, to which he gave a turbulence new in grave monuments (fig. 189). Earlier sculptors had used allegorical statues to honor the dead, but Bernini, who employed a plethora of such figures, gave them a new role, that of mourners for the departed. It is the emotional participation of these subordinate figures that gives the sepulcher the agitated unity basic in baroque design.

Bernini's phenomenal vogue, which caused him to be sought after outside Italy, especially in France, left little opportunity for other Italian sculptors, with a solitary exception, Alessandro Algardi, who was popular at the Vatican while Bernini was out of favor at the beginning of the pontificate of Innocent X. An increased interest in naturalistic detail marked Algardi's style. He was a meticulous realist, but his portraits on the whole are weaker emulations of a greater master.

In France portrait sculpture was the best in Europe, putting aside Bernini's work. Classicism as understood by Charles Le Brun, Louis XIV's court painter, permeated art. From the death of Richelieu's successor Mazarin in 1661 to the king's own death in 1715, classical elegance and formality, corresponding so closely to the literature of the time, marked every statue and bust. The consequent idealization did not, however, lend itself to a vigorous portrait style. Antoine Coysevox was the ablest of these portraitists. His bust of Louis XIV at Versailles displays the royal prerogative of haughty good looks, but the face is characterless. A slightly older contemporary of Coysevox, François Girardon, carved the effigy of Richelieu for the cardinal's tomb, which was probably designed by Le Brun (church of the Sorbonne, Paris). It shows originality in conceiving the top of the sarcophagus as the bed of death, at the foot of which Science laments the deceased and, at the head, Religion upholds the dying cardinal; but as portraiture the face is a stereotype.

There were other portrait sculptors at work, among them Nicolas and Guillaume Coustou, nephews of Coysevox. They belong partly to the 17th century and partly to the 18th century. They collaborated on a relief in Versailles showing Louis XIV crossing the Rhine, with allegorical figures reminiscent of Rubens's work for Marie de' Medici. But on the whole French sculptors contributed little of significance to the history of portraiture.

189. *Gianlorenzo Bernini.* Tomb of Urban VIII. *1628–47. Marble and gilt bronze. St. Peter's, Vatican.*

CHAPTER EIGHT

1660-1800: EUROPE AND AMERICA IN THE AGE OF ENLIGHTENMENT

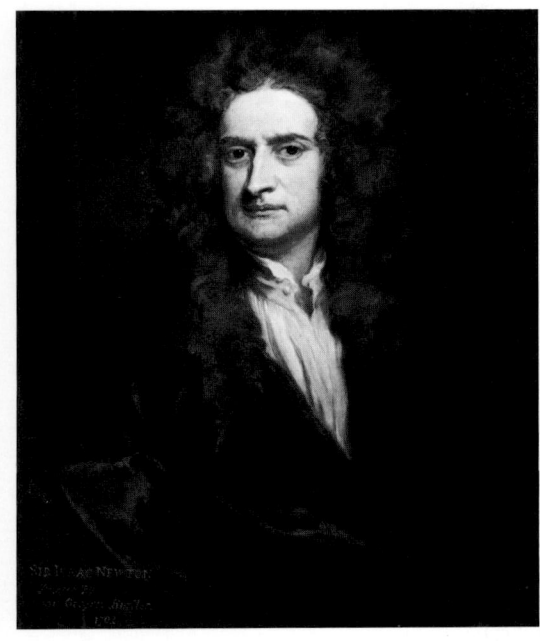

190. *Godfrey Kneller (c. 1649–1723).* Isaac Newton. *1702. Oil on canvas, 29 3/4 × 24 1/2". National Portrait Gallery, London.*

191. *William Hogarth (1697–1764).* The Graham Children. *1742. Oil on canvas, 63 3/4 × 71 1/4. The Tate Gallery, London.*

THE PAINTED PORTRAIT

I n the 18th century the finest portraitists were British and French, with a solitary exception, the Spaniard Francisco de Goya. He was the only genius among them. The others produced likenesses of high quality but failed to scale the heights attained by Leonardo, Raphael, Titian, Rubens, Van Dyck, Hals, Velázquez, and Rembrandt.

The British "phizmongers," to use Hogarth's term, were more numerous than the French and their work was more varied and original. For some time they have been unjustifiably denigrated. Recently, taste has changed and they are now beginning to be appreciated at their true worth.

It was not until the long and triumphant premiership of Robert Walpole, from 1721 to 1742, that the English aristocracy as a whole recovered the prosperity and self-assurance destroyed in the Civil War. It was then that the culture of the squirearchy received the definite form that was destined to become the distinguishing characteristic of English life. Continental portraiture during the 18th century might be described as urban since it was intimately connected with the metropolitan centers of taste: Paris, Rome, and Venice. English portraiture, on the other hand, might be considered rural since it was commissioned by a landed gentry and intended chiefly for the adornment of their country houses. Consequently, the patron on the Continent was usually presented with more suavity, in a more conventional pose. The Englishman, when painted by an English artist, generally appears plain and blunt, with the practical common sense of the country squire. The rather waxen pallor of female complexions in French and Italian portraits is unlike the more natural flesh tones of women in British portraits; moreover, rouge and powder are less conspicuous, which makes their skin look less enameled. There is much to suggest an outdoor life. The setting of British portraits of both men and women is frequently an exterior, and the sitter is often placed in a realistically observed landscape, in marked contrast to the conventional stage scenery used on the Continent.

Yet English painting in the 18th century, as in the 17th century, was closely in contact with Continental art. Although there was no foreign artist working in England of the ability of Van Dyck, he had able followers, including the Fleming Peter Lely and the German Godfrey Kneller. Moreover, there were visits from numerous French and Italian painters: Francesco Zuccarelli, Philip Mercier, Hubert François Gravelot, Sebastiano and Marco Ricci, and, in a class above these, Canaletto, to name only the most famous. On the Continent the English milord, so often portrayed by Pompeo Battoni or caricatured by

192. *William Hogarth*. The Shrimp Girl.
*c. 1750. Oil on canvas, 25 × 20". The
National Gallery, London. Reproduced by
courtesy of the Trustees.*

193. *William Hogarth*. Simon, Lord
Lovat *(detail). 1746. Etching. British
Museum, London.*

Thomas Patch, was well known as a collector and traveller, and his connoisseurship built up the great English collections of old masters. Even the lower aristocracy and the country squires, who did not go abroad, resorted during part of the year to Bath, where their taste and manners were improved by contact with men like Beau Nash, and where they might sit for their portraits to Gainsborough.

The 18th century in England was a period of exquisite taste in applied art and domestic architecture, and the portraits of the time should be considered in connection with the rooms that they were to adorn. At their best, their compositions echo the decorative rhythm of the English interior as perfectly as the mythological scenes of François Boucher echo the more nervous and delicate rhythm of French rococo ornament. But because they are portraits, and so have a certain actuality, these paintings, which are essentially decorative, are often judged by standards that should not be applied to them. With some wonderful exceptions, the English 18th-century portrait has only a little more characterization than an allegorical painting by Giovanni Battista Tiepolo; but it always has the virtues of good decorative art, that is to say, fine design in relation to its setting, and, except for the pictures of Joshua Reynolds, fine craftsmanship.

The roots of the English portrait school of the 18th century are firmly planted in the paintings of Van Dyck. As he died in 1641, however, something must be said of his followers, whose work covers the second half of the 17th century. Peter Lely was the ablest of the Van Dyck emulators. His career in England extended from 1645 to 1680. Portrayal of character was not his major talent. His faces are monotonously similar. But his color is distinguished, his compositions impressive, and his handling of the rich impasto he used is a delight. Like many fashionable painters, however, he suffered from the criticism of his sitters. As Dorothy Osborne wrote of her own portrait (private collection), "He was condemned for making the first he drew for me a little worse than I, and in making this better he has made it as unlike as tother."

Six years before Lely's death in 1680, a German, Godfrey Kneller, arrived from Holland. He became the next chief portraitist of the world of fashion. His first likenesses are almost indistinguishable from Lely's, but his own style soon emerged. His thinner paint was put on more swiftly, and his compositions tend to the vertical rather than the horizontal.

Both he and Lely were in a literal sense "face painters." As Alexander Pope wrote Lady Mary Wortley Montagu, "[Kneller] thinks it absolutely necessary to draw the face first, which he says can never be set right on the figure if the drapery and posture be finished before. To give you as little trouble as possible, he proposes to draw your face with crayons, and to finish it up, at your own house in a morning; from whence he will transfer it to the canvas, so that you need not go to sit at his house."[11]

Once the likeness was painted—although Pope does not mention the procedure or perhaps he did not know it—the portrait was usually handed over to a drapery painter to be finished. The most famous of these artisans was a Fleming, Joseph Vanhaken, who flourished somewhat later, in the 1730s and 1740s. A Swiss visitor to England described "that extraordinary sight at Vanhaken's, where he used to have canvases sent him from different parts of London and by the stagecoaches from the most remote towns in England, on which one or more masks were painted, and at the bottom of which the painter who sent them took care to add the description of the figures, whether large or small, which he was to give them." The Swiss was shocked, as the sitters, had they known, also might have been, and closes with, "Nothing could be more ridiculous."[12] All portraitists did not avail themselves of such assistance. The most distinguished painters who finished their own work were Thomas Gainsborough, William Hogarth, Jonathan Richardson, and Joseph Highmore.

Until about 1730, when portraying a man, the face painter was limited to the small area he could see of his sitter's features. It was not a great deal, for men from the 1660s on were enveloped by wigs, usually in their full-bottomed form. A wit said of the series of likenesses painted by Kneller for the political sanctuary of the Whigs, the Kit Kat Club, that they represented a lot of wigs with Whigs inside them—a fair description of many portraits of the time.

As might be expected in portraits of bewigged models, subtleties of personality and often personality itself disappeared. Feminine portraits were not handicapped by extraneous hair, but they suffered from the fashion for insipidity. Women's faces were abstract patterns, with eyebrows curving into the contours of the nose, eyes symmetrical ovals, cheeks smoothly rounded, hair a mass of carefully arranged curls, and the head placed at an angle to the neck much as in Italian mannerist painting. The formula produced a stereotype in which likenesses were so suppressed that there is uncertainty among specialists whether certain portraits are of Nell Gwyn or of the duchess of Cleveland —both royal mistresses, but with nothing but the king's bed in common. Yet even their insipid looks cannot entirely obliterate the sex appeal evident in these portraits of the royal harem.

Lely, Kneller, Michael Dahl, and a host of followers filled country houses all over England with their pictures. The men look urbane, polite, and boring; the women gaudy, languid, and vapid. There were, of course, exceptions: Kneller's portrait of Isaac Newton, for example (fig. 190), in which the great mathematician appears without a wig. A hairpiece seems to dull the insight of the artist, blunting the keenness of his perception. To find a really great portrait of a bewigged sitter is virtually impossible.

A breath of fresh air enters the bewigged and bedecked corridors of portraiture with the advent of William Hogarth, who lived from 1697 to 1764. His work inaugurates the great period of British portrait painting, from 1740 on. As he received relatively few commissions for society portraits, he decided his rivals had conducted a deliberate and malicious campaign against him. "Phizmongers," he called them, and he said they had persuaded potential patrons that his portraits of men were "caricatures" and his women "harlots." On the contrary, his few commissioned portraits are alive, vivacious, and beautifully delineated. Note, for example, the sparkling vitality of *The Graham Children* (fig. 191). Nevertheless, his masterpieces are portraits done for his own pleasure. *The Shrimp Girl* rivals Frans Hals's pictures in its dexterity of brushwork and animation of features; the subject, too, is more enticing than anything painted by the Dutch master (fig. 192). It is a miracle of direct painting, unsurpassed by any 18th-century portraitist.

Hogarth's fame depends greatly on his series of engravings—*Marriage à la Mode, The Industrious Apprentice*, etc.—made after his paintings. To what degree the actors in these scenes with moral messages are related to actual people has been debated. But even if they are in a sense portraits, the likenesses have been pushed to the verge of caricature. This is not true, on the other hand, of the prints done for journalistic purposes. Hogarth's portrait of Sarah Malcolm, painted in Newgate Prison as she was awaiting execution, is an objective re-

194. Joshua Reynolds (1723–1792). Dr. Samuel Johnson. c. 1769. Oil on canvas, 29 1/8 × 24 3/4". National Portrait Gallery, London (on loan from The Tate Gallery).

OVERLEAF LEFT:
195. Joshua Reynolds. Lady Caroline Howard. c. 1778. Oil on canvas, 56 1/4 × 44 1/2". National Gallery of Art, Washington, D. C. Andrew W. Mellon Collection.

OVERLEAF RIGHT:
196. Thomas Gainsborough (1727–1788). The Honorable Mrs. Graham. 1777. Oil on canvas, 93 1/2 × 60 3/4". National Gallery of Scotland, Edinburgh.

cording of the features of the celebrated murderess. She looks like a cook resting her arms on the kitchen table after basting the roast. With the Jacobite rebel Lord Lovat, Hogarth had a subject of more sensational appearance, but his portrait is said to be very like (fig. 193). It, too, was engraved, and such was its success that Hogarth for some time made the remarkable sum of twelve pounds a day from the sales. In the 18th century this was probably the largest profit any artist ever made from a print after a portrait.

For a portraitist the yardstick of prosperity was the number of carriages lined up in front of his studio. Reynolds had a long queue and at the height of his popularity painted six sitters a day, giving to each one hour of his time. Later he reduced sittings to three, with appointments at nine, twelve, and two. The sitter was placed on a dais eighteen inches high. The octagonal studio was lit from a small window high above, which concentrated the light. Such carefully arranged illumination was customary in the 18th century.

Reynolds placed his canvas close to his model, and, as one sitter said, "He took quite a quantity of exercise when he painted, for he continually walked backwards and forwards. His plan was to walk away several feet, then take a long look at me and the picture as we stood side by side, then rush up to the portrait and dash at it in a kind of fury. I sometimes thought he would make a mistake and paint on me instead of the picture."[13]

In spite of his apparent frenzy, Reynolds's procedure had nothing of the slapdash about it. We have a contemporary description of how he worked: "On his light-colored canvas he had already laid a ground of white, where he meant to place the head, and which was still wet. He had nothing upon his palette but flake-white, lake, and black; and without making any previous sketch or outline he began with much celerity to scumble these pigments together, till he had produced, in less than an hour, a likeness sufficiently intelligible, yet withal, as might be expected, cold and pallid to the last degree. At the second sitting, he added, I believe, to the three other colors, a little Naples yellow, but I do not remember that he used any vermillion, neither then nor at the third trial."[14] One piece of advice Reynolds gave his students he always followed himself. He used to urge them to use as few colors as possible and to be sure that these colors were not rubbed into each other once they were laid.

In one respect English 18th-century painters usually differed from their Continental colleagues. They painted the whole likeness at one time, whereas on the Continent the tendency was to paint the face bit by bit. Reynolds himself described how Pompeo Battoni, the most fashionable portraitist in Italy, "finished one feature before he proceeded to another. The consequence was, as might be expected; the countenance was never well expressed; and, as the painters say, the whole was not well put together."

Sir Joshua, like other 18th-century portraitists, did not paint exactly what he saw, nor did he risk losing the general design of the face by copying in an imitative way each variation of light and shade. There was a general tone for flesh, and there were certain places where highlights and deep shadows were placed. Definite conventions were often employed, such as a touch of carmine in the nostrils and often in the corner of the eye. Like the use of cosmetics, these conventions were intended to improve the appearance of the sitter. The painter did not feel guilty in flattering his subject. That was his intention. He was paid to give definite form to the sitter's idea of himself. He was trained to show his sitter not as he was but as he ought to be. The cruel realism of much modern portraiture would have been considered a violation of good manners.

In the 18th century the painter and the sitter usually maintained the same lack of curiosity about one another that would have characterized their relations outside the studio. There was an interest in personality, but this interest was restrained by a sense of decorum.

Sometimes such detachment was too great. Reynolds did not always satisfy his patrons with his ability to get a likeness. John Hoppner, not himself a penetrating analyst of character, expressed amazement that Reynolds dared sometimes send home a portrait with so little resemblance to the sitter. Occasionally the portrait was returned, for 18th-century artists were willing to make alterations to please their clients.

Within these limitations Reynolds's portraits show what variety and occasionally what persuasive characterization he could achieve, especially with old men. His portraits of his friend Dr. Johnson (fig. 194) bring to life that monumental character.

"Damn him! How various he is!" Gainsborough exclaimed enviously of Reynolds. And it is true that his eclecticism and his control over different styles make his art more varied than that of any of his English contemporaries. He used the imaginative pictorial mode of the Venetians very much as Rubens had. He was less instinctive, more thoughtful than Rubens, but his ideals in portraiture were essentially the same. He had mastered Venetian light and shade; he knew the construction of the human form even though he drew it sloppily; he could group his figures with the ample rhythms of the baroque; and he broke through the formula that had chained British portraiture to a monotonous symmetry, with the sitter dead center, the face basically an oval, the mouth and eyes standardized. He painted with tonal modulations that permitted features to be submerged in shadow or brought forward in light. At his best his portraits are remarkably dramatic.

But all these accomplishments were hampered and almost destroyed by a single fault. Reynolds was forever trying the most disastrous technical experiments. He wanted to discover something that would enable him to work with the solid technique of the old masters, only more quickly. He had learned from his first teacher, Thomas Hudson, how to make surfaces hard and smooth. But this was not the flowing brushwork, the sensitive impasto he observed in Rubens; still less was it the tactile surface that Rembrandt ultimately achieved; and these two artists Reynolds admired. He tried to rediscover their processes and failed. He is an example of a great painter shipwrecked by a faulty technique, an early instance of a tragedy common enough in the 19th century.

Occasionally one of Reynolds's canvases, such as *Lady Caroline Howard* (fig. 195), has retained its original brilliance and freshness, so that it looks as it did when it left his studio. Such marvellous luminosity of tone all his portraits must once have had, and if only one could see them in their original state, criticism would vanish in admiration. In *Lady Caroline Howard* he caught the unstudied gracefulness of childhood; but more often his portraits of children echo Wordsworth's *Intimations of Immortality*, lapsing into cloying sentimentality. Such a picture as *Lady Charlotte Spencer and Lord Henry Spencer* (fig. 197) could only have been painted by a bachelor!

In 1768 Reynolds was made the first president of the Royal Academy of Arts. Shortly thereafter he began his fifteen *Discourses* to fellow members and students. They are the classical defense of the grand manner in painting. Helped by his friend Dr. Johnson, he set forth the doctrine of the rational ideal

197. *Joshua Reynolds*. Lady Charlotte Spencer and Lord Henry Spencer (The Young Fortune Teller). *1755. Oil on canvas, 54 3/4 × 42 7/8". The Henry E. Huntington Library and Art Gallery, San Marino, California.*

against that incipient romanticism to which Reynolds himself was later to succumb.

A basic intention of the *Discourses* was to establish once and for all that painting was more than a mechanical art and that painters were more than craftsmen. In this, Reynolds was part of a movement to bring painting and sculpture into the liberal arts by establishing academies in which practical instruction was supplemented by theory and by a corpus of rules. Almost a century earlier in France, Charles Le Brun had inaugurated the same academic system, based on theories we later find echoed in Reynolds's *Discourses*. Both in France and in England aestheticians propounded a hierarchy of pictorial subject matter. History painting was placed at the top and still life at the bottom, with portraiture somewhere in between. Reynolds was more pragmatic and less doctrinaire than Le Brun, but even so he found it difficult to discover a satisfactory place for his own profession.

Yet economics compelled painters to be phizmongers, for in the 18th century, much as today, there was an incessant demand for portraits but very little for history painting. One portraitist who never bothered about historical subjects was Thomas Gainsborough. He was satisfied to paint likenesses since he could not support himself painting landscapes, which he would have preferred to do.

If Reynolds is an echo of Rubens, Gainsborough is an echo of Van Dyck. Both Gainsborough and Van Dyck created handsome men and women, somewhat insubstantial in construction, but painted with the utmost delicacy of touch; and both idealized their sitters to a point where physical attractiveness takes the place of personal characterization. But there was one great difference between them: Gainsborough almost always finished his paintings himself. He rarely used assistants and avoided the ubiquitous drapery painters.

Few portraitists have so seductive a touch. Unlike Reynolds, who walked back and forth in front of his canvas placed beside his sitter, Gainsborough put his easel at a right angle to his model; and using very long brushes—some say six feet long, improbable as it seems—he stood still and touched the painting at the same distance as that from which he viewed his subject. In spite of these long-handled brushes, which one would think must have been awkward, his rendering of a piece of drapery, his rhythmic touch, the delicacy of his modelling, all of these give the joy and delight we experience from an exquisite performance by an accomplished musician. We know that Gainsborough was fond of playing the viola da gamba, and when he is at his best there is in his painting of women a gossamer delicacy, a quality as melodious as the music of that instrument.

The Honorable Mrs. Graham (fig. 196), for example, not only is a likeness of one of the most beautiful women ever painted but also shows Gainsborough's technical virtuosity. Few other painters—possibly Watteau—could have rendered a dress with such exquisite phrasing. All the crinkled folds are like notes of music blending harmoniously together. The portrait has a romantic history. Mrs. Graham was consumptive, and in the hope of finding a cure her husband took her to the south of France, where she died. Meanwhile, the French Revolution had broken out. Returning to England with the body of his beloved wife, Graham was stopped at the French frontier. The guards thought that he was smuggling gold and forced him to open the coffin. The shock of seeing the corpse was so shattering that on his arrival at his estate he ordered all likenesses of Mrs. Graham placed in storage and never looked on them again.

In technical matters Gainsborough was more fortunate than Reynolds, for he discovered an original and satisfactory method of painting. He used oils as though they were watercolors, painting very thinly with one transparent stroke of the brush laid over another or placed beside it. The surface quality of his painting precluded strong contrasts of tone or great vigor of brushwork, which would, in any case, have been as discordant in his style as the sudden intrusion of a cornet in a quartet of strings.

Gainsborough was an instinctive and loving landscapist, and the backgrounds of his paintings, when the sitter is posed out-of-doors, are enchanting. Mr. and Mrs. Andrews, in an early work, are posed under a tree in a countryside painted with the naturalism of a Dutch master (fig. 198). Later his foliage became more feathery, his scenery more poetic, the whole more a creation of the painter's imagination.

Speaking of *The Mall,* now in the Frick Collection, New York City (fig. 199), James Northcote remarked to William Hazlitt that the scene "is all in motion, and in a flutter like a lady's fan. Watteau is not half so airy." It is a dream of beauty, insubstantial as a vision, the essence of 18th-century refinement and urbanity. No other European painter has combined so felicitously portraiture and landscape.

It is impossible to mention in detail the host of British portrait painters of the 18th century, whose work fills houses on both sides of the Atlantic. More than a generation before Reynolds and Gainsborough there was Jonathan Richardson, a writer as well as an artist, who was the ablest defender of portraiture before Sir Joshua delivered his *Discourses*. Richardson handed on his heavy but competent technique to Thomas Hudson, who became the most fashionable portraitist of the 1730s and 1740s. There was Joseph Highmore, who depicted Mr. Oldham and his guests (Tate Gallery, London) drinking tea together in one of the first English conversation pieces, a genre that will be discussed later. There was Allan Ramsay, who was more influenced by French art than any of his contemporaries. Often a dull painter, he produced an enchanting portrait of his wife (National Gallery of Scotland, Edinburgh), a connubial tribute hard to match. Later came the febrile George Romney, who rivalled and threatened to surpass Reynolds in popularity. His fine sense of color, of design, and of craftsmanship was marred by an obsession with pre-

198. *Thomas Gainsborough*. Mr. and Mrs. Andrews. *c. 1749. Oil on canvas, 27 1/2 × 47". The National Gallery, London. Reproduced by courtesy of the Trustees.*

tiness and a fatal passion for Emma, Lady Hamilton, which led him to paint her in fifty seductively sweet portraits. There was Joseph Wright of Derby, who revived the chiaroscuro of Caravaggio and Honthorst, and after painting portraits as original as *Experiment with the Air Pump* (Tate Gallery, London) ended with such sentimental likenesses as that of Sir Brooke Boothby, gracefully recumbent in a park with a volume of Rousseau beside him (Tate Gallery, London). A generation later we find John Opie, who was also influenced by the Italian Tenebrists, and John Hoppner, whose shallowness in characterization is somewhat concealed by his fresh and skillful brushwork.

Two painters who lived well into the Regency should be mentioned. Being antithetical, they reveal the range of portraiture at the turn of the century. One is Henry Raeburn, who immediately calls to mind Scottish society as it is described in *Waverley;* the other, Thomas Lawrence, who is equally suggestive of the more polished, more cosmopolitan world of Byron.

Raeburn as a young man decided to record only what he saw in front of him. In Edinburgh the influence of Reynolds was less pervasive, and, working in the provinces, he found it easy to put aside the usages and formulas of portraiture established by tradition: that conventional arrangement of highlights and shadows, that preestablished tone of flesh which have been mentioned. Instead, like a modern portraitist he relied on observation; having blocked out the head with vigor, he copied the areas of light and shadow he actually saw on his model's face. Sometimes he exaggerated the deep shadows around the eyes, repainting them until the sockets seem cavernous and mysterious. Sometimes he seized the salient features of his sitter at the first go and painted without changing a brushstroke. Success in direct painting of this kind depends on the swiftness and certainty of the artist's hand. Raeburn's touch failed more often than not, and his work frequently suffers from the same faults we find in many salon portraits: either the pigment is thick from re-

working, or the shadows too black, or the colors dull. Like many fashionable portraitists, particularly in the 19th century, he often tried to romanticize his sitters, placing them, when painted out-of-doors, in a wild Highland setting or emphasizing the picturesqueness of their plaids, their kilts, and their dirks (fig. 200).

Romanticism, but of a different kind, may also be discerned in Lawrence's work. It is romanticism of the drawing room, of the sentimental intrigue, for he possessed the assurance and dash of a born society painter. His art descends from Van Dyck through Nicolas de Largillière and Hyacinthe Rigaud and anticipates Giovanni Boldini and John Singer Sargent. The romantic appeal of his women—the long lines of their necks, their complexions suffused with a slight blush, their eyes limpid with sentiment—and the brilliant rendering of their gowns are unrivalled in the history of fashionable portraiture. *Sarah Barret Moulton, "Pinkie"* is probably the most seductive likeness of a young girl ever painted (fig. 201). For Windsor Castle he depicted the leaders of the alliance against Napoleon and the generals who brought about his downfall at Waterloo. Since Lawrence no portraitist has created such splendid examples of the elegance of the aristocracy. Occasionally he placed his sitters out-of-doors in a landscape that seems covered with hoarfrost, but often, in accordance with romantic taste, he left the background unfinished.

Lawrence for all his brilliance represents the end of the most creative period of the English portrait school. The degradation of the formula so firmly established soon followed. Like all formulas it was bound to lead to mannerism, to a style of painting that is illustrated by an anecdote of James Northcote's: "Hoppner frequently remarked that in painting ladies' portraits he used to make as beautiful a face as he could, then give it a likeness to the sitter, working down from this beautiful state till the bystanders should cry out, 'Oh, I see a likeness coming!' whereupon he stopped, and never ventured to make it more like."[15]

Idealization of the sitter was common in 18th-century British portraiture, for flattery was what the patron wanted; but when it was a question of his surroundings, whether indoors or out-of-doors, he wished everything portrayed with clarity and exactitude. This led to the development of a new type of painting, the conversation piece, which flourished particularly in England. It derives from 17th-century Dutch pictures of social life by such artists as Gerard Terborch, Pieter de Hooch, and Gabriel Metsu. Conversation pieces are relatively small in scale and depict several individuals informally placed in an intimate environment. The distinction between the conversation piece and the group portrait is subtle; the former, as the name implies, portrays the participants in some common activity—conversing, playing cards, listening to music; the latter shows a number of people assembled together to be portrayed. The artist painting a conversation piece focuses on the attention paid by his models to each other and also to some interest outside themselves, whereas the group portraitist concentrates on individual likenesses. Hogarth established the genre of the conversation piece, which was to become increasingly popular and to reach its peak in the work of John Zoffany, a German who spent much of his life in England, though he also sojourned in India. His Indian pictures introduce an exotic note into English portraiture, a welcome change from Georgian lawns and Palladian temples. *Colonel Mordaunt's Cockfight* combines portraits of British and Indians engaged in watching a favorite sport, a contest on which all have gambled heavily (fig. 203). How skillfully

Zoffany conveys their restrained and well-mannered excitement over the outcome!

George Stubbs specialized in portraits of horses, but he often included riders and owners, and those canvases in which they are shown together might be considered conversation pieces. What conversation goes on seems to be between the sitter and his horse. Their companionship appears more intimate than any among fellow bipeds. A charming illustration is a picture of Colonel Pocklington's sisters feeding flowers to a favorite hunter (fig. 202).

American portraiture began as a transplanted version of English portraiture. As Benjamin Haydon said in his autobiography, "Wherever the British settle, wherever they colonize, they carry and will ever carry, trial by jury, horseracing, and portrait painting." Art in the New World proved the correctness of this generalization. By the end of the first quarter of the 18th century, portrait painters appeared sporadically from Boston to Charleston.

During the second quarter of the 18th century, a fairly accomplished colonial style of portraiture was established. The leading artists of this generation were John Smibert, a Scot who emigrated to Connecticut with Dean Berkeley, and Robert Feke, the first native-born painter of ability. Smibert was a pupil at James Thornhill's Academy in London, and a student of Italian painting. He came to America to teach art in a proposed college for Indian missionaries. The year of his arrival, 1729, he painted his patron, Dean Berkeley, and his entourage, with himself on the extreme left (fig. 204). The design is elementary and the attempt at characterization exaggerated. But in spite of these faults, the sincerity of the artist, his brave effort to master the complicated subject, to create the first group portrait painted in the New World, gives his large composition a certain impressive dignity.

There is nothing specifically American in Smibert's work, nor is there in the paintings of Robert Feke. He too has left us a group portrait, *Isaac Royal and His Family* (Harvard University Law School, Cambridge), painted in 1741. It is simpler and less agitated in composition. Feke was an able craftsman and a subtle colorist, but he was more a drapery painter than a portraitist. In his work the brilliant color of a flowered waistcoat or the silvery sheen of a lady's gown is rendered skillfully, but there is little character or individuality in those portrayed.

The American school really begins with the work of two artists of the next generation, Benjamin West and John Singleton Copley, who were born the same year, 1738. They stand as the prototypes of a basic division among American painters: on the one hand, those who have chosen to work in Europe, and, on the other, those who have done their best work at home. West, who left America at the age of twenty-one, was the precursor of the expatriates James Abbott McNeill Whistler, Mary Cassatt, and John Singer Sargent. Copley, until he left the Colonies in mid-career, during the Revolution, marked out the path that Thomas Eakins and other American realists were to explore.

Benjamin West was born of Quaker parents and encouraged the story that he was taught to paint by friendly Indians. But he would have acknowledged that they could not teach him much, and he would have agreed with Copley

in his lament, "I think myself peculiarly unlucky in living in a place into which there has not been one portrait brought that is worthy to be called a picture within my memory." For an American, to become a painter meant to become a student abroad. West in 1763 settled in England, where he remained the rest of his life. In spite of the Revolution he became an intimate friend of George III and succeeded Reynolds as the second president of the Royal Academy. He preferred to look on himself as a history painter, but he executed a number of portraits. In *The Death of Wolfe* he combined historical painting and portraiture (fig. 205). Although the legend has been discredited that West was the first to portray the participants in a contemporary military action in the dress of the day and not in classical clothes, his picture remains an example of the

OPPOSITE ABOVE:
201. Thomas Lawrence (1769–1840). Sarah Barret Moulton, "Pinkie". 1794. Oil on canvas, 57 1/2 × 39 1/4". The Henry E. Huntington Library and Art Gallery, San Marino, California.

OPPOSITE BELOW:
202. George Stubbs (1724–1806). Colonel Pocklington with His Sisters. 1769. Oil on canvas, 39 3/8 × 49 3/4". National Gallery of Art, Washington, D. C. Gift of Mrs. Charles S. Carstairs in memory of her husband, Charles Stewart Carstairs.

ABOVE:
203. John Zoffany (1733–1810). Colonel Mordaunt's Cockfight. c. 1784–86. Oil on canvas, 40 1/8 × 58 5/8". Private collection.

LEFT:
204. John Smibert (1688–1751). Dean Berkeley and His Entourage. 1729. Oil on canvas, 69 1/2 × 93". Yale University Art Gallery, New Haven. Gift of Isaac Lothrop.

new trend toward historical realism. But prevailing neoclassicism caused him to depict the expiring general in the graceful pose of the Hellenistic statue *The Dying Gaul*. An Indian broods like a Greek river god over the scene, for West whenever possible brought into his paintings one or more redskins. An unkind critic pointed out that there were no Indians with the British at Quebec, and if there had been they would never have gone into battle barefoot. As an authority on the American aborigines, West, in spite of his claims, left much to be desired. Nevertheless, Indians were a reminder that he came from America and shared with Rousseau an admiration for the Noble Savage.

Before his departure for Europe in 1774, John Singleton Copley perfected the American colonial portrait. He painted in a style so forceful and so direct that even the facile Gilbert Stuart admitted that "he knew more than all of us put together." Such knowledge was forced on Copley by the exacting demands of his patrons. With patience he recorded their shrewd Yankee countenances. To do this he needed many sittings. Luckily for him, life in the Colonies was boring and there were few social diversions. Posing for one's portrait was as amusing as anything else. Henry Sargent remarked that his mother, after posing for more than ninety hours, discovered that Copley had rubbed out everything and was starting over again; yet she continued to sit and the portrait was finished. What a contrast with English portraitists, who required from one to three sittings! Epes Sargent, another Copley patron, must have leaned against the column for days while every wrinkle, every knuckle, every joint of his arthritic hand was painted (fig. 206).

Copley realized that this willingness to pose was essential. He wrote that his pictures were "almost always good in proportion to the time I give them, provided I have a subject that is picturesque." For a portraitist to speak of a picturesque subject may seem strange. By picturesque Copley meant interesting to paint; and in portraiture it is true that some faces are exciting to an artist while others are equally dispiriting. To be successful Copley needed a model like Mrs. Thomas Boylston, with the shrewd eyes and the firm mouth of a colonial housewife (fig. 208). How long she had to pose we do not know—

less than ninety hours, one hopes; doubtless there were many sittings, since the shortcuts of European portrait painting were unknown to Copley. He had never learned, for instance, the formulas for depth and placement of shadows or for flesh tones, for touches of carmine in nose and mouth—all those mechanical procedures that simplify portraiture. He had only a penetrating power of observation. He produced a brusque, unadorned recording of the sitter that has more in common with the 15th-century artist's unflattering statement of personality than with the suave, graceful style of the 18th century.

Though Copley longed to go to Europe, he could not make up his mind until the Revolution decided him. As he said, he hated political contests, "being neither pleasing to an artist nor advantageous to the art itself." Moreover, he was married to the daughter of Richard Clarke, the irascible Tory merchant whose shipment of tea was unexpectedly watered in front of his office. The Boston Tea Party was too much for a conservative entrepreneur like Clarke. He left the Colonies in high dudgeon and low repute, taking with him his daughter and grandchildren, and in London joining his son-in-law, who had been studying in Italy. To celebrate the family reunion, Copley painted his wife surrounded by her children, with Grandfather Clarke holding the youngest Copley (fig. 207). The painter stands in the background clutching a sheaf of drawings, all that remained of his New England prosperity.

Copley must have realized that he had to change his whole approach to painting. The image of Richard Clarke, especially his hands and face, and the doll in the corner of the picture are among the last appearances of that tight delineation which characterized Copley's early work. The portraits of Mrs. Copley and the children and the composition of *The Copley Family* all show the influence of Reynolds, of West, of the grand manner of portraiture, which Copley forced himself to adopt.

How accomplished he became in the new style can be illustrated by scores of portraits. But Copley's popularity dwindled, he fell into debt, and he often

looked wistfully homeward, frequently inquiring whether it would be wise for him to return, for he always considered his stay in England to some extent an exile.

Gilbert Stuart's life was in many ways the reverse of Copley's. Born in Rhode Island, he began his career in England but did his most interesting work later in America. He settled in London in 1775 and for a time had to live on his meager savings. In desperation he finally wrote Benjamin West, "At the age of twenty-one . . . [I] find myself ignorant without business or friends, without the necessaries of life so far that for some time I have been reduced to one miserable meal a day and frequently not even that." Always benevolent, West was touched. He took the destitute young painter into his house and helped him get established as a successful portraitist.

After six years of study, Stuart was described as capable of making "a tolerable likeness of the face, but as to the figure he could not get below the fifth button." Stung by this criticism, he determined to do a full-length of his next sitter. When William Grant of Congalton appeared at the studio one day, it was bitterly cold, and Stuart remarked, "It is a better day for skating than for posing." And so painter and sitter went off to St. James's Park to amuse themselves. The outing suggested to Stuart's unconventional mind a portrait on ice (fig. 211). The success of the painting at the Royal Academy was so great that, years later, Stuart told Josiah Quincy that he was suddenly lifted into fame by a single picture.

From West, Stuart had learned the formula of portraiture. As he said himself, "When Benny teaches the boys, he says yellow and white there and he makes a streak . . . brown and red there, for a warm shadow, and another streak. But nature does not color in streaks. Look at my hand; see how the colors are mottled and mingled, yet all is clear as silver." He was not satisfied with the 18th-century procedure. "I wish," he said, "to find out what nature is for myself and see her with my own eyes."[16]

Such freshness of vision was easier to achieve in the Colonies than in the mother country, for in America no formula for portraiture had been established. Stuart returned, swept home by an avalanche of debts. As he said on leaving Ireland, where he had sought refuge from his English creditors, "I expect [in America] to make a fortune by Washington alone. I calculate upon making a plurality of his portraits, whole-lengths, that will enable me to realize; and if I should be fortunate, I will repay my English and Irish creditors."

Fortunate he was, but there is no record of his having repaid his creditors. Washington sat for him, and the first portrait he painted of the president has been identified as the Vaughan *Washington* in the National Gallery of Art. Later Washington was persuaded to pose for two other portraits, the full-length Lansdowne painting, now belonging to Lord Roseberry, and the unfinished Athenaeum head (fig. 212). Throughout his life Stuart earned a considerable income by making replicas of these paintings, especially the Athenaeum head, which he copied more than seventy times, referring to these replicas as his "hundred-dollar bills."

In America Stuart's originality increased. The notes of his theories taken by another painter, Matthew Harris Jouett, are astonishing when judged by 18th-century standards. "Drawing the features distinctly and carefully with chalk [is] loss of time; all studies to be made with the brush in hand"; and, "Good flesh coloring partook of all colors, not mixed, so as to be combined in one tint, but showing through each other like the blood through the natural skin."

Stuart's late paintings often have the indistinctness of unfocused vision, with the planes of the face adumbrated rather than defined, an effect Stuart explained in terms not unlike those of Leonardo da Vinci: "The true and perfect image of the man is to be seen only in a mist or hazy atmosphere." In carrying out these theories he departed from the 18th-century formula for portraiture and approached the style of the French impressionists. Had there been the artists and the tradition in America that there were in France, a painter capable of the portrait of Mrs. Perez Morton might have caused impressionism to appear in the New World generations before it revolutionized art in Europe (fig. 209).

Stuart was the most important artist helped directly by West; but there were other American painters who swarmed around him, accepting gladly his assistance and hospitality. Three of these artists, Charles Willson Peale, John Trumbull, and Ralph Earl deserve some mention.

From 1767 to 1769 Peale stayed in London studying with West. He made great progress, and when in 1795 he painted the portrait of his two sons climbing a staircase (fig. 210), he showed himself a master of illusionism and an artist of originality. But in the New World his was not a lucrative profession, and to increase his income Peale opened a portrait gallery. Upon the discovery of the bones of a mastodon, his business manager suggested that they be shown with the paintings, because, as he said with more frankness than tact, "There are many men like myself who would prefer seeing such articles of curiosity than any paintings whatever." And eventually objects of natural history crowded out the portraits in the first American museum.

The position of the artist in the New World was indeed a difficult one. When John Trumbull argued with his father that art was highly esteemed "in the

OPPOSITE ABOVE:
211. Gilbert Stuart. The Skater. 1782. Oil on canvas, 96 5/8 × 58 1/8". National Gallery of Art, Washington, D. C. Andrew W. Mellon Collection, 1950.

OPPOSITE BELOW:
212. Gilbert Stuart. George Washington. 1796. Oil on canvas, 39 5/8 × 34 1/2". Owned jointly by Museum of Fine Arts, Boston, and National Portrait Gallery, Washington, D. C.

ABOVE:
213. Ralph Earl (1751–1801). Chief Justice Oliver Ellsworth and His Wife, Abigail Wolcott Ellsworth. 1792. Oil on canvas, 71 × 64". Wadsworth Atheneum, Hartford.

glorious days of Greece and Rome," and should be so in America, he received the laconic reply, "You forget, sir, that Connecticut is not Athens." But Trumbull was determined to be a painter, and he finally received the most important commission in the young Republic, to paint for the Capitol portraits of the founders of the new nation. Although his pictures were not received with great enthusiasm, they have for 150 years appeared in practically every book on American history.

Ralph Earl devoted himself to the faithful portrayal of the Connecticut squires, their wives, their farms, and their homes. They took immense pride in their possessions. In Earl's double portrait of Oliver Ellsworth and his wife, for example, the sitters desired to be completely surrounded by their property, so that through the window beside which they are seated one can see the exterior of the house in which they are posing (fig. 213). This provincial style—naive, without technical facility, rude, and at times awkward—is reflected in the vast majority of 18th-century American portraits.

Portraiture in France during the reign of Louis XIV, from 1643 to 1715, was competent but not of exceptional distinction. Charles Le Brun, a protégé of the king's minister Colbert, was artistic dictator and ruled with an iron hand. French artists accepted his decree that portraiture ranked below history painting. They did not, however, all share his love of Raphael and his distaste for Rubens. The division between those painters who emulated Raphael, his draftsmanship and composition, and those who admired Rubens, his color and brushwork, divided French painters until the middle of the 19th century.

After Colbert's death, the king's painter was replaced in all his offices by Pierre Mignard. Under his authority color took precedence over drawing. Mignard, a sloppy executant, became the most fashionable portraitist of his time; this, along with the emoluments of the royal tapestry factory and other art industries of the state, plus the vogue for his saccharine madonnas and mediocre decorative work, combined to make an indifferent artist one of the richest painters in history.

Philippe de Champaigne, Mignard's contemporary, was his artistic antithesis. A Fleming, he was the ablest foreign artist to settle in France during the 17th century. His dignified portraits were painted with precision and probity. After 1643, when he took up residence in the convent of Port-Royal, the austerity of his Jansenist friends seems to have found expression in a strictly limited palette and severely simple likenesses. His usual detachment is less apparent in his portrait of Sister Catherine Agnes Arnaud and Sister Catherine Susanne de Champaigne, his daughter, which is so infused with serene piety as to become almost devotional painting (fig. 215).

An outstanding contribution to portraiture made by French artists in the 17th century was in portrait engraving. Usually painters provided the originals of these prints. To aid the engraver, they rendered structure and contour with exaggerated clarity, in a consequently tight style. The greatest of the engravers, Robert Nanteuil, however, drew his own likenesses for many of his prints, and these drawings and pastels, and the engravings made from them, are among the most probing characterizations to be found in the graphic arts (fig. 214).

With the approach of the 18th century, a more colorful palette replaced

214. Robert Nanteuil (1623/25–1678). César D'Estrées. 1660. Engraving. National Gallery of Art, Washington, D. C. Rosenwald Collection.

OPPOSITE ABOVE:
215. Philippe de Champaigne (1602–1674). Sister Catherine Susanne de Champaigne and Sister Catherine Agnès Arnaud. 1662. Oil on canvas, 65 × 90 1/8". Louvre, Paris.

OPPOSITE BELOW:
216. Nicolas de Largillière (1656–1746). Elizabeth Throckmorton. 1729. Oil on canvas, 32 × 25 7/8". National Gallery of Art, Washington, D. C. Ailsa Mellon Bruce Fund.

217. Maurice Quentin de La Tour (1704–1788). Self-Portrait. 1751. Pastel, 25 1/4 × 21 5/8". Musée de Picardie, Amiens.

the grays and browns favored by the portrait painters of the earlier part of the reign of Louis XIV, but the gayer spirit characteristic of the rococo did not flourish until the reign of Louis XV (1715–74). In the work of such transitional painters as Hyacinthe Rigaud and Nicolas de Largillière, the model is often posed in the solemn, pompous style fashionable in the last years of the Grand Monarque. Convoluted draperies in the background repeat the silhouette of the figure, making the whole painting into a single design and enhancing the grandiose impressiveness of the sitter. Eyes were painted more vivaciously, flesh and blood were no longer frozen by the statuesque ideals of the classicists. French taste, influenced by Mignard, had swung once more from Italy to the Low Countries, and the vitalizing warmth of Van Dyck and Rubens, never completely chilled by Le Brun, was again to be felt.

Largillière, who lived to be ninety, was the John Singer Sargent of the age of the Roi de Soleil. Everyone in society wanted to be painted by him. As a young man he had travelled to London to study under Lely, and Charles II wished him to remain; but anti-Catholic feeling in England decided his return to France, where he spent the rest of his life, except for a short stay in England during the reign of James II. He was particularly popular with the English recusants, families like the Throckmortons, staunch supporters of the pope and the Stuarts. He painted Elizabeth Throckmorton when she was thirty-five years of age (fig. 216). Her beauty proves that life in a convent could preserve feminine loveliness better than all the cosmetics of the secular world. Little wonder that in 18th-century novels and memoirs, the hero often falls in love with a nun.

This was the time when French portraiture established that hegemony it has held ever since in European art. Though still admitted in theory, the primacy accorded the painting of history was challenged in France, as it was also in England, by the new psychological interest of the age. The mood of the 18th century was not only airier and lighter but also more introspective. Letters, memoirs, confessions flourished and were copiously published, with the result that in spite of aesthetic theory, portraiture increased, and, being more remunerative, attracted artists away from the loftier pursuit of historical painting. The pastel, popularized in France by the Venetian Rosalba Carriera, offered a medium that was rapid, fragile, and delicate in color, a vehicle perfectly attuned to 18th-century taste. The difficulty of this technique—the impossibility of retouching and the necessity of arriving at the correct tone by hatching with different chalks on the paper itself—all contribute by their discipline to the elimination of the unessential and the seizure of the significant features of the model.

The two greatest pastellists were both French: Maurice Quentin de La Tour and Jean-Baptiste Perronneau. Only rarely, in such portraits as that of President Bernard di Rieux and Madame de Pompadour, did La Tour draw more than the head and bust of his sitters. Impelled, nevertheless, by a desire for the utmost expression without distortion, he sometimes pushed his pastels too far, losing the essential quality of freshness. His genius for capturing the "speaking likeness," is apparent in his own self-portrait (fig. 217).

Perronneau's portraits are more delicate than La Tour's and less aggressively alive. Eclipsed by his rival's fame in Paris, he was forced to seek commissions in the provinces and abroad. In England, Holland, and Russia his sympathetic insight into character was more warmly appreciated and his gentler spirit worked with more freedom.

A third pastellist of distinction was Jean-Etienne Liotard. Of French origin, he worked principally in Geneva, although he spent five years in Constantinople executing pastels of exotic beauties from the seraglio. His portrait of Madame d'Epinay is a fine example of his precise draftsmanship and his skill in rendering with his crayon the textures of silk and lace (fig. 218). Liotard conveys with psychological astuteness his model's wistful allure. She is an 18th-century *femme de lettres,* piquant yet diffident. Ingres said of this pastel, "Je ne sais pas s'il y a un plus beau portrait que celui-là en Italie."

The pastel as a medium aroused the jealousy of artists who painted in oil. By its lighter tonality, its bright, sparkling color, a pastel will often "kill" the effect of an oil painting when hung on the same wall. Since in a salon exhibition the primary object of each artist is to make his work "tell," the too exclusive success of the pastellists led the Academy in 1749 to refuse them admission. Perronneau, therefore, painted his reception piece in oil and was thus forced to work in both mediums, as was Liotard. Other artists who normally painted on canvas used pastel from time to time, and such painters as Jean Marc Nattier, François Boucher, and Antoine Coypel were attracted to it less because of its possibilities for the delineation of character than for its value as ornament in boudoirs and small painted rooms.

To this generalization there are two remarkable exceptions: a self-portrait of Jean-Baptiste-Siméon Chardin (fig. 220) and Chardin's portrait of his wife (Louvre, Paris). At the end of his life, prevented by increasing blindness from painting in oil, Chardin turned to the use of chalk, as Degas was to do a century later. The likenesses of himself and Madame Chardin are more than portraits of individuals. In their quiet dignity they stand as universal types—the very ideal of bourgeois character.

In the 18th century the hierarchy of subject matter gradually ceased to be sacrosanct. With the decreasing absolutism of the monarchy, the artistic dictatorship of the Academy lessened. Moreover, the rise of the middle class provided new patrons who gave artists greater freedom. But the traditional supremacy conceded to the painting of history continued to influence portraiture. This ascendancy was responsible to some extent for that hybrid genre mythological likenesses, by which portraiture was elevated to the rank of history painting. Such portraits also looked forward to neoclassicism. Typical is the painting of Madame de Caumartin (fig. 219). By representing his sitter as Hebe, the goddess of youth, Nattier enjoyed a double advantage. He flattered his model and raised himself to the rank of the historical painters. Nattier came to specialize in this transformation of pretty ladies into Greek divinities, but the mythological style encouraged such idealization that his portraits became practically indistinguishable, except as particular persons were associated with particular mythological beings. But when sitters, like saints in devotional paintings, could be told apart only by their attributes, and when the limited number of Greek goddesses threatened frequent duplication, the fashion soon died out.

François Hubert Drouais, who marks the transition in the fashionable mode from Nattier to Elisabeth Vigée-Lebrun, was a more consistent analyst of character than his contemporaries. He was likewise an astute sociologist. His large group portrait in the National Gallery of Art in Washington, D.C., is one of the most percipient 18th-century representations of upper-class life. The husband in the painting leans forward tenderly and smiles equivocally. He doubtless has a mistress, but his wife's complacency makes one imagine

218. *Jean-Etienne Liotard (1702–1790).* Madame d'Epinay. *1757–59. Pastel, 26 3/4 × 21 1/4". Musée d'Art et d'Histoire, Geneva.*

219. *Jean Marc Nattier (1685–1766).* Madame de Caumartin As Hebe. *1753. Oil on canvas, 40 3/8 × 32 1/8". National Gallery of Art, Washington, D. C. Samuel H. Kress Collection.*

he may also be a cuckold. Only the young daughter seems innocent, an innocence with probably little perdurability. The painting is appropriately inscribed "1 avril 1756"—April Fools' Day!

In the 18th century French portrait painters were in demand throughout Europe. Paris was the center of fashion, as it has been so often in the past, and French taste was accepted as preeminent. Such artists as Pierre Hubert Subleyras, who worked in Rome painting both portraits and religious pictures, Antoine Pesne and Charles Amédée Philippe Van Loo, who became court painters to the king of Prussia, Louis Tocqué, who worked in Russia and Denmark, Jacques André Aved, whose influence was felt chiefly in the Low Countries, and Louis Michel Van Loo, who became first painter at the Spanish court, and whose portraits must have been familiar to Goya, all contributed to the ascendancy of Gallic taste. Three of the greatest 18th-century French artists, François Boucher, Jean-Honoré Fragonard, and Jean-Baptiste Greuze, though best known for other types of painting, also executed portraits. There is no marked individuality in Boucher's likenesses of women. They all look a little like Madame de Pompadour, his principal patroness—but then, the same resemblance carries over to his innumerable goddesses and shepherdesses. There is more personality in his unusual portrait of Miss O'Murphy, although her face is not the most prominent feature of the painting (fig. 222).

In his astonishing virtuosity with the brush, Boucher was rivalled and even surpassed by Fragonard. The latter painted a series of young girls caught in moments of relaxation and solitude, reading a billet doux, turning the pages of a book, or lost in the world of private thoughts. Few paintings show such dexterity of handling as does figure 221. Note the certainty of the touches that render the bows, the ribbons, and the ruffles of the young girl's dress. There is a spontaneity in every stroke suggestive of the impromptu notes of a Mozart cadenza. A climax is reached in the slashing brushwork that models the cushion and suggests its soft, yielding volume. Painted predominantly in tones of burnt umber, the picture seems aglow with sunshine.

Diderot considered portraits by Jean-Baptiste Greuze to be worth their weight in gold, but portraiture was not responsible for his great reputation, and the French Academy confirmed this when they agreed to accept him only as a painter of genre. Yet, like Fragonard, he was an admirable portraitist. His likenesses epitomize the age of Louis XV, although he also lived through the reign of Louis XVI and the Revolution. All the refinement and charm of life that made l' ancien régime so attractive is embodied in his painting of Lalive de Jully, chef de protocole and a great collector (fig. 223).

Except for Fragonard and Greuze, the most accomplished portraitist working immediately before and after the French Revolution was Elisabeth Vigée-Lebrun. Her skillful rendering of the appealing attitude—in figure 224, the mother adored and adoring—and her instinct for public relations, which caused her to carry a portrait of Marie Antoinette, draped in crape, on her travels throughout Europe, both contributed to her prodigious success as an emigrée. Although a feminine sensitivity to changing fashions in dress and coiffure never permitted her portraits to fall behind the mode, as a painter Vigée-Lebrun remained as reactionary as the Congress of Vienna.

For signs of the future one must turn to Pierre-Paul Prud'hon. His work reflects the gathering clouds of melancholy that darkened the romantic spirit in the 19th century. But though he lived until 1823, and though his fame dated from the Salon of 1808, Prud'hon belongs to the 18th century, with those who

223. Jean-Baptiste Greuze (1725–1805). Ange-Laurent de Lalive de Jully. Probably 1759. Oil on canvas, 46 × 34 7/8". National Gallery of Art, Washington, D. C. Samuel H. Kress Collection.

224. Elisabeth Vigée-Lebrun (1755–1842). Madame Vigée-Lebrun and Her Daughter. 1786. Oil on canvas, 41 3/8 × 33 1/2". Louvre, Paris.

225. Pierre-Paul Prud'hon (1758–1823). Marguerite Lagnier (later Madame Versigny). 1796. Oil on canvas, 25 5/8 × 21 5/8". Louvre, Paris.

OPPOSITE:
226. Francisco Goya (1746–1828). The Marquesa de Pontejos. 1786 (?). Oil on canvas, 83 3/4 × 49". National Gallery of Art, Washington, D. C. Andrew W. Mellon Collection.

devoted themselves to the expression of the loveliness of women, of the charm of femininity, a principal quest of rococo artists. But he was the last to take up the search, and the type he discovered no longer possessed the frivolity of the ladies of Boucher and Fragonard; instead, harking back to Leonardo and Correggio—and here we catch the first sign of those revivals of style so common in the 19th century—Prud'hon created a type poignant rather than piquant, tender and mysterious rather than gay and ebullient (fig. 225). The sharp break in the tradition of painting, the revolution caused by Jacques-Louis David and neoclassicism, did not quite bring to the artistic guillotine every painter transitional between the 18th and the 19th centuries, and the art of Prud'hon remained to connect the style of l'ancien régime with the style of Eugène Delacroix.

Another and finer portraitist transitional between the 18th century and the 19th century was Francisco Goya, a genius who broke the long somnolence of Spanish painting following the death of Velázquez. He was the last of Spain's great artists until Picasso. He began his professional career in Madrid, working in the studio of Francisco Bayeu y Subias, the court painter, subsequently his brother-in-law, but he declared he had only three masters: nature, Velázquez, and Rembrandt. Nevertheless, in such early portraits as The Marquesa de Pontejos, there is a strong influence of British style (fig. 226). Although he knew the work of Reynolds and Gainsborough only from mezzotint engravings, such reproductions taught him how to convey the elegance and urbanity of the aristocracy. His society portraits, however, were flawed from the beginning by his inability to take his sitters seriously. The Marquesa de Pontejos, for example, is a fashion plate, as much the product of artificial selection as her pug dog. Goya took more pleasure in painting her tulle skirt than in rendering her characterless face.

This cynical note increased as he became familiar with the Spanish court. Ruled over by an otiose king and a lecherous queen, its corruption was horrific. Goya has depicted the royal pair as ugly manikins—he irresolute, she dissolute. A measure of their imbecility was their wish to distribute numerous replicas of these unenticing portraits to their friends. One of Goya's sitters was their niece Maria Theresa, later known as the Chinchón. He had painted her at the age of three, when she was still a beautiful child with large innocent eyes. Later her degenerate aunt and uncle forced her to marry Manuel Godoy, who was also the lover of her aunt, the queen, and was known to be the greatest libertine at a licentious court. After experiencing her husband's infidelities and cruelties, the Chinchón sat for Goya again. This second likeness is among the saddest portraits ever painted (fig. 227).

A change had come over portraiture. Goya's concept is different from that of earlier masters. Velázquez, for instance, imposed no mood on his sitters, painting them with complete detachment and allowing the spectator to make his own judgment. Rembrandt often inflicted on his subjects his own tragic view of life. Hals presented his men and women with a photographic superficiality that makes them seem acquaintances, people one knows casually without the insight that comes from friendship. Goya, by contrast, studied character in relation to the subject's background and environment. This type of analysis, a combination of sociology and psychology, is well illustrated in the portraits of Don and Doña Sureda (figs. 228, 229). Sureda, an artist and Goya's

227. *Francisco Goya*. Condesa de
Chinchón. *1800. Oil on canvas, 83 1/8 ×
54 3/4". Prado, Madrid.*

OPPOSITE ABOVE LEFT:

228. *Francisco Goya*. Doña Teresa Sureda.
*c. 1805. Oil on canvas, 47 1/8 × 31 1/4".
National Gallery of Art, Washington, D. C.
Gift of Mr. and Mrs. P. H. B. Frelinghuysen,
in memory of her father and mother, Mr.
and Mrs. H. O. Havemeyer.*

OPPOSITE ABOVE RIGHT:

229. *Francisco Goya*. Don Bartolomé
Sureda. *c. 1805. Oil on canvas, 47 1/8 ×
31 1/4". National Gallery of Art,
Washington, D. C. Gift of Mr. and Mrs.
P. H. B. Frelinghuysen in memory of her
father and mother, Mr. and Mrs. H. O.
Havemeyer.*

OPPOSITE BELOW:

230. *Francisco Goya*. José Pio de
Molina. *c. 1827–28. Oil on canvas, 23 5/8
× 19 5/8". Collection Oskar Reinhart,
Winterthur.*

close friend, with whom many late and companionable evenings were spent, doubtless encountered on his return the resentment of his wife, conveyed in her portrait by her stiff back, her hard, staring eyes, and her sullen mouth. Here, in the portrait of an icy, outraged woman, Goya has painted not only a likeness but a point of view—the intolerance of uncompromising rectitude. The portraitist has taken on the role of the novelist.

Among authors, the closest to Goya is Dickens. In both painter and writer there is the power of presenting the individual with persuasive actuality. But there is also an element of exaggeration, a tendency to caricature. Both have a streak of humor that constantly appears, for England and Spain are nations with strongly developed senses of humor. But since the spearhead of English humor is optimism, of Spanish humor pessimism, Dickens when incensed at human wrongs becomes sentimental; Goya equally aroused by social injustice becomes ironical. In Goya's portraits this element of the sardonic inevitably colors his likenesses of the brainless officials who so tragically misgoverned Spain.

In 1792 Goya was taken ill, and when he finally recovered in 1794 he was totally deaf. The gay, cynical frivolity of his early work, objective and uncomplicated, gradually gave way to the subjective and complex portraits of his last years. To use a musical analogy: the change resembles the difference between the music of Mozart and that of Beethoven, for Goya, like Beethoven, was at the end of his life engulfed in the romantic movement. His sensationalism, his cloudy symbols, his rebellion against authority, his humanitarianism, and his egotism, all are part of a new emotional impetus that was to mold the art of the 19th century into so many dissimilar yet kindred shapes.

In his portrait of *José Pio de Molina* (fig. 230), painted when he was eighty-two, Goya went beyond 19th-century romanticism. The wavering outline of the face, the summary drawing of eyes and ear, and the arbitrary modelling of the other features anticipates the style of such a 20th-century painter as Oskar Kokoschka. Comparison between *The Marquesa de Pontejos* and *José Pio de Molina* discloses a range of expression equalled perhaps only in the work of the 20th-century Spaniard Picasso.

THE SCULPTURED PORTRAIT

It was not until the 18th century that the French talent for realism in sculpture emerged from the heavy classicism of Le Brun. Jean Baptiste Lemoyne carved a series of busts that are convincing, direct, and without affectation, but one must equally admit they lack much inspiration. Jean Jacques Caffieri was a more interesting portraitist. His busts have a nervous vitality, their gaze peculiarly penetrating. Caffieri carved a number of portraits of Benjamin Franklin, and they were frequently copied in the United States, where they were much more popular than Houdon's likeness.

The ablest and most popular portraitist of his generation, however, was Jean-Baptiste Pigalle. His tombs are the culmination of the sepulchral drama. He surpassed Bernini in the range of dramatic roles given to the allegorical figures surrounding the portrait of the deceased. The monument of Comte de Saxe, for example, shows Death holding up the lid of the sarcophagus, while Hercules, a symbol of bravery, mourns the departed (fig. 231). A seductive and partially draped figure of France tries vainly to defend the

CURLANDIÆ ET SEMIGALLIÆ DUCI
SUMMO REGIORUM EXERCITUUM PRÆFECTO
SEMPER VICTORI
LUDOVICUS XV:
VICTORIARUM AUCTOR ET IPSE DUX
PONI JUSSIT
OBIIT XXX NOV. AN. MDCCL. ÆTATIS LV

marshal from death. His victories over England, Flanders, and Austria are symbolized by the obvious discomfiture of the lion, leopard, and eagle. A disconsolate cupid weeps in front of the banners of the general's army, perhaps recalling his victories in arms and in amours. The count himself, superbly portrayed, standing in stately yet graceful posture, seems about to walk with nonchalance toward his coffin.

Allegorical figures on sepulchers were fashionable everywhere. Like actors in a repertory theater, they were called on sometimes for serious drama, sometimes for melodrama. The tomb in Westminster Abbey by Louis François Roubiliac, a Frenchman who worked in England, is an example of the melodramatic (fig. 232). Death emerges from the doors of a rusticated grave to aim a spear at Lady Nightingale, who swoons on the shoulder of her husband. Her consort, overacting the role of protector, grimaces and stretches out his arm to deflect the thrust of the skeleton's weapon. The scene declines into bathos; but as portraiture the figures of the Nightingales are excellent. Roubiliac in numerous busts shows more verve, style, and sense of individuality than any English sculptor of the time.

Although sepulchral monuments were a principal occupation of sculptors, individual busts became so popular in the third decade of the 18th century that they threatened the livelihood of painters. They were known as bustoes, and at their best they rival Roman work. The portrait of Robert Walpole by John Michael Rysbrack might be placed with honor beside any bust of the Augustan age (fig. 234). The prime minister appears as he was: cynical, ruthless, a master of political intrigue. It was his genius for patronage that restored prosperity to the aristocracy, or at least to those members of it who were his friends. It is said he asked an innocent young man about to enter politics, "Well, are you to be an old Roman? A patriot?" And then he added, "You'll soon come off that and grow wiser."

Jean Antoine Houdon, the greatest sculptural portraitist of the 18th century, preferred doing bustoes to tombs. Since the Renaissance no other sculptor, not even Bernini, has realized so well the true aim of portraiture: the combination of the individual and the universal. His portraits are basically realistic—even the pockmarks are shown on the faces of Gluck and Mirabeau—and the actuality of his likenesses is increased by the vivacity of glance he gave the eyes and by the expressiveness he gave the lips. But this realism is tempered by idealism and ennoblement. In his portrait of Voltaire in the Musée Fabre, Montpellier (fig. 233), he rendered the philosopher's sardonic smile in a way unique in sculpture.

Over Houdon's style passed the first chill of neoclassicism. A new ice age of classical imitation was about to begin. Rome became once more the artistic capital of the world. No artist could aspire to preeminence who had not studied there, for it was thought more important to be familiar with ancient statues than to perceive actuality, except as it was reflected in these prototypes. Never have aesthetic theorists so dominated creativity, and never has their influence been more sterile.

Houdon's instinctive realism provided a protective warmth against neoclassicism. But there was no realistic instinct in his artistry to warm Antonio Canova, the leading practitioner of neoclassical theory. His sculpture is frozen in imitations of the antique. It is a relief when even a glacial sensuality can be discerned, as in his portrait of Napoleon's sister Pauline Bonaparte (fig. 235). Her features are coldly idealized, but her body was of such exquisite and delec-

231. Jean-Baptiste Pigalle (1714–1785). Tomb of Marshal Maurice de Saxe. 1777. Marble. St. Thomas, Strasbourg.

table loveliness that her sexual charms seem as irresistible in marble as they were in flesh.

Portraiture held a low position in neoclassical aesthetics, which were based on the imitation of generalized and idealistic types. But patronage demanded portraits, and, to find an excuse to violate the dogmas of the cult, sitters were portrayed as classical gods and goddesses. In a statue in the Borghese Gallery, Rome, Pauline Bonaparte became Venus Victrix, thus permitting the sculptor to show her popular and well-known beauty. In the colossal nude statue at

LEFT:

233. Jean Antoine Houdon (1741–1828). Voltaire. 1781. Marble, lifesize. Musée Fabre, Montpellier.

ABOVE:

234. Joan Michael Rysbrack (1693–1770). Sir Robert Walpole, First Earl of Orford. c. 1726. Detail of a lifesize terra-cotta bust. National Portrait Gallery, London.

235. *Antonio Canova (1757–1822).*
Pauline Borghese Bonaparte. *1804–8.*
Marble, 78 3/4″ long. Galleria Borghese,
Rome.

OPPOSITE LEFT:
236. *Bertel Thorvaldsen (1768–1844).*
George Gordon, Lord Byron. *1817.*
Detail of a lifesize marble bust. Collection
H. M. The Queen, St. James's Palace,
London.

OPPOSITE RIGHT:
237. *Francis Chantrey (1781–1841).*
Washington. *Marble, over lifesize. State*
House, Boston.

Apsley House, London, Napoleon became a Roman emperor, and his mother at Chatsworth appears as the Agrippina of the Capitoline Museum, both more than a little ridiculous in their classical roles.

Neoclassicism in sculpture endured well into the 19th century, but for convenience we will conclude mention of its few noteworthy but incompetent practitioners here. Of these the Dane Bertel Thorvaldsen was the most

popular, though it is hard to discern in him anything to admire. His bust of Byron, for example, denies all character to one of the most vivid personalities the world has known (fig. 236). The rigid dogma of the imitation of the antique has congealed the poet's features. In England, on the other hand, neoclassicism was less doctrinaire. Two practitioners of this fashionable style, John Flaxman and Francis Chantrey, carved portraits of public figures ad nauseam. To increase the spiritual effect of his sculptures, Chantrey placed them on unusually high pedestals. His *Washington* in the State House, Boston (fig. 237), is evidently intended to be an American *Demosthenes,* but for a measure of the failure of neoclassicism in sculpture, compare it with figure 31. It can be fairly said that no English sculptor of the 19th century made a significant contribution to portraiture.

The American sculptor Horatio Greenough of Boston carved the preposterous statue of Washington on view at the Smithsonian Institution. A sense of the ridiculous was something the neoclassical sculptors obviously lacked, and although it was fashionable to undress celebrities and show them naked or half-naked in the guise of ancient gods and goddesses, there seems today something sublimely ludicrous in posing the Father of His Country in the attitude of the Phidean Zeus. That millions of tourists each year look at this seated statue without bursting into gales of laughter shows a disturbing lack of humor on the part of the American public. The portrait would at least have caused Jefferson to laugh, for he wrote Washington, "I think a modern in an antique dress as just an object of ridicule as a Hercules or Marius with a periwig and a *chapeau bras.*" In a few words our third president has justly demolished neoclassical portraiture.

CHAPTER NINE

1790-1914: EUROPE AND AMERICA IN THE BOURGEOIS AGE

THE PAINTED PORTRAIT

Why certain countries at certain times should be centers of genius remains a mystery. But it is undeniable that the quality of French painting from the time of the French Revolution until about 1930 is so far superior to the work done elsewhere that the greater part of any discussion of 19th-century portraiture must be devoted to France. There, a series of masters from Jacques-Louis David to Vincent van Gogh, French by birth or adoption, created one of the most brilliant epochs in art.

The latter part of the 18th century saw the rise of neoclassicism. Antiquities discovered at Pompeii and Herculaneum affected taste everywhere, and the French Revolution provided an added stimulus to a revived classicism. The birth of the French republic was looked on as the rebirth of the republics of Greece and Rome. To paint the Revolutionary leaders realistically was to paint the heroes of the past, of whom they were the reincarnation. Thus, in French painting classicism and realism were reconciled and cold imitation of the antique was avoided.

The leader of French painters from the mid-1780s until the fall of Napoleon was Jacques-Louis David. His work reflects one of the most significant changes in art, a transformation that can be illustrated by two of his paintings from different periods of his life. In the early portrait of Antoine-Laurent Lavoisier and his wife, painted in 1788, the composition is a zigzag, a design popular during the rococo period (fig. 238), whereas later, neoclassical taste favored straight lines. The sitters themselves also belong to the past. Lavoisier, France's great scientist, came under attack by Marat and was guillotined in 1794. The previous year Marat himself was murdered in his bath (fig. 239). His portrait showing him in the throes of death was also painted by David. The composition is rectilinear. Gone is the charm and urbanity of the portrait of the Lavoisiers; instead there is a brutal realism. Rococo style has vanished completely.

David became an important political figure and the artistic dictator of France, the first painter to regain the authority of Le Brun. Dictatorships, political or artistic, are always much the same, and the doctrine established by David in the midst of the Revolution was nearly identical to that established by Le Brun under Louis XIV. Art should serve the state; noble subject matter should be chosen; the antique should be used as a guide to the most beautiful aspects of nature; and color should be subordinated to clarity of draftsmanship, which meant clarity of contour. With these four dogmas David tore out the immediate roots of painting, which had grown deep as a result of the liberty of painters in the reigns of Louis XV and Louis XVI. He told his pupils, "Paint as you like and not like me," but art teachers always say this, and the student who takes them at their word is soon dismissed. David was actually as ruthless in art as was his close friend Robespierre in politics. He severed the tradition of rococo painting as sharply as the guillotine cut off the heads of the aristocratic patrons of Boucher and Fragonard—patrons whom David himself had been pleased to serve before the Revolution, as many portraits, including that of the Lavoisiers, indicate.

238. Jacques-Louis David (1748–1825). Antoine-Laurent Lavoisier and His Wife. 1788. Oil on canvas, 102 1/4 × 76 5/8". The Metropolitan Museum of Art, New York. Purchase, Mr. and Mrs. Charles Wrightsman Gift, 1977.

Under David's authority the appearance of portraits changed. In contrast to work of the previous generation, color is colder, contours firmer, and the surface of pictures more vitreous. The delicate, crinkled draperies of the rococo were ironed out into simple, unbroken folds. When David portrayed men and women he turned them into statues, whereas during *l'ancien régime* even the statues in paintings seemed of flesh and blood.

On the surface these doctrines and the changes that grew out of them may seem merely a return to the conservative principles of the 17th century. But in one important respect this is not true. The 17th-century artist painted largely from memory, and initially David followed this traditional procedure. But with the Revolution came a revulsion against this tradition, particularly as practiced by the artists of David's youth, who were associated with *l'ancien régime*. David developed a hatred of the facility of Boucher, for example, who could render a figure without glancing at the model. This drove David to paint only what he saw in front of him. Hals, Velázquez, and Vermeer had done the same, but their scrutiny of the model was transposed into idiomatic styles: the

239. *Jacques-Louis David*. The Death of Marat. *1793. Oil on canvas, 65 × 49 5/8″. Musées Royaux des Beaux-Arts, Brussels.*

quick, jagged brushstrokes of Hals, the adumbrated contours of Velázquez, the perfectly related tones of Vermeer. David, on the other hand, was more imitative, more literal in his rendering of the model. His power to transcribe appearance was strong; his ability to transform what he saw into a personal style of painting was weak. Therein lies an important difference between the masters of visualistic painting in the past and the academic painters of more recent times.

The paradox of David is that in spite of his classicism he was basically a realist. His portraiture is at its best when depicting the terrible dramas of contemporary life. *The Death of Marat* and *Joseph Bara Dying* (Musée d' Avignon) have the brutal sincerity of seicento naturalism. Madame David, whose devotion saved the painter from the guillotine when his revolutionary friends turned against him, is portrayed with beady eyes, a red nose, and a firm, thin-lipped mouth (fig. 240). Few marital likenesses have been so cruel. Confronted by this portrait, she may well have wondered why she had bothered to come to her husband's rescue.

Among David's followers, one alone became his peer, Jean Auguste Dominique Ingres. He, too, assailed the virtuosity of rococo artists. He was against their set vocabulary of forms and their worship of the Venetians and Rubens. He was instead in search of the principles to be found among those Italian masters the culmination of whose work for him was Raphael. However, Ingres's search was hampered by a paradox that also confronted David. Whereas Renaissance painting was based on a vocabulary of expression, on stock forms for rendering the figure, on abstract statements, Ingres would have none of them. He would trust only his eye, and, remaining faithful to it, discover for himself the exact appearance of his subject. But his realism was different in another way from that of the Renaissance painters. They were guided by anatomical dissection, from which they learned how the body worked. For example, in the 15th century Alberti said in a treatise usually referred to as *Della pittura*: "In painting the nude, begin with the bones, then add the muscles, and then cover the figure with flesh in such a way as to leave the position of the muscles visible. It may be objected that a painter should not represent what cannot be seen, but this procedure is analogous to drawing a nude and then covering it with draperies."[17] Ingres was not interested in studying anatomy, "cette science affreuse," as he called it. The reality he wished to express was based not on knowledge but on visual observation. Thus, to show the mechanics of the body concealed by its envelope of skin was not his goal. Instead it was to show the envelope itself, with all its subtle undulations of flesh. His probing brush sought to render the contours of the body as the eye observed them, not as touch and the science of anatomy might indicate their appearance to the mind. The marvellous conjunction of Ingres's hand and eye, for example, can be seen in Madame Moitessier's portrait, where every variation of contour in her fat arms is precisely rendered (fig. 241). He once remarked, "Line is probity itself," and each line in his portraits is scrupulously true to his observation.

Character may be lacking in Madame Moitessier's somnolent face, but her features and fleshy body were an inspiration to Ingres, recalling the canons of classical proportion as we know them from the sculpture of Greece and Rome. Fashions in the beauty of women are as variable as fashions in clothes. Today many people would consider Madame Moitessier an ugly woman, corpulent and bovine; but Théophile Gautier, the great 19th-century French critic,

240. *Jacques-Louis David*. Madame David. *1813. Oil on canvas, 28 3/4 × 23 3/8". National Gallery of Art, Washington, D. C. Samuel H. Kress Collection.*

wrote after watching her pose for her portrait, "Never did beauty more regal, more magnificent, more stately, and of a more Junoesque type, offer its proud lines to the tremulous pencil of the artist."

In portraying men Ingres was not distracted by any resemblance to classical sculpture (fig. 242). He wanted to show character, and he made it as explicit as it is in a portrait by Holbein. The solidity of his figures, the massive dignity he gave his sitters, and the sense of their existence and reality are so overpowering that his portraits are worthy of Raphael.

Ingres's pencil sketches, which number in the hundreds, form a unique portrait gallery (fig. 243). No major artist has equalled these drawings in quantity and quality. Attention is focused on the features of the sitter, which are worked out in detail, while the body is often indicated with a few cursive lines. In each case, the individual likeness is recorded with a precision impossible to match in the work of any other 19th-century painter except Degas. As a portrait draftsman Ingres ranks with Holbein and the Clouets.

Only one painter, Théodore Chassériau, was a worthy follower of Ingres, and even he abandoned the teachings of his master and ended his career under the influence of Delacroix. *Father Lacordaire* is the exemplar of the silent, contemplative monk, whose eyes seem to search into the spectator's soul (fig. 244). It is a portrayal so sensitive yet so striking that it seems a symbol of asceticism and the serene certainty of monastic life.

The stern admonition of Ingres to his pupils never to paint without the model, to ignore color and to concentrate on drawing, to forget about beauty of touch and handling, and to seek a smooth, vitreous finish had on the whole disastrous consequences. His work provided the foundations of 19th-century academic portraiture. Ingres's influence appears in the portraits of Hippolyte Flandrin, Armand Cambon, Eugène Emmanuel Amaury-Duval, and a host of other regular exhibitors at the annual Salons. But it also helped to form the style of Degas, and it had a strong and beneficial effect on modern painting.

The authority of David was too absolute to endure, and the next generation produced painters who, unlike Ingres, wished to recover the qualities neoclassicism had sacrificed, particularly brushwork, color, and movement. This revolt was begun, it would seem almost unconsciously, by David's favorite pupil, the Baron Gros. Antoine-Jean Gros was attached to Napoleon's suite, and in portraying the emperor among the pest-stricken soldiers at Jaffa or encouraging his generals on the snow-swept field of Eylau, he found little time to consult the antique as a guide to the beautiful in nature (fig. 245). He drew away from neoclassicism and involuntarily betrayed the precepts which, as director of the Academy, he had sworn to uphold. His personal remorse, which led to suicide, however, did not stop younger artists from considering his paintings a treaty of alliance, a support for their attack on neoclassicism.

This assault was led for a time by the short-lived and brilliant Théodore Géricault. In search of brushwork, color, and movement, he was first attracted to Rubens and then went to Italy to study the Italian masters. On his return to Paris he is known to have interviewed survivors of the ill-fated ship the "Medusa," and *The Raft of the "Medusa"* probably included some of their likenesses; but this, his most famous work, has little to do with the history of portraiture. More consequential for this book was a commission he received from Dr. Georget of the Salpêtrière Hospital to make physiognomic studies of the insane (fig. 246). The project absorbed him in his later years, and the

J. INGRES PINXIT.
1832.

LE BERTIN.

likenesses that resulted represent the first use of portrait painting in the service of science.

As the mantle of David fell on Ingres, so the mantle of Géricault fell on Eugène Delacroix. Géricault had admired David and even made a trip to Brussels to visit him during his exile, but Delacroix disliked Ingres, and their bitter antagonism divided French painters. It was not a matter of romanticism versus classicism. Ingres would have agreed with the remark Delacroix made repeatedly, "The more talent the painter has, the more beauty the calmness of study will add." Their hostility grew out of their practice of painting. It was part of the old battle of Rubenists against Poussinists, of the pictorial style of one against the sculptural style of the other.

Delacroix, like earlier Rubenists, fought for freedom of handling and richness of color; Ingres, like the Poussinists, for firmness of contour and clarity of drawing. In composition one sought to make the whole effect melt together, the other to maintain the structural solidity of the separate volumes. The illumination of one was dramatic, with stormy bursts of light and lowering shadows; of the other clear, cold, uniform. Delacroix infused into portraits warmth and informal charm; Ingres's figures are frozen in rigid postures. The differences between the two artists are more apparent in figure painting than in portraiture, but even when confronted with a sitter their styles differed basically. The precise recording of the model's appearance, which marked the realism of David and Ingres, is in Delacroix's work transformed into a more casual, more desultory rendering. At his best, as in the portrait of Paganini (fig. 247), Delacroix fuses subject and style into a unity that makes this little picture a symbol of the fervor and emotion of romantic art. How could the virtuosity, concentration, and brio of a great musician, his whole body twisting and pulsating with the music he is playing, be better shown? Nothing could be further from the static portraiture of neoclassicism.

Nor could there be a greater departure from neoclassicism than occurred in the next generation, in the painting of Gustave Courbet. Art in France in the 19th century is marked by sudden transformations, one movement succeeding another: first neoclassicism, then romanticism, next realism, and finally impressionism, changing into postimpressionism and modern art.

Yet the artists of one movement understood, if they did not approve, the work of the next. Both Ingres and Delacroix applauded the realism of Courbet's *Après-dîner à Ornans* (Musée Courbet, Lille), although the first was in search of an ideal beauty and the second worked largely from his imagination. Of his aesthetic goal Courbet said, "I will give you real nature with all her crudities and violence." Painting, he held, was an art of sight and consisted only in "the representation of real and existing things."

With such beliefs, Courbet was bound to be an accurate documentor of appearance, admitting no subjective response to the sitter's personality. In his famous *Funeral at Ornans* (Louvre, Paris) the artist seems only to say, "This is how it was." In this vast group portrait of village worthies, all the participants in a burial have their attention focused on the grave, some absorbed in their sorrow, others looking on with indifference. It is noteworthy that no one makes contact with the viewer, as was customary in group portraits. This would have implied a spectator outside the picture and would have introduced an element of artificiality. The mood is somber and reverent, as one might expect at a burial. No emotion seems forced; no interpretation is suggested by the artist.

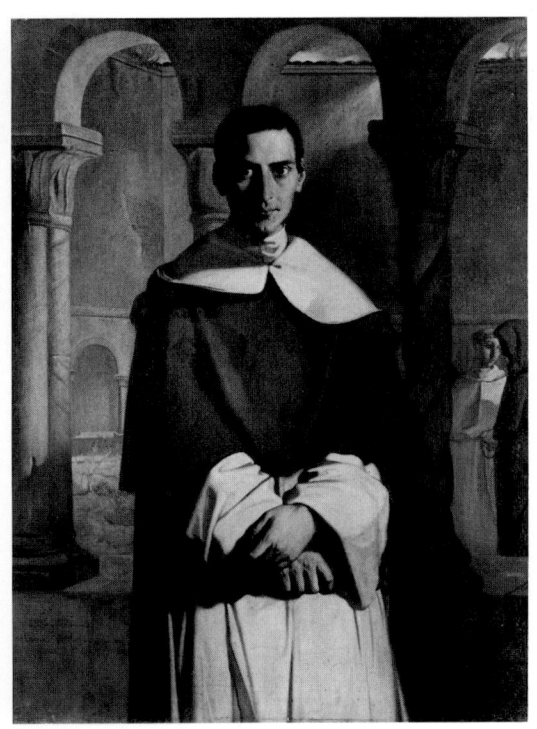

But Courbet, however, was inconsistent. For his other enormous group portrait, of friends and models, *Interior of My Studio* (fig. 248), he devised a subtitle: *A Real Allegory Summing Up Seven Years of My Life As an Artist.* "Real allegory" is a contradiction in terms, but no matter. The portraits are so admirable, so beautifully spaced, the whole composed so skillfully and lighted so adroitly, that a suspension of disbelief is easy to achieve. Again, as in *Funeral at Ornans,* there is no concession to the presence of the viewer, no one looks out of the canvas to establish the traditional contact. With these immense compositions Courbet has given the group portrait a new actuality and a new informality. In years to come, scores of artists would look at *Interior of My Studio,* buy large canvases, and paint their friends visiting them at work.

An example is *A Studio at Batignolles* by Henri Fantin-Latour (fig. 249). He was a friend of Courbet's and was doubtless inspired by his painting. A significant difference is noticeable, however, between the two group portraits, for the earlier picture is painterly, the later one photographic. Although in still-life painting Fantin-Latour created delicate and beautiful chromatic harmonies, in portraiture his subdued colors and fondness for brown tones suggest sepia photographs, snapshots that are arresting documents of human physiognomy, fascinating as identification but boring in the end.

Camille Corot and Jean François Millet were not primarily portraitists. They nevertheless did some distinguished work in this genre. For many years both were poor. Taste had deteriorated, and lack of artistic discernment in the middle class made patronage difficult to obtain. Corot's eventual success was due to his willingness to compromise. His nebulous canvases were a concession to the pseudo-poetic scenery popular with clients, who wanted landscapes vague, sentimental, and romantic. The compromise paid off, and he received wealth, honors, and finally admission to the jury of the Salons. When it seemed as though his real qualities of honesty, penetrating vision, and inspired color might be swallowed up in a gray mist, he miraculously painted a series of figure pictures unsurpassed in the art of the 19th century for richness of color, texture, and modelling (fig. 250). Painted from models sometimes standing in solitary grandeur, sometimes playing musical instruments, some-

ABOVE:

244. Théodore Chassériau (1819–1856). Father Lacordaire. 1840. Oil on canvas, 57 1/2 × 42". Louvre, Paris.

RIGHT:

245. Antoine-Jean Gros (1771–1835). Napoleon at Eylau. 1808. Oil on canvas, 209 7/8 × 315". Louvre, Paris.

OPPOSITE:

246. Théodore Géricault (1791–1824). A Kleptomaniac. c. 1822–23. Oil on canvas, 23 5/8 × 19 5/8". Musée des Beaux-Arts, Ghent.

times leaning on an arm in meditation, these are likenesses of specific individuals and deserve to be classed as portraits. They are more generalized than some of the sitters Corot delineated, for Corot could paint conventional portraits when he wished, but even in what are essentially figure studies his models have their own personalities. They are likenesses, although idealized as they might have been in Greek sculpture.

Unlike Corot's, Millet's portraits were painted at the beginning rather than at the end of his life. They helped him to stave off starvation as a young artist, and probably for that reason he always looked on them as potboilers. Yet in many ways they are better than the peasant subjects on which his prosperity ultimately depended. Since color is less important in portrait painting than in figure painting or landscape, Millet's outstanding weakness is less apparent there. Also, while his portraits show his magnificent draftsmanship and power of construction, they are free from the anecdotal, from the tiresomely repeated illustrations of peasant life that became his preoccupation. Certain of his likenesses, that of Leconte de Lisle, for example, rank with the best 19th-century portraits (fig. 251).

The economics and nature of portraiture were gradually changing. After 1850 a number of French masters of the first rank, like the Florentine artists of the 15th century, painted portraits more or less as a sideline. Their major interest was in figure compositions, landscapes, and still lifes. Moreover, after Courbet's attacks on the artistic establishment, progressive painters were determined to achieve complete liberty, some at the risk of destitution. Such independence, however, is difficult to maintain between the professional portraitist and his sitter. Consequently, portraiture as a way of earning a living fell to the lot of those artists willing to accept a degree of subjugation. Second-rate they might be, but if paid sufficiently they would paint the most irascible and unreasonable of patrons. Thus, a division in portrait painting was established, and the separation between conservative, fashionable portraitists like Franz Xavier Winterhalter and more advanced, innovative artists like the im-

OPPOSITE ABOVE:
247.   Eugène Delacroix (1798–1863).
Paganini. 1832 or 1842. Oil on panel,
17 5/16 × 11 1/2". The Phillips Collection,
Washington, D. C.

OPPOSITE BELOW:
248.   Gustave Courbet (1819–1877).
Interior of My Studio, a Real Allegory
Summing Up Seven Years of My Life
As an Artist. 1855. Oil on canvas,
55 7/8 × 92 1/2". Louvre, Paris.

ABOVE:
249.   Henri Fantin-Latour (1836–1904).
A Studio at Batignolles. 1870. Oil on
canvas, 67 3/8 × 80 3/4". Musée de
l'Impressionnisme, Paris.

Instead, his paintings often caused a scandal. Two of his first portraits were of a model, Victorine Meurent. He painted her nude in *Le Déjeuner sur l'Herbe* (Louvre, Paris) seated beside two friends fully dressed, and again in *Olympia* (Louvre, Paris) with a negress looking on, holding a bunch of flowers. Neither composition is impressionistic. The first is based on an engraving after Raphael and the second on Giorgione's *Sleeping Venus*. Both paintings were considered a public affront. Later Manet put some clothes on Victorine and got her into the Salon of 1874, in a portrait entitled *Gare Saint Lazare* (fig. 254). It is in some inexplicable fashion one of the gayest paintings ever devised. Perhaps this gaiety comes from Manet's skill as a portraitist of dogs. Where in art is a more entrancing puppy than the little spaniel in Victorine's lap? His favorite model looks at the spectator with the candid gaze of a woman to whom shyness is unknown; and her charge, a child seen from behind, stares through the fence at the railroad tracks below, conveying through her pose alone, the rapture of childhood at the smoke, steam, and power of trains.

The composition of the picture, which was painted largely out-of-doors, has the immediacy of a snapshot, the general appearance of a scene apprehended in an instant of time. This is true impressionism. For greater speed, Manet omitted the transitional values of conventional modelling and described with extraordinary precision of brushwork the main relationships of light and shade. Shadow is suppressed, and the flesh tones have a dazzling paleness.

In the painting *Le Balcon*, we have another seemingly spontaneous grouping (fig. 255). The lovely Berthe Morisot, who would become Manet's sister-in-law, is seated leaning on the iron railing, staring into the street below. Her two companions stand behind her. The modelling is flat, as in the work of Vélazquez, whom Manet studied assiduously, with the light falling directly on the figures from behind the artist's head. Again there are no cast shadows. The flesh tones are blond, and the three people portrayed are shown as pale

254. *Edouard Manet (1832–1883). Gare Saint Lazare. 1873. Oil on canvas, 36 3/4 × 45 1/8". National Gallery of Art, Washington, D. C. Gift of Horace Havemeyer in memory of his mother, Louisine W. Havemeyer, 1956.*

silhouettes against the dark background. Through this arbitrary suppression of shadow Manet was able to state local color more positively and to attain beautiful chromatic harmonies that have strongly influenced modern painting.

Edgar Degas, like Manet, sought in his portraits a fortuitous arrangement. He once said he intended to do "portraits of people in familiar and typical attitudes, above all giving to their faces the same choice of expression as one gives to their bodies." To do this meant to transcribe appearance accurately, and in the 19th century there was no one, not even Ingres, Degas's spiritual master, capable of achieving this degree of actuality. Degas's paintings look as though a camera had just clicked and the artist had transferred to the canvas his exact mental picture. Although a likeness lends itself less than a figure subject to such momentary vision, Degas, with his unorthodox compositions, influenced as they were by his knowledge of Japanese prints, attained a remarkable sense of immediacy, even in portraiture. An example is the painting entitled *Woman with Chrysanthemums* (fig. 256). The composition is emphatically asymmetrical, as it might have been in the work of a Japanese. This enhances the effect of a momentary glimpse, a sudden impression. Actually, in this case, Degas had previously painted on the same canvas a still life of flowers, which may have seemed to him a boring picture. Inspired by the originality of the designs he had seen in Japanese woodcuts, he later added the portrait of an unidentified lady. The result is a seemingly casual arrangement, which makes one feel the artist has unexpectedly entered the room. The model, caught in a moment of abstraction, holds her hand to her cheek. Her fingers appear to tremble with nervous energy. She is vividly alive. Degas has caught a gesture as in a snapshot, but he has given it a vibrancy beyond the power of photography. He has also eliminated all extraneous detail, which the camera can only omit or blur but not selectively eradicate. Attention is concentrated on the pose of the sitter, on the glowing color of the flowers, and on the pitcher and cloth, which, because they are placed so far from the central axis, bring the whole design into equilibrium. Degas was the last artist able to combine so photographic a likeness with so much aesthetic perception.

The rendering of movement preoccupied him. For example, in *La Répétition de Chant* everything is in motion (fig. 257). The pianist and the two singers are so united in their music that it seems almost audible. The spectator is caught up in the action and shares with the actors an instant of ecstatic performance. It is a snapshot of a concert, but Degas has given the scene a vividness far outside the range of photography. Although the camera can photograph objects in movement, except in cinema they remain static.

This mastery of significant representation was not attained without many years of study, of constant copying in the Louvre and in Italian museums and churches. Degas once said to George Moore, "No art was ever less spontaneous than mine." The effect of casual appearance in his portraits grew out of long hours of reflection. From a tireless inspection of the old masters he developed his own analytical vision. It was from them he learned how to express the essential gesture that brings the sitter alive. He was a genius who ranks undoubtedly with the greatest of all portraitists; yet he seems never to have accepted a commission to paint a portrait, and he made no effort to sell those he had painted.

Degas had two followers, two antithetical artists who greatly admired him: Henri de Toulouse-Lautrec and Mary Cassatt. One had the handicap of being a crippled dwarf, the other of being a conventional American. One came from

OPPOSITE ABOVE:
255. *Edouard Manet. Le Balcon. 1868. Oil on canvas, 66 1/2 × 48 1/2". Louvre, Paris.*

OPPOSITE BELOW:
256. *Edgar Degas (1834–1917). Woman with Chrysanthemums. Signed and dated twice: 1858, 1865. Oil on canvas, 29 × 36 1/2". The Metropolitan Museum of Art, New York. Bequest of Mrs. H. O. Havemeyer, 1929. The H. O. Havemeyer Collection.*

257. *Edgar Degas. La Répétition de Chant. c. 1865. Oil on canvas, 31 7/8 × 25 5/8". Dumbarton Oaks Collections, Washington, D. C.*

the aristocracy, the other from the middle class. Although Toulouse-Lautrec painted society, a world into which he was born, for he was a descendant of the counts of Toulouse, he preferred models drawn from the stage, the races, cabarets, and brothels, even the vicious and their victims—faces where genius had left the strong lines of character, or degradation the numb look of indifference. He was the portraitist of spontaneous wickedness. Yvette Guilbert, a favorite singer and model, called him the genius of deformity. Mary Cassatt, by contrast, painted the elaborate and fragile refinement of her friends and relations from Philadelphia, seen with their children and nurses, glimpsed at tea, observed on the beach, driven in their carriages, and rowed in their boats. Different as were these two artists, far apart as were the worlds they depicted, both drew their inspiration from the same source, from Edgar Degas.

Toulouse-Lautrec was a superb draftsman, but his figures lack the substance Degas learned from a study of the old masters. By comparison, his portraits, although penetratingly characterized, are two-dimensional silhouettes with little volume or solidity. This is evident in his famous painting *At the Moulin Rouge,* in which most of the people are identifiable (fig. 259). The artist himself

258. *Mary Cassatt (1844–1926).* Girl Arranging Her Hair. *1886. Oil on canvas, 29 1/2 × 24 1/2". National Gallery of Art, Washington, D. C. Chester Dale Collection, 1962.*

is seen passing across the back of the room with a tall, round-shouldered man, his cousin, Dr. Tapié de Céleyran, who was his constant companion. The bizarre green face of the woman at the right, which seems to float above her dress, gives a sinister air to the scene, makes it seem somehow hallucinatory.

Toulouse-Lautrec probably knew Mary Cassatt since they had many mutual friends, but her principle theme, mothers with their babies or young children, would scarcely have appealed to him. He would have understood, however, her portrait of a young girl arranging her hair (fig. 258), recognizing in it a witty adaptation to modern life of the famous pose of Michelangelo's *Dying Slave*. He would also have esteemed the realism with which this buck-toothed but nevertheless charming adolescent was painted. It is a portrait done under the direct inspiration of Degas, whose work Mary Cassatt saw in the window of a picture dealer when she first came to Paris. "I used to go," she wrote a friend, "and flatten my nose against the window and absorb all I could of his art. It changed my life." She finally met her hero, who was flattered by her admiration, and for a number of years he imposed his high standards on her painting. Unfortunately they quarrelled, and after the break in their friendship, Mary Cassatt succumbed to the sentimentality and overrefinement always latent in her work.

The other leading impressionists, Claude Monet, Camille Pissarro, Alfred Sisley, and Berthe Morisot painted occasional portraits, but their major interest was in landscape and figure compositions. Among the postimpressionists Georges Seurat can scarcely be considered a portraitist. But Paul Cézanne, Paul Gauguin, and Vincent van Gogh each had a different but lasting impact on portrait painting. With their work a bifurcation begins that characterizes portraiture in the 20th century. Cézanne was the progenitor of cubism, which paved the way for abstract painting. Gauguin and Van Gogh experimented with the use of color for emotional expression, and their work in turn leads in a direction away from Cézanne, to Teutonic expressionism.

Cézanne's late portraits foreshadow the disappearance of the realistic likeness. With the work of his admirers, the fauvists and the cubists, the accurate portrayal of the sitter faded like the Cheshire cat, leaving behind only a smile. Gauguin's portraits are less abstract and more traditional than Cézanne's. It is his Polynesian subject matter rather than his style that is exotic. Van Gogh delineated specific individuals but distorted his sitters' features for intensity of portrayal.

Cézanne's picture of his father, an early work done when he still wished to reveal personality, is one of the most powerful portraits ever painted (fig. 260). The sitter, oblivious of the artist, clutches a newspaper in his massive hands, appearing slowly to absorb its contents. His body, turned slightly in his chair, conveys a sense of weight and solidity equalling the ponderousness of the figures of Masaccio. Executed largely with a palette knife, the portrait is a monochrome of grays and blacks.

Later, color preoccupied Cézanne. He still produced recognizable likenesses but they gradually became more abstract. The sitter in front of him was the source of what he called "my little sensations." These his intelligence organized into a work of art. The model often had to pose for days on end while Cézanne refined the sensations he received from his observation. He changed the image on the canvas repeatedly to enhance volume and to increase chromatic resonance. Thus, the motif as registered by his acute vision was transformed into a monumental design of refulgent yet perfectly controlled color.

OVERLEAF LEFT:
259.   Henri de Toulouse-Lautrec (1864–1901). At the Moulin Rouge. 1892. Oil on canvas, 47 1/2 × 55 1/4". Art Institute of Chicago.

OVERLEAF RIGHT:
260.   Paul Cézanne (1839–1906). The Artist's Father. 1866. Oil on canvas, 78 1/8 × 47". National Gallery of Art, Washington, D. C. Gift of Paul Mellon.

The subject was no more than a three-dimensional object offering an opportunity to solve certain pictorial problems, to work out, for instance, complicated spatial relationships. In this transmutation, the personality of the sitter was unimportant and gradually disappeared. The result was not portraiture in the conventional sense. It was pictorial architecture. The portrait might equally have been a landscape or a still life.

This was not true of the portraits of Gauguin and Van Gogh. Gauguin was never detached from his subject matter. He was a human being of intense feelings, and his passionate nature drove him toward an exotic world, first to Panama, where he worked as a digger on the canal, then to Martinique, where the climate nearly killed him, and finally, after seventeen months of poverty spent largely in Brittany, to the tropics again. It was after his return to France that he painted Annah, a thirteen-year-old Javanese halfcaste, whom the dealer Vollard found for him (fig. 262). She soon became his mistress. He has painted her enthroned in a chair which he designed, confronting the spectator as a queen, the ruler of carnal desires. The colors, the model's brown flesh against the blue upholstery, the vivid yellow with touches of red, and the rose background, are used as arbitrarily as a composer uses sounds. In Mallarmé's words, such a painting is "a musical poem; it needs no libretto."

Van Gogh, too, felt color expressed something in itself. Red and green, for instance, in certain circumstances, he believed could bespeak "the terrible passions of humanity," though at other times these colors were merely decorative. This idea of the expressive power of color determined the palette he would use. He no longer depended on a close observation of the model but painted instead his own images, based on his interior vision. It was this vision, he felt, that would enable him to penetrate to the inner life of the individual as this was shown by his outward appearance. For example, he wanted to paint a portrait of Dr. Gachet, in whose care he had placed himself on his release from the asylum at St.-Rémy, because he read in the doctor's face "the heartbroken expression of our time" (fig. 263). He was always in search of the psychic significance of the subject he was portraying. This quest for the hidden personality of the sitter required intense mental effort and exhausted Van Gogh.

In 1890, the year of his death, he wrote his brother: "That which excites me the most, much, much more than the other things in my work—is the modern portrait . . . I would like to make portraits that, a century later, might appear to people of the time like apparitions. Accordingly I don't try to do that by way of photographic resemblance but by the way of impassioned expression, using as means of expression and exaltation of character our science and modern taste for color."

The excitement that painting aroused in Van Gogh was beyond Dr. Gachet's ability to control. It represented a cruel dilemma no psychologist could resolve. Vincent's letters to his brother Theo became less coherent, permeated with a deepening melancholy. He found he could only portray sadness and the extreme of loneliness, as he said. His self-portraits of these last months are haunting, the eyes seeming to appeal for an escape from despair (fig. 261). Painting he knew excited him and always brought on madness. But paint he would, if it destroyed him. He wrote his brother, "Well, my own work, I am risking my life for it and my reason has half foundered in it—that's all right." He was resigned. "Painters have more and more their backs to the wall," he admitted. When he could no longer stand the torture of ineluctable insanity, he shot himself.

OPPOSITE:
261. Vincent van Gogh (1853–1890). Self-Portrait. 1890. Oil on canvas, 25 1/2 × 21 1/4". Louvre, Paris.

OVERLEAF LEFT ABOVE:
262. Paul Gauguin (1848–1903). Annah the Javanese. c. 1894. Oil on canvas, 45 3/4 × 32 1/8". Private collection.

OVERLEAF LEFT BELOW:
263. Vincent van Gogh. Dr. Gachet at a Table with a Sprig of Foxglove in His Hand. 1890. Oil on canvas, 26 3/4 × 22 1/2". Louvre, Paris.

OVERLEAF RIGHT:
264. John Constable (1776–1837). Maria Bicknell (later Mrs. John Constable). 1816. Oil on canvas, 11 15/16 × 9 7/8". The Tate Gallery, London.

With his death the creative surge of French 19th-century portraiture was nearly finished. From 1860 on, portrait painting by the most significant artists was almost without patronage; but the masterpieces that resulted, perhaps for that reason, were marked by a sublime originality. No period in the history of art has ever produced works of greater genius.

In Germany painters were less creative, and England, too, after Lawrence, produced no portraitist of the first rank, though the number of likenesses shown each year at the Royal Academy is staggering. John Constable, for example, executed numerous portraits, competent but uninspired, to help him make a living. Once, however, love brought with it inspiration. His likeness of his fiancée, Maria Bicknell, ranks among the most beautiful portraits painted in the 19th century (fig. 264). For many years their marriage was prevented by her parents, and Constable had to console himself with this painting, of which he wrote, "I never had an idea before of the real pleasure a portrait could offer." He delineated Maria with a limited palette, the brushwork delicate and certain, and with a sensitive response to her angelic character. If the portrait had been shown along with his landscapes when they were displayed at the Salon of 1824, it would have proved to his French admirers that he was more than a landscapist. Maria's beauty would have enchanted Paris. But the portrait was too personal, too involved with his frustrated passion for him to allow its exhibition during his lifetime.

Of the many British practitioners of portrait painting, John Everett Millais was the best. His likeness of John Ruskin standing beside a rushing stream is distinguished; and the artist's Victorian and exiguous lovemaking with Mrs Ruskin while her husband posed adds an ironic interest (fig. 265).

Dante Gabriel Rossetti, a fellow Pre-Raphaelite, painted and drew innumerable portraits of the lovely Lizzie Siddal, before his infidelities caused her suicide. After burying his poems in her coffin and then exhuming them, he turned to painting the still more ravishing Mrs. William Morris and other beauties (fig. 266). These likenesses are less portraits than symbols of feminine attraction, paeans to the enticement of sex. They will always be a delight to any lover of beautiful women.

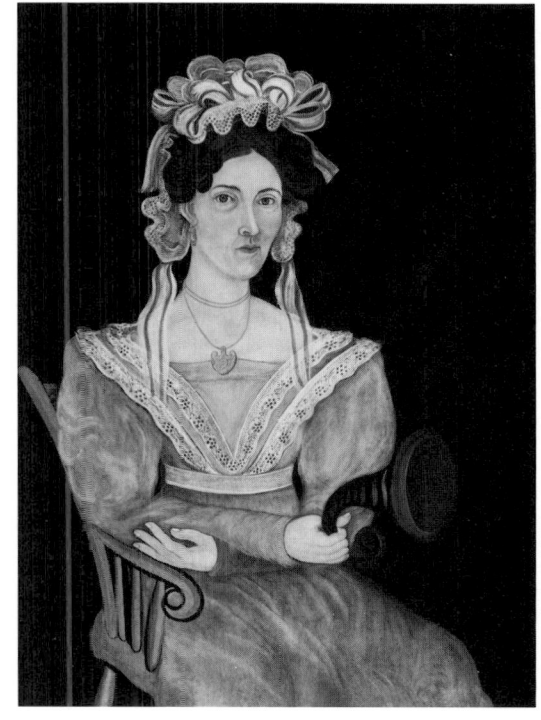

Whistler and Sargent, the two outstanding 19th-century portrait painters, who lived much of their lives in England, are labelled in English museums "British School"; but in spite of their long sojourns in England they remained American citizens and are discussed here with other American portraitists.[18] On the whole (apart from France), the best portraiture in the 19th century was done in the United States or by Americans living abroad.

Like the Dutch in the 17th century, Americans have unceasingly commissioned portraits of themselves. As John Neal wrote in 1829, "You can hardly open the door of the best room anywhere without surprising or being surprised by the picture of somebody, plastered to the wall and staring at you with both eyes and a bunch of flowers." Patronage was divided between the more sophisticated artists, who were often trained in Europe, and the more naive painters, commonly called "primitives," who were usually self-taught and are frequently no longer remembered by name. Their method of delineation was realistic but not naturalistic. They painted what they saw, to which their lack of facility added a touch of fantasy. Part of the charm of these portraits lies in the tension between a recalcitrant image and the artist's determination to get it down on canvas or panel. In the process there was a search for significant detail: the set of a mouth, which tells the character of an individual, or even an attribute such as an ear trumpet, which implies deafness and the warping of a personality (fig. 267). These singularities are stressed, thrust awkwardly but touchingly at the spectator so as to convey in the most emphatic way the message of the artist. Yet, because the primitive painter's intention is basically realistic, he manages to convey the specific character of his subject with a vividness that the academic painter, trained to generalize and to idealize, often loses.

Chester Harding is an excellent example of a self-trained American artist who was determined to pass beyond the technical limitations of the primitives. He eventually managed to produce portraits almost photographic in their realism, an ability that made him popular with the notables of his day, from Daniel Boone to General William Sherman. His likeness of Amos Lawrence, the Boston merchant (fig. 268), indicates that he could compete with the

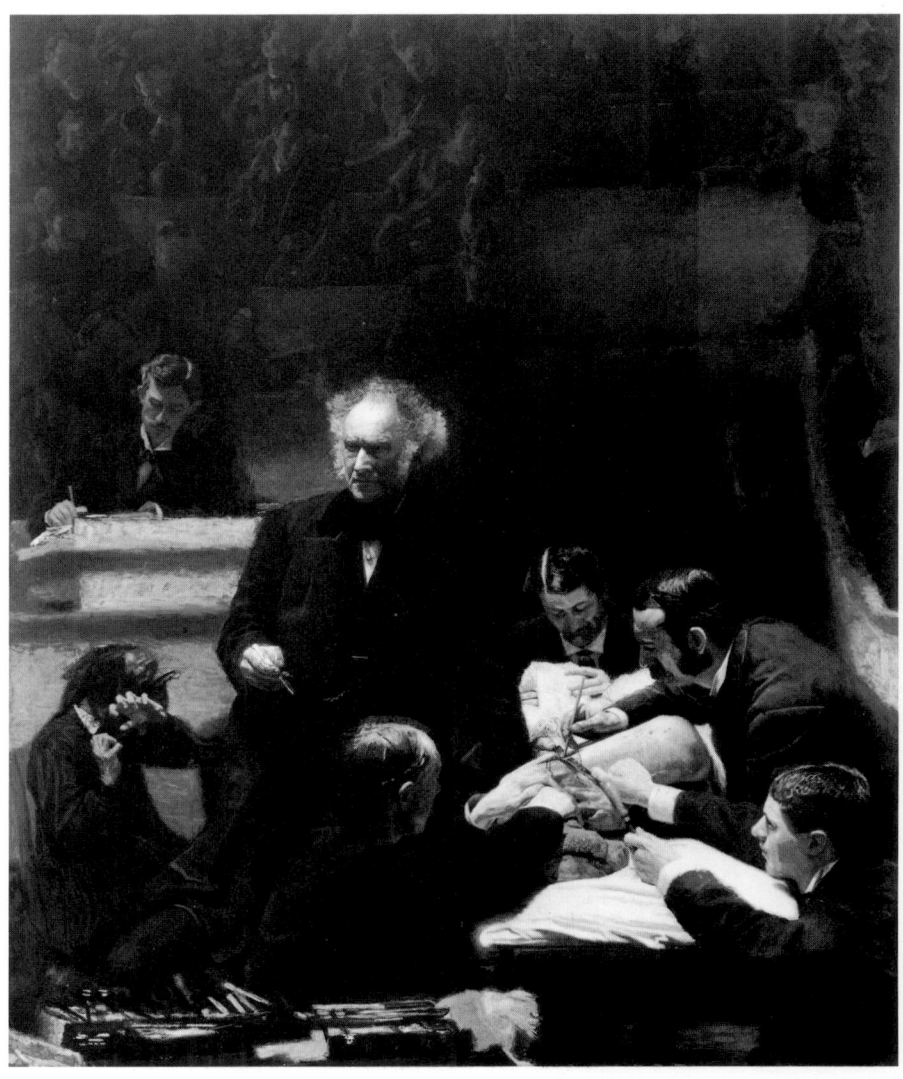

269. *Thomas Eakins (1844–1916). The Gross Clinic. 1875. Oil on canvas, 96 × 78". Jefferson Medical College, Philadelphia.*

270. *James Abbott McNeill Whistler (1834–1903). Arrangement in Flesh Color and Black: Portrait of Théodore Duret. 1883. Oil on canvas, 76 1/8 × 35 7/8". The Metropolitan Museum of Art, New York. Wolfe Fund, 1913. The Catharine Lorillard Wolfe Collection.*

best English portraitists of the time, and with confidence he went to London, where he spent three successful years. Had he been less ambitious and retained more of the naiveté with which he began his career, his portraits would probably seem less pedestrian.

Thomas Sully, Harding's contemporary and rival, was not self-taught. He received his first instruction in Charleston from Jean Belzone and Lawrence Sully, the miniaturist, and later studied with Gilbert Stuart, whose laconic advice to the struggling young painter was, "Keep what you have got, and get as much more as you can." This counsel he took to heart, leaving behind more than 2,600 portraits of the leading men and women of the time. His earliest likenesses are his best. They reveal a sound craftsmanship and a satisfactory characterization of the sitter. Later his style became slick and degenerated into a genteel formula. He seems endlessly to have delineated upper-class American society, where, to judge from his portraits, all women were languishingly beautiful and all men languidly well-bred. During his long life, which extended from 1783 to 1872, he saw the rise of Stuart, the passing of the men who studied under West, and the beginning of the new realism of Thomas Eakins.

Eakins had a hard, uncompromising sense of actuality typically American. Walt Whitman, whose portrait he painted, said, "I never knew of but one artist, and that's Tom Eakins, who could resist the temptation to see what they thought ought to be rather than what is." It was the simplicity and sincerity of this austere realism that made Eakins one of the great portraitists of the 19th century.

He was indifferent to impressionism, to postimpressionism, to all the movements of art of his day. In spite of the obviously 19th-century appearance of his pictures, Eakins bears a fundamental resemblance to the 15th-century Italian realists. He had the same burning passion for reality and, like them, he studied anatomy, worked out the mathematics of perspective, and investigated the optical effect of movement.

His two group portraits of doctors at work, *The Gross Clinic* (fig. 269) and *The Agnew Clinic* (University of Pennsylvania, Philadelphia), also challenge comparison with Rembrandt. More dramatic than *The Anatomy Lesson of Dr. Tulp* (fig. 178) or *Dr. Deyman's Anatomy Lesson* (fig. 186), *The Gross Clinic* has a photographic immediacy, as though a camera's flashbulb had just gone off, which is a quality not found in any painting of the 17th century. The eyes of the spectator are riveted on the action of the surgeon rather than on the personalities of the participants, and in this Eakins again departs from Rembrandt. But there is in the works of the American and the Dutch artist the same nobility of concept, the same moving tribute to the profession of medicine.

Eakins's hard, angular characterizations, as unflattering as the most candid of snapshots and as revealing as the most analytical of psychiatric reports, were not popular in his birthplace, Philadelphia, where he spent most of his life. He taught at the Pennsylvania Academy until, on his insistence that his female students draw from a nude male model, he was forced to resign. His reply to his critics was a portrait of William Rush, the greatly admired local sculptor, carving a statue with a naked model posing. Perhaps with a tinge of irony the painter placed a chaperone, Mrs. Rush, seated nearby knitting and keeping an eye on her husband. Deprived of his position as a teacher, Eakins would not have been able to support himself had it not been for his portrait commissions. These came from friends and from those outside the circle of Philadelphia society. Many of his sitters were priests, for the Catholic church, like Eakins, was socially taboo.

By contrast, the American painters James Abbott McNeill Whistler and John Singer Sargent, who lived most of their lives in England, portrayed the rich or socially acceptable. Whistler was a peculiar combination of charlatan, dandy, wit, and artist. He sought to combine the asymmetrical and subtly balanced designs of the Japanese printmakers with the visual realism of Velázquez. From the great Spanish master he learned to paint portraits low in tone and with quiet colors, to narrow the planes of the picture, to make the silhouette count in the design, and to adumbrate rather than to define form. This exotic and refined eclecticism Whistler embodied so skillfully in his delicate portraits and preached so effectively in his stinging aphorisms that, for a time, English taste was strongly affected by his theories.

One of his ideas seems at first anomalous in portraiture. He wrote dogmatically: "I insist on calling my work 'arrangements' and 'harmonies.' Take the picture of my mother, exhibited at the Royal Academy as an *Arrangement in Grey and Black*. Now that is what it is. To me it is interesting as a picture of my mother; but what can or ought the public to care about the identity of the

271. *John Singer Sargent (1856–1925). Asher Wertheimer. 1898. Oil on canvas, 58 × 38 1/2". The Tate Gallery, London.*

portrait?" Put this way, the idea seems startling, but it contains a basic truth about likenesses. The sitter's identity in most cases is soon forgotten. What remains is the "arrangement" and the "harmony." Whistler's portrait of Théodore Duret, for example, does not hold the attention of the spectator because it represents a famous critic (fig. 270). It is fascinating because of its elegance and distinction and the chromatic beauty of rose and black played together with such taste. We can see a reflection of Whistler's portrait in Edouard Vuillard's painting of Duret's study (fig. 277). Though the features in the mirror are so blurred as to make identification of Whistler's model difficult, yet the charm and refinement of his portrait persist indestructibly.

John Singer Sargent was trained in Paris by Emile Auguste Carolus-Duran. He developed an extraordinary talent for realizing at the first glance the tone and structure of a face. Few painters could surpass his manual dexterity, nor could any artist of his generation penetrate more cruelly on occasion into the character of his sitter. When he let the first statement stand, as in his portrait of Robert Louis Stevenson (J. H. Whitney Collection), he achieved the freshness and spontaneity of an instantaneous effect. When the sitters' character was obvious—vulgar, voracious, predatory (Asher Wertheimer in figure 271 is an example) or witty, brittle, incredibly chic (Madame Pierre Gautreau in the Metropolitan Museum portrait, for instance)—Sargent caught it without hesitation. But with personalities less salient he was lost. In a desperate effort to get a telling likeness he often painted and scraped out his portraits thirty or forty times, and these alterations and reworkings impaired the purity of his tone and blurred the sharpness of his vision.

An 18th-century painter would have handled Sargent's endless stream of sitters more easily. He would have modelled the head according to an established procedure, and after giving his subject a suggestion of individuality, which is all that a fashionable portraitist can hope to do, he would have passed on to the more important matters of design, of phrasing, and of color. But Sargent, like most of his academic contemporaries, was tied to the model. He was intent on copying each accidental variation in depth of shadow, each reflected light as it happened to appear. Worn out by this rigorous imitative technique with which he tried to portray his swarm of clients, he had little energy left for the serious problems of painting. Gradually he tired of portraiture and toward the end of his life he reduced the number of his sitters and turned more and more to sketching and mural decoration.

Sargent lived well into the 20th century, and with his death academic portrait painting lost one of its outstanding practitioners. He died, however, under a cloud of adverse criticism. Sixty years ago the postimpressionists began their triumph, eulogized by the ablest critics everywhere, who despised professional portraitists. Time, however, has restored much of Sargent's luster, and we now look with considerable delight at many fashionable painters working at the turn of the century, among these Sargent's friend Giovanni Boldini, who caught so perfectly the chic of the Edwardian world.

These fashionable portraitists have a nostalgic charm. The dexterity of their brushwork is a joy that has been lost in the work of the more advanced artists of our time. Portraiture, as the next chapter will show, has become probing, analytical, distorted at times to the verge of caricature, and almost always grim and solemn. The urbane blitheness and the social opulence that marked fashionable portraits hung in the French Salons and the Royal Academy before World War I have vanished from art. Even professional portraitists today,

272. *Auguste Rodin (1840–1917). Balzac. 1897. Bronze, 113 3/4" high. Boulevard Raspail, Paris.*

looked down on or ignored as they are by most critics, are as grave as their more radical colleagues. This unrelieved earnestness makes one occasionally long for the dash and brio of the chic portraitists of the past. The likenesses hanging today in drawing rooms, board rooms, club corridors, and judicial chambers would all gain from a little more vivacity, a little more elegance. It is sad that the tradition that began with Van Dyck should have ended with Sargent. But given the dire conditions of our times, the disappearance of all delectation from portrait painting is, one supposes, to be expected.

THE SCULPTURED PORTRAIT

In a general history of portraiture the temptation to pass over 19th century sculptors until reaching Auguste Rodin is almost irresistible. The production of those manufacturers of effigies, however, was prodigious. It was the age of monuments, of memorials to famous men and to historic events. Such statues were so multitudinous that in some cities legal restrictions to prevent their erection were contemplated and should have been carried out. One sculptor, however, in the second half of the 19th century, stands high above the mutations of fashion. Rodin was the most inventive, the most esteemed, and the most influential sculptor of modern times. It goes without saying, however, that his statue of Balzac, the outstanding sculptural portrait of the entire 19th century, was rejected by the authorities who had ordered it (fig. 272). The battle over this monument to the great novelist, which was fought between middle-class detractors and artistic admirers, parallels in a different medium the struggle of the impressionists and postimpressionists. The statue remained in plaster for many years until, in 1930, it was finally cast in bronze— not for a French museum, but for the museum of Antwerp. Nine years later a bronze casting paid for by friends of the artist at long last appeared in Paris. The stupidity of official French taste has lasted into this century!

Rodin's portrait of Balzac illustrates two characteristics of his style. First, only the parts of the figure that are significant are defined. Thus, the author's immense cape conceals his body, placing greater concentration on his head. Second, the modelling bears out Rodin's precept that sculpture should consist of bosses and hollows. The features of the face—scowling, imperious, and threatening—are effectively rendered by the tortured surfaces of the bronze.

Rodin was one of the few 19th-century sculptors to achieve successfully the goals of likeness and aesthetic quality. Toward the end of his life he devoted himself almost entirely to portrait busts. These go beyond mere verisimilitude. They are searching inquiries into the nature of the sitter. Rodin was probably the greatest modeller in clay in the history of sculpture. He rendered the inner personality of his subjects with a marvellous coordination of eye and touch. Marcel Tirel tells how in modelling the face of the duchess of Choiseul (fig. 273), he made her lie on the floor on her back. He then turned her head toward the light and held her neck between his knees, "while he modelled, with his thumb still warm, so to speak, from her skin." The result is a bust every hollow and protuberance of which describes the essential structure of the features of the duchess. He has given the bronze an infectious vitality. The portrait is almost too alive, and one feels an intimacy that verges on the embarrassing. Among great artists Rodin is the most disconcerting. His treatment of sex is often too explicit and his probing of personality sometimes too intrusive. But these are the faults, if they are faults, of an independent, astonishing genius.

In Germany in the second half of the 19th century the work of two portrait sculptors should be noted: Adolf von Hildebrand and Max Klinger. Hildebrand was not only an artist but the aesthetician of a group of sculptors. His book on the problem of form once exerted a wide influence. Even his portraits, impassive, simple, objective, were affected by his study of form. He revived classical standards without the imitative faults of neoclassicism. For him the nude body was the theme most worthy of representation, and some of his followers even carved naked portraits, as for example, Hermann Hahn's somewhat absurd likeness of Goethe in Chicago.

Klinger was at the opposite pole from Hildebrand. His work is subjective,

deeply personal, and romantic. He was less interested in form than in the pictorial and decorative. He was a practitioner of polychromatic sculpture using different materials—stones of strange and delicate color, various metals, and, for eyes, amber, with precious gems for accents of light. Klinger was an interesting sculptor, but today, outside of Germany, he is an almost forgotten artist.

America at this time was a backwater in sculpture, but it did produce one mild portraitist, Augustus Saint-Gaudens. Although not of the first rank, he created some well-characterized and at times poetic portraits. He was a master of *rilievo schiacciato*, a form of low relief, moderately impressionistic and much admired in the Renaissance. His delicacy of technique and general sobriety lend his bas-reliefs, like the portrait of Robert Louis Stevenson, an austere, yet touching beauty.

273. *Auguste Rodin*. La Duchesse de Choiseul. *1908. Bronze, 13 3/8″ high. Victoria and Albert Museum, London.*

CHAPTER TEN

1900-1983: MODERN EUROPE AND AMERICA

Artistic judgments are so dependent on historical perspective that to write about modern portraiture is difficult. When we look at a work of contemporary art our vision is apt to be blurred, as though we were astigmatic, or as though our eyes were farsighted and we were too close to see clearly. We need spectacles to bring everything modern into focus. These our immediate ancestors evidently lacked, considering the bad judgments they often made. The lenses the critics offer today appear to dim rather than to sharpen our vision. One critic, John Berger, writes, "It seems unlikely that any important portrait will ever be painted again." Another, Robin Gibson, affirms that portraiture "has not only survived but has produced many of the greatest masterpieces of this century."

It is an argument that will never be settled, least of all with statistics, but the following are nevertheless revealing. In the Pelican History of Art, a series of books with each volume the work of a distinguished art historian, the volume covering painting and sculpture from 1780 to 1880, written by Fritz Novotny, has 192 pages of illustrations. Of these, 72 reproduce portraits either painted, drawn, or sculptured. The succeeding volume, covering the period from 1880 to 1940, by George Hamilton, has the same number of illustrations but only 17 pages of portraits. It is evident that these two greatly respected authors consider that in the earlier period compared to this century more than four times as many significant likenesses were executed, all by the ablest artists. This may seem surprising, but it would probably be the consensus of the best critics.

At least three factors explain the decline of portraiture in our times: photography, abstraction, and patronage. All three are connected. The spread of photography impelled the more creative artists toward abstraction; the financial success of abstraction made them unwilling to submit to the tedious demand of patrons for realistic likenesses. Of the first, photography, Walter Richard Sickert, himself an excellent portraitist, remarked, "The retouched photograph has massacred serious portraiture." Although exaggerated, there is truth in this statement. Again statistics bear it out. In 1861 London alone had more than two hundred photographic portrait studios, one of which employed roughly one hundred people. From this glut of photographs all painters suffered, but the portrait miniaturists suffered most. In 1810 more than two hundred miniature paintings were shown at the Royal Academy. In 1863 there were only sixty-three and by 1870 a mere thirty-three. The camera had taken over. The miniaturists had to become photographers or photographic colorists.

But it was not only with miniaturists that the photographer competed. In Roger Fry's opinion the photographic portraits of Juliette Margaret Cameron "bid fair to outlive most of the work of the artists who were her contemporaries." She photographed Browning, Tennyson, Longfellow, Carlyle, Trollope, Darwin, and many other distinguished Victorians. She said of her own

274. *Henri Matisse (1869–1954).*
Femme au Chapeau. *1905. Oil on canvas, 31 3/4 × 23 1/2". Private collection.*

work, "When I have such men before my camera, my whole soul has endeavored to do my duty toward them, in recording faithfully the greatness of the inner, as well as the features of the outer, man." Her soul, however, took its time, and to sit for her was, we are told, pure agony. She was a tyrant who would not let anyone out of her clutches until she was satisfied that she had what she judged to be a good photograph. When Tennyson took Longfellow to pose, he warned his friend: "You will have to do whatever she tells you. I shall return soon and see what is left of you." It was worth the suffering, for her photographs are better than any paintings done of either poet. Whereas most photographers of her time let the light stream in from all sides to minimize the length of exposure, Mrs. Cameron, disregarding her sitter's comfort, concentrated the light to model features and opened her lens for as long as necessary, probably at least five minutes, during which the model could not move. The effect she got was similar to a photograph of a painting by Rembrandt (fig. 275).

In France, Nadar (Gaspard Félix Tournachon) photographed the illustrious French as Mrs. Cameron did the English, and he was only one of many able Parisian photographers. The study of Baudelaire by Etienne Carjat, for example, evokes the extraordinary modernity of the poet's face. His portrait of Rossini, so suggestive of Ingres, is also a masterpiece of interpretation.

To turn again to England, there was Lord Somers, who made a haunting photograph of his sister-in-law, Mrs. Cameron; there was Thomas Annan, a Scot, who photographed in a simple and straightforward way the professors of Glasgow University; and there was Lewis Carroll, whose camera recorded his obsession, little girls with and without clothes. All of them took superb photographs. There is no doubt that the 19th-century photographers made better portraits, in spite of the limitations of their equipment, than their successors.

Except for the addition of color, which is of doubtful artistic consequence, and the rapidity of exposure and development, the modern camera has not proved particularly advantageous for portraitists. One of the few 20th-century photographers to approach in quality the masters of Victorian times was Alfred Stieglitz, who chiefly employed old-fashioned equipment. His innumerable likenesses of his wife, Georgia O'Keeffe, taken when she was a young woman, rival the work of the early photographers (fig. 276).

The success of the camera in the hands of the really talented practitioners, from Louis Jacques Mandé Daguerre, the inventor of the daguerreotype, to Mathew Brady, photographer of the Civil War, had a strong impact on painting. It is thought that Ingres used daguerreotypes, and his portraits have a definite resemblance to these primitive photographs. Evidently Degas and Manet benefitted from a study of photography, gaining from it compositional inspiration and certain effects of immediacy. But the paintings of these three artists so far transcend photographic prints that the influence of the camera on them is only of some historic interest.

For lesser artists photography was a tool that facilitated their work, a short cut that dispensed to some extent with drawing from the model. But as Walter Sickert wisely observed, "The camera like alcohol . . . may be an occasional servant to a draftsman, which only he may use who can do without it."

More significant is the negative effect of photography on painters at the beginning of this century. André Derain, when shown an album of photographs taken by Mrs. Cameron, exclaimed, "It is the perfection of the camera that has spoiled everything." On another occasion he said, "It was the era of photography that may have influenced us and contributed to our reaction

against anything that resembled a photographic plate taken from life." He was referring to the time when he was a fauvist; the emphasis placed by him and his companions on color led gradually to the omission of the object. Wassily Kandinsky, explaining the inner enrichment possible through abstraction, wrote, "The impossibility and, in art, the purposelessness of copying an object, the desire to make the object express itself, are the beginning of leading the artist away from 'literary' color to artistic, i.e., pictorial aims." And much later André Breton summed up the issue, saying, "The invention of photography has dealt a mortal blow to the old way of expression, in painting as well as in poetry."

It took time for pure abstraction to gain ascendancy, but its monopoly of art for many years began with the fauvists, who "treated color like sticks of dynamite, exploding them to produce light." The emphasis on color, which can be traced to Cézanne, had a baneful effect on significant portraiture. The talented artists who became portraitists grew fewer and fewer. Fortunately, as this chapter will show, portrait painting was saved by the work of a few outstanding masters. Abstraction, however, captured many of the best artists of recent times. They were delighted to surrender the making of likenesses to photography and to devote themselves to patterns of color and shape. In the last few years painters have begun to return from this blind alley, and a number of younger artists have refused to enter it. For a lover of portraiture this is encouraging. But the problem of the patron remains irksome. His demands are not always aesthetically feasible. The finest artists among the impressionists painted few commissioned portraits. There was, of course, the alliance of a number of critics against the more advanced painters from 1860 to the end of World War I. Such hostility probably put off patrons of means. Exceptions there were—collectors like Chocquet, Caillebotte, Charpentier, and Camondo and dealers like Durand-Ruel and Vollard. But well-to-do friends and courageous entrepreneurs were not numerous enough to provide the more creative artists with patronage. The traditional harmonious relationship between patron and painter disappeared and has not yet been resumed on any satisfactory scale. The best portraitists today have become highly selective about sitters. In the 18th century sufficient money was all that was necessary to gain the immoratlity of being portrayed by Reynolds; and in the 19th century there were skillful purveyors of portraits like Sargent, of whom this was still true. But today the artist of significance will probably choose his sitter rather than the other way round. As Robin Gibson has pointed out, the finest portraits are now self-portraits or likenesses of the painter's family, his friends, or his models.

The difficulties of patronage have always existed. They cannot be entirely blamed on photography. Nevertheless, although the camera has not adversely affected the more innovative artists, the society and the official portraitists have suffered a blight from photographic competition. To be painted, say, by Pietro Annigoni is expensive and requires numerous sittings; to be photographed by someone like Cecil Beaton, though expensive, is cheaper and takes less time. The brilliant photographer Yousuf Karsh photographs Sir Winston Churchill—his family are delighted and the world accepts this photographic likeness as the image of a great leader. One of the best contemporary portraitists, Graham Sutherland, paints Sir Winston—Lady Churchill burns the portrait. Little wonder that we have few distinguished paintings of the great figures of our time.

279. *Pablo Picasso (1881–1973).*
Gertrude Stein. *1905. Oil on canvas,*
39 1/4 × 32". The Metropolitan Museum
of Art, New York. Bequest of Gertrude Stein
1946.

During the first quarter of the 20th century France retained its artistic leadership. In Paris there were able artists, transitional between impressionism and the modern styles, of whom the best as a portraitist was Edouard Vuillard. His likeness of Théodore Duret, dated 1912, is a beautiful example of modern portraiture; moreover, it is also a remarkable study of the effect of age (fig. 277). Reflected in the mirror in the background is another portrait of Duret as he was painted by Whistler when still a young man-about-town (fig. 270). Thirty years passed and Duret posed once more. He has totally changed. His body is now meager, his hands seem to tremble, his eyes are red. Vuillard painted directly on cardboard, which absorbed the paint, leaving it dry and brittle so that it conveys exactly the texture of Duret's desiccated flesh. The critic's weightless and insubstantial body is rendered with the same adumbrations, the same imprecisions, as his surroundings. Thus, the figure of the old man becomes one substance with all the other details of the scene, united with them by the blurred outlines so consistently rendered throughout in books, papers, and pictures. The conformity of the brushwork makes the portrait remarkably homogeneous. There is also a sadness about the painting, overtones of loneliness and solitude. Duret, at the end of his life, withdrawn from the world, is now reduced to the companionship of his cat. No other painter of Vuillard's generation has explored with such tender sympathy the increasing fragility and infirmity of old age.

Pierre Bonnard, Vuillard's lifelong friend and associate in the Nabis group, also painted occasional likenesses. His double portrait of Misia and Thadée Natanson—an intimate study in the drawing room of their house in Paris—shows the leading Parisian hostess and the editor of the *Revue Blanche* with cruel perception (fig. 278). She stands superbly elegant, with a sibylline smile, dominating her husband, who slouches in a chair playing with their dog. It is a perfect revelation of a woman confident of her conquests, those past and those yet to come. Bonnard himself was one of these. He wrote her, "The artist must think himself very lucky to have you for a model, someone who has never been painted by anyone worthy of her."

Vuillard and Bonnard with their sensitivity and intimacy are a part of the past. The "modernist revolution" was to find other leaders, of whom Henri Matisse and Pablo Picasso were the most influential. The first shock of the new movement occurred in the Salon of 1905, when Matisse showed a portrait of his wife, *Femme au Chapeau* (fig. 274). Her features are modelled in bright green with touches of yellow and pink. Even the Steins, Leo and Gertrude, who bought the picture, were unenthusiastic. Leo referred to it as "a thing brilliant and powerful but the nastiest smear of paint I had ever seen."

As a portraitist Matisse is heterodox. He once wrote, "I do not insist upon the details of the face. I do not care to repeat them with anatomical exactness. Though I happen to have an Italian model whose appearance suggests nothing but an animal existence, yet I succeed in picking out among the lines of his face those which suggest that deep gravity which persists in every human being." We are used to abstraction, so Matisse's portraits do not disturb us; but in 1905 the president of the Salon, Frantz Jourdain, begged the jury to reject *Madame Matisse au Chapeau*, not to preserve the reputation of the Salon but for the sake of Matisse, to protect him from his own folly. The jury declined and a new chapter in the history of portraiture began.

The solitary artist of the School of Paris equal in originality and inventiveness to Matisse was Picasso. One of his early works, and probably his greatest portrait, is a painting of Gertrude Stein. After ninety sittings he considered it still deplorable. In despair one day, painting from memory, he found his solution in his recollection of an Iberian mask (fig. 279). Gertrude Stein's friends could see no resemblance but Picasso was unperturbed. "Everybody thinks she is not at all like her portrait, but never mind, in the end she will manage to look just like it." And time proved him right.

With Georges Braque, Picasso initiated the cubist experiment. The new movement represented an even more violent break with tradition than had David's neoclassicism a century earlier. While it lasted, cubism represented the demolition of portraiture. Recognizable likenesses held on for a time, but often hidden under a pattern of angles and triangles. The result was unsatisfactory. Noses, eyes, and mouths shifted around by such violent if skillful surgery leave us unmoved. They have as little emotional effect as the shattered fragments of apples and mandolins. Personality, a major goal of portraiture, has vanished.

Paris at the beginning of this century swarmed with skillful and interesting portraitists, but only one painter of the School of Paris, Amedeo Modigliani, devoted himself almost exclusively to portraiture. As a portraitist he was probably the ablest of all. The combination of a formal stylization with a telling likeness was his goal, as it was also the goal of the great Renaissance masters he admired. They would have accepted him as one of themselves, for they too were absorbed in the problem of how to represent a face, both as a likeness and as an element of a formal design. Modigliani's whole life was devoted to this study. Even his rare and beautiful nudes are essentially likenesses of the model.

His portrait of Chaïm Soutine illustrates his objectives (fig. 281). The sitter is rendered in an idiomatic style as a formal pattern within the rectangle of the canvas. Modigliani also caught the dichotomy of Soutine's appearance, that of a coarse proletarian with thick nose and rough, asymmetrical features joined to that of a sensitive artist with long, tapering fingers. Soutine's hands are clasped nervously in a way suggestive of insecurity and diffidence.

Soutine, himself a portraitist, shared with Modigliani a Polish picture pedlar, Zborowski, who tried to sell their paintings to the more successful dealers, but without success. Both suffered from extreme poverty; at one time they lived in a filthy, insect-ridden attic, taking turns to sleep in the only bed. But Soutine was fortunate in gaining the patronage of the well-to-do Monsieur and Madame Marcel Castaing. The Castaings first enountered him at the Café de la Rotonde in 1919 and asked if they could buy a picture; but Soutine, though starving and desperately in need of support, imagined that they were being merely charitable and stormed out in a rage. Five years later there was a more successful meeting, and Soutine gradually drew close to the couple, often spending his summer months working at their château near Chartres. His portrait of Madeleine Castaing, distorted as it is, has an extraordinary vitality (fig. 280). The sitter comes alive with the nervous energy the portraitist poured into each stroke of his heavy impasto.

There were other portraitists of ability working at the same time in Paris. André Derain, already mentioned, portrayed objectively and with facile skill many of the leading Parisians; Salvador Dali united meticulous likenesses with the staffage of the dream world; Kees Van Dongen evoked with portraits of fashionable ladies an ineluctable sexual attraction, giving them with the help of floodlights the decadent appearance of the demimonde; and Pavel Tcheli-

280. Chaïm Soutine (1894–1943). Madeleine Castaing. c. 1928. Oil on canvas, 39 3/8 × 28 7/8". The Metropolitan Museum of Art, New York. Bequest of Miss Adelaide Milton de Groot (1876–1967), 1967.

OVERLEAF LEFT:
281. Amedeo Modigliani (1884–1920). Chaïm Soutine. 1917. Oil on canvas, 36 1/8 × 23 1/2". National Gallery of Art, Washington, D. C. Chester Dale Collection.

PAGE 249 ABOVE LEFT:
282. Edvard Munch (1863–1944). Puberty. 1894. Oil on canvas, 59 5/8 × 43 1/4". Nasjonalgalleriet, Oslo.

PAGE 249 ABOVE RIGHT:
283. Edvard Munch. The Cry. 1893. Oil on canvas, 33 × 26 1/2". Oslo Kommunes Kunstsamlinger, Munch-Museet, Oslo.

PAGE 249 BELOW:
284. Edvard Munch. Jealousy. 1895. Oil on canvas, 26 1/4 × 39 1/2". Rasmus Meyers Samlinger, Bergen.

tchew, with his austere vision, delineated such writers as James Joyce and Edith Sitwell, creating portraits stylish and accurate. These and other artists of the School of Paris had the support of the two most eloquent critics writing in English during the 1920s, Roger Fry and Clive Bell. Due to them and to a consortium of dealers, attention in England and America has been concentrated on contemporary French painting. Prices of works by these painters have risen inordinately until today they are probably much overvalued.

Because of this, collectors until recently have been less aware of the portraiture of Teutonic countries. Their inexperience is also due partly to the retention in Norway for nationalistic reasons of so many works by Edvard Munch, who was the greatest exponent of expressionistic portraiture. Expressionism has never been a style particularly congruent with Latin taste. The difference of interpretation and outlook between a French artist and one from a northern country is evident if one compares two nudes: Gauguin's portrait of Annah, his Javanese mistress, and Munch's *Puberty*, both probably painted the same year—1894 (figs. 262, 282). Gauguin's frank sensuality makes Annah's sexual attraction as explicit as possible; Munch's young model seems by contrast nervous and unhappy, at once coy and innocent. In Gauguin's portrait the symbolism of the monkey is related to promiscuity and carnal pleasure; in Munch's the dark shadow behind the girl is an obvious reference to death. One painting reflects a joyous acceptance of the pleasures of the flesh; the other a neurotic rejection of its temptations. Gauguin's mistress looks out of the canvas with no more psychological complications than a healthy animal; Munch's shivering adolescent stares at the spectator with pathetic and questioning shyness. The two paintings are worlds apart. They represent a basic difference between French painting and Teutonic painting. Yet Munch owes his early artistic inspiration to a visit to Paris, where the work of Seurat, Gauguin, Van Gogh, and Redon was a revelation. These artists taught him how to convey emotion through color and how to employ distortion for expressive purposes. Like Van Gogh, Munch's predominant disposition was despairing. The mood of depression that overhangs Munch's painting arose from adolescent illness, intensified by the death of his mother and sister when the artist was fourteen, and aggravated by the excessive piety of his father. Sickness, loneliness, disenchantment with love, alcoholism drove him to a mental breakdown. He recovered but the scars remained.

The curious portrait of his friend the Polish poet and novelist Pzybyszewski, entitled *Jealousy*, is typical of the allegories so often to be found in Munch's work. While in Berlin, he introduced a Norwegian student, Dagny Juell, to his circle of Bohemian writers and artists. She is represented in figure 284 as Eve tempting the painter, a fully dressed Adam. Her infatuated lover, Pzybyszewski, stares out of the picture with an expression of sullen anger. The red outline of the figures and the red cloak of Dagny symbolize the jealousy of the two men. The dilemma of the friends was finally resolved when Dagny chose to marry her Polish admirer, whose unpronounceable name she apparently mastered.

The Cry, Munch's most famous and characteristic picture, is in a sense a bizarre self-portrait (fig. 283). It also expresses the anguish and torment that inform his best work. He wrote of it: "I stopped and leaned against the balustrade, almost dead with fatigue. Above the blue-black fjord hung the clouds, red as blood and tongues of fire. My friends had left me, and alone, trembling with anguish, I became aware of the vast, infinite cry of nature." It would seem from this description that Munch himself is the screaming figure who hears in terror nature's dolorous and awful roar. Lines like the lash of a whip, lurid colors, violent distortions, all combine to express the inner horror of the artist. This is the ultimate in expressionistic painting. Here, portraiture of the individual vanishes into an interpretation of his state of mind.

In Vienna a portrait style different from postimpressionism as represented by Van Gogh and expressionism as we see it in Munch was being practiced by their contemporary Gustav Klimt. He is a recent hero of museum directors in England and America, one they ignored for half a century. His first important commission was to decorate the new Burgtheater in Vienna with a series of ceiling paintings. When these canvases were satisfactorily completed, he was asked by the city council in 1887 to paint a picture of the interior of the old Burgtheater before it was replaced by the new house. The councillors wished not only the theater shown but also a typical audience, and the commission was destined to provide a gold mine for Klimt. Depicting the stalls, boxes, and balconies as they would have looked during an intermission, he created what is probably the largest group portrait in number of individual likenesses ever painted (Historisches Museum der Stadt Wien). There are more than one hundred portraits of prominent and rich Viennese, who were eager for the social distinction of being immortalized as patrons of the Burgtheater; and Klimt showed them all, from Katherina Schratt, the emperor's mistress, to Karl Lueger, the future mayor. Everyone in Vienna clamored for a sitting and doubtless rewarded the portraitist accordingly.

Klimt was the obvious choice when the University of Vienna decided to commission three murals depicting the three major disciplines: philosophy, medicine, and jurisprudence. Here, Klimt's murky philosophical ideas and his explicit erotic ones got him into trouble, first with the faculty and then with Catholic conservatives. Both were opposed to allegories vaguely based on the doctrines of Schopenhauer and Nietzsche, and both strongly objected to the lubricity of his orgiastic nudes. He found himself disgraced, a disgrace all too apparent when the ministry refused his appointment as a professor of art. The combination of public obloquy and professional rejection caused Klimt's withdrawal from government commissions, and during the last fifteen years of his life he devoted himself largely to painting the portraits of women, most of them from wealthy Jewish families, and to the decoration of their houses.

Klimt, who was always close to the Wiener Werkstätten, the center of the Austrian arts and crafts movement, intended his portraits to be decorative elements in beautiful rooms. All his women—and he scarcely ever painted men—are the essence of refinement and elegance, but the artist has shown in these likenesses no psychological interest whatever. Klimt had been deeply impressed by the mosaics of Ravenna, and some of his portraits, such as that of Adele Bloch-Bauer (fig. 285), could easily take their place on the walls of S. Vitale, where they would reveal about as much character as appears in the face of the empress Theodora (fig. 67). These are society portraits, effective as decoration and of fine design, but they are as far from expressionism as it is possible for paintings to be. They prove, however, that in a milieu as cultivated as Vienna before World War I the portraitist, no matter how innovative, and his patron still enjoyed a happy relationship.

Egon Schiele, a Viennese artist of greater promise and more psychological insight, looked on Klimt as his father. He died in 1918, the same year as his master. He was only twenty-eight. His double portrait of the Benesches, father and son, is a touching family group (fig. 286). Otto, the son, became a great authority on Rembrandt; the elder Benesch, who was in the Austrian civil service and was devoted to Schiele, helped the painter when he was jailed for making indecent drawings. For, like Klimt, Schiele was obsessed with erogenous nudes, which he drew exquisitely. His sitters, as here, are often placed in stiff, ungainly poses. The father has his arm outstretched, seemingly protective of his son. Both have hands that are unusually large and bony, an idiosyncrasy of Schiele's style, while their eyes are tragic with distant visions. All Schiele's portraits are permeated with such sadness that death perhaps was not unwelcome, even to one so young. However, given the gifts manifest in this strange portrait group, his early demise was a great loss to modern art.

Klimt remained a father figure for other Austrian artists, but the decorative style he promulgated was dead even before his own death. The impact of Freud had turned painters in another direction. Intellectual circles in Vienna became deeply interested in psychoanalysis. Oskar Kokoschka was the leader of a new movement that ran on lines parallel to the expressionism of Edvard Munch. Under the sway of Klimt, members of the Secession had devoted themselves to creating in the houses of the wealthy "the life beautiful." Now, led by Kokoschka, younger painters attacked the elite and sought to destroy in the name of truth the artificiality of their environment. Kokoschka dowered his models with his own neurosis (at one time he was known as "the mad Kokoschka") and showed them in apparent psychotic states of mind. As he said, he revealed in his sitters "their closed personalities," and his own search for mental stability gives his portraits insight and sympathy. He managed to paint the socially prominent without becoming, like Klimt, a society painter. His portrait of the marquis of Montesquieu is an image as descriptive of the French aristocracy as anything in Proust (fig. 287). No portraitist in this century has equalled Kokoschka's analysis of the nervous anxiety characteristic of modern intellectual life.

In Germany as in Austria, modern portraiture, unrealistic as it was to become, had its roots in a 19th-century tradition of naturalism. Lovis Corinth was a bridge between the past and more recent painters. His likeness of the dramatist Gerhart Hauptmann makes a revealing contrast with Vuillard's portrait of Duret (figs. 277, 288). In the French painting the critic's study is filled with a diffused light, which illumines the colorful walls, books, and pictures. There is a subdued harmony of roseate tones with warm areas of darkish brown. Corinth has also placed his sitter at a desk. But here dark shadows obscure the background of books and paintings. Hauptmann's head is in full light to form a strongly contrasted chiaroscuro Corinth learned from Rembrandt. The hands of the author are beautifully painted, far better rendered than the tentative appendages Vuillard gave to Duret. But the French painting has a feeling of modernity, a stimulating originality; whereas the German picture is traditional, distinguished, but dull.

The best German painters of the 20th century have been expressionists, a movement that during the Weimar Republic became the so-called Neue Sachlichkeit (New Realism). The nature of the change is conveyed succinctly by two slogans, that of the earlier German expressionists, which was "Man is good," and that of the later painters, who, embittered by the war, used as their slogan the words of George Grosz, "Man is a beast." In the 1920s Germany produced a number of exceptional New Realist portraitists: Otto Dix, whose tightly and carefully drawn sitters seem frozen, as if hypnotized by the

285. *Gustav Klimt (1862–1918)*. Adele Bloch-Bauer. *1907. Oil on canvas, 54 3/8 × 54 3/8". Osterreichische Galerie, Vienna.*

painter; George Grosz, whose mordant drawings and paintings are made still more acrid by occasional surrealism; Christian Schad, whose realism recalls the precision of Albrecht Dürer, but with strange overtones of evil. There were many other accomplished practitioners of Neue Sachlichkeit, but one artist, Max Beckmann, rises above any particular movement. Like his progenitors, Van Gogh and Munch, he devoted himself to expressing his sitter's state of mind. But whereas the average person's mental state is on the whole stable and offers the artist little if any visible sign of his emotional condition, the sitters Beckmann chose usually reflect some type of psychological tension. His likenesses show people with nerves stretched taut. His compositions are tightly confined, as though his subjects were psychologically imprisoned. He himself in his many self-portraits reveals a square, enigmatic face (fig. 290). His appearance accords well with the style of his portraits, which are brutal and disturbing but always mysterious. The inscrutability of his sitters, however, leaves the spectators baffled and unsatisfied. Failure of communication is a basic problem of expressionism and of Neue Sachlichkeit.

With the advent of Hitler, creative art in Germany and Austria died a sudden and tragic death. The Nazis destroyed all significant portraiture, labelling it decadent. Some painters were killed, some committed suicide, some went into exile. When art is thus uprooted, time must pass until it flowers as before. Portraiture in Germany and Austria must germinate longer before it can produce the distinguished painters and sculptors of the Weimar Republic and of the Vienna that existed before Hitler's homecoming.

Although among British portraitists of this century no geniuses are to be found, there are many artists of talent. Walter Sickert was one of these. Painters of his generation looked up to him as author, artist, and founder of the Camden Town Group. In 1900 he moved to France and when he returned five years later he was one of the few English painters familiar with impressionism. He began his artistic career as an assistant to Whistler, but later repudiated his master, whose work he felt showed an oversimplification. He, on the other hand, was "avid of complications" and yet he also believed that "to demand more than one sitting for a portrait is sheer sadism." Consequently, because he worked with such swiftness, the "complications" in his paintings were not always completely solved. But few artists were more able to capture the mood of a place or scene. One can scarcely look at his double portrait entitled *Ennui* without yawning, so effectively does the monotony implied by colors, gestures, and surroundings nauseatingly strike the viewer (fig. 289).

William Orpen, who belongs to the next generation, and who made more money painting portraits than any artist of his time (he earned more than $200,000 in 1921 and nearly $300,000 in 1929), was once heard to say, "Twenty years after I die no one will remember me—but he [Sickert] will live forever." For a time it seemed Orpen was right about himself, if not about Sickert, but recently there has been a renewed interest in Orpen's work. Now his hard, polished style, which made him the favorite of the rich and eminent, has again become fashionable.

He and Augustus John for a time ran their own art school, housed in Dante Gabriel Rossetti's old studio. But John was not interested in teaching, only in painting, and the school faded out of their lives. But it could claim one dis-

OPPOSITE ABOVE:
286. *Egon Schiele (1890–1918)*. Otto and Heinrich Benesch. *1913. Oil on canvas, 47 5/8 × 51 1/8". Neue Galerie der Stadt Linz.*

OPPOSITE CENTER:
287. *Oskar Kokoschka (1886–1982)*. Le Marquis de Montesquieu. *1909–10. Oil on canvas, 31 1/2 × 24 3/4". Statens Konstmuseet, Moderna Museet, Stockholm.*

OPPOSITE BELOW:
288. *Lovis Corinth (1858–1925)*. Gerhart Hauptmann. *1900. Oil on canvas, 34 1/4 × 41 3/4". Städtische Kunsthalle, Mannheim.*

tinguished graduate, Henry Lamb. His portrait of Lytton Strachey (Tate Gallery, London) will assure him a limited immortality, both because of the fame of the subject and because of the extraordinary physique of his model. Unfortunately, his other portraits are not of equal quality. Lamb's masters, Orpen and John, were professional portraitists in the sense that they accepted work from anyone with sufficient money. John had an assertive, slightly vulgar virtuosity, which gained him many commissions. Occasionally he painted a brilliant likeness: for example, the portrait of Joseph Widener in the National Gallery of Art in Washington, D.C., and occasionally he had an inspiring model, like the actress Tallulah Bankhead, whom he painted so flatteringly that his portrait caused the theatrical producer Arthur Hopkins to say it proved Tallulah had a soul (fig. 291). No sitter could ask for more; few portraitists could provide so much.

Gwen John, the elder sister of Augustus John, though less famous than her brother, was probably the finest British portrait painter of her generation. Her psychological range was limited but she could convey with the utmost clarity emotions gentle and serene. Her likeness of Chloë Boughton-Leigh is one of many small pictures she painted, all of which convey a tranquil stillness, a quietude that refreshes the viewer (fig. 292).

Since World War II, calmness of this kind is rare. More characteristic is the work of Francis Bacon, the leading British painter of recent years. In his portraits the whole physiognomy of the sitter is deformed, the features twisted, each lineament warped. The tortured beings in his pictures who crouch naked and spotted on floors of empty rooms or lie huddled on unmade beds are repellent. But the dire impact of Bacon's paintings is a measure of their exceptional quality. No one can see them without a feeling of revulsion; yet once seen they cling to the memory like unforgettable nightmares. In a self-portrait of 1956 he snarls at the viewer very much as Rembrandt does in his early etching (figs. 176, 293). But Bacon has not yet attained—and doubtless never will—the humanity and compassion Rembrandt achieved in later life.

The brutality of Bacon's work is not suitable for commissioned portraits. These, however, continue to be painted and can be seen in their myriads and their mediocrity at the annual shows of the Royal Academy. Professional portraiture, a staple of British art since the 18th century, has sadly declined, not in numbers but in quality. Today most of the Royal Academicians are teachers, and the Summer Exhibitions are filled with the work of their pupils. The portraits shown are on the whole much better than the other paintings, but once people are no longer interested in the sitters, these Academy likenesses will soon be forgotten.

But the demand for portraits is there, the patronage exists; the difficulty is to find painters of ability to execute these potential commissions. Graham Sutherland is greatly admired. Some of his portraits justify this admiration, for example that of Somerset Maugham (fig. 294). But when he portrayed Mrs. Reginald Fellowes, who was considered one of the best dressed women between the two wars, he produced a dumpy, foreshortened figure with a disproportionately large head.

Commissions seem to have a deadening effect on modern painters. One artist who could carry them off with discernment and with exceptional actuality is David Hockney, the most gifted of younger portraitists, but he will paint only his friends and family (fig. 296). Patrons who want to hand on their features to posterity have a difficult problem facing them. There is Gardner

RIGHT:
291. Augustus John (1818–1961).
Tallulah Bankhead. *1930. Oil on canvas,*
48 × 24 1/2". National Portrait Gallery,
Smithsonian Institution, Washington, D. C.
Gift of the Hon. and Mrs. John Hay
Whitney.

OPPOSITE:
292. Gwen John (1876–1939). Portrait
of Chloë Boughton-Leigh. *c. 1910–14.*
Oil on canvas, 23 5/8 × 15". Leeds
Galleries, England.

Cox in America and Derick Hill in England, both adroit in rendering a likeness and probably the ablest professional portraitists available; but to be painted by them is no guarantee of the immortality that resides in canvases by Reynolds and Gainsborough. As Roger Fry judged that Mrs. Cameron's photographs "bid fair to outlive most of the work of the artists who were her contemporaries," so the finest photographs of our time may well outlast most contemporary portraits in other mediums.

America during World War II and after became what France had previously been, the center of creative painting. But the particular contribution of the

293. Francis Bacon (1909–   ). Self-Portrait. 1956. Oil on canvas, 78 × 54″. Private collection, Switzerland.

294. Graham Sutherland (1903–   ). Somerset Maugham. 1949. Oil on canvas, 54 × 25 1/2″. The Tate Gallery, London.

295. Andrew Wyeth (1917–   ). Christina's World. 1948. Tempera on gesso panel, 32 1/4 × 47 3/4″. The Museum of Modern Art, New York.

New York School, abstraction and color painting, are the antithesis of portraiture. Hardly any American portrait painter is known outside America.

Andy Warhol is one of the few who have achieved international fame. He was trained as a commercial artist, and his work in advertising has strongly affected his painting. His multiple-image series—portraits of such American folk heroes and heroines as Elvis Presley, Marilyn Monroe, and Jackie Kennedy, repeated in frames like those of a film clip—are an innovation (fig. 297). Based on photographs, they are executed in polymer paint and silk screen transferred to canvas. These repeated images, varied in color and lighting, have a remarkable power of fixing a likeness in the viewer's mind. It is fascinating how much they convey compared to the photographic print from which

they are mechanically derived. In their way they are an interesting proof that the camera can never replace the artist.

Andrew Wyeth is another painter whose work is known outside the United States. His portrait of the crippled Christina Olson lying on the ground looking toward a desolate house on the crest of a hill is such a moving study of help-lessness and loneliness that it has been widely seen in reproductions (fig. 295). Wyeth, who was trained by his father, an illustrator, has held himself aloof from the various movements of modern art and continued to paint in his own idiomatic, precisely realistic way.

With the opening of the 20th century, there was a revival of bronze portraits. The influence of Rodin was paramount. It was a strong factor in the work of the American Jacob Epstein, later knighted, and a Frenchman, Henri Gaudier-Brzeska. Both chose to live in London rather than in New York or Paris, a tribute to the vitality of art in England. Epstein's bust of Jacob Kramer in the Tate Gallery has the typical tortured bronze surface

OPPOSITE:
296. David Hockney (1937–   ). My Parents. 1977. Oil on canvas, 72 × 72". The Tate Gallery, London.

ABOVE:
297. Andy Warhol (1930?–   ). Sixteen Jackies. 1964. Synthetic polymer paint silkscreened on canvas, each panel 20 × 16". Walker Art Center, Minneapolis.

roughened by tools and fingers, derived from Rodin; but the depth of the eye sockets, the twisted, bitter lips, and the deep undercutting of the hair are exaggerations that go beyond the master's style (fig. 298). Epstein is the only 20th-century sculptor who produced official portraits that rise above the merely competent. He was tough enough to face commissions without a loss of integrity.

Gaudier-Brzeska's active life as an artist lasted only from 1912 to 1914. His death in World War I cut short one of the most promising careers in modern art. Much of the time during the short period he was at work was spent on commissioned likenesses, where he was clearly inhibited. But he modelled two busts of friends, Alfred Wolmark (fig. 299) and Horace Brodsky, which are so powerful in concept that they still startle the viewer. By forcing Rodin's hollows and bosses into geometric shapes in the cubist manner, he attained in his portraits a personal style, original and impressive. In these two busts his ferocious expressionism transforms the sitter into a symbol of intellectual strength. Had Gaudier-Brzeska lived he might have become the greatest portrait sculptor of our time.

The effect of Rodin on Epstein and Gaudier-Brzeska is self-evident, but much more remarkable is his influence on the finest of all abstract sculptors, Constantin Brancusi. Brancusi considered Rodin's statue of Balzac "the starting point of modern sculpture." His admiration for Rodin was immense, but in one important respect he differed from the master. Rodin himself never carved his marbles. This was done by professionals, one of whom for fifteen years was the well-known sculptor Emile-Antoine Bourdelle. Brancusi, on the other hand, insisted that direct carving was "the true road of sculpture"; and, working tirelessly over stone and wood, he gave these materials surfaces of shining beauty. In an extraordinary way he was able to combine abstraction and portraiture. His likeness of the dancer Mademoiselle Pogany, executed in 1912, which exists in eight versions in bronze and marble, has the grace of a ballerina with hands pressed to cheek—a dancer portrayed in a moment of stillness (fig. 300). The rhythm of curving lines—eyes, eyebrows, and the contours of the head and the suggested body—produces an effect of ineluctable charm. Although the elision of planes is even more evident than in the work of Francesco Laurana, the Renaissance sculptor may have been Bran-

299. *Henri Gaudier-Brzeska (1891–1915). Alfred Wolmark. 1913. Bronze, 25 5/8" high. Southampton Art Gallery and Museums, England.*

cusi's inspiration (fig. 112). Seventeen years after finishing the portrait of Mademoiselle Pogany, Brancusi carved a likeness of Agnes Meyer (National Gallery of Art, Washington, D.C.). All the subject's features have vanished, and yet in the curves of polished black marble, for those who knew the sitter, there is an intangible resemblance.

George Segal, an American sculptor, is the antithesis of Brancusi. Distortions for him are nonexistent. His portraits literally mirror the sitter. He bandages his live models with fabric saturated in hydrastone, a substance used for making industrial casts. When dry, it closely resembles plaster of paris but is less fragile and more resilient. The exposed parts of the sitter's body are protected by Vaseline and Saran Wrap. The nostrils, of course, are left open for breathing. When the cast has hardened, it is cut away. The result resembles those life masks such as we have seen in Roman and medieval royal portraits, except that recently Segal has used color on his figures.

The novelty of Segal's technique has placed him with the avant-garde, but he is actually a conservative sculptor working with great ability in a realistic style. Realism has continued a way of expression with some of the best modern portraitists. Harry Jackson's *The Foreman (Portrait of Cal Todd)* (fig. 301) is a penetrating likeness of an American type. The sculptor has found and expressed nobility in the face of a cowboy. He has conveyed the self-reliance and the dignity of men whose days and nights are spent in solitary vigil herding their cattle. Jackson's wrangler is traditionally rendered, yet its modernity is unmistakable. Thus, it seems a fitting conclusion to an artistic history that reaches back five thousand years.

300. Constantin Brancusi (1876–1957). Mademoiselle Pogany. *1913. Marble, 17 1/2" high. Philadelphia Museum of Art.*

OPPOSITE:
301. Harry Jackson. (1924–   ). The Foreman (Portrait of Cal Todd). 1981. Polychromed bronze, 13" high. Courtesy of the artist.

PORTRAITURE
TO THE YEAR 2000

Foolhardy as it is to prophesy the future of portraiture, the temptation is ineluctable. Everywhere the type of likeness produced in Europe, America, and Australia is being imitated. Thus, we need concern ourselves only with Western and Westernized artists. What are they likely to do? Though the creations of outstanding genius are unpredictable, it is not entirely futile to speculate on the nature of work by less prodigious artists, who are more influenced by their environment. In general, I would predict two things: an increased use of photography and the introduction of cassettes into portraiture.

The invention of photography has had a strong effect on art. At one time it impelled painters away from representation and toward abstraction, but among recent portraitists it has also had the opposite effect. For them it has been a major means of achieving a close resemblance. It has become a tool on which they increasingly depend. With a ready-made image available, the artist can work more rapidly, and increased celerity means a reduction in the time the model will have to pose. This is of great importance because patrons are more and more reluctant to give up the many hours the modern portrait painter demands. Faced with the necessity of greater speed, many of the best artists have more or less abandoned commissioned portraits and limited themselves to sitters with plenty of time to pose. Official portraits are increasingly handled by swifter but second-rate painters.

There is nothing new in the use of the camera as a shortcut for the portraitist. Snapshots have been constantly employed by painters since the invention of photography, but until recently major artists have turned to the photographic print less as a means of attaining a likeness than as a stimulating source of ideas for design. An able portraitist, Degas would have said, should depend for resemblance on his own vision. But today many capable artists are using photographs to reduce or even dispense with sittings. The likeness they then achieve is a photographic one.

There are serious disadvantages to such a procedure. When a portraitist employs photography exclusively, or virtually so, beauty of brushwork tends to disappear. Brian Organ, an English artist of exceptional ability, works largely from photographs, though he also makes drawings of his model. His pictures, admirable as likenesses, have, however, flat surfaces with no feeling for paint as a medium. Like all work based predominantly on the camera, the modelling looks as though the artist had copied precisely the light and shade in a photographic print. The use of the mechanical chiaroscuro of a snapshot is a dispiriting break with tradition; yet the trend toward painting from photographs will doubtless increase in the future. This in itself is a sad prediction for the development of portraiture in the next decades.

On the other hand, modern technology has opened up new, revolutionary possibilities for portraitists. These innovations have just begun to be explored and much remains to be done, but the prospect of an entirely different kind of portrait is foreseeable. Assuming that the object of the patron is to record for posterity not only his appearance but his whole personality, then it is conceivable that the video cassette may have an important role to play. The cassette, for example, might offer an interview with the sitter, discussion of his character, his opinion on matters of interest, and possibly public statements he has made. These would reinforce the visual image, the picture painted or drawn by the artist, which might be shown in a number of frames resembling Warhol portraits (fig. 297). Between now and the 21st century, the technique of combining the visual and the auditive is sure to be further developed. The painter with his palette and cassette will then be able to lend greater permanence to individuality, and thus, as never before, to satisfy his patron's desire to hold oblivion at bay.

The analysis of character will remain, however, the prerogative of the portraitist. The sitter's words will be merely a commentary to reinforce the nature of the image seen by the viewer. In the artist's search for the essential human being, advances in psychology, which have disclosed the working of the human brain to an extent unimaginable fifty years ago, will be of immense assistance.

Thus, portraiture during the next two decades seems likely to develop in fascinating and unexpected ways. But the desire of the person portrayed will usually remain what it has been from the beginning—a wish for a vicarious immortality. This, the sitter trusts, will be gained through the enduring statement of the artist's image:

> So long as men can breathe or eyes can see
> So long lives this and this gives life to thee.

NOTES

1. When I was a young man I lived with Bernard Berenson, the great expert on Italian art. We used to play a game when visitors came to his villa, I Tatti. We would try to decide who should have painted him or her. Sometimes it was Botticelli, sometimes Titian, occasionally a Fleming like Memling or a German like Cranach, more frequently a Pre-Raphaelite or a modern artist like Augustus John. It is amusing how often we agreed on the painter. After numerous museum visits and with the help of the illustrations in this book, the reader may enjoy the fun of attributing faces and categorizing in artistic terms the appearance of his friends.

2. Adolf Erman, *The Literature of the Ancient Egyptians,* trans. A. M. Blackman, London, 1927, p. 72.

3. Choice of the drill depended also to a great extent on the nature of the marble. Some marbles were easier than others to chisel; among these, Pentelic marble was one of the easiest. Marbles from Asia Minor, by contrast, responded better to the drill. The great increase in the use of Asian marbles during the Antonine period created a fashion for "drilled work" that continued in the Byzantine period.

4. *Rome, the Late Empire: Roman Art* A.D. *200–400,* trans. P. Green., London, 1971, p. 19.

5. Whether or not, as some believe, the imprint on the Turin Shroud came to be there because it was the burial cloth in which Jesus was wrapped, the portrait of the man on the linen closely resembles the traditional bearded likeness.

6. For further discussion of the group portrait, see Chapter Seven and pages 178–79.

7. Quoted in Erwin Panofsky, *Albrecht Dürer,* 3d ed., 2 vols., Princeton, N. J., 1948, vol. 1, p. 44.

8. Erwin Panofsky, *The Life and Art of Albrecht Dürer,* Princeton, N. J., 1955, p. 5.

9. Quoted in Seymour Slive, *Rembrandt and His Critics,* The Hague, 1953, p. 98.

10. *A History of European and American Sculpture,* 2 vols., Cambridge, Mass., 1921, vol. 2, p. 8.

11. David Mannings, "At the Portrait Painter's," *History Today,* May 1977, p. 279.

12. Mannings, "Portrait Painter's," p. 280.

13. Mannings, "Portrait Painter's," p. 285.

14. Ibid.

15. Quoted in D. S. MacColl, *Eighteenth-Century British Portraits,* Glasgow, 1902, p. 28.

16. These quotations, and the ones that immediately follow, are taken from Lawrence Park, *Gilbert Stuart,* 4 vols., vol. 1, New York, 1926.

17. Quoted in Kenneth Clark, *Leon Battista Alberti on Painting,* Annual Italian Lecture to the British Academy, London, 1944.

18. By the same token, Mary Cassatt should also be in this chapter, but her close association with the impressionists makes it difficult to separate her from her French colleagues.

BIBLIOGRAPHY

Groenewegen-Frankfort, Henrietta Antonia, and Ashmole, Bernard. *Art of the Ancient World: Painting, Pottery, Sculpture, Architecture, from Egypt, Mesopotamia, Crete, Greece, and Rome.* New York: Abrams, 1972.

Smith, William Stevenson. *The Art and Architecture of Ancient Egypt.* Reprinted with corrections. Pelican History of Art. Harmondsworth and Baltimore: Penguin Books, 1965.

Walker, John. *Egyptian Sculpture from the Gulbenkian Collection* (exhib. cat.). Washington, D.C.: National Gallery of Art, 1949.

Woldering, Irmgard. *The Arts of Egypt.* Trans. Ann E. Keep. London: Thames and Hudson, 1967.

CHAPTER ONE

Groenewegen-Frankfort, Henrietta Antonia, and Ashmole, Bernard. *Art of the Ancient World: Painting, Pottery, Sculpture, Architecture, from Egypt, Mesopotamia, Crete, Greece, and Rome.* New York: Abrams, 1972.

Parrot, André. *Sumer: The Dawn of Art.* Trans. Stuart Gilbert and James Emmons. London: Thames and Hudson, 1960; New York: Golden Press, 1961.

Strommenger, Eva, and Hirmer, Max. *Five Thousand Years of the Art of Mesopotamia.* Trans. Christina Haglund. London: Thames and Hudson; New York: Abrams, 1964.

CHAPTER TWO

Hinks, Roger Packman. *Greek and Roman Portrait Sculpture.* 2d ed. London: British Museum, 1976.

Richter, Gisela M. A. *The Portraits of the Greeks.* London: Phaidon, 1965.

Robertson, Martin. *A History of Greek Art.* 2 vols. Cambridge: University Press, 1975.

The Search for Alexander (exhib. cat.). Washington, D.C.: National Gallery of Art, 1980.

Stewart, Andrew Ferguson. *Attika: Studies in Athenian Sculpture of the Hellenistic Age.* Society for the Promotion of Hellenic Studies, Supplementary Paper no. 14. London, 1979.

CHAPTER THREE

Bianchi-Bandinelli, Ranuccio. *Rome, the Centre of Power: Roman Art to A.D. 200.* Trans. P. Green. London: Thames and Hudson; New York: Braziller, 1970.

————. *Rome, the Late Empire: Roman Art A.D. 200–400.* Trans. P. Green. London: Thames and Hudson; New York: Braziller, 1971.

Flinders Petrie, William Matthew. *Roman Portraits and Memphis.* London: School of Archaeology in Egypt, 1911.

Goldscheider, Ludwig. *Roman Portraits.* London: Phaidon, 1940.

Heintze, Helga von. *Roman Art.* London: Weidenfeld and Nicolson; New York: Universe Books, 1972.

Hinks, Roger Packman. *Greek and Roman Portrait Sculpture.* 2d ed. London: British Museum, 1976.

Maiuri, Amedeo. *Roman Painting: Ancient Painting in Rome, Pompeii, Herculaneum, Stabiae, Paestum, Cumae, and Ruvo.* Geneva: Skira; London: Zwemmer, 1953.

Mathew, Gervase. *The Character of the Gallienic Renaissance.* Oxford: Clarendon Press, 1943.

Moretti, Mario, and Maetzke, Guglielmo. *The Art of the Etruscans.* Trans. Peggy Martin. London: Thames and Hudson, 1970.

CHAPTER FOUR

Pallottino, Massimo, and Hürlimann, Martin. *Art of the Etruscans*. London: Thames and Hudson, 1955.

Rosenbaum, Elisabeth. *A Catalogue of Cyrenaican Portrait Sculpture*. Oxford: University Press, 1960.

Strong, Eugénie. *Roman Sculpture from Augustus to Constantine*. London: Duckworth, 1911.

Toynbee, Jocelyn Mary Catherine. *The Ara Pacis Reconsidered and Historical Art in Roman Italy*. Proceedings of the British Academy vol. 39, London, 1953.

Walker, Susan, and Burnett, Andrew. *The Image of Augustus*. London: British Museum, 1981.

CHAPTER FIVE

Abbott, Dean Eric et al. *Westminster Abbey*. London: Annenberg School Press, in association with Weidenfeld and Nicolson, 1972.

Aubert, Marcel. *La sculpture française au moyen age*. Paris: Flammarion, 1946.

Bovini, Giuseppe. *Chiese di Ravenna*. Novara: Istituto Geografico de Agostini, 1957.

Busch, Harald, and Lohse, Bernd, eds. *Gothic Sculpture*. Introduction, commentaries by Hans Weigert. Trans. Peter George. London: Batsford, 1963.

Clark, Kenneth. *Feminine Beauty*. London: Weidenfeld and Nicolson, 1980.

Dalton, Ormonde Maddock. *Byzantine Art and Archaeology*. Oxford: Clarendon Press, 1911.

Hanfmann, George M. A. *Classical Sculpture*. London: Michael Joseph, 1967.

Hinks, Roger Packman. *Carolingian Art*. Ann Arbor: University of Michigan Press, 1962. (Originally published London: Sidgwick and Jackson, 1935.)

Marle, Raimond van. *The Development of the Italian Schools of Painting*. 19 vols. The Hague: Nijhoff, 1923–38.

The Medieval Face (exhib. cat.). Introduction by Amanda Tomlinson. London: National Portrait Gallery, 1974.

Meiss, Millard. *French Painting in the Time of Jean de Berry*. London: Phaidon, 1967.

Van der Meer, Frédéric. *Early Christian Art*. Trans. Peter and Friedl Brown. London: Faber & Faber, 1967.

Walker, John. *The National Gallery of Art*. New York: Abrams, 1975.

CHAPTER SIX

Berenson, Bernard. *Italian Pictures of the Renaissance: Venetian School*. 2 vols. London: Phaidon, 1957.

Foskett, Daphne. *A Dictionary of the British Miniature Painters*. London and New York: Faber & Faber, 1972.

Freedberg, Sydney. *Parmigianino: His Works in Painting*. Cambridge, Mass.: Harvard University Press, 1950.

Friedländer, Max Julius. *Early Netherlandish Painting*. 8 vols. Leiden: Sitjhoff, 1967. (Originally published as *Die altniederländische Malerei*. Berlin and Leiden: Paul Cassirer, 1924–37.)

Friedländer, Max J., and Rosenberg, J. *Die Gemälde von Lucas Cranach*. Berlin: Deutscher Verein für Kunstwissenschaft, 1932.

Ganz, Paul. *Hans Holbein the Younger: Paintings*. London: Phaidon, 1950.

Goldscheider, Ludwig. *El Greco: Paintings, Drawings, and Sculptures*. 3d ed. London: Phaidon, 1954.

Manzini, Giana. *L'opera completa del Greco*. Milan: Rizzoli, 1969.

Marle, Raimond van. *The Development of the Italian Schools of Painting*. 19 vols. The Hague: Nijhoff, 1923–38.

Panofsky, Erwin. *Albrecht Dürer*. 3d ed. 2 vols. Princeton: University Press, 1948.

Pope-Hennessy, John. *The Portrait in the Renaissance*. London: Phaidon, 1967.

Post, Chandler R. *A History of European and American Sculpture from the Early Christian Period to the Present Day*. 2 vols. Cambridge, Mass.: Harvard University Press, 1921.

Reynolds, Graham. *English Portrait Miniatures*. London: Victoria and Albert Museum, 1952.

—————. *Hilliard and Oliver*. London: Victoria and Albert Museum, 1971.

Ring, Grete. *A Century of French Painting: 1400–1500*. London: Phaidon, 1949.

Santos, Reynaldo dos. *Nuño Gonçalves: The Great Portuguese Painter of the Fifteenth Century and His Altar-Piece for the Convent of St. Vincent*. Trans. Lucy Norton. London: Phaidon, 1955.

Schade, Werner. *Die Malerfamilie Cranach*. Dresden: Verlag der Kunst, 1974.

Strong, Roy Colin. *Holbein and Henry VIII*. London: Routledge and Kegan Paul, 1967.

Walker, John. *The National Gallery of Art*. New York: Abrams, 1975.

CHAPTER SEVEN

Clark, Kenneth. *Rembrandt and the Italian Renaissance*. London: John Murray, 1966.

Gluck, Gustav. *Van Dyck*. Klassiker der Kunst. Stuttgart, Berlin, and Leipzig: Deutsche Verlags-Anstalt, 1931.

Hinks, Roger Packman. *Michelangelo Merisi da Caravaggio*. London: Faber & Faber, 1953.

Hubala, Erich. *Die Kunst des 17. Jahrhunderts*. Propylaen Kunstgeschichte. Berlin: Propylaen Verlag, 1970.

Lopez-Rey, José. *Velázquez' Work and World*. London: Faber & Faber; Greenwich, Conn.: New York Graphic Society, 1968.

Mauqoy-Hendrickx, Marie. *L'iconographie d'Antoine Van Dyck*. 2 vols. Brussels: Académie Royale de Belgique, 1956.

Meldrum, David Storrar. *Rembrandt's Paintings*. London: Methuen, 1923.

Müller, Joseph-Emile. *Rembrandt*. Trans. Brian Hooley. London: Thames and Hudson, 1968.

Oldenbourg, Rudolf, and Rosenberg, Adolf. *P. P. Rubens*. Klassiker der Kunst. Stuttgart, Berlin, and Leipzig: Deutsche Verlags-Anstalt, 1931.

Post, Chandler R. *A History of European and American Sculpture from the Early Christian Period to the Present Day*. 2 vols. Cambridge, Mass.: Harvard University Press, 1921.

Ricart, José Guidol. *Velásquez*. London: Secker and Warburg, 1974.

Slive, Seymour. *Frans Hals*. 3 vols. London and New York: Phaidon, 1970–74.

—————. *Rembrandt and His Critics 1630–1730*. The Hague: Nijhoff, 1953.

Walker, John. *The National Gallery of Art*. New York: Abrams, 1975.

Walker, John. "The Nation's Newest Old Masters." *National Geographic*, Nov. 1956, p. 656.

CHAPTER EIGHT

Alberts, Robert C. *Benjamin West: A Biography*. Boston: Houghton Mifflin, 1978.

Bassi, E. *Canova*. Bergamo, Milan, and Rome: Istituto Italiano d'Arti Grafiche, 1943.

Hayes, John. *Gainsborough: Paintings and Drawings*. London: Phaidon, 1975.

Hazlitt, William. *Collected Works of William Hazlitt*. Ed. A. R. Walker and

Arnold Glover. 12 vols. Vol. 6 (Conversations with James Northcote). London: J. M. Dent, 1903.

Hind, Arthur M. *A History of Engraving and Etching*. London: Constable, 1923.

MacColl, D. S. *Eighteenth-Century British Portraits*. Glasgow: James Maclehose & Sons, 1902.

Mannings, David. "At the Portrait Painter's." *History Today,* May 1977, pp. 279–87.

Mason, G. C. *Life and Works of Gilbert Stuart*. New York: Scribners, 1879.

Millar, Oliver. *The Later Georgian Pictures in the Collection of Her Majesty the Queen*. London: Phaidon, 1975.

Osborn, Max. *Die Kunst des Rokoko*. Propylaen Kunstgeschichte. Berlin: Propylaen Verlag, 1929.

Park, Lawrence. *Gilbert Stuart*. 4 vols. New York: William Edwin Rudge, 1926.

Paulson, Ronald. *Hogarth: His Life, Art, and Times*. 2 vols. New Haven and London: Yale University Press, 1971.

————. *Hogarth's Graphic Works*. Rev. ed. 2 vols. New Haven and London: Yale University Press, 1970.

Piper, David. *The English Face*. London: National Portrait Gallery, 1978. (Originally published London: Thames and Hudson, 1957.)

Post, Chandler R. *A History of European and American Sculpture from the Early Christian Period to the Present Day*. 2 vols. Cambridge, Mass.: Harvard University Press, 1921.

Prown, Jules David. *John Singleton Copley*. 2 vols. National Gallery of Art Ailsa Mellon Bruce Studies in American Art. Cambridge, Mass.: Harvard University Press, 1966.

Ricart, José Guidol. *Goya*. London: Thames and Hudson, 1966.

Rocheblave, Samuel. *French Painting in the XVIII Century*. Trans. George Frederick Lees. London: Commodore Press, 1937.

Ternois, Daniel. *François Boucher*. Trans. Anita Brookner. London: Purnell, 1966.

Walker, John. *The National Gallery of Art*. New York: Abrams, 1975.

Walker, John, and James, Macgill, *Great American Paintings from Smibert to Bellows*. New York: Oxford University Press, 1943.

Waterhouse, Ellis Kirkham. *Painting in Britain 1530–1790*. 4th ed. Pelican History of Art. Harmondsworth and Baltimore: Penguin Books, 1978.

————. *Reynolds*. London: Routledge and Kegan Paul, 1941.

Weisbach, Werner. *Die Kunst des Barock*. Propylaen Kunstgeschichte. Berlin: Propylaen Verlag, 1929.

The World of Goya. Time-Life Library of Art. New York: Time-Life Books, 1968.

CHAPTER NINE

Descharnes, R., and Chabrun, J. P. *Rodin*. London: Macmillan, 1967.

Dobbs, Brian and Judy. *Dante Gabriel Rossetti: An Alien Victorian*. London: Macdonald & Janes, 1977.

Escholier, Raymond. *Delacroix*. 3 vols. Paris: H. Floury, 1926–29.

Gibson, Robin. *Twentieth-Century Portraits* (exhib. cat.). London: National Portrait Gallery, 1978.

Hamilton, George Heard. *Painting and Sculpture in Europe 1880–1940*. Pelican History of Art. Harmondsworth and Baltimore: Penguin Books, 1972.

House, John, and Stevens, Mary Anne, eds. *Post-Impressionism: Cross-Currents in European Painting* (exhib. cat.). London: Royal Academy, in association with Weidenfeld and Nicolson, 1979.

Larkin, Oliver Waterman. *Daumier: Man of His Time*. New York: McGraw-Hill, 1966.

Millais, Geoffroy. *Sir John Everett Millais*. London: Academy Editions, 1979.

Novotny, Fritz. *Painting and Sculpture in Europe: 1780–1880*. Pelican History of Art. Harmondsworth and Baltimore: Penguin Books, 1970.

———. *Toulouse-Lautrec*. London and New York: Phaidon, 1969.

Peillex, Georges. *Nineteenth Century Painting*. Trans. Angus Malcolm. London: Weidenfeld and Nicolson, 1964.

Post, Chandler R. *A History of European and American Sculpture from the Early Christian Period to the Present Day*. 2 vols. Cambridge, Mass.: Harvard University Press, 1921.

Raynal, Maurice. *The Nineteenth Century: New Sources of Emotion from Goya to Gauguin*. Trans. James Emmons. Geneva: Skira, 1951.

Schapiro, Meyer. *Vincent van Gogh*. New York: Abrams, 1950.

Walker, John. *The National Gallery of Art*. New York: Abrams, 1975.

Walker, John, and James, Macgill. *Great American Paintings from Smibert to Bellows*. New York: Oxford University Press, 1943.

Barr, Alfred H., Jr. *Matisse: His Art and His Public*. London: Secker and Warburg, 1975. (Originally published New York: Museum of Modern Art, 1951.)

Berger, J. P. *The Moment of Cubism and Other Essays*. London, 1969.

Crone, Rainer. *Andy Warhol*. London: Thames and Hudson, 1970.

Gibson, Robin. *Twentieth-Century Portraits* (exhib. cat.). London: National Portrait Gallery, 1978.

Goldscheider, Ludwig. *Kokoschka*. London: Phaidon, 1963.

Hamilton, George Heard. *Painting and Sculpture in Europe 1880–1940*. Pelican History of Art. Harmondsworth and Baltimore: Penguin Books, 1972.

House, John, and Stevens, Mary Anne, eds. *Post-Impressionism: Cross-Currents in European Painting* (exhib. cat.). London: Royal Academy, in association with Weidenfeld and Nicolson, 1979.

Marck, Jan van der. *George Segal*. New York: Abrams, 1979.

Moravia, Alberto, and Lecaldano, Paolo. *L'opera completa di Picasso blu e rosa*. Milan: Rizzoli, 1979.

Neue Sachlichkeit and German Realism of the Twenties (exhib. cat.). Essay by Wieland Schmied. London: Arts Council of Great Britain, 1979.

Newhall, Beaumont. *The History of Photography from 1839 to the Present Day*. New York: Museum of Modern Art, 1949.

Photography 1839–1937 (exhib. cat.). Introduction by Beaumont Newhall. New York: Museum of Modern Art, 1937.

Rothstein, John. *Modern English Painters*. Rev. ed. 3 vols. London: Macdonald and Janes, 1976.

Rothstein, John, and Alley, Ronald. *Francis Bacon*. London: Thames and Hudson, 1964.

Tucker, William. *The Language of Sculpture*. London: Thames and Hudson, 1977.

Vergo, Peter. *Art in Vienna 1898–1918: Klimt, Kokoschka, Schiele, and Their Contemporaries*. London: Phaidon, 1975.

Walker, John. *The National Gallery of Art*. New York: Abrams, 1975.

CHAPTER TEN

INDEX

Page numbers in *italic* type refer to illustrations. Names of artists are in CAPITALS. Titles of works are in *italics*.

PHOTO CREDITS

PROJECT DIRECTOR: *Margaret L. Kaplan*
EDITOR: *Ellyn Childs Allison*
DESIGNER: *Judith Michael*
RIGHTS AND REPRODUCTIONS: *Ann Levy*

LIBRARY OF CONGRESS CATALOGING IN PUBLICATION DATA

Walker, John, 1906 Dec. 24–
Portraits: 5,000 years.

Bibliography: p. 271
Includes index.
1. Portraits. I. Title.
N7575.W34 1983 704.9'42 82–24368
ISBN 0-8109-1450-6

PAGES 2–3
Henri de Toulouse-Lautrec (1864–1901).
At the Moulin Rouge. *1892. See figure*
259.

PAGE 4
El Greco. The Burial of Count Orgaz.
1586–88. See figure 146.